Pioneer Women
of
Faith and Fortitude

Volume III

INTERNATIONAL SOCIETY DAUGHTERS OF UTAH PIONEERS

Printed by Publishers Press

Because we want the histories to be as close to the donors' original texts as possible, we have tried to keep the thoughts and language as submitted. Some histories needed more information and some were long, requiring much editing. Since we have tried to keep the pioneer feeling, please overlook the grammatical and structural errors and read for the spirit of these dedicated women and the lives they lived.

Printed in the United States of America

ISBN 0-9658406-1-1

First Printing 1998

10 9 8 7 6 5 4 3 2 1

The accomplishments of the Utah Pioneer women merit hearty praise for these women in their own rights for these women were real builders in Deseret. When the pioneer father crossed the plains by ox team or by pulling a handcart, the pioneer mother was by his side. At the journey's end the man went forth to plow, sow, irrigate and harvest the crops, but the pioneer woman was in her home spinning, weaving, fashioning dresses, pants, coats, shoes, and articles for home adornment, or she was making soap, lye, drying fruits and vegetables—in every way a true partner.

In the heart of every pioneer woman was a determination to assist in the conquering of the desert. Her influence spread beyond the home, reaching out into the cultural fields of religion, art, education and literature. Throughout the Territory, in every settlement, these women of Deseret were ready to serve both in the home and in the community.

— Kate B. Carter

HESTER (ESTHER) CHALKER MABEY

BIRTHDATE: 1 May 1813
Loscombe, Dorsetshire, England
DEATH: 14 Sep 1889
Bountiful, Utah
PARENTS: Joseph Chalker
Mary Hoskins Chalker
PIONEER: 5 Oct 1862
Ansel P. Harmon Wagon Train
SPOUSE: Thomas Mabey
MARRIED: 7 May 1837
DEATH: 8 Mar 1863
Bountiful, Utah

CHILDREN:
Maria
Jane
Albert
Joseph Thomas
Esther
John James

Hester (Esther) was born in England in 1813. She married Thomas Mabey 4 May 1837, in England. They became the parents of six children who were all born in England. Hester was 49 years old when she and her husband and family emigrated to the United States and Utah.

They joined the Ansel P. Harmon Company and made the journey to the Salt Lake Valley by wagon. They suffered all the hardships and challenges of the early pioneers. Their possessions filled their wagon so Hester walked most of the way across the Plains. They arrived in the Salt Lake Valley 5 Oct 1862. They were in the Fourth Church Train. Their wagon and outfitting were provided by the Church's Perpetual Emigration Fund. They made their home in the new settlement of Bountiful, Utah.

Hester's husband died 8 Mar 1863, only five months after they entered the Salt Lake Valley. This was a bitter blow for Hester. She never entirely recovered from this great sorrow in her life. She was a widow for 26 years and raised her six children. Hester died at the age of 76 years, 14 Sep 1889. She is buried beside her husband in the Bountiful City Cemetery.

ELIZABETH GRAHAM MACDONALD

BIRTHDATE: 12 Jan 1831
Perth, Perthshire, Scotland
DEATH: 11 Jul 1917
St. George, Washington, Utah
PARENTS: John Graham
Ellen Kennock (MacKenzie) Graham
PIONEER: 30 Sep 1854
Capt. Daniel Carus Wagon Train
SPOUSE:
Alexander Findlay Macdonald
MARRIED: 20 May 1851
Scotland
DEATH: 21 Mar 1903
Chihuahua, Mexico

CHILDREN:
Alexander Findlay, Jr, 12 Feb 1855
Graham Duncan, 3 Jul 1856
Joseph Booth, 23 Dec 1857
Aaron Johnson, 12 Jul 1859
Samuel Whitney, 16 Nov 1860
Israel Hope, 25 Sep 1862
Heber Chase, 4 Jul 1864
Macrae, 4 Feb 1866
Brigham Alma, 19 Feb 1868
Smith, 12 Jan 1870
Abram Owen, 3 Apr 1871

Elizabeth was born in Scotland in 1831. She was the fifth of ten daughters. She married Alexander Findlay Macdonald 20 May 1851 in Perth, Scotland. They were both converts to the Church. They served the Church first in Scotland, and then in Liverpool, England. They sailed from there in March 1854, aboard the "John M. Wood." They arrived in the Salt Lake Valley 30 Sep 1854.

There were eleven sons born to this couple. The last three died in infancy. This family were involved in both church and civic activities. They first went to Springville, and in 1862 they moved to Provo. In 1872 they were called to help settle and assist in the temple construction in St. George, leaving the graves of five of their sons in Provo. Elizabeth was independent, and made most of her own living and assumed the leadership of the plural families during frequent absences of her husband. She was elected president of the "Ladies' Co-op Store." For three years, while her husband and two sons were on missions in Scotland, Elizabeth was called to manage the "Lorenzo Snow Big House" to board brethren working on the temple. She rose at 3 a.m. to make lunches for 60 to 70 men, as well as getting breakfast for as many as 80 men before 7 a.m. She was skilled in millinery and dressmaking. She had to earn money for her family's support, since she received no pay at that time for her boardinghouse service.

In 1879, her husband was appointed to preside over the Arizona Mission, so they moved to Mesa, Arizona. The Maricopa Stake was organized in 1882, and Elizabeth served for five years as the Stake Relief Society President. In about 1885, her husband went into Mexico to help establish colonies there. He lived there from then on. Elizabeth elected to return to Salt Lake City, and she lived first in a small adobe house at the East Gate of Temple Square, with responsibility for the dining room at the Temple Annex. In Salt Lake, she raised five of her motherless grandchildren.

With her eyesight failing, she spent her final days in St. George, where she died 11 Jul 1917 at the age of over eighty-six years. She is buried in Provo, Utah.

ELLEN HANCOCK BURNS MACDUFF

BIRTHDATE: 19 Jun 1812
Chesterfield, Derbyshire, England
DEATH: 11 Aug 1885
Salt Lake City, Utah
PARENTS, Joseph Hancock
Mary Jackson Hancock
PIONEER: 1864
Wagon Train
SPOUSE I: Joseph Burns
MARRIED: 20 Mar 1831
Brampton, Derbyshire, England
DEATH: 1831
Jamaica, West Indies

CHILDREN:
Charles, 3 Dec 1831

SPOUSE II: John Robertson MacDuff
MARRIED: September 15, 1839
Nottingham, England
DEATH SP: 17 Oct 1871
Salt Lake City, Utah

CHILDREN
Mary Ellen, 5 Apr 1840
Malcolm, 17 May 1842
Sarah Hanna / Anna, 16 Oct 1844
John Robertson, 20 Apr 1847
Ada Alice, 15 Nov 1850
Jane Rowan, 20 May 1855

Ellen was born in England in 1812. She was the second of six children. She married Joseph Burns on March 20, 1831 in the Old Church at nearby Brampton, Derbyshire, England. Shortly after their marriage, Joseph left for West Indies in search of employment and to make a home for Ellen. Joseph contracted yellow fever and died on the island of Jamaica. He never learned of the birth of his son, Charles, who was born December 3, 1831.

Ellen remained in Nottingham and worked as a dress-maker to support herself and her infant son. She married John Robertson MacDuff, a widower, on September 15, 1838 in the St. Paul's Church in Nottingham, England. They converted to the LDS Church. Ellen was baptized on June 8, 1845. They immigrated to America on May 21 1864, sailing on the "George B. McClellan."

They lived in Bountiful, Syracuse, and Salt Lake City, Utah. Ellen enjoyed singing and was a faithful member of the Bountiful Choir. Ellen died on August 11, 1885 in Salt Lake City, Utah.

ELIZABETH ARMSTRONG MACE

No
Photo
Available

BIRTHDATE: 2 Apr 1819
Seneca, Ontario Co., New York
DEATH: 12 Aug 1902
Fillmore, Millard, Utah
PARENTS: Alexander Armstrong
Grissel Chapman Armstrong
PIONEER: 1851
Wagon train
SPOUSE: Hiram Mace, Sr.
MARRIED: 4 Apr 1837
Nauvoo, Illinois
DEATH: 20 Aug 1896
Fillmore, Millard, Utah

CHILDREN:
Lamire, 14 Jan 1840
Fidelia Jane, 2 Jun 1842
Cordelia, 4 Apr 1844
Elizabeth Aramitta, 18 Feb 1846
Marietta, 23 Mar 1849
Hiram Jr., 17 Jan 1851
Emily Jane, 23 Jul 1853
James Henry, 28 Dec 1855
Edwin, 15 Feb 1858
Celestia, 3 Feb 1861
Charles Alexander, 4 Feb 1864

Elizabeth was born in New York State and married Hiram Mace, Sr. 4 Apr 1837. Their marriage was sealed in the Nauvoo Temple 21 Jan 1846. This couple had eleven children born to them. Two daughters died as small infants.

This family crossed the plains for Utah in 1851 in a wagon train. They settled in Fillmore, Utah. They endured many of the hardships which were common to the pioneer era. Five children were born to them while they lived in Utah.

Elizabeth was an excellent cook. She especially made delicious donuts.

Elizabeth outlived her husband by six years. She passed away 12 Aug 1902 in Fillmore, Utah where her husband also died. They spent most of their lives in Utah in that same area, valiant pioneers who had endured much for their religion which they loved. A great posterity honor their names.

MARY ANN GREENHALGH MACE

BIRTHDATE: 21 Apr 1848
Bolington, Manchester, England
DEATH: 21 Nov 1934
Kanab, Utah
PARENTS: Thomas Greenhalgh
Mary Moorcraft Greenhalgh
PIONEER: 1868
Wagon Train
SPOUSE: George Mace
MARRIED: 21 Jun 1869
Salt Lake City, Utah
DEATH: 10 Mar 1924
Kanab, Utah

CHILDREN:
Wandle Henry, 20 Aug 1872
George, 15 Aug 1874
Margaret Mary, 3 Jun 1878
Charles Abraham, 20 Oct 1881
William Merklee, 12 Jul 1884
Elizabeth Emily, 26 Apr 1887
Sarah Jane, 8 Oct 1889

Mary Ann was born in England in 1848. She came to Utah in early 1869. She married George Mace in the Endowment House 21 Jun 1869 in Salt Lake City, Utah.

This family moved to Kanab, Utah where seven children were born to them. They lived most of their life there. Her husband George, died in Kanab 10 Mar 1924 at the age of over 79 years. Mary Ann died 21 Nov 1934. She was 86 years of age, and had been a widow for over ten years.

ANE KIRSTINE PEDERSEN HANSEN HANSEN MACK

No
Photo
Available

BIRTHDATE: 3 Mar 1829
Toagerup, Denmark
DEATH: 3 Aug 1902
Tetonia, Idaho
PARENTS: Peder Jorgensen
Ane Larsen Pedersen Jorgensen
PIONEER: 1 Oct 1862
Joseph Horne Wagon Company
SPOUSE I: Rasmus Hansen
MARRIED: 11 Nov 1849
Denmark
DEATH: 1 Sep 1864
Smithfield, Utah

CHILDREN:
Annie Christina (Ahrens), 4 Apr 1852
Sophia Fredicka (Mack), 30 Aug 1856
Josephine Maria, 11 Feb 1859
Hans Peter Brigham, 26 Dec 1861
Rasmus Jr., 25 Oct 1863

SPOUSE II: John Fredrick Mack
MARRIED: 28 Nov 1866
Salt Lake, Salt Lake, Utah

DEATH: 3 Nov 1888
Smithfield, Utah

CHILDREN:
Mary Ann (Swensen) 15 Aug 1868

Ane Kirstine was born in Denmark, 1829. When she was seven years old she was hired out to herd sheep and geese in the summertime. She married Ramus Hansen in 1849. She was twenty years old. They became the parents of five children. They joined the LDS Church in 1855. Their desire was to emigrate to Utah and they began to make preparations for the journey. They sold their home but were prevented from leaving because war broke out in their country. It wasn't until 1862 that they set sail.

Ane and her seven month old baby were sick when they arrived in Florence, Nebraska. He died and was buried at Florence. They had to wait for seven weeks before they could leave because of high water. While on the Plains, they buried their little girl. Ane and her daughter were able to ride in the wagon but her husband and their other daughter had to walk. They arrived in Salt Lake in 1862 and stayed on the public square one week. They moved to Cache Valley and made their home in Hyrum.

In 1864 the family moved to Smithfield. Her husband worked on a farm. He went to work on 31 August, at noon he was brought back ill from drinking some bad water. On 1 September he died. She was left alone with three small children to raise. Her husband had told her to visit John Fredrick Mack for counsel. He was the leader of the Scandinavian Saints in Utah. Later she married him for time only. They had one daughter, Mary Ann. Her daughter, Sophia, also married John, they had five children. Ane died in 1902.

CHARLOTTE JAMES DAVIS MACKAY

BIRTHDATE: 20 Aug 1830
Langyndeyrn, Carmarethenshire, Wales
DEATH: 7 May 1901
Taylorsville, Utah
PARENTS: Mary James Davis
PIONEER: 1850
Dan Jones Company
SPOUSE: Thomas Sloan Mackay
MARRIED: 26 Jul 1853
Salt Lake City, Utah
DEATH SP: 19 Feb 1880
Taylorsville, Utah

CHILDRNE:
Hyrum, 1 Jun 1854
Margaret Ellen, 31 Jan 1856
Joseph, 1 Sep 1858
Mary Alice, 7 Jun 1860
David, 10 Jun 1863
Edward S., 6 Jul 1865
Heber, 13 Sep 1868

Ida Charlotte, 20 Apr 1871
Jane Eliza, 10 May 1872

Charlotte was born in Wales. Her father was very unkind to her mother and deserted her when Charlotte was just a baby. Her grandfather, Evan James, took Charlotte and her mother to live with him. Charlotte was told nothing about her father and grew up as Charlotte James. The James family joined the Mormon Church about 1848.

They soon made plans to emigrate to the United States with Dan Jones. While waiting for a wagon train to take them to the Salt Lake Valley, Charlotte's mother and grandfather died of a cholera epidemic.

Charlotte was left in the care of an Uncle David. He left with a small group of men who wanted to go on to California in search of gold. She did not hear from him again. Alone, she joined one of Dan Jones' Welch Companies going to the Salt Lake Valley. She had lost her family and she had a hard time understanding the English language. Charlotte went to work for Feramorz Little on a farm in Granger, Utah for about two years.

She married Thomas Sloan Mackay in the Salt Lake, City Endowment House 26 Jul 1853 in plural marriage. She was the second Wife. She lived with him and his first wife, Ane. Four years later, Thomas married his third wife, Sarah Franks. Charlotte and Sarah shared a room. They lived like sisters.

Charlotte was a small, shy, frail woman who suffered much pain from rheumatism and arthritis most of her life. She was a hard worker, inside and outside the home. She milked the cows, took care of the milk and cream. She fed and took care of the poultry, gathered eggs and made large quantities of butter. Her work was done in a cold, damp, dirt cellar that brought on her arthritis and eventually led to her being confined to a wheelchair. She also did handwork such as quilting, knitting and mending. Charlotte was a very good woman, very meek and quiet. Her childhood was full of sorrow, but her life with Thomas Mackay was a happy one. She loved and respected him. She was active in the Church all of her adult life. She died 7 May 1901 in Taylorsville, Utah. She is buried in the Salt Lake City Cemetery.

SOPHIE MARGRETHE HANSON SORENSON MACKELPRANG

BIRTHDATE: 2 Mar 1820
Brandersleve, Denmark
DEATH: 28 Nov 1908
Cedar City, Iron, Utah
PARENTS:
Christian Julius Sorensen
Margrethe Hanson
PIONEER: 20 Sep 1856
Knute Peterson Wagon Train
SPOUSE:
Peter Mathiasen Mackelprang
MARRIED: 23 Dec 1840
Rudby, Lowland, Denmark
DEATH:

CHILDREN:
Christina Johanne, 5 Sep 1844
Christian Erik, 16 Feb 1846
Kirstina Johanne Margrethe, 28 Dec 1847
Soren Wilhelm, 10 Oct 1849
August (Gus), 16 Aug 1851
Julius, 5 Dec 1853
Anna Eva Augusta, 3 Oct 1855
Mary M., 3 Sep 1857
Margaret, 19 Sep 1860
Peter, 21 Jul 1863

Sophie's mother died when she was three weeks old. She was raised by her mother's sister until her father remarried when she was ten years old. She married Peter Mathiasen Mackelprang of Rudby, Lowland, Denmark, who was a tanner and shoemaker. Rudby was their first home, but they soon moved to the country and became farmers. Margrethe accepted the gospel of the LDS Church and was baptized in the spring of 1854. After the harvest was completed, Peter also joined the church and they moved to Copenhagen where they lived for one year. Peter was called and served as a missionary for the last six months they were in Copenhagen. In 1855 they started on their ocean voyage to America. Their family was the only one which came across without losing a member. Upon reaching the Missouri River, they joined the Knute Peterson Wagon Company and completed the journey by ox teams. They arrived in Salt Lake City in 1856.

The Mackelprangs were sent to Old Fort northwest of Cedar City. They arrived on November 14, 1856. They lived there for many years, then moved to Cedar City and built one of the first homes in Cedar City. They were hospitable people and sold their produce to travelers passing through. They were hosts to many leaders going through to the St. George area as well as California. Margrethe was an excellent cook and a skilled dressmaker. She was a devoted Relief Society worker. She did a great deal for the poor and needy. Her love for the Gospel was boundless and her devotion to family and honesty was unsurpassed. She lived until November 28, 1908.

ALISON ARCHIBALD MADSEN

No
Photo
Available

BIRTHDATE: 6 Sep 1862
Abbey, Paisley, Lanark, Scotland
DEATH: 4 Feb 1885
Provo, Utah County, Utah
PARENTS: David Archibald
Janet (Jessie) Allan Archibald
PIONEER: After 1866
SPOUSE: Andrew Madsen
MARRIED: 20 Feb 1884 or April
DEATH: 9 Nov 1927
Provo, Utah

CHILDREN:
Tessie, 28 Jan 1885
Ellison (Alison), 28 Jan 1885

Alison was born in Scotland, 1862. She was the youngest of 12 children all born in Scotland. She came to Zion with her family when she was a very young girl. The Archibalds made their home in Little Cottonwood, where her father passed away 20 Dec 1876, when Alison was just fourteen. Her mother married again to William/David Powell.

Alison married Andrew Madsen when she was twenty-one, in 1884. She and Andrew made their home in Provo where they became parents of twins, born 28 Jan 1885. Alison did not regain her strength. One twin passed away at birth and the other passed away along with Alison on 4 Feb 1685. This was very hard for Andrew, as within one year he was a widower without children.

Andrew Madsen passed away 9 Nov 1927 and is buried beside Alison in Provo. Alison was only twenty-two at her passing.

ANE MARGRETHE PEDERSEN MADSEN

BIRTHDATE: 7 Aug 1818
Bileroyd, Sealon, Denmark
DEATH: 10 Apr 1896
Honeyville, Utah
PARENTS: Jeppersen Sorensen
Ann Pederson
PIONEER: 12 Sep 1857
Mathias Cowley Wagon Train
SPOUSE I: Johan Eliason
MARRIED: 24 Apr 1847
Esbonderup, Frederksborg, Denmark
DEATH: 23 Aug 1849
Tikob, Denmark

CHILDREN:
1 son
Laurine Wilhelmina, 19 Nov 1847

SPOUSE II: Jens Madsen
MARRIED: 27 Dec 1850
Denmark
DEATH: 3 Nov 1910
Honeyville, Utah

CHILDREN:
none–raised two grandsons

"Annie Margaret" was born in Denmark in 1818. When she was young, she married Johan Eliason. They were the parents of two children. The son died and some years later the husband died. Annie was left with her daughter to raise. She worked very hard to support herself and her child. Some time after, she married Jens Madsen, in Denmark.

They heard the Mormon missionaries and became members of the Mormon Church. Annie and Jens did not have children.

They emigrated to America in Nov 1854, but the ship broke and they drifted back to Norway. Three months later, they left Liverpool, England on the ship "James Nesmith." They landed in New Orleans on 23 Feb 1855. They lived in Kansas about two years to work to get means to travel to the Salt Lake Valley. Annie took in washing and did all that she could to help.

They crossed the Plains by ox team. One of their oxen died and they had to hitch up their milk cow. While at Fort Laramie, Wyoming, their ox and cow both gave out and they came into the Salt Lake Valley with another Company from Texas, driving cattle. They arrived 12 Sep 1857. They stayed in Salt Lake a short time and then moved to Scoll Valley to help take care of the cattle of Homer Dunklin. When the call to move South came they moved to Grantsville. They stayed there one year and then moved to Brigham City where Jens worked for Lorenzo Snow. Jens was a shoemaker by trade. They lived in Brigham City eight years. Annie had a loom and spun her own yarn and did her own sewing.

They moved to Honeyville, Utah and started farming. The stage drivers often stayed with them and ate their meals there. Annie was a very industrious woman. She always helped the poor and sick. Her daughter, Laura, became the second wife of Jens Madsen. She had three children by him. When Josephine was six months old Laura left Jens and married Nels Knudsen. She took Josephine with her, leaving the two boys to be raised by her mother, Annie. She raised the two boys to manhood and was very good to them.

She had been suffering with a tumor of the stomach and died 10 Apr 1896 in Honeyville, Utah.

ANNE METTE ERICKSEN MADSEN

No Photo Available

BIRTHDATE: 15 Dec 1839
Morkholt, Gaarslev, Veijle, Denmark
DEATH: 11 Feb 1934
Willard, Box Elder, Utah
PARENTS: Soren William Ericksen
Bodil Kirstine Kyhn Ericksen
PIONEER: 1863
John R. Young Wagon Train
SPOUSE: Hans Peter Madsen, Sr.
MARRIED: 19 Dec 1863
Salt Lake City, Utah
DEATH: 4 Nov 1906
Willard, Box Elder, Utah

CHILDREN:
Hans Peter, Jr., 25 Oct 1864
Anne Mette, 25 Apr 1867
Christina, 1 Mar 1869
Mathew, 12 Aug 1871
Serena Katherine, 29 Oct 1873
Charles, 25 Oct 1875
Zina, 30 Oct 1878

Anne Mette was born in Denmark in 1839. As a young girl in Denmark, she learned to milk cows, make butter and cheese. She raised chickens, geese, sheep, cattle and hogs. They raised hay, grain, vegetables, fruit and flowers. She learned to sheer the sheep, card the wool, spin, weave it, and sew the cloth into clothing. She learned to butcher hogs and cattle, make sausage, cure meat, and make head cheese. She also learned to make soap, to bottle fruit, make jams and jellies and to cook. She was not happy to be called a peasant. The skills she learned helped her much in her pioneer living, even though they were thought to be 'peasant' skills.

Anne Mette had seven children, the first three were born in the Cottonwood area of the Salt Lake Valley. The last four were born by 1871 when they lived in Willard, Box Elder County. Anne had come to Utah in 1863, and she was married in December of that year.

Anne served as a Relief Society visiting teacher for many years. She loved to dance, and it is said that even in her seventies she could waltz with a glass of water on her head. She was a great pioneer woman whose early skills and training stood her well in the new land of the West in her new homeland. Anne died in 1937.

BERTHA KNUDSEN MADSEN

BIRTHDATE: 26 Feb 1860
Ostre Sveen, Loten, Hedemarken, Norway
DEATH: 13 May 1949
Lakeview, Utah Co., Utah
PARENTS: Hans Knudsen
Bergitte Larsen Johnsen Knudsen
PIONEER: Oct 1864
John Smith Independent Company
SPOUSE: Peter Madsen, Jr.
MARRIED: 2 Jun 1881
Salt Lake City, Utah
DEATH: 11 Apr 1942
Lakeview, Utah, Utah

CHILDREN:
Hans Peter, 5 May 1882
John William, 22 Apr 1884
Anna Pearl, 3 Apr 1887
Clara, 8 Nov 1890
Evelyn, 12 Jun 1893
Spencer, 4 Nov 1895
Raymond Lamar, 22 Apr 1901

Bertha was born in Norway in 1860. Her father had been educated for the ministry of the Lutheran Church. Her mother had had an earlier marriage. They were introduced to the LDS Church and the parents were baptized in Jan 1863. They became the object of much persecution, and decided, therefore, to sell their possessions, and leave their beloved homeland for Zion, with their eight children. They had considerable silver, china, woolens ready for the journey. They traveled to Denmark, Hamburg, and then crossed the ocean. Her father purchased the best team and wagon available to make the journey across the plains. Along the way they were asked to leave their valuable treasures, with an understanding they would get them back, but they never saw them again.

They traveled to Provo in Oct, six months after leaving Norway. The family began farming without any implements to work with. Bertha worked alongside her brothers, came home and cut grass for their twelve oxen, and then assisted with the housework, and did the washing by hand. She cut and dried apples and peaches which she sold by the bushel. Her schooling was limited, but she did attend school long enough to learn to read and write.

Bertha married Peter Madsen, Jr., 2 Jun 1881 in the Salt Lake Endowment House. She had declared when asked to marry him, "There will be but one wife!" And there was. They built a small home which was added to from time to time. Their seven children were born and raised there. She was an ardent Relief Society visiting teacher, having a perfect thirty year record. This family spent their summers at the Madsen fishing camp in Strawberry, but she returned to Lakeview monthly to do her visiting teaching. She crocheted and tatted, was very quiet, was always prayerful, and attended church regularly. She never had running water in her home. She was a loving wife and mother. She lived most of her life in Lakeview,

Utah where she passed away 13 May 1949 at the age of eighty-nine years. Her husband had passed away seven years earlier. She was a wonderful, loving mother who raised a good family. She was industrious, a hard worker, and loved order and beauty.

BIRGITHE POULSDATTER / JENSEN MADSEN

BIRTHDATE. 23 Jul 1853
Dronninglund, Hiorring, Denmark
DEATH: 15 Sep 1932
Salem, Utah, Utah
PARENTS: Poul Martines Jensen
Mette Kjerstine Olsdatter Jensen
PIONEER: 8 Oct 1866
Andrew Scott Wagon Train
SPOUSE: James Ephraim Madsen
MARRIED: 6 Jul 1869
Salt Lake City, Utah
DEATH: 26 Mar 1915
Salem, Utah, Utah

CHILDREN:
James Ephraim, 24 Aug 1870
Enoch Martines, 3 Jul 1873
Mads Jonathan, 20 Sep 1875
Joseph Lorenzo, 4 Sep 1877
Ervin Erastus, 11 Dec 1879
Franklin Oliver, 18 Nov 1881
Bodelia Christine, 12 Dec 1883
Elmer LeRoy, 8 Jul 1889

Birgithe was born in Denmark in 1853. At the age of thirteen, Bergithe left Denmark with her parents and sister for the sake of the Gospel. At Omaha they were met by wagons from Utah and left with the Scott wagon train. Thirty members died during the crossing of the plains. Birgithe walked most of the way, their feet becoming sore and bleeding as they wore out shoes made from old hats. This family settled in Spanish Fork, Utah where they dug a dugout to store their belongings and lived in a tent until they could build a two room log house. Birgithe's father made the adobe and she and her sister mixed the mud and water with their bare feet.

Birgithe had gone to school just one year in Denmark, and she did not have the chance to attend in America. She worked until she was married at the age of sixteen to James Ephraim Madsen. He had come to America on the same ship she had, but they did not know each other until meeting in Spanish Fork, Utah. They moved to Salem, and lived in a wagon until they could build an adobe house. They added to their one room and finally built a large ten room brick house. Birgithe became the mother of nine children.

She was set apart as treasurer of the Relief Society in February 1884 and maintained that position for twenty-seven years. She spent many hours making temple clothes for the dead and other sewing that was needed. She helped lay out the dead and did much waiting upon the sick. She

had a cheerful, happy disposition, and was a good wife and mother.

Although she had many trials, she tried to look on the bright side. In her later years she would visit her children and teach her granddaughters to crochet and tat. She always loved to dance and her sons would see that she had a partner at the dances. Birgithe's husband died in 1915. He served many years as chairman of the Board of Education and was an active church worker. Birgithe passed away 15 Sep 1932 at the age of seventy-nine years in Salem, Utah.

CAROLINE KNUDSEN (KAREN JENSEN) MADSEN

BIRTHDATE: 3 Apr 1838
Toreby, Maribo, Denmark
DEATH: 20 Feb 1919
Lake View, Utah, Utah
PARENTS: Knud Jensen
Bodil Olsen Jensen
PIONEER: 15 Sep 1859
Robert F. Neslen Wagon Train
SPOUSE: Peter Madsen
MARRIED: 25 Apr 1860
Salt Lake City, Utah
DEATH: 20 Aug 1911
Provo, Utah, Utah

CHILDREN:
James, 7 Jan 1861
MaryAnn, 3 Oct 1862
Caroline, 25 Oct 1864
Ephraim, 28 May 1867
Bodil Margaret, 6 Mar 1869
Sarah Elizabeth, 15 Jul 1872
Dorthy (Dorthea), 9 Mar 1875
Charles Alfred, 23 Oct 1877
Eliza, 22 Mar 1880

Caroline (Karen Jensen) was born in Toreby, Denmark in 1838. She came to Utah in 1859. Her parents were also pioneers who came to Utah 1862. Caroline had left Denmark with three of her sisters 1 Apr 1859, traveled by steamboat, rail, sailing ship, ox team, wagon train and foot to reach the Salt Lake Valley. Soon after her arrival, she met Peter Madsen and entered into plural marriage as his third wife. She bore nine children, seven of whom grew to adulthood and married.

Caroline was very active in the Church and her husband was a bishop. She served as Relief Society President and counselor. She did her share of the farm work while her husband fulfilled two missions for the Church. Following the Manifesto, Caroline remained in Lake View while her husband moved to Provo with his fourth wife. Caroline depended on her children for help and support. She spent the last ten years of her life in a wheelchair.

Peter Madsen died in Provo 20 Aug 1911. His last two wives, Caroline and Wilhelmina, died within twenty four hours of each other Feb 19 and 20, 1919. A joint funeral service was held for them and they were buried side by side in the Provo City Cemetery. A newspaper clipping dated Friday, Feb 21, 1919 follows:

"With their lives closely interwoven for more than half a century in which they shared each other's joys and sorrows, the two remaining widows of the late Peter Madsen, identified with the interests of Utah County and one of the pioneer characters of this section, have passed to the great beyond. Mrs. Wilhelmina Madsen passed to her rest Wed, and Thurs. morning Mrs. Caroline K. Madsen was called. Both had suffered much in their declining years and the solicitation of each for the other's health brought joy to the hearts of the children who survived them.

"As a fitting tribute to their long association a double funeral will be held in the Second Ward Chapel, Sunday at one o'clock. . . ."

CHRISTINA PEDERSEN MADSEN

No Photo Available

BIRTHDATE: 17 Sep 1823
Vadum, Aalborg, Denmark
DEATH: 8 Oct 1902
Willard, Box Elder, Utah
PARENTS: Christian Pedersen
Berthe Jensdatter
PIONEER: 1860
Wagon train
SPOUSE: Hans Peter Madsen Sr.
MARRIED: Before 14 Apr 1858
Denmark
DEATH SP: 4 Nov 1906
Willard, Box Elder, Utah

CHILDREN: None

Christina Pederson was born in Denmark in 1823. She married Hans Peter Madsen in 1858 in Denmark. They came to Utah in 1860 by wagon train.

Christina was not blessed with children. Her husband married Edith Ella Robbins in 1888, (6 children); and married Evangeline Brig Ida Nielsen in 1872, (8 children). The family lived in Big Cottonwood in Salt Lake County, then moved to Willard in Box Elder County about 1868. He was a carpenter, farmer and stockraiser. Christina was the field superintendent on the Madsen farm. She died in Willard in 1902, and Hans died in 1906, also in Willard, Utah.

DOROTHEA KIRSTINE HANSEN MADSEN

BIRTHDATE: 11 Jan 1817
Skibsted, Aalborg, Denmark
DEATH: 5 Mar 1891
Bloomington, Bear Lake, Idaho
PARENTS: Hans Jensen
Anna Christensen
PIONEER: 13 Sep 1857
Mathias Cowley Co. &
Christian Christiansen Handcart Co.
SPOUSE: Jacob (Christensen) Madsen
MARRIED: 16 Apr 1838
Skibsted, Aalborg, Denmark
DEATH: 10 Jun 1879
Bloomington, Bear Lake, Idaho

CHILDREN:
Christen, 19 Jun 1838
Hans, 30 Jan 1840
Anna, 22 May 1842
Christen, 14 Nov 1844
Niels, 4 Dec 1846
Eliza, 22 Apr 1849
Anton Peter, 16 Jun 1851
Inger Marie, 24 Jun 1854
Franklin, 1 Dec 1856
Jacob Madsen, 5 Jan 1860

Dorothea was raised on a farm. She learned to make flax into linen, to sheer sheep, to use the wool to make bedding and winter underwear. She married Jacob Christensen and they settled in Skibsted, Denmark where eight children were born to them before they heard the gospel of the LDS Church and became members. They began their emigration in the winter of 1856-57 and were in Hurup, Denmark when their son, Franklin, was born. On April 18, 1857 the family boarded the "L. N. Hvidt Steamer" with a company of 536 fellow saints headed for Grimsby, England. They went by rail to Liverpool where they boarded the "Westmoreland" to cross the ocean and arrived in Philadelphia, Pennsylvania on May 31, 1857. They continued their journey westward by rail from Philadelphia to Iowa. The railroad cars they traveled in were rough cars or cattle cars. One evening they had to wait for another train all night while standing in the cold rain. Their son, Franklin, died.

From Iowa, they were crossing the Plains with the Mathias Cowley Ox-team Company and the Christian Christiansen Handcart Company. Their journey was full of the usual physical hardships plus a great anxiety because just across the river traveling parallel with them was the Johnston Army headed west to "wipe out the Mormons." On the 13th of September, 1857 they arrived in Salt Lake Valley where they camped on the North side of the city for three days.

Because of the threat of the army, Brigham Young sent all other saints down into southern Utah for safety. Dorothea and Jacob stayed the winter of 1857-58 in Nephi, Utah. When peace was declared between Utah and the United States, they moved to Ogden, Utah. Another son was born in Ogden. Years later, they moved to

Bloomington, Idaho where they lived the rest of their lives. They had ten children. Dorothea died in 1891, at the age of seventy-four.

GUSTAVA AMALEA LUNDSTROM CAPSSON MADSEN (MADSON)

BIRTHDATE: 17 Feb 1836
Sandakra, Skona, Sweden
DEATH: 16 Aug 1914
Gunnison, Sanpete, Utah
PARENTS: Neils Henry
Christina Bendicta
Swenson Lundstrom
PIONEER: 7 Sep 1855
SPOUSE I: Nils Capsson
MARRIED: 5 Feb 1854
aboard "Benjamin Adams" at sea
DEATH: 10 Sep 1863
Virgin, Utah

CHILDREN:
Mary Magdalena, 1 Sep 1856
Sarah Christina, 31 Jul 1858
Emma Ulrica, 17 Mar 1862

SPOUSE II: Bishop Christian A. Madson
MARRIED: 3 Jul 1864
Gunnison, Utah

Gustava Amalea (Amelia) Lundstrom was born in Sandakra, Skona, Sweden in 1836 to Neils and Christina Lundstrom. Nils Capsson was in Sweden as a student and missionary from his home in Denmark. The first branch of the church in Sweden was organized in Malmo and he was made president of this branch. He converted and baptized Gustava who was the second lady converted to the Church in Sweden. He was eventually driven out of Sweden by the police because of his missionary activities. He went to Kiel, Germany, reached Liverpool, England on 16 Jan 1854. Nils and Gustava Amelia set sail for America 2 Feb 1854. They were married 5 Feb 1854 while on board the ship "Benjamin Adams." Nine couples were married on the ship. They landed at New Orleans 22 Mar 1854, reached St. Louis 4 April, and finally arrived in the Salt Lake Valley 7 Sep 1855, after a year in St. Louis. In Salt Lake City, they took up farming and he planted trees around the Tabernacle block.

Their first year in Utah was spent on his brother's farm in Millcreek. Because of the crickets, their first month's meals were mainly composed of greens.

On 2 Apr 1861, they moved to Ephraim, Sanpete Co., and were then called to move to Dixie by Nov 1861. Their life in Virgin City, Dixie Co., was not for long. Nils Capsson died from pneumonia 10 Sep 1863, from exposure wading the Virgin River for straying cattle. He had been a large, powerful man of six ft., with black eyes and black curly hair. His widow and three small daughters were left to face their pioneer lives in Virgin City alone. Their home

had been a cave in the hillside. Gustava and her daughters managed to make their way to Gunnison in Sanpete Co. Here she entered into a polygamous marriage with Christian A. Madsen (Madson) for time only. She provided for her family by working as a servant for Christian's first wife.

Gustava Lundstrom was sealed to Nils Capsson in the Manti Temple 15 May 1889. Following her marriage to Bishop Madsen, Gustava's father Neils Lundstrom came to America to Gunnison in July 1864. He made a home for his daughter and granddaughters and lived in Gunnison until his death in 1888.

Gustava enjoyed accompanying her grandchildren to Provo and Salt Lake when they attended school at the Brigham Young Academy or the University of Utah. She enjoyed the environment of these campuses and enjoyed being a homemaker for these grandchildren. Her home in Gunnison was where she lived until her death. It was always referred to as "Grandma Capsson's."

Gustava was a beautiful woman, with brown eyes and lovely brown wavy hair. She wore a poke-bonnet style of hat all of her life, with her wavy hair beneath it, and the strings tied under her chin. In winter the hat was plush with tips of feathers and ribbon for trim. In the summer it was straw and had a trim of flowers. In her later years, her children loved the beauty of her hair as they combed it with its waves, evenly spaced all down the full length of her soft white hair.

Gustava was a Relief Society Councilor and a teacher for more than 40 years as she lived in Gunnison. She passed away there 16 Aug 1914 and was buried in the Gunnison Cemetery. She was over seventy-eight years of age, having had a life of hardships, trials, and tribulations that accompanied the lives of these early pioneer women. Truly she was among the women of great faith and fortitude.

JOHANNA (HANNAH) ANDERSEN MADSEN

BIRTHDATE: 1 Jan 1853
on board ship "Forest Monarch"
DEATH: 12 Apr 1938
Manti, Sanpete, Utah
PARENTS: William Andersen
Henrietta Laurentze Berntzen
Andersen
PIONEER: 30 Sept 1853
Wagon Train
SPOUSE: Jorgen Madsen
MARRIED: 12 Dec 1870
DEATH SP: 17 Oct 1936
Manti, Sanpete, Utah

CHILDREN:
Ernest, 30 Sep 1871
Evelyn, 12 Apr 1873
Ida Ardell, 6 Feb 1875
Ellice, 4 Dec 1876

Spencer William, 20 Mar 1878
Mary Henrietta, 23 Jan 1883
Lowe, 5 Nov 1884
Leslie Jorgan, 17 Jun 1896
Clifton Vernon, 19 Apr 1898
daughter, 4 Jun 1900

Johanna (Hannah) Andersen was born in 1853 on board the ship "Forest Monarch." During rough seas, the first few days, the baby was tossed from the bed. She had been wrapped in a long piece of cloth that unwound as she rolled away. They found her unharmed, but blue with cold.

The group arrived in New Orleans 19 Mar 1853, and after a hard, trying trip by wagon train, they arrived in the Salt Lake Valley 30 Sep. On Oct 4, they left for Spring City (little Denmark) where they intended to make their home. But on 15 Dec, orders were received from President Brigham Young to leave at once and move to Manti because of Indian troubles. It was a cold afternoon when they arrived and Elisha Edwards shared his one room home. They were eleven in number. In the spring, the family moved into a cellar and later into an adobe home. Their diet consisted mainly of vegetables, including segoes, and pig weed later in the season.

Johannah had met Jorgan Madsen in 1863 as he helped unload the family treasures his family had brought from Denmark. She prepared for her marriage during the spring and summer of 1870 by making her wedding clothes by hand. She made the ruffles on the sheer white wedding dress and the fine tatted lace. Her petticoats were embroidered by hand. She made a supply of nice wedding quilts, two down pillows, a straw tick and some rugs. They were married 12 Dec 1870 in the Endowment House in Salt Lake City. Their first home was in Manti, and in 1872, they moved into their brick home using the lumber they had saved for two years. Eight of their ten children were born there.

Hanhah had the only sewing machine in Manti. She sometimes sewed buckskin for the Indians but she was uneasy if Jorgen was away, and felt very relieved when the sewing was finished.

Johannah was truly a great pioneer woman. She had extreme faith and was a devout member of the LDS Church. She died 12 Apr 1938 at the age of eighty-five years. Her husband had passed away in 1936.

LENA JOHNSON MADSEN

BIRTHDATE: 9 Dec 1846
Loiten, Hedamarken, Norway
DEATH: 3 Sep 1915
Vineyard, Utah, Utah
PARENTS: John Johnson
Birgetta Larson Johnson
PIONEER: 1 Oct 1864
John Smith Wagon Train
SPOUSE: Peter Madsen
MARRIED: 2 Sep 1865
Salt Lake City, Utah
DEATH SP: 20 Aug 1911
Provo, Utah, Utah

CHILDREN:
Julia, 27 Nov 1866
John Joseph, Feb 1868
Ellen Bergitta, 29 Nov 1870
Hyrum, 2 Nov 1872
Marie (Maria) 23 Dec 1874
Alma Theodore, 18 Apr 1877
Parley William, 22 Oct 1879
Inger Bertha Christina, 20 Mar 1883
Edwin Anton, 18 Jul 1885

Lena was born in Norway in 1846, the second daughter. Lena's father died of appendicitis when Lena was just three years old. Her mother then married Hans Knudsen and five more children were added to this extended family.

Lena's stepfather was a successful farmer. They had servants to help both inside and outside the home. Lena loved the outdoor life. She was in the fields and around their animals as much as possible. She warmed water in the winter for the animals and put grain on the top of the barn on Christmas Eve so the birds could have a good Christmas breakfast. This is still a Norwegian custom. Lena always had the best of health and she had unusual strength. She attended school until age fourteen. Elders from the LDS Church called at their home. Her father was well read and studied a great deal and became interested in this new religion. He witnessed the healing of their young daughter, and this influenced him greatly.

When they decided to be baptized, Father Knudsen marched his whole family to the frozen pond, cut a hole through the ice and the baptisms took place there. Lena was not old enough to be baptized. She was troubled about their talk of emigrating to America, but she did leave with her family. They traveled on the ship, "Monarch of the Sea," crossed the plains and Lena walked all the way driving the cattle.

One day walking back of the wagon train, she found a little girl who had fallen out of a wagon, and the parents had not been aware that she had been left. The child was very ill with measles, but her life was saved by Lena's actions. Her younger sister died of measles and was buried in Echo Canyon just above Salt Lake Valley. The group reached the valley in 1864. Lena did get baptized 24 Nov 1864.

In 1865, in the fall, Lena married Peter Madsen as his fifth wife. The families all lived together in one home. Dances and community parties were often held in this home.

Peter was called on a mission to Hawaii. He spoke to Lena about going with him, but she felt it would be better for her to remain in Lake View with her family. This upset Peter and he did not enter Lena's home after his return. His property was divided among his other wives.

Lena's children often recalled their mother with a hymn book in her hand singing the songs of Zion. She especially liked "O My Father" and "O Babylon, We Bid Thee Farewell." She gave great support and love to her children and their families throughout her life. She died 3 Sep 1915 in the home of her son Joseph in Vineyard, Utah, surrounded by her family. She was indeed a great and good pioneer woman of faith and fortitude. She was nearly seventy-nine years old when she passed away.

MARTHA MARIA HANSEN MADSEN

BIRTHDATE: 14 Sep 1816
Skorenge, Maribo, Denmark
DEATH: 18 Mar 1896
Brigham City, Box Elder, Utah
PARENTS: Niels Hansen
Catherine Sophia Jacobsen
PIONEER: 10 Aug 1860
Warren Walling Co
SPOUSE: Nels Madsen
MARRIED: 25 Oct 1839
Denmark
DEATH: 18 May 1891
Brigham City, Box Elder, Utah

CHILDREN:
Adolphus, 12 Jun 1841
Peter F., 10 Aug 1843
Sophia Karen, 3 May 1846
Caroline, 11 Jan 1848
Trene, 1851
Nels, 14 Aug 1853
Josephina, 1 Oct 1855
Naphena Melissa, 4 Oct 1858

Martha's father died when she was just an infant. Her mother married Peter Rasmussen who had two daughters. When Martha was eight years old, she was sent to live with her stepfather's sister. She returned home when she was fourteen and completed her education from the priest. For the next eight years, she lived at different homes until she married Nels Madsen. They made their home in Maribo, Denmark. They had six children by the time they heard the gospel of the LDS Missionaries. They were baptized on March 26, 1854. They were poor, but desired to immigrate to Zion. A friend helped to pay their fare. In the spring of 1857, they sailed from Copenhagen and landed in Philadelphia in July. The family settled in Fairfield, Iowa for three years where they worked to earn the provisions

needed for the remainder of their trip across the plains. As they were crossing the plains, Martha's skirt became entangled in the wheel. She was pulled under the wagon wheel which ran over her breast and head. Through the blessings of the Lord, she recovered. She carried the scars for the rest of her life. They arrived in Salt Lake City on August 10, 1860.

They stayed a short time in Big Cottonwood Canyon, then decided to settle in Brigham City. That winter, they lived in a cellar until they could purchase a lot and build a small adobe home for their family the following spring. This was their home for many years. Martha was a great friend to the Indians and when called, she always gave them food and visited with them.

Nels and Martha traveled to Salt Lake to the Endowment House and were sealed on June 28, 1867. Martha died at the age of eighty, in 1896.

MARY ANN MADSDATTER MONK MADSEN

BIRTHDATE: 7 Oct 1815
Bredstrup, Vejle, Denmark
DEATH: 18 Apr 1881
Lake View, Utah, Utah
PARENTS: Mads Jensen
Anne Marie Olesdatter
PIONEER: 5 Oct 1854
Hans Peter Olsen
SPOUSE: Peter Madsen
MARRIED: 12 Nov 1847
Bredstrup, Bejle, Denmark
DEATH SP: 20 Aug 1911
Provo, Utah, Utah

CHILDREN:
Mads Peter, 5 Aug 1848
Ane Marie, 25 Jun 1850
Hans Ole, 15 Jan 1853
John, 5 May 1855
Peter, Jr., 2 Jun 1858

Mary was married to Peter Madsen in November of 1847. From 1848 to 1849, Peter fought in the Danish-German War. They had three children by the time they joined the LDS Church on June 11, 1853. On Christmas Day in 1853, they sailed for Hull, England on the small steamer, "Eideren." From Hull, they took a train to Liverpool. During the trip, an unidentified fever caused the deaths of their two youngest children. They continued their journey on the sailing ship, "Benjamin Adams," arriving in New Orleans. From there, they sailed up the Mississippi River. They arrived in the Salt Lake Valley on October 5, 1854.

First they lived in Sanpete County near Mt. Pleasant for about a year. Then they settled near the mouth of the Provo River. Due to the generosity of Peter and Mary Ann, many people were fed during the grasshopper period of 1855-56.

People came from as far away as Sevier on the south and Salt Lake on the north. They came with wagons, barrels, and salt to prepare fish for the winter. They fished day and night until they had enough salted or dried fish for the winter. Scores of barrels of fish were also sent to the neighboring settlements to be distributed among the poor. They were also generous with the Indians and were on friendly terms with them, often supplying them with fish. From 1859 to 1862, Mary Ann and Peter lived with three other families in a sort of fort with a house in each corner near the mouth of the Provo River. In 1862, the lake overflowed and they were forced to move to higher ground. Peter built a home nearly a mile upstream on the bank of the river. In this home was conducted the first school in Lake View. It was here the neighbors came from some distance for dances, parties, and food. New and younger wives were accepted into the family. They outgrew the original home and three additional houses were built, one for each of the newer wives. Mary Ann supported him all the years he served as bishop of Lake View Ward and when he was called on a mission to Denmark. She was much loved and respected by the other wives, and all of the children called her "mother." Mary Ann died in 1881.

METTE JOHANNA ANDERSON MADSEN

No Photo Available

BIRTHDATE: 29 Aug 1834
Thorby, Denmark
DEATH: 18 Apr 1896
Manti, Utah
PARENTS: Anders Westeson
Karen Sorenson Swenson (Svendson)
PIONEER: Fall 1863
SPOUSE: Ole Madsen
MARREID: Fall 1864
Manti, Sanpete, Utah
DEATH SP: 17 Mar 1881
Manti, Sanpete, Utah

CHILDREN:
Peter James, 25 Sep 1865
Ole, 4 Aug 1867
Annie, 21 Dec 1869
Andrew "O," 4 Oct 1874

Mette Johanna was born in Denmark in 1834. As a young woman Mette had learned to cook and knew all the processes of caring for and curing meat. She made especially good sausage. She knew what herbs and greens to use to make meals especially good which helped a great deal when she was crossing the plains. She was always on the lookout for wild berries and onions which pleased those she cooked for.

When she heard the Mormon Elders, she believed, was baptized, and decided to emigrate to America. She joined two other maiden ladies from a nearby town, Ole and Ann Madsen and their children. Mette was baptized 25 May 1862. Their journey first took them across the North Sea,

England by rail, and from Liverpool by ship. When they were ready to sail, Mr. and Mrs. Madsen were compelled to go ashore with a sick baby. They also kept with them their youngest child and asked the maiden ladies to take their other children to Utah with them. They were seven weeks on the Atlantic and the water supply had become almost unbearable. They landed at New York, went up the Hudson with beds made on the deck, and at Albany they boarded a train for Florence, Nebraska. Bodell bought a cow so the children would have fresh milk. The three ladies and the oldest Madsen, Christena, walked the distance both looking for berries and greens and prodding the cow.

When the Madsens arrived, they were directed to Manti where Brigham Young felt there was a need for a blacksmith. The Madsens had buried their baby and had then traveled with the next company from England. Ann's health was poor and she lived only two months after their arrival in Utah. After struggling for a year trying to keep his family intact, Ole Madsen sent his son Jorgen from Manti to Gunnison with a letter of proposal of marriage to Johanna. She had stayed with a friend in Gunnison. Ole waited for her acceptance letter and returned with it the same day. Ole and Mette Johanna were married that fall in 1864.

With Ole's blacksmithing, carpentry and farming talents, and Johanna's skill in cooking, curing meat, sewing, flower and herb raising, they soon had a beautiful home built with a yard with all kinds of fruit trees. It was a nice change from the first dugout home they had occupied. She was a true pioneer woman who had given up much for her religious beliefs but who was always thankful for the opportunities she had in this new land. She died at sixty-one years of age

METTE MARIE CHRISTENSEN MADSEN

BIRTHDATE: 13 Sep 1815
Lerbjerg, Randers, Denmark
DEATH: 16 Mar 1896
Manti, Sanpete County, Utah
PARENTS: Christen Hansen
Kirsten Nielsen Christensen
PIONEER: 5 Sep 1863
John Frank Sanders Company
SPOUSE: Niels Madsen
MARRIED: 19 Oct 1838
Denmark
DEATH: 25 Sep 1878
Manti, Utah

CHILDREN:
Mads Nielsen, 4 Sep 1838/39
Christen Nielsen, 11 Jun 1840
Kirsten Marie Nielsen, 2 Feb 1842
Inger Kirstine Nielsen, 7 May 1844
Jens Peter Nielsen, 22 Feb 1847
Inger Kerstine Nielsen, 3 Apr 1849
Jens Christian Nielsen, 27 Mar 1851
Marie Kirstine, 13 Jun 1853
Jens Peter, 9 Jun 1860

Mette Christensen Madsen was born in Denmark, near the Baltic Sea. Little is known of her childhood. She married Niels Madsen 19 Oct 1838. They owned farmland and dairy cattle and a home in Vorup on the Jutland Peninsula. Mette Marie joined the Church of Jesus Christ of Latter-day Saints. She was baptized 20 Apr 1862; her husband joined a month later. The family farm provided a good living. They decided to sell their farm and emigrate to the Valley of the Great Salt Lake in America. They had plenty of money to pay the costs of moving the family to Salt Lake City, Utah.

In the Spring of 1863, Mette Marie, her husband and children traveled by train to Hamburg, Germany and by sailing vessel to England. They sailed from Liverpool, England on board the sailing ship "B.S. Kimball" under the charge of Hans Peter Lund. The trip across the ocean was in stormy weather, lasting five weeks. Most of the passengers were seasick. They had insufficient, unbalanced meals and rancid water.

They arrived in the New York harbor and traveled by train and steamer to Florence, Nebraska. Here they rested two weeks, making preparations to make the 1,000 mile trip to the Salt Lake Valley. Mette Marie's second oldest son, Christen, died during their stay in Florence. He was twenty-two years old. They joined the wagon-train Company of John F. Sanders. The trail to Zion was one of death, stretching across the Plains and over the Rocky Mountains. Mette Marie met the trials of a pioneer woman's life with courage and unwavering faith. She was as the Danish people: honest, thrifty, hospitable and God-fearing. She endeavored to do right all of the time. She taught her family the principle of ambition, to make the most of their circumstances and to live and walk justly before their God.

Mette Marie, her husband and children, walked the entire distance from Florence, Nebraska to the Salt Lake Valley. The Company left Florence 6 July and arrived in the Salt Lake Valley on 3 October 1863. The family walked because their wagons carried all their earthly possessions and supplies. After their arrival in the Salt Lake Valley, the family spent about two weeks resting and preparing to move to their new home in Sanpete County. They lived, at first, in Ephraim, Utah and then found their permanent home in Manti, Utah. All of their children accompanied them to Manti. Mette Marie and her husband spent the remainder of their lives as early settlers of Manti. Mette Marie passed away 16 March 1896 and was buried beside her husband in the Manti City Cemetery. She had been a widow for almost eighteen years.

WILHELMINA JORGENSEN (NEILSEN) MADSEN

BIRTHDATE: 5 Nov 1847
Hjerup, Odense, Denmark
DEATH: 19 Feb 1919
Lakeview, Utah County, Utah
PARENTS: Neils Jorgensen
Johanna Peterson Jorgensen
PIONEER: 1863
Wagon Train
SPOUSE: Peter Madsen
MARRIED: 14 May 1864
Salt Lake City, Utah
DEATH: 25 Apr 1911
Provo, Utah

CHILDREN:
Nels Christian, 7 Oct 1865
Rosema (Minnie), 16 Mar 1868
Johanna, 11 Jan 1871
Brigham, 15 Jun 1873
George Abraham, 25 Nov 1875
Emma, 11 Aug 1878
David Heber, 12 Feb 1881
Mary Josephine (May), 28 Apr 1883
Albert Ephraim, 5 Aug 1884
Annie Juline, 24 Sep 1887
Clarence Elmer, 5 May 1893

Wilhelmina was-born in Denmark. She lived there until she became a member of the LDS Church. In 1863 she walked all the way from the Missouri River to the Salt Lake Valley. The Company she traveled with is not given. The next year after her arrival she married Peter Madsen and settled with him in Lakeview, Utah County, Utah. She was an active Church worker in Lakeview for many years. She moved to Provo, Utah about fifteen years before her death and made Provo her home.

She married Peter Madsen in plural marriage. His first wife, Mary Ann, was very wise and patient. All of the younger wives went to her for counsel and advice. All of the families lived in one home. They all shared the large living room which was often used as a community dance hall. They hosted a reunion twice each year for the Scandinavian Pioneers. They came from far and wide to attend this gala affair. His wives were busy preparing for these large groups. All the wives got along well and shared household work. They raised and sheared sheep, dyed the wool, carded, spun and wove it into fabric. They made all the family clothing. Peter Madsen was called on a mission to Hawaii at the time the Federal Authorities were interfering with men taking care of more than one wife and family. He was in Hawaii from 1886 until 1889. Wilhelmina accompanied him to the Islands. His property was divided among his families. Upon their return to Utah, Peter lived with Wilhelmina and another wife, Caroline, and their families until his death in 1911.

Wilhelmina and Caroline lived together more than half a century. They were the two remaining widows of Peter

Madsen. Their lives were closely interwoven with love and devotion. They were two beloved women in the community. They contributed much to their Church and community. Wilhelmina died 19 Feb 1919. The following morning Caroline passed away. As a fitting tribute to their long association a double funeral was held. Many floral offerings decorated the caskets. The two women were buried in a double grave at the Provo City Cemetery.

ANNA HENRIETTA THERESE MEITH MAESER

No Photo Available

BIRTHDATE: 4 May 1830
Dresden, Saxony, Germany
DEATH: 2 Apr 1896
Salt Lake City, Utah
PARENTS:
Karl Benjamin Immanuel Meith
Henrietta Christian Backhaus Meith
PIONEER: 1 Sep 1860
John Smith Wagon Train
SPOUSE: Karl Gottfried Maeser
MARRIED: 11 Jun 1854
Neustadt, Dresden, Germany
DEATH: 15 Feb 1901
Salt Lake City, Utah

CHILDREN:
Karl Frederick Reinhard, 19 Mar 1855
Karl Franklin "D," Feb 1857
Anna Ottilie (Delia), 1 Aug 1859
Mamie, 8 Feb 1862
Anna Camilla, 25 Apr 1863
Karl Emil, 29 Mar 1866
Evelyn (Eva), 21 Jun 1876
Helen Janette, 20 Jul 1873

Anna Henrietta was born in Germany and attended schools where she learned scholastic knowledge as well as homemaking skills of cooking and sewing. Her father was director of a school of higher learning. She married Karl Gottfried Maeser in 1854, who succeeded her father as director. They learned of the LDS Church. They were aware of the risk of imprisonment for investigating another Church. Anna was the first woman in Germany to be baptized. After she and her husband were baptized the extreme caution and slow communication with Church Leaders increased their desire to go to Zion.

In the middle of the night 6 Jun 1856, they secretly left Germany with as much as they dared take with them. Anna, Karl, three children and a son-in-law made their way to England. When Karl was called on a mission for the Church Anna supported him. In the middle of May 1857, they sailed for America. Many became ill and their baby died two days before reaching New York on 4 Jul 1857. Anna was thankful that they could bury their baby on the promised land. Their funds were exhausted. Karl was called on another mission to Virginia. Anna supported their family by sewing, mending and altering clothing. After the mission they journeyed by train to Florence, Nebraska.

They spent the Winter at Winter Quarters. In Jun 1860 they left for the journey across the plains to Utah. They arrived in the Salt Lake Valley 1 Sep 1860, four years and three months from the time they left Germany.

Karl was an educator and the pay was very little. Anna's greatest challenge in Zion was to make a cheerful home with less than the necessities. She always set the table with her best china from Germany, mended and pressed Karl's suit every night. Anna's responsibilities increased when Karl was called on a third mission. This time he went to England, Switzerland and Germany. Anna consented to plural marriage when the leaders of the Church asked Karl to marry a second wife. It was Anna's hardest challenge. The families moved to Provo when Karl was called to establish the Brigham Young Academy. She will always be remembered as a witty and vivacious person and a faithful, stalwart Latter-day Saint. She and Karl became the parents of eight children; three died in infancy. Anna died 2 Apr 1896 in Salt Lake City, Utah.

CAROLINE PENN MAIBEN

BIRTHDATE: 14 Mar 1817
Brighten, Sussex, England
DEATH: 14 Oct 1864
Salt Lake, Salt Lake, Utah
PARENTS: Thomas Penn
Sarah Edwards Penn
PIONEER: 30 Sep 1853
Jacob Gates Wagon Train
SPOUSE: Henry Maiben
MARRIED: 18 Dec 1845
Church of St. George,
Hanover Square, England
DEATH SP: 8 Oct 1883
Salt Lake, Salt Lake, Utah

CHILDREN:
Alice Penn (Squires) 16 Oct 1847
William Penn 26 Oct 1850
Marion 8 Jun 1853
Sarah Josephine 9 Sep 1855
Caroline (Lucas) 24 Apr 1857

Caroline was born in England, 1817. She married Henry Maiben in 1845 in England. She became a head dressmaker in a large dress shop in London. They prepared to leave London Feb 1853 on the ship "International" with Captain David Brown. After ten weeks of travel they landed in New Orleans. They traveled by ox team & wagon, the wagons were so full of provisions that many had to walk. Not long after leaving Keokuk, Iowa, Caroline gave birth to a daughter and later on she suffured with Mt. Fever. They arrived safely on Sept. 30, 1853. Her husband later became an actor in Old Salt Lake Dramatic Co. Caroline had charge of designing & making costumes. Rachel Ivans assisted her and they could authentically costume any play.

Caroline and her husband were sealed in the Endowment House 12 Mar 1854. They had five children, two of whom died young.

Caroline died at age forty-seven on 14 Oct 1864 in Salt Lake City, Utah. She was so well liked she had several poems written in her honor. Brigham Young spoke at her funeral.

The Deseret Dramatic club said of her, "She was our most worthy and usefull member. A lady of whom virtue, modesty and amiability won for her affection & esteem from all who had the pleasure of her acquaintance."

ELIZABETH RICHARDS MAIBEN

BIRTHDATE: 12 Apr 1821
Pater Pembroke, South Wales
DEATH: 10 Mar 1902
Manti, Utah
PARENTS:
James Williams Richards
Eleanor Williams Richards
PIONEER: 28 Sep 1855
Moses Thurston Wagon Train
SPOUSE: John Maiben
MARRIED: 22 Apr 1856
Salt Lake City, Utah
DEATH SP: 10 Mar 1910

CHILDREN:
Twin boys- died in infancy

Elizabeth was born in South Wales, one of four children. She met her husband, John Maiben, while investigating the Mormon Church. She was baptized in 1853 by John Maiben who was the husband of her sister, Phebe. Elizabeth was also known as Lizzie. On 22 Apr 1855, she and Phebe and John embarked for America on the ship "Samuel Curling" After reaching Council Bluffs, Iowa, they outfitted their wagons, bought supplies and began the arduous trip across the Plains. John served as a chaplain on the journey. They arrived in the Salt Lake Valley 28 Sep 1855.

There is some confusion as to the exact date that John and Elizabeth were married, but it was during the early part of their stay in the Valley. Their endowments were taken on 22 Apr 1856. In 1875, John was called to a mission in Manti, Utah to help settle Sanpete County. John built a large two-story home on "Maiben Street" where they lived the remainder of their lives. Elizabeth and her sister, Phebe, who was John's first wife, and John lived together. Elizabeth and John had twin boys, who only lived a short time.

Elizabeth and Phebe were well-educated and were gracious hostesses. They entertained early Presidents of the Mormon Church including Brigham Young, John Taylor, Wilford Woodruff, Lorenzo Snow, Joseph F. Smith and many other officers of the Church. They were involved with the Young Ladies' Mutual Improvement Association and the Primary Organization. They were also involved with the organization of the Relief Society in Manti. There was endless entertaining of guests in their home, which became the center of social affairs of the area and the showplace of Manti in its time.

Elizabeth was interested in the Women's Suffrage Movement in Utah and was an early advocate of women's rights. She was the bookkeeper and social secretary to her husband. She also administered to the sick and needy in the community. She did exquisite embroidery, handmade laces and fine drawn work. She won prizes at State Annual Exhibitions for the best embroidered work and for the best white shirts for gentlemen.

Elizabeth died in Manti, Utah 10 Mar 1902 and was buried in the Salt Lake Cemetery. She was loved and respected by all those who knew her.

FLORA LOUISA MADDISON LONG MAIBEN

BORN: 25 Feb 1835
Ghent, East Flanders, Belgium
DEATH: 11 Jun 1922
Salt Lake City, Salt Lake, Utah
PARENTS:
John Francis Maddison
Maria Susannah Merrick Maddison
PIONEER: 2 Oct 1851
Alfred Cardon Wagon Co.
SPOUSE I: Emanuel Long
MARRIED: 23 Jan 1855
Salt Lake City
DEATH: Unknown

CHILDREN:
Henry Joseph William Maddison Long, 4 Nov 1855
(known as Henry Joseph Maiben)

SPOUSE II: Henry Maiben
MARRIED: 20 Jul 1855
Salt Lake City
DEATH: 10 Oct 1883
Salt Lake City

CHILDREN:
John Bray 20 Nov 1857
Rosina Maria (Jones) 28 Nov 1859
Emily May (Robbins) 23 May 1863
Catherine Mary (Candland), 11 Sep 1865
James, 4 Mar 1867
Phebe (Candland) 5 Jan 1868
George 5 Aug 1870
Flora Louise (Bates) 2 Sep 1872
Alfred Henry 30 Jul 1874
Hubert C. 25 Oct 1877
Elizabeth Harriet(Magelby) 27 Jun 1879

Flora Louisa was born in Belgium, 1835. She was named after the flowers grown in Belgium, where she was born. She was a well educated cultured woman, raised in a wealthy English family.

At the age of eight, it was discovered she had a cataract on one eye. She had many operations. When she and her mother joined the church her father told them to renounce their religion or leave their home. She, her mother, and two brothers chose to come to Utah. Flora Louisa was sixteen. She became ill with Mt. Fever, but recovered. She taught school in Salt Lake, while she and her family had to move into a small log house that had been used for a chicken coop. They sold many of their fancy clothes for necessities.

Flora Louise married Emanuel Long. They were divorced the same year. She then married Henry Maiben. They lived in Salt Lake until 1858 when Johnston's Army came. They moved back in 1873 when she and her husband were called to settle Provo. She had twelve children. She was widowed for forty years, and took in boarders to provide for her family. Her son's wife died, and she took her twelve-day-old granddaughter, and nursed her along with her own six-month-old baby.

She was an excellent seamstress, who also did knitting, especially knitted lace. She was an excellent cook. She grew roses, and had a vegetable garden. She was ever ready and willing to help anyone. She was an ardent church and temple worker.

LOUISA EVELINE HARRISON MAIBEN

BIRTHDATE: 9 Apr 1861
St. Joseph, Missouri
DEATH: 13 Apr 1912
Los Angeles, California
PARENTS: William Harrison
Hannah Adams Harrison
PIONEER: 30 Sep 1862
Wagon Train
SPOUSE: Henry Joseph Maiben
MARRIED: 30 Dec 1880
Salt Lake City, Utah
DEATH SP: 19 Apr 1907
Provo, Utah County, Utah

CHILDREN:
Louie
Myrtle, 24 Feb 1883
Warren Henry, 12 May 1884
Dora, 8 Dec 1886
Olive, 13 Nov 1888
Ada Blanche, 4 Aug 1890
Grover George, 12 Aug 1892
Heber John, 26 Apr 1895
Fenton Maddison, 6 Jul 1897
Afton, 11 Mar 1899

Louisa Eveline was born in Missouri, while her parents were on their way to the Salt Lake Valley. They had been converted to the Mormon Church in England. They left Omaha, Nebraska, June 1862 for their journey across the Plains, after a final outfitting and buying of supplies.

Louisa was too young to remember the eventful journey, for she was just one and a half years old when they finally arrived in the Salt Lake Valley in 1862. Louisa spent her early girlhood in Salt Lake City, living in a home on the corner of Fifth South and Second East. She attended school in the Ninth Ward. She was a beautiful girl with golden curly hair, blue grey eyes, vivacious and happy, slight of figure.

Louisa was reared in a home of order and discipline and with strict observance of the religious principles of the Church. She was taught to sew, knit, cook and keep house. She was most proficient in all the domestic arts. Besides her regular share of the housework, Louisa was required to make a quilt block, or knit a certain length on a stocking or sew a pound of carpet rags each day. All the clothing, washing, ironing, soap and candle making, rag carpets and quilts were made by hand. Louisa was a talented singer, dancer and actress. She appeared often in the Home Dramatic Club. To add to the family income she did nursing, sewing and crocheting.

Three months before she was twenty years old she married Henry J. Maiben. They were married in the Endowment House in Salt Lake City 30 Dec 1880. They had a whirlwind courtship, but one that lasted all their lives. Henry was a most loving and thoughtful man, providing Louisa with every necessity and more of the luxuries than most people enjoyed at that time.

She was active in Church Auxiliaries, serving as Primary President and Relief Society teacher. Her family was always her highest priority. She and Henry became the parents of thirteen children; one died in infancy and three died at birth.

Louisa's husband died after twenty-six years of marriage. She survived him by five years. Her own health began to fail due to an asthmatic condition. She died 13 Apr 1912 at a son's home in Los Angeles, California. She was buried in the Provo City Burial Park.

PHEBE ELEANOR RICHARDS MAIBEN

BIRTHDATE: 13 Aug 1824
Milford-Haven, Pembrokeshire,
South Wales
DEATH: 9 May 1906
Manti, Utah
PARENTS:
James Williams Richards
Eleanor Williams Richards
PIONEER: 28 Sep 1855
Moses Thurston Wagon Co.
SPOUSE: John Bray Maiben II
MARRIED: 9 Apr 1855
St. Giles Cripplegate, London
DEATH SP: 10 Mar 1910

CHILDREN:
Three children- all lived a short time

Phebe Eleanor was born in South Wales. She met her husband, John Bray Maiben, while investigating the Mormon Church. They were married and assigned to assist in preparing new converts for the emigration to the Salt Lake Valley. John, Phebe and Phebe's sister, Elizabeth, embarked 22 Apr 1855 for America, sailing on the ship "Samuel Curling."

After reaching Council Bluffs, Iowa, they outfitted their wagons, bought supplies and began the arduous trip across the Plains. They left Council Bluffs 3 Jul 1855 and arrived in the Salt Lake Valley 28 Sep 1855. They traveled in the Moses Thurston Independent Company and John served as a Chaplain on the journey. John married Phebe's sister, Elizabeth, soon after they all arrived in the Valley.

In 1875, John was called to a mission in Manti, Utah to help settle Sanpete County. He built a large two-story home where he, Phoebe and Elizabeth lived the remainder of their lives. The street they lived on was named "Maiben Street." There was endless entertaining of guests in this gracious home, which became the center of social affairs of the area and the showplace of Manti.

Phebe and Elizabeth were well-educated and were gracious hostesses. They entertained early Presidents of the Mormon Church, including Brigham Young, John Taylor, Wilford Woodruff, Lorenzo Snow, Joseph F. Smith and many other leaders.

Phebe was involved with work in the Young Ladies' Mutual Improvement Association and the Primary Organization. Many lovely parties were given for the youth of Manti in the Maiben home. Phebe was interested in the Women's Suffrage Movement in Utah and was an early advocate of Women's rights. She busied herself with Church work and entertaining, and accomplished much exquisite embroidery, handmade laces and fine drawn work. She won prizes at the Annual Exhibitions in Salt Lake City for the best lady's collars. She enjoyed the ballet and theater and the many cultural events. Phebe and John had three children, all lived a short time.

Phebe died in Manti, Utah at the age of eighty-two on 9 May 1906.

VIRGINIA FAITHFUL MCMASTER MAJOR

BIRTHDATE: 9 Jul 1850 Dunfermline, Fifeshire, Scotland
DEATH: 18 Apr 1904 Layton, Utah
PARENTS: William Athol McMaster—Margaret Drummond Ferguson McMaster
PIONEER: 1 Oct 1854 Daniel Garn Wagon Train
SPOUSE: Wm. Duncombe Major
MARRIED: 30 Aug 1869 Salt Lake City, Utah
DEATH SP: 7 Jul 1925 Layton, Utah

CHILDREN:
Grace Millicent, 15 Sep 1870
William Duncombe, 27 Jun 1872
Margaret Elvina, 6 Jun 1874
Harriet, 4 Feb 1876
Albert Athol, 13 Mar 1878
Donald Henderson, 6 Mar 1881
Dora Elizabeth, 6 Mar 1881
Robert Bruce, 13 May 1883
Leona, 30 Nov 1885
Fredrick Raynaldo, 21 Jul 1888
Heber LeRoy, 14 Jun 1891

Virginia Faithful was born in Scotland in 1850. Her people were among the first in Scotland to join the LDS Church. Her family moved to England in 1851 when Virginia was nine months old. They lived in England for three years then left England to emigrate to Utah in 1854. They had a long, hard journey over the ocean and crossed the Plains by wagon. Her father was Captain over a company when crossing the Plains. They arrived in the Valley 1 Oct 1854.

Their first home was a small, adobe house in the Tenth Ward in Salt Lake City. When eight years of age she was baptized into the Church.

When Virginia was nineteen years of age she married William Duncombe Major, 30 Aug 1869. They were married by Apostle Wilford Woodruff in Salt Lake City, Utah. In 1876, she with her husband and children moved to Kaysville, Utah. They lived there ten years and in 1886 they moved to Bountiful, Utah where they resided for six years. In 1892, the family moved to Layton, Utah. When the West Layton Ward was organized, Virginia was appointed President of the Relief Society, a position she filled with ability until they moved to Thatcher, Arizona in 1900. Here, she was a Counselor to the President of the Ward Relief Society. She was later called to be a Counselor in the Relief Society Stake Presidency. In 1902, the family returned to Layton, Utah. She resumed her activity in the Relief Society and other Ward activities. She fed the hungry, nursed the sick and comforted the distressed. No matter what the hour of night, the condition of the weather, or the distance, she was always ready to respond to a call. She died in Layton, Utah, 18 Apr 1904. Her husband died in 1925. They are both buried in the Kaysville, Utah Cemetery.

PAULINE COMBE MALAN

BIRTHDATE: 4 Aug 1805
Angrogna, Torino, Italy
DEATH: 23 Jun 1864
Ogden, Weber, Utah
PARENTS: Jean Combe
Marie Madeleine Ricca Combe
PIONEER: 29 Oct 1855
James Harper Wagon Train
SPOUSE:
Jean (John) Daniel Malan
MARRIED: 28 Apr 1825
Angrogna, Torino, Italy
DEATH: 6 May 1886
Ogden, Weber, Utah

CHILDREN:
Jean Daniel, 6 Mar 1828
Mary Catherine, 10 Jul 1829
Jean Daniel, 29 Jun 1832
John Stephen, 8 Jan 1835
Madeleine, 25 Sep 1839
Emily Pauline, 25 Sep 1839
Jean Louis, 17 Oct 1842
Jane Dinah, 20 Sep 1844
Bartholomew, 22 Apr 1848

Pauline was born in Italy in 1805.. She married Jean Daniel Malan when she was nineteen years old. She and her husband were the first family in Italy to accept the missionaries and be baptized as members of the LDS Church. A few days later, many of their neighbors also joined the church. Pauline sang in tongues and then gave the interpretation. Their house became the mission headquarters for Italy. In 1855, the family sailed on the ship, "Jeventa," for Philadelphia and arrived there on the 6th of May. They then traveled to Mormon Grove to get outfitted. They arrived in Salt Lake City on October 29, 1855. On their way, her wagon had capsized going down a dugway. It was feared that Pauline and her twin daughters had been crushed under the large box of the company's glass and chinaware. Pauline was given the strength to lift her two young children from the overturned wagon and went about her domestic duties as usual.

They arrived in the year of the "grasshopper war" and suffered much from cold and hunger. By spring they subsisted mostly on weeds, bran, and the fish her husband caught in the Ogden River by using willow traps. Pauline was content to support her husband, raise children with great faith and firm understanding of truth. Pauline died in 1864, at the age of forty-nine.

SARAH MARY CHESTNUT SLADE FOY TRULOCK MALAN

No Photo Available

BIRTHDATE: abt 1845
DEATH: 24 Jul 1886
PARENTS: William A. Chestnut
Johanna Chestnut
PIONEER: Not given
SPOUSE I: Jefferson Slade
MARRIED: 20 Nov 1860
DEATH SP: 28 Dec 1915
Eager, Apache Co., Arizona

CHILDREN:
Jefferson Chestnut, 11 Apr 1862

SPOUSE II: John Moroni Foy
MARRIED: 13 Dec 1862
Salt Lake Endowment House, Utah
DEATH SP: 5 Dec 1900
CHILDREN: None

SPOUSE III: Dr. Aquilla Trulock
MARRIED: Nov 1865
DEATH SP: Date not given

CHILDREN:
Aquilla Jr., 6 May 1866
Priscilla Chesnut, 13 Jan 1868

SPOUSE IV: Stephen Malan
MARRIED: 20 Dec 1869
Logan, Cache Co., Utah
DEATH SP: 15 Aug 1926

CHILDREN:
Stillborn,
Pauline Amaelia, 3 Aug 1872
Stephen Eugene, 26 Jun 1874
Wilford Augustus, 12 Jan 1877
Cora Maud (Hileman), 2 Mar 1880
Ada Lettitia, 10 Sep 1883

Sarah Mary was born about 1845. When she was about five years old, traveling west with her parents and sister, Ann Catherine age eight, and brother, Alfred age two, their parents were murdered by two men that her father had hired as teamsters to take them west.

The three children were spared but the cruel men tied them to a cow and sent it on its way. At this time they were outside Echo Canyon. The confused cow and the frightened children were left to wander until they were rescued by Samuel Jefferson Adair, widower of eight children, also on his way to Zion. Being very shocked and amazed when he found them, he released them from the cow, took them in his arms and did his best to comfort the distraught children. He brought them on to the Salt Lake Valley, arriving on September 21, 1848.

When they arrived, the Chestnut children recognized that fine wagon that belonged to their parents. They started to shout, but were quickly silenced when two rough men told Samuel to shut them up or they would be shut up for good. The men were soon gone and the children remained with Samuel as he raised them as his own.

They moved south to Payson and then on to Manti. Then Brigham Young sent Samuel to Washington County to grow cotton. They arrived on April 15, 1857, first settling at Adair Springs and then Pine Valley.

Sarah Mary went to live with Bishop and Sister Bingham in Riverdale, Utah.

She was living there, when at age fifteen, she married Jefferson Slade. By the time her first child was born the couple had been separated, possibly over polygamy. After some time passed, she reconciled with Jefferson, but he would have no part of it. She left without telling Jefferson that she was pregnant.

She later married John Moroni Foy in the Salt Lake Endowment House on December 13, 1862. Her son was about eight months old at that time. The marriage lasted only two years and there were no children.

On January 13, 1868, Sarah Mary married Dr. Aquila Trulock. Shortly after the birth of their second child, Dr. Trulock passed away.

On December 1869, in the Logan Temple, Sarah married Stephen Malan. They became the parents of six children. Three years after the birth of their last child, Sarah Mary passed away at age forty-one.

FLORA HAYDEN DRAKE MALLORY

No Photo Available

BIRTHDATE: 11 Jul 1817
Pompey, Onandaga, New York
DEATH: 1850
While crossing the plains
PARENTS: Allen Hayden, Jr.
Betsy Gilson Hayden
PIONEER: 1850
Bennett Independent Wagon Co.
SPOUSE: Jacob Drake
MARRIED: 1 Jul 1834
Pompey, Onandaga, New York
DEATH: Abt 1843
Nauvoo, Illinois

CHILDREN:
Willis, 10 Jul 1836
Warren, 23 Nov 1837
Richard, 22 Nov 1839
Medelson DelRio, 6 Mar 1841
Jacob Moroni, 10 Mar 1843

SPOUSE II: Lemuel Mallory
MARRIED: 6 Feb 1846
DEATH SP II: 28 Jul 1893
Logan, Utah
CHILDREN: None

Flora Hayden was born in New York State in 1817. She was the oldest of ten children. At age sixteen she married Jacob Drake. They made their home in New York where three sons were born to them. They were converted to the LDS Church and joined the Saints in Nauvoo. Two more sons were born in Nauvoo.

Flora was a good woman who served her family well. She loved the Church and did all she could to stay close to it. Her trials were hard, especially after her husband died. She later married Lemuel Mallory in polygamy, and started across the plains with him and her family. However she died on the journey in 1850, and is buried on the plains. She was age thirty-three at her passing.

HANNAH PERSSON MALMBERG

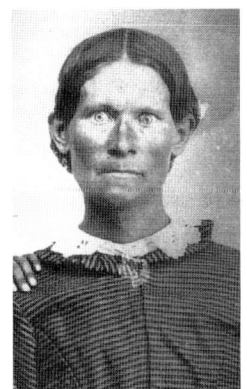

BIRTHDATE: 18 Jan 1821
Lunnarp, Bonderup,
Malmohus, Sweden
DEATH: 30 May 1895
Santaquin, Utah, Utah
PARENTS: Per Olsson
Kjarsti Nilsdotter
PIONEER: 10 Sep 1863
William W. Cluff Co.
SPOUSE: Samuel Carlsson Malmberg
MARRIED: 28 Dec 1847
Sweden
DEATH SP: 10 Jul 1877
Santaquin, Utah, Utah

CHILDREN:
Elna, 24 Aug 1848
Carl Peter, 3 Apr 1851
Elna Laurentia, 31 Mar 1852
Emma Christina, 22 May 1853
Peter August, 29 Jun 1854
Anna Maria, 25 Mar 1856
Otto Ferdinand 14 May 1859
Charles Ephraim 24 May 1864

Hannah was born in Sweden in 1821. Hannah was married to Samuel Carlsson Malmberg, 28 Dec 1847 in Sweden. They had eight children, and the first six died before the next one was born. The first seven were all born in Sweden. Hannah and her husband had joined the Mormon Church 17 Mar 1862, and were persecuted by the clergy because they had been dissenters. They immediately prepared to join the Saints in America. She, her husband, and their son, Otto, boarded the steamship "Aurora" 23 Apr 1863, docked at Grimsby, England, and traveled by train to Liverpool where they joined other converts on the "John G. Boyd" sailing 1 May 1863. They arrived in New York and disembarked 1 Jun. They went by train to Missouri, by steamer to Florence, Nebraska. They had stopped at Palmyra to see the Hill Cumorah, and the place where Joseph Smith had lived. They left Nebraska the first part of July and arrived in Salt Lake City 10 Sep 1863. Otto always remembered seeing a herd of buffalo stampede during their journey.

Hannah and Samuel moved to Provo for a year where their last child was born. They then moved to Santaquin where her baby died, and in 1877, her husband died after being thrown from a horse. When Otto was married in 1879, he and his family lived with Hannah for eight years before moving to their farm. He took care of Hannah as long as she lived. After having a stroke, she lived with this family for the last five years of her life.

In a letter written in 1881 to her oldest granddaughter, to be sealed in the Jubilee Box in Provo and to be opened 50 years later, she wrote, "To my dear grandchildren. I am now 60 years and 63 days old. My health is good, and I am glad I am a member of the Church of Jesus Christ of Latter-day Saints, and I can bear testimony to this work. I know it is the work of God. I will now say–if you have not a testimony for yourself, search the Holy Scriptures and ask God to help you read understandingly that you may get a testimony that this work is true. May God bless you. Be faithful to the Latter-day Work.

Yours in the Grave, Amen

Hannah Malmberg"

Hannah's husband had passed away in 1877, and Hannah passed away 30 May 1895. She loved this new-found religion and lived it throughout her life time. Having lost most of her children, the gospel of salvation must have been a consolation to her. She was a great pioneer woman who had faith and fortitude to live an active life and to be a great example for those who have followed her.

JOHANNA MARIA MAGNUSSEN MALMBERG

BIRTHDATE: 16 Mar 1830
Bjorland, Elborg, Sweden
DEATH: 8 Feb 1923
Logan, Cache, Utah
PARENTS: Johanes Magnusson
Johanna Olson / Olsendatter
Magnusson
PIONEER: 1863
SPOUSE:
John Peter (Petterson) Malmberg
MARRIED: 16 Oct 1857
Lindby, Sweden
DEATH SP: 16 Jul 1881
Clarkston, Utah

CHILDREN:
Johanna Christian 2 Apr 1856
Eveline Josephine 27 (31) Jan 1858
Hulda Emile 24 Dec 1859
Matilda (Tilda) 11 Aug 1861
Hilda Charlotte 26 Aug 1863
Joseph Peter 10 Jun 1865
Anna Marie 10 Dec 1866
John Ephraim 6 Aug 1868
Minnie 16 Apr 1870

Johanna Maria was born in Sweden in 1830, the oldest daughter in her family. The village was on the coast of the North Sea. Maria's father was a farmer. Maria attended the village schools. She could read well in Swedish, and although she learned to speak English, she could not read it. When Maria was sixteen her brother died of cholera. A few days later her mother died, and a week later her father also died, making three deaths from cholera within two weeks. After the funeral of her mother, Maria returned home to find her father stricken. He was in such pain he rolled from the bed to the floor; she tried to put him back on the bed but could not do so alone. Neighbors were afraid of the disease and would not help. She and her younger brother were left alone to care for him until he passed away. Four children were left orphans. The home and farm were sold for funeral expenses. The children went to live with people in different homes. Maria was a good cook so she was able to get work in a wealthy family. They would go to the sea to do their washing, wash all day and then they would dance at night. Sometimes their dresses would be frozen so hard when they took them off they would stand alone. It was at one of the dancing parties that she met her husband. Her sister joined the LDS Church and emigrated to Utah. Johanna Maria also emigrated to Utah and was near her sister who had settled in Logan.

Johanna Maria married John Peter Malmberg from Genarp, near Malmo, Sweden. Their first four children were born in Sweden. Their fifth child was born on the plains of Wyoming as they were on their trek west. Four other children were born in Utah. One child died very young and another died at age sixteen. The other seven grew to maturity. John Peter had joined the LDS Church in Sweden, but Maria did not. He wanted to come to America. Before they left Sweden, Maria had asked a minister of her Lutheran Church what she could do to get along if she remained in Sweden. The minister told her she would have to make her own way or go to the poor house, so she said she would go with her husband. She had been in Utah for some time before she joined the Church. Later she reflected "The Lord was good to me when he brought me to Utah. I know this is the true church." She was a pioneer woman who endured a lot by leaving the homeland she loved and coming to a new land. She died at almost ninety-three years of age in Feb 1923 in Logan, Utah.

JOHANNAH PERSSON ROSEQUIST MALMGREN

BIRTHDATE: 1 Jul 1843
Fossie, Malmohus, Sweden
DEATH: 5 Jan 1923
Salt Lake City, Utah
PARENTS: Pehr Trulsson Rosequist
Ingeborg Anderson Larson
PIONEER: 23 Sep 1862
Capt. Christian Madison Co.
SPOUSE:
Sven Peter Bengtsson Malmgren
MARRIED: 24 Apr 1864
Ephraim, Utah
DEATH: 12 May 1912
Salt Lake City, Utah

CHILDREN:
John Peter 11 Jan 1865
Sven Edwin 21 May 1866
Amanda Josephine 20 Apr 1868
Johannah Cecelea 28 Jan 1870
Henry 22 Jul 1871
Rosetta Ingaborg 29 Jan 1874
Emma Ottomina 7 Aug 1876
Mary Rosanell 7 Dec 1878
Herman Albert 17 Jan 1881
Minnie Amelia 11 Apr 1883
Oscar Laurence 11 May 1886
Jennie "V" 4 Dec 1888

Johannah Persson was born in Sweden in 1843. She had brown eyes and dark hair. Her father died when she was seven years old. She and her mother and brother joined the LDS Church when Johannah was fourteen. She worked with her mother in the glove factory to obtain money to come to Utah. They sailed from Hamburg, Germany, when Johannah was seventeen, on the ship "Franklin" with Elder Christian A. Madison in charge. They landed in Castle Gardens 31 May 1862. They left New York, went to Quincy, Illinois and then by boat to Florence, Nebraska on 9 Jun. They pitched tents north of Florence and waited for a month for the teams to come from Utah to help them across the plains. They left Florence 14 Jul 1862, and Johannah walked most of the way beside her brothers and sister.

While crossing the plains, Johannah met Sven Peter Malmgren from Malmo and they were married two years later on 24 Apr 1864 in Ephraim, Utah. They eventually settled in Levan, Utah where she lived most of the rest of her life. Johannah worked alongside her husband Sven, in farming. They raised twelve children, six of whom preceded her in death. Johannah had the first sewing machine in Levan which was purchased for $99.00. She sewed for people at various times. She first lived in a dugout, then an adobe house, and finally a brick home. She raised a beautiful flower garden and was a wonderful cook. She always had a strong testimony of the gospel and was a valiant pioneer woman maintaining her great faith and fortitude always.

Johannah's husband, Sven, passed away 12 May 1912 in Salt Lake City. Johannah died 5 Jun 1923 just ten years later, also in Salt Lake City. She was seventy-nine years old when she died. They left a great posterity to honor them for this great faith, of leaving their homelands and braving the trials and tribulations of the new land for their religion that they loved.

MARY ANN ADAIR MANGUM

BIRTHDATE: 5 Jul 1822
Pickens, Pickens Co., Alabama
DEATH: 9 May 1892
Georgetown, Kane, Utah
PARENTS: Thomas Adair
Rebecca Brown
PIONEER: Aug 1862
Jacob Bigler Wagon Train
SPOUSE: John Mangum III
MARRIED: 1841
Alabama
DEATH SP: 23 May 1885
Bushvalley (Alpine), Arizona

CHILDREN:
William Perry Oct 1841
Rebecca Frances 10 Oct 1843
Laney Ann 1845
Martha Elizabeth 1847
Joseph Eslan 12 Dec 1850
John Wesley 31 May 1852
Lucinda 8 Jul 1854
Cyrus (twin) 29 Jun 1856
Harvey (twin) 29 Jun 1859
Mary Abigail 2 Jun 1858
Amy Caroline 13 Feb 1860
Julia 13 Feb 1861
David Newton 13 Oct 1862
Sarah Ellen 17 Nov 1864

Mary Ann Adair was born in Alabama in 1822. The Adair family and the Mangum family were closely associated. Four of the Adairs married four of the Mangums, John and Mary Ann being the last of the couples to marry in 1841.

A missionary by the name of James Richey converted the two families and urged them to gather with the Saints, so they sold their belongings and moved to Nauvoo, Illinois. Almost immediately they were forced out of Nauvoo to Mt. Pisgah where they built a cabin to shelter the two families. Some family members lost their lives at this time, but all was not sadness. Daughter Lucinda married the missionary, James Richey, and he helped them with a team and wagon and provisions. However it was almost five years before they could come to the Salt Lake Valley, which they did in 1852.

Mary Ann was set apart by Brigham Young as a midwife not long after reaching Utah. Mary Ann and John were among the first settlers in Payson, Nephi, Washington

County, and Kanab, Utah. They later were sent to Alpine, Arizona to settle. While in St. George they helped with the growing of cotton. Mary Ann taught her children how to pick cotton seed out of the cotton balls. They spun and wove the cotton into cloth. John took a second wife, Ellen Bardsley, while in Payson, and Mary Hamblin, the adopted Indian daughter of Jacob Hamblin, became his third wife. John died in Bushvalley, (Alpine) Arizona in 1885. Mary Ann died at Georgetown, Kane, Utah in 1892.

LINA MENIZA JONES MANHARD

BIRTHDATE: 14 May 1833
Dresden, Tennessee
DEATH: 6 Jan 1910
Kanosh, Utah
PARENTS: Calvin Townsend Jones
Diana Louisa Jolley Jones Dorrity
PIONEER: About 1852
SPOUSE: William Henry Manhard
MARRIED: Apr 1853
Kanosh, Utah
DEATH SP: 11 Mar 1905
Kanosh, Millard Co., Utah

CHILDREN:
Mary Lovina 9 Feb 1855
Charles William 5 Feb 1857
Calvin Henry 27 Nov 1859
Louisa Temperance 5 Oct 1860
Dina Jane 23 Oct 1862
Sarah Ellen 20 Oct 1865
Dennis Bryant 16 Nov 1867
Albert Feb 1869
Meniza Elnora 1871
John Albern 1873
Ada Elmire 1875

Lina was born in Tennessee, in 1833, the only child of her parents. Her father died before she was born. Her mother married Dennis Dorrity, whose family owned a platation and slaves in Tennessee.

In 1842 the Mormon Elders visited Grandfather Jolley's farm. Most of the family was baptized and soon left for Nauvoo. They had to abandon their home when the mobs came. In 1848 they were in Council Bluffs, Iowa, and about 1852 they crossed the plains.

After their arrival the family moved south. Lina Meniza married William Henry Manhard in 1853 in Kanosh, Utah. She was his third wife, and they lived in Spanish Fork until 1868 when they moved to Kanosh. She was the mother of eleven children. William was a farmer and they did much to develop the new country. They were cherished friends to the Indians, feeding them and helping them in many ways. William died in 1905, and Lina passed away in 1910 and is buried in Kanosh.

ANNIE MARIA BUSBY MANN

BIRTHDATE: 28 Aug 1847
Birmingham, Warwickshire, Eng.
DEATH: 21 May 1924
Woods Cross, Davis, Utah
PARENTS: William Busby
Maria Meadows Busby
PIONEER: Prior to 1863
Wagon Train
SPOUSE: Charles William Mann
MARRIED: 4 Nov 1863
Salt Lake City, Utah
DEATH SP: 26 Oct 1901

CHILDREN:
Moroni Busby 15 Nov 1864
Sarah Jane 23 Sep 1866
Annie Elizabeth 14 Sep 1868
Alice Maria 28 Oct 1870
Lavina 22 Feb 1873
Charles Busby 25 Jul 1875
Jessie 8 Sep 1877
Ephriam Busby 17 Jan 1880
George Busby 1 Apr 1881
Ira Busby 11 Feb 1883
Chloe 6 Apr 1886
Lottie 23 Jul 1888
John Busby 28 Feb 1892

Annie Maria was born in England in 1847. It is not known when she came to Utah but it was before 1863. Annie Maria was married to Charles William Mann on 4 Nov 1863 in the Endowment House when she was sixteen years of age. She was his second wife. He later took a third wife in 1871.

Charles William purchased several acres of land in West Bountiful, Utah where he grew cabbages and onions. He sold this produce to the Army stationed at Fort Douglas, and sometimes traded the produce for mules or other items. The street on which they lived was called Onion Street, because when the onions were harvested and left on the ground to dry, the odor could be smelled for miles.

Annie Maria was the mother of thirteen children, two of whom died as infants, one who drowned at age two, and one who died at age fifteen. Her daughter Alice had gone out picking strawberries, became wet and cold, which developed into pneumonia. She became ill and died shortly thereafter. The other nine grew to maturity.

Annie Maria died in Woods Cross, Davis, Utah in 1924, at the age of seventy-seven years. Her husband passed away in 1901.

MIRIAM CUNNINGHAM MANN

No Photo Available

BIRTHDATE: 14 Feb 1838
Townsend, Toronto, Canada
DEATH: 20 Feb 1867
Union, Salt Lake, Utah
PARENTS:
Rev. Henry Cunningham
Mary Slaght Cunningham
PIONEER: 2 Sep 1861
Joseph Pingrey Wagon Co.
SPOUSE: Oscar Mann
MARRIED: 6 Sep 1860
Iowa
DEATH SP: 18 Nov 1919
Orem, Utah Co., Utah

CHILDREN:
Matilda, 30 Nov 1861
Nancy Jane, 7 Feb 1864
Oscar Leslie, 1 Mar 1866

Miriam was born in Canada in 1838. She married Oscar Mann in 1860 at the age of twenty-two years in Iowa. They came across the plains with the Joseph Pingrey Company in 1861, and settled in Union, Salt Lake Co., Utah.

Oscar was a miller by trade and managed the grist mill at Union. Miriam and Oscar received their endowments in September 1863 in the Endowment House. She passed away at the age of twenty-nine in 1867, leaving three small children, the youngest only a year old. Her husband remarried and settled in Arizona in 1879.

DEBORAH HOLLIST MANNING

BIRTHDATE: 25 Jul 1846
Brighton, Sussex, England
DEATH: 2 Jun 1928
Farmington, Davis, Utah
PARENTS: Henry Hollist
Elizabeth Chandler Hollist
PIONEER: 13 Sep 1861
Joseph Horne Wagon Co.
SPOUSE: Eli Manning
MARRIED: 24 Mar 1865
Salt Lake City, Salt Lake, Utah
DEATH: 6 Aug 1923
Farmington, Davis, Utah

CHILDREN:
David Eli 6 Sep 1866
Elizabeth 5 Sep 1868
William Henry 29 Mar 1871
John Chandler 1 Aug 1873
George Callard 5 Nov 1875
Charles Edward 7 May 1878
Alice Deborah 16 Dec 1880
Annie Susan 6 Jul 1883
James Elliott 20 Oct 1885
Joseph Walter 25 Nov 1890

Deborah was only two years old at the time her parents were converted and baptized as members of the LDS Church in 1848. She could remember how her father came home late from conducting branch meetings, bruised and ill from attacks from mobsters. Their family sailed from Liverpool, England on the ship, "George Washington," and arrived in the Boston Harbor on March 28, 1857. They were quarantined in Boston Harbor for a month, due to a measles outbreak. They lived in Boston for two years in order to earn enough money to buy provisions for their westward journey. On May 2, 1859, they left Boston and traveled by train to Florence, Nebraska. They had to remain in Omaha, Nebraska until they could afford to move further west. Deborah was now thirteen and secured work as a nurse girl and went into different homes to care for small children. Finally, in 1861, they were able to cross the plains. They arrived in Salt Lake City on September 13, 1861.

They went to Ogden to live for a year. In 1862, Deborah's father was asked to move to Farmington and serve as a mechanic in the area. They enjoyed their new home for a little while until Deborah's mother died in December 1864. In 1865, Deborah married Eli Manning in the Endowment House at Salt Lake City. They lived with his parents in North Farmington where the father and son continued to work together on the farm. Deborah accepted this way of living until their third child was born in 1871. Then Eli built a house of their own where seven more children were born to this union. They met the challenges of each day and passed through the joys and sorrows that time brought to them. Deborah died in 1928.

ELIZABETH ELLIOTT MANNING

No Photo Available

BIRTHDATE: 22 Nov 1818
Buckfastleigh, Devon, England
DEATH: 3 Nov 1901
Farmington, Davis, Utah
PARENTS: John Elliott
Ann Webber
PIONEER: 16 Oct 1853
By wagon
SPOUSE: Willard Callard Manning
MARRIED: 12 Jun 1843
In England
DEATH SP: 7 Sep 1887
Farmington, Davis, Utah

CHILDREN:
Eli 15 Apr 1844

Elizabeth was born in England in 1818. She married William C. Manning in June 1843 and they had one son. William was a sea captain and gone from home for long periods of time. During one of his journeys Elizabeth was taught the gospel and baptized into the Church. When William returned he was greatly surprised at her actions, but after he investigated he too was baptized.

They emigrated to America in 1853, traveling with an Independent Company led by C. E. Bolton, and arriving in Salt Lake on 16 Oct 1853. They settled in Farmington, Davis, Utah.

When her son, Eli, married he brought his bride home to live, but as time passed Elizabeth became quite jealous of her daughter-in-law and her babies. This made life unpleasant and so Eli and his family moved into a home of their own. Elizabeth died 3 Feb 1901 in Farmington at the age of eighty-two years.

MARGARET GALBRAITH MANNING

BIRTHDATE: 10 Dec 1835
Glasgow, Lanark, Scotland
DEATH: 12 June 1909
Hooper, Weber County, Utah
PARENTS: George Galbraith
Ann Wilkie Galbraith
PIONEER: 1 Jul 1854
Daniel Cairns Wagon Train
SPOUSE: Henry William Manning
MARRIED: 14 Mar 1855
Salt Lake City, Utah
DEATH: 28 Apr 1916
Salt Lake City, Utah

CHILDREN:
Ann Wilkie 19 Feb 1856
Joseph George 15 Apr 1857
Margaret Ann 11 Jun 1859
Henry William, Jr. 6 Aug 1861
Mary Ann 14 Feb 1864
Jane Wilkie 19 May 1866
George Galbraith 24 Oct 1868
Violet 1 Feb 1872
David 15 Feb 1874
Laurence Galbraith, 16 Jul 1875

Margaret was born in Scotland, in 1835. When she was five years of age her father died of Yellow Fever on St. Kitts Island in the West Indies. He was serving the British Crown as a civil engineer. Her mother was also stricken with Yellow Fever, but survived. After returning to England, Margaret's mother married John Hooper and had four more children.

In helping to care for her new brothers and sisters, Margaret began the chief vocation of her life, that of mothering and caring for countless children. Besides rearing her own ten children, she was helpful with her husband's orphaned brothers and sisters, rearing some of the children of her husband's second wife, and two orphaned boys from England. Her husband met these boys when on a mission to England.

Margaret and her mother and family left England with an LDS group of converts under the direction of President Dorr Curtis. After landing in New Orleans, La., on 16 Mar 1854, they sailed up the Mississippi River to St. Louis, Mo. From there, they went to Kansas and joined a company of five hundred with fifty wagons, under the direction of Captain Daniel Cairns. They left for the journey 1 Jul 1854 and arrived in the Salt Lake Valley 3 Oct 1854. Her future husband

Margaret married Henry William Manning on 14 Mar 1855 and was later endowed and sealed in the Endowment House in Salt Lake City, Utah 6 Dec 1862. She was for many years the President of the Relief Society in Hooper. In the winter of 1896, she developed an abdominal cancer and was operated on for the lesion on the dining room table of her niece, Mrs. George E. Browning, in Ogden, Utah. She recovered in spite of a surgical accident which caused cruel suffering for the rest of her thirteen years of life. She continued to serve as a nurse until she died 12 Jun 1909. Her husband survived her, dying 28 Apr 1916. The entire community of Hooper honored Margaret at her funeral.

MARY VOWELS MANNING

BIRTHDATE: 14 Jun 1810
Poulton, Somerset, England
DEATH: 14 July 1854
near Laramie, Wyoming
PARENTS: John Vowels
Mary Carter Vowels
PIONEER: Jul 1854
Daniel Cairns Wagon Train
SPOUSE: Joseph George Manning
MARRIED: 1829
Bristol, England
DEATH: 9 Jan 1850
Bristol, England

CHILDREN:
Joseph George, Jr. 15 Jan 1832
Henry William 28 Feb 1834
Frederick James 14 Apr 1836
Mary Ann (Marianna) 3 Apr 1838
Frederick Charles 5 Aug 1840
Hyrum John 9 Aug 1844
Alfred Edward 30 Oct 1847

Mary was born in England in 1810. She was baptized into the Mormon Church by Elder Wilford Woodruff, 26 Jan 1841. She was the first woman in Bristol to join the LDS Church. She had married Joseph George Manning in Bristol, England in 1829. They were the parents of ten children, four of whom died in infancy. Their home was always open to the Mormon missionaries, even to lending them considerable money when needed. She had the gift of tongues and her testimony was often heard through this gift.

On 9 Jan 1850, her husband died. Each of her sons worked as apprentices to earn enough money to finance their journey to the Salt Lake Valley. Mary and five of her children went to Liverpool and booked passage with Captain Kerr on the ship "Golconda" and sailed 4 Feb 1854. They arrived in New Orleans, then took a Mississippi River boat and landed in St. Louis, Mo. 1 Apr 1854. They joined the company of Captain Daniel Cairns in Kansas City and on 1 Jul 1854, the company of five hundred began the long, hard trek across the Plains.

As there were only fifty wagons, all who were able walked the entire way to the land of Zion. They suffered hardships and Indian trouble. As they neared Wyoming, Mary became very ill of Cholera, and in a short time, died 14 Jul 1854, just one month after her forty-fourth birthday. The oldest child was about twenty-two and the youngest was six years old. She was wrapped in a clean sheet, no casket, and buried. The grave was heaped with stones on which a fire was built as a safeguard against desecration by animals or Indians. The noble character of Mary Vowels Manning is an inspirational pattern and steadfast ideal for her numerous posterity. Margaret Galbraith's family helped to care for the Manning orphans and on 14 Mar 1855 Margaret, then nineteen years old, married Mary's son, Henry William.

JOHANNA CHRISTINA WINBERG (PARSON) PETERSON MANSFIELD

BIRTHDATE: 3 May 1824
Lund, Sweden
DEATH: 26 Mar 1887
St. George, Washington, Utah
PARENTS: Sven Winberg
Elna Winberg
PIONEER: 1855
SPOUSE I: Peter Peterson
MARRIED: 18 Nov 1842
Sweden
DEATH SP: 20 Jun 1855
En-route

CHILDREN:
Peter, 17 Nov 1843
Peter, 18 Mar 1845
Niles Fredrick Christen, 20 Jan 1847
Sven Edward, 5 Jul 1849
John August, 23 Dec 1851
Ephraim Millenium, 3 Mar 1855

SPOUSE II: Matthew Mansfield
MARRIED: 17 Jun 1856
Mill Creek, Salt Lake Co., Utah
DEATH SP: 6 Mar 1891
Mill Creek, Salt Lake Co., Utah

CHILDREN:
Isabelle Marie, 3 Jun 1857
Mary Ann, 11 Apr 1859
Matthew Winberg, 15 Jan 1862
Sarah Ellen Josephine, 7 Apr 1867

Johanna was born in Sweden, 1824. She was called Joan by her family. She, being the eldest, had many tasks to fulfill; washing and baking for the family. There was little time for pleasure. She was of a deeply religious nature.

In 1842, she married Peter Parson. Her first son died, and her second son was named Peter, too. Joan and her husband were baptized on June 7, 1852. This decision caused them much persecution. Their families were angry so they moved to Denmark, changing their last name to Peterson. They saved their money for three years, then sailed with their four sons to America. Their son, Sven, died and was buried at sea. While sailing up the Mississippi River, another son was born.

The hard journey across the Plains was too much for her husband; he died enroute and was buried in a wayside grave. She brought her family on alone. She arrived in the Salt Lake Valley with her four young boys with no place to stay.

Matthew Mansfield offered his home, and they were married in polygamy in 1856. Johanna did the carding, spinning and weaving, and made clothes for other people, and to barter and sell the material.

Matthew took another wife, Margaret, in 1857. Joan had four more children. In 1861, they were called to build up the Dixie Mission. In December, they made camp in a large tent on a dry, hard, white clay campsites. She had a child born there, but she never fully recovered. She had another child, her tenth, who only lived six months.

Her husband and one of his wives moved back to Mill Creek, where he died in 1891. Joan lived with her daughter, Mary Ann Bentley. She passed away at the age of sixty-three, 1887, in St. George.

Mary Ann was industrious, temperate and devoted to her family and Church. She did much work in the temple for her kindred dead.

LUCINDA BYBEE LAYNE MANSOR

BIRTHDATE: 20 Jun 1805
Glasgow, Barren, Kentucky
DEATH: 10 Jul 1896
Salt Lake City, Utah
PARENTS: Lee Allen Bybee
Jerusha Jane Atkerson
PIONEER: 24 or 27 Sep 1852
Benjamin Gardiner
Layne Bybee Wagon Co
SPOUSE I: David Layne
MARRIED: 27 Sep 1827
Barren County, Kentucky
DEATH: 18 Aug 1840
Clay County, Indiana

CHILDREN:
Martha Jane 26 Jul 1827
Sarah Ann or Sally 21 Feb 1829
Robert Lee 21 Oct 1830
Mary Elizabeth 24 Dec 1832
David Leland 1833/1834
Jonathan Ellis 13 Jan 1835
Elihu Preston 18 Oct 1837
Nancy Mariah 14 Feb 1838
Jerusha Emeline 18 Mar 1841

SPOUSE II: Barnett Mansor
MARRIED: Nov 1847
Mount Pisgah, Iowa
DEATH: not known

CHILDREN:
Stephen 13 Jun 1851

Lucinda was born, raised and married in Barren County, Kentucky. She resided there until about 1831 when she and her husband, David Layne, their three children, along with extended family on both sides, moved to Clay County, Indiana. A cabin was built, the land cleared. They were plagued by wild animals, bears, and great packs of wolves. Mormon missionaries came through the region in 1838 and the family was converted. Before Lucinda's husband was baptized he took sick and died after a two week illness. Lucinda was baptized in 1841.

She was left to care for seven children, the oldest but thirteen years of age. Another child was born six months after her husband's death. She was also $500.00 in debt. The home was sold, the debt paid, and they moved into a smaller home near her father. Lucinda passed through many trials in trying to provide for her family until some of the children became older and able to assist her. In 1842 she, with her children, left their home in Indiana and traveled toward Illinois in company of her father and other family members. They settled on property located five miles south and a little east of the city, close to the road leading from Warsaw to Nauvoo. Because of the mob action, they saw much of violence and of sadness at the death of the Prophet Joseph Smith and his brother, Hyrum. When the Saints were expelled from Nauvoo, Lucinda's small brick home and 10 acres of good land were sold for $11.00, paid with black flour that was too bitter to eat. In May 1846, Lucinda and her children left Nauvoo, ferried across the Mississippi River and headed into the the Iowa territory. They located at Mt. Pisgah for about eighteen months. Lucinda met Barnett Mansor and was married to him in Nov 1847. They had one son. They journeyed west, arriving in the Salt Lake Valley Sep 1852. She was a pioneer in the truest sense, to have carved a home from the wilderness for herself and her family. Upon their arrival in the Salt Lake Valley, they were called to help settle Nephi, Utah. After her husband's death she lived with a daughter in San Bernardino, California. She died at the age of ninety-one years, in 1896.

SARAH MARINDA HANCHETT MARBLE

BIRTHDATE: 18 Feb 1835
McKern, Erie, Pennsylvania
DEATH: 21 Sep 1899
Inverory, (Central) Utah
PARENTS: Martin Hanchett
Sarah (Sally) Mecham Hanchett
PIONEER: abt 1850
Appleton Harmon Independent
SPOUSE: William Lorenzo Marble
MARRIED: 1852
DEATH: 21 Oct 1916
Central, Sevier County, Utah

CHILDREN:
Mary Almeda 5 Jul 1854
William Lorenzo 29 Jun 1855
Martin Nathaniel 31 Jan 1857
Ealum Sylvester 22 Mar 1859
Sarah Marinda 27 Sep 1861
Henry Myron 11 Jan 1866
George Benjamin 8 May 1868
Appleton Milo 8 Feb 1872
Emma Jane 11 Apr 1874
Joseph Austin 12 Feb 1877

Sarah Marinda was born in Pennsylvania in 1835. When she was nine years old her mother died. At this time, Sarah Marinda was put in the care of another family. The mother of this family had cancer and her own daughter refused to dress her cancerous sore. Sarah Marinda cared for the mother. Her father refused to deny Mormonism so the mobs burned their house down. By the time Sarah Marinda turned thirteen she was without both her parents. After her father's death, she and her sister lived with George and Polly Stringham and came with them to Utah. The Stringhams were good to the girls and later Sarah Marinda's children referred to them as "Grandma and Grandpa Stringham."

In 1852, when Sarah Marinda was seventeen years old, she married a friend of her childhood, William Lorenzo Marble. He was seven years her senior. They became the parents of ten children; two died in infancy, a daughter died at eight years of age. Sarah Marinda had a natural gift and talent for home nursing and caring for the sick. She was a quick-spoken woman, fearless in asserting her rights. Once, a group of Indians, dressed in war paint, came to her house asking for meat. She told them she didn't have any. The Indians saw some hams hanging in the rafters and asked again for meat. She told them the meat was not hers, it belonged to her brother. At that point an Indian took a knife and stepped toward the meat. She picked up a chair and holding it over her head went toward the Indian saying if he took another step she'd break the chair over his head. He left the house and told the other Indians that she was a "heap brave squaw." Those Indians never returned to her house.

Sarah Marinda probably had no schooling. She could write a little but seldom did. She was a good cook and her main interests were her home and raising her family. She was a small woman, only four feet tall, slender, not very strong, and in her prime had very dark hair and dark eyes. She was faithful to her religion and a caring, loving mother to her children. She died at the age of sixty-four, 21 Sep 1899.

ANNA PEARSON MARCHANT

BIRTHDATE: 10 Dec 1854
Kylestorp, O Espinge,
Malmohus, Sweden
DEATH: 21 Jan 1941
Peoa, Utah
PARENTS: Ola Pearson
Sisa Bengston Pearson
PIONEER: 29 Aug 1862
Lewis Brunson Co.
SPOUSE: Franklin Wm. Marchant
MARRIED: 15 Feb 1875
Salt Lake Endowment House
DEATH: 11 Jan 1937
Peoa, Utah

CHILDREN:
Franklin Orson 1 Nov 1875
Ginevra May 5 Feb 1880
Abraham Pearson 1 Apr 1882
Amasa Ray 16 May 1886
Katherina Sisa 7 Jul 1888
Harold Grant 14 Mar 1893

While Anna was quite young, she learned the domestic arts from her mother. She made butter, raised chickens, ducks, and turkeys. She sold all of these items in order to pay an honest tithing. She made beautiful lace, knitted stockings and socks for the family. She always milked the cows, as the men in her area in Sweden never learned to do the milking. She was known as the best quilter in Peoa.

Anna married Franklin William Marchant and bore him six children. She had the full responsibility of raising the children for several years while her husband served missions for the church. She was very gifted in helping with the sick and would attend the sick night and day if needed.

Anna served for twenty three years as a counselor in Primary. She was always a visiting teacher for the Relief Society. After caskets were made, she lined them with white velvet or satin.

CHARLOTTE UNDERHLLL CLARKE GIBBS MARCHANT

BIRTHDATE: 24 May 1827
Tetbury, Gloucester, England
DEATH: 24 Nov 1878
Salt Lake City, Utah
PARENTS: William Underhill
Maria Nixon
PIONEER: 1854
SPOUSE I: William Clarke
MARRIED: about 1853
England
DEATH: 1854
Devil's Gate, Wyoming

CHILDREN:
Stillborn boy, on the Plains

SPOUSE II: Horace Dewitt Gibbs
MARRIED: 10 Jan 1855 (2nd wife)
Salt Lake City, Utah
DEATH SP II: 18 Aug 1875
Salt Lake City, Utah

CHLLDREN:
Hannah Maria Gibbs, 21 Nov 1856

SPOUSE II: Edmund Marchant
MARRIED: unknown (3rd wife)
DEATH SP: 16 May 1885
Rockport, Utah
CHlLDREN: unknown

Charlotte was born in England, in 1827. At age twenty-five, she married William Clarke. They became members of the LDS Church, along with her parents. Soon after their marriage in England, they determined to emigrate. They sailed for America on the "Marshfield" from Liverpool, 8 Apr 1854, landing in New Orleans.

They started for Utah with a wagon and ox-team. During a stampede of buffalo, their wagon was overturned and Charlotte later gave birth to a stillborn baby boy. After burying the baby and fixing their wagon, they were on their journey again. William Clarke became ill from exposure and died. He was buried at Devil's Gate, Wyoming. The young widow came into the Salt Lake Valley alone.

Charlotte went to work in the Gibbs home. On 10 Jan, 1855, she became the second wife of Horace DeWitt Gibbs. To this union, one daughter was born 21 Nov 1856. Charlotte and Horace were later divorced and she married Edmund Marchant as his 3rd/4th wife and went to Rockport, Summit Co., Utah to live. Charlotte remained active in the church, holding positions as Secretary of the Relief Society and as a teacher.

Charlotte cut wool from the sheep and spun it to make clothing. She had a hard life and died at the early age of fifty-one years on 24 Nov 1878. She is buried in the Salt Lake City Cemetery.

HANNAH MARIA RUSSELL MARCHANT

BIRTHDATE: 6 Aug 1850
Tetbury, Gloucester, England
DEATH: 22 Feb 1893
Peoa, Utah
PARENTS: Richard Russell
Hannah Maria Underhill Russell
PIONEER: 26 Oct 1864
William Hyde Wagon Company
SPOUSE: John Alma Marchant
MARRIED: 30 Nov 1867
Salt Lake City, Utah
DEATH: 27 Jan 1908
Peoa, Utah

CHILDREN:
John Alma Russell 14 Sep 1868
Abraham Henry 22 Apr 1871
Franklin Richard 31 Mar 1874
Austin William 4 Sep 1876
Hyrum 1 Mar 1879
George 7 Feb 1882
Albert Charles 20 Sep 1883
Willard 1 Feb 1886
Hannah Maria 9 Jan 1889
Myrtle Gladys 4 Feb 1890
stillborn daughter Feb 1893

Hannah Maria Russell Marchant was born in England. She was a sweet, red-headed baby who joined a family of two brothers and five sisters. By 1861, her family moved and located in Upton, Gloucester, fifteen miles north of Tetbury, in an area of well-to-do farms. Her father was a groomer of horses. Hannah Maria's mother died when Hannah Maria was ten years old. She was baptized a member of the Mormon Church by her father. At age thirteen, she and her father, some of her sisters, and her little brother sailed from London to America 3 Jun 1864 aboard the ship "Hudson." The group suffered the usual privations and pleasures of other emigrating Saints, arriving in New York 19 Jun 1864. Her father had remarried enroute. At Wyoming, Nebraska he became ill with cholera and died. His new wife, and now widow, brought the children on to the Salt Lake Valley and then to Peoa, Utah.

Hannah Maria married John Alma Marchant 30 Nov 1867 in the Salt Lake City Endowment House. They became the parents of eleven children; three died in infancy, a son died at age eight, and a daughter was stillborn. The other children all lived to marry and raise families. Hannah Maria welcomed into the family Jane Ann Maxwell, who was almost twenty years younger than she was, and she became her husband's second wife in 1879. Hannah Maria was a faithful, dedicated member of the Church. She was present when the Peoa Ward Relief Society was organized 13 Sep 1875. She served as Assistant Secretary and later as Secretary. She also served as an appraiser. The appraisers were to assess the value of the non-cash donations given by members. The Relief Society meetings were held in the school house or in private dwellings. Annual dues were instituted and were set at twenty-five cents.

Hannah Maria was a small woman with reddish hair. She had a jolly disposition and was known as an exceptionally neat housekeeper. She died 22 Feb 1893, following the birth of her eleventh child, a stillborn daughter. She and her baby were buried in the Peoa Cemetery. Her husband died 27 Jan 1908 and was also buried in Peoa, Utah.

HARRIET MATILDA CASPER MARCHANT

BIRTHDATE: 9 Nov 1849
Lexington, Platte, Missouri
DEATH: 24 Oct 1921
Peoa, Utah
PARENTS: Duncan Spears Casper
Matilda Allison Casper
PIONEER: 5 Sep 1855
John Hindley Independent Co.
SPOUSE:
Albert George Henry Marchant
MARRIED: 17 Feb 1873
Salt Lake City, Utah
DEATH: 18 Aug 1920
Peoa, Utah

CHILDREN:
Albert George 22 Mar 1874
Duncan William 9 Oct 1875
Lydia Maria 14 Aug 1877
Matilda 6 Apr 1879
Robert Henry Casper 21 Dec 1880
Alonzo Justice 23 Sep 1882
Abraham Franklin 30 Sep 1884
Mary Ann 19 Jul 1886
Edward Casper 31 Jul 1888
Steven Casper 10 Jan 1890
Harvey Allison 8 Oct 1891
Harriet Casper 5 Jul 1894
LeRoy Casper 22 Apr 1896

Harriet Matilda Casper Marchant was born in Missouri. When she was five years old her parents joined the John Hindley Independent wagon train, arriving in the Salt Lake Valley 5 Sep 1855. When Harriet was a small child, she had a severe case of smallpox. She later said that as she grew into womanhood her pockmarked face was ever present in her mind, so that she was never vain. Her mother was in poor health and died when Harriet was about twenty years of age. She assumed many family responsibilities during her early years.

She joined the Relief Society as a young single woman. She and her mother and sisters are all listed as contributors of quilt blocks. Harriet took an active part in meetings and bore strong testimonies. She asked that people would tell her if she did anything wrong so she could improve. She married Albert George Henry Marchant in the Salt Lake Endowment House 17 Feb 1873. They made their home in Peoa, Utah, about 45 miles east of Salt Lake City, on the Weber River, where her husband's family had been pioneers. They became the parents of thirteen children; two boys died in infancy and a daughter died at seven years of age. The other ten children grew to maturity, married, raised families, and all out-lived their parents. They were all active Latter-day Saints; six of their sons and one daughter filled honorable missions.

Harriet had taught school before her marriage and she now taught night school for members of her own family and others. Sacrifices had to be made to obtain the needed books. She was a good seamstress and made most of the clothes for her family. She was always active in her Church. When the Peoa Relief Society was organized 13 Sep 1875, Harriet was appointed Secretary, serving until 25 Aug 1881. She later served as First Counselor and again as Secretary. Her minutes, in beautiful handwriting and with excellent spelling, were meticulously kept. She was also Secretary to the Young Ladies and the Primary organizations.

As Harriet grew older she developed rheumatism and became quite heavy. She busied herself with crocheting, tatting, knitting and making quilts. She made yards and yards of lace for family members. The last few years of her life were more free from pain. She lived a little more than a year after her husband died. She was lonely without her companion and died at Peoa 24 Oct 1921. They are both buried in the Peoa Cemetery.

LUCY ANN PETTEGREW CUTLER MARCHANT

No Photo Available

BIRTHDATE: 26 Apr 1817
Columbia, Lorain, Ohio
DEATH: 17 Dec 1896
Salt Lake City, Utah
PARENTS: David Pettegrew
Elizabeth Alden Pettegrew
PIONEER: Sep 1852
Harmon Cutler Wagon Company
SPOUSE I: Harmon Cutler
MARRIED: 29 Aug 1842
Zarahemla, Iowa
DEATH SP I: 28 Jan 1869
West Jordan, Salt Lake, Utah

CHILDREN:
Susannah 27 Aug 1844
Harmon 6 Dec 1847
Zacheriah 17 Apr 1849
Lucy Ann 31 Mar 1851
Matilda 2 Jan 1853

SPOUSE II: Edmund Marchant
MARRIED: 15 Mar 1857
Salt Lake City, Utah
DEATH SP II: 16 May 1885
Rockport, Summit County, Utah

CHILDREN:
none

Lucy Ann was born in Columbia, Ohio, the first of eight children in the family of David and Elizabeth Pettegrew. Her family moved from Ohio to Dearborn County, Indiana where they joined the Mormon Church. They were persecuted and driven from their home by the mobs for doing so. They suffered greatly and were often very sick. They traveled on to Nauvoo, Illinois where the good Saints helped them. They then moved across the Mississippi River to help establish the city of Zarahemla, Iowa.

Lucy Ann married Harmon Cutler 29 Aug 1842 at Zarahemla. He was a prominent man. His wife had died leaving seven children. He was a wagon maker and Brigham Young called him to assist in preparing the wagons for the Saints to travel to the West. Harmon Cutler was the Captain of a company of 262 Saints traveling with 63 wagons pulled by horses and oxen. When they were near Fort Laramie, Wyoming the wagon train was attacked by Indians, who captured all their horses, leaving them to travel with only the oxen. They arrived in the Salt Lake Valley Sep 1852. They eventually went on to West Jordan to make their home. They were later divorced.

Lucy Ann married Edmund Marchant 15 Mar 1857. He died 16 May 1885. Lucy Ann survived him by fifteen years. She had suffered through all the persecution and sickness which the Saints had to endure at the hands of wicked men, but was strong and lived to have a family of five children. Her first child was born at Nauvoo, Illinois, three more were born in Iowa. Her last child was born after she arrived in the Salt Lake Valley and she and her husband and family had settled in West Jordan, Utah. Lucy Ann was a noble, strong and brave pioneer. She died 17 Dec 1896 in Salt Lake City, Utah.

LYDIA JOHNSON MARCHANT

BIRTHDATE: 8 Mar 1814
Bath, England
DEATH: 24 Jun 1892
Peoa, Utah
PARENTS: John Johnson
Mary Dowsing Johnson
PIONEER: 28 Oct 1854
Robert L. Campbell Company
SPOUSE: Abraham Marchant
MARRIED: 7 Feb 1837
Bath Hampton, Somerset, England
DEATH: 6 Oct 1881
Peoa, Utah

CHILDREN:
Robert Abraham (died in infancy) 19 Feb 1838
Mary Ann 17 Mar 1839
Sarah Mitilda 1 Sep 1841
Abraham Robert 5 Apr 1843 (died in infancy)
Albert George Henry 3 Jan 1845
Lydia Elizabeth 27 Oct 1846
John Alma 7 May 1848
Joseph Hyrum 2 Feb 1850

Maria Louisa 12 Oct 1851
Franklin William 20 Sep 1853
Gilbert Johnson 10 Feb 1858

Lydia Johnson Marchant was born in England. She was trained as a milliner while a young woman in Bath, and it was presumably through her work that she met her husband, Abraham Marchant, who was an apprenticed tailor. Lydia was a slight figure of a woman, weighing less than 100 pounds. Abraham was very tall. They were married in Bath Hampton, Somerset, England 7 Feb 1837. They became the parents of eleven children; two died in infancy.

They were converted to the Mormon Church in 1844. They left Bath in 1852 for the industrial city of Birmingham where they could more easily accumulate the money to emigrate to America. They left England on the ship "Windermere" from Liverpool 22 Feb 1854. They arrived at the mouth of the Mississippi River on 24 Apr and were beset with adversity from the beginning. They traveled up the Mississippi River to St. Louis, Mo. They joined the Robert L. Campbell Company and began their long trek westward by wagon with a team of oxen 14 Jul 1854. They arrived in the Salt Lake Valley 28 Oct 1854, the last company of the season to reach the Valley. They settled first in South Cottonwood, where they remained for seven years. They were called to settle on the upper Weber River with a party of 12 to 14 other families and moved to Peoa, Utah in 1861, where they lived the rest of their lives.

Their first home was very crude, a one-room log cabin with dirt floors, built fortstyle on a small creek. Abraham was appointed presiding Elder in 1862, a year after establishing themselves in Peoa. As the years went by, they built a better home more suited to their needs. Lydia was known as an able, exacting housekeeper and excellent seamstress. The Post Office and general store were run out of their home. Both John Taylor and Brigham Young were accommodated in their home.

When the Relief Society was organized in 1875, Lydia became First Counselor. In 1877, she became President, a position she help for fifteen years until 2 Feb 1892, shortly before her death. She also served in the Young Ladies Mutual Improvement Association and was the first President of the Primary Organization. She was a constant support to her husband in farming, merchandising, establishing the first school, building the first Church house, running the Post Office and Store and raising her large family. After her husband died, she opened a millinery shop and ran it until her death, 24 Jun 1892. Her greatest joy was going to the Logan Temple with her adult children and completing the temple work for herself and her husband and children. The hardships and inconveniences that she experienced in her newly adopted country did not destroy her strong spirit or discourage her, for she felt she was in Zion.

MARY ANN BARTER (COSSEY) MARCHANT

No Photo Available

BIRTHDATE: 5 Aug 1850
Tredegar, Wales
DEATH: 9 Jan 1873
Peoa, Summit County, Utah
PARENTS: William Barter
Emma Walden Barter
PIONEER: before 1867
by wagon
SPOUSE:
Abraham Robert Marchant
MARRIED: 12 Jan 1867
Peoa, Utah

CHILDREN:
Mary Ann 15 Nov 1868
Abraham Robert Johnson 25 Dec 1870
Marian Jerusha 1 Jan 1873

Mary Ann was born in Wales. Her mother married a second time to a man by the name of Joshua Cossey. Mary Ann also went by the name of Cossey, taking the name of her step-father. Little is known about their journey to Utah or their becoming members of the Mormon Church. Mary Ann made her home in Peoa, Summit County, Utah in the very early years of that settlement. She was well acquainted with the rigors of pioneer life. Settlers were called from the Salt Lake Valley to settle Peoa in 1861. She was there by 12 Jan 1867, when it is recorded that she married Abraham Robert Marchant in Peoa. She was only sixteen years old at the time of her marriage.

The couple lived in the original Peoa Fort in a log cabin, as did the other settlers. It was in 1867, the year of her marriage, that the townspeople moved their cabins about a mile south where they built a second Fort, known as the Sagebottom Fort. The people from the Kamas area joined with them for protection during an Indian scare. Later, the Peoa people moved their log houses and Church cabin, also used as a school, back to the original settlement on Fort Creek.

Mary Ann and Abraham became the parents of three children. Mary Ann gave birth to her first child 15 Nov 1868. This was a little girl whom they named Mary Ann. They next had a son, Abraham Robert Johnson, born on Christmas Day, 1870. He lived less than one month and died 15 Jan 1871. It is interesting to note that the last two children were born on holidays. The third child was named Marian Jerusha, born on New Year's Day 1973. What a sadness and trial of the faith of the young couple to lose two of their three children.

Mary Ann must have had complications with this birth because she lived only about one week after the third child was born. She died 9 Jan 1873. The baby lived six months before she passed away. Abraham took his little four-year old Mary Ann into the home of his parents. Throughout Mary Ann's life she was known as "Dolly," the loving name given her by her grandparents. Mary Ann, her mother, though her own life of twenty-two years was very short, is today held in grateful remembrance by a large posterity because her daughter had ten children.

MARY ANNE OLPIN MARCHANT

No
Photo
Available

BIRTHDATE: 24 Dec 1808
Cambridge, Gloucester, England
DEATH: 7 Oct 1871
Weber County, Utah
PARENTS: Samuel Olpin
Mary Curnock Olpin
PIONEER: abt 1850
by wagon
SPOUSE: Edmund Marchant
MARRIED: 8 Oct 1850
England
DEATH: 16 May 1885
Rockport, Summit County, Utah

CHILDREN: none

Mary Anne Olpin Marchant was the fifth child born to Samuel and Mary Curnock Olpin. She was one of eight children in their family. She was thirty-five years old when Mormon missionaries taught her family the true Gospel. She was baptized 7 Feb 1843, the first of her family to embrace the religion. Mary Anne found work at Leighterton, Gloucester, England. She apparently was a housekeeper for Edmund Marchant. His wife had died and left a daughter, Sarah. Edmund had joined the Mormon Church 7 Aug 1846.

The last of Sep or the first of Oct 1850, Edmund Marchant booked passage on the ship "James Pinnal" for himself, his daughter, Sarah, age eleven years old, and Mary Anne Olpin. The ship was to set sail 2 Oct 1850, but he cancelled out and transferred to a later ship. He obtained a license and he and Mary Anne were married 8 Oct 1850. They sailed on the "Joseph Badger" on 17 Oct 1850 under Captain Scholfield. They arrived in New Orleans, La. 22 Nov 1850. They later came by wagon train to Utah. Five years after arriving in the Salt Lake Valley, they were sealed and received their endowments in the Salt Lake City Endowment House 21 Sep 1855. Mary Anne was a good mother to his daughter, Sarah. Mary Anne did not have children of her own. Her husband married four wives in plural marriage.

Mary Anne continued faithful to her religion. She enjoyed activity in her Ward and was willing to help anyone in need. She had endured the hardships and challenges of pioneer life and never murmured or complained. She supported her husband in all of his activities. Mary Anne died 7 Oct 1871 and is buried in Weber County, Utah. Her husband died 16 May 1885 and is buried at Rockport, Summit County, Utah.

CHARLOTTA WHITEHEAD TAYLOR MARCROFT

BIRTHDATE: 17 Mar 1817
Saddleworth, Yorkshire, England
DEATH: 16 May 1887
Salt Lake City, Utah
PARENTS: Robert Taylor
Mary Whitehead Taylor
PIONEER: Fall 1859
By wagon
SPOUSE: John Marcroft
MARRIED: abt 1834
England
DEATH: 16 Oct 1898
Salt Lake City, Utah

CHILDREN:
William Aug 1835 (died as child)
James May 1837/8 (died as child)
Sarah abt 1840 (died as child)
John, Jr. 25 Apr 1843
Robert 28 Feb 1846
Joseph 9 Apr 1849
Thomas 1 May 1852 (died as child)
Benjamine and Mary Ellen- twins May 1855 (died in childhood)
Hyrum Taylor 25 Aug 1860

Charlotta Whitehead Taylor Marcroft was born in England. Her mother died when she was young. She was raised by her father and step-mother (name unknown). In England, they used to call the Mormon missionaries "The Dippers" because the Mormon Church baptized by immersion. Charlotta, before she was married, would go after her work to the street meetings of the missionaries. John Marcroft, her sweetheart, found out about it and was very angry. He followed her one night to a meeting, intending to make a fuss, but instead he became interested in the Mormon Church. They both accepted the true Gospel and were among the first converts in England. Charlotta was baptized 13 Mar 1842. John was baptized first, 6 Jul 1841.

Charlotta and John were married about 1834 in England. Charlotta give birth to seven children between 1835 and 1852 in England. They lost three of their children in infancy. She and her husband and four sons emigrated to America 19 Nov 1854. They landed at New Orleans, La. They proceeded on to St. Louis, Mo. where they were forced to stay because of sickness and not having finances to continue. While in St. Louis two children (twins) were born and three of their children died.

Charlotta, John and three sons came to Salt Lake City, Utah in the Fall of 1859. They traveled with one of the poorer companies. Their horses and wagons were not in good condition. All those who could walk did so. They were surrounded several times by Indians and had their cattle stampeded and driven off. When they arrived in the Salt Lake Valley, they were sent to a house in the Fifth Ward. In Aug 1860, another son was born. In all, ten children were born to them, but only four sons survived. Charlotta and John were sealed to each other 28 Mar 1860.

Charlotta was blessed with the Gift of Tongues. She was a very fine, faithful woman. Her children were all active Church members all of their lives. Charlotta died 16 May 1887 at seventy years of age. Her husband died 16 Oct 1898.

ELLEN MARGRETHE HANSDATTER PEDERSEN MARKER (MARCHER)

No Photo Available

BIRTHDATE: 9 Feb 1802
Klemensker, Bornholm, Denmark
DEATH: 31 Dec 1879
Manti, Sanpete, Utah
PARENTS: Hans Pedersen
Karen Kirstine Berildsen
PIONEER: 30 Sep 1853
John E. Forsgren Ox and Wagon Co.
SPOUSE I: Peder Pedersen
MARRIED: 11 Jul 1821
Klemensker, Denmark
DEATH SP: 6 Feb 1845
Vester Marie, Bornholm, Denmark

CHILDREN:
Peder, 29 Oct 1821
Hans, 30 Oct 1823
Soren Peder, 23 Nov 1825
Johan Peder, 8 Aug 1827
Catherine Christine, 25 Jan 1830
Andreas Peder, 17 Mar 1831
Lauritz Peder, 12 Aug 1834
Karen Kirstine, 25 Jan 1837
Helene, 12 Dec 1840
Janus Peter, 2 May 1842
Hans Peter, 6 Dec 1844

SPOUSE II: Jens Pedersen Marker
MARRIED: 7 Apr 1849
DEATH: 29 Aug 1885
Manti, Sanpete, Utah

Ellen Margrethe Hansdatter was born in Denmark in 1802. She married Peder Pedersen on 1821 and they were the parents of 10 children. Her husband died in 1845, and she remarried in 1846, to Jens Pedersen Marker.

When the gospel came to Denmark and the Book of Mormon was translated into Danish, Ellen Margrethe and many of her children joined the Church. Persecutions at that time were very severe. She wanted to come to Zion, and prepared to do so. However two of her sons were away at sea, and she had to leave without them. All her life she tried to contact them, but her letters were never answered. If her relatives in Denmark ever knew of the boys' fate, they never told her.

She sailed in 1853 with the first group of Scandinavian Saints to leave Denmark, on the ship "Forest Monarch." They arrived in Salt Lake City 10 Sep 1853. They continued on to Lehi, Utah, and later to Manti, Utah. Ellen Margrethe died in Manti, Sanpete, Utah in 1879.

MARY CURTIS HOUGHTON MARKHAM

BIRTHDATE: 15 Nov 1832
Highland, Oakland, Michigan
DEATH: 6 Oct 1900
Spanish Fork, Utah, Utah
PARENTS: Jeremiah Curtis
Ruth Stratton
PIONEER: 1 Oct 1850
Stephen Markham Company
SPOUSE I: Ornon Houghton
MARRIED: July 1845
Montrose, Lee, Iowa
DEATH SP: 18 Aug 1847
Nauvoo, Hancock, Illinois

CHILDREN:
Edgar Stratton Houghton, 10 Oct 1846

SPOUSE II: Stephen Markham
MARRIED: 5 Oct 1850
Salt Lake City, Utah
DEATH SP: 10 Mar 1878
Spanish Fork, Utah, Utah

CHILDREN:
Orville Sanford, 23 May 1851
Mary Lucy, 2 Apr 1853
William don Carlos, 6 Jan 1855
Sarah Elizabeth, 12 Jul 1857
Atta Ruth, 12 Aug 1859
Hosmer Merry, 3 Dec 1861
Emily Aurelia, 4 Jan 1864
Margaret Eliza, 21 Mar 1866
Joseph, 27 Aug 1869
Charlotta Julina, 5 Nov 1870
Ira Meacham, 20 Dec 1873
Clarissa Maretta, 4 Feb 1876
Caroline Louisa, 3 Oct 1878

Mary Curtis was born in Iowa in 1832. Her father was baptized into the Church three days after her birth. Many of the Curtis family were with Zion's Camp and in Missouri during the persecutions. In 1834 her oldest sister, Aurelia, married Ornon Houghton. Their baby died during those difficult times, so they adopted four-year old Mary as their own.

Later the family lived in Nauvoo where Aurelia had five more children before her death in 1845. Only two of the children survived. Eventually Ornon married his stepdaughter in Montrose, Iowa. He died in 1847 leaving Mary at age fifteen, with a son and his two surviving children to care for.

Mary's real parents and other family members decided to follow Lyman Wight to Texas, and begged Mary to go with them. But Mary believed that the mantle of the Prophet had fallen on Brigham Young, and wished to go West. She joined the Company of Stephen Markham, and five days after their arrival in the Salt Lake Valley she became the plural wife of Stephen. They had thirteen children and settled in the Spanish Fork area. She also raised his son Stephen Jr., and a foster Indian girl. Mary died in Spanish Fork, Utah in 1900.

PRUDENCE FENNER KINYON FAIRCHILD MARKHAM

BIRTHDATE: 25 Mar 1799
Hapkinton, Washington County, Rhode Island
DEATH: 5 Jan 1895
Grantsville, Tooele, Utah
PARENTS: Boen Fenner
Betsy Kinyon
PIONEER: 1 Oct 1852
David Wood Wagon Train
SPOUSE I: Aldric Kinyon
MARRIED: Not known
DEATH: Not known

CHILDREN:
son
daughter

SPOUSE II: Joshua Fairchild, Jr.
MARRIED: 1827
Marion, Ohio
DEATH: 15 Jan 1891
Basin, Cassia, Idaho

CHILDREN:
Elizabeth (Betsy), 28 Mar 1828/30
Alma Fenner, 7 Apr 1833
Moroni Fenner, 19 Sep 1835

SPOUSE III: Stephen Markham
MARRIED: 30 Jan 1846
Nauvoo, Hancock, Illinois
DEATH: 10 Mar 1878
Spanish Fork, Utah
CHILDREN: None

Prudence grew up and married Aldric Kinyon and bore him a son and a daughter. He died leaving her a widow. About 1827, she married Joshua Fairchild, Jr. in Ohio. She bore him three children. They moved to Missouri and suffered much persecution. Their home was burned by the mobs. They lived together for eight years, then due to a disagreement, Joshua and Prudence parted. Prudence had a desire to stay with the Saints and Joshua did not.

Prudence met Stephen Markham and they were married and sealed in Nauvoo, Illinois on the 30th of January 1846. She never lived with him. In 1852, she and her children came west with the Sixth company under the command of Captain David Wood. They arrived in Salt Lake Valley on October 1, 1852. They settled in Grantsville, Tooele County, Utah. Some of her family pioneered to Idaho, but Prudence remained and died in Grantsville.

She settled in Grantsville, Tooele County, Utah. She dropped the name Markham and went by the name of

Fairchild the rest of her life. She died September 5, 1895 in Grantsville, Tooele County, Utah.

HARRIET HEATH MARLER

BIRTHDATE: 15 Oct 1813
DEATH: 22 Dec 1869
PARENTS:
Adolph (Adolphus) Heath
Julia Ann Mayers
PIONEER: 2 Oct 1850
James Lake Independent wagon
SPOUSE: Allen Marler
MARRIED: 2 Feb 1832
Port Gibson, Claibourne, Mississippi
DEATH: 29 Apr 1850
North Ogden, Weber, Utah

CHILDREN:
Elizabeth Ann, 27 Dec 1832
Sarah Jane, 12 Nov 1834
William Norton, 18 Sep 1836
Susan (Harmon), 25 Jan 1839
George Washington, 22 May 1841
Allen Jr, 8 Jun 1843
Francis, 20 Sep 1845
Mary Magdalene, 17 Nov 1847
Lydia, 15 Apr 1850

Harriet was born in Port Gibson, Mississippi, in 1813, the fifth of twelve children, born to wealthy plantation owners. Harriet was taught the art of Southern Hospitality. At age 18, 2 Feb 1832, she married Allen Marler. They soon owned a small plantation that employed twenty slaves. All but the last of their nine children were born on the South Fork of Bayou Pierre Plantation.

Harriet's father was converted to the LDS church and spoke of this religion to his family, converting Harriet. After an unusual experience Allen was converted and they were baptized in 1845. By 1850 Allen sold his holdings at a loss and the Marler family proceeded to St. Joseph, Mo. They boarded a boat at Grand Gulf, Mississippi and went to St. Joseph. On board cholera broke out. They lost a daughter and Allen died, then their eldest daughter died, followed by little Mary Magdalene. On 15 Apr Harriet gave birth to her ninth and last child, Lydia, who died the same day. Harriet decided that those of her remaining family would press on to Utah. She could not even write her name at this time. On the way her hired driver taught her to write and some reading was learned. They arrived 2 Oct 1850 in the James Lake independent wagon train. Harriet joined others and took her family to Pleasant Grove, being one of the first settlers there.

On Christmas, Bailey Lake married 16-year-old Sarah Jane and took her to Ogden. One year later Sarah Jane sent Bailey to bring her mother to North Ogden. Harriet, along with three sons and daughter went, and made a new start. Bailey was killed the last of Mar 1858 on a mission to Fort

Lemhi. President Young told Pleasant Green Taylor to marry Sarah Jane and look after her. He took her to Harrisville to live near his other three wives. Harriet often rode horseback down to see Sarah Jane. It was about four miles. Harriet died at North Ogden on 22 Dec 1869, and was buried there beside Bailey Lake at the foot of Ben Lomond Peak. At her passing she was fifty-six years old and had been a widow for nineteen years. She literally gave up a fortune for the Gospel's sake and never regretted her decision.

LUCETTA MARIA GATES MARLER

BIRTHDATE: 2 Oct 1837
Livonia, Wayne, Michigan
DEATH: 12 Nov 1879
Clifton, Oneida, Idaho
PARENTS: Samuel Gates
Lydia Downer
PIONEER: 27 Sep 1852
By ox team
SPOUSE: William Norton Marler
MARRIED: 12 Oct 1856
Lynn, Weber, Utah
DEATH SP: 26 Jun 1889
Clifton, Oneida, Idaho

CHILDREN:
William Norton 22 Sep 1857
Samuel Gates 19 Jan 1859
Lucetta Maria 28 Mar 1860
George Allen 11 Jun 1861
Harriet Eliza Ann 3 Oct 1862
Charles John 15 Jan 1864
Susan Elizabeth 26 Mar 1865
Lydia Ernestine 15 Sep 1867
Adolph Albertus 20 Sep 1869
Nancy Jane 20 Dec 1870
James Levi 4 May 1872
Milton David 25 Nov 1873
Mary Isabella 25 Jul 1875
Orson Lewis 12 Nov 1879

Lucetta Maria Gates was born in Michigan in 1837. Her mother was converted by an inspired dream in which she read the Book of Mormon through before ever seeing it. The whole family joined the Church and came to Utah in 1852.

Lucetta married William Norton Marler in Oct 1856 at Lynn, Weber, Utah. They lived at Lynn, or Bingham's Fort, where they engaged in farming. The Indians were very friendly and William learned to speak their language.

In 1867 the Marlers moved to Cache Valley, where they also farmed. The children looked forward to Conference when the General Authorities came to Logan. They would meet them on the road and wave handkerchiefs and sometimes strew flowers in the road. The men would raise their hats and bow. Then they would all go to confer-

ence. The children wore homespun clothing and were nearly all barefoot, but they loved the gospel.

The family made another move in 1871 to Clifton, Idaho, which was sparsely populated. School was only held for three months in the winter. Lucetta had worked hard all her life, preserving fruits, vegetables and meats for winter use. She was the mother of fourteen children. Death came at the age of forty-two in 1879 at Clifton, Idaho. Her husband died in 1889 of a heart attack, also at Clifton. The family had been devoted to the Church.

MARY MATHEWS MARLER

BIRTHDATE: 26 Apr 1847
Swansea, Glanmorgan, South Wales
DEATH: 9 May 1831
Providence, Cache, Utah
PARENTS: Hopkin Mathews
Margaret Morris
PIONEER: 1856 Handcart Company
SPOUSE: George W. Marler
MARRIED: 6 Dec 1863
Providence, Cache, Utah
DEATH SP: 8 Jan 1922
Providence, Cache, Utah

CHILDREN.
George Washington, 10 Jan 1865
Alemeda, 16 Sep 1866
Margaret Lucetta, 23 Oct 1868
Harriet Elizabeth, 2 Oct 1870
Joan, 18 Mar 1873
Hopkin Allen, 10 Mar 1875
Sarah Jane, 16 Dec 1876
Annie May, 5 May 1879
Helen Gertrude, 14 May 1884
Maurice Mathews, 28 Feb 1890

Mary Mathews was born 26 Apr 1847 in Swansea, Glanmorgan, South Wales, to Hopkin Mathews and Margaret Morris. Her parents had received the gospel prior to their marriage so Mary was brought up in the Church, but there was much persecution of the Saints in their area.

Mary was nine years old when the family embarked on the ship "Samuel Curling" for America. They were all sick on the voyage, and very glad to be on land when they landed in Boston. After they arrived in Iowa City they started their trek with handcarts, arriving in Salt Lake 4 Oct 1856. The family settled in the Ogden area.

Mary married George W. Marler on 6 Dec 1863, and they became the parents of ten children. One of her greatest trials was when she was asked to share her husband with another wife. For fifteen years she and the sister wife lived and raised their children together, until the other wife was compelled to leave the home, because of the enemies of the Church.

For many years the work that Mary performed was to lay out the dead. She was a member of the Relief Society and served in many positions. She was also an officer in the Daughters of the Utah Pioneers organization. After a lingering illness she passed away at her home in Providence, Cache County, Utah on 9 May 1931 at the age of eighty-four years.

HELEN MAR CUTLER HENDERSON MARLEY

BIRTHDATE: 15 Feb 1838
Clymer, Chautauqua, New York
DEATH: 6 Mar 1904
Clifton, Oneida, Idaho
PARENTS: Perley Cutler, Jr.
Caroline Sophia Freeman Cutler
Thompson Hawkins Van Valkenburg
PIONEER: Aug 31 1850
Milo Andrus Wagon Company
SPOUSE:
Samuel Goforth Henderson, Jr.
MARRIED: 6 May 1855
Salt Lake Endowment House
DEATH SP: 29 Oct 1904
Osmond, Lincoln, Wyoming

CHILDREN:
Melvin Cutler, 23 May 1856
Samuel Parley, 26 May 1858
Marion Cutler, 28 Apr 1860
Adelbert, 11 Jul 1862
Oscar Sheldon, 6 Oct 1864 (died young)
Emma Louisa, 7 Aug 1866
Caroline Sophia, 31 Dec 1868
Hannah Jeannette, 15 Apr 1871
Sylvester, 19 Dec 1875 (died young)
Theodore, 25 Apr 1877

SPOUSE II: William Marley
MARRIED: After 1886
DEATH SP II: Unknown
CHILDREN: None

Helen Mar Cutler Henderson Marley crossed the plains at the age of twelve, driving an ox-team and wagon in order to help pay for the travel expenses of her mother and baby brother. At night, she and her mother would knit stockings for others. On one occasion while walking behind a wagon, a gentleman called to her to quickly jump behind a tree. She obeyed instantly and found that a hoopsnake was aiming at her, but hit the tree and fastened itself into the tree. The man caught it and killed it.

After reaching the Salt Lake Valley, they lived in Sugar House Ward. Helen did the heavier and rougher work, as her mother was not very strong. She helped her mother sew, knit, spin, cook, wash, iron, etc. From this experience she became efficient in housekeeping and grew into a beautiful, useful woman. She was seventeen years old when she married Samuel Goforth Henderson in the Endowment House. In 1855, Samuel built a beautiful two story adobe house in

Kays City, now known as Kaysville. It was probably the first house built there. Three sons were born there, and during the spring of 1860, they moved to Provo while Johnston's Army took over the Valley. While in Provo, she gave birth to a son. They moved back to their home about three months later. Their crops were ruined except they salvaged enough wheat to make about five pounds of flour, which they shared with their neighbors. This house was purchased by the family of Governor Henry Blood and was restored and is still occupied by one of Governor Blood's sons, Alan Blood (Sep. 1994). The Henderson family sold their home and moved north to Brigham City where they raised fruit trees, vegetables, wheat, hay, grain, and sugar cane. They built a mill and made their own molasses.

She was the mother of ten children, was a wonderful housekeeper; cook, preserving fruits and vegetables for home and market; seamstress, carded, spun, and wove wool into jeans-cloth, knit stockings, sewed pants, dresses, shirts and blankets; nurse, and midwife. She gave of her time and strength willingly. She died at sixty-six years of age in Clifton, Idaho of apoplexy, 6 March 1904.

PHYSICAL DESCRIPTION: Dark grey eyes, long black hair, white soft skin, 5 feet 7 1/2 inches tall, weighed 140 pounds, wore a size 5 shoe and size 7 glove.

ELIZABETH STEWART MARRIOTT

BIRTHDATE: 12 Apr 1829
Colmsworth, Bedfordshire, England
DEATH: 10 Feb 1914
Marriott, Weber, Utah
PARENTS: Charles Stewart
Sophia Tingey Stewart
PIONEER: 15 Sep 1853
Moses Clawson Wagon Company
SPOUSE: John Marriott
MARRIED: 26 Feb 1854
Endowment House,
Salt Lake City, Utah
DEATH: 10 Jun 1899
Marriott, Weber, Utah

CHILDREN:
Elizabeth Stewart, 22 Apr 1855
Moroni Stewart, 31 Oct 1857
Annie Tresa, 7 Aug 1859
Frances Sophia, 22 Feb 1861
Louisa, 28 Oct 1862
Hyrum Willard (twin), 6 Dec 1863
Esther Amelia (twin), 6 Dec 1863
Caroline Emma, 8 Apr 1866
Ellen Maria, 6 Mar 1868
David Charles, 13 May 1872

When Elizabeth was five years old, her mother died. When she was ten years old, she left home to be a nurse for a wealthy family. In this home she taught herself to read and how to cook. Her father died in 1845 and testified to her the LDS Church was true. She joined the LDS Church in 1848. When she was nineteen years old, she worked to buy a ticket so she could sail to America. On the day they were to sail, she was fifteen shillings short of her fare. She sold her black silk dress and good shawl for enough to board the ship. She and her brother sailed on the ship, "James Pennel," and landed in New Orleans on October 22, 1849. Her brother and his wife went on to Zion. She was working to earn her way west when she had an accident with a kerosene lamp which exploded. She was badly burned. Her sweetheart ran in and saved her life, but he died eighteen days later from inhaling the fumes. After she recovered, she decided to cross the plains with the Moses Clawson Wagon Company. She was fortunate enough to get passage to cross the plains if she would do the cooking for a man who had an invalid wife and his family. Her burns were not completely well for three years. She arrived in Salt Lake City on September 15, 1853.

Elizabeth went to Kaysville where her brother had located. She met John Marriott and they were married in February of 1854. She was one of four wives. They moved to Marriott (part of Ogden by 12th Street). She and John became the parents of ten children. John's first wife, Susan, died and left six other children that Elizabeth raised along with her own. She was a very strong woman who believed in living a life of truth. She helped her husband form Marriott, Utah in 1855. She was called to be the Primary President of the first Primary organization in the community and remained in this position until she was seventy five years old. She had also been serving as a counselor in the Relief Society at the same time she was in the Primary. She resigned from that position when she was eighty years old. She also worked in both the Salt Lake and Logan temples for about twenty years. She was a remarkable woman who would do anything for the Lord and her fellow man.

MARGARET BURTON MARRIOTT

BIRTHDATE: 4 Apr 1839
Bradford, Yorkshire, England
DEATH: 30 Sep 1918
Ogden, Weber, Utah
PARENTS: James Burton
Isabella Walton
PIONEER: Fall of 1855
Milo Andrus Company
SPOUSE: John Marriott
MARRIED: 17 Dec 1857
Kaysville, Davis, Utah
DEATH SP: 10 Jun 1899
Marriott, Weber, Utah

CHILDREN:
James Ephriam, 24 Apr 1859
Annie, 27 Feb 1861
Isabella, 29 Apr 1865
Robert, 10 Sep 1867
Margaret, 3 Sep 1873
Mary, 22 Feb 1875
Rose, 5 Jan 1878
Lucy, 16 Oct 1880

Margaret Burton was born in England in 1839. In 1855 she sailed on the ship "Samuel Curling" with her mother and six of her brothers and sisters. They joined the Milo Andrus Company traveling under the Perpetual Emigration Fund, and arrived in Utah in Sep 1855. They traveled on to Kaysville to stay with a brother who had emigrated earlier.

Their first winter in Kaysville was a hard one, with very little to eat. They had no bread for six weeks, and had to dig green sego roots to supplement their meager diet. They also killed an old cow, that was so weak it could not stand up.

Margaret married John Marriott as a plural wife in 1857 and moved to Marriott, Weber, Utah. She was the mother of eight children. Margaret was always busy with community and Church activities. She taught in Relief Society, was a midwife, visited the sick, and laid out the dead. She died in Ogden, Weber, Utah in 1918.

SUSANNAH HOUGHTON FOWKES MARRIOTT

No Photo Available

BIRTHDATE: 31 Jul 1821
Bohnhurst, Bedfordshire, England
DEATH: 15 Dec 1858
Marriott, Weber, Utah
PARENTS: Samuel Fowkes
Martha Houghton
PIONEER: 15 Sep 1851
Livingston-Kinkead Company
SPOUSE: John Marriott
MARRIED: 18 Mar 1842
Bedfordshire, England
DEATH SP: 10 Jun 1899
Marriott, Weber, Utah

CHILDREN:
Caroline Swanton, 15 Jan 1843
Lorenzo, 26 Oct 1844
John III, 24 Oct 1846
Susannah, 15 Oct 1848
Rebecca Isabelle, 19 Jun 1852
Martha Isabell, 16 Jun 1854
Joseph (twin), 21 Oct 1856
William (twin), 21 Oct 1856
Benjamin, 15 Dec 1858

Susannah Houghton Fowkes was born in England in 1821. She married John Marriott in England in 1842. They left England on the ship "Swanton" in January 1843. Susannah's first baby was born the day before the ship sailed, but died within hours. On board ship the Saints were divided into two groups, with the priesthood over them to see that prayers were said, meetings held, and to aid in the comfort and cleanliness of each person.

They arrived in Nauvoo in April. John and Christopher Layton built a 10 by 12 foot room where they both lived until another house could be built. The floor was dirt, but

Susannah wove a rug and placed straw under it. Here they lived until they were forced out of Nauvoo.

They arrived in Utah in September 1851. Two Mormon companies traveled with an Oregon-bound company, and John was one of the teamsters. At first they lived in Kaysville, then in 1854 John was called to settle in Weber County by the Ogden and Weber Rivers, or the Ogden Bottoms, as it was called. Susannah died in 1858, and John died in 1899, both in Marriott, Weber, Utah.

TERESA SOUTHWICK MARRIOTT

BIRTHDATE: 8 May 1840
Dudley, Worchester, England
DEATH: 6 Dec 1920
Ogden, Weber, Utah
PARENTS: Joseph Southwick
Mary Ann Martin Southwick
PIONEER: 3 Sep 1855
John Hindley Company
SPOUSE: John Marriott
MARRIED: 5 Nov 1855
Marriott, Weber, Utah
DEATH: 10 Jun 1899
Marriott, Weber, Utah

CHILDREN:
Mary Ann, 10 Sep 1860
Edward, 13 Nov 1862
Eliza, 4 Dec 1866
David, 18 Aug 1868
Charles Arthur, 6 May 1870
Brigham, 31 Dec 1872
Ida May, 8 Aug 1875
Israel, 25 Jun 1878

Teresa's family had accepted the gospel and were baptized in England before they came to America. They sailed on the ship, "Ashland," in February 1849. At age nine, just two and one half weeks after arriving at St. Louis, her father died from cholera. When she was fourteen she joined her older sister and others to cross the plains. Her sister became ill and wished to return to St. Louis. On the way back, the sister died. Teresa was left alone in St. Louis with no one. She worked out an agreement with Bishop Whorley who agreed to take her with his family if she would help his wife with the work while crossing the plains. She did so willingly. She had two pairs of shoes when she began the trek and wore one pair out. She saved the other pair for use in the Salt Lake Valley. She arrived in the Salt Lake Valley on September 3, 1855.

Teresa became a polygamous wife to John Marriott on November 5, 1855. They were the parents of eight children. She spun flax into warp for making jeans for her family. She supplied her own lye and made soap for her family. She helped the other wives of her husband to raise their children. Teresa was loved and respected by all who knew her. She was very compassionate and unselfish. It was her goal to be of service to her fellow men.

ELLEN COTTAM PILLING WILLIAMS MARSDEN

No
Photo
Available

BIRTHDATE; 15 Nov 1825
West Bradford, Yorkshire, England
DEATH: 3 Oct 1901
Salt Lake City, Utah
PARENTS: John Cottam
Catharine Livesay Cottam
PIONEER: 1855
SPOUSE I: Edmund Pilling
MARRIED: 31 Aug 1845
Burnley, Whaley,
Lancashire, England
DEATH: 25 Sep 1853
West Bradford, Yorkshire, England

CHILDREN:
John 8 Jun 1846
Thomas Cottam 24 Mar 1848
William Alma 12 Dec 1849
Catherine Margaret 22 Aug 1852

SPOUSE II: Ebenezer Albert Williams
MARRIED: 21 Jun 1857
Salt Lake City, Utah
DEATH: 18 Feb 1917
Kaysville, Utah

CHILDREN:
Jenny Cottom 25 May 1858

SPOUSE III: William Marsden
MARRIED: 2 Sep 1865
Salt Lake City, Utah
DEATH: 5 Aug 1878
Salt Lake City, Utah

CHILDREN:
Rachael Ann 10 Dec 1865
George Thomas 10 Dec 1868
John Cottom 20 Feb 1870

Ellen Cottam was raised in an ancestral home called the Meadowland. Although the family was notable, Ellen's mother entertained lavishly and was anxious to help people. She nearly ruined her husband financially with her generosity. They lost their ancestral home when Ellen was young. While her mother moved from their fine old manor in a stoic stance, the children cried as they loaded their belongings into the wagon. Ellen was not able to read or write which was evidenced by her signature on her marriage certificate to Edmund Pilling in 1845. She signed her marriage certificate with an X.

Ellen and Edmond had four children before he died. Two of their children died also. She was left to make her voyage and cross the Plains as a widow. She had assistance from the Perpetual Fund Program. Her little daughter Catherine died in Kansas on the way to Utah, leaving her with one child, William Pilling. They arrived in Utah in 1855.

Two years after she arrived in Salt Lake City, she married Ebenezer Albert Williams in a plural marriage. They had a daughter, Jenny Williams. Then Ellen left the polygamist situation.

Several years later, she married William Marsden and together they had three more children and raised them in Salt Lake City.

JANE ROSETTA ANDREWS MARSH

BIRTHDATE: 25 Sep 1836
Randolph, Chantaugue County, New York
DEATH: 1 Mar 1908
Ogden, Utah
PARENTS: Charles Amos Andrews
Keturah Button Andrews
PIONEER: 4 Oct 1848
Willard Snow Wagon Train
SPOUSE: George J. Marsh
MARRIED: 27 Feb 1854
Salt Lake City, Utah
DEATH: 24 Oct 1917
Ogden, Utah

CHILDREN:
George Ames, 7 Jan 1855
Jane Keturah, 16 Apr 1857
Josiah, 31 Aug 1859
Salley Ann, 11 Nov 1861
Lovisa Roseabel, 16 Oct 1863
Clinton, 25 Feb 1867-twin
David Richard, 25 Feb 1867-twin
Geneva Alwilda, 30 Aug 1869
Effie Nancy, 18 Nov 1871
Lottie Clotilda, 11 Dec 1873

Jane Rosetta was born in New York in 1836. She was the third of three daughters. Her parents were converted to the Mormon Church. Shortly after Jane's birth the family moved to Kirtland, Ohio. Jane was baptized in a branch of the Ohio River when about eight years of age. She remembered well the building of the Kirtland Temple and the trials of the Saints there.

They later moved to Nauvoo, Illinois. She knew the Prophet Joseph Smith and his brother Hyrum. They gave her a ride in their carriage when she was just a little barefoot girl on her way home from helping her father with the work on their share-cropping farm. When they reached her home, Joseph Smith lifted her down from the carriage and said that all would be well with her. After that, she prayed many times that she could have a vision like the Prophet.

Jane left Nauvoo with her parents in the year of 1846 when the Saints were driven from their homes and spent the Winter at Council Bluffs, Iowa. In the Spring of 1848, they started on their journey to the Salt Lake Valley. Jane was just twelve years old but she drove two yoke of oxen across the Plains. The family arrived in Salt Lake in Sep 1848 and lived in Pioneer Square durinq the Winter of 1848-49. They passed through all the hardships incident to early pioneer

life in Utah. Jane and her father worked with a team and wagon on a farm for a peck of bran and shorts a day. Some days all she would have to eat was one pancake, and sometimes she would faint for the want of nourishment.

Jane was married to George J. Marsh in the Salt Lake Endowment House 27 Feb 1854 by Elder Heber C. Kimball. During their first year of marriage her husband built toll bridges in Idaho. They lived among the Indians who were friendly to them because they knew Jane's father who was an interpreter and guide. It was a very difficult for Jane when her husband was called to a mission in England. They lived on a farm in Willard, Utah and she could barely make ends meet. She and her eight-year-old daughter knitted socks and sold them to the immigrants. During this time she buried one child. When her husband returned she had sufficient provisions on hand to last them the balance of the Winter.

In 1867, Jane gave birth to twin boys. One soon died and it was through the help of the Lord that the other lived. For eighteen long months Jane lay ill in bed. While she was sick she was blessed with the strength to endure. She was shown many wonderful things and had a strong testimony of the Gospel. She gradually regained her strength. Jane, through all of their trials and tribulations, remained a faithful member of the Church. She passed away 1 Mar 1908 in Ogden, Utah at the age of seventy-two.

MARTHA EVINS ALLEN OWENS MARSHALL

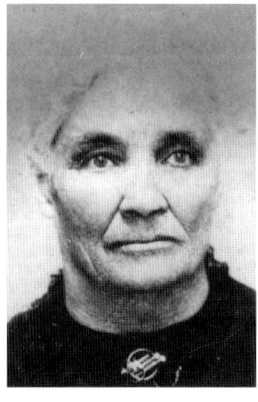

BIRTHDATE: 2 Mar 1823
Pulaski, Kentucky
DEATH: 4 Jul 1897
Smithfield, Cache Valley, Utah
PARENTS: Rial Allen
Margaret Moore Evins Allen
PIONEER: 25 Sep 1847
A. 0. Smoot Wagon Train
SPOUSE I: Robert Owens
MARRIED: 7 Mar 1850
Somerset, Pulaski, Kentucky
DEATH: 9 Nov 1883
Los Angeles, California

CHILDREN:
Margaret, 20 Dec 1850
Mary, 26 Feb 1852
William, 6 Feb 1853
Joseph, 10 Nov 1858
Rial, 10 Nov 1858

SPOUSE II: William Marshall
MARRIED: 1862
San Bernardino, California
DEATH: Feb 1894
CHILDREN: none

Martha Evins Allen Owens Marshall was born in Kentucky. She and her three brothers had heard the Gospel preached by Elder Wilford Woodruff in Kentucky. Martha joined the Mormon Church when she was fifteen years old. She and her brother, Andrew, made the journey across the Plains and into the Salt Lake Valley arriving about 25 Sep 1847.

Martha met Robert Owens and married him in plural marriage. They were sealed by Heber C. Kimball. They were blessed with five children; two were blind. Soon after the birth of their third child, Robert received a call to fill missions to Madris, India and Sydney, Australia. He left home 26 Apr l853. Martha had the care of her five young children. Times were hard and her challenges were many.

Shortly after her husband returned from his missions, Robert took Martha and her children to California. The twin boys, Joseph and Rial, were born on the way. When they arrived in San Bernardino, Martha and her husband had some misunderstanding. Martha told Robert to go on his way alone and she and the children would go on alone. They separated and Robert settled in Los Angeles. Martha started back to Utah. She met William Marshall, a convert from Australia and he brought her and her children back to Utah. They were married in San Bernardino, California in 1862. He had a son who was older than Martha's boys.

William Marshall died in 1894. Martha went to live with her son, William, and his wife in Smithfield, Utah. She died there 4 Jul 1897. Martha and Robert left scores of descendants blessed with testimonies of the Gospel. They have a strong love for the land that gave their parents and grandparents the peace they sought in coming so many miles across the desert waste to find. They are determined to carry on in the footsteps of these brave parents; true and faithful pioneers.

MARY JANE ALDER GOASLIND MARSHALL

BIRTHDATE: 7 Aug 1853
near Sweet Water River, Wyoming
DEATH: 14 Mar 1922
Franklin, Franklin, Idaho
PARENTS: George Alder
Mary Ann Hamilton
PIONEER: 9 Sep 1853
David Wilkin Company
SPOUSE I:
John Henry Goaslind, Jr.
MARRIED: 29 May 1867
DEATH SP: 30 Apr 1879
Franklin, Franklin, Idaho

CHILDREN:
George John, 8 May 1869
Levi, 1 Dec 1870
Mary Jane, 6 Nov 1871
Joseph Henry, 10 Nov 1872
Matilda Ann, 6 Apr 1875
Alfred Edmond, 2 Feb 1877
William James, 15 Sep 1879

SPOUSE II: George Thomas Marshall
MARRIED: 9 Nov 1882
Salt Lake City, Utah
DEATH SP: 20 Jul 1931
Preston, Idaho

CHILDREN:
Francis, 9 Aug 1883
Mary Jane, 23 Nov 1884
Charles Frederick, 27 Dec 1886
Priscilla Alder, 14 Jul 1888
Bart Alder, 31 Dec 1891
Don Carlos, 14 Jan 1894
LaVon Alder, 5 Jun 1896
Lola Alder, 2 Aug 1898

Mary Jane Alder was born on the banks of the Sweet Water River in Wyoming in 1853, while her parents were crossing the plains by ox team. Her mother rested only one day before traveling on.

The family first lived in Kaysville, Utah, then in 1860 moved to Franklin, Idaho. At the age of sixteen she married John Henry Goaslind, and to them were born seven children. John Henry drowned in the Cub River at Franklin, Idaho in 1879.

Mary Jane then married George Thomas Marshall in 1882 and had more children. One son, LaVon was killed on the battlefield in France during World War I. She lived most of her married life in Franklin, Idaho and died there in 1922.

SARAH BEDFORD BOOTH RUDD PILLING MARSING

BIRTHDATE: 29 Apr 1834
Liversige, Yorkshire, England
DEATH: 1 Apr 1911
Cleveland, Emery, Utah
PARENTS: John Bedford
Charlotte Truelove Bedford
PIONEER: 27 Aug 1860
Daniel Robinson Wagon Train
SPOUSE I: George Booth
MARRIAGE: date unknown
Divorced 25 Dec 1855

CHILDREN: None

SPOUSE II: Lorenzo Dow Rudd
MARRIED: unknown
DIVORCED: Unknown
CHILDREN: None

SPOUSE III: John Pilling
MARRIED: 15 Oct 1864
Salt Lake City, Utah

CHILDREN:
John, 24 Jul 1865
Ellen, 29 Nov 1867
Willie, 18 Aug 1869

SPOUSE IV: Niels Larson Marsing
MARRIED: 5 Sep 1870
Kanosh, Utah
DEATH SP: 2 Nov 1913
Price, Carbon, Utah

CHILDREN:
Hyrum, 3 Aug 1871
Sarah Bangta, 5 Feb 1873
Alma, 31 Oct 1875
Mary Jane, 26 Sep 1878

Sarah Bedford was born in England in 1834. Her twin brother died at birth. She married George Booth, date unknown, but when he found out she had been baptized into the LDS Church he threw her out. This was on Christmas Day in 1855. She trudged to Halifax and found employment in a clothing factory. For several years she worked to save to come to America. By 1860 she had saved enough to sail on the ship "Underwriter."

In Florence, Nebraska she was assigned to the 9th Handcart Company under Captain Daniel Robinson. Sarah pulled a cart all that first day, and when evening came she took off her shoes. The next morning her feet were so swollen she could not get her shoes back on, and so traveled the thousand miles in her bare feet. The company arrived in August 1860.

In Salt Lake City Sarah married Lorenzo Dow Rudd, but would never tell her children about her marriage or divorce to him. She found employment with the family of William Goddard. They helped her to learn pioneer ways; how to plant and raise a garden, and to preserve food for winter's use. She continued with her skill in knitting, crocheting and weaving. Sarah was an ardent Church worker, serving in the Primary and Relief Society.

She married John Pilling in 1864 in the Endowment House. They settled in Fillmore, Utah and had three children. John died in 1870. She then became acquainted with Niles Larson Marsing, a widower with five small sons. They were married in Sep 1879 and lived in Kanosh, Utah, where four more children were born to her. Niels later took another wife, Harriet Harmon, and the family moved to Joseph, Utah. The two wives worked together to make their large home comfortable. Later Niels moved his families to Desert Lake in Emery County. When the Manifesto came into effect Sarah told Niels to remain with Harriet since she had a young family of thirteen children. Niels and Harriet moved to Price, Utah and Sarah remained in Desert Lake. In her last years she lived with daughter Bangta, in Cleveland, Utah, where she died in 1911.

ELIZABETH SMITH MULLINER JONES MART

BIRTHDATE: 7 Mar 1836
Chinquacousy, Ontario, Canada
DEATH: 7 Aug 1883
Salt Lake City, Utah
PARENTS: Samuel Mulliner, Sr.
Katharine Nisbet Mulliner
PIONEER: 26 Sep 1850
Warren Foote Wagon Company
SPOUSE I: John Markland Jones
MARRIED: 23 Jul 1853
Salt Lake City, Utah
DEATH: 23 Dec 1871
St. George, Utah

CHILDREN:
Catharine (Kate) Jones 17 Jul 1854
Elizabeth Amelia 11 Mar 1856
John Markland 9 Dec 1858
Samuel Henry 8 Mar 1860
Edward William 18 Mar 1862
Nettie 12 Jun 1864
Louisa May 22 Jun 1867

SPOUSE II: Mr. Mart
MARRIED: not given
DEATH SP: not given
CHILDREN: None

Elizabeth Smith was born in Ontaria, Canada, in 1836. Her Scottish-born parents joined the Mormon Church when Elizabeth was a year old. They soon joined the body of the Church and became well acquainted with the Prophet Joseph Smith. Elizabeth was given a second name of Smith in honor of the Prophet.

Elizabeth was fourteen when the family began their journey across the Plains to Utah. She witnessed constant hardship, sickness and death. In Winter Quarters her father outfitted many wagons and teams for other travelers. Finally, they left Kanesville, Iowa with the Warren Foote Wagon Company in June 1850 and arrived in the Salt Lake Valley 26 Sep 1850. When Elizabeth was seventeen years old she married John Markland Jones 24 Jul 1853 in Salt Lake City. They were later sealed in the Endowment House 5 Mar 1857. They became the parents of seven children. Elizabeth was not well after her first baby was born. She was given a Patriarchal Blessing which promised her that she would have better health from that time forward. She was able to have six more children. Their son, John, was tragically drowned in Lehi, Utah at the age of two.

Elizabeth's husband was a fine musician and she had a lovely singing voice. Together they performed at State occations. At least once they performed at the home of Brigham Young. The family moved to Vancouver, Washington and San Francisco, California looking for work. John was a musician. There was not enough work in his field and the wages were poor. By June 1864, they were back in Utah where Elizabeth gave birth to her sixth child.

The years had been years of struggle and hardships for Elizabeth. As her husband was traveling in the St. George area he died of injuries from an accidental fall which were complicated by an attack of pneumonia, 23 Dec 1871. Their last child was five years old. Elizabeth's greatest skill was ironing and she made a business of it since there was a demand for well-ironed shirts to go with formal dress for men. She was dissatisfied with her life and work.

It was at this time that Mr. Mart, a traveler on his way to California came into Salt Lake. Elizabeth met him and a courtship developed. When he asked Elizabeth to marry him Elizabeth's father discouraged her. But Elizabeth went ahead with the marriage. She found homes for her children with friends, hoping to regain them once she got situated in California. That was never possible. She remained in California only a short time. She returned to Utah alone and broken in health. She was never able to get on her feet and take her children back. She died when she was just forty-six years of age, of what might have been ovarian cancer or perhaps a broken heart. Her youngest child, Louisa, was with her when she died 7 Aug 1883. She was buried in the Salt Lake City Cemetery.

ELIZABETH JENKINS MARTELL

BIRTHDATE: 9 Aug 1842
Llansaint, South Wales
DEATH: 2 Oct 1880
Spanish Fork, Utah Co., Utah
PARENTS: Morris Jenkins
Margaret Reese
PIONEER: Dec 1856
John A. Hunt Wagon Company
SPOUSE: Thomas C. Martell
MARRIED: 15 Jan 1858
DEATH SP: 23 Sept 1905
Spanish Fork, Utah Co., Utah

CHILDREN:
Elizabeth Margretta, 18 Oct 1858
Thomas Charles Jr., 10 Jul 1860
Morris Jenkins, 19 Nov 1861
William Charles, 14 Oct 1863
Lucy Ann, 1 May 1866
Margaret, 21 Jan 1869
Catherine, 15 Feb 1872
Eve, 28 Jul 1873
James Arthur, 23 May 1877
Mary Ellen, 29 Feb 1880

Elizabeth was born in South Wales in 1842, the first child born in the family. Eliza's family was taught the gospel of the Church of Jesus Christ of Latter-day Saints by the missionaries and they joined the new Church.

On April 19, 1856, they joined with many other converts in sailing from Liverpool, England on the ship "Samuel Curling." Her brother, David, age seven was left with his aging Jenkins grandparents as a comfort and help for them.

The Jenkins family crossed the Plains with Captain John A. Hunt's Wagon Company. They were directly behind the ill-fated Martin Handcart Company; they encountered much hazardous weather, also. They arrived into the Salt Lake Valley in late December, 1856. They went directly to Spanish Fork, where many of their friends and former neighbors lived.

Elizabeth, at age sixteen, married Thomas Charles Martell in polygamy on January 15, 1858 and they were sealed in the Endowment House in Salt Lake. Elizabeth was a gentle and loveable woman. Thomas claimed she was the most beautiful woman that he had ever seen. She was industrious and neat. She was kind and happy and loved to have the young people come over to her home.

The family went through trials and hardships in settling a new land, making a home and rearing a family. Elizabeth was religious and took part in auxiliaries of the Church. Thomas served a mission to Wales, leaving his wife and five children, ages seventeen to two on their own. She was a relief Society teacher at the time of her death.

Elizabeth had never fully recovered from the birth of her tenth child and she passed away on October 2, 1880 at the age of thirty-eight years. Her husband passed away on September 23, 1905 in Spanish Fork, Utah County, Utah.

These faithful pioneers left a great legacy of strength in following their religious convictions, a heritage they proudly left for the generations who have followed them.

ANN CLARK MARTIN

BIRTHDATE: 14 Oct 1835
Stroud, Gloucester, England
DEATH: 4 Feb 1909
Scipio, Millard County, Utah
PARENTS Thomas Clark
Elizabeth Boulton Clark
PIONEER: 12 Sep 1857
Jesse Bigler Martin Wagon
SPOUSE: Jesse Bigler Martin
MARRIED: 20 Dec 1857
DEATH SP: 17 Oct 1908

CHILDREN:
Elizabeth 27 Feb 1859
Esther twin 15 Apr 1862
Esdras twin 15 Apr 1862
Elzina 15 Jun 1865
Mariette 8 Nov 1869
Rose Ann 17 Aug 1872
Lucy May 16 May 1875
William 29 Dec 1877

Ann was born in England, 1835. She was the third of six children. Her parents heard the LDS doctrine in the spring of 1842. They became members of the Cheltenham Conference. Ann speaks of her early life: "My early home life was very comfortable. Our parents were kind and tender. Each morning father brought up our polished shoes and hot water, calling us to get washed and dressed and roll our hoops around the block to get an appetite for breakfast. They emigrated to America in 1857. I left my parental home and all my relations on the 28th of March for Liverpool. We set sail on the ship "George Washington" on April 1. We had a tolerably pleasant voyage. We landed in Boston on the 23rd of the same month. From there we traveled by railroad to Iowa City. We stayed there for five weeks, then traveled by ox team to Florence, Nebraska. I walked two hundred fifty miles of the three hundred miles distance. We suffered from blistered and bleeding feet for awhile, but later overcame that. We started to cross the plains about the last of June. Our Captain was Jesse Bigler Martin, a returning missionary from the British Mission. We arrived in Salt Lake City on Sep 13, 1857."

As was the custom, Ann was invited to stay with friends and acquaintances until she was permanently settled. Her history reads, "I stayed there until December, when I returned to Brother Martin's. He asked me to be his wife. His family consisted of wife and three children, who were willing that he take me as a second wife in obedience to the law of plural marriage. I was sealed to Jesse B. Martin on Dec 20, 1857 by President Brigham Young in his office. We lived in the city until 1860. In the spring of that year my husband bought a farm in Lehi, where we lived three years and were getting along quite nicely, but in the fall of 1863, he was called to Scipio, Millard County. Thither he went. He took part of his family, but I went to Provo and stayed with relatives until the following spring."

Jesse was called to preside over the newly formed branch of Scipio. During the first winter, he and his family lived in a dugout in the fort. In 1866, Ann was appointed to teach day school in Scipio. She taught for 33 years, receiving meat, butter, eggs and all kinds of commodities which she shared with Sophronia Martin's family. She did sewing, washing, and ironing far into the night in order to keep her little family neat and clean. She was always immaculate herself, and although a very small woman she must have had a wonderful reserve of energy or determination. She was secretary in the Relief Society for seven years, President of the Primary for twelve years and counselor for four years, taught Sunday School for 18-20 years and sang in the choir for 25 years. After the Manifesto she lived amongst her children. On one trip back to Scipio, while staying witb her daughter Lucy, she became ill and died 4 Feb 1909. Jesse died 17 Oct 1908.

CATHERINE FAHY MARTIN

BIRTHDATE: 26 May 1826
Knocktoper, Kilkenny, Ireland
DEATH: 17 Sep 1897
Galeana, Chihuahua, Mexico
PARENTS: Mihael Fahy
Margaret O'Niel Fahy
PIONEER: 4 Sep 1859
George Rowley Handcart Co.
SPOUSE: Josiah Fleming Martin
MARRIED: 3 Nov 1859
DEATH: 13 Apr 1881
Salina, Sevier County, Utah

CHILDREN:
Hannah Jane 30 Jul 1860
Nancy Ellen 2 Jul 1867

Catherine Fahy Martin was born in Ireland. She and her sister joined the Mormon Church in Ireland and wanted to emigrate to Utah. Times were hard. Catherine decided to use her money to send her sister, Jane, to Utah ahead of herself. When she had earned enough money Catherine journeyed to America and on to Utah alone. She crossed the Atlantic Ocean of the ship "William Tappscott." They arrived in New York. Theirs was the first group to travel from New York to Florence, Nebraska by way of Albany, New York to Niagara, Canada to Detroit, Michigan and on to St. Joseph, Missouri. Catherine was a thirty-two year old spinster traveling alone. She joined the George Rowley Handcart Company. This was the eighth handcart company to cross the Plains to Utah. They arrived in the Salt Lake Valley 4 Sep 1859.

When Catherine arrived in the Valley she learned that her sister, Jane, had died shortly before she arrived. Catherine married Josiah Fleming Martin 3 Nov 1859. She was his fourth wife in plural marriage. They helped settle Salina, Sevier County, Utah. Catherine was industrious. She braided hats and trimmed them. She wove many beautiful baskets. She was an officer in the Silkworm Association of Utah. She not only raised the silkworms, but she wove the silk into cloth. She had worked in the Mills in England and was an excellent seamstress.

She and her husband were the parents of two daughters.

While Catherine was in Church in Ireland she was given the gift of tongues. When she spoke in tongues a member present gave the interpretation. She said that Catherine would travel to five nations: Ireland, Scotland, England, the United State and Mexico. This came true. Catherine pioneered in Colonia Juarez, Colonia Dublan, Colonia Pacheco and Colonia Hidalgo (Galeana), Chihuahua, Mexico. Her greatest love was for God, Jesus Christ and her Church. Catherine died 17 Sep 1897 in Galeana, Mexico and is buried there.

ELIZA SALMON MARTIN

BIRTHDATE: 29 Nov 1832
London, Middlesex, England
DEATH: 10 Nov 1913
Salt Lake City, Utah
PARENTS: John Salmon
Charlotte Pratt Salmon
PIONEER: 30 Nov 1856
Edward Martin Handcart Co.
SPOUSE: Edward Martin
MARRIED: 1855
sealed 3 Oct 1863
Salt Lake Endowment House
DEATH: 8 Aug 1882
Salt Lake City, Utah

CHILDREN:
George, 12 Aug 1856
Emma, 6 Aug 1858
Charlotte, 11 Dec 1862
Edward Thomas, 12 Jul 1864
Eliza (Aubrey), 8 Jun 1866
John Salmon, 4 Mar 1868
Joseph Hyrum, 3 May 1869
Napoleon Bonaparte, 23 Jul 1871
Josephine, 6 Jul 1872
Earnest, 28 Apr 1874

Eliza was born in England, 1832. At age twenty-two, she married Edward Martin. They made their home in England, while getting ready to emigrate to Zion. Eliza came to the U. S. in March 1856 as an expectant mother. Her first child was born 12 Aug 1856 in Iowa City, Iowa while waiting for the handcart journey to begin.

The ill-fated Martin Handcart Co. left Iowa City 25 Aug and finally arrived in Salt Lake City 30 Nov 1856. After their arrival, they made their home in Salt Lake City where they became parents of nine more children. Eliza was also called upon to raise two of her husband's children from two other wives after their deaths. These children were Brigham Martin born 11 Jan 1859 (mother-Alice Clayton) and Martha Martin born 4 Aug 1858 (mother-Jane Gray). Eliza was a remarkable woman. Her home was on Main Street between 1st and 2nd South, where the Kearns Building now stands. She had a talent for making bonnets and beautiful hats for the pioneer women of the valley. She taught this trade to her step-daughter, Martha, who worked in millinery for many years.

Edward passed away 8 Aug 1882, when their youngest child was just eight. This was a hard time for Eliza, making a living and raising her large family. She remained active in church, serving well in her callings and raising her family. She passed away a few weeks before her 81st birthday, in Salt Lake City, having been a widow for thirty years.

JANE STARLEY MARTIN

BIRTHDATE: 16 May 1842
Bolney, Sussex, England
DEATH: 9 Jan 1925
Salt Lake City, Utah
PARENTS: James Starley
Caroline Mitchell Starley
PIONEER: 17 Nov 1855
Hooper & Williams Mercantile
Wagon Train
SPOUSE: Anthony Martin
MARRIED: 4 Feb 1859
Fillmore, Utah
DEATH: 1 Nov 1905
Salt Lake City, Utah

CHILDREN:
Mary Jane, 1 Jan 1860
Sarah Hanna, 1 May 1861
Anthony H., 25 Oct 1862
Thomas J., 22 Nov 1864
Caroline Elizabeth, 16 Nov 1865
Lulu, 7 Jun 1868
Charles, 23 Dec 1869
Minnie, 27 Jan 1872
Edith A., 29 Nov 1873
Tottie-twin, 17 Jun 1875
Fredrick-twin, 17 Jun 1875
Henry A., 20 Mar 1878
Midge, 14 Mar 1880
Leah, 31 Jan 1882
Frank, 10 Dec 1883

Jane Starley Martin was born in England, the eldest child of James and Caroline Starley. Theirs was a quiet, rural life where the father pursued agricultural work as his fathers before him. On 29 Jan 1854, Jane and her parents were baptized into the Mormon Church. The family made preparations to leave their home and to make the long, hazardous journey to Utah. When they left England 7 Dec 1854 both Jane and her mother were ill. They arrived in New Orleans, La. 11 Jan 1855. On the steamer "Oceana" that was taking them up the Mississippi River to St. Louis, Missouri, Caroline and a daughter, Julia, were ill and grew steadily worse. Both died and were buried along the Mississippi River.

Jane's father was able to get employment with the wagon train of Hooper and Williams, a mercantile firm, and they allowed him to have Jane accompany him. After hardships and suffering they arrived in the Salt Lake Valley 17 Nov 1855. Jane was thirteen years old. They made their home in the 16th Ward, near the Temple Block. Jane's father worked in the gardens and orchards of Brigham Young. He married before he was called to a ten year mission to establish a nursery in Fillmore, Utah. A new life was beginning for Jane. Three months before her seventeenth birthday she married Anthony Martin, a native of England. They made their home in Provo, Utah. They became the parents of fifteen children; three died in infancy and three died in childhood. Because of a disagreement between Brigham Young and Anthony they traveled to

California. They lived in San Francisco and then Sacramento.

Sometime in the Spring of 1871, Anthony decided they would return to Utah, following the Central Pacific Railroad tracks. Each night camp was made and the five children were settled to sleep in the wagon and Jane and Anthony made their bed on the ground beneath it. Jane made a good home for her family in the many places they lived. She taught her family well and joined them in their games. Each child had his duties which were assigned according to ability. The mattresses were periodically emptied and refilled with fresh straw and on Saturdays all shoes were polished and made ready for Church the following day.

In Salt Lake City, they made their home in an apartment building across from what was then Washington Square or Emigration Square. It wasn't until Jane was fifty-one years of age that she was able to purchase her first home. Here she had a garden and soon established bee hives so she could supply the family with honey. Jane was a quiet, loving and caring person. Her life had spanned a colorful period in the settling and development of Western America. She played a quietly modest but steadfast part as daughter, wife and mother. She faced trials, tribulations, sorrow and tragedy with courage. She died at the age of eighty-two in Salt Lake City, Utah.

MARY ANN STOCKDALE CARTER MARTIN

BIRTHDATE: 6 Mar 1805
Penryn, Cornwall, England
DEATH: 1 May 1898
Stone, Oneida, Idaho
PARENTS: William Stockdale
Avis Francis Stockdale
PIONEER: 12 Sep 1861
Milo Andrus Wagon Train
SPOUSE: Edwin J. Carter
MARRIED: 1830
Devonshire, England
DEATH SP: 10 Jun 1841
Prince Rock Quarry, Devon., England

CHILDREN:
Ellen, 28 Sep 1831
Edwin John, 28 Sep 1833
Ellen, 24 Jun 1835
William James, 29 Jun 1837
Jane, 16 Feb 1840
Mary Ann, 31 Jul 1841

SPOUSE II: James Martin
MARRIED: 1846
DEATH: unknown

CHILDREN:
James, Jr. 7 Jun 1846
John

Mary Ann was born to William and Avis Francis Stockdale on March 6, 1805 in Penryn, Cornwall, England. She married Edwin J. Carter when she was twenty-five years old. From this union there were five children born. She had a very kind and loving disposition. She was a hard working woman. Her husband worked in a stone quarry and was accidentally killed on June 10, 1842. This was a terrible shock to her, leaving her with five small children to support. She did washing, ironing, and cleaning to support her family. She married James Martin in the year 1846. They had two children born to their union. John died as a small child. She accepted the gospel in her native land and was baptized a member of the LDS Church in Ledbury, England in 1851. Her husband took sick with a stroke and was bedfast about seven years before his death. She sailed for America on the ship, "Thornton," with her children, Jane, Mary Ann, and James. Her sons, Edwin and William, had left England to find work. She never heard from them again.

Mary Ann lived in New York for five years until she could save enough money to go on to Zion. Three of her daughters had married, two of which had already gone to Utah. In 1861, she started her journey. She went 2,000 miles by rail to Florence where the saints prepared the wagons and handcarts to come the last 1,000 miles. Her son, Jimmy, and her daughter, Ellen and her husband, traveled with her. Mary Ann pushed a handcart until they arrived in Kaysville, Utah on September 12, 1861, very happy to be reunited with her children who had come before. She made her home with her children. She did washing and cleaning for people until she was seventy-two years old. She then made her home with her son, James, in Farr West, Ogden, Utah. When she was about eighty-five years old, she had typhoid fever and was very ill. She went to live with her daughter, Jane, at Stone, Idaho. She passed away on May 11, 1898 at the age of ninety three.

SARAH ANN SARGENT MARTIN

BIRTHDATE: 18 Dec 1836
Newbury, Berkshire, England
DEATH: 25 Oct 1911
Wilson, Weber County, Utah
PARENTS: John Sargent
Ann Allen Sargent
PIONEER: 16 Oct 1852
Eli B. Kelsey Wagon Train
SPOUSE: John Martin
MARRIED: 3 Jun 1855
Salt Lake City, Utah
DEATH: 24 Mar 1915
Wilson, Weber County, Utah

CHILDREN:
Sarah Ellen, 21 Jun 1856
John, 1 May 1858
Louisa (Branson), 16 Jun 1860
Janet (Jenet), 22 Aug 1862
Mary Ann (Cazier), 11 Mar 1864

Genevra (Bingham), 30 Aug 1866
William, 3 Nov 1868
Lenora, 16 Jan 1871
Joseph Albert, 3 Nov 1873
Rachel (Staker), 10 Dec 1875
Elizabeth, 17 Jun 1878
Idella Louvisa (Johnson), 12 Jan 1882

Sarah Ann was born in England, 1836, the second of five children and first daughter. Her father was a prosperous builder and member of the Burgess, a leading citizen of the town. When she was nine her mother died, and although a housekeeper was employed, Sarah helped with the housework and care of her younger brother and sisters.

In 1850 her father converted to Mormonism and the following year she was baptized. The family sailed from England 10 Jan 1852 aboard the ship "Kennebec," bound for Zion in the Salt Lake Valley. Arriving in New Orleans two months later, they continued their journey up the Mississippi River. At St. Louis the emigrants were placed on an old dilapidated steamboat called the "Saluda" for the remainder of the trip by water to Council Bluffs. At Lexington, Missouri, about 250 miles up the river, a tragic accident occured. The boat blew up and sank within ten minutes, killing about 100 passengers. Sarah Ann's father was among the dead and the body of a younger brother was lost in the River. Three of the orphaned Sargent children continued on to Utah with other Mormon Pioneers. Their sister, Ellen, remained in Lexington with a kind family who later adopted her. Mr. Sargent had paid in advance for wagons and supplies for the trip across the plains, but now that there were only three of them the extra wagon and provisions were given to others in need. They left Iowa in the Eli B. Kelsey Company and arrived in Salt Lake City 16 Oct 1852. After their arrival the children were left to shift for themselves. In the spring of 1855, Sarah Ann met John Martin, a British emigrant and orphan like herself. They were married three weeks later, on Jun 3rd. That first winter of their marriage was the historic "Hard Winter." They nearly starved. They obtained some land west of Ogden and there remained the balance of their lives. Although their first home was a dugout in a side hill of the Weber River, their land soon became productive and they built a large two-story home and became parents of twelve. They were active in church and Sarah Ann was in the Relief Society presidency for twenty-one years. She laid out the dead, hid polygamous wives in her home, was a polygamous wife herself and was a sociable, pleasent woman, always well groomed and well dressed. She passed away at age seventy-four, in Wilson, Weber County, Utah. Sarah Ann Sargent Martin died of pneumonia at her home in Wilson on 25 Oct 1911. She and her husband are buried in the Ogden City Cemetery.

SARAH ANN (HANNAH) TABERER OWEN (WRAGG) MARTIN

No
Photo
Available

BIRTHDATE: 27 Mar 1842
Warbourough, England
DEATH: 5 Jun 1877
Salt Lake City, Utah
PARENTS: George Taberer
Mary West Taberer
PIONEER: 17 Oct 1862
Henry W. Miller Wagon Company
SPOUSE: Oswald Owen or Wragg
MARRIED: 21 Dec 1859
Stafford, England
DEATH: Winter 1862/3

CHILDREN:
Joseph Hyrum, 1861

SPOUSE II: Ezra Francis Martin
MARRIED: 20 Jun 1863
DEATH SP: 28 Sep 1912
Salt Lake City, Utah

CHILDREN:
Rose Hannah (Moss), 5 May 1865
George Eli, 19 Feb 1867
Emma Sophia (Derrick), 20 Aug 1868
Samuel Beesley, 13 Sep 1869
Mary Alice, 18 Jan 1872
William Henry, 20 Nov 1873
Harriette Maude (Moss), 8 Nov 1874

Sarah Ann (Hannah) was born in England in 1842. At age 17, she married Oswald Owen or Wragg 21 Dec 1859 in England. Shortly after their marriage they emigrated to America. Their first child was born after they landed in New York. This was in 1861. They made their way to Florence, Nebraska, joining the Henry W. Miller Wagon Train, leaving 8 Aug and arriving in Salt Lake City 17 Oct 1862. Not long after they arrived, Oswald passed away during the winter of 1862/3.

As a young widow of 21, Sarah Ann married Ezra Francis Martin as his second wife, in polygamy, 20 Jun 1863. Together they had 7 children. Sarah Ann's Health failed and she passed away 5 Jun 1877 at age 35, when her youngest child was three.

Ezra had two other wives, Eliza Oliver Cook and Eliza Goodsell Griffin Jenkens. They raised Sarah Ann's children. Ezra passed away in Salt Lake City 28 Sep 1912. They are buried in the Salt Lake Cemetery. His first wife was Sophia Packer.

SOPHRONIA MOORE MARTIN

No
Photo
Available

BIRTHDATE: 17 May 1832
Orange, Franklin, Massachusetts
DEATH: 17 Nov 1915
Provo, Utah County, Utah
PARENTS: Samuel Moore
Eunice Sibley Bliss
PIONEER: Before Dec 1848
by Wagon Train
SPOUSE: Jessie Bigler Martin
MARRIED: 17 Dec 1848
Salt Lake City, Utah
DEATH SP: 17 Oct 1908
Provo, Utah County, Utah

CHILDREN:
Jessie Bigler, 19 Nov 1849
Isabella, 8 Aug 1851
Sophronia Lydia, 4 Jul 1853
Eunice Sylvia, 21 July 1858
John Snyder, 19 Oct 1860
Matilda, 3 Sep 1862
Samuel Moore, 12 Nov 1854
Marintha Althera, 15 Jul 1866
Stephen Erastus, 15 Dec 1868
Orson Lorenzo, 25 Oct 1871
Harriet Maria, 17 Mar 1873

Sophronia was born in Massachusetts in 1832, the second of seven children. Her parents joined the LDS Church in 1841. Her family moved to Iowa and were in Nauvoo for the Exodus. At age sixteen, Sophronia, with her family, crossed the Plains to Utah. They settled in Salt Lake City. That same year Sophronia married Jesse Bigler Martin.

SUSANNAH THOMPSON MARTIN

BIRTHDATE: 15 Dec 1842
Somersham, Huntingdonshire,
England
DEATH: 4 Jul 1918
Cowley, Big Horn, Wyominq
PARENTS: Edward Thompson
Sarah Chapman Thompson
PIONEER: Aug or Sep 1860
Horton Haight Handcart Company
SPOUSE: Robert Martin
MARRIED: 30 Jun 1863
Salt Lake City, Utah
DEATH: 5 Aug 1891
Meadow, Millard County, Utah

CHILDREN:
William Edward, 17 Apr 1864
James Richard, 3 Nov 1866
Susannah Elizabeth, 24 Mar 1868
Sarah Maria, 22 Mar 1870
Anna Matilda, 17 Sep 1872
John Thompson, 7 Mar 1875
Martha, 28 Dec 1876
Benjamin Franklin, 29 Jan 1879
Rebecca Isabel, 8 Sep 1881
Minnie, 28 Mar 1885

Archie Carlos, 16 Mar 1886
David, 7 Aug 1890

Susannah was born in England, the second child and the first daughter of ten children. She and her parents joined the Mormon Church 17 Jan 1852 and became prominent members of the Somersham Branch. They always welcomed the missionaries into their home and were generous about taking care of them. They emigrated to Utah in 1857, sailing on the ship "Tuscarora" from Liverpool, England. Susannah's mother and twin babies died on the journey. They were buried in New Jersey. They traveled to Omaha, Nebraska and prepared to cross the Plains. Susannah was fifteen years old. Sorrow came again. Two of her little sisters were burned to death when their clothing caught fire. They were buried in Omaha. Susannah's father had insufficient funds by this time to buy a wagon and oxen. With no other choice, he purchased a handcart and joined a handcart company that accompanied a freight wagon train. The Captain was Horton Haight. With so little room in the handcart, most of their possessions had to be discarded or sold.

The four remaining members of the Thompson family pushed and pulled their handcart across the Plains. Susannah walked most of the way, but had such bad headaches she was often allowed to ride in one of the wagons. At sixteen she was a very pretty girl. She had long black hair that she could sit on and big blue eyes. Her father refused to trade her to an Indian Chief for twenty ponies. Susannah could have been the squaw of the Chief! The family arrived in the Salt Lake Valley in Aug or Sep of 1860. Susannah lived in Brigham Young's home and worked for his wives until her marriage 30 Jun 1863 to Robert Martin, a widower and a Scotsman. She was twenty. He was thirty-three. His wife had died leaving him with a son. Susannah cared for him as if he were her own. They left Salt Lake City to settle on a ranch in Rush Valley, Tooele County, Utah. Susannah learned early in life to cook and sew well. She was always an excellent homemaker, keeping the house immaculate. All of these attributes she taught her daughters. She and Robert became the parents of twelve children; four died in infancy.

They helped settle Meadow, Utah. They were part of the first Sunday School and Relief Society. All the family sang in the choir. With a daughter and her husband and family she helped settle the Big Horn Basin of Wyoming. Susannah's husband became ill with comsumption. Susannah had to work hard all of her life, the more so when her husband became ill. She raised fruits and vegetables and Robert took them to the mining towns to sell. One day tragedy struck. A storm came up and Robert caught pneumonia and died a few months later. Susannah was a widow at the age of forty-nine. Susannah died in her sleep on 4 Jul 1918 in her home. The coroner put silver coins on her eyes to hold them closed. She had lived a life of extreme hardship but she remained faithful to her religious beliefs. She was a woman of faith and fortitude.

KINDNESS ANN HAINES JOHNSON BADGER MARTINDALE

BIRTHDATE: 12 Jun 1830
Green County, Tennessee
DEATH: 2 Feb 1929
Salt Lake City, Utah
PARENTS: Azariah Haines
Polly Ann Newman Haines
PIONEER: 9 Oct 1852
James C. Snow
SPOUSE: Thomas Smith Johnson
MARRIED: 4 Feb 1849
DEATH SP:

CHILDREN:
None

SPOUSE II: John Chamberlain Badger
MARRIED: 1855 (divorced 23 Oct 1865)
Grantsville, Tooele County, Utah
DEATH SP: 15 Nov 1888
Kelton, Utah

CHILDREN:
Electa Ann, 14 Mar 1855
Kindness Ann, 23 Dec 1856
Lydia Ann, 22 Oct 1858
John Haines, 20 Jun 1860
Nathan Bradley, 28 Oct 1862
Martha Bradley, 28 Oct 1862
Margaret Ann, 6 Jun 1866

SPOUSE: William Addington Martindale
MARRIED: 5 Jun 1865
Salt Lake City, Utah
DEATH: 14 Feb 1873
Duncan Retreat, Washington County, Utah

CHILDREN:
Rebecca Ann, 30 Apr 1869

The Haines family moved from Tennessee to Ohio when Kindness Ann was three months old. The family settled on land covered with timber. As the children grew older, the children had to help clear the land of timber. Kindness Ann joined the LDS Church and moved to Nauvoo. She ran away from home and started West with the first company of saints to leave Nauvoo. She traveled in the last buggy that crossed the iced river. She helped with the cooking. Rattlesnakes were many and bothered the people at Garden Grove. Food was scarce and often artichokes were dug for meals. Many people died from black leg. In 1849, she married Thomas Smith Johnson and they were later divorced. She spent two years in Winter Quarters and then on to the Valley of the Great Salt Lake in the James C. Snow Wagon Company.

Kindness Ann married for a second time and had seven children. She moved from place to place and eventually got a divorce and moved to Duncan Retreat to live with her sis-

ter and her husband. Her sister died a short time after she arrived. Soon after her death, Kindness married her sister's husband and helped him raise his children. They had one child born to this marriage.

She served as the first President of the Relief Society at Duncan Retreat. Soon after the death of her husband, she returned to Salt Lake City to live with a daughter. She lived to the age of ninety-nine years and eight months.

MATILDA JANE MCMURRAY MARTINDALE

BIRTHDATE: 17 Jul 1836
Sharon, Beaver County, Pennsylvania
DEATH: 7 Jan 1899
Oakley, Idaho
PARENTS: John McMurray
Mary Hutton McMurray
PIONEER: Oct 1852
Warren Snow Wagon Company
SPOUSE:
William Clinton Martindale
MARRIED: 5 May 1854
Grantsville, Tooele County, Utah
DEATH: 9 Jul 1911
Oakley, Idaho

CHILDREN:
Matilda Alfradine 27 May 1855
Rebecca Ann 11 Jun 1857
William Clinton 26 Apr 1859
Martha Mahalia 12 Jul 1861
Mary Lydia 25 Apr 1863
John Clinton 23 Aug 1865
James Alma 19 Jul 1867
Henriette 3 Sep 1869
Charles Edgar 26 Aug 1871
William Addington 29 Sep 1873
Joseph Alonzo 11 Mar 1876
Francis Marion 6 Jun 1880

Matilda Jane McMurray Martindale was born in Pennsylvania. She was the eighth of ten children of John and Mary Hutton McMurray. Her family had moved from several places in Pennsylvania. In 1830 the family moved to Ohio, but moved back and forth across the border of Ohio and Pennsylvania for the next few years. It is not known when Matilda Jane's parents joined the Mormon Church or when they left Ohio. The fact remains that they did join the Mormon Church. They sold their possessions in Ohio and arrived in Nauvoo, Illinois just at the time the bodies of the Prophet Joseph Smith and his brother Hyrum were brought to Nauvoo from Carthage, Illinois.

The family went through the many persecutions of the Saints in Nauvoo. They took refuge in Council Bluffs, Iowa. The McMurray family finally were ready to leave Kanesville, Iowa in Jun 1852. Matilda Jane was sixteen years old. After walking 1300 miles across the Plains, the family arrived in the Salt Lake Valley in Oct 1852 with the

Warren Snow Wagon Company. Following the death of her father in 1853, the family moved to Grantsville, Utah.

Matilda Jane married William Clinton Martindale 5 May 1854 in Grantsville, Utah. They became the parents of twelve children, all born in Grantsville. In 1880, they moved to Goose Creek Valley, Idaho. The name Goose Creek was later changed to Oakley. Again, Matilda Jane and her husband went through the challenges and difficulties of settling a new area. Matilda Jane died 7 Jan 1899 in Oakley. Her husband died in Oakley 9 Jul 1911.

REBECCA ANN HAINES MARSHALL MARTINDALE

No Photo Available

BIRTHDATE: 3 May 1825
Green County, Tennessee
DEATH: 9 Dec 1865
Duncan Retreat, Washington, Utah
PARENTS: Azariah Haines
Polly Ann Newman Haines
PIONEER: 9 Oct 1852
James C. Snow Wagon Train
SPOUSE: George W. B. Marshall
MARRIED: 25 Jan 1842
Clinton County, Ohio
DEATH SP: unknown

CHILDREN: None

SPOUSE II: William Addington Martindale
MARRIED: 24 Apr 1854
Salt Lake City, Utah
DEATH SP: 14 Feb 1873
Duncan Retreat, Washington, Utah
CHILDREN: None

Rebecca was one of the oldest children in the family, so she was required to help clear the land of trees so gardens could be planted. She was the first in her family to join the LDS Church. She married George W. Marshall and the two of them emigrated to Nauvoo.

With her second husband, William Addington Martindale, she crossed the Plains in the James C. Snow Wagon Company and arrived in Salt Lake City on October 9, 1852. She endured many hardships such as rattle snakes, black leg, and hunting for food. Rebecca and William were called to help settle Dixie in the little town of Duncan Retreat. The river would flood and wash away the crops in their fields. She worked long tiresome hours to try to tame this wild country. Rebecca passed away at forty years of age having no children. She is buried on a hillside above what was once Duncan's Retreat, Utah.

HANNAH GARDNER PARKER MASON

No Photo Available

BIRTHDATE: 19 Dec 1824
Washington, Erie, Pennsylvania
DEATH: 10 Apr 1861
North Ogden, Weber, Utah
PARENTS: Benjamin Gardner
Electa Lamport
PIONEER: 20 Sep 1852
Benjamin Gardner Co Wagon Train
SPOUSE I: J. W. Parker
MARRIED: abt 1846
Maine
DEATH: unknown

CHILDREN: unknown

SPOUSE II: George Sterling Mason
MARRIED: 22 Mar 1855
Birchs Mill, (Riverdale) Utah
DEATH: 10 Jul 1888
Willard, Box Elder, Utah

CHILDREN:
Jesse 27 Dec 1855
Electa (MacFarlane) 7 Jan 1858
Rebecca (Nisb) 22 Aug 1859

Hannah was born in Pennsylvania in 1824. At about age twenty-one she married J. W. Parker. They were married in Maine. Nothing is known about this marriage. At age twenty-seven, she emigrated to Utah in her father's wagon train. As a young woman, she worked for a wealthy family in Warsaw for quite some time. She also worked for the Alenders. While her family was living south of Nauvoo and had settled on Bear Creek on the Green plains north of Morley's Settlement in 1845, early in the morning before sunrise, the mob rode up and ordered them out of their house or they would burn the house over their heads. They did get out, and the mob did set fire to their house, crops, and destroyed everything, and Hannah and her mother cooked a little breakfast over the hot coals of their burned house.

After their journey across the plains, arriving in Salt Lake City 20 Sep 1852, Hannah made her home in Riverdale, where she married George Sterling Mason on 22 Mar 1855, at age thirty. They became parents of three children. Hannah passed away at age thirty-six when her youngest child was nineteen months old. In Jun 1861, George married Margaret Townsend Bradbury. They became parents of fourteen children and together they raised Hannah's three children.

MARY ANN CANTWELL MATHER

BIRTHDATE: 9 Sep 1853
St. Louis, Missouri
DEATH: 26 Mar 1928
Smithfield, Utah
PARENTS: James Sherlock
Cantwell—Elizabeth Cotterell
Hamer Cantwell
PIONEER: 4 Dec 1856
James G. Willie Wagon Train
SPOUSE: Thomas Mather
MARRIED: 5 Dec 1870
Salt Lake City, Utah
DEATH: 23 Oct 1917
Smithfield, Utah

CHILDREN:
Mary, Elizabeth 3 Oct 1871
James, 5 Apr 1873
William, 12 Jan 1875
Alice, 8 Apr 1877
Ellen, 13 Nov 1879
Rachel, 20 Sep 1880
Thomas Edgar, 18 Feb 1883
Zina May, 12 Mar 1885
John, 23 Sep 1887
Elias, 31 Dec 1889
Ethel, 9 Apr 1892

Mary Ann Cantwell Mather was born in St. Louis, Missouri. Her parents had joined the Mormon Church in Dublin, Ireland. The family left their homeland in 1850, coming by way of New Orleans, La. They settled in St. Louis for five years to earn the needed funds to complete their journey to Utah. Mary Ann was the third of four children to be born in St. Louis. She was their tenth child.

In 1856, the Cantwells took passage to Florence, Nebraska on the steamboat "Arabia." They purchased a good team of oxen and a wagon and joined the James G. Willie Company on 17 Aug 1856. Theirs was one of only a few wagons of a company mostly comprised of handcarts which had been hurriedly thrown together and ill-outfitted. Mary Ann's father recorded in his journal that the company was too ill-prepared for the conditions they would find in the mountains as it was too late in the year. Mary Ann was three years old when they made the ill-fated trip.

They suffered greatly with hunger and cold. When at Devil's Gate their oxen gave out and they joined the wagon of another family. Rescued at Fort Bridger, they made the ascent through the summit coming into the Salt Lake Valley through 18 feet of snow and bitterly cold conditions.

They arrived 4 Dec 1856 and settled in a dugout in Cottonwood, Utah. In 1858, as the family was preparing to leave their home at the warning of Johnston's Army, Mary Ann's mother died in childbirth. Seven children were left for her father to raise, including the newborn son. Two months later their dugout in Utah County burned with all their possessions and clothing. The children were sent to live with friends. Mary Ann and her younger sister would not leave their father. In May 1862, James gathered his

family and headed for Cache Valley, northern Utah. With no mother in the home, Mary Ann's help was greatly needed. Her father taught her to read and write. She attended school for a short time. Mary Ann married Thomas Mather in the Salt Lake Endowment House 5 Dec 1870. She was seventeen years old. They made their home in Smithfield, Utah. They became the parents of eleven children; two died in infancy, one died as a teenager. Mary Ann also cared for her husband's parents from the time of her marriage until their deaths. At times, thirteen people lived under her roof. She carried water from a creek a block away. Cooking was done on a wood stove. She rendered honey from three hives, carded wool, spun and knit, made soap, dried fruit and made cheese and vinegar and forty gallons of molasses each year. Theirs was one of the few homes with an organ, which gave hours of enjoyment. Mary Ann was a devoted mother and Church worker. She was a Visiting Teacher in the Relief Society for thirty-eight years. To this calling came the duty of gathering the Sunday eggs at the time of the completion of the Logan Temple. Mary Ann died on 26 Mar 1928 at the age of seventy-five -at Smithfield, Utah.

MARY DITCHFIELD MATHER

No
Photo
Available

BIRTHDATE: 28 Oct 1811
Culcheth, Lancashire, England
DEATH: 25 Dec 1892
Smithfield, Utah
PARENTS: William Ditchfield
Hannah Higginson Ditchfield
PIONEER: 7 Sep 1855
Noah T. Guyman Compapy
SPOUSE: James Higginson Mather
MARRIED: 3 Mar 1840
Manchester, Lancashire, England
DEATH: 17 Nov 1893
Smithfield, Utah

CHILDREN:
William Ditchfield, chr. 6 Mar 1836
John, 11 Jul 1838
Alice, 3 Jan 1842
Thomas, 28 Apr 1846
Hannah, 11 Nov 1847
James, 24 Oct 1851

Mary Ditchfield Mather was born in England. She married James Higginson Mather 3 Mar 1840 in Manchester, Lancashire, England.

James and Mary were both baptized on 11 Feb 1851. They were members of the Leigh Branch in Lancashire. They soon desired to emigrate to Utah.

On 16 Mar 1855 they left England on the ship "Juventa" with five children, the youngest being three years old. They arrived in Philadelphia on 7 May and went by train to the end of the line which was Council Bluffs, Iowa. They traveled by wagon with the Noah T. Guyman Co. and arrived in the Salt Lake Valley 7 Sep 1855. During the journey, their thirteen year old daughter, Alice, died.

Shortly after arriving in Salt Lake, daughter Hannah died. She was eight years old.

At the coming of Johnston's Army, the Mather family were sent south to Lehi, Utah and from there to Cedar Fort. During this time, their youngest son died. Upon the family's return to Salt Lake City, Mary's husband became very discouraged and longed for the green, lush land of England. James returned to their homeland, but Mary would not go. Their nineteen year old son headed for the gold fields of California. Assuming herself now a single woman, and being left alone with only her eleven-year-old son Thomas, Mary was married to a man named John Oldfield 27 Dec 1857. This marriage was soon absolved and she then married Ezekiel Hopkins 16 Nov 1861.

In 1859, Ezekiel and Mary and her son Thomas settled on the banks of the Summit Creek in Smithfield, Cache County, Utah and were some of the first to settle the area. They lived in the old Fort. Thomas was the first child to live there. Ezekiel was excommunicated from the Mormon Church and Mary obtained a divorce from him in 1867. Her first husband, James, had found England strange and disappointing and in 1861 he had returned to Utah. Eventually he found his family in Smithfield and took up a homestead there next to his son Thomas who married in 1870. Mary was living with her son and his wife. Former husband James lived next door in a tiny one room home, but he took his meals with Thomas' family.

Mary was proficient in the art of making cheese and in caring for the milk. She carded wool from the sheep, spun yarn, made quilts, knitted stockings, made soap, dried fruit, corn, hops and sage, churned butter and made dutch cheese. Large jars of mince meat were prepared. Forty gallons of molasses were made each year. Bread was baked, honey separated from the wax, rags dyed, stripped and sewed to be woven into carpets. They made their own vinegar. Everything was done over a wood stove. Mary and James were remembered by their grandchildren as Grandma and Grandpa Mather. They died just one year apart. Mary was eighty-one years old. She was sealed to James Mather after their death in 1897.

MARY JOHNSON MATHER

No Photo Available

BIRTHDATE: 1 May 1811
Whitefield, Lancashire, England
DEATH: 8 Apr 1875
Hamblin, Washington, Utah
PARENTS: Mathew Johnson
Esther Cherry
PIONEER: 2 Feb 1850
SPOUSE: John Mather
MARRIED: 20 Dec 1829
Duffield, Derby, England
DEATH: 11 Feb 1854
Salt Lake City, Utah

CHILDREN:
Charles, chr 1 Feb 1831
Hannah, chr 3 Dec 1832
William Elliott, chr 24 Mar 1835
Harriet, chr 11 Oct 1836
Sarah Ann, chr 19 Dec 1838

Mary was born in England in 1811. She was one of at least twelve children. At age eighteen, she married John Mather, 20 Dec 1829. John was also born in Whitefield. After their marriage, they made their home in Lancashire, where they became parents of at least five children. Mary and John were baptized into the LDS church on 3 May 1840 in Broughton, Lancashire, England. A few years later, they left England to join the Saints in Salt Lake.

The Mather's left England and according to family records, they arrived in Salt Lake City 2 Feb 1850. They brought their youngest daughter, Sarah Ann, with them. Shortly after arrival, 11 Feb 1854, John passed away at age thirty-eight. After his death, Mary lived with Sarah Ann, who married Newton Daniel Hall 7 Feb 1851 in North Ogden. Their first of eight children was born there in 1856. They were in Santaquin at the time of Johnston's Army, returning to North Ogden, then moving to Providence 1862/1869. They then settled permanently in Fort Hamblin, Washington County, Utah. Mary was active in church and helped much with Sarah Ann's family. She was a widow for twenty-one years, passing away at seventy-three.

CATHERINNE TREASURER MATHESON

BIRTHDATE: 24 Sep 1804
Dundee, Angus, Scotland
DEATH: 4 Jan 1896
Cedar City, Iron Co., Utah
PARENTS: Kenneth Treasurer
Mary Bain Treasurer
PIONEER: 24 Sep 1862
Homer Duncan Wagon Train
SPOUSE: Daniel Matheson
MARRIED: 20 Nov 1823
Creich/Avock, Sutherland, Scotland
DEATH: 22 Mar 1884
Parawan, Iron Co., Utah

CHILDREN:
Kenneth, 30 Aug 1826
David Hogg twin, 6 Aug 1828
infant twin, 6 Aug 1828
John Nathanial, 30 Oct 1830
Daniel, 28 May 1833
Catherine Ross, 20 Mar 1835
Hugh, abt 1837
infant daughter twin, abt 1839
infant son twin, abt 1839
Simon Anderson, 4 Apr 1841
Alexander, 7 Sep 1843
Catherine Ross, 8 Aug 1845
Ellen McKell (Wardle), 7 Dec 1848

Catherine was born in Scotland, 1804. At age nineteen, she married Daniel Matheson, 20 Nov 1823, in Scotland. Their marriage was prearranged, which she resented, but gradually accepted and made the most of it. When she and her husband heard the gospel of the LDS Church they accepted it and were baptized. While they made their home in Scotland, they became parents of thirteen children, six growing to adulthood. Catherine worked and supported the family while Daniel labored as a missionary, before they emigrated to Utah. Her traveling companions were Daniel and their three youngest children Simon, Alexander, Ellen McKell. The Matheson's left Florence, Nebraska 22 Jul with the Homer Duncan Ox-train, arriving in Salt Lake City 24 Sep 1862. From Salt Lake City, Catherine, Daniel and Ellen McKell went to Weber, and the two boys went to Southern Utah.

Catherine, Daniel, son Alexander and his wife Lydia, were then called to help settle Fairview (then in Iron Co. and later renamed Panguitch in Garfield Co). Because of the Indian troubles of the Black Hawk War, they returned to Parowan and made it their home. Simon disappeared and was never heard of again. Ellen McKell married Solomon Wardle, had a family and helped to colonize in both Nevada and Arizona. Catherine was proud of her children. Two of the older ones, David Hogg and John Nathanial, followed their parents to Utah, David settling in Parowan and John in Salt Lake City.

After the Indian trouble in Fairview, they returned to Parowan, Daniel to his loom and garden, and Catherine to work in different homes. When Daniel died, she left Parowan and went to live in Cedar City in the home of a cousin, although, by then, she was beyond seventy years old. She kept her clothes clean and ironed, did her share of the housework, and insisted on always washing the dishes.

Among other accomplishments she nursed the ill, often including midwife duties, and whatever other household work was required. She passed away 4 Jan 1896 (while Bells were ringing for Utah Statehood) at age ninety-one, having been a widow for over eleven years. Although Catherine passed away in Cedar City, she is burried in Parowan beside Daniel.

LYDIA EVANS MATHESON

BIRTHDATE: 14 Feb 1844
New Market,Flintshire, Wales
DEATH: 30 May 1912
Parowan, Iron Co.,Utah
PARENTS: Hugh Evans
Phoebe Jones Evans
PIONEER: 24 Sep 1862
Homer Duncan Wagon Train
SPOUSE: Alexander Matheson
MARRIED: 1 Aug 1864
sealed 13 Aug 1864
Salt Lake Endowment House
DEATH: 16 Aug 1932
Parowan, Utah

CHILDREN:
Alexander Gordon, 9 May 1865
Simon Anderson, 18 Sep 1867
Hugh Edward, 1 Aug 1870
Daniel Enoch, 14 May 1874
David Kenneth, 5 Aug 1876
William John, 6 Oct 1878
Lorenzo, 26 Dec 1880
Owen, 24 Sep 1882
Barnard White, 24 Dec 1885

Lydia was born in Wales in 1844. She had four younger brothers, one of whom died when three years of age. She had the care of her brothers, before and after her father remarried, following her mother's death. Lydia's father heard the gospel, joined the Church and was baptized in 1849. Her stepmother, Jane Ellen Roberts was baptized in 1851, and Lydia in 1854. One of her brothers was a sickly child, and during their journeys, she carried him constantly to keep him from crying and disturbing others which caused her to have round shoulders and made her subject to asthma attacks from then on through the rest of her life. In her later life, she carried a small china saucer with dried Cannabis leaves on it, and a small pack of sulphur matches. She would light the Cannabis and the fumes would relieve her asthma attacks.

Her family emigrated from Liverpool, England, on the square rigged sailing vessel, the "John J. Boyd," arriving in New York 1 Jun 1862. From New York they traveled in a circuitous route to Florence, Nebraska where they joined others in the Homer Duncan Ox-train and left Florence 22 Jul 7 arriving in Salt Lake City 24 Sep 1862. Her family left Salt Lake City and went to Kamas, Utah to make their home. In Aug 1864 Alexander Matheson returned to Salt Lake City to collect his sweetheart, Lydia Evans and make her his wife. They made their home in Panguitch in a small roughly built cabin. Here their first son was born. They moved to Parowan, where they had eight more sons. She made friends with the Indians and they helped her to know to boil the unripened grain for food. There was no flour, only wild meat and such wild vegetable-type foods as could be found.

Lydia's activity in the church consisted mainly in music. She sang with the choir and for funerals and special events. She raised her boys in the church and all were active. When Church Authorities were in Cedar City, where the Matheson's later made their home, they generally added to Lydia's responsibilities of providing housing and food. Lydia passed away 30 May 1912 from a severe asthma attack. She was sixty-eight; Alexander was a widower for twenty years, passing away 16 Aug 1932, in Parowan.

MARGARET MORRIS MATHEWS

BIRTHDATE: 26 Aug 1821
Pontyates, Carmarthenshire, Wales
DEATH: 14 Nov 1882
Providence, Cache, Utah
PARENTS: Richard Morris
Elizabeth Jones Morris
PIONEER: 2 Oct 1856
Edward Bunker Co
SPOUSE: Hopkin Mathews
MARRIED: 17 Jun 1844
Merthyr, Tydfil,
Glamorganshire, Wales
DEATH: 17 Jul 1903
Providence, Cache, Utah

CHILDREN:
Elizabeth, 1 Mar 1845
Mary, 26 Apr 1847
Margaret, 11 Jun 1849
Joan, 15 Jul 1851
Emily, 26 Dec 1853
Alma Morris, 21 Dec 1855
John Hopkin, 17 Sep 1858
David Richard, 17 Sep 1858
Sarah Jane, 8 May 1861
Anne Maria, 8 May 1861
Louisa Jane, 17 Aug 1863
Susannah, 11 Mar 1866
Joseph Moroni, 29 Sep 1867

When Margaret was a very young child, her mother passed away and Margaret was taken to the home of an uncle in Merthyr, South Wales. Her early life was full of hardships, hard work, and no advantage of an education. Margaret became a member of the LDS Church on April 2, 1844. She married Hopkin Mathews the following June. About three years after their marriage, Hopkin was called on a seven year mission in other parts of their native country. Margaret accompanied him. She aided him by singing songs of the gospel's truth. In April 1856, the couple with their five children sailed on the ship, "Samuel Curling." Six weeks later, they arrived in Boston and continued their journey by train to Iowa City. They remained there for three weeks before they joined the Edward Bunker Handcart Company. They shared the task of pushing and pulling their handcart. Provisions were scarce and they were often exposed to cold and hunger. While crossing the plains, her husband was taken with rheumatism in his feet, and for many days he had to be pulled in the wagon. Margaret walked every step of the way. They arrived in Salt Lake City on October 1, 1856. Their dreams had come true.

The family settled in Ogden, Utah, where for a time, they lived in a dugout house built on the banks of the Ogden River. Two years later, they were advised to move south to avoid confrontation with Johnston's Army. They moved to Provo where they remained for six months. They moved back to their willow home in Ogden where twin boys were born. They spent much of their time that winter burning green willows and sage brush to keep their family warm. In the spring of 1859, they moved to Providence, Utah where

they built a nice home. The Mathews family were members of the first choir formed in Providence. Margaret endured all the hardships and poverty of a pioneer. She instructed the Relief Society Sisters to do all they could toward drying fruit and laying up food for another year. They grew flax, and she learned how to spin, weave, and make clothing. She became an excellent dyer using herbs, barks of trees, and roots. She served as counselor in the Relief Society for two years, then became president for thirteen years. She also learned the use of herbs for making medicines. Margaret was best known for her work as a midwife in Providence, a position she held for twenty-three years until her death. She was ever ready to aid the sick and suffering. She was the mother to thirteen children, ten of whom lived to adulthood. She was a courageous and noble woman.

MARY ANN QUINNEY WHIPPLE MATHEWS

BIRTHDATE: 19 Aug 1833
Witham, Essex, England
DEATH: 1 Dec 1910
Provo, Utah
PARENTS: John Quinney
Susannah Moss Quinney
PIONEER: 26 Sep 1856
Edmund Ellsworth Wagon Co.
SPOUSE I: Edson Whipple
MARRIED: 26 Apr 1857
Salt Lake City, Utah
DEATH: 10 May 1894
Colonia Juarez, Mexico

CHILDREN:
Mary Unita, 26 Jan 1858
Blanch, 20 Feb 1861
John Quinney, 7 Jul 1863
Matilda, 19 Jun 1866
George Hutchens, 19 Jun 1869

SPOUSE II: James Mathews
MARRIED: 17 Oct 1892
DEATH: not given
CHILDREN: none

Mary Ann Quinney Whipple Mathews was born in England. She was the youngest of a family of three sisters and one brother. When she was four years old her mother died. Her father remarried when she was eight years old and at twelve years she lived with her oldest sister, Susan, and her husband. At fifteen Mary Ann and a friend started attending the meetings of the Mormon Missionaries that were held on the street corner twice a week. Mary Ann decided to be baptized. Her sister was very angry when she heard of Mary Ann's baptism and told her she was no longer welcome in her home. Because it was night, Mary Ann asked if she could stay until morning. The answer was no. She took what few pieces of clothing she had and started out. She decided she would pray for help, as the missionaries had taught her to do. A policeman came to her rescue and helped her obtain a position as nurse to an infant. The baby's mother was happy to have her and treated her kindly. When Mary Ann had saved enough money to emigrate to Utah, which took her five years, her employer gave her clothing and money to help her on her way.

Mary Ann and a girlfriend took the same ship to America. When they landed they had to sell a lot of their belongings to buy groceries. They made their way to Iowa City, Iowa and obtained a handcart with which to make the journey across the Plains to Utah. Mary Ann and her friend, Hester, pulled the handcart all across the Plains. They were caught in a terrible blizzard and snow storm. Some of Hester's toes were frozen and she begged Mary Ann to cut them off. Although it was hard to do, Mary Ann cut them off and healed them by putting axle grease on them. They were in the first handcart company that came across the Plains in 1856. (Probably the Edmund Ellsworth Company that left Iowa City 9 Jun 1856.) Hester died a year later in Salt Lake City.

Mary Ann married Edson Whipple in 1892. She was his fifth wife in plural marriage. They were among the first to settle Provo, Utah. The city was surrounded by a Fort to protect them from the Indians. She made straw hats, wove cloth on looms to make clothing, made soap, butter and cheese. Pioneer life was very hard. She always tried to live her religion as she understood it. She chose to remain in Provo when her husband and two wives went to Mexico. She raised her family of five children by herself. She married James Mathews in 1892. After he died she lived with a daughter. Mary Ann died at the age of seventy-eight 1 Dec 1910 in Provo, Utah.

RUTH PERKINS MATHEWS

BIRTHDATE: abt 1849
Glamorganshire, Wales
DEATH: 25 Dec 1932
Salt Lake City, Utah
PARENTS: William Perkins
Jane Mathews Perkins
PIONEER: 5 Oct 1867
Leonard C. Rice Independent Co.
SPOUSE: Joseph Davis Mathews
MARRIED: 7 Mar 1868
Salt Lake City, Utah
DEATH: 27 Aug 1904
Pleasant View, Utah

CHILDREN:
Martha Jane, 16 Jan 1869
William, 17 Apr 1870
Louise, 16 Oct 1871
Nephi Perkins, 10 Jul 1873
Daniel, 29 Mar 1875
Namomis, 10 Dec 1876
Hyrum P., 3 Sep 1878
John P., 10 Mar 1880
Sophia, 21 Nov 1881
Daisy, 14 Sep 1883

Caddie, 26 Mar 1885
Ruth, 30 Aug 1886
Kate, 10 Feb 1888
Leonard B., 25 Dec 1889
Maude, 3 Mar 1892
Mazy Lacelle, 11 Jul 1895

Ruth Perkins Mathews was born in Wales in the little town of Treboth. She was the tenth of fourteen children. When her parents joined the Mormon Church her father lost his job because of persecution. The family suffered much. Ruth was born in the poor house. She was baptized at the age of eight. She lived the principles of the Gospel all of her life. At the age of sixteen she was cured of cholera by a priesthood blessing. The family sailed from Liverpool, England, 21 Jun 1867 on the ship "Manhattan," under the direction of Archibald N. Hill. There was much sickness so the young girls cheered the sick with their sweet voices singing Church hymns. They arrived in North Platte, Nebraska by railroad. They then traveled by ox team in the Company of Leonard C. Rice, an Independent Company. After leaving North Platte 8 Aug 1867 they arrived at their final destination of the Salt Lake Valley 5 Oct 1867. Ruth had carried on her back part of the way across the Plains a baby whose mother was not in good health.

Upon Ruth's arrival in Salt Lake City, she did housework in private homes. On 7 Mar 1868, Ruth married Joseph Davis Mathews in the Salt Lake Endowment House, as his second wife in plural marriage. Joseph was thirty years her senior and a brother of her mother. She loved and admired his strength of character and sterling qualities. She lived in the same house with Joseph and his first wife for seven years. She learned to control her sharp Welsh temper by deferring to the first wife when there was a disagreement. Ruth remained in Salt Lake City until after the birth of her sixteen children. She witnessed the baptism of her youngest daughter in the Tabernacle font.

On 10 Mar 1904, the family moved to the Pleasant View Ward of Weber County, Utah. Joseph was in his eighty-fifth year and an invalid. He passed away on 27 Aug 1904, leaving Ruth at the age of fifty-five with four unmarried children. Her integrity and devotion to the Mormon Church continued through all of her life. She worked in the Relief Society during its beginning in Salt Lake City and continued in the Pleasant View Ward for many years. Ruth's developed character of nobility was attributed to her many and varied experiences as a pioneer. She was afforded many rays of sunshine as well as the seasons of sorrow. In her family of sixteen children she witnessed the spirits of nine of them depart this life before reaching their growth; seven with diptheria, one with whooping cough and one with convulsions.

Living near the Salt Lake Temple allowed her to do much Temple work. Hundreds of spirits will greet her with happy rejoicing augmenting the stars in her crown of eternal glory. Because Ruth had lived a good, clean life and was faithful, she was greatly rewarded. She was able to read, write and maintain her own home until the day of her death. Death came quietly and quickly to her on Christmas Day 1932.

ELIZABETH ROSS MATHIS

No
Photo
Available

BIRTHDATE: 12 Mar 1804
Guileford County, North Carolina
DEATH: Aug 1891
San Bernardino, California
PARENTS: Andrew Jackson Ross
Mary Ann Kimmons Ross
PIONEER: 12 Oct 1852
Charles C. Rich Wagon Co.
SPOUSE: Isaac Mathis
MARRIED: 20 Feb 1822
Paris County, Tennessee
DEATH: 22 Jul 1852
near Fort Laramie, Wyoming

CHILDREN:
Eliza, 3 Jan 1823
John, 25 Sep 1825
Allen, 8 Sep 1827
James Henry, 13 Nov 1829
Robert, 17 Jan 1832
Mary Elizabeth, 18 Aug 1834
Sarah Ann, 7 Dec 1836
Isaac Benjamin, 22/27 Feb 1839
Thomas William, 25 Jul 1841
Martha Jane, 12 Oct 1844

Elizabeth Ross Mathis was born 12 Mar 1804 in Guileford County, North Carolina. Her parents were Andrew Jackson and Mary Ann Ross. She was the second child in a family of nine. She grew up on her father's large plantation in North Carolina. She learned to read and write. A severe illness in her younger life caused her to lose her hair which never fully grew back. She always wore a black lace trimmed cap over her bare head.

She met and married Isaac Mathis. They were married 20 Feb 1822 in Paris County, Tennesee. Elizabeth was eighteen years old. They became the parents of ten children; four daughters and six sons. Two of their children died in infancy. In the Spring of 1852, the family started their journey across the Plains to Utah. Their three oldest children were married at this time. Their son Allen's wife died of cholera along with her baby boy, leaving Elizabeth to care for a grieving son and a little granddaughter.

On 22 Jul 1852, while camped near Laramie, Wyoming, her husband, Isaac, became very ill and passed away. Morning found the older children building a casket out of boards from their wagon. Isaac was buried along the side of the road and the family moved on with the wagon-train. They were traveling with the Charles C. Rich Company. They arrived in the Salt Lake Valley 12 Oct 1852. When her son, Isaac, lost his life Elizabeth moved into his home and helped raise a large family of young children. She endured the many hardships of pioneer life with-

out any complaining. Her life was one of caring for others. Elizabeth was proud of being a descendent of Betsy Ross who made the first United States flag. Elizabeth died in San Bernardino, California in Aug of 1891. She had been a widow for thirty-nine years.

SARAH ANN DOWDLE MATHIS

BIRTHDATE: 31 Jan 1828
Franklin, Lawrence, Alabama
DEATH: 3 Dec 1908
San Bernardino, California
PARENTS: Robert Dowdle
Sarah Ann Robinson Dowdle
PIONEER: 3 Sep 1852
Abraham 0. Smoot Wagon Train
SPOUSE: John Thomas Mathis
MARRIED: 1849
Council Bluffs, Iowa
DEATH: 15 Apr 1910

CHILDREN:
John Thomas, 28 Apr 1849
Elizabeth (Anderson), 1851
Julia (Cooper/Guggesberg), 1853
Elvira Jane (Angerson), 1855
Robert, 1855
Robert Francis William, 1857
Martha. Ann (Sinclair), 1859
James H., 11 Aug 1861
Sarah Ann, 1863
Joseph Franklin, 9 Sep 1866
Allen, 1871

Sarah Ann was born in Alabama in 1828. She was the fifth child in a family of nine. Her family was converted to the LDS church in 1844. They joined the Saints in Nauvoo, enduring the depredations of the mobs, and then traveled on to Council Bluffs. It was here, at age twenty-one, that Sarah Ann married John Thomas Mathis. Their first two children were born in Council Bluffs. They joined the Abrabam 0. Smoot Wagon Train and entered the Salt Lake Valley 3 Sep 1852.

After a third child was born in 1853, they were sent to settle in Payson, Utah County. They made their home there for about six years and added four more children to their family. Saran Ann's mother and brothers settled in Santaquin and they were able to visit, which was mutually enjoyable. In about 1860, The Mathis family moved to Provo. Here their last four children were born. About three years after their youngest was born, Sarah Ann's family moved to Franklin, Idabo and Cove, Cache County. In 1875 her mother passed away. This was very hard for Sarah Ann. She and John had a good life but worked very hard to support their family and were active in church. They were visiting in San Bernardino, California when Sarah Ann passed away. She was age eighty at that time. John followed her in death two years later.

JENETTE BROOM HILL VINCE MATTHEWS

No
Photo
Available

BIRTHDATE: 10 Mar 1811
Glasgow, Lanark, Scotland
DEATH: 23 Dec 1900
Lehi, Utah County, Utah
PARENTS: Robert Broom
Jenette Gavin Broom
PIONEER: abt 1852
SPOUSE: Alexander Hill
MARRIED: 10 Oct 1834
DEATH: unknown

CHILDREN:
William Brown, 19 Oct 1836
Mary, 1838

SPOUSE II: Moses Andrews Vince
MARRIED: 30 May 1854
Salt Lake Endowment House
DEATH: 20 Dec 1859
Moroni, Sanpete, Utah

CHILDREN:
Betsy (Yates), 11 May 1847
Rebecca (Matthews), 6 Mar 1853

SPOUSE: Abel Matthews
MARRIED: 10 Feb 1865
Salt Lake City, Utah
DEATH: 24 Apr 1891
Lehi, Utah Co., Utah
CHILDREN: None

Jenette was born in Scotland in 1811. At age twenty-one she married Alexander Hill. They were blessed with two children. They converted to the LDS Church and came to the U. S. after 1838. They gathered with the Saints in Illinois. It is unknown when or how Alexander died. Jenette married Moses Andrews Vince. Their first daughter was born 11 May 1847 in Weston, Platte, Missouri. The Vince family made their way to Utah probably by 1852, as their second daughter was born 6 Mar 1853 in Lehi, Utah County, Utah. Jenette and Moses were sealed in the Salt Lake Endowment House 30 May 1854. They were making their home in Moroni, Utah at the time of Moses' death, 20 Dec 1859.

Twice widowed and mother of four, Jenette, with the help of her oldest son Willian, made a living for her family. When her youngest was nearly twelve, Jenette married for a third time to Abel Matthews, 10 Feb 1865. Some records say 1862. She was his second wife. They made their home in Lehi. Abel was born and raised in England, father of nine children. Theirs was a happy union for over twenty-five years. Abel passed away 24 Apr 1891. Jenette lived nine more years, passing away 23 Dec 1900 at age eighty-nine in Lehi, Utah.

RHODA CARROLL MATTHEWS

BIRTHDATE: 16 Mar 1818
Johnston County, North Carolina
DEATH: 12 May 1896
Pima, Graham, Arizona
PARENTS: James Carroll
Rhoda Stevens Carroll
PIONEER: 21 Sep 1848
Brigham Young Wagon Company
SPOUSE: Joseph Lazarus Matthews
MARRIED: 14 Jul 1832
Johnston, North Carolina
DEATH: 14 May 1886
Glenbar, Arizona

CHILDREN:
Mahala Ann Rebecca, 30 Apr 1833
Julia Antoinette, 18 Sep 1836
Ann Horton, 15 Dec 1838
Anson, 1840 (died an infant)

Rhoda was born in Johnston County, North Carolina to James and Rhoda Stevens Carroll. When she was fourteen years old, she married Joseph Lazarus Matthews. Soon after their marriage, they moved to Noxubee County, Mississippi where their children were born. She and her husband were baptized as members of the LDS Church and moved to Nauvoo, Illinois. They were driven by mobs from Nauvoo a year after their arrival and went to Winter Quarters to live. Her husband was chosen by Brigham Young as a scout for the first Company of saints to cross the plains. Rhoda and her children remained in Winter Quarters with little to sustain them. After her husband returned for his family, they traveled across the plains and entered the Salt Lake Valley in 1849.

Winter was upon them before they could build suitable shelter for themselves and provide food for their families. Rhoda was a frontier wife and mother to three little girls. They eventually took farms near the mouth of Big Cottonwood Canyon and built nice homes. She endured the hardships and was very industrious. She supported her husband in his callings and gave her permission for him to marry in polygamy. She and her daughters were alone much of the time while her husband was called to serve as a scout for Brigham Young. He was called to explore the Rio Virgin and St. Clara River Country and to locate suitable valleys for Pioneer settlements. They were called to establish a colony in California in 1851. They endured the blizzards and mud in Utah, the thirst of the desolate sunbaked desert through Nevada, over the Sierra Nevada Mountains into California. They lost a considerable number of horses and cattle to the Indians when they were attacked. They helped to settle San Bernardino, California. At the time of Johnston's Army, they were called back to Utah to help in the expected war efforts. They went as far as Santaquin, Utah, and formed a settlement and were later called to Pima, Arizona. Rhoda was at his side in all of his labors as they settled these communities. She was a stalwart soul until her death in May of 1896 in Pima.

JANE HAYNES (HAINES) JAMES MAUDE

No
Photo
Available

BIRTHDATE: 1 Jan 1815
Brickalanton, Wostershire, England
DEATH: 11 Aug 1911
Provo, Utah
PARENTS: James Randall
Celia Cecilia Haynes Randall
PIONEER: 9 Nov 1856
James G. Willie Handcart Company
SPOUSE I: William James
MARRIED: Pinvin, England
15 Jun 1835
DEATH: 23 Oct 1856
Crossing the Sweetwater River,
Wyoming

CHILDREN:
Sarah, 16 Aug 1837
Emma, 8 Jun 1840
Rueben, 15 Jun 1842
Mary Ann, 16 Dec 1844
Martha, 8 Jun 1846
George, 16 Jun 1849
John Parley, 12 Aug 1852
Jane, 16 Aug 1855

SPOUSE II: Mathew Maude
MARRIED: not given
DEATH: Nov 1934

CHILDREN:
William Moroni, 30 May 1862

Jane was born in England. She was an infant when her mother died. She was raised by her grandmother. Her childhood was spent in poverty and she had no opportunity to attend school. As soon as she was old enough she was obliged to make her own living. She felt that it was an answer to prayer that led her to join the Mormon Church. Jane had married William James in England in 1836. They became the parents of eight children.

With an invalid husband and eight children, Jane sailed to America to join the Saints. Sadly, she had to bury her baby girl, Jane, at sea. When they arrived in America, they joined the Willie Handcart Company in 1856. More hardships came as they traveled across the Plains with handcarts enduring snow, cold and hunger. In 1856, Janet's husband died as they were crossing the Sweetwater River in Wyoming. Jane was left with the responsibility of caring for their eight children and getting them safely to Utah. After many hardships and challenges they arrived in the Salt Lake Valley 9 Nov 1856.

Her life continued to be hard in the Valley. With hard work and the help of her children she was able to find some security and comfort. She was an expert seamstress and very proficient in glove making. She produced beautiful needle work and enjoyed doing darning and mending for her friends. She married a Mr. Maud but the date was not indicated. They had one child, a son William.

During her life, which was for the most part filled with sorrow, she never murmured against her Maker, always feeling that His will be done. She was a faithful Relief Society worker and was always willing to do any task she was asked to do and she did it in a willing and cheerful way. Jane died 11 Aug 1911 in Provo, Utah.

BARBARA MORGAN MAUGHAN

BIRTHDATE: 14 Dec 1833
Merthyr Tydfil, Glamorganshire,
Wales
DEATH: 19 Sep 1888
Wellsville, Cache, Utah
PARENTS: Morgan Morgan
Cecilia Lewis Morgan
PIONEER: 1851
SPOUSE:
William Harrison Maughan
MARRIED: 25 Dec 1853
Tooele, Tooele, Utah
DEATH: 29 Aug 1905
Wellsville, Cache, Utah

CHILDREN:
Ruth Cecelia, 7 Oct 1854
Mary Elizabeth, 8 Dec 1856
Peter Morgan, 18 Oct 1858
William Harrison, Jr., 17 Oct 1860
Sarah Ann Morgan, 12 Dec 1862
Agnes, 19 Mar 1865
Thomas Morgan, 14 Jun 1869
Joseph Morgan, 26 Sep 1872
Brigham Morgan, 26 Sep 1878

In October of 1847, Barbara and her parents were baptized into the LDS Church. They sailed for America on February 25, 1849 from Liverpool, England on the ship, Buena Vista. They landed in New Orleans on April 19th, traveled up the Mississippi River, then worked their way to Pottawatamie County, Iowa. They arrived in Utah by wagon in 1851 or 1852 and were sent to Tooele to settle. Indian troubles and scarcity of food caused some suffering, but they were happy to be living among their fellow saints.

On Christmas Day in 1853, Barbara became the wife of William Harrison Maughan. The following year, the newlyweds moved to Salt Lake City where they were sealed in the Endowment House for time and eternity. In 1856, William and Barbara left Salt Lake City with their baby girl, Ruth, and went to Cache Valley to help establish settlements there. Their first settlement was called Maughan's Fort. In 1857, everyone from the Fort moved south because of the arrival of Johnston's Army. In 1859, they returned to the Fort and Barbara's life was much the same as other pioneer mothers. Foods was scarce, so roots were dug and cooked. Wool was sheared from the sheep and the women washed and carded it. It was then spun into yarn and woven into cloth for suits and dresses. Barbara was determined that her children would go to school. The family paid for the schooling with produce, flour, etc., or the teacher would live at their home. Her husband served as the bishop of the ward for forty years. In 1875, he went on a mission to England leaving Barbara with seven children. They were blessed with good health during his absence. She became the mother of nine children. She shared her husband with five other wives. In 1885, he was forced to go to Mexico to escape Federal Agents. William was forced to leave Wellsville for Mexico. He returned in 1888 since Barbara was very ill. Barbara died that same fall and her husband was arrested shortly after the funeral services were over.

ELIZABETII BRYCE HILL GARDNER MAUGHAN

No Photo Available

BIRTHDATE: 14 Feb 1838
Tosorontio Twp., Ontario, Canada
DEATH: 3 Oct 1908
Wellsville, Utah
PARENTS: Daniel Currie Hill
Elizabeth Bryce Hill
PIONEER: 15 Sep 1853
Moses Clawson Wagon Company
SPOUSE I: John Gardner
MARRIED: Jan 1856
DEATH SP: Dec 1856
Maughan's Fort, Cache Valley, Utah

CHILDREN:
Emmerine Elizabeth, 5 Nov 1856

SPOUSE II: William Harrison Maughan
MARRIED: 2 Jun 1860
Wellsville, Utah
DEATH: 29 Aug 1905

CHILDREN:
Margaret Ann, 9 Feb 1861
John, 30 Nov 1862

Elizabeth was born in Canada. She was the third child in a family of ten children. Her parents were baptized and joined the Mormon Church 8 Jan 1841. The following Spring, the family journeyed to Nauvoo, Illinois, arriving there 30 Sep 1842. They remained until 1846, leaving when the Saints were driven from Nauvoo by murdering mobs. The Hill family went to Waterloo, Iowa, and then moved to Warsaw, Illinois. Here Elizabeth's father learned the trade of a miller by working in a flour mill. It was two years later before he had accumulated sufficient means and felt prepared to make the journey to Utah. Elizabeth was fifteen years old. They joined a group of Saints leaving Keokuk, Iowa May 1853. They traveled with the Moses Clawson Company by wagon. They arrived in the Salt Lake Valley 15 Sep 1853. They were advised by President Brigham Young to settle in Mill Creek, Utah where her father was employed as a miller in Gardner's Flour Mills.

Elizabeth met and married John Gardner in Jan 1856. The marriage was tragically cut short in Dec of the same year. John decided to visit his parents who had settled in Cache Valley. He froze to death just a short distance from his destination. Elizabeth and John had one daughter. After the death of her husband, Elizabeth moved with her parents to Wellsville and became acquainted with Bishop William Harrison Maughan. She became his second wife 2 Jun 1860. They became the parents of two children.

During her life in Wellsville, Utah Elizabeth held many important leadership positions in the Ward. She was a First Counselor in Wellsville Relief Society for 18 years. She was thoroughly converted to prayer and never omitted family prayer and taking her husband's place when he could not be there. She owned and operated the first sewing machine in Wellsville. She was expert in sewing and needlework, such as stitching men's shirt fronts by hand, embroidering children and baby's clothes. She was also engaged in the milliner's business. Her home was always open to the missionaries.

Elizabeth passed away on 3 Oct 1908, just three years after her beloved husband, Bishop Maughan, who died 29 Aug 1905.

HANNAH WHITE HIBBARD MAUGHAN

BIRTHDATE: 20 Aug 1851
Llanellan, Monmouthshire, England
DEATH: 12 Jan 1929
Logan, Cache County, Utah
PARENTS: Thomas Jones White
Hannah Williams White Hibbard
PIONEER: 1854 by wagon
SPOUSE:
Hyrum Weston Maughan
MARRIED: 5 Apr 1875
Salt Lake City, Utah
DEATH SP: 3 Sep 19833
North Logan, Cache, Utah

CHILDREN:
Hyrum H., 28 Jun 1878
Mary Ann, 13 Mar 1881
George Weston, 26 Jun 1885
James Edwin, 25 Jul 1888

Hannah Maughan was born in England. She was the youngest of three children. Her parents were converts to the Mormon Church. Her father had emigrated to Utah earlier to prepare for the family to come. Hannah, her mother, a brother and a sister, and her grandfather left England 8 Apr 1854, crossing the ocean on the ship "Marshfield." Hannah was three years old. They arrived in New Orleans, La. and traveled up the Mississippi River to St. Louis, Mo. Her grandfather contracted cholera, became very ill and passed away. The little family was left alone to face the trials and hardships as they continued on to St. Louis and then westward to the Salt Lake Valley. They arrived in the Fall of 1854. Hannah's mother was divorced from Thomas Jones White and married George Hibbard in 1855. The family lived in Farmington, Willard, and Logan, Utah. As a young girl, Hannah did housework to support herself.

On 5 Apr 1875, Hannah married Hyrum Weston Maughan in the Endowment House in Salt Lake City. They were blessed with four children; three sons and one daughter. They lived in Logan until about 1884. They moved to North Logan, among the first to settle that area. They worked hard and with much interest to build a home and community life. Sorrows came their way. On 23 Jan 1892, their oldest son was stricken with diptheria and died suddenly. The following year, Hannah's husband became ill from an earlier injury. He had suffered a crushed lung in a logging accident in the canyon. He died at the age of forty-one on 3 Sep 1893. Hannah was truly courageous as she returned to her home with her three children, determined to carry on.

In addition to her many acts of kindness and love of her family and home, Hannah's greatest endeavor was to make her farm a success. She was the first to grow sugar beets in North Logan. On the small farm they also grew many kinds of fruits, berries and grains. Fowl and other animals were also produced in order that her family would be self-sustaining. Their smoke house produced hams and bacon. Their neighbors were invited to use the smoke house for their own meat.

Hannah made many sacrifices in her life to help others. When her sister died, leaving a six-week old baby, Hannah took the little girl into her home and reared her to womanhood, sharing the same interest and affection that she gave her own children. Hannah held many offices in the Church and the community. She was a member of the Ralph Smith Camp of the Daughters of Utah Pioneers. She held a life membership in the Genealogical Society of Utah. During her later years she worked faithfully in the Temple. One of her greatest pleasures was her flower garden. It was small but perfected with loving care. Her grandchildren delighted to visit her home. The open door, her smile, the special attention each one received made a lasting welcome for all. Hannah died 12 Jan 1929 at Logan, Utah.

MARY ANN WESTON DAVIS MAUGHAN

BIRTHDATE: 10 Mar 1817
Corse Lawn, Gloucestershire, England
DEATH: 15 Feb 1901
Logan, Cache, Utah
PARENTS: Thomas Halford Weston
Elizabeth Walker Thackwell Weston
PIONEER: 15 Sep 1850
William Wall Wagon Company
SPOUSE I: John Davis
MARRIED: 23 Dec 1840
DEATH SP I: 6 Apr 1841
England

CHILDREN: None

SPOUSE II: Peter Maughan
MARRIED: 2 Nov 1841
DEATH: 24 Apr 1871

CHILDREN:
Charles Weston, 24 May 1844
Peter Weston, 20 May 1847 (died age 3)
Joseph Weston, 25 Mar 1850
Hyrum Weston, 15 Apr 1852
Willard Weston, 31 Aug 1854
Elizabeth, 27 Sep 1856
Martha Weston, 4 Nov 1858
Peter Weston, 16 Jun 1861

Mary Ann attended the schools of her day and was trained in millinery and dressmaking. She became an apprentice to Miss Phelps from whom she learned about the LDS Church. She was baptized in 1840 in a village pond at midnight. On December 23, 1840, she married John Davis; but just months later he died from injuries received from an angry mob. She arranged to sail on the ship, Harmony, to Quebec, Canada. They took the steamer to Pa Prairie, where they boarded a train for St. Johns. They continued on to Kirtland, Ohio. Here she became acquainted with Peter Maughan who was a widower with five small children. They were married November 2, 1841 in Nauvoo, Illinois. The Maughans prepared for the trek west to the Salt Lake Valley. They traveled with the William Wall Wagon Company. They endured many hardships, the worst of which was when their three year old son, Peter, was run over by a wagon and killed. They arrived in the Salt Lake Valley on September 15, 1850.

The Maughan family was sent to Tooele to settle. They were assigned land and built a two room log house. Mary Ann received a letter from Dr. Willard Richards appointing her as midwife for Tooele. She did sewing for others outside her home in order to help with the family budget. Mary Ann was one of the first Sunday School Teachers in Tooele. Indians stole their cattle. Grasshoppers ate their crops. In 1856, Mary Ann was the first woman to enter Cache Valley as she accompanied her husband and others called to settle this region. She was called to be the first president of the Relief Society in that community and continued to serve as midwife and nurse for many years. Her husband, Peter, died in 1871. For over thirty years, she was a widow carrying the responsibilities of rearing her large family with courage and unwavering faith. During her later years, she worked faithfully in the temple and received much satisfaction from doing the work for her departed loved ones. She died at the age of eighty-four.

MILDRED CAROLINE UTLEY MAUGHAN

BIRTHDATE: 8 Jun 1851
Council Bluffs, Iowa
DEATH: 12 Feb 1930
Preston, Idaho
PARENTS: Little John Utley
Elizabeth Rutledge Utley
PIONEER: 12 Oct 1852
Allen Weeks Wagon Co.
SPOUSE:
Joseph Weston Maughan
MARRIED: 20 Dec 1872
Salt Lake Endowment House
DEATH: 12 Feb 1912
Logan, Cache, Utah

CHILDREN:
Sarah Matilda, 5 Oct 1873
Joseph Grey (Dode), 18 May 1875
Elizabeth, 23 Sep 1878
Little John, 24 Feb 1886 (died an infant)
Alta, 6 Feb 1887
Georgia, 24 Apr 1890

Mildred's parents heard the Prophet Joseph Smith speak while they were visiting with friends. They were converted to the truthfulness of the gospel and were baptized as members. They went to live in Nauvoo until they were driven from the town. They went to Council Bluffs where Mildred was born. While they were crossing the plains in the Allen Weeks Wagon Company, Cholera broke out. Millie's mother and two siblings died as a result of Cholera. At the time of her mother's death, Millie was only thirteen months old. An older sister took charge of Mildred. They arrived in the Salt Lake Valley on October 12, 1852 with the Allen Weeks Wagon Company.

They settled in Tooele where her father worked as a mechanic. They were well to do and were able to avail themselves of about all the educational and social advantages of the times.

Millie married Joseph Weston Maughan in the Endowment House in Salt Lake City, Utah when she was seventeen years old. Joseph and Mildred made their home in Wellsville for a year and a half then moved to Logan. They made another home in Glendale, Idaho where Mildred was the first Primary President Of the ward. She was also a teacher in the Relief Society. While she was living in Logan, she witnessed the completion of the temple and tabernacle. They lived in tents to be with Joseph as he traveled about working on the Utah & Northern Railroad. They went to live in Glendale where she served as the first Primary President. She was also a teacher in the Relief Society. She was a pastry chef for a cafe in Preston and was also an excellent seamstress. This enabled her to take in sewing to help provide for her children. She had a desire to help others and did so even when she needed help herself. She was a good singer and enjoyed reading. She had been able to acquire many good books from men who came from the east to survey for the railroad. In her last years,

she was living with her daughter when the home caught on fire. She saved her grandson, but she was badly burned and scarred for the rest of her life. She died on February 12, 1930.

SARAH MARIAH DAVENPORT MAUGHAN

BIRTHDATE: 22 Nov 1836
Fentonville, Genesse, Michigan
DEATH: 19 Nov 1914
Weston, Franklin, Idaho
PARENTS: James Davenport
Almira Phelps Davenport
PIONEER: 1851
Phileman Merrill Wagon Co.
SPOUSE:
John Harrison Maughan
MARRIED: 24 Jul 1853
DEATH: 31 Oct 1912
Weston, Franklin, Idaho

CHILDREN:
Sarah Agnes, 26 Jul 1854
Mary Almira, 5 Aug 1856
John Davenport, 10 Jan 1859
Harrison Davenport, 17 Sep 1861
William Davenport, 21 Oct 1863 (died as infant)
Ruth Emma, 15 Oct 1865
Peter Davenport, 15 Mar 1868
Martha Ann, 2 Jan 1870
Hyrum Davenport, 17 Dec 1871 (died age 27)
George Davenport, 17 Dec 1873
Ambrose Davenport, 15 Sep 1875
Elsie Medora, 4 Oct 1878
Margaret Alice, 9 Jan 1881

Shortly after the LDS Church was organized, the Davenport family became members. They were living in Nauvoo, Illinois in 1845 and were driven from their homes. Her father was called to go with the first company of saints across the plains to serve as their blacksmith. After a short stay in the valley, he returned to Winter Quarters for his family. It was almost three years before they were financially able to travel west by wagon train. At this time Sarah Mariah was thirteen years old. She met John Harrison Maughan in the wagon company.

When the Davenports arrived in the Valley, they were sent to Grantsville. The Maughan family was settled in nearby E. T. City. John and Mariah were married on July 24, 1853. The years spent in Tooele Valley were fraught with hardships, with frequent Indian scares, and crop failures. Mariah and John with their two little daughters were among the first seven families to settle permanently in Cache Valley under the leadership of Peter Maughan. Ten years later, they went with the first company to settle Bear Lake Valley where they remained for one and one half year. In 1866, they were sent to settle Weston, Idaho. The demands of the Indians often far exceeded the ability of the settlers to give. Mariah also faced the challenges of polygamy. When John was advised to move south for a while, he took his second wife and they served as missionaries to the Zuni Indians in northwestern New Mexico. This wife and her child died in childbirth. While they were gone, Mariah and their children managed the farm and a one room store. She was the mother of thirteen children. She had learned tailoring in her youth and was able to take in sewing to help provide for her family. She was an excellent cook and served church workers, railroad officials, and even some prisoners as they slept on the floor of Mariah's home during the years her husband served as Justice of the Peace. She was the first Relief Society President in the Weston Ward. She always went to the aid of those in distress.

KEZIAH MILES GOODMAN WARNER MAW

BIRTHDATE: 2 May 1834
Hallston, Leicestershire, England
DEATH: 14 Jul 1914
Ogden, Weber, Utah
PARENTS: Job Goodman
Ann Miles
PIONEER: 2 Nov 1855
Isaac Allred Wagon Train
SPOUSE I:
William Goodman Warner
MARRIED: 30 Nov 1854
Atlantic
DEATH SP: 26 Jul 1863
Ogden, Utah

CHILDREN:
William Goodman, 14 Aug 1856
Job Goodman, 11 May 1858
Heber Goodman, 20 Jan 1860
Margaret Ann Goodman, 12 Jul 1862

SPOUSE II: Edward Maw
MARRIED: 7 Mar 1864
DEATH: 9 Aug 1893

CHILDREN:
Edwin Goodman, 24 Jul 1865
Ephraim Goodman, 19 Feb 1868
Aaron Goodman, 24 Jan 1871
Ellen Keziah Goodman (Poulsen), 20 Nov 1873

Keziah was born in England in 1834. She was baptized 4 Mar 1854, in England, at the age of twenty. On 24 Apr she sailed from Liverpool on the "Clara Wheeler." While on board, 30 Nov 1854, she married William Goodman Warner. She was still twenty. After landing in New Orleans, all the Saints took a river boat up the Mississippi River to St. Louis. Christmas Day was spent on board the boat. 17 Jan 1855 they reached St. Louis. The women all stayed here until April, while William, along with others went to find work. Later Keziah went up the Missouri River to the Atchessions Camp. Here many of the people, with her, took sick with Cholera. She was very ill for several weeks. William heard of this and he returned and took care of her until she recovered. He worked on a farm until 25 Jul and they went to Mormon Grove, Kansas, leaving 31 Jul 1855 to cross the plains in the Isaac Allred wagon train, arriving in Salt Lake City 2 Nov 1855.

They were sent to settle Cache Valley to the Ch. Ranch located between Wellsville and Logan. They left and came to Ogden on 22 Jul 1856 where their first child was born in August. In the spring of 1857 they moved up on the bench. In the fall, William left for Echo Canyoa to fight and was there until Winter. Keziah, along with the baby, was left in the little pen made out of willows. William returned to the farm and three more children joined their family. William was killed in a cave-in. He died 26 Jul 1863. Keziah was a widow until 7 Mar 1864 when she married Edward Maw in polygamy. He had three other wives. William also had another wife, so this was nothing new. They tore down the little willow house and went to live in another. They became parents of four making a total of eight for Keziah. When Keziah married Edward, he had a small girl named Alice. Keziah took this child and raised her as her own. Edward Maw passed away 9 Aug 1893. Keziah was left alone again, after twenty-nine years of marriage. She was treasurer in the Relief Society for over ten years and spent many years working in the temple. She was small in stature, very neat and always dressed in black. She always wore cute little bonnet hats. She passed away 14 Jul 1914 at age eighty-two and was buried in the Ogden Cemetery, between her two husbands. She had been a widow for twenty years.

MARIA ALIDA (MARY ALICE) CHRISTINA BESS MAWSON

BIRTHDATE: 12 Feb 1852
Amsterdam, the Netherlands
DEATH: 20 Feb 1937
Salt Lake City, Utah
PARENTS:
Johannes Henricus Dykman
Olive (Aaltje) Ages Dykman
PIONEER: 2 Nov 1864
Warren S. Snow Wagon Co.
SPOUSE: James Lawrence Bess
MARRIED: 14 Mar 1870
Salt Lake Endowment House
DEATH: 1 Aug 1912
Taylorsville, Utah

CHILDREN:
John Henry, 10 Dec 1870
Georgina Lucinda, 13 Jul 1872
Mary Olive, 30 Mar 1874 (died age 6)
Annie Isabelle, 25 Dec 1876 (died infant)
Laurabelle, 21 Dec 1877 (died age 5)
Lola Eliza, 4 May 1879
Juel Franklin, 15 Jan 1882 (died age 1)
William Franklin, 24 Jul 1884
Alma, 28 Apr 1887 (died age 1)
Delbert, 31 Jul 1889 (died age 2)
Clara, 6 Jul 1982 (died 7 mo.)

SPOUSE: Robert Mawson
MARRIED: unknown
DEATH: unknown

Mary Alice and her family were converted to the gospel of the LDS Church. They began making plans to come to America to join the main body of the Saints. Before their plans could be realized, Mary Alice's mother died. Her father brought his five children across the ocean on the ship, "Hudson," to America. She was eleven years old at the time of this adventure. After they landed in New York, the Saints went up the Hudson River by steamboat as far as Albany, New York. Then they took the train until they reached St. Joseph, Missouri. This detour was necessary because the Civil War was still raging. When they reached Wyoming, Nebraska, they joined the Warren S. Snow ox-train, the last one of the season leaving in mid August, 1864 to cross the plains. They arrived in Salt Lake City on 2 Nov 1864. Their family settled in a little adobe home on a dry farm on the west side of the valley in an area known as Granger.

Mary Alice married James Lawrence Bess as his third wife. They were the parents of eleven children of which only four grew to adulthood. She also raised three of her sister, Cornelia's, children because Cornelia had been institutionalized. Then she raised a granddaughter from age five until she married. Mary Alice was very active in the LDS Church, serving in the Granger Ward for thirty years in the Relief Society Presidency. For twenty years she baked the sacrament bread for the ward. After her husband, James, died she moved to a home in Salt Lake City. She could walk from her home to her daughter's home every afternoon. She married Robert Mawson in 1917. They had a lot of birthday parties and family gatherings. There was always a lot of good food, especially her angel food cake. Mary Alice loved shopping and going to town.

HELEN ALCY TANNER MAXFIELD

BIRTHDATE: 18 Dec 1839
New Liberty, Rope County, Illinois
DEATH: 17 May 1915
Lyman, Wayne County, Utah
PARENTS: Nathan Tanner
Rachel Winter Smith Tanner
PIONEER: 19 Oct 1848
Amasa Lyman Wagon Company
SPOUSE: Elijah Hiett Maxfield
MARRIED: 24 Aug 1856
South Cottonwood, Utah
DEATH: 7 Sep 1925
Salt Lake City, Utah

CHILDREN:
Hiett Elijah, 7 Feb 1859
Helen Alcy, 8 Sep 1860
Nathan, 15 Sep 1862
Juliette, 18 Dec 1864
John Schuerman, 28 Feb 1867

Francis Quincy, 9 May 1870
Junetta, 19 Jun 1872
Archelaus Warren, 19 Oct 1876
Ethel Mae, 11 Oct 1879

Helen was born in New Liberty, Illinois. Her family journeyed to Winter Quarters, Iowa, leaving Montrose, Iowa the last part of Jun 1848. They traveled with the Amasa Lyman Company by wagon and arrived in the Salt Lake Valley 19 Oct 1848. Helen was nine years old. The family settled in South Cottonwood, Utah.

Helen married Elijah Hiett Maxfield 24 Aug 1856 in South Cottonwood, Utah. She was sixteen years old. They became the parents of nine children; five sons and four daughters. Helen possessed a natural talent for nursing and caring for the sick. In 1861, Marion Lyman set her apart to be a midwife. She attended school in Salt Lake City, Utah and was always searching for knowledge from every available source on the subject of nursing. In 1892, she took a special course from a Dr. Sorenson and received her diploma. In compliance with the laws of the Territory of Utah she was licensed to practice obstetrics in said Territory. This was over the signature of seven medical men who were the Board of Medical Examiners. Helen delivered over 2,000 babies throughout the Valley of Wayne County where she resided.

She also served as President of the Primary and the Relief Society. She was an expert seamstress and quiltmaker. She made suits and coats for men, and women's and children's clothing. She ginned the cotton, dyed it, and spun the yarn to make clothes for her family and others. Helen's home was a place where friends and neighbors loved to visit. The latch string was always out and a feeling of "Welcome My Brothers" existed. The traveler always felt refreshed and happy after being with them. They helped settle South Cottonwood, Toquerville and Loa, all in Utah. While Helen was positive in her views and stood firmly in her convictions as to what she thought was right, she was kind and affectionate, never imposing an injustice on others. She was wise and foreseeing. Her council and judgment were sought by many.

Helen died at the age of seventy-six years, 17 May 1915 in Lyman, Utah. Her husband died in Salt Lake City, Utah 7 Sep 1925.

MARY MARIA BATES MURRAY KELLEY MAXFIELD

BIRTHDATE: 6 Jun 1853
Warwickshire, England
DEATH: 1 Apr 1935
Stockton, Utah
PIONEER: Fall 1866
John Kain / Thomas Stenhouse Co.
PARENTS: Joseph Bates
Maria Redding Bates
SPOUSE I: John Murray
MARRIED: 21 Jun 1872
probably Stockton, Utah
DEATH SP: date not given
Black Hills, North Dakota

CHILDREN:
John June, 24 Jun 1874

SPOUSE II: James H. Kelley
MARRIED: abt 1876
Utah
DEATH SP II: 2 Feb 1905
Stockton, Utah

CHILDREN:
Theodore Carl, 1 Jun 1877
Pearl Elizabeth, 18 Oct 1880
Elsie, 24 Aug 1883
Joseph T., 24 Nov 1888
Mary Maria, 13 Nov 1891

SPOUSE III: Jessie LeRoy Maxfield
MARRIED: 1926
Stockton, Utah
DEATH SP III: not given

CHILDREN:
4 step-children

Mary Maria was born in England. She was about thirteen years old when she came with her parents to America. Mary Maria, her parents, one brother and two sisters boarded the wind vessel "Arkwright," under the leadership of Daniel P. Caulkin. They left England in May with four hundred fifty immigrants and arrived in America 6 Jul 1866. The Bates family came to Utah in the John T. Kain and Thomas B. H. Stenhouse Company. They shared a wagon, drawn by oxen, with another family. Mary Maria, along with the other children, walked across the Plains and into the Salt Lake Valley in the Fall of 1866.

After a short stay in Salt Lake City, the Bates family moved to Tooele, Utah where the father became a farmer. Mary Maria and an older sister were sent to Salt Lake City to further their education. Upon completion of her training, Mary Maria went to the mining town of Stockton, Utah to work in the Stockton Hotel. She spent the rest of her life in Stockton. She married John H. Murray 21 Jun 1872. They had one son, John June Murray. Her husband was killed by Indians in the Black Hills country of North Dakota.

Following the death of her husband, Mary Maria married James H. Kelley. They became the parents of five children; two boys and three girls. Her husband, James, died in Stockton, Utah 2 Feb 1905. Their daughter, Mary Maria, died 24 Apr of the same year. Mary Maria was a petite lady, very quick in her actions. She was adept at caring for the sick, a kind and generous woman. She was always willing to help in times of sickness or trouble. She enjoyed her lovely flower gardens. She kept active all of her life. Mary Maria had a special calling card by which everyone in town knew of a visit. She always placed the broom (which was always kept on the stoop in those days) crossways in the door frame.

She married Jessie LeRoy Maxfield in 1926. He was a widower with four children. Mary Maria died in Stockton on 1 Apr 1935. She is buried in the Stockton, Utah Cemetery next to her second husband, James H. Kelley,

SARAH CAHOON MAXFIELD

BIRTHDATE: 7 Aug 1846
Winter Quarters, Nebraska
DEATH: 30 Oct 1931
Los Angeles, California
PARENTS: Daniel Stiles Cahoon
Jane Amanda Spencer Cahoon
PIONEER: 24 Sep 1849
Orson Spencer Company
SPOUSE: Robert Quorton Maxfield
MARRIED: 7 Jan 1864
Salt Lake City, Utah
DEATH: 5 Jul 1880
South Cottonwood, Utah

CHILDREN:
Sarah-twin, 24 Dec 1864
Mary -twin, 24 Dec 1864
Daniel Styles, 19 Dec 1867
James Appleton, 14 Nov 1868
Sophia, 27 Sep 1871
Martha Ellen, 3 Jan 1873
John Amos, 23/27 Jan 1875

Sarah Cahoon Maxfield was born in Winter Quarters, Nebraska 7 Aug 1846. Sarah accompanied her parents from her birthplace at Winter Quarters, Nebraska across the Plains to Salt Lake City as a three-year-old. The family arrived in the Salt Lake Valley 24 Sep 1849 by wagon with the Orson Spencer Company. After a short time in Salt Lake City, her family moved to a home in South Cottonwood, now Murray, Utah. The home had been built by Andrew Cahoon, a brother of her father. Little is known of her early childhood. She was baptized a member of the Church of Jesus Christ of Latter-day Saints 3 Aug 1855.

Sarah married Robert Quorton Maxfield 7 Jan 1864 at Salt Lake City, Utah. They were endowed and sealed in the Endowment House in Salt Lake City 26 May 1866. They became the parents of seven children. Sarah lived through the attack upon their crops by the crickets. She learned how to make a home in a desert environment and did all the usual work of a pioneer wife and mother of seven children. Her husband died 5 Jul 1880. He was buried in the Murray City Cemetery. In later years, when a widow, Sarah went to California to live with some of her children. She was a widow for fifty-one years. Sarah died at the age of eighty-five years in Los Angeles, California. She is buried at the Forest Lawn Cemetery in Los Angeles.

MATILDA RUSSELL MAXHAM

BIRTHDATE: 7 Jan 1820
Dutchess, New York
DEATH: 19 Oct 1904
Colonia, Morelas, Mexico
PARENTS:
George Washington Russell
Anna Cole Russell
PIONEER: 13 Aug 1852
James W. Bay wagon train
SPOUSE: Charles Maxham (Maxam)
MARRIAGE: 8 Jan 1841
DEATH SP: 12 May 1885
Smithfield (Pima), Arizona

CHILDREN:
Cynthia Sildona, 29 Aug. 1843
Heber Kimball, 20 Feb 1849
Eliza Snow, 6 Jun 1853
Jane Lucinda, 18 Jun 1860

Matilda Russell was born in New York in 1820. Her childhood contained incidents that defied reason and explanation. When she was eight years old and her father was away, her mother became ill, so ill it was feared she would die at any moment. Friends and neighbors gathered in the front yard with sympathy and offers to help. James, her golden-haired two-and-a-half year old brother was taken to be cared for by a strange man who carried him away–they were never seen again. It was learned next day that the young man, a traveling sales man, had left in the night taking James with him. When Matilda's father returned and learned of his baby's disappearance he began a search that lasted many years. The boy was never found and her mother never ceased grieving for her lost child.

She always recounted the time her father, visiting neighbors, witnessed the curing of the neighbor's child's blindness. A strange man had appeared at the door. He followed a process of washing the blind child's eyes with his own saliva, clean water and clean cloth until the child shouted "I can see everybody in the room!" The stranger turned to Matilda's father and, saying that he "had a little girl who would some day learn all about me," went to the door and, as he stepped outside, suddenly disappeared. Unappreciated at the time, the incident gave her a strong testimony of the gospel in her adult life.

Matilda, grew up in an area about eighty miles from Palmyra, New York when religious fervor was strong.

After seeing neighbors the calibre of Wilford Woodruff turning to the new religion and listening to the message, Matilda was baptized 26 Oct 1838 by her husband Charles when she was twenty-five years old.

Matilda and Charles followed the Saints as they were forced westward and by 1846 were living in Nauvoo, with Charles working on the Temple as a mechanic trying feverishly with the other men to complete it after their beloved prophet was martyred so that as many as possible could partake of the endowments before they were forced again from their homes. She would tell her grandchildren how, when driven out of Nauvoo, they crossed the Mississippi river on the ice on a cold winter night with her three year old baby girl and nothing but the things they could carry. How they camped at Montrose and in great hunger pled with the Lord for help and how he sent the quails like manna from heaven to ease their hunger.

Charles and Matilda with their four children left Kanesville, Iowa along with 192 others at the end of May in 1852, the first wagon train of that season to reach the Salt Lake Valley that year. She contributed time and effort to her religion in Utah, being a counselor in the Relief Society when it was organized 29 Aug, 1868 and she was Primary President in Santaquin in 1879.

The Maxham family was called to help settle Arizona in 1879, they went by way of St. Johns County, and did not reach Smithville (Pima) until 1882. It was here that Charles passed away on 12 May, 1885. After a brief return to Utah, she lived with her daughter Lucinda's family in Pima, Arizona and traveled with them to Morelos, Sonora, Mexico with Brigham Young and Heber J. Grant and others to open this country for the Mormon Missionaries. It was while living in Mexico that she passed away at the age of eighty-nine.

ELIZABETH DONELY MAXWELL

No Photo Available

BIRTHDATE: 28 Dec 1804,
Kilman, Antrim, Ireland
DEATH: Sep 1857—near Cache Cave in Echo Canyon, Summit, Utah
PARENTS: Arthur Donely
Catherine Hyde
PIONEER: 1857
Daniel D. McArthur Handcart Co.
SPOUSE: Ralph Maxwell, Sr.
MARRIED: 13 Jul 1823
Carlisle, Cumberland, England
DEATH SP: 1852
Glasgow, Lanark, Scotland

CHILDREN:
Arthur, 22 Apr 1824
Catherine, 15 Apr 1829
John, 1 Jul 1834
Elizabeth (Betsy), 7 Jan 1835
Ralph, Jr., 30 Apr 1837
George, 24 May 1840
Ann, 5 Apr 1843

Elizabeth was born 28 Dec 1804 at Kilman, Antrim, Ireland. She married Ralph Maxwell, Sr. on 13 Jul 1823 in Carlisle, Cumberland, England. They were the parents of seven children and lived on a farm at Kirkfield Bank until 1851. They then moved to New Lanark where the whole family began working in the textile mills in Scotland and later in England. In emigration records they were all listed as weavers.

Elizabeth's husband died in 1852. In 1856, she and five of her children sailed on the ship Enoch Train and came to America, landing at Boston, Massachusetts. They traveled in steerage class and were assisted by the Perpetual Emigration Fund.

By railroad they traveled from New York to Dawn City, Iowa and joined a handcart company led by Daniel D. McArthur. When they reached Fort Bridger Elizabeth was too ill to travel and remained at the Fort while her family went ahead. She then tried to continue the journey, but died and was buried on the trail near Cache Cave in Echo Canyon.

ELIZABETH MCAUSLIN MAXWELL

BIRTHDATE: 16 Feb 1832
Baronry Parish, Brighton, Lanark, Scotland
DEATH: 10 Nov 1911
Peoa, Summit County, Utah
PARENTS: William McAuslin
Jane Kennedy McAuslin
PIONEER: 26 Sep 1856
Daniel D. McArthur
2nd Handcart Co.
SPOUSE: Arthur Maxwell
MARRIED: 8 May 1856
DEATH SP: 30 Oct 1871
Peoa, Summit Co. Utah

CHILDREN:
Arthur Jr., 14 Dec 1857
Jane Ann, 22 Jan 1860
Elizabeth, 30 Apr 1862
Agnes, 22 Jun 1864
Catherine, 14 Feb 1867
Ann, 25 Jul 1869
Elizabeth Durrah, adopted age 4

Elizabeth McAustin was born in Scotland in 1832. She was converted to the L. D. S. Church and heeding the call to gather in Zion, at twenty-four, took the opportunity to emigrate to America using the Perpetual Emigration Fund set up by the Church to help those converts who wished to come to Utah.

On the 23rd of March, 1856, Elizabeth boarded the ship "Enoch Train," and sailed with 534 other converts led by James Ferguson bound for Boston.

Toward the end of their six week voyage, Elizabeth married Arthur Maxwell and departed ship, a new wife in a new country. Their honeymoon was the 108 day trek of 1,000 miles pushing and pulling a handcart to Utah. (Perhaps it made the going more joyful?)

Within the year the newly married couple were faced with uprooting and moved south because Johnstons's Army was threatening the Mormons. Expecting war Brigham Young sent the citizens south for safety.

The Maxwell's settled permanently in Peoa, Wasatch Co. and if not accosted by Indians themselves, would hear about and worry of the Indian raids of stock and the killing of the men sent to retrieve them in the Heber area in 1866-67. Could they leave their cabins unattended by sons or husbands was a real worry. Could Elizabeth, carrying her fifth child, get help safely when it came time to deliver?

When that baby, Catherine, was four and baby Ann was two years and three months old, in late October, Arthur died, leaving Elizabeth with six children, the oldest, their only son Arthur, not quite fourteen. Arthur's cousin's child, Elizabeth Durrah, had been adopted by them.

The strength to walk one thousand miles helping pull a handcart, did not desert her. She had fortitude to surmount this tragedy and carry on. In her later life she enjoyed working in the temple and died at the age of seventy-nine having cared for her family alone for forty years.

JANE HIRD MAXWELL

BIRTHDATE: 30 Sep 1832
Thorpe, Yorkshire, England
DEATH: 19 Oct 1916
Salt Lake City, Utah
PARENTS: Stephen Hird
Jane Throup Hird
PIONEER: 27 Aug 1860
Franklin Brown's Wagon Company
SPOUSE: John Lambert Maxwell
MARRIED: 6 Mar 1860
Keighly, Yorkshire, England
DEATH: 28 Jul 1905
Salt Lake City, Utah

CHILDREN:
Mary Ellen Hird, 8 Mar 1861
John Stephen, 11 Feb 1863
Jane Elizabeth, 8 Mar 1865
Sarah Ann Maxwell, 2 May 1867
James Hird Maxwell, 28 Jul 1868
Margaret Hird, 13 Oct 1870
Thomas Hird, 31 Aug 1872
Alice Marie, 7 Nov 1874
Camelia Hird, 7 Nov 1877
William Hird, 8 Jul 1879

Jane, in her early womanhood, left Liverpool, England with her husband and came to this land of freedom and religious liberty where she could worship her Heavenly Father according to her faith. They settled in Salt Lake City where she taught her family to be hard-working. She and her children helped mold adobe bricks for their pioneer home. She motivated her sons to take an interest in the family nursery business until they became widely recognized florists in Salt Lake City. She often wore a beautiful flower on her dress as a means of encouraging her children in good grooming and appreciation of the beauties of nature. Her daughters were taught to beautify their surroundings by cultivating and growing beautiful flowers, plants, trees, and shrubs in their own homes and gardens. She also taught them the fine art of homemaking and sewing well made and attractive clothing.

Frontier life took its toll, but in her later years she could still crochet. She could still contribute to beauty and the enjoyment of cherished possessions. When her stitching was finished, she would present to loved ones an article of beauty. After the death of her husband, she was elected honorary President of the John Lambert Maxwell Genealogical Association which is still functioning. She was a devoted, loyal, and faithful member of the LDS Church and exemplified the teachings of our Savior.

When this noble woman died in 1916, she left a large posterity who were truly very devoted to her and so appreciative of having this wonderful lady as their mother, grandmother, and great grandmother.

JESSIE LAVINA RANDS MAXWELL

BIRTHDATE: 13 Mar 1862
Cape Town, South Africa
DEATH: 28 Feb 1945
Salt Lake City, Utah
PARENTS: Joseph Rands
Sarah Anderson Rands
PIONEER: 15 Sep 1868
John Gillespie Wagon Company
SPOUSE: James Maxwell
MARRIED: 25 Dec 1879
Salt Lake Endowment House
DEATH: 3 Mar 1941
Salt Lake City, Utah

CHILDREN:
James Gavin, 19 Oct 1880
Joseph Rands, 27 Oct 1881
William Edward, 24 Apr 1883
Martha Elizabeth, 13 May 1886
Sarah Lily, 2 Aug 1887
Hyrum James, 14 Feb 1889
Margaret LaVina, 15 Sep 1890
John McMillan, 27 Oct 1892
Jessie Ruth, 24 Dec 1884
Charles Henry, 25 Aug 1896
Mary Ellen, 3 Apr 1894
Samuel, 11 Sep 1898

Jessie LaVina was born in Capetown, South Africa. Her father had gone to Africa to work in the diamond mines. When he joined the Mormon Church he lost his job. In Africa Jessie was aware of wild animals and their roaring at night. In 1868, the Rands family left Africa for America.

They spent two months on the water. Jessie enjoyed watching the ship plow through the large waves. One day the Captain grabbed her as a wave nearly washed her into the sea.

After landing in New York, the family was detained for two more months. They left for Benton, Wyoming in a cattle car and then on to the Salt Lake Valley by ox-team with the John Gillespie Company. There were fourteen children and four adults in the wagon so Jessie had to walk most of the way. They arrived in the Salt Lake Valley 15 Sep 1868 and settled in Salt Lake in a converted barn. Her father found work out of town and her mother had to take local work. Jessie and her brother were left alone with a slice of bread and water for their lunch. The fire went out in the small stove and the children were cold. They climbed into the cold fireplace, somehow thinking they would keep warm. A friend found them nearly frozen. Jessie woke up finding herself being rolled in the snow to bring her to.

A couple persuaded their parents to let Jessie stay with them. They treated her harshly and made this little girl do all the family wash. When she had to go for milk her father saw her. She was crying. He took her home and never let her go back again. The Rands lived on a farm early in 1869. Their crops were eaten by the grasshoppers. They lived on pig weeds, red root weeds and sego lily bulbs, for a time. The family moved to 12th East and lived in a dugout until a home could be built. Jessie was baptized in Oct 1872. In 1875 her father was killed in an accident at the Z.C.M.I. department store where he was working. Jessie helped take care of his wounds until he died. She went to the Relief Society for clean clothes, so she got started in Relief Society before she was old enough to be a member. Jessie was a Sunday School teacher for a few months and at the age of fourteen she worked for prominent Church leaders, including President John Taylor, where she met her future husband.

She married James Maxwell 25 Dec 1879. They had twelve children; three died in infancy. They attended the Dedicatory Services of the Salt Lake Temple 6 Apr 1893. In 1902 James was called to be the Bishop of their Ward. Jessie was made Relief Society President. She was called to be an officer in the Ensign Stake Relief Society. She served forty-three years in the Relief Society organization. She was a worker in the Salt Lake Temple for ten years. Jessie was personally acquainted with all the Presidents of the Mormon Church from Brigham Young to Heber J. Grant, who was present at her 60th wedding anniversary. She died 28 Feb 1945 in Salt Lake City, Utah.

MARTHA ALLEN MAY

BIRTHDATE: 26 Sep 1839
Rochester, West Parmer,
Lorain, Ohio
DEATH: 17 Nov 1923 –Harper
Ward (Honeyville), Box Elder, Utah
PARENTS: Jude Allen
Mary Ann Nicholas
PIONEER: 25 Sep 1852
Benjamin Gardner/Jude Allen's 10
SPOUSE: James May
MARRIED: 24 Aug 1856
Sessions (Bountiful), Davis, Utah
DEATH: 29 Mar 1910 –Harper
Ward (Honeyville), Box Elder, Utah

CHILDREN:
James Ira, 29 Nov 1857
Jude Allen, 14 Oct 1859
George, 28 Nov 1861
Henry Lyman, 25 Jan 1863
Martha Ellen (Hunsaker), 14 Mar 1865
Sarah Margret (Bernard), 22 Sep 1867
Eveline (Hunsaker), 26 Jun 1869
Andrew, 22 Feb 1871
Frank, 18 Nov 1872
Harriet (Kelly), 7 Aug 1874
Richard 'C', 27 Jun 1876
Mary Ann (Arbon), 20 Apr 1878
Emma (Harper/Hanson), 19 Sep 1880
Joseph Eugene, 24 May 1882

Martha was born in Ohio, 1839. Her parents had joined the LDS church in 1831. They lived peacefully in West Parma until 1843, when the Allen family (four children) moved to Nauvoo, Illinois. Martha's father was one of the bodyguards of the Prophet. They suffered the persecutions and made the exodus from Nauvoo in 1846 settling on Indian lands with the Ponca Indians at Fort Vermillion. They were part of the Pawnee tribe. Then on to Kanesville for about two years, then to North Pigeon Creek, Iowa for four years. In 1852 they came west. They now had eight children. They left Kanesville, Iowa 15 May with the Benjamin Gardner Wagon Train with her father being captain of their ten. They arrived in Salt Lake City 25 Sep 1852, where, after two months, they were sent to the Sessions Settlement, now Bountiful, Utah. Martha never did learn to read and write. She was too busy helping her mother, who, before she died in 1860 had added four more children to the family, making twelve. Martha learned to do arithmetic, adding and subtracting sums in her head accurately, and she had an excellent memory. She learned to cook, spin wool, knit clothing, care for the sick and had an air of grace, was self-reliant, busy and productive. She was a tall woman, well built, very strong, had a clear complexion, long artistic looking hands, and a steady gaze from blue-grey eyes.

Martha married James May on 24 Aug 1856 when she was sixteen. They made their home in Call's Fort where their first child was born. Martha would endure James' absence off and on for most of her married life. In 1862,

the May family had become prosperous enough to move into a one-and-a-half story two room log home. They farmed for a living and James worked at his saw mill. After the seventh child was born, James was called on a mission. Martha stayed home and kept things going. After four more children, James took a second wife in polygamy. He married Rhoda Ann Lang, 2 Nov 1877 in St. George and they had eleven children. Martha added three more children, making a total of fourteen. The May families went through the government persecution of the Mormon Polygamists. During the ten years Martha shared her husband with Rhoda, she helped Rhoda bear six children and bury one. James passed away 29 Mar 1910. During the last years of their marriage, Martha had eight children living with her. She labored alone to raise them. She served as a midwife, counselor in the Relief Society and Y.W.M.I.A. She passed away 17 Nov 1923 at age seventy-four, having been a widow thirteen years.

ELIZABETH HARFORD MAYALL
(MAYAL, MAYALL, MAYBE, MAILES)

No
Photo
Available

BIRTHDATE: 5 Jul 1786
Eastnor, Herefordshire, England
DEATH: 1860-64
PARENTS: John Harford
Mary
PIONEER: 24 Sep 1848
Heber C. Kimball Wagon Co.
SPOUSE: Thomas Mayall(Mailes)
MARRIED: 12 Oct 1815
Eastnor, Herefordshire, England
DEATH SP: 19 Nov 1833
Eastnor, Herefordshire, England

CHILDREN:
Mary Ann, 25 Oct 1816
Hannah, abt. 1818
Eliza, 23 Jul 1820 died as child
John, 13 Jun 1825
Thomas, 24 Jul 1829
Elizabeth, 1 Oct 1832 died as child

Elizabeth Harford was born in England between 1786-90, where she grew to adulthood and in her twenties married Thomas Mayall. They were an illiterate couple and were not certain even to the spelling of their surnames, according to Parish records at least four different spellings are used.

Their children were born in England, (Eliza and Elizabeth died in childhood), and the couple were married seventeen years when Thomas died leaving forty-six-year-old Elizabeth and four children, Mary Ann 16, John 7, Thomas 3 and Elizabeth. (Was she born after her father died ?)

The four surviving children were in ages between 24 and 11 when the family was converted to the Mormon

Church and baptized by Wilford Woodruff in Herefordshire, in 1840. Within two years Elizabeth had made the necessary preparations and with her family sailed for America to join the Saints. On the same ship was Thomas English Jones and his small son, William Parsons. The two families became acquainted and gave each other assistance on the voyage. The party left New Orleans for Commerce, (Nauvoo), where Thomas Jones and Mary Ann were married by Willford Woodruff.

When the Mormons made the exodus from Nauvoo, Elizabeth traveled with her daughter and son-in-law, to St. Joseph, Missouri by river boat, leaving in early spring. They spent the summer and survived that terrible winter of 1846-47 in St. Joseph.

When they joined the wagon trains west, they were among the 662 Saints led by Heber C. Kimball on a very primitive journey to the Salt Lake Valley. Elizabeth and Mary Ann walked beside the wagons for 116 days. On the 24th of September 1848 the exhausted pioneers reached their destination.

The first winter was spent living in their wagon box and a brush-covered dugout on City Creek. The next year they were instructed to leave that colony and settle in Holliday. The family moved from Cottonwood (Holliday) to Kays Creek sometime between late 1850 and May 1851, still living out of the wagon box and a dugout.

Early in 1861, the Thomas Jones family moved from Kays Creek ten miles north and a little west of Ogden where they built their first substantial home of logs. They established a farm on the flat plain along the west bank of the Weber River in the community of West Weber.

Grandmother Elizabeth Mayall, age seventy-three was losing the battle of life. She succumbed on the Weber in 1864. The exact date is unrecorded.

LOUISA STARKEY MAYCOCK

BIRTHDATE: 6 Jul 1832
Bloxwich, England
DEATH: 13 Jan 1908
Salt Lake City, Salt Lake, Utah
PARENTS: William Starkey
Hannah Perry
PIONEER: 4 Sep 1859
George Rowley 8th Handcart Co
SPOUSE: Thomas Maycock
MARRIED: 11 Apr 1859
DEATH SP: 16 Apr 1900
Salt Lake City, Salt Lake, Utah

CHILDREN:
Louisa Maria, 31 Dec 1860
Hannah Elizabeth, 7 Apr 1863
Thomas Joseph, 6 Jan 1865
Mary Emile, 4 Mar 1867
James, 13 Jul 1868
Brigham William, 26 Sep 1869

Phillip Starkey, 23 May 1872
Lucy Eveline, 10 Mar 1874
George Edward, 27 Jan 1876

Louisa Starkey was born in England in 1832. She was baptized into the Church when she was twenty-four years old, 15 April 1856. It took great financial sacrifice to save enough money to get to America and great courage to leave family, friends, and home.

Louisa had that courage and more; by 11 April 1859 she set sail for America on the William Tapscott with 725 souls bound for New York and Utah. The brown haired, blue-grey eyed Louisa married Thomas Maycock aboard ship two days into the voyage.

From New York they traveled by steamer and train until they reached Florence, Nebraska. Two months later they had completed the preparation and on 9 June 1859 took their first step pulling a handcart for a seventy-five day trek to Zion. Louisa was in the only handcart company to cross the plains that year.

Indians were a concern and they had some frightening incidents, food became scarce and the last of the flour was rationed at eight pounds a man three weeks away from Salt Lake City. By August 22 the starving company of 225 people decided the faster ones should go ahead to meet the rescue wagons that were sure to be coming from Salt Lake. Louisa, being pregnant, was left behind with the slower group. The provisions and the first group met at Hams Fort. Thomas, taking precious food, hurried back to Louisa.

As the Handcart Company trudged down Immigration Canyon they were met by a great concourse of citizens cheering, welcoming the tired travelers.

One day, after living in the city for several years, looking up from her household duties, Louisa saw Indians coming down the street. Remembering the instructions to "feed the Indians, don't fight them" she began slicing bread and buttering the slices. Taking her baby in her arms she greeted them at the door. Grunting, one crowded past her. Crossing the room the Indian picked up the bread knife, tossed it into the air and caught it by the handle, and advanced menacingly toward her! She was frightened and backed toward the door. Louise and Harriet, playing on the floor set up a loud crying and the Indian dropped the knife and fled to the street. There the two were met by three more Indians. Crossing the road and entering a pottery shop they began to wreck every thing they could, stopping only when men were called in from the fields to use force to drive them away.

As the years passed they had six more children for a total of nine and raised their family in the city.

Louisa and Thomas made one trip back to England in their later years to gather genealogy. Both returned to die in Salt Lake City. Louisa died at the age of seventy-five living nearly eight years longer than Thomas.

MARY JANE HURST CRANDALL MAYCOCK

BIRTHDATE: 7 Nov 1832
South Hampton, Hampshire, Eng.
DEATH: 30 Aug 1914
Pleasant View, Weber, Utah
PARENTS: William Hurst
Susanna Webley Hurst
PIONEER: 21 Sep 1852
St. Louis Independent Company
SPOUSE I: Myron Nathan Crandall
MARRIAGE: 13 Mar 1857
Salt Lake City, Utah
DEATH SP: 4 Aug 1860
Springville, Utah Co., Utah

CHILDREN:
Isabel, 1 Feb 1858
William, 17 Jun 1860
Melbourne, died as a child

SPOUSE II: Martin Pardon Crandall (Myron's brother)
MARRIED: 4 Oct 1862
DEATH SP II: 2 Apr 1895
Springville, Utah
CHILDREN: unknown

SPOUSE III: Amos Maycock
MARRIED: 1 Sep 1875
DEATH: 20 Jul 1889
North Ogden, Weber, Utah

CHILDREN:
Mary Helen, 3 Mar 1877
Emma Elizabeth, 14 Nov 1878
Susannah Vermel, 11 Dec 1882

Mary Jane Hurst was born in England in 1838, the fifth child in a family of eight children. After accepting the gospel, the Hurst family traveled aboard the "Ashland" bound for America and New Orleans. They took a paddle boat up the Mississippi River to St. Louis, Missouri, and followed the same route the Saints used to get to Council Bluffs, Iowa where they purchased a wagon, a cart, two horses, three yoke of oxen and one yoke of cows.

Because of the hardships so far endured their family had been pared to the father and mother, Philip 16, 13-year-old Mary Jane, baby Emma, born after arriving in America, and a cousin Richard Westwood.

Mary Jane said of the trip across the plains that it was a pleasure trip for her. She was excited and happy coming to America and her main job was to tend the new baby sister. It was on the wagon train that she made her first boy acquaintances and learned to sing and dance around the campfire at night. They lived in what is now Liberty Park in the wagon box and a tent while her father worked for Brigham Young and helped build Chase Mill. The family soon moved into their own house their father built. It was adobe with a lean-to on the back and a wood floor.

Hard times hit the family when William died. The family moved to Springville (was it the evacuation for Johnstons's Army?) where Mary assumed the responsibility of providing for her family doing work for neighbors and giving her meager wages to her mother.

Encouraged by her cousin and brother Philip, she performed on the stage and attracted many beaus. At the age of eighteen she became the third wife of Myron Crandall for a brief marriage of three and one half years, years of security, stability and three darling children. Then misfortune and grief came to her once more when, at the age of 22, she was widowed.

Now she worked to support her children, teaching school in Fairview, Sanpete Co., and then housekeeping in Salt Lake City for one of Brigham Young's wives. She had to leave her children in the care of her mother who had remarried and was living in North Ogden. Just when things were looking up, her littlest boy Melbourne was bitten by a rattlesnake and died within eight hours! Only her faith in God and strength of character helped her now.

For fifteen years she supported herself and two children. At the age of thirty-seven, at her mother's house in Ogden, she met and married Amos Maycock to become his second wife. They lived in Pleasant View and three girls were born there. When the Edmond Tucker act was enforced Amos chose to go to prison rather than have his legal fatherhood denied to his children. He never recovered from confinement and died July 20, 1889 and at the age of fifty-one, Mary Jane was again a widow. To the end of her life she taught her children and grandchildren to have faith in God, a belief she exercised by working in the Church as Relief Society President, Sunday School teacher and with Ward Dramas.

She died at age seventy-six after a life of service to God, family and community.

SUSANNAH WEBLEY HURST MAYCOCK

BIRTHDATE: 30 Nov 1812
Bromsgrove, England
DEATH: 14 Nov 1878
Pleasant View, Weber, Utah
PARENTS: Richard Webley
Jane Danby Webley
PIONEER: 21 Sep 1852
St. Louis Independent Wagon Co.
SPOUSE: William Hurst
MARRIED: 11 Jul 1830
England
DEATH: 14 Mar 1853
Salt Lake City, Salt Lake, Utah

CHILDREN:
Thomas, 23 Dec 1831
Susannah, 3 Oct 1832
William, 11 Jan 1834
Philip, 15 Sep 1836
Mary Jane, 7 Nov 1838

Solomon, 18 Mar 1841
Betsy Ann, 1 May 1848 (died 11 months)
Emma Jane, 19 Jul 1851

SPOUSE II: Robert Singleton
MARRIED: 5 Feb 1854
DEATH: Divorced
CHILDREN: None

SPOUSE: James Maycock
MARRIED: 1857
DEATH: 18 Feb 1869
Pleasant View, Weber, Utah
CHILDREN: None

Susannah was the daughter of a shoemaker. She married John Hurst and they made their home in Worcestershire. He was a railroad contractor. The family moved around to where the roads were being built. Of their eight children, only three lived past infancy. They became members of the LDS Church and on February 6, 1849, William, Susannah, and their three children left Liverpool, England on the ship, "Ashland," and landed in New Orleans after five weeks on the ocean. They were traveling with Joseph and Ann Westwood with their eight children. They were traveling up the Mississippi River to St. Louis, Missouri when Cholera broke out. Their daughter, Betsy Ann, Mr. and Mrs. Westwood, and their baby died of this disease. Now Susannah was responsible for nine children. They spent the next three years in St. Louis. William worked hard to get sufficient money to immigrate to Salt Lake Valley. Their daughter Emma Jane was born in St. Louis. They left St. Louis in 1852 and traveled 200 miles up the river by steamboat to Alexander, and then on to Council Bluffs. They joined the St. Louis Independent Wagon Company with James Jeperson as the captain. They arrived in Salt Lake Valley on September 21, 1852.

They made their home near the "Big Field" which later became Liberty Park. Her husband obtained work on the Chase Mill. He built a large adobe room and used the lumber from his high wagon box to put a floor in the house. Six months after arriving in the valley, William ate a poison parsnip and died. A few years later, Susannah moved her family to Springville, Utah because she wanted her family to become landowners. Besides caring for her family, she cared for the sick people when they needed her. Her children worked wherever they could.

On February 5, 1854, she married Robert Singleton. They were soon divorced. In 1857, she married James Maycock who was thirty four years older than she, but was kind and considerate. After Johnson's Army came to Utah, Mr. Maycock traded property with Mr. Henry Mower of North Ogden and the Maycocks moved there. They planted the first apple orchard in the region and raised many cattle and good horses. Susannah labored in the fields with her children. Susannah was active in the community. She taught Primary and Sunday School. She took good care of

her family and her step-father-in-law. She was a hard worker and a courageous woman who never lost her faith.

ANN YOST MAYER

BIRTHDATE: 11 Dec 1809
Reading, Berks, Pennsylvania
DEATH: 26 Dec 1893
Salt Lake City, Salt Lake, Utah
PARENTS: Abraham Yost
Erasma Guillam Yost
PIONEER: 23 Sep 1848
Heber C. Kimball Wagon Co.
SPOUSE: George Mayer
MARRIED: 4 Mar 1828
Pennsylvania
DEATH: 24 Jul 1896
Spanish Fork, Utah, Utah

CHILDREN:
Rachel Ann, 9 Feb 1829
Elizabeth Ann, 4 Feb 1831
Mary Ann, 9 Apr 1833
Catharine, 3 May 1835
Maria, 8 Sep 1837
Benjamin Franklin, 16 Mar 1842 (died age 4)
Sarah Jane, 16 Mar 1845
Diantha, 9 Oct 1848
George Yost, 7 Mar 1852

Ann's father was of German descent and her mother was Irish. On March 4, Ann married George Mayer in Pennsylvania. She had made her own wedding dress. She had woven all her linens and material for sheets and pillowcases. She also made doughnuts for all the wedding guests. George and Ann made their first home in Bucyrus, Crawford, Ohio. They moved to Logansport, Indiana where their fifth and sixth children were born. In the autumn of 1843 the family members were baptized into the LDS Church and moved to Nauvoo, Illinois. After being driven from Nauvoo by the mob, they moved to Council Bluffs on the bank of the Missouri River in western Iowa. Her husband, George, made a living by making plows. The Mayers were among the twenty families who left to live with the Indians that winter. Ann experienced all the hardships, heartaches, and persecutions of early pioneer life. They crossed the plains with the Heber C. Kimball Wagon Company and arrived in the Salt Lake Valley on September 23, 1848.

They went immediately to Sessions Settlement (Bountiful). George built a sod "hut" in which they lived that winter. In the spring, he built a log house in Salt Lake City. Then George was called in 1852 to serve a three-year mission in Germany. Ann was both mother and father to her family during this time as she supported her family while he was away. After his return from his mission, George entered into plural marriage. He was called to a mission to settle Las Vegas. He took his new sixteen-year-old wife with him. This second marriage was a troubled one, but Ann always opened her home and heart to the children of this marriage. Ann was the mother of nine children. She died at the age of eighty-four.

JANE LOVENIA LITTLEWOOD RIGBY MAYER

No
Photo
Available

BIRTHDATE: 1 Oct 1813
Whitehaven, Isle of Man, England
DEATH: 23 Apr 1899
Fairview, Sanpete Co., Utah
PARENTS: John Littlewood
Francis Martin Littlewood
PIONEER: 18 Oct 1850
Edward Hunter Co.
SPOUSE: James Rigby
MARRIAGE: 7 Oct 1832
Stockport, Cheshire, England
DEATH SP: 23 Nov 1849
Agusta, Iowa

CHILDREN:
Lavenia Jane, 17 Mar 1833
Ann, 14 Sep 1834 died 3 years
Mary, 21 Oct 1836
Lavenia, 17 Jul 1838
Marie, 22 Feb 1841
Martha Jane, 12 Feb 1843
James, 8 Oct 1844
Margaret Melissa, 20 Mar 1846
Charles, 1 Sep 1847
Sophia Ellen, 2 Aug 1849

SPOUSE II: John Mayer
MARRIED: 20 Jan 1851
Fairview, Sanpete, Utah
DEATH SP II: unknown

CHILDREN:
Teresa, 22 Jun 1852
Millie Frances, 16 Oct 1856

Jane Lovenia Littlewood was born in England, and in her youth she was a chambermaid and seamstress in the palace of Queen Victoria at Kensington, England. She married James Rigby when she was nineteen and they left the upland of England, (Rigby Heights).

The couple had four girls, when, in the eighth year of their marriage, after being converted to the L.D.S. Faith, they decided to leave England for America and the Church. Taking their surviving daughters with them they boarded the sailing vessel "Lea High" in the late autumn for a six week voyage, one that ended sadly with the death at sea of their daughter Lavenia, December 1840, where she was slipped into the dark ocean for a grave.

Their fifth girl, Marie, was born in St. Louis shortly after they landed. The next nine years would see this family grow with five more children, but the baby Marie died at a

year and a half while still in St. Louis, a place rife with malaria and cholera in the summer time.

James and Lovenia followed the Saints from city to city, thinking that they had found a safe haven at last. Each time the building and planting were in progress, they were driven from their home into more meager and more meager circumstances until at the last they had little more than survival provisions. Then in the winter of 1849, in the middle of preparations to join the wagon trains to Utah, James died in Agusta, Iowa, leaving Jane with four children, between sixteen years and the four month old Sophia Ellen.

Jane and her family of small children, aided by friends, made their way across the plains and arrived in the valley amid the 261 pioneers in the Hunter company. Within three months she would have help in raising her family; the small, always neat in work and appearance Jane, married John Mayer the January after her arrival. They became parents of two daughters.

A few years before her death Jane Lovenia moved to Fairview, Sanpete Co. to live with her children. Known by her friends as Lady Jane, she passed her last days with her daughter, Margaret Turpin, at Birch Creek. There she died and is buried in the Fairview Cemetery.

ANN ROGERS MOORE MAYHEW

BIRTHDATE: 3 Aug 1832
Morsgreen, England
DEATH: 22 Apr 1874
Pleasant Grove, Utah
PARENTS: William Rogers
Rebecca Adams
PIONEER: 3 Oct 1862
Wagon Train
SPOUSE: Joseph Moore
MARRIED: before 1862
England
DEATH SP: date unknown
England

CHILDREN: None

SPOUSE II: Elijah Mayhew
MARRIED: 18 Apr 1868
Salt Lake, Salt Lake, Utah
DEATH: 17 Jan 1896
Pleasant Grove, Utah

CHILDREN:
Lydia Ann (Kirk), 7 Feb 1869
Elisha, 19 Feb 1871
George, 22 Apr 1874

Ann was born in England in 1832. Her father died when she was two years old leaving her mother with six children to raise. Ann was a bright-eyed happy child but suffered from an attack of rheumatic fever at an early age, which left her in frail health.

Her brother brought the missionaries to their home. Ann was baptized at the age of twenty. They desired to come to America, but had to make the trip one at a time. Thomas came in 1853; Susannah in 1860; then in 1862 Ann and her sister, Emma made the trip. They crossed the plains in the hot summer months. It was often stifling and dusty. The Indians, accustomed now to seeing the white men, were friendly most of the time, often begging for food from the emigrants. Families visited one another in camp at nights and often the banjo and violin would be tuned up for a party and Ann and Emma enjoyed this sociability. Trouble and sickness often visited the group, and sometimes even death. The prairie was gay with flowers and the girls gathered them for the graves.

They went to Pleasant Grove to live with her sister, Susannah. Her mother and the rest of her family came in 1864. Her mother died one day after arriving in the Valley.

In 1868 Ann married Elijah Mayhew, who was twenty-five years older than she, in polygamy. He was a prominent citizen, but had little time to spend with his new wife. Ann gave birth to three children. Ann always had poor health from her childhood, and giving birth to her third child took her life. The baby also died on the same day, 22 Apr 1874. They are buried in Pleasant Grove. Her sisters took the children and raised them.

LYDIA FARNSWORTH MAYHEW

No Photo Available

BIRTHDATE: 5 Feb 1808
DEATH: 5 Feb 1896
PARENTS: Reuben Farnsworth
Lucinda Kent
PIONEER: Sep 9 1853
John A. Miller / John J. Cooley Co.
SPOUSE: Elijah Mayhew
MARRIED: 2 Oct 1832
DEATH: 17 Jan 1896

CHILDREN:
Lucinda, 2 Nov 1833
Laurana, 20 Dec 1834
Otto Lyman, 2 Oct 1836
Austin Ship, 24 Oct 1838
Elijah (twin), 3 Dec 1841
Elisha (twin), 3 Dec 1841
Caroline Abigail, 18 Dec 1842
Elijah Warren, 1 Nov 1844
Walter Franklin, 27 Jan 1848

Lydia Farnsworth was born Feb 5, 1808 in Dorset, Vermont. She had four brothers; Stephen Martindale, Reuben Lafayette, William Jackson, Philo Taylor and five sisters, Laura, Lucinda, Eliza Ann, Anna Maria and Louisa Caroline.

The Farnsworths came to America from Lancashire, England about 1584. They settled in Maine to begin with, then through five generations slowly moved west settling in Indiana.

Lydia joined the Church of Jesus Christ of Latter-day Saints and emigrated to Utah in 1853, with her husband Elijah, and their children. A family of six, with two wagons and nine cattle. She had a hard journey of over 1,700 miles in a wagon before reaching their destination, being six months and one day from the time of leaving their comfortable home in Indiana. Their day-to-day journal tells of some of the hardships they encountered. They lost one of their oxen, a buffalo herd turned over their wagons, but they picked up all their supplies and moved on. They traveled anywhere from four miles a day to eighteen miles a day. They were all called together morning and evening for prayer. There were ten rules and regulations of the camp, such as: Wake up time was 5 a.m., no swearing, no card playing. The horn sounded at 4 p.m. which meant that they could visit with one another.

They arrived in the Valley September 9, 1853. She did the cooking, washing and other necessary labors in Camp life for eight persons during the greater part of the entire journey.

They made their home in Pleasant Grove, Utah. She was a hale and hardy lady and one respected by the whole community. All her life she served family, church and community. Hard work did not shorten her life span for she died at the age eighty-eight, on February 5, 1896, and is buried in the Pleasant Grove Cemetery.

CATHERINE ANN BICKMORE MCADAMS

BIRTHDATE: 16 Jul 1849
Near Council Bluffs,
Pottawottomie, Iowa
DEATH: 14 Jun 1948
Coquille, Coos, Oregon
PARENTS: William Bickmore
Christine Bagley Bickmore
PIONEER: 6 Sep 1852
Joseph Outhouse Wagon Co.
SPOUSE: Samuel S. McAdams
MARRIAGE: 10 May 1866
DEATH SP: 1904
Coquille, Coos, Oregon

CHILDREN:
Samuel Henry, 19 Apr. 1876
Female, apx. 26 Oct. 1868 (died 3 days)
James Carl, 29 Sep. 1871
Edward A., 9 Nov. 1873
Thomas Jefferson, 30 Nov. 1875
Sarah Hanna, 27 Dec. 1877
John Robert, 17 Jan. 1880
George Francis, 27 Jan. 1884
William L., 24 Jun. 1886
Nancy Jane, 24 Jun. 1886
Mary Agnes, 23 Feb. 1889

Catherine Ann was a three year old toddler when she came across the plains with her mother and father in 1852. Their journey west was three months of living outdoors, of sun and dust and hurriedly packing the wagon to beat coming rain storms. A journey of riding in a bumpy wagon all day, trying to find something to keep a three-year-old occupied in a wagon bed so she would not beg to walk with her sisters constantly.

The Joseph Outhouse Co. entered a valley bustling with opportunity for all who would work to attain their goals, but also to meager supplies to divide between those living there, those newly arrived, and those passing through to more distant destinations.

The Bickmore family went first to Fillmore, where in letters home, Catherine's mother Christina, expected "to spend her days in the best and richest country in this world." Christina, eternally homesick for the family she had run away from at Fredricktown, New York, may have overstated the conditions in this frontier town that was barely outgrowing the fort necessarily built for protection against the Indians.

Within two years the Bickmores had been sent to San Bernardino, California as a Church Agent to that newly organized community. He had, according to Catherine's mother's letters home, "sold his property in Utah and had a good property here."

They had, besides considerable cattle and Ranch property, "one house and lot in San Bernardino City, 40 acres on the Rancho of San Bernardino worth to the amount of 20,000 dollars."

Catherine Ann was six years old and went to school with the other pioneer children in one of the little one room school houses, built so close together they were later connected by a larger building erected between them.

Her mother also declared in the letters, "there are no winters here" and "I have thought of visiting the old country again but I don't know that I ever shall."

By the time Catherine Ann was seventeen, she had met and married Samuel S. McAdams, twenty-one years her senior. He was a farmer in the Corralitas District in Watsonville, near Santa Cruz,

The wedding was a special celebration, a double wedding. She to Samuel and her brother Thomas to his fiancé Martha Cullumber on 10 May 1866.

The couples remained in Watsonville for the next seven years, where Samuel, James and Edward were born, and where Catherine and Samuel lost their second child, a dear little girl three days old.

The couple's friendship extended to other facets of life. The Tom Bickmore family and the McAdams family moved to Jackson Co., Oregon together where Thomas Jefferson was born.

Their final move was to Coquille, Coos, Oregon where they remained the rest of their lives. Catherine and William had six more children. There were fraternal twins and their last child when Catherine was forty years old.

William died at seventy-six leaving Catherine a fifty-five-year-old widow with her youngest child fifteen. She lived forty-four years after William, and died one month short of her one-hundredth birthday.

ANN THOMPSON MCAFFEE (MCFIE)

BIRTHDATE: 9 Apr. 1825
Ballynears, Billy, Antrim, Ireland
DEATH: 14 Nov 1903
Lehi, Utah Co., Utah
PARENTS: Samuel Thompson
Sarah Lyons Thompson
PIONEER: 26 Aug 1864
John R. Murdock Wagon Co.
SPOUSE: John Sharp McAffee
MARRIED: 25 Apr 1841
DEATH SP: 20 Feb 1903
Lehi, Utah Co., Utah

CHILDREN:
Samuel, 4 Aug 1842
Samuel, 10 Jul 1844
Sarah, 24 Oct 1846
Infant son, 1848
Infant son, 1850
Infant daughter, 1852
Joseph Smith, Nov 1853 died 3 yrs.
Infant daughter, 30 Mar 1854
Moroni Smith, 28 Jun 1858
Eliza, 9 Aug 1860

Ann Thompson was born in Ireland in 1825 and she married John when she was nineteen years old. The first few years of their marriage were good years with the two babies to love, then what sad, traumatic circumstances caused the deaths of her next four children, and how great the grief to be overcome, the failure of spirit and belief that might send one in search of a meaning.

At some time during this period in their lives they heard the Mormon missionaries and took the gospel to their hearts. John was baptized in June, Ann was baptized on a cold December day, the 20th, in 1849.

To emigrate to Zion was a desire the family were willing to sacrifice for. They began saving everything they could spare to travel to far away Salt Lake City.

Brigham Young, needing skilled tradesmen, heard that John Sharp McAffee was a master stone mason and sent for him, but for lack of funds, only him, so John sailed away on the "Manchester" in 1862. Ann age 39 and her children Samuel 22, Sarah 17, Ephraim 8, Moroni 5, and Eliza 3 followed two years later leaving Liverpool on the 28th of April, 1864 on the ship "Monarch of the Sea" with nearly 1000 converts all with the same dream, to reach Zion.

Ann and her family continued their journey leaving from Wyoming, Nebraska in the John Murdock Co. of 78 people. It was a faster journey, 58 days compared to the 74 days the large companies of 400 took.

When the McAffee family entered the Valley that August day, it was a touching reunion for the husband and wife and children. John and Samuel chose Lehi for their first home but in a short time John bought land and developed a ranch just south of Charleston on the upper Provo River. It was a wonderful place for this hospitable couple to rear their children. Visitors could depend on a warm welcome and a plentiful meal. Sometimes the visitors were Indians, camping in the back yard as they traveled back and forth through the valley. Although the Indian raids in Wasatch Co. lasted only a year and a half, (Spring 1866-Aug. 1867) caution and fear were in everyone's minds when Indians appeared.

Ann McAffee, a caring, loving person, was of medium height, quite slim. A very beautiful woman who wore her hair parted in the middle and pulled back into a bob with a queenly way about her.

As she became too old to work on the ranch their son Ephraim persuaded them to move to Lehi, Utah so he could care for them better. Thus it was that this wonderful pioneer woman who had given so much for the good of her family, her fellowman and her church, passed away in Lehi, Utah November 14, 1903 at the age of eighty-one and was laid to rest there.

MARY HAIG MCALISTER

BIRTHDATE: 24 Jul 1826
Leuchars, Fifeshire, Scotland
DEATH: 16 Aug 1911
Logan, Cache Co., Utah
PARENTS: Robert Stein Haig
Helen Henderson Haig
PIONEER: 4 Oct 1863
Thomas E. Ricks Wagon Co.
SPOUSE:
Charles Houston Maxwell McAlister
MARRIAGE: 1849/50
DEATH SP: 25 Jan 1898
Logan, Cache, Utah

CHILDREN:
John Archibald, 22 Aug 1851
Helen Mary, 31 Mar 1853 (died age 1)
William Glover, 10 Jun 1855

Mary Haig was born in Scotland in 1826. Her father was Robert Stein Haig of "The Haigs of Bemerside Castle." Until she was seventeen, she lived in and around Dundee and then moved to Newcastle-on-Tyme. It was there she met Charles and fell in love.

As her great granddaughter was told, while preparing graves for the next day's Decoration Day one year, Mary had gone to the McAlister Estate to work as a dairy maid.

She was from the lowlands, and against all tradition, she and Charles, her employer's son, a Highlander, fell in love. When their love for each other was discovered she was banished back to her home and had to leave on the morrow. She was determined to marry the man she loved. She plunged her hand into scalding water, thus delaying the trip, and so they were married.

Their first son was born in New Castle, their second, a little daughter Helen, named after her two grandmothers, was born in Bykerhill. The little girl lived one short year dying eight days after her birthday.

Mary joined the LDS Church May 24 1853, one month after her husband was baptized. The couple moved. Sometimes the "Mormons" were persecuted in England as badly as they were in America. For the next few years they moved around in the Wallsend and New Castle areas.

They sailed from Liverpool on the ship "Cynosure," May 30, 1863 with 754 others under the leadership of D. M. Stuart to dock in New York City after eight weeks at sea.

Except for two days, the thirty-eight year old Mary, with determination as a strength, walked all the way from Missouri to Utah arriving October 4, 1863. The next year the McAlister family was sent to the four-year-old settlement of Logan, Utah.

When she was fifty years old Mary was called to study Obstetrics in Boston, Massachusetts, under Dr. Alaxander. She returned to the Logan Community and delivered 1,838 babies, including 38 sets of twins. Her first delivery was her own grandson, John Archibald McAlister Jr. She rode in a buggy pulled by her horse called "Old Pet" night and day in every direction, to deliver babies, and always carried her black bag. With her busy schedule she did a tremendous amount of Temple work for relatives and friends.

"Grandma McAlister is No More," was the headline of the Logan "Journal," dated Thursday, August 17, 1911. "Grandma" Mary McAlister, Logan's "grand old woman" is no more. The end which had been looked for for some time came at about two o'clock yesterday afternoon. She was a woman beloved of all her descendants and by thousands of others to whom she had ministered. Practical and somewhat blunt in manner, she had a heart of gold within her breast, and no soul ever made a vain appeal to her for help. She was a woman any community might be proud of."

ELIZABETH ELEANOR BELL MCALLISTER

BIRTHDATE: 22 Oct 1822
New Castle, New Castle, Delaware
DEATH: 27 Oct 1899
Salt Lake City, Salt Lake, Utah
PARENTS: John Bell
Susanna See Bell
PIONEER: 13 Sep 1861
Joseph Horne Wagon Company
SPOUSE:
Richard Wesley McAllister
MARRIED: 1844
Philadelphia, Pennsylvania
DEATH: 17 Oct 1904
Salt Lake City, Salt Lake, Utah

CHILDREN:
William James Frazier, 16 Aug 1845
John Daniel Thompson, 13 Sep 1848 (died 4 months)
James William Thompson, 17 Feb 1850 (died age 8)
Richard Wesley, 31 Jan 1853 (died 4 months)
Joseph Warrington, 6 Nov 1854
Susanna Bell, 11 Jan 1858
Mary Jane, 29 Jul 1860
Elizabeth Bell, 1 Jul 1863 (died age 4)

Elizabeth Eleanor was only three years old when her mother died. She was eight years old when her father died. She and her brothers moved into the home of her father's brother, James Bell, where they were cared for, educated, and trained for their life's work. She was working as a tailor in her uncle's shop when she met Richard Wesley McAllister. They were married and her skills were an asset to her husband's work as a shoemaker. She made the bindings, linings, and the facings around the tops and fronts of the shoes. Their family members were baptized into the LDS Church on January 1, 1861 along with her husband's mother and sister, Mary Jane. Her husband, Richard was deeply involved in politics as the Civil War was brewing. Elizabeth Eleanor pressured him to move west at this time. On the 18th of June, 1861, they left Philadelphia by train until they reached St. Joe, Missouri, then a three day trip on a steamboat to Florence, Nebraska where they became part of an active community busily preparing for means and equipment to move further west. Richard arranged for his mother, his sister, and his son, Will, to travel with a Mrs. Ottinger who needed another family to travel with her. Will was responsible for their safety as they went on with the Milo Andrus Wagon Company. The rest of Elizabeth Eleanor's family traveled in the Joseph Horne Wagon Company and arrived in the Salt Lake Valley on September 13, 1861.

Two years after their arrival, their daughter Elizabeth Bell was born. She lived to be four years old. Eleanor was called upon to share her husband with nineteen year old Emma Smith Walling. When Eleanor's children were grown and married, she insisted that Richard make his home with his younger family and provide for them. She went to live with her married daughter, Susanna. Elizabeth

Eleanor died in Salt Lake City on October 27, 1899 at the age of seventy seven.

ELIZABETH THOMPSON MCALLISTER

BIRTHDATE: 17 Aug 1803
Lewes, Sussex, Delaware
DEATH: 31 May 1872
Salt Lake City, Salt Lake, Utah
PARENTS: James Thompson
Mary Blades Abbott Thompson
PIONEER: 12 Sep 1861
Milo Andrus Wagon Company
SPOUSE:
William James Frazer McAllister
MARRIED: 4 Apr 1822
DEATH: 21 Aug 1857

CHILDREN:
James William Thompson, 3 Dec 1822
Richard Wesley, 19 Oct 1824
John Daniel Thompson, 19 Feb 1827
Mary Jane Abbott, 2 Feb 1829

Elizabeth Thompson was born in Lewes, Delaware. Her father and brother, James, were both fishermen and were lost at sea on the ship Oscar Davis, when a hurricane struck the Delaware Coast on September 3, 1821. On April 4, 1822, Elizabeth married William James Frazer McAllister. They moved to Philadelphia where he worked as a blacksmith with a large ship building company. They had three fine sons and an unusually gifted musical daughter. They were not rich, but were comfortable and able to educate their children well. William's legs were both broken when a ruffian twisted his stool around in the Village Pub. William's knees were caught between the stool and the counter. He was a helpless invalid for the remainder of his life. Elizabeth was faced with the care of an invalid and the support of their family. With the help of a black servant, she raised pigs and geese to support the family. Their oldest son, James, carried his father downstairs in the morning and upstairs in the evening for nine years until he caught cold and passed away in an epileptic seizure on June 24, 1857. Her husband dwindled after that until he died on August 21, 1857. Her son John D. T. had disgraced the family in 1851 by joining with the "Mormons" and moving west with them. In December 1860, he came back to visit them with a few of his friends. They introduced them to the gospel and the whole family was baptized into the LDS Church by the end of January, 1861. John D. T. went on to England to fulfill a mission. They had plans to wait for him until he returned from his mission and all would travel back to Salt Lake City together. However, the soldiers were marching past their home in preparation for the Civil War. Her son, Richard Wesley, and his family, took Elizabeth and his sister, Mary Jane, and made preparations to travel to Salt Lake City. They left Philadelphia on June 18, 1861 and traveled by train until they reached St. Joe, Missouri. Then they went by steamboat to Florence, Nebraska where they became part of an active community preparing to take them further west. Her son, Richard, placed Elizabeth and Mary Jane with Mrs. Ottinger who needed companions to travel with before they would permit her to take her wagon across the plains. Richard put his sixteen-year-old son, Will, in charge of the wagon and sent them with the Milo Andrus Wagon Company which arrived in the Salt Lake Valley on September 12, 1861.

Friends met them in Salt Lake City and took them to their home to stay until her son, Richard, and his family arrived in the John Horne Wagon Company. Three days later, her son, John D. T., arrived home from his mission. The McAllister family were all together and accounted for in the place called Zion. She lived with her son, John D. T. until her death in 1872.

MARY ANN MILLER MCALLISTER

BIRTHDATE: 13 Apr 1857
Norwich, Norfolk, England
DEATH: 28 Feb 1936
St. George, Washington, Utah
PARENTS: William Miller
Ann Winter Miller
PIONEER: 1868
SPOUSE:
Joseph Warrington McAllister
MARRIED: 14 Feb 1876
Salt Lake Endowment House
DEATH: 25 Mar 1930
St. George, Washington, Utah

CHILDREN:
Joseph William, 26 Nov 1876
Alma Warrington, 8 Mar 1878 (died infant)
Elizabeth Eleanor, 7 Apr 1879
Emily Lewis, 17 Apr 1881
Lovinia, 4 Feb 1883
Manita, 16 May 1885 (died age 1)
Richard Wesley, 23 Jan 1887
Agnes Maude, 10 Nov 1888
Mary Ann, 11 Jan 1892
Viola Victorious, 25 Sep 1893
Wesley Miller, 10 Sep 1896 (died 5 months)

Mary Ann's father was a bookbinder and shoe cobbler. She helped him by sewing the shoe tops to the bottoms before she was ten years old. The family was converted to the LDS Church. They sailed from England on the sailing ship, "John Bright." Her father was drowned in the New York Harbor the day after they arrived. Her baby brother died ten days later. The family buried their dead and traveled by train to Omaha, Nebraska. Her uncle, John Daynes, sent the family money enough to travel to the Salt Lake Valley. They traveled by wagon train from Omaha to the Salt Lake Valley in 1868.

Their family went to live with her Uncle John Daynes and family. She was one of the witnesses to the driving of the Golden Spike in the railroad track in 1869. She sang in Brother Goddard's choir of children for the 24th of July celebration. She also sang with the 20th Ward choir with her uncle John Daynes leading the music and her cousin Joseph J. at the organ. She also sang many solos in the Tabernacle. She worked for Becky, who was the second wife of John Daynes. Her uncle wanted to send her to the East to study music, but she married Joseph Warrington McAllister instead. They lived first in Salt Lake City, then in Kanab, and then moved to St. George. They became the parents of eleven children. Mary Ann put her training as a seamstress to good work earning money for her large family. Leaving the younger children in care of the older children, she went to various homes to spend the day making dresses, suits, and burial clothes. She was known for her lovely flowers and hand work. She participated in the local theatrical groups, and sang in many programs, meetings, concerts, and funerals. She died young in spirit on February 28, 1936 "without being a burden to anyone."

ELIZABETH BULLOCK MCARTHUR

BIRTHDATE: 22 Sep 1841
Lanark, Canada
DEATH: 28 Jan 1913
St. George, Washington Co., Utah
PARENTS: James Bullock
Mary Hill Bullock Spencer
PIONEER: 21 Sep 1848
Brigham Young Wagon Company
SPOUSE: Daniel D. McArthur
MARRIED: 13 Feb 1857
Salt Lake Endowment House
DEATH: 3 Jun 1908
St. George, Washington Co., Utah

CHILDREN:
Eugenia, 4 Dec 1860
George, 16 Jun 1866
Isabelle, 13 Jul 1868
James, 29 Jan 1871
Emmaline, 24 Feb 1874
Moroni, 25 Apr 1877

Very soon after Elizabeth's birth in Canada, her parents moved to Nauvoo, Illinois where she spent her early years. Her parents were dissenters of the Methodist church and had joined the John Taylor Society. Elders Parley P. Pratt and Samuel Lake were instrumental in their conversion to the LDS Faith. In Nauvoo, the family was driven from their home, beaten by mobs, and suffered greatly. James Bullock assisted in the construction of the Nauvoo House and Temple. They left Nauvoo with the Saints in 1846 and lived in Winter Quarters, Nebraska until the spring of 1848. Then moving to Utah, they settled in Salt Lake City.

In 1857, she and her cousin, Mary Hill were sealed to Daniel D. McArthur as polygamous wives in the Endowment House. She was only fifteen years old. The McArthur family was among the earliest called to settle St.

George, Utah. Just before entering the valley, she helped deliver her cousin's baby girl.

Elizabeth was a quiet, kind, unassuming person who didn't take offense at others in the family relationships. She always did her part in the work in the McArthur home as she raised her children. Each wife had specific assignments. Elizabeth supervised the garden work of planting, weeding, and watering. This was no little job in the early Dixie settlement. She always prepared the dinner and often helped with breakfast. She took care of the milk, made cheese, vinegar, and pickles. She made apple cider and dried the fruit. Some of the dried fruit was hauled by wagon to Milford to be sold and shipped on the train. She had the job of helping with the warp and rags for rugs that were made on the McArthur's large loom. She knit stockings, sewed many of the men's suits, and also made hats of warp and straw.

She accepted church responsibilities by teaching Primary, Sunday School, and doing Temple work.

SARAH ELIZABETH ABBOTT McARTHUR

BIRTHDATE: 12 Nov 1850
Keg Creek, Iowa
DEATH: 24 Aug 1916
Wilford, Idaho
PARENTS: Jacob Farnum Abbott
Martha Jane Bickmore Abbott
PIONEER: 15 Oct 1852
John B. Walker Wagon Co.
SPOUSE: John Dickson McArthur
MARRIED: 13 Jan 1865
Salt Lake City, Utah

CHILDREN:
John Abbott, 13 Feb 1868
Elizabeth Dickson, 28 Mar 1870
Jacob Farnum Abbott, 16 Nov 1871
Minerva, 19 Aug 1873
Daniel Duncan, 26 Nov 1875
George Abbott, 7 Apr 1878
Joseph Stephen, 3 Jan 1880
Sarah Jane, 24 Oct 1881
David, 13 Jan 1885
Mary Agnes, 13 Apr 1886
Florence, 13 Dec 1887
James, 24 Jul 1890
Danford, 5 Aug 1893
Edith, 12 Sep 1896

Sarah was born in Iowa in 1850. She was two years old when she and her parents arrived in the Valley in a wagon train. Their first home was in Grantsville. They later moved to Wilford, Idaho and to St. Anthony, Idaho. Sarah married John Dickson McArthur in 1865 in the Salt Lake Endowment House. They had seventeen children; the first three were premature and died.

Sarah was a wonderful homemaker and had full responibility of her family when her husband frequently worked away from home. When her husband and two sons worked in the coal mines in Rock Springs, Wyoming, she lived on the homestead in Bennington, Bear Lake, Idaho. The family moved to Wilford, Idaho in 1896. Sarah helped care for the sick and was a counselor in the Relief Society. She cared for her grandchildren when her children's spouses died. While her husband was jailer at the Fremont County Courthouse for two years, Sarah cooked for the prisoners and assisted in janitorial work there. Her home was always open to anyone in need.

Her husband, John, died in 1913 in St. Anthony, Idaho. Sarah died three years later in Wilford, Idaho, in 1916.

SUSAN McKEEN McARTHUR

BIRTHDATE: 10 Oct 1801
Corinth, Orange County, Vermont
DEATH: 4 Jul 1866
Mt. Pleasant, Sanpete County, Utah
PARENTS: David McKeen
Sarah Libby McKeen
PIONEER: 1849
Daniel Duncan Wagon Co.
SPOUSE: Duncan McArthur
MARRIED: 1 Jan 1818
Holland, Erie County, New York
DEATH: 29 Oct 1864
Mt. Pleasant, Sanpete County, Utah

CHILDREN:
Silas, 7 Oct 1818
Daniel Duncan, 8 Apr 1820
Orange Niles, 16 Jul 1822
Washington Perry, 24 Dec 1825
Sarah Libby, 28 Feb 1827
Henry Morrow, 21 Feb 1829
Ira James, 18 Dec 1830
Jennett Emerline, 17 Oct 1832
Mary Jane, 14 Nov 1834
Annis Marsh, 21 Nov 1836
Roxana Margaretta, 7 Feb 1839
Emma Lodoski, 22 Apr 1842
Susan Amanda, 22 Sep 1844
Joseph Smith, 12 Sep 1846

Early in Susan's life, her family moved to western New York. In 1818, she married Duncan McArthur and they began farming. They came into contact with brethren preaching the LDS gospel of Jesus Christ. In 1835, they were converted and baptized by Elder Hicks. Duncan was called to be the leader of the Holland Branch which was established before the Freedom conference in 1835. They left for Kirtland in that same year where Susan gave birth to one of her children. With those noble pioneers, they lived in Adam-ondi-Ahman, Far West, Payson, and Nauvoo, Illinois. When driven from Nauvoo, they were in Garden Grove when Susan lost her last baby. Of her fourteen children, only four lived to begin settling Utah with them.

After their arrival in Utah in 1849, they lived in Salt Lake for a short time before they were sent to settle in Utah County. American Fork was first named McArthurville after her husband. They had property near the fort in Pleasant Grove. Then they established a home and farm between American Fork and Pleasant Grove. By 1860, they had been sent to pioneer Mt. Pleasant where they remained the rest of their lives and are buried there.

Susan spent her life pioneering, moving, raising her family, and being loyal and true to her religion.

ABIGAIL MEAD MCBRIDE

No
Photo
Available

BIRTHDATE: 29 Jan 1770
Nine Partners, Dutchess, New York
DEATH: 12 Mar 1854
Ogden, Weber, Utah
PARENTS: Gideon Mead
Martha Fiske Mead
PIONEER: 29 Sep 1847
Edward Hunter Wagon Company
SPOUSE: Daniel McBride
MARRIED: 1787
Saratoga District, Albany, New York
DEATH: 1 Sep 1823
LeRoy, Genesee, New York

CHILDREN:
John, 5 Jan 1788
Samuel, 25 Aug 1789
Daniel, Jr., 19 Mar 1791
James, 9 Jul 1793
Margaret Ann, 1 Jun 1795
Hyrum, 5 Jun 1798
Cyrus Gideon, 17 Aug 1800
Reuben, 16 Jun 1803
Martha, 17 Mar 1805

Abigail's parents were descendants of the prolific colonial Mead family of Greenwich, Fairfield, Connecticut. She married Daniel McBride about 1787 in Saratoga District, Albany, New York. By 1795, they had moved north to Washington County, New York where they were still living when their last child was born. Abigail's husband was a Campbellite minister. Sometime between 1805 and 1823, they moved to LeRoy, Genesee, New York where Abigail's husband died. Ten years after his death, Abigail was baptized a member of the LDS Church on June 28, 1833 in Villanova by William F. Cahoon. Eventually, six of Abigail's children also joined the LDS Church. The McBrides sold their thriving farms in New York and journeyed to Kirtland, Ohio by stage coach and canal boat to be with other Saints. They contributed generously to the building of Kirtland and the new Temple. When they were driven from Ohio, Abigail joined in the migration to Nauvoo, Hancock, Illinois. She lived in Iowa about five miles from Nauvoo with her son, Samuel McBride. In 1847, she was with the Edward Hunter Wagon Company as they crossed

the plains and arrived in the Great Salt Lake Valley on September 29th.

There were about two thousand saints in the valley and they barely had enough food for the winter. Food had to be rationed and many lived on sego lily roots and thistle weeds. A fort had been built and the pioneers used the inside walls to build a small shed in which to live. In 1850, Abigail was living with Samuel's family in Davis, County. Later, she moved to Ogden to live with her grand-daughter. She died there at the age of eighty four.

AGNES ARCHIBALD KERR PARKINSON MCBRIDE

BIRTHDATE: 19 Dec 1851
Hart Hill, Scotland
DEATH: 6 Jan 1902
Wellsville, Cache, Utah
PARENTS: David Hamilton Kerr
Agnes Archibald
PIONEERS: 10 Oct 1861
By handcart
SPOUSE I:
Henry Fielding Parkinson
MARRIED: 23 Feb 1869
Salt Lake City, Utah
DEATH SP: 29 Jan 1923
Wellsville, Cache, Utah

CHILDREN:
David Kerr, 27 Dec 1871
Mary Agnes, 17 Jan 1873
Sarah Ann Kerr, 13 Oct 1874
Charles Kerr, 29 Jan 1877
Amos Kerr, 16 Aug 1880

SPOUSE II: Peter McBride
MARRIED: Sep 1898
Utah
DEATH SP: 10 Jun 1914
Utah
CHILDREN: None

Agnes Archibald Kerr was born 19 Dec 1851 at Hart Hill, Scotland, the daughter of David Hamilton Kerr and Agnes Archibald. She came across the plains at the age of ten with a handcart company. She arrived in the Salt Lake Valley 10 Oct 1861.

Agnes married Henry Fielding Parkinson in the Endowment House 23 Feb 1869 as a plural wife. She had five children by this union. She was a strong-willed woman who raised her children to be independent. In Sep 1898 she married a second husband, Peter McBride. He died 10 Jun 1914 in Utah. Her first husband, Henry Parkinson died 29 Jan 1923 in Wellsville, Cache, Utah. Agnes preceded him in death on 6 Jan 1902, also in Wellsville, Cache, Utah.

BETSY MEAD MCBRIDE

No
Photo
Available

BIRTHDATE: 6 Feb 1802
Chester, Washington, New York
DEATH: 8 Oct 1881
Hyrum, Cache, Utah
PARENTS: Isaac Mead
Deborah Mead Mead
PIONEER: 1851
Company unknown
SPOUSE: James McBride
MARRIED: 1818
DEATH: 13 Aug 1839
Pike County, Illinois

CHILDREN:
Henrietta, 1 Sep 1821
Reuben D., 12 Dec 1822
Harlum, 8 Dec 1824
George, 21 Dec 1826
Roxena, Jan 1829 (died at 4 months)
James, 17 Nov 1830
Oliver Stephen, 29 Aug 1835
Nathaniel Knight, 13 Jan 1840 (died age 18)

Betsy Mead was the eighth of twelve children born to her parents Isaac Mead and Deborah Mead. Her parents were second cousins. She was married to James McBride in 1818 and eight children were born to this union. On June 13, 1833, Betsy was baptized into the LDS Church in Villanova, Chautauqua, New York by Amasa M. Lyman. Her husband was baptized three days later. In 1837, they moved to Kirtland, Ohio where most of the saints had gathered. The next year, the family moved to Missouri. They suffered much persecution from the mob violence and were driven out of the state to Illinois. Betsy's husband died five months before her last child was born. They moved to the west side of the Mississippi River where a branch of the church had been organized. They remained there until 1846 when they had to move further west. Betsy crossed the plains with her daughter, Henrietta, and her sons, James and Nathaniel in 1851. They lost their oxen and a cow, so they had to leave their wagon behind. Another man in the company lost part of his oxen. Betsy's family hitched their cows with his oxen and they continued on across the plains. They arrived in the fall of 1851.

Betsy made her first home in Farmington. Then she lived for some time in Springville, Utah where her son Harlum had settled after returning from the Mormon Battalion. Betsy was one of the early school teachers there. She taught reading, writing, and spelling from the old Blue Back Speller. She went to Hyrum to live with her sons. She had lived as a widow for forty-two years and had seen many tragedies, but the gospel brought her comfort and peace. She died on October 8, 1881.

ELIZABETH CLARK MCBRIBE

BIRTHDATE: 1 Oct 1846
Wolverhampton, Stafford, England
DEATH: 25 Sep 1935
Pima, Graham, Arizona
PARENTS: Edward Watkins
Lucy Ashby Clark
PIONEER: Sep 1852
covered wagon
SPOUSE: James Andrew McBride
MARRIED: 18 Feb 1866
Santaquin, Utah Co., Utah
DEATH: 22 Dec 1922
Pima, Graham, Arizona

CHILDREN:
James Andrew, 11 Dec 1866
William Edward, 25 Oct 1868
Don Carlos, 13 Jan 1871
Frank Ashby, 10 Jul 1873
Sarah Elizabeth, 10 Dec 1875
Jessie Burt, 17 Apr 1878
Lucy Agnes, 19 Sep 1880
John Henry, 20 Jul 1883
Phebe Leila, 30 Apr 1886
Rolla, 14 Jun 1888
Susan Nellie, 15 Nov 1890
Julia Ellise, 4 Mar 1893

Elizabeth was born in England in 1846 to Edward and Lucy Ashby Clark. She was a tiny girl with blue eyes and brown hair and a sunny disposition. Her parents became dissatisfied with conditions in England and decided to move to Australia. They traveled to London to embark. While there they were converted to the LDS Church by missionaries. They postponed their trip for two years and were missionaries for the Church in their own home town. In 1851, they joined 400 Saints, working people, craftsmen who left not for Australia, but for America to Utah to join the Saints.

The first night, the small ship, in a severe storm, collided with another. Three weeks later, after repairs were made on the ship, they continued. Elizabeth was five years old at the time. The group was organized and the leaders supervised provisions, worship services and the care of the sick. Morale was good among them. They arrived at New Orleans, traveled up the Mississippi River to St. Louis, then the Missouri River to Council Bluffs, Iowa. Here arrangements were made for the westward trek. Their outfit consisted of one yoke of oxen, one cow, and the trip seemed exciting to Elizabeth. On the trip a sister of Elizabeth's fell from the wagon, was run over and died. They stopped long enough to bury her and then moved on. Wagons broke down, storms engulfed them, people became ill, and Indians were a problem along the way. Their strong faith sustained them through these trials.

The Lord blessed the Clark family and sustained them. Such problems in her childhood helped Elizabeth be prepared for greater challenges in her later life. In Santaquin, Utah, she met James Andrew McBride. They were married

17 Feb 1866. They lived in Santaquin. Elizabeth became a good cook, seamstress, and hostess. She had children as they moved sometimes from place to place. In 1880 the family moved to Marysvale, and in Oct of that year James decided to move to Arizona. Elizabeth was uncertain about this move. Her father gave her a blessing and promised that "angels would attend her, and she would be blessed with faith and courage." She went with the family. She fell at one point and dislocated her arm. That night she dreamed someone came, took her arm and pulled on it. In the morning she was able to use it.

Elizabeth gave birth to twelve children, two of whom died as children. They later decided to travel north into New Mexico. She stopped along the way to visit a Zuni Indian village. These were friendly Indians with soft voices, and gentle ways. They arrived at Pima in Dec 1881. They first lived in a tent, then a one room adobe house with a board floor, window and shingled roof. One day each week was given to washing, one to ironing, as the irons were heated on the stove. Sometimes the women even had to tend the livestock, milk the cows, do irrigating of crops and other chores in addition to their regular duties.

Clothes were made from yardage purchased at the general store. Sometimes underwear was made from flour sacks. There was always the duty of food preparations for the large family.

Elizabeth Clark McBride was a tiny, cute little lady, who was pleasant and fun to be around. She had snow white hair fixed in a bun on top of her head. She always wore a pretty apron; she loved baking pies and cookies and sharing them with her grandchildren. A grandson or her younger brother often lived with her. She enjoyed entertaining the visiting authorities as they came to Pima.

Elizabeth was always a staunch Latter-day Saint and she served as Primary and Religion Class leader and was a Relief Society visiting teacher. She loved to visit the sick and was frequently found at the bedside of a child or grandchild who was ill.

James McBride passed away 22 Dec 1922 at Pima, Arizona. Elizabeth lived until 26 Sep 1935 when she also died at Pima, Arizona, having been a widow for thirteen years. She was truly a stalwart pioneer woman of great faith and fortitude. She never gave up on her chores, and of living the best way she could. She and her husband had participated in the United Order for five years so she knew the value of working together and of sharing with all. Her life was typical of pioneer women of her day.

She had backbreaking work to do lifting tubs of water for the washing on washboards, and ironing with the metal irons, of chopping wood, cooking and preparing food–responsibilities she never shirked,. A great posterity honor her for her faithfulness, her tenacity, and her love and charity for: all qualities which made her a great pioneer woman of faith and fortitude in Utah's pioneer annals.

ELIZABETH HARRIS BALL BORAM MCBRIDE

BIRTHDATE: 7 Jan 1812/13
Hamilton, Warren, Ohio
DEATH: 1 Oct 1899
Salt Lake City, Utah
PARENTS: Andrew Boram
Sarah Harris
PIONEER: 19 Oct 1848
Willard Richard's wagon train
SPOUSE: William McBride
MARRIED: 1 Sep 1831
Randolph, Montgomery, Ohio
DEATH SP: 8 Mar 1895
Salt Lake City, Utah

CHILDREN:
Sarah Elizabeth, 7 May 1832
Mary Jane, 15 Feb 1834
Susan Ellen, 29 Jul 1836
Rebecca Ann, 28 Aug 1838
James Andrew, 29 Nov 1840
Harriet Eugenia, 7 May 1843
Mary Jane, 1846
Elizabeth Deseret, 22 Jul 1850
William Booram, 12 May 1853

Elizabeth was born 7 Jan 1812 at Hamilton, Warren, Ohio. On 1 Sep 1831 she married William McBride. On 25 Apr 1833 she was baptized and became a member of The Church of Jesus Christ of Latter-day Saints. Her husband was baptized ten years later. They lived at Kirtland and Nauvoo and there Elizabeth was sealed to William on 24 Jan 1846 by Brigham Young. They were among the Saints driven from their homes in Nauvoo and crossed the plains in 1848 in Willard Richard's wagon train.

Elizabeth's first home was in Salt Lake City, but they later lived at Santaquin, Grantsville, and Richfield, Utah. Her husband was ordained a seventy in 1845 and was called to serve a mission. This left Elizabeth with four children to provide and care for, plus a new baby that was born while he was away. She endured the trials of plural marriage, and then in 1880 gave up home and friends to help colonize an unknown area of the Gila Valley in Arizona. In October of 1890 they returned to Salt Lake City for their final home. Her husband passed away in 1895 and Elizabeth died at her daughter Susan's home in Salt Lake City on 1 Oct 1898

OLIVE MEHETABLE CHENEY MCBRIDE

BIRTHDATE: 5 May 1817
Freedom, Cataraugue, New York
DEATH: 4 Apr 1904
Oakley, Cassia, Idaho
PARENTS:Aaron Cheney
Mehetable Wells
PIONEER: 4 Oct 1850
Joseph Young Wagon Company
SPOUSE: James McBride
MARRIED: 7 Mar 1844
Nauvoo, Hancock, Illinois
DEATH SP: 6 Jan 1881
Grantsville, Tooele, Utah

CHILDREN:
Brigham, 6 Feb 1846
Thomas Aaron, 10 Jul 1848
Amos Orin, 2 Jan 1850
James Orson, 5 Sep 1852
Elam Wells, 18 Sep 1854
Heber Kimball, 16 May 1857
Catherine Mehetable, 20 Nov 1862

Olive was born 5 May 1817 in Freedom, New York. She married James McBride in Nauvoo, Illinois on 7 Mar 1844. Her first child was born 6 Feb 1846, just as many of the Saints began to cross the Mississippi, being forced out of Nauvoo. They named him Brigham. In April they left Nauvoo and traveled into Iowa. During that fall and winter there was much sickness and her little baby died. Olive gave birth to two more sons while they were in Iowa waiting to cross the plains.

In 1850 they crossed the plains in the Joseph Young company, arriving in Salt Lake on 4 Oct 1850. They settled at what is now Grantsville, Tooele, Utah. Here they built the first house and did the first plowing in that area. They had very little means with which to support themselves that first winter, and endured many difficulties, including the Indians driving off all their cattle in March of 1851.

Olive gave birth to three more sons, and then one daughter who died less than six weeks after she was born. In the early years at Grantsville there was little water for crops and many were forced to live on the greens and roots they could gather. As things got better Olive and her husband lived in peace and relative comfort for many years with their children near them. In 1856 her husband entered polygamy. His first plural wife died in 1875, and later that year he married again and this wife lived only until 1879. He passed away in 1881 and Olive lived until 1904. She passed away just one month short of her eighty-seventh birthday in Oakley, Idaho where her sons Aaron, Elam and Heber had all moved.

RUTH ANN MILLER MCBRIDE MCBRIDE

BIRTHDATE: 30 Mar 1834
Quincy, Adams, Illinois
DEATH: 31 Dec 1910
Swan Lake, Bannock, Idaho
PARENTS: Henry William
Elmira Pond Miller
PIONEER: 1852
Henry Wm. Miller Wagon Co.
SPOUSE I: George McBride
MARRIED: 27 Mar 1855
DEATH: 25 Feb 1858
Fort Lemhi,

CHILDREN:
James Henry McBride, 27 Feb 1856
David George, 25 Mar 1858

SPOUSE II: James McBride
MARRIED: 13 May 1859
Farmington, Davis,Utah
DEATH SP II: 6 May 1899

CHILDREN:
Nathanial James, 30 Jan 1860
Harlum Mead, 19 Mar 1861
Hyrum Silas, 22 Nov 1862
Reuben Marion, 12 May 1864
Charles Daniel, 11 Jun 1866
Laura Ann, 27 Jun 1868
William Oliver, 14 Oct 1870
Delia Elmira, 21 Jul 1872
Ruth Betsy, 5 Nov 1874
Lucy Maria, 30 Aug 1876
Loran Dyphus, 19 Jan 18 1880

Ruth Ann Miller was born in 1834 in Quincy, Illinois, to Henry William and Elmira Miller. Ruth Ann was married to Georrge McBride 27 Mar 1855. They had two sons. George died 25 Feb 1858 at the Fort Lemhi, Salmon River Mission in Idaho. This left Ruth Ann with two small sons to raise, one born after George's death.

On 13 May 1859, Ruth Ann married James McBride in Farmington, Davis County, in Utah. Ruth Ann had eleven more children from this marriage. In addition to her own children, she raised three step-children and one grandson. After her second husband had died, she sent two sons on missions.

Ruth Ann was a faithful Latter-day Saint. She told of seeing the Prophet Joseph Smith, and about the hardships they went through crossing the plains and after their arrival in Utah. Ruth Ann was a very industrious woman. Besides caring for her family, she raised a large garden. She always saved plenty of seeds for the next spring for herself and her neighbors.

She had traveled to Utah in 1852 in a wagon train. She and her husband must have been sent to Idaho to the Salmon River area to help settle there, and it was there her husband died. She married a second time in 1859 in Farmington, Utah. They must have also moved to the Idaho area where Ruth Ann died in 31 Dec 1910 at over seventy-six years of age at Swan Lake, Idaho. Having raised thirteen children she left a great posterity to honor her for her devotion to her religion, and her faith and fortitude in helping "tame" the wilderness of Utah and Idaho.

SARAH JOHNSTON MCCANN

BIRTHDATE: 17 Mar 1819
Ballinderry, Antrim, Ireland
DEATH: 2 Apr 1892
Garden City, Rich, Utah
PARENTS: Arthur Johnston
Sarah McGee
PIONEER: 1 Oct 1850
Stephen Markham Company
SPOUSE:
Thomas Ravenhill McCann
MARRIED: 11 May 1835
Stockport Parrish, Lancashire, Eng.
DEATH SP: 3 Oct 1882
Fish Heaven, Bear Lake, Idaho

CHILDREN:
Elizabeth, 10 Mar 1836
Caroline, 10 Jun 1838
Thomas Ravenhill, 10 May 1840
Joseph Nephi, 1 Apr 1844
Brigham, 13 Oct 1886
Sarah (Larsen), 20 Nov 1849
Mariah Jane (Pope), 20 Mar 1853
Emiline (Oderkirk), 9 Jun 1855
Deseret (Hobbs/Farney), 28 Sep 1857
Hyrum Johnston, 9 Mar 1860

Sarah was born in Ireland on 17 March 1819, the daughter of Arthur Johnston and Sarah McGee. Her father died when she was twelve, and she and her mother moved the family to England a year later. Sarah and her mother worked in a calico factory to earn a living for the family. Sarah was small of stature, with black hair and eyes and had a cheerful personality and great sense of humor, which proved to be helpful later in life.

She met and married Thomas R. McCann at Stockport Parish, Lankenshire, England on the 11th of May, 1835. They were baptized members of The Church of Jesus Christ of Latter-day Saints on March 26, 1839. In 1843 they sailed from England to America aboard the ship "Swanton."

They endured many hardships, including the death of three children. Her husband was a bodyguard for the Prophet Joseph Smith, and in Nauvoo he, too, was harassed by mobsters.

In May of 1846 they began their journey westward. While her husband left the family to seek work to obtain food, Sarah, her mother, and her children went on to Council Bluffs, arriving in time to put in crops.

In 1850 the family left Council Bluffs with the Stephen Markham company which arrived in the valley 1 Oct 1850. They lived in Salt Lake until 1854 when they were called to Ogden. Later they helped settle Franklin, Idaho and built the first house there. Later they were called to help settle Smithfield and then Bear Lake County where Sarah died in Garden City on the second of April 1992.

MARY JANE BENNETT MCCAUSLIN

No
Photo
Available

BIRTHDATE: 1 Jan 1821
Sumner Co, Tennessee
DEATH: 25 Jun 1852
Between Kanesville, Iowa and
Salt Lake City
PARENTS: William J. Bennett
Elizabeth Bell Bennett
PIONEER: Eratus Snow Co.
Graves Along The Way
SPOUSE: Jesse McCauslin
MARRIED: By 1848
DEATH: 6 Mar 1884
Provo, Utah, Utah

CHILDREN:
Sally McCauslin, 1848
William McCauslin, 1850

Mary Jane Bennett was born 1 Jan 1821 in Sumner Co, Tenn. She was one of eleven children born to William J. Bennett and Elizabeth Bell. Both of her grandfathers had been soldiers in the Revolutionary War. By the time she was eight the family had homesteaded in Shelbyville, Illinois. It was here the family heard the gospel. The Church requested that all members should come to Hancock County, Illinois, and the Bennetts, except for one brother, went to Nashville, Lee Co., Iowa. After her father's death, 30 Oct 1846, the family made their way to Kanesville Iowa. Here she met Jesse McCauslin, a widower with two little girls. Their mother, Tempey Durham, passed away 16 Apr 1842, after the birth of her second child. Mary Jane's two children were born while in Kanesville.

In April 1851 the family left Kanesville for the trip west. It was on this arduous journey that Mary Jane and her daughter Sally died just one day apart–25 Jun 1851 and 26 Jun 1851. They were members of the Erastus Snow Company. Mary Jane was thirty years of age when she was buried in a "grave along the way."

Her younger sister, Nancy Ellen, became the third wife of Jesse McCauslin and raised Mary Jane's son, William, along with eight children of her own.

NANCY ELLEN BENNETT MCCAUSLIN

No Photo Available

BIRTHDATE: 4 Jul 1833
Shelbyville Illinois
DEATH: 20 Mar 1909
Provo, Utah, Utah
PARENTS: William J.Bennett
Elizabeth Bell
PIONEER: 7 Oct 1851
Erastus Snow Company
SPOUSE: Jesse McCauslin
MARRIED: Oct 1851
DEATH: 6 Mar 1884
Provo, Utah, Utah

CHILDREN:
Mary Jan, 16 Apr 1854
Sarah Ann, 29 Aug 1855
Lydia E., 1 May 1857
Jesse B., 1860
George A., 6 Dec 1862
Alonzo, 1 May 1865
Elizabeth Mahalia, 6 Jan 1867
Caroline, 9 Oct 1859

Nancy Ellen Bennett was born 4 Jul 1833 in Shelbyville, Illinois. She was the youngest of eleven children born to William J. Bennett and Elizabeth Bell. After the family had joined the Church they moved to Lee County, Iowa. Her father died in 1846 and the family moved to Council Bluffs, Iowa.

Nancy's sister, Mary Jane, had married a widower, Jesse McCauslin who had two little girls, then she had two children of her own. On the trip to the Salt Lake Valley, Mary Jane died, and also her little daughter, Sally, and both were buried in a "grave along the way." Nancy took on the responsibility of caring for the children, and when they reached Salt Lake City she and Jesse were married, just two weeks after arriving. This was in Oct 1851, she was eighteen and her husband 34.

They moved for a time to Cedar Valley, then in 1852 moved to Provo, Utah. They farmed while raising eight children, and she helped her husband become a pioneer merchant in Provo. He was also Provo City Treasurer and Sheriff. Jesse died 6 Mar 1884 in Provo, Utah

Nancy Ellen was a widow for twenty-five years. She continued to farm and do Church work, along with raising her children. She took care of Jesse's father, Younger McCauslin until his death, and also her mother Elizabeth Bell Bennett. Nancy died 20 Mar 1909 in Provo, Utah. She was full of faith and service to others.

ALMEDA DAY MCCLELLAN

BIRTHDATE: 28 Nov 1831
Bastard, Leeds, Canada
DEATH: 22 Jun 1933
Salt Lake City, Salt Lake, Utah
PARENTS: Hugh Day
Rhoda Ann Nichols Day
PIONEER: 1 Oct 1850
Joseph Young Wagon Company
SPOUSE:
William Carroll McClellan
MARRIED: 19 Jul 1849
Little Pigeon, Pottawattamie, Iowa
DEATH: 28 Apr 1916
Colonia Juarez, Chihuahua, Mexico

CHILDREN:
Mary Almeda, 1 1 May 1850
William Hugh, 24 Mar 1852
Maria Matilda, 2 May 1854
Cynthia Lovesta, 2 May 1856
James Jasper, 28 Dec 1858
Sarah Evaline, 10 Feb 1861
John Henry, 12 Apr 1863
David Alvin, 16 Jun 1865
Samuel Edwin, 23 Jul 1867
Rhoda Ann, 27 Oct 1869
George Alma, 13 Jun 1872
Charles Eli, 8 Feb 1872

Almeda Day lived a life of relative poverty. Shortly after her father's baptism into the LDS Church in December of 1836, the Day family crossed the frozen St. Lawrence River from Canada to settle in the state of New York. From age seven to age twelve, Almeda attended school, and though she obtained scarcely five years of formal education, she remained an avid reader. At age twelve, the family relocated to Sun Prairie, Wisconsin where Almeda was employed as a housekeeper by her Aunt Lydia Nichols Brazee. In the fall of 1844, the Day family moved to Nauvoo. Already a fine seamstress, Almeda helped sew garments and temple clothing for the Nauvoo Temple. When her mother died in childbirth in November of 1844, the family left Nauvoo and lived for a time in Iowa and later went to Florence, Nebraska. This is where Almeda met and married her husband William C. McClellan who had just returned with the Mormon Battalion. In June of 1850, they left their home in Nebraska and traveled west with the Joseph Young Wagon Company. She had given birth to her first child, Mary, just five weeks before they began their trek. She not only nursed her daughter along the trail, but two more children as well.

Soon after their arrival in Salt Lake City, the family was called to pioneer Payson, Utah. Almeda lived the principle of plural marriage and in April conference 1877, the family was called to join the United Order at Sunset, Arizona. In 1881, they family moved to Brigham City, Arizona, then to Forest Dale, Arizona, and later to Pleasanton, New Mexico. The passage of the Edmunds-Tucker Bill necessitated a move to Juarez, Mexico. With the outbreak of the Mexican Revolution in 1912, the family returned to Payson for a while. They returned to Juarez in 1916 where her husband died. Her children later moved her to Utah where she lived the rest of her life which ended when she was one hundred one years old.

ALMEDA STEWART MCCLELLAN

BIRTHDATE: 8 Feb 1841
Fox River, Van Buren, Iowa
DEATH: 7 Feb 1912
Payson, Utah, Utah
PARENTS: Benjamin Franklin Stewart—Polly Richardson Stewart
PIONEER: 25 Sep 1847
Abraham O. Smoot Wagon Co.
SPOUSE:
Samuel Wilburn McClellan
MARRIED: 28 Dec 1856
Payson, Utah, Utah
DEATH: 10 Jul 1912
Payson, Utah, Utah

CHILDREN:
Samuel Wilburn, Jr., 12 Nov 1857
James Franklin, 20 Jun 1859
Jasper Cyrenous, 28 May 1860
George Edward, 27 Apr 1862
Harrison Whitman, 16 Aug 1863
Cynthia Arathusa, 18 May 1865
Myron Oscar, 16 Aug 1866 (died age 18)
Orla, 25 Sep 1868 (died age 16)
Sarah Lovena, 1 Mar 1872
Pollie Dean, 6 May 1874 (died age 2)
Lynn Stewart, 14 Nov 1876 (died as infant)
Ivy Almeda, 8 Oct 1878
William Clyde, 9 Apr 1882

Almeda's parents were baptized as members of the LDS Church and later moved to Nauvoo, Illinois to be with the Saints. They were then driven from Nauvoo and went to live in Council Bluffs. They joined with the Abraham Owen Smoot Wagon Company to cross the plains and arrived in the Salt Lake Valley on September 27, 1847. Their family lived in a small log house.

Shortly after, they moved to Mill Creek and built a thatched roof home. They planted crops and were expecting a bounteous harvest when thousands of crickets began devouring their crops. They experienced the miracle of the seagulls which saved a good portion of the grain. In 1851, they moved to Peteetneet or Payson where they farmed. They had a great deal of trouble with the Indians. On December 18, 1856, Almeda was married to Samuel Wilburn McClellan and moved to Payson. She performed her duties as a typical pioneer wife and mother, making her candles and soap, drying fruit and corn for winter use, besides doing all the other chores of a housewife of that time. She became the mother of thirteen children. She made all the clothing for her family. Her eyesight began to fail, so she traded work with others, having them do for her what she could not see to do for herself. She would encour-

age her children to develop their talents. She was always ready to help her family and neighbors when there was sickness or trouble in their homes. There was no need of calling a doctor when she was there because she knew just what to do. Almeda was one of the first to join the parent's class when it was organized in Sunday School and she attended it regularly.

The life of this real pioneer came to a close on February 7, 1912.

CYNTHIA STEWART MCCLELLAN

BIRTHDATE: 28 Apr 1810
Sumner County, Tennessee
DEATH: 29 Apr 1862
Payson, Utah, Utah
PARENTS: Samuel Stewart
Ann Wallace Stewart McCall
PIONEER: 1 Oct 1850
Joseph Young Wagon Company
SPOUSE: James McClellan
MARRIED: 18 Jan 1826
DEATH: 10 Feb 1881
Payson, Utah, Utah

CHILDREN:
William Carroll, 12 May 1828
Matilda Elizabeth, 15 Dec 1829
Mary Jane, 22 Aug 1831
Samuel Wilburn, 23 Aug 1833
Hugh Miles, 4 Feb 1835
Hugh Jefferson, 13 Nov 1836
John Jasper, 6 Aug 1838
Louisa Ann, 11 Apr 1840
Sarah Amanda, 5 Nov 1844
James Travers, 19 Aug 1848
Cynthia Selena, 22 Aug 1850
Arrninta Zerada, 11 Aug 1852

Cynthia was just four years old when her father was killed during the battle of New Orleans in 1814. Her mother married James A. McCall in 1822. Shortly before her sixteenth birthday, Cynthia married James McClellan and they shared the land of her mother and stepfather in Bedford County, Tennessee. Four children were born to them in that area. They sold hogs, cattle, coonskins, dressed turkey, venison, and hams to St. Louis and Chicago and were living a very comfortable life. The Elders of the LDS Church found them and both Cynthia and James were baptized on May 13, 1839.

In the fall of 1841, they moved to Nauvoo after selling all they had. James worked as a blacksmith and paid his tithing by working on the temple as often as was possible. Cynthia and James had the opportunity of being endowed and sealed in the Nauvoo Temple before they were expelled from Nauvoo. They were in Council Bluffs when their oldest son volunteered to serve with the Mormon Battalion. Cynthia and James worked very hard to make the preparations to move further west. As they were traveling with the Joseph Young Wagon Company toward Salt Lake Valley, their son, James, died. On August 22, 1850, she gave birth to her eleventh child, Cynthia. They arrived in Salt Lake Valley on October 1, 1850.

Her husband was asked to be a blacksmith in Payson. They arrived there on March 18, 1851. Here, their twelfth child was born. Her husband was called to be second counselor in the branch presidency. Cynthia had a strong faith in her church and supported her husband and children in their many church activities and callings. She was very charitable to the sick and those in need. She died the day after her fifty second birthday.

LYDIA GOLDTHWAITE BAILEY KNIGHT DALTON MCCLELLAN

BIRTHDATE: 9 Jun 1812
Sutton, Worcester, Massachusetts
DEATH: 3 Apr 1884
St. George, Washington, Utah
PARENTS: Jesse G. Goldthwaite
Sally Burt Goldthwaite
PIONEER: 13 Oct 1850
Edward Hunter Wagon Co.
SPOUSE: Calvin Bailey
MARRIED: 1828
DEATH: 1835

CHILDREN:
Rosanna, 3 Nov 1830
Edwin, 12 Feb 1832

SPOUSE II: Newell Knight
MARRIED: 23 Nov 1835
Kirtland, Ohio
DEATH: 11 Jan 1847
Niobrara, Knox, Nebraska

CHILDREN:
Sally, 1 Dec 1836
James Philander, 29 Apr 1838
Joseph, 18 Oct 1840
Newell, 14 Oct 1842
Lydia, 6 Jun 1844
Jesse, 6 Sep 1845
Hyrum Helaman, 26 Aug 1847

SPOUSE III: John Dalton
MARRIED: 18 Sep 1851
DEATH: Divorced 1858

CHILDREN:
Artemesia, 22 Jun 1852

SPOUSE IV: James McClellan
MARRIED: 1860 Payson, Utah, Utah
DEATH: 12 Feb 1880
CHILDREN: None

Lydia's father was a prosperous farmer. Her mother was better educated than most and was very ambitious for her children. Lydia attended boarding school and met Calvin Bailey. At age sixteen, she married him. He began drinking and abusing her. They were parents to one daughter and Lydia was expecting another child when Calvin left her. She suffered the deaths of her infant son and her daughter at age three. She moved to Mt. Pleasant, Canada with her friends, Mr. & Mrs. Freeman Nickerson. She was in their home when she first heard the gospel message from the lips of Joseph Smith. She was baptized a member of the LDS Church and went back to Kirtland to be with other saints. She was married to Newell Knight by the Prophet Joseph Smith on November 23, 1835. They were living with the Hyrum Smith family while her husband assisted in finishing the lower room of the temple. They purchased a forty acre farm in Caldwell County near Far West. Lydia suffered from much illness and persecution during these years. In 1838, Newell built a log cabin in Nauvoo for his family. Lydia was one of the first members of the first Relief Society and actively participated in that organization the rest of her life.

On April 17, 1846, Lydia's family joined a group of saints leaving Nauvoo, leaving their mills, houses, barns, and all their possessions to mobsters. They wintered with the Ponca Indians that year. After her husband's death that same winter, she went back to Winter Quarters where they were organized into the Edward Hunter Wagon Company. They arrived in the Salt Lake Valley on October 13, 1850.

Lydia's sons learned how to make adobe bricks and helped to build their home. As soon as the home was finished, Lydia started a small school. John Dalton asked her to marry him in polygamy and take her sons to work on his farm. Five years later, he asked her to return to the city. Brigham Young granted her a divorce from John. During the exodus south which was caused by the arrival of the Johnston Army, Lydia was asked to move to Provo. She became acquainted with James McClellan who was a widower with two young girls. They married and were later called to settle in Santa Clara. Lydia was called to be one of the attendants in the St. George Temple. After her husband, James, died, she continued working in the temple. She always took an active interest in raising and caring for silkworms and worked on the production of raw silk.

CATHERINE ORTHELIA KIDD McCLENAHAN

No Photo Available

BIRTHDATE: 25 Dec 1820/24 Dec 1819, Ohio County, Virginia
DEATH: 12 Jul 1912
Mt. Pleasant, Sanpete, Utah
PARENTS: Thomas Kidd
Susannah McKittrick
PIONEER: 3 Sep 1852
Abraham 0. Smoot Company
SPOUSE:
James Kemp McClenahan, Sr.
MARRIED: 13 Mar 1853
DEATH SP: 24 Dec 1872
Mt. Pleasant, Sanpete, Utah

CHILDREN:
James Kemp, Jr., 26 Jun 1856
Elijah Thomas, 24 Jul 1862
Susannah Elizabeth, 3 May 1867

Catherine was born 25 Dec 1820 at Ohio County, Virginia, a part of Virginia that is now West Virginia. The family later left that area and at Waffen County, Ohio they encountered Joseph Smith and his Mormon followers. Most of the members of the family were converted to The Church of Jesus Christ of Latter-day Saints and were baptized by Franklin D. Richards. Catherine, her parents, and brothers and sisters, were among the Saints in 1845-56 as they were driven from one county to another.

Catherine crossed the plains with her brother Alexander Kidd and his family in the Abraham 0. Smoot company. They had two large government wagons filled with provisions and seed. They reached the Salt Lake Valley in September of 1852

In Salt Lake City Catherine was married to James Kemp McClenahan on 13 Mar 1853. He was fifty years old and she was thirty-three. They lived in Salt Lake for a while, then moved to Provo where their first child was born in 1856. By 24 Jul 1862 they moved to Mount Pleasant. Here her husband operated a flour mill and Catherine sacrificed the material in her white silk wedding dress for use in the mill as there was a scarcity of good bolting cloth available.

Catherine's husband died at Mt. Pleasant on Christmas Eve in 1872. She was left with three children to rear and also took some responsibility in the management of the mill. She passed away at Mt. Pleasant on 12 Jul 1912 at the age of 92.

NANCY (ANN) POLLOCK McCLENAHAN

No Photo Available

BIRTHDATE: 14 Sep 1813
Townland of Barran, Ireland
DEATH: 4 Nov 1852
Fort Union, Salt Lake City, Utah
PARENTS: Thomas Pollock
Rebecca Simpson Pollock
PIONEER: 1 Oct 1850
Joseph Young Co. Wagon Train
SPOUSE:
James Kemp McClenahan
MARRIED: 21 Apr 1840
Stark County, Illinois
DEATH: 24 Dec 1871
Mt. Pleasant, Utah

CHILDREN: none

Ann Pollock McClenahan was lovingly called Nancy. She was a beautiful lass, described as having blue eyes and hair as fair as the flax that waved in the Irish meadows. The Pollock family was descended from a steward who faithfully served William The Conqueror (1075 to 1153). They were a very prominent and distinguished family, recognized and admired by royalty. Nancy's father was rightful heir to large estates in Derry County, Ireland, which had been given to the family by Queen Ann of England.

When Nancy was in her teens her father, Thomas, died, leaving her mother with six children to feed, clothe, shelter and nourish through hard times. Twelve years later, Nancy's mother died, leaving the children to fend for themselves. Nancy helped in the home with the children. Her brother, Samuel, went to the farmlands of Shropshire, England in search of work and food. He came into contact with Mormon missionaries and was baptized into the Church. He shared the Gospel message with Nancy who became a member of the Mormon Church and left with her brother to emigrate to Utah. They sailed from Liverpool, England on the ship "Swanton" with 212 Mormon converts in charge of Lorenzo Snow. They arrived in Nauvoo, Illinois 12 Apr 1843.

Somehow, the lovely Nancy met a handsome man, James Kemp McClenahan. He had accepted the Gospel and joined the Church in Illinois. He and Nancy were married 21 Apr 1840 in Stark County, Illinois. Nancy was twenty-seven years old and James was thirty-seven years old. Their circumstances and trials of life had evidently kept them single longer than most pioneer couples. Their marriage was not blessed with children. Nancy and James and her brother, James, with his family, traveled together on the trek West. The McClenahans and Pollocks were among the families who settled the Little Cottonwood-Fort Union area of the Salt Lake Valley.

On 30 Aug 1852, Nancy and James went to the Salt Lake City Endowment House and were sealed for time and eternity. It is not known what illness fell upon Nancy, but her earthly pilgrimage ended just a few months later, 4 Nov

1852, at the early age of thirty-nine years. She is buried in the pioneer cemetery at what then was called Fort Union.

AMELIA LAVILLA BROWN MCCOMBS

BIRTHDATE: 30 Jan 1840
Greene Township, Pennsylvania
DEATH: 31 Aug 1909
Logan, Utah
PARENTS: Ezekiel Brown
Catherine Slawson (Slauson)
Brown
PIONEER: 24 Oct 1855
Milo Andrus Wagon Train
SPOUSE: Andrew McCombs
MARRIED: 19 Apr 1857
Salt Lake City, Utah
DEATH: 2 Aug 1902
Grover, Wyoming

CHILDREN:
Catherine Amelia, 3 Aug 1858
Alma Thomas, 24 Oct 1860
Ezra David, 7 Apr 1863
Eliza Susan, 5 Aug 1867
Malvina, 12 Sep 1869
Effie Deborah, 25 Oct 1875
Ida Adell, 14 Jun 187

Amelia McCombs was born in Pennsylvania. Her parents gave her a good education and they were a prominent family in their community. When Amelia was eight years old her father fell dead in a restaurant while having breakfast. The Brown home became the headquarters for the missionaries of the Mormon Church in that area. Amelia was baptized 18 Aug 1850 as a member of the Church. The family decided to emigrate to Utah in 1855. Amelia and her sisters Lucy and Jane and Jane's two children left Mormon Grove to travel to Utah Jul 1855. Her mother and the rest of her family waited until another year. Amelia was able to ride in a carriage some of the way; most of the company walked. She also cooked meals for other families. They arrived in the Salt Lake Valley 24 Oct 1855.

Upon arriving in Utah, Amelia went to work for the Ezra Clark family in Farmington, Utah. She was there at the time of the grasshopper war in 1856 and knew the pangs of hunger and want. For some time she lived on greens and roots. Amelia next went to Salt Lake City in 1856 and worked out for different people until 19 Apr 1857 she married Andrew McCombs as his second wife in plural marriage. Her sister, Lucy, was his first wife. In 1857 the families moved up to the Weber Valley where Andrew herded cattle for the Church. They moved back to Salt Lake City and Andrew worked in the tannery during the Winter of 1858. In the Spring of 1862 they moved to Logan, Utah to begin pioneering in that new area. From Logan they moved to a triangle of towns where they lived the next thirty-seven years; Smithfield, Clarkston and Trenton.

During the Winter of 1868 Amelia's eight year old son died. The following Sep a daughter also died. In Nov 1869, her sister, Lucy, died in childbirth. Amelia took the little baby and nursed him, having just lost a baby in infancy. Amelia then became the mother of her sister's six children as well as her own three. It is said that no one could tell but that all nine children were her own.

In 1870 the family moved into Trenton and lived in a dugout for a year. Amelia was the first white woman to live there. Her boys helped their father build a two-story rock house. This house was the center of life for Trenton. Church meetings were held there. Amelia was the first Relief Society President. When her husband was called on a mission for the Church Amelia and her children earned the money to clear their debts and keep him on the mission. Amelia was a true pioneer; she made her own soap, spun wool and flax into thread and yarns, wove the cloth and made clothing for her family. In 1898 she went with her husband to Star Valley, Wyoming to start another home. After her husband's death she made Logan, Utah her home. Amelia died 31 Aug 1909 in Logan and is buried by her husband in the Smithfield, Utah Cemetery.

ANN DAVIDSON MCCULLOCH

BIRTHDATE: 31 Oct 1832
Penston, Haddington
East Lothian, Scotland
DEATH: 17 May 1902
Logan, Cache, Utah
PARENTS: Robert Davidson
Margaret Duncan Davidson
PIONEER: 1863
SPOUSE:
William Johnson McCulloch
MARRIED: 19 Mar 1852
Gladsmuir, E. Lothian, Scotland
DEATH: 27 May 1905
North Logan, Cache Valley, Utah

CHILDREN:
George Davidson, 1853
Robert, 12 Nov 1855
William, 25 Jun 1857
John, 15 Apr 1860
David, 10 May 1862
Henry, 16 Aug 1864
Davidson (David), 3 Nov 1866
Margaret Ann (Hincks), 10 Oct 1869
Richard, 31 Aug 1872
Marian (Hurst), 2 Jun 1874

Ann was born 31 Oct 1832 in Scotland. She was baptized into the LDS Church 17 Dec 1848 at age sixteen, in Hunterfield, Scotland. In 1852 she was married to William Johnson McCulloch. He had been baptized 7 May 1849, in Trancnt, Scotland. Their first five children were born in Penston or Tranent, Scotland. Ann and her husband were faithful members of the church in Scotland. They were both rebaptized in the spring of 1857.

By the spring of 1863, they were ready to join the Saints in Zion. They sailed on the ship "B. S. Kimball" on

8 May 1863. Their youngest son, David, died and was buried at sea. They continued their journey to the Great Salt Lake Valley, and in 1865 they moved to Logan, Cache Co., Utah. They erected a humble log cabin there where the rest of their ten children were born. After living in the log cabin for a few years, they replaced it with a two-story frame house which is still standing on the same corner of Third East and fourth North. They also had a farm near the foothills north of the University there.

Ann was always a faithful member of the Logan Fifth Ward. Her husband and sons helped haul rock to build the Logan Temple, and they worked on the East Logan and Smithfield Canal.

Ann and William experienced all of the hardships and trials of pioneer life as they had left their homelands for the sake of their religion. They remained strong in their faith all their lives. Ann passed away 17 May 1902 in Logan at the age of sixty-nine. She is buried in the Logan City cemetery beside her husband. She is a fine example of a pioneer woman of faith and fortitude whose life was a great example for others to follow.

MARGARET MCNEIL MCCULLOCH

BIRTHDATE: 1 Jan 1834
Penston, Haddington, Scotland
DEATH: 23 Nov 1927
Rexburg, Madison, Idaho
PARENTS: Charles McNeil
Marion Dobie
PIONEER: 27 Aug 1860
9th Handcart Company
SPOUSE:
John Black McCulloch
MARRIED, June 1852
In Scotland
DEATH SP: 20 Oct 1893
Rexburg, Madison, Idaho

CHILDREN:
George, 23 May 1855
Charles, 14 Aug 1857
Maria/Marion, 23 May 1860
John Henry, 12 Nov 1862
Isabelle, 3 Mar 1865
Alexander, 29 Apr 1868
Margaret, 9 Dec 1870
Agnes, 8 Jun 1873
Annie, 25 Jun 1881

Margaret McNeil was born in Scotland in 1834. She married John Black McCulloch in Jun of 1852 in Scotland. John was a coal miner by trade, and in 1854 he took his young wife and sailed for America where he hoped to find work in the Appalachian Mountains. They were living in Kentucky when their first child was born. Margaret missed her parents so much that they decided to return to Scotland.

At this time the Mormon Missionaries were spreading the gospel and offering free transportation and land to new converts who wished to immigrate to the Utah Territory.

The McCullochs and the McNeils were converted and once again Margaret and John set sail for the United States, this time with two small sons. In Nebraska they joined with the 9th Handcart Company to cross the plains. Margaret's third child was born along the "Mormon Trail." They arrived in the valley in August 1860.

After a short stay in Salt Lake City they moved to Logan, Cache, Utah where they lived for many years. About 1883-84 they moved to Rexburg, Idaho where they lived the rest of their lives. John died in Rexburg in 1893. Margaret continued to make her home with a son or daughter. She was hard-working and frugal, and spoke with a Scottish brogue. Her favorite expression was "My faith!." She was a tiny woman who lived to be ninety-three years of age. Margaret died in Rexburg, Idaho in 1927, and is buried beside her husband.

MARY SMITH MCCULLOCH

No
Photo
Available

BIRTHDATE: 22 Sep 1836
Penston, Edinburgh, Scotland
DEATH: 14 Feb 1894
Weston, Oneida, Idaho
PARENTS: Robert Smith
Margaret Archibald
PIONEER: 24 Nov 1864
SPOUSE: Henry McCulloch
MARRIED: 27 Feb 1857
Penston, Edinburgh, Scotland
DEATH SP: 3 Nov 1883

CHILDREN:
George, 4 Aug 1857
Robert, 19 Apr 1860
Margaret, 6 Jan 1862
William Albany, 22 Jul 1864
James, 15 Oct 1866
Marion Agnes, 26 Sep 1868
Henry Richard, 24 Sep 1870
Mary, 21 Oct 1872
Isabelle, 18 Feb 1875
Euphemia, 24 Dec 1878

Mary was born 22 Sep 1836 at Penston, Edinburgh, Scotland. When she was twenty years old she married Henry McCulloch. Two years later they heard the missionaries and Henry joined The Church of Jesus Christ of Latter-day Saints. They sailed to America on the ship "Hudson," leaving on 3 Jun 1864 arriving in New York in July. They made their way to St. Joseph, Missouri where they bought a wagon and supplies and joined a wagon train under the command of Captain Holiday. Mary was ill and confined to her bed in the wagon. Her little four year old son Robert fell while playing and the wagon wheel passed over his neck. He died from the injuries and was buried on the plains.

After many hardships and trials on the journey, they at last arrived in Salt Lake City on 24 Nov 1864. Mary did not join the Church until after they were in Utah for two years. They moved to Logan where they lived in a dugout until they could build a house. They later settled on some land in a place called Utida, on the boundary line of Utah and Idaho, and after some time moved to Weston in Idaho.

Henry worked as a contractor and built the railroad from Franklin to Big Hole Basin. While returning from St. Paul, Minnesota with the payroll, he was attacked and killed by two of his own men. Mary was left a widow with nine children. She worked as a nurse and mid-wife and spent much time caring for the sick. She would also make cheese to sell, and candles from beef tallow and starch from potatoes. She served as first counselor in the Relief Society for many years and was a visiting teacher. She passed away at age fifty-seven and was buried in the Weston cemetery.

HELEN MAR CALLISTER MCCULLOUGH

BIRTHDATE: 26 Sep 1846
Winter Quarters, Nebraska
DEATH: 13 Jun 1930
Delta, Utah
PARENTS: Thomas Callister
Helen Mar Clark
PIONEER: 26 Sep 1847
Daniel Spencer Co. Wagon
SPOUSE:
Henry Judson McCullough
MARRIED: 22 May 1864
Fillmore, Utah
DEATH SP: 17 Dec, 1911
Delta, Utah

CHILDREN:
Helen Mar, 12 Mar 1865
Carolina Eliza, 13 Nov 1866
Clarinda Atlana, 20 Nov 1867
Frances Melissa, 1 Nov 1870
Henry Judson, Jr., 12 Jun 1874
Clarabell, 19 Jan 1877
Esther, 7 Dec 1879
Levi Hamilton, 27 Mar 1883
Thomas Clark, 15 Dec 1885
Eleanor, 26 Mar 1888

Helen Mar was born in a covered wagon on 26 Sep 1846 at Winter Quarters, Nebraska. The first eight months of her life were spent in Winter Quarters, where the Saints were preparing to make the long trek across the plains. Her father became seriously ill, so they were unable to join the first company. They traveled with the Daniel Spencer company that arrived in the Salt Lake Valley on 26 Sep 1847. They spent the first winter in the fort in Salt Lake and in April moved out to Mill Creek on a ten-acre farm. Here they experienced the devastation of large black crickets destroying their crops. With her parents and sister she witnessed the coming of flocks of seagulls which destroyed the crickets and saved the people from starvation.

Her early life was spent much the same as other pioneer children. She learned to spin and knit and to help with the household tasks. Her early school days were spent in Salt Lake. There were few books and the children used slates to write on. They sat on long benches, holding their slates on their laps.

In 1861 the family moved to Fillmore, Utah. Here she met Henry Judson McCullough and on May 22, 1864 she became his bride. Their wedding reception and dance were held in the old state House. Her husband owned and operated a small farm north and west of Fillmore. In the spring of 1867 he was called to serve a mission to Great Britain.

In April of 1885 they sold their farm in Fillmore and moved to Coyote (Antimony) Garfield, Utah. There were no doctors in this little valley and she often went into the homes to help care for the sick. Throughout the valley she was lovingly called Aunt Helen Mar. In the fall of 1906 they returned to Fillmore and later moved to Delta where she passed away on 13 Jun 1930.

CHRISTINA BONNER MCCURDY

BIRTHDATE: 7 Sep 1852
Whitburn, West Lothian, Scotland
DEATH: 22 Apr 1930
Vernal, Uintah, Utah
PARENTS: George Bonner
Margaret Edmundston
(Edmiston, Edmunston)
PIONEER: 12 Sep 1861
Capt. John R. Murdock Wagon Co,
SPOUSE: Albert Gallatin McCurdy
MARRIED: 15 Sep 1869
Midway, Wasatch, Utah
DEATH SP: 24 Jan 1892
Vernal, Uintah, Utah

CHILDREN:
Almedia Loretto, 19 May 1870
Albert Gallatin, 8 Feb 1872
George Bonner, 4 Apr 1874
Mary Jane, 5 May 1882
Tina Lucretia, 19 Aug 1884
John Robert, 18 May 1887
Margaret Edmundston, 1 May 1876
Elizabeth Lindsay, 29 Apr 1888
Annie, 6 Apr 1878
Ethel May, 12 May 1891
Dezzie, 24 Feb 1880

Christina came to America at age four with her mother, Margaret, and two brothers, George and William. Her father had gone eight months earlier to raise enough money to send for them. They left Liverpool on 8 Nov 1856. The voyage took ten rough, cold, long weeks. When they were living in St. Johns, Illinois in 1857 there was a large earthquake seventy miles away. The house rolled back and forth, dishes rattled, the lids flew off the stove and during all this commotion her baby sister was born.

She was baptized in April of 1860. July 1861, five years since arriving in America and now age nine, she left Florence, Nebraska for Utah with the Murdock Company and entered the valley 12 Sep 1861. She settled at Mound City, Wasatch Co., with parents, brothers and sisters. The winter was very bad with five to six feet of snow. They could not get to the flour mill so they had to live on boiled wheat.

Her father went back east for a year. Christina helped her mother glean potatoes, helped with the chores, and helped take care of the three younger children, one being a baby.

Many times they were frightened by the Indians because they would try stealing their cattle and horses. Later this area of Mound City was renamed Midway.

Christina married Albert Gallatin McCurdy 15 Sep 1869 in Midway, Utah. On November 13, 1879 they went to the Endowment House in Salt Lake and took out their endowments and were sealed for time and eternity. While living in Midway she had seven children. They later moved to Vernal, Utah where another four children were born to this union.

Christina knew pain and sorrow when she lost her husband at the young age of forty-eight after only twenty-two years of marriage. Her oldest child was married. She managed to hold her family together with the help of the older children with ages from twenty to one year old. Sadness and pain came again when Elizabeth died at age six and Ethel May at age ten.

After being widowed for thirty-eight years Christina died in Vernal at the age of seventy-seven, buried next to her husband.

CHRISTINA STOKER MCDANIEL

BIRTHDATE: 24 Aug 1815
Bloomfield, Jackson, Ohio
DEATH: 10 May 1854
Mountainville (Alpine) Utah
PARENTS: David Stoker Sr.
Barbara Graybill
PIONEER: 28 Aug 1852
Isaac Stewart Company
Oxteam & Wagon Train
SPOUSE: John McDaniel
MARRIED: 8 Feb 1835
Ohio
DEATH SP: 11 Nov 1884
Alpine, Utah

CHILDREN:
Electa Jane, 3 Nov 1835
Tabitha, 29 Jan 1837
John Riley, 20 May 1839
Matilda, 24 Oct 1840
Katherine, 24 Jul 1842
George Washington, 25 Jul 1844
James William, 13 Sep 1847
David Stoker, 18 Apr 1849
Silvester, 26 Apr 1854

Christina was born 24 Aug 1815 at Bloomfield township, Jackson, Ohio. She was the eldest of seven children born to David Stoker, Sr., and Barbara Graybill. On 8 Feb 1835 she married John McDaniel. They lived in Ohio during their early married life, and it was here they first heard of the Mormon Church and were among the first people to join.

They later moved to Hancock Co., Illinois. They were greatly persecuted, along with the other Saints, and were driven out of their home several times by mobs. On one occasion they were forced to flee their home, both with a child under each arm, and watch while the home was destroyed by fire. John was a bodyguard for the Prophet Joseph Smith, and was captured by the mob before Joseph and Hyrum. They knew he was a good friend and also a very good shot. He was missing for three days and was found tied up and gagged in a corral way out of town, in manure up to his knees.

They left Illinois with the other Saints and moved to Iowa, and from there crossed the plains by ox-team in 1852. By then Christina had eight children. She helped her husband and older children drive a flock of 500 sheep across the plains.

They stopped at Salt Lake for a short time, then went on to Mountainville, now Alpine, where they were one of the first families to settle. Here they endured many privations of early pioneer life, at one point going without bread for three months. During that time they lived on roots and wild berries with the meat her husband provided by hunting game.

Christina died two years after moving to Mountainville from the complications of child birth, leaving the new-born infant in the care of her older children until the father remarried. Christina was a beautiful woman with red hair, pleasing good looks, and a serene countenance.

DURITHA HADDEN HOFHEINS DODGE MCDANIEL

BIRTHDATE: 23 Apr 1843
Fairfield, Wayne, Illinois
DEATH: 27 Dec 1897
Cleveland, Emery, Utah
PARENTS: Alfred Sidney
Julia Ann Hall Hadden
PIONEER: 1851
SPOUSE I: Jacob Hofheins
MARRIED: 4 Jan 1859
(div. 10 Jan 1862)
DEATH: 25 Aug 1887
Levan, Utah

CHILDREN:
Julia Ann, 26 Jul 1860

SPOUSE II: Nathaniel Morgan Dodge
MARRIED: 1862/63

DEATH: 11 Feb 1873
Glenwood, Utah

CHILDREN:
Viola Melissa, 17 Nov 1863
Nathan (child), abt 1865
Zenous Wayne, 23 Apr 1867
Louisa Frances, Feb 1870
Reuben Alexander, 17 Jun 1871

SPOUSE III: Samuel James McDaniel
MARRIED: abt. 1873
DEATH SP: 21 May 1907
Cleveland, Utah

CHILDREN
Samuel James, 8 Sep 1874
Charlotte, 24 Aug 1876
John Henry, 1878 or 1879
George Oscar, 29 Apr 1882
Lorenzo (Stillborn), 1884
Ida May, 24 Sep 1885
Effie Pearl, 15 Aug 1889

Duritha Hadden was born in 1843 in Illinois to Alfred and Julia Hadden. She was born into a newly converted Mormon family. Little is known of her mother, except that she died on the Plains. Duritha's (pronounced Duh-ree'-tha) father married two plural wives before beginning the trek across the plains. Their journey to Utah was delayed for some time while they remained in Iowa. They arrived in the Valleys of the Mountains in 1851. Duritha was eight years old when the family arrived in Provo, and when she was eleven they moved to Parowan. For the rest of her growing up years, Duritha's father was pioneering in Parowan, Harmony, and Beaver.

Duritha was just sixteen when she married Jacob Hofheins at his home in Parowan. Jacob was thirty years her senior and this marriage lasted only three years before she obtained a divorce from him. Her daughter was named for Duritha's deceased mother, and she used the surname of her stepfather Dodge, until she married.

When her marriage to Nathaniel Morgan Dodge took place is not known, but their first child was born 17 Nov 1863 in Beaver. Nate died in the winter of 1872-3, leaving Duritha with five young children to raise. Less than a year after his death, she was married to Samuel James McDaniel, by whom she had seven more children. Family tradition has it that Mr. McDaniel had difficulty dealing with strong-minded teenage girls, and both of Duritha's daughters by her first two husbands married at early ages–Julia at age sixteen, and Viola at age thirteen.

Both of Duritha's husbands moved about a great deal. Her thirteen children were born in at least eight different towns. Finally, after all of the children were born, the last of them in Idaho, they settled in Cleveland, Emery County, Utah, where they remained until their deaths. Duritha was just fifty-three when she died 27 Dec 1897. As with so many of our pioneer women, it is a miracle that she lived as

long as she did when we consider that her mother died when she was just five, she was reared by stepmothers, married three times, the first time at age sixteen, bore thirteen children in primitive conditions, and she rarely had a place she could really call home for more than two or three years at a time during those difficult years. She was truly a great pioneer woman of faith and fortitude to be honored and revered by all who have followed her.

ANN THOMPSON LESLIE STEWART MCDONALD

BIRTHDATE: 14 Jul 1805
Arbroath, Angus, Scotland
DEATH: 15 Feb 1882
Springville, Utah, Utah
PARENTS: William Thompson
Jane (Jean) Cant Thompson
PIONEERS: 21 Sep 1852
H. W. Miller Wagon Company
SPOUSE I: Andrew Leslie
MARRIED: 12 Jul 1829
Montrose, Angus, Scotland
DEATH: 31 Jan 1840
Montrose, Scotland

CHILDREN:
David, 2 Apr 1830
George(child), 22 Oct 1831
Jane(child), 5 May 1833
Mary Ann, 8 Aug 1834
Helen, 2 May 1836
Andrew, 13 Jul 1838

SPOUSE II: John Martin Stewart
MARRIED: 2 Mar 1857

SPOUSE III: Duncan McDonald
MARRIED: 29 Jul 1865
Utah

Ann was born in Scotland in 1805 to William and Jane Thompson. Her father was a flax dresser. She had two brothers who joined the army and the navy when they were young men. Ann was fond of them and told her grandchildren what fine men they were. Ann was given schooling and religious instructions and was taught how to work with her hands. When she was quite young her mother died. Her father took a second wife and they had two sons and two daughters.

When Ann was a young lady, she left her parents' home and married Andrew Leslie who was a grain dealer, and purchased cargoes of wheat from the Baltic. He also had a bakery shop in Montrose where they made their home. They were very thrifty people. They had a beautiful home with upholstered furniture and lovely drapes. They had a library with plenty of books where they could spend many happy hours reading. They became the parents of six children.

The Leslies went to the Church of England to worship. One morning Andrew read about the Latter-day Saint missionaries traveling in Scotland without purse or scrip. This impressed Andrew very much. Andrew did not live very long after reading this news. His family felt that he would have joined had he heard the gospel preached by these missionaries. He died 31 Jan 1840 at the age of thirty-four.

Ann was anxious to learn more about this new religion and attended their meetings and took some of her children with her. The oldest boy, David, refused to have anything to do with this new religion. Ann's half sisters came to visit and became interested and listened to the missionaries. One of her half sisters along with Ann, and her three children were baptized 1 Sep 1849. They moved to Edinburgh, and then sailed from Liverpool 10 Nov 1849 on the "Zetland" with 250 Saints. The ship headed for New York, but finally landed at New Orleans. They traveled to St. Louis, and finally reached Utah 21 Sep 1852. They settled in Springville, Utah.

It is said she married John Martin Stewart 2 Mar 1857 in Utah. No further information is available. On 29 Jul 1865, Ann married Duncan McDonald and they moved to St. George, Utah.

When her first husband died in Scotland, Ann kept a small store which she maintained for seven years. She kept her children at the best schools, and gave them the education she could afford. Before leaving Scotland, she took down her beautiful drapes and put them into her trunk, thinking to hang them in her Utah home. They ended up being used to make clothing for her and her children.

Ann taught her children by examples of faith and good works. She was always good to the poor. She preferred the Gospel to any earthly treasures and she always remained true to her Latter-day faith. Had she remained in Scotland, she would have had enough to keep her comfortable the rest of her life. Her property, however, fell into the hands of her oldest son, David. She was a true Latter-day Saint who endured the trials and tribulations of pioneer life, counting her faith in the Gospel of Jesus Christ as her most prized possession.

NANCY ELIZABETH CUMMINGS MCDONALD

BIRTHDATE: 7 Sep 1843
Nauvoo, Hancock, Illinois
DEATH: 18 Oct 1881
Heber City, Wasatch, Utah
PARENTS: John Cummings
Rachel Canada (Canardy) Cummings
PIONEER: 1 Oct 1852
Uriah Curtis Wagon Company
SPOUSE: Joseph Smith McDonald
MARRIED: 1863
Heber, Wasatch, Utah
DEATH: 15 Feb 1930
Daniel, Wasatch, Utah

CHILDREN:
Sarah Jane, 24 Dec 1864
Joseph C., 8 Oct 1866
Rachel, 15 Nov 1868
James X, 15 Feb 1872
Mary Ann, 22 Dec 1873
John, 26 Feb 1876
Isaac David, 14 Jul 1879

Nancy's parents were already members of the LDS Church and were living in Nauvoo, Illinois at the time of Nancy's birth. The Cummings family was among those who were expelled from Nauvoo in 1846. They crossed the state of Iowa that year and established themselves at Gallows Grove, about five miles from Kanesville, which was adjacent to Council Bluffs. They remained there five years. In the spring of 1852, they were among the saints who traveled west with the Uriah Curtis Wagon Company which arrived in Salt Lake Valley on October first.

Nine years later, the Cummings family joined with those who had begun the colonization of Provo Valley, now known as Heber City. Here Nancy met Joseph Smith McDonald and after a courtship of two years, they were married in 1863 in Heber. They had seven children born to them in Heber. They had little of worldly goods to begin with, but with determination and energy, they were soon comfortable in a cabin the McDonald brothers helped Joseph build. Nancy was a helpful companion to Joseph, and a cheerful, loving mother to her children. When her youngest child was two years old, Nancy died at the age of thirty eight.

RACHEL BURKE TAAFFE MCDONALD

No
Photo
Available

BIRTHDATE: 6 Apr 1806
Lurgan, Armaghshire, Ireland
DEATH: 28 Apr 1863
Salt Lake City, Utah
PARENTS: John Taaffe
Nancy Trainor
PIONEER: Fall of 1850
Warren Foote Company
SPOUSE:
John Kilpatrick McDonald
MARRIED: Apr 1823
in Ireland
DEATH SP: 31 Aug 1874
Salt Lake City, Utah

CHILDREN:
Elizabeth Taaffe, 27 Dec 1823
William, 13 Dec 1825
William Taaffe, 10 Dec 1827
John Taaffe, 11 Apr 1830
Alexander Taaffe, 8 Apr 1833
Washington Taaffe, 9 Aug 1835
James Kilpatrick, 4 Aug 1837
Jane Taaffe, Mar 1840
Joseph Taaffe, 1 Jan 1842

Rachel Taaffe was born in Ireland in 1806. She met John Kilpatrick McDonald when he became apprenticed to her father as a cabinet maker. They were married in Apr 1823; he was twenty-four and she was fifteen. To them were born nine children, but several of them died as children. John was of the Presbyterian faith and Rachel was Catholic.

In 1831 John had the urge to emigrate to Canada where his type of work was better. They placed their oldest daughter in a nunnery and sailed with two sons. Because of cholera in Canada they moved to Philadelphia, then to Pittsburg in 1840. This is where they learned of the Church and were baptized in 1842. They moved to Nauvoo only to be run out in 1846. Finally in 1850 they came across the plains with the Warren Foote Company arriving in Sep 1850.

In 1852 John was called on a five-year mission to Ireland. While he was gone Rachel had no means of support. She wrote to her son John, in San Bernardino, that they were hungry and were in danger of losing their home. He immediatley sent her money and started for Salt Lake with flour and cash, however along the way Indians robbed him of his horses and food. When he arrived Rachel didn't recognize him since he had been gone for four years. He remained in Salt Lake with her.

Rachel died in Salt Lake City in 1863, leaving a husband and four children; Elizabeth (the nun in Ireland), William, John and James. After her death John Sr. embraced polygamy, marrying a widow and her two daughters. He died in 1874 in Salt LakeCity.

SARAH FERGUSON MCDONALD

BIRTHDATE: 13 Oct 1802
Crawfordsburn, Down, Ireland
DEATH: 8 Mar 1883
Heber City, Wasatch, Utah
PARENTS: Samuel Ferguson
Mary Alderdice
PIONEER: 12 Sep 1850
Aaron Johnson Wagon Train
SPOUSE: James McDonald
MARRIED: 1826
Crawfordsburn, Down, Ireland
DEATH SP: 17 Jun 1850
On the trail

CHILDREN:
Jane, 17 Jul 1827
John, 1829
Eliza, 15 Dec 1831
John, 12 Dec 1833
William, 16 Nov 1834
Robert, 1836
Mary, 4 May 1837
David, 1840
Joseph Smith, 15 Oct 1842
Hyrum, 1845

Sarah Ferguson was born in Ireland in 1802. She married James McDonald in late 1825 or early 1826, and they were the parents of ten children, three of them dying very young. All of them were born in Ireland except the youngest who was born in Nauvoo.

In 1841 the gospel was preached to the family in Ireland and they were among the first to be baptized there. The family came to America in 1844 on a sailing ship, landed in New Orleans, and took the "Maid of Iowa" up the Mississippi to Nauvoo. That first summer they prepared and planted new ground, not only to feed themselves but to help other newcomers to Nauvoo. They were cast out of Nauvoo with the rest of the Saints, and spent three years in Kanesville preparing for the journey across the plains.

In June 1850 they left Kanesville with the Aaron Johnson Company, but only five days on the trip, cholera broke out and James McDonald was one of its victims. Sarah was prostrate with grief and it was necessary for Jane to take her father's place as head of the family. They managed to arrive in the valley in Sep 1850.

Sarah never remarried. In 1860 she moved with her sons to Heber Valley and remained there the rest of her life. She died in Heber City in 1883.

SUSANNAH HAMILTON GRANT MCDOUGAL

No Photo Available

BIRTHDATH: 8 Mar 1801
Bo'ness, Linlithgow, Scotland
DEATH: 27 Feb 1879
Willard, Box Elder, Utah
PARENTS: Richard Hamilton
Agnes Snaddon
PIONEER: 10-15 Dec 1856
John A Hunt Co. Wagon Train
SPOUSE: Robert Collier Grant
MARRIED: 23 Mar 1823
DEATH SP: between 1844/1849
Scotland

CHILDREN:
John, 28 Oct 1824
Agnes, 1826
Walter, 28 Jan 1829
Richard, 3 Sep 1830
Ellen (Pendelton), 15 Mar 1834
Susan, 11 Jul 1835
Thomas Torrance, 18 Jul 1838
Elizabeth, 18 May 1844

SPOUSE II: Isaac McDougal
MARRIED: 13 Jul 1867
DEATH: Unknown

Susan was a widow living in Scotland when elders from The Church of Jesus Christ of Latter-day Saints came to her home. She was baptized 2 June 1851. Five years later, on March 23, 1856, she brought her two youngest children Thomas and Elizabeth to America on the ship "Enoch Train." They traveled in the ship's steerage. Once on board the ship, the Saints were organized much the same as a ward, under the direction of James Ferguson. There were classes for the children and lectures on the gospel for adults.

When they landed at Boston, they were soon aware that pick pockets and thieves were roaming the wharf and they had to keep a constant vigil over their belongings. They traveled from there to Florence, Nebraska where they were assigned to Captain John A. Hunt's company which left on 1 Aug to cross the plains.

Young Thomas was assigned to harness and drive a team of oxen. He had never seen an animal such as these and was fearful of the seemingly untrained animals with their wide-spread horns. Susan was grateful to have a wagon to carry their possessions, although she and Elizabeth walked most of the way.

Their journey was slow and extremely difficult. They followed the Martin handcart company for much of the way and suffered many of the same hardships as those with the handcarts. They were the last to enter Salt Lake City, coming in sections that arrived between December 10th to the 15th.

Susan's first home was in Salt Lake City. On July 13, 1867 Susan was married to Isaac McDougal. They later moved to Three Mile Creek (Perry, Utah). She passed away on 27 February 1879.

MARY SMITH MCEWEN

BIRTHDATE: 5 Apr 1814
Hillsborough, Derry, Ireland
DEATH: 15 Oct 1899
Mancos, Montezuma, Colorado
PARENTS: John Smith
Mary Matthews
PIONEER: 1852
Fillmore Company Wagon Train
SPOUSE: Matthew McEwen
MARRIED: 13 May 1833
Tollcross, Barony, Lanark, Scotland
DEATH SP: 12 Dec 1875
Beaver, Beaver, Utah

CHILDREN:
Mary, 5 Apr 1834
Matthew, 12 Jan 1836
Martha, 22 Jun 1838
Eliza, 21 Dec 1840
Margaret, 21 Dec 1843
Hannah Marian, 5 Aug 1846
Moroni, 2 Feb 1849
Elizabeth, 11 Jun 1851
Joseph Smith, 7 Jan 1854
James, 23 Feb 1856
Hyrum (twin), 12 Dec 1859
Matilde Julia (twin), 12 Dec 1859

Mary Smith was born in Ireland in 1814. She married Matthew McEwen in Scotland in 1833. They were the parents of 12 children, including a set of twins.

The family came to Utah in 1852 by wagon with the Fillmore Company. At first they settled in Fillmore, Utah where they lived the United Order. Later they moved to Beaver, Utah. Mary boarded the man who brought the first telegraph to Beaver, and she was later honored by the Telegraph Company for this fact.

Mary had a lovely singing voice, and was an excellent knitter, even after she went blind. She died in Mancos, Colorado in 1899. Her husband died in Beaver, Utah in 1875.

HANNAH BOYACK MCFARLAND

BIRTHDATE: 12 Mar 1835
Dundee, Forfarshire, Scotland
DEATH: 31 Jan 1915
Wilson, Weber, Utah
PARENTS: James Boyack
Elizabeth Mealmaker
PIONEER: 24 Oct 1855
Milo Andrus Ox Team
SPOUSE: James McFarland
MARRIED: 6 Dec 1855
West Weber, Weber, Utah
DEATH SP: 12 Nov 1915
Wilson, Weber, Utah

CHILDREN:
Elizabeth, 18 Jan 1857
William Boyack, 22 May 1858
Margaret, 12 Mar 1860
Mary, 12 Nov 1861
Hannah, 30 Apr 1863
James Boyack, 7 Aug 1866
Peter Fenton, 1 Jun 1868
Robert Boyack, 1 Jun 1870
Isabel, 7 Mar 1872
Anne Ririe, 1 May 1874
Rose, 16 Nov 1878

Hannah Boyack was born in Scotland in 1835. The family was deeply religious and often had the local minister to Sunday dinner. They were introduced to the gospel by friends who had embraced it. Hannah's father joined right away but her mother waited for six years to be baptized.

The family emigrated to America on the ship "Samuel Curling" in 1855. They crossed the plains with the Milo Andrus Company, arriving in Salt Lake City on 24 Oct 1855. Hannah's brother had come on ahead and met them. They first settled in Spanish Fork where her father built a two-story home. Within a year Hannah and her four sisters were married. Hannah married James McFarland in Dec 1855. They lived in American Fork, Utah before moving to West Weber, Utah where she spent the remainder of her life

Hannah was the mother of eleven children. She never lost her Scottish accent and reminisced of her beautiful Scotland. She and her sisters all married Scottish men, and so were surrounded in their new homeland by rich Scottish influences. She was an articulate housekeeper and a devoted mother. Hannah died in Wilson, Weber, Utah in Jan 1915, and her husband died just ten months later in Nov 1915.

ISABELLA MITCHELL MCFARLAND

BIRTHDATE: 5 Mar 1837
Little Mill, Old Kilpatrick parish,
Dumbartonshire, Scotland
DEATH: Died: 10 April 1925
West Weber, Weber, Utah
PARENTS: William Mitchell
Isabella Nimmo
PIONEER: 25 Sep 1855
Richard Ballantyne Wagon Company
SPOUSE: Archibald McFarland
MARRIAGE: 3 August 1854
Boness, West Lothian, Scotland
DEATH SP: 14 Dec 1915
West Weber, Weber, Utah

CHILDREN:
William, 25 Jan 1856
Robert, 2 Jan 1858
James Rankin, 20 Dec 1859
Charles Blair, 8 Apr 1862
Isabella (Hogge), 25 Sep 1864
Archibald, 15 Jan 1867
John, 31 Dec 1868
Albert Rae, 1 May 1871
Margaret Elizabeth (Nelson), 13 Oct 1873 infancy)
Mary Ann, 6 Mar 1877
Janet (Faddis), 29 Jun 1879
Daniel McFarland, 17 May 1882

Isabella Mitchell was born on March 5th, 1837, in Scotland. She wrote, "My first recollections were in the town of Linlithgow, West Lothian, Scotland, where my father and mother had moved while I was yet a child. I, being the oldest child of my mother, was very much made of by her relations. I attended school in the vicinity of Linlithgow until my mother died, I being then in my fourteenth year. I had then to assume the care of my two younger brothers and a sister five years old."

Belle, as she was called, said she had been trained in "all the seriousness of the Presbyterian faith," yet after hearing the message of the Mormon missionaries, she was converted and was baptized in January of 1853 at the age of fifteen. About a year later, at a Mormon meeting, she met Archibald McFarland, another young Scottish convert. They were married on the 3rd of August 1854, in Boness, Scotland, by Elder William Heaton, president of the LDS Edinburgh Conference or district.

Belle's honeymoon was a long journey across oceans, plains and mountains, in the company of her husband's family, to Zion in the Salt Lake Valley. They sailed from Liverpool on January 17, 1855, with a large company of Mormon Saints, on the ship "Charles Buck." They crossed the plains in the Richard Ballantyne Company, arriving in Salt Lake City September 25, 1855.

Isabella and her husband settled first in Salt Lake City in the old 18th Ward on the Avenues. Her first child, born there, lived only seven months. Belle said they were under very trying circumstances that winter, were at times without any bread in the house, and knew not where to get any. "There were only a few houses there then and women and children from the lower parts of the city would come up in the spring to dig sego bulbs for food. They also boiled the roots of a thistle that grew in the lower parts of the city.

They remained only a year in Salt Lake City and then moved to American Fork where Archie's parents had settled. At the time of the Johnston Army occupation they heard, from Saints who had moved south the spring of 1858, that there was a large expanse of land on the Weber River west of Ogden which had not been settled, so, wishing to secure more land the entire McFarland family moved north in the early spring of 1859 and were among the first group of pioneers to settle West Weber.

Their first winter there was another of great suffering. Because they had spent the summer in feverish effort to get water from the Weber River onto their lands in order to grow food,, their cabin was only partially completed when winter struck. It was very cold. They were without window or door coverings and their clothing and bedding were insufficient to keep them warm. Under those miserable conditions Belle gave birth to another baby son in the month of December. She became the mother of twelve children and raised two grandsons whose mother had died following childbirth while on an LDS mission with her husband in Alberta, Canada.

Belle was very supportive of her husband, an active man in church and civic affairs. Even when he married two other wives in polygamy she shared her home with them unselfishly and took over the responsibility of raising her children alone and operating the family farm when he was absent on two foreign missions.

Archie left for his first mission in 1873 when their ninth child was seven days old. Their oldest surviving son was thirteen. Belle wrote that while he was away "we pursued the even tenor of our ways, making improvements, planting orchards, and raising our family, and did not run him in debt one dollar." Again in 1886 she had the full responsibility at home when he went on another mission and after his return when he was incarcerated in the Utah Territorial Prison for "unlawful cohabitation."

Belle was a rather small woman, dignified, capable, efficient, organized and intelligent. She was a quick, clean housekeeper, a good cook, and punctual in her habits. Her descendants have remarked that "No one could make a better pie," and "There was order and system in her home."

Along with her husband, Belle had a great interest in genealogy. She wrote, "While struggling to obtain a home and wrest from the desert a living I have not forgotten my forefathers who had died without hearing the everlasting Gospel, but through research have obtained many names of my ancestors and have had ordinances done for them in the temples of our God, numbering many hundreds." She was one of the first members of Weber County Daughters of the Utah Pioneers Camp 34 in West Weber.

Isabella Mitchell McFarland died at her home in West Weber on April 10, 1925. She is buried beside her husband in the West Weber Cemetery.

MARGARET MCCORMICK MCFARLAND

BIRTHDATE: 11 April 1804
Kilmany, Fifeshire, Scotland
DEATH: 10 January 1886
West Weber, Utah.
PARENTS: James McCormick
Janet Mitchell
PIONEER: Richard Ballantyne Co.
25 Sep 1855
SPOUSE: William McFarland
MARRIAGE: 9 Jan 1832
Dysart, Fifeshire, Scotland
DEATH SP: 27 Jan 1890
West Weber, Utah

CHILDREN:
Archibald, 17 Dec 1832
James, 25 Oct 1835
William, Jr., 14 May 1838
Mary Ann (Petterson), 22 Oct 1841
Robert McEwan, 19 Sep 1844
Janet, 8 Sep 1846

Margaret McCormick was born on a farm called New Cairnie, Kilmany parish, Fifeshire, Scotland. Her father, James McCormick, was of Irish descent and her mother, Janet Mitchell, descended from some of the oldest families in Fifeshire.

Margaret, also called Maggie, was married on January 9, 1832, at Hawkleymuir, Dysart parish, Fifeshire, to William McFarland, a widower nine years her senior. She raised his eight-year-old son and fourteen-year-old step-daughter along with her own children. Her husband's mother, Mary Blair, also made her home with the family. They lived in the hamlet of Boreland in a stone cottage on the estate of the Earl of Rosslyn, where her husband was employed as a coal miner.

The McFarlands were among the first in the area to join the LDS Church, being converted by George D. Watt, the first convert baptized in England. Margaret's baptism took place in the North Sea on the 24th of June 1842. She taught her children Christian principles and supported her husband as he served as Presiding Elder of the Pathhead Branch of

the Church until they were able to leave Scotland and join the Saints in Utah.

Margaret, her husband, six children, and a daughter-in-law, sailed from Liverpool on January 17, 1855, on the ship Charles Buck. They crossed the plains in the Richard Ballantyne Company, arriving in Salt Lake City on September 25th of the same year. They first settled in American Fork where they had old friends from Scotland, moving to Weber County in the spring of 1859. Her husband and sons took up a large tract of land in what is now West Weber on the low lands south of the Weber River. Living conditions were very primitive and difficult for the first few years there. One of her greatest sorrows was the death of her youngest child, daughter Janet, that first winter in West Weber, due to exposure in a frigid unfinished cabin.

Margaret was a fine mother and homemaker. One of the grandsons said she was "the sweetest, cleanest smelling woman I ever knew. She went Quietly along, doing what she intended to, a natural born peacemaker." She passed away at her home in West Weber on 10 Jan 1886 at age eighty-one. She and her husband are buried in the Ogden City Cemetery.

MATILDA POOL WESTERN MCFARLAND

BIRTHDATE: 29 Mar 1838
Malaga, Malaga, Spain
DEATH: 1 Nov 1903
West Weber, Weber, Utah
PARENTS: Thomas Pool
Eliza McCormick
PIONEER: 17 Oct 1853
John Brown Company
SPOUSE I: John Western
MARRIED: 26 Oct 1853
Salt Lake City, Utah
DEATH SP: 1864
Meadow, Millard, Utah

CHILDREN:
Elizabeth Jane, 29 Dec 1854
Mary Ann, 15 Dec 1856
Emma Florence, 9 Jan 1860
John Francis, 29 Jan 1862
Sarah Ellen, 5 Apr 1864

SPOUSE II: James McFarland
MARRIED: 3 Jun 1867
Salt Lake City, Utah
DEATH SP II: 14 Dec 1915

CHILDREN:
Thomas Pool, 8 Mar 1868
Alexander, 5 Jun 1870
Archibald Charles, 12 Aug 1872
Francis Joseph, 20 Jun 1874
Matilda, 28 Sep 1875

Matilda (Tillie) Pool was born in Spain in 1838 of English parents. Her father was helping with the iron industry in Spain, but they returned to England in 1850. She joined the LDS church in 1851. Her mother was a member and her father gave his consent, but never joined.

Matilda sailed for America with the John Western family, on the ship "Camillus" in 1853. They left Kanesville with the John Brown Company to cross the plains. Matilda's sweetheart, George Martin, died on the plains, and so she was persuaded to marry John Western as a plural wife. They arrived in the valley 17 Oct 1853, and she married John on 26 Oct 1853. The family settled in the Cedar City area and Matilda bore five children before John died in 1864.

Matilda then went to West Weber to be near her mother's sister Margaret Mitchell McFarland. A few years later she married James McFarland, son of Margaret, as his second wife, and had five more children. Matilda was a good homemaker, cook, seamstress and mother. She was also an active Relief Society and community worker. She served hot meals to men working on the railroad near her home. She always stood up for the principle of polygamy. Besides her ten children, she raised two grandchildren when her daughter died. Matilda died in 1903 at West Weber, Weber, Utah after a painful fight with cancer.

MARTHA ANN SMUIN MCFARLANE

BIRTHDATE: 8 Aug 1847
Abbington, Berkshire, England
DEATH: 13 Nov 1913
prob Salt Lake City, Utah
PARENTS: John Smuin
Jane Honey Smuin
PIONEER: 1866
by wagon
SPOUSE: James McFarlane
MARRIED: 5 Oct 1867
Salt Lake Valley, Utah
DEATH: 13 Mar 1921
Salt Lake City, Utah

CHILDREN:
James, 1 Aug 1868
Mary Jane, 7 Jun 1870
Martha Ann, 29 Sep 1872
Joseph Clark, 1 Oct 1874
John Clark, 24 Mar 1877
Louisa, 19 May 1879
William Carl, 23 Sep 1881
Arthur, 12 Nov 1883
Harriet Ellen, 20 Feb 1886
Florence Elizabeth, 17 Feb 1888
Lawrence Clyde, 14 Aug 1896

Martha Ann Smuin McFarlane was born in England. She was the second child of thirteen children. Only four grew to maturity. Martha Ann was the first of the family to leave for Utah. She was eighteen years old. Her parents went with her to Liverpool, England to see her board the ship. Two of her girlfriends were going with her. They traveled in the care of Brother and Sister Andrews who were close friends of Martha Ann's parents. It was in the early Spring of 1866 that their great journey started. The ship was six weeks in crossing the Atlantic Ocean. They were met at Florence, Nebraska by teamsters and covered wagons, with provisions and food for the trip.

It was during the journey that her life's romance began. Because her shoes were worn and thin, James McFarlane noticed her predicament. He was driving a yoke of oxen, having been called on a mission to go to Florence, Nebraska and bring a load of freight to Utah. He invited Martha Ann to ride in his wagon. A few years later they were married. Martha Ann often related an experience she had on the last night before entering the Salt Lake Valley. Her shoes had worn out and her feet were raw and bleeding. When the people of the camp were asleep, and as soon as it was light enough to see, she set out for the City. As soon as the stores were opened she purchased a new pair of shoes and went back to meet the caravan as it moved toward the City.

Martha Ann and James had eleven children; a son died when he was but three years old. They made their home in Ogden where Martha Ann was a member of the Ogden Tabernacle Choir. When her husband was transferred to Salt Lake City in 1896 they made their home there. In 1896, as Utah entered statehood, the Salt Lake Women's Democratic Club was organized. Martha Ann was one of the original members of this club. Martha Ann was five feet two inches tall. She weighed about 105 pounds. She had dark brown hair, blue eyes, thin lips and a pleasant personality. She served in the Relief Society for more than forty years. She also did a great amount of Temple work. Martha Ann died 13 Nov 1913.

MARY ANN NEAS MCFERSON

BIRTHDATE: 29 Jan 1824
Butler County, Pennsylvania
DEATH: 12 Apr 1906
Lewiston, Cache, Utah
PARENTS: Peter Neas
Lucinda Ellen Martin
PIONEER: 6 Oct 1851
Orson Hyde Company
SPOUSE:
Dimon Runnels McFerson
MARRIED: 29 Nov 1845
Nauvoo, Illinois
DEATH SP: 14 Feb 1875
Kaysville, Davis, Utah

CHILDREN:
Sarah Ellen, 20 Oct 1846
William, 10 May 1848
Abner, 14 Sep 1849
Delilah, 5 Jan 1852
Lydia, 26 Aug 1853
Israel, 14 Sep 1855
Jedediah, 7 Dec 1856
Miriam, 12 Oct 1858
Mary Ann, 4 Nov 1860

Rhoda Marilda, 6 May 1863
Dolly, 7 Mar 1865
David, 31 Mar 1867

Mary Ann Neas was born in Pennsylvania in 1824. She was fifteen when she first heard the gospel, and seventeen when she was baptized into the Church. In May 1844 Mary Ann and her sister started for Nauvoo, and were there soon enough to hear the Prophet preach before he was killed.

Mary Ann married Dimon Runnels McFerson in 1845. He was a widower with a small daughter, Amilla Jane, and was fifteen years older than Mary Ann. They had twelve more children, two of them dying as infants.

In 1851 they started for the Salt Lake Valley with the Orson Hyde Company. On the trail they were robbed by some prowling Indians. Mary Ann did not sleep well after this, but felt more like standing guard. They traveled for days without making a fire. They finally arrived in the Valley on October 6th, and went on to Kaysville to settle. They lived in a dugout until a home could be built.

Mary Ann was one of the women who organized the Kaysville Ward Relief Society, and she served as a teacher for twenty-five years. She later was President of the Primary organization. Mary Ann was devoted to the gospel, had a pleasing disposition and was always ready to help those in need. Her husband passed away in 1875 in Kaysville. Mary Ann was a widow for thirty-one years and died in Lewiston, Cache, Utah in 1906 at the age of eighty-two years. She is buried in Kaysville, Utah.

MARGARET CALDWELL CLARK RHODES MCGARY

BIRTHDATE: 6 Nov 1840
Paisley, Renfrewshire, Scotland
DEATH: 17 May 1876
Silver City, Grant, New Mexico
PARENTS: John Clark
Lillias Barbour
PIONEER: 1852
Independent Wagon Company
SPOUSE I: Joseph Rhodes
MARRIED: 1859
Logan, Cache, Utah
DEATH SP: 19 Jan 1860
Salt Lake City, Utah

CHILDREN:
Joseph Rhodes, Jr., 9 Jun 1860

SPOUSE II: William Henry McGary
MARRIED: 7 Mar 1868
Salt Lake City, Utah

CHILDREN:
William, 1869
Son (twin), 1871
Son (twin), 1871

Charlotte Lillias, 7 Mar 1874
Maggie May, 2 May 1878

Margaret Caldwell Clark was born in Scotland in 1840. Her parents were among the first converts to the Church in Scotland in 1837, prior to her birth. In 1841 the family set sail for America on the ship "Rochester." On this same ship were Brigham Young and other apostles returning from their missions to Great Britain.

Arriving in Illinois, the Clark family settled in LeHarpe, Illinois, about 22 miles from Nauvoo. After the martyrdom they crossed the Mississippi and finally settled at Winter Quarters in Iowa. They came across the plains in 1852 with an Independent Company, and after arriving in Utah they went North to the Ogden area. Margaret's father died just two years after coming to Utah.

In 1859 when Margaret was nineteen years of age, she married Joseph Rhodes, who had come into the territory with Johnston's Army. He was from Texas. Their happiness was shortlived when he was killed by a cattle rustling gang on 20 Jan 1860. Her son, Joseph Jr., was born the following June.

Eight years later Margaret married William Henry McGary in the Endowment House in Salt Lake City. She had five more children but they all died at birth or soon thereafter, leaving only Joseph Jr. surviving. In 1872 the family moved to Silver City, New Mexico, where silver had been discovered. On 17 May 1878, just fifteen days after the birth of her last child, Margaret McGary died. Her last words were, "Take my boy back to Utah." She was thirty-seven years old.

ELIZABETH COLLINS MCGHIE

BIRTHDATE: 1 May 1807
Ireland
DEATH: 24 April 1897
Millcreek, Utah
PARENTS: Barney Collins
Elizabeth Farrell Collins
PIONEER: 10 Oct 1854
By Wagon
SPOUSE: William McGhie
MARRIED: 29 July 1831
Kirkoswald, Ayr, Scotland
DEATH: 17 May 1866
Millcreek, Utah

CHILDREN:
William, 8 Jan 1830
Elizabeth, 6 Jan 1832
Sarah, 21 Dec 1833
John, 9 Jan 1835
Sarah, 9 Jan 1840
Agnes, 24 July 1843
Henrietta, 2 Mar 1846
Henrietta, 1 Mar 1849

Elizabeth was born in 1849 in Ireland. She was the fourth of seven children. She moved to Scotland with her parents in 1813. She married William, who was almost four years her senior, in 1831. She joined the LDS Church 4 Sep 1843. She sailed for America on the Ship "Windermere" 22 Feb 1854. Elizabeth arrived in the Salt Lake Valley 1 Oct 1854. She had buried five of her eight children before 1854, while still in England.

Their daughter Elizabeth was married in St. Louis at the start of their journey. She gave them nine grandchildren, the delight of their lives. They were in Utah twelve years when William passed away. Elizabeth was a widow for thirty years, passing away at age ninety on 24 April 1897.

ISABELLA LINDSAY MCGHIE

BIRTHDATE: 17 Oct 1834
Glasgow, Lanarkshire, Scotland
DEATH: 20 Apr 1910
Sugar House, Utah
PARENTS: Alexander Lindsay
Annie Mathie Lindsay
PIONEER: 16 Sep 1861
Ira Eldredge Wagon Company
SPOUSE: James McGhie
MARRIED: 28 Sep 1858
Scotland
DEATH: 16 Jul 1920
Sugar House, Utah

CHILDREN:
Isabella, 15 Dec 1859
Annie Rebecca, 22 Aug 1861
James, 24 Mar 1864
Helen, 14 Mar 1867
Robert Lindsay, 14 Apr 1874
Catherine Curtis, 11 Aug 1877

Isabella Lindsay McGhie was a woman of faith and courage. While still a young girl, she left school to work in a woolen mill. Soon after, she was put aboard a ship for America to teach girls to weave during the voyage. The ship was wrecked and drifted back to Ireland. Isabella ran away and returned to her sister's home in Scotland. While she was there, two Mormon missionaries preached the Gospel to her. When they came to the doctrine of the hereafter and baptism for the dead, Isabella became vitally interested. During the period of the shipwreck, her mother, who had died several years earlier, appeared to her in vision and asked for her help. Isabella believed that the LDS doctrine was an answer to her mother's request. She soon was baptized a member of the Mormon Church.

When Isabella and her husband, James, whom she had married in Scotland, arrived at Florence, Nebraska with their twenty-month-old daughter, Isabella was expecting another child. Seven weeks later she gave birth to her second daughter, Annie Rebecca, in Wyoming Territory, near Independence Rock during a mid-morning stop. Three weeks later, 16 Sep 1861, the emigrant company entered the Salt Lake Valley.

Isabella and her family first lived in the Twentieth Ward in Salt Lake City. They then moved to Sugar House, southeast of Salt Lake City. While there, Isabella's husband was called on a mission to Indiana, leaving Isabella to support and care for her four children who still lived at home. Letters that she wrote to James during this period have been preserved. They tell of difficult financial circumstances and of Isabella's accepting a call, against James' advice, to become President of the Sugar House Ward Primary.

Isabella had strong opinions which she wrote in letters to her husband. She wrote of a man whom she believed to be a "perfect infidel." He did not believe in a personal God nor a resurrection of the body. Isabella told him that she would rather lay her girls in their graves than see them marry one like him. She also had great faith. She wrote of her son, James, being nearly barefooted, who found a splendid pair of boots while he was cutting oak brush. They fit him even though he was hard to fit. She asked, "What do you think of that? Where do you think they could have come from?" Isabella believed in the providences of God.

She participated in both Relief Society and Primary in the Sugar House Ward. She lived a full life. She continued to correspond with her children. A final letter to a daughter concludes with a sad note, "I can't see what I write, so goodbye." Isabella died 20 Apr 1910 in Sugar House. Her husband died in 1920.

MARY MCBLAIN MCGHIE

BIRTHDATE: 27 Jul 1832
Scotland
DEATH: 11 May 1921
Butlerville, Utah
PARENTS:
Alexander McBlain (McBlane)
Mary McMaster
MARRIED: 1 Oct 1854
Daniel Garn Wagon Train
SPOUSE: William McGhie Jr.
MARRIED: 31 Dec 1850
Scotland
DEATH: 21 Nov 1902
Butlerville, Utah

CHILDREN:
William, 20 Dec 1851
Alexander, 8 Nov 1853
Mary (Butler), 25 Oct 1855
Agnes (Miller/Covert), 2 Sep 1857
John, 15 Aug 1859
Joseph, 9 Aug 1861
Thomas twin, 22 Jul 1863
Elizabeth (Blair), 22 Jul 1863
Sarah Jane (Colbrook), 8 Nov 1865
Henrietta (Hansen), 19 Mar 1868
Jane/jean (Buehler), 7 Oct 1870
Margaret Annie (Staker), 27 Mar 1873

Mary was born in Scotland, 1832. At age eighteen she married twenty-year-old William McGhie, Jr., 31 Dec 1850. He was a member of the LDS church, baptized Dec 1843. They made their home in Scotland for the birth of two children. They made plans to emigrate to America. Mary was not a Mormon, however she was willing to leave her family and friends in Scotland and come with her husband and his family to Salt Lake City, Utah.

They left Liverpool 22 Feb 1854 on the ship "Windermere." A Terrible epedemic of Small Pox broke out among the passengers. Little William was a victim to it. He and his father were quarantined in the bottom of the ship until better. On the morning of Apr 20 the ship entered the mouth of the Mississippi River and arrived at New Orleans Apr 23. They went up the Mississippi River on the steamboat "Grand Tower" to St. Louis, Missouri and continued on to Kansas City, Missouri. The McGhie families were assisted financially by their friend Thomas Boam who married Elizabeth McGhie in St. Louis, Missouri. On 2 Jul 1854 the Daniel Garr Co. left Kansas City. They arrived in Salt Lake City 1 Oct 1854. The McGhie's along with the other families were advised to settle east and a little south of the city proper, in what was known as Mill Creek. They stayed one year and left for Provo Valley to work in a saw mill. They returned to Mill Creek for ten or eleven years where five more children were born to them.

About 1867 they moved back to Salt Lake county where they took up a homestead at the mouth of Big Cottonwood Canyon. They built a nice log cabin and developed the land into a fine place. It had a natural spring on it, so there was plenty of water for a large garden and orchard of all kinds of fruit trees and berry bushes. There was a lush pasture for the cows and horses. The small community of Big Cottonwood soon became known as Butlerville. Here the last three of their family of twelve children were born. William was the Postmaster for some years and Mary aided in this responsibility. She was a large woman. She had dark brown hair, parted in the middle, and a bob in the back. She had blue eyes, always wore dark clothes, and wore a little black bonnet tied under her chin. She was a kind and happy woman, and a clean housekeeper. She was a good cook and made the best bread in town. She sold and/or traded her special yeast for supplies.

She was a widow for nineteen years. She passed away 11 May 1921 at the age of eighty-nine in Butlerville, the result of cancer in the gland of her neck. She was buried beside William in the Murray Cemetery.

ANN HOSSACK MCGREGOR

BIRTHDATE: 7 Feb 1822
Balfrone, Sterlingshire, Scotland
DEATH: 4 Feb 1899
Salt Lake City
PARENTS:
Archibald John Hossack
Agnes Gurley Hossack
PIONEER: Sep 1852
David Wood Wagon Company
SPOUSE: William McGregor
MARRIED: 28 Dec 1892
Scotland
DEATH SP: 10 Sep 1892
prob Salt Lake City, Utah

CHILDREN
son, died at birth
Agnes, 13 Aug 1843
Campbell, 7 Jun 1845
Jane Matilda, 21 Sep 1847
James, 10 Mar 1850
Ann Maria, 21 Aug 1853
William, 2 Nov 1855
Isabelle, 15 Oct 1858
Sarah Emily, 10 Feb 1861
Daniel Wells, 28 Aug 1865

Ann was born in Scotland, the second child of a family of three. Her parents were of moderate circumstances and as young girl she worked in a calico print company. The wages were small. In 1848, when the Mormon missionaries were preaching in Scotland, Ann studied the Gospel against her parents' wishes and knew by the power of prayer that the Church was true. On 28 Dec 1841, Ann married William McGregor in Glasgow, Scotland and the same year she was baptized into the Church. Ann and William became the parents of ten children; four were born in Scotland.

During these years, there was opposition from her family which she bore with faith. She would take her babe in her plaid shawl and walk seven miles to the Church meetings and then walk home more cheerful then before going. They emigrated to America in 1849. They arrived in Missouri and stayed there for a time making preparations to cross the Plains. On 18 Mar 1850, another son was born. After three years of preparation, Ann and William bought a wagon, an ox and a cow to begin their journey West. In Council Bluffs, Iowa they were assigned to Captain David Wood's Company. Ann with her little girls and two boys, trudged happily along. She put her children to sleep at night with a lullaby in Scottish. When her children's shoes wore out, Ann would make shoes from whatever they had, sometimes from her dress or burlap to keep their feet from burning in the sand. Their provisions were low but when the cow was milked the milk was divided with the needy.

They arrived in the Salt Lake Valley in Sep 1852 only to find brush and a few homes built. Their first home was adobe brick and one long room. When Johnston's Army caused the Saints to go South, Ann took the children alone because William remained as an officer to help guard Salt Lake City. They returned to their home in 1858 in the Second Ward.

Ann was the first Sunday School Teacher of a bible class of girls, all of whom loved her. She was a Counselor in the Ward Relief Society. She was secretary of the Wheat Fund until the wheat was placed in the general storehouses. There were several hundred bushels to be accounted for. During her early years in Utah she worked hard and at one time emroidered on a baby's dress for six months for a farmer who gave her one hundred pounds of flour. The flour was $25.00 per hundred and calico a dollar a yard. When her husband took another wife, Brigham Young gave him a recommend and said, "Brother McGregor, never forsake your first wife for she is truly a noble woman." Ann was considered to be the "mother" of the Ward. She was always ready to care for the distressed. She bore many wonderful testimonies. Ann died 4 Feb 1899, and was buried 7 Feb, on her seventy-seventh birthday. Her husband had died seven years earlier.

SARAH FISH SMITH MCGREGOR

BIRTHDATE: 24 Oct 1828
Compton, Sherbrook, Quebec, Canada
DEATH: 5 May 1905
Parowan, Iron County, Utah
PARENTS: Horace Fish
Hannah Leavitt Fish
PIONEER: 21 Sep 1848
Brigham Young Wagon Company
SPOUSE: John Calvin LaZelle Smith
MARRIED: 12 May 1846
Nauvoo Temple, Nauvoo, Illinois
DEATH SP: 30 Dec 1855
Parowan, Iron County, Utah

CHILDREN:
Horace Calvin, 25 Mar 1849
Sarah Jane, 16 Mar 1851
Nancy Francetta, 4 Mar 1851
John LaZelle, 8 Jul 1855

SPOUSE: William Campbell McGregor
MARRIED: 28 Apr 1857
Endowment House, Salt Lake City, Utah
DEATH SP: unknown

CHILDREN:
Adelbert Fish, 4 Apr 1858
Ellen Elnora, 6 Aug 1860
William Campbell, 5 Jan 1863
Julia Hannah, 18 Jun 1865
Joseph Franklin, 16 Aug 1868
Donald Alpine, 9 Apr 1876

Sarah's family was converted to the LDS Church in Canada and eventually moved to Nauvoo, Illinois. Sarah was sixteen years old at the time of the martyrdom of Prophet Joseph Smith and Hyrum Smith. She had vivid memories of that terrible and dark time. She was a bride of eleven days when she and her husband, John Calvin LaZelle Smith, left Nauvoo. Her father had made the family wagon, but had no team. He borrowed a team and hauled the wagon down to the river where they crossed on May 23, 1846. In later years, Sarah boasted how she had made their first home after they were married. They had gone down the Des Moine River and camped near Farmington. Her husband had built a shelter with four poles. The top was covered with willows and leaves to protect them from sun and weather. Then her husband became ill with chills and fever. It was then Sarah proceeded to build a sod house around the poles. She took a shovel and cut pieces of sod from near the creek. She laid them on a calf or deer hide and dragged the sod up to the poles and placed the sod one on top of another until she had all four walls built up. There were no windows, only a front door. John was sick a long time. They lived there close to a year.

In 1847, she, her husband, and her parents left Farmington and went to Council Bluffs. They left Winter Quarters, Nebraska on May 26, 1848 with Brigham Young's Wagon Company and arrived in Salt Lake Valley on September 21, 1848. They helped to settle Centerville, Utah. They were later called to settle Parowan on May 8, 1851. Shortly after their arrival in Parowan, her husband was called upon to serve as the first Stake President and served until his death in December of 1855.

Sarah was left with four children, a large home, and part owner of the flour mill. She took in boarders and acted as a midwife and nurse for the sick in the community for years. In 1856, William Campbell McGregor was sent to Parowan to help build the fort. He boarded at Sarah's and fell in love with her. He had cows and horses and was very industrious. They were married and Sarah bore him six children. After her mill burned down, Sarah decided to sell milk, butter, cheese, soap, and honey. She was famous for her homemade sage cheese.

For many years she served as an officer in the Relief Society. She believed in charity and visits to the sick. She loved people and loved to help people whether white or Indian. She lived a most unselfish life. She caught cold one day while she was making soap and it developed into pneumonia. She died and was buried in Parowan, Utah.

TAMAR STOKES MCGUIRE

BIRTHDATE: 11 Jan 1848
Bolsover, Derbyshire, England
DEATH: 13 Apr 1938
Riverton, Salt Lake, Utah
PARENTS:
Jeremiah (Stocks) Stokes
Fanny (Frances) Walker Stokes
PIONEER: 29 Aug 1859
James S. Brown III Wagon Co.
SPOUSE: John William McGuire
MARRIED: 14 Sep 1867
Salt Lake Endowment House
DEATH: 16 Oct 1879
Draper, Salt Lake, Utah

CHILDREN:
John William, Jr., 15 Jun 1868
Fannie Louisa, 4 Mar 1871
James Benjamin, 18 Jan 1873
Maud Eveline, 10 Mar 1875
Robert Alvin, 22 Oct 1876
Louis Miles, 16 Sep 1878

The Stokes family joined the LDS Church in Bolsover, England and were baptized when Tamar was one year old. Tamar was baptized on April 11, 1856. After they became "Mormons," the children were refused admittance to the local school, so their mother taught them at home. The family left England for America on May 22, 1856 on the ship, "Horizon," and arrived in Boston Harbor on June 30, 1856. They lived in Boston for three years to earn sufficient funds to come to Utah. In 1859, they crossed the plains in the James S. Brown III Wagon Company and arrived in Salt Lake Valley on August 29.

They spent the winter in Salt Lake City and then moved south to Draper in March of 1860. Tamar met John William McGuire who had come to Draper as a volunteer blacksmith with Johnston's Army. When Johnston's Army left the valley, John decided to remain and bought a thirty acre farm in Draper. Tamar married John in the Endowment House in Salt Lake City. They built an adobe house of two rooms and became the parents of six children, all born in Draper. Tamar became widowed at the age of thirty-one after just twelve years of marriage. John was killed by a run-away team of horses. Tamar continued to run the farm, raise her children, churn and sell butter, take in washing, or any other kind of work to earn a living. She always paid her tithing and most of the time, it was paid with butter, eggs, or what little cash could be earned. She was a Relief Society Visiting Teacher for many years. She helped to sew rags together to be used for making rugs. She donated beautiful hand work, and made many other sacrifices for her family and church. After the children were grown, she became a nurse and midwife. She helped to bring three hundred children into the world before her death at age ninety.

ANNIE BIRCH MCINTIRE

BIRTHDATE: 26 May 1852
Manchester, England
DEATH: 2 Jan 1935
Salt Lake City, burial Price, Utah
PARENTS: Joseph Flitcroft Birch
Dorothy Chambers
PIONEER: 1855
Richard Ballantyne Company
SPOUSE:
Erastus William McIntire
MARRIED: 23 Nov 1874
Salt Lake City, Utah
DEATH SP: 8 Jan 1902
Price, Carbon, Utah

CHILDREN:
Annie Dora 31, Oct 1875
Margaret Frances, 3 Sep 1877
Caroline Isabell, 13 Feb 1880
Edith Viola, 29 Dec 1881
Madelina Alice, 25 Sep 1883
Artemisa, 8 Sep 1885
Erastus William Jr., 21 Jul 1887
Jennie LaSell, 5 Dec 1890
Joseph Birch, 5 Dec 1890
Wallace Ezra, 1 Apr 1892
Otto, 5 Aug 1894

Annie Birch left England in 1855 with her parents, baby sister and grandmother. Annie had her 3rd birthday on the ship "Chimborazo." They joined with the Richard Ballantyne Company under the Perpetual Emigration fund to come to Utah. Tragically, her little sister took ill and died on the way, and was buried near the Sweetwater River.

Annie was married to Erastus William McIntire in 1874 in Salt Lake City. At first they lived in Paragonah, Utah, where they had three children. In 1881 they were among the first settlers in Price, Utah. Her father helped to build the railroad through Price and Spanish Fork Canyons. He built an eating house, store and rooming house along the railroad tracks in Price, and Annie helped with these businesses. He also was known as Dr. Birch and practiced medicine from a railroad car. Annie developed midwife skills and helped deliver many of the new town's babies.

Annie's husband was the Justice of the Peace and Annie was involved in helping him with his duties. Annie and her sister Isabell planted poplar trees that lined Main Street in Price for many years. They also planted fruit trees that produced abundantly. Annie died in 1935 in Salt Lake City, but is buried in Price, Utah. Her husband passed away in 1902.

MARIA CALDWELL MCINTOSH

BIRTHDATE: 17 Feb 1824
Lanark, Landrick, Ontario, Canada
DEATH: 17 Jul 1897
Mt. Pleasant, Sanpete, Utah
PARENTS: David Caldwell
Mary Ann Vaughn Caldwell
PIONEER: 23 Sep 1851
John Smith Wagon Company
SPOUSE: William McIntosh
MARRIED: 17 Sep 1841
Toronto, York, Canada
DEATH: 4 May 1899
Mt. Pleasant, Sanpete, Utah

CHILDREN:
John Ephraim, 13 Jun 1842
Mary Ann, 27 Jul 1845 (died age 2
David Hyrum, 5 Sep 1847 (died an infant)
William Henry, 18 Apr 1849
James Franklin, 8 Jan 1852
Melissa Jane, 27 Jul 1854
Alice Maria, 16 Sep 1857
Abraham Edward, 4 Mar 1860
Lillian Elizabeth, 11 Jan 1863
Caroline Janette, 1 Nov 1865
Joseph Alber, 8 Mar 1869

Maria Caldwell was baptized a member of the LDS Church on January 2, 1837 in Lanark, Canada when she was thirteen years old. When she was seventeen, she married William McIntosh in Toronto, York, Canada. Maria and her husband left Canada on foot with their possessions in bundles under their arms to gather with the saints. They suffered much sickness and poverty. They went by canal from Toledo, Ohio to Cincinnati. From there they went to St. Louis where they remained for two years. They went to Council Bluffs on the steamer, Monroe and Light Foot. Many people fell victim to Cholera. Maria and William were shoved from the boat at Savanna, a few miles from St. Joseph, Missouri where they stayed for another two years. William obtained work to earn the provisions they would need for their trek across the plains. They started with John Freeman on May 1, 1851 through rain and mud until they reached Council Bluffs. They joined a group with Brother Smith as the Captain of 100 and Brother David Lewis appointed as captain of their ten. They arrived in the Great Salt Lake Valley in September of 1851.

They moved to Sessions Settlement (Bountiftil) to live with her father-in-law, John McIntosh. Then they bought a farm in West Jordan. Due to lack of water and lost crops, they moved to Rush Valley, Utah. Maria cared for her own children, her widowed mother, and her dead sister, Jane Leonard's, two children. She also served in her church. Their family was called to the Dixie Mission in Panaca, Utah. When the Nevada state line was drawn, it included Panaca in the state of Nevada, so they were released from their mission. They lived in Panguitch and then moved to Tooele. In 1892, she and her husband moved to Mt.

Pleasant to live near their son, Abraham. In her later years, her health declined and she preceded her husband in death.

MARY ELIZABETH BANCROFT HARPER TAYLOR MCINTOSH

BIRTHDATE: 21 Feb 1832
Shaw, Lancashire, England
DEATH: 19 Nov 1907
Basin, Cassia, Idaho
PARENTS: Richard Bancroft
Jane Harper
PIONEER: Fall of 1860
By wagon
SPOUSE I: William Taylor
MARRIED: Abt 1851
in England (later divorced)
DEATH SP: date unknown
in Pennsylvania

CHILDREN:
Ruben William 28 Dec 1851
Martha Jane, 4 Oct 1854

SPOUSE II: Solomon Parks McIntosh
MARRIED: 21 Dec 1860
Grantsville, Tooele, Utah
DEATH SP: 6 Jan 1902
Basin, Cassia, Idaho

CHILDREN:
Margaret Floranza, 1 Jan 1862
Polly Ann, 15 Mar 1863
Mary Elizabeth, 4 Dec 1864
Solomon Parks Jr., 6 Jul 1866
John William, 3 Mar 1868
Samuel, 25 Oct 1869
Lousiana, 27 Oct 1871
James Stanley, 15 Oct 1873
Hyrum, 14 Sep 1875

Mary Elizabeth Bancroft was born in England in 1832, the seventh of seven children. She first married William Taylor about 1850, either in England or in Pennsylvania. They were soon divorced and she took her mother's maiden name of Harper. There were two children. She joined the LDS Church and traveled across the plains with a wagon train in 1860.

Solomon was told by his first wife as she was dying at Winter Quarters, that he would meet his next wife on the plains and she would be standing by a wagon with a child on each side. On his next to the last trip across the plains, freighting, he met Mary exactly as Polly had told him. They were married in Grantsville in 1860.

With a large group of Saints their family pioneered in Basin, Cassia, Idaho in 1861. They built homes and established a branch of the LDS Church. Mary was a good mother, raising a large family. Solomon had two children by his previous marriage, and Mary had two children by her first marriage. She and Solomon had nine children making thirteen in all. Both of them passed away in Basin, Cassia, Idaho; Solomon in 1902 and Mary in 1907.

HELEN (ELLEN) OMAN MCKAY

BIRTHDATE: 14 Aug 1807
How, Thurso Parrish, Caithness, Scotland
DEATH: 12 Dec 1887
Pleasant Grove, Utah
PARENTS: David Oman
Isabella Sutherland Oman
PIONEER: 29 Aug 1859
James S. Brown Wagon Co.
SPOUSE: William McKay
MARRIED: 12 Jan 1839
Giese, Thurso, Caithness, Scotland
DEATH SP: 3 Jun 1893
Ogden, Weber, Utah

CHILDREN:
Isaac, 2 Nov 1839
Isabella, 26 Aug 1842
David, 3 May 1844
Barbara, 30 Oct 1846
Williamena, 30 Oct 1846
John George Sinclair, 18 Nov 1848
Catherine, 4 May 1850

They were anxious to join with the Saints in Zion and made arrangements to sail on the ship, "Thornton," to cross the ocean. They arrived in Castle Gardens, New York on June 12, 1856. Because they had been defrauded of most of their money, they were forced to stay in New York for two years. They then went to Iowa City, Iowa, where they stayed another year gathering goods for the trip west. If it had not been for this forced delay, they would have crossed the plains with the ill-fated Willie Handcart Company. They joined the James S. Brown wagon train at Council Bluffs. Their captain approached them and told them of a lame widow and her daughter who were stranded. Ellen offered to let the woman take her place on the wagon, so she and her family walked across the plains. They arrived in the Salt Lake Valley on August 29, 1859.

The family settled in Ogden permanently and also helped to settle Huntsville. Ellen was adept in spinning, coloring and making cloth. Her husband made a loom for her and hired a weaver so she could make linsey for dresses, jeans for pants, blanket covers, and lids for beds.

She was the grandmother of David O. McKay, Prophet and President of the LDS Church. She died in Pleasant Grove, Utah on 12 Dec 1887, at age eighty.

JULIA SOPHIA RAYMOND MCKEE

BIRTHDATE: 9 Feb 1831
Hempstead, Long Island, New York
DEATH: 12 Nov 1901
Huntington, Emery, Utah
PARENTS: Samuel James Raymond
Elizabeth Dean
PIONEER: 15 Sep 1852
John Tidwell Company
SPOUSE: Hugh McKee
MARRIED: 22 Nov 1847
Council Point, Iowa
DEATH SP: 2 Feb 1897
Huntington, Emery, Utah

CHILDREN:
Mary Elizabeth, 13 Dec 1851 d. infant
Julia Alvira, 2 Jun 1854
Eliza Jane, 7 Sep 1856
Persis Minerva, 9 Oct 1858
Clarinda Rosella, 17 Jan 1861
Louisa Marinda, 5 Jun 1863

Julia Sophia Raymond was born in New York State in 1831. As a child she attended the Methodist Church. In 1841 the Mormon Elders came into their community to preach the gospel, and her parents joined the Church. Becuse her parents were Mormons, Julia was persecuted by her schoolmates. Julia was baptized in 1845 and soon after her father was called to Nauvoo to assist in building the Temple.

They made many friends in Nauvoo, but all too soon had to leave that beautiful city. Julia was married in 1847 to Hugh McKee. In 1850 she was given her mother's baby, Sheavas Annie, who was fifteen months old, to raise when her mother died. In 1851 her own baby was born and died soon after birth.

Julia and Hugh came across the plains and arrived in Salt Lake City 15 Sep 1852. They settled in Spanish Fork, where Hugh built the first adobe house. She passed away in Huntington, Utah, in 1901, at the age of seventy years. Her husband died in 1897.

MARY TWEED MCMILLEN MCKEE

No
Photo
Available

BIRTHDATE: 1 Jun 1795
Westmoreland Co., Pennsylvania
DEATH: 10 Nov 1851
Council Bluffs, Pottawattamie, IA
PARENTS: Daniel McMillen
Elizabeth Robb
PIONEER: Died along the way
SPOUSE: David Daniel McKee
MARRIED: 11 Jul 1816
Slippery Rock, Butler, Pennsylvania
DEATH: 1 May 1847
Mt. Pisgah, Union, IA

CHILDREN:
Thomas, 1 Apr 1817
Daniel, 25 Jul 1818
James, 6 May 1821
Jonathan, 22 Dec 1821
Hugh, 2 Nov 1824
William, 7 Oct 1825
Priscilla, 2 Jun 1827
Letty, 14 Apr 1828
Eliza Ann, 28 Aug 1833
Martha Jane, 2 Jun 1835

Mary and David accepted the gospel and were early converts to the Church of Jesus Christ of Latter-day Saints, having been baptized together on May 15, 1837. Although we have little detailed information of this family's movements from 1837-1846, we know that they eventually felt the spirit of gathering and desired to relocate to Nauvoo, Hancock County, Illinois to be with others who shared their faith. Here Mary and her family spent a number of very happy and productive years. Their children had the benefit of growing up for a time in a well organized and spiritually rich atmosphere. The family had the benefit of mingling with the Prophet, Apostles and other Church leaders as well as assisting in the construction of the Nauvoo Temple. Mary and her family were acquainted with the prophet Joseph Smith and his brother Hyrum. After their assassination, two of Mary's sons were given the assignment to assist in secretly transporting the bodies of Joseph and Hyrum back to Nauvoo from Carthage. In the cold of winter, February 1846, the larger part of the Church fled their homes in Nauvoo under the threat of death from the Illinois mobs. They traveled on together and finally found the beautiful location of Mount Pisgah on the Grand River, Iowa, 172 miles from Nauvoo, where many saints camped. Companies of saints were organized and moved on to the Missouri River and Winter Quarters as fast as they could supply or outfit for the trip. Although it was possible to be moderately comfortable in this place, it soon came to an end for the McKee family as it did for the others whose hearts were set on following the body of the Church to the Rocky Mountains. Because of hardships and deprivations, and the ever present unsanitary situations, diseases broke out often, and here again the Cholera had a death hold on its victims. Mary's husband David McKee, contracted this killer and passed away on 1 May, 1847.

Sorrow and death again hit this family on 10 Nov. 1851. The family's dear mother, Mary Tweed McKee had taken ill and left her earthly cares for a crown of Glory in heaven. Perhaps Cholera was the grim reaper again. Since they left their home in Nauvoo and while on this agonizing journey, one brother and both parents had died and left the rest to mourn the loss, while only half the journey had been completed. Mary could now peacefully attend to her Father in Heaven's business knowing that in spite of her death, the children she left behind made it safely to Zion.

PERSIS MOORE SWEAT MCKEE

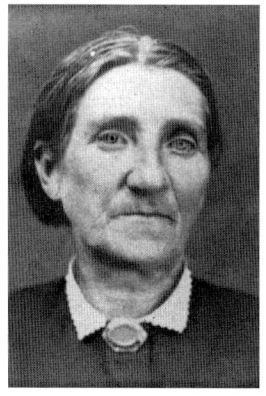

BIRTHDATE: 29 Jun 1820
Andover, Maine
DEATH: 4 Oct 1918
Spanish Fork, Utah
PARENTS: John Sweat
Mary (Polly or Molly) Marston
PIONEER: 15 Sep 1853
by Wagon
SPOUSE: Thomas McKee
MARRIED: 14 Jan 1841
Bloomfield, Illinois
DEATH SP: 30 Aug 1875
Salina, Utah

CHILDREN:
Mary Elizabeth, 22 Nov 1841
Louisa Matilda, 13 Jan 1844
David Thomas, 11 Feb 1847
Polly Marston, 25 Aug 1849
Harriet Persis, 20 Feb 1852
Eliza Ann, 23 Dec 1854
Sarah Lotecia, 26 Jun 1858
Elizabeth Jane, 20 Apr 1860
Susan Sophia, 15 Dec 1862

Persis lived near Andover, Maine in a sugar maple grove. She was the fifth child in a family of twelve children, five sons and seven daughters. She was taught to spin cotton, flax and wool, and make her own clothing and household materials. When the making of maple sugar season was on, the children would travel many miles on horse back to the different maple groves. Persis liked to ride horse back.

She came from a very religious family. Her parents never allowed them to work on a Sunday. They heard the gospel at a meeting held at the Sweat home. The spirit was so strong that many were converted. Persis was baptized August 15, 1833, with family members and a large number of others who attended the meeting. Not long after they joined the church, they were forced to sell their nice home and farm and gather with the saints in Kirtland, Ohio. She left Kirtland July 6 1838 with 529 souls for Far West. Traveled 870 miles through the heat, dust, storms, unfriendly settlers with little food. They reached Far West 2 Oct 1838. Far West was at the height of persecution, and they were forced on to Illinois where they helped build the city of Nauvoo.

Persis, still a young girl, worked at the printing office. She folded the leaves to the second edition of The Book of Mormon. One morning while working, she noticed that the type was set wrong and told the Editor. The press was stopped, the mistake was found and corrected. The Prophet Joseph Smith gave her a book of her own, folding and autographing it for her. She prized it dearly and would never part with it.

She married Thomas KcKee and they had five children born in Illinois. Her oldest daughter was buried there.

They came to Utah in 1853. The journey lasted from June 15 to Sept 15, 1853. With their four children they made a home in Palmira (Spanish Fork), Utah. Persis became known for her bravery with the Indians. In Spanish Fork she had four more children. Sometime later they moved to Salina, Utah where her husband died in 1875 at age fifty-eight. Persis never remarried but remained a widow for forty-three years. She lived many years with her youngest daughter and husband.

She was very industrious, always willing to aid in the progress of the Church. For each missionary who went into the field, she would knit them socks, for which she had corded the wool and spun it into yarn herself.

When she died at ninety-eight years of age, she had a strong testimony of The Book of Mormon, had all her faculties, could always see some good in everyone, do little jobs around the house, darn and mend, read small print without glasses, had a good sense of humor, a loving smile and kind words of advise. She is buried in the Spanish Fork Cemetery.

She was best known to the people of Spanish Fork as "Grandma" and had the distinction of being the oldest resident of the city.

HELEN WHYTOCK MONCUR MCKELL

BIRTHDATE: 12 Nov 1819
Auchtermuchty, Fife, Scotland
DEATH: 5 Feb 1856
Palmyra, Utah, Utah
PARENTS: John Whytock
Katherine Whytock
PIONEER: 15 Sep 1852
John Tidwell Wagon Company
SPOUSE I: Robert Moncur
MARRIED: 14 Aug 1838
Dundee, Angus, Scotland
DEATH SP: 15 Dec 1845
Dundee, Angus, Scotland

CHILDREN:
Robert, 24 Feb 1839
Katherine Lovet, 18 Oct 1841 (died 3 months)

SPOUSE II: Robert McKell
MARRIED: 26 Jan 1846
Dundee, Angus, Scotland
DEATH SP: 8 Jun 1903
Spanish Fork, Utah, Utah
CHILDREN: None

Helen was born in Auchtermuchty, Fife, Scotland to John and Katherine Whytock. She married Robert Moncur of Dundee, Scotland in 1838 when she was eighteen years old. They were the parents of two children. Helen's husband was not physically well and died just seven years after they were married. The following year after his death, Helen married Robert McKell who had worked with Robert in his trade of building coaches and carriages. Helen was a

seamstress and made a living at it. When she married Robert, they pooled their savings and purchased a store selling groceries. She also sold her homemade scones which became very popular. It was in their store that someone left a pamphlet about their religion. They did some inquiring around about the pamphlet and in this way became interested enough to join the LDS Church. After they joined, the minister of their former church was so upset with them that he led the others in their town to quit patronizing the McKell establishment. They sold their business and home and left for America on an old ship, "Argo," in January of 1850. After arriving in New Orleans on March 8, 1850, they took a river boat to St. Louis. Then they continued to Council Bluffs, Iowa. Some time was spent in preparation before they went on to Green River where they joined the John Tidwell Wagon Company. They arrived in the Salt Lake Valley on September 15, 1852.

They went to Palmyra, Utah and since it was late in the fall, a cave was found to house them until better weather came and a house could be built. For the next three-and-a-half years, she practiced her trade as a dressmaker. She died at the age of thirty-seven years.

FANNY GUNN MILLER MCKENZIE

BIRTHDATE: 6 Dec 1837
Beer, Devonshire, England
DEATH: 22 Jun 1892
St. George, Washington, Utah
PARENTS: John Gunn
Mary Emma Smith
PIONEER: 18 Oct 1862
Henry W. Miller Company
SPOUSE I: Henry William Miller
MARRIED: 25 Oct 1862
Salt Lake City, Utah
DEATH SP: 9 Oct 1885
Farmington, Davis, Utah

CHILDREN:
James Gardner, 19 Sep 1863
George Albert, 16 Oct 1865
Lovenia Ellen, 14 Dec 1867
John Henry, 11 Sep 1870
Albert Edwain, 9 Jan 1873

SPOUSE II: John Robert McKenzie
MARRIAGE: date unknown
CHILDREN: None

Fanny Gunn was born in England in 1837. In England she was a business woman, who did fancy doll dressing. She even had a business card which advertized her talents dressing English and foreign dolls.

Fanny left her home in England and traveled to the United States by herself. She joined the Henry W. Miller Company at Winter Quarters and walked most of the way across the plains. She married Henry W. Miller just one week after arriving in Salt Lake City. She was his second wife. In 1864 they were called to make a settlement at Beaver Dam, Arizona. Here she made friends with the Indians, and sometimes the Indian boys would help her with chores and her garden. Their pay was a slice of "White Woman's" bread. When a flood washed away the dam in 1867 they moved to St. George, Utah

In St. George she had a nice home where Relief Society, Church and Civic Leaders were entertained. She was active in Relief Society, and helped to make the rag carpets for the aisles and stairs in the tabernacle and temple. She developed a recipe for "Pickled Grapes," which consisted of a syrup made of vinegar, molasses and spices.

After her husband died in 1885 she married John Robert McKenzie, who helped to finish the rearing of her children. The date of marriage is not known. She died in St. George, Utah in 1892.

MARY ANN CROWTHER MCKENZIE

BIRTHDATE: 10 Nov 1840
Duffield, England
DEATH: 10 Jun 1910
Salt Lake City, Utah
PARENTS: John Crowther
Mary Taylor
PIONEER: 2 Sep 1857
Jesse B. Martin Company
SPOUSE: David McKenzie
MARRIED: 28 Feb 1859
Salt Lake City, Utah
DEATH SP: 10 Mar 1912
Salt Lake City, Utah

CHILDREN:
Alpha, 8 Nov 1859
David Jupiter, 30 Mar 1861
John, 5 Mar 1863
Mary, 3 May 1864
Joseph, 12 May 1866
Philip, 24 May 1868
Samuel, 1869
Elizabeth, 13 May 1870
Brigham, 9 Mar 1872
James A., 18 Sep 1873
Christina Isabella, 7 Feb 1875
Gene Bell, 7 Feb 1875
Julia, 18 Dec 1877
William, 9 Mar 1880
Nephi, 13 May 1885

Mary Ann Crowther was born in England in 1840. She was baptized in 1851, at the age of eleven, and when she was sixteen she left England on the ship "George Washington" to come to Utah. In Iowa City she was assigned to the Jesse B. Martin Handcart Company, and they arrived in Salt Lake City on 2 Sep 1857.

Mary Ann married David McKenzie on 28 Feb 1859 in Brigham Young's office, and they became the parents of fifteen children, several of them dying very young.

Mary Ann was a beautiful woman, and very close to her daughters. She supplied all the medicine for the family. She made pills and rolled them in flour, and one family member said they tasted "awful." She also made a hair tonic which she bottled. The family never washed their hair with water, but used this tonic, and it would lather and then would be rubbed dry. She never gave anyone her recipes. She was also a good cook and famous for her pound cake.

Mary Ann was very well educated and one always had to use one's very best manners when she came to visit. She died in Salt Lake City, Utah on 10 June 1910. Her husband died 10 Mar 1912, also in Salt Lake City, Utah.

MARY HAMILTON MCKINLAY

No
Photo
Available

BIRTHDATE: 12 Jan 1808
Bo'Ness, Linlithgow, Scotland
DEATH: 26 Mar 1887
Provo, Utah, Utah
PARENTS: Thomas Hamilton
Mary Forsyth
PIONEER: 26 Oct 1864
William Hyde Company
SPOUSE: George McKinlay
MARRIED: 9 Apr 1824
Tanent, East Lothian, Scotland
DEATH SP: 14 Nov 1876
Provo, Utah, Utah

CHILDREN:
James, 2 Mar 1823
George Jr., 6 Aug 1825
Mary, 16 Jun 1828
James, 23 Dec 1830
Robert, 22 Oct 1832
George Hamilton, 6 Jan 1835
Archibald, 1 Mar 1837
Jeanette, 1839
Peter, 1841
William, 1843

Mary Hamilton was born in Scotland in 1808. She married George McKinlay in 1824 at the Inveresk Church in Tanent, East Lothian, Scotland. They became the parents of ten children, all of them born in Scotland, and several of them dying as children.

George was a coal miner in Scotland, but through an accident he lost the use of his left arm. While crossing the plains he met with another accident, breaking both legs. This was quite a hardship for Mary as she had to take over the many things he could not do.

The family came to America on the ship "Hudson," and across the plains with the William Hyde Company by ox team and wagon in 1864. They settled in Provo, Utah, where George became engaged in herding cattle and sheep. Mary dried fruit and sold it and made soap for those who could afford the luxury, and they soon had a humble little adobe house, which stood near the area where the BYU Campus is now located.

Three of their sons, Peter, Archibald and Robert remained in Scotland and never embraced the gospel. George died in 1876, and Mary died in 1887, both of them at Provo, Utah, Utah.

SARAH ANN LEHMAN EWINGS MCKINNEY

No
Photo
Available

BIRTHDATE: 27 Sep 1803
Montgomery, Pennsylvania
DEATH: 1 Aug 1867
Camp Floyd, Cedar Valley, Utah
PARENTS:
Joseph Lehman (Leighman)
Ann Streeper
PIONEER: Sep 1850
John Bair Independent Company
SPOUSE I: Alexander Ewings
MARRIED: Abt 1820/21
DEATH SP: 18 Nov 1831
Philadelphia, Pennsylvania

CHILDREN:
Robert Alexander, 21 Oct 1821
John, 14 Aug 1823
Charles, 11 May 1825
Thomas Bradford, 16 Mar 1828
Eliza Ann, 4 Apr 1830
Elias & Elizah (twins), no date given, died as infants

SPOUSE II: Hugh McKinney
MARRIED: 30 Apr 1832
Montgomery, Pennsylvania

CHILDREN:
William, 4 Feb 1833
James, 25 Jun 1835
Henry, 20 Jun 1837
Sarah Jane, 30 Oct 1838
Hugh, 25 Aug 1840
Jacob Leighman, 16 Mar 1843
Joseph Edson, 16 Apr 1846

Sarah Ann Lehman (Leighman) was born in Pennsylvania in 1803. She married Alexander Ewings in about 1820/21, and they had six sons and one daughter. Alexander died in 1831 in Philadelphia, Pennsylvania.

After his death Sarah Ann married another Irishman, Hugh McKinney in 1832, and was later endowed in the Nauvooo Temple in 1846. Sarah Ann had six more sons and one daughter with this marriage also. They came to Utah in Sep 1850 with the John Bair Company, and settled in Cottonwood, Salt Lake County. Only two children from her first marriage, Eliza and Thomas came to Utah with the family.

When the soldiers of Johnston's Army were in Utah, the family moved to Camp Floyd, where they kept a boarding house. They also had a store and sold cakes and pies. Sarah Ann was President of the Relief Society at Camp Floyd, and the meetings were held in her home. They had

their own sheep and carded and spun the wool into cloth. Sarah Ann died 1 Aug 1867 at the age of sixty-three, and is buried at Camp Floyd, Cedar Valley, Utah.

JANE BROUGH MCKINNON

BIRTHDATE: 22 Feb 1860
Longton, Staffordshire, England
DEATH: 14 Sep 1927
Randolph, Rich, Utah
PARENTS: Samuel Brough
Elizabeth Bott
PIONEER: 15 Oct 1863
By wagon
SPOUSE: Archibald McKinnon
MARRIED: 10 Jul 1879
Salt Lake City, Utah
DEATH SP: 18 Apr 1915
Randolph, Rich, Utah

CHILDREN:
Arthur, 21 Apr 1880
Nephi, 8 Aug 1881
Jane, 5 Oct 1882
Sarah, 10 Nov 1864
William George, 24 Oct 1867
Katherine, 23 Sep 1888
Ernest Archibald, 28 Sep 1890
Ada Prudence, 8 Sep 1893
Phoebe, 29 Sep 1895
Benjamin, 11 Nov 1897
Ray Baxter, 12 Jan 1901

Jane Brough was born in England in 1860. She was a pioneer from the age of three when she left England with her parents on the ship "Cynosure" in 1863. The family crossed the plains with the Samuel D. White Company. Jane was allowed to ride in a wagon because she had been crippled with polio when very young and could not walk.

They arrived in Salt Lake City in Oct 1863, and lived first in a dugout in Porterville, Utah. Later they moved into a two-room log home.

The Brough family was called to settle in Bear River Valley, or Randolph, Utah, in 1870. Even though she had to use a crutch Jane always did her share of the work. In 1879 she married Archibald McKinnon Sr. in the Endowment House, as a plural wife. He was twenty-three years older than she was. They had a family of eleven children, whom she loved dearly, and also the children from the first wife, who called her Aunt Jane.

Jane did a lot of fancy work, worked in the Church, and sang in the Ward Choir. She always wore a long black dress with a spotless white apron. Her hair was long and bound up in a bob at the back of her neck. Her crutch was highly polished. She was sorrowed by the death of her husband in 1915, but kept busy with her duties to her children, Church, and community. Jane died at the family home in Randolph in 1927 and is buried in the Randolph Cemetery.

MARY MCKAY MCKINNON

BIRTHDATE: 16 Nov 1838
Glasgow, Scotland
DEATH: 4 Aug 1925
Randolph, Rich, Utah
PARENTS: Robert McKay
Agnes Shields
PIONEER: 4 Sep 1859
George Rowley Company
SPOUSE: Archibald McKinnon
MARRIED: 9 Aug 1861
Salt Lake City, Utah
DEATH SP: 18 Apr 1915
Randolph, Rich, Utah

CHILDREN:
Donald, Abt 1862
Robert, 2 Dec 1863
Archibald, 26 Jul 1865
Peter, 7 Feb 1868
Malcolm, 26 Oct 1869
Randolph Stewart, 29 Sep 1871
Samuel, 3 Sep 1873
Lemuel, 17 Jul 1875
John Francis, 22 Sep 1877
Donald, 26 Oct 1879
Mary (Rees), 9 Dec 1881

Mary McKay was born in Glasgow, Scotland in 1838. When she was young her parents joined the LDS Church and as a result suffered much bitterness from their friends. In 1855 they boarded the ship "Isaac Wright" and came to America. A brother and sister of Mary's had come to Utah earlier.

Mary and her parents stayed in Massachusetts for three years and worked in the cotton mills to earn money to finish their trek to Utah. They came with the George Rowley Company in 1859, arriving on 4 Sep in Salt Lake City. It wasn't long before Mary fell in love with Archibald McKinnon, who was also from Scotland. They lived in Salt Lake City for ten years, then were asked to settle in the Bear River Valley at Randolph, Utah.

Mary loved her flowers and rose bushes but found that they did not survive in the harsh winters in Randolph. She finally found other plants that were more suited to the climate. She was a Relief Society worker for many years. She had a beautiful singing voice and sang in the Ward Choir. In 1877 Archibald took a crippled girl to be his second wife. This was hard on Mary but she did her best to cope. After the Manifesto, it was decided that Archibald would live with his second wife since she had small children. Archibald died in 1915, and Mary died in 1925, both in Randolph, Rich, Utah

CORNELIA ANN STILSON MCKNIGHT

No
Photo
Available

BIRTHDATE: 22 May 1836
Little Beaver, Beaver, Pennsylvania
DEATH: 28 Jun 1865
Kingston, San Bernardino, Calif.
PARENTS: William B. Stilson
Susannah Young
PIONEER: 17 Oct 1849
SPOUSE: James McKnight
MARRIED: 17 Mar 1854
DEATH SP: 6 Apr 1865

CHILDREN:
James Arthur, 15 Dec 1854
Fanny Young, 8 Oct 1856
Willard Henderson, 23 Sept 1858
Susan Rebecca, 29 Mar 1861

Cornelia Ann Stilson, born 22 May 1836, Little Beaver, Beaver Co., Pennsylvania, the only daughter of Susannah Young to grow to maturity. As a child she lived with her mother in Nauvoo, Illinois, then in St. Louis, Missouri. In 1849 when thirteen years old, with her mother and brother, James A. Little, she crossed the plains in a wagon drawn by oxen, arriving in Salt Lake City in October of the same year. At the early age of sixteen she was an orphan without the love and guidance of a mother.

On 17 Mar 1854 she married James McKnight, son of John and Rebecca (Henderson) McKnight, in Salt Lake City. He was born 11 December 1828, Rathmullen, Donegal, Ireland. He died 6 April, 1906, at Portston, Townsend, Jefferson Co., Washington. She died 28 June 1865, Kingston, San Bernardino Co., California. Records in the Genealogical Archive show that McKnight married three other wives: 5 March 1857, Alvina Mackley; 20 December, Harriet Painter; 18 July 1863, Mary Ann Fielding.

Cornelia grew to womanhood, was a spirited lady fair to look upon and capable, but unhappily married. In order to free herself from a smooth-tongued, tyrannical husband she went away to California where she died.

–From Stilson Family Record

LYDIA PILCH THROWER BLACKBURN MCKNIGHT

BIRTHDATE: 6 Oct 1824
Hampton, Norfolk, England
DEATH: 7 Aug 1897
Minersville, Utah
PARENTS: James Pilch
Mary Leverage Pilch
PIONEER: 24 Sep 1862
Homer Duncan Wagon Company
SPOUSE: Thomas Thrower
MARRIED: 1 Sep 1845
Norwich, Norf., England
DEATH SP: 8 Aug 1862
Florence, Nebraska

CHILDREN:
Leah (Pyne), 21 Dec 1841
Ester/Esther, 1846 (died an infant)
John, 8 Feb 1848 (died an infant)
Lydia (Holdaway), 19 Oct 1849
Rachel (Marshall), 13 Feb 1854

SPOUSE II: Jehu Blackburn
MARRIED:
DEATH: 17 Mar 1879
Nephi, Juab, Utah
CHILDREN: None

SPOUSE: James McKnight
MARRIED: 1884
Minersville, Beaver, Utah
DEATH: 4 Oct 1908
Minersville, Beaver, Utah
CHILDREN: None

Lydia's father was a successful butcher. He built a large home and purchased a herd of cattle to fatten and sell. Her mother died when Lydia was thirteen which left Lydia with the responsibility of her father's home. On January 10, 1841, she was married to Thomas Thrower, who was a shoemaker by trade. They lived in Elham where their oldest child was born. Then they moved to Norwich where they heard the LDS Gospel. Lydia was baptized a member of the LDS Church in 1851. On April 23, 1862, Thomas and Lydia Thrower and their two little girls, Lydia and Rachel left England to go to America. They sailed on the "John J. Boyd" with 701 Saints. They arrived in New York on 1 June 1862. They crossed the plains in the Homer Duncan Wagon Company. One wagon was provided for twelve people. One evening, a terrible storm arose. The women and children were taken into the wagons. Thomas remained outside so there would be more room. He died three days later of pneumonia. Left without her companion, Lydia and the two little girls came on and arrived in Salt Lake City on September 24, 1862.

Lydia worked as a housekeeper in the home of Elias Blackburn. She later married Elias' brother Jehu Blackburn as his fourth wife. She lived with him on his ranch which was about seven miles from Minersville. They had a herd of cows to take care of. Forty pounds of cheese were made each day for ten days. Then butter was made the next ten days. They had sheep which had to be sheared. They had to pick the wool, spin, and weave it. She was a good nurse and helped deliver the babies of the other wives. She did not bear Jehu any children. At the time of the establishment of the United Order at Blackrock, Lydia was again in charge of making cheese and butter. It was hard work, but no matter what the church asked of her, she gave her best. When the Order was broken, she came out with practically nothing. When Jehu died, he left her with a small home where she worked at nursing, sewing, or anything she could. She nursed in many homes in Minersville. She had nursed the wife of James McKnight who had several children.

His wife died in childbirth which left him with all of his own children and the children of his daughter who had died leaving three children in his care. She stayed to help care for all of these children and eventually married James McKnight. They had a large home and ran a camp house where people could park their covered wagons and camp as they were on their way to the railroad in Milford. They also furnished accommodations in their home for those who did not camp. She sold her bread, butter, eggs, and home cured meat to the campers. She would also cook up a meal if they wanted one. She did marvelous quilting sewing. She loved music and would have her grandchildren sing. She served as President of the Relief Society for five years, and as a counselor for several years. She was a teacher in the Sunday School, a President of the Y.W.M.I.A. She was held in the highest esteem by all who knew her because of her willingness to help those who were in need. She died on 7 August 1897.

DESDEMONA WADSWORTH FULLMER SMITH BENSON MCLANE

BIRTHDATE: 6 Oct 1809
Huntington, Luzerne, Penn.
DEATH: 9 Feb 1886
Salt Lake City, Salt Lake, Utah
PARENTS: Peter Fullmer
Susannah Zerfass Fullmer
PIONEER: 19 Oct 1848
Willard Richards Wagon Co.
SPOUSE: Joseph Smith, Jr.
MARRIED: 1842
Sealing date 21 Jan 1846
Nauvoo, Hancock, Illinois
DEATH: 27 Jun 1844

CHILDREN: None

SPOUSE: Ezra Taft Benson
MARRIED: 21 Jan 1846
Nauvoo Temple, Nauvoo, Hancock, Illinois
DEATH: 3 Sep 1869
Ogden, Weber, Utah
CHILDREN: None

SPOUSE: Harrison Parker McLane
MARRIED: 1853
Salt Lake City
DEATH: Unknown

CHILDREN:
Sarah Desdemona, 24 Aug 1855 (died an infant)

Desdemona had many spiritual experiences in her early life and was eager to join the LDS Church when she first heard about the Gospel in 1836 in Richland County, Ohio with her parents and other family members. She followed the church and its members as they were persecuted and driven from Ohio, to Missouri, and on to Illinois. She was present at Haun's Mill when the 1838 massacre took place, but was protected as she hid in the woods with her sister-in-law and her children. She lived in the Prophet's home for a period of time after moving to Nauvoo. Desdemona was one of the eighteen charter members of the first Relief Society that was organized on March 17, 1842 by the Prophet Joseph Smith and his wife, Emma. She was a fine seamstress and made the Prophet a white suit to wear at public events. She was one of the first members of the church to accept plural marriage and was married to the Prophet in 1842. She had many challenges to her support of Joseph Smith, but told detractors that "the Lord convinced me that he was a true prophet, and he has not told me he has fallen yet."

After his death and the completion of the Nauvoo Temple, Desdemona was sealed for eternity, by proxy, to the Prophet Joseph Smith by Brigham Young on January 21, 1846. On the same day, she was married for time only to Ezra Taft Benson. She traveled across the plains with the Willard Richards Wagon Company and arrived in the Salt Lake Valley on October 19, 1848. She lived with Ezra Taft Benson and his families until their marriage was canceled about 1852. She married Harrison McLane and had a daughter, Sarah Desdemona, by him. The baby lived only a month. A short time later, Desdemona and Harrison separated. She took her first married surname and was known as Desdemona Smith, widow of the Prophet Joseph Smith for the remainder of her life. She had moved near her brother, David Fullmer, and his family in Salt Lake. The rest of her life was dedicated to service and participation in many social and church activities in the Salt Lake Sixth Ward. Desdemona was a quiet and unassuming woman. She was greatly admired for her sweet humility, integrity, and love manifested by her support of the Gospel and the Prophet who brought the Gospel into the world.

SUSAN MORRIS GUILLIFORD MCLATCHIE

BIRTHDATE: 15 Jun 1834
"Neen Savage," Shrophire, England
DEATH: unknown
PARENTS: Mr. Morris (poss John)
Mrs Morris (poss Letitia)
PIONEER: by 1867
SPOUSE I: Mr. Guilliford
probably in England
MARRIED: unknown
DEATH: unknown

No Photo Available

CHILDREN: none

SPOUSE II: Samuel Russell McLatchie
MARRIED: 4 Oct 1869
Salt Lake Endowment House
DEATH: 2 Nov 1906
Kanosh, Millard County, Utah

CHILDREN:
raised four of other people

Susan was born in England, 1834. She was a widow with no children of her own when she emigrated to America in 1864 from England. She was probably baptized in England. She left no record. She brought with her a young nephew who was six years old by the name of William Henry Reynolds.

They first settled in Newark, New Jersey for two years. William was baptized at the age of eight in the East River, underneath a bridge late at night because of mob violence.

Susan and her nephew William crossed the plains in 1867 by ox team and settled in Wanship, Summit County, Utah. On 4 Oct 1869, Susan married Samuel Russell McLatchie in the Endowment House in Salt Lake City, becoming his third wife. In 1872, the family moved to Kanosh, Millard County, Utah. In Kanosh, the family consisted of Samuel and Susan, two teenage boys, William and Peter Nielson, and also two orphaned twin baby boys, Andrew and James Cortsen. Susan and Samuel were sealed and endowed in the St. George Temple 23 Jan 1884. Susan died in Kanosh, but there is no date of her death recorded. Samuel died 2 Nov 1906 and is buried in Kanosh, Utah.

Susan Morris Guilliford McLatchie was a true, Christian, pioneer woman of Utah. She served others by caring for the motherless and giving them good homes and the care and love they needed. She is to be honored for her pioneer spirit and a life lived well amidst trials and tribulations.

ELIZABETH SMITH MCLEAN

BIRTHDATE: 21 Dec 1828
Boness, W-Lthn, Scotland
DEATH: 24 Mar 1895
West Weber, Weber, Utah
PARENTS: Thomas Smith
Anne Smith Smith
PIONEER: 1861
Wagon train and Ox team
SPOUSE: Daniel McLean
MARRIED: 16 Apr 1847
Boness, W-Lthn, Scotland
DEATH SP: 1 Nov 1886
West Weber, Weber, Utah

CHILDREN:
Anne, 1847
Daniel, 19 Oct 1848
Mary Ann, 1850
Thomas, 1851
James, 17 May 1853
Agnes Owen, 7 Sep 1855
Hugh Owen, 19 Sep 1857
Margaret, 28 Oct 1859
Eliza, 1861

Elizabeth Smith was born in Scotland in 1828. She married Daniel McLean in Scotland, and they became the parents of nine children. Several of her children died as infants, and she was only able to raise three of them to maturity.

Elizabeth and her husband came to Utah in 1861 with a wagon train. Her last child, Eliza, was born while crossing the plains but only lived for three days. Elizabeth was a hardworking housewife. Her husband had been hurt in the mines prior to coming to Utah so she had to work hard to help provide for her family. When a very dear friend from Scotland died while crossing the plains leaving a small baby, Elizabeth took the baby and raised him as her own for a year of two. She was very active in the Church, especially in the Relief Society organization. Daniel McLean died in 1886 and Elizabeth died in 1895, both in West Weber, Weber, Utah.

EMMA RUTH STRAW MCLING

BIRTHDATE: 14 Sep 1845
Sheffield, Yorkshire, England
DEATH: 21 Apr 1888
Wanship, Summit Co. Utah
PARENTS: William and Mary
Richardson Straw
PIONEER; Sep 1863
Wagon train
SPOUSE: James(Jackson)
Wilford McLing
MARRIED: 19 Apr 1865
DEATH SP: 1888
Uintah Mts.

CHILDREN:
Eliza Ruth, 20 May 1866
Alice Rebecca, 15 Jun 1871
James Wilford, 22 Feb 1874
Joseph Hyrum, 8 Oct 1876

Emma Ruth Straw was born in 1845 in England to William and Mary Straw. She had an older sister Alice. Emma's father made scales and tools for measuring. The family had lived in the same house for forty years. Her family members were converted and baptized into the LDS Church. Emma was baptized in 1857. When she was a pretty young woman of eighteen years, she crossed the ocean with her mother on the ship "Amazon," and crossed the plains to join the Utah Saints in 1863. At that time, the writer, Charles Dickens, was working for a newspaper whose editor sent him to investigate the Mormon converts who were leaving England for Utah. He found the group aboard the "Amazon" to be very clean, very organized, were teaching school for their children, and were having a choir practice. He was most favorably impressed by what he witnessed.

Emma married Dr. James McLing in Coalville, Summit Co., Utah in 1865. James moved around a lot because he found it difficult to earn a living as a doctor. People paid what they could with produce, and very little cash. He worked for the Union Pacific Railroad, he homesteaded, and he even worked as a deputy sheriff in New Mexico for a time. It was on one of his journeys to Green River, Wyoming, that he disappeared. The family waited so anxiously for his return because Emma had become ill. As hopes for his safe return dimmed, Emma refused to see any other doctor, and consequently she died 21 Apr in 1888. She was just forty-three years old and she left her four children orphans. The oldest was nearly twenty-two years of age. Emma was a true pioneer woman who left her homeland for the gospel of Jesus Christ and endured the many hardships of pioneer life in Utah.

MARGARET DRUMMOND FERGUSON MCMASTER

BIRTHDATE: 15 May 1822
Greenock Renfrewshire Scotland
DEATH: 21 Apr 1894
Salt Lake City, Utah
PARENTS: John Ferguson
Margaret Drummond Ferguson
PIONEER: 1 Oct 1854
Daniel Garn Co. Wagon train
SPOUSE:
William Athol McMasters
MARRIED: 2 Sep 1842
Middle Parish, Paisley, Scotland
DEATH sp: 22 Jan 1887
Salt Lake City, Utah

CHILDREN:
John Brigham, 15 Aug 1843
Margaret Drummond, 15 Jan 1845

Grace Henderson, 6 Dec 1846
William Athol, 8 Jan 1848
Virginia Faithful, 9 Jul 1850
Isrellous (child)(Isralis), 14 Sep 1852
Donald Henderson, 16 Aug 1855
Alexander (child), 12 Aug 1857
James Bruce, 1 Jul 1859
Hannah Elizabeth, 16 Mar 1861
Mary Ann, 28 Apr 1863
Joseph Heber, 30 Jul 1865

Margaret Drummond Ferguson was born in Scotland in 1822. Her childhood days were spent among the hills and braes of bonny Scotland. She was brought up in the environment of religious and pious parents who were members of the Methodist Church. Her parents were kind and loving to their children and so her disposition was sweet and gentle. She had sympathy for all God's children, and was never too busy to render aid to her friends or to anyone in trouble or distress. Many came to her to seek comfort and advice. They never went away without feeling much better than when they came.

Margaret married William Athol McMasters, 2 Sep 1842, by Thomas Joap of the Middle Parish, Paisley, Scotland. The joined the Church of Jesus Christ of Latter-day Saints in her native land. She was the mother of fourteen children. The first five were born in Scotland, one was born in England, and the rest were born in Salt Lake City, Utah. Two children must have died. They lived in England for some time before coming to America. Isralis who was born in England, died while they were crossing the plains of America. In great sorrow and grief, she left her baby and faced the desert heartbroken and sick. They arrived in Salt Lake City 1 Oct 1854 after a long and very weary journey over land in a foreign country among strangers. Her first home in the valley was a small adobe house, infested with bugs and beetles. Here her first baby was born in America- a fine twelve pound boy, Donald Henderson. Margaret was half starved and weak. Her life was almost dispared of as she nursed him until blood came from her body. With good care, she soon gained back her health. They bought property just off Brigham Street and built a home with two rooms. Just as they were getting comfortable, another son was born. This family gathered their possessions and left for the southern part of the territory when word came that the government was sending an army to destroy the lawless Mormons. All was peaceful shortly and they returned to their home.

Margaret was a member of the choir for many years and she loved to sing the songs of Zion. Her husband was away from home often, working for the Church. She had much responsibility and care for her large family. John, her oldest son, was a great help and a blessing to her. Her husband left on a mission to England just before her last baby was born; the child was three years old before his father saw him.

Margaret was president of the 11th Ward Relief Society for many years and was loved for her kindness, charity and advice. Her life was made up of kind acts and deeds. She was never impatient or cross though her burdens were heavy and her cross hard to bear, and she never complained. She was a true friend and devout Christian. She always remembered she was a lady, never raised her voice in anger, or gave way to fault finding or fretting. She was always tidy in her appearance, her hair was always combed before she left her room in the morning.

ELIZABETH CATHERS MCMENEMY

No Photo Available

BIRTHDATE: Dec 1771
Londonderry, Ireland
DEATH: 20 Aug 1864
Salt Lake City, Utah
PARENTS: Francis Cathers, Sr.
Ann Patterson Cathers
PIONEER: Oct 1857
Wm. G. Young Ox Train
SPOUSE I: John McMenemy
MARRIED: abt. 1798
DEATH: Feb 1850
New Castle Co., Delaware

CHILDREN:
Ann, 11 Feb 1799
Elizabeth, 26 Dec 1801
Mary, abt 1803
Maria, 3 Dec 1806
Margaret, abt 1813

Elizabeth Cathers was born in Ireland in Dec of 1771. She came to America during the early years of this new nation. Whether she married in Ireland or her new country is unknown. She and her husband, fellow Irishman John McMenemy, lived in Cecil County, Maryland where their oldest children were born. Her last child was born in Delaware. It is not known exactly when the family moved to Delaware. It was in Delaware that she heard the LDS missionaries and joined the Church along with several of her married daughters.

Elizabeth journeyed with her daughter Ann McMenemy Mousley and other family members to Utah in 1857 when she was eighty-six years of age. She continued to be active, and went to the Endowment House in 1859. She finally died of "old age" in her ninety-third year while in Salt Lake City.

Elizabeth Cathers McMenemy's life was one of movement and change. She adapted to many circumstances in her lifetime with courage and with an inate toughness of mind and body. She was a true, faithful pioneer woman of Utah.

MARY MURDOCH MAIR TODD MCMILLAN

BIRTHDATE: 23 Nov 1819
Gaswater, Ayrshire, Scotland
DEATH: 5 Dec 1900
Heber City, Wasatch, Utah
PARENTS: James and Mary
Murray Murdoch
PIONEER: Oct 1866
Andrew Scott's Wagon Train
SPOUSE I: Allan Mair
MARRIED: 4 Jun 1841
Scotland
DEATH SP: 2 May 1897
Scotland

CHILDREN:
John, 6 Sep 1841
James M., 17 Dec 1843
Allan Foulds, 25 Dec 1845
Mathew, 3 Jan 1847
William, 3 May 1849
Mary (Lindsay), 31 Jul 1852
Jessie, 4 Nov 1854
Andrew, 18 Feb 1856
Alexander, 17 feb 1859

SPOUSE II: Thomas Todd
MARRIED: 1 Dec 1866
DEATH SP: 5 Oct 1909

SPOUSE III: Daniel McMillan
MARRIED: 26 Jun 1871
Salt Lake City Temple
DEATH SP: 29 Apr 1902
Heber, City, Utah

Mary Murdoch was born in 1819 in Scotland. Her father died when he was overcome by damp gas while trying to rescue a fellow worker from a well. This made it necessary for Mary to seek employment as soon as she was old enough. She worked mostly at farm homes, where she learned to milk cows, make butter and cheese, and at harvest time she worked in the field, binding the grain by hand. During the winter she attended school along with her sister Veronica. She helped to knit the family stockings. When she was about twenty years of age, she married Allan Mair, whom she had known since childhood. He was a steady, sober, young man who worked on the farm and herded the sheep. They were strictly religious people, observing the Sabbath and attending the Kirk regularly. They had a comfortable home, and although its furnishings were plain and simple, they were happy and contented and enjoyed it very much. They were blessed with nine children.

In 1850, the Mormon Elders came to Scotland preaching a new and strange doctrine. After their message, Mary and her mother were baptized by her brother John M. Murdoch, who had previously joined the Church and now had the authority to officiate in that capacity. Her husband refused to hear the new Gospel or to have anything to do

with it or anyone who had an interest in it. He had given his consent for his wife to be baptized, but it caused friction in the home, where all had been peace and harmonious before. The Savior had said while here on the earth that His gospel would have just such an effect as it did on this family.

Mary's brother John and his family and her mother had gone to Utah, and she felt left quite alone. She received an abiding testimony of the gospel, which gave her much comfort. She had tried to convert her husband, but to no avail. She lived in this manner for fifteen years. Her two older sons, James and John, had gone to America and made homes for themselves in the state of Maryland. Another son, Foulds, was married. She had not been able to teach the Gospel to any of them, and for this she sorrowed greatly–it was the most earnest desire of her heart that her three younger children would become members of the Church and she could see no other way than to leave her husband and home and to go to Utah in order to accomplish this. She confided this to her daughter, Mary, who was fourteen years old at the time. Mary agreed to assist all she could, and soon the plans were made for their going. Mary, the daughter, carried bundles when the mother got them ready, and took them to a home of a friend, to be ready when the time came for them to leave. The friend, John Aird, secured passage for them on the ship "Saint Mark." They lead the father to believe they were going to visit friends for a short time, so he had given his permission. The mother, Mary, Andrew and Alex reached Liverpool safely, boarded the ship in company with other LDS emigrants bound for New York. The crossing took four weeks, and was a fairly good voyage. A few days after their departure, the father learned of their real whereabouts and sent a cablegram to his sons in Maryland asking them to meet the ship and see if they could persuade their mother to return, and if not, to at least prevent the children from going to Utah.

The boys went to New York, only to find the emigrants had started their westward journey a few days previous. This family crossed the plains in the Andrew Scott's wagon train and passed through all the trying experiences of the pioneers making their dreary, tiresome journey of 1,000 miles. They reached their destination at Heber Valley in October 1866. They went to the home of her brother John M. where they were royally welcomed.

Not long after her arrival in Heber, she met Thomas Todd whom she married in polygamy. They were later divorced. She then met Daniel McMillan, a widower, whose family was grown. He was the village blacksmith and was a hard worker, and made good wages. He had very little property when she married him, but through her thrift, economy and hard work, she managed to save enough of his means to build them a very nice, red sandstone home, where they lived comfortably for many years.

Mary served as a practical nurse and helped many families in the community. She did beautiful handwork. She had a stroke and was bedfast for the last fourteen years of her life. She was paralyzed from her waist down. Even through this she was cheerful, and most always kept her hands busy doing beautiful netting lace. Mary Murdoch McMillan died 5 Dec 1900, at the age of eighty-one years. She was loved and respected by all who knew her and she never lost her faith in God or in the Gospel for which she had suffered so much, a true faithful pioneer woman of great fortitude and strength

JANNET DAVIES MCMILLEN (MCMULLAN)

BIRTHDATE: 24 Dec 1814
West Derby, England
DEATH: 21 Apr 1869
Heber City, Utah
PARENTS: William Davies
Phebe Roughley Davies
PIONEER: 4 Oct 1863
Thomas E. Ricks Wagon Co.
SPOUSE: Daniel McMillen
(McMillan/Mc Mullan)
MARRIED: 8 Dec 1844
Walton-on-the-Hill, England
DEATH: 29 Apr 1902
Heber City, Utah

CHILDREN:
Phebe Hannah, 18 Nov 1846
Ephraim, 14 Mar 1848
William, 9 Dec 1849
Mary Ellen, 30 Jun 1851
Margaret, 1853
Janett, 1855

Jannet Davies Mc Millen was born in England in 1814. She was baptized into the LDS Church in March 1857. She, her husband and two girls (the two youngest had died) left England May 20, 1863 on the packet ship "Cynosure" with the 125th company. There were 775 emigrating saints on board. Jannet left her two boys behind to finish their apprentice training and provisions were made for them to come to Utah later. Jannet's health was not good and the worry of leaving her sons along with the difficult trip passage and crossing the plains, took its toll. She rode in a wagon half the day and walked half a day crossing the plains. After they arrived the family settled in Heber City. Three years after her arrival, she passed away when just fifty-five years old.

MARY PIERCE MCMULLIN

BIRTHDATE: 27 Sep 1819
Vinyl Haven, Knox Co. Maine
DEATH: 30 Oct 1896
Heber City, Wasatch Co., Utah
PARENTS: Josiah and Susanna
Trundy Luce Pierce
PIONEER: 1855
Ox Team and Wagon Train
SPOUSE: Henry McMullin
MARRIED: 21 Apr 1842
Vinyl Haven, Knox, Maine
DEATH: 2 May 1885/1886
Heber City, Wasatch, Utah

CHILDREN:
Calvin Pendleton, 3 Nov 1843
Albert Ells, 15 Jul 1847
Alphonso Payson, 6 Nov 1849
Henry Lufkin, 4 Sep 1852
Edwin Pierce (child), 6 Jun 1854
Sarah Jane, 21 Oct 1856
Susan (child), 22 Jun 1858

Mary Pierce was born in 1819 to Josiah and Susanna Pierce in the state of Maine. She grew up on the beautiful Fox Islands off the coast of Maine. Mary married Henry McMullun in 1842. They had seven children, the first five were born in Maine, and the last two were born in Utah, one in Weber, and the other in Provo. This family were partners in helping build a pioneer community and in using their talents. He was a carpenter and ship builder. Mary, Henry, Mary's father and her brother Edwin were converted to the Church of Jesus Christ of Latter-day Saints by the missionaries in 1845. This family decided to remain in Maine and to not leave their beautiful home and island and loved ones and to live their religion to the best of their ability there.

The spirit of gathering came upon them, and they received a great desire to go to Zion with the Saints, and they were not content until they made up their minds to do so. Mary is quoted as saying, "I would have walked every step of the way, if necessary." They arrived in the valley of the Great Salt Lake in 1855. By the fall of 1861, they bought land in Heber City. With Henry's expertise as a carpenter and ship builder they became an integral part in building up the new community. They also became involved in building coffins; Henry made the coffin, Mary and her daughter would carefully trim the interior of the coffin to make it look as beautiful as possible with the materials available. This was more than a business, for they knew in advance that many would not be able to pay for their work or materials.

They first built a small home, then a larger one that served many purposes, and people, including the Heber City branch of the US Post Office. It also became the "McMullin House," the first hotel in the city. Travelers always planned on having good rooms, kept up by Mary, and first class meals which were cooked by her. The work of running the hotel required much effort. This big home had a large well built right into her kitchen. She did not have to go outside to get water like most others did. A pully was fastened to the ceiling directly above the well, making it easy to draw fresh cool water. Henry built a shelf above this area where butter, milk, cream and other perishable foods could be stored and reached easily. Henry died in 1886 which left Mary with the full responsibility of the hotel as her only means of livelihood. She continued her wonderful baking and cooking.

Mary was a kind, dignified, understanding woman who was a good employer to many boys and girls, and she helped many homeless, unfortunate persons. She was also an excellent seamstress and found time to card and spin wool, weave cloth, and make fine clothing for others as well as for herself. With a dose of Yankee independence learned early in her life, she was able so sustain herself. She also served in Church callings in the Relief Society in Wasatch Stake.

Mary's son Henry and family lived through the block from her, and she helped his wife and children when he was called on a mission. A bond of love was forged through mutual respect and admiration, an inspiration to all around them. Mary's death occurred 30 Oct 1895(96) and her son (on his mission) wrote "Go in peace. You have endured faithfully to the end and your reward is waiting you." A true pioneer woman of faith and extreme fortitude, she is an example to all.

SARAH ANN KAY MCMURDIE

BIRTHDATE: 2 Jul 1841
Pilkington, England
DEATH: 16 Feb 1919
Paradise Cache, Utah
PARENTS: John Rushton
Sarah Chatterley Kay
PIONEER: 1851
John Brown Company
SPOUSE: Samuel McMurdie
MARRIED: 5 Mar 1856
Cedar City, Utah
DEATH: 4 Jun 1922
Paradise, Cache, Utah

CHILDREN:
Harriet Elizabeth(child), 9 Mar 1858
Samuel Thomas Kay, 25 Nov 1859
Robert Kay, 17 Feb 1862
John Chatterley Kay, 17 Nov 1865
Mary Ann (Olsen), 16 Feb 1867
James Kay, 28 Aug 1869
Sarah Dorothy (Mills), 27 Aug 1871
Lillian Kay (Allen) 26 Jan 1874
Barnard Kay(child), 10 Dec 1875
Matilda Jane Kay(Allen), Oct 1879
Joseph Kay, 1881
Amy Kay(Neilson/Allen), 3 Dec 1888
Florence Alverna (Hughert), 21 Oct 1893

Sarah Ann Kay was born in England in 1841 to John and Sarah Kay. She was ten years old when she came to America in 1851. She traveled with the John Brown Company with her parents, a seven year old brother, a three year old sister and a new baby brother who was born in St. Louis, Mo., and her grandfather. They settled in the Salt Lake Valley until her father was called to help colonize Cedar City in 1854. She met and married Samuel McMurdie there in 1856. In 1860 they moved to Wellsville to help colonize that area. Two more children were born there. In 1864 they moved to Petersburg, then to Paradise where they built a two story log cabin as the family home. A large fireplace was in the kitchen where kettles hung. They also had a bake oven and no finer food could have been prepared that Sarah cooked. She had been skilled in the homemaking arts by her mother.

Sarah made sheets of fine white muslin. She made patchwork quilts with an outing flannel lining with carded wool batting between. She also made mutton tallow lights with cotton wicks spun from yarn, which were called bitches'and were lighted with matches.

Sarah was loved by the Indians as well as by the others in the community. She learned to speak the Indian language as well as she spoke English. She was very charitable to the Indians as she shared her delicious food with all. The Indian women would jump off their horses and run and hug Sarah. She was also good to the hired men on the ranch and would walk miles to take a bucket of lunch to them. She also carried food to the sick on many occasions. This family had a large dairy on their ranch. Sarah made and delivered butter and cheese to Logan and shipped processed milk for many years–all in a white-topped buggy. She was very charitable and loving to others.

Sarah had thirteen children, the last ten of them were born as they lived in Paradise, Utah. Sarah lived for fifty-five years of her life in Paradise. She died there 16 Feb 1917(19). Her husband lived until 4 Jun 1922. A great posterity honor these humble pioneers who so willingly helped settle the valleys of Utah, and who had great faith and fortitude to continue through trials and tribulations to colonize these areas. We honor them and pay a great tribute to their names.

MARY HUTTON MCMURRAY

No
Photo
Available

BIRTHDATE: 6 Nov 1801
Warrington Twp., York Co., Penn.
DEATH: 31 May 1896
Liberty, Bear Lake Co., Idaho
PARENTS: Simon Hutton
Mary Underwood Hutton
PIONEER: Oct 1852
Warren Snow Company
SPOUSE: John McMurray
MARRIED: 18 Aug 1821
Warrington Township, York, Penn.
DEATH SP: 4 Oct 1853
Salt Lake City, Utah

CHILDREN:
Ann (infant), 21 Jul 1822
Sarah(child), 12 Mar 1824
William(infant), 3 Oct 1826
Arabella (Wetherbee), 4 Nov 1827
James Hutton, 24 Dec 1829
Joseph, 13 Apr 1832
Mary Jane(child), 23 May 1834
Matilda Jane (Martindale/Mckennie), 17 Jul 1836
Charles K, 24 Jun 1838
Harriet Lucinda (Fairchild), 18 Jul 1840

Mary Hutton was born in 1801 in Pennsylvania to Simon and Mary Hutton. In 1820, John McMurray went to work for Simon Hutton in Warrington as a farmhand. The Huttons were Quakers. Mary married John McMurray on 18 Aug 1821 by a magistrate. Mary was censured for marrying outside the church. John had been born in Cumberland County, Pennsylvania in 1798. After their first two children were born, the family moved to Hogestown, Cumberland, Pennsylvania. Here these two children died. Their third child, a son, was born there, but died six days later. In 1826, John was on the tax records of Silver Springs Township, Cumberland, Pennsylvania, as a tailor and had no property. In 1827, Mary was admitted to membership in the Silver Springs Presbyterian Church, Cumberland, Pennsylvania. Their fourth child, a daughter, was christened at that church. Four more children were born there. In 1830, the family moved to Ohio, but moved back and forth across the border of Ohio and Pennsylvania for the next few years. They built a home, and seemed to have prospered. John worked at farming, while his wife ran a hotel, a wayside inn or tavern as they called it.

It is not known when or where the family joined the Church of Jesus Christ of Latter-day Saints or when they left Ohio. Their son, James, was baptized in Beaver Co., Pennsylvania in March 1844. The parents joined the Church, sold their possessions in Ohio, and arrived in Nauvoo just at the time the bodies of the Prophet Joseph Smith and his brother Hyrum were brought to Nauvoo from Carthage, where they had been martyred. They laid in state in the Nauvoo Mansion House, viewed by a constant throng of people who filed in and out of the Mansion rooms.

James took care of their household goods while the parents went to see the bodies of the martyred men.

Mary often spoke of attending the meeting where Brigham Young was sustained as President of the Church, of how he looked like Joseph Smith as he spoke. Everyone at that meeting said that the mantel of the Prophet Joseph had fallen on Brigham. That meeting was held 8 Aug 1844, when Brigham Young, president of the twelve, was chosen to lead the Church.

John and Mary received patriarchal blessings from John Smith, uncle of the Prophet, at Macedonia, on 23 Sep 1844, and they were endowed in the Nauvoo Temple 6 Feb 1846. This family experienced many persecutions with the Saints in Nauvoo, and they took refuge in Council Bluffs, Iowa, with thousands of other homeless Saints. They built what shelter they could, and made the best of their conditions until such time as they could leave for the valleys of the mountains. They left Kanesville, Iowa, in Jun of 1852 as a part of the Warren Snow company. The hard and tiresome journey was difficult, but Mary rejoiced that she, her husband, and her family of six living children came safely through and made it to the Great Salt Lake Valley, arriving early in Oct 1852.

Mary's husband passed away 4 Oct 1853, in Salt Lake City, just one year after their arrival. He was a stalwart in the Church, holding the office of High Priest at the time of his death. Following his death, the family moved to Grantsville, where a daughter was living. Apparently, Mary stayed with family in Ogden and Oakley, Utah and Liberty, Bear Lake Co., Idaho. Mary passed away 31 May 1896 at the age of ninety-four-and-a-half years at Liberty, and was buried there. Mary McMurray was a true Mormon Pioneer woman, and should always be honored for her faith and fortitude, having given up much for her religious beliefs, and living as a widow for forty-three years, as she experienced the development of Utah from its very early years until its statehood in 1896. A great heritage is passed to her posterity.

JANET REID MCNEIL

BIRTHDATE: 2 Aug. 1824
Tranent,East Lothian,
Haddingtonshire, Scotland
DEATH: 6 Dec 1900
Logan, Cache Co., Utah
PARENTS. Peter Reid
Margaret Martin Reid
PIONEER: 4 Oct 1859
Wagon Train
SPOUSE: Thomas McNeil
MARRIED: 19 June 1845
Tranent, Scotland
DEATH SP: 9 Feb 1891
Logan, Cache Co., Utah

CHILDREN:
Margaret, 14 April 1846
Thomas Reid, 8 Dec. 1847

Emily, 19 June 1849
Peter Reid, 28 Feb. 1851
John Reid, 24 Feb. 1853
James Reid, 24 Oct. 1854
Charles Thorton, 1 May 1856
Joseph Reid, 14 Jan. 1859
Janet Jane, 14 March 1861
William Reid, 3 May 1863
Hiram McNeil, 30 Oct. 1864
George McNeil, 17 Oct. 1866

Janet was the fourth child of a family of nine girls and one boy. Her father died when she was thirteen so she worked to help her family in the coal pits of Scotland. In 1843 when a law was passed prohibiting female labor in the coal mines she obtained a job as a house maid for two years until she married Thomas McNeil. Her husband was the President of the LDS Branch in Scotland. Just before her seventh child was born he was released allowing them to leave for America. On board the ship "Thorton" in the Liverpool Harbor her son Charles Thorton was born. When Capt. Charles Collins and the Doctor found a baby had been born aboard the ship they felt it was good luck for the voyage.

They landed at Castle Garden, New York after a trying six-week trip. They were sent to St. Louis until spring, which is where their three-year-old son, John, died. When spring came President Snow asked them to make a settlement 100 miles west of Florence, Nebraska. While on the boat to Missouri all the children except Margaret came down with the measles. They established the settlement of Genoa, where they lived for two years. They then went 100 miles west to settle Woodriver but their stay was short due to hostile Indians. They arrived in Ogden on 4 Oct 1859. They left Ogden for Cache Valley 20 Oct 1859. She carded, spun, dyed and wove wool for their clothes, and raised chickens, pigs, and sheep. She worked by his side in the garden. She helped with the family income by selling rhubarb, vegetables, fruits, butter and eggs. She served as visiting teacher and a counslor in the Relief Society. She was known as a woman who never spoke a vulgar word nor ever gave ear to lightmindedness or vulgarity. She was always plesant but determined and independent. She was quick, active, and graceful. She was taken to her daughter Janet's and confined to bed for two years before her death 9 Dec 1900 in her seventy-sixth year. Her funeral was held in the Logan Tabernacle. She is buried in Logan Cemetery.

MARY ANN SMITH MCNEIL

BIRTHDATE: 2 Jul 1853
Newton Heath, Lancashire, England
DEATH: 30 May 1944
Showlow, Navajo, Arizona
PARENTS: William Smith
Mary Hibbert Smith
PIONEER: 1863
Ansel Harmon Wagon Train
SPOUSE: John Corbet McNeil
MARRIED: 12 Sep 1868
Salt Lake City, Utah
DEATH. 20 Aug 1909
Colonia Mirales, Mexico

CHILDREN:
Sarah Alice (Mills), 7 May 1870
Daniel, 2 Mar 1873
Ephraim, 2 Sep 1874
Lillias (Datton), 6 Mar 1876
Hannah (Goodman), 18 Feb 1878
Angus Smith, 6 Jul 1879
Benjamin, 16 Dec 1881
Althera (Peterson/Evans), 22 Mar 1883
James Hibbert, 3 Apr 1885
Jesse S., 4 Nov 1887
Annie Frances(Thompson), 25 Apr 1889
Willie Smith, 9 Aug 1892
Frederick, 25 Dec 1893
Don Carlos, 22 Feb 1896

Mary Ann Smith was born in 1853 in England to William and Mary Hibbert Smith. This family lived in a comfortable home in Manchester, England. When she was three years of age, her family left England on the ship "Fleetwell," bound for America. Following, they prepared for their travel to Missouri where they remained for several years as they prepared for their westward trek. They secured a team of oxen and a wagon and traveled with the Ansel Harmon wagon train with the family walking most of the way. Mary Ann was just ten years of age, and when she became very tired, she could ride on the long reach pole that stuck out behind the wagon. This was neither comfortable nor safe, but they finally reached the Salt Lake Valley in 1863.

They first settled in Bountiful, Utah, in a one room dugout. When fifteen years of age, Mary Ann married John McNeil in the Endowment House in Salt Lake City. This couple lived in Bountiful until 18 Nov 1878 when they began their journey to Arizona to make their home. Mary said, "The trip down was a long, hard journey and I was sick most of the time because of the cold weather and I was very sad because I had to leave my beloved parents and relatives to come to a country that was unsettled, without a home, or friends, and where the Redmen roamed at will. By this time I had five children to care for. My baby was only nine months old and was sick most of the time. She couldn't stand the jolting of the wagon so the children and I took turns walking and carrying her in our arms. Our outfit consisted of a wagon and a span of horses in the lead. We put the milk cows in the team as we had no one to drive them. Travelling by team was slow and we hadn't gone far when it began to snow. When we got to the canyon eighteen miles from Kanab, my husband had to leave us and go on to town for help, as our poor team was give out and we could go no farther. There was eighteen inches of snow on the ground and it was bitter cold. I am sure we would have all frozen to death before he got back had not two men happened along travelling our way. At first I was afraid of them as they asked a lot of questions but when they learned of our plight they brought wood to make a camp fire and camped close to our wagon all night. They went on next morning and wanted to take the children and me to Kanab but all we had was in the wagon and I did not want to leave it. My husband had left me there and there I would remain until he came to get me, which he did that night. On Christmas day we reached Kanab, glad to be alive. We lived that winter in a cellar and next spring rented a house from Jacob Hamblin. We stayed there until fall raising a good garden and lots of apples. When the crop was gathered we started again for Arizona. People told us that apples would bring a good price so we left our cook stove and many other things so we might load our wagon with apples but long before we reached our destination they were all frozen and we got nothing for them. We had to cook over a campfire for a year before John returned to Kanab to get our stove."

They arrived in SnowFlake, Arizona in December of 1879. Their neighbors all shared their tools and equipment. John was a shoemaker and went to town to trade services for food. They had very little food for most of that year. They became trusted by the Indians, and Mary Ann did a lot of sewing for the Indian Squaws. Their skirts had ten widths of material in each one, besides trimming by the yards. In her own words, "I had to use my own thread. I used up two boxes of thread that I brought from Utah. When it was all gone I could not sew any more and was glad, for they pestered me continually to sew for them. One day an Indian man came and asked me to make him a shirt. I told him I was sick and couldn't. He kept coaxing me so I told him I had no thread. He got awful angry and called me names he had learned from the soldiers at Fort Apache, so John told me I had better make him a shirt." Occasionally the Indians gave them scares, but her husband was always a friend to them. Some of them were the San Carlos, Apache, and Chief Geronomo, but they did not have any serious problems with them.

Food was scarce for her family most of the time. In 1900, the family moved to Old Mexico. John died there in 1909. Following this, Mary Ann returned to Arizona where her son bought a lot with a log house for her where she could walk where she wanted to go. He later built a home of which she said, "This is the best home I've ever had." It was built among the flowers and trees, and it was here she spent the last years of her life.

Mary Ann gave birth to fourteen children all together. When she turned eighty-three years old a party was held where 73 of her 178 descendants attended. Nine of her children met together for the first time in twenty years. Another party was held for her ninetieth birthday. She enjoyed it by dancing with two of her sons. Mary Ann had very little school training, however, she had a fine mind and sought learning through extensive reading, observation of nature and the people with whom she met. She, therefore, became a fairly well educated woman, informative, and was a good conversationalist.

Mary Ann Smith McNeil passed away at over ninety-one years of age. Great sadness was felt by those around her, but they expressed great gratitude for the exemplary life of this noble pioneer woman of great faith and fortitude. We honor her name.

LYDIA LITTLEFIELD MCNIVEN

BIRTHDATE: 6 Sep 1851
Portsea, Hants, England
DEATH: 2 Nov 1944
Burlington, Wyoming
PARENTS: William David
Ann Toomer Fry Littlefield
PIONEER: 2 Nov 1864
Warren C. Snow Wagon Train
SPOUSE: James Scott McNiven
MARRIED: 15 Jan 1872
Salt Lake Endowment House
DEATH: 25 May 1925
Burlington, Big Horn, Wyoming

CHILDREN:
James Robert, 15 Feb 1873
Lydia Ann (child), 15 Aug 1874
John Scott (child), 5 Feb 1876
Joseph William (child), 5 Dec 1877
Violet Nettie, 6 Jan 1880
Annie Josephine (child), 15 Nov 1882
Don Carlos (infant), 12 Oct 1884
Jessie Mar (child), 10 Oct 1886
Jane, 1 Mar 1889
May, 14 Feb 1893
Sylvia Dell, 18 Oct 1896

Lydia Littlefield was born in 1851 in England to William and Ann Littlefield. Her father was much opposed to the Gospel after her mother joined the church, so he withheld his wages. There was much turmoil in the home until her mother took Lydia and the rest of the children and went to Utah. Lydia was eleven years old when she left England. When she got to Utah, she lived in the home of her sister who was married to William Eddington, who was the only caterer for Brigham Young's entertainments. Lydia accompanied them and served behind the tables for them. She was impressed with the entertainments she saw at that time.

Lydia married James Scott McNiven in the Endowment House in 1872. He was from Morgan, Utah, and they went to live on a farm there where her first seven children were born. Three of the first four died during a diptheria epidemic in 1880. She grieved so that she told the Lord that she couldn't feel any worse if he took her son, Jim, too. She heard a voice say, "Jim will live to be a comfort to you in your old age." Lydia also told that one day during her great grieving, she looked out the window and saw her three little children playing in the yard; she was greatly comforted by this vision.

Lydia had three more children while living in Morgan. Her husband, James, was called to pioneer in St. Johns, Arizona. He left ahead of Lydia as she was expecting her seventh child. After the birth of Don Carlos, and shortly before leaving for Arizona, she awoke in the morning to find that the baby sleeping with her had died in the night. She felt she had smothered him, and she blamed herself the rest of her life.

Lydia left for Arizona with her three children. Life was hard in Arizona, and after two years her husband was released from this call. Before they returned to Utah, Annie Josephine died of scarlet fever. They moved to Emery County, Utah, residing the first two years in Huntington where her daughter, Jessie Mar was born. While there, her six year old, Violet, accidentally swallowed a pen point, which lodged in her throat, formed an abscess, and nearly cost her her life. It was weeks before the pen point came out.

They then moved to Lawrence where they lived for nine years. In May 1890, Jessie Mar died of scarlet fever and Lydia gave birth to two more daughters while there. Their farm was not good ground; upon hearing of the Big Horn Basin in Wyoming, they took their four remaining children in a wagon and started for northern Wyoming. They met Indians on the way, who wanted to trade beads, etc., for their year-old baby daughter, May.

Lydia was forty-two when she reached Mormon Bend on the Greybull River. They stayed the winter camping alongside the river, and the next spring they moved to the Burlington Flat. Her last child was born there. They eventually built a nice home on his farm.

Their five children grew to adulthood there. Her husband was Bishop for eighteen years, and she hosted the General Authorities in her home on many occasions. She took part in all the activities of the ward and town. Her life was centered in her family and in beautifying her home. She made straw ticks for mattresses, wove carpets for the floors, taught herself to read, and enjoyed reading the scriptures, Shakespeare and historical biographies throughout her life. She enjoyed pretty dishes, handmade doilies and was a good cook. One afternoon while baking pies, the chimney caught fire and her lovely home burned to the ground. She and her husband moved to town and built another home.

One of Lydia's grandsons grew up in her home. She had four other grandchildren in her home after their mother died from an appendicitis. They got typhoid fever. Lydia was a widow for the last nineteen years of her life after James died 25 May 1925. Lydia died with a farm and home unencumbered by debt and three of her eleven children sur-

vived her, one of whom was Jim, the one the Lord had promised her so many years before, that he would live to be a comfort to her in her old age. The night before her death, Jim gave her a blessing. Her daughter May was by her side as she took her last shallow peaceful breath on 2 Nov 1944, at ninety-three years of age. She was truly a devoted, great, faithful pioneer woman who had experienced much by her mother's joining the LDS Church and coming to Utah. She lived through many trials and tribulations of her pioneer life, never losing her strong testimony and her great love for the Lord.

JANE ANN OLLERTON MCPHERSON

BIRTHDATE: 2 Jan 1841
Eccleston, Lancashire, England
DEATH: 19 Mar 1933
Nephi, Juab, Utah
PARENTS: John Ollerton
Alice Dandy
PIONEER: 30 Nov 1856
Martin Handcart Company
SPOUSE:
James Ramsey McPherson
MARRIED: 15 Jul 1860
Nephi, Juab, Utah
DEATH SP: 16 Mar 1920
Nephi, Juab, Utah

CHILDREN:
Mary Lavina (Wright), 27 Nov 1861
James Ramsey, 6 Apr 1863
Alice Ann (Riches), 28 Oct 1864
John William, 28 Jan 1868
Seth Ollerton, 13 Jul 1869
Jane Ann, 25 Feb 1871
Elizabeth Helen (Sowby), 1 Nov 1872
Rose (Card), 8 Jun 1874
Thomas Witson, 28 Jan 1876
Janette, 27 Feb 1877
Isabell Estella, 15 Jul 1878
Heber Ernest, 28 Jun 1880
Amelia Lula, 15 Aug 1882
Bertha, 2 Jan 1884
Ruby, (Bigler), 23 Nov 1886

Jane Ann Ollerton was born in England in 1842. Her parents were baptized in 1837 prior to her birth. In 1856 the family prepared to leave their native land and come to America. They sailed on the ship "Horizon," but the ship was blown back to port three times before they actually got under way.

They joined with the Martin Handcart Company to come across the plains. Because of the delay and the early snows, several family members died on the journey, including Jane Ann's grandparents. They finally arrived in the Salt Lake Valley in November, 1856.

Jane Ann married James Ramsey McPherson in 1860 in Nephi, Utah. She was the mother of fifteen children, and also raised two motherless nephews, Alan and Colin

McPherson. She was an accomplished seamstress, making underwear, dresses, shirts, and knitted stockings. Her favorite Church call was as a Relief Society Visiting Teacher. She loved parties, especially for birthdays and Christmas. James died in 1920, and Jane Ann lived until 1933. Both are buried in Nephi, Juab, Utah.

CAROLINE AMELIA OWENS WEBB MCRAE

No Photo Available

BIRTHDATE: 9 Jul 1821
Warren, Trumbull, Ohio
DEATH: 1 Sep 1895
Fillmore, Millard, Utah
PARENTS: James Clark Owens
Abigail Cordelia Burr
PIONEER: 1 Oct 1852
Uriah Curtis Company
SPOUSE I: Edward Milo Webb, Sr.
MARRIED: 12 Dec 1839
Nauvoo, Hancock, Illinois
DEATH SP: 31 Jul 1852
On the trail

CHILDREN:
Cordelia Amanda(Warner), 2 Oct 1841
Horace Marcellus, 5 May 1843
Estelvin, 1845
Edward Milo Jr., 8 Mar 1847
Caroline Amelia (Reed), 5 Jul 1849
Francis Adelbert, 20 Mar 1853

SPOUSE II: Alexander McRae
MARRIED: Dec 1855
Salt Lake City, Utah
DEATH SP: 20 Jun 1891
Salt Lake City, Utah

CHILDREN:
Albert 1 Oct 1856
Julia Estella (Beauregard), 12 Oct 1858

Caroline was born in Ohio in 1821. The family joined the Church in 1831, moved to Missouri, but they were expelled by the mobs. Caroline was baptized in 1834.

In Dec 1839 Caroline married Edward Milo Webb, Sr. and they became the parents of six children. They lived in Nauvoo and had a comfortable home until the persecution became so great that they feared for their lives. Caroline's husband was offered employment in Missouri as a carpenter. This enabled them to have money for provisions for the trip west. But, near the Platte River in Nebraska tragedy struck, and the husband and father, died from cholera on 31 Jul 1852.

Caroline had no choice but to go on with her little family. She was expecting her sixth child, who was born in Big Cottonwood, Salt Lake County, after they arrived in Utah.

Caroline spent one winter in Provo, Utah, then moved to Fillmore, Millard, Utah. She was a good seamstress and

did much custom sewing. She raised a little garden, made butter and cheese, and was able to provide for her family without outside help. In 1855 Caroline married Bishop Alexander McRae as a plural wife. To them were born two children, Albert and Julia Estella. Caroline was a beautiful singer and loved to sing to her family. She was cultured and refined, with a pleasing personality. She died in Fillmore, Millard, Utah in 1895.

MARTHA JONES MEACHAM

BIRTHDATE: 7 Aug 1834
Warren, Jefferson Co., Ohio
DEATH: 14 Jul 1903
Park Valley, Box Elder Co., Utah
PARENTS: Elisha Jones
Margaret Talbot Jones
PIONEER: 3 Sep 1850
Mathew Caldwell Wagon Co.
SPOUSE: Erastus Darwin Mecham
MARRIED: 4 Feb. 1849
DEATH SP: 7 Jun 1899
Park Valley, Box Elder Co., Utah

CHILDREN:
Sylvia Ameretta, 17 Dec. 1849
William Henry, 31 Dec. 1851
Erastus Darwin Jr., 17 Mar. 1854
Martha Maria (Burton), 19 Feb. 1857
Elisha Jones, 15 Sep 1859
Margaret Elizabeth(Garrard/Coleman), 27 Mar. 1862
Stephen Peabody, 7 May 1864
Francis Carter, 10 Mar. 1866
John Hyrum, 10 Nov. 1870
Richard Lafayette, 21 Jul 1873

Martha Jones was born in Ohio in 1834. Her father was a blacksmith and wheelwright and when her family joined the Mormon church, because of the persecutions, they were baptized in the night. The Mecham's gathered with the saints at Nauvoo and Martha was a girl of ten when the Prophet and his brother were murdered. As a teenage daughter she shared all hardships when they were forced from their houses and into Winter Quarters, Nebraska, into Kanesville, Ohio and then Council Bluffs.

Her father set up his blacksmith shop in Council Bluffs, a town teeming with pioneers, gold seekers, adventurers and farmers leaving the "gateway to the west" and in need of wagons and conveyances to take them there. He hired twenty-year-old Erastus Meacham to work as his apprentice and fourteen-year-old Martha caught Erastus' eye. Volunteering for the Mormon Battalion in 1846, Erastus left on the record march and did not return to Council Bluffs for two years. He went to work for Elisha again, their love rekindled and Martha and Erastus were married in February of 1849.

In the spring of 1850, with their firstborn a few months old, the couple traveled with the independent Matthew

Caldwell Co. and reached Utah 3 Sep 1850. They first settled in Little Cottonwood (Union) where a son was born. Later they lived in Springville, Provo, then Fairview.

The year in Fairview was a horrid experience for Martha; the Black Hawk war had started, Erastus was on duty with the volunteer army to fight the Indians, and Martha was often alone with the children. There had been no time to complete their cabin and there was no roof over the loft. One night the Indians attacked the cabin, Martha saw a hand reaching over the top log of the cabin wall, with a mighty whack of a hatchet she chopped off the hand of the Indian. Their fourteen-year-old son William, armed with another hatchet, split open the head of another Indian who was attempting to crawl over another wall. Astonished by the defense of this roofless cabin with a woman and children, the Indians left. In Fairview, her baby Stephen died. Erastus moved the grieving woman into the more secure Salt Lake City and for two years Martha led a more pleasant life.

It was not the end of their moving however. For twenty-seven years they moved, made a home and moved again. Their permanent settlement was in 1877 in Dove Creek (Park Valley).

In 1870 Franklin D. Richard blessed Martha and set her apart to care for the sick and the dead. For the rest of her life she performed this mission in every community where she lived. In Park Valley she was the only nurse for a hundred miles and along with bringing babies into the world, washed and dressed the dead, lined their homemade caskets and comforted the living.

She was seventy-one when she died peacefully in her log cabin home with one of her sons at her bedside and a daughter nearby. A special lady, loved by all.

EMMA LUCY HOBBS MEADS

BIRTHDATE: 21 Feb 1843
Hersham, Surrey, England
DEATH: 17 Dec 1927
Los Angeles, California
PARENTS: William Down Hobbs
Mary Ann Pope
PIONEER: 4 Oct 1863
John W. Woolley Company
SPOUSE:
Alexander Mangus Meads
MARRIED: 19 Oct 1864
Salt Lake City, Utah
DEATH SP: 15 Mar 1914
Los Angeles, California

CHILDREN:
William Henry, 7 Aug 1865
George Alexander, 1868
Alice V. (Hall), 1 Apr 1870
Ida May (Royal), Abt 1873
John Franklin, 30 Jan 1877
Charles, 1882
Ora Leora, 11 May 1885
Ray Renzo, 28 Sep 1886

Emma Lucy Hobbs was born in England in 1843. She was sixteen when she came to the United States with her two sisters, Tryphena and Mary Ann, on the ship "Amazon." They traveled by train to Quincy, Illinois, crossed the Mississippi, then by train again to Florence, Nebraska.

Nothing is written about their personal hardships on the plains; however, Alexander Meads was in the company just ahead of the John Woolley Company, and he left her love notes in the sunbleached heads of dead oxen along the trail. They were married in the Endowment House in October 1864. Prior to her marriage, she was a governess for the children of Brigham Young.

The family settled in Parowan, Utah and three children were born to them while in Utah. In the Spring of 1872 they moved to Bishop, Inyo, California, where they homesteaded some land. Five more children were born in California. Sometime between 1898 and 1900 they moved to Los Angeles. Lucy was very talented at handwork. Even when she lost her sight, she continued to crochet. She made dark fruitcake for Christmas, until she died.

Alexander died in 1914, and Lucy died in 1927, both in Los Angeles, California.

LYDIA ABY PRESLEY MEAD

BIRTHDATE: 20 Feb 1835
Shardon, Geauga, Ohio
DEATH: 22 Jan 1919
Price, Carbon, Utah
PARENTS:
William Hawkins Presley
Eleanor Johnson
PIONEER: Fall of 1852
By wagon train
SPOUSE: Orlando Fish Mead
MARRIED: 27 Jun 1853
Salt Lake City, Utah
DEATH SP: 26 Feb 1897
Price, Carbon, Utah

CHILDREN:
Eleanor Hepsibath, 14 Dec 1853
Annie Eliza, 13 Aug 1855
Zina Percinda, 19 Oct 1857
Theresa Amelia, 13 Nov 1859
Lydia Kiziah, 13 Jun 1861
Emily Jane, 31 Mar 1864
Louisa Mary, 17 May 1866
Amanda Aurelia, 19 May 1868
Frances Idona, 17 Mar 1871
Orlando, 27 Dec 1873
George Carlos, 29 Jan 1877

Lydia Aby Presley was born in Ohio in 1835. Her parents had joined the Church in New York State, and suffered all the hardships of being driven from Kirtland, to Missouri, to Illinois. Lydia's mother and three siblings died in Nauvoo. Lydia, her father and brother Joseph, started across the plains, but her father and brother died from cholera on the trail.

Lydia Aby arrived in Salt Lake City in the fall of 1852. She settled in Parley's Canyon where she met Orlando Fish Mead. He had been a member of the Mormon Battalion march, and was several years her senior. They were married 27 Jun 1853 in Salt Lake City, and became the parents of 11 children. The family lived in Salt Lake, Spanish Fork, and Price, Utah. Lydia died in Price, Carbon, Utah in 1919. Her husband died in 1897, also in Price.

ANN ELIZABETH BOVEE MECHAM

BIRTHDATE: 18 April 1827
Hanover, Chattanuga, New York
DEATH: 17 October 1869
Milton, Morgan, Utah
PARENTS: Matthias Bovee
Waitstill Hill Bovee
PIONEER: 1852.
SPOUSE: Joseph Mecham
MARRIED: 29 January 1845
Nauvoo, Hancock, Illinois
DEATH: 6 March 1894
St. George, Washington, Utah

CHILDREN:
Josephine, 1847 (died in infancy)
Arianiah (Arthavah), 18 April 1849
Joseph, 16 February 1851
Ammon Earth, 1853 (died in infancy)
Ammon, 6 December 1855
Emma Waitstill, 18 October 1858
Brigham Bovee, 18 February 1860
Lucian Mormon, 16 February 1862
Seymour Brunson, 14 December 1864
Deseret, 5 November 1865
Elizabeth Vilate, 7 November 1867

Ann Elizabeth Bovee descended from a religious ancestry, being of French Huguenot descent, Protestants who were driven from France to Holland and later emigrated to America for their beliefs. Ann Elizabeth became an early member of the LDS Church, being baptized with her father and other members of her family some time before 1845. She enjoyed many of the events pertaining to the gathering of the saints and the building of Nauvoo. She knew the Prophet Joseph Smith, saw the building of the Nauvoo temple, experienced its blessings, suffered the agonies of the martyrdom of the Prophet and the driving of the saints from Nauvoo. Her father and future husband were personal friends of the Prophet and shared his confidence and bore many of his burdens.

The beautiful dark-haired Ann Elizabeth was the second wife of Joseph Mecham, he having first married Hannah Ladd Tyler on February 10, 1827. They had ten children at the time Joseph, age thirty-nine, married Ann Elizabeth, age seventeen, on 29 January 1845. A year later

on January 22, 1846 both Hannah and Ann Elizabeth were sealed in the Nauvoo Temple to Joseph Mecham.

Driven by the mob from Nauvoo, the Mecham family moved to Council Bluffs, Iowa, where Ann Elizabeth's first child was born and died, and where Hannah passed away 7 December 1846 leaving Ann Elizabeth with the care of Hannah's children. She became a true mother to them, showing no partiality between them and her own children who came to grace her home. Joseph and Ann Elizabeth's next two children were born in Harris Grove and Woodbine, Iowa, while Joseph was presiding over the settlements and helping prepare for the emigrating saints as they passed on their way to Salt Lake. The Mechams crossed the plains in 1852.

Ann Elizabeth had three other homes. First was Salt Lake where her fourth child was born. The next three children were born in Pine Canyon in east Tooele in a log cabin. Those were the hard times. They stayed indoors five to six months during the winter except for the times they had to feed their sheep and chop wood for the fireplace. Ann Elizabeth made their clothes from the sheep's wool, baked coals on brick and baked bread in a baking kettle. They cut wheat with a cradle, pressed it with a club, and ground their wheat in their coffee mill. They lived on boiled cracked corn which was made into bread. And the children had no shoes, risky when they were chopping wood.

The family recalls a time when all the children came down with measles. One night a severe rain storm occurred and their dirt roof collapsed on them. They all ran outside in their night clothes, but fortunately all survived the unforgettable experience without injury.

The last four children came to her happy and loving home in Milton, Morgan County, Utah. Two years after Elizabeth Vilate's birth, and still suffering from complications due to the lack of adequate medical skills, Ann Elizabeth died at age forty-two leaving her family to the devoted care of Sarah Marie Tuttle, Joseph's third wife, who had a family of seven children. She, in turn, blessed the lives of all the families.

ELVIRA DERBY MECHAM

BIRTHDATE: 6 Nov 1811
Canan, Grafton, New Hampshire
DEATH: 28 Apr 1866
Provo, Utah Co., Utah
PARENTS: John Derby
Sarah Currier Derby
PIONEER: 16 Oct 1853
Moses Worthen Mecham
Independent Wagon Company
SPOUSE:
Moses Worthen Mecham
MARRIED: 8 Nov 1827
DEATH SP: 22 Jul 1878
Provo, Utah Co. Utah

CHILDREN:
Leonidas Clinton, 20 Aug 1828
Sarah (Burdick), 20 Aug 1829
Samuel, 9 Feb 1831
Mormon, 17 Apr 1832 died same day
Polly (Packer, Sr.), 15 Nov 1833
Emily (Haws), 9 Jun 1835
Americus, 20 Dec. 1836
America (Orser), 11 Oct 1837
Martha (Bigelow), 23 Feb 1839
Lucinda, 13 Mar 1841
Elvira Jane (Bigelow), 4 Mar 1843
Moses Moroni, 8 Jul 1854
William Wallace, 22 Apr 1847
Celestia Ann (Mendenhall), 12 Sep 1848
John Derby, 30 Apr 1850
Donna Maria (Meacham), 15 Apr 1852
Marcus Layafette, 9 Feb 1855

Elvira Derby was born in New Hampshire in 1811 and was left motherless at two years of age. Her father, left with Elvira and the new three-month-old baby, Polly, soon married his wife's sister Anna (Mary?) Currier who was a good mother to the children and raised them as her own.

Elvira was two days past her sixteenth birthday when she and Moses Mecham were married. Moses had a thriving mercantile business and being an energetic and ambitious man, moved his business as he saw opportunity for growth. His family lived in various new eastern towns, moving westward as glowing reports of the western frontier piqued his interest and that of other members of his family.

Elvira was a mother in the finest sense; she gave birth to seventeen children (nine girls and eight boys) under every condition and in many towns from Hanover, New Hampshire to Lehi, Utah. She used her homemaking skills to care for and teach her children. Her nurturing sense was passed through the generations for her children married well and had fine families of their own.

When his parents joined the Mormon Church, Moses and Elvira, after much investigation to decipher why his parents would join a church whose members were harassed and persued, and after fervent prayer, had an experience with the "gift of tongues" which converted them and they were baptized. From their baptism onward they shared the experiences of all the Saints, thrust upon them by mobs and persecution.

They crossed the plains as an independent company following the Harmon Co. and the Brown Co. with two wagons, one yoke of oxen, two yoke of unbroken steers, and four cows. "There were thirteen of us children and mother and father, with one wagon and one tent" wrote Lucinda, their tenth child. She wrote of the company's traveling together to protect each other from the Indians, of hunger because the Indians were given the food to pacify them, and that the children walked all the way and were given time to keep clean. She recalled that her mother gave all their spare milk to the other travelers to save them from

starving. Their lives in Utah were spent in Provo, used up in work and deeds for their family and community.

Elvira cared for her family, suffered the grief of losing her last born and outlived her husband by eight years. She died at seventy-five and was buried at the side of her beloved husband in the Provo Cemetery.

LYDIA WELLS MECHAM

BIRTHDATE: 6 Aug 1817
Skaneateles, Onondaga, New York
DEATH: 20 Oct 1890
Provo, Utah
PARENTS: Judah Wells
Temperance Meacham Wells
PIONEER: 9 Oct 1852/1851
James C. Snow Co. Wagon Train
SPOUSE: Lewis Mecham
MARRIED: 5 Apr 1836
Mercer, Pennsylvania
DEATH SP: 21 Mar 1895
Provo, Utah

CHILDREN:
Emeline (Sweet), 6 Apr 1837
Mosiah, 24 Jul 1838
Margaret Marie (Ross), 24 Feb 1840
Joshua Josiah, 24 Mar 1842
Almira Ann (Meeks), 10 Feb 1844
Melissa, 1 Dec 1845
Brigham, 24 Nov 1847
Lydia Knight (Rowland), 28 Nov 1849
Martha Jane (Wall), 29 Jan 1852
Lewis, 28 Mar 1854
Samantha Louisa (Fausett), 12 Dec 1856
Jonathan James, 6 Nov 1858
Judah, 16 Feb 1860
Sarah Temperance (Duke), 4 May 1863

Lydia Wells Mecham was born in New York, a daughter of Judah Wells and Temperance Meacham Wells. Little is known of her childhood and adult years. She married Lewis Mecham 5 Apr 1836. She became a member of the Mormon Church early in her life. Her husband was also a member of the Mormon Church. They moved to Nauvoo, Illinois where Lydia and her husband received their Endowments in the Nauvoo Temple 30 Dec 1845. They suffered the hardships and trials of the early members of the Church as they were driven from place to place.

Lydia and her husband became the parents of fourteen children; three died in early childhood. Their first two children were born in Delaware, Mercer, Pennsylvania. Their third child was born in Illinois, the fourth and fifth children were born in Iowa. The sixth was born in Illinois. The next three children were born in Iowa, through 1847 to 1852. The tenth through fourteenth were born in Provo, Utah. Although very little information is known about Lydia and her husband, the birthplaces of their children give evidence of how they moved from place to place until they reached the Salt Lake Valley. The had traveled by wagon with the James C. Snow Company. This Company arrived in the Valley 9 Oct 1852. Some records show the Mecham's arriving in 1851.

Even though little is known about Lydia's life, her life could not have been easy having fourteen children while moving from place to place. She experienced the sorrow and sadness that came with losing to death three of her children in their early childhood. She was busy fixing meals, keeping clothes in repair for her large family, and being with child so much of the time. Lydia died 20 Oct 1890. It is recorded that she told her family, "Children, I want you to remember the Church, and stay with it. The principles are true and never abandon them. Let come what will, still hold fast to the everlasting Gospel."

MARGARET EMMA CHAMPLIN MECHAM

BIRTH DATE: 11 Jun 1833
Susquehana Co., Pennsylvania
DEATH: Feb 1909
Preston, Idaho
PARENTS: Wm. Sisson Champlin
Mary Ring
PIONEER: Sep 1852
Ox Team
SPOUSE: Leonidas Americus
Likurkus DeWitt Clinton Mecham
MARRIED: 25 Feb 1851
Kanesville, Iowa
DEATH: 20 Aug 1883
Riverdale, Idaho

CHLDREN:
Mary Elvira (Packer), 18 Sep 1852
Leonidas Americus, 19 Oct 1854
Clinton, 20 Nov 1856
Sarah Avilda (Packer), 17 Nov 1858
Emma Almita (Neeley), 30 Nov 1860
Emily Jane (Evans), 19 Apr 1863
Louisa Maria (Vail), 1 Dec 1865
Moroni, 25 Mar 1867
William, 18 Apr 1870

Margaret Emma Champlin Mecham was born 11 Jun 1833 in Susquehana County, Pennsylvania.

When five years old, Margaret and her family were present at the Haun's Mill Massacre on 30 Oct 1838. Her family was the only one present which escaped death or injury.

Margaret was a devoted mother and homemaker. She was a wonderful seamstress and sewed for the dead.

Margaret served as Relief Society President and as a visiting teacher in the Riverdale Ward in Idaho.

MARY ANN CLARK MECHAM

BIRTHDATE: 18 Nov 1842
Colchester, Essex, England
DEATH: 4 Apr 1930
PARENTS: William Nichols Clark
Mary King Clark
PIONEER: 19 Oct 1864
William Hyde Wagon Co.
SPOUSE: Lorenzo Dow Mecham
MARRIED: 9 Sep 1865
Salt Lake Endowment House
DEATH: 16 Apr 1906
Grouse Creek, Box Elder, Utah

CHILDREN:
Mary Ann (Lee), 27 Nov 1866
Lorenzo William, 29 Jun 1868
Annie Louisa (Paskett) 13 Feb 1870
Emma Elizabeth (Rohwer), 24 Mar 1872
Martin Daniel, 23 Aug 1874
Sarah Ruth (Cooke), 9 Aug 1876
Lusina Clark, 18 Jun 1878

Mary Ann Clark Mecham was born in Colchester, Essex, England. She was the daughter of William and Mary King Clark. The records do not indicate when Mary Ann became a member of the Mormon Church. She did arrive in the Salt Lake Valley 19 Oct 1864 with the William Hyde wagon-train Company. She married Lorenzo Dow Mecham 9 Sep 1865, probably in Utah, one year after arriving in the Valley.

They became the parents of seven children; five daughters and two sons. Their life as pioneers in a desert Valley was filled with many challenges, hardships and trials. Mary Ann was a devoted mother. She was a homemaker in the true sense of the Gospel. She developed the necessary skills of washing and carding wool, sewing, weaving, quilting, knitting, embroidering. She was very efficient in homemaking skills. She also supported her husband in all of his work, helping in the garden with all that was needed to be done. She was an excellent cook. Her desire was to be a loving mother and wife.

They lived in the remote area of Grouse Creek in Box Elder County, Utah. Her resourcefulness was both spiritual and temporal. She was active in furthering the work of the Lord in her home and Church callings. She served as a Relief Society teacher for many years. Mary Ann died 4 Apr 1930. Her husband had died in 1906. Mary Ann was a widow for twenty-four years. She was always faithful and had a strong testimony of the truthfulness of the Gospel. She is revered as a pioneer of faith and fortitude by all of her posterity.

PERMELIA CHAPMAN MECHAM

No
Photo
Available

BIRTHDATE: 25 Jan 1777
Hanover, New London, Connecticut
DEATH: 19 May 1866
Heber, Wasatch, Utah
PARENTS: Samuel Chapman
Hannah Fox Chapman
PIONEER: 1850
SPOUSE: Joshua Mecham
MARRIED: 5 Apr 1793
Canaan, Grafton, New Hampshire
DEATH SP: 8 Oct 1846
Bonaparte, Van Buren, Iowa

CHILDREN:
Joshua, 10 Dec 1795
Samuel, 23 Jan 1798
Permelia, 15 Feb 1800
Edward, 22 Feb 1802
Leonidas Moses Worthen, 19 Feb 1804
Elizabeth, 20 Jan 1806
Ephraim, 8 Mar 1808
Caleb, 15 May 1810
Lewis, 4 Sep 1814

Permelia had one sister, Hannah, and her brothers were Amos and Samuel. Her father and brother, Amos, served in the War of 1812. Permelia moved with her parents to Canaan, New Hampshire, where she met Joshua Meacham. They were married in Canaan and became the parents of nine children. They left New Hampshire for New York, then went to Mercer, Erie, Pennsylvania in 1827. In 1836, they heard the Gospel preached by LDS missionaries. Perinelia and her husband and four of her sons and their wives joined the LDS Church in 1837. On all of the church records since that time, their name has been spelled "Mecham." Permelia and her husband started for Nauvoo in 1838, but were stopped by a mob in Quincy where they wanted to cross the Mississippi River. When they finally arrived in Nauvoo, they became personally acquainted with Prophet Joseph Smith. They did their part in helping to build the city and the temple. They were sealed in the Temple on Christmas Day of 1845. Permelia did the temple work for many of her family before the saints were driven from their homes.

The Mechams were ill-prepared for the arduous journey. Their journey was slow because they had to stop along the way to secure food. When they reached Bonaparte, Iowa, her husband, Joshua and one of her granddaughters died from exposure. With the help of friends, Permelia was able to go on and reached the Salt Lake Valley in the fall of 1850.

She was the first of her family to arrive in the valley, so she lived with friends. When her son, Edward, came the following year, she made her home with him in Lehi. She was a courageous woman, a great example to her family, and was much loved by her family. As her other children arrived in the valley, she spent her years living with each

family. She lived in many places in the valley–Lehi, Provo, Wallsburg, and Heber. She died at the age of eighty-nine.

POLLY DERBY MECHAM

BIRTHDATE: 13 Aug 1813
Hanover, Grafton, New Hampshire
DEATH: 1 Dec 1898
Wallsburg, Wasatch, Utah
PARENTS: John Derby
Sarah Currier Derby
PIONEER: 17 Oct 1853
John Brown Wagon Company
SPOUSE: Ephraim Mecham
MARRIED: 29 Nov 1828
Mercer, Mercer, Pennsylvania
DEATH SP: 6 Jul 1891
Wallsburg, Wasatch, Utah

CHILDREN:
Amos, 5 Oct 1830 (died an infant)
Permelia, 11 Sep 1832
Lewis, 18 Dec 1835
Elvira, 23 Dec 1837 (died age 8)
Emma Maria, 9 May 1840
Hyrum Moroni, 20 Aug 1842
Sarah Ann, 16 Feb 1844 (died age 3)
Ephraim Don Carlos, 14 Aug 1846
Mary Henrietta, 10 Apr 1848
Polly Celestia, 12 Apr 1852
John Albert, 21 Jun 1854
Adelia Vilate, 26 Dec 1856

When Polly was only three months old, her mother died. Her father remarried and the family moved to Erie County, Pennsylvania. Polly had an older sister, Elvira. These two sisters became lifetime friends and neighbors as they married brothers, and joined the LDS Church. She married Ephraim Mecham and they had four children born to them in Pennsylvania before they heard and accepted the gospel of Jesus Christ and joined the LDS Church in 1837. They gathered with the saints in Missouri and suffered many persecutions with the rest of the saints and were driven from place to place. Polly and her family settled in Kanesville where they farmed and worked close to her sister Elvira and her family. In 1847, a flood came just as they were getting settled and washed away many of their precious possessions. In the spring of 1853 they started for the Salt Lake Valley in the John Brown Wagon Company. They arrived on October 17, 1853.

They settled in Lehi where two more children were born, making a total of twelve. They moved to Wallsburg, Wasatch Co. Polly lost her first child as a baby, and while crossing the plains, three more died. They endured many hardships. Polly was the first doctor in Wallsburg and used herbs, faith, and prayer in caring for the sick. She did beautiful sewing and handwork. She was active in many organizations and was President of the Relief Society in Wallsburg in 1887. She did temple work for many of her ancestors in the St. George Temple. She and her husband lived to celebrate their sixty-second anniversary. She maintained her love for poetry mingled with a strong love of the gospel. She was eighty-five when she died.

SARAH MARIA TUTTLE MECHAM

No
Photo
Available

BIRTHDATE: 25 Jan 1825
North Haven, New Haven, Conn.
DEATH: 24 Feb 1880
Milton, Morgan County, Utah
PARENTS: Edward Tuttle
Sarah Maria Clinton Tuttle
PIONEER: Sep 1852
Allen Weeks Wagon Co.
SPOUSE: Joseph Mecham
MARRIED: 5 Jan 1853
Salt Lake City, Utah
DEATH SP: 6 Mar 1894
St. George, Utah

CHILDREN:
Leander, 18 Dec 1854
Joseph Lyman, 26 Sep 1856
Ann Eliza, 29 Nov 1858
Daniel Lester, 7 Jan 1861
Luman Lehi, 14 Jul 1863
Mary Emeretta, 24 Apr 1865
Sarah Emily, 26 Feb 1868

Sarah Maria Tuttle Mecham was born 25 Jan 1825 in Connecticut. She was the third of five children. Sarah Maria was five feet nine inches tall with black hair and blue eyes. She developed into an ambitious, high strung, conscientious young lady who loved children and young people and had many friends. She was reared in a home of culture and refinement. She received a good education and learned early in life the saving value of honest toil. She developed into a beautiful woman, full of grace and truth and thus was well able to meet the great issues of her life.

Sarah Maria was the first one of her family to be baptized into the Mormon Church, 5 Apr 1843. Sarah's father died in 1845 at North Haven, Connecticut two years after he had joined the Church, leaving her mother a widow with a young family. other members of her mother's family joined the Church in 1843. They journeyed westward to Utah in 1848. The Tuttles, who were a prosperous family, gave up their beautiful home and surroundings for oxen and wagons to cross the Plains. They arrived at Winter Quarters 1 May 1848. They crossed the Plains in the Summer of 1852 with the Allen Weeks Company, arriving in Salt Lake City in Sep 1852. Also in this company was the family of Joseph Mecham.

The Tuttles and the Mechams settled at Pine Canyon, Tooele County, Utah. Sarah Maria became the third wife of Joseph Mecham on 5 Jan 1853. They were married in the Council House in Salt Lake City by Brigham Young. They became the parents of seven children; one died in infancy and one died in childhood. In 1861, the family moved to Milton, Morgan County, Utah. They were some of the first

settlers of that Valley. They homesteaded about 240 acres of land and built the first sandstone house in the town and were comfortable. All the washing was done by hand or on the washboard. Sarah did all the knitting and sewing for her family. Her artistic nature was displayed in her children's clothing, mittens and etc.

Sarah Maria taught school in Peterson, five miles from her home. She walked the distance morning and night, carrying her baby. She used the money she earned to buy a little furniture made by a carpenter of the town and to add to their food supply. When her husband's second wife died, Sarah Maria took the five motherless children into her heart and home, often working until two o'clock in the morning taking care of all her responsibilities. Truly this large family called her blessed for her life was one of sacrifice and love. She was also President of the Milton Ward Relief Society for three years, where she put her many talents and leadership abilities to good use. She was a woman talented and cultured in the arts of life; beautiful needle work, wrote poetry, her hand-writing was beautiful. She was modest in dress and conduct. She was thoroughly genuine. She gave service freely to others and taught by example as well as precept. Sarah Maria died 24 Feb 1880 at the age of fifty-five at Milton, Utah. Her large posterity appreciate the heritage she left them.

VASHTIA EMILY JOHNSON MECHAM

No
Photo
Available

BIRTHDATE: 4 Sep 1842
Kirtland, Lake County, Ohio
DEATH: 19 Jan 1865 Utah
PARENTS: Luke S. Johnson
Susan Arminda Poteet Johnson
PIONEER: 1853 by wagon
SPOUSE: Lewis Mecham
MARRIED: 29 Aug 1868
Salt Lake Endowment House
DEATH SP: 14 oct 1907
Wallsburg, Wasatch, Utah

CHILDREN:
Lewis Lafayette, 30 Sep 1862

Vashtia was born in Kirtland, Lake County, Ohio, in 1842. Her father was the local constable and one of the first Apostles of the Mormon Church. Family life was important; parents and children often enjoyed the evening together singing, playing, studying and discussing topics of common interest. Her parents and family stayed in Kirtland after most of the members of the Church had gone to Missouri because of the persecutions of the Saints in Ohio. When Vashtia was three years old, her family left Kirtland to join the members of the Church in Winter Quarters, Nebraska. The trip was long and hard. Winter came before they completed their journey. Vashtia's mother died from exposure and was buried in an unmarked grave outside St.

Joseph, Missouri. Because they were Latter-day Saints they were not permitted to bury her in the town.

Vashtia and her brothers and sisters stayed in Council Bluffs, Iowa while their father went west with Brigham Young to the Salt Lake Valley in 1847. He returned for his family and in 1853 they left for Utah by ox team. They were one of fourteen companies to leave Iowa from May through July and arrive in the Valley in September and October. Vashtia was nine years old. Little is known of Vashtia's life during those early days in the Salt Lake Valley. She met the challenges and hardships of pioneer life.

Vashtia married Lewis Mecham. They settled in Rush Valley, Utah. Vashtia was blessed to be able to be near her family who were also settled in Southern Utah. She gave birth to her only child, Lewis Lafayette Mecham, 30 Sep 1862. He was only three years old when his mother died at a very young age. Vashtia died at the age of twenty-two years in 1865

SARAH ANN GIBSON MEEARS (MEARS, MIERS, MEERS)

No
Photo
Available

BIRTHDATE: 9 Jan 1806
Birmingham, Wrwcks, England
DEATH: 28 Jul 1869
Salt Lake City, Utah
PARENTS: James Gibson
Elizabeth Reynolds Gibson
PIONEER: 1851/63 Wagon Train
SPOUSE: George Meears
(Mears, Miers Meers)
MARRIED: 8 Nov 1828
St Philips Parish, Birrminham,
Wrwcks, England
DEATH SP: 28 Dec 1891
Salt Lake City,Utah

CHILDREN:
Mary Ann (Taysum), 15 Nov 1828
Elizabeth (Hawkins), 3 Jul 1833
Sarah (Amerson), 20 Sep 1835
Jane (Smith), 7 Jan1838
Emma (Roberts), 09 Sep 1840
Selina (Blunt), 21 Jan 1843
George Alfred, 16 Nov 1846
Louisa (Rogers), 2 Sep 1849
Eliza, 1851

Sarah Ann was born in England in 1806. She was one of five children. She was the baby in her family and was much loved. She grew up in Birmingham, where she met and married George Meears at age twenty-two.

They made their home in that area, where eight of their nine children were born. In 1849 they heard the gospel and were converted. They decided to emigrate. The exact date of their arrival into the valley is not known. Two of their daughters, Elizabeth and Jane were married in Salt Lake City in 1864 & 1863. Sarah Ann and George were sealed in

the Endowment House 30 Nov 1868. They made their home in Salt Lake, where Sarah Ann passed away 28 Jul 1869 at the age of sixty-three.

George married again, to Elizabeth Romney sometime before 1876.

ELIZABETH ELLEN HICKMAN MEECHAM

BIRTHDATE; 13 Apr 1833
West Paris, Randolph, Missouri
DEATH: 1914
Baker, White Pine, Nevada
PARENTS:
William Adams Hickman
Brendetta Waters Burkhard
PIONEER: Abt 1855-56
SPOUSE: Jerimiah Emery Meecham
MARRIED: 1 Apr 1854
DEATH SP: 31 Aug 1894
Baker, White Pine, Nevada

CHILDREN:
Katherine M., abt 1855
Emery William M., 25 Jun 1856
Elizabeth M., abt 1857
Addie M., 6 May 1858
George M., 12 Aug 1862
Nettie M., 14 Jul 1864
Emma Jane M., 25 Jun 1866

Elizabeth Ellen Hickman was born 13 Apr 1833 in West Paris, Randolph, Missouri, the daughter of William Adams Hickman and Brendetta Waters Burkhard (Burkhardt). Elizabeth was raised in polygamy, as her father had nine wives.

She married Jerimiah Emery Meecham on 1 Apr 1854. The family lived in West Jordan, Utah for a number of years where all their children were born. Then they moved to Baker, Nevada where her husband was a rancher.

Emery, as he was known, died in Baker, White Pine, Nevada on 31 Apr 1894, and Elizabeth died in 1914, also in Baker, Nevada. Both are buried in Garrison, Millard, Utah.

ELIZABETH WOOL HILLYARD MEEKS

BIRTHDATE: 21 Apr 1810
Doddington, Cambridgeshire, Eng.
DEATH: 1 Jun 1891
Smithfield, Cache County, Utah
PARENTS: Moses Wool
Elizabeth Neagus Wool
PIONEER: 10 Oct 1853
Joseph W. Young Company
SPOUSE I: Thomas Hillyard
MARRIED: abt 1830
Doddington, Cambridgeshire, Eng
DEATH: 26 Jan 1840
Doddington, Cambridgeshire,
England

CHILDREN:
Thomas, 3 Dec 1831
Elizabeth, 15 Jan 1833 (died in infancy)
William, Feb 1835 (died in infancy)
Elizabeth, Jan 1837

SPOUSE II: Murfitt Meeks
MARRIED: 1853
England
DEATH: 1864
Richmond, Utah
CHILDREN: none

Elizabeth Wool Hillyard Meeks was born in England. Little is known of her childhood. She married Thomas Hillyard of Doddington, England when she was twenty years old. They became the parents of four children; two sons and two daughters. Two of her children died soon after birth. Her husband died in 1840, ten years after they were married, leaving her a widow with two small children. She was thirty years old. Her son, Thomas, was age nine and her daughter, Elizabeth was nearly three years old.

Elizabeth opened a store near Doddington, enjoying a good business for a time. Her two children attended school and helped her at the store. In 1847, Elizabeth was baptized and confirmed a member of the Mormon Church. She married Murfitt Meeks early in 1853. He was also a member of the Mormon Church. Change now came into her life. She was no longer content to live in England. Friends who had joined the Church were leaving England and going to Utah. The desire grew within her. They disposed of the store and what little holdings they had in England and were ready to leave Liverpool on 23 Jun 1853.

Elizabeth and her husband and her daughter left with a company of 321 Saints on the ship "Galconda." They arrived in America safely, but the next time the vessel crossed the ocean, it sank. It was a witness to Elizabeth that the Lord protects His Saints. They crossed the Plains with ox teams but were obliged to walk all the way. There were six persons and their luggage to every wagon. It was the year that the Church brought the Saints West for ten pounds of English money. They traveled with the Joseph W. Young Company and arrived in the Salt Lake Valley 10 Oct 1853. They had little money left, but with two other fami-

lies they rented a home with two rooms. They found work at the Public Works, trimming beets for making molasses. After a year, Elizabeth's son, Thomas, and his wife and their son arrived in the Valley. This was a great blessing to Elizabeth for he was able to get better employment. Elizabeth and her husband moved to Richmond, Cache Valley, Utah in 1860. She lived there in peace and happiness until her husband died in 1864, leaving her a widow once again.

She moved to Smithfield, Utah to live with her son's family for the rest of her life. She was young enough to be of great help with so many small children in the family. She was always faithful to attend her Sacrament Meetings, pay her tithing, and even attend General Conferences of the Church in Salt Lake City. She enjoyed meeting with old friends. She continued to do temple work for her dead relatives until she was seventy-five years old. She was an influence for good all her days to her children, grandchildren and all who knew her. She died 1 Jun 1891 at the age of eighty-one years in Smithfield. She was remembered as a valiant pioneer with a heart full of charity.

MARY ELIZABETH RHODES MEEKS

BIRTHDATE: 23 Jan 1820
Boone, Warwick, Indiana
DEATH: 29 Mar 1900
Thurber, Wayne, Utah
PARENTS: Henry Rhodes
Elizabeth Nicinger (Noffsinger)
PIONEER: Fall of 1852
Captain Nicinger Company
SPOUSE: William Meeks
MARRIED: 5 Oct 1837
Warwick County, Indiana
DEATH SP: 30 Nov 1877
St. George, Washington, Utah

CHILDREN:
Harvey Henry, 9 Apr 1838
Henry Rhodes, 23 Mar 1840
Mary Elizabeth (Cummings/Bullock), 11 Jun 1842
Mary Ann (Cummings), 23 Nov 1844
William 18 Feb 1846
Joseph Brigham 8 Jan 1848
Mary Jane (Pearce), 2 Dec 1851
Mary Ellen 16 Jan 1854
John 1855
Mary Melissa (Snow), 22 Aug 1856
Mary Louise (Gardner), 23 Aug 1859

Mary Elizabeth Rhodes was born in Indiana in 1820. She married William Meeks in 1837 in Indiana and they became the parents of eleven children.

William and Mary Elizabeth and their family joined the Church and came west with Captain Nicinger's (Noffsinger) Independent Company, arriving in Salt Lake City in the fall of 1862.

The family settled in Thurber, Wayne County, Utah, where Mary Elizabeth died in 1900. William died in St. George, Washington, Utah in 1877.

MARY MCLACHLAN MEIKLEJOHN

BIRTHDAY: 28 Apr 1812
Darleith, Bonhill, Dumbarton, Scotland
DEATH: 4 Nov 1878
Tooele, Tooele, Utah
PARENTS: Colin McLachlan
Agnes McCrone
PIONEER: 24 Oct 1855
Milo Andrus Company
SPOUSE: Robert Meiklejohn
MARRIED: 17 May 1835
Banns
DEATH SP: 7 May 1895
Tooele, Tooele, Utah

CHILDREN:
Peter, 10 April 1836
Agnes, 15 Mar 1838
Janet, 13 Apr 1840
Mary, 29 Jul 1842
Jane, 13 Feb 1845
Catherine, 16 Aug 1851
Robert, 17 Apr 1872 (adopted)

Mary McLachlan Meiklejohn was born 28 April 1812 in Scotland. She married Robert Meiklejohn in 1835 (the banns were published on 17 May of 1835). To this union were born six children. Three children died in their youth. A seventh child born in 1872 was adopted while they were in Tooele, Utah.

Mary and her husband Robert were baptized on 18 July 1841 at Bridge of Weir, Renfrew, Scotland by Elder Robert Hamilton and confirmed that same day also by Elder Hamilton. They were later sealed on 10 Sept 1859 by Heber C. Kimball with Orson Pratt and William W. Phelps as witnesses.

The family left Liverpool for America on 22 Apr 1855, on the "Samuel Orling" with 581 other saints. They arrived in New York, May 27, 1855 under the leadership of Israel Barlow. They continued by rail to Pittsburgh. They went by steamboat down the St. Lawrence River to St. Louis and then on to Mormon Grove, Kansas. This was the place the Saints made preparation for their long journey across the plains.

They started the last part of their journey August 5, 1855, in the Milo Andrus Company. Travel was slow. There were 48 wagons to carry all the belongings of the company. They walked all the way. When they reached the Platte river, the water was so high it was impossible to cross, so they were delayed for some time until the water receded. When they were able to cross, they found they had escaped a terrible massacre.

They arrived in Salt Lake on October 24, 1855. They were were happy to get to the end of their long walk of 1000 miles. They came to Tooele in the spring of 1856 and built a home of adobe which was still standing in 1957 as their history was written.

Robert Meiklejohn was a good musician, and played the violin and Scottish bagpipes. He entertained all the way across the ocean while his three daughters, Janet (Jeanette), Mary and Jane did Scottish dances. In an autobiography written by Barbara Gowans Bowen she commented "On board were three little girls, Mary, Janet and Janie Meiklejohn, who took great interest in me and were continually quarreling as to who of the three would be responsible for my care."

Mary died in Tooele, Tooele County, Utah on 4 November 1878.

On 10 Aug 1893 five of the children were sealed to their parents. Zina Diantha Huntington Smith Young was proxy for Mary McLachlan Meiklejohn. Mary and Zina were close friends. Zina D. Young was at that time general president of the Relief Society. Mary Meiklejohn Smith was proxy for Catherine, Janet Meiklejohn DeLaMare was proxy for Agnes, and Clarence Philip DeLeMare was proxy for Peter. Jane Meiklejohn Shields and Robert Meiklejohn were sealed to the family 29 Oct 1958.

MARY ANN PAYNE MELLOR

BIRTHDATE: 23 Jan 1819
Warwick, Warwickshire, England
DEATH: 15 Sep 1895
Fayette, Utah
PARENTS: Charles Payne
Charlotte Squires Payne
PIONEER: 30 Nov 1856
Edwin Martin Handcart Co.
SPOUSE: James Mellor
MARRIED: 14 Mar 1838
DEATH SP: 19 Dec 1903

CHILDREN:
Selena Ann, 1 Oct 1837 (died age 1)
Louisa, 23 May 1840
Charlotte Elizabeth, 16 Jan 1842
Mary Ann, 3 Mar 1846
James, 8 Oct 1848
William Charles, 15 Apr 1853
Emma (twin), 1 Oct 1857
Clara (twin), 1 Oct 1857
John Carlos, 1 Feb 1860

Mary Ann and James Mellor were living in Bradford, England when they heard the gospel as preached by the Elders and were both baptized in April 1844. They opened their home for the missionaries to teach in. This family relied upon the Church Emigration Fund in order to come to America. Her husband had already been in prison for being poor and out of work. They had moved from Leicester to wait in Liverpool until it was their turn to board a boat. As they were waiting, Mary Ann gave birth to Siamese twins and was too ill to board ship. The ship, "Horizon," was ready to leave the next morning. During the night James smuggled her aboard ship, sick or not. The saints had already made the decision to start late in the season to cross the ocean rather than remain in England any longer. When they arrived in Boston, Massachusetts, they traveled by train and arrived in Iowa City, Iowa on July 8.

They were advised at that time that it was too late to cross the Plains because winter would overtake them. The company again voted to go on. They left Florence, Nebraska with the Edward Martin Handcart Company on August 25, 1856. They suffered countless hardships. Mary Ann was still very ill and had to ride in a handcart part of the time with her babies. By October 31, when the rescue wagons finally met their handcart company at Greasewood Flats, more than a hundred saints had already died in their company. They were so grateful to receive food and help. It was November 30, 1856 when they arrived in the Salt Lake Valley. Several members of her family were severely frozen on the trek, but the whole family arrived in the valley as had been promised by Franklin D. Richards in a blessing upon their family in England prior to departure.

Their family settled in Springville, Utah where their last three children were born. Another move was made to Warm Creek where they built their permanent home. On September 15, 1895 Mary Ann died in Fayette, Utah. She received much happiness in service to her family, church, and community. In faith, courage, bravery, and endurance, Mary Ann proved herself as a stalwart giant among women.

IMOGENE JOSEPHINE GIBBS MELVILLE

BIRTHDATE. 6 Sep 1850
Chemung, McHenry County, Illinois
DEATH: 6 Nov 1942
Salt Lake City, Utah
PARENTS: William Gibbs
Elizabeth Dana Gibbs
PIONEER: 26 Sep 1857
William G. Young Co. Wagon Train
SPOUSE: James Andrew Melville
MARRIED: 12 Oct 1869
Salt Lake City Endowment House
DEATH SP: 21/24 Dec 1926
Salt Lake City, Utah

CHILDREN:
James Alexander, 19 Jul 1870
William Francis, 21 Feb 1873
Albert Bernard, 1 Aug 1875
John Harvey, 9 Feb 1878
Josephine, 21 Sep 1881
Lois Geneva (Greenwood), 1 Apr 1883
Mary Evelyn (Brown), 8 Mar 1886
Grover Cleveland, 22 Aug 1889

Imogene was born 6 Sep 1850 in Chemung, Illinois. In 1857 when Imogene was just seven years old, she crossed the Plains with her family. One frightening incident in which she, her twelve year old brother Josiah; and younger sister, Dora participated in was told of by Josiah. As the children sat in their covered wagon, their oxen were frightened by another balky oxen. The oxen ran down the road until within a few feet of a bridge then swerved toward a wash. Mitton Musser flashed his red flannel-lined cloak in the faces of the oxen, who then reared and fell, the wheelers on top of them, and the wagon partially on top of the prostrate oxen, scarcely ten feet between the oxen and the vertical wash. Except for a few bruises, everyone was unhurt. They arrived in the Salt Lake Valley on 26 Sep 1857, just ahead of Johnston's Army.

The family lived in Salt Lake for five years with the exception of the winter of 1858 when they moved to Summit Creek (now Santaquin) to get away from Johnston's Army. They then moved to Fillmore City, Utah where Imogene grew up.

Imogene tells the following story: "William Gibbs, my father, made me a dumb telegraph keyboard out of empty wooden spools. I practiced at home. At fourteen I learned the telegraph code. I went back to school one year and then I took the telegraph office at Fillmore. I was called to Scipio to take the telegraph office, but the fleas nearly ate me up, and I got so homesick I nearly died, so I took the buckboard back to Fillmore after three days. The telegraph office called all day and no one was there to answer, so they called Fillmore and wanted to know where the operator had gone. Mary, my sister, took the office at Scipio."

"Mary got married soon after we got into the telegraph office and I had it to myself. When in the office, I felt so tied and I wanted to go play ball and run around. We opened at 8:00 a.m. They paid me $25 a month. I quit the office in Fillmore to get married. "

Imogene married James Andrew Melville in 1868. She joined the Fillmore choir and Athenaeum Club, a dramatic society. Once she asked her brother, Josiah Gibbs why he gave her the leads so often. He replied, "because you are so graceful."

Imogene was a charter member of the Fillmore Relief Society.

When her husband took her sister, Dora, as his second wife, Imogene made the following remarks: "Dora and I never quarreled. I think I would have felt better if I had someone other than a sister in polygamy because I could have brushed over and relieved myself some. Not many men know how to handle polygamy after they get into it. They are pulled one side then the other; a lot of us will have to be converted to polygamy."

After the Melvilles moved to Salt Lake City in 1904, Imogene became involved in genealogy and temple work. At ninety-one she could still remember the telegraph alphabet. She passed away on 6 Nov 1942 and was buried beside her husband in Mount Olivet Cemetery in Salt Lake City, Utah. She often repeated the saying, "You learn how to live when you are ready to die."

JANE ANN DUTSON MELVILLE

BIRTHDATE: 10 Mar 1827
Lugwardine, Herefordshire, Eng.
DEATH: 11 May 1911
Fillmore City, Utah
PARENTS: John Dutson
Ann Green Dutson Carling
PIONEER: 21 Sep 1852
Henry W. Miller Wagon Co.
SPOUSE: Alexander Melville
MARRIED: 29 May 1848
Winter Quarters, Nebraska
DEATH: 6/19 Dec 1911
Fillmore City, Utah

CHILDREN:
John William, 21 Jun 1849
James Andrew, 3 Mar 1852
Mary Jane (Kelly), 4 Jun 1854
Ann Elizabeth (Bishop), 20 May 1856
Brigham, 15 Mar 1858
Francis Cannon, 1 May 1860
Daniel Dutson, 31 Dec 1862
Eleanor Green (Tomkinson), 27 May 1865
Joseph Matthew, 6 Aug 1867
David Alexander, 24 Aug 1869
George Edward, 25 Jan 1873

Jane Ann was born on 10 Mar 1827 in Lugwardine, England. Her father disappeared while on a business trip and was never heard from again. In 1840 she was baptized into the Mormon Church. Two years later, Jane Ann, fifteen years old, emigrated to Nauvoo with her mother and brother. For the next ten years she experienced many of the joys and tragedies experienced by the Saints in Nauvoo.

While in Nauvoo, Jane took care of the Cannon children, whose parents were deceased.

When Jane, along with other Mormons, was forced to leave Nauvoo, she and David Cannon, the youngest Cannon child, crossed the broad Mississippi River by holding hands and jumping from one block of ice to another. Later, she joined her family in St. Louis. Here she learned the art of binding the tops of shoes.

In 1849 at Winter Quarters, Jane married Alexander Melville, a widower. Alexander's first wife, Elizabeth Adamson, and small baby boy, Joseph Alexander, had passed away; and Jane Ann became the stepmother to his small daughter, Margaret. Jane and Alexander returned to St. Louis, then moved to Mosquito Creek, Iowa, having children born in both areas.

"At Canesville (sic), when the Saints had scurvy," wrote Alexander, "my wife sat up half of every night with the sick. So many died that they had to sew night, and they

had to set a candle on a white sheet to see." Mary Ann was faithful in her responsibility for "laying out the dead."

The family joined the Henry W. Miller Company wagon train, arriving 21 Sep 1852 in the Salt Lake Valley. Jane Ann and her mother, Ann Green Dutson Carling, carried the baby, James Andrew, in a clothes basket most of the way across the Plains.

After living in Provo for one year, Alexander and Jane Ann moved to Fillmore settling in the old fort. For the Fourth of July celebration in 1853, Jane Ann and her Aunt Elizabeth Richmond made the first flag to fly over the fort. The flag was made of Alexander's red Nauvoo Legion sash, a sheet and some blue quilt blocks.

In 1859 Alexander and Jane moved into a two room log cabin and later in a comfortable brick home. Here six more children were born. The house is still standing today (1995).

In Fillmore Jane continued to bind the upper parts of shoes as well as tailor men's suits. She raised cane for molasses, bleached straw and braided it into hats. She also made her own lye, soap, candles and brooms.

Jane was a member of and enjoyed singing in the Fillmore Choir. She was a charter member of the Fillmore Relief Society and counselor in the Fillmore Ward Relief Society. She donated money for the Perpetual Emigrating Fund in order for others to come West and worship together.

In her later years cataracts formed over Jane's eyes, taking her sight. She died 11 May 1911 and was buried in Fillmore, Utah.

ANN WILSON MEMMOTT

No
Photo
Available

BIRTHDATE: 11 August
1814 Whiston, Yorkshire, England
DEATH: 30 January 1902
Scipio, Millard Co., Utah
PARENTS: James Wilson
Martha Wilkinson
PIONEER: 12 Sep 1861
Milo Andrus Wagon Train
SPOUSE: William Memmott
MARRIED: 30 Nov1835
Yorkshire, England
DEATH SP: 3 Dec 1895
Scipio, Millard Co., Utah

CHILDREN:
Thomas, 27 Feb 1838
Martha, 21 Oct 1839
James Wilson, 25 Feb 1841
John William, 3 Dec 1845
William, 4 Oct 1847
Samuel Hemmott, 18 Jul 1850
Sara Ann, 6 Nov 1854

Ann was born in England, 1814. She was the fourth of ten children. She joined the LDS church in 1847. Her sister Julia joined in 1849. These sisters were close all of their lives. After each married and had their families, they emigrated to Utah and settled in Scipio, Millard Co., Utah

JULIA WIILSON MEMMOTT

BIRTHDATE: 11 Jun 1819
Whiston, Yorkshire, England
DEATH: 26 Aug 1898
Scipio, Millard, Utah
PARENTS: James Wilson
Martha Wilkinson
PIONEER: 29 Oct 1855
Capt. Charles A. Harper Company
Wagon Train
SPOUSE: John Memmott
MARRIED: 16 Mar 1846
Eccles Birelow, Yorkshire, England
DEATH: 29 Oct 1866
Scipio, Millard, Utah

CHILDREN:
Sarah (Probert), 18 Jan 1847
Martha (Memmott/Ivie), 19 Oct 1848
Thomas William, 21 Jul 1850
John Alma, 23 Sep 1852
Anna Laura, 18 Aug 1854
James Ammon, 22 Oct 1856

Julia was born 11 Jun 1819 in Whiston, England. At the age of eight, Julia went to work for a wealthy land owner to tend three small children. She later made pics for him for a fox hunt. He was so impressed he hired her as his cook. Her cooking skills were later used in cooking for large crowds. Julia also took a dress making class which proved helpful as she raised her family.

When nineteen, Julia trained with five other girls and six boys to become a doctor for Queen Victoria. A Dr. Davis, who won the position, later came to America and moved to Manti, Utah. He said he had to "work like a Britain to beat Julia" and highly praised her abilities. After coming to Utah, Julia used this training in helping to deliver many a baby and help nurse the ill back to health.

Julia joined the LDS Church on 28 Oct 1849 and sailed with her husband and five children on 22 Apr 1855. They came to America on the ship "Samuel Curling." While camped with the pioneers at Mormon Grove, Kansas her two youngest children, John Alma and Anne Laura, died of malaria. They were buried there, which was a heart breaking experience for Julia.

Julia and her family went to Beaver and while there she became very ill from eating nothing but bran bread. They moved to Cedar City and her last baby was born there. Later they moved to Round Valley (Scipio), lived in a dugout there and later a log cabin. While living in the fort she was widowed at the age of forty-seven.

Julia was always active in the LDS Church, willing to help in whatever capacity she could. A faithful, stalwart,

wonderful mother and wife, she sacrificed much for her testimony of the Gospel of Jesus Christ.

LOUISA FLEET SMART MENDENHALL

BIRTHDATE: 11 Oct 1845
Pavilly, Seine-Maritime, France
DEATH: 20 Aug 1922
Franklin, Franklin, Idaho
PARENTS: Henry Fleet
Ann Hayter Fleet Smart
PIONEER: 12 Oct 1852
Allen Weeks Wagon Company
SPOUSE: Thomas Mendenhall
MARRIED: 31 Mar 1863
Franklin, Oneida, Idaho
DEATH SP: 21 Mar 1909
Logan, Cache, Utah

CHILDREN:
Catherine Ann, 29 Dec 1863
Thomas George, 7 Jun 1865 (died age 1)
Mary Ann, 3 May 1867
Rhoda Kessiah, 25 Jul 1869
Susannah Matilda, 29 Nov 1871
William Henry, 21 Nov 1873
Lorin Matthew, 18 Mar 1876
Ada Louisa, 12 Jan 1878
Ruby May, 16 Nov 1880
Nettie Pearl, 7 Mar 1883
Leo Smart, 7 Apr 1886
Bert Smart, 4 Jul 1888

Louisa was born in northern France to English parents who divorced before she was born. Her mother subsequently married Thomas Smart, a brick maker. She was raised as his daughter, adopted by him, and sealed to him. She was just a baby when her parents emigrated to the United States settling in St. Louis, Missouri. There, her parents heard the gospel message and were baptized members of the LDS Church. Louisa was seven years old when her family arrived in Utah in October of 1852 with the Allen Weeks Wagon Company. The family first settled in the American Fork area. Then they joined the first pioneers settling Franklin, Idaho when Louisa was fourteen. As one of the older children in the family, Louisa learned many skills to assist the family. She gleaned wheat, gathered herbs, spun yarn, wove cloth, knit stockings, made candles, soap, butter, and cheese.

Louisa married Thomas Mendenhall, Jr., a pioneer of Franklin where they lived for their first few years. They helped settle several outlying communities in that area. They were parents to twelve children. In later years, Louisa turned her home into a hotel which she ran for many years. Her husband was a farmer and cattleman. She was a teacher and counselor in the Relief Society and worked on the Missionary Committee. She died at the age of seventy five.

MARIA CATHERINE BOYER MENDENHALL

BIRTHDATE: 13 Oct 1850
Frieburg, Union, Pennsylvania
DEATH: 28 Mar 1915
Mapleton, Utah Co., Utah
PARENTS: Augustus Sell Boyer
Catherine Houtz Boyer
PIONEER: 1853 ox team
SPOUSE: Richard Lovell
Mendenhall
MARRIED: 5 Dec. 1870
DEATH SP: 8 Aug 1821
Mapleton, Utah Co., Utah

CHILDREN:
Irena Boyer, 13 Dec 1871
Richard Lovell, 15 Nov 1873

Maria was born in Pennsylvania in 1850, the youngest of seven children to parents of German decent.

When Maria was seven months old, her father died of an infection to his jaw bone, it having been broken through the extraction of a tooth.

Jacob Houtz, Maria's uncle, returning from a mission in Germany, convinced his sister (Maria's mother) to go to Utah with him. Her friends and family thought her foolish to even consider leaving her home and parents but she had been studying the Gospel and felt it was true. She gathered her children and left their home never to return.

Maria entered the Salt Lake Valley as a three year old toddler, a valley growing visibly every day with wagon trains full of saints arriving once a week through all of September and October. She was six when the threat of Johnston's Army and concern for the survival and safety of the Mormons caused Brigham Young to call the Saints to gather and send the families south for their protection. She was sixteen when the Black Hawk War erupted making the presence of Indians a fearful threat, and she was twenty years old when she and Richard Lovell Mendenhall were married by Joseph F. Smith.

Her mother taught her all the duties of a pioneer woman, to spin and weave, to sew, and beautify her home with beautiful handiwork. She raised chickens, milked cows and made butter. Because Maria's health did not permit her to do heavy work, she spent her efforts in all the things she could do in every way she could to help her family. In serving her community, she was an officer in the Primary for many years and cared for the older people and others in need. She spread kindness and cheer wherever she went and had many staunch friends.

Richard and Maria homesteaded a sixty acre farm in Mapleton and built a large two story home on it. It was one of the first permanent homes in this little town. It still stands as a monument to them and the pioneers who were Utah's founders.

MARY ELLEN DEAL MENDENHALL

BIRTHDATE: 3 Oct 1845
Quincy, Adams Co., Illinois
DEATH: 30 Jun 1910
Springville, Utah Co., Utah
PARENTS: John Wesley Deal
Eliza Crandall
PIONEER: 2 Sep 1850
Aaron Johnson Wagon Train
SPOUSE: Thomas Mendenhall
MARRIED: 15 May 1864
Springville, Utah Co., Utah
DEATH SP: 24 Aug 1926
Springville, Utah Co., Utah

CHILDREN:
Thomas Deal, 7 Feb 1865
Seymour Lovell, 2 Apr 1867
Guy Wesley, 19 Jan 1870
John Fenmore, 10 Jul 1872
Jessie Eliza, 11 Dec 1876
Willioam Bayard, 18 Dec 1878
Nettie Zoe, 14 Jan 1883
Stephen, 16 Dec 1884
Berne Monroe, 13 Apr 1886
Mary Leona, 6 Jul 1889
Sarah Arline, 21 Oct 1891

Mary Ellen arrived into the Salt Lake Valley with her family by wagon train on September 2, 1850, at the age of five years. After a short rest they were sent to Springville, Utah, arriving there on September 18, 1850, as one of the first ten wagons to settle there. She well remembered jumping down from the wagon with relief into the tall grass that was growing there.

Her wedding dress was the first dress that she did not help spin and weave the material for. Her family started a mercantile business and she would stay up late at night making men's pants and jumpers to be sold over the counter the next day. She dried tons of fruit to be hauled to the markets of Salt Lake to be sold. She had a great love for flowers and grew many of them.

She served several years in the Primary Presidency and was a visiting teacher in the Relief Society for many years. She raised her large family of children pretty much by herself as her husband worked away from home a great deal of the time doing freighting, construction of railroads and working at building the St. George Temple.

SARAH LOVELL MENDENHALL

BIRTHDATE: 2 Mar 1818
Weaverthorpe, Yorkshire, Eng.
DEATH: 17 Oct. 1899
Springville, Utah Co., Utah
PARENTS Richard Lovell
Francis Sawdon Lovell
PIONEER 10 Oct 1852
Wagon Train
SPOUSE: William Mendenhall
MARRIED 21 Feb 1838
DEATH SP: 3 Jun 1906
Springville, Utah Co. Utah

CHILDREN:
Mary Francis, 29 Sep 1839
Thomas Lovell, 29 Oct 1841
Abraham, 22 Apr 1844 died 5 days
Richard Lovell, 19 Aug 1845
John, 7 Sep 1847
Elizabeth Wells, 3 Apr 1850
Sarah Lovell, 12 May 1853
William Amasa, 2 Jan 1856
Hannah Matilda, 12 Jun 1858

Sarah Lovell was born in England and came to America in her parents' arms as a one-year-old baby. The family settled in New Castle, Delaware where she was raised. Sarah fell in love with William Mendenhall and they married just nineteen days before her twenty-first birthday.

She was expecting her second child when she heard and was moved by the message of the restored gospel and was baptized in June of 1841. Their move into Nauvoo was in May of 1843, into a city expanding every day with new saints gathering to the church, reclaiming the swamps to build "a singular and most beautiful city," according to Colonel Kane. They lived there through the shock of the Prophet's assassination, the time of persecution and the order of extermination of all Mormons issued by Governor Boggs.

They suffered as all refugees when driven from the warmth and security of homes into the cold and despair of winter and hunger, carrying their babies and hurriedly salvaging what they could, crowding onto fields and in woods, trying to erect some sort of shelter in the dead of winter.

Six of her nine children were born under these diverse conditions, some in a belief of security, some in defiance to persecution and some in joy of the potential future, all in faith of the Gospel and its guidance.

They crossed the Mississippi River in June of 1846, across Iowa to Kanesville and Council Bluffs, remaining in Pottowatamie County until the last of the saints left in a final exodus from that place.

After crossing the plains by ox team they settled in Springville, arriving in the fall of 1852. Unknowingly, adversity was still to come, the threat of Johnston's Army,

and the Black Hawk War. Through it all their everyday lives were full of family, friends and church, raising their children, milking cows, helping neighbors, all the things that make a fruitful life.

She was treasurer and assistant Secretary to the Relief Society in Springville for many years and performed ordinance work for the dead in the old Endowment House, and the Salt Lake City, St. George, Logan, and Manti Temples.

Sarah Lovell passed away peacefully on 17 Oct 1899 at the age of 81 years, 7 months and 5 days. She had nine children, 51 grandchildren and 22 great grandchildren.

Hers was the path of the just, never faltering from the hour of her baptism, a loving mother, devoted wife and her example was a shining light to all.

ELIZABETH BARNES MERCHANT

No
Photo
Available

BIRTHDATE: 9 Jun 1805
Highworth, Wiltshire, England
DEATH: 10 Jun 1863
Beaver, Beaver County, Utah
PARENTS: William Barnes
Mary Dodds
PIONEER: 1897
Augustus Farnham Wagon from Calif.
SPOUSE: Richard Merchant (Bapson)
MARRIED: 30 Dec l827
Christ Church, Newcastle,
New South Wales, Australia
DEATH SP: 19 Sep 1862
Australia

CHILDREN:
William, 28 Jun 1828
Richard, 26 Sep 1829
Sarah Ann, 26 Aug 1831
Jane (Parker/Eardlev), 13 May 1833
James, 16 May 1835
Thomas, 17 May 1837
Harriet (Grant), 30 Jan 1839
Caroline (Wilson), 12 Jan 1841
Charles Edward, 9 Oct 1843
Susan Matilifa (Parrish), 18 Jun 1844
Mary (Bemis), 24 Dec 1846
John, 29 Jan 1850

Elizabeth was born in England in 1805. At age nineteen, her mother died and Elizabeth was in charge of her younger brothers. Her father was hired by the Australian Agriculture Company to transport Saxon and French Merino sheep to Port Stephens, Australia. William and his children boarded the "York" for Australia. The passengers on this ship were the first large group who came to Australia as free settlers.

Elizabeth, nicknamed Betsy, met and married Richard Merchant or Bapson (his father was William Bapson) 30 Dec 1827 at Christ Church, Newcastle, New South Wales. They left Telligherry in 1832 with their three children and sailed on the "Lambton," the Australian Agriculture

Company cutter, to Newcastle on their way to Maitland. They located near Vacy, New South Wales. Here, Laufiet Sheperd and his companion, Elder Davis taught the family the gospel. Elizabeth was baptized 1 Mar 1853 in the Allyn River. After their conversion, Richard and Elizabeth planned to emigrate to Zion. Aboard the ship, after a dispute, Richard disembarked, leaving Elizabeth to sail alone with her six youngest children. They were parents of twelve. They sailed from Sydney, Australia on the American ship, the "Jenny Ford," on 29 May 1855. They arrived in San Pedro California 19 Aug 1855, where they were greeted by Laufiet Sheperd, the elder who had baptized them. They travelled inland to San Bernardino, where Elder Sheperd had purchased a small farm for the family. They cultivated the land and planted fruit trees. After awhile, Elizabeth received an offer to sell her farm. She traded it for a team and wagon to go to Utah. Elizabeth joined the Augustus Farnham wagon train in 1857 with her two youngest sons and daughter, Caroline. They settled in North Creek, Beaver County, which became known as Merchant Valley. Elizabeth and her two sons homesteaded the land and again established a small farm. Elizabeth was very lonely. Richard did not come to Zion. She was scrubbing on the washboard one day, when blood started spurting from her nose and mouth. She died from cerebral hemorrhage on 10 Jun 1863 and is buried in Mountain View Cemetery, Beaver, Utah. She was age fifty-eight at her passing. Richard had passed away 19 Sep 1862 in Australia.

MARIA JOSEPHINE STOCK ALLRED MERKLEY

BIRTHDATE: 3 Sep 1858
Port Elizabeth, Cape Colony, South Africa
DEATH: 27 Jun 1954
Logan, Cache, Utah
PARENTS: John Stock
Jane Adams
PIONEEER: 5 Oct 1860
William Budge Company
SPOUSE I:
Medwin Newton Allred
MARRIED: 31 May 1875
Salt Lake City, Utah
DEATH SP: 21 Jul 1895
Fairview, Uinta, Wyoming

CHILDREN:
Medwin Alvin, 17 Jul 1876
Edith Marie, 11 Dec 1877
Asa Newton, 15 Aug 1879
Seymour Bertie, 5 Jul 1881
Edwin Nelson, 5 Mar 1883
William Lyle, 8 Feb 1885
John Edgar, 15 Jan 1887
Rollin Leslie, 5 Jan 1889
Arlin Richard, 15 Jul 1890
Darrel Stock, 9 Jul 1893

SPOUSE II: Christopher Amos Merkley
MARRIED: 28 Nov 1917

Maria Josephine Stock was born 3 Sep 1858 in Port Elizabeth, Cape Colony, South Africa, the daughter of John Stock and Jane Adams. Her parents were converted to the Church prior to her birth, and when she was two years old they came to America with their nine children. They came across the plains with the William Budge Company, arriving in the Valley 5 Oct 1860.

They lived in Salt Lake for a time, then moved to Bear Lake Valley in Idaho where her parents were asked to settle. It was a very cold area and wheat had a hard time ripening. The children, including Maria, would glean all they could from the fields, and they were paid a small amount. When she had earned enough money she bought some calico to make herself a dress.

Maria married Medwin Newton Allred in the Endowment House on 31 May 1875, and they became the parents of nine boys and a girl. Her first great sorrow was her little daughter being run over by a loaded wagon and killed. Then she was left a widow at the age of thirty-seven when her husband died on 29 Jul 1895, leaving nine sons, ages two to eighteen. The family lived in Fairview, Uintah, Wyoming (Star Valley) where Maria ran a grocery store and was Post Mistress. She was also Primary President, and served in other Church callings. She married a second time to Christopher Amos Merkley on 28 Nov 1917.

Maria died 27 Jun 1954 at age ninety-six years in Logan, Cache, Utah.

SARAH DAVIS MERKLEY

BIRTHDATE: 19 May 1810
LaShute, Lower Canada
DEATH: 7 May 1893
Salt Lake City, Utah
PARENTS: Nathaniel Davis
Sarah Jacobs
PIONEER: 10 Oct 1848
Amasa Lyman Co Wagon Train
SPOUSE: Christopher Merkley
MARRIED: 18 Feb 1828
Williamsburg, Dundas, Ontario Canada
DEATH SP: 2 May 1893
Salt Lake City, Utah

CHILDREN:
Nelson Jr, 11 Nov 1828

Sarah was born in Canada in 1810. At age seventeen, she married Christopher Merkley. They were both born in Canada, as was their child, Nelson Jr. There they were converted to the LDS church.

Nelson was her only child. In her Patriarchal Blessing, she was promised a large posterity. When her son married Sarah Jane Sanders they became parents of thirteen so her blessing was fulfilled. The family followed the Saints into Missouri, Nauvoo, Council Bluffs and eventually into the Salt Lake Valley. During this time Christopher was helping others move, hunting lost horses, going on many missions. In Council Bluffs in 1848, their horses were again stolen and Christopher could not complete two outfits to bring his two wives to Utah. It was decided to send Sarah and her son Nelson on alone in the spring of 1848. Christopher built her a nice home in Salt Lake when he arrived in 1849. It had one-and-a-half stories, five rooms and 72 panes of glass. Sometime in 1849-50 they took into their home a one-year-old girl whose mother had died shortly after her birth, 3 Aug 1848 at Deer Creek Platte River on the way to Utah. They called her Louisa Marie (Thompson) Merkley. She stayed with them about sixteen years. She married and moved to the Uintah Basin. Christopher's second wife divorced him.

Her husband having completed eight missions for the church and having followed many different lines of work, Sarah was left alone much of the time. She encouraged her husband, age fifty, to marry a third wife, Xarissa Fairbanks, age 20, which he did on 17 Jan 1859. Sarah felt the marriage would be an answer to her prayers. The two women were congenial and happy together. Each tried to help the other. Xarissa bore eight children, three pairs of twins and two single births, a total of three sons and five daughters. Later, children said they had never heard an angry word between the two women. Sarah, who was never strong, tended the children (who called her Grandma), spun the wool, knitted socks, and did light housework. Xarissa did the heavy outdoor work, cooking and washing. When polygamy was declared illegal, Xarissa and her family moved to a ranch in St. Charles, Bear Lake, Idaho, where she died 28 Nov 1904 and was buried there. In 1893, when Sarah was told that her husband had died she said that he could not go and leave her. She turned her face to the wall and died five days later. They were buried in the Salt Lake City Cemetery where they share a common gravestone that reads "In Memory, Christopher Merkley born 18 Dec 1810, Upper Canada, Died 7 May 1893. Died in full faith of the Gospel. They were one in life and in death they were not divided." Sarah was nearly eighty-three at her passing.

CHILDREN:
Nelson Jr, 24 Mar 1897
George Davis, 14 Jul 1899
Sarah Jane (Coltharp), 24 Aug 1861
Susan Maria (Britt), 28 Oct 1863
Christopher Ellis, 26 Aug 1865
Mary, 19 Jan 1867
Charles Albert, 11 Jan 1869
Elizabeth (Hall), 29 Dec 1871
John, 29 Aug 1874
Henry, 3 Dec 1877
William Sanders, 1 Jul 1880
Rachel Ellen (Murray), 2 Sep 1882
Jacob, 5 Feb 1886

Sarah Jane was born in Delaware in 1841. She came with her parents to Nauvoo in about 1842 and the home they had built and lived in is still standing there. She crossed the plains as a child when her parents came to the Salt Lake Valley in the Heber C. Kimball Wagon train. She "skipped along and had a wonderful time."

At age fourteen she married Nelson Merkley Sr., 25 Mar 1856 in the Salt Lake City Endowment House. He was thirteen years her senior, at age twenty-seven. Nelson was his mother's only child, so it is remarkable that this couple had thirteen children. Their first child, Nelson Jr., was born one day before their first wedding anniversary in the Carson Valley area which is now Genoa, Nevada, but would have been in the State of Deseret then. Nelson was back and forth in that area with his father. They were called back at the time of Johnston's Army.

They appeared to live in Cedar Fort for about thirteen years. Then Sarah Jane went with her husband to help settle the Ashley Valley . . . no small task for a woman with a large family. Her son Nelson Jr. had gone in 1879 and staked out some property and survived a cold winter. Sarah Jane and Nelson Sr. followed later. Her first child born in Vernal was Rachel Ellen in 1882. She bore eight sons and five daughters, with one child dying in infancy. Sarah Jane lived to age eighty-six and was a widow for twenty-six years. A stately granite stone marks the couple's burial place in the Vernal Memorial Park Cemetery.

SARAH JANE SANDERS MERKLEY

BIRTHDATE: 15 Dec 1841
Wilmington, New Castle, Dela.
DEATH: 14 Aug 1928
Vernal, Uinta, Utah
PARENTS:
Ellis Mendenhall Sanders
Rachel Broom Roberts
PIONEER: 23 Sep 1848
Heber C. Kimball Wagon Train
SPOUSE: Nelson Merkley Sr.
MARRIED: 25 Mar 1856
Salt Lake Endowment House
DEATH: 21 Jan 1902
Vernal, Uinta, Utah

MARTHA ANN CAMPKIN MERRELL

BIRTHDATE: 15 Jan 1854
Biggleswade, Bedfordshire, England
DEATH: 30 Dec 1936
Lewisville, Jefferson County, Idaho
PARENTS: Isaac Campkin
Martha Webb
PIONEER: 9 Nov 1856
James G. Willie Handcart Co
SPOUSE: Joseph Merrell
MARRIED: 6 May 1872
Salt Lake Endowment House
DEATH SP: 18 May 1921
Blackfoot, Idaho

CHILDREN:
Charles Me, 22 May 1873
Isaac George, 24 Sep 1874
Joseph Leonard, 28 Jan 1876
Jonathan, 10 Sep 1877
Martha Henrietta (Wood), 17 Mar 1879
Archebald, 5 Aug 1881
James Reuben 25 Jul 1883
Sarah Sophia (McDonald Tucker), 26 Dec 1884
Nancy Marinda, 11 Oct 1886
Benjamin Sylvester Campkin, 14 Aug 1888
Emma Luella (Hancock), 8 Jul 1890
Eliza Vilate, 8 Apr 1892
Albert Ervin 28 Mar 1894

Martha Ann was born in England, 1854. She was fifth of seven children. Her mother and many of her siblings came to Utah. Martha Ann was only two years old when they came in the ill-fated Willie Handcart Co.

At age eighteen she married Joseph Merrell in the Salt Lake Endowment House. They made there home in Perry, where their first child was born. They moved to Portage, where five more children were born. Their last move was to Brigham City where their last seven children were born.

Martha said "I have always been a pioneer, always moving to new territories, and have never had anything much but the bare necessities. I was a Relief Society teacher for years, driving my own horse and buggy and gathering many a bushel of wheat for the Relief Society storage program. I never did anything great in my life. All I had time for was to have babies, wash, and sew and mend and bake bread."

Martha Ann passed away 30 Dec 1936 at age eighty-two having been a widow for fifteen years. She was the mother of a "Baker's Dozen" (13 children). Her last days were spent in Idaho with her children, Martha, Sarah and Isaac, who all made their homes in Idaho.

MARY ANN SAXTON MERRELL (MERRILL)

No Photo Available

BIRTHDATE: 10 Sep 1908
Bridgewater, Oneida, New York
DEATH: 29 Apr 1861
Paradise, Cache, Utah
PARENTS: Joseph Saxton
Ann Haskins (Hoskins)
PIONEER: 24 Sep 1851
Tarry Walton Co Wagon Train
SPOUSE: Hosea Merrell
MARRIED: 25 Apr 1825
Bridgewater, Oneida, New York
DEATH: 5 Feb 1864
Paradise, Cache, Utah

CHILDREN:
George Clarence Jan 1826
Charles twin, 20 Feb 1827
Sally Jerusha (Davis/Coupe), 20 Feb 1827

Edna Marie (Reynolds), 29 Dec 1828
Alonza Clark, 3 Jun 1831
Joseph Jackson, 12 Nov 1832
Jerusha, Aug 1834
Joseph, Sep 1839
John Elwin, 25 Jan 1841
Silas Jerome, 28 Oct 1843
Porter William 10 Sep 1846

Mary Ann was born in New York in 1808. She was the oldest of five children. Just before her seventeenth birthday, she married Hosea Merrell (Merrill). Hosea joined the LDS church in 1837 and Mary Ann joined in 1844. They made their home in Butler, Wayne Co., New York, where their first five children were born. They made several moves, to Michigan and Iowa, all the while adding to their family, becoming parents of eleven. They eventually journeyed to Nauvoo, Illinois, just in time to bear the brunt of the persecutions and the exodus. They were living in Garden Grove when they joined the Harry Walton Company leaving 17 May and arriving in Salt Lake City 24 Sep 1891. Six children came with them.

They settled in the Big Cottonwood area, where many of the new arrivals were locating. Their family was then called to Cache Valley, where they settled in Paradise. Here, Mary Ann worked hard and faithfully to make a comfortable and happy home for her husband and children. Her father passed away in 1862, in Payson, where many of her family settled. She endured much but was faithful to the Church. She buried Hosea in Paradise, in 1864. She was a widow for five years, passing away 29 Apr 1869 at age sixty, in Paradise, Cache County, Utah.

ANNA CLAUDIA ANDERSEN (FREDRIKSEN) OLSON MERRILL

No Photo Available

BIRTHDATE: 21 Dec 1820
Froya, Norway
DEATH: 15 Jul 1885
Salt Lake City, Utah
PARENTS: Anders Fredriksen
Christine (Kristen) Pedersen Fredriksen
PIONEER: 1 Oct 1862
Joseph Horne Wagon Co.
SPOUSE I: Christen Olson

CHILDREN:
Kristine, 1852

SPOUSE II: Samuel Merrill
MARRIED: 8 Nov 1862

CHILDREN:
Phoebe, 10 Nov 1863
Rebecca, 12 May 1866

Anna came from a family of seven children. She was raised in a loving home and taught to work hard. She was nearly ten when her father, a fisherman, was lost at sea. Anna's stepfather read the Bible and said there would be a Prophet raised up for the true church.

Anna married Christen Olson and had a daughter in about 1852. He deserted Anna and her baby. She moved from Bakken to Trondheim. While living here she heard the missionaries, and was baptized 2 Aug 1860. On 13 Mar 1862, Anna and her nine-year-old daughter left on the ship "Athenia." Having buried her daughter at sea, along with all other children on that voyage under the age of twelve, she arrived in New York.

She traveled with Soren Christofferson's Co. from New York to Nebraska. She came with a wagon train arriving in the Valley in 1862. Anna walked all the way.

She went to work as a houseworker for Samuel Merrill, who had just lost his wife. They married and she had two daughters. Her husband had a stroke. Anna cared for him for for ten years.

They had an orchard. Anna picked the fruit, dried it and sold it to Teasdale's store. She also sold butter and eggs, carded wool, spun yarn and made clothing for the family. She raised her daughters, and managed to save enough money to add a kitchen to the two-room home at 437 No. Second West in Salt Lake. She died at the age of sixty-five.

BATHSHEBA SMITH MERRILL

BIRTHDATE: 14 Aug 1841
Nauvoo, Hancock Co., Illinois
DEATH: 22 Dec 1920
Crescent, Salt Lake Co., Utah
PARENTS: George Albert Smith
Bathsheba Bigler
PIONEER: 17 Oct 1849
Elisha Everett (Silas Richards)
SPOUSE: Clarence Merrill
MARRIED: 3 Jan 1861
Salt Lake City, Utah
DEATH: 21 Feb 1918
Salt Lake City, Utah

CHILDREN;
Anella, 19 Dec 1861
Leila (Allen), 6 Sep 1863
George Albert, 2 Feb 1866
Alice (Thorne), 2 Jan 1868
Maud (Lloyd), 7 Feb 1870
Margaret May (Fisher), 5 Feb 1872
Clarence, 7 Jan 1874
Irene, 4 Jun 1876
Alton, 15 Jul 1878
John Henry, 28 Feb 1880
Joseph, 8 May 1882
Thomas, 6 Mar 1884
Lewis Bigler, 30 Jul 1887
Charles, 27 Apr 1890

Bathsheba was born in Illinois in 1841. She was eight or nine when, with her family, she crossed the plains to Utah. She was called Kate by those who knew her. She told of "house-keeping of the family wagon on the trek" and how she and her brother, George, nestled in the buffalo robes her father had purchased from some Indians for them. She recalled the singing and dancing of the Pioneers, when gathered at nightfall around the campfire. Her family settled in Salt Lake City, where at age nineteen, she married Clarence Merrill, a dear friend of her brother George, who was killed while on a mission to the Indians. They married and moved to Fillmore, where her father had a "honeymoon cabin" erected for them. In a couple of years, her father oversaw the erection of a fine brick home for them. Their first two children were born in Salt Lake City, six more joined their family in Fillmore. Clarence had a fine bass voice and would sing, while Bathsheba was artistic and very ingenious. Clarence said "she could create anything: Fancy shoes, hats, coats and dresses." She could devise them and design as well as execute the costumes and they made a big hit with them, also painting scenery for their local theatrical productions in the community of Fillmore. Her scissors were magical with her innate skill. She would make shadow-box scenes of cut paper figures and then delighted the children with stories to accompany these treasures. She had a flower garden, a fruit orchard and a vegetable garden for her growing family from which they were often able to sell some of their produce which was shipped into Nevada. Bathsbeba was also asked to live the law of Polygamy.

In 1882 her mother purchased property for a home for the Merrill family to move to Salt Lake City. Here the last of their fourteen children were born. She was very busy with a large family, and could knit a pair of socks or mittens in just one day. She also had great faith. One day she called her children to her and told them that their cow was ill and was going to die. The cow lay immobile on the ground before them. She explained how disastrous it would be not to have this cow . . . they would no longer have milk or butter or products they were used to having which the cow provided for them. Bathsheba directed the children to kneel with her and they would pray for the cow's life to be spared. She anointed the cow and they prayed. The cow lived and continued to bless their little family with needful items. She was a loving, devoted, creative mother and wife. She passed away at age seventy-nine in Salt Lake City.

CYRENE STANDLEY MERRILL

BIRTHDATE: 1 May 1840
Nauvoo, Illinois
DEATH: 24 Nov 1917
Lewiston, Utah
PARENTS:
Alexander Scoby Standley
Philinda Upson Standley
PIONEER: 30 Oct 1852
Joseph Howell Co.
SPOUSE: Marriner Wood Merrill
MARRIED: age 16
Salt Lake Endowment House
DEATH SP: 6 Feb 1906
Richmond, Utah

CHILDREN:
Nathan Alexander, 26 Oct 1857
Healen (Jackson), 10 Nov 1859 (Pronounced Heel-Ann)
Parley, 24 Nov 1861
Ella Rebecca (Kerr), 10 Dec 1863
Olonzo David, 13 Dec 1867
Ida Philinda (Van Orden), 29 Aug 1870
Ezra Jay, 20 Nov 1873
Alice, 13 Mar 1876

Cyrene Standley was born 1 May 1840 in Nauvoo, Illinois. She was the seventh child of Alexander Scoby Standley and Philinda Upson Standley. She was twelve when she started across the plains in the Joseph Howell Company, arriving 30 Oct 1852. She and her older sister Elizabeth (fourteen) were in charge of herding the sheep. They would have to catch a big buck and pull him into the water to get the rest of the sheep to follow across a stream. They walked all the way.

Cyrene married Marriner Wood Merrill as his second wife in the Endowment House at the age of sixteen.

In the spring of 1860 Cyrene moved to Richmond and lived the first few months in a wagon box. By fall a new home was ready and her husband took her and baby Healen to Bountiful by ox team to get the other wife and her three children. At first the two families lived together, but by 1867 Cyrene had a home of her own.

The pioneer arts of her girlhood came to good use for she carded and spun wool, wove cloth and carpets, sewed coats, dresses and pants, knitted socks and mittens. She also made straw hats by gathering the straw, soaking and braiding it, and finally sewing it into hats. She knew animal husbandry and dairying.

Marriner married eight wives. There were no divorces, and all the wives got along well. She was a devoted and loyal wife. She passed away 24 Nov 1917 in Lewiston, Utah, and is buried beside her husband Marriner, who passed away 6 Feb 1906 at Richmond.

ELIZA JANE VANLEUVEN MERRILL

BIRTHDATE: 25 Aug 1845
Ruth, Davis Co., Illinois
DEATH: 4 Mar 1930
Tropic, Garfield Co., Utah
PARENTS:
Ransom VanLeuven (VanLeuben)
Lucinda Harvey
PIONEER: 1 Oct 1852
John Wimmer Wagon Co
SPOUSE: John Elwin Merrill
MARRIED: 17 Apr 1862
Paradise, Cache, Utah
DEATH: 9 Dec 1909
Tropic, Garfield Co.,Utah

CHILDREN:
Mary Eliza, 2 Apr 1863
John Elwin Jr., 5 Jun 1865
Lucinda Jane (Alvey), 17 Feb 1868
Edna Josephine (Roundy), 2 Feb 1870
Christina (Smith), 11 Jul 1872
Margaret Ann, 31 Aug 1875
Hosea, 24 Jun 1878
Minerva (Caffell), 7 Mar 1881
Elizabeth (Swapp), 4 Sep 1883
Frances, 21 Nov 1886

Eliza Jane was born in Illinois, 1845. Some records indicate her birthplace as Rath Dams, Mason Co, Illinois and others indicate Ruth, Davis, Illinois. When she was seven, she crossed the plains with her family. They left Kanesville in July and arrived in Salt Lake City 1 Oct 1852. Her family moved into the fort at North Ogden. Later they moved to Paradise, Cache where she met her husband, John Elwin Merrill. They were married 17 Apr 1862 in Paradise. They were parents of one child when, on 5 Nov 1864 they were sealed in the Salt Lake City Endowment House, at which time John also married Margaret Davis Owens, by whom he had three children. After their second child was born in Paradise, the Merrill family was called to settle the "muddy Mission." After much hardship in that area, they were released and thereafter lived in several places, all the while adding children to their family. They became parents of ten.

They finally settled in Tropic, Garfield County, where they perfected a homestead and lived out their lives. Eliza Jane attended the dedication of the Salt Lake Temple 6 Apr 1893. She served as a Relief Society teacher at Leeds, Utah and as a Sunday School teacher and Primary President at Clifton, Utah. John passed away 9 Dec 1909 in Tropic. Eliza Jane continued faithful in church and her community for another twenty years as a widow. She passed away at age eighty-four, in Tropic.

LAURA WILDER HARRIS MERRILL

BIRTHDATE: 21 Dec 1810
Chesterfield, Hampshire, Mass
DEATH: 19 Sep 1883
Smithfield, Cache, Utah
PARENTS: Joseph Harris
Martha Wilder
PIONEER: 21 Sep 1848
Brigham Young Co Wagon Train
SPOUSE: Austin Shepherd Merrill
MARRIED: 26 Mar 1827
New England
DEATH: 16 Jan 1874
Smithfield, Cache Co.,Utah

NE# 4339

CHILDREN:
Ledgard Dalenska, 12 Jun 1831
Laura Cordelia (Cox Jr.), 5 Aug 1833
Ira Elias, 21 Apr 1835
Horatio Harris, 3 Jan 1837
Andrew Colburn, 1 Dec 1839
Solyman Sylvanus, 7 Dec 1840
Sarah Cornelia (Noble Sr), 29 May 1843
Austin Taylor, 10 Aug 1845
Freeborn Sheperd, 25 Sep 1848

Laura was born in Massachusetts in 1810. Her family joined the LDS Church in 1838 in New York. They were called to go to Missouri and suffered through the wrongs done to the Saints there.

At age sixteen, Laura married Austin Shepherd Merrill, born 25 Sep 1802 in East Windsor, Hartford, Conn. He was eight years her senior. They made their first home in New York, where four of their nine children were born. Their fifth child was born in Illinois, after they had joined with the saints. They then moved to Nauvoo, were able to have a good house, and they enjoyed a few years of rest there. She and her family gave much of what they had to the work on the Nauvoo Temple, where she and her husband were endowed 28 Jan 1846. Two more children joined their family in Nauvoo. Laura was in Nauvoo when the tragedy of the Prophet's death reached the saints and she and her family were there when the Mantle of Prophet fell on President Brigham Young. She and her family were in the Young Company under Elder Lorenzo Snow. While her family left with very adequate provisions, the journey and the need to share with others caused them to arrive with almost nothing.

Laura and her family settled in Salt Lake County and were blessed with their ninth child there. They were there when the Army threatened the Saints. Because they had been blessed, they again shared what they had with their neighbors and all were able to survive that difficult period. She suffered the loss of her son Solomon to the Indians.

The Merrill family were later called to settle what would become known as Smithfield in Northern Utah. Her son Ira was also killed by the Indians. He was the first to be buried in Smithfield. Her husband Austin passed away there, 16 Jan 1874. Laura was generous and helpful to all,

active in all the Relief Society activities and died proclaiming her love of her God, His Church, and her Family. She passed away at age seventy-two, having been a widow for nine years. Laura also lived the law of Plural Marriage as Austin married Martha Sprague as a second wife.

LUCINDA POTTER BROWN MERRILL

BIRTHDATE: 9 Apr 1847
Adams Township, Seneca, Ohio
DEATH: 24 Jan 1924
Pima, Graham Co., Arizona
PARENTS: Bartlett Brown
Joanna Austin Leach
PIONEER: 4 Aug 1854
Bartlett Brown Indep. Wagon Co.
SPOUSE:
Philemon Christopher Merrill II
MARRIED: 11 Jan 1868
DEATH: 29 Oct 1897
Pima, Graham, Arizona

CHILDREN:
Joanna Sabrina (Marshall), 25 Feb 1869
Philemon Christopher III, 16 Nov 1870
Timothy, 16 May 1872
Bartlett, 29 Sep 1873
Gerald, 7 May 1875
Susannah (Crockett), 19 Mar 1877
Rhoda Asenath, 9 Oct 1879
Cyrena, 8 Jan 1881
Josephine (Follett), 17 May 1884
Seaman, 8 Aug 1887
Ray, 11 Jul 1890
Ralph, 27 Jun 1892

Lucinda was born in Ohio in 1847. At age seven, she came to Utah with her family in her father's independent wagon train in a Prairie Schooner. Her family settled in Centerville. After much death and hardship, and her father not joining the church, he left the family and returned to Ohio. Lucinda went through the typical pioneer life for a child. She received little schooling in Ohio, but received enough in Centerville that she qualified to become a school-teacher. Lucinda went to Morgan City when she became qualified and taught school. There, she met and married Philemon Christopher Merrill II and they made their first home in Morgan, where their first child was born.

They were called to settle in Idaho, first in Nounan for a child, then Soda Springs, for a third child, back to Centerville for a fourth then to Montpelier, Idaho for a fifth, to Richfield, Utah for two more then finally settling in Arizona, in St. David for three children and finally Pima for their last two. It was hard on Lucinda to move so much. No doubt it would have been her cheerful disposition that carried her through her many trials. She was a large woman but she was always happy. People loved to be around her. She is remembered for the beautiful flowers she always raised around her home in Pima. She always kept in close touch with her sisters in Idaho and in Utah. Her husband,

Philemon passed away 29 Oct 1897 in Pima. She never married again. As a widow, she raised a fine family. Lucinda passed away 19 Jan 1924 at age seventy-six having been a widow for twenty-six years.

MARGARET ANN RICHISON MERRILL

No Photo Available

BIRTHDATE: 15 Nov 1816
New York City, New York
DEATH: 30 Mar 1903
Salt Lake City, Utah
PARENTS; William Richison
Ann Jones
PIONEER:
Thomas D. Howell Wagon Train
SPOUSE: Captain Albert Merrill
MARRIED: 21 Mar 1836
New York City, New York
DEATH SP: 1 Nov 1873
Salt Lake City, Utah

CHILDREN:
Amanda, 11 Sep 1837
Alonzo, 27 Jul 1839
Clarence, 15 May 1843
Franklin/Frances, 17 Mar 1843
Austin, 28 Oct 1844
Alfred, 6 Aug 1846
Albert Jr, 10 Oct 1848
Margaret Eleanor, 19 Dec 1850
Marion, 29 Mar 1853
Melville, 11 May 1855
Irene, 23 Jan 1857
Alice, 28 Sep 1859

Margaret Ann was born in New York, 1816. At age nineteen she married Albert Merrill. They made their home in Connecticut, where their first four children were born. They joined the LDS church and gathered with the Saints in Nauvoo. Margaret Ann had a lovely lyric soprano voice and often sang to "lift her spirits" and those around her. They suffered the Nauvoo Exodus and came to Utah in the fall of 1852. Three of her children died on the Plains from exposure and a lack of adequate food and were buried in shallow graves.

Margaret and Albert became parents of twelve children, five of them born in Utah. She sang in choirs in Salt Lake when they settled there. She was tall and beautiful, and warm in her companionable spirit. She was a master at salesmanship and after the death of Albert, 1 Nov 1873, she carried on her financial life by being a seamstress and by being a saleswoman. Loving people as she did, she was interested in talking with them about their lives, and would often return from a day's work filled with her conversations with the people she had met. She would remark that she "just was interested in people and in their lives''. An early proponent of psychology, and family life, she carried local lore and fascinating stories companionably with her.

She and Albert were the first converts in Brooklyn, New York. Although early to leave Nauvoo in 1846, Margaret Ann's health had caused their staying back from their company, when she had delivered a baby and could not travel. They had problems sustaining themselves alone on the frontier. Finally, their difficulties with their health restrained the family from driving on to Zion and they remained in Winter Quarters and were able to grow crops and fruits and vegetables that aided other traveling "trains" in their western trek, an assignment given in time from the church leaders. They joined a west-bound company in 1852. Margaret passed away 30 Mar 1903 at age 86, having been a widow for 30 years.

MARGARET DAVIS OWENS MERRILL

BIRTHDATE: 30 Jun 1837
Liverpool, Lancashire, England
DEATH: 22 Dec 1926
Panguitch, Garfield, Utah
PARENTS: John Davis
(Jonathan Davis Jr)
Margaret Grace Davis
PIONEER: Fall 1851
Wagon Train
SPOUSE: Horace Owens
MARRIED: 4 Oct 1856
cancelled in 1859
DEATH: 20 Jun 1897
Woodruff, Navajo, Arizona

CHILDREN:
Hannah Elizabeth, 13 May 1858

SPOUSE: John Elwin Merrill
MARRIED: 17 Apr 1862 (sealed 5 Nov 1864)
Salt Lake City
DEATH: 9 Dec 1909
Tropic, Garfield, Utah

CHILDREN:
Joseph John, 2 Apr 1865

Margaret was born in England in 1837. Her family joined the LDS church in England and emigrated to the United States in 1850. Her father, brother, sister and an aunt came together. They spent the winter in Cincinnati, Ohio, waiting until the following spring for her mother to arrive so they could continue their journey to Salt Lake City in the fall of 1851.

Margaret crossed the plains at age fourteen. She walked most of the way, and helped drive cattle. She was baptized while crossing the plains. After arriving in Salt Lake, she lived in the house of President Brigham Young for a short time, which she enjoyed very much. At age nineteen, she married in Polygamy to Horace Owens, father of twelve children by his first wife, Sarah or Salley Ann Layne. They made their home in Nephi, where they became parents of a daughter, Hannah Elizabeth, who was crippled and died at the age of twelve. Her sealing was cancelled in 1859.

In 1862, she married John Elwin Merrill in Polygamy. A son, Joseph John, was born in Paradise, Cache Co., Utah. The Merrills were called to settle the "Muddy Mission" in southern Utah. Near Nephi, Margaret broke her foot and stayed with relatives. Eventually, she went to Panguitch to join her husband. In Panguitch she helped clear land and took in washing to keep herself and her two children. Her husband also had another wife and children to care for. The Merrill's also helped settle Hillsdale, Garfield Co. When John took his other family to settle in Tropic, Margaret stayed in Panguitch near her son. She lived a hard pioneer life. John passed away 9 Dec 1909 in Tropic. Margaret was a widow for seventeen years, passing away at age eighty-nine and is buried in Panguitch, Garfield Co., Utah.

MARY JANE SMITH MERRILL

CHILDREN:
John Smith, 4 Mar 1853
Jedediah Grant, 14 Dec 1857
Hannah Ann (Collett), 24 Jan 1860
Cyrena Imogean, 5 Nov 1861
David Elmer, 4 May 1863
Joseph Lott, 5 Jun 1865
Henry Morgan, 4 Mar 1867
Peter Herbert, 6 Jun 1869

BIRTHDATE: 27 Jul 1833
Jacksonville, Morgan, Illinois
DEATH: 2 Jun 1871
Bear Lake (Onieda) Idaho
PARENTS: J. Smith—Hannah Ann Dubois(DeBoise) Dibble
PIONEER: Between 1847-50
Wagon Train
SPOUSE:
Philemon Christopher Merrill
MARRIED: 5 Apr 1851
Salt Lake Endowment House
DEATH: 16 Sep 1904
Safford, Graham, Arizona

Mary Jane was born in Illinois in 1833. Not much is known of her childhood. An early Rhoads Scholar, she passed her love for books to her children. She lived for a time in the Mansion House with her mother, who later married Philo Dibble. She came to Utah probably between 1847/50 with a wagon train, because at age seventeen, she married Philemon Christopher Merrill as a plural wife 5 Apr 1851. Her first child was born in Salt Lake City.

The Merrills moved to Farmington, Davis County, where two more children joined their family. They next moved to Morgan, where Philemon helped build the railroad. There, Mary Jane's last five children were born. In 1869, the Merrill's were on the move to settle Idaho. On this journey, according to the journal of Cyrena, Philemon's first wife, Mary Jane's life ended. She wrote of the move to Liberty, Bear Lake, Idaho in July, 1869. "This was a hard trip for all of us, though it was only a hundred miles. Mary Jane's baby Herbert was only six weeks old, and Mary Jane was not strong." She continues, "I took little Lot in my wagon. He was just recovering from Typhoid Fever and was peevish and fretful, and I could do more with him than anyone else." He would have been four years old, having been born 1865. "We felt worn out when we reached our destination. We had lived here only two years when, on June 2, 1871 Mary Jane died, leaving seven children, who now looked to me for a mother's care, the oldest being eighteen and the youngest only two years old." She finishes simply, "I prayerfully undertook this charge."

Only one photograph of Mary Jane survived. In it, she has a sober expression. Hers was a brief, hard, exciting life. She passed away at age thirty-seven, apparently buried "at the mouth of Emmigration Canyon, on the way to Liberty, in an unmarked grave." Other records indicate she passed away near Liberty, Bear Lake, Idaho.

PHOEBE ODELL MERRILL

No Photo Available

BIRTHDATE: 24 April 1788
Cambridge, Washington, New York
DEATH; 26 January 1862
Salt Lake City, Salt Lake, Utah
PARENTS: Jonas Odell (Odle)
Lucy Weaver
PIONEER: 1847
Edward Hunter Ox Team
SPOUSE: Samuel Merrill
MARRIED: 10 Sept 1802
Oneida, New York
DEATH SP: 25 Sept 1878
Salt Lake City, Salt Lake, Utah

CHILDREN:
Emily Phelps(Merrill/Dustin), 8 Feb 180?
Justin Jared , 18 Feb 1806
Lucy Ann (Gillman), 12 Mar 1808
Philemon C, 16 Mar 1810
Samuel Bemis, 4 Jan 1812
Ferdinand Daniel, 8 Dec 1814
Polly Matilda(Colton), 15 Oct 1816/1817
Melissa Ruth, 12 Nov 1818
Philemon Christopher, 12 Nov 1820
Daniel Morgan, 28 Dec 1823
Albina Mariam (Williams), 25 Jul 1826
Phoebe (Phebe) Lodema(Collett), 15/25 Aug 1832

Phoebe Odell was born in Byron Genesee County, New York on 29 April, 1788, the daughter of a soldier of the American Revolution, Jonas Odell (Odle) and Lucy Weaver. They lived in Cambridge, New York until 1791. They moved to Albany, New York. In 1800, they again moved to what is now Utica, New York in Oneida County. At age fifteen, Phoebe married Samuel Merrill on 10 September 1802. They moved into a new, one room log cabin (built by the men and boys of the community). Her father was killed in 1804 by Indians, leaving her mother with three small children and one yet unborn. Phoebe helped her mother raise the little ones. In 1819 and 1820, the Merrills and Odells moved to Genesee County. New York. The journey was made in the winter because of the threat of Indian attacks. Phoebe's baby boy died that winter. (Death date on the fourth child is 1812 which may have been the correct moving year). Samuel and Phoebe settled in Alabama, New York (near Byron), then moved again to Shelby, (now Utica), Michigan. Here her daughter Polly Matilda married, three sisters were married and her mother died (12 August 1836). Samuel and Phoebe accepted the teachings of Mormon Missionaries with faith and unity, moving once again to establish homes in Nauvoo and Carthage, Illinois in 1838. They lived there six years until they were forced to abandon their home in the dead of winter. Phoebe was active in giving comfort and help to the sick. With the frontier training and knowledge of herbs and their uses, she was called upon day and night to help the many sick people in the camps. Samuel and Phoebe were among the first to arrive in Utah, reaching the Salt Lake Valley 1 October 1847 in Captain Foutz's Company. They had two sons and five daughters that helped to settle Utah. Phoebe Odell Merrill died in Salt Lake City on 26 January, 1862, and was buried in the Salt Lake City Cemetery.

SARAH ANN ATKINSON MERRILL

BIRTHDATE: 28 Sep 1834
Sackville, Canada
DEATH: 16 Oct 1917
Richmond, Utah
PARENTS: William Atkinson
Phebe Campbell
PIONEER: 11 Sep 1853
Independent Wagon Train
SPOUSE: Mariner Wood Merrill
MARRIED: 11 Nov 1813
Bountiful, Davis Utah
DEATH: 6 Feb 1906
Richmond, Utah

CHILDREN:
Phebe Ann (McNeil), 24 Oct 1854
Marriner Wood Jr, 19 Jan 1957
Thomas Hazen, 11 Jun 1859
Alma, 9 Nov 1861 Richmond
Rhoda Louisa (Hendricks), 9 Nov 1863
Clarissa, 20 FED 1866
William, 23 May 1868
Louis Edgar, 11 Sep 1870
Carrie Jane, 27 Jan 1873
Amos Newlove, 15 Mar 1875

Sarah Ann was born in Canada in 1834. She enjoyed life in New Brunswick. She became self-reliant and self-less. She longed to be able to learn, but her education opportunities were very limited. She attended school for a very brief time, and so her education came from living. She would read and ponder and listen and write. She was religiously inclined and in 1850, when the Gospel was brought to her father's house, she knew the message was true. She

liked to tell the story of how cold the water was, but how warm her heart felt after her baptism in the winter of 1851.

In the early spring of 1853, she gathered her meager earthly possessions and with her father's family, and her future husband, started on their long journey across the plains with ox-teams and heavily loaded wagons. She helped those around her and they finally arrived in Salt Lake City 11 Sep 1853, and settled in the little Mormon town of Bountiful a few miles north. At age nineteen, she married Marriner Wood Merrill, 11 Nov in Bountiful. Apostle Ezra T. Benson performed the marriage ceremony. She went to work for Apostle Benson's family, and her young husband went to the canyon to get logs to begin building their new home. Sarah Ann was a devoted young bride. Her first home was one log room with a fireplace. She lived there for four and a half years, having three children.

In the spring of 1860, Marriner and Saran Ann left Bountiful and moved to Cache Valley and settled in Richmond. She would roam through the fields with her children and tell them stories of when she was a child. The cold long winter evenings offered time for the family to gather and read and talk together. She lived in the "Fort" until her home was complete. 24 Dec 1861 she moved from the fort to a home they had built on the lot where she lived the remainder of her life. On 4 Jun 1868, the first Relief Society of the Richmond Ward was organized and Sarah Ann was sustained as President which position she held for seven years. When Marriner was called to be Bishop, she became a most loving and considerate "Bishop's wife". Seven more children joined their family. For fifty-five years, she was the center of activities of the Richmond Ward. When the practice of polygamy was introduced, Sarah Ann did much fasting and praying to try and understand and accept this policy as her husband would take seven other wives. She became Known as "Auntie" and her home became the hub of family discussions and activities. Marriner passed away 6 Feb 1906 at age seventy-four. Sarah Ann passed away at age eighty-one, having been a widow for nine years. They are buried in Richmond Utah.

EMMA NAYLOR MERRITT

BIRTHDATE: 18 Dec 1846
Radford, Nottingham, England
DEATH: 30 Jul 1922
Bedford, Lincoln, Wyoming
PARENTS: William Naylor
Diana Ireland Naylor
PIONEER: 13 Oct 1863
Rosel Hyde Co. Wagon Train
SPOUSE: Samuel Swift Merritt
MARRIED: 1 Jul 1865
Little Cottonwood Canyon,
Salt Lake, Utah
DEATH: 21 Feb 1918
Bedford, Lincoln, Wyoming

CHILDREN:

Samuel Alonzo, 1 Apr 1866
George William, 5 Sep 1867
Elizabeth Diana, 27 Dec 1869
Levi Edward, 16 Mar 1872
Perry, 20 Apr 1874
Emma Jane, 28 Apr 1875
Archibald James, 21 Aug 1877
Sarah Ellen, 28 Aug 1879
Charles Augustus, 4 Aug 1881
Delila May, 20 Sep 1882
Gertrude Alice, 10 Oct 1884
Edna Eveline, 6 Dec 1886
Martha Vinnie, 15 Apr 1889

When Emma was three years old, the LDS Missionaries baptized her parents into the LDS Church. She learned to read, write, add, and subtract. When she was eight, she went to work in a stocking factory. Later, she worked in a lace factory where they made famous Nottingham Lace Curtains. The desire for most church members in England was to go to America. When Emma was sixteen, her parents had enough money to take their family to Utah. Her father was crippled and her mother was not well, so Emma had the responsibility of taking care of them, both on the ship and crossing the plains. They were almost shipwrecked, they were swept off course, and they had only salt pork, sea biscuits, and tea to eat. When they landed in New York, they traveled by train to Florence. They joined the Rosel Hyde Wagon Company and pushed their handcart across the plains. They arrived on October 13, 1863.

They lived in a dugout for some time. Emma met Samuel Swift Merritt at one of the dances and after a short courtship, they were married. Sam and Emma became the parents of thirteen children. First they lived in a dugout in West Jordan, then they moved to Peoa where they lived on a dry farm. Even though they had to carry water one and one half miles, she was able to raise a small garden with wash and dish water. Then the family moved to Bedford, Wyoming where they all lived in a one room log cabin until they were able to build a larger cabin. Emma got starts for strawberries, raspberries, rhubarb, and gooseberries. She picked and cleaned the berries, and sold them for ten cents a quart. She was very thrifty, making clothes and knitting stockings for her family. She also did sewing for other people. She helped those who were sick and took care of new mothers and their babies. Emma worked long and hard hours, but her home was always a special place. She lived a full and active life benefiting all who were around her until she died at the age of seventy five years.

JEANNE ROBERT MESERVY

BIRTHDATE: 30 Jun 1811
St. Laurens Isle of Jersey England
DEATH: 16 Jun 1894
Wilford, Fremont, Idaho
PARENTS: John(Jean) Robert
Elizabeth De La Cour Robert
PIONEER: 10 Oct 1853
Joseph W. Young Co
Wagon Train
SPOUSE: Joshua Meservy
MARRIED: 3 Oct 1832
DEATH SP: 3 Apr 1871
Hooper, Weber, Utah

CHILDREN:

Joshua Jr, 30 Jun 1833
Jane, 24 Dec 1834
Henrietta, 20 Mar 1836
John, 26 Dec 1838
Joseph Robert, 30 Apr 1842
Jane, 18 Apr 1844
James, 1 Apr 1846
Laurens, Aug 1848
Elizabeth, Sep 1849
Jacob, 11 Dec 1850
Ann Elizabeth, 20 Dec 1852

Jeanne's father was a Methodist Minister and also a cabinet maker by trade. She married Joshua Meservy on October 3, 1852. Joshua was a very industrious man and they owned a large home on the Isle of Jersey, England. Jeanne and the children managed the farm with the aid of some hired help. She also collected the debts and paid the bills. She and her husband were baptized as members of the LDS Church in 1851. They sailed from Liverpool, England on the ship, "Golconda" to America. Jeanne was very ill from the motion sickness and couldn't nourish her very young baby. The baby had to suck on pound cake. They landed in New Orleans on April 12, 1853. They traveled by steamboat up the Mississippi River as far as Keokuk, Iowa. Their son, Jacob, died while crossing the plains. They were harassed by Indians the major distance across the plains. In Sweetwater, so many cattle died that more cattle had to be brought from the Valley in order to bring the wagon train into the Salt Lake Valley. They arrived on October 10, 1853 after traveling for nine months.

The family remained in Salt Lake City for a while and then moved to Tooele, Utah where they bought and cultivated ten acres of land. During the winter of 1855-56, the family burned charcoal made of cedar wood. They suffered hunger and privations in common with other settlers because the crops had been destroyed by grasshoppers. In the fall of 1856, the Meservy family moved to Santaquin, Utah where they farmed fifteen acres of land. In 1858, they moved to Goshen, Utah. In 1860, they moved to Franklin, Idaho where they started a sawmill business. They moved to Fish Haven, Idaho in 1864 and lived for four years. Then they moved to Hooper, Utah. After her husband's death, she lived with her son, Joseph Robert Meservy. She attended the Logan temple where she attended to her parent's temple work. She was a very brilliant woman and had a wonderful memory. She was very thoughtful of the sick and the poor. She died at the age of eighty three while visiting her daughter.

MARY ANN REEDER METCALF

BIRTHDATE: 15 Jan 1835
Linstead, Parva, Suffolk, England
DEATH: 18 Nov 1916
Malad, Onieda, Idaho
PARENTS: David Reeder
Lydia Balls Reeder
PIONEER: 24 Sep 1853
Claudius V. Spencer Wagon Train
SPOUSE: Anthony Metcalf
MARRIED: Apr 1853
St Louis, Missouri
DEATH: 20 Nov 1888
Elkhorn, Onieda, Idaho

CHILDREN:
Emma, 9 Feb 1854
Mary Ellen, 16 Mar 1856
Anthony George, 10 Mar 1858
William David, 27 Feb 1860
Charles Heber, 26 Mar 1862
Margaret Jane, 1 Jan 1866
Eliza Agnes, 14 Dec 1866
Robert, 19 Oct 1867
Ida, 19 Aug 1869
Frank, 26 Nov 1871
Sarah, 23 Mar 1874

Mary's mother died when she was four years old. She lived with her family in the Reeder Cottage on the Thomas Reed Estate. Mary joined the LDS Church in 1851 at the age of sixteen. At the age of eighteen, she left her homeland of England and sailed on the ship, Mary Ellen on January 17, 1853. She was traveling with the William Seamons family. While at sea, she met Anthony Metcalf and fell in love. They were married in April of 1853 in St. Louis, Missouri by Orson Pratt. They traveled to Keokuk, Iowa with the Claudius V. Spencer Wagon Company and arrived in Salt Lake Valley on September 24, 1853.

When they arrived, they had only two blankets, one quilt, and the clothes they had on their backs. They lived for the next three weeks on potatoes and water. They lived in Salt Lake City for two years. Then they moved to Hyde Park where they lived for the next ten years. Then they moved to Malad, Idaho where she spent the rest of her life. She became the mother to eleven children. She was a devoted wife, mother, and home maker. Mary Ann and Anthony did their full share in helping to start three settlements. Her husband died in November of 1888 at Elkhorn, Idaho. She died on November 18, 1916.

MARY ELIZABETH WASLIN METCALF

BIRTHDATE: 15 Jul 1810
Skidby, Yorkshire, England
DEATH: 26 Mar 1884
Fayette, Sanpete, Utah
PARENTS: Christopher Waslin
Ann Nelson Waslin
PIONEER: 17 Sep 1853
Claudius Spencer Wagon Co.
SPOUSE:
John Edward Metcalf Sr.
MARRIED: 23 Dec 1832
In England
DEATH SP: 4 Feb 1887

CHILDREN:
Jane Ann, 15 Mar 1834
Elizabeth, 15 Aug 1835
Anthony, 26 Sep 1837
John Edward Jr., 23 Jun 1839
Elizabeth, Feb 1841
Anthony, Jan 1842
Anthony, 5 Sep 1843
Mary Elizabeth, 24 Oct 1845
Metcalf (son-stillborn)
James, 12 Jan 1847
Eliza Roxie, 17 Aug 1850
William, 5 May 1855

Mary Elizabeth Waslin was born in England in 1810. She married John Edward Metcalf Sr. in 1832, and they were the parents of twelve children, several of whom died when very young.

Mary and her husband set sail from Liverpool in Jan 1853 on the "Ellen Marie," with six of their surviving children, from Jane Ann to Eliza Roxie. In Iowa they obtained a wagon, oxen, and supplies for their journey west. They arrived in the Salt Lake Valley in September 1853, and lived in the 4th Ward. In 1855 Mary gave birth to her twelfth and last child, William.

In 1856 they moved to Springville, then in 1863 Brigham Young called them to settle in Fayette, Sanpete, Utah, where John was asked to build a grist mill and operate it the year round. Here they lived in a dugout. Mary tried to beautify her dugout house by wetting down and tamping the dirt floor, then she made designs on it with charcoal and lime.

John took a second wife, Cecelia Anderson, in 1869. When he was called on a mission (1877-1879), Mary helped her sons operate the grist mill while caring for her family's needs. Three years after his return home, he was thrown from a buggy and blinded. She cared for him until her death in 1886. John died in 1887, in Fayette, Sanpete, Utah.

SYLVIA ELIZA SANFORD METCALF

BIRTHDATE: 16 Nov 1845
Hancock County, Illinois
DEATH: 12 Aug 1947
Gunnison, Sanpete, Utah
PARENTS: Cyrus Sanford
Sylvia Elmina Stockwell
PIONEER: Oct 1850
William Snow Co.
SPOUSE: Anthony Metcalf
MARRIED: 27 Aug 1862
Springville, Utah, Utah
DEATH SP: 28 Mar 1924
Gunnison, Sanpete, Utah

CHILDREN:
Mary Eliza, 15 Oct 1863
Sylvia Elmina, 4 May 1865
Anthony Edward, 29 Jun 1867
Cecelia Elmira, 6 Mar 1869
Melissa Elvira, 10 Feb 1870
Clara Evangeline, 30 May 1872
Emma Elizabeth, 12 Apr 1874
Cyrus William, 26 Nov 1875
Arthur Velorus, 8 Dec 1877
Ettia Happolona, 28 Feb 1880
Waslin, 26 Sep 1881
Otho Young, 23 Nov 1883
Guy Henry, 5 Jul 1885
Ina, 10 Sep 1889
Jane Ann, 5 May 1892

Sylvia Eliza Sanford was born in Hancock County, Illinois in 1845. At the tender age of four she left Council Bluffs with her parents headed for the Rocky Mountains. They arrived in the Valley in October 1850.

Sylvia married Anthony Metcalf in 1862, and bore him fifteen children. They lived in Sanpete County, Utah, in a one-room log cabin with an open fireplace where she cooked. Their furniture was sparse and homemade. Sylvia spun her own yarn and wove her own cloth.

One time during an Indian uprising, when the women and children were alone in the Fort, their food ran short, so Sylvia and four other women yoked up a team to a wagon and drove five miles to Fayette, where they gathered vegetables from their gardens and other foods, and returned before dark, unmolested. The Indians were too busy to notice them; they were trying to keep out of the way of the men from the Fort.

Sylvia raised ten children to maturity without the help of a doctor or medicines. She used castor oil, olive oil, essence of peppermint, and other remedies such as grated rhubarb root. They had their good times too; spelling matches, dances, amateur plays, and reading clubs. The reading club met at night, and by candlelight, Sylvia would read for hours, history, literature and fiction, while the other ladies kept busy with their knitting needles. Sometimes the men would join them. Anthony Metcalf died in 1924, and Sylvia died in 1947, both in Gunnison, Sanpete, Utah.

EMELIE CAROLINE HANNIBAL MEYER

BIRTHDATE: 24 Apr 1846
Copenhagen, Denmark
DEATH: 6 Oct 1918
Salt Lake City, Utah
PARENTS: Peter Christian Hannibal
Sophia Marie Siversen
PIONEER: 30 Sep 1853
J. E. Forsgfen Co. Wagon Train
SPOUSE:
Fredrick August Englebert Meyer
MARRIED: 8 Jan 1872
Salt Lake City, Utah
DEATH SP: 6 Oct 1918
Salt Lake City, Utah

CHILDREN:
Rosa Emelie (Ryckman), 6 Oct 1872
Fredrick Hannibal, 1 Nov 1874
Dellie, 6 Sep 1876
Eugenie Sophia Louise (Madsen), 9 Jun 1879
(girl), 18 Dec 1881
Ernest Emil, 1 Sep 1883
Emelie Josephine (Babe) Rasmussen, 3 Nov 1885

Emelie Caroline Hannibal was born 24 Apr 1846 in Copenhagen, Denmark, the daughter of Peter Christian Hannibal and Sophia Marie Siversen. When Emelie was six years old she sailed with her parents to America on the ship "Forest Monarch." They came across the plains with the J. E. Forsgren Company, by ox team and handcart, arriving in the Valley on 30 Sep 1853.

The family lived for a while in Spring City, Sanpete County, then moved to Centerville, Davis, Utah, then to Salt Lake City. She married Fredrick August Englebert Meyer on 8 Jan 1872. They were the parents of seven children.

Emelie and her husband had a beautiful home in Salt Lake, which was well kept and a showplace. They had a Blue Room, a Gold Room, a Red Room, a dining room, a large kitchen, plus a summer kitchen, and four bedrooms upstairs. Fredrick was a buyer of mens wear for ZCMI, and made two buying trips each year, and he would always bring Emelie something beautiful for their home. She insisted that her children go to college and learn to play a musical instrument. She did a lot of entertaining.

Emelie cared for her mother after her father passed away. Emelie died in Salt Lake City on 6 Oct 1918 at the age of seventy-two years.

JAMIMA HUTCHENSEN MEYRICK

BIRTHDATE: 28 Oct 1843
Mt. Pleasant, Fifshire, Scotland
DEATH: 21 Sep 1922
Mt. Pleasant, Sanpete, Utah
PARENTS: David Hutchensen
Jeanette Crockston
PIONEER: Oct 1861
John Murdock Co
SPOUSE: John Meyrick
MARRIED: 28 Oct 1861
American Fork, Utah, Utah
DEATH SP: 22 Apr 1899
Mt. Pleasant, Sanpete, Utah

CHILDREN:
Jennette, 4 Aug 1862
James David, 10 Nov 1864
John Thomas, 11 Sep 1866
Anna, 30 Sep 1868
Jamima, 1 Jun 1870
George, 31 Oct 1871
Elizabeth Jane, 14 Feb 1873
Mary, 14 Dec 1875
Christina, 13 Aug 1877
Cyrus, 21 Mar 1878
Hyrum, 24 Apr 1881
Joseph, 10 Jan 1883
Eliza, 27 Jan 1885
Brigham, 2 Sep 1887
Donald, 11 May 1891

Jamima Hutchensen was born 28 Oct 1843 in Mt. Pleasant, Fifshire, Scotland. When only eight years old she went to work in the linen mills, winding shuttles. Because she did not realize how dangerous the machines were, she caught her hand in the belt, severing two fingers. Her parents were among the first in their area to accept the gospel, and Jamima was baptized at eight years by her father.

The Hutcheson family came to America in 1861 when Jamima was seventeen years old, traveling with the John Murdock Company. One of the young men who helped to guard the wagon train was John Meyrick. He had been in Utah for eight years and was now thirty years old. He let Jamima ride in his wagon, or on his horse, and this is how their courtship developed. They were married on Jamima's eighteenth birthday, 28 Oct 1861 in American Fork.

John had a small home in Mt. Pleasant, Utah where they lived. He worked on the Manti Temple, and made several trips to help the Saints. They donated money and material to help build the temple, and attended the dedication in 1888. Of their fifteen children only seven lived to maturity.

John died 22 Apr 1899 when a rock fell on him while he was digging a well in Mt. Pleasant. Jamima was a widow for twenty-three years. She crocheted, tatted and sewed clothes. She was very religious, paid tithing, and prayed night and morning. She never complained of poor health. She died in Mt. Pleasant, Sanpete, Utah, 21 Sep 1922.

MAREN MICHELSEN THORSEN MICHELSEN

No Photo Available

BIRTHDATE: 16 Mar 1795
Voersaa, Albaek, Hjorring, Denmark
DEATH: 1856
Crossing the plains
PARENTS: Michael Pedersen
Maren Madsen
PIONEER: 1856 William
Hodgett Co. Wagon Train
SPOUSE I: Jens Thorsen
MARRIED: 23 Nov 1823
Albaek, Hjorring, Denmark
DEATH SP: 16 Mar 1842
Albaek, Hjorring, Denmark

CHILDREN:
Thor Jensen, 3 Aug 1829
Else Marie Jensen, 11 Feb 1833
Johanna Marie Jensen, 17 Apr 1835

SPOUSE II: Ole Michelsen
MARRIED: 16 Oct 1842
Albaek, Hiorring, Denmark
DEATH SP: unknown
CHILDREN: None

Maren Michelsen was born 16 Mar 1795 in Voersaa, Albaek, Hjorring, Denmark, the daughter of Michel Pedersen and Maren Madsen. Both of her parents died when she was eleven years old.

Maren was twenty-eight when she married Jens Thorsen. When he died in 1842 she was left a forty-seven year old widow with two young girls. Her second husband was nineteen years her junior. They joined the Church about 1855, and in 1856 they sailed on the ship "Thornton" for the New World. From New York they traveled to Iowa City where daughter Johanne went ahead with the Willie Handcart Company. Maren and Ole followed later with the William Hodgett Ox train Company. Maren died on the plains and only Ole survived the trip, arriving in the Salt Lake Valley in Dec 1856.

ELIZA ANN HELENA MICHIE

No Photo Available

BIRTHDATE: 11 Apr 1860
East Boston Massachusetts
DEATH: 26 Aug 1861
Sweet Water River, Wyoming
PARENTS: Robert Michie
Frances Potts Michie
PIONEER: 1861
Died on the Plains
SPOUSE:
MARRIED:
DEATH:

Eliza Ann Helena Michie was one year old when she came across the Plains with her parents, Robert Michie and Frances Potts Michie and her three year old sister, Agnes. They left Florence, Nebraska in July 1861 by ox team to travel across the Plains to Utah with an independent company. All the men and women who could walked the distance.

Without proper food for small children, little Eliza Ann Helena became ill with black canker and died at Ice Spring on the Sweet Water River on August 26, 1861 at sixteen months of age. They were just two hundred forty miles away from Salt Lake City. Her mother dressed her in a freshly washed white nightgown and placed her in a casket that her father had made from a piece of the wagon box. She was buried on the Plains and her sorrowful parents continued with the company toward Great Salt Lake where they arrived in September 1861.

FRANCES POTTS MICHIE

BIRTHDATE: 22 Dec 1835
Barton, Feversham, Kent, England
DEATH: 20 Jul 1904
Woodland, Summit, Utah
PARENTS: Thomas Potts
Harriett Pullen Potts
PIONEER: Sep 1861
Wagon team
SPOUSE: Robert Michie
MARRIED: 16 Mar 1857
Preston, Kent, England
DEATH: 20 Apr 1909
Woodland, Summit, Utah

CHILDREN:
Agnes Catherin Harriett, 4 Sep 1858
Eliza Ann Helena, 11 Apr 1860
Robert Moroni, 11 Nov 1861
Harriett Frances, 11 Jan 1864
Alice Matilda, 6 Jan 1866
John Thomas, 14 Jun 1868
Mary Ellen, 9 Feb 1870
Della, 28 Jul 1872
William George, 19 Oct 1875
Christianna, 1 Jun 1878

When Frances was eleven years old, her mother died leaving her to care for her brothers and sisters when the youngest child was two years old. As soon as Frances was old enough, she worked as a servant to help support the family. At twenty one, she married thirty-seven-year-old Robert Michie on 16 Mar 1857. Six days later, she was baptized a member of the LDS Church. She and her sister, Alice, were married on the same day and together the two couples sailed from Liverpool, England for America on the ship "George Washington" on March 28, 1857. They lived in Boston for four years. In 1861, she, her husband, and their two children left Florence, Nebraska in July 1861 with ox teams to cross the Plains. The men of the group walked all the way and the women walked most of the way.

Frances was pregnant as she walked across the Plains. Her little daughter Eliza Ann Helena became ill with black canker and died at Ice Spring on the Sweet Water River. They arrived in Utah in September 1861 and in November 1861 gave birth to her son, Robert.

Frances was a hard working woman who bore ten children in twenty years and moved at least eight times. She was a great teacher and example to her children. She raised six children to maturity and enjoyed her many grandchildren. She was active in her church duties. Frances was very considerate of her friends and neighbors. She worked in the post office in one end of their home. She invited many of the people to come in and get warm after walking in the cold to get their mail. She had many friends and loved to talk. She had the good pioneer hospitality. Everyone who came to her home was invited in and offered food.

She died of cancer of the stomach on July 20, 1904 at her home in woodland and was buried in the Heber City Cemetery.

ANE NIELSEN MICKELSEN

BIRTHDATE: 27 Apr 1825
Orslov, Maribo, Denmark
DEATH: 22 Jan 1908
Parowan, Iron, Utah
PARENTS: Niels Christensen
Ane Margrethe Rasmussen
PIONEER: 5 Oct 1854
Hans Peters Olsen Co Wagon Train
SPOUSE: Rasmus Mickelsen
MARRIED: 3 Sep 1848
Maribo, Denmark
DEATH: 22 Oct 1903
Parowan, Iron, Utah

CHILDREN:
Ane Rasmussen, 31 Oct 1848
Niels, 28 May 1850
Michael, 26 Aug 1851
Johannas, 26 Sep 1852
Anna Maria 7 Apr 1855
Joseph, 1 May 1857
Peter, 23 Oct 1858
Magdalena, 9 Dec 1860
Rasmus, 28 Oct 1863
Mary Sophia, 13 Apr 1866

Ane's parents were weavers by trade and her mother wove very fine linens during the daytime and knit socks in the evening. Ane, as a child helped with the knitting. Her father died when she was eight years old. She went to live with an Uncle whose family was very good to her. He raised geese and Ane's job was to herd them during the day. Some years later, she went to work at a large dairy where she milked cows, did most of the housework, made butter, cheese, etc. Ane loved to dance and more than once the dance lasted until early morning, and she would have to hurry home, change her clothes, and be ready to milk the cows at 4:00 in the morning. While working there, she met Rasmus Mickelsen and they courted eight years before they were married. They heard the gospel from Erastus Snow and became baptized members of the LDS Church. Rasmus served a mission in Denmark for the church before they left for America. Four of their children were born to them in Denmark. Niels was the only child still living when they arrived in America. They stayed in St. Louis until they had earned enough to purchase provisions to cross the plains. They crossed the plains with the Hans Peters Olsen Wagon Company and arrived in the Salt Lake Valley on October 5, 1854.

Soon after their arrival, they were sent to Cedar City to help settle that part of the country. They lived there for six years. From Cedar City, they moved to Parowan where Rasmus was engaged in fanning and sheep raising. They made their own clothes from the wool of their sheep. They made a lovely wool carpet which they used for fifty years. Whenever any new Saints arrived to make their home in Parowan, Ane would welcome them by giving them a leg of mutton, butter, milk, etc. After her husband died in 1903, she lived with her daughter, Lena Bently. When her strength permitted, she would knit socks, card wool, or sew carpet rags. Her family loved her dearly.

KAREN SOPHIA ERICKSEN NIELSEN MICKELSEN

BIRTHDATE: 22 Oct 1815
Westgaard, Hjorring, Denmark
DEATH: 7 Aug 1888
Spanish Fork, Utah, Utah
PARENTS: Erik Larsen Nielsen
Christance Bartelson Larsen
PIONEER: 13 Sep 1857
Christian Christiansen's
Handcart Co.
SPOUSE: Niels Christen Nielsen
MARRIED: 25 Jan 1842
Jetsmark, Hjorring, Denmark
DEATH: Spring 1857
St. Louis, Missouri

CHILDREN:
Christance, 17 Sep 1839
Bartel, 22 Sep 1841
Annie Catherine, 18 Apr 1845
Karen Maria, 3 Jan 1846
Erick Christian, 18 Mar 1848
James Andrew, 29 May 1849
Erick, 14 Mar 1852
Anna Maria, 29 Aug 1853
Nielsena Christena, Jul 1855

SPOUSE: Jens Mickelsen
MARRIED: 1857 or 1858
DEATH: 10 Oct 1884

Karen and Erik had grown up as neighbors in Westgaard, were married, made their home near their parents, and had nine children. They had very happy lives. They heard of a new religion and embraced the Gospel. Soon they were saving money to enable them to join with the Saints in America. It took them two years to save enough to send their two oldest children. Two years later, they were able to board the ship "John H. Boyd" headed for America. Their voyage was full of tribulation. They landed in New York after fifteen months of hardships, rough seas, hunger, and death among many families on board. They had to stay in New York for three weeks before they could move on to St. Louis. It took them from the last of February until May to travel to St. Louis. They had been in St. Louis only a short time when a dreadful epidemic broke out with sickness and death everywhere. Karen's husband, Niels, was taken ill, died, and was buried in St. Louis.

Karen and five little fatherless children left with the Morton Lund Company to go up the Missouri River to Florence, Nebraska. From there they came to Salt Lake with the Christian Christiansen's Hand Cart Company and arrived in Utah on September 13, 1857. The mother in the Mickelson family passed away near Echo Canyon. Jens Mickelson and Karen married soon after they arrived in Salt Lake City. They learned her two oldest children had been sent to Fillmore to settle, so their family walked down to Fillmore.

Karen, Jens, and their family settled near the Spanish Fork River and built a fishing industry there. Karen and the girls made the fish nets for the men to fish with. In the winter, the women would spin thread for the nets. They had sheep, cows, ducks and chickens to care for and to provide for their needs. Whatever was surplus, they took to market in Spanish Fork.

LAURA JOHANNA INGMANN MICKELSEN

BIRTHDATE: 27 Aug 1844
Trondheim, Sor-Trondelag, Norway
DEATH: 9 Jan 1934
Salt Lake City, Salt Lake, Utah
PARENTS: Johan Henrik Gabrielsen Ingmann
Bergithe Johnson Berg Ingmann
PIONEER: 12 Sep 1861
John R. Murdock Co Wagon Train
SPOUSE: Niels Mickelsen
MARRIED: 9 Aug 1862
Salt Lake City, Salt Lake, Utah
DEATH: 17 Jan 1894
Logan, Cache, Utah

CHILDREN:
Ane Mary, 4 Mar 1864
Emma Bergetta, 14 Nov 1865
Niels Henry, 17 Oct 1868
Soren, 9 May 1871
Laura Jennet, 28 Aug 1873
George Albert, 11 Sep 1875

Willard, 13 Mar 1878
Anne Christina, 15 Aug 1880
Orson, 13 May 1883

Laura was born in Norway in 1884. Her mother died when Laura was nine years old. Her father, a captain of a sailing vessel, drowned at sea a year later, leaving five children orphaned. At age seventeen, Laura heard the gospel message taught by missionaries in Norway and was baptized a member of the LDS Church. She soon emigrated with a large group of Scandinavian Saints on the ship, Monarch of the Sea, from Liverpool to New York City. The Company traveled by rail and steamboat to Florence, Nebraska. She crossed the Plains in the John R. Murdock Company arriving in Salt Lake Valley in September 1861, walking all the way. Laura first served as a domestic servant with a Hyrum family, who had helped finance her passage. A short time later, she was sent to the home of Niels Mickelsen in Logan to help care for his ailing wife and two children. At the suggestion of Brigham Young, Laura became Niels' second wife. They had a family of nine children. Her husband was more than twenty years older than Laura, and she became a widow at the age of forty-nine.

Laura was a hard worker and accomplished in pioneer skills, such as carding and weaving wool, knitting, and making soap and candles. She was a skilled practical nurse who assisted local doctors. She also had a knowledge of home medicines. She served as a counselor and then president of the Logan Fourth Ward Relief Society for forty years. She assisted with many births, helped the sick, and prepared the bodies of the dead.

Laura lived to see the 100th Anniversary of the organization of the LDS Church, which was her desire. She died in 1934 at the age of eighty-nine, having lived a life of devotion to the church and service to her family and fellow men.

SENA CATHERINE JOHNSON MICKELSEN

No
Photo
Available

BIRTHDATE: 14 May 1837
Vester Marie Klemmen, Bornholm, Denmark
DEATH: 9 May 1923
Logan, Cache, Utah
PARENTS: John Jorgenson Johnson—Karen Kirstine Jensen
PIONEER: 5 Oct 1854
Hans Peter Olsen Co
SPOUSE: Niels Mickelsen
MARRIED: 1855
Brigham City, Box Elder, Utah
DEATH SP: 17 Jan 1894
Logan, Cache, Utah

CHILDREN:
Caroline, 24 Aug 1856
Ephraim, 22 Jul 1858/9
Sena Catherine, 17 Aug 1860

Sena was born on the island of Bornholm, Denmark where she received the gospel with her family. Persecution was severe in their area, and the family decided to immigrate to Zion. Sena's father sold his farm and financed the journey of his own family plus twenty other saints, beginning their journey in December 1854. They arrived in New Orleans in January 1854. They started their journey westward in June, arriving in Salt Lake City in October 1854. The Johnson family made their home in Brigham City where Sena's parents lived the rest of their lives.

Sena met and married Niels Mickelsen in Brigham City, where they settled for the first year or two. This was where their first child, Caroline, was born and died. Their second child, Ephraim, was born in Sanpete County while the Saints were moved south when Johnston's Army approached Utah. They returned to Brigham City, but soon moved on to Logan where they made their permanent home. Their last child was born there. Niels became a prominent settler and farmer in Cache Valley.

Sena accepted polygamy with a true spirit. She welcomed the second wife, Laura, into her home where both families lived together in harmony for fourteen years before building separate homes. Sena served faithfully in the LDS Church as a counselor in the Relief Society Presidency of the Logan Fourth Ward and as a teacher for twenty years in the Logan Seventh Ward. She died in Logan at the age of eighty six.

MARIA CHRISTINA RATH JENSEN MICKELSON

BIRTHDATE: 14 Aug 1831
Reisdorf, Preetz, Schlesvig-Holstein, Germany
DEATH: 6 Nov 1916
Manti, Sanpete, Utah
PARENTS: Heinrich Christian Rath
Gide (Ida) Petersen/Rasmussen Rath
PIONEER: 29 Sep 1866
Peter Nebeker Co. Wagon Train
SPOUSE: Lars/Louis Jensen
MARRIED: 1858
Copenhagen, Denmark
DEATH: 11 Sep 1866
Sweetwater County, Wyoming

CHILDREN:
Frederick, 27 May 1860
Jens Julius Christian, 12 Sep 1861
Carl/Charles Edward, 6 Apr 1863
Annie Edith, 19 Dec 1864/5

SPOUSE: Peter (Anderson) Mickelson
MARRIED: 24 Nov 1866
Manti, Sanpete, Utah
DEATH: 5 Mar 1924
Manti, Sanpete, Utah

CHILDREN:
Christine 7 Sep 1867
Laura 21 Aug 1869

Louis Peter 21 May 1871
Andrew 26 Dec 1873

Maria worked on a large dairy farm in Denmark and learned the art of making cheese and butter. After her marriage to Louis Jensen, they worked on a very large dairy farm. He was trusted with buying the cattle and traveled much of the time. Maria had charge of twenty-five girls who milked three hundred cows and made all the butter and cheese. She was baptized into the LDS Church on July 21, 1865. The following year, she and her husband and their four small children began the journey to Zion. On May 25, 1866, they sailed from Hamburg, Germany on the ship, Kenilworth, which docked in New York on July 16 after a fifty two day passage. After reaching Wyoming, Nebraska, they crossed the plains with the Peter Nebeker Wagon Company. At Sweetwater River in Wyoming, the teamster asked her husband and another man to wade the stream to keep the cattle from going downstream as they crossed. That night both men became ill with pneumonia and died during the night. Maria and her children sorrowfully traveled on and arrived in Salt Lake City on September 29, 1866.

They traveled on to Manti because Louis' parents were already living there. A month later, she married Peter Mickelson with whom she had four more children. Maria was a very thrifty person going through all the trials of an early pioneer. At the time of the "grasshopper war" in 1867, they had planted ten acres of wheat. This was entirely devoured by the grasshoppers, despite all effort to burn or drown the insects. One time, when all the wheat was gone, she made bread out of ground pears. She also made butter out of squash and molasses out of beets. She continued to use her expertise in making cheese with her special tubs and cheese presses. During the building of the Manti Temple, people would bring their milk to Maria every Monday morning and she would make it into cheese. She would take this to the Bishop's Storehouse to be given out to the workers or taken to Salt Lake City to be traded for hardwood. Credit is given to her and her husband for operating the first cheesery in Manti.

ABIGAIL KEELER MIDDLEMAS

No Photo Available

BIRTHDATE: 22 Mar 1810
Dartmouth, Nova Scotia, Canada
DEATH: 24 Jun 1855
Little Nemaha, Nebraska,
PARENTS: John Henry Keeler
Elizabeth Tufts
PIONEER: Graves 1855
SPOUSE: Edward Middlemas
MARRIED: 15 Aug 1835
Saint Andrews Church, Halifax, N.S.
DEATH: 9 Dec 1877
Salt Lake City, Utah

CHILDREN:
Simeon, 16 Jun 1836
Anna (Bird Foizey/Foosey), 12 Sep 1837
Sarah, 28 Sep 1839
Abigail (Walker Atkin), 1 Feb 1842
Emma Charlotte, 21 Oct 1845
Edward Robert, 25 Jan 1848
William Mark, 22 Nov 1849
Joseph Hyrum, 11 Feb 1853

Abigail was born in Canada, 1810. She was fifth of eleven children, all born in Dartmouth, Halifax, Nova Scotia (Canada). At age twenty-five she married Edward Middlemas, born 20 Sep 1807 in Durham, England. They made their home in Popes Harbor, Halifax where they became parents of eight, raising three to adulthood. They converted to the LDS church in 1843/44 and by 1855 they emigrated to the United States.

They joined a Wagon Train for the trek. Abigail contracted cholera and passed away 24 Jun 1855 at Little Nemaha, Nebraska where she became a "Grave along the Way." Edward and family arrived in Salt Lake City Fall 1855 and he married Jane Jackson 2 Aug 1856. She raised Abigail's family and added eleven children of her own.

ELLEN HINCHLIFFE MIDGLEY

No Photo Available

BIRTHDATE: 24 Dec 1801
Upperthong, Almondbury,
Yorkshire, England
DEATH: 4 Sep 1855
PARENTS: John Hinchliffe
Hannah Collier
PIONEER: 1855
Milo Andrus Co. Wagon Train
SPOUSE: Thomas Midgley
MARRIED: 30 Sep 1821
Almondbury, York, England
DEATH SP: 9 Sep 1870
Nephi, Juab, Utah

CHILDREN:
Jonathan, 28 Feb 1822
John, 28 Jan 1824
Ann, 6 Sep 1826
Hannah Hinchliffe, 6 Sep 1828
Mary Ellen, 15 Sep 1831
Joshua, 15 Oct 1832
Thomas, 30 Dec 1835
Martha, 24 Jan 1837
Elliot, 13 Feb 1838
Ephriam, 20 Jan 1840
Benjamin, 19 May 1843

Ellen Hinchliffe was born 24 Dec 1801 in Upperthong, Almondbury, Yorkshire, England, the daughter of John Hinchliffe and Hannah Collier. She married Thomas Midgley on 30 Sep 1821 in England, and they were the parents of eleven children, four of whom died before the age of four years.

The entire family joined the Church and wanted to come to Utah. Ellen's two sons, Jonathan and Joshua, and her husband came ahead in 1850 and 1853, Ellen came with the other children sailing on the ship "Samuel Curling" in 1855.

In Mormon Grove, Kansas they were elected to travel with the last group to leave, and this was Milo Andrus's Company. On the plains many became sick with cholera. She helped treat others until she also became sick with cholera and lung fever. She passed away 4 Sep 1855 near Ash Hollow, Wyoming, Nebraska Territory. Her remains were wrapped in a sheet and buried deep in the ground. The Midgley children went on to Salt Lake City and were happy to be with their father and brothers again. Thomas Midgley died 9 Sep 1970 in Nephi, Juab, Utah.

JEMIMA RUSHBY HOUGH MIDGLEY

BIRTHDATE: 20 May 1834
Wooden Box, Leicestershire, England
DEATH: 5 Aug 1917
Salt Lake City, Utah
PARENTS: William Hough
Jemima Drabwell Rushby Hough
PIONEER: 10 Sep 1852
James Jepson Co. Wagon Train
SPOUSE: Joshua Midgley
MARRIED: 8 Apr 1853
DEATH SP: 30 Apr 1912
Salt Lake City, Salt Lake Co., Utah

CHILDREN:
Joshua Hough, 8 Jan 1854
Ellen, 13 Oct 1855
John George, 20 Dec 1857
Thomas William, 1 Apr 1860
Jemima Hough, 18 Sep 1861
David Hough, 16 Nov 1863
Daniel Hough, 19 Mar 1866
Joseph Hough, 7 Mar 1868
Ann Hough, 31 Oct 1869
Jessie Hough, 19 Nov 1870
Edward Paul, 29 Oct 1872
Edith Ann, 30 Jul 1877

Jemima Rushby Hough was born in England in 1834 and was six years old when missionaries began their first work in England. The missionary work was met by some who were antagonistic, some who listened, some who weighed the evidence and grew to agree with the message and some few, who, having a dream, a forewarning, knew the moment they heard the courier, that it was the message they had been foretold of and immediately accepted that Gospel they had been awaiting.

Jemima and her family, having heard, agreed and accepted the gospel of the Mormon missionaries, boarded a ship early one year and suffered the weeks-long voyage of crowded, malnourished, illness-causing conditions to come to America to gather with all the Saints.

Nine days after her eighteenth birthday, Jemima began the long, arduous, one-hundred-and-eleven-day journey of over one thousand miles overland to Utah. Wagons so overloaded with survival equipment had little room for riders and most everyone walked the days they were not sick or injured.

After spending the first winter in the most primitive of circumstances, Jemima married Joshua, a boy from her own country, in the spring the next year. We know of her life by the dates each of her twelve children were born.

Their first was born in the middle of a cold January. By spring food was either foraged for or bartered for. Conditions improved with each passing year. Her third child was born under the fear of what Johnston's Army would do to the weary saints and the migration to the south.

By the time Thomas William was born, Jemima could have received word with the Pony express of relatives and friends who could be joining them and news of the Civil War would chill many who had come from the south upon hearing of the destruction back home.

Joseph Hough, her eighth child could have seen the brand new Deveroux House and would have been carried through the new Z.C.M.I.

The world was changing. Salt Lake City was growing by leaps and bounds with the entrance of the railroad when Ann was born. Polygamy, always a conflict with every other society, was causing hardships in many households. By the time her twelfth baby was born, the old was passing away. President Brigham Young died when Edith was a month old, leaving many heartsick.

We know Jemima was a fine seamstress, loved music, sang in the old First Tabernacle Choir and held leadership positions in Relief Society for many years. She was a widow for five years and died at the age of eighty-three, having given her life to her beliefs.

SARAH GIBBONS JACKSON MIDGLEY

No Photo Available

BIRTHDATE: 9 Jul 1848
Chesterfield, Kent, England
DEATH: 9 Feb 1920
Salt Lake City, Utah
PARENTS: Thomas Jackson
Joyce Staples
PIONEER: 1864
SPOUSE: Benjamin Midgley
MARRIED: 15 Dec 1866
Salt Lake City, Utah
DEATH SP: 15 Nov 1925
Salt Lake City, Utah

CHILDREN:
Ellen Joyce, 29 Nov 1867
Benjamin, 19 Nov 1868

Edith Ann, 13 Feb 1872
Sarah Gibbons, 23 Feb 1872
Beatrice Winnifred, 28 Aug 1877
Hannah H., 17 Sep 1878
Leo Leroy, 3 Mar 1881
Bertha Eliza, 30 Aug 1882
Thomas Jackson, 6 Dec 1885
Edna, 16 Jan 1887
Kenneth, 26 Aug 1888
Leonard Jackson, 12 Feb 1891

Sarah Gibbons Jackson was born 9 Jul 1848 in Chesterfield, Pratt's Bottom (Brumley), Kent, England, the daughter of Thomas Jackson and Joyce Staples. She was sixteen years of age when she came across the plains. Her parents and brother and sister came two years later.

Sarah married Benjamin Midgley on 15 Dec 1866 in the Endowment House in Salt Lake City. They made their home in Nephi for twenty-two years where most of their twelve children were born. Her husband was thrown from a horse and suffered a broken leg which was never set properly, and her eleven-year-old son Benjamin was dragged behind a horse over rocks and dirt, which caused his death. Five other children also died young.

In 1889 the family moved to Salt Lake City where Benjamin worked for the Salt Lake Tribune for seventeen years. He was musically inclined, as were his two daughters who sang with the Tabernacle Choir. Sarah and Benjamin celebrated their 50th wedding anniversary in 1906.

Sarah died in Salt Lake City on 9 Feb 1920, and Benjamin died 15 Nov 1925, also in Salt Lake City, Utah.

CATHERINE MIKESELL MIKESELL

No
Photo
Available

BIRTHDATE: 11 Oct 1784
Franklin County, Pennsylvania
DEATH: 20 Jul 1851
Salt Lake City, Utah
PARENTS: Jacob Mikesell
Mary Bast Mikesell
PIONEER: 21 Sep 1848
Brigham Young Co Wagon Train
SPOUSE: John Aylor Mikesell
MARRIED: 12 Dec. 1807
DEATH SP: 2 Dec.1858
Payson, Utah Co., Utah

CHILDREN:
Mary, 1808
Garret Walls, 18 May 1810
Hiram Washington, 13 Jun 1812
Amelia Delilah, 27 Jul 1813
John Harrison, 29 Mar 1815
Jacob, 1817

Catherine Mikesell was born in Pennsylvania in 1784, the fourth child born into the family of six children. Her father was a soldier in the Revolutionary War and for some reason Catherine was the only child born in Pennsylvania; the three older than she and her youngest sibling were all born in Maryland.

When she was twenty-three Catherine Mikesell and Jacob Micksell, her first cousin nine months older than she, were married. The marriage endured forty-four years and produced six children–four boys and two girls.

When western land and better opportunities showed themselves, Catherine and John, unafraid of work and eager to better their lives, moved to Kentucky where their first child was born in the year after they married.

Within two years they had moved to Cynthaiana, Harrison, Kentucky where Garret was born. One more move, to Liberty Montgomery, Ohio where Hiram Washington was born as the war of 1812 began, and they remained there for the next few years and the births of the last three children. Their oldest daughter, Mary and their youngest son, Jacob, died in childhood.

When they were about fifty-one years old they heard and accepted the Gospel of the Mormon Church and cast their lot with the Saints, following the Prophet from place to place to "find a place of suitable refuge."

They were fifty-five when they were expelled from Missouri, driven from their home during the winter of 1838-39 and with their children and grandchildren followed along to Nauvoo, Illinois. Hiram, their third son, married in Nauvoo that winter and Amelia, their fourth child, married Mr. Campbell there four years later, in 1844.

Catherine joined the Relief Society in Nauvoo on 28 September 1842 and enjoyed her life there. The city was growing into a prospering, social area, a circus visited in 1843, private excursion boats brought visitors up the river. But for the most part visiting each other and dancing, rag bees and quilting bees or corn husking bees and harvest bees were the most widely enjoyed.

When the Mormons were forced again to flee their city, the Mickesell's left also, finding refuge with their neighbors and friends. When Brigham Young traveled back to Illinois from his first sojourn into Utah to direct the main body of the church back to Salt Lake City, Catherine's family went to the Utah Territory with his company of 1,220 people. It was a train so large that shortly into the journey it was divided into four sections so as not to deplete the natural resources of grasses and water.

Over two thousand pioneers entered the Valley in 29 days that fall of 1848, the Mikesells among them.

Catherine lived only two winters in the valley; she passed away in the summer not quite three years after reaching her destination, at the age of sixty-six. John lived seven years after the loss of his companion to die at the age of seventy-four.

RUTH CUNNINGHAM MIKESELL

BIRTHDATE: 9 Jan 1811
Cincinatti, Hamilton, Ohio
DEATH: 10 Nov 1869
Richville, Morgan, Utah
PARENTS: John Cunningham
Frances Jones
PIONEER: 4 Sep 1863
A. H. Patterson Wagon Train
SPOUSE: Garrett W. Mikesell
MARRIED: 20 Jun 1830
DEATH SP: 20 Apr 1888
Richville, Morgan, Utah

CHILDREN:
Louise Cathern, 17 Apr 1831
George W., 20 Dec 1832
Delilah, 19 Oct 1835
John Cunningham, 4 Aug 1837
Independance, 4 Jul 1839
Cynthia Ann, 12 Aug 1841
James Miles, 12 Apr 1843
Frances Maranda, 15 Apr 1845
Brigham Young, 3 Apr 1849
Heber C., 20 Jan 1850
William Richards, 18 Jan 1853

Ruth Cunningham was born 9 Jan 1811 at Cincinatti, Hamilton, Ohio, the daughter of John Cunningham and Frances Jones. She married Garrett W. Mikesell on 20 Jun 1830 in Clark County, Illinois. In the year 1835 the family joined the LDS Church and moved to Missouri. They were driven out with the rest of the Saints in the winter of 1838/39, and settled in Quincy, Illinois. Again they had to move, this time to Council Bluffs in Iowa. They came across the plains with the A. H. Patterson wagon train, and arrived in Salt Lake City 4 Sep 1863.

The family evidently settled in Richville, Morgan County, Utah. Little is known of her activities there, but she died in Richville on 10 Nov 1869, and was buried in the Mikesell family plot in Salt Lake City, Utah.

SENA CATHERINE JOHNSON MIKKELSEN

BIRTHDATE: 14 May 1837
Klemmensker, Bornholm, Denmark
DEATH: 9 Mar 1921
Logan, Cache Co., Utah
PARENTS: John Johnson
Karen Kristine Anderson
PIONEER: 5 Oct 1854
Hans Peter Olson
SPOUSE: Niels Mikkelsen
MARRIED: 15 Apr. 1855
DEATH SP: 17 Jan 1894
Logan, Cache Co., Utah

CHILDREN:
Caroline Catherine, 26 Aug 1856

Ephraim, 21 Jul 1858
Sena Catherine, 17 Aug 1860

Sena Catherine Johnson was born in Denmark in 1837, the oldest daughter of prosperous farmers. She was fourteen when she first heard the gospel and two years later, along with her family, was baptized in the big pond in back of their house. (9 June 1853)

With acceptance of the gospel came harassment and abuse from their friends and neighbors, some of the worst was from their own relatives. One grabbed her hair by the braids, holding her while others whipped her back with a switch and when the persecution worsened her father decided to sell his farm. Taking much less than it was worth, he took his family to America, sailing from Liverpool, England on the ship "Jessie Munn" with other converts.

There were 335 saints crowded into the vessel for forty-three days on a voyage with inadequate water, food or space. They suffered malnutrition among other illnesses. Armed with faith they landed in New Orleans and were joined by additional Saints from another ship to travel up the Mississippi to St. Louis where they would stay until spring.

Cholera broke out; of the combined group of 687 emigrants, 200 lost their lives to the dreaded disease while camped at Westport, Missouri.

About the month of June they had finally begun their journey, traveling on the wrong trail for six weeks over valley and mountains so steep the men had to lower the wagons down the mountain sides with ropes.

Sena walked every step of the way. She waded the Green River up to her armpits in mush ice. She walked gathering buffalo chips in her apron so as to have a fire when they camped. Their prayers for food were answered by ravens so tame they were caught by hand and buffalo that wandered straight toward the wagon train.

Sena's family was sent to Box Elder (Brigham City) but seventeen-year-old Sena stayed in Salt Lake City working for a family for six months, (not understanding a thing they did the first few days). Shortly after joining her family in Box Elder she met Niels Mikkelsen and they were married that spring.

Crickets were a scourge to the early settlers causing near starvation. Sena foraged for thistle, water cress and pig weeds in the fields. Sego Lily roots were dug by the thousands each day. Eaten raw or dried they tasted like butternuts, boiled they tasted like a potato. Bulbs were frequently ground and bread was made from the starchy meal.

To escape Johnston's Army, Sena and Niels moved south to Goshen where Ephraim was born in a dugout with clean dry straw spread for a floor.

In Goshen Sena wove straw hats she sold to soldiers for enough to buy a fifty pound sack of flour. They returned to Logan. The constant moving, less than perfect living conditions and food, contributed to Sena's poor health and it was necessary to find help for her. Hearing of a girl working in servitude in Hyrum, Niels called at that home, and in agreement paid the debt, and returned home with Laura Ingels. The young girl became the second mother and then the second wife to the household, eventually adding her own family of nine children to Sena's two, melding both into one unit of love and friendship.

Sena lived seven years a widow, dying at seventy-four and being buried in the cemetery located on their original property which had been given to the town.

ANNIE GEORGE SMITH MILES

BIRTHDATE: 9 Nov 1859
Dundee, Forfar, Scotland
DEATH: 21 Jan 1950
Smithfield, Cache County, Utah
PARENTS: George Young Smith
Johann Luckie Smith
PIONEER: 1862
Jacab Gates Co.
SPOUSE: Edwin Ruthven Miles
MARRIED: 9 Jan 1859
DEATH: 31 Oct 1914
Smithfield, Cache County, Utah

CHILDREN:
George Edwin, 25 Dec 1879
Jane Ruth,, 3 Mar 1882
Edwin Ruthven, 9 Jul 1884
Leonard Smith, 17 Jul 1887
Johann Pearl, 30 May 1890
Hazel Vern, 12 Nov 1892
Maurice Kent, 21 Jan 1899

Annie arrived in the Salt Lake Valley with her parents and family in October 1862. They settled in Smithfield, Utah, 3 Nov 1862, just six months after leaving their home in Scotland. Life was not very pleasant for the children. The other children called them "Scotchies." One day some boys filled Annie's head full of porcupine quills. She thought Zion was a pretty hard place in which to live.

The family's first home was a one room structure with a dirt roof that leaked. There seemed to be more Indians than white and Annie was afraid of them. She endured all the hardships of a new country, having to sometimes go hungry. When Annie was five years old she fell into a creek and was nearly drowned. Annie had a good education for the times and taught school. She also made lace collars for which she found a ready market. At the age of sixteen she helped make Temple Clothes for the dead. She sang in the ward Choir, taught Sunday School and was a member of the Sunday School Dramatic Association.

Annie married Edwin Ruthven Miles, Jr. 9 Jan 1879. She continued her work in all the organizations of the Church, from Primary to Relief Society. She was President of her ward Relief Society for nearly twelve years. Also,

Annie served on the Stake Board. She worked with the American Legion Auxilliary, sat up with the sick, washed and dressed the dead. She was a member of the Daughters of the Utah Pioneers. She helped with dramatic entertainments to help pay for the First Ward organ in Smithfield. She had fond memories of having seen four United States Presidents. She entertained in her home two L.D.S. Church Presidents: Joseph F.Smith and his wife, Heber J. Grant and his wife, and also Counselor Charles Penrose. She also had entertained all of the twelve Apostles, other Church Officials and leading men in political circles.

Annie lived in Smithfield all of her life. She watched it grow from a sage brush flat covered with log houses and dugouts into an established city. She knew the days of ox teams and the days of automobiles, radios, electric lights and airplanes. She lived a life of service both in public and among her family. She said that she was happier doing something for somebody rather than herself. She passed through many sorrows, burying her parents, her husband, and many of her children. But through all the sorrows she had always been optimistic, very active and interested in life. Her family remember her as a truly remarkable woman. Annie died 21 Jan 1950 in Smithfield, Utah. She was ninety-one years old.

HANNAH DANIELS JOB MILES

BIRTHDATE: Chr 5 Mar 1829
Llanpumsaint, Carmarthenshire, Wales
DEATH: 19 Apr 1892
Mink Creek, Franklin, Idaho
PARENTS: John Daniels
Anne Thomas
PIONEER: 2 Oct 1856
Edward Bunker Co.
SPOUSE I: Thomas Job
MARRIED: 2 May 1848
Llanpumsaint, Wales
DEATH SP: 23 Dec 1890
Goshen, Utah, Utah

CHILDREN:
Mary, 21 Sep 1848
Elizabeth, 9 May 1851
Anne, 17 Sep 1853

SPOUSE II: Albert Miles
MARRIED: 13 Jan 1857
Salt Lake City, Utah
DEATH SP: 12 May 1886
Glendale, Franklin, Idaho

CHILDREN:
Mari ah (Powell), 11 Dec 1857
Thomas, 15 Jun 1858
Hannah (Montrose), 10 Aug 1861
John, 26 Jan 1863
Daniel, 4 Mar 1865
Davis, 7 Jun 1867
James, 25 May 1869
Dianna, 19 May 1871

Hannah Daniels was born in Wales in 1829. She married Thomas Job in 1848, and to them were born three daughters, however the last died as an infant. Hannah's uncle, Daniel Daniels, was a prominent leader of the Church in Wales and converted them to the gospel. Thomas wanted to go to Zion, but at the last minute Hannah backed out and refused to go. So Thomas took their daughter Elizabeth, and sailed on the ship "Golconda" in 1854.

Two years later Hannah had a change of heart and wrote to her uncle, Daniel Daniels, that she would now like to come to Utah with her daughter Mary and her sister Anne. Thomas was delighted and wrote back that he would pay their way. They came with the Edward Bunker Company by handcart in 1856.

In the meantime, Thomas had married Elizabeth Davies, another Welsh convert. Hannah did not know this until she arrived in Salt Lake. She would not accept the principle of plural marriage and so left Thomas. She married a widower, Albert Miles in 1857, and with him had eight more children. They lived in Cottonwood for a time, then moved to Smithfield in Cache County.

Hannah was known for her quick wit and dancing feet. She entertained ward members with her Welsh step dancing and folk songs. Although her trials were great, she was a happy person. Even after she lost her eyesight, the result of an unsuccessful operation to remove a cataract, she would tease her sons and grandchildren. Hannah died in 1892 in Mink Creek, Idaho.

JANE RUTH WAKEFIELD MILES

BIRTHDATE: 3 Feb 1840
Springfield, Illinois
DEATH: 14 Mar 1878
Smithfield, Cache County, Utah
PARENTS: Thomas Wakefield
Mary Clarke Wakefield
PIONEER: 1 Oct 1852
Uriah Curtis Company
SPOUSE:
Edwin Ruthven Miles, Sr.
MARRIED: 11 Mar 1857
Salt Lake City, Utah
DEATH SP: 2 Apr 1912
Smithfield, Utah

CHILDREN:
Edwin Ruthven, 3 Oct 1858
Thomas, 7 Sep 1860
Mary Jane, 20 Sep 1861
William Albert, 7 Apr 1864
Loretta Lucinda, 29 Mar 1866
Harriet Ann, 16 Jul 1868
Alice Mariah, 22 Dec 1869
Sylvia May, 12 May 1872
Eleanor, 25 Jan 1874
Franklin Wakefield, 16 Mar 1876
Stillborn baby, 14 Mar 1878

Jane Ruth Wakefield Miles was born in Springfield, Illinois. She moved with her parents and sister to Nauvoo, Illinois when she was an infant. Her father died of Malaria in Warsaw, Hancock County, Illinois in 1842, leaving her mother a widow with two small children. About one year later, May 1843, her mother married William Ainscough, a young convert from England. Jane Ruth was about six years old when her mother and stepfather and their three daughters were forced to leave Nauvoo because of the severe persecution of the Saints. They sold Thomas Wakefield's chest of carpenter tools to buy provisions, oxen and wagon as they made hasty arrangements to leave Nauvoo. They lived in the area of Winter Quarters for several years. Jane Ruth grew up with the hardships of that very early frontier pioneer life.

On 24 Jun 1852, when Jane Ruth was twelve years old, the family began the journey from Elk Horn River, Nebraska to the Salt Lake Valley. They were with the Sixteenth Company with Uriah Curtis as Captain. They had a wagon, two oxen and two cows. They had many hardships on their journey. Their white flour ran out and they only had bran to eat, causing the children to become very ill. A lady in the Company traded white flour for their bran; this gruel saved their lives. They arrived in the Valley 1 Oct 1852. They settled in Big Cottonwood in Salt Lake County. Here, Jane Ruth met Edwin Ruthven Miles, Sr. They were married in the Salt Lake Endowment House 11 Mar 1857. Jane Ruth was seventeen years old.

In the Spring of 1860, they moved to Smithfield, Cache Valley, Utah. On the day of an Indian raid, Jane Ruth ran for shelter, carrying her baby under her arm. Because of her fright and excitement, she was taken ill and lost her second child. They lived in a house with a dirt roof, which let the water wash into the house. Pans were held over the bed in which Jane Ruth was lying ill, to prevent the mud and rain from soaking her. After they moved out of the Fort, her husband built her the first hewed log house in the town. Her husband bought her a chain-stitch sewing machine, the first in Smithfield. Jane Ruth earned a little money by sewing. She received six cents per yard for stitching, which was used as a trimming. She also made endowment clothes for the Temple.

The family moved into a large two-story house, one of the best homes in town. They had a prayer room which was set-apart for the purpose of a prayer circle, which was held every Sunday morning. Jane Ruth lived the law of polygamy for the last thirteen years of her life. She died 14 Mar 1878 at the age of thirty-eight from an accident. She left a young family of eight children. Everyone spoke of Jane Ruth as cheerful and lovable, so good to those in need. Hers was the highest type of womanhood. Her life was one of endless service. No sacrifice was too great to make for the Gospel. She was true, unselfish and faithful to the end of her life.

JOHANNE KRISTINE "JANE" MOURITSEN MILES

BIRTHDATE: 29 Jan 1853
Ronnousholm Tileworks, Vrejlev, Hjorring, Denmark
DEATH: 8 Oct 1946
Smithfield, Cache County, Utah
PARENTS: Lars Mouritsen
Maren Sorensen Mouritsen
PIONEER: 12 Sep 1859
George Rowley Handcart Co.
SPOUSE: Edwin Ruthven Miles
MARRIED: 3 May 1870
Salt Lake City, Utah
DEATH: 2 Apr 1912
Smithfield, Utah

CHILDREN:
Lettie Luella, 20 Jan 1877
Ruth, 19 Mar 1879
Jeddie LeRoy, 1 Mar 1881
Mina, 30 Nov 1884
Leone, 25 Aug 1887
Beth, date not known
Ruby Mouritsen, 23 Jul 1895

Johanne Kristine Mouritsen Miles was born in Denmark. Her parents joined the Mormon Church in 1858. Johanne was just five years old. Baptisms had to be done in a very quiet fashion; there was an edict against emigration. When the edict was recalled the family started their journey to America in 1859. Johanne was six years old. They sailed on the ship "William Tapscott." The company was blessed with a most pleasant and agreeable voyage which lasted only thirty-one days. They arrived in Florence, Nebraska 25 May 1859. They left Florence 26 June with the George Rowley Handcart Company. Johanne's father had a team and wagon, which was part of the Company. Johanna told of the long walk across the Plains and how her little feet would get so dry and cracked that they would bleed. Sometimes, her father would put her on the wagon to ride for a little way. As the children walked, they pulled grass to feed the animals to keep them moving.

They arrived in the Salt Lake Valley 12 Sep 1859. They first made a home in Sessions' Settlement (now Bountiful, Utah). In 1861 they moved to Plain City, near Ogden, Utah and then to Smithfield in Cache Valley, Utah. She was baptized in 1862, probably in the Weber River in Utah. Johanne married Edwin Ruthven Miles 3 May 1870 in the Endowment House in Salt Lake City; it was a long trip by wagon from Smithfield to Salt Lake City. They lived in a log house while they were homesteading a ranch in Smithfield. Johanne was Edwin Miles' plural wife. His first wife died 14 Mar 1878, leaving eight children ages two to twenty years. Johanne was a faithful wife and mother and loved both families very dearly. When her husband was called to serve a mission Jane took care of her two families. Her little daughter, Ruth, died when she was nearly five years old. It was a sad time for Johanne. She spent several years in Franklin, Idaho. Her last child was born there. She later returned to Smithfield.

Jane had a natural talent for nursing the sick and studied and learned all the natural remedies for different illnesses. She healed animals, too. When a dog's toes were accidently mowed off, Johanne carefully put the toes in place and wrapped them in sugar and turpentine and they grew back. Johanne loved music. She played the accordion and could make everyone want to dance.

She could fix everything; wire and glue chairs back together and fix the holes in the plaster. She served in all capacities that women were able to serve in the Church. She was an excellent teacher and wonderful cook. She fell on the ice getting out of a car. She lived several weeks but was in intense pain all the time. Her death was a sweet passing from this life into a much more beautiful life with all of her family who had preceeded her in death. She died 8 Oct 1946. She left 200 plus descendents who all loved and revered her life and memory. She was one of the very finest spirits God ever created.

MARGARET MARIAH VIETS MILES

BIRTHDATE: 31 Jan 1810
Southington, Trumbell, Ohio
DEATH: 20 Oct 1856
Big Cottonwood, Salt Lake, Utah
PARENTS: Benjamin Viets
Sally Donaldson Viets
PIONEER: 23 Sep 1848
Heber C. Kimball Co.
SPOUSE: Albert Miles
MARRIED: 1833
Phlanx Station, Southington, Trumbell, Ohio
DEATH: 12 May 1886
Glendale, Franklin, Idaho

CHILDREN:
Henry Albert, Dec 1833
Benjamin Adarian, 3 Dec 1835
Edwin Ruthven, 25 May 1838
Franklin, 10 Dec 1841 (died, age 9)
Sally Ann, 6 Oct 1843
Mariah Louisa, 18 Sep 1849

Mariah was born and grew up in Southington, Trumbell, Ohio. As a beautiful young woman of twenty three, she married Albert Miles at Phlanx Station in Southington, Ohio. They went to live in Parkman, Ohio where her husband's parents and family lived. Her first three children were born there. During this time, she and her husband were baptized members of the LDS Church. To be with the saints, they moved to Mendon, Adams County, Illinois where two more of their children were born. She supported her husband in his duties as a member of the Nauvoo Legion which included protecting the Prophet Joseph Smith. He also served as a Seventy, as a carpenter on the construction of the Nauvoo Temple, and the Nauvoo House. When they were forced to leave the beautiful Nauvoo area, their family went west with the Heber C. Kimball Wagon Company and arrived in the Salt Lake Valley on September 23, 1848.

They lived in the Big Cottonwood area of Salt Lake Valley where their last child was born a year after their arrival. Mariah cared for her family alone much of the time because her husband was a member of the Regiment Mounted Rangers, Nauvoo Legion, involved in the Expedition against the Utah Indians near the Provo River. He was also called on a mission to Las Vegas, Nevada. Mariah finally had to write him and advise him of the awful plight she was in with the drought, the devastation to the crops by the crickets, and no supplies. Mariah served in her community by assisting in the care of the sick people. She nursed some who had smallpox. She contracted the dreaded disease and died on October 20, 1856 at the age of forty-six.

RACHEL MAHULDA LOCKHART MILES

BIRTHDATE: 24 Feb 1836
Monroe, Monroe, Mississippi
DEATH: 13 May 1912
Peoa, Summit, Utah
PARENTS: John Lockhart
Margaret Maria Towery
PIONEER: 19 Oct 1848
Heber C. Kimball Company
SPOUSE: Benjamin Adrain Miles
MARRIED: 28 May 1856
Salt Lake City, Utah
DEATH SP: 5 Dec 1888
Peoa, Summit, Utah

CHILDREN:
Benjamin Franklin, 5 Jan 1858
John Lockhart, 1 Apr 1859
James Henry, 28 Dec 1861
Edwin Hezikiah, 1 Jan 1863
Margaret Maria, 15 May 1864
Mary Alice, 24 Dec 1865
Adrain Edgar, 5 Dec 1867
Albert, 5 Jul 1869
Don Carlos, 10 Jan 1871
Luchious Marion, 24 Jun 1872
Ida May, 25 Jan 1874
Eva Maud, 20 Jul 1876

Rachel Mahulda Lockhart was born in 1836 in Mississippi. She was twelve years old when she came to the Utah Territory with the Heber C. Kimball Company in 1848.

Rachel married Benjamin Adrain Miles in 1856. They were sent by Brigham Young to settle in the Peoa, Summit county area about 1862. She had three little boys at the time, and later had nine more children. Rachel, with her husband and brother-in-law, Orrin Lee, owned and operated the first dance hall or amusement hall in Peoa. She had a very good education and spoke French, taught to her by her mother.

During the Black Hawk War in 1865, the family had to live in the fort for protection. She was a very religious person, and served as the first Relief Society President in Peoa. Benjamin died in 1888, and Rachel died in 1912, both in Peoa, Summit, Utah.

ALICE HIGGENBOTHAM ASHTON MILLER

BIRTHDATE: 25 Oct 1814
Denton, Lancashire, England
DEATH: 16 Feb 1897
Provo, Utah Co., Utah
PARENTS: John Higgenbotham
Rebecca Lees
PIONEER: 1852
SPOUSE I: Richard Ashton
MARRIED: 17 Dec 1837
in England
DEATH SP: unknown

CHILDREN:
Mary, d. in infancy
Hannah, 23 Feb 1840
John, 1843
Thomas, 1846
Sarah, 1848

SPOUSE II: Charles Dutton Miller
MARRIED: 16 Jan 1853
DEATH SP: 24 Jan 1878
Provo, Utah, Utah

CHILDREN:
Alice Rebecca, 25 May 1854
Elizabeth, 16 Sep 1856
Charles, 12 Sep 1858

Alice Higgenbotham was born England in 1814. She married Richard Ashton 17 Dec 1837. They emigrated to America with daughter Hannah in 1840 New Jersey, where the other children were born.

In 1852 the Elders preached the gospel to them and converted Alice and daughter Hannah. Richard could not accept the gospel and later returned to England with the youngest daughter, Sarah.

Alice and three children, Hannah, John, and Thomas, came across the plains in 1852 with the Horace Eldridge Company. Alice drove her own team and wagon. She settled in Salt Lake City. Her sons, John and Thomas, left their mother for the California gold rush. She never heard from them again.

In Salt Lake she met Charles Dutton Miller, a widower with three children. They were married 16 Jan 1856. For a time they lived in Farmington in a sod house, however snakes had infested the walls of the house and it was necessary for them to move. 1855 they moved to Provo, where they resided the rest of their lives. Charles died 24 Jan 1878, and Alice died 16 Feb 1897, both in Provo, Utah, Utah.

AMANDA MORGAN MILLER

BIRTHDATE: 10 Aug 1795
Essex, Chittenden, Vermont
DEATH: 16 Oct 1879
Nephi, Juab, Utah
PARENTS: Daniel Morgan
Abigail Jones
PIONEER: 20 Oct 1847
SPOUSE: Josiah H. Miller
MARRIED: About 1816
DEATH SP: 29 Jul 1865
Nephi, Juab, Utah

CHILDREN:
Evaline, 2 Nov 1817
Miles, 26 Jul 1819
Daniel Morgan, 19 Nov 1821
Harriet, 9 Jan 1824
Emily, Jul 1825 d. age 2
Emily Louisa, 16 Apr 1827
Clarissa Amanda, 8 Oct 1829
Abigail, 18 Mar 1836 d. 18 mos

Amanda Morgan was born in Vermont in 1795. She married Josiah H. Miller about 1816, and they became the parents of eight children. Amanda was baptized in 1836 in Kirtland, Ohio. They came to the Salt Lake Valley in 1847 with the Jedediah M. Smith Company. Both Amanda and Josiah were fifty years old at the time.

The family was sent to Nephi, Juab Co., Utah to settle. Amanda carded and spun the wool for her family's clothing. She made her own dyes from sagebrush, dogwood, indigo and other herbs. All sewing was done by hand, and their stockings and gloves were hand knit. Rags were made into rugs; nothing was wasted.

Times were hard, with bad weather, grasshoppers, and Indian troubles. Her son Daniel was killed by an Indian, and his thirteen years old son wounded in 1872. Amanda lived to be eighty-four years old and died in 1879. Josiah preceded her in death in 1865, both in Nephi, Juab, Utah.

AMELIA CAROLINE SMITHSON MILLER

BIRTHDATE: 4 Aug 1848
On the Plains
DEATH: 26 Feb 1919
White Pine County, Nevada
PARENTS: William Cox Smithson
Lucinda Wilson Smithson
PIONEER: 1848
Wagon Train
SPOUSE: Hyrum Smith Miller
MARRIED: 8 May 1870
Utah
DEATH: 31 Dec 1932
Nevada

CHILDREN:
Hyrum William, 30 Jun 1872
John Bartley, 22 Feb 1874
Gregg Henry, 3 Jun 1875
Elvira Almina, 11 Mar 1878
Charles Sterling, 19 Apr 1880
Rowland Hugh, 23 Feb 1882
Caroline Lucinda, 20 Apr 1884
Charles Sterling, 19 Apr 1886
Herbert Arnold, 24 Jul 1887

Amelia Caroline was born in a wagon during her parents' journey across the Plains to the Salt Lake Valley. Her parents were early converts to the Mormon Church. Her father had joined the Church in Munroe, Mississippi, 1 Sep 1843. Her parents answered the call to emigrate to the Utah Territory. They traveled by wagon. Amelia bumped and jostled in her mother's womb most of the way until she was born in a wagon. They arrived in the Salt Lake Valley the Fall of 1848.

Little is known of her childhood. Amelia and her parents experienced all the trials of frontier life. They were in the San Bernardino, California Colony of 1850. Amelia would have been two years old. When the Colony was closed down they were called to help settle the Southern Dixie Mission. They built new homes and planted crops in the area.

Amelia married Hyrum Smith Miller 8 May 1870. He was a freighter, farmer and colonizer. They settled in St. George, Utah and then homesteaded in the Snake Valley. They finally settled on a ranch near Silver Creek, North of Baker, Nevada in 1871. Life was hard for the young Amelia. They experienced trouble with the Indians in the area so they decided to return to Washington County, Utah. There they lived until 1890. They became the parents of nine children. They then returned to their ranch in Nevada where they made their home and lived out their lives. Many of the ranch buildings are still standing today. Amelia was a faithful, compassionate and loving mother and wife. She educated her children in the Gospel.

ANN SHEPHERD MILLER

BIRTHDATE: 8 May 1825
Depford, Kent, England
DEATH: 27 Mar 1910
Coltman, Idaho
PARENTS:
Nathaniel John Shepherd
Mary Andrews
PIONEER: Sep 1866
Thomas E. Ricks Co.
SPOUSE: John Hawkins Miller
MARRIED: 17 Mar 1841
DEATH SP: 16 Dec 1905
Coltman, Idaho

CHILDREN:
Harriet Hawkins, 17 Mar 1841
Alice Ophelia, 19 Jul 1845
John Shepherd, 12 Mar 1848

Ann Shepherd was born 8 May 1825 in Depford, Kent, England, the daughter of Nathaniel John Shepherd and Mary Andrews. She married John Hawkins Miller on 17 Mar 1841 in England, and they were the parents of three children, one who died at age three years.

The Miller family, after they joined the Church, sold their beautiful home in Southampton, England, and sailed on the ship "Caroline" for America. They traveled across the plains with the Thomas E. Ricks Company wagon train and arrived in Salt Lake City 4 Sep 1866.

They lived in Salt Lake for one year then moved to Willard, Utah. John practiced carpentry and cabinet making, and built a lovely home for his family. For a time their daughter Alice, and her son lived with them. Ann was musically inclined with a beautiful singing voice. She gave lessons to many students in Willard, one of which was Evan Stephens, the noted LDS hymnast.

Ann was also artistic and loved gardening. She learned to make wax flowers, and made intricately beaded cushions. In the 1880's they moved to Plain City, then in 1904 moved to Coltman, Idaho. John died in Coltman, Idaho on 16 Dec 1905, and Ann died 27 Mar 1910, also in Coltman. They are both buried in the Central Cemetery, not far from Idaho Falls, Idaho.

ANNA DOROTHEA ELIZABETH JENSEN MEYER MILLER

BIRTHDATE: 17 Apr 1816
Flensburg, Schleswig, Germany
DEATH: 20 Feb 1890
Salt Lake City, Utah
PARENTS: Christian Jensen
Elise Maria Christiansen
PIONEER: 23 Sep 1862
SPOUSE I: Fredrick Heinrick
Johannes Meyer
MARRIED: 21 Sep 1836
DEATH SP: 25 Jan 1857

CHILDREN:
Joseph Christian, 29 Sep 1833
Carl Ludwig Friedrick, 8 Mar 1836
Heinrick Friedrick Emmanuel, 17 Feb 1837
Wilhelm Carl Agnes, 8 Sep 1842
Anna Margaretha Juliane, 9 Aug 1845
Johannes Christian Ludwig, 3 Nov 1846
Fredrick August Englebert, 23 Jun 1849
Maria Margaretha Doris, 2 Mar 1854
Josephine Henrietta, 21 Mar 1856

SPOUSE II: Eleazer Miller
MARRIED: 10 Nov 1866
DEATH SP: 12 Apr 1876
Salt Lake City, Utah
CHILDREN: None

Anna Dorothea Elizabeth Jensen was born 17 Apr 1816 in Flensburg, Schleswig, Germany, the daughter of Christian Jensen and Elise Marie Christiansen. She married Fredrick Heinrick Johannes Meyer on 21 Sep 1836 in Germany. She states in her history that she was the mother of twelve children, but only nine of them have been listed on the records, and several of these died very young.

Anna was fair skinned with beautiful blue eyes and blonde hair, like her Danish parents, but her husband was very dark, for he was a Hebrew and an Orthodox Jew. He was killed by some German soldiers who were patrolling on 25 Jan 1857.

Anna had previously joined the LDS Church in 1852 and desired to come to Zion. In the spring of 1862 a son, Fredrick, and daughter Josephine, sailed with her on the ship "Athenia." Two older sons remained in Germany. They arrived 23 Sep 1862 in Salt Lake City, where she built a home a few years later. On 10 Nov 1866 she married Eleazer Miller in the Endowment House in Salt Lake City.

Anna was well acquainted with the scriptures, and was a faithful member of the Church. She passed away 20 Feb 1890 and is buried in the Salt Lake City Cemetery.

CAROLINE MARGRETE KIRSTINE LARSEN MILLER

BIRTHDATE: 1 Sep 1840
Ostermarie, Bornholm, Denmark
DEATH: 23 Jun 1923
Gunnison, Utah
PARENTS: Thomas Larsen Nielsen
Margretha Jensen
PIONEER: 29 Aug 1863
John Murdock Co
SPOUSE: Hans Peter Hansen Miller
MARRIED: 22 Jun 1861
Florence, Nebraska
DEATH SP: 7 Aug 1894
Richfield, Sevier County, Utah

CHILDREN:
Maria Margaret, 27 Oct 1863
Hans Peter, 3 Oct 1865
Janus Thomas, 28 Jan 1867
Caroline Margaret, 16 Dec 1868
Ane Kirstina, 2 Sep 1871
Martha Johanna (twin), 22 Feb 1874
Margaret (twin), 22 Feb 1874
Eleanora Elizabeth, 17 Mar 1876
Laura Antionette, 14 Jul 1878
John Clarence, 13 Nov 1880
Eudora Augusta, 8 Aug 1883

Caroline was born in Denmark in 1840. She emigrated to Utah in 1863. When they had arrived at Ellis Island, New York for quarantine, Caroline's husband was in charge of their group as he was the only one who spoke English. She married Hans Peter Hansen Miller in Florence, Nebraska 22 Jun 1861. They had been sweethearts in Denmark and married on the way to Utah. They traveled with a wagon-train company with Herman Sylvester as Captain. They arrived in the Salt Lake Valley 29 Aug 1863.

Their first home was in Mt. Pleasant, Utah. They were the first settlers in Richfield, Utah. Her first home was a dugout. It was a cellar with a willow-dirt roof with steps out of the soil leading to the entrance. With tears in her eyes she asked, "Is this home?" There was no window and no door, merely a cloth hung up to keep out some of the cold. She had tiny children to take care of and a new child to be born in mid spring! This was the sort of home that greeted these wives and families who had left fairly comfortable homes to come to the "land of promise." Her first son, Hans Peter, was the first white child born in Richfield, Utah.

Caroline could read and write. One year she was chosen as Mrs. Utah and rode in the Fourth of July Parade. She looked beautiful dressed in all white with her crown resting on her white hair. Behind her was a banner of Utah. In front of her was a bed of flowers which read, "Utah, We Love Thee." In Sep 1914 she was honored during the 50th year celebration of the founding of Richfield, Utah as one of nine original pioneers of Richfield. She acted as secretary to her husband for the receiving of tithing.

Everyone brought things they had raised and she was held responsible for them. She was responsible in all of her dealings and callings in the Church. Her husband died in 1894. She was a widow for twenty-nine years. Caroline died at the age of eighty-three years, 23 Jun 1923. She and her husband were the parents of eleven children; two died in infancy and one died in childhood. Caroline was a loving mother and wife and a faithful member of the Church.

CHRISTINE JORGENE/GEORGINA NORR MILLER

BIRTHDATE: 14 Sep 1853
Melby, Frederiksborg, Denmark
DEATH: 19 Apr 1941
Ogden, Utah
PARENTS: Anders Pedersen Norr
Frederikke Pedersen Norr
PIONEER: 1867
walking with a wagon-train company
SPOUSE: Hans Koford Miller
MARRIED: 1871
Salt Lake Endowment House
DEATH: 5 Sep 1907

CHILDREN:
Minnie Almina, 16 Nov 1871
Hans Oscar, 13 Jan 1875
Peter William, 14 Jul 1876
George Wilford, 14 Dec 1878
Emma, 9 Nov 1883
Arthur G., 24 Mar 1886
Mabel Eliza, 15 Jan 1889
Illa, 18 Apr 1895
Leona, 2 Apr 1898
Child, died in infancy

Christine Jorgene was born in Denmark in 1853. Her parents were honest and hard working. Her father died when she was nine years old and Georgina worked to help support the family. During the winter she knitted stockings and did cross stitch and in the summer she herded geese for farmers.

Shortly after her father's death Georgina's mother joined the Mormon Church and Georgina was baptized when she was ten years old.

They were persecuted because of their new religion. In 1867 a good friend offered to take one of her mother's children to Utah with him. Georgina was chosen. She was fourteen years old. It was a trial for her to part from her mother and it was very difficult for her widowed mother to give up her child.

She traveled to England where she embarked on her long sea voyage, but unfortunately her baggage was lost in transit. She was left with only the clothes she was wearing. She borrowed clothing from other children to wear when her own needed washing.

The sea voyage lasted nearly two months and was hard and disagreeable, but her travels across the Plains were more difficult. Towards the end of the journey food was scarce and she often went to bed hungry. Her shoes were worn out before the end of her journey and her stockings fell into the fire ashes and burned. She wrapped her feet in rags. Many times her feet were so sore that she could hardly move them. They arrived in the Salt Lake Valley the fall of 1867. A family took her in and treated her kindly. Two years after her arrival in Utah her mother emigrated to Utah to join her. She never told her mother of the hardships she had on her trip to Zion.

Georgina was seventeen years old when she married Hans Miller in the Endowment House. They lived in Salt Lake City, Brigham City and then moved to San Pete County to be near the St. George Temple. They joined the United Order, but their community was dissolved two years later, leaving them destitute. They moved to Idaho where they endured many hardships

She was the First Counselor to the Primary President in Snowville for six years, taught Sunday School in Mayfield and worked for many years in the Relief Society.

In August of 1907 her husband was injured in an accident and died nine days later. Following his death she moved to Brigham City, Utah and lived in that city until her death in 1941. Georgina wrote in her autobiography that through all her trials God had been with her and guided and led her to a true testimony of the Gospel. Her greatest ambition in her youth was to be married to a good man, have a home and children and that was all realized and she rejoiced in the goodness of the Lord.

ELLEN (ELEANOR) WILLIAMSON WANDLESS MILLER

BIRTHDATE: 29 Sep 1826
Easington Lane, Durham, England
DEATH. 26 Feb 1864
Farmington, Davis, Utah
PARENTS: Thomas Williamson
Hannah Robinson
PIONEER: 26 Sep 1856
Daniel McArthur Handcart Co.
SPOUSE I: Thomas Wandless
MARRIED: 28 Mar 1847
Durham, England
DEATH SP: unknown

CHILDREN:
John Williamson, 24 Jun 1847
Ellen (Eleanor), 28 Apr 1849
Jane, 1851

SPOUSE II: Daniel Arthur Miller
MARRIED: 27 Mar 1857
Salt Lake City, Utah
DEATH SP: 4 Dec 1851
Farmington, Utah

CHILDREN:
Rubin, 21 Jan 1858
Claryse Ruth, 28 May 1859
Charles Arnold, 22 May 1861
Frederic Septimus, 26 Feb 1864

Ellen (Eleanor) was born in England in 1826, the daughter of Thomas Williamson and Hannah Robinson. She married Thomas Wandless on 28 Mar 1847 in Durham, England, and they had three children, one of whom died at birth. Her husband evidently died in England.

Ellen came to America on the ship "Enoch Train" with her daughter Ellen, age 6. They came across the plains with the second handcart company, under the Perpetual Emigration Fund, and arrived in Salt Lake in Sep 1856.

On 27 Mar 1857 she married Daniel Arthur Miller in the Endowment House in Salt Lake City. They lived in Farmington, Davis, Utah, and were the parents of three children. The first, Rubin, was stillborn, and when baby Frederic was born she contracted childbed fever and died at his birth, 26 Feb 1864. Little Frederic Septimus died the following May 1864. Ellen was buried in Farmington, Davis, Utah.

ELMIRA POND MILLER

BIRTHDATE: 14 Feb 1811
Barlow, Washington, Ohio
DEATH: 3 Sep 1904
Syracuse, Salt Lake County, Utah
PARENTS: Thaddeus Pond
Lovissa Miner
PIONEER: 21 Sep 1852
Henry W. Miller Wagon Train
SPOUSE: Henry William Miller
MARRIED: 19 Jun 1831
Quincy, Adams, Illinois
DEATH SP: 9 Oct 1885
Farmington, Davis, Utah

CHILDREN:
Elizabeth Ellen (Quigley), 25 Sep 1832
Ruth Ann (McBride), 30 Mar 1834
Lucy, 10 Jan 1837
William Henry, 22 Dec 1838
Alma, 20 Jan 1841
Mary Elmira (Hess), 10 Sep 1843
Freelove (Hammond), 24 Jul 1845
Hyrum Smith, 4 May 1847
Satah Jane (Carbine), 22 Mar 1849
David, 14 Feb 1851
Arnold Daniel, 2 Mar 1852

Elmira was born in Ohio in 1811. Elmira was number eight of eleven children. She read the New Testament often and wondered why they didn't have the same gifts and blessings as in the time of Christ and his apostles. Her mother and some of the children belonged to the Methodist Church.

In 1831 she married Henry Miller who wasn't a religious man. A few years later they met people that had been driven from their homes in Missouri. They started having religious meetings in their home and Elmira was the first one wanting baptism. She, with her husband, was baptized in 1837. She was soon challenged by the adversary and through faith and prayer was given the gift of tongues and assurance it was the true church. She witnessed many miracles. Her husband was also a staunch believer from then on.

In 1841 they went up the Black River to get lumber for the temple. Elmira and their five children accompanied her husband and several men. The river froze over so they continued by oxen. At night fifteen of them would sleep in the sleigh that had to be shoveled free from snow. She cooked and washed for all of them for ten months. Supplies ran low and for weeks there was nothing to eat but potatoes and salt. She had been given a blessing by one of the apostles that her children wouldn't cry for bread while on this mission. None did.

She stayed with her husband to help outfit the people coming west and they finally left for Utah in 1852. They left Kanesville, Iowa in June, with her youngest child being only three months old. The trip was hard and she walked most of the way.

In 1862 her husband took another wife. Although it was not to her natural feeling she accepted it for the Gospel's sake. In 1866, Elmira and children joined her husband who was in Southern Utah. When health problems developed they moved back to Farmington. They were living here when he died in 1885.

In May, 1899 Elmira received a manifestation while living at her daughter Ruth's home in Hyrum, Utah. Writing appeared on the wall and Henry told her of his love for her, how lonely he was, about a granddaughter's impending death, for her to do temple work for some dead relatives, how to dispose of property, etc. He said he would come to get her but couldn't tell her when.

Elmira lived with children and grandchildren until her death in 1904. She is buried by the side of her husband at Farmington, Utah.

HANNAH BIGLER MILLER

BIRTHDATE: 24 Jun 1820
Harrison County, Virginia
DEATH: 13 Mar 1905
PARENTS: Jacob Bigler
Elizabeth Harvey Bigler
PIONEER: 4 Sep 1848
Brigham Young Company
SPOUSE: Daniel A. Miller
MARRIED: 29 Dec 1844
DEATH: 6 Dec 1881

CHILDREN:
Isabell Clarinda, 21 Jan 1846
Joseph Smith, 12 1847
Emeline Elizabeth, 24 May 1849
Sarah Lovina, 24 Jul 1850
Ruth Abigail, 27 Jul 1852
Hannah Malinda, 23 Jun 1854
Bathsheba, 12 Jun 1855
David Edger, Oct 1857
Daniel Gardner, 29 May 1859
Henry W., 5 Oct 1860

Hannah's mother died when she was three years old, leaving her three children to stay with their Grandmother Harvey until their father remarried. Her opportunities for schooling were limited due to the fact that children on the frontiers were expected to help on the farm and in the home for the maintenance of the family. In 1838 the Jacob Bigler family accepted the gospel of the LDS Church and moved to Far West where the body of the Church was located. The following year, the Saints were exterminated from the state of Missouri and went to Illinois. They endured persecution and the privations incident to the establishment of the Church at that time.

Hannah was a girl beaming with a cheerful disposition, sympathy for others, and was ever ready to assist those in need. In the early summer of 1844, she went into the home of Daniel A. Miller whose wife lay seriously ill. She nursed the sick mother, cared for the children, and kept up the work of the home. Months after his wife, Clarysa, died he asked Hannah to become his second wife to help him raise his children Louisa, Jacob, James Thaddeus, Susan Hilda, Clarysa Jane, and David Arnold. On March 1, 1846, Daniel disposed of his property and fitted up wagons to move westward with the Saints to the Rocky Mountains with Hannah, his five children by Clarysa, and their new baby girl. Their progress was slow because they were in the advance company which had to make roads and build bridges over streams. They also formed temporary settlements along the way for those Saints who could go no farther and for those who should follow later on. They stopped at a place they called Miller's Hollow (later named Kanesville after Captain Kane of the Mormon Battalion, and now known as Council Bluffs). Hannah not only shared the hardships connected with that long, tedious journey, but she also carried the greater responsibility of her large family while her husband was in charge of fifty persons and twenty wagons. They arrived in Salt Lake Valley on 4 Sep 1848.

HELEN AURELIA HINMAN MILLER

BIRTHDATE: 20 Sep 1840
West Stockbridge, Berkshire,
Massachusetts
DEATH: 12 Nov 1911
Syracuse, Davis, Utah
PARENTS: Lyman Hinman
Aurelia Lewis
PIONEER: 21 Sep 1848
Brigham Young Company
SPOUSE:
Henry William Miller
MARRIED: 2 Mar 1858
Salt Lake City, Utah
DEATH: 2 Jul 1922

CHILDREN:
Edna Mosella, 20 Dec 1859
William Morgan, 12 Feb 1861
Helen Louisa, 23 Mar 1863
Lyman Henry, 27 Apr 1865
Lucy Aurelia, 25 Apr 1868
Seymour Lewis, 1 Nov 1870
Evelyn Elmira, 2 Sep 1872
Maud Mary, 5 Mar 1875
Amy Christine, 24 Dec 1876
Arnold David, 12 Oct 1879
Harriet Acenith, 20 Aug 1881
Rhoda Ann, 11 Feb 1884

Helen was born into a home of wealth, culture, and refinement, governed by the strict rules of her Puritan ancestors. When Helen was one year old, her parents were converted and baptized as members of the LDS Church. In the fall of 1843, Lyman Hinman sold his store, donated his home to the city and emigrated by rail and steamship to Nauvoo with his wife and children. They purchased a dry farm from Daniel H. Wells and lived happily until they were driven from their home. When the weather permitted, they traveled to Winter Quarters where they stayed until they joined the Brigham Young Wagon Company and arrived in the Salt Lake Valley on September 21, 1848.

They spent their first winter in part of the old fort, and lived in Salt Lake City for several years. Helen attended school for only a few weeks, but learned to read and write at home. She became a lover of good literature. Helen was taught the finer arts of homemaking and was skilled in knitting, embroidery, dying her threads, quilting, spinning, crocheting, netting, and tatting. The Hinmans moved to Farmington, Utah where her father built and operated mills. She had many suitors, but chose William Henry Miller to marry. They were married in the Salt Lake Endowment House. Due to the threat of Johnston's Army, they moved to Mona with his parents until they could move back to Farmington. Helen gave birth to twelve children between the years of 1859 and 1884. She raised five other children who were left without mothers. Helen was a good cook and kept a well furnished home. She had one of the first sewing machines and washing machines and organs. Her home was a gathering place for the young people. She became

famous for her great success as a skilled nurse with her use of native herbs and plants. In 1882 they filed for a homestead on one hundred sixty acres in Syracuse and Helen again faced the rigors of pioneer life without the assistance of her husband. He was called on a mission to South Carolina. She served as the president of the Syracuse Primary for thirteen years.

HELEN MAR CHENEY MILLER

BIRTHDATE: 25 Jul 1835
Sandusky, New York
DEATH: 13 Aug 1913
Farmington, Davis County, Utah
PARENTS:
Nathan Calhoun Cheney
Eliza Anne Beebe Cheney
PIONEER: 6 Oct 1850
William Snow Company
SPOUSE: Jacob Miller
MARRIED: 16 Mar 1856
prob Farmington, Utah
DEATH: 11 Oct 1911
Farmington, Utah

CHILDREN:
Jacob Franklin, 10 Dec 1856
Eliza Ann, 13 Jan 1859
James Bertram, 22 Apr 1860
Helen Vestina, 10 Nov 1861
Nathan W., 23 Mar 1864
Bertina Nathalia, 21 Aug 1865
Daniel Thomas, 15 May 1870

Helen Mar Cheney Miller was born in New York. She moved from New York with her parents when she was one year old. Her parents had joined the Mormon Church and moved to Kirtland, Ohio. The family suffered hardships and persecutions and were eventually forced to leave their home and possessions and move to Nauvoo, Illinois. They were among the first pioneers who settled there. Helen Mar saw the Prophet Joseph Smith many times and listened to his teachings. Her family was one of the last to leave Nauvoo in 1846 because her father had been called to look after the aged and the widows and get them started on their journey west. The family lived at Benton's Port, Iowa for two years and then moved to Winter Quarters, Nebraska and then to Jefferson, Missouri. They finally made the journey to Utah, arriving 6 Oct 1850 with the William Snow Company.

Helen's father bought a farm in Centerville, Davis County, Utah. He built a log house which was covered with willows and had a dirt floor. Helen was fifteen years old. They slept in the wagon bed the first winter. only one year later, 6 Oct 1851, Helen's mother died and her father died four months later. Helen assumed a mother's role when she was sixteen years old. She had to work to help keep four brothers and sisters. She found work in Farmington, Utah, working for Evelyn Potter. She was able to attend school during the winter months. She met Jacob Miller in

Farmington. They were married when Helen was twenty years old.

Her husband was called away on a mission to the Salmon River for two years. He was able to return in 1856 when their first child was born. They lived in a two-room house with her sister and brother-in law. Helen had her bed in the room where the fire was, but she learned that her sister was also giving birth that night. Helen insisted that her sister go into the room where the fire was. To keep peace, they granted her request. Only three of Helen's seven children lived to be adults. Despite her sorrow at the loss of four children over the years Helen fulfilled her Church responsibilities. She was a Sunday School teacher and Treasurer of the Farmington Ward Relief Society. She was a first Counselor to Aurelia Rogers in the first Primary Association formed on 11 Aug 1878 and held that position until 1887. She served in the Presidency of the Davis Stake M.I.A. and was President of the Relief Society for twelve years.

Helen was noted for her good cooking. She made wedding cakes and furnished the bread for the Sacraments. Fremont Island, in the Great Salt Lake, was first known as Miller Island. Jacob Miller kept sheep there. Helen carded the wool, spun it, made cloth and clothes for her family. They lived in a log house until 1869. Jacob completed their rock home, one of the first rock homes in Farmington. Her husband died in 1911. Helen died 13 Aug 1913 in Farmington, Utah.

LUCINDA MATHENA WADSWORTH MILLER

BIRTHDATE: 28 Jan 1851
Council Bluffs, Iowa
DEATH: 3 Oct 1933
Salt Lake City, Utah
PARENTS: Abiah Wadsworth
Elizabeth Hardy Wadsworth
PIONEER: 23 Sep 1851
John G. Smith Co.
SPOUSE: William Miller
MARRIED: 12 Nov 1865
Utah
DEATH: 28 Jan 1928
Salt Lake City, Utah

CHILDREN:
Eliza Jane, 31 May 1870
William W., 9 Jan 1874
Lucinda Ann, 31 Jan 1876
George W., 11 Jul 1878
Rose May, 17 Jun 1881
Abiah Wadsworth, 7 Jul 1883
Mahonri, 15 Jul 1885
Catherine, 3 Oct 1887
Josephine, 31 Oct 1892

Lucinda Mathena was born at Council Bluffs, Iowa while her Parents and family were getting ready to cross the Plains to Utah. The family left the following Spring on 10 May 1851 with the young baby on her mother's lap as her mother drove a buggy pulled by two ponies, arriving in the Salt Lake Valley 23 Sep 1851. The family was sent to East Weber (Uinta) to live. As a child, Cindy knew the struggles that were common to pioneers in Utah.

When she was fifteen years old, Cindy married a young man who had been working for her father in the carpentry trade. He had met Cindy when she was ten years old and had waited five years to marry her. Her husband was called on a mission to Iowa and Missouri. When they returned to Utah they made a home in Morgan. Cindy's first baby was born there. They became the parents of nine children, born in Morgan, Hooper, Salt Lake City and Hunter, Utah. Just as they were getting more of the comforts of life her husband felt that they needed more land to provide for their growing family. They moved to Hunter, Utah where the family of five children lived in a one-room house until a better home was built. They went through many hardships: hauling their water from a neighbor a half mile away; attending Church five miles away; having only a buggy for transportation.

William farmed, taught school and was the Bishop of their Ward. Cindy supported him in every way that she could while assuming her other responsibilities. She took as active part in the Church.

Pioneering was difficult. Cindy assumed chores outside of her home as well as inside. An orchard was planted and provided fruit for many. Cindy preserved the fruits for the Winter. She raised chickens and traded eggs and butter for things she needed. She bought cloth and made the children's clothes. An Uncle came to live with them until he died. In 1902 they purchased a home in Stirling, Alberta, Canada. They also homesteaded in Claresholm, Alberta, about eighty miles from Stirling. The winters were severe and it was a very lonesome time for Cindy. She said that she felt that she was in Prison. By the Spring of 1909 they decided to return to Salt Lake City. They bought a small home and for the first time in her life Cindy had electricity and electric heat to cook with, a bathroom and running water. Her husband suffered a stroke and Cindy nursed him for seven years. After he died, Cindy stayed in her home until the last six weeks of her life. She died at a daughter's home in Draper, Utah 3 Oct 1933, at the age of eighty. She had been a mother who had given her life for her husband, her children and anyone in need. She has shown great faith and support to her family and fulfilled her calling as a mother in Zion. She is honored by a goodly posterity who appreciate her memory and the valiant person that she was.

MARGARET FIFE EASTON MILLER

BIRTHDATE: 25 Jul 1829
Devon, Clackmannan, Scotland
DEATH: 1 Jan 1915
Greenville, Beaver County, Utah
PARENTS: Adam Fife
Helen Sharp Fife
PIONEER: abt 1851
Joseph Wilkies Co.
SPOUSE I: John Easton
MARRIED: before 1851
Grovie, Missouri
DEATH: not given

CHILDREN:
John, 15 Dec 1850
Ellen, 7 Oct 1853

SPOUSE II: David Miller
MARRIED: 7 Feb 1854
Salt Lake City, Utah
DEATH: 8 May 1890
Greenville, Utah

CHILDREN:
Chales Adam, 28 Nov 1856
Margaret Agnes, 4 Feb 1860
Mary Jane, 5 Feb 1862
Sarah Elizabeth, 11 Jul 1864
Martha Ann, 22 Oct 1866
Catherine Jennette, 25 Jun 1869
David James, 30 Dec 1871
William Archable, 11 Mar 1875

Margaret Fife was born in Scotland. She was the second child of fifteen, eight sisters and six brothers. Her parents joined the Mormon Church when they heard the Gospel from missionaries who had come from America. Margaret was baptized into the Church 13 Sep 1848 at the Clackmannan, Scotland Branch. The family left Scotland in 1849 and sailed to New Orleans, Louisiana. From there they traveled to St. Louis, Missouri before crossing the Plains to the Deseret Territory to be with the Saints. Before leaving Scotland, Margaret's father worked as a coalminer and Margaret worked in the mines as a child growing up. It was a hard life.

Margaret met John Easton, they were married and lived at Grovie, Missouri before coming to Deseret. They had a son named John while living there. They traveled across the Plains with the Joseph Wilkies Company, arriving in the Salt Lake Valley about the Fall of 1851. They moved to Cedar City, Utah where their daughter, Ellen, was born. While there, John decided to go to California during the gold rush. The leaders of the Church had asked the pioneers not to go to California for gold, but John went anyway. He left Margaret with two small children to raise by herself. Margaret and John had been sealed in the Endowment House 30 Jul 1853, but were later divorced.

Margaret moved to Ogden, Utah where her parents lived. She married David Miller 7 Feb 1854 at Salt Lake City, Utah. They were later married and sealed by Brigham Young in the Endowment House. They were called by Brigham Young to go colonize Greenville, in Beaver County, Utah. They built a home and David farmed. He later was the second Postmaster of Greenville. They became the parents of eight children. They were valiant members of the Church and endured their trials well. They were happy and satisfied. They raised a wonderful family. Margaret's husband preceded her in death. He died 8 May 1890. Margaret died 1 Jan 1915, due to a burning accident. They were both buried at the Greenville Cemetery.

MARGARET GARDNER MILLER

BIRTHDATE: 11 Sep 1844
Warwick, Kent, Canada
DEATH: 14 Oct 1930
Millcreek, Salt Lake, Utah
PARENTS: Robert Gardner
Jane McKeown
PIONEER: 1 Oct 1847
Edward Hunter Wagon Co.
SPOUSE: Reuben Parley Miller
MARRIED: 10 Oct 1868
Salt Lake City, Utah
DEATH SP: 29 Mar 1901
Murray, Salt Lake, Utah

CHILDREN:
Reuben Edgar, 30 Oct 1869
Robert Gardner, 20 Apr 1872
David Osro, 19 Jun 1873
Uriah George, 28 Nov 1874
Maggie May, 7 May 1878
Edith Lyle, 7 Aug 1879
Melvin Parley, 30 Apr 1882
Ernest Fay, 30 Apr 1884

Margaret Gardner was born in Canada in 1844. She came to the Salt Lake Valley at the age of three with her parents. They arrived in Oct 1847 and settled in the Millcreek area of Salt Lake County.

As a child Margaret learned to spin and weave. She also herded cows, driving them from pasture to pasture. When her parents were called to help settle Utah's Dixie in 1861, she divided her time between them and her married sister who still lived in Millcreek. At times Indians were a problem, and Margaret was frightened of them, but she was taught to whistle and not to be afraid.

Margaret married Reuben P. Miller in the Endowment House in 1868. They lived with his parents until her first child was born, then they moved to a two-room adobe house on State Street.

Her days were busy caring for her family, making tallow candles, her own soap, drying fruits and vegetables, caring for cows and chickens. She would take butter and eggs into Salt Lake to sell them. She was one of the first in the area to have a sewing machine, and made shirts for neighbors as well as her own family. While she had many hardships, there were also many pleasures, such as quilting and rag bees, dances and parties. She was lovingly called "Aunt Maggie."

Reuben died in Murray, Utah in 1901, and Margaret lived until 1930, passing away very quietly and peacefully.

MARGARET JANE NEIBAUR MILLER

BIRTHDATE: 20 Feb 1836
Preston, England
DEATH: 29 Jan 1928
Evans, Box Elder, Utah
PARENTS: Alexander Neibaur
Ellen Breakell
PIONEER: 21 Sep 1848
Brigham Young Co.
SPOUSE: William Miller
MARRIED: 5 Jun 1856
Salt Lake City, Utah
DEATH SP: 5 Jul 1910
Spring Glen, Carbon, Utah

CHILDREN:
Ellen, 29 Mar 1857
Rebecca Jane, 24 Nov 1859
William Perry, 7 Jan 1860
Van Ransler, 3 Jan 1860
Alice, 5 Jul 1862
Gilbert, 31 Oct 1863
Sabrina, 3 Jul 1865
Harrison, 6 Feb 1867
Elliot, 21 Nov 1868
James Nathan, 3 Mar 1870
Isaac Alexander, 26 Sep 1871
Heber John, 8 Sep 1873
George, 28 Spr 1875
Margaret, 25 Feb 1879

Margaret was born in England in 1836. Her father was the first Jewish convert to accept the gospel. The family sailed from England on the ship "Sheffield" in 1841. Margaret was baptized while they lived in Nauvoo, but they were soon forced to leave that beautiful city.

In Winter Quarters the Neibaur family made preparations to cross the plains. In 1848 they joined with Brigham Young in his second trip to the Rocky Mountains, arriving on 21 Sep 1848.

Margaret married William Miller in 1856. They lived in Salt Lake for a time, then moved to Coalville, where William worked in the coal mines. Later they moved to Carbon County and lived in Spring Glen, where Margaret was President of the Relief Society. In 1890 she lost three sons in the Scofield Mine explosion. They were Van Rensler, Harrison and Isaac.

William later took a second wife, who bore him two sons, but she decided she did not like polygamy, and divorced him. William died in Spring Glen in 1910. Margaret then moved to Ogden, Utah and lived with her son George. She passed away in Evans, Box Elder, Utah in 1926 at the age of ninety-two years.

MARY ANN HIGGINS LYON MILLER

BIRTHDATE: 14 Apr 1826
Kilmarnock, Ayrshire, Scotland
DEATH: 26 Feb 1891
Salt Lake City, Utah
PARENTS: James Higgins
Jeanie Smyth Higgins
PIONEER: 16 Sep 1956
Edward Stevenson Co.
SPOUSE I: Thomas Lyon
MARRIED: 1 Jan 1849
Kilmarnock, Ayrshire, Scotland
DEATH SP: 20 May 1863
Salt Lake City, Utah

CHILDREN:
Jeanie Smith, 29 Mar 1849
Jessie Campbell, 17 Mar 1851
Mary Ann, 23 Jul 1853
Christina Enock, 20 Mar 1856
Francis Stenhouse, 21 Feb 1858
Lillias Stains, 20 May 1861
Georgina, Aug 1862

SPOUSE II: John Miller
MARRIED: 20 Apr 1866
Salt Lake City, Utah

CHILDREN:
Thomas John, 14 Aug 1866

Mary Ann was in her early twenties when she met Thomas Lyon, who was serving a mission for the LDS Church. She became interested in the Gospel and was converted to Mormonism. As a result of her conversion, her parents disinherited her and would have nothing more to do with her. They spent the first eight years of their married life in Scotland, but during these years they were making preparations to come to America. Early in the year of 1856 they and their three children began the ocean voyage. Sailing through the English Channel their fourth daughter was born. The ship was named The Enock Train so they named the new baby Christina Enock Lyon.

While they were in New York waiting and saving for a chance to come west. Thomas was called on a mission to the British Islands. After he left Mary Ann gave birth to another daughter. She and her five daughters lived in a tenement house in New York City until Thomas had completed his mission. Then they began their journey westward. Thomas died though still a young man, leaving Mary Ann with very little money and seven girls to care for. The oldest was fourteen years and the youngest just nine months old. Thirteen months later the youngest child died and was buried beside her father.

Later Mary Ann married and had a son but the baby only lived two weeks. The marriage was not a happy one, so they decided to separate.

Mary Ann was a good seamstress, and with the help of the older girls she took in sewing. They also had many fruit trees and would sell much of the fruit.

It was through some Mormon Missionaries from Salt Lake City, that Mary Ann's brother James Higgins, heard of the trouble and hardship that she had been having and he wrote to her. He told her that their parents were dead, and that they had never forgiven her for joining the Church. She had not been mentioned in their last will, and being the oldest son, he had inherited most of the estate, and he wanted to help her financially. From that time until he died, he sent her fifty pounds a year, which was equal to about $250 American dollars. This money was certainly an answer to her prayers.

Mary Ann had many hardships and sorrows but if she could speak today, she would say that she had no regrets, and was happy for the part she played in pioneering this great land of Zion.

MARY HANNAH PEAKE PARKES MILLER

BIRTHDATE: 14 Apr 1834
Derby, Derbyshire, England
DEATH: 26 Mar 1883
Nephi, Juab, Utah
PARENTS: Samuel Peake
Mary Harrison
PIONEER: Oct 1863
By wagon train
SPOUSE I: Thomas Parkes
MARRIED: Abt 1850
In England
DEATH SP: Nov 1861
Derby, Derbyshire, England

CHILDREN:
Elizabeth Jamima, 11 Apr 1851
Alma John, 21 Nov 1852
Eunice Ida, 17 Nov 1854
Mary Ann, 1 Dec 1856
Georgania, 24 Dec 1858
Thomas Henry George, 27 May 1861

SPOUSE II: Thomas Miller
MARRIED: 1865
DEATH SP: Sep 1884
Nephi, Juab, Utah

CHILDREN:
Alphus, 4 Mar 1866
Angus, d. infant
William, d. infant

Mary Hannah Peake was born in England in 1834. She married Thomas Parkes in Derbyshire, England about 1850 and they were the parents of six children, all born in England. Her third child died when very young, and her husband died in Nov 1861 in Derbyshire, England.

In May 1863 Hannah, with her five remaining children, started out for Utah. Her son Alma had an accident before they left Derby where he had fallen on the ice and broken his back. This caused him some great difficulty while crossing the plains and he died and was buried near Green River, Wyoming. The family arrived in the valley in October 1863.

Hannah married Thomas Miller in 1865 and had three more sons, Alphus, Angus and William. Her two youngest children died as infants. Her daughters, Elizabeth (Lizzie), Mary Ann and Georgania had beautiful singing voices and performed on many programs. Hannah died in March 1883, and Thomas died the following September, both in Nephi, Juab, Utah.

MARY JANE GARDNER MILLER

BIRTHDATE: 13 Feb 1843
Warwick, Kent, Ontario, Canada
DEATH: 8 Dec 1929
Murray, Salt Lake, Utah
PARENTS: Robert Gardner
Jane McKeown Gardner
PIONEER: 1 Oct 1947
SPOUSE: James Robison Miller
MARRIED: 20 Feb 1859
Salt Lake City, Utah
DEATH SP: 5 Apr 1903
Salt Lake City, Utah

CHILDREN:
Rhoda Ann, 12 Dec 1859
Reuben Gardner, 7 Nov 1861
Robert Letts, 30 Dec 1863
James Robison, 7 Apr 1866
Mary Jane, 20 Sep 1868
Henry (twin), 11 Mar 1871
William Edgar (twin), 11 Mar 1871
Baby, Oct 1873
Leroy Cromwell, 29 Dec 1874
Maud Luella, 15 Sep 1877
Ernest Gardner, 6 Feb 1881
Leonard Malore, 14 Aug 1882
Albert Elmo, 9 Aug 1886
Eva Merl, 1 Oct 1889

Mary Jane was born in Canada in 1843. She crossed the plains with her parents at the age of four arriving in the Valley in Oct 1847. The family settled in Millcreek where her father operated a saw mill. As a child she had to milk cows and do other chores, and as she grew older she began working out for others. One of her prize possessions was a pine chest, which was used to store flour when the family went South because of Johnston's Army. This chest is still owned by a family member.

Mary Jane married James Robison Miller in 1859 at the age of 16. They lived in the Cottonwood area of Salt Lake County. The Indians always camped just below their house, and she often fed them, and was never afraid of them even if she was alone. She made her own cloth by carding and spinning and weaving the wool. Her husband planted mulberry trees so she could help with the silk industry in Utah. She was the mother of fourteen children, however six of them died when very young.

After years of hard work and thrift their log cabin was replaced by a beautiful home on the same site. She had a dining room large enough to seat fifty guests at the table. She also had a spare bedroom for guests or travelers. William died in 1903; and Mary Jane lived for twenty-six more years, still directing the activities of the home and farm. She passed away in 1929.

REBECCA VAN ZANT MILLER

No Photo Available

BIRTHDATE: 20 Oct 1797
Coeymans, Albany, New York
DEATH: 23 Jun 1886
Coalville, Summit County, Utah
PARENTS: Gilbert Van Zant
Rachel Lucas Van Zant
PIONEER: 21 Sep 1848
Brigham Young Co Wagon Train
SPOUSE: Eleazer Miller
MARRIED: abt 1816
New York
DEATH SP: 12 Apr 1876
Salt Lake City, Utah

CHILDREN:
Gilbert, 14 Aug 1817
Van Renslar, abt 1819
Perry, 20 Nov 1822
Sabrina, abt 1823
Harrison, abt 1825/24
Elliott, 8 Apr 1829
Child Miller, abt 1831
William, 10 Jun 1832
Emma, 1834
Rachel, 1836

Rebecca Van Zant Miller was born in New York. She married her hometown sweetheart, Eleazer Miller, about 1816 and bore him eight children. They lived in and around the Bradford area of Pennsylvania for many years. Rebecca and her husband joined the Mormon Church Dec 1831. The Church was in its infancy with only two hundred members. She supported and sustained her husband as he went forth as a missionary in Canada and the Eastern States to preach the Gospel. Rebecca's sacrifice allowed her husband to leave home and make a great contribution to the Mormon Church. He baptized future leaders Brigham Young and Heber C. Kimball. Rebecca and her husband were in the elite group of Saints and highly respected.

Rebecca again became both mother and father to her family when her husband went to Zion's Camp in Missouri. Eleazer was a Captain in the group. Most of the leaders of the Church were chosen from this group of men. Eleazer was called to serve as a Seventy because of his faithfulness and was ordained 5 Jan 1839 at Adam-ondi-Ahman, Missouri. It is possible they lived in the settlement of Adam-ondi-Ahman that existed during that time period. After the Saints were driven out of Missouri, Rebecca and Eleazer moved their family to Nauvoo, Illinois. Rebecca passed through the persecutions and tribulations which the Saints underwent prior to their expulsion from Nauvoo. She remembered the scenes connected with the martyrdom of the Prophet Joseph Smith and his brother, Hyrum Smith. She participated in the general exodus from Nauvoo. They traveled to Winter Quarters where they spent the Winter of 1847-48. Additional responsibilities were given to Rebecca as a wife and mother when her husband served on the Committee to expedite the removal of the Saints from Illinois and assumed the role of Captain to further help the Saints in the Westward movement.

Rebecca and Eleazer and their family left Winter Quarters 26 May 1848 in the Brigham Young Company. Eleazer was made Captain of 50. They arrived in the Salt Lake Valley 21 Sep 1848. They made their home in Salt Lake City in the 12th Ward. Rebecca became a First Counselor's wife when her husband was made First Counselor to the Bishop. She also cared for the family while her husband ran the Church Farm which was southeast of the City. In 1849, Rebecca was sealed to her husband for time and all eternity 18 Dec by President Young. Her husband married five wives in plural marriage.

Rebecca received her Patriarchal Blessing in 1860 from Patriarch Charles W. Hyde. Her husband died in 1876. She moved to Coalville, Utah to live with her son, William Miller. She died firm in the faith of the Gospel at her son's home 23 Jun 1886. She was buried in the Salt Lake City Cemetery alongside her husband, Eleazer Miller.

SARAH JANE RICH TOBIN MILLER

BIRTHDATE: 11 Feb 1838
Quincy, Illinois
DEATH: 5 Aug 1926
Salt Lake City, Utah
PARENTS: Charles Coulson Rich
Sarah DeArmon Pea
PIONEER: 2 Oct 1847
C. C. Rich Artillery Company
SPOUSE I: John Tobin
MARRIED: Salt Lake City, Utah

CHILDREN:
Ella, 14 Sep 1857

SPOUSE II: Thomas Rudolph Miller
MARRIED: 19 Sep 1863
Salt Lake Endowment House

Sarah Jane Rich was born in 1838 in Quincy, Illinois. She remembered the Prophet Joseph Smith picking her up and kissing her. He was on his way to Carthage Jail at the time.

Sarah Jane came to the Salt Lake Valley in 1847. Her father was in charge of the "Artillery Company," and was responsible for the cannon, boat and Nauvoo Bell. They arrived on 2 Oct 1847.

Sarah Jane was an attractive and popular young lady. Her mother taught her household skills and she was an expert seamstress. While her father was away colonizing in San Bernardino, California, Mary Jane met John Tobin, and married him. They had one little girl. Her father was unhappy at this, but accepted her choice. Later John went with his father-in-law on a mission to the British Isles, but was excommunicated for a moral transgression. The marriage was cancelled in 1861.

Sarah Jane married Thomas Rudolph Miller in 1861, but this was an unhappy union and they were divorced in 1893. There were no children. For a while they lived in the Bear Lake area, where her father was sent to colonize. She later returned to Salt Lake with her daughter and mother. She adopted a boy named Alfred Curtis, and was a matron at the county infirmary for many years. She enjoyed going to the temple with her mother to do work for the dead. In 1926, at the age of eighty-seven, she fell from the porch at her home and never fully recovered. She died 5 Aug 1926 and is buried in Salt Lake City Cemetary. Her daughter Ella, never married.

NANCY JANE BEAL MILLET

BIRTHDATE: 22 Oct 1846
Portsmouth, Scioto, Ohio
DEATH: 23 Feb 1921
Provo Bench (Orem), Utah
PARENTS: William Beal
Clarissa Allen Beal
PIONEER: prob 1848
Heber C. Kimball Co
Wagon Train
SPOUSE I:
William George Parker
Divorced 1862

CHILDREN:
Sophronia Jane, 13 Apr 1863

SPOUSE II: Artemus Millet, Jr.
MARRIED: 4 Oct 1865
Glenwood, Utah
DEATH: 31 Oct 1902
Provo Bench (Orem), Utah

CHILDREN:
Artemus, 4 Dec 1866
Franklin Nelson, 23 Sep 1868
Charles William, 18 Apr 1871
Emily Maria, 4 Nov 1873
Susan Harriett, 15 Aug 1876
Eliza Lemira, 4 Nov 1878
Paul Alma, 12 Dec 1880
Clarice Effie, 21 Jun 1883
Sarah Jane, 19 Apr 1885
Ella Augusta, 15 Aug 1887
Lenora Nancy, 8 Feb 1890

Nancy Jane Beal Millet was born in Ohio in 1846. She was the ninth child. She crossed the Plains with her family at a very young age. They came with the Heber C. Kimball Company by wagon. Nancy's mother died before crossing the Plains, a few days following the birth of a pair of twins. There is information that Nancy married William George Parker and was divorced in 1862. No other information is given. However, it appears that they had one daughter, Sophronia Jane. Nancy was married to Artemus Millet, Jr. 11 Oct 1865 at Glenwood, Utah. Under the direction of President Brigham Young, they moved to Spring Valley, Pioche, Nevada. Nancy raised twelve children, plus two small boys. Their mother died and their father left them with Nancy until he got a place for them a couple of years later.

Nancy did all her own sewing for her large family, underwear and all. She knitted socks for the men as well as the children. While nursing her children she was able to keep up with her knitting. With the leftover material from her quilts and other sewing projects, she was able to make rugs and carpets for her home. She had quilting bees when a few neighbors would come in and help. She made her laundry soap and tallow candles. She would take care of the milk, make cheese and churn butter to sell. At hog-killing time she would make sausage for her family that would last through the winter. Nancy raised her family without the help of a doctor. She always had a bottle of campher and turpentine ready for use when needed. She often rode in a wagon or buckboard twenty to twenty-five miles to deliver babies. She would be gone for ten to twelve days at a time.

Everyone was welcome who came under her roof. She would make beds on the floor for the children and give others her own and her children's beds. She would make visitors as comfortable as she could under the circumstances. Nancy's stature of five-foot-five inches accompanied sparkling, dark gray eyes, black braided hair and a friendly disposition that won her many lasting friendships. She was light on her feet while dancing the jig and enjoyed teaching her children how to dance. She would always make sure that the blessing was said on the food three times a day and had family prayer night and morning. She taught the Gospel in her home through example and by word and deed.

She and her husband and family moved to Provo Bench, Utah in 1900, where she lived for nineteen more years. Her husband died in 1902. Nancy died at the home of one of her daughters 23 Feb 1921. She was buried in the Provo City Cemetery alongside her husband.

SARAH ELIZABETH GLINES MILLETT

BIRTHDATE: 14 Aug 1830
Franklin, Merrimack,
New Hampshire
DEATH: 4 Oct 1889
Springdale, Washington, Utah
PARENTS: James Pearson Glines
Ruth Brown Glines
PIONEER: 20 Sep 1856
Canute Peterson Co. Wagon Train
SPOUSE: Joseph Millett
MARRIED: 26 Mar 1854
Lowell, Middlesex, Massachusetts
DEATH SP: 31 Oct 1911
Cedar City, Iron, Utah

CHILDREN:
Artemus, 22 Jun 1855 (died an infant)
Aldura Artimissa, 1 Dec 1856 (died age 13)
Joseph, Jr., 16 Nov 1858
Sarah Elizabeth, 9 May 1861
Byron Glines, 1 Mar 1863
Mary Jane, 21 Jun 1865
George Alma, 15 May 1868
Araannah Ruth, 8 Sep 1870
Marion Martin, 10 Aug 1872

Sarah Elizabeth was twelve years old when her oldest brother, James, left home and set up his own tailoring shop in 1842. He was baptized into the LDS Church in 1843 much to his parents' disappointment. Joseph Millett was serving a mission in the area where Sarah lived. They fell in love and he baptized her as a member of the church and they were married the next day. After their marriage, Sarah lived with an aunt in Petersboro, New Hampshire while Joseph completed the last of his mission in the Eastern states. Sarah and Joseph started on their journey to Utah in October of 1854. They stopped in Iowa where Joseph worked for winter supplies and they stayed until the baby was born. The baby died when he was three months old. Sarah and Joseph arrived in Salt Lake City on September 20, 1856 with the Canute Peterson Wagon Company.

Brigham Young assigned the new couple to help settle Manti, Utah where two of their children were born. In 1860, Sarah returned to Spanish Fork to stay with her brother James and his family while Joseph continued working in Manti. A son and daughter were born during her stay there. Their next move was to Gunnison, Utah where she and Joseph were called to help settle the Sevier Valley. They lived there for four years. In 1866, they were called to Utah's Dixie by President Young. Their next move was to Spring Valley, Nevada. Sarah's life was one of continual moving and pioneering in new areas. She endured many hardships through her life. They moved again to Show Low, Arizona, then to Taylor, Arizona. When the Navajo

tribe went on the warpath, they moved to Springdale, Utah at the mouth of Zion's Canyon. Sarah was a valiant spirit who stood by her husband through Indian attacks, floods, droughts, and the taming of a great wilderness. Sarah died at age fifty-nine and was buried in the Springdale Cemetery.

ELIZA HARRIET BAILEY MILLS

BIRTHDATE: 22 Sep 1838
Fareham, Hampshire, England
DEATH: 28 May 1910
Hoytsville, Summit, Utah
PARENTS: Francis William Bailey
Eliza Smith Bailey
PIONEER: 11 Oct 1861
Wm Wright Indep. Freight Company
SPOUSE:
Charles Edmond Thomas Mills
MARRIED: 26 Jan 1861
Southampton, Hampshire, England
DEATH: 6 Jan 1910
Hoytsville, Summit, Utah

CHILDREN:
Charles Frank, 14 Dec 1861
Alonzo Alvin, 31 Aug 1863
Eliza Jane Crittenden, 23 Aug 1865
Mary Ellen, 4 Jun 1867
Samuel James, 2 Oct 1869
Ella Louisa, 5 Oct 1871
Maud Elizabeth (Peterson), 6 Apr 1873
Albert Edmond, 8 Nov 1874
Walter Louis, 18 Jul 1876
Ezra Thomas, 15 Jan 1878
Amy Clara, 9 Nov 1879

Eliza Harriet was born in Fareham, Hampshire, England. She married Charles Edmond Thomas Mills on January 26, 1861 in Southampton, Hampshire, England. They became members of the LDS Church and desired to go to America to live with the main body of Saints. They sailed from England on the ship, Manchester, on April 16, 1861 and arrived in New York on May 15, 1861. They proceeded from Castle Gardens by rail to Florence, Nebraska. Then they traveled by wagon to Salt Lake City arriving on October 11, 1861 with the William Wright Independent Freight Company.

They lived first in Kaysville, Davis County, Utah. In 1870, Eliza helped pioneer the community of Hoytsville, Utah. They bought a piece of land and a two room house. Later they added two rooms to this log cabin. She was well known for her fine cooking. Eliza had eleven children and raised an honorable and respected family. She was no stranger to sorrow having lost five of her children in their youth. She died at the age of seventy-one and was buried in Hoytsville.

ELIZABETH HALL MILLS

BIRTHDATE: 10 Nov 1816
Chatham, Kent, England
DEATH: 20 Jan 1900
Soda Springs, Idaho
PIONEER: Fall 1852
by Wagon Train
PARENTS: William Hall
Mary
SPOUSE: John Mills
MARRIED: abt 1836
England
DEATH SP: 1 Nov 1857
Sacramento, California

CHILDREN:
Mary Jane, 19 Mar 1837
Elizabeth (Oakden), 7 Mar 1839
Thomas, 6 Nov 1841
Mary Alice (Collier), 22 Sep 1842
William, 5 Jun 1844
Martha, 8 Jan 1850
Alice(Smith), 1846

SPOUSE II: George Rowley
MARRIED: abt 1859
DEATH: 1901/2
Soda Springs, Caribou, Idaho

CHILDREN:
George, 29 Feb 1861
Daniel Hall, 21 Jan 1865

Elizabeth Hall Mills was born in England. She married John Mills about 1836. They were the parents of six children; four daughters and two sons. Three of their children died in childhood. The couple lived on Douglas, Isle of Man. It was here the Mormon missionaries taught them the Gospel and they were converted and baptized into the Mormon Church. They left England for America on the ship "Rochester." They then lived in Nauvoo, Illinois; Fort Madison, Iowa; Drakesville, Iowa; Des Moines Iowa. They finally settled in Council Bluffs, Iowa and lived there for two years. In 1852, they left for the Salt Lake Valley with the St. Louis Freight Company, Fort Larrimers Company and the Independent Company. This was to help keep the Indians at bay. Elizabeth and her two boys were in one company and her husband and daughter in another company, four miles ahead. The two boys died during the course of the journey. The family reached the Valley in the Fall of 1852. When entering the Salt Lake Valley they saw only two horses besides the Fort.

John Mills was killed in California 1 Nov 1857. The powder magazine he was soldering exploded. Times were very hard for the family for a time after his death. In about 1859, Elizabeth married for the second time and moved to Soda Springs, Idaho. Two sons were born to this marriage. Elizabeth died in Soda Springs, Idaho 20 Jan 1900.

FRANCES FARR MILLS

BIRTHDATE: Aug 1816
Westbourne, Sussex, England
DEATH: Aug 1889
Enterprise, Morgan County, Utah
PARENTS: Thomas Henry Farr
Frances Phoebe Bone Farr
PIONEER: Fall 1863
by wagon
SPOUSE: Charles Edmond Mills
MARRIED: 17 Apr 1832
Lancashire, England
DEATH: 2 May 1863
Southhampton, England

CHILDREN:
Frances, 12 Sep 1830
Jane Ruth, 26 Aug 1841
Martha, 29 Jan 1832
Ann Mariah, 22 Apr 1844
Harriott, 22 Jan 1834
George M.D., 12 Jul 1845
Mary, 5 Apr 1836
Phebe Sarah, 12 Oct 1848
Charles Edmund Thomas, 7 Jan 1838
Louisa Harriott, 10 Dec 1849
Emma Roseona, 4 Feb 1840

Frances Farr Mills was born in England. She married Charles Edmond Mills 17 Apr 1832. They became the parents of eleven children, all born in England and Ireland. Six of their children died in infancy. Frances' husband was a British soldier. Frances traveled with him to every English Colony, including India. She assisted with hospital work, attending to soldiers on duty. Frances was converted to the Mormon Church by missionaries in 1850. They called on her family when her baby was seriously ill and, by a priesthood blessing, the baby was made well. Frances became an ardent defender of her religion and often defended the various missionaries from violent mobs. In 1857, she was fasting and praying for the Mormons in the United States to be delivered from Johnston's Army, at the request of President Brigham Young. She became so weak from fasting that she fainted while ironing clothes.

President Young advised the British Saints to come to Utah, and he further asked families to emigrate one at a time if finances would not allow them to come all together. Frances and her husband sent their two oldest children to America in 1861 and in 1862 they sent a daughter. They planned for a daughter to emigrate in 1863 and they decided they would be able to make the journey in 1864. However, Frances' husband suddenly died of a heart attack before their daughter Sarah left England. Frances sold all of her possessions and she and her daughter emigrated to Utah. They traveled to New York, then to Albany and St. Joes, then up the Mississippi River to the place where they spent several weeks preparing to make the journey to the Salt Lake Valley.

The Company they journeyed across the Plains with is not known. They arrived in Utah in the Fall of 1863. They lived first in Kaysville, Utah and then made their home in Enterprise, Utah in the Morgan Valley. Frances worked at housekeeping, farming and nursing. She was the first midwife in that part of the Valley. She is credited with controlling Smallpox by vaccinating most of the people in the area. She understood the use of herbs and used them in caring for the sick. She received her Patriarchal Blessing from the Church Patriarch, John Smith, about 1877. She gave birth to eleven children; three died in Ireland, four came to America and the others remained in England. Frances died in Enterprise, Utah in Aug 1889. She was buried in the family lot in the Enterprise Cemetery.

JANE SANFORD MILLS

No
Photo
Available

BIRTHDATE: 11 Apr 1808
Kitley, Leeds, Ontario, Canada
DEATH: 26 Jan 1893
Provo, Utah, Utah
PARENTS: Solomon Sanford
Eleanor Barry Sanford
PIONEER: 28 Sep 1851
Morris Phelps Wagon Co
SPOUSE: John Mills
MARRIED: 13 Mar 1827
Markham, York, Ontario, Canada
DEATH: 20 Mar 1876
Provo, Utah, Utah

CHILDREN:
Sarah Eleanor, 1 Mar 1828
Martin Walderfin, 30 Aug 1830
Barbara Belinda, 1 Jan 1836
Daughter, 15 Jul 1837 (Stillborn)

In 1827, Jane was married to John Mills. Three children were born to them as they resided in Upper Canada. This was a wild new country where her husband built two saw mills. After her last child was born, they sold their place with the intentions of moving to warmer country for her husband's health. About this time, John Taylor brought the message of the restored gospel to their family. They were converted, and were baptized in February 1837 in their mill pond after they had broken the ice. They traveled with John Taylor to Kirtland. Then they moved to Farr West, and eventually to Nauvoo, enduring all the persecutions and hardships the early members went through. They were driven out of Nauvoo by the mobs and stopped for a time at Winter Quarters. Jane's oldest daughter died after childbirth, so Jane raised Sarah's son as her own. Her husband, John, went to Salt Lake Valley in 1850 to prepare a home for them. He left provisions for her to come the next spring with the Morris Phelps Wagon Company. They arrived in Salt Lake Valley on 28 September 1851. She was met by her husband and they went to Lehi. They then moved to Provo where they made their home.

In 1874, Jane and her husband traveled to St. George where John worked on the temple. Shortly after returning home to Provo, John died. Twice more, Jane traveled to St. George to work in the temple. She never wearied in doing good for others. This faithful lady lived in her own little apartment, caring for herself, cheering her neighbors, and helping her grandchildren right up to a week before she died. She died just before her eighty-fifth birthday, beloved and faithful to the end.

LOUISA AVALINA SLEATER MILLS

BIRTHDATE: 22 Dec 1832
Sligo, Sligo, Ireland
DEATH: 30 Jan 1836
Salt Lake City, Utah
PARENTS: Robert Sleater
Mary Marchant
PIONEER: 24 Oct 1855
SPOUSE: William Gill Mills
MARRIED: 25 Apr 1856
DEATH SP: 14 May 1895
Salt Lake City, Utah

CHILDREN: none

Louisa Avalina Sleater was born 22 Dec 1832 in Ireland, the third of twelve children born to Robert Sleater and Mary Marchant. The family was fairly well-to-do and lived in Bath, England. The children had a governess and were well educated. Louisa became an accomplished pianist.

Louisa heard the missionaries and fell in love with one, Elder William Gill Mills. She was baptized 30 Sep 1850 in Bath, England, but did not come to Utah until 24 Oct 1855. On 25 Apr 1856 she received her endowment and was sealed to her husband.

Louisa was not blessed with children. She had a lovely home and furniture, and was able to travel a lot. She was very thrifty in her nature. In her late 80's she suffered a broken hip but insisted on using a crutch instead of a wheelchair. She lived to be ninety-three years of age, and died on 30 Jan 1936. Her husband preceded her in death. Both are buried in Salt Lake City, Utah.

LOUISA CHRISTINA BICKMORE MILLS

BIRTHDATE: 20 Mar 1844
Hancock Co. Illinois
DEATH: 30 Nov 1900
Gonzales, Monterey, Califorina
PARENTS: Wliliam Bickmore
Christine Bagley Bickmore
PIONEERS: 6 Sep. 1852
Joseph Outhouse Co. Wagon
SPOUSE: John Boardman Mills
MARRIAGE: 19 Aug 1860
Santa Cruz, California
DEATH SP: 1 Jul 1887
Gonzales, Monterey, California

CHILDREN:
Sylvina (Vine), 31 Jan 1863
Rosetta Christina (Rose), 2 Apr 1864
Oliver, 7 Apr 1866
Clara, 24 Jan 1868
John Boardman, Oct 1869
Drusilla May, 16 Oct 1870
Mills, 1872
Edgar, 1873
Mary Jane (Mazie), 10 May 1876
George Washington, 1878
Phoebe, 13 Mar 1880
Rachel, May 23 Jan 1882

Born to parents recently converted to the Mormon Church, Louisa Christina's birth came at the time of great upheaval in the Church. John Bennet's plan to assassinate Joseph Smith and the ensuing rift caused over 200 Saints to go with the Law Brothers to organize a new church, but the Bickmore family stood fast in their new religion and followed the Saints. Her mother's letters place them in Hancock Co. during the murder of Joseph and Hyrum; she was a babe about four months old.

She was one of those babies who lived through the expulsion of the Saints and William and Christina Bickmore, her parents, were among those families who stayed in Pottawattomie. Some were chosen to stay behind and grow wheat to help provide for the emigrants that were without the supplies necessary for a year's sustenance, supplies enough to see them three months across the plains and enough to eat through the winter until a crop could be raised.

Louisa Christina was eight years old when her parents decided it was time for them to go to Utah. She walked much of the way because the wagons were filled with all they could take of their past life and provisions enough to ensure a new one. Cows were herded along for the milk to help feed the families and some were driven for beef to eat. To her the trek was both fearful and an adventure, Indian raids were ever on their minds, but camp time was often play time for the younger ones. The three month arduous journey was at times a great adventure.

The family went first to Fillmore where nine-year-old Louisa Christina would have helped prepare their food, brought in wood for the cooking, and carried water in a bucket from the spring into the house for drinking or bathing. She would have cleaned the chimney or the coal oil lamp if they were fortunate enough to have one.

Their sojourn in Fillmore was brief, because her father William Bickmore was called as a Church agent to the embryo town of San Bernardino, California and by 1855 they were established there. Her father had sold his property in Utah and bought the "Rancho Ucipe." He had 1500 head of cattle and 124 Mustang horses.

The family owned a city lot in San Bernardino and she attended a one room school house. She was about eleven years old when they moved there.

Louisa Christina met John Boardman Mills,, fell in love and they were married in Santa Cruz California when she was sixteen years old. John had been a crewman on a sailing ship and had come to California about the same time as she. John was a brewer, teamster, woodman and in later years a carpenter and farmer. They lived in Corralitos, near Watsonville where seven of their children were born in nine years time. They moved to San Miguel Canyon near Prunedale, by Monterey, California, where Edgar their eighth child was born. In that same year they lost their little four year old son John. The next four children were born at different locations in that area. Louisa Christina had her twelveth child when she was thirty-eight years old lacking two months.

John Boardman died when she was forty-three years old. Her three oldest children were married and Clara, nineteen, married the next year. Seven children were now her full responsibility–from Drucilla seventeen, to Rachel who was five years old. Louisa Christina lived thirteen years longer than her husband. She died leaving only her youngest daughter unmarried. She was laid to rest next to John Boardman in Pioneer Cemetery in Watsonville California.

ANN CATHERINE JARVIS MILNE

BIRTHDATE: 27 Oct 1848
London, Middlesex, England
DEATH: 8 Oct 1956
Salt Lake City, Utah
PARENTS: George Jarvis
Ann Prior
PIONEER: 15 Aug 1860
Jesse Murphy Wagon Train
SPOUSE: David Milne
MARRIED: 3 May 1870
DEATH SP: 5 Jul 1895

CHILDREN:
David M. Young Jarvis, 3 Jul 1871
Susan, 20 Feb 1873
George Jarvis, 16 Jun 1875
Athole Jarvis, 19 Aug 1877

Erastus Jarvis, 13 Nov 1879
Margaret Jarvis, 15 Oct 1882
Josephine Jarvis, 29 Dec 1884
Joseph Jarvis, 27 Sep 1889

Ann Catherine Jarvis was born 27 Oct 1848 in London, Middlesex, England, the daughter of George Jarvis and Ann Prior. She was only twelve when she walked across the plains carrying her books in a knapsack that her father had made. These represented her love of learning which she had throughout her life.

As a young girl in St. George she was asked to help care for the ailing wife of David Milne. A few years later she became the second wife of David, marrying him on 3 May 1870. She worked at gathering cotton, and making cloth for the clothing for the family. She also worked in the silk industry, caring for the silk worms in her home. She furnished the new St. George Temple with upholstery; in addition she made carpets, and hung curtains and drapes. She worked in Relief Society, laid out the dead, and cared for the sick.

Ann Catherine lost sight in both eyes at age seventy, and learned to read by the Braille method. At age ninety she had cataracts removed and regained her sight. She was grateful she could then read and do housework. She lived to be 107 years of age, one of the oldest living pioneers at the time. She was priviledged to fly over the pioneer trail at the of ninety-two years. She died on 8 Oct 1956. Her husband died 5 Jul 1895, sixty-one years earlier.

ANNA HESS MILNE

BIRTHDATE: 8 Mar 1854
Afeltrarigen, Thurgau, Switzerland
DEATH : 10 Oct 1921
St. George, Washington, Utah
PARENTS: Johannes Hess
Anna Maria Dietschweiler
PIONEER: 24 Sep 1860
Stoddard Handcart Company
SPOUSE: David Milne
MARRIED: 9 Oct 1871
Salt Lake City, Utah
DEATH SP: 5 Jul 1895
Salt Lake City, Utah

CHILDREN:
Fanny Hess, 5 Jul 1872
Mary Hess, 9 Jul 1874
Kenneth Hess, 4 Oct 1879
Elizabeth Hess, 27 Nov 1881
Jessie Hess, 1 Mar 1884
Anna Hess, 7 Mar 1886
Catherine Hess, 28 Mar 1888

Anna Hess was born 8 Mar 1854 in Afeltrangen, Thurgau, Switzerland, the daughter of Johannes Hess & Anna Maria Dietschweiler. Her father passed away before she was born. When Anna was three years of age her moth-

er joined the Church, and in 1860 they emigrated to America with her mother, sister and crippled grandfather. They joined with the Stoddard Handcart Company to cross the plains, and arrived in the valley 24 Sep 1860.

After her mother remarried they were called to go to the Dixie Mission and settled in Santa Clara, Utah. At age seventeen Anna married David Milne on 9 Oct 1871 in the Endowment House, as his third wife. Her husband was busy in Church and civic affairs. She went with him to Manti in 1884 when he was called to supervise the painting of the Manti Temple.

At the time of the Manifesto she had to take over the support of her family. She went to Salt Lake and was trained as a midwife, graduating with high honors. She returned to St. George and delivered many babies in Southern Utah. The Bishop said he could tell how many babies had been delivered by Anna by the amount of tithing she had paid.

David Milne died 5 Jul 1895, and Anna Hess Milne died 10 Oct 1921 in St. George, Washington, Utah.

ESTHER (ELIZABETH) YARDLEY THURMAN MILNER

BIRTHDATE: 24 Jan 1825
Tanworth, Warwick, England
DEATH: 29 Sep 1911
Provo, Utah
PARENTS: Thomas Yardley
Mary Rose Yardley
PIONEER: 19 Sep 1853
Cyrus H. Wheelock Wagon Co.
SPOUSE I:
Thomas Edward Thurman
MARRIED: 6 Nov 1848
Dudley, Worcester, England
DEATH: 23 Dec 1851
Birmingham, England

CHILDREN:
Ellen, abt 1849
Thomas Edward, abt 24 Jul 1850

SPOUSE II: John Brewitt Milner
MARRIED: Mar 1854
Salt Lake City, Utah
DEATH: 17 Oct 1912
Provo, Utah

CHILDREN:
Benjamin Franklin, 19 Sep 1855
John William Seaton, 8 Nov 1857
George Brewitt, 28 Feb 1861
Sarah Ann, 29 May 1862
Mary Victoria, abt 1864
Lillie Jane, 4 Mar 1866
Isabelle Yardley, 17 Oct 1868

Esther was born in England, the first child of thirteen children. Esther helped her mother with the duties of raising a large family. She became a good cook and house-keeper. As a young woman, she went to Birmingham to take charge of her bachelor Uncle's household and servants. She learned of a new religion and went to hear the Mormon missionaries preach the Gospel. She heared the hymn "O My Father" sung, which helped to convert her. She met Thomas Edward Thurman whom she married 6 Nov 1848 in England. He told her he was going to be baptized into the Mormon Church. They were both baptized 7 Mar 1849 in the Birmingham Branch. They became the parents of two children; one son and one daughter. Their daughter died a few weeks after her birth. Esther's husband died of tuber-culosis but before his death he asked her to go to Utah to be with the Mormons.

It was now necessary for Esther to earn her own living. She opened a pastry shop and had housekeeping rooms upstairs in her place of business. She did well. One of her customers was Charles Dickens, the author. They had many chats together. He portrayed her in a novel as a pleasant, plump and rosy-cheeked young matron who kept an Inn. Esther sold her property to pay her passage and expenses to emigrate to Utah. She left England 5 Feb 1853 on the ship "The Jersey" and after six weeks on the water arrived in New Orleans, La. She made her way to Keokuk, Iowa where she outfitted herself with a horse to ride and a cow for milk and teamed them up to a wagon. She walked all the way across the Plains so her son and others could ride. She joined the Cyrus H. Wheelock Company. They arrived in the Salt Lake Valley 19 Sep 1853. A year later she mar-ried a young man in the Salt Lake Endowment House who had been in the same company. They made their home in Provo, Utah. They became the parents of seven children; a daughter died in infancy.

Her husband became a prominent lawyer and judge. Esther loved music and art and had brought one of her paintings with her from England. When it became possible she bought an organ and her daughters learned to play it and sing. She kept a boarding house where prominent people stayed. She was an excellent cook and always set a fine table. She was hospitable to her many friends. All through the trials of pioneer life Esther loved her home and family and was content to live her life in Utah. She faced her trials and worked out her problems with a courageous and happy disposition. She was kindhearted and extremely generous to anyone in need. She assisted many poor people with food and clothing. Esther was nearly eighty-eight years of age when she died at the home of her son, Thomas Edward Thurman, in Provo 29 Sep 1911.

NANCY ELIZABETH CHASE MINER

BIRTHDATE: 1 Nov 1845
North Rochester, Lorane, Ohio
DEATH: 3 Jun 1928
Springville, Utah, Utah
PARENTS: Solomon Drake Chase
Lydia Ann Thorn Chase
PIONEER: 9 Sep 1853
John A. Miller Wagon Company
SPOUSE: Moroni Miner
MARRIED: 3 Feb 1861
Springville, Utah, Utah
DEATH: 14 Aug 1935

CHILDREN:
Moroni Albert, 27 May 1862
Charles Alonzo, 30 May 1864 (died age 2)
John Wallace, 29 Oct 1865 (died age 17)
Abner Delacey, 21 Apr 1867
Solomon Chase, 22 Oct 1869 (died age 12)
Ralph Chase, 26 Mar 1871 (died age 11)
Marian Francis, 23 Mar 1873
Nancy Elizabeth, 10 Jan 1875
George Chase, 28 Jul 1876
Ruth Ada, 7 Feb 1878
Austin Clinton, 30 Nov 1880
Emmaline, 25 Dec 1882
Floyd Lee, 16 Jan 1884
Thom Chase, 1 Jan 1887
Paul Chase, 5 Jan 1889

Nancy's parents were among the first saints to accept the gospel and become baptized as members of the LDS Church. Her father was a carpenter who worked hard mak-ing many wagons that were used for crossing the plains. Nancy was eight years old when her parents crossed the plains with Joseph Thorn as Captain and as part of the John A. Miller Wagon Company. They arrived in the Salt Lake Valley on September 9, 1853.

Their wagon company settled in Springville, Utah. At the age of fifteen, she married Moroni Miner and became the proud mother of fifteen children. Her role as a mother took precedence over public life, yet she still found time to serve in the Relief Society as a teacher and a teacher and counselor in the Primary. She and her husband did temple ordinance work and genealogical research. She and her husband moved to their farm where their nearest neighbor was two miles away. Many Indians camped nearby. She learned to treat them kindly and fed them from her store-house. She was able to converse with them. Nancy suf-fered all the hardships incident to the life of Pioneer moth-ers trying to keep her children dressed, fed, clean, and healthy. She was known far and wide for her hospitality. Her home was a stopping place for years for friends and rel-atives traveling from the south to Salt Lake City and back. Her home was ever open to the immigrant saints. Many families stayed at her home until they found places to settle. She took several motherless children into her home until other arrangements could be made for their care. She was blessed to the last of her life with a keen intellect and strong mentality. She and her husband were very active in temple work. They gave freely of their means to search out records and have them compiled in proper books.

ANN DALTON LEFEVRE MITCHELL

No
Photo
Available

BIRTHDATE: 28 Feb 1804
Crowland, Lincoln, England
DEATH: 30 Aug 1864
Parowan, Utah
PARENTS: Luke Dalton
Elizabeth King Dalton
PIONEER: Sep 1852
Captain David Wood Wagon Co.
SPOUSE I: John LeFevre
MARRIED: 21 Jun 1829
England
DEATH: 25 Jan 1849
Liverpool, England

CHILDREN:
Sarah, 22 May 1830
Daniel, 1832
William, 31 Aug 1833
Luke Dalton, 19 Nov 1835
Susanna, 7 Aug 1837
Susanna, 18 Feb 1839
Amy Elizabeth, 16 Oct 1840

SPOUSE II: Willliam Cook Mitchell
MARRIED: 26 Sep 1852
Salt Lake City, Utah
DEATH: 20 Jun 1857
Parowan, Utah
CHILDREN: none

Ann was born in England. She married John LeFevre 21 Jun 1829. They became the parents of seven children. She and John were baptized the same day, 22 Dec 1847 in Crowland, Lincolnshire, England. They began to prepare to emigrate to Utah to join the body of the Saints. They took the train to Liverpool, England where her husband became ill and died. He was buried in Liverpool. At that time Ann had only two living children, Sarah and William. They sailed on the ship "Zetland" under the presidency of Elder Orson Spencer. They arrived at New Orleans, La. 2 Apr 1849 and then traveled to Kanesville, Iowa. They had suffered much from cholera while passing up the Missouri River. This was when Ann, Sarah and her nephew contracted cholera. Sarah died, but Ann and her nephew recovered.

When they arrived at St. Louis, Mo. they rented a house and Sarah and William and Tom found work. By each person working and accumulating what they could they were able to travel to Council Bluffs, arriving 20 May 1850. They secured a yoke of oxen and in company with a Mr. Jacob Morris, a lone man who had a good wagon and a yoke of oxen and two cows they started their trek to the Salt Lake Valley. They traveled with the David Wood Company. Ann met William Cook Mitchell who had been a

missionary in England. He had traveled on the same ship and with the same company crossing the Plains. He persuaded Ann to marry him and to settle in Parowan, Utah. They arrived in Parowan 20 Oct 1852. Before leaving for Parowan, Ann was sealed to her first husband in the Salt Lake City Endowment House 26 Sep 1852. She was married to her second husband for time only on this date.

Ann died 30 Aug 1864 in Parowan, and was buried in the Parowan Cemetery. Ann was always a small woman, never weighing over ninety pounds at any time in her life. She endured many sorrows, trials and hardships in her life. Her faith never waivered.

CAROLINE NEWMAN MITCHELL

BIRTHDATE: 16 May 1849
Worcester, England
DEATH: 9 Jun 1928
Parowan, Iron County, Utah
PARENTS: John Newman
Mary Ann Williams Newman
PIONEER: 9 Nov 1856
James G. Willie Handcart Co
SPOUSE: John Thomas Mitchell
MARRIED: 25 Jun 1875
Salt Lake City
DEATH SP: 12 Mar 1938
Parowan, Iron County, Utah

CHILDREN:
Gwendolynn (Benson), 12 Feb 1876
Maud Mary (Stewart), 29 Mar 1878

Caroline was born in England in 1849. As a girl of seven, she left home in England, with her widowed mother and her five brothers and sisters. They emigrated to America 1 May 1856. They landed in New York 14 Jun traveled by train to Iowa City and headed west 15 Jul with the James G. Willie Handcart Co, arriving in Salt Lake City 9 Nov 1856. Some mornings their hair was frozen to the ground. Their mother heated rocks in the campfire at night and put them in the bed to keep the children warm. Sometimes their clothes froze from the damp cold.

As a young woman, Caroline worked for Brigham Young in his home in Salt Lake City and at one time the Lion House. At age 26 she married John Thomas Mitchell 25 Jun 1875. They lived at Blackrock, near Garfield in a large rock home with four rooms downstairs and two upstairs. Their first child was born there. Later they moved to Rush Lake, Tooele County, where their second child was born. In 1880 they moved to Deseret Millard County and in 1881 moved to Parowan, Iron Co, where they permanantly settled. When Caroline's sister, Mary Ann Warren died, she raised her four children also.

As a wife and mother raising a family in Parowan, she would be left alone quite a bit with her husband freighting, before they opened their Post Office and General Dry Goods Store. It was a small Mom & Pop operation and was located in the corner of their home. They also operated a ranch at Panquitch Lake where they cut and sold the wild grass for hay and also had a farm outside of Parowan City limits. Many stories tell of how the Indians would come and walk right in the homes demanding food and sugar, and how the children there, would try to hide for fear of being kidnapped, which was quite common. Caroline assisted her children and grandchildren and the latchstring of their home always hung out to their friends and acquaintances and to anyone in need.

Caroline passed away at age seventy-nine in Parowan. John passed away almost ten years later. They are buried in the Parowan Cemetery.

CHRISTIANNA GERTRUDE CORNELIA CLEGNET (VAN EETVELDT) FROST MITCHELL

BIRTHDATE: 7 Sep 1842
Uitenhage, South Africa
DEATH: 6 Mar 1896
PARENTS: Van Eetveldt
Christianna Van Lilyveldt Frost
PIONEER: 4 Sep 1863
A. H. Patterson Wagon Company
SPOUSE:
David Alexander Mitchell
MARRIDE: 1858
DEATH SP: 9 Mar 1891

CHILDREN:
Hester Elizabeth, 3 May 1859
Marian Elizabeth, 4 Sep 1860
Amelia, 12 May 1862
David Alexander, 23 Apr 1864
Phillip John, 11 Mar 1866
James Archibald, 20 Jan 1868
Robert McKenzie, 31 Jan 1870
Gertrude, 10 Apr 1872
Ephraim Arthur, 4 Aug 1874
Cornelia, 19 Feb 1876
Henrietta, 19 Aug 1879
Rachel Ann, 27 Jan 1882
Nora, 10 Mar 1885

Christianna Gertrude Cornelia Clegnet was born a van Eetveldt. Her father left her mother shortly after her birth. She was raised by Philip John Frost and her mother, Christianna van Lilyveldt Frost. She was well trained in music and became an accomplished pianist. She received training from her father as she assisted him in developing his medicines.

When Christianna was sixteen years of age, she married David Alexander Mitchell of Scottish descent. She was married, moved to a small house in town, baptized a member of the L. D. S. Church, and disinherited from her family - all in the year 1858. Her husband, David, joined the

church in 1860, and in March of that year they left South Africa to sail to America. It was a long three month voyage across the Atlantic Ocean. They joined an Independent Wagon Train led by Captain Patterson and arrived in Salt Lake Valley September 4, 1863. Their daughter Amelia died as they crossed the Plains. When they arrived in the valley, they were then directed by Brigham Young to go to Payson to help settle that area.

Through all their hardships, David managed to buy an organ for Christianna so she could teach organ lessons. One of her pupils was John J. McClelland who later became a Tabernacle organist. She used the education her father gave her in medicines by making poultices and dressing wounds. She was said to have a God-given talent as a nurse.

After David's death, Christianna was left alone at age forty-eight with four children to care for. Her own health was failing. She died five years later of cancer on March 6, 1896.

ELIZABETH BOWERS MITCHELL

No
Photo
Available

BIRTHDATE: 9 Apr 1829
Burslem, Staffordshire, England
DEATH: 3 Apr 1889
Salt Lake City, Utah
PARENTS: Daniel Bowers
Dinah Joinson (Johnson)
PIONEER: 30 Nov 1856
Edward Martin Handcart Co.
SPOUSE: Hezekiah Mitchell
MARRIED: 31 Dec 1856
Salt Lake City, Utah
DEATH SP: 25 Sep 1872
Salt Lake City, Utah

CHILDREN:
Brigham William, 23 Dec 1857
Hezekiah, 11 Aug 1860
Heber Daniel, 30 Mar 1864
Margaret Salina Theresa, 29 Mar 1867

Elizabeth left Iowa City, Iowa July 28 1856 with the Edward Martin Handcart Company with five hundred and seventy-six saints. Going through all the hardships and suffering they endured by being so late getting started is said to have been the worst in all the history of western settlement. One hundred and fifty souls were lost in this company.

After being in the valley less than a month, Brother and Sister Richards introduced her to Hezekiah Mitchell of Simmondley Parish, Glossop Derby, England who had been in the valley for two years with his wife and family. Brother Richards suggested to Hezekiah that he marry this young woman. Hezekiah, being nineteen years older than she, suggested marriage to Elizabeth, but she did not give an answer at that time.

He returned home and discussed the matter with his first wife, Sarah Mallinson Mitchell, who rebelled at first but finally agreed. The two returned to Salt Lake and

Elizabeth was sealed to Hezekiah on Wednesday, Dec. 31, 1856 by Brigham Young. On January 2, 1857, all three started back to E. T., a small farming area southwest of Garfield, where he had a home on a city and garden lot with ten acres to farm. They traveled in a heavy snowstorm and were compelled to stop for the night in the storm. When Johnston's Army came into the valley the families moved to Lehi for four months until the danger was over. A potato crop had been planted before leaving so on their return it was ready to be harvested. Times were getting hard at E. T. and her husband thought he would make a better living where land was better. In 1859 he moved his first wife to Ogden and his journal reads as though Elizabeth with her first child remained in Salt Lake where living quarters were provided for them. In 1867 they returned to Salt Lake to live. In March of 1867 Elizabeth was blessed with a daughter after having three sons. Sarah was midwife to her and tended the three older children.

Elizabeth died April 3, 1889 just one week prior to her sixtieth birthday.

ELLEN LEGG MITCHELL

BIRTHDATE: 25 Feb 1800
Outseat Par. Gamrie, Banff, Scotland
DEATH: 22 Apr 1875
Payson, Utah County, Utah
PARENTS: William Legg
Elizabeth Leddingham (Ledikan)
PIONEER: 25 Sep 1866
John D Holladay 4th Train
SPOUSE: William Mitchell
MARRIED: 30 May 1826
Old Machar, Aberdeen
DEATH: Mar 1865
Blyth, Northumberland, England

CHILDREN:
Isabelle, 5 Dec 1819
Helen or Ellen (Mathewson), 7 Nov 1827
Barbara (Mathewson), 7 Apr 1830
Mary, 24 Dec 1832
Jane (Cowan) 24 Jul 1835
Eliza or Elizabeth (Barnett), 30 Nov 1840
Jessie, 1844

Ellen was born in Scotland in 1800. By age twenty, she was married to William Mitchell, and living in McDuff Parrish and had one child. They moved to Aberdeen where six more daughters were born to them. William was a skilled artisan who was a stone mason and did contracting in England and Scotland for building wharves for ships to load and unload. This took engineering skill and he was so well qualified that he mainly supervised on his contracts. They were of the middle class in England and did not know the poverty that many of that time experienced. They joined the LDS church and were very active until a wayward missionary caused William to be incensed and unforgiving and wanted nothing more to do with the church and tried to dissuade his family. Ellen began making preparations for moving to Zion. First she got the older single girls off to America. Mary and Helen came as far as St. Louis. Helen married and stayed there. Mary started on with the company but was stricken with cholera and died. Eventually all of the girls had left for America with Ellen's help. Barbara, the third daughter, left her unbelieving husband in Scotland and came to Utah. William died in 1865 and Ellen left England with a company of Mormons making the 6500 mile trip by sea, by rail and then across the plains. She was sixty-six years old and since she survived the trip she must have been in good health. She crossed the plains with the John D. Holliday Co. arriving in Salt Lake City 25 Sep 1866. On this trek, due to the hot weather, they traveled in the mornings and rested in the middle of the day and then often drove to near sundown. After her arrival, she went to Brigham Young's office where she signed notes of obligation to pay $180.00 for transit across the plains, 28 pounds for sea and rail fare.

Ellen went to Payson, Utah County, where three of her daughters lived. She died there 22 Apr 1875, at age seventy-five, having been a widow for ten years. Her descendants are grateful for her faithfulness in the gospel and for assisting her daughters to come to Zion.

JANET FIFE MITCHELL

BIRTHDATE: 7 Feb 1822
Sauchie, Scotland
DEATH: 12 Apr 1899
Hooper, Utah
PARENTS: John Fife
Margaret Hunter Fife
PIONER: 21 Sep 1851
David Walker Co Wagon Train
SPOUSE: James Mitchell
MARRIED: 13 Jan 1840
Clackmanan, Scotland
DEATH SP: 4 Mar 1890
Riverdale, Utah

CHILDREN:
James, 4 Feb 1841
John, 31 Dec 1842
Andrew, 1844
Jannette, 1846

Janet was born in Scotland, 1822. She was the youngest of eight. Her father worked in the Coal fields. At age seventeen, she married James Mitchell, born 24 Jun 1817 in Newton,Clackmanan, Scotland. They made their home in Clackmanan, where four children were born to them. Two survived to adulthood. The family was attracted to the LDS religion but had to meet secretly because of the great persecutions at that time. Janet felt James' hair one night and found it to be wet because he had been baptized. She, too, was soon baptized. Janet and James soon made preparation to come to Zion. They joined the David Walker company in 1848. Her sister and brother and their families also came. They arrived in Salt Lake City 21 Sep 1851.

The Mitchells were called to settle in the southern part of the state. They went to Cedar City, Iron County. Food was scarce and they lived on squash almost all winter. In 1855, Janet and James and family were some of the first to settle in Riverdale, Utah. They became restless, joined the gold rush, and went to California.

They missed the LDS church while in California and soon moved back to Riverdale, Utah. Here they planted a big fruit orchard. In 1863, fifteen years after leaving Scotland, they went to Salt Lake City to do their share of taking care of immigrants who had no place to stay for the winter. They took in a girl named Maren Jensen. Before long, Janet gave her consent for James to marry Maren. They had nine children.

Janet then moved to Hooper, Utah, to live with her son, John and his wife, Ann. Janet often went to Clinton, Davis County to see Maren, James' second wife. Once, when she went to visit, she became ill and Maren took care of her until she died on 12 Apr 1899 at age seventy-seven. She had been a widow for nine years.

LOIS JUDD PAGE MITCHELL

BIRTHDATE: 15 Sep 1825
Bostontown, Leeds, Upper Canada
DEATH: 9 Jun 1912
Draper, Salt Lake County, Utah
PARENTS: Azra Judd
Lucinda Adams
PIONEER: Fall 1848
Independent Wagon Train
SPOUSE I: John Edmond Page
MARRIED: unknown
DEATH SP: unknown

CHILDREN:
Rachel Minerva, 1846

SPOUSE II: Benjaman Thomas Mitchell
MARRIED: 1 Jan 1848
Winter Quarters, Dougland, Nebraska
DEATH SP: 7 Mar 1880
Salt Lake County, Utah

CHILDREN:
Mary Lois, 10 Feb 1849
Ruth Todd (Trotter), 25 Feb 1851
Daniel Judd, 18 Jan 1853
Ann, 8 May 1855
Nathaniel, 2 Nov 1857
Fannie, 12 May 1861
Lucb Content, 10 Aug 1868
Byron Teancum, 28 Mar 1872

Lois was born in Upper Canada in 1825. She grew up with a close extended family. The Judd family lived in the country, so the children had quite a walk to school. Sunday was considered "The Sabbath," a day of rest, and the children were expected to put away their toys and be sober and serious. Lois was one of ten children, with her mother dying in childbirth with child number ten. Her father married Jane McMann (McMahon) Stoddard in 1835 (widow of Nathaniel Stoddard) who had four boys of her own. Jane was very good to the children and treated them like her own. When the Judd's were first moving to Nauvoo, her father Azra died of Malaria fever. Lois first married John Edmond Page and had one child, Rachel Minerva in 1846. When she married Benjaman Thomas Mitchell in 1848, he had Rachel Minerva sealed to him.

Lois was age twenty-two when she married Benjaman and they became parents of eight. She was his fourth wife, in Plural Marriage. They were married on the first day of the New Year, Jan 1, 1848 at Winter Quarters by Brigham Young. She always referred to him as Mr. Mitchell. They came to Utah in 1848. Benjamin brought Lois to Salt Lake City. Later they went to Kamas to live. They first lived on the Old Jensen Place, then Mr. Mitchell built Lois a home on the place where the canal crossed in back of Frank Fitzgerald's home. Lois' seventh child, Lucy, was crippled in the hip and could not walk. She had a table built that Lucy could stand in and she could wheel her in. She had to weave carpets to make her living. She wove carpets for 10 cents per yard. Five yards was the amount she could weave in a day. She made the first carpet for the Kamas Church and Relief Society House. Lois was Treasurer for the Kamas Relief Society. She was a faithful woman and always took a bucket of flour to Testimony Meeting to pay her fast offering. When her children were grown, she moved to Francis in a litttle log house built for her by her son Bishop Dan Mitchall. She lived on the Reservation when it was first opened up. She never liked to have anything fancy to wear. She died 9 Jun 1912 in Draper, Utah at age eighty-seven, having been a widow for thirty-two years.

MAREN JENSEN MITCHELL

BIRTHDATE: 1 Apr 1845
Norre Amme Ring, Kjobing, Denmark
DEATH: 23 May 1907
Clinton, Davis County, Utah
PARENTS:
Jens Christian Christensen
Christiane Jensen
PIONEER: Jul 1863
John Smith Handcart Company
SPOUSE: James Mitchell
MARRIED: 12 Dec 1863
Salt Lake City, Utah
DEATH: 8 Mar 1890
Riverdale, Weber County, Utah

CHILDREN:
Jennette, 27 Nov 1864
Mary Ann, 24 Aug 1866

Charles, 25 Oct 1868
Hector, 6 Dec 1870
Joseph Clements, 12 Jan 1872
Ellen Christiana, 24 Jul 1874
James Franklin, 29 Aug 1876
George Christian, 22 Feb 1879
Fredrick Ewin, 17 Aug 1881

Maren Jensen Mitchell was born in Denmark. Two cities are listed: Norre Amme Ring, Kjobing or Skrupstrup. She was the eighth of eleven children. She was a frail, sickly child, but did what she could to help on her father's farm. Once while she was herding sheep, an electric storm suddenly came up. She thought she had been struck by lightning. She was revived by the rain falling in her face. She may have just fainted. At the age of eight years she went to work for a woman as a milkmaid's apprentice. After milking, she skimmed the cream from the pans of milk to make butter and cheese. She would scrape off the cream that stuck on the sides of the pans and eat it; she felt this helped to restore her health. In return for work, she learned the art of sewing and tailoring women's and children's clothing and men's suits. She was an excellent seamstress. She went from house to house doing family sewing. With the money she earned she sent part of it to her folks to help them with their large family.

She went to school, as much as they had at that time. In about 1862, she heard about the Latter-day Saint religion. She and her cousin, Christian L. Oleson, were the only ones of the family who accepted the true Gospel. She and Christian left Hamburg, Germany 15 Apr 1862 on the ship "Franklin" and arrived in New York 29 May 1862. She joined the handcart company of Captain John Smith and arrived in the Salt Lake Valley in Jul 1863. She walked over 1,000 miles, most of the way pushing a handcart. She sunburned her arms so badly that she was left with deep scars for the rest of her life. She arrived in the Valley with no money and no place to go. At immigrant Square she met James Mitchell and his wife Janet. They invited Maren to go with them to their home in Riverdale, Utah, to live in their home and help on the farm. Not long afterwards, James asked Maren to be his second wife. His wife gave her consent.

After their marriage 12 Dec 1863, Maren first lived in a little one-room log cabin along the Weber River near Ogden. She and James became the parents of nine children; three died as children. She moved to Clinton, Utah in 1890. Her husband died a month later in Riverdale. Maren bought land and her boys helped her farm. They planted mostly hay and grain. They had cows and ten acres of orchard and berries of all kinds. When Relief Society was first organized in Clinton, she was President from 1892 until 1906. She was the midwife in this area, bringing many children into the world without one death. She also taught Sunday School. She raised a good family and also took into her home a little English convert, William Burt, who died of pneumonia when a young man. Her husband's first wife lived with her until her death in 1899. Maren was a small woman who had a beautiful singing voice. She had business foresight and was a success in all she undertook. She suffered a stroke when she was sixty years old. She died in the home of her eldest daughter 23 May 1907.

SARAH MALLINSON MITCHELL

BIRTHDATE: 16 Nov 1810
Sheffield, Yorkshire, England
DEATH: 10 Apr 1883
Salt Lake City, Utah
PARENTS: John Mallinson
Mary Shaw
PIONEER: 3 Oct 1854
James Brown Co
SPOUSE: Hezekiah Mitchell
MARRIED: 7 Oct 1832
Manchester, Lancashire, England
DEATH: SP 25 Sep 1872
Salt Lake City, Utah

CHILDREN:
Martin Luther, 11 Aug 1833
Frederick A.H.F., 14 Jul 1835
Lovina, 22 Jul 1837-27
Priscilla Victoria, 19 Oct 1839
Martha Ann Millinson, 21 Mar 1842
Maria 14 Apr, 1844
Elizabeth, 14 Apr 1846
Ebenezer Israel, 9 May 1849
Sarah Ann, 31 Mar 1851

Sarah did not accept the gospel at the time of her husband's baptism. She joined the church fifteen months later about February 1846. They were disowned by the family members and friends. He could not find employment. Sarah was compelled to do dressmaking to help support the family. They had been members of the Methodist faith, he being a preacher for eight years. She entertained Orson Hyde, Parley P. Pratt, John Taylor and others in her home. She was supportive to his callings and took care of the children and home while for five years he served as Branch President over one to three branches at a time.

They lost three children–Martin at age three, Martha Ann at nearly two months, and Ebenezer at one month. She knew pain and sorrow over this loss.

On Tuesday, October 30, 1849, they left Sheffield by railway for Liverpool. Saturday, November 10, they boarded the ship "Zetland" and left Liverpool for America and arrived in New Orleans December 24, 1849. Because of lack of funds they were not able to continue on to Utah. When they got to St. Louis they only had 35 cents in their pocket. As soon as they could they opened a small store. Sarah assisting with her sewing. While in St. Louis a daughter, Sarah Ann, was born. A few months later they moved to Jersey Co. Illinois where they settled on a farm. They stayed there until 1854. On June 17, 1854 they left Kansas City with the James Brown Company, facing several hardships and obstacles. The trip was hard and tedious not only for the saints but the animals were showing effects of the strain. While crossing they picked three quarts of choke cherries and Sarah made jam. Her family was always pleased with her cooking and how she made many tasty things that others did not bother with. She milked the cow and made delicious butter. They arrived in the valley October 3, 1854, and settled at E. T. which was a small farming area southwest of Garfield. On April 15, 1855 Sarah, her husband, Priscilla, Maria and Elizabeth were rebaptized. Sarah was endowed June 4, 1856. On December 31, 1856 her husband took a second wife. Sarah shared her home with Elizabeth. Looking for better land and a larger community they moved to Ogden in 1859 taking all their possessions. It was a five day trip. His second wife remained in Salt Lake where living quarters were provided for her. Sarah remained in Ogden until late 1867 and moved back to Salt Lake.

The second wife had a daughter in March of 1867 and Sarah served as Midwife and tended to all the children, of Elizabeth Bowers Mitchell. Sarah was a devoted, supportive and patient and loving person. She was a mother of nine children; six she was able to raise to adulthood. She also received her patriarchal blessing in 1875. She died April 10, 1883 at nearly seventy-three years of age. Sarah is buried in the Salt Lake City Cemetery.

SUSANNA HOUSTON MATLOCK MITCHELL

BIRTHDATE: 11 Feb 1826
Jackson, Pennsylvania
DEATH: 6 May 1900
Salt Lake City, Utah
PARENTS: James Houston
Mary Ettelman Houston
PIONEER: 1855
Benjamin Thomas Mitchell Co.
Wagon Train
SPOUSE:Gideon Cooper Matlock
MARRIED: 1848
Council Bluffs, Iowa
DEATH: abt 1849

CHILDREN:
Cameron Alexander, 12 Jun 1849

SPOUSE II: Benjamin Thomas Mitchell
MARRIED: 6 Mar 1857
Salt Lake Endowment House
DEATH: 7 Mar 1880
Salt Lake City, Utah

CHILDREN:
Thomas Houston, 22 Jan 1858
Edward Hunter, 17 Aug 1859
Erastus Snow, 22Jan 1862
Charles James, 31 Jul 1864
Lehi Houston (twin), 7 Sep 1866
Nephi Houston(twin), 7 Sep 1866
Walter Houston, 8 Nov 1869

Susanna Houston Matlock Mitchell was born in Jackson, Stark County, Pennsylvania. She was the sixth child in a family of seven children. Her parents and other relatives joined the Mormon Church soon after it was organized in 1830. Susanna was seven years old when her family left Canton, Ohio to travel to Adams County, Missouri, then to Caldwell County, and from there to Nauvoo, Illinois. Some of these moves were caused by anti-Mormon mobs driving the family from their home. In 1846, the Houston family, with thousands of other Saints, found themselves in makeshift homes in Winter Quarters. After all kinds of privations, exposure to cold and inadequate diet, Susanna's parents died.

In 1848, after surviving so many trials and hardships, Susanna's life was made happy with her marriage to an intelligent young lawyer, Gideon Cooper Matlock. On 12 Jun 1849, their son, Alexander C. Matlock, was born in Council Bluffs, Iowa. Susanna's husband was familiar with some of the Indian languages and had often acted as an interpreter. He was sent on a mission by the U. S. Government to an Indian tribe. Weeks lengthened into months and Susanna received no word from him. To support herself and her son, she began to sew for some of the families in the neighborhood. She tried every way possible to get some word of her husband, but communication was slow. Perhaps he was being held by the Indians, but would somehow escape and return home.

Most of the Saints had left for the West, but Susanna refused to leave her home. She thought that her husband might come and find her gone. Finally, after six long years, she decided to make the journey to Utah and join the other members of her family. She later learned that her husband had died of Smallpox on his journey into the Indian Country. Susanna met Benjamin Thomas Mitchell in 1855 when she was in the emigrating party that he led across the Plains. She was a widow with a six year-old son. Benjamin was returning from a three-year Church mission. Susanna became his sixth wife on 6 Mar 1857. Seven sons were born to this couple. Her husband tried to deal fairly with his wives and children and they were congenial and happy with each other. His families grew so large that he had to have land to till in order to raise food for over fifty people. As a result, he helped settle Kamas, Utah. Here, they farmed and raised cattle and sheep. Benjamin died in Salt Lake City on 9 March 1880 at the age of sixty-four.

Susanna, who was ten years younger than her husband, lived for twenty years after he died. Her grandchildren remember the large orchard in front of her house, her pantry shelves that were always stocked with goodies, fruit and pies for those who visited her often and were always made to feel welcome. Susanna died on 6 May 1900 in Salt Lake City. She left a large posterity who honor her name.

CAROLINE THIRKELL MITTON

BIRTHDATE: 17 Feb 1844
Hutton Bushel Yorkshire, Englan
DEATH: 31 Jan 1937
Wellsville, Utah
PARENTS: John Pinnock Thirkell
Mary Baynes Brown Thirkell
PIONEER: 26 Sep 1853
Jacob Gates Wagon Company
SPOUSE: Edwin Crowther Mitton
MARRIED: 2 May 1861
Wellsville, Utah
DEATH: 14 Sep 1906
Wellsville, Utah

CHILDREN:
Edwin Crowther, 29 Oct 1862
John William, 16 Sep 1865
Harriet, 2 Oct 1867
George, 7 Aug 1870
Mary Thirkell, 31 May 1873
Emily Thirkell, 18 Nov 1875
Parley, 24 Jun 1878
Ann - twin, 1 Oct 1879
Hannah - twin, 1 Oct 1879
Emery Thirkell, 1 Jun 1882
Ezra, 2 Nov 1886
Minnie Thirkell, 18 May 1891

Caroline Thirkell Mitton was born in Yorkshire, England in 1844. She was the third daughter of John and Mary Thirkell. She came to America with her family when she was nine years old. They sailed across the Atlantic Ocean on the "Ellen Maria" and arrived in New Orleans, La. 7 Mar 1853. They continued up the Mississippi River to Keokuk, Iowa. From there, they crossed the Plains with the Jacob Gates wagon-train Company. They arrived in Salt Lake City 26 Sep 1853. Brigham Young directed them to continue on another 27 miles west to Grantsville, Utah.

Caroline moved to Wellsville, Cache Valley, Utah with her family in the Spring of 1859. She married Edwin Mitton on 2 May 1861. They lived throughout their lives in Wellsville. They were the parents of twelve children. Six lived to adulthood. Three daughters died within a month during a diphtheria epidemic in 1888. There were also good times. She must have been happy in her three room log home surrounded by her roses, peonies, trailing vines and other colorful flowers. They grew their own vegetables and bottled hundreds of quarts each year. She dried corn, peaches and apples. She cured meats which were home grown. In their pasture were milk cows and sheep, pigs and chickens. They made cheese and butter.

Caroline was a good neighbor and her neighbors were good to her. As was common in those days, she helped with the birth of babies. She taught her children to be responsible and how to work. She supported them in their special moments. She was always a faithful member of the Church. She and her family enjoyed musical times together because her husband and his brothers were involved in music and drama through the years. Her husband died in 1906 at the age of sixty-six years. This left Caroline a widow for over thirty years. She cared for herself and children who were still at home. In 1930, she had a stroke. Her last seven years were spent with her sister, Emily Johns, and her daughter, Mary Gunnell. Caroline died in 1937 at the age of ninety-three.

HANNAH CROWTHER MITTON (DODDIS)

No
Photo
Available

BIRTHDATE: 1 Apr 1811
Sawhill, Sowerly, Yorkshire,
England
DEATH: 12 Nov 1864
Wellsville, Utah
PARENTS: William Crowther
Rhoda Hansen Crowther
PIONEER: Oct 1859
James S. Brown Wagon Company
SPOUSE: William Mitton
MARRIED: 12 Feb 1832
England
DEATH: 27 Sep 1849
Moose, Illinois

CHILDREN:
Harriet, 6 Jul 1832
John Crowther, 3 Jul 1834
Samuel Crowther, 27 Play 1836
Emma, 4 May 1838
Edwin Crowther, 15 Apr 1840
Sarah, 28 Jan 1842
William Crowther, 22 Jun 1844
Hannah Doddis, 8 Jul 1850

SPOUSE II: Harry Doddis
MARRIED: not given
DEATH SP: not given

CHILDREN:
Hannah, died in 1856

Hannah Crowther Mitton was born in England. Little is known of her childhood. She married William Mitton 12 Feb 1832 in England. Hannah and her husband heard the Mormon missionaries preach the true Gospel and joined the Mormon Church in 1847. They were anxious to join the Saints in Utah. The missionaries recommended that William go to America to earn the money to send for his family to make the trip. He went to the United States as soon as he could, but on the Plains in Illinois he suffered chills and fever and died before he could send for his family. After William's death, Hannah married Harry Doddis and they had a daughter, Hannah, who died in 1856. There is no further mention of Mr. Doddis.

The family continued their quest to go to America. On 31 Mar 1855, Hannah's sons, John and Samuel, sailed on the "Juventa." They worked in the Eastern States and within eighteen months Samuel had the money to send for Hannah and the rest of the family. Hannah, Harriet, Edwin, Sarah and William sailed on the "George Washington," an old sailing vessel. They arrived in Boston, Mass. after encountering rough seas, sandbars, a fire, and many other hardships. Hannah's daughter, Emma, and her husband came at another time. Hannah rented a room in Boston and wrote to Samuel for funds to get to St. Louis, Missouri.

By June 1859, they had saved enough money to join the James Brown wagon-train, heading for Zion. The wagons were not in such good shape and broke down often, causing some delays and discouragements. Hannah would often say, "We are going to Zion, and we'll surely get there." They were greeted by the Saints along the way and given food and help. They arrived in the Salt Lake Valley the Fall of 1859. They were befriended by a kind man, Mr. Openshaw, who invited them to his home until they could move into an adobe home. The following Spring, he loaned them oxen to pull their wagon to Cache Valley, Utah. They settled in Wellsville in a little log cabin with no floor or windows. The sod roof leaked badly when it rained. In a few years they were able to move this cabin closer into town and add floor, windows and a lumber roof.

Hannah was very proud of her children. The girls had lovely singing voices and her sons could play most any musical instrument. They also acted in plays and minstrels around the Valley. Her sons were some of the first carpenters in the area and built many homes. Hannah had a lot of faith and worked so hard to get her family to Zion. She and her children have been an asset to the Church and to their communities. Hannah had been ill for some time and passed away 12 Nov 1864. She was only fifty-three years old.

ELIZABETH FRANCINE RUSHTON MOESSER

BIRTHDATE: 15 Oct 1841
Leeks, Stafford, England
DEATH: 9 Oct 1920
Granger, Utah
PARENTS:
Frederick James Rushton
Jane Wood Rushton
PIONEER: 25 Sep 1855
Richard Ballantyne Company
SPOUSE: Joseph Hyrum Moesser
MARRIED: 28 Aug 1864
Salt Lake City, Utah
DEATH: 10 Dec 1928
Salt Lake City, Utah

CHILDREN:
Emma Elizabeth, 16 Jan 1866
Joseph Henry, 5 Jun 1868
Minnie Jane, 17 Mar 1870
Edwin Frederick, 22 Dec 1872
Franklin Dewey, 22 Sep 1874
Charley Everett, 10 Apr 1876
Martha Maria, 17 Jun 1881
Ida Maud, 31 Jul 1882
Belle Marie, 16 Apr 1885

Elizabeth Francine Rushton Moesser was born in Leeks, England. She emigrated to America with her parents and her grandfather when she was two years old. They sailed from Liverpool, England 8 Mar 1843 on the "Yorkshire." They arrived in Nauvoo, Illinois 31 May 1843. Elizabeth's mother died in 1849 in St. Louis, Missouri. Elizabeth lived with her Aunt Diana Bullock.

The Bullock family came to Utah with the First Division of the Perpetual Emigration Fund Company. Richard Ballantyne was the Captain. They arrived in the Salt Lake Valley 25 Sep 1855. Times were very hard. Elizabeth learned to make candles. It seemed she always had to work hard so she could furnish all her own clothing and needs. She was always asked to sing at parties and dances. She had a sweet voice and people liked to hear her sing. On 28 Aug 1864, she married Joseph Hyrum Moesser. For the first few years they lived with Joseph's mother in the Sixth Ward in Salt Lake City. Later, they acquired a farm on the west side of the Jordan River (north of present day Rose Park). Her father lived with them for some time. They became the parents of nine children; four boys and five girls. Two of their children died as young children.

Later, they homesteaded a section of land in Hunter, Utah. This land was called the dry farm area. They had a good water well so they were able to have a good farm and a good life. Elizabeth was a good wife and mother. She was a good cook and always kept a neat and clean home. She was always busy; sewing, cooking, knitting. In the Summer of 1914, Elizabeth fell while going down cellar steps and hurt her hip. It was three months before she could walk. She used a crutch for nearly two years before she could walk naturally. Her children were born and raised under the influence of two loving parents. Elizabeth died 9 Oct 1920 after a short illness. She was seventy-nine years old.

JANET LEISHMAN MOFFAT

BIRTHDATE: 10 Sep 1816
Crichton County, Edinburgh, Scotland
DEATH: 19 Jan 1891
Meadowville, Utah
PARENTS: William Leishman
Janet Donaldson Leishman
PIONEER: 27 Aug 1860
Daniel Robinson Co. Hancart
SPOUSE: David K. Moffat
MARRIED: 1 Jul 1842
Scotland
DEATH SP: 14 Oct 1885
Meadowville, Utah

CHILDREN:
Janet (Jessie), 7 May 1843
Catherine, 4 Nov 1844
Joseph Smith, 16 Jun 1846
William, 11 Feb 1848
Christine, 26 Mar 1850

Alexander, 22 May 1852
Marion, 4 Jun 1854
Millen Atwood, 9 Oct 1856
Mary Jane, 9 Sep 1859

Janet Leishman Moffat was born in Edinburgh, Scotland. Her father was a ploughman and Janet became a domestic servant. She secured much credit and esteem arising from her extensive knowledge in the dairy department and every other department connected with the duties of a female servant. Her character was unmarred, very temperate, chaste and of a religious disposition.

Janet married David K. Moffat 1 Jul 1842 in Scotland. They became the parents of nine children; six were born in Scotland and three in Pennsylvania. They became interested in the Mormon Church and Janet was baptized 9 Jun 1844; David was baptized 2 Jun 1844. Janet was pleased and their life was much happier because of this. The family emigrated to America in 1853. They settled in Pennsylvania where David worked in the coal mines.

After selling their home and household goods for a very small sum, they bought a team and wagon and with other Latter-day Saint converts they left Pattersville, Pennsylvania for Florence, Nebraska to join three hundred converts who had gathered there to make a train to journey to Utah. Here they exchanged their team and wagon for two handcarts and joined the Daniel Robinson Company. What a trial and heartache this must have been for this dear little mother and the children. Joseph Smith, the eldest son, then about fourteen, pulled or pushed a handcart every day along with his father for ninety-two days, except Sundays, starting about 7 Jun 1860 and ending 27 Aug 1860, when they reached the Salt Lake Valley. Janet and the children walked most of the way, enduring many hardships and privation.

They lived in Salt Lake City where Janet made a lovely home for her family. In 1869, Brigham Young called hundreds of families from Salt Lake to colonize other parts of Utah. Janet and David and their family help to settle Meadowville, Utah in the Bear Lake Valley. The settlers were like a big family. All, helped each other. The home built for Janet and family was good for that time. Janet was a lovely homemaker, wife and mother. They used one of the rooms of their home as a store and post office, the first in the community. It served the people of Meadowville, Round Valley and Laketown for many years. Janet would give her grandchildren a piece of candy, even though their mothers did not like it.

When the Relief Society was organized 6 Jun 1879, Janet became a Counselor. The presidency had great responsibilities in those days. The families worked hard and long overcoming many trials. As families grew and children married many started leaving the area. However, Janet and David stayed until their deaths and were buried in the Meadowville Cemetery. David died 14 Oct 1885. Janet died 19 Jan 1891.

MARY PATTERSON HUNTER MOFFAT

BIRTHDATE: 18 Nov 1849
Deven, Scotland
DEATH: 14 Aug 1926
Afton, Wyoming
PARENTS: Adam Patterson Hunter
Elizabeth Patterson Hunter
PIONEER: 13 Aug 1852
John Higbee Wagon Company
SPOUSE:
Archibald (Archie) Russell Moffat
MARRIED: 4 Jun 1875
Salt Lake City, Utah
DEATH: 12 Dec 1933
Afton, Wyoming

CHILDREN:
Elizabeth (Bessie) Patterson, 6 Jun 1876
Allison (Fallie) Archibald, 29 Dec 1877
James Theodore, adopted

Mary Patterson Hunter Moffat was born in Deven, Scotland. She was six weeks old when she left Scotland with her mother, two sisters, one brother, a grandmother and other close relatives to emigrate to America where her father was waiting for them. They sailed on the ship "Josiah Bradley" out of Liverpool, England in late Feb 1849. When the ship was well underway an epidemic of smallpox broke out among the passengers. Mary became ill as the disease spread rapidly and many were dying. The Captain decided the dying should be cast overboard in order to get rid of the infection. Mary's mother hid her under the feather tick of the bunk when the Captain came to inspect their cabin. With this vigilance, loving care and many prayers Mary lived. Their ship landed in New Orleans, La. They then traveled up the Mississippi River to St. Louis, Missouri. The family was soon united with their father and preparations were made to join the Saints in Utah.

In the Spring of 1852, the Hunter family headed west with a party of ten wagons under the direction of Captain John Higbee. They arrived in the Salt Lake Valley 15 Aug 1852. They lived in a wagon and a dugout in Red Butte Canyon. There was not much food so the children gathered weeds and Sego lily bulbs to eat. Mary had little formal schooling, but was skilled in all the necessary things of life. She did housework for other people to earn money to help her family. Mary attended the celebration of the first railroad car to come to Salt Lake City, she played on the foundaton of the Salt Lake Temple and attended other events in the early days of the City.

Mary met Archibald Russell Moffat at a Scottish people gathering. They were married by Wilford Woodruff in the Endowment House 4 Jun 1875. They moved to Almy, Wyoming where Archie found work in the coal mines. Mary had an accident in her wagon while crossing a deep ditch. Serious injuries to her legs and hip would give her pain for the rest of her life. From Wyoming they moved to Park City, Utah and Snyderville to share a farm with her husband's brother. Mary helped her husband on the farm.

Here they adopted a son, James Theodore. Mary followed her husband to Star Valley, Wyoming in Nov 1887. They joined three or four other families to help settle that area. People remembered the Moffat's garden, where Mary would work seated on a chair and would teach her children to do the work she was unable to do. For the rest of her life she used a crutch and had to learn how to do everything with her left hand. That didn't stop her playing with her children, singing with them and even using her hands to teach them to dance.

Mary was always cheerful and smiling. She was a good singer and always had music in her home. She and Archie often sang together. Her home was the center for the young people of the area. Mary was a guiding star to everyone who met her. She never complained and was always attentive to others who needed her help or advice. She was an excellent cook and a gifted seamstress. She made her family's clothes and made beautiful quilts and burial clothing. In Star Valley, she served in the First Stake Relief Society as third Vice President and as Treasurer. Mary died in Afton, at the age of seventy-seven, 14 Aug 1926. She was laid to rest in the Afton Cemetery, mourned by her loving husband daughters Bessie and Allison, son Jim, 21 grandchildren and 2 great Grandchildren.

MARY JANE EMMETT HOLDEN MOFFETT

BIRTHDATE: 26 Dec 1825
Shellyville, Shelly County, Indiana
DEATH: 23 Sep 1909
Porterville, Morgan County, Utah
PARENTS: James Emmett
Phoebe Jane Simpson Emmett
PIONEER: 1850 by wagon
SPOUSE I : Willey Howard Holden
MARRIED: 11 May 1843
Navoo, Hancock, Illinois
DEATH:

CHILDREN:
James Hyrum, 1 Jun 1844

SPOUSE II: Armstead Moffett
MARRIED: 1845
Indian Country
DEATH: 27 Mar 1891
Eden, Weber, Utah

CHILDREN:
Phoebe Jane (McBride), 14 Dec 1846
Martha Marin, 5 Jan 1848
William Armstead, 6 Aug 1850
Mary Jane (McBride), 1 Oct 1852
Malinda Ann (Rawson), 9 Oct 1854
Carlos Smith, 21 Aug 1856
Benjamin Franklin, 17 Sep 1858
Bethsina, 11 Sep 1860
Alvin Smith, 25 May 1862

Elizabeth Ann (Froirer), 19 Apr 1864
Sariah (Carter), 15 May 1866

Mary Jane Emmett Moffett was born in Shelly County, Indiana. When she was about eight years old she moved with her parents to Jackson County, Missouri. Her father had worked one year on the Kirkland Temple prior to their moving to Missouri.

They experienced mob persecutions and violence in Missouri and their home was burned to the ground before the eyes of the family. Mary Jane's father hid in the woods nearby to escape certain death by the mob. They all walked to Clay County where they hoped for relief from the mob terror. Most were barefoot on this trip and even walked on hands and knees part way to relieve their bleeding bare feet. After three years of peace at Caldwell, they were again driven out and lost everything again. They journeyed to Nauvoo. While they were traveling and about to perish with hunger, quail in countless numbers entered their camp. They were able to catch them by hand and thus their starvation was ended. They believed that through the power of God they were able to have this blessing and other blessings and safety from the mobs.

Mary Jane loved to go to Church and listen to the Prophet Joseph Smith and other presiding authorities. She was present and saw Joseph and Hyrum Smith after they were murdered at Carthage Jail. Later they were in the expulsion from Nauvoo. In 1844, the family with others stopped in an unsettled section called the Indian Country. Here they raised corn for their support. Mary Jane met a young man whom she married, Armstead Moffett, about 1845. In 1850, they crossed the Plains to Utah and settled in Ogden among the pioneers of that place. Later, they assisted in settling Ogden Valley where they raised a large family of eleven children. On 23 Sep 1909, Mary Jane died at the home of her youngest daughter, Sariah Carter, in Porterville, Utah.

REBECCA GALLOWAY MOLLAND

No Photo Available

BIRTHDATE: 4 Apr 1818
Worcester, England
DEATH: 9 or 12 Jan 1883
Near Downey, Bannock, Idaho
PARENTS: Robert Galloway
Martha Galloway
PIONEER: 15 Sep 1968
John Gillespie Wagon Train
SPOUSE James William(s) Molland
MARRIED: 23 Sep 1837
Liverpool, Lancashire, England
DEATH: 23 Oct 1872
Poulton cum Seacombe, Cheshire, England

CHILDREN:
Hannah (Byington), 21 Jul 1838
John, 12 Apr 1840
Maria, Jan 1842
Sarah, 27 Dec 1843

Maria, 25 Mar 1845
James, 14 Feb 1847
Charles, 26 May 1848
Mary Ann, 31 May 1851
Elizabeth, 31 Jan 1853
William James, 15 May 1854
James, 18 Aug 1855
Martha, 12 Sep 1856
William, 10 Aug 1864

Rebecca was born in England in 1818. At age nineteen, she married James William(s) Molland. They made their home in England, where they became parents of thirteen children, with only three living to adulthood. Her daughter, Hannah married 27 Feb 1864 in Salt Lake City.

Rebecca converted to the LDS church and decided to emigrate. Her husband, James chose not to come. He passed away in 1872 in England. She came to America in 1868, made her way to Benton, Wyo joining the John Gillespie Wagon Train, arriving in Salt Lake City 15 Sep 1868.

She was an early settler of Oxford and Marsh Valley, Idaho. She helped care for her daughter Hannah's children. She passed away in 1883 at age sixty-four, having been a widow for ten years.

Rebecca and James were early British converts in 1841. It is unknown, why James did not come to Utah.

FRANCES GATSEY JOLLEY MONCUR

BIRTHDATE: 8 Oct 1845
Nauvoo, Hancock County,Illinois
DEATH: 17 Oct 1914
Acequia, Minidoka, Idaho
PARENTS:
Henry Bryant Manning Jolley
Brittanna Elizabeth Mayo Jolley
PIONEER: 15 Sep 1852
Henry B. M. Jolley Wagon Co.
SPOUSE: Robert Moncur
MARRIED: 30 Sep 1860
Pond Town (Salem), Utah
DEATH: 26 Feb 1932
Acequia, Minidoka, Idaho

CHILDREN:
Robert Bryant, 14 Aug 1861
William Franklin, 25 Oct 1863
Harvey, 14 Apr 1866
Heber, 14 Nov 1868
George, 9 Dec 1871
Wallace, 22 May 1874
Frances Helen, 14 Apr 1877
Donald Wesley, 15 Jul 1879
Reuben L, 16 Oct 1882
Charles Marion, 24 Nov 1886 (died as child)

Frances Gatsey Jolley Moncur was born in Nauvoo, Illinois. Her parents had joined the Mormon Church in Dresden, Tennessee in 1842 and soon left to join the Saints in Nauvoo, Illinois. Frances was only four months old when the Saints started to leave Nauvoo early in 1847. The family remained in Iowa at the request of President Young and produced food for the members as they outfitted themselves for the trek across the Plains westward. Finally, on 10 Jun 1852, it was time for them to leave for Utah.

Frances' father, Henry Bryant Manning Jolley, was Captain of the Seventh Company and they arrived in the Salt Lake Valley 15 Sep 1852. Family records indicate that Henry rode a horse most of the time. The mother and the two smaller boys rode in a horse-drawn carriage across the Plains. This was quite a luxury in those days. Frances was not quite seven years old so she probably was able to ride some of the way in the carriage. The Jolley family settled in Palmyra and then on to Spanish Fork, Utah.

On 30 Sep 1860, Frances married Robert Moncur, a member from Dundee, Scotland, and a friend of the family. She wasn't quite fifteen years old. Frances had a great love for her parents and siblings. She and her husband helped settle many towns. She and Robert and their large family of nine boys and one girl would all have homes in the same area for the next twenty-seven years. These two families lived in Spanish Fork, Dixie, Long Valley and Mt. Carmel, Utah. With large families and large herds of cattle they left Mt. Carmel and moved to Lovell, Wyoming in the early 1900s. Later, they were early settlers in Minidoka and Cassia Counties in Idaho.

Frances and Robert settled on a farm in Acequia, Idaho. She was loving, kind and truly devoted to her home, husband, family and friends. Many is the stranger, the sick and unfortunate who have felt the blessing of her thoughtful and kind administration. She endured the hardships and privation of pioneer life and was identified with many ventures in the growth and development of Southern Utah. Frances and Robert shared joy and sorrow for over fifty years. Frances died at age sixty-nine and is buried in the Rupert City Cemetery in Rupert, Idaho.

ANNA (ANNIE) CATHERINE PETERSON MONSON

BIRTHDATE: 25 Sep 1831
Fulstop, Flemsbad, Denmark
DEATH: 13 Aug 1869
Richmond, Cache, Utah
PARENTS: Christian Peterson
Anna Bendtson
PIONEER: before 1860
Company unknown,
SPOUSE: Christian Hans Monson
MARRIED: 26 Apr 1861
Richmond, Cache, Utah
DEATH SP: 23 Sep 1896
Richmond, Cache, Utah

CHILDREN:
Joseph, 2 Feb 1862
Annie Catherine, 10 Dec 1863
Hans, 6 Jun 1866
Elizabeth, 10 Jun 1868

Anna (Annie) Catherine Peterson was born 25 Sep 1831 in Fulstop Flemsbad, Denmark, the daughter of Christian Peterson and Anna Bendtson (Benston, Benson). Little is known of her early life. She married Christian Hans Monson on 26 Apr 1861 in Richmond, Cache, Utah as a second wife. She had been a friend of the first wife, Nelsine, in Denmark. Later Christian and Nelsine divorced and Christian then married a young seventeen-year-old girl Ellen Persson Manssen, who had been hired at first to help out in the household. Anna's health had not been good, and she died soon after her last child was born on 13 Aug 1869 in Richmond, Cache, Utah.

ELLEN PERSSON MANSSON MONSON

BIRTHDATE: 5 Sep 1850
Langarod, Malmohus, Sweden
DEATH: 11 Apr 1924
Preston, Franklin County, Idaho
PARENTS: Pehr Mansson
Hanna Persson Mansson
PIONEER: 28 Sep 1862
John Murdock Company Wagon
SPOUSE: Christian Hans Monson
MARRIED: 16 Mar 1867
Salt Lake City, Utah
DEATH SP: 23 Sep 1896
Richmond, Cache County, Utah

CHILDREN:
Parley Herman, 26 Oct 1868
Charles Andrew, 2 Mar 1870
Ellen Marinda, 14 Dec 1871
Hyrum Moroni, 19 Nov 1873
Walter Peter, 30 Jun 1875
Brigham, 30 Aug 1877
Aaron Abraham, 11 Apr 1879
Otto Junius, 20 Jun 1881
Bertha Maria, 9 Aug 1883
Lafayette, 4 Nov 1886
Emma Cherste, 19 Aug 1888

Ellen Persson Mansson Monson was born in Langarod, Sweden. Her father died before she was born. When she was seven years old, her family accepted the teachings of the Mormon Church. They sailed for America on the ship "Humbolt" on 2 Apr 1862. Ellen was very ill on the ship and was unconscious for three weeks. She was twelve years old. Ellen walked across the Plains barefooted. They arrived in the Salt Lake Valley 28 Sep 1862 with the John Murdock Company.

When they got to Utah the family located in Hyrum, Cache County, Utah. Ellen had to work for her board and received no wages. She still did not have any shoes and had to carry water to the cattle in bad weather. The exposure caused her much suffering in her later years. James Unsworth took her away from the people who were unkind to her. He made her a pair of wooden shoes. She gathered wool the sheep left on fences and brushed and spun it into yarn and knitted stockings for herself. Brother Unsworth made her a wooden box to keep her clothes in. She treasured this box very much. She was able to go to school for only one month, but she never stopped learning and learned to write after she was married.

Ellen's mother married a man who would not accept Ellen into his family and even took away her precious box for payment of her board. It was returned to her after she married. She went to work for a Brother Monson because his wife was ill. Ellen and Christian Hans Monson were married 16 Mar 1867 in the Endowment House in Salt Lake City, Utah. Ellen was sixteen years old. Christian Monson's first wife died two years later. Ellen cared for her three children and two of her own by the time she was nineteen years old. She and her husband became the parents of eleven children. He married three more wives. The families all lived together in a large home in Richmond, Cache County, Utah. The house was built by Christian without nails, only wooden pegs. Ellen was the seamstress for the families. She gathered the wool, washed it, corded and spun it into yarn, wove the yarn into cloth and sewed the clothing. It was very hard for the family when Christian Monson went on a mission to Sweden, and in 1888 when he was sent to the Utah State Penitentiary for unlawful co-habitation. The family was stricken with Typhoid Fever, but all recovered. Ellen stayed in the big house while the other wives moved to separate quarters. Her husband died in 1896. In 1901, Ellen's children, Bertha and Lafayette, died of Diptheria.

Ellen cared for her blind grandmother, Christina, until she died. She had been like a mother to Ellen when they lived in Sweden. In 1924, Ellen died at the home of a daughter in Preston, Idaho, and was buried in the Richmond, Cache County, Utah Cemetery.

SARAH JANE LAMOREAUX MONTAGUE

BIRTHDATE: 13 Dec 1840
Springville, Illinois
DEATH: 7 May 1917
Panguitch Utah
PARENTS:
David Burlock Lamoreaux
Mary Ann Gribble
PIONEER: 10 Sep 1850
Indep. Wagon Train by Ox Team
SPOUSE: James Shepard Montague
MARRIED: 30 Jan 1859
Payson, Utah County, Utah
DEATH SP: 11 Dec 1912
Panguitch, Utah

CHILDREN:
Mary Jane (Ann), 23 Apr 1860
Josephine Lovina, 22 Aug 1861
Sarah Jane (Gould), 7 Jan 1863
Julia Ann (Worthen), 6 Nov 1864
James Albert, 6 Feb 1867
Mary Louisa, 30 Nov 1867
Aurelia Rozella (Worthen) 13 Feb 1872

Abigail Iva (Dowdell), 15 Jan 1875
David West, Mar 1877
Angie L. (Hudson), 9 May 1880
Laura May (Bartlett), 18 May 1883
Charles Andrew, 16 Jan 1886

Sarah Jane was born in Springville, Illinois 1840. Her parents were early members of the LDS church. In 1846 they were living in Nauvoo and in 1848 they were in Iowa City. In the summer of 1850 her family left for Utah in their covered wagon pulled by an ox team. Sarah Jane at about ten, walked, skipped, danced, and sang as she walked across the plains. She enjoyed the company of the other pioneer children as they made up and played games as they walked along the trail. Sarah Jane helped her father with the oxen and any other chores that were asked of her. She helped collect dried buffalo chips for the nightly fires. They arrived in Salt Lake City 1850 and after a short time, settled in Farmington.

Her parents moved to Ogden Hole in 1855, then back to Farmington. In 1856 her father took a second wife and her mother was left to raise the family alone. Sarah Jane was sixteen when they left Farmington. When they arrived in Payson, her mother taught the children to pick potatoes gather the cat-tails to make pillows, gather sage brush for firewood and glean wheat, also using the wheat grasses to make straw flats for the sixty-five men in the Payson Ward. Sarah Jane was attractive with beautiful large gray-blue eyes, small frame, well groomed and fun loving. She also loved to dance and sing. She was courted by James Shepard Montague and they were married by his father on 30 Jan 1859 in Payson. In Dec 1859 they buried their first child and soon moved to Carson City, Nevada. After her second child died in Nevada they moved back to Payson with sad hearts and empty arms. Soon they were called to settle Paragonah, Iron County, Utah. Sarah Jane worked side by side with James to clear the land for them to farm and have a garden. She loved flowers and probably had a beautiful garden. James engaged in farming, cattle raising, and ranching. The rest of their family of twelve children were born in Payson, Paragonah, and Panguitch, where they put down roots and lived on and off, for the remainder of their lives. In Paragonah, Sarah Jane joined the first Relief Society when it was organized. In 1871 they were in Panguitch. Sarah Jane was active in the community and was an expert seamstress. She also made quilts, carpets, candles, soap, lotions and medicines from herbs, ointments, feather ticks, and all other necessary things for her growing family. They were sealed in the Endowment House 30 Oct 1871. They settled in Woodville, Idaho for awhile and had a wonderful home on the banks of the Snake River.

They were very active in the Woodville Ward, holding offices in the organizations and singing and playing their wonderful Organ. They came back to Panguitgh and James died one week after he arrived home. In spring 1917, Sarah became ill and passed away 7 May 1917 at age seventy-six.

ANN CHADWICK MONTGOMERY

BIRTHDATE: 8 May 1847
Council Bluffs, Iowa
DEATH: 5 Feb 1926
North Ogden, Utah
PARENTS: Abraham Chadwick
Mary Burton Chadwick
PIONEER: 1851 by wagon
SPOUSE:Robert Montgomery Jr.
MARRIED: 23 Mar 1864
North Ogden, Utah
DEATH SP: 11 Sep 1912
Yost, Box Elder, Utah

CHILDREN:
Robert Wilson, 1 Feb 1866
Alice Mary(Rose), 6 May 1867
William Abraham, 2 Jan 1869
Joseph Albert, 15 Jul 1870
John Edward, 19 Mar 1873
Hyrum Smith, 13 Oct 1874
Margaret Ann (Lee), 10 Sep 1876
Eva Lily, 4 Aug 1878
James Nathaniel, 27 Jun 1880
Charles Andrew, 1 Apr 1882
Isabell Jane (Oman), 25 Jan 1884
Olive Pearl (Brewerton), 20 Nov 1885
Bessie Irene (Eames), 6 Apr 1888
Sarah, 12 Apr 1891
Heber Alma (Jones), 6 Feb 1893

Ann Chadwick Montgomery was born at Council Bluffs, Iowa, where the Mormons had gathered to begin their trek west. A cholera epidemic broke out and Ann's mother died in 1850. Her father soon married Mary Foxall in Dec 1850 and she cared for his children and four born to them. They arrived in the Salt Lake Valley in 1851. The name of the Company they had traveled with is not known.

As a child, Ann was very active and a good runner. Walking was too slow for her and she went on the run until old age overtook her and her legs gave out. Family members remember her running about as she worked. She loved to dance and was a good step-dancer. She had a cheerful disposition.

At the age of seventeen, Ann married Robert Montgomery, Jr. on 23 Mar 1864. They lived in North Ogden where they raised fifteen children, eleven of whom grew to adulthood. They filed on land in the Cold Water area of North Ogden, about a mile east of Robert's family home. A spring of clear, cold water irrigated an orchard of apple trees and grapevines.

In 1877, the dreaded desease of diptheria invaded their home. Her oldest son died. He was eleven years old. In 1896, thinking that North Ogden was becoming too crowded, Robert and Ann and their children who were still at home moved to George Creek Canyon in Box Elder County, a place now known as Yost, Utah. They first lived in a one-room log cabin with a dirt floor, but later built a good four-room log home among pine, cedar and mahogany trees. Wild bluebell flowers grew nearby. In the fall they would gather pine nuts and roast them in the oven to eat on long, cold winter evenings.

Ann raised her large family of children with love and devotion. She helped settle Yost, Utah. She served in the Relief Society Presidency and as a Visiting Teacher. She and her husband taught friends and neighbors how to dance the "French Four" and gave dancing demonstrations in Yost. She was known for her help in times of sickness in her community. One time, she gave one of her coats to an Indian woman. The next time she saw the coat it was being worn by the Indian woman's husband. After her husband's death in 1912, Ann gave up housekeeping and lived in the homes of her children. She was living with her son, Will, in North Ogden at the time of her death on 5 Feb 1926. A headline above her obituary stated, "Utah Pioneer Expires. Large Family Survives Mrs. Ann Chadwick Montgomery." Funerals were held in both North Ogden and Yost, where she was buried.

MARY WILSON MONTGOMERY

BIRTHDATE: 20 April 1811
Greenock Renfrew, Scotland
DEATH: 17 May 1876
North Ogden, Utah
PARENTS: Robert Wilson
Isabel Pettigrew Wilson
PIONEER: 20 Sept. 1850
Warren Foote's Co. Wagon
SPOUSE: Robert Montgomery
MARRIED: 6 Sept. 1830
Paisley (Low), Renfrew, Scotland
Death SP: 17 April 1863
North Ogden, Weber, Utah

CHILDREN:
James, 1 April 1831
John, 3 June 1832
Isabella (Cazier), 16 July 1834
Robert, 8 May 1837
Margaret (Gardner), 31 July 1839
Nathaniel, 3 May 1842
Mary Elizabeth (Bailey/Spackman), 23 May 1843
William, 17 Sept 1845
Joseph Smith, 24 May 1848
Hyrum Smith, 29 Jan 1850
Alma, 1 Jan 1852

Mary Wilson was born in Scotland. She loved and missed that country all her life, so much that she named a Utah mountain Ben Lomand after her beloved mountain in Scotland.

She and Robert married when she was nineteen years old. They were a courageous, decisive couple determining to have as good a life as they could make for each other and their first act was to move to America.

Their son James was born in the New York Harbor, a dramatic omen for their new life.

They moved into Montreal, moving back and forth between upper United States and Canada every two or three years as circumstances demanded. They had eight of their eleven children in this area.

By 1848 they had heard a new religious message and decided their happiness lay with joining the Latter-day Saints. They moved to Farmington, Iowa where their two sons Joseph Smith and Hyrum Smith were born.

It took two and a half years to accumulate the provisions necessary, and they readied themselves for the three month trip west, joining the more than five thousand Saints who emigrated to Utah that year.

Mary was thirty-nine when they entered the Valley on September 1850, She had one more child, Alma, who was born in North Ogden where they settled. She was forty-one when he was born, making twenty-one childbearing years.

The fact that all were raised to adulthood is attributed to her incessant demand for cleanliness. Her reputation of never touching a clean dish unless she had a tea towel in her hand has been passed down for generations.

Before starting across the plains, Mary got barm from a nearby still, put hops with it and made yeast cakes which were thoroughly dried and lasted all the way to Utah.

They made their home for the rest of their lives in north Ogden, there Robert died in 1863 leaving Mary for thirteen years alone until she followed him in death at the age of sixty-five. Both are buried in the North Ogden Cemetery

NANCY MARIA CLARK MONTGOMERY

BIRTHDATE: 14 Jan 1849
Highland Grove, Pottawattamie Co., Iowa
DEATH: 23 Jun 1923
North Ogden, Utah
PARENTS: John Clark
Lillias Barbour Clark
PIONEER: 1852
Independent Wagon Company
SPOUSE: Nathaniel Montgomery
MARRIED: 1 Jan 1868
North Ogden, Utah
DEATH SP: 3 Nov 1913
North Ogden, Utah

CHILDREN:
Nathaniel Robert, 15 Oct 1868
John Clark, 20 Feb 1870
Hyrum Smith, 2 Oct 1872
Mary Lillias, 12 Aug 1874
Margarct Isabcll, 13 Oct 1877
Kate Olive, 30 May 1881
Florence Alberta, 1 Oct 1885
Grace Irene, 28 Mar 1889

Nancy Maria Clark Montgomery was born in Highland Grove, Iowa. When she was three years old, the Clark family left Council Bluffs early in 1852 for the Great Salt Lake Valley with an Independent Wagon Company. Although it was a long and difficult journey, all members enjoyed good health and they were prepared well. Nancy remembered how rough it was in the wagon where she was permitted to ride and how tired she would get when she had to walk. She remembered seeing large buffalo herds along the way and the Indians who visited their camp during the evenings. They arrived in the Salt Lake Valley in 1852.

The family moved north to Ogden, settling in Brigham's Fort. Nancy's father passed away in the Spring of 1854. Her widowed mother remarried in 1856 to William Gibson. They moved to the Provo area during the invasion of Johnston's Army. When they returned to Brigham's Fort another family was occupying their home. They had no title for the land and were left homeless. In 1859, Nancy's stepfather was called on a three-year mission to Europe. After his return, he never lived with the family again. The children had to help earn a living for the family. Nancy learned to weave cloth. She became a first class weaver and wove cloth for many families in the area. When she was twelve years old, she went to Salt Lake City and lived with a family doing housework, cooking and weaving. While visiting an Aunt in North Ogden she met Nathaniel Montgomery. They kept company for a couple of years and were married 1 Jan 1868. They became the parents of eight children; two boys died in infancy. Nancy and her husband were able to purchase a 40-acre farm in 1873. More land was purchased and Nancy cooked for hired farm help.

Nancy was a home-loving wife and mother. She joined the Relief Society in Aug 1868. Her husband was frequently away from home, taking part in Church and Civic affairs. Nancy stayed at home to care for the farm and family. She cooked meals for guests her husband brought home. She supplied a home for her mother for the last fourteen years of her mother's life. She became skilled in drying fruits; she dried apples, peaches and apricots by the hundreds of pounds. She sold dried fruit to buy clothes and food for her family. About two years after her marriage, Nancy suffered a severe sick spell. Her health was poor for the rest of her life.

Her husband died in 1913, leaving her a widow for ten years. She lived some of those years in California where she enjoyed improved health at the lower elevation. She passed away in her home in North Ogden 23 Jun 1923. She was buried in the North Ogden Cemetery beside her husband.

ELIZABETH POOL MOODY

BIRTHDATE: 6 Sep 1838
Manchester, England
DEATH: 18 Apr 1918
Thatcher, Graham, Arizona
PARENTS: Daniel Pool
Elizabeth Miller Pool Blazard
PIONEER: Fall of 1852
SPOUSE: John Monroe Moody
MARRIED: 23 Jan 1856
Salt Lake City, Utah
DEATH SP: 27 Jan 1884
Thatcher, Graham, Arizona

CHILDREN:
John Monroe, 8 Oct 1856
Francis Winifred, 26 Aug 1858
Urilda (Paxman), 28 Mar 1860
Edward, 20 Mar 1862
William Alphonz, 8 Mar 1864
Elizabeth Dorinda (Cluff Sr.), 19 Sep 1866
Thomas Epps, 23 May 1869
Susan Ann (Claridge), 5 Oct 1871
Emma Rosezilla (Cluff), 16 Mar 1874
Charles Daniel, 29 Mar 1877
Henry Owen, 10 Feb 1879

Elizabeth Pool was born 6 Sep 1838 in Manchester, England, the daughter of Daniel Pool and Betsy Miller. Elizabeth's mother, without her husband, joined the Church in 1838, the same year as Elizabeth's birth. Betsy took her three children to Nauvoo, Illinois with the first company of Saints from England.

After a short time the children were all 'farmed' out. Elizabeth came across the plains at the age of twenty-four years, arriving in the Valley in the Fall of 1852. She worked out a living in Salt Lake City, and was married 23 Jan 1856 to John Monroe Moody as his second wife. Together they had eleven children, one dying in infancy.

Elizabeth lived in the same house as the first wife, but she had to suffer through the divorce from the first wife, which brought much moving and finally losing her own residence. John also had two other wives.

After living in Salt Lake City for a time, the family moved to St. George, Utah where eight of her children were born, one of them being born in an underground dugout. From there the family moved to Thatcher, Arizona. Elizabeth was the first Relief Society President in Thatcher. She had a firm testimony of the gospel, and died in Thatcher 18 Apr 1918. Her husband preceded her in death on 27 Jan 1884, also in Thatcher, Graham, Arizona.

LOLA ELIZA BESS MOODY

BIRTHDATE: 1 Mar 1837
Stuben County, New York
DEATH: 6 Dec 1923
Salt Lake City, Salt Lake, Utah
PARENTS: Juel Bess
Laura Richardson Bess
PIONEER: 23 Sep 1848
Heber Chase Kimball Wagon Co
SPOUSE:William Cresfield Moody
MARRIED: 20 Dec 1857
Salt Lake Endowment House,
DEATH: 26 Sep 1906
Santa Monica, California

CHILDREN:
Laura, 23 May 1859
Eliza Lucinda, 21 Oct 1860
William Warren, 27 Jul 1863
Mary Ellen, 1 Dec 1864
Joseph Moroni, 17 Dec 1866
Helen, 27 May 1868
Juel, 20 Apr 1870
Luella, 27 Jul 1873
Benjamin Epps, 26 Aug 1875
Annie, 23 Aug 1878
Oliver, 21 Jun 1880

When Lola Eliza was six years old her parents became members of the LDS Church. The following year, her father died leaving her mother to rear seven children. Four years after her husband's death, she took her family of seven children to cross the plains. Soon after they reached Winter Quarters, they were all very sick with Scarlet Fever. They arrived in the Salt Lake Valley on September 23, 1848 with the Heber C. Kimball Wagon Company.

Lola was married to William Cresfield Moody on December 20, 1857 in the Endowment House in Salt Lake City. She was his second wife. He also married Cinthia Elizabeth Damron the same day he married Lola Eliza. They lived in Salt Lake City where their oldest child, Laura, was born. Then they moved to Ephraim where William owned and operated a general store. When he was called on a three year mission in 1860, he moved Lola back to Salt Lake City. Soon after his departure, Lucinda was born. William was then called to help colonize St. George, Utah where they lived for eight years. They were called to go to Spring Valley, Nevada to colonize and William was to be the Presiding Elder. The family lived in spring Valley, Dry Valley, and Eagle Valley until 1881 before they were released. They moved to Deseret, Utah. Lola Eliza adjusted herself rapidly and well to pioneer conditions. She was a source of great help and strength to her husband and children. She was an exceptionally fine seamstress and made her husband's and children's clothing. She also made buckskin gloves to sell. She served ten years as President of the Primary Association and fifteen years as the President of the Relief Society. Besides raising her own eleven children, she raised an Indian boy William had brought home. She

also raised five children of the third wife who had passed away. She died at the home of her daughter in Salt Lake City at the age of eighty-six.

LYDIA MOON MOON

No
Photo
Available

BIRTHDATE: 9 Oct 1811
Eccleston, Lancs, England
DEATH: 9 Jul 1868
Salt Lake City, Utah
PARENTS: Mathias Moon
Alice Plumb Moon
PIONEER: 5 Oct 1850
Independent Wagon Train
SPOUSE: Henry Moon
MARRIED: 30 Jan 1841
Pine Township, Pennsylvania
DEATH SP: 14 Nov 1894
Farmington, Davis, Utah

CHILDREN:
Alice Ann, 17 Sep 1842
John Thomas, 13 Sep 1844
Joseph Henry, 30 Jul 1847

Lydia was born in England in 1811. She was one of four daughters and five brothers. After their conversion to the LDS church, they made preparations to leave for Zion. They sailed in 1840 with the first company of saints to sail from England to America. At age twenty-nine Lydia married Henry Moon in Pennsylvania. They were married by Captain John Moon. Following, came hard work, sickness and sorrow as Lydia buried her only daughter one day following her birth in Iowa. As they continued to travel, they had two more children.

Lydia's little boys were six and three when they began the trek arriving in Salt Lake City 5 Oct 1850. Lydias home was in Salt Lake City. Here, Henry was ordained a High Priest and set apart as a Bishop by President Brigham Young on 21 Oct 1855. He held this office for fourteen years. Knowing the responsibilities and activities of any bishop and his wife, we see a period of unselfish service and work in the church for Lydia.

On 18 Mar 1856 Henry married Temperance Westwood as his second wife. She was much younger than Lydia. Lydia always treated her with love and kindness and was like a mother to her in teaching and helping her in many ways. Henry made a home for Temperance in Farmington but four of her children were born in Lydia's home in Salt Lake City. On 1 Jan 1860 Henry also married Mary Ann Thayne.

Lydia passed away 9 Jul 1868 at the early age of fifty-seven. Her youngest child married Alice Jane Pulley and they gave Lydia grandchildren.

TEMPERANCE WESTWOOD MOON

BIRTHDATE: 19 Aug 1839
Bromsgrove, Worchestershire,
England
DEATH: 21 Sep 1922
Farmington, Davis County, Utah
PARENTS: Joseph Westwood
Ann Webley
PIONEER: 10 Sep 1853
Jesse W. Crosby Wagon Train
SPOUSE: Henry Moon
MARRIED: 18 Mar 1856
Salt Lake City, Utah
DEATH: 14 Nov 1894
Farmington, Davis, Utah

CHILDREN:
Robert Henry, 17 May 1858
Joseph Hyrum, 23 Sep 1859
Hannah Temperance (King), 7 Oct 1861
Elnora (Hess), 9 Oct 1863
Rowane (Udy), 20 Dec 1866
Henry Moroni, 22 Mar 1868
Edmund, 21 Apr 1870
Phillip Westwood, 10 Aug 1872
Lelia Olive (Potter), 15 Oct 1874
Mercy Evaline (Udy), 2 Jan 1877
Louise Westwood (Moon), 24 Jun 1879
Albert, 14 Oct 1881
Franklin Everett, 19 Nov 1889

Temperance was born in England in 1839. Her family were early converts to the LDS church. Her grandmother left England first, alone and came to Nauvoo. The family never heard from her again. Early in the year of 1849, the Westwood family with some brothers and their eight children walked from Bromsgrove to Liverpool to board a sailing vessel for America. The crew said they would rather take Mormon passengers than anyone else because they never had any accidents with saints aboard. This ship sank on its way back to Liverpool. At the mouth of the Mississippi River the passengers were transferred to a steamer for the trip up the river to St. Louis, where they found an epidemic of Cholera Fever was raging. Their father Joseph died, next, the infant daughter and then the mother, followed by another child. Seven little children were left alone in the strange country. Temperance lived with a kind woman who gave her a foster home. Temperance's older sister Mercy, sixteen , obtained employment as a cook in the home of Roswell M. Field, father of Eugene Field, who grew up to become a famous poet. One day when Temperance was visiting her sister Mrs Field told the eleven year old girl, "I want you to stay here and take care of Eugene, who is getting to be a big boy." Temperance had the entire charge of Eugene, sleeping with him in the nursery and looking after him all day long.

In 1853, when Temperance was almost fourteen, she left the Field home in St. Louis to cross the plains with her brother in the Jesse W. Crosby Co. The oxen pulled the wagon and Temperance and her brother walked until a painful stone bruise on her heel allowed her to ride until it

broke and healed. Upon reaching the valley, the Westwoods first went to Springville. Here Temperance married Henry Moon 18 Mar 1886. He was the Bishop of the first ward in Salt Lake City from 1856 to 1870 and later Bishop of the Woodland Ward. Temperance and Henry became parents of thirteen children. He also had two other wives. Henry's first wife, Lydia was like a mother to Temperance and as she grew older they were like sisters. Lydia was to die a young woman and Temperance nursed her in her illness with loving care. Henry was twenty years older than Temperance. After Lydia's death, he married Mary Ann Thayne and moved her to Woodland. In 1888 Henry suffered a stroke which rendered him an invalid for the last six years of his life.

Temperance nursed him until his death 14 Nov 1894. She loved to read, raised a beautiful garden, had a sweet face, gentle voice and later, snowy white hair. She was a widow for twenty-seven years, passing away at age eighty-three. She was remembered by poet Eugene field as his "nurse" with love.

ALICE YOUNG MOORE

No
Photo
Available

BIRTHDATE: 23 May 1814
Lesbury, England
DEATH: 9 May 1884
Slaterville,Utah
PARENTS: James Young
Sarah Anderson
PIONEER: 5 Oct 1863
Wagon Train
SPOUSE: James Moore
MARRIED: 1838 England
DEATH: 11 Feb 1876
Hooper, Utah

CHILDREN:
Joseph, 17 Feb 1839
James I, 21 Jul 1840
James, 1 Jul 1842
Mary (Howell), 25 Nov 1845
John, 4 May 1848
Sarah (Smout), 20 Jun 1850
Thomas, 20 Oct 1853

Alice was born in England in 1814. Her girlhood days were spent there. She had but very little schooling, but learned to be a good cook. At age twenty-four, she married James Moore in England and was the mother of seven children, one dying young. They were converted to the LDS church by John Taylor and Joseph Stanford. They were both baptized in England, 5 Oct 1851.

They left England, 26 Mar 1863. When they got their clothes and things down to the ship it was so crowded they had to leave part of their clothing and put some in gunny sacks. Part of them were thrown into the ocean as they came. Two of their sons stayed in England. Two boys and two girls came to this country with them and also a niece.

They arrived in Salt Lake City on Oct 1863. They went to Ogden and lived on 28th street on Watson's Farm. James worked in Taylors mill. Then they moved to Newey's Farm and stayed until 1868, when they moved to Riverdale.

In 1871 they moved to Hooper to homestead land and-make their home. About this time, Alice's second son came from England. On 11 Feb 1876. James Moore died and buried in the Hooper cemetery. In 1877 Alice and Mathew Young and his three daughters came from England. Alice was of a charitable disposition and liked her friends to stay to tea.

She went to Slaterville to live with her youngest daughter Sarah Moore Smout, where she died 9 May 1884 and was buried in the Hooper cemetery. She was age almost seventy at her passing, having been a widow for eight years.

CLARISSA JANE DROLLINGER MOORE

BIRTHDATE: 12 Sep 1824
Springfield, Butler, Ohio
DEATH: 10 Jan 1905
Payson, Utah, Utah
PARENTS: Samuel Drollinger
Rachel Koch (Cook)
PIONEER: 17 Sep 1852
Thomas D. Howell Wagon Train
SPOUSE: John Harvey Moore
MARRIED: 6 Oct 1841
Nauvoo, Hancock, Illinois
DEATH: 15 Nov 1899
Payson, Utah, Utah

CHILDREN:
Melinda Rachel (Hancock Tyler), 6 Aug 1842
Rebecca Estella (Tanner), 13 Nov 1844
John Harvey, 28 Mar 1847
Clarissa Jane (Tanner), 7 Oct 1849
Sarah Francis (Wimmer), 28 Jan 1853
Samuel Drollinger, 2 May 1855
Annie Mary Bistle (Huish), 12 Mar 1857
Andrew Cook, 17 Oct 1859
Franklin Edward, 27 Apr 1862
George Barton, 8 Jan 1870

Clarissa Jane was born in Ohio, 1824. Her parents moved to Indiana when she was three. They were baptized into the LDS church 8 Jul 1831. In the fall of 1833, they moved to Missouri. They camped at Lafayette that winter on a farm her father bought. They then moved out on the Tabor Prairie. In June following, they moved to Clay County. Her father went to enter a piece of government land where he was taken sick and suffered until 16 Aug 1834 when he died, leaving her mother and his mother and six children, all sick. In Feb 1838, they moved to Caldwell County. Clarissa was in Far West at the time Joseph Smith was delivered up to the mob. They left 28 Feb 1839 and moved to Quincy, Illinois. She had to walk every step of the way through mud, rain and snow.

At age 17, Clarissa married John Harvey Moore at Nauvoo. She became a member of the Relief Socityy 1 Aug 1842. Her first child was born 6 Aug 1842. Her second child was born 13 Nov 1844, ten miles south of Nauvoo. In 1846 they left Illinois with the rest of the saints because of the mob. They stopped in Lee County, Iowa where their third child was born. In the spring of 1848 they moved to the Big Pidgeon, where John left her and the children in a tent and was gone four months in the Government Service. Their fourth child was born there in 1849. They left their home the first of Jun 1852. Clarissa drove a three horse team across the plains and arrived in Salt Lake City 27 Sep 1852. They went on to Payson, Utah County, where they permanently settled and had six more children.

In May 1856 John took a second wife. In Feb 1858, he took a third. John and Clarissa had their sealings and annointings at the Endowment House. Clarissa labored faithfully in the Relief Society for many years In 1873, she went to Salt Lake City and studied midwifery and was a practicing midwife afterward. In 1878, she was set apart under the hands of Joseph S. Tanner to the office of second Counselor to the President of Third District Relief Society Payson Second Ward. John passed away 15 Nov 1899, leaving Clarrissa a widow for five years. She passed away at age eighty, 10 Jan 1905. They are buried in the Payson Cemetery.

DIANNA HERRICK CLARK MOORE

No
Photo
Available

BIRTHDATE: 29 Sep 1832
Jackson Co., Missouri
DEATH: 8 Aug 1905
Ogden, Weber County, Utah
PARENTS: Lemual Herrick
Sally Judd Herrick
PIONEER: 12 Sep 1850
Aaron Johnson Co Wagon Train
SPOUSE: Isaac Clark
MARRIED: 10 Jun 1851
DEATH SP: 24 Jan 1854

CHILDREN:
Isaac Lemuel, 10 Sep 1853

SPOUSE II: David Moore
MARRIED: 7 Apr 1854
Ogden, Utah
DEATH SP: 26 Jan 1901
Ogden, WeberCo,Utah

CHILDREN:
Lester James, 25 Oct 1855
George Albert, 14 Mar 1858
Henry David, 24 Dec 1860
Clara Diana(Fronk/Martin), 5 Apr 1863
Parley Pratt, 14 Nov 1865
Kate Maybelle, 14 Feb 1870

Dianna was born in Missouri in 1832. She was the youngest of ten children. Her family were early members of the LDS church. Their story is the "Mormon" story. They left Kanesville, Iowa 12 Jun 1850 in the Aaron Johnson Co, arriving in Salt Lake City 12 Sep 1850. Her family settled Ogden, Utah. Her mother had died 17 Nov 1841 in Nauvoo and her father died 1 Sep 1861 in Ogden, Utah. At age eighteen, Dianna married Isaac Clark in Ogden. His other wife was Mary Lemmons. They made their home in Ogden, where they became parents of one son in 1853. Their happiness was short lived, as Isaac passed away 24 Jan 1854, leaving Dianna a widow at age twenty-two. She worked to support their young son and on 7 Apr 1854, she married David Moore in Salt Lake City. They made their home in Ogden, where they became parents of six. David Moore was also married to Susan Maria Vorce and Sarah Barker.

Dianna helped to construct dwelling places for her family both in Ogden and a three-year period in Ogden Valley. She also helped put in crops of wheat and corn. She helped put in a willow fence and helped construct adobe bricks by mixing mud with her feet. She was a very devoted mother, Diana was a very diligent worker in the LDS church. At the time of her death, she was President of the Relief Society of the Mound Fort Ward. David passed away 26 Jan 1901. Dianna passed away at age seventy-two, having been a widow for four years.

ty-three, Eunice married Samuel Moore. They became parents of nine children. When the missionaries brought the gospel into their lives, they embraced it wholeheartedly. They desired to be with the Saints. Leaving a comfortable home, and with Eunice large with child, they journeyed west. While camping in Van Buren County, Iowa, their fourth child was born. They were living in Nauvoo, for the fifth and sixth children. In Nauvoo, they were rebaptized on 15 Aug 1841. On 2 Jan 1846, both Eunice and Samuel had their endowments and were sealed on 30 Jan 1846.

On 15 Jun 1847 a camp was organized to come to Salt Lake City. It was the first hundred, Daniel Spencer was Captain. The third Ten with Elijah K. Fuller as Capt and William M. Lemon as clerk was the company the Moore family was listed with. They left Winter Quarters 17 Jun and arrived in Salt Lake City 24 Sep 1847. Eunice was once again with child. On 7 Mar 1848, she gave birth to twin girls. Both died young.

With the commandment to practice polygamy, Samuel took a second wife, seventeen-year-old Mary Caroline Hawk on 7 Apr 1850. Five children were born to them, three dying as children. Eunice had one more child, a son who died at age four and a half. Records also show that Samuel had two more wives without more children. Samuel passed away 11 Oct 1883 in Provo. Eunice passed away at age eighty-three in Scipio, Millard County, having been a widow for six years.

EUNICE SIBLEY BLISS MOORE

BIRTHDATE: 2 Mar 1807
Concord, Essex, Vermont
DEATH: 4 Apr 1890
Scipio, Millard County, Utah
PARENTS: Stephen Bliss
Ester Wait Bliss
PIONEER: 24 Sep 1847
Daniel Spencer Wagon Train
SPOUSE: Samuel Moore
MARRIED: 7 Apr 1830
DEATH: 11 Oct 1883/21 Oct 1882
Provo, Utah County, Utah

CHILDREN:
Ann, 2/6 Dec 1830
Sophronia (Martin), 17 May 1832
Stephen Bliss, 29 Feb 1836
Harriet (Kelly), 17 Apr 1840
Russell, 1842
Bernice Sibley, 1844
Eunice twin, 7 Mar 1848
Ester twin, 7 Mar 1848
Samuel, 18 May 1851

Eunice Sibley was born in Vermont in 1807. She was the first child born to her parents, followed by seven brothers, and two sisters. When she was seven, her parents moved to Orange, Franklin, Mass. It was there, at age twen-

MARY ANN DAVIS MOORE

BIRTHDATE: 20 May 1832
Wolverhampton, Staffordshire, Eng.
DEATH: 23 Dec 1870
Heber City, Wasatch, Utah
PARENTS: Thomas Davis
Sophia Peers (Pearce)
PIONEER: 23 Sep 1861
Joseph W.Young, Ansel P. Harmon
SPOUSE: George Sharrett Moore
MARRIED: 11 Aug 1851
St Peter,Wolverh
DEATH: 9 Dec 1923
Utah County, Utah

CHILDREN:
Olivia Sophia (Bancroft), 31 Aug 1852
Caroline Eliza, 14 aug 1854
Henry Thomas, Dec 1856
George Cagnight, 8 Jan 1858
Joseph Lorenzo, 4 Jul 1860
William Davis, 1 Jan 1862
Albert Davis, 4 Feb 1864
Anne Eva (Jennings), 6 Aug 1865
Warren Davis, 1 Jan 1869
Samuel Davis, 13 Apr 1870

Mary Ann was born in England in 1832 She joined the LDS church and was baptized 30 Jul 1850. At age nineteen, she married George Sharrett Moore in Wolverhampton, in the Collegiate Church which was over six hungred years old. Two daughters were born in Willenhall, Staffordshire, England.

The Moore family sailed from Liverpool 18 Feb 1856 on the ship "Caravan" landing in New York 27 Mar 1856. They lived in New York for five years. Three of their children, two boys and a daughter died and are buried in the Greenwood Cemetery.

Mary Ann, husband George, daughter Olivia and son George Cagnight walked across the plains while her husband drove the team and wagon for the company. They left Florence, Nebraska 11 Jul 1861 with the Joseph W. Young Company under Ansel P. Harmon arriving in Salt Lake City 23 Sep 1861. They lived in Salt Lake for two years and then moved to Provo. Mary Ann received her endowments and was sealed to her husband 25 Feb 1865. She received her Patriarchal Blessing 20 May 1832.

They moved to Heber City, Utah where son Samuel was born.

Mary Ann's health began to fail. She died 23 Dec 1870, leaving George with five small children to care for. She was buried in the Provo City Cemetery, 26 Dec 1870. George married Agnes Ann Bancroft 15 May 1871. They had eleven children and Agnes raised Mary Ann's along with her own.

SARAH BARKER MOORE

BIRTHDATE: 7 Aug 1829
Diss, Norfolk, England
DEATH: 12 Jul 1908
 Ogden, Weber, Utah
PARENTS: Frederick Barker
Ann Blygh Barker
PIONEER: 1 Oct 1849
Allen Taylor Wagon Company
SPOUSE: David Moore
MARRIED: 6 Sep 1850
Salt Lake City, Salt Lake, Utah
DEATH SP: 19 Jan 1901
North Ogden, Weber, Utah

CHILDREN:
David Moulton, 1 Jul 1851
Mary Ann, 17 Mar 1853
Joseph Byron, 9 Feb 1855
Ellen Louisa, 26 Apr 1858
Franklin, 22 Nov 1861
Leonard, 2 Jun 1863

Sarah's parents, two sisters, and one brother sailed for America on March 23, 1830 on the ship, New Brunswick. They located in Le Rayville, Jefferson, New York and later moved to Watertown. While living in Watertown, the family joined the LDS Church. They moved to Council Bluffs on June 8, 1849 where they met with a large company of saints who were preparing to move to Salt Lake Valley. They traveled in the same company with David Moore,

Sarah's future husband. They arrived in Salt Lake Valley on October 1, 1849.

The family stopped that first winter in a group of cabins near the junction of Ogden and Weber River. In the spring of 1850, they moved cabins and all their belongings into Farrs Fort. On September 6, 1850, Sarah was married to David Moore by Brigham Young. Their first home was on Washington Avenue near 14th Street. She was a great lover of flowers, so this first home was made beautiful with her old fashioned flower garden. Later they moved into North Ogden. At the foot of the tall majestic mountains, they built the old rock farm house. She was very busy raising her six children. She still found time to work in her garden and cultivate beautiful flowers. She lived until she was seventy nine years of age and died on September 10, 1908.

SUSAN MARIAH VORCE MOORE

No
Photo
Available

BIRTHDATE: 5 Feb 1810
Winsor County, Vermont
DEATH: 2 Mar 1882
Mound Fort, Weber County,Utah
PARENTS: Warren Vorce
Amanda
PIONEER: 20 Oct 1849
Allen Taylor Wagon Company
SPOUSE: David Moore
MARRIED: 19 Aug 1839
Eardley, Ottawa Co. Canada
DEATH SP: 26 Jan 1901
North Ogden, Weber County, Utah

CHILDREN:
Catherine Smith, 17 Nov 1842

Susan Maria was born in Vermont in 1810. At age twenty-nine, she married David Moore. Their only child was born in 1842, while they were living in Addison, Vermont. They were converted to the LDS church and joined the Saints. She witnessed and patiently shared the sufferings, persecution and expulsion of the Saints from Nauvoo. She developed self-reliance, patience, fortitude and faith in God during the early days in Utah. Left Kanesville, Iowa 12 Jul 1849 and arrived in Salt Lake City 20 Oct 1849 with the Allen Taylor Wagon Train.

Susan Mariah presided over the Relief Society of the Mound Fort Ward in Weber County (Ogden) for many years. One of only three women to accompany twenty-seven men, members of the LDS church who were called to establish the Salmon River Mission. Susan was one of the missionaries and although it was one of the hardest experiences of her life, she was always patient and willing to do her part in teaching the gospel to the Indians.

David and Susan Mariah lived the law of Polygamy. He married Sarah Barker and Diana Herrick. She was kind and helpful throughout. She passed away 2 Mar 1882 at age seventy-two in Mound Fort, Weber County, Utah. David passed away 26 Jan 1901 in North Ogden, Utah.

CATHERINE JARMAN MORGAN

No
Photo
Available

BIRTHDATE: 12 Sep 1830
Disserth, Radnor, Wales
DEATH: 25 Mar 1873
Tooele, Tooele County, Utah
PARENTS: John Jarman
Margaret Price Jarman
PIONEER: 2 Oct 1856
Edward Bunker Handcart Co.
SPOUSE: William Samuel Morgan
MARRIED: 20 Jun 1856
Iowa City, Iowa
DEATH: 5 May 1877
Tooele, Tooele, Utah

CHILDREN:
Sarah Elizabeth, 26 Nov 1857
Margaret Catherine, 1 Jul 1859
William David, 19 Nov 1861
Evan Samuel, 27 Mar 1863
Annie Arbella, 23 May 1866
Thomas Vaughan, 1 Sep 1868
John Franklin, 23 Oct 1870
Daniel Osborn, 20 Mar 1873

Catherine's father was a yeoman and an agricultural laborer. All the men in the area knew coal mining which was a very important occupation to the people of Wales. Catherine became baptized as a member of the LDS Church in January 1853. On April 18, 1856, she sailed with her brother and his family on the sailing vessel, "Samuel Curling." Catherine met William Samuel Morgan on the boat. They fell in love by the time the boat landed in New York. They came by rail to St. Louis, then by steamboat up the Mississippi River to Iowa City. They were married just three days before they began their trek across the plains. They were fitted out with handcarts and under the leadership of Edward Bunker, they pushed their handcart across the plains. Catherine pushed a blind man, whose name was Giles, most of the way in a handcart. If anyone became ill, they had to ride the handcarts. They arrived in Winter Quarters on July 19, 1856 and stayed until July 30. Then they pushed on and arrived in Salt Lake Valley on October 2, 1856.

Catherine and William Morgan settled in Rush Valley in the small town called Shambip, which is now Tooele, Utah. The men and women worked for potatoes, wheat, butter, etc. They didn't have very many worldly goods, but they were most contented with what was theirs. Catherine became the mother to eight children. She and William bought a large piece of land in Shambip. William's brother, Evan, helped them to build a small adobe home on this land. Catherine died of childbirth with her last child at the age of forty three. William continued to care for the family, but also met his death at age forty eight while digging in an old well. The children were put into the care of relatives by the courts. Caroline and William are both buried in Tooele, Utah Cemetery.

CECELIA LEWIS WILLIAMS MORGAN

No
Photo
Available

BIRTHDATE: 1 Mar 1803
Tredegar, Glamorganshire, Wales
DEATH: 19 Aug 1888
Mt. Pleasant, Sanpete, Utah
PARENTS: Jenkin Lewis
Cecelia Lewis
PIONEER: Between 1850 and 1852
SPOUSE: William Williams
MARRIED: 21 Nov 1825
Merthyr Tydfil, Wales
DEATH SP: 1831
Merthyr Tydfil, Wales

CHILDREN:
James, 1 May 1826
William Jenkin, 29 Apr 1828
Elizabeth, 2 May 1831

SPOUSE: Morgan Morgan
MARRIED: 16 Feb 1833
Merthyr Tydfil, Wales
DEATH SP: 12 Sep 1878
Oneida County, Idaho

CHILDREN:
Barbara, 14 Dec 1833
Mary, 16 Dec 1835
Sarah, 1838
Morgan, Jr., 1840
Thomas William, 28 Feb 1842

Cecelia was the daughter of a farmer. On November 21, 1825, she married William Williams and to this union were born three children. James probably died young since he is not with his mother in the 1841 census. Her husband, William, died after their third child was born. On the 16th of February, 1833, Cecelia married Morgan Morgan and they had five children. In the 1840's, missionaries from the LDS Church were proselyting throughout the British Isles. Morgan and Cecelia embraced the gospel and were anxious to join the saints in America. On February 25, 1840, the family consisting of Morgan, Cecelia, Elizabeth Williams, Barbara, Mary, Sarah, and Thomas sailed from Liverpool aboard the ship, Buena Vista. They arrived in New Orleans on April 19, 1849. It is likely the Morgans didn't start for the Salt Lake Valley until 1851.

Following their arrival in the Salt Lake Valley, the Morgans settled in Tooele. Times were hard, food was scarce, grasshoppers had destroyed most of the crops, living conditions were less than desirable. When Brigham Young asked Peter Maughan to explore Cache Valley as a suitable site for a new settlement, Morgan Morgan accompanied him to the Valley. Due to some disappointment, Morgan changed his mind and the family remained in Tooele. In 1870, they moved to Cherry Creek, Oneida, Idaho and lived there until Morgan died in 1878. Then Cecelia returned to Tooele and lived with her son, Thomas. The two of them did temple work in the St. George Temple for several members of their family. Later, Cecelia moved to Mt. Pleasant, Utah to live with her daughter, Elizabeth Williams Winters who had a large home on Main Street. They hauled water from the creek in large buckets. They made soap and sold it for additional income. Cecelia liked to make down pillows and would patiently gather the down to fill them. She died and is buried in the Mt. Pleasant Cemetery.

CLARISSA ADELAIDE BAXTER MORGAN

No Photo Available

BIRTHDATE: 22 Aug 1849
Independence Rock, Nebraska
DEATH: 10 Jan 1890
Wellington, Utah
PARENTS: Zimri Harford Baxter
Eunice Seavey Baxter
PIONEER: Dec 1849
SPOUSE: Daniel A. Morgan
MARRIED: 9 Nov 1867
Salt Lake Endowment House
DEATH SP: 6 Oct 1902
Wellington, Utah

CHILDREN:
Daniel Seavy, 5 Sep 1868
Clarissa Adelaid, 25 Sep 1870
William Henry, 14 Nov 1872
Eunice Abigail, 28 Feb 1874 (died 9 months)
Martha McGill, 28 Feb 1876
Zimri Harford,, Jr. 2 Jul 1879
John Athos, 8 Jul 1881 (died an infant)
Edward Nelson, 29 Jun 1882
Joseph Albert, 11 Sep 1884
James Oscar, 28 Jan 1887
Ira Roy, 12 Oct 1889

Clarissa Adelaide was a twin to Charles Albert Baxter. They were number eleven and twelve in their family. Their family had experienced much hardship and persecution at the hands of the mobs in Illinois. They were driven with the rest of the saints across the Mississippi River into Iowa where preparations were made to cross the plains to the Rocky Mountains. The Baxter family arrived in the Salt Lake Valley in December of 1849.

The Baxters settled in Big Cottonwood where Clarissa's father built a flour mill on the Cottonwood Stream. He also farmed there. When Clarissa was nearly two years old, her family moved to settle Salt Creek, now Nephi, in Juab County. Clarissa attended the schools the town founders provided. Her mother taught her the ways of pioneer home-making. Some of her chores were spinning and carding wool, coloring the cloth with herbs, knitting stockings, etc. They suffered through the war with the Indians in 1855, then the war with the grasshoppers. She married Daniel A. Morgan in the Salt Lake Endowment House. After their marriage, they moved to various towns to help the southern area of Utah. Wherever Clarissa lived, she made many friends. She was diligent in church activi-

ties, especially in Relief Society. She served as president of the Relief Society. She shared her talents with the other sisters. Her home was made cozier and more comfortable with her handwork of doilies, carpets, rugs, and lovely quilts. Clarissa and her husband later moved to Wellington where they made their home. She died on 10 Jan 1890 leaving a family of nine living children, the youngest only a few months old. She was only forty-one at the time of her death. Her husband died at the age of fifty-eight in 1902.

ELIZABETH (BETSY) DAVIS MORGAN

No Photo Available

BIRTHDATE: 3 Aug 1793
Builth, Brecon, Wales
DEATH: 27 Dec 1855
Brigham City, Utah
PARENTS: David Davis
Jane Evans Davis
PIONEER: Summer 1854
SPOUSE: William Morgan
MARRIED: 29 Jan 1820
Cardiff, Gla. Wales
DEATH SP: 4 Oct 1861
Brigham City, Utah

CHILDREN:
Ann, 1819
Mary, 5 Nov 1821
Jane, Apr 1823
Elizabeth, 3 Sep 1825
Sarah, 1827
David, 8 Feb 1829
William, 1831
William, 2 Aug 1833
Hannah, 1835
Sarah Ann, 10 Jun 1837
Susan, 19 Oct 1840

Elizabeth (Betsy) Davis Morgan was a year older than her husband. They had eleven children. Betsy emigrated to Utah with her husband when she was sixty years old. They brought with them their younger children, David at age twenty three, Hannah age twenty, Sarah Ann age sixteen, and Susan age fourteen. They crossed the Plains without one quarrel. As soon as they arrived in the valley, they joined a married daughter, Mary, in Brigham City. Elizabeth (Betsy) died a year after her arrival in Utah.

HANNAH TURNER MORGAN

BIRTHDATE: 12 Mar 1814
Hall Green, Staffordshire,
England
DEATH: 3 Jun 1883
Fairfield, Utah, Utah
PARENTS: William Turner
Hannah Smith Turner
PIONEER: 22 Aug 1861
Ira Eldredge Wagon Company
SPOUSE: David Morgan
MARRIED: 1832
DEATH: 6 Oct 1890
Grouse Creek, Utah

CHILDREN:
Mary, 19 Aug 1833
Olive, 3 Jun 1835
Olive, 29 Jun 1840
Jesse, 23 Jan 1843
David Jr., 25 Feb 1845
Agatha, 30 Mar 1850
Amanda, 27 Apr 1852
Clara Eudora, 4 May 1855
Benjamin Llewellyn, 20 Dec 1859

Hannah was born in Hall Green, Sedgely Parrish, Staffordshire, England. She married David Morgan and nine children were born to this union. Hannah and her mother, Hannah Smith Turner, both joined the LDS Church about 1852. Her mother was living with her at the time they joined the church. As soon as she was baptized, she started saving money to bring her family to Zion. After her mother died, Hannah moved to Broadwaters in 1855. Her husband still was not a member of the church and he discouraged her from emigrating. Finally, Hannah sailed from Liverpool with her husband and children, Jesse, David, Amanda, and Agatha. They sailed on the ship, "Underwriter," on April 23, 1861. The ship was crowded and they had to live on hard sea biscuits, corn beef, and salt pork. They arrived in New York on May 22, 1861. They traveled by rail to Florence, Nebraska and from there they crossed the plains in the Ira Eldredge Wagon Company.

When they arrived in Utah, Captain Eldredge invited them to his home for bread and milk. They camped on the Eighth Ward Square where the Federal Building now stands. A friend of Hannah's came and took them to his house until they could get a house to live in. Her family moved to Fairfield in 1863 where they battled grasshoppers that fall and again in 1867. Her life was very hard. In her later years, she became disaffected and apostatized from the church. After her death, her daughter, Amanda, was strongly impressed by Hannah's spirit until her baptism and temple work had been redone.

HELEN MELVINA GROESBECK MORGAN

BIRTHDATE: 7 Feb 1852
Springfield, Illinois
DEATH: 15 Jun 1930
Oakland, Alameda, California
PARENTS: Nicholas Groesbeck
Elizabeth Thompson Groesbeck
PIONEER: 1 Oct 1856
John Banks Wagon Company
SPOUSE: John Hamilton Morgan
MARRIED: 24 Oct 1868
Salt Lake Endowment House
DEATH SP: 14 Aug 1894
Preston, Idaho

CHILDREN:
Helen Melvina, 19 Jan 1870
Elizabeth, 7 Oct 1872
Eliza Ann, 8 Feb 1875
Ruth, 4 Oct 1878
John, 12 Feb 1881
Flora, 19 Sep 1882
Nicholas Groesbeck, 9 Nov 1884
Gail Hamilton, 3 Apr 1888
Bessie, 11 Jan 1891
Garrard Earl, 8 Oct 1892
John Hamilton, 7 Feb 1894

Melvina (Mellie) was only four years old when her parents left Illinois for the Great Salt Lake Valley. The thing that seemed to impress her the most were all of the buffalo. She often talked about how frightened she was of them. They traveled with the John Banks Wagon Company as they crossed the plains. They arrived in the Great Salt Lake Valley on October 1, 1856.

When she was fifteen, her parents enrolled her in a commercial college. Her father owned the property on which the college was located and had rented it to a young convert named John Morgan. She was only sixteen when she and John were married. Mellie was a beautiful seamstress. She made by hand many beautiful christening outfits. She also crocheted many shawls and did beautiful hand work. Her father arranged to have a baby grand piano shipped across the plains and Mellie became a wonderful pianist. Her piano is now exhibited in the Daughters of Utah Pioneer's Museum. While John served in the mission field off and on for fifteen years, Mellie was raising their family. She had little time for other callings. She stood beside her husband in every call he had, not only while he was in the mission field, but many other church and stake callings. Her parents died in 1884 and left her a substantial sum. John convinced Mellie to build a hotel which was called Morgan Hotel. They had mortgaged their lovely home and other properties in order to build the hotel. It had been in operation two years when the "Cleveland Panic" hit. John passed away in 1894 leaving Mellie homeless and penniless with five children to support. She used her skills as a seamstress to support her family. She was a wonderful daughter, wife, mother, sister, and grandmother.

MARTHA MATILDA McGILL NELSON MORGAN

BIRTHDATE: 19 Nov 1824
Midlden, Ivemess, Scotland
DEATH: 26 Dec 1906
Levan, Juab, Utah
PARENTS: Edward Nelson
Catherine Banks Nelson
PIONEER: 1851
SPOUSE: William Morgan
MARRIED: 23 Apr 1841
Hallbath, Fife, Scotland
DEATH SP: 19 Nov 1876
Levan, Juab, Utah

CHILDREN:
Catherine Banks, 27 May 1842
Daniel, 16 Jul 1844
Agnes Beverage, 20 Aug 1846
Jane
Mary Ann Elizabeth, 30 Sep 1853
William Thomas, 2 Mar 1856
Edward Nelson, 1 Oct 1857
John Athos, 22 Jan 1860
Martha Etta, 24 Aug 1862
James Nathaniel, 2 Oct 1864
Ira Robert, 25 Feb 1868

Martha was the daughter of Edward Nelson and Catherine Banks Nelson. When she was sixteen years old, she married William Morgan. He had been taught to work and help in the fields. As he became older, he worked in the coal mines. Martha and William heard the message the humble missionaries brought to the area. They were baptized into the LDS Church in the year of 1847. Because they suffered much ridicule from their friends and family, they became anxious to emigrate to America. On July 13, 1849, William, Martha, and their four children crossed the ocean. After landing at New Orleans, the Saints were loaded on sail boats which were tugged up the river to Kanesville, Iowa. They were provided crude housing to wait until the following spring to cross the plains. In the spring they joined a wagon company and suffered fatigue, overexertion, and weakness due to lack of food. It is not known which of the companies the Morgan family traveled with.

Shortly after their arrival in the Salt Lake Valley, they were sent to help settle Nephi, Utah in the spring of 1851. Because William had mining skills, his family was sent to the Iron Mission in 1851 where he helped with the mining of iron ore. The Morgans lived in Cedar City until 1859 when they were called to move to help establish the church and community in Beaver. In 1861, they moved to Chicken Creek in Juab County. The soil was too poor, so they moved east to what is now known as Levan. Martha was so glad to be able to stay in one place. She did her part as a pioneer mother and home maker. She did her part to help settle these different areas. She supported her husband in his church and civic callings. She enjoyed the association of her neighbors and was a friend to all. She was widowed for twenty years before she died at the age of eighty-two.

MARTHA WILLIAMS HOWELL MORGAN

BIRTHDATE: 8 Jun 1813
Cefn, Pennor, Aberdare, Glamorgan,
South Wales
DEATH: 27 Sep 1879
Wellsville, Utah
PARENTS: Reese Williams
Alice Lewis
PIONEER: Oct 1852
Wagon Train
SPOUSE: William Howell
MARRIED: 26 Sep 1829
Aberdare, Glamorganshire, So Wales
DEATH SP: 21 Nov 1891
Kanesville(Council Bluffs) Iowa

CHILDREN:
Ann (Jones/Burt), 23 Jul 1840
William, 19 Apr 1843
Martha Ann, 19 Jun 1845
Reese, 9 Sep 1848
Louis Williams, 20 Jun 1851

SPOUSE II: William Morgan
MARRIED: 13 Nov 1855(Divorced)
DEATH SP: Mar 1889
Willard, Box Elder, Utah

CHILDREN:
Edmund, abt 1855
Joseph Williams, 17 Feb 1857

Martha was born in South Wales in 1813. Her parents were wealthy as they owned coal and iron-stone mines. They gave each of their children a regular monthly allowance. This allowance helped to keep Martha's husband on his mission to France. Martha, at age sixteen, was married to William Howell, a Baptist Minister. They became interested in the LDS Church from a missionary, Dan Jones. After being baptized, William was sent on his mission and Martha used her allowance to support him, but her father was very angry and was going to exclude her from his will. He passed away before this could be accomplished.

4 Mar 1851, the Howells sailed from Liverpool on the ship "Olympus" landing in New Orleans. They went by steamer "Atlantic" to St. Louis arriving 8 May 1851. They made their home at Kanesville (Council Bluffs) for the winter. After a month at Kanesville, Martha gave birth to the last of their five children. During the winter, they prepared to go west the following year and busily prepared for the trip. Tragedy struck 21 Nov 1851, as Martha's husband passed away. Griefstricken though she was, this did not stop her from this journey. In the Spring of 1852 she started across the plains in the company with others, and with her four living children. Again tragedy struck. One morning as

they started, the wagon ran over Henry. He had got under the wagon to rest in the cool tall grass. No one knew this. After a few days of suffering, although Martha did all that was possible under the circumstances, he died and Martha had the sorrow of having to bury him by the trail as they traveled on with the others. They reached Salt Lake City in Oct 1852. After living in Salt Lake City for eighteen months, she and her three children moved to Brigham City.

At age forty-two, she married William Morgan, a widower with a son, Edward. They married 13 Nov 1855 in Willard, Box Elder, Utah. They became parents of two sons. This marriage ended in divorce. Martha raised her children on her own. Later she moved to Wellsville, where she lived out her days. While living at Wellsville, Brigham Young lent her the money to return to England to obtain her money from her father's estate. As she returned to America, she paid the way for thirteen converts to come to Salt Lake City.

Martha died 27 Sep 1879 at age sixty-six. She was always active in the Church, showing great faith and endurance in times of stress and trials. She was continually helping those in need. Hers was a true spirit of a Saint.

CYNTHIA ABIAH BRADLEY MORLEY

BIRTHDATE: 14 Sep 1833
Clarence, Erie, New York
DEATH: 11 Mar 1926
Price, Carbon, Utah
PARENTS: Thomas J.Bradley
Elizabeth Kroll Bradley
PIONEER: 21 Sep 1848
Brigham Young Wagon Co
SPOUSE: Isaac Morley
MARRIED: 3 Oct 1851
Manti, Sanpete, Utah
DEATH: 21 May 1908
Moroni, Sanpete, Utah

CHILDREN:
George Franklin, 30 Sep 1852
Thomas Jefferson, 12 Feb 1854
Betsey Abiah, 3 Jan 1855
Lucy Amanda, 20 Dec 1857
Theressa Arthursa, 24 Apr 1859
Lena Margretta, 29 Apr 1861
Arletta, 15 Feb 1863
Isaac, Jr., 7 Apr 1865
Amarillis, 20 Jan 1867
Daniel Henrie, 3 Oct 1868
Evelyn, 20 Aug 1870
William Alfred, 21 May 1872
Heber Chase, 28 Feb 1874
Ann Mary, 21 Feb 1876
Son, 20 Feb 1877
Jerome Bonaparte, 26 Mar 1878

Cynthia's father died before she was born. Her mother married his younger brother, George Washington Bradley who raised the children as his own. Cynthia joined the LDS Church at the age of ten and along with her family, moved to Nauvoo. They lived on Joseph Smith's farm and rented from him. She vividly remembered the mob taking Joseph and Hyrum away, and saw Brother Richards bring the bodies back to their loved ones. She was fourteen years old at the time. Their family was driven from Nauvoo and they came across the plains with the Brigham Young Company. They arrived in the Salt Lake Valley on 21 Sep 1848.

Her family and about fifty other families were called to settle the Sanpitch Valley. The site of Manti was selected as the frontier town of central and southern Utah. The first camp was made on November 22, 1849. She married Isaac Morley. They were the second couple to be married in Manti. They were the parents of sixteen children. The large family she raised was accomplishment enough for this good woman, but along with this challenge came the many hardships and trials experienced on this mission. They suffered hard cold winters, hunger, sickness, blazing trails, and Indian problems. They were called to help settle Moroni. Besides raising her own family, she went among the sick acting as a doctor. She was the only midwife in the area. After her husband's death in 1908, Cynthia lived until she was ninety two years old and met death in Price, Utah. She was buried in Moroni Cemetery beside her husband.

HANNAH B. FINCH MERRIAM MORLEY

BIRTHDATE: 19 Mar 1811
Woodbridge, Fairfield, Connecticut
DEATH: 16 Apr 1874
Manti, Sanpete, Utah
PARENTS: Daniel Finch
Mary Blakesley Finch
PIONEER: 21 Sep 1848
Brigham Young Wagon Co.
SPOUSE: Edwin Parker Merriam
MARRIED: 5 Nov 1831
DEATH: Sep 1842

CHILDREN:
Amasa Edwin, 25 Oct 1832
Joseph Newell, 13 Feb 1838
George Francis, 20 Aug 1841

SPOUSE II: Isaac Morley
MARRIED: 1844
Nauvoo, Hancock, Illinois
DEATH: 21 Jul 1864
Fairview, Sanpete, Utah

CHILDREN:
Joseph Lamoni, 15 Jul 1845
Simeon Thomas, 12 Jun 1849
Mary Lenore, 26 Mar 1852

When Hannah was twenty years old, she married Edwin Parker Merriam who was a farmer from Litchfield, Connecticut. They moved to New Hartford, New York where their first son Amasa was born. They became converted to the LDS Church and joined the exodus of saints to the Kirtland, Ohio area where they were active church members and helped in building the Kirtland Temple. Hannah's second son, Joseph, was born in Kirtland and shortly thereafter, they decided to move to Missouri and began making preparations to travel with the "Kirtland Camp" which left Kirtland on Saturday, July 7, 1838. About two months later, the baby died and was buried where they camped in Indiana. The family arrived at Adam-Ondi-Ahman on October 4, 1838 and farmed almost two years before persecution drove them to Illinois. They settled in Springfield, Illinois, where Hannah gave birth to George Francis. Early in 1842, their family moved to Nauvoo where her baby, George, died and five weeks later, her husband died. All she had left was her ten year old son.

In 1844, Hannah became the second wife of Isaac Morley, Patriarch to the LDS Church. They were endowed and sealed to Isaac in the Nauvoo Temple. She gave birth to another son, but he also died and was buried in Nauvoo. Hannah traveled with the Saints to Winter Quarters, Iowa where she gave birth to another son, Simeon. They crossed the plains in the Brigham Young Wagon Company and arrived in the Salt Lake Valley on September 21, 1848. In the following spring, her husband had been called by Brigham Young to lead a group of 224 people to settle Manti, Utah. They arrived in mid-November and spent a very cold, hard winter. Hannah's last child was born in Manti. Hannah was a good mother, a loyal wife, and a faithful daughter of her Heavenly Father through all the trials and adversity in her life. She remained in Manti for the rest of her life and died at the age of sixty three.

NANCY ANN BACHE BUCHANAN MORLEY

No Photo Available

BIRTHDATE: 25 Feb 1790
Lexington, Fayette, Kentucky
DEATH: 17 Aug 1884
Manti, Sanpete, Utah
PARENTS: Harmon Bache
Martha Bache
PIONEER: 27 Sep 1852
Thomas D. Howell Wagon Co.
SPOUSE: John Buchanan
MARRIED: 12 Apr 1812
Lexington, Kentucky
DEATH SP: 1839
Lima, Adams, Illinois

CHILDREN:
Jane, 1813
Elizabeth, 1 Jul 1815
Lorenzo Dow, 14 Jul 1817
Emmeline, 1 Mar 1820
Catherine, 1822 (died age 15)
John, 25 Jan 1825
Mary Ann, 1 Aug 1827
Eleanora, 1828 (died age 10)

Archibald Waller Overton, 9 Feb 1830
Martha Maria, 2 Mar 1833

SPOUSE II: Isaac Morley
MARRIAGE: 22 Jan 1846
Nauvoo Temple, Nauvoo, Hancock, Illinois
DEATH: 24 Jun 1865
Fairview, Sanpete, Utah
CHILDREN: None

Nancy Ann was raised in Lexington, Kentucky where she was born and later married. She and her husband, John Buchanan made their home there. In 1830, Nancy, John, and their family of nine children moved to Tazewell County, Illinois where their tenth child was born. It was at that time, the LDS Missionaries introduced them to the LDS Church and were baptized in 1835. Two years later, she and her husband joined the saints in Caldwell, Missouri where they endured much suffering. Nancy Ann saw her husband arrested in November of 1838 and had to nurse him the best she could after his release. She helped to get her children and sick husband across the Mississippi River back into Illinois and to Lima, Adams County where they made a new home. John died in 1839 in Lima. Again in 1845, persecution increased, so the family moved into Nauvoo where they could be with the Saints.

On January 22, 1846, Nancy Ann was married to Isaac Morley, a very good friend of her husband. Even though she was married to Isaac, she maintained her own home. In February 1846, the mobs forced the saints from Nauvoo. Nancy and her younger children crossed into Iowa. They made their way to Mt. Pisgah where they remained while her son, John, went with the Mormon Battalion. As soon as John returned, Nancy had the family ready and they crossed the plains with the Howell Company on September 13, 1852. Almost immediately, they were advised by President Brigham Young to travel south and help build up the settlement in Manti. Nancy's first home in Utah was very primitive, but she succeeded in making it a "haven of peace" for her family. Though they had little food that winter, she realized the Indians were hungry, suffering and in need, so they shared their scanty food supply with them. Nancy took an active part in the church and served in many capacities. She was also very interested in the civic and community affairs of Manti.

DORTHEA MARIE JULIA JACOBSEN (JORGENSEN) MORRELL

BIRTHDATE: 16 Jan 1832
Kirkesoby, Fyn, Denmark
DEATH: 11 Nov 1913
Fremont, Wayne County, Utah
PARENTS: Jacob Jorgensen
Gertrude Marie Hansen Jorgensen
PIONEER: 12 Sep 1863
John R. Young Wagon Company
SPOUSE: William Wilson Morrell
MARRIED: 16 Apr 1864
Salt Lake Endowment House
DEATH SP: 14 Jan 1907
Fremont, Wayne County, Utah

CHILDREN:
Carl Rudolph Hoist, 26 Nov 1858
William Henry, 27 Nov 1866
George, 4 Jul 1869
Hyrum, 1 Feb 1871

Dorthea embraced the gospel and was baptized a member of the LDS Church on December 13, 1860. She had a burning desire to emigrate to Zion. She was with a group of saints who left Denmark on April 23, 1863. They traveled by rough, simple conveyances until they reached England. From Liverpool, they sailed on the ship, "John J. Boyd." After twenty nine days at sea, they landed in New York Harbor on June 1, 1863. There they boarded a train which took them to St. Joseph and from there they sailed up the Missouri River to Florence, Nebraska.

Dorthea Marie and her small son, Charles Rudolph Holst, joined the John R. Young Wagon Company to cross the Plains to the Salt Lake Valley. Upon arrival in Great Salt Lake Valley, Dorthea and her son were alone without relatives or sponsorship. Single people were assigned to the custody of a bishop. On April 16, 1864, she was married to William Wilson Morrell as his third wife. She was married and sealed to him at the Endowment House by Heber C. Kimball.

William and his families were called to settle Kamas Valley. In 1876, he moved his family to Rabbit Valley, Wayne County. They lived at the sawmill for several years, then moved back down to Fremont and settled on a bend of the Fremont River and made a lovely home. Being away from the populace of Salt Lake Valley, Julia had to depend upon what she could raise, make, or obtain from the land to provide for her family's needs. They had plenty of milk, cream, butter, cheese. They raised their own grain. She gathered herbs in the fall to use for winter. She made her own starch for clothing from potatoes. She had one hundred laying hens. She had her own garden and was well known for her delicious bread and Danish dumplings. She washed and carded wool from their sheep and spun it into yarn and made their own clothing. She dried gooseberries and sold them for five cents a quart.

Julia was a very religious woman and donated a large amount to the building of the Manti Temple. She spent her later years doing a great deal of genealogy and temple work for her relatives. Her children and grand children were a source of great joy and comfort to her.

SALINA JOHNSON MORRELL

BIRTHDATE: 26 Aug 1823/4
Dartford, Kent, England
DEATH: 12 Apr 1886
Logan, Cache, Utah
PARENTS: Thomas Johnson
Ann White Johnson
PIONEER: 22 Sep 1861
Samuel Wooley Wagon Co.
SPOUSE: Thomas Morrell
MARRIED: 18 Dec 1846
St. Philip's Church, Friars Mt.,
Bethnal Green, Middlesex,
England
DEATH SP:

CHILDREN:
Thomas, 25 Nov 1847
Henry, 14 Jul 1850
Salina, 11 Jan 1852
Caroline, 23 Nov 1854
Joseph, 11 Feb 1856
Heber George, 18 Jan 1858
Fredrick William, 18 Nov 1860
Walter Charles, 30 May 1863
Sarah Ann, 26 Jul 1865
Camilla Mary, 12 Mar 1868

Born and raised in England, Salina learned and followed the trade of making dress trimmings such as fancy buttons, tassels, fancy cords, and lace trimming. She married Thomas Morrell in the St. Phillips Church at Friars Mt, Bethnal Green, in Middlesex, England. Recognized as an expert in her field, she opened a millinery store in England. A successful business woman, Salina employed as many as 18 to 20 girls at a time. Many of the dress trimmings were made out of the silk which her husband produced. Salina also understood the use of herbs in treating medical problems and spent much time aiding the sick and giving service whenever needed.

After joining the LDS Church, the family left England on the sailing ship, Monarch of the Sea. The trip took six weeks on the ocean. Also traveling with the family were Salina's adopted daughter, Mary Ann Johnson; Mary Ann's husband, Joshua Jarier; Salina's sister-in-law, Sarah; and Sarah's husband, J. Curtis. Two of Salina's children had died as babies in England. Another of her children became ill on the journey and died between New York and Chicago and was buried by the train tracks. They traveled with the Samuel Wooley Wagon Company and arrived in the Salt Lake Valley on September 22, 1861.

They moved to Logan in Nov 1862. Salina wove hair nets from silk threads brought from London and supplied the local stores. She sewed shirts, overalls, and fancy baby hoods. At one time, she was the head dry-goods clerk at the United Order Store in Logan and did the buying for that department. She was quick to make friends with the local Indians. She was a faithful member of the LDS Church and a teacher in the Relief Society from the time it was organized in Logan. She was an officiator in the Logan Temple.

POLLY LUCINA SHEFFIELD TINDRAL MOORE MORREY

BIRTHDATE: 4 May 1837
Bethany/Batavia, Genesee, New York
DEATH: 12 Dec 1908
Kanosh, Millard County, Utah
PARENTS: Anson Sheffield
Maria Howe Mott
PIONEER: Sep 1852
Harmon Cutler Wagon Train
SPOUSE: Ferney Fold Tindral
MARRIED: Mar 1853
Payson, Utah, Utah
DEATH SP: Santaquin, Utah, Utah

CHILDREN:
Fernie Francis (Hatton/Robison), 27 Feb 1854

SPOUSE II: John Harvey Moore
MARRIED: 9 May 1846 (divorced)
DEATH SP: 15 Mar 1899
Payson, Utah, Utah

CHILDREN:
Joseph Andrew, 16 Jul 1857
John Harvey, 1861

SPOUSE III: John Morrey
MARRIED: Oct 1864
Payson, Utah, Utah
DEATH: 15 Feb 1885
Kanosh, Millard, Utah

CHILDREN:
Lucina Elizabeth, 21 Oct 1866
Wesley, 22 Feb 1868
John Ferney, 27 Feb 1869
William Anson, 22 Jan 1871
Charles Henry, 14 Nov 1872
Mary Maria "Mae," 23 Jul 1874
Assa Romanzo, 14 May 1876
George Albert, 3 Dec 1878

Polly Lucina was born in New York, 1837. She was the seventh of nine children. She was "loaned" to a childless couple. There she was pampered and given everything a child could desire. It was a great trial to her to be claimed by her parents when they joined the LDS church and prepared to move west. Her foster parents kept all her clothes and possessions. It was hard to adjust to a large family of limited means. The Sheffields stopped in Wisconsin for awhile before proceeding on to Utah. The family arrived in Salt Lake City Oct 1852 in the 12th Company under Captain Harman Cutler. Lucina traveled in the company but as her grandparents were with her parents there was no room in their wagons. She hired out to come with a family where the mother was an invalid. As she came along, she picked up wood or buffalo chips to make the fire over which she did the cooking. Her last duty before breaking camp was to make an inspection of the wagon tongue and grounds to see that nothing was left behind. She was fourteen years old.

In Payson, Lucina worked for Tanners, possibly the ones she had traveled with. Also working there was a widower, Ferney Francis Tindral. Lucina and Ferney were married Mar 1851 in Payson. He was sixteen years older. They were building a house and had the roof ready to put on when tragedy came. While harvesting potatoes in Santaquin 12 Oct 1853, Indians swooped down from the mountains and killed Ferney. Some time later an Indian came begging at Lucina's door. He was wearing Ferney's boots. On 27 Feb 1854 Lucina gave birth to their child. In 1855 a neighbor, Clarissa Moore, asked Lucina if she were willing to marry Clarissa's own husband as a second wife. Lucina married John Harvey Moore and they had two children. Trouble arose when Lucina wanted to be sealed in the Endowment House to her first husband. At age twenty-three she was widowed and divorced. She married John Morrey in 1864. They made their home in Payson for two children and then moved to Kanosh Millard County for the remainder of their days and added six more children to their family. Life in Kanosh was hard. John passed away there in 1885. Lucina's children were energetic, taking the lead in building their mother a new adobe house. She was well provided for the rest of ber life

She was a studious person who loved reading and was especially interested in politics and the issues of the day. Sbe studied obstetrics but her health failed. She passed away at age seventy-one. She was a widow twenty-three years.

LYDIA ANN DAVIS MORRILL

BIRTHDATE: 19 Oct 1833
New Castle, Ontario, Canada
DEATH: 22 Sep 1893
Junction, Piute, Utah
PARENTS: Isaac Davis
Sarah Salisbury Davis
PIONEER: 1851
Levi Calvin Independent Wagon Co.
SPOUSE: Laban Morrill
MARRIED: 17 Oct 1854
DEATH: 8 Dec 1900
Junction, Piute, Utah

CHILDREN:
Calvin, 16 May 1855
Edgar, 9 Oct 1856

Alexander, 8 Dec 1858
Emily Francis, 8 Dec 1860
Mary, 31 May 1862
Edward Davis, 2 Nov 1865
Henry Chancy, 10 Mar 1868
Lydia Ann, 13 Mar 1871
Luther Lewellyn, 27 Apr 1874
Jonathan Davis, 17 May 1877

Lydia Ann was born in New Castle, Ontario, Canada. At the age of eighteen, she came to Utah in an Independent Wagon Company led by her brother-in-law, Levi Calvin. She had a mild disposition and was very helpful to others. She often sacrificed her own pleasure to make others happy. She loved the great outdoors, and was never happier than when wandering through the fields or woods gathering wild berries or fishing in the rivers or mountain streams. While living in Utah, she had to support herself by working in private homes as a seamstress or by doing general housework. She was working for Laban Morrill's second wife, Pennelia Handmore Drury and her five sons. Laban's first wife, Esther Lorraine Brown and her three children had died previously. Lydia became his third wife on October 17, 1854.

Laban and his first wife had helped to build a fort at Johnson's Springs which became known as Johnson's Fort. He was to help protect cattle from frequent Indian raids. They made their home in Cedar Fort where seven of her ten children were born. She lived in harmony with Permelia and her family. When Laban married Mary Elizabeth Lemon Buchannan, she and her children also became part of a large happy family. Laban was called on a mission to the north central states in 1872. After his return, he was called to go to Springdale on the Virgin River and help establish the United Order there. When the United Order was later disbanded, he returned to Fort Johnson. They moved to Circleville where they tried to help the struggling community survive. Then they moved to Junction in 1877 where he built a home on City Creek, a mile from town and planted orchards. They later moved into the town and built two houses, one for Permelia's family and one for Lydia's. Perrnelia died of an unfortunate accident on September 6, 1892. The following year, Lydia died on September 22, 1893 at the age of sixty years. She was known as Aunt Lydia among the people in the community.

PERMELIA HANDMORE DRURY MORRILL

BIRTHDATE: 20 Aug 1821
Wendell, Franklin Co., Mass
DEATH: 6 Sep 1892
Junction, Utah
PARENTS: Joel Drury
Tirzah Winters Drury
PIONEER: 24 Oct 1852
Daniel McArthur Wagon Company
SPOUSE: Laban Morrill
MARRIED: 22 Feb 1844
Nauvoo, Illinois
DEATH SP: 8 Dec 1900
Junction, Utah

CHILDREN:
Horatio, 25 Oct 1845
John, 21 Feb 1848
Laban Drury, 4 Oct 1850
Joseph, 27 Feb 1853 (died 36 days)
Charles, 13 May 1854
Hyrum, 14 Jan 1856
George Drury, 18 Sep 1857
Sarah Permelia, 22 Nov 1860
Horace, 18 Jul 1863

When Permelia was a very young child, she contracted what was known as hip-joint disease and had to use crutches in order to walk. As a young woman she became converted to the LDS religion. She wanted to be baptized immediately, but her parents feared she would become ill. At twenty-one years of age, she was baptized and as she came up out of the water, she said it was not necessary for her to use crutches again. Those who witnessed this miracle accepted it as a case of divine healing. Their family emigrated to Nauvoo to be with the body of the Church. Permelia became acquainted with a young widower, Laban Morrill. They were married in Nauvoo, Illinois on February 22, 1844.

Laban and Permelia purchased a forty acre farm about twenty five miles from Nauvoo where they made improvements and a good comfortable home. They were living there when the martyrdom of Joseph and Hyrum Smith occurred. They passed through the persecutions and hardships shared by the Saints in those times. Part of their property was spent assisting others who had previously taken their journey westward. Due to various stops along the way, they arrived in Salt Lake Valley with the Daniel McArthur Wagon Company on October 24, 1852 which was five and a half years since their departure from Nauvoo. When they arrived in Utah, they settled in Springville where Laban built a comfortable home, a blacksmith shop, a dance hall, and other buildings, and secured a farm. Brigham Young called them to go to Southern Utah to help settle what is now Iron County. They arrived in Cedar Fort in the fall of 1853. Then they were sent to Johnson Settlement, Summit Creek, Springdale, Rockville, and Circleville. This noble pioneer mother had moved and established new homes for her husband and children nineteen times during her marriage.

In 1877, Laban moved his families from Johnson's Fort to Junction. When the Relief Society was organized in Junction, Permelia was selected as the President, and she remained in this position until her death eight years later. She was a ministering angel to the poor, the sick, and the afflicted. Nobly had she ever performed the duties of a wife, mother, sister, and friend.

ANNE MATHEWS MORRIS

BIRTHDATE: 12 Aug 1840
Nottingham, England
DEATH: 28 Dec 1913
Salt Lake City, Utah
PARENTS:
William Mathews (Matthews)
Hepzibah Jarvis
PIONEER: 4 Oct 1863
Haight, Woolley, or Ricks Ox team
SPOUSE: George Morris
MARRIED: 26 Dec 1863
Salt Lake Endowment House
DEATH SP: 29 Jan 1897
Salt Lake City, Utah

CHILDREN:
Annie Mathews, 18 Mar 1865
Elizabeth Mathews, 13 Jan 1867
Minnie Mathews, 7 May 1869
William Charles, 16 Jun 1871
David Henry, 3 Apr 1873
Albert George, 18 Feb 1876
Orson, 9 Sep 1878
Mercy Mathews, 28 Jan 1881
Nathan, 28 Jan 1881
Belva Mathews, 27 Mar 1883

Anne was born in England in 1840. She was seventh of eleven children. She came to Utah with her family, arriving 4 Oct 1863. They made their home in Salt Lake City, where her father passed away in 1874 and her mother in 1879. At age twenty-three, Anne married George Morris, nearly twenty-three years her senior, who was also from England. Anne was his fourth wife in polygamy. He had a total of five wives, one of whom (Maria Allen) is a sweet story of a sealing. They made their home in Salt Lake City where they became parents of ten children, three of whom were raised to adulthood. They lived on City Lot at 252 North 100 West adjacent to Temple Square in the Seventeenth Ward.

A young plural wife who dutifully and lovingly nurtured her young ones during many trials of sickness and death, especially following the passage of the Edmund Tucker law which prohibited a man to live with his plural wife. She and three of her young children had been able to accompany her husband and visit with her sister Eliza when he was called in Oct 1874 to work on the St. George Temple. William passed away 29 Jan 1897 in Salt Lake

City. Anne passed away at age seventy-three, having been a widow for sixteen years. Both are buried in the Salt Lake City Cemetery along with their seven small children and her parents.

ELISABETH ALEXANDER MORRIS

BIRTHDATE: 23 Mar 1806
Vernham, Hamps.,England
DEATH: 21 Feb 1878
Salt Lake City, Utah
PARENTS: William Alexander
Mary Noyes Alexander
PIONEER: 20 Aug 1860
Jesse Murphy Ox-team Company
SPOUSE: Richard Morris
MARRIED: 20 Mar 1827
Vernham, Hamps., England
DEATH SP: 23 Feb 1863
England

CHILDREN:
Maria, 5 Sep 1830
Elisabeth, 20 Mar 1834
Ann, 20 Jun 1836
Richard, 24 Jun 1837
William, 20 Jun 1838
Joseph, 22 Jun 1839
Robert, 10 Nov 1842
Susan, 19 May 1844
Mary, 25 Dec 1845

Elisabeth Alexander Morris was born in England to a very wealthy family. Her parents were William and Mary Alexander. Elisabeth received a very good, liberal education. She also learned such practical skills as cooking and sewing.

Elisabeth married Richard Morris 20 Mar 1827 in Vernham, Hamps., England. He was a boot fitter and shoemaker. Elisabeth learned to bind and line the boots. They became the parents of nine children; all born in England. Elisabeth and her children were baptized by President John Taylor. Her two older sons soon emigrated to America. The following year, 1857, Elisabeth and Richard and five of their children sailed for America. In 1860, they left New York to make the long journey across the Plains to Utah. Elisabeth's husband, Richard, returned to England. Elisabeth and her children joined the Jesse Murphy ox-train Company, leaving Florence, Nebraska 10 June 1860 and arrived in the Salt Lake Valley 20 Aug 1860.

Upon arriving in Salt Lake, Elisabeth was asked to teach school because of her well educated background. She built a cabin on 4th South between 6th and 7th East in Salt Lake City. The Church had begun a silk industry and Elisabeth raised silkworms. She kept the silkworm cocoons under her bed to keep them warm. Her grandchildren gathered the mulberry leaves for the silkworms to eat. She also made hats to sell. She split wheatstraws, bleached them, braided them and sold them to the local millinery shops.

Elisabeth was a very capable and faithful pioneer. She died in Salt Lake City, Utah 21 Feb 1878. Her husband did not come to Utah but died in England 23 Feb 1863.

ELIZABETH WILLIAMS MORRIS

No
Photo
Available

BIRTHDATE: 15 May 1828
St. Asaph, Flints., Wales
DEATH: 25 Oct 1865
Salt Lake City, Salt Lake, Utah
PARENTS: John Roland Williams
Mary Roberts Williams
PIONEER: 10 Oct 1853
Joseph W. Young Wagon Company
SPOUSE: Isaac Conway Morris
MARRIED: 16 Oct 1852
Abergele, Denbighshire, No. Wales
DEATH SP: 22 Nov 1868
Richville, Morgan, Utah

CHILDREN:
Sarah Elizabeth, 13 Sep 1853
Mary, 25 Oct 1855
William, 23 Sep 1857
Isaac, 23 Aug 1859
Elizabeth Ann, 18 May 1861
Priscilla, 30 Nov 1862
John, 18 Sep 1864 (Stillborn)
Thomas, 21 Oct 1865 (died an infant)

Elizabeth was born to John Roland and Mary Roberts Williams on May 15, 1828 in Engleways, Denbighshire, England or North Wales. She married Isaac Conway Morris on October 16, 1852 in Abergele, Denbighshire, North Wales. They were baptized as members of the LDS Church and sailed from Liverpool on February 5, 1853 on the ship, "Jersey." After they arrived in New Orleans, they traveled by steamer to Keokuk, Iowa. They traveled from there with the Joseph Young Wagon Company. At Sweetwater, Wyoming, their first daughter, Sarah, was born. They arrived in the Salt Lake Valley on October 10, 1853.

They settled in Salt Lake City where their next seven children were born. Elizabeth was a mother who suffered many hardships as they tried so diligently to provide food, clothing, and shelter for her family. She died four days after her son, Thomas, was born. She was only thirty-seven years old when she died. She was buried in Salt Lake City beside her son, Thomas.

HANNAH MARIA NEWBERRY MORRIS

BIRTHDATE: 13 Mar 1823
Strongsville, Cuyshoga, Ohio
DEATH: 6 Nov 1893
Salt Lake City, Salt Lake, Utah
PARENTS: James Newberry
Mary Smith Newberry
PIONEER: 21 Sep 1848
Brigham Young Wagon Company
SPOUSE: George Morris
MARRIED: 23 Aug 1843
Nauvoo, Hancock, Illinois
DEATH: 29 Jan 1897
Salt Lake City, Salt Lake, Utah

CHILDREN:
Lavina Newberry, 13 Jul 1844
Julia Ann, 28 Aug 1846
Rosella Newberry, 29 Mar 1848
George Vernon, 15 May 1850
Maria Jane, 17 Sep 1851
Joseph Newberry, 15 Apr 1853
Mary Ann, 29 Jun 1855
James Newberry, 1 May 1857
Ellen Newberry, 20 Feb 1859 (died an infant)
Franklin Newberry, 21 Mar 1860
Harriet Newberry, 10 Apr 1862
Ephraim Frederick Newberry, 25 Jul 1864

Hannah was baptized a member of the LDS Church in 1840. She married George Morris in 1843 when she was twenty years old. Their first home was a lean-to built against the home owned by William Anderson. As George was working on the Nauvoo Temple, they were requested to donate two-thirds of their wages to the church. They eventually were able to build a nice little brick house, but were compelled by the mob to dispose of it. They received their endowments on January 30, 1846. George, Hannah, their daughter, and Hannah's sister, Harriet, crossed the Mississippi River and camped while George found work to obtain more supplies. They moved on and found a stable in which to live. George earned a living by digging wells. Because of overwork and anxiety, he became very ill. Hannah gave birth to a second daughter and became very ill from yellow jaundice. Harriet nursed them and took care of the children. When George recovered, they moved from place to place in whatever poor shelter they could find and George sank several more wells. Harriet went with her brothers and a sister. Hannah gave birth to a third child and was ill again. They were both terribly ill when they left with the Brigham Young Wagon Company, but they felt Satan was working against them. They arrived in the Salt Lake Valley on September 21, 1848.

George built an adobe home for them and worked at various jobs farrning, building houses–fifty houses in all, sunk seventy-five wells, made and mended shoes, did police work, and road work, anything he could do to pay expenses. Hannah and George had twelve children. They added improvements to their home as years went on. In 1857, they had to move their family to the Provo River Bottoms until the Johnston Army threat was settled. After they returned, George served as a counselor in the bishopric and served in this office for fourteen years. Hannah raised her children and prepared them to be an influence for good, caring for and sharing with their fellow men. Hannah suffered from ill health most of her life, but lived until she was seventy.

MARIA ALLEN MORRIS

No Photo Available

BIRTHDATE: 31 Dec 1833
England
DEATH: 16 Jan 1856
Salt Lake City, Utah
PARENTS: Mr. Allen
Mrs Allen
PIONEER: 1855
by Handcart
SPOUSE: George Morris
MARRIED: 15 Jan 1858
Salt Lake City, Utah
DEATH SP: 29 Jan 1897
Salt Lake City, Utah

CHILDREN:

Maria was born in England in 1833. She had a sister named Ellen. They joined the church in England and emigrated to Utah in 1855.

This is her story: Being ill from overexposure to adverse weather Maria Allen was cared for in a home in George Morris' Block Teaching District where he visited and administered to her several times. Learning more of the Sealing Ordinances of the LDS church and the plurality of wives, Maria requested that she be sealed to her Block Teacher. After an interview with her and permission granted by President Brigham Young, George Morris and Maria Allen were sealed by Apostle Franklin D. Richards at a private house in the seventeenth Ward in Salt Lake City. She died the following day at 5 a.m.

Maria Allen was sealed in the Endowment House to George Morris on 26 Dec 1863 with Hannah Maria Morris standing proxy. From George Morris' Journal: "'I was unable to learn anything more of the history of Maria Allen and her sister Ellen, only that they received the gospel in England and gathered up with the saints to the valleys of the mountains coming with handcarts and this is recommendation good enough for anybody of their worthiness."

George Morris married first, Hannah Marie Newberry, Maria Allen Anne Mathews, Jane Higgenbotham and Harriet Newberry. He was born 23 Aug 1816 in Hanley, Cheshire, England, and died 29 Jan 1897 in Salt Lake City.

MARIA BILLINGS LINNEY MORRIS

BIRTHDATE: 12 Nov 1806
So., Witham, England
DEATH: 17 Nov 1889
Salt Lake City, Salt Lake, Utah
PARENTS: John Linney
Sophia Billings
PIONEER: 24 Sep 1866
Wagon Train Company
SPOUSE: John Morris
MARRIED: 1832
England
DEATH SP: 29 May 1882
England

CHILDREN:
Charles, 13 Aug 1833
John, 18 Nov 1834
John, 17 Jan 1836
Emma (McMurrine Caffell), 29 Jan 1838
Harriet (Bishop), 2 Nov 1839
Louisa (McCullough), 29 Jul 1841
Robert, 13 Sep 1843
William, 26 Jan 1846

Maria was born in England in 1806. She was an only child. She married John Morris in 1832 and they had eight children. Her second child died at one year of age.

In 1845/1846, missionaries from the Church of Jesus Christ of Latter-day Saints came to their home. Her husband was opposed to the teachings, but she was baptized on December 10, 1848, with her sons, Charles and John. The rest of her children were baptized later. The Elders brought small pox to their home; every one of the family caught it.

They lived in a poor neighborhood. She helped clean and prepare tripe for the children to sell from door to door. In 1855/1856, two of her sons emigrated to America. They earned enough to send for the rest of the children. In 1866, her son, Robert, sent enough money for her passage. She arrived in the Salt Lake Valley in September, 1866 and went to live with her daughter, Louisa.

Maria was an expert seamstress and good cook. After she came to Utah at the age of sixty, she did nursing and family washings to support herself. She had good health. She died in November, 1889 in Salt Lake City, at the age of eighty-three.

MARY LOIS WALKER MORRIS

BIRTHDATE: 14 May 1835
Leek, Stafford, England
DEATH: 19 Nov 1919
Salt Lake City, Salt Lake, Utah
PARENTS: William Gibson Walker
Mary Goodwin
PIONEER: 10 Oct 1853
Joseph W. Young Wagon Company
SPOUSE: John Thomas Morris
MARRIED: 5 Sep 1852
St. Louis, Missouri
DEATH SP: 22 Feb 1855
Cedar City, Utah

CHILDREN:
John Walker Morris 17 Oct 1854

SPOUSE II: Elias Morris
MARRIED: May 1856
Salt Lake City, Salt Lake, Utah
DEATH: 17 Mar 1898
Salt Lake City, Salt Lake, Utah

CHILDREN:
Effie Walker, 10 Jan 1859
Marion Adelaide, 26 Feb 1861
John Conway, 22 Aug 1863 (died age 4)
Nephi Lowell, 2 Oct 1870
Ray Godwin, 22 Jun 1872 (died 7 months)
George Quayle, 22 Feb 1874
Katherine Vaughn, 10 Apr 1876
Richard Vaughn, 20 Jul 1882 (died an infant)

Mary Lois was born in Leek, Stafford, England where she learned the skills of sewing and millinery from her mother. Their family had become converted to the LDS Church. When she was fifteen, Mary Lois and her parents boarded the ship, Josiah Bradley, in Liverpool and emigrated to America to be with the Saints. They landed in New Orleans in April of 1850 and traveled by steamship up the Mississippi River to St. Louis. Her mother died in St. Louis and her father decided to return to England. Mary Lois married John Thomas Morris in St. Louis and they traveled west across the plains with his family in the Joseph W. Young Wagon Company. John was ill when they married, but this did not stop them from traveling to Salt Lake. They arrived in the valley on October 10, 1853.

John's family continued on to Cedar City to join an older brother, Elias and his wife on the Iron Mission. A baby was born on October 17, 1854, but had contracted his father's disease. They both died and Mary Lois was alone again. On his death bed, John asked his brother, Elias, to take care of his wife and raise a family for him. He did so and eight children were born to this union. Elias moved his families to Salt Lake City. Mary worked as a seamstress and milliner to buy the things her family needed. She was a fine teacher, training her sons to work diligently and only allow the best of companions in their lives. She was a member of the ward choir, worked in Relief Society, was

Primary President in her ward and Sunday School. She supported her family while her husband served a mission to England for five years. She was devoted to the church, its leaders, and the Lord. Prayer was her constant companion. Premonitions alerted her to be watchful. Elias brought both of his families to Salt Lake to make their permanent home.

MARY PARRY MORRIS

BIRTHDATE: 21 Dec 1834
Flintshire, New Market, No. Wales
DEATH: 4 Mar 1919
Salt Lake City, Salt Lake, Utah
PARENTS: John Parry
Elizabeth Parry Parry
PIONEER: 2 Nov 1852
Philip DeLamar Wagon Company
SPOUSE: Elias Morris
MARRIED: 23 May 1852
Council Bluffs, Iowa
DEATH SP: 17 Mar 1898
Salt Lake City, Salt Lake, Utah

CHILDREN:
Barbara Elizabeth, 30 May 1853
Winnifred Jane, 26 Oct 1855
Harriet Ann, 3 Sep 1857
Elias Parry, 23 Sep 1859
Mary Ella, 11 Mar 1862
Edward Parry (twin), 20 Sep 1864
Rosa Frances (twin), 20 Sep 1864
John Parry, 23 Mar 1870
Ernest Edwin, 21 Jun 1872
Albert Conway, 8 Jun 1874
Jessie Pearl, 22 Aug 1876
Josephine Edna, 22 Oct 1879

Between the years of twelve and sixteen, Mary attended school in Liverpool while she was living with relatives. She would return home for an occasional visit. The Parry family was converted to the LDS Church and Mary was baptized on March 3, 1850. Mary sailed on the vessel, "Ellen Maria," on the first of February, 1852 arriving in New Orleans ten weeks later around Easter time. She traveled to Kanesville where her uncle, Joseph Parry was located. Her fiancé Elias Morris arrived a month later and they were married on May 23, 1852 in Council Bluffs, Iowa. They began their trek across the prairie with the Philip DeLamar Wagon Company with Elias acting as a captain of ten in the company. There was a constant vigil for Indians and stray cattle. They arrived in the Great Salt Lake Valley on November 2, 1852.

Her husband had been placed in charge of bringing sugar beet refining machinery to Deseret. They continued their journey to Provo where Elias' business was settled with John Taylor and his responsibility for the machinery was completed. Elder Taylor offered them the use of his granary in which to live until February when they could move into a log house. In April 1853, Elias was appointed by Brigham Young to go to Cedar City to help build the

Pioneer Iron Works. They remained there for seven years and returned to Salt Lake in 1860 where Elias was the chief mason of the Salt Lake Temple, the Salt Lake Theater, and other important buildings. In 1865, Mary cared for her five children while Elias served a mission in Wales. After his return, she supported him as he served as bishop for many years and as he served his community in business and civic affairs during the remainder of his life. Mary was always kind and thoughtful of the poor and helped wherever she could. She had a strong testimony and faithfully filled numerous church callings. She died of influenza at the age of eighty four.

OLIVE (ALIDA) CORNELIA DYKMAN MORRIS

BIRTHDATE: 12 Jul 1857
Amsterdam, Holland
DEATH: 10 Nov 1910
Provo, Utah, Utah
PARENTS: Johannes Henricus
Aaltje Ages Dykrnan
PIONEER: 2 Nov 1864
Warren S. Snow Wagon Co.
SPOUSE:
Samuel Abraham Morris
MARRIED: 1876
DEATH SP:

CHILDREN:
Ann, 14 Jan 1877
John S., 21 Jul 1879 (died age 2)
James Hyrum, 23 Nov 1881
George Abraham, 10 Sep 1886

Olive was born on July 12, 1857 in Amsterdam, Holland. Her mother died when she was five years old. After her mother's death, her father joined the LDS Church and emigrated to Utah with his five children. They sailed on the ship, "Hudson," then traveled by rail and ox team. They arrived in the Salt Lake Valley with the Warren S. Snow Wagon Company on November 2, 1864. Olive was seven years old at the time they crossed the plains.

Their family settled on the west side of the Jordan River in an adobe home. Her father and brother worked on the Salt Lake Temple and were very skilled in the use of tools. Olive was baptized a member of the LDS Church on May 6, 1866. She married Samuel Morris in approximately 1876. Census records indicate the family lived near Corinne, Utah and that Samuel was a baker at that time. Olive had four children but was not able to complete raising them. Her son John died and was buried in the Salt Lake City Cemetery. A few years later, at the age of thirty-one, Olive was admitted to the State Mental Hospital in Provo, Utah. The cause of her collapse is unknown and what happened to her husband is unknown. At the time she was admitted to the hospital, her youngest child was only two years old and the oldest was eleven. Her sister, Mary Alice

Dykman Bess Mawson, took her children and raised them as her own. Olive died November 10, 1910 after being confined for twenty two years. We can never know the agonies Olive endured. We love and honor her as a courageous pioneer woman.

SARAH DURHAM MORRIS

BIRTHDATE: 6 Jun 1825
Oldham, Lancashire, England
DEATH: 3 Jul 1916
Parowan, Iron, Utah
PARENTS: John Durham
Isabella Thompson Durham
PIONEER: 27 Sep 1862
John R. Murdock Wagon Company
SPOUSE: William Morris
MARRIED: 20 Aug 1848
Fallsworth, Lancashire, England
DEATH SP: 7 Nov 1900
Parowan, Iron, Utah

CHILDREN:
Mary Ann, 20 Dec 1849
Sarah Jane, 8 Feb 1852 (died age 10)
Emma, 6 May 1854 (died an infant)
Elizabeth, 30 Jul 1856
Emma, 27 Jan 1859
William Thomas, 17 May 1861
Joseph (twin), 30 Nov 1863 (died 7 months)
John (twin), 30 Nov 1863 (died 7 months)
George Durham, 16 Jul 1866

When Sarah was a young girl, she worked in the Nottingham Cotton Factory. The Durhams were influential people and were well educated in music. Sarah had a beautiful alto voice and sang with her brother Thomas in a choir for the United Brethren Church. Sarah and her brother were in attendance at a meeting where Elder Wilford Woodruff spoke and converted most of the congregation, among them Sarah and Thomas. She was baptized at the age of eighteen. When she was twenty three, she married William Morris. He was a convert to the LDS Church and a shoemaker by trade. Sarah helped all she could by sewing in the linings. They were very active in their branch of the Church and made preparations to emigrate to Utah as their finances would permit. On May 2, 1862, the Morris family of seven went to Liverpool and sailed on the sailing vessel, Manchester, for America. It was a long and hazardous voyage where the ship came very near being wrecked by icebergs. After their arrival in Castle Gardens, New York, they traveled up the Hudson River to Albany, into Canada, across Lake Erie to Detroit, then on to St. Louis, Missouri and Florence, Nebraska where the railroad ended. They crossed the plains with the John R. Murdock Wagon Company and arrived in Salt Lake on September 27, 1862. Their daughter Sarah Jane had died of Typhoid Fever as they crossed the plains.

They moved on to Parowan where they made their first home inside the fort. Later her husband secured a farm. Sarah was proficient in the homemaking skills needed in that time. She soon had a good garden growing to help with their food supply. She made butter and had eggs to trade at the store for merchandise. She and her husband had nine children. She was well read on history, politics, religion, and world events in general, and had an excellent memory. She took a great interest in politics and urged everyone to vote. She was steadfast in her religion. She loved to attend to her church duties in the Parowan Stake Primary Presidency, in the Relief Society, and Sacrament Meetings. She was known as an excellent cook. She and her brother were singers in the Parowan Choirs. In 1870, their choir was invited to sing in the October 1870 Conference. They were also invited to sing for General William T. Sherman when he came to investigate the "Mormon Question." She died at age ninety one.

MARY MARGARET FORQUHAR CRUICKSHANK MORRISON

BIRTHDATE: 5 Jun 1823
Aberdeen, Scotland
DEATH: 10 Jan 1910
Mt. Pleasant, Sanpete, Utah
PARENTS: William Cruickshank
Mary Forquhar Cruickshank
PIONEER: 20 Sep 1856
Canute Peterson Wagon Company
SPOUSE: William Morrison
MARRIED: 22 Dec 1843
Aberdeen, Scotland
DEATH: 26 Aug 1889
Sevier County, Utah

CHILDREN:
Anthony Bruce, 31 Oct 1844
Andrew Cruickshank, 25 Sep 1848
Sarah Allen, v15 Sep 1850
Mary Isabella, 16 Jan 1852
Mary Margaret, 3 Jan 1855
William George Cruickshank, 9 Dec 1856
Williamina Henrietta, 13 Mar 1859
Clementina Marion, 15 Feb 1863

Mary Margaret received a common school education until she was fourteen years old. Then she stayed home to assist her mother in her domestic duties. She married William Morrison in Aberdeen, Scotland. Her husband received a government appointment in Her Majesty's Dockyard, in Shermess, Kent, England. Five years later, they became members of the LDS Church and had a firm conviction they should gather with the Saints in Zion. While living in Scotland, their first two children died. They sailed from Liverpool on the ship, Germanicus on 6 April, 1854 and arrived in New Orleans eleven weeks later. Then they sailed up the Mississippi River to St. Louis. No one in their company was ill, but they were required to be quaran-

tined. In one week's time, eighty persons died of Cholera before they were allowed to leave that dreadful place. Two of her children and one of her nephews died there. Mary Margaret's faith remained strong. She believed the Lord was with her in the midst of her affliction. They joined the Canute Peterson Wagon Company and crossed the plains. They arrived in the Salt Lake Valley on September 20, 1856.

They bought a good city lot and house in the Fifth Ward in Salt Lake City. At the time of the approach of Johnston's Army, she moved to Ephraim with friends while her husband served in defense in Echo Canyon. She was called to share her husband with three other women. They moved to Mt. Pleasant where she stayed for the rest of her life. She was the first Relief Society President in Mt. Pleasant and served in that capacity for over forty years. It is said that over one thousand of those who had died and were buried in Mt. Pleasant Cemetery were dressed and laid out for burial by her without charge. She assisted the needy and distressed often from her personal resources. Of her eight children, only two of them lived beyond the age of twenty-nine. Through all of her trials and tribulations, she remained valiant to the end of her life.

SARAH MARK MORRISON

BIRTHDATE: 15 Jan 1817
Crepmolmeshire, Mayo County, Ireland
DEATH: 26 Jun 1870
Spanish Fork, Utah
PARENTS: Thomas Mark
Rebecca Bray Mark
PIONEER: 16 Oct 1852
Eli B. Kelsey Co. Wagon Train
SPOUSE: John Morrison
MARRIED: 1834/5
Endowments, Nauvoo 7 Feb 1846
DEATH: 7 Apr 1881
Preston, Franklin County, Idaho

CHILDREN:
Jane (Pine), 5 Sep 1836
Andrew, 10 Sep 1838
Sarah, 1840
Mark, 1840
Matthew, 1842
John Jr., 15 Aug 1844
Joseph, 18 Dec 1846
Ellen (Clayton), 15 Aug 1848
Thomas, 3 Apr 1850

Sarah was born in Ireland in 1817. Some records indicate 10 Aug 1820. At age sixteen, Sarah married John Morrison, who was sixteen years her senior. They were early converts to the LDS church and by 1840, they were living in Nauvoo, Illinois. Their story is the "Mormon" story.

They came to Salt Lake City with the Eli B. Kelsey Wagon train, leaving Kanesville, Iowa in July and arriving

16 Oct 1852. While living in Nauvoo, they helped build the temple. In Utah, they settled in Palmyra. Their oldest daughter, Jane married in 1855 in Salt Lake City. They farmed for a living and raised their family. Sarah passed away at age fifty-three in Spanish Fork, Utah.

John went to Idaho to be with four of their children that helped settle Idaho. He was a pioneer to Franklin. He passed away 7 Apr 1881 in Preston, Franklin County, Idaho, at age eighty, a widower of ten years.

ALICE LEWIS MORSE

BIRTHDATE: 22 Jul 1836
Merthyr Tydfil, Glamorganshire, Wales
DEATH: 7 May 1911
Hyde Park, Cache, Utah
PARENTS: Hugh M. Lewis
Mary Wilzabeth Williams
PIONEER: 4 Sep 1866
Thomas E. Ricks Wagon train
SPOUSE: John Morse
MARRIED: 21 May 1855
Vaynor Church, Merthyr Tydfil
DEATH: 1 Jan 1901
Hyde Park, Cache, Utah

CHILDREN:
Sarah Ann (Brown/Cushing), 22 May 1856
Martha, 11 Jun 1858
Richard, 20 Oct 1860
Hyrum, 23 Jul 1862
Jane, 18 May 1864
John Lewis, 7 Dec 1866
Brigham Lewis, 31 Aug 1869
Alice Elizabeth (James/Maxwell), 8 Sep 1872
James Edward, 21 Oct 1875
Berkley Hugh, 22 Feb 1878

Alice was born in Wales, 1836. At age eighteen, she married John Morse, a thirty-three-year-old widower with four children: Mary, eleven; William, seven; Joseph, four; and Margaret, two. John accepted the LDS faith and was baptized in 1846. Alice around 1853/55. They felt it would be better for them if they accepted the encouragement from John's two brothers asking them to come to America and Zion where the brothers had already located for two years. Religious persecution was creating problems for the Saints in Wales and John needed to get out of the coal mines so it was decided to go as soon as possible.

Except for John's first daughter, Mary, now twenty, who chose to stay in Wales, the family now totaled seven children plus parents who made their way to Liverpool, England where they set sail on the "Bellewood" 29 Apr 1865 landing in New York. This ship sank on her return voyage. They made their way to Wyoming, Nebraska, joining the Thomas E. Ricks wagon train, leaving 6 Jul and arriving in Salt Lake City 4 Sep 1866. They went to settle in Logan, where another child was born. They next moved to settle Hyde Park, Cache County, where their last four

children were born and they built their home and lived out their days. They were active in their church and community. John passed away at age seventy-seven on 1 Jan 1901 leaving Alice a widow for ten years. She passed away at age seventy-four on 7 May 1911. They are both buried in the Hyde Park Cemetery.

ESTHER JENKINS MORSE

BIRTHDATE: 1 Feb 1845
Abercanoid, Glamorganshire, Wales
DEATH: 21 Jul 1913
Pleasant View, Oneida, Idaho
SPOUSE: David Jenkins
Anna Evans
PIONEER: 4 Sep 1866
Thomas E. Ricks wagon train
SPOUSE: Joseph Bennett Morse
MARRIED: Oct 1868
Logan, Cache County, Utah
DEATH SP: 13 Jul 1916
Pleasant View, Idaho

CHILDREN:
David Joseph, 12 Aug 1869
John Twin, 25 May 1872
William twin, 25 May 1872
Evan Jenkins, 6 Aug 1873
Ann (Davis), 30 Sep 1876
Anna (Evans), 26 Dec 1878
Richard Jenkins, 2 Dec 1880
Mary Esther, 21 Feb 1883
Jane (Thomas), 11 Sep 1885
Margaret (Wilson), 15 May 1890

Esther was born in Wales, 1845. She grew up in industrial Merthyr Tidfil, the coal center of the world. She was seven when her father was killed in a mine explosion. After 1858, when her step-father was no longer in their home, Esther worked as a waitress to help make a living for the family of eight children. Before her father's death, the family had joined the LDS church and made plans to earn money to emigrate. Finally Esther and older brother, David went ahead, leaving Liverpool 30 Apr 1866 on the, "John Bright" arriving in New York 6 Jun and arriving in Wyoming, Nebraska 19 Jun 1866. They joined the Thomas E. Ricks wagon train, leaving 6 Jul and arriving in Salt Lake City 4 Sep 1866. David worked odd jobs and Esther worked in homes to send money to the family. They finally arrived in Aug 1868, for a joyful reunion.

In Salt Lake City, Esther met and fell in love with Joseph Bennett Morse. They married in Logan in Oct 1868 when she was twenty-three and Joseph was eighteen. They lived in Logan until after their first son was born, then they moved to Samaria, Oneida, Idaho where Esther's mother and brothers had homesteaded. They, too, homesteaded and endured the trials of pioneering in a new land among both their families in the Welsh community. They had chickens, pigs, cows, horses, and always a large garden of potatoes, corn, onions, and rhubarb. In the fall, after grain harvest, Esther would fill mattress ticks with fresh, clean straw.

Indians from Pocatello valley often stopped to sharpen their knives. The squaws would beg through the village. People were generous with them. Esther was active in community and church work and a Relief Society teacher for many years. She sang with her husband in church and at many funerals. The children were taught the Welsh Language, speaking it in their home and singing many songs in their native tongue. Esther was like a doctor to many people and always had a bottle of camphor and potash on hand. Many times she used her tongue to remove foreign objects from people's eyes; she took care of many who were ill with diptheria. She did have the healer's art, which was a fulfillment of her blessing.

She and her husband acted as undertakers; she washing and laying out the female dead and he the males. They seemed to have a sense that something was wrong before a death and often felt they received a warning at times. Esther was the mother of ten children, raising six to adulthood. She passed away 21 Jul 1913 in Samaria at age sixty-eight, after nearly forty-five years of marriage, having given a full measure during her life.

MARGARET EVANS MORSE

BIRTHDATE: 10 Oct 1826
Con Wil Elvet Carmarthen Shire, Wales
DEATH: 11 Aug 1893
Samaria, Utah
PARENTS: Ebenezer Evans
Amy Williams Evans
PIONEER: 4 Oct 1863
Thomas E. Ricks Handcart Co.
SPOUSE: William Morse
MARRIED: 8 Oct 1859
DEATH SP: 15 Apr 1904
Samaria, Utah

CHILDREN:
Mary Jane Morse, 26 Jun 1860
Ann, 9 Aug 1862
Emma, 17 Jun 1865
William Evans, 31 Oct 1867
Margaret, 24 Mar 1870
Rachel, 26 Nov 1872
Sara, 19 May 1876
Sophia, 22 Jan 1880

Because Margaret married a Mormon, she was disowned by her family and was known as their lost child. The ship "Amazon" brought not only Margaret and William's family to America, but Charles Dickens also. He had boarded the ship to get material for a negative article about the Mormons, but left the ship declaring that they were the "Pick and flower of England."

Margaret and William walked across the plains with the Rick's handcart company, carrying her year old baby Ann Welch-fashion in her shawl, which left her arms free to do chores and care for three-year-old Mary Jane who was riding in the handcart.

Her personal treasures, her metal cooking ware and other possessions, she was told "Were too heavy for the oxen," and the teamster hauling them had to unload them on the plains. Margaret's tears were more for the last shred of her childhood, her family connection and memories of Wales, left in a pile beside the trail, than for the loss of a cooking pot.

They arrived in Utah in October, going on to Logan where other Welsh emigrants they knew had settled. The Davis family took them in until her first home in America was ready, a dugout. Here she had her third baby. One day she found a lizard in bed with little Emma! Even at that she said it was better than living in a wagon box. A few months later she moved into her own log cabin with dirt floors and a sod roof.

The larger cabin they built after moving to Samaria also had a dirt floor and dirt roof. She had a knack for "making do" and her broom was a sage brush. To white wash the walls, since no brush was available, her brush was sheep skin. Her furniture was homemade from rough lumber and she scoured them with sand and ashes to make them smooth. She was an excellent knitter and used one strand of cotton with the wool to knit the toes and heels of the hose she made for her family.

In Logan, they broke the ice to baptize her. She did not catch cold which strengthend her testimony, and she was very active in her ward, and in the Relief Society for many years. It was said she "mothered the ward." She loved Temple work, many times spending the night in Logan to do another session the next morning.

When she was sixty-four years old she had the means to go back to Wales and see her family. Most of them treated her with reserve; she was still the lost one.

She returned to Logan ill, never to regain her health or live long enough to see her dream house finished, (a two story frame house, still standing).

She suffered deep depression after going to Wales, and died 11 Aug 1893. When William died eleven years later he was buried in the Samaria Cemetery beside his beloved Margaret.

ANE KJERSTINE POULSEN MORTENSEN

BIRTHDATE: 9 Sep 1839
Vestervig, Thirsted, Denmark
DEATH: 9 Jul 1878
Levan, Juab County, Utah
PARENTS: Poul Andersen
Else Kirstine Jensen
PIONEER: 29 Sep 1866
Peter Nebeker Wagon Train
SPOUSE:
Hans Christian Mortensen, Sr
MARRIED: 22 Apr 1866
Denmark
DEATH: 30 Aug 1927/02 Jun 1931
Levan, Juab County, Utah

CHILDREN:
Hans Christian, 22 Apr 1866
Johanna Kirstine (Lawson/Holmes), 12 Sep 1870
Maria (Finney/McCormick), 20 May 1873
Adolph, 29 Oct 1874
William, 9 Jul 1878

Ane Kjerstine was born in Denmark, 1839. At age twenty-six, she married Hans Christian Mortensen, Sr. They became parents of five. Her deep-seated faith in Heavenly Father and her love for the scriptures was ever a constant joy and strength for her. She was a very devoted Lutheran in Denmark and participated in a program to increase her skills through the Church. All remarks and homes she stayed in were recorded in a small book which she kept. She worked as a hired girl doing baby sitting, cooking, sewing and cleaning. She also read her scriptures daily and received many awards for her knowledge of them. She met and fell in love with Hans Christian Mortensen, married him and came to America with him but did not join his new church. He was baptized in Denmark. Just being a newlywed she was able to help young mothers and their children all during the journey across the ocean and across the plains. She was baptized 5 Aug 1877 after the arrival of her fourth child. She was soft spoken, industrious, had a delightful sense of humor, and was a most loving wife and mother. She was a great strength to Hans and backed him all the way. She taught her children to be industrious, loving and to stay close to our Heavenly Father. She was only thirty-seven years of age when she died in childbirth with her fifth child, William.

CORNELIA LEE DECKER MORTENSEN

BIRTHDATE: 15 Jan 1846
Nauvoo, Hancock, Illinois
DEATH: 26 Dec 1937
Sanford, Conejos, Colorado
PARENTS:
John Doyle Lee
Nancy Bean
PIONEER: by 1849
Wagon Train
SPOUSE: Lars Mortensen
MARRIED: 29 Dec 1863
Parowan, Iron County, Utah
DEATH SP: 29 Jun 1910

CHILDREN:
Cornelia Adella (Mickelsen), 24 Jan 1865
Nancy Evelyn (Adams), 17 Dec 1866
Helena Laurette (Peterson), 11 Oct 1868
Lars Hamner, 9 Nov 1870
Alice Gertrude (Hyde), 22 Dec 1872
Minnie Montez (Adams), 21 Sep 1874
Arlington Peter, 20 Feb 1877
Rulon Erastus, 18 Aug 1879
Martin Junius, 29 Sep 1881
Golda Georgett (Clayton), 7 Nov 1883
Wilford Woodruff, 9 Mar 1886
Pearl Caroline (Driggs), 22 Apr 1889

Cornelia was born in Illinois, 1846. At age three, she came with her family to Salt Lake City. She learned all the pioneer skills from her mother. By age seventeen, she married Lars Mortensen and they made their home in Parowan, Iron County, Utah where eleven of their twelve children were born. They were living in Sanford, Colorado for child number twelve. Cornelia was President of the Sanford Stake Relief Society. She was a benefactor, a teacher and a monument of truth and integrity. She was an excellent nurse. She understood most diseases and could apply a helpful remedy. She helped hundreds of mothers in child bearing. Her work and skill was done in a reverential way, asking for and depending on divine power to help her.

Lars Mortensen passed away 29 Jun 1910 in Parowan, Iron Co.,Utah. Cornelia passed away at age ninety-one, having been a widow for twenty-seven years. The name Decker was given her from her mother's third husband. She used this as a legal name.

DIONITIA EMILY ALEXANDER MORTENSEN

BIRTHDATE: 18 Oct 1843
Nauvoo, Hancock, Illinois
DEATH: 24 Oct 1879
Parowan, Iron County, Utah
PARENTS:
Horace Martin Alexander
Nancy Reeder Walker Alexander
PIONEER: 10 Nov 1847–Ox Train
followed lst 6 companies
SPOUSE: Hans Jorgen Mortensen
MARRIED: 16 May 1859
Parowan, Iron County, Utah
DEATH SP: 17 Jan 1912
Parowan, Iron County, Utah

CHILDREN:
Hans Lyman, 6 Feb 1860
Nancy Dionita, 16 Aug 1861
William Henry, 16 Sep 1862
Francis Marion, 19 Dec 1863
Lena Losana (Owens), 25 Feb 1866
Sarah Eveline, 8 Dec 1867
Horace Martin, 21 Mar 1870
Jesse Leonidas, 21 Apr 1873
William Wallace, 23 Apr 1875
Junius Denton, 12 Aug 1877
James Peter, 24 Oct 1879

Dionitia Emily was born in Illinois, 1843. Her family were early converts to the LDS church. Dionitia, the fourth daughter was born in Nauvoo. Her parents left Nauvoo with their family because of the mob's persecution. They went to Winter Quarters, the first part of the journey across the plains. The summer of 1846, Horace joined the Mormon Battalion. In Winter Quarters 1 Jan 1847, Nancy, in the rudest of log huts gave birth to a son Horace Martin Alexander Jr. The weather was bitter cold and there were not enough blankets to keep the babe and mother warm and dry. On 28 Jan, Nancy died. Three days later the baby died. Dionitia was three years old at this time. A young orphan girl, Catherine Houston, aged nineteen, had been staying with Nancy during her confinement. Dionitia, her sister, and Catherine went to live with their mother's sister. Together they crossed the plains. They were met somewhere in Wyoming by her father Horace, who had been released from the Mormon Battalion and returned to Salt Lake City 10 Oct 1847. The ox train arrived in Salt Lake City 10 Nov 1847. This was a joyful reunion with his family. The Alexander family stayed with the Henry Rollins Family. In 1849, Horace married Catherine Houston and Martha Burwell. In 1851 the family were sent to settle Parowan, Iron County.

Dionitia grew up in Parowan with two stepmothers having known her own mother for only a short time. On 16 May 1859, at age sixteen, Dionitia married a young Danish Hans Jorgen Mortensen, aged twenty-two. They made their home in Parowan, where they became parents of eleven, six of whom died in childhood. Dionitia died in Parowan, the

same day her last child, James Peter, was born and died. She was age thirty-six at her passing. Hans survived her by thirty-three years. He died 17 Jan 1912. They are buried in Parowan cemetery.

DORTHEA JENSEN MORTENSEN

BIRTHDATE: 26 Apr 1840
Thorby, Maribo, Denmark
DEATH: 12 Nov 1916
Central, Graham, Arizona
PARENTS: Knud Jensen
Bodil Olsen
PIONEER: 15 Sep 1859
Robert F. Neslen Wagon Co.
SPOUSE: Morten Peder Mortensen
MARRIED: 10 May 1859
aboard ship, "William Tapscott"
DEATH: 6 Jun 1891

CHILDREN:
Jens Peter, 5 Apr 1860 (died an infant)
Diantha Elizabeth, 18 Mar 1861
Martin, 28 Oct 1862
Elsie Margaret, 16 Aug 1864
Helena, 26 Feb 1866 (died 8 months)
Maria Helena, 11 Oct 1867
Peter, 29 Nov 1871
Knud Hyrum, 24 Nov 1873
Ellen Bodelle, 29 Apr 1877

Dorthea was the daughter of Knud Jensen and Bodil Olsen who were prosperous and well respected because of their honesty, energy, thrift, and careful work habits. Her family received the LDS Missionaries into their home and were baptized as members on December 31, 1859. Morton Peder Mortensen was one of the local missionaries who converted her. They boarded the ship, "William Tapscott," and were married just a few days before landing in America. They joined the Robert F. Neslen Wagon Company in which to cross the plains and arrived in Salt Lake Valley on September 15, 1859.

They were called to move several times and lived in Parowan, Ephraim, and Gunnison. Morten was called on a second mission to Denmark while Dorthea stayed with her children. On his return, he was asked to take two young converts as his wives. He took his three wives and moved to Scipio. In the spring of 1875, Morten and his families were called by President Brigham Young to do missionary work with the Indians near Tuba City, Arizona. In 1880, Morten moved his three families to Sunset, Arizona where they lived the United Order for four years. Dorthea and her boys took the dairy cows up in the mountains to pasture and back each day, milked them, and made cheese, butter, and other dairy products. In 1885, the Mortensen families moved to Colonial Diaz in Old Mexico for the next twenty five years to protect Morten from authorities who were trying to arrest polygamists. Dorthea was an excellent cook.

She made most of the clothing by spinning, weaving, and knitting. They became the parents of nine children. Dorthea was active in the Relief Society. After Morten died, Dorthea stayed in her home in Mexico and was cared for by her son, Peter, and his wife. In 1912, due to the Mexican Revolution, Dorthea moved to the home of her oldest daughter in Central, Graham County, Arizona. She died there on November 12, 1916 and was buried in Thatcher, Arizona.

ELIZABETH ANN ANDERSON FRANKLAND MORTENSEN

BIRTHDATE: 7 Jan 1851
Glenisla Angus, Scotland
DEATH: 29 Feb 1892
Grover, Wayne, Utah
PARENTS: Alexander Anderson
Catherine McKenzie Anderson
PIONEER: 15 Sep 1868
John Gillespie Wagon Company
SPOUSE I:
William Richard Frankland
MARRIED: 11 Oct 1870
Salt Lake Endowment House
DEATH: 30 Mar 1930
Teasdale, Wayne, Utah

CHILDREN:
William Richard, Jr., 17 Sep 1872 (died age 20)
John Dye, 4 Jan 1874
Catherine, 29 Sep 1875
George Samuel, 20 Aug 1877 (died age 15)
Margaret Isabella, 13 Dec 1878

SPOUSE II: Peter Mortensen
MARRIED: 15 Aug 1888
DEATH: Not listed

CHILDREN:
Lillie Elizabeth, 26 Sep 1889 (died age 3)
Parley Peter, 6 Apr 1891

When Elizabeth was young, she was expected to work and help with the living. She herded cows when she was a small child. At the age of fourteen, she obtained employment in a factory where she learned to spin wool and cotton, and she learned to weave it into different kinds of material for making clothing. She was baptized a member of the LDS Church in 1859. Elizabeth Ann and her mother worked and saved until they were able to sail to America in 1868. They joined the John Gillespie Wagon Company. They were met at the North Fork of the Platte River with supplies and assistance. William Richard Frankland was one of those sent by President Brigham Young to the assistance of the immigrants. This is were they met and fell in love. They arrived in Salt Lake City on September 15, 1868.

Elizabeth and William were married in the Endowment House on October 11, 1870. They lived in Salt Lake near her mother. William worked for Brigham Young helping with the Gardo House and the Bee Hive House. He also worked as a cook for 40 men while they were building road above Stockton. Her mother had remarried and moved to Levan, Utah. Elizabeth and William moved back and forth from Salt Lake to Levan several times. They eventually became divorced. Elizabeth worked at any kind of work she could get, raising a garden and fruit. Several years later, a neighbor, Peter Mortensen, persuaded her to marry him as his second wife. They were married August 15, 1888. Because of trouble with the Federal Marshall, they moved to Wayne County where they felt safe. They had two children together before their family contracted Diphtheria. Elizabeth had worked as a nurse, helping the settlers in times of illness and tried to care for her family as the disease ravaged through their home. But Elizabeth died on February 29, 1892 as well as three of her children. They were all buried in Grover.

ELIZABETH CARSON LEWIS LEWIS MORTENSEN

No
Photo
Available

BIRTHDATE: 10 Aug 1833
Carrelltown, Pickens, Alabama
DEATH: 23 Jun 1901
Parowan, Iron, Utah
PARENTS: Samuel Carson
Eliza Jane Adair Carson Pearson Price
PIONEER: 1851
SPOUSE I: David Lewis
MARRIED: 4 Aug 1852
Salt Lake Endowment House
DEATH: 2 Sep 1855
Parowan, Iron, Utah

CHILDREN:
Eliza, 18 Jun 1853
Elizabeth Ann, 29 May 1854

SPOUSE II: Tarleton Lewis
MARRIED: 1856
Parowan, Iron, Utah
DEATH: 22 Nov 1890
Teasdale, Wayne, Utah

CHILDREN:
Benjamin, 1 Feb 1858
William, Feb 1860

SPOUSE III: Neils Otto Mortensen
MARRIED: 1862 Parowan, Iron, Utah
DEATH: 7 Apr 1912

CHILDREN:
Martin H., 5 Mar 1863
Neils Otto, 14 Mar 1865
Samuel Carson, 11 Sep 1867
Olive Melissa, 2 May 1869
Joseph Edgar, 4 Apr 1871

Elizabeth was converted to the LDS Church as a young woman in Mississippi. She left Mississippi in November of 1845 with her mother; step-father, John Price; her brother, Valentine Carson; and two half sisters. They arrived in Nauvoo on March 6, 1846 and moved on to Winter Quarters where they put in crops and worked at various jobs to get some means to travel to the Salt Lake Valley. They were finally able to start for the valley in the spring of 1851 and arrived in late summer of that same year.

Elizabeth married David Lewis in the Salt Lake Endowment House on August 4, 1852 and they had two children before she was left a widow at the age of twenty two with two small daughters. They had also purchased two Indian boys to save them from slavery. Elizabeth learned to understand and speak the Indian language and raised these boys to adulthood. She married her brother-in-law with the idea that he would take care of her. He was called to establish and supervise other settlements and left her in Parowan. They had two sons together, but she needed to go to work to support her family which now consisted of six children. One of her employers was Neils 0. Mortensen. She was providing care for his invalid wife. After his wife died in early 1862, the church sanctioned her marriage to Neils. They made their home on a farm west of Parowan. She was known as a welcoming hostess to the young people of the area, often having musical evenings and dancing parties in her home. She was an excellent cook.

HELENA SANDERSON MORTENSEN

BIRTHDATE: 8 Mar 1808
Fanefjord, Moen, Prasto, Denmark
DEATH: 24 Aug 1890
Parowan, Iron, Utah
PARENTS: Peder Sanderson
Ane Christine Jorgensen
PIONEER: 9 Nov 1856
James G. Willie Handcart Company
SPOUSE: Peder Mortensen
MARRIED: 9 Nov 1827
Fanefjord, Moen, Prasto, Denmark
DEATH: 9 Apr 1866
Parowan, Iron, Utah

CHILDREN:
Morten Peder, 27 May 1829
Annie Kirstine, 12 Aug 1831
Anders Jergen, 21 Sep 1833
Hans Jorgen, 11 Apr 1837
Peder, 5 Aug 1839 (died age 16)
Lars, 25 Jul 1842
Mette Kirstine, 2 May 1845
Mary, 3 Jul 1847
Caroline, 16 May 1850

Helena (Lena) was born to a family who owned their own homes and farm, who were well respected, and who were skilled as high classed tradesmen. She married Peder

Mortensen and they became the parents of nine children. In 1855, two LDS Missionaries came to their home and the family was convinced of the truthfulness of their gospel message. All of the family were baptized as members of the LDS Church. They were no longer respected, but persecuted instead for their strange beliefs. They decided to emigrate to be with the main body of the church. Their oldest son, Morton, had been asked to serve a three year mission and would follow them to America later. In 1856, they and their seven children sailed on the ship, Thornton, to New Orleans. They went up the Mississippi River. When they got to Iowa City, they were told the equipment was not ready for them. They had to wait until handcarts were built for their trip west which caused their start across the plains to be August 25th. Peter had the means to purchase an ox team and wagon, but was advised that he should divide his means with those less fortunate. He did so and was promised that he and his family would have strength, health, and wisdom as they traveled and the whole family would reach their destination in safety. Peder had been crippled for many years and had to be pushed in a handcart the entire distance. Many hardships were endured during this well-known, ill-fated handcart journey. Seventy seven people died, but the entire Mortensen family reached the Salt Lake Valley on November 9, 1856.

Less than a month after their arrival, they continued their journey by handcart to Parowan, Utah where they lived the remainder of their lives. Helena was ever attentive to Peder. After Peder's death on 5 Apr 1872, Helena was cared for by her daughters until her death on 24 Aug 1890. She was much loved and revered by all who knew her.

INGEBORG PEDERSEN MORTENSEN

BIRTHDATE: 27 Apr 1821
Blaustrod, Frederiksborg, Denmark
DEATH: 10 Jan 1900
Huntsville, Utah
PARENTS: Peder Christensen
Kristen Christiansen Christensen
PIONEER: 28 Sep 1864
William B. Preston Wagon Co.
SPOUSE: Andreas Peder Mortensen
MARRIED: 25 Jun 1848
Sollerod, Copenhagen, Denmark
DEATH: 29 Jul 1913
Huntsville, Weber, Utah

CHILDREN:
Annie Sophie, 24 Mar 1849
Sina Marie, 15 Jul 1851
Niels Wilhelm, 28 May 1853
Jens Christian, 22 Oct 1859
Adam Anders, 5 Jun 1863

Ingeborg Pedersen Mortensen was born in Denmark. She married Andreas Peder Mortensen about 1848. They became the parents of five children, all of whom were born at Sollerud. Ingeborg and Andreas lived and worked on a large estate. She was the head of the Manor House staff and Andreas was the foreman of the farm. They were skilled in their work. Ingeborg set the finest of tables with the beautiful linens, china and silver. She planned the menus and did some of the fancy cooking. In addition to his other duties, Andreas was a skilled butcher.

Sometime before 1860, missionaries from the Mormon Church taught Ingeborg and Andreas the true Gospel. They accepted baptism in Nov 1860. They secretly planned to emigrate to Utah. Secrecy was necessary because they were being severely persecuted by their neighbors. They spent most of the next two years trying to save enough money to emigrate. In the middle of the night, late in Apr 1864, the family left their comfortable home and set sail for America on the clipper ship, "Monarch of the Sea." There were 974 Mormons aboard, the largest company to cross the ocean. The ship was the largest to transport Mormon immigrants. They sailed from Liverpool, England 28 Apr 1864. There was much sadness on the journey. Measles broke out among the children. Their baby died the day before they docked, thirty-five days later, at Castle Gate, New York.

The large company made its way to Mormon Grove, where they remained a month getting outfitted. They then walked 1200 miles to the Salt Lake Valley. They traveled in the William B. Preston wagon-train Company. They arrived in the Salt Lake Valley 28 Sep 1864. They went almost immediately to Huntsville, Utah, a small settlement only three years old. It was situated in a beautiful, green valley some fifteen miles east of Ogden, Utah. The first winter was spent in a dugout. Andreas constructed furniture and cabinets. Ingeborg decorated with flowered material she had brought from Denmark. She had to have things pretty. They were warm and they had privacy. How wonderful that was after six months of travel. The next Spring, Andreas built a beautiful cabin, which stands preserved in Huntsville today. It has been restored and furnished in the style of the period. Later, he built a fine home for Ingeborg and their family.

They prospered and raised their family in Huntsville. They were sealed in the Endowment House 28 Jul 1867. Their children were sealed to them in the Logan Temple 15 Jul 1885. They did the Temple work for their kindred dead in both the Logan and Salt Lake Temples. They were present for the dedication of the Salt Lake Temple. They thanked their Father in Heaven that they had been privileged to gather to the Rocky Mountains. Ingeborg lived to be nearly eighty years old. She was loved and respected by all who knew her.

JENZINA (ZINA) CATHERINE LIND MORTENSEN

BIRTHDATE: 14 Mar 1853
Jylland (Jutland) Alborg Denmak
DEATH: 10 Aug 1929
Moiese Lake, Montana
PARENTS:
Jens Christian Anton Lind
Mariana (Mary Ann) Nielsen
PIONEER: 1868
Jessie Smith Ox Teams
SPOUSE: Peder (Peter) Mortensen
MARRIED: 30 Oct 1871
Endowment House Salt Lake
DEATH SP: 12 Apr 1931
Los Angeles, California

CHILDREN:
Peter Alonzo, 19 Nov 1872
George Anthon, 15 Jun 1875
Eliza Marie, 28 Feb 1878
Mary Elizabeth (Hutchinson), 10 Aug 1880
Lewis Waldmer, 27 Dec 1883
John Henry, 11 Jul 1885
Christina May (Harmon), 6 May 1888
Robert Benjamin, 28 Apr 1894

Jenzina was the fourth child born to Jens Christian Anton Lind and Mariana Nielsen. The family came to America from Denmark and arrived in Utah in 1868 with the Jesse Smith Ox Team Company.

The family was sent to Sanpete County, but Jenzina returned to Salt Lake where she worked as a maid and it was here that she met Peter Mortensen. Their families had made the voyage from Denmark on the same ship. They were married 30 October 1871.

Jenzina and Peter settled in Levan and at times lived in Nephi and also Grover in Wayne County. Peter, having always lived in a city, didn't do well as a farmer, so Jenzina helped the family by sewing for others. She was also a midwife and traveled many miles to help families. The ranches were far apart and many of the people were very poor, so often she was not paid for her work. She often gave the families a quilt she had made. Both she and Peter were generous and shared what few possessions they had.

Peter married Elizabeth Ann Franklin as his second wife and went into hiding, leaving Jenzina to raise the family. He returned after Elizabeth died of diphtheria, bringing their child Parley for Jenzina to raise.

In about 1893 the family moved to Cama Meadows, Idaho and the last years of her life, Jenzina lived with her children. She was an avid reader and helped the children with their school work. She died 10 August, 1929 at Moiese Lake, Montana.

KAREN MARIA CHRISTENSEN MORTENSEN

No
Photo
Available

BIRTHDATE: 23 Apr 1824
Wensysel Co. Denmark
DEATH: 20 Apr 1891
Salt Lake City, Utah
PARENTS: Peter Christensen
Anna Catherine (Katrina) Jensdatter
PIONEER: 1856/1862
SPOUSE: Diedrick Mortensen
MARRIED: 23 May 1863
DEATH SP: 30 Dec 1872
Fairview, Utah

CHILDREN
Andrew Christian, 1855
Anna Katherine (Rasmussen), 11 Nov 1865

Karen Maria was born in Denmark in 1824. She was the oldest of four children. Her brother Jens Christian Christensen married in 1856 in Keokuk, Iowa.

Karen was age forty when she had her last child born in Richfield Utah. She was living the law of polygamy, as Diedrick married Maren Jensdatter 20 Oct 1831 in Denmark and they had nine children.

Diedrick was eighteen years older than Karen. It may be that Karen Maria was a widow with one child when he married her, as the family records show that she had two children, first a son and then their daughter Anna Katherine. Diedrick and his wife, Maren were living in Spring City, when he received a call to settle Sevier County, some 75 miles south to a new town called Richfield. It seems that most of his sons and daughters and their mates participated in this move which was about 1863. By this time he had married a second wife, Karen Maria and she was also living in Richfield with them. Because of Indian troubles, they came back to Mt. Pleasant to live. Their last move was to Fairview. It was there, 30 Dec 1872 that Diedrick passed away leaving Karen Maria a widow once again. Family records show that Maren lived to be seventy-six. In her declining years she was cared for by her children. Karen Marie passed away three days shy of sixty-seven years, having been a widow for eighteen years.

KAREN MARIE NIELSEN MORTENSEN

BIRTHDATE: 18 Sep 1815
Gudum, Aalborg, Denmark
DEATH: 22 Dec 1897
Logan, Cache, Utah
PARENTS: Jens Nielsen
Maren Christensen
PIONEER: 23 Sep 1862
Christian A. Madsen
Independent Co.
SPOUSE: Anders Mortensen
MARRIED: 11 Nov 1837
Hurup, Aalborg, Denmark
DEATH: 1873

CHILDREN:
Morten, 18 Dec 1837
Karen (Klingbeck), 1 Jul 1839
Mary (Maren) (Olsen), 13 Oct 1840
Ane Katherine (Nielsen), 30 Oct 1842
Jens Anders, 17 Aug 1844
Christiana (Olsen), 1 Dec 1846
Karen Marie (Saunders), 21 Dec 1848
Mariane, 2 May 1851
Inger Katharine (Jensen), 13 Aug 1852
Josephine, 16 Feb 1855
Sarah Nielsen (Larsen), 2 Sep 1856
Carl, 22 Jun 1859

On Sunday, April 6, 1862, Karen Marie left Als Parish in Denmark with eight of her twelve children, ranging in ages two to twenty-one years, and started her journey to America. Her husband did not accompany her.

Her youngest child, Carl, died 22 Apr 1862 and was buried at sea. They sailed on the ship "Franklin," with Christian A. Madsen in charge of the company, arriving in New York City May 28th.

Traveling by steamboat and train they arrived at Florence, Nebraska on June 9th. It was here that Karen faced more tragedy. Three of her young daughters died of the dreaded cholera. In Florence the Scandinavian emigrants were split into two companies. The Mortensens remained with Elder Madsen. They left 14 Jul 1862 and arrived in the Salt Lake Valley the 23rd of September. Karen's daughter Ane Katherine was there to meet her. Her daughter Karen had died leaving a small baby.

Karen lived in Salt Lake until 1865 where she earned money by weaving. In the spring of 1865 she walked to Logan with her two youngest daughters.

In Logan Karen worked hard to make a living. She wove carpets and cloth and acquired nursing skills. She took care of many sick people and delivered over 500 babies. The city blessed and revered her name for her many kind acts and valuable service.

Karen Marie Nielsen Mortensen died 22 Dec 1897, at the age of eighty-one and was buried in the Logan, Utah cemetery.

LEENE PEDERSEN MORTENSEN

BIRTHDATE: 28 Mar 1804
Fanefjord, Denmark
DEATH: 24 Aug 1890
Parowan, Iron, Utah
PARENTS: Peder Sandersen
Ane Kirstine Jorgensen
PIONEER: 9 Nov 1856
Willie Handcart Company
SPOUSE: Peter Mortensen
MARRIED: Abt 1826/27
in Denmark
DEATH SP: 9 Apr 1866
Parowan, Iron, Utah

CHILDREN:
Morten P., 27 May 1828
Ann Kirstine, 12 Aug 1831
Anders Jorgen, 21 Sep 1833
Hans Jorgen., 11 Apr 1837
Peter, 5 Aug, 1839
Lars, 25 Jul 1842
Meete Kistena, 2 May 1845
Mary (Maria), 3 Jul 1847
Caroline, 16 May 1850

Leene Pedersen was born 28 Mar 1804 in the village of Fanefjord, Parish of Dame Haarbolle, Praesto ampt, Denmark. Her parents were Peder Sanderson and Ane Kirstine Jorgensen. She married Peter Mortensen about 1826/27, and they became the parents of nine children. One son, Peter, died in Denmark at the age of ten years.

She and her husband were ostracised as they left their home in Denmark to come to America. Their oldest son, Morten was asked to stay in Denmark as a missionary, leaving the burden of the trip on three younger sons and Leene, since she had to do the work for herself and her crippled husband. There were intense hardships as they crossed the plains, food was low and travel was slow, but with unswerving faith they reached the Salt Lake Valley on 9 Nov 1856, traveling with the J. G. Willie Handcart Company. They settled in Parowan, Iron county, Utah.

When the St. George Temple was dedicated, Leene took her family to St. George to be sealed together. Though her son, Peter had died in Denmark, all the other children were present, and they were the first complete family to be sealed in that temple. Peter Mortensen died in Parowan on 9 Apr 1866, and Leene lived for many more years, passing away 24 Aug 1890, at the age of eighty-four years. Both are buried in Parowan, Iron, Utah.

MARIANNA CHRISTIANSEN MORTENSEN

BIRTHDATE: 27 Mar 1835
Follerup, Aarhus, Denmark
DEATH: 3 Dec 1907
Ogden (Eden), Weber, Utah
PARENTS: Christian Mortensen
Anna Katherine Peterson
PIONEER: 1 Oct 1864
John Smith Co. Wagon Train
SPOUSE:
Niels (Neils) Christian Mortensen
MARRIED: 4 Nov 1864
Huntsville, Weber Utah
DEATH SP: 26 Sept 1898
Huntsville, Weber, Utah

CHILDREN:
Emma Marie Elizabeth, 29 Dec 1865
Josephine Andrina, 15 Feb 1868
Neilsena Christena, 26 May 1870
Mary Ann (Mariana), 14 Aug 1871
Niels Christian, 4 Jul 1875
Elvina Caroline, 16 Feb 1878
Ingar Sophia Amelia, 29 Jun 1880

Marianna was five years old when her father died. She went to work at age five tending to chickens and herding geese. When a few years older she was hired as a dairy maid. Many jobs she had were strenuous and unpleasant. She said she sang a lot to keep from thinking about jobs assigned to her. There were no free schools in Denmark so the family earnings were much needed to pay for her schooling.

Marianna met the Mormon missionaries and became interested in their message. Convinced of its truthfulness, she was baptized by Elder Andrew Hansen in 1860. Now her great desire was to go Zion. She started saving as much as she could. She was then working as a cook in the King's Palace.

In 1864 when war broke out between Denmark and Grermany there was danger of the harbor being closed. Word was sent that those wanting to go to Zion should go to Copenhagen and board the steamer for Grimsby where the Church had a very large sailing vessel. On the 28th of April Marianna with 973 Saints left Liverpool, England on the "Monarch of the Sea," under the direction of Patriarch John Smith. It was aboard this ship she met Neils (Niels) Christian Mortensen who had been baptized a member of the church in 1856.

After thirty-five days on a comparatively calm ocean they reached New York on June 3, 1864. They traveled by train to Buffalo. It was slow progress to Wyoming, Nebraska but they made it safely, then left there with the John Smith Independent Company in July with about 150 Saints. Marianna and Niels walked all the way to Salt Lake. Food and water were scarce. They had to improvise coverings for their feet; many were barefoot. There was sickness and death. The friendship between the two had grown to courtship. Before reaching the valley Niels proposed marriage to her. They arrived in the valley October 1 1864.

They were married November 24 1864 in Huntsville, Utah by Bishop Hunt. Two years later they went to the Endowment House in Salt Lake. They acquired some land in Huntsville where they planted crops and built a small home. She managed the home, fed and cared for the animals and chickens, sheared the sheep, washed the wool and spun it into yarn. She dyed some with a log wood dye she made. She dried and stored wildberries for winter, made tallow candles, was a good cook and would cook meals during the planting and harvesting time and carry them out to the fields so the men would not lose day light hours. She made their clothes, quilts, and carpets for the floor with fresh straw under them to keep the floors warmer. They had an egg and butter business which she took care of when her husband went to Denmark on a mission in 1883-1885. She was kind and loveable, and made everyone welcome and comfortable that came to visit. She entertained many Church Authorities when they came for special affairs.

She died December 2, 1907 at the home of her daughter Mary Ann, in Eden, Utah, and was buried beside her husband in the Huntsville Cemetery.

METTE MARIA HANSEN MORTENSEN

BIRTHDATE: 27 Jun 1830
Emb, Hjorring, Denmark
DEATH: 17 Jun 1905
Salina, Sevier, County, Utah
PARENTS: Hans Christen Thomsen
Johanna Maria Poulsen Thomsen
PIONEER: Oct 1862
Wagon John R. Murdock Co.
SPOUSE: Jens Fredrick Mortensen
MARRIED: abt. May 1862
On ship "Franklin," Atlantic Ocean
DEATH: 9 Jan 1886
Koosharem, Sevier County, Utah

CHILDREN:
Christian Jorgensen,, 29 Jan 1860
Annie Catherine (Ivie), 26 Nov 1863
Johanna Marieh (Olsen), 14 Mar 1868
Martha Marie (Ronnow), 6 May 1871
James Fredrick, 28 Nov 1873

Mette Maria Hansen Mortensen was born in Denmark. Her first baby was born after bans had been posted. After she joined the Mormon Church, Mette was disowned and disinherited by her parents and her husband-to-be. Mette came from a wealthy family in Denmark. She had been trained as a weaver and was able to take a spinning wheel, loom and many supplies with her when she emigrated to America to live with the Saints in Utah. Some who boarded the ship on which she sailed had measles and it quickly spread. Many became ill and by the time they reached New York forty-eight people had died, most of them children.

Mette met and married Jens Fredrick Mortensen on board the ship. He gave away most of her supplies to help those who were ill and in need. Few of her possessions were left by the time they reached America.

They were able to purchase a wagon before crossing the Plains but shared it with another family. There was little room for the families to ride in the wagon so Mette walked all of the way to the Salt Lake Valley. Most of the time she walked bare-footed to save her shoes from wearing out. When they crossed streams, Mette was able to ride on the tongue of the wagon. They arrived in Utah with the John R. Murdock Company Oct 1862. They spent the first winter in Mt. Pleasant, Utah in a dugout, where their first child was born. While in Mt. Pleasant Mette was very ill for a long time with Mountain Fever. Later, they were called to help settle Salina, Utah, largely because of Mette's weaving skills. They were among the first five families to settle there. Because of Indian problems they had to move to Gunnison, Utah where they spent nearly five years before returning to Salina. Mette was a faithful worker in Relief Society from its beginning in Salina and was always ready and willing to help those in need. She was described as a peaceful, unoffending woman.

After her parents'death, she was given some inheritance which she used for genealogy research for her family and her husband's family. Because her husband practiced polygamy, he had to leave Salina with a group of men and when they had gone only as far as Koosharem he contracted pneumonia and died at the age of fifty-three. President Wilfred Woodruff said of him that he was a martyr to the cause. Mette continued to live in her home in Salina with her youngest son until her oldest daughter and her family came to live with her and take care of her until she died 17 Jun 1905. She was seventy-five years old. She had been a widow for nineteen years.

WILHELMINA CHRISTINE IPSEN MORTENSEN

BIRTHDATE: 20 Jan 1836
Vestermarie, Bornholm Denmark
DEATH: 8 Jul 1885
Manassa, Conejos Co., Colorado
PARENTS: Hans Ipsen
Bodil Kjerstine Schroeder Ipsen
PIONEER: 26 Aug 1864
Wagon John R. Murdock Co.
SPOUSE:Anders Jorgen Mortensen
MARRIED: 15 Jul 1865
Salt Lake City, Utah
DEATH: 13 Oct 1884
Parowan, Utah

CHILDREN:
Holm Andreas, 17 Oct 1866
Francis Ipsen, 5 Jan 1869
Laura Andrea, 27 Jun 1873
Hemming Carl, 29 May 1879

Wilhelmina Christine Ipsen Mortensen was the first-born of five children. She spent her childhood on Bornholm, an Island off the Danish coast. When she was old enough, she worked on a neighbor's dairy farm where the cold, wet conditions were so unhealthy that she developed a type of rheumatism. She had to return to her parents' home to recover. The family was Lutheran, and Elmina was the lead soprano in the Church choir. She was tall and good looking with dark hair and eyes. She was very serious minded and sincere in her beliefs. The family had many discussions about religion and felt something was missing in the doctrines of the Lutheran Church. Wilhelmina (Elmina) and her sister, Andrea, went to a meeting to hear the doctrine of the Mormon missionaries. The talks were given in English, but both Elmina and Andrea understood every word. This was a testimony to them. They returned home to tell their family of this inspiring experience. Elmina was baptized 20 May 1856, and the family started making plans for the girls to travel to Zion.

Andrea was the first to leave Denmark. When she arrived in the Salt Lake Valley she went to Minersville, Utah to work. In 1864, Elmina joined a group of Saints bound for America via Liverpool, England. They landed at New Orleans , then went up the river to St. Louis. There she joined a company led by Captain John R. Murdock. There was not space in the wagons for all to ride and the girls who were walking were very glad when Captain Murdock would take them across the streams on the back of his mule.

When Elmina arrived in the Salt Lake Valley 26 Aug 1864, she went to her sister in Minersville. She was hired to do housework during the threshing season. One of the threshing crew, Anders Jorgen Mortensen, and Elmina were attracted to each other. On 15 Jul 1865, she was endowed and sealed as the second wife to Anders in the Endowment House in Salt Lake City. His first wife was Christine Andersen. Anders built a small adobe house in Parowan, Utah and Elmina lived there and had their four children. As she aged, she became more crippled and could not dress herself or comb her hair. She managed her home with strict discipline and cleanliness. Her family was never late for a meeting. Elmina and her children were always neatly dressed.

On 13 Oct 1884, Anders died suddenly. In 1885, his two wives and their children decided to move to San Luis Valley, Colorado, where Anders' brothers were living. Elmina, Christine and the four youngest children went by train. The older children moved their possessions by wagon which took six weeks. They were unaware that Elmina had died in Colorado on 8 Jul 1885, while they were traveling. Elmina is buried in the Manassa Cemetery in Colorado. She lived nine months longer than her husband.

BARBARA MATILDA NEFF MOSES

BIRTHDATE: 28 Oct 1822
Lancaster County, Pennsylvania
DEATH; 29 May 1890
East Mill Creek, Utah
PARENTS: John Neff II
Mary Barr Neff
PIONEER: 2 Oct 1847
Jedediah M. Grant Wagon Co.
SPOUSE: Julian Moses
MARRIED: 25 Mar 1845
Nauvoo, Illinois
DEATH: 12 Apr 1892
Salt Lake City, Utah

CHILDREN: none

Barbara Matilda Neff Moses was born in Lancaster County, Pennsylvania. She joined the Mormon Church along with her parents when the Mormon missionaries visited Strasburg sometime before the Summer of 1841. Barbara had the privilege of meeting Joseph Smith when she and her parents were guests of the Prophet in the Nauvoo Mansion House in May 1844. They spent time in conversation and they heard him speak many times from the pulpit. They returned to their home and sold their goods and possessions so they could join the Saints in Nauvoo, Ill.

While in Nauvoo, Barbara met Julian Moses. They were married 25 Mar 1845. They crossed the Plains with the Jedediah M. Grant wagon train Company, leaving Winter Quarters, Nebraska 17 Jun and arriving in the Salt Lake Valley 2 Oct 1847. They first settled in Sugarhouse area in southeast Salt Lake and began farming. Her husband was called on a mission for the Church for two years and when he returned he found that the farm had been sold for taxes. They started anew on another piece of land near the mouth of Mill Creek Canyon. They did very well on this farm of 160 acres. Skyline High School stands on the old Julian Moses farm.

When Barbara was young an accident injured her back. She grew up to be "hunched-back" and did not achieve an appreciable height. She was never able to bear children of her own. In order to have a family, she consented to the marriage of her husband and a young girl who had been working for them in their home. It was agreed that the first child from this marriage would be given to Barbara to raise. A son was born and named Julian Neff. Barbara raised him as her own.

Barbara was a pioneer of faith and fortitude. She died in East Mill Creek, Utah 29 May 1890.

ANN MITCHELL MCCLUSKEY MOSS

BIRTHDATE: 1 Jan 1813
Birmingham, Warwickshire, Eng.
DEATH: 10 Jan 1887
Salt Lake City, Utah
PARENTS: Michael McCluskey
Ann Mitchell McCluskey
PIONEER: 26 Oct 1864
William Hyde Wagon Company
SPOUSE: William Jackson Moss
MARRIED: 1 Dec 1828
St. George, East London, Surrey, Eng.
DEATH: 26 Jan 1893
Salt Lake City, Utah

CHILDREN:
Ann, 7 Oct 1829
Catherine, 15 May 1831 (died 2 mo)
William, 10 Nov 1832 (died age 22)
John, 5 Dec 1834 (died age 6)
Catherine, 4 Feb 1837 (died age 3)
James, 16 Jun 1838 (died age 3)
Jane, 25 Feb 1840 (died age 22)
Thomas, 25 Oct 1841
James, 17 Apr 1843 (died age 19)
Mary Ann, 4 Sep 1845 (died age 18)
Eleanor, 12 May 1847
Sarah, 31 Jan 1849 (died age 4)
Emily, 9 Jun 1851
Elizabeth, 19 Feb 1853 (died age 1
Joseph, 8 May 1855

Ann was from a very large and poor family. She was fifteen when she married William Jackson Moss. He worked as a harness maker. They had fifteen children of their own and raised two adopted children. They became members of the LDS Church in January 1851. Her husband was the Presiding Elder of that branch of the church. Ten of their children had died of various causes by that time. It is difficult to imagine the heartache she endured.

Her testimony of the truthfulness of the gospel led to a desire to come to Zion. Ann was blessed with the means to come with her companion to help build up the Kingdom of God. Her son, Thomas', wife came to America first and worked to send money for Tom, all of his family, as well as her own parents. They emigrated to America with their remaining children in 1864 on the sailing ship, "Hudson." They crossed the Plains with the William Hyde Wagon Company and arrived in Salt Lake Valley on October 26, 1864. Her husband obtained work with the Jenkin Brothers Harness Makers in the valley. They resided on Ninth East between South Temple and First South in the eleventh Ward. On November 9th, 1868, she and William received their endowments in the Endowment House.

She shared her husband in polygamy with Maria Barrett. She gave her clothes to the needy, and opened her doors to the Elders. She and William had the privilege of celebrating their 58th Wedding Anniversary in the Eleventh Ward December 1, 1886 before she died on January 10, 1887.

EMMA ALEXANDER MOSS

BIRTHDATE: 14 Apr 1846
Calne, Wiltshire, England
DEATH: 11 Jan 1922
Bountiful, Davis, Utah
PARENTS: Able Alexander
Sarah Alexander Alexander
PIONEER: 26 Oct 1864
William Hyde Wagon Company
SPOUSE: John Moss
MARRIED: 25 Mar 1865
Salt Lake City, Utah
DEATH: 4 Aug 1884
Bountiful, Davis, Utah

CHILDREN:
David, 8 Jan 1867
Alma, 21 Jan 1868
Sarah, 13 Sep 1870
Eveline, 14 Jun 1872
Abel Alexander, 6 Jun 1874
Robert, 15 Apr 1876
Stephen, 30 Mar 1879
Margaret, 5 Nov 1882

Emma and her parents became converted to the LDS Church while living in England. Their family sailed from London on June 3, 1864 on the ship, "Hudson." There was much sickness and misery on their voyage across the ocean. From Wyoming, Nebraska they joined the William Hyde Wagon Company and arrived in Utah on October 26, 1864.

As soon as they reached the valley, they went to Bountiful to join with other English immigrants. Emma's father hired out to John Moss to herd his sheep. Eventually, John asked Emma to join his family in plural marriage. They were married in the Endowment House in Salt Lake City, Utah. Emma was a very good English cook, and a tidy clean housewife. She possessed a jovial disposition and was a faithful church member. She and her father often bore their testimony in word and in song. Emma was an active Relief Society teacher for many years. She cared for her parents for the rest of their lives.

Emma was one of the first group of Visiting Teachers of the South Bountiful Ward when Visiting Teachers was a separate organization from the Relief Society. She had a fine voice and sang in many choral groups and in the choir. On February 11, 1892, the Davis County group of the National Suffrage Association for Women was founded in Bountiful with Emma Moss as one of the Executive Committee. She was zealous in her effort to promote the cause of suffrage and attended the great mass meeting of Utah Suffragists held in the Salt Lake Tabernacle on March 18, 1885. At this time, women in the Territory of Utah were granted the privilege of voting. Emma Moss was a devoted daughter, loving helpmate to her husband, and a caring mother.

FANNIE ELIZABETH GOODMAN MOSS

BIRTHDATE: 29 Dec 1839
Aspley, Bedfordshire, England
DEATH: 2 Mar 1913
Salt Lake City, Utah
PARENTS: William Goodman
Matilda Crisp Goodman
PIONEER: 15 Oct 1862
Isaac Canfield Wagon Company
SPOUSE: Thomas Moss
MARRIED: 17 Feb 1860
near London, England
DEATH SP: 29 Oct 1909
Salt Lake City, Utah

CHILDREN:
William Thomas, 15 Aug 1861
Jane Elizabeth (Caldwell), 9 Jun 1864
Mary Lavina (Boam), 2 Oct 1866
Annie Francis (Castleton) 5 Mar 1869
Matilda Ellen (Webley) 14 Mar 1871
Katie Loretta (Boam), 24 Aug 1873
James Edward, 4 Sept 1875
Joseph Henry, 27 Feb 1879
Maude Edna, 16 Oct 1881
George Quincey, 12 Oct 1882

Fannie was an only child, born in Aspley near London, England. Her grandfather was an English nobleman's son who married the cook. He was cut off from any claim to the family estate. Fannie married Thomas Moss in 1860, near London, England. Both were born to parents who had accepted the gospel of Jesus Christ and were members of the Mormon Church. It was their desire to immigrate to Utah to be with the Saints. Both families were poor so only one could come first while the others worked to save the money so the rest could follow.

Fannie, with an eight month old baby boy, came first. At Winter Quarters she was assigned to the Isaac Canfield Company of 125 people. Fannie walked across the plains carrying her baby. Because of the baby she was allowed to ride in a wagon every other day. Six months after leaving England she arrived in Utah, 15 Oct 1862. She worked as a maid at the Townsend House for travelers to earn the money for the rest of her family to immigrate to Utah. One year later Tom and his parents and Fannie's parents arrived in the Salt Lake Valley.

Fannie and Tom had ten children. In 1875 they were called to go south and settle Grass Valley, near Koosharem, and to live the United Order. The family had many experiences with the Indians. After six years they returned to the Salt Lake Valley. Fannie died at the age of seventy-four of heart failure, five years after Tom had passed away.

Fannie had a cheerful, sunny and optimistic personality. She was always looking on the bright side. She could endure hardships and cheerfully go on full of courage and faith. She made friends everywhere. Her posterity honor her memory.

SARAH MATTHEWS MOSS

No Photo Available

BIRTHDATE: 18 Jan 1843
Hatch, Northill, Bedfordshire, Eng.
DEATH: 8 Jun 1874
Portage, Box Elder, Utah
PARENTS: Jeremiah Matthews
Ann Martin Matthews
PIONEER: 1865
Wagon Train
SPOUSE: Patterson Moss
MARRIED: abt 1865 on the Plains
or in Salt Lake City, Utah
DEATH SP: Apr 1888
Portage, Box Elder, Utah

CHILD (born out of wedlock):
Sarah Jane, 17 Nov 1860

CHILDREN (by Patterson Moss):
Mary Ann, 4 Sep 1867
George Riley, 13 Mar 1869
John William, 23 Oct 1871
Perry Samuel, 4 Oct 1872

Sarah Matthews Moss was born in England. She was the third daughter and sixth child of the eight children born to Jeremiah Matthews and Ann Martin Matthews. She was baptized into the Mormon Church at the age of nine. As Sarah grew older, she helped her mother braid straw for making hats. At the age of seventeen, Sarah gave birth out of wedlock to a daughter, Sarah Jane. They emigrated to America together in 1865.

The names of Sarah Mathews and Sarah Jane Matthews can be found on the record of the ship "Caroline." They left London, England 5 May 1865 and sailed from Liverpool, England 6 May 1865. They reached New York on 11 Jun. It is said they walked every step of the way from the Platte River. It is thought they started near Council Bluffs, Iowa, as they traveled along the Platte River for a long way. Brigham Young had sent teams and wagons to help the emigrants. One of these wagons was driven by Patterson Moss, a widower. He had lost his first wife in Iowa before coming to Utah. He had two children, a boy and a girl. Sarah and Patterson were married either on the way across the Plains or soon after reaching Utah. They went to Kaysville, Davis County, Utah to live. While living in Kaysville, three children were born. They also lived in Brigham City, Utah where Patterson was a tanner and worked for the Mormon Church. They moved to Portage, Box Elder, Utah where their fourth child was born.

Sarah was endowed and sealed to her husband 2 Feb 1869 in the Endowment House. Sarah died 8 Jun 1874 in Portage, leaving behind a family of very small children.

She was buried in Portage, Utah. Her husband also died in Portage Apr 1888, and is buried there.

CAROLINE MATILDA LEE MOTT

BIRTHDATE: 20 Jan 1828
Unadilla, Otsego, New York
DEATH: 30 Mar 1867
Chicken Creek, Juab County, Utah
PARENTS: Hatheway Lee
Aurilla Evans Lee
PIONEER: 1854
Independent Wagon Company
SPOUSE: John Wentworth Mott
MARRIED: Jan 1847
New York
DEATH SP: 7 Apr 1903
Vernal, Utah

CHILDREN:
Julia Ann, 27 Mar 1848
Charles Alverado, 12 Jan 1850
John Romanzo, 2 Dec 1851 (died as child)
Samuel Dwight, 20 Sep 1853
Electa Anthony, 22 Sep 1855 (died as infant)
Caroline Alvira, 11 Dec 1858
Myron Oscar, 27 Mar 1860
Vicena Augusta, 7 Nov 1862
Wesley Harrison, 6 Nov 1864 (died as child)
Edman A., Jul 1866 (died as child)

Caroline Matilda Lee Mott was born in Unadilla, New York. Her parents were Hatheway and Aurilla Lee. Caroline was baptized a member of the Mormon Church 4 Apr 1851 in Wisconsin. In Jan 1847 she had married John Wentworth Mott in New York. They became the parents of ten children; three died as children and one as an infant. Four of their children were born in Decature Green, Wisconsin. The rest were born in Utah.

Caroline and John and their family made the decision to cross the Plains and join the members of the Mormon Church in the Salt Lake Valley. They joined an Independent wagon-train Company in 1854. They helped settle the Spanish Fork, Utah area. Three of their children were born in Spanish Fork. They then settled in Payson, Utah where their last three children were born. Caroline and her husband were sealed in the Endowment House, Salt Lake City, Utah 24 Mar 1854. Caroline also received her Patriarchal Blessing. She was of Spanish descent. Her Spanish lineage was from Castilla, Spain unknown from her father or mother's line. It is not known if she had brothers or sisters. She once made the remark that no one would be able to find her ancestors.

Caroline died almost a year after giving birth to her tenth child. She had lived in Chicken Creek, Payson and Spanish Fork, all in Utah. She died in Chicken Creek 30 Mar 1867. Her husband died 7 Apr 1903 in Vernal, Utah. Caroline was buried in the Payson City Cemetery.

ELIZABETH DWIGHT MOTT

No
Photo
Available

BIRTHDATE: 18 Mar 1790
Great Bearington, Massachusetts
DEATH: 6 Jul 1865
Payson, Utah, Utah
PARENTS: Israel Dwight
Susannah Gerry Dwight
PIONEER: 1854
Independent Wagon Company
SPOUSE: Samuel Mott
MARRIED: 24 Dec 1807
Rutland, Orwell, Vermont
DEATH: 5 Apr 1867
Payson, Utah, Utah

CHILDREN:
Maria Howe, 20 Sep 1808
Wesley, 1810 (died age 19)
William Harisson, 1812
Jeremiah (twin), 1814
Harmond (twin), 1814
Ann, Sep 1818
Mary, 27 Nov 1820
Samuel, 1821 (died age 3)
John Wentworth, 20 Dec 1822
Daniel Richmond, 23 Apr 1826
Electa, 1 Jul 1828
Susannah, 16 Sep 1830
Thomas, 19 Jun 1832
Simeon, 1834
Wesley

Elizabeth was born in Great Bearington, Massachusetts. Her parents kept moving west with the frontier. On December 24, 1807, she married Samuel Mott in Rutland, Orwell, Vermont. Their first children were born in Vermont. The Mott family moved to New York between 1814 and 1817. They were acquainted with Joseph Smith. Elizabeth, her husband, and daughter, Maria, were among the converts to the new religion in the first year the church was organized. Her husband, Samuel Mott, was listed as a presiding elder over a meeting of the LDS Church in New York.

They followed the church in the moves westward. The family was of a pioneering heritage, so they continued with the course of the LDS emigration to the Salt Lake Valley. Samuel and Elizabeth came across the Plains with their daughter and her family. Samuel was sixty nine and Elizabeth was sixty four when they arrived in Salt Lake in 1854 in an Independent Wagon Company. They were directed to settle on the banks of Peteetneet Creek at what is now the town of Payson. The Motts built their house just two blocks from their daughter, Maria and her husband Anson Sheffield's home.

EUPHEMIA ANN CARROLL MOULTON

BIRTHDATE: 9 Jun 1856
Cumberland Co.,York, New Brunswick
DEATH: 18 Apr 1914
Heber, Wasatch, Utah
PARENTS: Patrick Carroll
Margaret Euphemia Robinson
PIONEER: 1861
Francis Brown Company
SPOUSE: James Heber Moulton
MARRIED: 28 Sep 1874
Salt Lake City, Utah
DEATH SP: 29 Mar 1934
Salt Lake City, Utah

CHILDREN:
Euphemia Lucretia, 31 Aug 1875
Sarah Margaret, 10 Feb 1877
James Heber, 22 Mar 1879
Emily Jane, 19 Mar 1881
Thomas Henry, 28 Jul 1882
Patrick Robinson, 26 Nov 1884
Lula Pearl, 16 Jul 1886
Edmund Roy, 11 Sep 1888
Robert Merrill, 19 Nov 1890
Rolland Carroll, 16 May 1893
Grant, 18 Oct 1896
Ida May, 12 Nov 1900
Cecil, 19 Aug 1903

Euphemia Ann Carroll was born 9 Jun 1856 in Cumberland Co., York, New Brunswick, the daughter of Patrick Carroll and Margaret Euphemia Robinson. Her parents came to Utah Territory in 1861 while Euphemia was still a young child, traveling with the Francis Brown Company.

Euphemia married James Heber Moulton on 28 Sep 1874 in Salt Lake City. They made their home in Heber City where all of their children were born. She worked hard to make her home an attractive place, raised a nice garden, and helped care for the farm animals. She cared for a twelve-year-old sister when her parents moved to Ashley Valley. She was secretary to the Relief Society, and a teacher in other organizations of the Church.

Euphemia died on 18 Apr 1914 in Heber city. Her husband died 29 Mar 1934 also in Heber City, Wasatch, Utah.

ISABELL TONKS THACKER MOULTON

BIRTHDATE: 12 Jul 1858
Philadelphia, Pennsylvania
DEATH: 2 Mar 1925
Heber, Wasatch Co., Utah
PARENTS: William Thacker
Rachel Tonks Thacker
PIONEER: 1 Oct 1862
Joseph Horne Wagon Company
SPOUSE: John Ephraim Moulton
MARRIED: 23 Mar 1882
Salt Lake Endowment House
DEATH SP: 3 Feb 1915
Heber, Wasatch, Utah

CHILDREN:
Charlotta Elizabeth (Giles), 5 Jan 1883
John Thomas, 24 Dec 1884
Fredrick William, 22 Jan 1887
Addison Charles, 30 Apr 1889
Deyce Dell (Robbins), 3 Feb 1893
Albert Thacker, 17 Feb 1895
Ernest Dewey, 7 May 1898
Ethel Fern(Watson), 19 Sept 1901

Isabell remembered very well walking a good part of the way across the Plains. They were traveling across the Plains with the Joseph Horne Wagon Company at the time she was four years old. She also remembered the episode where her father, William, found what he thought were mushrooms. He gathered a hat full of toadstools and cooked them for dinner. Everyone, except the baby, ate some and became very ill. They had to be administered to and after vomiting, they were soon relieved of the poison. They were very thankful to be well again.

She and her parents lived in a home on North Temple Street just west of the Temple Block. Her family lived in Salt Lake for three years, then moved to Cache Valley. They lived in Logan for a year, then moved to Clarkston. During the Blackhawk War, they moved again. They lived in Smithfield for two years and from there went to Peoa. From Peoa, they moved to Heber City, then moved to Daniel and took up a homestead. Isabell went out doing day work for people in their homes. She bought the first sewing machine in the family. She helped the family all she could. She paid her own tuition, went to school, and was one of the first school teachers in Daniel. While she was working at William Knowlton's Ranch which was north of Heber, she met John E. Moulton. They were married in the Endowment House in Salt Lake City on March 1882. They raised seven of their eight children to adulthood.

MARY ELIZABETH GILES MOULTON

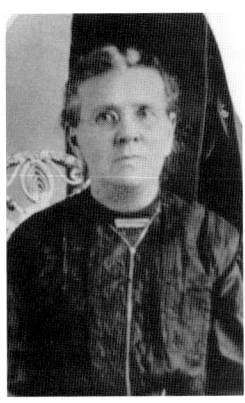

BIRTHDATE: 30 Jul 1852
Burlington, Des Moines, Iowa
DEATH: 21 May 1932
Heber City, Wasatch, Utah
PARENTS: George Giles
Mary Greenwood Giles
PIONEER: 15 Aug 1856
E. B. Tripp Wagon Company
SPOUSE: Joseph Moulton
MARRIED: 15 Dec 1868
Salt Lake Endowment House
DEATH SP: 6 Mar 1935
Heber City, Wasatch, Utah

CHILDREN:
Sarah Elizabeth, 14 Nov 1869
Joseph Giles, 12 Apr 1871
Thomas William, 8 Oct 1872
George Wilford, 2 Sep 1874
Charles, 12 May 1876
John William, 7 Jul 1878
Alma Moroni, 22 Nov 1880
Brigham Nephi, 12 Aug 1883
Mary Malinda (Lindy), 5 Jul 1885

Mary Elizabeth was born while her parents were waiting for other family members to arrive from England so they could all cross the plains together. Her parents were recent converts to the LDS Church and her father was a blacksmith. After the remainder of the family arrived, they were assigned to the E. B. Tripp Wagon Company. They arrived in Salt Lake City on August 15, 1856, but camped at Emigration Square until arrangements were made for them to go to Provo on the 19th. They purchased land near the mountains east of Provo and helped each other build homes and plant gardens. All of the wagon train stayed together, helping each other until everyone had a home.

In 1860, the Giles family moved to Heber City where they lived at the fort until they could build a home of their own. Mary Elizabeth (Lizzie) had to weed in the grain fields; learn to spin wool, make flannel, and make her dresses. She was a little over sixteen when she married Joseph Moulton in the Salt Lake Endowment House. Their first home was in Heber and was enlarged as their family increased. Joseph was called to practice polygamy and took two additional wives. He tried hard to be fair to the three families, but there was jealousy and bad feelings. The families had to go into hiding to avoid having Joseph arrested for practicing polygamy, so they moved to New Dublan in Old Mexico. Life was miserable for them and Lizzie insisted on moving back to the green pastures of Heber. In 1893, all three wives were in their own homes and all went out to work when they could find it, washing, sewing, house cleaning, and nursing. She became an excellent midwife. They raised fruit and sold it. What they didn't sell, they prepared for winter use. Lizzie was of fine moral character and generous to all she knew. Through all her trials she showed unshakable faith in God and humanity, with love for the good and comfort of others. She died 21 May 1932.

SARAH DENTON MOULTON

BIRTHDATE: 5 Jun 1817
Rushden, Northampton, England
DEATH: 7 Jul 1888
Heber, Wasatch, Utah
PARENTS: Charles Denton
Charlotte Bassfield
PIONEER: Nov 1856
Willie Handcart Company
SPOUSE: Thomas Moulton
MARRIED: 18 Apr 1840
Irchester, Northampton, England
DEATH SP: 17 Apr 1892
Heber, Wasatch, Utah

CHILDREN:
Mary Ann, 5 May 1841
William Denton, 17 Jul 1843
Joseph, 22 Aug 1845
James Heber, 1 Jul 1848
Charlotte, 7 Jun 1851
Sophia Elizabeth, 30 Oct 1853
Charles Alma, 6 May 1856
Thomas Denton, 29 Oct 1858
John Ephriam, 16 Sep 1860
George Franklin, 19 Mar 1863

Sarah Denton was born 5 Jun 1817 in Rushden, Northampton, England, the daughter of Charles Denton and Charlotte Bassfield. She married Thomas Moulton 18 Apr 1840 in Irchester, Northampton, England, and they became the parents of ten children, all but the last three born in England.

After reading a pamphlet by Parley P. Pratt, "The Voice of Warning," she and her husband joined the Church. She secretly saved small amounts of money in a fruit jar until they had enough to come to America. Her son, Charles Alma, was born on board ship three days after they set sail. They joined with the Willie Handcart Company in Iowa City, but had to leave behind many posessions because there was no room on the carts.

Their first home was in Provo, then in 1860 they moved to Heber City, where they lived the rest of their lives. Sarah was a thrifty homemaker, and a very faithful member of the Church. Besides her own large family she raised a daughter of her husband's deceased wife, Esther Marsh, who was also named Sarah.

Sarah D. Moulton died in Heber City on 7 Jul 1888, and Thomas Moulton died 17 Apr 1892, also in Heber City, Wasatch, Utah.

MAREN SORENSEN MOURITSEN

BIRTHDATE: 22 Apr 1824
Guldager, Vrejlev, Hjorring,
Denmark
DEATH: 16 Feb 1904
Smithfield, Cache, Utah
PARENTS: Soren Christian Hansen
Johanne Christiansen
PIONEER: 4 Sep 1859
George Rowley Handcart Company
SPOUSE: Lars Mouritsen
MARRIED: 12 Sep 1848
Bronderslev, Aalborg, Denmark
DEATH SP: 1 Feb 1913

CHILDREN:
Johanna Maria (adopted), 17 Jun 1846
Mourits/Lars, 28 Jan 1849
Maren, 11 Nov 1851
Johanne Kirstine/Jane, 29 Jan 1853

Maren was born to Soren Christian Hansen and Johanne Christiansen in Guldager, Denmark on April 22, 1824. When she was twenty-four, she married Lars Mouritsen in Bronderslev, Denmark. Her husband was a brick mason who owned his own kiln and had a prosperous business. They lived well and happily. They had many friends until they were baptized as members of the LDS Church. Disappointed, but continuing faithful to their beliefs, Lars sold his fine business for a substantial sum of money to buy passage on the ship, "William Tapscott," for his family. They left Liverpool, England on April 11, 1859. The ship's financial register also records that Lars had purchased wagons and cattle to make the journey west to the Salt Lake Valley. After arriving in Castle Gardens, New York Harbor on May 14, 1859, this emigrant company steamed up the Hudson River to Albany, went on to Windsor, Canada, and then crossed over to Detroit. From there, they traveled by train to St. Joseph, Missouri and boarded the Steamboat, "St. Mary" on May 21. Four days later the vessel discharged the passengers at Florence, Nebraska.

The man from whom Lars purchased wagons and cattle did not deliver them. Therefore, Maren and her family heroically chose to walk across the plains in the George Rowley Handcart Company which departed from Florence, Nebraska on June 9, 1859 and arrived in the Salt Lake Valley on September 4, 1859. Maren persevered as her children hungered for food by digging for sego lily bulbs, catching wild game, and grinding grains in a wooden bowl with two large rocks in order to make flour for pancakes. Her entire family survived the rigorous journey and later settled in Smithfield, Utah. Maren helped her husband and family faithfully live the gospel and build a new business of brick making. She died February 16, 1904.

SUSAN ELIZABETH WILDMAN MOURITSEN

BIRTHDATE: 24 Mar 1862
Norwood, Asphodel, Peterbro,
Canada
DEATH: 9 Nov 1946
Bennington, Bear Lake Co., Idaho
PARENTS: Edward Wildman
Jane Baxter Wildman
PIONEER: 2 Sep 1868
Simpson A. Molen Wagon Train
SPOUSE: Mourits Mourtisen
MARRIED: 22 Oct 1885
Logan Temple , Cache Co., Utah
DEATH: 23 Sep 1922
Bennington, Bear Lake Co., Idaho

CHILDREN:
Edward, 19 Jul 1886
Vara (Lindsay), 28 Jul 1888
David, 24 May 1890
Gwendolyn, 19 Mar 1892
Glendale, 19 Mar 1892
Daughter (stillborn), 7 Jan 1898
Bertie (Rich), 18 May 1899
Alnora, 23 Mar 1901
Roy, 28 Jul 1903

Susan Elizabeth was born in Canada, 1862. At age six, she was the oldest of four children, when her family immigrated to Utah. They left Canada 24 Jul 1868, met other saints in New York and traveled six, weeks and three days, arriving by ox drawn wagon at Salt Lake City, then on to Smithfield where she grew to womanhood. At age twenty-three she married Mourits Mourtisen, a widower of five years. This was a polygamous union, as he married Karen Hansen on the same day. Soon after he was called to a mission in Denmark. Susan's first son was born while he was there.

They were living in Idaho by 1907 and each wife had borne eight children, when "Aunt Carrie" died in child birth. The two families were then combined as one and Susan reared this large family. Susan was a natural diplomat, had a strong will and deep faith. Many turned to her for help in times of illness or distress, and much of her service was to the sick in the homes of her sisters and later her children.

Susan was a productive genealogist and an active temple worker for many years. She was also a counselor in M.I.A., Primary and Relief Society. She was the first religion teacher in Bennington, Idaho, and taught Relief Society, off and on, for over forty years. Her talents were many. She was an excellent seamstress; she sewed for the large combined family and in her later years made an average of twenty-six quilts a year to assist her children and grandchildren. Many benefited from her long, productive life. Susan was independent and faithful. She passed away 23 Sep 1922 in Bennington at age eighty-four at the home of her daughter Vara Lindsey, having been a widow for twenty-four years.

ELIZABETH HALL BILLS MOWER

BIRTHDATE: 20 Nov 1820
Surry County, North Carolina
DEATH: 17 Mar 1897
Milburn, Sanpete, Utah
PARENTS: Harrison Hall
Rebecca East
PIONEER: 21 Sep 1848
Brigham Young's Wagon Co.
SPOUSE I: Mr. Porter (Divorced)
MARRIED: Date not known

CHILDREN:

SPOUSE II: John Bills
MARRIED: 6 Jan 1848
Nauvoo, Illinois
DEATH SP: 19 Feb 1850
Pacheco Pass, San Joaquin, California

CHILDREN:
Martha, 18 Feb 1848
Wesley, 6 Mar 1850

SPOUSE III: Henry Mower
MARRIED: 24 Jul 1851
DEATH: 20 Feb 1902

CHILDREN:
George Harrison, 25 Jun 1852
William Ezra, 10 Nov 1854
John Lisbon, 9 Jan 1859

Elizabeth grew up in North Carolina to hard working, energetic, and religious parents. She was baptized into the LDS Church in 1842 and lived in Nauvoo. She became an excellent seamstress and made clothing for the Prophet Joseph Smith. Tradition says she made the suit of clothes the prophet was wearing when he was martyred. She also made the cloak that belonged to his militia uniform.

After a brief marriage to Mr. Porter, she became the second wife of her employer, John Bills. Their first child, Martha, died and was buried in Winter Quarters. They made arrangements to cross the Plains with the Brigham Young Wagon Company and arrived in Salt Lake Valley on September 21, 1848. The following year, John heard of the gold fields in California and because his family was so destitute, he left in search of gold. He died of pneumonia in California. Later on, Elizabeth became the second wife of Henry Mower, Jr. whom she had known in Nauvoo.

After the death of Henry's first wife, Susan, Elizabeth reared Susan's two small children, William Henry and John Albert.

In the spring of 1854, Henry and Elizabeth sold their belongings at Union Fort and moved to Springville, Utah. There they bought a small farm. Henry took a third wife,

Alice Burton. She later left Henry their two small sons, took her baby with her, and divorced Henry. Elizabeth also raised these two children, Henry (Hank) and Charles Albert (Cheal). In the year of 1862, Elizabeth and Henry, along with their eight boys moved to Fairview, Sanpete County. Elizabeth also reared two foster children, Emma Jane Weller and a handicapped boy, Jimmy Dewitt. Elizabeth was very compassionate. She was also a wonderful story teller. She passed away at the age of seventy-seven years, beloved by all who knew her.

LOIS COON STEVENS JORDAN WOODWARD MOWER

BIRTHDATE: 10 Mar 1811
Leeds, Ontario, Canada
DEATH: 30 May 1897
Fairview, Sanpete County, Utah
PARENTS: Abraham Coon
Sabra Halliday Coon
PIONEER: 5 Oct 1851
Daniel H. Wells Wagon Company
SPOUSE I: Arnold Stevens
MARRIED: 5 Nov 1828
Leeds, Ontario, Canada
DEATH SP: 27 Mar 1847
Pueblo, Pueblo County, Colorado

CHILDREN:
Byron, 29 Feb 1830
Elizabeth, 25 Dec 1831
Lois Ann, 15 Dec 1833
Rachel Matilda, 25 Jul 1836
Arnold, Jr., 22 Aug 1838
Ransom Abraham, 27 Sep 1839
Erastus Snow, 31 Mar 1842

SPOUSE II: Nathaniel Jordan
MARRIED: 27 Nov 1847
Pottowattamie County, Iowa
DEATH: 1853
Spanish Fork, Utah

CHILDREN:
Nathaniel Heber 14 Feb 1849
Justus Perry 26 Dec 1851

SPOUSE III: James Woodward
MARRIED: 16 Feb 1854
Spanish Fork, Utah
DEATH: not given
CHILDREN: None

SPOUSE IV: Henry Mower, Jr.
MARRIED: 11 Jul 1863
DEATH: 3 Aug 1866
CHILDREN: None

Lois Coon was born in Canada. She was only three years old when her mother died; later her father married Sylvia Sly, and they had ten children. Lois grew up in a large family. When she was seventeen years old, she met and married Arnold Stevens 5 Nov 1828. They moved about many times in their young married life. They became the parents of seven children; two died in infancy and three died in childhood. They were converted to the Mormon Church and baptized 18 Nov 1836.

In Mar 1837, they made their way southward to Kirtland, Ohio to be with the main body of the Saints. They knew the Prophet Joseph Smith and his brother, Hyrum. They were on their way to Missouri when Lois gave birth to their fifth child. They never did live in Missouri, for the mob drove the Saints from Missouri and Lois and Arnold moved to Springfield, Illinois. Lois endured with saintly patience all the hardships and challenges. She suffered the plundering of the Saints in Nauvoo. With the great exodus out of Nauvoo, they journeyed across Iowa. While at Council Bluffs, Iowa her husband enlisted in the Mormon Battalion in Jul 1846. She was left with their children encamped in a wagon to get along as best they could. Lois drove her own team of oxen from Council Bluffs, Iowa to Winter Quarters, Nebraska. Here they spent the winter with wives and families of other Battalion volunteers. It is difficult to describe the hardships they endured.

In the Spring of 1847, she learned that her husband had been kicked by a mule causing his death 27 Mar 1847 in Ft. Pueblo, Colorado. Being left alone, she needed help and protection to get her family to the Salt Lake Valley. She married Nathaniel Jordan, a good man she had known in Canada, 27 Nov 1847 in Pottowattamie County, Iowa. Lois had two sons from this marriage. She was saddened by the death of her daughter, Rachel, at Council Bluffs. She was thirteen years old. The family entered the Salt Lake Valley on 5 Oct 1851 with the Daniel H. Wells Company. They moved to Spanish Fork, Utah. Her husband died before they could get a house built. Again, Lois had to provide for her children.

From Spanish Fork she moved in 1859 to Fairview in Sanpete County, Utah and resided there until her death.

Lois was small, even less than five feet tall, but matronly. She had sparkling brown eyes, a sweet face that in her later years was surrounded by snowy white hair. She knitted, worked in her garden which produced great corn and cucumbers, made quilts, made melt-in-your-mouth pies, churned butter, carded wool and spun yarn. She was very gracious and sweet. She taught her children at school. She was calm and patient. She had a cow and did her own milking; she had chickens and a huge pig so she was very independent. She wore a little white lace cap and always a shawl with fringe and a little old silk vest that was her husband's. She married two more times; she had four husbands. She always had pie and doughnuts for the children and could always discuss freely the current events with visitors. She had a fireplace and she would sit in her rocker and rock her black cat by the hour. Toward the end of her life her eyesight failed and she had poor health. She fell on the ice and hurt her hip, from which she never recovered. She died as she had lived, in a quiet way, 30 May 1897 at Fairview, Utah. She was eighty-six years old. She was buried in the Fairview Cemetery, loved and mourned by many. She remained firm in her faith all of her life. She enjoyed all family members, friends and relatives.

LUCRETIA HUPPER MOWER

BIRTHDATE: 15 Sep 1818
Lincoln, Penobscot, Maine
DEATH: 29 Jul 1915
Springville, Utah Co., Utah
PARENTS: William Laud Hupper
Margaret Craig
PIONEER: 20 Nov 1851
Abraham Day Wagon train
SPOUSE: Henry Mower, Sr.
MARRIED: 5 Feb 1847
Council Bluffs
DEATH SP: 4 Apr 1878
Springville, Utah Co., Utah

CHILDREN:
Matilda, 22 Mar 1848
Orson Hyde, 29 Nov 1849
Oscar Middleton, 25 Apr 1852
Lucretia twin, 29 Aug 1854
Eliza (Singleton), 29 Aug 1854
Delilah Jane (Hanson), 8 Sep 1859

Lucretia was born in Maine, 1818. She became an early member of the LDS church. She was living in Council Bluffs, where, on 5 Feb she married Henry Mower, Sr. widower. His first wife, Mary Ameck by whom he had 10 children, passed away in 1846 in Council Bluffs. They made their home in Council Bluffs (Kanesville) where their first two children were born. They Joined the Abraham Day wagon train and arrived in the Salt Lake valley 20 Nov 1851. They settled in Ogden, Weber Co where the third child joined their family. In 1854, in North Ogden, they were blessed with a set of twins.

Lucretia was asked to live the law of polygamy, when, on 5 Sep 1856 Henry took a third wife, Elmera/Almera Jane Wheeler, by whom he had nine children. The Mower's then went to settle in Springville due to Johnston's Army, and it was here, in 1859, that Lucretia's last child was born, making a total of six. They decided to stay and settle permanently in Springville. It was here, in 1878, that Henry passed away. Lucretia was independent and continued to help provide for herself and her family. Her sister wife, Jane, passed away in 1899 in Lewiston, Cache Co., Utah where she was residing with children. Lucretia loved poetry and during her lifetime, she wrote more than 100 poems concerning the events of her life. She was active in her community and her church until her passing at age ninety-six. She was a widow for thirty-seven years. She is buried in the Springville Cemetery.

SARAH ANN BIDWELL MOWER

BIRTHDATE: 12 Jul 1830
Farmersville, Caltargus County,
New York
DEATH: 7 Jan 1915
Pleasant View, Utah
PARENTS: Robert William Bidwell
Elizabeth Roe Bidwell
PIONEER: 25 Sep 1850
by wagon
SPOUSE: John Mower
MARRIED: 11 Apr 1850
Council Bluffs, Iowa
DEATH SP: 20 Mar 1896

CHILDREN:
daughter (died in infancy), 1851

Sarah Ann Bidwell Mower was born 12 Jul 1830 in Caltargus County, New York. She was the oldest of seven children. At the age of five or six, Sarah Ann left New York with her family and moved to Kirtland, Ohio. She was baptized a member of the Mormon Church when she was eight years old. She witnessed the sufferings and persecutions of the Saints in Missouri and Nauvoo, Illinois. She and her family lived in Nauvoo for six years.

Sarah Ann married John Mower 11 Apr 1850 in Council Bluffs, Iowa. They journeyed across the Plains to Utah by ox-team. They arrived in the Salt Lake Valley 25 Sep 1850. The Company they traveled with is not known. They went to Bountiful, Utah to live for a short time. While living in Bountiful, a baby girl was born to them. Sadly, she died in infancy. She was the only child born to Sarah Ann and John.

In the Fall of 1851, they moved to North Ogden, now known as Pleasant View, in Weber County, Utah. They kept a Stage Coach Station on their farm in Pleasant View, starting sometime in the 1860s. It operated until into the 1870s. It served the Holliday Overland Lines, which ran 950 miles to the Dalles, Oregon. There was also a branch to Virginia City, Montana. It was at the Stagecoach Station that the horses were fed and pastured and fresh horses changed for the tired ones. Sarah Ann cooked meals for the passengers. She became well known for her butter-making and buttermilk and her salt-rising bread. They raised poultry and had a duck pond, which helped in part for the delicious meals she served. They also raised a fine garden.

Sarah Ann and her husband were very hospitable people. Having no living children of their own, they took into their home and cared for nieces, nephews and the unfortunate and homeless. Sarah Ann was very patient, and never complained, although she suffered with rheumatism. She was bedfast for many years. Sarah Ann had a firm testimony of the gospel. She loved to tell of her experiences in the early days of the Church. She died at her home in Pleasant View, Utah 7 Jan 1915 at the age of eighty-four years. Her husband, John Mower, passed away 20 Mar 1896. She was a widow for nineteen years.

MARTHA JANE SARGENT SHARP MOWREY

BIRTHDATE: 24 Sep 1827
Floyd County, Indiana
DEATH: 20 Dec 1920
Vernal, Utah
PARENTS: Abel M. Sargent
Sallie Edwards Mowrey Sargent
PIONEER: 24 Jul 1847
Mormon Battalion Company
SPOUSE: Norman Sharp
MARRIED: Sep 1845
Nauvoo, Illinois
DEATH SP: abt 1846
near Pueblo, Colorado

CHILDREN:
Sarah Ellen 1846

SPOUSE II: Harley Mowrey, Jr.
MARRIED: 4 Jul 1847
Independence Rock, Wyoming
DEATH: 19 Oct 1920
Vernal, Utah

CHILDREN:
Angeline, 30 Jul 1848
Harley, Jr., 21 Feb 1850
Martha Jane, 1 Mar 1855
Ruth Caroline, 28 Nov 1858
Harried Ann, 15 Sep 1859
Ella Drucilla, 4 Sep 1864
Barton Charles, 15 Jun 1866
Thomas Uriah, 9 Feb 1869
David Sargent, 9 Jul 1872

Martha Jane was born in Floyd County, Indiana. While she was a very young child, her parents became members of the Mormon Church and gathered with the Saints in Jackson County, Missouri. Although Martha Jane was very young at the time, she remembered well the gathering of the mobs and the experiences of the banishment of the Saints from Jackson County, Clay County and Far West Missouri. She witnessed the arrest of the Prophet Joseph Smith and other Church leaders. Not knowing where to seek refuge, her family made their way to Indiana to the home of her mother's parents, arriving there in destitute circumstances. Soon after their arrival, her mother died from exposure, leaving the children to Martha Jane's care, as she was the eldest.

Three years later, the family gathered again with the body of the Church in Nauvoo, Ill. where they resided until the Saints were again driven out in Feb 1846. Before leaving Nauvoo, Martha Jane married Norman Sharp in Sep 1845, and in 1846 to them was born one daughter, Sarah Ellen. During their flight westward from Nauvoo, while stopping at Council Bluffs, Iowa temporarily, her husband became a member of the Mormon Battalion. Martha Jane accompanied her husband to Pueblo, Colorado. Here, he met with a gun accident and died after four long and weary days.

On 4 Jul 1847, Martha Jane married Harley Mowrey, Jr. at Independence Rock, Wyoming. He was a member of the escort group from the Mormon Battalion. They continued with their group on the trek and arrived in the Salt Lake Valley 24 Jul 1847. Martha Jane's labors with her husband as pioneer and colonizer in the states of Utah, California and Idaho were often related to their children with tearful eyes. In the early days in Utah, she had listened helplessly to the piteous cries of her children for food. They subsisted for weeks at a time on roots dug from the earth and sage gathered from the hills of the Salt Lake Valley.

Martha Jane was a woman of the highest and noblest character. She was an active worker in the Church. Her life was adventurous and eventful and even after she had reached the age when most people thought she should lay aside all physical activity she kept house for her husband. She was ninety-one years old and her husband was ninety-seven. One winter their little home was partly destroyed by fire and they found shelter with their daughter, Sarah Ellen. They were living at Vernal, Utah at the time and had resided there for thirty-five years.

Martha Jane always befriended the poor and needy, and cared for the sick and afflicted. She was a very sympathetic and loving mother of ten children. She died 20 Dec 1920, two months after the death of her husband. He was the last survivor of the Mormon Batallion

ELIZABETH HUTCHISON MOYES

BIRTHDATE: 17 Mar 1814
Lastillion, Donegal, Ireland
DEATH: 16 Aug 1906
Ogden, Weber County, Utah
PARENTS: William Hutchison
Mary Spears Hutchison
PIONEER: 26 Sep 1866
Daniel Thompson Wagon Co.
SPOUSE: Robert Moyes
MARRIED: 22 May 1836
Paisley, Scotland
DEATH SP: 11 Jul 1861

CHILDREN:
James, 13 Apr 1838
William, 17 May 1841
Robert, 1 Jan 1844
John Hutchison, 22 Mar 1846
Stewart Hutchison, 11 Aug 1848
Alexander Hill, 22 Mar 1851
Margaret, 28 Sep 1853

Elizabeth Hutchison Moyes was born in Ireland. She was the daughter of William and Mary Hutchison. Little is known of her childhood. She married Robert Moyes by proclamation 22 May 1836 with the Banns published in Abey Parish. They became the parents of seven children; six boys and one girl. Her husband died 11 Jul 1861 in Paisley, Scotland. She was left alone to care for her children.

After the death of her husband, Elizabeth brought John, Stewart, Margaret and a nephew, William L. Hamilton, on the long journey to join the main body of the Saints in Utah. Her oldest son, James, had emigrated earlier. Elizabeth and her family left Liverpool, England 30 May 1866, sailing on the ship "Arkwright." They joined the Daniel Thompson Ox-team Company and left Wyoming, Nebraska 25 Jul 1866. They arrived in the Salt Lake Valley 26 Sep 1866.

Shortly after arriving in the Valley they made the long trek to Oregon and settled in Oregon City. Here, the boys found work in the woolen mills. They worked there for two years and were able to send enough money back to Scotland for the rest of the family to come to Salt Lake City, Utah. Elizabeth settled in Ogden and filled all of her Church assignments with a smile. She died 16 Aug 1906 in Ogden, Utah. She had been a widow for forty-five years. Elizabeth became a pioneer when she was fifty-two years old. She overcame many hardships and challenges. Elizabeth was truly a woman of faith and fortitude.

MARY EASTCOTT MOYES

BIRTHDATE: 23 Apr 1817
Jacobstow, Cornwall, England
DEATH: 26 Apr 1874
Beaver, Beaver, Utah
PARENTS: William Eastcott
Elizabeth Vendall
PIONEER: 15 Feb 1858
Via San Bernardino from Australia
SPOUSE: William Moyes
MARRIED: 3 Oct 1840
Jacobstow, Cornwall, England
DEATH SP: 16 Feb 1909
Beaver, Beaver, Utah

CHILDREN:
William, 26 Mar 1841
Elizabeth, 23 May 1843
Eliza, 4 Mar 1844
Joseph John, 11 Feb 1845
John, 17 Jun 1846
Richard, 5 Jan 1848
Mary Jane (Grimshaw), 6 Jun 1850
Elizabeth Ann (Cale), 6 Mar 1852
Martha Maria (Williams), 24 Sep 1854
Joseph, 16 Nov 1855

Mary was born in England, 1817. She was one of five children all born in Cornwall. At age twenty-three, she married William Moyes in England. They traded their home in Cornwall, where their first child was born. They had the opportunity to go to Australia in 1842. They made their home there, adding nine more children to their family. They were converted to the LDS church, while in Australia and decided to come to Zion. They sailed from Australia to San Bernardino, California, joining a wagon train and arriving in Beaver, Beaver County, Utah 15 Feb 1858. They made their home in Beaver.

Mary was a good homemaker and they were happy in their new home. Their children married and moved away from home; their youngest settling in Thatcher, Graham, Arizona. Mary passed away in Beaver, 26 Apr 1874. She was age 57, just 3 days alter her birthday.

William took a second wife, Zelpha Hunt. They made their home in Beaver, where he passed away 16 Feb 1909, 34 years after Mary. They are buried in the Beaver Cemetery.

ELIZABETH WOOD MOYLE

BIRTHDATE: 20 Dec 1839
Mt. Sterling, Brown County, Illinois
DEATH: 26 May 1908
Salt Lake City, Utah
PARENTS: Daniel Wood
Mary Elizabeth Snyder Wood
PIONEER: 23 Jul 1848
Brigham Young 2nd Wagon Co.
SPOUSE: James Moyle
MARRIED: 22 Jul 1856
Salt Lake City, Utah
DEATH: 8 Dec 1890
Salt Lake City, Utah

CHILDREN:
James Henry, 17 Sep 1858
Mary Elizabeth, 25 Jan 1860
John Alma, 2 May 1862
Phillipa Ann, 4 Dec 1863
Bertha May, 15 May 1865
Daniel Wood, 13 Dec 1866
Oscar Wood, 20 Jan 1868
Stephen Lawrence, 12 Dec 1869
Deseret Blanche, 19 Feb 1872
Ida, 25 Sep 1873
Walter Wood, 25 Sep 1876
Mahonri, 8 Aug 1878
Ellen, 29 May 1880
Louise Rebecca, 11 May 1881

Elizabeth Wood Moyle was born in Mt. Sterling, Illinois during the time of the mob persecutions of the members of the Mormon Church. Before she was two years old her family was forced to move from their home. They settled in the Nauvoo area. She could see from a second story window of their home mobs burning Mormon houses in the distance. In 1846, her family was forced to move again, this time across the frozen Mississippi River, across Iowa, to the banks of the Missouri River where they settled at Winter Quarters. When Elizabeth was eight years old, her family joined the Brigham Young 2nd Company for the journey across the Plains. They arrived in Salt Lake City 23 Jul 1848.

In Apr 1856, James Moyle, a young stonemason, came to Woods Cross to work for her father. After a short two

month courtship she and James were married 22 Jul 1856 by Brigham Young. They lived for a time with her parents in Woods Cross. They then rented a small house in the 17th Ward in Salt Lake City, soon moving to the 15th Ward. When Johnston's Army was approaching the Valley, Elizabeth was left alone when James joined the Nauvoo Legion and left for Echo Canyon to help hold off the army. James was grateful for the warm shirt that Elizabeth had made for him from her woolen petticoat. During the Spring of 1858, as Johnston's Army approached the Valley, Elizabeth, though pregnant, fled the City with most of the townspeople in the great "move South" while James returned to Salt Lake City to help stand guard and burn the city, if necessary.

They had the largest vegetable garden in the 15th Ward, 3.5 acres with an abundant orchard. Elizabeth was skilled at spinning, weaving, soap and candle making, etc. Her son, James, called her "the good angel" of the 15th Ward; she cared for the sick and baked bread for each new neighbor. Her home was the center where neighbors gathered to discuss the news. On 31 Jan 1870, her husband took a second wife in plural marriage. Elizabeth served as midwife at the birth of their first child. James built both wives a house in the 18th Ward. Elizabeth and James became the parents of fourteen children; eight of whom died. Four died of diphtheria during the month of May 1880. In Apr 1903, Elizabeth joined the Daughters of the Utah Pioneers as one of the founding members. Her application was Number 25. She lived in her home on 3rd Avenue in the 18th Ward until her death on 26 May 1908 at the age of sixty-eight. She had been a widow for eighteen years.

MARGARET ANNA CANNELL MOYLE

BIRTHDATE: 26 Jun 1845
Onchan or Douglas, Isle of Man, Eng.
DEATH: 22 Jun 1920
Cottonwood Canyon, Salt Lake City, Utah
PARENTS: Thomas Cannell
Esther Jane Corlett Cannell
PIONEER: 1868
walked from Cheyenne, Wyoming
SPOUSE: James Moyle
MARRIED: 31 Jan 1870
Salt Lake City, Utah
DEATH: 8 Dec 1890
Salt Lake City, Utah

CHILDREN:
Edith, 4 Apr 1871
Florence, 5 Jan 1873
Seth, 12 Mar 1874
Alfred, Jan 1875
Franklin Cannell, 4 Sep 1876
Nelson, 27 Sep 1878
Wilford, 4 Mar 1880
Gertrude, 27 Oct 1883
Angus Dermode, 26 Jan 1888

Margaret Anna Cannell Moyle was born on the Isle of Man, England. She and her mother and sisters joined the Mormon Church. Before her mother died, she insisted that her husband promise her that he would take the girls to Utah where they could marry men of their own faith. He agreed. In the early 1860s Thomas Cannell and his three daughters left the Isle of Man to emigrate to America. After three weeks on the Atlantic Ocean they took passage on a train for the West. They reached the end of the line in Cheyenne, Wyoming and walked the remainder of the way into Salt Lake City, Utah.

They took up residence in the 15th Ward. In 1870, Margaret married James Moyle in the Endowment House as a plural wife. She lived next door to his first wife. Her children remembered the delicious apples and pears from her orchard and the Pottowatamie plums from which Margaret made wonderful jam. Her husband built his two wives and families houses on 3rd Avenue in the 18th Ward. In 1866, James was arrested and served six months in the Utah Territorial "Pen" and paid a fine of $300.00. After James died in 1890, Margaret had no income and was left to care for her six children, the youngest less than two years old. She and her husband had nine children; four died in childhood. She decided to rent some of the rooms of her home. She was an excellent cook and boarded some of the students from the University. She was able to support her family in this way.

In later years, she took care of her ailing father until his death in 1910. When her son Frank's wife died, Margaret moved into his home and cared for his three children. It was in Cottonwood, Frank's home, that she died in 1920, just before her seventy-fifth birthday. A family friend once had said of Margaret, "Maggie, a Manxman isn't worth a damn, but a good Manx woman is a jewel beyond compare." This was a fitting tribute for Margaret. She was a small woman. The tallest of her children was ten inches taller than she was. She was an accomplished cook. Her hands were always busy with food preparation; peeling carrots, mixing her white sponge cake, kneading her loaves of round bread. Her quilts were distinctive. The blocks were made from men's dark wool suits but the backing was of flowered cotton. Margaret is loved and honored by her posterity.

MARY ANN WILLIAMS WEST MOYLE

BIRTHDATE: 15 Apr 1848
Haverfordwest, Pembrokeshire,
South Wales
DEATH: 20 June 1902
Salt Lake City, Utah
PARENTS: Benjamin Williams
Margaret Thomas Williams
PIONEER: before 1867
Company not known
SPOUSE: Jesse West
MARRIED: 31 Aug 1867
Salt Lake City, Utah
DEATH SP: 24 Dec 1906
Salt Lake City, Utah

CHILDREN:
Sarah Ester West, 13 Sep 1868

SPOUSE II: John Rowe Moyle
MARRIED: 3 Oct 1868
Salt Lake City, Utah
DEATH SP: 15 Feb 1889
Alpine, Utah

CHILDREN:
George William, 13 Mar 1870
Eleanore, 23 Nov 1872

Mary Ann Williams West Moyle was born in Southern Wales in the area known as "little England." She had little if any education as she was never able to read or write. It is not known what company she traveled with to come to Utah. She was in Utah by 1867. At the age of nineteen, she married Jesse West 31 Aug 1867 in Salt Lake City, Utah. They were married in the Endowment House and she became his plural wife. She had one child by Jesse West, a daughter named Sarah Ester, born the following year. She was apparently divorced from Mr. West as she married John Rowe Moyle in the Endowment House 3 Oct 1868, becoming his plural wife. She moved to Alpine, Utah to join the Moyle family there.

Mary Ann had two children by John Rowe Moyle, George William and Eleanore. Only George grew to adulthood. Her daughter, Sarah West, died in 1872 at four years of age. Eleanore Moyle died young, also.

In 1880, she was living in Salt Lake City caring for her elderly widowed Aunt Esther Twigg and her handicapped cousin, Ann. She was listed on the census as divorced and she was using her maiden name. By 1900, she was living in Salt Lake City with her son, George, and his family. She was still caring for her cousin, Ann Twigg. Mary Ann's life was one of great hardship and suffering: the death of all but one of her children, two marriages and for over twenty years caring for an elderly Aunt and a severely handicapped Cousin Ann. Mary Ann died of cancer in the Holy Cross Hospital in Salt Lake City, Utah 20 Jun 1902. She is buried in the Salt Lake City Cemetery.

PHILLIPA BEER MOYLE

BIRTHDATE: 13 Dec 1816
Devonport, Devonshire, England
DEATH: 21 Jan 1891
Alpine, Utah
PARENTS: William Beer
Elizabeth Cook Beer
PIONEER: 26 Sep 1856
Edmund Ellsworth Handcart Co.
SPOUSE: John Rowe Moyle
MARRIED: 23 Feb 1834
St. Peter Port, Guernsey, England
DEATH SP: 15 Feb 1889
Alpine, Utah

CHILDREN:
James, 31 Oct 1835
Elizabeth, 12 Jan 1837
Henry, 23 Jan 1839
Stephen, 27 Nov 1840
Phillipa, 12 Dec 1842
Henry, 3 Jan 1844
Alfred, 11 Oct 1846
William, 13 Nov 1848
John, 25 May 1851
Joseph Edward, 19 Nov 1857

Phillipa Beer Moyle was born in England. She was the eldest of nine children. She spent her early years in the Plymouth, England area. She and her friends would take their lunches down to the shore to watch the ocean waves. At age nineteen she was married to John Rowe Moyle. His work as a stonemason necessitated Phillipa moving the family frequently from one job location to the next. They became the parents of ten children; nine were born in England and one in Utah.

In 1851 they converted and were baptized into the Mormon Church. On Apr 11, 1856 Phillipa and her husband and five children left Plymouth to join their son, James, in the Salt Lake Valley. They sailed on the "Samuel Curling" to Boston, then by rail in box cars to Iowa where they were outfitted with a handcart. They were allowed 14 pounds of baggage which necessitated leaving much clothing and bedding behind. When Phillipa was refused permission to take a pillow which had been given to her by her father and mother she said that she would take the pillow if she had to carry it all the way under her arm. She did just that. The grueling trip of this first handcart company ended on their arrival in the Salt Lake Valley 26 Sep 1856.

They spent their first year in the Valley in Salt Lake City. She and her family were at the 24 Jul 1857 celebration in Cottonwood Canyon when the news arrived of the coming of Johnston's Army. Later that fall, just before the birth of her last child, she stood at her door and watched two of her sons marching with the other members of the militia up Brigham Street (South Temple) on their way to Echo Canyon.

In 1858, Phillipa and her husband and family moved to Alpine, Utah. Her first home there was a dugout they called "the cave." Later, they lived in a rock house that her husband built with two foot thick walls made of granite boulders with an adjoining rock tower built to protect the family. There was an orchard with apple trees, grape vines and mulberry trees. These leaves were fed to the silk worms Phillipa raised in her kitchen and contributed the silk to the silk industry of Utah. There were areas along Dry Creek where the sand had leveled pretty places which made her very homesick for the Devonshire Coast. Phillipa adapted well to the difficult life in the West. She traded thirteen chickens to buy her son, Henry, a gun. When a wild cat was killed by one of her sons, she made a fur neckpiece for herself out of the pelt. She was an active member of the Mormon Church and was serving as President of the Relief Society teachers at the time of her death at age seventy-four. She died about two years after the death of her husband of fifty-five years.

MARY HAUENSTEIN MUHLESTEIN

BIRTHDATE: 26 Nov 1835
Koelliken, Canton, Aargau,
Switzerland
DEATH: 20 Jan 1892
Provo, Utah County, Utah
PARENTS: Johannes Hauenstein
Verena Aschbaugh
PIONEER: 25 Sep 1863
Peter Nebeker Co wagon train
SPOUSE: Nicholas Muhlestein
MARRIED: 6 May 1858
Kolliken, Aagau, Switzerland
DEATH SP: 9 Jun 1916
Provo, Utah Co., Utah

CHILDREN:
Mary Louise, 24 Jul 1859
Rosalie, 5 Sep 1860
Emma, 23 Dec 1861
John Nicholas, 23 Sep 1864
Emil, 28 Nov 1866
Joseph Aaron, 10 Aug 1868
Christian Hyrum, 1 Sep 1870
Friedrich Bernhard, 2 Sep 1872
Martha Josephine (Hasler), 12 Mar 1875

Mary was born in Switzerland, 1835. She was one of four children all born in Koelliken. At age twenty-two, she married Nicholas Muhlestein 6 May 1858 in Koelliken and they made their home there, where two children were born to them. They moved to Kerchenthurnen, where, in 1861, their third child was born. They converted to the LDS church and emigrated. They joined the Peter Nebeker wagon train, leaving Florence, Nebraska 25 Jul 1863 and arrived in Salt Lake City 25 Sep 1863. They settled in Provo, where the rest of their nine children were born.

In the spring of 1868, Mary was asked to live the law of polygamy when, on 13 Apr 1868, Nicholas married Anna

Caroline Wintch, also from Switzerland, by whom he had nine children. These wives and families were compatible and Mary worked hard to make life pleasant and comfortable for her family. Mary was a devoted and affectionate wife and mother. She left a strong handwritten testimony of the truthfulness of the church of Jesus Christ of Latter-Day-Saints. She knew Joseph Smith, Brigham Young, and John Taylor were chosen by the Lord to guide and lead his people. She believed that polygamy was right and a commandment of God. She abided and lived this principle for thirteen years. She forsook her native land, her beloved ones and came to Utah, obedient to the call of the Lord that she might fulfill his commandments better.

Nicholas passed away 9 Jun 1916 in Provo. Mary passed away at age fifty-six, 26 Jan 1892. They are buried in the Provo Cemetery.

CHRISTINA HOWIE LINDSAY MUIR

BIRTHDATE: 3 Jul 1821
Craighall, Ayrshire, Scotland
DEATH: 25 Jul 1906
Heber City, Wasatch, Utah
PARENTS: William Howie
Jane Blackwood
PIONEER: 21 Sep 1862
Homer Duncan Company
SPOUSE I: William Lindsay
MARRIED: 19 Jul 1844
Craighall, Scotland
DEATH SP: 17 Oct 1861
In Scotland

CHILDREN:
Robert, 19 Apr 1845
William, 11 Feb 1847
James, 17 Feb 1849
George, 3 Mar 1851
Samuel, 3 Mar 1851
Andrew, 14 Apr 1853
Jane Blackwood, 11 Jul 1855
Elizabeth, 1 Dec 1858
Isabella Blackwood, 14 Nov 1860

SPOUSE II: George Muir
MARRIED: 13 Jun 1863
Heber City, Wasatch, Utah
DEATH SP:

CHILDREN:
John Lindsay, 24 May 1864
George Lindsay, 6 Feb 1868

Christina Howie was born in Scotland in 1821. Her parents were poor and it was necessary for her to go out to work at an early age. She mostly did work on a farm, doing milking and helping with the harvest. Christina married William Lindsay in 1844. They moved around a lot because William was a coal miner and took contracts to sink shafts and open new mines.

While living in Lanarkshire, Scotland they heard the gospel and joined the Church, though her family strongly objected. They desired to come to Utah, and tried to save money, but in 1861 William was killed in a coal mine accident. She was brokenhearted but determined to make the trip. She wrote to George Q. Cannon and asked if she could borrow the money needed and he wrote back saying, be ready in four days. She quickly disposed of her property and sailed with her eight children on the ship "John J. Boyd" in Apr 1862.

Christina joined with the Homer Duncan Company, and arrived in Heber City in Sep 1862. Shortly after arriving her little daughter Elizabeth, who had been ill most of the way, died and was buried in Heber. Christina was thankful she didn't have to be buried along the way. They were welcomed by George and John Muir, whom she had known in Scotland. In 1863 Christina became a polygamist wife to George Muir, and had two more sons. She had one of the first sewing machines in Heber, and did sewing for herself and others. She also learned to be a mid-wife. She cooked for the railroad construction men in Echo Canyon, and later kept boarders in Evanston, Wyoming. She built a lovely home in Heber with money she had saved. She died in Heber in 1906 and is buried in the Heber City Cemetary.

ELLEN BEVERIDGE MUIR

No
Photo
Available

BIRTHDATE: 1 Sep 1789
Dalgety, Fifeshire, Scotland
DEATH: Oct 1869
Beaver, Beaver, Utah
PARENTS: George Beveridge
Janet Muir Beveridge
PIONEER: 1848/5 2 Wagon Train
SPOUSE: Walter Muir
MARRIED: 1812
Scotland
DEATH SP: Apr 1858
Cedar City, Iron, Utah

CHILDREN:
Janet, 22 Jan 1813
Montgomery (Cook), 25 May 1816
Thomas, 30 May 1818
Betty, 26 Mar 1821
George, 18 Jul 1823
Grace (Muir), 3 Mar 1825
David, 2 Jun 1829
Mary (Murie), 28 Oct 1831

Ellen (Eleanor/Helen) was born in Scotland, 1789. She was one of eight children, all born in Scotland. She was the youngest and was doted upon. At age twenty-three she married Walter Muir. He was one of thirteen children, all born in Scotland. They made their home in Colliery Fifeshire, where two children joined their family. They next moved to Fordel, Fifeshire, where six more children joined their family. They were converted to the LDS church and decided to emigrate to Zion. Sometime between 1848 and 1852, they came by wagon train to Utah, settling in Beaver, Beaver County, Utah. They suffered through the Grasshopper plague, the Indian Depredations and Johnston's Army. Ellen lost Walter in 1858 while in Cedar City, Iron County, Utah. She remained independent, visiting her children and being active in her church until her death in Oct 1869 at age seventy, having been a widow for eleven years.

MARGARET HANNAH MUIR

BIRTHDATE: 1 Jan 1830
Kilmarnock Ayrshire, Scotland
DEATH: 10 Aug 1882
Heber City, Utah
PARENTS: William Hannah
Jane Howie Hannah
PIONEER: 26 Sept 1856
McArthur Handcart Co.
SPOUSE: George Muir
MARRIED: 19 April 1852
Kilmarnock, Scotland
DEATH SP: 25 May 1908
Heber City, Utah

CHILDREN:
Mary, 15 April 1853
Jane Howie, 5 July 1854
James, 22 Sept 1856
Margaret, 4 Oct 1858
Isabella, 21 June 1860
Elizabeth, 11 June 1862
George, 10 May 1864
Christina, 31 Jan 1866
Agnes, 7 Mar 1870

Margaret's father was a traveling carpenter so they moved around a lot. He died when Margaret was only twenty months old. Although her mother's family were well to do they would not help her because they hadn't wanted her to marry Margaret's father. Margaret had three sisters Ann, Mary, and Jane, and one brother William, only three months old. Her Mother's brother owned a ship yard but would not help her. A short time later they all died in a fire. So her mother worked at anything she could to support her family and died from Typhus Fever when Margaret was twelve years old. When Margaret was fourteen she and her sister went to work in a factory. Margaret was later chosen to be houskeeper, which she did until she was eighteen. Then she became sick and was taken to the hospital.

Margaret joined the LDS Church 15 Oct. 1849. While attending church she met George Muir. They were married in April 1852. He was a coal miner.

They left Scotland for America Feb. 1856 on the ship "Enoch Train." After arriving in New York they traveled by train to Iowa. Then went to Florence, Neb. and stayed three months. They left in May with the McArthur Handcart Co. Margaret walked all the way to just beyond

Fort Bridger, Wyoming, where she gave birth to a son. She then rode the rest of the way on one of the supply wagons. All she had to eat for four days was broth from buffalo meat.

They lived with his parents until they could build the adobe home in 10th ward. In 1847 when soldiers were coming Margaret and the children went to Provo with his parents. Margaret drove the ox team and wagon with her family and posessions and two cows tied to the tailgate. It was only a short time until they returned to Salt Lake City.

George was called in 1859 to go settle in Sanpete Co. to open the first mine. They settled on the western side of the valley in a place called Coalbed, later changed to Wales. He lost the sight in one eye and it took three weeks to walk to Salt Lake City to the Doctor. While he was gone there was a big storm and flash flood that flooded the dugout while Margaret was asleep. By the time she woke up water was already up to her knees. She ran out and called for help. Thomas Campbell helped her and the children get out but she caught a bad cold that settled in her head and caused her to be deaf in one ear. They moved to Heber City the next spring.

In 1863 George married Margaret's cousin as his second wife. She was a widow with eight children. After the fall of 1874 they all moved to Grass Creek, Wyoming where they lived for six years, then moved back to Heber and their farm, where Margarert died in 1882 and is buried in Heber City Cemetery.

MARY BELL ROSS MUIR

BIRTHDATE: 9 May 1815
Levenseat, West Calder, Scotland
DEATH: 27 Nov 1888
Mendon, Cache, Utah
PARENTS: John Bell
Mary Paterson
PIONEER: 9 Oct 1866
Daniel Thompson Company
SPOUSE: Walter Muir
MARRIED: 15 Nov 1835
West Calder, Midlothian, Scotland
DEATH SP: 25 Aug 1860
Whitburn, Scotland

CHILDREN:
Mary, 28 Aug 1836
Agnes, 17 Apr 1838 d. 1852
Jane, 14 Apr 1841
Janet, 7 May 1843
Walter, 25 Jul 1844
Margaret, 25 Oct 1845
Annie, 27 May 1848
Robert, 1850 d. prior 1855
Agnes, 26 Jan 1853
Elizabeth Wright, 18 Mar 1855
James Ross, 31 Aug 1857

Mary Bell Ross was born 9 May 1815 in Levenseat, West Calder, Midlothian, Scotland, to John Bell and Mary Paterson. She was born as Mary Bell but later took on the Ross name, either because she was adopted or just taken in by the Ross family.

She married Walter Muir on 15 Nov 1835 in West Calder, Midlothian, Scotland. He was an iron miner. He died of consumption on 25 Aug 1860 at Whitburn, Scotland, leaving Mary with eight children under seventeen years of age.

In 1866 Mary and five small children sailed on the ship "Arkwright" for America. Under the direction of Daniel Thompson they crossed the plains, with Mary walking and guiding the oxen the entire way to the Salt Lake Valley, arriving 9 Oct 1866.

She traveled on to Cache County where her daughter Jane had settled. She began working as a midwife and nurse, relying on knowledge from childhood as she had observed her mother in the same profession. Mary died in Mendon, Cache, Utah on 27 Nov 1888 at the age of seventy-three years.

MARY MURRAY REED MUIR

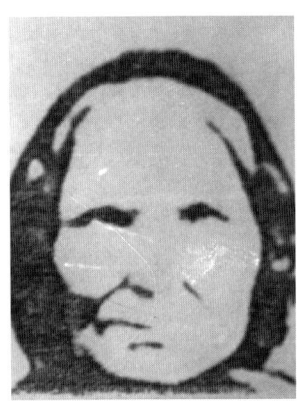

BIRTHDATE: 25 Dec 1790
Ench, Wgth, Scotland
DEATH: 27 June 1872
Salt Lake City, Utah
PARENTS:
James William Murray
Isabelle Montgomery
PIONEER: Nov 1850
Appleton, Harmon ox team.
SPOUSE: John Reed
MARRIED: 8 April 1815
DEATH: Lost at Sea

CHILDREN:
John Reed

SPOUSE II: James Muir
MARRIED: 11 June 1836
DEATH: 29 Oct. 1873
Salt Lake City, Utah

CHILDREN:
John, 8 Jan. 1830
George, 16 Oct. 1832
Mary, 3 June 1835
Isabella, 15 Aug. 1837

Mary was a small woman of dark complexion and very quiet and well respected. She was a good housekeeper and very religious. She even paid her tithing from the milk and cream from one cow.

Mary's first husband was lost at sea. They had one son, John Reed Jr. Mary married James Muir in 1826.

Mary joined the LDS Church 27 April 1844 at age fifty-two. James and Mary and their four children arrived in Salt Lake Nov 1850. They built their home on 2nd East between 3rd and 4th South Streets in Salt Lake City. Brigham Young hired her husband to make his families' shoes.

At the time of Johnston's Army, they were sent south until the incident was over. Then they were called back to Salt Lake City to make shoes.

Mary died at age eighty-two in Salt Lake City, Utah and is buried in the Salt Lake City Cemetery.

ANN CAPSTICK ROYLE MERCER MULLINER

BIRTHDATE: 26 Jul 1812
Oldhutton Bridgend, Wstmrl, Eng.
DEATH: 7 Jul 1879
Lehi, Lehi, Utah
PARENTS: Christopher Capstick
Ann Allsom
PIONEER: 21 Sep 1848
Brigham Young wagon train
SPOUSE: Henry Royle
MARRIED: 3 May 1848
Winter Quarters, Douglas, Nebraska
DEATH: 8 Jul 1852
Lehi, Utah County, Utah

CHILDREN:
Sarah Ann (Olmstead), 22 Sep 1849
Henry Moroni, 22 Jun 1851

SPOUSE II: John Mercer
MARRIED: 9 Nov 1852
DEATH SP: 8 Mar 1860
American Fork, Utah County, Utah

CHILDREN:
Martha (Kirkham), 6 Oct 1852

SPOUSE III: Samuel Mulliner
fourth polygamous wife
MARRIED:
DEATH SP:
CHILDREN:

Ann was born in England, 1812. Her birthplace was a beautiful green area in the Lake District, just a short walk from the William Wordsworth estate. A small chapel is just down the hedged lane, where records show the Capstick family worshiped there. Behind the huge Yew trees is the two story house belonging to the Capsticks today.

Ann and her sister Jane came to America in 1842 following the death of their parents. Ann was baptized a member of the LDS church 30 Jul 1843 in Newark, Connecticut. Her bible, purchased in 1839 is a record of early dates, names and events. Recorded in that bible is Ann's marriage to Henry Royal at Winter Quarters. President Brigham

Young performed the marriage 3 May 1848 in his office and sealed them for time and eternity, though Ann had not yet received her endowments (3 Jun 1856 in the Salt Lake Endowment House).

Following the marriage, the honeymoon was a trek across the plains traveling in the first division of Brigham Young's Company in 1848, leaving Winter Quarters 26 May and arriving in Salt Lake City 21 Sep 1848. They made their home in Salt Lake City where their first child was born. While Ann and the baby remained in Salt Lake City, Henry went to explore Utah Valley. They decided to settle there. Brigham Young advised them not to go around the point of the mountain as it dropped sharply into the Jordan River, so they went due south through the low draw, arriving at Dry Creek (Lehi) 10 Sep 1850.

It was spring of 1851 and the first crops consisted of wheat, corn, potatoes, squash and a few vegetables. The Indians insisted on turning their ponies loose in the growing fields, claiming the grass and water was theirs. They took delight in frightening the women and children. Not long after, Ann's second child was born, being the first male child born in Lehi. After four short years with Ann Henry died. Ann, with two small children, cut hay and grain and hauled it by ox team to Johnston's Army in Fairfield to sell for money to pay government duty on the land her husband had surveyed in 1850. She married John Mercer in 1852. They had one daughter by the time he passed away 8 Mar 1860. Ann was a widow again, with three children. She married Samuel Mulliner in Polygamy, being his fourth wife. Nothing is known of this union. Ann passed away at almost sixty-seven years of age, 7 Jul 1879 in Lehi, Utah Co., Utah.

KATHARINE NISBET MULLINER

No Photo Available

BIRTHDATE: 6 Jun 1804
No. Berwick, East Lothian, Scotland
DEATH: 1 Apr 1881
Orderville, Kane County, Utah
PARENTS: John Nisbet
Janet Runciman Nisbet
PIONEER: 26 Sep 1850
Warren Foote wagon company
SPOUSE: Samuel Mulliner, Jr.
MARRIED: 4 Dec 1830
No. Berwick, East Lothian, Scotland
DEATH SP: 23 Feb 1891
Lehi, Utah County, Utah

CHILDREN:
Janette (Jennette), 28 Feb 1833
Katherine
Elizabeth Smith, 7 Mar 1836

Katharine Nisbet Mulliner was born in Scotland. Little is known of her childhood. She married Samuel Mulliner, Jr. in North Berwick, East Lothian, Scotland 4 Dec 1830. Soon after their marriage, they planned to move to Australia. Later, they changed their plans and emigrated to Canada. While living in Ontario, Canada, two girls were born. There they heard the Mormon missionaries tell of the restored Gospel when Samuel attended a street meeting. He went home and told his wife that he had heard something "good and sweet." The next night, after again attending a street meeting, he announced to Katharine that all he had in Canada was for sale. They were going to move to Kirtland, Ohio to the headquarters of the Mormon Church.

Katherine accepted this desire of her husband and supported him in the move and all through the remainder of their life together. When her husband was the first missionary to be sent back to Scotland, their homeland, she remained at home and supported him by doing ironing for several customers, one of whom was President Abraham Lincoln in Illinois. They were called upon to make many changes and sacrifices. They prepared wagons and outfits to cross the Plains into Utah for other families. Their most urgent desire was to support the leaders of the Mormon Church. They, after preparing many wagons and outfits, finally arrived in the Salt Lake Valley 26 Sep 1850 by wagon, part of the Warren Foote Perpetual Emigrating Fund Company.

After arriving in Utah, Katharine was the one who acted as nurse and assisted in the recovery of those pioneers who had frozen feet when at the end of their journey. They lived on property they had purchased where the future Walker Bank Building was located for many years. Later, they were asked to move to the Lehi, Utah area where they established a grist mill. Katharine's husband was a tanner and leather man. Brigham Young asked them to move to Orderville, Utah where the United Order began. Katharine was helpful in being a nurse to all those who needed her. By this time, Katharine's husband had his third wife in plural marriage. When it was time to leave Orderville, Katharine chose to remain and assist in the work there. Her husband and his second wife returned to the American Fork area.

During her remaining years, Katharine performed services for others by nursing, doing laundry and ironing for the members of the Church and remaining true to the Gospel teachings which she had been taught. Her death came while at Orderville on 1 April 1881. She is buried there among the pioneers for whom a monument was erected to honor them.

ASENETH HARMON GHEEN STOUT MUMFORD

BIRTHDATE: 12 Nov 1823
Indianapolis, Indiana
DEATH: 20 Jun 1899
Pleasant Grove, Utah County, Utah
PARENTS: Henry Harmon
Agnes Green Harmon
PIONEER: 1849
Moses M. Markham Wagon Company
SPOUSE: William Gheen
MARRIED: 1841
DEATH SP: 19 Aug 1852
Sacramento, California

CHILDREN:
boy, 1841 (died age 1)
Louise, 28 May 1843
William, Jr., 1845
Thomas, 1847
Ruth, 1849

SPOUSE II: Hosea Stout
MARRIED: 9 Jan 1854
Salt Lake City, Utah
DIVORCED: 7 Jul 1854

SPOUSE III: Edward Thomas Mumford
MARRIED: 15 Apr 1856
DEATH SP:

Aseneth married William Gheen in 1841. While living in Indianapolis, they had two children. Their little boy died when he was a year old. The family moved to Nauvoo, Illinois where William fought in the Nauvoo Battle in September 1846. Aseneth was very ill, so she was moved to a position under the river's bank so she could be protected from the fighting. After the battle, her husband became baptized into the LDS Church. Aseneth refused baptism until they could get to the Salt Lake Valley. Their next move was to Sararah Mission in Savanna, Missouri where they became prosperous as hotel keepers. They employed a nurse, Harriet Dilworth, to care for the babies while they worked.

The family then crossed the Plains with the Moses M. Markham Company in 1849. They were able to afford a four horse team to pull their wagon. Equipped as they were, they were able to make better time than the rest of the column. When they arrived in Salt Lake City, they bought a small home on the corner of Main and Broadway and opened a butcher shop just north of it. They had trouble selling their meats because people were so poor, they were unable to pay. So discouraged, Aseneth's husband went alone to California.

In 1851, Aseneth and her eight year old daughter were baptized and then went by stage to join William in Sacramento, California. They established another hotel and a big tent boarding house. William became ill with rheuma-

tism in May of 1852 and died the following August at the age of forty. Now a widow, Aseneth sold their property and returned to her little home in Salt Lake City. In January 1854, Aseneth became the wife of Hosea Stout who was a widower with several children. She moved back into her own home in March and was divorced from him in July of 1854. She was married a third time to Edward Thomas Mumford on April 15, 1856. Aseneth died at the age of seventy-five in Pleasant Grove, Utah.

SUSAN FLITTON MUMFORD

BIRTHDATE: 22 Sep 1848
Flamstead, England
DEATH: 19 Oct 1947
Ogden, Weber Co., Utah
PARENTS: Joseph Flitton
Hannah Hansty
PIONEER: Aug 1868
McGaul Handcart Company
SPOUSE: George Mumford
MARRIED: 11 Dec 1871
Salt Lake City, Salt Lake, Utah
DEATH SP: 16 Jun 1896

CHILDREN:
Louisa, 9 Sep 1872
George Authur, 21 Apr 1874
Daisy, 20 Jun 1877
Dottie Susan (Grange), 2 Apr 1879
Emily (Stuart), 17 Jul 1881
Homer Louise, 1 Apr 1884
Thomas Allen, 15 Oct 1885
John Flitton, 16 Jul 1888
Joseph Lawrence, (sep 1890
Albert, 8 Sept 1892

Susan was born in England in 1848. She received little education; she worked in her father's hat factory as a young girl.

At the age of eight, her father baptized her. It was cold and they had to break a hole in the ice. They were persecuted for their membership in the Church of Jesus Christ of Latter-day Saints. Susan was in ill health as they prepared to emigrate to America. She was eighteen years old. She was attractive, small built, with beautiful hair, worn in ringlets, and had blue eyes.

In 1868, they sailed from Liverpool on the ship "John Bright." They arrived in August and traveled by train, in cattle cars, to Laramie, Wyoming.

Captain McGaul took charge and decided to take the Bitter Creek route. The water was so bitter they could not drink it. The trek was very hard. Susan walked the entire distance.

They settled in the Salt Lake Valley, then moved to Kaysville. Susan moved back to Salt Lake and lived with the Duncan McCallister family, until she was married to

George Mumford in 1871, in the Salt Lake Endowment House. They made their home in Ogden.

Susan rode the first train from Salt Lake to Ogden. Three of her ten children died when very young. George died in 1896, leaving her a widow with seven children to care for. She took in boarders and did washing and ironing.

At the age of seventy-three, she took her son and his three children into her home, when his wife died. For her ninety-ninth birthday a testimonial dinner was held in her honor, but she was too ill to attend.

In her last years, she lived with her daughter, Dottie. She spent much of her time crocheting. She was known for her happy temperament and service to others. She worked many years in the Relief Society. She had a hard pioneer life, but was a strong and determined lady. Susan passed away in 1947.

FREDERIKKA CHRISTENSEN MUNK

No
Photo
Available

BIRTHDATE: 10 Jun 1825
Tolstrup Aarhus, Denmark
DEATH: 17 Sep 1899
Manti, Sanpete Co., Utah
PARENTS: Christen Rasmussen
Maren Rasmussen
PIONEER: 20 Sep 1858
Iver N. Iverson Wagon Train
SPOUSE: Christian Ipsen Munk
MARRIED: 12 Nov 1859
Salt Lake City, Utah
DEATH SP: 23 Oct 1908
Manti, Sanpete Co., Utah

CHILDREN:
Maria Christina, 24 Sep 1860
Ana Maria, 11 Apr 1862
Louise, 17 Nov 1863
Petrea (Nazer), 4 Jul 1865

Frederikka was born in Denmark, 1825. At age thirty-three, she emigrated. She sailed from Liverpool 22 Mar 1858 on the ship "John Bright" under Iver N. Iverson landing in New York. From there by rail to Florence Nebraska, leaving in July, again with the Iver N. Iverson wagon train, arriving in Salt Lake City 20 Sep 1858. One year later, 12 Nov 1859, she married Christian Ipsen Munk, also from Denmark, in polygamy. His first wife was Ane Marie Rasmussen by whom he had nine children. Frederikka and Christian made their home in Manti, Sanpete county where they became parents of four. Christian married a thrid wife, Margrete Hansen.

Frederikka was a homemaker maintaining her Danish customs as remembered by a grandson. Her faith in the gospel was a great comfort to her, especially at the time her three oldest children died of a contagious disease in one week in May 1869 leaving her youngest child to grow to maturity. She had a quiet, retiring nature. She passed away at age seventy-four in Manti. Christian passed away in 1908 at age eighty-six in Manti.

MAREN (MARY) CHRISTINE CHRISTENSEN MUNSON

No
Photo
Available

BIRTHDATE: 28 Oct 1844
Roholt, Praesto, Denmark
DEATH: 10 Mar 1930
Moreland, Bingham County, Idaho
PARENTS: James Christensen
Maria Kirstine Anderson Christensen
PIONEER: 12 Sep 1863
John R. Young Wagon Train
SPOUSE: John Munson
MARRIED: 22 Feb 1864
Salt Lake City, Utah
DEATH SP: 9 Apr 1903
Salt Lake City, Utah

CHILDREN:
John Henry, 9 Apr 1865
James Nephi, 23 Aug 1867
Charles Lehi, 23 Aug 1867
Lorenzo, 5 Jun 1874
Martha Christine, 12 Oct 1882

Maren Munson was born in Denmark. During her teen years, she learned the hat-making profession. At age sixteen she heard the Mormon missionaries preach the true gospel and believed their message. Her father forbade her to listen to the missionaries. At the age of eighteen she was baptized. Consequently, her father asked her to leave his home. Peter Christiansen was planning to emigrate to Utah and he agreed to pay her passage in return for her services helping his family. They came to Utah with the John R. Young Wagon-Train, arriving in the Salt Lake Valley 12 Sep 1863. She left the Peter Christiansen family and went to work elsewhere. She tells of buying a pair of shoes for $3.00. This price was a whole month's salary.

She became acquainted with John Munson and they were married 22 Feb 1864. They went to Hyrum, Utah to make their home. They became the parents of five children; four boys and one girl. Maren and John were called to Arizona to proselyte among the Navajo Indians. Maren became good friends with them and they exchanged remedies for illnesses. The Indians loved her and rewarded her with some of their nicest bead work. After returning from Arizona, they were called to help settle Overton, Nevada. This mission was soon recalled by the Church but not before they had buried their two-week-old daughter, Martha, under the drifting sand. She was their only daughter. It was a time of great sadness for Maren.

Maren was known as Mary. She and her husband worked hard. Her husband worked building railroads and Mary was a mess cook. She had a large tent for her cook house. She was an excellent cook and was especially noted for her mouth-watering donuts. Mary and John eventually settled in Moreland, Idaho. Mary was active in the auxiliaries of the Church. She was the secretary of the Relief Society when the Moreland Ward was organized. Her husband died 9 Apr 1903 in Salt Lake City, Utah. He was buried in the Moreland, Idaho Cemetery. After his death, Mary became active in genealogical and Temple work. She also did dressmaking for family and friends. Mary was a widow for twenty-seven years. She died 10 Mar 1930 at Moreland, Idaho.

ANNE STEELE MURDOCH

BIRTHDATE: 27 Oct 1829
Kirkconnel, Dumfrieshire, Scotland
DEATH: 15 Dec 1909
Heber City, Wasatch County, Utah
PARENTS: James Steele
Elizabeth Kerr Steele
PIONEER: 3 Sep 1852
Abraham 0. Smoot Wagon Company
SPOUSE: John Murray Murdoch
MARRIED: 15 Feb 1848
Kirkconnel, Dumfrieshire, Scotland
DEATH: 6 May 1910
Heber City, Utah

CHILDREN:
Elizabeth, 21 Nov 1848
James, Jun 1850
Mary Murray, 20 May 1851
Ann, 14 Sep 1854
Janett Osborne, 20 Dec 1856
Sarah Jane, 15 Jan 1859
Jacobina, 7 Nov 1860
John Murray, Jr., 4 Jan 1863
Isabella Lovina-twin, 2l Apr 1864
William-twin, 21 Apr 1864
Thomas Todd, 4 Mar 1866
Lucy Veronica, 25 Nov
Joseph A., 11 Mar 1870
David Steele, 31 May 1872
Millicent Sophia, 21 Aug 1874

Anne Steele Murdoch was born in Scotland. She lived on a small farm with her family. On 25 Feb 1848 she married John Murray Murdoch, also of Scotland. Anne's first child was a daughter, Elizabeth. Their first son, James, was also born in Scotland. Anne's brother, James Steele, had become a member of the Mormon Church in England. When he preached the Gospel to Anne and John they were baptized members of the Mormon Church 29 Nov 1850.

When a call came for two sheepherders and their dogs to go to Utah and herd sheep for President Brigham Young, John was about the only one of the members who was qualified to do this and he was instructed to emigrate to Utah. He and Anne sold all their belongings and put what money they could into the Church Emigration Fund. They boarded the ship "Kennebec" in Liverpool, England 10 Jan 1852. It took nine weeks to travel to New Orleans. Their son, James, died because of lack of food and brackish water.

They buried him on the banks of the Mississippi River 12 miles from Columbia. When they landed in St. Louis, Mo. they were put under the direction of Abraham 0. Smoot. Their daughter, Elizabeth, was extremely sick and, despite the loving care she was given, she too died. The next month, Anne gave birth to a baby girl. She carried her baby almost every foot of the way to Utah. On 3 Sep 1852, they reached the Salt Lake Valley, safe but very weary after seventeen weeks in crossing the Plains. Theirs was the first Company that had come to Utah aided by the Perpetual Emigration Fund. On 28 Mar 1856, Anne and John received their endowments and were sealed to each other.

In 1854, the grasshoppers destroyed most of the crops and many people had very little to eat. Anne, along with others, went to the hills and dug sego and thistle roots to help appease their hunger. They lived in Salt Lake City until 1860. They learned that land was available in the Provo Valley by merely paying the surveyor's fees, and irrigation water was plentiful. They moved to Heber City, Utah. Their first home was a dugout built at the old Heber Fort located in the northwest part of Heber. Meals had to be cooked in an open fireplace. Their soap was homemade and cloth for clothing was homespon from wool. Candles for lights were made out of mutton tallow. The children would gather cattails to make feather mattresses. The family went through trials of poverty, living in mud-roofed houses and enduring the trouble with Indians.

In Jun 1869, a Relief Society was established and Ann was chosen as a Counselor to the President. She was President of the society for many years. Anne was worn out with having labored for over eighty years. She grew feeble from the strain and burdens of years of sorrows, cares, and troubles of a long and active life. She died 15 Dec 1909. Her husband died a few months later. They had accumulated a great deal of wealth. They were both buried in the Heber City Cemetery.

ISABELLA CRAWFORD MURDOCH

BIRTHDATE: 11-2 Apr 1836
Blantyre, Lanarkshire, Scotland
DEATH: 10 Apr 1916
Heber City, Wasatch, Utah
PARENTS: Andrew Crawford
Margaret McClure
PIONEER: Fall 1858
Wagon Train
SPOUSE: John Murray Murdoch
MARRIED: 9 Aug 1862
Salt Lake Endowment House
2nd wife in Polygamy
DEATH SP: 6 May 1910
Heber City, Wasatch, Utah

CHILDREN:
Margaret Ann (Hawkes), 19 May 1863
Catherine Campbell (Hicken), 15 Nov 1864
James Crawford, 11 Feb 1869
Brigham, 2 Nov 1870
Robert, 12 Sep 1872

John Murray, Jr., 1 May 1874
Isabella Crawford (Nicol), 8 Jan 1876

Isabella was born in Scotland, 1836. Her mother died when she was six years old. Her father joined the British Army and went to Canada. She lived with relatives and was baptized 16 Aug 1855. She was driven out of her home and migrated to America. She became an expert weaver of fine linens. She walked all the way across the plains and arrived in Salt Lake City with no family to greet her in the fall of 1858.

At age twenty-six, she married John Murray Murdoch as a plural wife 9 Aug 1862. in the Salt Lake Endowment House. The two wives lived in harmony and love with each, raising a large family. John's first wife, Ann Steele, married 24 Feb 1848, had fifteen children. With Isabella, he had seven children, all born in Heber City, Wasatch County, Utah where they made their home. Isabella did much weaving to help support her family and remained active in her faith. Ann, her sister wife, passed away in 1909 in Heber. John passed away 6 May 1910 and Isabella passed away 10 Apr 1916 two days shy of her eightieth birthday. She was a widow for five years. They are all buried in the Heber Cemetery.

MARY MURRAY MURDOCH

BIRTHDATE: 13 Oct 1782
Glencairn, Dumfrieshire, Scotland
DEATH: 3 Oct 1856
Chimney Rock, Scottsbluff, Neb.
PARENTS: John Murray
Margaret McCall Murray
PIONEER:
Edward Martin Handcart Co.
SPOUSE: James Murdoch
MARRIED: 10 Jan 1811
Auchinleck, Ayrshire, Scotland
DEATH SP: 20 Oct 1831
Gaswater, Ayrshire, Scotland

CHILDREN:
Janet, 8 Dec 1811
Mary, 16 Jun 1813 (died an infant)
James, 29 Jul 1814
Veronica, 16 Jun 1816
Mary, 3 Oct 1818
John Murray, 28 Dec 1820
Margaret, 30 Dec 1822 (died as child)
William, 3 Jul 1825

Mary was born to John Murray and Margaret McCall Murray at Glencairn, Scotland. On January 10, 1811, she married James Murdoch. They became parents of eight children. Two of her children died in childhood. Her husband was employed at the Lime Works in Gaswater, Scotland and lost his life trying to rescue a man who had become a victim of poisonous air in a mine shaft. She and her children were already accustomed to hard work. Her energy and thrifty disposition was a great help to her in raising and providing for her fatherless children. Her son-in-law, James Steel, visited from England and shared his message of the restored Gospel of the LDS Church. After he returned to England, he sent missionaries to their home. They were baptized and held many church meetings in her home. She was baptized on December 22, 1851. Her son, John, and his wife emigrated to Utah in 1852. In 1856, he sent money for his mother's fare to join him in Zion. She was seventy-four years old, but she bravely sailed on the ship, "Horizon," on May 25, 1856. They arrived at New York on July 8, 1856, then took a train to Iowa City, Iowa. She received her handcart and supplies to cross the plains under the direction of Edward Martin, who was just returning from a mission to England.

They had to stop in Florence, Nebraska longer than they had planned due to so many axles on the handcarts. They left very late in the season. They didn't have enough warm clothing and bedding for the cold temperatures. Due to scarcity of food, they were becoming weaker. They were hit by an early winter storm and weren't able to drive their stakes into the ground in order to put up their tents for protection against the elements. They had to camp at Chimney Rock for a few days because so many were too weary and sick to travel. On the morning of October 3, 1856, word was sent through the camp that sister Mary Murray Murdoch and many others had passed away during the night from these hardships. Her spirit was strong, but her body was not able to finish the desire of her heart to join her son, John, in Zion.

ELIZABETH HUNTER MURDOCK

BIRTHDATE: 17 Apr 1839
Clackermannan,
Clackermannanshire, Scotland
DEATH: 11 Jun 1935
Heber City, Wasatch, Utah
PARENTS: Robert Hunter
Agnes Ann Hunter Hunter
PIONEER: 13 Aug 1852
James W. Bay Wagon Company
SPOUSE: Joseph Stacy Murdoch
MARRIED: 11 June 1854
Salt Lake City, Salt Lake, Utah
DEATH: 15 Feb 1899
Heber City, Wasatch, Utah

CHILDREN:
Jonathan Robert, 19 Aug 1855
Alva Moroni, 26 Apr 1857
Parley Alexander, 3 Feb 1859
James Stacy, 8 Dec 1861
Alphonso Brigham, 15 Mar 1864
Elizabeth Ann, 5 Jun 1866
Nelson, 1 Oct 1868
Eunice Clara, 7 Mar 1873
Joseph Gideon, 26 Mar 1876
Erastus Coridon, 31 May 1879
Andrew Hunter, 14 Nov 1881

Elizabeth's mother, Agnes, was baptized in 1847 by John Sharp, President of the LDS Mission Branch. The following year, her husband, Robert, and daughter, Elizabeth, were baptized into the LDS Church. They began planning and saving to go to Zion. Her father found the ridicule from his friends was more than he could bear, so he allowed his wife and four children to go to America with the thought that he would support them and come later after selling his store. They sailed on the sailing vessel, "North Atlantic," from Liverpool, England on September 4, 1850. They landed in New Orleans on November 1, 1850. After traveling up the Mississippi River by steamboat, they arrived in St. Louis on November 8, 1850. They went to a small mining town of Gravies where Elizabeth's mother died one year later. One of Elizabeth's sisters, Margaret, married David Love who had become widowed due to an outbreak of Cholera. He promised Margaret if she would help him care for his little children, he would help her bring her younger siblings to Utah. In 1852, they crossed the plains with the James W. Bay Wagon Company and arrived in Salt Lake Valley on August 13th.

When they arrived in Utah, people knew they were orphans and gave them work to do and whatever help they could. Elizabeth went to work for a Mrs. Nicholson where they had good food and shelter. One of her duties was to gather, clean, and sell vegetables to emigrants as they came from Emigration Canyon. Later, she went to Mill Creek to work, cutting beets for molasses. In 1853, they received word of the death of their father in Scotland. Elizabeth, at age fifteen, went to work for Joseph S. Murdock at the Church Pasture where she helped to milk thirty-four cows night and morning. They sold the milk to the men who worked at the Red Butte Sandstone Quarry. On June 11, 1854, Elizabeth married Joseph Stacy Murdock as his second wife. In 1856, they were called on a colonizing mission to Carson Valley, Nevada. They kept many cows and made a little money by making butter and selling it to emigrants. At the time of the Johnston Army threat, they were called back to Utah and settled in American Fork.

SALLY STACY MURDOCK

BIRTHDATE: 22 Apr 1788
New Salem, Franklin, Mass.
DEATH: 25 Sep 1864
Salt Lake City, Salt Lake, Utah
PARENTS: Nymphas Stacy
Sarah Gibbs Stacy
PIONEER: 22 Sep 1847
Daniel Spencer Wagon Co.
SPOUSE: Joseph Murdock
MARRIED: 15 Apr 1818
Hamilton, Madison, New York
DEATH: 9 Oct 1844
Nauvoo, Hancock, Illinois

CHILDREN:
Betsy, 1819 (died an infant)
son, 1820 (died an infant)

Joseph Stacy, 26 Jun 1822
John Deans, 28 Jul 1825 (died age 21)
Sarah Salome, 22 Nov 1828 (died age 4)
Nymphas Coridon, 12 May 1833

Sally's father had served as a Captain in General George Washington's command. She was born in New Salem, Franklin, Massachusetts. On April 15, 1818, she married Joseph Murdock as his second wife. They farmed in Hamilton, New York to make a living. They owned a large tract of sugar maple trees as well as orchards and farmlands where hops were a major part of their crop. Sally taught many women to spin and weave. Her husband had been crippled and was often bedfast due to a ruptured blood vessel in his back. When the LDS Missionaries visited and taught them the gospel, he asked for a blessing and was completely healed. They were soon baptized as members of the LDS Church. They sold their beautiful home and traveled across New York, Pennsylvania, Ohio, and Indiana to Nauvoo, Illinois. Hatred grew daily in Nauvoo and it was becoming apparent they would have to journey further west. Sally's husband died in 1844 and she received several offers from her relatives to return to the east. As she was traveling east, her husband's spirit appeared and asked her where she was going. She quickly returned to Nauvoo and made arrangements to travel west with the saints. Her son, John, died of pneumonia he acquired while helping other saints, cattle, and horses across the icy Mississippi River. Sally now had only twelve year old Nymphas. She lost her husband, her homes, one of her sons. Her son, Joseph had been chosen to care for the Church owned livestock. He traveled with the advance party led by Brigham Young. Sally and Nymphas were assigned to the Daniel Spencer Wagon Company. Thus Sally, Nymphas, and Joseph and his family and his stock tenders were between the Advance Party and the Spencer Company. She had to drive her own wagon. She had tied a buck and two ewes to the back of her wagon. She was the first woman to bring sheep into the Salt Lake Valley.

Sally and her son lived in the back of their wagon inside the fort that first winter. She and her son built a two story home on the ground where the New House Hotel was built. They also had a farm. Sally was a thrifty, energetic, and courageous woman. She was generous and kind to others; sympathetic and helpful in times of sickness and death among the people. She died at the age of seventy six years.

SARAH MELISSA BARNEY MURDOCK

BIRTHDATE: 30 Mar 1834
Amherst, Loraine County, Ohio
DEATH: 21 May 1911
Heber City, Wasatch County, Utah
PARENTS: Royal Barney
Sarah Bowen Esterbrook
PIONEER: 13 Oct 1850
Edward Hunter Wagon Train
SPOUSE: Nymphus Murdock
MARRIED: 31 Oct 1853
Salt Lake City Endowment House
DEATH SP: 19 Apr 1917
Heber City, Wasatch County, Utah

CHILDREN:
Nymphus Coridon, 2 Aug 1854
Sarah Melissa, 15 Nov 1856
Joseph Royal, 11 Aug 1858
Betsy Emaline, 28 Mar 1860

Sarah Melissa was born in Ohio in 1834. She was the third child of five. Her family were early members of the LDS church. The story of the church is their story. They lived in Kirtland, Ohio and Nauvoo. They left Nauvoo in 1850 and came to Utah. Some records say they travelled with the Edwin Wooley Merchandise Ox Train. Melissa was sixteen and she walked all the way to Salt Lake City. At age nineteen, she married Nymphus Murdock who gave her a Mexican dollar to seal his proposal. They set up housekeeping in their own meager way, in a wikiup made of willows, their total equipment being a butcher knife, a frying pan and an axe. As soon as Nymphus was able, he built an adobe house and they invited his mother to share it with them.

They became parents of four, but raised only Joseph Royal to adulthood. When Plural marriage was practiced, Nymphus married Esther Mariah Davies, a lovely Mormon girl Melissa chose for him. She was presented to Nymphus as Sarah presented Hagar to Abraham. They were married in the Endowment House 6 Dec 1857. The trauma and fears of Utah the summer of 1858 were particularly hard for Melissa. She was seven months pregnant when the family moved south, however all ended well. Diptheria claimed three of her four children. As the families grew, it became advantageous to make a separation. Esther Mariah's family was left in the home in Salt Lake City and Melissa went with her husband to Charleston, Utah. They purchased land for a home a mile and a half south of town. They were an enterprising couple and started a store in the kitchen of their home, the items for sale being sold out of a large dry good box. A large part of the running of the store naturally fell upon Melissa. In addition she assumed the responsibilities associated as the wife of the Bishop. Later, they removed the store to the central part of Charleston, adding a lumber mill and a creamery to the store and a school was held in an upstairs room of the store.

Melissa served in the Relief Society, where she was a counselor and President of the Charleston ward for many years. She supported Nymphus on his mission to the Eastern States and while he served in the Utah State Legislature. They moved to Heber City in 1908 where they built a lovely home. Melissa suffered with diabetes, which affected her eyes. She did not see well the last years of her life. She passed away 21 May 1911 at age seventy-seven. Nymphus passed away five years later.

ELIZA ANN LAMBORN MURPHY

BIRTHDATE: 16 Apr 1858
Clarmont Building, Bath, England
DEATH: 19 Apr 1949
Upalco, Duchesne, Utah
PARENTS: John Lamborn
Ellen Jane Bailey
PIONEER: Fall 1864
Wagon Train
SPOUSE: Emanuel Bird Murphy
MARRIED: 16 Oct 1876
Salt Lake Endowment House
DEATH: 19 Apr 1943
Upalco, Duchesne, Utah

CHILDREN:
Nancy Ellen, 20 Oct 1877
Eliza Ann (Michie), 4 Dec 1878
Emily Elizabeth, 26 Jan 1881
Josephine, 26 Jun 1883
Emanuel Masters, 29 Nov 1885
Edwin Leslie, 8 Jan 1887
Ada Melinda, 26 Aug 1889
Paul, 19 Feb 1892
Beatrice (Fitzgerald), 11 May 1894
George Amos, 30 Sep 1896
Rhoda, 9 Nov 1897
Agnes Maud (Williams), 25 May 1900
Pearl Geneva, Living

Eliza Ann was born in England, 1859. She was fifth of five children all born in Bath, England. Her mother and her siblings came to Utah in 1864. They left London on the ship "Hudson" 3 Jun 1864 and landed in New York. They made their way to Wyoming, Nebraska and joined an Independent wagon train, arriving in Salt Lake City in the fall of 1864. On the ship Hudson, Eliza Ann's brother was badly burned in an accident and his mother had to carry him across the plains nearly every step of the way. Eliza was then six years old, and she walked beside her mother the greater part of the way. After their arrival, they went to live with her grandmother and brothers in the Bear Lake Area. They were called by President Brigham Young to help settle that area.

On one of her trips to Salt Lake to buy shoes, Eliza met Emanuel Bird Murphy. They were married in the Old Salt Lake Endowment House by President Daniel H. Wells 16 Oct 1876, when she was seventeen. Their first home was in Mill Creek. They lived there twenty years. Then they moved to Woodland, Utah. Eliza Ann was Relief Society President for fifteen years. She was also a midwife, and delivered many babies and took care of many new mothers. Emanuel then took employment in the Uintah Basin. They moved there and remained until they both died. She again served as Relief Society President for nine years. She served in many other church callings also. She was known as Grandma Murphy to everyone. She had thirteen children and outlived all but three. Three died within a few days of each other of Typhoid. She had many trails in her faith, but she was a great leader and example to every one. She passed away in Upalco, Duchesne County, Utah 19 Apr 1949 at age ninety.

GRACE BROADBENT MURPHY

BIRTHDATE: 11 Jun 1836
Dukenfield, Cheshire, England
DEATH: 18 Feb 1924
Salt Lake City, Utah
PARENTS: William Broadbent
Mary Greenwood
PIONEER: 21 Sep 1857
Jacob Hofheins Wagon Train
SPOUSE: Jesse Easters Murphy
MARRIED: 28 Apr 1857
St. Louis, Missouri
DEATH SP: 25 Mar 1916
Mill Creek, Salt Lake, Utah

CHILDREN:
Jesse Emanuel, 7 Sep 1858
William Francis, 19 Nov 1860
Mark, 5 Jul 1862
Charles Howard, 28 Aug 1864
Mary Etta (Horne), 12 Dec 1866
Louise, 13 Dec 1869
Grace Viola, 8 May 1872
Hyrum, 17 Aug 1874
Joseph Twin, 17 Aug 1874
Alice Maud (Hovey), 28 Apr 1877
Samuel Leslie, 30 May 1880

Grace was born in England, 1836. She was the oldest child.

In about 1844 she emigrated with her family to America, first settling in Mason County, Kentucky and then locating in Cincinnati, Ohio where church records indicate that Grace was baptized 22 Oct 1854 by Orson Spencer. In 1857, Grace was in St. Louis, Missouri, where she met Jesse Easters Murphy, who was on his way to Utah to prepare and arrange for his parents and brothers and sisters to come west. Grace and Jesse were married after a brief courtship of five days, and on the advice of Erastus Snow.

The Murphy newlyweds left for Utah from Iowa City in June 1857 in the wagon company of Captain Jacob Hofheins. Records indicate that Jesse and Grace were endowed 14 Mar 1860 in the Salt Lake City Endowment House. They became parents of eleven children. After

arriving in Salt Lake, Grace and Jesse built a small home on the corner of 'C' Street and South Temple. Her husband was called as a guard during the Johnston's Army troubles, and in early 1860 he returned East to head a wagon train bringing his parents and family to Utah in Jun 1860. In 1864 Jesse and his father bought property in the Millcreek area (about 36th So.) on what is now known as Murphy's Lane. Jesse and Grace's home still stands on the corner and is on the register of Utah Historic Sites (3605 South 13th East). Grace was asked to live the law of plural marriage. Jesse married Robina Sproul 15 Feb 1862. She died 1871 in Millcreek in childbirth and Grace helped raise these children. He also married Lovina Ann Murphy and Elizabeth Sproul. Grace was small, dark haired, alert and competent. Her husband told folks what a "first class" wife she was. Grace died on 18 Feb 1924 at the home of her daughter Alice Maud Hovey and is buried in Wasatch Lawn cemetery. She was referred to as a 'pioneer of 1857.' She was age eighty-seven at her passing, widowed for seven years.

NANCY JUDD EASTERS MURPHY

BIRTHDATE: 30 Jul 1813
Chester, Union Co.,So.Carolina
DEATH: 25 Feb 1898
Millcreek, Salt Lake Co.,Utah
PARENTS: Robert Easter
Celiz Hiatt
PIONEER: 3 0 Aug 1860
Jesse Easters Murphy
SPOUSE:
Emanuel Masters Murphy
MARRIED: 5 Apr 1831
Union County, So. Carolina
DEATH SP: 23 Jul 1871

CHILDREN:
Jesse Easters, 27 Jun 1832
Holly Ann, 30 Mar 1834
Mark B., 6 Jul 1837
Louisa Jane (Almond), 3 Jun 1840
William Columbus, 1 Apr 1842
Martha Francis, 11 Dec 1843
Hyrum, 3 Mar 1846
Thomas Gaden, 12 Jan 1848
Charles, 15 May 1851
Emanuel Bird, 14 Oct 1813

Nancy was born in South Carolina, 1813. She was the fifth child. She was baptized by Wilford Woodruff in Tennessee, 1836 and she and her family lived in Far West during the Missouri Persecutions.

Nancy married Emanuel Masters Murphy on 5 Apr 1831 at age seventeen. They made their home in Union, South Carolina for the birth of their first child. They were in Tennessee for their second child, and their conversion to the LDS church. They were in Far West for their third child and after the depredations, returned to Union, So Carolina for their fourth child. Their next move was to Fayette,

Georgia and peace for five more children. Their last child was born in Weakly, Tennessee. They decided to emigrate to Zion with their son Jesse E. Murphy who had been to the Salt Lake Valley earlier and went East to bring the wagon train. They arrived in Salt Lake City 30 August 1860. Nancy was asked to live the law of plural marriage, when Emanuel married Sarah Elizabeth Alexander 12 May 1861 in Salt Lake City. They had six children. He also married Margaret Dennings Apr 1864 and Elizabeth Irving Aug 1864. Nancy was a very small woman weighing no more than 100 pounds, had deep blue eyes and dark hair. She was raised on the large southern plantation of her father, Robert Easter, who was considered wealthy with many slaves but Nancy learned to spin and weave making many beautiful items for her home. She had a widespread reputation as a wonderful cook. The Murphy's lived on Murphy's Lane (35th So. between 13th E. and Highland Drive for many years. Emanuel died there 23 Jul 1871. Nancy passed away 25 Feb 1898 at the age of eighty-four, having been a widow for twenty-seven years. She had received her Patriarchal blessing at Far West, Missouri in 1837 under the hands of Joseph Smith, Sr. Faithful to the gospel to the end, she left a great heritage for hundreds of descendants.

KAREN MARIA NIELSEN MURRAY

BIRTHDATE: 3 Jan 1846
Rusgaard, Hjorring Amptt, Denmark
DEATH: 12 Jun 1897
Jensen, Uintah County, Utah
PARENTS: Niels Christian Nielsen
Karen Sophia Ericksen
PIONEER: 13 Sep 1857
Christian Christensen Handcart Co.
SPOUSE: Jeremiah Hatch Murray
MARRIED: 6 Feb 1863
Spanish Fork, Utah
DEATH SP: 5 Sep 1909
Spanish Fork, Utah

CHILDREN:
Jeremiah, 7 Dec 1863
Sarah Helen, 28 Jul 1866
Andrew Rich, 15 Jul 1868
William Riley, 4 Oct 1870
Elizabeth Caroline, 6 Jan 1873
Rebecca, 25 Dec 1875
Stephen Robert, 3 Dec 1877
Hyrum Smith, 22 Jul 1880
Jonathan Moyes, 8 Nov 1882

Upon hearing the teaching of the gospel of Jesus Christ of the LDS Church, Karen's family was baptized and left their native homeland to make their new home in America with Elder Knud Peterson who had just completed a mission in Norway. It took them fifteen months to arrive in St. Louis, Missouri. They suffered many hardships due to high winds, rough weather, sickness, hunger, two fires which destroyed many of their possessions, thirty deaths and burials at sea. Shortly after arriving in America, Karen Maria's

father died of Cholera. Karen's mother and seven little children joined the Christian Christensen Handcart company and they had to walk the entire distance. Her oldest brother and sister had come to Utah two years earlier and had settled in Fillmore, Utah.

Karen married Jeremiah Hatch Murray on February 6, 1863 in Spanish Fork. They made their home in Lealand, Utah. Several years later, they moved to the Ashley Valley by the Green River where they homesteaded six hundred acres and put it into farm land, raised livestock, and raised a lot of fruit. She was a very intelligent woman with a great love for music. She was always kind and gentle, a beautiful seamstress and homemaker, a wonderful cook and mother. Her main virtue was sharing her faith and her home to the needy. Their door was always open. She had a heart attack and died while she was doing the family wash on the scrubbing board.

LOVINA HEATON NEBEKER MURRAY

No Photo Available

BIRTHDATE: 5 Nov 1855
Bradford, Wilsden, England
DEATH: 19 Jan 1938
Marysvale, Piute, Utah
PARENTS: Rebecca Heaton
adopted and raised Henry Nebeker
22 Jul 1865
PIONEER: Aug 1864
Independent Wagon Company
SPOUSE: Franklin C. or
Wm Murray
MARRIED: Mar 1873 Utah
DEATH SP: 1902
Piute County, Utah

CHILDREN:
Lovina Lauretta (McCarty), 4 Apr 1874
Frank, 5 Sep 1875
Patrick, 17 Mar 1877
William Raymond, 26 Jan 1879
Francis L., 5 Nov 1881
Sidney Manning, 1883
Franklin, 16 Feb 1886

Lovina was born in England, 1855. She was the oldest of ten children. All others were born in Utah or Nevada after her mother married Henry Nebeker and he adopted Lovina. Her mother married in polygamy and her next younger sibling was born 13 Jun 1866 in Payson, Utah Co., where they made their home. In 1868 they were living in Nevada and in 1872 they were in Glenwood, Sevier County.

At age seventeen Lovina married Franklin C. or William Murray. He was born in New York Jun 1840. He was fifteen years older than Lovina. They became parents of seven children. From her mother, she had learned many household tasks which she put to good use taking care of her large family. She made a happy home for her children.

Lovina was active in the LDS church, whereever she and her family were living. She also kept in touch with her large, extended family. Franklin passed away in 1902, when their youngest child was sixteen. Lovina continued to raise their family and make a living for them. She passed away in Marysvale, Piute County, Utah at age eighty-two, having been a widow for thirty-six years.

MARY ANN MALLEY RILEY MURRAY

No
Photo
Available

BIRTHDATE: 20 Nov 1816
Preston, St. Mary, Lancashire, Eng.
DEATH: 21 Jan 1881
Spanish Fork, Utah County, Utah
PARENTS: Benjamin Malley
Mary Caton Malley
PIONEER: 30 Nov 1856
Edward Martin Handcart Company
SPOUSE: John Riley
MARRIED: 22 May 1849
Preston, Lancashire, England
DEATH SP:

CHILDREN:
Thomas Caton, 30 Apr 1844

SPOUSE II: John Murray, Jr.
MARRIED: 13 Dec 1862
Salt Lake Endowment House
DEATH SP: 1894
Lapoint, Uintah County, Utah

Mary Ann and her father were among the first to recognize the true church when it was presented to them. They were baptized in the River Ribble just two months after the first missionaries arrived in England. She was baptized August 15, 1837 by Joseph Fielding and confirmed by Orson Hyde in September 1837. Without the support of her father who died in January 1855, life became very difficult for Mary Ann. The Saints were advised to go to Zion as soon as ways and means could be arranged, so she determined to take her son to Utah. While she was making preparations for the journey, her husband's sister kidnapped and hid Thomas. He was returned in time to sail on the ship "Horizon" on the May 25, 1856 with 856 English Saints on board under the direction of Edward Martin. Her husband stayed in England.

Mary Ann had very little money. The Edward Martin Handcart Company was the fifth group to use this means of transportation. They began the 1,300 mile trek poorly out-fitted. Their carts were made of green wood and required major overhauls along the way. Even though they reached Florence, Nebraska in less than four weeks, it was late August before they arrived at the Missouri River. October found them at the Platte River with early frost. There was bitter cold and winter winds. Food allotments were cut. Many were ill and exhaustion overcame them. Their tents would freeze to the ground and many of them were forced to chew rawhide to reduce their hunger pains. On October 28, help arrived from Salt Lake City. They had lost fifty-six

people in the past nine days. Though their clothing was worn out and provisions nearly gone, the only way to escape death was to keep moving on. When they finally reached Salt Lake Valley, Mary Ann and her son, Thomas were taken to Spanish Fork to the home of John and Sarah Bates Murray and their nine children.

Mary Ann was married and sealed to John Murray, Jr. who was twenty years younger than she. John Murray was also sealed to Rachel Allred seven years later in the Endowment House. They had two children who died young and are buried next to Mary Ann in Spanish Fork, Utah.

What gratitude we as her descendants have for this faithful lady who had a testimony of the truthfulness of the gospel of Jesus Christ strong enough to sustain her through countless obstacles and hardships.

MARY ASHBY MURRAY

BIRTHDATE: 1 Apr 1851
West Leicester, Leicestershire,
England
DEATH: 16 Jan 1922
Vernal, Uintah, Utah
PARENTS: Samuel Ashby
Hanna Ward Ashby
PIONEER: 20 Sep 1864
Jos. S. Rawlins Wagon Company
SPOUSE: Jeremiah Hatch Murray
MARRIED: 4 Mar 1865
DEATH SP: 5 Sep 1909

CHILDREN:
John Richard, 14 May 1867
Elizabeth Hannah, 27 Apr 1869 (died 1 mo.)
Thomas Ward, 6 Aug 1870
Mary Lovina, 27 Jan 1873
Samuel Ashby, 25 Sep 1874
Margaret "M," 9 Sep 1876
Jeremiah Hatch, 2 Apr 1878
Joseph Smith, 19 Jun 1880
William Ashby, 21 Jun 1882

Mary was three years old when she was first put to work in a box factory stacking boxes. Each member of the family had to work due to the ill health of their father. When she was a little older, she helped her mother with glove making. The Ashby family heard the message of the gospel from missionaries and were baptized as members of the LDS Church. When the call from the General Authorities of the church came for the Saints to gather in Utah, the Ashby family could only afford passages for Mary to go with her grandparents, Thomas and True Love Lathan Ward.

They traveled to Liverpool and sailed from there to America on the ship "General McClellan." As soon as they could, they arranged to join the Jos. S. Rawlins Wagon Company to cross the Plains. Mary's parents had scraped enough money together to buy her a nice pair of leather boots to wear across the Plains. They were stolen even before they left England. So much of the time, Mary was walking across the Plains in bare feet. The driver of the water wagon would let her ride on the back of his wagon when his load was not too heavy. They arrived in Salt Lake on September 20, 1864. When she arrived, she was told that Sister Murray in Spanish Fork needed help until she and her baby regained their health. Their love for each other grew until Jeremiah took his first wife, Karen Maria, the baby, and Mary to the Endowment House in Salt Lake to be married and sealed for time and eternity.

In 1865 their families were called with fifty other families on a mission to the Muddy, by St. George. They had a very difficult time getting down there. When their mission was finished, they moved back near Spanish Fork where they farmed. Jeremiah then moved Mary and her family to Maiser (Vernal). Here he planted a three acre orchard of fruit trees. Jeremiah eventually accumulated the means by which he sent for Mary's family in England to join them in Utah.

SARAH BATES MURRAY

BIRTHDATE: Jun 1808
Drafton, Tyrone, Ireland
DEATH: 24 Jan 1882
Spanish Fork, Utah, Utah
PARENTS: Richard Bates
Sophia Anderson Bates
PIONEER: 15 Sep 1852
John Tidwell Wagon Company
SPOUSE: John Murray
MARRIED: 28 Oct 1833
DEATH SP: Sep 1879
Spanish Fork, Utah

CHILDREN:
Christian, 25 Aug 1834 (died 9 mo.)
John, 19 Jul 1836
Edward, 23 Dec 1837 (died infant)
Richard, 16 Dec 1839
Elizabeth, 24 Dec 1840
Robert, 15 Aug 1842 (died age 8)
Jeremiah Hatch, 11 Jul 1844
Joseph Albert, 8 Sep 1846 (died infant)

Sarah's parents lived in Drafton, Ireland until the potato famine. They went to America and located in New Hampshire where her father worked in the lumber industry. He had the pioneering spirit which urged him further west to Buffalo, New York. At the time Sarah was a young lady, she and a group of other young ladies met some soldiers from the British Army who were stationed near Toronto, Quebec, Canada. She took a liking to John Murray. John and Sarah were married October 28, 1833 and made their home in Lucerne, Monroe, Michigan where seven of their children were born.

When their seventh child was nearly ten days old, the LDS Missionaries met this family and told them of the gospel. They baptized the family and blessed the son naming him Jeremiah Hatch Murray after one of the missionaries. They were inspired to leave their home and journey to be with the Saints in Nauvoo, Illinois. John and Sarah went forth with undaunted courage, took necessary steps to outfit themselves for migration, and responded to Brigham Young's call for the Saints to settle in Kanesville. Their last child had been born during this move. After living in Kanesville for a time, they prepared to enlist in the John Tidwell Wagon Company which arrived in Salt Lake Valley in September of 1852. They moved to Spanish Fork to farm.

In 1865, the family was called to colonize "The Muddy," an area seventy miles southwest of St. George. It is actually in Nevada. They were greeted by a barren desert, occupied by Indians who were always ready to attack weak, defenseless travelers and neglected no opportunity to prey upon the animals in the area. They were one of fifty families sent to settle the area. The entire enterprise was abandoned early in 1871 and Sarah and John went back to Spanish Fork for the rest of their lives.

MARY ELIZABETH WHITE MUSSER

BIRTHDATE: 7 Nov 1846
Garden Grove, Pottawattamie, Iowa
DEATH: 24 Feb 1932
Salt Lake City, Utah
PARENTS: Samuel Dennis White
Mary Hannah Burton White
PIONEER: 24 Sep 1851
Harry Walton Indep. Wagon Train
SPOUSE: Amos Milton Musser
MARRIED: 1 Oct 1864
Salt Lake Endowment House
DEATH SP: 24 Sep 1909
Salt Lake City, Utah

CHILDREN:
Samuel White, 4 Feb 1866
Franklin White, 13 Nov 1867
Don Carlos White, 26 Aug 1869
Joseph White, 8 Mar 1872
Willard White, 7 Aug 1873
Mary White, 17 Apr 1875
Gertrude White (Howard), 21 Jun 1877
Barr White, 10 Aug 1879
Blanche White (Lewis), 8 Aug 1882
Burton White, 10 Jul 1886

Mary Elizabeth was born in Iowa, 1846. Her family was settled there after they were forced to leave Nauvoo. When Mary was born, it was not a pleasant experience. Her mother lay on a bed in a crude one-room log house with a dirt floor and a dirt roof. In every corner of that room were beds on which lay sick people. The crude log house did not succeed in shutting out the winter. When it rained, the roof leaked so badly that buckets and pans had to be shifted around to catch the water.

On May 17, 1851, her family joined the Harry Walton Independent Wagon train and left Garden Grove for Utah, arriving 24 Sep 1851. After a short rest, the family moved to Lehi where they settled for four years. They were then sent to settle Cedar City and then moved north to Beaver where they settled. About this time, Amos Milton Musser, a young elder who had just returned from a round-the-world missionary tour, was made Traveling Bishop of the Church under President Brigham Young. One of his duties was to collect tithes from outlying communities. While in Beaver he was often entertained at the White home, and in 1864, when he returned to Salt Lake City, he brought with him Mary Elizabeth White.

At age seventeen, 1 Oct 1864, Mary Elizabeth married Amos Milton Musser in the Salt Lake City Endowment House by Heber C. Kimball. Their first home was in the 13th ward, where their first five children were born. They then moved to the 1st ward where the last four were born. Mr. Musser's first wife died in 1876 and his third wife in 1893. Mary cared for their children with her own, and they loved her as a mother. This was a tremendous responsibility because Mr. Musser was away much of the time.

The "underground" days were trying for everyone. Mr. Musser served six months in the penitentiary for polygamy. During this time his prison fare was supplemented with smuggled delicacies. Mary served in the ward organizations. In the 13th ward, she served as treasurer of the Relief Society. After their move to the 1st ward, she served in the Primary first as a counselor and then as President. She also served as one of the six counselors in the Retrenchment Association which later became the YWMIA. In 1896 she became a regular temple worker in the Salt Lake Temple where she served for thirty years. Mr. Musser passed away 24 Sep 1909 in Salt Lake City. Mary passed away 24 Feb 1932 in Salt Lake City at age eighty-five, having been a widow for twenty-two years.

EMMA ELIZABETH GODFREY MYLER

BIRTHDATE: 6 Apr 1856
Stoke Prior, Worcestershire, England
DEATH: 6 Dec 1943
Clarkston, Cache, Utah
PARENTS: John Godfrey
Mary Pittaway
PIONEER: 10 Oct 1862
Henry Miller Company by Ox team
SPOUSE: Joseph Elias Myler
MARRIED: 10 Oct 1872
Salt Lake City, Utah
DEATH SP: 17 Jun 1922
Clarkston, Cache, Utah

CHILDREN:
John Elias, 27 Jul 1875
Mary Emma, Sep 1876

Sarah Ann, 5 Feb 1878
Katherine Lovina, 2 Feb 1881
George Joseph, 2 Jul 1884
Orrin Frank, 23 Oct 1887
James Thomas, 26 Jan 1890

Emma Elizabeth Godfrey was born in Stoke Prior, Worcestershire, England on 6 Apr 1856, the daughter of John Godfrey and Mary Pittaway. In May 1862, when Emma was six years old, the family sailed to America on the ship "William Tapscott."

They crossed the plains with ox teams in the Henry Miller Company. Emma walked a lot of the way by her father's side, picking up buffalo chips for fuel as they went. They arrived in Salt Lake City on 10 Oct 1862, and stayed that winter in a log cabin that her brother, who came the year before, had prepared for them. Later they moved to Cache Valley and finally settled in Clarkston.

Emma stayed with an aunt in Wellsville for a time, and became very homesisck. She walked bare-foot from Wellsville to Mendon, then caught a ride to Clarkston. The family at that time was living in a dug-out. She and her brother cared for the gardens, chickens, pigs, and other animals.

She was married to Joseph Myler 10 Oct 1872 in the Endowment House in Salt Lake City, and they became the parents of seven children. She joined the Relief Society as a young girl and was a very faithful visiting teacher for over forty years. Emma died in Clarkston, Cache, Utah on 6 Dec 1943 and is buried there.

JULIA ANN BROWNELL MYLER

BIRTHDATE: 12 Feb 1826
Dayton, Ohio
DEATH: 27 Jan 1898
Lewisville, Idaho
PARENTS: Gideon Brownell
Elizabeth (Betsy) Wheeler Brownell
PIONEER: 22 Sep 1849
William P. Miller's 5th Company
SPOUSE: James Myler
MARRIED: 5 Oct 1843
Bertrand, Berrien County, Michigan
DEATH: 21 May 1894

CHILDREN:
William Oscar, 25 Sep 1844
Joseph Elias, 31 Jan 1846
Calvin, 1848 (died age 1)
James Russell, 19 Nov 1850
Julia Elzina, 25 Jul 1852
John Young, 14 Jun 1854
Orin Main, 14 Sep 1856
Margaret Lavina, 2 May 1859
Charles C., 22 Apr 1861
Rosetta Sophrona, 15 May 1863
George Frank, 10 Aug 1865

Julia was taught early to be thrifty, honest and industrious. Her family moved many times and she lived in many states traveling by covered wagon and walking. Julia's family joined the LDS Church when they were living in Dayton, Ohio. She was baptized by her father in May of 1841. While they were living in Berrien County, Michigan, she met and married James Myler. Her parents, her brother, and her little family moved to Nauvoo to be with the Saints. While there, her family knew President Joseph Smith and they received their endowments in the Nauvoo Temple. They were faced with many mob threats until they were forced to leave one night in February 1846 in weather that was 26 degrees below zero. They camped with the Saints at Montrose, Iowa until spring, then traveled on to Winter Quarters on the outskirts of Omaha, Nebraska.

While they were in Winter Quarters, the government called for 500 men to go to Mexico to fight the war. Julia's husband was one of the men called to go. Julia and her two sons lived in a wagon bed which had the wheels removed and was placed under some trees. They lived there for the eighteen months her husband was gone. After James was released in San Diego, California, he walked to Winter Quarters during the winter months, gathered up his family, and made preparations to join Captain William P. Miller's 5th Wagon Company to cross the Plains. They arrived in Utah on September 22, 1849.

They settled in North Cottonwood (Farmington) for ten years. They moved south when Johnston's Army came. They moved again to Logan, Utah, then Clarkston, Utah. Later they, with five of their married children, settled a farm in Lewisville, Idaho. She suffered the hardships of every woman of that era without complaint. Her home was a haven for all her loved ones.

MARY AERNY FREY NAEF

BIRTHDATE: 9 Apr 1840
Schoftland, Aarau, Switzerland
DEATH: 1 Jan 1903
Providence, Cache Co., Utah
PARENTS: Johann Jacob Frey
Ann Barbara Aerny
PIONEER: 3 Sep 1860
James D. Ross Wagon Train
SPOUSE:
Johannes J. (Ira) Naef
MARRIED: 29 May 1860
Florence, Nebraska
DEATH SP: 12 Feb 1921
Sugar City, Madison Co., Idaho

CHILDREN:
Mary Lucinda, 14 May 1861
Jacob David, 11 Jan 1864
Robert Henry, 7 Mar 1866
Lydia Emma, 20 Dec 1867
Annie Eliza, 8 Apr 1870
John Albert, 7 Apr 1872
Joseph William, 5 Mar 1874
Rudolph Gootlieb, 9 Mar 1876
Elsbeth "Elsie" Barbara, 5 Apr 1881

Mary Aerny Prey Naef was born in a little village in Switzerland. When she was about fifteen years old she and her family moved to St. Gallen where a branch of the Mormon Church had recently been established. Mary was baptized a member of the Church of Jesus Christ of Latter-day Saints, October 17, 1856. The Frey family was neighbors of and grew to be very friendly with the family of Johannes Naef. The elder son of the family, Johannes, had been ordained Presiding Elder of the Branch.

He and Mary became sweethearts but shortly before they were to have been married Johannes Naef died of consumption. At that time all converts of the Church were urged to gather in Utah.

On March 15, 1860, Mary and her family began the journey to Utah. They were thirty-two days crossing the ocean. During the crossing, Mary's mother sickened and died and was buried at sea. This was a great sadness to Mary and the family. They landed in New York and then traveled to St. Joseph, Missouri. They went by steamer up the Missouri River to Florence, Nebraska. There they spent about five weeks in preparation for their journey of over 1,000 miles westward.

While at Florence, Mary was married on May 29, 1860, to Johann Jacob (Ira) Naef, brother of her former sweetheart. Their intentions were to cross the Plains with handcarts. A kind friend, John Diem, had purchased four new wagons with eight head of oxen to each wagon and he gave them the opportunity to take one of these wagons for their long journey.

Mary walked much of the way helping to drive the loose stock. She was often very tired but did not consider it a hardship as they were young and happy and anxious to get to Zion. They arrived in the Salt Lake Valley on September 3, 1860 and went to Providence, Utah, to live.

Work was immediately started on their first house which was partly in the form of a dugout. This was finished shortly before Christmas, until then, they slept in a covered wagon box. Jacob worked on the farm cutting the grain. Mary would prepare a hot dinner for him. With the dinner in her hands and her new baby strapped to her back she would walk to the field and help shock up the grain.

Mary became a member of the Providence Relief Society. She was appointed a teacher and served for thirty-two years. Her health improved and she was able to journey to the St. George Temple and do work for her kindred dead.

Mary was a faithful wife and loving mother, thinking and doing for everyone but herself. She was a true pioneer, always making the most of the resources at hand, and while careful, was generous almost to a fault.

Mary passed away January 1, 1903, at the age of sixty-three and was buried in Providence, Utah.

MARIA "MARY" HUERNI NAEGLE

BIRTHDATE: 12 Apr 1831
Wenzikon, Switzerland
Salt Lake City, Salt Lake, Utah
DEATH: 31 Dec 1907
Santa Clara, Washington, Utah
PARENTS: Johannes Huerni
Maria Buechi
PIONEER: 1862
SPOUSE: Conrad Naegle/Naegeli
MARRIED: 8 Jan 1863
DEATH SP: 19 May 1920
Bunkerville, Clark Co., Nevada

CHILDREN:
Mary, 14 Feb 1864
Bertha Margaretta, 4 Jun 1866
Conrad, 6 Dec 1869

Maria was born in Wenzikon, Gachnang, Switzerland, 1831. After joining the Church of Jesus Christ of Latter-day Saints, she crossed the ocean with a group of Saints. Then she traveled by wagon to the Salt Lake Valley. The name of the company is not known, but she arrived in the Valley in 1862.

She married Conrad Naegle / Naegeli on January 8, 1863. They were early pioneers of Santa Clara, Washington County, Utah. It is said of her that "she took more pleasure in work than going out socially." Her habit of cleanliness was well developed.

She was an excellent cook with home grown nutrients, a devoted wife and mother. On December 31, 1907, she died in Santa Clara, Utah.

PAULINE BECK NAEGLE

BIRTHDATE: 31 Aug 1846
Aichelberg, Germany
DEATH: 5 Oct 1927
Miramonte, Cochise Co., Arizona
PARENTS: Johannes Beck
Christiana Carolina Holl
PIONEER: Oct 1863
Wagon Train Company
SPOUSE: John Conrad Naegle
MARRIED: 22 Apr 1865
Salt Lake City, Salt Lake, Utah
DEATH SP: 10 Sep 1899
Colonia Oaxaca, Sonora, Mexico

CHILDREN:
Samuel, 23 Jul 1872
Davis, 23 Mar 1875
Daniel Conrad, 23 Mar 1875
Lydia Ann, 3 Apr 1879
Marion Beck, 16 May 1881
Parley Paul, 16 Oct 1887

Pauline Beck Naegle was born in Germany. Little is known of her childhood.

Her brother, John, joined the Church of Jesus Christ of Latter-day Saints and then introduced it to the rest of the family. The family began their journey to the Salt Lake Valley in 1863. They had a harrowing trip which began on May 12, 1863.

They traveled first to Hamburg, Germany where they literally clung to each other and the Mormon missionaries traveling with them so they would not be captured and sold as slaves. They finally reached London, England and sailed to America on the ship "Hudson Liverpool." They were six weeks crossing the ocean; food was very scarce, a fire broke out and a hostile warship came into sight. They were grateful to finally reach America. They stayed at an old warehouse while preparations were made to cross the Plains to Utah. Here, they became infected with body lice which they carefully picked out of their clothing until they were finally free of them.

Pauline walked all the way across the Plains except one day when she was sick. She crawled into the back of the wagon, thinking she would rest for a few minutes. She fell asleep and when camping time came the teamster was very angry with her because she didn't have her apron full of buffalo chips, as usual.

When they came to the Platte River, Pauline tried to lead their cow across the water. The cow followed her through water so deep that it came up to her armpits. When she made it to the other side, the company gave three cheers for the little Dutch girl. They arrived in Utah in October, 1863, six months after leaving their home in Germany.

Pauline became the sixth of seven plural wives of John Conrad Naegle. They were married April 22, 1865, by Heber C. Kimball. After their marriage they returned to Lehi, Utah, where the other wives had prepared a wedding feast. Pauline said she wished she could have dropped through the floor.

Pauline had no children for seven years after her marriage. She raised to maturity a little German boy who needed a home. She and her husband finally became the parents of six children; three died in infancy. Three children were born in Lehi, Utah.

Pauline lived most of her married life in Toquerville. She was a very hard worker, especially during summer months when there were so many peaches, apricots, plums, grapes and other fruits to be dried and taken care of.

Pauline was very careful about her religion. She kept a careful account of her eggs, butter and other produce so she could pay an honest tithing. She shared what she had with her neighbors and friends. On fast day all the family would attend. Pauline was a Relief Society teacher and also a First Counselor in the Primary Association. All of her children attended Primary on Saturday afternoon.

Pauline died October 5, 1927, in Miramonte, Arizona. She outlived her husband by twenty-eight years.

REGULA BENZ NAEGLE

BIRTHDATE: 1 Jul 1839
Weininger, Zurich, Switzerland
DEATH: 20 Oct 1920
Toquerville, Washington, Utah
PARENTS: Heinrich Benz
Elizabetha Lang
PIONEER: 1855 Wagon Train
SPOUSE: John Conrad Naegle
MARRIED: 6 Oct 1860
Salt Lake City, Salt Lake, Utah
DEATH SP: 10 Sep 1899
Colonia Oaxaca, Sonora, Mexico

CHILDREN:
Joseph Richard, 19 Feb 1863
Elizabeth Anna, 13 Nov 1865
Hyrum Conrad, 28 Jun 1869
Francis Regula, 25 Sep 1871
Enoch Nephi, 11 Aug 1875

Regula Benz Naegle was born in Switzerland. She and her older sister, Anna, learned the art of silk weaving when they were very young. They were taught by their mother who kept a loom in their home and she demanded perfection from the girls.

Regula and Anna were baptized April 29, 1854, into the Church of Jesus Christ of Latter-day Saints. They had a great desire to emigrate to Utah to be with other members of the Church. They were able to begin their journey to America early the following year. They arrived in the Salt Lake Valley in 1855. It is not known which Company they traveled with but they probably came with a wagon-train but walked the 1,300 miles across the Plains.

Regula was married to John Conrad Naegle on October 6, 1860, in Salt Lake City. She was a plural wife. They were sealed in the Endowment House in Salt Lake City, January 19, 1861. She was wife number five. She and John became the parents of five children; their eldest was born in Lehi, Utah. The other children were born in Toquerville, Utah. Their second child died the day she was born.

Regula spun the first silk material while living in Toquerville. She was also a skilled midwife. She was paid two or three dollars for ten days of nursing care.

Regula died in Toquerville, Washington County, Utah on October 20, 1920. She outlived her husband and all five of her children. She is buried in the Toquerville Cemetery.

EMMA EVANS NALDER

BIRTHDATE: 13 Jul 1848
Cardiff, Glasmorganshire, Wales
DEATH: 29 Aug 1926
Layton, Davis Co., Utah
PARENTS: Thomas Evans
Ann John
PIONEER: 2 Oct 1856
Edward Bunker Company
SPOUSE: William New Nalder
MARRIED: 3 May 1869
Salt Lake City, Salt Lake, Utah
DEATH SP: 27 Dec 1918
Layton, Davis Co., Utah

CHILDREN:
William Butler, 13 May 1870
Mary Esther, 1 Jan 1872
Thomas Stephen, 1 Mar 1873
Francis Henry, 22 Dec 1874
Emma Jane, 25 Nov 1876
Daniel Hyrum, 11 Sep 1878
Albert Oscar, 9 Aug 1880
Melvina Evaline, 19 May 1882
Walter Alvin, 23 Jun 1884
George Chester, 5 Feb 1886
Charles Evans, 17 May 1887
Luella Ann, 24 May 1889
Leland Rudger, 6, Nov 1890
Byron Joseph, 1 Jul 1893

Emma Evans was born in Wales in 1848. She was the second of four children, all born in Wales. She came to the Utah Territory in 1856 with the Edward Bunker Handcart Company, when she was eight years old. She celebrated her eighth birthday on the Plains.

Emma was orphaned at the age of nine. She had very little schooling, but a kind neighbor taught her to spin and she became very skillful at this.

She married William New Nalder in 1869 in the Endowment House, and they became the parents of fourteen children. She learned to be a great help in times of sickness and was often called upon to care for those who were ill.

Emma was the first President of the Young Women when the Layton Ward was organized. She was also a Sunday School teacher.

As the family was able to increase the size of their home, she made it a lovely place, inside and out, with lawns, flowers, trees, and a grape arbor.

William Nalder passed away in 1918 in Layton, and Emma passed away in 1926, also in Layton, Davis County, Utah.

ESTHER NEW NALDER

BIRTHDATE: 29 Mar 1813
Chievely, Berkshire, England
DEATH: 19 Dec 1898
Layton, Davis Co., Utah
PARENTS: Daniel New
Rebecca Butler
PIONEER: 1853
Joseph W. Young Wagon Train
SPOUSE: Stephen Nalder
MARRIED: 29 Nov 1846
Newbury, Berkshire, England
DEATH SP: 19 Dec 1880
Layton, Davis Co., Utah

CHILDREN:
William, 25 Jun 1848
Sarah Elizabeth, 28 Dec 1852 (died as an infant)
Henry Hacel, 16 Dec 1855

Esther New was born in England in 1813. She married Stephen Nalder in 1846 in England. They came to the Utah Territory in 1853 with the Joseph Young Wagon Company. There were two children at the time, however, her daughter Sarah Elizabeth, who was just a few months old, died on the trip and was buried near the Platte River. One more child was born in 1855, in South Cottonwood, Salt Lake County.

Esther spent most of her life in Utah taking care of her family and home. She was an excellent cook. She kept bees and was never stung, though others who came near were not so fortunate. She was always willing to help those in need, but firmly believed that one should work for what he received.

It is a strange coincidence that she and her husband were both born on March 29, and both died on December 19. Stephen passed away in 1880, and Esther passed away in 1898, both in Layton, Davis County, Utah.

ELIZABETH CORNELL NATE/NEATE

BIRTHDATE: 23 Sep 1839
Endfield, Middlesex, England
DEATH: 13 Feb 1917
Dingle, Idaho
PARENTS: Frederick E. Cornell
Emma Minton
PIONEER: 1863
McCarthy Co., Wagon Train
SPOUSE: Sampson Nate
MARRIED: 17 Feb 1864
Salt Lake Endowment House
DEATH SP: 4 Apr 1921
Dingle, Idaho

CHILDREN:
Emma Elizabeth, 6 Jan 1865
Frederick Ebenezer, 24 Apr 1866
Louisa Adelaide (Dayton), 14 Oct 1868
Henry William, 18 Nov 1870
Mary Ellen (Bridges), 18 Jul 1872
Charles Cornell, 13 Jun 1874
Ettie Rebecca (Bird), 13 Mat 1880

Elizabeth was born in England. She was of English-Irish descent. She was the only girl in the family. She had two brothers. Elizabeth was the only member of the family who accepted the Gospel and joined the Church of Jesus Christ of Latter-day Saints.

Elizabeth left England to emigrate to America on the ship "Amazon." She traveled with two very close girl-friends. They arrived in New York harbor July 18, l863.

Upon arriving, Elizabeth and her friends rode in a cattle car with no place to lie down and very little to eat. Then they rode in a flat boat down the Missouri River for three days and nights. It was the time of the Civil War and the boats were often showered with bullets. When they finally landed, they were met by Saints from Utah.

They began their long journey by ox-team across the Plains. Five hundred miles, by the Platte River Crossing, were traveled by foot. The journey held its pleasures aside from its trials and heartaches.

The Salt Lake Valley was entered with awesome weariness on the part of Elizabeth. They had traveled with the McCarthy Wagon Company and arrived in the Fall of 1863. Elizabeth went to Lehi, Utah, thirty-one miles from Salt Lake City.

There, in Lehi, she met a young family by the name of Kemp. They became her dearest friends. Sometime later, Mrs. Kemp died, leaving an infant baby. Elizabeth cared for the baby boy, keeping him with her, loving him like a mother would. Later, she received a proposal of marriage from Mr. Kemp, but she refused.

On February 17, 1864, Elizabeth was married in plural marriage to Sampson Nate in the Endowment House in Salt Lake City.

In October, 1864, they were called by the Church to settle Paris, Idaho, in Bear Lake County. They homesteaded. They became the parents of seven children, six of them were born in Paris, Idaho. Their eldest, Emma Elizabeth, died of Scarlet Fever and was buried in the Paris Cemetery.

Elizabeth and her husband's first wife were very congenial. For several years they braided hats from straw to assist Sampson in making a living. Elizabeth braided the hats and Mary Ann blocked them. They sold very well. They presented one of their hats to Apostle Charles C. Rich, which he appreciated very much.

In 1867, Sampson moved his families to Peg Leg Island (now called Dingle) where they built their homes and lived the remainder of their lives.

Elizabeth became Secretary of the Relief Society where she labored for years, faithfully and well. She wrote many poems and gave readings. She had an appreciative nature and had many friends. She was a woman of very strong faith and righteous inclinations. She taught not only by precept, but by worthy example.

Elizabeth passed away on February 13, 1917, at Dingle, Idaho, leaving a heritage to her six children and forty-six grandchildren. She is honored and dearly loved as a worthy progenitor.

MARY ANN COTTRELL NATE

BIRTHDATE: 23 Dec 1831
Upton-on-Severn, England
DEATH: 6 Nov 1895
Dingle, Bear Lake, Idaho
PARENTS: Benjamin Cottrell
Hannah Cottrell
PIONEER: 11 Oct, 1853
Cyrus H. Wheelock Wagon Train
SPOUSE: Samson Nate
MARRIED: 7 Dec 1852
Worchester, England
DEATH SP: 4 April 1921
Montpelier, Idaho

CHILDREN:
Sampson William, 24 Oct 1854
Mary Ann, 4 Mar 1857
Sarah Jane, 1 Mar 1859
Willard Benjamin, 18 Apr 1861
Elizabeth Hannah, 6 May 1863
George Thomas, 1 Jun 1866 (died as a child)
Lucy Ann, 17 May 1868
Rosina Margaret, 19 Jun 1870
Effie Minerva, 27 Dec 1872

Mary Ann was born in Upton-on-Severn, Worchester, England, 1831. After the death of both of her parents, Mary Ann lived with an aunt and uncle at Strensham. There she and her dear friend, Jane Ann Fowler, heard the gospel message of the Church of Jesus Christ of Latter-day Saints. They walked seven miles to Pershore on Sundays to attend the meetings.

Mary Ann met Samson Nate at Pershore. They were both baptized on May 23, 1850. On January 7, 1853, one month after their marriage in the Strensham Church, Worchester, England, they sailed from England on the "Ellen Maria" under Captain Whitmore, with Moses Clawson as company leader. Jane Ann Fowler and Alfred Sparks were also on board and were married at sea. On March 7, 1853, they landed in New Orleans.

At Keokuk, Iowa, the two young couples arranged to share a wagon in the Cyrus H. Wheelock Wagon Company. The Indians were hostile and many of the cattle and oxen died from lack of forage. The company was not well supplied and the people suffered from hunger. They arrived in the Salt Lake Valley on October 11, 1853, and lived at Ft. Harriman and then Lehi.

Mary Ann and Samson were sealed in the Endowment House on December 20, 1862. Mary Ann agreed that Samson should take another wife. On February 17, 1864, he married Elizabeth Cornell. The following October, they were called to go to Paris, Idaho, where they spent the winter of 1864 in a one-room dugout. In 1867 the family moved to Dingle, then known as Peg Leg Island.

Mary Ann was first counselor to the Relief Society President, Jane Ann Fowler Sparks. When President Brigham Young gave the commandment for the women of the Relief Society to store wheat, Mary Ann arranged for the Primary children to go into her husband's fields and glean so the Relief Society could start their storage. Mary Ann helped make the original carpets for the Logan Temple. She and Elizabeth made straw hats and quilts for sale to raise funds for the temple.

When Mary Ann had a stroke during the harvest of 1895, the Relief Society gathered in her home for a prayer and testimony meeting. She passed away on November 6, 1895, at the age of sixty-three.

THANKFUL LUCY PINE PACKARD KELLY NAY

BIRTHDATE: 4 Nov 1830
Stockhome, New York
DEATH: 29 Jul 1897
Monroe, Sevier Co., Utah
PARENTS: Joseph Pine
Adelia Ann Sparrow Winn
PIONEER: 3 Apr 1850
Indep. Wagon Train
SPOUSE I: Orren Packard
MARRIED: 9 Nov 1851
Springville, Utah Co., Utah
DEATH SP: 3 Nov 1852
Springville, Utah Co., Utah

CHILD:
Joseph Dudley Packard, 1 Sep 1852

SPOUSE II: Joseph Kelley / Kelly
MARRIED: 22 Apr 1856

DEATH SP: 11 Aug 1886
CHILDREN: None

SPOUSE III: John Nay, Jr.
MARRIED: 1859
Springville, Utah Co., Utah
DEATH SP: 1 Oct 1892
Monroe, Sevier Co., Utah

CHILDREN:
Myron Windslo, 22 Aug 1860
George John, 27 Dec 1862
Ormund Russell, 23 Mar 1864
Elmer Carr, 9 Jul 1867
Samuel, 1869

Thankful Lucy Pine Packard Nay was born in Stockhome, St. Lawrence County, New York. She was very fortunate to spend her childhood in New York and to be a witness to the early days of the Restored Church, the Church of Jesus Christ of Latter-day Saints. Her parents were early converts of the Church and were close friends and supporters of the Prophet Joseph Smith. Her family moved with the body of the Church to Kirtland, Ohio and then to Nauvoo, Illinois.

In 1849, Lucy's father passed away but told his sons to take the family to the Salt Lake Valley. On April 3, 1850, at the age of twenty, Lucy began her trek across the Plains with her mother and brothers and sisters. They arrived in the Salt Lake Valley, April 3, 1850, in the independent wagon-train company of her brothers, Samuel and Dudley Pine. The family settled in the Southern part of the State and Lucy married her first husband, Orren Packard, November 9, 1851.

Her first son, Joseph Dudley, was born in Springville, Utah. Her husband passed away and Lucy was left a widow with a young son to care for. Her second marriage was to Joseph Kelley and there is no available information.

Lucy married a third time in 1859 to John Nay, Jr. She bore five more sons, one of which died in infancy. In later years, Lucy bore the burden of caring for her aging husband. She had to make the decisions about the purchase of property and the raising of funds to do so.

Lucy endured to the end and passed away in 1897, a stalwart pioneer wife and mother. She had prayed earnestly to the Lord on behalf of her sons, that they might remain true to the Gospel and her prayers were answered.

ALICE SUTTON NAYLOR

No
Photo
Available

BIRTHDATE: 9 Feb 1837
Parr, St. Helens, England
DEATH: 21 Sep 1917
Salt Lake City, Salt Lake, Utah
PARENTS: John Sutton
Mary Ellison
PIONEER: 10 Oct 1853
John W. Young Wagon Train
SPOUSE: Thomas Naylor
MARRIED: 4 Sep 1857
Salt Lake City, Salt Lake, Utah
DEATH SP: 7 Jan 1872
Salt Lake City, Salt Lake, Utah

CHILDREN:
Sarah Ellen, 18 Oct 1857 (died as a child)
Ellen Marian, 1 Oct 1859
Fanny, 27 Jul 1861
Alice, 6 Apr 1863
Caroline, 11 Oct 1865
Thomas George, 9 Oct 1867
Katie, 28 Oct 1869
Eliza, 11 Jan 1871

Alice Sutton was born in Parr, St. Helens, Lancashire, England in 1837. Her father was a grocer and all of the children helped in the store. She was baptized in 1851, and in 1853 came to America with her parents.

They sailed from England on the ship "Elvira Owen," crossed the Plains with the John W. Young Company, and arrived in the Salt Lake Valley in October, 1853.

Alice married Thomas Naylor, September 4, 1857 as his second wife. She was the mother of eight children, her first dying as a child. Her last child was born four days after her husband died. Alice had a hard time raising her children. She did sewing, took in washings, and did house-work. As the children grew they helped with the finances. They all helped in sending Thomas on a mission to the Southern States.

Alice made many braided rugs and was busy all the time. She spoke with an English accent, and wore her hair pulled straight back in a bob, with a little black bonnet around her bob. She was a widow for forty-five years.

She died in 1917 in Salt Lake City at the age of eighty years.

DIANAH IRELAND NAYLOR

BIRTHDATE: 12 May 1811
Chillwell, Nottingham, England
DEATH: 23 Nov 1889
Lovendahle (Murray), Utah
PARENTS: Moses Ireland
Eleanor "Ellen" Ballard
PIONEER: prob 1863
Rosel Hyde Co. Wagon Train
SPOUSE: William Naylor
MARRIED: 24 Mar 1839
Attenborough, England
DEATH SP: 24 Feb 1903
West Jordan, Salt Lake Co.,
Utah

CHILDREN:
Levi, 29 Oct 1839
William Jr., 31 May 1843
Emma, 18 Dec 1846
Ellen, 10 Jun 1849

Dianah was born in England. When she was about seven years old, her father died. Her mother remarried.

Dianah married William Naylor in the Parish Church of Nottingham. Neither William or Dianah could write as they signed the Certified Entry of Marriage with an X.

They became the parents of four children, all born in England. Dianah was baptized into the Church of Jesus Christ of Latter-Day Saints one year after her husband, on February 18, 1850.

They wanted to emigrate to America, and therefore decided that the boys would emigrate first and earn the money for the parents and sisters to come. The boys gave President Brigham Young enough money in 1862 to see their parents and sisters safely to America. Their voyage was a difficult one.

William had to have his leg amputated due to an infection in England before they made their journey. Dianah was not well. Bad weather seemed to be their lot. It took them seven weeks and four days to cross the Atlantic. Their food supply was almost exhausted and they arrived in the United States weary and ill but grateful for the blessing which was theirs in being this much nearer their goal.

They were disappointed to find that they had not enough means to purchase an ox-team and wagon for the family. They were able to put their possessions in some wagons of fellow travelers. They had faith enough to start the long trek across the continent on foot. William's stub of a leg became more and more irritated and inflamed and he finally had to ask to be taken into a covered wagon.

At one point along the trail, the girls missed their mother, Dianah. They went back along the trail and found her so ill that she could not call for help. A family made room in their wagon for Dianah to ride until well. She hung between life and death for a long time and was still very ill when the company arrived in the Salt Lake Valley, in the Fall of 1863.

Since they arrived with no means, they were not able to build a regular log cabin but found shelter for the winter in a dugout. It was a far cry from a home, but they could be warm and out of the winter storms. Their first Christmas was a sad one. Dianah's son, Billy, went to Salt Lake to pay their tithing. On his return he was met with a very bad snow storm and blizzard. He could not find the door of the dugout and found shelter in the cow shed nearby. On Christmas day, the family found his frozen body by the side of the cow shed.

Dianah's life was never easy, but for her and her family being in Zion was enough. She left this life, November 23, 1889 and was buried in Murray. The gravesite is not known. However, it is thought that she is buried in the West Jordan Cemetery by the side of her husband, William.

ANN ELIZA DALTON NEAL

BIRTHDATE: 2 Sep 1833
Rochester, New York
DEATH: 31 Jul 1920
Salt Lake City, Salt Lake, Utah
PARENTS: William Dalton
Ann Eliza Savage
PIONEER: 16 Oct 1862
Canfield's Co. Wagon Train
SPOUSE: William Cooley Neal
MARRIED: 9 Jun 1852
DEATH SP: 11 Nov 1912
Salt Lake City, Salt Lake, Utah

CHILDREN:
Josephine "Josie" Asenath, 28 Aug 1853
Ann Eliza, 19 Nov 1866
William Dalton, 31 Jan 1869
Emma Elbertine, 18 Dec 1873

Ann Eliza was born in Rochester, New York in 1833, her father died when she was three years old and her mother, taking her five daughters, moved to Cambria, New York to be among relatives who helped the young widow raise her children.

Ann Eliza married William Neal when she was eighteen years old, the same year his parents (who had been baptized into the Church nine years earlier) moved to Salt Lake City. William and Ann remained in Cambria.

Ann left a record of her life in the journal that she kept and writes of her own interest in religion, of her wish, eight years after her marriage, to attend services, the desire for William to accompany her and the pleasure it would give her to sit beside him in meetings. But he would not.

Ann's first baby, Josie, contacted what must have been polio as a child and despite Ann's efforts and use of remedies, Josie's arm remained paralyzed. Her education however continued with her mothers teaching of decency as well as her school work. Ann pampered the little girl with pretty clothes and she sewed for other people as well.

Her handicraft skills were many, her specialty was "hair pictures." They were so beautiful that William's mother sent hair bushings to New York by Pony Express which Ann worked into a wire mesh. One hair picture hangs in the D.U.P. Museum in Salt Lake City.

Ann was aware of the coming Civil War and wrote fearfully of it, leaving it to God's care wrote, "If we are not deserving of peace, we must submit to war and all it's attendant horrors."

In 1862, they set off for Utah, intending to visit only, they stayed for the rest of their lives. Reaching the mouth of Immigration Canyon, William rode ahead to find his family in the City. Ann wrote how her spirits fell as darkness descended and no William, how they lost their way but soon were set right. William returned with his mother, his sister and his pockets full of peaches, and Ann wrote how she liked them all. "I find William much like his mother. I think she will seem near to me."

William became a freighter between Utah and the Eastern States and Ann and Josie lived with his family because of his many absences. She longed for her own home and she was extremely anxious about his travels, for there were many occasions where freighters and Pony Express riders were ambushed and massacred by the Indians.

Their first baby born in Utah, thirteen years after Josie, died of whooping cough, and much to her disbelief, shortly after the little girl was buried William was called to a mission to the Eastern States. He was also just recovering from bloody dysentery.

But she believed, so much so that her letters home state of the lonely times but that she felt comforted and blessed all the time and was glad for William mission call. She writes of the paralysis her husband was stricken with and his nineteen years of suffering. Of her joy in upholding the church positions in Relief Society she was given, and that after his death she worked tirelessly in the temple.

Ann Eliza, age eighty-six years, eleven months, died at the home of her daughter, Mrs. W. H. Schluter, (Josie) "a favorite of all who knew her."

ASENATH COOLEY NEAL

No Photo Available

BIRTHDATE: 27 Aug 1798
Pittsford, Rutland Co., Vermont
DEATH: 1 Oct 1872
Salt Lake City, Salt Lake, Utah
PARENTS: Samuel Cooley
Polly Dike
PIONEER: 21 Sep 1852
Henry D. Miller Wagon Train
SPOUSE: George Augustus Neal
MARRIED: 30 Jan 1820
DEATH SP: 15 Oct 1874
Salt Lake City, Salt Lake, Utah

CHILDREN:
Mary Melissa, 3 Jul 1824
William Cooley, 1 Jul 1828

Asenath was born in 1798 in Vermont, her family being one of the early Vermont families. She married George Augustus Neal and had two children. She and her husband were early converts to the Church of Jesus Christ of Latter-day Saints in Niagara County, New York.

They were stalwart members who contributed to the building of the Nauvoo Temple, the relief of the persecuted Saints, foreign missionaries, and emigrating Saints. Her husband served as presiding Elder in the Cambria Branch from 1843 to 1852. Asenath was a frequent hostess to the missionaries serving in Canada and New York State.

She also endured much of the persecution that was heaped upon her husband and other members of the small branch of the church. She stood beside her husband and supported him in every calling and duty he performed.

They crossed the Plains in 1852 trying to escape the persecution and to join the Saints in the Salt Lake Valley. They made their home in Salt Lake City one block north and west of Temple Square.

Her husband was called to go back east for two years as a missionary. While he was gone, Asenath cared for her family and was active in the church helping immigrants until they could sustain themselves. She was skillful in making pictures formed from hair.

Asenath continued to be faithful and endured to the end which came for her in October, 1872, at the age of seventy-four.

DELIA LANE NEBEKER

BIRTHDATE: 30 Jun 1845
Jamestown, Grant, Wisconsin
DEATH: 7 Feb 1901
Logan, Cache Co., Utah
PARENTS: Hyrum Mead Lane
Naomi Chase
PIONEER: 23 Jul 1853
Independent Company
SPOUSE: Ira Nebeker
MARRIED: 15 Nov 1861
Salt Lake City, Salt Lake, Utah
DEATH SP: 24 Apr 1905
Los Angeles, California

CHILDREN:
Delia N., 1862
John , 23 Jan 1864
Hyrum, 3 May 1866
Ira, Mar 1868
Frank Knowlton, 15 May 1870
Lucy, 12 Jan 1872
Naomi, 13 Jan 1874
Clara, 14 Apr 1876
Horace Greeley, 30 May 1878

Ella Nora, 28 Mar 1880
Effie, 9 Apr 1882
Laura Ethel, 1 Oct 1885
Ruth Leith, 7 Jun 1889

Delia was born June 30, 1845, in Jamestown, Grant County, Wisconsin. Her father died when she was a child. She emigrated to Utah with her mother and siblings with an independent company, arriving July 23, 1853.

Delia married Ira Nebeker, November 15, 1861, in Salt Lake City. They lived in several different places; Toquerville, New Harmony, Parowan, back to Salt Lake City, then were asked to assist in the settlement of the Bear Lake area.

Ira was called as Bishop in the Laketown Ward, and Delia was a Relief Society Counselor, and Sunday School teacher in Laketown. She was a wonderful hostess, had a refined nature, was a lover of flowers, and had tender feelings for the sick and the afflicted. She was the mother of thirteen children, three of then dying in infancy.

Delia passed away on February 7, 1901, in Logan, Cache County, Utah, and Ira passed away, April 24, 1905, in Los Angeles, California.

ELIZABETH DILWORTH NEBEKER

BIRTHDATE: 3 Jan 1829
West Chester, Pennsylvania
DEATH: 6 Feb 1911
Salt Lake City, Salt Lake, Utah
PARENTS: Caleb Dilworth
Eliza Wollerton
PIONEER: 1848
SPOUSE: George Nebeker
MARRIED: 13 Feb 1851
DEATH SP: 2 Dec 1886
Salt Lake City, Utah

CHILDREN:
Ida Elizabeth, 11 Jan 1852
George Dilworth, 24 Mar 1853
John Leonard, 1 Nov 1854
Mariah Louise, 7 Nov 1856
Aurelia, 6 Sep 1858
Anna Mary, 13 May 1860
Elizabeth Dilworth, 6 Sep 1861
Martha Luella, 28 Feb 1864
Vilate Kimball, 21 Jan 1866
Ernest Elwood, 15 Apr 1870
Byron Dilworth, 23 Apr 1872

Elizabeth was born in West Chester, Pennsylvania. She was baptized as a member of the Church of Jesus Christ of Latter-day Saints in the Brandywine River, and later went to Nauvoo, Illinois in 1845. When the Saints were forced out of Nauvoo she went to Winter Quarters, then came across the Plains with her brother, John Dilworth, in 1848.

On February 13, 1851, she married George Nebeker. She accompanied him on a mission to Carson Valley in 1855, returning to Salt Lake in 1857.

In 1863, her husband took a second wife, her sister, Maria Louisa Dilworth Leonard, who was a widow.

In 1864, George was called on a mission to the Sandwich Islands, and he took Maria Louisa with him, leaving Elizabeth with the care and responsibility of her family of small children. She was the mother of eleven children, three of them dying as infants.

Her special mission was to visit among her kin and administer for their consolation and comfort; also to attend the laying out the dead, in which capacity she labored with kindness and efficiency.

George Nebeker passed away in 1886, in Salt Lake City, and Elizabeth passed away on February 6, 1911, also in Salt Lake City.

ELIZABETH JANE DAVIS NEBEKER

No
Photo
Available

BIRTHDATE: 27 Mar 1829
Llanfoist, Monmouth, Wales
DEATH: 10 Nov 1851
Salt Lake City, Salt Lake, Utah
PARENTS: James Davis
Elizabeth Sykes
PIONEER: 26 Sep 1847
A. 0. Smoot Co. Wagon Train
SPOUSE: Peter Nebeker
MARRIED: 13 Feb 1847
DEATH SP: 25 May 1885
Willard, Box Elder Co., Utah

CHILDREN:
Susannah Elizabeth, Apr 1848
Peter Alma, 31 Mar 1850

Elizabeth Jane Davis was born March 27, 1829, in Llanfoist, Monmouth, Wales. She was married to Peter Nebeker on February 13, 1847, just prior to coming across the Plains. They were with the Abraham 0. Smoot Company which came by wagon train, and arrived in the Valley on September 26, 1847.

Elizabeth's first child was born in the Old Fort with its leaky roof. They settled in the area where West High School is now located. Here they grew some of the first apples grown in the valley.

Elizabeth was fatally injured in an accident involving a team of oxen. She passed away on November 10, 1851, in Salt Lake City, Utah.

A year later, Peter married her sister, Mary Maria Davis, who took care of Elizabeth's children and went on to have eleven children of her own. Peter Nebeker died in Willard, Box Elder County, Utah in 1885.

HARRIET ANN VAN WAGGONER HAVENS NEBEKER

BIRTHDATE: 25 Mar 1817
Pompton, Bergen, New Jersey
DEATH: 26 Jul 1899
Payson, Utah Co., Utah
PARENTS: John Van Waggoner
Mary Van Waggoner
PIONEER: 26 Oct 1847
A. 0. Smoot Wagon Train
SPOUSE I: John Havens
MARRIED: 13 Feb 1839
New Jersey (later divorced)

CHILDREN:
Ann Havens, 10 Dec 1839
William Henry Havens, 31 Mar 1841
Mary Ann Havens, 25 Feb 1844

SPOUSE II: Henry Nebeker
MARRIED: 4 Jan 1847
Winter Quarters, Iowa
DEATH SP: 17 Aug 1891
Sigurd, Sevier Co., Utah

CHILDREN:
Ammon, 29 Feb 1848
George Washington, 25 Oct 1850
Florence, 16 Mar 1854
Susanna, 3 May 1856
Henry Jr., 3 Jun 1859
John Cush, abt 1845 (Lamanite)

Harriet Ann Van Waggoner was born in Pompton, Bergen, New Jersey. She married John Havens in New Jersey, February 13, 1839, and they had three children, then were divorced.

Harriet married Henry Nebeker, January 4, 1847, at Winter Quarters. They came across the Plains in the Abraham 0. Smoot Company by ox-team, arriving in the Valley, October 26, 1847. Harriet's baby, Ammon, was born in the Old Fort during a rainstorm and leaky roof.

They later made their home in Payson, Utah, except for a time when Henry was called to the Muddy Mission. Harriet learned from the Indians how to make baskets. She was a teacher and treasurer in Relief Society in Payson.

She also raised a Lamanite boy named Cush, whom they adopted. Henry also adopted children by John Havens. Henry married a second wife, Rebecca Heaton, in 1865.

Henry passed away August 17, 1891, in Sigurd, Sevier County, Utah, and Harriet passed away July 26, 1899, in Payson, Utah County, Utah.

LURENA FITZGERALD NEBEKER

BIRTHDATE: 25 Apr 1819
Monongahela, Pennsylvania
DEATH: 7 Feb 1898
Salt Lake City, Salt Lake, Utah
PARENTS: John Fitzgerald
Leah Phillips
PIONEER: 26 Sep 1847
Abraham 0. Smoot Wagon Train
SPOUSE: John Nebeker
MARRIED: 25 Oct 1835
Riley, Butler Co., Ohio
DEATH SP: 25 Oct 1886
Laketown, Rich Co., Utah

CHILDREN:
William Perry, 5 Sep 1836
Ira, 23 Jun 1839
Aaron, 28 Dec 1840
Ashton, 23 Sep 1843
Rosella, 3 Oct 1845
Samuel, 12 Apr 1847
John, 17 Jun 1848
Almira Jane, 9 Mar 1850
Wiley, 8 Mar 1852
Presinda, 18 Apr 1854
Laura, 19 Nov 1856
Jacob, Nov 1857
Aquilla, 17 Jun 1859
Richard, 1856 (Lamanite)

Lurena Fitzgerald was born in Monongahela, Washington County, Pennsylvania. As a child she was a student of the Bible, and had valuable instruction from her mother in sewing skills.

At the age of sixteen, Lurena was married to John Nebeker, October 25, 1835. The family was baptized into the Church of Jesus Christ of Latter-day Saints in 1842. In company with her husband and five children she crossed the Plains, arriving in Salt Lake City, September 26, 1847, traveling with the A. 0. Smoot Company.

With her husband they planted many seeds in the Valley, and grew the first apples near where West High School is now. Her training in sewing was an asset to her with her large family.

She was the mother of thirteen children and also took in an Indian boy, whom she raised as her own. She also cared for her weakly sister, Barbara, and raised three motherless grandchildren. She was very fond of poetry, and took a great interest in current events.

Her husband took a second wife, Mary Woodcock, in 1854 by whom he had eight children.

John Nebeker died in Laketown, Rich County, Utah, October 25, 1886, and Lurena died February 7, 1898, in Salt Lake City, Utah.

MARIA LOUISA DILWORTH LEONARD NEBEKER

BIRTHDATE: 14 Jan 1834
Chester County, Pennsylvania
DEATH: 29 Dec 1905
Salt Lake City, Utah
PARENTS: Caleb Dilworth
Eliza Wollerton
PIONEER: 2 Oct 1847
Jedediah Grant Company
SPOUSE I: John Chatfield Leonard
MARRIED: 22 Feb 1855
DEATH SP: 21 Nov 1857

CHILDREN:
John Chatfield, Jr., 13 Jul 1856

SPOUSE II: George Nebeker
MARRIED: 29 Aug 1863
DEATH SP: 2 Dec 1886
Salt Lake City, Utah

CHILDREN:
William George, 28 Jul 1864
Elizabeth Dilworth, 13 Aug 1866
Ella Maria, 7 Oct 1867
Marcellus Leonard, 21 Oct 1869
Walter Dilworth, 21 Aug 1872
Albert Lucas, 20 Dec 1874

Maria Louisa was born 14 Jan 1834 in Chester County, Pennsylvania, the daughter of Caleb Dilworth and Eliza Wollerton. She came west with her parents at the age of 13, arriving in the valley 3 Oct 1847. She attended the first school taught in Utah, her sister, Mary Jane Dilworth being the teacher. Later she assisted her sister as a teacher

She was married to John Leonard on 22 Feb 1855, and a son was born to them, John, who only lived one year. Not long after this her husband passed away leaving her a widow, about the time Johnston's Army came into the Utah Territory.

On 29 Aug 1863 she married George Nebeker. In 1865 George was called to a mission in the Sandwich Islands (now Hawaii), and Maria Louisa accompanied him along with their son William. She learned the Hawaiian language, and worked in a store, buying and selling to the native people. She had the task of caring for the many travelers and missionaries who came to Laie, in her home. Three children were born to her while in the Islands. After they returned to Utah about 1870 two more children were born. She was always an active and faithful member of the Church.

George Nebeker died 2 Dec 1886 in Salt Lake City, Utah, and Maria Louisa died 29 Dec 1905, also in Salt Lake City, Utah.

MARY ADELMA DIXON NEBEKER

BIRTHDATE: 25 Apr 1852
Kirtland Lake, Ohio
DEATH: 30 Jun 1934
Payson, Utah Co., Utah
PARENTS: Christopher F. Dixon
Jane Elizabeth Wightman
PIONEER: 16 Oct 1862
Isaac Canfield Wagon Train
SPOUSE: Ammon Nebeker
MARRIED: 23 Feb 1874
Salt Lake City, Utah
DEATH SP: 19 Sep 1921
Rock Springs, Wyoming

CHILDREN:
Mary Jane, 17 Mar 1875
Ann, 2 Nov 1875
Ammon, 22 Nov 1878
Aurora, 15 Jan 1881
Leo Volmer, 3 Apr 1883
Erastus, 7 May 1885
Alberta, 1 Feb 1887
Claudius, 12 Aug 1889

Mary Adelma was born in Kirtland Lake, Ohio. She was only ten years of age when the family made the long trip across the Plains. They traveled with the Isaac Canfield Company, and came by wagon, arriving in the Valley on October 16, 1862. The family was asked to help settle Utah County, and they made their home in Payson, Utah.

She married Ammon Nebeker on February 23, 1874, in the Endowment House in Salt Lake City. She was the mother of eight children, all of them born in Payson.

Mary served as one of the first Primary Presidents in Payson, was secretary in the Relief Society, and an officer in the Retrenchment Society (the forerunner of the YWMIA), but first and foremost was a devoted wife and mother. One of her favorite sayings was, "Don't find fault."

At quarterly conference time she always extended an invitation to dinner to all those who had not been invited elsewhere, and during the depression she gave many meals to transients traveling through the area.

Ammon Nebeker passed away in Rock Springs, Wyoming on September 19, 1921, and Mary Adelma Dixon Nebeker passed away on June 30 1934.

MARY MARIA DAVIS NEBEKER

BIRTHDATE: 13 Apr 1834
Llanfoist, Monmouth, Wales
DEATH: 30 Oct 1886
Willard, Box Elder Co., Utah
PARENTS: James Davis
Elizabeth Sykes
PIONEER: 26 Sep 1847
A. 0. Smoot Co. Wagon Train
SPOUSE: Peter Nebeker
MARRIED: 31 Jan 1852
Salt Lake City, Salt Lake, Utah
DEATH SP: 25 may 1885
Willard, Box Elder Co., Utah

CHILDREN:
Mary Maria, 25 May 1853
Olive Davis, 6 Nov 1855
George Washington, 25 Oct 1857
Thurza, 25 Oct 1857
Brigham, 22 Oct 1860
Reuben, 8 Sep 1862
Jasper, 1 Oct 1864
Naomi, 19 Nov 1866
Luella Elmira, 3 Nov 1869
Chloe N., 21 Jan 1871
Alfreda N., 24 Nov 1874

Mary Maria was born April 13, 1834 in Llanfoist, Monmouth, Wales. Her parents were James Davis and Elizabeth Sykes. She came to the Salt Lake Valley with the Abraham 0. Smoot Wagon Company, by wagon train, arriving on September 26, 1847. Peter Nebeker also came to the Valley about the same time.

Peter was married to Elizabeth Davis, a sister of Mary Maria's. Elizabeth died in 1851, leaving behind two small children. The following year Peter and Mary Maria were married on January 31, 1852. Mary Maria was the mother of eleven children of her own, and helped to raise six children belonging to her brother, whose wife had died. They lived in Salt Lake City near West High School where they had an orchard, and poultry farm. They raised some of the first apples grown in the valley. In 1876, they moved to Willard, Box Elder County to make their home, where they raised cattle and crops.

Mary Maria loved to sing, and took part in most of the entertainments in the community.

Peter died May 25, 1885, and Mary Maria died October 30, 1886, both in Willard, Box Elder County, Utah.

MARY WOODCOCK NEBEKER

BIRTHDATE: 19 Sep 1830
Pilly Green, Yorkshire, England
DEATH: 12 Feb 1902
Laketown, Rich Co., Utah
PARENTS: William Woodcock
Hannah Stones
PIONEER: 14 Oct 1863
Cyrus Wheelock Handcart Comp.
SPOUSE: John Nebeker
MARRIED: 10 Sep 1854
Salt Lake City, Salt Lake, Utah
DEATH SP: 25 Oct 1886
Laketown, Rich Co., Utah

CHILDREN:
Encora Lurena, 17 Dec 1855
William Woodcock, 30 Dec 1856
Alfred Woodcock, 19 Sep 1858
Sarah Ann, 24 Dec 1860
Susannah Adelia, 26 Nov 1863
George Washington, 16 Oct 1864
Mary Luella, 30 Mar 1867
Zettie May, 29 May 1869

Mary was born in England, the daughter of William Woodcock and Hannah Stones. She was baptized into the Church of Jesus Christ of Latter-day Saints in 1852. She worked doing cooking and camp duties for an emigrating family, to pay her way to America, and across the Plains.

On board ship she caught a severe cold which affected her legs, nevertheless she walked all but fifty miles on the journey to Utah. She arrived in the Salt Lake Valley, October 14, 1863, having traveled with the Cyrus Wheelock Handcart Company.

Mary was set apart by President Brigham Young as a midwife, and she worked at nursing and housekeeping until she became the plural wife of John Nebeker on September 10, 1854. They lived in Bountiful, Utah, for a time, then were called to Southern Utah, where they lived from 1861 to 1871. The family was then called to settle in the Bear Lake area. Mary was the first Relief Society President in Laketown, Utah, and also delivered many babies, for which she was paid $2.50 for delivery and extended care.

Mary passed away in Laketown, Rich County, Utah, on February 12, 1902. Her husband preceded her in death, October 25, 1886, also in Laketown, Rich County, Utah.

NANCY MARIA GARDNER NEBEKER

BIRTHDATE: 15 May 1831
Melson, Portage Co., Ohio
DEATH: 29 Dec 1906
Richfield, Sevier Co., Utah
PARENTS: Elias Gardner
Ann Prichard
PIONEER: 1851
SPOUSE: Lewis Nebeker
MARRIED: 5 Nov 1853
Salt Lake City, Salt Lake, Utah
DEATH SP: 12 Feb 1894
Richfield, Sevier Co., Utah

CHILDREN:
Lewis Elias, 13 Sep 1855
Don Carlos, 13 Jan 1858
Adelmon, 17 Oct 1860
John Henry, 29 Feb 1864
Nancy Almira, 6 Oct 1870
LeNora, 9 Sep 1876

Nancy Maria was born May 15, 1831, in Melson, Portage County, Ohio, the daughter of Elias Gardner and Ann Prichard.

She married Lewis Nebeker on November 5, 1853, in Salt Lake City as his second wife, and was the mother of six children. While the family lived at Cedar Fort she helped her husband quiet the Indian disturbances since she could speak the Indian dialect.

In 1864, they moved to Richfield, but because of Indian problems there they moved back to Payson, Utah. Later they moved again to Richfield and she helped her husband with their farm. They both loved music, and had fine singing voices. Dances were held in their home.

Lewis Nebeker passed away February 12, 1894, in Richfield, Sevier Co., Utah, and Nancy passed away on December 29, 1906, also in Richfield, Utah.

REBECCA HEATON NEBEKER

BIRTHDATE: 28 Feb 1834
Little Orton, Bradford, England
DEATH: 24 Apr 1896
Sigurd, Sevier Co., Utah
PARENTS: Jonathan Heaton
Frances A. O'Dwyer
PIONEER: Aug 1864
SPOUSE: Henry Nebeker
MARRIED: 22 Jul 1865
Salt Lake City, Salt Lake, Utah
DEATH SP: 17 Aug 1891
Sigurd, Sevier Co., Utah

CHILDREN:
Lovina Heaton, 5 Nov 1855
Samuel Meredith, 13 Jun 1866
Jedediah, 1868 (died as an infant)

Wilford Franklin, 17 Sep 1869
Maggie Alberta, 4 Mar 1872 (twin)
Daughter, 4 Mar 1872 (twin-died as an infant)
Frances Maude, 29 Mar 1873
Dora Selina, 2 Sep 1874

Rebecca was born February 28, 1834 in Little Orton, Bradford, Yorkshire, England, the daughter of Jonathan Heaton and Frances A. O'Dwyer. She came to the Utah Territory as a convert from England in August of 1864, with her daughter, Lovina.

On July 22, 1865, she married Henry Nebeker in Salt Lake City, as his second wife. In 1867, Henry was called on a second mission to The Muddy, and she accompanied him.

When the mission broke up they moved to Sevier County, where he built a home for Rebecca in Sigurd, Utah. His first wife had remained in Payson, Utah. He adopted Rebecca's first child, Lovina, also an Indian boy named Cush. Rebecca was a counselor in Relief Society; she made butter to sell; and she had great faith in the answers to prayers.

Henry Nebeker passed away in Sigurd, Sevier County, Utah on August 17, 1891, and Rebecca passed away on April 24, 1896, also in Sigurd, Sevier County, Utah.

ANN JOHNSON MILNER NEEDHAM

No Photo Available

BIRTHDATE: 2 Oct 1802
Gringley-on-the Hill, England
DEATH: 30 Nov 1882
Provo, Utah Co., Utah
PARENTS: George Johnson
Sarah Brewitt
PIONEER: 16 Oct 1853
Cyrus H. Wheelock Wagon Train
SPOUSE I: John Milner
MARRIED: 10 May 1825
Mattersey, Nottingham, England
DEATH SP: 9 Sep 1829
Mattersey, Nottingham, England

CHILDREN:
George Johnson, abt 1826
daughter, abt 1828
John Brewitt, 27 Jan 1830

SPOUSE II: Thomas Needham
MARRIED: sealed 24 Nov 1860
DEATH SP: 25 May 1880
Provo, Utah Co., Utah
CHILDREN: None

Ann was born in Gringley-on the Hill, Nottingham, England, an only child. Her father died two days before Ann's third birthday. When she was five years old her mother married George Justice; a happy marriage that lasted for forty-seven years.

Ann, at the age of twenty-three, married May 10, 1825 John Milner, a shoemaker from Mattersey, Nottingham. They became the parents of three children. Her husband passed away on September 9, 1829.

Ann accepted the gospel of the Church of Jesus Christ of Latter-day Saints and was baptized February 4, 1844. She was active in her Church and looked forward to the time when she could emigrate to Utah. Ann had sufficient funds from inherited property to make the journey so she and her son could live among the people who had accepted the Gospel.

They left for America on the ship "Ellen Marie," January 17, 1853. It took some time to reach Keokuk, Iowa. They traveled on to Winter Quarters, then journeyed across the Plains with the Cyrus H. Wheelock Wagon Company.

With others, they suffered hardships during the long and tedious journey across the trail. Her son, John, was not well.

Ann is described as 5'16" tall, dark brown hair and dark brown eyes. Her features were long and her expression pleasant and smiling, yet sober. She always wore a cap, the custom in those days. Well-educated and wealthy, she paid the fare of several families to Utah, and helped others after they were in the Salt Lake Valley. They arrived on October 16, 1853.

Her home on 3rd East and 1st South in Provo was built and paid for with her own money. It was a home, built of adobes and plastered white on the outside. Ann was a neat and excellent housekeeper, a fine cook, and enjoyed setting a nice table using her favorite table linens, china and silverware. She was very kind to children. A jar of cookies was always kept to delight them. Ann's son, John, became a prominent lawyer, active in civic and religious affairs in Utah County. She raised her oldest grandson who came to live with her when he was quite young. He was much adored by his grandmother. He was well taken care of and given strict but kind training.

Ann married Thomas Needham, a widower, and was sealed to him November 24, 1860. He was an experienced farmer, dependable and a good husband.

Thomas passed away on May 25, 1880, when he was nearly eighty-one years old. Ann passed away on November 30, 1882 at Provo. She was eighty years old.

CLARA ST. LEDGER MARSDEN MCDONALD NEEDHAM

BIRTHDATE: 16 Sep 1857
Sheffield, Yorkshire, England
DEATH: 25 Jul 1924
Salt Lake City, Salt Lake, Utah
PARENTS: William Marsden
Sarah Johnson
PIONEER: Fall of 1862
SPOUSE I: John K. McDonald
MARRIED: 26 May 1872
Salt Lake City, Salt Lake, Utah
DEATH SP: 31 Aug 1874
Salt Lake City, Salt Lake, Utah

CHILDREN:
Flora Jane, 29 Nov 1873 (died as an infant)
Maybeth Laurel, 12 Sep 1896 (died as an infant)

SPOUSE II: David Stafford Needham
MARRIED: 17 Feb 1898
Salt Lake City, Salt Lake Co., Utah
DEATH SP: 25 Jan 1931
Salt Lake City, Salt Lake Co., Utah

CHILDREN:
Boy, Dec 1898 (stillborn)
Sarah Jessie (Morton), 19 Jul 1900
Clara Alberta, 22 May 1903 (died as an infant)

Clara St. Ledger Marsden was born in Yorkshire, England in 1857. She came to Utah with her mother and sister in 1862.

While crossing the Plains four year old Clara fell into a stream and caught a cold in her eyes, later causing cataracts to form. For most of her life she was blind, or nearly blind.

In 1863, her mother married John Kilpatrick McDonald, a widower, who was a good step-father to Sarah's two daughters, Harriet Zelnora and Clara. Clara's mother gave her consent for John to marry each girl at the age of fifteen.

Clara and John were married in 1872, and one daughter was born who died at eleven months. John suffered an accident which caused his death in 1874, leaving three widows; Sarah, age forty-seven, Harriet Zelnora, age twenty, and Clara, age seventeen. Times were very difficult for the family .

In 1886, an intruder came to Clara's home and raped her. The baby girl born from this rape lived only a few days. After twenty-three years of widowhood, Clara married David Needham in 1898. They parented three children in a polygamous marriage which ended in divorce.

Clara's mother lived with her until her death in 1900. Clara lived twenty-three years after her mother's death and passed away in 1924 of heart trouble at the age of sixty-seven years.

ELIZABETH MILLER NEELEY

No Photo Available

BIRTHDATE: 4 Apr 1808
Coleraine, New York
DEATH: 2 Feb 1847
Winter Quarters
PARENTS: Oliver Miller
Sophronia Nobles Miller
SPOUSE: Lewis Neeley
MARRIED: 20 Apr 1828
Vermillion County, Illinois
DEATH SP:

CHILDREN:
Alanson, 18 Apr 1829
William Noble, 29 Aug 1830
Armenius, 30 Apr 1832
Mary Jane, 8 Oct 1833
Armenius Miller, 7 Jan 1836
Lewis Arnold, 1838
Harriet, 10 Sep 1839
Lewis, 1 Aug 1841
John, 29 Jan 1843
Hyrum Smith, 7 May 1844
Elizabeth, 1846
Elizabeth Ann, 25 Jan 1847

Elizabeth Miller was born April 4, 1808, in Coleraine, New York, the daughter of Oliver Miller and Sophronia Nobles Miller. When she was young, her family moved westward, settling in Vermillion County, Illinois. There in 1832 the family was taught the restored gospel and baptized into the Church of Jesus Christ of Latter-day Saints. Her parents "gathered" to Missouri with the early Saints, where they both died.

Elizabeth married Lewis Neeley April 20, 1828, in Vermillion County. They were the parents of twelve children. Elizabeth and Lewis received their endowments in the Nauvoo Temple on 6 February 1846 just before leaving Nauvoo. They left Nauvoo and crossed the Mississippi River on the ice on February 26th. Just eight days after her last child was born, Elizabeth died of exposure on February 2, 1847, at Winter Quarters. Five of her children lived to finish the journey west to the Great Salt Lake Valley.

HELEN CRAVATH NEELEY

BIRTHDATE: 7 Oct 1835
Weathersfield, Wymn, New York
DEATH: 7 Sep 1889
Brigham City, Box Elder Co., Utah
PARENTS: Austin Cravath
Eliza Doty Cravath
PIONEER: 1850
Warren Foote Wagon Company
SPOUSE: William Neeley
MARRIED: 18 Sep 1852
Salt Lake City, Utah
DEATH: 24 Jan 1913
Neeleyville, Power County, Idaho

CHILDREN:
Viroqua Vilate, 17 Oct 1853
Esther Lauretta 18 Mar 1855
William, 30 May 1857
Laura Eliza, 2 Oct 1859
Mary Elizabeth, 24 Nov 1861
Lewis Austin, 18 Feb 1863
Harriet Helen, 6 May 1866
Lucille Sariah, 1 Feb 1869
Arthur Cravath, 8 Jan 1872
Horace Doty, 10 Apr 1874
Ira Jonathon, 8 Apr 1877
Marian Alferatta, 3 Oct 1883

Helen Cravath Neeley was born in New York. Her parents became members of the Mormon Church about 1843/4. They sold their comfortable home and farm lands in New York and joined the Saints in Nauvoo. Her father died that same year of a fever prevalent in that locality. Helen was fourteen years old when the family began their trek across the Plains to Utah; her mother was alone with six children. Helen and her sisters performed heroically the tasks that fell to their lot while on the trail. Helen and her family had arrived in the Salt Lake Valley the Fall of 1850 with the Warren Foote Company. They appreciated to the fullest the kindness of Apostle Heber C. Kimball in providing a home for them in Utah when otherwise they would have had no shelter or protection. It was while Helen was a member of the Kimball household that she met William Neeley. He was a fine, upright, handsome man who had come to Utah with his parents in one of the 1850 wagon-trains.

After a short courtship, Helen and William were married 19 Sep 1852 in Salt Lake City, Utah. Their first home was in Bountiful, Utah, a log cabin with a dirt roof, a quilt hung up for a door and white cloth nailed over the window frames instead of glass. Helen and William became the parents of twelve children. William played the violin for dances after his hard day's work to help support his family. Helen often put her little girls to bed early at night so that she could wash, iron and mend their clothes ready for another day. During hard times the family lived entirely on greens and sego lilies. They had a cow that gave milk which was a blessing to them. The family moved to Brigham City, Utah and lived there during the hard winter of 1855/86.

In 1862, William married a second wife and went to live in Bear River, spending only part of his time in Brigham City from then on. Helen had no desire to leave her lovely home in Brigham City. She and her daughters were practically self-supporting. They were thrifty and frugal. They always planted a garden in which they raised sweet corn. They would extract the starch from the corn which made delicious puddings. They were always willing and ready to assist others in times of need.

About 1880, Helen was called to go to Salt Lake City to study obstetrics and become a mid-wife. She had a natural talent for this work. When she was making a rag rug for her frontroom she injured her knee and it pained her badly and she walked with a limp after that. Helen traveled to Logan, Utah to care for someone in need of a nurse. She had Helen Mar Kimball Whitney in her home for one winter and gave her the medical care she needed. Helen was a handsome woman. She had a light complexion with beautiful hair. She was a striking, aristocratic-looking woman. She created an atmosphere of refinement and culture. She encouraged others to appreciate the Gospel and its principles which she faithfully lived and honored. As her health began to give her problems, she lived with her daughters who did all they could to make her comfortable. She died at the home of her daughter Viroqua on 7 Sep 1889.

SUSAN MORGAN NEELEY

BIRTHDATE: 19 Oct 1840
Whitmore Lane, Cardiff,
Glamorganshire, England
DEATH: 31 Dec 1877
Franklin, Idaho
PARENTS: William Morgan
Elizabeth "Betsy" Davis
PIONEER: 1854
SPOUSE: Armenius M. Neeley
MARRIED: 8 Dec 1856
Brigham City, Box Elder, Utah
DEATH SP: 28 Sep 1908
Franklin, Idaho

CHILDREN:
Armenius Miller, Jr., 30 Sep 1857
Orson David, 23 Dec 1859
Dora Isabell, 26 Jun 1862
Lauretta Geneva, 14 Apr 1863
William Lewis, 7 May 1865
Jonathan Harvey, 2 Sep 1867
Lorenzo Hezikiah, 8 Jun 1869
Eli Davis, 5 May 1871
Ezra Elias, 5 Jun 1872
Mary Myriam, 19 Sep 1874
Sarah Jane, 14 Sep 1876
Susan, 31 Dec 1877

Susan Morgan was born in Wales to a family of early converts of the Church of Jesus Christ of Latter-day Saints. She was baptized when she was eight and a half years old.

They emigrated to Utah in 1854 through the help of the Emigration Fund. They sailed on February 4, 1854 for America on the ship, "Golconda," under the direction of Dorr P. Curtis.

Two years after coming to Utah, she met and married Armenius Neeley when she was sixteen years old. He had heard her sing and had fallen in love with her voice before he met her. They were called to colonize Franklin, Idaho. There was much trouble with the Indians. The terrible war with the Shoshone Indians was fought on the Bear River during their first years there.

She bore twelve children before she died at the birth of her twelfth child. She was thirty seven years old when she died.

Susan loved to dance and sing. She raised her children where they could play in the Cub River Canyon, fish in the river, and sing together. Her home was always open to people who needed help. She took in several homeless children besides raising her own big family.

MARY MAGDALENE GOSSAUER NEESER

No
Photo
Available

BIRTHDATE: 21 Dec 1822
Riesbach, Zurich, Switzerland
DEATH: 3 May 1872
Monroe, Sevier Co., Utah
PARENTS: Johannes Gossauer
Anna Barbara Schreiber
PIONEER: Fall of 1862
Wagon Train Company
SPOUSE: Rudolf Neeser /Naser
MARRIED: 10 Jan 1844
Switzerland
DEATH SP: 29 Aug 1902
Monroe, Sevier Co., Utah

CHILDREN:
Caroline, 23 Oct 1844
Robert, 19 Jul 1847
Susan, abt 1848
Rudolph, abt 1850
Marie, abt 1851
Mary Magdalene, 14 Jun 1853
Edward, 1 Feb 1857
Rudolph, 25 Mar 1858
Emilie, 20 May 1860
Martha, 19 Dec 1860
John Charles, 30 Jul 1868

Mary Magdalene was born in Switzerland in 1822. She married Rudolf Neeser (Naser) in 1844 in Switzerland. Most of her children were born in Alstetten, Zurich, Switzerland, however the last two were born in Manti, Utah. Some of them evidently died young, as the family group sheet only list eight children.

Mary Magdalene and her husband and children came to the United States on the ship "Windermere" in 1862, then by covered wagon from Florence, Nebraska, to the Salt Lake Valley. They settled in Monroe, Sevier County, Utah, where she used her homemaking skills as she helped her family adjust in the change from the mother country to a pioneering life in Utah.

Mary Magdalene passed away in Monroe in 1872. Her husband, Rudolf, passed away in in 1902, also in Monroe, Sevier County, Utah.

ANN ELIZA BENEDICT NEFF

BIRTHDATE: 8 Feb 1845
Canaan, Litchfield, Connecticut
DEATH: 8 Nov 1930
Salt Lake City, Salt Lake, Utah
PARENTS: Joshua N. Benedict
Fidelia Moses
PIONEER: Sep 1861
SPOUSE: John Neff, III
MARRIED: 31 Jan 1863
Salt Lake, Endowment House
DEATH SP: 6 Jan 1918
Salt Lake City, Salt Lake, Utah

CHILDREN:
Delia Benedict, 16 Apr 1864
Marian Barr, 10 Jun 1866 (twin)
Mary Bitner, 10 Jun 1866 (twin)
Ruth Irene, 14 Jan 1869
Frances Emeline, 31 Mar 1872
Esther Eliza, 29 Sep 1874
Lillian Edna, 22 Mar 1877
Susan Eugenia, 31 Aug 1882
Laurance Elaine, 21 May 1886

Ann Eliza was born of sturdy New England stock at Canaan, Connecticut. Her grandfather Moses heard about some people in western New York who were being severely persecuted for their religion. He became intrigued because the Constitution gave to every man the right to worship as he pleased. Then he investigated the Church of Jesus Christ of Latter-day Saints then sent his sons to invite the missionaries to Canaan to preach. Their families were converted and baptized members of the Church of Jesus Christ of Latter-day Saints.

When Ann Eliza was four years old, she started to school, was a diligent student, and continued her school work until she was sixteen years old. Their family then crossed the Plains in wagons that were well supplied with tools, implements, and provisions.

During the journey, Ann Eliza was stricken with the measles and had to remain in one of the covered wagons. In September 1861, the wagon train entered the Salt Lake Valley.

They moved to the mouth of Mill Creek Canyon. Ann Eliza found work as a teacher for two years after her arrival in the Salt Lake Valley.

In January of 1863, Ann Eliza and John Neff were married in the Endowment House. They lived with John's parents until after their first three children were born. John homesteaded and farmed about seventy five acres of land. They kept cows and made butter. They made sorghum syrup from sugar cane. During the 1870's, John was called on a mission to England where he stayed for one and one-half years. While he was gone, Ann Eliza and the girls took care of the farm.

Nine children were born of this union, seven of whom grew to maturity. Ann Eliza served as President of the East Mill Creek Ward Relief Society for nearly forty-three years. When she resigned, the ward relief society had amassed the largest wheat fund in the Church. She often went out to help the sick. She was always ready to assist those in need.

Ann Eliza and John contributed the land for the construction of a new ward meeting house where the East Mill Creek Chapel stands.

When her daughter, Delia, was widowed, she moved back into the home with her two children, Ann Eliza helped to raise them.

After a lifetime of service and devotion, Ann Eliza passed away on November 8, 1930 at the age of eighty-five.

CATHERINE ELIZABETH THOMAS NEFF

BIRTHDATE: 4 Apr 1843
Pencaecelyn, Altween, Wales
DEATH: 12 Mar 1917
East Mill creek, Salt Lake, Utah
PARENTS: Davis Thomas
Mary Davies
PIONEER: Sep 1854
SPOUSE: Amos Heff Neff
MARRIED: 17 Dec 1864
DEATH SP: 1 Feb 1914

CHILDREN:
Harriet Seymour, 16 Sep 1865
Amanda Baff, 16 Oct 1867
Samuel, 13 Jun 1871 (twin)
David, 13 Jun 1871 (twin)
Catherine A., 1 Oct 1873
Aldus Dilworth, 16 Jul 1875
Alice May, 18 May 1877

Catherine was born to a family of moderate means. Her father ran a butcher shop in a coal mining district. Her mother taught her the joys of cooking, gardening, games, songs, and other traditions native to the Welsh.

When her parents were converted to the Church of Jesus Christ of Latter-day Saints, they sold everything and sailed with their family to America. After several weeks at sea, the family began the trip by river boat up the Mississippi River to St. Louis, and then up the Missouri River to Council Bluffs, Iowa.

In the Spring of 1854, they obtained a wagon and necessary supplies to cross the Plains. Cholera struck the camp and in less than a week, Catharine's family died. She was the lone survivor of her family. Fellow travelers carried her across the Plains to the Salt Lake Valley.

She spent the next ten years living with many different families in Utah and Idaho. One of the last families with whom she lived was Susanna Neff Pierce who was a sister of Amos Heff Neff. She met Amos Neff through her participation in church and community activities. He was a widower with seven children.

Catherine was twenty when they were married. When her husband was called on a mission in 1869, she was left to care for nine children. After his return they had five more children.

In December of 1875, Amos married Eliza Anne Hughes with whom he had seven more children. When polygamy was outlawed, Amos was jailed. When he was released, Catherine felt that Amos should stay with the younger wife and his younger children.

Catherine lived across the street from Amos and his third family. Catherine and her children worked diligently to provide for their needs. They raised and marketed a variety of fruits, butter, milk, and took in boarders. Catherine made and provided the sacrament bread every Sunday for the East Mill Creek Ward for many years. She was a wonderfully charitable woman who earned the love and respect of her family and those she served.

Catherine passed away on March 12, 1917, having been faithful in all of the trials set before her.

ELIZABETH MUSSER NEFF

No
Photo
Available

BIRTHDATE: 7 Dec 1825
Lancaster, Pennsylvania
DEATH: 24 Feb 1853
Salt Lake City, Salt Lake, Utah
PARENTS: Samuel Musser
Anna Barr
PIONEER: Spring 1848
Wagon Train Company
SPOUSE: Franklin Neff
MARRIED: 5 Mar 1847
banks of Des Moines River, Iowa
DEATH SP: 17 Nov 1882
East Mill Creek, Salt Lake, Utah

CHILDREN:
Martha Elizabeth (Eldridge), 16 Apr 1848
Letitia, 21 Feb 1853

Elizabeth was born in Lancaster, Pennsylvania. When she was ten years of age her father passed away, leaving her mother with four children to raise. In 1837, her mother married Abraham Bitner and the family moved to Illinois and settled near Quincy. A few years later, because of Mr. Bitner's ill health, the family moved back to Pennsylvania where he passed away. Elizabeth's mother was a widow for the second time.

There had been more children added to the family and she struggled to clothe and feed them. Each child had to do his/her share to help provide for the family. They learned to work and care for themselves at a very early age. They became a close family.

During this second widowhood some elders from the Church of Jesus Christ of Latter-day Saints called at their home. Her mother converted to this faith. Her sister and her husband had joined the Mormon Church a few years earlier. Elizabeth was baptized at this time.

In 1846, Elizabeth, her mother, and the other children moved to Nauvoo, Illinois. It was here that Elizabeth met Franklin Neff, her cousin, and they were married on the banks of the Des Moines River, March 6, 1846. They were later endowed and sealed in the office of Brigham Young in Salt Lake City, Utah on March 6, 1851.

Elizabeth and Franklin became the parents of two daughters, Martha Elizabeth and Letitia. Martha Elizabeth was born, April 26, 1848, at Winter Quarters, Iowa. Letitia was born in East Mill Creek, Utah, February 2, 1853.

After Letitia's birth, Elizabeth became very ill and passed away a few weeks later on February 24, 1853. She was only twenty-eight years old. She was buried in the Salt Lake City, Utah Cemetery.

Her baby, Letitia, was not a healthy child and struggled to live after the death of her mother. She passed away at the age of eight months on October 18, 1853. She was buried by her mother's side in the Salt Lake City Cemetery.

FRANCES MARIA STILLMAN RUSSELL RUSSELL NEFF

No Photo Available

BIRTHDATE: 29 May 1830
Westmoreland, Ostego Co.,
New York
DEATH: 13 Sep 1903
East Mill Creek Salt Lake, Utah
PARENTS: Jason Stillman
Harriet Elizabeth Seymour
PIONEER: 1850 Wagon Train
SPOUSE I: Samuel L. Russell
MARRIED: 20 Jan 1846
Nauvoo, Hancock Co., Illinois
DEATH SP: 1850
Died crossing the Plains

CHILD:
Daughter,

SPOUSE II: Isaac Nelson Russell
MARRIED: 1850
Salt Lake City, Salt Lake Co., Utah
DEATH SP: 1921
San Francisco, California

CHILD:
Harriet Ida (Bolton), 29 Oct 1851

SPOUSE III: Franklin Neff
MARRIED: 1 Jan 1855
Salt Lake City, Salt Lake Co., Utah
DEATH SP: 17 Nov 1882
East Mill Creek, Salt Lake Co., Utah

CHILDREN:
Frances Mariah, 29 Sep 1855
Mary Minerva (Fisher), 6 Sep 1857
John Franklin, 7 Aug 1859
Barbara Matilda, 15 Mar 1861
Rosella Salome, 27 May 1863
May Seymour (Wilson Sharp) 30 Oct 1866
Alice Amelia, 22 Nov 1868
Seymour Howard, 23 Dec 1870
Alfaretta (Seely), 18 Jan 1873

Frances Maria was born in New York, the month after the Church of Jesus Christ of Latter-day Saints was organized. She grew up in a home where there was great love between her father and mother. Most of the work and responsibility was on the shoulders of her mother. Her father became ill with tuberculosis, and died.

Frances' mother and the three children joined the Church of Jesus Christ of Latter-day Saints and moved to Nauvoo, Illinois.

Frances, at the age of sixteen, became the plural wife of Samuel Russell in the Nauvoo Temple. They began their trek to the Salt Lake Valley but her husband died while crossing the Plains.

Frances married her husband's cousin, Isaac Nelson Russell. They became the parents of two little daughters. one died in infancy. This marriage did not work out well. Isaac left to seek gold in California. Frances and her little daughter stayed in Salt Lake City to be close to her mother.

Frances met Franklin Neff and they were married on January 1, 1855. They added to their family of two nine more children. three of these children died of dyptheria the same year. This was a great sadness for the parents. Another daughter died of cancer at the age of twenty-seven.

They made their home at the Neff Mill in East Mill Creek, Utah. They homesteaded a quarter section of land and took over the grist mill, a shingle mill and a molasses mill. They built an adobe home, four rooms in a row with a porch along the front. The house was whitewashed. The present Neff's Lane was named after the Franklin Neff family.

Frances was an active worker in the Church and in civic affairs. She was one of the first school teachers in the district, having taught, in the first old log school house. She had a good education and often entertained her children by reading to them. She took active part in social gatherings, often writing sketches of those prominent in the ward and gave many of the readings herself. She held offices in the Relief Society, YLMIA and the Primary.

She was hospitable and took many immigrants into her home until they could provide for themselves. She fed the many Indians who came to her door. She nursed the sick and delivered babies. She entertained and provided for Church Authorities when they visited their community. She was a skilled horse-woman.

After her husband died, she operated the grist mill for a time. She moved to a lovely two-story frame home with a parlor with a fire-place and a grand staircase.

Frances passed away on September 13, 1903, and was buried at her husband's side in the Salt Lake City, Utah, Cemetery.

MARIA ANN BOWTHORPE BAKER NEFF

No
Photo
Available

BIRTHDATE: 6 May 1843
Norwich, England
DEATH: 18 Mar 1925
Salt Lake City, Salt Lake, Utah
PARENTS: William Bowthorpe
Mary Anne Tuttle
PIONEER: 16 Oct 1853
Cyrus Wheelock's Wagon Train
SPOUSE I: Job Baker
MARRIED: 6 Oct 1859
Salt Lake Endowment House
DEATH SP: Unknown

CHILD:
Job Baker

SPOUSE II: Benjamin Barr Neff
MARRIED: 7 Oct 1870
DEATH SP: 18 Feb 1883

CHILDREN:
Virtue Leonora, 28 Feb 1872
William Cyrus, 22 Dec 1873
Franklin Tuttle, 4 Sep 1876
Deseret Charlotte, 22 Sep 1878
Maria Pearl, 27 Apr 1880

Maria Ann was born May 6, 1843, not far from London, Norwich, England. She was the third of six children in her family.

Maria's family left Liverpool, England, on February 15, 1853, on the ship, "Elvira Owen," which arrived in New Orleans after a voyage of five weeks. The trip to Utah was made by wagon in the Cyrus H. Whealock's Company. An Indian interpreter traveled with the company and they had a peaceable journey to the Valley.

Maria Ann married Job Baker in the Endowment House in Salt Lake City, Utah. They were the parents of one son, Job Baker. Her husband was accidentally killed in the Bear Lake region.

To support herself, Maria Ann and her son went to live in the home of Squire Daniel Wells. She served as a seamstress for his wife Martha. Martha died, July 24, 1868, leaving her four children in the care of Maria Ann.

On October 7, 1870, Maria Ann married Benjamin Barr Neff for time only, as a plural wife. On the same day, Mary Ellen Love also married Benjamin. They worked together raising fourteen children. Maria Ann was an excellent cook and a skillful dressmaker. She had been trained in domestic arts and was a very good manager.

After Benjamin's death, Maria Ann moved to Holladay to live near her parents. Her small farm and her skill as a seamstress supported her for years. When her daughter, Virtue Leonora, married she invited Maria Ann into her home.

Maria Ann passed away in 1925.

MARTHA ANN BITNER NEFF

No
Photo
Available

BIRTHDATE: 13 Nov 1840
Lancaster Co., Pennsylvania
DEATH: 24 Jul 1868
Dry Creek (Crescent), Utah
PARENTS: Abraham Bitner
Anna Barr Musser
PIONEER: 1852
SPOUSE: Benjamin Barr Neff
MARRIED: 26 Feb 1858
DEATH SP: 18 Feb 1883
Dry Creek (Crescent), Utah

CHILDREN:
Martha Louise Bitner, 22 May 1859
Anna, (died at age 4)
Benjamin Barr, Jr., 2 Nov 1862
Mary Elizabeth (Hall), 11 Jun 1866

Martha Ann was born November 13, 1840, in Lancaster County, Pennsylvania. She was the youngest of her family and was "accustomed to the tender devotion of her mother and brothers." She crossed the Plains when twelve years of age and became intimately acquainted with the hardships of such an experience.

Benjamin Barr Neff and Martha were married for eternity in 1858. They settled in East Mill Creek and remained there for ten years. All of their children were born there.

After the birth of their second child, Benjamin was called to serve in the Mormon Military under Captain Lot Smith. Martha was left to care for her two young children. Upon her husband's return they were blessed with the birth of a son and daughter.

They moved from East Mill creek to Crescent, Utah. Here the family obtained a license enabling them to run a hotel for the year beginning May 1, 1868.

It wasn't long after that Martha passed away on July 24, 1868. She left behind her four children, ranging in age from nine to two years.

MARTHA ANN DILWORTH NEFF

No
Photo
Available

BIRTHDATE: 9 Jan 1826
Uwchlang, Chester, Pennsylvania
DEATH: 5 May 1862
East Mill Creek, Salt Lake, Utah
PARENTS: Caleb Dilworth
Eliza Woolerton
PIONEER: 2 Oct 1847
Jedediah M. Grant Wagon Train
SPOUSE: Amos Herr Neff
MARRIED: 15 Apr 1848
Salt Lake City, Salt Lake, Utah
DEATH SP: 1 Feb 1914
East Mill Creek, Salt Lake, Utah

CHILDREN:
Ida (Russell), 25 Feb 1849
Eva (Huffaker), 4 Dec 1850
Amos Barr, 13 Aug 1853
Cyrus, 22 Apr 1855
Martha Ann (Smith), 8 Aug 1857
Mary Barr (Young), 16 May 1859
John Dilworth, 11 Jul 1861

Martha Ann was born January 9, 1826, in Pennsylvania. She came to the Salt Lake Valley with the Jedediah M. Grant Wagon Train.

Fortunately for the pioneers of 1847, the Winter of 1847-48 in the Salt Lake Valley was a mild and short one. It was long enough, however, for Amos Herr Neff to convince Mrs.Dilworth that he would make a good husband for one of her daughters. On April 15, 1848, in the old Salt Lake Fort, Amos Herr Neff and Martha were married.

Immediately after their marriage, they traveled by horseback to the East to obtain supplies for the pioneers in the Valley. They traveled to Philadelphia where they purchased goods and shipped them to Council Bluffs. They stopped to visit Martha's father, Caleb Dilworth, who had refused to come West with the Saints. He passed away the following year.

She was a skilled homemaker, preserving food, making candles and soap, and was a fine seamstress, especially skilled in tailoring.Martha Ann also would clip, wash and card wool, then spin and weave it into cloth.

Martha Ann had been raised in a home with emphasis on education and culture. Her family brought books across the Plains and her sister Mary Jane Dilworth was called as the first school teacher in the Valley.

MARY BARR NEFF

BIRTHDATE: 1 Dec 1801
Bart Township, Pennsylvania
DEATH: 1 Dec 1875
East Mill Creek, Salt Lake, Utah
PARENTS: Christian Barr
Susanna Brenneman
PIONEER: 2 Oct 1847
Jedediah M. Grant Wagon Train
SPOUSE: John Neff, II
MARRIED: 12 Jan 1822
Strasburg, Pennsylvania
DEATH SP: 9 May 1869
East Mill Creek, Salt Lake, Utah

CHILDREN:
Barbara Matilda, 28 Oct 1822
Franklin, 18 Feb 1824
Amos Heff, 20 May 1825
Cyrus, 16 Jan 1827 (died at age 20)
Mary Ann, 5 Aug 1829
Susanna, 26 Mar 1831
Benjamin Barr, 6 May 1834
Amanda, 7 Jun 1836
John Neff, III, 28 Dec 1837
Elizabeth, 15 Nov 1840

Mary was born in Bart Township, Lancaster County, Pennsylvania. Her parents were Mennonites. She grew up in a large, well built, brownstone house, learning to cook, weave cloth, sew, keep a clean house, and tend the garden and livestock. As her mother cared for the sick, Mary learned home nursing and the use of herbs as medicine.

She married John Neff, II in Strasburg, Lancaster, Pennsylvania, with whom she bore ten children. They became prosperous by owning woolen shops; flour, shingle, and molasses mills; plus a brewery. She was a gracious hostess and often entertained her husband's personal friend, President James Buchanan in her large fifteen-room rock home in Pennsylvania.

In 1842, missionaries converted and baptized them as members of the Church of Jesus Christ of Latter-day Saints. In 1844, John and Mary traveled to Nauvoo to become acquainted with the Church leaders to see if they wanted to move there. They were favorably impressed, returned to Pennsylvania to sell their property, and returned to Nauvoo in time to learn the Saints had been turned from the city. They hurriedly crossed the Mississippi River and joined the Saints in Winter Quarters where their son, Cyrus, died of the plague.

They joined the Jedediah M. Grant Wagon Company to cross the Plains and arrived in the Salt Lake Valley on October 2, 1847, spending their first winter in the Old Fort.

John built the first flour mill in Utah and moved his family to a home near the mill. They also developed a fine orchard. Mary was a staunch supporter of her husband, a good wife and mother, an example of good homemaking, and thrift. She was generous with what they had and was especially kind to the poor and to strangers. Those in need were always welcome in her home.

In addition to her own children, she raised an Indian boy and an Indian girl rescuing them from a life of slavery.

Mary passed away on her seventy-fourth birthday and was buried in the Salt Lake City Cemetery.

ELLEN BREAKELL NEIBAUR

BIRTHDATE: 23 Feb 1811
Preston, Lancastershire, England
DEATH: 14 Dec 1870
Salt Lake City, Salt Lake, Utah
PARENTS: Richard Breakell
Alice Bannister
PIONEER: 14 Sep 1848
SPOUSE: Alexander Neibaur
MARRIED: 16 Sep 1833/34
Preston, England
DEATH SP: 15 Dec 1883
Salt Lake City, Salt Lake, Utah

CHILDREN:
Joseph William, 6 Jan 1835
Margaret Jane(Miller) 20 Feb 1836
Samuel Breakel, 7 Jan 1838 (died as a child)
Isaac, 30 Mar 1839
Alice(Rosenbaum), 22 May 1841
Bertha Breakel (Pangburn Fillmore), 14 Dec 1842
Hyrum Smith, 30 Nov 1844
Leah Breakell, 29 Aug 1846
Rachel, 12 Dec 1847 (stillborn)
Sarah Ellen (O'Driscoll) 2l May 1849
Rebecca Ann (Nibley), 30 Mar 1851
Mary Esther, 4 Dec 1852
Matilda Isabell (Lorden), 30 Jan 1854
Nathan Alexander, 14 Sep 1855

Ellen Breakell was born in 1811 in England. Her father was a weaver but took up farming to support his family. They belonged to the Church of England and attended their meetings about five miles west of Preston on the River Ribble.

By 1834, Ellen met Alexander Neibaur who was of the Jewish faith. His parents wanted him to become a Rabbi, but he wanted to go into dentistry. Ellen and Alexander were married on September 16, 1834.

They were taught the Gospel of Jesus Christ and joined the Church of Jesus Christ of Latter-day Saints in 1838. They desired to join the Saints in America.In February, 1841, they sailed on the ship, "Sheffield" with three young children and arrived in St. Louis in April.

Moving to Nauvoo, they acquired a lot and built a home. They became close friends with the Prophet Joseph Smith, and Alexander taught him German and Hebrew.

In 1846, Ellen and Alexander received their endowments in the Nauvoo Temple and were sealed. They were forced to leave Nauvoo in September, 1846, and they arrived in Winter Quarters where Ellen gave birth to a little girl who was stillborn.

By May, 1848, they began their journey across the Plains. Ellen guided a pair of lead cows, walking most of the way. Much of the time she had to carry a sick baby in one arm and guide the cows with the other and then when they stopped at night she would wash the cows to cool them and then milk them. They arrived in the Salt Lake Valley, September 24, 1848.

They spent their first winter in a tent which frequently blew down in the winter winds and snow storms. They acquired a lot on 2nd South and 2nd East and constructed a small home. Her husband started his dentistry practice, and Ellen assisted a Dr. Anderson a great deal, by nursing the sick.

She was a very pretty woman, having won beauty contests in England, Nauvoo, and in Salt Lake. Ellen was the mother of fourteen children Their first son, Isaac, died in England, three came with them from England, four more were born in Nauvoo, one in Winter Quarters who was stillborn, and the remainder were born in Salt Lake City, Utah. She raised eleven of them to adulthood.

In 1860, Ellen became ill and was bedfast for several months. She continued to have ill health for about ten years before she passed away of a cerebral hemorrhage, December 14, 1870, at nearly sixty years of age.

Ellen was a great pioneer woman who had tremendous faith, courage and fortitude throughout her lifetime. She left a great posterity who honor her name for the great woman she was, an example for all.

MARION ROBERTSON NEIL

BIRTHDATE: 2 Apr 1837
Tollcross, Lanarkshire, Scotland
DEATH: 8 Aug 1896
Heber, Wasatch Co., Utah
PARENTS: John Robertson
Agnus Lawson
PIONEER: 29 Sep 1866
Daniel Thompson Wagon Train
SPOUSE: William Neil
MARRIED: 31 Dec 1863
Rutherglen, Scotland
DEATH SP: 11 Jun 1905
Charleston, Wasatch Co., Utah

CHILDREN:
Agnes, 1 Jan 1865 (died at age 1)
Rachel Clark, 26 Aug 1866 (died at age 20)
Marion R., 18 Jul 1870
William R., 14 Sep 1872
Martha Ann, 1 Sep 1874
Jane, 26 Aug 1877
John Alexander, 4 Nov 1879

Marion's mother's family were wealthy in Scotland. She married William Neil in Rutherglen, Lanarkshire, Scotland. He was their poor gardener whose first wife had died two years previously. Then her family disowned her.

They became members of the Church of Jesus Christ of Latter-day Saints and decided to emigrate to America on the ship, "Arkwright."

They joined the Saints in the Daniel Thompson Wagon Company to cross the Plains to Utah. Marion's trip across the Plains was a very difficult ten weeks, due to the death of her beloved small child somewhere in Wyoming. Two weeks later, their wagon train stopped again so she could give birth to another baby. They arrived in the Salt Lake Valley on September 29, 1866.

John hauled granite thirty miles for the Salt Lake Temple. Marion was very active in the Relief Society. In Heber, she gleaned wheat for the Relief Society Work Fund as well as being a busy mother. Education was very important to this family. Two of her sons attended the University, one becoming a medical doctor and another one a mining engineer at the University of Utah. The girls were also given extended schooling.

She raised her children to be strong in the Gospel and her testimony of the Church held strong until her death.

ANE / ANNA MARIE HOLM SORENSEN NEILSON

No Photo Available

BIRTHDATE: 21 Jun 1818
Hals, Aalborg, Denmark
DEATH: 25 Aug 1895
Salt Lake City, Salt Lake, Utah
PARENTS: Andreas Jacob Holm
Meatte Jensdatter
PIONEER: 5 Oct 1854
Hans Peter Olsen Wagon Train
SPOUSE I: Nicolai Sorensen
MARRIED: 12 May 1838
Hals, Aalborg, Denmark
DEATH SP: 22 May 1849
Coast of Denmark (drowned)

CHILDREN:
Marie Kirstine Andreasine, 6 Jun 1838
Caroline Elizabeth (Pedersen), 20 Jul 1840
Johan Henrik, 26 Jan 1844
Mette Jacobine Petrine, 28 Sep 1846

SPOUSE II: Nels Neilson
MARRIED: 7 Aug 1857
Salt Lake, Endowment House, Utah
DEATH SP: Unknown
CHILDREN: Unknown

Ane (Anna) was born in Denmark in 1818. She married Nicolai Sorensen on May 12, 1838. They were the parents of three girls and one boy.

Ane's husband was so set against her daughter, Caroline, joining the Church of Jesus Christ of Latter-day Saints, that he sent her to fend for herself when she was about thirteen years old.

When Ane was thirty-five years old her husband, Nicolai, drowned off the coast of Denmark, on May 22, 1849, leaving her with three girls, Mary (fifteen), Caroline (thirteen), and Mette (seven).

Caroline had saved some money to help pay the passage for her, her mother and two sisters to the Salt Lake Valley, in Utah. They left Coppenhagen, Denmark, December 9, 1853, went to Liverpool, England, there they boarded the ship, "Jesse Munn," January 3, 1854. They landed in New Orleans, February 20, 1854. Then they went to Kansas City, where they joined the Hans Peter Olsen Wagon Train, arriving in the Salt Lake Valley, October 5, 1854, after ten months from leaving her home in Denmark.

Ane died in Salt Lake City, August 25, 1895, at the age of seventy-seven.

ANN CHRISTINE MORTENSEN CLAPP NEILSON

BIRTHDATE: 14 Sep 1837
Nederby, Viborg, Denmark
DEATH: 12 Apr 1898
Annabelle, Sevier Co., Utah
PIONEER: 19 Sep 1856
Benjamin L. Clapp Wagon Train
PARENTS: Diderich Mortensen
Maren Jensen
SPOUSE I: Benjamin L. Clapp
MARRIED: 12 Oct 1856
Salt Lake City, Salt Lake, Utah
DEATH SP: 31 Oct 1865
Woodbridge, California

CHILDREN:
Elijah Charles 11 Dec 1857 (twin)
Elisha Drown, 11 Dec 1857 (twin)

SPOUSE II: Lars Neilson
MARRIED: 1859
Ephraim, Sanpete Co., Utah
DEATH SP: 25 May 1916
Hollbrook, Oneida Co., Idaho

CHILDREN:
Lorenzo, 18 Apr 1860
Mary Ann Helena (Allred Jones), 18 May 1861
Morten Didrich, 7 Dec 1862
James Didrich, 19 Mar 1864
Christine, 13 Nov 1865
John Fullmer, 9 Dec 1866
Emma Amelia (Weaver), 14 Jun 1868
Lars Ferdinand, 28 Mar 1870
Lorette Christine (Robinson), 27 Sep 1871
Dozinda Christiana (Berrestensen), 10 Apr 1873
Raymond Anton, 25 May 1875
Minnie May (Collings), 23 Apr 1877

Viola Nickolina, 7 Apr 1879
William Dare, 14 Jul 1880

Ann Christine was born in Denmark in 1837, she joined the Church of Jesus Christ of Latter-day Saints when she was sixteen years old and came with her parents and family to America aboard the ship, "James Nesmith," two years after her baptism, leaving Liverpool on January 7, 1855, with 440 converts bound for New Orleans, and Utah.

She was with the wagon train captained by Benjamin L. Clapp. They arrived in the Salt Lake Valley on September 19, 1856, and nineteen year old Ann Christine was married to Benjamin not long after their journey ended. She bore Benjamin twin sons the next year but it was not enough to keep the couple together and they divorced.

Ann, two years later, entered into a plural marriage with her sister Dorothy Marie's husband Lars Neilson and went to live in Sanpete County with them.

Dorothy Marie died, May 3, 1864, leaving twenty-seven year old Ann Christine and Lars with a combined family of eight children, all under seven years of age. The family lived in Sanpete and Sevier Counties most of their lives, engaged in farming for their livelihood.

Ann and Lars had fourteen children together, seven boys and seven girls and the large family was very musical, accomplished musicians and singers. They had the first public dance hall on their property in Annabelle, Sevier County, Utah.

Ann Christine passed away in Annabelle, Utah, at the age of sixty and is buried in Richfield, Sevier, Utah. Lars, living eight years longer, died in Hollbrook, Oneida County, Idaho, and is buried in Richfield also.

AGNETA / ANNETTA BENGTSSON NILSSON / NELSON

No Photo Available

BIRTHDATE: 9 Dec 1832
Oringe Hallands, Sweden
DEATH: 4 Nov 1873
Logan, Cache Co., Utah
PARENTS: Nils Bengtsson (Benson)
Johanna Johansson
PIONEER: 15 Sep 1864
William Preston's Wagon Train
SPOUSE I: Unknown
MARRIED: In Sweden
DEATH SP:

CHILDREN: (Adopted and sealed to second husband
Botilda (Matilda), 31 Dec 1853 (died at age 11)
James Peter, 13 Dec 1355

SPOUSE II: John / Johannes Nelson / Nilsson
MARRIED: 17 Nov 1855
Veinge, Hallands, Sweden

DEATH SP: 26 Nov 1902
Logan, Cache Co., Utah

CHILDREN:
Nels August, 18 May 1357
Josephine, 5 Feb 1860 (died as a child near Omaha, Nebraska
Amanda, 26 Dec 1862 (died as a child buried at sea)
Annette Josephine, 18 Nov 1864
Joseph Hyrum, 14 Jun 1868
Jacob Nelson, 9 Dec 1870 (twin)
Jacobina, 9 Dec 1870 (twin)
Charlotte Abigail, 16 Dec 1872
Moses, 25 Oct 1873

Agneta was born on December 9, 1832 in Oringe Hallands, Sweden. Agneta was the oldest child in a family of eight children.

On Thursday, April 28, 1864, with 973 emigrants aboard, the ship, "Monarch of the Sea," sailed from Liverpool, England. Patriarch John Smith was President of the company. At Florence, Nebraska, they traveled by teams under the Company Captain William B. Preston, to Salt Lake City, arriving September 15, 1864.

The Gospel of the Church of Jesus Christ of Latter-day Saints came to their home in 1862, and Agneta, her mother and some of her brothers accepted the message gladly. But it wasn't until the Spring of 1864, that Johannes and Agneta were ready to leave Sweden for America and the West.

The voyage was long and stormy with much sickness aboard. The rations were meager; raw beef, lard, and hard crackers, water, mustard and salt. Many times they would wait all day for their turn to cook the meat, and sometimes the turn never came. Agneta saw several bodies being lowered into the deep ocean; and then it was her turn to watch eighteen month old with a rock tied to her feet, slipping into the ocean.

Laying to rest little ones in unknown territory was to be Agneta's experience two more times. Matilda, in New Jersey, near the Delaware River, and four year old Josephine near Omaha, Nebraska.

During these trials, she valiantly went forward, giving birth to her sixth child in a cold, stark dugout in Logan, Utah.

Arriving in late October, most homes in Logan that fall were underground, about five feet deep, with a rock chimney in corner. Fuel was willows from the Logan River bottom. It was quite warm, until spring thaw caused the room to fill with water about two feet. The cold of Cache Valley became known to all new settlers that winter.

The next winter found John and Agneta in a snug log cabin, with cows, sheep, a yoke of steers, and 120 bushels of wheat raised on their six acres. Agneta also gleaned wheat from the field. She sheared the sheep, washed, carded, spun and wove the wool into clothing for her family; and with her gleaning, she was able to provide nice clothes for herself, and children.

On October 4, 1867, three years after their arrival in Utah, John and Agneta traveled to Salt Lake City, to be sealed in the Endowment House. In the next six years she gave birth to five more children, with only two surviving beyond the age of accountability.

Just nine years after her entering Utah, Agneta gave birth to her last child, Moses Nelson, born October 25, 1873; and she did not survive this birth. Moses died November 12, 1873. A mother had sacrificed for a child of God.

ANNA "ANNIE" SOPHIA NETTERSTROM NELSON

BIRTHDATE: 7 Dec 1841
Karlsham, Biekinge, Sweden
DEATH SP: 2 Oct 1927
Tooele, Tooele Co. Utah
PARENTS: Erik Netterstrom
Sophia Maria Ekstrom
PIONEER: 15 Sep 1866
William Chipman Wagon Train
SPOUSE: Peter Nelson
MARRIED: 7 May 1865
DEATH SP: 15 Jan 1915
Tooele, Tooele Co, Utah

CHILDREN:
Selma Helena, 8 Feb 1866
Mary Ann, 4 Jan 1868
Hilda Matilda, 30 Nov 1869
Peter William, 1 Feb 1872
Charles Erik, 12 Dec 1873
Hannah, 21 Oct 1875
Nils Wilford, 20 Sep 1877
Edward Harrison, 15 Nov 1879
Louis, 24 Dec 1881
Fredrick Brock, 23 Mar 1884
Gilber Helman, 28 Jun 1886

Anna Sophia Netterstrom was born in Sweden in 1841, the oldest of seven children she learned compassion and responsibility.

She joined the Church of Jesus Christ of Latter-day Saints and as a young woman of twenty-three boarded the ship, "Monarch of the Sea," April 8, 1864 with 974 converts for the voyage to America to join the people of the Church in Utah.

She married Peter Nelson one month into the voyage. They were accompanied on their ship board wedding by forty-nine other couples. The overcrowding had one reasonable solution, to double up the living quarters.

Their first born came to them in Mt. Pleasant, Cass, Nebraska. They left Wyoming, Nebraska, July 13, 1866, with five month old Selma Helena for sixty-three days of a plodding trek completely at the mercy of nature.

In Utah, the couple were sent to Tooele where they built their home and raised their children.

Anna and Peter were married for fifty years and raised eleven children in a harmonious home. Two of her daughters died leaving nine children which she reared for several years.

Anna lived twelve years after Peter passed away, she was eighty-six, at the time of her death.

BERETA "BERTHA" PEHRSSON NELSON

BIRTHDATE: 6 Jun 1811
Gustav, Malmahus, Sweden
DEATH: 31 Dec 1896
Pleasant Grove, Utah Co., Utah
PARENTS: Par Jonsson
Kerstine Magnusson
PIONEER: 25 Sep 1868
John G. Holman Wagon Train
SPOUSE: Ole Nilsson /Nelson
MARRIED: 27 Dec 1840
DEATH SP: 13 Jun 1891
Pleasant Grove, Utah Co., Utah

CHILDREN:
Else "Ellen," 15 Mar 1841
Kjersti, 31 Dec 1842
Nels Oleson, 25 Jan 1845
Mangur Oleson, 31 Mar 1847
Jens Oleson, 21 Jun 1849
Johanna Oledotter, 31 Dec 1851

Bereta "Bertha" Pehrsson was born in Sweden in 1811, she married Ole Nelson two days after Christmas and six months before her thirtieth birthday. The couple's six children were born and raised in Denmark.

Bereta was active in the Church of Jesus Christ of Latter-day Saints in Sweden. She and Ole worked and saved to send a son and daughter ahead to Utah. They waited, coming last of all to Zion. "And the Lord called his people Zion, because they were of one heart and one mind, and dwelt in righteousness; and there were no poor among them." (Moses 7:18). It was a call that warmed the heart and fed the soul.

At the age of fifty-seven, Bereta and Ole sailed from Liverpool on the ship "Emerald Isle," with 876 souls for a crowded but orderly voyage of fifty-two days, landing in New York. They had brought a seven year old granddaughter with them.

The company of converts traveled by train to Benton, Wyoming. About 650 Saints were in the John G. Holman Wagon Company, the last official church train to arrive into the Salt Lake Valley. Mostly everyone walked the twenty-six days it took to come from Benton, the wagons being too full of provisions, bedding and personal belongings to permit otherwise.

The Nelson's settled first in Bountiful, Utah for seven years, then moved to Pleasant Grove, Utah to live for the rest of their lives.

Bereta never learned English. She was a home maker, raised a garden and animals and sold eggs, butter and cheese. She served in the Church by making quilts and rugs and baking and cooking for church events. She was a faithful tithes payer and attended Relief Society, Fast Meetings and Church Services.

Bereta lived twenty-eight years in Utah, passing away at the age of eighty-five.

CAROLINE DOMGAARD NIELSEN / NELSON

BIRTHDATE: 29 Aug 1846
Hals, Aalborg, Denmark
DEATH: 10 Feb 1908
Manti, Sanpete Co., Utah
PARENTS: Niels P. Domgaard
Else Kirstine Nielson
PIONEER: 30 Sep 1853
Justesen's / Shurtliffe Company
SPOUSE: Fritz E. Nelson
MARRIED: 14 Apr 1863
DEATH SP:
Manti, Sanpete Co., Utah

CHILDREN:
Fritz Emanuel, 21 Jan 1864
Caroline Elizabeth, 23 Jan 1866
Mary Christina, 22 Jun 1868
Annie Margaret, 2 Sep 1870
Alice Victoria, 28 Feb 1873
Charles Christian, 29 Dec 1875
Ethel Elfrieda, 13 Sep 1878
Ida Maria, 21 Mar 1881
Edwin Alvin, 29 Nov 1883
Lawrence Niels, 12 Sep 1886

Caroline was born in Denmark in 1846 and came to America and Utah as a little girl six years old, leaving all that was dear and familiar behind, clinging to one favorite toy for comfort. Her story is found through the diary of her future father-in-law, Christian Nelson.

The company of Saints left Copenhagen on the steamer "Abotric" (Obotric) at 12 o'clock and "a great crowd of people bid us good by swinging their hats and with hand-kerchiefs, two fine psalms were sung before we sailed away."

He writes of the wind that came up on the Baltic Ocean, and blew some passengers to the other side of the boat, among them his son, Fritz, age fourteen, (Caroline's future husband). In Germany, they traveled by train to Alton near Hamburg, and 11,300 persons strong marched through that city much to the citizens surprise in seeing so many.

On the double decked Aiel ship "Lion," going to Liverpool, "such wind came up--a wave broke the deck, water came down, women and children screamed, afraid we would all drown, the captain said in twenty-five years he had never seen such a 'hurricane.' We all prayed to God for his protection and he mercifully heard our prayer."

They sailed from Liverpool on the "Forest Monarch," and docked in New Orleans after fifty-one days on the Ocean. (Caroline's little brother, Laurice Eliase, died on the voyage and was buried at sea.)

The group was delayed in St. Louis, four months and four days, then they took a steamer to Keokuk, Iowa, to camp in a place where many other emigrants were gathered, including some from England. Finally, May 21, they began the trek to Salt Lake City.

On September 15, they are at the Green River, having traveled through rain and mud, poor roads and better ones, crossed the La Platte River on a ferry, traveled through places where grass was rich and lush, the oxen well fed. Other times, some oxen weakened by starvation were killed by wolves.

After reaching Salt Lake City, they left for another 150 mile journey to Denmark Fort (Spring City) where they stayed for a while. On December 16, 1853, they were at the Manti Fort, "met by friendly generous people willing to share their homes and food with them."

Caroline was sixteen when she and Fritz Emanuel were wed in Manti, the town where they established their home and their lives. The Nelson's were married for thirty-five years and had ten children and contributed greatly to that settlement.

She wrote beautiful letters, showing love and compassion and concern for the welfare to those she was writing.

Caroline passed away at sixty-one years of age in Manti, having gone through many hardships in her life. She was truly a Pioneer.

CHRISTIANA HAILSEN LARSEN NELSON

BIRTHDATE: 29 Mar 1804
Mosbjerg, Hjorring, Denmark
DEATH: 21 Aug 1897
Bloomington, Idaho
PARENTS: Lars Hailsen
Ana Knudsen
PIONEER: 20 Sep 1856
Canute Peterson's Handcart Com.
SPOUSE: Soren Nelson/Nielsen
MARRIED: 6 Oct 1827
Elling, Hjorring, Denmark
DEATH SP: 15 Apr 1896
Bloomington, Bear Lake, Idaho

CHILDREN:
Niels Christian, 26 Jan 1828
Karen Marie, 19 Feb 1832

Lauritz Antona, abt 1835 (died in Denmark)
Soren Christian, 5 Nov 1837
Charlotte Amelia, 21 Jan 1841
Christiana, abt 1843 (died in Denmark)
Otena, 20 Nov 1846

Christiana was born March 29, 1804, at Mosbjerg, Denmark. In 1827, she married Soren Nelson. They were converted to The Church of Jesus Christ of Latter-day Saints in Denmark and left for America, sailing from Liverpool, England on December 12, 1855, aboard the sailing vessel "John Boyd."

It was a difficult journey of eleven weeks and three days, during which they suffered a fire, a broken mast during a bad storm, and an out-break of measles. Their daughter, "Tena," nine years old, was the youngest child to survive the measles. Five adults and sixty children died and were buried at sea.

They crossed the Plains with the Knud (Canute) Peterson Handcart Company. Christiana walked the entire distance to Salt Lake City. They arrived on September 20, 1856. From Salt Lake City they moved to Goshen, Utah, where they lived in a dugout. In 1860, they moved to Hyde Park, Utah, and lived there for four years, then moved with a group of Saints to settle Bloomington, Bear Lake, Idaho, in the spring of 1864.

On November 20, 1865, the wedding of her daughter, Tena, to James Claybourne Thomas was the first wedding in the settlement.

Christiana and Soren retained their Danish way of life in both dress and speech. Christiana passed away at the home of her daughter, Tena, on August 21, 1897, and is buried in the Bloomington Cemeery.

ELIZA SNOW BRYSON NELSON

BIRTHDATE: 13 Jun 1854
Glasgow, Lanark, Scotland
DEATH: 21 Apr 1935
Woods Cross, Davis Co., Utah
PARENTS: Samuel Bryson
Sarah Ann Conrey
PIONEER: 24 Oct 1855
Milo Andrus Handcart Company
SPOUSE: Jens Christian Nelson
MARRIED: 22 Nov 1869
Salt Lake City, Salt Lake, Utah
DEATH SP: 6 Aug 1910
Woods Cross, Davis Co., Utah

CHILDREN:
Jens Knud, 2 Dec 1870
Samuel Roy, 4 Oct 1873
David Melvin, 7 Jun 1876
Sarah, 25 Dec 1879 (twin)
Sylvanus, 25 Dec 1879 (twin)
Eliza, 10 Jul 1883
Hyrum, 3 Jul 1885
Lawerence N., 10 Scp 1866 (twin)

Clarence C., 10 Sep 1866 (twin)
James Everett, 7 Dec 1889
Harold Clyde, 18 Feb 1894

Taken from the writings of Eliza Snow Bryson Nelson;

I was born to Irish parents and the following year they came to Utah, crossing the ocean in a sailing vessel which took eleven weeks. While crossing the Plains at one time when we are camped my mother left me alone when an Indian came and was going to steal me when my father, who had just returned from hunting leveled his gun at him. The Indian dropped me and rode away causing no more trouble.

My early days were spent in the home of my parents and after my marriage went to Nevada to live for a short time returning the next summer. In, 1874, we moved to Rich County, living on a ranch raising cattle. We were gone three years. Upon our return, I spent much time in the YLMIA.

In February, 1893, I was called to work as a Relief Society teacher in the South Bountiful Ward. For many years I was an active worker and always enjoyed doing what I could to help those in need

I am the mother of eleven children, having reared ten to maturity, and also a niece, Mary Emma Bryson, daughter of James and Mary Emma Oliver Bryson. Her mother died when she was three weeks old and she lived with me until her marriage.

In 1915, I visited the World Fair in San Francisco and also the State Fair in San Diego and had the most enjoyable trip. I feel that I have been greatly blest of the Lord in having one of the best men for a husband also a loving, kind father to his children. I have had six sons fulfill honorable missions and a son, Harold, who served two years in the world war. I am enjoying fairly good health at this time being seventy-seven years of age and still trying to do my bit to help the world along.

ELIZABETH DOBINSON THOMPSON NELSON

No
Photo
Available

BIRTHDATE: 20 Oct 1786
Weatheral, Cumberland, England
DEATH: 15 Mar 1874
Buysville, Wasatch Co., Utah
PARENTS: Thomas Thompson
Elizabeth Dobinson
PIONEER: 1852 (or before)
SPOUSE: Thomas Nelson
MARRIED: 20 Jan 1805
Wetheral, Cumberland, England
DEATH SP: Aug 1846
Near Mt.Pisgah, Iowa (en route)

CHILDREN:
William, 24 Mar 1805 (died as a child)

John, 1807 (died as a child)
Thomas, 1809 (died as a child)
William, 18 Oct 1812
Richard, 2 Jul 1815 (died as a child)
Henry, 23 Jul 1818 (died as a child)
Isaac, 23 May 1821
Jane (Mulford Jones), 26 Sep 1823
Henry, 6 Sep 1826

Elizabeth Dobinson was born in England in 1786 to Thomas Thompson and Elizabeth Dobinson, who did not marry. As a child she was known by both names, Dobinson and Thompson.

She married Thomas Nelson, two years older than she and the couple lived in his home village of Moreland, Westmoreland, England. The first of nine children were born to Elizabeth when she was nineteen years old.

Isaac, Jane and Henry, the last three children , survived. All had lived past the age of three, the year that seemed to be the critical year for all the other babies, and all the children were raised in Morland, England.

Elizabeth was fifty-two when she and Thomas, with their three teenage children and William, about twenty-six, set forth for America about 1838, to settle for a short time in Cayuga County, New York. Between 1839 and 1841, the entire family joined the Church of Jesus Christ of Latter-day Saints and left for Nauvoo to be with the Saints where the Thompson family worshiped in the Nauvoo Fourth ward, There both William and Henry received their Patriarchal Blessings from Hyrum Smith.

The Nelsons were driven from Nauvoo and some where near Mt. Pisgah, Iowa, in August 1846, Thomas died and was buried on the Plains. Elizabeth and her sons and daughter stayed in Winter Quarters for a time, then Elizabeth continued on to the Valley with her four adult children. Both William and Isaac married before coming to Utah, The entire family made their homes in Provo.

Henry moved to Buysville (Center Creek) Wasatch County, and during her last years Elizabeth made her home with him. She died at the age of eighty-eight years probably in Buysville, but there is no record of her burial in Provo, nor in the Heber Cemetery, where both William and his wife are buried. There is room for another grave between their graves and the road, perhaps Elizabeth was buried there and the tombstone has worn away and disappeared through the years.

ELIZABETH JOSEPH NELSON

BIRTHDATE: 1 Nov 1819
Muff, Donegal, Ireland
DEATH: 12 May 1902
Smithfield, Cache Co., Utah
PARENTS: John Joseph
Martha Carr
PIONEER: Sep 1852
Harmon Cutler Co. Wagon Train
SPOUSE: Robert Nelson
MARRIED: 12 Dec 1842
Muff, Donegal, Ireland
DEATH SP: 10 Feb 1902

CHILDREN:
Samuel, 22 Jan 1845
Robert, 4 Jun 1847
Joseph, 6 Jan 1850
Mary Elizabeth (Hatch), 4 May 1852
John Alexander, 17 Oct 1854
Robert James, 17 Jun 1856
David William, 1 Jan 1860
Eliza Jane, 1861 (died at 4 days old)
Jane Margaret (Tidwell), 12 Sep 1862

Elizabeth and her husband, Robert, were both born in the same town in Ireland. They grew up, became sweethearts, and were married December 12, 1852. Due to the potato famine, they moved to Scotland where their first three children were born.

They heard the gospel preached here and were baptized as members of the Church of Jesus Christ of Latter-day Saints on December 13, 1849. With the help of the Perpetual Emigrating Fund, the Nelson family joined a group of Saints who were going to Liverpool. They were on the ship, "Manchester," for six weeks.

They docked in New Orleans for three days and boarded a riverboat which took them to St. Louis. This is where their first daughter was born. When they were able, they went to Kaneville, Iowa, where they joined the Harmon Cutler Wagon Company. They traveled over the Mormon Trail and arrived in Salt Lake City in September of 1852.

After their arrival, they rested a short period before President Young sent them to Farmington, Davis County, Utah, where they made their home. The next four children were born in Farmington. The family then moved to Smithfield, Cache County, Utah, where their youngest daughter was born.

Robert and Elizabeth were able to be married, endowed, and sealed in the Endowment House on November 15, 1855. They both died and were buried in Smithfield, Utah.

ELMYRA "MYRA" PURSER NELSON

BIRTHDATE: 5 Oct. 1860
Lawrenny, Pembrokeshire, Wales
DEATH: 24 Aug 1915
Treasureton, Franklin Co., Idaho
PARENTS: Francis Purser
Frances "Fanny" Eynon
PIONEER: Aug 1868
SPOUSE: Soren Joseph Nelson
MARRIED: 29 Dec 1877
DEATH SP: 17 Sep 1930

CHILDREN:
Almira Ellie, 23 Oct 1879
Soren, 13 Aug 1880
David, 17 Jul 1882
Pearl Frances, 3 Sep 1884
James, 16 Dec 1886
Mary, 14 Jan 1889
Frank, 6 Dec 1890
Lenard, 30 Dec 1892
John, 27 Oct 1893
Etta Belle, 22 Oct 1894
Bertha, 26 Dec 1896
Earl Glen, 3 Nov 1898
Ruby Frances, 10 Jan 1900
Edith, 3 Feb 1903
Harold, 28 Jan 1905
Stanley, 12 Apr 1906

"Myra" was born in Wales in 1860 and was not yet eight years old when, on June 6,1868, her parents with her brothers Peter and Phillip, and she and her sister Maria, left Liverpool, England with 722 others on the ship, "John Bright" for the voyage to America. Three short days into the crossing her mother died and was slipped into her watery grave.

The family landed in New York nearly two months after boarding and took a train as far as the line went, then in Laramie, Wyoming, they joined a wagon train to complete their five month journey, arriving toward the end of August into Salt Lake City.

Frank Purser took his motherless children to Hyde Park, Cache County where his sister in law was living, and Myra was raised in that little settlement.

She was seventeen when she and Soren Joseph were married on December 29th. Their first child was born in Hyde Park but they moved to Smithfield before the birth of their next child ten months later and lived there for the next nine years. The next four children were born in Smithfield.

Their last venture was to Treasureton, Idaho, where they built their home permanently and completed their family of sixteen children. There were times when Myra could have felt as though she was raising three sets of twins, her first two only ten months apart, John and Etta Belle only

twelve months apart and Harold and Stanley fourteen months.

Her life was given over to motherhood. Of her thirty-seven years of marriage, in all but nine she was tending a baby or expecting one. In grief she lost six babies in infancy, nine grew to adulthood, her youngest child was nine years old when Myra passed away at the age of fifty-five.

She gave the gift of her life to her children, and they returned the gift as decent men and women who settled the frontier.

ELVIRA VAIL NELSON

BIRTHDATE: 25 Apr 1839
McLean Co., Illinois
DEATH: 12 Mar 1932
Riverdale, Idaho
PARENTS: Gamaliel Vail
Martha Bartholomew
PIONEER: 1851
James Holms Co. Wagon Train
SPOUSE: William G. Nelson
MARRIED: 25 Nov 1855
DEATH SP: 30 Oct 1922
Riverdale, Idaho

CHILDREN:
William Isaac, 31 Aug 1856
Elvira, 18 Jan 1858 (died at age 5)
Martha, 25 Oct 1859
Luna, 18 Sep 1861
Emmaline, 14 Sep 1863
George Goforth, 25 Sep 1865
Rhoda, 28 Oct 1867
Brigham Young, 20 Jul 1869
Gamaliel Vail, 8 Dec 1871
Angelina, 11 Jan 1872
Rachel, 8 Dec 1876
Taylor, 23 Dec 1878
Ezra, 5 Sep 1881

Elvira was born in Illinois in 1839. Her mother, Martha Vail, brought the family from Clarksville, Illinois to Council Bluffs Iowa after the father died. The family lived there five years before immigrating to Utah in 1851.

She was twelve years old when her family left the past and history of the persecuted to traveled across the Plains on a three month plodding trek into a future and a life, the best life that hard work and strong faith would allow. It was a scary trip for a twelve year old. The Frontier Guardian newspaper of June 13th, was urging everyone who intended to cross the Plains to leave immediately and not to cross the Missouri River later than the 20th of the month, and to keep a strong guard at night so as to protect themselves from Indians depredations, for it was reported that Pawnees and other tribes were bent on mischief and theft.

She was close to seventeen when she and William were married in their own log house in the middle of the fort at Mountainville (Alpine) Utah. The winters of 1855 and 1856 were very harsh. Their cattle died and in 1857 grasshoppers killed over half their crops.

When Johnston's army threatened and the settlers were sent south, Elvira's husband went to Payson in 1858 and was able to raise crops there. The couple were asked to colonize in Cache Valley and they moved there. They went first to Richmond, but were told to go on to Franklin, about five miles north. On April 14, 1860, their wagon drove into Franklin, the sixth wagon to enter that day. Trouble with the Indians pushed the first settlers into a fort to live for a while.

In the Spring of 1863, William was called to help immigrants from Missouri and returned six months later to a new baby daughter, Emmaline, and to grief, four days after his return his daughter, Elvira, sickly from birth, died at the age of five years.

The family moved to Oxford near Franklin, Idaho in 1864 and finally to Riverdale in 1879. William died twenty-six days before they were to celebrate their sixty-seventh wedding anniversary. Elvira lived with her daughter, Angela, the last few years of her life.

Her son, Taylor, said of her "She was a good mother, she ruled with kindness. She was a good cook, a wonderful housekeeper and went about her work cheerfully, usually singing. She was religious and interested in temple work."

FREDRICKA JORGANSON NELSON

BIRTHDATE: 19 Jun 1840
Malmo, Sweden
DEATH: 13 Apr 1919
Tooele, Tooele Co., Utah
PARENTS: Philip Jorganson
Lanamaya "Lena" Maria Brock
PIONEER: Nov 1865
Wagon Train Company
SPOUSE: Swen Nelson/Nielsen
MARRIED: May 1865
on ship B. S. Kimball
DEATH SP: 11 Dec 1910
Tooele, Tooele Co., Utah

CHILDREN:
Matilda Helena, 11 Dec 1866
Anna Fredricka, 12 Oct 1868
Amelia, 28 Jul 1870
Sven Philip, 12 Mar 1872
Oscar, 30 Oct 1873 (died as a child)
David, 12 Apr 1875
Alfred Mathias, 12 Jun 1878
Edward Oliver, 13 Nov 1879
Clara Edna, 22 Jul 1882
Ada Cadilla, 16 Feb 1885

Fredricka was born June 19, 1840, in Malmo, Sweden to Philip and Lanmaya "Lena Maria" Jorganson. She became a Lady in Waiting to the Queen of Sweden, and was used to the luxuries of the day. She chose, however, to run away from home as her parents were against her joining the Mormon faith.

She was able to allude the detectives her father had hired, took a small boat to Copenhagen, Denmark, and from there to Liverpool where she joined the missionary who had taught her, and other Saints. The ship, "B. S. Kimball" left for America, May 8, 1865, bound for New York with 553 passengers aboard.

Fredricka and her missionary, Swen Nelson were married by the president of their group on board the ship along with Swen's brother, Peter and his fiance. They traveled the stormy sea for five weeks. They then crossed the Plains, walking most of the way, in a wagon train led by President Winberg. It is said that Fredricka had different colored kid gloves which she put on to carry wood during their trip across the Plains.

These couples proceeded to Tooele where Swen's brother, Mathias, was waiting for them. It was November of 1865 when they arrived in Utah. By 1875, Swen was called on another mission to Sweden. He left Fredricka with four children and another on the way. During his absence Oscar died.

After her departure from Sweden, Fredricka had had no direct word from her parents. She knew her mother had died and that her Father had remarried. He died in 1830. His widow was very gracious and sent Fredricka money to come to Sweden to collect her inheritance. The entire town turned out to get her ready, and she left in April, 1881, and remained in Sweden for one year. She returned with trunks full of china, linens, glassware, materials, silver sleigh bells, and with $35,000. Fredricka used her money to build a beautiful home which was still standing in Tooele, and she entertained lavishly.

Fredricka had ten children all together, and all but Oscar lived to adulthood. Fredricka was a large lady and spoke with a heavy accent. She wore taffeta petticoats and she could be heard coming a long way off. She was always very stylish and dignified and always well dressed.

Fredricka had strong faith which never failed her. She was always active in the Church and held many positions including being Primary President. She was a strong woman who endured many trials and tribulations and she gave up great wealth and security for her new religion and new life.

Her husband passed away in 1910, and she passed away April 13, 1919, at almost seventy-nine years of age. They are both buried in Tooele,Utah.

Fredricka was truly a great pioneer woman of faith and fortitude who is an example for those who have followed.

JANE TAYLOR NELSON

No
Photo
Available

BIRTHDATE: 1 Jan 1804
Tamis, Williamson, Tennessee
DEATH: 2 Jun 1872
Franklin, Idaho
PARENTS: Billington Taylor
Mary Modglin
PIONEER: 9 Sep 1850
Thomas Johnson Wagon Train
SPOUSE: Edmond Nelson
MARRIED: 3 Oct 1820
Waterloo, Illinois
DEATH SP: 13 Dec 1850
Mountainville (Alpine), Utah

CHILDREN:
Price William, 17 Nov 1822
Elizabeth, 5 Jun 1824
Martha, 17 Feb 1826
Rhoda, 19 Apr 1828
Hyrum, 29 Dec 1829
William Goforth, 10 Jun 1831
Mary Jane, 8 Mar 1832
Thomas Billington, 9 May 1835
Joseph Smith, 20 Dec 1836
Nancy, 1840 (died as a child)
Edmond, 22 May 1842
Mark, 5 May 1844
Anna, 8 Mar 1847

Jane's father was a farmer, landowner, and a frontiersman who moved often. These moves took the family from North Carolina to Tennessee where Jane was born. They then moved on to Ohio and then to different areas in Illinois.

Jane married Edmond Nelson when she was sixteen years old. They had eight children by the time they heard the gospel of the Church of Jesus Christ of Latter-day Saints. Jane was baptized in 1838 and from this time forth, her entire life was built around her faith and service to the Church.

The persecution in Nauvoo increased and forced her family to leave their home, their stock, and most of their belongings. Her ninth child was born at Shoal Creek which is near Far West.

Jane, her husband, and children came across the Plains in a covered wagon traveling alone at first and then joined with more Saints. On July 4, 1850, Thomas Johnson was chosen as the captain of their company which was made up of fifty wagons and a fairly good supply of stock. They arrived in Salt Lake Valley on September 9, 1850 and were directed by Brigham Young to go thirty miles south to Mountainville (Alpine).

They established a home and just three months later, Edmond passed away at age fifty-one. He had contracted mountain fever while crossing the Plains. Jane faced tremendous hardships and challenges as a widow with her several young children yet to raise.

In 1851, her oldest son persuaded the family to move to Brown's Fort in Ogden. In 1856, she moved to Payson with her son, Edmond. In 1860, she moved to Cache Valley and then was invited to help settle Franklin, Idaho. She taught her children the gospel, family unity, and to love and care for each other.

Jane was a faithful wife, a great mother, and a devoted and faithful member of the Church. Jane spent the last few years of her life serving her family and community. She enjoyed the accomplishments of her children and grandchildren. She passed away while living at Franklin, Idaho.

JOHANNA MARIE CHRISTINA RIGTRUP NELSON

BIRTHDATE: 10 Mar 1842
Randers, Randers, Denmark
DEATH: 17 Dec 1884
Spanish Fork, Utah Co., Utah
PARENTS: Peder Rigtrup
Johanna Elizabeth Korsgaard
PIONEER: Oct 1859
Wagon Train Company
SPOUSE: Andrew E. Nelson
MARRIED: 15 May 1859
Omaha, Nebraska
DEATH SP: 15 Nov 1900
Spanish Fork, Utah Co., Utah

CHILDREN:
Andrew V., 14 Feb 1860
Peter E., 12 Aug 1861
Ephraim E., 14 May 1863
Hyrum H., 23 May 1865 (died as a child)
Henry J., 4 Jun 1867
Hanna O., 21 Jul 1869 (died as a child)
Emma M.., 3 Oct 1871
Oliver W., 7 Dec 1874
James O., 11 Mar 1876
John E., 16 Apr 1878
Fanny M., 16 Mar 1880 (died as an infant)
Charles F., 23 Jul 1881

Johanna Marie Christina Rigtrup was born in 1842 in Denmark to Peder and Johanna Elizabeth Rigtrup. She had two brothers and one sister. Her family came to the United States in 1855 settling in Burlington and St. Louis, and then Omaha, Douglas County, Nebraska.

Johanna married Andrew Eklund Nelson on May 15, 1859, in Omaha. A few weeks after their marriage they started for Utah in a covered wagon. They arrived in Salt Lake City in October of 1859. They moved on to Spanish Fork in Utah County where their twelve children were born. Nine of these children grew to adulthood.

Johanna Marie was proud of her heritage, and, like her brave parents, was not afraid of any task, but made each task a stepping stone to something higher. She was very generous and a friend of the poor. For many years she was a very active worker in the Relief Society.

Johanna Marie passed away in December, 1884, at the age of forty-two years and nine months. She left small children in their home and some older family members who could help in rearing these children. Her husband Andrew lived until 1900, sixteen years after Johanna died. They both died in Spanish Fork, their home in Utah.

These were noble pioneers who left a great legacy of faith and fortitude for those who have followed them.

KAREN MARGRETTE CHRISTENSEN JENSEN NELSON

BIRTHDATE: 28 Nov 1803
Gunderup, Aalborg, Denmark
DEATH: 10 May 1873
Richmond, Cache Co., Utah
PARENTS: Christen Jensen
Mette Christensen
PIONEER: 29 Sep 1853
John Forsgren Co. Wagon Train
SPOUSE: Knud C. Nelson
MARRIED: 21 Jun 1829
Gunderup, Aalborg, Denmark
DEATH SP : 11 Apr 1862
Bountiful, Davis Co., Utah

CHILDREN:
Christiana, 6 Jan 1830
Chresten, 19 Nov 1831
Bergetta, 5 Aug 1833
Mette Marie, 3 May 1835
Peder, 15 Sep 1836
Ann, 17 Mar 1839
Jens Christian, 8 May 1841
Nels, 19 Apr 1842
Peder, 19 Apr 1843
Christian, 24 Jan 1845
Karen Marie, 21 Apr 1847

Karen Margrette was born in 1803 in Denmark to Christen and Mette Christensen Jensen. As a young child, she learned the art of weaving, and she helped her mother make clothing for the family. This was a talent she used throughout her life.

In 1829, she married Knud Christensen Nelson and they moved to Kjellgaarden where they had eleven children, three of whom died in infancy.

In 1851, the family joined the Church of Jesus Christ of Latter-day Saints, and they made plans to go to America. What courage and testimony it took to leave a comfortable home and go to the western wilderness. They sailed with the John Forsgren Company on the "Lion," headed for Liverpool. Karen became ill during the trip, and her father died and was buried in Liverpool.

They sailed to America on the "Forest Monarch," leaving Liverpool on January 16, and landed in New Orleans. They crossed the Plains and finally reached the Salt Lake Valley, September 29, 1853, many months after leaving their homeland.

The family moved to the Woods Cross area and bought a small farm. Here Karen again took up her weaving skills to provide clothing for the family. Her life as a pioneer mother was one of sacrifice and thrift. The excellent management of Knud and Karen helped sustain the family, as well as provide passage money for several other converts to emigrate to America.

This kindly, stalwart pioneer mother died on May 10, 1873, at the home of her daughter, Ann, in Richmond, Cache County, Utah. She was sixty-nine years of age and had been a widow for eleven years.

A great posterity honor this great pioneer couple who gave up much for their religious beliefs, including their homeland, and their comfort to help develop and establish a new land-the state of Utah. We honor them.

LYDIA ANN LAKE NELSON

BIRTHDATE: 13 May 1832
Camdon, Ontario, Canada
DEATH: 14 Jan 1924
Eager, Apache Co., Arizona
PARENTS: James Lake Jr.
Philomelia Smith
PIONEER: 1850
SPOUSE: Price Williams Nelson
MARRIED: 13 Dec 1850
Ogden, Weber Co., Utah
DEATH SP: 1902
Sonora, Mexico

CHILDREN:
Edmond, 30 Oct 1851
Samantha, 28 Oct 1853
Price William, 29 Aug 1855
Lydia Ann, 12 Dec 1856
Lorana, 10 Mar 1859
Jane, 22 Mar 1861
Hyrum, 10 Jan 1863
James Mark, 12 Aug 1865
Allen David, 7 Jan 1868
Thomas George, 12 Aug 1865 (died as an infant)
Levi, 4 Apr 1872
Wilford B., 26 Apr 1874
Philomelia, 20 Feb 1876 (died as an infant)

Lydia Ann Lake was born in Camdon, Ontario, Canada, in 1832 to James and Philomelia Smith Lake.

Her ancestors, through hard work and industry, had accumulated a goodly share of life's necessities, after being expelled and burned from their homes during the American Revolution. Their ability to survive adversity and to move on, try again, was a trait characteristic of the Lake family and became a dynamic force in Lydia's life.

Lydia's parents had both been widowed, with a total of ten living children between them, when they were married to each other. Of the ten born to this union, Lydia was the sixth. She would have been less than a year old when they joined the Church of Jesus Christ of Latter-day Saints in 1833. They moved with most of the family to Kirtland, Ohio, about that time. There they built homes, planted crops and helped finish the temple during the next three years. They were again forced to leave when angry mobs rushed to ransack and burn the city there. For Lydia this was only the first in a life-long series of such events.

Her family was living near Carthage when Joseph and Hyrum were martyred and were among those Saints who crossed the Mississippi on ice during their dramatic escape from Nauvoo. She was fifteen when her family went to Missouri and worked to earn enough for their journey to Utah. She had a job in a tavern and was nearly burned to death when her clothes caught fire over the fireplace. She was miraculously healed after two Elders administered to her.

In 1850, while crossing the Plains, she met Price Nelson, her future husband, as their two companies were trying to cross the Green River. She was impressed when he jumped to rescue a mother and her child who were being washed down stream in a run-away wagon box.

Lydia and Price were married in Ogden soon after their arrival in Utah. They were married on December 13, 1850, in Ogden, Utah. Her life with Price continued on a familiar pattern as they contributed to the building up of new colonies all over the West. Their itinerary included such difficult places as San Bernardino, California; Franklin, Idaho; the Muddy Mission in Nevada, several places in southern Utah, the Missions of Arizona and the Mormon Colonies in Mexico.

Along the way, Lydia gave birth to thirteen children, and lost two at birth. Though less than five feet tall, she was a tower of strength and virtue and remained faithful to her Church.

One of her sons wrote of life on the trail, "I wonder why we did not help mother with the cooking. She made flapjacks over the coals in a frying pan, then fried bacon and made gravy while we just sat around and watched. This was our every day fare, and no food ever tasted better."

Some of their married children accompanied their parents when they went to Mexico, and stayed to raise their own families in the Mormon Colonies there. Lydia and Price had a nice home and ranch at Oaxoca, in the state of Senora, where they were living when Price took sick and died in 1902. She remained in her home until 1905, when the area was completely destroyed by flood waters, then she moved in with her children.

In 1912, when the Mormons were forced out of Mexico, she traveled to Arizona and lived with a son until her death on January 14, 1924, at the age of ninety-one.

Lydia was truly a noble woman who endured to the end, with a posterity both numerous and righteous. We honor her name.

MARGARET WHISTANCE NELSON

BIRTHDATE: 15 May 1825
Brecon, Breconshire, Wales
DEATH: 23 Sep 1904
Provo, Utah Co., Utah
PARENTS: Edward Whistance
Mary Lewis
PIONEER: 30 Sep 1353
Vincent Shurtliff Wagon Train
SPOUSE: Isaac Nelson
MARRIED: 23 Feb 1854
Provo, Utah Co., Utah
DEATH SP: 23 Feb 1894
Provo, Utah Co., Utah

CHILDREN:
Isaac Phillip, 13 Jan 1855
Elizabeth Jane, 20 Mar 1856
Margaret Anna, 13 Dec 1857
Sarah Ellen, 11 Mar 1859
John Edward, 2 Jul 1862
Mary Eliza, 13 May 1861
Frances Emily, 14 Dec 1864
Rosina, 22 Sep 1866
David Thomas, 17 May 1868
Joseph Hyrum II, Apr 1870 (died as a child)

Margaret Whistance was born in 1825 in Wales to Edward and Mary Lewis Whistance. Her parents died early, and Margaret, the youngest of three children, was raised by an uncle and aunt. After hearing the Mormon Elders, she was converted and baptized into the Church of Jesus Christ of Latter-day Saints in 1853 by Charles Tysome. She was about twenty-eight years old at the time.

She was willing to give up home and family for the gospel. Leaving behind a brother, Edward, and a sister, Mary, she came to Utah shortly after her baptism. She traveled across the Plains in a wagon train that left Keokuk, Iowa, July 13, 1853. Encountering the usual hardships of crossing the Plains, the company arrived in the Salt Lake Valley on September 30, 1853.

She met Isaac Nelson who was from Morland, Westmorland, England, and they were married in Provo, Utah, February 23, 1854. They became the parents of ten children all born in Provo.

Isaac and Margaret made their home on a corner lot in Provo, located on what is now 313 West 500 South. The home has been continuously owned by a member of the Nelson family and was still in use in 1995. The children were raised to be good Latter-day Saints, honest, law-abiding citizens, and supported the large family by farming and raising a large garden. The Nelson farm consisted of thirty acres just off the state highway in Lakeview, with another piece of land owned by the State Hospital, today.

Isaac passed away in 1894, at the age of seventy-three years. Margaret survived him by ten years, living until September 23, 1904. They are both buried in the Provo Cemetery.

They are great examples of pioneers who had great faith in their new found religion and whose lives exemplified true pioneer traits. They are honored by a great posterity.

MARY CATHERINE WELKER NELSON

BIRTHDATE: 12 Jan 1832
Madison, Jackson Co., Ohio
DEATH: 8 Dec 1920
Thatcher, Graham Co., Arizona
PARENTS: James Welker
Elizabeth Stoker
PIONEER: 31 Dec 1852 or
28 Aug 1852
Isaac Stewart Wagon Train
SPOUSE: Thomas B. Nelson
MARRIED: 27 Mar 1853
Willow Creek, Box Elder, Utah
DEATH SP: 19 Feb 1918
Thatcher, Graham Co., Arizona

CHILDREN:
Elizabeth Mary Jane, 1 Apr 1854
Thomas James, 19 Oct 1855
Charles Edmond, 23 Dec 1857
John William, 11 Aug 1860
Margaret Ann, 1 Nov 1862
Martha Emiline, 2 Oct 1865
Joseph Aaron, 1 Apr 1868
Adam Heber, 11 Jun 1870
Effie Rosina, 14 Sep 1872
Dora Rebecca, 28 Feb 1875
Hyrum Jacob, 1 Sep 1877

Mary Catherine was born in Madison, Ohio, and spent her early childhood there. She was baptized a member of the Church of Jesus Christ of Latter-day Saints in Hancock County, Illinois, in March 1844.

As a young girl, she and her family were victims of the many persecutions by the mobs as they moved about with the Saints. Her father died from broken health at Nauvoo when she was twelve years old. Her mother was left to care for six young children.

They were forced to leave Nauvoo with just enough money to get to Council Bluffs where they lived until 1852. Mary Catherine's family crossed the Plains from Illinois to Utah with the Isaac Stewart Wagon Company.

Three months after her arrival in Utah, she married Thomas Billington Nelson. They established their home in Logan, Utah, where five children were born to them. In 1864, they moved to a farm in Bloomington, Bear Lake County, Idaho. Thomas entered into plural marriage with Dortha Christina Sorenson and made a nice large house with two apartments exactly alike for each of his families.

In 1890, for the safety and protection of his families and himself, they moved to the Arizona Territory where they pioneered again and helped to build a thriving community that supported and sustained their families.

Thomas, Mary, and Dortha lived the balance of their lives in Arizona in good faith in the gospel.

Mary Catherine lived about two years past her husband and passed away just short of her eighty-eighth birthday on December 8, 1920.

MARY ELLEN MCMILLEN / MCMILLAN NELSON

BIRTHDATE: 30 Jun 1851
West Derby, England
DEATH: 5 Mar 1918
Victor, Idaho
PARENTS: Daniel McMillen
Janet Davies
PIONEER: 4 Oct 1863
Thomas E. Ricks Wagon Train
SPOUSE: Henry Thomas Nelson
MARRIED: abt 1876
DEATH SP: 15 Nov 1927
Victor, Idaho

CHILDREN:
Mary Janette, 13 Jan 1874
Phebe Hannah, 2 Mar 1877
Henry Thomas, 25 May 1878
Margaret, 7 Nov 1879
Emma Mae, 28 Jul 1881
Daniel, 13 Apr 1884
Sarah Ann, 29 Jun 1886
William, 12 Nov 1888
Joseph, 9 Jul 1890
Rose Ellen, 19 Sep 1892
Jessie Richmond, 9 Dec 1894
Jean, 10 Nov 1898

Mary Ellen joined the Church of Jesus Christ of Latter-day Saints along with her family in England. When she was twelve years old, she crossed the Plains, walking much of the way. Her parents settled in Heber, Wasatch County, Utah.

It was while Mary Ellen was in Heber, that she met and married Henry Thomas Nelson. They lived in Buysville (Now called Daniels), where all of their children were born except for her first daughter, Mary Jeanette who was born in Salt Lake City.

Most of Mary Ellen's time was taken up with the raising of her large family. She served in the Church as counselor to Mary McDonald, Relief Society President. Mary Ellen remained in Buysville for thirty years, then moved to Victor, Idaho.

Mary's husband never had the opportunity to attend school so she taught him to read and write.

Mary was an influence for good throughout her life. There was much happiness and humor in her home.

MATILDA HANSINA PETERSEN NELSON

BIRTHDATE: 19 Apr 1863/64
Aaker Landsogn, Bornholm,
Denmark
DEATH: 18 Feb 1907
Daniel, Wasatch County, Utah
PARENTS: Hans Peter Pedersen
(or Mortensen)
Christina Margrethe Christensen
PIONEER: 25 Sep 1868
John G. Holman Wagon Train
SPOUSE: Wilford Nelson
MARRIED: 1 Dec 1881
Salt Lake City, Utah
DEATH: 7 May 1933
Daniel, Wasatch County Utah

CHILDREN:
Hyrum, 16 Mar 1883
Christina Margrett, 5 Oct 1884
Matilda Ann, 12 Aug 1887
Mary Emily, 31 Mar 1890
Elfy, 2 Dec 1892
Wilford Osmond, 26 May 1895
Carl Henry, 18 Apr 1898
Caroline, 10 Sep 1901
Minnie Jenette, 9 Jul 1904
Nymphus Alma, 5 Jan 1907

Matilda was born in Denmark in 1863/64. She left Denmark for America when she was four or five years old with her mother and six-year-old sister, Caroline Pretronella, 28 May 1860. Her sister Caroline was pulled into the ocean attempting to get a bucket of water.

Matilda and her mother came to the Salt Lake Valley by wagon. Her mother became ill and died when they reached Emigration Canyon, leaving Matilda an orphan.

Sarah Tonks Duel had heard there was an orphan on the wagon train and met them at the arrival point and took Matilda home. They soon became very close. With Sarah being a frail person Matilda helped her a lot.

In 1879 they moved to Heber and then to Buysville. In Buysville she met Wilford Nelson and they married on 1 Dec 1881 in Salt Lake City, Utah. They were the parents of ten children.

Matilda loved flowers and worked very hard to have them around her home. She served as Primary President from 1901-03. Then she was called to be Relief Society Counslor. She served until her death 18 Feb 1907 at age forty-three or forty-four.

NICOLENA "LENA" CHRISTENSEN NELSON

BIRTHDATE: 23 Dec 1857
Sessing, Hjorring, Denmark
DEATH: 19 Mar 1935
Brigham City, Box Elder, Utah
PARENTS: Anders Christen
Kirstine Marie Peaersen Jensen
PIONEER: 7 Oct 1866
SPOUSE : Charles F. Nelson
MARRIED: 1 Feb 1875
Salt Lake City, Salt Lake, Utah
DEATH SP: 20 Jul 1913
Brigham City, Box Elder, Utah

CHILDREN:
Charles, 18 Jan 1887 (twin - died as an infant))
Mary, 18 Jan 1887 (twin - died as an infant)
Alphonzo Jensen, 30 Mar 1889
Lana Geska, 2 Dec 1876
Joseph Scott, 14 Aug 1892
Carlos Fredrick, 10 Apr 1879
Norman, 22 Dec 1893 (died as a child)
Clarence LeRoy, 14 Nov 1881
Bergetta Marie, 19 Jan 1885
Joseph Scott, 14 Aug 1892
Percy Lamont, 14 Sep 1895

Nicolena "Lena" Christensen's parents had joined the Church of Jesus Christ of Latter-day Saints, and Lena was abused at school because she was a Mormon. Her parents removed her from the school because of this treatment.

When she was nine years old in 1866, she came to America with her parents Kirsten Marie and Anders and her little sister, Marianne. They traveled on the sailboat, "Kenilworth," which left Hamburg, May 25, 1866, and arrived in New York City.

They traveled to Wyoming, Nebraska, and joined Captain Scott's Wagon Train which then arrived in Salt Lake Valley October 8, 1866. There had been 684 passengers on the ship crossing the ocean, and there were 300 in the company which crossed the Plains.

The Deseret News newspaper stated, "The best looking group ever to arrive." Along the way, the travel was not always pleasant, but, because of Lena's cheery disposition, she always said, "It was the happiest time of my life." Upon their arrival in Utah, this family were sent north to help settle Brigham City.

During the year, Nicolena's father was infected with tick fever and became very ill. By summer he was recovering, but was thrown from a hay wagon and killed. Thirty-nine days later, her mother gave birth to a little boy, who died less than two years later.

Being alone in a strange country with a strange language, her mother, Kirsten, and the little girls struggled to survive. With bags filled with eggs and vegetables hung on their shoulders, they walked each morning seven miles to Corinne and back to sell their produce.

Corinne was a city filled with gambling houses for the railroad men, but there was money there. Kirsten's beauty attracted the wealthy men. Nicolena prayed that her mother would not marry out of the Church.

Kirsten made her own adobe bricks and built her own home which still stands in 1995. Nicolena and Marianne helped carry and place the bricks. The girls also learned to weave and spin, but soon a knitting factory in town took their livelihood away. People urged Kirsten to remarry, and she finally did.

Nicolena was "the most remarkable and beautiful woman I ever knew," her granddaughter said. Her stepfather wanted to marry her, so he forbade her to leave the house. Nicolena had fallen love with Charles Frederick Nelson (Nielsen), so one night she stuffed her bed with pillows so that her stepfather would think she was in bed, and then she climbed out the window. Her stepfather, discovering her absence, met Charles and Nicolena at the gate with a gun. "Shoot me if you will!" shouted Charles, "but this girl is not going into that house again." In spite of the hour, President Lorenzo Snow took them into his home and gave them a recommend to be married in the Endowment House in Salt Lake City. They were married on February 1, 1875, when Nicolena was eighteen and Charles was twenty-one.

Nicolena had eleven children born to her, five did not live to maturity. On the wall of her home hung an embroidered needlework which read "God Bless Our Home." Their's was a home of faith, and love and laughter. They were a happy family.

Early in their marriage, Charles was called on a mission to herd sheep under the United Order in Brigham City. He helped build the Box Elder Tabernacle, the architectural gem in Brigham City. Most of the people there were poor at that time, but President Lorenzo Snow helped the area to prosper.

Charles was accidentally killed July 20, 1913. Nicolena was a widow for twenty-two years. Even though her phlebitis legs could hardly carry her, she did a great service in caring for others. She is remembered bending over an aching body with her little saucer of alcohol and oil warmed on the Monarch coal range. She rubbed aches away.

She took flowers daily to loved ones in the cemetery and she tearfully asked, "Who will put flowers on our graves when I am gone?"

Nicolena Nelson died March 19, 1935 at over seventy-seven years of age. Her granddaughter wrote, "She is as alive to me as if she never left. I am proud to be named for my dear Grandma Lena. What a rich heritage I have! I have always tried to live worthy of her name."

She was a great example of a brave pioneer woman who had great faith and fortitude and left a great legacy to those who have followed her.

SARAH ANN POOL NELSON

BIRTHDATE: 2 Jun 1844
Nauvoo, Hancock Co., Illinois
DEATH: 14 Jul 1925
Ogden, Weber Co., Utah
PARENTS: William Pool
Elizabeth Stockton
PIONEER: Sep 1852
Wagon Train Company
SPOUSE: James Horace Nelson
MARRIED: 1 Aug 1859
Ogden, Weber Co., Utah
DEATH SP: 27 Apr 1924
Ogden, Weber Co., Utah

CHILDREN:
James Horace, Jr., 21 May 1860
David George, 24 Nov 1862
Sarah Elizabeth, 30 Dec 1865 (died as a child)
Mary Martha, 10 Apr 1868
William Francis, 21 Sep 1871
Chester Pool, 16 Feb 1874
Roscoe Miller, 30 Mar 1876 (died as a child)
Sumner Parker, 7 Jun 1879
Maynard Elliott, 7 Jan 1882
Leland Kay, 6 Apr 1884

Saran Ann was born in 1844 in Nauvoo, Illinois. She walked nearly every step of the way from Winter Quarters and was eight years of age upon arrival in Salt Lake Valley, in September, 1852. She was baptized shortly after.

Her family remained at the original settlement for about a year, then moved to Grantsville, Tooele County, Utah, where they remained for about two years before moving to Ogden in 1855, the year of the crickets. Sarah remembered the crop shortage of the following winter and spring. Dandelions and Sego lily roots were used to stay alive. She also remembered threshing wheat by pounding and tromping. When Johnston's Army came in 1858 to put down the "Mormon Rebellion," the family moved with the rest of the Saints to a location south of Utah Lake and subsisted largely upon trout from the lake.

It was after that experience, when they returned again to Ogden, that she married James Horace Nelson on August 1, 1859. They lived by farming in the early years, then James opened the first real estate office in Ogden. Sarah Ann gave birth to ten children, two of whom died as children. James took a second wife under polygamy which was an acceptable relationship to Sarah and caused her no great distress.

After the federal government passed the anti-polygamy law in 1882, and the 1884 commission was sent to stop co-habitation, Sarah had an unusual incident. Two U.S. Marshalls came to her door demanding entrance to see if

James was cohabiting. She demanded to see their search warrant, which they did not have; so one of them tried to force his way past her in the doorway. She pushed him bodily off her porch, then pulled a picket from her fence and beat the two marshalls across their backs until they departed.

Ultimately, James had to choose to live with one family, and he decided to live where he was most needed, with the younger family. So, after 1885 Sarah became a polygamy widow. She supplemented whatever support James was able to provide by dressmaking and nursing sick people and mothers with babies. Her services as a midwife came to be in considerable demand.

Early in 1925, she became ill so her daughter, Mary, took her into her home to care for her. Sarah died there on July 14, 1925, and was buried in the Ogden City Cemetery.

Sarah Ann was truly a pioneer woman of faith and fortitude who is to be honored for her pioneering spirit and faith.

SARAH WARBY NELSON

BIRTHDATE: 5 Mar 1854
Raymond Terrace, NSW, Australia
DEATH: 3 Jun 1887
Beaver, Beaver Co., Utah
PARENTS: James Warby
Mary Blanch Warby
PIONEER: 1866 Wagon Train
SPOUSE: Daniel M. Nelson
MARRIED: 8 Oct 1876
Beaver, Beaver Co., Utah
DEATH SP: 3 Jun 1932

CHILDREN:
Daniel Edward, 27 Jul 1877
Sarah Ann, 23 Jan 1879
Mary Jane, 22 Feb 1881
William L. James, 25 Jan 1883
Harvey Eddy, 14 Feb 1885
Ray, 14 Dec 1886 (died as a child)

Sarah was born March 5, 1854, in Raymond Terrace, NSW, Australia to James and Mary Blanch Warby. Her mother had left England when nine years of age bound for Australia. While there she met and married James Blanch who had also come from England. They were converted to the Gospel while living there. Sarah was just seventeen days old when her family left Australia for America under the supervision of Elder Hyde. They landed in San Pedro, California, after an arduous crossing of eighty-one days. They then went to the Mormon community of San Bernardino.

In the Spring of 1857, with three other families, they drove their wagons to the settlement of Beaver, as the first four families to settle there. The settlement grew rapidly.

Among the new arrivals was a tall, Scottish lad named Daniel Morgan Nelson. He had been born in St. Louis, had walked across the Plains as his parents pulled a handcart. This family then traveled to Beaver where Daniel's father began a shingle mill.

Sarah married Daniel Morgan Nelson, October 8, 1876, in Beaver and in January, 1877, they were sealed in the St. George Temple by Erastus Snow.

Sarah bore two daughters and four sons, the last one died a few days after Sarah. Sarah suffered a lingering illness during and after her last pregnancy. In the six months previous to her death, her younger sister, Matilda, came to assist in caring for her, her baby and her five growing children.

Sarah passed away June 3, 1887 in Beaver, Utah. A brave pioneer woman who had experienced thirty-three years of pioneering new places and new lands.

Following Sarah's death, Daniel proposed marriage to Matilda and she accepted. They were married, September 30, 1857, in Beaver.

In 1896, Daniel led a group of Beaver settlers to Lucern Valley. The family lived in a small dugout the first winter, but a two-room log house the next. Eventually he built a larger house for his family of twelve children. This home became the center of the social life for the citizens of Manila.

Daniel and Matilda moved to Vernal, after the children were married. Daniel died in June, 1932, and Matilda followed December 27, 1932, leaving a large posterity who honor both Sarah and Matilda Warby Nelson and Daniel their spouse.

SARAH ANN RICHMOND NELSON

BIRTHDATE: 20 Nov 1829
Bettsford, Lester, England
DEATH: 4 Sep 1902
Buysville, Wasatch Co., Utah
PARENTS: Thomas Richmond
Sarah Burrows / Burrah
PIONEER: 1851
Wagon Train Company
SPOUSE: Henry Nelson
MARRIED: 16 May 1848
Nauvoo, Hancock Co., Illinois
DEATH SP: 12 Sep 1897
Buysville, Wasatch Co., Utah

CHILDREN:
Henry Thomas, 28 Oct 1850
Elizabeth Ann (Gordon), 29 Feb 1852
Jesse Richmond, 29 Dec 1853
William Richard, 29 Mar 1856
Wilford, 12 May 1858
Sarah Alice (Baird), 2 Dec 1859
Marcy Jane (Moss), 1 Dec 1861
Joseph Everett, 26 Aug 1863
Margaret (Vincent), 16 May 1865

Emma, 11 Jan 1867
John Benjamin, 14 Sep 1868
Hyrum, 20 Jan 1870
Emily (Gappmayer), 29 Dec 1871

Sarah Ann, along with the rest of her family, joined the Church of Jesus Christ of Latter-day Saints in June of 1839. She was ten years old. She could relate many interesting stories of violence, privations and other dangers peculiar to the following of the Prophet Joseph Smith and Brigham Young.

She knew the Prophet well and remembered when he organized the Relief Society, of which she attended. Sarah Ann was a faithful member of the Relief Society all of her life. Sarah Ann was sealed to her husband in Salt Lake City on September 6, 1852 with Heber C. Kimball officiating.

Originally, Sarah Ann settled in Provo and then fourteen years later they moved to Heber City in Wasatch County, Utah. From Heber, in 1878, Sarah Ann and her family moved to Buysville, Utah

She helped in the fields fighting the crickets. Almost at the point of exhaustion, she knelt in the fields with Henry and the others and prayed to God for assistance. He answered their prayers by sending the seagulls.

Her mother-in-law lived with her for many years. When she passed away a newspaper article headlined, "A well known and highly respected resident of Buysville, Sarah Ann Nelson, has passed away."

Sarah Ann was so kind. A mother dropped two of her girls off for her to watch and the mother never came back. She raised these two girls like her own. She also raised a granddaughter for several years.

SUSANNAH CUTLER NELSON

BIRTHDATE: 27 Aug 1844
Nauvoo, Hancock Co., Illinois
DEATH: 21 Sep 1909
Fish Haven, Idaho
PARENTS: Harmon Cutler
Lucy Ann Pettegrew
PIONEER: Sep 1852
Harmon Cutler Co. Wagon Train
SPOUSE: John Lowry Nelson
MARRIED: 17 Nov 1860
DEATH SP: 21 Mar 1906
Fish Haven, Idaho

CHILDREN:
Lydia Ann, 11 Sep 1861
Susannah, 12 May 1863
Jeannette, 4 Mar 1865
John Lyman, 10 Jan 1867
Hyrum Alden, 15 Feb 1871
David Frederick, 16 Dec 1873
Eva Bertha, 10 Jan 1876 (died at age 4)
Ida Suetha, 30 Sep 1880
Elsie Mina, 8 Sep 1883

Effie Estelle, 10 Jun 1885
Veda, 29 Aug 1887

Susannah's parents were members of the Church of Jesus Christ of Latter-day Saints who suffered greatly at the hands of the persecutors of the Mormons until they were forced to leave Nauvoo. Her father, who was a wagon maker by trade, was called by Brigham Young to assist companies of Saints in their journey across the Plains. He was assigned to be captain of a group of 262 Saints with sixty-three wagons.

Near Fort Laramie, they were attacked by Indians and all except five horses were stolen. They had to continue with oxen. Susannah was eight years old when they arrived in the Salt Lake Valley in September, 1852.

When Susannah was sixteen years old, she married a good looking Danish immigrant named John Lowry Nelson on November 17, 1860. They rented a home on the John Taylor Farm in the Sugar House Ward where they began their family.

John's brother had been called to settle at Fish Haven. They welcomed John and Susannah's family to join them. They homesteaded land at Bear Lake, clearing the land, building their homes, and working hard to take care of their families. Susannah was a very ambitious and energetic woman who worked hard and loved her family.

Susannah passed away on September 21, 1909, and is buried at the Fish Haven Cemetery, Bear Lake County, Idaho.

ELIZABETH DUNN NERDIN

BIRTHDATE: 24 Sep 1814
St. Giles, Rowley Regis, England
DEATH: 2 Nov 1889
Pleasant Grove, Utah Co., Utah
PARENTS: Joseph Dunn
Phebe Watchorn
PIONEER: 15 Sep 1853
Moses Clawson's Wagon Train
SPOUSE: Thomas Nerdin
MARRIED: 22 Oct 1837
New Town, Dudley Parish,
Worchestershire, England
DEATH SP: 21 Jul 1885

CHILDREN:
Mary Ann, 23 Sep 1838
George, 14 Aug 1840
Harriet, 12 Nov 1841
William, 1 Feb 1843
Thomas, 10 Jan 1845
Joseph, 25 Mar 1847
Martha, 3 Dec 1849
Enoch, 1 Jan 1851
Caroline, 22 Jun 1853
Phebe, 27 Mar 1855
John Heber, 12 Jul 1857
Elizabeth Charlotte, 29 Oct 1860

Elizabeth was born in St. Giles, Rowley Regis, Staffordshire, England, 1814. She married Thomas Nerdin October 22, 1837 in New Town, Worcestershire, England. They joined the Church of Jesus Christ of Latter-day Saints in Prielg Hill, Worcestershire and decided to join the Saints in Utah.

They sailed from Liverpool under the Ten Pound Plan on the vessel, "Horizon" or "Swanton" and landed in New Orleans. They went to Winter Quarters, then on to St. Clair, Missouri. They lived there for four years with much mob violence and persecution. They left for Utah in June, 1853, in Captain Moses Clawson's Wagon Company. They walked most of the way and suffered many hardships.

Elizabeth's one-room log house was later donated as a school house. She and Thomas donated to the city of Pleasant Grove both the old and the first section of the present city cemetery.

Elizabeth passed away in November, 1889, and is buried next to her husband.

ELEANOR STEVENS TREWELLA NESLEN

No Photo Available

BIRTHDATE: 12 Mar 1833
Hale, Cornwall, England
DEATH: 5 Apr 1870
Salt Lake City, Salt Lake, Utah
PARENTS: Jacob Stevens
Eliza Simons
PIONEER: 15 Oct 1859
Robert F. Neslen Wagon Train
SPOUSE I: John Trewella
(Trewhela-Trewheel)
MARRIED: 25 Dec 1853
DEATH SP: 1856

CHILD:
Mary Elizabeth, 3 Oct 1854

SPOUSE II: Robert Francis Neslen
MARRIED: 15 Mar 1859 Scotland
DEATH SP: Not given

CHILDREN:
Eleanore Stevens (chr.), 6 Jul 1860
Robert Francis, 10 Jul 1862 (died as a child)
Samuel Stevens, 4 May 1864
Florence, 6 Apr 1866
Richard Franklin, 29 Feb l868 (stillborn)
Richard Franklin, 22 Jun 1869

Eleanor Stevens was born March 12, 1833 in Hale, Cornwall, England to Jacob and Eliza Symons Stevens. She was born of goodly parents and was raised in the Church of Jesus Christ of Latter-day Saints.

She is listed as first being married to a John Trewolla on Christmas Day in 1853. One daughter was born to this union. John died in 1856.

Eleanor emigrated to Utah on the ship "William Tappscott," a few months after her marriage to Robert Francis Neslen. He was apparently on a mission to Scotland in 1859. Her husband was the captain of the company of Saints on that ship and was also the captain of the ox-team with which Eleanor traveled to Utah.

They arrived in the Salt Lake Valley on 15 October, 1859, and lived in Salt Lake City the remainder of their lives. Eleanor gave birth to seven children, but one was stillborn, and two died at two years of age. The other four children were talented and grew to maturity and raised a noble posterity. Eleanor was well loved, talented in the arts, and provided for her family with grace and distinction.

Eleanor passed away on April 5, 1870, leaving children from under one year in age to almost ten years of age. Her parents had also emigrated to Utah, and they both lived eight years longer than Eleanor.

Eleanor Neslen was an exemplary pioneer woman of great faith and fortitude and left a great heritage to those who have followed, even though she was just over thirty-seven years of age at her death.

EUNICE FRANCIS NESLEN

BIRTHDATE: 8 Jun 1808
Lowestoft, Suffolk, England
DEATH: 22 Feb 1891
Salt Lake City, Salt Lake, Utah
PARENTS: Robert Francis
Rachel Burgess
PIONEER: 24 Sep 1853
Claudius Spencer Wagon Train
SPOUSE: Samuel Neslen
MARRIED: 13 Jul 1829
Lowestoft, Suffolk, England
DEATH SP: 29 Aug 1887
Salt Lake City, Salt Lake, Utah

CHILDREN:
Susanah, 13 Sep 1830
Samuel, 30 Sep 1831
Robert, 10 Oct 1832
Eunice, 13 Jan 1834 (died age 2)
Elizabeth Burgess, 4 Jun 1835
Ester, 3 May 1837
Eunice, 15 Jul 1838
Phoebe, 27 Sep 1839
William, 5 Jan 1841
Hannah Rebecca, 1 Jan 1844

Eunice was reared from childhood as a Wesleyan Methodist in Lowestoft, England. She married Samuel Neslen on July 13, 1829, at Lowestoft, Suffolk, England.

They had been married twenty years and had ten children when Samuel, at age forty-two, was baptized into the Church of Jesus Christ of Latter-day Saints in 1849. He was a prominent carpenter, contractor, and a Methodist minister. Eunice was not baptized until three years later.

By November, 1852, their whole family had become members of the Church.

On January 17, 1853, they left London, England in the sailing vessel, "Golconda." After heavy storms at sea, they arrived at New Orleans on April 1, 1853. They traveled up the Mississippi and Missouri Rivers by Steamboat. Samuel paid the fare for forty-three other persons in addition to his own family. They crossed the Plains in the Claudius V. Spencer Wagon Company and arrived in the Great Salt Lake Valley on September 24, 1853.

The family lived in a log cabin while Samuel was building an eight-room adobe house at the corner of A Street and South Temple. Samuel and Eunice received their endowments and were sealed on November 18, 1856, in the Old Endowment House.

In the exodus of the Saints, Samuel moved his family to Springville. They learned their son, Samuel, died of consumption in Williamsburg, New York, in 1858, as he was returning from a mission. They moved back to Salt Lake City after the Johnston's Army threat subsided.

Eunice was very supportive of her husband in his endeavors as missionary and teacher. She helped to raise a very fine family.

WILHELMINA JACOBSEN NESSEN

No Photo Available

BIRTHDATE: 24 Jan 1835
Fredericia, Vejle, Denmark
DEATH: 9 Mar 1910
Smithfield, Cache Co., Utah
PARENTS: Neils Peder Jacobsen
Julie Henriette Thiessen
PIONEER: 1863 Wagon Train
SPOUSE: Jens James Nessen
MARRIED: 27 Sep 1863
DEATH SP: 27 Sep 1907
Logan, Cache Co., Utah

CHILDREN:
James "Jens," 4 Nov 1864 (died as an infant)
Alma, 11 Nov 1865 (died as a child)
Nephi, 28 Aug 1867
Wilhelmina, 4 Oct 1869
Julia, 29 Feb 1872
Thomas. 28 May 1874

Wilhelmina Jacobsen was born in 1835 in Denmark. She was baptized February 20, 1859, when she was fourteen years of age. She came to New York in 1862, on her way to Utah. It was at this time that she met her future husband, who helped to bring her to Utah. They left New York in 1863, traveled by ox-team and arrived in the Salt Lake Valley by September, 1862.

Wilhelmina married Jens James Nessen September 27, 1863, in Logan, Utah. They received their endowments December 13, 1866, and were sealed the same day. They

made their home in Logan, Utah. Wilhelmina gave birth to six children.

There were Indians who lived in the same area as the Nessens, and they were friendly with Wilhelmina's children. This family later homesteaded a farm in Newton, Utah, where they raised sheep, cows, chickens and did general farming.

Jens passed away in 1907 in Logan. Wilhelmina passed away on March 9, 1910, two years after Jens. She was seventy-four years of age when she died. They are buried in Logan, Utah.

They were brave pioneers of Utah who experienced all the hardships and trials of leaving their homelands and coming to the new world for their religious beliefs; great pioneers of faith and fortitude who had experienced forty-four years of marriage on the frontier of the West.

ANN LYDIA WEST NEVILLE

BIRTHDATE: 1 May 1850
Stoke, Middlesex, England
DEATH: 14 Jul 1930
Byron, Big Horn Co., Wyoming
PARENTS: Charles Henry John
Eliza Dangerfield West
PIONEER: 1 Oct 1856
Wagon Train Company
SPOUSE: Joseph Hyrum Neville
MARRIED: 5 May 1873
Salt Lake City, Salt Lake, Utah
DEATH SP: 16 Feb 1924
Byron, Big Horn Co., Wyoming

CHILDREN:
Joseph William, 11 Jan 1876
Eliza Amanda, 29 Apr 1878
Annie May, 19 Oct 1880 (died as a child)
Charles Lafayette, 27 Feb 1883 (died as a child)
Nora Jessie, 11 Oct 1885
Leo Jennings, 8 Oct 1887
Daniel West, 10 Feb 1890
Jabez Edward, 26 Jan 1892
Ralph Milton, 21 May 1895
Solon James, 16 Sep 1898

Ann Lydia West was born in 1850 in England to Charles and Eliza West. When she was six years of age, she sailed with her sister Caroline who was about ten, from Liverpool on the ship, "William Tappscott," which landed in New York. She traveled in the wagon train of John Banks, and walked most of the way across the Plains. She and her sister were under the care of a Brother King, his wife, mother and sister. The wife and mother died on the journey, and the sister did not care for the girls.

When they arrived in the Salt Lake Valley, October 1, 1856, a Bishop William Miller took the girls into his home in Provo. His first wife cared for Caroline, and the second wife, Sarah, cared for Annie as if she were her own. The parents of Ann and Caroline arrived a year later from England, and the family moved into a one-room adobe house with only a sea chest for a table, one chair, a bake skillet, some boxes and their bedding.

They remained in Provo for awhile, then they moved to the Salt Lake Valley near the Jordan River. Her father worked for Brigham Young and got tithing for pay. She walked fourteen blocks carrying things home for the family. Ann learned to read when they moved into the 6th Ward, and then to the 11th Ward where an uncle lived.

On May 5, 1873, Ann was married to Joseph Hyrum Neville in Salt Lake City, Utah. They first moved north to Woodruff, where most of their children were born. For a short time they lived in Bountiful, and then Brigham Young called them to help settle the Big Horn Country in Wyoming, so they settled there, where they remained the rest of their lives. Ann gave birth to ten children, two died as children.

Ann Lydia West Neville was a talented singer. She and her sister earned extra food as they traveled to America on the ship, and from a teamster while they crossed the Plains by singing for them. She sang in choirs all of her life, and was in productions at the Salt Lake Theater as a young lady. She later served as Primary President for fourteen years, and then as Relief Society chorister, and as a Sunday School teacher for twenty-five years, then in the YWMIA, and finally as Relief Society President. She knew how to care for the sick, and to attend women at childbirth, and was called to do so often. She had a strong testimony of the Gospel, and had a great love for her family, which motivated and sustained her during her lifetime.

Ann's husband, Joseph, passed away in 1924, in Byron, Big Horn County, Wyoming. Ann passed away, July 14, 1930, six years later at the age of about eighty years.

Coming to Utah at the age of six years, Ann Neville experienced much of the development of the Western United States. She was continuously active in the Church as long as she lived. She was a true, faithful pioneer woman who contributed much during her lifetime.

RACHEL JENNINGS NEVILLE

BIRTHDATE: 7 Jun 1809
Sherborne, Hampshire, England
DEATH: 22 Sep 1902
Woodruff, Rich Co., Utah
PARENTS: William Jennings
Hannah Moss
PIONEER: 15 Sep 1866
SPOUSE: William Neville (Stiff)
MARRIED: 27 Sep 1826
DEATH SP: 9 Sep 1880
Woodruff, Rich Co., Utah

CHILDREN:
Elizabeth, 2 Nov 1828
Sarah, 27 Feb 1831
Rachel, 3 Sep 1833
William, 20 Sep 1836
Anne, 19 Mar 1839
Charles, 16 Jul 1841
George, 19 May 1844
John, 13 Jan 1847
James, 28 Nov 1849
Joseph Hyrum, 31 Aug 1851

Rachel Jennings was born in England in 1809. She married William Neville in England, and they became the parents of ten children. William was also known as William Stiff, but Rachel and her children generally went by the name of Neville.

The family left England in 1866 on a sailing vessel with 359 Saints. They landed in New York, June 11, 1866, and came across the Plains by ox-team and handcart.

They reached the Salt Lake Valley, September 15, 1866, and settled in Davis County. In 1871, they moved to Woodruff, Rich County, Utah, where they lived the remainder of their lives.

William passed away in September, 1880, and Rachel passed away on September 22, 1902, both in Woodruff, Rich County, Utah.

MARIA LOUISA ROBERTS NEWELL

BIRTHDATE: 11 Nov 1829
Montesuma Pike Co., Illinois
DEATH: 15 Sep 1904
Provo, Utah Co., Utah
PARENTS: Horace Roberts
Harriet McEvers
PIONEER: 7 Oct 1852
Wagon Train Company
SPOUSE: Elliot Alfred Newell
MARRIED: 4 May 1851
Council Bluffs, Iowa
DEATH SP: 14 Jan 1893
Provo, Utah Co., Utah

CHILDREN:
Luella Isola, 2 Apr 1852
Elliot Alfred Jr., 7 Jul 1853
Arthur Pembrose, 12 Oct 1854
Myron Clark, 26 Sep 1856
Cealy, 26 Apr 1859
Charles Ephraim, (chr.) 6 Feb 1860
Ida Olive, (chr.) 23 Oct 1862
Frank Ernest, 21 Jun 1864
Maria Louisa, 29 Feb 1867
Lucy Edith, 25 Apr 1871
George, 8 Nov 1872 (died as an infant)

Maria Louisa was born in 1829 in Illinois. Maria was about eight years old when she, her mother, and her father were baptized in the Church of Jesus Christ of Latter-day

Saints. Because of their conversions, they were driven from their homeland their property was taken from them in Ripley, Illinois.

In February, 1838, the family of mother, father, seven children and a wagon driver traveled in one wagon to Nauvoo. The Prophet Joseph Smith advised them to build a pottery and make crockery for the Saints, which they did.

Maria said, "Indeed they were dark and trying times. I saw Joseph and Hyrum after their martyrdom in their coffins with their wounds. We were forced to leave our home and go into strange lands among strangers and seek a home and subsistence upon the extreme borders of civilization with nothing to recommend us to the charities of the frontiersmen or the savage Indian except the good Spirit or influence we carried with us." They settled in Council Bluffs after being driven from Nauvoo, after the temple had been built.

Maria met and married Elliot Alfred Newell in 1851. They left for the Salt Lake Valley, June 6, 1852, in a wagon with a team of oxen. Elliot had the use of one hand only (due to felons), so Maria had to yoke and unyoke the cattle and drive them a great part of the way. They arrived October 7, 1852.

Maria endured many hardships which continued after their arrival in Utah. She cared for her family while Elliot was away defending the Saints against Johnston's Army, and again when he was called to southern Utah to protect the Saints from hostile Indians, and later when called to settle in Provo, and when Elliot served a mission in his native state of New York.

Maria and Elliot were always faithful, humble servants of the Lord. They participated actively in Church and community activities in Provo.

Maria was selected to be the main speaker at the celebration of the 50th anniversary of the organization of the Relief Society on March 17, 1892. The following is taken from her speech at that time.

"After 50 years, we are only now recovering from long years of toil, hardships, and trials that have taken from us many of our strongest pillars, our brightest stars and most noble minds. Many times it appeared as though we were adrift upon an ocean of trouble without a landmark to steer to, but in our darkest hours, we sought refuge in our Heavenly Father's care. He had heard the cries of His Saints, through His aid we were enabled to surmount the greatest obstacles that at times almost overpowered us. Our hearts should swell with gratitude this day that we are permitted to assemble under so favorable circumstances to commemorate so great an event as occurred 50 years ago today." (Her speech in its entirety is in the DUP historical department.)

Maria Louisa Roberts Newell was a great pioneer woman who experienced first hand the early history of the Saints in Nauvoo, and continued to participate to a great extent in the history of Utah. She passed away, September 15, 1904, in Provo, Utah, at almost seventy-five years old. Elliot Alfred Newell had died January 14, 1893, ten years prior, also in Provo. We honor them for their great faith and fortitude.

OLIVE COMSTOCK NEWELL

No Photo Available

BIRTHDATE: 1808/1809
Williamstown, Oswego, New York
DEATH: Feb 1846
West of Mississippi River
PARENTS: Thomas Comstock
Olive Hamilton Comstock
PIONEER: died on the way
SPOUSE: Almon Newell
MARRIED: 1829
DEATH SP: 1887
Mona, Sanpete County, Utah

CHILDREN:
Elliot Alfred, 1830
Orris Comstock, 1834
Cealy, about 1838
Sarah Olive, 1844

Olive Comstock was born 1808 or 1809 in Williamstown, Oswego, New York. Her parents were Thomas Comstock born 7 May 1775 in Smithfield, Rhode Island and her mother Olive Hamilton Comstock born 13 October 1781 in Williamstown, New York.

Olive Comstock married Almon Newell in about 1829. He was born 28 June 1800 in Amboy Otsego, New York. His parents were Moses Newell and Mahitable Griffin Newell of Otsego, New York.

In 1835 near Amboy, New York they heard of and joined the Church. Taken from their history, "We have been unable to trace the route they took to Nauvoo, Illinois, we can only imagine they followed the trails which were prescribed by the Prophet, going by wagon train whenever necessary, or using the river boats as often as possible. We know the journey was very hazardous and certainly uncomfortable. They enjoyed a very short time of peace and rest before the mobs came in and drove them out of their homes. They were forced to cross the Mississippi River in the bitter cold of February, and find what shelter they could on the other side. It was during this trying time that Olive died, 1845-46. We have no record of the cause, but many of the pioneers had pneumonia and many others cholera."

Almon was left homeless and alone to care for their three children. He married a widow, Rachel Bunn Lundy Jerman with two children Daniel and James Alonzo Jerman. From this marriage a son, Geraldus Newell, was born.

Almon Newell arrived in the Salt Lake Valley in 1851 or 1852. Records show him a member with his family in the Provo Second Ward in 1852. He died 1887 at Mona, Sanpete, Utah.

RACHEL BUNN LUNDY JERMAN NEWELL

No
Photo
Available

BIRTHDATE: 5 Jun 1808
Warren, New Jersey
DEATH: After 1852
Utah
PARENTS: Jesse Lundy
Phoebe Bunn
PIONEER: 1851/52
SPOUSE I: James A. Jerman
MARRIED: abt 1843
DEATH SP: abt 1846/47

CHILDREN:
Daniel Smith, 13 Jul 1844
James Alonzo, 16 Apr 1847

SPOUSE II: Almon Newell
MARRIED: abt 1848
DEATH SP: 29 May 1878
Mona, Sanpete Co., Utah

CHILD:
Geraldus, 1 Jun 1849

Rachel was born in 1808 in Warren, New Jersey. She married James Alonzo Jerman in about 1843 and they had two sons, Daniel and James Alonzo. James died from causes unknown.

Rachel then married Almon Newell in about 1848 in Iowa. Almon's first wife, Olive Comstock, died leaving three children for Almon to care for. She had died from cholera or pneumonia. These two tragedies led to the marriage between Rachel and Almon.

The two combined families crossed the Plains and endured all the hardships from Iowa to the Salt Lake Valley. Their exact arrival date is not recorded, but the Church records of the families, along with the new son born to them are listed as being members in the Provo Second Ward lists of 1852.

This family lived in Provo for a short time, and then moved to Mona, Juab County, Utah.

"Pioneering was difficult in any area and we can assume that Mona was no exception. Almon probably built the typical log cabin for their first dwelling. This could be constructed quickly, using available materials in the area. The thick log walls and sod roof were nice and warm in the winter and were a special blessing in the summer as insulation against the hot desert sun and wind. Almon and Geraldus died in tragic deaths in the Mammoth Utah mine. It seems that Geraldus got caught in the mine cage. His father, Almon, tried to pry the cage to free his son, but he was impaled on the shovel handle and both of them died on May 29, 1878. They were both buried in the Mona City Cemetery." (excerpt from a history written about them)

The date of Rachel's death is unknown.

They were great pioneers who suffered great losses but who carried on in the face of much tribulation.

ELIZABETH HUGHES NEWMAN

No
Photo
Available

BIRTHDATE: 16 Sep 1811
Alrewas, Staffordshire, England
DEATH: 4 Jun 1906
Holladay, Salt Lake Co., Utah
PARENTS: Joseph Hughes
Ann Partridge
PIONEER: 1853
Claudius Spencer Wagon Train
SPOUSE: Joseph Newman
MARRIED: 27 Oct 1834
Wolverhampton, England
DEATH SP: 21 Jul 1877
Salt Lake City, Salt Lake, Utah

CHILDREN:
Samuel, 25 Dec 1836
John, 27 Jan 1838
Ann Elizabeth, 29 Jun 1840
William Hughes, 21 Jul 1842
Joseph Partridge, 20 Feb 1845
James, 4 Apr 1847
Thomas Samuel, 8 May 1852
Elizabeth Ann, 6 Apr 1863
(Stepdaughter Joseph Newman's divorced wife-Elizabeth Payne)

Elizabeth Hughes was born in 1811 in England. She married Joseph Newman on October 27, 1834 in the "Old Church," Wolverhampton, England.

Elizabeth and her family landed in the United States of America on May 8, 1853, the day their son, Thomas, was one year old. They emigrated to Utah with the Spencer Company. They stayed in Salt Lake City for a few weeks and then moved near the mouth of Big Cottonwood Canyon, on a country road near 62nd south and Hillsden Drive. They built a log cabin, raised a good garden, and some very fine green onions.

One day the Indians came begging. Elizabeth gave them some food and all turned to go, but one saw the green onions growing in the garden and demanded some of them. He was told the onions were too small to pull, and he would have to wait until they were larger. The Indian began to be nasty about it, and was going to pick them himself. Elizabeth picked up the long bread knife and went after him telling him to leave the onions alone and go on with the other Indians. They were all surprised that this little five foot tall, 100 pound woman would threaten such a big man. They told their chief about it and he came the next day to tell her she was a brave woman. After that he brought their next Indian baby to her to be named, and Elizabeth named her Phoebe. The Indians continued to bring Phoebe to visit the Newmans every year.

Elizabeth and Joseph moved to a home on Fourth South in Salt Lake City shortly before Joseph passed away, July 21, 1877. After his death, Elizabeth made her home with her sons, Joseph, then James and Thomas. She assisted her daughters-in-law by peeling apples, preparing freestone peaches for drying and with any other work she could sit to do.

Elizabeth would tell stories of her life in England. When her granddaughter asked her why she was so old, she answered that she was old because she always honored her father and mother.

Elizabeth passed away at her son, James', home June 4, 1907, at the age of ninety-four years, eight months. She is buried beside her husband in the Salt Lake City Cemetery; a great pioneer woman of faith and fortitude.

HANNAH SELLEY NEWMAN

BIRTHDATE: 20 Apr 1860
North Moulton, England
DEATH: 24 Apr 1917
Salt Lake City, Salt Lake, Utah
PARENTS: William Selley
Hannah Lake
PIONEER: 25 Sep 1866
SPOUSE: Stephen J. Newman
(a.k.a. Stephen James Newman)
MARRIED: 27 Dec 1877
Salt Lake, Endowment House
DEATH SP:

CHILDREN:
Mary Emily, 2 Jun 1879 (died as an infant)
Sarah Martha (Twitchell), 8 Jan 1881
Hannah Bell (Emery), 1 Apr 1883
Stephen Burton, 11 Dec 1891
Wendell Allan, 15 Mar 1893
Lucy, 31 May 1896
Lyle Jespersen, 9 Mar 1900

When Hannah was six years old, her family left England on the sailing vessel, "Caroline" on Saturday, May 5, 1866, under the Presidency of Samuel H. Hill. Her family, her grandparents were emigrating to America along with 339 members of the Church of Jesus Christ of Latter-day Saints or Mormons. They landed in New York City, June 11, 1866, after being on the water for thirty-eight days.

Part of the journey from New York to the Missouri River was made in cattle cars with planks for seats; the last part of the journey on the river was by steamboat. Under Captain John D. Holladay, with ox-teams, they traveled across the prairies following the 'Oregon Trail' to Fort Laramie. From there they crossed hill and stream to the bridge. The Mormon immigrants of 1847 had built a ferry near Casper, Wyoming. They traveled to Devil's Gate, to the Sweetwater where they left the Oregon Trail and then followed the Mormon Pioneer Trail. They reached Echo Canyon, went over the mountain through Parley's Canyon where they entered the Salt Lake Valley on Saturday, September 25, 1866, a sixty-nine day journey.

In Hannah's own words, "Our family left London, England 5 May 1866, with 389 Saints under the presidency of Samuel H. Hill, sailing on the ship 'Caroline' and arrived in New York 11 Jun 1866. We reached Salt Lake City on the 25th day of Sep 1866. After arriving in Salt Lake City, my father, William Selley, worked for Phillip Pugsley at his tannery and we lived in one his houses. It was an adobe house with one large room in front and a slope at the back. The slope was decaying and the adobe was full of holes so we had but one large room to live in. We had a large box that held all we owned which was used for a table. We did not have chairs to sit on and our bedding was rolled in canvas on the floor. Soon after, mother bought a bedstead but it took a long time to save the $25.00 which it cost. Living expenses were high and wages low. Rent was $6.00 a month, flour $6.00 a 100 weight and father earned but two dollars a day. We purchased a tiny cook stove that was brought in by ox team. After the death of Mr. Pugsley in March 1873, the tannery was closed down and we moved. I was 13 and went to work, doing housework and taking care of children for a small wage. I cannot remember just when I met my husband. It must have been when I was sixteen. I was married on the 27th of December, 1877, at the age of 17 to Stephen Jackson Newman. We were married in the Endowment House at Salt Lake City, Utah, by Daniel H. Wells. The morning of our wedding we had to walk through a heavy snow storm to be at the Endowment House by seven o'clock."

"Our first home was only three rooms, one finished. . . We had a hundred pounds of flour, a load of wood, a cow, a small pig and two chickens. My husband had gotten the cow in exchange for labor. It proved to be a poor cow, which might have been the reason for the willingness to get rid of it. Our first winter was difficult, but we managed. When work began to open up in the spring, my husband got a job working in the Assembly Hall. One day when he was getting in the wagon, the horses started up suddenly and threw him to the ground. He was laid up for some time . . . On June 2, 1879, our first baby was born. I was very ill and my grandmother and aunt took care of Mary Emily, but she died two months later. My sickness kept me in bed and helpless for two months . . . I had seven children all together."

Hannah Newman participated with the Daughters of the Utah Pioneers. She was the Chaplain of her camp. Those in her camp said of her, "We have been thrilled many times as she has revealed in her prayers her love of the Gospel and we will cherish always this faith, especially when she would say 'God is good'!"

In May, 1942, she was presented at the County Camp Meeting and gave a short talk on her life as a pioneer. She said, "I do not think my life as a pioneer was one of hardship because I was always happy to be here in Utah with the Latter-day Saints."

When Hannah Newman passed away it was said of her, "In as much as her work was finished and she has been called home, we are sure she is being welcomed, not only by her loved ones, but by that immortal band of Pioneers who have preceded her." Another spoke how she directed her home--"how she influenced her children for good, how she loved them and how she bore testimony time and time again with deepest feeling and with sweetness of disposition and soul to the gospel of Jesus Christ. . . . God doesn't make any better people than the children of Sister Newman." Her children were always raised as true sons and true daughters of God. Another said, "It was a pleasure to know Sister Newman and her family. She was so clean and so precise. I looked upon her as I looked upon my mother-one to be respected, revered and cherished."

Hannah Newman passed away April 24, 1917 in Salt Lake City, Utah. She was truly a great pioneer woman of faith, fortitude and endurance as she experienced life in the United States from the age of six years to fifty-nine in the new area of the West-the territory and state of Utah. She passed to those who have followed a great heritage, one to be admired and followed.

MARIA LOUISA PENN NEWMAN

BIRTHDATE: 10 Jul 1829
London, Middlesex, England
DEATH: 15 May 1902
PARENTS: John Penn
Hannah Brookwell
PIONEER: 13 Dec 1856
John A. Hunt Co. Wagon Train
SPOUSE: Henry J. Newman
MARRIED: 30 Mar 1851
St. Giles Parish, Middlesex,
London, England
DEATH SP: 23 Dec 1888
Ogden, Weber Co., Utah

CHILDREN:
Maria Louisa, 5 Jan 1852
Henry James, 22 Jul 1853
Priscilla Penn, 28 Feb 1855
Hannah, 13 Nov 1856 (died day of birth)
Deseret Lincoln, 11 Mar 1858
Emily Jane, 30 Nov 1860
Annie Louvena, 18 Aug 1863 (twin)
Brigham Penn, 18 Aug 1863 (twin)
Heber John, 21 Dec 1865
Hannah Elizabeth, 20 Apr 1868
William Edward, 22 Mar 1871
Ida Josephine, 20 Nov 1873

Maria Louisa was the youngest of seventeen children in her family. Although she was a sickly child, she thrived because of gentle care. Every advantage was given her including a good education.

She married Henry James Newman who was a member of the Church of Jesus Christ of Latter-day Saints and soon Maria Louisa became converted and was baptized. They were both disowned by their parents for joining the Mormons.

They had three children before they were able to join the Saints. As they were preparing for their journey to America, Henry tried to persuade Maria Louisa to purchase a bolt of silk so she could have a lovely new dress in the new country. They returned to the store three times to look at the cloth, but Maria Louisa opted instead for a bolt of warm Welsh Flannel.

In 1856, they left England on the ship, "Horizon." While on the ship, Maria Louisa made everyone in the family some coveralls which had long arms and legs with drawstrings that closed over their hands and feet. When they landed in Boston, the family traveled by rail to Iowa City where they joined the John A. Hunt Wagon Company which was following behind the Edward Martin Handcart Company.

Henry's oxen broke loose and scattered their food and belongings from their wagon. This caused a lack of food and warm clothing later in their journey. Maria Louisa gave birth to her fourth child on the Plains and it died the same day.

The Willie Handcart Company and Hodgett Wagon Company were a day or two ahead of them. All four companies suffered from terrible snow storms, cold winds, lack of food, and lack of warm clothing. When Maria was most disheartened and wanted to die, rescue parties arrived from Salt Lake City with food and blankets.

They were assisted into the Salt Lake Valley and warmly welcomed by the Saints in that bitter winter of December, 1856. To the amazement of everyone, their family arrived with no frostbite damage nor need of amputations. Many people from the four groups suffered from death, frostbite, and eventual amputation of fingers, toes, feet, or arms. Maria Louisa was confident the warm Welsh flannel had protected her family.

During their residence in Salt Lake City, Henry took his tin repair kit from house to house trying to find someone who needed repairs on their metal household items, but many times he returned home with no earnings for the day.

After an attempt at farming in Lehi and then again in Plain City, they moved to Ogden where Henry opened a successful tinsmith business. Maria Louisa gave birth to twelve children and did all in her power to care for the needs of her husband and children. She was called to provide medical assistance to ailing ward members and comfort the distressed people of her ward.

Mary Louisa was a beacon to all who knew her and stood strong in her faith of the truthfulness of the gospel until her death.

MARY ANN JACKSON NEWMAN

BIRTHDATE: 3 Jun 1810
Langtoft, Lincolnshire, England
DEATH: 10 Mar 1886
Salt Lake City, Salt Lake, Utah
PARENTS: John Burton Jackson
Ann Bellars
PIONEER: 19 Sep 1853
Claudius Spencer Wagon Train
SPOUSE: William Newman
MARRIED: 11 Mar 1839
South Witham, England
DEATH SP: 8 Feb 1851
St. Louis, Missouri

CHILDREN:
Stillborn, 17 Apr 1839
Thomas, 30 May 1840 (died as a child)
William John, 25 Feb 1840
Sarah Ann Dorothy (Reid), 17 May 1844
Martha May, 26 Aug 1846
Stephen James, 8 May 1851
Allen Jackson, 13 Jul 1849
Allen Jackson, 23 Apr 1850

Mary Ann Jackson was born in 1810 in England. She had one sister, and two brothers. Mary Ann's mother died when Mary Ann, the eldest of four children, was only thirteen years of age. Mary Ann had considerable responsibility until her father married Alice Arms, who lived only nine years after her marriage, leaving John again with older, but unmarried children.

For many years, Mary Ann was a school mistress. It is thought that she taught or tutored children in wealthy families.

Mary Ann married William Newman, March 11, 1839, in South Witham, Lincolnshire, England. They had a small farm as well as a bakery. William was a baker as well as a slater by trade. They were educated people.

They both embraced the Gospel of Jesus Christ about eleven years after the missionaries were first in England, being baptized in November, 1848. William was soon appointed to preside over their branch of the Church. William's brothers and sisters joined the Church also, but his parents were deceased before the family had heard the Gospel.

On October 17, 1850, this family, including Mary Ann's children, Williams's relatives, left for America. They traveled on the ship, "Joseph Badger," with English and Irish passengers. They arrived in New Orleans, went up the Mississippi River and arrived in St. Louis, December 4, 1850. This ship had carried 227 passengers.

In St. Louis, they rented a house, and a bakery, but William became ill from cholera, from which he never recovered. William died at the age of thirty-three on February 8, 1851, and their eldest son Thomas, died two days later. They were both buried in the same grave in the Episcopal Church Cemetery.

There was just one male family member who had left England who lived to come to Utah. Mary Ann was left penniless upon the death of William. Her son, William, was about ten years of age at that time. He attended school some, and worked long hours as he was apprenticed to a hat maker. A son, Stephen J., was born 8 May 1851, about three months after the death of his father. Being weak and sickly, he required much of Mary Ann's time.

They finally left St. Louis, May 8, 1853, with the Claudius V. Spencer Company. Stephen, had to be carried most of the way across the Plains by his mother. His feet became turned out and he had difficulty trying to walk. He finally had special shoes made for him to help support his weak ankles and legs. They arrived in the Salt Lake Valley, September 19, 1853. They lived for a time on South Temple St. and Mary Ann taught school.

With Johnston's Army problems, Mary Ann and her family moved for a time to American Fork. During their first years in Utah, food was very short. They gathered roots and sego lily bulbs to eat. Once when they had little food, Stephen was crying for something to eat and Mary Ann walked almost three miles to the pioneer flour mill to try to get some flour for food for him.

Returning to Salt Lake City, they eventually moved to North Temple between 600 and 700 West. Here Mary Ann opened the first store and bakery west of Main Street to support her family. Her daughter and her son-in-law assisted in the store.

At one time, Stephen was west of the Jordan River herding cows, when he became surrounded by Indians who held him captive. One in the group of Indians recognized him as being the son of the woman who operated the bakery and reminded them that she had often befriended them and fed them. After Indian Tom told them who Stephen was, he was released and allowed to go home.

In her later life, since Mary Ann had to earn her living and could not leave the store to go out, she daily entertained her friends at tea in the store. On one occasion a friend asked her why she always wore the big white baker's apron all the time. Mary Ann told her that she wore it out of gratitude. She said that without the apron, she would not have been able to carry Stephen to Utah. She then picked up the two bottom corners of the apron, and tied them around her waist and said that she had carried him in the fold of her apron and that it had made it possible for her to walk and carry him.

Mary Ann passed away at the age of seventy-five on March 10, 1886, loved and respected by the people of the community where she lived. She is buried in the Salt Lake City Cemetery.

Her obituary notice which appeared in the Deseret News read: "Wednesday, March 10, 1886, Newman: In Salt Lake, March 10, of Bright's Disease, Mary Ann, relect of the late Elder William Newman, in the 76th year of her age. Funeral services will be conducted in the 16th Ward, where on Sunday, March 14, at 10:00 a.m. Friends of the family are invited to attend."

Mary Ann Jackson Newman was a faithful, stalwart pioneer woman who experienced many trials and tribulations, but who continued to work hard to survive and to be able to provide a living for family even in the most desolate circumstances. She is to be honored for her great faith and fortitude.

SARAH MATILDA MARCHANT NEWMAN

BIRTHDATE: 1 Sep 1841
Bath, Somerset, England
DEATH: 20 Jan 1910
Milo, Jefferson Co., Idaho
PARENTS: Abraham Marchant
Lydia Johnson
PIONEER: 28 Oct 1854
Robert L Campbell Wagon Train
SPOUSE: John Newman
MARRIED: 26 Dec 1859
Salt Lake City, Salt Lake, Utah
DEATH SP: 18 Jul 1902
Milo, Jefferson Co., Idaho

CHILDREN:
John Henry, 16 Oct 1860
Abraham William, 16 Sep 1862
Sarah Matilda, 7 Jan 1864 (died as an infant)
Lydia Maria, 13 Mar 1865
Joseph Alma, 3 Dec 1866
Elizabeth May, 23 May 1869
Robert Marchant, 24 Feb 1871
James Johnson, 11 Jan 1873
Albert Samuel, 2 Dec 1874
Mary Ann, 27 Sep 1876
Amelia Sophia, 11 Jul 1878
Emily Florence, 13 Oct 1880
Franklin Hughes, 26 Sep 1885

Sarah Matilda was born in 1841 in England. As a girl of thirteen, Sarah and her family boarded the ship, "Windermere," chartered by the Saints of the Church of Jesus Christ of Latter-day Saints to sail from Liverpool to New Orleans.

During the voyage, there was a terrible storm which lasted eighteen hours. The 477 Mormons of the 572 passengers, fasted and prayed, and the storm abated. Smallpox broke out and some of the Marchant children contracted the disease but survived. Next, March 17, a fire broke out in the ship's galley, which caused a loss of food and shortened the fresh water supply. After their landing at New Orleans, some of them were afflicted with cholera.

This family traveled with the Robert L. Campbell Ox-Train, and arrived in the Salt Lake Valley, October 28, 1854, and made their home in South Cottonwood, which is now Murray.

It was here, in Murray, that Sarah met John Newman, who had arrived September 24, 1853. They were married

December 26, 1859, and after spending their first year in Big Cottonwood, they moved with Sarah's family to Peoa, Summit County, Utah, where they lived for the next thirty-five years. Their children were all born in Peoa except the first who was born in the Cottonwood area.

Twelve of their children grew to maturity, married and raised families. Sarah and John experienced the hardships of pioneer life in the Salt Lake Valley and again in Peoa.

In 1875, Sarah became second counselor in the Peoa Ward Relief Society and served in that position for eight years. In 1893, she became president of the Peoa Ward Primary, and held that position until 1896.

In 1896, she and her husband and children moved to Idaho, homesteading a piece of land adjoining that of two of her sons. For the third time, Sarah and John were to experience the difficulties of helping to settle a new area.

The first house John and Sarah built was of logs and was destroyed by fire. Because of this, he selected stone as the building material for their next home. It is still being lived in today, and is located on the south side of the Ririe highway, (US26), between the Milo Road and the Buck School Road Junction. Their children married and settled in the area, most of their homes within the boundary of the Milo Ward.

Sarah passed away on January 20, 1910, at the age of sixty-eight years. John had passed away in 1902. Both are buried in the Milo Cemetery in Jefferson, Idaho.

They were valiant pioneers who helped settle three different areas of the West. They left a great posterity to honor their names.

ANN JAQUES NEWTON

No
Photo
Available

BIRTHDATE: 16 Dec 1813
Shackestone, Leicester, England
DEATH: 1 Nov 1892
Harrisburg, Washington, Utah
PARENTS: William Jaques
Mary Jaques
PIONEER: 30 Nov 1856
Martin Handcart Company
SPOUSE: John Newton
MARRIED: England
DEATH SP: 18 Jun 1865
Harrisburg, Washington, Utah

CHILDREN:
John, 30 Jul 1838
Caroline (Gifford), 25 Dec 1839
Thomas, 15 May 1847
Mary Ann, 4 Nov 1851
Elizabeth Ann, 12 May 1860

Ann Jaques was mother of five children, four of whom were born in Leicester, England. In 1851, she was baptized and became a member of The Church of Jesus Christ of

Latter-day Saints. She soon began making plans to go to America to be with the main body of the Church. By borrowing money from the Church Emigration Fund she was able to make the trip with her only living child, Caroline.

They sailed from Liverpool, England, on May 25, 1856, on the ship "Horizon." When they arrived in New York they went by train to Iowa City and there joined the Martin Handcart Company.

She endured the hardships of traveling with little food and in snow and extreme cold, as did the other members of this company.

After arriving in Utah, she married John Newton. To them was born a daughter, Elizabeth Ann, born May 12, 1860, at Moroni, Utah. She was sealed to her husband in the Endowment House on May 23, 1863.

They moved south to help settle Harrisburg, (near St. George) Utah. Here her husband passed away on June 18, 1865. Tragedy again struck in 1866 with the passing of her daughter, Elizabeth Ann.

Ann was a very religious person and when the Relief Society was first organized in Harrisburg, 1877, she was the second counselor in the presidency. When it was later reorganized in 1883, she again served as the second counselor.

Ann passed away on November 1, 1892, at Harrisburg and was buried beside her husband John and little daughter, Elizabeth Ann.

HELEN NIBLETT

No Photo Available

BIRTHDATE: 10 Dec 1822
Avening, Gloucestershire, England
DEATH: 3 Sep 1911
Payson, Utah
PARENTS: John Niblett
Mary Ann Hopkins
PIONEER: 4 Sep 1861
Job Pingree ox team company
SPOUSE: James William Huish
MARRIED: 14 Feb 1842
Avening, Gloucestershire, England
DEATH SP: 1 Dec 1897
Payson, Utah

CHILDREN:
Eduard Alexander, 21 Apr 1843
Joseph Walter, 25 Jul 1846
Fanny, 4 Dec 1848
Orson Pratt, 9 Sep 1851
Franklin David, 27 Nov 1854
Lorenzo Snow, 27 Nov 1854
Heber C., 15 Nov 1857
James William, Jr., 11 May 1860
Florette, 29 Jun 1863
Frederick Augustus, 9 Jun 1866

James emigrated leaving Helen in England with five children and one yet unborn. After two years he sent money to emigrate the family. When the money came the smaller children had the whooping cough but Helen immediately bought tickets and prepared to go to America. As they boarded the Dreadnaught, she cautioned the children not to cough as they passed the inspectors; if they did they could not go to America where their father was. After being on the ship a few days, the baby became worse, died and was buried at sea. They would not let her watch the burial but her oldest son watched and reported the event to her.

After arriving in New York they went to Frankfort, Missouri, where they lived until they started across the plains in May 1861 with the Job Pingree ox team co. She walked two-thirds of the way carrying her thirteen-month-old baby in her arms. They went directly to Payson Utah arriving 4 Sep 1861.

She joined the Relief Society 20 Jan. 1869 and was made a teacher in March which position she held until she was made president in 1878. She was then president for fourteen years.

She practiced obstetrics for thirty years and assisted in the birth of some 500 babies.

JEAN WILSON NIBLEY

BIRTHDATE: 12 Jun 1815
Newbattle, Scotland
DEATH: 20 Mar 1899
Wellsville, Cache Co., Utah
PARENTS: Charles Wilson
Mary Chalmers
PIONEER: 1 Sep 1860
J. D. Ross Wagon Train
SPOUSE: James Nibley
MARRIED: 17 Apr 1836
Newbattle, Scotland
DEATH SP: 18 Dec 1876
Wellsville, Cache Co., Utah

CHILDREN:
James, 23 Apr 1837
Mary, 12 May 1838
James, 22 Feb 1841
Margaret, 21 May 1843
Henry, 8 Jul 1845
Charles, 5 Feb 1849
Henry, 9 Aug 1851
Euphamia, 6 Feb 1855

Jean Wilson was born in Scotland in 1815. She married James Nibley in 1836 in Scotland, and they became the parents of eight children, all of them born in Newbattle, Scotland.

Jean worked along by her husband's side in the coal mines of Scotland until six weeks before her third child was born. When the Government stopped women from working in the mines, she sold baked goods from one of the two rooms of her home. After the family joined the Church of Jesus Christ of Latter-day Saints in 1839, she let the Elders use this room as a meeting room.

The family came to America in 1860. Several families had worked in the woolen mills to save money for the trip to Utah. They came to the Salt Lake Valley with the J. D. Ross Company, and arrived September 1, 1860.

After arriving in Utah, Jean sold her rare cook stove to buy twenty-five acres of land in Wellsville, Utah. She worked along side her husband in the fields as she had done in the coal mines. She did washing for a few pounds of flour a day, and also dug potatoes for a share. She was a woman of untiring industry and thrift.

James Nibley passed away in 1876, and Jean passed away in 1899, both in Wellsville, Cache County, Utah.

ANN RACHEL MARSH NICHOLES

No Photo Available

BIRTHDATE: 16 Oct 1823
St. Helens, Isle of Jersey, Europe
DEATH: 9 Mar 1909
American Fork, Utah Co., Utah
PARENTS: James Marsh
Anne Esther Clements
PIONEER: 16 Oct 1853
Cyrus H. Wheelock Wagon Train
SPOUSE: Josiah Nichols
MARRIED: 25 Dec 1853
Salt Lake, Endowment House
DEATH SP: 27 Feb 1893
American Fork, Utah Co., Utah

CHILDREN:
Josiah, 19 Sep 1854
James, 12 Dec 1855 (died as an infant)
Elizabeth Harriet (Woods), 9 Jul 1857
John, 25 mar 1859
Joseph, 23 Apr 1861 (twin)
David, 23 Apr 1861 (twin)
Daniel, 8 May 1864 (died at age four)
Ann Rachel (Torgersen), 23 Jul 1867

Ann Rachel was deprived of the loving care of a mother at birth, she was raised by a step-mother until the age of fifteen, when her father died, leaving her an orphan.

She learned the trade of tailoress and followed that for almost six years, then an opportunity came for her to enter Major Pace's homes as a cook. It was here that she met Mary Hallet, who had heard the gospel of the Church of Jesus Christ of Latter-day Saints then investigated its principles. This new religion interested Annie and she brought home a Book of Mormon to read. She quickly became convinced of its truthfulness and was baptized.

In January, 1853, Ann and several other converts from the French mission, sailed from Liverpool for New Orleans on the ship, "Elvira Owen." It took six weeks to cross.

Annie was extremely sick for the entire six weeks, except for the very last day when she said that she could smell land and the next morning they arrived at their destination.

She then sailed up the Mississippi to Keokuk, Iowa, then was outfitted for the journey, she crossed the Plains, arriving at the Salt Lake Valley, October 6, 1853.

Ann was taken home by a Sister Sarah Britton. It was here that she met Josiah Nicholes and consenting to his request, she followed him to American Fork to be his housekeeper. After one month as his housekeeper, Josiah took her to Salt Lake and they were married by Brigham Young.

The year of 1854 and 1855, when the crickets came, devouring all of the crops, Josiah had managed to save a small amount of the barley. Grinding up the barley, Annie would make it into cakes. The cakes were green in color and the husks had to be picked out while being eaten. These cakes were much better than nothing with their diets of pig weed greens and thistle roots.

Annie, with her natural skills of nursing, gave unending service to those sick and in need of her assistence. She used remedies of herbs and poultices, and was known to have a very "healing and comforting touch."

In her last years, her struggle against illness was a courageous one. She maintained her cheerfulness and was very appreciative and thankful for those who cared for her. Annie met death with same heroic spirit that she had exhibited throughout her life, she passed away on March 9, 1909, surrounded by her family.

ELLEN WHITE NICHOLS

BIRTHDATE: 20 Jan 1832
Bishop Middleham, England
DEATH: 12 Feb 1901
Coalville, Summit Co., Utah
PARENTS: George White
Catherine Gibbons
PIONEER: 15 Sep 1868
John Gillespie Co. Wagon Train
SPOUSE: William Nichols
MARRIED: 19 Mar 1854
Kelloe, Durham, England
DEATH SP: 16 Aug 1885
Coalville, Summit Co., Utah

CHILDREN:
John George, 16 Apr 1855 (died as an infant)
Catherine Jane, 13 Apr 1856
William, 8 Jul 1858 (died as an infant)
Margaret, 20 Oct 1860 (died as an infant)
George, 9 May 1862 (died as an infant)
Isabell, 13 Mar 1865
Mary Ellen, 19 Sep 1867
Elizabeth Ann, 8 Jan 1870
Barbara, 16 Feb 1872
Benjamin Thomas, 2 Aug 1875

Ellen White Nichols was born in Bishop Middleham, Durham, England, in 1832. She married William Nichols in 1854 and they were the parents of ten children, seven of them born in England. Four of these children died as infants. William previously had two other wives, and three other children, but all of them had died before he married Ellen.

The family sailed from England in 1868 on the ship, "Constitution" for America. William was a violinist and played for the Saints on their way over the pioneer trail. They arrived in Utah in September, 1858, and settled in Coalville, Summit County, Utah, where William plied his trade as a skilled carpenter.

William sent to New York for a little hand organ. Ellen would play the organ while William played the violin. This combination formed the dance music for early day dances throughout Summit County. The little hand organ is still in possession of the family.

Ellen was a midwife, bringing many babies into the world, including three more for herself. William passed away in 1885, and though all was calm and quiet, for some unknown reason notes were heard from his violin. Ellen passed away in 1901, both of them in Coalville, Summit County, Utah.

EMILY SEWELL NICHOLS

BIRTHDATE: 23 Jun 1841
Yarmouth, Norfolk, England
DEATH: 19 Oct 1918
Salt Lake City, Salt Lake, Utah
PARENTS: Joseph Sewell Jr.
Emily Ellett
PIONEER: Oct 1861
Wagon Train Company
SPOUSE: Henry W. Nichols
MARRIED: 3 Mar 1860
London, Middlesex, England
DEATH SP: 9 Feb 1933
Vandergrift, Pennsylvania

CHILDREN:
Henry William, 21 Mar 1863
George Edward, 27 Jun 1865
James Arthur, 3 Nov 1867
Emily, 28 Sep 1870
Clara Louise, 26 Feb 1873
Francis Joseph, 2 Jul 1875
Mary Isabell, 25 Oct 1877

Emily Sewell was born in England in 1841. The Sewell family and the Nichols family were members of the same branch of the Church of Jesus Christ of Latter-day Saints in London, England. Emily became a special friend to young Henry William, and they had many happy times at the theater, church events, and in their homes. He left for America when she was fifteen, but he returned after three years.

While waiting for him, Emily worked as a dressmaker during the day and took singing lessons at night. She belonged to a chorus which gave public concerts. She also sang in the branch choir.

A few months after Henry's return he and Emily were married and set sail for America with her parents. They crossed the Plains in 1861 and lived in Salt Lake City in a variety of places until her husband designed and built their permanent home. Here they raised their family and continued to enjoy the same sort of things they had liked in London; the theater and home life, though they gave up church attendance.

It was at this home where she died in 1918, leaving her husband and six living children.

MARY ANN JOHNSON NICHOLS

BIRTHDATE: 23 Jul 1841
Vester Maria, Denmark
DEATH: 10 Jan 1918
Brigham City, Box Elder, Utah
PARENTS: Jorgen Jorgensen
Karen Kirstine Jensen
PIONEER: 5 Oct 1854
Hans P. Olsen Wagon Train
SPOUSE: Alvin Nichols
MARRIED: 8 Apr 1857
Salt Lake City, Salt Lake, Utah
DEATH SP: 18 Sep 1899
Brigham City, Box Elder, Utah

CHILDREN:
George Washington, 10 Aug 1859
Hyrum, 3 Jan 1862
Lewis, 22 Jul 1864
Mark Leslie, 3 Apr 1866
Willard Stephen, 22 Jun 1868
Hattie Caroline, 29 Apr 1871
Ada Susannah, 4 May 1878

Mary Ann Johnson (christened Ane Marie Jorgensen) was born in Vester Maria, Bornholm, Denmark in 1841. Her parents, John Johnson (christened Jorgen Jorgensen) and Karen Kirstine Jensen, were hard-working people who owned a farm. She remembered that at age eleven she carried food and drink to the workmen in the fields. When she was twelve she was baptized at midnight, because of the persecution from friends and other family members.

Mary Ann sailed with her parents in 1854 on the "Jesse Munn" from Liverpool. In Kansas they joined the Hans Peter Olsen Wagon Train. Mary Ann walked the entire 1,500 miles to the Salt Lake Valley, in Utah.

She married Alvin Nichols, a native of Canada, when she was sixteen, as his second wife. She was the mother of seven children. Mary Ann was small in stature, only 4 feet and 11 inches. She was a marvelous cook and nurse. She was an accomplished seamstress and enjoyed doing embroidery and fine stitchery. She was a counselor in the

Relief Society, and also a teacher. She helped her husband, who was Bishop, with the tithing and fast offerings brought in the form of produce.

Alvin Nichols passed away in 1899, and Mary Ann passed away in 1918, both at Brigham City, Box Elder County, Utah.

HULDA CHAPMAN NICKERSON

No Photo Available

BIRTHDATE: 19 Aug 1780
Tolland Co., Connecticut
DEATH: 22 Mar 1860
Provo, Utah Co., Utah
PARENTS: Eliphalet Chapman
Abigail Chase
PIONEER: 24 Sep 1850
Jackson Stewart Wagon Train
SPOUSE: Freeman Nickerson
MARRIED: 19 Jan 1801
Cavendish, Windsor, Vermont
DEATH SP: 12 Jan 1847
Chariton, Lucas Co., Iowa

CHILDREN:
Data, 1 Sep 1802
Moses, 9 Mar 1804
Eleazer Freeman, 12 Apr 1806
Caroline Eliza, 25 Jun 1808
Uriel Chittendon Hatch, 14 Nov 1810
Samuel Stillman, 22 Sep 1812 (died at 6 months)
Levi Stillman, 2 Apr 1814
Hulda Abigail, 16 Apr 1816
Eliphalet Seneca (Sullivan), 5 Mar 1818

Hulda was born to Eliphalet and Abigail Chase Chapman on August 19, 1780, in Connecticut. She married Freeman Nickerson in Cavendish, Windsor County, Vermont, on January 19, 1801. Six of her nine children were born in Cavendish, Vermont. In 1814, they moved to Springfield, Pennsylvania. Ten years later, they moved to Buffalo, New York. After the Erie Canal was finished in 1825, they moved to Perrysburg, New York.

In 1833, Hulda, Freeman, and seven of their children were baptized into the Church of Jesus Christ of Latter-day Saints by Elder Zerubbabel Snow. That same year, Hulda's husband was sent on his first mission to Kirtland, Ohio.

Hulda was often left alone as her husband served four missions and accompanied the Prophet to Zion in Jackson County. Her husband took two more wives in polygamy. They moved to Kirtland where they helped to build the temple. Huldah suffered many hardships during the pioneer exodus to Quincy, Commerce, and Peoria, Illinois. In November 1840, they moved again to Commerce. They were driven again from their home.

Her husband died on January 22, 1847, of dropsy and congestive chills at the Pioneer Crossing of the Chariton River in Iowa. He was buried in Winter Quarters.

In 1850, accompanied by her daughter, Caroline and her son, Levi, Hulda crossed the Plains with the Jackson Stewart Wagon Company. They arrived in Salt Lake City on September 24, 1850.

Once the Saints reached the Salt Lake Valley, Hulda lived with her children in Provo, Utah. In the Fall of 1852, they moved to Provo, Utah.

Hulda passed away on March 22, 1860, after an illness of two weeks, in Caroline's home. She left a faithful testimony of the truths of the Everlasting Gospel. She is buried in the Provo City Cemetery.

JOHANNA CHRISTINE MAGDALENA HANDBERG NICOL

BIRTHDATE: 11 Mar 1839
O'dense, Fyen, Denmark
DEATH: 14 Dec 1919
Heber City, Wasatch Co., Utah
PARENTS: John J. Handberg
Marie Christine Trane
PIONEER: 13 Sep 1857
C. C. A. Christensen Handcart
SPOUSE: Thomas Nicol
MARRIED: 11 Mar 1858
Salt Lake City, Salt Lake, Utah
DEATH SP: 23 Dec 1909
Heber City, Wasatch Co., Utah

CHILDREN:
Josephine Marie, 25 Jan 1859
Thomas Handberg, 20 Jan 1861
Johanna Christina, 25 Dec 1863
Jennette Elizabeth, 14 Nov 1864
Rachel Ann, 6 Mar 1866 (died at age 16)
Sarah Matilda, 18 Apr 1868
Adolphus Alexander, 9 May 1870
Moroni, 9 Jun 1871
Joseph Alma, 7 Jan 1873
Hyrum Chase, 9 Feb 1876
Gabriel Blake, 29 Oct 1878

Johanna Christine became converted to the Church of Jesus Christ of Latter-day Saints by the missionary Erastus Snow. On December 14, 1850, a hole was chopped in the ice on the river at Bogense, Denmark and Joanna was baptized there.

She traveled with a group of Danish Saints to England, then sailed on the ship, "Westmoreland." They arrived in Philadelphia on June 2, 1857. They reached Iowa City by rail and were taken to a small grove west of the city were handcarts were provided them for their 1,334 mile trek to Great Salt Lake Valley.

They traveled with the C.C.A. Christensen Handcart Company who gave them courage and good cheer as they struggled with their handcart loads. Johanna and three other Danish girls were ever serving and aiding those who needed help. On September 13, on Sunday, they marched with feelings of thankfulness into the Valley of the Saints.

She went to work for Thomas Nicol whose wife had died and left two baby boys. She married him on her nineteenth birthday. She was a natural nurse and studied under Ramonia B. Pratt Penrose in nursing and medicine at Salt Lake City. Johanna became the leading midwife of Wasatch County having 800 births to her credit.

Johanna and Thomas became the parents of eleven children. Her step-daughter, Dora, was an invalid for many years and every night, even in weather much below zero, Johanna trudged through the snow with a lantern to light her path to care for Dora and make her as comfortable as possible for the night.

She had a keen sense of humor. She loved to sing, dance, and make everyone happy. She also served as a counselor in the Primary for many years and had a wonderful influence on children.

She was a kind, helpful, tender, thoughtful wife and mother. All who knew her loved her for her unselfish service to those in need of her help, offering courage and good cheer to others.

JOHANNA KIRSTINE JENSEN NICOL

No Photo Available

BIRTHDATE: 18 Apr 1840
Rakkeby, Hjorring, Denmark
DEATH: 1 Oct 1865
Heber City, Wasatch, Utah
PARENTS: Jens Hansen
Christine Nielsen
PIONEER: 23 Sep 1861
Joseph W. Young Wagon Train
SPOUSE: Thomas Nicol
MARRIED: 17 Dec 1864
Salt Lake Endowment House
DEATH SP: 23 Dec 1907

CHILD:
Dora Elizabeth, 29 Sep 1865

Johanna's friends described her as refined and lovely. She became interested in the gospel of the LDS Church through her uncle who was active in the Danish Mission. She was the only member of her family to join the Church of Jesus Christ of Latter-day Saints. They were unhappy with her choice and disowned her. She was baptized on February 14, 1860. She was interested in joining with the Saints as they emigrated to America.

Johanna sailed from Denmark on the steamer, "Waldemar," on May 9, 1861 with 565 other Scandinavian Saints until they reached Kiel. From there, they traveled on until they came to Liverpool, England. They sailed from Liverpool on the "Monarch of the Sea" with 955 souls aboard. They arrived in New York on June 19, 1861 and traveled by rail and steamboat until they reached Florence,

Nebraska. Preparations for their journey west were made at once. Johanna was assigned to the company under the leadership of Joseph W. Young which was hauling mostly cargo and machinery consigned to Brigham Young. The driver of the wagon to which she was assigned was Thomas Nicol. Their company arrived in Salt Lake City on September 12, 1861.

Thomas and Johanna became friends and courted until they married in the Salt Lake Endowment House on December 17, 1864. Her health seemed to fail and a few days after the birth of her daughter, she passed away on October 1, 1865.

ANNA MARY BAULDRY WEEKES NIELD

No Photo Available

BIRTHDATE: 1 Dec 1799 East
Wickham, Suffolk, England
DEATH: 26 Oct 1888
Smithfield, Cache Co., Utah
PARENTS: James Bauldry
Elizabeth Hall
PIONEER: Sep 1853
SPOUSE I: Robert Weekes
MARRIED: 3 Apr 1818
DEATH SP: 14 Sep 1853
Fort Laramie, Wyoming

CHILDREN:
Robert, 19 Jul 1819
John, 1821 (died at age 9)
Elizabeth, 1 May 1824
Mary Ann, 26 Aug 1826
Eunice, 1827 (died as a child)
Samuel, 12 Apr 1829
Eunice, 14 Oct 1831 (died at age 2)
Benjamin, 16 Feb 1834 (died at age 18)
David, 9 Jul 1836
Edith, 12 Dec 1838
Sidney, 8 Mar 1841
Emma, 18 Apr 1846

SPOUSE II: Luke Nield
MARRIED: 13 Feb 1855
Fillmore, Millard Co., Utah
DEATH SP: Not given
CHILDREN:

Anna Mary was born to James and Elizabeth Hall Bauldry in Suffolk, England. At the age of eighteen, she married Robert Weekes. They became the parents of twelve children. Three children died as young children and a son died at age eighteen. Robert and Anna Bauldry Weeks were aristocrats of England owning a large estate on which grains, hay, potatoes, fruits, animals, and fowl were raised.

They were converted to the Church of Jesus Christ of Latter-day Saints by elders who were proclaiming the gospel in England. They and their four youngest children left their home in England in February 1853, crossing the ocean in the ship, "International." They arrived in New Orleans in April of the same year, then traveled to Keokuk, Iowa by steamer.

In May, 1853, they left Council Bluffs with a company of Saints for Salt Lake City. Their perilous journey lasted five months. Due to severe hardships and exposure, Robert became ill and died at Fort Laramie, Wyoming. Anna Mary continued on with her family and settled in Salt Lake City.

On February 13, 1855, she married Luke Nield in Fillmore, Utah. They were divorced and Anna Mary moved to Smithfield where she and her sons, David and Sidney, planted a couple of crops. which were destroyed by grasshoppers and crickets. They seldom had enough to eat.

Ann Mary was very industrious and thrifty. She constantly planned for the future. She brought enough tea from England to last until they could buy it in the United States. She served it only to the sick. Sidney assisted his mother in supporting the family until 1864 when he married. He built her a home beside his own and continued to care and provide for her needs as he grew older.

Anna Mary passed away in 1888 and her body was laid to rest in the Smithfield Cemetery.

ELIZABETH GREEN HAMILTON RICHMOND NIELD

BIRTHDATE: 3 Oct 1804
Lucwardine, England
DEATH: 7 Feb 1883
Fillmore, Millard Co., Utah
PARENTS: William Green
Jane Prosser
PIONEER: Oct 1851
Orson Hyde Wagon Train
SPOUSE I: Eli Hamilton
(More information not available)
MARRIED: Unknown
DEATH SP: Unknown

CHILDREN: Unknown

SPOUSE II: Thomas Richmond
MARRIED: After 15 Jan 1844
St. Louis, Missouri
DEATH SP: 1851 en route to Utah
CHILDREN:

SPOUSE III: Luke Nield
MARRIED: 7 Feb 1859
DEATH SP: 23 Jul 1869
CHILDREN: Not given

Elizabeth was one of ten children in her family of origin. Her family joined the Church of Jesus Christ of Latter-day Saints and came to America. They settled in St. Louis. Elizabeth married Eli Hamilton about whom nothing

is known other than she raised his children from his first marriage to adulthood.

She married Thomas Richmond, a widower who had a previous family which stayed in St. Louis. Elizabeth decided she wanted to go with Thomas and her children to Zion to be near her sister and other Saints in Fillmore. They were traveling with the Orson Hyde Company. En route, Thomas died leaving her to finish the task of crossing the Plains alone with her first husband's children.

Elizabeth was a special friend of the widows and orphans, taking them into her home, caring for them, nursing them in sickness, clothing them, and feeding them. She took in motherless, Eliza Ann Trucket when she was but a few days old and raised her to womanhood. She boiled buckskin, stretched it over the neck of a bottle, punctured small holes in it and used this to bottle-feed the tiny baby. She was able to take what little was available and serve attractive appetizing dishes. Her sister, Ann Dutson, was a midwife and Ruth would help her whenever she was called upon for help. She helped to design the first flag to fly over Fillmore. It was made of a white sheet, a military sash, and patchwork stars.

She was in regular attendance in the Relief Society from 1868 until her death. She also contributed to the Emigration Fund.

On February 7, 1859, she was married to another widower, Luke Nield whose companionship she enjoyed for ten years before he passed away.

Elizabeth passed away at the age of seventy-seven and is buried in the Fillmore Cemetery beside her sister, Ann.

JANE PARKER NIELD

BIRTHDATE: 18 Aug 1861
Earlville, Delaware Co., Iowa
DEATH: 9 Nov 1952
Logan, Cache Co., Utah
PARENTS: William Parker
Ruth Gibbs
PIONEER: 1865
SPOUSE: John Edward Nield
MARRIED: 19 Sep 1877
Fillmore, Millard Co., Utah
DEATH SP: 13 Aug 1925
Afton, Lincoln Co., Wyoming

CHILDREN:
John William, 10 Oct 1878
Ben, 16 Apr 1880
Sarah Jane "Sadie," 27 Nov 1884
Daniel, 13 Mar 1886
Martha Opal, 21 Jul 1890
Van Luke, 22 Jun 1893 (died at age 19)
Ellis, 25 Feb 1898
Elworth, 1900

When Jane was four years old, her father sold his home in Iowa and started with an Independent Wagon Company to cross the Plains. After traveling with them for many miles, they separated from the main group who were headed for Oregon. They traveled on to Salt Lake City alone. Her father traveled further south to a place called Meadow Creek where he made a dugout for his family.

Her father was a mason and soon built them a home of adobe. He was killed by a runaway team of horses when Jean was eleven years old. She gleaned grain from the fields to help the family get the things they needed.

When Jane was sixteen, she married John Nield and they moved to Star Valley to help a group of men open the road. They moved back to Deseret to live with his parents when their second son was born. They had built their own home by the time Sarah Jane was born. They moved to Afton, Wyoming, then to Rockland, Idaho, where they lived on a ranch.

She made diapers by tearing up old sheets or her chemise. She made overalls for her sons from the backs of the worn out men's overalls. She made them suits for Sunday from suit good they purchased. She would wash the girls clothes on Saturday night after they had bathed and use the same water to scrub the floors because they had to haul all of their water into their home.

Her husband passed away in August of 1925. Jean lived to be ninety-one years old, passing away on November 9, 1952 in Logan, Cache Co., Utah.

MARTHA WILDE NIELD

No Photo Available

BIRTHDATE: 8 Feb 1797
Oldham, Lancashire, England
DEATH: 25 Jun 1854
Kansas City, Jackson, Missouri
PARENTS: Benjamin Wilde
Mary Jones
PIONEER: 1854
died en route
SPOUSE: Luke Nield
MARRIED: 30 Jun 1817
Prestwich, Oldham, England
DEATH SP: 23 Jul 1869
Spring City, Sanpete Co., Utah

CHILDREN:
Benjamin, 21 Aug 1817
Joseph, 5 May 1819 (died at age 2)
Joseph Merrick, 4 Jul 1822
Rebecca, 31 Aug 1824
Hannah, 18 Mar 1827 (died at age 8)
Mary, 15 Jul 1829 (died as an infant)
Daniel, 25 May 1831 (died as an infant)
John, 23 Feb 1834
Alice, 20 Oct 1836
Ann, 1838 (died as an infant)

Martha was born in Oldham, Lancashire, England. She married Luke Nield June 30, 1817, in Prestwich, Oldham, Lancashire, England. Their children were all christened at Oldham even though Shaw was much closer to their home. They lived in Cowlishaw, Shawside, Longfield for five years, and then Glodwick.

Luke was a spinner at the time his family was baptized into the Church of Jesus Christ of Latter-day Saints. The Nields decided to apply for help from the Perpetual Emigration Fund to enable them to emigrate to the United States.

Soon Luke and Martha were on their way with their youngest children, Alice, and John with his wife and baby. They sailed from Liverpool on the ship "Marshfield" and were on the water for seven weeks. They were taken to Quarantine Island (five miles south of St. Louis) where many contracted cholera and passed away.

When released, they traveled up the Missouri River to where Kansas City now stands. Martha caught Cholera and died on June 25, 1854. Luke continued across the Plains with his children traveling in the William Empey Wagon Company which arrived in Salt Lake Valley on October 24, 1854.

After he arrived in Utah he eventually married three more wives. One of those wives was Sarah, a sister to Martha.

SARAH BROADBENT NIELD

BIRTHDATE: 19 Jul 1833
Saddleworth, Yorkshire, England
DEATH: 10 Jun 1901
Afton, Uintah Co., Wyoming
PARENTS: Joseph Broadbent
Elizabeth Scofield
PIONEER: 24 Oct 1854
William Empey
SPOUSE: John Nield
MARRIED: 23 May 1863
Prestwich, Oldham, England
DEATH SP: 14 Dec 1913
Afton, Lincoln Co., Wyoming

CHILDREN:
Orson William, 8 Dec 1853 (died at 6 months)
John Edward, 24 Nov 1855
Hannah, 28 Feb 1858
Joseph Luke, 9 Jul 1860
Daniel Broadbent, 19 Feb 1863 (died at age 13)
Benjamin Franklin, 2 Apr 1865 (died as an infant)
Thomas Taylor, 28 Aug 1866
James Wild, 2 Jun 1869
Sarah Elizabeth, 28 Nov 1872
Seth Broadbent, 2 Jul 1875

Sarah was baptized a member of the Church of Jesus Christ of Latter-day Saints by Luke Nield, the father of John

Nield on January 12, 1848. She and John lived in the same branch of the Church.

Five years later, Sarah and John were married in Prestwich, Oldham, Lancashire, England. They decided to save something each week until they had enough means to emigrate to America.

They sailed from Liverpool, England on the ship, "Marshfield," on April 8, 1854. They had their little boy, Orson, with them. Sarah developed an infection in her breasts and being unable to nurse the baby, he died and was buried at sea. They arrived on Quarantine Island, five miles below St. Louis, Missouri where sickness got started among them and many of their group died of Cholera. They were treated well by old friends until they were ready to go up the Missouri River. They landed near Kansas City on June 17, 1854.

They traveled West with the William Empey Wagon Company and arrived in Salt Lake City on October 24, 1854. They moved on to Lehi, Utah, October 29, 1854.

They went to work digging potatoes and any other kind of job they could find. They lived in a cellar until they were able to build their home. They planted fields only to have the grasshoppers eat everything that was green. They came close to starvation.

Later, they moved to Fillmore where her husband worked at farming on shares, making adobes until 1859 when they moved to Moroni, Sanpete County, where they could have land and water in trade for their fur. They built their home and ran a little store out of their home.

Years later, they moved to Afton, Wyoming and started over again, laboring hard to make their home comfortable, raising their family, and participating in church callings the remainder of their lives.

ANDREA JENSEN NIELSEN

BIRTHDATE: 9 May 1842
Gjo, Hjorring, Denmark
DEATH: 23 Nov 1922
Weston (Oneida), Franklin, Idaho
PARENTS: Jens (Ron) Jensen
Else Nielsen
PIONEER: 23 Sep 1862
0. N. Liljenquist Wagon Train
SPOUSE: Thomas L. Nielsen
MARRIED: 22 Apr 1862
Atlantic Ocean
DEATH SP: 28 Apr 1905
Weston (Oneida), Franklin, Idah

CHILDREN:
Lauritz, 24 May 1864
Thomas, 22 Jun 1866
Andrea Eliza, 13 Jul 1868
James, 9 Dec 1870
Peter Adolph, 22 Nov 1873
Antone Edwin, 29 Oct 1874
Mary Anne, 6 Feb 1877 (died at age 5)

William, 10 Oct 1879
Sarah Elienora, 26 Apr 1882 (died at age 10)
Myra Amelia, 11 Jan 1885

When Andrea was very young, she was bound out for $3.00 a year and was very homesick.

Andrea was baptized a member of the Church of Jesus Christ of Latter-day Saints on May 12, 1861. She was disowned by her parents and went to work for a well-to-do family where she worked until they learned that she was a Mormon.

In the Spring of 1862, Andrea put her trust in God, decided to leave her homeland, and go to Zion. She boarded a ship where she became quite ill. Each day, she grew worse and needed special care.

Thomas Nielsen had charge of seeing to the needs of her group. He cared for Andrea and pleaded with her to marry him so he could give her more attention and better care. They were married on board ship by the ship's captain on April 22, 1862. Andrea's illness developed into Typhoid Fever, and Thomas did everything possible for her, never leaving her side.

Upon their arrival in New York, Andrea was placed in a hospital where she received very poor care. While there, her legs were so swollen, they burst open and water ran out. When she recovered enough to travel, Thomas and Andrea traveled with a group of Saints to Florence, Nebraska where they made preparations for their journey West.

They traveled with the O. N. Liljenquist Wagon Company and arrived in the Salt Lake Valley on September 23, 1862. They were sent north to settle in Logan, Utah. They lived on a farm and raised hay, grain, sugar cane, and vegetables.

After the birth of their first two children, they moved to Hyde Park and shared the humble home of their friend Lars Fredricksen. They received a call to settle Bear Lake area. They lived in a humble one-room log cabin for a few years and homesteaded eighty acres. Later he built a two-room log home.

She loved to read and composed several poems. She was secretary in the Relief Society for a number of years and helped to prepare burial clothes for the dead. She loved music and was always singing while she worked. She had a great love for flowers.

She took loving care of her good husband, Thomas, who was very ill for such a long time. He passed away in April, 1905, in Weston after forty-three years of marriage.

Andrea remained faithful and active in the Church until her death at the age of eighty. She was loved and respected by all who knew her.

ANE BENEDICTA ENGELBRECHT HANSEN NIELSEN

BIRTHDATE: 6 Nov 1833
Horby, Odense, Denmark
DEATH: 14 Jul 1924
Richfield, Sevier Co., Utah
PARENTS: Hans Peterson
Hedevig Lucie Englebrecht
Sorensdatter
PIONEER: 5 Oct 1854
Hans Peter Olsen Wagon Train
SPOUSE: Augustinus Nielsen
MARRIED: 5 Feb 1854
on ship "Benjamin Adams"
DEATH SP:

CHILDREN:
Ephramine Benedicte, 11 Jul 1855
Augustinus, 3 Mar 1857
Hedevig Hansine Caroline, 27 Oct 1858
Mary Sophia, 27 Nov 1860
Caroline Louise, 13 Nov 1862
Ana Josephine, 14 Nov 1864
Rephina Sevine, 10 Apr 1867
George Christian, 14 Jun 1869
Niels Peter, 23 Oct 1871 (died age 14)
Joseph Hans, 16 Dec 1873
Clarinda Leonie, 2 Aug 1876
LeRoy Benone, 9 Mar 1878

Ane's father died while serving in the army when she was a small child. Her mother was a doctor of Obstetrics and had a large practice in her country. Ane was educated in a private school and sent to a finishing school where she attended classes with the Crown Prince and his sister.

When she was seventeen years old, the first Mormon missionaries visited her home. She and her stepfather had little to do with them until she was stricken with a fever. After the missionaries administered to her, she was healed and this eventually led to her conversion to the Church of Jesus Christ of latter-day Saints.

In February, 1852, she left her native land and sailed on the ship, "Benjamin Adams." She and the missionary she fell in love with, Augustinus Nelson, were married aboard ship as they crossed the ocean.

After an eight week voyage, they landed at New Orleans, then sailed up the Mississippi River to St. Louis. They remained there until mid March to complete their preparations for their journey across the Plains to Salt Lake Valley. They traveled with the Hans Peter Olsen Wagon Company and arrived on October 5, 1854.

They settled in Big Cottonwood where her first two children were born. They were then sent to Mt. Pleasant where four more children were born. In 1863, they were called to settle Sevier Valley. They were among the first ten families to settle in Richfield. In 1863, the Indians caused the people to move back to Sanpete County. Some time later, they returned to Richfield and remained there the rest of their lives.

She endured all the hardships incidental to pioneer life with courage and patience. She was an industrious woman. With a family of twelve children, she still found time to help her husband care for the mail station for several years. She was active in the church and was the first secretary of the Relief Society in Richfield. She took a keen interest in politics and never failed to cast her ballot. She possessed a remarkable memory and could relate historical events with accuracy until the last year of her ninety-one years of life.

ANE KJERSTINE ANDERSEN NIELSEN

BIRTHDATE: 24 Nov 1836
Vinisburg, Hjorring, Denmark
DEATH: 27 Oct 1914
Ephraim, Sanpete Co. Utah
PARENTS: Soren Andersen
Anna Maria Jensen
PIONEER: 1850
Hans P. Olson's Handcart
SPOUSE: Jens Nielsen
MARRIED: 16 Apr 1858
DEATH SP: 14 Apr 1814
Ephraim, Sanpete Co. Utah

CHILDREN:
Maren Marie Kjerstine, 24 Mar 1859
Jensine Petrine Brighamine, 9 Sep 1861
James (Jens) Peter, 24 Jun 1864
Ane Kjerstine Caroline, 2 Oct 1866
Marie Magdalena, 28 Mar 1868
Thomas Louis, 11 Dec 1870
Louis Brigham Young, 15 Dec 1873
Neils Heber Daniel, 20 Jan 1876
Gertrude Marie Elnore, 28 May 1878
Joseph Henry, 12 Jan 1880

At the age of fourteen, Ane walked over 1,000 miles to Utah, the trek through Plains and mountains, over rocks and through rivers, took about three months. Sometimes she pushed and sometimes she helped her father pull the hand-cart that carried all their past and the beginning of the rest of their lives. Both of them missing the mother they had left behind in a grave in Denmark.

When the Pioneers reached the Salt Lake Valley, they were sent on to Ephraim to settle in the Sanpete County. She and her father built a house out of adobe bricks they made themselves, a three-room house with rocks carefully laid down for the floor and it had a dirt roof. Later it was given wood floors and a tin roof.

It was the house she would live in all her married life, the one she would raise ten children in, card wool and spin thread in, and both joy and sorrow would visit.

Ane often told about her experiences when she was a young mother in this wild country. One day she had to go for water, a block and a half away. As she left the house, an Indian lurking in willows saw her leave, he entered her cabin finding a five-year-old daughter, her three-year-old sister and baby brother alone in the house. The Indian begged for bread and meat, the daughter fearfully gave him all they had and hoped he would leave. Instead he went over to the crib and would have stolen her little brother but Ane returned just in time. She could speak the Indian language fluently, and wasted no time in telling the Indian to leave, which he did, hurriedly!

She told us about the time the Indians had stolen all the cows the pioneers owned. Word came that their cows were being driven up to the mountains. The men quickly grabbed their weapons, saddled up their horses and rode off in hot pursuit. They overtook the Indians and rescued their cattle and returned them to the settlement.

On Ane's house doorstep, was written the words "Vielcome," not in print but in spirit. No one ever came to her home without receiving something, either a piece of cake, a slice of bread and butter, or even a lump of sugar.

Ane left a large posterity to mourn her passing. She was so dear to all our hearts.

ANE JOHANNE JOHANSEN NIELSEN

No Photo Available

BIRTHDATE: 22 Feb 1812
Svendstrup, Aalborg, Denmark
DEATH: 2 Apr 1890
Fish Haven, Idaho
PARENTS: Johan C. Andreasen
Ane Hansen Blikfeld
PIONEER: 30 Sep 1853
John E. Forsgren Wagon Train
SPOUSE: Anders Nielsen
MARRIED: 22 Oct 1830
Aalborg, Denmark
DEATH SP: 21 Feb 1847
Svendstrup, Aalborg, Denmark

CHILDREN:
Anna Christina, 26 Jan 1832
Niels Christian, 5 Feb 1834
Johan Laurits, 27 Jun 1836 (died as an infant)
Johan Laurits, 4 Jul 1837
Horace Peter, 4 Nov 1840
Ane Marie Dorothea, 23 Mar 1843

Ane Johanne was born in Svendstrup, Aalborg, Denmark to parents who were quite wealthy. At the age of eighteen, she married Anders Nielsen who was a poor man. Her parents disinherited her for her choice. Instead of having plenty of means to rear and educate her family, she lost the portion of wealth that was her right by birth.

Anders built a comfortable home and they became the parents of six children. Anders passed away in 1847, leaving her with a great deal of responsibility with five children to care for.

In 1850, they heard the gospel of the Church of Jesus Christ of Latter-day Saints. They joined the Church and made preparations to emigrate to America. All the children were able to go except Niels Christian who had apprenticed

to work for someone. Ane and her four children left Denmark to travel to England.

They had a very treacherous time on the North Sea in a storm which sank more than one hundred vessels. They crossed the Atlantic Ocean on the ship, "Forest Monarch," in mid-January and arrived in New Orleans on March 7, 1853. They sailed up the Mississippi River to St. Louis, Missouri.

They left Keokuk to cross the Plains with the John E. Forsgren Wagon Company which finally arrived in Salt Lake City on September 30, 1853.

After their arrival, the three older children went to work for families in the city. Ane settled in Salt Lake City where she lived during the grasshopper famine. She saw many marvelous changes take place in the area.

Her son, Horace Peter, was called to help settle the Bear Lake Valley in Idaho. Ane and her two widowed daughters and her son, John, with his family moved to Fish Haven to be near Horace Peter and his family. Horace built a small home close to his where they could provide for her in her later years.

Ane Johanne loved to walk and would sometimes walk several miles to visit friends, enjoyed good health until the day she passed away on April 21, 1890.

ANE MARGRETHE JENSEN CHRISTENSEN OR NIELSEN

BIRTHDATE: 22 Jun 1805
Seden Odense, Denmark
DEATH: 16 Mar 1883
Mt. Pleasant, Sanpete Co., Utah
PARENTS: Jens Madsen
Karen Nielsen
PIONEER: 13 Sep 1857
C. Christensen Handcart Comp.
SPOUSE: Christian Nielsen
MARRIED: 20 Mar 1842
Tanderup, Odense, Denmark
DEATH SP: 11 Dec 1880
Mt. Pleasant, Sanpete Co., Utah

CHILD:
Karen Marie, 22 Jul 1842

Ann Margrethe was born to Jens Madsen and Karen Nielsen in Seden, Odense, Denmark on June 22, 1805.

She was the first wife of Christian Nielsen or Christensen. They were married in Tanderup, Odense, Denmark and became the parents of Karen Marie.

Ane Margrethe and her husband were converted to the Church of Jesus Christ of Latter-day Saints and brought their daughter to America with a large group of Danish emigrants.

When they arrived in Iowa City, Iowa, they became a part of the Christian Christensen Handcart Company with whom they crossed the Plains. They arrived in the Salt Lake Valley on September 13, 1857.

In the Spring of 1859, they moved to help establish the new settlement of Mt. Pleasant in Sanpete County, Utah. Her husband took three more women as his wives in polygamy.

Ane's last years were spent with her only daughter and family where she passed away on March 16, 1883.

ANNA HANSEN NIELSEN

No
Photo
Available

BIRTHDATE: 16 Nov 1800
Voldby, Aarhus, Denmark
DEATH: Feb 1886
Weston, Franklin Co., Idaho
PARENTS: Hans Jensen
Maren Mogensen
PIONEER: 29 Aug 1859
James S. Brown Wagon Train
SPOUSE: Niels Nielsen
MARRIED: 25 Oct 1842
Hammel, Skanderborg, Denmark
DEATH SP: 25 Sep 1858
Burlington, Iowa

CHILDREN:
Maren, 23 Jul 1827
Hansine, 28 Mar 1831

Anna was born on November 16, 1800 in Voldby, Aarhus, Denmark. She married Niels Nielsen on October 25, 1842 in Hammel, Skanderborg, Denmark.

They had begun their family when they heard the gospel as preached by the missionaries. They were baptized as members of the Church of Jesus Christ of Latter-day Saints. They were listed on the Fredericia Conference Immigration List to leave Denmark and sail to America with other Saints in the Spring of 1857.

Anna, her husband, her daughter, Hansine, and a five year old grandson were on the list. Anna was the mother of another daughter, Maren, but it is not known when she came to America. The family sailed on the ship, "Tuscarora," with Richard Harper as their leader.

After they arrived in Philadelphia, they went on to Burlington, Iowa where Niels died in 1858. They waited for two years for Hansine's fiance to immigrate to America. After his arrival in 1859, they traveled with the family of Christopher Funk who was a captain in James Brown's Wagon Company. They arrived in Salt Lake City with no food.

Brigham Young directed Bishop Edward Hunter to have the tithing yard cleared for their cattle and ordered a meal cooked for all who needed food. They first camped in Union Square.

After their arrival in Utah, Anna lived with her daughter, Hansine, and her husband Rasmus Nielsen. They

first lived in Bountiful, then in Weston, Franklin County, Idaho. She insisted on having the care of the home as her daughter did the spinning and weaving.

Anna passed away in Weston in February, 1886, and is buried there.

ANNA MARIA CHRISTENSDATTER ANDERSEN NIELSEN

BIRTHDATE: 18 Jun 1837
Orso, Dronninglund, Denmark
DEATH: 28 May 1872
Moroni, Sanpete Co., Utah
PARENTS: Christen Andersen
Ane Catrine Pedersen (datter)
PIONEER: 22 Sep 1856
Knute Peterson Wagon Train
SPOUSE: Jens Christian Nielsen
MARRIED: 2 Oct 1856
Big Cottonwood, Salt Lake Co., Utah
DEATH SP: 26 Dec 1920
Moroni, Sanpete Co., Utah

CHILDREN:
Daniel Christian, 28 May 1858
Andrew, 22 Jan 1860
Joseph, 30 Dec 1861
Mary Minerva "Maria" (Johnson), 30 Oct 1863
Ephraim, 30 Sep 1865
Jens Christian, 24 Sep 1867
Annie Nora (Hyler), 3 Sep 1869
Boy, May 1872 (Stillborn)

The children's surname was legally changed to Nelson.

Anna Maria was born June 18, 1837, in Orso, Dronninglund, Hjorring, Denmark. She emigrated with her family from the Vendsyssel Conference on the sailing ship, "James Nesmith," January 7, 1855. In America the children all took the surname of Andersen which was their father's surname.

Anna Maria's parents died of chills and fever in Iowa late in 1855, leaving the children to care for themselves. Anna Maria and her sister, Elsie, had opportunity to cross the Plains with the families of Morten Lund and Samuel Lee.

Jens Christian Nielsen, who was friendly with Anna Maria gave her the $30.00 she needed to make the journey, and she arrived in September, 1856. They lived with Jens' brother, Augustinus, in Big Cottonwood. Within two weeks, Anna Maria married Jens after she told him in her honest way..."If you want me you better be at, for there is others that are offering a home."

Maria was a good wife in those days of poverty, not having much but cornbread, skimming of molasses, and the flour of one bushel of wheat.

Finding it not safe for a woman to be alone in the Big Cottonwood Canyon they moved to Spanish Fork making their camp at the West Wall. This wall was made of dirt and built eight feet high to protect people from the Indians. In July, they left for Sanpete Valley. The journey was very hard on Anna Maria and her baby, but Jens and two teams helped get them to Ephraim.

In 1859, Brigham Young ordered Mt. Pleasant and Moroni settled so Anna Maria's family moved to Moroni and bought a farm. After building homes and a meeting and or school house, Brigham condemned the ground and they were counseled to move to higher ground.

We have no details of the life of Anna Maria through the Indian fighting and the trials of building and rebuilding but we know she had a large family and kept the home going while her husband was fighting, farming, building and rebuilding. We do know she possessed many wonderful talents and contributed much to not only her family but the society she lived in and the myriads of people influenced by her children whom she loved, taught and brought up in honesty and integrity.

Anna Maria passed away in 1872, after her last child was born; a little boy born dead who is buried in the Moroni Cemetery.

ANNIE HANSEN NIELSEN

BIRTHDATE: 23 Mar 1854
Torby, Maribo, Denmark
DEATH: 10 Apr 1940
Salina, Sevier Co., Utah
PARENTS:
Hans Hansen (Cook Hans)
Annie Johansen
PIONEER: Fall 1863
SPOUSE: Hans C. Nielsen
MARRIED: 21 Nov 1883
St. George, Washington, Utah
DEATH SP: 20 Feb 1935
Salina, Sevier Co., Utah

CHILDREN:
Mary Bertha, 21 Dec 1880
Trena Alvilda, 10 Nov 1885
Daniel, 28 Jul 1887
James Terry, 13 Apr 1890
Onest Christian, 22 Jan 1893
Parley Deloy, 12 Jul 1902

Annie was one of nine children in her family. Her father was an all around carpenter. He served in the war between Denmark and Germany.

When the Hansen family arrived at Florence, Nebraska, they joined a wagon company to help them cross the Plains. Shortly after they left Florence, her youngest brother, Johanes, died. They arrived in Salt Lake Valley in the Fall of 1863.

Annie became the second wife of Hans Christian Nielsen. They traveled by horse and wagon to the St. George Temple to be sealed on November 21, 1883. The

first family lived "over the river" on the farm west of Salina. Hans was imprisoned because of polygamy.

In later years, Annie moved to Salina from the farm. She and her parents had homes on the same lot on West Main Street.

After his release from prison, Hans took his first family to Oak City in Millard County. He brought a load of rock salt to Annie from the Redmond Salt Mines so she could use it to trade or barter for other items needed by her family.

Annie had a flock of chickens, a cow, and usually a pig to feed. She had currant and gooseberry bushes from which she made jams. She had a parsley patch from which she plucked a tasty herb for her Danish dumpling chicken soup. She had a nice garden which helped with her living. She would trade her extra eggs at the store for sugar, soda, thread, and other necessities. She crocheted and visited with family members.

Annie passed away at the home of her daughter, Alvilda, in Salina, Utah.

CAROLINE AMELIA MORTENSEN NIELSEN

BIRTHDATE: 20 Mar 1821
Koboley, Skov, Denmark
DEATH: 3 Apr 1900
Springdale, Washington, Utah
PARENTS: Morten Andersen
Else Justesen
PIONEER: 1857
Seventh Handcart Company
SPOUSE: Ole Nielsen
MARRIED: abt 1841
Denmark
DEATH SP: 23 Dec 1892
Arizona

CHILDREN:
Hans Jorgen, 18 Oct 1842
Wilheimine Kristine (Sanders), 14 Jul 1847
Frederik Ferdinand, 31 May 1849
Dorthea Olevia (Lemmon Durfee), 28 May 1851
Ludvig Bernhard, 7 Jul 1854
Caroline (Clark), abt 1856
Joseph Smith, abt 1858
Ole, 12 Jun 1862

Caroline Amelia was born in Koboley, Skov, Maribo, Denmark. While living in Falster, Denmark with her parents, Caroline and her husband were baptized on August 11, 1853. Because of mob violence, the baptism was performed secretly at night in a stream.

In a short time the Nielsens became dissatisfied in their native country and began to plan to join the Saints in Utah. They sailed, April 18, 1857, on a steamship to Britain. As they left Denmark, Caroline's mother wrung her hands as she cried bitterly and said, "Oh Ole, my son, you are taking your young family among those wicked, wicked Mormons."

Caroline and Ole's family than sailed from Liverpool, England, April 25, 1857, on the ship "Westmoreland." Matthias Cowley was the president of this company of 544 converts and four missionaries. They reached Philadelphia on May 31, 1857. In June they began the trek westward in the company which included sixty-six handcarts, and four mule-drawn wagons under the command of James P. Park. Because Captain Park could not understand Danish, Christian Christiansen consented to serve as captain. Caroline walked the entire trip while Ole rode part way in a cart because of his poor health.

Three weeks after the Seventh Handcart Company arrived in the Salt Lake Valley, Caroline gave birth to her child. After a short stay in Salt Lake City, the family moved to Southern Utah. Caroline worked for the James Abbott Lemmon family, the two families decided to move to Short Creek in southern Arizona and then to Toquerville, Utah. Later the two families settled in Northup.

Caroline passed away on April 3, 1900, Springdale, Utah. She was a great pioneer woman who gave up much for her religious beliefs. She is honored for her great faith and endurance.

CAROLINE CHRISTENSEN NIELSEN

BIRTHDATE: 5 Sep 1848
Ugilt, Hjorring, Denmark
DEATH: 24 May 1928
Salt Lake City, Salt Lake, Utah
PARENTS:Christian Christensen
Ane Marie Nielsen
PIONEER: 1867
Kesco Group
SPOUSE: Niels Peder Nielsen
MARRIED: 13 Dec 1868
Salt Lake City, Salt Lake, Utah
DEATH SP: 17 Apr 1923
Ephraim, Sanpete Co., Utah

CHILDREN:
Neils Peder, 8 Sep 1869
Stillborn son, Apr 1871
Heber Peter, 19 Mar 1872
Hans Frederick, 18 Aug 1874
David Waldemar, 13 Nov 1876
Abel Christian, 7 Nov 1878
Aurelia Christine (Otterstrom Mattson), 28 Aug 1880
Aaron Godtfred, 24 Jun 1882
Moses Marion, 22 May 1884
Anna Marinda Adina (Clark), 13 Feb 1886
Caroline Matilda (Anderson), 26 Dec 1888
Ernest Hyrum, 6 Feb 1891
Joseph Richard, 30 Jan 1893

Caroline was born in 1848 in Denmark. Caroline's family accepted the gospel of the Church of Jesus Christ of Latter-day Saints when the missionaries brought it to their home in Denmark. She was baptized in 1863 at the age of fifteen.

Her family were faithful members and many times walked eighteen miles to attend conferences of the Church, leaving home at 4 a.m. to get there for the afternoon meeting.

The family decided to join the Saints in the New World but couldn't all afford to come at once. Caroline, now age nineteen, and her half sister, Johanne Sine Fredericke Pederson (Tante), came first, leaving in 1867. The next year her father and younger sister, Ane Katrine, came over, and a year later, her mother came and the next year her brother, Niels Christian, came as the last of the family to leave Denmark.

Caroline walked all the way across the Plains. Many emigrants from Denmark went to Ephraim, Utah, so that's where she settled. She lived with a family and did housework to earn her board and room. In December of 1868, she married another emigrant from Denmark, Niels Peder Nielsen in the Endowment House in Salt Lake City. They.made their home in Ephraim and raised a fine family of sons and daughters, many of whom attended Snow Academy. She gave birth to thirteen children; ten sons and three daughters.

Caroline was industrious and wove rugs, took in boarders and cooked for weddings to help the family income. She made candles and soap, dried fruits and vegetables, made butter and cheese and of course planted a large garden, raised wheat for bread and had cows for milk and meat. She had a special 'loom room' in her home where she spent many hours, sometimes weaving by candlelight until late at night. She carded the wool, colored it and wove it, using very fine thread. She wove cloth for towels, sheets and temple clothes by the hundreds of yards.

When she had been married nine years, her husband took a second wife. Later, he was called to go back to Denmark on a mission and she supported the family while he was gone. When the Manti Temple was built, they took the records of their Danish ancestors and did the temple work for hundreds of them.

Caroline died at the age of seventy-nine in Salt Lake City. She was a faithful member of the Church, was the mother of many, and had endured the hardships of pioneer life. Her family honor her name.

CHRISTINA MARIE CHRISTIANSEN NIELSEN

BIRTHDATE: 13 Mar 1848
Saeby, Hjorring, Denmark
DEATH: 15 Apr 1924
Fairview, Sanpete Co., Utah
PARENTS: Peter Christiansen
Marie (Larsar) Rasmussen
PIONEER: 25 Sep 1868
John G. Holman Wagon Train
SPOUSE: Niels Nielsen
MARRIED: 28 Mar 1870
Salt Lake, Endowment House
DEATH SP: 12 Dec 1924
Fairview, Sanpete Co., Utah

CHILDREN:
Wilhelmina, 29 Jan 1871
Diantha Marie, 3 Dec 1873
Niels Peter, 17 May 1876
Johanna, 16 Dec 1878 (died as a child)

Christina Marie was born in 1848 in Denmark. She was seven years old when her mother joined the Church of Jesus Christ of Latter-day Saints. It was a time of great distress for Christina and her brothers and sisters, as their father was bitter against the Church and forced their mother to leave their home. He subsequently became ill and sent for her to return home where he passed away three years later.

As a teenager, Christina went to work for a woman on a large estate. She was baptized on November 8, 1863. At that time the Branch Records listed her as being from Odstrup.

Christina, her mother and her sister, Dorthea, left Copenhagen, Denmark, June 13, 1868, for America. They sailed on the ship "Emerald Isle," and were on the water for fifty-five days. Conditions were very poor and there was a lot of sickness and many deaths.

They crossed the Plains in Captain John G. Holman's Ox-Train Company and arrived in the Salt Lake Valley on September 25, 1868. They were able to place their luggage in a wagon, but it was necessary for them to walk most of the way. Christina recounted in later years that the happiest time of her life, although she had to walk all the way, was when crossing the Plains. She loved the singing and the dancing.

While living in Salt Lake City, she supported herself by doing housework for people. It was here that she met and married Niels Nielsen on March 28, 1870, in the Endowment House. He and his mother had also come from Denmark.

Niels was an excellent carpenter and had been working on the Salt Lake Temple. They were called to go to Sanpete County to settle in Fairview where their children were born.

For the first few years everything went well, and then her husband took a second wife. Christina received very little, if any, financial support from him after that time. She made a living by taking in washings and doing other household work. She spent a great deal of time on "The Mountain" cooking for the saw mill workers and milking cows. She made wool bats for quilts for many of her friends and neighbors. She would wash, pick and card the wool bats for a quilt for fifty cents.

Christina learned to speak English quite well, but continued to speak Danish whenever one of her Danish speaking friends visited her. She always read her Danish newspaper. Christina devoted her entire life to her family and to the Church. She was a wonderful woman who was loved by all who knew her.

Christina passed away on April 15, 1924 at the age of seventy-six years. She had been a valiant pioneer woman, one of great faith and with great strength to move forward regardless of the circumstances. Her posterity honor her for her greatness.

DOROTHEA PAULSEN NIELSEN

No Photo Available

BIRTHDATE: 25 Feb 1825
Kaarup, Godstd Maribo, Denmark
DEATH: 16 Nov 1868
Milton, Morgan Co., Utah
PARENTS: Hans Paulsen
Karen Marie Jorgensen
PIONEER: 1861
SPOUSE: Anders Nielsen
MARRIED: abt 1849/50
Denmark
DEATH SP: 3 Jun 1911
Milton, Morgan Co., Utah

CHILDREN:
Hans Peter, 1850/51
Theodore, 24 Oct 1852
Theodore Waldemar, 15 Feb 1854
Matilda Marie, 23 Oct 1855
Laura Nicolina, 31 Jun 1858
Joseph, 20 Feb 1860
Hyrum, 10 Dec 1861
Emma, 23 Sep 1865
Mary, 23 Sep 1866
Willard, 1 Nov 1868

Dorothea was born February 25, 1825 in Kaarup, Godstd Maribo, Denmark. She met Anders Nielsen when she worked in a wealthy doctor's home as a cook and he was a master craftsman in the flour mill near Copenhagen.

After they were engaged, Anders left to fight in the war between Denmark and Russia and was taken prisoner. Before he left he had saved several hundred dollars which he entrusted to Dorothea.

When he returned they were married at her village near Maribo, Lolland, Denmark. Their early married life was one of comfort. Six children were born to them during the first ten years. The first two died in infancy.

In 1859, Dorothea joined The Church of Jesus Christ of Latter-day Saints. Her husband was resentful at first, but later was converted and baptized on August 15, 1859. In May, 1861, they left Copenhagen, unlike most convert families, they had ample means to emigrate to Zion.

While crossing the Plains, Dorothea and her little children were very ill. They were sent to help settle Milton in Morgan, Utah. Two months after they arrived in Milton, Dorothea gave birth in the covered wagon to their seventh child.

The first two years in Milton were times of bitter cold, hunger, and hardship. Dorothea worked beside her husband in hard physical labor. She supported and encouraged him in his decision to mary Sophia Christensen as a second wife in June of 1866.

In 1868, Dorothea experienced a difficult tenth pregnancy and died sixteen days after the baby was born.

ELIZABETH ERIKSEN NIELSEN

No Photo Available

BIRTHDATE: 28 Sep 1842
Sangsee, LaSalle Co., Illinois
DEATH: 4 Oct 1891
Hyrum, Cache Co., Utah
PARENTS: Henry S. Eriksen
Melinda Jonasen
PIONEER: Before 1852
SPOUSE: Andrew B. Nielsen
MARRIED: 1 Apr 1865
Hyrum, Cache Co., Utah
DEATH SP: 5 Feb 1913
Hyrum, Cache Co., Utah

CHILDREN:
Mary Elizabeth, 23 Mar 1866
Andrew Henry, 5 Jan 1869
Anna Melinda, 5 Sep 1871
Margaret Maria, 5 Jun 1875
Emily Christine, 4 Mar 1878
Joseph Ilard, 10 Sep 1882

Elizabeth was born September 28, 1842, in Sangsee, Illinois, the youngest of eight children. Six of the older children were born in Norway and came with the parents to Illinois sometime before 1839. Her parents were converts to The Church of Jesus Christ of Latter-day Saints and had the privilege of receiving their endowments and being sealed in the Nauvoo Temple.

The Eriksen family came to the Salt Lake Valley and settled in the Mill Creek area before 1852. Her mother died when she was just nine years old and her stepmother was said to be very particular and strict.

Elizabeth was married to Andrew B. Nielsen on April 1, 1865, by Bishop O. N. Liljenquist. They later received their endowments in the Endowment House and were sealed

in the Logan Temple. They made their home in Hyrum, but later moved to the area that was developed into the College and Young wards.

As the wife of a farmer, Elizabeth often cooked for the threshing crews. She directed the washing, picking, and carding of wool when their sheep were sheared. She then would spin the wool for their clothing. She also cared for bees for the production of honey. One time she was stung so bad that she became very ill from the poison.

Elizabeth was forty-nine years old when she died at Hyrum and was buried in the Hyrum Cemetery.

HANSINE NIELSEN

BIRTHDATE: 28 Mar 1831
Randers, Jutland, Denmark
DEATH: 15 Oct 1909
Weston, Franklin Co., Idaho
PARENTS: Soren Christiansen
Anna Hansen
PIONEER: 29 Aug 1859
James S. Brown Wagon Train
SPOUSE: Rasmus Nielsen
MARRIED: 12 Jun 1859
Florence, Nebraska
DEATH SP: 17 May 1896
Weston, Franklin Co., Idaho

CHILDREN:
Rasmus, 13 Mar 1862
Ane Marie (Campbell), 20 May 1864
Ane Kirstine "Stena" (Montgomery), 20 Apr 1868
Hans Christian, 19 Jun 1870

Hansine was born in Randers, Denmark in 1831. She started working out when she was quite young and did hard manual labor as she grew older. The family converted to the Church of Jesus Christ of Latter-day Saints in 1855, and they carefully saved their money so they could come to America.

She and Rasmus Nielsen fell in love while in Denmark, but decided not to get married until they emigrated. Hansine came first in 1857, and was followed by Rasmus in 1859. Hansine knew Rasmus was coming, but was very surprised one evening when she visited a nearby camp in Florence to see Rasmus there. Rasmus and Hansine were married on June 12, 1859

They made their first home in Bountiful where a son was born in 1862. They were called to help settle Cache County, so they first settled in Richmond, then moved to Weston, Idaho as the first settlers of that community.

Rasmus took a second wife Maren Christina Jensen on March 17, 1869. He spent time in a Detroit, Michigan prison for being a polygamist, which left the wives to care for themselves. Polygamy was difficult for Hansine.

While Rasmus was incarcerated, Hansine's mother died and her husband wrote her a letter of comfort, and urged her to find consolation with her sisters, her blood sister, Maren, or his other wife, Maren.

Hansine earned money for support by weaving cloth, making carpets, and some of her weaving was used in the Logan Temple. Her yarn was of her own making. She carded, cleaned the wool, dyed it, and then wove it. One bed covering she made is white, orange and blue.

Hansine was active in the Church serving as counselor in the Relief Society presidency for many years. As a visiting teacher, she often walked six or seven miles to complete her teaching, usually taking most of the day to do it. One time when one of her children was ill and nothing seemed to help, she promised Heavenly Father she would stop drinking coffee if He would spare the child's life. The child recovered, and though it was very difficult to break a lifelong habit, she had given her word, and she quit.

Hansine passed away in Weston, Idaho, on October 15, 1909 at the age of seventy-nine years and seven months. Her husband, Rasmus, had passed away in 1896, leaving her a widow for over thirteen years.

Hansine had lived a good Christian life, was loving to her family and devoted to the Church which meant much to her throughout her life. She was a true, devoted, faithful Latter-day Saint pioneer woman.

INGEBORG SOPHIA HANSEN NIELSEN

BIRTHDATE: 13 May 1816
Munkerjirgby, Soro, Denmark
DEATH: 25 Sep 1908
Brigham City, Box Elder, Utah
PARENTS: Hans Christofferson
Ane Catherine Larsen
PIONEER: 1857
SPOUSE: Neils H. Nielsen
MARRIED: 26 Feb 1847
Haugerup, Pedersborg, Soro,
Denmark
DEATH SP: 10 Mar 1893
Cleveland, Bannock, Idaho

CHILDREN:
Maren "Mary" Kirstine (Neeley), 17 Jun 1847
Hans Peter, 24 Apr 1849
Karen Sophia (Ralphs), 23 Feb 1853

Ingeborg Sophia was born in Denmark in 1816. In 1845, she married Niels H. Nielsen. She was the mother of three children. Her parents were considered to be wealthy, so she was accustomed to a comfortable home and surroundings.

Her husband, Neil came home one day and suggested her joining a new Church. This was most unpopular at that time, and she realized it would be necessary to dispose of their comfortable home, furniture valuables, jewelry, etc. and come to a new country. It was a momentous decision. Ocean travel was most uncertain, all were sailing ships and when a ship set out, there was no indication of how long it would take to make a trip.

Ingeborg had three small children the youngest being a babe in arms. From what is known about her, Ingeborg was anything but an adventurous type, but she did consent to come, although it took a lot of courage.

This family disposed of their possessions, saving only enough money to pay their transportation, and to buy a small home in Salt Lake City, which they had purchased sight unseen, from a missionary before leaving Denmark. The rest of their money was turned over to the Emigration Fund. The family arrived in Salt Lake City in 1857, so much in debt that they had to sell the home they had bought while in Denmark and move to Brigham City. Brigham City was the home of Ingeborg for the remainder of her life.

Through all their hardships, she remained steadfast to her faith. She was a good financier, and always had a way of making a little money. She planted mulberry trees when the silk worm industry was introduced. She always kept a few pigs.and chickens, and the eggs bought most of her groceries.

Ingeborg loved children and seemed to understand them. A child never left her home without something special. It-might be only a lump of sugar. Her bread was made famous by her special baking of it in a "crock." It had extra flavor.

Many young emigrant girls found refuge at her home. She was immaculate housekeeper and always looked neat as a pin herself. She wore a long black dress with a high necked basque, a black cap on her head and always had on clean, white aprons, some with wide crochet on the bottom. She wore a pair of round gold earrings that hung from her pierced ears, nearly to her shoulders. She always displayed culture and refinement, even in her advanced years.

Ingeborg's health was generally good. She lived to be nearly ninety-three years of age, and did her own house-work until she was past ninety. She had a very independent nature.

Her husband passed away on March 10, 1893, and she was a widow for over fifteen years. Ingeborg passed away at her home on Second West in Brigham City on September 25, 1908 and was buried in the Brigham City Cemetery, a great pioneer woman who is honored by her family.

JOHANNE CHRISTINE ANDERSON HANSEN ALLERUP NIELSEN

BIRTHDATE: 16 Sep 1818
Belgholm, Denmark
DEATH: 30 Jan 1901
Egin, Fremont Co., Idaho
PARENTS: Anders H. Allerup
Inger Margerthe Larsen
PIONEER: 17 Sep 1861
J. Woolley Handcart Company
SPOUSE: Hans I. Nielsen
MARRIED: 4 Dec 1841
Strobelev, Denmark
DEATH SP: 11 Oct 1911
Hyrum, Cache Co., Utah

CHILDREN:
Jensine Christine, 17 Feb 1842
Inger Nielsen, 27 Oct 1843
Dorthea Nielsen, 6 Sep 1846
Marthine Nielsine Matenia, 28 Mar 1849
Bregitte Nielsen, 19 Jun 1852
Anne Christine Nielsen, 17 Apr 1854

Johanne Christine was born, September 16, 1818, in Belgholm, Denmark. She married Hans I. Nielsen on December 4, 1841 at Strobelev, Denmark. She was the mother of six daughters, all of them born in Denmark. They arrived in Utah in 1861, having traveled with the John Woolley Company, and settled in Hyrum, Cache County, Utah.

Johanne made yeast for the entire town of Hyrum. The town people would bring a cup of flour in exchange for a cup of yeast. She was a fine seamstress and passed her talents on to her six daughters. She could do anything from sewing to butchering poultry, dairy stock, and could make all kinds of head cheese. She also cut and cured meat. She loved the gospel and served in many positions in the Church.

Johanne passed away, January 30, 1901, at Egin, Fremont County, Idaho, and her husband, Hans, passed away on October 11, 1911 at Hyrum, Cache County, Utah.

JOSEPHINE CHARLOTTE ERICKSON NIELSEN

BIRTHDATE: 10 Apr 1839
Gotteburg, Sweden
DEATH: 10 Dec 1924
Hyrum, Cache Co., Utah
PARENTS: James A. Erickson
Catherine Erickson
PIONEER: 1860
SPOUSE: Hans I. Nielsen
MARRIED: 5 Nov 1866
Salt Lake City, Salt Lake, Utah
DEATH SP: 18 Oct 1911
Hyrum, Cache Co., Utah

CHILDREN:
Hans Peter, 27 Nov 1867
Joseph I., 12 Feb 1868
Lize Christine, 28 Mar 1872 (twin)
Anna ELiza, 28 Mar 1872 (twin)
Levi, 28 Mar 1873
Josephine Charlotte, 10 Oct 1874
Gustav Nielsen, 18 Apr 1875
Doris Amanda, 9 Apr 1877
Hyrum Isaac, 25 May 1879

Josephine Charlotte was born on April 10, 1839 at Gotteburg, Sweden. Little is known of her early life, but she came to the Salt Lake Valley in 1860.

She was married to Hans I. Hansen on November 5, 1866 in the Endowment House in Salt Lake City, Utah, as a plural wife. She was the mother of eight children.

Her husband, Hans, passed away in Hyrum, Cache County, Utah on October 18, 1911, and Josephine passed away on December 10, 1924, also in Hyrum, Utah.

KAREN "CAROLINE" NEILS SORENSEN NIELSEN (NIELSON)

BIRTHDATE: 23 Feb. 1821
Flemming, Scandaborg, Denmark
DEATH SP: 29 Jul. 1901
Washington, Washington, Utah
PARENTS: Soren Nielsen
Anna Jensen
PIONEER: 5 Sep. 1855
Jacob F. Secrist Wagon Train
SPOUSE: Peter Nielsen Sr.
MARRIED: 14 Jan. 1855
aboard ship
DEATH SP: 9 Apr. 1883
Washington, Washington, Utah

CHILDREN:
Isreal, abt 1850 (stepson)
Peter II, 1 Dec 1856
Anna Marie, 8 Oct. 1858 (died same day)

Karen "Caroline" Neils Sornsen was born in Flemming, Hornborg Parish, Scandaborg County, Denmark in 1821 and grew up in a small white farm house with a red roof, nearby was a thatched barn to house the animals that every family owned on their own tiny farm. Her education was to the compulsory age of fourteen and their family worship was of the Catholic faith. (though the established church of Denmark was Lutheran).

As she grew she watched three cousins die from tuberculosis and because of her own poor health, lived in constant fear that she had that disease. She wrote in her journal that she had decided to join a Catholic Nunnery so as to spend "what few years she might still live" with their help.

At the time she was working for Peter Nielsen whose wife needed constant care and looking after their small son along with the household duties.

In 1850, missionaries from the Church of Jesus Christ of Latter-day Saints were spreading through much of Denmark and Caroline was one of the first to hear the beautiful message. The Elders were welcomed into the Nielsen home and he too listened. Ten months after Mrs. Nielsen died, Caroline was baptized, she wrote "it was an icy cold day; as I came out of the waters of baptism, I felt cured and sweetly healed by the Gospel from that dreadful disease."

Peter Nielsen was not baptized until a year later. Once baptized he went out doing missionary work and by 1854 was preparing to emigrate to Utah.

On November 26, 1854, the "Cimbria" set sail from Copenhagen with thirty-four year old Caroline, Peter forty-two and his son Isreal among it's passengers. The voyage was horribly troubled, fainter souls would have given up. Under raging wind and rain storms to the point of capsizing the ship, they were knocked about the North Sea, ship broken by waves, cargo washed overboard, and a wind so erratic that in three weeks time they found themselves blown back to Denmark, almost where they had started.

Again they set out, again raging storms, the crew pumped with all their might to keep from going under, the brethren carried coal to renew the furnace, some thought they would go down. By 6 o'clock Christmas Eve, they reached Hull, England. A sailor came to them congratulating them for their work and divulging the secret that the captain had risked a ship and all on it for the sake of money. They shared their secret, "The Lord had spared all their lives because they were His people." Other dangers met them face to face as they crossed the ocean, disease accosted all, bad luck caused loss of faith and "five were buried and it kept on us hard, Oh so hard."

Then, with a visit from Brother Erastus Snow, a chastisement for their poor spirits, and a blessing at their repentance and renewal of faith, they were given a promise that the scourge would be cast from their midst: and the sick healed. And it was so.

Captain Secrist, leader of the wagon train, came among them with strict rules and demanding for absolute obedience from every person and animal, "and more than this he said but I don't remember the interpretation" but that night he became ill and soon died of cholera. Another was sent to lead us, Brother Gisiman, and from then on we got along pretty well."

Caroline's life in Utah reflects the history we all know. She accepted a polygamous wife, Harriet Amanda Brown, moved again and again as they were called, suffered grasshopper invasion and lack of essentials. She was also beloved by her community. Her husband, and her children called her blessed.

KIRSTEN ANDERSEN NIELSEN

BIRTHDATE: 30 Mar 1808
Systofte, Falster, Denmark
DEATH: 7 Nov 1867
Ephraim, Sanpete Co., Utah
PARENTS: Anders Jorgensen
Bodil Mortensen
PIONEER: 1862
Horn Co. Wagon Train
SPOUSE: Peder Nielsen
MARRIED: 9 Dec 1831
DEATH SP: 14 Sep 1862
Sweetwater River, Wyoming

CHILDREN:
Inger Christine (Kudsk), 4 May 1827
Jorgen, 31 Mar 1832 (died as a child)
Maren, 9 Feb 1834
Karen, 22 Oct 1835
Anne, 30 Dec 1837 (died at age 14)
Bodil, 16 Apr 1840 (died as a child)
Niels Peder, 13 Feb 1847

Kirsten was born in 1808 in Denmark. Missionaries from the Church of Jesus Christ of Latter-day Saints came to the town in Denmark where Kirsten and Peder lived and Kirsten was the first of the family to be baptized. This was in December, 1859, when she was fifty-one years of age. About two years later, her husband joined the Church, and in March of 1862, their son Niels Peder, age fifteen was baptized. The two older daughters did not join the Church and stayed in Denmark when the family came to America.

When they sailed from Hamburg, Germany on April 8, 1862, Kirsten was fifty-four years old. They sailed on the ship "Humboldt" with their son Niels Peder, and they arrived in New York City, May 20, 1862. They continued on west, traveling by railroad to Florence, Nebraska, and then traveled by ox-team with the Horn Company to Utah. They arrived on October 1, 1862 after leaving Nebraska July 29th.

Kirsten's husband died while they were in the Sweetwater River country, in Wyoming. He was buried in an unmarked grave. Kirsten and her teenage son, Niels, continued on and settled with other Danish emigrants in Ephraim, Sanpete County, Utah.

Kirsten Andersen Nielsen, faithful pioneer, passed away in November of 1867 at the age of fifty-nine years, only five years after arriving in Utah. She is buried in the old pioneer cemetery in Ephraim, Utah.

Kirsten was a true pioneer woman of great faith and fortitude, who gave up much for her religious beliefs, and endured the trials and tribulations which these brave souls encountered. We honor her for her great devotion.

KIRSTEN LARSEN NIELSEN

BIRTHDATE: 28 Apr 1826
St. Hans, Odense, Odense, Isle of
Fyn, Denmark
DEATH: 21 Sep 1905
Spanish Fork, Utah Co. Utah
PARENTS: Lars Larsen
Ane Marie Thomasen(datter)
PIONEER: 8 Nov 1865
Miner Atwood Co. Wagon Train
SPOUSE: (Peder) Peter Nielsen
MARRIED: 4 Apr 1857
DEATH SP: 23 Mar 1912
Spanish Fork, Utah Co. Utah

CHILDREN:
Lars, 5 Jun 1857
Ane Marie, 24 Oct 1859
Maren Kirstine, 6 Nov 1863 (died at age 1)
Emma, 15 Nov 1867-69
Caroline, 15 Oct 1870

Kirsten Larsen was born in Denmark in 1826 and it was told in the family that Kirsten was a lady-in-waiting to the queen of Denmark. Kirsten became pregnant and a husband was found for her. Twenty year old Peter Nielsen was given a ninety-nine year lease on twenty-four acres of land in exchange for marrying thirty year old Kirsten.

Kirsten was given a wooden chest by the queen which contained her dowry a small black trunk which she brought all the way to Utah. A marriage with such an inglorious beginning lasted forty-eight years, yielded five children, a life of worship, and took the couple halfway round the world.

Their second child was not quite three years old when Kirstine, having heard the missionaries of the Church was baptized, August 8,. 1862, with Peter following two months later on October 7, 1862.

Their third child was one and a half when all the preparation had been made, supplies paid for and with a crowd of 484 souls, they left Copenhagen on the Steamer "Aurora," by rail from Kiel, and were joined by seventy-three in Hamberg to board the "B. S. Kimball" for a voyage with 654 others to New York.

The weather was good the whole of the voyage but the drinking water was so foul that vinegar was added to quell the taste, when this made them sick whisky was taken as an antidote and that proved a temptation to many and the sickness increased, no ventilation except that coming down the stairwell, caused such a stench the odor overcame many, and vermin of all kinds increase and infested the quarters. Measles proved villainous and the combination of all caused the death of three adults and twenty-five children. One of those children buried at sea was Kirsten's little one year old, Maren.

Once in America, there were times of waiting to begin traveling again, five weeks were required in Wyoming, Nebraska just to be ready for the wagon train. Seven more died by the time they were able to start the way west with the Atwood Company.

Several incidents made this journey memorable, after seven weeks of travel the train was met at Fort Laramie by United States Army officers who informed them through three interpreters in three languages that they could go no further, the Indians were on the warpath. They would be given transportation to any other destination in America they wished to go. A vote was taken and unanimously decided, Utah or nothing, so on they went completing a trek of another six weeks.

Food had to be rationed, teams ran away and sister Louise Nelsen from Aalberg, was run over and killed. An Indian attack wounded seven brothers with arrows, all survived. A freight company traveled with them for protection and was greatly appreciated. Still, campfires at night cast shadows of young and old dancing to the strains of an old violin and songs were sung for comfort and strength as they walked beside the wagons.

On November 8, wallowing through two feet of snow in the canyons, the company arrived into the Salt Lake Valley. The Nielsens went to Spanish Fork to winter through in a doorless, windowless adobe home. Two children were born to Kirsten and Peter in Utah.

Kirsten passed away in Spanish Fork at the age of seventy-nine, having lived a selfless life obedient to God.

KIRSTEN SVENDSEN PEDERSEN NIELSEN

BIRTHDATE: 25 Mar. 1828
Thune, Copenhagen Denmark
DEATH: 2 Dec. 1899
Brigham City, Box Elder, Utah
PARENTS: Svend Pedersen
Sidne Sorensen
PIONEER: 7 Sep. 1855
Secrist & Guymon Wagon Train
SPOUSE I: Hans Pedersen
MARRIED: Feb-Jun 1855
DEATH SP: 5 Nov 1859
Brigham City, Box Elder, Utah

CHILDREN:
Kirstine Mary, 29 Jan 1857
Sarah P., 9 Jan. 1859

SPOUSE II: Niels Hans Nielsen
MARRIED: 19 Feb 1860
DEATH SP: 10 Mar. 1893

CHILDREN:
Hans Hyrum, 30 Nov. 1860 (died at age 4)
Erastus William, 11 Apr. 1864 (died at 15 months)
Anne Sophie, 20 Aug. 1867
Nilaine Christine, 23 Apr. 1872 (died at 11 months)

Kirsten was born in Denmark in 1828. She was baptized on July 17, 1853 in the LDS branch of Ishoj, eleven miles southwest of Copenhagen, Denmark.

At the age of twenty-seven she joined a group of Danish Converts who boarded the ship "James Nesmith" in November of 1854, immigrating to Utah with other Scandinavian converts. Among the passengers on the forty-five day voyage was Hans Pedersen.

They shared the crowded ship, the rancid water and the shortages of food with the four hundred and forty people and some how found the privacy to fall in love. Some where after landing in New Orleans on the 18th of February and leaving Mormon Grove, Kansas for Utah, 13 June, Kirsten and Hans were married.

The couple joined Captain Jacob F. Secrist Company. He died on the plains leaving Noah T. Guymon to bring the group into Salt Lake Valley. Kirsten and Hans went to Brigham City, in Box Elder County where many of the Danish Saints had settled. Hans found work in a sand pit there and built his family a home and there the couple's two girls were born.

A friendship developed between Hans and their neighbor, Niels Nielsen, such a close bond that each promised the other "if something happened to one, the other would take care of his family."

Four years after arriving in Utah, Hans was killed in a cave in at his work and true to his word, Niels married Kirsten a few months later. He moved them to Bear River City where Niels had a farm. Kirsten was the second of his five wives.

The couple had four children, two boys and two girls. Grievously, when Hans was four and a half years old he died and three days later the second son, a baby fifteen months old died also.

Of the two girls, only Anne lived to adulthood. Only through the hope and faith that exists in the heart.

Kirsten was a homemaker with many talents; cooking, canning, drying fruits, and the making of special rock candy on a string. She sewed beautiful clothing by hand for her girls and other family members and also knitted and crocheted many beautiful items.

In her later years, she moved to Brigham City, to a home built by her son-in-law, James Peter Olsen, so she could be close to her daughter, Mary, and their family.

Kirsten passed away on December 2, 1899 and is buried in the Brigham City Cemetery.

MAGDALENA RASMUSSEN NIELSEN

BIRTHDATE: 17 Apr 1822
Thirsted, Maribo, Denmark
DEATH: 12 Feb 1903
Vernal, Uintah Co., Utah
PARENTS: Rasmus Nielsen
Ane Catherine Johansen
PIONEER: 22 Oct 1866
Abner Lowry Co. Wagon Train
SPOUSE: Peter C. Nielsen
MARRIED: 28 Dec 1844
Skjorringe, Maribo, Denmark
DEATH SP: 6 Aug 1879
Holladay, Salt Lake Co., Utah

CHILDREN:
Niels, 9 Mar 1845
Anne, 19 Mar 1847
Petrasanne Christine, 1 Sep 1850
Rasmus, 19 Mar 1852
Johanne Catrine, 26 Mar 1854
Thom, 1 Jul 1862

Magdalena was born in Thirsted, Maribo, Loiland, Denmark, 1822. When she was old enough, she went to work on a dairy farm and learned the skills of making good butter and cheese. She also became a fairly good practical nurse and midwife.

She married Peter Christian Nielsen. He was a farmer and was skilled in carpentry. They were introduced to the Church of Jesus Christ of Latter-day Saints and most of the family were baptized. After leaving the state church, people turned against them, refusing them water from the well belonging to the community, and refusing employment to her husband. At times, Magdalena was called upon to help the sick people because she was needed, so they managed to exist.

Eleven long, hard years after joining the Church, a Mr. Gregsen who was well-to-do, sold his property and donated money to buy the passage for all seven of their family. Later, the missionaries returned and told them the fares had been raised, so it was arranged for her sons Niels and Rasmus to stay until they could send for them.

They crossed the ocean by ship, "Cavour" and landed in New York. They traveled by rail and by boat until they reached Florence, Nebraska. There, they joined the Abner Lowry Wagon Train with whom they crossed the Plains.

Some of the people became ill with cholera and many died. Magdalena went among them and helped all she could until she also became ill. However, she recovered and no other member of her family caught it. The parents of two other families died from the cholera and Magdalena took their children and cared for them until they reached Salt Lake where they went to live with others. They went to live in Big Cottonwood for two years.

They moved to Brigham City and Peter was called upon to work in Weber Canyon for the railroad. Magdalena was left with two small children to care for as well as she could. When he returned, Peter used his money to send for their son, Rasmus. He arrived in August, 1869, having ridden all across the United States on the train.

In 1871, they received a letter from Denmark telling them their oldest son, Neils, had died. Her married daughter, Petrasanne, came home for a visit and died of black canker while she was there.

Magdalena's life was filled with many hardships and sorrows. It was a struggle all of her life just for a meager existence. After her husband died, she lived with her son, Rasmus, until she died.

MAREN SOPHIA CHRISTENSEN NIELSEN

No Photo Available

BIRTHDATE: 2 Sep. 1820
Winneberg, Jtln, Denmark
DEATH: 15 Mar. 1904
Preston, Franklin, Idaho
PARENTS: Peder Christensen
Anne Nielsen
PIONEER: Handcart Company
SPOUSE: Andreas Nielsen
MARRIED: 30 Jun. 1866
DEATH SP: 3 Jun. 1911
Milton, Morgan Co. Utah

CHILD:
Annie Nielsen, 2 Jun. 1867

Maren Sophia was born in Denmark in 1820 and joined the Church of Jesus Christ of Latter-day Saints at a time when Mormons were harassed there, some times so extensively that they either gave up their religion or hurried their departure from their native land. Their faith was stronger than their need for security and comfort.

The journey was a ten month ordeal over the North Sea to Liverpool England, over the Atlantic Ocean to (possibly before 1855), New Orleans. So many converts died from malaria or cholera that by February of 1855 the immigrants were sent to New York. The journey over land was longer but healthier.

Sophia was full of expectations and willing to work to fulfill her dreams, and work she did. Sophia pushed a hand-cart the entire distance.

She married at age forty-six becoming the second wife of Andreas Neilsen and had their first and only child at the age of forty-seven. Approximately two years later, Andreas' first wife died in child birth, leaving Sophia the duties of caring for her ten children as well as Sophia's one year old daughter, Annie.

Sophia was a very small woman with beautiful brown curly hair, large gray eyes, and fine features. (no pictures were taken of her, but all who knew and remembered her say she was very beautiful). She spent much of her life caring for and feeding the sick and poor in the village of Milton, Utah.

She often wore a full petticoat that had numerous pockets sewn into the skirt. In these pockets she would have small bottles of cream, pats of butter and homemade cheese. Sometimes the pockets contained homemade soap and other hard to obtain articles. All of these she freely gave to the widows and needy friends she visited.

She was brave also, when Indians came to her home, she would place the children in a back bedroom, then go out and face the Indians, giving them food as Brigham Young had instructed the people to do. When her little children would ask her if she was afraid, she would calmly reply, "There is no need for fear when you put your trust in the Lord."

When Sophia was in her late seventies, she moved to Preston, Idaho, with her daughter, Annie, and Annie's husband. Sophia passed away there on March 15, 1904 at the age of eighty-three.

MARIA THOMSEN POULSEN NIELSEN

BIRTHDATE: 25 Mar 1824
Vausted, Hjorring, Denmark
DEATH: 20 Jan 1901
Brigham City, Cache Co. Utah
PARENTS: Niels Thomsen
Caroline Karen Hansen
PIONEER: Nov 1855
SPOUSE: Martin Poulsen
MARRIED: abt 1851
DEATH SP: abt 1853
Alborg, Denmark

CHILDREN:
Caroline Christine (Cutler), 27 Aug 1852
Martin, 27 Nov 1853

SPOUSE II: James Nielsen
MARRIED: 20 Dec 1855
DEATH SP: 16 Jan 1911
Perry, Box Elder Co., Utah

CHILDREN:
James Nelson Jr., 3 Feb 1857
Marie, 10 Oct 1858
Joseph, 21 Jan 1861
Mary Ann (Wight), 12 Jan 1862
Sarah, 24 Nov 1863
Rebecca (Cutler), 5 Sep 1865
Brigham, 10 Sep 1867

Maria born in Denmark in 1824, one of five children born to Niels and Caroline. Her father's health was poor and for the family to survive the children hired out to work at very early ages.

Maria herded geese for a farmer a few miles away, too far for a little five or six year old to walk and so she lived on that farm but was so homesick she cried every day. Sleeping with the older girls did not stem her tears. At a neighbor's behest, she returned home to be with her mother for two more years.

Her parents died and the orphan went to work where ever she could. In her later teens she went to the city of Alborg, Denmark where she kept house and worked in a store for a very old man and his daughter who treated her kindly. She worked for them until she and Martin Poulsen married about eight years later. He was a milk man and had courted her for five years.

When their baby daughter, Caroline, was seven months old, both father and baby developed cholera, Martin died. Six months later Maria gave birth to a baby boy she named Martin.

James, Maria's brother, had encouraged her earlier to hear the missionaries from the Church of Jesus Christ of Latter-day Saints but plural marriages made her reluctant to investigate. However, after Martin's death, James came to live with her and her interest in the Gospel was ignited.

By November, 1854, they set sail for England. The ship was wrecked and towed back to Denmark where she waited at a sister-in-law's for three weeks for another ship.

When they left England it was a terrible journey, the ship drifted around the Atlantic ocean all winter and all spring. Caroline's greatest asset was to remain well amid all the sicknesses, in caring for those in need she met James Nielsen and his mother, who helped Maria care for her children.

On the trek to Utah, Maria took care of James's mother in his absence (he had broken his leg on Christmas Eve pulling down the masts during a terrific storm and had been sent back to England on another boat). She was a frail little thing, became ill and on her death bed ask Maria to care for James when he did reach Utah. Maria's little one, Martin, was buried someplace beside the trail during the trek also.

James caught up with the wagon train two days after his mother's burial on the Plains. He blamed himself for his mother's death and all his life could never speak of it with out crying.

In Utah, James and Maria married. Their first winter, 1855-56 was a hard one. Animals froze while still standing. James and Maria with her brother James and his wife, built a dugout to live in. It was a hole 15 feet square, a fireplace at one end, a table and chairs and two beds, with willows and dirt for a roof.

One day, an ox seeking warmth from the stove pipe crashed through the flimsy roof and had to be killed to remove it. They weathered the winter and life's storms together, they endured Indians, Johnston's Army, many uprootings and still they endured.

Maria passed away at seventy-seven years of age and was buried in Brigham City, Utah.

"MARY" JOHANNA MARIA BECKSTROM NIELSEN

BIRTHDATE: 18 Aug 1856
Caroli, Malmo, Sweden
DEATH SP: 23 Jan 1928
Spanish Fork, Utah Co. Utah
PARENTS: Hogan Beckstrom
Fredrica Eleonora Ekelund Bauer
PIONEER: 29 Aug 1863
J.R. Murdock Wagon Train
SPOUSE: Lars Nielsen
MARRIED: 13 Feb 1879
DEATH SP: 27 Sep. 1941
Spanish Fork, Utah Co. Utah

CHILDREN:
Lars William, 18 Dec 1879
James, 25 Mar 1882
Peter Elias, 1 Apr 1884
Mary Elnora, 19 Dec 1885
Rebecca Elizabeth, 7 May 1888
Annie Christine, 17 Mar 1890
Eleanor Nielsen, 2 Aug 1892
Harvey Alexander, 8 Mar 1894
Ralph John, 10 Jun. 1896
Clarence Beckstrom, 23 Sep 1898
Nellie Ardella, 9 Jan 1902

Mary Johanna was born in Caroli, Malmo, Malmohus, Sweden in 1856, the third of five children in the Beckstrom family of two boys and three girls.

Her parents and their two oldest children, joined the Church of Jesus Christ of Latter-day Saints in Sweden but Mary, William Oliver and Johanna Matilda were not eight years old. Soon after joining the Church, they were treated so bitterly by the community, her parents decided to emigrate to Utah.

In April, 1863, when Mary Johanna was almost seven years old, her family left Sweden and began their journey to America. Crossing the North Sea to England, they boarded the "John J. Boyd," in Liverpool and sailed away.

On the one month voyage, Johanna Matilda, the youngest child, was taken ill, died and was buried at sea. Then Mary was given her sister's name Johanna.

From Florence, Nebraska they joined the Murdock Wagon Company for a month long bumpy, dusty, trek into the Salt Lake Valley. Other than creating a shortage of horses and materials, the Civil war raging in the East was of little consequence to the travelers but the Black Hawk Indian War was still to come and Indians were a concern to everyone on an unprotected trail.

At first they settled in Milton, Utah, by spring they moved to Spanish Fork. The last Indian attack occurred

June 26, 1866 in Spanish Fork Canyon, calling all the Minute Men, under the command of Col. Creer for a forty-eight hour fight. Two men were killed, Al Dimmick and John Edmundson. It was the last of the serious Indian trouble in Spanish Fork.

Mary Johanna met Lars Nielsen, fell in love with him and they were married. Their first home, an adobe, was later changed to the house that sits at 411 East 100 North in Spanish Fork. Eleven children graced this home, all were taught the simple rules of work and faith.

Mary Johanna was thrifty, hard working and made her own lye with ashes; her own starch by grating potatoes and letting them dry on a sheet; and her own soap. She carded wool, spun it and knit all the families' sox and sewed all the clothes and underwear her family wore. She was on the ward committee to entertain the old and to sew for and lay out the dead. Her friends were life long friends sharing joys and sorrows , helping each other as sisters in quilting bees, rag bees, and carpet bees.

In 1911, Lars and Mary built a new home at 91 East 200 North and made more friends. During the later part of her life her daughter, Nellie and her husband William Creer and their children lived with them in the new house.

Mary Johanna passed away from a heart ailment at the age of seventy-two years., doing the thing she loved best and that warmed her heart, she was rocking a beloved grandchild.

MARY LAVENDER BATEMAN NIELSEN

No
Photo
Available

BIRTHDATE: 10 Mar 1838
Bedford Beds, England
DEATH: 20 Dec 1875
West Jordan, Salt Lake Co., Utah
PARENTS: Thomas Lavender
Charlotte Apthorpe
PIONEER: 27 Aug 1860
D. Robinson Handcart Company
SPOUSE I: Thomas Bateman Jr.
MARRIED: 18 Sep 1861
West Jordan, Salt Lake Co., Utah
DEATH SP: 4 Oct 1868
West Jordan, Salt Lake Co., Utah

CHILDREN:
Mary Elizabeth (Dimond), 4 Dec 1862
Harriet Alice (Peterson), 2 Jun 1864
John Thomas, 18 Jul 1866
Joseph William, 15 Sep 1868

SPOUSE II: Frederick Nelson / Nielsen
MARRIED: 1869
Cottonwood, Salt Lake Co., Utah
DEATH SP: Unknown

CHILDREN:
Four children, the youngest died at birth along with Mary.

Mary was born in England, 1838, as the fourth of six children. Her father was a "fancy" gardener, and they were very well-to-do. Mary and her sister, Elizabeth, attended a sewing school, becoming the best seamstresses in the school. They graduated and sewed for the "Gentry" and the higher class of people, earning and saving a little money.

When Uncle James Lavender returned to a mission to Bedford, staying with Mary's family, they were baptized. When he was released from his mission, it was decided that Mary and her two sisters, Susan and Elizabeth should emigrate to Utah.

Early in 1860, they sailed on the ship "Underwriter," leaving March 30, 1860 from Liverpool, England, landing at New York.

They journeyed by train to Florence, Nebraska, where they joined others preparing to cross the plains. They remained there for almost four weeks, purchasing a limited amount of necessary supplies, and awaiting completion of the handcarts. When everything was ready, the Lavender's girls joined the Ninth Handcart Company, under Captain Daniel Robinson. They left Florence, June 9, 1860, and about 121 weeks later they arrived in the Salt Lake Valley, August 27, 1860. Uncle James Lavender found homes for Mary and her sister, Susan, to help out in West Jordan, to earn room and board.

While Mary was living in West Jordan, she met Thomas Bateman and on September 18, 1861 they were married. The following year, on December 4, 1862, Mary had her first child. three more children followed. Tragedy struck this little family on October 4, 1868 when Thomas, her husband, passed away. This left Mary as a young widow of thirty, with four young children, one of which was a two-week old baby.

Not long after, in 1869, she married Frederick Nielsen or Nelson in Cottonwood, Utah and they had three children. Then just before Christmas on December 20, 1875, Mary died in childbirth along with the child, and was buried on December 23, 1875, leaving seven motherless children.

Mary's brother-in-law, William Bateman and wife Sophronia, took the four Bateman children into their home and raised them along with their own twelve. The last three were raised by their father.

METTE KIRSTINE DITLEVSEN HANSEN NIELSEN

BIRTHDATE: 11 Apr 1823
Herringe, Svendborg, Denmark
DEATH: 23 Nov 1890
Scipio, Millard, Utah
PARENTS: Hans O. Ditlevsen
Apelone Jacobsen
PIONEER: 8 Oct 1866
Andrew Scott Co. Wagon Train
SPOUSE: Peter Nielsen
MARRIED: 2 Apr 1854
Herring, Svendborg, Denmark
DEATH SP: 19 May 1911
Scipio, Millard Co., Utah

CHILDREN:
Johanna Sophia, 9 Jan 1851
Hans Christian, 14 Jun 1853
Neils Ditlov, 4 Mar 1855
Marie Abelone, 10 Jun 1857
Trine Nielsen, 19 Jul 1860
Jensine, 9 Aug 1862

Mette was born in Denmark, 1823, to Hans Ottlevson or Ditlevsen and Apelone Jacobsen. Mette married Peter Nielsen in Herring, Denmark. They were very poor. Peter worked for eight cents a day flailing wheat, while Mette worked to harvest fields or did cooking for the neighbors. She was given a drink of whiskey and sandwiches for lunch. She traded the whiskey to some of the men for their sandwiches then took the sandwiches home to her children. Her pay as a cook was usually a pail of skimmed milk and some wheat bread.

Peter and Mette were converted to the Church of Jesus Christ of Latter-day Saints and were baptized on April 3, 1861.

Before leaving Denmark, Mette traded a piece of furniture for enough home-spun material to make clothes for the entire family. This meant one suit each. When washday came, each child was placed in bed while their clothes were washed and dried.

In 1866, they borrowed $500.00 from friends and made arrangements for passage for their family of six children to go to America. They crossed the ocean in the ship, "Kenilworth," from Hamburg Germany. They crossed the Plains in the Andrew H. Scott Wagon Company. Their eleven year old son, Neils, died two days after leaving Omaha, Nebraska. They arrived in the Salt Lake Valley on October 8, 1866.

They were sent to Moroni, Salina, and then Richfield where they were driven out by the Indians in 1867. So they moved to Gunnison. In February, 1868, they settled in Scipio where they lived in a cellar until Peter could build a home.

Peter worked as a rock mason and farmer. Mette was a quiet housewife and member of her ward. She worked hard and managed their home well. Mette passed away at the age of sixty-seven years.

NANCY MARGARET OSBORN NIELSEN

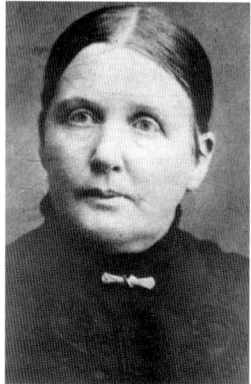

BIRTHDATE: 8 Mar 1840
Bloomfield, Green Co., Indiana
DEATH: 2 Feb 1906
Hyrum, Cache Co., Utah
PARENTS: David Osborn
Cynthia Butler
PIONEER: 9 Sep 1852
Thomas D. Howell Wagon Train
SPOUSE: Hans Enoch Nielsen
MARRIED: 11 Feb 1857
DEATH SP: 22 Jul 1889

CHILDREN:
William Enoch, 19 Apr 1858
Cynthia Elnora, 1 Mar 1860
Margaret Elizabeth, 26 Jan 1862
Rebecca Christina, 24 Jan 1864
Mary Ann, 2 Jan 1866
Hans Benjamin, 31 Dec 1867
David Osborn, 12 Jan 1880
Edgar, 23 Feb 1872
Harriet Jane, 13 Feb 1874
Albert Henry, 13 May 1876
Clarence Charles, 31 Jan 1878

Nancy Margaret Osborn was born in Indiana in 1840. She kept a diary of her life and leaves record of her experiences rich with her own thoughts and feelings. She tells of living five miles from Nauvoo, that they rode the five miles in a wagon every Sunday to attend meetings. She writes of the births of brothers and sisters, tells of the death of her brother, John, and that when he died of black cancer at the age of two, "mother was sick in bed and father and a neighbor put him in a box and carried him in the rain to the grave and buried him. It seemed to me that it rained all the time."

"At one time," she writes "all the family was sick in bed with fever and ague except me, I was four or five at the time and I would take a little pail and go to the spring and get a drink for them."

"I remember well when the Prophet Joseph was killed and wondered why father cried as I never saw him shed tears before. I had seen the Prophet and thought him a grand man."

She remembered well when they were driven from Nauvoo, how they put all they had in a wagon, piled the children on top and traveled through storms and mud to Garden Grove, there they stopped and raised a crop. That winter the family went to Missouri where her father and brother Jefferson broke hemp to make money to feed and cloth the destitute family.

They moved to Potpuatomi (Pottawattamie) near Kanesville (Florence) and stayed five years raising crops, provisions for those moving West. "We attended school most of the time walking one and a half miles, the snow was very deep in winter but the boys went ahead and broke the road and the girls stepped in their tracks."

Their clothing was thin, poor factory cloth colored with oak bark dye their mother made. Their father made all their shoes "and he was no shoe maker, we never saw overshoes or hoods or warm wraps of any kind, we were just as happy with our johnny cake and bacon as the children are now with all their luxuries."

She wrote of their journey across the Plains with two yoke of oxen and two cows the children had to drive, how they could ride on a good road that would not tax the oxen but on hills and rough roads they walked. That her mother was sick in the night and a new baby was shown to them the next morning, "but she was dead, after a day or two mother got worse and suffered terrible when she died. They wrapped her in a quilt. Poor mother, I shall never forget how I felt when they put her in the grave."

Nancy Margaret survived the experience of thirst that swelled her tongue so she could not talk, the mothering she did for her brothers and sisters, and her own family of eleven children.

Nancy Margaret lived an industrious life of faith and example, contributing to the world in the very best way, being a mother.

NELSINA KIRSTINE NIELSEN NIELSEN

BIRTHDATE: 29 Aug 1855
Rusagers Mark, Denmark
DEATH: 10 Jul 1932
Spanish Fork, Utah Co., Utah
PARENTS: Niels C. Nielsen
Karen Sophia Ericksen
PIONEER: 13 Sep 1857
Christiansen's Handcart Comp.
SPOUSE: Peter Nielsen
MARRIED: 22 Sep 1872
Salt Lake City, Salt Lake, Utah
DEATH SP: 23 Mar 1912
Spanish Fork, Utah Co., Utah

CHILDREN:
Caroline Christine, 2 Nov 1874
Peter, 18 Nov 1876
Joseph Alexander, 10 Jul 1878
William Henry, 12 Jan 1881
Albert Christian, 19 Jan 1883
Christence Amelia, 25 Mar 1884
Elizabeth Rebecca, 30 Nov 1885
Andrew Lauritz, 11 May 1888
Melvine Loretta, 23 Apr 1890
Hannah Elnora, 1 Oct 1892
Annie Laurina, 15 Jan 1895
Elmer Francis, 24 Aug 1896

Sarah Elsine, 16 Jul 1898
Jemima Marie, 17 Mar 1900

Nelsina was born in Rusagers Mark, Ketsmark, Hjorring, Denmark. Her family were people of moderate means and lived a very normal life. They had a comfortable home where there was love, work, and the chatter of little children with Father Niels often taking his fiddle down and playing some of the tunes of the day.

The family was converted to the Church of Jesus Christ of Latter-day Saints in January of 1852, by Chris Janson Christence. In November, 1855, the family left Denmark for America. They crossed the ocean on the ship, "John J. Boyd," a voyage which lasted sixty- five days.

After landing in New York, they traveled by train to St. Louis, Missouri. Nelsine's father died of cholera while they were in St. Louis. The family came with Morton Lund and other Saints up the Missouri River to Florence, Nebraska. They crossed the Plains with the Christian Christianson Handcart Company. Nelsina was two years old when they arrived in Salt Lake City on September 13, 1857.

Nelsina's mother married a widower with two children shortly after their arrival in the Salt Lake Valley. They lived near Provo River where her stepfather engaged in fishing. Karen and the girls made the fishing nets for the men to fish with.

Nelsina Kirstine married Peter Nielsen on September 22, 1872. They had fourteen children. Nelsina was the second wife of Peter Nielsen. His first wife lived in Spanish Fork while Kirsten and her family lived in Palmyra on a farm. Nelsina was kept busy taking care of the children and household duties. Peter learned to play the violin and would play for dances in homes for the enjoyment of his family and friends. Nelsina learned to render oil from some of the fish they caught. The oil was sold by the barrel. Later, they moved to Spanish Fork where they spent the rest of their lives.

Nelsina Kirstine was widowed twenty years before she died at the age of seventy-seven.

SIDSEL PEDERSEN NIELSEN

BIRTHDATE: 2 Mar 1826
Edgelev, Norre Vedby, Denmark
DEATH: 1 Nov 1901
Leamington, Millard Co., Utah
PARENTS: Peder Mikkelsen
Bertha Jensen
PIONEER: 5 Sep 1863
Saunder's Co. Wagon Train
SPOUSE: Lars Nielsen
MARRIED: 18 May 1853
Idestrup, Maribo, Denmark
DEATH SP: 5 Feb 1924
Leamington, Millard Co., Utah

CHILDREN:
Niels Peter Nielsen, 19 Jun 1854

Jens Christian Nielsen, 7 Feb 1856
Annie Margaret Nielsen, 20 Mar 1858
August Nielsen, 6 Aug 1860
Bertha Marie Nielsen, 8 Aug 1863
Son Nielsen, Jan 1866
Louis Nielsen, 18 Apr 1867
Joseph Hyrum Nielsen, 18 Oct 1871

Sidsel was born March 2, 1826, at Edgelev, Norre Vedby, Maribo, Denmark. She married Lars Nielsen on March 18, 1853, at Idestrup, Maribo, Denmark.

The Nielsen family joined the Church of Jesus Christ of Latter-day Saints in 1860 and immigrated to the United States in May of 1863. They brought with them four young children. At Florence, Nebraska they joined the Saunder's Wagon Company and arrived in the Salt Lake Valley on September 5, 1863.

Sidsel and her husband lived in many places in southwestern Utah. They finally settled in Leamington, Utah. Sidsel had poor health a good part of her married life. She went through many trials and hardships. She was a Bishop's wife for seventeen years.

Sidsel passed away in November 1, 1901, in Leamington and Lars passed away on February 5, 1924. Both are buried in the Leamington Cemetery.

ELSA NILSSON JONSSON NIELSON

BIRTHDATE: 12 Feb 1819
Getinge, Gardstanga, Sweden
DEATH: 4 Mar 1915
Millville, Cache Co., Utah
PARENTS: Nils Olsson
Hanna Akesson
PIONEER: 29 Sep 1866
Peter Nebeker Wagon Train
SPOUSE I: Jons Jonsson
MARRIED: 15 Jul 1842
Gardstanga, Malmohus, Sweden
DEATH SP: 25 Jan 1865
Sweden

CHILDREN:
Elna, 25 Oct 1843
Hannah, 29 Nov 1844
Elna (Olson), 21 Jun 1847
Hannah (Mickelsen) 5 Feb 1850
Anna (Hjorth), 15 Aug 1853
Caroline (Carlson) 12 Oct 1856

SPOUSE II: Ola Nielson
MARRIED: 29 Nov 1867
Salt Lake, Endowment House, Utah
DEATH SP: 5 Dec 1917
CHILDREN:
None

Elsa was born in Getinge, Gardstanga, Malmohus, Sweden 1819. She inherited the 'right' to the family farm and fortune. She used her money to help emigrate fourteen other Saints. She took care of her aging father and younger siblings.

At age twenty-three she married Jons Jonsson. They made their home in Gardstanga, where they became parents of six children, losing two in infancy.

After her husband died in 1865, she and family emigrated. Together with two of her family, Elsa left her native land to come to Utah in 1866 with her own family; four daughters and her only living brother, Ake (Ohie,) and her youngest sister, Sissa, with her three sons and her niece Elna Jonsson.

All walked across the Plains as their wagons were so loaded there was no room to ride. They arrived in Salt Lake City, September 29, 1866, and came to Millville, Cache County to settle October 6, 1866. That was Elsa's home ever after.

In 1867, Elsa married Ola Nielson. He bought a lot in Millville below the new Post Office near 2nd North and 1st West and built a one room and a lean, adding two more rooms later. They raised Elsa's family having no children of their own.

Elsa was an ambitious woman and she and her daughters sheared sheep for a share of the wool which they spun into yarn. They husked corn and picked potatoes on shares to help provide food for the family. She was very fond of reading, especially the Church works and sermons until her eyes got bad.

Elsa was very active in life until the year of 1892 when she had a bad sick spell that left her an invalid afterward and she made her home with her daughter, Anna. She had a privilege to live to be very old. Elsa passed away on March 4, 1915 at the age of ninety-six years, the oldest of any of the family.

ELSIE RASMUSSEN NIELSON

BIRTHDATE: 29 Jan 1830
Stokkemarke, Maribo, Denmark
DEATH: 16 May, 1914
Bluff, San Juan Co., Utah
PARENTS: Jorgon Rasmussen
Maren Mason
PIONEER: 9 Nov 1856
Willie Handcart Company
SPOUSE: Jens Nielson
MARRIED: 18 May 1850
Denmark
DEATH SP: 24 Mar 1906
Bluff, San Juan Co., Utah

CHILDREN:
Jens Niels, 29 Oct 1850
Mary, 3 Oct 1860
Julie Ann Mariah, 13 Apr 1862
Agnes, 14 May 1865

As an infant, Elsie was taken into the home of the Beaboum family and had no recollection of her parents. She attended school until she was age fourteen, then hired out as a farm hand.

She met Jens Nielson, also a farm hand. They were married when she was twenty years old. When they joined the Church of Jesus Christ of Latter-day Saints, they were shunned and persecuted by family and former friends.

In 1856, they sailed from Liverpool, England on the ship, "Thornton" and landed at New York. They traveled by train to Iowa where they joined the Willie Handcart Company. With them was their six year old son, Jens, and a little Mortensen girl thought to be about ten years old.

The company was overcome with cold and hunger in Wyoming. Both children died on October 23, 1856, along with twelve others of the company. Jens' feet were frozen and he urged Elsie to leave him, but she pulled him in the cart as they struggled towards Zion. They were met with rescue teams and supplies at Fort Bridger where they left their worn out carts.

After resting a short time in Salt Lake they were instructed by Brigham Young to help settle the communities of Parowan, Paragonah, Circleville, and Panguitch, then Cedar City. Their final move was to Bluff in San Juan County.

Jens had promised Elsie if she would consent to living in polygamy she would be blessed with more children. This was fulfilled with the birth of three daughters.

Elsie was frugal and resourceful. She planted mulberry trees to raise silk worms, extracted honey from beehives and wove many beautiful strips of carpet for her home and her neighbors. She made countless hand-sewn buckskin gloves and most boys in town had a baseball covered with buckskin by "Aunt Elsie."

Elsie passed away on May 16, 1914, and is buried in the Bluff Cemetery beside her husband.

FLORENCE VIRGINIA DUTSON NIELSON

BIRTHDATE: 22 Feb 1857
St. Louis, Missouri
DEATH: 12 Feb 1948
Oak City, Millard Co., Utah
PARENTS: John William Dutson
Elizabeth Jane Cowley
PIONEER: 20 Sep 1857
Delaware/St. Louis Wagon Train
SPOUSE: Niels Peter Nielson
MARRIED: 14 Mar 1878
Salt Lake Endowment House
DEATH SP: 24 Apr 1900
Oak City, Millard Co., Utah

CHILDREN:
John Lewis, 5 Feb 1879
Peter N., 14 Jan 1881
Edgar, 22 Nov 1882
Ellen Jane, 15 Nov 1884
Frank, 19 Dec 1886
Clarence, 27 Apr 1889
Florence Vern, 14 May 1891
Margaret Edna, 2 Sep 1893
Zella Mirinda, 23 Sep 1895

Florence Virginia Dutson was born in St. Louis, Missouri, February 22, 1857. She was the daughter of John William Dutson and Elizabeth Jane Cowley.

Florence was only three weeks old when the family left their home in St. Louis to begin their trek West. Her mother walked most of the way and carried Florence in her apron. They arrived in the Salt Lake Valley, September 20, 1857, coming with the Delaware and St. Louis Wagon Train. She moved with her family to Fillmore, Utah, then stayed in Fillmore with her sister Rebecca, when her parents moved to Oak City.

In 1873, she joined her parents in Oak City. Here she met Niels Peter Nielson and they fell in love. They were married in the Endowment House, March 14, 1878, and nine children were born to them.

She cared for her own family and others in the community that needed her help. She was a natural born nurse. Most of her church work was done in the Relief Society organization. She served in many positions there and was a visiting teacher for over fifty years.

Niels passed away on April 24, 1900, at Oak City. Florence was a widow for forty-eight years. She passed away on February 12, 1948, in Oak City, at the age of ninety-one years.

HANNA ANDERSON NIELSON

BIRTH: 11 Feb 1854
Gislov, Malmo, Sweden
DEATH: 24 Mar 1919
Millville, Cache, Utah
PARENTS: Nils Anderson
Arna Larsson Martensson
PIONEER: 1867
SPOUSE: Ake Nielson
(Oke Nels Olson Nielson)
MARRIED: 1 Nov 1875
Salt Lake Endowment House
DEATH SP: 17 Oct 1896
Millville, Cache, Utah

CHILDREN:
Hanna Matilda, 22 Dec 1873
Anna Augusta, 7 Feb 1875
Emma Beata, 2 Apr 1876
Hilma Amanda, 1878
Joseph Alvin, 14 mar 1881
Lydia Josephine, 13 Dec 1884
Orson Alma, 26 Dec 1888
John William, 12 May 1891
Selma Alta, 15 Apr 1896

Hanna was born 11 Feb 1854 in Gislov, Malmo, Sweden. Her family was converted to The Church of Jesus Christ of Latter-day Saints in Sweden and emigrated to Utah in 1867. They settled in Millville, Cache, Utah, where their first home was a dugout.

In 1873 when Hanna was just nineteen years of age she married Ake Nielson. He was thirty-eight years old. Three years later he married her younger sister Louisa as a plural wife. He built a four-room log cabin for his two wives and as the families grew in number more rooms were added.

Louisa was the mother of four children and on 18 Dec 1886, when her youngest child was only two and one-half years old, she died. Hanna took the children and raised them along with her own.

It was a very hard life for Hanna When her baby Selma was only six months old, her husband came home from his dry farm in Clarketon with a terrible pain in his side. He died of appendicitis on 17 Oct 1896. Louisa's oldest was nineteen-and-a-half, but he died two months later. Hanna's oldest living daughter, Emma, was twenty years old and married and she and her husband did all they could to help.

Hanna had no indoor plumbing and all the water had to be carried into the house in buckets. She had cows, chickens and raised a pig for butchering. She dried and canned fruit and vegetables and baked her own bread. Her son Joseph Alvin and Louisa's son Niels both went to work on the railroad to earn wages which they sent home to help pay the bills and keep the farm going.

Hanna died at age sixty-five in Miliville on 24 March 1919 and is buried by her husband and her sister in the Millville cemetery.

HULDA FRANZISKA LASSEN NIELSON

No Photo Available

BIRTHDATE: 25 Jan 1840
Schwerin Branden, Germany
DEATH: 5 Oct 1874
Peterson, Morgan Co., Utah
PARENTS: Rasmus K. Lassen
Marie Elizabeth Spaeth
PIONEER: 22 Sep 1861
Wagon Train Company
SPOUSE: Peter Nielson
MARRIED: 8 Mar 1862
Salt Lake, Endowment House
DEATH SP: 25 Jan 1886
Colonia, Juarez, Chouch, Mexico

CHILDREN:
Peter Erastus, 21 May 1863
Mary Elizabeth (McNeil), 19 Jul 1865
John Thomas, 5 May 1867
Alberta Franciska (Hatch), 30 Apr 1869
Agnes Ashcroft), 11 Jan 1873
Son, 5 Oct 1874 (stillborn)

Hulda Franziska was born in 1840 in Schwerin Branden, Prussia, Germany. She was born into a large family. As a young girl she had deep blue eyes and long black hair which she braided and tied with a big ribbon or wound around her head; she was beautiful.

In 1855, she came with her parents and brothers and sisters to Denmark. It was here they heard about the Gospel of Jesus Christ. She was an apprentice tailor in a shop and her project for graduation was to make a beautiful alpaca cape with black fringe. She put such tiny stitches on it and it wore well. She became a graduate seamstress.

As she listened to the missionaries she knew the Gospel was true. One evening in her home there was loud talk and much scolding from her father. She would cry when she went to bed at night. She prayed and knew the Church was true. One day she put on her beautiful cape. When her father demanded to know where she was going, she said, "To a cottage meeting." He said, "No you're not! Don't you dare leave this house again to go to those meetings. If you do, don't ever come back to my house!" She stood there frightened for a few moments, then turned and went to her room. She put a few things in a small valise and walked to the door. She hated to leave her father, mother, brothers and sisters. She loved them all.

A kind lady at church that evening, took her home and said, "We'll find a place for you." At a branch conference, the Branch President, Peter Nielson was there. He met Hulda and learned of her problem. He took her to his home to live with his wife and son. He felt she could be of help to his wife because he was gone so much on Church business. They became good friends to Hulda and she was like an older sister to Frihoff, she being eleven years older than he. She loved the Church she had joined and was soon happily working in it.

Peter was released from his mission after seven years service. He was home more, always making suits, coats and shoes for his family and other members. They were going to America; Hulda too. She was very happy, but would miss her family. They boarded the steamship "Wladamar," to Keil on May 9, 1861, then traveled by train to Liverpool and sailed on the "Monarch of the Sea" on May 16th. The old ship was loaded and passengers had to throw some clothing and bedding overboard to lighten the ship.

From her own journal, "On Jun 19, 1861 at 2:00 p.m. we arrived at Castle, New York harbor. Erastus Snow, one of the twelve spoke to us that evening. We were so grateful to be here. Jun 20, went to New Jersey by boat. Left here at 5:30 by train, arrived at Dunkirk at 10:00 a.m. changed trains at 4:00 p.m . . .finally arrived in Quincy on the 25th of Jun at noon. . . We arrived in Florence on July 1. The Brethren rented us rooms to stay in. From the time we left Copenhagen until July 3, 17 children and 3 women have died and 6 children have been born. July 7, Sunday we received our oxen to drive about 4 miles Peter Nielson was a captain of one of the 4 companies."

"We arrived in Salt Lake September 22, 1861 in the afternoon where we were welcomed.Oct 26, 1861 we attended our first dance in the valley."

On March 8, 1862, Hulda received her endowments and was sealed to Peter Nielson. He and his wife Marie received their endowments and were sealed also. They still had trials and stated that "Satan is tempting us."

Hulda had her first child on May 21, 1863; Peter Erastus.

INGAR NILSSON NIELSON

No Photo Available

BIRTHDATE: 4 Apr 1810
Getinge, Gardstanga, Sweden
DEATH: 27 Nov 1883
Millville, Cache Co., Utah
PARENTS: Nils Olsson
Hanna Akesson
PIONEER: 25 Sep 1868
John G. Holman Wagon Train
SPOUSE: Jon Nielson
MARRIED: 12 Nov 1834
Gardstanga, Malmobus, Sweden
DEATH SP: Unknown

CHILDREN:
Nils, 3 Aug 1835
Ake, 7 Sep 1837
Hanna, 28 Jun 1840
Elsa (Olson), 2 Nov 1842
Ohla, 21 May 1845
Elna (Anderson), 8 May 1848
Anders, 17 Mar 1851

Ingar was born in Getinge, Gardstanga, Malmobus, Sweden, 1810. She was named after her maternal Grandmother. Ingar was the oldest in her family of nine children. At age twenty-four she married Jon Nielson. They became the parents of seven children.

They converted to the Church of Jesus Christ of Latter-day Saints and left Copenhagen, Denmark, on June 13, 1868, arriving in Hull, England on Tuesday, June 16th. On the 19th of June they boarded the sailing vessel, "Emerald Isle," and arrived at the New York harbor on August 11th.

The emigrants landed at Castle Garden, New York on August 14th and the same day they were taken by steamer up the Hudson River. Then by rail on the 17th via Niagara, Detroit and Chicago to Council Bluffs, by steamboat up the Missouri and rail again to Benton, Wyoming, by August 25th. Ingar and her family were met by church teams which took them across the Plains by ox-team with the John G. Holman Wagon Company, arriving in the Salt Lake Valley, September 25, 1868.

Ingar and her family went to Millville, Cache County, where they were greeted by her sisters and her only living brother, Ake. They all settled in Millville.

In January, 1871, Ingar made the long trip to Salt Lake City to the Endowment House where they took out their endowments and made their marriage eternal on January 30, 1871.

Ingar passed away at age seventy-three and was buried in the Millville Cemetery.

KAREN KIRSTINE HANSEN NIELSON

BIRTHDATE: 18 Nov 1850
Odense, Denmark
DEATH: 8 Apr 1928
Richfield, Sevier Co., Utah
PARENTS: Hans Larsen
Maren Larsen
PIONEER: 5 Oct 1867
Leonard G. Rice Wagon Train
SPOUSE: Carl Henrick Nielson
MARRIED: 26 May 1867
Odense, Denmark
DEATH SP: 1 Aug 1912
Richfield, Sevier Co., Utah

CHILDREN:
Alice Christine, 29 Jul 1867
Charles Nephi, 3 Aug 1870
Clara, 27 Oct 1872
Martha, 26 May 1875
Ammon Alma, 17 Sep 1877
Joseph Alma, 19 Sep 1879
Eleanora Christine, 2 Nov 1881
Henry Richard, 11 Jun 1885
Wilford Leo, 17 Jan 1888
Juanita Miralda, 3 Oct 1890

Karen married Carl Henrick Nielson on May 26, 1867. They left Denmark for America on June 21, 1867 on the steamship, "Manhattan." After a voyage of thirteen days, they arrived in New York on the 4th of July. What a sight to see; fireworks, something they had never seen before.

They arrived at North Platte and were outfitted with a wagon and four mules. The captain of the company was Leonard G. Rice. They arrived in Salt Lake Valley on October 5, 1867.

Karen and Carl lived in Levan, Richfield, and were the first settlers of Elsinore, Utah. Kristine gathered rabbit brush, tied them together to make a broom to sweep the dirt floor in her dugout.

One day, she and another lady took their children for a walk. They saw something in a garden that looked very beautiful to them. They could not ask what they were and the people could not understand them because of the language barrier, but they gave them some. They took them home and put them on the table for decorations. These beautiful items turned out to be tomatoes. The next year, they planted some tomatoes for the same purpose, not knowing they could eat them.

Karen would gather ashes and put them in a fifty gallon barrel of water. This would soften her wash water.

Karen moved back to Richfield and lived there for the rest of her life. Kristine loved to raise vegetables and loved her flower garden.

Karen passed away on April 8, 1928, in Richfield, Sevier County, Utah.

KIRSTEN JENSEN NIELSON

BIRTHDATE: 29 Aug 1834
Blans, Stokkemnarke, Denmark
DEATH: 19 Dec 1908
Bluff, San Juan Co., Utah
PARENTS: Peder Jensen
Kirsten Weaver
PIONEER: 13 Sep 1857
Christianson's Handcart Comp.
SPOUSE: Jens Nielson
MARRIED: 4 Oct 1857
Salt Lake City, Salt Lake, Utah
DEATH SP: 24 Apr 1906
Bluff, San Juan Co., Utah

CHILDREN:
Jens, 13 Nov 1858
Hans Joseph, 24 Jan 1860
Jens Peter, 9 Feb 1862
Margaret Christine, 1 Apr 1864
John, 18 Jul 1866
Francis, 11 Oct 1868
Lucinda Diantha, 6 Mar 1872
Caroline, 21 Jul 1874
Hyrum, 10 Nov 1878 (stillborn)

Kirsten was born in Blans, Stokkemnarke, Maribo, Denmark, 1834. She became trained as a dressmaker and tailor. She earned a good salary and was able to give financial help to her parents.

Her parents gave missionaries from the Church of Jesus Christ of Latter-day Saints food and shelter one night, heard their message, and the family was converted to the Church. Her friends spurned her and she was dismissed from her employment.

Her father, mother, and two brothers left for America before Kirsten, her sister, and one brother were able to obtain the necessary money to travel. When Kirsten, her sister, and her brother arrived in St. Louis, they learned their mother and one of their brothers had died of cholera six months before.

In 1857, they were able to secure the necessary provisions to travel across the Plains and they joined the Christianson Handcart Company. They suffered from lack of water which caused her brother, Hansey, to die as they were crossing the Plains. Kirsten and her father pulled their handcarts 1,300 miles to Salt Lake City. They arrived in Salt Lake Valley on September 13, 1857.

Kirsten would wash all day for a little food or a cup of molasses while they were adjusting to their new life.

Kirsten became the second wife of Jens Nielsen who had baptized her in Denmark. They were called by the Church to help settle five towns in central Utah. Their nine children were born in Parowan, Circleville, and Cedar City.

Kirsten would work in the fields shocking hay. At night, she made gloves and took in sewing and tailoring.

They were called from their home in Cedar City to settle in San Juan County. She and Jens pioneered San Juan County with the "Hole in the Rock" expedition in 1879. She raised chickens and her son, Joseph, would take the eggs and other produce to Durango, Colorado, and sell them for her. She used the money to buy fabric so she could make clothing for her family. The Lord's protecting power was with them through Indian perils, accidents, sickness, and floods of the San Juan River which washed away their fields and irrigation system.

Kirsten served as Second Counselor in the Relief Society in Bluff for four years, then as president for twenty years. They built a Relief Society meeting house and purchased a herd of sheep to use for the welfare of the members. She did many things for the young people and had a soothing influence on them. A lifetime of tribulations faded into a triumph of faith as she died surrounded by her loved ones.

MARIANE "MARY ANN" ANDERSON JENSEN NIELSON

No Photo Available

BIRTHDATE: 16 May 1822
Elling, Hjorring, Denmark
DEATH: 17 Jan 1897
Hyrum, Cache Co., Utah
PARENTS: Jens (Skraoder) Andersen
Henne Marie Jensen
PIONEER: abt Fall 1859
Independent Wagon Train
SPOUSE: Jens Christen Jensen
MARRIED: 1 Jan 1846/1848
DEATH SP: 15 Jul 1859
crossing the Plains

CHILDREN:
Jens Anton, 20 Aug 1841
Jens Peter, 15 Jul 1848 (died in 1855)
Maren "Mary," 18/20 Jun 1853 (died in 1855)
Louisa/Lovisa (Wray), 26 Aug 1857
Ludvig, 26 Aug 1857 (died same month)

Mariane was born in Denmark, 1822. At age eighteen, she married Jens Christensen. They made their home in Elling, where their first child was born, moved to Astrup, where a second child joined their family. Their final move was to Sindal, where their last three children were born. They buried three of their little family in Denmark.

They joined the Church of Jesus Christ of Latter-day Saints and made plans to come to America. Mariane, Jens and their infant daughter, surviving twin, emigrated.

They were sharing a wagon with another emigrant who was going to Utah. Apparently they were not in a wagon train. Stampeding buffalo killed Jens, and the other man in the wagon said he could not care for her, and her baby. He left her and her daughter and a few belongings on the trail, to be picked up by another immigrant.

Soren Nielson, another Danish convert bound for Zion, came along the wagon trail. He took Mariane and Louisa in, and they came to Utah, settling in Hyrum, Cache County, Utah. Mariane eventually married Soren Nielson on November 14, 1862 in the Salt Lake Endowment House. Soren married a second wife, Caroline Andersen, August 24, 1867 in Salt lake City, Utah.

Mariane had a son in Denmark who had not joined the Church. She always encouraged those who went to Denmark to look him up and teach him. Eventually her son, Jens Anton Jensen, was introduced to the gospel and he and his wife and family came to Utah. Mariane had only two children grow to adulthood.

Mariane passed away on January 17, 1897 at the age of seventy-four.

MARIANE JENSEN HANSON NIELSON

BIRTHDATE: 21 Apr 1844
Sterup Mark, Jerslev, Denmark
DEATH: 5 Feb 1899
Elsinore, Sevier Co., Utah
PARENTS: Thomas C. Jensen
Karen Marie Iverson
PIONEER: 22 Oct 1866
Abner Lowry Wagon Train
SPOUSE I: Niels C. Hanson
MARRIED: 5 May 1863
Denmark
DEATH SP: 1881
Ephraim, Sanpete Co., Utah

CHILDREN:
Christian Dorius, 6 Feb 1864
John Brown Kenelworth, 29 May 1866
Dorthea Marie, 29 May 1868
Mary, 6 Apr 1871
Niels Sena, 25 Nov 1873
Christian Peter, 24 Apr 1876
Josephine, 27 Dec 1878

SPOUSE II: Thomas Nielson
MARRIED: 11 Jan 1882
DEATH SP: 2 May 1923
Elsinore, Sevier Co., Utah

CHILDREN:
Allie Marinda, 14 Dec 1882
Ada Lena, 14 Dec 1882
Elvina, 19 Aug 1885

Mariane was born in Sterup Mark, Jerslev, Hjorring, Denmark, 1844. She was an unselfish, patient person who was quick, alert, and always willing to help others. As a child, when she was not in school, she worked out doing housework and herding geese and cows.

Mariane joined the Church of Jesus Christ of Latter-day Saints in October, 1860. She married Niels Hanson in 1863. She, her husband, and son left Denmark with a group of Saints on May 25, 1866. The voyage lasted seven weeks and five days. She gave birth to her second son while crossing the Atlantic Ocean.

They traveled by freight steamer to New Haven, Connecticut, then went by train northward to Montreal, Canada. They traveled by steamer to St. Joseph and from there took a steamboat up the Missouri River to Wyoming, Nebraska, where they met her parents and siblings.

They crossed the Plains in the Abner Lowry Wagon Company and arrived in Salt Lake City on October 22, 1866. They lived at first in Ephraim, then moved to Elsinore, Utah in 1876.

Mariane was devoted to her religion and did her part in pioneering the west in a cheerful way, never complaining of the hardships she endured. She helped to support the Relief Society by donating wheat, eggs, butter, and script. She was a very caring wife and mother. She raised seven children with her first husband. She raised three daughters with her second husband.

MARY DOROTHEA CATHERINE DAVIDSON NIELSON

BIRTHDATE: 22 Feb 1853
Majollie, Olsen Isles, Schleswig, Denmark
DEATH: 25 Apr 1933
Sigured, Sanpete, Utah
PARENTS: Hans Christian Davidson
Anne Maria Jensen
PIONEER: 20 Sep 1858
Captain Ivan Iverson Company
SPOUSE: Niels Peter Nielson
MARRIED: 22 Mar 1875
Mt. Pleasant, Sanpete Co, Utah.
DEATH SP: 17 May 1913
Indianola, Sanpete Co, Utah

CHILDREN:
Mattie Lnora Christine, 9 Apr 1876
Nathaniel Voltaire Peter, 31 Mar 1878
Arstanus Humbolt Socrates, 11 June 1880
Aurelius Newton Cortez, 5 Dec 1881
Grace Darling Georgina, 24 Mar 1884
Charlesmagne Eprhaim Gladstone, 7 Mar 1886

SPOUSE II: Thomas Thompson

Mary was the daughter of Hans Christian Davidson and Anne Maria Jensen. They arrived in the Salt Lake Valley on 20 September 1858 in the Captain Ivan Iverson Company.

She married Niels Peter Nielson 22 March 1875 at Mt. Pleasant, Sanpete Co, Utah. Mary was a home maker and mother who took great pride in her children. She loved to sew and weave rugs and make Danish cheese. She died 25

Apr 1933 at age seventy. Niels died 17 May 1913 at Indianola, Sanpete Co, Utah. No other information is given about Mr. Thompson.

PERNELLA BAUM CHRISTENSEN NIELSON

BIRTHDATE: 21 Apr 1818
Viby, Gustaf Adolf, Sweden
DEATH: 20 Dec 1898
Fairview, Sanpete Co., Utah
PARENTS: Nils C. Bomb
Karna Jonsdotter
PIONEER: 5 Sep 1863
John F. Sanders Wagon Train
SPOUSE: Ole Nilsson/Nielson
MARRIED: 4 Aug 1844
Gustaf Adolf, Sweden
DEATH SP: 17 Feb 1875
Fairview, Sanpete Co., Utah

CHILDREN:
Sissa, 10 Aug 1845
Peter, 30 Apr 1848
James, 6 Jun 1851
Ole Swen, 1 Jan 1854
Lars Peter, 3 Jun 1855
Sena, 6 Jul 1859
Ole, 10 Feb 1862 (twin)
Son, 10 Feb 1862 (twin)
Ole, Jr., 16 Sep 1863

Pernella was born on April 21, 1818 in Viby, Gustaf Adolf, Kristianstad, Sweden. She was a school teacher in her early years. She married Ole Nielson in 1844 in Gustaf Adolf, Kristianstad, Sweden. They had four children born to them in Sweden. In 1855, she moved to Denmark to be with her husband who had been working there for some time. She gave birth to four more children in Vanderup, Denmark.

It was in Vanderup that they were converted and baptized as members of the Church of Jesus Christ of Latter-day Saints. As there was not enough money for all the family to come to America together, they came at separate times. Pernilla came with her three youngest children. Her youngest daughter, Sena, died and was buried at the Loup Fork of the Platte River. They were traveling with the John F. Sanders Wagon Company and arrived in Salt Lake City on September 5, 1863.

They went directly to Mt. Pleasant where she reunited with the rest of her family. Eleven days after her arrival, she gave birth to a son in Mt. Pleasant. They had their first home in a dugout.

She carded wool, spun it, and wove it into clothes. She made candles and worked very hard to care for her family. In 1867, they were called to go to Fairview where they suffered through the Blackhawk Wars. Her son, Peter, drowned in Green River after being called by the Church to help new emigrants enter the Valley.

Her husband suffered a prolonged illness which caused him blindness. He eventually died in February of 1877 and Pernella worked for people doing odd jobs.

She was ever faithful, helped others with her skills of sewing, cooking, spinning wool, and weaving cloth. She often bore her testimony of the truths of the Restored Gospel.

At one time, her son, Ole Jr., had seen some people enter their home. He rushed home to see the company. When he found no one there, his mother informed him the people he saw were members of their departed family who came to ask that Pernella do their temple work.

Pernella did the work for many of her relatives in the Manti Temple before she passed away on December 20, 1898, in Fairview, Utah.

BOTILDA PAULSSON NELSON NILSON

BIRTHDATE: 23 Jun 1834
Ria Nonrviding, Sweden
DEATH: 21 Dec 1916
Mt. Pleasant, Sanpete Co. Utah
PARENTS: Ake Paulson
Anna Jonsson /Johnson
PIONEER: 15 Sep 1859
Robert Neslan Wagon Train
SPOUSE I: Lars Nelson
MARRIED: 1860
DEATH SP: 4 Feb 1863
Tooele, Tooele Co., Utah

CHILD:
Louise Amanda (Peterson), 7 Feb 1861

SPOUSE II: Peter Nilson
MARRIED: 1866
Mt. Pleasant, Sanpete Co., Utah
DEATH SP: 1900
CHILDREN:

Botilda Paulson was born in Ria Nonrviding near Malmo, Sweden in 1834, the youngest of eight children, the family divided equally, four boys and four girls. They were a religious family and a singing family, all of them had good singing voices.

When Botilda was eighteen years old she heard the Elders of the Church of Jesus Christ of Latter-day Saints and believing the Gospel, was baptized as were others in her family. Her brother, Paul, deciding to come to America with his wife, promised his parents to look after Botilda and take good care of her if she could come with them. They agreed and the little family and Botilda left Sweden.

With Johnston's Army no longer a threat, local affairs assumed normal conditions, but only 809 Saints sailed from

Europe that year. Paul, his wife and child, and Botilda among them. They had thought of pushing a handcart across the Plains but because of the small baby and several other women beside his sister to take care of, Paul sold his wife's jewelry and added to what he had, bought a wagon with a team of oxen and joined the Nearlen Wagon Train Company.

Botilda, twenty-five years old, acted as interpreter for some of the Swedish people as they traveled. She understood English well and one joy was to be the communicator between a Swedish boy and an English girl who depended on her to help them declare their love for each other.

Once in the Salt Lake Valley, she moved to Tooele where she lived with her sister, Olivia, until the next year when she married twenty-eight year old Lars Nelson (also from Malmo Sweden) as his polygamous second wife.

They had been married three years when Lars, a well educated man who spoke several languages was working as an auditor for one of his clients, a brewing company, when he slipped on ice and fell into a vat of hot syrup and was scalded to death.

His two widows comforted each other and lived harmoniously with Botilda's only child, Louise, and his three other children until Botilda moved to Mt. Pleasant to be near her brother, Paul.

In 1866, she married Peter Nilson who was a shoe maker by trade. They did not have children.

A compassionate person all her life, Botilda showed this side of her nature by caring for anyone who desired her help. Many people found a good home with her. When Paul's wife died, she cared for his five children in her own home. John, the baby, never had another home but hers, and he was sent to school and on a mission. Christen Swenson, a friend's daughter in Sweden, became an orphan and Botilda sent for her and harbored the girl until she married some years later. Addie Hackensen shared the same good fortune as Christen and Ann Monson was taken from the infirmary and given loving care by Botilda until Ann died eight years later.

Botilda was lovingly called "Aunt Tildy" by her nieces and nephews, and eventually by her own little girl, in fact she was known in Mt. Pleasant as "Aunt Tildy."

Botilda passed away at the age of eighty-two. Peter preceded her in death by sixteen years and her own daughter by four years. Seven grandchildren survived her.

"Aunt Tildy" was loved for her cheerful disposition, her hearty laugh her kindness in all her Church Callings and her unwavering faith in the Gospel.

BOTILDA TYKESON NILSON

BIRTHDATE: 15 May 1812
Fulltofta, Melmohus, Sweden
DEATH: 7 Apr 1894
Smithfield, Cache Co., Utah
PARENTS: Jon Tykesson
Elna Olasson
PIONEER: 29 Aug 1859
James Brown Wagon Train
SPOUSE: Nils Nilsson / Nilson
MARRIED: 26 May 1837
Kvssarum, Malmohus, Sweden
DEATH SP: 16 Oct 1886
Smithfield, Cache Co., Utah

CHILDREN:
Else, 17 Jul 1838
Pehr (Peter), 18 Nov 1840
Nils, 30 Jul 1843 (died at age 6)
Elna, 17 May 1846 (died at age 10)
Ola, 14 Apr 1849
Bangta, 28 Aug 1854 (died as an infant)

Botilda "Boel" was born May 15, 1812, in Sweden; a country without religious freedom. She was blessed with the gift of faith and discernment, and upon hearing the gospel of the Church of Jesus Christ of Latter-day Saints she accepted its truths and followed her husband and priesthood leaders.

On May 26, 1837 Boel and Nils Nilsson / Nilson were married in Kvssarum, Sodra Rorum, Malmohus, Sweden. In the Fall of 1855, Boel, her husband, and their five children left their home in Sweden to Come to America. While crossing the ocean their baby daughter, Bengta, died and was buried at sea. Their ten year old daughter, Elna, was ill on board the ship and in March of 1856. she died in Iowa.

They left Florence, Nebraska in the early part of May, 1859, with the James S. Brown Wagon Company and arrived in the Salt Lake Valley about the middle of August. It was a difficult journey. At one time their own oxen were without water for twenty-four hours.

They spent the first winter living in Brigham City with their daughter, Else, who had left Iowa two years earlier. In March of 1860, Boel and her family moved to Smithfield, Cache County, Utah.

They first built a house, but because of Indian trouble they were forced to live in a fort for about four years. When land was divided in Smithfield, her husband got twenty acres and a city lot where he built a two-room log house.

She was happy and content in her twilight years, knowing she had chosen the right religion and prepared the way for future generations.

Botilda passed away on April 7, 1894, and was buried by the side of her husband in Smithfield Cache County, Utah.

SVENBORG "SENA" TUFVESON NILSON

BIRTHDATE: 14 Dec 1833
Osby, Kristianstad, Sweden
DEATH: 14 Mar 1917
Smithfield, Cache Co., Utah
PARENTS: Tufve Johnson
Pehrnila Pehrson
PIONEER: Summer 1862
SPOUSE: Pehr (Peter) Nilson
MARRIED: 12 Oct 1862
Logan, Cache Co., Utah
DEATH SP: 11 Nov 1927
Smithfield, Cache Co., Utah

CHILDREN:
Samuel Peter, 13 Jul 1863
Emma, 18 Apr 1865
James "R," 24 May 1867
John Nephi, 6 Feb 1869 (died at age 2)
Eliza Nelle, 16 May 1871
Ellen, 29 Jun 1873
Zina Matilda, 11 Apr 1875 (died at age 2)
Daniel, 25 Feb 1877 (died at age 1)

Svenborg "Sena" Tufveson, as a young woman in Sweden, chose to be baptized a member of the Church of Jesus Christ of Latter-day Saints; come to Zion, be married, and live a life of service to God and her fellow-men.

Sena was industrious and raised a nice garden to provide for her family and the stranger's needs. Because of the scarcity and expense of goods, she used her talents to card, spin, weave, and knit articles of clothing for her family.

She was left alone with her children while her husband, Peter, went on two missions to Sweden. With the work of her sons, Sena was able to be the source of the entire expense money for his second mission.

She showed her sterling qualities when she welcomed into her home her husband's second wife, giving her a room and teaching her home-making skills, also caring for her and her two children while their husband had left to serve on his second mission.

In the early years, she opened her home for many gatherings, meetings, and recreation for the people of Smithfield. The missionaries were always welcome in her home.

At the death of her daughter, the grandchildren moved in with her when she was sixty-three years old. Sena was a visiting teacher for the relief Society, serving on the "Danish Visiting Teaching Committee."

JOHANNA NILSSON (NILSSDOTTER)

No
Photo
Available

BIRTHDATE: 19 Sep 1824
Vastra Broby, Kriatianstad,
Sweden
DEATH: 1898-99
Oakley, Cassia Co., Idaho
PARENTS: Nils Pehrsson
Bengta Olssdotter
PIONEER: 29 Sep 1866
Peter Nebeker Wagon Train

CHILD:
Charles "Carl" Scharling, 13 Jun 1856

Johanna Nilsson was born in Sweden in 1824, she was the fifth child born to Nils and Bengta. Conditions were very difficult for the Nilsson family, it is not known how old Johanna was when her father died (after 1829) but her mother, Bengta Olssdotter, died on the 19th of June in the Yattighus (Poor House).

When Johanna was thirty-one she moved to 240 Halsingborg to work for Johannes Christian Scharling, a book binder by trade. It was here she gave birth to her son Carl the next year and was absolved by the Lutheran Church for having a child. After a court case, Johannes Scharling was named the father of the child and ordered to pay support until he was sixteen years of age.

It was an emotional, traumatic time for Johanna as court records portray and she welcomed the message of the missionaries as a source of strength and comfort and was baptized into the Church of Jesus Christ of Latter-day Saints.

When the "Humbolt" sailed from Hamberg, Germany on June 6, 1866, forty-one year old Johanna and Carl, age ten, were among the throng of passengers determined to reach Utah. The voyage was organized and orderly but crowded for the 328 converts.

The food, became sour, soggy and a miserable substitute for nourishment but was eaten. The water, taken from the Elbe River and put into barrels that had been burned out inside, was black as coal but was drunk. It was all they had to sustain them for the six week voyage to America. The beds were made from common lumber, four people to a bed and two tiers high.

The Humbolt docked at Castle Garden, New York and the passengers boarded a train (dirty cattle cars) for many days to reach St. Louis, then Florence, Nebraska and finally to walk with some freedom along side a wagon in the open air. Still a courageous way to go.

In Utah, they joined with group of Swedish emigrants who were settling in Grantsville, Tooele County, Utah and there both mother and son were re-baptized on October 28, 1866.

In 1879 and 1880, they moved to the lush green valley in southern Idaho. (Oakly). Carl nearly twenty-four and Johanna, now fifty-six. Johanna bought a log cabin.

Charles daughter, Iva Scharling Sullivan, remembered when she was three years old and Johanna handed over the fence, a small pail and shovel for her to play with. Iva remembered also that when her grandmother died the casket had to be taken from the house through a window. It must have been built in the house and would not fit through the door.

Johanna passed away when she was about seventy-five and is buried in the Oakly Cemetery with her son, Charles, his wife, Carolina Augusta Clausson Scharling and their five children who died in childhood.

AGNES WILSON NISH

No Photo Available

BIRTHDATE: 15 Jan 1837
Newart Hill, Scotland
DEATH: 30 Jan 1919
Franklin, Idaho
PARENTS: John Wilson
Elizabeth Mallace
PIONEER: 25 Sep 1855
Richard Ballantyne Wagon Train
SPOUSE: Robert Nish
MARRIED: 16 Jan 1855
Liverpool, England
DEATH SP: 30 Sep 1919
Franklin, Idaho

CHILDREN:
Elizabeth (Spencer), 2 Jul 1855
Agnes (Durrant), 10 Feb 1857
Robert, 11 Oct 1858
Thomas, 30 Jun 1860
Isabella (Durrant), 14 Jan 1862
Malcolm William, 17 Mar 1864
Mary Ellen, 30 Apr 1867 (died as an infant)
David, 26 Nov 1868 (died as an infant)
Margaret (Wheeler), 17 Mar 1872
Euphemia, 25 Mar 1874
Ida Martha, 28 Jan 1875 (died as a child)
Nephi, 18 Jan 1877
Alma Wilson, 23 Sep 1878
Joseph Smith, 11 Jan 1881 (died at age 8)
Ann Maud, 2 May 1888

Agnes was born in Scotland in 1837. As a young woman she and her sweetheart, Robert Nish, were on their way to buy some candy when they stopped at a street meeting and listened to the Elders preaching. They were interested and were later baptized, much against their parents wishes.

Agnes and Robert were married on board the ship "Charles Buck" on January 16, 1855, with Richard Ballantyne performing the ceremony. Robert often said he married her to save cabin fare. The ship sailed the next day for America.

They arrived in the Salt Lake Valley in September, 1855, and settled in Cedar City, Utah for a time. They also lived in Portage, Box Elder County; Clarkston, Cache County; and finally several places in Idaho, the last place, Franklin, Idaho.

Agnes was a quiet person, but said she could never get a word in edgewise because her husband did all the talking. He was the "life of the party," a very cheerful person who loved to call square dances.

Agnes was the mother of fifteen children, the last one was born when she was about fifty years of age.

Agnes passed away in January, 1919, at the home of her daughter in Franklin, Idaho. Robert died in October, 1919, also in Franklin, Idaho.

SARAH SLUSSER NISONGER

BIRTHDATE: 26 Apr 1816
Clear Creek, Warren, Ohio
DEATH: 2 Apr 1900
Santaquin, Utah Co., Utah
PARENTS: Peter Slusser
Mary Deam / Diehm
PIONEER: Fall of 1856
Milo Andrews Company
SPOUSE: Henry Nisonger
MARRIED: 3 Mar 1836
DEATH SP: 27 Nov 1872
Salt Lake City, Salt Lake, Utah

CHILDREN:
David, 16 Dec 1837
Mary, 12 Mar 1840
Chester, 18 Oct 1842
Carmen, 1 Aug 1844
Airon, 21 Mar 1845
Sarah Jane, 15 Oct 1846
Lydia Ellen, 14 Jan 1849
Phebe, 4 Feb 1851
Elisie, 12 Jan 1854

Sarah Slusser was born April 26, 1816, near Dayton (Clear Creek), Warren, Ohio, the daughter of Peter Slusser and May Deam (Diehm). She married Henry Nisonger on March 3, 1836. They lived in the woods where her husband cut wood for a living. She cooked for the men who worked with him. About this time they met the Elders and joined the Church of Jesus Christ of Latter-day Saints.

They moved to St. Louis but her husband could not get work, so she worked in a shirt factory to support the family. Finally Henry got a contract to cut wood for the railroad. In this way they were able to earn money to bring them to Utah. They came with the Milo Andrews Company by wagon and ox-team in the Fall of 1856.

They lived in Ogden for a while, then moved to Payson where they lived in a brush shack. Then they moved to Camp Floyd. Here she washed for the soldiers and baked pies and sold them. She also corded wool, spun the yarn, and wove the cloth to make clothes for her family. Later they moved to Santaquin, Utah.

Sarah's husband passed away November 27, 1872, in Salt Lake City, Utah, and Sarah passed away, April 2, 1900, in Santaquin, Utah County, Utah.

SARAH LANE ELSEY NIX

No
Photo
Available

BIRTHDATE: Chr. 11 Sep 1803
Semperinghem, Lancashire, England
DEATH: 5 Nov 1855
Tooele, Tooele Co., Utah
PARENTS:
PIONEER:
Milo Andrus Wagon Train
SPOUSE I: Joseph Elsey
MARRIED: 8 Jon 1827
Semperingham, England
DEATH SP: 14 Apr 1839
England

CHILDREN:
Mary Ann, 25 Jun 1829
William, (chr.) 15 May 1831
Joseph, 7 Oct 1832
Sarah, 22 Mar 1834
Susannah, 25 Oct 1835
Richard, (chr.) 20 Mar 1838

SPOUSE II: James Nix
MARRIED: 20 May 1840
DEATH SP: 6 Dec 1878

CHILD:
Samuel, 5 Aug 1842

Sarah was christened in Semperingham, England on September 11, 1803. She had five sisters and four brothers. When she was twenty-four years old she married Joseph Elsey and they were the parents of six children.

After the death of her husband, she met and married James Nix. From a previous marriage he had three children. Sarah and James had one son born in 1842.

In 1850, Sarah and James were baptized and became members of The Church of Jesus Christ of Latter-day Saints. Sarah was one of the first converts in Lincolnshire. Her daughters, Mary Ann and Susannah, were baptized at the same time and were sent to America.

In 1854, Sarah and James boarded the ship "Helios," but it sprang a leak and six weeks later passage was secured aboard the ship "Charles Buck." They set sail on January 17, 1855. They were fifty-six days on the water and Sarah was sick all the way across the ocean.

They landed at New Orleans and traveled by boat to St. Louis where they waited a week for the ice to clear from the river. A steamboat had been engaged by Apostle Erastus Snow to take them to Atcheson, Kansas. When it was inspected by Richard Ballantyne, their company leader, he found it was unsafe and arranged for them to travel on the "Michigan." The first boat they chartered met with an accident and sank.

At Atcheson, Kansas, four companies were formed of about four hundred people in each and James and Sarah went with the Milo Andrus Company. They reached Salt Lake in November of 1855. Her daughters, Mary Ann and Susannah with their husbands had come from Tooele to greet the family and take them to Tooele. They arrived at Tooele on November 5, 1855, around five o'clock in the evening. Sarah died that night at eleven o'clock.

Sarah Lane Elsey Nix was a courageous woman and faithful Latter-day Saint to the end.

ELIZABETH HURSILLAR JOHNSON NIXON

BIRTHDATE: 1 Nov 1849
Council Point, Iowa
DEATH: 20 Sep 1938
Holden, Millard Co., Utah
PARENTS: Richard Johnson
Husseler Bevan
PIONEER: Fall of 1851
SPOUSE: George William Nixon
MARRIED: 24 Oct 1868
Salt Lake City, Salt Lake, Utah
DEATH SP: 5 Dec 1923
Holden, Millard Co., Utah

CHILDREN:
Harriet Ellen, 7 Feb 1870
George William, 15 Feb 1873
Ira Alvin, 5 Feb 1875 (died as a child)
Elizabeth H., 2 Oct 1877 (died as a child)
Richard Stephen, 12 Sep 1880
Frances Charlotte, 1 Nov 1883
Marion, 19 Jan 1887 (died as a child)
Carl, 29 May 1889
Flossie, 18 Oct 1892

Elizabeth was born in Iowa in 1849. The family came to Utah in the Fall of 1851, and settled in Fillmore, Millard County, Utah. In 1855, they moved to Cedar Springs (Holden) in Millard County. They slept in dugouts and wagon boxes, and when some other families joined them, they built a fort as protection against the Indians. They called it "Fort Butterworth," because the women made butter and saved the buttermilk in a cool place to refresh the weary travelers.

Elizabeth was baptized in 1860. She had very little education because she had to milk cows night and morning, as well as help plant crops and harvest them. She carded and spun wool, knit stockings, and made beautiful lace on very fine needles.

Elizabeth married George William Nixon in 1868 in the Endowment House. George built a large brick home in Holden.

Elizabeth was famous for her hospitality, and many friends called on her just to sample her famous salt-rising bread. She kept her children busy with chores, telling them that "idle hands are the devil's workshop."

George passed away in Holden in 1823 and Elizabeth passed away in 1838, also in Holden, Millard County, Utah.

HANNAH ISABELL FAWCETT NIXON

BIRTHDATE: 17 Jan 1845
Nauvoo, Hancock Co., Illinois
DEATH: 31 Oct 1929
St. George, Washington, Utah
PARENTS: William Fawcett
Jane Comer Smith
PIONEER: 15 Sep 1850
David Evans Co. Wagon Train
SPOUSE: James William Nixon
MARRIED: 21 Feb 1876
Salt Lake City, Salt Lake, Utah
DEATH SP: 19 Feb 1882
St. George, Washington, Utah

CHILDREN:
Mary Johannah (Washington), 8 Nov 1876
Franklin, 22 Feb 1879
Elizabeth Jane "Jennie" (Foster), 9 Dec 1879
Eva Jennetta, 12 Jul 1880

Hannah was born January 17, 1845 in Nauvoo, Illinois, one year before her family was evicted by anti-Mormon mobs. She survived for four years living in temporary shelters in Iowa and Missouri while her family was preparing to cross the Plains.

With her parents, Hannah, at age five, set out in 1850 to travel across the Plains to Salt Lake City. She remembers being frightened crossing streams and during encounters with animals. Hannah endured the many hardships that came with making a new home. She was sixteen when she helped drive cattle as her family moved to the Dixie Cotton Mission.

She married James Nixon as a second wife. Hannah spent several years living with other members of the Nixon family at Trumbull Sawmill where lumber was cut for the building of the St. George Temple. This sawmill complex was part of the United Order in the Cotton Mission. She cooked for the workers and her husband's families. Hannah was often responsible for caring for many children. When the workers and her husband and his other families would leave in the autumn, she was left alone to face dangers from Indians, accidents, illness and starvation.

After Hannah's husband died in St. George, she lived with her parents and did so until they died. She taught classes in Sunday School and the Young Women's MIA, She served as a counselor in the Primary and then as

Primary President. She was a teacher in the Relief Society for many years and did temple work. In addition, she served as a recorder for her father, who was a Patriarch, when he gave Patriarchal Blessings.

She was a dedicated and hard working woman. She wrote a long, detailed history of her life. Hannah passed away in St. George at the age of seventy-four.

JOHANNA MARIE SHULTZ NIXON

BIRTHDATE: 1 Apr 1844
Honsinge, Denmark
DEATH: 13 Mar 1922
Provo, Utah Co., Utah
PARENTS: Christian J. Schultz
Ane Dinesdatter
PIONEER: 29 Aug 1859
James Brown Co. Wagon Train
SPOUSE: James William Nixon
MARRIED: 26 Oct 1859
Salt Lake City, Salt Lake, Utah
DEATH SP: 19 Feb 1882
St. George, Washington, Utah

CHILDREN:
Mary Anne, 2 Jan 1861
Emma Amelia, 22 Dec 1862
Hannah Maria, 22 Oct 1864
James William, 7 Sep 1866
Sena Lenora, 4 Dec 1871
Adelia Matilda, 16 Mar 1874
Josephine May, 30 Jun 1876
Delia Maude, 27 Mar 1879

Johanna Marie Shultz was born in Denmark in 1844. She was only eleven when the missionaries from the Church of Jesus Christ of Latter-day Saints came into their village and converted the family. They suffered much abuse because of their membership and finally the family left Denmark for Utah in 1859.

Johanna's father died at sea, and her mother and three other siblings made their way to Burlington, Iowa. Here her mother died, as well as a younger brother and sister. Johanna walked the entire way to Utah.

Soon after she arrived she married James William Nixon. She was only fifteen at the time. Her first home was in East Weber, and six miles from the nearest neighbor. The threat of Indians coming into her home brought terror to her heart.

Then a call came for the family to help settle Utah's Dixie. She was the mother of six children, the last five born in St. George, Utah. Her husband was a very prosperous merchant and one of the Bishops in St. George. Johanna was a great example of faith, industry and obedience.

Her husband passed away in St. George in 1582, and Johanna passed away in 1922 in Provo, Utah County, Utah.

ELIZABETH WILCOX MEAD NOAKES

No
Photo
Available

BIRTHDATE: 7 Jan 1784
Halifax, Windham, Vermont
DEATH: 3 Apr 1881
Brigham City, Box Elder, Utah
PARENTS: Nathan Wilcox
Rebecca Moon
PIONEER: 1 Oct 1852
Uriah Curtis 16th Wagon Train
SPOUSE I: Ezra Mead
MARRIED: 1811
DEATH SP: 26 Sep 1861/8

CHILDREN:
Sophia Burnham, 12 Jul 1812
James Parish, 10 Jun 1814
Ezra William, 12 Oct 1815
Henrietta, 5/17 Oct 1818
Sally Ann, 2 May 1820
Minor Moss, 10 Dec/Jan 1822
Charles Clark, 1825

SPOUSE II: Thomas Noakes, Sr.
MARRIED: 18 Mar 1852
Salt Lake City, Salt Lake Co., Utah
DEATH SP:
CHILDREN:
None

Elizabeth was born January 7, 1784, in Vermont. Not much is known about her growing up years but she did make her living at tailoring.

Elizabeth married Ezra Mead who was a violin maker, There was not much call for that instrument at the time, so he did not bring much money into the home. At one time he was putting the finishing touches on a violin for a wealthy woman when Elizabeth, in a fit of anger, picked it up and smashed it to pieces. Her husband was so shocked and stunned that he picked up his hat, walked out of the house and out of Elizabeth's life forever. For many years, Elizabeth supported her family as a tailoress.

Later, she married Thomas Noakes. Her son James Parish died in Ohio and is believed to have been buried on the temple grounds in Kirtland.

The Noakes family joined the other Saints and crossed the Plains to the Salt Lake Valley. They eventually settled in Brigham City, Utah.

Elizabeth did not have an easy life. But she must have had an abiding testimony of the truthfulness of the Gospel which was the glue in her life helping her to endure the heartaches and problems that she faced.

EMMA INKPEN NOAKES

No
Photo
Available

BIRTHDATE: 25 Oct 1789
Ringmer, Sussex, England
DEATH: 22 Apr 1851
Salt Lake City, Salt Lake, Utah
PARENTS: Edward John Inkpen
Sussanah Cossaw
PIONEER: 1847 Wagon Train
SPOUSE: Thomas Noakes
MARRIED: 30 Mar 1810
England
DEATH SP: 1 Sep 1871
Springville, Utah Co., Utah

CHILDREN:
George, 4 Sep 1811
Thomas, 29 Oct 1813
Emma, 17 Jan 1815
Edward Inkpen, 3 Mar 1816
William, 23 Oct 1818
John, 26 Sep 1821
Frances, 21 Aug 1824
Robert, 24 Sep 1827
John Hubbard, 7 Aug 1832

Emma Inkpen was born in England in 1789. She was tall and slender with brown eyes and medium black hair.

She married Thomas Noakes in 1810, when she was twenty-one and he was nineteen. They lived in Udimore, which is near the English Channel. Several of their children were born and died here.

Their oldest son, George, stowed away on a vessel bound for America. The captain of the ship befriended him and helped him get employment on a lake boat on Lake Erie. George saved his money so that he could bring his parents and siblings to America. They arrived about 1827/28 and lived in Litchfield, Ohio for several years. They joined the Church of Jesus Christ of Latter-day Saints about 1842 and moved to Nauvoo, Illinois, where Thomas helped to build the Nauvoo Temple.

It is thought that the family came to Utah in 1847. Thomas said they came into the Salt Lake Valley with a team made up of two oxen, two cows, and two heifers. They settled in Salt Lake City.

Emma passed away in Salt Lake City in 1851. Thomas lived for another twenty years and passed away in 1871 in Springville, Utah County, Utah.

SUSAN AMELIA CHILDS NOAKES

BIRTHDATE: 5 Mar 1839
Mexico City, Oswego, New York
DEATH: 3 Aug 1914
Springville, Utah Co., Utah
PARENTS: Moses Childs
Molly Patten
PIONEER: 12 Sep 1852
John D. Parker Company
SPOUSE: John Hubbard Noakes
MARRIED: 25 Feb 1855
Springville, Utah Co., Utah
DEATH SP: 3 Oct 1910
Springville, Utah Co., Utah

CHILDREN:
Verona Amelia, 30 Jun 1856
Emma Arathusa, 16 Oct 1858
Polly Ann, 2 Mar 1861
Susan Agnes, 17 Oct 1863 (died as an infant)
John Thomas, 16 Feb 1865
Eunice Alberta, 13 Nov 1867
David Patten, 26 Aug 1870
Moses Adelbert, 18 Dec 1872
George Hubbard, 20 Feb 1875
William Inkpen, 5 Nov 1878
Ann Amanda, 10 Apr 1885

Susan Amelia Childs was born in New York State in 1839. Susan's mother Polly, had joined the Church of Jesus Christ of Latter-day Saints in 1834, right after her marriage to Moses Childs. They first moved to Kirtland, Ohio, then to Nauvoo in 1844.

In the exodus of Saints from Nauvoo in February 1846, and over the frozen Mississippi River, her father's wagon was the last one to cross before the ice broke up. Her mother recalled how the ice would crack under her feet as she hurried over it.

The family came across the Plains with the John D. Parker Company, arriving in September, 1852. They were asked to take only the bare necessities, but Susan could not part with her favorite doll. She strapped it under the wagon so tight that no one knew it was there until they arrived in Utah. The family went to Springville to live.

Susan married John Hubbard Noakes in 1855 when she was fifteen years of age. He was frequently gone fighting Indians and such, and Susan had to care for the children and the farm during his absences. She was the mother of eleven children, one of them who died at birth.

She went with her husband when he was called to go to San Bernardino, California, for a time, then they returned to Springville. Susan worked hard doing washings for the railroad men and their families. She was a great help when people were sick or in need of assistance.

John passed away in 1910, and Susan passed away in 1914, both in Springville, Utah County, Utah.

REBECCA SQUIRE NOALL

BIRTHDATE: 14 Feb 1826
Lynton, Devonshire, England
DEATH: 6 Jun 1886
PARENTS: Phillip Squire
Agnes Parker
PIONEER: 7 Nov 1854
Capt. James Wagon Train
SPOUSE: Simon Noall
MARRIED: 18 Mar 1854
DEATH SP: 21 Jun 1896

CHILDREN:
Phillip Squire, 19 Feb 1856 (died at age 10)
Rebecca Jane, 25 May 1858
Mary Agnes Parker, 20 July 1859 (died as an infant)
William Thomas, 21 Dec 1860
Sarah Eliza Squire, 12 Jan 1863 (died as an infant)
Mathew, 1 Feb 1864
Catherine Cogar, 14 Sep 1865 (died at age 1)
John Simon, 25 Feb 1865 (died as a child)

Rebecca was the seventh of ten children, five girls and five boys. She had a very studious nature, but never had a formal education. In her teen years she was a "Lady-in-Waiting" to two girls in the home of a titled gentlemen in London. Here she learned much of culture, refinement, courtesy, and proper etiquette. She was loved by the family, they even had portrait painted of her. She was sixteen years old.

The father and some of the family joined the Church of Jesus Christ of Latter-day Saints, August 15,1853. They then decided to join the Saints in America. It was decided Rebecca's mother would stay with Rebecca's older sister until her baby was born. They never saw them again.

Nine family members, Phillip the father, son William and his wife and two children, daughter Sarah and her husband, and daughters Mary and Rebecca boarded the sailing ship, "Windermere," February 15, 1854.

One day out the wind died and they set for five days just rocking with the waves. On the sixth day the wind came and they were able to travel again. Rebecca's father who was grieving over leaving his wife became very ill and at 8 o:clock that night he passed away, and was buried at sea the next morning in a violent storm.

The storm worsened, large boxes tied to berths broke loose, pots and pans rolled with terrible force and there was great confusion. The captain came to Daniel Garn and told him to pray to see if the Lord would hear them, if not he was afraid they would go down. They did, the storm abated and they all felt better.

But their troubles were not over. There was small pox on the ship, and early one morning while many were still asleep fire broke out under the cooking gally. In great haste buckets were filled and passed to the sailors and the fire was put out.

They landed in New Orleans on May 2, 1854. After a few days quarantine the Squire family boarded a steamboat, "The Grand Towee" and went to St. Louis, then to Kansas City. They bought a covered wagon and oxen and joined Captain James Wagon Company.

One time Rebecca tried to get out of the moving wagon and fell and the wagon run over her leg, giving her an injury that lasted the rest of her life. They reached the Valley, November 1, 1854. The family bought a home on the same block where Simon Noall lived. Not long after he and Rebecca met they were married, March 18, 1854.

The family lived in a very comfortable home on the corner of 4th North and 4th West. It was a half acre lot, with many fruit trees and berry bushes, with a deep well giving cold fresh water. They grew vegetables and flowers.

Amidst all the chores Rebecca suffered constantly with the leg injured on the Plains. She used to put it on a chair and push it around the kitchen to ease the pain. Rebecca was very generous, constantly watching for those in need. She made soap from scraps of fat, starch from potatoes, and molasses from beets.

In 1858, they were among the Saints moving south because of Johnston's Army. Due to the stormy weather, they stopped in American Fork for a while. Here on the May 24, Rebecca gave birth to her daughter Rebecca Jane in her covered wagon home. When she was six weeks old they returned to their home in Salt Lake.

Rebecca passed away in June 1886.

SUSAN HAMMOND ASHBY NOBLE

No Photo Available

BIRTHDATE: 28 Aug 1808
Marblehead, Massachusetts
DEATH: 15 May 1851
Salt Lake City, Salt Lake, Utah
PARENTS: Edward Hammond
Rebecca Flack
PIONEER: 20 Sep 1848
Erastus Snow Wagon Train
SPOUSE I: Nathaniel Ashby
MARRIED: 30 Nov 1826
Salem, Essex Co., Massachusetts
DEATH SP: 23 Sep 1846
Bonapart, Iowa

CHILDREN:
Robert Reed, 17 Aug 1827
Benjamin, 19 Dec 1828
Susan Ann, 1 Feb 1830
Elizabeth Rebecca, 17 May 1831
Martha Ellen, 28 Aug 1832
Harriet Maria, 8 Apr 1834
Nathaniel, 25 May 1835
Richard Hammond, 25/26 Dec 1836
William Hardin, 16 Jul 1839
Mary Jane, 20 Oct 1841

Emma Smith, 14 Mar 1843
John Jefford, 9 Dec 1845

SPOUSE II: Joseph Bates Noble
MARRIED: 11 Feb 1847
Winter Quarters, Iowa
DEATH SP: 17 Aug 1900

CHILD:
Louisa Adeline, 13 Dec 1849

Susan was born in Marblehead, Essex County, Massachusetts. Her father was a merchant seaman. At the age of eighteen, she married Nathaniel Ashby. They were honest, thrifty, hard working people. They became prosperous shoe manufacturers owning their own business and several houses in Salem which they rented.

When Erastus Snow came to Salem as a missionary, the Ashbys were among the first to accept the gospel and were baptized as members of the Church of Jesus Christ of Latter-day Saints on December 9, 1841. One of her daughters married Erastus Snow. They permitted the Snow family to live rent free for two years in one of their houses.

After Erastus Snow returned to Nauvoo, the Ashbys sent money to help build the Nauvoo Temple and bought half of Erastus Snow's lot. Brother Snow had a double brick home built for himself and the Ashby family at the corner of Parley and Hyde Streets. The home continues to stand today in Nauvoo. They moved into their new home in Nauvoo in January of 1844. Susan donated her large mirror, a dresser, two beautiful home made rugs, and a Brussels carpet as furnishings for the Nauvoo Temple.

One year after their arrival, the Prophet Joseph Smith, was murdered. The Ashbys along with many other Saints were driven from their homes in August of 1846.

Nathaniel became ill and died in September 1846 on the Plains near Bonapart, Iowa. This left Susan with twelve children to bring to Utah. She arranged for the children to be provided for. One daughter was taken into the family of Lorenzo Young, one with Joseph Bates Noble, and still another traveled with the family of Brigham Young. One son drove a team for Brother Haven. Susan still had six children to look after and care for their needs. Her oldest son drove the team and acted as a father to the younger children.

While in Winter Quarters, Susan married Joseph Bates Nobel. They all arrived in Salt Lake Valley on September 20, 1848 in the Erastus Snow Wagon Company. They lived in a vacated room in the old fort. In December of 1849, she gave birth to her thirteenth child.

Susan was a woman of great faith spending much time among the sick, where she was very capable. Being always cheerful and optimistic, she scattered happiness along her path.

Susan passed away on May 15, 1851, leaving several young children. "Her integrity and patience in the face of poverty and death, sets forth a standard that urges us forward."

CAROLINE MATILDA HAMILTON NOKES

BIRTHDATE: 15 Oct 1851
St. Joseph, Missouri
DEATH: 14 Sep 1925
Riverton, Salt Lake Co., Utah
PARENTS: James L. Hamilton
Mary Ann Campbell
PIONEER: 15 Sep 1852
Robert Weimer Wagon Train
SPOUSE: Charles M. Nokes
MARRIED: Sep 1879
Salt Lake City, Salt Lake, Utah
DEATH SP: 8 Apr 1932
Salt Lake City, Salt Lake, Utah

CHILDREN:
Mary Caroline, 31 Oct 1880
Matilda Ellen, 8 Jan 1883
Charles Mormon, 20 Jul 1885
James Robert, 21 Aug 1887 (died at age 1)
Benjamin Hamilton, 12 Dec 1889
Harold Templeton, 1 Jul 1893

Caroline Matilda Hamilton was born October 15, 1851, in St. Joseph, Missouri, the daughter of James Lang Hamilton and Mary Ann Campbell. She came across the Plains with her parents and was only eleven months old when they arrived in the Valley. They came with the Robert Weimer Company, by wagon, arriving on September 15, 1852.

As a young woman she learned how to wash, card, and spin wool into yarn for clothing. She was an expert at knitting socks and mittens for family members. In 1875, her father passed away, leaving a good farm. She helped milk the cows, make butter, and dress chickens.

She had chances to marry into polygamy but didn't want second best. She married Charles Mormon Nokes in September, 1879, in the Endowment House. He later took a second wife, which was a great trial for Caroline.

Charles spent six months in the penitentiary, then when released he took his second wife and fled to California, leaving Caroline to run the farm in Riverton. Later Charles returned to live with her in Riverton.

The last fifteen years of her life Caroline endured poor health. She passed away on September 14, 1925, in Riverton.

CAROLINE TERRELL NORRIS

No
Photo
Available

BIRTHDATE: 26 Aug 1824
Wicken, England
DEATH: 16 Aug 1894
Randolph, Rich Co., Utah
PARENTS: Jacob Terrell
Elizabeth Billings
PIONEER: 25 Sep 1866
J. D. Holladay Company
SPOUSE: William Norris
MARRIED: 18 Jan 1844
Wicken, England
DEATH SP: 7 Nov 1907
Randolph, Rich Co., Utah

CHILDREN:
Alfred James, 29 Dec 1844 (died as an infant)
Walter, 17 Feb 1846
Elizabeth, 10 Jun 1847
Reuben, 7 Jan 1850
Hyrum Job, 15 Apr 1852
Emily, 9 Aug 1854
Heber Willard, 23 Oct 1856 (died as an infant)
Joseph, 21 Mar 1860 (died as an infant)
Lorina, 13 Mar 1864 (died as an infant)

Caroline Terrell (also spelled Tyrell, Turrell, Tirell) was born in Wicken, Northhampshire, England in 1824. When but twelve years of age she went to work in a lace factory making lace, and working ten to twelve hours each day.

She married William Norris in 1844 when she was nineteen in Wicken, Northhampshire, England. They were the parents of nine children.

Wilford Woodruff taught them the gospel of the Church of Jesus Christ of Latter-day Saints and they were baptized. They left England on the ship "Caroline," and in Nebraska they joined the J. D. Holladay Company to cross the Plains, arriving in September, 1866.

The family was sent to help settle Morgan, Morgan County, Utah. About 1872, they moved to Randolph, Rich County, Utah, where they took up land to farm and built a home.

Caroline was a neat housekeeper, she loved flowers and had every kind that would grow in that climate. She also had an herb garden. She was a super seamstress and made beautiful clothing, mens and women. She was a tall, slim woman, walking very straight, until she was struck with arthritis.

Caroline was in bed for more than a year before she passed away in 1894. William died thirteen years later, in 1907. Both are buried in Randolph, Utah.

ALBERTINE JOSEPHINE JOHNSON NORTH

BIRTHDATE: 31 Jan 1837
Tjerby, Halland, Sweden
DEATH: 23 Sep 1922
Taylorsville, Salt Lake Co., Utah
PARENTS: Bertel Johnson
Margaret Larsson
PIONEER: Sep 1859
Rowley Handcart Company
SPOUSE: Charles Addison North
MARRIED: 27 Jan 1861
Salt Lake City, Salt Lake, Utah
DEATH SP: 31 Jan 1906
Mill Creek, Salt Lake Co., Utah

CHILDREN:
Charles Levi, 25 Oct 1861
John Addison, 9 Sep 1863
Hyrum King, 5 Sep 1865
Albertine Ariminta, 22 Dec 1867
Alice Almira, 9 Jan 1870
Ada Alvira, 9 Jan 1870
Levonna Diana, 27 Jun 1872
Melinda, 15 Apr 1874
Lilly Ann, 1 Mar 1876
Nellie Josephine, 17 Feb 1879
Emily Deseret (Daisy), 18 Feb 1881

Albertine Josephine Johnson was born on January 31, 1837, in Tjerby, Halland, Sweden, the daughter of Bertel Johnson and Margaret Larsson. At a young age she was farmed out to relatives because her father had died, and her mother was too ill to care for her.

She sailed for America at the age of twenty-two aboard the ship, "William Tappscott." Because she could speak some English and German, as well as Swedish, she earned her way by being an interpreter. She joined with the Rowley Handcart Company, and served as a cook for the supply wagons, arriving in the Salt Lake Valley, September 10, 1859.

Albertine married Charles Addison North, January 27, 1861, and they became stalwarts in the Mill Creek community. They ran a store, had charge of the Post Office, and for many years had the only telephone in the area.

Albertine served as secretary for the Relief Society, and also wrote articles for "The Exponent." She had many talents, a beautiful singing voice, and helped her children cultivate their own musical talents. Of her eleven children, seven lived to adulthood.

Albertine's husband passed away in 1906 in Mill creek, Utah, and Albertine passed away on September 23, 1922, in Taylorsville, Salt Lake County, Utah.

PRISCILLA JANE BLAIR NORTH

BIRTHDATE: 13 Feb 1853
Adams Co., Illinois
DEATH: 13 Jun 1927
Midway, Wasatch Co., Utah
PARENTS: Harrison Blair
Mary Ann McNutt
PIONEER: Aug 1857
Homer Duncan Wagon Train
SPOUSE: Hyrum Bennett North
MARRIED: 5 Apr 1869
Salt Lake City, Salt Lake, Utah
DEATH SP: 28 May 1915
Charleston, Wasatch Co., Utah

CHILDREN:
William Harrison, 14 May 1870
Webster Howard, 21 Jul 1872
Arthur Mormon, 30 May 1874
Ashael Albert, 2 Jul 1876
Milton Blair, 27 Sep 1878
Edith Priscilla, 16 Feb 1881
Alma, 22 Jan 1883 (died as an infant)
George Addison, 23 Jul 1884 (died as an infant)
Royal Exile, 29 Aug 1886 (died in 1898)
Warren Lyman, 22 Aug 1888
Lorin Harvey, 4 Apr 1890

Priscilla Jane Blair was born in Illinois in 1853. When she was three months old her parents and two brothers left Illinois and went to California. They lived there until 1857 when they joined the Church of Jesus Christ of Latter-day Saints. They came to Utah with the Homer Duncan Company in 1857 and located in the Mill Creek and Cottonwood area of Salt Lake County.

At the age of sixteen, Priscilla married Hyrum Bennett North in the Endowment House, as his second wife. She became the mother of eleven children, ten boys and one girl.

They moved to Midway in Wasatch County, where she had to climb the hills for wild berries and dig sego roots for food. Priscilla made her own soap, candles, and dye for the wool she spun.

Priscilla got along well with the first wife. She loved flowers and worked hard to have beautiful ones around her home. She made bouquets of flowers for church meetings, and was always sharing them.

Hyrum passed away in 1915 in Charleston, Utah. Priscilla passed away in 1927 in Midway. Both are buried in the Midway Cemetery, Wasatch County, Utah.

ELIZABETH BENEFIELD OR PENEFIELD NORTON

No
Photo
Available

BIRTHDATE: 9 Aug 1801
Montgomery Co., Ohio
DEATH: 1867/68
Lehi, Utah Co., Utah
PARENTS: James Benefield
Elizabeth Newton
PIONEER: 20 Sep 1848
Brigham Young Wagon Train
SPOUSE: David Norton, Jr.
MARRIED: 10 Feb 1820
Fayette Co., Indiana
DEATH SP: 2 Jun 1860
Lehi, Utah Co., Utah

CHILDREN:
John Wesley, 6 Nov 1820
James Wiley, 6 Aug 1822
Melissa Isabel (Allred), 23 Dec 1824
Henry Elliot, 23 Oct 1827
Hyrum Fletcher, 8 Jul 1829
Isabella (Judd), 14/22 Aug 1836

Elizabeth was born August 9, 1801, in Ohio. It is not known how Elizabeth met her husband but they were married in Indiana and all of their six children were born there.

Elizabeth and David joined the Church of Jesus Christ of Latter-day Saints at an early date and moved to Missouri in 1836, buying property near Haun's Mill. Unfortunately the persecution of the Saints escalated in Missouri. The night before the terrible Haun's Mill Massacre the Norton family had sought refuge at the Mill. But Elizabeth's husband, David, had a premonition and decided to return to his own farm. As a result they escaped the terrible massacre. Some of the other people who were able to escape also sought refuge at the Norton farm. Elizabeth and her family were glad to serve these sorrowing people.

Soon they were forced to move into the state of Illinois. Here, too, the enemy followed and they again suffered much persecution until they were compelled to abandon their home, their Prophet and their temple. They stopped in Council Bluffs to refurbish their supplies. Here their daughter, Melissa, was married and they all continued into the Salt Lake Valley in September, 1848.

Now they were free from persecution from the enemy but here they were faced with the challenge of a barren uncultivated land with little food and clothing. So they struggled with this challenge of sharing not only their food with their neighbors but also the Indians.

Elizabeth was an industrious, ambitious person but she was glad when they finally settled in Lehi. However she had one constant worry; her loved ones who were fighting in the Civil War. This caused her health to fail and she passed away at the age of sixty-six.

LUCY WILKINSON NORTON

BIRTHDATE: 3 Mar 1789
Chatham, Connecticut
DEATH: 17 Sep 1851
Coalville, Utah
PARENTS: Thomas Wilkinson
Sarah Hall
PIONEER: 23 Sep 1851
John G. Smith Co. Wagon Train
SPOUSE: Allen Norton
MARRIED: 31 Dec 1809
Granville, New York

CHILDREN:
Alanson, 26 Mar 1814
Betsy Susanna, 10 Dec 1816
Charles, 29 Aug 1819
Delinda Amelia, 27 Apr 1822

Lucy was born in Chatham, Middlesex County, Connecticut, 1789. When she was fifty-three years old, her husband died leaving her with three unmarried children and one married son, Alanson.

Arrangements were made to join Alanson, his wife, and two children in Clymer, New York. While living there, they learned about the Gospel of Jesus Christ of Latter-day Saints and were baptized in February of 1843.

Alanson was appointed a Branch President of the Church in 1844. Lucy was eager and earnest to share her knowledge of the Gospel with others. Alanson was able to baptize a number of people whom Lucy had converted.

In 1845, this combined family gathered with the Saints in Nauvoo. Here they found more unrest and persecution than at Clymer, New York. The Prophet had been killed and Saints had been driven from New York, Ohio, and Missouri. Now they were being expelled from Illinois. Both of Lucy's daughters died during that year.

In the Spring of 1851, with the John G. Smith Company, the family started across the Plains. They reached Salt Lake Valley, September, 1851, and were asked to settle in Provo, Utah.

In January, 1852, Alanson's wife died shortly after giving birth. Now the duties of being a grandmother and mother rested upon Lucy as she continued her spinning of yarn and thread, knitting stockings, weaving carpets, and countless other useful duties that had to be performed in pioneer life.

When Alanson married again and began a new family with his wife, Julia, they moved to Sugarhouse area, then to Parley's Canyon. When her son Charles died, he left his home in Coalville, Utah to Alanson, so they all moved to Coalville, Utah. It was here that Lucy spent the remaining years of her life serving her family and her church.

Lucy passed away September 17, 1851, and was laid to rest in Coalville, Utah.

MAREN JENSEN CUTLER NORTON

BIRTHDATE: 28 Jan 1846
(Borgium) Hjorring, Denmark
DEATH: 26 Jan 1921
Salt Lake City, Salt Lake, Utah
PARENTS: Mads C. Jensen
Maren Hansen
PIONEER: 30 Sep 1853
John E. Forsgren Wagon Train
SPOUSE I: Sheldon Bela Cutler
MARRIED: 2 Mar 1861
Salt Lake City, Salt Lake, Utah
DEATH SP: 11 May 1870
Brigham City, Box Elder, Utah

CHILDREN:
John, 29 Apr 1863
Mads Christian, 22 May 1865
Parley, 2 Jun 1866
Andrew Oscar, 27 Apr 1869

SPOUSE II: Alanson Norton
MARRIED: 5 Feb 1872
Salt Lake City, Salt Lake Co., Utah
DEATH SP:

CHILDREN:
Elvin Jensen, 6 Jan 1877
Joseph Asa, 14 Feb 1882

When Maren was five years old, her parents joined the Church of Jesus Christ of Latter-day Saints. Persecution of the Elders and any who joined the Church was so strong, many of the members couldn't stand such treatment any longer.

They sold their homes and prepared to emigrate in 1852. In November, they left their home and went to Copenhagen. From there, they sailed to England in the first company of Mormon emigrants from Scandinavia.

From Hull, England, they sailed across the Atlantic Ocean on a sailing vessel called, "Forest Monarch." It took eleven weeks and three days with very little food. A steamboat took them up the Mississippi River to St. Louis. From there, they went by rail to Iowa and prepared to cross the Plains. They traveled with the John E. Forsgren Wagon Company and arrived in Utah on September 30, 1853.

Their first home was a dugout in Kaysville, Utah, for a short time. Then they moved to Salt Lake City for a time, then to Ogden for two years, then to Brigham City where her parents lived the remainder of their lives. Maren met and later married Sheldon Bela Cutler, March 2, 1861, in Salt Lake City. They had four sons before Sheldon died in 1870.

Until the boys could take care of themselves, Maren supplemented her farm with earnings at her carpet loom. She was employed at the woolen factory in Brigham City.

It was while she was living in Brigham City that she met Alanson Norton, Superintendent of the mill. They were married on February 5, 1872, in the Endowment House in Salt Lake City for time only.

When it was necessary, Maren, Elvin, and Joseph lived with Alanson, his other wife, Julia, and family. But she mostly stayed on her farm north of Brigham City. When her sons married, she would spend winters with her Cutler sons in Idaho.

Maren passed away on January 26, 1921 in Salt Lake City, Utah, where she spent the last two months of her life with her son, Elvin.

MARTHA ANN COVINGTON GAY NORTON

No
Photo
Available

BIRTHDATE: 8 Dec 1818
Rockingham, North Carolina
DEATH: 24 Aug 1871
Salt Lake City, Salt Lake, Utah
PARENTS: Thomas Covington
Jane Thomas
PIONEER: 25 Sep 1851
Capt. Brown Handcart Company
SPOUSE I: Alexander Gay
MARRIED: 24 Aug 1841
DEATH SP: 11 Oct 1846
Mt. Pisgah, Iowa

CHILDREN:
Eliza Jane, 27 Sep 1838
Susan Ann, 13 Jun 1841
John Franklin, 28 Mar 1843
Benjamin, 31 Jul 1845

SPOUSE II: John Norton
MARRIED: Jun 1847
Mt. Pisgah, Iowa
DEATH SP:

CHILDREN:
Mary, 5 Mar 1848
Nancy Elvina, 27 Apr 1850
Martha, 23 Jan 1853

Martha Ann was born in Rockingham, Richmond County, North Carolina. She married Alexander Gay in North Carolina, when she was about twenty years old. Some of their relatives had moved to Mississippi by 1840 and Alexander and Martha followed them. Here, in Mississippi, they became members of the Church of Jesus Christ of Latter-day Saints.

They left Mississippi for Nauvoo in 1846 only to find the city deserted. They then followed the Saints into Iowa, where tragedy struck them. Alexander and the baby, Benjamin, became ill with mountain fever and died just one day apart. Martha was left with three small children and not much means of support.

She married John Norton, a widower with seven small children. They came across the Plains with a handcart company in 1851.

Martha and John were among the first settlers in Alpine, Utah, but because of Indian troubles they moved back to Salt Lake City.

John was called to serve a mission in Australia and was gone seven years. He and Martha drifted apart and Martha was known as "Widow Gay," in the community.

She possibly married a third time to a Benjamin Gibson, but little, if anything, is known of this union. Martha was sealed to Alexander Gay in 1869.

Martha passed away at the age of fifty-two years, and is buried in Ogden, Weber County, Utah.

NANCY HAMMER NORTON

BIRTHDATE: 14 Oct 1829
Putnam Co., Ohio
DEATH: 13 Jul 1898
Lehi, Utah Co., Utah
PARENTS: Austin Hammer
Nancy Jane Elston
PIONEER: 24 Sep 1848
Brigham Young Wagon Train
SPOUSE: James Wiley Norton
MARRIED: 8 Jul 1846
Florence, Nebraska
DEATH SP: 7 Feb 1897
Ammon, Idaho

CHILDREN:
Amanda Melissa, 19 Apr 1847
Nancy Fedelia, 22 Jan 1849
Sarah Jane, 17 Apr 1852 (died as an infant)
Rufus Wiley, 14 Aug 1853 (twin)
James Riley, 14 Aug 1853 (twin)
Julia Isabel, 23 Jul 1855 (died as an infant)
Marietta, 29 May 1856
Leander David, 17 Feb 1859
John Franklin, 27 Apr 1860
Rebecca Rosetta, 3 Feb 1862
Elizabeth Ann, 20 Apr 1864 (died as an infant)
Elmira Ceretta, 19 Jul 1865
Alfred Squire, 30 Dec 1867

Nancy Hammer was born in Putnam County, Ohio, in 1829. Her parents were baptized into the Church of Jesus Christ of Latter-day Saints in 1835 and moved to Shoal Creek in Missouri, where they had 180 acres of farm land. Her father was killed in the Haun's Mill Massacre in 1838. Three weeks after the massacre they were told to be out of the State in ten days.

Nancy helped to load the wagon with what they could, leaving the rest behind, and they started off for Quincy, Illinois. She walked the entire way, her feet wrapped in rags, and with rain or snow most of the journey. They were glad to be with the Saints again.

Nancy married James Wiley Norton in 1846. They had one child when they crossed the Plains with the Brigham Young Company in 1848. When Johnston's Army came into Utah they moved to Lehi, where they lived several years. Then they moved to Ammon, Idaho, where some of their family had homesteaded.

Nancy was a small woman, only 5 feet 2 inches, and weighed less than 120 pounds. Her husband was a stonemason, and he built a house of stone, making the window sills wide, where she proudly placed her geranium plants.

James passed away in Ammon, Idaho in 1897, and Nancy passed away in Lehi, Utah, in 1898. Both are buried in the Ammon, Cemetery in Idaho.

CAROLINE CHLOE NORTON PICKUP NORWOOD

BIRTHDATE: 6 Sep 1836
Shelby Co., Tennessee
DEATH: 15 Mar 1901
Porterville, Morgan Co., Utah
PARENTS: John Warren Norton
Dorothy Osborn
PIONEER: 28 Sep 1851
John Brown Co. Wagon Train
SPOUSE I: George Pickup
MARRIED: 17 Apr 1851
Alpine, Utah Co., Utah
DEATH SP: 1860/61
San Bernardino, California

CHILDREN:
James Edward, 23 Aug 1853
John William, 18 May 1855
Rebecca, abt 1857

SPOUSE II: Richard Smith Norwood
MARRIED: 5 Dec 1857
Salt Lake City, Salt lake Co., Utah
DEATH SP: 18 Jan 1898
Orderville, Kane Co., Utah

CHILDREN:
Adelia, 8 Jun 1859
Dorothy, 13 May 1861
Sarah Jane, 12 May 1863
Caroline Matilda, 23 Aug 1865
Richard, 17 Jan 1867
David, 12 May 1870
Smith, 21 Oct 1872
Isaac, 19 Sep 1878

Caroline Chloe was born in Tennessee in 1836. Because of persecution to the members of the Church of Jesus Christ of Latter-day Saints, her parents moved around frequently, first to Alabama, then to Mississippi, finally to Nauvoo in 1846.

Her mother died in Iowa, and when her father remarried all seven children in the family were "farmed out."

Because they were all separated, they did not see each other for years.

Caroline came to Utah with her foster family and settled in Alpine, Utah County, Utah. She married George Pickup in 1851, and they had three children. George went to California during the gold rush and never returned. Caroline divorced him prior to his death about 1861.

Caroline then married Richard Smith Norwood in 1858, as his second wife, and had eight more children. The family moved to Porterville, in Morgan County where they homesteaded. They lived the United Order for two years, then moved to Orderville, Utah, where they again lived the United Order.

In 1890, Caroline left Richard and moved to Huntington, Emery County, Utah, and lived with some of her children. Later she returned to Porterville, where she died in 1901.

ELIZABETH STEVENSON BAILEY NORWOOD

BIRTHDATE: 11 Feb 1823
Colony of Gibraltar, Spain
DEATH: 3 Oct 1878
Porterville, Morgan Co., Utah
PARENTS: Joseph Stevenson
Elizabeth Stevens
PIONEER: 12 Oct 1848
Amasa Lyman Wagon Train
SPOUSE I: Job T. Bailey
MARRIED: 24 Jun 1845
Charleston, Lee Co., Iowa
DEATH SP: 7 Feb 1848
Charleston, Lee Co., Iowa

CHILDREN:
Bethany, 27 Jun 1846
Elizabeth, 8 Feb 1848

SPOUSE II: Richard Smith Norwood
MARRIED: 13 Oct 1850
Salt Lake City, Salt Lake Co., Utah
DEATH SP: 18 Jan 1898
Orderville, Kane Co., Utah

CHILDREN:
Mary Melinda, 1 Nov 1851
Brigham, 1853 (died at 9 months)
Martha, 27 Jul 1856
Nancy Areta, 29 Jun 1859 (died at 16 months)
Eliza, 29 Nov 1860
Phoebe Ellen, 1 Aug 1863

Elizabeth was born to English parents living in Gibraltar, Spain. She emigrated to the United States with her family when she was four years old. Her family was pioneering in Michigan when her father died. She was seven years old at this time.

Her mother and her third brother joined the Church of Jesus Christ of Latter-day Saints in 1833. In 1836, her mother took three of her children to Missouri to join with the Saints there. They experienced the persecutions and mobbing in Clay County, in Caldwell County, and finally left Missouri for Clarksville, Iowa.

Elizabeth married Job T. Bailey when she was twenty-two years old. In 1846, her family left the area to live in Winter Quarters. She wanted to go also, but Job had joined the Strangites after the martyrdom of Prophet Joseph Smith. He became ill and died just one day before her second daughter was born. Her brother and brother-in-law came back for her and her children and took them to Winter Quarters just in time to go West with the Amasa M. Lyman Wagon Company, arriving in the Valley on October 12, 1848.

In 1850, Elizabeth married Richard Smith Norwood. Richard and Elizabeth lived in Salt Lake City and Big Cottonwood for ten years. In 1858, Richard took another wife and in 1860 the two families moved to Morgan County.

Elizabeth and her children lived in the town of Porterville and the third wife, Caroline, and her children lived with Richard on the farm at Norwood's Hollow. Elizabeth was active in the Porterville Relief Society after it was organized in 1868.

In September, 1878, Elizabeth became ill and passed away at the age of fifty-five. She lived and died true to the principles of the Everlasting Gospel.

SARAH ANDERSON NOWERS

BIRTHDATE: 4 Dec 1828
Murfreesboro, Tennessee
DEATH: 6 May 1909
Beaver, Beaver Co., Utah
PARENTS: Miles Anderson
Nancy Face
PIONEER: 1 Oct 1851
Alfred Cordon Wagon Train
SPOUSE: Willson Gates Nowers
MARRIED: 23 Jun 1855
DEATH SP: 17 May 1922
Beaver, Beaver Co., Utah

CHILDREN:
Willson Edward, 14 Mar 1856 (died at age 4)
Nancy Kathleen, 22 Apr 1857
William Gates, 27 Jun 1859
Sarah Susannah, 25 Mar 1861
John Alfred, 5 Mar 1863
James Albert, 29 Nov 1864
Edward Lorenzo, 26 Jan 1867 (died at age 2)
Joseph, 15 Dec 1868 (died as an infant)

Sarah "Sally" was born in Murfreesboro, Rutherford County, Tennessee in 1826. Her parents were baptized into the Church of Jesus Christ of Latter-day Saints in 1836. They reached Nauvoo in the Spring of 1842, and Sally was baptized by her father in the Mississippi River in 1845.

After they were expelled from Nauvoo, and living in Kanesville, Iowa, Sally met Willson Gates Nowers, who came from Kent, England. They traveled across the Plains together and had many opportunities to get well acquainted, however fate separated them for four years.

Sally arrived in Salt Lake with her family in 1851 and then went to Parowan to live. Willson remained in Salt Lake until 1853 then went to Parowan where he again met Sally. They were married in 1855; he was twenty-seven and she was twenty-six.

Their first home was in Parowan, then they moved to Beaver, in Beaver County. Sally was the mother of eight children, and all but three of them lived to maturity. She was very systematic, a good manager, loved and highly respected by family, friends and acquaintances.

Sally passed away in Beaver in 1909, and Willson passed away in 1922 also in Beaver, Beaver County, Utah.

ELIZABETH CLARKSON NUTTALL

BIRTHDATE: 28 Apr 1836
Hyson Green, England
DEATH: 19 Jul 1902
Provo, Utah Co., Utah
PARENTS: Thomas Clarkson
Cathrine "Kitty" McCoy
PIONEER: 12 Oct 1852
Allen Weeks 21st Wagon Train
SPOUSE: Leonard John Nuttall
MARRIED: 25 Doc 1856
Provo, Utah Co., Utah
DEATH SP: 23 Feb 1905
Salt Lake City, Salt Lake, Utah

CHILDREN:
Elizabeth Ann (Shumway), 1 Apr 1858
Leonard John, 5 Dec 1857/59
Thomas Clarkson, 19 Oct 1861
Joseph William, 16 Dec 1863
Mary Clarkson (Holdaway), 27 Dec 1865
George Albert, 24 Sep 1867
Daughter, 10 Oct 1869 (stillborn)
Eleanor Clarkson (Warner Mahlon), 2 Sep 1870
Lenora, 12 Feb 1873/75
Clara Clarkson (Giles), 25 Mar 1875
Heber Clarkson, 8 May 1877 (died day of birth)
Wilford Clarkson, 29 Mar 1878

Elizabeth was born April 28, 1836, in England. Her father was a grocer. By February, 1847, the family had been converted and baptized into the Church of Jesus Christ of Latter-Day Saints.

In the Summer of 1849, Elizabeth left England with her parents on the ship, "Berlin," arriving in New Orleans, October 23, 1849.

The Clarkson family resided in St.Louis, Missouri and Kanesville, Iowa until 1852 when they crossed the Plains. They moved to Provo, Utah, where Elizabeth was a member of and participated in a theatrical company with her future husband and some of his family.

Elizabeth received her own endowments in the Endowment House, December 14, 1855. One year later she married Leonard John Nuttall in Provo. They lived in Provo for eighteen years except for a short time when they moved to Spring Lake as the first settlers there.

One Sunday morning in September, 1870, while her husband was at Springville attending church meetings, the home and all the household effects (plus the hay and grain) were destroyed by fire.

In June of 1874, Elizabeth's husband left for a mission to England, leaving her with eight children and pregnant. She was filled with sorrow when their youngest child, Lenora died.

Elizabeth moved to Kanab November, 1875, when her husband was called as bishop of the Kanab Ward. There she made and sold women's hats. She selected, braided and dyed the straw shaping it into the hat and made flowers. Elizabeth made gloves for men and women. She also tanned coyote skins, some of which she made into a robe for President Wilford Woodruff.

Elizabeth was president of the Relief Society of Kanab Stake in June, 1878. Her husband was gone a great deal of the time due to his church responsibilities. By June, 1879, he was called to be President John Taylor's private secretary. Elizabeth moved to Salt Lake City with all but her three oldest children who remained to care for the farm, except Elizabeth Ann who was married,

In May of 1880, Elizabeth attended Mrs. Pratt's School of Obstetrics in Salt Lake and passed the exam to be a midwife. She did not do much as a midwife but did help a few.

When Elizabeth's husband went into exile with President Taylor in 1885, she moved to Provo with her children. In December, 1890, Elizabeth went to Washington D. C. to join her husband who had been called as a missionary. She stayed for five months enjoying a trip down the Potomac River and along the coast to New York, sight seeing before the train ride home.

Elizabeth passed away suddenly in Provo while her husband was in Canada. He returned quickly for her funeral.

MARY LANGHORN NUTTALL

BIRTHDATE: 22 Dec 1798
Shap., Westmorland, England
DEATH: 20 Apr 1880
Wallsburg, Wasatch Co., Utah
PARENTS: John Langhorn
Eleanor Taylor Langhorn Miller
PIONEER: 2 Nov 1852
Philip De La Mar Wagon Train
SPOUSE: William Nuttall
MARRIED: 8 Jul 1822
St. Mary, Lancaster, England
DEATH SP: 14 Mar 1864
Provo, Utah Co., Utah

CHILDREN:
William Ephraim, 29 Oct 1825
Richard, 24 Apr 1833
Leonard John, 6 Jul 1834
Joseph, 31 Aug 1836
Eleanor Jane, 13 Jan 1839

Mary was the first child of John Langhorn and Eleanor Taylor. Three months after her birth, he became an excise officer and was sent to Liverpool for seven months. Then he moved his family to Bradford, Yorkshire where he worked until his death in January, 1801. At this time, Mary was just two years old and her mother was expecting a second child within the month. Her mother took Mary to live with her parents near Carlisle, Cumberland.

When Mary was twenty-six, she married William Nuttall. Her husband was a dock worker for the Navy. Mary's cousin, John Taylor, returned to England from America as a missionary for the Church of Jesus Christ of Latter-day Saints and was instrumental in converting the family to the Church. The family was baptized in July 1850.

They emigrated on March 6, 1852, on the ship, "Rockwell," and were part of the group that John Taylor had organized to bring machinery for the manufacture of sugar in Utah. Forty large prairie schooners were used to transport the 5,000 to 9,000 pounds of iron machinery across the Plains with Captain DeLaMar. They arrived in the Salt Lake Valley in November of 1852.

The family moved to Provo to make their home. Mary was fifty-four years old and was learning pioneer life. Although she kept the home fires burning under the most primitive conditions, she never lost the refinement and culture so characteristic of her own home.

Mary was a widow for sixteen years before she passed away at the age of eighty-two in Wallsburg, Utah, where she was living with her son, William Ephraim.

ROSAMOND WATSON NUTTALL

BIRTHDATE: 28 Jun 1829
Liverpool, Lancashire, England
DEATH: 22 Oct 1916
Ogden, Weber Co., Utah
PARENTS: George Watson
Mary Dyson
PIONEER: 2 Nov 1852
Philip DeLaMar Wagon Train
SPOUSE: William E. Nuttall
MARRIED: 4 Aug 1851
Liverpool, Lancashire, England
DEATH SP: 5 May 1899
Wallsburg, Wasatch Co., Utah

CHILDREN:
Infant, Apr 1852 (died on ocean)
William George, 4 Mar 1853
John Horatio, 14 Dec 1854
Joseph Brigham, 9 Oct 1856
Richard James, 19 Sep 1858
Mary Eleanor, 22 Sep 1860
Walter Henry, 5 Jul 1862 (died as an infant)
Martha Agnes, 8 Sep 1863
Rosamond Emily, 7 Mar 1865
Ruth Caroline, 6 Nov 1866
David Watson, 14 May 1869
Elizabeth Ann, 1 Feb 1871 (died as an infant)
Laura Alice, 29 Jun 1873

Rosamond Watson came from a very wealthy family. Her father was a rich tea dealer and made furniture for ships. During the early 1850's, John Taylor, a cousin of the Nuttall family, had been to America. While there, he heard of and joined the Church of Jesus Christ of Latter-day Saints and returned to England as a missionary.

Rosamond heard and received the new gospel, and was baptized a member of the Church. Her parents were hostile to this new religion and asked her to renounce this religion or leave home.

She went to live with her married sister, Caroline, until she married William Ephraim Nuttall, who had also joined the Church. They were married in the Church of St. John the Baptist on August 4, 1851.

Rosamond, her husband, his parents and two unmarried brothers left Liverpool on March 6, 1852, on the ship, "Rockaway," with the Elias Morris Company of Saints.

Rosamond's first child was born, died, and buried as they crossed the ocean. This group of converts were known as the Sugar Company because they were also carrying the sugar refining machinery for beets grown in the Salt Lake Valley. John Taylor had purchased the machinery for the Church. It was left in charge of Elias Morris and the Nuttall brothers. Special wagons were ordered to carry this heavy machinery across the Plains.

Green and unseasoned lumber was used, so the wagons soon began to break down. They purchased forty-two Santa

Fe Wagons to complete their trek across the Plains. They arrived in Salt Lake Valley on November 2, 1852.

Rosamond and William Ephraim settled in Provo where they lived until about 1870, then moved to Wallsburg, Wasatch County, Utah. They bought a farm near the center of Wallsburg where they lived for the rest of their lives.

William Ephraim passed away in Wallsburg, on May 5, 1899. Rosamond passed away at the home of her daughter, Laura, in Ogden, Weber County, Utah.

HEDVIG LUCIE ENGELBRECHT SORENSDATTER HANSEN / PETERSEN NYBOLLE

No Photo Available

BIRTHDATE: 20 Sep 1808
Odense, Odense, Denmark
DEATH: 3 Nov 1867
Mt. Pleasant, Sanpete Co., Utah
PARENTS: Andreas Sorensen
Anne Benedicte Ericksen
PIONEER: 13 Sep 1887
Matthias Cowley Wagon Train
SPOUSE I: Hans Petersen
MARRIED: abt 1832/33
DEATH SP: 24 May 1835
Denmark

CHILD:
Ane Benedicta, 6 Nov 1833

SPOUSE II: Rasmus Nybolle
MARRIED: abt 1835/36
DEATH SP: 29 Jul 1863
Mt. Pleasant, Sanpete Co., Utah

CHILDREN:
Hansine Jacobine, 3 Jul 1836
Karen, 2 Jun 1839
Jens Christian, 23 Aug 1846

Hedvig Lucie Engelbrecht Sorensdatter was born in Denmark in 1808. She married Hans Petersen in about 1832/33. They had one daughter, then Hans was killed in 1835 in the service of his country when little Ane was eighteen months old.

Hedvig then married Rasmus Nybolle in Denmark about 1835/36. They had three children, all born in Denmark. When the missionaries taught them the gospel of the Church of Jesus Christ of Latter-day Saints, Hedvig and Ane slipped away separately and were baptized, unbeknown to each other. Later they confessed to joining the Church.

Three years later, in 1857, the family left Denmark for America. They sailed on the ship "Westmoreland," under Matthias Cowley, who also accompanied them across the Plains. The Nybolle family settled in Mt. Pleasant, Sanpete County, Utah.

Little is known of her activities in Mt. Pleasant, but daughter Ane, stated that Hedvig had been a doctor of obstetrics in Denmark and was licensed to practice in a large district.

Hedvig passed away in Mt. Pleasant in 1867 of consumption at the age of fifty-nine. Her husband passed away in 1883, also in Mt. Pleasant, Utah.

ALBERTINA AXELINA LOVING NYMAN

BIRTHDATE: 18 Jun 1851
Lund, Stadsforsamling, Sweden
DEATH: 26 Jul 1925
North Logan, Cache Co., Utah
PARENTS: Andreas Loving
Bengta Hansson
PIONEER: 29 Aug 1863
John R. Murdock Wagon Train
SPOUSE: Carl Nyman
MARRIED: 11 Jan 1870
Salt Lake City, Salt Lake, Utah
DEATH SP: 18 Aug 1931
North Logan, Cache Co., Utah

CHILDREN:
Sarah Helen, 20 Oct 1870
Carl Andrew, 20 Oct 1871
Willard Ezra, 10 Feb 1874
Golden Alfred, 23 Apr 1876
Albert, 27 Nov 1878
Annie Elizabeth, 7 Nov 1880
Abbie Camille, 13 Apr 1882
Bendine, 20 Jun 1883 (died as an infant)
Andrew B., 14 Dec 1884
Ida, 23 Nov 1886 (twin)
Idella, 23 Nov 1886 (twin)
Walter, 5 Jun 1889
Christine, 3 Jul 1891
Vilate, 23 Jan 1893
Ernest Leslie, 14 Oct 1895

After Alberta Axelina's family joined the Church of Jesus Christ of Latter-day Saints they decided to come to Utah, but could not come all at once. Albertina came with a neighbor, Mrs. Swensen, in 1863, when she was twelve years old. The voyage across the North Sea was rough and they had to wait while the damaged boat was repaired. In April, they crossed the Atlantic Ocean. Albertina did not experience any sea-sickness on the voyage. They landed in New Orleans, then up the Mississippi River to Iowa, thence to Florence, Nebraska.

In Florence, Albertina joined with the John R. Murdock Company and walked the entire distance across the Plains. She enjoyed the trip and especially the new scenery. In the same company was her future husband, Carl Nyman.

Years later Carl saw her in her mother's yard in Logan and recognized her as the little girl he talked to while crossing the Plains. They were married in the Endowment

House in 1870, and Albertina became the mother of fifteen children.

Albertina was a very talented lady. She learned to spin, weave, sheer wool from the sheep's back, and take it through the different processes for the making of clothes. The family lived in Logan for many years, then moved to North Logan (Greenville) for the rest of their lives. She was very happy that all her married children had been married in the temple.

Albertina passed away in North Logan in 1925, in North Logan, Cache County, Utah.

SARA CARLSSON QUARSTROM (SARAH QVARNSTROM) NYMAN

No
Photo
Available

BIRTHDATE: 13 Jun 1813
Gallsjon, Sunborn, Sweden
DEATH: 12 May 1893
North Logan, Cache Co., Utah
PARENTS: Carl O. Qvarnstrom
Ann Hansson
PIONEER: 29 Aug 1863
John R. Murdock Wagon Train
SPOUSE: Anders Nyman
MARRIED: 23 Aug 1839
Sweden
DEATH SP: 15 Oct 1876
North Logan, Cache Co., Utah

CHILDREN:
Anna, 23 Jan 1840
Anders, 21 Mar 1842 (died as an infant)
Anders, 5 Jan 1844 (died as a child)
Elisabeth, 14 Apr 1845
Carl, 11 Mar 1847
Sara Helena, 22 Jul 1849
Ulrica Margreta, 8 Dec 1851
Bror Anders, 6 Oct 1853

Sara was born in Gallsjon, Sunborn, Kopparberg, Sweden in 1813. She married Anders Nyman in 1839 and they had eight children, but only two of them survived childhood.

In the Spring of 1863, they sold their farm and possessions and started for Utah with their two sons Carl, age sixteen and Andrew (Bror Anders), age nine.

The seas were very rough and they had to turn back three times, and were detained while the boat was being repaired. Finally they reached Liverpool, then St. Louis, and Fort Leavenworth. Here they joined with the John R. Murdock Company arriving in Salt Lake City in August, 1863.

Little is known of their activities here in Utah. They evidently settled in North Logan in Cache County. Sara and Anders were sealed in the Endowment House on October 4, 1867.

Anders passed away in North Logan in 1876, and Sara passed away in 1893, in North Logan, Cache County, Utah.

MARIE ANN OLSEN OAKASON

BIRTHDATE: 29 Jan 1844
Gjerperod, Idd, Ostfold, Norway
DEATH: 10 Jan 1920
Salt Lake City, Salt Lake, Utah
PARENTS: Svend Arnt Olsen
Ellen Marie Syversen
PIONEER: 1 Oct 1862
Joseph Horne Co. Wagon Train
SPOUSE: Hans Oakason
MARRIED: 21 Sep 1865
Salt Lake City, Salt Lake, Utah
DEATH SP: 22 Jan 1924
Salt Lake City, Salt Lake, Utah

CHILDREN:
Emma Elvira, 8 Jul 1866
Heber William, 7 Feb 1868
Sarah, 1 Jul 1871
Eliza Marinda, 28 Aug 1873
Albert Frank, 26 Jan 1876
Lillian Hannah, 1 Jan 1879
John Edmund, 21 Aug 1881
Alice, 31 Jul 1884
Mary Ellen, 27 Dec 1888

Marie's people were of royal descent. Her parents were members of the Lutheran Church, and although they never did join the Church of Jesus Christ of Latter-day Saints, they were not opposed to its teachings.

Four of their daughters joined the Church, Mary Ellen being baptized on July 19, 1860, and soon after they left their parents and came to America. Marie was the youngest, being fifteen years of age at that time.

They crossed the ocean on a German sailing ship, and, as was common with most sailing vessels, their progress was very slow. Sometimes they were blown by the wind farther behind than they came the day before. After being on the water for six weeks , the three girls landed safely at St. Louis, Missouri.

Here, they joined the Joseph Horne Wagon Company and began their walk across the Plains. Trials and hardships were many, but they also had time for recreation and enjoyment.

The sisters had been raised in a home of plenty and were well cared for when they left Norway, but as the emigrants were allowed to carry only a certain amount of luggage, most of their belongings were disposed of. When they reached the Salt lake Valley, nearly all of their clothing was gone.

Hannah, her older sister,was stricken with Mountain Fever, died, and was buried in Coalville. The two remaining girls were met in Salt Lake City by the missionaries who had converted them.

Marie worked in the home of President John Taylor as a nurse for his aged mother and later in the home of Daniel H. Wells.

Marie married Hans Oakason, as his second wife. Hans' first wife had crossed the Plains but passed away before Marie and Hans were married. Their first home was very crude; a hole in the side of a hill. They owned very few possessions. Later they built a small, two room adobe home. It was a great improvement over their first home and was one of the nicest homes in the area for quite some time. As the family grew to nine children Hans built a large red-brick home at 936 East and 1st South.

Marie often told of the devastation of the crickets, and how she would step on the ugly creatures and feel them squish between her toes.

Marie was a hard worker and made life pleasant for her family. She was a good teacher, and a fine example for her children.

PRUDENCE TREMAYNE BARKDULL OAKES

No Photo Available

BIRTHDATE: 9 Jun 1807
Westfield, Tiago, Pennsylvania
DEATH: 13 Mar 1859
Farmington, Davis Co., Utah
PARENTS: John Tremayne
Elizabeth Judd
PIONEER: 15 Sep 1852
Henry Jolley Co. Wagon Train
SPOUSE I: Michael Barkdull
MARRIED: 6 May 1824
Akron, Portage Co., Ohio
DEATH SP: 25 Jul 1839
Quincy, Adams Co., Illinois

CHILDREN:
Isaiah Jones, 6 Feb 1825
Solomon Michael, 5 May 1827
Peter Samuel, 3 Apr 1830
Sarah Elizabeth, 27 Apr 1832
Mary Prudence, 27 Apr 1832
Jason Nicholas, 17 Jan 1834
Jasen, 17 Jan 1835
Martha Ann, 26 May 1837
Alvin Tremayne, 12 Aug 1839

SPOUSE II: Henry Oakes
MARRIED: 12 May 1842
Nauvoo, Hancock Co., Illinois
DEATH SP: Not given

CHILD:
Permelia Louise Oakes (Barkdull), 11 Oct 1845

Prudence was married at the age of seventeen. Michael and Prudence made their first home in Akron. Later they moved to New Portage, Wayne County, Ohio. They joined the Church of Jesus Christ of Latter-day Saints and were very humble and sincere in their belief. The Barkdull family moved to Far West along with many other families.

In 1839, the Missouri mobs were forcing the Mormons from their homes. The refugees began arriving along the banks of the Mississippi river and established temporary camps on the opposite shore.

Prudence's husband had been imprisoned in Missouri and from the exposure and ill treatment received from the mobocrats, he contracted a disease which terminated in his premature death.

Prudence became very ill and was not expected to live. She was expecting her eighth child. The weather was stormy, and she and her children were only sheltered from the storms by an improvised tent made from bed quilts. President Heber C. Kimball administered to her and she was healed. Eighteen days after Michael's death she gave birth to a son.

In 1840, Prudence moved her family to Nauvoo. The temple records show that Prudence and her sons did baptisms for the dead for family members. On March 17, 1842 the Relief Society was organized and she became a member.

While residing in Nauvoo, Prudence married for a second time to a man named Henry Oakes.

It is believed that on June 14, 1852, Prudence departed from Kanesville Iowa. After she came to Utah, she lived in Farmington, Davis County, Utah.

Prudence was highly respected by all members of the family and all who knew her.

ANN COLLETT OAKEY

No
Photo
Available

BIRTHDATE: 12 Jan 1812
Pendock, Worcester, England
DEATH: 14 Apr 1892
Paris, Bear Lake Co., Idaho
PARENTS: William Collett
Elizabeth Bromage
PIONEER: 09 Nov 1856
James G. Willie Handcart Comp.
SPOUSE: Thomas Oakey
MARRIED: Aug 1836
England
DEATH SP: 15 Aug 1890
Paris, Bear Lake Co., Idaho

CHILDREN:
Ann, 8 Nov 1833
Charles, 25 May 1837
Jane, 8 Apr 1839
Heber Thomas, 30 Jan 1841
Joseph Lorenzo, 9 Aug 1843
Rhoda Rebecca, 28 Oct 1845
Reuben Hyrum, 20 Aug 1847
James William, 27 May 1849
Sarah Ann, 9 May 1852
Walter John, 27 Jun 1854.

Ann and her husband made their home in Eldersfield, Worcester, England where all their children were born. In 1840, they were taught the gospel of Jesus Christ by Elder Wilford Woodruff. They were impressed by his teaching and were among the first 600 converts who were baptized. They had an earnest desire to come to America to join with the Saints and they worked hard to try to save enough money to make the journey.

In 1856, their dreams came true with help from the Perpetual Immigration Fund that the Church had made available for those desiring to come to America. In May, they left family and friends and boarded the ship "Thornton," and were finally on their way.

They landed at Castle Garden, New York, six weeks later and from there they went to Iowa. They were advised that they should wait until the next spring to make their journey, but they were anxious to be amongst the Saints, so they started out with two handcarts and a limited amount of supplies. The journey was long and hard and they suffered much from fatigue, hunger and cold. There was also much illness among the company.

To add to their trials, a few days after their journey had begun, they discovered one day that their son, Joseph, had disappeared. They searched amongst the company but no one knew what had happened to him. Some twenty years later, through the efforts of Apostle Charles C. Rich, he was located and later he came to Paris to visit his parents.

Thomas' health began to fail and many times he was forced to drop out of the train of immigrants and rest by the roadside. When he did his, Ann would continue and get the children all settled in camp and then would go back to where they had left him and help him into camp.

Ann also was often called upon to go among the sick of the company doing whatever she could to help them. They looked upon her as a doctor and nurse for the sick.

When they reached Wyoming the company encountered snow and cold weather. Their food supplies were low and they did not have sufficient clothing and bedding to keep them warm. The suffering was particularly great at Rock Creek and on one morning fifteen people were found dead.

When the brethren in Salt Lake heard of the plight of the Handcart Companies in the mountains, they sent help in the form of wagons, food and warm clothing. Ann and the other Saints were relieved when the rescue teams arrived and took them to Salt Lake. They lived with Ann's brother, Don Collett and his family for awhile and then moved to Kaysville and later to Lehi, Utah.

In the Spring of 1865, they moved to Paris, Idaho where they resided the rest of their lives. Ann served as a midwife and assisted in bringing many babies into the world. She and her husband did much to build up the Bear Lake Valley.

They were Pioneers in every sense of the word and were true and faithful to the religion that they loved and had sacrificed so much for.

MARY COOPER OAKEY

BIRTHDATE: 5 Mar 1814
Greasley, Nottingham, England
DEATH: 28 Mar 1893
Dingle, Bear Lake Co., Idaho
PARENTS: Matthew Cooper
Mary Burrows
PIONEER: 2 Oct 1862
James S. Brown Co. Wagon Train
SPOUSE: James Oakey
MARRIED: 6 Jan 1840
Radford, Nottingham, England
DEATH SP: 31 Jan 1897

CHILDREN:
Thomas, 6 Jul 1840
Mary, 9 Jun 1843
Lucy, 23 Feb 1845
James, 31 Mar 1847
Alfred, 10 Apr 1849
Joseph, 9 Apr 1851 (died as an infant)
Sarah, 31 Mar 1854
Hyrum, 11 Nov 1859

Mary was born in Greasley, Nottingham, England. She married James Oakey on January 6, 1850 in Radford, Nottingham, England. They were the parents of five children before they joined the Church of Jesus Christ of Latter-day Saints. Missionaries and several of the apostles were welcomed in their home.

Her husband, James, was active and was assigned as presiding elder in many of the small congregations. Their lives were centered around church activities. By the time they decided to emigrate to Zion, they had eight children.

It was decided that James would remain to sell the property. Mary and her children, except her daughter, Mary, sailed on the ship called "John J. Boyd." The children broke out with measles and were very sick. By the time they landed in New York, they were very hungry. It took them thirty-nine days on the ship, six days on the rail cars, and two days on a steam ship to get to Florence, Nebraska.

They joined the James S. Brown Wagon Company. Her daughter, Lucy, died the day after they left Florence. Mary's sons hired out to drive teams for others. Her oldest son, Tom, carried four year old Hyrum on his shoulders. They arrived in Salt Lake Valley on October 2, 1862.

After their arrival, they lived in a dugout in Caseward, Utah Territory. When her husband, James, arrived in 1863, he was called to help settle Paris, Idaho. Mary and the rest of the family joined him there after a very severe winter.

In England, James was a lacemaker. In Paris, Idaho he did carpentry work. When he took a second wife, Mary moved to Dingle.

When they cleaned house in those days, they took everything out of the house, emptied the straw ticks, and whitewashed the house with lime. This made the walls a pure white. To clean the floors, the carpet was taken up, the old dirty straw was removed, the floor was scrubbed, and a straw was put on the floor before they laid the carpet back down. It was fastened with carpet tacks.

In the summer they rented their cows on shares. Their pay came in round, flat, 12 to 30 pound molds of cheese. They would kill a fat cow and two big hogs every winter to provide their food each winter.

Mary passed away in Dingle, on March 28, 1893.

MARY ANN PASSEY OAKEY

BIRTHDATE: 28 Mar 1844
Strensham, Worcester, England
DEATH: 12 Jan 1925
Paris, Bear Lake Co., Idaho
PARENTS: William Passey
Sarah New Neat
PIONEER: 13 Sep 1861
Joseph Horne Co. Wagon Train
SPOUSE: Charles Oakey
MARRIED: 17 Jan 1862
Lehi, Utah Co., Utah
DEATH SP: 16 May 1903
Paris, Bear Lake Co., Idaho

CHILDREN:
Charles Lorenzo, 6 Nov 1862
Elthura Roseltha, 30 Jul 1864
William Thomas, 7 Sep 1866
Rhoda Jane, 25 Oct 1868
John Herbert, 1 Feb 1871
Reuben George, 5 Jul 1873
Joseph Heber, 21 Jun 1875
Edwin Arthur, 30 Oct 1877
Mary Ann "Polly," 11 Oct 1878
Sarah Elizabeth, 28 Feb 1881
Hyrum James, 15 Jun 1883
David Wilford, 13 Jan 1885

When Mary Ann was six years old, her parents became members of the Church of Jesus Christ of Latter-day Saints. From that date forth, their dream was to go to America and join with the Saints in Utah.

On March 28, 1856, the family boarded the ship, "George Washington," and sailed for America. They landed in Boston on April 19, 1856. The Passey family settled in East Cambridge, Massachusetts for the next five years while they earned enough money to continue their journey west.

In June of 1861, her family began their journey west with the Joseph Horne Wagon Company. They arrived in the Salt Lake Valley on September 13, 1861. They first settled in Lehi, Utah with other relatives.

Mary Ann met a young man named Charles Oakey who had come from England and was in the Willie Handcart Company in 1856. They were married on January 17, 1862. In 1864, they moved to Bear Lake Valley and settled in

Paris, Idaho. Like many other early settlers in Paris, they knew what it was like to go hungry.

Mary Ann and Charles became the parents of twelve children. Diphtheria robbed her of three children in one year.

Mary Ann took the time to lend a helping hand to a neighbor who had a new young baby and was very sick. She cared for both the baby and the mother. She also took two other children into her home. Mary Ann loved the Gospel very much. She was active in Church activities and did much temple work.

Mary Ann suffered many years from crippling arthritis. In spite of this, her crippled fingers were always busy. She made many beautiful temple aprons, quilts, doilies, lace, and rugs which she shared with her children and grandchildren. She also assisted with making many Relief Society quilts and rugs, and she helped Sister Ashley make burial clothes. She loved flowers and had many beautiful house plants.

Her husband died in 1903. After twenty-two years of living as a widow, Mary Ann passed away on January 12, 1925.

ELIZABETH DEGROAT / DEGROOT OAKLEY

BIRTHDATE: 16 Jan 1795
Castleton, Staten Isle., New York
DEATH: 26 Dec 1885
Salt Lake City, Salt Lake, Utah
PARENTS: John DeGroot
Mary Wood
PIONEER: 29 Sep 1847
Edward Hunter Co. Wagon Train
SPOUSE: Ezra Oakley
MARRIED: 1816
Gravesend, Long Isle., New York
DEATH SP: 29 Jan 1879
Salt Lake City, Salt Lake, Utah

CHILDREN:
Henry DeGroot, 18 May 1818
John DeGroot, 12 Nov 1819
Mary Ann DeGroot, 20 Mar 1826
James DeGroot, 5 Sep 1827
Margaret Simonson, 13 Aug 1835.

In 1840, Elizabeth and her immediate family were the first to embrace the gospel of the Church of Jesus Christ of Latter-day Saints in Long Island.

After her marriage to Ezra they lived in a comfortable home on the shore of the Atlantic Ocean and they were able to set a bounteous table as a result of the daily work. In their home all the sewing, washing and ironing was done by hand. They were the only members of the Church in the village of Flatlands, up to the time they left to migrate to Nauvoo in 1842.

They met the Prophet Joseph Smith for the first time and gloried in his association. Their daughter, Mary Ann, was asked to become the fourth wife of John Taylor, who later became president of the Church. The family felt great sorrow when they learned of the martyrdom of their beloved prophet and his brother Hyrum, and the wounding of their son-in-law.

In February, 1846, the Oakleys packed everything they could into their covered wagon and crossed the ice to the other side of the river. They remained at Winter Quarters until June 10 1847. In Salt Lake they made their home in the old Fort. A log house was built for the family and the yards and garden were clean and orderly and well laid out.

Elizabeth was a remarkably healthy woman all her life, scarcely knowing what sickness was. She received a patriarchal blessing under the hands of Father Joseph Smith in Nauvoo, in which she was blessed she would live until satisfied with life. She was always noted for her activity, vivacity and youth. She retained all her faculties up to the time of her death which occurred at the age of ninety-five.

FANNY PALFREYMAN OAKLEY

BIRTHDATE: 22 May 1852
Denby, Derbyshire, England
DEATH: 23 Jun 1935
Springville, Utah Co., Utah
PARENTS: Richard Palfreyman
Hannah Butler
PIONEER: Jun 1863
SPOUSE: James D. Oakley
MARRIED: 19 July 1869
Salt Lake City, Salt Lake, Utah
DEATH SP: 30 Apr 1915
Springville, Utah Co., Utah

CHILDREN:
Richard Delos, 12 Sep 1871
Lilly Ann, 23 Sep 1875
Phebe Loretta, 27 Sep 1877
Carrie, 19 May 1881
Ernest, 22 Jul 1883
Leo, 2 Oct 1886.

Fanny attended school in England and was taught to sew and make quilt blocks. Their home in England was filled with the comforts of life. When Fanny was only eleven years old she and her older sister, Selina, left their home in England (under the care of Mr. and Mrs. Hatfield) on the ship "Sinieshore," to come to America to live in Utah.

Fanny lived with Jim Miller at Cottonwood awaiting her mother's coming to America the following year. She met her mother, three sisters, and one brother in Salt Lake City. It was a happy reunion. It was almost more than her young heart could stand when her mother left her there and went to reside in Springville.

As soon as her mother was located and obtained work she sent for Fanny. She assisted her mother by gleaning in the fields and doing house work at many different homes, such as the Birds, Deals and Johnson's. While working for Cecelia Oakley, she met James and he became her husband,

She was a wonderful cook and anyone felt it a privilege to be a guest at her table and enjoy the rich hospitality of her wonderful home. She was always kind to those in distress and shared her last bite with the unfortunate. One of her sayings was "Pity without relief, was like mustard without beef."

Fanny was a teacher in Relief Society and always paid a full tithing, she was very good to remember the missionaries. Her testimony was strong and she always raised her voice in defense of that great principle of polygamy.

She was a lover of songs and poetry and said many lessons were taught by them. She hated weeds, both physical and mental weeds. Gossip never escaped her lips. Her favorite song was "Nay Speak No Ill." To raise a good family, to be honest and fair with friends and neighbors, and to teach by example the importance of faith and a true knowledge of the mission of the Savior are values Fanny instilled in her children and grandchildren.

ABIGAIL MARY REYNOLDS OAKS

BIRTHDATE: 2 Sep 1842
Nunda, Lyngat Co., New York
DEATH: 23 Dec 1912
Santa Monica, California
PARENTS: William P. Reynolds
Melissa Bardwell
PIONEER: 1853
Ammon Brown Co. Wagon Train
SPOUSE: David Martin Oaks
MARRIED: 2 Mar 1869
Salt Lake City, Salt Lake, Utah
DEATH SP: 27 Oct 1894
Vernal, Uintah Co., Utah

CHILDREN:
William Hyrum, 22 Jul 1872
Sarah Melissa, 20 Jan 1874
Edwin Martin, 6 May 1877

As the oldest child of fourteen, Abigail learned that industry and service are paths of joy. In 1848, her family moved to Adrian, Michigan. By this time they had joined the Church of Jesus Christ of Latter-day Saints. They stayed in Michigan for five years. In 1853, they loaded their possessions into a wagon and headed West.

When they arrived in Salt Lake Valley they stayed for two years and then moved to Provo. The family in 1862 moved to Heber Valley. Abigail was then nineteen years old and she taught school. It was here she became acquainted with David Martin Oaks who became her husband.

On November 14, 1879 in the Oak's cabin at the mouth of Daniels Canyon above Heber Valley, there was a party with anticipation and also sadness at farewells that were soon to be spoken. The next morning a party of nineteen (Abigail, her family and her two brothers and one sister and their families) began their trek to the Uintah Basin, much too late in the season, but with high courage. They spent an almost disastrous winter of 1879-80 in Ashley Valley in bitter cold, living mostly on deer meat and coarse, black flour. All ten of their milk cows froze to death. The next summer Abigail's parents were among more settlers who came to join them to help establish a community in what later became Vernal, Utah.

Abigail taught Ashley Valley's first school and was very active in community life. She was called as the Primary President and then was called to serve as the first Stake Primary President. She served in that position for over sixteen years.

After the death of her husband she assuaged her loneliness in offering comfort to the sick. She applied herself to the study of midwifery. She drove a one-horse rig to all parts of the settlement and filled her days and nights in service to others.

As she became elderly she developed high blood pressure and heart disease and was persuaded to go to California to avoid the rigors of the harsh winters in the Uintah Basin and passed away in Santa Monica, California and was buried in Vernal, Utah.

SARAH ANN WATSON OAKS

BIRTHDATE: 28 Dec 1858
Glatin, Iowa
DEATH: 29 Jan 1933
Vernal, Uintah Co., Utah
PARENTS: James Watson
Jannett Campbell
PIONEER: Not given
SPOUSE: Hyrum Edwin Oaks
MARRIED: 20 Mar 1878
DEATH SP: 30 Mar 1930
Vernal, Uintah Co., Utah

CHILDREN:
Edwin L., 22 Apr 1879
Sarah Janet, 29 Jan 1881 (died at age 4)
James Watson, 11 May 1885
William Wallace, 28 Mar 1888
Lindsay, 6 Apr 1903

Sarah Ann was born on December 28, 1858 at Glatin, Pottawattomie County, Iowa. Her father was James Watson born in 1820, her mother was Jannett Campbell born in 1824; they were born in Series, Fifeshire, Scotland.

Sarah Ann married Hyrum Edwin Oaks on March 20, 1878. He was born in American Fork on January 6, 1854.

For awhile they lived in the Heber City area moving to Center Creek, then to Daniels Creek. While living in this area they had four children born to them.

Jennie (Sarah Janet) died at the age of four in Center Creek. After which they moved to Vernal and settled in Maeser. Winters were hard and the Indians were not friendly.

When her husband bought fifty acres of ground, Sarah bought herself a sewing machine. She was a beautiful seamstress and did sewing for other people much of the time. Their fifth child was born in Vernal, Uintah County, Utah. They named him Lindsay.

Sarah Ann was an exceptional home maker. Helping neighbor and rearing grandchildren when her oldest sons wife passed away. She passed away at her home on January 29, 1933. Her husband had passed away three years before on March 30, 1930.

SARAH ANN WOOD OAKS

BIRTHDATE: 8 Apr 1827
Cornwall, Innbrg, Canada
DEATH: 8 Apr 1906
Vernal, Uintah Co., Utah
PARENTS: David Wood
Catherine Critz / Crites
PIONEER: 1851 Wagon Train
SPOUSE: Hyrum Oaks
MARRIED: 6 Dec 1846
Council Bluffs, Iowa
DEATH SP: 19 Mar 1903
Vernal, Uintah Co., Utah

CHILDREN:
David Martin, 2 Jan 1848
William Henry, 16 Jul 1849
Martha, 1850
Catherine Almida (Harry Jackson), 2 Oct 1851
Hyrum Edwin, 6 Jan 1854
John Osborn, 18 May 1856
Sarah Ann (Dennis Curtis), 22 Oct 1860
Mary Agnes (Burgess), 30 Nov 1861
Margaret Rozilla (Fullmer), 25 Oct 1862
James Sidney, 22 May 1864
Oscar Alonao, 20 Mar 1865
Amanda Elizabeth, 6 Jun 1866
Forte Alonzo, 2 Apr 1867

Sarah Ann was born in Canada, 1827. She was baptized as a member of the Church of Jesus Christ of Latter-day Saints in April of her thirteenth year.

On the 4th of July, 1840, with her parents, she crossed the St. Lawrence River on their way to Nauvoo. That trek took three months and they made their home in Nauvoo until they were driven out by the mobs in 1845. They crossed the Mississippi River into the state of Iowa and camped on the banks of the river for a few days, then moved on to Winter Quarters in Iowa.

Sarah Ann and Hyrum Oaks were married on the 6th of December in that bleak time, perhaps the one bright spot in that sadness.

When the Saints left Winter Quarters, they crossed the Missouri River into Pottawattamie County in the year of 1848. Here they remained until 1851. They moved through Nebraska, across the plains to the Salt Lake Valley.

Their first home in the valley was in American Fork, where they lived and raised their family for a time, moving on to Provo and then Heber, where their last seven children were born. In 1889, they moved to the Ashley Valley, now Maeser.

Sarah was always serving in the Church as well as serving her neighbors and community. She was one of that immortal band to whom the inhabitants of this once desert but now fruitful land, will ever owe a debt of gratitude. She was a woman of highest character and is universally loved and respected by all who knew her.

She was well acquainted with the Prophet Joseph Smith Jr. and was at the meeting in the grove where, by divine witness the "Mantle of Joseph" fell on the shoulders of Brigham Young who was President of the Twelve Apostles.

Hyram Oaks was born in 1820 in Susquehanna County, Pennsylvania. He always served faithfully in the Church. He passed away on March 19, 1903 at the age of seventy-seven years. Sarah Ann passed away on April 8, 1906, on her birthday, in Vernal, Uintah County, Utah, at the age of seventy-nine years.

CAROLYN BRENCHLEY OBRAY

BIRTHDATE: 6 May 1830
Borden, East Kent, England
DEATH: 20 Nov 1910
Paradise, Cache Co., Utah
PARENTS: William Brenchley
Caroline Weller
PIONEER: 10 Dec 1856
John A. Hunt Co. Wagon Train
SPOUSE: Thomas L. Obray
MARRIED: 2 Aug 1857
Salt lake Endowment House
DEATH SP: 21 Oct 1899
Paradise, Cache Co., Utah

CHILDREN:
Samuel Brenchley, 27 Jun 1858
Sarah Ann, 27 Sep 1859
John William, 22 Dec 1860
Robert Henry, 15 Jul 1862 (died as an infant)
Marian B., 13 Sep 1865 (died at 9 months)
Joseph Brenchley, 15 Apr 1867
Ezra Thomas, 26 Oct 1869
Ida Brenchley, 18 May 1872

Caroline's mother was a strict Methodist. Her father professed no religion, but they taught their children good moral principles based on reading from the Bible. She did not receive much schooling as she was obliged to work at an early age.

About 1850, a friend of the family came to their home and told them about the new religion that was being preached in a town two miles from their home. Soon after the family heard the message of missionaries from the Church of Jesus Christ of Latter-day Saints. The whole family was converted and baptized by a young man named Thomas Obray.

As a young woman, Caroline went to London to care for the blind daughter of Dr. Wiseman. She came to America with this family on May 25, 1856 on the ship, "Horizon." They landed in Boston, then went by steamboat to Iowa and joined the John A. Hunt Wagon Company.

Due to the late start from Iowa and the early winter weather, many immigrants died en route. Caroline walked the entire distance across the Plains, arriving in Salt Lake Valley in early December of 1856. Her feet were badly frostbitten, but she suffered no ill consequences regarding her feet after reaching the Valley.

After arriving in Salt Lake City, she met Thomas Obray, the young man who converted her family to the gospel. She became his third wife on August 2, 1859 in the Salt Lake Endowment House. They settled in Spanish Fork after their marriage.

They lived in Tooele, North Ogden, and Wellsville. They moved with several other families to a settlement called Petersburg, which is now known as Paradise. This is where Thomas and Caroline resided the remainder of their lives. They became the parents of nine children.

Caroline was a faithful, true, Latter-day Saint, always willing to do a kindness to others. She was patient and trusting through all the troubles of persecution to those entering plural marriage. Her husband spent five months in prison in Salt Lake City during 1887, and three months in 1890, for being a polygamist. These trials she bore patiently and lived righteously all the days of her life.

Caroline quietly passed away on November 20, 1910 in Paradise, Cache County, Utah.

ELEANOR BAINBRIDGE OBRAY

BIRTHDATE: 29 May 1832
Durham, England
DEATH: 2 Apr 1902
Paradise, Cache Co., Utah
PARENTS: Joseph Bainbridge
Jane Welch
PIONEER: 1854 Wagon Train
SPOUSE: Samuel William Obray
MARRIED: 1852
St. Louis, Missouri
DEATH SP: 5 Jun 1910

CHILDREN:
Thomas William, 11 Apr 1848
Joseph Bainbridge, 18 Sep 1850
Ellen Jane (Lloyd), 15 Jun 1853
Louisa (Smith), 16 Aug 1855
Emma Bainbridge (Smith), 5 Dec 1857
Hannah Maria (Oldham), 21 Nov 1859
Elizabeth (Bankhead), 13 Feb 1862
Adalaid (Miles), 17 Mar 1864
Sam Napolean, 24 Sep 1867
May (Henning), 27 Apr 1869

Eleanor was born on May 29, 1832 in Durham, England, the daughter of Joseph Bainbridge and Jane Welch. In 1847, her mother passed away leaving Eleanor with the responsibility of caring for the younger children at the age of eighteen.

In 1851, the family sailed from Liverpool aboard the ship, "Ellen Maria." The Bainbridge family consisted of Joseph, five children, and Eleanor's four month old son, Joseph. On board the ship, Eleanor met Samuel William Obray and his three year old son, and they became good friends.

They remained in St. Louis, for four years, working to obtain enough money to continue to Utah. Eleanor and Samuel were married in St. Louis about 1852, and their first child was born there. By 1854, they had saved enough money for the journey but had to leave some of the Bainbridge family behind.

They settled first in Tooele, later moving to Ogden, then to Cache Valley. Samuel built a two-room log cabin for Eleanor in Paradise, Utah, where she lived the rest of her life. In 1869, Samuel took another wife and built a lovely two-room home for his new bride.

Eleanor was a typical little English lady, small in stature, with her hair parted in the middle and pulled back in a bun. She was always ready to lend a helping hand when needed. She was active in the Church and the Gospel.

Eleanor passed away in her little log cabin on April 27, 1902; at the age of seventy years.

MARY VICKERS OGDEN

BIRTHDATE: 6 Oct 1819
Hall-ith-wood, England
DEATH: 28 May 1893
Richfield, Sevier Co., Utah
PARENTS: William Vickers
Mary Greenhaulgh
PIONEER: 24 Sep 1868
Edward Mumford Wagon Train
SPOUSE: William Ogden
MARRIED: 11 Aug 1844
Bolton, Lancashire, England
DEATH SP: 20 Apr 1888
Richfield, Sevier Co., Utah

CHILDREN:
James, 7 Jan 1845

Mary Ann, 26 Dec 1846
Thomas, 25 Sep 1849
Jane, 26 Jan 1852
William, 25 Aug 1854
John, 31 Jan 1857
Joseph, 31 Aug 1859

Mary and her twin sister, Alice, were born in Hall-ith-wood, Lancashire, England, which was a large mansion near Bolton. The mansion was transformed into living quarters for poor families who worked in the calico weaving industry. The twins were so much alike they would fool even their suitors until their voices betrayed them.

Mary married William Ogden on August 11, 1844. They lived in the same building where she had lived all her life and all seven of her children were born there.

William was baptized a member of the Church of Jesus Christ of Latter-day Saints in 1848 and Mary was baptized in 1849. In 1868, they had finally saved enough money to emigrate to America.

They sailed on the ship, "Emerald Isle," on June 20, 1868. Thirty-seven deaths occurred on the ship due to bad drinking water and poor food. They arrived in New York where they were quarantined for four days. The family journeyed by train to Benton, Wyoming where they were met by Edward T. Mumford's Mule Team Company from Salt Lake City. They arrived in the Salt Lake Valley on September 24, 1868. They were met by a relative and were taken to Santaquin, Utah to live.

They first lived in a rented log cabin while various members of the family took any job they could such as digging potatoes, drying fruit on shares, husking corn, etc. in order to obtain their winter's store of provisions.

In 1872, they joined in the resettlement of Sevier County. Richfield was the place they chose for their home. William became very active in church and community affairs. Mary was a great support to him, making a home that was a haven of peace. She raised a big garden and had many fruit trees.

In 1887, her son John died leaving a wife and two small children. In 1888, her husband, William, died and her daughter Mary Ann died leaving a husband and seven children. Mary was grief stricken and soon became very ill and blind. Her daughter, Jane, and her family moved from Arizona to live with her and run the farm.

Mary passed away on May 28, 1893. She had set a wonderful example of faith, thrift, and hard work for her loved ones.

SARAH ROOTH GARRETT OGDEN

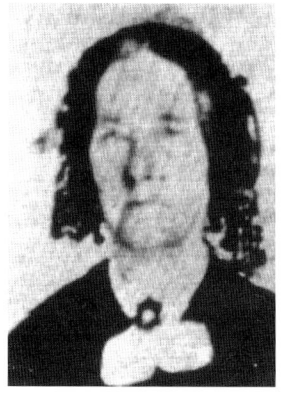

BIRTHDATE: 1 Apr 1808
Youlgrave, Derbyshire, England
DEATH: 20 Jun 1890
Kaysville, Davis Co., Utah
PARENTS: William Garrett
Sarah Goodwin Rooth
PIONEER: 17 Oct 1853
John Brown Co. Wagon Train
SPOUSE: Edward Ogden
MARRIED: 11 August 1834
DEATH SP: 7 Sep 1853
Bear River, Uintah, Wyoming

CHILDREN:
Esther, 17 Jun 1835 (twin - died 6 months)
Samuel, 17 Jun 1835 (twin)
William, 26 Aug 1837
Esther Emily, 6 Aug 1839 (twin)
Lucy Ann, 6 Aug 1839 (twin)
Sarah Rooth, 3 May 1841 (died at 5 months)
Elizabeth, 26 Sep 1842
Edward, 21 Jul 1847
Mary, 20 Jun 1849

Sarah, her husband, and family resided at Mottram, Cheshire, England and were the proprietors of the Angell Inn. Her husband became blind, so Sarah with her good management skills began running the inn with the aid of her husband.

Missionaries from the Church of Jesus Christ of Latter-day Saints asked to rent their hall in which to hold their meetings. Their request was granted and eventually Sarah and all of her family were baptized as members of the Church.

The spirit of gathering came upon them and they began planning for the move to the valley of the mountains. They sold the Angell Inn, and in March 1853, Sarah, her husband, and their seven surviving children crossed the ocean.

Upon their arrival in America, Sarah bought oxen, cows, wagons, and supplies for their journey across the Plains. They traveled with the John Brown Wagon Train. Before reaching the Salt Lake Valley, Sarah's husband became ill with mountain fever and died. He was buried near the Bear River (east side). Now bereft and sorrowing, she gathered her children and continued on until they reached the Salt Lake Valley on October 17, 1853.

The winter following was a very trying one. Sarah did her best, but had a hard time getting food for her children. She found work outside the home and her younger children were often left alone.

In 1858, Sarah and her family moved south with the rest of the Saints, locating in Spanish Fork, where they lived in a wagon until they got a dugout. With the passing of Johnston's Army through Salt Lake City, the Saints returned to their homes.

The Ogdens moved to Kaysville, Utah. Sarah lived there the rest of her life. She passed away at the age of eighty two.

BARBARA ELIZABETH MATTATAHL CAMPBELL OGILVIE

No
Photo
Available

BIRTHDATE: 12 May 1797
Tatamongouche, Nova Scotia
DEATH: 14 Apr 1857
Spanish Fork, Utah Co., Utah
PARENTS: Levi Mattatahl
Margaret Forcing
PIONEER: 12 Sep 1855
Noah T. Guymon Wagon Train
SPOUSE I: Alexander Campbell
MARRIED: abt 1817
DEATH SP: 14 Apr 1827
Musquodoit River

CHILDREN:
Mary Ann, 1818
Benjamin, 1820
Nathaniel, 1822
Margarete Jane, 9 Apr 1824

SPOUSE II: George Byers Ogilvie
MARRIED: 11 Aug 1827
St. Pauls Church, Halifax, Nova Scotia
DEATH SP: 31 Aug 1885
Pleasant Valley, Elko Co., Nevada

CHILDREN:
Barbara Elizabeth, 29 May 1829
Elizabeth, 19 May 1830
Ester Eunice, 12 Jun 1832
George, 24 Apr 1834
Ann, 1835
Alexander, 1836
Louisa Ellis "Alice," 28 Dec 1838
William, 25 Dec 1845

Barbara Elizabeth was born on May 12, 1797 to Levi Mattatahl and Margaret Forlong Mattatahl at Tatamongouche, Halifax, Nova Scotia.

She married Alexander Campbell who was a widower with three children. Alexander was about forty-nine years old when he left home to go to Musquodoit Harbour where he apparently drowned. Four months later, his body was found on the banks of the River.

Barbara married George Beyers Ogilvie on August 11, 1827. They had seven children together. The entire Ogilvie family was taught the gospel of the Church of Jesus Christ of Latter-day Saints by Brigham Young and were convinced of the truth.

They left Nova Scotia and joined the Saints. George Beyers Ogilvie and his son, George, were teamsters with the Noah T. Guyman Wagon Company and arrived in the Salt Lake Valley on September 12, 1855. They located in Big Cottonwood.

The family endured all the hardships of pioneer life, but the most severe hardship was the lack of food when the grasshoppers devoured most of the crops. The family existed on roots, weeds, and sego lilies since all the other rations were gone.

In July of 1856, Bishop Reuben Miller's fall wheat was harvested by the Saints and he shared the harvest according to the size of each family. Their share was five bushels of wheat for their family of ten. It was the first taste of wheat they had seen in six to eight weeks.

They lived in Big Cottonwood from 1855 until 1857 when they moved to Spanish Fork, Utah. Barbara Elizabeth didn't live long enough to enjoy the fruits of their labors, as she passed away on April 14, 1857 at sixty years of age.

ELIZA ANN HALES OGILVIE

BIRTHDATE: 27 Nov 1840
Quincy, Adams Co., Illinois
DEATH: 4 Jan 1899
Richfield, Sevier Co., Utah
PARENTS: Charles Henry Hales
Julia Ann Lockwood
PIONEER: Sep 1852
Edward Hunter Wagon Company
SPOUSE: Dr. George Ogilvie
MARRIED: 2 Mar 1857
DEATH SP: 23 Sep 1918
Richfield, Sevier Co., Utah

CHILDREN:
Eliza Ann, 16 Apr 1858
George William, 15 Mar 1860
Mary Isabella, 28 Jul 1862
Charles Henry, 13 Mar 1865
Joseph, 8 Jul 1867 (died at 9 months)

Eliza became a responsible person very early in life since she was the oldest of twelve children in her family. She helped her mother wherever she could during very trying times. Her family experienced the persecution of the mobs before and after the murder of the Prophet Joseph Smith and his brother, Hyrum Smith.

Eliza endured hardships of pioneer life and the sorrow of losing her beloved Grandmother, Mary Ann Hales, on the journey to Utah. The Hales family was traveling with the Edward Hunter Wagon Company and arrived in Salt Lake Valley in September 1852.

Eliza married Dr. George Ogilvie and they became the parents of five children. They were some of the original settlers of Richfield, Utah. She was called to be Relief Society President during the time the silk industry was started and continued in the presidency for eight years.

During the Indian troubles, the settlers of Richfield were advised to move north to larger settlements for safety.

They moved back to Spanish Fork from about 1867 until 1870 before they returned to Sevier Valley. Eliza's son, Charles Henry, was shot and killed instantly when he was twenty years old.

Eliza's life was one of hard work and service to others. Her children and grandchildren loved her and enjoyed the biscuits she made for breakfast every morning. She and her husband did a lot of temple work in the Manti Temple. She remained faithful to the principles of the gospel until her death on January 4, 1899.

ANNA BRITTA MARTINSSON OHLSON

BIRTHDATE: 8 Mar 1845
Eknar Dalhand, Sweden
DEATH: 19 Nov 1920
PARENTS: Martin Martinsson
Maria Larsen
PIONEER: 1867-walked
SPOUSE: Gustave A. Ohlson
MARRIED: 4 Jan 1868
Salt Lake Endowment House
DEATH SP: 11 Dec 1912

CHILDREN:
Rosoly, 3 Oct 1868
Emma Augusta, 2 Feb 1870
Selma Eleanor, 2 Feb 1872
Charlotte, 28 May 1874
Ida Corneala, 14 Apr 1876
Elvira Valate, 18 Jul 1878
David H., 5 Aug 1880
Eveline, 26 Feb 1882
John Edgar, 1 Jun 1884

Anna Britta was born in 1845 in Sweden to Martin and Maria Martinsson. She first heard the Gospel preached by a lady missionary who sang the beautiful hymn "O, My Father." She was very touched by the message of that song. She studied and was converted to the faith and was baptized as a member of the Church of Jesus Christ of Latter-day Saints on May 19, 1864. When she was twenty-two years of age, she left her parents and brothers and sisters to come to Zion.

Arriving at Gotenborh, Anna boarded the steamer Vensborg and sailed to Copenhagen. By sailing over the North Sea, they reached Liverpool, England. There she boarded the "Manhattan," for New York. It was the first steamer to take Mormon converts across the ocean. She arrived in New York on July 4, 1867, took a boat up the Hudson River, then went by rail to Omaha, Nebraska. From there to the North Platte they stayed for four weeks waiting for supplies to continue. She walked every step of the way to Salt Lake City.

On January 4, 1868, Anna married Gustave A. Ohlson in the Endowment House. She had nine children born to her and Gustave. Gustave passed away on December 11, 1912.

Anna held positions as Relief Society teacher, Sunday School teacher, and counselor in the Relief Society. She owned a carpet loom and made beautiful carpets from the rags that people brought to her. She was the second wife of Gustave Ohlson. Anna and Ellen, Gustave's first wife, were like sisters and were dear friends.

Anna passed away on November 19, 1920, almost eight years after the death of her husband. She left a great legacy of faith for those who have followed.

JOHANNA ANDERSON OHLSSON

No Photo Available

BIRTHDATE: 27 Oct 1810
Bastasen-Varsas, Sweden
DEATH: 30 May 1899
Huntsville, Weber Co., Utah
PARENTS: Anders Mansson
Maria Svensson
PIONEER: 5 Sep 1864
Wagon Train
SPOUSE: Gustave Ohlsson
MARRIED. 20 Feb 1840
DEATH SP: 27 Dec 1910
Lynn, Weber Co., Utah

CHILDREN:
Maria Kaisa, 1 May 1840
Mary Charlotte, 27 Sep 1843
Sophia, 4 Feb 1847
Gustava Fredrica, 21 Mar 1849
Matilda Christina, 16 Mar 1854
Johan Gustaf, 14 Jan 1857

Johanna was born on October 27, 1810 in Bastasen-Varsas, Skaraborg, Sweden. Johanna and her husband, Gustave Ohlsson joined the Church of Jesus Christ of Latter-day Saints about 1860. They were among the first to join in their small community in Sweden. Gustave was called to be president over that part of the mission field.

On one occasion the Ohlssons were holding a meeting in their home when a mob broke in threatening to kill the Elder conducting the meeting. Johanna took the church books that lay on the table and hid them under her arm. The mob began breaking the furniture. One of the mob members saw the books, asked her what they were, at the same time snatching them from her and threw them into the fireplace. Johanna acted quickly and retrieved them from the fire. The books were not even scorched. This was a strong testimony to Johanna that the Lord will protect his truths. She bore testimony to this fact many times throughout her life.

In 1864, Johanna and Gustave decided to leave Sweden. They traveled to England. From there, they sailed on the "Monarch," with 973 other converts under the direction of Patriarch John Smith. The Ohlsson family reached New York on June 3, 1864. From New York they traveled by train to Wyoming, Nebraska where they waited for church wagon teams to meet them.

Johanna and her, family started across the Plains on July 1, 1864. The Ohlsson family arrived in the Salt Lake Valley on September 5, 1864 and later settled in Huntsville, Weber County, Utah.

BENGTA PEHRSDOTTER CARLSON OKERLUND

BIRTHDATE: 1 Aug 1832
Riseberga, Kristianstad, Sweden
DEATH: 28 Apr 1915
Loa, Wayne Co., Utah
PARENTS: Pehr Carlsson
Kersti Jonsdotter
PIONEER: 22 Sep 1861
Samuel A. Wooley Wagon Train
SPOUSE: Ola Jeppasson
(changed to Ole Okerlund)
MARRIED: 16 Nov 1856
Vittskovle, Tofflosa, Sweden
DEATH SP: 13 Nov 1909
Loa, Wayne Co., Utah

CHILDREN:
Carl Peter (Charles Perry), 28 May 1856
Hilda Josephine, 21 Feb 1859
Mat(h)ilda Ephramina, 14 Oct 1860
George William, 9 Nov 1862
Lydia "Eleda," 11 Jul 1864
Hannah, 23 Apr 1866
Albertina, 1 June 1868
Ole Albert, 17 Sep 1870
Mary Ellen, 12 Feb 1873
Orilla Bengta, 31 Mar 1876
Edward, 18 Sep 1879.

Bengta had a monumental year in 1856 when she was baptized as a member of the Church of Jesus Christ of Latter-day Saints, married Ola Jeppasson (changed to Ole Okerlund), and had her first child.

Being among the first to embrace the restored gospel of the Church in the Scandinavian countries, Bengta and Ole suffered great persecution. Bengta and Ole were both imprisoned at different times for their religious beliefs. When their baby, Hilda, died at age six months, they suffered great sorrow. Enduring all these trials required great faith and determination.

Desirous to join the Saints in Zion, Bengta, Ole, and their two children Charles and Matilda boarded the ship "Monarch of the Sea" and set sail for America.

Twelve hundred miles to travel and she walked every step of the way and carried her baby Matilda. When her shoes wore out, she continued walking and left bloody foot tracks behind her. She never complained and would often say, "Walking had its advantages, and there were many scenes on the Plains never to be forgotten."

They were called to establish Mt. Pleasant where Bengta gave birth in a dugout during the wintertime. Then they were called to settle Circleville, and then Salina where she gave birth on the bank of the Sevier River to the first baby born in that area.

To keep the family from starving, Bengta prepared nourishment from greasewood greens, thistles, and sego lily roots. She cooked over an open campfire as stoves were not available. Ole built the first house in Salina and she was happy for this one-room adobe house with dirt floors and dirt roof.

Bengta did much weaving of linen, cotton, and woolen cloth. She planted the flax seed, cultivated it, and then worked the flax into linen thread which she wove into cloth making stripes, plaids and different patterns, her fabric was a work of art. Bengta also owned fourteen sheep which she sheared. She was a very good seamstress.

On one occasion after Bengta had washed the family clothes and hung them out to dry, an Indian squaw came along and took them. Bengta couldn't afford to lose her family's clothing, so she followed the squaw right up Salina Canyon and into the Indian camp. Her bravery impressed the Chief and he ordered the clothes be returned.

The Indians were preparing for war and the settlers had to flee for their lives. Leaving everything they owned behind, she and her family again faced starvation. The family started over again in Gunnison where they joined the United Order and lived there for ten years. When the Order broke up they moved to Scipio. Again the family struggled upward from poverty's pit. She would often say, "The Lord fits the back for the burden." The family's last move was to Loa where they were among the first to enter the Fremont Valley in Utah.

Bengta was a liberal giver of the often meager amount she had. She was the first Relief Society President and her daughter (who she had carried across the Plains) was her secretary. Bengta had a beautiful singing voice and sang at funeral and entertainments. They did much research and performed temple work for their dead ancestors.

At the time of her death, Bengta had served the Relief Society for fifty years. In the hour of her death Bengta said, "The Lord hears and answers my prayers and I know that He lives."

MARY ELLEN CLARK OKEY

BIRTHDATE: 12 Sep 1856
Pinxton, Debyshire, England
DEATH: 16 Dec
Lehi, Utah Co., Utah
PARENTS: George E. Clark
Catherine Gascoigne
PIONEER: 8 Oct 1863
Horton Haights Co. Wagon Train
SPOUSE: Edwin Okey Jr.
MARRIED: 19 Jan 1874
Salt Lake City, Salt Lake, Utah
DEATH SP: 28 Oct 1904
Alpine, Utah Co., Utah

CHILDREN:
Harriet Ada, 7 Nov 1874
Catherine, 1 Oct 1876
Mary Ruth, 15 Mar 1879
Charlotte Ellen, 5 Oct 1881
Sarah Adelaide, 28 Aug 1883
George Edwin, 21 Jan 1886
Lucy Elizabeth, 21 Jun 1888
Harvey Clark, 6 Dec 1890
Lovina, 22 Nov 1892
Martha Hortence, 15 Jan 1895
Lester Clark, 1 Dec 1897

Mary's parents heard the gospel of the Church of Jesus Christ of Latter-day Saints through the humble missionaries before she was born and knew that they had found the truth. The Elders were always welcome at their home and many times her parents gave their own bed to the missionaries.

Like many of the converts they desired to join the Saints in Zion and ten years after their baptism on May 30, 1863 the family left for a home in a new country. They landed in New York and went directly to Florence, Nebraska.

There were men and boys with ox-teams and big covered wagons from Utah ready to take them across the plains. After arriving in Salt Lake they remained in the campgrounds for two weeks and then stayed with a Walker Family while Mary's father went south looking for work. He was gone for six weeks and then moved the family to American Fork. In the spring they moved to Alpine which became their permanent home.

Mary's childhood days were spent weeding, gleaning wheat, planting corn and potatoes and helping to clear and burn sage brush from the land. She joined the Relief Society when she was sixteen years old. Many times she went to meetings bare foot, but they were happy and thankful for all that they had.

After her marriage, Mary and Edwin's first home was a log room. Through hard work and careful management they were able to care for their children as they came along and the happiness they found together seemed to really compensate for their labors.

For thirty years they faced trials and enjoyed the sunshine of their life together but upon his death she felt the added responsibility of being both father and mother in training the children as well as earning a livelihood. But through it all she trusted in her Heavenly Father.

She took care of an invalid mother for four years and upon the death of her daughter took in the youngest of five children to raise until her marriage. Another daughter died leaving six little children.

In 1914, she began Nursing and assisted in bringing 185 babies into the world as well as taking care of the mothers. She also devoted a great deal of time to Church and Public work. She was an assistant secretary and then secretary for the Ward Relief Society for a total of thirty-seven years. Mary also served as a teacher in the Sunday School and Primary and was set apart to help care for the dead and assist in making burial clothes especially aprons and veils. She was a member of the Genealogical Committee and was also in charge of the Temple Excursion work for both Baptism and Endowment. Mary was a Deputy Tax Collector and was Register of vital statistics for four years. She was a member of the Daughters of the Utah Pioneers.

It was always Mary's desire to do all the good she could for those with whom it was her privilege to associate and to work for the Lord as long as she had life and strength.

MARY PITT OKEY

BIRTHDATE: 19 May 1820
DEATH: 20 Feb 1906
PARENTS: William Pitt
Marion "Mary" Guest
PIONEER: 1848 or 1849
SPOUSE: Edwin Okey Sr.
MARRIED: 26 Feb 1840
Gloucester, Gloucester, England
DEATH SP: 10 Oct 1855
Salt Lake City, Salt Lake, Utah

CHILDREN:
Daniel, 25 Nov 1840
Mary Elizabeth, 23 Nov 1843
Hyram William, 28 Oct 1846
Sarah Celestia, 5 Sep 1848
Edwin Okey Jr, 10 Mar 1852
Joseph Moroni, 27 Mar 1855

Mary and Edwin Okey were still newly weds when they heard missionaries from the Church of Jesus Christ of Latter-day Saints preach in their neighborhood. Mary's parents told her if she joined with those people she need never step inside their door again. However Mary and Edwin were converted and baptized just one year after their marriage.

Soon after they embraced the Gospel they had a desire to emigrate to America. When this young couple chose to leave England they sacrificed wealth, family and friends. They set sail together with a new baby of three months for America. Upon arrival they went directly to Nauvoo where they made their home for about three years.

Mary was personally acquainted with the Prophet Joseph Smith and his wife Emma and Hyrum Smith. Mary assisted her husband in making shoes and some of the shoes they made the Prophet wore. Mary suffered the persecutions of the Saints at the hands of wicked men. Mary has often told the interesting and inspiring story of being present at the meeting when the Prophet's mantle fell upon Brigham Young.

The family moved to Iowa in late 1843 or early 1844, and remained there till 1848, when they desired to move to Utah. The family managed to get a wagon, a yolk of cows, and a yolk of oxen to haul their belongings.

In 1855, Mary was left a widow with five small children to raise, the youngest only seven months old. The rearing of the family amid poverty and distress was not an easy task, but through it all this good woman instilled into the hearts of her children, the principles of the Gospel and the value of living honest lives. Many times the family would gather thistles and greens for their breakfast. When asked by her Bishop if she needed help, she always replied, that as long as she had health and strength she could get along.

Mary's oldest son, John, took his turn standing guard when Johnson's Army came through Utah and it was not long after this incident that Mary was counseled to go to the country with her children. She moved her family to American Fork in 1858, which became her home for the rest of her life.

Mary lived as a widow for fifty-one years, but through all the hardships, she trusted in her maker and said, "The Lord giveth and the Lord taketh away, Blessed be His name."

CHILDREN:
Catherine, 9 Apr 1842
Archibald, 4 Jan 1844
John, Jul 1846
Andrew, Jul 1847

SPOUSE II: Peter Liddle Oldroyd
MARRIED: Aug 1850
Glasgow Lanark, Scotland
DEATH SP: 22 Jul 1907
Fountain Green, Sanpete Co., Utah

CHILDREN:
William, 22 Nov 1850
Janet, 22 Nov 1850 (adopted)
Peter Meicklejohn, 25 Nov 1854
Ellen Jane, 14 Nov 1856
Isaac Robert, 18 Jan 1859
Sarah Agnes, 7 Jul 1861

Catherine Mary was of Scottish descent, born in Yoker, Scotland in 1822. When she was eighteen years old she married Andrew Todd in Glasgow, Scotland.

Their first child, a daughter, Catherine was born at Gorbals in Lanark County, Scotland. Of the three boys, John died shortly after birth in 1846, and Andrew, born six months after his father's death, died at fifteen months. Catherine, her daughter, died in August, 1847, seven months after her father's death. Only Archibald, the second child and first son, remained to live with his mother.

Catherine Mary married Peter Liddle Oldroyd in August, 1850, while still in Glasgow, Scotland. Their first child, William, was born in Glasgow in 1850. They also adopted a little girl, Janet, who was also born the same day as William. William died shortly after birth, and little Janet died ten months later.

The four other children born to Catherine Mary and Peter Liddle, two boys and two girls, were all born at Ephraim, Sanpete County, Utah after the couple came to Utah. Baby Sarah Agnes died when she was two years old.

CATHERINE MARY MEICKLEJOHN TODD OLDROYD

BIRTHDATE: 4 Aug 1822
Yoker, Renf, Scotland
DEATH: 1 Apr 1897
Fountain Green, Sanpete, Utah
PARENTS: Peter Miecklejohn
Janet Wilson
PIONEER: Oct 1852
Appleton Harmon Wagon Train
SPOUSE: Andrew Todd
MARRIED: 13 Nov 1846
Glasgow, Lanark, Scotland
DEATH SP: 20 Jan 1847
Glasgow, Lanark, Scotland

MARIA "MARY" ANDERSON OLDROYD

BIRTHDATE: 20 Sep 1845
Slimminge, Malmohus, Sweden
DEATH: 15 Aug 1936
Glenwood, Sevier Co., Utah
PARENTS: Ola Anderson
Anna Borkerson
PIONEER: 7 Sep 1855
Noah Guyman Co. Wagon Train
SPOUSE: Archibald T. Oldroyd
MARRIED: 4 Jan 1864
Ephraim, Sanpete Co., Utah
DEATH SP: 6 May 1917
Glenwood, Sevier Co., Utah

CHILDREN:
Mary Ellen, 22 Feb 1865
Archibald Todd, 19 Oct 1866

Peter Micklejohn, 29 Nov 1869
Catherine Ann, 7 Jan 1871
Andrew, 5 Feb 1873
Isaac Robert, 18 Nov 1874
Niels William, 25 Jan 1877
John David, 27 Jan 1879
Hannah Jane, 28 Jan 1881
Agness Caroline, 14 Nov 1882
Albert, 10 Nov 1884

Mary was baptized into the Church of Jesus Christ of Latter-day Saints in Sweden when she was nine years old.

After coming with her family to America, they settled in Ephraim, where they underwent trials and hardships of pioneer life in those early days. Her father died when she was eleven years old, leaving the family with no means of support. The children then had to go into other homes to work or be cared for so that their mother could work to support her family. Mary was taken into the home of Peter Madsen in Provo, where she lived for three years. She returned to Ephraim, working for different families.

Mary married when she was nineteen years old. She was a petite woman and good looking, with dark hair which was parted in the middle and combed straight down and behind her ears, with a small bob at the back of her neck. She always wore small gold earrings.

In 1865, they moved to Glenwood, Sevier County, where she helped to settle this valley. Her first home here was a dugout or cellar with thick rock walls and a dirt floor.

During the Indian trouble in Sevier Valley many settlers were killed and others barely escaped with their lives. One day Mary was sitting on the doorstep of her home and an Indian fired from the hillside and the arrow struck at her feet and bounced into her lap. In the year of 1867, the Indian trouble became so bad the settlers of Glenwood were forced to leave their homes and Mary and her husband moved their family to Fountain Green, returning to Glenwood in 1874.

Mary's adobe house was always kept spotless. There were handmade rugs on the floor and lace curtains at the sparkling windows and flowers in bloom on the window sills. She also knitted socks, and did extensive quilting. She knitted beautiful petticoat skirts in pretty colors and designs for her daughters and older grandchildren. She washed, dried and hand carded her own wool into beautiful white, fluffy batting for her handmade quilts. Her bed was made tall and soft by a feather 'tick' which she also sewed and stuffed and kept beaten up until it was soft and downy. She always had four stuffed down pillows on each bed. The pillowcases had wide crocheted lace on them, made by her own hands. She always had homemade bread, usually 'salt-rising', and homemade jam ready for visitors, especially grandchildren.

Mary was always busy. She was quiet and reserved, a good listener, but often talked fluently about her life experiences, especially those when she lived with different families. She was a pleasant person, and enjoyed life. She was a devoted and faithful wife and mother and a true friend to every one.

MARY JOLLEY OLDROYD

BIRTHDATE: 18 Jul 1847
Thornley, Durham, England
DEATH: 22 Feb 1942
Fountain Green, Sanpete, Utah
PARENTS: John Jolley
Susan Carter Oldroyd
PIONEER: 19 Oct 1862
Horton Haight Co. Wagon Train
SPOUSE: Peter Oldroyd
MARRIED: 5 Apr 1863
Salt Lake Endowment House
DEATH SP: 22 Jul 1907
Fountain Green, Sanpete, Utah

CHILDREN:
John Jolley, 9 Aug 1865
William, 26 Jul 1867 (died as an infant)
Thomas Jolley, 16 Jan 1869

Mary's family joined the Church of Jesus Christ of Latter-day Saints and desired to join the Saints in America.

They left England on the "William Tappscott," the Scottish ship arrived in America forty-two days later. They joined the Horton Haight Handcart and Wagon Company on their way to Utah.

Two days out of Winter Quarters, a new baby boy was born to the Jolley family. The long ocean voyage, and the land journeys, had been too much for her—she passed away and was buried at Shoal Creek on the plains of Nebraska. The grave was covered with buffalo chips, and set on fire to keep the wolves away.

"I Mary had just turned 15 years of age, and had the responsibility for the new baby." She cared for him as best she could, but he too, died on October 13, at Needle Springs. Mary helped by taking her turn at traveling, walking and pulling the handcart. These pioneers suffered much for their love of the Gospel. The Jolley family arrived in Utah on October 19, 1862.

Mary's first years in Utah were also difficult with helping to fight the thousands of grasshoppers, crickets, and their constant fear of the Indians.

On April 5, 1863, Mary married Peter Oldroyd in the Endowment House in Salt Lake City. She had three sons born to her, the middle one died in infancy.

Mary always had a great love for her religion, and lived it honestly and with all her belief that it was the one and only true church on the face of the earth at that time. She shared her many talents and served in the Relief Society for over thirty years. She served her home city and its people by sharing and giving of her time, talent, and material things of life.

Mary raised a few sheep, sheared their wool, carded it, and spun it into cloth. Gathering straw from the grain they raised, she cured it and made hats for the family. She homesteaded ground at the foot of the West Mountain, and there raised a fine garden of vegetables and fruits. Walking to town daily and sometimes several times a day, she carried some of her produce and shared with friends along the way. She raised chickens, and the eggs helped buy her groceries. Her jersey cow became almost a pet to her. From its milk and cream, she churned many pounds of butter, some to sell. She was always willing to share with friends and relatives.

Mary had many talents, including love for music and drama. She and her friend did a lot of entertaining at the theatre. She often held song fests in her garden or inside her home where friends and neighbors were welcome. The children loved her, and visited her often. She did beautiful handwork, especially knitting, using four steel needles, making stockings, sweaters, caps and booties. She was a wonderful cook.

One of Mary's great loves was her love of life, which included her family, her friends, her church, and her new country. She was a very jolly, happy person. She shared some of her faith-promoting and inspirational incidents and thoughts with others. Never did she complain about her health nor hardships she had experienced. She enjoyed dancing, singing, and loved to listen to her music recordings. She also loved and appreciated the city band which included her son as a member.

Mary liked to cut rug rags and make her own rugs. That meant that she liked to have her friends, neighbors, relatives come to rag-rug-making bees. She had the misfortune of losing her eye sight due to cataracts in 1925. Though she was in darkness for the remainder of her life, the sunshine glowed in her heart. She was always an inspiration and joy to those around her, was cheerful and enthusiastic. She cared for herself in her own home until ninety years, when she loved spending time with her children, grandchildren and great grandchildren.

Her husband, John died in July 1907 in Fountain Green, Utah. Mary continued on alone, doing all the good she could for others, and enjoying her posterity. Her sons filled missions for the Church, as have many of her posterity.

Mary Jolley Oldroyd passed away on February 22, 1942 in her ninety-fourth year of life. She died at the home of her son in Fountain Green, Sanpete County, Utah. Fountain Green was where she had lived most of her life in America.

Mary was among the noble people, with qualities of culture, personal dignity, and pride. They were industrious people, faithful and humble. They were our Pioneers.

MARGARET LANCASTER OLER

No Photo Available

BIRTHDATE: 1824 or 1826
Philadelphia, Pennsylvania
DEATH: Unknown
Leeds, Washington Co., Utah
PARENTS: Levi Lancaster
Margaret Hinckel
PIONEER: btwn 1861-1863
SPOUSE: George Oler
MARRIED:
DEATH SP: 1 Oct 1886
American Fork, Utah Co., Utah

CHILDREN:
Mary, 13 Mar 1843
Margaretta (Baldwin), 20 Oct 1846
George Jr., 29 Aug 1848
Susan (McCleve), 2 Jun 1851
Mary (Souse), 13 Mar 1853
Elizabeth (Lewis), 24 Feb 1861

Margaret was born in 1824 or 1826 in Pennsylvania to Levi and Margaret Lancaster. Margaret married George Oler, a rope maker in about 1842. Both of them were from Philadelphia, Pennsylvania.

Between 1861 and 1863 this couple came to Utah. They had six children, all born in Philadelphia. Margaretta, George and Susan lived to maturity, passing away at ages sixty-one, sixty-seven, and thirty-four years of age. No further records are found for the other members.

Margaret's accomplishments include joining the Church of Jesus Christ of Latter-day Saints, and of giving up the comforts of living in a large city with its goods and services, and of coming to the Utah Desert to raise her family under the extreme hardships.

Margaret passed away at Leeds, Washington County, Utah and was buried there, the date is unknown.

ANN MARIE EBBESEN OLESEN

BIRTHDATE: 11 Nov 1780
Meisling, Vejle, Denmark
DEATH: 6 Feb 1870
Mt. Pleasant, Sanpete Co., Utah
PARENTS: Ebbe Knudsen
Anna Michelsen
PIONEER: 7 Sep 1855
Wagon Train Company
SPOUSE: Jes Olesen
MARRIED: 16 Oct 1800
Fredericia, Vejle, Denmark
DEATH SP: 26 Aug 1842
Meisling, Vejle, Denmark

CHILDREN: (Children's name were all Jessen)
Ebbe, 13 Jan 1802 (died young)
Ann, 30 Sep 1804

Maren, 9 Jul 1807
Ole, 24 Jan 1809
Margrethe Dorthea, 6 May 1813
Ebbe, 8 apr 1816
Dorthe, 3 Mar 1820
Mads Peter, 22 Apr 1822
Dorthea Johanne, 2 Mar 1825
Jes, 18 Sep 1826
Johanne Marie, 12 May 1829

Anne was born in 1780 in Denmark. She was the third child born in the family. Her father was a farmer living in the village of Meisling, Denmark, an area known for the good quality of potatoes grown there. Little is known about Anne's early life.

Anne married Jes Olesen on October 16, 1800 in the city of Fredericia, Denmark. They had eleven children. The oldest son died young, and three others probably died young. Seven of the children grew to adulthood and were married according to the records.

Anne's husband, Jes, died in 1842, at the age of sixty-four. Anne was sixty-two years old, a widow, with her youngest child just thirteen years old.

Anne did some work as a house maid and seamstress to support herself and her young daughter. Missionaries from the Church of Jesus Christ of Latter-day Saints came from Copenhagen to Jutland in 1850. Anne and at least two of her sons were baptized in 1851. Saints in Denmark suffered much persecution from members of the country's Lutheran Church at that time.

Four of Anne's sons, Ebbe, Mads, Peter, Jes, and Ole emigrated to America in 1854. Soon after this, Anne began making plans to join them and their families in Utah. By that time her youngest child, Johanne was married and had a three year old son.

On January 7, 1855, Anne, Johanne, her husband and child, left Liverpool, England together with 440 Scandinavian Saints on the ship "James Nesmith" with Peter O. Hansen presiding. After forty-seven days on the ocean, they arrived at New Orleans. From there the group traveled on a steamer to St. Louis, Missouri. Cholera claimed the lives of twenty-nine Saints just after the steamer docked at Leavenworth, Kansas.

Due to the sickness of many of the Saints, and also to lack of funds, the group delayed their journey from Kansas until June. While at Leavenworth, Johanne contracted cholera and died. This was difficult for Anne, at the age of almost seventy-five years, losing her youngest daughter and still facing the long wagon train journey to Utah.

The company of faithful Saints finally arrived in the Salt Lake Valley on September 7, 1855. Two of Anne's sons had settled in Mt. Pleasant, so Anne went to be near them. No records are found of Anne from this time until her death on February 6, 1870 at Mt. Pleasant.

Anne Marie Ebbesen Olesen was eighty-nine years old when she died. She is buried in Mt. Pleasant Cemetery. She was truly a pioneer woman of faith and fortitude to venture from her homeland at the age of seventy-four years for her religious beliefs. She was a great woman to be honored by those who have followed after her.

CAROLINE ROBERTS OLIVERSON

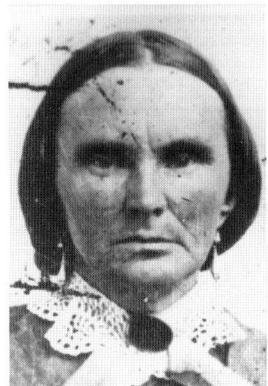

BIRTHDATE: 30 Oct 1838
Deerhurst, England
DEATH: 29 Jul 1901
Franklin, Franklin Co., Idaho
PARENTS: Levi Roberts
Harriet Ann Hefford / Efford
PIONEER: Fall 1850
Pearson Indep. Co. Wagon Train
SPOUSE: James Oliverson
MARRIED: 30 Sep 1856
Kaysville, Davis Co., Utah
DEATH: 28 Feb 1911
Franklin, Franklin Co., Idaho

CHILDREN:
Ellen Esther, 22 Sep 1857
Theodosia Ann, 16 Mar 1859
Harriet Ann, 22 Oct 1860
Lucy Mary, 1 Jul 1862
Jennetta, 24 Aug 1864
James Henry, 11 May 1866
Levi Roberts, 3 Mar 1868
Matilda, 31 Mar 1870
John Besley, 22 Feb 1872
Richard Thomas, 31 Mar 1875
Christopher, 29 Dec 1876
William, 12 Aug 1879

Caroline was born in England in 1838. Her parents heard the Gospel and joined the Church of Jesus Christ of Latter-day Saints in 1840. In 1841, Caroline, at the age of two, with her parents emigrated to America.

They traveled on the ship "North America" the second ship to leave England with new converts. They landed in New Orleans, traveled by boat up the Mississippi River to Nauvoo. When she was twelve years old, she crossed the Plains with the Pearson Independent Wagon Company and arrived in Salt Lake City in the fall of 1850. Her family moved to Kaysville, Davis County, where she lived until she married James Oliverson.

Caroline and James Oliverson were married on September 30, 1856 in Kaysville. They stayed there until they had two of their children. Brigham Young then asked a few brethren to go north into Cache Valley and establish a new settlement. On June 15, 1859, they arrived in the new area. They thought they were settling in Utah and didn't find out until months later they had settled the first white settlement in Idaho, known as Franklin.

While living in Franklin, Caroline had ten children. She had six daughters and six sons. When she was expecting one of her children, she was in need of diaper flannel. A gentile came by selling goods and Caroline bought some diaper flannel from him. The Bishop said that she had to return the flannel to him because he was a gentile.

Caroline was a faithful wife and a good mother. She passed away on June 29, 1901, at the age of sixty-three. Her husband passed away almost ten years later. They both died in Franklin, Idaho and are buried there. Caroline lived most of her life in the United States. She had had the many experiences of pioneering-crossing the ocean, the Plains, and moving to the different areas of the West in helping colonize these areas.

Caroline was truly a great pioneer woman of faith and fortitude.

ALICE DANDY OLLERTON

BIRTHDATE: 4 Oct 1802
Croston, Lancas., England
DEATH: 20 Nov 1856
Crossing the Plains
PARENTS: James Dandy
Elizabeth "Betty" Ogden
PIONEER: 1856
Martin Handcart Company
SPOUSE: John Ollerton
MARRIED: 4 Feb 1826
Eccleston, Lanc., England
DEATH: 12 Nov 1856
Sweetwater crossing the Plains

CHILDREN:
Elizabeth, 1825 (died as an infant)
Jane, 5 Mar 1826
Seth, 11 Dec 1827
Esther, 20 Mar 1830
John Dandy, 8 Jul 1831
Elizabeth (Wilson), 23 Dec 1832
James, 2 Jun 1834 (died as an infant)
Ellen, 10 Sep 1835
Hannah, 1836 (died as a child)
Alice, 3 Mar 1837 (died at age 19)
Hannah, 17 Aug 1838
Jane Ann (McPherson), 2 Jan 1841
Margaret, 15 Mar 1844 (died as an infant)
Henry, 1847 (died at age 7)
Sarah Gullie (Eatough), 5 Nov 1850

Alice was born in 1802 in England. She was born in the middle of the family having an older sister and brother, and two younger brothers and one younger sister. The family lived in Croston, Lanc., England where all were born and christened.

Alice met John Ollerton in Eccleston, and they were married there on February 4, 1826 when she was twenty-three years of age. Their first child was born there, and they lived many years within a ten mile area of their first home. Alice gave birth to fifteen children all together, three died

the same day or within a short time of their births, one died just under eight years of age. Nine grew to maturity, married and have a great posterity who honor this couple.

The Ollerton family learned about the Church of Jesus Christ of Latter-day Saints in 1836 or 1837. John was the first to be baptized on November 6, 1837, followed by Alice on February 8, 1838. Many of their children were baptized at various ages and at different times, the strong faith of Alice and John being a strong religious influence for their family.

On May 22, 1856, John, Alice, and their three daughters-Alice age nineteen, Jane Ann age fifteen, and Sarah five, sailed from Liverpool aboard the ship "Horizon," under the leadership of Edward Martin with 856 souls aboard. They arrived in Boston, traveled to Iowa City where they secured their handcarts and provisions to cross the Plains.

They left on August 25, 1856 with 575 in the company, many of whom were older. This was the 5th handcart company that year. They pushed along the Platte River, and finally reached Ft. Laramie on October 8, after much toil and hard travelling. Their provisions were becoming scant and rations were cut to starvation proportions. By October 19, they reached the last crossing of the North Platte River, near Red Buttes, where some wagon trains helped them cross, but many had to wade the river themselves. Many were the hardships of the crossing and shortly following, a bad snow and sleet storm hit. Many of these pioneers died the next month.

John Ollerton was one who did not survive the terrible cold and privations of the time. He passed away on November 12, 1856, just fifty-six years of age, at about the area of the Sweet water River. His beloved wife, Alice, followed him eight days later, on November 20, 1856, at just fifty-four years of age. She died just ten days before this company of handcart pioneers entered the Salt Lake Valley.

This left their three daughters alone in this new country. About two days after they arrived in the Salt Lake Valley, Alice, the oldest girl died.

Jane Ann married in 1860 and had a large family. She died in Nephi, Utah in 1933. Sarah married Martin Gullies and had one son. She then married George Eatough in about 1874, and had ten children. Sarah died in 1903.

This brave pioneer couple, John and Alice Dandy Ollerton were young at the times of their deaths, but they had suffered the last months of their lives more than most people experience in a life time. They were true to their faith, and died in full fellowship with strong testimonies of the truthfulness of the Gospel of Jesus Christ they had embraced. Honor is given to them.

ANN DEE OLPIN

BIRTHDATE: 3 May 1828
Westbury-Severn, England
DEATH: 18 Sep 1893
Pleasant Grove, Utah Co., Utah
PARENTS: James Dee
Mary Grassing
PIONEER: abt 1860
SPOUSE: Joseph Olpin
MARRIED: 23 Oct 1861
Salt Lake City, Salt Lake, Utah
DEATH SP: 17 Jan 1880
Pleasant Grove, Utah Co., Utah

CHILDREN:
Joseph William, 25 Jul 1863
Edwin Dee, 8 May 1865
Alma James, 20 Nov 1867
Albert Henry, 11 Aug 1870

Ann was born in 1828 in Westbury-Severn, Gloucester, England. She was the second child of five girls and one boy. Some time before 1860, the missionaries from the Church of Jesus Christ of Latter-day Saints visited England where the Dee's lived. Ann and her younger sister, Emily, accepted the Gospel and began saving their money to emigrate to Utah. Their father disinherited them for joining the Mormon Church.

Ann and Emily met Joseph Wadley, a missionary in England. Emily's friend was married to Joseph Wadley from Pleasant Grove, Utah, and it was her friend's desire that Emily come to Utah and become a plural wife to her husband.

By 1860, they had saved enough to pay passage on the ship "William Tappscott." On May 11, 1860 they set sail with 731 passengers aboard. Of these 312 were Scandinavians. Smallpox broke out aboard ship, so they were placed in quarantine when they arrived in the New York harbor. They left finally, and continued on to Florence, Nebraska, where Joseph Wadley met them.

Arrangements were made for crossing the Plains. Ann paid $40.00 for her board, but had to walk all the way. Emily and Joseph Wadley were married on November 5, 1860. This left Ann alone. She sought housework to sustain herself. She went to work for President Penrose, and on her days off, Ann would walk to Pleasant Grove to visit Emily.

Ann met Joseph Olpin and they fell in love. He was also from England. Joseph was a tall broad-shouldered man, very gentle in his nature and the Gospel really influenced his life. He was a stone mason, trained by his father in England. They were married on October 23, 1861, in Salt Lake City. They went to the Endowment House and were sealed on February 14, 1863. (This was an important day for the Olpin family as Joseph's parents were also sealed.) Their first child was born on July 25, 1863 in Salt Lake City.

Before 1865, they moved to the town of Rockport, a settlement near the Weber River. Joseph Wadley persuaded the family to move to Pleasant Grove so Joseph could build a home for them. He was to build the home in exchange for some land. He built a one-room log cabin for Ann. Later, he built a large two-story rock home.

Ann's husband, Joseph passed away at his home of Rocky Mountain Fever in 1880, one month before his forty-fourth birthday. Ann was very poor at this time. Their home was not finished, but Ann, being a good manager, and with the help of her older sons, made a good living on their small farm.

Ann Dee Olpin passed away on September 18, 1893, at the age of sixty-five in Pleasant Grove, Utah. She had given up her family and her homeland for her religious beliefs.

Her one sister and her only brother did come to America and they gratefully enjoyed having family in the new land. They were all great pioneers who helped settle Pleasant Grove in Utah County.

FRANCES HIGGENBOTHAM / HIGGINBOTTOM CLAYTON OLPIN

BIRTHDATE: 25 Oct 1830
Sheffield, York, England
DEATH: 9 Jan 1907 or 1808
Morgan, Morgan Co., Utah
PARENTS: James Higginbotham
Elizabeth Leatherbarr
PIONEER: 1861-1862
Wagon Train Company
SPOUSE I: Albert Clayton
MARRIED: 10 Jul 1851
England
DEATH SP: 24 Jul 1860
Hanover, Connecticut

CHILDREN:
John, 20 Oct 1852
Mary Ann, 30 Jan 1855
Albert Jr., 10 Jul 1857 (died as a child)
Sarah Elizabeth, 17 Sep 1860 (died as a child)

SPOUSE II: Henry Olpin
MARRIED: 2 Jan 1862
Salt lake City, Salt Lake Co., Utah
DEATH SP: 28 Dec 1879
Morgan, Morgan Co., Utah

CHILDREN:
Henry Alfred, 10 Jul 1863 (died at age 13)
Clara Alice (Simmons), 30 Sep 1865
Josephine (Crouch), 10 Aug 1869

Frances was born in England in 1830. She grew up in a home where the Bible was studied and she was taught the skills and arts of the household.

When missionaries from the Church of Jesus Christ of Latter-day Saints preached the gospel in Sheffield, she embraced the truth and was baptized on March 8, 1849. On July 10, 1851, in Sheffield, Frances married Albert Clayton. Two children were born there, John and Mary Ann.

Frances and Albert had a great desire to leave England and to join with the Saints in America. As soon as they could obtain money for their passage they left family, friend and homeland behind and with their two children and the few possessions they could bring with them, they set sail for America to begin a new life.

Landing in New York Harbor, they lacked the necessary funds to outfit themselves to continue their trek across the Plains. Albert found work and began to make plans to go West. Frances gave birth to their third child in Greenfield, Massachusetts.

The family moved to Connecticut in 1860, for Albert's work. The wet climate was something they were not used to, and after two and a half months, Albert became ill and died at the age of twenty-nine on July 24, 1860. There was hardly time for Frances and the children to mourn as Albert Jr., three years old, became ill and died seventeen days later on August 10, 1860. He was buried beside his father in Connecticut far from their native England and far from the Saints in the West.

This was a dark and difficult time for this young grieving mother. One month later, Frances gave birth to her fourth child, Sarah Elizabeth, who was born in Plymouth, Litchfield County, Connecticut. She lived for one year only. Times and conditions were very hard on little children, too. We don't know why Frances made this difficult journey half way across the state in her condition.

Frances prepared for and crossed the Plains with her two remaining children by 1862, driving a team and wagon in one of the companies. Her small children walked nearly all the way. Frances had finally completed her dream when they joined the Saints in Utah.

One record states that on January 2, 1862, Frances married Henry Olpin, a widower. Their first child was Henry Alfred who was born in Salt Lake City in 1863.

They family later moved to Morgan, Utah and Frances became a pioneer in settling this county. Henry Olpin died in December of 1879, leaving Frances at the age of fifty, alone, to raise their children, the youngest child being ten years old.

Frances remained true and faithful to her religion all her days. Frances had gone to the Endowment House in Salt Lake City and was sealed to Albert on February 3, 1897. She lived to raise her children, and to enjoy her grandchildren before her death on January 9, 1908.

She was truly a valiant woman who had endured much as she helped pioneer the Morgan area of Utah. She is honored by the posterity who have followed her.

SARAH ANN WHITE OLPIN

No Photo Available

BIRTHDATE: 19 Aug 1805
New Parsley, England
DEATH: 11 Sep 1859
Salt Lake City, Salt Lake, Utah
PARENTS: Daniel White
Sarah Savage
PIONEER: 4 Sep 1859
Rowley Handcart Company
SPOUSE: Henry Olpin
MARRIED: 25 Oct 1835
Coaley, Gloucester, England
DEATH SP: 28 Dec 1879
Morgan, Morgan Co., Utah

CHILDREN:
Mary Ann, 8 Mar 1824
Louisa, 9 May 1824 (died as a child)
Daniel, 1 Nov 1832 (died as a child)
Joseph, 10 Feb 1835 or 1836
Ellen (Gibby), 2 Jul 1838
(Wooley) Alfred, 2 May 1841 (child)
Sarah Ann (Cooper), 27 Mar 1844
Dorcas (Gibby), 15 Jun 1847
Julia (Bluemel), 31 Jul 1850

Sarah Ann was born in England in 1805. She was the last of seven children born in the family. She was christened in the Methodist Church when she was sixteen days old, and eighteen days later her mother died leaving her seven children. Five months later, her father married a widow who cared for the motherless children and had four children of her own. Daniel had eleven children to raise.

Sarah married Henry Olpin on October 25, 1835 in England. Henry was a stone mason in England and also later in America. Henry and Sarah had nine children, three of whom died as children. All of their children were born in England and attended school there to the age of twelve.

In 1839, Elder Woodruff was in England teaching the Gospel in the midlands, and he was told by the spirit to go southward where many people were praying for light and truth. He opened three counties for the preaching of the Gospel. Church membership increased and new branches were formed. Missionaries came to teach the Olpin family.

Henry's sister, Mary Ann, was the first to hear the Gospel, and Sarah White Olpin followed being baptized in May, 1843. She influenced Henry to listen to the missionaries. Henry bore testimony that when he heard the gospel of Jesus Christ, he knew it was true. He thrilled to the message of the Book of Mormon. He was baptized August 25, 1843. About six weeks later, Henry's mother died and his father came to live with him and Sarah, so he was also taught the gospel, and was baptized in his seventy-ninth year of age on August 19, 1854.

This family had the desire to emigrate to America. Because Henry's father was too old to travel, they stayed to care for him. By 1850, a daughter, Mary Ann, along with Henry's sister sailed for America; they were followed by

Joseph, a son who left in 1856. Henry's father passed away in 1859.

On February 18, 1859, Henry, Sarah and their daughters began to make their plans to emigrate. They said goodbye to families and friends and went to Liverpool where they boarded the ship "William Tappscott," on April 18, 1859 with 725 saints aboard.

The rough waters they encountered made many passengers ill. The crew assured the passengers, that with so many Mormons aboard the ship would not sink. From New York Harbor, they took the train, reached Florence, and joined the George Rowley Handcart Company which was leaving two weeks later.

They traveled with the handcart company on June 9, 1859 with 235 souls, sixty carts and six wagons. Sarah was diligent with making sure her family was fed first and often took little for herself. One day she came upon a buffalo that had been killed, as she was gathering wood. She cut a piece of the meat and took it back to camp. She cooked it and tried it herself. It tasted good at first, but then she became ill, grew worse and had to be placed in a wagon.

Returning missionaries and supply wagons sometimes passed the handcart company and would bring word into the Salt Lake Valley about the conditions of the pioneers. Henry sent word to Ann and Joseph of their mother's condition. They prepared a wagon, and supplies, and Joseph set out to meet them. His mother was critically ill and a sister, Dorcas, had Mountain Fever. They were happy to meet him and laid aside their handcarts without regret.

Sarah Ann passed away one week after reaching the Salt Lake Valley.

ern terminus of the railroad. They left Florence on July 3, 1857 with the Christian Christiansen Handcart Company, marching over the trails which the pioneers had made ten years before.

While the Saints were pulling their crude handcarts on the north side of the Platte River the soldiers of Johnston's Army were marching along the south bank, going to Utah. As they reached the Sweet Water, one of Uncle Sam's fat oxen had one of its feet crushed by a wagon. The captain gave the oxen to the pioneers for food.

For several weeks they had been without meat and were very low of flour. On August 22, they arrived at Devil's Gate, within about thirty miles of Salt Lake City. They were met by teams that brought bread, cake and fruit. These provisions not only gave strength to their bodies, but filled their hearts with courage and gave them assurance of the loving welcome they would receive when they clasped the hands of their brothers and sisters in their new homes. The mules were so weak, the emigrants had to help them over the last steep hills of the mountain-sides by the aid of ropes. On September 13, 1857, a Sunday, they marched with feelings of thankfulness and grand expectations into the city of the Saints. One out of every ten of their group had died on the journey.

This band of sturdy, enthusiastic emigrants possessed the courage that comes from religious hope. Most of them would have lain down by the roadside and passed into eternity if they had not had the faith and courage to reach the goal of their religious ambition.

Ane and Peter were among the first settlers in Moroni, Sanpete County, Utah.

Ane passed away on March 4, 1914 and was buried in Moroni, Sanpete County, Utah.

ANE ANDERSEN OLSEN

BIRTHDATE: 18 Oct 1823
Flensted, Laasby, Denmark
DEATH: 04 Mar 1914
Moroni, Sanpete Co., Utah
PARENTS: Anders Knudsen
Else Jacobsen
PIONEER: 13 Sep 1857
Handcart Company
SPOUSE: Peter Olsen, Sr.
MARRIED: Jul 1847
Denmark
DEATH SP: 12 Jun 1888
Moroni, Sanpete Co., Utah

CHILD:
Peter Olsen, Jr. 23 May 1861

Ane was born in Flensted, Laasby, Skanderborg, Denmark, 1823. Ane and her husband joined the Church of Jesus Christ of Latter-day Saints in Denmark and joined a company of emigrants bound for Utah in April, 1857. They arrived in Philadelphia, Pennsylvania on June 2, 1857. They were soon on their way, reaching Iowa City, the west-

ANNA CATHRINE CHRISTENSEN OLSEN

BIRTHDATE: 13 Oct 1841
Jyland, Denmark
DEATH: 10 Aug 1923
Ogden, Weber Co., Utah
PARENTS: Hans Christensen
Johanna Christensen
PIONEER: Sep 1855
P. O. Hansen Company
SPOUSE: Jens "James" Olsen
MARRIED: 19 Oct 1859
DEATH SP: 16 Oct 1883
Manti, Sanpete Co., Utah

CHILDREN:
James, 9 Oct 1860 (died as a child)
James Peter, 12 Mar 1862
Annie Catherine (Johnson), 17 Sep 1864
David, 14 Sep 1866
Ingeborg Diantha, 14 Apr 1869
Alma, 1 Apr 1872 (died at age 8)
Heber C., 23 Jul 1877 (died at age 2)
Hans Christian, 11 Sep 1880

Anna Cathrine was born in 1841 in Denmark. She attended school from age seven until she was twelve years old. She helped in the house and watched the sheep on her school vacations. Her father was daily under the influence of liquor. Her mother prayed that something would transpire to help him change his ways.

Two Elders came to their door. They were invited in to share dinner with the family. Their conversation drifted into the Gospel of Jesus Christ of Latter-day Saints. Her father became interested. He learned of the first principles of the Gospel and of the gathering of the Saints. The Elders returned many times and taught this family.

One of the Elders had had a dream that they went out tracting and came to a house where there was a hen with a brood of little white chickens in the front yard. They went there and the people embraced the Gospel. The next morning they went looking for this house and after walking for quite awhile, the other Elder exclaimed "I am afraid we won't find the chickens today." The first Elder replied "Yes, we will, we are going to keep on going until we find them." After more walking, they came to the Christensen home and there in the front yard were the chickens. "This is the place; this is proof that if we will go to our Heavenly Father in earnestness, he will help us overcome our trials and troubles." Thus Anna's mother's prayer and the prayer of the Elder were both answered. They became members of the Church and were baptized the winter of 1852 when Anna was eleven years old. Her father never touched liquor or tobacco after he joined the Church. They were the only family in that town who joined.

They finally sold their home and belongings, and began to prepare to go to Zion. They left Denmark for Liverpool, England where they embarked for America on January 1, 1855 on the ship "James Nesmith," with 440 Scandinavian Saints.

One day a storm came up when Anna was standing on the middle of the deck holding onto a large barrel. She felt impressed to move over under the deck, and just as she did so, a mast beam broke and fell, breaking the barrel to pieces. She learned how necessary it is to heed the promptings of the Spirit at all times.

The family arrived in New Orleans, traveled up the Mississippi River to St. Louis, then went to Leavenworth, Kansas and finally reached Mormon Grove. They cleared away snow to pitch their tents, while they awaited the arrival of oxen. Cholera broke out in the camp, and they had to move farther from the town. Her mother became ill and many of the young people of the camp died.

When the oxen arrived the family started their trek across the Plains, travelling with the P. O. Hansen Wagon Company. They had to walk most of the way due to their supplies they took with them.

They encountered Indians, herds of buffalo, and they could feel the ground tremble as they passed over the road. They crossed the rivers, the best they could. Her mother

was stung by a scorpion or some poisonous insect which caused her arm to swell. The poison spread throughout her body, and she became very sick. She passed away the day after they reached the Salt Lake Valley without seeing the place she had gone through so much to reach. They had difficulty finding anyone to understand them, so they buried her that same day by themselves.

ANNA ELLINGSON OLSEN

BIRTHDATE: 21 Dec 1835 Aker, Akershus, Norway
DEATH: 22 Jan 1900 Weston, Onieda Co., Idaho
PARENTS: Elling Anderson Gudbior Erichsdau
PIONEER: 1859 or 1860
SPOUSE: Christian Olsen
MARRIED: 20 May 1859 en route by ship's captain
DEATH SP: 23 Feb 1916 Weston, Franklin Co., Idaho

CHILDREN:
Orson, 11 Nov 1860
Christian, 28 Sep 1862
Agnes, 11 Apr 1864
Annie Marie, 12 May 1866
Joseph, 27 Mar 1868
Nephi, 20 Sep 1870
Hyrum, 17 Mar 1873
Martha Elizabeth, 7 May 1875
Wilford, 26 Nov 1877
Amelia 10 Sep 1879

Anna was born in 1835 in Norway. She married Christian Olsen while they were en route to America aboard the ship. The captain of the ship performed the marriage.

Anna was the mother of ten children. All of her children who were raised and married, were sealed in the temple.

She and Christian lived for a short time in Salt Lake City, where Orson was born. They then moved to Logan, Cache County, Utah in 1861 or 1862. In 1867, they moved to the new settlement of Weston, Oneida, Idaho, which was first settled in 1865, and was the second settlement in Idaho. Weston was one of the six settlement sites on the west side of the Bear River, determined by a scouting expedition under Marriner W. Merrill of Richmond, and sent out by Apostle E. T. Benson in 1864. The fast growth of the east side of the valley showed the necessity of these new Cache Valley northern and west-side settlements. Other sites included Petersburg, Clarkston, Dayton, Oxford and Stockton. Companies of colonists were selected that fall and winter and in late 1864 and early 1865 all sites were occupied. Indian resistance forced abandonment of all the new villages in 1866 except Clarkston, Weston, Dayton and Oxford.

Anna and Christian were farmers, with farming at that time being as much by brute force as by skill. Their children were raised by hard work and ingenuity. Christian Sr., and Orson, the oldest, were among a group selected to go into the mountains west and south of McCammon in January 5 1879, to cut ties for the railroad.

In 1886, her husband accepted a mission call to his Norwegian homeland; this left Anna responsible for the nine children still at home.

Anna and Christian had gladly given up their homeland as well as their homes and families for the gospel. Both were rejected by their families.

Anna was all that a faithful pioneer woman could be. She passed away on January 22, 1900, sixteen years before her husband. Her posterity are proud of the heritage they have from Anna and they honor her name.

ANNE DORTHEA NIELSEN OLSEN

BIRTHDATE: 10 Aug 1836
Rorbeck, Maribo, Denmark
DEATH: 18 Jun 1914
Wanship, Summit Co., Utah
PARENTS: Niels Rasmussen
Grethe Jensen
PIONEER: 25 Sep 1868
John Holman Co. Wagon Train
SPOUSE: Lars Olsen
MARRIED: 3 Jul 1864
Denmark
DEATH SP: 1883

CHILDREN:
Hannah M. Christine, 19 Dec 1865 (died as a child)
Julia Augusta (Redden), 17 Aug 1867
Hannah Christine (Olsenlegger), 1 Jan 1870
Louise Andrea (young), 17 Apr 1871
William Lars, 29 Nov 1872 (died at age 15)
George Albert, 28 Jul 1874
Anna Elizabeth, 2 Jul 1876 (died as a child)
Carrie Marie (Anderson), 30 Mar 1878 (twin)
Elmire Elsie, 30 Mar 1878 (twin - died as an infant)

Anne Dorthea was born in 1836 in Denmark. At that time, Denmark had a very good school system and each girl and boy was required to go to school for a certain length of time. Upon graduation they were given a job, and they had to work at that place for a certain period of time no matter how good or how bad they were. It was quite a disgrace to fail at their work.

On July 3, 1864, Anne married Lars Olsen. He had joined the Church of Jesus Christ of Latter-day Saints two years before their marriage. Anne did not join the Church until nearly five years later. In 1868, a strong effort was made to assist the Saints who wished to emigrate, especially faithful Saints of many years standing. Besides this, the Church sent for the last time teams out to the terminus of

the UPRR to bring members through the deserts and mountains. There were 820 souls who emigrated from the Scandinavian countries that year.

Anne and Lars left Denmark with their two children, and his brother's sweetheart, on June 13, 1868. They crossed the English Channel to Liverpool, and on June 19th they boarded the ship "Emerald Isle," bound for America. The emigrants received very rough treatment from the officers and the crew. Theirs was the last company of Scandinavians to cross the Atlantic in a sailing vessel; steamers were used after that time.

On board, the water became stagnant and unfit for use. This caused much sickness among the passengers, and no less than thirty-seven deaths occurred on the voyage. Many other deaths were caused by measles among the children. Among them was Anne's daughter, Hannah.

On August 11, the ship arrived at New York harbor, they resumed their trip travelling by railway to Council Bluffs where they arrived on August 31st. They took up the westward trek by ox-team led by Captain John C. Holman. They walked most of the way to Salt Lake.

Sickness continued to rage and about thirty people died between New York and Salt Lake City. They arrived in the valley on September 25, 1868. With this company ended the emigration of LDS Saints from Europe by sailing vessels and ox-teams.

Anne and Lars spent their first year in Hoytsville, then moved to Marion. Later they moved to Wanship where they homesteaded some ground. They had seven more children in Utah.

Anne's husband died in 1883. His death left a great burden on the family, especially Anne. Six children were left to support and care for.

Anne passed away June 18, 1914, leaving a great heritage to those who followed this valiant pioneer woman of great faith and fortitude.

ANNE NIELSEN PEDERSEN OLSEN

BIRTHDATE: 18 Mar 1803
Volstrup Mark, Denmark
DEATH: 11 Mar 1895
Brigham City, Box Elder, Utah
PARENTS: Niels Pedersen
Kirsten Sorensen
PIONEER: 5 Oct 1854
Hans P. Olsen Co. Wagon Train
SPOUSE: Christen Jensen Olsen
MARRIED: 27 Sep 1829
Budolphi Parish, Denmark
DEATH SP: 28 Oct 1869
Brigham City, Box Elder, Utah

CHILDREN:
Mette Kirstine, 3 Feb 1830
Karen Marie "Caroline," 27 May 1832
Christine, 13 Aug 1834

Nicoline, 16 Apr 1836
Jens "James," 27 Mar 1839
Else Marie, 24 Feb 1841
Ane Margurethe, 30 Jan 1844 (died at age 2)
Niels Christin, 3 Oct 1846

Anne was born in Oster Homum, Aalborg, Denmark, 1803. She married Christen Jensen Olsen on September 27, 1829. They had eight children but lost Ane Margurethe at the age of two.

Ane became a member of the Church of Jesus Christ of Latter-day Saints in 1851 and by 1852, her husband became a missionary in his own land. After serving for a year, he was released so they could leave for Zion.

Their son, James, had the opportunity to go to America earlier in the year of 1853. Anne, her husband, their daughter, Mette Kirstine, and two younger children left Denmark on December 15, 1853. They left three of their older daughters in Denmark to come later. The family arrived in Hull, England after spending Christmas on the turbulent North Sea.

They left Liverpool on the old sailing vessel, "Jessie Munn," on January 3, 1854. After arriving in New Orleans, they took an old steamer up the Mississippi River to St. Louis. Here, her oldest daughter, Mette, died of cholera after being sick for only six hours. They remained in St. Louis for several weeks before they continued on to Kansas City. They traveled across the Plains in the Hans Peter Olsen Wagon Company and arrived in Salt Lake Valley on October 5, 1854.

After they met their son, James, they moved to Elder Fort which is now known as Brigham City. In 1857, they were overjoyed when they were reunited with their three daughters from Denmark. They all had to move south when Johnston's Army came through the valley, but returned to their homes in the fall of 1858.

They built two rooms of the Olsen home on First East and Forrest Street in Brigham City. They were farmers. She supported her husband in all he did.

After Christen Jensen Olsen's death, she did a great deal of temple work for her ancestors in the Salt Lake Endowment House.

At age eighty five, she fell on the ice and broke her hip leaving her feeble for the next seven years until she passed away in 1895 at the age of ninety-two. She was buried in the Brigham City Cemetery.

BODEL "KRISTINE" LARSEN OLSEN

No Photo Available

BIRTHDATE: 21 Jan 1840
Aagerup (Orup), Denmark
DEATH: 11 Jan 1898
Ferron, Emery Co., Utah
PARENTS: Lars Larsen
Birthe Catherine Larsdatter
PIONEER: 1858
SPOUSE: Andrew Niels Olsen
MARRIED: 1857
DEATH SP: 24 Oct 1919

CHILDREN:
Brighamina Hancena, 30 May 1858
Andrew Niels, 18 Apr 1860 (died as an infant)
Andrew Christian, 20 Aug 1861
Lewis Napoleon, 7 Apr 1864
Mary Catherine, 24 May 1866
Niels, 8 Jun 1868
Edward, 24 Feb 1872
Frederick A., 13 Nov 1873
George Alexander, 27 May 1878

Bodel "Kristine" was born in 1840 in Aagerup (Orup), Frederiksborg, Denmark. Bodel was the second of five children. She was baptized into the Church of Jesus Christ of Latter-day Saints on June 12, 1857. Her parents, a brother and sister also joined the Church, but did not come to America. Bodel did her mother's temple work in the Manti Temple on January 1, 1891.

Bodel married Andrew Niels Olsen of Venslev, Frederiksborg in 1857. They emigrated to America in 1858. Their first child was born in Iowa City, the stopping point of the railroad and the beginning of the wagon train crossings at that time. Upon their arrival into the Salt Lake Valley, they were sent to Sanpete County to settle.

Ephraim was a little Danish Community, first settled in 1854. They also lived in Gunnison before choosing Spring City for a home. While living there, Bodel and Andrew went to the Endowment House to be sealed on August 16, 1875. The following December, Niels was sealed to his second wife, Jorgina Mathieson, a Norwegian girl just a year and a half older than his oldest daughter. When Jorgine had three children, both families moved to Emery County, Utah.

Bodel was very active in the Church, and loved her family. Three of her sons returned to her homeland as missionaries. Bodel loved animals-kittens, cats, puppies, birds, chickens.

Bodel worked hard to keep the home clean and to maintain a loving atmosphere there. She made sassafras, peppermint and sage brush teas for tonics and treatment of illnesses. They had animals for their use; chickens, pigs, sheep and cows. The wives raised the gardens, put up fruit, and did their own sewing. Wheat and corn was taken to the mills to be ground for flour and cereals. Hunting and fishing also supplied some of their food.

Bodel passed away in Ferron, Utah and was buried there in 1898.

The life of Bodel Larsen was an example of one who recognized the truth of the Gospel of Jesus Christ, accepted it even though there was much persecution and ridicule for those who did. She made a hazardous trip to Zion, and pioneered a new land. Her posterity honor her faith, courage, and her fortitude as a great pioneer woman.

EVELINE BENSON SMITH OLSEN

BIRTHDATE: 28 Feb 1835
Lexington, Lafayette, Missouri
DEATH: 1 Jan 1925
Safford, Arizona
PARENTS: Jerome M. Benson
Mary Rhodes
PIONEER: 1850
Heber C. Kimball Wagon Train
SPOUSE I: Leonard I. Smith
MARRIED: 1852
(divorced in 1856)
DEATH SP: Not given

CHILDREN: None

SPOUSE II: Charles Canute Olsen
MARRIED: Fall 1856
Salt Lake City, Salt Lake Co., Utah
DEATH SP: 12 May 1887
Safford, Graham Co., Arizona

CHILDREN:
Charles Messenger, 25 Jun 1857 (died as an infant)
Mary Caroline (Bartholomew), 30 Aug 1858
Oscar Alfred, 4 Aug 1860
Eveline Amelia (Hall), 28 Nov 1862
Logena Norwenda, 22 Sep 1864 (died at age 19)
Roselia Cosena, 26 Nov 1866 (died at age 17)
Lucinda, 22 Jun 1868 (died at age 16)
Alma, 10 Feb 1870 (died as an infant)
Vendee Clorinda, 13 Jul 1871 (died as a child)
Elam Melando, 26 Feb 1873
Virginia Arilla (Curtis), 9 Feb 1875
George Leo, 24 Jun 1878 (died as a child)

Eveline was born in 1835 in Missouri. She was a member of the Church of Jesus Christ all of her life. She was a faithful and consistent worker in the Church and was a strict observer of the Word of Wisdom.

Although a young child at the death of the Prophet Joseph Smith, she remembered the martyrdom, and the consequent expulsion of the Saints from their homes and the trek across the Plains.

Eveline, with her parents and family, traveled in covered wagons and endured the hardships and sufferings incident of the trip at such a time. They arrived in Utah in 1850 with the Heber C. Kimball Wagon Company.

Eveline was married a short time to Leonard Smith and was divorced. She married Charles Canute Olsen in the Fall of 1856, in Salt Lake City, Utah. To this family were born twelve children. Many of their children did not survive to adulthood. Four of them died as infants the day they were born, or as young children from the age of a few months to a few years. Three of their children died within a few weeks of each other at ages from sixteen to nineteen years.

Charles was a cabinet maker from Norway. At some time they were sent to settle in the state of Idaho. Later they were called to settle in Arizona. Eveline became one of the citizens of Graham County's early pioneers who helped in the reclaiming of the Gila Valley from a desert wash. They endured the many hardships and trials incident to such experiences.

Charles had passed away thirty-seven years prior to Eveline's death. During her long life, she was well and active until the last year.

In July of 1924, she was honored at the Annual Pioneer Meeting as being the second oldest woman in Graham County and was always one of their honored guests. Eveline passed away on January 1, 1925 in Safford, Arizona at the age of eighty-nine years. At the time of her death, only five of her twelve children survived her.

Eveline was a great pioneer woman to be honored for her faith and fortitude and contributions to the development of the West.

GUNNEL / GUNILD SEVERSEN OLSEN

BIRTHDATE: 27 Apr 1851
Royken, Norway
DEATH: 17 Feb 1933
Mantua, Box Elder Co., Utah
PARENTS: Halver Seversen
Mattie / Mathie Evensen
PIONEER: 29 Sep 1866
Peter Nebeker Co. Wagon Train
SPOUSE: Ole Olesen
MARRIED: 30 May 1868
Salt Lake City, Salt Lake, Utah
DEATH SP: 18 Jan 1922
Mantua, Box Elder Co., Utah

CHILDREN:
Levi, 9 Apr 1869
Martena, 7 Aug 1870
Ole, 14 Nov 1873
Martha, 16 Oct 1875
Annette, 7 Aug 1878
Albert, 9 Sep 1881 (twin)
Alvilda, 9 Sep 1881 (twin)
Josephine, 7 Aug 1884 (twin)
Joseph, 7 Aug 1884 (twin)
Merie, 7 Apr 1887
Abner Scott, 19 Apr 1889

Gunnel was born in Norway, 1851. She was the eldest of ten children. She was baptized into the Church of Jesus Christ of Latter-day Saints in 1865 in Norway, and the following year she came to Zion with her parents and family.

The family pushed a handcart across the Plains even though they were not with a handcart Company. After their arrival into the Salt Lake Valley, they settled in Big Cottonwood.

Gunnel worked for several families for two years before her marriage to Ole Olesen, who was one of the teamsters who helped the immigrants to Utah in 1866. They were married in the Salt Lake Endowment House in 1868. She was the mother of eleven children including two sets of twins; four of her children died young. One daughter died after being scalded.

The Olsens moved and then settled in Mantua, Box Elder County, where Ole did farming for a living. In 1892, her husband was called on a mission, and at that time Gunnel was very poor in health. But she was promised that she would be healed while her husband was gone, and she was.

Ole passed away very suddenly in 1922, after doing a hard days work. At the age of seventy-one, Gunnel was left alone with one daughter, Annette "Nettie," who had been injured at birth. To help finances she churned butter and sold it. She and Nettie were custodians of the Mantua Chapel for many years.

Gunnel was a wonderful cook and homemaker, and a very spiritual person. She was a counselor in the YWMIA and also a counselor in the Relief Society for many years.

Gunnel passed away on February 17, 1933, at her home in Mantua, Box Elder County, Utah.

INGEBORG SORENSEN LARSEN OLSEN

No Photo Available

BIRTHDATE: 23 Dec 1812
Stensby, Praesto, Denmark
DEATH: 6 Jun 1883
Ephraim, Sanpete Co., Utah
PARENTS: Hans K. Sorensen
Else Knudsen
PIONEER: 1858
SPOUSE I: Jens Larsen
MARRIED: 11 Nov 1829
Praesto, Denmark
DEATH SP: 1835
Denmark

CHILDREN:
Catherine, 7 Feb 1830
Maren Catherine, 20 Feb 1832
Anna, 17 Apr 1835

SPOUSE II: Rasmus Olsen
MARRIED: 4 Aug 1836
Denmark

DEATH SP: 7 May 1888
Ephraim, Sanpete Co., Utah

CHILDREN:
Jens, 4 Aug 1835
Ole, 9 Mar 1839
Jens, 14 May 1841
Hans Peter, 1843
Kirsten, 27 Feb 1844
Hans Rasmussen, 16 Dec 1850
Hans Peter, 18 Sep 1858

Ingeborg was born in Denmark, 1812. She was the eighth of ten children. At age sixteen, she married Jens Larsen. They became parents of three before he passed away in 1835. She then married Rasmus Olsen in 1836. They became parents of seven, the last child born in Utah in 1858.

The Olsen family converted to the Church of Jesus Christ of Latter-day Saints in Denmark and came to Utah by 1858. They made their home in Ephraim for the remainder of their lives.

Ingeborg was a worthy citizen and used her talents and energy in caring for her large family and church work. She was endowed and sealed in the Endowment House on November 11, 1858. She passed away at age seventy in Ephraim. Rasmus followed her in death, five years later.

JOHANNA CARLSEN DANIELSON OLSEN

BIRTHDATE: 13 May 1848
Medelplana, Sweden
DEATH: 16 Dec 1937
Paradise, Cache Co., Utah
PARENTS: Carl Danielson
Maria Persson
PIONEER: 15 Sep 1864
William B. Preston Wagon Train
SPOUSE: Gideon Elias Olsen
MARRIED: 4 Mar 1865
Salt Lake City, Salt Lake, Utah
DEATH SP: 1 Nov 1919
Paradise, Cache Co., Utah

CHILDREN:
Franklin Christopher, 14 Sep 1866
Gideon Elias, Jr., 19 Dec 1869
Julia Maria, 17 Feb 1872
Charles James, 11 Oct 1874

Johanna was born in Sweden, 1848. She was baptized as a member of the Church of Jesus Christ of Latter-day Saints on July 24, 1859, at the age of eleven. In 1864, at the age of sixteen, she and her sister, Anna, left Sweden and emigrated to America. When crossing the Plains, she met her future husband, Gideon Elias Olsen. She walked the entire way.

Upon her arrival into the Salt Lake Valley, she went to Logan and worked for Peter Jorganson family. She again met Gideon, when she was seventeen, and they were married in Logan. Later, they were sealed in the Endowment House.

Their first home was in Hyrum. They made a home in a granary with cracks large enough to see through. That year they raised enough sugar cane to fill a forty gallon barrell full of molasses. They moved to Paradise in 1866. Johanna had six children, two died very young. They lived with Gideon's brother and family until his brother died. He married his brother's wife. Johanna said she would never forget that day, she sat in the cellar all day.

Johanna was an excellent cook, always taking a pot of chicken soup and dumplings to a family whenever a new baby was born. She was close to her married children. When her son's wife died, she moved in and cared for their five children until he remarried.

Johanna was the first Primary President in the Paradise Ward, and served there for thirteen years. She also worked in the Relief Society. She always attended Church in a black suit and a white wool shawl.

Her children and husband preceded her in death. She loved to read, and at the age of seventy, began genealogy work. She hired a researcher in Sweden, who acquired 100 names. She did temple work for all of them before her death at the age of eighty-nine. She was a faithful church member and had a strong testimony.

JOHANNAH JOHANSON BENGTSSON OLSEN

BIRTHDATE: 15 Feb 1813
Oringe, Veinge, Halland, Sweden
DEATH: May 1897
Spring City, Sanpete Co., Utah
PARENTS: Johan Swensson
Ingjard Esbjornsson
PIONEER: 30 Sep 1862
Joseph Horne Co. Wagon Train
SPOUSE I: Nils Bengtsson
MARRIED: 4 Jul 1830
Veinge, Halland, Sweden
DEATH SP: 12 Mar 1859
Veinge, Halland, Sweden

CHILDREN: Unknown

SPOUSE II: Christoffer Olsen
MARRIED: After they came to Utah
DEATH SP: Unknown

CHILDREN:
Agneta (Nelson), 9 Dec 1832
Lars Nilsson, 11 May 1835
Ingjard Nilsson (Rollins), 17 Feb 1839
Christina (Jorgensen), 21 Jun 1840
Bengta (Samuelson), 19 Mar 1843
Nils / Nels, 23 Aug 1846
Borta, 6 Apr 1849 (died as a child)
Johan Peter, 31 Aug 1855

Johannah was born in 1813 in Sweden. She was born during a time when many religious denominations found roots in Swedish soil, and congregations sprang up in various parts of America. The Church of Jesus Christ of Latter-day Saints was one of these. Many families earned their livelihood by farming or fishing. Only about ten percent of the people lived in cities.

During her seventeenth year of age, Johannah married Nils Bengtsson on July 4, 1830 in Sweden. To this union were born eight children. One died as a child.

Sometime prior to March, 1859, two Elders from the Church of Jesus Christ of Latter-day Saints called at the home of Johannah and Nils. She invited them in and as she sat talking to them, Nils, being ill in an adjoining room with only a curtain between, listened intently to what was being said. He called to his son, Nels, and informed him that what the Elders were saying was true and that the family should plan to go to America. He knew he wouldn't be able to go. He passed away on March 12, 1859.

This family worked and saved their money for passage to America. Lars, the oldest son, was a great help to Johannah throughout the preparation and the trip.

Johannah together with six of her children boarded the ship "Electric," April 18, 1862. Soren Christoffersen was in charge of the 336 emigrating Saints. Rough seas kept them from leaving as they intended, and disease ravished the ship. Many passengers died of measles or diphtheria. They arrived safely in New York Harbor on June 6, 1862, where they joined Saints from the ship "Athenia."

Both companies left New York via train for Florence, Nebraska. Lars purchased an oxen team, wagon and provisions for the trek. They were assigned to the Third Company with Captain Joseph Horne.

The journey took sixty-five days of trial, adventure, and excitement, challenging Johannah to the limit. Nels, seemed to be adventurous and he and others decided to explore along the Missouri River while they were camped for the night. One spotted an island in the river and suggested they swim out and investigate. Off came their clothes, and to the island they swam. Talking and resting, they found themselves drifting away. They couldn't get to shore due to rocky cliffs and infestations of snakes. At evening they finally found an area to get out. Their clothes had been found with no sight of the boys. They hid from the searchers embarrassed without their clothes. Nels peeked from a bush and his sister-saw him and screamed, "ghost." Johannah was thankful he was alive. She felt punishment was in order but seeing his sunburned, scratched body, and his suffering, that was enough punishment.

Another incident was when they stopped to pick berries. Nels lingered too long, and the wagons were quite a distance ahead. An Indian on horseback came along, tried to grab him. Nels dodged him for a time, but became exhausted and was barefoot. Men came along riding to the rescue, and the Indian left.

Johannah endured many challenges in looking after her energetic children as well as those incident to pioneer life.

JOHANNE CHRISTENSEN THOMPSON NIELSEN OLSEN

BIRTHDATE: 14 Jun 1823
Tarrs, Hjorring, Denmark
DEATH: 17 Oct 1897
Pleasant Grove, Utah Co., Utah
PARENTS: Christian H. Hansen
Inger Marie Pederson
PIONEER: 25 Sep 1868
John Holman Co. Wagon Train
SPOUSE I: Niels Thompson
MARRIED: 1846
DEATH SP: Unknown

CHILD:
Niels Christensen Nielson, 28 May 1847

SPOUSE II: Mads Pehr Nielsen
MARRIED: 1850
DEATH SP: Unknown

CHILDREN:
Nine Marie Madsen, 22 May 1851
Henrietta Magdelene, 3 Feb 1855 (died as a child)

SPOUSE III: Johannes "John" Olsen
MARRIED: abt 1856
DEATH SP: 30 Oct 1889
Pleasant Grove, Utah Co., Utah

CHILDREN:
Charles John, 6 Jul 1857
Ane Christine, 2 Jun 1859 (died at age 9 - on Plains)
Lars, 28 Aug 1862 (died at age 6 - at sea)
Joseph, 25 Mar 1865 (died at age 3 - at sea)

Johanne was born in 1823 in Denmark to Christian Henrick Hansen and Inger Marie Pederson. On September 25, 1868 she sailed on the "Emerald Isle" boat to America. She then took a train to Benton, Wyoming. From there she traveled with the John G. Holman Wagon Company to the Salt Lake Valley. Like many other pioneers, she walked most of the way to the Valley.

Johanne had married Niels Thompson in 1846 in Denmark. She had the one child who lived just one year. By sometime in 1850 she married Mads Pehr Nielsen. She had two children from this union. These two daughters lived to maturity and were married. Nine married Anders Christian Peterson and she lived until 1930. Henrietta married John Nelson. Her death date is unknown.

Johanne married a third time in 1856. She had four children from this marriage. The first, Charles John was the only one to live to maturity. Johanne brought some of these

children with her to America, but two died at sea, and one died while they were crossing the Plains of America.

Johanne was very active in spreading the Gospel in Denmark and held missionary meetings in her home. She had to leave two daughters in Denmark to emigrate later.

She and John left with their four children, but arrived in Utah with just the one. John Olsen lived until 1889 and was buried in Pleasant Grove.

They settled on a farm in Pleasant Grove, Utah. Johanne did not learn English, but she was active in working with the Danish people in Pleasant Grove. She was a house wife, mother, gardener, giving compassionate service to her neighbors and the church she loved. Of her seven children, just three grew to adulthood.

Johanne passed away on October 17, 1897 in Pleasant Grove, Utah at the age of seventy-four years. She was a true pioneer who gave up much for the Gospel of Jesus Christ which she deeply loved.

KAREN MARIE HANSEN JENSEN OLSEN

BIRTHDATE: 14 Jan 1821
Vejby, Fredricksborg, Denmark
DEATH: 2,Nov 1889
Clarkston, Cache Co., Utah
PARENTS: Hans Neilsen
Karen Anderson
PIONEER: Aug 1863
John R. Young Co. Wagon Train
SPOUSE I: Ole Jensen
MARRIED: 18 Nov 1843
Tibirke, Fredricksborg, Denmark
DEATH SP: 30 Jul 1863
On the Plains

CHILDREN:
Hanne Jensine J., 27 Sep 1847 (died in 1852)
Karen Marie J., 12 Oct 1849
Ane Kirstine J., 11 Oct 1852
Hanne Jensine J., 7 Nov 1855
Hans J., 25 Dec 1857
Caroline J., 21 Feb 1860

SPOUSE II: Jorgen Olsen
MARRIED: 14 Dec 1863
DEATH SP: Not given
CHILDREN: Not given

Karen Marie was born, January 14, 1821, in Fredricksborg, Denmark. She married Ole Jensen, in Tibirke, Fredricksborg, Denmark on November 18, 1843. They were the parents of six children, all born in Denmark.

The family joined the Church of Jesus Christ of Latter-day Saints about 1860, and by 1863 they were ready to come to Zion. The trip across the ocean was uneventful.

Ole bought a yoke of oxen in Florence, Nebraska, and they started across the Plains. At Laramie, Wyoming the horses and oxen stampeded and Ole was thrown from the wagon and run over by two wagons. This injury caused his death on July 30, 1863. Karen wrapped him in a sheet to bury him, covered his grave with willows, and came on with the next company. After arriving in the Salt Lake Valley, they moved on to Brigham City, Utah.

On December 14, 1863, Karen married Jorgen Olsen and they lived in a dugout in Hyrum, Utah. Once some Indians came to the door and almost killed Karen because she did not have enough bread to give them each a slice.

Later they moved to Clarkston, Utah. Karen and Jorgen eventually separated because he did not treat the children well. She even had to hide food for them to eat.

Karen passed away on November 2, 1889 in Clarkston, Cache County, Utah.

KAREN OLSEN OLSEN

BIRTHDATE: 16 Oct 1807
Winnes, Leir, Norway
DEATH: 2 Mar 1890
Murray, Salt Lake Co., Utah
PARENTS: Ole Tromsen
Margarethe Pedersen
PIONEER: 12 Sep 1863
John R. Young Co. Wagon Train
SPOUSE: Johan Olsen
MARRIED: 4 Jan 1830
Norway
DEATH SP: 21 Aug 1879
Levan, Juab Co., Utah

CHILDREN:
Martin M., 17 Nov 1833
Olaus Johnsen (Nordstrand), 17 Nov 1833
Amfion Johnsen, 18 Dec 1835
Lillie Johnson, 24 Feb 1840
Julin Johnsen, Mar 1845
Jullin Johnsen, 2 Mar 1846
Julin Johnsen, 2 Mar 1846
Glagehart Johnsen, 28 Feb 1848
Hagbart Jullin Johnsen, 28 Feb 1848
Kalo Ingelin (or Charles), 9 Jun 1849

Karen was born on October 16, 1807 at Winnes in Leir, Norway. She married Johan Olsen, son of Ole Jacobsen and Anna Marie Jensen, on 4 Jan 1830. Prior to their marriage Johan had been a shoemaker, but later decided to become a fisherman for a trade. He purchased ground and built a house near the seashore called Nordstrand. Here twin sons were born, Olaus and Martin. Their mother, Karen taught them how to spin fish nets for their father, and gave them the only education they had.

The family also had another home in Roken Buskerud, Norway, with enough land to raise the necessities of life. They were thrifty and able to save what they earned by fishing, living on what the farm produced. Other children were born to Karen and Johan in Norway.

While sailing along the Danish shore, Johan learned about the Church of Jesus Christ of Latter-day Saints from missionaries, and by humble prayer obtained a testimony of the true gospel. They decided to leave Norway and emigrate to Utah for their new religion. They sold their two homes and obtained enough money to go to Zion.

On April 30, 1863, they boarded the steamship "John J. Boyd" at Liverpool, captained by J. H. Thomas. They were twenty-nine days on the ocean, arriving in New York, May 29, 1863. All members had to remain on board ship until the doctors had examined them to make sure no diseases were spread.

They were sent by rail across the Hudson River for a start across the States. Due to the Civil War, they were transferred several times to different trains and sometimes had to ride in dirty cattle cars which had no seats. Many times their luggage was broken into and items stolen, so it was necessary to post guards.

They arrived at Florence, Nebraska on June 12th, and joined the John R. Young Wagon Company which left on July 6th. Three days before the company came into the Salt Lake Valley, their son, Olaus, was married to Helena Amundsen, in Echo Canyon, Weber Valley. They arrived in Salt Lake City on September 12, 1863.

Johan and Karen settled in the Mill Creek area. They did all of their own work because there were no masons or carpenters to hire, nor money to do it. At one point they decided to move to the Bear Lake area then changed their minds.

Later they did move to Levan, Utah where Johan passed away on August 21, 1879, and was buried. Karen moved in with her daughter-in-law, Paulina, who cared for her until her death on March 2, 1890.

Karen is buried in the Murray City Cemetery, in Utah.

MAREN "MARY" MORTENSEN KNOWLTON OLSEN

BIRTHDATE: 13 Oct 1840
Hurup, Aalborg, Denmark
DEATH: 24 Oct 1934
Logan, Cache Co., Utah
PARENTS: Anders Mortensen
Karen Marie Nielsen
PIONEER: 23 Sep 1862
Christian Madsen Wagon Train
SPOUSE I: Sidney A. Knowlton
MARRIED: 17 Jan 1863
DEATH SP: 20 Apr 1863
Salt Lake City, Salt Lake, Utah

CHILDREN: None

SPOUSE II: Christian "L" Olsen
MARRIED: 17 Jun 1865
Salt Lake City, Salt Lake Co., Utah

DEATH SP: 29 Apr 1922
Logan, Cache Co., Utah

CHILDREN:
Christian, 31 Mar 1866
Ezra, 22 Jul 1867
Heber, 29 Nov 1868
Mettina (Lindquist), 28 Jul 1870
Carrie Marie (Niebusch), 15 Feb 1872
Alma, 11 Jul 1873
John, 18 Jun 1875
Moses Andrew "Anders," 25 Jan 1877
Aaron Brigham, 15 Nov 1879
Mary Lovina (Fredrickson), 22 Apr 1882

Maren "Mary" was born in Denmark in 1840 to Anders and Karen Marie Mortensen. Mary crossed the Plains of America with her mother with the Christian A. Madsen company that arrived in the Salt Lake Valley on September 23, 1862.

On January 17, 1863, Mary married Sidney Algernon Knowlton as his sixth wife. Sidney and Mary did not have any children. He died on September 20, 1863 in Salt Lake City, Utah.

On June 17, 1865, Mary married Christian "L" Olsen in Salt Lake City. They were the parents of ten children. Christian was also born in Denmark and had emigrated to America.

Mary had been baptized a member of the Church of Jesus Christ of Latter-day Saints on January 8, 1863. She was endowed on January 17th, and sealed to Christian "L" Olsen on October 31, 1888 in the Logan Temple. Christian and Mary had moved to Logan shortly after their marriage. All ten of their children were born in Logan, Cache County, Utah. All of these children lived to maturity, married, and lived for many years. Some moved to other states and some remained in Logan near their parents.

Christian Olsen passed away on April 29, 1922 in Logan and is buried in the Logan Cemetery. Mary lived until October 24, 1934, to the age of ninety-four years.

Mary had come to America at the age of twenty-two years, and had participated in the development of the Logan area. She was a great pioneer woman who left a legacy of faith and fortitude for all her posterity who have followed her.

MAREN OLSEN OLSEN

No Photo Available

BIRTHDATE: 20 Aug 1812
Udsholdt, Frederiksburg, Denmark
DEATH: 26 Aug 1887
Geneva, Utah Co., Utah
PARENTS: Ole Olsen
Maren Madsen
PIONEER: 1862
SPOUSE: Lars Olesen
MARRIED: Denmark
DEATH SP:
Geneva, Utah Co., Utah

CHILDREN:
Martine, 17 Nov 1840
Ole, 30 Sep 1847
Samuel, 1851

Maren and Lars joined the Church of Jesus Christ of Latter-day Saints in Denmark, and came to Utah to be near the main body of the Church.

They lived in Big Cottonwood when they first arrived in 1862, and later settled on a farm in Mantua, Utah. She was primarily a homemaker.

MARY CARLSEN OLSEN

BIRTHDATE: 10 Sep 1850
Jutland, Copenhagen, Denmark
DEATH: 5 Sep 1927
Brigham City, Box Elder, Utah
PARENTS: Ole Carlsen
Ane "Annie" Margaret Hansen
PIONEER: 5 Oct 1860
William Budge Co. Wagon Train
SPOUSE: Christian Olsen
MARRIED: 28 Mar 1868
Salt Lake City, Salt Lake, Utah
DEATH SP: 21 Feb 1920
Brigham City, Box Elder, Utah

CHILDREN:
Christian Jr., 7 Jan 1869
Annie Margaret (Peirce), 3 Feb 1871
Orson James, 4 Nov 1873
Oliver Woodruff, 11 Apr 1876
Wilford Lorenzo, 3 Apr 1879
Mary Rebecca (Korth), 14 Jan 1881
Jonathan Carlos, 17 Apr 1885
Birdie Lavon (Hansen), 21 Dec 1886
Ira Joseph, 28 Dec 1889 (died as a child)
Eunice Ivera (Fuller), 7 Jul 1891

Mary was born in 1850 in Denmark. It was in a small village near Copenhagen. She had two sisters and one brother and a baby sister who died on the ship while crossing the ocean. Other siblings were born in this family after their arrival in Utah.

Mary's parents became members of the Church of Jesus Christ of Latter-day Saints in the early days of the Church in Denmark. (One baptism date is March 10, 1856 and another says in the forties.) Mary, her brothers and sisters joined the Mormons and suffered persecutions. In 1860, this family left their native Denmark and all that was lovely and dear to them, and began their journey to Zion.

They left Liverpool on May 11, 1860. Smallpox broke out while they traveled, and many emigrants died from the disease. The ship landed in New York after six long and tedious weeks on the water. They journeyed on to Nebraska. Few wagons were available, and the wild and dreary waste of the plains lay like a mighty wall between them and Zion of their dreams. But with courage born of God, the journey was begun.

Mary was ten years of age when they came to America. Theirs was the last ox-team of the season and this family walked most of the way. They arrived in Utah on October 5, 1860, they went directly to Brigham City, and soon moved to Bear River City where they lived in a dugout. They remained there until they were able to buy a small home in Mantua, Box Elder County, Canyon.

Mary and her sisters worked in the homes of the Saints making fifty cents a week as their wages. At the time of her death, Mary still owned a small table which she had worked seven weeks to pay for , and it could be bought then for around a dollar and a half. (An interesting fact is that about 1867 Ole and Ane Margaret along with a son James, apostatized and moved to Iowa and joined the Josephite Church. They later returned to Utah and to the Church.)

At the age of eighteen, Mary married Christian Olsen in the Endowment House in Salt Lake City, March 28, 1868. To them were born ten children. At this time Christian was in charge of the church cattle in Box Elder County. When the co-op system was abandoned, they moved to a farm at Paradise. After 1886, they moved back to Brigham City and took care of Christian's parents until they died. They then moved to the old Barnard Farm six miles north of Brigham City where they lived and raised their family. They also took care of Mary's parents.

Christian was a successful farmer and stockman and a good provider for his wife and family. Mary was a wonderful homemaker and cook, usually making wonderful food without using a written recipe. She did her own sewing, making everything for the daughters, and shirts and clothes for the sons. She is quoted as saying, "My oldest boy was twenty-five years old before he had a boughten suit." She also did many pieces of beautiful handwork including a beautiful baby dress which had solid eyelit embroidery half way up a long skirt.

In 1898, Christian went on a mission back to Denmark for two years. Mary, with the help of her son and the farm, supported her family. Mary was never very active in public work, due to defective hearing she had. In 1913, they sold the farm and moved back to the family home in Brigham City.

Christian passed away from the flu in 1920. After eight years, Mary passed away on September 5, 1927 at the age of seventy-seven years. Their oldest daughter died shortly after her father.

These were devoted Latter-day Saint pioneers who helped develop Box Elder County in Utah. They are greatly honored for their contributions to Utah Heritage.

MARY NIELSON OCKERMAN OLSEN

BIRTHDATE: 29 May 1861
Gustav, Skurup, Sweden
DEATH: 29 Apr 1952
Pleasant Grove, Utah Co., Utah
PARENTS: Peter C. Ockerman
Else "Ellen" Nelson
PIONEER: 25 Sep 1868
John Holman Co. Wagon Train
SPOUSE: Charles John Olsen
MARRIED: 5 Feb 1880
Salt Lake City, Salt Lake, Utah
DEATH SP: 24 Aug 1933
Pleasant Grove, Utah Co., Utah

CHILDREN:
Mary Ellen, 23 Aug 1880
Charles Alvin, 13 Dec 1882
Anna Christina, 7 Jan 1885
Albert John, 7 Feb 1887
Ernest Wilford, 6 Aug 1889
Ephraim Leonard, 23 Nov 1891
Reuben Leslie, 15 Jan 1894
Ida LaVina, 8 Nov 1897
Herman DeWayne, 22 Nov 1901

Mary was seven years old when she sailed with her grandparents on the ship, "Emerald Isle." After arriving in New York, New York, they traveled by train to Benton, Wyoming where they were met by the John G. Holman Wagon Company.

Mary walked all the way to the Salt Lake Valley arriving in Salt Lake City on September 25, 1868. They first settled in Bountiful for seven years, then they moved to Pleasant Grove. She went to Salt Lake City at age fifteen where she worked as a servant for four years for a wealthy family.

Mary returned to Pleasant Grove where she married Charles John Olsen and began life on his farm and became mother to nine children.

Mary served on the Relief Society Board and was a visiting teacher for over fifty years. She served on the Old Folk's Committee for fourteen years. She did beautiful needlework and quilts. She received many awards for her beautiful flowers and garden. She was honored as the oldest living pioneer in Pleasant Grove in 1950.

Mary passed away at age ninety-two while still doing her own housework. She is buried in the Pleasant Grove Cemetery.

MATILDA JENSEN JUSTESEN OLSEN

BIRTHDATE: 16 Feb 1840
or 2 Jan 1840
Kofor, Soro, Denmark
DEATH: 16 Oct 1892
Ferron, Emery Co., Utah
PARENTS: Peder Jensen
Anna Hedvig Maria Malling
PIONEER: 30 Sep 1853
John E. Forsgren Wagon Train
SPOUSE: Lars A. Justesen
MARRIED: 25 Oct 1862
DEATH SP: 4 Apr 1868
Sevier Co., Utah

CHILDREN:
Don Carlos, 7 May 1858 (died as an infant)
Maria Elizabeth, 2 Apr 1860
Carolina, 31 May 1862
Diantha, 21 Dec 1863
Marie, 1865
Matilda Frances, 2 Mar 1867

SPOUSE: Frederick Olsen
MARRIED: 31 May 1869
Salt Lake Endowment House, Utah
DEATH SP: 13 Feb 1906
Ferron, Emery Co., Utah

CHILDREN:
Louis Alexander, 1 Mar 1870
Mary Veletta, 6 Aug 1873
James Frederick, Jr., 29 Feb 1876
Sarah Ellen, 17 Apr 1878
Matilda Jensine, 1880 (died as an infant)
Matilda Annena, 1882 (died as an infant)
Allen Deloss, 19 Jul 1883

In 1852, Matilda, her parents, and her sister, Elizabeth Karadine, were baptized as members of the Church of Jesus Christ of Latter-day Saints. Elder John E. Forsgren arranged their passage on the sailing vessel, "Forest Monarch."

After arriving in New Orleans, Louisiana, they boarded a river boat and went up the Mississippi River to Keokuk, Iowa. There they began their journey to Salt Lake City with Elder Forsgren as captain of the wagon company in which they traveled. They arrived in Salt Lake City on September 30, 1853.

After their arrival, Brigham Young sent the Jensen family to settle in Sanpete County. They went to Springtown, then moved to Manti because of Indian hostilities.

Matilda married Lars Alexander Justesen as his fifth wife. They were the parents of five children. The families lived in Ephraim, Moroni, and Spring City. Matilda was left a widow at the age of twenty-eight. Lars was killed by Indians in a battle in Sevier County. Matilda took her small children and went to Ferron, Emery County, Utah to stay with, Mary Olsen, and her husband, Frederick.

Matilda became a plural wife to Frederick and they became the parents of six children. Matilda supported and encouraged her husband in his duties as bishop of Spring City, a position he held for twenty-five years.

Matilda gave needed support to her family and others in times of sickness. She had a talent in art. She was greatly respected by all who knew her.

Matilda passed away as she had lived; true and faithful to the covenants she had made.

SENA KATRINA CHRISTENSEN OLSEN

No
Photo
Available

BIRTHDATE: 25 Jan 1861
Bolderup, Denmark
DEATH: 30 Apr 1952
Spanish Fork, Utah Co., Utah
PARENTS: Mickle Christensen
Johanna Katrina Christofferson
PIONEER: 1863
SPOUSE: Hans Olsen
MARRIED: 15 May 1879
Salt Lake City, Salt Lake, Utah
DEATH SP: 11 Nov 1931
Spanish Fork, Utah Co., Utah

CHILDREN:
George, 6 Sep 1880
Joseph Michael, 26 Feb 1882
Albert, 23 Dec 1883 (died as a child)
Hanna Christina (Evans), 5 Feb 1885
Christiana (Briggs), 19 Jan 1887
Leonil "Leo," 16 Apr 1891
Lorin, 11 May 1893
Etta Sena (Carson), 30 Mar 1895
Hazel Lavern (Tall), 12 Feb 1898
Selma Mary Ann (Bertelsen), 4 Apr 1900

Sena Katrina was born in 1861 in Denmark. Her family were members of the Church of Jesus Christ of Latter-day Saints.

When Sena was two years old her family crossed the ocean on a sailing vessel for America. Sena was sick all the way. Upon arriving in Utah, they moved south to Spanish Fork, Utah County, Utah.

Their first house was a dugout in the ground with a cane roof covered with dirt, and with canvas for windows. Later, a one-room log cabin was built with windows and doors. How happy they were when they could see out the windows. Sena said it was like heaven to her family.

Sena gleaned wheat from the fields, then her father would thresh it with a flail, throw it into the air, the wind would blow the chaff away leaving the wheat. This made the bread coarse to eat. They travelled to the Morgan-Hughes molasses mill to get the skimmings, would let this settle, and good molasses was always found at the bottom. Thinning it a little they then spread it on their bread. This made it taste better.

Sena was nine years old when her mother died. Sena helped with the family until her father married again. Part of Sena's childhood and youth was spent working for Harriet B. Young, one of Brigham Young's wives. She milked cows night and morning where the Eagle Gate now stands. She always sent money home to her parents. This pleased them very much.

When Sena went home to be married, her stepmother, who had saved all the money Sena had sent her, gave it all back to Sena to help buy her trousseau.

Sena Katrina, age eighteen, and Hans Olsen were married on May 15, 1879 in the Endowment House in Salt Lake City. This couple first lived in one room of his mother's home until after their first child was born. They then moved into a one-room log house where a second son was born. They built a five-room family home where their other children were born. (A daughter, Selma, still lived in that home at the age of ninety, in 1995.)

Sena was very ambitious. She helped her husband milk cows until her sons were old enough. From the milk she made butter and cheese to sell at the co-op store in town. When a child was asleep, Sena would go out and gather grease wood and sagebrush to burn in their fireplace where she cooked meals. She did a lot of sewing by hand. She saved pockets from worn out overalls to make pantie-waists for the children. She knit stockings, corded and spun the yarn. She knit six pair of new socks to send with her son, Joseph, when he went on his mission to their native land of Denmark from 1907 through 1910.

Sena worked in the primary for twenty-seven years, and in the Relief Society and as a visiting teacher until the age of ninety. She nursed, help bathe mothers and babies of thirty-six grandchildren and twenty-four neighbors. Besides raising her own ten children, she raised a granddaughter from the age of seventeen months to maturity after the child's mother died. In later years she did a lot of genealogy and temple work. She traveled by horse and buggy to do baptisms, endowments and sealings.

She worked making burial clothes for the dead for over thirty years. In her ninety-second year she fell and broke her hip which left her an invalid for three months. Sena passed away on April 30, 1852 in Spanish Fork, Utah County, Utah.

ANNA PERSSON OLSON

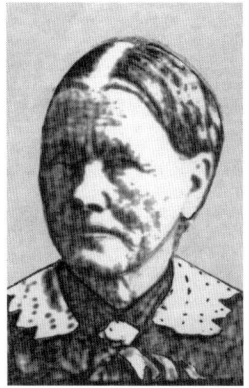

BIRTHDATE: 19 Jun 1819
Sweden
DEATH: 4 Mar 1898
Moroni, Sanpete Co., Utah
PARENTS: Pehr Pehrsson
Johanna Bengtsson
PIONEER: 15 Sep 1859
Neslin Wagon Train Company
SPOUSE: Sven Olson
MARRIED: 17 Jun 1841
Svalov, Sweden
DEATH SP: 19 Jun 1883
Moroni, Sanpete Co., Utah

CHILDREN:
Ola "Ole," 1 Apr 1843
Johannes (John), 23 Sep 1845
Johanna "JoAnn (Anderson), 14 Jan 1848
Kirsta 3 Feb 1850 (child)
Hannah (Cloward), 11 Nov 1852
Bengt (Benjamin), 7 Aug 1856
Anna, 12 May 1859 (died as a child)

Anna was born in Sweden in 1819. She had piercing dark blue eyes and dark brown hair. She was plain spoken, honest, quick with all she had to do, and was an expert weaver, owning her own loom.

As a young girl, Anna belonged to the Lutheran Church along with her family. When she was only four years old, her mother died. Little is known of her childhood.

At age twenty, Anna met a young man named Sven Olson and they were married on June 17, 1841 in Svalov, Sweden. They began their family in Malmohus, Sweden. Anna had six children.

One day, an Elder from the Church of Jesus Christ of Latter-day Saints knocked on their door and taught them the Gospel. They were impressed with this message. Anna joined the Church and was baptized in December, 1858.

She wanted to join the Saints in America, so she gathered her family together and made plans to leave Sweden. They worked on their emigration papers, received their vaccinations, and began packing for their journey. They left their home on April 1, 1859 on the steamer "L. N. Hvidt," for England, and on April 7, 1859 they boarded the ship "William Tappscott," which held 725 passengers. They left for America on April 11, 1859.

Anna was expecting her sixth child when the ship arrived on May 12, 1859. During this time that the ship was docked, Anna delivered a baby girl she named Anna. The family went on to Florence, Nebraska arriving on May 25, 1859.

Sven had a hard time finding wagons, so he purchased handcarts. Shortly before the company was to leave, they found and purchased a wagon, ox-team and a cow. They bought supplies, packed the wagon with their belongings, and traveled with the Neslin company. At this time Sven decided to be baptized in the Church. They arrived in Salt Lake City, September 15, 1859.

They moved to Mt. Pleasant where the missionary who taught them lived, but stayed a short time. They then moved to Moroni where they built a two-room adobe house. Anna was a wonderful cook so her sons built a fine Swedish brick oven outside, built a corral, and bought more cows. Anna was a generous woman. When a new immigrant came to town, she supplied them with a free quart of fresh milk a day until they were settled. She taught her family to work hard, and they acquired several acres of land. They planted alfalfa and wheat, and Anna helped even with the irrigating.

During the Indian troubles, her older sons joined the minute men to help out. Anna gave each of her sons a shrill whistle to use to signal if there were Indians in the area or if there was any trouble. Her daughters helped while they were gone in the garden and in preserving food for later use. Anna raised chickens for eggs, and wool from their sheep. She did all the steps of making wool into clothing, and she also made gloves, socks, scarfs and caps.

Anna and Sven were both students of the Bible and loved to read scriptures and taught them to her children. She paid an honest tithing to the last penny. They took their whole family to the Endowment House and had their temple work done on November 14, 1863.

MAREN CHRISTENSEN WESTERGARD OLSON

BIRTHDATE: 4 May 1843
Viesby, Thested, Denmark
DEATH: 27 Jul 1931
Moroni, Sanpete Co., Utah
PARENTS:
Christen Eneval dan Christensen
Anne Christine Jensen
PIONEER: 29 Sep 1866
Peter Nebeker Co. Wagon Train
SPOUSE: Swen Olson
MARRIED: 17 Jun 1866
aboard ship on Atlantic Ocean
DEATH SP: 27 Sep 1917
Moroni, Sanpete Co., Utah

CHILDREN:
Ane Sophia, 30 Mar 1868
Olive Chatrine, 30 Sep 1869
Elizabeth Margrethe, 27 Oct 1870 (died at 11 months)
Swen Magness, 11 Oct 1871
Maren Amanda, 13 Jan 1873
Isaac Christian Junius, 26 Jun 1875
Elizabeth Lillian Louise, 9 Jun 1877
Anine Rosine Lette, 19 May 1879 (died as a child)
John Ludvia Severeen, 1 Apr 1881
Lettine Seveline Gjerstine, 17 Dec 1882
Mary Leone Winnifred, 8 Apr 1885

Maren and her brothers were converted to the Church of Jesus Christ of Latter-day Saints and came to America in 1866. They went by the surname Westergard because the part of the village they came from was Vestergard.

On board the ship, Maren met Swen Olson. They fell in love and were married by Elder Martin Lund. They arrived in America and made arrangements to travel across the Plains in Captain Peter Nebeker's Wagon Company. She and Swen settled in Mt. Pleasant where they became the parents of eleven children.

In 1881, they moved on a 200 acre farm which was located between Mt. Pleasant and Moroni. There was a great deal of work to do to built up their farm. They had to clear the land, build their home, plant their crops, and take care of their sheep and cattle. Maren was a grand home maker. She was the best cook and anyone who dropped by was welcomed to eat. Even the Indians were treated with respect in her home.

Maren lived a very happy and productive life.

MARGARETRA NILSON OLSON

No Photo Available

BIRTHDATE: 21 Jul 1826
Vidtskofle, Sweden
DEATH: 11 Aug 1866
Crossing the Plains of Nebraska
PARENTS: Nils Freid Sjoberg
Hannah Olson
PIONEER:
Joseph S. Rawlins Wagon Train
SPOUSE: John N. Persson Olson
MARRIED: abt 1849
Sweden
DEATH SP: 31 May 1905
Soda Springs, Caribou Co., Idaho

CHILDREN:
John Nils, 22 Sep 1850
Andrew, 7 Jul 1856
Mary (Lemmon), 31 Mar 1859
Charles Frederick, 28 Apr 1863

Margaretha was born in 1826 in Vidtskofle, Christianstad Lan, Sweden. She was very happy, living in Sweden.

Missionaries from the Church of Jesus Christ of Latter-day Saints taught her the Gospel, she and her family were baptized. She then desired to emigrate to America and to raise her children with the Saints in Zion. She thought that all would go well and they could live the Gospel better in Utah.

Margaretha had a lonely feeling as the time came to leave her beloved land, her possessions, her family and her friends. She worked hard to get ready to go, spinning yarn and weaving cloth to make clothing for her husband and children. She also made many loaves of bread to dry, so they could eat them on their way.

On May 25, 1866, Margaretha and her family left from Hamburg, Germany where they boarded a squeaky, condemned ship called the "Kenilworth." She was pregnant with another child, and was in ill health. One day little three year old, Charles, stood up to walk over to his mother who was lying sick in bed, but the tossing ship made it hard for him to walk. The motion pushed him over and he bumped his head on the deck. He cried, but his mother didn't come; she was too ill.

They were one month, three weeks on the ocean and then they landed in New York on July 17, 1866. They found a cheap hotel in the suburbs. Their rooms were upstairs and the stairway, without a railing, was on the outside of the building.

During the night, in an effort to get to the outside toilet, Margaretha fell from the narrow stairway to the ground. In spite of the concern of her family, she insisted she would be all right and after a rest of about two days, arrangements were made for the long journey across the Plains to the Salt Lake Valley.

The many hardships she endured and the jolting of the wagon, proved too much for Margaretha. She had already lost the baby, and one night, under the lonely sky of the Nebraskan Plains, she died, leaving her family to go to Zion without her. A crude coffin was fashioned of boards taken from the wagon box, and Mary and her brother, Charles, stayed by the wagon and watched as their father and two older brothers, John and Andrew, took their mother and laid her to rest.

Her children never got over the loss of their beloved mother. They could not speak of her without tears, but they received the blessings of the Gospel and of being raised in Utah among the Saints. Her posterity honor her for this blessing.

RADINE GUNDERSON OLSON

BIRTHDATE: 6 Sep 1848
Grefsengerie, Norway
DEATH: 4 Jun 1906
Santaquin, Utah Co., Utah
PARENTS: Gunder Larsen
Tonetta Poulsen
PIONEER: 8 Oct 1866
Andrew H. Scott Wagon Train
SPOUSE: Lars Olson
MARRIED: 9 May 1866
Christianna, Norway
DEATH SP: 23 Dec 1913
Santaquin, Utah Co., Utah

CHILDREN:
Lauritz, 30 Nov 1867
Joseph Ludwig, 24 Jan 1869
Thea Christina, 26 May 1871
Lars L. Jr., 14 May 1874
Olof Gilbert, 28 Oct 1876
Amanda Josephine, 13 Jan 1879
Dena Louisa, 29 Mar 1881
Alvin Edward, 5 Aug 1883

Clara Marinda, 20 Sep 1885
Anna Pearl, 7 Sep 1888
David Martin, 11 Jan 1891

Radine was born in Norway, 1848. Her father died when she was five years old. Her mother struggled to support the four children. Her mother heard missionaries from the Church of Jesus Christ of Latter-day Saints and was determined to emigrate to America.

Radine married Lars L. Olson, from Sweden, in 1866. They left for America with her mother and aunt. They sailed on the ship "Humbolt," arriving in New York on July 18, 1866. After seventeen days on the train and river they joined a wagon train. Thirty of the company died on the Plains, the remainder arrived in the Salt Lake Valley in October, 1866.

Radine's first child was born in Provo in 1867 and died the next year. Ten other children were born to them in Santaquin. They purchased a small farm there, and she supplemented the family income by weaving carpets. She also made potato flour and starch to sell. She walked several miles to scrape saleratus from the ground near Goshen for leavening. It had to be washed and strained many times before it could be used as soda or lye. Bread was baked everyday.

They were a strict, religious and exemplary family. On one occasion they had pledged a certain amount of corn as tithing, it got blight. They were unable to fulfill their commitment, they gave their only family cow.

Radine was an industrious woman, getting up at 4:00 a.m. every morning to do chores and to weave. She was a faithful Relief Society worker and was called upon many times to sew clothing for the dead.

One evening, after doing her visiting teaching in the rain, while rethreading her loom, she took a chill, it turned to pneaumonia. She passed away in 1906.

ELNA JONSSON OLSSON

BIRTHDATE: 10 May 1817
Skeglinge, Malmohus, Sweden
DEATH: 9 Jul 1884
Millville, Cache Co., Utah
PARENTS: Jons Pehrsson
Kirstina Andersson
PIONEER: Sep 1864
William B. Preston Wagon Train
SPOUSE: Knut Olsson
MARRIED: 29 Dec 1834
Skeglinge, Malmohus, Sweden
DEATII SP. 16 Nov 1880
Millville, Cache Co., Utah

CHILDREN:
Anna (Hunt), 20 Sep 1835
Hanna A., 9 Feb 1837 (died at age 3)
Hans, 15 Mar 1839

Hanna, 11 Apr 1841 (died at 6 months)
Ola, 18 Dec 1842
Hanna, 6 Feb 1845 (died at 7 days)
Anders, 28 Jan 1846
Jons "James," 4 Aug 1848
Nils, 12 Oct 1850 (died at age 4)
Hanna, 27 Feb 1853 (died at age 2)
Nils, 8 Jun 1855
Johanna, 27 Jul 1857 (died at age 5)
Maria (Humphrys,) 3 Feb 1860
Carl "Charles," 22 Mar 1862

Elna was born in 1817 in Sweden. She was the youngest daughter and she had one brother and two sisters.

At the age of seventeen, Elna married Knut Olsson. They knew sorrow, as six of their fourteen children died before the age of five. The Olssons were farmers in a small village of Vidorp. Here they were baptized into the Church of Jesus Christ of Latter-day Saints, Knut being baptized in August, 1858, and Elna nine months later.

Desiring to emigrate to Utah, they sold their belongings at an auction and on April 10, 1864, they left for America bringing with them their five youngest children. They crossed the Plains with the William B. Preston Wagon Company which consisted of fifty wagons with Joseph Baker as second captain. They arrived in the Salt Lake Valley in September, 1864, and settled in Millville, Cache County, Utah. The next year, the three older children joined them and they became the first Scandinavian family to have settled in Millville.

Elna supported polygamy, and her husband, Knut, married another wife, Elin Anderson, on June 15, 1874.

Knut and Elna were sturdy and faithful pioneers who left a legacy of faith and perseverance for their descendants. They persevered many trials and gave up much for their religious beliefs.

Elna passed away at the age of sixty-seven on July 9, 1884 and is buried in the Millville Cemetery in northern Utah. Her husband preceded her in death about three years.

KJERSTINA PERSDOTTER OLSSON

BIRTHDATE: 9 Jun 1801
Hylteberga, Sjorup, Sweden
DEATH: 27 Apr 1888
Mt. Pleasant, Sanpete Co., Utah
PARENTS: Per Akesson
Lisbeth Borjesson
PIONEER: 29 Sep 1866
Peter Nebeker Co. Wagon Train
SPOUSE: Hans Olsson
MARRIED: 12 Dec 1827
DEATH SP: 1895
Mt. Pleasant, Sanpete Co., Utah

CHILDREN:
Bengta (Svensson), 17 Sep 1828

Elisa (Neilsson), 6 Apr 1830
Ola, 3 Oct 1832
Johanna (Allred), 10 Nov 1834
Ingar (Neilsen), 24 Nov 1836
Per / Pehr, 16 Feb 1839
Nils, 16 Mar 1841
Hanna (Seely), 27 Nov 1842

Kjerstina was born in 1801 in Hylteberga, Sjorup, Malmohus, Sweden, the second child in her family. She had two brothers and two sisters. Nothing is known of her childhood until she married Hans Olsson, a widower, whose wife had died on December 20, 1826. On June 9, 1828, Kjerstie celebrated her twenty-seventh birthday, and her oldest child was born the following September.

It was a cold winter night when Kjerstina and her youngest daughter, Hanna, quietly slipped out of their home to walk six miles to Slemeing, Sweden, where the Elders chopped a hole in the ice to baptize this mother and her thirteen year-old daughter at midnight on October 18, 1855. They had been members of the Lutheran Church.

Kjerstie's husband was bitterly opposed to this new religion she and Hanna had joined, but before long, Elisa, too, had been converted and baptized. Like other converts of their time, they began to make plans to emigrate to Utah. With this in mind, the two girls found jobs polishing china dishes in a factory in Copenhagen. They visited their home as often as possible. When Hanna was nineteen years old, she and Elisa decided that the time had come to leave their home and join the Saints in Zion.

Their parents dreaded to have the girls leave, travel alone, and cross the ocean and cross the barren wastes of the American frontier. Their father begged them not to go and told them if they would wait another year, he and their mother would go with them. Elisa consented, but Hanna, would not change her mind and started out, left Sweden in April, 1862. Elisa, Johanna, and Ingar joined her in Mt. Pleasant the following year.

Kjerstie longed more and more to be with her four daughters and members of her beloved Church in America. Communication between the families was rare. Occasional word from her daughters about marriages, grandchildren and the challenges of their frontier life made Kjerstie's heart yearn for her far away families.

The struggles and sacrifices endured by Kjerstie and Hans to acquire enough means to join their children were endured and on September 29, 1866, in Peter Nebeker's Wagon Company, they arrived in the Salt Lake Valley from Sweden with other immigrants. They settled in Mt. Pleasant, near their children.

After sixteen long years since her own baptism, Kjerstie's husband, Hans Olsson was baptized on her seventieth birthday, June 9, 1871 in Mt. Pleasant, Utah. This was an answer to Kjerstie of many, many years. Four years later she and Hans went to the Endowment House in

Salt Lake City and received their endowments and were sealed for time and eternity.

ANNA ELIZABETH JENSEN OMAN

No Photo Available

BIRTHDATE: 25 Feb 1841
Rogen, Skanderborg, Denmark
DEATH: 16 Mar 1896
Mt. Pleasant, Sanpete Co, Utah
PARENTS: Jens Laursen
Mette Kristine Jensen
PIONEER: 22 Sep 1861
Samuel A. Woolley Wagon Train
SPOUSE: Aaron Gustaf Oman
MARRIED: 4 Nov 1861
Mt. Pleasant, Sanpete Co., Utah
DEATH SP: 14 Jul 1916
Mt. Pleasant, Sanpete Co., Utah

CHILDREN:
Aaron Nelson, 12 Apr 1863
Andrew, 12 Apr 1866
Anne Elizabeth, 24 May 1868 (died at age 10)
Antomina (Tidwell), 4 Aug 1870
John Williams, 14 Aug 1873
Daniel, 29 May 1876
Cyrus, 20 May 1879
James Larsen, 18 Apr 1882

Anna Elizabeth was born in 1841 in Rogen, Skanderborg, Denmark. This city was located in the Jutland Peninsula of Denmark. Anna's father owned a lot of property in Rogen, and was considered well-to-do. They had servants helping in the home and in the fields. Seven children made up this family, and Ann was the youngest.

She was baptized into the Church of Jesus Christ of Latter-day Saints, July 29, 1860, in Denmark. Her brother baptized her. They were the only members of the family to join the Church. Their father disinherited them because of this action. Her brother was three years older than Anna.

On May 9, 1861, Anna, age twenty, emigrated to Zion alone. Her brother Soren, remained in Denmark until 1865. Anna, in a company of 565 Scandinavian Saints, sailed from Copenhagen, crossed the North Sea, and arrived at Hull, England. Two days later, May 14th, they took a special train to Liverpool.

They boarded the clipper ship "Monarch of the Sea," which left May 16th, at 11:00 a. m. for America. Three decks housed the passengers with single individuals cramped together. Many marriages were performed when the captain suggested this would alleviate some problems of the close quarters. This was the largest ship which carried Saints to America-it measured 1,979 tons and was 223 feet long. The weather was favorable most of the time. They passed large icebergs, one of which was judged to be 200 feet above the water, and the vessel escaped collision. They arrived June 19th, at New York.

They traveled by rail and steamboat from New York to Florence, Nebraska, where preparations began immediately for the trek across the Plains.

Anna, left Florence, July 13, 1861, with the Samuel Woolley Wagon Company of 338 Saints, 70 wagons, 277 oxen, 81 cows, 6 mules and 2 horses. They arrived in the Salt Lake Valley on September 22, 1861. Many of these Scandinavian settlers moved to Sanpete County.

Anna became better acquainted with Aaron Gustaf Oman who had crossed the ocean on the same ship. They were married November 4, 1861 in Mt. Pleasant, Utah. Anna was twenty and Aaron was twenty-one years of age. They later received their endowments, October 12, 1869, at Salt Lake City.

Aaron filed on a homestead of 160 acres in Mt. Pleasant where they made their home and raised their eight children. In addition to farming, Aaron freighted and was employed in the timber industry as a sawyer for twenty-five years. He helped prepare the wood for the interior of the Manti Temple. In 1886-1887, he worked in the saw mill at Manti six days a week and ten hours a day.

Anna's family, being well-to-do one in Denmark, left Anna unaccustomed to the hardships and privations of pioneer life. She was a small lady, weighing about 120 pounds.

She was ill for a long time after the birth of her first baby, but eventually her health returned to normal. Anna had brought beautiful clothes and fabrics with her from Denmark. Ladies in her area borrowed her dresses for important events in their lives. Dancing was a popular form of amusement and helped them forget their hardships. Her friends could be seen adorned in her dresses doing the grand right and left, and it was known that she never refused a request for the use of her clothing.

ANNA MARIA TOBIASSON OMAN

No Photo Available

BIRTHDATE: 13 Dec 1804
Algutsrum, Kalmar, Sweden
DEATH: 12 May 1864
Mt. Pleasant, Sanpete Co., Utah
PARENTS: Tobias Persson
Helena Persson
PIONEER: 5 Sep 1863
John F. Sanders Wagon Train
SPOUSE: Peter Nilsson Oman
MARRIED: 15 Jul 1827
Kalmar, Sweden
DEATH SP: 24 Dec 1880
Mt. Pleasant, Sanpete Co., Utah

CHILDREN:
Anna Lena, 12 Apr 1828
Nils John, 28 Jul 1829
Tobias Alfred, 7 Mar 1831
Anders Peter, 10 Jul 1833
Olof Fredrick, 10 Aug 1835
Maria Charlotta, 15 Apr 1838

Aaron Gustav, 1 Jul 1840
Christina Charlotta, 25 Oct 1844
Maria Matilda, 10 Apr 1847
Tobias Alfred Oman, 4 Nov 1849

Anna Maria was born on the Island of Oland just off the south eastern coast of Sweden. Her birthplace of Algutsrum is located in central Oland.

She married Peter Nilsson Oman on July 15, 1827, and in the next twenty-one years they were blessed with ten children in the same town. Peter was a mason by trade, and in their early married years, they were considered "well-to-do."

In 1852, they were baptized as members of the Church of Jesus Christ of Latter-day Saints by missionaries in that area. They were hard working faithful members of the church and did all they could to further the gospel. They did all they could to protect the missionaries from the mobs.

The entire family was active in the Church. Their sons, Anders and Nils served missions in Sweden and their thirteen year old son, Aaron, was appointed as a local missionary in Denmark.

As funds became available, the older children emigrated to Zion. In 1863, Peter, Anna, and the two youngest children left Liverpool on the ship, "B. S. Kimball." On June 6, 1863, they left Florence, Nebraska in the John F. Sanders Wagon Company to cross the Plains. They arrived in the Salt Lake Valley on September 5, 1864.

They went to Mt. Pleasant to settle. Anna passed away on May 12, 1864 in Mt. Pleasant, Utah at the age of fifty-nine, less than a year after arriving in the Salt Lake Valley.

Anna had done a great deal to further the work of the Lord as she supported her husband and her sons in their priesthood positions after their conversion to the Church. She also did a great deal for the missionaries who were serving in their area.

At one time the family was destitute for food, a knock at the door was answered by Anna Maria. A hand thrust through the door opening and placed five dollars in her hand and left without being identified. Thus was the testimony given of the Lord's goodness to His children. "As you do unto others, so too, you shall be given."

Anna had a great devotion to the Church and a deep love for her family.

ELIZA ROSANNAH PEARS SUMMERS O'NEIL

BIRTHDATE: 5 Feb 1842
Bedford, Yorkshire, England
DEATH: 5 Aug 1909
Uintah, Weber Co., Utah
PARENTS: John Pears
Rosanna Whitehead
PIONEER: 30 Nov 1856
Martin Handcart Company
SPOUSE I: Nicholas Summers
MARRIED: 2 Jan 1857
DEATH SP: 25 May 1865
Salt Lake City, Salt Lake, Utah

CHILDREN:
John Charles, 4 Dec 1857
Sarah Ann, 5 Dec 1859
Rosanna, 17 Nov 1861
Elizabeth, 24 Feb 1864

SPOUSE II: Timothy O'Neil
MARRIED: Not given
DEATH SP: Not given
CHILDREN: Not given

Eliza was born at Bedford, England and was baptized into the Church on January 11, 1853. She left England with her father, mother and one sister in 1856. They brought with them many personal belongings, including bolts of silk and woolen goods. They sailed from Liverpool on the ship "Horizon."

They crossed the Plains in the Martin Handcart Company. They suffered many hardships from cold and hunger. Eliza's father died and was buried on the Plains. Her mother's feet were frozen so bad she was unable to walk. They lost most of their possessions while crossing the Plains.

On January 2, 1857, Eliza married Nicholas Summers. They were the parents of one son and three daughters. Nicholas passed away on May 29, 1865, leaving her with four small children to care for. She worked wherever she could to provide for her children.

She later married Timothy O'Neil in Uintah, Utah. He was a railroad worker and she helped support her family by cooking for the men who worked on the Union Pacific Railroad.

They owned a fifteen acre farm, raising some fruit, berries and hay. While helping load fruit crates on a wagon for market, Eliza was badly injured.

Later, Eliza was diagnosed with cancer and was given treatments, but they were not successful and she passed away on August 5, 1909 at Uintah. She was preceded in death by two of her daughters, Sarah Ann and Rosanna.

ANN WALMSLEY GREENHALGH OPENSHAW

BIRTHDATE: 9 May 1806
Bolton, Lancashire, England
DEATH : 31 Mar 1895
Santaquin, Utah Co., Utah
PARENTS: Robert Greenhalgh
Ellen Walmsley
PIONEER: 30 Nov 1856
Martin Handcart Company
SPOUSE: William Openshaw
MARRIED: 20 May 1833
Bury, Lancashire, England
DEATH SP: 21 Dec 1882
Santaquin, Utah Co., Utah

CHILDREN:
Roger William, 22 Oct 1829
Samuel, 1 Nov 1833
Eli, 1 Feb 1835
Levi, 2 Feb 1837
Mary, 25 Mar 1839
Eleanor, 15 Apr 1842
MaryAnn, 16 Sep 1845

Ann was the fourth child and youngest daughter of her parents. Life was hard in Bolton, England and all of the family worked in the linen mills, twelve hours a day. Ann married William Openshaw on May 20, 1833 in Bury, Lancashire, England, and they were blessed with four sons and three daughters, all born in Breightmet, England.

William and Ann embraced the gospel in 1840, and the spirit of gathering to Zion was very strong with them. Their sons, Roger and Eli, were the first to leave England. Roger left behind his new young bride, Eliza Booth, with his mother. They lived on meager rations to save money to send for the rest of the family.

William and Ann, their five remaining children, and Roger's bride left Liverpool on May 16, 1856 on the ship "Horizon." They joined with the Willie Martin Handcart Company, which left Iowa City on July 15, 1856.

This company was caught up in the early snows in the mountains and nearly half of the group died of cold and hunger. When Ann's sons heard of the plight of the Martin Company, they rushed up the eastern trails through waist deep snows to bring meat to the starving group.

Roger's heart was greatly saddened when he learned that his bride, Eliza, had been too frail to withstand the journey and had died along the way.

They finally arrived in the Salt Lake Valley on November 30, 1856. After a short stay in Salt Lake to recuperate, they traveled to Santaquin to the two-room log home Roger and Eli had built for them.

With great faith Ann helped her husband work the small piece of land. They planted an orchard and garden and struggled with crop failures. Yet, in all, Ann's testimony never wavered. Ann and William traveled to Salt Lake and were sealed in the Endowment House on December 7, 1867.

William passed away on December 21, 1882, and Ann passed away on March 31, 1895, both in Santaquin, Utah County, Utah.

ELIZABETH "BETTY" RAMSBOTTOM OPENSHAW

BIRTHDATE: 11 Oct 1841
Oldham, Lancashire, England
DEATH: 21 Mar 1911
Santaquin, Utah Co., Utah
PARENTS: Henry Ramsbottom
Mary Sykes
PIONEER: Fall of 1862
SPOUSE: Roger W. Openshaw
MARRIED: 25 Oct 1862
Moroni, Sanpete Co., Utah
DEATH SP: 19 Jul 1909

CHILDREN:
Mary Ann, 25 Dec 1863
Rosetta, 29 Sep 1865
Elizabeth, 22 Dec 1867
Eliza, 19 Oct 1870
Sarah Jane, 7 Mar 1872
Matilda Ellen, 13 Feb 1874
Minnie, 29 Feb 1876
Ellenor, 6 Jan 1878
Henry Roger, 4 Jun 1880
Zina Euzella, 8 Aug 1881
Zelpha Celesta, 4 Nov 1883

Elizabeth was the last born child of her parents. Her mother and sisters accepted the restored gospel and were baptized in 1849. Her mother, Mary, had poor health all her life and died when Elizabeth was ten years old. Elizabeth then had to go to work in the linen mills with her siblings.

In 1853, her father, Henry, remarried a widow with two children, but Elizabeth could not get along with these new family members. Her older sisters had married and gone to Zion, so Elizabeth and her sister Mary worked long, hard hours to save enough so that they could join them.

On April 23, 1862, Elizabeth and Mary sailed on the ship "John J. Boyd," for America, and traveled with the other Saints to Utah in the Fall of 1862.

She met Roger Openshaw at dance held in Moroni for new arrivals. She danced in her stocking feet because she had no shoes. After a brief courtship she and Roger were married on October 25, 1862 in Moroni.

Roger took his bride to Fountain Green where he had built a small two-room home. She found the smaller room filled with fleece of wool which Roger had shorn. She threw up her hands and declared, "What do we do with this?" He replied, "You make clothes with it. " "But I know nothing of making clothes from fleece." "You will learn." And she did.

During the Black Hawk War with the hostile Indians, Elizabeth and Roger moved in with Roger's parents in Santaquin, Utah. Later they bought property and built a home there. When Roger took a second wife, Mary Gledhill, Elizabeth supported her husband and extended the hand of love and sisterhood to Mary, who was actually her niece.

Elizabeth passed away at her home on March 21, 1911, at age seventy and is buried next to her husband in the Santaquin Cemetery.

NANCY INGHAM OPENSHAW

BIRTHDATE: 23 Jan 1821
Heywood, England
DEATH: 24 Mar 1875
Salt Lake City, Salt Lake, Utah
PARENTS: Jonathan Ingham
Esther Whitworth
PIONEER: 6 Oct 1853
Cyrus Wheelock Wagon Train
SPOUSE: George Openshaw
MARRIED: 2 Feb 1845
Bury, Lancashire, England
DEATH SP: 5 Jun 1906
Salt Lake City, Salt Lake, Utah

CHILDREN:
John Thomas, 23 Nov 1848 (died as a child)
Esther Ellen (Crofts), 30 Oct 1851
Alice, Apr 1853 (died as an infant)
George Ingham, 9 May 1855
Joseph, 6 Aug 1857
Mary Nancy (Squires), 8 Dec 1859
Sarah Elizabeth (Wiscombe), 11 Jul 1861

Nancy was born in 1821 in England. Her father was a merchant and the family owned their own merchant ship by the name of "Ingham." The ship was lost at sea in a severe storm. Nancy was born in the small town of Heywood near the manufacturing district of Manchester, and she followed the popular occupation of the area by working in the mills, manufacturing cloth.

George Openshaw was a weaver and lived in the nearby village of Heap. In 1845, Nancy married George at St. Mary, Bury, Lancashire, England, in the Church of England. He was not very religious. Nancy belonged to the Church of England, she sang in the choir and taught in the Sunday School. When the Elders of the Church of Jesus Christ of Latter-day Saints called on them, she was the first to join, July 3, 1847. A little over a year later, October 7, 1848, her husband was also baptized.

In November, 1848, they were happy to have a son born to them, and in 1851 a daughter. They sold their house and made preparations to set sail for America on the ship "Ellen Maria." They were to sail, November 23, 1852, but the ship was moored until January 17, 1853.

They crossed to New Orleans, March 6th, went up the Mississippi River to St. Louis. Another daughter was born, but lived only a short time. They were in St. Louis for several weeks and George was able to get work to earn money to help them along their way.

Continuing to Keokuk, Iowa, they started across the Plains by ox-team with the Cyrus H. Wheelock Wagon Company. When they reached Echo Canyon, John Thomas became very ill and died. They brought him to Salt Lake and George made a casket and buried him in the City Cemetery.

It was six months before Nancy wrote home to England with the news because her mother had wanted her to leave this boy behind and had predicted that if she took him away she would lose him.

This family arrived in the Basin, October 6, 1853, and occupied a room in a log cabin belonging to the Walker's on Main street and Fourth South. They stayed there for two winters and then bought a two-room adobe house. Here their other four children were born. George was overseer or toll keeper of Brigham Young's wood yard. He also ran the first planing mill in Utah.

Nancy taught her children the truths of the Gospel. She encouraged education and all of her children went to school as far as possible. They studied mathematics, public speaking and history, and the girls studied music, including organ and singing. They moved to Canyon Road between 3rd and 4th Avenue. This was a more roomy home and they were able to furnish it better. Fire burned this home to the ground later, and Brigham Young built them another home on the west side of the street.

For several years before her death, Nancy had poor health. She had a quiet, retiring nature, and never cared to be in the public eye. She remained true and faithful to the Gospel for which she had sacrificed so much. Her death occurred, March 24, 1875, at the age of fifty-four years. She was shopping where the Joseph Smith Building now stands, when she had a heart attack. She died suddenly.

Nancy was indeed, a great, faithful pioneer woman who left a great heritage to those who have followed her.

SUSANNAH HARDING ORCHARD ORCHARD

BIRTHDATE: 27 Jan 1809
Rudge Farm, Froxfield, England
DEATH: 1 Nov 1889
Lewiston, Cache Co., Utah
PARENTS: William Harding
Martha Watts
PIONEER: 21 Sep 1868
Capt. Gillespie Co. Wagon Train
SPOUSE I: James Orchard
MARRIED: abt 1837
DEATH SP: abt 1845

CHILDREN:
Martha Ellen (Barshaw), 2 Jan 1838
Sarah Ann (Kelsey), 5 Feb 1840
Naomi (Sanders), 21 Nov 1843

SPOUSE II: Jacob Orchard
MARRIED: abt 1844/1845
DEATH SP: 10 Jun 1864

CHILDREN:
William Joseph, 16 May 1846
Ruth (Fawcett), 25 Aug 1847
Clara Jane (Day), 25 Jan 1849
Samuel, 5 Aug 1851
Elnora "Lenora" (McDonald), 1 Nov 1853

Susannah was born in 1809 in England. She married twice. After the death of her first husband, James, she married his brother, Jacob. She had three daughters by the first marriage, and three daughters and one son by the second marriage. One record shows a second son who may have died at birth.

Susannah joined the Church of Jesus Christ of Latter-day Saints early in 1845, and although she was very faithful, her husband, Jacob, never joined. She often anointed her sick husband, and all the family knelt to pray for his health.

When Jacob, her second husband, died in 1864, Susannah decided to bring her youngest children with her to Salt Lake City. She was very devoted to her children and they to her. A widower in Salt Lake wanted her to marry him. "No," she answered, "I have my children and can live with them."

She was a religious, God-fearing woman who attended to her church duties at all times and she set an excellent example for her children.

Susannah went to Dixie for two years to help care for her daughter, Ruth's young family. She was a great spiritual help to the small community of Price, exhibiting her great faith in the Gospel in Fast Meetings and Relief Society. She was a splendid public speaker with her sincerity and love of the Gospel.

She returned to Salt Lake City to live with her daughter, Naomi, and then went to Lewiston in Cache Valley to live out her last years with her son, William.

Susannah did a great many endowments and sealings for the Orchard and Harding families in the Logan Temple.

Susannah passed away on November 1, 1889, just two months before her eightieth birthday. She passed away in Lewiston, Cache Valley, Utah.

Susannah was a great, faithful pioneer woman endeared by those who have followed her.

ELEANOR GRANT ORD

BIRTHDATE: 14 Jun 1828
Leichestershire, England
DEATH: 13 Aug 1914
Nephi, Juab Co., Utah
PARENTS: John Grant
Mary Hall
PIONEER: 30 Nov 1856
Martin Handcart Company
SPOUSE: Thomas Ord
MARRIED: 4 Mar 1856
Leichestershire, England
DEATH SP:

CHILDREN:
Mary Eleanor, 23 Aug 1857
Thomas George, 5 Sep 1859
Isabella Maria, 7 Mar 1844
Elizabeth Ann, 1 Nov 1861
John William, 5 Oct 1863
Samuel Grant, 13 Oct 1868
Robert James, 13 Nov 1871

Eleanor's mother died when she was two years old. Her father remarried and they had more children. Eleanor attended school in Leicester, England, but she was forced to abandon her studies and go to work. She obtained employment as a frame work knitter. She would work during the day and go to school at night.

Eleanor became converted after hearing the gospel message of the missionaries from the Church of Jesus Christ of Latter-day Saints. She was baptized, May 4, 1847, after much opposition from her father, and many prayers to her Heavenly Father. She was baptized by Crandal Dunn and confirmed by Thomas Sevenson.

Eleanor met Thomas Ord. He was a traveling Elder. He asked Eleanor to marry him and go to Zion with him. They were married on March 4, 1856. As newlyweds, they sailed on the vessel, "Horizon," on May 25, 1856. After six weeks on the ocean, they landed at Boston, Massachusetts and traveled by rail to Iowa City where handcarts were being made for their journey across the Plains. They were members of the Edward Martin Handcart Company.

Eleanor walked and pulled a handcart, also an eight year old crippled child which belonged to another woman. The crippled child eventually died from exposure. Later, Eleanor and her husband pulled a sick man, who was left on the trail too ill to go on, the rest of the way to Salt Lake City. The rations had become so low and the divisions of flour were so small, they had to stir it in water and drink it.

Eleanor arrived in the Salt Lake Valley, Sunday, November 30, 1856, after more than three months of pulling her handcart. After two weeks, she and Thomas Ord were sent to Nephi, Juab County, Utah. There they spent the rest of their lives.

They participated in the building of the town of Nephi and building the wall around the city that acted as a protection against the Indian attacks. They built a home in the northwest corner of the old fort. The roof of their home in the fort was made of willows, sod, and thatch. When it rained, the mud and water would come through.

After the Indian troubles were over, the city was enlarged and they obtained a portion of a block situated one block north of the old fort. She was very active in Relief Society. She loved to sing, to teach, to speak, share her testimony, and do temple work.

JOHANNA CHARLOTTA GRANNE ORELL

BIRTHDATE: 16 Aug 1824
Kimstad, Ostergotland, Sweden
DEATH: 10 Jan 1906
Hyrum, Cache Co., Utah
PARENTS: Jonas P. Granne
Britta Catrina Andersson
PIONEER: 29 Sep 1866
Peter Nebeker Co. Wagon Train
SPOUSE: Carl Fredric Orell
MARRIED: 12 Oct 1851
Sweden
DEATH SP: 17 Oct 1864
Sweden

CHILDREN:
Josephine Charlotta, 26 Aug 1852
Albertina Wilhelmina, 2 Feb 1855
Charles Ernest, 1 May 1858
Gustaf Philip, 30 Sep 1859
Josephine Amanda, 4 Sep 1861

Johanna Charlotta was born in 1824 in Sweden. She was baptized into the Church of Jesus Christ of Latter-day Saints in Sweden on September 11, 1863. She opened her home often to the missionaries and supplied them with clothing.

Johanna married Carl Fredric Orell on October 12, 1851 in Sweden. They had five children born to them.

Carl was a dairy farmer and Johanna helped in that work. She was also a skilled weaver and made men's and women's clothing as well as blankets, sheets and carpets.

Carl passed away in 1864 leaving her with her five children ranging in age from three to twelve, to raise a great responsibility.

Johanna emigrated to Utah arriving in Utah September 29, 1866, with the Peter Nebeker Wagon Company. She walked most of the way across the Plains, and endured the many hardships accompanying such an experience. She moved to Hyrum, Utah where she was a member of the first Relief Society of Hyrum ward. She was a teacher in the Relief Society did much temple work for the dead in the Logan Temple. She had the temple work done in the Endowment House in Salt Lake City for her husband and children. She also wove cloth for burial clothing and helped prepare burials.

Johanna was very generous with whatever money she had. She loaned money to seven immigrants to come to Zion in Utah. She was a wonderful mother and grandmother and is a great example for the posterity who have followed.

Johanna Orell passed away on January 10, 1906 in Hyrum, Cache County, Utah, a great pioneer woman of faith and fortitude.

ANNA "ANNIE" ELIZA BUSENBARK ORISON

BIRTHDATE: 7 Sep 1849
Honey Creek, Iowa
DEATH: 17 Jun 1936
Huntington Park, California
PARENTS: Isaac Busenbark
Abigail Manning
PIONEER: 1852
David Wood Co. Wagon Train
SPOUSE: David Franklin Orison
MARRIED: 1869
DEATH SP: 16 Oct 1909
Logan, Cache Co., Utah

CHILDREN:
Chloe Abigail, 12 Aug 1870 (died as a child)
Samuel David, 15 May 1872
Amie "Annie," 28 Sep 1876 (died at age 17)
Millie May, 18 Nov 1879
Charles Henry, 17 Jan 1882
Letha Jane, 11 Aug 1884
Lophelia, 19 Dec 1886

Anna Eliza was born at Honey Creek, Pottawattamie County, Iowa in the fall of 1849, and became a pioneer child who crossed the Plains without her mother.

Her father (Busenbark was of Prussian origin) and mother had lived in New York state when they learned of the restored Gospel and cast their lot to live with the Saints. They had eight children at that time, all of whom were living. When they moved to Nauvoo, they added one more child, and when they were driven from that beautiful city they camped at Winter Quarters in Iowa and Nebraska, and added three more children to their family including Anna Eliza who was the eleventh born into this family. A twelfth child was also born in Winter Quarters, but died six months later,crossing the Plains, along with the mother of all these children, Abigail Manning Busenbark. They were buried at Winter Quarters in Florence, Nebraska.

Remaining was a family of five children (the older four were married, and two others had died) who finally crossed the Plains in the summer of 1852 with their father. Annie's father chose to settle first in Weber County in North Ogden, then to Cache Valley near Richmond. They were happy to be in Zion. In 1853, Annie's father married again to bring a mother into the family.

Annie grew to adulthood, met and married David Franklin Orrison in 1869. When their first child was born, they dropped one "r" in the spelling of their last name. In December of 1878, Annie and David were sealed in the Endowment House in Salt Lake City. Their seven children were born in the beautiful Cache Valley, where they lived and farmed until he died in 1909.

At some time after her husband's death, Annie went to live with one of her married children, and died at Huntington Park, California at the age of eighty-six years. Thus ended the life of a sturdy, brave little pioneer woman, one of great faith and courage who experienced many of the pioneer adversities of helping settle the West.

AMY "MARY" KIRBY ORME

BIRTHDATE: 13 Jan 1804
Burbage, Hinckley, England
DEATH: 19 Mar 1893
Salt Lake City, Salt Lake, Utah
PARENTS: John Kirby
Charlotte Reddles
PIONEER: 30 Nov 1856
Martin Handcart Company
SPOUSE: Samuel Orme
MARRIED: 7 Dec 1825
St. Martins, Leicester, England
DEATH SP: 6 Feb 1843
Coalville, Leicester, England

CHILDREN;
Sarah Ann, 18 Aug 1826
Eliza, 26 Oct 1827
Amy Kirby, 21 Jul 1830
Samuel Washington, 4 Jul 1832
Caroline, 14 Apr 1835
Rebecca, 17 Jan 1838
Elizabeth, 1840 (died at age 6)
Martha, Oct 1842 (died at age 4)

Amy was born in Burbage, Hinckley, Leicester, England, as one of thirteen children. She married Samuel Orme of Silesby, Leicestershire in 1825. They moved several different times as their children were born.

In 1831, Amy, her husband, and three small children went to America and settled in Ohio to be with her brothers and parents in America. Her son, Samuel, was born in Ohio. Around the year of 1834, their family returned to England where her husband worked as a bookkeeper for the Midland Railroad Office. When her husband, Samuel, died on February 10, 1842, she was left with eight children.

Soon after his death, she heard the gospel of the Church of Jesus Christ of Latter-day Saints preached by the missionaries. She and her family were baptized and were anxious to join the rest of the Saints in America.

Her second daughter, Sarah Ann, married in 1847. Sarah Ann and her husband took her sister, Caroline, to America with them in 1849. In 1856, Amy, her two daughters, and son sailed from Liverpool to Boston. They went by rail to Iowa City where they joined with the Edward Martin Handcart Company.

They endured extreme suffering on the Plains. Her son was so weak, the women of the family shared their portion of food with him. They were in the process of starving when they were reached by an advance scout sent out by Brigham Young. He brought them buffalo meat to sustain them until the rest of the rescue party came. They finally reached the Salt Lake Valley on November 9, 1856. Shortly afterward, the Orme family moved to E. T. City in Tooele County.

After her children married, Amy took turns living with each of her children. Amy's daughters, Sarah Ann, died in 1866 and Rebecca, died in 1871 leaving three small sons. Amy moved to Salt Lake City where she raised the boys.

As they married, she visited and lived with one and then another of her children or grandchildren until she died in March, 1893 in Salt Lake City.

Amy spent her life serving others and was a very noble pioneer.

SARAH CROSS ORME

BIRTHDATE: 3 Mar 1833
Quomdon, England
DEATH: 24 Feb 1903
Tooele, Tooele Co., Utah
PARENTS: John Cross
Keziah Marshall
PIONEER: 11 Sep 1857
Israel Evans Handcart Company
SPOUSE: Samuel W. Orme
MARRIED: 8 Nov 1857
E. T. City, Tooele Co., Utah
DEATH SP: 19 Jul 1889
Tooele, Tooele Co., Utah

CHILDREN:
Samuel Washington, Jr. 19 Sep 1858
Joseph Cross, 1 Aug 1860
John Kirby, 3 Oct 1862
Silas Cross, 26 Dec 1864

Arthur Orrne, 4 Oct 1867
Charles Alvin, 21 Oct 1869
Lafayette, 14 Mar 1872
Edwin Marshall, 19 Jul 1874

Sarah was born in Quomdon, Leicestershire, England. Her father was a farmer and livestock man who preferred sheep. She was the youngest of her family and received much attention while growing up. Her older sisters did the household work, so little was expected of Sarah in the way of work. Every evening, her mother would read to her from the Bible.

Her mother died when she was ten years old. Her father suffered a paralytic stroke, became an invalid, and died when she was fourteen years old. Her brother, Silas brought his wife and family to the farm, but he died when she was sixteen. Since she and her sister-in-law were not congenial, Sarah went to Loughborer where she worked in a hosiery factory.

Here, in Loughborer, she heard the gospel and was baptized a member of the Church of Jesus Christ of Latter-day Saints on December 18, 1851 by John Wilson. By doing so, her kindred were all opposed to her; but with the help of the elders, she was able to convert her sister, Katie.

At a church conference, she met Samuel Washington Orme. They courted until 1856 when he and his mother went to Zion with the understanding that Sarah would follow the next year.

On March 28, 1857, she sailed from Liverpool on the ship, "George Washington," and landed in Boston. She traveled by rail to Iowa City. Then she went from there to Florence, Nebraska by ox-team and was fitted out with a handcart to cross the Plains with the Israel Evans Handcart Company. They arrived in the Salt Lake Valley on September 11, 1857. To her dying day, she thanked the Lord that she was permitted to gather in Zion.

Samuel met her in Salt Lake City and took her to E. T. City, which is now known as Lake Point in Tooele, Utah. They were married by Hezekiah Mitchell shortly after her arrival.

In the Spring of 1858, they moved to Tooele to live in a one room log cabin. They hardly got settled into this environment, when the word came that all inhabitants must move south to Lehi because the Johnston's Army was approaching the area. After the threat was over, they returned to Tooele.

For a number of years, it was a hard struggle for existence. She became the mother of eight sons. She encouraged the family to work together and they became successful in the farm and livestock industry. Food and clothing were scarce. She was not a public worker, but a wonderful homemaker and teacher to her children. She was kind and charitable to those in distress or less fortunate than herself.

ELIZABETH JANE GREEN ORR

BIRTHDATE: 19 Feb 1840
Newport, Monmouthshire, Wales
DEATH: 2 Apr 1890
Clover, Tooele Co., Utah
PARENTS: Richard W. Green
Anna Phillips
PIONEER: 1862
MARRIED: 1863
Clover, Tooele Co., Utah
SPOUSE: James Copeland Orr
DEATH SP: 5 Jun 1890
Clover, Tooele Co., Utah

CHILDREN:
James Copeland, 1 Jan 1864
Charley Edward, 17 Nov 1865
Osbourne Llewellyn, 20 Nov 1867
Malcolm Campbell, 30 Aug 1870
Walter Scott, 9 Dec 1873
Richard Robert, 27 Jan 1876
Ernest Eugene, 28 Feb 1879
Daughter, died at birth

Elizabeth was a little Welsh girl who came to the land of Zion to become a faithful member of the Church. She endured the many hardships of a pioneer to raise a fine family of wonderful sons.

Sometime before 1853, a missionary from the Church of Jesus Christ of Latter-day Saints converted the Green family. The father forsook one of the great honors he held as Grand Master of the Independent Order of Odd Fellows in Newport when he heard this great truth and readily gave up his earthly possessions to join the Saints in America. They sailed aboard the ship, "Martha Whitmore," in 1853.

Little did the Green family realize when they undertook this trip that it would be nine long years before they could get to Utah. After eleven weeks on the ocean, the boat anchored at New Orleans. We know nothing of their trip from there but we do know they arrived in Utah in 1862. After General Conference that year they decided to go to Grantsville, Utah.

They settled in Clover Creek, Utah where Elizabeth's father engaged in rope making. Shortly after their arrival she met and married James Orr. They were married in 1863 and some records say in the old Endowment House. They were the parents of seven handsome sons and a daughter who died at birth. This was great heartbreak for Elizabeth who was never very well after the birth.

Elizabeth played the violin and often would play for others to dance the "Highland Fling." She was a wonderful mother who left her sons a rich heritage. She taught them the worth of hard work, the value of education, and the love of music.

James and Richard both had college degrees. James taught school in Avon and Highland, Utah. The Media Center in the Highland school is named after him. Ernest,

Walter and Osborne were successful farmers. Charlie drowned at Bear Lake while fishing. Malcolm, the youngest left home and was never heard from again, although the family never quit looking for him.

She and her husband are buried in the St. John's Cemetery in Tooele County, Utah.

ELIZABETH MCQUEEN ORR

BIRTHDATE: 15 Jun 1806
Killyleagh, Down, Ireland
DEATH: 27 Jul 1880
Grantsville, Tooele Co., Utah
PARENTS: Osborne McQueen
Elizabeth Copeland
PIONEER: 16 Oct 1853
Appleton Harmon Wagon Train
SPOUSE: Robert Orr
MARRIED: 16 Apr 1828
Kilbumie, Ayrshire, Scotland
DEATH SP: 7 Nov 1887
Grantsville, Tooele Co., Utah

CHILDREN:
Marian "May," 14 Nov 1827
Thomas, 2 Aug 1829
James Copeland, 6 Jun 1830
Robert Copeland, 6 Apr 1833 (died at age 1)
Robert, Jr., 10 May 1835
Matthew, 12 May 1837
Elizabeth, 18 Aug 1840
John M., 10 May 1841 (died age 1)
Annie, 14 Aug 1843
John, 26 Jul 1845

Elizabeth was born in Ireland, but raised in Scotland. When she was twenty-one, she married Robert Orr. They had ten children losing two in childhood.

Elizabeth was trained as a midwife and nurse. She spent much of her time among the sick. Robert was an engineer in a factory that produced thread. All the factory workers lived in small cottages which were built close together in a court near the factory.

Elizabeth heard Willard Richards preaching on a street corner and soon applied for baptism and joined the Church of Jesus Christ of Latter-day Saints. She opened her home to the elders and extended every hospitality to them. Robert and some of the children joined the Church in 1847.

On February 28, 1853, Robert, Elizabeth, and their children James, Robert Jr., Matthew, Elizabeth, Ann, and John sailed from Liverpool, England aboard the ship, "Falcon." Robert signed on as an engine keeper and her son, James, signed on as a cook.

Their family made their way to Kanesville, Iowa where they prepared to travel with the Appleton M. Harmon Wagon Company to cross the Plains. They arrived in the Salt Lake Valley on October 16, 1853.

Robert and his sons were employed as stone cutters on the temple. At General Conference in October 7, 1853 an appeal was made for fifty families to move to the Tooele Valley. They needed volunteers to strengthen the Grantsville Fort. The Orrs moved to Grantsville and built a log house on the corner of Clark and Cooley Streets where they started and operated a store for many years.

In addition to operating the store, Elizabeth continued caring for the sick. Her services as a nurse and midwife were constantly in demand. Elizabeth also prepared meals for freighters as they passed through Grantsville. She was blessed with a beautiful singing voice and participated in duets locally and in Stake Conference. She was also a great student of law and history. She was gifted in poetry.

Elizabeth and Robert often expressed their gratitude for the gospel message. Their first thought was to serve and to do their part in church affairs. They loved their home in the United States and took great pride in assisting in civic duties.

CLARA VIRTUE BARNETT ORTON

BIRTHDATE: 7 Nov 1857
Steeple Ashton, England
DEATH: 23 May 1919
Ogden, Weber Co., Utah
PARENTS: George Barnett
Mary Ann Mathews
PIONEER: 2 Nov 1864
Warren S. Snow Wagon Train
SPOUSE: Joseph Orton
MARRIED: 20 Dec 1875
DEATH SP: 24 Apr 1919
Ogden, Weber Co., Utah

CHILDREN:
George Henry, 27 Apr 1877
Mary Ann, 28 Oct 1878
Jo Barnett, 1 Dec 1879
Charles Edward, 30 Jul 1881
James Alma, 22 Jul 1883 (died at 5 months)
William Lorenzo, 10 Nov 1884
Francis Heber, 12 Dec 1886
Clarence Victor, 26 Aug 1888
Thomas Delbe, 14 May 1890
Clara Virtue, 25 Dec 1892
Luella May, 1 Mar 1895
Ellen Alean, 4 Apr 1898

Clara was born in Steeple Ashton, Wiltshire, England. She spent her first years in Steeple Ashton where her father and grandfather had been farmers on the same estate.

Missionaries from the Church of Jesus Christ of Latter-day Saints came to this area and converted the family and several others. After her parents were baptized, her father presided over the Steeple Ashton Branch of the Church from 1861 to 1864.

On June 3, 1864, they sailed on the ship, "Hudson," to America. After a voyage of nearly seven weeks, they arrived in New York and went to Wyoming, Nebraska where they were outfitted to cross the Plains with the Warren S. Snow Wagon Company.

There were a number of deaths before they reached the valley. Clara's mother died at Blade Butte, Wyoming. Her youngest sister died on the Sweetwater, and her grandmother died at Big Muddy.

On November 2, 1864, they arrived in Salt Lake Valley. Clara's father and children went to live in North Ogden where a cousin, Alfred Berrett, lived.

When Clara was eleven years old, her father married Eliza Miller. Clara worked in the home of John and Rachel Woodfield. She was industrious and thrifty.

Rachel married Joseph Orton on December 20, 1875. They made their home North Ogden, Utah where they had a farm. Twelve children were born to them. With this large family, there was much work to be done. However, Clara's work was always well organized. She was a hard worker even though she suffered a serious knee injury when she was a young girl.

Work and pleasure were combined. She had many rag rug and quilting bees where friends came to sew, chat, and eat a hot meal. She loved flowers and tenderly cared for them both inside and outside her home.

The last years of their lives were spent Ogden where Joseph passed away in April of 1919. Clara followed in death one month later. They were both laid to rest in the North Ogden Cemetery.

ELIZABETH MIDDLEFELL BENTLEY ORTON

No Photo Available

BIRTHDATE: 10 Feb 1814
Salford, Ulverston, England
DEATH: 9 Apr 1877
Parowan, Iron Co., Utah
PARENTS: William Middlefell
Mary Witters
PIONEER: 20 Aug 1868
Chester Loveland Mule Train
SPOUSE: John Bentley
MARRIED: 1831
DEATH SP:: 9 Feb 1867
Salford, Lancashire, England

CHILDREN:
Edward, 31 Jul 1832
Frederick, 20 Sep 1834
Elizabeth Hannah (Jones), 15 Sep 1836
Mary Ann (Lawrence), 9 Jun 1839
Lucy, 1 Aug 1841 (died as a child)
Matilder, 7 Nov 1843 (died as a child)
Sarah Jane, 11 Nov 1845 (died as a child)
John, 26 Nov 1847

William, 8 Aug 1850
Joseph, 26 Nov 1853

SPOUSE II: William Orton
MARRIED: 1870 or 1872
Parowan, Iron Co., Utah
DEATH SP: 3 Jan 1877
American Fork, Utah Co., Utah
CHILDREN: None

Elizabeth was born in Salford, Ulverston, Lancashire, England, 1814. (Different records show different birth dates for Elizabeth.) She was the eldest of five daughters in this family. Nothing is known of her childhood or of her parents' lives.

She met John Bentley probably in Bolton, a town near Salford. They were married about 1831 and lived in Salford. Their first two sons were born in 1832 and 1834. Two daughters were born in 1836 and 1839. Her next three were daughters but unfortunately, they all three died very young.

Elizabeth did not leave any written word of her family but she must have heard about the Church of Jesus Christ of Latter-day Saints through friends or the missionaries. She was baptized on November 10, 1842. Her husband was not baptized. The Manchester Branch to which she belonged was a good sized branch by the time she was baptized. Her oldest son was baptized in 1848 at the age of fifteen, and the next year their two oldest daughters were baptized.

Three more sons were born to Elizabeth and John. Her husband died very suddenly on the street, probably from a heart attack, 1867, in Salford. With only her youngest boys at home, Elizabeth decided to emigrate to Utah to be with the Church Members. She received help from the Perpetual Emigration Fund of the Church of twenty-eight pounds, and they sailed from Liverpool in the steamship "Minnesota," on June 30, 1868.

After their arrival to the Salt Lake Valley on August 20, 1868, they were persuaded to move to Parowan. They had traveled with the Chester Loveland's Wagon Company. They had continued by wagon to Parowan. Some family traditions say the boys worked on the Salt Lake Temple for a time. After their move to Parowan, her sons married and settled there.

In Parowan, Elizabeth married again, to William Orton sometime between 1870 and 1872. He had lost his wife in 1870 (Hannah Taylor Orton). Elizabeth went to Salt Lake City to receive her endowments in the Endowment House October 10, 1872, her name then was Elizabeth Orton. William passed away on January 3, 1877, and Elizabeth passed away either in April, 1876 or 1877, and is buried in Parowan, Utah.

Elizabeth was a good, hard-working woman, and was a good-natured, chubby, English woman. She desired the best for her family and suffered a lot-first from the loss of three daughters, then her husband, and the sacrifices she must have made leaving her family and friends in England to start over in the United States. She was a big help in a new, pioneer community of Parowan, and was especially helpful with the ill, and she worked as a midwife in Parowan.

Elizabeth must have been taught beautiful handwork. Her daughter has handed down to her family a square of very lovely needlepoint that she did when she was just nine years old. The family members take turns keeping it for a year at a time.

Elizabeth and John Bentley were the parents of ten children, seven growing to maturity with families of their own. Their posterity are proud of these pioneers and their accomplishments.

HANNAH TAYLOR ORTON

No Photo Available

BIRTHDATE: 12 May 1803
Arnold, Notts. , England
DEATH: 16 May 1870
Parowan, Iron Co., Utah
PARENTS: George Taylor
Mary Brown
PIONEER: 15 Sep 1861
Ira Eldredge Co. Wagon Train
SPOUSE: William Orton
MARRIED: 9 Jun 1834
Arnold, Notts. , England
DEATH SP: 3 Jan 1877
American Fork, Utah Co., Utah

CHILDREN:
Ann Taylor, 19 May 1822
Thomas Taylor, 1 Jul 1824 (died as a child)
Samuel Taylor, 1 Jul 1832
Sidney, 25 Aug 1834
Alexander, 20 Apr 1837
Harriet Victoria (Buckwalter), 12 Jan 1840
Byron, 12 Jun 1842/1843 (died at age 2)
William, 3 Oct 1844

Hannah was born in 1803 in England, the second of six children. Nothing is known of her childhood, or where she met William Orton. Hannah's mother died just four months after her last child was born. Hannah would have been only twelve years of age. She had much of responsibility with the other children until her father remarried.

Hannah had three children when she married William Orton. She married William while they lived in England, and they must have emigrated as a family. They moved first to Parowan, Utah where they had five more children born to them. One child, Byron died at two years of age, and her first son, Thomas had died as a child.

They spent their life in America residing in Parowan. It was here that Hannah died in 1870. Her husband, William, married again. He married Elizabeth Middlefell Bentley in 1870 or 1872. She was a widow from Lancastershire, England, who had brought her three sons to Utah in 1868.

At her death, Hannah's children put this saying on her stone: "Gone, dear Mother, but not forgotten." She had been a faithful wife, mother and pioneer who helped to settle the area around Parowan, Utah.

JANE HOLMES ORTON

BIRTHDATE: 7 May 1839
Birmingham, England
DEATH: 8 Mar 1909
Parowan, Iron Co., Utah
PARENTS: Josiah Holmes
Jane Gilbert
PIONEER: 11 Sep 1857
Israel Evans Handcart Company
SPOUSE: Alexander Orton
MARRIED: 1 Nov 1857
Cedar City, Iron Co., Utah
DEATH SP: 11 Jun 1915
Parowan, Iron Co., Utah

CHILDREN:
Harriet Maria (Wardell), 30 Mar 1859
Jane Ann (Eyre), 3 Dec 1860
Elizabeth Ellen (Benson), 6 Aug 1862
Alexander Holmes, 6 Feb 1864
Albert Holmes, 7 Nov 1865
Laura (Thornton), 23 Aug 1868
Laurette(Mitchell) 6 Nov 1871
Rosabelle (Durham), 17 Jan 1874
William Henry, 10 Feb 1876
Oscar Josiah, 2 Feb 1878 (died as a child)
Florence May (Mitchell), 27 May 1880
Emma, 4 Feb 1882 (died as an infant)

Jane was born in 1839 in England. She was the fifth of six children born into this family. When Jane was ten her mother was converted and baptized a member of the Church of Jesus Christ of Latter-day Saints, and just a year later her father was baptized along with Jane and her older sister, Elizabeth.

As a young lady, Jane went to work at the Nottingham Lace factory where she worked at the stretchers preparing lace curtains for market. While there, she met a loom worker named Alexander Orton, fell in love and determined to marry.

Both being Mormons, they decided to join the Saints in Utah and then get married. Alex emigrated first in 1856 while Jane kept working. Early in 1857, Alex sent word for Jane to join him in Utah.

At the age of eighteen, Jane and her mother set out for America. They sailed on the ship "George Washington," from Liverpool on March 28, 1857.

Arriving in Boston, they then traveled by train to Iowa City, procured a handcart to hold all the pretty things Jane had made for her dowry and were assigned to the Israel

Evans Handcart Company, and walked and pushed the cart the 1,300 miles to Utah.

Records say this company made a fairly smooth crossing of the Plains. It included 154 souls and thirty-one carts. They arrived in the Salt Lake Valley on September 12, 1857. Jane stayed in Salt Lake City until a handcart company was organized to go south.

They arrived in Cedar City on October 31, 1857. Alex met her there and they were married the next day, November 1, 1857. They lived at Johnston's Fort (Enoch) for two years in a dugout home, and then they moved to Parowan. Here their twelve children were born. By 1863, Jane's father also had come to Parowan, so this couple were surrounded with family members for the remainder of their lives.

Jane Orton was a woman of great faith, courage and talents. She corded, spun, and wove wool and cotton and made it into clothing, including underclothing and her husband's shirts. According to grandchildren, she made the best bread in the world. Her seven daughters learned from her the fine arts of homemaking, cooking, sewing, and housekeeping. She was kind and loving to her family including her husband's other wife and children. She worked in the Primary presidency and as a primary teacher for many years with a reputation for being a great story teller.

Jane was an older woman when electricity finally came to Parowan. A favorite story is told of her listening patiently to her children as they explained her new light switch and how the dial turned round and round, showing the words 'on' and 'off' and how the current was regulated with this wondrous switch. She finally broke in "Oh, I hunderstand all that," in her thick Birmingham English, "but when you come 'ome of a dark night, 'ow do you tell if it's 'hon' or 'hoff?' " We love you Grandma Orton.

Jane passed away in Parowan on March 8, 1909 at the age of sixty-nine years. Her husband lived six years longer. Both are buried in the Parowan Cemetery. They were both brave pioneers who willingly left their homeland for the Gospel they loved.

MARY ANN WARD ORTON

BIRTHDATE: 10 Oct 1814
Burton Avery, Leicester, England
DEATH: 14 Dec 1883
North Ogden, Weber Co., Utah
PARENTS: Bryan Ward
Jane Rice
PIONEER: 10 Oct 1853
Joseph W. Young Wagon Train
SPOUSE: John Orton
MARRIED: 24 Dec 1840
Leicester, Leicester, England
DEATH SP: 9 Jun 1873
Ogden, Weber Co., Utah

CHILDREN:
Sarah Jane, 13 Jun 1842
Joseph, 5 Jan 1845
Thomas "A," 1850 (died in 1851)
Bryan William, 30 Sep 1852
Hyrum James, 2 Jan 1856

Mary Ann was born into a very wealthy family in Leicester, England. She met her future husband at a ball where many of the nobility of England had gathered. On December 24, 1840, they were very quietly married. Her family objected to their wedding because John had been attending the street meetings conducted by Elders from the Church of Jesus Christ of Latter-day Saints.

Mary Ann and John were baptized as members of the Church on April 14, 1844. On February 5, 1853, she and her husband with her three small children, sailed from Liverpool, England. They arrived in New Orleans on March 21, 1853.

From New Orleans, they traveled up the Mississippi River to St. Louis, and then to Keokuk, Iowa. They joined the Joseph W. Young Wagon Company. Most of their journey was made on foot by both the children and adults. They reached Salt Lake Valley on October 10, 1853, just a little more than eight months since they left their homeland.

They moved to E. T. City in Tooele County where they lived until they were advised to move south due to the invasion of Johnston's Army. After the threat was over, they moved the family to North Ogden.

John Orton passed away in June, 1873. Mary Ann grieved so badly at his passing that the bishop gave her a blessing which promised her that she would be consoled.

Mary Ann accomplished a great deal of temple work for her many relatives in the Endowment House. Ten years later, she passed away and was buried at her husband's side in the North Ogden Cemetery.

SARAH ANN DALLEY ORTON

BIRTHDATE: 22 Feb 1848
Keg Creek, Pottawattamie, Iowa
DEATH: 9 Jun 1909
Beaver, Beaver Co., Utah
PARENTS: William Dalley
Mandana Hillman
PIONEER: 21 Sep 1852
Henry Miller Co. Wagon Train
SPOUSE: William Owen Orton
MARRIED: 1 Jan 1865
Summit, Iron Co., Utah
DEATH SP: 9 Nov 1924
Parowan, (buried in Beaver, Utah

CHILDREN:
Harriett Elizabeth (Wilcock), 26 Oct 1865
William Owen Jr., 16 Sep 1866
Moroni Alexander, 2 Nov 1867
Sarah Ann, 26 Mar 1869 (died at 16 months)

Adalinda (Thornton), 25 Nov 1870
Julia Anne (LeFevre), 10 May 1872
Byron Mayhew, 15 Aug 1874
Hannah Mandana (Haycock), 13 Dec 1875
Henry Saddler, 18 Aug 1877
Sylvanus Cyrus, 9 May 1879
Luella Rowena (Linford), 26 Mar 1881
Lenora Caroline, 6 Apr 1883
Grover Cleveland, 7 Feb 1885
Joseph Lawrence, 15 Aug 1886
Walter Fredric, 17 Jul 1888
Celeste (Talbot), 11 Dec 1889
Mary, 21 Apr 1892 (died at age 2)

Sarah Ann was born in 1848 in Keg Creek, Iowa, the eldest child in the family. Her father had heard the Gospel preached in his native England when he was twenty years of age. He was converted, and made plans to sail to America. Sarah Ann was born at a trading point, Kanesville, Pottawattamie, Iowa.

Her parents were living in Nauvoo at the time of the martyrdom of the Prophet Joseph Smith. They left Nauvoo with the body of the Saints and migrated to Utah, settling in Pleasant Grove. Later they helped settle southern Utah.

When Sarah Ann was ten years old, they moved to Summit, Iron County, Utah, where she resided the balance of her childhood. Six children blessed her parent's home and Sarah Ann was given many responsibilities at an early age. She contributed much toward making her the pioneer mother she was destined to become by learning early in life to do her share and more.

On January 1, 1865, Sarah Ann married William Owen Orton at Summit; their marriage was later solemnized in the Endowment House in Salt Lake City on April 3, 1876. They lived in and near Summit until 1882, by which time Sarah Ann had given birth to eleven children.

She was an ambitious and industrious person. She also possessed a sweet and pleasant disposition. During some of the summers, they spent 'ranching' on Summit Mt., where they milked cows and made butter and cheese.

One frightening experience was when her husband had gone to town on business and left her alone with three small children. He was gone longer than expected, so Sarah Ann took her two babies in her arms and, with the other hanging to her skirts, walked to Summit, several miles away. Through the thick timber, she heard the cry of a panther. Afraid that it might attack her, she ran and walked as fast as she could until she was beyond the sound of it. When she and her husband were reunited and returned home, they saw the large footprints of the beast that had followed her down the canyon.

The family owned a farm east of Summit. Sarah Ann made all the clothing worn by the family from the wool from the sheep. She sheared the wool, washed, corded and spun it on her old spinning wheel, then made it into cloth on her hand loom, and then made the clothes by hand. She made her own candles, soap, and took pride in it. She also made quilts, with beautiful patterns which were filled with wool from the sheep. She also covered the floors of their home with homemade carpets. She used everything to its maximum usefulness. She was thrifty, economical, and industrious to the extreme.

In 1882, their home burnt to the ground. They moved to Parowan and established a home for their ten children plus the three born while they lived there. They later traded this farm for land near Panguitch. Moving in March it took three days to make the thirty mile trip because of heavy snow. They hadn't lived there long when this home, too, burned to the ground.

The people of Cleveland a few miles away, came to their rescue and took this family of fourteen children into their homes, provided food, clothing and shelter. They were soon established once again in a home.

This home was on a main highway, so a front room became a small store. The post office was also at this place. Their last two of seventeen children were born here. Their small daughter, Mary, the last of their children, died at the age of two and a half years. By this time, five of their children were happily married with homes of their own. Ten children remained in the home to receive the care and love their mother could give them.

In about 1909, Sarah Ann's health began to fail and she moved to Beaver to the home of her son, Vene. She was diagnosed with a bad heart and dropsy. On June 9, 1909, she passed peacefully to the next life at the age of sixty-one years. She had lived fully and had enjoyed life. At her passing, she left fifteen living children, forty-nine grandchildren, and one great-grandchild. She was buried in the Beaver City Cemetery. Her husband lived until 1924. These were brave pioneers who helped settle Utah. We honor them.

The verse on Sarah's gravestone reads "We shall meet again, sweet mother, in a brighter clime than this. Where the anguish of this world of ours, is lost in deathless bliss':

Her posterity think of her as the Mother in the following poem:

"God made a wonderful mother,

A mother who never grew old.

He made her smile of the sunshine,

And He molded her heart of pure gold.

In her eyes he placed bright shining stars,

In her cheeks, fair roses you see.

God made a wonderful mother,

And he gave that mother to me. "

Author Unknown.

CYNTHIA BUTLER OSBORN

No
Photo
Available

BIRTHDATE: 19 Nov 1811
Gatha, Galia Co., Ohio
DEATH: 2 Jul 1852
Plains near Ft. Carney
PARENTS: Thomas Butler
Mary Robinson
PIONEER:
Thomas D. Howell Wagon Train
SPOUSE: David Osborn
MARRIED: 10 Apr 1828
Owen Co., Indiana
DEATH SP: 12 Jun 1893
Montpelier, Idaho

CHILDREN:
Thomas Jefferson, 20 Feb 1829
Mary Eleanor, 26 Aug 1831
Elizabeth, 31 Aug 1833
William, 29 Nov 1835 (died at age 3)
David, 19 Apr 1838
Nancy Margaret, 8 Mar 1840
Rebecca Ann, 25 Oct 1842
John, 8 Feb 1844
Harriet Jane, 8 Feb 1847
Cynthia Adeline, 4 Oct 1849

Cynthia was the second of eleven children born to her parents. When she was about ten years old, her family moved to Green County, Indiana.

Cynthia married David Osborn when she was sixteen years old. David was a farmer and raised flax as one of his products. He raised sheep, cows, hogs, and had ten beehives. He cleared land for orchards and grazing land.

He provided a wheel and loom for Cynthia so she could provide clothing for her family. After investigating several churches, the doctrine in the Church of Jesus Christ of Latter-day Saints received their attention in 1835, and they were baptized in Black Creek.

In the Fall of 1836, they moved to Missouri. Cynthia's health was greatly affected by the hardships and birth of most of her children. She was confined to her bed many times. Their family and friends begged them to return home and accept their help, but Cynthia and David always refused with reasons of devotion to the Church.

They were driven from Nauvoo and went to Garden Grove where they built a cabin and put in a crop. They did not reach Council Bluffs until June 5, 1847 where they remained for five years and where Cynthia gave birth to her tenth child.

In 1852, they joined the Thomas D. Howell Wagon Company and were on their way to Salt Lake Valley. Cynthia's health worsened and they delayed their start in hopes she would improve. She gave birth to an stillborn infant in June of 1852, and two weeks later, she died along the Platte River about 250 miles west of the Missouri River.

Her husband said of her, "This terminated the life of my old and worthy companion. . . a life which had been checkered with many afflictions, hardships, and anxieties and now she is where the weary pilgrims are at rest. We lived together twenty-four years, two months, and twenty-two days. . . and justice here requires that I should say, she was kind-hearted, an affectionate mother, and was truthful, industrious, cleanly and strictly virtuous."

ELLEN STANDLEY OSBORN

No
Photo
Available

BIRTHDATE: 8 Apr 1833
Suffield, Portage Co., Ohio
DEATH: 17 Jun 1861
Bountiful, Davis Co., Utah
PARENTS: Alexander Standley
Philinder Abalona Upson
PIONEER: 9 Sep
Capt. Howell Co. Wagon Train
SPOUSE: Thomas J. Osborn
MARRIED: 14 Sep 1851
Garden Grove, Iowa
DEATH SP: 10 Jun 1861
Echo Canyon

CHILDREN:
Cynthia Adaline, 26 Oct 1852 (died as a child)
Martha Ellen, 15 May 1854 (died as an infant)
Mary Elizabeth, 12 May 1855 (died as a child)
Lydia (Hall), 3 Jan 1857
Sarah (Wilson), 5 Jul 1859
Thomas Jefferson, 1 Jun 1861 (died as an infant)

Ellen was born in Ohio in 1833. When she was a child,her family moved to Far West, then Nauvoo in the spring of 1840. Ellen was baptized on April 8, 1841.

The family left Nauvoo, in February, 1846, to cross the Plains. They started with George Miller's Wagon Company. They stayed for a time in Pottawattamie County, Iowa, where Ellen taught school before her marriage and worked very hard to make her own clothes with a great deal of hand work to make them attractive.

Ellen was married on September 14, 1851 to Thomas Jefferson Osborn, in Garden Grove, Iowa. They finally arrived in the Salt Lake Valley on September 9, 1852. They first settled in Weber County, and put up a house there where their first child was born.

They soon moved to the fort because of the Indian troubles. Her husband took a second wife, Ellen's sister, in 1854. Their second child was born on May 14, 1854 and died on May 31st. In that same year in December, Ellen's father died. Soon after, their daughter, Cynthia, became ill and died leaving them without a child. On May 12, 1855, Mary Elizabeth was born. Ellen and Thomas received their endowments on March 8, 1856. Thomas was called to be a Bishop and performed his first wedding ceremony, December 25, 1857.

In 1859, Ellen's father had died, and there was a division of his estate. From this, Ellen and her sister, Elizabeth, received $713.00 and ten acres of land, one house, one steer, and one cow, one wagon and harness.

While he was on duty in Echo Canyon in 1861, Thomas contacted a very bad cold. He passed away, June 10, 1861, leaving a new born son just ten days old. His death was too much for Ellen in her weakened condition, and child fever set in. After his burial, she went to her mother's place in Bountiful. She only lived until the next day and died on June 17, 1861, at the age of twenty-eight years. The baby, Thomas Jefferson Jr., lived only until October 31, and died and was buried by his parents' side.

Ellen was a very industrious woman, made almost everything she used for her family. She had given birth to six children and two only survived to adulthood. Lydia and Sarah were cared for by their mother's mother, and were married in 1873 and 1876.

Ellen Osborn went through untold trials and for her religious beliefs. She was a great pioneer woman of faith and fortitude indeed.

NANCY THORN OSBORN

No
Photo
Available

BIRTHDATE: 24 Oct 1841
Summerhill Twp., Pennsylvania
DEATH: 6 Apr 1918
Rexburg, Madison Co., Idaho
PARENTS: Asahel Thorn
Sarah Lester
PIONEER: Sep 1853
Joseph Thorn Co. Wagon Train
SPOUSE: David Osborn, III
MARRIED: 25 Dec 1857
3 Mile Creek, Box Elder, Utah
DEATH SP: 4 Feb 1917
Rexburg, Madison Co., Idaho

CHILDREN:
David Ashael, 4 Sep 1859
Cynthia Abigail (Bird), 6 Jan 1861
Sarah Blanca (Young), 1 Feb 1863
Mary Marvelia (Phelps), 13 Jan 1865
Lydia Jane (Thomson), 11 Mar 1867
Nancy Adaline (Orson), 26 Apr 1869
Margaret Ann (Eckersley), 20 Jul 1871
Jefferson Lester, 18 Oct 1873
William Wallace, 14 Feb 1876
John Richard, 18 Nov 1877
Issac Melvin, 7 Apr 1880
Glen Milton, 1 Jan 1887

Nancy was born, October 24, 1841, in Summer hill Township, Crawford County, Pennsylvania, the seventh of ten children. The family moved to Illinois, settled near Nauvoo and later joined the Church of Jesus Christ of Latter-day Saints. Nancy's father helped complete the Nauvoo Temple and the family left with the Saints in 1845, to Mt. Pisgah, staying in Iowa for seven years. After her

father and brother returned from the California gold rush, her mother died in 1851. In 1853, the family continued to the Salt Lake Valley.

Nancy's family settled in Three Mile Creek (Perry), Box Elder County, Utah, where she met her David Osborn, III, whom she married in 1857, she being sixteen and he nineteen years old. They packed their joint possessions in a wash tub and traveled to their first home in Uintah, Utah.

Nancy was well and ambitious and knew the hardships as well as the arts of pioneer life such as shearing sheep, carding and spinning yarn, dying and weaving cloth and making clothing and carpets. She made tallow candles, soap and molasses, cheese and butter.

In Uintah, they were among the pioneers who went south during the threatened invasion of Johnston's Army. They returned to Hyrum, Cache Valley, being called to pioneer the area.

In 1865, Nancy moved with her husband and four children to Montpelier, Idaho. Here they completed their family of twelve children when Nancy was forty-six years old and at fifty-one, she took her grandson, David Robert Young, to raise as her own after the death of her daughter, Sarah.

Moving to a larger home, Nancy's husband tried to provide things to make her work lighter and life more enjoyable for all. They were first in that community to have a cook stove to cook on instead of a fireplace, a kerosene lamp instead of candles, an organ, a sewing machine and a white top buggy to ride in, which was a luxury in those days.

In 1895, they moved to Rexburg, Idaho where they operated a hotel, The Osborn House. Her greatest joy was having her family and grandchildren around her on all occasions.

Osborn was a good neighbor and friend to all and is remembered as one of God's ideal women. She did not have the educational advantages that her children had, but she read a great deal, especially the church works, so that she became well versed in Mormonism which was very dear to her. She had the privilege of going to the   temple and serving chiefly in the Relief Society and it's presidency.

On April 6, 1918, she passed away in her sleep, just as peaceful in death as she was in life. She was buried in Rexburg, Idaho.

ANNE BRYAN or BRAND OSBORNE

No
Photo
Available

BIRTHDATE: 22 May 1812
Baronville, Glasgow, Lanark,
Scotland
DEATH: 11 Sep 1868
Coaville, Summit Co., Utah
PARENTS: No record
PIONEER: 8 Aug 1851
John Gillespie Co., Wagon Train
SPOUSE: Allen Osborne
MARRIED: 26 Nov 1830
Kilmarnock, Ayr, Scotland
DEATH SP: 25 Jul 1854
Scotland

CHILDREN:
Cunningham C., 5 Sep 1831
Allen, 7 Nov 1833
Annie (Clark), 30 Mar 1842
James, 14 Jul 1844
John, 18 Sep 1846
Mary, 7 Jul 1849
George, 8 Aug 1851

Anne was born in May 22, 1812, in Glasgow, Lanark, Scotland. She married Allen Osborne November 26, 1830 in Kilmarnock, Scotland. They had seven children, all born in Scotland except for their daughter, Annie. She was born in New London, Ontario, Canada.

Anne had gone to Canada as a young bride to be with her husband who was a wool commissioner or buyer for the government.

Anne and her husband joined the Church of Jesus Christ of Latter-day Saints on December 14, 1848, in Glasgow, Scotland. Allen passed away on July 25, 1854, in Scotland.

After his death, Anne age fifty-six, immigrated to America on June 24, 1868 on the ship, "Constitution," with her daughter, Annie, age twenty-five. They traveled to Utah with John Gillespie Wagon Company in 1868.

Anne did not live to see the Salt Lake Valley. She passed away en route to the Salt Lake Valley, in Coalville, Summit County, Utah of cholera. She was buried in an unmarked grave at the campsite.

Anne, her daughter, continued on the next morning alone. The company arrived on September 15, 1868, in Salt Lake City, Utah.

Seven children had been born to Anne and Allen. Only Annie, their first daughter, lived to maturity.

PHILINDA UPSON STANDLEY OSBORN

BIRTHDATE: 1 Aug 1814
Randolph, Ohio
DEATH: 27 Jan 1892
Richmond, Cache Co., Utah
PARENTS: Freeman Upson
Sarah Culver
PIONEER: 27 Sep 1852
Thomas D. Howell Wagon Train
SPOUSE I: Alexander Standley
MARRIED: 19 Mar 1829
Suffield Ohio
DEATH SP: 29 Dec 1854
Bountiful, Davis Co., Utah

CHILDREN:
Eliza, 16 Apr 1830
Franklin, 19 Aug 1831
Ella, 8 Apr 1833
Martha, 20 Sep 1834
Alexander Henry, 28 Apr 1836
Elizabeth (Benson), 7 Mar 1838
Cyrene (Merrill), 1 May 1840
Philinda (Burnham), 19 Mar 1842
Sarah Alvira (Pace), 26 May 1844
Lydia (Burnham), 13 Dec 1846
Michael. 7 May 1849

SPOUSE II: David Osborn
MARRIED: Not given
DEATH SP: Not given
CHILDREN: None

Philinda was born in Ohio, 1814. She married Alezander Scoby Standley in 1829. She had eleven children. Two of her children died young.

Tradition says that she was a member of the first Relief Society organized by President Joseph Smith. Her name is not on the original role. However, minutes of the second year show her name listed as proposing "that she would give every tenth pound of flax and also one quart of milk per day for the building of the temple." She and her husband were able to receive their endowments in the Nauvoo Temple on January 30, 1846.

The family left Nauvoo in 1846 and went to Punca, Nebraska. In the Spring of 1847, they went to Winter Quarters, then in 1848, they moved across the Missouri River into Iowa. Here they accumulated twenty milk cows and sheep. They crossed the Plains in 1852, arriving on October 30, 1852. They brought the first dairy herd into Utah.

Two years after arriving in Utah, Philinda's husband passed away, 1854, in Bountiful, Utah. She and her family were left with the dairy farm to manage.

In 1865, she married David Osborn and moved to Hyrum. Later, they were separated, by mutual consent. Philinda passed away on January 27, 1892, in Richmond, Cache County, Utah.

LYDIA ROPER OSGUTHORPE

BIRTHDATE: 4 Feb 1828
Sheffield, Yorkshire, England
DEATH: 2 Mar 1915
East Mill Creek, Salt Lake, Utah
PARENTS: Abel Roper
Sarah Mosley
PIONEER: 4 Sep 1853
Charles Wilkin Co. Wagon Train
SPOUSE: John Osguthorpe
MARRIED: 13 Oct 1846
Sheffield, Yorkshire, England
DEATH SP: 13 Apr 1884
East Mill Creek, Salt Lake, Utah

CHILDREN;
Sara Ann (Bitner), 23 May 1847
Emma, 18 Aug 1850 (died at 8 months)
Priscilla Miranda, 21 May 1852
Hannah, 20 Dec 1854 (died at age 16)
John Henry 2 Feb 1857
Lydia (Stillman), 6 Aug 1859
Abel Roper, 16 Mar 1862 (died at age 2)
Thomas, 8 Jun 1864
Joseph, 14 Dec 1866
Selina, 11 Aug 1869
Irvin Kitson, 26 Jan 1872 (died as a child)

Lydia was born in 1828 in England; one of seven children in this family. When two years of age, Lydia and her parents came to America and settled in Philadelphia, Pennsylvania. While the children were still small, Lydia's father died and was buried in Pennsylvania. Her mother, having no means of support for her small family, returned to England. There, at the age of nine years, Lydia was hired out as a nursemaid to help support the family. Later she worked in the polishing room of a cutlery establishment in Sheffield. It is said she met her future husband there.

Lydia married John Osguthorpe in England on October 30, 1846, when she was eighteen years of age. Their first child, Sara Ann, was born while they were living in England. When she was eighteen months of age, the family again crossed the ocean for America. They lived in Pennsylvania to be near Lydia's sister. Lydia's three ocean voyages had been enjoyable for her, and she claimed she was never seasick and hoped she could make the voyage again someday. Two daughters were born to them in Philadelphia, and one died at nine months of age.

In 1851, Elders from the Church of Jesus Christ of Latter-day Saints converted John and Lydia to the Church. By April, 1853, this family began their journey to the Salt Lake Valley with the Charles Wilkins Company. They arrived in the Salt Lake Valley on September 4, 1853 and settled in the East Mill Creek area.

They first lived at the Alexander Place, a hollow, by the creek. They later moved into their own home which was quite luxurious for that day. The bedroom had bright blue woodwork with white washed walls, with white Swiss curtains at the windows, and they had a four poster bed with a white valance and a dressing table with a cover and valance of Dolly Varden material.

Lydia often walked ten miles to Salt Lake City. She was a woman of courage, and is credited with saving the mill which caught fire. They were half owners in the mill on the Mill Creek stream. When it caught fire, she jumped into the cold water up to her waist, and threw water on the flames. Another day she had nothing to feed her family, so she trudged to Neff's mill, a mile and a half away to see if she could get some meal. They had sold out. Starting back home with a heavy heart, she stopped to pray to ask the Lord what to do. When she looked up, before her in the road was a large bag of meal that had been split open and some of the contents were on the ground. She did not take the bag, but gathered some of the spilled contents and put them into her apron, but left the bag for its rightful owner. She was able to feed her family that night.

Their mill was operated for many years. Lydia took an active part in the Church, and worked and helped build the community. She sang in the choir for thirty-five years, and was counselor in the Relief Society for thirty years. She was ever faithful to her duties, and had an ever abiding faith in her religion which meant so much to her.

MARY GEORGINA HUCKVALE OSMOND

BIRTHDATE: 7 May 1836
Oxford, England
DEATH: 14 Mar 1922
Bloomington, Idaho
PARENTS: James Huckvale
Mary Worville
PIONEER: 1856
SPOUSE: George Osmond
MARRIED: Jul 1855
St. Louis, St. Louis Co., Missouri
DEATH SP: 25 Mar 1913
Afton, Wyoming

CHILDREN:
Clara, 4 Dec 1856
Anson, 18 Apr 1858
Alfred, 5 Oct 1861
Rosabell, 8 Jan 1864
Ira, 2 Mar 1866
Ida Ann, 26 Feb 1869
Ella, 18 Jan 1872
Nellie, 2 Jun 1875
Georgina, 2 Jul 1877 (died at 5 months)
Alice Maud, 16 Sep 1879

Georgina remembered living on a farm when she was six or seven years of age. Her father leased the grazing land for his large herd of sheep. When she was nine years of age, the family fortunes changed. The sheep were stricken with a strange disease and losses were heavy.

When she was thirteen, Georgina was apprenticed to a dressmaker where she learned to knit lace and other needlecraft that was popular at the time. She met George Osmond who was a convert to the Church of Jesus Christ of Latter-day Saints and was determined to emigrate to the United States. He converted Georgina, then went alone to the states where he worked a year to pay for her passage to America.

When Georgina arrived in St. Louis, they were married in July of 1855. George drove a team of oxen to the Salt Lake Valley where he arrived in 1856.

They went to live in Bountiful with Anson Call. George helped out on Anson's farm and Georgina helped in the house. They found a small house in Bountiful and George became a teacher. Georgina helped out by sewing and doing extra work. They later homesteaded at Willard.

Georgina attended meetings in Willard and became involved in Relief Society, especially in nursing and caring for the sick. In 1864, they were called by the authorities to go to the Bear Lake Valley. Their first winter was spent at North Creek which is now called Liberty.

They soon moved to Bloomington, where George spent most of the winter teaching school in Bountiful. Georgina was a good cook and manager. She enjoyed helping in the community and church. She often gave of her time and means.

When plural marriage was emphasized and George was requested to take another wife, it took years for Georgina to give her consent. When the second wife moved into her own home, Georgina attended her at the birth of her first child. George and Amelia moved to Star Valley when a call came to George to do so. Georgina and her children stayed in Bloomington.

Georgina's health began to fail and she passed away on March 14, 1922, shortly after her daughters had provided an eighty-sixth birthday celebration for her. She was a devoted wife and mother, a nurse to the sick and ailing, and a woman of faith and high ideals.

MARY ANN TAYLOR OSTERHOUT

BIRTHDATE: 8 Sep 1844
Keokuk, Lee Co., Iowa
DEATH
PARENTS: Benjamin Taylor
Mary Ann Fenner
PIONEER: 1859
Ellwood Stevenson Wagon Train
SPOUSE: John Osterhout
MARRIED: 8 Mar 1862
Willard, Box Elder Co., Utah
DEATH SP:

CHILDREN:
John Carlos, 27 Jan 1864
Benjamin, 12 Apr 1866
Betsy Ann (Allen), 26 Aug 1868

Thomas, 8 Dec 1870
Mary Ann Bigler), 2 Nov 1873
Sarah Eveline, 1 May 1876 (died as an infant)
Rosa Ethel, 10 Nov 1878 (died as a child)
Jesse Appolos, 21 Oct 1882
Merritt Adelbert, 20 Mar 1888

Mary Ann's parents joined Church of Jesus Christ of Latter-day Saints in England and united with the Saints in the move to Zion.

Mary Ann left Nauvoo and traveled with her family in the Ellwood Stevenson Company and settled at Willard, Utah in 1859. Enroute Mary Ann and some other girls went swimming. It made Mary Ann ill, and she was sick for the remainder of the trip.

Mary Ann and John remained in Willard after their marriage where there first four children John, Benjamin, Betsy, and Thomas were born. They moved north to Portage where Mary Ann was born. In 1876, they moved to Snowville where Eveline and Rosa were born. How Mary Ann's heart must have ached when these two babies both died.

The Osterhouts next moved on to the Snake River to a place called Bonanza Bar. Sometime between 1879 and 1882, the family moved to Elba and filed on a homestead. It was here the last of their nine children Jesse and Merritt were born.

Mary Ann was a very industrious woman. Her quilt linings and carpet rags were very beautiful and dyed with the yellow blossoms of the match weed. She made her soap and candles with beef or mutton tallow. She poured the hot fat into molds that held several candles. She churned all her own butter, and when there was some to spare it was sold to buy other supplies,

Mary Ann was a very good cook. She was especially noted for her cakes, which she often served with butter instead of icing because John preferred them that way. She helped cure their own hams and smoke the bacon. Salt brine was used for preserving meat.

Mary Ann operated the Post Office from her home. She was kept busy cleaning up the mud people tracked in. The mail came from Kelton, Utah at the time. Mary Ann was most hospitable. Everyone was welcome at their table and also offered lodging.

When John brought home a plural wife, Mary Ann informed him, "Either she goes or I do." So, he turned the buggy around and took his second wife back to Willard.

Mary Ann passed away on October 8, 1914, Elba, Cassia County, Idaho. She is buried in the Elba Cemetery. The following is inscribed on the grave marker,

"No pains, no griefs, no anxious fears

can reach our loved one sleeping here."

ANNA BEAGLEY OSTLER

No
Photo
Available

BIRTHDATE: 14 Aug 1842
Newton Valence, England
DEATH: 18 Aug 1874
Nephi, Juab Co., Utah
PARENTS: William Beagley
Mary Ann Feilder
PIONEER:
SPOUSE: David Ostler
MARRIED: 1861
DEATH SP: 9 Sep 1911
Salt Lake City, Salt Lake, Utah

CHILDREN
Sarah Ellen, 16 Nov 1862
Mary Ann, 30 Apr 1864
Oliver, 21 Aug 1865
Agnes, 16 Sep 1866 (died at age 2)
Emily, 29 May 1868
David John, 4 Mar 1870
Joseph, 16 Nov 1872
Annie, 8 Aug 1874 (died at 1 month)

Anna Beagley was born in Newton Valence, Hampshire, England in 1842 in a humble thatched cottage to poor parents who farmed for their livelihood. It was a life that trained her from childhood to be able to face the trials and hardships that would come to her on the frontier.

When Anna, at age sixteen, joined the Church of Jesus Christ of Latter-day Saints, her sisters were so furious with her they turned her out of their home. (Later her mother and two brothers would join the Church, also).

In 1961, when she was nineteen, the strong minded Anna sailed from Liverpool, England on the ship "Manchester," April 16th, in a group of three hundred and eighty converts for a one month voyage to New York. She traveled alone having promised Mr. Burmingham she would marry him upon her arrival in Utah.

The group of travelers reached Florence, Nebraska and faced a dilemma. The Perpetual Emigration Funds were depleted and they must find work and money to live on and outfit themselves for their trek. The shock was softened by the information that Mr. Burmingham had taken himself a wife, and she was free, she could marry David Ostler. The two young people had fallen in love. By mid-summer they were ready and began the journey across the land. Before they reached the Valley, David and Anna were married by Captain Hooper who was in charge of their company on the Plains.

When Mr. Burmingham arrived with his first wife on his arm to claim Anna as his second, she surprised him instead, by introducing him to her husband, David Ostler. There was another reunion, David's two brothers, William and George had come to Utah two years before.

After the first winter, spent in Salt Lake City, they were called in the spring to Nephi with other members of the Ostler family.

They built a one-room home with one window, one door and left the hardened earth for a floor. Their bed was made from poles, rope for springs and a straw filled tick was their mattress. In this humble place Anna gave birth to the first of her eight children. When it rained pans were set to catch the water coming through the roof near the new mother. David did the washing by candle light after his chores were done and his consideration allowed Anna to fully regain her health and strength.

They built a larger home complete with a carpeted floor and later on a cellar for the preservation of food. They cleared sage brush and began a small farm. Even the children participated in the venture.

Life dealt them stunning blows along with their successes. Their little Agnes died from the scarlet fever epidemic of 1868 when she was two years old, the next year, little Emily nearly drowned in an irrigation ditch.

Anna had her eighth child when she was thirty-two years old, she had passed through too many hardships and she died ten days after Annie's birth. The baby, without a mothers tender care was called to join her mother in about six weeks.

David remarried to have a mother for his orphaned children who grew to adulthood and had families that contributed to their communities and to history, evidence of their parents sacrifice and faith.

DOROTHY HOWARTH BEAGLEY OSTLER

BIRTHDATE: 7 Jun 1849
Manchester, Lancashire, England
DEATH: 28 Mar 1920
Tooele, Tooele Co., Utah
PIONEER: 3 Sep 1868
Wagon Train Company
PARENTS: Benjamin Howarth
Ellen Gregory
SPOUSE I: John Beagley
MARRIED: 24 Dec 1868
Divorced 29 Oct 1871
DEATH SP: Not given

CHILDREN:
Mary Ellen, (died as an infant)
John William, 14 Nov 1870

SPOUSE II: John C. Ostler
MARRIED: 9 Jun 1873
Salt Lake City, Salt Lake Co., Utah
DEATH SP: 17 Aug 1913

CHILDREN:
Earl Howarth, 8 Sep 1873
Willard Howarth, 1 Feb 1876

Fredrick Howarth, 5 Aug 1878
Mary Ellen, 2 Sep 1880
Moroni Howarth, 9 Jun 1883
Elizabeth Ann, 18 Jan 1886
Alice, 1 Jan 1889
Ephraim Howarth, 14 Dec 1891

Dorothy Howarth Beagley Ostler was born April 7, 1849, in Manchester, Lancashire, England.

Dorothy went to work in the woolen mills at the age of six years. Sometime during her very tender years she was caught in some machinery and cut from hip to hip. The law of England required that a doctor was to be called in case of accidents, so the doctor came, taped her body together and left. He had concluded that she could not live.

Her family had joined the Church of Jesus Christ of Latter-day Saints before this time and they believe that it was through their faith and the power of the priesthood that she was healed.

Later on, a sickness broke out among the children of the community and many died. The father, Benjamin, had no faith in the medicine left by the doctor. He dumped it out and gave the children consecrated oil instead.

Father, Benjamin, left for America with two of the older children before his wife and the younger children were able to go. He was able to rejoin them soon after they reached the Salt Lake Valley.

When the mother, Ellen, crossed the Plains with her children, she buried one of her daughters along the trail at a place called 'The Muddy'. Within a few days of her arrival in the Valley, another child, the youngest, died and was buried in the cemetery in Salt Lake City.

The father was soon able to join the family. He had worked his way to Utah by driving sheep from the east for Brigham Young. The city of Nephi, Utah became the home of this family.

Soon after they had settled there, Dorothy married John Beagley one of the teamsters who had driven them across the Plains. Her first home was a dugout, and her first cupboard was a box with a curtain made from one of her skirts. Her first child, a little girl named Mary Ellen died soon after birth. The second child, a son, John William, survived and lived to raise a large family.

Difficulties arose between Dorothy and her husband after he had married a second wife. They were divorced on October 29, 1871. John William was given to Dorothy's parents to raise.

After some time, Dorothy married John C. Ostler as his second wife. He already had one wife, Mary Ann Prince, and several children. Dorothy and John became the parents of eight children. Dorothy's life was hard with little financial support, but she very seldom complained.

Dorothy loved the church. She loved the beautiful church hymns, which gave her hope and she sang them often. She was a strong believer in the word of wisdom and

passed this belief on to her children. No matter how hard times were for her or how limited her finances, she paid tithing to the last required penny. She was as generous as it was possible for her to be with her fast offering. She served for nine years in the presidency of the Fountain Green Relief Society.

Dorothy passed away on March 28, 1920 in Tooele, Tooele County, Utah.

SARAH ENDACOTT GOLLOP OSTLER

BIRTHDATE: 7 May 1809
Stoke Abbott, England
DEATH: 24 Apr 1872
Nephi, Juab Co., Utah
PARENTS: Thomas Gollop
Agnes Endacott
PIONEER: 1861
Claudius Spencer Wagon Train
SPOUSE: John Ostler
MARRIED: 6 Jun 1830
Bridport, Dorset, England
DEATH SP: 25 Aug 1869
Salt Lake City, Salt Lake, Utah

CHILDREN:
Jonathan, 23 Feb 1831
William, 14 May 1833 (died as an infant)
William Golakher, 3 Mar 1835
Sarah A., 26 Feb 1837 (died as an infant)
John, 5 Jun 1838
George Gallacher, 21 Feb 1840
David, 28 Sep 1842
Oliver Radford, 10 Oct 1844
Sarah Ann, 28 Aug 1846
Mary, 28 Sep 1849

Sarah's parents were not married. She was raised with the name of her mother, Endacott. Her mother had sued Thomas Gollop for the keep of her child.

On June 6, 1830, Sarah married John Ostler in Bridport, England. Sarah, her husband, and many of their relatives joined the Church of Jesus Christ of Latter-day Saints in 1847 and were a part of the Bridport Branch of the Church.

In the Spring of 1859, two of the sons, William and George, left for Utah. John, Sarah, and the rest of their family sailed on the ship, "Manchester," in 1861 landing in New York on May 14, 1861. They sailed up the Missouri River on their way to the outfitting point at Florence, Nebraska, where they learned the funds they had paid at the General Office at Liverpool for their outfits to cross the Plains had not arrived due to a mistake. They were without food, shelter, or means with which to cross the Plains.

Their leader Claudius V. Spencer arranged for their employment with the Telegraph Company. They worked and earned good wages as they traveled by wagon across the Plains. Her husband, John, worked for the Telegraph

Company Salt Lake City setting up this communication system.

They stayed in the Salt Lake Valley for the first winter. In the Spring of 1862, they moved to Nephi in Juab County. They lived on a piece of ground that was referred to as "Ostler Block" between 1st and 2nd East and between 4th and 5th South.

Sarah and John went to Salt Lake City for medical help for John inasmuch as he suffered from consumption, but the disease took his life on August 25, 1869. Sarah returned to Nephi where she passed away three years later.

MARIA KAISA JOHNSON OTTERSTROM (MAJA CAJSA JONSSON)

BIRTHDATE: 25 Jan 1825
Nyed, Vaffnland, Sweden
DEATH: 2 Sep 1897
Ephraim, Sanpete Co., Utah
PARENTS: John Nielson
Maria / Maja Jonsson
PIONEER: 20 Sep 1856
Canute Peterson Wagon Train
SPOUSE: Jonas Otterstrom
MARRIED: 1845
Sweden
DEATH SP: 1884
Ephraim, Sanpete Co., Utah

CHILDREN;
Johan, 6 Aug 1846
Stine Marie (Hyde), 16 Mar 1848
John Henry, 24 Mar 1850
Augusta, 5/6 Aug 1852
Augusta Kaisa, 19 Aug 1853
Josephine (Cramer), 21 Oct 1855
Louisa (Oveson), 16 Feb 1858
Joseph, 14 Dec 1859
Caroline, 13 Sep 1861
Brigham, 29 Jan 1864

Maria Kaisa was born on January 25, 1825 in Sweden. Maria was the first of four wives of a polygamous marriage. She bore ten children, four of whom reached adulthood.

As early settlers in Ephraim, they often contended with Indians. Doors in many homes were equipped with heavy wooden bars to guard against Indian intruders when the men were absent.

Maria Kaisa spent many hours making beautiful watch fobs, necklaces, flowers and pictures from human hair. It was such a fine art it required an excellent eye to accomplish it. She was precise in all her work and even the mending and darning were done to perfection.

Maria Kaisa passed away at the age of seventy-two on September 2, 1897 in Ephraim, Sanpete County, Utah.

ELSIE CHRISTINE ANDERSEN OTTESEN (ELIZAH / ELESE KRISITINE JENSEN)

BIRTHDATE: 24 Jul 1825
Borup, Vraa Parish, Denmark
DEATH: 10 Dec 1914
Fountain Green, Sanpete, Utah
PARENTS: Jens Andersen
Anne Jensen
PIONEER: 7 Sep 1855
Capt. Jacob Secrist Wagon
Train
SPOUSE: Christen Ottesen
MARRIED: 1854
on board ship to America
DEATH SP: 28 Sep 1906
Fountain Green, Sanpete, Utah

CHILDREN:
James "Jens," 18 Jan 1857
Joseph Smith, 15 Dec 1858
Christian, 12 Mar 1861
Antone, 6 Oct 1862
Stenie Lorinda, 12 Mar 1864
John Christian, 9 Sep 1866
Anna (Bigler), 6 Nov 1870

Elsie Christine was born July 24, 1825 in Borup, Vraa Parish, Hjorring, Denmark. Elsie joined the Church of Jesus Christ of Latter Day Saints while living in Denmark. Her father, who owned a distillery, disapproved of her joining the Church. He gave her what was to be her share of the business and told her good-bye.

Elsie left Denmark in 1854 at the age of twenty-nine and sailed for America. She became ill while on the ship. Elsie met and married Christen Ottesen as they traveled en route to America and Zion.

After arriving in the Salt Lake Valley in 1855, they were asked to establish a town called Uintah Creek, later known as Fountain Green, Utah.

While raising their family they had many encounters with the Indians. They were known for their fine crops, gardens, horses and dairy products which Elsie would often sell. She gathered wool, carded it, wove it and made clothes for her family.

When polygamy was introduced, Christen took another wife. Elsie lived alone and worked hard to support her family. She later lived with her sons.

Elsie died at the age of eighty-nine in Fountain Green, Utah.

JOHANNA SORENSSON OTTESEN

BIRTHDATE: 15 Oct 1839
Aarrarp, Malmohus, Sweden
DEATH: 20 Feb 1922
Manti, Sanpete Co., Utah
PARENTS: Nils Sorensson
Anna Marie Nilsson
PIONEER: 24 Sep, 1860
Oscar Stoddard Handcart Comp.
SPOUSE: Jens Ottesen
MARRIED: 18 Nov 1860
DEATH SP: 27 Apr 1884
Goshen, Utah Co. Utah

CHILDREN:
Anne Martina, 15 Nov 1861
Otto 27 Jul 1863
Jessie (Crista), 31 Mar 1866
Nephi, 17 Apr 1870

Johanna Sorensson was born in Sweden in 1839, one of ten children. The Sorensson's were of the Lutheran Faith however, upon hearing the Gospel from the Mormon Elders, they accepted it, but not Johanna. When she could see that her family was determined, she too was baptized and came to America.

She was twenty-one years old when her family joined the Handcart Company in Florence, Nebraska for the long, long trek across prairies, through rivers over muddy trails when it rained and dusty trails when it did not. At the last, after eleven weeks and three days they came into the Salt Lake Valley, worn, tired and in triumph, the last of the pioneers to cross with handcarts.

Her family settled in Goshen, Utah where she met, was courted by and married the widower Jens Ottesen within two months of her arrival. Their first two children were born in Goshen, then, moving to Salina in 1865-1866, they fashioned a dugout on their small farm and were ready for the birth of their third child, Jessie "Crista."

The Indians fought the settlers fiercely for two years, burning them out, and driving off the live stock. Jens Sorensson was killed, and the John Given family was found. The parents had been shot, the adult son and three little girls killed with tomahawks and all had been stripped of their clothing, their food and bedding was gone. The settlers were told to abandon their farms and retreat to Fort Gunnison where Johanna and Jens had their last child.

When later, Jen's brother, Hans, offered to rent Jens his farm in Manti, the offer was quickly accepted and in 1873 they were, at last, settled.

Johanna was a surprising woman. She had a skill with the hand loom and wove all kinds of cloth and carpets. She was handy with the knitting machine making socks of all kinds, and she had great strength. She was in constant demand during the sheep shearing season. It was said that she could shear more sheep than any man in that part of the country and she would walk from her home to the shearing corral before day break, then back home in the evening.

She was paid for her work with wool, which she would wash, card and spin into a fine thread of wool yarn. All the members of her family wore stockings and socks knit from this wool. The cloth she wove was used for mens and women's clothing. The soap she made was bought by others and the carpets she walked on were made by her own hand

Johanna did Temple work as fervently as she did physical work, doing the temple ordinances for about 1,500 people in the Manti Temple.

She passed away at the age of eighty-three years in the winter of 1922 and those that dressed her in her burial clothes remarked upon the callous marks on her shoulders, worn there by the straps of the handcart she had pulled across the Plains those many years ago.

JENSINE CHRISTINE JENSEN OVERSON

No
Photo
Available

BIRTHDATE: 17 May 1841
Frederickshaven, Denmark
DEATH: 19 Aug/Sep 1879
Oak City, Millard Co., Utah
PARENTS: Jens Larsen
Christiane Marie Jacobsen
PIONEER: 1 Oct 1862
Joseph Horne Wagon Train
SPOUSE: Christian Overson
MARRIED: 16 Nov 1862
Mt. Pleasant, Sanpete Co., Utah
DEATH SP: 12 Jun 1924
Leamington, Millard Co., Utah

CHILDREN:
Joseph, 18 Sep 1863
Hyrum Frederick, 11 Aug 1865
Emma (Nielson), 23 Apr 1868
Mary Ann (Strange), 17 Dec 1871
Sine Christine, 25 Jul 1874
James Christian, 10 Jan 1876

Jensine was born May 17 1941 in Denmark. She grew up in Denmark where she was converted to the Church of Jesus Christ of Latter Day Saints along with her family.

When her mother, brothers and sisters emigrated to Utah, Jensine and Kirsten remained in Denmark to earn money for the trip. They came the following year with their Uncle Frederick Jacobsen's family. They sailed on the ship "Franklin" with the John Murdock Company. Three adults and forty-three children died on the journey.

At Florence, Nebraska, Christian Overson was assigned to look after the sick. He discovered both girls in bed. Kirsten was dead and Jensine was very sick with cholera. Kirsten was buried and he took care of Jensine until she recovered. They left to cross the Plains on July 29, 1862 and arrived in Salt Lake City, October 1, 1862.

Jensine and Christian Overson were married at the home of her mother in Mt. Pleasant, Utah on November 16, 1862. They made their home in Fillmore and then were called to settle Deseret where they helped build a fort.

While her husband was away working in the mines in Nevada, Jensine managed to stretch her supplies and care for her family. She saved an accidentally chopped off finger from young Frederick, drove away a bold cowboy who came to steal a cow from her yard and sent a rebellious Indian from her home with the big six gun.

They lived the United Order while they were in Oak City.

Jensine was a courageous and dedicated woman. We are not sure what caused her death at the young age of thirty-eight years, but her oldest son, Joseph, was ill with typhoid fever shortly afterwards. Jensine passed away in 1879 in Oak City, Millard County, Utah.

SALLY RAE WHITLOCK ROGERS OVIATT

BIRTHDATE: 9 Oct 1828
Nashville, Bedford, Tennessee
DEATH: 15 Oct 1905
Cleveland, Emery Co., Utah
PARENTS: Andrew H. Whitlock
Hannah Caroline Allred
PIONEER: 15 Sep 1852
John Tidwell Wagon Train
SPOUSE: Mark Rogers
MARRIED: 11 Jan 1849
DEATH SP: May 1849

CHILD:
Amanda Azelia, 28 Oct 1849

SPOUSE: Henry Herman Oviatt
MARRIED: 1 Feb 1853
Spring City, Utah
DEATH SP: 8 Apr 1919
Elmo, Emery Co., Utah

CHILDREN:
Henry Herman, 1 Dec 1853
Ruth Adeline, 19 Jul 1856 (twin)
Hannah Adelaide, 19 Jul 1856 (twin)
Andrew Adelbert, 7 Sep 1859
Mary Angeline, 21 Sep 1861
Beman Lewis, 12 Dec 1863
Agnes Evaline, 17 May 1866
George Travis, 18 Oct 1868
Nora Emmeline, 4 May 1871

Sally Rae's parents joined the Church of Jesus Christ of Latter-day Saints and moved to Clay County, Missouri to be with the Saints. Sally Rae was very much a part of the persecution that took place in Missouri. She was living in Nauvoo with her parents at the time of Joseph Smith's death.

She met Mark Rogers in Council Point, Pottawattamie County, Iowa and married him on January 11, 1849. They were married only a few months when Mark died in May, 1849. She gave birth to a baby girl in October of that same year which made her a bride, widow, and mother all in the same year. Sally's mother had died in childbirth, so she had much of the responsibility of helping her father with the rest of her brothers and sisters. Her father, brothers, sisters, and little daughter crossed the Plains together in Captain Tidwell's Wagon Company.

After their arrival, they were sent to settle Ephraim, Utah and were the early settlers of Sanpete County. It was there she met Henry Herman Oviatt. She married him February 1, 1853 in Spring City. Her sister, Mary Jane, and her brother, Charles, and Sally Rae were all three married on the same day.

She raised all her children to be loving and faithful to the Church. She worked along side her husband on the farm in Ephraim. Many times she was left alone when he had to go fight the Indians. They were later called to settle in Emery County where she was a real helpmate to Henry in all of his civic duties. She was known as a hard worker.

Sally Rae lived to be seventy-seven years of age. She passed away in Cleveland, Emery County, Utah and is buried in Cleveland City Cemetery.

SARIAH RAWSON OWEN

BIRTHDATE: 15 Mar 1834
Lafayette Co., Missouri
DEATH: Dec. 13, 1914
Ogden, Weber Co., Utah
PARENTS: Horace S. Rawson
Elizabeth Coffin
PIONEER: Oct 1850
Wilford Woodruff Wagon Train
SPOUSE: James C. Owen
MARRIED: 1851
Ogden, Weber Co., Utah
DEATH SP: 26 Jan 1914
Ogden, Weber Co., Utah

CHILDREN:
James Albert, 2 Nov 1852
William Franklin, 5 Aug 1854
Joseph Henry, 14 Oct 1857
Daniel Warren, 5 Oct 1859
Horace Nathaniel, 8 Jan 1862
Sariah Emily, 4 Feb 1864
Mary Elizabeth, 1 Jan 1867
Charles Hanford, 13 Aug 1869

Sariah was born after the Saints left Jackson County, Missouri, so she suffered the hardships along with her family during the mob uprisings in Missouri as they moved from place to place. By the time she was ten years old they had moved to Nauvoo and the prophet had been slain and the Saints were being forced to leave Nauvoo.

Sariah can remember the Prophet Joseph Smith preaching, standing on a platform in front of the trees. He spoke of the Savior coming and said he would come in a cloud. Many were the times both the Prophet and his brother, Hyrum, passed on the road running in front of their place. She remembers well the Prophet dressed in his uniform, riding his horse. He was Major General of the Nauvoo League.

Sariah suffered many hardships along with the rest of the Saints. She was sick a lot. She walked most of the way across the Plains barefooted. She helped her brothers drive the cows. Cracks would come under her toes so wide they would be hard to heal. She would draw the cracks together with needle and thread so they would heal faster.

In 1850, they started again for the trip to the Mountains. They traveled with oxen and wagons in the Wilford Woodruff Wagon Company. There was a great deal of sickness in the fall part of their journey, especially of the Cholera. They traveled about five miles a day and had lots of rain in the fall part of their journey. They reached Salt Lake Valley in October, 1850 and their provisions gave out. They had some bread and beets sent to them from the Valley. It looked good, but when they tasted it, it was bitter. The sunflower could not be gotten out of the wheat as it is now-a-days.

They moved to Ogden, Utah, when there were only a few families there. She married James Colegrove Owen in 1851.

Sariah was a wonderful cook. Her home was always so clean and homey with the aroma of her good cooking in the air, although she was sick a lot through many years of her life, no doubt caused from the sufferings and hardships she went through as a child with the hardships of the Saints during the mobbings and while crossing the Plains. She was loved and admired by all who knew her.

ABIGAIL CORDELIA BURR OWENS

No Photo Available

BIRTHDATE: 22 Nov 1799
Kingsboro, Fulton, New York
DEATH: 27 Nov 1862
Fillmore, Millard Co., Utah
PARENTS: Horace Burr
C. Hungerford
PIONEER: Nov 1852
Capt. Hodges Co. Wagon Train
SPOUSE: James C. Owens Sr.
MARRIED: 1816
DEATH SP: Jan 1846

CHILDREN:
Rebecca Cordelia, 1817
Horace, 23 Jul 1819
Caroline Amelia, 1 Jul 1821

Levi Benjamin, 1823
Charles, Jan. 1826
Julia Minerva, 17 Oct 1828
John, 1830
James Clark, 7 Jul 1832

Abigail was born in New York in 1799 and as a young girl of seventeen, she married James. The young couple were among the first fifty members of the Church of Jesus Christ of Latter-day Saints in their area.

They followed Joseph Smith where he moved, they followed (their last child was born in Independence, Missouri), and what he asked, they did. Abigail was there during the violent times in the early days of the Church, caring for her children during James many absences.

She was at Haun's Mill seeking refuge when the mobs attacked the Mormons there. Abigail, clutching six year old James and hiding him under her skirt, hid themselves in a corn field for hours, James made not one sound.

She was at Farr West, Missouri when she and James became acquainted with the Prophet, she visited the jail and talked to the brethren and to Joseph through the bars of the prison. She was at the meeting in the Grove when the mantle of Joseph settled on Brigham Young and she knew that he was indeed the one chosen to lead the Church.

During the winter of 1846, James left for Mt. Pisgah to get work, he lost his way in a heavy blizzard and for three days weathered the storm. Some ranchers found the badly frozen man and took him to their camp. James, barely able to talk, told them his name, gave them his gun and belongings and ask them to tell his wife and family and then he died.

Abigail, after the loss of her husband, became ill and it would take six long years of frugal living to earn enough to supply themselves with the things needed for the trip west.

Food had to be saved, enough to last them the three months to cross the prairies and mountains with enough to sustain them after reaching their destination until work could be found and food grown. James Jr. procured enough wood to build a wagon and finally they obtained a team of oxen.

Abigail's family, James Clark Jr., daughter Julia and her children, Caroline, her husband Edward Milo Webb and their four children, set out with Captain Hodges Wagon Company for the long journey. Before they had traveled far, Edward was stricken with Cholera and died as did a granddaughter.

They went to Provo for a winter of poverty but in the spring they moved to Fillmore where James Jr., a rock mason like his father, found work quarrying rock for the stake house there. He was a leading figure to the building up of the city of Fillmore.

As he was laying the rock foundation of the Joseph Robisons home, he was laying the foundation for his own life. He and Lucretia Robison fell in love and were married.

When her husband passed away, Abigail had received a blessing of peace and happiness and it came true in Fillmore. Secure with her daughter-in-law and son James, she gave of her time and talents to the Church, her family and the community.

Abigail passed away at the age of sixty-three, leaving her greatest contribution to God, her obedient children.

ANN WILLIAMS HARRIS OWENS

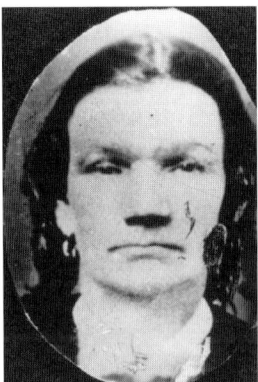

BIRTHDATE: 31 Dec 1818
Llansantfraad, Aberstwith, Wales
DEATH: Aug 1872
Salt Lake City, Salt Lake, Utah
PARENTS: Thomas Williams
Mary Lewis
PIONEER: 1863
SPOUSE I: Thomas Harris
MARRIED: 1 Mar 1844
Abarystruth, England
DEATH SP: 29 Dec 1917
Henefer, Summit Co., Utah

CHILDREN:
Thomas William, 13 Dec 1844
Son, abt 1846
Micah Francis, 3 Aug 1847
Jane, abt 1849
Joseph, 18 Oct 1850 (twin)
Hiram, 18 Oct 1850 (twin)
Mary Jane, 28 Nov 1851
Dan Richard, 5 May 1853
Eldora Ann, abt 1856

SPOUSE II: William John Owens
MARRIED: 29 Feb 1868
Salt Lake Endowment House, Utah
DEATH SP: Unknown
CHILDREN: None

Ann was born in Llansantfraad, Aberstwith, Brenah, Wales, 1818. She married Thomas Harris on March 1, 1844 in Abarystruth, Monmmouth, England.

Of the eight children born to Ann and Thomas only three sons, Thomas, Micah and Dan survived. A daughter was born during the time the family spent in Nebraska while working their way West. She lived for only about three years.

Ann and Thomas lived in a dugout at Chalk Creek, later at Grass Creek, then Anderton's Canyon and finally at Henefer, all in Summit County. Sometime before 1866, Thomas and their son went to the Gold Field's of Montana to earn money for the family. Thomas made one brief trip home, then returned to Montana. When the next winter passed without his return, Thomas was presumed dead and Ann struggled to survive. Ann married William J. Owens on February 29, 1868 in the Salt Lake Endowment House.

Thomas returned home later in 1868, a very angry man to find his wife married to another man. No postal service existed. Lack of ability to communicate had a tragic effect on his family.

Surely her fifty-four years of life were shortened by the hardships she endured. She was loved and admired by all who knew her, including a grandson, Joseph B. Harris, who paid tribute to her faithfulness to the gospel which brought her from Wales so many years before.

LAURA FARNSWORTH FRAMPTON OWENS

No Photo Available

BIRTHDATE: 11 Jan 1806
Milton, Chittenden Co., Vermont
DEATH: 24 Jun 1881
Pleasant Grove, Utah Co., Utah
PARENTS: Reuben Farnsworth
Lucinda Kent
PIONEER: 13 Aug 1852
James W. Bay Wagon Train
SPOUSE: Nathaniel Frampton
MARRIED: 27 May 1824
Burlington, Lawrence Co., Ohio
DEATH SP: 8 Jul 1883
Lexington, Ray Co., Missouri

CHILDREN:
Adeline, 7 Apr 1825 (died as an infant)
Sarah Montgomery, 5 Sep 1826 (died as an infant)
Adolphus, 8 May 1829 (died as an infant)
William Martindale, 20 Sep 1831

SPOUSE II: Owen Asa Owens
MARRIED: 1838
DEATH SP II:

CHILDREN:
Harvey, 1839
Harrison, 1841
Son, 1844

Laura was about nine years of age when her parents moved to Zanesville, Ohio. They later moved to Burlington, Lawrence County, Ohio where she met Nathaniel Frampton. They were married and she soon learned of his previous habits of drinking and gambling. Despite her pleading, he returned to his habits. She clung to her husband for years. Laura finally procured a divorce.

Too proud to be dependent, she became skillful with her needle and used it to earn some means of support for her son and herself. She had been educated and was able to teach school.

She met Owen Asa and they were married in 1838. Two years afterward, on May 24, 1840, Laura was baptized a member of the Church of Jesus Christ of Latter-day Saints. Owen also joined the Church, but forsook the cause and gave his wife the choice of leaving the church or leaving him and their two young sons, Harvey and Harrison.

This was a supreme test of faith. The gospel meant more to her than life itself. She managed to hold the other two sons close to her heart through letters, and with the help of friends and family.

Her husband loaded her and her son, William, with supplies and helped them with the means necessary for the trek across the Plains. She brought with her one of the few organs to arrive in the territory with the early pioneers. She had two wagons and hired a man to drive one of them for her. She started out with a horse team, but later changed to oxen. They arrived in the Salt Lake Valley with the James W. Bay Wagon Company on August 13, 1852.

Old Pleasant Grove was soon to feel the uplifting influence of this courageous woman. She became an active worker in the Relief Society and helped to make the first American Flag used in the town on the occasion of the first Pioneer Day celebration. She lived with her son, William, the rest of her life and joined with him in teaching in their Pioneer School. Her home was ever a center of helpfulness and culture, radiant with the Spirit of the Gospel.

LUCRETIA PROCTOR ROBISON OWENS

BIRTHDATE: 18 May 1841
Shroeple, New York
DEATH: 24 May 1929
Snowflake, Arizona
PARENTS: Joseph Robison Jr.
Lucretia Hancock
PIONEER: 5 Oct 1854
Peregrine Sessions Wagon Train
SPOUSE: James C. Owens Jr.
MARRIED: 16 Jan 1856
DEATH SP: 1 Feb 1901
Woodruff, Arizona

CHILDREN:
James Clark III, 12 Jan 1857
Marion Alfred, 15 Jul 1860
Lucretia Adelpha, 20 Sep 1862 (died at 1 year)
Clarence Edwards, 12 Jan. 1865
Elsie Abigail, 1 Feb 1867
Joseph Alonzo, 14 Jan 1869
Mary Amelia, 14 Nov. 1871
John, 20 Apr 1874 (died at 4 days)
Lillis Alvira, 3 Jun 1876 (died at 4 months)
Zina, 27 May 1878
Franklin Horace, 17 Jan 1881
Adelia, 15 Jun. 1883

Lucretia Proctor was born in New York in 1841, the eighth in a family of thirteen, (two older sisters died earlier) with five older brothers.

Her parents had joined the Church of Jesus Christ of Latter-day Saints three months before she was born and when she was three years old the family moved from New York to Crete, Will County, Illinois, about thirty miles from Chicago, onto 160 acres.

Her father ambitious, hard working seemed to always accumulate and prosper in his efforts and soon had a home and live stock to sell at a profit. He was contented in his surroundings but his wife was determined to move with the main body of the Church.

The Robisons, with fourteen in their family left Crete on April 12, 1854 with three ox-teams and one horse team, joining the Perigren Sessions Company. The fourteen wagons making up the company had a safe journey, no illness, no lose of life occurred in cattle or people. After five and a half months of travel, they entered the Salt Lake Valley. Their first act as soon as they could go to the city, was to pay their tithing.

They were sent to Fillmore and lived in the fort while the Indians were hostile and causing trouble, but the next year her father began building his house. He hired a young man just newly arrived to quarry the rock and lay the walls for the new home.

James Clark Owens "Jim" was twenty-two years old, brave and strong with a tender side that did not go unnoticed by Lucretia and they were married in January of the next year.

Their first child, James the III, was a month old when, in fulfilling the call to cut temple stones, the Owens family went to Little Cottonwood canyon near Salt Lake to live in tents and sheds. Their pay was the sustenance given as tithing paid by the members of the Cottonwood Ward and brought by Bishop Holliday. At times there was not enough food or clothing.

They returned to Fillmore. There were shortages in every necessity including medical attention and during her years in Fillmore, four little ones died. Her two-room adobe house harbored her six children, her mother-in-law, her sister-in-law and two children, until the sister-in-law remarried. Jim's mother lived with them for eleven years until she passed away.

In December of 1878, they moved to Arizona,, first Show Low then Bush Valley (Alpine). Crops failed, Indians raided their cattle. Then they were called to Woodruff, where they lived in an adobe room 16 by 20 with a dirt roof that flooded the dirt floor and covered the beds with muddy rain.

Her last years, after her husband's death and her children's marriages, were spent living in a little home built next to her son Clarence's home in Snowflake, Arizona. Here she lived until at the age of eighty-six.

MARY THOMAS OWENS

BIRTHDATE: 5 May 1834
Merthyr Tydfill, South Wales
DEATH: 14 Mar 1887
PARENTS: Richard Thomas
PIONEER: 10 Oct 1853
John W. Young Co. Wagon Train
SPOUSE: John Edward Owens
MARRIED: 15 Feb 1853
DEATH SP: 3 Nov 1895

CHILDREN:
Richard Thomas, 21 Apr 1854
Sarah, 16 Nov 1855
Margaret, 21 Feb 1858
John Thomas, 21 Jul 1860
Edward Thomas, 14 Apr 1863
Mary Blanch, 14 Nov 1865
Catherine Elizabeth, 27 Dec 1868
Charlotte Jane, 12 Oct 1871

Mary was born in Merthyr Tydfill,Glamorgan, South Wales in 1834 and was nine years old when missionaries of the Church of Jesus Christ of Latter-day Saints first entered that country. She was two years older when Elder Dan Jones concentrated his mission work in the part of Wales in which she lived.

As the message of the Gospel flourished and more converts grew, so did the opposition of the other churches in Merthyr Tydfill until at one point Elder Jones was set upon by the officials of the town to have him arrested. The lies swirled around him, "You are saying the end of the world is near and scaring everyone senselessly they said." "You are taking all they have removing them to another country to sell into slavery" they accused.

Against all these false hoods and the condemnent of the church officials, Mary saw through to the truth, accepted the messages of the missionaries and was baptized.

She was nineteen when she boarded the ship "John Bright," with other Scandinavian converts who were leaving from Liverpool, England eager to go to Utah.

It was a voyage of scarcity of material things but full of excitement for Mary, she married John Edward Owen aboard ship, a comfort, a sharing of hearts for eternity.

The couple would make their way to Kanesville, Iowa where on July 11th, their company of 321 pioneers would begin their journey of three months duration. Many times, when they realized that Salt Lake would be in their view on the morrow, sleep would not come. Some anxious to look as good as possible made extra effort to do so, never the less a group of travel weary souls would wind their way down the canyon and into the future.

Mary and John's first of their eight children would be born in the spring, and she would live thirty-three years in this frontier. Johnston's Army was yet to threaten, Indians would worry them, there were children to be born and crops to raise.

Mary passed away at age fifty-two, having been steadfast in her religion, in her duties and in her love for her children.

ANN MORIAH REDD PACE

BIRTHDATE: 26 Jul 1830
Onslow, North Carolina
DEATH: 29 Nov 1908
New Harmony, Utah
PARENTS: John Hardison Redd
Elizabeth Hancock
PIONEER: 20 Sep 1848
James Pace Co. Wagon Train
SPOUSE: Wilson Daniel Pace
MARRIED: 22 Aug 1852
Spanish Fork, Utah Co., Utah
DEATH SP: 30 Oct 1899
Thatcher, Graham Co., Arizona

CHILDREN:
Mary Elizabeth, 30 May 1853
Mary Moriah, 21 Feb 1855
William Wilson, 8 June 1857
Lemuel Alexander, 19 Apr 1859
Clarisa Ann, 10 Jun 1861
Keziah Evelin, 23 Mar 1863
Sarah Caroline, 27 Mar 1865
lrminda, 23 Feb 1867
lcevinda, 23 Feb 1867
Almarene, 25 Mar 1869
Francel Marene, 25 Mar 1869
John Granville, 10 May 1870

"Aunt Moriah," as everyone called her, was about five feet two inches tall, of average weight with black hair and grey eyes. She was very neat in appearance, and was a proud spirited woman. She was humble, brilliant, cheerful and ambitious; she was hospitable and uncomplaining.

As with those pioneer women she worked for her family for years, cording, spinning and weaving wool into cloth. With this she made clothes for her family including suits for the men.

In 1875, she was asked to be the Relief Society president, a position she held until 1905. For eighteen of those years her husband Wilson Daniel was the bishop of New Harmony ward.

She gave birth to twelve children, including two sets of twins. Even with that large family she was set apart to be the midwife in the New Harmony area. She carried on that work for thirty-five years.

In 1868, Wilson Daniel entered into the law of polygamy with Ann Moriah's consent. The second wife, Elizabeth Lee bore twelve children, eight of whom Ann Moriah attended at birth.

Ann Moriah gave her all to the gospel. It meant very much to her. Her parents had been well to do southern plantation owners and so with this background she was used to the luxuries of those early days and the help of slaves. To give all this up for the gospel and for the things she knew to be truer, was a real sacrifice.

Ann Moriah was a Utah pioneer, a good companion to her husband, an exemplary mother, a cheerful and hospitable neighbor. She was the best medicine anyone could ask for when ill; she was a devout member of the church, a patriotic citizen and had a keen sense of humor.

ANN WEBB PACE

BIRTHDATE: 17 Apr 1833
Studham, Bedford, England
DEATH: 18 May 1918
Thatcher, Graham Co., Arizona
PARENTS: William Webb
Emma Stokes
PIONEER: 1855
SPOUSE: James Pace
MARRIED: 4 Dec 1855
Payson, Utah Co., Utah
DEATH SP: 6 Apr 1838
Thatcher, Graham Co., Arizona

CHILDREN:
Emma Ann, 29 Oct 1856
James Orlando, 16 Apr 1858
Margaret Leonora, 27 Feb 1860
Adalaide, 15 Jun 1862
Mary Adelia, 18 Sep 1864
Ruth Elmina, 13 Dec 1866
Amanda Elena, 9 Jul 1869
Sarah Ellen, 12 Mar 1872

According to a will of Ann's Grandfather, John Stokes, we read concerning Ann Webb:

"My dear fun loving Ann is also in America. I gave her a pewter pitcher and bowl used by her great-grandmother and 25 lbs. Ann is good with children and has a special fondness for her brother Willie. She could always find something good to do for loved ones and give them pleasure. She waited for dusk to come so they could sing and tell stories. She was so good at making up stories. She could draw pictures of flowers and birds and deer. They looked real. She could run like a deer and move with the grace of a queen. She was always spiritual like her mother and joined the Church at the time Emma joined. She was humming and singing all the time. I miss her smiling sweet face and manner and her serious talk. She too has children I will never see. I have missed her sorely this past 6 years. I do love her. "

Ann came to the Salt Lake Valley in the fall of 1855. On December 4, 1855, she married James Pace as his third wife. The ceremony was performed in the Pace home in Payson by President Brigham Young.

In November, 1882, James Pace moved his wife, Ann Webb and family to Southern Arizona, settling on the Gila River. He had previously been to the area as a member of the Mormon Battalion, and wanted to return to it.

James passed away on April 6, 1888, and Ann passed away on May 18, 1918, both at Thatcher, Arizona.

ELIZA BALDWIN PACE

No
Photo
Available

BIRTHDATE: 8 Apr 1806
Otis, Berkshire, Massachusetts
DEATH: 1863
Bountiful, Davis Co., Utah
PARENTS: Samuel Baldwin
Mehitable Kingsley
PIONEER: 20 Sep 1848
Lorenzo Snow Co. Wagon Train
SPOUSE: Elisha Pace
MARRIED: 25 Mar 1827
Newark, Licking Co., Ohio
DEATH SP: 1 Oct 1845
Nauvoo, Hancock Co., Illinois

CHILDREN:
Samuel, 1828 (died in 1829)
Edwin C., 3 Dec 1831
Benjamin, 1834 (died in 1835)
George Milton, 3 Jan 1836
Sarah, 1840 (died at age 4)
Amanda Melvina, 11 Sep 1842

Eliza was born in Otis, Massachusetts until her family moved to Granville, Licking County, Ohio.

She met Elisha Pace and married him on March 25, 1827 in Newark, Ohio. Six children were born to this union, three of whom died in their childhood.

Eliza and Elisha received the gospel and were baptized as members of the Church of Jesus Christ of Latter-day Saints in 1837. They moved to Nauvoo, Illinois where they had the opportunity of knowing the Prophet Joseph Smith and enjoyed their association with the Saints. But they also suffered many hardships.

Her husband, Elisha, died in Nauvoo on his fortieth birthday in 1844. After his death, Eliza took her three small children and moved from Nauvoo to the Punca Indian Village which was about 200 miles away from Winter Quarters. The family endured the severe trials incidental to the winters of 1846 and 1847.

In the Spring of 1848, the family went to Omaha where they joined the Lorenzo Snow Wagon Company bound for Salt Lake Valley. Eliza's widowed sister, Sarah Baldwin Smith, joined her. They were fortunate to have an old wagon, two yoke of cattle, and one horse. They arrived in the Great Salt Lake Valley on September 20, 1848.

They quickly moved to Sessions Settlement where they spent the winter in a cave in a hill. Her son erected a shelter of willows, rushes, and grass sod over the mouth of the cave. Pasturing was available in the Jordan River bottoms. They lived mainly on mustard greens. It was necessary to ration themselves with what food they had, but they were blessed with the milk from their cows.

Through ingenious means, Edwin met the grasshopper plague by plowing three furrows around the planted area. The insects were shooed into these trenches and were forced into bags at ends of rows, and covered in pits. A good grain crop materialized which was not typical in the area. They had to move south during the invasion of Johnston's Army. When they returned home, they continued their struggle of daily living.

They cut wild hay and stacked it for winter use, made butter and cheese for trade. They clipped, washed, carded, and spun the wool from their sheep. When they killed an animal, they divided the meat among the neighbors. Each year, living became a little better.

Eliza lived long enough to see Edwin, George, and Amanda married and many of her grandchildren born. At her funeral, it was said of her, "She was the hardest working woman I ever knew and an excellent manager."

Eliza suffered greatly from cancer of the face until her death, but was usually cheerful and always eager to be helpful to her neighbors.

LOUISA MARY PHILLIPS PACE

BIRTHDATE: 18 Jan 1848
Cardiff, Glamorgan, South Wales
DEATH: 18 Sep 1934
Spanish Fork, Utah Co., Utah
PARENTS: Charles Phillips
Priscilla Merriman
PIONEER: 30 Sep 1854
Darwin Richards Wagon Train
SPOUSE: William Franklin Pace
MARRIED: 30 Nov 1868
Salt Lake City, Salt Lake, Utah
DEATH SP: 22 Dec 1918
Spanish Fork, Utah Co., Utah

CHILDREN:
Louisa Caroline (Angus), 4 Aug 1870
Priscilla Margaret (Boyack), 1 Aug 1872
James Thomas, 9 Apr 1873
William Franklin, 16 Oct 1875
Mary Ann (Stewart Reynolds), 10 Oct 1877
Jane Elizabeth (Stewart), 9 Nov 1879
Maggie Davidson, 6 Oct 1881
Charles Phillip, 22 Aug 1883
Rebecca Amelia (Nielsen), 9 Apr 1886
Martin Eli, 30 Jun 1888
Son, 22 Mar 1890

Louisa Mary was born in South Wales in 1848. She started reading at the age of three, and when six years of age she won a fifteen pound butter lion at school for reading the Bible the best. She was a Bible scholar and could recite any verse from memory.

Louisa came across the Plains when six years of age with the Darwin Richards Company. She went to school nights; gathered offerings for the poor; and cooked for the men working on the railroad. She taught Sunday School at age eighteen and in 1865 helped form a theater group in Spanish Fork and presented plays in the group for many years.

Louisa married William Franklin Pace in 1868 in the Endowment House and they became the parents of eleven children. The family lived in the Spanish Fork area all their lives. Besides rearing her large family Louisa served faithfully in many Church callings.

William passed away in 1918, and Louisa passed away in 1934, both in Spanish Fork, Utah County, Utah.

LUCINDA GIBSON STRICKLAND PACE

No
Photo
Available

BIRTHDATE: 16 Jun 1805
Abbeyville, South Carolina
DEATH: 11 Mar 1897
Washington, Washington, Utah
PARENTS: Warren G. Strickland
Mary Anderson
PIONEER: 1850 Wagon Train
SPOUSE: James Pace
MARRIED: 21 Mar 1831
Tennessee
DEATH SP: 6 Apr 1888
Thatcher, Graham Co., Arizona

CHILDREN:
William Byram, 9 Feb 1832
James Finnis, 20 Feb 1834
Mary Ann, 20 Oct 1835
Warren Sidney, 28 Dec 1837
Martha Elmina "Alvira," 15 Apr 1840
Margaret Angeline, 14 Sep 1842
John Ezra, 12 Jul 1845
Amanda Lucinda, 18 Feb 1850

Lucinda was well educated and an accomplished musician. She was able to teach her children their reading, writing, arithmetic and music. They first lived in Tennessee, then moved to Shelby, Illinois. They endured many hardships and sickness, causing the death of their second child, James, and Lucinda's mother. Three more children were born there.

In 1839, they joined the Church of Jesus Christ of Latter-day Saints and moved to Nauvoo. She was in Nauvoo at the time of the Prophet's death. They were forced to leave Nauvoo in February, 1846, and crossed the Mississippi River to the home of her husband's brother, William. They later continued their journey to Mt. Pisgah where they stayed to raise a crop to help others who would be traveling West.

Her husband and son, William, were called to be in the Mormon Battalion. Lucinda had to care for the family by herself until he returned in December, 1847. The family reached Utah in September, 1850. They were called to settle on Peteetneet Creek; later named Payson for the Pace family. They built a home fortified with pickets of cottonwood.

In 1852, James went on a mission to England, and for three more years Lucinda managed the household, which had been enlarged by a plural wife, Margaret Huitt Pace.

On his return from his mission, he married another wife, Ann Webb.

In 1861, the families were called to settle New Harmony in Southern Utah. They spent the winter in a dugout, cooking in the dugout and sleeping in a wagon box.

In November, 1882, James and Ann, his third wife, moved to Arizona, Margaret stayed in New Harmony and Lucinda stayed in Washington, Utah. Much of her spare time was spent in knitting. She also did embroidery work and netting.

She was well loved by all who knew her. From the lips of those who knew her comes the tribute,

"She was a real lady."

Lucinda passed away on march 11, 1897 in Washington County, Utah.

MARGARET GRINDER CALHOUN HEWITT PACE

BIRTHDATE: 16 Aug 1825
Brandywine, Pennsylvania
DEATH: 2 Apr 1918
Loa, Wayne Co., Utah
PARENTS: Hugh Calhoun
Elizabeth Grinder
PIONEER: 1850 or 1851
SPOUSE I: Wilkerson Hewitt
MARRIED: Unknown
DEATH SP: Before 1852

CHILD:
Child drowned while a child

SPOUSE II: James Pace
MARRIED: 2 Jan 1852
Endowment House, Salt Lake City, Utah
DEATH SP: 6 Apr 1888
Thatcher, Graham Co., Arizona

CHILDREN:
James Wilkerson, 25 Dec 1852
Jeff, 1854
Willard, 13 Aug 1856
Wilford Woodruff, 8 Feb 1858
Eugenia Ruth, 17 Jul 1860
Naomi Euginia, 7 Jul 1861
Jefferson Davis, 18 Feb 1863
Lucinda Alvira, 21 Sep 1864
Margaret Dixie, 18 Sep 1866
Ann Louise, 3 Apr 1868

Margaret was born in Brandywine, Westchester County, Pennsylvania on August 16, 1825 to Hugh and Elizabeth Calhoun. Margaret married Wilkerson Hewitt. They were planning to move west. He was working on a ferry boat and told Margaret he would make one more trip across the river before they continued their journey. On that one extra trip, he drowned. Margaret was left with a small boy to bring across the Plains. She continued across the Plains with friends in 1850 or 1851.

After Margaret arrived in the Salt Lake Valley, she went on to Peteetneet (Payson) where she met James Pace. She became his second wife on January 2, 1852.

On August 28, 1852, he was called to serve a three year mission to England. Their first child was born in his absence. While her husband was serving a mission, her first child from her first marriage drowned in Peteetneet Creek. After James returned from his mission, they had seven more children. They farmed and he built houses in the Payson area.

In 1861, Brigham Young called James Pace to go to the St. George area. They lived in New Harmony for the next twenty years. Margaret had a very busy life raising her children and doing all the necessary chores to keep a household in those frontier conditions. In 1875, she served as a counselor in the Relief Society.

In 1882, James and his third wife moved to Thatcher, Arizona. Margaret's sons worked at the Silver Reef mines to help support her. They eventually moved to Loa, Wayne County, Utah where she remained the rest of her life.

Margaret passed away on April 2, 1918.

MARGARET NICHOLS PACE

BIRTHDATE: 30 May 1808
Logan Co., Kentucky
DEATH: 21 Sep 1887
New Harmony, Utah
PARENTS: Daniel Nichols
Mary Alexander
PIONEER: 20 Sep 1848
Brigham Young Wagon Train
SPOUSE: William Franklin Pace
MARRIED: 2 or 21 Oct 1828
Double Springs, Tennessee
DEATH SP: 30 Oct 1876
New Harmony, Utah

CHILDREN:
James Byron, 12 Aug 1829
Wilson Daniel, 27 Jul 1831
Harvey Alexander, 12 Oct 1833
William Franklin, 19 May 1836
Granville Madison, 6 Nov 1838
John Alma Lawrence, 2 Feb 1841
Joseph Randolph, 24 Dec 1842
Parley Pratt, 8 Sep 1844
Eli Nichols, 18 Sep 1849
Mary Ann, 17 Feb 1852 (died as an infant)

Margaret's parents were what was called southern thoroughbred people. She was a kind lovely young woman who attracted William Pace and married him in Double Springs, Rutherford, Tennessee.

They followed in the footsteps of their forbearers and acquired much land in Rutherford County, Tennessee. To run their plantation, it was necessary to have slaves and they became very well to do.

In 1842, John D. Lee, a missionary for the Church of Jesus Christ of Latter-day Saints, taught William, Margaret, and their family about the restored gospel. They were baptized and because they wanted to be near the Prophet Joseph Smith and the main body of the Saints, the Pace family sold their beautiful plantation, home, and their slaves.

In Nauvoo, William and Margaret secured land and built a beautiful nine-room home. Their trials and tribulations while in Nauvoo were many, including the martyrdom of the prophet. They were sealed in the Nauvoo Temple on January 30, 1846. When the members of the church were driven out of Nauvoo in 1847, they went with other Saints to Council Bluffs, Iowa. They persevered through that winter of 1847-48, while preparing for the long journey to cross the Plains. They arrived with the Brigham Young Wagon Company which arrived in the Salt Lake Valley on September 21, 1848.

They prepared a crude shelter in Cottonwood, Utah area to get them through that winter. Then they were sent to Utah Valley by Brigham Young to find and settle new country.

They helped with the founding of Provo in 1849. In the spring of 1850, they moved on to settle the area of Spanish Fork. Her husband served as bishop until he was called to serve a mission in England in 1856. While living in Palmyra, Utah for more protection from the Indians, Margaret gave birth to her only daughter who lived only seven days. They helped to build the big fort which they had to build their homes for protection from the Indians. They endured many hardships while her husband was in England, but they survived and were so happy upon his return.

In early 1861, they were called to assist in settling in New Harmony, Washington, Utah which was the most southern settlement in Utah. Her husband opened the first store and served as the Postmaster from 1861 to 1875.

Margaret served faithfully in her church callings until she died in 1887.

MARY JANE ATKINSON PACE

BIRTHDATE: 13 Sep 1838
St. Johns, Canada
DEATH: 2 Mar 1881
Bountiful, Davis Co., Utah
PARENTS: William Atkinson
Phoebe Campbell
PIONEER: 10 Sep 1853
Jesse W. Crosby Wagon Train
SPOUSE: Edwin Pace
MARRIED: 1 May 1855
Salt Lake City, Salt Lake, Utah
DEATH SP: 13 Feb 1917
Bountiful, Davis Co., Utah

CHILDREN:
Launa, 2 Dec 1855
Sarah Jane, 6 May 1857
Eliza Melvina, 8 Jan 1859
Phoebe Priscilla, 26 Sep 1860
Rose Belle, 27 Nov 1862
Myra, 29 Aug 1864
Ida May, 25 Oct 1866
Rhoda, 16 Jun 1868
Edwin, Jr., 18 Jan 1870
Clara, 10 May 1873
Effie, 15 May 1876
Deserett, 28 Sep 1880

Mary Jane was the fourth child of fifteen born. She was baptized a member of the Church of Jesus Christ of Latter-day Saints on July 4, 1852.

In the Spring of 1853, Mary Jane and her parents left their home to move to the Salt Lake Valley. They were members of the Jesse W. Crosby Wagon Company. They were stopped by a large band of hostile Sioux Indians who placed themselves across the road, stopped the ox-teams, and demanded food. After they were given food, they reluctantly let the pioneers pass.

Another incident of great fear was when their teams stampeded. They encountered many large herds of wild buffalo which nearly stampeded the teams again. They arrived in the Salt Lake Valley on September 10, 1853.

After settling in South Bountiful, Mary Jane fell in love with Edwin Pace. They were married the next spring on May 2, 1854. All twelve of their children were born in South Bountiful. Mary Jane lived to see five of her children married and some of her grandchildren born.

Unfortunately, she passed away at the young age of forty-three, just six months after her last child was born.

JESSIE BELLE STERLING PACK

BIRTHDATE: 26 Sept 1845
Forforshire, Dundee, Scotland
DEATH: 27 Dec 1925
Bountiful, Davis Co., Utah
PARENTS: Thomas Sterling
Elizabeth Bell
PIONEER: 20 Oct. 1862
Horton Haight Co. Wagon Train
SPOUSE: John Pack
MARRIED: 16 Jan 1864
DEATH SP: 4 Apr 1885

CHILDREN:
William Elmer, 15 Nov 1865
David Thomas, 19 Sep 1868
Nettie Elizabeth, 27 Nov 1870
Hyrum Osmer, 15 Nov 1872
Roy Greenleaf, 10 Mar 1875
Gerald F., 9 Mar 1878
Jessie Belle, 31 Mar 1882

Jessie became a member of the Church of Jesus Christ of Latter-day Saints when she was thirteen years old. When she was sixteen, she and some of her girl friends left Scotland to come to Utah. None of her immediate family came across at this time.

When they arrived in the Salt Lake Valley she went to work at the home of Ward Pack who had helped bring the wagon train to Utah. While she was staying there Ward's father, John, came to visit. In the Spring she went to help John's wife on the farm in Kamas, Utah. Later she married John as his sixth wife.

Her husband established a good home for her in Bountiful, Utah. There she raised her seven children. Her family was still young when her husband died but with the help of her sons they maintained themselves on that farm.

JULIA IVES PACK

BIRTHDATE: 8 Mar 1817
Watertown, Jefferson, New York
DEATH: 23 Jun 1903
Kamas, Summit Co., Utah
PARENTS: Erastus Ives
Lucy Paine
PIONEER: Sep 1848
Heber C. Kimball Wagon Train
SPOUSE: John Pack
MARRIED: 10 Oct 1832
Watertown, Jefferson, New York
DEATH SP: 4 Apr 1885
Salt Lake City, Salt Lake, Utah

CHILDREN:
Ward Eaton, 17 Apr 1834
Lucy Amelia, 24 Jun 1837
George Caleb, 6 Nov 1840

John, Jr., 5 Oct 1843
Julia, 5 Oct 1845 (died at 5 months)
Don Carlos, 22 Aug 1847
Eleanor Philotte, 22 Aug 1849
Erastus Frederick, 17 Jun 1853
Merritt Newton, 1 May 1856
Sedenia Tamsen, 20 May 1858
Joel Ives, 9 Sep 1860 (died at age 11)

Julia Ives was born in New York State. She married John Pack in 1832, and they joined the Church of Jesus Christ of Latter-day Saints in 1836. In 1837, with their first child they located in Kirtland, Ohio, then later in Davies County, Missouri. The mobs forced them out of Missouri and into Illinois, then onto the plains of Iowa.

Julia came to the Salt Lake Valley in 1848 with her husband, two other wives and several children, arriving in September, 1848. They settled in Salt Lake City.

In 1849, her husband was called on a mission to France and was gone three years. All the family worked hard to sustain themselves. Her oldest son, Ward Eaton was a great help, though but fifteen years of age.

In 1853, her husband was called on another mission to the Carson Valley to help settle that area. This was the year of the famine, and rations were very scanty. They all gleaned wheat and dug roots to eat.

Julia was an ardent Relief Society worker, having joined the Society when in Nauvoo, Illinois. She was 1st Counselor to Bathsheba W. Smith in the 17th Ward in Salt Lake, until she moved to Kamas, Summit, Utah in 1896.

Julia passed away in Kamas in 1903. Her husband preceded her in death in 1885 in Salt Lake City, Utah.

BETSY ELIZABETH SCOTT A.K.A. MARY ELIZABETH MARSHALL PACK

BIRTHDATE: 22 Sep 1846
Albany, New York
DEATH: 10 Aug 1936
Kamas, Summit Co., Utah
PARENTS: William Scott
Ann Sinclair
PIONEER: July 1848
W. S. Muir Co. Wagon Train
SPOUSE: John Pack Jr.
MARRIED: 20 Dec 1865
Salt Lake City, Salt Lake, Utah
DEATH SP: 20 Nov 1921
Kamas, Summit Co., Utah

CHILDREN:
John, 24 Jul 1866
Willard Ives, 11 Sep 1867
Daniel Sinclair, 18 Oct 1869
Zoa, 14 Jun 1872
Ernest, 26 Apr 1874
Edna Ann, 12 Mar 1876
Julia Thyrza, 2 Feb 1878

Robert, 1 Oct 1880
Jeanette Lynn, 6 Nov 1885

During the early part of her life, Mary Elizabeth had two different names. She was an only child. At the time of her birth, her father's two maiden sisters promised to remember her in their wills if she was named after them. She was named Betsy for the one and Elizabeth for the other giving her the name of Betsy Elizabeth Scott.

Shortly after, her parents moved to Wheatland, Monroe County, New York and a year later to Winter Quarters with the Sinclair family. Throughout the winter months the suffering was great among the destitute Saints camped along the river banks and they became acquainted with more misery than they had ever known.

This was a sad time for her mother, Ann Sinclair Scott, because her young husband had become dissatisfied with the new religion and announced that he would go no further west with them. Ann left her husband behind although he had been good and kind to her for the two years of their marriage, never to see or hear from him again.

A few days out from Winter Quarters Daniel Sinclair, Ann's father was stricken with cholera and died, leaving Ann, her mother and her baby to travel on alone.

A young Scot by the name of Robert Marshall often helped them with many of their heavy tasks and Ann's mother hired him to drive their oxen and wagon the remainder of the way across the Plains.

In 1849 Ann Sinclair Scott married Robert Marshall. At this time Betsy Elizabeth Scott, now three years old, lost her identity because her name was changed to Mary Elizabeth Marshall. It is thought that Ann did this to prevent William Scott from ever contacting his daughter.

Mary thought a great deal of her new stepfather. She helped him with the farm work, rode the range to gather the cattle and helped plant and harvest the crops. Being a member of a large family of half-brothers and a half-sister, Mary learned all the arts of home making from washing and carding wool, spinning it into yarn and weaving it into cloth, braiding straw for hats, making soap, candles and preserving peaches in molasses.

At the age of nineteen she married and lived in Salt Lake City and Woods Cross until 1870, when they moved to Kamas, Utah. At first they lived in a tent.

Mary took her turn each week making cheese in the cheese factory built by her father-in-law. She had the honor of making the cheese that took the prize at the first fair in Utah.

She witnesses much change in her life time. She lived to see the United States pass through three wars and voted for fourteen presidents.

MARY JANE WALKER PACK

BIRTHDATE: 3 Apr 1835
Devonport,, Stoke Damerel,
Devon, England
DEATH: 5 Apr 1908
West Bountiful, Davis Co., Utah
PARENTS: James Walker
Jane Shepherd
PIONEER: 13 Aug 1852
James W. Bay Co. Wagon Train
SPOUSE: John Pack
MARRIED: 15 Sep 1852
DEATH SP: 3 Apr 1885

CHILDREN:
Geneva Harriet, 22 Jul 1853
Kamelia Luella, 17 Dec 1855
Quince Rufus, 29 Nov 1857
Walker Xenophon, 17 Feb 1860
Annie Jane, 28 Sep 1862
Edith Olive, 17 Mar 1865
Flora Inez, 10 Dec 1867
Phylotte Green, 7 Dec 1869
Hattie, 30 Sep. 1872
Frederick James, 2 Feb 1875
Harold Rantler, 7 Aug 1882

Mary Jane Walker was born in 1835 in Devonport, England. Her family moved within a short time to Helier, Jersey in England.

Her father was a seafaring man and the captain of an English merchant ship who was absent from home for long periods of time. He left for China just before Jane was born and returned after she was five years old. During a visit home in 1852, he died after a short illness leaving his seven year old daughter with few memories of him, save those of a big kindly man who had visited them once in a while bringing gifts and precious things from far off countries.

He had been a good provider which allowed Jane to attend a private school where she was taught the genteel manners of a lady.

Twelve year old Jane, her mother and stepbrother were converted to the Church of Jesus Christ of Latter-day Saints on December 20, 1847.

Jane came alone to the United States with Missionaries and a group from the St. Helier Branch of the Church. At not quite seventeen years of age she embarked on the vessel "Kennebec," bound for New Orleans.

Six months later she set foot in Salt Lake City, travel weary and grateful to be invited into the Dunbar home to rest and get her bearings.

Four weeks after arriving she kept her promise given to Elder John Pack, who had been among those coming from St. Helier, she became his plural wife. John had three wives, the first of whom had a son older than Jane.

At seventeen, Jane went to live at the Pack home at the corner of West Temple and 1st North where her initiation into pioneer life was begun. Spinning, making soap and tallow candles and in the summer, on the farm in Kamas, they made butter and cheese.

When Johnston's Army threatened the Mormons, Jane packed her wagon, and with Quince in her arms, and Geneva and Luella at her side she drove to Utah County. After the army had passed without incident, many returned to their homes. Jane and her sister wife, Ruth, remained for about five or six months selling butter and cheese to the soldiers. They returned home with money enough to buy some things they had long wanted.

Eventually an adobe house was built on the farm in West Bountiful, large enough for Jane and her eleven children. From this time on her life was substantial and secure. She had hay fields plowed and planted into early potatoes and tomatoes for a nearby cannery. Melons and three acres of strawberries went to the Salt Lake market. There was nearly an acre of large red currents and in the autumn, onions to harvest and sell.

In her seventy-third year, after twenty-three years of widowhood, and two days after the anniversary of her husband's death, she passed away.

Mary Jane had died as she had lived, peacefully, reverently, and with good will toward all and a supreme faith in God's goodness to her.

RUTH MOSHER PACK

BIRTHDATE: 12 Apr 1824
Prescott, Canada
DEATH: 10 Sep 1914
Kamas, Summit Co., Utah
PARENTS: Silas Mosher
Martha Van Cura
PIONEER: Oct 1848
Heber C. Kimball Wagon Train
SPOUSE: John Pack
MARRIED: 21 Jan 1846
Nauvoo, Hancock Co., Illinois
DEATH SP: 4 Apr 1895
Salt Lake City, Salt Lake, Utah

CHILDREN:
Silas Mosher, 20 Oct 1849
Catherine DeValah, 8 Jun 1853
Irving James, 16 Apr 1855
Orson Parley, 2 Nov 1856
Ursula Vilate, 22 Aug 1858
Yoma Zenith, 2 Mar 1860
John Ambrose, 2 Sep 1862
Mary Martha, 13 Mar 1865
Benjamin Van Cura, 11 Jun 1867

Ruth Mosher was born in Canada in 1824. When she was three years old the family moved to New York State. At the age of ten she learned that there were Mormon Missionaries in the area, and secretly went to hear them.

She continued to attend their meetings and when she was twenty she was baptized as a member of the Church of Jesus Christ of Latter-day Saints. One night she ran away and joined a family that was going to Nauvoo.

In Nauvoo Ruth met Jesse Crosby, the missionary who baptized her. He was leaving for a mission and asked her to wait. He also gave her a promise ring. However President Heber C. Kimball told her it was the will of the Lord that she marry John Pack, and they were married right away. When Jesse Crosby returned she gave him back his ring, but always remembered him with the tenderest of feelings.

Ruth was the second wife of John Pack. He also had a third wife, and all three wives came across the Plains with the Heber C. Kimball Company in 1848.

In the Spring of 1849, John was sent on a three year mission to France, and the wives got along the best they could. When he returned he built a large adobe house in Bountiful, Utah.

In 1863, John obtained a ranch in Kamas, Summit County, Utah, where Ruth would spend one summer, then trade off with Jane, the third wife. Here they made butter and cheese, which they sold. One year Ruth made two 100 pound cheeses which won first prize at the State Fair. Ruth added some rooms to the house in Kamas and rented them out.

She was a counselor in Relief Society, and was a very effective fund-raiser. She had the gift of healing, and also the gift of tongues.

Ruth passed away in Kamas, Summit County, Utah in 1914 at the age of ninety years.

ANGELINA AVILDA CHAMPLIN PACKER

BIRTHDATE: 8 Jan 1820
Hartland, Windsor Co., Vermont
DEATH: 7 Jan 1893
Colonia, Juarez, Mexico
PARENTS: William S. Champlin
Mary Ring
PIONEER: 21 Sep 1848
Brigham Young Wagon Train
SPOUSE: Johnathan T. Packer
MARRIED: 1840
DEATH SP: 26 Jan 1889
Safford, Graham Co., Arizona

CHILDREN:
Alonzo Hamilton, 14 Apr 1841
Lorenzo James, 27 Jul 1843 (died at age 6)
Sarah Elizabeth, 19 Oct 1845 (died at age 1)
William Jefferson, 26 Oct 1848
Pleasant Deseret, 21 Feb 1851 (died at age 20)
Mary Angeline, 9 Sep 1852
Avilda Verona, 25 Sep 1855 (died at age 3)
LeVema Sonora, 19 Apr 1858
Eva Ellen, 30 Sep 1860 (died at age 2)

Avilda and her parents were taught the gospel by Martin Harris in 1832. They became baptized as members of the Church of Jesus Christ of Latter-day Saints and were with the Saints in Kirtland, Missouri, Far West, Hauns Mill, and Nauvoo, Illinois. They experienced the joys of being associated with the prophet Joseph Smith and experienced the joys of watching the church grow, but also suffered greatly through much persecution due to their choice of religion. Her father was one of the surviving blacksmiths at Haun's Mill.

When they were in Nauvoo, Avilda met and married Johnathan Taylor in 1840. He was a young widower with a year old son named Nephi. They built a fine home in Nauvoo and for the next five years, they prospered and added three more children to their family.

Due to more persecution, they headed for Winter Quarters, Nebraska in freezing temperatures. Food was so scarce, Avilda dug sego roots to cook for food. She pulled pigweed for a make shift house. Their daughter, Sarah, died that winter. The following year, they came with the Brigham Young Wagon Company to the Salt Lake Valley. They were given a large lot in Salt Lake and built the first home in their ward. They raised a garden and small animals there.

Avilda unselfishly shared her husband in polygamy. The responsibility of providing for two families became so great, they moved to Brigham City where Avilda with the help of her children opened a boarding home. Johnathan was the first manager of the Co-op Mercantile store in Brigham City. While working as a member of the police, he was shot in the leg and limped the rest of his life.

In 1883, they were called to colonize in Arizona. She was living with her daughter, Sonora. Her family had to sleep in the wagon box for the first year. Sonora's husband, Lorenzo Wright, was killed by Indians in December of 1885. Avilda tended the children while Sonora went to work. Sonora married into polygamy and they all had to move to Mexico where they helped to build a settlement called Colonia in Chihuahua, Mexico. Avilda was always busy with her garden, the grandchildren, the chickens and the cows.

Avilda passed away one day prior to her birthday and was buried on her seventy-third birthday in Colonia, Juarez, Chihuahua, Mexico.

ELIZABETH TAYLOR PACKER

BIRTHDATE: 6 Dec 1812
Payette Co., Pennsylvania
DEATH: 17 May 1887
Franklin, Oneida Co., Idaho
PARENTS: Samuel M. Taylor
Mary Shaffer
PIONEER: 23 Sep 1850
David Evans Co. Wagon Train
SPOUSE: Nathan W. Packer
MARRIED: 31 Mar 1829
Perry, Richland Co., Ohio
DEATH SP: 27 Oct 1875
Riverdale, Oneida Co., Idaho

CHILDREN:
Lewis William, 15 Mar 1831
Martha Jane, 6 Apr 1832
James, 10 Oct 1833
Isaac Hopmier, 27 Apr 1835
Samuel, 29 Apr 1837 (died as an infant)
William, 22 May 1838 (died at 4 months)
Mary Ann, 18 Oct 1839
Elizabeth, 25 May 1842 (died at age 2)
Emma, 19 Apr 1844
Mary Eliza, 8 May 1846
Nathan Taylor, 8 Aug 1848
Walter McFarland, 23 Apr 1850
Moses, 9 Jul 1852
Jonathan Taylor, 20 Jan 1854
Edson Whipple, 14 May 1857

Elizabeth was born in Pennsylvania. Her parents moved their family to Ohio.

In 1828, Nathan William Packer met Elizabeth. They were married on March 31, 1829. His description of her was, "She was beautiful, intelligent, feminine, a busy lady, loved music, enjoyed a good sense of humor, and was a tremendous homemaker and wife."

They lived in Perry, Ohio when they heard Sidney Rigdon preach the gospel. They became members of the Church of Jesus Christ of Latter-day Saints and were very anxious to go with the Saints to Nauvoo.

They began their journey in May, stopping in Vigo, Indiana for the birth of her sixth child. Another child was born in October of 1839 in Illinois as it took them over two years to reach Nauvoo. After they arrived, her husband was called on two short missions. Elizabeth and Nathan received their ordinances in January, 1846, in the Nauvoo Temple prior to their exodus from Nauvoo.

The month Mary Eliza was born, they were driven from their home. With a few other families, they drove to Andrew, Missouri where they found an abandoned log cabin where they lived while two more children were born.

In 1850, the Perpetual Emigration Fund made it possible for them to procure equipment and supplies so they could join the Saints in the Great Salt Lake Valley. They joined David Evans Wagon Company and arrived on September 15, 1850.

In the spring of 1851, the Church sent them into Utah County to settle in a place called Middleville (now Alpine).

Nathan Packer and Lorenzo Hatch built the first flour mill in Utah County and ran it for many years. In 1860, they were called to help settle Cache Valley. Indians were a constant menace, so they had to live inside a fort. They sent for assistance from Fort Douglas Military Post in Salt Lake City. Many Indians were killed which caused the other tribes to withdraw from the valley.

When her husband brought a second wife home, Elizabeth was so hurt, she took her four youngest sons and moved to Franklin. Later, she moved to Riverdale where she lived with her son, Nathan, for the rest of her life.

Elizabeth passed away, May 17, 1887, having served her fellow men well in all of her undertakings.

LUCY CHARLOTTE BERRY PACKER

BIRTHDATE: 16 Oct 1838
Stockport, Lincolnshire, England
DEATH: 13 Jun 1919
Shelley, Bingham Co., Idaho
PARENTS: Edmond Berry
Charlotte Rose Berry
PIONEER: 23 Sep 1854
St. Louis Co., Missouri
SPOUSE I: Peter Poole
MARRIED: 1857
Salt Lake City, Salt Lake, Utah
DEATH SP: Not given

CHILD:
Mary Elvira

SPOUSE II: Isaac Hoffmire Packer
MARRIED: 18 Nov 1864
Salt Lake City, Salt Lake Co., Utah
DEATH SP: 10 Apr 1908
Parker, Fremont Co., Idaho

CHILDREN:
Isaac Alma, 2 Aug 1865
Nathan Edmond, 22 Nov 1866
William Walter, 24 Jan 1869
Lucy Luella, 25 Dec 1870
Samuel Delbert, 9 Nov 18721
Lewis Edgar, 10 May 1874
Edson Berry, 9 Mar 1876
George Franklin, 11 Mar 1878
Nellie Louise, 26 Nov 1879
Lafayette Hatch, 2 Apr 1883.

When Lucy was very young the family left England for Australia, after a few years they went to Auckland, New Zealand. Not liking the country they went on to South America. They spent three years in Valparaiso and then left to return to England. In 1848, the family embarked for North America on the steamer "European." Lucy was almost ten years old and remembered well the passage.

In 1849, cholera broke out in St. Louis and Lucy's mother was a victim of that dread disease. Lucy lost a devoted mother. Her father married a widow, Thurza Booth.

In 1854, Lucy started for Utah in the company of her brother Samuel and his family. Lucy was fifteen and did not get along well with her stepmother and was ready for a new adventure.

Lucy joined the Church of Jesus Christ of Latter-day Saints after she arrived in the Salt Lake Valley. She settled in Kaysville, Davis County, Utah with Samuel and his family.

Lucy married Peter Poole in 1857 in Salt Lake City and one daughter was born to them Mary Elvira. Lucy and her family joined Samuel's family and a small company of Saints to establish a new settlement in the north end of Cache Valley. In June, 1860, they arrived at what is now Franklin, Idaho. Thus she was one of the first settlers of Idaho. She later separated from Peter Poole.

Lucy married Isaac Hoffmire Packer in 1864 in Salt Lake City and they left for California in a prairie schooner, drawn by a yoke of oxen. They traded their oxen for a team of horses which made their journey more pleasant. They finally reached San Bernardino, California. They lived there about eight years then returned to Idaho. They settled at Franklin, Idaho where Lucy raised a large family.

Lucy loved to sing and spent many hours singing with her children and grandchildren. Her children remembered well her singing and compared it to the voice of an angel. Her son, Samuel Delbert, remembered that she had sung for the Queen of England and that she had sung in a competition with Jenny Lind.

She went with her husband to participate in the Black Hawk Indian War. She traveled with the men to cook and be a nurse.

Lucy passed away at the age of eighty-one years.

Orpha Maria, 21 Dec 1859 (died in 1861)
Ossian Leonidus, 10 Dec 1861
Ann Eliza, 27 Dec 1863 (died in 1867)
Albert Taylor, 2 Sep 1865 (died in 1867)
Wilford, 10 May 1868 (died as an infant)
Polly Sameda, 1 Mar 1870
Walter, 23 May 1872 d. 1872
Josia George, 24 Jun 1874

Polly Mae was born in Pennsylvania in 1833. Her parents had heard about the wonderful Oregon Territory, and in 1836 decided to go there. One night as they camped by a stream they were joined by members from the Church of Jesus Christ of Latter-day Saints fleeing from a mob.

After hearing about the gospel they decided to cast their lot with the Saints. They lived for a time in Lee County, Iowa, then in Nauvoo, where Polly was baptized when she was ten. They were driven from Nauvoo when Polly was fifteen, and came across the Plains in 1853, with the Appleton Harmon Company. She walked barefoot most of the way.

Polly married James Packer, Sr. in 1854 in Lehi, Utah County, Utah. They were the parents of eleven children, several of them dying very young. In 1860, the family moved to Franklin, Idaho.

After they had been there nine years James took a second wife. Two sons, Alfred and Nathan, were born to this union. However the young mother, being very inexperienced, got discouraged and went away leaving Polly to raise her boys. Polly also reared a grandchild when the mother died.

James went away contracting, leaving Polly to care for the farm, and died in Monterey, Mexico in 1892.

Polly was always busy with some kind of work. She pieced quilts, made braided rugs, and was a faithful Latter-day Saint. Her skin was wrinkle free beacuse she always washed it in buttermilk.

Polly passed away in Preston, Idaho in 1920.

POLLY MAE MECHAM PACKER

BIRTHDATE: 15 Mar 1833
Mercer Co., Pennsylvania
DEATH: 17 Nov 1920
Preston, Idaho
PARENTS: Moses W. Mecham
Elvira Derby
PIONEER: 16 Oct 1853
Appleton Harmon Wagon Train
SPOUSE: James Packer
MARRIED: 14 Feb 1854
Lehi, Utah Co., Utah
DEATH SP: 15 Jul 1892
Monterey, Mexico

CHILDREN:
Samuel Lewis, 9 Jun 1855 d. 1855
James, 21 Jul 1856
Elvira Elizabeth, 3 Mar 1858

ANNE CHRISTENSEN PEDERSON JENSEN PADRIGH / PADRETHA

BIRTHDATE: 10 Jul 1802
Resen, Viborg, Denmark
DEATH: 17 Jul 1891
Gunnison, Sanpete Co., Utah
PARENTS: Christen Hansen
Dorthe Laursdatter Hansen
PIONEER: 11 Nov 1856
James Willie Handcart Company
SPOUSE: Mr. Pedersen
MARRIED: Not given

CHILD:
Hans Peter Pederson, 26 Feb 1837

SPOUSE II: Anders Jensen
MARRIED: 31 Aug 1844
DEATH SP: 29 Aug 1856
Sweetwater, Wyoming

CHILDREN:
Peder Christian Jensen, 11 Apr. 1843
Michael, 5 Feb 1845 (died at age5)
Antonin Jensen, 30 Jun 1847

SPOUSE III: John William Padrigh / Padretha
MARRIED: before 9 Aug 1859
DEATH SP: 9 Aug 1887
Manti, Sanpete Co., Utah
CHILDREN: None

Anne's family emigrated from Denmark with the help of the Perpetual Emigration Fund. They arrived in Iowa City, June 26, with complete faith in the organization that had brought them half way around the world.

Their arrival at Iowa City, was totally unexpected by the church agents outfitting the pioneers in helping them travel West, and while they were frantically trying to get 764 people equipped and on the road, the city was swamped by another influx of emigrants waiting for supplies and help to cross the Plains also. Construction of 250 handcarts, gathering wagons, teams and basic supplies for 1,500 people for three months was an almost impossible task.

Anne, close to fifty years old, was nearly to her new home, and with her husband pushing the yoke of a hastily built, inadequately supplied handcart, was prepared to walk the whole way to Salt Lake Valley, unknowing, unsuspecting the disasters that were to befall them.

Every delay in time was critical. They searched for their first missing person, lost all night in drenching rain, They stopped to make graves for travelers who had been killed by Indians a few days earlier.

Tragically, one night, buffalo stampeded through and over their camp, when they crawled out from under their carts and wagons they found no one hurt, but many draft animals and thirty head of cattle, their beef for the trip, were gone! They searched for two days to no avail, they went on with hardly enough animals to pull their supply wagons. They reached Ft. Laramie expecting to buy more provisions, able to buy only a barrel or two of crackers. By necessity supplies were rationed, and still less was given as they plodded on.

They learned to eat prickly pear cactus, boiled leather broth made of odd pieces of thongs or hides, hoping for some little nourishment. Fathers gave to their children and wives, pushing their carts until they were worn unto death, as the strong died, the weak were left weaker. Winter came early with a vengeance and when the rescue wagons arrived they found a camp of people having gone two days without food.

They were rescued! Anders was so weak they tied his handcart to the back of one wagon and with Anders walking between the handcart holding onto the back of the wagon they went on, but he slipped on wet ground, the handcart rolled over him Anders, badly hurt, died the next morning. He was buried beside the trail near Sweetwater, Wyoming.

Anne, sitting on an upturned kettle was weeping bitterly, a man came by with a walking stick, he struck her across the back and said sternly, "Get up and go on! You can't sit here crying, we have to go on at once or we shall all die!"

There was still two hundred miles to travel through the snow before reaching Salt Lake and Sustenance. Material goods and food were so scarce, but this did not influence Anne to marry an unloved Suitor. Nor did she allow Michael to work in Brigham City for an extremely hard task master.

John William Padrigh, in Manti, needed some one to care for his motherless daughter. They married and melded into a happy family needing nothing for the rest of their life he did not give them, including love.

ELEANOR ESTHER LEADER PAGE

BIRTHDATE: 22 Mar 1818
Manthorpe, England
DEATH: 30 Mar 1889
Salt Lake City, Salt Lake, Utah
PARENTS: Henry Leader
Ann Laughton
PIONEER: 3 Oct 1852
John B. Walker Co. Wagon Train
SPOUSE: John Page
MARRIED: 1 Jul 1835
England
DEATH SP: 12 Jul 1895
Salt Lake City, Salt Lake, Utah

CHILDREN:
Eleanor Esther, 16 May 1836
William Henry, 25 Aug 1838
John Jr., 25 Jan 1841
Emma, 19 Nov 1843
Mary Ann, 14 Apr 1851
Lydia Leader, 15 Feb 1856
Sarah Eleanor, 15 Mar 1861

Eleanor was born in Manthorpe, Lincolnshire, England, into a family of wealth. She had one sister and one brother. Her Aunt, Eleanor Bembridge, whom she was named after, was supposed to have left her a large sum of money, but due to her coming to Utah and losing track of them she received none of it.

She married when she was seventeen and said she loved John from the first time she saw him. Eleanor's parents were not willing for her to marry. Eleanor and John were afraid they might try to stop the wedding so they had a horse and buggy, or "fly" as they called it, ready to leave for the next town for the ceremony. But it turned out all right and they didn't have to use it.

Eleanor gave birth to four children in England. The first one died as an infant. Eleanor's parents, grandmother, she and her husband and three children, and her Aunt Eleanor emigrated to America on November 10, 1849 on the ship "Zetland."

They settled in Iowa after arriving in New Orleans, and with her relatives moved on to Council Bluffs where Eleanor gave birth to another child, Mary Ann.

They came to Utah just five years after the first pioneers. One year after the grasshopper plague on February 15, 1856, Lydia was born. This plague caused untold suffering for the family. Eleanor had nothing to make clothes with. She would take lining out of her dresses to make clothes for her children. Her daughter, Lydia, said she had a shirt made out of muslin that was joined fifteen times and its weight was that of a pocket handkerchief However they were thankful for being able to keep warm. Eleanor gave birth to her last child Sarah Eleanor in 1861. She had six living children out of seven born.

Her husband's health became poor and Eleanor had to work hard to make ends meet. She took in washing and ironing until she could not work anymore then her daughters continued to work for the three years she was sick.

She and her family knew this Gospel was true and that was all she and her husband wanted on this earth. She kept the faith and taught her children true principles.

LOUISA GRAVES PAGE

BIRTHDATE: 20 Dec 1820
Birmingham, England
DEATH: 22 Mar 1864
Bountiful, Davis Co., Utah
PARENTS: John Graves/Glaves
Mary Ann Glaves
PIONEER: 13 Sep 1861
Joseph Horne Co. Wagon Train
SPOUSE: James Page
MARRIED: 16 Oct 1837
Aston Parish, England
DEATH SP: 6 Jan 1892
Lamoni, Decatur Co., Iowa

CHILDREN:
William, 5 Aug 1838
Martha, 28 Jun 1840
Mariah, 26 Mar 1842
Thomas John, 14 Dec 1843
Samuel James, 8 Apr 1845 (died at age 2)
Louisa, 8 Jan 1847 (died at 22 months)
Louisa, 7 Feb 1849 (died at 3 months)
Hyrum, 14 Jul 1850
Alma, 30 Sep 1852
Cyrus, 3 Nov 1854
Orson, 30 Nov 1856

Lorenzo, 27 Dec 1858
Louisa, 15 May 1860 (died as an infant)
James, 12 Feb 1862

Louisa Glaves (also spelled as Greaves, Gleaves, and Graves) was born on December 20, 1820 in Birmingham, Warwickshire, England. Her father was a brazier (one who works with brass.)

She married James Page on October 16, 1837 in Aston Parish, Warwickshire, England. James was a railway worker and Louisa kept a little grocery store and was a watch chain maker. Louisa was kept very busy as her family continued to grow to fourteen children.

James and Louisa accepted the message of the Gospel and were baptized as members of the Church of Jesus Christ of Latter-day Saints on June 6, 1848. They became very active members and welcomed the elders to their home.

Louisa's son, William, was the first to emigrate. On May 11, 1860, their family boarded the "William Tappscott," ship and sailed for America. Louisa gave birth to her thirteenth child on board the ship.

The baby died during their one year stay in New York. James and some of his children found employment to help build a suspension bridge in Williamsburg. He also employed many Saints who needed more money to continue their journey.

In the Spring of 1861, they traveled to Florence, Nebraska where they joined the Joseph Horne Wagon Company. They arrived in Salt Lake City on September 13, 1861.

They were invited by William Muir to move to Bountiful, Utah. Brother Muir took the Page family into his home and gave James employment on his farm.

In 1863, the family moved to Three Mile Creek near Brigham City in Box Elder County where they lived nearly one year. They returned to Bountiful where Louisa passed away and was buried in the spring of 1864, at the age of forty-four.

MARY ANN CLARK PAGE

BIRTHDATE: 5 Jul 1841
Leamington, England
DEATH: 11 Jun 1925
Bountiful, Davis Co., Utah
PARENTS: James Clark
Hannah Tustin
PIONEER: 19 Oct 1862
Horton D. Haight Wagon Train
SPOUSE: William Page
MARRIED: 24 Mar 1863
Bountiful, Davis Co., Utah
DEATH SP: 28 May 1893
Bountiful, Davis Co., Utah

CHILDREN:
Louisa Clark, 23 Mar 1864

Caroline Hannah, 10 Feb 1866
Martha Jane, 20 Nov 1867
Avilda Lucene, 7 Mar 1870
Rose Ellen, 19 Mar 1872
William James, 17 Jan 1874
George Albert, 14 Nov 1875
Mary Annie, 9 Nov 1877
Agnes Amelia, 23 Sep 1879
Mabel, 30 Oct 1881
John Henry, 4 May 1884

Mary Ann was born in Leamington, Warwickshire, England. She was the eldest living child in her family. The town of Leamington, England was a summer resort for the wealthy people of the Shire. She was educated in the Baptist school and was a member of the Independence Church.

Mary Ann was asked by a friend to go with her to hear the Mormons speak and she was impressed with the truth and was baptized, leaving parents and native land for Utah. She sailed from Liverpool on the ship "William Tappscott," having on board 808 Saints.

Mary Ann crossed the Plains enduring many hardships and she often said the hardest thing she had to do was to gather buffalo chips in her dress skirt.

After arriving in the Salt Lake Valley, she was first taken to the home of President Hess. It was dark when she arrived. When she went in the house, there was a dirt floor and roof, a drygoods box was used for the table and stumps of trees for the chairs. The bed had been made by putting in posts and using the corner of the house for the other legs, raw hide was stretched over and across for springs. The mattress was a straw tick. She was not too worried, for she thought that in the morning she would get better lodging.

In the morning, Ann was up early and went out doors. To her surprise, all the homes were like the one she was in, and she couldn't help crying. President Hess came out and comforted her and blessed her and promised her she would never regret coming to America.

Mary Ann went to live with Sister Roberts in Bountiful and while visiting at the home of William Muir she met and fell in love with William Page. After their marriage her husband's parents lived with them. Her mother-in-law was very ill and they lived in one room. Grandmother Page died on the night of March 22, 1864 and Mary Ann gave birth to her first baby in the opposite corner of the room.

They had suffered many hardships. The grasshoppers ate all their grain leaving them without much food. She had five little girls when her husband was called on a mission to Arizona. He took the wagon and horses but with the help of good neighbors and her little girls she managed the farm.

She worked in the Relief Society from 1877 and was the president in 1891. During this time she prepared many bodies for burial and sat many nights with the sick and helping those in need. She was forced to resign on account of poor health in 1899. She was elected the first Lady Trustee of the District School and held that position for seven years, and was a member of the Old People's Party for about twenty years serving as the secretary.

Mary Ann was loved by everyone.

MARY LEAVER PAGE

BIRTHDATE: 26 Aug 1837
Brooklyn, Kings, New York
DEATH: 4 Mar 1896
Payson, Utah Co., Utah
PARENTS: Samuel Leaver
Mary Ann Hartlett
PIONEER: 10 Sep 1852
James Jepson Co. Wagon Train
SPOUSE: Jonathan Socwell Page
MARRIED: 12 Aug 1855
Salt Lake City, Salt Lake, Utah
DEATH SP: 15 Oct 1924
Payson, Utah Co., Utah

CHILDREN:
Jonathan Socwell, Jr., 14 May 1856
Anna Maria, 26 Apr 1858
Samuel Leaver, 16 Nov 1859
Mary Losana, 2 Jan 1862
Ruth Ellen, 28 Mar 1864
Elizabeth Hannah, 27 Jan 1866
Joseph Edmond, 21 Feb 1868
William Henry, 21 Sep 1869
Nellie Ingram, 8 Aug 1872
George Milton, 1 Oct 1874
Hartlett Hall, 9 Feb 1877
Ethel Adele, 7 Mar 1879
Cora Verena, 27 Mar 1881

Mary's parents had emigrated to America about 1829 from England and were living in New York when she was born.

Her parents joined the Church of Jesus Christ of Latter-day Saints in March 1840 and were among the forty persons baptized by Apostle Parley P. Pratt. Her family gathered in Nauvoo with the Saints in 1844 where they suffered many persecutions. They crossed the Mississippi River in 1846 where they were forced to live in tents for several weeks. They suffered hunger, cold weather, sickness, and distress. They experienced the miracle of the quails which fed the camp.

During the next six years, their family endured the hardships of Winter Quarters, Council Bluffs, and Savannah, Missouri before they were prepared to cross the Plains. Since there were no boys old enough to help their father, Mary was taught to drive a team of oxen hitched to a wagon, how to make camp, and build fires. Mary observed her fifteenth birthday a month before they entered the Salt Lake Valley, September 10, 1852, with the James J. Jepson Wagon Company. The Leaver family settled in Salt Lake City where her father built a log home and supported the family as a tailor.

Mary married Jonathan on August 12, 1855. In 1858, Mary and Jonathan moved to Payson where he operated the Payson Cooperative Institution (store). He also owned and operated a steam mill in Payson Canyon.

Her husband was mayor of Payson for twenty years, was Justice of the Peace, was County Commissioner for fifteen years, was in the State Legislature, served in the bishopric, and as a Patriarch. He was also a captain in the cavalry in the Walker and Black Hawk Indian Wars, in the Utah militia, and also participated in the Echo Canyon campaign.

Mary fitted well her role of devoted mother to thirteen children and supported her husband in his activities as mayor, merchant, and patriarch.

She passed away, March 4, 1896, at the age of sixty-two in Payson, Utah.

MARY SOCWELL PAGE

BIRTHDATE: 26 Apr 1805
Dividing Creek, New Jersey
DEATH: 04 Apr 1884
Mt. Pleasant, Sanpete Co., Utah
PARENTS: Jonathan Socwell
Lorana Whitaker
PIONEER: 6 Sep 1852
Joseph Outhouse Wagon Train
SPOUSE: Daniel Page
MARRIED: 18 Apr 1822
Newport, New Jersey
DEATH SP: 17 Aug 1882
Mt. Pleasant, Sanpete Co., Utah

CHILDREN:
Ruth, 1 May 1823
David, 17 Nov 1824
Daniel, 23 Jun 1828
Joseph, 6 Feb 1830
Lucy Ann, 3 Sep 1831
Jonathan Socwell, 4 Jun 1833
Mary Ellen, 1 Mar 1835
George Washington, 15 Nov 1836
William Whitaker, 15 Feb 1839 (died at 5 months)
Lorana, 17 Aug 1843
Jeremiah Day, 21 Feb 1847

Mary was the sixth child born to Jonathan Socwell, Jr. and Lorena Whitaker Socwell. When she was seventeen, she married Daniel Page. They farmed and had eight children by the time the financial panic of 1837 affected them.

During this time, Daniel lost his property. Daniel and his sons went west to find a new home. They found work in the forests, cutting timber until they reached Illinois. Mary and her oldest daughter found work in a cotton factory in Pennsylvania.

While her husband and sons were in Illinois, they joined the Church of Jesus Christ of Latter-day Saints.

After being apart for four years, Daniel and his son, Daniel, returned and persuaded Mary and the rest of the family to return to New Jersey. In 1843, the missionaries came to their home and Mary became baptized a member on September 29, 1843.

In January of 1850, Daniel and Mary decided they were ready to join the Saints. They went to Council Bluffs, joined the Joseph Outhouse Wagon Company, and crossed the Plains to Salt Lake City. They had difficulties with Cholera, storms, oxen stampedes, rattlesnakes, thirst, wagon breakdowns, killing buffalo, and Indians stealing their horses. Mary and Daniel settled in Provo where they lived in their wagon by the Provo River for many months.

In 1853, they settled in Payson. Daniel was often ill, suffering from rheumatism. Mary and her daughter, Ruth, assisted with the family's support by taking in washing, knitting, and sewing. They also took wool to work on in shares. They washed it, picked it, and spun it in order to keep one half of it. Mary and Ruth would glean the fields for wheat for their own use after the wheat was harvested. They helped with the raising of gardens, pigs, and cattle. Eventually, they settled permanently in Mt. Pleasant.

Mary was an educated woman. She wrote several poems to her daughters. She valued education and saw to it that her children could read and write.

Mary and Daniel enjoyed taking trips to the temples to do work. She had a great prosperity and an abiding faith in the gospel.

Mary passed away on April 4, 1884 in Mount Pleasant, Utah just twenty-two days short of being seventy-nine.

ELIZABETH NUTTAL BRADSHAW PAINTER

BIRTHDATE: 15 Jul 1843
Manchester, Lancashire, England
DEATH: 12 May 1913
Wellsville, Cache Co., Utah
PARENTS: Charles H. Bradshaw
Ann Nuttal
PIONEER: 03 Sep 1860
James D. Ross Co. Wagon Train
SPOUSE: William Painter
MARRIED: 21 Mar 1861
Bountiful, Davis Co., Utah
DEATH SP: 17 Feb 1892
Wellsville, Cache Co., Utah

CHILDREN:
Mary Ann, 3 Sep 1862
Martha, 1 Oct 1864
William Charles, 21 Mar 1867
Sarah, 22 Jul 1869
Emeline, 18 Nov 1871
Matilda, 15 Apr 1874
George, 6 Aug 1876
Thomas, 13 Aug 1879
James, 10 Dec 1881

Elizabeth was ten years old when she and her parents left England and immigrated to America. They crossed the ocean on the ship, "Clara Wheeler." They left Liverpool on April 24, 1854 and after spending ten weeks and one day on the water, arrived in New Orleans on July 3, 1854. There were only twenty-nine LDS passengers on board this ship.

From New Orleans they took another vessel up the Mississippi River and onto St. Louis, some 1,200 miles. Latter-day Saints were counseled if they could pay their own way to St. Louis to do so, for they could obtain an outfit there easily. Due to lack of money the Bradshaws were forced to remain in St. Louis and obtain employment.

Elizabeth, now eleven years old was sent each day to the coal pits with dinner for her father and his three brothers. Cholera broke out, and within one day of each other her parents died leaving their children, Elizabeth age eleven, Ruth age six, and Thomas age three. Her uncle, Thomas Bradshaw, took Elizabeth and her brother Thomas, Uncle George Bradshaw took Ruth. Six years later the families had saved enough money, to continue their journey to Utah.

Elizabeth was a very cheerful girl and would sing with others as they walked on their way. Elizabeth, along with the other girls in the company, milked the cows. The milk was used throughout the camp. Any milk not used would be put in a tin churn and strapped on the side of the wagon. By noon it would be thoroughly churned and butter could be molded and the buttermilk drank for lunch.

Elizabeth tells of a harrowing experience with an Indian. She and Margaret Nibley (Maughan) were walking along side by side talking, when an Indian rode up and threw his lasso rope around the girls and was pulling them to him. Their screams attracted the teamsters who opened fire on the Indian and frightened him away.

On Monday, September 3, 1860, the company came out of the canyon and onto the bench near Fort Douglas. Elizabeth was full of joy to see the little growing city of Salt Lake and felt that all of their troubles and trials were mostly at an end.

Elizabeth married William and in the year 1862, they moved to Logan and later in that year settled in Wellsville, in the old Fort, which was called "Maughan's Fort." They later received a parcel of land in the west part of Wellsville and built a home on it.

Elizabeth loved her family and together she and her husband taught them the principles of the Gospel and to be honorable men and women.

MARY ANN BROOKS PAINTER

BIRTHDATE: 6 Jun 1843
Coventry, England
DEATH: 5 Oct 1888
Provo, Utah Co., Utah
PARENTS: Charles Brooks
Mary Ann Wilson
PIONEER: 26 Sep 1862
James Wareham Wagon Train
SPOUSE: John Scoffins Painter
MARRIED: 21 Apr 1862
On board ship
DEATH SP: Not given

CHILDREN:
John Charles, 20 Nov 1863
William, 2 Jul 1865
Mary Jane, 22 Apr 1868 (died in 1869)
Harriet Ann, 1 Aug 1870 (died in 1870)
George, 9 Feb 1872 (died in 1881)
Mary Ann "Mae," 14 Sep 1875

Mary Ann Brooks was born in England in 1843. When she was eight years old she fell down a flight of stairs, which impaired her health for the rest of her life. Also while a child she worked in a button factory, and later as a weaver of fine cloth. She was baptized as a member of the Church of Jesus Christ of Latter-day Saints at the age of thirteen.

Mary Ann left England in 1862 with three friends, sailing on the ship "John J. Boyd." On board ship she met John Scoffins Painter, a widower with a two year old daughter, Elizabeth. They were married on April 21, 1862, while at sea.

A calamity nearly befell her when Elizabeth came up missing one day. Mary Ann was accused of throwing her overboard, and the captain put her in chains for a time. The little girl was found asleep under her bed, unharmed.

The company arrived in Salt Lake in September, 1862, and with some of their friends they traveled on to Nephi, Juab County, Utah to live.

John eventually built a seven-room house, where they had a family orchard, a fine garden, flowers, a chicken coop, and stable and corral. All of her children were born in Nephi.

John and Mary Ann saved money so that Mary Ann's mother, sister and two brothers could emigarate from England.

In 1870, John married her sister, Sarah, but there was much jealousy, so John moved Mary Ann and her son, George, into a small home, and supplied her with some commodities. She later gave birth to her last daughter, Mae. There was much bitterness and John refused to even acknowledge this daughter until years later when he asked forgiveness from her.

Mary Ann had a cerebral hemorrhage and passed away in 1888, at the age of forty-five years.

HANNAH BUTLER PALFREYMAN

BIRTHDATE: 18 Nov 1824
Denby, Derbyshire, England
DEATH: 18 Feb 1892
Springville, Utah Co., Utah
PARENTS: Joseph Butler
Mary Chapman
PIONEER: 4 Oct 1864
William S. Warren Wagon Train
SPOUSE: Richard Palfreyman
MARRIED: 22 Jan 1842
Denby, Derbyshire, England
DEATH SP: 20 Apr 1907
Denby, Derbyshire, England

CHILDREN:
Selena, 24 Sep 1843
Charles, 17 Feb 1845
Thomas, 13 Nov 1846
Sarah, 25 Feb 1849 (died at age 1)
Richard, 19 Sep 1850
Fanny, 22 May 1852
Annie, 12 Jan 1854
Joseph Henry, 12 Jun 1855 (died at age 7)
Mary "Polly," 19 Aug 1857
Esther, 31 Jan 1859
Hannah, 16 Mar 1861 (died at age 2)
Dennis, 29 Mar 1863

Hannah's childhood was spent in Denby where she received her education which qualified her to become a most efficient homemaker.

At the age of seventeen years, she married Richard Palfreyman and to them were born twelve children, nine of whom grew to maturity. Richard earned a living as a coal miner while Hannah tended to her home duties. Their home in England was filled with comforts of life.

Hannah was baptized into the Church of Jesus Christ of Latter-day Saints on April 14, 1851 in the Belper Branch in Derbyshire, England. She accepted the teachings with her heart and soul. Her husband received the missionaries into his home and treated them kindly, but never joined the Church.

Hannah felt the urgency to leave England and gather with the Saints. Her husband and sons, Charles, Thomas, and Richard remained in England. The two oldest girls, Selina and Fanny were sent to Utah in 1863 under the care of Mr. and Mrs. Hatfield. Hannah and the remainder of her children came to America in 1864. They traveled West with the William S. Warren Wagon Company and arrived in the Salt Lake Valley on October 4, 1864.

They settled in Springville, Utah. Hannah wove rag rugs, gleaned the wheat fields, and used her culinary skills to support her family. Her bread, buns, currant loaf, rolly polly pudding, potato pie, and pork pie became famous among her family, friends, and neighbors. She often took tasty dishes to those who were sick. Hannah enjoyed helping others and was the first one there to help them in times of sickness, births, or death.

In 1866, her husband sent their son, Richard to America to assist her. Richard brought a large box of rare provisions with him, including fancy apparel, a feather bed, gun, and other articles. Hannah sold some of these things and with the money, she purchased land upon which to build a home. Her children helped her to purchase the logs.

She was blessed with a fine singing voice and took great joy and comfort singing the songs of Zion. She was very industrious and took great delight in growing all kinds of fruit, vegetables, flowers, until her health failed.

Hannah passed away on February 18, 1892 in Springville, Utah County, Utah.

ANN ELIZABETH HODGKINSON WAMSLEY PALMER

No Photo Available

BIRTHDATE: 24 Aug 1807
Chipping, Lancashire, England
DEATH: 16 Nov 1888
Bloomington, Bear Lake, Idaho
PARENTS: Francis Hodgkinson
Jane Malley
PIONEER: 1849
SPOUSE I: Thomas Wamsley
MARRIED: 25 Dec 1826
DEATH SP: 16 Nov 1842
Nauvoo, Hancock Co., Illinois

CHILDREN:
John, 25 Mar 1830
Franciscus, 2 Jan 1833
William, 13 Apr 1834
Thomas, 1835 (died at age 4)
Marinda, 5 Jun 1838 (died as an infant)
Nancy Marinda, 11 Dec 1839
Heber Chase Kimball, 1841 (died at age 22)

SPOUSE II: Isaac Palmer
MARRIED: 1844
DEATH SP: After 1853
Pottawattamie Co., Iowa

CHILDREN:
Journal, 10 May 1847
Isaac, 12 Oct 1848
Rhoda, 23 Apr 1850 (died at age 4)

Ann Elizabeth was married to Thomas Wamsley and was one of the first nine converts to the Church of Jesus Christ of Latter-day Saints in the British Isles. Heber C. Kimball entered their home as a missionary and learned she was very ill with consumption from which she had suffered for several years. She was converted to the gospel and was carried to the water where she was baptized and partially healed. At the time of her confirmation, the Elders rebuked her disease in the name of the Lord and promised she would be completely healed. Within a week, she was well enough to perform her household duties.

Ann Elizabeth and Thomas brought their family to America with the first company of Saints in 1842, settling in Missouri. They shared the persecutions and privations of those trying times. They moved to Nauvoo, Illinois where Thomas died.

In 1844, Ann Elizabeth married Isaac Palmer and three children were born to this union. Ann gave birth to her son, Journal, just ten days out of Winter Quarters on the journey to the Salt Lake Valley. She drove an ox and two cows across the Plains. They arrived in the Salt Lake Valley in 1849 and worked with the Saints to build homes.

After their daughter, Rhoda's, birth and death, Isaac Palmer left his family and went to the gold fields of California. Ann Elizabeth took back the surname of Wamsley. She and her children moved to Bloomington in Bear Lake Valley to settle and to be near her oldest son, John. Even though her home was a crude one, she was a neat, orderly, and splendid housekeeper.

Ann Elizabeth passed away in Bloomington, Idaho on November 16, 1888.

FRANCIS FARR MILLS PALMER

BIRTHDATE: Chr. 1 Sep 1811
Westbourne, Sussex, England
DEATH: 3 Feb 1891
Enterprise, Morgan Co., Utah
PARENTS: Thomas Henry Farr
Francis Pheobe Bone
PIONEER: 1863
Roswell Hyde Co. Wagon Train
SPOUSE I: Charles E. Mills
MARRIED: 17 Apr 1832
Prescott, Lanks, England
DEATH SP: 19 Apr 1863
Southampton, England

CHILDREN:
Francis, 20 Sep 1831
Martha, 29 Jan 1832
Harriett, 22 Jan 1834
Mary, 5 Apr 1836
Charles Edmund Thomas, 14 Jan 1838
Emma Rosina, 4 Feb 1840
Ruth Jane, 26 Aug 1841
Ann Maria, 22 Apr 1844
George William David, 12 Jul 1846
Phoebe Sarah, 12 Oct 1848
Louise Harriet Susan, 10 Dec 1849
Sarah Ellen, 17 Mar 1852

SPOUSE II: Thomas Palmer
MARRIED: 9 Feb 1865

DEATH SP: 21 Nov 1900
Enterprise, Morgan Co., Utah
CHILDREN: None

Francis was raised on a small farm in Westbourne, Sussex, England. She was a servant girl before her marriage. She was married at the age of sixteen.

Her family lived in Winchester for eight years, then moved to the seaport town of Southampton. Here the family heard the gospel. The gospel came when Francis' baby, Harriet Louise, was laying at death's door. She had been given up by ministers and the doctor. She heard a knock on the door and it was two missionaries from the Church of Jesus Christ of Latter-day Saints. She asked them to hurry as she had a dying baby. Brother Savage asked to see the baby. He said, "In the name of the Lord, the child should not die." With her permission, Brother Savage administered to the baby in the name of the true and living God. Francis gave her permission, but asked them to hurry before her minister returned.

In 1860, President George Q. Cannon counseled the Saints to come to Zion. If they did not have means, they were instructed to send their family in shifts. In 1863, after the death of her husband, Francis sold everything and she and her daughter, Sarah, came to America.

She sailed from Liverpool and landed in New York; then traveled overland to Albany and on to St. Joes, up the Mississippi River to Florence, Nebraska which was the outfitting place for the Saints. Several weeks were spent in preparing for the journey to the Great Salt Lake Valley.

Once in the Valley, she was met by her son, Charles, and taken to his home which was a dugout on Kay's Creek, Kaysville, Utah. The following spring she went to Enterprise, Morgan County, Utah to keep house for Thomas Palmer whose wife had died and left him with four small children. His home was a log house with a dirt floor and roof. She swept the floor with willows for a broom.

Francis married Thomas Palmer. In February, 1865, she permitted Thomas Palmer to marry her daughter, Harriet Louisa, and Francis always lived with them. She helped him and her daughter clear land of sage brush and assisted with the regular farm work.

She was the first midwife and nurse in that part of the state. Much credit is due her in helping to control small pox because she vaccinated practically all the population in that area. She knew every herb and their use and each year she would gather herbs from early spring until winter, each in their greatest medical value, to be used in caring for the sick. When called to the sick, she would evaluate the condition, then make medicine from her supply.

She was a pleasant, loving person. She was a true Latter-day-Saint and the mother of twelve children. Three died in Ireland in one year. Four came to America and the remainder stayed in England

LOUISA HARRIET MILLS PALMER

BIRTHDATE: 10 Dec 1851
Winchester, Hampshire, England
DEATH: 15 Nov 1930
Clearfield, Davis Co., Utah
PARENTS: Charles E. Mills
Francis Farr
PIONEER: 9 Oct 1862
Dan Miller Co. Wagon Train
SPOUSE: Thomas Palmer
MARRIED: 14 Feb 1865
Salt Lake City, Salt Lake, Utah
DEATH SP: 17 Nov 1900
Enterprise, Morgan Co., Utah

CHILDREN:
George David, 3 Dec 1865
Charles Edmond, 28 Nov 1867
Harriet Louisa, 6 Jan 1869
Walter Welrose, 27 May 1871
Joseph Hyrum, 2 May 1873
Ernest Edward, 7 Aug 1875
Fredric, 22 Jun 1877
Tracy, 12 Jul 1879
Francis Rosina, 22 Dec 1880
Thomas Henry, 23 Mar 1883
Sidney, 16 May 1884
Clara Pearl, 13 May 1886
Oliver Alonzo, 22 May 1888
Nellie Corel, 4 Sep 1894

Louisa's family was in Winchester when they first heard the gospel of the Church of Jesus Christ of Latter-day Saints and she was lying at death's door. There came a knock on the door by two missionaries and her mother told them she had a dying baby in the house.

Brother Charles R. Savage asked to see the baby. He said "in the name of the Lord this child shall not die." He asked permission to administer to the child in the name of the True and Living God. Mother gave her consent, but with instruction to be quick, before her clergyman returned. In his blessing he told Louisa that she would live and be a savior to her people and they would be gathered to the land of Zion.

She attended public school for a short time but forced to leave school because of poor health. Later she attended a Catholic School where she learned to crochet, knit, and other subjects taught in the school.

She remembers that John Taylor and Erastus Snow were missionaries in their town, and it was at this time she learned to love music. At this time her family moved to St. James Street to be near the Church and after a few years she was baptized by President Henry Passey.

President George Q. Cannon was in charge of the European Mission and he counseled the Saints to come to Zion. "If all can't come at once, come as you can." Her brother and sister came in 1861, and in 1862 at eleven years old she traveled without a relative to Liverpool where she set sail for America.

Now ahead of them; the great hardship of crossing the Plains. Travel was slow and George Q. Cannon had great concern for Louisa and checked on her daily. Her brother Charles Mills met her in Salt Lake City and after a while took her to their sister Mary Mills Hibbert in Morgan County, Utah. While staying here she met her future husband and was his fourth wife.

Her mother, three stepsons and Louisa helped clear the farm in Enterprise of sagebrush. Grasshoppers and crickets were bad. For weeks older members of the family went without bread in order that the younger children could eat.

She was president of the Young Womens for seventeen years, Treasurer of the Relief Society of Peterson Ward for eleven years and counselor to the Superintentent of the Sunday School for a number of years. She was mother of ten boys, four girls; stepmother to five other childen of Thomas Palmer by former marriages.

In 1902, she moved to Ogden with her family, because of little employment and a small farm would not sustain them. She began a career as a nurse working with a number of doctors. It was necessary to work long hours to keep her family together. She had a happy home.

Louisa sang until she was eighty years old. Her life as a polygamist wife was happiness all around.

LUCINDA ANN AYERS PALMER

BIRTHDATE: 1 Apr 1851
Kanesville, Iowa
DEATH: 19 Sep 1833
Cherry Creek, Nevada
PARENTS: Caleb Ayers
Lucinda Catherine Hagerty
PIONEER: 1852
SPOUSE: David Moroni Palmer
MARRIED: 1 Jan 1869
Springdale, Washington, Utah
DEATH SP: 4 Oct 1930
Ely, Nevada

CHILDREN:
William George, 3 Jun 1870
David Henry, 29 Oct 1872
Musetta, 31 Aug 1874
Heber Caleb, 27 Jun 1876
Victoria, 22 Sep 1878
Lottie, 16 Apr 1881
Albert, 30 Oct 1882
Jennie Blanche, 22 May 1885
Mary, 9 Feb 1888
Irene Louisa, 31 Mar 1889
Daisy Amanda, 27 Jan 1891
Ruby, 2 Feb 1893
Arthur, 6 Jan 1895
Dora Evelyn, 2 May 1898

Lucinda Ann was born on April 1, 1851 at Kanesville, Pottawattamie County, Iowa as the seventh child.

Lucinda's parents were in Iowa preparing to come West with the Saints. Her father died, March 14, 1852, at Council Bluffs, so she, along with her mother, two sisters and two brothers, continued the long, hard journey to Utah. They arrived in the Salt Lake Valley in 1852. The family settled in Manti, Sanpete County, Utah, but later moved to Rockville, Washington County, Utah.

In 1868, she met David Moroni Palmer when he stopped in Rockville to visit an uncle. They were married on January 1, 1869 at Springdale, Washington County, Utah. They were the parents of fourteen children:

Lucinda was left alone a good deal of the time while David was in Richfield cutting ties for the railroad. It was hard because she had five little children at that time. When he came home he found them all down with chills and fever.

They loaded up the wagon to go back to his job, but decided to go to Deseret instead, to visit relatives. They never left there. Times were hard at Deseret also, with the water dams washing out. Lucinda and her two small boys bound willows to help save the dams, and to pay for her husband's water rights. He was away working at the mines.

Her religion always came first. Lucinda was a faithful Relief Society teacher for many years. Her husband passed away on October 4, 1930 at Ely, Nevada; and Lucinda passed away on September 19, 1933 at Cherry Creek, White Pine County, Nevada. She is buried in the Deseret Cemetery, in Utah.

MARY ELLEN PURDUN PALMER

BIRTHDATE: 1829
Ohio
DEATH: 24 Aug 1902
PARENTS: David Purdun
Hannah Purdun
PIONEER: 1856
SPOUSE: Wiliam G. Palmer
MARRIED:
DEATH SP: 14 Apr 1891
Provo, Utah Co., Utah

CHILDREN:
Hannah Saloma Jane (Smith), 25 Apr 1847/1848
David Moroni, 10 Aug 1849
George Alma, Jun 1851 - 1853

Mary Ellen Purdun was born in Ohio in 1829. She was the second of five children of David Purdun and Hannah (last name unknown at this time).

Mary Ellen was the second wife of William George Palmer, who was born August 25, 1821 in Haldimand, Northumberland, Ontario, Canada, They moved to Sycamore, DeKalb County, Illinois and then to Jackson County, Missouri. Mary Ellen and George became the parents of three children while living there.

Undoubtedly, they went through the persecutions of the Saints for several years before going to Utah and settling in Draper, Utah in 1856.

William passed away on April 14, 1891 and was buried in Provo, Utah County, Utah. Mary Ellen passed away on August 24, 1902.

MARY JANE EWER PALMER

BIRTHDATE: 30 Apr 1846
Banbury, Oxfordshire, England
DEATH: 4 Jul 1934
Grantsville, Tooele Co., Utah
PARENTS: John Ewer
Hannah Taylor Weaver
PIONEER: 15 Sep 1866
SPOUSE: James Palmer
MARRIED: 10 Aug 1867
Salt Lake Endowment House
DEATH SP: 6 Oct 1905
Grantsville, Tooele Co., Utah

CHILDREN:
Henry Ewer, 12 Jul 1869 (died at age 18)
Alonzo Ewer, 30 Dec 1870 (died at age 3)
Hannah Ewer, 13 Sep 1872
Joseph Ewer, 12 Feb 1874
Levi Ewer, 4 Mar 1876
Wilford Ewer, 3 Jun 1878
David Ewer, 24 Mar 1880
Alice Ewer, 26 Sep 1882
Daisy Ewer, 13 Oct 1884
Richard Ewer, 5 Aug 1886
Ada Ewer, 27 Jun 1888 (twin)
Fannie Ewer, 27 Jun 1888 (twin)
Heber Ewer, 10 May 1890

Mary Jane's father was a weaver by trade and had two looms in his home. Mary Jane started her steady work of weaving at the age of six. Her first job was to wind the bobbins for the weavers. When her brother, George, went to work in a dye factory, Mary replaced him on the loom at ten years of age. At the age of fourteen, her family moved to Coventry, England where Mary hired out as a weaver to help support her family.

Her family heard the gospel preached by Charles W. Penrose. They soon embraced the gospel and were baptized as members of the Church of Jesus Christ of Latter-day Saints.

Mary Jane obtained a job in an impressive factory where it took her five years to save the necessary money for her trip to Utah. She sailed on the ship, "Belle Wood," and was sea sick most of the time. They landed in New York on June 1, 1866. She decided to join the Nixon family as they were crossing the Plains. They went by boat and train to Wyoming, Nebraska and camped there until the teams were ready for the journey. Their company was under the leadership of William Henry Chipman. They arrived in the Salt Lake Valley on September 15, 1866.

Mary Jane worked for Bishop A. Milton Musser, attended church regularly, and was a member of the Tabernacle Choir.

On August 10, 1867, she became the plural wife of James Palmer. They were sealed in the Endowment House in Salt Lake City. They rented Delle Ranch in Skull Valley, Tooele County, where their crops failed twice in succession. They filed claim on land eight miles south of the ranch where they built a comfortable cabin and began their own ranch near a good stream of water. Mary Jane's greatest desire was to have a large family and over a period of years, they had thirteen children.

Because they lived so far from any town, Mary Jane had to be very versatile in helping her children to survive. She knitted stockings for the family from the wool she gathered. She washed it, carded it, and made her own yarn. She also made the quilts for their beds. Their old clothing was used in the quilts or rugs for the floor.

They made their own pillows from the down of ducks they killed. She made her own yeast and starch. They enjoyed making dandelion pop and buttermilk. They made soap, cured hams, corned beef, jerked beef and venison. Plain boiled wheat was their most used cereal. She raised her own vegetable garden.

During the evenings, James taught the children how to read and write. He was musically inclined and taught the children to sing parts, do simple dance steps, and how to read music.

Mary became friends with the Indians and learned the use of each herb from them. She found these to be very useful remedies. In 1890, they sold their ranch and moved to Grantsville where she lived until she was eighty-eight years old.

No task was too difficult and no sacrifice was too great for Mary Jane as she filled, so well, the role of a pioneer, a devoted wife, and a mother.

PATIENCE DELILA PIERCE PALMER

BIRTHDATE: 15 Feb 1809
Oswegatchie, New York
DEATH: 25 Mar 1894
Aurora, Sevier Co., Utah
PARENTS: Rev. Isaac Pierce
Elizabeth Taylor
PIONEER: Spring of 1852
Company unknown
SPOUSE: Abraham Palmer
MARRIED: 10 Jul 1825
Oswegatchie, New York
DEATH SP: 24 May 1875
Dover, Sanpete Co., Utah

CHILDREN:
Isaac Pierce, 25 Apr 1826
Luther Moses Morris, 5 Jul 1827
John Quincy, 11 Jan 1829
Elizabeth, 13 May 1831
Ann Eliza, 28 Aug 1834
Susan Charlotte, 15 Oct 1835
Abraham P., 19 Feb 1838
James Albert, 25 Dec 1841
Patience Delila, 11 Nov 1844
William Moroni, 10 Dec 1846
Hyrum Smith, 9 Feb 1849

Patience Delila was born on February 15, 1809, at Oswegatchie, St. Lawrence County, New York.

She married Abraham Palmer; son of Noah Palmer and Tirzah Whitney Palmer, on July 10, 1825, at Oswegatchie, St. Lawrence County, New York.

In 1834, two elders came to their home preaching the gospel of the Mormon Church, which they accepted. In May, 1838, they left New York to gather with the Saints in Far West, Missouri.

Their lives ran parallel to the early history of the Church. They were at Haun's Mill the night of the massacre, had their wagons searched and their books and guns taken by the mobs. Tired and hungry, they stopped for awhile in Springfield, Illinois, where her husband worked as a carpenter on the state-house. Soon after they were called to Nauvoo to work on the temple. Before long they were driven into Iowa, as winter was approaching, leaving their homes and all they had.

Very late in the Fall of 1848, they arrived upon Pottawattamie Creek, at an Indian village, which was fifty miles from Kanesville. The snow had become so deep they could travel no farther.

In the Spring of 1852, they left Kanesville for Utah. They arrived in the Salt Lake Valley in October, 1852, moving to Ogden City, Utah. Patience was made the first Relief Society president in Weber County. She worked diligently helping the poor during the grasshopper ravages.

Again they were told to leave their homes as Johnston's Army was coming. The family moved to Spanish Fork where she lived all summer in a willow shack. Then the government found out that the stories of disloyalty were all lies and their family returned to Ogden, later, moving to Sanpete County where some of their children were located.

Here Abraham Palmer, her husband, passed away on May 24, 1875, at Fayette. Patience then lived with her son, William M. at Glenwood and later in Aurora, Sevier County where she passed away on March 25, 1894, and was buried by the side of her husband in Fayette, Sanpete County, Utah.

All during Patience's strenuous life she acted as a midwife and doctor, administering help and comfort to all in need. Of the hundreds of women she waited on she never lost one woman or child which she ascribes to the fact that a prayer was always on her lips for divine assistance whenever she waited on the sick.

She was also a school teacher of considerable success, having taught in Annabel, Sevier County; Deseret, Millard County; and Chicken Creek, Juab County. She was a very genial, kind person, beloved by all and especially the children. Truly a more righteous, patient, and humble woman never lived. She had devoted her whole life to the gospel of Christ and had now gone to her reward.

SALLY KNIGHT PALMER

BIRTHDATE: 1 Dec 1836
Gallatin, Clay Co., Missouri
DEATH: 1 Oct 1916
Orderville, Kane Co., Utah
PARENTS: Newel Knight
Lydia Goldthwait
PIONEER: 3 Oct 1850
Edward Hunter Co. Wagon Train
SPOUSE: Zemira Palmer
MARRIED: 1 Dec 1851
Provo, Utah Co., Utah
DEATH SP: 22 Oct 1880
Orderville, Kane Co., Utah

CHILDREN:
Alma Zemira, 12 Jun 1853
Mary, 1 Jan 1855 (twin - died day of birth)
Martha, 1 Jan 1855 (twin - died at 7 days)
Lydia Amelia, 20 Jan 1856
Phebe, 18 Feb 1858
James William, 23 Sep 1860
George Asahel, 1 Nov 1861
Jessie Milo, 11 Dec 1864
Emma, 30 Jun 1867
Newel Knight, 9 Jul 1870
Joseph, 20 Nov 1874
Chloe, 31 Jan 1878

Sally's parents was the very first marriage ceremony performed by the Prophet Joseph Smith in Kirtland, Ohio at the home of the Patriarch Hyrum Smith.

Sally was named for her grandmother, Sally Goldthwait. She was going on three when her parents settled in Nauvoo.

She was the oldest child in the family and was baptized in 1844. Sally witnessed the persecutions heaped upon the Saints.

Sally, with her family, left Nauvoo at age nine. A month following her tenth birthday, her father became suddenly ill and died. She saw him buried on the Plains in a rude coffin made from a wagon box. A few months later her baby brother, Hyrum, was born. They lived in a dugout and log cabin in Pottawattamie and Winter Quarters for three years.

Now, at age thirteen, Sarah's family left Kanesville, Iowa with the Edward Hunter Company for Utah. She walked a great part of the way, arriving on October 3, 1850.

While attending school, she met Zemira Palmer who was born in Canada. They were married on her fifteenth birthday, he being twenty. Later sealed in the Endowment House on September 18, 1855 by Heber C. Kimball. Her first six children were born in Provo. When the twins were born, Mary died that day and was buried. Martha followed her in death on January 8, 1855. Mary was removed from her grave so the two could be buried together.

About 1861, they moved to Heber City where George and Jessie were born. While living in Provo, Sally became a plural wife when Zemira married Caroline Jaques in 1856.

Sally made many moves when her husband was called to different areas. To Panaca at the head of the Muddy Creek in Nevada where her daughter, Emma, was born and then to Eagle Valley where Newel was born. Later they moved again to Springdale in Washington County, where Joseph was born. Then to Orderville to help and to live the United Order.

In December, 1877, Caroline died after the birth of her three day old child, Ann, leaving her younger children in the care of Sally; in all making nine children to care for in one room. Sally was taken to Santa Clara to stay with her mother where the last child, Chloe was born.

Because of her husband's health problems they moved back to Orderville. Here he died at the age of forty-nine. Sally, nearly forty-four years old, was left to care for the children of both families.

She did her share of work for the Order, spinning, weaving, braiding straw and making hats, etc., and then at night by the light from the fireplace she would mend and make clothes. She could make attractive new clothing out of old used material. She was thrifty, industrious, resourceful, an excellent cook and seamstress. She sewed carpet rags and at one time, she and her youngest son milked as many as forty-seven cows, night and morning. She was never too strict with her children, but was able to maintain mastery over her family.

Sally labored about twenty years at the St. George and Salt Lake Temples doing 1,400 names for the dead. At age seventy-seven years she fell and broke her hip, and after recovering from that she continued her work at the temple.

Sally was living with her daughter, Emma, in Orderville when she died shortly before her eightieth birthday. She is buried next to her husband.

ELIZABETH TAVENER PAPWORTH

BIRTHDATE: 3 Jan 1827
Cambridge, England
DEATH: 7 Jan 1907
Crescent, Salt Lake Co., Utah
PARENTS: Osborne D. Tavener
Ellen Watson
PIONEER: 1864
SPOUSE: James Papworth
MARRIED: 25 Dec 1847
Chesterton, Cambridge, England
DEATH SP: 23 Mar 1898
Crescent, Salt Lake Co., Utah

CHILDREN:
Susannah (Covell), 4 Dec 1848
Ellen Watson, 23-Oct 1850
Richard, 14 Feb 1852
Emma Elizabeth (Kemp), 10 Dec 1853
James Robert Hull, 8 Apr 1856
Clara (Whitehead Hadlock), 2 Apr 1858
Frances Washington, 18 Mar 1860
Mary Ann, 19 Jun 1862
Henry Tavener, 24 Oct 1864
Osborne Tavener, 27 Jan 1865
George Washington, 7 Jan 1869

Elizabeth was born in Cambridge, Cambridgeshire, England in 1827. She and James were married on Christmas Day in 1847, two weeks before her twenty-third birthday. Their first eight children were born in England; five girls and three boys.

Eleanor Watson, Elizabeth's mother, joined the Church of Jesus Christ of Latter-day Saints with Elizabeth and James in the years when it was an act of courage and strength. Friends, neighbors and family members were against the Mormons. Newspapers printed greatly exaggerated stories against them and other clergymen denounced them from the pulpit. Sometimes the feelings of the community were so intense that a few chose the night time to become baptized.

The family left Liverpool, England on June 3, 1864, for America, sailing on the "Hudson" with 863 Saints. Crossing the ocean includes shortages of every kind. One daughter died and was slipped to her eternal rest at sea.

It was to be no better crossing the Plains as they pulled away from Wyoming, Nebraska with their wagon train company. A second of Elizabeth's daughters died and was buried beside the trail. The day before the company arrived in the Salt Lake Valley, the third of Elizabeth's daughters passed away, but fate was not yet through because shortly after their arrival, the fourth of Elizabeth and James' five daughters, burned to death.

Never did Elizabeth loose faith in God or the Mormon belief that had motivated her journey. With her remaining daughter and the three boys, the Papworth family settled in Crescent, between Sandy and Draper, in the valley. Three

more sons were born to the couple. In October of the year they entered Salt Lake, George Washington, was born. She was forty-two years old.

Elizabeth was a woman of endurance who overcame great obstacles in her path, some put there by her husband who was an alcoholic. She was a midwife, which at that time often meant ten days of caring for the mother and child. She practiced that calling hundreds of times delivering babies in Sandy, Draper, South Jordan and Riverton.

Elizabeth passed away four days after her seventy-ninth birthday, serving her community, her family and God to the best of her ability.

SARAH THOMAS JONES PARISH

No
Photo
Available

BIRTHDATE: 8 Oct 1811
Abersychan, Trevethin, Wales
DEATH: 19 Oct 1891
Springville , Utah Co., Utah
PARENTS: Evan Thomas
Ann Sarah Thomas
PIONEER: 27 Aug 1860
9th Handcart Company
SPOUSE I: Robert Jones
MARRIED: Unknown
DEATH SP: 1865
Pennsylvania

CHILDREN:
Sarah, 1837
Margaret Emma (Savage Evans Hancock), 29 Dec 1839
Gomer Thomas, 22 Aug 1840
Ann Elizabeth (Kirkman), 10 Feb 1849
Sarah Rebecca (Avery Bird), 22 Dec 1852

SPOUSE II: Samuel Parish
MARRIED: 1 Mar 1861
Springville, Utah Co., Utah
DEATH SP: 12 Oct 1873
Centerville, Davis Co., Utah
CHILDREN: None

Sarah Thomas was born in Abersychan, Trevethin, Monmouth, Wales in 1811. She married Robert Jones in Wales and they had five children.

The family left Wales with the intent to gather to Utah, but Robert settled his family in Schuylkill County, Pennsylvania, and went to work in the mines. Their last two daughters were born in Pennsylvania.

Sarah finally decided it was time to gather with the Saints in Utah, and so joined the 9th Handcart Company, under Captain Daniel Robinson. Robert was content to stay in the East. He died in 1865 in a mining accident.

Sarah entered the Salt lake Valley in August, 1860, and settled in Springville, Utah County, Utah. She was a midwife in Springville for many years.

In 1861, she married Samuel Parish in Springville, Utah. Their marriage was sealed in the Endowment House on September 2, 1865. There were no children.

Sarah passed away in Springville, in 1891, when eighty years of age.

AGNES FINDLEY PARK

BIRTHDATE: 10 Sep 1825
Lanark, Ontario, Canada
DEATH: 1 Jan 1908
Fairfield, Utah Co., Utah
PARENTS: John Findley
Jennet /Janet McDonald
PIONEER: 1848
SPOUSE: James Pollock Park
MARRIED: 21 Sep 1849
Big Cottonwood, Salt Lake, Utah
DEATH SP: 30 Dec 1890
Fairfield, Utah Co., Utah

CHILDREN:
Agnes Jane (Young), 22 May 1852
James, 15 Jun 1859
Andrew, 2 Nov 1861
Jannette (Carson Harrison), 17 Apr 1864

Agnes' parents moved from Darvel, Ayrshire, Scotland to Lanark, Canada where she was born. When Agnes was about seventeen she was visited by missionaries from the Church of Jesus Christ of Latter-day Saints. Her parents and five of their children were baptized in 1845 and moved to Nauvoo in order to associate with others of their faith.

Agnes was twenty-one years old when the pioneers began their preparations for the difficult journey to the Rocky Mountains. She wished to make the trip West with the first group of pioneers, but Brigham Young persuaded her and a brother and sister to wait until the following year when they would be better prepared to make the journey. They followed his council and remained in Winter Quarters until 1848.

Soon after arriving in the Salt Lake Valley, Agnes married James Pollock Park, a veteran of the Mormon Battalion. They settled at Big Cottonwood, Salt Lake County, where they resided until 1869.

Agnes was left alone with her first child while her husband served a five year mission in England, Scotland and Wales. He returned home in 1857 as a leader of a company of immigrants on the Atlantic Ocean on the ship "George Washington."

Agnes allowed James to take a second wife, Sarah Ann Pymm by whom he had six children. Sarah Ann divorced him and she married William 'T' Sanford.

Agnes passed away in January of 1908 of what the coroner called "old age." She was buried by the side of her husband in the Fairfield, Utah Cemetery.

AGNES STEELE PARK

BIRTHDATE: 3 Apr 1827
Kilborne, Scotland
DEATH: 21 Feb 1896
Salt Lake City, Salt Lake, Utah
PARENTS: John Steele
Jennette Alexander
PIONEER: 1852 Wagon Train
SPOUSE: Hamilton Gray Park
MARRIED: Apr 1843
Kilbirnie, Ayre, Scotland
DEATH SP: 1 May 1913
Salt Lake City, Salt Lake, Utah

CHILDREN:
Hamilton Gray, 10 Mar 1845 (died as a child)
Janette Alexander (Heber Clayton), 30 Oct 1846
Marion Martha, Nov 1847 (died as a child)
Isabella Gray (Kenner), 23 Feb 1848
Sarah Agnes, 9 Oct 1852 (died as a child)
John Samuel, 18 Nov 1854 (died as a child)
Edwin Alma, 24 May 1856 (died as a child)
Annie Alexander (Midgley), 24 Jul 1858
Arthur Hamilton, 9 Apr 1865
Mable Gray (Meade), 5 Feb 1868

Agnes Steele was born in Kilborne, Scotland in 1827, when she was sixteen she married Hamilton Gray in Kilbirnie, Ayre, Scotland. Their first four children, a boy and three girls, were born in their native land.

Agnes would have been twelve when missionaries from the Church of Jesus Christ of Latter-day Saints first set foot on Scottish soil on December 20, 1839. Alexander Wright and Samuel Mulliner had returned to the country of their birth to spread the Gospel.

On January 14, 1840, not quite a month into their mission call, they baptized Alexander Hay and his wife Jessie, the first fruits of Scottish labors.

As the missionary work progressed and conversions grew, resistance to the messengers grew also and the two missionaries were forced to leave Kilpatrick under a shower of stone and rubbish. Ministers warned their flocks, workers were threatened with dismissal if they attended Mormon meetings. Despite it all, many of the honest in heart heard, were convinced and baptized. Agnes and Hamilton Gray Park were among them.

The young couple had other worries beside their beliefs, their little children fared badly. Of their first four children, their first born and the third, a little girl, died as children and the couple knew grief intimately.

The young family, Agnes now age twenty-four, would heed the earnest call issued by the First Presidency of the Church in Utah "to come to the gathering place." The Perpetual Emigrating Fund enabled many to board the ships leaving Liverpool, England for a half a year or more of travel before they would reach Utah. The courageous, the determined, the stout of heart responded and left all they knew and loved. They came to Zion.

Agnes and Hamilton had six children after they reached the Salt Lake Valley, the first three, a boy and two girls died as children but the last three, Annie, Arthur and Mable grew up, married and along with Janette and Isabella, who crossed the Plains as children, gave their gifts of knowledge and physical work fortified by their beliefs to help settle this territory.

Agnes lived forty-four years after reaching the Valley. She passed away at the age of sixty-eight, and is buried in Salt Lake City, Utah.

ANN BROOKS PARK

No Photo Available

BIRTHDATE: May 1811
Cambuslang, Lanark, Scotland
DEATH: 25 Feb 1889
Carson City, Douglas, Nevada
PARENTS: James Brooks
Barbara Newbigging
PIONEER: 29 Sep 1847
Edward Hunter Co. Wagon Train
SPOUSE: David Park
MARRIED: abt 1829
DEATH SP: 22 Jul 1884
Mottsville, Douglas Co., Nevada

CHILDREN:
Barbara, 11 Sep 1830
Marion Allen, 25 Sep 1831
Jane, 15 Apr 1834
James, 20 Jun 1835
Mary Ann, 24 Jan 1837
David Brooks, 24 Dec 1839
James, 31 Aug 1841
Hugh, 23 Feb 1843
Martha, 3 Feb 1845
John, 16 Feb 1847
Joseph Hyrum, 17 Dec 1849
Margaret Ellen, 8 Mar 1852
William Nephi, 3 Jan 1854

Ann was a lovely Scottish girl who married David Park and emigrated to Canada. There, she went through the hardships of a pioneer woman.

Two of her children were born in Dalhousie, Ontario, Canada. From there, they went to Warwick, Kent County, Canada where five more children were born. They moved to West Plympton, Kent County, Canada where two more children were born.

It was here that she met the Elders of the Church of Jesus Christ of Latter-day Saints and became converted to their teachings. They moved to the United States in 1846. Two of her children were born in Missouri.

Ann endured the sufferings of the Latter-day Saints at Winter Quarters before she traveled to the Salt Lake Valley

in 1850 with the Edward Hunter Wagon Company. They first settled in Millcreek, Salt Lake County, Utah. They moved to Jordan, then Ogden.

Ann was a patient loving woman with many talents which she needed to endure continual pioneering. She was a noble wife. She became the mother of thirteen children. When her restless husband again wanted to move to Nevada, she gathered her family of little ones and pioneered in Nevada. She experienced the joy of seeing their farms develop into a permanent home where for years she lived surrounded by her children and grandchildren.

After her husband's death, she lived with a son until her death on February 25, 1889. She was buried in the Mottsville Cemetery.

ISABELLA GRAY PARK

No Photo Available

BIRTHDATE: 1 Oct 1791
Newton Stewart, Tyron, Ireland
DEATH: 21 Dec 1879
Skull Valley, Tooele Co., Utah
PARENTS: Robert Gray
Margaret McFarland
PIONEER: 26 Sep 1856
D. McArthur Handcart Company
SPOUSE: Samuel Park
MARRIED: 18 Aug
Ireland
DEATH SP: Apr 1833
Ireland

CHILDREN:
John, 1821
William, 20 Mar 1823
Hamilton Gray, 25 Nov 1825
Mary Jane, 17 Sep 1827
Samuel, Jr., 14 Aug 1828
George, 1832

Isabella was born and raised in Ireland. She married Samuel Park who was a weaver of pure Irish linen. They were well to do financially and highly respected in the community.

Her husband had signed a note to help his brother. Then his offer to pay the note was not accepted, yet as soon as he was taken in death, they took possession of all the many bolts of pure linen which was many times the amount of the note. He died in 1833, leaving Isabella with six small children to care for.

She took her little family to Kilbumie, Ayershire, Scotland where her parents were living. It was there she heard the message of the missionaries and joined the Church of Jesus Christ of Latter-day Saints in 1851. Her daughter, Mary Jane, and her sons Samuel and Hamilton Gray also joined the Church. They immediately began making plans to travel to Utah.

The three children left for Zion in 1855. The following year, Isabella came to Boston on the ship, "Enoch Train."

From Boston, she traveled to Iowa by rail and arrived in time to join McArthur's second company of handcart pioneers. She had an accident where the fore wheel of a wagon struck her, threw her down, and passed over both her hips. Before she could be pulled away from the wagon, her ankles were run over by the hind wheel. Although the wagon had nearly two tons of equipment on it, a load for four yoke of oxen to pull, she didn't have a single broken bone. Although she was terribly sore for several days, she got well enough to continue walking with her friend.

Her son, Samuel, was sent out to meet the Handcart Company with some supplies. When he saw her, he rushed up to her and hugged her, she gave him a sound whack because she didn't recognize him due to the beard he had grown since she last saw him. They arrived in the Salt Lake Valley on September 26, 1856.

From that time on, she lived with her children in turns going from Salt Lake City, Plain City, to Skull Valley. She died at the home of her son, Samuel, in Skull Valley at the age of eighty-eight. She was buried in the Salt Lake City Cemetery.

JANE ANN ELLISON PARK

BIRTHDATE: 18 Mar 1859
Parr, Lancashire, England
DEATH: 1 Jun 1917
Holladay, Salt Lake Co., Utah
PARENTS: James Ellison
Alice Halliwell
PIONEER: 16 Oct 1853
Cyrus Wheelock Wagon Train
SPOUSE: Andrew Duncan Park
MARRIED: 14 Mar 1868
DEATH SP: 19 May 1920
Holladay, Salt Lake Co., Utah

CHILDREN:
Alice Ellison, 16 Mar 1869
Martha Jane, 26 Oct 1871
William Andrew, 22 Jun 1874
James Henry, 9 Apr 1877
Ethel Gertrude, 23 Nov 1880
Lilly May, 11 May 1883
Fern Amanda, 28 Jan 1885
Pearl Lyle, 10 Nov 1889
Clive Peter Sutton, 29 Apr 1895

Jane Ann Ellison was born in England in 1849. When only a child she came from England with her parents who had embraced the gospel of the Church of Jesus Christ of Latter-day Saints there. This family arrived in Salt Lake City in the year 1853, bringing six children with them.

Their first home was in Kaysville, Davis County, where they passed through a very hard winter. The Weber River froze over and when the under nourished, thirsty cattle went for water they would slip on the ice and in their weak condition could not struggle up. The men would have to

kill them and use them for food and skin them for hides. To help her family get provisions, six year old Jane Ann tended a baby for several weeks and received a chicken as pay.

Because of Johnston's Army, the Ellison family joined others in moving south, settling in Nephi. When Jane Ann's parents went into the fields to cradle wheat, she remained at home to care for the younger children, often having to feed Indians who stopped by.

Once when she went to bring in the cows, she couldn't find them and searched for a very long time. Finally she returned to the fort only to find the gates in the stone wall locked and she could not get in. She somehow climbed to the top of the wall to alert the watchmen she was there.

One day delivering the laundry her mother did for the officers of Johnston's Army, Jane found a $2.50 gold piece on her way home. She returned to the officers quarters trying to find the rightful owner of the money. The Officer patting her head, told her she had found it and so it was hers to keep. She used the $2.50 to buy new dresses for her mother and herself.

As she grew she learned to dye and spin wool to make clothing and some times she would dance in her new dress with bare feet as she could not make shoes.

At the age of nineteen, Jane Ann married Andrew Duncan Park and moved with him to Millcreek in the south part of the Salt Lake Valley. She lived there until the last years of her life when she lived in Holliday, Utah.

She was a Relief Society teacher for many years and was president of the Primary Association. She was very kind to the sick and those who were less fortunate than she. She was a quiet, unassuming person who never cared for public honor.

Jane Ann passed away at the age of sixty-six. A speaker at her funeral praised her as living a life nearly perfect, always willing to serve someone.

JANE DUNCAN PARK

BIRTHDATE: 19 Feb 1808
Alton Lanark, Scotland
DEATH: 20 Nov 1873
Millcreek, Salt Lake Co., Utah
PARENTS: John Duncan
Agnes Thompson
PIONEER: 29 Sep 1847
Edward Hunter Co. Wagon Train
SPOUSE: William Park
MARRIED: 1828
DEATH SP: 3 Jul 1893
Millcreek, Salt Lake Co., Utah

CHILDREN:
Agnes Thompson, 16 Dec 1828
James Duncan, 26 Jul 1830
John Duncan, 18 Jun 1832
Marion Ellen, 5 May 1834

Jane, 16 Feb 1836
William Duncan, 25 Mov 1837
Hugh Duncan, 24 Feb 1840
Mary Duncan, 30 Mar 1843
Andrew Duncan, 24 Mar 1845
Joseph Duncan, 18 Aug 1848
Martha Hannah, 19/22 Sep 1850 (died at age 15)

Jane Duncan was born in Scotland in 1808 and was twelve years old when the Duncan family, along with thirty-three other families from Glasgow and Paisley, Lanarkshire, Scotland, sailed to Canada,, settling on the Dalhouseie frontier in Ontario, Canada.

William Park's family was also one of those thirty-three pioneering families and by the time Jane was twenty, the two had become sweethearts and married. Their first six children were born on the Dalhousie Frontier, then moving to Warwick, Township (Kent County), three more children were born.

Missionaries from the Church of Jesus Christ of Latter-day Saints reached their area and on April 11, 1844, Jane and William were baptized as were two of William's brothers and soon there was an organized branch with about twenty-five members.

Two members journeyed to Illinois to see the Apostles that summer, then the following winter, John A. Smith traveled to Canada with the message of persecutions and to see if they wanted to join the Saints traveling west. If so, there was no time to lose.

Most of the branch left that spring arriving at Nauvoo in April 1846, after so many families had already left. Available supplies and oxen had been purchased by the departing Saints and time was spent outfitting themselves for the trek, finally they arrived at Winter Quarters where they stayed until the following spring.

Joining the John Taylor Wagon Company group were the William, John and David Park families. Jane was traveling with eleven children, the youngest two years old, on a three month journey that was not with out it's own pleasures. William was a good fiddler and often played around the camp fires at night for the dances, amazingly the pioneers had energy still to enjoy.

Their first winter in the Salt Lake Valley was lived in the fort, when spring came William planted grain where the Salt Lake Penitentiary would be built (21st South and 13th East). The next year they moved to Big Cottonwood Creek (Mill Creek) into a log home and there the last two children were born.

Their existence was meager, many meals would consist of Sego bulbs, mustard greens and one pint of meal a day. The next home was sun dried adobe. Jane kept her home intact through all the many months her husband and older sons traveled back and forth to the East bringing supplies and now immigrants into the valley.

William married two plural wives and as the first and more experienced, she was the one to oversee family affairs and care for the sick. She was a midwife delivering hundreds of babies. Her large, blue dumpling bowl was a symbol of her consideration. It was delivered full of   chicken and dumplings to many, including neighbors and friends, who were in need of sustenance and comfort.

JANET MCDONALD FINDLAY PARK

BIRTHDATE: 2 May 1823
Perth, Canada
DEATH: 3 Jul 1893
Mill Creek, Salt Lake Co., Utah
PARENTS: John Findlay
Janet McDonald
PIONEER: Fall of 1848
Wagon Train Company
SPOUSE: William Park
MARRIED: 7 Apr 1850
DEATH SP: 3 Jul 1893
Mill Creek, Salt Lake Co., Utah

CHILDREN:
David Findlay, 12 Mar 1851
Janet McDonald, 3 Oct 1852
Duncan Findlay, 4 Nov 1854
Allen Thomas, 26 Sep 1857
Catherine Findlay, 26 Aug 1860

Janet was born in Perth, Canada in 1823. She moved with her parents to Nauvoo, Illinois in 1845, at the invitation of the Church missionaries to "join with the Saints, all who would travel into the unknown went with them."

She came to Utah with her brother Alexander, and a sister, Agnes, in 1848. (Her parents stayed in Nauvoo, to come at a later date.)

A faith promoting experience happened to Janet on the trail. A team of cattle had stampeded and she was called out of a sound sleep to help with the children while others went after the cattle. Groggy from sleep, she went out into the open field where she was run over by two teams of oxen and wagons. She was thought dead. She was picked up and brought back to camp severely hurt and unconscious. A strange lady came into camp and ask the attending woman if she was the girl's mother. The answer was no. The unknown woman gave Janet a blessing, saying she would recover and reach her destination safely and fulfill the mission she was sent on earth to do. She then disappeared and was never seen in camp again.

One year and a half after entering the Salt Lake Valley, Janet became the second wife of William Park who was seventeen years older than she. The couple was married in the home of Brigham Young.

Because William must divide his time between his church duties, his work and his three wives with their multiplying families, Janet took responsibility for her own and her children's welfare. She made her living by nursing, farming, and what ever work was necessary. She made braided hats, and steamed and blocked hats too

During the latter part of her life she took in boarders, men who worked at the brick yard and at the Murray Smelter. Janet, her oldest daughter, fell in love with and married one boarder, William Tate.

During these years Janet hired a young girl to help do the housework and left her in charge while she rode into Salt Lake to visit her youngest daughter, Kate. After some days, the girl became tired of the work and just walked away, leaving the men to fend for themselves until Janet's return.

She was a compassionate, protective mother and during one period of scarcity, defied William and the sign posted on the pit of seed potatoes that were in the back of her house , warning all to "Keep Out." She and William's third wife, Mary Gordon, decided that they could not let their little children go hungry and took turns getting a bucket of potatoes from the pit. Toward spring the pit became empty and they had William's wrath to face but their children had survived the winter.

Janet passed away at home two months after her eightieth birthday.

JEAN HARVEY PARK

BIRTHDATE: 25 Aug 1831
Kilbumie, Ayshire, Scotland
DEATH: 18 Jan 1920
Tooele, Tooele Co., Utah
PARENTS: David Harvey
Margaret Law
PIONEER: 1855
Gill Green Indep. Wagon Train
SPOUSE: Samuel Park
MARRIED: 31 Dec 1849
Kilbumie, Ayshire, Scotland
DEATH SP: Not given

CHILDREN:
Isabela, 17 Jul 1851 (died as a child)
Samuel, 3 Jun 1853 (died at age 2)
Mary Jane, 26 Aug 1856
David Harvey, 26 Aug 1856
Sir Agnes, 26 May 1858 (died at age 4)
Hamilton Gray, 15 Sep 1860
John William, 4 Jul 1862
Margaret Ann, 9 Aug 1864
George Albert, 25 Sep 1866
Janet Alexander, 25 Dec 1868
Joseph Robert, 12 Oct 1871
Ellen Hannah, 18 Jan 1874

Jean was the youngest of ten children. As a girl, she worked in the factory, weaving linen. At the time cholera

broke out, she nursed the sick and prepared the dead for burial. One night, thirty died and it was not possible to do more than just cover them in a trench.

She was led by her father to hear Elders from the Church of Jesus Christ of Latter-day Saints preach the gospel. She was baptized in 1852 and was turned from her home by her mother.

She married Samuel Park, who was also a member of the Church. She and her husband were "one in all things; sorrow and sacrifice." They left Scotland on January 17, 1855. They reached St. Louis on March 22, 1855. After the death of her little son, she and her husband joined the Gill Green Independent Wagon Company to cross the Plains.

After reaching the Salt Lake Valley, she pioneered with her husband, ever at his side in all he undertook to do for the benefit and betterment of the community. In August of 1856, their crop was not yet ready for harvesting, so she cooked weed greens. She became very ill from starving, so her husband went out to see if he could find any potatoes. He hurried home with what he could find and she laid on the floor and cooked them. Five days later, she gave birth to twins.

After living in Salt Lake City a short time, they moved to Utah County, then moved to Weber County, and finally to Tooele in the year 1872. Jean was in the Relief Society in Weber when they decided to buy a knitting machine and pledged to save the Sunday eggs for the fund. She was the mother of twelve children. She assisted at the birth of more than one hundred babies.

Samuel passed away twenty-one years before Jean. Jean passed away at the age of eighty-eight, two weeks after suffering a fall from complications due to the fall.

MARY GORDON PARK

BIRTHDATE: 22 Mar 1832
Bridge of Weir, Scotland
DEATH: 27 Jun 1895
Mill Creek, Salt Lake Co., Utah
PARENTS: Joseph Gordon
Jean Stewart
PIONEER: Unknown
SPOUSE: William Park
MARRIED: 11 Jun 1854
Salt Lake City, Salt Lake, Utah
DEATH SP: 11 Mar 1890
Mill Creek, Salt Lake Co., Utah

CHILDREN:
Elizabeth, 29 Mar 1855
Margaret Ellen, 20 Aug 1859
Charles Sutton, 12 Feb 1861
Annie Hannah, 28 Dec 1862 (died young)
Rachel, 14 Oct 1864
Alexander, 29 Jan 1866
Janie, (died as a child)

Hannah, 4 Aug 1867
Annie, 24 Dec 1868

Mary Gordon was born in Bridge of Weir, Renfrew, Scotland in 1832, the daughter of Joseph Gordon and Jean Stewart. It is not known when she came to Utah, but she married William Park in 1854 in Salt Lake City as his third wife, and was the mother of several children. Some of them died as infants.

Little is known of her activities in Utah. The family settled in the Mill Creek area of Salt Lake County. It seems that William Park was considering taking a fourth wife, but Mary Gordon, thought otherwise. She locked him in a room for several days, giving him only bread and water. That cured him of thinking about another wife.

Her husband passed away in 1890 in Mill Creek; and Mary passed away in 1895, also in Mill Creek, Salt Lake County, Utah.

SARAH JANE TAYLOR PARK

No Photo Available

BIRTHDATE: 15 Mar 1843
Urcy, Adams Co., Illinois
DEATH: 29 Mar 1904
Pleasant Grove, Utah Co., Utah
PARENTS: Joseph Taylor
Cecilia Harvey
PIONEER: August 1850
Captain Cook's Wagon Train
SPOUSE: Samuel Wallace Park
MARRIED: 18 Mar 1860
Lindon, Utah Co., Utah
DEATH SP: 10 Jun 1917

CHILDREN:
Samuel Joseph, 6 Jan 1861
Celia Jane, 6 Sep 1862
John Wallace, 22 Jan 1864
Robert Addison, 27 Jan 1866
William Taylor, 19 Feb 1868
Sarah Matilda, 19 Apr 1870
Cyntha Elizabeth, 20 Oct 1872
Mary Louisa, 10 Jan 1878
Mariah Janette, 18 Oct 1883

Sarah Jane's mother was converted to the Church of Jesus Christ of Latter-day Saints and joined against the wishes of her husband. This caused a divorce and division of the family. Her father took her with him back to Adams County while her little brother, Lorenzo, went with her mother on to Nauvoo.

In 1850, just after gold was discovered in California, Sarah's father left her with a friend and went to California. He died there.

The friend with whom Sarah had been left wrote to Sarah Jane's mother and told her to come for her little girl if she wanted her. Sarah's mother immediately saddled her horse and went after Sarah Jane.

Just shortly after they returned back to their home, they made preparations to cross the Plains in Captain Cook's Wagon Train Company. Sarah crossed the Plains with her mother, her brother, and her grandparents Sarah B. Harbert and Jonathan Lewis Harvey. They arrived in the Salt Lake Valley in August of 1850.

Sarah Jane was seventeen when she married Samuel Wallace Park in Lindon, Utah. Their home life was one of happiness and full of life. She was a member of the Relief Society and acted as a teacher until the time of her death. If there were any sick that needed her help, her services were freely given. Many people blessed her name for the help, love, and sympathy she gave them.

Sarah passed away on March 29, 1904 in Pleasant Grove, Utah County, and is buried by her husband there.

CATHERINE COX PARKER

BIRTHDATE: 23 Mar 1856
St. Pancras, London, England
DEATH: 14 Jun 1933
Hooper, Weber Co., Utah
PARENTS: Levi Ashton Cox
Mary Sharp
PIONEER: 13 Oct 1863
Rosel Hyde Co. Wagon Train
SPOUSE: Edwin Parker
MARRIED: 31 Oct 1870
Salt Lake Endowment House
DEATH SP: 18 Oct 1935
Hooper, Weber Co., Utah

CHILDREN:
Eliza Burningham, 20 Aug 1871
Edwin George, 6 Apr 1873
Susan 15 Dec 1874
Louise May, 3 Mar 1877
William Charles, 23 Oct 1878
Mary Catherine, 5 Jan 1881
Anna Ray, 4 Mar 1883
Lutisa Maria, 4 Aug 1885
Levi Cox, 16 Jul 1887
Minnie Irene, 18 Feb 1890
Robert Parel, 29 Feb 1892
Leet Grant, 1 Nar 1895
Vern Cassio, 1 Nov 1897

Catherine Parker was born in England. She was blessed on March 22, 1857 at the age of one year. A part of the blessing read as follows: "You are to be a great woman in Zion and stand in the Kingdom of God as a mother, and a stay and comfort to your parents."

When she was seven years old, Catherine sailed for America with her parents and brother on board the sailing vessel "Amazon." She walked the entire distance across the Plains from Winter Quarters to Salt Lake City, most of the way barefooted. They arrived in the Salt Lake Valley with the Rosel Hyde Wagon Company on October 13, 1863.

They went to Franklin, Idaho, where their first winter was spent in dugout. Here she endured the hardships of pioneer life and raids from Indians. In 1867, the Cox family moved from Franklin to Wilson Lane, Utah. Catherine walked all the way driving the cows and sheep. A year later, they moved to Hooper, Utah. Again, their first home was a dugout.

Catherine helped her father make the adobes for their first house built in Hooper. When she was thirteen years old she helped her father dig a mile of ditch. They received for their pay a wood stove, the first one in Hooper. The first hat Catherine bought in Utah was made out of straw. She paid for it with the course salt she gathered out of the slough.

When she was thirteen years old, Catherine married Edwin Parker, and they became the parents of thirteen children; two died before maturity.

Their first home was a one-room adobe house. Since they had no bed they slept on wheat. Catherine worked very hard to make a comfortable home for her family. She had no formal schooling in England. She taught herself to write. She developed good penmanship. She learned to read after her children started school and shared with her what they had learned. She became a good reader and was able to read the scriptures, newspaper, etc.

Catherine was a member of the Hooper theatrical troop which traveled from town to town to put on plays. She also coached others. She was known as the "old favorite." She had a lovely voice and took part in several Choirs.

Catherine was honored by the Daughters of the Utah Pioneers as an original pioneer of Hooper. She was active in Relief Society activities and assisted anyone in need. She was devoted to her religion, home, community and her adopted country of America. She was a wonderful cook; her filled cookie bars were superb. She was a tall, very dignified, cultured lady, beloved by her family who often sought her council and advice. She was thought of as a public-spirited woman, a devoted wife and mother and a person who radiated good throughout her entire life.

Catherine pased away in Hooper on June 14, 1933. Her husband passed away two years later.

DRUCILLA DICKSON HARTLEY PARKER

BIRTHDATE: 23 Jul 1824
Mercer, Pennsylvania
DEATH: 16 Mar 1891
Salt Lake City, Salt Lake, Utah
PARENTS: Benjamin Hartley
Mary Dickey
PIONEER: 15 Sep 1852
Robert Weimer Co. Wagon Train
SPOUSE: Joshua Parker
MARRIED: Aug 1844
Hancock Co., Illinois
DEATH SP: 17 Jul 1880

CHILDREN:
Robert Martin, 30 Sep 1842
Orson Hyde, 15 Nov 1845
Joshua, 21 May 1847
Benjamin Alma, 22 Jan 1849
Francis William, 2 Sep 1850
Mary Melissa, 21 May 1852
Hannah Jane, 25 Mar 1855
Parley Pratt, 19 Aug 1857
Frederick Albion, 9 Dec 1859
Charles Henry, 31 Mar 1861
Elizabeth Ann, 21 Jan 1863
Daniel, 3 Mar 1866
Joseph Almon, 4 Dec 1869

Drucilla Parker was born in Pennsylvania. At the age of twelve, Drucilla became an orphan, following the death of her mother in 1834 and the death of her father in 1836, both in Merced, Pennsylvania.

It is likely she may have been taken in by her older brother and his wife because she travelled West with them to Illinois. Drucilla's baptism into the Church of Jesus Christ of Latter-day Saints is given as December, 1846.

She was married to Joshua Parker in August of 1844 in Illinois. When the Saints were driven from Nauvoo, Illinois in 1846, it appears that the Parker family must have gone to St. Louis, Missouri, probably to obtain work and the means to begin the long trek across the Plains to the Salt Lake Valley.

In 1848, they joined with the Saints in Kanesville, Iowa where they remained until July 13, 1852, when they joined with the Robert Weimer Wagon Company.

It was a long, hard trip for Drucilla with her baby of less than two months of age, and three other children ranging in ages from two to nine years. She had given birth to and buried two other children after leaving Nauvoo and while residing in St. Louis, Missouri and Kanesville, Iowa. They arrived in the Salt Lake Valley on September 15, 1852.

In Salt Lake City she went on bearing children, grateful that she was permitted the privilege of motherhood. Seven more children were added to the family, making a total of thirteen. Her last child was born when Drucilla was forty-five years of age.

Drucilla was not one to seek public notice. Keeping her family fed, clothed, and making her home a happy place for her children was her duty and pleasure. She supported her husband in his church callings and in his occupation as a carpenter and cabinet maker. She was industrious, a careful manager and taught her children the value of work through guidance and by her own example. She taught them to stay close to the Church and it's teachings as a guide for right living. She helped and encouraged them in educational pursuits. It was her greatest pleasure to have her children and grandchildren nearby.

Drucilla lacked a few days of being fifty-six years old when she was left a widow having six children still at home to care for. She lived out the rest of her life in Salt Lake City and died there at sixty-six years of age.

Drucilla and her husband, Joshua, had been endowed and sealed in the Endowment House in Salt Lake City August 24, 1855.

ELIZA ANN GROVER SIMMONS PARKER

BIRTHDATE: 13 Mar 1839
Palmyra, Missouri
DEATH: 2 Mar 1920
Parker, Idaho
PARENTS: Thomas Grover
Caroline Whiting Grover
PIONEER: Oct 1847 with
Charles C. Rich Wagon Train
SPOUSE I: William A. Simmons
MARRIED: 9 May 1856
DEATH SP: 30 Sep 1857
Echo Canyon, Summit Co., Utah

CHILD:
Elsena, (died at 18 months) 3 May 1857

SPOUSE II: Wyman Miner Parker
MARRIED: 15 Jan1860
Farmington, Davis Co., Utah
DEATH SP: 1907
Parker, Idaho

CHILDREN:
Eliza Ann (Stoddard), 27 Mar 1861
Julia Marie, 30 Sep 1862
Thomas Grover, 14 Sep 1864
Emeline (Winger Brower), 1 Feb 1867
Henry M., 5 Feb 1869
David Grover, 23 Jan 1870
Lionel, 26 Dec 1870
Melrose, 8 Dec 1872
Joel, 31 Dec 1874
Mary Adel (Moon), 17 Jun 1878
Lucy Caroline, 9 Mar 1880
Albert B., 14 Jun1882

Eliza Ann was born on March 13, 1839 in Palmyra, Missouri. Her father was a member of the Church of Jesus Christ of Latter-day Saints' first High Council and a close friend of the Prophet Joseph Smith.

When Eliza was only two, her mother died and the family moved to Nauvoo, Illinois where they were neighbors of the Smiths. Joseph Smith was especially kind to the motherless Eliza Ann, letting her ride with him on his horse, "Duncan." In 1846, when the Saints were driven from Nauvoo, the family made their way to Winter Quarters, Nebraska.

As they crossed the Mississippi River in the winter, the oxen broke through the boat and it sank. All were saved but Eliza Ann; she appeared to be drowned. They worked with Eliza Ann and prayed for her for twelve hours before she was resuscitated.

In the Fall of 1847, they joined Company 3 which was led by Eliza Ann's brother-in-law Charles C. Rich. They reached the Salt Lake Valley in October and spent the hard first winter with the near-starving Saints in the old Fort.

Eliza Ann married William A. Simmons in 1856 at the age of seventeen. They had one daughter who died at eighteen months. William was killed in a training accident when the Saints were arming themselves to repel Johnston's Army. Eliza Ann lived in East Weber but later lived with her father in Farmington, Utah for three years.

On January 15, 1860 she married Wyman Miner Parker whose wife had died leaving him with four children. They settled in Morgan, Utah where they prospered. In addition to his four children, twelve children were born to Eliza Ann and Wyman

Four of Eliza Ann's children had died in infancy so she was eager to learn how to prevent suffering and death. When a doctor arrived prepared to conduct a medical school she provided her home and eagerly took the training that would prepare her for her later life in the Idaho wilderness.

They were called by the Church to colonize in Idaho in 1881. They sold their beautiful home, land and business and with three wagons, one "spring wagon," thirty horses, some cows and enough provisions for a year they went first to Star Valley and then to Swan Lake. Wyman's oldest son had explored the upper Snake River Valley and persuaded them to settle on the Egin Bench. Their quarter section of land there is now in the village of Parker, named for Wyman who was the first Bishop and Patriarch in the area.

After the death of their son, Thomas, they sold the original homestead and moved another two miles away where they built a beautiful home and lived out their lives, sharing with and serving their community.

Eliza Ann loved to help others and with her medical training she soon became indispensable to the health of the community; extracting teeth, setting bones, sewing wounds, performing minor surgeries and delivering hundreds of babies.

In 1897, she lost one eye but continued in her medical services. In 1907, her husband passed away and in 1908 her daughter also passed away, leaving three children; this would be the fourth family she would raise.

Eliza Ann passed away on March 2, 1920 after a year's illness. She was loved and revered throughout the area. In 1942, The Daughters of the Utah Pioneers named their Upper Snake River Valley Camp the "Eliza Ann Camp."

ELLEN BRIGGS DOUGLAS PARKER

BIRTHDATE: 7 Nov 1806
Downham, Lancashire, England
DEATH: 24/25 Feb 1888
Virgin, Washington Co., Utah
PARENTS: Father - unknown
Isabella "Bella" Briggs
PIONEER: 28 Aug 1852
John Parker Indep. Wagon Train
SPOUSE I: George Douglas
MARRIED: abt 1823/1824
Downham, Lancashire, England
DEATH SP: 12 Jul 1842
Nauvoo, Hancock Co., Illinois

CHILDREN:
Ralph, 28 Dec 1826
Richard, 27 Feb 1828
William, 3 Nov 1829
Ann (Robbins), 7 Oct 1831
Isabella (Pincock), 1 Nov 1833
Mary (Curry), 19 Oct 1835
George, 27 Feb 1838
Ellen Vilate (Romney), 19/29 Nov 1840

SPOUSE II: John Parker, Jr.
MARRIED: 23 Jan 1846
Nauvoo, Hancock Co., Illinois
DEATH SP: 24 Mar 1886
Virgin, Washington Co., Utah

CHILDREN:
Alice (Isom), 8 Jan 1848
John Samuel, 2 Nov 1851

Ellen was born on November 7, 1806 in Downham, England. Ellen's mother later married Robert Douglas and Ellen was sealed to this couple.

About 1823/1824, Ellen married George Douglas in Downham, England. He was the younger brother of her stepfather, Robert. This was a unique relationship as Ellen's mother was also her sister-in-law.

Ellen and George were blessed with eight children. The family was converted and baptized into the Church of Jesus Christ of Latter-Day Saints by Heber C. Kimball. The Douglas's emigrated to America in 1842, crossing to New Orleans and up the Mississippi River to Nauvoo.

George, who was a mason by trade, worked on both the Nauvoo Temple and the Nauvoo House. When the work slowed he went to work in the harvest on Joseph Smith's farm. George was not used to the humid summer heat when compared with the coolness of England. About noon on July 12, 1842, George became very ill and died six hours later of heat exhaustion.

Within three months of arriving in America, Ellen was a widow with seven children. She and the three oldest children got jobs to support the destitute family; leaving Isabella, not yet nine years old, as primary housekeeper and care giver for the three youngest children.

Ellen and her family suffered much privation and sickness during the next four years. But she was not known to murmur for she had deep faith in the Gospel and was supported and cared for by the Relief Society and her own children. The young family saw the bodies of the martyred Prophet Joseph Smith and his brother Hyrum.

On January 23, 1846, in the Nauvoo Temple, Ellen married John Parker, Jr., a widower whom she had known in England. She sold her cow for beef and suet with John donating his only fifty cents for currants to make plum pudding for their wedding dinner. Together they had ten children with six being under the age of ten. Ellen provided motherly love and care to John's children: William, age nine; Elizabeth, age seven; and Mary Ann, age five.

Ellen and John didn't have the funds to go with the Saints leaving Nauvoo. As conditions worsened Ellen's family took refuge in St. Louis. Here they found jobs, kind people and John learned the business of soda water, root beer and summer drinks, Ellen gave birth to two children while in St. Louis.

John sold his prosperous business and outfitted his own independent wagon /oxen company. Ellen and John were blessed and generous to provide the means to bring all their children, extended family including John's two sisters and families. Their crossing the Plains was without incident of any kind and was spoken of as a pleasure trip. Ellen and company arrived in the Salt Lake Valley on August 28 1852.

For ten years the Parker and Douglas families lived in Salt Lake City. Here they built homes, started the first wheat threshing and cleaning business, enjoyed community dancing, harvested salt from the Great Salt Lake, farmed crops, gathered berries, started a sawmill, hauled logs from Bingham Canyon, continued making syrups and soda water, raised sheep for food and wool, weaved cloth and did all to be self sufficient while giving to and aiding the less fortunate.

Ellen and her family were stalwarts in the Gospel. They endured the threats of the invading Johnston's Army and were among those who relocated to Utah County and were ready to burn all if necessary in order to defend their rights to worship and colonize as they wished.

In 1862, John was called to Dixie to raise cotton. Ellen moved her family to Virgin, Utah, living in a dugout at first. They were successful in growing cotton, weaving beautiful white cloth and raising sheep for weaving wool fabric. John and Ellen were first to set up a co-op store in their home in Virgin. They also relocated the wheat threshing business, started a cattle co-op in Kolob, ran a flour mill on the Virgin River and were active in civic and social activities.

Always dedicated and faithful to the Lord, Ellen was appointed first president of the Virgin Ward Relief Society in 1868. Her husband was ordained the first bishop, a position he held for eighteen years. The years of service were long and hard but their faith never wavered.

In 1877, the St. George Temple was dedicated. Ellen, John, and families performed many ordinances for all their progenitors that they could remember or find record of, Ellen was experienced writer. Through her letters sent to families in England, we know much of her life, church history, pioneer traditions, gospel teachings and her firm testimony of the Gospel of Jesus Christ.

Ellen Briggs Douglas Parker passed away on February 24, 1888 in Virgin, Utah. She was a devoted and loving wife to two husbands.

Ellen taught her children both by example and precept to be honest, law abiding, industrious and to live by the principles of the Gospel. Ellen will be remembered as a sincere, faithful, talented, generous, serving and loving woman.

MARIA BLAKE PARKER

BIRTHDATE: 13 Feb 1809
Preston Candover, England
DEATH: 23 May 1869
Ogden, Weber Co., Utah
PARENTS: Charles G. Blake
Mary Marsh
PIONEER: Oct 1863
Wagon Train Company
SPOUSE: William Parker
MARRIED: 28 Apr 1829
Preston Candover, England
DEATH SP: 23 Jan 1883
Ogden, Weber Co., Utah

CHILDREN:
George, 20 Mar 1830
Charles, 12 Feb 1832
Mary, 21 Feb 1834
Gilbert, 18 Jan 1836 (died at age 19)
Charlotte, 20 Feb 1838
Maria, 27 Jun 1840
Edwin, 1 May 1843
William, 3 Jan 1845
Edith, 14 Feb 1847 (died an infant)
Anna, 7 Sep 1849 (died at age 15)

Maria was born in Preston Candover, Hampshire, England, 1809. When she was fifteen years old, her mother died.

Maria married William Parker with whom she had ten children. Maria had a good education and became a school teacher for the Church of England and ran the school at the rectory under the direction of the clergy. She taught many years at the school. She was an avid reader of the Bible and could quote scripture fluently.

She heard missionaries from the Church of Jesus Christ of Latter-day Saints conducting a street meeting and knew what they said conformed with the scriptures. She was baptized into the Church on February 14, 1852. She was instrumental in spreading the gospel to her family and friends.

Her unwavering attitude led to her dismissal as a teacher. Her husband lost his jobs as a parish clerk and at the brickyard. Maria ran a small bakery and taught sewing and weaving of straw hats to earn money to support the family. William worked on the roads for a shilling a day.

Some of Maria's children emigrated at intervals to Utah. Finally, in June 1863, Maria, William, and the three youngest children sailed from London in the ship, "Amazon," to New York City. They crossed the Plains with an ox-team. William was very ill on the journey which left a heavy responsibility of Maria to care for the family's needs.

They made their home in Wellsville for a time where they purchased a city lot and lived in a log house. Maria was one of the first school teachers in Wellsville. They had no books, so she used the Bible as a text. The family later moved to Hooper.

Mary did whatever she could in church and community service. She was a kind compassionate woman and always willing to help those in need. She was a hard worker and had many trials come her way. She was an intelligent, noble woman who carried a true testimony of the gospel throughout her life. She lived to be sixty years of age.

MARIA JACKSON NORMINGTON PARKER

BIRTHDATE: 25 Dec 1820
Haggate, England
DEATH: 19 Mar 1881
Virgin, Washington Co., Utah
PARENTS: Robert Jackson
Jane Thornton or Susan Jackson
PIONEER: 30 Nov 1856
Martin Handcart Company
SPOUSE: Thomas Normington
MARRIED: 29 Sep 1839
England
DEATH SP: 6 Nov 1856
On the Plains near Platte River

CHILDREN:
Joseph, 27 Jun 1840
Mathew Heber, 16 Aug 1841
Jane Ann, 10 Aug 1843

Lovinia (Wright), 16 May 1846
Mary Ellen (Cook), 5 Jun 1847
Hannah or Ann (Ott), 10 Aug 1849
Ephraim Robert, 21 Aug 1851
Daniel, 12 Dec 1854

SPOUSE II: John Parker
MARRIED: 15 Nov 1857
DEATH SP: 24 Mar 1886
Virgin, Washington Co., Utah

CHILDREN:
Richard, 21 Jan 1859
Maria (Hilton), 19 May 1862

Maria Parker was born in Haggate, England, on Christmas Day, December 25, 1820. Little is known of her childhood.

She married Thomas Normington September 29, 1839 in England. They became the parents of eight children. One died in childhood.

Maria and Thomas became members of the Church of Jesus Christ of Latter-day Saints in Burnley, England. They desired to join the body of the Church in Utah. They emigrated to America in 1856. They reached Iowa City, Iowa on July 8, 1856. Here they made a handcart to push across the Plains to the Salt Lake Valley.

They started West on July 28, 1856 with the Edward Martin Handcart Company. During the trip her husband died on the Plains near the Platte River. She also suffered the grief of having two of her sons die, her two youngest. When the Company could travel no further due to hunger and fatigue, they were rescued by scouts sent by President Brigham Young.

Maria survived that long, difficult journey across 1,300 miles. They arrived in the Salt Lake Valley on November 30, 1856. Maria was taken to the home of John Parker, Jr.

On November 15, 1857, Maria married John Parker, Jr. They became the parents of two children; Maria and Richard. The family was called to help settle the Virgin, Washington County, Utah, a barren desert in Southern Utah.

Her husband built the first flour mill and cotton gin in Virgin. He organized the first cattle co-op and the first store. Maria was the storekeeper while her husband worked at his other jobs. She also supported him as the first bishop of the ward and president of the United Order. Maria was a devoted wife and mother. She gave much service to the people of the community.

Maria passed away on March 19, 1881, in Virgin, Washington County, Utah; the country she helped colonize. Her husband passed away five years later. They were true pioneers.

MARY ELIZABETH ROSS PARKER

BIRTHDATE: 4 Mar 1845
Nauvoo, Hancock Co., Illinois
DEATH: 22 Oct 1909
Joseph, Sevier Co., Utah
PARENTS: Thomas Ross
Rachel Smith
PIONEER: 6 Sep 1850
Aaron Johnson Co. Wagon Train
SPOUSE: Joseph F. Parker
MARRIED: 30 Jun 1861
DEATH SP: 14 Jan 1936
Joseph, Sevier Co., Utah

CHILDREN:
Huldah Jane, 1862
Joseph William, 19 Nov 1864
Thomas Bryant, 12 Nov 1866
John Alma, 20 Dec 1869
Mary Susannah, 18 Aug 1872
Anna Elizabeth, 26 Feb 1875/6
Amy Elinor, 6 Feb 1879
Stella, 18 Jun 1881
Ella, 11 Dec 1883
James Marion, abt 1885
Alta, 15 Apr 1891

Mary Parker was born in "Beautiful Nauvoo," Hancock County, Illinois on March 4 1845. She and her family lived on the outskirts of the City.

When the Saints were driven out of Nauvoo, her family went with the Saints to Winter Quarters, Iowa. They suffered much sickness, hardships and challenges in that temporary city. Mary was only five years old.

They joined the Aaron Johnson Wagon Company. They had two wagons; one was drawn by oxen and the other by a team of cows. They arrived in the Salt Lake Valley on September 6, 1850.

Mary married Joseph Faulconer Parker on June 30, 1861 in Joseph, Sevier County, Utah. She was sixteen years old. They became the parents of eleven children; seven girls and four boys.

Mary was an active Church worker. She was President of the Ward Relief Society. The women built the Relief Society Hall by donating eggs and other donations.

While her husband served a mission for the Church, Mary managed the farm, home, and family. She sent her husband money so he could fulfill his mission. Mary attended a school of Obstetrics for six months in Elsinore, Utah.

In addition to her midwife duties, she washed, carded and spun into thread the wool from the sheep. She wove the thread into cloth, cut the cloth out of the loom and made it up into suits, dresses, etc., to suit the needs of her family. Her life was busy as she served the community along with her large family.

Mary was a beautiful, loving woman. She passed away on October 22, 1909 in Joseph, Sevier County, Utah, which she and her husband had helped settle. Her husband passed away on January 14, 1936, also in Joseph, Utah.

NANCY WOOD RILEY PARKER

BIRTHDATE: 20 May 1817
Blackburn, Lancashire, England
DEATH: 13 May 1879
Wellsville, Cache Co., Utah
PARENTS: John Riley
Elizabeth Wood
PIONEER: 13 Oct 1850
Edward Hunter Co. Wagon Train
SPOUSE: Henry Miller Parker
MARRIED: 29 Jan 1844
Nauvoo, Hancock Co., Illinois
DEATH SP: 28 Jul 1887

CHILDREN:
Joseph Hyrum, 27 Feb 1845
Vilate Ellen, 30 Jun 1847
Heber Thomas, 30 Aug 1849
Ruth Elizabeth, 30 Dec 1851
Willard Richard, 7 Oct 1854
Sarah Jane, 16 Feb 1857
Henry Abraham, 11 Aug 1859 (twin)
Nancy Ann, 11 Aug 1859 (twin)

Nancy was born in England. She was among the earliest of British converts to the Church of Jesus Christ of Latter-day Saints. She was nineteen at the time of her baptism in November, 1837, by Heber C. Kimball in the Ribble River near Preston, England. This was just four months following the first baptisms in that country.

Nancy and her family had a great desire to join with the main body of the Church in Utah. They sailed for Zion in February of 1841 on the ship "Sheffield," and arrived in Nauvoo, Illinois on April 18, 1841.

Three years after settling in Nauvoo, Nancy married a widower with two young sons, Henry Miller Parker, January 29, 1844. She was twenty-six years of age at the time. Their home was located two blocks north of the temple site.

As the Nauvoo Temple was being built the Saints were asked to sacrifice their time and means to this worthy cause. Nancy and Henry donated her wedding ring to this worthy cause. They were blessed to receive their Endowments in the Nauvoo Temple on January 29, 1846. Shortly after, they were forced to leave Nauvoo when the Saints were driven from their homes. They experienced many trials as they traveled across the state of Iowa in the cold, snow and mud.

They established a home in Council Bluffs, Iowa and lived there until 1850. They traveled to Utah with the Edward Hunter Company. This was the first group to be financed through the Perpetual Emigration Fund. They arrived in the Salt Lake Valley, October 13, 1850.

They became the parents of eight children; one died in infancy and one died in childhood. The family lived for a short time in Salt Lake City and then moved to Lehi, Utah. Two years later they moved west of Lehi to the new settlement of Cedar Fort. The family was there when the first ward was organized in 1853. In 1858, Johnston's Army established Camp Floyd just two miles south of Cedar Fort. This led to many problems for the settlers.

In the Spring of 1860, the Parker family moved north to Cache Valley and settled in Wellsville, Utah. The family of eleven lived in a one-room dugout the first year. During the Winter, Nancy was deeply saddened when three of her children died within a three week period.

In 1878, Nancy gave her support to her husband when he was called to serve a short mission to England. She suffered many trials and hardships in her life for the sake of the Gospel, but she was faithful to the end.

Nancy passed away on May 13, 1879 in Wellsville, Cache County, Utah at the age of sixty-two.

SARAH ANN COOPER PARKER

BIRTHDATE: 26 Jun 1851
St. Louis, Missouri
DEATH: 28 Apr 1932
Wellsville, Cache Co., Utah
PARENTS: James Cooper
Christena Guest
PIONEER: Sep 1853
John Tingey Co. Wagon Train
SPOUSE: Heber Thomas Parker
MARRIED: 8 Jan 1872
Salt Lake City, Salt Lake, Utah
DEATH SP: 23 Jun 1914

CHILDREN:
Eliza, 2 Oct 1872
Heber, 3 Nov 1874
Christena, 25 Jan 1877
Sarah Ann, 3 Apr 1879 (died at age 3)
Henry (Harry), 15 Feb 1881
James, 8 Dec 1882
Caroline, 2 Jun 1885 (died at 15 months)
Violet, 19 Dec 1886
Frederick, 27 Dec 1888
Orson, 19 May 1891
Melvin, 20 Jul 1893 (died at age 1)

Sarah was a child of two when she crossed the Plains with her parents and family. After arriving in the Salt Lake Valley, they went to Grantsville for four years and then settled in Maughan's Fort (Wellsville). Sarah Ann was six years of age at the time.

Sarah Ann began her church service at an early age. She taught Sunday School at the age of sixteen and sang in the ward choir. She was taught the art of homemaking by her mother. She also was taught how to make straw hats. When her father passed away in 1868, she remained with her mother, assisting in every way possible to lighten the load placed on her mother's shoulders.

At the age of twenty-one she was married to Heber Thomas Parker in the Endowment House in Salt Lake City. They traveled by horse and sleigh through the snow to get there. Sarah Ann and Heber lived their entire lives in Wellsville.

Sarah Ann was very energetic and full of life and happiness. She was very kind and gave her services willingly whenever needed. She served as the Relief Society President of the Wellsville ward while the Tabernacle was being constructed. Under her direction the sisters made one hundred yards of carpet for the Relief Society Room. They earned money to buy seventy-five chairs and window blinds for the room. They purchased the silver sacrament service sets. Many acts of charity were performed by her and she was always alert to the needs of others. Sarah Ann later served as treasurer of the Hyrum Stake Relief Society Board.

Sarah Ann was very active in civic as well as church affairs. She served on the first committee for the Wellsville Old Folks Party. She did extensive work in the temple for her kindred dead. She lived a long and fruitful life. She is buried in the Wellsville Cemetery beside her husband and three little children.

SARAH BEBBINGTON EDGELEY PARKER

BIRTHDATE: 19 Feb 1835
Bulkeley, Cheshire, England
DEATH: 7 May 1899
Riverdale, Weber Co., Utah
PARENTS: William Edgeley
Sarah Bebbington
PIONEER: Sep 1854
Robert Campbell Wagon Train
SPOUSE: William Cope Parker
MARRIED: 13 May 1855
Salt Lake City, Salt Lake, Utah
DEATH SP: 27 Apr 1917
Riverdale, Weber Co. Utah

CHILDREN:
William Henry, 10 Jan 1856
Sarah Jane, 22 Apr 1857
George William, 19 Feb 1859 (twin)
Mary, 19 Feb 1859 (twin)
Thomas, 31 Dec 1860
Elizabeth, 18 Feb 1863
Joseph, 20 Aug 1864
John, 3 Oct 1866
Richard, 31 Jul 1867
Edwin Bebbington, 18 Jun 1870
Robert, 8 Dec 1872
James William, 2 Feb 1876
Daniel, 22 Apr 1877

Sarah was born in England. She was baptized a member of the Church of Jesus Christ of Latter-day Saints by her friend, William Cope Parker on June 18, 1853.

She wanted to join other members of the Church in Utah but her parents would not give their consent. Every day, as she went to the home of her Aunt and Uncle to get milk for her family, she would wear an extra item of clothing until she had enough clothing to take with her to America. She left home without saying anything to her family.

Sarah traveled to America on the ship "Windermere," which left Liverpool, England on February 22, 1854. She was with four members of her mother's family plus one young man by the name of William Cope Parker. They landed at New Orleans, Louisiana on April 23, 1854. They traveled by steamboat to St. Louis, Missouri, where they were outfitted for the trip across the Plains.

They joined the Robert Campbell wagon-train Company. William Cope Parker was the teamster who drove the oxen for their family. The terrain was rough and they had to walk part of the time to lighten the load for the oxen. Once, while crossing a deep gully, Sarah jumped out of the wagon and almost went under the wheel of the wagon. She was rescued by her "sweet William." They arrived in the Salt Lake Valley in September, 1854.

Sarah married William Cope Parker on May 13, 1855 in Salt Lake City, Utah. They spent their first night on a straw tick mattress in their covered wagon. They became the parents of thirteen children; four died in infancy, two in childhood and one at birth.

William and Sarah both worked for a miller, Archibald Gardiner. They ran a mill for the Parker family in Riverdale, Weber County, Utah. They bought forty acres of land and raised fruit which was a very successful business so they could buy more land. They also raised tomatoes and sugar beets.

Sarah acted as a midwife and delivered many of the babies of Riverdale. The Parkers had a large home and after a baby was delivered mother and baby would stay with them to be taken care of until they were strong enough to go back to their own home.

The Parkers were active members of the Church. Sarah was the Relief Society President in the Ogden 2nd Ward, before the Riverdale Ward was organized. She was an active member of the Riverdale Ward Relief Society. She is mentioned often in the Riverdale Ward Relief Society minutes for her donations and help. One note of mention was that Sister Sarah Parker can make corsets and would be glad to help anyone who would like to make their own. Sarah was an excellent homemaker.

Sarah passed away on May 7, 1899 in Riverdale at the age of sixty-four. She is buried in the Ogden City Cemetery.

ELIZA FOULDS PARKIN

BIRTHDATE: 7 Dec 1839
Holdbrook, Morr, England
DEATH: 11 Jun 1889
Bountiful, Davis Co., Utah
PARENTS: James Foulds
Sarah Saxton
PIONEER: 1863
Kimball & Lawrence Wagon Co.
SPOUSE: William John Parkin
MARRIED: 18 Aug 1864
Bountiful, Davis Co., Utah
DEATH SP: 16 Feb 1919
Bountiful, Davis Co., Utah

CHILDREN:
Sarah Elizabeth, 16 May 1865
Harriet, 15 Apr 1867
William John, 27 Jun 1869
James Henry, Nov 1871
George, 2 Mar 1873
Stephen, 20 Oct 1875
Zipporah, 14 Apr 1878
Eliza Jane, 4 Jun 1880
Grace Hannah, 3 Oct 1883
Mary Olive, 4 May 1886

Eliza heard the gospel from a missionary preaching on the street corner. She was the only one of her family to join the Church of Jesus Christ of Latter-day Saints. Her sisters objected to her joining the Church; her father thought it was the right thing to do, although he did not join.

On May 30, 1863, Eliza left Liverpool, England and sailed to America. Her traveling companion was Hannah Randall. While crossing the ocean, she met William John Parkin and fell in love with him. When they reached New York, they were separated and did not meet one another until later in Utah. She came to Utah with the Kimball and Lawrence Company with James Brown in charge.

Eliza was working for a family in Salt Lake City and was out for a walk one day when she accidently met William driving an ox-team. They began their courtship again and were married, August 18, 1864, in Bountiful, Utah. She and her husband were blessed with ten children.

Eliza was a home loving woman. She always made home a pleasant place for her husband and children. She and her daughters did their own knitting, sewing, churning, and other household tasks. She prepared large suppers for members of the ward choir when her husband brought them to their home to practice. She prepared food and took it to the sick with her husband during a diphtheria epidemic in Bountiful. She attended church regularly and was an active member of the Relief Society.

ELIZA SNOW COOPER PARKIN

BIRTHDATE: 20 Jul 1852
Eastwood, Nottingham, England
DEATH: 29 Sep 1926
Woods Cross, Davis Co., Utah
PARENTS: William Cooper
Millizer Robinson
PIONEER: 19 Oct 1862
Horton D. Haight Wagon Train
SPOUSE: Joseph H. Parkin
MARRIED: 14 Feb 1870
Salt Lake City, Salt Lake, Utah
DEATH SP: 23 Oct 1935
Bountiful, Davis Co., Utah

CHILDREN:
Joseph Hyrum, 26 Nov 1871
Zebulon, 10 Mar 1874
Millezer, 4 Aug 1876
Mary Evalyn, 11 Mar 1880
Ulysses Henry, 4 Aug 1882
Amy Maude, 22 Feb 1885
Stella, 10 Jul 1887
Harriet E., 30 Jun 1888
Gertrude, 17 Feb 1891
Irene, 3 Aug 1892
Ione, 3 Aug 1892

Eliza Parkin was born in Holdbrook, Morr, Derbyshire, England in a poor but loving family. When she was nine, she came with her family across the Plains to Utah, walking most of the way. When she was about fourteen, she was able to find a job and work to help her parents. As a result, she had very little formal schooling. This was just a few years before her father died, leaving her mother with seven children to raise.

Eliza endured many hardships as she was growing up. She learned the value and necessity of hard work. They had crossed the Plains with the Horton D. Haight Company, arriving in the Salt Lake Valley on October 19, 1862.

Eliza married Joseph H. Parkin, February 14, 1870, in Salt Lake City, Utah. After her marriage, her husband taught her to read and write in the evenings after supper.

Eliza was a wonderful seamstress and cook. She did all the sewing for her family and much for her neighbors and friends. She bottled many gallons-of blue plum jam from their own orchard. Her bottled peaches were a favorite of her son, Ulysses, for many years.

The year that her oldest son, Joseph, was called on a mission, she and her husband did much to take care of his wife and children while he was away.

In the Fall of 1878, during the Diphtheria epidemic in Bountiful, Eliza prevented her husband from contracting the disease by boiling his clothes each time he came home from burying the dead.

In her later years they moved to Salt Lake City. Eliza served as a Relief Society Visiting Teacher, something she had longed to do for some time. She was a faithful member of the Church. She attended church services and General Conferences whenever possible.

Eliza passed away at Woods Cross, Utah, September 29, 1926. Her husband passed away in Bountiful, Utah in October, 1935.

ELIZABETH SELENA THURGOOD PARKIN

BIRTHDATE: 29 Apr 1863
Camberwell, London, England
DEATH: 22 Apr 1949
Salt Lake City, Salt Lake, Utah
PARENTS: Thomas Thurgood
Sarah Ann Banks
PIONEER: 13 Oct 1864
Capt. Hyde's Co. Wagon Train
SPOUSE: William John Parkin
MARRIED: 24 Apr 1884
Salt, Lake City, Salt Lake, Utah
DEATH SP: 16 Feb 919
Woods Cross, Davis Co., Utah

CHILDREN:
Sarah Laura, 5 Feb 1885
Alice Elizabeth, 9 Jul 1887
Thomas Cornelius, 21 Feb 1890
Rilla Ann, 3 Feb 1892
Roland Thurgood, 22 Mar 1894
Edith Lucille, 5 Sep 1896
Lincoln Dewey, 6 Jan 1899
Carrie Ardell, 12 Mar 1901
Clifford Foulds, 28 Feb 1902
Erma, 13 Aug 1906

Elizabeth was born in England in 1863. When she was one year old she came across the Plains with her parents in Captain Hyde's Company arriving in October, 1864.

The family moved to Bountiful, Utah, where they had a little farm. Grasshoppers were a problem. Her father and mother would lay sheets on the ground, and when the grasshoppers lit, they would gather them and bury them in trenches.

Elizabeth learned to make tallow candles and also to crochet. Her mother died when she was seventeen, leaving six children for her father and herself to care for.

At the age of twenty-one, she married William J. Parkin Sr., in the Endowment House as his second wife. He was twenty-one years older then Elizabeth. She continued to live with her father and to care for his household.

William's first wife had ten children, many of them about the same age as Elizabeth, and they seemed to resent her. Elizabeth had to go underground when Federal Marshals were looking for polygamous men. William was caught and put in jail for fifty days and fined $50.00. When the first wife died, Elizabeth cared for her last five children, and then went to her husband's home to live. She was the mother of ten children, two who died early in life.

Elizabeth worked in the Relief Society in Bountiful, and also in the 18th Ward Relief Society in Salt Lake City after her husband's death in 1919. She did temple work for many years before she passed away in 1949.

ELIZABETH WRIGHT BROWN PARKIN

BIRTHDATE: 18 Mar 1821
Loscoe, Codnor, England
DEATH: 4 Apr 1887
Bountiful, Davis Co., Utah
PARENTS: John Brown
Ann Wright
PIONEER: 4 Oct 1863
Thomas E. Ricks Wagon Train
SPOUSE: John Parkin
MARRIED: 28 Feb 1839
Duffield, Derbyshire, England
DEATH SP: 14 Nov 1885
Bountiful, Davis Co., Utah

CHILDREN:
William John, 19 May 1839
George, 15 Dec 1841 (died as an infant)
Harriet, 30 Jun 1843
John, Jr., 20 May 1847
Joseph, 6 Jun 1850
Hyrum, 4 Feb 1854
Heber, 19 Jun 1861

Elizabeth was born in Loscoe, Codnor, Derbyshire, England. She married John Parkin on February 28, 1839 in Duffield, Derbyshire, England. They were baptized into the Church of Jesus Christ of Latter-day Saints on December 15, 1850.

The family left England on May 26, 1863 on the ship, "Cynosure," in company with 754 other members of the Church. They arrived in New York on July 19, 1863 and continued on their journey to Florence, Nebraska by train. They joined the Thomas E. Ricks Wagon Company and traveled by ox-team, arriving in Salt Lake City on October 4, 1863.

They settled in South Bountiful where her husband built her a log home with three rooms. He also built a white picket fence surrounding it. In their south room, Elizabeth and John kept a small store where they sold candles, groceries, candy, and prize boxes for children. They milked several cows, made butter and cheese, and raised chickens. They had one of the nicest gardens in the area and peddled their fruit, vegetables, cheese, butter, and eggs to regular customers in Salt Lake City every Friday.

He would also go to Park City which was a mining town east of Salt Lake City. To arrive in Park City was not an easy trip since the steep grade of Parley's Canyon had to be traversed. Traveling there usually took two days going one direction.

Elizabeth was quiet, good to children, and kept everything neat and clean around the house and yard. She attended church regularly and always bore her testimony. She was a faithful worker in the Relief Society. She was endowed and sealed to John on February 9, 1867. She shared her husband with three other wives.

Elizabeth did much genealogy and temple work before her death on April 4, 1887 in South Bountiful and was buried in the Bountiful City Cemetery.

MARY ANN LEWIS PARKIN

BIRTHDATE: 7 Dec 1853
Fleur De-Lis, Monmouth,
Wales or England
DEATH: 30 Dec 1925
Salt Lake City, Salt Lake, Utah
PARENTS: David Lewis
Ann Lewis
PIONEER: 2 Oct 1856
E. Bunker Handcart Company
SPOUSE: John Parkin Jr.
MARRIED: 26 Dec 1870
DEATH SP: 2 Apr 1936
Salt Lake City, Salt Lake, Utah

CHILDREN:
David John, 4 Mar 1871
Heber Brown, 18 Sep 1872
George Edmund, 31 Dec 1874
Ann Elizabeth, 13 Nov 1876
Lafayette, 12 Jan 1879
Don Carlos, 10 Aug 1881
Elias, 9 May 1884
Mary Jane, 1 Mar 1886
Mazella, 3 May 1888
Owen, 14 Oct 1890

Mary Ann Parkin was born in England, the first girl born to David and Ann Lewis. Her parents joined the Church of Jesus Christ of Latter-day Saints and desired to emigrate to Utah.

They left Liverpool, England April 18, 1856 on the ship "Samuel Curling." While out to sea many people died of chicken pox; twelve children and seven adults, and were buried at sea. Mary Ann and her family were blessed to survive. They landed in Boston, Massachusetts and made their way to Iowa City, Iowa to meet with 300 other Welsh Saints.

They joined with the Edward Bunker Handcart Company and on June 23, 1856, started West with brave and determined hearts and great faith. Mary Ann was two and one half years old and rode on the handcart. When they stopped for the evening, she and her brother would scamper to find wild flowers to brighten their day and sticks and buffalo chips to help kindle the fire. Hunger and hardships were forgotten while her parents sang Welsh lullabies to soothe and cheer them. They arrived in the Salt Lake Valley on October 2, 1856.

They traveled on to Willow Creek, later known as Willard, Utah and stayed for more than a year. They moved to Bountiful, Utah and then made their home in Salt Lake City, Utah.

Mary Ann loved to go with her father and watch as he cut stones for the Salt Lake Temple. Mary Ann was over ten years old before she had a pair of leather shoes or saw and ate an apple.

Her mother died when she was thirteen years old and Mary Ann had the responsibility of taking the place of her mother; five children to care for, cook for, sew clothes for and teach them the right things. The privilege of going to school was never hers.

She did meet the man of her dreams at the young age of seventeen, John Parkin, Jr. They were married on December 26, 1870. Mary Ann and John built a two-story home in Bountiful, Utah. They became the parents of ten children; seven sons and three daughters. All of their children grew to maturity and married except their first and seventh babies.

Mary Ann was always neat and clean and kept her home and children clean. She was a wonderful mother and housekeeper, an excellent cook and tailor. On Sunday she would wear a clean, white apron trimmed with crocheted lace over her dress and tied around her waist. Black currant pie was one of her specialties along with her roast beef, milk gravy and Yorkshire pudding. There was always a demand for her butter; she always gave a big pound.

In 1892, her husband was called to serve a mission to England. The older children went to work to support their father and help with the finances of their own home. Mary Ann did her part, as well. Her husband served over two years, baptizing many of his and Mary Ann's kinfolk.

Mary Ann served as a Relief Society visiting teacher for many years. She may have been deeply hurt but she would never talk of it, or ever talk about anyone else that wasn't good. She had a very remarkable memory and was a wonderful mother. She loved to sing to her children and grandchildren.

Mary Ann endured to the end and remained faithful to the Gospel of the Church of Jesus Christ of Latter-day Saints. She passed away on December 30, 1925 at the age of seventy-two after a brief illness at the LDS Hospital in Salt Lake City, Utah.

MARY JANE BARNES PARKIN

BIRTHDATE: 24 July 1856
Iowa City, Iowa
DEATH: 16 Dec 1910
Holladay, Salt Lake, Co., Utah
PARENTS: George Barnes
Jane Howard Barnes Barnes
PIONEER: 30 Nov 1856
Martin Handcart Company
SPOUSE: Fred Parkin
MARRIED: 8 Oct 1872
DEATH SP: 10 Mar 1931

CHILDREN:
Fredrick William, 14 Aug 1873
Charles Henry, 7 Nov 1875
George Herbert, 16 Apr 1878
Jedidah, 20 Oct 1880 (died 18 Mar 1881)
Jane Ann, 13 Feb 1882
Margaret May, 30 Sep 1884 (died 20 May 1888)
Martha, 2 Apr 1888
Albert, 30 Apr 1890
Arthur, 18 Mar 1896 (died 26 Aug 1899)
Mida Pearl, 15 Jun 1898 (died 10 Oct 1899)

Mary Jane's family sailed from England May 25, 1856 on the ship "Horizon." They arrived at Iowa City, Iowa on July 8th, Mary Jane was born on July 24th, and they set out for Zion on July 28th, with the Martin Handcart Company.

Of the 576 souls who began the journey, 150 died on the way. Mary Jane's father was one who died when the company was caught in a terrible storm at Martin's Cove in Wyoming.

Mary Jane was the fifth girl and the sixth child. They arrived in Salt Lake Valley on November 30, 1856. William Barnes, her father's brother, had come earlier and had a home ready for them. In the Spring, Mary Jane's mother and William were married.

On October 8, 1872, at the age of sixteen, Mary Jane married Fred Parkin. Their first home was in the Salt Lake Valley near where Murray is today. Here four sons were born to them.

In 1882, a baby girl was born and, that same year, they moved to Willow Creek, Idaho near Idaho Falls. They took, up a homestead and Mary Jane was a true pioneer, helping her husband "prove up" the land. Winters were severe and wresting a living from the soil was hard. Three more children were born here.

In 1892, they traded the farm for a place on the outskirts of Nephi, Utah. Two more children were born but both died at an early age. Of Mary Jane's ten children, only six grew to maturity.

ARABELLA ANN CHANDLER PARKINSON

BIRTHDATE: 27 Feb 1824
Cheltanham, England
DEATH: 9 Aug 1894
Franklin, Idaho
PARENTS: George Chandler
Esther Glover
PIONEER: 23 Sep 1854
Job Smith Co. Wagon Train
SPOUSE: Samuel R.
Parkinson
MARRIED: 1 Jan 1852
St. Louis, Missouri
DEATH SP: 23 May 1919

CHILDREN:
Samuel Chandler, 23 Feb 1853
Charlotte Chandler, 1 Aug 1855 (twin)
William Chandler, 2 Aug 1855 (twin)
George Chandler, 18 Jul 1857
Franklin Chandler, 7 Jul 1859
Esther Arabella, 2 Feb 1862
Albert C., 15 Aug 1863
Clara Jenette, 18 Apr 1865
Caroline Chandler, 10 Nov 1866

Arabella was born to George and Esther Glover Chandler in Cheltanham, England on February 27, 1824. She became a professional dressmaker and milliner. After the death of her father in 1836, she was the main support of her widowed mother and younger brother.

In 1842, the three of them joined the Church of Jesus Christ of Latter-day Saints and became active members in spreading the gospel. In 1849, her mother died. She worked hard and was able to save enough for her brother and her to emigrate. They left Liverpool on the ship, "George W. Bourne."

When they arrived in New Orleans, they were taken by riverboat to St. Louis. She went to work again as a dress maker and milliner in an effort to acquire the necessary means to continue their journey to Utah.

Arabella met Samuel Rose Parkinson. They were married in St. Louis, Missouri on January 1, 1852, where they remained until after the birth of their first child. They crossed the Plains with the Job Smith Wagon Company and arrived in the Salt Lake Valley on September 23, 1854.

Their first home was a one-room log hut with a dirt floor and dirt roof. The following summer she gave birth to twins. In 1860, they moved to Cache Valley which later became Franklin, Idaho. They lived in their wagons until their log home was built, then began their gardening and farming in preparation for the coming winter.

Arabella prepared their meals with the most primitive utensils and they had only the bare necessities of food. She made soap, molded candles, and cured meat. She made buckskin pants and shirts for her husband and boys, using horse hair for thread.

In 1862, they began to operate a small store in part of their home. She took an orphaned Indian boy to raise. In 1866, she became a plural wife and was known as the "peace maker" for the three families. When her husband was imprisoned for polygamy, she looked after his large family and guarded carefully his financial interests. She taught her children to be industrious and self-supporting.

Arabella started and maintained during her lifetime a charity benefit for the aged, the widows, orphans and unfortunate of the Franklin area and entertained them in her home annually until she died.

BETSY BARNES WOODWARD PARKINSON

BIRTHDATE: 3 May 1841
Nauvoo, Hancock Co., Illinois
DEATH: 15 Dec 1898
Wellsville, Cache Co., Utah
PARENTS: Joseph Woodward
Margaret Barnes
PIONEER: 1852
SPOUSE: Henry F. Parkinson
MARRIED: 2 Jan 1860
Wellsville, Cache Co., Utah
DEATH SP: 29 Jan 1923
Wellsville, Cache Co., Utah

CHILDREN:
Henry Woodward, 16 Dec 1861
Margaret Ann (Jones), 29 Nov 1864
Rose (Brown), 9 Aug 1865
Julia Woodward (Grant), 6 Nov 1867
Martha Woodward (Johnson Woodward), 14 Feb 1871
Joseph Woodward Parkinson, 6 Dec 1873
Timothy Woodward Parkinson, 17 Mar 1876
Chauncey Woodward Parkinson, 16 Mar 1879
LeRoy Woodward Parkinson, 14 Jun 1882
Sylvia Pearl (Darley), 21 Jun 1885
Ross Woodward Parkinson, 21 Aug 1887
Bessie Parkinson, 30 Jun 1890

Betsy was born in Nauvoo, Hancock County, Illinois on May 3, 1841. Her parents were Joseph Woodward and Margaret Barnes.

Betsy and her mother were some of the first Saints to see the martyred body of the Prophet Joseph Smith at the Carthage jail.

The family arrived in Utah, entering the Salt Lake Valley in 1852 when Betsy was about eleven years of age.

Betsy married Henry Fielding Parkinson on February 2, 1860 in Wellsville, Cache County, Utah. They were later sealed in the Endowment House in Salt Lake City. Betsy was the mother of twelve children. She was a hard working, thrifty soul.

Betsy passed away in Wellsville, Utah on December 15, 1898; her husband passed away on January 29, 1923, also in Wellsville, Cache County, Utah.

ELIZABETH KING PARKINSON

BIRTHDATE: 15 Feb 1823
Clapham, England
DEATH: 4 Sep 1909
Portage, Utah
PARENTS: James King
Mary Nowell King
PIONEER: 17 Oct 1853
John Brown Wagon Co.
SPOUSE: Thomas Parkinson
MARRIED: abt. 1846
DEATH SP: abt. 1882

CHILDREN:
John, 27 Aug 1847
James, 6 May 1850
Thomas, Mar 1852
Isaac, 15 Mar 1855
Mary Ann (Harris), 9 Aug 1858
Son, 8 Dec 1860
Elizabeth (Gibbs), 26 Oct 1861
Hyrum, 20 Nov 1863
David, 31 Jan 1866

Elizabeth was born in England in 1823. She and her brother, Isaac, were very devoted to each other. She was of medium height, with light brown hair and blue eyes.

Her mother taught her all the social graces of the day, and she had a private tutor for a time. As a small child she learned a stated number of scriptures. As she grew older, she continued this practice until she had most of the New Testament memorized.

She married Thomas Parkinson in England, but the date is unknown. They were converted to the Church and baptized in 1853. At this time they had three small boys.

The family boarded the ship "Camillus" in April 1853 and set sail. The arrived at Keokuk, Iowa in June. Elizabeth walked by the side of her husband, carrying her baby most of the way. The baby became feverish, but the company could not stop because of it being so late in the season. He died and was buried in his best little dress, in a coffin made of bark and limbs, in a shallow grave.

The Parkinson family lived in Salt Lake for the first year, then moved to Grantsville in 1854. Two years later they moved to Ogden, then in 1859 to a farm in Wellsville. Her husband was a boot maker. Many times she helped him finish an article so the order would be on time. In 1867, they moved to Portage where she was hired as clerk of the Co-op Store and her husband kept the books. Her husband became disillusioned with some of the people and went to seek gold in Idaho. In 1882, she received her last letter from him. She never knew what happened to him.

Elizabeth was the first Relief Society President in Portage. Her motto was, "A place for everything and everything in its place." She was the mother of nine children, four of whom died very young. She took an active part in church and social events. She helped make the U. S. flag of Portage. She had a deep affection for others, and showed kindness and courtesy toward her associates. She was an ideal woman to all who knew her and beloved by her family. She died in 1909, at the age of eighty-six.

HANNAH MARIA CLARK PARKINSON

BIRTHDATE: 8 Jul 1832
Herefordshire, England
DEATH: 17 Mar 1869
Grantsville, Tooele Co., Utah
PARENTS: Thomas H. Clark
Charlotte Gailey
PIONEER: 1850 Wagon Train
SPOUSE: Charles G. Parkinson
MARRIED: 15 Oct 1855
Grantsville, Tooele Co., Utah
DEATH SP: 4 Jan 1907
Grantsville, Tooele Co., Utah

CHILDREN:
Charles Graham, Jr., 18 Aug 1856
Timothy Henry, 3 Mar 1858
Charlotte Ann, 16 Dec 1859
John William, 9 Dec 1861
Mary Ann, 17 Oct 1862
Hannah Maria, 12 Jul 1865
Ellen Ann, 6 Feb 1867
Joseph Thomas, 23 Jul 1868

Hannah Maria was born on July 8, 1832, the daughter of Thomas H. Clark and Charlotte Gailey. Hannah Maria was the fourth of nine children. Her family joined the Church of Jesus Christ of Latter-day Saints and came to America in about 1840. Her youngest sisters were born in Nauvoo. Her parents received their Endowments there in 1846. They suffered the pursecutions and in 1850 they came by wagon to the Salt Lake Valley. her father was a polygamist and his families settled in Grantsville, Utah.

At age twenty-three, Hannah married Charles Graham Parkinson on October 15, 1855 in Grantsville, Utah. She became the mother of eight children, and was a woman of courage and integrity.

Charles took a second wife, Sarah Hill, by whom he had eight children. Hannah became a second mother to these eight children.

Hannah passed away, March 17, 1869, at Grantsville, Tooele, Utah, at the age of thirty-six. Her youngest child was only ten years old. Her husband passed away on January 4, 1907, also at Grantsville, Tooele County, Utah.

MARIA BLACK PARKER PARKINSON

BIRTHDATE: 27 Jun 1840
Preston, Candover, England
DEATH: 3 Nov 1891
Wellsville, Cache Co., Utah
PARENTS: William Parker
Marie Black
PIONEER: 1862
SPOUSE: Timothy F. Parkinson
MARRIED: 5 Jan 1863
Salt Lake City, Salt Lake, Utah
DEATH SP: 20 Oct 1898
Wellsvilee, Cache Co., Utah

CHILDREN: None

Maria was born on June 27, 1840, at Preston, England, the daughter of William Parker and Marie Black.

Maria came to the Salt Lake Valley in 1862. On January 5, 1863, she married Timothy Fielding Parkinson, Jr. in the Endowment House in Salt Lake City, Utah. They were not blessed with children, but she did raise a niece, Ellen Ann Parkinson.

Maria and Timothy settled in Wellsville, Cache County, Utah, where Maria held many church positions in her ward. She was secretary and visiting teacher in the Relief Society and Primary President. Maria also worked as a 'clerk' in the Wellsville Co-op store where she was fondly called "Auntie."

Maria passed away on November 3, 1891, and Timothy passed away on October 20, 1898, both in Wellsville, Cache County, Utah.

MARTHA HARVILLE BICKMORE PARKINSON

BIRTHDATE: 4 Jan 1808
Kainey, North Carolina
DEATH: 26 Oct 1883
Wellsville, Cache Co., Utah
PARENTS: Squire James Harvel
Mary Monette
PIONEER: 5 Oct 1852
John B. Walker Co. Wagon Train
SPOUSE I: Isaac M. Bickmore
MARRIED: 1 Mar 1829
Friendship, Knox Co., Maine
DEATH SP: 6 Jul 1852
Loop Fork, Nebraska

CHILDREN:
John Jackson Bickmore, 1829
Martha Jane Bickmore, 24 Jan 1832
Isaac Danfor Bickmore, 24 Sep 1838
Mary Ann Bickmore, 1 Feb 1840
Sarah Elizabeth Bickmore, 31 May 1842
David Newman Bickmore, 1 Aug 1844
Daniel Marion Bickmore, 10 Mar 1847

SPOUSE II: Timothy Graham Parkinson Sr.
MARRIED: 4 Jun 1856
Salt Lake City, Salt Lake Co., Utah
DEATH SP: 20 Oct 1891
Wellsville, Cache Co., Utah
CHILDREN: None

Martha Harvel or Harville was born on January 4, 1808 in Kainey, North Carolina. Her parents were Squire James Harvel and Mary Monette. She married Isaac Motor Bickmore in 1858 and they became the parents of seven children, all born in Illinois.

In 1852 they joined with the Walker Company to cross the Plains. Her husband Isaac, died at Loop Fork, Nebraska on July 6, 1852. Martha arrived in the Salt Lake Valley with her children on October 5, 1852.

On June 4, 1856 she married Timothy Graham Parkinson Sr. in the Endowment House in Salt Lake City, Utah. She helped to raise his two young sons, Henry Fielding Parkinson and Timothy Fielding Parkinson. They also adopted a son together, who they named Henry Parkinson.

Martha co-owned and operated a dairy farm in Wellsville, Utah. She made butter and cheese, which she proudly stamped with a big letter "P." She was a mid-wife and helped deliver many babies, traveling on horseback for each delivery. She was a good Latter-day Saint, who was generous with her time and money. She donated a portion of her farm to the town of Wellsville to be used as the Wellsville Cemetery.

Martha passed away on October 26, 1883 in Wellsville, Cache County, Utah. She was buried in the cemetery she donated the land for. Her husband, Timothy , passed away in 1891 also at Wellsville, Cache County, Utah.

MARY ANN BRYANT PORTER PARKINSON

BIRTHDATE: 13 May 1824
Rolvenden, Kent, England
DEATH: 6 Sep 1905
Beaver City, Beaver Co., Utah
PARENTS: Samuel C. Bryant
Sarah Stapley
PIONEER: 15 Feb 1858
William Moyes Wagon Train
SPOUSE: John Porter
MARRIED: 16 Apr 1844
New Castle, NSW, Australia
DEATH SP: Not given

CHILDREN:
William Frederick, 6 Jan 1845
Elizabeth Ann, 11 Dec 1847
John, 31 Jul 1849
Samuel, 8 Dec 1851

SPOUSE II: Thomas Parkinson
MARRIED: 12 Jun 1855
San Bernardino, California
DEATH SP: 3 Mar 1906
Beaver City, Beaver Co., Utah

CHILDREN:
Mary Jane, 15 Oct 1855
Eliza Ellen, 8 Sep 1857
Thomas James, 2 Sep 1859
Joseph Henry, 22 Dec 1861 (died at age 9)
Reuben, 7 Mar 1864
George Arthur, 21 May 1866
Sarai Alice, 18 Jul 1868

Mary Ann was born in Rolvenden, Kent, England. When she was a child, their family crossed the ocean to live in Australia.

She married John Porter on April 16, 1844 in Maitland, NSW, Australia. They had four children before he died. She brought her four children to America aboard the maiden voyage of the ship, "Julia Ann." They landed in San Bernardino.

She married Thomas Parkinson on June 12, 1855 and they became early San Bernardino colonizers. Their family traveled from San Bernardino to Beaver Utah with the William Moyes Wagon Company. Mary Ann helped her husband establish a homestead in the town of Beaver in 1858.

She raised eleven children. She was an active member in the Beaver First Ward, beloved by her friends and neighbors, and known as "Mother Parkinson" to all. She was a charter member of the famous "Beaver Choir" and participated in that choir for nearly forty years.

MARY NUTTALL HASLAM PARKINSON

No
Photo
Available

BIRTHDATE: 4 Jan 1802
Summerset, Lancashire, England
DEATH: 31 Dec 1853
Grantsville, Tooele Co., Utah
PARENTS: Edmund Nuttall
Martha Hoyle
PIONEER: 16 Oct 1853
Cyrus Wheelock Wagon Train
SPOUSE I: Robert Haslam
MARRIED: 19 Oct 1828
Prestwich, England
DEATH SP: Unknown

CHILDREN:
Mary Haslam, (chr.) 26 Oct 1824
John Robert Haslam, (chr.) 10 Jan 1828
William Haslam, 17 Jul 1832
Betsy Haslam, (chr.) 3 May 1835

SPOUSE II: Timothy Graham Parkinson, Sr.
MARRIED: 20 Aug 1849
Bury, Lancashire, England

DEATH SP: 10 Oct 1891
Wellsville, Cache Co., Utah
CHILDREN: None

Mary Nuttall was born on January 4, 1802 in England, the daughter of Edmund Nuttall and Martha Hoyle. She married Robert on October 19, 1828 in Prestwich, England. They became the parents of four children all born in England. The death date of her husband in not known.

Mary was married a second time to Timothy Graham Parkinson, Sr., August 20, 1849 at Duty, Lancashire, England. They came across the Plains with the Cyrus Wheelock Wagon Company and Captain George Kendall Company, arriving in Salt Lake City on October 12, 1853.

Mary was a weaver by trade and she was accomplished as a fine lace maker. She was wounded by an Indian arrow shot into her chest, during an attack on the Grantsville Fort. She died in the Grantsville Cemetery. Her death occured on December 31, 1853.

Thomas remarried again and moved to Wellsville, Cache County, Utah. He died in Wellsville in 1891.

PRISCILLA JANE WILLIAMS PARKINSON

BIRTHDATE: 2 Feb 1861
Coventry, Warwickshire
England
DEATH: 10 Aug 1957
St. Anthony, Fremont Co., Idaho
PARENTS: Thomas P. Williams
Jane Fawson
PIONEER: 30 Sep 1861
Ira Eldredge Co. Wagon Train
SPOUSE: Timothy H. Parkinson
MARRIED: 3 Mar 1881
DEATH SP: 16 Feb 1941
Grantsville, Tooele Co., Utah

CHILDREN:
Esther Jane, 11 Mar 1882
Hannah Priscilla, 26 Jan 1884
John Henry, 20 Sep 1886
Thomas Franklin, 29 Apr 1889
Charles Leslie, Nov 1891
Sedlie William, 25 Jul 1894
James Ezra, 27 Sep 1896
Clarence Cleone, 27 Jan 1900
Joseph Earl, 30 May 1902
Sarah Luana, 24 Dec 1904
Eva Leone, 2 Apr 1908

Priscilla Jane was born in England in 1861. She came across the Plains in 1861 with the Ira Eldredge Company, and was carried in her mother's apron. She was only three months old at the time. The family arrived with few possessions and only one penny in her father's pocket. But with faith and hard work her father was able to provide a good home.

Priscilla married Timothy Henry Parkinson in 1881, and became the mother of eleven children. She was a cheerful person with a good sense of humor. She held various Relief Society positions. Her home was neat and clean, and the evenings were filled with music from the children as she quilted or mended by lamplight. The children entertained with their music at public and church dances, and Priscilla herself loved to dance the reels and the polkas. Timothy and Priscilla served in the Logan Temple for fifteen years.

Timothy passed away in 1941 in Grantsville, Tooele County, Utah; and Priscilla passed away in 1957 in St. Anthony, Fremont County, Idaho.

REBECCA SHAW WOOD GREEN PARKINSON

BIRTHDATE: 17 Apr 1817
Slaughet, Yorkshire, England
DEATH: 30 Aug 1900
Murray, Salt Lake Co., Utah
PARENTS: Joseph Shaw
Mary Whitwam
PIONEER: 5 Oct 1852
John Walker Co. Wagon Train
SPOUSE I: George Wood Sr.
MARRIED: 25 Feb 1838
Huddersfield, Yorkshire, England
DEATH SP: 1850
died at sea

CHILDREN:
Alice (Eddins), 29 May 1837
George Shaw, 2 Feb 1839
John, 20 Nov 1842
Mary (Wilson), 2 Nov 1844

SPOUSE II: Thomas Green
MARRIED: 3 May 1862
DEATH SP: Unknown
CHILDREN: None

SPOUSE III: Timothy Graham Parkinson Sr.
MARRIED: 4 Oct 1869
Salt Lake City, Salt Lake Co., Utah
DEATH SP: 10 Oct 1891
Wellsville, Cache Co., Utah

Rebecca Shaw was born in Slaughet, Yorkshire, England on April 17, 1817. Her parents were Joseph Shaw and Mary Whitwam.

She married George Wood Sr. on February 25, 1838 at Huddersfield, Yorkshire, England. They were the parents of four children, however, George Wood, Sr. died in 1850, while at sea coming to America.

Rebecca brought her children to Zion, leaving Kanesville, Iowa on July 5, and arriving in the Salt Lake Valley on October 5, 1852 in the John B. Walker Wagon Company.

She was an accomplished weaver, making beautiful rag rugs and broadcloth. Because of her situation it became necessary for her to raise four children alone.

There is no available information for her second marriage to Thomas Green.

On October 4, 1869, she married Timothy Graham Parkinson Sr., in the Endowment House in Salt Lake City. He passed away on October 10, 1891 in Wellsville, and Martha passed away on August 30, 1900 in Murray, Salt Lake County, Utah.

SARAH ANN PARKINSON

No Photo Available

BIRTHDATE: 25 Aug 1834
Holcombe, Lancashire, England
DEATH SP: Jun 1853
Omaha, Nebraska
PARENTS: Timothy Parkinson
Ann Fielding
PIONEER:
Cyrus Wheelock Wagon Train
SPOUSE: Never married

Sarah Ann Parkinson was born on August 25, 1834 in Holcombe, Lancashire, England, the daughter of Timothy Graham Parkinson Sr. and Ann Fielding.

Sarah was a calico printer of fine silks, and an accomplished lace maker. The family had joined with the Cyrus Wheelock Company to cross the Plains in 1853.

Sarah Ann Parkinson passed away in Omaha, Nebraska in June, 1853, just after they started the journey. She was nineteen years of age, and had never married.

ANGELINE SANFORD TAYLOR PARKIS

No Photo Available

BIRTHDATE: 8 Mar 1831
Near Toronto, Canada
DEATH: I Feb 1870
Spring City, Sanpete Co., Utah
PARENTS: Solomon Sanford
Ellenor Barry
PIONEER: Fall of 1866
Independent Company
SPOUSE I: William Pim Taylor
MARRIED: 4 Apr 1852
DEATH SP: 1860
New Canton, Pike Co., Illinois

CHILDREN:
Robert Ephriam, 25 Jan 1853
Charles Henry, 1 Jan 1855

SPOUSE II: Stephen Parkis
MARRIED: abt 1865

DEATH SP: Not given
CHILDREN:
Katie Keanie, abt 1866
Elmer, abt 1869

Angeline was born near Toronto, Canada in 1831. She married William Pim Taylor in Illinois in 1852 and they had two children. Angeline supported William in his service as a country doctor. William was drowned in the Missouri River in 1860 near New Canton, Pike County, Illinois.

Angeline cared for her two sons after her husband's death and before her marriage to Stephen Parkis, who was from Leeds, Ontario, Canada. Little is known of this marriage except it produced two more children.

Angeline drove a team most of the way across the Plains in 1866, with an Independent Company of Pioneers. It is said she helped fight off Indians and swam a river.

Angeline settled in Spring City, Sanpete County, Utah, where she passed away in 1870.

FRANCES "FANNY" DACK PARRISH

BIRTHDATE: 29 Oct 1795
Wicklow, Wicklow, Ireland
DEATH: 29 Sep 1851
Centerville, Davis Co., Utah
PARENTS: William Dack
Jane Code
PIONEER: 22 Sep 1847
Parley P. Pratt Co. Wagon Train
SPOUSE: Samuel Parrish
MARRIED: 13 Feb 1820
Elizabethtown, Leeds, Canada
DEATH SP: 12 Oct 1573
Centerville, Davis Co., Utah

CHILDREN:
Sarah, 23 Nov 1820
Mary, 21 Feb 1822
Lydia, 16 Nov 1823
Jane, 25 Oct 1825
Joel, 6 Nov 1827
Priscilla, 20 Mar 1833

Frances "Fanny" Dack was born in Ireland in 1795. In 1817, the family emigrated to Canada, settling in Elizabethtown Leeds, Ontario, Canada.

She married Samuel Parrish in 1820 in Elizabethtown, Leeds, Ontario, Canada and to them were born five daughters and one son.

Samuel engaged in farming but the soil was poor in that area, and so they moved to Stark County, Illinois about 1839.

While living there they met missionaries from the Church of Jesus Christ of Latter-day Saints, whose message was just what they had been looking for. They were baptized in 1840 and moved to Nauvoo, Illinois.

The family suffered much from sickness and privation from Nauvoo to Utah. Three of their daughters died and were buried in Iowa. They came to Utah with the Parley P. Pratt Company arriving on September 22, 1847. The first winter was spent in the old adobe fort in Salt Lake City. In 1848, they moved to Centerville, Davis County, Utah, where Fanny spent the rest of her life.

While residing in Centerville, Fanny was a midwife. She was rather large of stature, sandy complexioned, considerate in disposition, a good business woman, and loved by all who knew her.

Fanny passed away in Centerville on October 29, 1851. Her husband passed away in 1883, also in Centerville, Davis County, Utah.

CHRISTINA "KITTY" STEVENS SCOTT PARROTT

BIRTHDATE: 1 Jan 1853
Sunderland, Durham, England
DEATH: 16 Feb 1936
Nampa, Idaho
PARENTS: Alfred Stevens
Christina Lynd
PIONEER: Oct 1866
Alfred Stevens Co. Wagon Train
SPOUSE I: Robert Griffin Scott
MARRIED: 5 Aug 1872
Salt Lake City, Salt Lake, Utah
DEATH SP: 28 Aug 1877
Ogden, Weber Co., Utah

CHILDREN:
James G., 4 Jan 1875
Walter, 16 Jan 1876
Mary, 1877 (died as an infant)

SPOUSE II: William Edward Parrott
MARRIED: abt 1878
DEATH SP: 21 Jul 1896 Albion, Idaho

CHILDREN:
Maholey Ella, 1875 d, 1878
William E., 27 Jan 1880
John Henry, 27 Mar 1882
Jennie Louise (Gransbury), 19 Feb 1883
Alfred E., 10 Feb 1886 (died as an infant)
Wilford A., 27 Aug 1887
Joseph Franklin, 29 Apr 1888
Samuel Monroe, 25 Jul 1891
Anna (McKay), 9 Oct 1893
Ezra, 1896

Christina "Kitty" was born in England in 1853. Kitty came to America on the ship "St. Mark" in 1866 with her parents. She was thirteen at the time. The family settled in Slaterville, Weber County, Utah. Her father taught school there, and so Kitty had a good education.

In 1872, Kitty married Robert Griffin Scott as his second wife. They had three children before died he in 1877.

She then she married William Edward Parrott (called Edward) in 1878, and they became the parents of ten children. They lived in Albion, Idaho, where Edward died in 1896 of Scarlet Fever, Kitty's last child was born after his death.

Kitty took in washings and did housework to support the family. Life was always hard for her. Four of her sons never married as adults. Ezra was kicked in the head by a horse and had to have special care for the remainder of his life. Another, son spent time in a mental hospital in Blackfoot, Idaho. As she got older, she and her sons went to Nampa State School to live in a home for the poor.

Kitty passed away in Nampa in 1936 at the age of eighty-three years.

CATHERINE VAUGHN EVANS PARRY

BIRTHDATE: 14 Dec 1825
Trawscoed, Guilsfield, Wales
DEATH: 20 Nov 1893
Marriott, Weber Co., Utah
PARENTS: Edward V. Evans
Margaret Williams
PIONEER: 27 Oct 1849
George A. Smith Wagon Train
SPOUSE: Caleb Parry
MARRIED: 26 Feb 1849
Liverpool, England
DEATH SP: 19 Sep 1871
Birmingham, England

CHILDREN:
Caleb Evans, 16 Feb 1850
Bernard Evans, 1 Mar 1852
Arthur Evans, 9 Jan 1854 (twin - died in 1856)
Llewelyn Evans, 9 Jan 1854 (twin - died in 1854)
Brigham Evans, 14 Mar 1857
Anewin Vaughn Evans, 27 Feb 1859
Leo Victor Evans, 9 Nov 1861
Rose Winifred, 7 Apr 1864
Rodolph Roy Evans, 22 Feb 1867

Catherine Vaughn was born in Trawscoed, Guilsfield, Powys, Wales in 1825. She married Caleb Parry the day the ship, "Buena Vista," departed for America with a large number of Welsh immigrants and captained by Dan Jones.

They arrived safely in New Orleans, and then to St. Louis, but after that many of the company fell victim to the dreaded cholera epidemic. Included in this was her mother-in-law, Mary William Parry, who was buried on the river bank at Council Bluffs.

Catherine and Caleb joined with the George A. Smith Company to cross the Plains, arriving in the Salt Lake Valley in October, 1849. Caleb and Catherine settled in Salt Lake City at first where their first four children were born. The twins died very young and were buried in Salt Lake.

About 1856/1857 the family was asked to move to Marriott, Weber County, Utah, to settle. This was a lonely area for Catherine, and the Indians were a problem. Catherine was appointed Secretary in the first Relief Society in Marriott. She was also a Sabbath School teacher.

Caleb was called on a mission to England and Wales, and he died in Birmingham, England in 1871 of smallpox, at the age of forty-seven. Catherine was now left alone to raise her family. The older children helped, and Catherine taught school for a time.

Catherine passed away in Marriott, Weber County, Utah in 1893, at the age of sixty-eight years.

HARRIET JULIA ROBERTS PARRY

BIRTHDATE: 2 Jan 1829
Ruthin, North Wales
DEATH: 30 Sep 1902\
Logan, Cache Co., Utah
PARENTS: Robert Roberts
Margaret Owen
PIONEER: 2 Oct 1856
Edward Bunker Co. Wagon Train
SPOUSE: John Parry, Jr.
MARRIED: 26 Dec 1853
Ruthin, North Wales
DEATH SP: 26 May 1882
Logan, Cache Co., Utah

CHILDREN:
Brigham Bernard, 26 Ap 1855 d. 1856
Lavinia Charlotte, 24 Nov 1857
Mary Anron, 24 Oct l859
Aimenia Julia, 14 Nov 1862
Sarah Celestia Harriet, 27 Feb 1866
John Marari 26 Jun 1869

Harriet Julia was born in Ruthin, Denbigshire, North Wales in 1829. She lived with her Aunt Mary Mason of Wrexham, where she attended school and learned to sew. Her aunt and uncle often told her that she would possess their home and business when they died.

At the age of twenty-two, she attended a meeting of the Church of Jesus Christ of Latter-day Saints, and eventually embraced the new gospel. Her aunt was furious, so she moved back with her family.

Harriet met a Welsh missionary, John Farry, Jr. and they were married in 1853. Her family was so opposed to the marriage that they did not attend the wedding.

Harriet and John embarked from Liverpool in l856 with their first child. Many children on the trip had the measles, but it wasn't until they reached Iowa City that little Brigham came down with them and died. He was buried at Chicago.

Their handcart company, of Edward Bunker, arrived in the Salt Lake Valley in October, 1856. In Salt Lake they stayed with John's father, John Parry, Sr.

Harriet was able to sew in exchange for things they needed. She would boil carrots until she could obtain a sweet syrup which she used to sweeten other foods. In 1865, John went on another mission to England for four years. Again Harriet sewed to support herself and children. John was called in 1877 to labor on the Logan Temple and they set up a new home in Logan.

John died four years later. Harriet was an officiator in the temple, and did much temple work until her death in 1902 in Logan, Cache County, Utah,

HARRIET PARRY PARRY

BIRTHDATE: 18 Oct 1822
St. Asaph, Flintshire, Wales
DEATH: 4 Apr 1901
Salt Lake City, Salt Lake, Utah
PARENTS: William Parry
Ellen Foulkes
PIONEER: 10 Oct 1853
Joseph W. Young Wagon Train
SPOUSE: John Parry
MARRIED: 2 Apr 1854
Salt Lake City, Salt Lake, Utah
DEATH SP: 13 Jan 1868
Salt Lake City, Salt Lake, Utah

CHILDREN:
Joseph Hyrum, 8 Aug 1855 (twin)
Bernard Llewellen, 8 Aug 1855 (twin)
Louisa Ellen, 22 Sep 1857
Edwin Francis, 11 Jun 1860
Henry Edward, 11 Feb 1862

Harriet Parry was born in Wales in 1822. She was in her late twenties when she heard the gospel, and was the only one of her family to join the Church of Jesus Christ of Latter-day Saints. Her family was bitterly opposed to the Church and would not even say goodbye to her when she left Wales.

At Council Bluffs she joined the Joseph W. Young Company to cross the Plains, arriving in the Salt Lake Valley in October, 1853. For a while she lived in the home of Daniel H. Wells.

Harriet married John Parry in 1854 in the old Council House. They had lived within five miles of each other in Wales, but did not meet until they got to Utah. Harriet became the mother of five children, all born in Salt Lake City, Utah.

John was a lover of flowers and trees, a gardener by nature. He sold much of the produce from his orchards. Harriet dried a lot of the fruit for her own use. She was a hard-working woman. She had a mulberry tree in her yard, and raised silk worms for one year, but that was enough, she said.

After her husband died in 1868 she started to nurse, especially maternity cases, and was very much in demand. She always paid her tithing and gave extra for the building of the temples being built in Utah. She always paid for an item in cash or went without.

Harriet passed away in 1901, in the home she had lived in for forty-eight years. She was seventy-nine years of age.

MARY WIILLIAMS PARRY

No
Photo
Available

BIRTHDATE: 1784
Belan, Mold, Flintshire, Wales
DEATH: 17 May 1849
near Missouri River
PARENTS: William Williams
Mary Williams
PIONEER: 1849
died near Council Bluffs, Iowa
SPOUSE: John Parry Sr.
MARRIED: 1808
New Market, Flintshire, Wales
DEATH SP: 13 Jan 1868
Salt Lake City, Salt Lake, Utah

CHILDREN:
Bernard, 9 Oct 1809
Elizabeth, 21 Jul 1811
Mary, 4 May 1813
Sarah, 3 May 1815
John, 13 Oct 1817
William, 16 Oct 1820
Caleb, 9 Oct 1823

Mary Williams was born in Wales in 1784. Mary married John Parry in 1808, and they were the parents of seven children. Mary and her husband raised their family in New Market, North Wales, but in 1846 moved to Birkenhead, England, near Liverpool.

Mary's husband and son John had been traveling preachers for the Scotch Baptists, and then Campbellites. But in 1846, after attending one of the Church of Jesus Christ of Latter-day Saints meetings, they gave their names for baptism. Mary, John and their son, John, were baptized on September 12, 1846.

John, Mary and two of their sons, Caleb and William, left Liverpool, England, February 25, 1849 on the ship "Buena Vista," with other Welsh Saints. They were under the direction of Captain Dan Jones and reached New Orleans on April 19th. The group took a steamer, the "Highland Mary" up the Mississippi and Missouri Rivers.

Cholera claimed sixty of the Welsh group, Mary being one of them. She was buried in Council Bluffs, Iowa. Mary was sixty-five years old at her death in 1849.

PATTY BARTLETT SESSIONS PARRY

BIRTHDATE: 4 Feb 1795
Bethel, Oxford Co., Maine
DEATH: 14 Dec 1893
Bountiful, Davis Co., Utah
PARENTS: Enoch Bartlett
Anna Hall
PIONEER: 24 Sep 1847
Daniel Spencer Wagon Train
SPOUSE: David Sessions
MARRIED: 28 Jun 1812
Newry, Oxford Co., Maine
DEATH SP: 11 Aug 1850
Salt Lake City, Salt Lake, Utah

CHILDREN:
Perrigrine, 15 Jun 1814
Sylvanus, 5 Jun 1816 (died at age 16)
Amanda, 19 Mar 1817
Sylvia, 31 Jul 1818
Asa, 1819 (died at age 6)
Anna "B," 21 Mar 1820 (died at age 5)
Porter, 31 Jul 1822
David, Jr., 9 May 1823
Anna "B," 16 Mar 1825 (died at age 7)
Bartlett, 1 Aug 1827 (died at 6 months)
Amanda, 14 Nov 1829 (died at age 4)

SPOUSE II: John Parry
MARRIED: 14 Dec 1851
DEATH SP: Unknown
CHILDREN: None

Patty was born in Bethel, Oxford County, Maine. Immediately after her marriage to David Sessions, her mother-in-law introduced her to the practice of midwifery. The two women worked together for some time.

While Patty was establishing her practice of midwifery, she was also having babies herself and assisting her husband in establishing large farms, a sawmill, and a hotel or tavern. Of all her children, only three of them lived to adulthood.

Patty and David had been baptized as Methodists, but when they were introduced to the gospel as taught by the missionaries from the Church of Jesus Christ of Latter-day Saints, they were baptized in July, 1834, by Daniel Bean.

They were called upon to sacrifice a considerable amount of property and bid farewell to many friends and relatives as they joined the main body of Saints in Kirtland, Ohio in June, 1837.

Less than five years after establishing a home and livelihood in Nauvoo, Patty and her family were again uprooted and began the long journey West by crossing the Mississippi River on February 13, 1846.

Patty continued to serve as a midwife often under most unfavorable conditions. Brigham Young felt her services would be needed more by the second company of pioneers, so she departed from Winter Quarters on June 5, driving a four-oxen team.

Patty delivered four babies during the trek. She baked, washed, ironed, picked and dried berries, sewed, held meetings, doctored the sick all across the Plains and into the Rocky Mountains. They arrived in the Great Salt Lake Valley on September 24, 1847 and the following day, she helped Lorenzo Young's wife deliver the first white male into the Salt Lake Valley.

The greatest trial of her life was when her husband, David took two other women in plural marriage, but she never wavered. He passed away in August, 1850, and Patty sturdily continued delivering babies.

Patty passed away on December 14, 1893 in Bountiful, Davis County, Utah.

TEMPERANCE KETURAH HAIGHT McFARLAND PARRY

BIRTHDATE: 15 Sep 1844
Nauvoo, Hancock Co., Illinois
DEATH: 25 Feb 1929
Cedar City, Iron Co., Utah
PARENTS: Isaac C. Haight
Eliza Ann Snyder
PIONEER: 12 Sep 1847
Daniel Spencer Co. Wagon Train
SPOUSE I: Daniel S. McFarlane
MARRIED: 12 Feb 1862
Cedar City, Iron Co., Utah
DEATH SP: 25 Oct 1914
Cedar City, Iron Co., Utah

CHILDREN:
Daniel Sinclair, 12 Dec 1862 (died at 7 months)
Leonora Caroline, 31 Mar 1864
Isaac Chauncey, 29 Mar 1866
May, 2 May 1868
Keturah "Kate," 17 Sep 1870 (died at age 7)
Annabella, 25 Jan 1875
Eliza Ann, 1 Jan 1876
John, 1 Jun 1879 (twin - died as an infant)
Mary, 1 Jun 1879 (twin - died as an infant)
Emelina, 10 Jul 1880
Caleb William, 18 Jan 1882
Kanneth Haight, 21 Dec 1884

SPOUSE II: Edward Parry
MARRIED: 1919
DEATH SP: Not given
CHILDREN: None

Temperance Keturah was born in Illinois in 1844. Her father, mother, sister and herself left Nauvoo in 1846 when the Saints were driven out. They traveled on to Winter Quarters, where Keturah had black canker so bad that all the skin in her mouth peeled off and her lips were raw. Because of this sickness her gums were eaten away leaving her with out teeth throughout her entire life.

Her family traveled with the Daniel Spencer Wagon Company arriving in the Salt Lake Valley in September, 1847. In 1855, they moved to Cedar City, Iron County, Utah.

Keturah married Daniel Sinclair McFarlane in 1862 when she was eighteen. They were the parents of twelve children.

Keturah was an attractive person, with blue eyes and wavy, brown hair. She had a beautiful singing voice, and encouraged all her children to sing. She taught school, was a postmistress for ten years, a faithful Church member, and always interested in community affairs. Her husband served a three-year mission to Scotland, and while he was gone one daughter died. On his return he took another wife.

After Daniel's death in 1914, Keturah married Edward Parry in 1919. She passed away in 1929 at the age of eighty-four years.

MARY CHRISTINA JOHNSON PARSONS

No
Photo
Available

BIRTHDATE: 7 May 1849
Ovdrup, Denmark
DEATH: 1 Nov 1910
Koosharem, Sevier Co., Utah
PARENTS: Johan Larson
Johanne Kirstine Lausten
PIONEER: 30 Nov 1856
Martin Handcart Company
SPOUSE: Elijah Parsons
MARRIED: 11 Jan 1869
Salt Lake City, Salt Lake, Utah
DEATH SP: 2 Dec 1930
Salina, Sevier Co., Utah

CHILDREN:
Arthur Stanley, 26 Jun 1869
Anna Louise, 12 Oct 1871
Elijah John, 4 Mar 1876
William Henry, 2 Mar 1878
George Edward, 16 Mar 1881
Mary Ellen, 20 Feb 1884
Sarah Hannah, 1 Jan 1887

Mary Christina was born in Denmark in 1849. Her father was a prosperous farmer, owning large farmlands, cattle, sheep, fine horses and barns. They also ran a tavern and an inn. The family had been Lutheran prior to joining the Church of Jesus Christ of Latter-day Saints in 1853. They had to sell their properties at auction, then in 1854 they secured passage on the ship "Nesmith" to America.

They traveled on to Mormon Grove, but things were discouraging there because they did not speak the language. Cholera was rampant at the time, and both her father and her mother and a brother died. The other children were assigned to families in different handcart companies.

Mary Christine left Omaha with a childless couple from England named Onion. They were with the fifth handcart company and the last to leave that season. The company was caught in the early snows in the mountains and had to be rescued. Mary Christina's legs were frozen and had to be amputated after they came into the Salt Lake Valley.

Mary Christina lived in the home of Brigham Young for several years where she learned housekeeping skills, cooking, knitting, crocheting, millinery and sewing. President Young had a sewing machine altered so that she could operate it with her knees.

Mary Christina married Elijah Parsons, who was from England, in 1869. They had seven children.

Mary Christina was well versed in the scriptures. She helped make quilts, and washed for families. She was known to walk for two miles on her knees to help someone in need. It always hurt to walk on her legs. She had scabs and running sores most of the time.

They lived in Richfield for a time, then in Koosharem, Utah where she passed away in 1910. Her husband passed away in 1930 in Salina, Sevier County, Utah.

ELIZABETH BUXTON PARTRIDGE

BIRTHDATE: 5 May 1840
Sheffield, Yorkshire, England
DEATH: 8 Sep 1898
Fillmore, Millard Co., Utah
PARENTS: John Buxton
Elizabeth Carnall
PIONEER: 10 Sep 1852
James J. Jepson Co. Wagon Train
SPOUSE: Edward Partridge Jr.
MARRIED: 15 Feb 1862
Salt Lake City, Salt Lake, Utah
DEATH SP: 17 Nov 1900
Fillmore, Millard Co., Utah

CHILDREN:
Emily, 1 Dec 1862
John Clisbee, 29 Jul 1866
Charles, 15 Jun 1867
George Arthur, 12 Mar 1869
Don Carlos, 14 May 1871
Clara, 4 Aug 1873
Frank Harvey, 12 Aug 1875
Mary Aloha, 13 Nov 1877
Lydia Maud, 19 Oct 1879

Elizabeth Partridge was born in England, the oldest of five children. Her parents were among the first to join the Church of Jesus Christ of Latter-day Saints in Sheffield, Yorkshire, England. They often held cottage meetings in their home and were ardent missionaries for the Church.

Before the family could emigrate to Zion her father died. His last request was that his wife and chidren should go to Utah to be with the Saints. Elizabeth was baptized on her eighth birthday, just one month after her father's death.

In 1849, Elizabeth traveled with her mother and brother across the ocean on the splendid ship "Zetland." After a safe voyage they traveled to New Orleans, Louisanna and then on to St. Louis, Missouri. They stayed with her father's brother for a year. Her mother died here in 1852.

Elizabeth and her brother were orphans at twelve and nine years. Some friends who had crossed the ocean with them took them in charge and brought them to Utah with them. They crossed the Plains with the James J. Jepson Wagon-train Company, arriving in the Salt Lake Valley on September 10, 1852.

The children found their uncle but he was in very poor circumstances. Elizabeth's first employment netted her one dollar per week, from which she deducted her emigration expenses. What little she had went for the barest necessities and none for luxuries.

Elizabeth became the second plural wife of Edward Partridge, Jr. on February 15, 1862 in Salt Lake City. She was twenty-two years old. They lived for a time in Farmington, Utah and then moved to Fillmore, Millard County, Utah.

They opened a mercantile business for a short time in Deseret, but when her husband was called as a Mission President she moved with her children back to Fillmore. She had the responsibility of raising their children alone. While her husband was serving his mission she experienced real hardships and trials. Not once did she neglect family prayers nor fail to teach her children the principles of the Gospel. Her diligence and faith were rewarded when she was promised in her Patriarchal Blessing that not one of her children would ever go astray. This promise was fulfilled.

Elizabeth had a beautiful voice and sang in the ward choir for many years. She worked in the Primary for many years and was also a Sunday School teacher. She was very spiritual and prayerful. Many times her prayers were answered.

Although Elizabeth was very religious, she loved amusement, innocent jokes and fun. She had a great sense of humor. She could dance beautifully and waltz and dance the old style dances with ease and grace. She was industrious. She did her own sewing and knitting, made soap, dried fruit, made her own carpets and helped raise the vegetables.

Elizabeth passed away on September 8, 1898 in Fillmore, Utah. She fulfilled her mission nobly and her memory will live on as one of the noble women to live on this earth during the Fullness of Times.

MARY ANN YATES PARTRIDGE

BIRTHDATE: 12 Dec 1833
South Stake, Somerset, England
DEATH: 5 Jan 1919
Salt Lake City, Salt Lake, Utah
PARENTS: William Yates
Hannah House
PIONEER: 1855 Wagon Train
SPOUSE: Jonathon W. Partridge
MARRIED: 5 Jan 1857
Salt Lake City, Salt Lake, Utah
DEATH SP: 20 Jan 1904

CHILDREN:
Emma Louise, 17 Apr 1858 (died at age 19)
Mary Ann, 25 Mar 1861
Lafayette, 7 Jun 1863 (died at 3 months)
Hannah Elizabeth, 6 Feb 1865 (died at age 12)
Henry Jarvis, Feb 1867 (died at birth)
Sarah Keziah, 7 May 1869 (died as an infant)
Minnie, 30 May 1871 (died at age 4)
William Elmer, 1 Jun 1873 (died at 3 months)
Joseph Smith, 10 Mar 1877

Mary Ann was the sixth child in a family of eight. In 1849, the missionaries from the Church of Jesus Christ of Latter-day Saints were teaching the gospel. They were convinced that this was the true church and so the parents and the four youngest children were baptized. Because of this, the children were expelled from school, but they studied at home and became well informed and beautiful penmen

Mary Ann was a dainty, beautiful young lady and it was difficult for her to leave her family to come to America. She packed her belongings and came with a group of Saints on a sailing vessel. It took six weeks to cross the ocean. Then she came West in a covered wagon, enduring all of the hardships of the pioneers.

In 1918, she wrote a letter to her niece, Louise Y. Robinson, General President of the Relief Society, telling of the birth and death of each of her nine children.

Mary Ann was a very lonely, sweet, little old lady who had lost her husband and all of her nine children.

MARY ANN WARMBY / WHARMBY PASS

BIRTHDATE: 8 Jan 1812
Chorley, England
DEATH: 15 May 1888
Nephi, Juab Co., Utah
PARENTS: James Warmby
Elizabeth Warmby
PIONEER: 25 Sep 1863
Peter Nebeker Co. Wagon Train
SPOUSE: Thomas Pass
MARRIED: 28 May 1837
England
DEATH SP: 2 Jul 1899
Nephi, Juab Co., Utah

CHILDREN:
Elizabeth, 1 Apr 1839
Ellen, 1 Mar 1841
Sarah, 25 Nov 1843
Susannah, 11 Jan 1846
John, 6 May 1848 (died as an infant)
Martha, 20 Nov 1849 (died as an infant)
Mary Eleanor, 28 Jul 1851
Rachel, 6 Apr 1854
Thomas Jr., 18 Jan 1856
Mary Ann, 3 Mar 1861 (died as an infant)

Mary Ann Warmby or Wharmby was born in England in 1812. She married Thomas Pass in 1837. They lived in Stockport on the Mersey River, which empties into the Irish Sea. Three years after their marriage they joined the Church of Jesus Christ of Latter-day Saints, and for many years entertained the missionaries in their home.

Two girls in the family, Elizabeth and Rachel came to America ahead of the family. In 1863, Mary Ann, Thomas, and their children, Ellen with husband and small baby, Susannah, Thomas Jr., and Mary Eleanor, set sail. Sarah, at the last minute, decided to stay in England. They joined the Peter Nebeker Wagon Company to cross the Plains, arriving in the Salt Lake Valley in September, 1863. They went on to Nephi, Utah where daughter, Elizabeth, lived.

Mary Ann befriended many people in times of sickness and death. She had a great testimony of the gospel to the extent that she was able to speak in tongues.

Mary Ann passed away in Nephi in 1888. Her husband then lived with Thomas Jr. and passed away in 1899, also in Nephi, Juab County, Utah.

ANN NEW PASSEY

BIRTHDATE: 20 Oct 1817
Upton on Severn, England
DEATH: 6 Apr 1911
Paris, Bear Lake Co., Idaho
PARENTS: William New
Elizabeth Collins
PIONEER: 13 Sep 1861
Joseph Horne Co. Wagon Train
SPOUSE: John Passey
MARRIED: 17 Apr 1836
St. Nicolas, England
DEATH SP: 21 Mar 1883
Paris, Bear Lake Co., Idaho

CHILDREN:
Thomas, 23 Sep 1837
William, 29 Dec 1838
Frederick, 7 Sep 1842
George, 14 Dec 1844
Herbert, 7 Nov 1847 (died at age 2)
Mary, Sep 1848 (died as an infant)
John Parley, 12 Jun 1851

Ann was born in the small village of Upton-On-Severn in England. When she was eighteen, she married John Passey in St. Nicolas, Worcestershire, England. They made their first home in Strensham where their seven children were born. They joined the Church of Jesus Christ of Latter-day Saints in 1850 and were severely persecuted for not attending the village church.

They moved to Birmingham, England where all the men in the family worked in the coal mines to earn sufficient funds to pay their way to America. Her oldest son, Thomas, went to the United States in 1856.

John, Ann, and the rest of their family sailed for America on the ship, "Underwriter," on March 30, 1860. From New York, they took the steamer to Boston where her sister was living with her family. They stayed there one year to earn money to enable them to cross the Plains.

In the Spring of 1861, the family took the train to Omaha, Nebraska and a steamer to Florence, Nebraska. They joined the Joseph Horne Wagon Company. John helped to provide the evening entertainment across the Plains as he played his fiddle for the saints to dance around the fire. They arrived in the Salt Lake Valley on September 13, 1861.

They were met by Ann's nephew who took them to Lehi where Ann's sister and family settled. John and Ann went further south to Cedar Fort in 1863.

In 1865, they were asked by President Young to go to the Bear Lake Valley in Idaho to settle. They obtained land and built a nice log two-room home where they lived the remainder of their lives.

John passed away on March 21, 1883 and Ann passed away April 6, 1911. They are both buried in the Paris City Cemetery in Idaho.

DRUSILLA THEOBALD PASSEY

BIRTHDATE: 22 Oct 1842
Freshwater, England
DEATH: 23 Oct 1915
Paris, Bear Lake Co., Idaho
PARENTS: William Theobald
Martha Lane Theobald
PIONEER: 3 Oct 1854
Allred & Kelsey Wagon Train
SPOUSE: Thomas Passey
MARRIED: Aug 1858
Salt Lake City, Salt Lake, Utah
DEATH SP: 10 Dec 1910
Paris, Bear Lake Co., Idaho

CHILDREN:
John Thomas, 24 Jan 1860
William Theobald, 6 Jun 1862
Florence May, 1 Nov 1863
Charles Herbert, 30 Nov 1865
George Henry, 16 Feb 1867
Ann Selina, 25 Mar 1869
Clara Andaline, 23 Mar 1871
Cora Francis, 13 May 1873
Arthur, 28 Jan 1875
Drucilla, 18 Mar 1877
Margaret Katie, 20 Nov 1878
Ernest Frank, 28 Mar 1880
Edgar, 20 Mar 1882

Drucilla was born in Freshwater, Isle of Wight, England. Sometime after her birth the family moved to Newport and it was here that they became acquainted with missionaries from the Church of Jesus Christ of Latter-day Saints.

They were taught the Gospel by missionaries from the Church of Jesus Christ of Latter-day Saints and they were baptized.

They sailed to America when Drusilla was eleven years old. They landed at New Orleans, Louisanna and then traveled by boat up the Mississippi River to St. Louis, Missouri. From there the family went to Winter Quarters, Iowa. Here they joined with the Allred and Kelsey Companies and proceeded on their journey to the Salt Lake Valley, arriving on October 3, 1854

In August 1858, Drusilla married Thomas Passey, a young Englishman who had traveled to Utah with the first Handcart Companies two years earlier. They made their first home in Salt Lake City, Utah and then moved to Farmington, Utah where their first three children were born. They became the parents of thirteen children; seven sons and six daughters.

In 1866, they moved to the Bear Lake Valley where they were to remain the remainder of their lives. Ten more children were born to Drusilla here so they had to work very hard to support their family of thirteen children. They became the managers of the Union Dairy and later the Cooperative Dairy in Nounan. This gave them good experience and after awhile they were able to purchase a farm which was located between Montpelier and Paris, Idaho and established a Dairy of their own.

To help out with expenses, Drusilla would leave her oldest daughter to tend the other children and she would go out and do house cleaning for other people. After they started up their own dairy, it was her responsibility to deliver the milk to their customers in Montpelier. She did this for thirty years. They also ran a roadside stand where they sold butter and cheese along with other items. She was responsible for making these items to sell.

In her backroom, Drusilla had a carpet loom and here she would weave rags into carpets. She not only made carpets for her own home but she would also make carpets for others. She sold the carpet for ten cents a yard. In about 1910, they sold their dairy and moved back to Paris, Idaho.

Her husband passed away on December 10, 1910. Drusilla continued to live in their home in Paris until her own death on October 23, 1915. Drusilla and her husband, Thomas, are both buried in the Paris City Cemetery.

ELIZABETH ANN CLIFTON PASSEY

BIRTHDATE: 31 Jul 1852
Crowle, Lincolnshire, England
DEATH: 13 Jun 1934
Paris, Idaho
PARENTS: John Clifton
Hannah Pettinger
PIONEER: 13 Sep 1861
Joseph Horne Co. Wagon Train
SPOUSE: John Parley Passey
MARRIED: 28 Sep 1874
Salt Lake City, Salt Lake, Utah
DEATH SP: 30 Dec 1927
Paris, Bear Lake Co., Utah

CHILDREN:
Frederick William, 1 Nov 1875
George Alvin, 8 May 1877
Harry, 9 Jun 1879
Ada Elizabeth (Budge), 13 Mar 1881
Edward John, 18 Feb 1883
Parley Clifton, 19 Jun 1886
Ezra Thomas, 24 Aug 1888
Joseph Seth, 23 Dec 1890 (died as a child)
Oliver, 13 Feb 1892
Ida Ann (Ward), 21 Oct 1893
David Russell, 20 Nov 1897

Elizabeth Ann was born in England during Queen Victoria's reign. She was the oldest child of John and Hannah Clifton At the age of eight, in 1860, she left England with her family for America. Her parents had joined the Church of Jesus Christ of Latter-day Saints and wanted to live with the Saints in Zion. After nine weeks they arrived in New York. Here they stayed until the Spring of 1861.

They traveled by steamboat to Florence, Nebraska. Here they were met by a Utah emigrant train of wagons and ox teams. Joseph Horne was the company captain. Elizabeth and her brother walked the entire 1,000 miles across the Plains, riding in wagons only when fording deep streams. Their chore was to fill a sack full of buffalo chips for the camp fires at night. At night, the children slept on the ground under the wagons and were lulled to sleep by the howling of coyotes and the flapping of the loose canvas on the wagon.

They arrived in Utah in September, 1861; her father was the sole possessor of one ox, a cow and an old wagon. These things made it possible to go to the Bear Lake Valley in Idaho to help settle the valley. They arrived in Paris, Idaho on October 6, 1863.

A crude house was built out of cottonwoods found growing nearby. The house had a dirt roof, a hard dirt floor which became unpleasant when it rained. Food was very scarce for their family of eight. Her father went to the St. Charles Creek and caught a sack full of fish. The fish was cured and was their only food for many weeks. It was like manna from Heaven to them.

When Elizabeth was fourteen years old she supported herself by tending babies for busy mothers and doing houswwork and nursing. At fifteen years she was given a spinning wheel for work she had done. She hired out by the week, spinning cloth for underwear, dresses and sheets. She worked for $2.00 a week and her dinner.

She met and married John Parley Passey on September 28, 1874 in the Salt Lake City Endowment House. Her husband had come to Utah on the same boat and wagon train as Elizabeth and her family. However, they had never met until they were living in Paris, Idaho.

They owned a homestead north of Paris where they raised many vegetables and supplied many stores with fresh produce. Her husband became ill and was too ill to work anymore. Elizabeth took care of him for twenty years.

For several years, Elizabeth was the oldest living person in the valley. The Daughters of the Utah Pioneers Organization in Paris named their camp "Camp Elizabeth" in her honor. She passed away on June 13, 1934, a few weeks before her eighty-second birthday.

SARAH NEW NEAT PASSEY

BIRTHDATE: 9 Sep 1810
Pershore, England
DEATH: 6 Mar 1896
Paris, Bear Lake Co., Idaho
PARENTS: William New
Elizabeth Collins
PIONEER: 13 Sep 1861
Joseph Horne Co. Wagon Train
SPOUSE I: Richard Neat
MARRIED: 1831
Pershore, England
DEATH SP: 9 Sep 1841
Ponty Pool, Monmouth, Wales

CHILDREN:
George, 22 Aug 1832
Samson Nate, 8 May 1834
Emma, 25 Mar 1836 (died at 9 months)

SPOUSE II: William Passey
MARRIED: 1 Aug 1841
Strensham, Worcestershire, England
DEATH SP: 9 Nov 1873
Paris, Bear Lake Co., Idaho

CHILDREN:
Sarah Emma, 8 Jan 1843 (died at 2 months)
Mary Ann, 28 Mar 1844
John, 1 Jul 1849 (died at 3 months)

Sarah was born in Pershore, Worcestershire, England, 1810. As a child, she attended school and helped in her parents' produce and confectionery store.

Sarah's first marriage was to Richard Neat with whom she had three children before she left him and returned to her parents.

After Richard died in 1841, Sarah married William Passey. They were baptized as members of the Church of Jesus Christ of Latter-day Saints in 1850. On March 28, 1857, they sailed from Liverpool on the ship, "George Washington." They landed in Boston and settled in New Cambridge to earn money and wait for more of their family members to arrive.

In May of 1860, Sarah's sister, Ann, and her family arrived from England and the two families prepared to travel West with the Joseph Horne Wagon Company. Her son, Samson Nate, met them in Salt Lake City when they arrived on September 13, 1861 and took them to Lehi in Utah County to live. In 1864, Sarah's family was called to help settle Bear Lake Valley. William died nine years later.

She was an ever-ready friend to the sick and those in need, and sympathetic in time of death. She was noted for her expertise as a seamstress and was always invited to the sewing circles and parties by Apostle Rich's family. She was especially fond of dances and theater. She welcomed grandchildren into her home as they arrived from England. She also had grandchildren living with her as they attended Fielding Academy.

Sarah loved the gospel and lived a life of service until she passed away on March 6, 1896.

ELIZABETH RANDALL PATERSON

BIRTHDATE: 24 Dec 1815
Ministerworth, England
DEATH: 20 Sep 1906
Spanish Fork, Utah Co., Utah
PARENTS: Joseph Randall
Betty Whittle
PIONEER: 28 Sep 1851
John Brown Wagon Train
SPOUSE: Samuel Paterson Jr
MARRIED: 11 May 1851
Kanesville, Iowa
DEATH SP: 15 Sep 1893

CHILDREN:
Joseph Randall, 12 Aug 1852
Hyrum Smith, 2 Mar 1854
Dorcus (Warner), 4 Apr 1855
Ann Bell (Jarvis), 4 Mar 1857
Samuel, 8 Feb 1860
James Cummings Randall, 5 Apr 1863

Elizabeth was born in Ministerworth, Gloucester, England in 1815. Elizabeth worked as a maid in the manor house of nobleman in Ministerworth, Gloucester, England. She actually met Queen Victoria who stayed there for awhile as a house guest.

Elizabeth was a single woman, thirty-six years old when she boarded the ship "George W. Bourne" and sailed to America. When she arrived in Kanesville she met and married Samuel Patterson Jr. before traveling to Utah with the John Brown Wagon Company.

Upon their arrival on September 28, 1851, they moved into a dugout in Blooming Grove, South Fork, Holmes Creek, Davis County, Utah. They lived in that dugout seven years before moving to Spanish Fork in 1858. Elizabeth gave birth to six children, three of whom survived to adulthood. She was known throughout the community for her knowledge of herbal remedies and her beautiful garden.

Elizabeth passed away in Spanish Fork, September 20, 1906, at the age of ninety-one.

MARTHA HARRIET DEAN PATERSON

BIRTHDATE: 15 Sep 1857
Burnley, Lanshire, England
DEATH: 4 Nov 1944
Beaver, Beaver Co., Utah
PARENT: John Dean
Martha Holdsworth
PIONEER: 28 Sep 1865
Joseph Rawlins Co. Wagon Train
SPOUSE: Edward N. Patterson
MARRIED: Feb 1878
DEATH SP: 25 Oct 1926
Beaver, Beaver Co., Utah

CHILDREN:
John Edward, 23 Nov 1878
Thomas Morgan, 26 Aug 1880
Lettie Mable (Bowden Thompson), 16 Jan 1883
Martha Jane (Morgan), 29 Nov 1884
Heber, 28 Mar 1887
Edgar LeRoy, 24 Jun 1888
Alice Maud 12 Sep 1890
Wilford Elmer, 21 Dec 1893
Dean, 15 Jul 1895
Edna Darle, 17 May 1897
Viola (Smith), 23 Mar 1899
William Chester, 9 Sep 1901

Martha was born in England in 1857. When Martha was five years old she went to work in a factory, where she learned to knit. When she was seven on March 14, 1864, her parents and two brothers left Liverpool on the ship "Virginia City."

They landed in New York, then went up the Hudson river about 100 miles to Riften Glen, Ulster County, where they lived for fifteen months. Then left for Utah in July of 1865.

They joined the Joseph Rawlins Wagon Company arriving in the Salt Lake Valley on September 28, 1865. They then went to Sugar House. Where they lived until June, 1870 when they moved to Beaver, Utah. When Martha was fourteen she went to work at the Beaver Woolen Mills for five years.

Martha married Edward Nielson Patterson on February 7, 1878. They were the parents of twelve children, seven boys and five girls, four of whom died young.

On the morning her daughter, Martha Jane, was born at 8 a. m., Martha cooked breakfast for forty thrashers. When she was thirty-six years old she fell across the front door and broke her arm. When she was thirty-nine a cow hooked her and broke her nose. When she was seventy, she was operated on for Gall Stones, the rest of her life she was healthy.

Martha walked across the Plains, rode behind an ox team, and a mule team, rode horses, rode in autos, and flew in an airplane. She was a good singer and sang in public.

Martha passed away on November 4, 1944 in Beaver, at the age of eighty-seven.

RACHEL BAIRD PATRICK

BIRTHDATE: 31 Oct 1836
Northern Ireland
DEATH: 27 Apr 1914
Salt Lake City, Salt Lake, Utah
PARENTS: Humphrey Baird
Elizabeth Hethrington
PIONEER: 4 Oct 1863
Wagon Train Company
SPOUSE: Robert Patrick
MARRIED: 29 Dec 1859
Scotland
DEATH SP: -31 Aug 1918
Salt Lake City, Salt Lake, Utah

CHILDREN:
Elizabeth (Pringle), 18 Sep 1860
Robert Jr., 30 Jun 1862
Sarah, 1864
Rachel, 22 Aug 1866 (twin)
Martha, 22 Aug 1866 (twin)
William George, 29 Apr 1868
Mary Ellen (Morris), 6 Mar 1871
Laura Baird (Corey Nicholson), 16 Jul 1873
Joseph Humphrey, 30 Apr 1876
Eliza Maud Baird (Barnes), 7 Sep 1879

Rachel Patrick was born in Northern Ireland, the youngest of ten children. When she was four years old both parents died and she was left an orphan. She lived with an older sister, Martha. When Martha and her husband emigrated to America they left Rachel with friend. Rachel also was baptized into the Church of Jesus Christ of Latter-day Saints with her sister.

Rachel earned her own living when she was thirteen years old. Rachel felt that Heavenly Father had been mother, father and all to her; he blessed and protected her all the days of her life. She was a devoted member of the Church and a strict payer of tithing.

She met and married Robert Patrick on December 29, 1859 in Glasgow, Scotland. They became the parents of ten children. When their second baby was a few months old, the family made plans to emigrate to Zion.

Early in 1863, they sailed on the ship "Cynosure" to America. They finally arrived at Castle Gardens, New York City and started their long trek across the great Plains to the Salt Lake Valley. They traveled by ox-team, arriving at Emmigration Square in Salt Lake City on October 4, 1863.

They were met by friends and experienced great joy that they were at last in Zion. They lived in different homes on the Avenues in Salt Lake City.

Rachel made all the clothes for her family, knitted the stockings, made soap and candles and did all the cooking and baking for her large family. They always made room for friends. All were asked to join in family prayers. They kept a large garden. They were grateful for the fruit and vegetables they could raise. When the diptheria epidemic struck their family, one of the twin girls died. She was thirteen years old. Want and poverty was known by them. When the children were crying for bread and there was none in their house, Rachel's husband prayed to know where he could get work. He met a man on the street who offered him work and gave him a sack of flour. They were ever grateful for the answer to their prayers.

Rachel served as first counselor in the Ward Relief Society Presidency for twenty-seven years. She was also a visiting teacher. She nursed the sick and when death came helped wash the body for the undertaker and often made the burial clothes. She also played a very prominent part in caring for the poor. In 1905, a testimonial was given in honor of the retiring Relief Society Presidency. Rachel was given a dozen sterling silver spoons.

She had a strong character and great determination, yet she was gentle, modest, humble, kind, charitable and patient beyond belief. She never compromised on matters of principle. She would not allow the spirit of adverse criticism to enter her home. She always sustained her husband in all of his Church and civic duties.

Rachel's last days were spent in prosperity, with the comforts of life. Her devoted husband and loving children ministered to her. Her friends were many and she had no enemies. She suffered with a heart ailment during the last three years of her life then passed away on April 27, 1914 at the age of seventy-seven years.

HANNAH INGERSOLL PATTEN

No
Photo
Available

BIRTHDATE: 11 May 1788
Hamer, Onondaga, New York
DEATH: 4 Apr 1853
Manti, Sanpete Co., Utah
PARENTS: Peter Ingersoll
Polly Miller
PIONEER: 22 Aug 1849
Charles C. Rich Wagon Train
SPOUSE: Dr. John Patten
MARRIED: 25 Apr 1824
DEATH SP: 18 Apr 1847
Winter Quarters, Iowa

CHILDREN:
John Jr., 20 Jun 1825
Hannah, 20 Sep 1826
Thomas Jefferson, 10 Apr 1828
Deborah (Billings), 11 Apr 1830
Edith, (Billings), 15 Mar 1832

Hannah Ingersoll was born in Hamer, New York on May 11, 1788. She married Dr. John Patten on April 25 1824. To them were born five children.

The family joined the Church of Jesus Christ of Latter-day Saints in 1830, and endured all the persecution of the early Saints. In 1847, they moved to Winter Quarters and were preparing to leave for the Rocky Mountains when Dr. John Patten suddenly passed away, on April 18, 1847. This delayed their journey for two years.

Hannah and her children arrived in the Salt Lake Valley on August 22, 1849, in the Charles C. Rich Wagon Company.

Soon the family was called to make Manti their home, where she lived until her death on April 4, 1853.

LUCINDA MARIA PATTERSON PATTEN

BIRTHDATE: 19 Nov 1859
Bennington, Minnesota
DEATH: 4 Dec 1923
Payson, Utah Co., Utah
PARENTS: Alvus H. Patterson
Martha Fillmore
PIONEER: Unknown
SPOUSE: Charles Moroni Patten
MARRIED: 19 Feb 1878
Payson, Utah Co., Utah
DEATH SP: 7 Feb 1913

CHILDREN: None

Lucinda Maria was born in 1859 at Bennington, Minnesota, the sixth of eleven children. She was just six weeks old when she left Florence, Nebraska with her parents and six sisters.

The family settled in Payson, Utah County, Utah where they lived in a dugout until a home could be built. Her father had a wonderful garden and sold some of the produce, and later the fruit from their orchard. The little girls would accompany him when he went to the Mercur Mining District to sell his vegetables. The family was called to go to St. Johns, Arizona for a time, then they were called back to Payson. By now Lucinda was a young lady.

Lucinda met and married Charles Moroni Patten in 1878. He was a blacksmith by trade. Lucinda and Charles took up a homestead at Star Ranch. Their property was across the street from his father's ranch, and he had three brothers who had farms close by.

About this time the Church called for all the young women that liked nursing to take a course to be taught in Salt Lake City. Lucinda took this course, and after graduating served as a midwife, and nurse, and also did some doctoring.

Lucinda and Charles spent a few years at Dublan, Mexico, but later moved back to Payson where they built a home. They had no children, but adopted a little boy at birth. She called him Leland, and he was a great joy to her, but he passed away at the age of two from pneumonia.

When her husband was called to the Tintic Mining District to be a tool sharpener, she went with him, and served as a midwife at Mammoth, Silver City, and Diamond for many years. She had plenty of milk, and her own chickens, and would prepare chicken broth for her sick patients.

In her declining years, when she was a widow, she sold her home in Payson and built a small home next to her nephew, who cared for her until she passed away in 1923. She is buried in Payson next to her adopted son.

MARY JANE NELSON PATTEN

BIRTHDATE: 8 Mar 1832
Jefferson Co., Illinois
DEATH: 6 Jul 1896
Payson, Utah Co., Utah
PARENTS: Edmond Nelson
Jane Taylor
PIONEER: 9 Sep 1850
Thomas Johnson Wagon Train
SPOUSE: George Patten
MARRIED: 20 Feb 1851
Mountainville (Alpine), Utah
DEATH SP: 16 Feb 1914
Payson, Utah Co., Utah

CHILDREN:
Joseph Cornwall, 17 Dec 1851
George Washington, 13 Jan 1853
William Henry, 18 Sep 1854
John Edmund, 3 Sep 1856
Charles Moroni, 17 Apr 1858
Mary Jane (Loose), 5 Jan 1863
Julia Ann (Colvin), 10 Aug 1867
Sarah Elizabeth (Wimmer), 20 Mar 1870

Mary Jane Nelson was born, March 8, 1832, in Jefferson County, Illinois, the eighth child of Edmond Nelson and Jane Taylor. After her parents were baptized they started for Missouri to join with the Saints. They suffered many hardships along with the other Church members at that time.

In the Spring of 1850, the family started West with Captain Thomas Johnson Company, and arrived in the Salt Lake Valley on September 9, 1850. Theirs was a pleasant journey, no Indian troubles and only three deaths during the trip, although her father contracted mountain fever from which he never fully recovered.

The family settled in Alpine, Utah. Here Mary Jane met George Patten, and they were married on February 20, 1851 in the Endowment House in Salt Lake City. In 1854, George and Mary Jane moved to Payson, Utah. She was the mother of nine children, all of them surviving to maturity.

In 1865, when a call came for them to help build up Southern Utah, they moved to St. Thomas on the Muddy River. Mary Jane had a great ability to nurse the sick, and lay out the dead. During their lifetime they built eighteen dwellings for themselves and sons. She was a wonderful cook and homemaker. She sewed tiny, fine stitches for hand-tucked shirts, and did beautiful darning. She made several trips to Old Mexico where one of her sons lived. Later in her life her husband built her a two-story home in Payson.

Mary Jane passed away on July 6, 1896 in Payson, Utah County, Utah and is buried there.

WEALTHY EDDY SHUMWAY PRATT PATTEN

BIRTHDATE: 24 Mar 1810
Salon, Somerset / Orange, Maine,
or Hampshire, Massachusetts
DEATH: 18 Jul 1892
Piano, Egin or Parker, Idaho
PARENTS: John Fuller Eddy
Rhoda Eddy (cousins)
PIONEER: abt 1851
Brown Co. Wagon Train
SPOUSE I: Stephen B. Shumway
MARRIED: 6 Jan 1831
DEATH SP: 8 Jan 1839
Hampshire, Massachusetts

CHILDREN:
Clarissa, 30 Nov 1831
Ammi Warren, 16 Dec 1832
Mary Amanda, 18 Oct 1838

SPOUSE II: William Dickinson Pratt
MARRIED: 1 Mar 1841
Kirtland, Ohio (later divorced)
DEATH SP: 15 Sep 1870
Salt Lake City, Salt Lake Co., Utah

CHILDREN:
Martha Marinda, 13 Dec 1841
William Jared, 22 Jun 1844
Stephen, 30 Jan 1847
Mirgo Lyona, 1849

SPOUSE III: William Cornwall Patten
MARRIED: 1854
Payson, Utah Co., Utah
DEATH SP: 9 Mar 1883
Bloomington, Idaho

CHILDREN:
Sarah Wealthy, 3 Nov 1857

Wealthy Eddy was born in Salon, Somerset or Orange County, Maine, or Hampshire, Massachusetts in 1810. She learned to spin and to weave and made many things for her hope chest but never got to use them. When her father found out she had joined the Church of Jesus Christ of Latter-day Saints she fled from home, and never went back.

She married Stephen Billings Shumway in 1831 and they had three children. He died in 1839 of appendicitis.

She then married William Dickinson Pratt in 1841 in Kirtland, Ohio, and they were later divorced. There were four children from this union.

In 1838, she and her first husband were on their way to Haun's Mill, but had to stop because she gave birth to a baby girl, and so escaped the massacre that happened there. She was a good seamstress and helped to make the burial clothes for the Prophet and his brother, Hyrum.

Wealthy and her fifteen-year old son, Ammi Warren came across the Plains in 1851 with the Brown Wagon Company.

She married William Cornwall Patten in 1854, and they had one daughter. William passed away in Bloomington, Idaho in 1883, and Wealthy passed away in Fremont, Idaho in 1892.

JEAN "JANE" NELSON /NIELSON MORGAN PATTERSON

No
Photo
Available

BIRTHDATE: 2 Feb 1817
Joppa, Duddingston, Scotland
DEATH: 28 Aug 1878
Beaver, Beaver Co., Utah
PARENT: Edward Nielson
Catherine Banks
PIONEER: 1 Jul 1852
Independent Wagon Train
SPOUSEI: Thomas Morgan
MARRIED: 26 Jul 1834
DEATH SP: 14 Aug 1838

CHILDREN: Unknown

SPOUSE II: Andrew Patterson
MARRIED: 1851
St. Louis, Missouri
DEATH SP: 1 Jul 1879
Beaver, Beaver Co., Utah

CHILDREN:
Edward Nelson, 16 May 1852
Catherine Banks (Sly), 30 Aug 1853
Alexander, abt 1854
Andrew, 1855
Thomas Morgan, 1 Jul 1857
John Nelson, 31 Jul 1859
Martha Jane (Morgan), 7 Aug 1864

Jean Nelson was born in Scotland in 1817. She met and married Thomas Morgan on July 26, 1834. He died April 14, 1838

While in St. Louis, in 1851, she met and married Andrew Patterson a widower with four children. They then started their journey West. Their first son was born in Council Bluffs, Iowa. He only weighed two and a half pounds and was too small to dress so Jane wrapped him in a blanket and carried him on a pillow in her apron as she

walked across the Plains. He wasn't dressed until they reached the Salt Lake Valley. After arriving in Salt Lake on July 1, 1852, they went to Big Cottonwood to a farm owned by Isaac Crosby.

In the Spring of 1853, they moved to Cedar City so Andrew could work in the mines. They built their first log cabin after living in a dugout all winter. On August 30, 1853, a baby girl, Catherine, was born.

In 1855, they had another son, Andrew, and in 1856 a son, Alexander, was born. However both Andrew and Alexander died this year of starvation.

After the tragic death of their two sons they moved to Beaver. First living in a dugout, they then built another log cabin. Before they had windows or doors another son Thomas was born on July 1, 1857. Three years later they had a five-room brick home. But Jane had no stove, she cooked in the fire place and had a brick oven for backing.

In 1859, their sixth child a son, John, was born and on August 7, 1864, just six months before Jane was fifty years old another baby girl, Martha, was born.

Jane was the first woman doctor in this area to hold a medical degree. She brought 500 babies into the Beaver area, while she doctored the people for all their ailments.

Jane passed away on August 28, 1878 at age sixty-one.

MARY THOMPSON PATTERSON

BIRTHDATE: 24 Feb 1853
Landum, Denmark
DEATH: 25 Nov 1947
Bloomington, Bear Lake, Idaho
PARENTS: Peter Thompson
Mary Jensen
PIONEER: 12 Sep 1861
Milo Andrus Co. Wagon Train
SPOUSE: Edward M. Patterson
MARRIED: 31 Oct 1868
DEATH SP: 25 Nov 1909
Bloomington, Bear Lake, Idaho

CHILDREN:
Mary Jane (Broomhead), 21 Jan 1872
Edward Thompson, 24 Mar 1874
William McGregor, 29 Aug 1876
Joseph Peter, 2 Apr 1879
Amy Eldora (Painter), 20 Sep 1881
Dorthy Ann (Painter), 24 Apr 1884
Rose Emily (Patterson), 10 Mar 1887
John Alma, 20 Dec 1889
James Willard, 19 Jun 1893

Mary was born in Denmark in 1853. She was the second of seven children. They left Denmark in the Spring of 1861 for Liverpool. They left Liverpool for New York on May 15 1861 on the ship "Monarch of the Sea" arriving in New York on June 19, 1861.

Mary's little brother, Joseph, passed away on August 17, somewhere in Wyoming. Thirteen days later August 31, 1861 a little sister, Josphine, was born.

They arrived in the Salt Lake Valley on September 12, and continued on to Brigham City. Here they lived with her mother's mother, Anna Christensen for four years.

In the Spring of 1862, Mary went to work for Mrs. Jensen in Mantua, they had a family of all boys. Mary worked for them for several years. One day while Mary was knitting an Indian came, wanting to trade her brass knitting needles for a butcher knife, after he had rubbed them on a stone to make sure they were brass. Mrs. Jensen promised she would buy her a new set. Shortly after, the Indian returned with brass rings on his ears and fingers, very proud of his trade.

In the Fall of 1867, Mary moved to Bear Lake, Idaho. She helped her mother work the loom, card wool, knit and learned to weave.

Mary married Edward M. Patterson on October 31, 1868. Fourteen years later Edward married her sister, Sarah. These sisters lived in the same house and brought their children together as one family. Mary had nine children and Sarah had six.

Edward was called on a mission to England in 1889, Mary's son John was born in December, 1889. Edward had built his wives a loom, they supported themselves by weaving at ten cents a yard. They also took care of the farm and garden, with ten children still at home.

Sarah passed away in 1906 and Mary took the responsibility of both families raising them as one.

Edward passed away on March 25, 1809, leaving Mary with seven children still at home. Mary broke her hip in 1917 and it never completely healed. She pieced quilts, crocheted lace, specialized in hairpin lace, hooked rugs and wove rugs, and was always busy. She did lots of reading.

Mary joined the Relief Society when it was first organized and belonged the rest of her life.

ANN WALKER PAUL

No Photo Available

BIRTHDATE: 28 Jan 1840
Gringley-on-the-Hill, England
DEATH: 14 Jan 1875
Mendon, Cache Co., Utah
PARENTS: George G. Walker
Mary Hopkin
PIONEER: Aug/Sep 1852
Walker Townsend Wagon Train
SPOUSE: Walter Paul
MARRIED: 25 Dec 1856
DEATH SP: 11 Nov 1916
Rexburg, Madison Co., Idaho

CHILDREN:
Annie Elizabeth, 19 Dec 1857

Walter George, 28 Sep 1859
William Henry, 30 Sep 1861
John Robert, 2 Dec 1863
Mary Jane, 11 Mar 1866
Priscilla, 6 Jan 1868 (died as an infant)
Edmund Young, 22 Mar 1869 (died as an infant)
Sarah Irvin, 22 Mar 1869 (died as an infant)
Frank Orson, 26 Sep 1870 (died at age 2)
Minnie Susan, 10 Jul 1873 (died at age 6)
Infant son, 14 Jan 1875 (stillborn)

Annie was born in Gringley-on-the-Hill, Nottingham, England, January 28, 1840. She lived in England for the first part of her life with her parents as members of the Wesleyan Methodist Church. Her parents heard about the Church of Jesus Christ of Latter-day Saints and Ann was baptized in 1849, by Claude Roger. The following year, in 1850, she left England to sail to America.

She arrived in 1850, with her family, and settled in St. Joseph, Missouri. Ann's father went into business almost immediately so that they could travel to Utah and join the rest of the Saints.

On May 3, 1851, the family joined the Townsend and Walker Company and left St. Joseph. There were ten wagons in their train as they started their journey for Salt Lake. They endured many trials on their trek westward.

When Ann and the family arrived in the Salt Lake Valley they settled in Cottonwood. After a few years, Ann's family moved into Salt Lake.

When she met Walter Paul it was true love and they were married on December 25, 1856. Ann and her husband lived on Soldier Road, named this because the soldiers used it to travel back and forth to the city.

After the birth and death of her last five children, Ann's health was very poor. Even though she suffered constantly, the family was adventurous and were interested in new territories.

In 1873 or 1874, they left Salt Lake and went to Cache Valley to help in that part of the Lord's vineyard. They settled in Mendon and brought to Cache Valley the first organ. They took the organ around to many churches and entertainments, their oldest daughter played and sang.

Ann continued in poor health and her body was very frail. The hardships of pioneer life were more than she could take. When she was only thirty-five, she gave birth to her eleventh child, both mother and child died.

With the death of Ann, the family suffered a great loss. She had always been a devoted mother and wife, who had suffered and endured much because of the poverty and hardships of pioneer life. Not only had she been a comfort to her own family, but also to any who were in need or suffering sorrow. She was a true Latter-day Saint throughout her short life.

CATHERINE HUGHES ROBERTS PAUL

No
Photo
Available

BIRTHDATE: 20 Aug 1807
Garthoffeiriad, Wales
DEATH: 10 Dec 1877
Salt Lake City, Salt Lake, Utah
PARENTS: Thomas Hughes Sr.
Mary Lloyd
PIONEER: Oct 1863
Wagon Train Company
SPOUSE I: Robert Roberts
MARRIED: 25 Aug 1842
DEATH SP: 31 Aug 1842

CHILDREN: None

SPOUSE II: James Patton Paal
MARRIED: 24 Mar 1866
Salt Lake City, Salt Lake Co., Utah
DEATH SP: 3 Apr 1891
Salt Lake City, Salt Lake Co., Utah
CHILDREN: None

Catherine was born in Garthoffeiriad, Llanddoget, Wales, 1807. She was the oldest of eight children. She and her youngest brother, Peter, were members of the Church of Jesus Christ of Latter-day Saints and came to Utah.

Catherine married Robert Roberts on August 25, 1842 in Wales. He died six days after their marriage.

After coming to Utah, Peter married Elizabeth Evans and they became parents of three daughters, one being Martha Hughes Cannon. Peter passed away on September 17, 1861 in Salt Lake City, Utah. This was very difficult for both Catherine and Elizabeth. In 1862, Elizabeth married James Patten Paul. They became parents of five more children. Elizabeth asked and gave permission for Catherine to become his fourth wife, which she did on March 24, 1866.

James Patton Paul was born 1817 or 1818 in Ayre, Scotland. He first married Robina Gribbon, in 1839. He came as a pioneer to Utah and married a second time to Sarah Wilson in 1861. He married his third wife, Elizabeth Evans Hughes, and his fourth wife became Catherine Hughes Roberts.

James worked for the Union Pacific Railroad as a cabinet maker for twenty years. He provided well for his large family. Catherine enjoyed being another mother to his growing family. They made their home in Salt Lake City, where, at the age of seventy, Catherine passed away on December 10, 1877.

ELIZABETH EVANS HUGHES PAUL

BIRTHDATE: 22 Mar 1833
8arston Warwickshire, England
DEATH: 17 Jan 1923
Salt Lake City, Salt Lake, Utah
PARENT: Joseph Evans
Maria Shervington
PIONEER: 13 Sep 1861
Capt. Horne's Co. Wagon Train
SPOUSE I: Peter Hughes
MARRIED: 4 Mar 1854
Llandudno, Deabigh, Wales
DEATH SP: 17 Sep 1861
Salt Lake City, Salt Lake, Utah

CHILDREN:
Mary Elizabeth (Neeley), 14 Dec 1854
Martha Marie (Cannon), 1 Jul 1857
Annie Lloyd, 4 Dec 1859

SPOUSE II: James Patten Paul
MARRIED: 25 Oct 1862
Salt Lake City, Salt Lake Co., Utah
DEATH SP: 3 Apr 1891
Salt Lake City, Salt Lake Co., Utah

CHILDREN:
Joshua Hughes, 20 Jan 1863
Joseph Evans, 20 Jul 1867
Lotta Robina (Baxter), 14 Feb 1873
Barbara (Ballif), 30 Oct 1873
Sarah Maude, 30 Dec 1875

Elizabeth was born in England in 1833. It is said she moved to Wales to become a handmaid to wealthy women.

Elizabeth married Peter Hughes in Llandudno, Carnarvanshire, North Wales. They were the parents of three daughters.

They sailed from Liverpool on the ship "Underwriter," March 30, 1860. For two years they lived in New York, During which time her husband was very ill and she earned the living for the family. It was during the Civil War and work was scarce. She made neckties for a large clothing establishment, at other times nursing and washing were undertaken to make the money.

The hope of going West seemed very slim at this time, but after serious prayer, Erastus Snow came to her home and said their arrangements had been made with Captain Horne's Wagon Company. Elizabeth walked most of the way so her invalid husband and three girls could ride in the wagon.

They reached the Salt Lake Valley in September, 1862. On the third day in the Valley her husband died. Elizabeth was living in a dugout without her husband and she was dreadfully lonely.

She married James Patten Paul on October 25, 1862, to them were born five children and they enjoyed twenty-nine years of marriage.

From the time it was organized, in the 10th Ward, Elizabeth was an active member of Relief Society. She later served twenty years as president. During this time she loved taking care of the sick, continuing until her eighty-first year.

Peacefully and without suffering, Elizabeth passed away on January 17, 1923, at the age of ninety.

ANN RUSHEN KEYS PAXMAN

BIRTHDATE: 11 Sep 1830
Danbury, England
DEATH: 10 Apr 1919
American Fork, Utah Co., Utah
PARENTS: Joseph Keys
Mary Ann Rushen
PIONEER: 13 Sep 1861
Joseph Horne Co. Wagon Train
SPOUSE: William Paxman
MARRIED: 3 Mar 1855
London, Middlesex, England
DEATH SP: 12 Oct 1897
Nephi, Juab Co., Utah

CHILDREN:
William Reed Horizon, 13 Jun 1856
Edgar Moroni, 25 Aug 1857
Emma Tryphena, 12 Jan 1859
James Walter, 12 Oct 1861
George Francis, 25 Apr 1863
Esther Elizabeth, 16 Feb 1865
Martha Eleanor, 2 May 1867
Joseph Hyrum, 26 Mar 1869
Alice Ann, 16 Sep 1870
Edwin Washington, 4 Jul 1872
Albert Reynolds, 19 Aug 1875

Ann Rushen Keys was born, September 11, 1830, in Danbury, Little Baddow, Essex, England. She married William Paxman on March 3, 1855 in London, England.

They set sail from Liverpool on May 25, 1856, and her first child, a son, was born on board ship on June 13, 1856. He was named William (for his father), Reed (for the captain of the ship), and Horizon (the name of the ship).

They came across the Plains by wagon train, Joseph Horne as captain, and arrived in the Salt Lake Valley on September 13, 1861.

Ann brought a supply of yeast cakes for the journey, and would mix her bread at night, and by morning she had delicious yeast dough for flapjacks for breakfast. She had many encounters with Indians during the great trek and also while living in Utah.

Living conditions were not the best, but in 1866 they finally moved into a regular house. She became the first wife when her husband married again in 1875. She was the mother of eleven children, most of them born in American Fork, Utah. Later she moved to Nephi, Juab County, Utah. In a short time there were three other wives, and the 'raid'

on polygamy had begun. Her husband went into hiding for two years and she was alone during that time.

It was said, by her children, that she walked erect, was youthful in spirit, clear in intellect, pleasing in appearance, and never idle. She spent much of her time in her eighties doing exquisite hand embroidery work, to give to her children as a remembrance of her.

William passed away on October 12, 1897 in Nephi, Juab County, Utah. Ann passed away on April 10, 1919 in American Fork, Utah County, Utah.

MARY GOBLE PAY

BIRTHDATE: 2 Jun 1843
Brighton, England
DEATH: 25 Sep 1913
Nephi, Juab Co., Utah
PARENTS: William Goble
Mary Penfold
PIONEER: 11 Dec 1856
John A. Hunt Co. Wagon Train
SPOUSE: Richard Pay
MARRIED: 26 Jun 1859
Nephi, Juab Co., Utah
DEATH SP: 18 Apr 1893
Leamington, Millard Co., Utah

CHILDREN:
Richard William, 11 Sep 1860
George Edwin, 4 Oct 1862
Edward James, 18 Sep 1864
John Henry, 11 Aug 1866 (died as an infant)
Joseph William, 16 Jun 1867 (died as a child)
Mercy Mary, 11 Aug 1869 (died as an infant)
Jesse, 11 Dec 1870
David Alma, 25 May 1873
William Goble, 8 Mar 1876
Mary Ettia, 25 May 1878
Sarah Eliza, 26 Jan 1881 (died at age 14)
Leonard, 14 Jun 1883
Phillip LeRoy, 14 Nov 1885

Mary Goble was born in England in 1843. She was baptized into the Church of Jesus Christ of Latter-day Saints at the age of twelve. In 1856, the family sailed from England on the ship "Horizon," for America. Her sister, Fanny, caught measles on board ship, but seemed to recover, however when they were in Iowa this same sister got wet during a thunderstorm and died. Mary was two years old at this time.

The company, leaving late to cross the Plains, followed one of the handcart companies. Indians were hostile, and at times they could not light a fire at night. Mary's mother had a baby girl who died at six weeks through lack of nourishment. The snows and cold weather came and Mary's feet were frozen. The company could not travel and had to wait for help sent from Brigham Young. Her brother was well when he went to bed one night, but in the morning he was dead. Her mother died just as they were coming into the Salt Lake Valley.

When Brigham Young saw the condition of their frozen limbs the tears rolled down his cheeks. The doctor wanted amputate Mary's feet, but President Young said, "No, just the toes." He promised Mary her feet would heal. Instead they got worse. Another doctor also wanted to amputate, but Mary told him that President Young promised her it would not be necessary. A kind sister came and put poultices on her feet every day and within three months they were healed. The family moved to Spanish Fork.

In 1856, Mary married Richard Pay, whose wife had died at Fort Bridger. They lived in Nephi for twenty-two years, then moved to Leamington in Millard County. Mary was a Counselor in Relief Society, and President of the Primary in Leamington.

Richard passed away in Leamington in 1893, and Mary passed away in Nephi, Juab County, Utah in 1913.

CATHERINE LOUISE NICHOLS PAYNE

BIRTHDATE: 1 Dec 1824
Eaton Socon, England
DEATH: 10 Jun 1906
Kaysville, Davis Co., Utah
PARENT: James Nichols
Sarah Barrington
PIONEER: 13 Oct 1849
Redic Allen Wagon Train
SPOUSE: William Lauder Payne
MARRIED: 7 Jun 1843
Nauvoo, Hancock Co., Illinois
DEATH SP: 22 Dec 1892
Kaysville, Davis Co., Utah

CHILDREN:
Sarah Jane (Layton), 22 Nov 1844
Emma, 25 Aug 1846
Mary Ann (Harris), 10 Sep 1848
Elizabeth Barnes (Deshazo), 26 Mar 1851
William Richard, 12 Apr 1853
James Levi, 7 Sep 1855
Orson Nichols, 14 Oct 1857
Catherine Amelia (Sardine), 2 Jul 1860
Priscilla Margaret (Van Orden), 30 Jul 1862
Esther Louise (Hedrich), 2 Mar 1864
Joseph Henry, 22 Mar 1867

Catherine Louise was born in Eaton Socon, Bedfordshire, England in 1824. She was the last of six children. Her father died three weeks after she was born. When she was seventeen her mother died, leaving her a small fortune. When she was eighteen, she sewed the gold coins in her corset and set sail for America, on the ship "Swaton" from Liverpool, June 16, 1843.

Catherine was very seasick and spent most of the time in her cabin. Although she never met William she wanted to put a hot potato in his mouth, because he was singing and

happy on deck. They landed in New Orleans. Catherine and William met on the way to Nauvoo, arriving June 6, 1843. They were met by the Prophet Joseph Smith.

Catherine and William were married on June 7, 1843. With Catherine's money they bought a twenty acre farm and built a home. Catherine was a lace maker by trade. Two daughters were born to them in Nauvoo, Sarah Jane and Emma.

In 1846, they left Nauvoo with the rest of the Saints. Little Emma died on the way and was buried at Winter Quarters. The family stayed in Council Bluffs, Iowa for three years, where another daughter, Mary Ann, was born.

They continued their journey West on July 5, 1849. Along the way, Catherine and Sarah Jane contacted small pox and were very ill. The captain ordered them back to Council Bluffs but they continued to travel a few miles behind the others. William walked back each night with food. Both recovered. They arrived in the Salt Lake Valley on October 13, 1849. In the Spring of 1850 they settled in Kaysville.

Catherine worked in the Presidency of Relief Society and as a district teacher. She was always visiting the sick and afflicted and giving comfort to those in sorrow. She did work in the Logan and Salt Lake Temple for her kindred dead. Catherine was the mother of eleven children, ten of whom grew to adulthood.

Catherine passed away, June 11, 1906, in Kaysville, Davis County, Utah at the age of eighty-two.

EMMA POWELL PAYNE

BIRTHDATE: 1 Mar 1838
Aldridge, Staffordshire, England
DEATH: 4 Sep 1927
Glenwood, Sevier Co., Utah
PARENTS: George Powell
Maria Mousley
PIONEER: 20 Sep 1864
Joseph S. Rawlins Freight Train
SPOUSE: Edward Payne
MARRIED: 16 Sep 1854 Dudley
Port, Worcester, England
DEATH SP: 27 Mar 1918
Glenwood, Sevier Co., Utah

CHILDREN:
George, 4 Dec 1855
Harry M., 3 Dec 1857
Lucy, 16 Mar 1860
Thomas, 10 Apr 1862 (died at age 2)
Elizabeth, 2 Oct 1864
Edward William, 2 Apr 1867
John Henry, 19 Aug 1869
Margaret Ann, 29 Nov 1871
Charles Willard, 2 Feb 1874
James Heber, 27 Feb 1876 (died an infant)
Emma Maria, 3 Jun 1877 (died as an infant)
Claude Brigham, 5 Oct 1878
Benjamin Franklin, 17 Nov 1881

Emma's parents were very poor, so Emma did housework and tended children at a very young age. When she was six years old, her parents joined the Church of Jesus Christ of Latter-day Saints. Emma was baptized on April 25, 1850, when she was twelve years old. She helped her father in his church assignments by leading the singing and distributing the tracts to all who attended the street meetings where her father preached.

Emma met Edward Payne when he came to board at her parents' home while he worked in the coal mines with Emma's father. Edward and Emma were married in 1854 when she was only sixteen. They moved from coal mine to coal mine for nine years in England before making the decision to come to America and join the Saints in Utah.

In 1863, Edward left Emma and their three small children in England while he went to America to earn money for the fare of his young family. Emma and her children came the following year.

They went on to Utah with her father and his family with the Joseph S. Rawlins Freight Wagon Train. Most of their family had to ride up on top of the freight. Emma's job was to make and bake bread for the company. When they were nearly half way, their son, Thomas, died. The rest of the family arrived safely in Heber City on September 20, 1864. Edward had stayed in Pennsylvania to repay his debts. Then he joined the family in Utah the following year.

Emma's family and her father's family went to Heber City to live. Emma gave birth to her daughter, Elizabeth, two weeks after their arrival. Emma found work in a boarding house and asked for the good table scraps from the kitchen to feed her family.

After Edward arrived, their faith was tested again by the grasshoppers and crickets which devoured their garden.

They moved to Sevier County where they built a small home and farm. Emma loved flowers and made her yard always full of beauty. While they were living in Glenwood, they were part of the United Order.

Emma owned one of the first sewing machines in the town. She was one of a group of four women who did the sewing to keep the Cooperative Mercantile stocked with overalls, jumpers, hats, buckskin suits, underwear, etc. She did much custom sewing.

She served as a second counselor in the Relief Society, then served in the Presidency for twenty-five years. She learned about using herbs and medicines from her husband. He had learned what he knew about herbs while he was working in a drug store in England. They were called upon to help whenever anyone was ill. Emma's special calling was to care for the dead, see they were properly dressed, and laid away.

Emma spent her later years with her children and passed away at the age of eighty-nine in Glenwood, Utah.

MARY MORRIS BROADHEAD PAYNE

BIRTHDATE: 21 Aug 1841
Duckenfield, England
DEATH: 28 Jan 1906
Fillmore, Millard Co., Utah
PARENT: James Morris
Mary Butterworth
PIONEER: 24 Oct 1855
Milo Andrus Co. Wagon Train
SPOUSE I: David Broadhead
MARRIED: 17 Feb 1856
Salt Lake City, Salt Lake, Utah
DEATH SP: 29 Jun 1905
Nephi, Juab Co., Utah

CHILDREN:
Mary Alice (Goodman), 15 Oct 1857
James Morris, 29 Jul 1860
John, 19 May 1862

SPOUSE II: James Payne
MARRIED: 25 Dec 1864
Nephi, Juab Co., Utah
DEATH SP: 17 Feb 1905
Fillmore, Millard Co., Utah

CHILDREN:
Emma (Sibley), 6 Oct 1865
Eliza Ann (Starley), 7 Apr 1867
James William, 19 Oct 1868
Sarah, 17 Nov 1870
Matthew Richard, 7 Apr 1872
Parley Morris, 17 Apr 1875
George, 1 Jun 1877
Mary Ellen, 7 Sep 1878
Catherine, 28 Jan 1881
Unnamed Female Child, 1882
Myrtle, 30 May 1884
Unnamed child, 1886

Mary was born in Duckenfield, Lancashire, England in 1841. Mary and her family left England in 1853 arriving in St. Louis, Missouri. Her father went into business and decided to stay awhile. In 1854, her mother died.

Mary's father sent her to her older brother, Charles, in Utah. He supplied her with plenty of food, clothes and several pair of shoes. Mary left Mormon Grove, Kansas on August 5, 1855. Mary walked all the way, dividing her food and clothing with those in the company in need. Her shoes wore out and her feet were wrapped in burlap to protect them. She had very little left when she reached the Salt Lake Valley.

She went to Nephi to her brother, but he couldn't support her so she went to live with the Biglers. She was grateful for a home and anxious to help all she could. She learned to cook, sew, card wool for yarn. Mary couldn't read or write, She was cheerful and sociable and made friends easily. She had a lovely voice and sang in the choir.

When Mary was only fifteen, she married David Broadhead on February 17, 1856, as his second wife. They lived with his first wife and family. In a short time she had three little children, making eight children and three adults in a one-room home. Mary took her baby and went to live with her father for two years, then divorced David.

Mary married James Payne on December 25, 1864, leaving her two older children with David a little longer.

In the Spring of 1865, they moved to Fillmore. Mary was thrifty, industrious, and not afraid of work. She made what is called "Hop Yeast" growing hops on the fence. She made a crock or two every day because they came from all over to buy it. She braided her own carpet taking several years to get enough rags, it measured 12' x 15' She never complained and was always glad she came to Utah.

Mary passed away on January 28, 1906 at the age of sixty-five in Fillmore, Utah

HENRIETTA CROMEANS PEARCE

BIRTHDATE: 1807
New River, Scott Co., Tennessee
DEATH: 17 Apr 1864
St. George, Washington, Utah
PARENTS: Josiah Cromeans
Nancy Mears
PIONEER: 9 Oct 1852
James Snow Co. Wagon Train
SPOUSE: Harrison Pearce
MARRIED: 25 Jul 1836
DEATH SP: 28 May 1899

CHILDREN:
John David, 5 Apr 1837
James, 6 Mar 1839
Amelia, 15 May 1841
Nancy Clark, 12 Dec 1842 (died at age 12)
Thomas Jefferson, 22 Feb 1845
Harrison, 24 Mar 1849
Henrietta, 15 Jun 1852

Henrietta met and married Harrison Pearce. Harrison became converted to the Church of Jesus Christ of Latter-day Saints and was baptized on November 2, 1845. The following day, Henrietta and several of their neighbors were baptized.

In February of 1846, they left Mississpippi for Nauvoo to be where the Saints were gathering. After resting one week in Nauvoo, they went to Pittsburg on the Des Moines River in Iowa. There her husband was able to work for provisions and clothing. That winter they suffered with the chills and fever.

In April, the family moved to Mt. Pisgah where Harrison was able to teach school. At that time, President Snow complimented the Pearces because they hosted parties and musical events for the community in order to keep their spirits high.

Three years later, they moved to Council Bluffs, Iowa. In 1852, they crossed the Plains with the James Snow Wagon Company and arrived in the Salt Lake Valley on October 9, 1852. Their daughter, Nancy, died of cholera as they were crossing the Plains. After arriving in Salt Lake, they were assigned to go to Payson, Utah to help settle the area.

In 1856, they moved to Dixie where they were to raise sugar cane, cotton, indigo, and madder. They also planted peach pits to start peach trees. They raised their cotton, picked the seeds out with their fingers, gathered dock roots to color the cotton, carded it, spun it, and then they would weave it into cloth.

Later they moved to St. George and were among the first to locate there. They moved the little peach trees to St. George with them. They were the first peaches grown in that area.

JEAN RIO GRIFFITH BAKER PEARCE/PIERCE

BIRTHDATE: 8 May 1810
London, England
DEATH: 21 Jul 1883
Los Gatos, California
PARENTS: John W. Griffiths
Susanna Ann Burgess
PIONEER: 29 Sep 1851
Griffiths Co. Wagon Train
SPOUSE I: Henry Baker
MARRIED: 24 Sep 1832
DEATH SP: 3 Sep 1849
London, England

CHILDREN:
Henery Walter Baker, 24 Jul 1833
William George, 10 Jun 1835
Charles Edward, 21 Dec 1836 (died at age 2)
Charles Edward, 5 May 1839
Elizabeth Anne, 20 Apr 1841
John Edye, 31 May 1843
Charles West, 21 Oct 1844 (died at age 9)
Josiah Elliott, 23 May 1846 (died at age 5)
Jean Rio, 7 May 1848 (died at age 1)

SPOUSE II: Edward Pearce / Peirce
MARRIED: 1864
DEATH SP: 1864
Ogden,
Weber Co., Utah
CHILDREN:

Jean Rio was born in London, England in the springtime, blessed with a great musical talent which she shared as she grew up by singing for audiences both in England and the United States. She also gave readings of Shakespeare and other fine writers.

She was twenty-two years old when she married Edward, settled into married life and motherhood. She and Edward had nine children, seven boys and two girls, sadly she lost four children in death, raising four sons and one daughter to adulthood.

Edward passed away in 1849 and with great courage and determination, Jean assumed the responsibility of bringing her six children to America. Traumatically, her one year old baby girl died on the voyage over and was buried at sea.

Their journey began January 4, 1851. They sailed from London, England on the George W. Bourne on the 7th day of January. Their long, arduous journey to reach the Salt Lake Valley by ship and wagon took nine months, almost a year of traveling.

Jean resided in Utah for eighteen years, first in Salt Lake City, then in Ogden where she supported her children and herself as a dressmaker.

There she married Edward Pearce /Pierce who passed away just six months after their marriage.

Jean later moved to Los Gatos, California to be with her children. She passed away there at the age of seventy-three.

MAGDALENA SCHNEIDER ITTEN PEARCE

BIRTHDATE: 6 Dec 1838
Switzerland
DEATH: 6 Jun 1896
St. George, Washington, Utah
PARENTS: Fredrik Scheider
Elizabeth Scheider
PIONEER: Btwn 1857 and 1861
Handcart Compnay
SPOUSE I: John Itten
MARRIED: 18 Oct 1861
Salt Lake City, Salt Lake, Utah
DEATH SP: 1862

CHILDREN None

SPOUSE II: Harrison Pearce
MARRIED: 3 Oct 1863
DEATH SP: 28 May 1889
St. George, Washington Co., Utah

CHILDREN:
Magdalena Elizabeth, 26 Jan 1867
Mary Abigail (Milexethen), 5 Oct 1870
Frederick Harrison, 22 Jul 1873
Mable Lucy (Laub), 12 Jul 1875
Emily Minerva (Atkin), 12 Apr 1880

Magdelena was born in Switzerland in 1838. Her mother died in 1841. It is unknown how and when she

came to Utah, but stories are told of how she pushed a hand-cart to Zion.

She married John Itten on October 18, 1861 in Salt Lake City, Utah. They were among the first Swiss settlers in Santa Clara. When John recieved a small inheritance of eighty dollars worth of musical instruments, they donated them to the town for a band. John became the first Swiss settler to die in Santa Clara, leaving Magdalena a childless widow.

Magdalena married Harrison Pearce as his third wife on October 3, 1863. They were the parents of five children but only two lived to adulthood.

In 1882, Harrison, Magdalena and the girls went to Taylor, Arizona. Here Magdalena served as the Primary President.

Harrison and Magdalena returned to St. George, where Harrison passed away on May 29, 1887. Magdalena was widowed again at the age of forty-nine. The hardships of frontier life placed Magdalena in a wheelchair the last part of her life.

Magdalena passed away in St. George on June 6, 1896 at the age of fifty-five.

MARY JANE MEEKS PEARCE

BIRTHDATE: 2 Dec 1851
Council Bluffs, Iowa
DEATH: 15 Oct 1941
Taylor, Arizona
PARENTS: William Meeks
Mary Elizabeth Rhodes
PIONEER: 1852
Nisenger Handcart Company
SPOUSE: James Pearce
MARRIED: 06 Mar 1867
St. George, Washington, Utah
DEATH SP: 17 Feb 1922
Taylor, Arizona

CHILDREN:
Lola May, 23 Jun 1868
James William, 27 Jun 1871
Joseph Harrison, 4 Sep 1873
Mary Jane, 11 Mar 1876
Elizabeth, 9 Jul 1878
Henrietta, 20 Apr 1881
John Henry, 22 Jan 1884
Jesse Harvey, 3 Dec 1886
Sylvia Amelia, 11 Mar 1889
David Earl, 18 Jul 1891
Perry Meeks, 28 May 1895

Mary Jane's parents were at Council Bluffs, Pottawattamie County, Iowa at the time of her birth which was after the exodus of the Saints from Nauvoo, Illinois.

In 1852, she was a babe in arms when her parents continued on, and arrived in Utah. They were called to go to Southern Utah in 1853 to help settle St. George and to help build the temple. Her childhood days were mostly helping her mother. She learned to weave cloth and to make clothing from hand woven cloth. She helped her mother with the household chores.

By the time she was sixteen, she had made all her bed ticks, pillow slips, and sheets all of which were corded, spun, and woven by her own hands. She learned the art of dying and was skilled in weaving striped and plaid materials. She was so expert at it, she was requested to do the weaving for wives of the high church officials of the LDS Church. She also learned about home remedies by using herbs, tree bark and leaves. She became a nature doctor and also a midwife.

Mary Jane was married to James Pearce in St. George. They were called to colonize Arizona. They camped first at Sunset, then Woodruff, and finally, Taylor. Eleven children were born to her. All illnesses in the family were attended by her. She seemed able to cope with any emergency in the wild unsettled section of Arizona. Mary Ann became so proficient in nursing and doctoring that the county of Yavapai in Arizona gave her a certification in nursing and midwifery. She brought over 100 babies into the world.

Mary Jane always kept up her work in the Church and other civic duties. She was the first post mistress at Shumway, Arizona and a member of the school board of trustees. She served as a member of the Ward Building Committee. In Liberty, Arizona, she was president of the Ward Relief Society and was Assistant Superintendent of the Sunday School.

SARAH BROWN PEARCE

BIRTHDATE:(chr) 22 Dec 1816
Porlock, Somerset, England
DEATH: 13 Apr 1898
Paradise, Cache Co., Utah
PARENT: John Brown
Sarah Bale
PIONEER: 10 Sep 1863
William B Preston Wagon Train
SPOUSE: Robert Pearce
MARRIED: 28 Dec 1844
Porlock, Somerset England
DEATH SP: 18 Oct 1885
Paradise, Cache Co., Utah

CHILDREN:
Elizabeth (Pope), 16 May 1845
Mary, 9 Dec 1846
Sarah, 23 May 1849
Robert, 24 Aug 1851
Mary, 3 Jan 1854
Thomas Joseph, 28 May 1857
Charles, 16 Sep 1860

Sarah was born in England in 1816. She was the fifth of seven children. When she was twenty-eight she married

Robert Pearce on December 28, 1844. Two years later they moved to Cardiff, Wales.

On April 30, 1863 Sarah, her husband and five children boarded the ship "John J. Boyd" for America. (Mary and Sarah had died of scarlet fever just nine days apart) They landed in New York then went on to Florence, Nebraska by railroad, then on to Utah.

They were among the first to settle in Old Paradise, Cache County, Utah. They arrived in the fall and the community helped them build a half dugout half cabin to live in. Four years later they had to move three miles north to protect themselves from Indians, having to start all over.

In 1874, the second Mary died and Elizabeth had married and moved to Randolph, leaving Sarah without the companionship of any of her daughters.

At age seventy-five, Sarah fell down the stairs in her home leaving her crippled for the remaining seven years of her life. She was independent to the end. The only thing that seemed to worry her was if her body would straighten out when she died. Which it did.

After being a widow for eighteen years Sarah passed away peacefully in her sleep on April 13, 1898 at the age of eighty-two. She experienced many hardships, sickness, and death, but always retained a spirit of optimism.

ROSE HANNAH WHITEHEAD PEARS

No
Photo
Available

BIRTHDATE: 26 Feb 1801
Bradford, Yorkshire, England
DEATH: 10 Feb 1864
Salt Lake City, Salt Lake, Utah
PARENTS: Lawrence Whitehead
Mary Brown
PIONEER: 30 Nov 1856
Martin Handcart Company
SPOUSE: John Burton Pears
MARRIED: 30 Jan 1822
St. Mary's Bishophill, England
DEATH SP: 21 Oct 1856
Crossing the plains

CHILDREN:
John, Jr., 1825
Mary, 1829
Margaret, 1831
Elizabeth, abt 1833
Eliza, 5 Feb 1842

Rose Hannah was born at Bradford, England. She was baptized and became a member of The Church of Jesus Christ of Latter-day Saints on January 24, 1844. With her husband and two daughters she came to America in 1856. One son and two daughters remained in England.

They were the owners of large silk and woolen mills and when they left England they brought with them many bolts of silk and woolen goods, enough, they thought, to last until they could make another trip to England.

It took twelve weeks to get to New York. From there they traveled by train to Iowa City where they were assigned to cross the Plains in the Martin Handcart Company.

They lost most of their possessions and suffered much from cold and hunger. On October 21st, her husband died and was buried in a grave with five other men. Brush was heaped on the grave and burned to keep the wolves from digging up the bodies. Rose Hannah and her two daughters continued on with the company. Her feet and legs were so badly frozen that she never walked again.

Rose Hannah and her daughters could not read nor write and were unable to get word back to England of the death of her husband and receive any help from her family.

Her daughter, Eliza, married Nicholas Summers on January 2, 1857, Rose Hannah made her home with them. She was very crippled and was cared for by Eliza until her death on February 10, 1864.

CHRISTINA KNUTTSON BECKSTRAND (PEHRSSON) PEARSON

BIRTHDATE: 24 Dec 1825
Granstarp, Jonkopings, Sweden
DEATH: 16 Oct 1916
Huntington, Emery, Utah
PARENTS:
Knut Johan Beckstrand
Ingierd Jacobson Beckstrand
PIONEER: 29 Aug 1863
John R. Murdock Wagon Co.
SPOUSE: Pehr Swenson Pehrsson
MARRIED: 26 Dec 1859
DEATH SP: 9 May 1902

CHILDREN:
Anna Maria, 5 Apr 1860 (died age 12)
John Peter, 16 Jan 1865
Josephine Christina, 5 Sep 1867 (died age 1)
Albertina, 23 Sep 1869 (died age 4)
Elvina Hancine Olsen, 15 May 1868 (adopted in 1874)

In her youth, Christina went through many trials and hardships which included a famine. She remembered grinding the bark from trees and straw from the fields in order to make bread. She lost both parents at an early age and was bound out to work for rich people as a servant. The heavy loads she had to carry caused her to become humped and stooped. As servants at the end of each year, they were asked to sign yearly contracts. They were either free to go or sign on for another year. She met and fell in love with Pehr Swenson Pehrsson who was also working as a servant in the same home. They set their wedding date, but were told by their employer that poor people should never be allowed to marry. Christina told them if the poor people should not be allowed to marry, it would not be long before they would have no one to work for them. At marriage, their

contract was broken and they were free to seek a home of their own.

They learned of the gospel of the Church of Jesus Christ of Latter-day Saints and were baptized June 9, 1861 by Niels Larsen. On April 14, 1863, they left Sweden bringing with them their little daughter. They boarded the steamer, "John J. Boyd," upon which they were six weeks crossing the ocean. They left Florence, Nebraska to cross the plains in the John R. Murdock Company which arrived in Salt Lake City August 29, 1863. Brigham Young soon sent them to settle in Deseret, Millard County.

They moved to Oak City which is about thirty miles away, where Albertina was born and Anna Maria, who was then twelve, was stricken with fever and died. She was the first to be buried in Oak City. When Albertina was four years old, she was playing on a hay rack, lost her footing, slipped, broke her neck, and died. Later that year, the family adopted a five year old Danish girl, Elvina Hancine Olsen who had been born in Nabro, Albury, Denmark. They loved her as their own.

In 1874, Brigham Young gave instructions for them to settle in Orderville to live the United Order. Christina had learned the trade of weaving and spinning to help make a living. She washed, carded, spun and dyed the wool. Then she made socks, mittens, and sweaters. She also used wool in making quilts, dresses, sheets and blankets. She dyed the yarns with roots and plants gathered from the fields. She successfully spun flax and it was woven into linen for tablecloths, sheets, towels, and clothes. She was so proficient at her trade that she was in demand to make clothing for others, including wedding dresses.

She and her husband did a lot of temple work in St. George and Manti. John was ordained an Elder at the age of fourteen, on April 25, 1879 in the St. George temple so he could help his parents with the many proxy names they had to do. Elvina was sealed to Christina and Pehr Pehrson that same day.

They left Orderville through an assignment by Brigham Young to go to Castle Valley on September 4, 1882. They settled in Huntington, Emery County. She and Elvina became well known for their spinning and weaving skills. Her husband died in Huntington on May 9, 1902. Christina died in Huntington on October 16, 1915, at the age of eighty-nine.

ELIZA MARY CURTIS PEARSON

BIRTHDATE: 30 Jul 1849
Bethnal, London, England
DEATH: 30 Apr 1939
Moore, Butte Co., Idaho
PARENTS: Joseph H. Curtis
Sarah Morrell
PIONEER: 23 Sep 1861
Ansel P. Harmon Wagon Train
SPOUSE: Benjamin A. Pearson
MARRIED: 27 Dec 1869
Salt Lake City, Salt Lake, Utah
DEATH SP: 18 Jun 1934
Moore, Butte Co., Idaho

CHILDREN:
Eliza Ellen (Davidson), 9 Nov 1870
Mary Etta (McGuire), 29 Feb 1872
Sarah Olive (Haney), 27 Sep 1874
Selina Maude (Lafever), 22 Oct 1876
Ida May (Haney Kerns), 31 Oct 1878
Benjamin Jesse, 7 Feb 1881
Joseph Harry, 30 Apr 1884
Roy Curtis, 3 Mar 1886
Albert Russell, 1 Mar 1888
Fredrick Rolla (Fred), 20 Jan 1890

Eliza was born in Bethnal, London, Middlesex, England in 1849. She had little opportunity for an education but what she received was very thorough.

She came to Utah on the ship "Underwriter," at age nine with her parents and family. They went to Philadelphia by train, where they stayed for one year. They came to Utah in the Ansell P. Harmon Company arriving on September 23, 1861.

When she was twenty years old she married Benjamin Pearson on December 27, 1869. They lived in Malad, Oxford, Garden Creek and McCannon, Idaho; Salt Lake and Harrisonville, Utah before they settled in the Lost River Valley.

Eliza and Benjamin celebrated their 50th and 60th wedding anniversary before Benjamin passed away in 1934. Eliza passed away on April 30, 1939 at age ninety.

SISSA JONSSON BENGTSSON PEARSON

BIRTHDATE: 6 Sep 1821
Fulltofta, Malmhus, Sweden
DEATH: 19 Feb 1910
Oakley, Summit Co., Utah
PARENTS: Jons Bengtsson
Elsa Petersson
PIONEER: 29 Aug 1863
John R. Murdock Wagon Train
SPOUSE: Ola Pehrson /Pearson
MARRIED: 31 Dec 1847
Fulltofta, Malmohus, Sweden
DEATH SP: 27 Sep 1847
Oakley, Summit Co., Utah

CHILDREN:
Ola, 18 Mar 1847
Nils, 24 Mar 1849
Elna, 10 Jan 1853
Elsie, 10 Jan 1853
Anna, 10 Dec 1854
Anders, 6 Jun 1857
Per "Peter," 26 Jul 1859
Jons, 26 Jul 1859
Andreas, 25 Aug 1862
Levi, 28 Apr 1866

Sissa was born in Sweden in 1821. She married Ola Pehrson /Pearson on December 31, 1847 in Sweden.

In Sweden, Sissa's family was required to work 200 days each month to pay rent on the small rocky ground where they grew their food. Sissa knew the burden of hard work.

Sissa's family decided to come to Utah and started saving money in 1855. In 1862, Sissa sent two of her children, Anna and Anders with her sister, Anna, because they were young enough for reduced rates. On the ship Anders contacted measles and died. He was buried at sea.

The next year, in 1863, Ola borrowed enough money to bring the rest of the family to Utah. They left Liverpool on the ship "John J. Boyd" on April 30, 1863, landing in New York, then arriving in the Salt Lake Valley on August 29, 1863. They lived in Cottonwood for a year then moved to Peoa in the fall of 1864.

While on the ship, Sissa served as a mid-wife to help those who needed care. After arriving in Utah she found people were still in need of her assistance. She was a humble unassuming person who was sought out for the sick because of her gentle soothing ways.

In the Spring of 1865 Ola Jr. received a cow and calf for a years work. Sissa and Ola walked the cow and calf 120 miles to Sanpete County to pay off the man who lent them the money to come to Utah.

Sissa had one more child in Utah. During the time she lived in Peoa her husband was Branch President, on February 2, 1893, Sissa was sustained as first counselor in the Relief Society. After her children married they all settled in Peoa so she was able to enjoy her grandchildren.

When Ann her youngest son's wife died she moved in with him and took care of his three children. She continued to live with him until her death in 1910 at age eighty-nine.

ELIZABETH CHRISTIANA ASHMENT PEART

BIRTHDATE: 23 Sep 1849
Crewkerne, Somerset, England
DEATH: 26 Aug 1926
Richmond, Cache Co., Utah
PARENT Thomas Ashment
Ann Huggins
PIONEER: Unknown
SPOUSE: Benjamin Loss Peart
MARRIED: 9 Aug 1869
Salt Lake City, Salt Lake, Utah
DEATH SP: 16 Nov 1929
Richmond, Cache Co., Utah

CHILDREN:
Sylvia Ann, 16 Oct 1870
Merelda, 17 Dec 1872
Joseph, 16 Mar 1875
Leander, 21 Jun 1877
Rhoda, 24 Sep 1879
Maud, 21 Jul 1882
Ada May, 25 May 1887
Olive Melora, 7 Nov 1889

Elizabeth was born in England in 1859. She was the oldest of nine children. Elizabeth found work in the same cinch factory her father worked in. She attended night school to learn to read and write. She learned some good cooking skills while working at a bakery.

Although the family wanted to come to America finances were poor. Finally Elizabeth said "If I can't go now - I won't go." Her parents took her Liverpool and bought her passage on the ship "Colorado," then they left her before the ship sailed. The ship was delayed a day after it was scheduled to leave. A kind lady took Elizabeth home with her and a kind young man helped her aboard the next morning. She was seasick all the-way across the Atlantic. After opening the porthole by her bed, she couldn't close it. So her bed was wet all the way, but she was too sick to care.

When she crossed the Plains isn't known but she talked about the wagon she rode in.

On arrival into the Great Salt Lake Valley, the missionary who converted her family, helped her get a job in Brigham Young's dairy. She later worked in the home of Squire Wells. She was happy in both places.

Elizabeth married Benjamin Loss Peart on October 9, 1869 in Salt Lake City. Their first child Sylvia was born in 1869 in Salt Lake City.

Benjamin and Elizabeth started for Soda Springs when their baby was six month old, stopping in Richmond to visit Elizabeth's family that came in 1869. Circumstances led them to remain in this home for two years. Elizabeth's mother died in March, 1873.

Elizabeth did sewing to help provide for the family. Benjamin bought a saw mill and shingle mill in High Creek Canyon. Elizabeth cooked for the mill hands. Benjamin lost all his property and they moved to Cottonwood Valley. The snow was eight feet the first winter and they were snowed in without any supplies. Neighbors helped dig them out.

After her mother's death, Elizabeth took care of her mentally retarded sister, Mary, she outlived Elizabeth by four months.

Elizabeth was a wonderful mother, very resourceful and ambitious, a clean and tidy housekeeper and always a friend.

Elizabeth passed away on August 22, 1926 at the age of seventy-seven.

ELIZA JANE BAKER PEAY

BIRTHDATE: 18 May 1834
Poole, Dorchester, England
DEATH: 17 Aug 1915
Provo, Utah Co., Utah
PARENTS: Jeremiah T. Baker
Mary Ann Harden
PIONEER: 26 Sep 1853
Jacob Gates Co. Wagon Train
SPOUSE: Francis Peay
MARRIED: 5 Mar 1853
aboard the ship "Golconda"
DEATH SP: 5 May 1906

CHILDREN:
Prudence (Holdaway), 7 Mar 1854
Francis Alfred, 28 Dec 1856
Eliza Jane, 25 Jan 1858
Mary Louisa, 23 Feb 1860
Emily Ann (Loveless), 30 Jul 1862
William Baker, 8 Jan 1863
Walter Blake, 12 Jul 1867
Arthur Edwin, 9 Aug 1869
Rosetta Priscilla (Wride), 3 Nov 1871
Freddie, 3 Jan 1874
Lily Frances, (Scott), 12 Aug 1875
Parley Gilbert, 28 Dec 1877

Eliza Jane was born in England in 1834. She was the first of three children. After Eliza Jane's mother died, she worked as a nurse maid.

When Eliza was eighteen years old her father sent her to America. She sailed on the ship "Golcondo," on January 23, 1853. She became reaquainted with Francis Peay and they were married aboard ship, March 5, 1853.

They arrived at the mouth of the Mississippi River and had to wait twelve days for a tug to take them to New Orleans. They then boarded a steam packet "Illinois" to St Louis, Missouri, then went to Keokuk, Iowa.

They left for the Salt Lake Valley on June 3, 1853 and arrived on September 26th. They had to leave most of their possesions behind because the wagons were too small.

Eliza and Francis settled in Southwest Provo. Although they moved into the fort during the Indian trouble they went back to the farm as soon as possible.

Eliza Jane was the mother of twelve children; ten of whom lived to maturity.

Eliza dried fruit and kept fruit and vegetables in a large celler. She made dye from dogwood berries, medicines from herbs, berries, candies. She made lye from wood ash to use in making soap. She carded wool to make quilts, read to her family at meal times. Eliza churned butter, packed it in ten pound buckets and shipped it to Salt Lake twice a week. She delivered butter and eggs to regular customers in Provo.

Her husband passed away on May 5, 1906. Eliza was confined to her bed for several years before she passed away on August 7, 1915 in Vineyard, Utah at the age of eighty-one.

KAREN MARIE SORENSEN PEAY

BIRTHDATE: 1 Oct 1850
Mygdal, Denmark
DEATH: 23 Feb 1944
Hinckley, Millard Co., Utah
PARENTS: Soren C. Sorensen
Maren Hansen
PIONEER: 8 Nov 1865
Miner G. Atwood Wagon Train
SPOUSE: George Thomas Peay
MARRIED: 2 Mar 1867
Salt Lake City, Salt Lake, Utah
DEATH SP: 4 Jan 1922
Provo, Utah Co., Utah

CHILDREN:
Louise Alice, 15 May 1869
Joseph Charles, 28 Jan 1872 (died as an infant)
Harriet Ada, 5 Sep 1873
Lydia Hortense, 1 Jan 1877 (died at age 11)
Emma Electa, 9 Sep 1879
Etta Marie, 12 Jun 1882
Edward Lott, 18 Jul 1885

Karen Marie was born in Denmark in 1850. Her parents were Lutheran, but when the gospel reached them, they were all interested. Her father was in poor health and died before he could be baptized with his family as members of the Church of Jesus Christ of Latter-day Saints.

Marie's mother made preparations to come to Zion. They left Denmark in the Spring of 1865, when Marie was fourteen years old. There was much sickness on the ship, causing about fifty deaths. Her mother was very sick, and died just the day before land was sighted. She was buried at sea.

They landed in New York, and traveled in cattle cars to Wyoming, Nebraska. Marie was sick all the way, and even while they waited in Nebraska for their company to be outfitted to cross the Plains. Marie's hair all came out, but after she recovered it came back in curly and beautiful.

There were many problems on the trail; oxen stampeded, Indians tried to steal the cattle, Marie's hand was run over with a wagon, and food became scarce and had to be rationed. A relief party was sent from Utah. George Thomas Peay was one of those who came with the supply wagons. They finally arrived in Salt Lake City in Nov 1865, and the children, four of them, were sent to various homes to live.

Marie married George Thomas Peay as his third wife in 1867 in the Endowment House. They lived in Provo, Utah, and after her third child was born she moved to a farm west of Provo and lived with the second wife, Hannah. Here they raised their families together.

They had a very trying time when the Saints were being tried and prosecuted for polygamy. Her husband was sent to prison for a time.

Marie lived in Randolph, Utah for a time; also in Hinckley, Utah. On her ninety-second birthday her great-grandson took her for an airplane ride. She enjoyed it so much she wanted to go again.

Marie passed away in Hinckley, Millard County, Utah in 1944, at the age of ninety-three years.

MARY BLAKE PEAY

BIRTHDATE: (chr) 4 Mar 1798
DEATH: 15 Mar 1853
Provo, Utah Co., Utah
PARENTS: Francis Blake
Mary Wingate
PIONEER: Oct 1852
Jedediah Grant Co. Wagon Train
SPOUSE: Francis Peay
MARRIED: 13 May 1820
England
DEATH SP: 15 Apr 1843
Chichester, Sussex, England

CHILDREN:
James Alfred, 31 May 1821
Louise, Feb 1823
Francis, 23 Sep 1825
Edward, 22 May 1829
Frances, 15 Sep 1833
Jane Elizabeth, 1834
George Thomas, 1 Jan 1837
Emily, 24 Apr 1842 (died in 1847)

Mary Blake was born in England in 1798. At the age of twenty-two she married Francis Peay, a widower with two small children, who Mary reared as her own. She became the mother of eight other children. She had a beautiful voice and sang sweet lullabies to her babies as they came along.

Francis Peay died in 1843, leaving Mary a widow with a family to care for. She moved to Portsmouth, England, where her older boys found work on the docks. It was here that she learned of the gospel and was baptized in 1848.

In 1851, Mary with three of her children; Edward, age twenty-one, Frances, age eighteen, and George Thomas, age thirteen, sailed from Portsmouth on the ship "G. W. Bourne" for America. Her son Francis helped with their fare, then remained in England for two years to earn enough for the passage for his own family.

Mary and her children arrived in Provo, Utah in October, 1852. It had been an exhausting trip for Mary and she passed away five months later, on March 18, 1853.

The wife of her son, Francis, and two of his three children died of the Black Plague just two weeks before they set sail in 1853. He was passenger number 111.

It is interesting to note that Eliza Lane Baker, an eleven year old girl, was passenger number 112. She was destined to become Francis's wife. They were married aboard ship en route to America. Francis and his new wife arrived in Provo just seven days after his mother had passed away.

CHARLOTTE AMELIA VAN ORDEN WEST PECK

BIRTHDATE: 13 Jan 1828
Windham, Green Co., New York
DEATH: 8 Sep 1895
Provo, Utah Co., Utah
PARENTS: William Van Orden
Julia Ann Haight
PIONEER: 24 Sep 1848
Brigham Young Wagon Train
SPOUSE: Ira Enos West
MARRIED: 8 Jan 1846
Nauvoo Temple
(sealing canceled 2 Dec 1851)
DEATH SP:

CHILDREN:
Julia Ann, 2 Mar 1846 (died at 17 months)

SPOUSE II: Martin Horton Peck
MARRIED: 2 Dec 1851
Salt Lake City, Salt Lake Co., Utah
DEATH SP: 17 Jun 1884
Salt Lake City, Salt Lake Co., Utah

CHILDREN:
Arthur Van Orden, 14 Aug 1854
Everett Van Orden, 6 Apr 1857
Davis Horton, 2 Mar 1859
Dorr, 10 Feb 1861
Charlotte Amelia, 23 Jan 1864
Cyril Van Orden, 6 Feb 1866
Heber 20 Aug 1870, (died as an infant)

Charlotte Amelia was born in New York State in 1828, the eldest, of eight children. They were taught the gospel of the Church of Jesus Christ of Latter-day Saints from her Uncle Isaac Chauncey Haight, and were baptized in 1839 along with other family members.

They gathered with the Saints in Nauvoo in 1843, where her father died just two weeks after the martyrdom of the Prophet Joseph Smith.

In 1845, Charlotte married Ira Enos West, and was sealed to him on January 28, 1846 in Nauvoo Temple. One daughter was born of this union, but the little girl died at Winter Quarters in Iowa, and is buried there.

Charlotte and her husband crossed the Plains in 1848 with the Brigham Young Wagon Company. In March, 1849, Ira was tried for stealing and fined $100.00. Her sealing was canceled by Brigham Young, and the same day, December 2, 1854, she was sealed to Martin H. Peck as his fourth wife.

They lived in Provo, Utah where he operated a sugar cane mill. In 1862, they moved to Haytsville, Summit County, Utah, where he worked as a blacksmith. Later they moved back to Salt Lake City, Utah.

Martin passed away in Salt Lake City, Utah in l884 and is buried there. Charlotte lived with some of her children until her death in 1895 in Provo, Utah, at the age of sixty-seven years. She is buried in Salt Lake City, Utah, next to her husband.

SARAH REASOR PECTOL

BIRTHDATE: 8 Apr 1810
Shelby Co., Kentucky
DEATH: 7 Jan 1861
Manti, Sanpete Co., Utah
PARENTS: Frederick Reasor
Sarah Kester
PIONEER: 26 Aug 1850
Wagon Train Company
SPOUSE: George Pectol
MARRIED: 2 Nov 1828
DEATH SP. 28 Sep 1869
Washington, Washington, Utah

CHILDREN:
Dorothy, 8 Oct 1829
Elizabeth, 9 Apr 1831
Eliza Ann, 18 Nov 1832
Eunice, 22 Sep 1834
Mary Jane, 24 Mar 1836
Jemima Belle, 31 Mar 1839
George Peter, 25 Aug 1841
James, 25 Nov 1846
William, 7 Apr 1850

Sarah was the daughter of a Baptist minister who performed her marriage to George Pectol on November 2, 1828. For the first five years of their marriage Sarah and George lived in Indiana and then moved to Madison County, Missouri where George ran a store.

It was here that they received a Book of Mormon and became interested in Mormonism. In 1846, they traveled to Nauvoo, Illinois to learn more about the gospel, and were baptized in the Mississippi River on March 29, 1846.

They endured much persecution in Missouri and Illinois and moved with the Saints to Council Bluffs, Iowa where they remained until June 2, 1850, when they started for Utah. Sarah gave birth to her ninth child while they were crossing the Plains at Pottawattamie County, Iowa.

They arrived in the Salt Lake Valley on August 26, 1850. Four days after arriving in Utah they left with a few other families for Sanpete County, arriving there September 6, 1850. The first winter in Manti they lived in a dugout and were bothered with snakes in the spring. In May, 1851, they completed a comfortable home.

Sarah was an industrious and ambitions woman. She was a successful homemaker. Many of her descendants filled missions for the Church of Jesus Christ of Latter-day Saints.

Sarah passed away at Manti, Utah on January 1, 1861. After her death, George moved to Washington Utah and married a second wife, Mrs. Blazzard, with whom he lived until his death on September 28, 1869.

ANE KIRSTINE MATHIASEN PEDERSON

No Photo Available

BIRTHDATE: 5 Aug 1798
Trendl, Hjorring, Denmark
DEATH: 9 May 1886
Hyrum, Cache Co., Utah
PARENTS: Mathias Jorgensen
Mette Kirstine Poulsen
PIONEER: 15 Sep 1864
William B. Preston Wagon Train
SPOUSE: Soren Aarup Pederson
MARRIED: 23 May 1825
DEATH SP: Oct 1877
Hyrum, Cache Co., Utah

CHILDREN
Petrine, 10 Sep 1827
Martina Aarup, 15 Jun 1830
son, 22 Jun 1833
Peder, 20 Jun 1834
Hedvig, 1837
Hedvig Kirstine, 20 Sep 1838
Maren, 12-18 Oct 1842

Ane Kirstine was christened in Denmark in 1798. At the age of twenty-six she married Soren Pedersen (Aarup) and had seven children in Denmark, five girls and two boys. It would seem their third child-and first son may have died an infant, having never been christened and perhaps their fifth child Hedvig died an infant also, because the next to be born was given the same name.

The Mormon missionaries reached the area of Hjorrig, in Denmark, a place of special people, humble and honest in heart, accepting of the ideals of the Gospel of Jesus Christ so much so that the "spirit of gathering fell upon them." The urge to comply with which made no sacrifice seem too great and no hinderance great enough.

Mormonism was not looked upon kindly during those years in Denmark, and converts were usually submitted to what ever devilment of persecution that could be dreamed up by opposing neighbors and people of the community. Family members were often times the very worst in trying to dissuade the newly baptized.

Ane's family were ready for the message of the gospel and with courage determined to join the Saints in Zion. All preparation was made and in the summer of 1864, having collected together from many countries, 2,797 Saints left the shores of Liverpool, England on one of three ships under such crowded conditions that on the ship "Monarch of the Sea," forty-nine couples were married in a single ceremony to help solve the problem of sleeping spaces. New York was the docking area of all Saints and they proceeded to Wyoming, Nebraska to continue their journey.

Between late June and early August of that summer of 1864, nine companies of stalwart pioneers left Wyoming, Nebraska at weekly intervals to travel across the Plains. The William Preston Wagon Company, they departed July 8, with 400 Saints and reached the Salt Lake Valley sixty-nine days later.

Most of Ane's family were married and came to Utah. Her youngest child Maren, then twenty-one, came with them and stayed in Salt Lake City, Utah.

Soren and Ane settled in Cache Co. Thirteen years after arriving, Soren died. Ane lived ten and a half years with out her mate, passing away at the age of eighty seven, she was a comfort and helped her other daughter Martena and family as they came to their new land and religion.

DORTHEA ANDERSEN THOMSON NIELSEN PEDERSEN

BIRTHDATE: 20 Oct 1808
Vikert, Falkerslev, Denmark
DEATH: 13 Mar 1854
St. Louis, Missouri
PARENTS: Anders Larsen Buch
Karen Rasmussen Belling
PIONEER: 1854
SPOUSE I: Thomas Neilsen
MARRIED: 17 Nov 1826
DEATH SP: 17 May 1837

CHILDREN
Jens Thomson, 7 Oct 1827 (died at age 1)
Jens, 6 Nov 1829 (died at age 7)
Andrew, 4 Dec 1831
Niels, 31 May 1835 (died at 4 years

SPOUSE II: Peter Pedersen
MARRIED 20 Oct 1837
DEATH SP. Not given

CHILDREN:
Maren, 13 Jul 1838
Thomas, 2 Jan 1841
Karen, 24 Oct 1843
Neils, 23 Jan 1846
Jens, 22 Dec 1848

Dorthea Andersen Thomson was born in Denmark in 1808. She met Thomas Neilsen, a man ten years older than she who was from the same town and when she was eighteen years old, the two were married.

The couple named their first born Jens, the little soul lived one year, one month and one day. Their second son, traditionally was given the same name as the deceased little one, Jens. Two more boys were added to the family in Falkerslev, Andrew and later Niels who was born in the Spring of 1835. Dorthea seemed predestined for tragedy. The second Jens passed away at the age of seven in the year 1836, and the next year her husband died also.

Left with her two young boys to provide for, five months later, grateful for some promise of a future she married Peter Pederson. It would seem that just as things began to better themselves, tragedy struck again. Her last son from the deceased Thomas passed away.

Of her marriage lasting ten years and begetting four children, only one child, Andrew, remained, a symbol of great tribulation.

Dorthea and Peter were converted by missionaries from the Church of Jesus Christ of Latter-day Saints in 1852, when she was forty-four years old. Early the next year, January, 1853, the only survivor of her first marriage, her son, Andrew, now twenty-one, set sail from Liverpool on the ship "Forest Monarch," for America and then Utah. His mother and her family would join up with him in the Salt Lake Valley the next year. Neither mother nor son would know this was their final farewell.

True to the plan, Dorthea and Peter with their five children sailed for America early the next year landing in New Orleans after a four week ocean voyage. At St. Louis, Missouri, Dorthea, falling prey to the cholera that had killed so many immigrating converts, died, March 3, 1854

Peter and the children arrived in the Salt Lake Valley in October of 1854, with the Hans Peter Olsen Wagon Company. They settled at Ephraim, Sanpete County, together with Andrew and many other Scandinavian Saints.

While Dorthea did not live to see the Valley, she has been remembered and revered through the years for her faithfulness and sacrifice by her many descendants and is honored for the heritage she has given them.

ELSIE MARIE LARSEN PEDERSEN

BIRTHDATE: 28 Mar 1828
Astrup, Hjorring, Denmark
DEATH: 23 May 1917
Logan, Cache Co., Utah
PARENTS: Lars C. Jensen
Mette Christiansen
PIONEER: 10 Sep 1863
William B. Preston Wagon Train
SPOUSE: Christian Pedersen
MARRIED: not married
DEATH SP: 15 May 1901
Holladay, Salt Lake, Utah

CHILD:
Line Christiansen, 10 Nov 1849

SPOUSE II: Soren Christiansen
MARRIED: Not married
DEATH SP:
CHILD:
Twins, 19 Feb 1854 (stillborn)

SPOUSE III: Soren Christian Pedersen
MARRIED: 22 Oct 1861
DEATH SP: 1 Oct 1895
Logan, Cache Co., Utah

CHILDREN:
Cecilie Mathilde, 10 Jan 1862 (died as an infant)
Soren, 4 Jul 1866
Theodore, 21 Feb 1869
Josephine, 9 Aug 1871

Elsie Marie was born in Denmark in 1828. The legal papers containing the statistics of Elsie Marie's life show a courageous, fiercely independent, very young woman trying to earn a living for herself. Papers reflect a woman who gave trust to two men and was not the best judge of character. Her pride and independance came to her rescue.

At the age of nineteen, she moved to Linderumgaard Ugilt where she made her living as a domestic servant for two years until she returned to Moobjerg to have her daughter, Lise. (The father, Christain, had shown interest in another woman and Elsie had been so hurt she left him. Many years later, in Utah, the humiliation was so strong she refused to let Christian see the girl.) The little girl was left with her grandmother, Mette, for the young years of her life while Elsie Marie continued to work in others homes.

In 1851, she moved to Ugilt as a domestic servant to Soren Christiansen, four years later giving birth to stillborn twins, a boy and girl, continuing to live with Soren, the father of the children. Within the year she realized the unfulfilled direction her life had taken and moved again, searching for employment and security. She moved three times in three years.

The third move was to St. Olai to work for Soren Christian Pederson who owned considerable commercial property. Soren fell in love with Elsie, threatening suicide if she would not marry him but she was reluctant.

The missionary work in Hjorring, Denmark was eagerly accepted by souls ready for the Gospel's message and Elsie Marie was baptized on August 10, 1861. Two months later, with a softened heart she married forty year old Soren, she was thirty-three. In January of the following year, their daughter was born.

In 1863, the couple with their year old baby and Lise, sailed from Hamburg on May 8, on the "B. S. Kimball," with 654 converts coming to Utah.

They joined the Preston Company of oxen drawn wagons leaving Florence, Nebraska, July 6, and arrived in the Salt Lake Valley on September, 10th. Their baby Cecilie was ill all the way. They moved to Cache Valley. At their teamster, Soren Sornenson's urging, they were sheltered and fed at his mothers home.

At first their home was a wagon box loaned to them by Niels Mickelson, then a cabin, rented from Brother Lander. It had no windows, a dirt floor and a sod roof. Just after moving into the cabin the baby, Cecilie Mathilda, died.

By November they had built a house of their own, it was mostly a cellar covered with a sod roof with the added luxury of a wood floor and a window with a fireplace to cook in and for heat. They shared this one room until spring, with another family just newly arrived and who had no place to live.

Elsie had three children in Logan in her home on Fourth North just below Main Street, living through scarcity of food, fear of the Indians who they fed to keep from fighting, and twenty-two years of widowhood, passing away at the age of eighty-nine.

HARTMANDINE NIELSEMINE PETRONELLA HURUP NIELSEN PEDERSEN

No Photo Available

BIRTHDATE: 1 Jan 1810
Thorslunde, Denmark
DEATH: 8 Jun 1887
Fairview, Sanpete Co., Utah
PARENTS: George Hurup
Anna Johanne Hoeg
PIONEER: 8 Oct 1866
Andrew H. Scott's Wagon Train
SPOUSE I: Niels Nielsen
MARRIED: 25 Sep 1838
Reerslev, Copenhagen, Denmark
DEATH SP: 22 Feb 1858
Reerslev, Copenhagen, Denmark

CHILDREN:
Niels, 10 Mar 1839
Jorgen, 4 Jul 1841
Peder, 21 Dec 1845

SPOUSE II: Jens Pedersen
MARRIED: 3 Jan 1860
Reersiev, Copenhagen, Denmark
DEATH SP: Unknown
CHILDREN: None

Hartmandine was born in Denmark in 1810. She married Niels Nielsen in 1838 and they were the parents of three children. Their youngest son died when he was two years old. Her husband died in February, 1858.

She married Jen Pedersen in 1860. They had no children.

After her conversion to the Church of Jesus Christ of Latter-day Saints, she and her son Niels wanted to come to the Salt Lake Valley, They left Copenhagen, May 18, 1866, then sailed from Hamburg on the ship "Kenilworth," May 25, 1866, arriving in New York on July 16, 1866. Then to New Haven, Connecticut, Where they took a train to Wyoming , Nebraska. There they joined the Andrew H. Scotts Wagon Company, arriving in the Salt Lake Valley on October 8, 1866. She lived with her son Niels in Salt Lake City, Utah.

Then in 1870, when he married Christine Marie Christensen they moved to Fairview, Sanpete County, Utah. Here her son built her a small log house where she lived until her death on June 8, 1887 at the age of seventy-seven.

JENSINE KIRSTINE SORENSEN PEDERSEN

BIRTHDATE: 2 Jan 1834
Asdahl, Hjorring, Denmark
DEATH: 24 Jan 1911
Holladay, Salt Lake Co., Utah
PARENTS: Soren Kristoffersen
Karen Jensen Sorensen
PIONEER: 29 Sep 1866
Peter Nebeker Co. Wagon Train
SPOUSE: Christian Pedersen
MARRIED: 26 Jun 1857
Denmark
DEATH SP: 15 May 1901
Holladay, Salt Lake Co., Utah

CHILDREN:
Bine, 27 May 1857
Caroline, 3 Sep 1859
Peder, 27 May 1862
Ida,
Peter, 11 Jan 1868
Christian, 10 Mar 1870
David, 26 Dec 1871
Heber, 18 Dec 1872

Jensine was born in Denmark, the second child in a family of seven. Little is known of her childhood.

On June 26, 1857, Jensine married Christian Pedersen in Denmark. He was a farmer. Shortly after their marriage, they heard missionaries from the Church of Jesus Christ of Latter-day Saints preach the true Gospel and they were baptized on August 21, 1862.

There was to be a large emigration of Saints in the Spring of 1866. Christian and Jensine made arrangements to join this group.

Early in May 1866, the family left their home and went to Copenhagen where the Danish emigrants were gathering to leave for the United States. They sailed on the ship "Kenilworth," leaving Hamburg, Germany on May 25, 1866. They landed at Castle Garden, New York and then made the long journey to Wyoming, Nebraska which was the outfitting place for the Saints who crossed the Plains in the years 1864 to 1866. It had taken them ten weeks and three days to reach this destination.

After spending five days at Wyoming organizing their Company, they were ready to begin the journey across the Plains to Utah on August 2, 1866. They were assigned to Peter Nebeker's Wagon Company.

Jensine suffered great sorrow when her little four year-old, Peder, died on September 6th. They wrapped him in a piece of sheet and buried him in a shallow grave by the side of the road. Six days later, her daughter, Ida, died of Scarlet Fever. Soon Bine died of the dread disease. All three of their children are buried between Ft. Laramie and the three crossings of the Sweetwater River in Wyoming. Eight days later the wagon train reached the Salt Lake Valley, on September 29, 1866.

They were befriended by a man who was a native of Denmark. He took them to Big Cottonwood and found a place for them to live in a dug-out. In the Spring, Christian and Jensine took up a piece of ground, about forty acres was good farming ground. They planted a crop but the grasshoppers took it. They built an adobe, one-room house in the fall. They were very frugal and by hard work they bettered their living conditions from year to year.

Jensine and Christian became the parents of eight children; five died in childhood. Jensine's husband and two sons herded sheep on the mountain east of their home. She washed and carded the wool and spun it into yarn, then knit the socks and stockings and mittens for the family. She also carded the wool for their quilts. She had her own spinning wheel.

Her husband passed away on May 15, 1901. Jensine continued to live in their home and keep house for herself; all their children were married. She was a very independent nature. She continued to make butter and would deliver it and eggs to neighbors in her nice top-buggy.

In the Fall of 1910, Jensine's health was failing. On the morning of January 24, 1911, she called her family to her bedside and told them she would be leaving soon, and that she was ready and happy to go. She died of dropsy that afternoon. She was buried beside her husband in the Big Cottonwood Cemetery in Salt Lake, Utah.

JULIANE SORENSDATTER SMITH PEDERSEN

No Photo Available

BIRTHDATE: 3 Jan 1815
Norre Sunby Parish, Denmark
DEATH: 13 Apr 1873
Brigham City, Box Elder, Utah
PARENTS: Soren Pedersen
Maria Catherine A. Cushauge
PIONEER: 5 Oct 1854
Hans Peter Olsen Wagon Train
SPOUSE I: Rasmus Smith
MARRIED: Unknown
DEATH SP: 30 Jun 1860
Vor Frue Parish, Odense Ary,
Denmark

CHILD:
Rasmus Julius, 20 Aug 1843

SPOUSE II: Jorgan Christian Pedersen
MARRIED: 3 Jul 1855
Salt Lake City, Salt Lake Co., Utah
DEATH SP: 25 Oct 1910
Snowville, Box Elder Co., Utah
CHILDREN:

Juliane was born in Denmark in 1815. She married Rasmus (Schmidt) Smith in Denmark. Little is known of this marriage except she had a son, Rasmus, born on August 20, 1843.

She saved her money and gave all that she had to bring herself and her son to America. They left Kansas City, June 15, 1854, in the Hans Peter Olsen Wagon Company for the Salt Lake Valley arriving on October 5, 1854.

Juliane married Jorgan Christian Pedersen, July 3, 1855, in Salt Lake City as his second wife. His first wife had died leaving him three children to raise. He also married Nicoline Olsen in 1858 and Sena Hansen as his fourth wife, but it isn't known when this marriage took place. They lived in Brigham City and Mantua.

They were in Brigham City when Julliane passed away on April 13, 1873 at the age of fifty-eight.

MAREN PEDERSEN

No Photo Available

BIRTHDATE: 16 Jan 1819
Snedsted, Thstd, Denmark
DEATH: 22 Mar 1897
Harrisville, Weber Utah
PARENTS: Peder Nielsen
Dorthe Pedersen Nielsen Larsen
PIONEER: 1863
SPOUSE: Berthel Christensen
MARRIED: Not married
DEATH SP:

CHILD:
Mariane Berthelsen, 20 Jul 1841

Maren was born in Denmark in 1819. Her daughter, Mariane was born on July 20, 1841.

When Maren was forty-four years old, she and her twenty-two year old daughter, Mariane, boarded the ship "B. S. Kimball" for America. Her daughter, Mariane, married P. C. Stephenson on board ship. They landed in New York then on to Salt Lake Valley arriving in the Fall of 1863.

Maren's daughter had twelve children and her husband had three other wives, so she lived with her to help take care of her large family. Maren's son-in-law had her sealed to him in 1867.

Maren was an industrious, courageous, and independent person. She passed away in Harrisville, Weber County, Utah on March 22, 1897 at age seventy-eight.

ELIZABETH LETITIA HIGGINBOTHAM PEERY

BIRTHDATE: 13 Jan 1846
Nauvoo, Hancock Co., Illinois
DEATH: 13 Dec 1938
Ogden, Weber Co., Utah
PARENTS: W. E. Higginbotham
Louisa Ward
PIONEER: 1 Sep 1864
Independent Co. Wagon Train
SPOUSE: David Harold Peery
MARRIED: 10 Apr 1865
Holiday, Salt Lake Co., Utah
DEATH SP: 17 Sep 1901
Ogden, Weber Co., Utah

CHILDREN:
David Henry, 13 Apr 1866
Joseph Stras, 10 May 1868
Nancy May, 5 Feb 1871 (died at age 3)
Horace Eldridge, 14 Nov 1873
Eleanor Virginia, 27 Apr 1876 (died at 9 months)
John Harold, 19 Feb 1878
Margaret Louise, 20 Feb 1881
Simon Francis, 18 Aug 1884
Louis Hyrum, 14 Nov 1887
Harman Ward, 23 Aug 1891

Letitia was born in Nauvoo, Hancock County, Illinois in 1846 to William Elliot Higginbotham and Louisa Ward. She was only two months old when her family had to leave their comfortable home in Nauvoo to flee across the Mississippi River and experience a long and extremely difficult trip across Iowa to Council Bluffs.

When they heard of the death of Louisa's father, they returned to Burke's Garden, Virginia hoping to claim an inheritance. The claim failed to materialize and they remained there to raise funds for the long trek westward.

The outbreak of the Civil War and an epidemic of typhoid fever plagued Southwestern Virginia. Her father, her sister, and two of her sister's children died of the disease.

Letitia was eighteen when her mother took her family with the James Harman family to cross the mountains between Virginia and Kentucky. Some renegades harassed them and pushed their wagons into the river. Her brother and Mr. Hannan obtained two flatboats and several armed men, retrieved the wagons from the river, and they were on their way again.

They met her widowed brother-in-law, David Harold Peery, and his daughter, Lettie, in Cattlesburg as planned. They took a steamboat to Omaha, Nebraska and on July 3, 1862 they began the western portion of their travels.

They joined an independent party of wagons that lacked organization and fellowship. Three times, they were attacked by Indians. At Fort Kearney, they were joined by a company of Missourians headed for the gold fields of California. Affairs were chaotic and they finally chose a captain, William Pritchett.

After many trials, they arrived in Salt Lake City on September 1, 1864. The Roby family who had settled in Heber Valley took them in and helped them build a small log cabin. When spring arrived, they joined David in Cottonwood where he had spent the winter teaching school.

On April 10, 1865, David and Letitia were married. He purchased a farm in Cottonwood and after a year of farming, they moved to Ogden where David became one of the most influential leaders in the community.

Letitia became an accomplished wife, mother, grandmother, and a leading hostess to a steady stream of guests of senators, judges, church leaders, and prominent merchants. Occasionally, whole families of pioneer immigrants were housed and cared for until they became located and found employment.

Elizabeth Letitia Peery was a remarkable woman who tried always to help others. She was known to say, "Every day, I try to help someone in need, or to make someone happier."

After her husband died, she was still an independent, enterprising woman. Her keen intellect remained with her to the end. She died just one month short of her ninety-third birthday.

ANNA SOPHIA ERIKSDOTTER JONSSON PEHRSON

BIRTHDATE: 3 Jul 1835
Mullersatter, Kvistbro, Sweden
DEATH: 10 Jan 1907
Vernon, Tooele Co., Utah
PARENTS: Erik Jonsson
Stina Lisa Pehrsdotter
PIONEER: 1861
Company unknown
SPOUSE. Eric Johan Pehrson
MARRIED: 16 May 1861
DEATH SP: 19 Oct 1916

CHILDREN:
Matilda (Bennion), 21 Jan 1862
Sophia, 29 Feb 1864 (died as an infant)
Heber, 8 Apr 1865
Emil, 3 Sep 1867
Elizabeth, 28 Apr 1873
Charlotte (Fawson), 4 Nov 1875

Anna Sophia was born in Mullersatter, Kvistbro, Orebro, Sweden in 1835 to Erik and Stina Jonsson. In 1861, Anna Sophia left Sweden betrothed to Erik Johan Pehrson. They were married aboard the ship en route to America and Zion.

Faced with the rigors of pioneer life in a new land, she developed the skills necessary to be self-sufficient using raw materials at hand. She and her husband's hearts, minds, and strength were dedicated to the Lord and to helping build up Zion in America.

Arriving in Utah in 1861, they settled in Vernon, Tooele County, Utah. She was eager and willing to learn, she worked diligently learning to read English well. They sent their children to Salt Lake to obtain all the education possible.

Anna polished her domestic skills of sewing, cooking, canning, weaving, gardening and working in the field beside her husband to help support her family. Anna had six children; four daughters and two sons. She fulfilled well her role as a true companion to her husband and a mother and teacher to her children.

When her husband served a mission to Sweden, she managed the farm with her three young children and the help of others. Sometimes she walked thirty-five miles to Tooele to mail letters to him.

She served her ancestors by doing their temple work in the Manti Temple. She always reached out her hand to those in need, and she was serving as Relief Society President in Vernon at the time of her death. She was a great pioneer woman of faith and fortitude-an example to her posterity who have followed her.

Her nearly seventy-two years of life were exemplary to all. Anna Sophia Pehrson passed away on January 10, 1907 in Vernon, Tooele County, Utah.

CHRISTINA KNUTTSON BECKSTRAND PEARSON PEHRSSON

BIRTHDATE: 24 Dec 1825
Granstarp, Jonkopings, Sweden
DEATH: 16 Oct 1916
Huntington, Emery Co., Utah
PARENTS: Knut J. Beckstrand
Ingierd Jacobson
PIONEER: 29 Aug 1863
John R. Murdock Wagon Train
SPOUSE: Pehr S. Pehrsson
MARRIED: 26 Dec 1859
DEATH SP: 9 May 1902

CHILDREN:
Anna Maria, 5 Apr 1860 (died at age 12)
John Peter, 16 Jan 1865
Josephine Christina, 5 Sep 1867 (died at age 1)
Albertina, 23 Sep 1869 (died age 4)
Elvina Hancine Olsen, 15 May 1868 (adopted in 1874)

In her youth, Christina went through many trials and hardships which included a famine. She remembers grinding the bark from trees and straw from the fields in order to make bread.

She lost both parents at an early age and was bound out to work for rich people as a servant. The heavy loads she had to carry caused her to become humped and stooped. As servants at the end of each year, they were asked to sign yearly contracts. They were either free to go or sign on for another year.

Christina met and fell in love with Pehr Swenson Pehrsson who was also working as a servant in the same home. They set their wedding date, but were told by their employer that poor people should never be allowed to marry. Christina told them if the poor people should not be allowed to marry, it would not be long before they would have no one to work for them. At marriage, their contract was broken and they were free to seek a home of their own.

They learned of the gospel of Jesus Christ of Latter-day Saints and were baptized June 9, 1861 by Niels Larsen. On April 14, 1863, they left Sweden bringing with them their little daughter. They boarded the steamer, "John J. Boyd," upon which they were six weeks crossing the ocean.

They left Florence, Nebraska to cross the Plains in the John R. Murdock Wagon Company which arrived in Salt Lake City August 29, 1863. Brigham Young soon sent them to settle in Deseret, Millard County.

They moved to Oak City which is about thirty miles away, where Albertina was born and Anna Maria, who was then twelve, was stricken with fever and died. She was the first to be buried in Oak City. When Albertina was four years old, she was playing on a hay rack, lost her footing, slipped, broke her neck, and died. Later that year, the family adopted a five year old Danish girl, Elvina Hancine Olsen, who had been born in Nabro, Albury, Denmark. They loved her as their own.

In 1874, Brigham Young gave instructions for them to settle in Orderville to live the United Order. Christina had learned the trade of weaving and spinning to help make a living. She washed, carded, spun and dyed the wool. Then she made socks, mittens, and sweaters. She also used wool in making quilts, dresses, sheets and blankets. She dyed the yarns with roots and plants gathered from the fields. She successfully spun flax and it was woven into linen for table-cloths, sheets, towels, and clothes. She was so proficient at her trade, that she was in demand to make clothing for others, even wedding dresses.

Christina and her husband did a lot of temple work in St. George and Manti. John was ordained an Elder at the age of fourteen, on April 25, 1879 in the St. George Temple so he could help his parents with the many proxy names they had to do. Elvina was sealed to Christina and Pehr Pehrson that same day.

They left Orderville through an assignment by Brigham Young to go to Castle Valley in September 4, 1882. They settled in Huntington, Emery County. She and Elvina became well known for their spinning and weaving skills.

Her husband passed away in Huntington on May 9, 1902. On October 16, 1915, Christina at the age of eighty-nine, also died in Huntington, Utah.

SISSA NILSSON PEHRSSON SORENSEN PEHRSSON

BIRTHDATE: 15 Nov 1830
Getinge, Gardstanga, Sweden
DEATH: 26 Oct 1918
Millville, Cache Co., Utah
PARENTS: Nils Olsson
Hanna Akesson
PIONEER: 29 Sep 1866
Peter Nebeker Co. Wagon Train
SPOUSE I: Ola Pehrsson
MARRIED: 10 Feb 1856
Sweden
DEATH SP: Not given

CHILDREN:
James, 26 May 1856
Nils, 12 Dec 1858
Ola, 19 Jul 1861

SPOUSE II: Nils Niels Sorensen
MARRIED: 21 Dec 1868
Salt Lake City, Salt Lake Co., Utah
DEATH SP: 17 Apr 1906
Bloomington, Utah

CHILDREN:
Josephine (Winberg), 8 Jan 1870

SPOUSE III: James Pehrsson
MARRIED: 1876
DEATH SP: 17 Sep 1920
Millville, Cache Co., Utah
CHILDREN: None

Sissa was born in 1830 in Getinge, Gardstanga, Malmohus, Sweden. When her father was fifty-one years old and her mother thirty-nine. She was the eighth of nine children born in her family. Five years later a brother was born into the family

One year after that Sissa's mother died leaving her father the responsibility of raising the infant son, plus others still at home. He never remarried, and the older sisters filled in as substitute mothers. Life was a little easier for this family because Sissa's father had received an inheritance from his wife's family.

Sissa's father died in 1848, leaving her on her own at the age of seventeen years. She used the skills she had learned on her father's farm to get jobs.

At one of these farms, she met her first husband Ola Pehrsson and they were married on Febraury 10, 1856 in the Lutheran Church in Sweden. Three sons were born to them.

In 1861, Sissa's oldest sister joined the Church of Jesus Christ of Latter-day Saints. Sissa and Elsa joined on February 24, 1864. Plans were made for the extended family to all go to Utah to be with other Saints.

Sissa borrowed money from the Perpetual Emigration Fund for herself and her three sons to emigrate to Utah. Her husband was to join her later in America. On May 28, 1866, nine members of their extended family with one servant and Sissa and her three sons, all left Copenhagen, Denmark, traveled to Hamburg, Germany because the English ports were closed because of a smallpox outbreak.

They then left Germany on the "Humboldt" for the United States, along with about 400 other emigrants. The captain of the ship said that he had never witnessed such a good and orderly company of Saints. It took forty-six days. There was a happy event on board when Sissa's niece was married. They arrived in New York on July 18, 1866.

From New York, they traveled by rail to Canada some-times in cattle cars. Then they went to Michigan, and then finally by rail to Quincy, Illinois. They then went by steamer across the river and to St. Joseph, then by steam-boat to Wyoming, Nebraska on August 1, 1866. This was the last year that emigrant trains traveled from the Missouri River to Utah by ox-teams.

After a few days rest, Sissa and her group joined the Peter Nebeker Wagon Company with about 400 British and Scandinavian emigrants in sixty-two wagons, each with two yoke of oxen, and each wagon loaded with merchandise and provisions and luggage. All able to walk did so. Sissa's two youngest sons rode in one of the wagons. Her ten year old son hung tightly to a horse's tail as they crossed the swift currents of the rivers. They traveled an average of ten miles per day. They arrived in the Salt Lake Valley on September 29, 1866. Sissa's family went to Millville, Utah almost immediately.

Because Sissa didn't have means of supporting herself, her family split up. Her oldest son, James spent the winter sleeping in haystacks. Two years later, Sissa's sisters and their families joined the family in Millville in the fall of 1868.

They brought word that Ola Pehrsson, Sissa's husband, had left the Mormon Church, and probably wasn't coming to Utah. Sissa entered into a polygamist marriage to Nils Sorensen two months later, December 21, 1868. Nils had emigrated from Denmark two years earlier with first wife, and two children.

Life for these two families and the very harsh winters made it difficult for all. Several years later, Sissa asked to be released from this marriage. The family then returned to Millville from the Bear Lake Valley where they had lived.

Two years later, Sissa married a third time in 1876 to James Pehrsson, a fellow Swede. She acquired a new step-daughter when James' only living daughter came from Sweden with James Pehrsson's father.

James and Sissa and their children made their home in Millville. In 1891, Sissa's daughter, Josephine, married John Winberg on April 16, in the Logan Temple and they made their home in Millville also, just one block from her mother. James and Sissa spent forty-two years of their lives together before death separated them.

Sissa always loved to attend Church and loved the Gospel of Jesus Christ. She was active in the Relief Society and enjoyed her association with her fellow sisters. She never learned to speak English very well, but her children spoke it fluently.

Sissa Pehrsson passed away on October 26, 1918 at the age of almost eighty-eight years, and was buried in the Millville Cemetery. Her husband survived her by almost two years, and at the age of nearly eighty years, died and was buried beside Sissa in the Millville Cemetery.

Josephine had spent much of her life looking after her mother and stepfather. Sissa was an exemplary pioneer woman of faith and fortitude, one to be honored by those who have followed after her.

NANCY RICHARDS PEIRSON

BIRTHDATE: 22 Nov 1792
Hopkinton, Massachusetts
DEATH: 14 / 15 Jul 1852
near Platte River
PARENTS: Joseph Richards
Rhoda Howe
PIONEER: 1852
died crossing the Plains
SPOUSE: William Peirson
MARRIED: 4 Mar 1819
Massachusetts
DEATH SP: 17 Apr 1862

CHILDREN:
Edwin Dwight, 10 Dec 1819
Eliza Ann (Richards), 14 Apr 1822
Amelia Elizabeth (Richards), 16 Apr 1825
Levi, 29 Mar 1827
Albert Howe, 8 Jan 1829 (died at age 10)
Susan Sanford (Richards), 13 Dec 1831

Nancy was born on November 22, 1792, the sixth child, in the town of Hopkinton, Middlesex County, Massachusetts. Her family was deeply religious, and it was only natural that they embrace the restored Gospel when her first cousin, Brigham Young, brought it to their home.

Her family was a picture of loving and kindly parents, brothers and sisters. It was a home of much sickness at times, of some strain and stress of life, but a feeling of love and goodness for one another and for neighbors, friends, and associates.

Nancy married William Peirson on March 4, 1819. Her husband never accepted the Gospel. He was a "selectman" of Richmond, Massachusetts. He was active in civic and religious denominations. Nancy was obliged to be the hostess of the minister of the parish her husband attended.

There was contention in their home, and it was a "thorn in her side" that her husband and sons rejected the Gospel. Six children were born into this home. Her son Edwin Dwight and the girls joined the Church of Jesus Christ of Latter-day Saints. Edwin later "grew cold to its teachings." Nancy grew in faith and knowledge of the Gospel, was a good wife and mother. She knew the value of work, thrift and courage. She contracted cancer, making it hard to do physical work keeping up her home and prudently taking care of the produce from their large farm.

Nancy had bad headaches, and had a tumor removed from her side. She took medicine for the cancer, given her by doctors and especially from "Uncle Willard Richards." She also received priesthood blessings.

Nancy's two daughters, Amelia and Eliza, left on April 19, 1840 to go West with the Saints which made Nancy happy they could go, but missing them terribly. En route, Eliza passed away on October 12, 1846.

In the Spring of 1852, Nancy and Susan Sanford left their affluent home and belongings, and traveled with a cousin, Franklin D. Richards, who was returning to Zion from a European Mission. She so desired to accomplish the journey to Zion, but her strength failed. She made it as far as the Platte River, probably in Wyoming or Nebraska, but passed away in July, 1852, and was buried near the "Liberty Pole."

Nancy's husband never joined the Church. After her death, he remarried. He passed away on April 17, 1862.

ALICE JEFFERY PENDLETON

BIRTHDATE: 15 Jan 1834
Watford, Northampton, England
DEATH: 21 Jul 1914
St. George, Washington, Utah
PARENTS: William Jeffery
Mary Crock
PIONEER: 1860/1861
Company unknown
SPOUSE: Benjamin F. Pendleton
MARRIED: 26 Oct 1861
Salt Lake City, Salt Lake, Utah
DEATH SP: 17 Nov 1881
St. George, Washington, Utah

CHILDREN:
Alice Jeffery 11 May 1863 (died as an infant)
Violet Jeffery (Church), 25Jan 1865
Gertrude Jeffery (Ipson), 4 Sep 1866
Benjamin Franklin, Jr., 30 Sep 1868
Mannette Jeffery, 6 Apr 1871
Minnie Jeffery (Church), 29 Jan 1873
WilfordWoodruff, 27 Nov 1876

Alice was born in 1834 in England. She was converted to the Church of Jesus Christ of Latter-day Saints and crossed the ocean on May 11, 1860 on the ship "William Tappscott," in company with her sister, Jane, her brother, Thomas, his wife, and their adopted daughter, Sarah Ann. She crossed the Plains in 1860 or 1861 with Jane.

Alice married Benjamin Franklin Pendleton in Salt Lake City on October 26, 1861. She had worked in his household, and within a few days left for a mission to St. George. Alice endured the hardships of settling in a country with heat, disease, crude shelters at first, Indian troubles and short supplies. She aided her husband in his horticultural work and sustained his business and community enterprises.

She was the second wife of Benjamin Franklin Pendleton, and the "Dixie wife" as Lavina Patten Pendleton chose to remain with the first family in Salt Lake City.

Alice was a fine seamstress and is listed, along with her brother and sisters, as a shoemaker in the 1850 English census, although there is no record that she practiced this trade in Utah. Alice worked in the St. George Temple in her later years.

She passed away in St. George on July 21, 1914 at the age of eighty years. Her husband had died in 1881, leaving Alice a widow for over thirty-two years. Their youngest child was just five years of age when his father died. At the time of his death, her children ranged in ages from five years to seventeen years which left a great burdon for Alice. She succeeded in raising her family to be faithful adults.

Alice loved the gospel of Jesus Christ, lived its principles, and loved the Lord. She taught her children to do the same-a great legacy.

ELIZABETH THACKER PENFOLD

BIRTHDATE: 24 May 1852
Willenhall, England
DEATH: 1 Mar 1912
Driggs, Teton Co., Idaho
PARENTS: William Thacker
Rachel Tonks
PIONEER: 13 Sep 1861
Joseph Horne Co. Wagon Train
SPOUSE: John Penfold
MARRIED: 1 Jan 1868
Peoa, Summit Co., Utah
DEATH SP: 23 Dec 1901

CHILDREN:
Elizabeth, 8 Jan 1868 (died as an infant)
John T., 16 May 1870
Algeroy, 19 Sep 1872
Farley, 19 Sep 1874
Emily Isabella (Belle), 16 Jan 1878
William Fredrick, 26 Mar 1880 (died at age 16)
Hannah, 16 Jan 1883
Horace, 12 Nov 1886 (died at age 15)
Mary Aurtense, 10 Jun 1889
Virgil, 8 Feb 1892

Elizabeth's family joined the Church of Jesus Christ of Latter-day Saints and came to America on July 6, 1856. The family moved on to Philadelphia, Pennsylvania to get work and remained there until Elizabeth was eleven years old. During this time, she attended school, got a good foundation of learning, and was taught singing.

In 1861, her family left Florence, Nebraska in the Joseph Horne Wagon Company. She recalled in later life the wonderful days on the Plains. They saw buffalo, antelope, deer, and many other animals that were new to them. After their arrival into the Salt Lake Valley, they settled in Salt Lake City for a time.

Elizabeth and her sister crossed City Creek Canyon to take lunch to their father who worked in Brigham Young's blacksmith shop making square nails for 'The Old Playhouse." She also attended the Brigham Young School which was on Canyon Road.

She married John Penfold when she was sixteen years old in Peoa where her parents were then residing. They started their married life on a big hay ranch owned by Barzee.

Her husband had a strong desire to go to Arizona, so they prepared their family to make a three month journey with oxen and wagon. The family went from place to place wherever there was work for the father and boys. Then they moved back to Utah, to Montana, to Idaho Falls, Idaho, then to Heber City, Utah where John bought a ten acre farm and built a four-room house for the family.

Elizabeth had lived in dugouts, tents, and a log cabin until this time. She had tried to nurse her sick family through bad colds and pneumonia using a quilt for a door in the log cabin and a flour sack on the window opening.

Elizabeth and her family loved singing together. Elizabeth loved reading and was a good reader. Many evenings she read aloud and went on with her knitting while the children kept the book in position and turned the pages for her. She made the best bread, corn meal mush, rice pudding, and sour cream cake. She was honest, frugal, industrious, and patient all her life. She loved good books, travel, people, and music.

ELLEN ELIZA DURFEE PENROD

BIRTHDATE: 18 Mar 1848
New Canton, Pike Co., Ohio
DEATH: 6 May 1925
Wallsburg, Wasatch Co., Utah
PARENTS: Thomas J. Durfee
Charlotte Amelia Sanford
PIONEER: 1861 Wagon Train
SPOUSE: Abraham Penrod
MARRIED: 5 Jun 1870
DEATH SP: 26 Dec 1893
Wallsburg, Wasatch Co., Utah

CHILDREN:
David Abraham, 9 Apr 1871
Elmer Leander, 26 Oct 1872
Delosse Wells, 10 Aug 1874
Ada Ellen (Gardner), 5 Aug 1876
Eva Elmina (Sabin), 12 Jun 1878
Minerva Ora, 13 Aug 1880 (died as an infant)

Ellen Eliza was born in 1848 in Ohio. She was raised in a loving home by caring parents. She attended school in her childhood and loved to read and she instilled this love in her own children. Her family joined the Church of Jesus Christ of Latter-day Saints and came to Utah by wagon train in 1861, when Ellen was thirteen years old. She walked most of the way. Their wagons were full of their precious belongings and necessities. Her mother had her and her sisters wear sunbonnets all the way so they would not be sunburned when they reached the Salt Lake Valley.

They surprised their cousins in Provo being brown as the sun could make them as they met them. It was a humorous sight.

One day during their trip to the West, Ellen was helping a three year old sister out of the wagon when she slipped and they both fell under the wagon wheel. Little Lola suffered a broken leg and the wheel ran over Ellen's chest. It broke something and she suffered all her life with it and had a large hump on her back in her older years.

Ellen worked in a boarding house near Lehi after she came to Utah. She met President Brigham Young many times. He liked bread and milk for supper in spite of the lavish meals Mrs. Green prepared just for him and his company.

Ellen met and was courted by Abraham Penrod and they were married on June 5, 1870. They lived in Provo for awhile and then moved to a homestead in Wallsburg where they lived the rest of their lives. Ellen worked hard to supply the needs of her family, spinning cloth, baking bread. She drew all the water she needed out of a good well near the corner of her home. She taught her children to read and write and to love to read. Her home was a haven for her children and their friends, and there was always a crowd there. There were picnics along the streams while the men fished and hunted for meat; games and activities kept active children happy. She held a family prayer circle every evening and they were taught to pray and to walk uprightly before the Lord. She raised a lovely flower and vegetable garden and had a nice orchard in her yard. She raised chickens for the meat as well as the eggs. They had a cow and they lived well and never went hungry. This in itself is a tribute to her industry and resourcefulness.

Ellen's hands were never idle, she knitted their stockings, mittens, wristbands to keep her children clothed and warm. She stayed up late at night to do these tasks while her children slept. She was a wonderful cook and taught her daughters to be good cooks, as well. She preserved and stored fruit, vegetables, meat, molasses, lard, soap which she made herself, all the items needed for the winter months.

After her husband's untimely death in 1893, her children rallied around her. Her grandchildren took turns staying at night and loved doing it. She was terrified of thunder and lightning and took them into a small room and covered them with a quilt during a storm.

Ellen passed away on May 6, 1925, thirty-one years after her husband. Both are buried in the Wallsburg Cemetery.

Ellen Eliza was dearly loved by her husband, children and grandchildren. She was gentle, loving, and kind, was an honest pioneer deserving of the richest of rewards. She left a great legacy for those who have followed.

TEMPERANCE KELLER PENROD

BIRTHDATE: 18 Nov 1817
Rowan Co., North Carolina
DEATH: 15 Nov 1893
Provo, Utah Co., Utah
PARENTS: Abraham Keller
Sarah "Sally" Hinkle
PIONEER: 1850 Wagon Train
SPOUSE: David Penrod
MARRIED: 14 Oct 1831
Jonesboro, Union Co., Illinois
DEATH SP: 26 Feb 1872
Provo, Utah Co., Utah

CHILDREN:
William Lewis, 27 Jul 1832
Solomon, 17 Mar 1834 (died at age 15)
Elizabeth (Wall), 9 Sep 1836
Israel, 13 Mar 1838
Sarah Evelyn, 15Apr 1840 (died as an infant)
Christina (Smith), 6 Mar 1842
Abraham, 12 Jul 1844
Polly Elmira, 23 May 1847 (died as an infant)
David Nephi, 24 Oct 1850
Temperance (Evans), 19 Sep 1852
Minerva Olive (Meldrum), 24Feb 1854
Ephraim, 11 Jun 1857 (died at age 8)
Amasa Lyman, 12 Nov 1858

Temperance was born in 1817 in North Carolina. Her family joined in the westward movement of settlers, first to Tennessee and later to southern Illinois.

She married David Penrod on October 14, 1831 at Jonesboro, Union County, Illinois, and several of their children were born there. They became acquainted with the missionaries and Temperance and her husband were baptized.

Because of the persecutions and mob violence, many Saints prepared to move westward and the Kellers were among them. They were asked to remain at the Missouri River for awhile so her husband could help repair the Saints' wagons. They left in 1850, under the direction of church officials but not in the ten major companies. They suffered many trials and hardships on the Plains. Their son, Solomon died, and they buried him in a grave along the trail. Temperance contracted cholera, and it was feared she would die.

After arriving in the Salt Lake Valley, they lived in Salt Lake City about a year before moving to the Old Fort in Provo, Utah. They later moved into an adobe house on Center Street.

Temperance was a good mother to her thirteen children; two died as infants, one died at age eight, and another at age fifteen.

She made clothing, stockings, shawls, from the wool from her husband's sheep, even doing the spinning and weaving. She took food and medicine to care for the sick.

She was always generous and willing to share with those less fortunate,and no one was ever turned away from her door.

Temperance and her husband David lived in Provo the remainder of their lives. He passed away in 1872 and Temperance was a widow for over twenty-one years. She remained a faithful pioneer woman and was a great example for her progenators who have followed her. She passed away in Provo on November 15, 1893 at age seventy-six.

LUCETTA STRATFORD PENROSE

BIRTHDATE: 15 Sep 1834
Malden, Essex, England
DEATH: 19 Jan 1903
Salt Lake City, Salt Lake, Utah
PARENTS: George Stratford
Eliza Barwell
PIONEER: 1861 Wagon Train
SPOUSE: Charles W. Penrose
MARRIED: 21 Jan 1855
Maldon, Essex, England
DEATH SP: 16 May 1925
Salt Lake City, Salt Lake, Utah

CHILDREN:
Charles Kimball, 2 May 1856
Ernest Stratford, 10 Dec 1857
Jessie Lucetta (Jones), 10 Dec 1858
Kate (Brown), 1 Mar 1860
Bertha, 12 Sep 1861 (died as an infant)
Alice Cecelia (Crawford), 21 Nov 1862
Clara Matilda, 2 Feb 1864 (twin - died as an infant)
Cora Eliza, 2 Feb 1864 (twin - died as an infant)
Lucetta, 31 Dec 1865 (died as an infant)
Emma Louise (infant), 21 Sep 1869
Lettie, 30 Jun 1870 (died as an infant)
George William, 14 Oct 1871
Ella Maude, 6 Nov 1872 (died as an infant)
Frederick Edgar, 19 Nov 1873 (died as an infant)
Lou Bell, 1874 (died as an infant)
Edwin Centennius, 4 Jul 1876
Wallace Harold, 19 Jul 1877 (died as an infant)
Lucile (Brown), 21 Jan 1880

Lucetta was born in England in 1834. At just over twenty-one years of age she married Charles William Penrose on January 21, 1855 in England.

At an early age, Lucetta, showed marked talent for designing clothes and bonnets which she would fit on her thumbs and fingers if she did not have a doll. In later years she became an expert in dressmaking and millinery.

She was determined and conscientious, the last to join the Church of Jesus Christ of Latter-day Saints in her family; she wanted to be sure before joining. Her whole family was converted and baptized by Charles W. Penrose, her future husband. Charles later became a member of the First Presidency of the Church with Joseph F. Smith and Heber J. Grant.

In 1861, Lucetta came to America on the ship "Underwriter," with about 624 people on the ship. With a group leaving Florence, Nebraska with the Captain Homer Duncan Wagon Company, they traveled to Utah taking eleven weeks to do so. They arrived in the Salt Lake Valley on September 13, 1861, after experiencing the trials and tribulations of that travel.

In 1864, this family was called to move to Cache Valley where Charles and Lucetta both taught school. When they moved to Logan across from the Logan Tabernacle, she secured the first wallpaper in the town and papered her front room herself. She also opened a millinery business. Her children gathered straw which she wove into hats.

Lucetta was the mother of eighteen children, with only seven growing to adulthood. She was always a loving mother, loyal wife and helpful neighbor. She was faithful and active in the Church and was supportive of her husband in his church callings.

Lucetta passed away on January 19, 1903 in Salt Lake City. Her husband survived until May 16, 1925. They were great pioneers who contributed much to the development of the West, particularly Cache Valley and Salt Lake City. She experienced much in her over seventy-eight years of life, a faithful, devoted member of the Church of Jesus Christ of Latter-day Saints.

MARY ANN GIBSON THURMAN PERKES

BIRTHDATE: 15 Oct 1820
North Rancely, England
DEATH: 22 May 1898
Hyde Park, Cache Co., Utah
PARENTS: William Gibson
Eleanor Charles
PIONEER: 17 Oct 1862
Henry Miller Co. Wagon Train
SPOUSE I: Edward Thurman
MARRIED: abt 1847
DEATH SP: 19 Mar 1892

CHILDREN:
Edward Moroni, 15 Dec 1848
Mary Elizabeth, 8 Apr 1850

SPOUSE II: James Perkes
MARRIED: 9 Dec 1854
DEATH SP: 22 May 1889
Hyde Park, Cache Co., Utah

CHILDREN:
William Lorenzo, 3 May 1856 (died as a child)
Ellinor Emily, 14 May 1858 (died as a child)
Katherine Sarah (Harris), 12 May 1861

Mary Ann was born in 1820 in North Rancely, Lincolnshire, England.

As the wife of a British nobleman, Mary Ann lived a very comfortable life with property, servants, and moderate wealth. Her cousin introduced her to missionaries from the Church of Jesus Christ of Latter-day Saints and she was greatly affected by their message. She was unable to get her husband to listen to her feelings and he forbade her to pursue the religion. They both felt very strongly about this.

The attraction of the message was so strong, Mary Ann eventually left him, his means, and his love. It was emotionally devastating to both of them, but he would not bend and she felt she must follow what she knew to be true. She made the eleven week journey across the ocean with her two small children, knowing she would never see her husband again.

While on the ship, she made the acquaintance of James Perkes, who was traveling with three small children. He had left his wife, with four other children, in England. She, too, had been unable to accept the teachings of the Mormon missionaries, which he accepted. Their friendship grew into a deeper relationship and they were married in Missouri.

They had three children together, two of whom died in 1869, before they arrived in Utah. They settled in Hyde Park, Utah, living in a dugout the first winter. They endured poverty and hardships, very new to the woman who had experienced all the amenities of a noblewoman. She was a small woman, with auburn hair and grey eyes and was an excellent pie maker. She also tended a beautiful garden which she loved.

After several years, James' first wife, Eliza, decided to come to America and Mary Ann willingly parted with her personal savings to finance the trip for Eliza, who became James' plural wife. Eliza's children stayed with Mary Ann and they loved her.

Mary Ann had been taught the social graces in her life as Edward Thurman's wife. Poise and graciousness were ingrained in her being and no matter how hard things became when she became a pioneer woman, she filled her roll with refinement. She even raised her own caraway seeds so she could make cookies for her grandchildren that were extraordinary. She never stopped loving her first husband, and prayed that he would join her beloved church. As poor as she was, she never communicated with him or asked him for anything, even though he was a wealthy man.

Mary Ann passed away on May 22, 1898 in Hyde Park, Cache County, Utah. James had died nine years before also in Hyde Park.

Mary Ann had truly given up much in life for her great beliefs in the religion she loved. She is known for being a great pioneer woman whose faith had brought her to Utah, a move she never regretted.

ANN MATHEWS PERKINS

BIRTHDATE: 2 Dec 1786
Loughor, Glamorgan, Wales
DEATH: 3 Jul 1868
North Ogden, Weber Co., Utah
PARENTS: Joseph Mathews
Margaret Beddow
PIONEER: 02 Oct 1856
Edward Bunker Handcart Comp.
SPOUSE: Thomas Perkins
MARRIED: 3 May 1808
Loughor, Glamorgan, Wales
DEATH SP: 23 Mar 1854
Aberdare Churchy, Wales

CHILDREN:
William, 16 Feb 1807
Ann, 6 Dec 1808
Thomas, 1811 (died an infant)
Margaret, 4 Apr 1814
Mary, 1817 (died age three)
Joseph Thomas, 24 Sep 1820
Mary, 1823 (died as an infant)
Ruth, 1825 (died as an infant)
Ruth, 12 Jun 1827
Elizabeth, 4 Apr 1829
Catherine, 18 Jul 1833

Ann was born and raised in Loughor, Wales. Her father died when she was about seven years old. She married Thomas Pergrine Perkins on May 3, 1808 in Loughor, Wales. Thomas worked in the mines in the area where they lived. Ann spoke English quite well and taught her children to speak both English and Welsh.

They joined the Church of Jesus Christ of Latter-day Saints in 1844 and were devoted to the Church. After most of their children married, they moved to Aberdare, Wales in 1845. Their children started emigrating to America as they could afford to.

In March, 1856, Ann's husband suffered a paralytic stroke and died. Almost immediately, at the age of seventy, Ann decided to join her children in Utah. She sailed from Liverpool aboard the ship, "Samuel Curling." After arriving in Boston, Ann traveled by rail to Iowa City where they were outfitted to cross the Plains with the Edward Bunker Handcart Company. They arrived in the Salt Lake Valley on October 2, 1856.

Ann was met by her children, Ruth and Joseph. She continued on to North Ogden with her family where she made her home and endured the hardships and privations along with the rest of the early pioneers.

She participated in the general move south when Johnston's Army was approaching Utah, but returned when the scare subsided. Ann received her endowments in the old Endowment House in Salt Lake City in 1865.

Ann's daughter, Elizabeth, cared for her in her old age, sickness, and death. Ann was an example of courage, faith, and fortitude. The principles of honesty, hard work, loyalty, as well as staying firm to religious convictions were taught to her family.

Ann stayed strong and firm in the gospel until she passed away at the age of eighty-two. She is buried at the foot of the majestic mountain peak, Ben Lomond, in the North Ogden Cemetery.

ANNA WARREN PERKINS

BIRTHDATE: 5 Jan 1813/1814
Rutherford Co., Tennessee
DEATH; 3 Oct 1908
Salt Lake City, Salt Lake, Utah
PARENTS: Thomas Warren
Winifred Bates
PIONEER: 17 Sep 1850
Warren Foote Co. Wagon Train
SPOUSE: Ute Perkins
MARRIED: 10/18 Feb 1835
DEATH SP: 23 May 1901
Salt Lake City, Salt Lake, Utah

CHILDREN:
Sarah Caroline"Caddie" (Tye), 9 Jul 1836
Amanda Ellen (Griffen), 15 Mar 1838
LoDica Ann (McIntyre), 8/18 Jul 1840
Joseph Smith, 11 Oct 1842
Hyrum Smith, 20 Sep 1845 (died as an infant)
William Alma, 28 Jan 1847
Ute Warren, 11 Feb 1849
Louisa Deseret (Perkins), 17 Aug 1852

Anna was born in 1813 or 1814 in Tennessee. Her's was a large family. Her father had gone off to serve in the war of 1812 and he never came back. The mother worked increasingly hard to keep her family together and to make them self-supporting. Anna was taught to cook, sew, keep house, card wool, spin yarn and to weave.

When it was impossible to keep the family together, they were bound out to work for their keep. Anna went to work in the household of Rachel Shell where she worked very hard as a servant. She was treated kindly and looked upon as almost one of the family. Anna became an expert tailoress, being very proficient with the needle. She was called upon to do sewing for other people.

Anna met Ute Perkins when he came to have her make a vest for him. He was delighted with her work, but more so with the tailoress. They were married on February 10, 1835.

Anna and Ute cleared land for a log cabin and farm. It was here the missionaries of the Church of Jesus Christ of Latter-day Saints found them and converted them.

After accepting the gospel, they decided to join the main group of the Saints and so moved to Macedonia, Illinois not far from Nauvoo. Here their first male child was born. They already had three daughters. This son was blessed and given the name of Joseph Smith Perkins by the

Prophet himself. After their second son was born, the persecution became so great they moved to Winter Quarters in Iowa.

This family expected to go West with the first company, but were asked to stay and plant and harvest crops to help others as they prepared for their westward treks.

Besides trying to save enough money and provisions for their trip, Ute was asked to help care for the wives and children of the men of the Mormon Battalion which had marched westward.

At one time when Ute was away, Anna and her five children, including a six week old baby, were forced from their home into the snow and cold by a mob. As a result, the baby died and Anna, still alone and frightened, had to prepare and bury the infant. The family finally left Winter Quarters after two more chidren were born to them. They entered the Salt Lake Valley on September 17, 1850 with Captain Warren Foote's Company.

It was a great struggle to establish a new home in a new country with a large family and no finances or anything. An eighth child was born, and their log cabin was too small so an adobe house was built. Anna was thrifty and frugal. She took wool as it was sheared from the sheep, washed, spun and wove it on shares. With her ability as a tailoress, she clothed her husband and family.

This family was fairly well established in the Valley when called to leave their home and help colonize Dixie. It seemed more than they could bare to leave, and they felt they had traveled enough. With faith in their leaders, and true to their pioneer spirit, they packed up their belongings they could take in wagons, and with their few cattle, sheep and chickens, they set forth. Each evening Ann prayed for guidance and protection, and they finally arrived at their destination. They planted alfalfa, cotton, sugar cane, and grapes. Anna also planted a few flowers beside the house. They dug wells and ditches to irrigate the gardens each morning for one hour. They had to hand dip what water they needed throughout the day.

When well advanced in years, Ute and Anna went to Nevada to the Muddy River to help their sons settle and make a start there. Anna's sight was impaired by cataracts, and later she became totally blind. Her widowed daughter, Louisa, came from Salt Lake and took her parents home with her.

Anna's life was one of love and devotion to others. As she became blind, her husband, Ute, devoted his life to her comfort, making her life pleasant and happy. Even though blind, Anna made rugs and knitted socks, to do something useful so she would not be dependent upon her daughter. Her work was not perfect due to her blindness, and after Anna was in bed, Louisa often had to unravel Anna's work and rewind the yarn for the next day. The dear old lady was happy and never knew. Louisa would pay her for the work and she would give it back saying, "I feel better if I can help you a little and pay my way."

Anna Warren Perkins passed away on October 3, 1908, and is buried beside her husband in the Salt Lake City Cemetery. Ute, had passed away in 1901, seven years before Anna.

This faithful pioneer couple left a great heritage to those who have followed them-one of great faith in the Lord, and fortitude of surviving many trials and tribulations of their day.

JANE BENSON FIELDING DALTON BOSNELL PERKINS

No
Photo
Available

BIRTHDATE: 4 Jun 1824
Wrightington, England
DEATH: 6 Dec 1900
Mancos, Montezuma, Colorado
PARENTS: Thomas Benson
Margaret Marsden
PIONEER: 1852
SPOUSE I: Amos H. Fielding
MARRIED: Mar 1860
(divorced 31 Mar 1870)
DEATH SP: Not given

CHILDREN:
Amos Hyrum, 17 Sep 1848

SPOUSE II: Edward Dalton
MARRIED: 9 Oct 1855 (divorced)
DEATH SP: Not given
CHILDREN: None

SPOUSE III: James Warner
MARRIED: 21 May 1856 (divorced)
DEATH SP: Not given

SPOUSE VI: John Perkins
MARRIED: Mar 1860
DEATH SP: 31 Mar 1870

CHILDREN:
Sarah Jane (Rogerson), 17 Jan 1861
Phoebe Madora (Guymon), 9 Jan 1863
Eva Estella, 18 Oct 1865 (died as a child)

Jane was born in 1824 in Wrightington, Lancashire, England, as one of eight children in the family. This family all accepted the Gospel, and joined the Church of Jesus Christ of Latter-day Saints. Jane was baptized in 1837 in England, by Heber C. Kimball. Her father joined later, after study and listening in secret to the teachings of the missionaries. Jane's grandmother, who was blind, came to live with them when Jane was young and it was her responsibility to lead her about.

In about 1847, Jane met Amos Fielding who had come from Utah to help the emigrating Saints. The two fell in love, and their son Amos Hyrum was born in September, 1848.

Amos's duties kept him in England for a longer time, so he sent Jane and her six weeks old son to America with an immigrant ship. They traveled on the ship "Horizon," with over 1,000 Saints, and Jane knew only an Elder she had met in England.

They crossed the ocean, traveled up the Mississippi to St. Louis. Jane found her brother, Richard, who had come to America earlier and lived in his home for four years where she learned to be a tailoress. She did this very well and was quick and neat. It was said that she could measure a man with a tape measure, then with shears cut out and make a man's suit by hand, finishing every seam of the pants, coat and vest, and press them with an iron heated in the fire place, and do this all in one day. This became the means of her livelihood for a great part of her life.

Amos finally called for her in 1852. He had met another woman and brought her with him. They all started across the Plains to Utah together with Amos and the other woman riding in a carriage, and Jane and her four-year-old son walking most of the way.

Jane ended up waiting on them, cooking their meals, which took courage for her to continue under these circumstances. Her knowledge that she was going to Utah to be with the Saints kept her buoyed up.

Heber C. Kimball met her and took her and her young son under his care. Brigham Young said he should pick her up. She met a man named Bosnell, they separated within the year. She later married a man named Dalton. Her son and his sons did not get along without quarreling, so she left again.

She lived alone for some time, but peace and real love came to her in John Perkins. He had come from Australia. His first wife had died in Australia.

John and Jane were married in March, 1860, and they were congenial and lived happily until his death in 1870. They first lived in the fort at Parowan, and later moved into a home in another part of town. Their third child lived just a very short time.

Their home had no windows. A storm came up suddenly and snow came into the room where Jane and the baby were lying. They later moved to a cabin with one large room. Here they had a nice flock of chickens, but wolves kept stealing them so they put poison out one night. The next morning they found five wolves dead.

Jane endured many hardships, and John having come from a big city, knew little of this kind of life, so they had great difficulty earning a living.

John passed away at the age of forty-nine years in March, 1870. Her daughters were still quite young which made it hard for Jane. With the help of her son, Hyrum,

who was then twenty-two years old, she was able to resolutely face the future.

Jane always did her share of the church work, being a Relief Society teacher for many years. Her knowledge of sewing came in handy and became the means of their livlihood for many years. At first she sewed by hand, then with her savings, she was able to buy a sewing machine, the first kind of machine made and one of the first in that locality. She would sew while her daughters were in school, and after they had gone to bed at night.

Her stepson, George, and her son, Hyrum, had moved away, but they returned often with presents and items to help make Jane's life easier.

Hyrum had moved to Mancos, Colorado. After some time, Jane moved to Mancos into a small home Hyrum and his brother-in-law had built for her. For a time there, she obtained work. She spent the Summer of 1889 in Monticello with her daughter. Her grandson took her home November 8, 1900, where she died a month later on December 8, 1900 at the age of seventy-six years. She had taken out her endowments and had been sealed to John Perkins on March 12, 1878 in the St. George Temple. She was buried in Mancos, Colorado.

Jane is honored and admired by those who have followed after her for her great faith and desire to learn and live the Gospel of Jesus Christ.

NANCY MARTIN PERKINS

No Photo Available

BIRTHDATE: 1 May 1799
Bedford Co., Virginia
DEATH: 11 Aug 1856
Salt Lake City, Salt Lake, Utah
PARENTS: Charles C. Martin
Susannah Richardson
PIONEER: 1 Oct 1849
Allen Taylor Co. Wagon Train
SPOUSE: Absalom Perkins
MARRIED: 1815
Sparta, White Co., Tennessee
DEATH SP: 18 Jan 1850
Salt Lake City, Salt Lake, Utah

CHILDREN:
Ute, 5 Mar 1816
Sarah, 28 Sep 1817
William Louis, 18 Jun 1819
Hyrum, 15 Apr 1821 (died at age 17)
David Martin, 23 Aug 1823
Levi, 29 Dec 1824
James Caffery, 15 Apr 1827 (died at age 16)
John Calvin, 25 Jul 1828 (died at age 19)
Susannah, 5 Apr 1830
Nancy Adeline, 5 Dec 1831
Francis Marion, 22 Jun 1833
George Washington, 1 Apr 1836
Christopher Columbus, 4 Jan 1838

Nancy's parents were of a hearty pioneer spirit and had moved their family to the frontier land of White County, Tennessee. The Perkins family moved into the area about this same time and their son, Absalom and Nancy became acquainted and eventually married. Their first son, Ute, was born in 1816 and within the next twenty-three years, she gave birth to a total of thirteen children.

Nancy worked hard along side her husband on their farm. They were a self-sustaining frontier family. They made clothing from the wool of their sheep and provided practically all their wants. They killed and cured the meat of twenty or thirty hogs in a year which provided most of the meat for the family. Nancy taught her daughters to spin, knit, make soap, make sugar from their maple trees, and cook for their large family.

In 1838, they were converted and baptized as members of the Church of Jesus Christ of Latter-day Saints. After the settlement of Nauvoo, the Prophet Joseph Smith and other church authorities visited the Perkins home frequently.

Nancy supported her husband and sons as they donated their time and talents in building the Nauvoo Temple. Their family was driven from Nauvoo and escaped into Iowa where her husband presided over a branch of members. In 1846, her sons, David and John joined the Mormon Battalion.

Nancy, Absalom, and four of their children crossed the Plains with the Allen Taylor Wagon Company and arrived in the Salt Lake Valley on October 1, 1849.

After their arrival in Salt Lake Valley, Nancy took on the responsibilities of helping her husband set up a home again and begin farming. They were happily involved in the ward until Absalom passed away of lung fever in 1850.

Nancy carried on with the help of her family. Although her life was short by today's standards, she lived a life of adventure, courage, faith, and love that will never be forgotten. She passed away on August 28, 1856.

SARAH JANE RICHARDS PERKINS

BIRTHDATE: 13 Jan 1833
Wales
DEATH: 15 Feb 1896
Pleasant Green, Utah
PARENTS: John Richards
Sarah Eynon
PIONEER: 1851
SPOUSE: William Louis Perkins
MARRIED: 27 Oct 1853
DEATH SP: 7 Jan 1899
Pleasant Green, Utah

CHILDREN:
Sarah Jane (Cozzens), 27 Aug 1854
John Absalom, 20 Sep 1856
William Louis, 19 Jul 1858 (died as an infant)

David Richards, 26 Apr 1860
Francis Marion, 2 Feb 1862
Mary Emma (Kesler), 30 Mar 1872
Nancy Adeline, 28 Jan 1864 (died as an infant)
Hannah Elizabeth (Hillier), 7 Sep 1865
Jesse Andrew, 1 Nov 1867
Isaac Munroe, 10 Dec 1869

Sarah Jane was born in 1833 in Wales. Her father was an Elder in the Baptist Penuel Chapel of Priory St., and was also a fisherman. Sarah was the third daughter in her family named Sarah, the two others died shortly after their births. Sarah was especially close to her brother, David.

When she was fifteen years old, in 1846, Sarah and a friend decided to attend a meeting held by Elders from the Church of Jesus Christ of Latter-day Saints. They attended with the intent of making sport and fun and annoying the Elders. Instead of making fun, however, they were so impressed they wanted to learn more about this religion. Upon returning home and reporting to her parents about the meeting, her father forbade Sarah to attend any more meetings. Sarah, wanting to hear more, attended two more meetings and decided she wanted to join the Church.

Sarah Jane's parents felt she must be made to give up this idea. They took various strong measures such as locking her in her room with a diet of bread and water, whipping her. They even placed her in a boarding school with strong discipline. Nothing changed her strong desire to join this Church. She was baptized in 1848, even though her friends and sweetheart made fun of her and even threw rocks at her. Her father put her bodily out of the house and told her she wasn't a daughter of his. She left without money, clothes or any belongings.

Sarah Jane procured work near Liverpool shoveling coal in the coal mines and began to save to go to Zion. One day at this work, her hand was broken and crushed so seriously that the Doctor insisted on amputation for it. She begged him to delay-he granted one day. She had complete faith she could be healed, and so she prayed constantly for the Elders to come and give her a blessing. That night they came, telling her she literally prayed them there. They administered to her, and their combined faith was so efficacious that the next day when the doctor arrived, he marvelled at the change and decided the operation was unnecessary. In later years the hand was as good as new; a crooked little finger was the only evidence of the accident.

By 1850, when she was seventeen years old, Sarah Jane finally obtained passage on a boat, "Badger," tending children as part of her payment for her fare. Her parents still begged her to give up this new religion, but she refused. The ocean crossing took six weeks.

Going up the Mississippi River, smallpox broke out and they were quarantined another six weeks at St. Louis. She became ill and was given up for dead, but finally recovered enough to roll off the low bed to where she could see a pail of water on the floor. She drank a good long drink and from then on she was better.

In later years she was able to do a great deal of good nursing those afflicted with that disease. Sarah Jane finally found work with a Jewish family. She contacted typhoid fever while there. It was 1851, before she managed to cross the Plains to Utah.

A family had taken her along to tend their children, and she walked most of the way driving cattle most of the time. One day, feeling sick and tired as they gathered chips for the fire, she sat down to rest. Her companions returned to camp not knowing she had been left behind. She became confused as to the directions and called out, but no answer came. As night was coming on, she became frightened. She saw the glaring eyes of some animal. She sat down and cried bitterly, wondering if she had gone through all her trials only to now be devoured by wild beasts. She heard a voice say, "Sarah, where is they faith?" She felt ashamed of this attitude, and immediately prayed once more with her old faith. Upon rising, she saw a light, followed it, and was guided back to camp by it, when it vanished.

When she arrived in Utah, she became the housekeeper for William Louis Perkins. His wife had died following the birth and death of their fourth child, leaving William wiih three young children to raise. Sarah Jane became a wonderful companion who loved his children, and they loved her, and William soon found he loved her too, and so asked her to be his eternal companion. They were married on October 27, 1853. He was thirty-four and she was twenty-two years of age. Besides raising his three children, she became the mother of ten children, all of whom were born in Salt Lake City, Utah.

Sarah Jane was a faithful church member who never tired of doing for others. She looked after her garden, orchard, bees, and nursed the sick among her neighbors, besides making cloth for their clothing. She wove and made straw hats and did lovely embroidery and hand work.

Sarah Jane loved to sing the songs of Zion, her favorites included "Come, Come Ye Saints," "Oh My Father," and "We Thank Thee O God for a Prophet." She spent many hours doing temple work for her people as well as being a Relief Society teacher for many years. Her husband worked setting stones on the Salt Lake Temple, and set rock walls along City Creek Canyon.

In 1887, Sarah Jane and William moved to Pleasant Green "Over Jordan" as it was sometimes called. They had a small milk farm, bees, fruit trees and a garden overlooking the Salt Lake Valley to the last.

Sarah Jane died suddenly, at age sixty-three, of pneumonia on February 15, 1896, and was buried on a little hill overlooking her beloved Salt Lake Valley. William died at age eighty, three years later and is buried beside his sweetheart on the same hill.

Sarah Jane Perkins was a great pioneer woman who left a great legacy for others. A favorite poem that Sarah Jane used to quote is:

"God has not promised sky ever blue,

Flower strewn pathway ever for you

God has not promised sun without rain

Joy without sorrow, peace without pain

But he hath promised strength from above,

Unending sympathy, Undying love."

SARAH LAUB PERKINS

BIRTHDATE: 10 Nov 1850
Caldwell, Clay Co., Missouri
DEATH: 9 Oct 1938
St. George, Washington, Utah
PARENTS: George Laub
Mary Jane McGuinnis
PIONEER: 20 Aug 1852
John Higby Co. Wagon Train
SPOUSE: Ute Warren Perkins
MARRIED: 16 Sep 1867
DEATH SP: 18 Apr 1903
Salt Lake City, Salt Lake, Utah

CHILDREN:
Eva Rosetta (Whitmore), 10 Nov 1868
Ute Vorace, 19 Oct 1870
LuEmma Elizabeth (Cox), 6 Mar 1872
Joseph Franklin, 15 Jan 1874
Pearl, 1 Apr 1876
John Fenton, 14 Feb 1878
George Elwood, 12 Oct 1880
Mary Virginia (Lytle), 21 Jun 1883
Fay, 28 Jan 1885
Ralph, 19 Nov 1886
Clara (Lytle), 28 Sep 1889
Sadie Sarah, 4 Oct 1893
Vivian (Hickman), 11 Jun 1895
Baby, (stillborn)

Sarah was born in Missouri in 1850. She came to Utah with the John Higby Wagon Company at the age of under two years. She attended school in Salt Lake City with Asenith Adams, mother of Maud Adams, the actress. She attended the first play "Pride of the Market" in the first theater in Salt Lake City, which her father helped build.

Sarah followed the example set by her mother, as quoted from her history, "The people were very hard put to find enough to eat. Some lived on bread made from ground cane seeds or bran. Many a time mother would send me with a little bucket of flour or a bit of tea or coffee to some poor sick lady. There were many women grateful to her for the kindness she did for them. Mother was quiet and unassuming in her charities . . . always cautioning me to say nothing about them."

Sarah's family was called to Dixie in 1862. She was the baby tender of her family, and spent many hours rocking the cradle as she knitted or read. She said, "I read a great deal. In fact, that was my principle means of education for the schools were poor then. Reading and writing were plenty for a girl to know. Arithmetic was only for boys."

Sarah learned the talents and skills necessary to run a household with a large family; cooking, baking, washing, ironing, sewing, mending, doctoring and caring for the sick, getting along with the Indians, and helping the neighbors.

In Dixie, she helped pick cotton, carded it to make her own bedding. She milked cows, made cheese, and resorted to many other ways to maintain a living.

Sarah met and married Ute Warren Perkins. They moved to Overton, Nevada, a little valley tucked out of the way and became a hide-out for some outlaws. (Black Jack, one of the most notorious of these, stopped many times at Sarah's place for a meal and a rest, sometimes with a posse not far behind him.) For a time her husband was the sheriff.

At Overton, Sarah became the first Relief Society President of the Overton Ward. She nursed the sick and afflicted and traveled many miles in a wagon in order to administer to the needs of her people.

Sarah had fourteen children; one was stillborn. She raised the thirteen to adulthood. Jim Peters, an Indian boy, was with her family for quite a long time. They lived in the same adobe house she and her husband had built until her death.

She was a widow for about thirty-four years but had good health until she fell and broke her hip about ten months before her death. She never recovered from the shock and was crippled after the fall. She could read without glasses, and she even had her own teeth.

Sarah passed away on October 9, 1938 at the age of eighty-eight years. She said, "I have been blessed with good health if not riches. I am very thankful for the health and there were times when I could have used a little of the riches." She died in the hospital in St. George, Utah and is buried beside her husband in the Overton Cemetery in Nevada.

She was a great pioneer woman of Utah who did much good for others and left a heritage of faith for the great numbers of people who have followed her.

ANNA MARIA HULET PERRY

BIRTHDATE: 11 Dec 1817
Nelson, Portage Co., Ohio
DEATH: 27 Jul 1884
Springville, Utah Co., Utah
PARENTS: Charles Hulet
Margaret Noah
PIONEER: 22 Sep 1850
Capt. Bennett Co. Wagon Train
SPOUSE: Stephen C. Perry
MARRIED: 18 Jan 1844
Nauvoo, Hancock Co., Illinois
DEATH SP: 16 Nov 1888
Springville, Utah Co., Utah

CHILDREN:
Mahonri Moriancumer, Jan 1845 (died same year)
Tryphena Rozaltha, 19 Jun 1847
Lewis Rozalvo, 31 Dec 1849
John Sylvester, 10 Mar 1852
Colista Ann, 10 Aug 1854
Sarah Elizabeth, 1850's (died in the 1850's)
Charles Asahel, 31 Dec 1858

Anna Maria was born on December 11, 1817 in Nelson, Portage, Ohio. She was married to Stephen Chadwick Perry on January 18, 1844 in Nauvoo, Illinois, and they became the parents of seven children, two of them dying in infancy.

Anna Maria and Stephen with their first two children, Tryphena and Lewis, came West with other relatives and arrived in Springville, Utah on September 22, 1850. It was a very trying journey and they had to walk most of the way. By hanging a bucket of cream on their wagon, they had butter churned by nightfall. They lived at first in a fort in the Springville area.

The children would go to the canyons and pick chokecherries and serviceberries. Sometimes their father would take them to Utah Lake to get fish, which they would dry in the sun for future use. Anna Maria worked hard at spinning, weaving, coloring wool, making straw hats and doing other duties of pioneer women.

Stephen was gone from home for several years doing missionary work. Anna Maria was patient and long suffering. Her husband entered into plural marriage with two other wives; Margaret Eleanor Stewart, three children; and Mary Boggs, eleven children.

Anna Maria passed away in Springville, July 27, 1884, and Stephen Chadwick Perry passed away in 1888, also in Springville, Utah County, Utah.

ARVILLA PRATT PERRY

BIRTHDATE: 13 Sep 1833
Greenfield, Erie, Pennsylvania
DEATH: 11 Feb 1912
Provo, Utah Co., Utah
PARENTS: Samuel Pratt
Louisa Tanner
PIONEER: 20 Sep 1852
James McGaw Co. Wagon Train
SPOUSE: Philander J. Perry
MARRIED: 27 May 1850
Mount Pisgah, Iowa
DEATH SP: 4 Oct 1902
Provo, Utah Co., Utah

CHILDREN:
Louisa Arvilla, 5 Apr 1851
Philander Franklin, 13 Mar 1853
Samuel Edgar, 5 Aug 1855
Clarissa Alvira, 26 Jan 1858
Zenos Orrin, 2 Oct 1860
Agatha Allula, 28 Feb 1863
Lelia May, 5 May 1866
Wilford Pratt, 14 Apr 1871
Maurice Elliott, 6 Jan 1874

Arvilla Pratt Perry was born in Pennsylvania, the second of ten children. Her parents moved from Greenfield to Thompson, Ohio and on to Noble Indiana.

It was at Noble that her parents were baptized into the Church of Jesus Christ of Latter-day Saints in 1842. Arvilla was baptized two years later. They joined with the Saints in Nauvoo, Illinois. When they were driven out of Nauvoo by hateful mobs they went to Mt. Pisgah, Iowa.

Here she met and married Philander Jackson Perry on May 27, 1850. Philander was a widower with a three year old son. Arvilla cared for him as her own. Arvilla's first child, Louisa, was born in St. Joseph, Missouri and died nine months later.

In June, 1852, Arvilla was in the beginning of her second pregnancy. Arvilla, her husband, and three year old son left Kanesville, Iowa in James McGaw's Wagon Company and arrived in the Salt Lake Valley on September 20, 1852. They traveled south to Springville, Utah, where her husband's parents, his brother and sister were living. Here, her second child, a son, was born.

Frightening experiences with Indians caused them to move to Provo in the Spring of 1860. They lived by Utah Lake which had fish, ducks and geese which helped in providing food for the family. Arvilla and her husband became the parents of nine children; two died in infancy and three in childhood.

Arvilla and her family were active in the Church. She was a good cook and helped with all the gatherings. In October, 1874, Arvilla and her husband began laying the walls of their new home. To start the new year in a new house was a great happening for their family. She was also active in community events and participated in the activities as the community grew, welcoming the new woolen mill and the railroad to the city of Provo.

She taught her children to love Jesus Christ and to follow his teachings. Her life was a good example of helping and serving her fellow men. She participated in the elections which showed her interest in her country. She maintained a garden which furnished the family with fresh vegetables during the summer and into the winter. She was able to utilize the garden produce in preparing healthy meals. Beautiful flowers surrounded her home and were her pride and joy.

Their last two children married in 1891 and 1892. Arvilla and Philander enjoyed ten years together before Philander passed away in 1902 at the age of eighty-one years. Arvilla continued to live in her Provo home until her death at seventy-eight of Bright's disease in 1912. She was survived by two sons and a daughter. She was buried beside her husband in the Provo City Cemetery.

CYNTHIA STEVENS YEAMAN PERRY

No
Photo
Available

BIRTHDATE: 10 Oct 1822
Hornell, Steuben, New York
DEATH: 1899
Idaho
PARENTS: Thomas Stevens
Mother unknown
PIONEER: 16 Aug 1861
David H. Cannon Wagon Train
SPOUSE I: Michael Yeaman
MARRIED: 7 Dec 1831
DEATH SP: 26 Jun 1865
Huntsville, Weber Co., Utah

CHILDREN:
John, 1832 (died age 7)
William, 26 Jun 1833
Richard, Dec 1834
Thomas, 11 Sep 1836
Maranda, 1838 (died as an infant)
Charles, 1840 (died at age 2)
Sarah Ann, 6 Jun 1843
Michael David, 26 Sep 1846
Cynthia Catherine, 1849 (died as an infant)

SPOUSE II: Steven Perry
MARRIED:
DEATH SP:
CHILDREN:

Cynthia was the daughter of Thomas Stevens. Her mother is unknown. She married Michael Yeaman on December 7, 1831.

They were living in Scarborough, York, Ontario Canada and had the privilege of hearing about the restored gospel from Parley P. Pratt. They were both baptized as members of the Church of Jesus Christ of Latter-day Saints.

While traveling from Canada to Kirtland, their daughter, Maranda, was born and died shortly afterward.

They arrived in Kirtland where conditions were impossible for them to remain, so they had to travel on to Far West, Missouri. They were exhausted and the weather was freezing. They kept moving until they came to Nauvoo, purchased a lot from Hyrum Smith, and built a long awaited happy home.

They worked hard in Nauvoo to help build that beautiful city and its temple before they were driven from their home. Cynthia and Michael were able to receive their endowments before they left Nauvoo. They traveled to Garden Grove where their eighth child, Michael, was born.

Their family was requested by Brigham Young to build wheels for wagons for the Saints who would come later. They moved from Garden Grove to White Breast River where they fulfilled President Young's request while their twelve year old son, Richard joined the Mormon Battalion. They had a farm and a lodge for those who were traveling west. Cynthia had to work hard to meet the cares for their travelers.

The Yeaman families farmed until the spring of 1861, then decided to immigrate to Utah. They loaded their wagons and traveled to Omaha, Nebraska where they joined the wagon train of Captain David Cannon. They arrived in Salt Lake City on August 16, 1861. They stayed there for a week and went to Ogden where they bought a farm. Their land became a part of Huntsville. Michael and his sons helped to build the school and church building there. In 1865, her husband passed away while on the way to Ogden to buy supplies.

Cynthia married Steven Perry who took her back to to Missouri. No records have been found about them after this.

ELIZABETH ZABRISKIE PERRY

BIRTHDATE: 20 Aug 1828
Vermillion Co., Indiana
DEATH: 23 Apr 1902
Rockland, Power Co., Idaho
PARENTS: Abraham Zabriskie
Susannah Holtz
PIONEER: 3 Sep 1855
John Hindley Co. Wagon Train
SPOUSE: Henry Elisha Perry
MARRIED: abt 1848
DEATH SP: 19 May 1875

CHILDREN:
Susan Amelia, 2 Jun 1849
Eunice Jane, 18 Nov 1854
Henry Morgan, 3 Dec 1856
Rosalie Elvira, 15 Feb 1859
Hyrum Elisha, 20 Mar 1861
Margaret Melvina, 9 May 1863

child, 1864
Heber William, 25 Oct 1866
Lucy Elizabeth, 11 Jun 1870

Elizabeth's father was one of the early settlers along the Missouri River. She met and married her husband in Platte County where he was hired as a hand to help on a 12,000 acre farm and was over seeing a freight outfit.

In 1854, her parents died leaving Elizabeth forty acres of land, some money, and household goods. Elizabeth could not sell the land, but with the money she had and the household goods together with what her husband had earned outfitted them very well for the trip West.

Their family joined the John Hindley Wagon Company which consisted mostly of Henry, his brother Alonzo and his family, several close friends and neighbors. Her husband and his brother were often sent out to get buffalo for the company to eat. They arrived in the Salt Lake Valley on September 3, 1855. They settled in Three Mile Creek (Perry), Box Elder County, Utah near members of her husband's family.

Her husband became the presiding Elder for several years before the town was divided into wards. He was also captain of a company of militia to guard against Indians.

Henry raised some sheep. Elizabeth would wash the wool, card and spin it, weave it into cloth from which she made suits and dresses for the family. Her husband also organized a cooperative store that was kept in a lean-to at his home. They raised their own fruit trees, grain, and vegetable garden.

Elizabeth was appointed as a Relief Society Teacher in Three Mile Ward. She was also on the committee to look after the storing of grain. She also served as first counselor for five years.

Henry was in very poor health during the last thirteen years of his life suffering from tuberculosis of the lung. He passed away, May 19, 1875, leaving Elizabeth with the family to raise. She lived her last eleven years with her daughter, Rosalie, in Rockland, Idaho.

Elizabeth was buried in Brigham City, Box Elder County, Utah.

EUNICE WING PERRY

No
Photo
Available

BIRTHDATE: 8 Jul 1797
Hinsdale, Massachusetts
DEATH: abt 1863
Three Mile Creek, B. E., Utah
PARENTS: Elisha Wing
Anna Boardman
PIONEER: 1852
John B. Walker Wagon Train
SPOUSE: Gustavus A. Perry
MARRIED: abt 1816
DEATH SP: 2 May 1868
Three Mile Creek, Utah

CHILDREN:
Orrin Alonzo, 11 Sep 1817
Rosalia Elvira, Nov 1819
Amanda Melvina, 11 Sep 1822
Lorenzo, 8 May 1824
Henry Elisha, 24 Aug 1827
Cornelia, abt 1830
Lucy, 20 May 1839

Eunice is a descendent of Deborah Wing, a widow, who came to America in 1632 with her four sons and father, the Reverend Stephen Bachiler. The family settled on Cape Cod and stayed for four generations. Eunice's parents went west to Hinsdale, Berkshire, Massachusetts, where Eunice was born and spent her childhood.

No record has been found of where and when she married Gustavus Adolphus Perry possibly when they were both nineteen. They lived and farmed in Lewis, Essex County, New York, where all but one of their children were born.

Eunice and Gustavus were baptized in 1832 soon after they met the missionaries of the Church of Jesus Christ of Latter-day Church.

Eunice and Gustavus Perry lived in Far West, Missouri. They were with the Saints when they were forced out of Missouri, in the vicinity of Nauvoo until 1846, across Iowa to Council Bluffs where they lived in the Lake Branch until 1852.

They came West in 1852; two daughters and a son-in-law were with them. One son, Lorenzo, came West in 1850. The other two sons came in 1855 when they had earned enough money to bring their families to Utah.

Eunice and her husband lived in Farmington, Utah, for almost two years. By 1854, they had moved to Three Mile Creek, now Perry, Box Elder County, Utah, where their son, Lorenzo, and his new bride had moved in 1853.

Gustavus was the first presiding elder of the Three Mile Creek Branch of the Church of Jesus Christ of Latter-day Saints. Eunice supported him and helped him in his calling when her health permitted.

GRACE ANN WILLIAMS PERRY

BIRTHDATE: 21 Feb 1801
Ashperton, England
DEATH: 14 Nov 1872
So. Bountiful, Davis Co., Utah
PARENTS: James Williams
Sarah Hooper
PIONEER: 3 Oct 1847
Charles C. Rich Wagon Train
SPOUSE: John Perry
MARRIED: 14 Nov 1822
Ashperton, England
DEATH SP: 18 Jul 1855
Mormon Grove, Kansas

CHILDREN:
James, 17 Aug 1823
Elizabeth, 15 Oct 1824
Grace, 26 Aug 1826
Eliza Ann, 39 Mar 1828
Thomas, 21 Dec 1829
Alice, 14 Jun 1831
William, 7 Nov 1833
Elizabeth Melissa, 27 Sep 1836
John, (chr.) 1 Jul 1839

Grace Ann was born into a good but unpretentious home in England. She was a beautiful, dark-eyed baby. She grew into a stately young woman whose early years were filled with homey tasks customary to young women of her day. She became an excellent homemaker; proficient in all duties. Her kindly eyes held the attention of all who met her.

Grace Ann and John Perry were married on November 14, 1822. They made their home at Castle Fromes, Herefordshire, England. They became the parents of nine children; four died in childhood.

They heard the Gospel of the Church of Jesus Christ of Latter-day Saints preached by Wilford Woodruff. Grace Ann was one of the first to recognize its truthfulness. She was baptized on March 27, 1840 in the pool on John Benbow's farm.

Grace Ann, John, and their five children emigrated to America on the ship "North America," sailing from Liverpool, England on September 8, 1840. Their son, William, became sick before America was sighted. Grace Ann buried her beloved son on Staten Island, New York.

Sadly, they continued their journey to Nauvoo, Illinois, arriving November 20, 1840. She had a home at last. She enjoyed joining with other sisters in church and assuming responsibilities in the community. She cared for her children and encouraged her husband as he worked to build the Nauvoo Temple as a master carpenter and joiner. Then came the "Swamp Fever" and much illness. They experienced sadness again as her daughter and son were taken from her and buried in the same grave in 1844.

Times did not improve and the mobs forced the expulsion of the Saints from Nauvoo. With trepidation,

Grace Ann awaited the return of her son, John, from Nauvoo when he with others went back to retrieve the Temple Bell. Her family then journeyed to the Elkhorn River where they camped. They were assigned to the Charles C. Rich Wagon Company with Edward Stevenson as their captain. They arrived in the Salt Lake Valley on October 3, 1847. Elizabeth Melissa was the only child to finish the trip with Grace Ann and John.

The "Old Fort" was her home the Winter of 1847-1848. In early April, 1848, Grace Ann and her family went with Perrigine Sessions to settle what is now Bountiful, Utah. Here, Grace Ann helped as she could to establish a home for her family and others. She experienced the miracle of the crickets and the seagulls.

Later, South Bountiful became her permanent home. She and her daughter, Melissa, took care of the farm while her husband was called on a mission to England in 1852.

Her husband passed away from cholera at Mormon Grove, Kansas while in charge of a company of English emigrants.

Grace Ann suffered with asthma and passed away in South Bountiful on November 14, 1873. She was buried in the family plot of her daughter, Elizabeth Melissa Hatch, Bountiful Cemetery.

LUCINDA COLE PERRY

BIRTHDATE: 07 Nov 1820
Sheffield, Ashtabula Co., Ohio
DEATH: 15 Jun 1905
Vernal, Uintah Co., Utah
PARENTS: Barnet Cole
Phebe VanAlstyne
PIONEER: Sep 1850
Capt. Lake Indep Wagon Train
SPOUSE: Josiah Henry Perry
MARRIED: 30 Nov 1845
Nauvoo, Hancock Co., Illinois
DEATH SP: 1 Sep 1891
Huntsville, Weber Co., Utah

CHILDREN:
Eliza Jane, 28 Sep 1846
Phebe Roxy, 13 Mar 1848
Adelade Almina, 26 May 1851
Sally Maria, 10 Feb 1853
Rosetta Lucinda, 08 Apr 1855
Lucetta Lovina, 08 Apr 1855
Joseph Josiah Dejalma, 13 Mar 1858
Vashti Survina, 8 Sep 1860
Sylvia Morilla, 9 Jan 1864

Lucinda Perry was born in Ohio. She was baptized into the Church of Jesus Christ of Latter-day Saints in 1831 at the age of eleven. They later moved to Nauvoo, Illinois.

Lucinda and her mother were members of the first Relief Rociety in Nauvoo. Her parents were among the first converts to the Church and remained faithful and supportive when the violence raged and the members were attacked by vicious mobs. Lucinda was a comfort to her mother when her father was dragged by mobs and whipped and beaten.

Lucinda married Josiah Henry Perry on November 30, 1845. The families emigrated to Utah in September, 1850 with Captain Lake's Independent Company. They settled in Ogden, Utah in March of 1851, then in Willard, Utah (then called Willow Creek) in 1851 or 1852.

In 1884, Josiah and Lucinda performed temple work in the Logan Temple while living with other Perry family members in tents at West Fields.

Lucinda and Josiah insisted that their home be filled with music, that being very important to the Perry family. President David 0. McKay, at the dedication of the new Huntsville Chapel in May, 1959, said he was well acquainted with the Perry family and he had taken music lessons from Lucinda's daughter, Sylvia. The younger girls played the organ and were good musicians. Two girls taught school.

Lucinda believed in the adage, "Educate a woman and you educate a generation." Another motto she loved was "service is our rent on earth." Lucinda paid her rent in abundance.

Lucinda was a strict disciplinarian and wanted her family to be strong, active Church members. She insisted and encouraged their participation in church and community affairs. Lucinda is remembered by many because of her integrity in living the Gospel principles.

Her husband passed away in 1891, leaving her a widow for fourteen years. Lucinda passed away on June 15, 1905 in Vernal, Uintah County, Utah.

MARION LECKIE SHANKS PERRY

BIRTHDATE: 19 Jul 1837
Paisley, Renfrew, Scotland
DEATH: 21 Apr 1890
Willard, Box Elder Co., Utah
PARENTS: James Shanks
Isabella Dock
PIONEER: 12 Oct 1855
Charles Harper Co. Wagon Train
SPOUSE: Alexander Perry
MARRIED: 21 Dec 1855
Salt lake City, Salt Lake, Utah
DEATH SP: 30 Aug 1889
Mexico

CHILDREN:
Isabella Dock, 27 Mar 1857
Alexander, 1 0 Feb 1859
Mary Turner, 11 Jan 1860
Marion Elizabeth, 29 Mar 1863
Mathew, 6 Apr 1865
James Shanks, 9 Sep 1868
Agnes Jane, 9 Sep 1868
Lucy Danridge, 4 Sep 1871

Marion was born in Scotland in 1837, When she was eighteen years old she came to the Salt Lake Valley arriving on October 12, 1855, with the Charles Harper Wagon Company.

Marion married Alexander Perry on December 21, 1855 in Salt Lake City, Utah. They moved to Three Mile Creek in Box Elder County, Utah. They were the parents of eight children.

Alexander was gone frequently and Marion had to keep large bonfires going all night to protect the colts and calves. Marion was a talented seamstress and made clothes for the people of the community. She later became a milliner. Marion worked hard and never complained.

Alexander passed away on August 30, 1889, while in Mexico. Marion passed away in Willard, Box Elder County, Utah on April 21, 1890, at the age of fifty-three.

MARION LINDSAY MCLEAN CAMP PERRY

No
Photo
Available

BIRTHDATE: 22 Jun 1829
Wanlockhead, Scotland
DEATH: 24 May 1878
Salt Lake City, Salt Lake, Utah
PARENTS: Robert M. Lindsay
Elizabeth Geddes
PIONEER: 4 Oct 1864
William S. Warren Wagon Train
SPOUSE I: John W. McLean
MARRIED: 15 Dec 1845
Patna, Ayshire, Scotland
DEATH SP: 30 Sep 1863
Patna, Ayshire, Scotland

CHILDREN:
Son, 1846
James K., 1848
Elizabeth, 1850
Robert, 1853
Joseph Booth, 1855
Nephi Lindsay, 1857
John, 1861
William, 1862

SPOUSE II: Williams Washington Camp
MARRIED: 1865
Salt Lake City, Salt Lake Co., Utah
DEATH SP: 21 Nov 1875
Salt Lake City, Salt Lake Co., Utah

CHILDREN:
Williams Lindsay, 8 Mar 1866
Margaret Lindsay, 11 Sep 1868

SPOUSE III: Joseph Perry
MARRIED: after Nov 1875
DEATH SP: Unknown
CHILDREN: None

Marion Perry was born in Scotland. She married John William McLean in 1845 in Patna, Ayshire, Scotland. They became the parents of eight children, all born in Ayshire, Scotland. Her husband passed away on September 30, 1863 in Scotland.

Marion married a second time to Williams Washington Camp in Salt Lake City, Utah 1865. They had two children; a boy and a girl. Her second husband passed away on November 21, 1875 in Salt Lake City, Utah.

Marion later married Joseph Perry in Salt Lake City, Utah. Marion's first husband and their oldest son were killed in a coal mine explosion on October 29, 1863 in Patna, Ayshire, Scotland.

Marion and John, along with their children, had joined the Mormon Church in Scotland. After becoming a widow, Marion and her seven children emigrated to America. They sailed on the ship "General McClellan" on May 21, 1864. Marion's parents had emigrated to America, previously. While crossing the Atlantic Ocean, her second son died and was buried at sea. This was a very sad occasion for her.

They made their way to Wyoming, Nebraska where they joined the William S. Warren Wagon Company. They arrived in the Salt Lake Valley on October 4, 1864.

Being without any financial support, Marion and her children went to live with her parents in Heber Valley, Utah. She found employment in the home of Williams Washington Camp and his wife Dinnah Greer Camp. Marion would work several weeks doing housework and launder by hand to get money to support her family. She would then walk back to Heber from Salt Lake City to assist her parents in caring for her children.

Williams was twenty-nine years older than Marion when they had a civil marriage in 1865. Marion was his seventh and last wife. He built Marion and their two children an adobe house on Camp Lane which is now Redwood Road. Williams died of pneumonia in 1875.

Later, Marion married Joseph Perry in Salt Lake City. Marion was stricken with appendicitis and passed away on the operating table of ruptured appendix on May 24, 1878.

Marion left two children, Williams age eleven and Margaret age nine. Joseph Perry and his daughter took care of these two orphaned children until they went to live with their half-brother, Richard C. Camp and his wife Jane Glen in Wallsburg, Wasatch County, Utah.

This courageous lady, Marion Lindsay Camp, endured many hardships and sorrows in her life, but remained faithful to the end. She was truly a pioneer to be remembered by her large posterity.

MARY ANN HIND DAND PERRY

No
Photo
Available

BIRTHDATE: 31 Mar 1790
Cumberland, England
DEATH: 30 Dec 1856
Utah
PARENTS: Wilfred Hind
Mary Arnold
PIONEER: 1852
SPOUSE I: Thomas Dand
MARRIED: 26 Jan 1807
Harrington, England
DEATH SP: 30 Dec 1832
Harrington, England

CHILDREN:
Ann, 1 Jul 1809
Sarah (Tibbitts), 6 Jul 1812
Mary, (chr) 5 Apr 1814
Isabella, (chr) 6 Jan 1816
Wilfred, (chr) 2 Aug 1817
John, 6 Mar 1819
Rebecca, 24 Nov 1820
William, (chr) 22 Feb 1828
Elizabeth, (chr) 1827
Jessie, (chr) 17 Jan 1829
Thomas (chr) 12 Aug 1830
Jemima (Wright), 10 Mar 1832
Rebekah (Dixon Barnes), chr 22 Feb 1828

SPOUSE II: William Perry / Parry
MARRIED: 12 Jul 1841
St. Nicholas, Liverpool, England
DEATH SP: Unknown
CHILDREN: None

Mary Ann was born in England, 1740. At age sixteen, she married Thomas Dand, January 27, 1807 in St. Marys Church, Harrington, England. Thomas was a mariner and miner by trade. They made their home in Harrington, where they became parents of thirteen children.

In the year 1840/1841, after Thomas' death, when Mary Ann had been remarried to William Perry, they were converted to the Church of Jesus Christ of Latter-day Saints and decided to emigrate to Zion.

They worked hard, saving their money helping their children to convert and their very small branch to grow in numbers. Dear William did not realize his dream as he passed away before the journey. Mary Ann made the journey with some of her children and was in the Salt Lake Valley in 1852.

Mary Ann passed away on December 30, 1856 at the age of sixty-six, having been in the Salt Lake Valley for about two years.

MAY WRAY WALKER PERRY

BIRTHDATE: 7 May 1838
Lapeer, Michigan
DEATH: 7 Jun 1913
Perry, Box Elder Co., Utah
PARENTS: William Walker
Elizabeth Wray
PIONEER: 1850 Wagon Train
SPOUSE: Lorenzo Perry
MARRIED: 1 May 1853
Farmington, Davis Co., Utah
DEATH SP: 9 Apr 1886
Three Mile Creek, B. E. , Utah

CHILDREN:
Gustavus Adolphus, 12 Mar 1856
Mary Elizabeth, 15 Feb 1858
Matilda Jane, 14 Feb 1860
Sarah Maria, 27 Jan 1862
Phebe Ann, 5 Jul 1864
Melissa Emeline, 24 Dec 1866
Lorenzo Dan, 6 Oct 1868
Ida Volette, 8 Sep 1870
Amos William, 13 Feb 1873
Hannah Marentha, 4 Mar 1877
Thomas Moses, 20 Feb 1880

May Perry was born in Lapeer, Michigan. She and her parents left Kanesville, Iowa in 1850 to cross the Plains and journey to the Salt Lake Valley. May was just twelve years old.

They may have been with an independent wagon-train. There were many independent companies that made the journey to the Salt Lake Valley in 1850. May did not have good health so her father bought her a muley cow to ride. She actually pulled the cow more than she rode it, however. They arrived in the Salt Lake Valley in the Fall of 1850. She was fifteen years old.

In 1853, she became the wife of Lorenzo Perry. She and her husband were one of the first two families to settle in Three Mile Creek, Box Elder County, Utah. The area is now known as Perry City. May had the talent and ability to learn languages. She was able to learn and speak the Shoshone language very rapidly. She became well known as a friend to the Indians.

She and her husband became the parents of eleven children, nine of whom lived to be adults. May also assisted in rearing several grandchildren. Her husband passed away abruptly in 1886. It is recorded that a visit from one of the "Three Nephites" brought her comfort.

At the age of thirty-seven she was sustained as Second Counselor in the Branch Relief Society. She served for sixteen years. When she was released, she was called as First Counselor and served until January of 1910, serving thirty-five consecutive years.

May passed away on June 7, 1913 in Perry, Utah. She had served her God, community, family and friends all of her life. She was loved by all who knew her.

NANCY ANN SHAFFER PERRY

BIRTHDATE: 14 Nov 1822
Rush, Indiana
DEATH: 19 Aug 1908
Slaterville, Weber Co., Utah
PARENTS: Henry Shaffer
Eve Beard
PIONEER: Fall 1851
Wood Co. Wagon Train
SPOUSE: Lyman Sylvester Perry
MARRIED: 22 Jan 1855
Bingham Fort, Weber Co., Utah
DEATH SP: 6 Jul 1908
Slaterville, Weber Co., Utah

CHILDREN:
Henry Sylvester, 27 Dec 1855
Mary Jane (Powlett), 24 Oct 1859
William Heber, 30 Jun 1862
Susan Arrenia (Singleton), 19 Oct 1864
Sarah Elizabeth (Stratton), 2 Oct 1867
Nancy Ann (Ross), 4 Aug 1870
Margaret Elle (Bybee), 29 Apr 1873

Nancy Perry was born at Rush, Indiana. Her family moved to Nauvoo, Illinois to be with the members of the Church of Jesus Christ of Latter-day Saints.

As a young girl, Nancy Ann was well acquainted with the Prophet Joseph Smith. She and her mother often visited in the Smith home and she liked to listen to the Prophet's sermons.

On the day Joseph and Hyrum Smith were martyrd, she and other family members were hoeing in their field. There was an air of tension and the very atmosphere seemed heavy and threatening. On their way home they were met by a messenger with the news of the events at Carthage.

Nancy Ann attended the meeting where the mantle of Joseph Smith fell upon Brigham Young, who was the President of the Quorum of Twelve Apostles. She was in camp when the Mormon Battalion was recruited, and also near when Colonel Kane visited the camp. He asked her for a drink of water.

They had traveled as far as Winter Quarters with the Heber C. Kimball Wagon Company. When they again started West it was in Captain Wood's Company. During the journey West she became ill with Cholera and her life was despaired of. Through the blessing of God, she was spared.

After reaching the Salt Lake Valley the Fall of 1851, she worked in the home of Ezra Clark at Sessions' Settlement, now Bountiful, Utah, until her marriage. She married Sylvester Lyman Perry. They became the parents of seven children.

Her husband was often away from home during the early years of their marriage. He was called several times to go meet Saints on the trail and help them with the rest of the trip. When the threat of Johnston's Army came, Sylvester was sent to guard Echo Canyon. While he was gone, Nancy Ann dug sixty bushels of potatoes with a hoe and carried them in a water pail to a pit she had dug. She also unloaded corn from the wagon. She had to keep her oxen hidden and carry water and feed to them each day because some white men were stealing and harassing the settlers. Indians often stole, too, but the white men were worse.

Her husband became too ill to continue at Echo Canyon, so he came home to recuperate. As soon as he was well enough, he returned to his post. Nancy Ann and her baby moved to Payson, Utah with the rest of the people. When the threat was gone, her husband walked to Payson and brought his family home. They moved to Slaterville, Weber County, Utah, where they lived the rest of their lives.

Nancy Ann was active in the Relief Society until failing health compelled her to give it up. She loved flowers passionately, and her home was a beautiful bower. She was skillful in making artificial flowers from feathers, wool, tarleton, paper, wax and hair. Some of her creations once hung in the Logan Temple. Nancy Ann and her husband spent much time in doing temple work.

Nancy Ann became bedfast before her death on August 9, 1908. Her husband had died on July 6, 1908.

POLLY CHADWICK PERRY

BIRTHDATE: 24 Jun 1789
Tyringham, Massachusetts
DEATH: 30 Dec 1878
Springville, Utah Co. Utah
PARENTS: Isaac Chadwick
Dinah Brewer
PIONEER: 20 Sep 1850
James Pace Co. Wagon Train
SPOUSE: Asahel Perry
MARRIED: 26 Mar 1806
DEATH SP: 16 Feb 1869
Springville, Utah Co., Utah

CHILDREN:
Isaac, 4 May 1807
Lucy Ann, 22 Feb 1809
Willard, 3 Aug 1810
William Chadwick, 26 Jan 1812
Orrin, 19 May 1814
Hiram, 29 Apr 1816
Stephen Chadwick, 22 Dec 1818
Philander Jackson, 29 Sep 1821
Lewis B., 13 Dec 1826 (died at 3 months)
Polly Maria, 16 Jun 1832

Polly's parents came from proud old New England lines. She was the second child in a family of eight children.

She married Asahel Perry on March 26, 1806 and they took up residence in Madison, Madison County, New York where they bought forty two acres of land. After the birth of six of their children, they moved to Middlebury, New York where the rest of the children were born. Polly was forty-three years old when she was baptized a member of the Church of Jesus Christ of Latter-day Saints on November 7, 1832.

In 1836, Asahel sold his property and moved his family to Kirtland, Ohio. They bought a farm and assisted in building the temple there. In 1838, he turned his farm over to the church to pay a debt against the church in New York. They moved to Missouri.

They were with the main part of the Saints being driven from place to place taking full share of the trials and difficulties of the time. Asahel served a short mission to New York and tried to convert his children who remained there.

They moved to Nauvoo where they helped to build another temple and were driven from their property again. They moved on to Council Bluffs and decided to cross the Plains with the James E. Pace Wagon Company. They arrived in the Salt Lake Valley on September 20, 1850.

In October, 1850, they went to Hobble Creek east of Springville and settled. They lived in a fort for a while, then later built homes and lived in Springville. She moved thirteen times since her marriage and bore ten children.

Polly was a hard worker, working in the home and in the garden; producing clothing and food for the family. She was very good at making ends meet. They enjoyed their home, their children, grandchildren, and great grandchildren for the next nineteen years.

After her husband died, she went to live with her son, Stephen, and died at age eighty-nine years.

RHOBY EDWARDS PERRY

No
Photo
Available

BIRTHDATE: 23 Jul 1793
Windsor Co., New York
DEATH: 12 Oct 1865
Ogden, Weber Co., Utah
PARENTS: Joseph Edwards
Olive Green
PIONEER: 20 Sep 1850
James Pace Co. Wagon Train
SPOUSE: Stephen Perry
MARRIED: 12 Apr 1816
Sherburne, Vermont
DEATH SP: 29 Dec 1886
Kanesville, Iowa

CHILDREN:
Josiah Henry, 5 Apr 1818
Susannah Irene, 3 Aug 1820
William Howard, 2 Aug 1823

Sally Sylvia, 1 Sep 1826
Stephen Washington, 9 Oct 1829
Sylvester Lyman, 2 Jan 1833
Alonzo Orson, 17 May 1836

Rhoby Edward's progenitors had been in the United States for several generations. Her father was a soldier in the Revolutionary War.

Rhody met Stephen Perry and they were married at Chester, Vermont. They moved to the town of Lewis, in Essex County, New York to make their home. They were raising their family of seven children as Methodist Episcopalians and brought them up with a strict code of morals.

Missionaries from the Church of Jesus Christ of Latter-day Saints came to Lewis with their message. Their daughter, Susannah, was the first of their family to become converted to their teachings. One by one, the rest of the family followed.

Ten years after joining the Church, the Perry family moved to Nauvoo, Illinois. They were able to receive their endowments and sealings in the Nauvoo Temple. As a wife and mother, Rhoby went through all of the excitement and hardship of the Nauvoo years.

Before they came west, her daughter, Sally Sylvia, died leaving her baby daughter for Rhoby to raise. After Rhoby's family left Nauvoo, they lived at some of the settlements along the way during a four year period. They were at Farmington, Iowa, at Mount Pisgah, and Winter Quarters. At each of these places they planted and then harvested crops to help the pioneers as they came West along the trail.

In June, 1850, they were able to come across the Plains with the James Pace Wagon Company. They arrived in the Great Salt Lake Valley on September 20, 1850. They moved to Bingham's Fort which is north of Ogden. Then they moved to Lynne and Slaterville. There was a close tie between the Perry families. They had great fun together and cherished their association.

Rhoby became an invalid with cancer. Her daughters and daughters-in-law took care of Rhoby and gave her the help she needed. She passed away in Lynne and is buried in the Ogden City Cemetery.

CAJSA CATHERINE CHRISTINA JACOBSSON CHRISTENSSON PERSSON

No
Photo
Available

BIRTHDATE: 13 Mar 1797
Arges-Hemse, Gotland, Sweden
DEATH: 1863
Florence, Nebraska
PARENTS: Jacob Classon
Anna Catharina Classon
PIONEER: Died along way
SPOUSE I: Bothel Christensson
MARRIED: 18 Oct 1820
Sweden
DEATH SP: 25 Sep 1827
Sweden

CHILDREN: I
Brita Kajsa, 22 Jul 1822
Anna Greta, 25 Oct 1824
Bathel, 9 Mar 1828 (twin)
Christian Gertrud, 9 Mar 1828 (twin)

SPOUSE II: Peter Micias Persson
MARRIED: Unknown
DEATH SP: Unknown
CHILDREN: None

Cajsa Batelsson Persson was born in Arges-Hemse, Gotland, Sweden. Her childhood was spent on the Island of Gotland.

She married Bothel Christensson and they became the parents of four children. Two of their children, Bathel and Christian, died in infancy. Cajsa's husband died in 1827.

She then married Peter Niclas Persson. When Cajsa and her children joined the Church of Jesus Christ of Latter-day Saints they decided to emigrate to Utah. Apparently Peter Persson, her second husband, did not emigrate with them.

Cajsa and her children traveled to Stockholm, Sweden with other family members, the Lars Petter Esklund family. After six months spent in Stockholm preparing for their journey, they sailed by small ship to Hamburg, Germany.

Here, they joined with other Danish and Swedish members of the Mormon Church to board the clipper ship "Electric" for their voyage to New York. The ship's progress was slow because of adverse winds and weather. The water became bad which caused many people to become ill; Cajsa included. They arrived in New York on June 5, 1863. From there they traveled by train to Florence, Nebraska.

Here the pioneers were outfitted with wagons and oxen to make the journey to the Salt Lake Valley. Cajsa was very ill due to the bad water she had drunk on the ship when they were crossing the ocean. As the time drew near for their departure, Cajsa passed away. She was not to realize her dream of joining other members of the Church she loved in the Salt Lake Valley. She was buried in Florence, Nebraska.

It is recorded that her daughter, Brita, continued on the journey to the Salt Lake Valley, then settled in Scipio, Millard County and died there in 1888.

Cajsa was a true and faithful pioneer.

LAURA JONES DAVIS PETERS

BIRTHDATE: 8 Feb 1817
Llanfair, Mirnth, North Wales
DEATH: 14 Dec 1899
Brigham City, Box Elder, Utah
PARENTS: John Davis
Loury "Laura" Jones Davis
PIONEER: Nov 1849
George A. Smith Wagon Train
SPOUSE: David Peters
MARRIED: 11 Apr 1840
North Wales
DEATH SP: 12 June 1898
Three Mile Creek, B. E., Utah

CHILDREN:
Sarah (Squires), 16 Feb 1841
Laura (Woodland), 16 Mar 1842
Elizabeth, 21 Jun 1845
John David, 10 May 1850
David, 23 Oct 1851
William, 30 Oct 1853
Morris Rees, 22 Nov 1855
Thomas Davis, 14 Dec 1857
Peter Hughes, 27 Nov 1860

Laura Peters was born in North Wales. She was the daughter of land owners raised in a home where the advantages of that time were plentiful and abundant. Laura was dark complexioned with dark sparkling eyes. She had a kind and loving disposition but was firm and truthful by nature.

On April 11, 1940, she became the wife of David Peters. He owned a successful textile business in North Wales. They became the parents of nine children. Their third baby lived only a few months and died October 2, 1846.

The same year Laura and David heard of a new Church which had been founded in America, the Church of Jesus Christ of Latter-day Saints. They were baptized on June 21, 1846. Laura was the third person and the first woman in North Wales to become a member.

Until Laura and David emigrated to America all of the Church meetings were held in their home. Laura was a woman of great faith and sought guidance from her Heavenly Father in prayer. When the time arrived for them to emigrate to America, Laura hestitated since she was not convinced it was the right time for them to leave. In answer to her prayer she received a vision wherein she was visited by three personages. She was told that she should go and would arrive safely. As a result, David sold the factory and they prepared for the journey.

They sailed from Liverpool, England on March 5, 1849 on the ship "Hartley," and fifty-four days later they arrived in America.

They left New Orleans, Louisianna on a steamship which was attacked by an epidemic of cholera. Many bodies were left buried along the banks of the Mississippi River. Laura was kept busy caring for the sick and preparing the dead for burial. She became prostrated with the dread disease. She never lost faith and knew that she would be healed by the power of the Lord. Laura kept walking, with help, to prevent her from going to sleep. So many had died while in their sleep. Through administration by the Elders she was immediately healed. Thus, the promise given to her by heavenly messengers was fulfilled.

The party landed at Council Bluffs and crossed the Plains in the George A. Smith Wagon Company. Laura and David and their girls arrived in the Salt Lake Valley in November, 1849, after nine months of travel by land and sea. They built their first home on or near the present site of the Denver and Rio Grande Depot in Salt Lake City. They were among the first settlers in Box Elder County. They made many contributions to that early community and to their Church.

David passed away on June 12, 1898, almost twenty months before Laura passed away on December 14, 1899.

MARY CATHERINE BARTON IVIE PETERS

BIRTHDATE: 30 Jun 1837
Shamokin, Pennsylvania
DEATH: 24 Dec 1888
East Fork, Blaine Co., Idaho
PARENTS: John Barton
Susannah Wilkinson
PIONEER: 1847
2nd Company Wagon Train
SPOUSE I: John Lehi Ivie
MARRIED: 16 May 1852
Bountiful, Davis Co., Utah
DEATH SP: 19 Mar 1909
Vermillion, Sevier Co., Utah

CHILDREN:
Joseph Alma, 21 May 1853
Phoebe Ellen, 25 Jul 1854
Mary Susannah, 7 Jun 1856
Rosella Ann, 2 Feb 1858
John Lafayette, 10 Nov 1860
James Oscar, 9 May 1863
Lillie Belle, 13 Oct 1865
Catherine May, 24 Feb 1868
Seymour Illif, 26 Aug 1870
Alden Salathiel, 4 May 1873
Ida Priscilla, 18 Oct 1875
Ray, 4 Jun 1878

SPOUSE II: Lyman Peters
MARRIED: 1881

DEATH SP: Not given
CHILDREN: None

Mary Catherine was born, June 30, 1837, Shamokin, Northumberland County, Pennsylvania, the oldest of eight children. She was ten years old when her family joined the second wagon train after the coming of Brigham Young in 1847. Her family settled in Bountiful, Utah, fifteen miles North of the Salt Lake Valley.

It was in Bountiful that she met and married John Lehi Ivie when she was fifteen years old. She had been very popular among the young people. In fact, it was said that her friends were sorry when she and her husband moved to Provo, Utah.

Mary Catherine was a nurse and a midwife. She had many pioneer remedies to treat the sick and heal wounds. One was a salve made from pine gum, bees wax and mutton tallow which saved the life of a great-grandson some eighty years later when he had blood poisoning in his heel from a blister.

One time she badly burned her own hands when she was making liniment and it caught on fire. She had her children grate potatoes and put them into two salt sacks which she put her hands into and they healed without a blister.

She knitted all of the socks, caps and sweaters for the family and could knit while she was walking around. She also did sewing for her family and for others. Mary Catherine was also interested in mining and staked out claims on many mines. One claim was jumped and it became the largest mine in Idaho.

Mary Catherine and her husband became the parents of twelve children. Her life was not without much sorrow as her first child died when just a day old and two little daughters died when they were one year old. A twenty year old son was carrying a sack of grain on his shoulder up some steep stairs to a loft when he became overbalanced and fell, injuring his back so badly that he died. A six year old son died of what was then called dropsy.

Her husband, who was a Lt. Colonel in the Militia, was often gone from home leaving most of the care of the home and family to Mary Catherine. They were divorced and she later married Lyman Peters 1881 and went to Idaho with him. There, she worked very hard to keep up her home and to help her children, both those who had stayed in Utah and the four who came with her.

In August of 1888, when she was just fifty-one years old, she was going to inspect one of her mines with her youngest son. Having gone as far as they could in a buck-board, she continued by horseback and something frightened the horse. She was a good horsewoman but her foot caught in the stirrup when the horse threw her and she was dragged for some distance with the horse kicking her in the head and chest. She finally got loose but was badly hurt and was unable to walk again because of a twisted knee.

She "took to her bed" in October and passed away on Christmas Eve. She was buried in Mt. Pleasant, Sanpete County, Utah.

ANE JENSEN PEDERSEN / PETERSEN

BIRTHDATE: 10 Sep 1823
Tureby, Praesto, Denmark
DEATH: 17 Feb 1901
Logan, Cache Co., Utah
PARENTS: Jens Hansen
Johanne Bendtsen
PIONEER: 9 Nov 1856
James G. Willie Handcart Comp.
SPOUSE: Jens "O" Peterson
MARRIED: 1 Nov 1845
Vollerslev, Praesto, Denmark
DEATH SP: 7 Jan 1900
Brigham City, Box Elder, Utah

CHILDREN:
Johanna Sophia, 24 Sep 1844
Maria, 9 Sep 1846
Hans Peter, 28 Aug 1848
Christen, 22 Aug 1850
Peter, 14 Mar 1852
James Christen, 24 Jun 1854
Mary Christina 17 Sep 1857
Abraham Fredrick, 18 Nov 1859
Anna, 2 Nov 1861
Isaac, 24 Dec 1863
Jacob, 14 Jan 1866
Nephi, 23 Apr 1868

Ane was born in Tureby, Praesto, Denmark. She became a house maid at the lessee Fischer of Juellund (Vollerslev). She married Jens Peterson on November 1, 1845 in Vollerslev, Denmark.

They joined the Church of Jesus Christ of Latter-day Saints and sailed for America from Liverpool, England on the ship, "Thornton." They were traveling with their six children ranging in age from one year to twelve years old.

They arrived in Iowa City where they had to wait for handcarts to be built before they could cross the Plains. They joined the James G. Willie Handcart Company.

When they camped at night, Ane would bake what bread the entire family was to eat the following day. On September 4th, their cattle were run off by a band of Indians, causing their food supply to become dangerously low. They were frightened by a herd of buffalo, suffered bitter frosts and cold weather which increased in severity day by day.

Ann did her part pulling the handcart and carrying the smaller children. Their last flour was used on October 19th, the same night that it snowed fourteen inches deep. A rescue team reached them two days later about 340 miles from the Salt Lake Valley.

At Fort Bridger, the company was met with fifty wagons and they were taken on to Salt Lake City arriving on November 9, 1856. By nightfall, everyone had been taken into homes to be cared for. There had been sixty-eight deaths, but all eight of Ann's family survived.

Ann and her family settled at Fort Ephraim, Utah in 1857, where Mary Christina was born. Then they lived in Brigham City for a couple of years, but finally settled in Logan where Ann's last four children were born.

Ane was thirty-eight when she set up her home in Logan and lived there until her death forty years later.

ANE MARIE CHRISTENSEN (PODER) PETERSEN

No Photo Available

BIRTHDATE: 25 May 1821
Daugbjerg, Viborg, Denmark
DEATH: 30 Nov 1896
Redman, Sevier Co., Utah
PARENTS: Christen Andersen
Kirsten Christensen
PIONEER: 1854
Handcart Company
SPOUSE: Peder C. Pedersen
MARRIED: 29 Oct 1848
DEATH SP: 16 Dec 1895
Levan, Juab Co., Utah

CHILDREN:
Mary Ann, 16 Oct 1847
Katherine,
Christine,
Mary Amelia (Acord), 20 Feb 18
Peter, 17 Dec 1865

Ane Marie was born in 1821 in Denmark. She was the first daughter and second child in her family of seven children. Her father died when she was seventeen years old, and her mother was married a second time to an Anders Pedersen.

Little is known of this family until their home was visited by Mormon Elders. Ane Marie and her husband were baptized members of the Church of Jesus Christ of Latter-day Saints on May 1, 1853. To these converts there seemed to grow a great desire of the 'Spirit of Gathering' into one great body with the Saints in the Rocky Mountains. Ane and Peder immediately planned to emigrate to Zion.

They, with their three little girls, Mary Ann, Catherine and Christine, the oldest barely seven, traveled across the Plains. They walked, pushed and pulled a handcart which contained their belongings. They endured the hardships with determination and unrelenting faith. They finally arrived in the Salt Lake Valley in 1854. On February 20, 1855, their fourth daughter Mary Amelia was born. They later had a son, Peter born in Salt Lake City.

Soon after their arrival, the family moved to Levan, Utah where they settled to raise their family.

Ane Marie's husband, Peder Christian, passed away in December, 1895, and was buried in the Levan Cemetery. Ane Marie passed away less than a year later on November 30, 1896 in Redmond, Sevier County, Utah. She is buried beside her husband in the Levan Cemetery, in Juab Co., Utah. They are buried under the name of Poder.

Ane Marie was a faithful, pioneer woman of faith and fortitude who is an example to those who have followed her.

ANNE ELIZABETH NIELSEN PETERSEN

BIRTHDATE: 12 Feb 1835
Helsingor Denmark
DEATH: 3 Dec 1887
Huntsville, Weber Co., Utah
PARENTS: Niels Johason
Elizabeth Olddater
PIONEER: 1861
W. W. Cluff Co. Wagon Train
SPOUSE: Soren Lind Petersen
MARRIED: May 1861
on board ship "B. S. Kimball"
DEATH SP: 25 Nov 1901
Huntsville, Weber Co., Utah

CHILDREN:
Anna, 29 Apr 1862
Caroline, 20 Jul 1864
Emma Louise, Jan 1866
Soren Lind Jr., 7 Feb 1868
Adam Lind, 2 Mar 1870 (twin)
Mary Elizabeth, 2 Mar 1870 (twin)
Matilda, 21 Jan 1872
Baby Girl, 6 Jun 1873

Anne was born in Denmark in 1835. She was the fourth of seven children. But she was the only one to join the Church of Jesus Christ of Latter-day Saints. Ann was well educated in the arts, poetry, and literature and knew the art of combing, carding and spinning wool, she made all her childrens clothes.

She was a fine homemaker and excellent cook. After she came to the Salt Lake Valley, she gleaned the fields with sons Soren and Adam in exchange for bricks and labor then built a nine-room house during 1874 through 1876, while Soren Sr. was serving a mission in Denmark.

Anne was gentle and kind, sharing her home with two other women her husband had married in polygamy. She passed away in Huntsville, Weber County, Utah on December 3, 1887 at the age of fifty-two.

ANNE MARGRETHA DORTHEA LORENTZEN PETERSEN

BIRTHDATE: 28 Oct 1829
Keil, Schleswig, Prussia
DEATH 17 Nov 1922
Hyrum, Cache Co., Utah
PARENTS: Lorentz Lorentzen
Margaretha Jacobsen
PIONEER: 15 Sep 1863
John R. Young Co. Wagon Train
SPOUSE: Hans Petersen
MARRIED: Mar 1851
DEATH SP: 6 Feb 1911

CHILDREN:
Josephine Margaret, 16 Apr 1852
Ernest, 30 Jan 1854
Lorentz, 15 Feb 1857
Hans, 1864
Ezra, 28 May 1866

Anne was born in Keil, Schleswig, Holstein, Prussia in 1829, She went all her life as Doris. Her mother and father worked for king Fredrick VI of Denmark.

In 1836, there was a war between Germany and Denmark and the king moved to Copenhagen. Doris and her mother moved with him, her father having died the same year.

Doris was taught with all the other children of the court and was excepted as a princess. She learned five languages and throughout her life gave evidence of this extensive education.

Doris left the courts in her teens. When she was twenty-two years old she married Hans Petersen in March, 1851. They had their own coachman, footman, and servants.

On April, 1863, they left Denmark for Zion. They financed the immigration of forty people from Denmark to America and then to the Salt Lake Valley.

They went from Copenhagen to Liverpool, England where they boarded the ship "John J. Boyd" to New York. They then went on to Florence, Nebraska where they joined the John R. Young Wagon Company, and arrived in the Salt Lake Valley on September 15, 1863. They settled in Hyrum where they had twenty acres of land. Doris and Hans were divorced in 1867. Hans moved half a block away with his new wife.

In 1870, Doris went to Salt Lake and got a job washing dishes in a hotel to support her family. But in 1878 she was back in Hyrum again. Brigham Young called her to be a mid-wife and after ten months of training, at age forty-nine, she began a long practice of forty-one years. Delivering about 1,200 babies in the Cache Valley area.

Doris passed away on November 17, 1922 in Hyrum, Cache County, Utah at the age of ninety-three.

CHRISTENA ANDERSON PETERSEN

BIRTHDATE: 2 Jan 1850
Malmo, Sweden
DEATH: 2 Jun 1936
Fairview, Sanpete Co., Utah
PARENTS: Andrew Anderson
Ellen Hansen
PIONEER: 29 Sep 1859
James Brown Co. Wagon Train
SPOUSE: Christian Petersen
MARRIED: 2 Jan 1867
Mount Pleasant, Sanpete, Utah
DEATH SP: 8 Jan 1926
Fairview, Sanpete Co., Utah

CHILDREN:
Annie Elnora, 8 Feb 1868
Amelia Henrietta, 24 Apr 1870
Hannah Christena, 12 Jan 1873
Alice Melinda, 20 Feb 1875
Andrew Christian, 10 Dec 1877
Caroline Elizabeth, 6 Jul 1880
James Lewis, 2 Sep 1882
Joseph Follett, 8 Jun 1885
Ellen Margaret, 4 May 1888
Sarah Minerva, 8 Jun 1891
Edward Justin, 13 Apr 1894

Christena was born in Sweden. She was the youngest child in a family of nine children. Christena was four years old when the Gospel of the Church of Jesus Christ of Latter-day Saints was brought into her home.

Her parents accepted its teachings with gladness and at once began working to emigrate to Utah. The family moved to Denmark in 1855 where they were baptized. Christena's father worked to save the money to bring his family the great distance from Denmark to Utah.

The family was crossing the Atlantic Ocean, landing at New York, leaving December 12, 1855 and arriving on February 15, 1856. They journeyed to Burlington, Iowa. Here, the family prepared for the trip to Utah. Christena's brother, Andrew, had the opportunity of driving a team for a man who had two wagons, so he arrived in the Salt Lake Valley before his family.

Her father found employment cutting timber. They lived in a little hut in the woods. After a year and a half, Christena's father became ill and died. Her mother worked hard to earn the money to pay for their journey across the Plains. They had eaten the last of their food when they came to the mouth of Emigration Canyon. They had walked all the way across the Plains, traveling with the James Brown Wagon-train Company. They arrived in the Salt Lake Valley on September 29, 1859.

Christena's brother, Andrew, had married and moved to Mount Pleasant, Utah. Christena and her mother went out to Brigham Young's farm and gathered wheat in exchange for bread. They walked all the way from Salt Lake City to Mount Pleasant, Utah.

Christena was only ten years old but she milked a cow every morning and night for her board and room. At the age of eleven, Christena worked for a family by the name of Winters. For her work they helped her to get her first schooling. Her mother was given a small home at the edge of town. The lot was covered with sage brush which they cleared and piled so they could use it for fuel in the winter. The next spring they planted a garden; among other things they planted melons. In the fall they gleaned the wheat. They had for lunch bread, butter and melons. They gleaned wheat for six weeks. Christena gathered thirteen bushels which she sold for $5.00 a bushel. With some of the money she bought a pair of shoes. She bought a cow for $30.00.

A few years later, while working in Mount Pleasant for a family named Peel, Christina met Christian Petersen. She fell in love with him and they were married on her birthday, January 2, 1867. They later traveled by wagon to Salt Lake City and were married in the Endowment House by President Joseph F. Smith. They became the parents of eleven children.

In 1869, they moved to Fairview, Utah and built a home where they lived in peace and contentment for fifty-four years. In 1917, they celebrated their Golden Wedding Anniversary.

They both lived exemplary lives, serving both their Church and community. Christena was a Relief Society worker for forty years.

She passed away on June 2, 1936 in Fairview, Utah. She was laid to rest by those she loved, her mother, a son, Follet, and her companion and husband, Christian Petersen.

CHRISTINA MARGRETHE CHRISTIANSEN PETERSEN

No Photo Available

BIRTHDATE: 16 Oct 1834
Pedersker, Bornholm, Denmark
DEATH: 24 Sep 1868
Emigration Conyon, Utah
PARENTS: Christean Larsen
Berthe Kierstine Poulson
PIONEER: Sep 1868
John G. Holman Wagon Train
SPOUSE: Hans Peter Pedersen
MARRIED: 28 May 1860
Aaker Landsogn, Denmark
DEATH SP: Unknown

CHILDREN:
Caroline Petronelia, 6 Oct 1860
Matilda Hansina, 19 Apr 1863/1864

Christina was born in Denmark in 1834. She married Hans Peter Pedersen or Mortensen May 28, 1860.

After she joined the Church of Jesus Christ of Latter-day Saints and wanted to come to America her husband wouldn't come, so Christina left Bernholm with her two daughters. Crossing the Atlantic Caroline was pulled into the Ocean trying to fill a bucket with water.

After arriving in America they started across the Plains for the Salt Lake Valley with John G. Holman Company. As they neared their destination, Christina became ill and died, at the last stop in Emigration Canyon, September 24, 1868. Her body was brought on to Salt Lake and buried.

Matilda her four or five year old daughter entered the Salt Lake Valley an orphan, and was raised by Sarah Tonks Duel Thacker.

ELSIE MARIE LARSEN PETERSEN

BIRTHDATE: 28 Mar 1828
Astrup, Hjorring, Denmark
DEATH: 23 May 1917
Logan, Cache Co., Utah
PARENTS: Lars C. Jensen
Mette Kristensen
PIONEER: 10 Sep 1863
William Preston Wagon Train
SIGNIFICANT OTHER I:
Christen Pedersen
DEATH S. O: Not given

CHILDREN:
Liza / Lise Pedersen, 10 Nov 1849

SIGNIFICANT OTHER II: Soren Christiansen
CHILDREN:
Daughter Sorensen, 19 Feb 1854 (twin)
Son Sorenson, 19 Feb 1854 (twin)

SPOUSE: Soren Christian Petersen
MARRIED: 22 Oct 1861
Hjorring, Denmark
DEATH SP: 1 Oct 1895
Logan, Cache Co., Utah

CHILDREN:
Cecilia Matilda, 10 Jan 1862
Soren, 4 Jul 1866 (twin)
Son, 4 Jul 1866 (twin)
Theodore, 24 Feb 1868
Josephine, 9 Aug 1871

Elsie Marie joined the Church of Jesus Christ of Latter-day Saints just one year after the gospel was brought to Denmark.

In 1863, she came to America with her husband, Soren Christian Petersen, their two living children, Liza and Cecilia Marie. They came across the Plains with William Preston's Wagon Company and arrived in the Salt Lake Valley on September 10, 1863. They were advised to go to Cache Valley and arrived there on September 12, 1863.

Shortly after their arrival, Cecilia died. She had been ill while they were crossing the Plains. They were very

grateful they could bury her in Logan instead of somewhere along the trail.

Elsie Marie was a faithful, humble, compassionate, energetic, loving woman with a beautiful spirit and sharing heart. She loved the gospel and was eager to leave her native country to come to America to live and to serve the Lord.

She sold her wedding ring to buy a cow. She made and sold butter and other things and walked many miles to take them to market to help provide a living. They gleaned the wheat fields to provide flour for their bread. When the Logan Temple was completed, she was called to help keep it clean. She walked with her bucket and cleaning materials on her arm to perform this duty. She made candles, knitted stockings for her family and others, made slippers with leather soles. She carded wool from their sheep, spun it into thread or yarn, then wove it into fabric for their clothing.

She gave of her love and compassionate assistance to her family and countless others who were in need of her help. She had a great sense of humor and was a fascinating story-teller. Elsie Marie loved people, shared her home with the homeless many times. She had a strong testimony of the gospel and loved sharing it with others. She was a visiting teacher for thirty years and was always active in the Church.

JACOBINE KIRSTINE MOGENSEN JENSEN JORGENSEN PETERSEN

No
Photo
Available

BIRTHDATE: 22 Aug 1836
Hornslet, Aarhus, Denmark
DEATH: 1866
Ovid, Idaho
PARENTS: Mogens Petersen
Maren Thomasen
PIONEER: 12 Sep 1861
John R. Murdock Wagon Train
SPOUSE: Christen Jensen
MARRIED: 2 Jun 1854
(later divorced)
DEATH SP: Unknown

CHILDREN:
Soren, 25 Sep 1856
Maren, 13 Dec 1858

SPOUSE II: Rasmus Jorgensen
MARRIED: 20 May 1861
On board ship "Monarch Of The Sea"
DEATH SP: 1865
Ovid, Idaho

CHILD:
Maria (Nielsen), 10 Apr 1862

SPOUSE III: Thomas Christian Petersen
MARRIED: Unknown
DEATH SP: 3 Sep 1903
CHILDREN:

Jacobine Kirstine was born in Hornslet, Aarhus, Denmark, 1836. After her divorce from Christen Jensen, on May 16, 1861, Jacobine, her eight year old daughter Maren, her neighbor Rasmus Jorgensen, his grown daughter Cecilia and a young man named Poul Michael Poulsen sailed for America on the ship "Monarch of the Sea." Rasmus having paid passage for them all.

This sailing vessel carried the largest group of Saints ever to leave England. There was difficulty housing the passengers. There was plenty of room for married couples but a great shortage of space for single passengers. It was proposed those planning on marrying later should marry now to alleviate the crowded conditions in the "single" area. Among them were Rasmus and Jacobine and Cecilia and Poul. Jacobine being twenty-five years old and Rasmus being fifty-eight.

They crossed the Plains in the John Murdock Wagon Company arriving in the Salt Lake Valley on September 12, 1861. They first settled in Brigham City where their daughter, Maria, was born.

In 1864, they moved to the Bear Lake Valley. They settled in the community of Ovid where many other Danish people were. The weather was severely harsh and cold. Jacobine's husband Rasmus passed away in the spring of 1865.

A short time later she married Thomas Petersen as his second wife. She passed away the following year 1866, at the age of thirty.

JOHANNA SOPHIA BACKMAN PETERSEN

BIRTHDATE: 26 Jun 1856
Gardhem, Sweden
DEATH: 29 Nov 1934
Huntsville, Weber Co., Utah
PARENTS: Oliver Backman
Inga Lena Johanesson
PIONEER: 29 Sep 1866
Capt. Nebeker's Wagon Train
SPOUSE: Jens Peter Petersen
MARRIED: 24 Feb 1873
Salt Lake City, Salt Lake, Utah
DEATH SP: 3 May 1906
Huntsville, Weber Co., Utah

CHILDREN:
Amelia Sophia "Millie," 9 Apr 1879
Helma Maria "Hilma," 8 Oct 1881
Anne Charlotte "Annie," 9 Nov 1883
Mary Fredrericka, 2 Nov 1885
Olga Olivia, 10 Feb 1888
Peter Adolph, 28 Mar 1889 (twin)
James Francis, 28 Mar 1889 (twin)
Selma Elvina 1891
George William, 15 Mar 1892
Josephine Alma, 25 Apr 1894

Johanna was born in Sweden in 1856. She emigrated to America with her parents when she was ten years old. They sailed on the ship "Humbolt" from Copenhagen Denmark landing in New York, then went to Florence, Nebraska where they joined with Captain Nebeker's Wagon Company, arriving in the Salt Lake Valley on September 29, 1866.

Her mother was sick throughout their journey, also her two year old brother, Karl, who died on the Plains, no date given. They settled in Huntsville.

When Johanna was sixteen, in 1872 or 1873, Johanna married Jens Peter Petersen in Salt Lake City, Utah. They were the parents of ten children.

In her younger years she was troubled a great deal with rheumatism.

Johanna's home was between both her parents and Jen's parents home. Leaving her to care for them in their old age. Many times she ran from one place to the other supplying their needs. Three of them died close together and four years later her husband died. Her mother lived another nine years. Death had visited her home several times, losing all but three daughters and one son.

Through all her trails and tribulations she had a sense of humor, liked to cut up and would play tricks. Johanna could play several instruments by ear. This helped her through the dark times. She was called to be a Relief Society teacher in 1903.

Johanna passed away on November 29, 1934 at the age of seventy-eight.

KJESTIE "KATY" LOFGREEN PETERSEN

BIRTHDATE: 10 Nov 1842
Hofterup, Sweden
DEATH: 1923
Huntsville, Weber Co., Utah
PARENTS: Paul Lofgreen
Anna Truesdotter
PIONEER: 20 Aug 1868
Chester Loveland Handcart Com.
SPOUSE: Soren Lind Petersen
MARRIED: 1864
Sweden
DEATH SP: 25 Nov 1901
Huntsville, Weber Co., Utah

CHILDPEN:
Niels, 2 Sep 1865
Josephine (Harris), 27 Dec 1870
Joseph, Mar 1871 (stillborn)
David, 13 Mar 1875
Hyrum, 15 Oct 1881

Katy was born in Sweden, 1842. At the age of twenty-one, she married Soren Lind Petersen in Sweden. They became parents of one son while living there. They converted to the Church of Jesus Christ of Latter-day Saints and emigrated in 1868.

They came by rail to Laramie, Wyoming, obtained a handcart and came to the Salt Lake Valley with the Chester Loveland Wagon Company arriving on August 20, 1868.

They made their home in Huntsville, adding four more children to their family, Katy gave permission for Boren to marry twice more. His second wife was Anne Elizabeth Nielson by whom he had nine children and third, Maren Louisa Pedersen by whom he had ten children.

Katy and Soren were sealed in the Salt Lake Endowment House on December, 1869. They farmed for a living in Huntsville. Katy had the sadness of a stillborn son in 1871. She was a good wife and mother, helping all within her extended family and her community.

Soren passed away in 1901. Katy did not marry again and remained independent until her passing in 1923 at the age of eighty-one, having been a widow for twenty-one years.

MAREN JENSEN SKOW PETERSEN

BIRTHDATE: 20 Dec 1830
Lime, Viborg, Denmark
DEATH: 30 Aug 1900
Ephraim, Sanpete Co., Utah
PARENTS: Jens Jensen Skow
Kirsten Nielsen Bertelsen
PIONEER: 29 Sep 1853
John E. Forsgren Wagon Train
SPOUSE: Niels Petersen
MARRIED: 10 Sep 1853
Ephraim, Utah Co., Utah
DEATH SP: 28 Mar 1897
Ephraim, Sanpete Co., Utah

CHILDREN:
Jens, 13 Feb 1855
Mary Christena, 6 Jan 1857
Niels Christian, 1 Jan 1859
Zinne, 28 Dec 1860
Annie Elizabeth, 24 Mar 1862
Niels Jospeh, 22 Apr 1864
Marie, 9 Apr 1866
Ephraim, 29 Mar 1869
Gertrude, 19 Dec 1870

Maren was born in Denmark in 1830. Maren left Denmark with her brother, Niels, for America. She met Niels Petersen on the boat leaving Denmark, they were married in Zions camp on September 10, 1853.

They arrived in the Salt Lake Valley on September 29, 1853, then went to Sanpete County. They called it "Little Denmark," later called Spring City. On Christmas day they were burned out and they moved to Manti for protection. When it was safe they moved to Pine Creek. Maren arranged her house and grounds like her home in Denmark.

Maren supplemented the family income by selling currants picked, cleaned and steamed for ten cents a gallon. She made butter and cheese selling the surplus for ten cents a pound. Maren and Niels raised sheep for food and Maren cleaned, carded, and spun wool into yarn for cloth and knitting. She was a faithful Relief Society worker and was a teacher for many years.

Niels passed away on April 28, 1897. Three years later Maren passed away on August 30, 1900 at age seventy.

MAREN JOHNSON (JOHANSDATTER) PETERSEN

No
Photo
Available

BIRTHDATE: 18 Feb 1829
Horslev, Viborg, Denmark
DEATH: 21 Feb 1890
Logan, Cache Co., Utah
PARENTS: Johan Christiansen
Johanne Knudsdatter
PIONEER: Btwn 1860 and 1863
SPOUSE: Niels E. Petersen
MARRIED: 7 Jun 1850
Viborg, Thistede, Denmark
DEATH SP: 27 May 1902
Logan, Cache Co., Utah

CHILDREN:
Johanne Marie, 27 Mar 1851
Johanne Marie, 1 Mar 1852
Anne Marie, 5 Oct 1854
Jens Johan "James," 27 Aug 1856
Wilhelm "William," 7 Oct 1858
Johan Peter, 16 Oct 1860
Hyrum Smith, 16 Oct 1863
Joseph Smith, 7 Jan 1865
Nephi Engaard, 4 Mar 1867
Sarah, 9 Mar 1869

Maren was born in Denmark in 1829. While she was younger she learned to tailor mens suits, from her father. She made the suit her husband was married in. When she was twenty-one years old she married Niels E. Petersen on June 7, 1850.

They left Denmark the end of 1860, Maren's mother, Johanne Knudsdatter, came with them and their children. They earned enough money to buy a wagon and supplies to start their journey to the Salt Lake Valley. There was no date given as to when.

Maren's mother, Johanne, never reached the Valley. She died of cholera in Wyoming. They arrived in the Salt Lake Valley before 1863 because their son, Hyrum Smith, was born in Logan, Utah in 1863.

Maren also learned at a young age to cook, sew, quilt, knit and weave, which helped her all her life.

Maren passed away on February 21, 1890 in Logan, Cache County, Utah at the age of sixty-one.

MAREN "MARY" PETERSEN THOMPSON PETERSEN

BIRTHDATE: 13 Jul 1838
Horbelev, Denmark
DEATH: 2 Jul 1917
Ephraim, Sanpete Co., Utah
PARENTS: Peter P. Thompson
Dorthea Andersen
PIONEER: 1854
SPOUSE I: David Thompson
MARRIED: 9 May 1855
Ephraim, Sanpete Co., Utah
DEATH SP: 20 Mar 1865
Ephraim, Sanpete Co., Utah

CHILDREN:
Mary Diantha, 13 Apr 1857
Elizabeth Marie, 28 Nov1858
Louisa Jane, 6 Oct 1860
David William, 1 Dec 1862
Annie Caroline, 14 Dec 1864

SPOUSE II: Peter Petersen
MARRIED: 4 Nov 1865
Ephraim, Sanpete Co., Utah
DEATH SP: 15 May 1939
Ephraim, Sanpete Co., Utah

CHILDREN:
Peter Christian, 24 Sep 1866 (died as an infant)
Hannah Ephraimine, 23 Dec 1867 (died at age 1)
Orval Erastus, 25 Nov 1871
Ellen Lorinda, 19 Mar 1874
Dora Ann, 2 Jul 1876 (died at age 2)
Sarah Jane, 18 Jun 1879

Maren was born to Peter Petersen Thompson and Dorthea Andersen in Horbelev, Denmark. When Mary was fourteen years old, her parents brought their family of five children to America. Their family arrived in the Valley of the Great Salt Lake in 1854. They continued on to Ephraim, Sanpete County, Utah to settle.

Maren married David Thompson on May 9, 1855, in Ephraim, Utah.

Maren was a true pioneer and was an expert in weaving, dyeing, cheese making, spinning wool, wool cording, sewing, and cooking. She knitted, canned food, and was very proud of her garden vegtables, her fruit trees, and her flowers.

Her husband passed away after ten years of marriage, leaving her with five young children.

Maren married again, this time to Peter Petersen on November 4, 1865, and six children were born to this union. Maren and Peter served a mission to Denmark in 1900 and brought back much genealogy.

Maren passed away at her home in Ephraim, Utah on July 2, 1917.

MARIE SORENSSEN PETERSEN

BIRTHDATE: 9 Oct 1823
Trige, Pannerup, Denmark
DEATH: 09 Jul 1899
Huntsville, Weber Co., Utah
PARENTS: Soren Jensen
Bodil (Pedersdatter) Peterson
PIONEER: 23 Sep 1862
Madsen Indepen Wagon Train
SPOUSE: Peder Petersen
MARRIED: 22 Oct 1850
Denmark
DEATH SP: 20 Feb 1897
Huntsville, Weber Co., Utah

CHILDREN:
Peder, 19 Mar 1851 (died at age 2)
Soren, 28 Apr 1852 (died at 3 months)
Soren Peter, 11 Aug 1853
Peter, 29 Nov 1854 (died at 2 months)

Marie was born in Trige, Pannerup, Aarhus, Denmark. Her father was a railroad worker, a farm hand, and owned a small farm. Her mother was a weaver and taught her daughters the weaving skills. Marie became a good weaver.

At the age of twenty-seven, she married a widower, Peder Peterson, who lived in the same small town. He had a four year old daughter. They had four sons and only one survived to adulthood.

When Marie and Peder heard the missionaries of the Church of Jesus Christ of Latter-day Saints, they felt at last they had found the true church and were baptized as members. They made the decision to emigrate to America, sold all their earthly goods, and left Denmark on April 27, 1862. They went to Germany, then sailed from Hamburg for the United States.

When they arrived in New York City, Abraham Lincoln was President and the Civil War was being fought. They traveled on train as far as St. Joseph, Missouri, then traveled by boat up the Missouri River to Florence, Nebraska. They crossed the Plains with an independent wagon train called the Madsen Company and arrived in the Salt Lake Valley on September 23, 1862.

The family lived in Salt Lake City for two years before moving on to Huntsville, Utah. Marie and her family lived in a dugout for the first two years before they built a log home in which they lived about ten years.

Marie was a wonderful mother and considered this her greatest achievement. Her son, Soren Peter, married and had three children before his wife died. Marie raised the children for the next three years until he remarried.

On February 20, 1897, Marie's husband died and two years later, Marie died at the age of seventy-six.

ALBERTINA ERICKSEN PETERSON

BIRTHDATE: 8 Sep 1850
Fredrickstad, Fred., Norway
DEATH: 10 Nov 1922
Santaquin, Utah Co., Utah
PARENTS: Engelbret Ericksen
Olena Mobee Olsen
PIONEER: Unknown
SPOUSE: Solomon Peterson
MARRIED: 8 Jan 1872
DEATH SP: 17 Dec 1924
Santaquin, Utah Co., Utah

CHILDREN:
Jennie Albertina, 28 Jan 1873
Solomon Alma, 7 Feb 1875
Joseph A., 12 May 1877 (died as an infant)
John Oliver, 19 Apr 1878
Peter Engebret, 11 Aug 1880
Emma S., 26 Feb 1885
Clara V. Dale, 7 Aug 1887
Brigham, 5 Jun 1890
Esther, 9 Nov 1893

Albertina was the oldest of six children born to her parents in Norway. The family was taught the gospel and joined the Church of Jesus Christ of Latter-dy Saints, Albertina being baptized in 1863. Her father died in 1864, leaving the family destitute.

Her mother emigrated to Utah in 1866 with the four younger children. She left Albertina and her sister, Emma, in Norway. The two girls endured many hardships working in the homes of strangers for their board and room.

On the handcart trek, the mother Olena, met Solomon Peterson, and told him of leaving the two girls behind in Norway. He offered to provide the money to bring them to Utah. So Albertina and her sister joined with some other Scandinavian Saints to cross the ocean and the Plains.

Albertina concented to marry Solomon only after her mother had a home and was able to care for her family without Albertina's help. They were married on January 8, 1872 in the Endowment House. To them were born nine children; eight of them living to maturity.

Albertina was a quiet woman, her home and children were her main interests.

She passed away on November 10, 1922 at age seventy-two and is buried in the Santaquin Cemetery.

ANN PATTEN PETERSON

BIRTHDATE: 18 May 1831
Chester Co., Pennsylvania
DEATH: 28 Jan 1909
Mesa, Arizona
PARENTS: William C. Patten
Julianna Bench Patten
PIONEER: 3 Oct 1850
Whipple Wagon Train
SPOUSE: Charles S. Peterson
MARRIED: 21 Jan 1849
DEATH SP: Not given

CHILDREN:
Alma, 17 Feb 1850
Nancy Ann, 30 Mar 1852
Charles, 18 Jan 1854
Sarah, 23 Feb 1856
Joseph Smith, 24 Jun 1858
Hyrum Smith, 29 Jun 1860
Julia Anna, 8 Jun 1862
Brigham Young, 17 Apr 1864 (died at age 3)
Heber Kimball, 22 Feb 1866
Jedediah Grant, 6 Sep 1868
Ann, 17 Apr 1873
Martha, 9 May 1875
William, 16 Jul 1880 (died as an infant)

Ann's mother died when was very young. Her grandmother Cornwell, came to help her father raise the children.

In the Fall of 1841, her father accepted the gospel of the Chuch of Jesus Christ of Latter-day Saints and was baptized as a member. He took his family and moved to Nauvoo, Illinois.

Ann became the second wife of Charles Shreeve Peterson. Her sister, Mary Ann, was his first wife. He took his first family to the Salt Lake Valley in 1849. Ann came the following year with her father's family with the Edson Whipple Wagon Company. They arrived in the Salt Lake Valley on October 3, 1850.

Ann's husband moved his families from place to place for years and in each place, houses were built for them. Everything was crude those early pioneering days, and it made life dreadfully hard for a mother with a large family. There were times when they lived on sego lily roots and other greens.

Ann was a good natured mother. She had a great deal of sewing to do by hand and stockings to knit. She washed the wool, carded it into rolls, spun it into yarn, wove it into cloth, and formed it into clothing. She became a nurse in hundreds of cases and learned midwifery by practice.

After the railroad came, Charles built a six-room house and ran a blacksmith shop and a small store. Ann and her daughter, Sarah, boarded the railroad workers. She was the mother of thirteen children and also raised some children of Charles' other wives.

Ann was President of the Relief Society of the Weber City Ward in Morgan Stake for ten years. They moved again to Bear River Flat (Fielding) where they homesteaded for a short time and then moved back to Peterson. In the summer of 1883, they moved to Mesa, Arizona where they homesteaded 160 acres. Charles later moved his young wife and family to Mexico leaving Ann and her family to work the homestead.

Charles passed away on September 26, 1889. Not long after his death, Ann's house burned and nothing was saved. She sold her land to provide shelter for herself and her single daughter.

As soon as Ann could earn money to pay for transportation, she took her daughter to Utah to do temple work in Utah several times. The altitude of Utah bothered her a great deal, so she continued living in Mesa and nursed people until just a few weeks before her death on January 28, 1909.

ANNA KATRINA (CAJSA) OLSSON PETERSON

No Photo Available

BIRHTDATE: 1 Jan 1811
Skalby, lmar, Kal, Sweden
DEATH: 21 Dec 1900
Clarkston, Cache Co., Utah
PARENTS: Peter / Pehr Olsson
Elin Carlsson
PIONEER: 7 Oct 1866
Capt. Scott Co. Wagon Train
SPOUSE: Johannes Peterson
MARRIED: 26 Nov 1834
Kalmar, Sweden (other records
show 5 Dec 1834)
DEATH SP: 14 Jul 1893
Logan, Cache Co., Utah

CHILDREN:
Johanna Mathilda, 11 Sep 1835
Johanna "Ann" Sophia, 17 Jan 1838
Amanda Mathilda, 30 Sep 1840
John (Johan), August, 15 Jul 1842
Carl Fredrik, 1841)
Carl Frederick, 21 Jun 1850
Johanna Mathildal, 23 Nov 1852

Anna Katrina was born on January 1, 1811 in Sweden. Her father had been married before and his wife had died leaving three children who were raised by Elin.

This family lived on a small farm. Elin was very industrious and she taught her children to do all kinds of work, saying it was a sin to be idle. Ann learned to care for wool, to spin and to weave cloth. She sometimes wove beautiful colored stripes. When their family cow died, she sold enough hand woven cloth to buy a cow to replace it.

The family was very religious. Each morning they knelt in prayer, sang a hymn and read from the Bible before partaking of breakfast. They grew flax, cut and treated it, spun and wove it into cloth for bed linen and other uses. It was two of these home-grown handwoven sheets that were sewn together to keep them warm as they crossed the plains.

When very young, Anna went out to work as a seamstress in different homes, made suits for men besides the other sewing. She stayed at a place where she had received steady work until she married Johannes Peterson 26 Nov 1834. Her mistress cried when she left after three years and said, "Where will I get anyone so good and so gifted as my Anna?" On her wedding day she wore the Golden Church Crown, rented from the church, which was considered a great honor. Old country people loved weddings, and a sizable crowd witnessed her marriage in the church.

They set up housekeeping but found it difficult to find work. Anna stitched shirt fronts and cuffs of men's shirts to help out. Johannes was a ship carpenter, and because times did not get any better, they decided to go to Denmark. They were able to buy a farm in Bornholm where most of their seven children were born. Three of the children died in infancy. Mormon Elders brought the Gospel to them. The whole family was baptized in 1852. They had always made the Elders feel welcome in their home and they held cottage meetings there. One day their thatched roof caught on fire when the family was away at a meeting. They lost everything but some papers and a trunk. The next spring they were able to build a comfortable home with the fire insurance and John's wages.

They raised vegetables, small fruit, cherries and apples. The had a cow, some sheep, ducks and chickens. They drained the wet, soggy ground, and had a wooded lot where they grew a garden and trees.

After joining the Church, their hearts were filled with joining the Saints in Zion. They sold their farm and booked passage on a steamer. They left Bornholm I May 1866 with Johannes, Anna, their son, John and his wife and daughter, Sophia 28, and Mathilda age 13. They borrowed money for one fare, but couldn't get enough money to bring 15 year old Carl. It was six years before Carl came to America. They sailed on the "Kenilworth" with 680 emigrants on the ship. It took 65 days as they encountered many storms. They had faith and said, "Don't be afraid. God is on the water as well as on the land." Anna's motto was "Hope and trust in God, do right, and you will be able to meet the storms of life."

ANNA MARGRETHE LARSEN PETERSON

No
Photo
Available

BIRTHDATE: 8 Aug 1818
Nykobing, Maribo, Denmark
DEATH: 4 Jun 1871
Huntsville, Weber Co., Utah
PARENTS: Lars Simonsen
Juliane Hansen
PIONEER: 1 Oct 1862
Capt. John Horne Wagon Train
SPOUSE: Hans Peterson
MARRIED: 17 May 1833
Bjorup, Maribo, Denmark
DEATH SP: 18 Nov 1900
Kaneville, Weber Co., Utah

CHILDREN:
Peter, 14 Apr 1834
Lars, 27Feb 1837
Hans Jorgen, 4 Apr 1839
Peter, 11 Jan 1841
Anne Kirstine (Cristiansen), 31 Mar 1843
Christian, 18 Sep 1845

Anna was born in Denmark in 1818. She had one older brother. Her childhood was spent in Nykobing.

At age fourteen she married Hans Peterson, Bjorup, Maribo, Denmark May 17, 1833. They were the parents of six children, five boys and one girl all born in Denmark.

When they came to America they boarded the ship "Humboldt," from Hamburg, Germany sailing to New York. Then they joined Captain John Horne's Wagon Company to cross the Plains. Arriving in the Salt Lake Valley on October 1, 1862, they settled in Huntsville, Utah.

Anna passed away eight years later on June 4, 1871, when she was fifty-three years old.

ANNA MARIE OLSEN PETERSON

BIRTHDATE: 11 Jan 1829
Oslo, Norway
DEATH: 9 Nov 1875
Ogden, Weber Co., Utah
PARENTS: Peter Olsen
Margarete Mathiasen
PIONEER: Oct 1866
SPOUSE: Peter C. Peterson
MARRIED: 15 Oct 1850
Oslo, Norway
DEATH SP: 16 Jan 1914
Plano, Madison Co., Idaho

CHILDREN:
Caroline, 4 Aug 1853
Peter, Jr., 4 Sep 1855
Edward, 10 Jun 1857
Maren Agnete, 1858
Mathilde, 1860
Hyrum, 1862
Elizabeth, 23 Mar 1868

William Franklin, 30 Jan 1870
Ephriam, 15 Feb 1872

Anna Marie was born in Norway in 1829. When she was twenty-one years old she married Peter Peterson on October 15, 1850.

They traveled from Oslo to Hamberg, Germany in 1866. Then sailed on the "Kenilworth," in April, 1866, for America. They arrived in the Salt Lake Valley in October, 1866. The company was unknown. They first settled in Bingham Canyon at Cottonwood. Peter soon built them a house out of logs.

They decided that Cottonwood didn't offer them the opportunities for their large family so they moved to Ogden in Weber County, Utah. They built their home on Main Street.

Ann Marie's health failed and she passed away in 1875, at the age of forty-six.

ANNE CHRISTINA NELSEN PEDERSON PETERSON

BIRTIIDATE: 11 Sep 1805
Denmark
DEATH: 14 Dec 1880
Salt Lake City, Salt Lake, Utah
PARENTS: Peder Hanson
Karen Jensen
PIONEER: 1867 Wagon Train
SPOUSE: Niels Pederson
MARRIED: 13 Oct 1833
Denmark
DEATH SP: 20 Sep 1867
Salt Lake City, Salt Lake, Utah

CHILDREN:
Peder George, 21 Mar 1833
Charles "Carl," 11 Jul 1834
Peder George, 3 Mar 1836
Johana Nicoline, 3 Dec 1837
Andrea Fredrike, 25 Jul 1839
Axeline Marie, 22 Dec 1840
Rudolph William, 3 Jul 1842
Thora Martine, 16 Aug 1844
Alvilda Elenora, 16 Feb 1846

Anne Pederson was born in Copenhagen, Denmark. Her mother died when she was small. She was raised by her grandmother. When her grandmother died, Anne worked to earn her own living.

She married Niels Pederson on October 13, 1833 in Denmark. They were both twenty-eight years old. When they came to America they changed the spelling of their name to Peterson.

Anne, along with her husband and family, joined the Church of Jesus Christ of Latter-day Saints and they were baptized in 1851. Anne and Niels became the parents of nine children; all born in Copenhagen, Denmark. Two of their children died in childhood. Their family names are all listed in the Copenhagen Branch records.

They had a great desire to emigrate to America to be with the members of the Church. They emigrated to America in 1867. All their living children, except Thora Martine, emigrated with their parents.

They crossed the Plains by wagon, but the name of the company is not known. They arrived in the Salt Lake Valley 1867. They were a tired and hungry group, having experienced many hardships and challenges on their journey. Anne's husband, Niels, died as they neared Big Mountain as they approached the Salt Lake Valley. He was buried near where the Pioneer Monument now stands. Later, when the family came back to reclaim his body, they could not find it. They believe it had been disturbed by animals. Anne was sixty-two years old when she became a widow. It is not known where the family settled in the Valley.

Anne passed away December 14, 1880 and was buried in the Salt Lake City Cemetery. The temple sealing for Anne and Niels was performed on August 24, 1894.

ANNE MARTINE ANDERSEN PETERSON

BIRTHDATE: 30 Dec 1826
Klemensker, Denmark
DEATH: 1 Nov 1908
Plain City, Weber Co., Utah
PARENTS: Anders Hansen
Karen Marie Hansen
PIONEER 30 Sep 1853
John E. Forsgren Wagon Train
SPOUSE: Hans Peterson
MARRIED: 3 Nov 1849
Ostermarie, Bornholm, Denmark
DEATH SP: 16 Sep 1881
Plain City, Weber Co., Utah

CHILDREN:
August Peder (Gus Petersen), 8 Jul 1850
Lovire Marie, 11 Jan 1852
Daughter, 1854
Emma, 29 Oct 1856
Joseph, 1859
Hans, 1860
Martena, 14 Oct 1864
Ellen, 11 Dec 1867
Caroline, 4 Jun 1871
Daughter, 1873
Laura, 6 May 1875

Anne Martine was born in Denmark in 1825. She married Hans Peterson three years after they met. Her parents gave them a little farm.

In the later part of 1852 they emigrated to America. While sailing on the ocean her two children came down with yellow fever, of which Lovire Marie died. Not wanting her buried at sea she said she wasn't dead. But her husband said they would find out so he with two other men took a life boat and found an island to bury her on. Bringing back some twigs and leaves to prove to her it was on land. During this time Anne received word her mother had also died.

While walking to the Salt Lake Valley Anne found a stray lamb. Hans put it in the wagon and from that they raised a large band of sheep.

They arrived in the Salt Lake Valley on September 30. 1853. They lived in Lehi, Utah until 1859 when they settled in Plain City, Utah.

Anne carded, spun, and knit all the wool stockings for her family. She was always willing to share what she had.

Hans was called to help other emigrants who were on their way, this left Anne alone with her family. Anne always said "We were blessed and protected while he was away."

Anne was the mother of ten children and lived to see seven of them married with children.

Hans passed away in 1881 leaving Anne the little ones to raise on her own. Anne passed away on November 1, 1908 in Plain City at the age of eighty-three.

ANNE MORIAH "ANE MARIE" HANSEN PETERSON

BIRTHDATE: 13 Mar 1822
Stove Lime, Norup, Denmark
DEATH: 31 Jul 1911
Fairview, Sanpete Co., Utah
PARENTS: Hans Olesen
Mette Jensen
PIONEER: 1853 Wagon Train
SPOUSE: Anders Pedersen
(Andrew Peterson)
MARRIED: 15 Oct 1854
Salt Lake City, Salt Lake, Utah
DEATH SP: 20 Jan 1873
Fairview, Sanpete Co., Utah

CHILDREN:
Christena, 15 Sep 1855
Andrew, 4 Jul 1857
Lorenzo, 29 Jul 1858
Peter, 27 Sep 1860
Mette Mary, 21 Nov 1862
Ane Marie Hansena, 3 Aug 1868

Ane Marie was born in Stove Lime, Norup, Vejle, Denmark. She was baptized into the Church of Jesus Christ of Latter-day Saints on December 2, 1851.

She left her home in Denmark and emigrated to America and then to the Salt Lake Valley for her love of the true Gospel. She arrived in the land of Zion by wagon, the Fall of 1853.

Anne Marie married Andrew Peterson (Anders Pedersen) on October 15, 1854 in Salt Lake City, Utah. Her husband married his first wife in Denmark; she died in July, 1853 on the Plains of Kansas as they were journeying to Utah.

Anne Marie and Andrew became the parents of six children; one baby died at the age of one day. They lived in Salt Lake City, Brigham City, Ephraim before permanently settling in Fairview, Sanpete County, Utah which was called at that time North Bend, Utah.

When they first came to North Bend they lived in a dugout. Their fourth child was born in that dugout. Later, they built a two-story, ten-room adobe house.

Anne Marie and Andrew were sealed in the Endowment House in Salt Lake City on November 28, 1863. She shared her husband when he took a second wife in plural marriage a year later.

Anne Marie was active in the Church, serving as a counselor in the Relief Society for many years. She assisted in gathering grain for the Church storehouse. She was a weaver. She corded, spun and dyed sheep wool and made yarn of which she wove many yards of linsey cloth. She used this cloth to make suits and shirts for the boys, and dresses, petticoats and aprons for the girls and women.

After her husband passed away on January 20, 1873, Ane Marie took in boarders, operating the first hotel in Fairview. This combination home and hotel stood at the south end of Main Street at a terminal where the main highway turned west. It faced north and looking from it you could see straight up Main Street. She also owned and took care of bees and continued to weave linsey cloth, carpets and rag rugs. She was thrifty and industrious.

Anne Marie enjoyed good health throughout her life. She was a widow for thirty-seven years. Anne Marie passed away at her home in Fairview at the age of eighty-nine years.

ANNIE CHRISTINA SORENSEN PEDERSON

BIRTHDATE: 8 Oct 1821
Oslo, Norway
DEATH: 28 Nov 1899
Preston, Idaho
PARENTS: Soren Hansen
Anne Christensen
PIONEER: 25 Sep 1863
Peter Nebeker
SPOUSE: Simon Pederson
MARRIED: 16 Dec 1842
Aker, Akerhus, Oslo, Norway
DEATH SP: 20 Jun 1895
Aker, Akerhus, Oslo, Norway

CHILDREN:
Bertha Serena (Jensen), 20 Aug 1841
Peter Olavis, 19 Feb 1844

Hans August, 29 Jul 1846
Christian Elvin, 12 Mar 1849
Julia Konstance (Jensen), 30 Aug 1851
Jendrick Emil, 29 Jan 1854
Gensine Antana or Jensina Antonia, 20 Nov 1856
Annettie Othilie (Olsen or Ollefsen Tollefsen), 2 Jul 1858
Carl Ferdinand, 19 Jun 1863

Annie Christina was born in Norway, 1821. At the age of twenty-one she married Simon Pederson. They made their home in the area of Oslo, Norway, becoming parents of ten children.

Annie Christina converted to the Church of Jesus Christ of Latter-day Saints and made plans to emigrate to Utah. Simon did not come, he returned to East Aker, Akerhus, Oslo, Norway where he passed away in 1895.

The Pederson family left Florence, Nebraska on July 25, 1863 in the Peter Nebeker Wagon Company, with seventy wagons and 500 immigrants. Some wagons also carried freight to Utah. They traveled by wagon and walked. Their baby, Carl Ferdinand, was carried by his mother Annie Christina. They arrived in the Salt Lake Valley on September 25, 1863 and made their home with family from Norway.

After a while, they settled in Idaho. Four of the Pederson children homesteaded in Idaho, in Preston, Rexburg, and Franklin. As they grew to adulthood, they helped their mother remain independent and active until her passing at age seventy-eight in 1899. She is buried in Preston, Idaho.

CAROLINE ELIZABETH SORENSEN PETERSON

No Photo Available

BIRTHDATE: 20 Jul 1840
Hals, Aalborg, Denmark
DEATH: 5 Nov 1858
Salt Lake City, Salt Lake, Utah
PARENTS: Nickolai Sorensen
Ane / Anne Marie Holm
PIONEER: 5 Oct 1854
Hans P. Olsen Wagon Train
SPOUSE: Samuel Peterson
MARRIED: 24 Aug 1856
Salt Lake City, Salt Lake, Utah
DEATH SP: 5 Mar 1906
Salt Lake City, Salt Lake, Utah

CHILDREN:
Maria Christina (Olsen), 19 Jun 1857
Baby son, 5 Nov 1858 (died at birth)

Caroline was born in Denmark. She was the first in her family to be converted to the Church of Jesus Christ of Latter-day Saints. She was thirteen years of age. Although her father demanded that she not listen to the Mormon Elders in the streets of Denmark, she knew it was the true restored Church and was baptized and confirmed a member. Her father sent her away to fend for herself. She found work in others' households. She saved her money and after her father died, she was able to help buy passage to America for herself, her mother and two other members of their family.

Caroline and her family lefts Hals, Denmark on December 9, 1853 with the Christian J. Larsen Company to New Orleans, arriving on February 20, 1954. By the way of two steamers they arrived in Kansas City on April 13, 1854. They left Westport, June 15, 1854, with the Hans Peters Olsen Company and after ten months of arduous journey by ocean, rivers, mountains and barren plains, they arrived in the Salt Lake Valley on October 5, 1854.

On August 24, 1856, Caroline married Samuel Peterson, an immigrant who crossed the Plains with oxen and wagon arriving in the Salt Lake Valley on September 30, 1853. He was in the first company of Scandinavian converts to leave Copenhagen for Zion.

They became the parents of two children. Caroline was sixteen years old when she married Samuel. Samuel earned his living by wood carving and building furniture for Brigham Young. Caroline's marriage was short and so was her life here on earth. She passed away in childbirth at the age of eighteen. She and her newborn son were buried together, November 5, 1858.

Her first child, Maria Christina, was cared for by her maternal grandmother until her father married two years later. Samuel Peterson died in Salt Lake City, Utah.

CHRISTINE WILHELMINE CATHERINE KROLL PETERSON

BIRTHDATE: 23 Mar 1833
Copenhagen, Denmark
DEATH: 22 Apr 1913
Salt Lake City, Salt Lake, Utah
PARENTS: Johan Joackin Kroll
Maren Dorthea Olsen
PIONEER: 15 Sep 1861
Joseph Horne Co. Wagon Train
SPOUSE: Charles C. Peterson
MARRIED: 3 Jul 1861
DEATH SP: 13 Oct 1874
Salt Lake City, Salt Lake, Utah

CHILDREN:
Charles Niels, 20 Jul 1862
Mary Wilhelmine, 18 Jun 1864
Anna Pauline, 8 Aug 1866
Thora Josephine, 26 Nov 1868
John William, 11 Jan 1871
Axeline Katherine, 19 May 1873

Wilhelmine was born, March 23, 1833, In Copenhagen, Denmark, the only daughter in a family of six children. As a child, "Meena" learned to be an excellent seamstress while helping her father in his tailor shop.

She was well educated and learned to speak and write English and French. Her mother died of typhoid fever when she was eight years old, her father eventually remarried.

Wilhelmine received a Book of Mormon from a missionary and after reading a few pages she was thoroughly convinced of its truthfulness. She was baptized into the Church of Jesus Christ of Latter-day Saints on February 20, 1854.

She was engaged to the missionary who had converted her. He went to serve in the army and when he returned he had apostatized from the Church and tried to convince her to also leave the church. She gave back his ring.

She encouraged her father, a devout Lutheran, to come to church with her but her stepmother was very much against the new religion and threatened to leave if he went to church with her. She also told Wilhelmine that she was no longer welcome in their home.

Wilhelmine left and went to work at the mission home. It was here that Wilhelmine met Charles "Carl" Christian Peterson, the choir leader. Wilhelmine and Charles left Denmark on May 9, 1861 and then sailed from Liverpool, England on the "Monarch of the Sea." They landed in New York on June 23, 1861.

They had to planned to marry when they reached the Salt Lake Valley, but since so many others were getting married they chose to marry along the way, July 3, 1861. They later were sealed in the Salt Lake Endowment House on October 4, 1862.

They joined the Joseph Horne Wagon Company in Florence, Nebraska, driving a team and walking with sore and bleeding feet for the majority of the way. They arrived in the Salt Lake Valley on September 14, 1861.

They borrowed a wheel barrow to carry their belongings in a large wooden box to their rented cabin. Later, they built a one-room adobe home at 133 South 7th East on a half acre of land they purchased. Wilhelmine helped make the adobe bricks. They added more rooms to this house where her six children were born.

Early in their marriage she moved with her husband to Ogden, Weber County, Utah and Charles helped build a meeting house. While living in Ogden, they stayed in a dugout where the snakes and Indians were troublesome.

In October, of 1874, Wilhelmine's husband said, "the home is paid for, we owe no one, and life will be easier now." He passed away the following week, leaving her a widow at the age of forty with six children. The oldest child was twelve years old and the youngest was 17 months.

Wilhelmine took in sewing to support her family, she knitted underwear and made beautiful fancy lace stockings which were greatly admired.

She worked in the Relief Society as a block teacher in the 11th ward. She had a firm testimony in the truthfulness of the Gospel. Her own words were, "I still rejoice in the Gospel and hope I will be able to be faithful forever."

Welhelmine was almost blind before she passed away on April 22, 1913 at the age of eighty in Salt Lake City, Utah.

ELIZABETH ESKLUND PETERSON

BIRTHDATE: 23 Apr 1857
Vemlingbo, Gotland, Sweden
DEATH: 21 Aug 1942
Scipio, Millard Co., Utah
PARENTS: Lars Peter Esklund
Catherine Christensen
PIONEER: 1863
J. R. Young Indep. Wagon Train
SPOUSE: Carl M. Peterson
MARRIED: 4 Nov 1880
DEATH SP: 1930

CHILDREN:
Anna Elizabeth, 11 Oct 1881
Emma Catherine, 24 Oct 1883
Edith Gertrude, 9 May 1886 (died at age 10)
Ina Isadora, 5 Apr 1889
Edward Carl, 6 Sep 1891 (twin)
Albert Mathias, 6 Sep 1891 (twin)
Genevieve Alice, 30 Jun 1894
Leon Hans, 17 Sep 1899

After having been converted to the Church of Jesus Christ of Latter-day Saints, Elizabeth's parents sold all their possessions and started for America in 1862. There were father, mother, grandmother, aunt, and five children in their group. After living in Stockholm for six months preparing for the voyage, they sailed from Liverpool with 336 other Scandinavians under the leadership of Soren Christopherson. A baby brother was born to the family three days after leaving Liverpool.

They reached New York on June 5, 1863 and took the train to Florence, Nebraska. Here the grandmother died and was buried. The Esklunds purchased a wagon, four oxen, and a cow. They joined an independent wagon company under the direction of J. R. Young, leaving Florence on July 7, 1863. Elizabeth walked most of the way.

After arriving in the Salt Lake Valley, the family was advised to go to Gunnison where several Scandinavian families were established. The Indians were troublesome, so after seven years, the Esklunds moved to Round Valley (now Scipio) in order to escape Indian problems. They soon had a pleasant new home.

Elizabeth's father died when she was a young woman, so Elizabeth taught school to help her mother support the younger children. Her school was in a log granary and the tuition was three dollars. The tuition was usually paid in grain, flour, or other necessities. Once, a child paid her with a pair of woolen socks.

At fourteen, Elizabeth was a member of the Relief Society. She was second counselor in the Primary, and was later president for eleven years. She also taught in the Sunday School.

On November 4, 1880, she married Carl M. Peterson who was a tailor. They raised eight children. One of their daughters died in later years leaving five children which Elizabeth and Carl raised.

ELSE MARIE JENSEN PETERSON

No
Photo
Available

BIRTHDATE: 11 Feb 1833
Albaek, Hjorring, Denmark
DEATH: 17 Oct 1862
Pleasant Grove, Utah Co, Utah
PARENTS: Jens Thorsen
Maren Michelsen
PIONEER: 23 Sep 1862
Christian Madsen Wagon Train
SPOUSE: Lars Peter Petersen
MARRIED: 26 Nov 1852
Albaek, Hjorring, Denmark
DEATH SP: 14 Aug 1906
Richfield, Sevier Co., Utah

CHILDREN:
Ane Marie, 16 May 1853
Jens Christian, 12 Dec 1854
Maren, 12 Jun 1856 (died at age 5)
Niels Peter, 9 May 1858
Ole Christian, 24 Jun 1859 (died at age 2)
Kristen, 17 Jun 1861 (died 11 months)
Elsie Marie, 9 Oct 1862 (died at 1 month)

Else and her husband, Lars, were well-to-do and highly respected in their native Denmark. Lars was a member of the King's Guard and represented King Frederick VII in the northeast area of Denmark where they lived. Else and Lars were considered to be of nobility. In addition to other luxuries, Else owned many beautiful dresses which she wore to court.

Else accepted the message of missionaries and was baptized a member of the Church of Jesus Christ of Latter-day Saints. This put an enormous strain on her marriage, almost resulting in a separation. Four years after her baptism, however, Lars was also baptized.

In April 1862, the family sold their home and belongings and prepared to emigrate to Zion. Just prior to their departure on the ship, "Franklin," from Hamburg Germany, her daughter, Maren, died of measles. With no time for a burial, she was the first passenger to be buried at sea. Forty other passengers subsequently died of measles and were buried at sea, including Else's two sons, Kristen and Ole Christian.

Else and her family traveled to Florence, Missouri and left from there to cross the Plains with Christian A. Madsen's Ox Train Company on July 7, 1862. They arrived in the Salt Lake Valley on September 23, 1862.

Immediately, the family settled in Pleasant Grove, Utah where Else gave birth to her seventh child. Else died a week later and the baby, Elsa Marie, died three weeks after. Both are buried in the Pleasant Grove Cemetery. Else's beautiful court dresses were sold to pay for her burial. Else had truly given her all for truth's sake.

EMMA MATILDA BACKMAN PETERSON

BIRTHDATE: 14 Jul 1853
Trollhattan, Sweden
DEATH: 24 Aug 1925
Huntsville, Weber Co., Utah
PARENTS: Olas A. Backman
Engelena Johannason
PIONEER: Oct 1866
Nebeker Handcart Company
SPOUSE: Christian Peterson
MARRIED: Feb. 13, 1869
Salt Lake Endowment House
DEATH SP: 13, 1893
Huntsville, Weber Co., Utah

CHILDREN:
Anna Matilda, 8 Mar 1870
Amelia Marie, 29 Mar 1892
John Christian, 28 Jan 1874
Emma Magdalina, 27 Dec 1875
Christian David, 5 Dec 1877
Margaret Elizabeth, 29 Apr 1880
Olivia Amanda, 4 Aug 1882
Carl Alfred, 21 Jul 1884
Fredrick William, 12 Oct 1887
Helga Charlotte, 19 Dec 1889
Adam Edwin, 16 Mar 1892
Moroni, 14 Apr 1893

Emma was the third child of six children and thirteen years of age as she accompanied her parents across the Plains. She stayed in Salt Lake for several years and then joined her family in Huntsville, Utah where she met Christian Peterson.

After her marriage she worked along with him in their small mercantile business. She was a devoted wife and mother of twelve children; six boys and six girls.

Emma taught her children that the greatest quality they could possess was that of unselfishness, denying self for the good of others. Her daughters were taught that motherhood was their first and greatest calling.

She was a gifted poetess and enjoyed writing poems for special occasions. She served for twenty-three years in the Primary and was also a diligent worker in YLMIA and Relief Society. She belonged to the Olive Camp of DUP.

Her dear husband, Christian, passed away in a tragic saw mill accident one month before their last son was born. She has left a posterity of hundreds in Western Canada and the United States and is loved and honored by all her descendants.

Emma was indeed a woman of great faith and courage.

HANSINE JACOBINE NYBOLLE HUFF PETERSON

BIRTHDATE: 27 Jun 1836
Haarby, Odense, Denmark
DEATH: 3 Sep 1916
Richfield, Sevier Co., Utah
PARENTS: Rasmus Nybolle
Hedevig L. Engelbrecht Petersen
PIONEER: 1857
SPOUSE I: James Huff
MARRIED: 1858
Manti, Sanpete Co., Utah
DEATH SP: 16 Oct 1903
Colonia, Juarez, Mexico

CHILDREN:
Julie Ann, 2 Sep 1859
James William, 1860 (died at 2 months)
Enoch Erastus, 1 May 1862

SPOUSE II: Sixtus Kjar
MARRIED: 3 Sep 1863
DEATH SP:
CHILDREN: None

SPOUSE III: Wilhelm Sanberg Peterson
MARRIED: 18 Jun 1864
DEATH SP: 5 Jan 1901
Richfield, Sevier Co., Utah

CHILDREN:
Hannah Wilhelmina, 6 Apr 1867
Christian George, 3 Sep 1870
Peter Niels, 1 Dec 1873

Hansine was born and educated in Denmark. She had an older brother and sister from her mother's first marriage. Her brother, Jorgen Erik, died at the age of nineteen. Her sister, Ann Benedict married the missionary who converted the family to the Church of Jesus Christ of Latter-day Saints.

Anne and her husband, Augustine Nielsen left for America shortly before the rest of the Nybolle family. Hansine's father was an artisan in metal work and her mother was a midwife. The Nybolle family boarded the ship, L. N. Hvidt, to reach Liverpool, England. Then they boarded the ship, "Westmoreland," to cross the ocean and landed in Philadelphia on May 30, 1857. On June 2, they continued their journey by rail to Iowa City. They proceeded on with a handcart to Council Bluffs. On July 2, 1857, they stopped for provisions and rest at Crescent City. They traveled on until they reached the Salt Lake Valley in the same year.

Shortly after arriving in Salt Lake Valley, they went to Mt. Pleasant where her sister, Anne, and her family had moved.

Hansine married James Huff in 1858 in Manti, Utah. They lived there a year, then moved to Mt. Pleasant where James became a cabinet and furniture maker. James' father had started a sawmill business in Upton, Summit County and invited James to join him.

James took his wife and infant daughter, Julia Ann, to Upton where they lived with the Huff family. Her second child was born there and died within six weeks. She gave birth to her third child in Ephraim in her parent's home and did not return to James. They were divorced.

Hansine married Sixtus Kjar on September 3, 1863 and soon divorced him. Then on June 18, 1864, she married and was sealed to her third husband, Wilhelm Sanberg Peterson. They lived in Santaquin where she bore three children to this union.

In 1880, after many years in this difficult marriage, Hansine took her children and moved to Richfield where she could be near her sister, Ann. She established a home in Richfield where she lived until her death in 1916.

JOHANNE THOMPSON PETERSON

BIRTHDATE: 3 Oct 1850
Harbelev, Maribo, Denmark
DEATH: 18 Dec 1877
Ephraim, Sanpete Co., Utah
PARENTS: Peter Peterson
Dorothy Thompson
PIONEER: 1854
SPOUSE: Peter C. Peterson
MARRIED: 2 May 1870
Salt Lake Endowment House
DEATH SP: 7 May 1932
Salt Lake City, Salt Lake, Utah

CHILDREN:
Sarah Dorthea (Jenson), 28 Feb 1871
Hannah Lillian (Peterson), 10 Aug 1873
Peter Canute, 23 Feb 1876

Johanne was born in 1850 in Denmark, the youngest of six children. They were a happy family living in a comfortable home and operating a little farm which provided most of their food. In 1850, Erastus Snow brought the Gospel to Denmark, and Johanne's parents were among the first to be interested. Her mother was the first to be converted, but her father wanted to know more.

"Mormonism" was very unpopular in all of Scandinavia; and when the Thompsons began thinking of emigrating to America, the relatives became really hostile and tried in every way to get them to give up their plans and not take their children to grow up among such people. When they failed, they even threw rocks through the windows, some of the glass falling on little Johanne as she lay in the cradle. This was the breaking point for Peter and Dorothy, and they made preparations to leave.

They sold their home and farm, and selected the date when they would sail for America. Dorothy's health being poor, she was afraid she could not live on the ship's food. She began to prepare smoked sausage, smoked beef, and smoked legs of geese. When all things were ready, they left for Copenhagen and America. The sailing was delayed for one day, so when they arrived in Copenhagen, they went to a hotel for the night, leaving their food and luggage at the dock. In the morning, they were terribly upset to find all of their food and part of their other possessions had been stolen.

They left Denmark on December 22, 1853 on the ship 'Slesvig'. Arriving at Liverpool, they boarded and then sailed on the ship, "Jesse Munn" across the Atlantic, and arrived at New Orleans on January 16, 1854. They arrived at St. Louis on March 11, 1854. Johanne's mother died before they reached St. Louis.

Peter, Johanne's father, purchased a wagon, a span of horses, harness, and other supplies. Before starting out for the mountains he hired a buggy and took the children out to the cemetery where they all knelt down by the grave and prayed, saying goodbye to their dear wife and mother. It took them three months to get to Utah. After their arrival, Brigham Young said the people from Scandinavia, were hardy people and were used to the cold so they could make a better life in Sanpete, 1,000 feet higher than the Salt Lake Valley. He called on them to colonize that area.

Johanne married Peter Cornelius Peterson on May 2, 1870. Three children were born to them.

Johanne passed away on December 18, 1877 in childbirth in Ephraim, Utah, a dedicated pioneer woman who gave her all for the religious beliefs she had. A great heritage is left to those who have followed her.

KAREN JENSEN PETERSON

BIRTHDATE: 3 Oct 1843
Haugerup, Soro, Denmark
DEATH: 26 Jan 1899
Salt Lake City, Salt Lake, Utah
PARENTS: Hans Jensen
Marie Jensen
PIONEER: 13 Sep 1857
C. Christiansen Handcart Comp.
SPOUSE: Samuel Peterson
MARRIED: 18 Jul 1860
Salt Lake City, Salt Lake, Utah
DEATH SP: 5 Mar 1906
Salt Lake City, Salt Lake, Utah

CHILDREN:
Samuel, Jr., 26 Sep 1861
John Jensen, 23 Mar 1864
Caroline Elizabeth (Wolcott), 23 Nov 1866
Eva Karen Sophia (Hansen), 11 Jul 1871
Alma Hans, 27 Nov 1874
Moroni Nephi, 1 Aug 1877
Joseph Alma, 14 Feb 1881

Ellen Maria Christensen), 23 Oct 1883
George Aaron, 1886

Karen Jensen was born in Denmark. Her parents joined the Church of Jesus Christ of Latter-day Saints on October 3, 1843. On June 17, 1856, Karen, her parents, and three brothers and a sister crossed the Atlantic Ocean from Denmark to the United States in a sailing boat. The journey took two months.

They made their way to Utah in the C. Christiansen Handcart Company. Her sister died along the way and was buried at Fort Bridger, Wyoming. They arrived in the Salt Lake Valley on September 13, 1857.

Karen was fifteen years old when she was hired to help out with the care of Caroline Peterson, her daughter Maria and an infant son. Both mother and son died in November, 1858. Karen married the husband of Caroline, Samuel Peterson, in the Salt Lake City Endowment House on July 18, 1860. He had been born in Denmark, also.

With the sewing Karen took in and from proceeds from the farm Karen was able to finance Samuel's four-year mission to Sweden and a one-year mission to Minnesota. When he returned, she supported him in his calling as Bishop of the Second Ward in Salt Lake City for thirteen years. Karen served as Relief Society President for twenty-five years. She was a caring step-mother to Maria and gave birth to nine children.

Karen was a faithful Latter-day Saint and she was loved by her family and all who knew her. She passed away on January 26, 1899 in Salt Lake City, seven years before the death of her husband in March, 1906.

MAREN HANSEN PETERSON

BIRTHDATE: 18 Feb 1823
Herstedoster, Denmark
DEATH: 22 Jun 1886
PARENTS: Hans Pederson
Kirsten Andersdatter / Anderson
PIONEER: 1861
C. Christiansen Handcart Comp.
SPOUSE: Ole Peterson
MARRIED: 5 Feb 1846
Sangelose, Kobenhaven,
Denmark
DEATH SP: 14 Apr 1891

CHILDREN:
Peder, 11 Feb 1847
Maren, 24 Oct 1848 (died at age 7)
Hans, 19 May 1851 (died at age 5)
Soren, 9 Oct 1853 (died at age 4)
Ane / Ann (Wilcox), 18 Mar 1856
Mary (Fisher), 14 Feb 1859
Joseph, 24 Apr 1861
Inger (Anderson), 28 Aug 1863
Laura Jane, 20 Nov 1865 (died at age 12)

James, 27 Feb 1868

Maren was born in 1823, as the third girl in her family. She had two older sisters and two brothers and a sister younger than she. Her family lived at Herstedoster, Denmark all of their lives.

Maren met and married Ole Peterson (Oedersen) on February 5, 1846 when she was twenty-three years old and Ole was thirty-one. They went to the town of Sengelose, Kobenhaven, Denmark, where they made their home. They were of the Lutheran faith. Maren's first child was a son, and twenty months later had a daughter.

On September 15, 1850, a mission branch of the Church of Jesus Christ of Latter-day Saints was established in Kobenhaven by Elder Erastus Snow. When Maren and Ole heard the gospel they joined the Church and were baptized on June 22, 1851. Maren and Ole had dreams of going to America and to the Utah territory, to join the other Saints. Many friends had already left for America. They saved and prayed for the day they could also journey to Utah.

The year 1856, brought both joy and sorrow to their family. Another daughter was born March 18, and a month later May 26, tragedy struck when two of their children died and were buried May 30, 1856, Maren and Hans.

Some good friends of Maren and Ole, the Martin Hansens, were leaving in April, 1857, for America, and Maren and Ole gathered what money they could and with a loan from Martin were able to get the $380.00 needed to be able to be on the same emigration list. They had $56.00 in American currency and $30.00 in foreign money. They traveled by boat from Denmark to Liverpool, England, were assigned to the ship "Westmoreland." Their passage cost $215.30. They were under the leadership of Mathias Cowley, and there were 544 passengers, mostly Scandinavians. They left England on April 25, 1857.

The voyage across the ocean took about five weeks and landed at Philadelphia on May 31, 1857. They traveled by train to Iowa arriving, June 9, 1857.

Maren and Ole were assigned to a handcart company. Getting their handcart and supplies ready to leave on June 15, made a busy time. The Cowley and Christiansen Companies were to leave on the same day. Some wagons were allotted to the handcart company to care for the elderly and sick. Handcarts were loaded with only the necessary things. Looking across the Plains it seemed so flat, but this was not to be. There were hills to climb, dust and heat were stifling, and on hot days the ground blistered their feet. Rains turned the dust to mud making pulling and pushing much harder, but was welcomed for their poor tired feet.

Maren and Ole's two small children made it hard, but Peter was a good help for his parents, and often carried his small sister, Ane. Rivers caused many problems as hand-carts had to be unloaded so the flour, clothing and bedding could be carried across. Many things were abandoned along the trail to lighten their load.

Each new day started with prayer, personal and group, asking that they would be watched over for that day. Their faith was still very strong. Little Ane became ill. It seemed she grew worse with each step. Maren was allowed in one of the wagons to make it easier, but Ane grew worse. Indians began to threaten the group so camp was made. Indians moved on, and the company moved forward. Ane was given a blessing but it did no good because she died. Indians again threatened, and there was no time for burying Ane, so she was wrapped in a blanket and put under some bushes and the group went on, later to make camp again.

After dark that night, Maren crept out of the camp and went back to bury her baby to protect her body from the wild animals. When Maren picked up the bundle from under the bushes, Ane was still alive. What joy Maren felt for this was surely a miracle. With many prayers of thanksgiving and loving care, Ane lived. Ane grew up to be a special person. Everyone who knew her loved her. She nursed the sick and attended the births of over 800 babies.

This trek with the handcarts was hard and began to take its toll on all of them. It made them stronger and their faith greater, but it didn't lessen their suffering. A few days from Omaha, Maren developed a bad leg. It grew worse each day. Maren and Ole had to leave the company at Omaha having pulled their handcart 281 miles. Ole got the family settled and went for a doctor. One finally was found, he checked her leg and told them if she was to live, the leg would have to be amputated, but Maren refused. In her troubled sick sleep, she dreamed she walked into the Salt Lake Valley on her own two feet. In time, after many prayers and much care, her leg finally healed.

This family had one more heartbreak in the year of 1857, Soren, their young son died. Ole was able to get work to get them through that fall and the winter. The next spring he farmed for himself and was successful. Life became a little easier and their dream was still to finish their journey to Salt Lake. The winter of 1858 and 1859 they moved back across the river to Council Bluffs. Here another daughter was born to them on February 14, 1859.

By the early part of 1861, their friend, Martin Hansen returned to Council Bluffs. Maren and Ole were happy to see their friend. Ole was also happy to have enough money to pay Martin the money they had borrowed in Denmark. Martin's group had stopped at Nebraska and had farmed for those years, so Martin asked if they wanted to join his group to continue to Utah. They were able to buy a wagon, a team of oxen, two cows and supplies to take them to the Valley. A son was born to them as they were preparing to leave.

The journey was easier after their hardships of the handcarts in 1861. At last the Salt Lake Valley was in view. Maren walked on her own two feet into the Valley. They stayed in Salt Lake but a short time and then went to American Fork then later to Lehi. Ole worked making molasses from sugar cane and adobe bricks from clay.

They moved farther west to Cedar Fort where they stayed the remainder of their lives. They had found their home.

They were very happy in Cedar Fort and were very active in their Church there. On February 10, 1865, Maren and Ole went to Salt Lake City for their endowments in the Endowment House and were sealed to each other for time and eternity. Their hopes and dreams of these many years were finally fulfilled. Three more children were born to them at Cedar Fort.

Their children who lived, were adults when Maren passed away on June 22, 1886 at the age of sixty-three years. Her youngest child was eighteen years at the time. She was buried in the Cedar Fort Cemetery.

Ole passed away on April 14, 1891 at the age of seventy-six years. Their children were pioneers also and Peter crossed the Plains twice more helping other emigrants, and settled in Vernal.

Ole and Maren have many descendants as their children all had large families.

On a gentle hill in Cedar Valley, Maren and Ole rest in peace, the dreams of their early years having been fulfilled. They are dearly loved by those who are their descendants. They were great pioneers who never lost their dream or their faith in its accomplishment.

A poem titled "The Wagon Train Incident," was written about their experience.

MAREN (MARY) LARSEN BENSON PETERSON

BIRTHDATE: 19 Dec 1843
Rostofte, Sjaelland, Denmark
DEATH: 21 Feb 1926
Mendon, Cache Co., Utah
PARENTS: Magnus Larsen
Maren Hanson
PIONEER: Aug 1863
SPOUSE I: Ezra Taft Benson
MARRIED: 15 Sep 1866
Salt Lake City, Salt Lake, Utah
DEATH SP: 3 Sep 1869

CHILDREN:
Walter Taft, 17 Jun 1867
Henry Taft, 19 Mar 1869

SPOUSE II: Peter Peterson
MARRIED: 1878
DEATH SP: 3 Jun 1914

CHILDREN:
Oliver Larsen, 22 May 1879 (twin)
Edward Larsen, 22 May 1879 (twin)
Levi Larsen, 1 Oct 1880
Fred Larsen, 19 Sep 1883
Willard Larsen, 24 Jan 1886

Jessie Larsen, 7 Oct 1887 (twin)
Miles Larsen, 7 Oct 1887 (twin)

As Mary grew up in Denmark, she worked for wealthy families in home management and food preparation. After she became a member of the Church of Jesus Christ of Latter-day Saints, she sailed on the ship, "John J. Boyd," from Liverpool, England to New York City. Then she traveled by rail and by boat to Florence, Nebraska.

From Florence, she was able to have her provisions and baggage hauled by a wagon which was pulled by oxen. She walked almost the entire distance to the Salt Lake Valley.

Three years after arriving in the Valley, Elder Ezra Taft Benson asked her to join him in plural marriage as his eighth wife. They were married in the Endowment House in Salt Lake City, Utah.

Mary made great use of her skills in home management and food preparation as she helped entertain prominent civic and church leaders in the Benson household. Mary managed food services for the firm of Benson, Farr, & West when the railroad was built west of Ogden. Six months after Henry was born, Ezra Taft Benson died in Ogden Utah. She used her skills in order to support her sons.

In 1878, Mary married Peter Peterson and they lived on his ranch where they raised their sons. She helped raise these nine sons to manhood. Their ranch became one of the finest integrated properties in Utah. Her contribution was so great that she shared equally with her husband and sons in managing the ranch.

Mary was immaculate in appearance. She was thrifty, punctual, strong willed, and a very dominating woman.

MARGARETHE LARSEN PETERSON

No Photo Available

BIRTHDATE: 14 Aug 1808
Nykobing, Denmark
DEATH: 4 Jun 1871
Huntsville, Weber Co., Utah
PARENTS: Lars Simonsen
Juliene Hansen
PIONEER: 1862 Handcart Com.
SPOUSE: Hans Peterson
MARRIED: 17 May 1833
Sweden
DEATH SP: 18 Nov 1900
Kanesville, Weber Co., Utah

CHILDREN:
Peder L., 14 Apr 1834 (died as a child)
Lars, 27 Feb 1837
Hans Jorgen, 4 Apr 1839
Peter, 11 Jan 1841
Anne Kristine, 31 Mar 1843 (died at age 15)
Christian, 18 Sep 1845

Margrethe was born in 1808 in Denmark. She married Hans Peterson on May 17, 1833, while living in Sweden.

Hans and Margrethe were a devout and serious minded couple.

The Scandinavian Mission was opened by Erastus Snow and the Peterson family were taught by the missionaries and they embraced the gospel of the Church of Jesus Christ of Latter-day Saints. They emigrated to Utah in 1862 and joined a handcart company to cross the Plains of America. The ox-teams and handcarts were loaded to capacity so her sons, Peter and Christian, took turns carrying her on their backs as they traveled West.

The family first settled in Farmington, Utah. Hans lost his right arm in a roller mill while extracting juice from sugar cane. Following this accident, the family decided to move to Huntsville. Peter and Christian built a one-room house for Hans and Margrethe in the southeast part of the town.

Margrethe passed away nine years after her arrival in that valley. She died January 4, 1871 at the age of nearly sixty-three years. She had suffered many trials and tribulations for the Gospel. She was a pioneer woman revered for her faith and fortitude in helping to develop the state of Utah.

MARIA CHRISTENSEN TYGESEN PETERSON

BIRTHDATE: 7 Aug 1830
DEATH: 25 May 1903
PARENTS: Christen Thygesen
Kirsten Sorensen
PIONEER: 15 Sep 1859
Robert F. Neslen Wagon Train
SPOUSE: Thomas Peter Peterson
MARRIED: 25 Sep 1859
Salt Lake City, Salt Lake, Utah
DEATH SP: 29 May 1873
Richfield, Sevier Co., Utah

CHILDREN:
Mary, 24 Jul 1861
Thomas E., 15 Mar 1863
Elsina, 9 Jul 1865
Joseph, 1867 (died same day)
Andrew Christian, 24 Sep 1870

Maria was a very spiritual person. She joined the Church of Jesus Christ of Latter-day Saints after her investigation of many other churches and after much study and prayer. She had a dream in which some men from the West came to Denmark and gave her the true gospel of Jesus Christ as taught in the Bible. Her parents were not as bitter as some when she decided to join the Church and journey to Utah, although, they wept bitterly.

Maria boarded the ship "William Tapscott," on April 8, 1859 in Liverpool, England. They arrived in New York on May 12, 1859. She traveled by train and steamship to

Florence, Nebraska, where she joined a wagon-train. Maria walked the entire distance and carried a small child of a friend who was too ill to walk. They arrived in the Salt Lake Valley on September 15, 1859. Ten days later she married Thomas Peter Peterson, a young man she had met in Denmark when he served a mission there.

After a short stay in Salt Lake, they moved to Ephraim, Utah, where Maria became a farmer's wife, helping her husband with the plowing and planting along with other farm chores and keeping her small home. Her life was much different from that of a wealthy family's daughter in Denmark.

Maria and Thomas were called by Brigham Young to go to Gunnison, Utah, to help put down an Indian uprising. Maria baked hundreds of loaves of bread to take to the Indians as they were told it was better to feed them than to fight them.

In 1870, they were released from the call in Gunnison and settled in Richfield where she cooked, sewed, cleaned, made soap, helped her husband on the farm and helped her neighbors and friends in times of illness and need. Her life was full of peace, joy and contentment as she taught her children the principles of the gospel, hard work, integrity and love.

After three years, tragedy struck and her husband was killed in a farm accident. Maria suffered a nervous break-down and she was bedfast for several months. Another spiritual experience came to her as she saw two men enter her room with the message that her husband had been called on a mission and she must carry on alone. She immediately arose from her bed and started to care for her family and help her son on the farm. She had a dream in which her husband came to her and told her to take the family and move to Arizona.

They left Richfield in the Spring of 1878 and after a long, difficult journey they arrived at Brigham City, Arizona (now Winslow). Here they were living the United Order so Maria joined her possessions to the Order. She lived here about two years and then withdrew her belongings from the Order and moved to "Meadows," a short distance from St. Johns.

In 1897, Maria sold what she had and went to Santaquin, Utah, to live with her daughter, Mary. Here she lived until she passed away on May 25, 1903. She was buried in the Santaquin City Cemetery. Maria's testimony of the gospel never wavered in spite of her many trials and she was one of the most faithful, stalwart pioneers.

MARNA ANDERSON PETERSON

BIRTHDATE: 27 Sep 1807
Vinteriet, Blentarp, Sweden
DEATH: 30 Apr 1879
Lehi, Utah CO., Utah
PARENTS: Anders Andersson
Sissa Christensen
PIONEER: 23 Sep 1862
SPOUSE: Anders Peterson
MARRIED: abt 1834
Sweden
DEATH SP: 20 Sep 1875
Lehi, Utah Co., Utah

CHILDREN:
Magnus Florentine, 20 Jun 1835
Johannah, 24 Aug 1837
Andrew, 13 Jan 1840
Anna (Christofferson), 23 Oct 1842
Christina (Miller), 31 May 1845
John, 8 Nov 1848

Marna was born in 1807 in Vinteriet, Blentarp, Malmohus, Sweden. She had one brother who died as a child, and seven sisters.

Marna married Anders Peterson on about 1834. He was a farmer and gardener. This family became early converts to the Church of Jesus Christ of Latter-day Saints and were members of the first branch organized in Sweden. The 'Spirit of the Gathering' came upon them and they desired to go to America.

Marna had six children born to her. The oldest child, Magnus, followed his father's footsteps and became an expert gardener and landscape artist. He was the first to join the Church. He moved to Copenhagen and prepared for his emigration.

Marna's oldest daughter, Johannah, a beautiful young lady of twenty years became a martyr to her new religion. She was riding with a young man in a carriage when people shouted and yelled and called her names. The horse became frightened and lunged. Johannah was thrown from the buggy, her skirt caught in the wheel and she was dragged to her death.

Their second son, Andrew, went to Denmark to work and from there was called on a mission to return to Sweden. While on this mission he met his future wife-to-be. He baptized her, and when he was released from his mission in 1862, he joined his parents to come to Utah. He met Anna Marie Pherson in Copenhagen, and they were married on the Elbe River in Germany before sailing for America.

The Peterson families emigrated under the direction of Ola N. Liljenquist, and after fifty-one days on the ocean, they arrived in New York City. It then took them seventy-one days of long hard travel over the Plains to reach the Salt Lake Valley where they arrived on September 23, 1862. As a whole they enjoyed good health.

After their arrival in Utah, following President Young's advice, some of these emigrants chose to make their home in Lehi, and others went to Mt. Pleasant. Their daughters married, some stayed in Mt. Pleasant, some moved to Idaho or Canada, and some spent most of their lives in Lehi. The first home in Lehi where Anders and Marna lived was the first adobe house erected in Lehi. It had two rooms with a door and a window in each room at the front of the house. Some family members were called to help settle in Arizona. Magnus was the only one of the family to stay in Mt. Pleasant.

Anders Peterson died as a result of injuries received from a fall from a wagon on September 20, 1875. After his death, Marna made her home with her son John and family. She passed away on April 30, 1879. Both are buried in the Lehi Cemetery. They were great pioneers who helped settle the Utah Valley and are honored by those who have followed them.

MARY ANDERSEN PETERSON

BIRTHDATE: 22 Jun 1856
Bredstrup, Odense, Denmark
DEATH: 22 May 1938
Thatcher, Graham Co., Arizona
PARENTS: Hans Andersen
Maren Jensen
PIONEER: 12 Sep 1863
John Young Indep. Wagon Train
SPOUSE: Peter "O" Peterson
MARRIED: 14 Feb 1876
Salt Lake City, Salt Lake, Utah
DEATH SP: 3 Nov 1927
Thatcher, Graham Co., Arizona

CHILDREN:
Mary "May" (Brown), 18 Nov 1876
Anna Janette, (chr.) 18 Mar 1879
Sena Lenore (Kempton), 21 Mar 1881
Peter, 10 May 1883
Wilford, 3 Oct 1885
Alma, 30 Dec 1887
Andrew, 21 Mar 1890
Emily, 4 Jun 1892
James Ammon, 20 Aug 1894
Sylvia, 9 Nov 1897
Lillian (Mullenaux), 21 Mar 1900

Mary was born in 1856 in Denmark. She spent her early childhood in Bredstrup learning to work early in life. Her mother, an excellent seamstress, taught her daughters these skills. The family worked with their farm animals and had responsibilities at very young ages to help with the chores.

When Mary was about two years old, the Elders first came to their home. They were impressed with the message but did not join the Church then. Elders who came to their island were welcomed and always had clean beds to sleep in. When Mary was five, her brother Andrew was kicked in the head by a horse, crushing his head badly. Mary's father went to a grove of trees near their home and knelt to petition God to save his child. He promised God he would join the Church and give and do all in his power to build up the Church. When he returned to the house, the boy was much improved. Through the Elder's priesthood blessing, he recovered rapidly with only a scar on his head which his hair covered. This event made a great impact on the family and Mary's parents were baptized as members of the Church of Jesus Christ of Latter-day Saints in March, 1861.

Two years later the family sold their holdings and in April, 1863, Maren and Hans with their seven children left Denmark for America.

They left Liverpool, England on April 20, 1863 on the ship "John J. Boyd," with 755 Saints. As they sailed, Mary, age seven, was in awe and wonder of the ship and the vast ocean. She told of the incident when a whale came up to the vessel, raised its head, and leaned against the boat. The captain ordered passengers to the opposite side of the ship so it would not tip over. He ordered men to bring buckets of potatoes which they poured into the whalers mouth until it finally slid back into the water and swam away.

The ship landed at New York and from there the family boarded a train for Missouri, a boat for Winter Quarters, and joined the wagon train. Hans brought $20,000 in gold coins with him. Mary's mother made slips of strong material to hang from their shoulders for the girls and herself to wear under their clothing to carry some coins. The rest were carried in a large bag.

As they left Nebraska, they had two wagons with four yoke of oxen each, plus one spring wagon drawn by a team of horses, to carry the women and provisions for fifteen people. They arrived in the Salt Lake Valley on September 12, 1863.

Mary's father, Hans, decided to go north, so they settled in Logan where Mary spent her childhood. Hans helped build the temple providing money and labor while her mother paid her egg money gathered on Sundays. Mary worked for other people in Logan so she could learn the English language faster. She attended school for a few months only. She told of running away from school to hide in a haystack when the children laughed at her Danish brogue. Mary learned to sew well. She and Andrew tended their cows and took care of the milk at the ranch in Logan Canyon. Since she loved to dance, and life on the ranch was quite lonely, she and Andrew occasionally walked the ten miles into town just for a dance.

Among the Danish families in Logan, Mary dated Peter "O" Peterson. He received a call from Brigham Young to get married and to help settle in Arizona. Peter asked Mary to share this call with him. Her parents did not approve, but since she was 20 years old and of age, they decided she could go. Her brother, Andrew and his wife, also were to go.

On February 7, 1876, Peter and Mary left Logan on bob-sleighs. They were married on February 14, 1876 in the Endowment House in Salt Lake City. They then left with a group of 200 people, forty families and some singles, headed for Obed, Arizona over the rough and long way. It took thirteen weeks.

They passed over "Lee's Backbone" with rocks so large there was barely room for the wagons to pass. It was so steep that ropes were tied to the back of the wagons to keep them from falling onto the horses. They crossed the Little Colorado by piling things high on the water barrel and floating the wagons and teams across. At Obed, a rock fort was built and all tried farming. They soon found the land was not good for farming so about 80% of the Saints returned to Utah.

While there at Obed, Mary gave birth to their first child whom they named Mary for her mother and grandmother, but they called her May. Peter wanted to return to Utah, but Mary wouldn't go (some might have called her stubborn), and Peter was finally persuaded to stay.

By 1879, they were sent back to Utah for supplies. Mary and her mother Maren had a nice reunion. It was especially sweet since Maren died the next year-November. May became ill, so they could not return, and when she finally was well it was too late in the season to travel. Mary was also ill carrying her next child, who was consequently born in Logan. They returned to Arizona to the settlement St. Joseph and the United Order.

Peter and Mary, with another family, were sent to Mormon Lake to care for cattle. During the time there Mary and the other wife made 1,300 pounds of butter, and 2,000 pounds of cheese for the Order. Having learned early to work hard, Mary always tried her best. They lived in the Order for about seven years. Peter then worked for awhile for the railroad. Mary earned a little money by providing cold milk for the railroad workers. She was always thrifty and saved money to buy a sewing machine.

By 1882, the family had moved to the Gila Valley near Thatcher and Safford, Arizona. Here, they first lived in a tent. They farmed the land. Just three weeks after their arrival, a daughter Anna Janette, died of spinal meningitis and was buried on the hill in the cemetery near Graham. Five months later, still living in the tent, Mary gave birth to her first son, Peter. As soon as they could they built a log house, lined with a muslin. Sometimes dirt leaked in from the roof. It was a hard life. The land was good for farming, and life improved with their crops, garden and orchard.

Mary served in church positions in the primary and as Relief Society President. She was always a good house-keeper, and a very good seamstress. She was a marvelous cook. She was always thrifty and did not like to see any-thing wasted. She taught her children to be strictly honest, to be dependable, and to do their best. She said, "Few can see how long it takes you to do a thing, but everyone can see how it is done."

Mary had many trials to endure during her lifetime. She had eleven children without a doctor's help. For a twelve year period of time she suffered from sciatic rheumatism so severely she sat in a big chair with heat applied to ease the pain every night, forcing herself each morning to walk around to exercise her leg.

After their children were all married, Mary and Peter moved closer to town. Peter became ill with cancer and she nursed him until his death in November, 1927. Her daughters took turns looking after her until she had a stroke on Mother's Day in 1938 and passed away two weeks later at her home in Thatcher.

She had lived eighty-two long and fruitful years and left a lasting legacy for her posterity. Mary Peterson left a great legacy for those who have followed her.

MATILDA MARIE NIELSON PETERSON

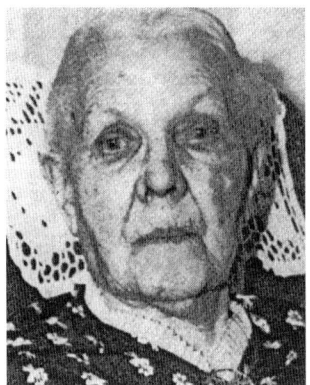

BIRTHDATE: 23 Oct 1855
Copenhagen, Denmark
DEATH: 22 Aug 1955
Morgan, Morgan Co., Utah
PARENTS: Andrew Nielson
Dorthea Hansen
PIONEER: 22 Sep 1861
Wagon Train Company
SPOUSE: Nels Peterson
MARRIED: 3 Dec 1878
Littleton, Morgan Co., Utah
DEATH SP: 12 Dec 1926
Milton, Morgan Co., Utah

CHILDREN:
Leanders Baltzar, 2 Sep 1879
Margaret May (Thursdon), 5 Feb 1882
Archibald Theodore, 20 Feb 1885
Edna Dorothy (Bertoch), 12 Jun 1887
Amy Laura (Randall), 1 Nov 1890 (twin)
Bertha (Anderson), 1 Nov 1890 (twin)
Cleveland, 13 Jun 1893
Bessie Virginia (Thurston), 21 Dec 1895

Matilda Marie Nielson was born in Copenhagen, Denmark in 1855. Her father and mother joined the Church of Jesus Christ of Latterday Saints and in 1861 started for Utah. It was a very hard trip.

In Matilda's own words, "I was sick all the way, both across the sea and Plains, many times when they looked in the wagon they thought I was dead, but father said, 'No, she will get well, because they promised me I should take my whole family to Zion,! He was able to do so. We sailed May 16, 1861 on the 'Monarch of the Sea' from Liverpool. The old ship was loaded, and we set out to sea. We had to throw a lot of our clothing and bedding overboard, as we were not allowed to have so much on the ship. We arrived in New York June 19th, went in cattle cars to Council Bluffs. They bought their supplies and father bought an old wagon, three cows and a yoke of oxen. We were now ready to start the long trip across the desert. The hardships of that journey are impossible to describe. Mother was sick but she walked all the way across the Plains. The company arrived in Salt Lake City September 22, 1861. We stayed there a few days, then moved to a little valley called Morgan County. The road was almost impassable. They were sent there to help settle Morgan County."

"We lived in a covered wagon most of the first winter, while father was getting our log cabin built. It had a dirt roof and dirt floor, but, Oh, how happy we were to move into it. Our first cabin door had a wooden latch and hinges were made of leather. A gunny sack covered the opening made for the window. When we got up in the morning, the first thing we would look out to see where there was smoke coming. Then we would take our fire shovel and go over to get coals to start our fire, to save matches.

"We had a heavy wooden box that we brought food in across the Plains. Father made two wooden stools of logs to set this box on. We used this for a table. We also had the same kind of stools to sit on. Their beds were made by driving four posts in the ground and placing other poles across them, then straw on top. The children's beds were made the same way only not stationary, and it was lower so it could be put under the larger bed in the daytime. Our fireplaces were made of rock or sandstone with an iron bar across and hooks hanging down from this, to hang our kettles on. For baking we had a heavy iron bake kettle. We would rake the hot coals out and put the bake ovens in the fire and then the hot coals on top of the lid. Our only light was a light from the fireplace. Mother would spin yarn by this light. Later on when we had a little grease, we would put a little in a plate and put a rag in it, then light the rag. Still later on when we had more grease or beef tallow, we made candles."

"It seems as though we didn't have any food. We boiled wheat mostly, some of it we ground with an old coffee mill. After they started to raise vegetables it helped so much. We gathered wild fruit and dried it for winter, we also dried wild rose leaves which we steeped for tea."

"The schools in those days were being held about three months of the year. The teacher would board around with different families spending about two weeks in each home. Church and parties were held in the same old building."

"There is another thing I can never forget, how kind the people were to help in sickness or trouble and would never think of asking for pay.

"When I was 11 years old I wove cloth to make myself a dress. Mother was so happy to know I could do so many things, but she was not here long to enjoy it.

"When I was 12 years old my mother died leaving a sixteen day old baby . . . Father had another wife, she took the baby and nursed him as her own, but he died when two years old. After mother's death, we children all had to get out and rustle for ourselves. I worked for 60 cents a week and had ten cows to milk night and morning. I had to go

barefooted to do it all . . . Father made something to wear on our feet. He often made wooden soles and put a strip of leather on the top, but we felt ashamed to wear them. More than once I left them under the bench and sat in my stocking feet.

"Dances were held often, I was never allowed to go, only with a married man. (That was the years when polygamy was practiced.)

"I can never forget how we used to celebrate the 24th of July. We would form an emigrant train to show just how we came across the Plains. We would walk and some of the women would have their aprons full of buffalo chips to build fires with when we camped at night. We would end up with a dance, and we would all have to dance in our bare feet.

"When I was 15 years old I went to Farmington to work. I worked 6 months and got $10.00 - some pay."

"I stayed home just a little while. While I was home I met Nels Peterson, a violin player. Then I went to Evanston to work, but I wrote to this friend all the time. I worked there 6 months then I came back home. The next winter on 3 Dec 1878, I was married. We lived in Richville that winter. That winter I spun yarn, wove the cloth and made my husband the first overcoat he ever had."

They moved to Preston, Idaho where Nels played for dances for 75 cents a night. They had hard times while there. She would go three miles to hunt her cows, come home spread her skirt out and lay her baby on it while she milked the cows. They then moved back to Morgan County to Richville.

She was a teacher in the Sunday School, and literary class leader in Relief Society. Her husband was the choir leader for twenty-eight years. Their daughters were organists.

"The World War was declared in 1914. My youngest son had to go. Then we had a different work to do. I knit 51 pairs of socks for the soldiers and I have forgotten how many sweaters. We also went without sugar and ate coarse bread."

Their children all married between 1903 and 1920. They were alone, but kept busy in the Church. They lived for 6 happy years in a new home, then "my partner died and I was left alone. My youngest son and wife came to live with me. I was quite well and getting along fine for I have some of the most wonderful children in the world. I am in my 79th year 1934 and I have found life is made up of little things; of sorrow, of joy, trials, pain and pleasure. I have tried to treat others as I would like to be treated, and to give service wherever it has been needed, it has not been a hardship but a pleasure. Today I feel that I haven't any enemies in this world, if I have I don't know it."

"In July, 1934, my daughter, Bertha and her son drove down from Montana to get me and my daughter Bessie and take us on a trip through Yellowstone National Park and parts of Montana. Since I had never been in that part of the country, I looked forward to the trip with a great deal of pleasure, which it proved to be." They drove through the Park, enjoying the wonderful sites, wildlife and scenery. They then went into Montana to her daughter's home in Great Falls where they had a chance to rest up, still a lot of things yet to see.

While on this trip, Matilda was asked if she would like a ride in a large twelve passenger plane that was in Great Falls taking people up in the air. It was the last day it would be there, so "I said Yes, I would like to go. " It was about 11:00 p.m. and the city looked beautiful all lighted up. Upon their landing she replied, "I didn't think we went very high and we didn't stay very long. I felt it was grand to have that thrilling experience. When the plane landed there was a news reporter waiting to talk to me, he was very much interested and talked quite a while. The paper next morning carried a long article about me. One thing he told was that I had ridden in every conveyance from a handcart to an airplane . . . On the Sunday before we came home, we had the radio on and an announcement was made that the next number to be sung was dedicated to Mrs. N. J. Peterson, who was visiting with her children . . . I spent two weeks there and enjoyed every minute of it, and then we had to leave."

Even though Matilda Peterson started out poor and had had such a hard young life, she ended up with eight children and a very nice home. She had twenty-five grandchildren and fifty-eight great-grandchildren. She made embroidered quilts for every one of her grandchildren. Her two oldest boys died after Matilda was ninety years old herself. That was pretty hard for her as she thought she should have been taken first.

She was very independent and used to say "I am enjoying life now, my older years have been my best years, and I'd like to live, as long as I don't become a burden." Matilda died just lacking two months of being 100 years old when she died in 1955.

METTE MARGRETE JUULSEN PETERSON

BIRTHDATE: 11 Jan 1834
Holme, Aarhus, Denmark
DEATH: 18 Jan 1919
Richville, Morgan Co., Utah
PARENTS: Juul Eskildsen
Karen Nielsen
PIONEER: 5 Sep 1863
John F. Sanders Wagon Train
SPOUSE: Baltzar S. Peterson
MARRIED: 30 May 1857
Holme, Denmark
DEATH SP: 21 Dec 1910

CHILDREN:
Niels Juul, 13 Oct 1857
Soren Baltzar, 16 Jan 1860

Laura, 24 Dec 1861 (died as a child)
James Joel, 1 Mar 1863
Joseph Juul, 5 May 1865 (died as a child)
Baltzar Jr., 29 May 1867
Charles Coulsen, 15 Jul 1869
George Lorenzo, 2 Jul 1871
Anna Eliza, 26 Nov 1873
William, 29 Feb 1876 (died as a child)
Frederick Leonder, 12 Feg 1879

Mette Margrete Juulsen was born in 1834 the seventh child of a family of eight children. Her father was a small lease-hold farmer and weaver. He died when Margrete was two years old. Her mother had a financial struggle, but she saw to it that the children were educated in the state school in Holme.

On May 30, 1857, Margrete was married in Holme, to Baltzar Sorensen Peterson. Sorensen was his Danish name as recorded in the Lutheran Church Register. When they came to Utah, he was known as Baltzar Peterson. The young couple made their home in Aarhus where Baltzar obtained work as a coach and transfer man, hauling freight and passengers to and from the ocean liners that docked at Aarhus. Three children were born to them there.

Baltzar's mother and sister had joined the Church of Jesus Christ of Latter-day Saint about 1852, and by November 20, 1852, Baltzar and Margrete were baptized. Baltzar's father was baptized about that same time and the two families began preparations to emigrate to Utah. Their son, James Joel, was born in 1863, and in March, 1863, their daughter, Laura, died.

On April 30, 1863, the two families boarded a steamer for Kiel, Germany, then to England. The journey was anything but a comfortable ride because of the forty steers, and several hundred sheep which were aboard, besides nearly 600 emigrating Saints. At Liverpool, 644 Scandinavian Saints and 13 English Saints boarded the "B. S. Kimball," and set sail for the United States. It was May 9, 1863. They arrived in New York on June 13, were held on board for fumigation and inspection for two days before they were allowed to board a train. Because of Civil War battles, the route was a northern one, and at times they rode in crowded freight cars. It was difficult for all, but especially so for Margrete because she had a three month old baby to hold and care for.

Upon their arrival at Florence, Nebraska, they found with the limited space in the wagon, they would be obliged to leave much of their bedding and heavy clothing. They left there in the Captain John F. Sanders Wagon Company. When their company camped near East Canyon Creek, just east of Big Mountain, Baltzar made his way down East Canyon to the settlement of Richville, where his brother Peter and his sister, had settled.

Arrangements were made for Peter and his brother-in-law Mads, to meet the emigrant train in Salt Lake City. Baltzar walked back to the head of East Canyon and rejoined the other. They arrived in the Salt Lake Valley on

September 5, and their baggage and supplies were hauled to Richville.

Their first two seasons were difficult as they lived in a dugout. In this shelter, two more children were born. Their food supply was adequate, but during the second winter they mostly ate cooked grain, and they even rationed that. On September 1, 1866, tragedy struck when fifteen month old Joseph drowned in the old Mill Race. The body was found on the screen where the water plunged off the later wheel of the grist mill at Richville.

A new log house was built, five more children were born, and in 1886, a two-story brick home was built.

William passed away on April 18, 1877, their two oldest sons had gone to southern Idaho fo homestead, but they still had a large family in Richville. Their home was a gathering place for the young folks for many years.

Margrete was a perfect hostess, always making everyone feel welcome and making sure there were plenty of good things to eat. Parties were livened by the violin music of Baltzar Jr. and Charles.

There was singing and dancing, and Margrete enjoyed life the most when the young folks came and participated in good home entertainment.

This family gradually became very prosperous, much credit being given to Margrete. She was well educated and had a natural ability to manage. She was resourceful; her judgment was sound; she gave advice when it was needed, and when it would do the most good.

She was an excellent seamstress and made all of her own clothes. When there was means to buy, she insisted on good quality, not only for herself, but for her family. She was not extravagant, for nothing was wasted or mis-used. Baltzar and Margrete were generous to family members that had remained in Denmark. They forwarded money and helped in other ways to enable a sister and a niece to emigrate to Utah as well as others.

In 1909, Anna Eliza and her family moved from Lyman, Wyoming, bought the family home and most of the farm, and moved in to take care of Baltzar and Margrete. Baltzar had had a severe stroke and Margrete was not well. Baltzar passed away on November 21, 1910. Margrete lived for eight more years.

Margrete became ill with congestive heart failure and had to remain in bed. Her legs became terribly swollen. She passed away on January 18, 1919 at the age of eighty-five years. Because the flu epidemic was still raging, no public meetings were allowed, her body was not embalmed. A short funeral was held out of doors, in front of the brick home. She was buried in the little cemetery in Richville,.

The cemetery was a small piece of land donated to the community by the Petersons. They were an integral part of the development of this area of Utah. Truly they were great pioneers of faith and fortitude.

SARAH ANN NELSON PETERSON

BIRTHDATE: 16 Feb 1827
Murray, Orleans Co., New York
DEATH: 20 May 1896
Ephraim, Sanpete Co., Utah
PARENTS: Cornelius H. Nelson
Kari Pedersdatter Hesthammer
PIONEER: 1849
Ezra T. Benson Co. Wagon Train
SPOUSE: Canute Peterson
MARRIED: 2 Jul 1849
east of Kanesville, Iowa
DEATH SP: 14 Oct 1902
Ephraim, Sanpete Co., Utah

CHILDREN:
Peter Cornelius, 22 Jun 1850
Canute, 1851 (died as an infant)
Sarah Ann (Lund), 4 Jan 1853
Parley Pratt, 29 Jun 1857
Canute Veiderborg, 5 Apr 1859
Nels, 26 Jan 1861
Martha Amelia, Apr l863 (died as a child)
Walber Herbertie, 29 Jan 1866
John Morset, 1 Nov 1868

Sarah Ann was born in 1827 in New York State, to Cornelius Nelson Hersdal and Kari P. Hesthammer, most prominent Scandinavian settlers in Utah. She was born in a Norwegian settlement.

Her parents were among the first group of Norwegian emigrants to journey to America in 1825 as religious dissenters seeking freedom to worship as Quakers.

Sarah Ann spent her early childhood in Murray, New York, before moving in 1836 with her widowed mother to a new Norwegian settlement on the Fox River in Illinois. At the age of eighteen she began teaching school. "It did not require much education to teach those country schools. I had some scholars who were from twenty to forty years old who came to learn the English language."

When Mormon missionaries arrived in the settlement in 1842, Sarah Ann was intrigued with their message, "Here, when 14 years of age, I first heard the Gospel, and at once believed in the divine mission of the prophet Joseph; but on account of the opposition of relatives, was prevented from joining the Church until four years later."

Despite close ties to family and friends, when the call came to gather in the West with the Saints, Sarah "left all that was near and dear to me" and set out for Utah on April 18, 1849 in a train of six wagons carrying twenty-two of her fellow Norwegians from the Fox River settlement. Sarah Ann lay sick in the wagon with cholera by the time they reached Iowa. Canute Peterson, a friend from childhood, went down to the woods near the creek to pray for her recovery. Canute stated "I became so filled with the Spirit of the Lord that I thought I hardly touched the ground while going from the place of prayer to the wagon." He reached his hand between the wagon box and cover and placing it on her head, he rebuked the disease and Sarah Ann was instantly healed.

After they arrived at the Missouri River, this young couple was married by Orson Hyde, July 2, 1849 at their camp five miles east of Kanesville. The next day they set out on their honeymoon journey to Zion, uniting with the Ezra T. Benson Wagon Company.

The couple spent eighteen months in the old Salt Lake fort, and then moved to Lehi where Canute worked to establish a farm.

Their early years in Utah were ones of pioneering, hard work and sacrifice. At the age of twenty-five, and pregnant with her third child, Sarah Ann bid goodbye to her husband when he was called on a mission to Norway. During his four year absence, she supported the family by working the farm. She fretted when her crops failed to appear in 1855, but then the grasshoppers descended, devoured each tender shoot of her neighbors' wheat. After the hoards had left, Sarah Ann's wheat appeared. She harvested sixty bushels that summer, along with potatoes and sixty bushels of corn. She was able to feed her own family along with seven orphans in another, while many were in destitute circumstances. Sarah Ann gave birth to nine children, seven of them lived to adulthood. The family also included two plural wives and their children.

In 1867, the Peterson families moved to Ephraim, Utah, where Canute had been called to serve as bishop and Sarah Ann dedicated herself to service in that community. As president of the Ephraim Ward Relief Society from 1869 to 1880, she championed the gleaning and storing of wheat, supervised the construction of a granary and meeting hall, organized a cheese-making project to help finance the Manti Temple, provided for the poor, and nursed the sick. She encouraged the Sisters to donate the money from their eggs laid on Sundays to the Perpetual Emigrating Fund.

In November, 1880, Sarah Ann was called to serve as a counselor in the Sanpete Stake Relief Society Presidency, a position she held until her death. She worked tirelessly to exhort and encourage the sisters in the stake, and was a particular advocate of storing grain, and home and cooperative industry. She also served as a worker in the Manti Temple.

 Sarah Ann passed away on May 20, 1896 at her home in Ephraim, Utah. She was eulogized by friends and family for her "gentle, amiable disposition," and her lively sense of humor, and her service to others.

REBECCA HOOD HILL PETIT

BIRTHDATE: 2 Apr 1845
Nauvoo, Hancock,Co., Illionis
DEATH: 16 Sep. 1922
Salt Lake City, Salt Lake, Utah
PARENTS: Archibald N. Hill
Isabella Hood
PIONEER: 20 Sep 1848
Abraham O. Smoot Wagon Train
SPOUSE: Edwin Pettit Sr.
MARRIED 29 Oct 1864
DEATH SP: 17 Apr 1924
Salt Lake City, Salt Lake, Utah

CHILDREN
Mary Isabel, 9 Jul 1866
Clara Hanna, May 1868 (died as a child)
Emeline, 31 Aug 1870
Edwin, 28 Feb 1872
Lillian, 5 Aug 1873
Daisy Elizabeth, 28 Feb. 1875
Florence, 25 Jan 1877 (died at 3 months)
Nellie, 10 Feb 1878
Fannie Rebecca, 9 Jul 1880
Archibald Newell, 18 Jun 1882
Elsie, 1 Aug 1884
Jesse Raymond, 25 Jul 1886
Winifred, 3 May 1888
William, 27 Jul 1890

Rebecca's family, wishing to follow the Saints, moved to Nauvoo in 1842 where Rebecca was born in the spring of 1845. Persecution of the Mormons forced them into Winter Quarters late in the autumn of 1846 where they spent the winter under severe conditions and her mother, Isabella died of exposure in March of 1847 leaving her husband and three small children.

Grandparents took Samuel age 6, Hanna age 4, went with Aunt Elizabeth Swapp and Aunt Mary Bullock took the year and a half old Rebecca, and brought her across the Plains. She lived with them until her father married four years later.

Rebecca grew up on the corner of West Temple and South Temple, and was baptized in City Creek Canyon which ran just north and west of her home. They broke the ice to get into water deep enough and though she immediately ran home, her clothes were frozen before she entered the house.

She was a quiet, bashful girl yet she was active in church activities. Living near the center of church head quarters, just three blocks from old pioneer fort and three blocks to church head quarters, made it easier to participate.

Edwin Pettit was thirty years old, a widower with three small children when Rebecca met and fell in love with him. She was only eighteen but not afraid of responsibility and hard work.

She possessed a natural beauty of mind, body and spirit, and conducted herself with dignity and self-reliance, an ability that helped her raise her three step children and their own fourteen children when ever Edwin was away on his many freighting trips.

Rebecca raised all but two of her children to adulthood. It was undoubtedly due to her natural sense of cleanliness and her untiring energy. Dishes were scrubbed clean, hands washed before every meal, mosquito netting over all windows and doors during summer. She was meticulous.

When Rebecca was sixty, her eldest daughter died in childbirth , she took the baby to raise along with her six children still at home.

Rebecca loved and enjoyed her family. They gathered often at her home to visit and bring their children. Her life was not spectaular, yet she fulfilled the most important calling a woman can have, that of raising a successful happy family.

ELIZABETH ALDEN PETTEGREW

No
Photo
Available

BIRTHDATE: 14 Oct 1791
Claremont, New Hampshire
DEATH: 27 Feb 1858
Salt Lake City, Salt Lake, Utah
PARENTS: John Alden
Keziah Holmes
PIONEER: Fall of 1848
SPOUSE: David Pettegrew
MARRIED: abt 1816
DEATH SP: 31 Dec 1863
Salt Lake City, Salt Lake, Utah

CHILDREN:
Lucy Ann, 26 Apr 1817
David Alden, 6 Mar 1819
Hiram King Solomon, 22 Nov 1820
Betsy Ann, 11 Feb 1823
James Phineas, 15 May 1825
Caroline Kezia, 22 Mar 1827
Lydia Louisa, 16 Feb 1829
George Frederick, 6 Feb 1831

Elizabeth Alden was born in New Hampshire in 1791. She married David Pettegrew about 1816, and they became the parents of eight children.

In 1832, they were living in Indiana and heard about the Mormons. David had been a very devout Methodist, but after much studying he became convinced that the Book of Mormon was true.

They boarded a steamboat on the Ohio River on their way to Kirtland, but the boat became lodged on a sandbar and would not move. Here Elizabeth and her son, Hirum, were very sick with cholera and nearly died. They recovered and resumed their journey.

David traveled on to Independence, Missouri where he had a home built, and the family was comfortable here until the mobs became unbearable and drove them out. They were also driven out of Clay County and Caldwell County in Missouri, and finally reached Quincy, Illinois, where her son, Hirum, became sick and died.

The Pettegrew family left Nauvoo with the rest of the Saints in 1846. In Council Bluffs the Mormon Battalion was being organized, and so her husband David, and her twenty-one year-old son, James Phineas, joined in that long march. After they were disbanded in San Diego they returned to get her and the rest of the family and she finally crossed the Plains in 1848, settling in Salt Lake City, Utah.

Elizabeth was a noble pioneer, and suffered many hardships. Her death occured in 1858 in Salt Lake City. Her husband died in 1863, also in Salt Lake City, Utah.

JANE CLOTILDA MARSH PETTINGILL

BIRTHDATE: 7 Jun 1828
Randolph, Catarragus, New York
DEATH: 6 Jun 1904
Willard, Box Elder Co., Utah
PARENTS: Josiah Marsh
Sally Powell
PIONEER: 1852
Company unknown
SPOUSE: Elihu U. Pettingill
MARRIED: 26 Oct 1849
Council Bluffs, Iowa
DEATH SP: 4 Apr 1899
Willard, Box Elder Co., Utah

CHILDREN:
John Christopher, 30 Aug 1850
Paulina Clarissa, 26 Sep 1851
Elihu Ulysses, 6 Mar 1853
Eliza Jane, 13 Sep 1854
Josiah Joseph, 24 Jan 1856
Sarah Clarinda, 15 Jun 1857
Clotilda Sally, 13 May 1859
Orinda Hannah, 20 Jan 1861
Emma Maria, 20 Apr 1862
Susan Elvina, 10 Feb 1864
Mary Amelia, 16 Jan 1866
Ida Melissa, 28 Oct 1867 (twin)
Ada Cirisca, 28 Oct 1867 (twin)
Almeda, 28 Sep 1869
Harriet Rosetta, 6 Oct 1871

Jane Clotilda was born in New York State in 1828. She married Elihu Ulysses Pettingill in 1849 in Council Bluffs, Iowa. They had two children when they crossed the Plains in 1852, but all in all she was the mother of fifteen children, three boys and twelve girls.

The family lived in Bountiful for three years, Ogden for two years, then in 1856 they moved to Willard in Box Elder County where they purchased a farm.

Jane never turned a hungry person away, and her door was always open to the homeless. Besides her own family she reared a number of orphans to man and womanhood.

Jane never knew what it was like to have plenty. With such a large family, clothing was often scarce. She cut up her wedding dress and underskirt to make baby clothes. She could put a patch on clothing as nice as any tailor. She seemed to have the gift of healing by just rubbing the pain from a person's body.

Jane's husband passed away in 1899, leaving her alone since all her children were married. She passed away in 1904 of pneumonia at her home in Willard, Utah, leaving a posterity of ten living children, ninety-eight grandchildren, and three great-grandchildren.

SUSANNAH YOUNG LITTLE OLIPHANT STILSON PETTINGILL

BIRTHDATE: 17 Jun 1795
Hopkinton, Massachusetts
DEATH: 5 May 1852
Salt Lake City, Salt Lake, Utah
PARENTS: John Young
Abigail "Nabby" Howe
PIONEER: 17 Oct 1849
Capt Perkins Indep Wagon Train
SPOUSE I: James Little
MARRIED: 1815
Aurelius, Cayuga Co., New York
DEATH SP: Nov 1822
Aurelius, Cayuga Co., New York

CHILDREN:
Edwin Sobieski, 23 Jan 1816
Eliza, Jan 1818 (died as an infant)
Feramorze, 14 Jun 1820
James Amasa, 14 Sep 1822

SPOUSE II: Richard Oliphant
MARRIED: Feb 1825
DEATH SP: 15 Mar 1862
Oswego, Oswego Co., New York

CHILD:
Charles Henry, 16 Nov 1825

SPOUSE III: William B. Stilson
MARRIED: 1829
Mandon, Monroe Co., New York
DEATH SP: 2 May 1844
Jefferson Barrac, St. Louis, St. Louis

CHILDREN:
Emeline, 1830 (died as a child)
William Lacy, 20 Sep 1833
Cornelia Ann, 22 May 1836

SPOUSE IV: Alonzo Pettingill
MARRIED: 1845
DEATH SP: Feb 1849
CHILDREN: None

Susannah was born June 7, 1795. She was a sister to Brigham Young. She married James Little in the year 1815 at Aurelius, Cayuga County, New York. Their home was on a farm in Auburn, New York where they raised vegetables, packaged the seeds, and put them on the market for sale. The governor of New York gave them permission to use tomatoes for eating because until that time, people thought they were inedible.

James was killed when his wagon load of lumber over-turned and pinned him beneath it. At the time, their youngest son was just two months of age. Susannah moved her children to Mendon, New York where she could be close to her father and siblings.

She married Charles Henry Oliphant in February of 1825 with whom she had a son. They were soon divorced. In 1829, she married William Stilson with whom she had three children.

Susannah was introduced to the gospel by her brother, Brigham Young, and was baptized a member of the Church of Jesus Christ of Latter-day Saints in 1834. William Stilson left his family and wasn't heard from for several years.

Susannah followed the Saints to Nauvoo where her son, James, built a log home for her. Later, her husband, William, wrote to her and informed her he had joined the army and he invited her to join him. She was able to scrape together enough money to join him in Jefferson Barracks, Missouri. William became ill and passed away in May of 1844.

Susannah married Alonzo Pettingill in St. Louis. They went to Nauvoo, but soon returned to St. Louis to find work where her son, Feramorz, had a grocery business and a boarding house. He hired Alonzo to help him. Alonzo was stricken with lung fever and died in February 1849.

Susannah came to the Salt Lake Valley on October 19, 1849 in Lorenzo Clark group of ten with the wagon company led by Captain Perkins.

Susannah passed away in Salt Lake City on May 5, 1852. She endured many trials of those pioneer days and much grief, but she remained true to the church.

LUCINDA ABRAMS PETTIT

BIRTHDATE: 15 Apr 1838
Lynbrook, Nassau, New York
DEATH: 11 May 1922
Salt Lake City, Salt Lake, Utah
PARENTS: Lewis Abrams
Martha Brower
PIONEER: Fall of 1862
SPOUSE: Brower Pettit
MARRIED: 17 Jan 1854
Lynbrook, Naussau, New York
DEATH SP: 15 Jul 1897

CHILDREN:
Susan, 31 Mar 1856
Martha Armenia, 9 Apr 1858
Blanchard Bradford, 21 Mar 1861
Arthusia "Susie," 28 Jul 1869
Lewis Sanford, 28 Apr 1872

Lucinda Abrams was born in New York State in 1838. She married Brower Pettit in 1854 and they lived close to her parents in Lynbrook, New York.

When Wilford Woodruff came to New York on a mission he converted the entire Pettit family. They desired to come West with the rest of the Saints. At the time they had three children, one a very sick baby. Lucinda prayed that he might live until they reached Utah, and he did, until he was twenty-four. They arrived in the Salt Lake Valley in 1862.

Lucinda "Cindy" felt very separated from her family in New York, and she made several trips back East to visit them. On the first trip she left the older children in Utah and took her two year old with her. She stayed for three years before returning to Salt Lake.

The family moved to Mendon, Utah for a time, but the grasshoppers were so bad that the only crop they had was onions. People would come from far and near to buy onions from them.

When the family moved back to Salt Lake, Cindy kept bees, and she was able to get the honey without getting stung.

Her last trip to the East was in 1917, but it was much easier to travel on the train than across the Plains in a covered wagon. Lucinda suffered a stroke in 1922, and passed away on May 11, 1922. Her husband preceded her in death in 1897.

JULIA ANN WRIGHT PETTY

BIRTHDATE: 2 Dec 1847
Birmingham, England
DEATH: 29 Apr 1939
Ogden, Weber Co., Utah
PARENTS: William H. Wright
Emma Taylor
PIONEER: Sep 1859
Capt Brown's Ind. Wagon Train
SPOUSE: Robert Thomas Petty
MARRIED: 22 Jan 1864
Salt Lake City, Salt Lake, Utah
DEATH SP: 23 Aug 1904
Richmond, Cache Co., Utah

CHILDREN:
Margaret Emma, 29 Oct 1865
Julia Vilate, 9 Dec 1867
Robert Thomas, Jr., 24 May 1870
William Henry, 27 Mar 1874
Martha Jane, 29 Jun 1876
Lewis James, 30 Aug 1879

Florence Louise, 2 Mar 1884
Angus Wright, 15 Feb 1886
Chrystabel, 27 Dec 1891

Julia Ann was born in England in 1847. She left England with her parents in 1854, at the age of seven. They landed at Philadelphia where they stayed for five years. She attended school here. In 1859, they crossed the Plains with the Independent Company of Captain Brown, arriving in the Valley in September, 1859.

The family lived in Alpine for a time, then moved to Richmond, Cache County, Utah in 1860. Julia Ann married Robert Thomas Petty in 1864 in the Endowment House, and to them were born nine children.

She always assisted with musicals in Richmond, was a member of the choir, and a teacher and counselor in Relief Society for many years. As a homemaker she could not be beat. She could spin, mend, cook and weave, and had nine babies to tend. In Richmond, they had a large home, which they turned into a hotel about 1882, to house and feed travelers. It was known as the Petty Hotel.

After her husband died she moved to Logan to be with her daughter Chrystabel, who was in school. While there her home in Richmond burned to the ground. Since some of her children lived in Ogden, she bought a little home there where she lived until her death in 1939 at the age of ninety-one years.

LUCINDA CATHERINE HAGGERTY AYERS PETTY

BIRTHDATE: 29 Jan 1816
Brenchville, Sussex, New Jersey
DEATH: 26 Jan 1906
Oasis, Millard Co., Utah
PARENTS: John Stoll Haggerty
Catherine Welch
PIONEER: Prob 1852
Wagon Train Company
SPOUSE I: Caleb Ayers
MARRIAGE: 11 Jan 1832
Stanhope, Wantage, New Jersey
DEATH SP: 14 Mar 1852
Council Bluffs, Iowa

CHILDREN:
Almira Murray, 23 Jun 1834
Marian /Morean, 8 Aug 1838
Victoria, 8 Nov 1839
Catherine Malinda, 29 May 1844
Ira George Haggerty, 31 Aug 1845
Heber Caleb, 23 Apr 1848
Lucinda Ann, 1 Apr 1851

SPOUSE II: Albert Petty
MARRIED: 5 Jun 1853
DEATH SP: 19 Jun 1869
Springdale, Washington Co., Utah

CHILDREN:
Amanda, 3 May 1854
Frank Haggerty, 26 Apr 1856
John Henry, 19 Jun 1859

Lucinda Catherine was born January 29, 1816 in Branchville, Sussex County, New Jersey. She married Caleb Ayers on January 11, 1832 in Stanhope, Wantage, New Jersey. They became the parents of seven children.

While they were waiting to cross the Plains, Caleb died in Council Bluffs, Iowa, March 14, 1852, leaving Lucinda a widow at age thirty-six, with a baby under one year. She came across the Plains with her children probably that same year, 1852.

Lucinda remarried on June 5, 1853 to Albert Petty, by whom she had three children. She and Albert also raised a foster daughter, a Lamanite girl named Martha, who later was sealed to her son, Ira George Haggerty Ayers, after his death.

Lucinda was widowed again at age fifty-three when Albert Petty passed away on June 19, 1869. She then went to live with her daughter and son-in-law, Victoria and William Valentine Black. Lucinda passed away on January 26, 1906 at Oasis, Millard County, Utah.

MARGARET JEFFERSON WELLS PETTY

BIRTHDATE: 2 Mar 1806
Edgecombe Co., North Carolina
DEATH: 20 Jan 1890
Lewiston, Cache Co., Utah
PARENTS: Leonard Wells
Sarah Barnes
PIONEER: Fall of 1850
Company unknown
SPOUSE: Robert Cowan Petty
MARRIED: 1832
Nashville, Tennessee
DEATH SP: Spring of 1856
Oklahoma Territory

CHILDREN:
Mary Pyrannah, 3 Jun 1833
Jane Caroline, 8 Jul 1835 (twin)
Kayzah Albine, 8 Jul 1835 (twin)
Martha Narcissa, 8 Nov 1837
Louisa Minerva, 27 Dec 1839
Robert Thomas, 22 Sep 1842
George Albert, 14 Feb 1846
Lewis James, 20 Mar 1848
Margaret Jefferson, 13 Sep 1849

Margaret was born in Edgecombe County, Tennessee in 1806. She married Robert Cowan Petty in 1832 and they made their home in Nashville, Tennessee. They were the parents of ten children; two boys died before they came to Utah in 1850.

The family lived in West Jordan (Herriman), Utah, and when Johnston's Army came through the Territory, Margaret and her daughters made pumpkin pies for the soldiers and sold them for twenty-five cents. They also sold them buttermilk and clothing they had made. In this way the army was a blessing to the family.

They bought a ten acre farm in Herriman, Utah, but the ground was hard and not easily farmed. They owned a yoke of oxen and two horses. When Robert was called on a mission to Oklahoma Territory he sold one of the horses to raise money for the mission and rode the other. He left his family with nothing.

Robert died in Oklahoma in the Spring of 1856 and is buried there. They were not able to bring his body home at that time. Margaret wove cloth to make her clothes and also for other people, to make money to support her children. In 1859 she moved with her son to Richmond, Cache, Utah, and they were among the first settlers there.

Margaret Jefferson Wells Petty passed away in Lewiston, Cache County, Utah in 1890.

HENRIETTA DRUZILLA WEYMOUTH PEW

BIRTHDATE: 8 Mar 1830
Olean, Cattaraugus, New York
DEATH: 22 Jun 1888
Mesa, Maricopa Co., Arizona
PARENTS: Daniel Weymouth
Sophia Burnham Meade
PIONEER: Oct 1850
Edward Hunt Co. Wagon Train
SPOUSE: Hyrum William Pew
MARRIED: 31 Mar 1852
Salt Lake City, Salt Lake, Utah
DEATH SP: 25 Feb 1903
Mesa, Maricopa Co., Arizona

CHILDREN:
William, 1853 d. 1852
Caroline Fidella, 10 Apr 1854
Marian Druzilla, 6 Apr 1856
James Hyrum, 21 Jun 1858
Charles Orrin, 11 Aug 1860
Elizabeth Sophia, 18 Sep 1862
Daniel Plummer, 8 Jun 1866
Walter Harvey, 14 Aug 1868
Arthur Lionell, 27 Dec 1870

Henrietta Druzilla Weymouth was born in New York State in 1830. Her father owned a saw mill and shipped lumber down the river to Cincinatti. When Druzilla was two years old her mother got very homesick, so when the next shipment of lumber was ready, her father lashed the logs together and built a little shelter on top, and she and her mother floated down the river together.

The Saints were living in Kirtland at the time, and Druzilla's mother learned about the gospel and joined the

Church of Jesus Christ of Latter-day Saints. Her father was very angry at this, and since the mother would not recant her membership, the father left them, went back to the sawmill and was never heard from again.

When Druzilla was eleven her mother remarried to William Plummer Tippets, who had five children. They came across the Plains in 1850 with the Edward Hunt Wagon Company. The family went to Brigham City, Box Elder County, Utah to live.

Druzilla was married to Hyrum William Pew in 1852 in the Endowment House.

In 1858, they moved to Richmond, Cache County, Utah, where they lived for twenty years. Then the Pew family was persuaded to move to Arizona, and took up an eighty acre homestead just north of Mesa, Arizona. They also had a bounteous orchard of fruit and nut trees, a garden, and chickens, turkeys and ducks. They also had a store where they sold things that could not be produced on the farm.

Druzilla enjoyed Mesa but did not get to live in her home for very long. She became ill, and was so sick, frail and delicate that she passed away in June, 1888, at the age of fifty-eight years. Her husband passed away in February, 1903, and is buried beside Druzilla in the Mesa Cemetery.

1853, then they traveled up the Mississippi River to Keokuk, Iowa. Hannah recalled looking across the river and seeing the ruins of the once beautiful Nauvoo Temple.

They joined the Cyrus Wheelock Company and arrived in the Salt Lake Valley in October of 1853.

In 1856, the Pexton family moved to Salt Creek (Nephi), Utah, and were among the first settlers there. For a while they lived in the fort that had been built.

James was a blacksmith and continued in this trade all his life until his health began to fail. Hannah was medium tall and slender with brown hair and blue eyes. She was a good cook, making excellent bread, cookies and jams. She often fed the Indians when they came to her door.

In 1865, James took plural wife, an immigrant from Sweden. He spent most of his time with this second family, which made Hannah very uncomfortable and caused trouble between her and James, resulting in their separation. Her two youngest sons went to Montana to work, but sent her money for her support.

In her later life she lived in seclusion near her son, James Dales. One night, in 1897, she got up and walked outside, and was later found dead, face down in the creek. Hannah Bullas Parrott Pexton is buried in Nephi, Juab County, Utah.

HANNAH BULLAS PARROTT PEXTON

BIRTHDATE: 6 May 1830
Whitgift, Yorkshire, England
DEATH: 13 Jun 1897
Nephi, Juab Co., Utah
PARENTS: Thomas Parrott
Ann Bullas(s)
PIONEER: 15 Oct 1853
Cyrus Wheelock Wagon Train
SPOUSE: James Pexton
MARRIED: 4 Jan 1853
Whitgift, Yorkshire, England
DEATH SP: 1 May 1887
Nephi, Juab Co., Utah

CHILDREN:
Ann or Hannah, 24 Dec 1854 (died in 1855)
Jamess Dales, 9 May 1857
Sarah Frances, 16 Feb 1859 (died in 1864)
Thomas Parrott, 11 Jun 1861
William Nathaniel, 13 Jun 1863
John Franklin, 26 Apr 1865
Hyrum Parrott, 2 Feb 1867
Robert Parrott, 22 Jan 1871 (died in 1871)

Hannah Bullas Parrott was born in England in 1830. She married James Pexton on January 4, 1853, and two weeks later embarked on the ship "Ellen Maria." Their honeymoon was also their emigration to Zion.

There was much sea-sickness on board ship; five births occured on the voyage, and also five deaths, and two marriages. The ship docked in New Orleans in March

ELIZA TAYLOR STEERS GALLIAN HOWELL PHILLIPS

BIRTHDATE: 17 Mar 1817
Mt. Pleasant, Ulster, New York
DEATH: 6 Apr 1899
Salt Lake City, Salt Lake, Utah
PARENTS: Thomas Taylor
Charity Sharpnet
PIONEER: 29 Aug 1859
James Brown Co. Wagon Train
SPOUSE I: William Steers
MARRIED: abt 1833
New York
DEATH SP: 2 May 1849

CHILDREN:
Harriet, 15 Sep 1834 (died as an infant)
Elijah Minerly, 11 Mar 1836
Sarah Frances (Broadbent), 3 Dec l838
Catherine Louise(child), 3 Jan l842 (died as a child)
Mary Virginia, 28 May 1845
Emma Jane, 29 Apr 1847 (died as a child)

SPOUSE II: Jesse Gallian
MARRIED: 2 Apr 1854
St. Louis, Missouri
DEATH SP:
CHILDREN: None

SPOUSE III: William John Howell
MARRIED: 3 Oct 1859
Salt Lake City, Salt Lake Co., Utah

DEATH SP: Unknown
CHILDREN: None

SPOUSE IV: William Phillips
MARRIED: 1887
Salt Lake City, Salt Lake, Co., Utah
DEATH SP: Unknown
CHILDREN: None

Eliza was born in 1817, in Pleasantville, Westchester County, New York, as the eighth child. In about 1833, she married William Steers, and she gave birth to six children, four of whom died in early childhood. After William had passed away, she married Jesse Gallian, on April 2, 1854, in St. Louis, Missouri, at thirty-seven years of age.

Eliza's daughter Frances, was preparing to leave for Utah, and she felt she did not want her to go that distance alone, but her husband would not give his consent for her to accompany Sarah. Eliza prayed earnestly that the way would be opened that she might go West with her daughter. The day before the company was ready to leave, Mr. Gallian came home very angry and told Eliza he was through with her and all her Mormon friends and she could get out of his home. Eliza felt this was an answer to her prayers.

Eliza went West with her only living children, Elijah Minerly and Sarah Frances. They crossed the Plains in Captain James Brown's Company, with Sarah Frances driving the ox-team for her mother, and Elijah driving for a lady who had lost her husband. The company left on Monday, June 13, 1859 with 353 souls, including men, women and children, with 59 wagons, 114 yoke of oxen, 11 horses, 36 cows and 5 more horses for a total of 387 people, 66 wagons. Their journey took about seventy-five days and they arrived in the Salt Lake Valley on August 29, 1859. They camped at Union Square where they were greeted by some of the Apostles, who advised them where to go, and what to do, in order for them to make preparations for the coming winter.

After their arrival in the Salt Lake Valley, Eliza married a widower, William John Howell on October 3, 1859. This romance had budded during their trek across the plains. No children were born to this union. After Mr. Howell died, Eliza married William Phillips in 1887 in Salt Lake City, Utah. She was seventy years old at that time.

Eliza had persevered through many trials for her religious beliefs. She had suffered the loss of four of her six children in their early lives, and the deaths of two spouses. She was a valiant example for those who have followed her. Eliza Phillips passed away on April 6, 1899 at the age of eighty-two years, in Salt Lake City, Utah.

Honor is given her as a great pioneer woman of faith and fortitude.

ELIZABETH ANN HEWITSON PHILLIPS

BIRTHDATE: 12 Apr 1852
Wakefield, York., England
DEATH: 20 Jul 1936
Monrovia, California
PARENTS: George Hewitson
Mary Hobson
PIONEER: 3 Nov 1864
WarrenSnow Co. Wagon Train
SPOUSE: John Campbel Phillips
MARRIED: 12 Apr 1875
Salt Lake City, Salt Lake, Utah
DEATH SP: 10 Feb 1937
Monrovia, California

CHILDREN:
John Edward, 23 Mar 1876
Arhur Alexander, 23 Dec 1877
Mary Elizabeth, 13 Mar 1880 (died as an infant)
Charles Henry, 13 Mar 1880 (twin)
Sidney George, 20 Apr 1882
Leila, 14 Mar 1884 (died as an infant)
Robert Wendell, 6 Jun 1885 (died at age 7)
Vincent Lee, 4 Jul 1888
Clarence Roy, 6 Jun 1892 (died at age 6)

Elizabeth Ann was born in England in 1852. Her only sibling was a brother two years older than she, Marmaduke. Elizabeth parents had been converted to the Church of Jesus Christ of Latter-day Saints a few years after their marriage. On June 3, 1864, this family left England for America on the ship "Hudson."

George was age fifty, Mary age forty-seven, Elizabeth age twelve, and Marmaduke age fourteen. The voyage took forty-seven days. They arrived on August 2, 1864, at Florence, Nebraska where they camped. Approximately 750 immigrants were divided into two companies and Elizabeth's family were in the second group with Captain Warren Snow. They left on August 11th or 13th. Twelve passengers were assigned to a wagon which was already loaded to capacity so the passengers were in name only-all had to walk.

Before leaving England, the Hewitsons had purchased an iron kettle along with the other necessary supplies, and they brought it all the way with them using it to cook in, wash in, fetch water in and even as a pail for the milk as they milked the cow. In Utah it was used for cooking and melting wax and dipping candles. Sometimes on the trail hunger and thirst had to be appeased by such berries and herbs as could be found along the way. Buffaloes became plentiful and became their meat supply. Many buffaloes had to be slaughtered at one time to prevent a stampede which would wreck their camp. At Ft. Laramie, the travelers were offered twenty-dollar gold pieces for a barrel of flour, but the captain realized how short their supply had become and they threatened to leave behind any driver who sold a "cupful of the precious flour." They arrived in the Salt Lake Valley on November 3, 1864, exhausted, cold and hungry.

Their first winter was difficult. Commodities were high priced, and the people were forced to exist on the least possible food. Flour sold at $25.00 a barrel and sugar $6.00 a pound. Elizabeth's father took up farming, and later added a sawmill to his farm.

When Elizabeth was in her late teens, her father took a young second wife. This caused trouble, and Mary took her two children and left George. Upset, Mary stopped going to the Mormon Church, and she and her two children began attending the Congregational Church. George remained active in the Church and lived in the Woodland, Utah area.

Elizabeth was living in the Mill Creek area near Salt Lake City when she met John C. Phillips. John had been born in Ireland. They were married in Salt Lake City, April 12, 1875, on her twenty-third birthday. Elizabeth's father was one of the witnesses.

John worked in the Park City mines. While they lived there, they took in boarders. These two were never idle. Elizabeth had her first children there. Elizabeth gave birth to nine children, but four of them died as young children. John and Elizabeth's children were blessed in the Mormon Church, but none was ever baptized.

John and Elizabeth had a grocery store in the Woodland area for awhile. They extended credit, and people didn't pay their bills, so they went broke. Between 1899 and 1901, John and Elizabeth and family, moved to Salt Lake City.

In 1912, John and Elizabeth moved to Los Angeles where they ran a grocery store. Their youngest son Vincent, accompanied them. In about 1916, they returned to Salt Lake and opened a grocery store. They had barrels of crackers, vinegar, molasses, bins containing beans and dried fruit, bananas hung in bunches, and glass jars with cheese.

About 1921, John and Elizabeth moved back to California. They bought three or four acres of land in Monrovia where they lived for the remainder of their lives. Many of the Park City people had settled in Monrovia and they would get together on July 4, for picnics. John and Elizabeth celebrated their sixieth wedding anniversary in April of 1935.

In her late years, Elizabeth had a growth on the back of her eye which caused her to go blind. She became ill and was in bed for over six months. It was said she just lay quiet and slept nearly all the time. She was not in pain, but had to be fed. John was older and not able to work and said, "Our time is short here now and the only thing that worries me now is that I will pass away before your granma, and then I wonder what will become of her, but we hope for the best."

Elizabeth passed away first on July 20, 1936 at the age of eighty-four years, in Monrovia, Los Angeles County, California. John's health failed, and seven months later on February 10, 1937, he passed away. Elizabeth and John were both buried at the Murray Cemetery near Salt Lake City.

Elizabeth and John are honored for the great pioneers they were in helping settle the Salt Lake Valley, and also Park City, and California.

HANNAH HENDERSON PHILLIPS

No Photo Available

BIRTHDATE: 1 May 1812
Cilycum, Wales
DEATH: 26 Oct 1899
Dayton, Franklin Co., Idaho
PARENTS: James Henderson
Martha Thomas Jones
PIONEER: 15 Oct 1854
William S. Phillips Wagon Train
SPOUSE: William S. Phillips
MARRIED: 21 Apr 1834
Wales
DEATH SP: 18 Dec 1876

CHILDREN:
James, 5 Mar 1835 (died as an infant)
Hannah, 21 Nov 1837
James Henderson, 24 Nov 1841
Thomas Joseph, 1 Sep 1844
Moroni Lorenzo, 13 Jul 1848
Sarah Ann, 7 Dec 1851 (died as an infant)
William Peter, 9 Dec 1854

Hannah was born in Cilycum, Carmarthenshire, Wales, 1812. She married William Samuel Phillips in 1834 in Wales. They had seven children born to them. Sarah died the day she was born, James died shortly after his birth, Hannah died at age twenty-seven, and Thomas died at age forty-two. James and Moroni and William lived to be mature adults. Hannah was of Scottish descent; her great grandparents left Scotland to settle in Wales.

In 1844, Hannah was baptized into the Church of Jesus Christ of Latter-day Saints. Her husband became the presiding Elder of the Merthyr Branch for four years, also serving for one and a half years over the Monmouthshire Conference.

In January, 1849, be was called to be the President in the principality of Wales where he served until the end of 1853. His positions caused extensive travel for him, and Hannah was left to manage the children and their home at 14 Castle Street in Merthyr Tidfel. The missionaries were always welcome in their home. Hannah often slipped money into the pocket of poor missionaries. Apostles stayed in there home when they visited that country.

After President Phillips was released, Hannah and four children, Samuel's mother and a friend sailed from Liverpool on the ship "Goloconda," on January 31, 1854. Six weeks later they landed at New Orleans. They wintered in St. Louis and journeyed to Kansas City in the Springtime. Indian troubles at Ft. Laramie were the only mention of their travels. Apparently her husband was in charge of this company which arrived on October 15, 1854 in the Salt Lake Valley.

President Snow called them to go to Box Elder County. They first lived in the Old Fort, later moving into a small house. Hannah helped her husband in working the land; new experiences for both of them. Their crops were frequently destroyed by insects. They moved several times and finally their home was located near Brigham City and Perry on the land where Maddox Restaurant now stands. The entire family worked hard to make a living. Hannah had wisely brought a supply of good clothing and fabric from Wales, most of which was traded for goods to keep them alive.

Frail and unfit for pioneer life, William suffered in many ways and died on December 18, 1876, at the comparatively young age of sixty-one years. Hannah was stronger, and lived in Perry for many more years, often visiting at the home of her son, William, in Dayton, Idaho.

It was there Hannah passed away on October 26, 1899, at the age of eighty-seven years, having been a widow for nearly twenty-three years. She was truly a grand matriarch, much beloved by those who have followed after a great pioneer woman of faith and fortitude.

HANNAH SIMMONDS PHILLIPS

BIRTHDATE: 13 Jan 1820
Dynock, Worstershire, England
DEATH: 12 Jan 1898
Kaysville, Davis Co., Utah
PARENTS: John Simmonds
Sarah Bryan
PIONEER: 22 Sep 1849
Orson /Spencer Co. Wagon Train
SPOUSE: Edward Phillips
MARRIED: 2 Aug 1842
Camp Creek, Illinois
DEATH SP: 1 Dec 1896
Kaysville, Davis Co., Utah

CHILDREN:
Sarah Francis, 9 May 1843
William Robert, 14 Feb 1845
John D., 29 Jan 1846
Mary Ann, 7 Mar 1848
Edward Charles, 29 Dec 1848
Heber James, 18 Sep 1850
Rebecca, 29 Oct 1852
Alma, 10 Dec 1853
Isabella, 15 May 1855
Thomas Henry, 2 Apr 1857
Hannah Maria, 5 Apr 1859
Daniel Maisy, 27 Nov 1860
Willard Richard, 15 Dec 1863
Infant, 11 Apr 1866
Infant, 11 Apr 1866

When Hannah was young, she attended Mrs. Benjamin Hill's finishing school in England. Here she learned all the arts of homemaking and etiquette.

Hannah, her friend, and Mr. and Mrs. Hill all joined the Church of Jesus Christ of Latter-day Saints when Wilford Woodruff baptized the six hundred people. Her parents gave their permission for her to come to America with the Hills. She was just eighteen years old. They crossed the ocean, traveled to Kirtland, Ohio, and then on to Nauvoo.

She met her old friend, Edward Phillips from England. They were married at Camp Creek, Illinois. They had two children born to them at Camp Creek before they were driven away from their home by the mobs in 1846.

In 1849, they had four small children with whom they traveled West to the Promised Valley with Captain Gulley's Wagon Company. When he died, Orson Spencer was in charge for the remainder of the trip. They arrived in Utah September 22, 1849. They settled Kaysville, Utah.

She taught her daughters many of the skills she learned in finishing school. She taught them to spin, weave, sew, make soap and candles, dry fruit, make home made dyes, and preserve fruit. She knew how to cure meat and cook it in such a way that it won her quite a reputation.

Hannah entertained Church authorities who came to Kaysville when her husband was in the Kaysville bishopric. She was noted for her hospitality. Her motto was "Speak no evil of any one," and she would not allow it in her home. She and her husband were still sweethearts in their old age. She always remained faithful to the gospel. She left a large posterity a great example to follow.

MARGARET LUKER PHILLIPS

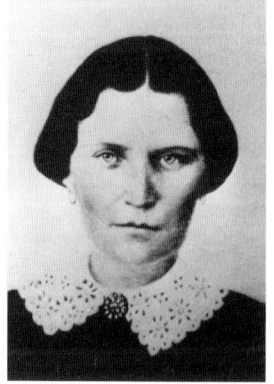

BIRTHDATE: 5 Feb 1818
Tom's River, Ocean, New Jersey
DEATH: 18 May 1867
American Fork, Utah Co., Utah
PARENTS: Thomas Luker
Margaret Luker
PIONEER: 13 Sep 1867
Milo Andrews Co. Wagon Train
SPOUSE: Richard Phillips
MARRIED: 1 Oct 1835
Monmouth Co., New Jersey
DEATH SP: 29 May 1885
American Fork, Utah Co., Utah

CHILDREN:
Mary Elizabeth, 1 Nov 1836
Elmira, 21 Oct 1838
Rachel, 29 Jan 1841
John Wesley, 17 Jun 1843
St. Lewis Lanc, 23 Jul 1847
Jacob Amazon, 23 Dec 1848
Elwood, 27 Sep 1850
Richard, 1851
Margaret Emma (Emeretra), 25 Dec 1854

Mary, abt 1855
Thomas Ivins, 2 Mar 1857
William Applebee, 8 Feb 1858
Benjamin, 9 Aug 1860
Sarah Ann, 2 May 1863

Margaret had three sisters and five brothers. She was a beautiful woman, and lived and exciting life on the sea shore taking trips on various boats of which her husband Richard was captain. They had a large home, with a large orchard and garden, and a bake house outside. This made it even harder when they they joined the Church of Jesus Christ of Latter-day Saints and gave it all up to join with the saints in Utah.

They left Florence, Nebraska in July, 1861. They were fortunate enough to have two wagons and a heavy carriage so a lot of the family could ride. Her oldest daughter and her two daughters joined them in Nebraska which gave Margaret added anguish, because she was expecting her third child and her husband didn't come with her.

One of the families in the wagon train was bringing a Negro boy with them, which was against the law because of the trouble over ownership of slaves at that time. Margaret gave them one of her daughter's dresses for him to wear.

Three weeks out of Salt Lake, Margaret's daughter, Libby, gave birth to a daughter named Sarah. They arrived in the Salt Lake Valley on September 12, 1861. Dick left his family with friends and went to American Fork to check out the land. He traded the mule team for a section of land with a small house. Margaret gave birth to her fourteenth child Sarah Ann, May 2, 1863, in American Fork. They took up a fourth section of land and began to build a bigger house. Their youngest son, Benjamin, died in November, 1865.

Margaret only enjoyed her new home for a few short years. She passed away on May 18, 1867 and is buried in the American Fork Cemetery.

MARIA ANN TUCKFIELD PHILLIPS

BIRTHDATE: 15 Jul 1843
Aberavon, Glamorgan, So. Wales
DEATH: 2 Oct 1902
Salt Lake City, Salt Lake, Utah
PARENTS: James Tuckfield
Maria Rendell
PIONEER: 1862
SPOUSE: William G. Phillips
MARRIED: 4 May 1861
Boston, Massachusetts
DEATH SP: I Mar 1911
Salt Lake City, Salt Lake, Utah

CHILDREN
Emma Francis (Romney), ll Feb 1862
Mary Lizey (Corbis), ll Feb 1864
Alice Valinda (Wright), 7 Apr 1866

Maria Ann, 18 Mar 1868 (died as a child)
Florence May (Robbins), 11 Jul 1869
William James, 4 Sep 1871
George Arthur, 6 Jan 1875 (died as a child)
Charles Albert, 1 May 1880 (died as a child)

Maria Ann was born in 1843 in South Wales. She was the youngest of seven children in her family. Her father was a shipwright. Maria spent her childhood in her native land, and about 1856, her family was introduced to the Church of Jesus Christ of Latter-day Saints by missionaries from America. Their one desire as a family was to be baptized and join the Saints in Salt Lake City, Utah.

Records show that Maria was baptized in December, 1856. Her family embarked on this journey. On board ship, she met a young man from Portsmouth, Hampshire, England named William George Phillips.

They spent time in Boston, Massachusetts where they were married on May 4, 1861. They traveled West by wagon train and arrived in the Salt Lake Valley about 1862 where their first child was born. They had three children born into their family, three of whom died young.

William was appointed City Marshall and Chief of Police in Salt Lake City from 1884 to 1892. In 1886, with four children still at home, William took a leave of absence and left to serve a mission in his homeland of Manchester, England. Maria was very skilled in management, and was able to maintain the home well in his absence.

Maria passed away on October 2, 1902 at the age of fifty-nine years. She died in Salt Lake City and is buried in the Salt Lake Cemetery. She was a devout member of the Church and helped build up the Church in the Salt Lake Valley, truly a pioneer woman of faith and fortitude to be honored by those who have followed her.

MARY ANN PRESDEE PHILLIPS

BIRTHDATE: 4 Dec 1774
Alfrick, Worcestershire, England
DEATH: 19 Jan 1872
Kaysville, Davis Co., Utah
PARENTS: James Presdee
Mary Purshull
PIONEER: 22 Sep 1849
Orson Spencer Co. Wagon Train
SPOUSE: William Phillips
MARRIED: 3 Dec 1793
DEATH SP: 29 Nov 1825
Suckley, Worcester, England

CHILDREN:
John, 26 Oct 1794
Thomas, 5 Apr 1797
William, 24 Feb 1800
Mary, 1 Nov 1804
Elizabeth, 1806
Richard, (chr.) 18 May 1807
Richard, (chr.) 24 Jan 1808

Harriet, (chr.) 26 Aug 1810
Ann, 1811
Edward, 2 Apr 1814
Susannah, 2 Nov 1816
James, 1820

Mary had been a member of the Methodist Church when she was younger. Then she joined the United Brethren. In 1793, she married William Phillips and they started their family. All of her children were born in England.

In 1825, she was widowed and left to care for her own family as best as she could. In 1840, she was baptized into the Church of Jesus Christ of Latter-day Saints by Wilford Woodruff. She emigrated to America when she was seventy years old together with her son, Edward, the John Green family, and her daughter Ann's son, James Burrup.

It took eight weeks for them to cross the ocean on the ship, "Caroline." They landed in Quebec, Canada. They went to Montreal by steamer and on to Lewiston where they boarded a mule drawn train to Niagara Falls. They went from Niagara Falls to Chicago on the ship, "Chesapeake."

In Chicago, they hired wagons and drivers to take them to Nauvoo and arrived in October 1841. They lived in an area fifteen miles from Nauvoo called Camp Creek. They suffered much persecution, illness, and loss of personal property through fire.

They started west in the wagon company led by Edward Phillips who died of cholera en route. The company was then led by Orson Spencer until it arrived in the Salt Lake Valley in September of 1849. A great many of the emigrants died of cholera. They also had to have escorts through the Indian country.

Mary moved to Kaysville in 1851 where she officiated in the capacity of midwife for forty-five years, until she was ninety-six years of age. She waited upon thirty women annually and never lost a woman under her administration.

When she was over eighty two years old, she gleaned over twenty bushels of wheat and raised thirty bushels of potatoes, dug them, and carried them into her cellar. She fattened two hogs and gave a yoke of oxen that year to help emigrate the poor people from England. She made a will of all the property she had, including fifteen head of horned stock to the emigration fund.

Mary had been true to her family, her friends, and her religion. She passed away in 1871 at the age of ninety-seven, Kaysville, Davis County, Utah.

MERAB HANCOCK GORDGE PHILLIPS

No
Photo
Available

BIRTHDATE: 13 Dec 1819
Dale, Pembrokeshire, Wales
DEATH: 5 Sep 1893
Beaver, Beaver Co., Utah
PARENTS: William Hancock
Ann Laidley
PIONEER: 1859
SPOUSE I: Samuel Gordge
MARRIED: 14 Nov 1847
DEATH SP: 25 Dec 1850
Australia

CHILDREN:
Ann (Lee Kennedy), 30 May 1849
David, 9 May 1851

SPOUSE II: John Phillips
MARRIED: abt 1855
Wales
DEATH SP: 1880
Beaver, Beaver Co., Utah

CHILDREN:
John Richard, 26 Sep 1856
Elizabeth Chestina (Washburn), 1859
Sarah (Meyers), 1860

Merab was born in 1819 in Wales. She was the oldest child of the family. She joined the Church of Jesus Christ of Latter-day Saints in Wales on February 14, 1842.

She married Samuel Gordge in 1847 in Wales. They later emigrated to Australia where their two children were born. While working in a shipyard, Samuel drowned in the harbor on Christmas Day, December 25, 1850, five months before David, their son, was born.

Through working hard, and with the generosity of friends, Merab had enough money to sail to California. There she met John Phillips of Toms River, New Jersey. He had come to San Francisco on the ship "Brooklyn" with Sam Brannan.

With others from the ship "Brooklyn" and from the Mormon Battalion, they settled in San Bernardino, California where their first child John Richard, was born in 1856.

Although Merab did not cross the Plains, she arrived in Utah before 1869, among the pioneers who came from California. Brigham Young had called the Saints to Utah in 1859, so the Phillips family moved to Beaver, Utah. Here John and Merab were sealed in the Endowment House on November 19, 1859.

Merab was always strong in the Church, but records of any church positions have not been available. When the Manti Temple was opened in 1888, Merab, her son, David and David's wife, traveled over the mountains from Beaver to Manti to perform a lot of temple work for their ancestors.

They even did work for close friends. Some of the endowments were done for people without their first name, such as Grandpa McMath and Grandma McBride.

Merab's daughter, Ann Gordge, became the nineteenth wife of John Doyle Lee, being married in the Endowment House on June 10, 1865. They had three children. Many years after John D. Lee's death, Ann married Frank Kennedy.

Merab Phillips passed away on September 5, 1893 in Beaver, Utah at the age of eighty-three years. Her husband preceded her in death. She was a brave pioneer woman who went through the trials and tribulations of the pioneer women of Utah.

SARAH ANN BRETT / BRATT WRIGHT CORBETT PHILLIPS

BIRTHDATE: 7 Nov 1825
London, Middlesex, England
DEATH: 12 Dec 1894
Nephi, Juab Co., Utah
PARENTS: John James Brett
Sarah Upstone
PIONEER: 30 Nov 1856
Edward Martin Handcart Comp.
SPOUSE I: Andrew Wright
MARRIED: 16 Dec 1849
Parish of Manchester, England
DEATH SP: 10 Jun 1924
Salt Lake City, Salt Lake, Utah

CHILDREN:
Thomas Brett, 23 Nov 1851
Emma Maria, 29 Sep 1854

SPOUSE II: Thomas Corbett
MARRIED: 23 Feb 1857
Payson, Utah Co., Utah
DEATH SP: Unknown
CHIIDREN: None

SPOUSE III: Samuel Phillips
MARRIED: Unknown
DEATH SP: 1 Sep 1874
Nephi, Juab Co., Utah

CHILD:
John William, 29 Jan 1863

Sarah Ann joined the Church of Jesus Christ of Latter-day Saints in 1842 when she was seventeen years old and was rebaptized on May 23, 1844. The father of her first child, James Brigham Brett (Wright),is unknown.

She married Andrew Wright on December 16, 1849 in Parish of Manchester, Lancaster, England. They had two children. After her husband left her in 1854 or 1855 she worked very hard in a factory trying to support her three children. They were in very poor circumstances and at one time the officials came and put them in the "Poor House."

It was a terrible trial for her and nearly broke her heart. However, they were only there nine days because a good Latter-Day-Saint friend of the family heard of her trouble and helped her out. The friend was Edward Chappell.

Sarah Ann journeyed to America with the help of the Church Perpetual Emigration Fund in 1844. She was accompanied by her three children and her mother, Sarah Brett Upstone Alcock. Her mother became ill and died. She was buried at sea.

They arrived at Boston, Massachusetts, then took the train to Iowa City, arriving July 8, 1856. On July 26, 1856 they started West with the ill-fated Edward Martin Handcart Company.

In the beginning of the trek the hot summer sun beat down upon them and mosquitoes swarmed about their heads. They trudged across Nebraska. Their boots were worn beyond repair. Their feet became swollen and blistered. They struggled on valiantly.

The company was late leaving Iowa City so they had great difficulty with early snowstorms. One day they awoke to a foot of new snow and had to break new trails. They camped in a ravine that was later called "Martin's Cove" in Wyoming. They made round beds with their feet together in the center to try to keep them from freezing. Emma Maria had her feet frozen and she limped the rest of her life. Many of the Saints died of exposure. One day Sarah Ann could see that her son, James, was becoming ill. She got a little stick and began to run him around the camp-fire until he was perspiring freely. Then she rolled him in a blanket and he was well the next day. Many times they had to shovel snow to make their beds. They were extremely short of food and were rationed to one quarter pound of meal a day for cakes or hotcakes.

It was November 30, 1856 when Sarah Ann and her children reached the Salt Lake Valley. They stayed with friends for a short while then settled in Payson, Utah. She married Thomas Corbett.

When Thomas died she married Samuel Phillips and moved to Nephi. They lived on roots and weeds for a time. She saw the seagulls eat the grasshoppers and save the crops. She delighted in telling the story.

Sarah Ann was a faithful Latter-day Saint all of her life. She passed away on December 12, 1894 in Nephi, Utah.

SARAH BODEN PHILLIPS

BIRTHDATE: 7 Mar 1850
Aberdare, Wales
DEATH: 5 Dec 1926
Dayton, Franklin Co., Idaho
PARENTS: James Boden
Annorah Coleman
PIONEER: 5 Oct. 1867
Capt. Leonard Rice Wagon Train
SPOUSE: Thomas J. Phillips
MARRIED: 17 Oct 1870
DEATH SP: 1 Dec 1886
Dayton, Franklin Co., Idaho

CHILDREN
Thomas James, 15 Oct 1871
Sarah Lottie, 25 Nov 1872
Hanna Annorah, 15 Jan 1875
Mary Elizabeth, 8 Jul 1876
William Boden, 9 Apr 1878
Ellen Jane, 5 Nov 1879
Martha May, 17 Sep 1881
James Boden, 25 Nov 1882
Emily, 14 Apr 1884
Vernon Moroni, 9 Feb 1886

Sarah was born in Aberdare, Glamorganshire, Wales in 1850 to parents who had been baptized into the Church of Jesus Christ of Latter-day Saints two years before her birth. The Bodens were among the first to be converted in Wales and were stalwarts in their faith. Her father was president of the Aberdare Branch of the Church, befriending missionaries and Church dignitaries was part of their life.

The family desperately wanted to go to Utah but did not have the means. Deciding that Sarah should go and join her sister, Polly Callan, she was sent to Utah with a company of 482 Saints. The seventeen year old girl, very frightened, (never had she stayed away from home overnight) left with her good friend Fannie Morgan and sailed from her homeland on the steam ship "Manhattan," June 21, 1867, reaching New York City on the 4th of July.

Traveling to North Platte by train they joined the wagon train of Captain Leonard Rice, the only wagon train to Salt Lake City that summer. Even though the journeys lessened in miles and time as the railroad crawled further west each year, it was a trek of considerable effort. Captain Rice, a kindly considerate man, kept everyone encouraged and cheerful. Still the rigors of the journey took ten who died and were buried beside the trail.

The company of about 500 people arrived in the Salt Lake Valley on October 5, just in time to attend the first conference held in the Tabernacle on October 6, 1867.

Sarah made her home in Brigham City with her sister Polly, at times staying with the Jensen and Jones families doing housework to earn her keep. She worked at whatever was at hand for money to contribute to her parents meager savings and help them come to Zion. She rented an acre of land and planted potatoes to sell. She cleared grub sage from a lot for $4.00 among other work. Her parents came to Utah the next year, at great loss.

A new baby born at Sweetwater, died in twelve days and Sarah's father died from Mountain Fever the day after he arrived into the Valley.

Sarah married Joseph Thomas, when she was twenty. The couple lived in Perry, before moving to Idaho where they settled in 1874 for the rest of their lives.

After sixteen years of marriage and one month after the birth of her tenth child, Joseph was injured in a runaway horse accident. It was bitter cold and he suffered from exposure and, among other injuries, a broken leg, which was frozen and had to be amputated. He did not respond to treatment and passed away.

Sarah's children worked to help their mother eke out a living on the farm and Sarah worked as a practical nurse and midwife. So much did she make herself a part of the community that she was called Grandma Phillips by the whole town and the Dayton Ward gave her a birthday party every year.

On December 5, 1926, Sarah Boden Phillips passed away. Her body had worn out.

ADAH STEWART PHIPPEN

No
Photo
Available

BIRTHDATE: 19 Jul 1798
Neversink, Ulster Co., New York
DEATH: 14 Apr 1870
Salt Lake City, Salt Lake, Utah
PARENTS: Luther Stewart
Esther Smith
PIONEER:
SPOUSE: Isaac Phippen
MARRIED: 15 Oct 1818
Springfield, Clark Co., Ohio
DEATH SP: 2 May 1875
Salt Lake City, Salt Lake, Utah

CHILDREN:
James Worthington, 12 Oct 1819
Joseph Freeman, 20 Sep 1822
Esther Permelia, 6 Sep 1824
Isaac Clark, 17 Dec 1827
Asa Stewart, 20 Apr 1832
Sylvester Smith, 20 May 1834
Almon Sherman, 6 Feb 1837
Adah Louise, 2 Sep 1842

Adah was born in New York in 1798. By age twenty, she was living in Springfield, Clark County, Ohio and had met and married Isaac Phippen. There the couple stayed for the next four years and two sons were born to them.

The couple then moved three states bordering the Great Lakes to the North East, into Vermont, for a short year or two. The first of their two daughters was born there. The next ten or twelve years were lived in Charlotte, Chautaqua County, New York where four more sons were born.

It was the period of religious revival among the people of the frontier area of America and the time of the Revelation to the Young Joseph Smith.

Adah was thirty-two, when, in Fayette, New York the Church of Latter-day Saints, was organized. Samuel Smith, the Prophet's twenty-two year old brother filled his knapsack with copies of the Book of Mormon and set off on a journey through the neighboring towns to acquaint people with the recently published scripture.

Isaac and Adah's last child, their second daughter Adah, was born in the fall of 1842, in Nauvoo, Hancock County, Illinois.

Very little information is available about her but the places of birth of their children indicate her involvement as a wife and mother in the early history of the church.

Their oldest son was very involved in the building of Nauvoo and the many things that happened there.

One child died at the age of three, another at age eleven and one at eighteen. Without the sacrifices such women made as wives and mothers the things that were accomplished would not have been possible.

Adah Stewart Phippen passed away at the age of seventy-two in Salt Lake City, Utah. Isaac passed away five years later.

JULIA ADELIA PRATT PHIPPEN

No
Photo
Available

BIRTHDATE: 13 Aug 1825
Newstead, Erie Co., New York
DEATH: 19 Jun 1885
PARENTS: Silas Pratt
Silence Phippen
PIONEER: 19 Jun 1885
SPOUSE: James W. Phippen
MARRIED: 9 Aug 1845
DEATH SP: 13 Dec 1907

CHILDREN:
Silas Lucien, 5 Dec 1846
Lenord Henry, 28 Nov 1853
Rosabel Adelia, 4 Nov 1855
Worthington Elmer, 10 Jan 1858
Elna Lodema, 21 May 1861
Frank Eugene, 7 Mar 1864
Julia Pamela, 18 Sep 1865
Sila Pearl, 3 Sep 1871

Julia Adelia was born in Newstead, Erie County, New York in 1825. She married James when she was twenty years old, in the same town of Newatead, but the couple had moved to Newton (Elmira), Chemung County, New York

by the time their first child, Silas, was born in December of the next year.

The next child, Lenord Henry, was born seven years later in Salt Lake City, Utah. Within those seven years the Church had sent missionaries to far corners of the earth with wonderful results of conversion. To gather with the Saints and live in a place peaceful to them was the goal of the newly baptized.

It was a goal requiring great preparation, determination and physical strength to accomplish and the young couple made all the sacrifices that enabled them to do so.

There is little information about her and her civic and church callings, as the one daughter who lived beyond her fifties seldom talked about her.

Five of her eight children died in infancy and of the three who survived, one died in his forties and the other in her fifties.

The couple built a home in Salt Lake City where, in her later years, because she was in poor health, her daughter that lived the longest, came with her family to live with Julia and care for her.

As a wife and mother she played a very important role in the history of the church, almost from it's beginning. She died just before her sixtieth birthday, old and frail from the hardships she endured for the cause of her religion, preceding her husband in death by twenty-two years. Certainly she is to be counted as a woman of great faith and fortitude.

CHARLOTTE REBECCA WHITE PICKETT

BIRTHDATE: 7 Oct 1849
Sweet Water, Fremont, Wyoming
DEATH: 11 Oct 1918
Logan, Cache Co., Utah
PARENTS: Jonathan White
Elizabeth Dodd White Clegg
PIONEER: 17 / 29 Oct 1849
E. T. Benson Co. Wagon Train
SPOUSE: John W. Pickett
MARRIED: 21 Dec 1866
Salt Lake City, Salt Lake, Utah
DEATH SP: 12 Apr 1936
Logan, Cache Co., Utah

CHILDREN:
George Mathew, 21 Sep 1867
Harriet, 25 Dec 1869
Mary Eliza, 23 Jul 1871
Charlotte, 17 Jan 1874
Henry Arthur, 29 May 1876
Lucy Lorena, 12 Sep 1878
Nellie May, 14 Jan 1881
Fred Ray, 6 Feb 1887
Theron Roy, 28 Aug 1889
Wade Hampton, 25 Aug 1893

Charlotte was born to her recently widowed mother by Pacific Springs in Wyoming as they were crossing the

Plains in the Ezra Taft Benson Wagon Company. She was born in a dugout on a night so cold that sixty head of the company's cattle froze to death. They arrived in Salt Lake City on October 29, 1849 where they lived in one of the small one-room huts of the fort. Her mother married Benjamin Clegg and their family moved to Tooele, Utah.

Charlotte had very little formal schooling. Her education consisted mainly of hard work. As she grew older, she worked in other people's homes. She was very ambitious and loved to sew clothes. Her brother-in-law, Alex, was a tailor by profession. Charlotte would help him occasionally with his tailoring. She was very thrifty, wasting neither food nor clothing.

Charlotte married John W. Pickett when she was seventeen years old. She became the mother of eleven children. Her life was one of hard work and self sacrifice. While living in Salt Lake City, she took in boarders and sewing in order to make a living for her family. She lived many years in polygamy.

They have been residents of Tooele City, Salt Lake City, Lake Town in Rich County, Providence, and Logan in Utah. They also lived in Manassa, Colorado, and the Teton County in Idaho.

She practiced all the pioneer arts and was a spendid cook, made good soap, butter, cheese, and candles. Her vegetable and flower gardens were second to none. She always had a profession of flowers to beautify her surroundings. She served as a Relief Society Teacher in Providence. That was the only public office she ever accepted because her heart was always with her children.

Charlotte Rebecca suffered from diabetes and a slight stroke of paralysis. She passed away four days after her sixty-ninth birthday.

HARRIET POCOCK PICKETT

BIRTHDATE: 2 Jun 1817
Long Lane, Berkshire, England
DEATH: 20 Feb 1898
Tooele Co., Utah
PARENTS: John Pocock
Ann Lailey
PIONEER: 16 Oct 1862
Isaac Canfield Co. Wagon Train
SPOUSE: Mathew Pickett
MARRIED: 1 Nov 1845
Chieveley, Berkshire, England
DEATH SP: 21 Aug 1892
Tooele Co., Utah

CHILDREN:
John, 2 Aug 1846
Moroni, 16 Oct 1848
Elizabeth, 3 Aug 1850
Rhoda, 21 Aug 1852
William Hyrum, 3 Dec 1854
Mathew, Jr., 2 Jun 1862 (died as an infant)

Harriet as a child was sent regularly to the village of Cuffidge, a trip of seven miles, for yeast (barm) for the family bread. During her later girlhood, she was at service in a home of wealthy people. She learned to read and write well.

She experienced a tragic romance when she became engaged to a young fellow who died. She remained single until she was twenty-seven years of age and then married Mathew Pickett.

On March 28, 1847, she was baptized a member of the Church of Jesus Christ of Latter-day Saints. The family, consisting of the parents and five children sailed from Liverpool on the ship, "John J. Boyd," which landed in New York on June 1, 1862. At the frontier town of Florence, Nebraska, their sixth child, Mathew, was born and died shortly thereafter. The family joined the Isaac Canfield Wagon Company and arrived in Salt Lake City on October 16, 1862.

They made a home on the deep black soil near the mouth of Settlement Canyon in Tooele City. He settled near his brother William A. Pickett who had settled there two years previously.

Mathew was a farmer who owned a lime kiln. They built a rock home above the creek. She had an accident while building a nest for a hen. She placed two stones together and a piece chipped off and struck her in the eye causing blindness in the eye.

She and her husband were good friends to the Indians. Her husband married a second wife, Millicent Rose, and subsequently was arrested and confined in the penitentiary. At these times, Harriet and her family had to support themselves and meet the needs of the second family.

After her husband died, Harriet lived with his second wife in Tooele City. The last five years of her life were spent in the home of her daughter, Rhoda.

MARY CASTLE PICKETT

BIRTHDATE: 1820
DEATH: 27 Dec 1889
PARENTS:
PIONEER: 1849
SPOUSE: William Armstrong Pickett
MARRIED:
DEATH SP: 11 Dec 1901

CHILDREN: None

Mary was born to a well-to-do family who left her an inheritance of seventeen pounds. She married William Armstrong Pickett who worked in a glass factory in

England. After their marriage, they went back to her old home in Hampshire.

When the Elders from the Church of Jesus Christ of Latter-day Saints presented their message to them, they were converted and baptized as members of the church in 1846.

With her inheritance money and the help her people could give them, they were able and prepared to take a journey to New Zealand. They changed their minds after their baptism. William and Mary Pickett booked passage on the ship, "James Pennell" in September 1848 and arrived in New Orleans on October 22, 1848. They crossed the Plains and arrived in the Salt Lake Valley in 1849.

They settled first in Tooele County in an area known as Clover Creek. This was twenty miles southwest of Tooele City. There were many rushes there. Her husband was a leader in the community taking an active part in all matters.

He and Mary were friends to the Indians and were brave enough to live away from the protection of the Tooele City Wall. They were later called to settle the Muddy River District in Eastern Nevada. They stayed there many years while her husband was a partner in a saw mill venture.

After his brother, George, died in St. Louis on his way to the Salt Lake Valley, William went back to St. Louis and brought George's children to Salt Lake Valley. His niece, Jane, came to live with them. She helped them a great deal in tending their sheep.

Mary was in poor health all of her life and never had children. She passed away on December 27, 1899.

JANE NANCY ROMRIALL / ROMMRELL HAMMOND PIERCE

BIRTHDATE: 23 Feb 1830
St. John, Jersey Islands
(Channel Islands)
DEATH: 4 Feb 1909
Ogden, Weber Co, Utah
PARENTS: Francois Romriell
Mary Billot
PIONEER: 22 Sep 1855
SPOUSE: Joseph Hammond
MARRIED 1858
DEATH SP. May 1859

CHILDREN
Mary Jane, 17 Mar 1858
Matilda, 20 Jul 1859

SPOUSE II: George Thomas Pierce
MARRIED: 20 Sep 1863
DEATH SP: 29 Nov 1897
Ogden, Weber Co., Utah

CHILDREN:
Caroline Sophia, 4 Sep 1867

George Thomas, 16 Dec 1869
Eliza Rebecca, 31 Oct 1871
Benjamin Franklin, 9 Sep 1873
Elizabeth, 8 Oct 1875 (died as a child)
Porter Marion, 21 Sep 1877
Fredrick Abraham, 15 Dec 1879
Bertha, 22 Nov 1881 (died as a child)

Jane Nancy was born on St. John, Jersey Island in 1830. She was the key to her parents introduction into the Church of Jesus Christ of Latter-day Saints through the missionaries teachings. Jane Nancy was eighteen when her family joined the Church.

Her family was enthusiastic and they were the catalyst in spreading the word of the Gospel on that Island, holding meetings in their home for the next seven years until in 1855, their preparations complete, they embarked for America.

After six weeks on the ocean where they experienced terrible storms, malnutrition (sea biscuits were the average fare deep into the voyage), stale water that grew scarce, and diseases that were inescapable, the company of Saints landed in New York.

Making their way to Mormon Grove, Kansas, the 305 souls left on July 28, 1855 to cross the Plains in Captain Harpers Wagon Company. Each wagon usually was stuffed so full of the necessities of the journey that only a privileged few were able to ride most of the way. Twenty-five year old Jane Nancy walked nearly the whole ninety-four day crossing, arriving into the Salt Lake Valley deep into fall weather with feet sore and bleeding. Her family settled in Little Cottonwood.

In 1858, when Jane Nancy was twenty-eight, she married Joseph Hammond (a much older man) as his second wife. Two girls were born of this marriage. That same year the Saints were advised to move north and Jane Nancy pushed her little girl in a handcart to Bingham Fort (Lynne Warde, Five Points, Ogden) where they settled.

Joseph died two months before the birth of their second little daughter, leaving Jane Nancy to survive and provide on her own. For four years she struggled to care for herself and her little ones then she married George Thomas Pierce in Ogden. Eight children were born of this marriage.

Pain and grief visited the family when they lost Elizabeth and then Bertha as young children, but joy in seeing the others grow and make families of their own was here also. Her children settled in the Ogden area, not too far away, and it comforted her to have her two oldest girls sealed to their stepfather in the Endowment House on June 19, 1871

Jane made her surroundings beautiful with flowers and trees. She sewed the families clothing, including her own, stitch by stitch and sold produce from her garden to support herself. She was educated in English and French and the Indians taught her the medical value of herbs.

It is said that she had the most beautiful parlor and furnishings on 2nd street in Ogden, where she lived in a big brick home, still standing.

SARAH SKINNER PIERCE

BIRTHDATE: 23 Mar 1840
Quincy, Adams Co., Illinois
DEATH: 5 Aug 1925
Idaho Falls, Bonneville, Idaho
PARENTS: Horace B. Skinner
Eleanor Cease
PIONEEER: 4 Oct 1852
John B. Walker Wagon Train
SPOUSE: George Henry Pierce
MARRIED: 6 Apr 1859
DEATH SP: 20 Jan 1905
Levan, Juab Co., Utah

CHILDREN:
Sarah Diantha, 17 Feb 1860
Phebe, 15 Jul 1861
George Washington, 14 Mar 1862
Brigham Horace, 28 Mar 1864
Lucy L., 27 Apr 1866
Eleanor, 7 Apr 1868
Isaac D., 6 Mar 1870
Samuel Elmer, 25 Aug 1871
Sylvester, 20 Jul 1873
Elizabeth Ester, 27 Feb 1875
Angeline S., Sep 1877
Emma Minerva, 20 Oct 1878
Orson Harvey, 14 Apr 1881

Sarah was born in Quincy, Illinois, the town that had taken in the Mormon refugees fleeing from persecution. The spring previous to her birth, Commerce (Nauvoo) Illinois, forty-five miles to the north, had been purchased and the Saints were relocating there as rapidly as their circumstances permitted.

However safe they felt in gathering with their Prophet Joseph, they could not escape the inevitable persecution that would persue them, nor the circumstances of starvation, diseases and exposure that took so many, until all were forced to flee to Utah.

She came into the Salt Lake Valley with her parents when she was twelve years old and spent her teenage years helping her family survive on the frontier. When she was two weeks past her seventeenth birthday she married George Henry Pierce at Provo. (Two years before, many had been sent south, to Provo and beyond to escape Johnston's Army and had remained.) In less than one year the teenage couple were sent to Fillmore and then Nephil where their first child was born.

Then came the calling to Deseret where their next five children were born. As farmers there they built a dam on the Sevier River in order to irrigate their crops, and every year for eight years when high water came, the dams were washed out, the crops dried up and the pioneers barely eked out an existence.

Indian raids on nearby settlements did little to encourage their staying and in 1869 they gave up and moved to the new settlement of Levan and took up 320 acres of land about nine miles from town for farming and stock raising. They lived there for years while the children married and one by one moved away until Sarah and her husband were all alone.

George Henry's health was not good and so they sold the farm and moved into Levan where he died early in January of 1905, and was buried there.

Sarah, age sixty-five and lonely, accepted the invitation of her youngest daughter, to come live with her. Emma Minerva, now twenty-seven, had married Edd Everett and they were raising their family in Idaho Falls, Idaho.

Sarah spent the remaining twenty years with their family, being as much help as she was given. She passed away at the age of eighty-five and was laid to rest at the side of her husband in the cemetery at Levan, Utah.

SUSANNAH BAIRD SMITH PIERCE

BIRTHDATE: 7 Jul 1832
Alabama
DEATH: 9 May 1887
PARENTS: Samuel Baird
Matilda Rutledge
PIONEER: 1867
Unknown Company
SPOUSE I: Theodore Smith
MARRIED: 24 Sep 1849
Quincy, Illinois
DEATH SP: 24 Jun 1890
Illinois

CHILDREN:
William Almarion, 21 Feb 1851
James Champion, 6 May 1853
Ida Irabella, 2 Dec 1855
Flora (Novey), 16 Feb 1859
Mary Matilda (Robinson), 12 Nov 1860

SPOUSE II: Robert Pierce
MARRIED: 25 Nov 1872
Salt Lake City, Salt Lake Co., Utah
DEATH SP: 27 Mar 1884
East Mill Creek Salt Lake Co., Utah

CHILDREN: None

Susannah was born in Alabama in 1832. She was the first child in the family. In 1846, she and her family moved to Adams County, Illinois. When Susannah was seventeen years old, she married Theodore Smith on September 24, 1849 in Quincy, Adams County, Ilinois. Theodore and Susannah moved to Jefferson City, Missouri.

Susannah and her husband were divorced and she came west with her two daughters, leaving Theodore and her two sons behind. Her first daughter, Ida Irabella died April 18, 1857. The company and the way she came is unknown, but she arrived about 1867.

After Susannah came to the Salt Lake Valley, she married seventy-five year old Robert Pierce, November 25, 1872, in Salt LakeCity, Utah, as his polygamist wife. She was forty years old at the time.

Robert passed away in 1884 when Susannah was fifty-one years old. She passed away on May 9, 1887 at the age of fifty-five.

KAREN KIRSTINE MADSEN PIHL

No
Photo
Available

BIRTHDATE: 16 Dec 1793
Pedersker, Bornholml Denmark
DEATH: 30 Nov 1853
Salt Lake City, Salt Lake, Utah
PARENTS Mads Hansen
Kirsten Jacobsen
PIONEER 13 Sep. 1853
John Forsgren Co. Wagon Train
SPOUSE: Henning Peel or Pihl
MARRIED: 16 Oct 1819
DEATH SP. 6 Aug. 1885
Mt. Pleasant, Sanpete Co., Utah

CHILDREN
Peder Madsen, 24 Aug 1820
Ann Kirstine Elaine, 14 Mar 1826 (died 2 days later)
Caroline, 14 Sep 1827 (died at age 7)
Caroline, 5 Mar 1836

Karen Kirstine was born in Denmark in 1793. Her father owned a large farm in the lovely village of Pedersker and she, being the oldest child, in a family of six children, learned very early how to take responsibility and how to care for younger children.

She grew into a lovely young lady and fell in love with the "hired hand" on her father's farm who was Henning Pedersen Pihl. He was from Povlsker, a village only two miles away.

Shortly after their marriage in the Luthern Church, the two were given permission to move and they located in Aaker where their first child was born. For five and a half years they waited for another child only to have the little girl die in two days time. Again she became pregnant and had Caroline who, when she was almost eight became sick and passed away.

Needing to fill the empty space in her heart, forty-three year old Karen had one more child, a daughter she also named Caroline.

The first Mormon missionaries came to Bornholm in June of 1851. In November of that year, Karen, Henning and Caroline, age fifteen, were invited to meet them at the

home of Jeppi Folkman, Peder's brother-in-law. It was an inspiring meeting and several people were baptized that night at the beach with the crowd watching. Three days later, November 10, 1851, Karen, Henning and Caroline were baptized also.

The persecutions started. There were beatings, men lost their jobs and were threatened with harm. At one time the Elders were literally carried out of the County and threatened with death if they came back. The mob was led by the Sheriff.

In the autumn of 1852, responding to the call to gather to Zion, all of the Pihls decided to leave. They got their outgoing permits on November 6, 1852, but lacking money enough for all, decided that Henning, Karen and Caroline should go and Peder's family would come next year. Led by Brother John Forsgren, these were the first Mormon converts from Scandinavia to come to Utah.

Sailing for England on December 20, via Kiel, they passed through a terrible storm on the North Sea and the "Lion" was pounded pretty badly. The emigrants boarded the "Forest Monarch" with 297 others for a two month crossing to New Orleans. Up river to St. Louis was the next step then to Keokuk, Iowa. The John Forsgren Wagon Company left for Utah early in the morning on May 21st with 294 for 132 days of toilsome journey.

Karen, now age sixty, and having been ill since they got on the boat in England felt no better. She had struggled through the stormy winter voyage, through the heat and mosquitoes of St. Louis and the struggling journey to Keokuk, and now endured a journey at the mercy of the elements and what ever else impeded their travel to come to the Salt Lake Valley.

The weariness never left Karen and forty-three days after reaching her destination, she passed away. She was buried in Salt Lake in an unmarked grave and when they returned to find it two years later, they could not. Nor to this day does any one know where this courageous lady is buried.

CHRISTIANE FOLKMAN PIHL/PEEL

BIRTHDATE: 17 Aug 1820
Aakersogn, Bornholm, Denmark
DEATH: 6 Nov 1899
Mt. Pleasant, Sanpete Co., Utah
PARENTS: Jorgen C. Folkman
Gjertrud Kristine Jeppesen
PIONEER: 5 Oct. 1854
H. P. Olsen Co. Wagon Train
SPOUSE: Peder M. Pihl/Peel
MARRIED: 27 Nov 1846
DEATH SP: 7 Nov 1900
Mt. Pleasant, Sanpete Co., Utah

CHILDREN
Christiane, 28 Apr 1847 (died at 10 days)

Christiane, 25 Jul 1848 (died at 9 months)
Christian Fredrick, 14 Nov 1850 (died at 3 years)
Christian Fredrick, 29 Jun 1854
Margaret Folkman, 1 Mar 1858
Annie, 5 Dec 1860
Hannah Elia, 8 May 1864 (died at age 1)

Christiane Folkman was born in Denmark in 1820, the second child in a family of eight, three of whom were buried in childhood. Christiane grew into a slender, dark haired vivacious young lady.

When she was twenty-six she married Peder, a man her age who worked for her father in his blacksmith shop. Their marriage lasted fifty-three years until their deaths.

In all the fifty-three years of hardship, uncertainty, and want, nothing that happened to them compared to the grief of losing their children.

Their first, a little girl, lived but ten days, and the second, given the same name of Christiane, died after burrowing a space into the heart that was left full of tears at her leaving, Tears that leaked out of Christiane's eyes at the most unexpected moments. Christian Fredrick was their first son.

Mormon missionaries came to Bornholm in June of 1851 and were so readily received that by August they were organizing a Branch. Her married brother, Jeppi, baptized on November 7, 1851, was the first in her family to be baptized. Brothers Chris and Peter followed in just days and she and Peder on August 3, of the next year. Peder's family left for Utah that same year of 1852. Christiane and Peder worked all year toward their goal and left on December 22, 1853 to join his parents in Utah.

On December 22, 1853, they sailed from Copenhagen on the ship "Sleavig" carrying 301 persons to Liverpool by way of Kiel, Gluckstaat and Hull. They left Liverpool on January 26, 1854 for more than six weeks on the ocean until they reached New Orleans. There was much sickness and several deaths on the voyage, her own little boy had been ill since they were in Liverpool and had languished weak and pale.

Little Christian, their only surviving child, died two days before they docked. Christiane could not bear to have her child buried at sea and prayed to God that if she could keep him until she reached land, she would not cry. The mother carried her son off the ship when they reached New Orleans and they buried him on a grassy knoll in a grove of trees. She was again without child, but this time she was pregnant.

Meeting other Scandinavians in West Port (Kansas City), they left on their journey across the Plains. Their wagons were so overloaded that a halt was called. It was there, fourteen days into the journey, that another little boy was born to Chriatiane, to be named the same as her lost child, Christian.

After their autumn arrival into the Salt Lake Valley, the couple hurried to Lehi to join Peder's father and sister, (his mother had died days after arriving.) Ephraim was the choice of settlement when the Pioneers were uprooted at the coming of Johnston's Army. By early spring of 1859, Peder and Christiane moved to Sanpete County and were among the first settlers in Mt. Pleasant.

The last of their lives were spent in their home that became a hotel for the "drummers" and others who came to Mt. Pleasant. They sheltered and fed the visiting Church dignitaries when they came and loved and pampered their grandchildren and if any grandchild passed without coming in, she ran out and got them.

CATHERINE ADAMS PILLING

BIRTHDATE: 9 Apr 1838
Quincy, Adams Co., Illinois
DEATH: 1 Oct 1935
Cardston, Alberta, Canada
PARENTS: Elias Adams
Malinda Railey
PIONEER: 7 Sep 1850
SPOUSE: Richard Pilling
MARRIED: 10 Mar 1856
DEATH SP: 28 Dec 1906
Cardston, Alberta, Canada

CHILDREN:
Richard A., 14 Oct 1857
John Adams, 5 Jan 1860
Joseph, 5 May 1862
Mary Catherine, 24 Apr 1865
Elias, 1 Nov 1867
Margaret Malinda 27 May 1870
George Edmond 5 Jan. 1873
James Henry 2 Sep. 1875
Rufus Elijah 26 Mar. 1878
Elizabeth Caroline 5 Jan. 1881

Catherine Adams was born in Illinois in 1838 into a family considered prosperous. Her father was a business man who owned a brick manufacturing company and a flour mill, and cared for a large farm.

After her family joined the Church of Jesus Christ of Latter-day Saints in 1843 they moved to Nauvoo, Illinois. Being only five years old, Catherine witnessed the shock and grief around her when the Prophet Joseph was assassinated in June, 1844. As a girl of seven or eight she was bundled into a packed wagon in fright but not understanding the hatred of people around them. She was grateful to live in a home when her father was asked to stay in Mt. Pisgah to grow crops to feed and supply those pioneers coming across the Plains.

In the Spring of 1850, they took their turn to join the body of the Church in the Rocky Mountains arriving at Council Bluffs where a wagon train was being organized.

Aaron Johnson was elected Captain over 100 wagons and her father was elected captain over ten of these wagons.

She was a mature, responsible twelve year old the morning of June 4, 1850, when at the signal, her father's wagon snapped forward on it's creaking, swaying journey to Zion. After seventy-three days in the wilderness the courage building, wearying, self reliant journey ended with a triumphant entry into the Salt Lake Valley and her parents settled in Kaysville.

Three weeks shy of her eighteenth birthday, Catherine, who had met and fallen in love with an English man, married him. Richard was five years older than his bride and their life together was industrious; a life of faith and satisfaction in their family of ten children.

In 1887, when the couple were in their fifties, they were one of forty families selected to settle the new country in Canada and left with a group of twenty-five. They arrived July 13, 1889, to a location near the route used by the emigrants from the south and everyone coming into Canada stopped to rest and "have a good meal" in the Pilling home.

Medical help was non existent and Catherine, because of her experience in caring for ten children through their many sicknesses and injures, was called often to the side of a sick bed. She brought 526 babies into this world with loving care and not one died.

Inheriting her fathers spirit of giving, she was an honest tithe payer and donated, even to the giving of her last pound of butter and a cheerful, comforting person any who came in need.

Richard was sixty-eight when he suffered a stroke. For five years Catherine cared for her paralyzed husband which resulted in many a sleepless night. With her new calling as aid to the Stake Relief Society demanding long trips and many other responsibilities, her life was one of hardship and endurance. Catherine was sixty-eight years old at Richard's death and lived another twenty-nine years to pass away at the age of ninety-seven.

MARGARET BANK PILLING

BIRTHDATE: 17 Jan 1799
Bolton By Bowland, Yorkshire, England
DEATH: 13 Sep 1853
Kaysville, Davis Co., Utah
PARENTS: Richard Bank
Margaret Harrison
PIONEER: 13 Sep 1853
Independent Co. Wagon Train
SPOUSE: John Pilling
MARRIED: 17 Oct 1818
DEATH SP: 20 Aug 1887
Kaysville, Davis Co., Utah

CHILDREN:
Susannah, 18 Oct 1818

Alice, 25 Nov 1820
John, 8 Dec 1822
Edmund, Jan 1825
John, 14 Jul 1827
Margaret, 1 Aug 1830
Richard, 28 Nov 183
Mary Anne, 31 Mar 1836
Joseph, 6 Apr 1839

Margaret was born in England in 1799 and married John Pilling when she was nineteen years old. The couple had nine children, four girls and five boys, all born in England. Naming her third and fifth boys with the same name of John, indicates perhaps the death of the first little one.

Margaret was thirty-eight and her eighth child born when missionaries from the Church of Jesus Christ of Latter-day Saints first entered England to begin their proselyting. The first messages were given from borrowed or rented churches and failing that, they were preached on street corners. The more successful the missionaries became in converting the citizens, the more bold and nasty were the reports against the Church both in the public press and from other ministries pulpits.

The men and women convinced enough to be baptized were in for ridicule and harassment by their fellow towns-people, some to the point of injury and some hounded from their homes to move again and again. Of all the things it was, it wasn't easy.

To "gather with the Saints in Utah" meant months of preparation, sometimes living to the point of penury to save enough. The nearly two months voyage was crowded, with poor water and food in short supply. Many meals consisted of rationed sea biscuits, (a salt and flour batter poured on a scrubbed step, with flour pounded into the batter until it would absorb no more. It was baked, broken into pieces with the smallest used as crackers. The petrified sea biscuits were soaked in a damp cloth the day before being eaten. Two or three weeks of this fare and some of the malnourished children died.).

Margaret was fifty-four and her youngest was age fourteen when they docked at New Orleans. They made their way to Iowa and crossed the Plains to complete a journey of six to nine months duration.

The Pilling family settled in Kaysville. They endured the threat of Johnston's Army, fed Indians who came asking for food and helped their community in any way they could and their church in every job they were called to do.

Margaret lived twenty-one years in Zion. She passed away at the age of seventy-five, convinced of her faith and the direction she took.

ISABELLA DOUGLAS PINCOCK

BIRTHDATE: 1 Nov 1833
Downham, Lancashire, England
DEATH: 15 Aug 1918
Ogden, Weber Co., Utah
PARENTS: George Douglas
Ellen Briggs
PIONEER: 28 Aug 1852
John Parker Ind. Wagon Train
SPOUSE: John Pincock, Jr.
MARRIED: 3 Feb 1851
St. Louis, St. Louis, Missouri
DEATH SP: 16 Dec 1905
Ogden, Weber Co., Utah

CHILDREN:
Mary Ellen (Stephens), 8 Nov 1851
John Edmund, 16 Dec 1853
Isabella Alice (Forbs), 5 Feb 1856
James Henery, 20 Jan 1858
Ann, 20 Aug 1860
Jane, 15 Nov 1863
Charlotte (Garner), 7 Oct 1861
George Albert, 1 Mar 1865
Vilate (Woodmansee), 24 Aug 1867
Charles, 22 Sep 1869
William Aaron, 17 Oct 1871
Josephine, 20 Jan 1874
Richard Douglas, 14 Mar 1876
Wealthy, 8 Mar 1879

(Much of the following text is taken from Isabella's autobiography which she, at age eighty-two, related at a meeting of the "Daughters of the Utah Pioneers.")

Isabella was born on November 1, 1833 in England. In March of 1838, her family was converted and baptized into the Church of Jesus Christ of Latter-day Saints by Heber C. Kimball. They emigrated to America in 1842 by way of New Orleans, up the Mississippi River to Nauvoo, Illinois where they became part of the early historical events of the church.

Isabella's father, a stone mason on the Nauvoo Temple, went to help with the harvest on the Prophet Joseph Smith's farm. Not used to the extreme beat of America, he became very ill and died of heat stroke, July 12, 1842.

Within three months of their arrival, Isabella's mother and the three oldest children went out to work leaving Isabella, not yet nine years old, as the primary housekeeper and baby sitter for the three youngest children. The next four years were filled with sickness and meager means for the family but little murmuring because of their great faith and generosity of the Saints.

Isabella related being greatly affected by Governor Ford's hollow promise of safety for the Prophet Joseph Smith when at the very time he and his brother Hyrum were martyred. She saw the wagon pass containing their bodies and viewed their remains at the Mansion House.

Shortly after the martyrdom, in 1846, Isabella's mother married widower John Parker who brought his three young children and elderly, ill father into the family. Isabella, now thirteen years old, was left to care for them when her parents went to St. Louis, Missouri to find refuge for the family . . . "All the responsibility of the home and family was in my care. We had no stove. We baked our bread in a bake kettle by a fireplace. We had no yeast cakes with which to make bread, but would set salt-rising bread and bake every day. Washing, ironing, mending and caring for the family depended entirely upon myself."

While in St. Louis, Isabella fell in love with her brother Richard's friend, John Pincock. They were married on February 3, 1851. In the spring of 1852, Isabella and John caring for a new baby born on November 8, 1851, crossed the Plains with her mother and extended family in Isabella's stepfather's independent wagon train, the John Parker Company. They traveled without incident calling their journey "a pleasure trip" arriving in the Salt Lake Valley on August 28, 1852.

In 1853, Isabella's family witnessed the laying of the corner stone of the Salt Lake Temple and forty years later attended the dedication. They were relocated to Utah County in 1858 for a short period because of the invasion of Johnston's Army. Upon returning to their home in Kaysville they found their home secure and a bumper volunteer wheat crop ready to harvest.

Isabella kept busy making all clothing, soap, candles and food stuffs for her family. In her words. . . "Our log cabin was clean and cozy, and although we were poor and I had much to do, I felt happy and contented in caring for my little ones, believing I was doing a mother's duty. . . "

Isabella's last move was to Ogden in 1874. There she continued raising fourteen children while loving, supporting and assisting her successful (much to her credit) husband, John.

Isabella's daughter, Charlotte, said this about her mother: "She was ambitious, frugal, thrifty, ingenious and resourceful. She had very little schooling but seemed to know just how to adjust herself to any condition that came up. She was a good cook and housekeeper, always having her work planned ahead of time. She was an expert darner, mender and was a beautiful sewer. She was gifted in caring for the sick, her touch bringing relief and comfort . . . she relieved many of her neighbors and friends in time of confinement."

Along with her firm testimony of the truthfulness of the Gospel of Jesus Christ and His church, Isabella expressed these words of experienced faith and gratitude at a meeting of the Daughters of the Utah Pioneers: . . "I am now in my 82nd year, and while I am not enjoying the best of health, I am able to be about the house and enjoy the comforts of my home, for which I am very thankful, I feel satisfied with my life's work, and after having passed through all the trials and hardships incident to pioneer life, and for the benefit of those who may read these memories that they may not forget what the pioneers had to pass through that make conditions such as they now enjoy."

Isabella Douglas Pincock, at age eighty-five, passed on August 15, 1918, in Ogden, Weber County, Utah.

ADELIA ANN SPARROW WINN PINE

BIRTHDATE: 1 Jan 1794
Lansingburg, New York
DEATH: 30 Dec 1874
San Bernardino, California
PARENTS: Mr. Winn
Thankful Winn
PIONEER: 3 Apr 1850
Independent Wagon Train
SPOUSE: Joseph Pine
MARRIED: 27 Sep 1814
New York
DEATH SP: 1849
Nauvoo, Hancock Co., Illinois

CHILDREN:
Delia Fanny, 1814
George, 1816
Jane Eliza, 7 Aug 1818
Dudley, 7 Jun 1821
Samuel Cook, 30 Jul 1825
Myron, 1827
Thankful Lucy, 4 Nov 1830
John, 6 Nov 1833

Adelia Ann was born in 1794 to Mr. and Mrs. Winn in Lansingburg, Ranseler County, New York. She married Joseph Pine in September, 1814.

She and her husband Joseph, gave up their membership in the Presbyterian Church when the news of a Latter-day Prophet came to their ears. They embraced the gospel of the Church of Jesus Christ of Latter-day Saints and its prophet, despite many clerical visits and much persecution designed to dissuade them. They were close personal friends of Joseph Smith and lent aid and support whenever possible.

This family moved with Joseph Smith to Kirtland, and then to Nauvoo. Delia received her personal endowment in the Nauvoo Temple on Febraury 2, 1846. She became the mother of eight children, and as her husband was often ill, she worked many times eighteen hours out of twenty-four so that she might provide them with food, clothing and comfortable circumstances.

Before her husband's death in 1849 in Nauvoo, he told his sons Samuel and Dudley to take the family to the Salt Lake Valley. On April 3, 1850, they fitted out a train and crossed the Plains. They first resided in Southern Utah, but in 1858, Dudley and Samuel moved to California. Delia went there in 1859, to try to induce them to return to Utah, but failed in her purpose. In August of 1863, she thought she would try once more to bring her children back from California, and started for that purpose. She lived with

them, doing all the good that her heart could think of all the time. Her sons never did return to Utah.

Delia passed away in San Bernardino, California at eighty years of age, a brave pioneer woman who had experienced much in crossing the Plains to the West, and doing all she could in the cause of the Church she loved.

Delia was a great pioneer woman of faith and fortitude to be honored by those who have followed her.

ESTHER HOOPER PINGREE

BIRTHDATE: 22 Sep 1839
Hallow, England
DEATH: 9 Dec 1912
Ogden, Weber Co., Utah
PARENTS: James Hooper
Susannah Hancock
PIONEER: 1861
Job Pingree Co. Wagon Train
SPOUSE: Job Pingree
MARRIED: 27 Sep 1861
Salt Lake City, Salt Lake, Utah
DEATH SP: 21 May 1928
Ogden, Weber Co., Utah

CHILDREN:
Samuel James, 30 Jan 1862
Joseph, 7 May 1876
William, 24 Dec 1863 (died as an infant)
Hyrum, 30 Jun 1878
Annie (Gale), 18 Apr 1865
Franklin, 15 Jul 1880
Charlotte Esther (Moyes), 7 Dec 1866
Pearl (Taylor), 7 Jul 1883
Ellen (Scowcroft), 26 Oct 1868
Elizabeth (Emmett), 16 Feb 1871
Charles, 10 Mar 1873 (died as a child)

Esther was born in 1839 in Hallow, Worchestershire, England. Her parents were quite poor and had a large family. It was necessary for Esther to earn her own living at an early age. Her father was a gardener for an English gentleman, and he secured a position for Esther in this man's home as a nurse girl. She caught scarlet fever while working there, and had to go stay with an aunt to regain her strength.

While there, she found some tracts and books pertaining to the Church of Jesus Christ of Latter-day Saints. She studied the Gospel and decided to join the Church. She hoped her family would join also, but they scoffed at her and were unkind. Returning to her job, they scoffed at her and were unkind, also, and tried to convince her she had done the wrong thing. She was always telling others about the hope she had in her new religion, and she defended it.

Their first Elder of the Church was Job Pingree. He baptized her, and she later became his second wife after she emigrated to America.

The spring following her baptism, she started her journey to Zion. She sailed on the ship "Underwriter." When she arrived in Iowa City, she joined Job's Wagon Company. She traveled with an aunt who had small children, so she walked all day, prepared camp and food for the members of the company at night. She endured these hardships without a murmur of complaint. She loved it when everyone raised their voices to sing praises to their Lord.

Arriving in the Salt Lake Valley, Esther became the wife of Job Pingree without the consent of his first wife. This created ill feelings throughout her lifetime with the first wife and her family. Their marriage was performed just one year before the government made the law against polygamy. These two families shared a home for a time, and eventually, Job built a second home of bricks and moved both families into it. By 1874, Job married his fourth wife.

Esther, with her caring heart, shared her home with this wife who suffered from lung disorder. She died a few years later leaving two little girls for Esther to raise. One of these girls was severely burned over half of her body to the extent that her bones were showing. Esther changed her dressings every day and cared for her constantly, and Job stayed with her during the night.

During this time, Job was arrested for co-habiting and was sent to the penitentiary. While he was there the little girl died. Some of his children were compelled to testify against their father, so, to avoid this, Esther went underground by moving from place to place, and never showing herself to anyone who wasn't directly responsible for her safety. Sometimes she posed as a sister or a servant in some households. Job spent five months in confinement, and she was compelled to take the place of both father and mother in the family. She did this with a brave heart and without any sign of complaint.

Between the years 1900 and 1902, three of her married daughters died leaving seven small children. This had such a sorrowing effect upon her that she never survived the shock. Her family meant everything to her.

Esther was a very religious person and found pleasure in attending Church meetings and studying the Gospel. She was a worker in the Relief Society and was secretary in the Ward and a visiting teacher. She was devoted to her friends.

During her last illness she suffered many months, but her faith never weakened. She left her children with her testimony. "The Gospel is true, be faithful and let not the acts of man change your testimony. If you see faults in others, you do better, but be faithful to the end of your days." Esther Hooper Pingree passed away in Ogden on December 9, 1912, a faithful, valiant pioneer woman of Utah.

MARY MORGAN PINGREE

BIRTHDATE: 19 Aug 1835
Bradley, Staffordshire, England
DEATH: 2 Nov 1921
Layton, Davis Co., Utah
PARENTS: David Morgan
Hannah Turner
PIONEER: 12 Sep 1857
Jesse B. Martin Co. Wagon Train
SPOUSE: Job Pingree
MARRIED: 27 Sep 1857
Ogden, Weber Co., Utah
DEATH SP: 21 May 1928
Ogden, Weber Co., Utah

CHILDREN:
Margery Adella, 5 Dec 1858
Job Jr., 6 May 1863
David Morgan, 28 Jan 1865
Mary Amanda, 26 Mar 1867
John Morgan, 13 Nov 1870
Clara, 9 Aug 1873 (died at age 2)
Lillian, 3 Aug 1877

Mary was born in Bradley, Staffordshire, England. At the age of twenty, she was converted to the Church of Jesus Christ of Latter-day Saints. She desired to migrate to Zion, but since she had no money, she became hired to Charlotte Pingree Banford in exchange for payment of her own transportation to Utah.

They left Liverpool, England on March 28, 1857 on the ship, "George Washington," with 817 people. After a voyage of twenty-three days, they landed in Boston Harbor, then traveled to Iowa City by train. They joined the Jesse B. Martin Wagon Company traveling the rest of the way by walking. They arrived in Great Salt Lake Valley on September 12, 1857.

Mary married Job Pingree just fifteen days after her arrival in Ogden, Utah. He was Charlotte's son by her first marriage. They lived on bread and potatoes unless Job could shoot some chicken, ducks, or rabbits. In order to obtain soap to wash her own family's clothing, Mary would wash all day for some other family. She cooked in a kettle which would hang over the fireplace. Her furniture was crudely home built beds. Their chairs were nailed to the wall. She had a dirt floor and roof.

Job was called on a mission to England and was gone for two years. Mary and her eighteen month old child, Adella, were left to work for whatever she could get to eat and wear. When her husband returned from his mission, he also brought another wife with him.

Throughout her life, Mary was an ardent worker in the Relief Society, giving help and assistance to anyone needing it. Her husband became a very successful business man and she was able to enjoy a fine home in Ogden.

Mary passed away at the home of her daughter, Amanda P. Cook, in Layton, Utah at the age of eighty-six.

JANET FREW PITKIN

BIRTHDATE: 31 Jan 1849
Parish of Darley, Scotland
DEATH: 6 Sep 1884
Miliville, Cache Co., Utah
PARENTS: John Frew
Jane Clotworthy
PIONEER: 26 Sep 1956
D. McArthur Handcart
Company
SPOUSE: George Orrin Pitkin
MARRIED: 18 May 1867
Salt Lake City, Salt Lake, Utah
DEATH SP: 27 Jan 1910
Logan, Cache Co., Utah

CHILDREN:
Mary Jane, 25 Jul.1868
John Orrin, 19 Mar 1870 (died at age 1)
Sarah Ann, 20 Nov 1871
Agnes Janet, 25 Jan 1874
Emily Lavern, 12 Feb 1876
Parley Parker, 20 Oct 1877 (died as an infant)
Charlette, 5 Sep 1879
Orson, 17 Jan 1882

Jane was born in Parish of Darley, Ayrshire, Scotland. She was seven years old when her family emigrated from Scotland. They sailed on the ship "Enoch Train" from Liverpool on march 23, 1856, arriving in Boston, May 1, 1856, then traveled to Iowa city by train. Jane's father and mother and three day old William, two year old Mary, seven year old Janet and nine year old James joined the McArthur Handcart Company.

Janet attended a special school in Ogden to get her teaching credentials. She was the first teacher in Franklin, Idaho. Later she taught in Millville, Utah where she married George as his second wife on May 18, 1867.

Janet sang in the choir, was a member of a dramatic club that performed all over the valley. She was secretaary of Relief Society for twelve years. She was an expert weaver and knitter. She cooked for the men who worked at the rock mill.

She contracted typhoid fever and passed away at the age of thirty-five leaving six children ages eighteen months to fifteen years. George's first wife raised the children.

MARTHA ANN STOUT PITTS

BIRTHDATE: 25 Jan 1848
Winter Quarters, Nebraska
DEATH SP: 8 Jul 1889
Ogden, Weber Co., Utah
PARENTS: Allen Joseph Stout
Elizabeth Anderson
PIONEER: 2 Oct 1851
Alfred Corden Co. Wagon Train
SPOUSE: Thomas Pitts
MARRIED: 28 Jul 1866
St. George, Washington, Utah
DEATH SP: 16 Nov 1890
Vernal, Uintah Co., Utah

CHILDREN:
Thomas Miles, 18 Apr 1867
James Alford, 9 Dec 1869
Charles Allen, 27 Feb 1872
Jonathan Edward, 9 Oct 1874

Martha Ann was born in 1848 at Winter Quarters, Nebraska. She crossed the Plains at about the age of three years with her family. They arrived in the Salt Lake Valley on October 2, 1851. They moved south with other Saints.

Martha Ann married Thomas Pitt on July 28, 1866 in St. George, Washington County, Utah. Born to them were four sons. The first, Thomas Miles, was born in Paragonah, Iron County, Utah the second James Alford was born in Beaver, and the third and fourth sons were again born in Paragonah. Martha's family must have moved to the various locations as they helped in the settlement of the southern parts of the state and the territory of Utah.

Because of their location, Martha Ann went through many of the Indian troubles encountered by the Saints. She was always an active member of the Church of Jesus Christ of Latter-day Saints and participated in the activities within the Church and in the communities in which they lived. Her influence and faith have been handed down for several generations.

Martha Ann Pitts passed away on July 8, 1889 in Ogden, Utah at the age of forty-one years. Her husband Thomas Pitts passed away a year later on November 16, 1890 in Vernal Utah.

Three generations have followed this brave pioneer couple in developing the state and territory of Utah. Those who have followed honor them for their devotion and examples to others.

SARAH JANE BEEDEN PITTS

No
Photo
Available

BIRTHDATE: Feb 1806
Old Sleaford, England
DEATH: 6 Oct 1881
Salt Lake City, Salt Lake, Utah
PARENTS: William Beeden
Rebecca Watson
PIONEER: 1865
SPOUSE: William Henry Pitts
MARRIED: 15 May 1834
Quarrington, England
DEATH SP: 22 Jan 1885
Salt Lake City, Salt Lake, Utah

CHILDREN:
Elizabeth, 9 Jul 1835
William Henry, Jr., 18 Sep 1837
James, 8 Feb 1839
Annie Elizabeth, 25 Mar 1840
John W., 29 Nov 1841
Martha, 10 Jan 1843
Edward, 5 Oct 1844
Sarah, 4 Mar 1846
Joseph, 3 Oct / Sep 1848

Sarah Jane was born on February 6, 1806 at Old Sleaford, Lincolnshire, England. She was christened that same day in the Church of England at Quarrington Parish.

Sarah Jane married William Henry Pitts on May 15, 1834 in the same parish where she was christened. They joined the Church of Jesus Christ of Latter-day Saints and were members of the Grantham Branch, in England. Sarah Jane was baptized on March 19, 1850 by Elder Bailey.

They crossed the Atlantic Ocean on the ship, "Bellewood," and arrived the Great Salt Lake Valley that same year.

They settled in the Sixth Ward Salt Lake City where Sarah Jane's husband was a druggist and a Veterinary Surgeon.

Sarah was fifty-nine when they arrived in the Salt Lake Valley. She had been a brave and valiant woman in the church which she displayed by leaving her home country to come to America with her husband and family.

Sarah Jane passed away on October 6, 1881 and was buried in the Salt Lake City Cemetery.

ELIZA HESTER PLATT

BIRTHDATE: 6 May 1832
Hamper Mills, Watford,
England
DEATH: 12 Jun 1914
Salt Lake City, Salt Lake, Utah
PARENTS: Edward Hester
Elizabeth Wellington Roles
PIONEER: 28 Sep 1853
SPOUSE: Francis Platt
MARRIED: 19 Nov 1853
Salt Lake City, Salt Lake, Utah
DEATH SP: 14 Dec 1895
Salt Lake City, Salt Lake, Utah

CHILDREN:
Lenora / Leonora Hester, 26 Aug 1854 (died as an infant)
Franklin Benjamin, 13 Oct 1856
Ephraim Frances, 1 Feb 1859 (died as an infant)
Charlotte Eliza, 3 Nov 1860 (died as a child)
Eva Isabella, 10 Jan 1863
Marie Louise, 28 Jun 1868
Jospeh Chareton, 31 Jan 1871
Alonzo Watson, 28 Nov 1872

Eliza Hester was born on May 6, 1832 in Hamper, Watford, Hertfordshire, England; the eleventh of fourteen children. Seven boys and seven girls.

Eliza had joined the Church of Jesus Christ of Latter-day Saints in England, when she was a young girl. This was against the wishes of her parents. She crossed the ocean with a company of Saints soon after, and started the journey across the Plains arriving in Salt Lake City, on September 1853.

She met and married widower, Frances Platt on November 19, 1853. He was born in Darlaston, Stafford, England to Francis Platt and Eliza Watson. He and his wife, Mary Ann White and their baby daughter, Mary Elizabeth came to America, and started the trek across the Plains, where Mary Ann died, eight miles west of Kansas City and Francis walked on to Salt Lake, carrying his baby girl in his arms. So Eliza became a new bride and step-mother at the same time. They married fifty-two days after her arrival.

It is interesting to note that both Eliza's parents passed away in Connecticutt 1870 and 1871, so they also came to America.

Francis and Eliza made their home in Salt Lake City, where he was a harness and sadderly maker by trade. Many times his pay was in wheat and corn. When the crickets devastated all the crops, they were able to share their stock with those who had nothing and also feed their family.

Eliza suffered the loss of three of her children, all before they were two years old. All eight children were born in Salt Lake City, Utah. Eliza was active in the Church and was sealed to Francis on April 1, 1855. She celebrated the Utah Statehood in 1896 and the Pioneer Jubilee of 1897.

She watched the 20th century come with its new fangled automobiles and electric lights.

Francis passed away on December 14, 1895, leaving Eliza a widow for eighteen years. Eliza passed away on June 12, 1914 in Salt Lake City, Utah. At the time of her passing three of her five living children had large families of their own.

Eliza was well loved and respected.

ELIZABETH MERCER PLATT

No
Photo
Available

BIRTHDATE: 26 Sep 1816
Prescott, Lancashire, England
DEATH: 21 Dec 1895
Nephi, Juab Co., Utah
PARENTS: Henry Mercer
Margaret Brown
PIONEER: 12 Sep 1862
John R. Murdock Wagon Train
SPOUSE: James Platt
MARRIED: 20 Jan 1834
Farnworth near Prescott,
Lancashire, England
DEATH SP: 16 Mar 1885
Mona, Juab Co., Utah

CHILDREN:
Margery (Mutch), 8 Feb 1834
Mary Ann, 1835
John, 18 Feb 1836
Margaret, 1837
James, 26 Sep 1838 (died at age 16)
John, 10 Feb 1839
Nancy Ellen (Harrison), 23 Nov 1839
Edward, 1842 (died at age 12)
Mary Ann, 1844 (died at age 14)
Johnathan Mercer, 19 Oct 1845
Joseph 1848
Henry 1849
Willie, 1850
Elizabeth (Yates), 6 Mar 1851
William Henry, 13 Feb 1855
Sarah Ellen (Vest), 8 May 1858
Marintha Altheria (Ostler), 26 Jul 1860

Elizabeth was born in Prescott, England in 1816 to Henry and Margaret Brown. She married James Platt on January 20, 1834 near Prescott, England. They had seventeen children born to them. Their eldest daughter married while they lived in England as well as her daughter Nancy Ellen.

Elizabeth was baptized into the Church of Jesus Christ of Latter-day Saints on September 26, 1849, six months after her husband had joined.

When they emigrated to Utah in 1862 Elizabeth had four children between the ages of two and eleven, plus a sixteen year old son. Their two married daughters and their families emigrated with them. They left their native England and came to Utah because of their commitment to their religion and they lived the best they knew how.

Their daughter, Sarah Ellen, said, "We used to see many Indians in Nephi, and we protected ourselves against them in the usual manner. The men had to stand guard all the time to protect their homes and cattle. Each man had to take his turn as guard and watchman. In Nephi they would get on top of the jail with spy glasses to keep an ever watchful eye on every movement of the Indians, and sound a warning cry of any suspicious actions on the part of the Indians. My mother and father were very kind to the Indians."

The family, therefore, lived in or near Nephi after their arrival in Utah. When such Indians came to their home begging for food, Elizabeth always gave them something to eat, saying it was better to be friends with them than to anger them. After the Platts moved to Mona, the Indians remembered her as "the woman who lived that way; (pointing toward Nephi)."

Elizabeth's daughters who crossed the Plains to Utah before 1869, making them pioneer women also include, Margery Platt Mutch, Nancy Ellen Platt Harrison, Elizabeth Platt Yates, Sarah Ellen Platt Vest, and Marintha Altheria Platt Ostler.

James Platt, Elizabeth's husband, passed in 1885 in Mona, Utah, over ten years prior to Elizabeth's death on December 21, 1895.

Elizabeth was over eighty-nine years of age. She had experienced much leaving her home in England, crossing the ocean and the plains of the United States for her religious beliefs. She was truly a valiant, faithful, pioneer woman who helped to settle Utah. She had lost seven of her children, but had a great posterity from the others of her family who honor her for her faithfulness.

EMILY PRICE PLATTS

No
Photo
Available

BIRTHDATE: 11 Mar 1832
DEATH: 29 Apr 1901
PARENTS: Thomas Price
Mary Ann Platts
PIONEER: 24 Oct 1854
William A. Empy Wagon Train
SPOUSE: John Platts
MARRIED: abt 1848
DEATH SP: 4 Jan 1889

CHILDREN:
Ann, 1850 (died at age 4)
Orson, 8 May 1851
Clara E., Jan 1853 (died at age 1)
John Parley, 23 Nov 1855
Charles, 29 Feb 1858
George Henry, 11 Jun 1860

Emily, 30 Oct 1862
Jane, 31 Oct 1862 (died young)
James, 19 Mar 1867
Lucy Ann, 11 Jun 1868 (died at 6 months)
Louise, 4 Jul 1872

Emily married John Platts about 1848 in Coleorton Leicestershire, England. In 1853, they were baptized as members of the Mormon Church. Less than a year later they began their long trek to Zion. They boarded the "Golconda" tn Liverpool wtth their three young children; Ann, Orson, and Clara.

The "Golconda" sailed from Liverpool, England on February 4, 1854 bound for New Orleans and St. Louis. Arriving in St. Louis on March 31, they joined the William A. Empey Wagon Company for the journey West. Equipment, supplies, and wagons were scarce and very expensive. The cholera that followed them from New Orleans continued to St. Louis and Kansas City and on the trail west. Many saints died here and on the immigrant trail.

Emily's two young daughters died somewhere along the Mormon Trail. No other company suffered more hardships, disease and distress on their long trek west with, the exception of the Handcart Companies of 1856. The company finally arrived in the Salt Lake Valley on October 24, 1854, four months and nine days after leaving Kansas City, Missouri.

Soon after their arrival, Emily, John and their three year old son, Orson., began to make their home in Salt Lake City. John built a cabin on the northeast corner of Apricot and Quince Street. They planted an orchard and large garden.

Emily and John were to raise their family in this home, seven of their children were born here. Emily was able to raise eight of her children to adulthood, and see them make homes of their own and give her twenty-four grandchildren. This pioneer home was enlarged to become a lovely, comfortable home which still stands today.

About 1960, this pioneer home was placed on the National Histortc Register of Historical Buildings. Emily and John were to live in their pioneer home until their deaths. John Platts passed away on January 24, 1889 and Emily passed away on April 29 1901.

Emily and John taught their children to be ambitous, hard workers and honest. Emily's and John's long hard journey for their church and their pioneer spirit and hard work gave their descendants a rich heritage and the opportunity to live, prosper, and enjoy their freedoms.

ELIZABETH "BETSY" OADES ROBBINS PLAYER

BIRTHDATE: 25 Sep 1829
Crowle, Lincolnshire, England
DEATH: 27 Oct 1912
Salt Lake City, Salt Lake, Utah
PARENTS: William Oads/Oades
Elizabeth Sowersby
PIONEER: 7 Oct 1852
James C. Snow Co. Wagon Train
SPOUSE I: George Robbins
MARRIED: 9 Dec 1848
St. Louis, Missouri
DEATH SP: early 1849
St. Louis, Missouri

CHILDREN: None

SPOUSE II: Charles Warner Player
MARRIED: 7 Mar 1850
Ferryville, Pottawattamie Co., Iowa
DEATH SP: 29 Aug 1884
Salt Lake City, Salt Lake Co., Utah

CHILDREN:
Sarah Ann (Harvey), 25 Nov 1850
Charles Warner, 7 Aug 1852
Joseph Hyrum, 21 Mar 1854
Betsy (Griffiths), 14 Dec 1855
William Warner, Jr., 24 Oct 1857
Henry, 7 Oct 1859
Vilate, 15 Mar 1861
Alma Oades, 12 Dec 1862
Hannah Rebecca (Skillicorn), 5 Nov 1863
Laura, 20 Sep 1864
Mary Annie (Jeffs), 16 May 1866
Fred, 29 Jun 1870
Hattie (Cowley), 18 Oct 1873

Elizabeth "Betsy" was born in 1829 in Crowle, England. She lived her early life in England. Her family had been baptized into the Church of Jesus Christ of Latter-day Saints in England. Betsy was baptized on September 26, 1846. The family had sailed on the boat "Erin's Queen" on September 7, 1848 bound for America with 232 passengers.

They arrived in St. Louis where she was married to George Robbins (Robins) the Elder who had taught them the gospel and baptized them in England. She and a sister were both married the same day. Early in 1849, a siege of cholera hit St. Louis. Betsy's husband became very ill, and was suddenly "Taken with violent cramps, and gave up all hope, and before nightfall he was a corpse." His death occurred shortly after their marriage.

Betsy later married Charles Warner Player on March 7, 1850 in St. Louis. He had left Nauvoo, being one of the remaining men to defend that city in its last stand. He had gone to St. Louis to visit his sister who resided there. There, he met Betsy. By the 1850 census, they were listed as living in the Pottawattamie County, Iowa. Many of the members of both of their families were also listed there.

In June of 1852, this family, now including their first child, left Winter Quarters, at Council Bluffs, Iowa, with the James C. Snow 18th Wagon Company along with 250 people. Their possessions included one wagon, two oxen, three cows. Betsy was expecting her second child. Their son, Charles Jr. was born in 1852 at Watch Creek near Lone Tree, Nebraska. Their wagon train party arrived in the Salt Lake Valley on October 9, 1852. The value of their property totaled $208.00 including horses, cows, wagons, furniture, stove and guns.

Charles began working as a stonemason in the Public Works Department; a trade he had learned from his father. He worked on the Salt Lake Temple. He soon built an adobe three-room home not far from Temple Square. The home still stands at 726 West 300 North. It was here they raised thirteen children, all of whom became hard working principled adults. They learned the work ethic young, and they also became refined men and women.

By the time the older children were getting married, their younger children were born. One daughter died near the age of twenty. Theirs was a close-knit family where parental influence was great. As their children formed their own families, many of them lived in homes nearby their parents. One daughter was 'chosen' to take care of her mother in her older years, and she never married, living with her mother in the family home.

Charles, Betsy's husband, passed away in August, 1884. This left Betsy a widow for about twenty-eight years. Her death occurred, October 27, 1912, at the age of eighty-three years. Her symptoms were acute cerosis and chronic gastritis.

Elizabeth "Betsy" left a great legacy through her numerous posterity. Having thirteen children was a challenge, and having one born while crossing the Plains, and the stuggles in the Valley qualify her to be called a true Pioneer Woman of Faith and Fortitude.

NANCY HAMER PLAYER

BIRTHDATE: 1 Apr 1828
Bolton, Lancheshire, England
DEATH: 28 Jun 1889
Salt Lake City, Salt Lake, Utah
PARENTS: Samuel Hamer
Jane Thornley
PIONEER: 2 Oct 1851
Alfred Cordon Wagon Company
SPOUSE: William J. Player
MARRIED: 24 Sep 1850
Ferryville, Iowa
DEATH SP: 10 Feb 1882
Salt Lake City, Salt Lake, Utah

No Photo Available

CHILDREN:
Zillah Jane (Riser), 13 Aug 1851

Nancy Ellen (Wright), 3 Mar 1853
Emma A., 24 Nov 1855 (died at age 9)
William Jeremiah, 8 Dec 1857 (died at age 7)
Samuel George, 12 Oct 1859 (died as a child)
Maggie (Janney), 18 Oct 1861
Florence Bell (Janney), 20 Jul 1864
Heber John, 12 Apr 1866
Amy A. (McIntosh), 20 Jan 1868
Lottie C. 25 Jan 1870 (died at age 11)

Nancy was born in 1828 in Bolton, England, the third of ten children. The Hamer family was converted to the Church of Jesus Christ of Latter-day Saints in about 1840 and emigrated to the United States on the ship "Hope" in 1842. Nancy turned fourteen years of age the day the Hope landed in New Orleans.

They traveled up the Mississippi River to Nauvoo. A few months after settling there, Nancy's young brother died, and before the family moved west her father had died. When the remaining members of her family fled Nauvoo, they settled on the east bank of the Missouri River in Ferryville.

While residing in Ferryville, Nancy married William Jeremiah Player on September 24, 1850. This was the same day that Nancy's brother, John Hamer, married Elizabeth Ann Wilding.

The next year, Nancy and William Player traveled West with the Alfred Cordon Wagon Company. The rest of Nancy's family also emigrated to Utah in 1851, as did William Jeremiah's sister, Zillah Allan, and her young family.

Along the Mormon Trail, Nancy gave birth to her first child, Zillah Jane near Lincoln, Nebraska. Their group of ten wagons with which Nancy and William Jeremiah were traveling, stopped long enough for Zillah Jane's birth, and then traveled on to cover fourteen miles that day. This company entered the Salt Lake Valley sometime in 1851 and Nancy and William settled in the 16th Ward. Here nine more children were born to them.

William prospered here in Utah, working as a blacksmith. He was a hard worker. He was called to the "Cotton Mission" in 1861, and tragedy seems to have beset the family. About this time, Nancy lost her son Samuel, whose death date, cause, or burial has not been located. Then in 1864, a few months after the birth of her seventh child, Nancy buried William Jeremiah Jr and Emma. Both of them died of disease.

After these deaths, Nancy gave birth to three more children and then Lottie died of typhoid in 1881, when she was eleven years of age.

Six months later, on February 10, 1882, at the age of fifty years, Nancy's husband passed away at his home in Salt Lake City of a brain abcess. He left his solitary wife, Nancy, with four children still living at home, before her own passing on June 28, 1889.

Eight years later, Nancy had experienced the deaths of a grandson, a son-in-law, a sister, several brothers, nieces, nephews, and her mother. She was just over seventy-one years of age.

Nancy Hamer Player's greatest accomplishment was her continued functioning as a wife, mother of ten, sister to many, daughter, grandmother, and widow, through many hard times of personal despair. Happily, and at least in part to her credit, her pioneer life of sadness is glorified by progeny with outstanding accomplishments in Utah.

She was indeed a faithful pioneer woman who loved the Lord and endured much for her religion. She is honored by those who have followed her as one who always showed much courage and fortitude. Her six children and their posterity honor this great couple for their examples of courage and for their part in helping settle the West.

ZILLAH SANDERS BROWN PLAYER

No
Photo
Available

BIRTHDATE: 15 Jul 1788
Bisham, Birkshire, England
DEATH: 3 Dec 1867
Salt Lake City, Salt Lake, Utah
PARENTS: Benjamin Sanders
Hannah Hudsin
PIONEER: 1862
SPOUSE I: Charles Brown
MARRIED: Not given
DEATH SP: Not given

CHILDREN:
Zilla, (died as an infant)

SPOUSE II: William Warner Player
MARRIED: 22 Jul 1821
St. Lukes, Finsbury, Middlesex, England
DEATH SP: 23 Feb 1873
Salt Lake City, Salt Lake Co., Utah

CHILDREN:
Ann (Grocutt Kirby), 29 Nov 1823
Zillah (Allan), 24 Jul 1825
Charles Warner, 19 Jun 1827
William Jeremiah, 13 Jul 1831

Zillah was born in 1788 in England. She was the fourth of five children in the family having three sisters and one brother.

She married Charles Brown and had one child, Zilla, according to Bisham, England records. Apparently both her husband and the child died.

Zillah Sanders Brown, widow, married William Warner Player on July 22, 1821 in Finsbury, Middlesex, England. William was a stone mason and worked in the potteries area probably helping to build St. James Anglican Church.

At some point William became a lay Methodist minister. Then the early Mormon missionaries began their proselytizing in 1840. This Player family became interested and invited the missionaries to teach them. Some of the missionaries who were there included Heber C. Kimball, Brigham Young, Wilford Woodruff, and George Smith. The missionaries stayed at the Player home often. Through their discussions, the Players became baptized. Zillah was baptized on September 11, 1840.

In 1842, Zillah and her family emigrated on the ship "Hanover" to St. Louis, then up the river to Nauvoo. William Warner had come to work on the Nauvoo Temple. He was the chief stone mason, so they settled in Nauvoo. They purchased property of one acre on Kimball street, lot 32. It's worth was $80.00.

In 1843, this family was assessed on $25.00 for horses, $7.00 cattle, $10.00 worth of watches, $15.00 wagons, and $13.00 for personal property valued at $70.00.

Just prior to leaving Nauvoo, Zillah and William Warner were endowed in the Nauvoo Temple, being numbers fifteen and sixteen of the third company. They received second patriarchal blessings by the patriarch John Smith just nine months after the martyrdom of Joseph Smith.

Two of the Player children with their families crossed the Plains in 1851 and 1852, but Zillah and William Warner did not move west for another decade. During this interim they lived in Savannah, Missouri, where they sometimes provided lodging for traveling Mormon friends. Their daughter, Ann, lived her life out in St. Louis, Missouri.

Zillah was seventy-four years old when she finally arrived in Great Salt Lake City. In Salt Lake City, Zillah and William Warner lived in the 17th Ward, close to the temple block where her husband cut stone for "yet another temple" which was his desire.

Zillah lived just over five years in the Salt Lake Valley. She passed away on December 3, 1867 over seventy-nine years of age.

She was a wonderful wife and mother. She remained a faithful Latter-day Saint and enjoyed the blessings of living in the Great Salt Lake Valley. William Warner Player also carved headstones for the cemetery. He inscribed the following on Zillah's stone which is in the hands of a great, great granddaughter. They were truly an integral part of the Mormon community, built their homes of the earth and labored for family, church and community.

> "Dear loving partner, fare thee well
> With whom it was my lot to dwell
> O Lord prepare me in the end
> To meet my loving wife and friend
> Dry up your tears and do not weep
> My sufferings now are past
> You gave me your kindest aid
> So long as life did last. "

SARAH CANADA KENNEDY PLUNKETT

No
Photo
Available

BIRTHDATE: 10 Mar 1800
County Dawn, Ireland
DEATH: 26 Aug 1891
Kanab, Kane Co., Utah
PARENTS:
PIONEER: 15 Sep 1852
Henry B. Jolley Co. Wagon Train
SPOUSE: William R. Plunkett
MARRIED: before 1830
Scotland
DEATH SP: after 1870
Plymouth, Amador, Georgia

CHILDREN:
William A., 15 Oct 1832
James, 17 Feb 1836
Mary Melinda, 4 May 1837
Ellen, 1839/1840
Isaac, 2 Mar 1841
Robert, Jr., 1842
Joseph Hyrum, Jul 1844 (died as a child)

Sarah was born in County Dawn, Ireland and moved to Scotland as a child. She was born March 10, 1800 or before.

Family tradition says she met and later married Robert Plunkett before 1830, and that they had two children born in Scotland, but there is no record of them.

In about 1830, the family emigrated from Glasgow, Scotland to Upper Canada making their home near Brockville, Leeds, Ontario, Canada. They were farmers. In 1840, Sarah and Robert were baptized into the Church of Jesus Christ of Latter-day Saints.

Together with their six children, they arrived in Nauvoo before the spring of 1843. Sarah had a baby boy right after the martyrdom of the Prophet Joseph Smith and his brother Hyrum and named him after these two brothers. He died June 30, 1845 and was buried in Nauvoo. Sarah and Robert received their endowments in the Nauvoo Temple on January 30, 1846.

Sometime in February, 1846, they moved across the Mississippi River leaving their home and belongings and property and persecution. They traveled about 300 miles and wintered in the Pottawattamie lands six miles north of Kanesville.

In the 1850 census, Sarah and family were living in Van Buren County, Iowa. Robert was working as a laborer.

In 1852 they sold their belongings and joined the Henry B. H. Jolley Wagon Company and began their journey. They left in June, 1852, with one wagon, four oxen and four cows for Utah.

Sarah and family arrived in the Salt Lake Valley on September 15, 1852 and went immediately to American Fork, Utah. On May 10, 1869, Sarah came in from Sacramento on the first train for the Golden Spike ceremo-

ny. She came alone and joined her daughter in American Fork. Her daughter, Mary Melinda Adams had been called to help build the settlement in Southern Utah. Sarah helped them pack up their belongings and their big family and she again left her comforts and home and went to Washington County and then later moved to Kanab Fort with her daughter and son-in-law and their family. A covered wagon was placed on each side of the cabin to use as bedrooms, one for the boys and one for the girls.

Sarah lived her last twenty years in Kanab. She passed away on August 26, 1891 there, in full faith in the Church.

Her year of birth and surname have not been documented yet, but are still being researched, as is the information on her husband.

LOUISA MOORE MITCHELL POGSON

BIRTHDATE: 5 Nov 1823(27)
Panton, Lincolnshire, England
DEATH: 12 Mar (11 May) 1897
Huntington, Emery Co., Utah
PARENTS: William Moore
Elizabeth Holvey
PIONEER: 27 Oct 1849
Orson Spencer Co. Wagon Train
SPOUSE I: William C. Mitchell
MARRIED: 18 Jul 1849
Kanesville, Kane Co., IA
DEATH SP: 20 Jun 1857
Parowan, Iron Co., Utah

CHILDREN:
Enoch, 10 Mar 1850
Thomas S., 14 Feb 1851 (died at age 12)
Joseph, May 1854 (died as an infant)
Mary Ellen (Wilcock), 8 Dec 1857

SPOUSE II: James Walker Pogson
MARRIED: 28 May 1864
DEATH SP: 6 Feb 1888
Cedar City, Iron Co., Utah

CHILD:
Ann Eliza (Sherman), 22 May 1865

Louisa was born in 1823 or 1827 in England. There is no information on her childhood or growing up years, or how she joined the Church of Jesus Christ of Latter-day Saints.

Louisa and her sister, Mary Moore, sailed from Liverpool on January 29, 1849 on the ship "Zetland" in company with 358 Saints in the Orson Spencer Wagon Company.

She met William Cooke Mitchell on the ship and they were married in Kanesville, Iowa in July, 1849. They reached Salt Lake City on October 27, 1849.

After about a year in Salt Lake City, William was called by President Brigham Young to go south and help settle the 'Little Salt Lake Valley.' On December 10, 1850, they went with President George A. Smith's Company to what is now called Parowan, and arrived there on January 13, 1851. A month later, Louisa had her first child, a son.

In the fall of 1852, William C. married Louisa's older sister, Mary, in polygamy. Louisa had her second son in May, 1854, but he died eight months later-on January 20, 1855.

In 1857, while getting out lumber from the mountain, cutting and hauling timber from the first left-hand canyon, William was accidentally killed. Pinning him beneath it, a wagon load of logs had tipped over near what is known as the Hogsback. He was killed on June 20, 1857, and was buried in the Parowan Cemetery. Louisa was four months pregnant with a daughter who was born on December 9, 1857.

Following William's death, Louisa had a hard time financially raising her two children. When Thomas was twelve years old he drowned in a swimming accident. This left Louisa with only one child. (Enoch is listed on their records, but nothing is known about him.)

As Mary Ellen grew up she was very good to her mother, and helped her take in washing to help support them. Louisa had a strong testimony of the gospel, and taught it to her children. She was a good mother and homemaker. After her daughter married, Louisa spent much time with Mary Ellen, helping her with her children.

A second spouse is listed for Louisa, James Walker Pogson. Records show they were married on May 28, 1864. One daughter is listed as being born to Louisa, Ann Eliza born on May 22, 1865. She married a Mr. Sherman.

Louisa Moore Mitchell Pogson passed away in 1897, date unsure. She died in Huntington, Emery County, Utah. She was in her mid-seventies when she died.

Louisa had experienced much during her lifetime from England to Utah and had helped settle different parts of the state or territory. She was a great pioneer woman who was faithful to her beliefs, one who had cause to mourn for her loved ones but who remained faithful and strong in the face of much adversity.

CHARLOTTE LONG POLL

BIRTHDATE: 29 Jun 1823
Wymondham, Norfolk, England
DEATH: 19 Feb 1903
South Weber, Davis Co., Utah
PARENTS: John Long
Elizabeth Minns
PIONEER: 26 Sep 1853
Jacob Gates Co. Wagon Train
SPOUSE: William Flint Poll
MARRIED: 2 Nov 1842
Wymondham, Norfold, England
DEATH SP: 7 Nov 1895
Salt Lake City, Salt Lake, Utah

CHILDREN:
William John, 11 Jul 1844
Ann Maria, 12 May 1846
Fredrick Robert, 8 Oct 1848
Elizabeth Flint, 5 Jan 1852
Elizabeth Janette, 4 Aug 1854
Martha Ann, 5 Jan 1857
Mary Ann, 29 Dec 1858
Alice Eliza, 19 Jan 1861
Harriet, 5 Apr 1863
Charles Henry, 28 Feb 1865
Joseph, 14 Mar 1868

At an early age, Charlotte learned to cut meat in her parents' butcher shop. Charlotte was baptized a member ' of the Church of Jesus Christ of Latter-day Saints on January 7, 1849.

She sailed from Liverpool on the "Golconda" on January 23, 1853. She started to cross the Plains in the latter part of May and arrived in Utah in September, 1853. Her first Utah home was on the hill in the Twentieth Ward.

Five days after the birth of her fifth child, a terrible rain storm washed the wagon box, which was being used as a bedroom, and its occupants down the hill to where the Salt Lake City and County building now stands. No one was injured.

In 1861, William and Charlotte were called to go to Dixie for five years. They lived in Grafton. In 1865, food was very scarce due to a drought. One day when Charlotte had used the last of the flour to make a few precious biscuits, a tall, well dressed, distinguished looking man came to the door and asked for bread. She told him if he would wait until the bread was baked, she would share it with him. He waited and when she gave him the bread, he blessed her and told her she would never want for bread. He walked down the path to the gate. Nothing obstructed Charlotte's view, but when she looked, he had completely vanished.

In 1866, Charlotte and her family returned to Salt Lake City and made their home in the Tenth Ward where she was active in the church and prosperous in business. She had a meat market on the comer of Fourth South and Ninth East in Salt Lake City.

Charlotte loved her home, but after William passed away, she lived the balance of her life with one or the other of her daughters until her death.

MARY ANN BAILEY POLLARD

BIRTHDATE: 1 Mar 1821
Lifton, Devon, England
DEATH: 21 Nov 1895
Salt Lake City, Salt Lake, Utah
PARENTS: James Bailey
Mary Brook
PIONEER: 21 Sep 1857
Jacob Hofheins Handcart Comp.
SPOUSE: Joseph Pollard
MARRIED: 27 Sep 1845
Kalherwhite, Surrey, England
DEATH SP: 25 Feb 1890
Salt Lake City, Salt Lake, Utah

CHILDREN:
Mary Ann (Allred), 26 Aug 1846
Louisa (Evans), 28 Jun 1848
Lydia (Puzey), 21 Jan 1852
Joseph James, 1854 (died as an infant)
Elizabeth (Boud), 12 Nov 1857
Lovinia (Holding), 28 Mar 1860
Alice (Johnson), 15 Apr 1862
Benjamin, 1864 (died as an infant)
Grace (Backman), 27 Nov 1867

Mary Ann was born in 1821 in England. On September 27, 1845, she married Joseph Pollard in England. While in England, Mary gave birth to three daughters and one son. (He died at five months of age.)

In the year 1848, Mary Ann and Joseph heard the Mormons preach. They were baptized being the only members of their family to accept Mormonism. On November 18, 1854, they left their home in England to emigrate with a group of 400 Saints on the ship "Clare Mueler" bound for America.

By December 30, they sighted land and January 9, they reached the Mississippi and traveled to St. Louis by January 22, 1855. Mary Ann was so ill she had to be carried off the boat.

They lived between St. Louis and Iowa City, Iowa until June 15, 1857. Joseph had built their handcart, and Mary and Joseph with their three young daughters walked across the plains, traveling from June until September 21, when they entered the Salt Lake Valley.

On the trail, the cattle took off on a wild stampede, stampeding through creeks, hollows and hills. Men, women, and children were thrown from the wagons. Some were picked up bruised and bleeding, some unconscious, yet their faith in God and with blessings bestowed, they were able to continue their journey, though sore, tired and bleeding. They were most anxious to reach the end of their hard journey. Mary was expecting her fifth child who was born 12 Nov of that year.

After settling in the Salt Lake Valley permanently, Joseph built for Mary Ann an 'interesting English cottage' which was considered very comfortable in comparison to some of their less fortunate neighbors. Four more children were born the them, but the son died the year he was born.

A frail looking English lady, Mary Ann, had walked across the Plains, had nine children, had buried two sons, had raised her family of seven daughters, who married and had numerous posterity. She supported and sustained her husband in his church callings as counselor and then bishop for thirty-one years. (There were times Mary Ann did not attend sacrament meeting as Joseph was quite outspoken and she didn't want to be embarrassed.) She loved gardening and raised a fine garden with the help of her daughters.

Mary Ann's husband, Joseph, passed away in February, 1890 in Salt Lake City, Utah. Mary Ann passed away almost six years later November 21, 1895 nearly seventy-six years of age. She had experienced much change in her lifetime from England to the unknowns of Utah. She was firm in her faith and is truly a great pioneer woman to be honored and revered.

ANN MEREDITH MATHEWS PEARCE POLLOCK

BIRTHDATE: 28 Sep 1836
Maesy Gollen, Wales
DEATH: 18 Apr 1882
Kanarra, Iron Co., Utah
PARENTS: James Meredith
Mary Owens (some records show Mary Williams)
PIONEER: abt 1852
SPOUSE I: Allen Mathews
MARRIED: abt 1854
Utah
DEATH SP: first year married

CHILD:
Allen Henry, died as an infant)

SPOUSE II: Harrison Pearce
MARRIED: 3 Aug 1856
Spanish Fork, Utah Co., Utah
DEATH SP: 29 May 1889
St George, Washington Co., Utah

CHILDREN:
Joseph Harrison, 13 Aug 1857 (died at age 5)
Harriet Ann, 16 Jul 1859

SPOUSE III: Samuel Pollock
MARRIED: 10 Oct 1865
St. George, Utah Co., Utah
DEATH SP: 1891
Kanarra, Iron Co., Utah

CHILDREN:
James Wallace, 17 Nov 1866
Daniel Allen, 5 Mar 1869
Almira A., abt 1873

Ann Meredith was born in 1836 to James Meredith and his wife. Some records say that Mary Williams was her birth mother and Mary Owens was a step mother.

Ann Meredith was born in Wales. Her family came to Utah in about 1852. Ann married Allen Mathews in 1854 in Utah. Their only child died during his first year of life, and her husband Allen died also within the first year of their married life. They lived in Payson during this time.

Ann's second marriage was to Harrison Pearce in Spanish Fork, Utah on August 3, 1856. They had one son born in 1857 and a daughter born in 1859. This son, Joseph Harrison died in 1862. Ann and Harrison were divorced when their sealing was cancelled in 1862.

Ann's third marriage was to Samuel Pollock on October 10, 1865 in Salt Lake City, Utah. They had two sons and a daughter. James Wallace and Daniel lived to adulthood. Little is known about Almira. Records also show that Mary Owens Meredith died while in Iowa.

Ann's father worked as a carpenter and wheelwright, which resulted in her family living in various places in Wales. She had one brother and one younger sister. Ann was baptized into the Church of Jesus Christ of Latter-day Saints late in 1845, when her father, stepmother, and her father's sister all joined the Church. This family became the first group of Welsh Saints to leave for America. When they arrived at Liverpool, England, the group was too large for the one ship, so, some, including the Meredith family, waited for the second ship.

They sailed on the "Hartley" on March 5, 1849 and reached New Orleans, on April 30, 1849. They traveled up the Mississippi River. Cholera took many lives including Ann's Aunt. It then claimed her father on May 25. Finally June 8, the much smaller Meredith family, reached Kanesville, Iowa.

Ann's family lived in Pottawattammie County, Iowa for some time. A Welsh branch of the Church had been established for those who were unable to continue to the Salt Lake Valley. Ann's step-mother Mary Owens Meredith married a widower there in Iowa. His wife had also died of cholera. Mary Meredith Jones also died before leaving Council Bluffs, Iowa.

Though orphaned, Ann and her sisters made it to Utah about 1852. Their brother ran away from the wagon train because of ill treatment. Many years later he did write to his sister from Montana. Ann's younger sister lived with Ann until she was married.

Ann first married in about 1854 in Payson, Utah. Her joy was short lived when both her husband and an infant son died during her first year of marriage. Ann's second marriage was as a plural wife. She was almost twenty and he was twenty-eight years older. She had a son and daughter by this marriage, the son passing away at age five years.

In April, 1857, Ann and Harrison and Ann's sister Mary, went to help settle in Southern Utah. Their first home there was a wagon and dugout. By 1861, Ann and Mary moved to St. George to help settle there. Her sister Mary was married to Thomas Cook and a daughter was born to her in 1865. She also married four other spouses and had seven children during her lifetime. She spent much of her married life in the mining towns of Utah.

When twenty-nine years of age, Ann married her third husband, a widower Samuel Pollock in Salt Lake on October 10, 1865. Samuel acted as proxy as Ann received an LDS sealing to her deceased first husband. Ann's sons from this marriage were born in Kanarra, Utah. She also had a daughter born about 1873 but no further information is known.

Ann passed away on April 18, 1882 in Kanarra, Utah at the age of nearly forty-six years. She had gone through many trials and tribulations by losing her parents, a spouse, and several children. She had helped settle the southern part of Utah with her husbands. She lived to see her daughter, Harriet Ann, married to William Willis Young in 1876. She was truly a pioneer woman who endured much for her religious beliefs. She is honored by those who have followed her.

ELIZABETH REEVES POLLOCK

BIRTHDATE: 26 Mar 1829
Faulsgreen, Shropshire, England
DEATH: 18 Feb 1864
Kanarra, Iron Co., Utah
PARENTS: William Reeves
Frances Long
PIONEER: 1 Oct 1850
Gardner Snow Co. Wagon Train
SPOUSE: Samuel Pollock
MARRIED: 5 Feb 1847
Nauvoo Temple, Illinois
DEATH SP: 1891
Kanarra, Iron Co., Utah

CHILDREN:
Hyrum, 28 May 1848
Joseph Henry, 15 Oct 1850
Samuel Josiah, 15 Apr 1853
William Ashley, 4 Sep 1855
Heber Thomas, 20 Mar 1857 (died at age 11)
John Franklin, 12 Apr 1860
Rebecca Jane, 21 May 1862 (died as a child)

Elizabeth was born in England in 1829. She was one of five children born in the family. Her father was a shoemaker by trade. Her mother was a beautiful, stately woman. Her family records show they were baptized in 1842 into the Church of Jesus Christ of Latter-day Saints.

Early in 1842, this family left their home to follow the leaders of their new-found Church. They sailed on the ship "Swanton" from Liverpool, England to New Orleans, with 212 Saints aboard. They traveled up the Mississippi River to St. Louis, took another boat to Nauvoo, where they arrived on April 12, 1843. There they met the Prophet

Joseph Smith and his brother Hyrum. Also on this trip was Samuel Pollock.

He had heard about the Church of Jesus Christ of Latter-day Saints in his home town in Ireland. He had had the Spirit testify to him that this message was true, so he had left Ireland and gone to England.

Samuel lived with the Reeves family there, and left with this family for America. Samuel and Elizabeth became close friend, their love grew from a childish admiration into a strong, enduring relationship. They were married in the Nauvoo Temple, February 5, 1847, by Lorenzo Snow. Samuel was twenty-three years old and Elizabeth was nearly eighteen years of age. He had worked on the Nauvoo Temple.

Elizabeth and Samuel, together with her family left Nauvoo, on January 20, 1849. They started West in a wagon and ox-team company. They marched with courage to the land of their dreams, a place remote from mobs, lawsuits, and persecutions. Parting was sad, but the future looked bright.

On June 12, 1850, the emigrating Saints left for the Great Salt Lake Valley. Anticipation grew as they neared the Valley. Emigration Canyon was arrayed in flaming colors of red and gold. A cool breeze and a bubbling stream filled the atmosphere with sweet repose. Their first son had been born in 1848, so as they approached the Valley, Samuel pulled Elizabeth and Hyrum close to him as they beheld Salt Lake City on October 1, 1850. Brigham Young greeted them and called the family to Little Cottonwood area.

Samuel's talents were many. He was a blacksmith, stone mason, and civic minded. He had beautiful handwriting which helped him keep excellent records. Other children were born to them, and Elizabeth was carrying her third child when they packed again and moved to Spanish Fork (then called Palmyra). Samuel helped construct a dam to help develop the rich farmland.

On April 15, 1852, Samuel and Elizabeth traveled to Salt Lake City and were sealed by Brigham Young in the Endowment House. By 1853, the family moved to Cedar City.

By 1858, they were in LaVerkin where he built the first log house in Toquerville, named for an Indian Chief. Samuel was called to testify in the John D. Lee trial.

By 1862, Elizabeth had her only daughter, but less than a year later she died. Just one year after that sadness, Samuel was called to mourn the loss of his beloved wife, Elizabeth Reeves.

Elizabeth passed away on February 18, 1864 and was buried in Kanarraville Cemetery. Left with a small family, Samuel found another companion Ann Meredith Mathews, a widow with one child. Samuel passed away in 1891 and is buried beside Elizabeth.

These were brave pioneers who indeed helped in the settlement of many cities and towns in Utah. They had been touched by their faith in the Lord and obeyed His calls. They are revered by those who have followed for their valiant service.

IRENE URSULA HASKELL POMEROY

BIRTHDATE: 1 Nov 1825 New Salem, Massachusetts
DEATH: 15 Jun 1860 Salt Lake City, Salt Lake, Utah
PARENTS: Ashbel G. Haskell Ursula Billingsly Hastings
PIONEER: Sep 1847
SPOUSE: Francis M. Pomeroy
MARRIED: 13 Jul 1844 Petersboro, New Hampshire
DEATH SP: 28 Feb 1882 Mesa, Arizona

CHILDREN:
Francelle Eugenia, 21 Sep 1845
Francis Ashbel, 10 Jan 1849
Elijah, 26 Jun 1850
John Haskell, 1 Sep 1852
Irene Ophelia, 28 May 1854
May Isabel, 18 Jun 1856
Ella Amelia, 16 Jun 1858 (twin)
Emma Adelia, 16 Jun 1858 (twin)

Irene was born in New Salem, Franklin, Massachusetts. She was a very intelligent child. Her mother was glad she was able to satisfy her daughter's thirst for knowledge by having her attend a nearby academy.

In order to supply the needs of the loggers who were cutting timber on their land, Irene and her mother opened an eating house. She and her mother were baptized on March 1, 1842.

Irene married Francis Martin Pomeroy on July 13, 1844. They were hoping for a better life for themselves and moved to Nauvoo where their first child was born. In 1846, most of the Saints left Nauvoo due to persecution. Francis and Irene remained there until her mother and brother, Thales, were on their way to join them in April.

They left Nauvoo on May 26, 1846. Her husband was chosen by Brigham Young be with the first 143 men who comprised the first company to lead the way into the Salt Lake Valley. This left Irene, her little girl, Irene's mother, with Irene's thirteen year old brother, Thales, to take charge of driving their ox-team and wagon. They left Winter Quarters on June 18, 1847 and arrived in the Salt Lake Valley in late September.

Irene and Francis became the parents of eight children. At the time of the move south to avoid Johnston's Army, Irene suffered a burned hand which did not heal. As a result she had to have her arm amputated. The shock undermined her health and she died at the age of thirty-five at the home of her dear friend, Emeline B. Wells. Some of her last words were, "Tell them to educate my children." Her husband had married two other women in polygamy by that time.

Irene's mother took full charge of Irene's children and kept the family together in Salt Lake City until Francis became well located in Paris, Idaho. In 1877, Francis moved to Arizona with most of his family.

SARAH MATILDA COLBURN POMEROY

BIRTHDATE: 4 Nov 1834
Rose, Wayne Co., New York
DEATH: 25 Dec 1926
Mesa, Arizona
PARENTS: Franklin T. Colburn
PIONEER: 24 Sep 1848
Heber C. Kimball Wagon Train
SPOUSE: Francis M. Pomeroy
MARRIED: 20 Apr 1853
Salt Lake City, Salt Lake, Utah
DEATH SP: 29 Oct 1882
Mesa, Maricopa Co., Arizona

CHILDREN:
Mary Ursula, 27 Jul 1861
Talmai Emerson, 6 May 1863
William Edley, 24 Mar 1866
Franklin Thomas, 15 Sep 1870
Sarah Rosina, 21 Mar 1873
Edward Leslie, 19 May 1876

Sarah was born in Rose, New York. Her mother's family line goes back to the Dutch in New York—and her father's people came from Scotland a few generations back. Both parents belonged to the Methodist Church.

They heard the Gospel preached by missionaries from the Church of Jesus Christ of Latter-day Saints, Brigham Young and his brother Joseph.

Sarah and her family traveled 650 miles to Nauvoo, Illinois. The Prophet Joseph Smith came to their home in Nauvoo to borrow $100.00 from Sarah's father to defend Porter Rockwell who was falsely accused of trying to kill the Governor of Missouri. Sarah's faith in the Prophet was made strong when he returned the money as promised in spite of a severe rain storm, arriving at their home at ten o'clock at night. Sarah remembered the scarcity of food in Nauvoo and that potatoes were plentiful and were eaten in place of bread.

Sarah was fourteen years old when they crossed the Plains to journey to the Great Salt Lake Valley. They traveled by wagon with the Heber C. Kimball Wagon Company, arriving in the Salt Lake Valley on September 24, 1848. The family lived in the Holliday settlement and then an adobe home was built for them in the Second Ward on a ten acre farm that was all planted.

While her father was on a two year mission to England and Germany, Sarah married Francis Martin Pomeroy in 1853 in plural marriage. Being a high-spirited girl, Sarah did not take very kindly to that principle. Brigham Young, who was familiar with all the circumstances surrounding the case, sent for Sister Pomeroy and gave her a blessing that fairly made the blood in her veins tingle. He promised her in the name of the Lord that if she would remain true to the covenants that she had made with her husband that she would bring forth a child whose posterity would be an influence for good throughout Zion. Shortly after, this prediction was fulfilled when her daughter, Mary Ursula, was born.

Her husband's first wife treated Sarah like a sister and Sarah respected her as a true Saint. They lived as one family for a number of years before a cottage was built on the same lot for Sarah and her children.

Twenty years later the families pioneered in Bear Lake County, Idaho. When they moved to Arizona, Sarah did her best to make a happy home in Mesa, Arizona. She, like many of the mothers in Zion, conquered self-control so that she could meet life with a smile and a great challenge. She was happy to have three of her sons fill missions. She was active in her Church work as long as she was able.

Sarah passed away at her home in Mesa on December 25, 1926 at the age of ninety-two. Although she had passed through many trials, she remained true and faithful to the true Gospel she had embraced so many years ago.

ABIGAIL THORN RUSSELL POND

BIRTHDATE: 2 Apr 1821
Lair Promise, Cayuga, New York
DEATH: 7 Mar 1904
Lewiston, Cache Co., Utah
PARENTS: Richard Thorn
Mary Anner/Ann Armstrong
PIONEER: 10 Oct 1847
John Taylor Co. Wagon Train
SPOUSE I: Major Samuel Russell
MARRIED: 1845 (later divorced)
Nauvoo
DEATH SP: Not given

CHILD:
Frances Maria, 18 Oct 1846

SPOUSE II: Stillman Pond
MARRIED: 8 Feb 1848
Salt Lake City, Salt Lake, Co., Utah
DEATH SP: 30 Sep 1878

CHILDREN:
Mary Anner, 1 Jan 1850
Charles Stillman, 19 Sep 1851
Brigham, 9 Jun 1853
Lewis Sumner, 25 Dec 1854
Abigail, 11 Jun 1857

Joseph Thorn, 19 Sep 1859
Martin, 21 May 1862
Zina Adaline, 7 Jun 1865

Abigail was converted to the Church of Jesus Christ of Latter-day Saints as a young lady and later the majority of her family joined. The 'Spirit of Gathering' touched Abigail and she went to Nauvoo to join the Saints.

She was a skilled seamstress. Once, Brigham Young had been given a suit and coat made by Abigail Thorn.

She married Major Samuel Russell in Nauvoo in 1845. Their only child, Frances Maria, was born in a covered wagon at Winter Quarters. The next year, they crossed the Plains in the Second Wagon Company to leave Winter Quarters called the John-Taylor Company. Major Russell often acted as a captain and Abigail, walking by his side, carried her young child nearly the entire distance from Missouri River to the Salt Lake Valley.

Major Russell insisted upon continuing on toward the gold fields in California. Abigail, firm in her faith, refused to go with him and divorced him after he left her.

She later married Stillman Pond. They had eight children as they lived in Salt Lake City, Spanish Fork, and Richmond, Utah. Since times were hard, the boys had to work in the fields without shoes. Their feet became chapped and bled. She bathed their sore feet in warm bran water.

As a Relief Society President of her ward, she served capably and well. She possessed a powerful and magnetic personality together with a great store of practical wisdom. She was intelligent and well informed. An outstanding achievement for which she enjoyed distinction was of being a clever fire-side conversationalist.

After her husband passed away, she continued for a short time to maintain her home in Richmond, then moved to Lewiston into a small home which her sons had built for her. She passed away March 7, 1904 at the age of eighty-three.

HARRIET BITTON POOLE

BIRTHDATE: 13 Apr 1846
Great Yarmouth, England
DEATH: 17 Nov 1929
Idaho Falls, Idaho
PARENTS: William F. Bitton
Jane Evington
PIONEER: 4 Oct 1863
Thomas E. Ricks Wagon Train
SPOUSE: John Rawlston Poole
MARRIED: 12 Dec 1864
DEATH SP: 16 Sep 1894
Menan, Idaho

CHILDREN:
John Walter, 8 Dec 1866

Lewis Henry, 2 Sep 1869
James Arthur, 22 Sep 1871
Benton Bitton, 25 Oct 1874
Ida Jane, 15 Aug 1877
Hubert Bitton, 25 Oct 1880
Ethel Rebecca, 2 Nov 1883
Emmett Bitton, 7 Apr 1886

Harriet had brown wavy hair and big brown eyes. She was five feet five inches tall and naturally very thin. She had a very loving disposition. She always said, "It was better to be hurt than to hurt someone else."

Her father had been injured in an accident at sea and had lost his eyesight so the children had to go to work to help support the family. So it was a great responsibility that she had to bear to help care for her elderly parents whom were in poor health. She worked as a seamstress, an art she learned from an aunt who had worked for Queen Victoria.

Harriet and her parents joined the Church of Jesus Christ of Latter-day Saints and were baptized in May, 1855. In 1863, Harriet came with her parents to America.

They left Florence, Nebraska, August 10, 1863, with the Thomas E. Ricks Wagon Company arriving in the Salt Lake Valley October 4, 1863.

When Harriet was crossing the Plains her feet got frozen and she suffered with severe foot problems the rest of her life.

When they got in the Valley they traveled to the home of her sister, Jane, who lived in Ogden. She had come earlier and had married a man by the name of John Rawlston Poole who owned and operated the Globe Hotel in Ogden, Utah. A year later Harriet also married this man on December 12, 1864. She lived in Ogden sixteen years, then moved to Idaho.

She lost her husband in 1894 and was a widow for thirty-five years. When she arrived at the age that she could no longer care for herself, she went to live with her daughter, Ida Jane, who lived in Idaho Falls. It was there she passed away on November 17, 1929, at the age of eighty-three. She is buried in the Annis Little Butte Cemetery with her husband, sister Jane and her mother.

JANE BITTON POOLE

BIRTHDATE: 3 Sep 1836
London, England
DEATHDATE: 23 Jul 1921
Rexburg, Madison Co., Idaho
PARENTS: William F. Bitton
Jane Evington
PIONEER: 30 Nov 1856
Edward Martin Handcart Comp.
SPOUSE: John Rawlston Poole
MARRIED: 12 Sep 1857
DEATH SP: 16 Sep 1894
Menan, Idaho

CHILDREN:
Hyrum Evington, 25 Dec 1858
Wyatt Alexander, 8 Dec 1860
Harriet Jane, 6 Feb 1863
Edith Roseltha, 16 Jul 1865
Emily Cordelia, 17 Jan 1867
Charles William, 12 Apr 1870
Minuann Durant, 13 Jul 1872
Ewalt, 26 Aug 1874
Mary Ann, 23 Feb 1877

Jane, was the fifth of ten children. When she was still very young, her parents and family moved to Great Yarmouth, Norfolk, England. Her father who had been injured in an accident at sea lost his eye sight. The children had to work to provide for the family. Jane went to work as a nursemaid at the age of nine years. Later she worked with a milliner and learned to braid and sew straw to make hats. She learned many crafts as sewing, knitting, netting and embroidery which helped her prepare for hard times in later years.

Jane, age nineteen, her older brother John and his wife Sarah, sailed from Liverpool, May 25, 1856, on the ship "Horizon" for America. After a voyage of thirty-seven days at sea they cast anchor in Boston Harbor, Massachusetts. They arrived at Iowa City, Iowa July 8, 1856. This was as far as the railroad extended. They remained here for twenty days while handcarts and tents were built, then left on July 28, 1856 with the Edward Martin Handcart Company, with 145 handcarts, 7 wagons, 30 oxen and 50 cows and beef cattle.

Winter came early causing so much hardship and suffering to be endured by this company that 150 persons died on the trail. When the relief wagons finally reached them Jane, her brother and his wife were assigned to the John Rawlston Poole rescue wagon. They arrived in the Salt Lake Valley on November 30, 1856.

Mr. Poole gave them shelter in his home in Ogden. The following year Jane married John Rawlston Poole on September 12, 1857. She bore him nine children.

She always had trouble with language. Even though she spoke English, she would cut off the letter at the beginning of most words.

Jane's husband, John, preceded her in death by twenty-seven years. Jane passed away at the home of her son Charles William Poole in Rexburg, Idaho on July 23, 1921, at the age of eighty-four. She is buried in the Annis Little Butte Cemetery next to her husband, her sister, Harriet, and mother.

JENNETTE BLEASDALE POOLE

BIRTHDATE: 10 Feb 1826
Thornley, Lancashire, England
DEATH: 20 May 1921
Menan, Jefferson Co., Idaho
PARENTS: William Bleasdale
Margaret Moss
PIONEER: 1 Oct 1850
Joseph Young Co. Wagon Train
SPOUSE: John Rawlston Poole
MARRIED: 6 Jul 1848
Farmington, Van Buren, Iowa
DEATH SP: 19 Sep 1894
Idaho Falls, Idaho

CHILDREN:
Mary Elizabeth, Sep 1849
Joseph Ewalt, 24 Feb 1851
Addaline Melinda, 24 Feb 1852
John Bleasdale, abt 1854
Rebecca Margaret, 29 Aug 1855
William Micajah, 17 Jan 1858
Jeanette Alice, 23 May 1860
Susanna Rosetta, 4 Jul 1862
Reuben Mack, 25 Nov 1864
Christine Jane, 18 Jan 1868
Milburn Benton, 24 Feb 1871

Jenette was born in Thornley, Lancashire, England. Little is known of her childhood. She married John Rawlston Poole on July 6, 1848 in Farmington, Van Buren County, Iowa. They became the parents of eleven children their first baby, Mary Elizabeth, died of cholera in July, 1850, while they were crossing the Plains on their way to the Salt Lake Valley. They had left Kanesville, Iowa, June 15, 1850, traveling with the Joseph Young Wagon Company. They arrived in the Salt Lake Valley on October 1, 1850.

Jennette was a supportive helpmate to her husband, John. John was the Presiding Elder from 1879 to 1884 in Menan, Bingham County, Idaho. It was called "Pooles Island." Jennette was a loving and compassionate mother and homemaker.

While her husband served a two year mission for the Church, she managed the home, farm and the Globe Hotel in Ogden, Utah. She was a capable midwife, doctor, nurse and counselor. She helped deliver 1,300 babies.

Jennette wrote the address presented at the 50th Anniversary of the Relief Society for the wards to present. She was known for the beautiful lace she knitted. She enjoyed piecing quilt tops. She made rag rugs, especially for all the rooms while operating the Globe Hotel in Ogden. She was an excellent cook; she especially loved to bake. She was very meticulous about her clothes. She was given the title of the best dressed woman in Nauvoo, Illinois. Jennette always raised a garden where and whenever possible.

Jennette's husband passed away in Idaho Falls, Idaho on September 19, 1894. Jennette was a widow for almost twenty-seven years. Jennette passed away in Menan, Jefferson County, Idaho on May 20, 1921. She was ninety-five years old.

CATHERINE MCBRIDE POPE

BIRTHDATE: 10 Jun 1821
Wayne County, Iowa
DEATH: 16 Jan 1878
Oakley, Cassia Co., Idaho
PARENTS: Thomas McBride
Catherine John McBride
PIONEER: 05 Oct 1852
John B. Walker Wagon Train
SPOUSE: William Monroe Pope
MARRIED: 1841
Nauvoo, Hancock Co., Illinois
DEATH SP: Not given

CHILDREN:
Wyatt, 1842 (died at age 4)
Charlotte, 19 Dec 1844
Oscar Monroe, 19 Aug 1846
Casanda, 19 Dec 1848
William Harrison, 26 Apr 1850
Mary Isabell, 10 Dec 1851
Martha Ellen, 28 Nov 1853
Sarah Catherine, 1854
Huldah Jane, 4 Aug 1857
Daniel LeGrande, 8 May 1860
Arminta, 23 Jul 1862

When Catharine was ten years old, missionaries from the Church of Jesus Christ of Latter-day Saints converted their family. As soon as they could, the McBride family turned their backs upon Ohio and went to find a settlement with the church members in Missouri.

In 1830, they had settled on Shoal Creek at the time of the Haun's Mill Massacre. Her father was killed in this incident. They were expelled from Missouri and went to settle in Nauvoo, Illinois. On the way there, a young man recently disinherited by his family because he had become a Mormon, joined their group. His name was William Monroe Pope. He and Catherine were married in Nauvoo in 1841.

Catherine had a beautiful, sweet voice and loved to sing the songs of Zion. She was a gifted singer. She had six children before they started their trek across the Plains with the John B. Walker Wagon Company.

When they reached the Salt Lake Valley in 1852, they went on to Grantsville, Utah where the McBride relatives had settled. The remainder of their family was born here.

They endured the trials of pioneer life as they helped to settle that area. They lost livestock to the Indians, suffered destruction of their crops by grasshoppers and crickets, suffered from the cold miserable winters, suffered from extreme drought, and had to eat roots and edible green weeds for weeks.

Catherine and William were noted for their hospitality and generosity. Often they would make up an extra sack of flour into bread and invite all their neighbors and friends to enjoy it.

Catherine passed away, January 16, 1878, in Oakley, Idaho, but was buried in Grantsville, Utah where she had pioneered.

SARAH LADUC POPE

BIRTHDATE: 21 Jul 1835
St. Cesaire, Montreal, Canada
DEATH: 13 Dec 1918
Vernal, Uintah Co., Utah
PARENTS: Charles LaDuc
Marguerite DuFaut
PIONEER: 26 Jun 1858
David Brenton Co. Wagon Train
SPOUSE: Robert Pope
MARRIED: 1 Oct 1851
Rosendale, Wisconsin
DEATH SP: 14 Jul 1915
Vernal, Uintah Co., Utah

CHILDREN:
Charles Holmes, 3 Oct 1852
Hattie Ann, 16 Sep 1855
Robe-rt Alexander, 20 Sep 1857
John Theadore, 2 Mar 1860
George Eugene, 25 Apr 1862
Richard Henry, 28 Sep 1864
William Franklin, 20 May 1867
Adaline Orno Orlando, 24 Sep 1869
Sarah Adell, 19 Sep 1872
Marcella Barnum, 26 Nov 1874
Rock Marcus, 20 May 1877

Sarah LaDuc Pope was born in St. Cesaire, Montreal, Quebec, Canada. Little is known of her childhood. She was married to Robert Pope on October 1, 1851 in Rosendale, Fon-du-lac, Wisconsin. Two years after her marriage, the family moved to Minnesota.

It was here that they met missionaries of the Church of Jesus Christ of Latter-day Saints. They were baptized into the Church of Jesus Christ of Latter-day Saints on June 6, 1857. They emigrated to Utah in 1858. They joined the David Brenton Wagon Company and arrived in the Salt Lake Valley on June 26, 1858. This was probably an independent wagon train company.

They first settled at Farmington, Utah where they lived until 1864. The family then moved to the Bear Lake Valley the Fall of 1864. They were among the first settlers of St. Charles, Bear Lake, Idaho.

In the Spring of 1870, they were called to help settle Randolph, Utah. Sarah and Robert owned and operated the first store in that city. After three years in Randolph, the family moved back to the Bear Lake Valley. They lived first in Laketown, Utah and then Fish Haven, Idaho where they engaged in the mercantile business.

On May 6, 1878, the Relief Society was organized at Fish Haven and Sarah was called to be the first President. She held this position until they moved to Garden City, Utah in June, 1881. Here she served as the secretary of the Relief Society.

In 1883, they were called as pioneers to the Ashley Valley in the Uintah Basin. They and their children were numbered among the first stalwart pioneers of that region, now it is known as Vernal, Utah.

Sarah was the first Stake Relief Society President and held that position for eighteen years. Sarah was an excellent self-taught nurse and midwife and was set apart as such by President Brigham Young. She kept a record of babies she delivered until they numbered over 500. She never lost a mother for which she gave thanks to her Father in Heaven. Sarah was also an excellent seamstress and did beautiful needle work. At the age of eighty she did needle-work that later took first place in several Utah State Fairs. She never wore eye glasses. During World War 1, she knitted over 150 pairs of socks for the war effort.

Her husband, Robert, passed away on July 14, 1915 in Vernal, Utah. Sarah died three years later, December 13, 1918. They are both buried in the Vernal Cemetery in Uintah County, Utah.

SARAH ELIZABETH HAMPTON PORRITT

BIRTHDATE: 13 Mar 1853
Big Pigeon, Pottawattomie, Iowa
DEATH: 29 Mar 1926
Pocatello, Idaho
PARENTS: Thomas J. Hampton
Martha Ruth Bracken
PIONEER: 30 Nov 1856
Edward Martin Handcart Comp.
SPOUSE: Thomas Porritt
MARRIED: 13 Nov 1868
Utah
DEATH SP: 13 Oct 1918
Ashton, Idaho

CHILDREN:
Thomas Hampton, 14 Oct 1869
Sarah Jane, 12 May 1872
Martha, 30 Aug 1874
James, 11 Jun 1877
George, 12 Nov 1878
Margaret, 1 Sep 1881

Levi, 7 Oct 1884
Nephi Nathaniel, 27 Jan 1887
John Martin, 4 Jun 1888
William Robert, 25 Apr 1891
Bertha, 18 Oct 1892
Leola, 24 Oct 1894
Rula Rebecca, 22 Oct 1896

Sarah was born in Big Pigeon, Pottawattomie County, Iowa, the fifth of six children. She walked all the way across the Plains when she was three years old. She and her family suffered the terrible hardships of the Martin Handcart Company, arriving in the Salt Lake Valley on November 30, 1856.

Her father had died in 1856 in Council Bluffs, Iowa Her mother re-married and her step-father wanted to marry Sarah Elizabeth as his second wife in plural marriage. Neither Sarah nor her mother wished it. Sarah had already fallen in love with Thomas Porritt. Her mother lowered her clothes out of the upstairs window on a rope so that Sarah could run away and marry Thomas. He had been born in England and crossed the Plains with the Martin Handcart Company, also. They were married on November 3, 1868 in Utah. They made their home in Franklin, Idaho. They moved to Dayton and then to Clifton, Idaho. In Clifton, her husband was a farmer and worked on the railroad. They became the parents of thirteen children; seven sons and six daughters.

For a short period of time, Thomas and Sarah lived in Lost River. On the trip to Lost River they ran into acres of crickets. They then moved to Ashton, Idaho where they lived until Thomas died of influenza on October 13, 1918.

Sarah moved to Pocatello, Idaho and lived with her daughter, Sarah Jane, and her husband and family. Sarah passed away on March 29, 1926. She had been a widow for eight years. She was buried in the Ashton Cemetery along side of her husband.

ELIZABETH BAILEY PORTER

BIRTHDATE: 8 Feb 1848
Charleston, Lee Co., Iowa
DEATH: 27 Oct 1927
Porterville, Morgan Co., Utah
PARENTS: Job T. Bailey
Elizabeth S. Bailey Norwood
PIONEER: 12 Oct 1848
Amasa M. Lyman Wagon Train
SPOUSE: Lyman Wight Porter
MARRIED: 5 Oct 1867
Salt Lake City, Salt Lake, Utah
DEATH SP: 31 Mar 1914
Porterville, Morgan Co., Utah

CHILDREN:
Elizabeth Adeline, 28 Nov 1868
Clarisse (Claracy), 5 Mar 1871 (died at 6 months)
John Riley, 14 Apr 1872
Zina, 2 Jul 1874

Rhoda Areta, 14 Sep 1876
Rachel, 16 Dec 1878
Job Bailey, 30 Jan 1881
Brigham Ernest, 17 Mar 1883
LeGrand Thatcher, 4 Oct 1885

Elizabeth's father died one day before her birth. Her mother left Winter Quarters in June, 1848, with her two year old sister, Bethana, and four month old Elizabeth. They were assisted by Ezra Thompson Clark. They traveled in the Amasa M. Lyman Wagon Company and arrived in the Salt Lake Valley on October 12, 1848. Her uncle, Edward Stevenson, provided a home for them in the Valley which was located in the Fifteenth Ward.

In 1850, her mother married Richard Smith Norwood. After their marriage, they lived in Big Cottonwood until about 1860. They moved to an area called Norwood Hollow in Porterville, Morgan County.

In 1867, Elizabeth became the third wife of Lyman Wight Porter when she was nineteen and he was thirty. In 1870, she went with Lyman when he accepted a mission call to settle Kanab. His other two families remained in Porterville to care for the farm and his aged father. After eighteen months, they returned to Porterville where Lyman built her a log cabin which was later replaced by a two-story brick home. They became parents to nine children.

Elizabeth was well known for her excellent quilt making and her rag rug weaving. She served as the Relief Society President of Porterville from 1890 to 1902. When they were building their new church house, the women helped where they could by painting, scrubbing, and cleaning windows. Each sister was asked to donate a ball of rags to make a rug. They held rag bees where they tore worn clothing into strips and sewed them together until they were long enough to go the full length of the chapel. Then they rolled the rags into a ball until it was time to weave them into the rug.

Elizabeth was admired for her strength of character, "faith and fortitude," and her many talents. She made clothing of hand woven linsey-woolsey for her children. She knit the stockings they wore. She was affectionately known as "Lizzie."

LYDIA ANN COOK PORTER

BIRTHDATE: 6 Aug 1830
Peoria, Illinois
DEATH: 20 Dec 1882
Orderville, Kane Co., Utah
PARENTS: Ahaz Cook
Hannah Sherwood Jennings
PIONEER: 19 Oct 1849
Willard Richard's Wagon Train
SPOUSE: Chauncey W. Porter
MARRIED: 28 Mar 1847
DEATH SP: 3 Mar 1867

CHILDREN:
Warriner Ahaz, 20 May 1848
Charles, 22 Jun 1850 (died as an infant)
Cynthia Cannes, 22 Jun 1850
Amy Zenora, 4 May 1852
Justin Rockford, 19 Oct 1853
Nancy Arvena, 20 Sep 1855
Mary Ziona, 25 Apr 1857 (died same year)
Edson Darius, 12 Apr 1859
Omni Lehi, 27 Jan 1861
Annie Ozina, 27 Apr 1863
Abinadi, 28 Mar 1865
Arval Marion, 20 Apr 1867 (died same year)
Lydia Bereft, 21 Jun 1868 (died as an infant)

Lydia's parents joined the Church of Jesus Christ of Latter-day Saints before 1836. Due to severe persecution of the Saints, Lydia's mother left the church and took her daughter, Irene, with her.

At the conference held in Farr West on October 6, 1836, her father volunteered as a missionary, but died as he reached home. Lydia was left as an orphan at age six.

She lived with various other families until she was invited to live with Chauncy Warriner Porter and his wife Amy. Amy became weaker due to the birth and death of so many of her children beside the persecutions they were enduring.

Before she died, she asked Lydia to marry her husband, Chauncy, in plural marriage. They were married on March 28, 1847 and Amy died on April 6, 1847. On February 10, 1848, Chauncy married a third wife, Priscilla Strong. In May of 1848, they were making preparations to cross the Plains.

Priscilla became ill, so Chauncy sent Lydia, his children by his first wife, and Lydia's new baby across the Plains with his parents and brothers. She was assigned to the Willard Richard's Wagon Company with Ezra T. Clark as the captain of her wagon division. They arrived in Utah October 19, 1848. Chauncy and Priscilla arrived the following year. He took his three families to Mill Creek Canyon which is south of Salt Lake City.

In 1860, after settling a while in Centerville, Utah, the Porter families moved to an area over the mountains from

Centerville. Their settlement was called Porterville, Utah. Lydia had kept her promise to Amy to raise and teach her children. Chauncy died in 1868 leaving her with eight children to raise.

Lydia Ann Cook Porter passed away on August 6, 1830 in Orderville, Kane County, Utah.

MARCIA MARIA BISBEE PORTER

BIRTHDATE: 24 Oct 1805
Covington, Massachusetts
DEATH: 24 Nov 1867
Ogden, Weber Co., Utah
PARENTS: Luther Bisbee
Sarah Whitmarsh
PIONEER: 7 Oct 1863
A. Canfield Ind. Wagon Train
SPOUSE: Abraham Porter
MARRIED: 1 Oct 1828
Ossian, Allegheny, New York
DEATH SP: 19 May 1884
Ogden, Weber Co., Utah

CHILDREN:
Luther Gilbert, 16 Nov 1829
Nahum Bisbee, 16 Jun 1831
Sarah Jane, 17 Jul 1833
Henrietta, 4 Feb 1835
Mary, 18 Jun 1838
Margaret Eleanor, 30 Oct 1840 (died at age 3)
Harriet Eleanor, 16 Oct 1848

Marcia was born in Covington, Hampshire County, Massachusetts, 1805. When she was two years old, her family moved to Albany, New York where her father was engaged in turnpike building. Her father and some of her brothers served in the War of 1812.

They later moved to Charlton, New York where her father was in the hotel business and cared for the grounds around Union College. They moved a few more times before they moved to Ossian, New York where she met Abraham Porter.

Marcia and Abraham were married on October 1, 1828. They farmed and she learned to spin, weave, sew clothing, and became gifted in nursing. She was known all over the county for her knowledge of medicine and her nursing ability. Abraham and Marcia Maria had seven children.

In the year 1843, a great change came to their home when the Elders of the Church of Jesus Christ of Latter-day Saints converted and baptized them as members of the Church. At once, there was unrest which never cleared until they began the long journey from western New York to Utah in May of 1863.

They traveled by train from New York to Omaha, Nebraska. Then they traveled by boat up the Missouri River to Florence, Nebraska where they stayed for six weeks. On the third of July, they left Winter Quarters in the Augustus Canfield Independent Wagon Company. They

separated from the company as they entered the Weber Canyon and went to Ogden where some of their relatives were living.

The following spring, they moved to Salt Lake City and settled on a farm on the Jordan River. They worked this farm until their youngest daughter, Harriet Eleanor, married. They went to live with her in Ogden until Marcia passed away.

Thus ended the life of one of God's handmaidens who had lived sixty-two years of pioneer and frontier life.

MINERVA ADELINE DEUEL PORTER

BIRTHDATE: 3 Mar 1843
Montrose, Lee Co., Iowa
DEATH: 10 Feb 1873
Porterville, Morgan Co., Utah
PARENTS: William H. Deuel
Eliza Avery Whiting
PIONEER: 2 Oct 1847
Charles C. Rich Wagon Train
SPOUSE: Alma Porter
MARRIED: 15 Nov 1855
Centerville, Davis Co., Utah
DEATH SP: 27 Oct 1903
Porterville, Morgan Co., Utah

CHILDREN:
Alma William, 16 Aug 1859 (died at 3 months)
Mary Minerva, 19 Sep 1860
Ann Eliza, 22 Oct 1862
Lewis Alfred, 14 Jan 1867
Nelson Warriner, 6 Jan 1867
Charles Worthy, 17 Dec 1867
Orson Merit, 26 Jul 1869
George Myron, 17 Mar 1871
Amy Vilate, 29 Jan 1873

Minerva Adeline was warmly welcomed by her parents on March 3, 1843, while they were living in Montrose, Iowa. Her parents brought her across the Plains with the Charles C. Rich Wagon Company when she was just four years old. They arrived in the Salt Lake Valley on October 2, 1847.

When they lived in the valley, the families of her father and his brother both shared the same small cabin. This same cabin is now situated between the Family History Library and the church Museum. Later the Deuel brothers moved to Deuel Creek, now known as Centerville. This is where Minerva grew up.

When she was fifteen years old, she was married to Alma Porter in her parent's home by Charles C. Rich. In 1881, the family moved to the little settlement of Porterville, Morgan County, Utah. It was rough pioneering and lean times. There were bad years when the grasshoppers devoured nearly every green thing.

Minerva became the mother of nine children. Twelve days after the birth of her last child, Minerva died. She and her husband's grandfather, Sanford Porter, died the same day. A double funeral was held for them before they were buried in the Porterville Cemetery.

NANCY RICH PORTER

No
Photo
Available

BIRTHDATE: 3/5 May 1821
Essex, Switzerland Co., Indiana
DEATHDATE: 14 Dec 1857
Centerville, Davis Co., Utah
PARENTS: Joseph Rich Sr.
Nancy O'Neal
PIONEER: 2 Oct 1847
Charles C. Rich Wagon Train
SPOUSE: John P. Porter Sr.
MARRIED: 5 Feb 1843
Lee Co., Iowa
DEATH SP: 28 May 1895
Portersville, Morgan Co., Utah

CHILDREN:
Joseph Rich, 29 Mar 1844
Sanford Colson, 25 Dec 1845
John President Jr., 4 Sep 1847
Nancy, 16 Mar 1851

Nancy was a sister to Charles Colson Rich, an Apostle to Brigham Young. She married John Porter February 5, 1843. Their two oldest sons were born in Charleston, Lee County, Iowa. They lived for awhile in Nauvoo, Illinois.

Nancy and John left Winter Quarters, Nebraska on June 17, 1847 with the Charles C. Rich Company. There were 126 people in the company. On September 2, they camped on the Sweetwater River and met there about thirty other wagons of pioneers and the balance of the twelve Apostles, who had been traveling with President Young. On the 4th of September, Nancy gave birth to a baby boy, whom they named John President Porter, Jr.

From here to Salt Lake Valley she traveled with her sister-in-law, Sarah Pea Rich. Nancy's parents were also traveling with this company, her mother being very ill at the time. On the 11th of September, they crossed the Green River and by the 20th they had crossed the Bear River where some of the wagons broke down. After making what repairs were necessary they continued on and reached the Old-Fort in the Salt Lake Valley of what is now Salt Lake on the 2nd of October. Nancy lost her mother just three days after entering the Valley. She was the second person to be buried in the valley.

For a short while Nancy and her family lived in Salt Lake and then in 1850 they moved to Centerville, Davis County, where her husband's father had settled earlier. In 1851, she gave birth to a baby daughter who lived only two months.

Nancy only lived another six years before she too passed away at the age of thirty-six. Her husband had married a second time, before Nancy's death, to Mary Palmer Graves. Nancy would never allow a picture to be taken of her, according to family tradition, she thought it was vain.

At the time of her death her sons were nearly fourteen, twelve and ten. Nancy was buried in Centerville, Davis County, Utah.

NANCY WARRINER PORTER

No
Photo
Available

BIRTHDATE: 29 Jul 1790
Vershire, Vermont
DEATH: 2 May 1864
Porterville, Morgan Co., Utah
PARENTS: Reuben Warriner
Sarah Colten
PIONEER: 2 Oct 1847
Charles C. Rich Wagon Train
SPOUSE: Sanford Porter, Sr.
MARRIED: 1 Jan 1812
Vershire, Vermont
DEATH SP: 7 Feb 1873
Porterville, Morgan Co., Utah

CHILDREN:
Chauncey Warriner, 20 Oct 1812
Malinda, 3 Nov 1814
Sarah, 11 Sep 1816 (died at age 24)
John President, 28 Jul 1818
Nathan Tanner, 10 Jul 1820
Reuben, May 1822
Sanford, Jr., 25 Jun 1823
Nancy Areta, 8 Aug 1825
Joseph, 1827 (twin - died as an infant)
Hyrum, 1827 (twin - died as an infant)
Justin Theodore, 18 May 1828 (died at age 12)
Lucinda, Aug 1831 (died as an infant)
Lyman Wight, 5 May 1833

Nancy Warriner and Sanford Porter lived half a mile apart as children, went to the same school when they could attend school, and became close friends while living in Vershire, Vermont. A short time after they were married, Sanford was called to serve in the War of 1812. When he was released from the army, they began homesteading in New York. They moved to Ohio and to Illinois.

It was in Illinois that two missionaries from the Church of Jesus Christ of Latter-day Saints visited their home and converted Nancy and Porter. They were baptized on August 10, 1831.

They sold their home and traveled by wagon through severe winter weather to Independence. There they built a home on a twenty acre farm only to be driven from it before they were really settled in. For the next fourteen years they suffered the persecutions and mobbing that the Saints were called to endure. They later moved on to Nauvoo where they helped to build the city and the temple.

Driven out again, they suffered the terrible experience of the winter of 1846 in Council Bluff. The following summer, the Saints began the migration West. It was three and one half months of hazardous travel for Nancy. She was now fifty-seven years old. Her life had known little rest. She had eleven children and moved from one frontier homestead to another.

Now Nancy was to help establish a home in a barren desert land. They lived in their wagon that first winter. Food was so scarce, Nancy had to ration out the little food they had only one fourth pound of flour per person a day. Sometimes the meat of a wild animal or a bird was added to their near starvation fare.

In spite of all her hardships, Nancy cared for the sick and was often the midwife when new babies came to the families in the settlements. She lent help and provisions for those in need wherever she found them. The next year after their arrival they moved to Centerville to help settle the area. They lived here for twelve years.

When Nancy was seventy-two, her husband couldn't resist the challenge for a new settlement. They moved east over the mountains to form a town which they called Porterville which was her last home.

PRISCILLA STRONG PORTER

BIRTHDATE: 11 Dec 1830
Sheldon, Genesee Co., New York
DEATH: 9 Jan 1895
Orderville, Kane Co., Utah
PARENTS: Ezra Strong
Olive Lowell
PIONEER: 1848
Capt. Cunningham Wagon Train
SPOUSE: Chauncey W. Porter
MARRIED: 10 Feb 1848
Winter Quarters, Nebraska
DEATH SP: 3 Mar 1868
Centerville, Davis Co., Utah

CHILDREN:
Chauncey Union, 17 Mar 1850
Daniel Dorath, 27 Jun 1851
Printha Priscilla, 29 Aug 1852
Francis Lysander, 4 Jul 1854
Mary Etta, 5 Jul 1856
Melvin Omer, 11 Jun 1858
Carmi Nephi, 31 Oct 1860
David Nathaniel, 23 Feb 1863
Wilford Woodruff, 22 Feb 1864
Olive Martha, 29 Apr 1866
Ezra Soloman, 1 Dec 1867

Priscilla was born the same year the Church of Jesus Christ of latter-day Saints was organized and in the same state.

At the age of eighteen, she married Chauncey Warriner Porter who was a widower eighteen years her senior. She was his third wife. They were making preparations to travel West with the Willard Richard Wagon Company when Priscilla became very ill. Her husband sent his second wife with her month old baby and his children by his first wife

on with this company because his other relatives were in the company and could assist them if need be. He and Priscilla stayed behind until she regained her health and they were able to come the following year.

His son, Alma, went to meet them in Echo Canyon with a fresh set of oxen to help them finish their trek. Chauncey then took his families four or five miles south of Salt Lake City along the Jordan River where they lived during the winter. He rented a saw mill twelve miles south of the city and eight miles up the canyon. It was here that Priscilla's first baby was born. They worked so hard to build a log cabin, plow the ground, and plant grain. Then the crickets came and ate almost everything.

She endured the hardships of hunger, hard work, moving from place to place, bearing eleven children, and providing their comfort. They moved to Millcreek, Centerville, Springville, Hardscrabble, and Porterville while her husband was alive. He was bishop in Porterville and was involved with the saw mill, building of homes, helping others to solve their problems. He was very busy.

When Chauncey passed away in 1868, she and Chauncy's second wife sold their property in Porterville and invested in the United Order in Orderville. She lived there until her death at age sixty-four.

Priscilla loved to write poetry. She was a loving mid-wife and nurse to many. She taught her children by precept and example to love and live the gospel.

JULIE JANE JEMMETT POTTS

BIRTHDATE: 17 Dec 1840
Faversham, Kent, England
DEATH: 23 Sep 1925
Woodland, Summit Co., Utah
PARENTS: William Jemmett
Mary Ann Browning
PIONEER: 6 Oct 1862
Ansell Harmon Co. Wagon Train
SPOUSE: Thomas Pullen Potts
MARRIED: 6 May 1860
Faversham, Kent, England
DEATH SP: 27 Jan 1909
Woodland, Summit Co., Utah

CHILDREN:
Charlotte Isabell, 12 Nov 1860
Thomas Henry, 18 Sep 1862
John William, 6 Aug 1864
William Edward, 8 Nov 1866
George Fredrick, 8 Feb 1869
Julie Jane, 12 Mar 1871
Albert Sidney 19 Oct 1873
Frank Nicholas 8 May 1876
Charles Robert 5 Jul 1879
Clarence 11 Sep 1883

Two years after their marriage Julie and her husband, Thomas Pullen Potts, with their little daughter Charlotte set sail for America, May 6, 1862, from Liverpool, England on the ship, "Manchester," with Henry Trask as their Captain.

They landed at Castle Garden, New York, June 21, 1862, and traveled on to Florence, Nebraska. They waited six weeks for the ox teams to be made ready. There were forty wagons in their company. While crossing the Sweetwater Territory in Wyoming her second child, Thomas Henry, was born.

Everything went well until the wagon train arrived at Echo Canyon. While traveling at night their wagon was thrown down an embankment and into the creek. They all suffered bruises and Julie's ankle was put out of place. They arrived at the Salt Lake Valley on October 6, 1862. Julie was very sick.

They lived in Cottonwood for four years. During this time they lived for one winter in Salt Creek (near Nephi). In 1865, they moved to Hyrum, Cache County and took a farm on shares. The grasshoppers were so bad they couldn't raise anything. They stayed only one year.

Julie was a small, energetic woman and her husband was tall and very distinctive looking. They were endowed and sealed to each other in the Endowment House on December 21, 1866.

In 1867, they moved to Bear River and then to Tooele. In 1870, they moved to Woodland, Utah and lived there for the remainder of their lives. They lived in a one-room house and in the summer the boys slept outside but in the cold winter they slept in the house. They later lived in a five-room house and Julie thought she was living in a mansion. The boys built a new outhouse and Julie put a lock and key on the door and claimed it for her own.

Julie attended her church meetings and participated whenever she found time from her busy home. She fulfilled the role of loving wife, mother, grandmother, neighbor and friend. She was loved by all who knew her. Her time was spent being a housewife and mother to her ten children. She was faithful to her religion and taught her children the same. Her sons were bishops or in bishoprics and one son became a Patriarch. Her children called her the best mother on earth.

Her husband passed away in 1909 at Woodland. Julie passed away on September 23, 1925, also at Woodland. She is buried at the Woodland Cemetery, next to her husband. Their homestead was given to the Church about 1962.

CECILIA (SIDSEL) JORGENSEN POULSEN

No Photo Available

BIRTHDATE: 19 May 1835
Grundfor, Denmark
DEATH: 27 May 1878
Petersboro, Cache Co., Utah
PARENTS: Rasmus Jorgensen
Karen Jensen
PIONEER: 12 Sep 1861
Woolley / Murdock Wagon Train
SPOUSE: Paul Michael Poulsen
MARRIED: 17 May 1861
aboard "Monarch of the Sea"
DEATH SP: 24 Jan 1911
Logan Cache Co., Utah

CHILDREN:
Michael,
Erastus,
John,
Hyrum,
Cecilia,
Kerstine,

Cecilia Poulsen was born in Denmark. She was christened the very day she was born which probably indicated that her parents feared for her life. Little is known of her childhood.

Cecilia was the first in her family to accept the gospel of the Church of Jesus Christ of Latter-day Saints and to be baptized into the Church. She was then twenty-four years of age. Her father joined the Church the following year. However, as so often happened, his wife did not accept the faith. Cecilia left Denmark along with her father and their neighbor, Jacobine Kirstine Mogensen Jensen, and her young daughter, Maren. Paul Michael Poulsen, a mason by trade, also came with them.

They sailed from Liverpool, England on May 16, 1861 aboard the ship "Monarch of the Sea." According to the journal history of the ship, the first few days at sea were very stormy ones and there was much sickness on board. Due to the over crowding of the area where those who were single were housed, the Church leaders asked that any on board who were planning to marry later do so as soon as possible in order to make quarters on the ship more comfortable for those on board.

So it was that Cecilia and Paul Michael were married on May 17, 1861 on board the ship. Her father married their neighbor, Jacobine Kirstine, the same day. After the ship docked, they made their way to Florence, Nebraska. They joined the combined Company of Samuel A. Woolley and John R. Murdock and traveled across the Plains by wagon, arriving in the Salt Lake Valley on September 12, 1861.

Paul and Cecilia settled in Petersboro, Cache Valley, Utah, just west of Logan, Utah. They established a fine farm. Paul used his skills as a mason to help with the building of the Logan Temple. It was said that Cecilia's health was very fragile and that she was slightly deformed.

Seventeen years after arriving in the Valley, Cecilia passed away, during the early years of the settlement of Cache Valley. She and Paul became the parents of six children. Her body was buried in the Logan Cemetery along with all of her six children who preceeded her in death. She was forty-three years old.

There are many today who owe her much for the part she played in influencing her family to accept the Gospel and to emigrate to America to become a pioneer who helped settle the wilderness called Zion.

DORTHEA CHRISTINE MIKKELSEN POULSEN

No Photo Available

BIRTHDATE: 3 Apr 1815
Lihmskov, Norup Parish, Vejle, Denmark
DEATH: 4 Apr 1854
Kansas City, Jackson, Missouri
PARENTS: Mikkel Pedersen
Ane Mortensen
PIONEER: 1854 Wagon Train
SPOUSE: Mads Poulsen
MARRIED: 26 Oct 1833
Denmark
DEATH SP: 27 Mar 1888
Goshen, Utah Co., Utah

CHILDREN:
Maren, 9 Oct 1835
Ane, 6 Jul 1839
Mikkel, 3 Dec 1842
Powel /Poul, 20 Feb 1846
Ane Johanne "Hannah," 6 Mar 1849
Sern /Soren, 27 Sep 1851

Dorthea was born in Lihmskov, Norrup Parish, Vejle, Denmark, 1815. Nothing is known of her childhood.

She married Mads Poulsen on October 26, 1833 in Denmark. They became the parents of six children; all born in Denmark. Dorthea was a deeply religious woman. When the family heard the Gospel preached by missionaries of the Church of Jesus Christ of Latter-day Saint, their daughter Maren was the first to be baptized. Dorthea was baptized on January 5, 1852 and her husband a year later. Joining the Church meant persecution from those who did not believe.

After her baptism, Dorthea's greatest desire was to gather with the Saints in Utah. When a group of Scandinavian converts to the Church were ready to leave their native land, Mads and Dorthea went with them, leaving on December 10, 1853. When they reached Liverpool, England, they boarded the ship that was to take them to America.

The family reached New Orleans in 1854, and cholera was raging and contagious. Many of the Mormons contracted this dreaded disease and died. There were Mormon men stationed at New Orleans to help the emigrants get aboard river boats to take them up the Mississippi River to Kansas City, Missouri. This was the outfitting station for the Saints to cross the Plains. At this place, death from Cholera again took a large toll of the people.

Their fond anticipations at the prospect of going to Zion were suddenly and unexpectedly cut short, and they were buried in that place. Such was the fate of Dorthea (Dorthe) Christine (Kirstine) Mikkelsen Poulsen (Powelsen). She passed away on April 4, 1854, at the age of thirty-nine in Kansas City, Jackson County, Missouri. This left her sorrowing husband with their six children to care for alone. They continued on their journey to Utah, arriving the fall of 1854.

It can be said of Dorthea that she paid the supreme sacrifice for the price of pioneering. Her descendents will ever be indebted to her for her faith and fortitude.

KAREN CHRISTENSEN OLSON POULSEN

BIRTHDATE: 5 Jul 1820
Jegindo, Thisted, Denmark
DEATH: 4 Nov 1902
Ephraim, Sanpete Co., Utah
PARENTS: Christen Oleson
Else Margrethe Christensen
PIONEER: 5 Oct 1854
Hans Peters Olsen Wagon Train
SPOUSE: Lars Poulsen
MARRIED: 15 Oct 1844
Jegindo, Denmark
DEATH SP: 17 Feb 1884
Ephraim, Sanpete Co., Utah

CHILDREN:
Poul/Paul, 24 Jul 1845
Else Margrethe, 19 Oct 1847
Elsie, 1849
Christen 1852
Jens Louis, 1855
Orson Hyde, 7 Sep 1860
Mary,

Karen Poulsen was born in Denmark. She and her future husband, Lars Poulsen, lived on neighboring farms.

Karen and Lars were married when she was twenty-four years old, and Lars was twenty-five years. They became the parents of seven children.

In 1851 the missionaries of the Church of Jesus Christ of Latter-day Saints found them; almost from the first conversation they were ready to receive the true Gospel. They and Karen's mother were baptized April 7, 1852. Persecution began immediately, so they sold their farm, valued at $65,000, for half price and left their Island on August 1, 1852, traveling down the Lim Fjorden for about 100 miles in an open boat as far as Aalborg. There they lived for most of a year in a hut outside the city because a cholera epidemic was raging.

They planned to travel with the Forsgren Company in January, 1853. However, while the family remained in Aalborg, Lars returned to their hometown of Jegindo as a missionary.

About a year later in November, 1853, Karen and Lars with their four children, Karen's mother and a hired girl traveled to Copenhagen and then to England en route to America. In Liverpool, Karen's mother became ill and was not allowed to travel. They entrusted two of their children to the care of a woman who did not keep her promise to look after them. They sailed on the ship "Jesse Munn" on January 3, 1854. Karen's mother died so Karen and her family sailed on the next ship, the "Benjamin Adams," on January 22, 1854. Their ship ran out of fresh water and they all nearly died of thirst. On the way, their baby, Christen, died and was buried at sea, a great sorrow to Karen and Lars.

In New Orleans, Louisiana, the hired girl, passed away. They made their way to Kansas City, Missouri, and joined the Hans Peter Olsen Wagon Company. They left Kansas City on June 15, 1854 and reached the Salt Lake Valley on October 5, 1854. Their joy at finding their two children safe in Kansas City was short-lived becaude their five year old daughter died half way across Kansas and was buried at Smokey Hills.

On the trek West they brought a cow along and tied her behind their wagon. The cow was appreciated on the trip as well as in Ephraim, Utah where they settled. They arrived in Ephraim destitute. They had used all of their money to aid many other emigrants to travel to Zion.

Their first home was their wagon, then a dugout which lined the inside fort walls. Karen drove a team to bring rocks to town to build fort walls and homes. They later built a two-room log house and later added two more rooms. The first years were very discouraging; no crops grew because of drought and grasshoppers. Sego lily roots were much sought after to keep them from starving.

Karen and Lars always had new emigrants stay with them until they could erect their own homes. They raised an abandoned Indian baby girl, who lived to be sixteen years of age. Karen loved her very much and had her sealed to them on November 12, 1859.

Karen passed away at eighty-two years of age, some eighteen years after her husband's death.

KAREN MARIE HANSEN POULSEN

No Photo Available

BIRTHDATE: 7 Apr 1820
Slagelse, Soro, Denmark
DEATH: 14 Feb 1888
Levan, Juab Co., Utah
PARENTS: Hans Jensen
Augusta Vilhelmine Maria Hansdatter
PIONEER: 1868
Jessie Smith Co. Wagon Train
SPOUSE: Morten Poulsen
MARRIED: 27 Jan 1843
DEATH SP: 18 Mar 1878

CHILDREN:
Niels Mortensen, 30 Jan 1843
Poul Mortensen, 19 May 1844
Poul Mortensen, 22 Sep 1845 (died as a child)
Peder / Peter Mortensen, 8 Aug 1847
Inger Marie Mortensen, 26 Dec 1849 (died as a child)
Hans Mortensen, 14 Apr 1851
Son, (died when a few weeks old)
Daughter, 13 Nov 1854 (stillbirth)
Son, 6 Dec 1855 (stillbirth)
Son, 7 Dec 1856 (died 3 days after birth)
Daughter, 18 Jan 1858 (stillborn)
Son, 11 Feb 1859 (died 2 days after birth)
Daughter, 20 Feb 1860 (twin - died 2 days after birth)
Son, 20 Feb 1860 (twin - died 2 days after birth)
Daughter, 14 Jul 1861 died soon after birth)
Marie Vilhelmine Mortensen, 29 Aug 1862 (died on day of birth)

Karen Marie and her husband, Hans, joined the Church of Jesus Christ of Latter-day Saints in Denmark. When they decided to leave their home to come to Utah their two oldest sons, Niels and Poul, stayed in Copenhagen, Denmark. Their son Hans came with them. Of the sixteen children born to Karen Marie, only four lived to adulthood.

Both Karen Marie and her husband were tailors. They had always lived in the city and their perfectly tailored suits and the men's tall silk hats set them apart from most of the immigrants.

They crossed the Plains in 1868 with the Jessie Smith Ox-Team Company and settled in Levan, Juab County, Utah. Karen Marie died there at the age of sixty-eight.

BODILLA KATHERINE LARSON POULSON

No
Photo
Available

BIRTHDATE: 3 Oct 1820
Lommaluv, Falster, Denmark
DEATH: Dec 1886
Sanford, Colorado
PARENTS: Peter Larson
Katherine Yorgensen
PIONEER: 30 Sep 1853
John E. Forsgren WAgon Train
SPOUSE: Anders Poulson
MARRIED: 29 Nov 1840
DEATH SP: 28 Nov 1901
Sanford, Conejos, Colorado

CHILDREN:
Ann Katherine (Christensen), 29 Dec 1840
Karen Kjerstena (Christensen Reid), 16 Jun 1844
Neils Peter, 18 Jul 1850
Poil, 20 May 1852
Joseph, 19 Dec 1854
Boletta Lucy (Jensen), 19 Aug 1857
Sarah (Rasmussen Lindburg), 3 Jul 1859
Mary, 29 Sep 1862 (twin)
Martha (Smith), 29 Sep 1862 (twin)

Bodilla Katherine was born in Denmark in 1820. When Bodilla was eleven years old, both parents died the same day of cholera. She worked as a farm helper at various locations until her marriage to Anders Poulson.

After reading a scripture in the Bible and listening to missionaries from the Church of Jesus Christ of Latter-day Saints, they were converted. When it became known their minister demanded they give up their bible, and when they refused they lost their jobs and couldn't get others. So they borrowed money to come to Zion.

While crossing the ocean her ten months old son, Poul, died and was buried at sea. They arrived in the Salt Lake Valley on September 30, 1853.

They lived in Manti; Bodilla gathered greens (pig weeds) off the hill to help with the food that winter. Bodilla loved gardening and always had a beautiful garden.

Anders married two other wives, Andrea Steck in 1863, and Barbara Gosshauer in 1869.

They lived in Manti, Sanpete County, Utah for twenty-seven years then moved to San Luis Valley, Colorado. There was a big celebration when the last of her family joined with them in 1880.

Bodilla was the mother of nine children.

Bodilla passed away in December of 1886, near Sanford Colorado at the age of sixty six.

DORTHEA LARSEN NIELSEN POULSON

BIRTHDATE: 18 Jul 1850
Mosbjerg, Hjorring, Denmark
DEATH: 31 Jan 1911
Redmond, Sevier Co., Utah
PARENTS: Hans Peter Larsen
Marie Larsen
PIONEER: 25 Sep 1868
John G. Holman's Wagon Train
SPOUSE: Peter Nielsen
MARRIED: 9 Aug 1868
On board ship "Emerald Isle"
DEATH SP: 18 Nov 1871
Weber, Utah

CHILDREN:
Elisina Maria, 20 May 1870
Emily Catherine, 6 Mar 1872

SPOUSE: William Poulson
MARRIED: 5 Feb 1872
Salt Lake City, Salt Lake Co., Utah
DEATH SP: 4 Mar 1916
Salt Lake City, Salt Lake Co., Utah

CHILDREN:
Wilhelm Peter, 21 Apr 1874
Sarah Ann, 3 Dec 1875
Johanna Brighamina, 5 Oct 1877
Joseph Francis, 14 Dec 1879
John Lorenzo, 27 Apr 1882
David Ernest, 23 Nov 1883
George Milo, 4 Nov 1884
Moroni Otto, 25 Sep 1886
Mary Alverita, 27 Jun 1889
Albert Nephi , 13 May 1891
Andrew Wilford, 20 May 1893

Dorthea was born in Denmark in 1850. Her only brother was twelve years younger than She.

On Saturday, June 13, 1868, Dorthea boarded the steamship "Hansia" at Copenhagen, Denmark arrivng at Hull, England. She went by train to Liverpool were she boarded the ship " Emerald Isle," June 20, 1868, landing in New York on August 12. Dorthea married Peter Nielsen while onboard the ship "Emerald Isle."

They left New York by rail August 17, arrived in Benton, August 25th, then joined Captain John G. Holman Wagon Company arriving in Salt Lake Valley on September 25, 1868. Dorthea and Peter settled in Sugar House. Their first daughter Eliza Maria was born May 20, 1870, but died on November 11, 1870.

Peter went to Weber County and while there became ill and died November 18, 1871. Dorthea being pregnant again had lost both of her loved ones in a little over a year.

About this time Dorthea met William Poulson. They were married on February 5, 1872. Emily was born March 6, 1872.

William, Dorthea, and Emily moved to Ephraim, Sanpete, Utah where they lived for a year or two then moved to Richmond, Utah. They had eleven children.

William started a salt mine were he worked for days at a time leaving Dorthea the family and farm to see to. When the boys were older they worked at the mine also. The oldest son worked too hard and became ill and died when he was sixteen years old. David E. was only a month old when he died. Making the death of three of the thirteen children Dorthea had.

One day in July, Dorthea was bit by a rattle snake in the field, her leg was always red and sore after that.

Dorthea passed away from stomach cancer on January 31, 1911 at the age of sixty-one.

MARGARETHE KIRSTINE CHRISTENSEN POULSON

BIRTHDATE: 6 Oct 1853
Harbolle, Presto, Denmark
DEATH: 22 Jan 1929
Sanford, Colorado
PARENTS: Frederic Christiansen
Mettie Kirstene Christophersen
PIONEER: 30 Sep 1861
John E. Forsgreen Wagon Train
SPOUSE: Niels Peter Poulson
MARRIED: 3 Dec 1869
DEATH SP: 11 Mar 1918

CHILDREN:
Andrew "P," 6 Aug 1870
Frederick Niels, 22 Oct 1872
Peter David, 20 Oct 1873
Christian Orson, 1 Mar 1875
Joseph Clarence, 13 Sep 1876
Metta Kirstine, 22 Sep 1878
William Francis, 9 Nov 1879
Maggie Maria May (Christensen), 29 Sep 1881
Peter Edwin, 25 Dec 1883
Sarah Kathrine (Mortensen), 3 Jul 1886
Frank George, 11 Apr 1888
Nellie (Peterson), 15 Nov 1889
Eugene Daniel, 8 Sep 1891

Margarethe was born in Denmark in 1853. She was the second of six children. They were all born in Denmark, except her youngest brother who was born on the ocean on January 11, 1861.

Margarethe was eight years old when her family left Denmark to come to Zion. They joined the John E. Forsgren Wagon Company and arrived in the Salt Lake Valley in September, 1861.

Her mother died in 1864. Margarethe helped raise the smaller children.

When she was sixteen years old Margarethe married Niels Peter Poulson on December 3, 1869, in Manti, Sanpete County, Utah. They were the parents of thirteen children. She also cared for an ill husband. She helped provide food for the Southern converts who were not used to the cold weather in the San Luis Valley of Colorado as she was.

Margarethe passed away on January 21, 1929 in Sanford, Conejoies County, Colorado at age seventy-six.

SIDSEL CATHERINE ANDERSON POULSON

BIRTHDATE: 6 Sep 1815
Vejby, Hjorring, Denmark
DEATH: 14 Dec 1878
Richfield, Sevier Co., Utah
PARENTS: Anders Pedersen
Maren Nielsen
PIONEER: July / Aug 1862
Independent Co. Wagon Train
SPOUSE: Peder Jensen Poulson
MARRIED: 12 Jul 1839
Vejby, Hjorring , Denmark
DEATH SP: 6 Jun 1900
Vejby, Hjorring, Denmark

CHILDREN:
Johanne Marie, 29 May 1840
Anders Peter, 8 Jan 1842
Anders, 8 Jun 1843
Poul, 19 Sep 1845
Christian Michael, 24 Mar 1847
Christian Michael, 28 Aug 1848
Niels, 16 Feb 1851
Son (stillborn) 2 4 Mar 1853

Sidsel was born in Denmark in 1815. She married Peder Jensen Poulson on Juy 12, 1839. They were the parents of eight children three of whom died in infancy Sidsel suffered a serious internal injury at the birth of one of her children that left her crippled the rest of her life. But she never ceased to do all she could to help her family and friends.

Sidsel's mother died in 1839. Sidsel's brother J. C. Anderson taught her the trade of tailor, and how to cut and draft her own patterns. There was a very close bond between these two.

Sidsel joined the Church of Jesus Christ of Latter-day Saints in 1859 along with her children but Peder didn't. In April of 1862, Sidsel with four of her children (Johanne, Andrew, Poul, Christian) left Denmark. Because of a Danish law she had to leave her youngest son Niels with her husband.

Peder gave Sidsel suffcent means to make the trip, so they were able to join an independent wagon train to come to the Salt Lake Valley, entering the Valley in July or

August, 1862. They settled in Pleasant Grove, then moved to Richfield.

Sidsel supported herself weaving cloth, carpet, and sewing , especialy mens clothing. Sidsel was loving and kind, industrious and courages. She and Peder never divorced or remarried. Sidsel's concern for her youngest son ceased when Niels, his wife and small daughter joined her in Richfield in 1871 or 1872.

Sidsel passed away of pneumonia on December 17, 1878, at the age of sixty-three.

CAROLINE STRUBELL POULTER

BIRTHDATE: 23 Jan 1820
West Molesey, Surrey, England
DEATH: 7 Nov 1887
Ogden, Weber Co., Utah
PARENTS: Richard Strubell
Mary Ann Davis
PIONEER: 29 Sep 1854
Captain Fields Co.
SPOUSE: William Poulter
MARRIED: 10 Mar 1844
Parish of St. Giles, England
DEATH SP: 7 Mar 1866
Ogden, Weber Co., Utah

CHILDREN:
William, 19 Mar 1845
George, 25 Nov 1846
Ephraim, 11 Mar 1849
Sarah Jane, Oct 1851
Thomas, 19 Jul 1853
Moroni, 6 Jan 1856
Rachel Caroline, 23 Sep 1858
Joseph, 1860

Caroline Strubell was born in England in 1820. She married William Poulter in Parish of St. Giles, London, England on March 10, 1844, and they became the parents of eight children. Caroline was baptized in 1846.

Their small family set sail in 1848 on the ship "Erin Queen." When they got to St. Louis they had to stop, because of lack of funds. In St. Louis they were both stricken with cholera, but their lives were spared. It took them six years of hard labor to obtain a wagon, three oxen, a cow, and the supplies necessary for the journey. They traveled with Captain Field's Company, arriving in the Salt Lake Valley on September 29, 1854.

In 1855, they moved to Ogden, Utah. The winter there was one of the worst ever experienced in Ogden. The night of January 6, 1856, the weather was so terrible that William brought their only milk cow into the house to keep it from freezing. As the cow stood in one corner of the dirt floor room, Caroline gave birth to their sixth child in the opposite corner. The next morning the chickens were frozen on the roost with little icycles hanging from their beaks. Much of the stock froze, and people chopped flesh off the carcasses to keep from starving.

During the summer at harvest time, Caroline would strap her baby on to her back, and glean from the wheat fields. Indians were a problem, but Caroline always fed them.

In 1857, William was just finishing an adobe house for the family when word came that Johnston's Army was en route to Utah. William was sent to Echo Canyon to harass the army. It was bitter cold and for warmth William had only a large woolen shawl that Caroline had spun and wove herself. It was later refered to as "Grandma Poulter's Shawl" by the grandchildren.

During the construction of a larger home for his family, William was killed by a falling tree. Then it was necessary for Caroline to do everything she could to make a living; housework, weaving cloth, making soap, caring for sick, etc.

Caroline was a widow for twenty-one years before she passed away in 1867 of pneunomia in Ogden, Weber County, Utah.

MARY ELIZABETH JACKSON POULTER

BIRTHDATE: 22 Jul 1851
Macclesfield, England
DEATH: 12 Aug l933
Odgen, Weber Co., Utah
PARENTS: Aaron Jackson
Elizabeth Horrocks
PIONEER: 30 Nov 1856
Martin Handcart Company
SPOUSE: George Poulter
MARRIED: 9 Feb 1874
Salt Lake City, Salt Lake, Utah
DEATH SP: 8 Jun 1922
Ogden, Weber Co., Utah

CHILDREN:
George Aaron, 4 Feb 1875
Grace Elizabeth, 5 Mar 1877
Claude Jackson, 4 Nov 1879
William Richard, 30 Aug 1882
Martha Caroline, 3 Nov 1885
Mary Frances, 17 Aug 1888

Mary Elizabeth Jackson was born in Macclesfield, Chestershire, England in 1851. She was four years old when she left England with her parents on the ship "Horizon."

In Iowa they joined with a handcart company to cross the Plains, and Mary Elizabeth had to walk most of the way. Because of the hardships of the trip, and an illness, her father passed away and was buried in the snow. The ground was too frozen to dig a grave. The handcart company had to be rescued by men and teams from Salt Lake City.

Upon arriving in the Salt Lake Valley they continued on to Ogden, Utah to make their home.

Mary Elizabeth started school in a little one-room adobe building. There were only wooden benches to sit on. No paper or pencils, but only broken slates for some of the children. She was taught reading, writing, and spelling from Webster's Spelling Book. In those days when you learned enough, you could teach others, which she did for three or four years.

In 1874, Mary Elizabeth married George Poulter in the Endowment House. They were the parents of six children. She opened a small store in her home to support George when he was called on a mission.

Sunday was always a family affair in the Poulter home. They spent Saturday cleaning and pressing clothing, shining shoes, and preparing for the Sabbath. She had a great testimony of the Gospel of Jesus Christ.

Mary Elizabeth passed away on August 12, 1933, at her home in Ogden. Her husband passed away in 1922, also in Ogden, Weber County, Utah.

ANE OR HANNAH DORTHEA ANDERSON POWELL

No Photo Available

BIRTHDATE: 7 Mar 1818
Raunsvad, Ikast, Denmark
DEATH: 4 Aug 1899
Lehi, Utah Co., Utah
PARENTS: Anders Westesen
Karen Svendsen / Swensen
PIONEER: Fall of 1854
Company unknown
SPOUSE: James Q. Powell
MARRIED: 1 Mar 1857
Salt Lake City, Salt Lake, Utah
DEATH SP: 4 Dec 1891
Lehi, Utah Co., Utah

CHILDREN:
Susanah Anderson, 27 Jan 1859
Benjamin Theodore, 27 Mar 1863

Ane or Hannah Dorthea Anderson was born in Denmark in 1819. She was baptized into the Church of Jesus Christ of Latter-day Saints on April 28, 1852 in the Lolland Conference, Denmark, and sailed from Liverpool in 1854.

She arrived in New Orleans, then came up the Mississippi River to St. Louis. It is not known which company she came across the Plains with.

Ane (sometimes known as Anna Dorothy Anderson), was sealed to James Quaintance Powell, March 1, 1857, in the Endowment House, as his third wife. They had two children, both born in Lehi, Utah County, Utah. She was known to be an excellent cook.

Ane passed away in Lehi, Utah County, Utah in 1899.

ANN TONGUE POWELL

BIRTHDATE: 9 Sep 1820
Clifton, Notts, England
DEATH: 4 Dec 1902
Upton, Summit Co., Utah
PARENTS: Richard Tongue
Bethia Francis
PIONEER: Fall of 1866
Wagon Train Company
SPOUSE: Edward Powell
MARRIED: 27 Apr 1846
Clifton, Notts, England
DEATH SP: 24 May 1898
Upton, Summit Co., Utah

CHILDREN:
John, 6 Feb 1847
Henry, 22 Jan 1849
Edward, 5 Dec 1850
William, 18 Dec 1852
Richard, 1 Feb 1855
Joseph Frederick, 23 Apr 1857
Bethia, 26 Apr 1859

Ann Tongue was born in England in 1820. She married Edward Powell in England and they were the parents of seven children, all of them born in England.

The family was converted to the gospel of the Church of Jesus Christ of Latter-day Saints in England, and emigrated to America on the ship 'St. Mark" in 1866. After reaching the United States, they traveled by train to Omaha, then by ox-team to the Salt Lake Valley, arriving in the fall of 1866.

They built their first home in Coalville, Utah, then later moved to Upton, ten miles east of Coalville. Here they homesteaded a farm at a place called Huff Creek. Their second son, Henry, was killed by lightning while they were living there. They lived in a little old log house where one end was living quarters, and the other part was a hay shed and a place for horses. They were always strict about having prayers every morning.

Ann was slightly heavy-set but not overly fleshy. She had a fiery disposition. She always took care of the house and did little outside work. They spent their life farming in Huff Creek.

Edward passed away in 1898, and Ann passed away in 1902, both in the little house at Huff Creek, Summit County, Utah. Ann was eighty years old.

ELIZABETH HARRIS POWELL

BIRTHDATE: 12 Oct 1821
Llanover, Gwent, Wales
DEATH: 6 Jan 1890
Payson, Utah Co., Utah
PARENTS: John Harris
Elizabeth Harris
PIONEER: 26 Sep 1856
Edmond Ellsworth Company
SPOUSE I: John Powell
MARRIED: 15 Nov 1840
Wales
DEATH SP: 9 Oct 1856
Salt Lake City, Salt Lake, Utah

CHILDREN:
William, 28 Jan 1841
Mary Ann, 2 Nov 1843
Joseph, 6 Jan 1845 (died at age 5)
Margaret, 12 Mar 1848
Elizabeth, 6 Aug 1849
Hannah Susan, 6 May 1851
Sarah Ann, 16 Apr 1855 (died at age 1)
David, 2 Mar 1856

SPOUSE II: James Butler
MARRIED: 1858 Later divorced
DEATH SP:

CHILDREN:
John James, 28 Dec 1859
Emma Jane, 25 Jan 1861

Elizabeth was born in Wales in 1821. She spent her childhood with her grandparents on a farm, while her parents went to England to find work. In 1840, she married John Powell who had come to work in Wales. He was a stonecutter.

They moved to Blaenavon and became acquainted with the Huish family who were members of the Church of Jesus Christ of Latter-day Saints. John and Elizabeth were converted and baptized in 1850. They kept an open house for the missionaries, and Elizabeth cooked for them and mended their clothes. She was the mother of eight children born in Wales.

The Powell family sailed from Liverpool on the ship "Enoch Train" in 1856. At Council Bluffs they joined a handcart company under Edmond Ellsworth, and walked all the way to the Salt Lake Valley, arriving in September, 1856. John started to work on the temple as a stonecutter, but after only two days work he took very sick with the Black Canker and died just two weeks after reaching Salt Lake City.

Elizabeth was now a widow with six children in a stange new land. She sold her handcart to buy food which was very scarce and of little variety, mostly cabbage, bran bread and toasted bran coffee. She was a good seamstress and learned to make gloves, and did some tailoring for prominent people in the city.

In the fall of 1857, she moved to Payson, Utah, and the next year married James Butler, by whom she had two children. She divorced him because he was mean and abusive. She refused to let her two children be called by his name, and she also took back the name of Powell.

After the children were all married she lived alone. Elizabeth developed cataracts on her eyes and spent her few remaining years in semi-darkness. She passed away in 1890 in Payson, Utah County, Utah.

ELIZABETH JANE CARTER POWELL

BIRTHDATE: 29 Aug 1833
Adams Co., Illinois
DEATH: 5 Oct 1918
Rye Valley, Baker, Oregon
PARENTS: Reuben M. Carter
Rachel Ann Campbell
PIONEER: 5 Oct 1852
John B. Walker Co. Wagon Train
SPOUSE: James Evans Powell
MARRIED: 14 Sep 1852
Independence Rock, Wyoming
DEATH SP: 9 Mar 1906
Huntington, Baker Co., Oregon

CHILDREN:
James William, 8 Aug 1853
Savilla Jane, 14 Aug 1854
Mary Elizabeth, 10 Feb 1857
David Levi, 27 Jun 1859
Francis Marion, 30 Jan 1861
Joseph Russell, 9 Nov 1863
Rachel Melissa, 12 Sep 1865
Julia Etta, 23 Oct 1866
Cornelia, 11 Sep 1869
John Eli, 6 Jul 1871
Reuben Eugene, 30 Oct 1872
Arminda Celia, 1 Jul 1877
Laura Eliza, 16 Aug 1877 (twin)
Lowa, 16 Aug 1877 (twin - died as an infant)

Elizabeth Jane was born in Illinois in 1833. Along with her parents and siblings she was driven out of Nauvooo by the mobs. They stayed at Winter Quarters for two years, gathering provisions to cross the Plains. They joined with the John B. Walker Wagon Company to come West.

This is where she met James Evans Powell. He had made several trips across the Plains, driving teams and helping the immigrants. As the journey wore on so did the fondness of James for Elizabeth. They were married at Independence Rock in Wyoming in September, 1852, before entering the Salt Lake Valley.

They settled at first in the Salt Lake Valley, but since James was gone for long periods of time helping other companies along the trail, Elizabeth was alone most of the time. She kept herself busy milking cows, planting or harvesting, spinning yarn or weaving cloth, and caring for her family's needs.

In 1853, they were called to the Provo, Utah, area where several children were born. James also rode for the Pony Express, and on one of his rides to California he was attacked by Indians and received arrow wounds in his hip and leg. He was laid up for six months.

The family lived in Parowan, Kanosh, and Monroe, Utah. About the time her last children, twins, were born, James contemplated taking a second wife. She was Sarah Carter, (Sally), a sister of Elizabeth's. Elizabeth objected very strenuously, and said she would move to Rye Velley in Oregon, where her son was living. James did not go through with his plans for a second marriage, and instead went with Elizabeth to Oregon. This is where they lived the remainder of their lives.

James passed away in 1906, and Elizabeth passed away in 1918, both in Huntington, Baker County, Oregon.

FANNY CHAMBERLAIN POWELL

BIRTHDATE: 14 Oct 1820
Bamstables, Devonshire, England
DEATH: 18 Aug 1872
Fillmore, Millard Co., Utah
PARENTS: James Chamberlain
Betsy Decker
PIONEER: 20 Sep 1856
Knute Peterson Co. Wagon Train
SPOUSE: John Powell
MARRIED: 13 Nov 1842
London, Middlesex, England
DEATH SP: 3 Jun 1902
Fillmore, Millard Co., Utah

CHILDREN:
Mary Ann, 16 Sep 1843
Fanny Louisa, 16 Jul 1845
John, 14 Sep 1847 (died at age 4)
Jessie, 3 Jun 1849
Mercy Mae, 15 May 1852 (died at age 1)
Samuel, 20 Apr 1855 (died as an infant)
Ephraim, 13 Oct 1856 (died as an infant)
Elizabeth "Bessie," 5 Nov 1858
Alice Jane, 15 Jun 1862 (died at 6 months)

Fanny's family moved to London when she was quite young. Her family were aristocrats so she and her sisters were privileged to attend a private girl's school.

She met John Powell while attending the Church of England. They were married at her home on November 13, 1842. They had three children while they were living on Bethel Green Road in London.

A friend of Fanny's loaned her a copy of "The Voice of Warning" which left her with a desire to know more. Fanny and John joined Church of Jesus Christ of Latter-day Saints on May 7, 1848.

They left Liverpool on January 1, 1851 and crossed the ocean on the ship, "Ellen." After landing in New Orleans, they steamed up Mississippi on the "Alleck" to St. Louis.

There was a great epidemic of cholera and they suffered much sickness on their way. She helped to nurse and care for many who were ill. She nursed a Mrs. Gasquin. As she was dying, she asked Fanny to raise her youngest child, Tho Gasquin as a part of her family. When they arrived in St. Louis, John found work in a bedstead factory to earn money to finance the remainder of their trip across the Plains.

At the request of their bishop, they took in a twenty-four year old girl, Henrietta Blyth, from Scotland. She was able to provide much help for Fanny. They left St. Louis with the Knute Peterson Wagon Company and arrived in the Salt Lake Valley on September 20, 1856.

They stayed in Salt Lake City for two years before they decided to settle in Fillmore. They first moved into a dugout which was completely ruined by a cloudburst. Neighbors helped them build an adobe home.

In 1860, they moved to help build a dam on the Sevier River in a town they named Deseret. Fanny was the first school teacher of Deseret. In 1863, when the dam washed out for the second time, they moved back to Fillmore. A year later, they moved to Cedar Springs (Holden) where John built a school. Fanny started teaching school in her home until the school was finished. She was paid mostly in farm products.

Fanny and John were both highly motivated to have their children well educated. Fanny worked among the sick and did all the good she could to help others. She was loved by all who knew her.

HANNAH MATILDA SNYDER POWELL

BIRTHDATE: 26 Feb 1847
Winter Quarters, Nebraska
DEATH: 7 Dec 1877
Salem, Utah Co., Utah
PARENTS: Robert Snyder
Almeda Melissa Livermore
PIONEER: 20 Sep 1848
Isaac Morley Co. Wagon Train
SPOUSE: John Ammon Powell
MARRIED: 13 Dec 1863
Kamas, Summit Co., Utah
DEATH SP: 14 Dec 1928
Salt Lake City, Salt Lake, Utah

CHILDREN:
John Ammon Jr., 4 Oct 1864
Mariah, 18 May 1867
Almeda Matilda, 29 Sep 1869
James, 14 Mar 1872
Leah Theresa, 23 Aug 1874
Robert Augustus, 4 Jun 1877

Hannah Matilda was born at Winter Quarters, Nebraska in 1847. She came to the Utah Territory with her parents in 1848 at the age of one year. They arrived on September 20, 1848.

Hannah Matilda married John Ammon Powell in Kamas, Utah in 1863, and they had six children.

She suffered from poor health most of her life. She passed away at an early age, leaving six children, from thirteen years to a baby, six months old. Hannah Matilda died in Salem, Utah County, Utah.

Her mother, Almeda Snyder, took the baby and raised him until he was eight years old, then his father came and took him to Price, Utah were he was living. This event nearly broke the Snyder's hearts, to have the child taken away from them.

JEMIMA WIMMER POWELL

BIRTHDATE: 14 Mar 1815
Hamilton Co., Ohio
DEATH: 13 Dec 1893
Price, Carbon Co., Utah
PARENTS: Peter Wimmer
Elizabeth Shirley Wimmer
PIONEER: 15 Sep 1852
Robert Weimer Wagon Train
SPOUSE: James Powell
MARRIED: 6 Oct 1833
Henry Co., Indiana
DEATH SP: 22 Jul 1856
Ogden, Weber Co., Utah

CHILDREN:
Elizabeth, 10 Mar 1835
Peter, 11 Jan 1838
Robert A., 13 Oct 1839
Simeon Comfort, 4 Sep 1842
John Ammon, 27 Nov 1844
Malinda, 13 Oct 1847
Martha Ellen, 13 Jan 1849
James, 25 Mar 1852
Abraham, 15 Jul 1855

Jemima's family was living in Hamilton County in Ohio at the time of her birth. Jemima married James Powell in Henry County, Indiana. They became members of the Church of Jesus Christ of Latter-day Saints and loved working on all church assignments. They were also called upon to make many moves with other members of the Church and experienced terrible persecutions through Missouri and Nauvoo.

Her husband, James, was beaten on his head with a gun by a mobster in Randolph County, Missouri. This left the left side of his body paralyzed and he suffered from seizures the rest of his life. Her eighth child was only four months old when they began their journey across the Plains with the Robert Weimer Wagon Company. They arrived in Salt Lake Valley on September 15, 1852.

They moved to Ogden where her ninth child was born. James was crossing the Weber River on his horse when he took a seizure, fell off his horse, and was drowned. They found his body the next day and Jemima had him buried in Ogden Cemetery.

Jemima took her children to Springville to be near her parents. After her mother died, she moved up to Summit County where she lived with her son, John Ammon.

Jemima served as a midwife and nursed the sick when called upon. She loved to cook, sew, and help people. When they were having trouble with Indians in Summit County, she moved her children to Salem, Utah.

Her greatest attribute was her ability to overcome the trials she had to endure in her life. She served her church faithfully and was a visiting teacher until her death.

Near the end of her life, she had moved to Price to be near her children, so her death occurred in Price, Utah. She was buried in the Salem Cemetery.

MARIA MOUSLEY POWELL

BIRTHDATE: 25 Mar 1819
Aldridge, Staffordshire, England
DEATH: 4 Jun 1903
Glenwood, Sevier Co., Utah
PARENTS: John Lunn
Elizabeth Mousley
PIONEER: 20 Sep 1864
Joseph S. Rawlins Wagon Train
SPOUSE: George Powell
MARRIED: 26 Feb 1837
Aldridge, Staffordshire, England
DEATH SP: 3 Feb 1893
Glenwood, Sevier Co., Utah

CHILDREN:
Emma, 1 Mar 1838
Ann, 2 Jun 1840
Edward, 12 Dec 1842 (died at 5 months)
Lucy, 1 May 1844 (died at age 2)
Margaret, 8 May 1847
Eliza, 12 Apr 1849 (died at age 8)
Rachel, 18 Nov 1851
Charles, 16 Jul 1854

Maria Mousley was born March 25, 1819 at Aldridge, Staffordshire, England to Elizabeth Mousley. Her father was John Lunn. Her mother married Thomas Gould when Maria was five years old.

Maria married George Powell who worked as a groomsman and shepherd to a wealthy Lord. Later he worked in a foundry and the coal mines to support his family. They became converted and baptized into the Church of Jesus Christ of Latter-day Saints by Elder George Hill. They were active in the missionary efforts in England.

The family desired to emigrate to America, but money was scarce. Her daughter , Emma, and her husband, Edward Payne, were leaving for America in 1863. George decided to go with them and work in the coal mines to earn money which would enable the rest of his family to join them in America.

Still in England, Maria worked day and night at her profession as a seamstress trying to support her family and save some money to help pay for their emigration. With some assistance from the Perpetual Immigration Fund of the Church, they were finally able to sail from Liverpool.

After they landed in New York, they traveled by rail to Omaha, Nebraska where they stayed to make preparations for the trip across the Plains. Maria supervised the making of wagon covers, tents, etc. Maria had sprained her ankle badly and could not walk, but she did all she could to care for the children and the daily chores. They arrived in the Salt Lake Valley on September 20, 1864 with the Joseph S. Rawlins Wagon Company.

They arrived in Heber City on October 20, 1864 where they lived in a one-room log house with another family. In the summer of 1866, Maria and George moved to Glenwood where the Indians were still quite troublesome.

Most people were forced to relocate to Fountain Green for three or four years. When they returned to Glenwood, they were active in the United Order for the years it was practiced. Maria was a dressmaker and sewed clothing by hand. She made burial clothing and many quilts. She brought quilt patterns from England and taught the art of quilt making to many of the sisters.

Maria served as a counselor and secretary in the Relief Society for many years. She was also a teacher in the Sunday School. She and her husband traveled to the Manti Temple several times to do temple work for their kindred dead. Maria was a widow for ten years before she died at the age of eighty-six in Glenwood, Utah.

MARY JANE COOPER POWELL

BIRTHDATE: 25 Oct 1810
Salisbury, Pennsyvania
DEATH: 16 May 1893
Lehi, Utah Co., Utah
PARENTS: Robert Cooper
Jane Marshall
PIONEER: 20 Sep 1848
Zera Pulsipher Co. Wagon Train
SPOUSE: James Q. Powell
MARRIED: Sep 1841
Philadelphia, Pennsylvania
DEATH SP: 4 Dec 1891
Lehi, Utah Co., Utah

CHILDREN:
Isaac, 2 Aug 1842 (died in 1847)
Naomi, 16 Aug 1844
James 15 Jun 1846 (died in 1847)
Augustus Napoleon, 1 Aug 1851
Thaddeus, 30 Sep 1854

Mary Jane Cooper was born in Salisbury, Lancaster County, Pennsyvania in 1810. Her parents died early in life, leaving Mary and seven siblings to be reared by their grandparents.

She married James Quaintance Powell in Senpenber, 1841. James had previously been married to Susanna Charlston, who died in 1840, leaving him with four children; Mary J., Albert, Ann, and William. James's mother, Tamsen Quaintance Powell, lived with James and Mary until her death in 1842, when they sold her farm and purchased another one near Nauvoo, Illinois. James's son, William, died in 1843, and two of Mary's children died in 1847.

After they were forced from Nauvoo by the mobs they joined with the company of Zera Pulsipher to come West. During the journey Albert disappeared, and was never heard of again. The rest of the family arrived in the Salt Lake Valley in September, 1848.

Mary was an excellent homemaker. Her husband had a herd of sheep, and she carded and spun the wool, and made cloth for their clothes. She had a garden and fruit trees, and loved to grow flowers. She was ever mindful of the sufferings of others.

Mary was active in Relief Society as a teacher and counselor. They lived for a while at the Point of the Mountain, then moved to Lehi, in Utah County in 1854. In 1857, James took a third wife, a Danish convert, Anna Dorothy Anderson, and by her had two more children.

Mary Jane passed away in Lehi, Utah in 1893.

SARAH JANE SHIELDS PLUM POWELL

BIRTHDATE: 29 Sep 1854
Pajaro, Monterey, California
DEATH: 5 Jan 1932
Price, Carbon Co., Utah
PARENTS: John Fenton Shields
Mary Howell
PIONEER: 1862
From California to Utah
SPOUSE: Jeremiah Plumb
MARRIED: 24 Jan 1870
Salt Lake Endowment House
DEATH SP: 20 Nov 1871
Salem, Utah Co., Utah

CHILDREN:
Mary Elizabeth, 6 Feb 1871
SPOUSE: John Ammon Powell
MARRIED: 6 Jan 1873
Salt Lake City, Salt Lake Co., Utah
DEATH SP: 5 Jan 1932
Price, Carbon Co., Utah

CHILDREN:
Sarah Jane, 13 Dec 1874
Lot Fenton, 14 Apr 1876
Florence Edith, 30 Sep 1878

Martha, 1 Dec 1880
Abraham, 6 Mar 1882
Joseph F., 1 Feb 1884
Pearl, 24 Nov 1886
Perse, 24 Nov 1886
Zoe Ellen, 6 Dec 1888
Earl, 6 May 1891
Hazel, 15 Aug 1893
Frank Irving, 12 Nov 1894 (died as an infant)
Jody, (living)

Sarah Jane's parents had been converted to the Church of Jesus Christ of Latter-day Saints and had arrived in the Great Salt Lake Valley with the John Brown Wagon Company in 1851. They were sent on to Pajaro, California to settle. It was in Pajaro that Sarah Jane was born. Sarah was eight years old when they were called to return to the Salt Lake Valley. She rode horseback most of the journey to help drive the cattle and keep them near the covered wagon. Her father bought a farm in Salem, Utah. In this thriving community, Sarah Jane grew up and attended school.

Sarah Jane married Jeremiah Plumb in the Endowment House in Salt Lake City. They had a beautiful little daughter who was nine months old when her father contracted typhoid fever and died. Sarah Jane helped her father on the farm doing many chores to earn enough to support her daughter and maintain her home.

Three years later, Sarah Jane became the second wife of John Ammon Powell. His first wife died five years later, leaving her six children in Sarah Jane's care. Fifteen children were born to this union. Only six lived to maturity. Several children died of Typhoid Fever and Jody was drowned in the Price River.

In 1879, John Ammon Powell and Sarah Jane rode horseback to Castle Valley. She was the first white woman to arrive in Price. They took up several homesteads in this area where the city of Price now stands. John freighted hauling supplies when the railroad was being built. Sarah Jane sold butter, eggs, milk, and cheese to feed the workers. Sarah Jane was a midwife and nurse, attending to many of the births in Price and surrounding areas.

She was a prominent figure, helping to build and develop the community. She served a number of years as first and second counselor in the Relief Society and was president of the Relief Society for eight years. She organized the Daughters of Utah Pioneers in Price. Her home was a stopping place for many people who came to Price for supplies that had come by railroad.

Sarah Jane passed away at her home in Price at the age of seventy-seven.

THURZA ANN POWELL POWELL

BIRTHDATE: 13 Apr 1835
Bradpole, England
DEATH: 31 Dec 1910
Salt Lake City, Utah
PARENTS: Thomas Powell
Mary Hodder Powell
PIONEER: 20 Sep 1864
John D. Chase Indep. Wagon Co.
SPOUSE: Joseph Powell
MARRIED: 13 Jun 1853
Allington, England
DEATH: 9 Mar 1925
Salt Lake City, Utah

CHILDREN:
Stillborn (boy), 1 Mar 1854
Mary Elizabeth, 9 Nov 1855
Emma Jane, 15 Sep 1857
Ellen Lovina, 3 Jan 1863
William Joseph, 2 Jan 1869
Thurza May, 2 May 1873

Thurza was born in England in 1835. She was the eighth of nine children. Most of Thurza's family joined the Church in 1847.

Thurza married Joseph Powell in 1853. One year later they sailed for Liverpool, on the ship "Windermere" to America. During a terrible storm at sea, Thurza gave birth to a stillborn baby. They had to bury him at sea. They were short on water and food when they reached New Orleans, after two months of sailing.

Thurza and Joseph lived in Council Bluffs, Iowa and Venice, Illinois. They arrived in the Salt Lake Valley in 1864, with Chase's Independent Mule Train. She brought two children with her; she had buried three children.

Thurza lived most of her life in Salt Lake City except for a brief time in 1896, when they moved to Castle Valley to help settle Desert Lake and help to build the Buckhorn Dam. It was a hard struggle. The dam broke and many had a narrow escape. Their farms were left swampy and the water unfit. Thurza and her family moved back to Salt Lake She had had a hard life. She died in 1910, at the age of ninety. She was remembered as a sweet, loving person.

ADELIA ANN BISHOP PRATT

BIRTHDATE: 5 Nov 1826
Crown Point, Essex, New York
DEATH: 29 Dec 1913
Salt Lake City, Salt Lake, Utah
PARENTS: John Fitch Bishop
Lucy Goff
PIONEER: Fall of 1851
Orson Pratt Co. Wagon Train
SPOUSE: Orson Pratt
MARRIED: 13 Dec 1844
Nauvoo, Hancock Co., Illinois
DEATH SP: 3 Oct 1881
Salt Lake City, Salt Lake, Utah

CHILDREN:
Lucy Adelia, 15 Sep 1847
Elzina, 26 Feb 1851
Lorum, 27 Nov 1855 (twin)
Lorus, 27 Nov 1855 (twin)
Eltha, 12 Dec 1858
Orthena, 31 Oct 1863

Adelia Ann was born in New York State in 1826. At the age of sixteen she had a strange dream where her deceased father came to her and said, "There is a here-after. I want you to prepare for it." Soon after, her mother met with missionaries from the Church of Jesus Christ of Latter-day Saints and was converted. Also Adelia Ann was baptized and came with her mother and other siblings to Nauvoo, Hancock County, Illinois.

In Nauvoo, Adelia Ann and her sister, Charlotte, both married Orson Pratt as plural wives in 1844. Charlotte was twenty years old and Adelia Ann was seventeen at the time. Charlotte abandoned the arrangement within a few months, but Adelia remained faithful all her life to her husband, who had a total of ten wives.

Adelia's first baby was born in Winter Quarters, and the second was born while Orson was on a mission to England. They came to the Salt Lake Valley in the Fall of 1851.

Times were difficult for Adelia and many other of the plural wives. In 1856, Brigham Young again sent Orson to England, so Adelia took her little family and moved to Tooele for a time. They lived on pig weeds, dandelion roots, sego lily bulbs, and on what they could borrow. Yet she never became bitter or let her testimony waver during all that time.

Her son, Lorus, became a well-known painter, who studied his art in Paris, France. He painted some of the murals in the Salt Lake Temple. Her daughter, Orthena, married well, and became one of wealthiest women in Salt Lake City. Adelia read many books, loved to go to the Salt Lake Theater, and loved to wear stylish clothes. Her favorite hobby was collecting new 'bonnets'.

Adelia Ann passed away in Salt Lake City, Utah on December 29, 1913.

ANN AGATHA WALKER PRATT

BIRTHDATE: 11 Jun 1829
Leek, Staffordshire, England
DEATH: 25 Jun 1908
Ogden, Weber Co., Utah
PARENTS: William G. Walker
Mary Godwin
PIONEER: 28 Sep 1847
Parley P. Pratt Company
SPOUSE I: Parley P. Pratt
MARRIED: 28 Apr 1847
Winter Quarters, Nebraska
DEATH SP: 13 May 1857
Van Buren, Crawford, Arkansas

CHILDREN:
Agatha, 7 Jul 1848
Malona, 15 Apr 1850
Marion, 28 Nov 1851
Moroni Walker, 10 Oct 1853
Evelyn, 8 Aug 1856

SPOUSE II: Joseph Harris Ridges
MARRIED: 4 Mar 1860
Salt Lake City, Salt Lake Co., Utah
DEATH SP: 7 Mar 1914
Salt Lake City, Salt Lake Co., Utah

CHILDREN:
Louie, 4 Aug 1861
Wilford Owen, 5 Sep 1866

Ann Agatha was born in England in 1829, of educated and refined parents. Her mother was the town milliner, and her father was a teacher and bookkeeper. By the time she was six she had read the Bible and many other books.

The family was living in Manchester, England when they heard the missionaries, among them Parley P. Pratt. They accepted the gospel and Ann Agatha was baptized as a member of the Church of Jesus Christ of Latter-day Saints on July 9, 1843.

When these missionaries returned to America in Jan 1847, Ann Agatha, age seventeen went with them. They sailed on the ship "America," and were very comfortable on the voyage. They chartered the second cabin and hired the ship's cook to prepare their meals.

Ann Agatha married Parley P. Pratt at Winter Quarters. She was his tenth wife, and came with his company to the Salt Lake Valley. Ann Agatha and Belinda Marden Pratt, his sixth wife, drove an ox-team together across the Plains, arriving in the Salt Lake Valley in September, 1847. She had five children by Elder Pratt.

Ann Agatha cooked for the men who were making a road through Parley's Canyon. She was also a milliner, like her mother, and made both women's and men's hats, some for the apostles and Brigham Young and their wives. She was an ardent church worker, serving twice as Relief Society President. She also sang in the Tabernacle Choir.

When Apostle Pratt was killed on his mission to Arkansas in 1857, Ann Agatha was twenty-eight years old. She married Joseph Ridges three years later and had two children by him. She later discontinued living with Ridges and moved to Ogden, Utah.

Ann Agatha passed away in Ogden in 1908, and is buried in Salt Lake City, Utah.

HANNAHETTE SNIVELY PRATT

BIRTHDATE: 22 Oct 1812
Woodstock, Shenandoh, Virginia
DEATH: 21 Feb 1898
Salt Lake City, Salt Lake, Utah
PARENTS: Henry Snively
Mary Heavnor
PIONEER: 25 Sep 1847
SPOUSE: Parley P. Pratt
MARRIED; 2 Nov 1844
Nauvoo, Hancock Co., Illinois
DEATH SP: 13 May 1857
Van Buren, Crawford, Arkansas

CHILDREN:
Alma, 31 Jul 1845
Lucy (Russell), 9 Mar 1848
Henriette (Russell), 26 Oct 1851

Hannahette was born in Virginia, in 1812. Hannahette was converted to the Church of Jesus Christ of Latter-day Saints by Erastus Snow.

With money from their father's estate, Hannahette and her sister Susan built a cozy brick home in Nauvoo. When cholera broke out this home became a veritable hospital for all who were in need of assistance.

Hannahette married Parley P. Pratt on November 2, 1844, in the Nauvoo Temple by Brigham Young. She was tall, of fair complexion, deep blue eyes and a sunny disposition, serene and humble demeanor. Her home was a haven of rest for many.

She went through the winter of 1846-1847 at Winter Quarters, arriving in Salt Lake Valley with her infant son on September 25, 1847.

She was the first white woman to settle in the Big Field. She built a two-story adobe home. Indians would often come to the adobe house.

In later years she made her home with family at 16 South and 4th West. Her room became the most interesting room in the house, especially at Christmas time. Here they told stories, sang and played games while Hannahette sewed.

She was active and energetic to the end. She wasn't a person to brood or complain.

Hannahette passed away on February 21, 1898 in her eighty-fifth year.

LOUISA BARNES PRATT

BIRTRHDATE: 10 Nov 1802
Warwick, Massachusetts
DEATH: 8 Sep 1880
Beaver, Utah
PARENTS: Willard Barnes
Dolly Stevens
PIONEER: Sep 1848
Brigham Young Wagon Train
SPOUSE: Addison Pratt
MARRIED: 3 Apr 1831
Durham, Canada
DEATH SP: 14 Oct 1872
Anaheim, Orange Co., California

CHILDREN:
Ellen Saphronia (McGary Coombs), 6 Feb 1832
Frances Stevens (Dyer), 7 Nov 1834
Lois Barnes (Hunt), 6 Mar 1837
Ann Louise (Willis), 6 Apr 1840
Ephriam Pratt, (adopted son)

Louisa was born in Warwick, Massachusetts, in 1802, one of eight children of Willard Barnes and Dolly Stevens Barnes. In 1810, she moved with her family to Dunham, Canada. There she attended school, was an excellent scholar and became a school teacher at an early age, often living away from home. She learned tailoring and set up her own business making men's clothing.

Louisa married Addison Pratt on April 3, 1831. They lived in Buffalo, New York, where Addison took a job sailing on the lake trade. They decided to farm at Ripley, New York. In 1837, they were converted and baptized into the Mormon Church.

They sold their farm and traveled to the New Zion in Missouri. Because of the expulsion of the Saints from that state, they stopped at Pleasant Gardens and then to Nauvoo, Illinois. Addison was called on a mission to the South Seas and Louisa was left to build a home in Nauvoo, take care of herself and her children. When the Saints were driven from Nauvoo she and her children made the trip across the Plains.

Louisa met her husband, Addison, in the Salt Lake Valley after a five and one-half years absence. Louisa had passed through many trials during that period. She had scurvy at Winter Quarters. She received only enough from their farm to get a wagon, oxen and a few supplies. She was given fifty dollars in Church aid during all the time that she was a missionary widow.

No sooner had Addison settled his family in the Salt Lake Valley in the 'Old Fort' he was called to return to the Society Islands. This time Louisa and her daughters joined Addison in the Islands. She learned enough of the new language to teach the women and children the gospel, and to teach English. When they finished their mission they settled in San Bernardino, California, Addison was called on a third and then a fourth mission to Tahiti. Again, Louisa was on her own financially.

They were called back to Utah to help defend against Johnston's Army. Louisa and her sister decided to settle in Beaver, Utah. Again she started over. She taught school in her own home. A garden, cow, pig and chickens and, eventually, some cattle on the range became her livelihood.

When her husband was released from his mission he went to live with their daughter, Frances. Louisa was again a "worse than widow," as she called it. She sold books, subscriptions to the Women's Exponent and taught school. Her three oldest grand-daughters attended her school and enjoyed her help with any project. She taught them to sew and introduced them to good books.

Louisa sold some of her cattle and made a trip by train to see her family in Canada. Although she was not able to convert any of them she felt it was a very worthwhile experience.

Louisa passed away in Beaver, Utah on September 8, 1880. She had traveled far and given much to the faith they had chosen. She left homes, sailed the seas, supported herself and her children against all odds and stayed true to her faith. Her descendants honor her name.

MARY ANN FROST STEARNS PRATT

BIRTHDATE: 14 Jan 1808/1809
Bethel, Maine
DEATH: 24 Aug 1891
Pleasant Grove, Utah Co., Utah
PARENTS: Aaron Frost
Susan Gray
PIONEER: Sep 1852
Harmon Cutler Co. Wagon Train
SPOUSE: Nathan Stearns
MARRIED: 1 Apr 1831
Bethel, Maine
DEATH SP: Dec 1832

CHILD:
Mary Ann Stearns, 25 Apr 1833

SPOUSE II: Parley Parker Pratt
MARRIED: 9 May 1837
DEATH SP: Not given

CHILDREN:
Nathan, 31 Aug 1838
Olivia, 2 Jun 1841
Susan, 17 Apr 1843
Moroni, 7 Dec 1844

After nearly two happy years of married life, Mary Ann was left a widow with a five month old daughter. In August, 1836, Brigham Young with five others of his Quorum came through Vermont, New Hampshire, and held a conference in Bethel, Maine. Many were converted and baptized at this time. Mary Ann was one of them.

Mary Ann prepared to make the journey with the little company which was returning with the elders. When she arrived in Kirtland, she and her little girl boarded for a time with Hyrum Smith's Family.

On May 9, 1837, in New York, Mary Ann was married to Apostle Parley Parker Pratt who was widowed with a small son. She and Parley had four children. They had experiences of great joy and also many persecutions as she served with him as his mission companion, first to New York and then to England where they remained two years. When he was imprisoned, she visited him in prison. She accompanied him on every assignment she could.

Mary Ann and her sister, Olive Gray Frost, were the first lady missionaries in this dispensation.

By 1847, Parly had acquired several wives and made his first trip to the Salt Lake Valley. He was frequently away from home on church business. Two of her young sons had died in Nauvoo. After being alone for years, Mary Ann applied for and secured a bill of divorcement from Parley in the Spring of 1852.

This left her with her daughter and two of Parley's children yet to raise. She and her daughter would bake bread and sell it to the California emigrants. They also made floursacks in which emigrants could store their provisions. In this way she was able to earn a living and save toward the day she could take her family to Utah.

In a miraculous answer to her prayers, she was able to obtain a team, wagon, provisions, and driver to join with Bishop Harmon Cutler's Wagon Company which arrived in September of 1852.

Mary Ann settled in Pleasant Grove (Grove Creek), Utah. She was a midwife to any mothers. She wrote articles for the original Women's Exponent and she was interested in the feminist movement of her day. She was a dainty, refined, educated, unselfish lady.

MARY CATHERINE MATHIS WOODARD PRATT

No Photo Available

BIRTHDATE: 25 Feb 1830
Dekalb, Green Co., Alabama
DEATH: 10 Feb 1885
Deseret, Millard Co., Utah
PARENTS: Thomas Mathis
Martha Ann Nicholas
PIONEER: 1 Oct 1847
Edward Hunter Co. Wagon Train
SPOUSE I: Francis S. Woodard
MARRIED: Jan 1848
Salt Lake City, Salt Lake, Utah
DEATH SP: Feb 1888
Silver Reef, Washington, Utah

CHILDREN:
Mary Elizabeth, 2 Jun 1850
Francis Jedediah, 18 Aug 1852
Martha Ann, 25 Jan 1855

Emily Amelia, 27 Sep 1859
Mahala Jane, 26 Jun 1861
George Thomas, 18 Sep 1864

SPOUSE II: William Pratt
MARRIED: Unknown
DEATH SP: Unknown
CHILDREN: None

Mary Catherine was born in 1830 in Alabama. Many court house records were burned during the Civil War so little is known about her family. Mary was one of four chidren. Her family made their way from Alabama to Winter Quarters, Nebraska. They left for Utah about June 17, 1847 in the Edward Hunter company and arrived in October, 1847.

Mary Catherine married Francis Snow Woodard in the Old Council House in 1848. He had been a member of the Mormon Battalion, Company D. They settled in Salt Lake City but later moved to Provo and Lehi, Utah.

They were very valiant in paying their tithing, which they did by counting off stacks putting nine coins of equal value in one stack, and one coin of equal value in another for tithing. They did not know mathematics.

Francis became a partner in a business venture with other men in the nature of a distillery of liquor. This caused disgrace on Mary Catherine and their children. Because of this, Mary Catherine and Francis separated. She lived in Lehi with her parents for many years. She later married again to William Pratt. They moved to Deseret, Millard County, Utah.

Mary Catherine passed away at the age of fifty-five in Deseret. She was severely burned when she fainted and fell into an open fireplace while she was cooking, and she died February 10, 1885.

Mary Catherine was loved by all who knew her. She was known to be a fine, loving woman who served her family and others throughout her lifetime.

MARY CHUGG PRATT

BIRTHDATE: 20 May 1854
Canton, Cardiff, Wales
DEATH: 31 Jan 1894
Fairview, Franklin Co., Idaho
PARENTS: John Chugg
Elizabeth Lovering
PIONEER: 1868 Wagon Train
SPOUSE: Moroni Walker Pratt
MARRIED: 27 Apr 1874
Salt Lake City, Salt Lake, Utah
DEATH SP: 28 Jun 1911
Salt Lake City, Salt Lake, Utah

CHILDREN:
Ellice, 14 Mar 1875
Mary Louie, 11 Apr 1877

Francis Moroni, 19 Oct 1879
Evelyn Violate, 13 Oct 1881
Cora Agatha, 21 Aug 1884
Mabel Elizabeth, 30 Jul 1886
Hazel, 30 Sep 1888
Florence, 21 Jan 1892

Mary was born in Canton, Cardiff, Glamorganshire, Wales in 1854. Her parents had moved to Canton Wales to find work on the shipping docks. While there, they were converted to the Church of Jesus Christ of Latter-day Saints, and Mary was baptized on February 18, 1864, when she was ten years of age.

Her father put his money into the Perpetual Emigration Fund and sent his eight children to Zion as he could afford it, spanning a nine year period. Mary came to America on June 30, 1868 on the ship "Minnesota" with her two brothers George age twenty and John age nineteen. Mary was fourteen years old at that time. Her mother arrived in America in 1871 and died after two months here.

Mary married Moroni Walker Pratt (son of Apostle Parley P. Pratt) on April 27, 1874 in the Endowment House in Salt Lake City and she was endowed the same day.

They spent the early years of their marriage on a small acreage in Sugarhouse in Salt Lake City. Two daughters were born there. They were then called to Meadowville near Bear Lake to settle. Four more children were born to them there. When Mary's husband was called on a mission to Indiana, she stayed in Meadowville and took care of her family while he was away. They later moved to Malad, Idaho, and then to Fairview, Idaho where Moroni was called to be Bishop, a position he held for seventeen years.

Mary was a beautiful homemaker and seamstress. She was a good cook, was very thrifty and often entertained many church authorities and civic leaders in their home.

She was the mother of eight children, and she died during childbirth at the age of thirty-nine years at Fairview, Idaho and was buried there. She was a faithful member of the Church who served well in her family, her church and the community, and is one who is revered by those who have followed her. She was truly a great pioneer woman of Utah and Idaho.

CECILIA PREECE

No
Photo
Available

BIRTHDATE: 20 Aug 1846
Ligntilia, England
DEATH: 27 Jan 1853
Salt Lake City, Utah
PARENTS: Richard Preece
Susanna Pritchard Preece Woolsey
Walker
PIONEER: 15 Sep
John Tidwell Wagon Train

Cecilia was born in England in 1846. At the age of five, she and her family sailed from Liverpool, on the ship "Ellen Maria," for New Orleans. Her baby sister, Sarah, died on the ship and was buried at sea. They went to St. Louis on the ship "Alex Scott" They traveled to Council Bluffs, Iowa, on the "Robert Campbell" where her father died.

Cecilia, her mother and two brothers came on to Salt Lake by wagon train. The oldest sister, Harriet, stayed in Council Bluffs with friends because she was too ill to travel. She came the next year.

Cecilia contracted Scarlet Fever the first winter and was sent to the "Pest House." Since her mother worked in other people's homes, she was not allowed to visit Cecilia for fear of carrying the disease to the families for whom she worked. Cecilia died at the age of six years on 27 Jan 1853.

ELEANOR (ELLEN) COMISH PREECE

No
Photo
Available

BIRTHDATE: 30 Dec 1840
Onchan/Conchan, Isle of Man
DEATH: 13 Nov 1871
Franklin, Idaho
PARENTS: William Comish
Elizabeth Kegg Comish
PIONEER: 3 Sep 1855
John Hindley Wagon Co.
SPOUSE: Mark Preece
MARRIED: 22 Nov 1862
Salt Lake City, Utah
DEATH SP: 13 Jan 1905
Cove, Utah

CHILDREN:
Susannah Elizabeth, 19 Oct 1863
Mark Henry, 26 Nov 1865
William Fredrick, 19 Nov 1867
Francis Chase, 24 Oct 1869
Isabel Ellen, 11 Nov 1871

Eleanor was born on the Isle of Man in 1840. When she was a small child she was badly burned on her cheek which left a bad scar. She was very sensitive of the scar and would never allow her photograph to be taken. She had long brown hair and hazel colored eyes.

She came to St. Louis in 1852, with her mother and seven brothers and sisters. They met her father and two other sisters, which had come in 1849. The family came West in 1856. They lived in Taylorsville and Kaysville until moving to Franklin, Idaho in 1860, to help settle this area. They lived in wagon boxes until they could harvest their crops.

Eleanor married Mark Preece in the Endowment House in 1862. They lived in a two-room log house with a dirt roof. One room was used as a granary. By 1869, they had a two-room log house with a shingled roof. Their furniture was all handmade. She had five children.

In the fall of 1871, Ellen had a bad fall while shopping. She was expecting another baby. The baby was born, but Ellen did not feel well. Two days later she was much worse. Her last words were, "Take care of the children, Mark." She died at the age of thirty-one years.

EMMA BLOOMFIELD VAIL PREECE

BIRTHDATE: 18 Mar 1827
Bungay, England
DEATH: 11 May 1887
Cove, Utah
PARENTS:
John Bloomfield (Blumfield)
Martha Riches Bloomfield
PIONEER: by Oct 1861
SPOUSE: Isaac Hawk Vail
MARRIED: 26 Oct 1861
Salt Lake Endowment House
DEATH SP: 7 Nov 1871

CHILDREN: None

SPOUSE II: Mark Preece
MARRIED: 27 Nov 1872
CHILDREN: None

Emma was born in England in 1827. She was a daughter of John Bloomfield and Martha Riches Bloomfield. At age six she learned to reel silk, even though she was so small she had to stand on a stool. Later she worked as a servant.

Emma left England 11 May 1860 on the "William Tapscott" to begin her immigration to Utah. She married Isaac Hawk Vail 26 Oct 1861 in the Endowment House in Salt Lake City, Utah. They did not have any children. He died 7 November 1871 and is buried in Franklin, Idaho.

On 14 February 1872, Emma went to work for Mark Preece whose wife, Ellen, had died just a week after Emma's husband died. Mark was left with five small children between the ages of eight years and three days old. They married later that year on 27 November 1872 and lived in Franklin. She was a good, faithful wife and mother to Mark's children. They did not have children of their own.

In the spring of 1873, they moved to what was called Southfield (Coveville), now Cove, Utah. They were the third family to move out of Franklin. When the branch was organized, Emma was chosen as the president of the Relief Society. She filled this position faithfully until she was released due to poor health.

According to Susie Preese Allen, her step-daughter, "Emma was a small, blue-eyed woman, very ambitious and clean and neat." Susie felt her step-mother was very kind and very good to her. She called her "Mother."

Emma died 11 May 1887 in Cove, Cache County, Utah and was buried in Franklin, Idaho.

MARGARET HOLDEN HARDMAN PRESTLEY

No Photo Available

BIRTHDATE: 4 Aug 1809
Wheelton, Lancashire, England
DEATH: 7 Apr 1873
Huntsville, Weber Co., Utah
PARENT'S: James Holden
Margaret Slater
PIONEER: 1852
SPOUSE I: Richard Hardman
MARRIED: 7 Jan 1828
Brindle, Lancashire, England
DEATH SP: 1846
Mississippi River

CHILDREN:
Betty, 24 Feb 1828 (died as an infant)
Alice, 4 Apr 1829 (died as an infant)
Betsy, 14 Mar 1831 (died as an infant)
Mary Ann, 18 Dec 1832 (died as an infant)
Alice, 9 Jul 1834 (died as an infant)
Alice Eliza, 9 Jul 1836
James, 18 Jul 1839 (died as an infant)
Mary Jane, 6 Jun 1840 (died as an infant)
Lehi Nephi, 12 Jun 1841
Richard, 27 Nov 1845

SPOUSE II: William Prestley
MARRIED: 1850
DEATH SP: 16 Jul 1852
on the plains

CHILD:
Jane Amanda, 17 Feb 1851

Margaret's entire childhood and youth were spent working in the cloth weaving industry located in Manchester, England. She did not have the privilege of attending school.

She married Richard Hardman in Brindle, Lancashire, England. They made their home in Manchester, England and worked as weavers in the local cotton mills.

Margaret was baptized into the Church of Jesus Christ of Latter-day Saints on November 25, 1838. She had

become crippled from her life of working under the adverse conditions that existed in the cotton mills. She was carried to the place of her baptism. She was healed of her afflictions from a blessing given to her from Wilford Woodruff.

On January 12, 1842, the Hardmans left Liverpool, England on the ship, "Tremont," which was bound for New Orleans. After their arrival in New Orleans, they traveled on the river boat, "Ariel," which was bound for Nauvoo. They experienced many joys, much hard work, and a great deal of persecution while living there. They received their endowments in the Nauvoo Temple in 1846.

Her husband went to New Orleans to meet his sisters who were coming to join the saints. He was murdered by the crew members on a riverboat somewhere between Saint Louis and Nauvoo.

On September 17, 1846, the sick, the aged, and the weary that were unable to leave Nauvoo were literally forced from their homes and driven to the Mississippi River at sword point.

In 1850, Margaret married William Prestley who was a widower with two children. The Prestley family, consisting now of three families, traveled by ox-team from Council Bluffs, Iowa headed for the Salt Lake Valley. On July 16, 1852, William and his son were stricken with Cholera and died. Margaret pressed on toward Salt Lake Valley with her five young children. They arrived in the Fall of 1852 and settled north on Camp Land, better known to us as north Redwood Road.

After arriving in the Valley and settling in, she was given a job spinning, weaving, and sewing for President Young. She then moved nearer to the center of Salt Lake City.

At the approach of Johnston's Army in 1857, they moved down to Payson for about two years. When they returned, they went back to their home on Jordan River for a brief time. Then they moved to Coalville, and last to Hunt's Fort (presently called Huntsville).

Margaret passed away in her sixty-fourth year of life.

JANE LANGSHAW PRESTWICH

BIRTHDATE: 2 Nov 1818
Wigan, Lancashire, England
DEATH: 16 Dec 1890
Moroni, Sanpete Co., Utah
PARENTS: George Langshaw
Dorothy Wood
PIONEER: 19 Oct 1862
Horton Haight Handcart Comp.
SPOUSE: Silliam Prestwich
MARRIED: 9 May 1816
Odenshaw, Lancaster, England
DEATH SP: 8 Dec 1892
Moroni, Sanpete Co., Utah

CHILDREN:
Dorothy, 20 Apr 1837 (died as a child)
Elizabeth Stevens Hardy, 16 Apr 1839
Sarah (Kellett), 10 Apr 1842
Caroline (Mallenson), 20 Jan 1845
Jane (Hutchinson), 9 May 1847
William, 3 Aug 1849
Cyrus Wheelock Hubert, 20 Jun 1852
George (Smith), 21 Apr 1855
Mary Ann (Draper), 9 Feb 1861

Jane was born in England in 1818. She left Liverpool, England, April 23, 1862 on the ship "John J. Boyd." She joined the Horton D. Haight Handcart Company and crossed the Plains arriving in the Salt Lake Valley on October 19, 1862.

Her family traveled to Moroni, Sanpete County, Utah, where they reared their family. There were nine children born to them, all in England before they traveled to America.

Jane was a noble pioneer woman of courage and great stamina. At age sixty-three, she took on the responsibility of her four grandchildren when her daughter, Sarah and her husband, John Kellett both passed away.

Jane Prestwich passed away at her home in Moroni, Sanpete County at the age of seventy-two on December 16, 1890. Her husband passed away just two years later on December 8, 1892.

Jane remained a faithful, courageous Latter-day Saint throughout her lifetime.

ANN POWELL PRICE

BIRTHDATE: 2 Jun 1840
Bromwich, England
DEATH: 20 Jul 1916
Charleston, Wasatch Co., Utah
PARENTS: George Powell
Maria Mousley
PIONEER: 20 Sep 1864
Joseph S. Rawlins Wagon Train
SPOUSE: James Price
MARRIED: 28 Mar 1857
Ludlow, Shorpshire, England
DEATH SP: 16 Oct 1914
Heber City, Wasatch Co., Utah

CHILDREN:
Annie, 21 Jun 1858
George, 6 Jan 1861
James Willard, 12 Feb 1863 (died at age 1)
Maria Rawlins, 22 Aug 1864
Sarah Jane, 28 Dec 1866
John Heber, 22 May 1869
Emma, 10 Jun 1871
Charles Edward, 1 Oct 1873
Rachel Mary, 18 Dec 1874
James William, 31 Dec 1877
Margret, 18 Apr 1879

Charlotte Rozine, 16 Aug 1881
Mary Bell, 25 Nov 1883

In her childhood, Ann did not have a chance to attend school, but had to work. She tended children for the rich and learned to read while in their homes.

Ann was nearly seventeen when she married James Price, Jr. He had worked in the coal mines since he was ten years old. They joined the Church of Jesus Christ of Latter-day Saints in 1861 and their dearest wish was to emigrate to America.

They sailed on the vessel, "General McClellan," and landed in New York on July 23, 1864. They traveled by train to Omaha, Nebraska. They joined the Joseph S. Rawlins Wagon Company and started West. After two weeks of traveling, her son, James Willard died. Her daughter, Maria Rawlins, was born at Ash Hollow, Nebraska. They arrived in the Salt Lake Valley on September 20, 1864.

They settled in Heber Valley and lived in an old stable their first winter until they could obtain a cabin. They later moved to Charleston, Wasatch County, Utah and lived there the remainder of their lives.

Ann was a devoted mother, a good neighbor, and lived to serve others. She made the Sacrament bread for the Charleston Ward for thirty years. She was Relief Society treasurer for many years. She made burial clothes for the dead and helped to prepare the bodies for burial. She was a wonderful cook and entertained her family and grandchildren in her home often.

Ann's husband was injured in a run away horse and buggy accident and passed away on October 16, 1914. Ann passed away on July 20, 1917 and is buried by her husband in the Charleston Cemetery.

MARY ANN WINGROVE PRICE

No Photo Available

BIRTHDATE: 1832
Scottswood Village, England
DEATH: Sep 1864
Sweetwater River, Wyoming
PARENTS: Richard Wingrove
Margaret Parker
PIONEER: Died crossing Plains
Snow Co. Wagon Train
SPOUSE: John Isaac Price
MARRIED: 1852
New York City, New York
DEATH SP: 20 Dec 1915
LeGrande, Oregon

CHILDREN:
Isaac Thomas, 26 Oct 1855
Margaret Caroline, (chr.) 13 Dec 1858
John Richards(infant) 7 Sep 1863 (died as an infant)

Mary Ann was born in 1832 in Scottswood Village East Denton, New Castle upon Tyne, Northumberland, England. She had four brothers. It is not known when she came to America or whether the entire family came with her. She and her brother Jacob lived in New York City where Jacob owned a jewelry store and Mary Ann worked for him.

She met and married John Isaac Price in New York in 1852. John worked in a sawmill and they later moved to Cincinnati, Ohio where their first son was born. This son was named after John's beloved brother Isaac, who had died a short time after John and Isaac had come to America.

In 1856, they heard the Gospel message from the missionaries of the Church of Jesus Christ of Latter-day Saints and were at once converted and baptized on February 27, 1857. This was a wonderful event in their lives which brought joy and happiness into their home.

After joining the Church, their great desire was to emigrate with the Saints to Utah. Being quite poor, they began to work, plan and prepare to go to Zion. A daughter was born to them, and within a year this daughter died of measles. A third child, a son, was born in 1863.

Before leaving for Utah, Mary Ann and John visited Jacob in New York. Jacob gave Mary Ann their mother's Bible, a treasure for them. Returning to Ohio, they completed their plans and left early in 1864 with other Saints in covered wagons heading for the town of Wyoming, Nebraska, the gathering place of the Saints.

The trip proved to be very strenuous, provisions became low. John drove their wagon loaded with sawmill equipment and heavy machinery, and their son, Isaac Thomas, age eight and a half years, drove the other team bringing the household supplies, his mother and baby brother riding by his side.

Cholera swept through the country, claiming many lives. Many Saints contracted the disease and there were numerous graves along the way. Little John Richards was ill only a few days, and soon a small mound was left for his burial. With sorrow and fatigue, they pressed on enduring all for the Gospel's sake, and the glorious hope for the future.

Travel was difficult and tedious. One morning, Isaac desired a drink of water and his mother climbed into the wagon to get a cup, thinking she could run back to the stream and then catch up. As she attempted to climb down from the moving wagon, her clothing caught on the brakerod, and threw her forward, with her head beneath the wheel of the heavily loaded wagon, crushing out her life instantly. This was in September, 1864, near Sweetwater, Wyoming.

Because of the imminent Indian troubles, the train stopped only briefly, while a shallow grave was made and the mortal remains of the lovely Mary Ann, wrapped in a dainty patchwork quilt made by her own hands were placed within the grave, soil was replaced, and a pile of rocks were left to mark the grave. At thirty-two years of age, this ended the life of a beautiful, courageous woman, a lovely mother and a true Latter-day Saint.

Gratitude is felt for the influence and inspiration Mary Ann Price left upon her young son, Isaac whose posterity is humbled by the hardships, sacrifices, heartaches, and disappointments their ancestors experienced to provide them a life in this great country. She was a true pioneer to be honored and revered by those who have followed.

MARY ELSA JOHNSON PRICE

BIRTHDATE: 8 Mar 1834
Kirtland, Lake Co., Ohio
DEATH: 25 Apr 1912
Nephi, Juab Co., Utah
PARENTS: Luke Johnson
Susan Arminda Poteet
PIONEER: 1852 Wagon Train
SPOUSE: Charles Price
MARRIED: 25 Nov 1847
Council Bluffs, Iowa
DEATH SP: 24 Mar 1905
Nephi, Juab Co., Utah

CHILDREN:
Laura Marinda, 27 Jul 1849
Mary Alice, 22 Jan 1851
Charles Henry, 16 Sep 1852
James William, 8 Oct 1854
Orson Albert, 17 Feb 1857
Frank Johnson, 2 Feb 1859
Alonzo Eugene, 25 Dec 1860
Emma Lavinia, 10 Nov 1862
Joseph Richard, 24 Mar 1864
Zina Geneva 14 Jan 1867
Olivia Urania, 11 May 1869
Edward Oliver, 11 May 1869
Emily Janet, 1 Sep 1870
Elsa Elizabeth, 13 Apr 1873
Fannie Belle, 28 Dec 1874

Mary Elsa was born in 1834 in Kirtland, Ohio. She and her family lived in Kirtland for several years after the Saints had left. In 1846, when the Saints were in Winter Quarters, this family joined them. Mary Elsa's mother died on the way from exposure. She was buried in an unmarked grave. Mary Elsa was only twelve years of age, but she was the oldest, and she had the responsibility of the five younger children.

Mary Elsa married Charles Price in Council Bluffs in a ceremony performed by her uncle, Orson Hyde in 1847. Her first two children were born there. In 1852, they left Council Bluffs for Zion. Their third child was born while they were crossing the Plains. They arrived some time in 1852 in the Salt Lake Valley.

Charles and Mary Elsa were called to help settle Nephi. They had a two-story adobe house in town, and a ranch in the hills at the foot of the Red Cliffs. Mary Elsa lived at the ranch in the summer with her family to- milk the cows and make butter and cheese to sell.

She was the mother of fifteen children, four of whom died in infancy. She raised a very close-knit family. After church on Sundays, her family would gather for dinner. All remember these Sunday dinners when they would sit at the long table on which there was always a clean whitetable-cloth.

Mary Elsa was a hard working, courageous, honest lady who, for fifty-one years, stood side by side with her companion. She sacrificed all for her children and her posterity.

Mary Elsa passed away, April 25, 1912, at the age of seventy-eight years. She had been a widow for seven years. She left a great posterity who honor this brave pioneer woman's courage, faith and fortitude.

MARY JANE BISHOP PRICE

BIRTHDATE: 7 Dec 1818
Berrieu, Wales
DEATH: 14 Mar 1904
Paradise, Utah
PARENTS: John Bishop
Catherine Evans Bishop
PIONEER: 13 Aug 1852
John S. Higbee Wagon Co.
SPOUSE: Edward Jeremiah Price
MARRIED: 30 Mar 1852
New Orleans, Louisiana
DEATH SP: 1 Jan 1906
Paradise, Utah

CHILDREN:
Mary Jane, 15 Apr 1853
Sarah Ann, 23 Feb 1855
Edward, 23 Aug 1856
James William, 19 Sep 1857
John Lloyd, 16 Jan 1859
Thomas, 1 Apr 1861
Joseph, 25 Nov 1862
Peter, 7 Nov 1864

Mary was born in Wales in 1818. She was devoted to her family. When her parents died, she cared for her four younger brothers. They were baptized in 1846. She and two of her brothers sailed from England on the ship, "Kennebec" in 1852.

Mary Jane met Edward, a sailor on the ship. Upon landing in New Orleans, he was baptized and they were married in 1852. Both were thirty-three years old. They continued on to Zion by wagon train and made their first home in Salt Lake City. She continued to care for her brothers. They moved to Provo in 1854, then to Cache Valley in 1860, and were among the first settlers of Franklin. Then in 1862 they moved to Paradise, where she lived to the age of eighty-six. Six of her eight children died as infants.

Mary Jane was an ambitious, strong minded, dominant woman but very tender and loving, a friend to everyone. Shessisted with many births and was always willing to help the sick and needy. She was an exceptionally fine seamstress, using her talent to sew burial clothes. She served in the Paradise Ward Relief Society for twenty years.

MARY JANE SHELTON PRICE

No
Photo
Available

BIRTHDATE: 2 Sep 1822
Great Stockley, England
DEATH: Date unknown
Lehi, Utah Co., Utah
PARENTS: John Shelton
Mary Shelton
PIONEER: 1851 Wagon Train
SPOUSE: Charles Price
MARRIED: 9 Oct 1841
Nauvoo, Hancock Co., Illinois
DEATH SP: Jan 1873
Harrisville, Weber Co., Utah

CHILDREN:
Benjamine P., 11 Aug 1842
Mary Jane (Hill), 22 Dec 1843
Sarah Ann, 5 Sep 1845
Sarah W., 1849

Mary Jane was born in Great Stockley, Huntington, England in 1822. When she was ninteen she married Charles Price, October 9, 1841, in Nauvoo, Illinois. Their first son, Benjamin P. was born in Nauvoo August 11, 1842.

Their next two little girls, Mary Jane and Sarah Ann were also born in Nauvoo. But Sarah Ann died in May 1846 and Benjamin died in October, 1850. Their next daughter Sarah W. was born in Kanesville, Iowa, nothing else is known of her.

Charles, Mary Jane, and eight year old Mary Jane joined an independent wagon train and came to the Salt Lake Valley in 1851.

Charles married Caroline G. W. Blaky and Ann C Oakey on February 19, as plural wives. Caroline had two children and Ann had five children. Charles took a fourth wife, Sally Andrus in 1870.

It is not known when Mary Jane passed away but she must have been a brave lady.

RHODA ELIZABETH WATKINS PRICE

BIRTHDATE: 12 Sep 1844
Nauvoo, Hancock Co., Illionois
DEATH: 30 Sep 1912
Tremonton, Box Elder Co., Utah
PARENTS: Robert Watkins
Mary Smallman
PIONEER: Sep 1852
Thomas Bullock Wagon Train
SPOUSE: Ezekiel Price
MARRIED: 16 Feb 1862
Alpine, Utah Co., Utah
DEATH SP: 24 Jan 1892
Draper, Salt Lake Co., Utah

CHILDREN:
Mary, 1862
Ezekiel, 6 Oct 1864
Henry Robert, 30 Jan 1866
Mary Matilda, 25 Jan 1868
James Evans, 27 Jan 1869
David Louis, 13 May 1870
George Franklin, 30 Oct 1871
Jane, 5 Apr 1873
Margaret Ann, 25 Apr 1874
Porter William, 22 Apr 1875
Angus Byard, 27 Nov 1878
Aaron Thomas, 7 Dec 1879
Charles Andrew, 3 Oct 1880
Ida May (Clements), 31 Dec 1882
Samuel Mason, 10 Apr 1890

When Rhoda was two and a half years old her family was driven from their home in Nauvoo. In 1846, they went to Council Bluffs, Iowa and lived there for six years because her father was asked to stay and manage the farming for the migrating saints.

In 1852, when she was eight years old, the family left Council Bluff and crossed the Plains, traveling fifteen to twenty miles a day. Rhoda and her sister Catherine walked most of those miles.

They first settled on 33rd South just west of State Street. In 1854, they moved to Alpine, Utah where Rhoda grew to womanhood. She was famous for beauty and her horsemanship. She could ride anybody's horse.

She met Ezekiel Price in Corner Canyon, just south east of Draper. Ezekiel was there looking for his live stock he had taken there to get them out of the way of Johnston's Army. Rhoda and Ezekiel fell in love and were married on February 16, 1862 in Alpine, Utah by David McOwley, with her parents and Ezekiel's sister Ann and her husband William Mason as witnesses.

RUTH WILLIAMS PRICE

No Photo Available

BIRTHDATE: 14 Apr 1816
Llandeilforfan, Breconshire,
South Wales
DEATH: 20 Sep 1873
Samaria, Idaho
PARENTS: Daniel Price Williams
Ruth Jones Williams
PIONEER: 25 Sep 1866
John D. Holladay Wagon Train
SPOUSE: John Evan Price
MARRIED: May 1841
DEATH SP: 25 Jun 1876
Samaria, Idaho

CHILDREN:
Esther, 30 Oct 1842
Isaac, 7 May 1845
David, 4 Mar 1847
Ruth, 16 Apr 1848
Mary, 1 May 1850
Daniel Evan, 17 Nov 1852
John Evan, 18 Jan 1855
Ann Maria, 14 Jun 1859

Ruth was converted to the Church of Jesus Christ of Latter-day Saints while she lived in South Wales. She was baptized on October 17, 1847 by John Griffith. She was always a stalwart member.

She and her husband, John Evan Price, spent many years as missionaries moving from place to place in Wales. They suffered many hardships and persecutions because of their religion. Ruth believed strongly in prayer and her faith never faltered. She was blessed with the gift of tongues both in speech and song. She was very patient and had a kind and loving disposition. She always wore the traditional Welsh hood and clothing.

One day while standing on a chair to wind her clock, she fell and broke several bones in her feet. Not having proper medical care, she was left with a crippled foot and leg the remainder of her life. Although she was on crutches and had poor health, she corded wool, spun yarn, and knit clothes for her family.

Ruth had a strong desire to come to America and raise her family in a land where there was freedom of worship. After much sacrifice, they left Liverpool, England in May, 1865, on the ship, "Bridgewater." After five weeks and two days, they arrived in New York. From New York, they traveled to Pittsburgh, Pennsylvania to join other Welsh emigrants.

From there, they went to Detroit, Michigan to join other converts. They left Wyoming, Nebraska on July 19, 1866 in the John D. Holladay's Wagon Company. On September 25, 1866, they arrived in the Salt Lake Valley. They were greeted by Brigham Young and treated very kindly by him and the other settlers. President Young encouraged them to go north to Brigham City when they were able.

They went to Brigham City and became ill with Mountain Fever and were unable to travel for two months. When they were well again, they continued north to Malad, Idaho. Later, they moved to an unsettled area that is known as Samaria. They were the first white people to live there among the Indians. Their first home was a dugout near a spring of water.

They welcomed other pioneer families who followed them. Together they formed a new community which was a good place to raise their families. Lorenzo Snow gave the town this name because the people were well known for their good will and kindness to all who came in contact with them Ruth contributed much to this valley in the posterity she left behind. They all took leadership positions in church and civic offices.

SOPHIA HOLLIS HILL CONNELL PRICE

BIRTHDATE: 9 Jan 1825
Birmingham, England
DEATH: 7 Dec 1880
Salt Lake City, Salt Lake, Utah
PARENTS: John Hollis
Mary Ann Rawlings
PIONEER: 4 Oct 1864
SPOUSE I: Samuel Hill
MARRIED: 10 May 1847
Birmingham, England
DEATH SP: 1849 England

CHILD:
Samuel, (chr.) 9 Apr 1849

SPOUSE II: William Michael Connell
MARRIED: 1859
DEATH SP: Unknown
CHILDREN: None

SPOUSE III: Edward Price
MARRIED: 26 Sep 1864
Salt Lake City, Salt Lake Co. Utah
DEATH SP: 20 Aug 1875
Salt Lake City, Salt Lake Co., Utah

CHILD:
Louie Lenore (Daniels), 11 Oct 1865

Sophia was born in 1825 in England. She was christened in the St. Phillip's Church on October 10, 1815. She was the seventh and last child born in this family. Her father was a tin and iron, spoon, fork manufacturer and also a silversmith. She grew up in Birmingham, England in the neighborhood of St. Mary's Chapel on Stafford St. Her mother died in 1826 when Sophia was nearly two years old. Her father remarried before 1830 and moved to a new home.

When Sophia became of age she worked as a female servant in a home of a family. While working as a servant,

Sophia met Samuel Hill who lived nearby. They were married in 1847 when Sophia was twenty-two years old. Neither of them could write their names so marked the marriage certificate with an "X." They had one son whom they named Samuel. Her husband died sometime in 1849.

In the Spring of 1858, Sophia heard the missionaries preach the restored Gospel, and she was baptized as a member of the Church of Jesus Christ of Latter-day Saints in April, 1853.

In the latter part of 1859, Sophia met and married William Michael Connell in Birmingham. As the years passed Sophia was not content with her living conditions and wanted to leave England to join the Saints in Utah. Her husband, did not want to leave England. Sophia made the decision to leave and emigrate to Utah. She traveled to Liverpool and on May 20, 1864, she boarded the ship "General McClellan" for America.

The following is quoted as being the feelings of one of the missionaries, "I suppose the countenances bear the marks of joy and gratitude for the deliverance which is afforded them by the Almighty, judging by the feeling with which they sing the verses of the hymn. We pray that our passage may be a safe, prosperous and happy one. It has been what thousands of our brethren and sisters have realized by their faith and trust in Him, and it is what we may realize , too, if we place our dependence upon God, who is the deliverer of his Saints and the great Capt. of our salvation. I hope, that I may be true to my holy calling and ever be found trying to work out my personal salvation. I have set out for this purpose. Nothing but my religion would ever have induced me to leave my native land with those prospects which are before me. I go to Zion to serve God, and I pray that when I get there I may do so."

Only one death occurred during their thirty-three day voyage, but a fierce storm did occur which lasted three days, icebergs were seen, and fear was felt among the passengers. The ship anchored in New York, and the Saints spent the night on board the ship.

After passing through emigration inspection, they continued on their journey. They finally arrived in Nebraska City, Nebraska. Sophia traveled in William Warren's Church train leaving on July 19, 1864. Two and one half months later, she arrived on October 4, 1864 in the Salt Lake Valley.

She met Edward Price who was working driving wagon teams and delivering goods from the Eagle Emporium a general merchandise store. Edward's first wife had died in 1864 two days after the birth of a son. Sophia and Edward were married on December 26, 1864.

Sophia became the mother to Edward's eight living children. On October 11, 1865, a baby girl was born to Edward and Sophia. Sophia and Edward went to the Endowment House and were sealed on February 17, 1866 by Wilford Woodruff.

Edward's health began to deteriorate, and on Friday morning, August 20, 1875, he died at the age of sixty-one years. Sophia continued in their home and was a good mother to the children.

During the winter of 1880, Sophia caught cold which turned to pneumonia. She passed away at the office of Dr. Seymour B. Young, on December 7, 1880.

Sophia had embraced the Gospel of Jesus Christ and it meant everything to her including leaving her family and and her homeland. She endured trials and tribulations but used the gospel to help her endure. Sophia was indeed a brave pioneer woman of Faith and Fortitude. She is an example to all.

SUSANNAH JUCHAU PRICE

BIRTHDATE: 6 Dec 1845
London St. Johns, England
DEATH: 10 Jan 1923
Paris, Idaho
PARENTS: Charles D. Juchau
Susannah Deighton
PIONEER: 16 Sep 1861
Milo Andrus Co. Wagon Train
SPOUSE: Robert Price
MARRIED: 2 Mar 1864
Salt Lake City, Salt Lake, Utah
DEATH SP: 6 Apr 1910
Paris, Idaho

CHILDREN:
Charles Juchau, 19 Nov 1864 (died as an infant)
Susan, 7 Jan 1867
Mary Ann, 12 Jan 1870
Elizabeth, 12 Dec 1872
Joseph Stanners, 22 Mar 1874
Ketty May, 9 Mar 1876
Heber James, 6 Oct 1888
George Benjamin, 4 Sep 1878
Emma Charlotte, 7 Sep 1880
Arthur David, 19 Nov 1882
Ilelvina Charlotte, 18 Aug 1884
Mercy Isabell, 26 Jan 1886

Susannah was born in 1845 in London, England. She was the eldest of three children. Her father and mother joined the Church of Jesus Christ of Latter-day Saints in England, and her father became President of a branch of the Church there. Susannah was baptized by her father in November, 1855 before she was ten years of age. Her mother had died in 1854, her father married again. A little girl, Annie was born to them. In 1856, Susannah came to America with her father and step-mother.

They lived in Brooklyn, New York for seven years. Susannah was a good reader and loved to spend a lot of time reading in secluded places where she would not be disturbed. She attended very little school, and by thirteen years of age she was sent out to do housework for others.

Susannah came to Utah at the age of fifteen with a Laker family in 1861, traveling with the Milo Andrus Wagon Company. Her family stayed in New York and were to come the following year. Trouble arose, her father was disfellowshipped, they never came West.

Susannah drove an ox-team across the Plains for Brother Laker and she walked most of the way. Her only pair of shoes were soon worn out, and she went on barefoot. Much of the way was through cactus-covered land and her feet bled much of the time. Upon their arrival in the Salt Lake Valley, they settled in Grantsville, and later Skull Valley.

Susannah was married on March 2, 1864 to Robert Price as his second wife. They were married in the Endowment House by Heber C. Kimball. They lived in Salt Lake City in the same house with the first wife, Matilda. Matilda was sickly and so Susannah did the hard work of washing, milking cows.

Her first child was born in November, 1864. On the third day after his birth, Susannah got up and did her own washing. Before she was strong enough to go outside to milk, the cow was driven up to the door so she could milk it. This child died at two weeks of age, and Susannah washed him, laid him out, and prepared him for the burial. About a year later she had a room of her own. Her second child was born in this new home in 1867.

By 1869, these families moved to Bear Lake Valley into Paris Idaho. While there Susannah got her first pair of shoes, having gone barefoot until that time.

They had a one-room log house with a fireplace and a shingled roof, the only one in town. The floor was kept spotlessly clean even without any covering. Her second daughter was born in her new home in 1870. Susannah's health was not as good.

In 1897, Susannah went to New York to visit her father and family, and spent three months there. Her father was again happy in the Gospel, and remained faithful until his death.

Susannah was a member of the Relief Society Presidency for seven years and was a class leader for many years. She visited and assisted those who had trouble, sickness or death in their homes. She was ambitious and energetic, was always doing needlework and crochet work.

Susannah was a woman of exemplary character, loyalty and was true to her convictions and her friends, a great pioneer woman who passed away on January 10, 1923, an example to all.

MARY JAMES PRIDAY

BIRTHDATE: 20 Jan 1813
Mathon, Worcestershire, England
DEATH: 30 Oct 1891
Salt Lake City, Salt Lake, Utah
PARENTS: William James
Elizabeth Stallard
PIONEER: 6 Oct 1863
Wagon Train Company
SPOUSE: Samuel Priday
MARRIED: 26 Dec 1841
England
DEATH SP: 30 May 1903
Salt Lake City, Salt Lake, Utah

CHILDREN:
Charles James, 4 Nov 1836
Martha Esther, 22 Oct 1842
Thomas Samuel, 11 Nov 1844
Jane Elizabeth, 25 Dec 1846
Mary Emily, 17 Nov 1848
William James, 4 Sep 1851
Sarah Ann, 8 Feb 1854

Mary was born in 1813 in England. She was the third child of eight born into her family. On December 26, 1841, Mary married Samuel Priday at the parish Church of St. John the Baptist in the city of Gloucester, England. Samuel was a stone cutter by trade. Samuel and Mary had seven children all born in England as they moved from place to place for Samuel's work.

Four years before her marriage, Mary had become a convert to the Church of Jesus Christ of Latte-day Saints being baptized November, 1837. Seven years after their marriage, Samuel embraced the Gospel and was baptized. Mary was rebaptized at that time.

At this time, the Saints had a great desire to emigrate to Zion. The Church called a superintendent or agent to look after the welfare of Mormon converts. They helped arrange passage, quarters that were cleaner, and better food for the emigrants. It was through this Emigation Program that the Priday family booked passage on the "Amazon," a vessel that was to leave on June 4, 1863 from Liverpool, England.

It was this day that the famous Charles Dickens met the Mormons and learned what they were like. He said, "No one is in an ill temper, nobody is the worse for drink, nobody swears an oath or uses a coarse word, nobody appears depressed, nobody is weeping . . . "

Dickens continued ". . it would be difficult to find 800 people together anywhere else, and find so much beauty and so much strength and capacity for work among them. . . I went on board their ship to bear testimony against them if they deserved it, as I fully believed they would; to my great astonishment they did not deserve it. . . "

Two of Mary's children remained in England, and one son, Thomas, was called to serve a mission in England at that time. Samuel, Mary and their four youngest children, embarked on this long-awaited voyage with 882 Saints. Six weeks later the ship docked at New York on July 18, 1863. They traveled by rail to Iowa City as arranged by the person who met them.

Mary's journal recorded, "Each child had a year's supply of shoes in a leather bag." After they arrived in the States and started their trek to Utah, Mary's shoe bag became lost. All she had was her dancing shoes and they were not made for walking, so Mary rode in the covered wagon most of the way.

One of their prize possessions was a little black hen which laid an egg every day while they travelled to Utah. Mary was ill all the way and the egg was her nourishment and saved her from serious sickness. Mary's father, was not seasick during the voyage, but did get landsick, so much so, that he went down by the river to die. While lying on the ground, a huge Indian came near him and he was so scared he ran back to the wagon and forgot about the sickness and death.

Crossing the Plains by covered wagon, they were ferried over some of the largest rivers. They finally arrived in Salt Lake Valley on October 6, 1863. Samuel went to work almost immediately cutting stone for the Salt Lake Temple. Thomas finished his mission in England, and joined the family in 1866 in Utah.

Mary is an outstanding example of a woman devoted to her church and to her family. She left family and friends in England to cross the ocean and settle in a new land. She was the first in her family to join the Church of Jesus Christ of Latter-day Saints and was the shining example which gathered her husband, children and many descendants into the fold.

Mary passed away of cancer on October 30, 1891 in Salt Lake City after two years of illness. She was buried in the Salt Lake City Cemetery. She had witnessed great changes in her life.

Six years after her death, her husband Samuel, married again. He was seventy-seven years old at the time. He passed away in 1903 at his home in Salt Lake City and is buried in the Salt Lake City Cemetery.

These were both brave, valiant pioneers who helped in the development of the Church in Salt Lake and in the building of the great Salt Lake Temple. They are honored by their posterity for their lives.

SARAH ANN FULLMER PRIDAY

BIRTHDATE: 24 Jul 1848
Ft. Laramie
DEATH: 19 Nov 1928
River Heights, Cache Co., Utah
PARENTS: Almon L Fullmer
Sarah Ann Follet
PIONEER: 20-24 Sep 1848
Brigham Young Wagon Train
SPOUSE: Thomas S. Priday
MARRIED: 11 Mar 1869
Salt Lake Endowment House
DEATH SP: 12 Apr 1915
Logan, Cache Co., Utah

CHILDREN:
Thomas Samuel, Jr., 21 Jun 1870
Ida Roana, 2 Mar 1872
Sarah Florence Nellie, 9 Mar 1874
Charles DeWitt, 16 Oct 1876
Pearl Victoria, 30 Apr 1882
Dora Elizabeth, 22 Sep 1884
Ella Tryphena, 30 Jan 1887
Chloe Alvena, 3 Sep 1889
Sidney Preston, 11 Jan 1894

Sarah Ann was born in 1848 in Laramie, on the morning of July 24, 1848 just before the watchman cried, "Two o'clock-all is well." Her parents were traveling with the first division of organized emigration under the direction of the First Presidency. It was under the direction. of Brigham Young with Daniel H. Wells as Aid-de-camp.

They had left Elkhorn River on June 1, 1848 and arrived in the Great Salt Lake Valley, September 20-24, 1848. There were 1,229 souls and 397 wagons, 74 horses, 19 mules, 1,275 oxen, 699 cows, 184 loose cattle, 411 sheep, 141 pigs, 605 chickens, 37 cats, 82 dogs, 3 goats, 10 geese, 8 doves and 1 crow.

Sarah Ann lived in Salt Lake City and received a fine education with Karl G. Maeser and Milton H. Harding being two of her teachers. This schooling enabled her to later create in her own home an atmosphere of charm, culture and intellectual training.

She later taught school for two years. During this time she met Thomas Samuel Priday, a stone cutter who was working on the Salt Lake Temple. Thomas had recently emigrated from England.

Sarah and Thomas were married in the Endowment House on March 11, 1869 with Daniel H. Wells officiating. Their first home was in Salt Lake City. In 1871, this family moved to Providence, Cache Valley, at the extreme west end of Providence Lane near the sugar factory.

Sarah Ann was always a supreme optimist. After the horde of crickets had devoured everything in their garden but the onions, Sarah Ann turned to her husband and said, "Be grateful they did not eat the onions."

Thomas passed away in 1915 in Logan, Cache County, Utah and is buried in the city cemetery there. Sarah Ann passed away on November 19, 1928 at over eighty years of age. She had been a widow for thirteen years.

Sarah Ann was truly a great pioneer woman who had lived well, had learned much and used her knowledge and talents to share with others. Her optimistic outlook on life is a trait her posterity have emulated.

SARAH BOWMAN PRINCE

BIRTHDATE: 11 Jan 1819
Exning, Suffolk, England
DEATH: 13 Jul 1875
Middleton, Washington, Utah
PARENTS: Francis Bowman
Sophia Hammond
PIONEER: 5 Oct 1860
William Budge Co. Wagon Train
SPOUSE: George Prince
MARRIED: 10 Oct 1837
Exning, Suffolk, England
DEATH SP: 22 Jan 1905
Escalante, Garfield Co., Utah

CHILDREN:
Francis William, 16 Jul 1838 (died at 11 months)
Francis, 31 Jul 1840
Mary Ann, 3 Jun 1843
Richard, 26 May 1846
William, 23 Oct 1848
Sophia,
George, Jr.,
Sussannah,
Sarah Ann, 1858
Lucy Naomi,

Sarah was the fifth-child in the family. Her mother passed away when she was fourteen years old and her aunts helped to care for her. It is told in her girlhood, she was a "Lady in Waiting" to a member of the Royal Family of England. She was quiet, determined and had a good sense of humor. She had pretty brown expressive eyes. She loved people especially her English Queen, Victoria. She was frail and wasn't able to do real hard work.

Sarah was nineteen and George was twenty-two when they married.

In 1841, when the Queen, Victoria offered land grants in South Africa, this young couple with their baby were chosen to go. She lived there several years before she saw another white woman. Twice they were attacked by hostile natives and each time the Queen set them up in another home. Sarah had seven children while living in Africa.

When the family was baptized into the Church of Jesus Christ of Latter-day Saints they were criticized by their friends. They decided to go to America to join the Saints. Before they left Queen Victoria sent Sarah a beautiful carved oak rocking chair and a beautiful shoulder cape, covered with shiny black beads.

In the Spring of 1860, they left Algoa Bay on the ship "Alcrity." Sarah was expecting and the trip was hard. After three months they reached Boston, Massachusetts, then traveled to Florence, Nebraska. Leaving Nebraska on July 20, 1860 with William Budge Company, Sarah lost her twin babies that were born prematurely and they were buried on the Plains. Because of her poor health she was able to ride in the wagon.

When they arrived into the Salt Lake Valley, they went to Kaysville: While living here she had her last child born to her. Her health had improved but she suffered from rheumatism. Thinking the warm, dry climate would help her, they moved to Middleton, about three miles north-east of St. George. Here they lived in a dugout and wagon until their home was built.

Sarah raised geese. She made down pillows and a huge feather bed. She made pretty quilts and spun cotton. Her linens were edged with beautiful lace she crocheted and the pillowcases were delicate with her pretty handiwork. She grew beautiful flower beds. She raised her children with love and honesty.

She died in Middleton at the young age of fifty-seven on July 13, 1875.

ELIZABETH TIBBITTS RAY PRISBREY

No Photo Available

BIRTHDATE: 25 Dec 1836
Liverpool, Lancs. England
DEATH: 23 Oct 1888
Salt Lake City, Salt Lake, Utah
PARENTS: John Tibbitts
Sarah Dand
PIONEER: 1852 / 1855
SPOUSE: John Alexander Ray
MARRIED: 11 Oct 1855
Salt Lake City, Salt Lake, Utah
DEATH SP: 4 Jul 1862
Fillmore, Millard Co., Utah

CHILDREN:
Milton Sevier, 15 Oct 1856
Simeon Noble, 25 May 1859
James Wilford, 19 Aug 1861

SPOUSE II: Miner Jewett Prisbrey
MARRIED: 13 Jul 1867
Salt Lake City, Salt Lake Co., Utah
DEATH SP: 18 Sep 1888
Elsinore, Sevier Co., Utah

CHILD:
Myron William, 14 Jul 1863

Elizabeth was born in England, 1836. She was the third of seven, all born in Liverpool. Her grandparents and parents joined the Church when she was a small child. They made plans to come to Utah and emigrated by 1855.

They made their home in Salt Lake City, where Elizabeth met and married John Alexander Ray. She was eighteen. They were called to help settle Fillmore. While on their journey south, their first child was born on the Sevier River. They lived in Fillmore and helped this small community through the Indian problems, adding another child to their family.

By 1861, they were again in Salt Lake. They had a third child there, before returning to Fillmore where tragedy struck this small family. John passed away on July 4, 1862 in Fillmore. He was older than Elizabeth by nineteen years and also had other wives in polygamy. This was very hard for Elizabeth to lose John who was her protector and friend.

Five years went by and Elizabeth married Miner Jewett Prisbrey whom she had known in Fillmore. They made their home there and had a son. Life was good for them until Miner passed away in 1888. This time, Elizabeth followed. She passed away on October 23, 1888 in Salt Lake City, Utah. She was age fifty-one.

MARY GUNN PRISCOTT

No Photo Available

BIRTHDATE: 2 Aug 1830
Great Torington, England
DEATH: 5 Sept. 1904
Salt Lake City, Salt Lake, Utah
PARENTS: Mr Gunn
PIONEER: 15 Sep 1868
John Gallispie Co. Wagon Train
SPOUSE: James Priscott
MARRIED: 1854
England
DEATH SP: Unknown

CHILDREN:
James, 5 May 1859
Thomas, 8 Oct 1864
Mary Catherine (Ridd), 6 Dec 1866

Mary was born in Great Torington, Devonshire, England in 1830. She married James Priscott in 1854.

James, Mary and their three children left Liverpool, England for America about one o' clock Wednesday, June 24, 1868 on the packet ship "Constitution." The boat reached New York on August 5, 1868, not having lost a single soul. They then went on to Benton by rail. They joined the John Gallispie wagon train arriving in the Salt Lake Valley on September 15, 1868.

After they settled they helped in the development of farming. James also traveled a lot as a saleman, leaving Mary to take care of the farm and family.

Mary passed away on September 25, 1904 in Salt Lake City, Utah at the age of seventy-four.

ANN GIBBONS PROBERT

BIRTHDATE: 31 Jul 1815
Eyton, Herefordshire, England
DEATH: 29 Apr 1901
Croyden, Morgan Co., Utah
PARENTS: William Gibbons
Frances Blunt
PIONEER: 13 Oct 1863
Rawsel Hyde Wagon Co.
SPOUSE: William Probert
MARRIED: 1 Jun 1837
Edgaston, England
DEATH SP: 3 Jan 1894
Holden, Millard Co., Utah

CHILDREN:
Samuel, 21 Apr 1838
William Jr., 14 Mar 1840
Mary, 1 Apr 1842
Emma, 16 May 1844
Eliza Emma (Mitchell), 4 Dec 1846
Fanny Ann (Johnson Horton), 6 Feb 1849
George Joseph, 27 Feb 1851
Jane (Blackwell), 24 Jan 1853
Joseph, 26 Nov 1854
Anna Margaret, 2 Mar 1860 (twin)
Levi Richard, 2 Mar 1860 (twin)

Ann was born in England, 1815. At age twenty-one, she married William Probert. They made their home in England, where they became parents of eleven. They were converted to the Church of Jesus Christ of Latter-day Saints and emigrated to America.

They left Florence, Nebraska on August 11, 1863 and arrived in the Salt Lake Valley on October 13, 1863, with the Rosel Hyde Wagon Train.

The Probert family first settled in Holden, Millard County, where they farmed for a living and raised their large family. Their son, William Jr., and his wife Cleone, were leaders in the new MIA. William and his son worked on the new brick meeting house, where William Jr. was the General Manager of the project.

William passed away in Holden, on January 3, 1894. Ann went to live with others of their children. She passed away at Croyden, Morgan County, on April 29, 1901 at age eighty-five, having been a widow for seven years.

SARAH MEMMOTT PROBERT

BIRTHDATE: 18 Jan 1847
Sheffield, Yorkshire, England
DEATH: 27 Dec 1921
Scipio, Millard Co., Utah
PARENTS: John Memmott
Julia Wilson Memmott
PIONEER: Fall 1855
Wagon Train Company
SPOUSE: Samuel Probert
MARRIED: 12 Jan 1869
Salt Lake Endowment House
DEATH SP: 9 Nov 1918
Scipio, Millard Co., Utah

CHILDREN:
Sarah May (Walch), 5 Nov 1869
Samuel G., 22 Sep 1871
John William, 20 Mar 1873
Martha Eliza, 25 Apr 1876
Ann, 20 Jul 1878
Emma Julia (Thompson), 16 Oct 1880
Elizabeth Ellen, 24 Jan 1883
Marion James, 26 Aug 1884
Samuel Don, 7 Oct 1886
Daniel Grover, 13 Dec 1888

Sarah was born in England, 1847. She was the oldest of six children. Her family joined the Church of Jesus Christ of Latter-day Saints and sailed from England on April 14, 1855 on the ship "Samuel Curling," landing in New York on May 22, 1855. They traveled by rail to St. Louis, Missouri and then on to Mormon Grove Kansas, where they joined a wagon train, arriving in the Salt Lake Valley in the Fall of 1855.

At age twenty-one, she married Samuel Probert on January 12, 1869. They made their home in Scipio, Millard County, where they became parents of ten children. They buried all but three of them.

Sarah's life was one of hard work. She was an exemplary wife and mother, devoted to her family. She was never known to gossip or say any unkind word about anyone. She was known for her grace in dancing. When she was on old woman, she won a prize for the most graceful dancer in town.

In 1879, Samuel was called to serve in the new MIA. Their son, John William, played in the Scipio Brass Band and their two children Emma Julia and Marion James attended the Primary in 1889.

William passed away on November 9, 1918 from the 'great flu epedimic' and is buried in Scipio. Sarah passed away on December 27, 1921 at age seventy-four, having been a widow for three years. She is buried beside William in the Scipio Cemetery.

MARTHA E. GRAHAM PROCTOR

BIRTHDATE: 22 Jan 1832
Hope Pickens, Alabama
DEATH: 22 Mar 1904
Union, Salt Lake Co., Utah
PARENTS: Thomas Graham
Sarah Ann McCory
PIONEER: 1852
Howard Egan Co. Wagon Train
SPOUSE: David Proctor
MARRIED: 1855
Salt Lake City, Salt Lake, Utah
DEATH SP: 18 Feb 1919
Midvale, Salt Lake Co., Utah

CHILDREN:
Martha Ellen, 22 Dec 1856
Alice Elitha, 22 Sep 1858
David Alma, 9 Feb 1860
George William, 9 Feb 1862
James Francis, 19 May 1869

Martha was born in 1832 in Alabama. Her family traveled to Utah in the Howard Egan Wagon Company. His was an independent wagon train. He had first come to Utah in 1849 with just fifty-seven people and had arrived in August after leaving Iowa in April.

After her arrival in Utah, Martha married David Proctor. Their marriage was in 1855 in Salt Lake City, Utah. Martha gave birth to five children between December of 1856 and May of 1869.

Children were born in Salt Lake City, South Cottonwood, and Dayton, Nevada and Union, Utah. They therefore, moved around quite a bit during their years in the Utah territory.

Martha was a good mother and house keeper. She was also a very good cook. Their last home was in Union, Utah. Martha passed away there on March 22, 1904 at the age of seventy-two years. Martha's husband, David, passed away in Midvale in 1919, fifteen years after Martha.

These were faithful, pioneers of the Utah Territory who are honored for their faith, courage, and fortitude. Both Martha and David Proctor are buried in the Murray City Cemetery.

MARY LOUISE CHARLES PROCTOR

BIRTHDATE: 7 Jul 1867
Little Deans Hill, England
DEATH: 19 May 1935
Union, Utah
PARENTS: James Charles, Jr.
Louisa Amelia Williams Charles
PIONEER: 24 Sep 1868
E. T. Mumford Wagon Co.
SPOUSE: George William Proctor
MARRIED: 3 Nov 1886
Union, Utah
DEATH SP: 30 Mar 1935
Union, Utah

CHILDREN:
George Francis, 26 Mar 1887
Baby, Jul 1890
Verna Louise (Bishop), 10 Aug 1894
Clyde Charles, 17 Jun 1896
Roland Phillip, 7 Apr 1901
Grace Ann, 13 Mar 1904
Thelma Amelia (Hardman)

Mary was born in England in 1867. Her father died in England shortly before the family emigrated. Mary was called "Polly." She, with her mother and sister, left from Liverpool, 20 Jun 1868 on the ship "Emerald Isle." Arriving in Ireland, they remained for three days. They recieved very rough treatment from the ship's crew. The water was so rank they could hardly drink it, and it made them sick.

They arrived in New York and were quarantined for three days. By train they went to Council Bluffs, then to Benton, Wyoming. They were met by church wagons. They arrived in the Valley in Sept. Polly's mother died 12 days after their arrival. Bishop Phillips took them into his home.

Mary attended school in the Union Fort. As a young girl, she did farm chores. She did washing, ironing and cleaning house for other families.

In 1886, she married George Williams Proctor. They lived in Union Fort. They owned a store where she clerked. Three of her baby daughters died. She was a beautiful quilter, a good cook and a good housekeeper. She taught Sunday School, and was a counselor in a Religion Class. She was a visiting teacher for the Reief Society for thirty-five years. She was a wonderful mother and good friend to everyone who knew her. Her husband died in Mar 1935. She died 19 May of the same year.

ELIZABETH THOMAS REES / REESE PROTHERO

BIRTHDATE: 16 Apr 1846
Pontypool, South Wales
DEATH: 25 Mar 1916
Paragonah, Iron Co., Utah
PARENTS: Henry Thomas Rees
Elizabeth Powell
PIONEER: 1868
SPOUSE: Jonathan Prothero
MARRIED: 31 May 1869
Salt Lake Endowment House
DEATH SP: 26 May 1922
Paragonah, Iron Co., Utah

CHILDREN:
Margaret Elizabeth, 6 Jun 1870
John Henry, 31 Dec 1873
Joseph Reese, 31 Aug 1876
David Jonathan, 6 Sep 1877
Mary Alice, 7 Sep 1881
Johanna Rees, 10 Jan 1885
George Stanley, 17 Aug 1887

Elizabeth Thomas was born in 1846 in South Wales. Little is known of her life in Wales, except that her father was a coal miner, and her mother used to do big washings for her family and others, doing it all by hand, not even using a wash board.

When Elizabeth was old enough, she was hired out to the neighbors to tend and rock their babies in their cradles. She must have been schooled in her youth, because she was a good reader, a pretty writer, and had an outstanding knowledge of arithmetic especially figuring in her head.

The Rees parents joined the Church of Jesus Christ of Latter-day Saints in 1847 and Elizabeth was baptized on June 23, 1858 by her father.

A missionary from Cedar City, Utah had visited the Rees home often, and when he was released in 1863, he offered to bring two of the girls to America, and he married one of these sisters.

When Elizabeth was about twenty-two years old, it was her turn to emigrate. There was an old lady who wished to come with this group. She had two sons who previously had come to America and were in Salt Lake City. She sold her property and belongings and prepared to come if she could find someone to look after her along the way. Elizabeth became this person. When they reached New York, an elder wanted to show them some sights so Elizabeth and her companion went along with others and saw the Niagara Falls and had a good time.

As they became outfitted for the journey west, "Lizzie" was expected to walk,along with all able-bodied persons. They arrived in 1868 in the Salt Lake Valley and Lizzie left her old-lady friend safe in the care of her sons. Lizzie's sister and husband met Lizzie to take her to Cedar City with them.

A story is told that a friend from Iron County had jokingly told Jonathan Prothero that he would bring a wife back for him when he assisted others crossing the Plains. When he got back to Paragonah, he said he had kept his part of the bargain and had brought a girl for him, a young Welsh lassie, Elizabeth Rees by name. Jonathan needed no urging and won the fair lady, and brought her to Parogonah with him.

They were married in Salt Lake City in the Endowment House on May 31, 1869. Their first home was a little log house. Lizzie was at first lonesome for her homeland, but as she stood at her cabin door and looked toward the mountains to the east, she learned to love them as she did the valley in this Little Salt Lake City.

Elizabeth was busy cleaning and whitewashing her home frequently. She was excited when these sisters heard their parents were coming to America. A brother of hers, Joseph, was busy taking pictures of the train area when he was crushed and killed instantly when a train came too close to where he was standing. This was a great sorrow which marred the joy of the family's arrival. The family returned to the area around Cedar City where most lived and died.

Elizabeth was not too much in the public view, and was happy spending her time in her own home, and helping neighbors in some act of kindness. She was kind and good to the children who came to her home, and had cookies and other goodies for them. She enjoyed her Relief Society meetings, and she and her husband never missed a church meeting.

Elizabeth had seven children and as they married and made homes of their own they also lived near the family. Her daughter, Johanna, died from a ruptured appendix leaving an eight month old child for Elizabeth to care for. When this child, LaGrand was just four years old, Elizabeth passed away on March 25, 1915, at sixty-nine years of age.

Elizabeth was a great pioneer woman who had a great posterity who honor her faith and fortitude.

LODESKY ANN ROBERDS PROWS

BIRTHDATE: 28 Jul 1835
Monroe Co., Mississippi
DEATH: 2 Sep 1922
Salina, Sevier Co., Utah
PARENTS: John Roberds
Martha Tucker Walpole
PIONEER: 1848
Independent Co., Wagon Train
SPOUSE: William Cook Prows
MARRIED: 14 Apr 1850
Mary's River, Nevada
DEATH SP: 24 May 1894
Juarez, Chihuahua, Mexico

CHILDREN:
John Thomas, 12 Nov 1853
William Reform, 2 Jul 1855
Joseph, 24 Apr 1857
Francis Marion, 20 Sep 1860
Martha Ellen, 14 Mar 1862
Hyrum, 27 Jan 1866
Mary Elizabeth, 5 Jan 1868
Margaret Annie, 23 Jul 1869
Desky Lovina, 28 Feb 1872
Sarah Elmira, 7 Jun 1873
George Franklin, 18 Jun 1876

Lodesky was born in 1835 in Mississippi. When she was eleven, her family left Mississippi in wagons. The family numbered six children with one on the way. They arrived in the Salt Lake Valley by September, 1848, where her sister was born. The family made a log cabin and prepared for winter before heading to California.

In Salt Lake City, Lodesky met William Cook Prows, who had returned from the service in the Mormon Battalion. William decided to go along with her family on their trek to California. With two teams, they started in the spring of 1850 with William driving one of the teams. They traveled down the Humbolt River where they found the Indians troublesome. They stopped by Mary's River and panned for gold. William and Lodesky decided to get married, so on April 14, 1850, at the age of fifteen years, Lodesky was married to William, twenty-three. William panned out the first gold in Nevada.

The party reached California in July, settling Diamond Springs, and the Suisun Valley. They did very well panning for gold in Mill Creek, Mendocino County. At one point, a huge chunk was panned out which William made into a gold brooch for Lodesky. The couple got about $15,000 in gold from this area which they invested in brood sows intending to make a good business in the hog industry. The pigs got pig cholera, so their investment was lost. Discouraged, the couple left for San Bernardino where her parents were living. A call came from Brigham Young for the members of the Church in California to return to Utah, and the Prows did so with their three children in 1858. They were called to settle in the Pauvant Valley, and Lodesky's gold brooch was sold to make the trip possible. They helped settle in Deseret.

In 1867, a second wife joined this family and both families moved to Kanosh. William built two one-room homes with a large cellar under one which was a focal point for local activities. William would play the violin and Lodesky made tunes by blowing through a paper placed over a comb.

When the Edmunds Tucker Act was passed prohibiting polygamy, William Cook Prows spent three months in the penitentiary in 1889. To protect his family, they sold all in 1894 and moved to Mexico. Lodesky and her children were left in Mesa, Arizona while William settled his second family in Mexico. William fell ill and died shortly after their arrival there. Lodesky, with a Mexican permit, placed a tombstone on his gravesite. She returned with her children to Kanosh.

In 1907, at the age of seventy-three years, Lodesky lived with her oldest son, John Thomas. She passed away there in 1922 at the age of eighty-seven years.

Lodesky had eleven children, and was remembered by grandchildren as having a lovable disposition, always being kind and considerate and ever ready to give a helping hand. She loved life and all the good things in it, especially the Gospel of Jesus Christ. She was a faithful, valiant pioneer woman of the West.

ANN MOLYNEAUX ALSTON PRYE

BIRTHDATE: 3 Feb 1829
Birkdale, Lancashire, England
DEATH: 20 Nov 1899
Salt Lake City, Salt Lake, Utah
PARENTS: John Molyneaux
Elizabeth Howard
PIONEER: 9 Nov 1865
Henson Walker's Wagon Train
SPOUSE I: James Alston
MARRIED: 8 Nov 1852
England
DEATH SP: 26 May 1863
England

CHILDREN:
Christopher, 8 Sep 1853
John Molyneaux, 24 Dec 1855
Thomas, 24 Oct 1857
Elizabeth, 6 Sep 1859
Margery, 6 Nov 1861

SPOUSE II: John Isreal Prye
MARRIED: Dec 1865
Salt Lake City, Salt Lake Co., Utah
DEATH SP: 8 Aug 1908
Salt Lake City, Salt Lake Co., Utah

CHILDREN:
Mary Ann, 16 Nov 1866
Margaret Emma, 25 Nov 1868

Ann was born in 1829 in England. When just three weeks old, Ann was christened in the Anglican Church. As a young girl she became skilled in boot binding and putting fancy needlework on expensive shoes. She bound the shoes by hand and put buttonholes and needlework on them.

Ann's entire family joined the Church of Jesus Christ of Latter-day Saints; Ann was baptized in December, 1852.

Earlier in that same year, Ann had married James Alston. James was a cabinet maker in his father's mill. James had no interest in Ann's religious beliefs, and did not care to join the Mormon Church.

In the Spring of 1863, Ann's status was suddenly changed from wife to widow when James died. Ann supported her young family of three sons and two daughters by working as a seamstress for the gentry.

Now that she was a widow, Ann wanted to go to Utah. Her mother-in-law and brothers-in-law strongly opposed Ann's children being taken. They had been appointed executors of James Alston's will. Because of this, Ann had to make the necessary steps for her two oldest sons, to travel to Salt Lake City with a family friend. They were ages ten and eight years old at the time when they left Liverpool on May 21, 1864 on the ship "General McClellan," and they arrived in the Salt Lake Valley on September 20th, with the Joseph S. Rawlins Wagon Company.

Early in the Spring of 1865, Ann was able to emigrate to Utah with her three younger children. Thomas a cripple who used crutches was seven years old and the girls were ages five and three. She had sold her late husband's property which included a carpentry shop and a shipping place on the waterfront, to finance their journey.

Ann made all the arrangements for their trip including paying for the necessary wagons and livestock they would need. As they were about to board the ship, Margaret broke out with the measles and they were not allowed to go. Ten days later they joined a company of twenty other Saints on the ship "David Hoadley," which left Liverpool, England on May 10th.

En route they experienced a bad storm. Margery was ill with measles and almost died, but Ann's faith and prayers helped make her better. After six weeks on the ocean, they landed in New York on June 20th.

They rode in freight cars to St. Louis, steamboat to Nebraska. During a short stop, Ann found some plums and picked a bucketful which she made into some pies which were thoroughly enjoyed by all. They remained in Wyoming for weeks preparing for the trek. She had two teams of oxen, two steers, and two cows to insure an adequate supply of milk for the children. She gave a couple their board for driving one of her outfits, and she drove the other and walked much of the way.

Before leaving England, Ann had purchased silk and made four extra full dresses. She planned to sell much of the material in Utah. Later on she bartered one dress for enough calico to make much needed house dresses. She had also brought a set of beautiful china dishes thinking she could purchase common dishes in Utah. When she arrived in the Salt Lake Valley, she discovered that dishes were a scarce commodity, so she used her fine china for everyday use.

At a distance east of Ft. Bridger, the Walker Company was met by supply teams from Utah to help them. Ann was so anxious to arrive in Utah as soon as possible, she arranged for one of these men to escort her family to the Valley ahead of the main company. She left the team and wagon in charge of their driver, and drove to Salt Lake City with her three children. Before entering the Valley, Ann washed herself and her children, and all put on their best clothes. They were warmly greeted as they approached Temple Square. Ann was at last reunited with her family including her two older sons. They stayed at her sister's home and a short time later this sister moved to Summit County, leaving the house for Ann and her children.

Before the end of the year, Ann met and married a tall, young man named John Israel Prye from Pennsylvania. He had arrived in Salt Lake City in 1865 also, and had just joined the Mormon Church. Following the deaths of her parents in 1866 and 1867, Ann's family moved into her parents' home.

Ann encouraged her husband to take a second, younger wife in polygamy. Ann lived in her separate home at 21st East and 17th South, where she had five acres in orchard and garden. She was a good business woman, bought and sold land for a good profit.

Ann, a devout and conscientious Latter-day Saint, was extremely prayerful. She always paid a full tithing, even when she had only flour to give during her less affluent days. The day before her death, she sent her eldest daughter, Elizabeth, to pay her tithing and a small debt that she owed the pharmacist.

Ann was over seventy years of age when she died of pneumonia on November 20, 1899. Her daughter said, "My mother's chief ambition was to make good LDS members of her family. She never complained about the sacrifices she had made, or the hardships she had endured in pioneering. She was a peacemaker and was a hostess with her home open to relatives and friends, and because of her helpfulness and kindness she was much admired and loved by all."

Ann was truly a great pioneer woman who left a legacy of faith and fortitude for all of those who have followed her.

MARGARET PERREN PUCELL

No Photo Available

BIRTHDATE: 10 May 1802
Warrington, Chesire, England
DEATH: 27 Oct 1856
Crossing the Plains
PARENTS: Joseph Perren
Ann Basnet
PIONEER: 1856
Martin Handcart Company
SPOUSE: Samuel Pucell
MARRIED: 1 Aug 1825
Lymm, Cheshire, England
DEATH SP: 22 Oct 1856
crossing the Plains

CHILDREN:
James, 1823 (died as an infant)
William, 1826 (died as an infant)
Ann (Shepley), 1830
Samuel, 1831
Elizabeth (Dixon), 1834
Joseph, 1836 (died as an infant)
Margaret, 1838 (died as an infant)

Margaret (Walker), 1841-1916
Ellen (Unthank), 1846-1915

Margaret rejoiced to hear the glad tidings of the restoration of the Gospel of the Church of Jesus Christ of Latter-day Saints as preached by Apostles Heber C. Kimball and Orson Hyde. Ten days later, at the River Ribble she was baptized by authority. She held the distinction of being the second woman baptized into the Church in England and she was confirmed later that week. She was present at the first meeting held by the missionaries in England.

Fearing to tell her husband of her decision, she held her peace for three months until he surprised her and confessed that he had also been baptized the previous month. For nineteen years the couple saved for their emigration to Utah. In the meantime, they entertained the missionaries in their small home and often had to put their children to bed hungry in order to provide food for the Elders.

They sailed for Zion aboard the ship, "Horizon," and pulled their handcart toward Utah until they both passed away on the Plains. Margaret passed away five days after Samuel. Their daughters, Margaret and Ellen, were assisted by rescuers to finally make their way into the Salt Lake Valley with the survivors of the Martin Handcart Company.

These were devout members of the Church, who gave their all, literally, for the Church and the truths of the Gospel which they loved. Margaret had given birth to nine children, four of whom died in infancy. Four remaining daughters and one son carried on the pioneering spirit of their parents.

ELIZABETH KELLY PUGH

BIRTHDATE: 1 Mar 1849
Merden, Herefordshire, England
DEATH: 24 Aug 1917
Kanab, Kane Co., Utah
PARENTS: John Phillip Kelly
Eliza Long
PIONEER: abt 22 Sep 1862
James Wareham Wagon Train
SPOUSE: Edward Pugh
MARRIED: 5 May 1866
Salt Lake Endowment House
DEATH SP: 14 Sep 1900
Kanab, Kane Co., Utah

CHILDREN:
Edward Kelly, 18 Apr 1868
Eliza Ann, 27 Jan 1870
John Philip, 31 Dec 1871
Charles Robert, 28 May 1874
Emily Vilate, 18 Oct 1876
Mary Elizabeth, 21 Apr 1879
Leonard Bailey, 9 Nov 1880
David Long, 24 Sep 1882
Orsen Levi, 29 Nov 1884
Pearl Edna, 22 Mar 1886

Elizabeth left England at age thirteen with her parents and some members of her family on the "John J. Boyd," on April 2, 1862, with agent George Q. Cannon. The party of Saints arrived in Castle Gardens, New York, about June 3, 1862 and went immediately to Florence.

Here the women worked at making wagon covers while their father went to Council Bluffs with Edward Pugh, a returning missionary, who had taken passage on the same boat.

As Edward Pugh had crossed the Plains to Utah in 1853, he was a great help to Elizabeth's father. They bought supplies for the trip West.

At the age of seventeen, she married Edward Pugh and they made their home in Mill Creek, Utah where the first two children were born. They lived there until 1870 when they were called by the church authorities to go to Kanab, Kane County, Utah to help settle it. Upon arriving in Kanab, they lived in the Kanab Fort for the first winter.

Later, Edward built the first house outside the fort. It was a large one-room home of red sandstone and had port holes through which persons inside could look out in time of danger. It served as a refuge for neighbors outside the fort in times of Indian hostilities.

Elizabeth was very active in her ward and civic affairs of the city. To help out with the family income she sold milk, molasses and vegetables. Elizabeth was given a patriarchal blessing by Joel H. Johnson at Johnson Canyon on April 30, 1882, which stated that she would be able to heal the sick in the absence of her husband or the Elders of the Church and that she would be sought out by members of her own sex for counsel and advice. During her long service in the Relief Society these promises were fulfilled. She served for approximately thirty-six years as an executive in the Ward and Stake Relief Society. Elizabeth and Edward were very ardent workers in the St. George Temple.

Several people in Kanab took up the silk making industry. The sisters of the Relief Society also became interested and fostered the industry. She remarked that "she had never had a silk dress, but if they could raise the cocoons and manufacture the silk, she would not mind having one."

Elizabeth was a small, graceful woman and was known as a very good cook. She had a very full and satisfying life leaving a large posterity.

MARYANN ROCK WILLIAMS PUGH

BIRTHDATE: 2 Feb 1813
West Hide, England
DEATH: 1 Jun 1895
PARENTS: George Rock
Mary Ann Clarke
PIONEER: 1 Oct 1853
Henry Ettleman's Wagon Co.
SPOUSE: Benjamin Williams
MARRIED: 4 Jul 1837
England
DEATH: Dec 1844
Nauvoo, Hancock Co., Illinois

CHILDREN:
George A., 4 Nov 1837
Lucy Maria, 22 Sep 1840
Ephraim H., 2 May 1842.

SPOUSE II: Edward Pugh Jr.
MARRIED: 24 Jul 1847
Kanesville, Potawattomie Co., Iowa
DEATH SP: 14 Sep 1900
Kanab, Kane Co., Utah

CHILD:
Enoch Rock, 16 Jan 1848.

Mary Ann was born in West Hide, Herefordshire, England. She and Benjamin met Elder Wilford Woodruff in England and both were baptized by him on November 4, 1837.

By 1842, they were ready to travel to America on the ship "John Cummins" which sailed from Liverpool, February 20, with 200 Saints aboard. The Prophet Joseph Smith met them in Nauvoo on April 13, 1842 as they arrived by ship by way of the Mississippi River. The mobs were molesting the Saints and Benjamin was asigned to guard the door of the meeting house. He was weak from over work, so Mary Ann took his place and with a large stick, drove off men who came to do harm.

Mary Ann became a widow in December of 1844. She lived comfortably until September, 1846, when a company of armed men came to her door and told her she would be safe if she denounced the Mormon faith. She declined and they gave her twenty minutes to leave her home. She had no team, she gathered bedding, 112 bushel of meal, a small piece of pork, her three children and headed for the Mississippi River bank where she found many other Saints. They were loaded on a flat boat so heavily laden that they stood ankle deep in water as they crossed, praying that they would make it to the other side. By the time she reached the west bank, the mobsters had taken possession of the temple and they sent a cannon ball from there into the river. It caused a shower of mud and water to cover Mary Ann and her children.

Mary Ann lie sick with fever and "ague" on a bed of brush on the west bank for six weeks while her children cried with hunger. They had no shelter. Finally some brethren came from the Camp in Potawattomie, Iowa and took her with them. They built her a rough shelter without floor or chimney where she lived and fed her children cracked corn. By the end of the next summer she was so thin and feeble that light could almost be seen through her hands.

Mary Ann was taken to Kanesville, where she met and married Edward Pugh, Jr. Together, they moved to Council Bluffs where Mary Ann gave birth to a son. It took four years and two moves to prepare for their journey to Utah. She brought her spinning wheel, and butter churn with her and upon their arrival in the Salt Lake Valley they built a log cabin.

Mary Ann was a particularly good cook and entertained Brigham Young many times in her home.

CAROLINE NIELSON PUGMIRE

BIRTHDATE: 31 Oct 1840
Malmohus, Sweden
DEATH: 8 May 1913
St. Charles, Bear Lake Co., Idaho
PARENTS: Anders Nielsson
Ingar Olsson Nielson
PIONEER: 22 Sep 1861
Wagon Train Company
SPOUSE: Jonathan Pugmire
MARRIED: 13 Apr 1864
Salt Lake City, Salt Lake, Utah
DEATH SP: 16 Sep 1860
St. Charles, Bear Lake Co., Idaho

CHILDREN:
Henry Nelson, 11 Feb 1862
William Nelson, 16 Aug 1863
Ellen Nelson, 16 Jun 1865
Sarah Nelson, 3 Dec 1867
David Nelson, 11 Jan 1870
Alma Nelson, 11 Sep 1872;
Nora Nelson, 14 Jan 1875.

Caroline was born in Malmohus, Skoma Esrope, Sweden in October of 1840. She lost her mother while still in her tender years.

Her family all accepted the Gospel and planned to come West. She with her father and brother Peter and family set sail for America. After landing in New Orleans, they joined a company of Saints and started on their Westward trip.

While coming across the Plains, her father died and she saw them lower her father in an unknown grave. Now she was an orphan speaking no English. Caroline walked most of the way and her shoes wore out. Brigham Young gave her employment so she could buy some new shoes. The immigrants camped on the tithing yard. Caroline was very lonely and had become separated from her brother.

A friend, Mrs. Anna Swenson, from Sweden came looking for her and took the young girl home with her to live. She had a large family so it was necessary for Caroline to find work to support herself.

Caroline soon engaged in domestic services in different homes. One of the homes she went to work in was for the Jonathan Pugmire family.

She was a beautiful girl with red hair. Her outstanding character traits were patience, faith, kindness, sweet tempered, humility, purity, integrity, and love.

Caroline was the seventh child of nine; four brothers and four sisters, with three girls passing away in infancy. She wrote to her brother to tell him about two suitors she had, one was the polygamist named Jonathan Pugmire and, because of her faith in the Gospel, she was going to choose the proposal from him. Caroline's brothers and sister disowned her, even tried to pay her for not marrying in polygamy, and so by doing she lost contact with them all.

After her marriage, as a second wife, being seventeen years younger than her husband, they lived in Salt Lake. Then they were called to come to Bear Lake in 1864 to help Charles C. Rich colonize it. They left everything and went willingly. They settled in St. Charles, Bear Lake County, Idaho. They lived in a five-room log house with a dirt roof and a dirt floor with no windows or doors. A new home was built later with three stories; each wife had a section.

To support the families, a store named the St. Charles Cooperative Institute was built in 1869 and became known as the Pugmire Store.

At age forty, Caroline was a widow with a family to support. One of her sons died and eighteen months later his wife died leaving four children. Caroline took two of the older children, Matthew and Sidney Pugmire and raised them to manhood.

She was alone for thirty years without seeing any of her family kin. One time a traveling salesman came through and stayed at her place. He was watching her prepare his meal and visited with her. Soon he said, "I had a sister named Caroline and you remind me of her," but he had lost contact with her. He walked over to her and parted her hair and searched for a scar which his sister had carried since childhood. While young she had fallen and cut her head on a rock. When he found the scar he said, "I am your brother Nels Anderson presently living in Snake River, Idaho. He and his brother Olaf ran a freight business. Thus after thirty years she was united with her family. The family did not all come to America at the same time. Those that lived in Idaho took part of the father's name so were Anderson and the ones settling in Utah took as their last name Nelson.

Although Caroline had much sorrow in her life, her faith grew stronger as the years went by. Her faith and courage made her a true pioneer.

CLARISSA AMES MONJAR WILLIAMS PUGSLEY

BIRTHDATE: 16 Dec 1827
Shorham, Addison Co., Vermont
DEATH-. 24 July 1910
Salt Lake City, Salt Lake, Utah
PARENTS: Ira Ames
Charity Carter
PIONEER: 1851
SPOUSE I: Thomas Monjar
MARRIED: 1843
Vermont
DEATH SP: Unknown

CHILDREN:
Charity Caroline, 17 Jun 1846

SPOUSE: II John D. Williams
MARRIED: Dec 1850
DEATH SP: Unknown
CHILD:
Charles John, 1 Apr 1855

SPOUSE III: Philip Pugsley
MARRIED: 24 Aug 1855
Salt Lake City, Salt Lake Co., Utah
DEATH SP: 23 Jun 1903
Salt Lake City, Salt Lake Co., Utah

CHILDREN:
Sarah Isabel (Raleigh), 22 Jul 1856
Mary (Lambourne), 27 Jun 1858
Clarissa (Barlow), 31 Aug 1860
George, 29 Aug 1865

Clarissa's family joined the Church of Jesus Christ of Latter-day Saints in 1832 and the family moved from place to place with the Church.

The family were neighbors of the Prophet Joseph Smith in Kirtland, Ohio and Clarissa was baptized at the age of eight in the Mississippi River in the month of December. The ice had to be broken for her baptism.

Clarissa's mother was a close companion to Emma Smith, the Prophet's wife, who gave Clarissa a beaded necklace which she always cherished. Many times the Ames family would spend evenings at the home of the Prophet. She was proud of the fact that as a young child the Prophet would hold her on his knee. Clarissa attended a school which was called "the School of the Prophets," which convened at night in which the Prophet Joseph Smith was the teacher.

Her mother died from exposure, caused by traveling, when Clarissa was twelve years old. After the death of her mother, she went to live with Lydia K. Knight, who was the mother of Jesse Knight. She took care of the children while Mrs. Knight attended her millinery shop.

At the age of sixteen, Clarissa married Thomas Munjar. They had one baby who died. She left her husband as he failed to provide a living and returned to her fathers home. In December, 1850, she married John D. Williams and in the following Spring came with him to Utah. Her husband died two months before Clarissa gave birth to a baby boy.

Clarissa could spin, card, weave and knit, she also belonged to the first Relief Society in her ward.

When Philip Pugsley arrived in the Salt Lake Valley, he found work in a tannery which belonged to Ira Ames, Clarissa's father. They became good friends. Ira Ames decided to move to Logan, and he suggested to Philip that he might take Clarissa as his plural wife. His first wife, Martha Roach, gave her permission, and they lived together in polygamy happily for forty-eight years.

EVELYN ROSETTE HARMON PUGSLEY

BIRTHDATE: 6 May 1854
Genese, New York
DEATH: 19 Nov 1922
Salt Lake City, Salt Lake, Utah
PARENTS: Norton Harmon
Thankful Loretta Tanner
PIONEER: 1862
Wagon Train Company
SPOUSE: Joseph E. F. Pugsley
MARRIED: 23 Dec 1875
Salt Lake City, Salt Lake, Utah
DEATH SP: 10 Apr 1916
Salt Lake City, Salt Lake, Utah

CHILDREN:
Joseph Norton, 22 Oct 1876
Philip Roy, 10 Oct 1878
Mable Evelyn, 30 Sep 1880
Edna, 5 Dec 1882
Dora Estella, 23 Dec 1884
Elsie, 17 Jan 1887
Shirley Wilton, 10 Nov 1890
Martha Roach, 12 Jan 1896
Dewey Cresswell, 5 Apr 1898

Evelyn Rosette "Rosa" was born in 1854 in New York State, just about fifty miles west of Palmyra and the Hill Cumorah, the fifth of twelve children.

Norton Harmon joined the Mormon Church in 1847. His family opposed, and would not help him move west until in 1861, his brother agreed to look after the farm which had been Norton's responsibility.

Rosa was seven years old when they started their trek West. They crossed the Plains in the fall of 1862 in the Peter Nebeker train of fifty wagons. They camped in the circles in their wagons, oxen grazed and fed at night and each family prepared their own meals. To her the trip was not a hardship, but an adventure. She loved to hear the Saints sing "Come, Come Ye Saints." When they came to steep hills, her father put her up high to see how difficult it was.

Because one of their oxen took sick, her father walked to Coalville, the nearest settlement as they neared the Salt Lake Valley. A bishop found a home for them and advised them to stay the winter which they did.

They left Coalville and moved to Kaysville. Her father built a log cabin with a fireplace and a bed built against the wall at the other end of the room. They enjoyed spreading a big buffalo rug before the fire and sitting on it and listening to their father talk about the gospel or listening to their mother sing. Her father died in January, 1872, and the family had hard times following this. Rosa went to Salt Lake City to find work when she was eighteen years of age.

Rosa married Joseph Edward Franklin Pugsley on December 23, 1875. They bought a home in the city where nine children were born to them.

Joseph began mining by 1876 and was gone from home a lot of the time. She wrote letters to him. Quoting one, "The only pleasure I have is in taking care of my little darling and in looking forward to the time when you will come home." Rosa's sisters lived near by for quite awhile and they enjoyed each other. The oldest son, Jody, died of diptheria one month before his fourteenth birthday.

Rosa was good hearted and generous, was outspoken with strong likes and dislikes. She helped people and enjoyed doing it. She loved and helped her children throughout her life. She taught her family to be kind to others. She watched their language, nothing rude or vulgar should be spoken. She taught by example.

Rosa's husband passed away from a heart attack. She lived until 1922, when she passed away from cancer of the esophagus.

Rosa was a brave, valiant pioneer woman of Utah.

MARTHA ROACH PUGSLEY

BIRTHDATE: 14 Dec 1829
North Curry, Somerset, England
DEATH: 23 Jun 1906
Salt Lake City, Salt Lake, Utah
PARENTS: John Roach
Mary Knapp
PIONEER: 26 Sep 1853
Jacob Gates Co. Wagon Train
SPOUSE: Philip Pugsley
MARRIED: 28 Jun 1851
Bristol, Gloucestershire, England
DEATH SP: 7 Aug 1902

CHILDREN:
Joseph Edward Franklin, 15 Apr 1852
Elizabeth Ann (Hayward), 23 Dec 1854
Emily (Thompson), 30 Jan 1857
Martha Louisa, 10 Feb 1858 (twin - died as an infant)
Philip, 10 Feb 1858 (twin)
William Henry, 11 May 1861
Minnie (Barlow), 19 Aug 1863
Adelaide (Beesley), (twin) 26 Sep 1866 (twin)

Albert, 26 Sep 1866 (twin - died at age 13)
Eva 12 Jun 1869 (died as an infant)
John Roach, 14 Aug 1871

Martha was born in 1829 in England to John and Mary Roach. She was the third child of seven born in her family. Her father died when Martha was just thirteen years old. Two children had died and her mother took all five children to Bristol to live where there were better opportunities to make a living by sewing.

Martha wrote letters for neighbors who could not write, and she worked at a young ladies boarding school. When acting as a nursemaid in the home of a Mr. Green, Martha had gone with the maid of the house to have her fortune told by tea leaves. Martha was told she would soon meet the man she would marry, and that he would be at the door when she answered it. She was also told she would go into a new country and have a large family. She replied "Nonsense, I never answer the door." A few days later, in the maid's absence, Mrs. Green sent Martha to answer the door. Philip was there as he had been called by Mr. Green to go on an errand for him.

Martha was baptized into the Church of Jesus Christ of Latter-day Saints in 1850. She was married to Philip Pugsley in Bristol, England on June 28, 1851. Her family was opposed to the Church, and were very staunch Church of England people. Martha's mother died soon after her marriage. Martha took her youngest sister to live with her until Martha left Bristol for America.

The spirit of gathering was felt deeply by the Saints and Martha was especially anxious to leave before they had much family, so they took three young men into their home as lodgers in order to get the money needed to emigrate.

They crossed the ocean on the ship "Falcon," arriving at New Orleans eight weeks later. They had left England on February 28, 1853. In April of 1853, Martha's family left with the famous "Ten Pound Company," which was without any Church aid. (The ten pound was the money necessary for the entire trip.)

They arrived at Council Bluffs, Iowa and were outfitted for the trek. They traveled with the Jacob Gates Wagon Company, arriving in the Salt Lake Valley on September 30, 1853. Philip had ten cents, one very sick wife, one son and one small box containing all of their clothing.

Their first home was a one-room log house with dirt floors. There was a terrible storm which blew snow through the dirt roof. A quilt was tacked over the bed to keep it dry as Elizabeth Ann was born on December 23, 1854. Some time later Philip bought property on 4th North where nine more children were born to them, including two sets of twins.

During the Johnston's Army scare, Martha moved south but Philip remained in Salt Lake City as a guard.

In 1865, Philip was sent to the Sandwich Islands by the Church for the purpose of determining the advisability of starting a tannery there. This trip took six months. Philip was running a tannery and a flour mill as well as a butcher shop and other industries. Martha took care of his business and directed the drying of hundreds of pounds of fruit which was later shipped to Montana to the mines.

At the time of her death, Martha had six of her children living; four daughters and two sons. Three sons had died, one son at fourteen years of age, another son at twenty-one years, and one more at thirty-one years; she had also lost two infant daughters.

Philip and Martha celebrated their Golden Wedding anniversary in June, 1901. Philip passed away in August, 1903, and Martha passed away in June of 1906, at the age of seventy-six years.

Martha was a very reserved woman with but few intimate friends, but with the respect of many. She was always very generous to those in need. She never refused to share what she had with others, even in her own time of need.

Martha did not work in the Church organizations her early years being occupied with the care of eleven children and her later life being devoted to the care of her husband who was sorely afflicted with rheumatism.

Her Patriarchal Blessing was fulfilled when it said, "Her children shall rise up and call her blessed, and her name shall be handed down and revered by her posterity." One of her daughters-in-law said of her, "She was one of the best women that ever lived," a great tribute to a great, faithful, pioneer woman who truly lived her religion and was an examplar-for all.

MARY BROWN PULSIPHER

BIRTHDATE: 2 Mar 1799
Kent Litchfield, Connecticut
DEATH: 7 May 1885/1886
Hebron, Washington Co., Utah
PARENTS: John Brown
Sarah Fairchild
PIONEER: 23 Sep 1847/1848
Heber C. Kimball Wagon Train
SPOUSE: Zerah Pulsipher
MARRIED: 18 Aug 1815
Susquehanna, Pennsylvania
DEATH SP: 1 Jan 1870/1872
Hebron, Washington Co., Utah

CHILDREN:
Mary Ann, 30 May 1816
Iona Almira, 8 Sep 1817
Nelson, 28 Mar 1820
Mariah, 11 Jun 1822
Sarah Ann, 20 Nov 1824
John, 17 Jul 1828
Charles, 20 Apr 1830
Mary Ann, 20 Nov 1833
William, 21 Jan 1836
Eliza Jane, 26 Jul 1840
Fidelia, 13 Oct 1842

Mary was the fourth child of eight-children. She was raised in the Methodist Faith. At age six her family moved from Connecticut to Pennsylvania. Here she met Zerah Pulsipher and married. They lived in Pennsylvania seven years and had four children, later moving to New York State in Onendago County. Four more children were born here.

In 1832, they happened to see a Book of Mormon, borrowed it, read it, and-believed it to be true. It was not long before a Mormon Elder named Jared Carter came and taught them the gospel. The night before baptism, Mary became very lame with rheumatism. She was so sick she could not get around much. As they were fixing to go, Elder Carter told her, "Sister Pulsipher, If you will do your duty, you shall be healed." She took a cane and hobbled to the water and went in. It was a very cold day, but she came out well, left her cane, and went away rejoicing.

They moved to Kirtland, Ohio. Her son William was born here. They remained in Kirtland four years and helped,build the temple. Being driven from the area, they moved on to Missouri and stayed at Far West through that winter. They were in Bear Creek Woods nearly two years.

When the Saints began to settle in Nauvoo they moved and resided there for five years. Her two daughters were born here and the youngest died just shortly before they were driven out in February of 1846. While in Nauvoo, they helped to build the temple and received their endowments there.

After arriving in the Salt Lake Valley they built a home on block 82 on Jordan Street. It was 34 by 30 feet. The next season they built a large barn and made a farm over Jordan River where they were able to keep cattle.

In 1862, they were called to go to the Dixie Mission, so they sold their property and moved south, helping to establish a settlement called Hebron (near Enterprise, Utah).

On March 2, 1879, Mary went to a Relief Society meeting expecting to see ten or twelve sisters. To her great surprise, when she opened the door, she saw long tables loaded with cookies, cakes, cheese and other food. Nearly every family in town was there. The bishop stood and said, "This is in honor of "Mother Pulsipher." This is her eightieth birthday." She thanked them for the honor and respect that they had shown her.

Mary said that she had been in the Church over forty-seven years. She had passed through persecutions, mobbings and drivings with the Saints since the days of Kirtland. She rejoiced to be worthy to have a name and place with these people.

METTE SUSANNE RASMUSSEN (SORENSEN) PULSIPHER

BIRTHDATE: 14 June 1838
Vandlose, Bronshoj,
Copenhagen, Denmark
DEATH: 19 Apr 1893
Brigham City, Box Elder, Utah
PARENTS: Soren Rasmussen
Anne Haagensen
PIONEER: 1862
George Stringhouse (Stringham) Co.
SPOUSE: Orson Hyde Pulsipher
MARRIED: 8 Mar 1861
Brigham City, Utah
DEATH SP: 8 Mar 1878
Brigham City, Box Elder, Utah

CHILDREN:
Orson Henry, 26 Aug 1863
Susannah, 27 Jan 1865
Ephraim, 5 Oct 1866
William, 15 Jun 1868
Polly Ann, 2 Jul 1870
Lescine, 12 Mar 1872
Lena Olena, 12 Mar 1872
Elise, 12 Apr 1874
Elias, 19 Oct 1875

Mette was born 14 Jun 1838 in Denmark. She joined the Church in Denmark and came to Utah with her parents and two sisters. They came across the plains in the George Stringham Company in 1861, and she met her husband-to-be, Orson Hyde Pulsipher, when he was sent to meet the company and help them come into the valley. They were married 8 Mar 1862 in Brigham City, Utah.

Shortly after their marriage they moved to Brigham City. Their first home was a log hut with no floors or windows. Mette became treasurer of the Relief Society and also a teacher in that organization. She was very handy with needlework, for herself and others. When her husband died 8 Mar 1878 she had to raise her five surviving children alone, by farming and growing a garden. Mette died 19 Apr 1893 in Brigham City, Utah.

ROZILLA HUFFAKER PULSIPHER

BIRTHDATE: 24 Jan 1837
Bureau Co., Illinois
DEATHDATE: 9 Feb 1871
Enterprise, Washington Co., Utah
PARENTS: Simpson D. Huffaker
Susan Green Robinson
PIONEER: 6 Oct 1847
Wagon Train Company
SPOUSE: John Pulsipher
MARRIED: 4 Nov 1853
Salt Lake City, Salt Lake, Utah
DEATH SP: 9 Aug 1891
Enterprise, Washington Co., Utah

CHILDREN:
Sarah Elzina, 6 Nov 1854

Henrietta, 2 Dec 1856 (stillborn)
Emily Sariah, 14 Jan 1858
Mary Elizabeth, 20 Nov 1859
John David, 28 Dec 1861
Charles Zerah, 4 Feb 1863
William Lewis, 8 Jan 1865 (died at age 5)

Rozilla, with her parents, moved to Nauvoo in the year 1845. Here her mother died. Rozilla was nine years old and the oldest of five children. She witnessed the finishing of the Nauvoo Temple and the destruction of home and property. She came across the Plains at ten years of age.

Rozilla married John Pulsipher on November 4, 1853 in her fathers home at age sixteen. He was from New York and had come with the Saints in 1848. She was sealed to him in the Endowment House March 20, 1854, by Heber C. Kimball.

Rozilla was a brave, strong minded woman and was supportive of her husband. She made buckskin gloves which were sold readily in the local stores. Some were very elegant and brought in $25.00 a pair. She also helped teach school in Salt Lake.

She was the first white woman to go into Fort Supply at the time Johnston's Army was approaching. She suffered many privations there.

They were called to the Cotton Mission down south where St. George was to be built. Arriving on December 24, 1861, she gave birth four days later on the 28th to her fifth child which was their first son.

In time a log house was built. Because of a hard winter and lots of rain, the streams were overflowing and it was found necessary to move to Shoal Creek later known as Hebron (now Enterprise). Here, her second son was born, being the first white child born in Shoal Creek. Rozilla was good to the Indians and fed them often.

Rozilla's health became poor. She suffered from a consumptive cough. After a lingering illness of three and a half years she passed away on February 9, 1871 at the age thirty-four years and sixteen days.

LOUISA DRIGGS PURNELL

BIRTHDATE: 18 Sep 1841
Nauvoo, Hancock Co., Illinois
DEATH: 2 Aug 1923
Preston, Franklin Co., Idaho
PARENTS: Samuel Driggs
Elizabeth Ann Taylor
PIONEER: Sep 1850
Loran Andrew Co. Wagon Train
SPOUSE: Shem Purnell
MARRIED: 22 Sep 1855
Kaysville, Davis Co., Utah
DEATH SP: 6 Jun 1897
Franklin, Franklin Co., Idaho

CHILDREN:
Ernest Alphreda, 26 Nov 1856
Ida Evaline (Hobbs), 2 Feb 1859
Anna Jane, 12 Dec 1861 (died as an infant)
Hannah Maria (Head), 13 May 1862

Louisa was born in 1841 in Nauvoo, Hancock County, Illinois. She crossed the Plains to Utah in the Loran Andrews Ox-Team Company, arriving in the Salt Lake Valley in September, 1850, after a three months journey.

Louisa was baptized in Kaysville in February, 1854. Her parents were farmers and she learned early to spin and to perform the domestic duties of housekeeping. They resided in Kaysville until April, 1860, when they moved to Franklin, Idaho. They lived all summer in a covered wagon box, and built a log room in the fall. Their homes were built in the form of a fort for protection from the Indians, who were numerous and troublesome.

In September of 1855, Louisa had married Shem Purnell. They had their endowments and were sealed in the Salt Lake Endowment House in October, 1856. At first it was hard to make a living, as money was scarce. Louisa, being ambitious and willing to do all she could to help, set up a milliner shop; the first in Preston, Idaho. This was in her home. She was unique in making and trimming women's hats. Also being an excellent seamstress, she took in dressmaking. She became renowned in these two fine arts, and this won for her much distinction. This proved to be a great help after the death of her husband when the responsibility of earning a livelihood for her children fell on her shoulders.

Louisa was a good housekeeper, keeping her home immaculate. Her homemade braided rugs were clean and placed wherever needed to protect her shiny linoleum. They put skim milk in the water they mopped with to give a shine to their floors.

Her husband's sudden death was a severe shock to her. She was in Kaysville visiting her mother when she received word of his death. This was in 1897. About 1903, Louisa had a fall and broke her hip. She was compelled to use a crutch the rest of her life. She, as well as her two sisters, all died of strokes. They were tall and stately women. They kept in close touch with each other all their married lives.

Louisa passed away at the home of her daughter in Preston, Idaho on August 2, 1923 of a stroke. She had married at age fourteen and had lived almost forty-two years when her husband passed away.

At the time of Louisa's death, her posterity numbered 3 living children, 32 living grandchildren, 102 great-grandchildren and 1 great-great-grandchild for a total of 138 living descendents and 11 deceased.

Louisa was a great, valiant pioneer woman who experienced much during her lifetime of nearly eighty-two years of age. Her posterity honor her name.

LYDIA POLLARD PUZEY

BIRTHDATE: 21 Jan 1852
Depthford, Kent, England
DEATH: 19 Apr 1940
Spring City, Sanpete Co., Utah
PARENTS: Joseph Pollard
Mary Ann Bailey
PIONEER: 22 Sep 1857
Jacob Hofheins Handcart Comp.
SPOUSE: William Henry Puzey
MARRIED: 19 Oct 1874
Salt Lake Endowment House
DEATH SP: 1887
Spring City, Sanpete Co., Utah

CHILDREN:
Frederick, 4 Sep 1875
Joseph Henry, 26 May 1877
Albert Edward, 2 May 1879
Lavina (Mott), 12 Mar1881
Mary Alice (Neilson), 23 Dec 1882
William, 27 Jun 1885

Lydia was born in 1852 in England. She was the youngest of her family of five children, and she left England when just three years of age. They crossed the Atlantic on the ship "Clara Wheeler," and she recalled vividly crossing the Atlantic as many lost their lives.

They arrived in St. Louis, Missouri in January, 1855, and stayed there for two years. While there, her father worked for Captain James Eades, as a carpenter working on steam ships and other ships.

The family joined the Jacob Hofheins Party at Florence to come to Utah in June of 1857. On their way they witnessed a stampede of animals hitched to the wagons and her father and her family were severely hurt, being run over by one of the wagons. By faith and prayer, Lydia's father was healed and able to travel, and they arrived in the Salt Lake Valley on September 22, 1857.

They lived in the 15th Ward where her father worked for twelve years for President Young as a carpenter. He was a bishop for many years, and was ordained a High Priest by Apostle Erastus Snow on October 5, 1856, when he was a member of the St. Louis Stake of Zion High Council.

Lydia married William Henry Puzey on October 19, 1874 in the Salt Lake Endowment House. They moved to Spring City, Sanpete County, Utah. Her husband was a wheelwright and a carpenter, he owned his blacksmith shop and made wagons. Henry took pneumonia and passed away in 1887. He was just fifty-three years old. Lydia was left with a family of six children to raise alone. She never remarried. She was always a good mother and an excellent housekeeper. She did her washing on a board and never had a machine.

Lydia raised a garden, taught Relief Society for forty years. She belonged to the Daughters of Utah Pioneers

Camp in Spring City. She had twenty-seven grandchildren, and twenty-five great-grandchildren at the time of her death.

Lydia Pollard Puzey was a brave pioneer woman to be honored by all. At the time of her death, April 19, 1940, she was eighty-nine years of age. She passed away in Spring City where she had spent most of her adult life, after leaving her homeland in England to join with the Saints in their Zion.

CATHERINE DONALD RANKIN PYMM

BIRTHDATE: 21 Jun 1825
Dunfirmline, Scotland
DEATH: 1909
St. George, Washington, Utah
PARENTS: Malcolm Donald
Mary Shaw
PIONEER: 2 Sep 1860
Wagon Train Company
SPOUSE I: Richard Rankin
MARRIED: 28 Nov 1859
Scotland
DEATH SP: 12 Jul 1869
Salt Lake City, Salt Lake, Utah

CHILDREN:
Catherine (Pace), 15 Sep 1860
Mary Ann (Carter), 6 Oct 1864
Sarah (Dodge), 27 Feb 1866

SPOUSE II: John Pymm
MARRIED: 1870
DEATH SP: 12 Mar 1901
St. George, Washington Co., Utah
CHILDREN: None

Catherine married Richard Rankin in Glasgow, Scotland in 1859. He was a jeweler. When missionaries from the Church of Jesus Christ of Latter-day Saints brought the gospel to their area in the mid-1850's, they embraced it and began their migration to the Rocky Mountains in 1860.

They were seven weeks on the ocean leaving from Liverpool, England to New York. They then traveled by train and river boat to St. Louis, Missouri, where they were outfitted with a wagon and ox-team and headed for the Rocky Mountains.

Catherine was eight months pregnant when they left Missouri and they fully expected the baby to be born on the trek. The baby, however, arrived in the Salt Lake Valley two weeks after their arrival on September 2, 1860.

Richard, Catherine, her sister and her father were included in their group. Catherine's mother chose to remain in Scotland.

When they left Scotland they sold their jewelry store and as part of the pay they took silk, dress patterns, paisley shawls, fine linens and lace. They brought these with them to America, carrying them in three large chests.

In St. Louis the chests were fitted into a wagon box and made the trip all the way to Salt Lake. During their struggles in getting started in Utah, they sold those beautiful things to buy sheep. The following winter, all of the sheep died of a disease. Richard Rankin passed away on July 12, 1869, at seventy-three years of age.

In 1870, Catherine married John Pymm; husband of her sister, Agnes. He came to Salt Lake City on business and went home to St. George, Utah, with a new wife. He was postmaster and ran a hotel and a restaurant.

Catherine's life in St. George was one of real pioneering. Many of the workers on the St. George temple lived and ate at the hotel. Catherine fed many of the visitors to the temple as she helped run the hotel. When the temple was completed, she became an avid temple worker.

Catherine Donald Rankin Pymm passed away in St. George in 1909 at eighty-four years of age. She had experienced much from her home in Scotland to the newly settled area of Utah. She was a true faithful pioneer woman to be honored by her posterity.

CHRISTIANA DOLLINGER PYPER

BIRTHDATE: 31 May 1836
New York City, New York
DEATH: 21 Oct 1925
Salt Lake City, Salt Lake, Utah
PARENTS: Thomas J. Dollinger
Eliza Rhodes
PIONEER: 1 Sep 1859
Horton Haight Co. Wagon Train
SPOUSE: Alexander C. Pyper
MARRIED: 24 Dec 1855
Florence, Nebraksa
DEATH SP: 28 Jul 1882
Salt Lake City, Salt Lake, Utah

CHILDREN:
Julia Eliza, 6 Nov 1856 (died at age 15)
Robert Alexander, 9 Oct 1858
George Dollinger, 21 Nov 1860
Cathrine Dollinger (Preston), 10 Jan 1863
William Dollinger, 28 May 1865
Eleanor Dollinger (Thomas), 19 Aug 1867
Alexander Cruikshanks, 28 May 1873
Walter Thomas, 3 Aug 1876
Genevieve Alice, 14 Aug 1878

Christiana was born in 1836 in New York City. Mormonism was introduced in New York in the 1830's and some of Christiana's families joined this Church of Jesus Christ of Latter-day Saints.

Her parents joined the Church and moved to the City of Nauvoo in 1842 with a party of Saints. Her family was welcomed by brothers Joseph and Hyrum Smith. Joseph rented a little house he owned to them. Her father bought two lots and on one he built a store and on the other a home for his family. Her father passed away in 1845 at the age of

thirty-three, having lived just about three years in Nauvoo. Her mother was left to care for two daughters.

Christiana was asked to write her recollections of their life in Nauvoo. From her record is quoted, "The first company of Saints crossed the Mississippi River in the early part of Feb 1846. . . The remnant of Saints who were left remained longer to try and sell their property to get an outfit. My mother, then a widow with two little girls, were among the remnant. Having little means, she helped those she could and kept a little for her own needs. My mother was given notice to vacate and be gone in 10 days. . . We did not know where to go, and was at the mercy of a murderous community . . . On the 9 Sep we were taken from our home with just enough clothes and bedding for our needs, and rode in a lumber wagon down to the ferry, crossed the Mississippi. . . and taken to Nashville and remained there until Nov."

They eventually returned for a short period to Nauvoo, a very changed city, beautiful homes were desecrated, robbers, kidnappers and counterfeiters were roaming there.

When "Christy" was sixteen years of age, she and her sister left Nauvoo for Council Bluffs where they did housekeeping work. Her mother remained in Nauvoo, visited New York again and then died in 1854.

In 1855, Christiana married Alexander Cruickshanks Pyper in Florence, Nebraska where he had an outfitting company to assist immigration. Alex was a widower, and Christy raised their one daughter. This daughter married Truman O. Angell, Jr, son of the temple architect.

Christy and Alex began their journey across the Plains on June 7, 1859 in a church train of eighty-two wagons, and two yoke of oxen on each. They were in the Horton Haight Wagon Company. At night they stopped the wagons and formed the circle with the animals inside. Tents were pitched outside the wagons, fires were made, and suppers cooked.

They were traveling for three months and arrived at Emigration bench at noon on September 1, 1859. Alex was the captain of the first ten group. They first stayed in the front yard of a Bishop Cunningham and ate their first meal there. She reported it was the "sweetest supper we had had since we left our dear Old Florence."

Six years after his marriage to Christy, Alex took a second wife, Jane Puckett Tullidge, a daughter of an accomplished musician. Alex was the father of twenty-one children. His families were close, and were growing up together. Alexander passed away in 1882 at the age of fifty-four years.

Christy's third child George, served faithfully in the Sunday School organization for fifty years and was the Superintendent at age eighty-three of the Deseret Sunday School.

Christiana was an active church worker, served in the Relief Society. She was a devout temple worker, and she administered to the sick.

Christiana passed away at eighty-nine years of age in Salt Lake City in 1925, as a true pioneer and Mormon.

ELIZABETH ELLEN MILLER QUIGLEY

BIRTHDATE: 25 Sep 1832
Quincy, Adams Co., Illinois
DEATH: 2 Jan 1915
Swan Lake, Bannock Co., Idaho
PARENTS: Henry W. Miller
Elmira Pond
PIONEER: 21 Sep 1852
Henry Miller Co. Wagon Train
SPOUSE: Andrew Quigley
MARRIED: 30 Nov 1853
Salt Lake City, Salt Lake, Utah
DEATH SP: 23 Jun 1881
Salt Lake City, Salt Lake, Utah

CHILDREN:
Ellen Elmira (Koeford), 16 Jul 1854
Lucy Celestra (Hadley), 9 Jan 1855
Andrew Henry, 15 Oct 1857
David Thadius, 14 Apr 1860
Alma Miller, 14 Feb 1862
William, 8 Jun 1864
Mary Elizabeth (Burrup), 30 Jul 1868
Sarah Melvina (McClelland), 12 Jan 1870
Adelia (Butterfield), 21 Dec 1871
Eveline (Patterson/Petterson), 8 Dec 1873
Robert George, 13 Dec 1877
Richard Oliver, 21 May 1880

The Henry Miller family was in the advance wagon train out of Nauvoo. They spent three months traveling across Iowa in the rain, snow and cold. Building bridges and roads for the Saints that would follow. They were the first settlers of Miller's Hollow which later became Council Bluffs. Elizabeth helped her family with crops for the emigrating members.

Elizabeth's father was called to the Salt Lake Valley in 1852 and was the captain of the entire wagon train. They settled in Farmington, Davis County, Utah, where she met and married Andrew Quigley.

Elizabeth gave her approval of a second wife in 1856, Harriet Yates and again in 1865 to Almira Fifield.

Elizabeth had great courage and strength throughout her life in the face of tragedy. She traveled to Wisconsin to cut timber for the Nauvoo Temple and the Nauvoo House. She nursed her husband back to health when he was shot and beaten by Indians in 1858. She also survived her home in Bountiful being burned down in 1862 during a great wind storm.

In the 1860's, the Quigleys were called to live the United Order and settle the town of Newton, where they moved to Clarkston and back to Newton before finally settling in Swan Lake, Bannock County, Idaho. Here, they built the first log home.

ELIZABETH DAVIS DAY RADDON

BIRTHDATE: 15 Nov 1839
Avenbury, England
DEATH: 28 Jan 1929
Santa Monica, California
PARENTS: William Davis
Elizabeth Bishop
PIONEER: 1854 Wagon Train
SPOUSE I: David Day
MARRIED: 3 Apr 1857
Salt Lake City, Salt Lake, Utah
DEATH SP: 11 Jun 1876
Salt Lake City, Salt Lake, Utah

CHILDREN:
Elizabeth, 1858 (died as an infant)
James William, 19 Jan 1859
Sarah Eliza, 1 Mar 1861
David Franklin Davis, 25 Apr 1862
Abraham John, 22 Feb 1864
Joseph, 1865 (died at age 13)
Alice Vilate, 7 Mar 1868
George June, 1871 (died at 16 months)
Orson Davis, 8 May 1873
Mary Amelia, 12 Mar 1875

SPOUSE II: James Henry Raddon
MARRIED: 15 May 1877
DEATH SP: 24 Feb 1900

CHILDREN:
Josephine LePage, 8 Aug 1878
Clarissa, 23 July 1880
Albert Davis, 3 Feb 1882

Elizabeth was born in Avenbury, Herefordshire, England, 1839. Her parents were baptized in 1841 at Herefordshire, England, when Elizabeth was a baby.

She was fourteen years old in 1854, when the family left England on the ship "Windemere." They suffered five weeks of stormy weather and an outbreak of smallpox. Her two youngest brothers died from the disease and were buried at sea. She and her father escaped the disease. Her mother and the other children were quarantined in New Orleans for two weeks. During that time Elizabeth and her father lived in an abandoned vessel, and there they waited for the family.

They arrived in the Salt Lake Valley in 1854. The family first stayed in one-room in the Big Cottonwood area near her uncle's family. In 1855, they moved to Kaysville, and there on September 18, 1856, Elizabeth was baptized.

On April 3, 1857, she was endowed, and in a ceremony performed by President Brigham Young, she became David Day's second wife at age seventeen. Their first four children were born at Kaysville.

In 1862, Elizabeth and David moved to Salt Lake City to open a mercantile store. Six more children were born there. Elizabeth was thirty-six years old when David died.

Elizabeth later married James H. Raddon and moved the family to her farm in Kaysville. She had three children by James.

Elizabeth was a musician and taught her children to play the organ. She enjoyed growing beautiful plants in her conservatory.

David was often away on church assignments, and Elizabeth took full responsibility for their home and children. She also cared for Mary, her husband's first wife, who was ill with rheumatic fever. Her testimony was strong and she served in many church callings.

In her later years, Elizabeth was crippled with arthritis and was cared for by her daughter, Clarissa. For her comfort they moved to Santa Monica, California, where she died at the age of eighty-nine. She is buried in the Salt Lake City Cemetery in the Day family plot.

RACHEL LEAH SMITH ROSS RADFORD

BIRTHDATE: 30 Nov 1822
Gibson Co., Tennessee
DEATH: 13 Dec 1896
Shelton (Ririe) Bonneville, Idaho
PARENTS: Richard Smith
Deannah Braswell
PIONEER: 12 Sep 1850
Aaron Johnson Co. Wagon Train
SPOUSE: Andrew Jackson Ross
MARRIED: 21 Sep 1837
DEATH SP: 1843
Tennessee

CHILDREN:
James Richard, 18 Nov 1839
Melvin, 27 Mar 1842

SPOUSE II: John Whitlock Radford
MARRIED: 6 Apr 1846
DEATH SP: 14 Dec 1889
Liberty, Uinta Co., Wyoming

CHILDREN:
Nancy Jane, 14 Jan 1847
Catherine Elizabeth, 10 Dec 1848
John Franklin, 10 Dec 1850
Leah Ellen, 6 Apr 1853
Granville L., 13 Mar 1855
Daniel H., 6 Mar 1857
Deannah Rebecca, 6 Apr 1859

Rachel Leah (or Lear / Leer) Smith, third child, was born on November 30, 1822 in Gibson County, Tennessee. Her parents were among the first settlers in this area.

The Smith family lived in Tennessee for a number of years and when missionaries of the newly restored gospel contacted them, they recognized the truth and joined the Church of Jesus Christ of Latter-day Saints in 1842. They moved to Nauvoo, Illinois a year later, leaving behind the fruits of all their labors.

Leah was raised in the frontier country of Tennessee and at the age of fifteen, was married to Andrew Jackson Ross II. Leah and her husband also joined the Church and planned the move to Nauvoo. However, in 1844, Andrew Jackson was killed while logging in the Tennessee woods. Soon after her husband's death, Leah and her two small sons made the move to Nauvoo and joined her parents.

In Nauvoo, Leah met John W. Radford, a resident of the area who had recently joined the Church. They were married on April 6, 1846.

The Smith family were in Nauvoo at the time of the martyrdom of the Prophet and his brother. Both this family and the newly-established Radford family were among the Saints who were driven out of Illinois and across the Mississippi River into Iowa. Her family began the trek across the Plains in 1850. Somewhere along the North Platte River they buried little eighteen month old, Catherine Elizabeth.

Arriving in the Salt Lake Valley on September 12, 1850, the Radford family was sent immediately to the Provo area. Here they lived inside the fort for protection from the Indians.

Fillmore, in Millard County, was their next destination when Brigham Young sent John to that community as a missionary and also to oversee some of the building projects there. He was active in the early civic affairs in Fillmore, serving as an alderman in 1859. He also served in the Presiding Council of the 42nd Quorum of the Seventy. All of these callings put additional pressure on Leah as she was left to make a home on the frontier, raise and preserve the garden produce, as well as feed and clothe a large family.

Perhaps the faith of John and Leah was tested when they were asked, in 1855, to deed all their possessions to the Church and attempt to live the United Order. The United Order experiment in Fillmore was not successful.

Another test of faith came to Leah, in 1855, when John married Polly Stevens in plural marriage. Polly was also a "southern lady," a widow with two children. John and his new wife had three children (one of whom died shortly after her mother) before she passed away in 1863. Thus Leah was left with her own eight children and four of Polly's to raise. She was a faithful and devoted mother to all.

Deseret, further west in Millard County, was the next stop for the Radfords. Life was difficult here. Again it was a new area, Indians were a constant challenge as the Black Hawk War had erupted, and obtaining water became a continual problem. No stable supply could be secured because the Sevier River, the primary source, would come down each spring with such force that it would break the dams and flood the crops.

Finally, most of those who were called to settle Deseret moved to other areas. Several families, including the Radfords, went a few miles east and began again in the tiny hamlet of Oak City.

It was here, finally, that Leah and her family were able to live for many years, still struggling to establish a new area but finding happiness and joy in their accomplishments and in their family and church.

In Oak City, again, the family signed everything they owned over to the United Order proving their faith and obedience to the Church authorities. Here, too, it was not successful.

Leah was a hard working, industrious lady, with firm faith and a desire to do what was right. She was a woman with little or no formal education, but she taught her children to be honest, upright and honorable and to love the Lord. She was willing to serve where she could, helping others as the opportunity presented itself, and always sustaining her husband.

When Leah was sixty-seven years old, her husband decided to again go "pioneering. " They packed all of their belongings and started out with a long caravan of wagons, cows, chickens, pigs, etc., for Star Valley, Wyoming.

After one of Wyoming's extremely hard winters brought much trauma, including the death of Leah's husband, John, as well as cattle freezing and starving, they decided to continue on to the Upper Snake River Valley in Idaho. Leah had become very ill on the journey from Utah and was in no condition to go further. Her daughter, Leah Ellen, and family remained in Wyoming to care for her. Finally, when Leah was some better, the Lovells, followed the rest of their family and friends to Idaho, taking Leah with them.

In this new country, again facing the challenges associated with pioneering, but no longer a young, vigorous woman, Leah lived with her various children, helping out in any way she could.

Leah passed away on December 13, 1896 at Shelton, Bingham County, Idaho. She is buried in the Ririe-Shelton Cemetery. A number of years later, after the area was well established, several of her grandsons and a grandson-in-law moved the body of her husband from his lonely grave in Wyoming to the Ririe-Shelton Cemetery so that he could be at her side.

DOROTHY / DORITHY JANE DENNIS MCGEE RAINEY

BIRTHDATE: 16 Jun 1840
Pontatoc Co., Mississippi
DEATH: 18 Jul 1920
Santa Barbara, California
PARENTS: William T. Dennis
Talitha Cumi Bankhead
PIONEER: 22 Aug 1855
Gilbert & Garrish Wagon Train
SPOUSE I: Franklin McGee
MARRIED: August 1855
Salt Lake City, Salt Lake, Utah
DEATH SP: Unknown

CHILD:
Martha Jane, 25 May 1856

SPOUSE II: David Pinkney Rainey
MARRIED: 9 Feb 1857
Provo, Utah Co., Utah
DEATH SP: 6 Nov 1888
Richmond, Cache Co., Utah

CHILDREN:
David William, 6 Jan 1858
Margaret Minerva, 15 Sep 1860
Joseph P., 19 Sep 1861
Mary Elizabeth, 25 Aug 1863
George Washington, 2 Oct 1864
James Albert, 2 Feb 1866
Frederick Henry, 29 Oct 1868
Emma Catherine, 9 Aug 1870
Grace Ann, 15 Jan 1871
Talitha Dean, 18 Sep 1872
Sina Marie, 13 Nov 1873
Chloe Eugenia, 7 Dec 1875
Junius Roland, 24 Dec 1876
Jennie Bell, 23 Jun 1879
Inez Leona, 26 Jan 1882

Doritha Jane Dennis Rainey was born in Pontatoc County, Mississippi on June 16, 1840. Her father was a wealthy planter, owning a large plantation and many slaves, which enabled his family to enjoy social prominence in the aristocracy of the community in which they lived. She had eight brothers and sisters. Doritha's childhood was spent in ease and luxury. At thirteen she attended a boarding school ten miles from her home. She was an excellent horse woman and often took long rides through the beautiful countryside.

When Doritha was nine years of age, the family was visited by Elders Preston Thomas and Jolly who were preaching the gospel of Jesus Christ of Latter-day Saints. Doritha's father recognized the truth but his family did not do so until after their arrival in Utah. Doritha was always a firm defender of Mormonism and often engaged in heated arguments with her school mates in its defense. The faith of William T. Dennis was so strong that he remarked, "I would go to Utah if I knew it was only a barren rock."

In 1854, the family left their home and all that was near and dear to them there and started for the gathering place of the Saints. Doritha was fourteen years of age at the time, well developed and considered quite beautiful.

Doritha had many suitors, foremost among whom was one named Franklin McGee, a young man much older than herself. He followed the family from their home in Mississippi to St. Louis. Here he persuaded Doritha's father to allow him to accompany them to Utah. Doritha was a clever horsewoman and drove the family carriage most of the journey, being able to care for her team as well as any teamster. Franklin McGee had been very devoted to the family through many, many miles of early travel. He had been a timely assistant, being at hand when they needed him most. His acts of chivalry and seemingly untiring affection won Doritha's girlish heart, and in the latter part of August 1855, she became his wife. The ceremony was performed at her father's home by an Elder Stevens.

Doritha's life certainly changed. The child of luxury, at the age of fifteen she was a wife in a new and sparsely settled country. In the Summer of 1856, a baby girl was born. She watched the waning affection of her once devoted husband and when winter came, with her babe in her arms, she was obliged to return to her father's home in Lehi.

Doritha married David P. Rainey in February of 1857 and they moved to Provo. David had been a personal friend of the Prophet Joseph Smith and a worker in the Nauvoo Temple.

In the Spring of 1857, David was called on a mission to San Francisco to assist President George Q. Cannon in editing a paper there. Doritha and her baby girl were once more left alone. The summer was filled with hard work, hardships and privations. In the autumn the little girl sickened and died, leaving Doritha with a broken heart.

On the 6th of January, 1858, a son was born to Doritha and David. The family moved to Pond Town which was later called Salem. David was appointed bishop, holding the office until the Spring of 1860 when they moved to Cache Valley to make their home. They were some of the first settlers of Richmond.

Their home through the first spring and summer was a tent, then a dugout. During much poverty and hardship the family increased as well as decreased, babies came bringing their joyous welcome.

In the Spring of 1875, Elder Rainey was again called on a mission to the Southern States. He was obliged to return home on account of ill health. In 1888, he passed away and Doritha cared and provided for her remaining children until they were all married and had home of their own. One of the most severe trials of her life was the accidental drowning of her son, James, in the waters of the Snake River.

Doritha was the mother of sixteen children, of whom ten remained to comfort her in her declining years. Besides rearing so large a family, Doritha had been an active worker in the Relief Society and was present at its first organization in Richmond.

She procured for herself a comfortable home in Richmond in which she enjoyed many of the modern conveniences. Here she quietly spent the evening of her life surrounded by her children and grandchildren who loved to visit her and cheer and gladden her during her declining years.

A family reunion was held, June 16, 1920, in honor of Doritha's eightieth birthday. Her son, daughter, many grandchildren and great-grandchildren were there. At the program she recited the poem, "I Am the Monarch of All I Survey." The reunion was held in the Richmond Tabernacle and was a day of rejoicing for her family.

A short time later her daughter, Jennie Campbell, took her to California to spend the winter. Just before reaching Santa Barbara, Doritha had a stroke and on the 17th of July passed away. Jenny brought her home to the town and people she loved so much.

She was laid beside her husband and thus ended the life of a lovely, noble woman, a blessed mother and a true Saint.

SARAH JOHNSON RALPHS

BIRTHDATE: 3 Feb 1821
Ireland
DEATH: 14 Apr 1896
Brigham City, Box Elder, Utah
PARENTS: Joseph Johnson
Margaret Johnson
PIONEER: 29 Oct 1849
Ezra T. Benson Wagon Train
SPOUSE I: Thomas Ralphs
MARRIED: 10 May 1842
Missouri
DEATH SP: 11 Jun 1859
Brigham City, Box Elder, Utah

CHILDREN:
Georgina, 24 Jul 1842
Joseph, 5 Feb 1846
Ephraim, 19 Apr 1848
Sarah Ann, 5 Mar 1851
Thomas Heber, 29 Jan 1853
James Albert, 18 Dec 1854
Mary Frances, 15 Feb 1857
Lovinnia E., 12 Aug 1859

Sarah Johnson was born on February 3, 1821 in Ireland. Her parents were English and evidently were employed in a pottery in Ireland at the time of Sarah's birth. Both Thomas Ralphs and Sarah Johnson worked in a pottery in England. Thomas molded the clay and Sarah decorated it.

They were sweethearts in England and Thomas urged Sarah to be married but Sarah was desirous of going to America and joining the Saints before they married. When

reminiscing with her daughter, Mary, years later, she felt like that was a mistake, as she was extremely seasick on the long ocean voyage.

They were married, May 10, 1842, in Missouri. In the midst of the turmoil and the persecution of the Saints in Missouri, Thomas and Sarah ventured forth on their honeymoon. Their goal was to join the Saints in Nauvoo and this they did. Their grandson, Orestus, recalled that he heard his grandmother say that they lived across the street from the Prophet Joseph Smith and his family.

Sarah told her descendants that she was present at the meeting when the mantle of Joseph Smith fell upon Brigham Young. Both Thomas and Sarah received their Patriarchal Blessings from John Smith, uncle of the Prophet, in Nauvoo, September 15, 1845. Thomas received his endowments on February 7, 1846 in the Nauvoo Temple. Sarah would have been there, too, but her second child was born on February 5, 1846.

In April of 1848, they were in Bonaparte, Van Buren County, Iowa. Along the trek, death claimed their second child, Joseph, on July 27, 1848. Ezra T. Benson's Company "arrived in the city in Companies of Ten" on October 29, 1849.

The family of three located in the Tenth Ward in Salt Lake City. Sarah received her Endowments and was sealed to her husband in Salt Lake City, December 9, 1851. Thomas assisted in the building of the Salt Lake Temple by hauling rock for "a granite quarry some twenty miles to the southeast. The only means of transportation was by ox-team taking three or four days to make the round trip."

They continued to pioneer and suffered many privations and hardships, going two miles west of Brigham City to pull what were called water segos, which grew in the water. The segos were stewed and with a little bran or flour, made into porridge to subsist on.

Thomas passed away on June 11, 1859. He was less than forty years of age. Sarah was greatly grieved at the loss of her beloved companion. Two months later, she gave birth to a daughter.

Resolutely, she set forth to provide for and raise her family. She organized a school and taught in a room of her own home. Later she taught school in a public building in Calls Fort, almost five miles distant from her home and she commuted on foot. When Mary became old enough, she assisted her mother with the school. Sarah's sons all worked hard to help maintain the family.

Later Sarah was called to attend classes in Salt Lake City to train to be a midwife. She was set apart with others as a mid-wife and nurse on September 26, 1873.

Notwithstanding the many trials and privations endured, Sarah lived to be seventy-five years old. She passed away on April 14, 1896 and she and her husband are both interred in the Brigham City Cemetery.

ANE MARIE SOPHIE CLAUSEN JENSEN BRISTOL CAMBRON RAMBO

BIRTHDATE: 27 Apr 1851
Horsens, Skanderborg, Denmark
DEATH: 4 Nov 1929
Mt. Pleasant, Sanpete Co., Utah
PARENTS: R. Clausen or Jensen
Mette Marie Iversdatter Iversen
PIONEER: 27 Sep 1862
John Murdock Co. Wagon Train
SPOUSE I: Hans Gulbransen
MARRIED: 6 Jul 1867
Sealed in the Endowment House
DEATH SP: 26 Jun 1894
Woodruff, Navajo Co., Arizona

CHILDREN: None

SPOUSE II: William Bristol
MARRIED: prior to the Census of July 1870
DEATH SP: late 1874 or early 1875

CHILDREN:
Emma Elizabeth (Dodge), 15 Apr 1871
Margaret Ann (Jensen), 2 Aug 1872
Charles William, 25 Nov 1873
Christopher Columbus, 17 Apr 1875

SPOUSE III: Joseph Cambron
MARRIED: abt 1875
Nephi, Juab Co, Utah
DEATH SP: prior to 1891

CHILDREN:
Josephine (Mouritzen), 25 Nov 1876
Evelyn (Zabriskie), 13 Dec 1878
Eleeta or Electa Pearl, 6 Mar 1880
Patrick Henry, 17 Dec 1882
Abbie Gill (Waldemar), 24 Nov 1884

SPOUSE IV: Charles D. Rambo
MARRIED: 17 Jan 1891
Nephi, Juab Co., Utah
DEATH SP: Jun 1945
Mt. Pleasant, Sanpete Co., Utah
CHILDREN: None

Ane Marie Sophie Clausen (Jensen) was born on April 27, 1851 in Horsens, Skanderborg, Denmark to Rasmus Clausen (or Jensen) and Mette Marie Iversdatter Oversen. Ane had one brother, Ole Carl Christian Clausen (or Jensen).

When missionaries from the Church of Jesus Christ of Latter-day Saints came to Denmark to preach the gospel, Ane's mother gained a testimony of the truthfulness of what she heard; however, her father would not listen nor believe. This seemed to be the reason that Mette and Rasmus ended their short marriage. Mette Marie was baptized into the Church, and Ane and her brother Carl (Charles) were given blessings.

In the year 1862, there was a common desire among the Saints to emigrate to America and join the main body of the Church in the mountains of Utah. Mette Marie labored hard, and sold what few possessions she could in order to send her oldest child, Ane Marie to America with some of the other Saints.

Ane was eleven when she became a passenger on the ship "Humboldt." It sailed from Hamburg, Germany for America on April 9, 1862. The Humboldt arrived at New York, May 29th. Ane was listed as number 1,188. She was probably in the care of other emigrating Saints.

Ane now became an immigrant, and traveled by trains and steam boats to Florence, Nebraska. Here the people were reorganized into companies to cross the Plains. Eleven year old Ane was assigned to John D. Murdock's Ox-Company, which left Florence, July 24, 1862 and arrived in Salt Lake City, Utah on September 27, 1862.

Almost all of the Danish immigrants were sent south to Sanpete County to make their homes. Ane went along, and her final destination was in Mount Pleasant, where she was taken into the home of Bishop William Seeley.

Ane had to make many changes and adjustments. She had to learn to read, write and speak English. Her name was now spelled "Annie." She witnessed the hostile Indians during the Black Hawk Indian War, and the settlers of Fairview who had to move into the Mt. Pleasant Fort for protection.

A family that Annie was working with, had placed their baby by a nearby fenceline, where they could find it quickly, if necessary. Annie happened to look up and see Indians sneaking towards them, and screamed "Indians" as a warning to the others. Since she was near the fence, she swept the baby into her arms and ran for safety as fast as she could. At one point she felt a pain in her neck, as an arrow cut through the skin, but she kept running with the baby. When she reached safety an arrow was still embedded in her long skirt. The arrow that hit her neck left a life-long ugly scar on Annie's neck. She was always self-conscious of the scar and wore high collared dresses to cover it. Children and grandchildren always liked to look at the skirt with the arrow holes in it that she had saved.

Another family story says that Annie was pressured into marrying an old polygamist, but shortly after the marriage she ran away from him. Annie had just turned sixteen years old and Hans Gulbransen was forty-four. It is not known how long Annie lived with Hans, but there is a Cancellation date of July 30, 1870 in the Church Special Records.

Annie married William Bristol who had come from Upper Canada with his mother and family. This seemed to be a marriage of love and one of Annie's own choosing. They moved to Eureka where William began a new trade as a miner.

Annie's mother and brother were finally emigrated to Utah in 1870, however, no further record of Mette is found after she married seventy-one year old John Swenson, April, 1871 in the Endowment House.

Annie and William had four children. While Annie was pregnant with her fourth child, tragedy struck, William was working in a mine up a canyon near Nephi when he was to have met two other men and ride with them in a wagon down the canyon, to catch a train back to Nephi. Nobody knows exactly what happened, but when William was found he had frozen to death.

Shortly after William's death, Annie married Joseph Cambron who had come to the rich silver fields of Eureka as a miner. They had five children. Around 1880, Joseph's health began to decline and he was unable to work full time. Family stories stated that while Annie was trying to raise her family, she ran a boarding house, did a lot of cooking and was a very good cook. Eleeta or Electa died about 1887 when a lot of sickness and deaths was going through Eureka. Joseph died of miners consumption prior to 1891.

Annie met and married a man younger than herself, Charles D. Rambo. He was a carpenter and mason by trade. Annie's children didn't seem to care much for their new step-father. He drank and didn't like to have children around him. Some of the children left home to be on their own after this marriage. Annie and her family moved back to Mt. Pleasant, Utah, where Annie had been raised as a young pioneer girl. Annie bought some property and a home there and lived with Charles Rambo through thirty-eight years of marriage to him, until Annie, herself, passed away, November 4, 1929, in Mt. Pleasant, Utah at the age of seventy-eight.

Annie's life seemed to be one of trial of faith and courage one after another, but she was a fighter and a survivor! Even though Annie's children were not raised actively in the Church, almost all of them seemed to cherish the faith and sacrifices that their Danish mother and grandmother went through to become members of the Church. Most of them were later baptized and raised their own families actively in the Church.

CAROLINE BERGER RAMMELL

BIRTHDATE: 24 Aug 1846
Karlsruhe, Baden, Germany
DEATH: 24 May 1922
Tetonia, Teton Co., Idaho
PARENTS: Fredrick Berger
Elizabeth Barbara Braeuer
PIONEER: 1862
ship "Windemere" from France
SPOUSE: Charles H. Rammell
MARRIED: 14 Feb 1862
Providence, Cache Co., Utah
DEATH SP: 1906

CHILDREN:
Herbert Charles, 23 Feb 1864
William, 17 Dec 1866

Rhoda Ann , 30 Mar 1869
George Fredrick, 21 July 1871
Amy Sabrin, 18 Nov 1874
Caroline "Lena," 27 Jan 1877
Alma Henry, 14 Jun 1880
Parley Samuel, 4 Dec 1884

Caroline Berger Rammell was born on August 24, 1846 in Karlsruhe, Baden, Germany. Caroline's mother died shortly after her birth. When Caroline and her father, Fredrick, immigrated to America, they brought with them a boy named Henry Berger. He lived with them until his marriage. They also raised, as their own, Lydia Cantwell, whose mother had died and left the father with too many children to care for. She and Henry later married.

Charles and Caroline were very prominent in Providence. They owned much land and gave much away to those in need. She was a mid-wife and delivered many babies in Providence and later in Teton Valley, Idaho.

They immigrated to Teton Valley in 1900, where their grown sons had gone two years before. Here they homesteaded in the Haden area. Their youngest son, Parley, lived with them.

Caroline's husband passed away in 1906 and her son, Parley, died two years later. Parley's wife, Letitia J. Hegsted, lived with Caroline and continued the homesteading in that area and also on the west side of the valley.

Caroline served in many church positions and also continued in her midwifing service. She delivered over 300 babies and never lost a baby or a mother.

Caroline was a prayerful, humble servant.

SABRIN SOUTH RAMMELL

No
Photo
Available

BIRTHDATE: 12 Aug 1824
Pershon, England
DEATH: 23 Jan 1884
Providence, Cache Co., Utah
PARENTS: William South
Mary Combs
PIONEER: Btwn 1851 and 1853
SPOUSE: Charles H. Rammell
MARRIED: 20 Dec 1846
St. Marlin, Worchestershire,
England
DEATH SP: 4 Apr 1906
Tetonia, Teton Co., Idaho

CHILD:
Joseph, abt 1847

Sabrin South Rammell was born on August 12, 1824 in Pershon, Worchestershire, England to William South and Mary Combs South.

Sabrin married Charles Holling Rammell in St. Marlin, Worchestershire, England on December 20, 1846. She sailed, with her husband from England on the "Ellen

Marie," under Captain Whitman. They left England on February 1, 1951 and arrived in New Orleans on August 29, 1951. Charles worked up and down the Mississippi River on a "tug boat' to earn enough money to travel on to the Salt Lake Valley. Just when they arrived in Utah, is not certain. They were members of the Butterfield Ward in 1853.

They had no children, but raised an Indian boy, Joseph, born about 1847 of Providence, Utah. He was sealed to them on January 20, 1891 in the Logan Temple.

Sabrin was a "second" for her husband as he fought barefisted in the ring in England. When they heard the missionaries one night on the street corner, they knew immediately the church was true and immigrated to America, to Zion.

ADA ALICE MACDUFF RAMPTON

BIRTHDATE: 15 Nov 1850
Chesterfield, England
DEATH: 11 Sep 1910
Centerville, Davis Co., Utah
PARENTS: John R. MacDuff
Ellen Hancock
PIONEER: 1864
Wagon Train Company
SPOUSE: Henry Rampton
MARRIED: 1 Nov 1868
DEATH SP: 24 Nov 1903

CHILDREN:
George Albert, 15 Mar 1870
John Robertson, 16 May 1872
Jane Maude, 3 Apr 1874
Thomas, 19 Jul 1876
Nellie Eliza, 14 Oct 1878
Malcolm MacDuff, 4 May 1881
Elizabeth Ellen, 17 Mar 1883
Sarah Anna, 17 May 1885
Laura Olive, 25 Aug 1887

Ada Alice was born on November 15, 1850 in Chesterfield, Derbyshire, England to John Robertson MacDuff and Ellen Hancock MacDuff.

The MacDuff family was converted to the Church of Jesus Christ of Latter-day Saints by Elder Joseph F. Smith and Elder John Nicholson in England. Many of the Elders received hospitality in the family home until they emigrated to Utah in 1864. They left on the vessel, "George B. McLelland."

The vessel had to take a northern route because of the Civil War and possible molestation by vessels of the south. The vessel ran into huge icebergs and caused great fear and confusion. The women and children were crying and huddled together.

The mate of the vessel took his lantern to examine parts of the vessel for possible leaks and found Ada Alice and her sister, Jane, and said, "Little girls, aren't you afraid?" They answered, "No, we're not afraid, the Lord didn't bring us out here to be drowned in the sea." Then the mate, in joy, swung his lantern round and round and cried out very loudly, "Hurrah! this vessel won't sink, there is faith enough here to save our ship."

The vessel did not sink and they reached America safely. The next year this same vessel, was caught in a similar storm and every one on board was drowned in the Atlantic Ocean.

After Ada Alice was married she lived in Bountiful for about eighteen years. The family then moved to West Syracuse where the family was engaged in farming. She took care of the farm with the help of her children. The farm was close to the Great Salt Lake and the nearest neighbor was over a mile from their house.

Ada Alice was first Counselor in the Primary in the Syracuse Ward when the Primary was organized. She remembered that Sister Aurelia S. Rodgers and Sister Clark from the General Board Presidency visited their Primary quite frequently. She served as a counselor for about twelve years.

Ada Alice loved to read. She was self-educated. Nearly every night she read, the last thing before she turned off the lamp to sleep. She read from The Bible and Book of Mormon. She was fond of the English Classics; Scott, Burns, Dickens and other English Classics. She also liked Shakespeare and was acquainted with grand Operas and knew many lines and verses from memory.

Ada Alice possessed a beautiful voice and loved to sing. She was active in Relief Society, and Sacrament Meetings. She believed in the principles of the Gospel. Her religion was the most important part of her life.

MARY ANN CHESHIRE RAMSAY

BIRTHDATE: 28 Aug 1841
DEATH: 5 Nov 1922
Snowflake, Arizona
PARENTS: George Cheshire
Elizabeth Keys
PIONEER: 4 Oct 1863
Independent Co. Wagon Train
SPOUSE: Ralph Ramsay
MARRIED: 02 Aug 1869
Salt Lake City, Salt Lake, Utah
DEATH SP: 25 Jan 1905
Snowflake, Arizona

CHILDREN:
Mariam, 22 May 1871
Joseph, 11 Oct 1872
John, 2 Sep 1874
George, 27 Jun 1876
Rose Ann, 7 Jun 1878

Still born son, Nov 1800
Ralph Cheshire, 20 Apr 1883

Mary Ann was the oldest child in a family of eight children. She was sick when the brother next to her was born so she went to live with an aunt and uncle, and lived with them off and on until her aunt's death.

By the age of six, Mary Ann and her sisters went to school where they learned to braid straw and brought it home to sell. They entered school in the morning, braided eleven yards; went home for lunch, came back and braided eleven more yards, went home for tea, returning to braid nine more yards in the evening.

They were constantly concerned that it would be discovered they were Mormons and then would be expelled from school and the sale of their braid would stop and they would be held in derision by their associates. The entire family were working and trying to save to be able to go to Utah to be with the Saints.

When Mary Ann was twenty-one she received some money willed to her by the uncle she had lived with earlier and this money was used by the Cheshire family to come to America.

Her twenty-second birthday was spent on the Plains, and she traveled part of the way across the plains on a thrashing machine. They arrived to Salt Lake City and traded their wagon for a stove and the oxen for a city lot. They still owed a few dollars on the lot and Mary Ann and her sisters continued to braid straw and make hats to help with the family finances. She soon established a millinery store on Main Street and had six girls working for her.

She married Ralph Ramsay and they lived in Salt Lake until 1872 when they left for Richfield and joined the United Order there. She started to wait on the sick there. They moved to St. Johns, Arizona and then moved to Old Mexico in February, 1885.

While they lived in Mexico, she took three of her children and went to Salt Lake City to study midwifery under Sister Shipp. In 1891, they moved to Snowflake, Arizona where she practiced midwifery. On one of her trips to Salt Lake City she went to the temple and received a blessing regarding her work among the sick. This blessing was a big comfort to her. All together she spent about thirty-five years practicing midwifery. She was a wonderful midwife.

Mary Ann Cheshire Ramsey was always true to her Faith, always attended to her church duties and was a devoted Relief Society member.

ANN LEMON RANCK

BIRTHDATE. 7 Mar 1821
Earl, Lancaster, Pennsylvania
DEATH: 11 Dec 1884
East Mill Creek, Salt Lake, Utah
PARENTS: James Lemon
Catherine Keyser
PIONEER: 20 Sep 1852
Isaac Stewart Co. Wagon Train
SPOUSE: Peter Ranck Jr.
MARRIED: 25 Aug 1840
Pennsylvania
DEATH SP: 18 Nov 1895
East Mill Creek, Salt Lake, Utah

CHILDREN:
Robert Byers, 25 May 1841
Margaret Elizabeth, 4 Sep 1843
Mary Catherine, 17 Nov 1844
William Eicholtz, 5 Mar 1846
Joseph Gibson, 6 Feb 1848
Sarah Jane, 14 Dec 1849
Lydia Ann, 8 Mar 1852
Susanna Louise, 26 Dec 1854
Eudora Vilate, 4 Mar 1857
Harriet Irene, 6 Aug 1859
Peter Lemon, 25 Jul 1862

Ann was raised in a wealthy family by the name of Byers. She joined the Church of Jesus Christ of Latter-day Saints and was baptized by William I. Appleby. The river was frozen over with one foot of ice and it was necessary to cut away the ice to baptize her. To confirm her a member of the Church, she was seated on a sled. Ann was disowned by the Byers family when she joined the Church, but her testimony of the truthfulness of the gospel was stronger than her desire for wealth.

Ann endured many trails and hardships during the early years of the Church. Crossing the Plains one afternoon her two year old daughter Sarah, fell in front of a wagon heavily loaded with food and belongings of two families. Both wheels passed over her body, just above the knees. The captain called a halt and camp formed immediately. The Elders administered to her and a doctor in camp examined her and found that no bones had been broken. It was a miracle that she had not been killed and the whole Ranck family felt extremely blessed by the Lord.

During her trials she never complained. When the crickets came and ate every green thing, bread and molasses was their main food. Another time when Ann's husband was bringing a wagon train to Salt Lake and she was left alone, Ann divided her last baking of flour with her neighbors. She did not know where her next meal would come from, but the Lord blessed her and she was provided with enough corn meal to make bread for herself and her children.

Ann was a member of the Relief Society, from 1852 until six months before her death. She was called upon to nurse the sick and there was hardly a home in the valley that she did not visit to comfort and nurse the sick or prepare the dead for burial. She acted as a midwife at the birth of over five hundred babies and was looked upon as an "Angel of Mercy."

Ann was a very good member of the Church and passed away in full faith of the gospel she espoused to in her younger days.

EMMERETTE LOUISA DAVIS RANDALL

BIRTHDATE: 18 May 1818
Livonia, Livingston, New York
DEATH: 12 Mar 1898
Ogden, Weber Co., Utah
PARENTS: Asa Davis
Sally Richardson
PIONEER: 21 Sep 1848
Brigham Young Wagon Train
SPOUSE: Alfred Randall
MARRIED: 8 Jan 1834
Munsion, Ohio
DEATH SP: 21 Mar 1891
Ogden, Weber Co., Utah

CHILDREN:
Charles Franklin, 8 Feb 1835
Sarah LaVern, 25 Apr 1838 (died at age 19)
Alfred Jason, 8 Jan 1845
Emmerette Louisa, 21 Mar 1849 (died at age 1)
Levi Leander, 18 Nov 1850
Alison Roxana, 10 Jun 1853 (died at age 1)
Davis Richard, 30 May 1855 (died at age 1)
Charlotte Ann, 4 Sep 1858 (died at age 2)
Martha Jane, 2 Dec 1860

Emmerette's parents moved to Munson which is near Kirtland, Ohio. She was converted to the teachings of the Church of Jesus Christ of Latter-day Saints when she was fourteen years old.

She met and married Alfred Randall before she was sixteen. They lived in this area until 1838 when they were driven from the area. They moved to Quincy, Illinois where Alfred became a carpenter. In 1840, he was converted to the gospel. They were close to the Prophet Joseph Smith, and were willing to endure many hardships and all of the persecutions which plagued the membership of the Church.

They were all prepared to cross the Plains in 1847 when Alfred broke his leg. Heber C. Kimball asked him to donate his wagons and supplies for others to make the trip. Alfred, Emmerette, and their children came to the Salt Lake Valley on September 21, 1848 with the Brigham Young Wagon Company.

They first settled in Salt Lake Valley and lived in an adobe home until they were called by Brigham Young to go to Ogden and build a woolen mill.

Emmerette was a strong support to her husband and was willing to live the principal of polygamy. She gave her consent for Alfred to marry four additional wives.

The deaths of her five children all came within a period of about ten years. To sorrow, she was not a stranger, but the Lord knew her heart and desires and was with her in her trials. In her later years, she lived first with her son, Levi, and then with her daughter, Martha Jane.

Her eyesight became poor in her old age. She always loved the gospel and liked to attend Relief Society Meetings in the Ogden Fourth Ward. She often spoke in tongues during the meetings.

Emmerette's husband and her son, Levi, preceded her in death. She passed away at the age of eighty. She was loved and respected by all who knew her.

FRANCIS REBECCA BENNETT RANDALL

BIRTHDATE: 15 Aug 1854
Adams Basin, New York
DEATH: 30 Jan 1937
Centerville Davis Co., Utah
PARENTS: Winthrop Bennett
Sarah McQuarters
PIONEER: 1868
SPOUSE: Melvin Harley Randall
MARRIED: 15 Apr 1875
Salt Lake Endowment House
DEATH SP: 21 Apr 1930
Centerville, Davis Co., Utah

CHILDREN:
Harley Phelps, 8 Jan 1876
Mary Margaret, 20 Jun 1878
Melvin Howard, 10 Dec 1879
Elbert Eugene, 3 Oct 1881
Amelia Emerett, 23 Nov 1883
Ethel, 5 Jan 1886
Laura Sarah, 19 Aug 1887
Alice, 4 Jun 1889
Amy, 19 Jan 1892
Frankie, 8 Aug 1893
Rula, 30 Oct 1895

Francis "Frankie" was born on August 15, 1854 in Adams Basin, Monroe County, New York. Here her early child hood was spent, her parents dying when she was about five years of age.

She came to Centerville in the Fall of 1868 with her Uncle Joseph Phelps, commonly called Uncle Joddie, who adopted her. They lived for a short time in the home of Captain Witherell, the school master, then in the home of Bishop William R. Smith and later with Margaret Randall.

She spent most of her time giving music lessons throughout Davis County, but especially in Kaysville and Centerville.

She was baptized into the Church of Jesus Christ of Latter-day Saints in February, 1875, and was married to Melvin Harley Randall in the old Endowment House in Salt Lake City, Utah.

She acted as a counselor in the YLMIA, and was set apart to work in the Primary Association as First Counselor, on March 31, 1879, where she served in different offices from Organist to President for over thirty years.

Later, she worked on the Stake Primary Board for several years. She gave concerts with the children and young folks throughout Davis County, and in Centerville. She gave concerts to raise money to buy the first Church Organ, also song books for the Sunday School children to sing from. She was put in as Organist in the Sunday School in the year 1874, and worked as organist for over thirty years. She was always on time with her whole family of little children.

Frankie gave many concerts and social entertainments with the Primary children, showing unusual ability that will long be remembered by all who saw them or took part in them.

She was the mother of eleven children. She had fifty grandchildren and nineteen great-grandchildren (1934).

Her three sons and one daughter, Amelia, filled missions for the Church, and her second son, Melvin Howard, was President of the Morgan Stake.

She has ever had a kind and lovable disposition, making many friends and keeping them through the years. She was a kind and loving wife and mother always busy and never shirking any labor or duty that came her way.

In later years, she spent her time in doing beautiful handiwork of all kinds, but especially quilts, giving them to her children and grandchildren, who have long kept them as loving keepsakes of their mother and grandmother.

She passed away at 11:15 a. m. at her home in Centerville, Utah on January 10, 1937 and was buried in the Centerville, Utah Cemetery.

HANNAH SEVERN RANDALL

BIRTHDATE: 24 Mar 1841
Hucknal, Nottingham, England
DEATH: 24 May 1912
North Ogden, Weber Co., Utah
PARENTS: Enoch Severn
Ann Allen
PIONEER: 2 Oct 1862
James Brown Co. Wagon Train
SPOUSE: Alfred Randall
MARRIED: 7 Mar 1863
Salt Lake Endowment House
DEATH SP: 21 Mar 1891
North Ogden, Weber Co., Utah

CHILDREN:
James Enoch, 4 Oct 1864
Ann Severn, 6 May 1867
David Ephraim, 1 Jan 1869
Heber John, 12 Oct 1870
George Edward, 15 Apr 1873
Lucy, 8 Jun 1876

William Henry, 3 Aug 1878
Esther Louise, 19 Oct 1879
Samuel Moroni, 20 Oct 1881

Hannah was born to Enoch and Ann Severn in Hucknal, Nottingham, England on March 24, 1841. As a child she was brought up in a humble home that did not have many of the comforts of life, but their home was clean and orderly and her parents were strict. They were taught to be truthful, honest and industrious. Besides Hannah, there were three other children, William, Sarah and Joseph.

Her father, Enoch, worked in the mines all day. Hannah went to work as an apprentice dressmaker. Schools were few and her education was very meager as compared to today.

When Hannah was about seventeen years old, she and a friend, Eliza Folds (Brown), heard missionaries speaking in the street. She was impressed and went to church even though it was against the wishes of her parents. She was baptized as a member of the Church of Jesus Christ of Latter-day Saints on April 10, 1859, and told her parents she was going to Utah.

She saved her money for a couple of years and on April 23, 1862 she set sail for America on a small sailing vessel. James J. Boyd was in charge and they arrived in New York on June 1, 1862. James A. Brown, Joseph Rich and Brother Linsay were also in charge. Among the women, besides Hannah, were Elizabeth Giles, Eliza Lester (Brown) and Zella Green Smith. They soon went on to Florence, Nebraska where she awaited the wagon trains. They left on July 28, 1862 with James A. Brown in charge and they arrived in the Salt Lake Valley on October 2, 1862.

Hannah came to believe in the principle of plural marriage and married Alfred Randall on March 7, 1863 in the Endowment House. Alfred Randall was aged fifty-four and she was his fourth wife. They lived in Salt Lake for a few years and later moved to Ogden and then North Ogden.

Hannah and Alfred built a large home and had a very successful farm in the Randall district of North Ogden. They had nine children, one (William) died in infancy.

During Hannah's busy life of raising a large family, she found time to do many outside things. She made overalls for Z.C.M.I. Company in Ogden. She raised silk worms. She had a knitting machine and knit stockings for her own family as well as for others. She raised chickens and geese. With the help of her children she dried large quantities of fruit. They earned their winter clothes in this way.

Hannah was always a faithful tithe payer and worked very hard to clear the mortgage on the farm. She made pounds and pounds of fresh cream butter which supplied all of Alfred's families. As well, she took many pounds of butter to sell to customers in town.

She was a trustee in the Relief Society organization and later she spent many years as a Relief Society teacher.

Many a time, Hannah went around in her horse and buggy to gather needed supplies for the Relief Society.

In Hannah's later years her health was not too good and she passed away on May 27, 1912 in North Ogden. She was buried in the Ogden City Cemetery alongside of her husband.

Hannah raised a splendid and large family to whom she gave her first attention. She also had many friends and found time to help them and she was honored and loved by everyone. She left a memory rich in devotion and staunch in the faith and an everlasting love for the truth. Her posterity cherishes her memory.

LOUISA JANE HALL MILLER RANDALL

BIRTHDATE: 8 Sep 1844
Byron, Genesee Co., New York
DEATH: 11 Jul 1887
St. George, Washington, Utah
PARENTS: Newton D. Hall
Sarah Jane Busenbark
PIONEER: 12 Sep 1847
Wagon Train Company
SPOUSE: Alma Miller
MARRIED: abt 1861
Millersberg/Beaver Dam, Nevada
DEATH SP: 10 Feb 1871
Eagle Valley, Nevada

CHILDREN:
Alma George, 18 Dec 1868
Louisa Elmira, 25 Jul 1870

SPOUSE II: Joseph Henry Randall
MARRIED: 1881 prob
St. George, Washington Co., Utah
DEATH SP: 1 Mar 1909
St. George, Washington Co., Utah

CHILDREN:
Sarah Jane, 1882 (lived two weeks)
Mary Alice, 20 Aug 1884 (lived four months)
Henry, 9 May 1886

Louisa Jane was born in New York. Her parents were baptized members of the Church of Jesus Christ of Latter-day Saints on June 9, 1842 by John Smith, Uncle of the Prophet Joseph Smith. Her parents wanted to emigrate to the West with the Saints. Her father's parents objected but finally relented and told the young couple to fill up their supplies at their granary. It was frequently mentioned among the emigrants that they indeed would have often gone hungry had it not been for Louisa's parents' flour.

Louisa's life was saved in a miraculous way when she was three years old. She had fallen asleep on the top-most part of the load of flour. The wagon tipped over and the pioneers rushed to the wagon and succeeded in putting it upright. Then, they began to carefully lift the sacks of flour off Louisa's body, one sack at a time. Upon reaching the

tiny body, the sacks had so arranged themselves by parting in the center and thus prevented any injury to Louisa.

After leaving New York, they traveled as far as Winter Quarters, Nebraska. They entered the Salt Lake Valley on September 12, 1848. In 1859, they moved to Providence, Cache County, Utah. Louisa was fifteen. Her father worked in the Woolen Mills, did some farming and raised livestock.

In 1866, her father was called to colonize in the South. There were six wagons in the company and two mule teams. Louisa was twenty-two years old. Apostle Erastus Snow instructed them to settle in the Muddy Valley. They ended up at Millersberg, Arizona, the first settlers in Arizona.

Louisa married Alma Miller in 1861. After the flood of 1867, Louisa and Alma moved to Spring Valley. They lived in a tent. Louisa spun wool to make all their clothes. She braided straw hats for all the family. She was an excellent tailor.

While freighting in the mines, Alma was killed by Indians in Eagle Valley near the Nevada-Arizona border.

Louisa moved her small family to Mountain Meadows to be near her parents who lived at Hamblin, Utah. She then moved to St. George, Utah with her family and worked in the mills there.

In 1881, she married Henry W. Randall. They became the parents of three children, two died in infancy, Her health failed and her marriage, also.

Louisa Jane did temple work until her death in July, 1887. Her daughter's fondest memories of Louisa were of her unselfishness, her love of the Gospel, and always her prayerfulness which she faithfully taught her children.

MARGARET HARLEY RANDALL

BIRTHDATE: 13 Jan 1823
Chester Co., Pennsylvania
DEATH: 05 Apr 1919
Georgetown, Bear Lake, Idaho
PARENTS: Benjamin Harley
Elizabeth Rinehart
PIONEER: Sep 1848
SPOUSE: Alfred Randall
MARRIED: 29 Jan 1848
Winter Quarters, Nebraska
DEATH SP: 21 Mar 1891
North Ogden, Weber Co., Utah

CHILDREN:
Orrin Harley, 11 Jan 1850
Melvin Harley, 1 Aug 1852
Mary Elizabeth, 19 Jan 1855
Margaret Ellen, 31 Mar 1858
Thurza Amelia, 23 Dec 1860
Alice, 21 Dec 1863
Emily, 8 Apr 1869

In their Pennsylvania home, Margaret and her brother Edwin, four years her senior, were converted to the Church of Jesus Christ of Latter-day Saints, were baptized, and left the rest of their family as they headed for Nauvoo. She arrived after the death of the prophet, Joseph Smith.

Margaret hired out to work as a domestic servant for Alfred Randall and his wife, Emmerette. She traveled with the family to Winter Quarters, Nebraska. Alfred had been selected to accompany the first company of Saints to the Salt Lake Valley, but had an accident in which he broke his leg and was delayed until 1848.

Margaret heeded the council of the brethren and was married to Alfred Randall by President Brigham Young. They journeyed from Winter Quarters, Nebraska to Utah by ox-team and arrived in the Salt Lake Valley in September of 1848.

They spent the winter of 1848/1849 in Mill Creek Canyon just east of Bountiful in a dugout. She experienced many hardships and trying times, often going hungry as food was so scarce.

In 1862, Alfred bought a farm and home in Centerville and moved his families there. Margaret supported herself and family by caring for cows, selling milk and butter, raising hay, grain, chickens and other animals, and a vegetable garden. Margaret carded wool, spun and dyed cloth, made quilts and carpets, and sewed clothes. She also engaged in raising silk worms for the silk industry of Utah. A small amount of cash was obtained from the sale of dried fruits. Her sons cut and hauled wood from the canyons for fuel.

Margaret's life was a struggle of hardships and a fight against poverty. She was the mother of seven of her children who all lived to maturity. For nearly thirty years, Margaret served as President of the Centerville First Ward Relief Society. She was a very energetic and efficient worker, visiting the sick and afflicted, caring for the sick and preparing the dead for burial, and giving solace and comfort to those called to mourn.

The latter years of Margaret's life were spent in blindness caused by cataracts. She died in Georgetown, Idaho at the home of her daughter and was buried in the Centerville Cemetery.

MILDRED ELIZA JOHNSON RANDALL

BIRTHDATE: 5 Jul 1827
New Hope, Augusta, Virginia
DEATH: 19 May 1913
Salt Lake City, Salt Lake, Utah
PARENTS: Francis Johnson
Mary Jane Hall
PIONEER: 29 Aug 1859
James Brown Co. Wagon Train
SPOUSE: Alfred Randall
MARRIED: 30 May 1860
Salt Lake Endowment House
DEATH SP: 21 Mar 1891

CHILDREN:
Francis, 20 Mar 1863 (died as a child)
Eli Bradley, 28 Dec 1864 (died as an infant)

Mildred Eliza was born in 1827, in Virginia. This was a home of culture and refinement in the Shenandoah Valley of Virginia. Her father taught school, and she was scholastically inclined. She desired to follow the teaching profession and attended the Augusta Female Seminary in Stanton, Virginia. She also enjoyed doing fine needlework. She often traded her chores to her sisters so she could sew or pursue her studies.

When she was seventeen years of age, her father died. She requested two books he had written on English and math, and her share of the inheritance in money to enable her to pay for additional schooling.

After teaching in Virginia some years, she went to visit her brother, Cicero, in Council Bluffs. While there, she was converted and baptized into the Church of Jesus Christ of Latter-day Saints on May 22, 1859. She left shortly thereafter for the Rocky Mountains with Captain James Brown's Wagon Company. They arrived in the Salt Lake Valley on August 29, 1859.

Mildred went to Bountiful and lived with the Randall family. On May 29, 1860 she became Mrs. Alfred Randall, in the Endowment House. She returned to Salt Lake City and began teaching in the 17th Ward. To this marriage was born two sons, but both died soon after their births. She resumed her teaching.

In 1865, she and her husband were called on a mission to the Church Plantation in Laie, Hawaii. She sold her lovely home and gave her furniture to friends to help finance their mission. While there Mildred conducted two schools, one for foreign children and one for native children. Upon her return to Salt Lake, she took charge of Brigham Young's private school on his Eagle Gate property. She taught all classes from ABC's through reading, writing, spelling, arithmetic, geography, history and botany. She was well liked by her pupils.

On May 4, 1873, she was set apart for a second mission to the Sandwich Island, becoming the first woman in the Church to serve a 'foreign' mission without a husband. She borrowed money to finance this mission and went without 'purse or script,' teaching school to pay her expenses while there. Upon her return to Utah she not only did regular day teaching, but had night classes in her home and sold books to pay her mission debt.

Mildred Eliza had a lengthy, productive life of service and passed away at the age of eighty-six years in 1913. A Deseret News article concerning her death stated, "Community lost one of the most active and best loved of the state's pioneer women." She is to be honored for her devoted service to the Lord and to those around her.

RUTH CAMPKIN RANDALL

BIRTHDATE: 2 Jan 1845
St. Louis, St. Louis, Missouri
DEATH: 26 Apr 1929
Pine, Gila Co., Arizona
PARENTS: George Campkin
Elizabeth Bell
PIONEER: 1850 Wagon Train
SPOUSE: Alfred Jason Randall
MARRIED: 16 Nov 1867
Salt Lake Endowment House
DEATH SP: 26 Sep 1907
Willow Valley, Arizona

CHILDREN:
Annie Elizabeth, 21 Aug 1868
Alfred Bradley, 2 Dec 1870
Emmerette, 26 Sep 1872
George Camplin, 23 Aug 1874 (died as an infant)
Walter John, 8 Oct 1875
Frank Campkin, 28 May 1879
Bert Davis, 11 Apr 1882
Harry Jason, 29 Nov 1884
Howard L., 12 Feb 1887

Ruth was born to her parents just as they were arriving in St. Louis, Missouri from England. Her early childhood was spent in St. Louis. In 1850, the family traveled to Canesville, Illinois where they became prepared for their trek across the Plains with a company of Saints. They arrived in the Salt Lake Valley that fall. They established a home in the 17th Ward where she received some schooling.

When Ruth was twenty-two years old, she married Alfred Jason Randall. She and her husband had been called to help in the settlement of southern Utah. They settled in Harrisburg, Washington County for fourteen years until a call sent them to the Tonto Basin in Arizona.

Alfred left his family while he went with an exploring party to Arizona. He returned home and left again taking his cattle to his new settlement in Arizona. Shortly after he returned to Utah for his family, Ruth's sister, Annie, died leaving five children. Ruth helped to raise these five children until they were grown.

In 1879, her husband left again to help his brother-in-law take his cattle to Arizona. In 1881, they all moved to Arizona. Their first year there was spent in a small log room that had been a blacksmith shop. They used covered wagon boxes for bedrooms.

Alfred and Ruth were hospitable to all who came to their door. She was generous in sharing and helping the poor and unfortunate at any time. Ruth was often left at home with all of the children because it was necessary for Alfred to be away with the livestock.

Ruth was a good housewife and mother, supporting her husband in his public works in the church and community. Alfred was accidentally killed when his team of horses bolted and he was trampled to death. She was widowed for twenty-two years and died at the age of eighty-four and was buried in Pine near her beloved husband.

SARAH DARLING ROSS RANDALL

BIRTHDATE: 20 Jun 1858
London, Middlesex, England
DEATH: 25 Jan 1919
Salt Lake City, Salt Lake, Utah
PARENTS: James Darling
Sarah Elizabeth Smith Ross
PIONEER: 3 Sep 1860
James D. Ross Co. Wagon Train
SPOUSE: Brigham Y. Randall
MARRIED: 4 Aug 1877
DEATH SP: 10 Jul 1939
Salt Lake City, Salt Lake, Utah

CHILDREN:
William Brigham, 29 Mar 1879
Sarah Mary, 23 Mar 1881
Louise Adele, 2 Mar 1883
Ella May, 11 Apr 1885
George Ross, 21 Apr 1887
Flora Darling, 14 Mar 1889
Alice Grace, 7 Sep 1891
Emily Agnes, 20 Feb 1894
Alta, 1 Mar 1896 (twin)
Afton, 1 Mar 1896 (twin)
Isabelle, 15 Dec 1898

Sarah crossed the ocean and prairie with her parents as an infant to come to Zion. Sarah Darling was the mother of eleven children. Her daughter, Alice, died as a young child but she raised the others to adulthood.

Her husband, Brigham Young Randall, opened one of the first bakeries in Murray, Utah and this business thrived until his establishment burned down and wasn't rebuilt.

Sarah seldom raised her voice in anger, being patient with courage for the vissicitudes of life, and literally giving her life to help others.

In the terrible flu epidemic of 1919, she felt it necessary to nurse ill members of her family. Within a week she contracted the flu and passed away.

Sarah Darling Ross seemed like a mother hen with a large brood of chicks, always willing to care for and feed one more. Visitors were always received with warmth and open arms. There always seemed to be "enough stew" for one more. No task seemed too great nor any service too difficult to render.

SARAH ANDERSON RANDS

BIRTHDATE: 12 Apr 1829
Hampstead, Middlesex, England
DEATH: 20 Sep 1880
Salt Lake City, Salt Lake, Utah
PARENTS: William Anderson
Ann Cowley
PIONEER: 15 Sep 1868
John Gillespie Co. Wagon Train
SPOUSE: Joseph William Rands
MARRIED: 29 Mar 1847
DEATH SP: 11 Oct 1875
Salt Lake City, Salt Lake, Utah

CHILDREN:
Henry James, 30 May 1848
Sarah Rhodia (Neal), 14 Jan 1851
Joseph William, 29 Jan 1854
Lydia Jane (Weyland), 21 Dec 1856
Hyrum, 1 Jul 1859
Jessie Lavina (Maxwell), 13 Mar 1862
Helena Ruth (Maxwell), 31 Jul 1864
Elizabeth (Larsen), 28 Mar 1870 (twin)
Martha, 28 Mar 1870 (twin - died as an infant)

Sarah was born in England in 1829 as the second daughter. Little is known about her childhood years.

When she was seventeen years old, a young man named Joseph William Rands began courting her. Despite parent disapproval, the pair decided to marry. On March 29, 1847, they were married at the parish of St. John Hampstead. Sarah was almost eighteen and Joseph almost twenty.

The lure of adventure called the newlyweds to Capetown, Union of South Africa. They sailed in 1847, with William's brother and wife. The British government encouraged colonization in their empire, and wanted settlers in Africa to claim this as English territory. Joseph William was gardener by trade, and they did well in their new country. They prospered and enjoyed life. Their first children were born there. Along with their family duties, other changes came into their lives.

In 1853, missionaries from the Church of Jesus Christ of Latter-day Saints arrived in South Africa. They taught the Gospel well and baptized many converts. The Rands family were converted. Sarah was baptized on April 29, 1855, and Joseph William on September 9, 1855.

By 1859, the Rands family longed to be closer to the Church headquarters to enjoy the fellowship of the Saints. It was difficult for Joseph and Sarah to leave his brother and family, without expectations of ever seeing them again. They left for 'Zion' on March 16, 1868, after selling their belongings and taking only the bare essentials they could carry. Passage fees ranged from $14.40 to $24.00 which was one-third of a laborer's annual income.

Weather was often cold, quarters were crowded, and passengers were to bring their own supply of food. Despite the hardships, there were times of enjoyment and adventure. They finally docked May 16, 1868 at New York City. They spent about two months in New York, and the children attended school, for some this was their only schooling.

New York Newspaper reporters wrote the following about these immigrants, as quoted in the Deseret News of 1868, "The immigrants to Utah are inferior to non-Mormons who settle in their city. Yet these very people are building a thriving, flourishing state! Great credit must be given to a system that makes of them industrious, reliable, honest, self-sustaining and even wealthy citizens."

The Rands family traveled West with the John Gillespie Company with 500 saints, 50 wagons, and most of them walked most of the way. They encountered the usual hardships, including dust, insects, rain, winds, hot sun, rivers to cross, mountains to ascend, sagebrush, all before reaching the Salt Lake Valley on September 15, 1868. Their journey of half way around the world had been completed.

They first lived in Salt Lake City, and Brighton, Utah. This was a resort area. Logging was done from the canyon. William Brighton had taken a large homestead at Brighton in 1870 to build a resort. Two more children were born to Sarah at Brighton, the twins one of whom died very soon after birth in September.

They moved back to Salt Lake City near 5th Avenue and Virginia St. Indians often came to their homes begging for food. Wild animals came near also. Soldiers from Ft. Douglas also went by their homes.

The Rands worked hard developing their home and their lands. In 1875, construction was begun on ZCMI and Joseph worked there. Unfortunately, he fell from an elevator and was badly hurt. He passed away as a result on October 11, 1875.

Things were bad and Sarah had to sell the home. She lived only five years after her husband, passing away on February 11, 1874. This sweet pioneer mother left her posterity a noble example to follow. Her granddaughter wrote "I love this sweet Grandmother Sarah.

LOUISA ELIZABETH CUTLER RAPPLEYE

No
Photo
Available

BIRTHDATE: 16 May 1816
Lisle, Brown, New York
DEATH: 9 Mar 1854
Lehi, Utah Co., Utah
PARENTS: Alpheus Cutler
Lois Lathrop
PIONEER: 1853
SPOUSE: Tunis Rappleye
MARRIED: 17 Jan 1836
Kirtland, Ohio
DEATH SP: 25 Dec 1993
Kanosh, Millard Co., Utah

CHILDREN:
Emily Jane, 21 Dec 1836 (died as an infant)
John Alpheus, 22 Aug 1838 (died at 9 months)
Lauretta, 23 Mar 1840
Clarissa Cymanthe, 23 Mar 1842 (died at age 9)
Ammon Llewelyn, 23 Sep 1844
David Franklin, 22 Jun 1849
Harriet F. Melvina, 22 Jun 1849 (died at age 1)
Ezra Tunis, 23 Nov 1851
Edwin Richmond, 28 Feb 1854

Louisa Elizabeth was born in Lisle, New York. Her parents moved to Kirtland, Ohio where Louisa Elizabeth joined the Church of Jesus Christ of Latter-day Saints.

She married Tunis Rappleye on January 17, 1836. This marriage was performed by the Prophet Joseph Smith. Louisa and Tunis remained in Kirtland long enough to witness the completion and dedication of the Kirtland Temple. They traveled west to Crooked River, Missouri where they farmed and their first child was born.

They were driven from Missouri and went to Hancock County, Illinois. Louisa worked with Tunis at farming for five years. She gave birth to three more children while in this area.

When they moved to Nauvoo in 1845, Tunis was sent on a mission to the eastern states while Louisa and the children stayed in Nauvoo until the Saints were driven out of Nauvoo.

By the time Louisa and the children arrived in Council Bluffs, Iowa, they were all sick with Cholera and unable to go on. She remained in Council Bluffs for six years and had three more children there. She became very skilled in nursing. As more Saints arrived at Winter Quarters, many were too sick to go any further. Louisa was called upon to nurse them back to health.

In 1847, her husband was called to travel West as a driver of one of Brigham Young's teams. He made several trips back and forth helping others on their way to the Salt Lake Valley.

Finally, in 1853, Louisa and her four living children were able to travel West and arrived in Salt Lake Valley in the year 1853.

They were sent to Lehi to live and this is where their ninth child was born. Louisa passed away nine days after the birth of her little son.

ELIZABETH GILES RASBAND

BIRTHDATE: 11 Apr 1826
Loudham, England
DEATH: 15 Oct 1900
Park City, Summit Co., Utah
PARENTS: William Giles
Sarah Huskinson
PIONEER: 25 Aug 1856
Wagon Train Company
SPOUSE: Thomas Rasband
MARRIED: 25 Jan 1847
Lincoln, England
DEATH SP: 24 Jul 1884
Heber City, Wasatch Co., Utah

CHILDREN:
John R., 15 Apr 1848 (died as an infant)
Emily (Hicken), 20 Jun 1849
William Giles, 24 Dec 1852
Annie, 1855 (died as an infant)
Fredrick, 2 Sep 1856
Thomas Heber, 15 Jan 1859
George Wesley, 16 Jun 1861
James Franklin, 6 Aug 1862
Mary Elizabeth (McDonald), 30 Sep 1865
Joseph A. 17 Mar 1867
Charles, 21 Aug 1870

Elizabeth "Betsy" was born in 1826 in England. Betsy was a petite woman weighing ninety pounds and was about five feet tall. She had blue eyes and light brown hair. She moved in various places in England with her family.

In 1844, they moved to Lincoln, and it was while living there that Elizabeth met and married Thomas Rasband on on January 25, 1847 in the St. Mark's Church.

Elizabeth's mother and her brother went to Hull, England to visit relatives to learn more about a new religion, and while they were there, they were baptized on December 23, 1849 into the Church of Jesus Christ of Latter-day Saints. Her father, William, had been baptized on September 2, 1849. On their return, Elizabeth's mother taught them about this new religion, and they were baptized on August 30, 1850.

While living in England, Elizabeth had two children, but their first, John died at the age of two months, but Emily came to America with them. They emigrated in 1852, crossing the ocean on the ship, "North Atland," and stayed in Quincy, Illinois.

On May 4, 1854, Elizabeth's parents and family came to America and joined their daughter when they arrived in St. Louis, Missouri, May 6, 1854. Elizabeth was at the pier to meet them.

By 1856, Thomas, a hard worker and good manager, had obtained a team of oxen, a wagon, and supplies for the journey to the Salt Lake Valley. They arrived in Provo, Utah on August 25, and soon after, a son was born in a wagon box as they had not had time to build a home.

In April, 1859, Thomas left with some other men for what is now the Heber Valley. Crops were planted and then the men returned to Provo for their families. Elizabeth and Thomas were among the first eleven families to settle Heber City where they made their permanent home.

Elizabeth was also a hard worker and wonderful mother and homemaker. She made balls for the boys by collecting cloth and string and covering it with cloth and rag dolls for the girls at Christmastime. She also made molasses candy for a bit of sweet.

Thomas had many church callings and community responsibilities. He was a Bishop and also the Justice of the Peace. She supported him in his activities. Elizabeth served in the Relief Society when it was formed.

Thomas passed away on July 24, 1834 as the result of an accident with his team. Elizabeth then lived with her children. She lived with a daughter-in-law while her son, Joseph, fulfilled a mission in the Samoan Island, and she cared for her grandson while the mother worked in a store. While living with her son, Fredrick and family in Park City, Elizabeth developed pneumonia and passed away on October 15, 1900. She was buried in the Heber City Cemetery.

They were truly faithful pioneers who served the Lord, their family and their' communities, and who set great examples for those who have followed after them.

ANNE HAAGANSEN RASMUSSEN

No Photo Available

BIRTHDATE: 15 May 1813
Vandlose, Denmark
DEATH: 19 Apr 1893
PARENTS: Haagen Bentsen
Susanne Larsen
PIONEER: 1862
George Stringham (Stringhaus) Co.
SPOUSE: Soren Rasmussen
MARRIED: 9 Aug 1835
Copenhagen, Denmark
DEATH: 16 Dec 1870
Richfield, Utah

CHILDREN:
Rasmus, 10 Mar 1836
Mette Susanne, 14 Jun 1838
Emma Hansine Oline, 28 Aug 1843
Soren, 20 Dec 1846
Soren, 11 Jun 1848
Larsine Hannah Catrina, 21 Feb 1851
Brighamine, abt 1853

Anne was born in Denmark in 1813. She joined the Church there, and came to American with her family. They traveled across the plains with the George Stringham Company, and arrived in the valley in 1862.

They settled in Richfield, Utah where Soren farmed. Anne was a homemaker.

Her husband died 16 Dec 1870, the first pioneer to die in Richfield when it was re-settled after the Black Hawk war. Ann died 19 April 1893.

JENSINA JANSON CHRISTENSEN RASMUSSEN

BIRTHDATE: 10 Apr 1854
Taars Hjrring Jutland, Denmark
DEATH: 20 Feb 1940
Ephraim, Sanpete Co., Utah
PARENTS: Niels Jansen
Else Marie Christensen Andersen
PIONEER: Sep/Oct 1862
John R. Murdock Wagon Train
SPOUSE: Bent Rasmussen
MARRIED: 13 Nov 1871
Ephraim, Sanpete Co., Utah
DEATH SP: 2 Nov 1927
Ephraim, Sanpete Co., Utah

CHILDREN:
Mary Elizabeth, 3 Sep 1872
Elsena Malinda, 26 Sep 1874
Ben, 23 Mar 1877
Christine Dorann, 20 Sep 1879
Carrie Maretta, 24 Dec 1881
Johanna Marselda, 22 Feb 1884
Hans Fredrick, 30 Aug 1886
Clyde, 10 Jan 1889
Fern Josephine, 2 Mar 1891

Jensina was born in Denmark. She was eight years old when she emigrated to America with her mother. They left all they had and joined a group of Danish Saints in an unfamiliar, uncomfortable journey. Jensina never forgot the roughness of the ship as it pitched and rolled in heavy seas, scattering furniture, baggage and people across the rooms and over the decks. The Measle epidemic took the lives of most of the children. The sailing took six weeks. They docked at New York harbor May 29, 1862. They were in the C. A. Madsen Company.

They traveled by train to Florence, Nebraska where people were prepared for the arduous trek West. Because Jensina and her mother were without a family they were obliged to join wherever there was room with a family. She had a friend with whom she walked and played along the way. They traveled with the John R. Murdock Company, arriving in the Salt Lake Valley September or October, 1862. They went directly to Ephraim, Utah to live with her mother's father who had come several years earlier.

Her mother married in 1864 and John Larson became a loving step-father to Jensina. However, a few years later he gave his home and land to Jensina's mother and returned to the east. Jensina, a teenager, helped her mother keep up the house; preparing meat, planting and harvesting food, carding, spinning and weaving wool for socks and clothing. They were expert cooks and needle women, known for their handiwork. Jensina, at fifteen, received pay for her spinning and artistic weaving.

Jensina met Bent Rasmussen who was also a Danish emigrant who came to Ephraim in 1856. They were married on November 13, 1871. Jensina was seventeen and Bent was twenty-two. They became the parents of nine children; six daughters and three sons.

Their happy marriage lasted for fifty-six years when Ben passed away in 1927. The new couple lived for a few years with her mother until they could buy land of their own. Bent built a two-room adobe house then added a second floor later to accommodate their large family. The yard was large with apple and pear trees, lawn, flowers and a pole fence surrounding it. It was a favorite gathering place for grandchildren and grown-ups of all ages. Family was important.

Jensina and Bent celebrated their golden wedding anniversary with a big party and reception held at the Church. Invitations printed in gold were sent out to family and friends far and near. It was a grand occasion. Their posterity numbers hundreds and includes outstanding men and women who have worked hard to make the world a better place. Jensina and Bent would be proud.

Jensina passed away in Ephraim, Utah where she had lived all her married life. She was eighty-six years old.

JOSEPHINE THOMPSON RASMUSSEN

BIRTHDATE: 30 Aug 1861
Plains of Wyoming
DEATH: 31 Dec 1953
Bloomington, Bear Lake, Idaho
PARENTS: Peter Thompson
Mary Jensen
PIONEER: 19 Sep 1861
SPOUSE: Niels Peter Rasmussen
MARRIED: 20 Dec 1878
Bloomington, Idaho
DEATH SP: 11 May 1935
Bloomington, Idaho

CHILDREN:
Joseph Peter, 13 Nov 1879
Alma Lorenzo, 25 Jun 1882 (died as an infant)
Elmer, 16 Nov 1883 (died as an infant)
Julia Louvinia (Nelson), 8 Sep 1885
Edgar Alonzo, 7 Aug 1887
Morlain, 19 Feb 1890 (died as an infant)
Emma Althea (Hayes), 2 Jul 1891
Inger Cecilia (Hess), 5 Jun 1894
Marvin Ambert, 5 May 1897

Clifford Harvey, 9 Jul 1900
Leo Ephraim, 1 Apr 1904

Josephine was born in 1861 in a covered wagon on the plains of Wyoming just before her parents crossed the Platte River. They were delayed only one hour as they had to reach the rest of the company with whom they were traveling, before nightfall.

Josephine was named after her brother, Joseph Mouris, who had died after they left Nebraska, and was buried at Deep Creek, Wyoming. She arrived in the Salt Lake Valley when she was just twelve days old. They continued to Brigham City and arrived there on September 19, 1861.

After living there for four years they moved over the hill to the Bear Lake Valley to Bloomington, Idaho in 1865. Josephine grew to womanhood and lived the remainder of her life there.

On December 20, 1878, Josephine and Niels Peter Rasmussen were married. They went to the Endowment House in Salt Lake City on May 8, 1879. She was also sealed to her parents in the Logan Temple on October 12, 1899. Niels and Josephine had eleven children. Two of their children, Elmer and Morlain died the same day they were born, eight grew to maturity.

Josephine was active in the Church until her health failed. She helped make a living by sewing carpet rags and weaving rugs. She was a Relief Society teacher and helped care for the sick in her neighborhoods. She made most of her children's clothes, knit their socks and mittens. She enjoyed quilting and crocheting. She was generous and good to those in need. She helped care for her father and small half brother, when her mother passed away.

Niels Peter and Josephine celebrated their Golden Wedding anniversary in December of 1928. Niels passed away on May 11, 1935 in Bloomington, Idaho. Josephine, one of the last of the emigrant pioneers to live in this valley, passed away on December 31, 1953 at the age of ninety-two years. Both Niels and Josephine are buried in the Bloomington, Idaho Cemetery.

They were valiant, brave pioneers who suffered much in their lifetimes, but who witnessed many changes during their long lifetimes. They lived as great examples to those who have followed them.

KAREN MARIE CHRISTIANSEN RASMUSSEN

BIRTHDATE: 26 Jul 1842
Lunge, Fyen, Denmark
DEATH: 19 Mar 1900
Mt. Pleasant, Sanpete Co., Utah
PARENTS: C N. Christiansen
Ane Margrethe Jensen
PIONEER: 13 Sep 1857
C. Christiansen Co. Wagon Train
SPOUSE: Morten Rasmussen
MARRIED: 1 Apr 1859
Ephraim, Sanpete Co., Utah
DEATH SP: 28 Jun 1885
Mt. Pleasant, Sanpete Co., Utah

CHILDREN:
Martin, 6 Dec 1859
Maria Sophia, 12 Oct 1861
Lars Christian, 29 Oct 1863
John, 28 Nov 1865
Mary, 7 Feb 1868
Ane Margaret, 4 Feb 1869
Henry, 6 Aug 1871
Erastus, 21 Dec 1873
Daniel, 25 Feb 1876
George, 23 Jul 1878
Wilford Woodruff, 4 Apr 1881
Hyrum, 2 Apr 1884

Karen was born in Denmark. She was an only child. She joined the Church of Jesus Christ of Latter-day Saints in Denmark when she was eleven years old. She was forced to discontinue school at this time because of persecution. Her teacher, a Minister, gave her instruction after school. She had a beautiful singing voice and assisted the Mormon missionaries with her music.

In the Spring of 1857, she left Denmark with her parents to emigrate to Utah. They crossed the ocean and arrived at Philadelphia, Pennsylvania. They traveled by train to Iowa City, Iowa and then by handcart to the Salt Lake Valley, arriving on September 13, 1857. They were with the Christian Christiansen Handcart Company. Karen was plagued with poor health and was able to ride much of the way. She was fifteen years old.

The family spent a short time in Salt Lake City then joined their Danish friends in the newly settled Ephraim, Utah.

Here, in Ephraim, Karen met Morten Rasmussen who had emigrated from Denmark in 1854. They were married on April 1, 1859 and left the same day to make their home in Mt. Pleasant, Utah which was just being settled. This became their permanent home.

They lived in the fort where Karen's first two children were born. When it was safe to leave the fort they built a small house on their assigned lot on West Main Street. The erection of the big two-story house was a project in which Karen was much involved. The bricks were fired in a kiln

on the lot and Karen said that she handled every brick in the house at least twice. The house still stands as a monument to their labors. It is occupied by family and is listed on the State and National Registers of Historic Homes.

Karen was greatly respected in the community because of her ability to manage her affairs and her integrity in her dealings. She managed her family's affairs when her husband was serving a mission in their native land of Denmark.

When her husband passed away in 1885, Karen managed their accumulated properties, sought no special considerations. She paid her way, completed business matters and made a host of friends. She was firm in her testimony of the divinity of the Church of Jesus Christ of Latter-day Saints. When the hay was hauled she saw to it that the Lord's tenth was delivered to the tithing yard and also at threshing time the Lord's tenth was taken to the Bishop. In her efforts to make ends meet financially she sometimes rented rooms or took in boarders.

Her crowning achievement was to be the great-grandmother of a Prophet. Her grand-daughter, Nellie Rasmussen Hunter, is the mother of President Howard W. Hunter, ordained in 1994 as Prophet, Seer and Revelator and President of the Church of Jesus Christ of Latter-day Saints. Death came to Karen on March 19, 1900 in Mt. Pleasant, Utah at the early age of fifty-seven.

MAREN STEPHANSEN RASMUSSEN

BIRTHDATE: 11 Aug 1820
Praesto, Jutland, Denmark
DEATH: 1 Apr 1899
Ephraim, Sanpete Co., Utah
PARENTS: Not given
PIONEER: 16 Dec 1856
William Hodgetts Wagon Train
SPOUSE: Hans Rasmussen
MARRIED: 7 Jun 1844
Denmark
DEATH SP: 25 Aug 1887
Ephraim, Sanpete Co., Utah

CHILDREN:
Rasmus, 16 Feb 1845
Jens / James, 23 Jul 1847
Bendt / Bent, 14 Nov 1849
Karen / Caroline (Hansen), 25 Sep 1851
Annie (Jensen), 15 Aug 1854 (twin)
Christena, 15 Aug 1854 (twin)
Hans, 17 May 1858
Mary, abt 1860

Maren was born in Denmark. She married Hans Rasmussen who was the only son and heir to a beautiful estate on the Island of Shetland, Denmark. Maren was twenty-four years old and Hans was twenty-one.

They began their life together with all the comforts of a large estate. They had many servants to do all the work, inside and out-side. In 1854, they met the Mormon missionaries. They knew their Gospel message was true. They were baptized in June, 1855.

Almost immediately Hans began selling off his estate and by Spring of 1856 he and Maren and their six children were ready to journey to Utah with the main body of Church immigrants. The estate brought in enough money to pay all their expenses for passage on ships and trains and for outfitting them for the wagon-train. There was money left over which they used to pay for the passage of some thirty converts who had no means to go at that time.

Their children were young; ages eleven to two. One of their twin girls died in Iowa. The journey by sailing vessels, railcars, carriages, horses and oxen took from April 23, to December 16, 1856; a full eight months.

Their experience crossing the Plains is extremely well documented as they were in the William B. Hodgetts Wagon Company that followed the Willie and Martin Handcart Companies.

The Rasmussen family, though well outfitted, delayed their own departure in Iowa City and then in Florence, Nebraska in order to help their friends using handcarts. They were late in departing and the early storms left them stranded on the east side of the Continental Divide without food, warmth or shelter. Hundreds died. Hans abandoned all the extra thing he started out with to help the Saints. A stove for Maren was left on the trail. She never again had a stove to cook on. Rescuers from Salt Lake City finally found them and assisted them into Zion.

After a brief rest, Hans and Maren began another journey. This one was south to Ephraim, Utah where a small fort had been established for protection against Indian attacks. A wall of brick and adobe surrounded a two block square area within which their dugouts, tents and adobe houses as well as their livestock were safe. Maren's first home was a dugout. They were soon called to help settle Richfield, Utah. Again, Maren's home was a dugout. The Richfield settlement could not continue and they returned to Ephraim where they were given a city block of land on which Hans built another dugout. Later, Hans added a two-room adobe house but no cookstove.

Maren's life was hard as she coped with deprivations and dangers. She moved three times and gave birth to a son while living in dugouts and facing death at the hands of angry Indians. All of this happened within two and a half years after her arrival in Zion. She had one more child, Mary, who died as a baby.

Maren was faithful to the Gospel. She served in Relief Society and the Manti Temple. She lived to see her family grow to maturity and become honorable and useful men and women.

Maren passed away at home in Ephraim on April 1, 1988 at the age of seventy-nine. Blessed be her name.

MARY ANN MORRIS RASMUSSEN

BIRTHDATE: 20 Dec 1849
Duckinfield, Chester, England
DEATH: 8 May 1924
Provo, Utah Co., Utah
PARENTS: William Morris
Sarah Durham
PIONEER: abt 27 Sep 1862
John R. Murdock Wagon Train
SPOUSE: Niels Rasmussen
MARRIED: 28 Dec 1865
Parowan, Iron Co., Utah
DEATH SP: 7 Jan 1901
Parowan, Iron Co., Utah

CHILDREN:
Ann Kathrine, 23 Oct 1866
Niels William, 28 May 1868
John Thomas, 12 Oct 1869
Sarah Isabella, 21 Feb 1872
Carl Morris, 18 Sep 1877
George Leonard, 16 Sep 1886
Iva Varnum, 12 Sep 1888

Mary Ann was born in England one year after her parents had joined the Church of Jesus Christ of Latter-day Saints. They were eager to emigrate to Utah as soon as their finances would permit.

On May 6, 1862, Mary Ann with her parents, three sisters and an infant brother sailed from Liverpool, England. They arrived at Castle Garden, New York on June 12, 1862. They traveled to Florence, Nebraska, where the railroad ended. They started their 1,000 mile journey across the Plains on July 28, 1862 as members of the John R. Murdock Company. Twelve year old Mary Ann walked most of the way. Ten year old Sarah Jane died of Typhoid Fever on September 10, at Rocky Ridge in Wyoming. The weary pioneers arrived in the Salt Lake Valley about September 27, 1862. After a short rest they continued on to Parowan, Utah.

The family made their first Parowan home in the fort to protect themselves from the Indians. Mary Ann married Niels Rasmussen in Parowan on December 28, 1865. She was sixteen years old, her husband was thirty-six. They set up housekeeping in Parowan. They built a comfortable frame home with a nice orchard and big corrals. There was plenty of room to grow vegetables and feed for the animals. They became the parents of seven children; three daughters and four sons. One child died in infancy and another was stillborn.

Mary Ann did a lot of sewing and millinery. She was good at it. She sang in the choir. The choir members were honored to furnish the music for the General Conference in Salt Lake City on October 6 and 7, 1870, singing with the Tabernacle Choir under the direction of George Careless the next day.

Her husband served a mission in Denmark from 1882-1884, leaving Mary Ann to manage the farm and care for their young family. She supplemented the family income with her seamstress and millinery skills.

Her husband passed away of pneumonia on January 7, 1901. Her father had died just two months previously, leaving her with a grieving and sorrowful heart.

A call came for settlers to go to the Big Horn Basin in Wyoming. Mary Ann decided to go with her two oldest children and her two youngest. They traveled with ten or twelve other families in 1902. She made a down payment on twenty acres of land and raised oats and alfalfa and sugar beets. Her son, George, was just sixteen and not able to run the farm so she decided to sell the land, move to Cowley and run a millinery store. She sold hats for about two years from the living room of her home. She then sold her home in Parowan and purchased a lot for a store where she could have a more profitable business. She took her sewing machine to the shop. She had taught Iva to sew and they made a good living with their excellent dressmaking skills and millinery business. Mary Ann built a lovely home of lumber; three big rooms and an upstairs area. She worked hard all of her life.

Mary Ann passed away at her daughter's home in Provo on May 8, 1924, at the age of seventy-four. She was buried in the Parowan City Cemetery next to her husband and parents.

METTA KISTENA MORTENSEN RASMUSSEN

BIRTHDATE: 2 May 1845
Fanefiord, Praesto, Denmark
DEATH: 5 Jul 1935
Parowan, Iron Co., Utah
PARENTS: Peter Mortensen
Leene Pedersen
PIONEER: 9 Nov 1856
Willie Handcart Company
SPOUSE: Christen Rasmussen
MARRIED: 30 Apr 1863
Parowan, Iron Co., Utah
DEATH SP: 15 May 1915
Parowan, Iron Co., Utah

CHILDREN:
Christen Henry, 7 Aug 1865
Mettie Catherine (Matheson), 5 Sep 1867
Enoch, 30 Apr 1871
Ellen Melissa (Slaughter), 2 Jul 1873
John Amon, 28 Dec 1875
George Walter, 28 May 1878
Anna Olivia, 14 Dec 1880
James Peter, 24 Feb 1883
Joseph, 23 Apr 1885

Mette Kistena was born in 1845 in Denmark. After joining the Church of Jesus Christ of Latter-day Saints her parents sold their property and left their homeland in the face of an angry mob.

From Copenhagen their journey was by rail to Keil, Germany, then by steamer to England, and by boat from Liverpool. After arriving in New York,. they traveled by rail to Iowa City, Iowa. There they joined the J. G. Willie Handcart Company and left, July 15, 1856, and arrived in the Salt Lake Valley noon November 9th, of that year. The family settled in Parowan, Iron County, Utah. She traveled with her parents, four sisters and three brothers. Her mother's handwoven sheets were all used up as they covered the bodies of those who died along the way.

Mette married Christen Rasmussen on April 30, 1863 in Parowan. He had emigrated from Denmark and was twenty years older than Mette. He said he had never seen another woman he wanted to marry, so he waited for her to grow up and they were married when she was eighteen years old.

She was a gentle woman, very active in the Church, and was a homemaker for her husband and family of nine children. She instilled in each of them the principles of the Gospel which she lived fully. They moved to Cedar City and lived in the fort. He bought John D. Lee's cabin when the fort was abandoned about 1857, and he took the logs down one by one and hauled them to Parowan and rebuilt the cabin. He later built a three-room house on the front part of the lot. It was adobe, and had a nice porch with a railing around it. Mette lived in this house in Parowan until she died.

Mette remembered crossing the Plains and told how a band of Indians rode into their camp with the scalps of two white men tied to the end of their spears. Another time the children (she was just nine years old) gathered cupsful of colored beads from an ant hill, probably from the burial spot of an Indian. She often walked with an older woman who died one night. Metta took a crust of bread from that dead woman's pocket. She realized it wouldn't be eaten and she was so hungry she ate it. All of her life she lamented having stolen that crust of bread.

Their home in Parowan was filled with home-made furniture and homemade rugs covered the floors. Cooking utensils were mostly made by her husband. Their children were taught homemaking and gardening skills. She was thrifty and one of her mottos was, "Use what you have or do without."

A grandson remembers his grandmother as being a gentle and quiet lady. She and her husband were both very precise and orderly. Everything in the house, yard, and corral had to be in its place. People in Parowan knew it was 12:00 when they saw Christen come home from his farm for lunch.

Christen died when he was ninety years old, and Mette was seventy. She lived in the family home with her three unmarried children until her death.

Mette was a devout member of the Church, and held positions of leadership in the various church auxiliaries throughout her life. She passed away on July 5, 1935 at the age of ninety years and was buried in the Parowan Cemetery beside her life-long sweetheart.

These were true pioneers who had endured much for their religious beliefs. They were wonderful examples to those who have followed after them.

SINA MARIE MORTENSEN RASMUSSEN

BIRTHDATE: 15 Jul 1851
Sollerud, Copenhagen, Denmark
DEATH: 15 May 1917
Ogden, Weber Co., Utah
PARENTS: Andreas Mortensen
Ingeborg Mortensen
PIONEER: 28 Sep 1864
William B. Preston Wagon Train
SPOUSE: Jorgen H. Rasmussen
MARRIED: 25 Jan 1869
Huntsville, Weber Co., Utah
DEATH SP: abt 1915
Huntsville, Weber Co., Utah

CHILDREN:
Jorgina Cecilia, 12 Apr 1870
Anna Nielsina, 29 Jun 1872
Jorgen Peter, 2 Jul 1875
Andrew Christian, 18 Oct 1882
Amelia Ingeborg, 30 Oct 1882
Mary Elena, 7 Jun 1887
Elvena Mathilda, 10 Jun 1890

Sina Rasmussen was born in Denmark. She was twelve years old when she was baptized a member of the Church of Jesus Christ of Latter-day Saints. The following Spring she and her family emigrated to Zion.

They sailed from Liverpool, England on April 28, 1864 on the clipper ship "Monarch of the Sea." Sina Marie remembered the trip as long and full of sadness. Over fifty children died of measles, including her own baby brother.

They landed at New York and made their way to Mormon Grove, 1,200 miles from the Salt Lake Valley. They joined the William B. Preston Company. They all walked because the wagon carried needed machinery and goods as well as their belongings. Sina Marie's job was to gather buffalo chips or whatever was available for the cooking fires. They arrived in the Salt Lake Valley on September 28, 1864. They left almost immediately for Huntsville, Utah, a beautiful new settlement only three years old. They built a dugout where they spent the Winter. The next Spring her father built a fine cabin which is preserved today. It is the work of a master craftsman.

Sina Marie was bright and industrious as well as beautiful. She had learned to spin in her native land of Denmark. She went out spinning and was much in demand. Soon she earned enough to buy her own spinning wheel. She met the new shoemaker in town recently arrived from Denmark, Jorgen Hansen Rasmussen.

Sina Marie and Jorgen were married on January 25, 1869. It was a long and happy marriage. Seven children were born to them, all born in Huntsville, Weber County, Utah. They became farmers, homesteading a large tract of land.

They were active in the Church. Jorgen served in the Priesthood and Sina Marie in Relief Society. She went about doing much good; delivering steaming pots of her chicken and dumplings to new mothers and those who were ailing. She was a visiting teacher in Relief Society all of her married life. She was grateful that she had been able to raise all seven of her children to maturity. Her children remembered her as tender-hearted and kind and that she had a delightful sense of humor. She kept a lovely home, meticulously cared for. She had a splendid garden.

Sina Marie did a lot of temple work for her kindred dead and also for friends. She was in attendance at the dedication of the Salt Lake Temple. Sina Marie and Jorgen were close friends and neighbors of Bishop McKay, the father of the Prophet David O. McKay. They were home teaching companions for many years.

Sina Marie, a beautiful and loving wife, mother and grandmother passed away at the home of a daughter, Mary Webb, on May 15, 1917, following a massive stroke. Her beloved husband preceded her in death just two years before. She was loved and respected by all who knew her; a role model in every sense of the word.

ANN SKINNER RAWLINGS

BIRTHDATE: 13 Sep 1828
England
DEATH: 19 May 1909
PARENTS: John Skinner
Ann Beeley / Beely
PIONEER: Sep 1862
James Wareham Wagon Train
SPOUSE: Eber B. Rawlings
MARRIED: 31 Dec 1850
Daventry, Northampton, England
DEATH SP: 18 Sep 1908
Provo, Utah Co., Utah

CHILDREN:
Henry Eber, 15 Oct 1851
Zeda Emma (Lund), 1 Mar 1854
George Peleg, 27 Aug 1856
Levenia, 27 Nov 1858
Anne Marie (Holman), 27 Feb 1860
Bertha, Oct 1862
William Senior, 27 Nov 1863
Kate Estella (Pyne), 27 Jan 1868
John Earnest, 28 Oct 1870

Ann was born in England. She attended village schools and later attended the Church of England school. Having a beautiful voice, she sang for her school and church.

After completing her schooling, she worked as general housekeeper, supervising the servants in a home of one of the notables of England. During that time she had a desire to become a nurse. She was educated in obstetrics, for which she was grateful because it proved to be the mission of her life.

Ann listened to two Mormon missionaries and was baptized as a member o the Church of Jesus Christ of Latter-day Saints on June 17, 1850. Prior to her baptism, she had met Eber Brightwell Rawlings, they were married on December 31, 1850. They both were anxious to gather with the Saints in Zion, so four weeks after they were married they left their native England in 1851 on the ship "Ellen Maria," to emigrate to America. It was a rough voyage but Ann endured and proved herself a ministering angel among the people on board who needed assistance.

Shortly after arriving at Alton, Illinois, Eber was set apart as Branch President and Ann was set apart as midwife. After twelve years of missionary work at Alton, Ann and Eber decided to journey to Utah. She was then the mother of five children. She and Eber would become the parents of nine children.

They joined the wagon-train of James Wareham. Ann was blessed with an abundance of vitality and had real courage when it was needed. Although she was in delicate health herself at the time of their journey West, she unselfishly picked up the task of caring for the aged and nursing the sick. She walked a good part of the way across the Plains. On reaching Echo Canyon, she was overcome with fatigue and was unable to go any further. Several wagons were stopped by Ann but they said they were loaded to capacity and could not give her a ride. Later in the day, the captain of the wagon-train saw her plight and asked the last wagon to return and pick her up. She rode from there to the Salt Lake Valley, arriving on September 26, 1862. They made their home in Provo, Utah.

Soon after their arrival, Ann gave birth to a baby girl who died within a few hours after its birth. Ann was called on to help the sick. She asked no pay from the poor. From those who were in better circumstances, she charged the small sum of $3.00 for the care of mother and baby for ten days or more. Her self-sacrifice and helpfulness to others in time of need were greatly appreciated. She was an angel of mercy to the thousands whose eyes have beamed as she knelt over them ministering to their needs until they were nursed back to health.

When her eldest daughter died, Ann raised four of the six children she left. She often said, "We are creators of our own happiness; what we have may be largely dependent upon others, but what we are rests largely with ourselves.

Ann passed away on May 19, 1909.

JANE SHARP RAWLINS

No Photo Available

BIRTHDATE: 22 Mar 1794
Kentucky
DEATH: 5 Apr 1858
Big Cottonwood, Salt Lake, Utah
PARENTS: Robert Sharp
Elizabeth Forgy
PIONEER: 12 Oct 1848
Wagon Train Company
SPOUSE: James Rawlins
MARRIED: 19 Mar 1816
Harrison, Indiana
DEATH SP: 17 Oct 1874
Lewiston, Cache Co., Utah

CHILDREN:
Sarah, 3 Mar 1817 (died as a child)
Lucinda (Cunningham), 12 Mar 1819
Elizabeth, 27 Feb 1821 (died as a child)
Joseph Sharp, 9 Apr 1823
Harvey McGalyard, 14 Feb 1825
Leah (Day), 19 Sep 1827
Millie Jane (Carson), 16 Jul 1931
Elva Ann (Carson), 6 Jan 1834
Nelson, 1835 (died as a child)
Charlotte Melvina (Lemons), 9 Feb 1837

Jane was born in 1794 in the state of Kentucky. When she was about twenty-two years of age she married James Rawlins on March 19, 1816 in Indiana. He was a veteran of the Revolutionary War.

James became a member of the Church of Jesus Christ of Latter-day Saints in April, 1840, being baptized by David Evans. He received his patriarchal blessing from John Smith, the patriarch on August 23, 1845 in Nauvoo, Illinois.

This couple endured the persecutions and hardships of the Saints while they lived in Illinois, and when they began their westward trek, being among the first group to prepare to make that journey. They were assigned to the third division with Willard Richards as leader. In this group there were 526 people, 169 wagons, 50 horses, 20 mules, 515 oxen, 426 cows and loose cattle, 369 sheep, 63 pigs, 5 cats, 170 chickens, 4 turkeys, 7 ducks, 5 doves, 3 goats. They left the Elkhorn River on July 10, 1848, and part of them arrived in the Salt Lake Valley on October 19, 1848.

Jane and James became the parents of ten children; three of whom died as children. Upon their arrival in Utah they made their first home at Big Cottonwood, Utah.

In 1852 they moved to Draper, then in 1865 to Spring City. In 1871, they left Salt Lake and moved to Cache Valley to the city of Richmond and then to Lewiston, Utah. James was a farmer and loved to work in the good earth, producing life-giving food.

Jane had passed away on April 5, 1858 while living in the Big Cottonwood area. They had raised a noble family. They were middle aged when they left their home in the East but still forged ahead and made for themselves a wonderful heritage in this great western land to which their God had led them.

James also married five other women. He passed away on October 17, 1874 at Lewiston, Cache County, Utah.

These were early pioneers who had great faith and fortitude and contributed much to the development of the Utah Territory. One of their grandsons, Joseph Lafayette Rawlins became a United States Senator.

MARGARET ELZIRA FROST RAWLINS

BIRTHDATE: 28 Apr 1830
Knox, Tennessee
DEATH: 4 Apr 1920
Lewiston, Cache Co., Utah
PARENTS: McCaslin Frost
Penina Smith
PIONEER: 12 Oct 1848
A. Cunningham Wagon Train
SPOUSE: Harvey M. Rawlins
MARRIED: 3 Dec 1846
Nishnabothna, Missouri
DEATH SP: 9 Sep 1913
Lewiston, Cache Co., Utah

CHILDREN:
Margaret Elzirah, 30 Apr 1848
James McCaslin, 3 Jul 1850
Harvey McGalyard, 13 Dec 1851
Samuel Lafayett, 17 Jul 1854
Franklin Archibald, 22 Jan 1857
Pennina Jane, 6 Apr 1859
Mary Eveline, 19 Nov 1861
Joseph William, 4 Mar 1864
Alma Frost, 23 Oct 1866
Elva Arminta, 14 May 1869
Jasper Alfonzo, 1 Feb 1872
Nancy Ellen, 1 Aug 1874

Margaret Elzira was born in Knox, Tennessee. Her parents moved to Illinois after they joined the Church of Jesus Christ of Latter-day Saints. Her brother, Samuel, returned to Tennessee to serve his mission for the Church among his relatives. Margaret Elzira was baptized by her brother in 1842, after he returned from his mission.

Margaret found work helping a family in 1846. The mother of this family was sick. One day, the father tore a large hole in his coat going through the brush by their home. Margaret offered to mend the hole. She did such a nice job that other neighbors brought work for her to do.

Margaret married Harvey M. Rawlins on December 3, 1846. She was sixteen years old. When their first baby was about three weeks old they left their parents in Nauvoo and started West with the Andrew Cunningham Wagon Company. Margaret and her baby rode in the wagon which carried their supplies.

A pig-pen was built on the back of the wagon and a chicken coop was built on top of the wagon. The hens laid eggs every day. Their cow gave milk every day. They strained the cream and the jarring of the wagon made butter which was a luxury for them. They were never bothered by Indians nor did they see a buffalo stampede. They arrived in the Salt Lake Valley on October 12, 1848. They stayed in the fort their first night.

Many of their family members came into the Valley at this time and they moved to Big Cottonwood and on to Draper, Utah. In 1871, Margaret and their family moved to Lewiston, Cache County, Utah where Margaret lived the rest of her life.

They were blessed to attend the dedication of the Logan Temple on May 17, 1884. On January 6, 1876, the Relief Society was organized in Lewiston, Utah and Margaret was called to be the first president. There were twenty-three members at the beginning. She served as President for twenty-six years. On her fiftieth birthday, the Relief Society sisters had a surprise party for her. While she was the President she helped to bury about 125 bodies. She cared for the sick and the homeless.

Margaret ELzira took care of her father and mother until they died. She and her husband had some of their own family living with them at all times. Her oldest daughter married at the age of fifteen. Her first baby died in just a few weeks. At seventeen this daughter had her second baby and two weeks later this young mother died. This was the beginning of many sad sicknesses and deaths with the Frost and Rawlins families. Margaret wrote in her journal, "I just live with the dreads."

Margaret and her husband became the parents of twelve children, one died in infancy. Margaret and her husband lived together for sixty-seven years, until his death in 1913. He was blind for the last thirteen years of his life.

Margaret's journal states the Daughter of the Utah Pioneer Organization held their meeting at her home and lunch was served. She had her own home until she became sick a few months before she died. She lived to be ninety years old. She was always a very great example of a true Pioneer. Her faith never wavered.

MARY ELLEN FROST RAWLINS

BIRTHDATE: 28 Jan 1827
Knoxville, White Co., Tennessee
DEATH: 18 Jan 1917
Salt Lake City, Salt Lake, Utah
PARENTS: John M. Frost
Nancy Pate
PIONEER: 12 Oct 1848
Joseph S. Rawlins Wagon Train
SPOUSE: Joseph S. Rawlins
MARRIED: 1 Feb 1844
Hancock Co., Illinois
DEATH SP: 13 Oct 1900
Salt Lake City, Salt Lake, Utah

CHILDREN:
Nancy Jane, 5 Feb 1845
Mary Ellen "Helen," 1 May 1848
Joseph Lafayette, 28 Mar 1850

Mary Ellen was born in Tennessee. Her father was English and her mother was Irish. Mary Ellen and her brother, Lafayette, were the only members of the family to become converted to the Church of Jesus Christ of Latter-day Saints.

Mary Ellen married Joseph Sharp Rawlins on February 1, 1844 in Hancock County, Illinois. They began their westward trek to the Salt Lake Valley on May 12, 1848. At this time they had a three year old daughter and a twelve day old daughter. They remained camped at Council Bluffs during 1847 and 1848. There they planted and gathered corn, potatoes and other food products to provide for their journey West.

It was suggested to Mary Ellen that her departure for the trip across the Plains be delayed because of her illness after childbirth, but she stated, "We are going now." She endured the hazards and difficulties of the thousand mile journey with a staunch, uncomplaining courage which was to become typical of her throughout her life. They reached the Salt Lake Valley on October 12, 1848 and established a home in Mill Creek.

Two years later they were asked to move south to Draper, Utah where an adobe house was built. A well was dug north of the house and the fireplace was used for both cooking and heating of the house.

Mary Ellen had a spinning wheel-built. She hand carded sheep's wool and then spun the rolls into yarn on the spinning wheel. She dyed the wool various colors and set the warp on the hand loom. The yarn was then woven into cloth. The cloth was then cut into clothes to be sewn for her family. She also made shoes by cutting the soles from a hide tanned in the neighborhood to which she fitted and sewed the uppers.

It was necessary for Mary Ellen to manage without her husband for many months at a time during his church and government assignments. Her husband made seven trips to aid the Saints coming to the Valley in addition to other service. There were wolves, coyotes, bears, snakes and hostile Indians to contend with. Some of the precious live-stock were killed by wolves from time to time.

Mary Ellen clothed and fed her children, milked the cow, churned, spun, wove, cared for the animals, hauled gathered wood and fought off wild beasts. There were times when it was necessary to pacify the hostile Indians who surrounded and invaded her home, frightening the children. They wanted food which was very scarce. She was able to pacify the Indians, maintain her courage-before the children and carry on her many responsibilities until her husband returned.

Mary Ellen was noted for her gracious hospitality. She enjoyed entertaining visitors in their comfortable home.

Her life was filled with faithful service and devotion to the Church for which she gave up the security of her girlhood home and endured the hardships of the long trek across the Plains and the difficulties of pioneering a strange land.

Mary Ellen passed away on January 18, 1917 at Salt Lake City, Utah. She was ninety years old and had been a widow for seventeen years.

CATHERINE SMITH CROSLAND YOUNG RAWLINSON

BIRTHDATE: 8 Mar 1836
Ft. Lorney, Sarnia, Kent, Canada
DEATH: 03 Sep 1914
Holden, Millard Co., Utah
PARENTS: John A. Smith
Annie Anderson
PIONEER: 12 Oct 1849
Silas Richards Co. Wagon Train
SPOUSE I: Benjamin Crosland
MARRIED: 14 Jun 1852
Salt Lake City, Salt Lake, Utah
DEATH SP: 15 Jun 1860
Tooele, Toolel Co., Utah

CHILDREN:
James Smith, 14 Apr 1853
Sarah, 24 Oct 1855
John Smith, 12 Mar 1858
Benjamin, 15 Feb 1859

SPOUSE II: John Young
MARRIED: 12 Apr 1862
DEATH SP: (divorced)

CHILD:
Heber C., 31 Dec 1862

SPOUSE III: Charles Rawlinson
MARRIED: 14 Aug 1867
DEATH SP: 8 Apr 1903
Holden, Millard Co., Utah

CHILDREN:
Hannah, 13 Apr 1868
Rebecca, 15 Jul 1870
Annie, 20 May 1872
Ada, 3 Oct 1875
Nettie, (died as an infant)
Emma (died as an infant)

Catherine's parents had accepted the gospel of the Church of Jesus Christ of Latter-day Saints and were anxious to join with the body of the Church in Nauvoo, Illinois. By the time they were financially able to leave Canada, they were the parents of three sons and two daughters.

Catherine was baptized on June 4, 1848 in Nauvoo. Her mother brought the family across the Plains in the Silas Richards Wagon Company. Her father had crossed the

Plains the previous year when he was called to deliver the first mail to the Salt Lake Valley.

When Catherine was sixteen years old, she entered into plural marriage with Benjamin Crosland who came to Utah from England. Benjamin owned a farm and also worked at a sawmill in Cottonwood Canyon. Four children came to bless their union before her husband was killed in a sawmill accident.

With her four children, she went to Tooele, Utah. She entered into another plural marriage to John W. Young. They had one child, Heber, and soon after his birth, this marriage ended in separation.

President Young set Catherine apart as a midwife. She served in this capacity for forty years. Catherine was called upon to help settle Deseret in Millard County. They went through all the hardships of pioneering that isolated place.

She married Charles Rawlinson who was a widower with one son. He took then to Holden where six daughters were born to them making a total of twelve children. Catherine was also the town doctor and nurse until her death at age seventy-nine.

ELIZABETH COFFIN RAWSON

BIRTHDATE: 18 Oct 1807
Montgomery Co., Virginia
DEATH: 20 Apr 1890
Harrisville, Weber Co., Utah
PARENTS: William Coffin
Mary Dunkin
PIONEER: 14 Oct 1850
Wilford Woodruff Wagon Train
SPOUSE: Horace Strong Rawson
MARRIED: 9 Oct 1825
Washington Co., Indiana
DEATH SP: 10 Oct 1882
Ogden, Weber Co., Utah

CHILDREN:
Mary Ann Olive, 8 Oct 1826
Daniel Berry, 16 Dec 1827
Samanatha Priscilla, 26 Apr 1830
William Coffin, 13 Jul 1832
Oriah, 15 Mar 1834
Sariah, 15 Mar 1834
Chloe Ann, 15 Aug 1836
Caleb Linsey, 5 Mar 1839
Arthur Morrison, 17 Jun 1840
Sarah Arinda, 8 Feb 1844
Cyrus, 15 Jun 1846
Horace Franklin, 9 Oct 1848
Elizabeth, 21 Aug 1853

After Elizabeth was born, her family moved to Indiana where her father died. Elizabeth married Horace Strong Rawson on October 9, 1825. After her marriage, she helped her husband care for his twelve orphaned brothers and sisters.

In 1831, they were baptized into the Church of Jesus Christ of Latter-day Saints and moved to Jackson County. When they received the extermination order from Governor Boggs, they moved to Lafayette County, then to Clay County, Missouri. In 1839, they moved to Illinois where they enjoyed feasting on the teachings of the servants of God. In 1846, they were obliged to leave the state due to more persecution from mobs. They stopped in Council Bluffs where their son, Daniel, joined the Mormon Battalion.

They journeyed across the Plains in the Wilford Woodruff Wagon Company and arrived in Salt Lake Valley on October 14, 1850.

Daniel, their son, met them and took them to Ogden where he had prepared a home for them. Elizabeth's husband worked as a carpenter and did the work of a blacksmith when necessary. The family later moved to Farmington where they farmed until the Johnston's Army caused them to move south.

They lived in Payson from 1857 to 1860. While there, her daughter, Samantha, died leaving three children for her to care for until their father remarried. Elizabeth was always busy helping her married children with their families. She did their spinning, weaving, knitting of socks, caps, mittens, and other articles of clothing.

After her husband died in Ogden, she moved to Harrisville and spent the rest of her life with her children. Catherine passed away at the age of eighty-two.

MARY MELVINA TAYLOR RAWSON

BIRTHDATE: 22 Feb 1847
Council Bluffs, Iowa
DEATH: 8 Jun 1934
Ogden, Weber Co., Utah
PARENTS: Joseph Taylor
Mary Moore
PIONEER: 20 Sep 1850
James Pace Co. Wagon Train
SPOUSE: Daniel Berry Rawson
MARRIED: 10 Mar 1866
Salt Lake City, Salt Lake, Utah
DEATH SP: 18 Feb 1892
Farr West, Weber Co., Utah

CHILDREN:
Silas Daniel, 4 Dep 1867
David Ward, 17 Sep 1871
Joseph Horace, 6 Aug 1874
Wilford Woodruff, 1 Sep 1881

Mary Melvina was born in 1847 in Council Bluffs, Iowa. At the time of her birth, her father was with the Mormon Battalion and was not present. Her mother was living in the back of a wagon. When born, Mary was very ill and had to be administered to by the laying on of hands and through her mother's faith, Mary Melvina lived.

She was just three years old when she crossed the Plains with her family. She had a five year old sister and a two year old brother and a two week old brother. They left Council Bluffs, May 30, 1850, were with fifty wagons in the James Pace Wagon Company and they arrived in the Salt Lake Valley on September 20, 1850.

She suffered the hardships and horrors of Indian troubles. She was so frightened of the Indians, that her mother would bring her meals to her in the wagon on a tin plate. Mary never forgot that plate.

The Taylor family moved to Kaysward, now Kaysville, Utah. On April 4, 1852, Mary's mother went into premature labor, had convulsions and died shortly after a baby boy was born, but he died also. Mary Melvina was just five years old at the time. They buried her mother in a wagon box, which Joseph made into a coffin with the baby in her arms. It was heart-breaking for her to lose her mother when she was such a young age.

Mary's father married soon after, but the new stepmother could not take her mother's place. Mary Melvina had beautiful long, dark curls, that had been a joy to her mother who loved to take care of them. The stepmother thought these curls a lot of unnecessary work and cut them off. Mary never forgot how she felt when her beautiful long hair was cut.

When she was ten, the family moved to Payson. It was a bad winter, they had very little to eat and went barefoot for the entire winter. They moved back to their home after the Johnston's Army scare. Mary learned to spin and knit, and made the clothing worn by most of the family. She learned to cook and to dry corn and fruit. She knew how to care for everything they could raise in the summer in order to have food until the next harvest. Her father got some cows, and Mary, age thirteen, was the one to milk them, and make the cheese and butter to be sold to others.

Mary Melvina met Daniel Berry Rawson and they were married, March 10, 1866, in Salt Lake City. She was his third wife in plural marriage. They lived in Farr West, Utah. She had four sons. She lived in a log cabin. She made her son's clothing by hand, and even made them straw hats, dying the color, soaking and braiding them. She also made her own soap. She was very independent, was a hard worker and always found things for her boys to do.

Her husband went on a mission to the Mokie Indians. He was also sent to prison for co-habitation and was charged a fine. He passed away when Melvina was forty-five years old.

Melvina sold her home and land and settled on thirty acres of land in Idaho near her son, Silas. She lived there for sixteen years with her younger boys with her. She received a small government pension because her husband had served in the Mormon Battalion. She rented rooms to a school teacher, and she sold butter and eggs. Her son, Wilford, went on a mission and she supported him. Her last thirty years were spent living in her son's home in an apartment. Her health was good, and she loved spending time with her grandchildren.

Melvina passed away in her sleep when she was eighty-seven years old. She had four sons, eighteen grandchildren and thirty-two great grandchildren all who loved her dearly.

She was truly one of the great women of faith, who loved her religion and lived it to the best of her ability to the end, a great example for all.

NANCY BOSS RAWSON

BIRTHDATE: 26 Mar 1829
Lexington, North Carolina
DEATH: 20 Aug 1888
Farr West, Weber Co., Utah
PARENTS: Philip Abed Boss
Obedience Brown
PIONEER: 1849
Company unknown
SPOUSE: Daniel Berry Rawson
MARRIED: 26 Nov 1849
DEATH SP: 18 Feb 1892
Ogden, Weber Co., Utah

CHILDREN:
Nancy Emeline, 29 Jun 1851
Elizabeth Ann, 3 Feb 1853
Mary Ann Olive, 2 Jan 1855
Obedience Leonora, 23 Apr 1857
Polly Ann, 3 May 1859
Sariah Diantha, 28 Jul 1861
Daniel Heber, 8 Sep 1863
Charlotte, 18 Feb 1865
Samantha Dalena, 26 Aug 1867
Daniel Benjamin, 16 Nov 1869/70

Nancy was born in Lexington, Davidson County, North Carolina. When she was six years old, her father died and left her mother with nine children to raise. Her mother moved her family to Brown County, Illinois in 1838. They joined the Church of Jesus Christ of Latter-day Saints there and moved to Nauvoo in 1842. They encountered trouble along with other members of the Church. A mob burned their house.

Nancy was employed as a servant by Colonel Williams. She did not know at first that he was a leader of the Anti-Mormon forces. Knowing she was a member of the Church, he refused to let her out of the house on pain of death. She heard the men planning to kill the Prophet Joseph Smith. She had to cook dinner for these men before they started for the jail at Carthage. She said after they returned to the Williams' home that night after the prophet's death, they seemed chastened and frightened they had committed such a terrible crime. She managed to escape from the house by pretending to go for a bucket of water. She ran into the woods where a cousin mounted on a horse was waiting to help her escape.

She and her mother's family left Nauvoo with other members of the Church in 1846. They lived other places along the way as they traveled across the Plains. They arrived in Salt Lake Valley in 1849.

Nancy married Daniel Berry Rawson on November 26, 1849 in Salt Lake City. The couple helped to settle the Ogden area and Harrisville, Utah.

Nancy was a kind, honest, affectionate woman, a good mother to her ten children, and a kind friend to the poor. She labored many years as a counselor in the Relief Society of the Harrisville Ward. In March, 1866, she shared her husband, Daniel, as he married a plural wife, Mary Melvina Raylor.

Nancy passed away on August 20, 1888 in Farr West, Weber County, Utah.

SARAH CHANTRY RAWSON

BIRTHDATE: 31 Dec 1824
Mansfield, Nottingham, England
DEATH: 11 Sep 1902
Plain City, Weber Co., Utah
PARENTS: John Chantry
Marie Boughskill
PIONEER: 2 Sep 1868
Daniel McArthur Wagon Train
SPOUSE: John Rawsen/Rawson
MARRIED: 8 Apr 1844
Swanwick, Derbyshire, England
DEATH SP: 10 Jun 1668
Swanwick, Derbyshire, England

CHILDREN:
Francis, 26 Apr 1845
Joseph, 3 Apr 1847
John, 9 Apr 1849
Jane, 27 Aug 1851
William, 6 Jan 1854
George, 9 Mar 1856
Samuel, 13 May 1859
Hannah, 9 Nov 1861
Thomas, 6 Mar 1864
Harry, 11 Oct 1867

Sarah was raised in a beautiful place in England. She had no schooling. As a young woman she was tall with light brown hair and blue eyes. Her family was very bitter when she joined the Church of Jesus Christ of Latter-day Saints.

After her marriage she lived with her husband's parents. Sarah and John were the parents of ten children. They were saving and preparing to come to American when John became very ill. Their son came to tell them that he and his family were leaving for America and the death of his father occurred half an hour after he arrived.

John's passing left Sarah heartbroken she had no way of supporting those of her family too small to work. She was advised to take her four youngest children and

immigrate to America. She left on the steamship "Colorado," and arrived in New York.

After arriving in Salt Lake City, she was sent to Farmington, Utah, where friends and Church could help her. In January of that first winter she received word of the death of her son, George, the youngest child she left in England. As in other sorrows and trials of life, she met this bravely and without complaint, still she mourned deeply.

In the Spring of 1869, she moved to Coalville, a mining town, to be there at the arrival of her son, Francis and his wife and babe, sons John and William and daughter Jane, who arrived on October 6, 1869. With the boys working in the coal mines Sarah was able to keep her family together. In the Fall of 1871, her son, Joseph, who had married since she left England, with his wife and nine months old babe arrived this brought her family all together again.

In 1874, Sarah moved to Plain City, Weber County, Utah where she made her permanent home. With the help of her family she bought a comfortable home and a city lot, from which by thrift and industry, the sale of fruit and vegetables and the pay she received from working out at house work, she was able to gather around her more of the comforts of life than she had ever known before. It was here that she learned to read. She labored as a Relief Society visiting teacher for many years and was always generous to those less fortunate

CELIA HALL RAYMOND

BIRTHDATE: 20 Apr 1825
Liberty Falls, New York
DEATH: 22 Oct 1898
Kaysville, Davis Co., Utah
PARENTS: Bradley Hall
Elizabeth Reynolds
PIONEER: Aug 1852
Wagon Train Company
SPOUSE: Grandison Raymond
MARRIED: 12 Aug 1849
New York
DEATH SP: 28 Feb 1898

CHILDREN:
Martha, 21 Jun 1850
Emma, 23 May 1852
Alice, 17 Jan 1854
Asenath, 12 Nov 1855
Grandison, 29 Sep 1857
David, 21 Jan 1860
Walter, 9 Oct 1861
Bradley Lemual 04 Dec 1863
Acenith or Elizabeth "Bessie," 16 Apr 1865
Celia, 1 Apr 1868

Celia was born in Liberty Falls, Sullivan County, New York. Her father died when she was fourteen years old. Her mother was expecting a baby; it was a sad time.

When Celia was growing up she and her mother and two brothers were in comfortable circumstances but lived a life of thrift and industry. Celia was industrious and studious. Her work was to milk about eight cows night and morning. In between she did the spinning. While her mother did the housework she would spin what was estamated a day and a half's spinning. She could do this and than have all the time she wanted to go and see the neighbor girls or read.

Though Celia belonged to no Church, she read the Bible through while still a girl. She loved poetry and recited long poems by heart.

At the age of twenty-four, she married Grandison Raymond. They became the parents of ten children; seven sons and six daughters. Two died in childhood. Very early in their married life they heard missionaries from the Church of Jesus Christ of Latter-day Saints preach the true Gospel. They traveled to Council Bluffs, Iowa to learn more about the Mormon Church and the members. They both were baptized into the Mormon Church.

In the Spring of 1852, they started across the Plains with ox-teams. It is not known if they traveled with a wagon-train. Celia had two children at this time, the youngest only ten days old. The journey was a hard one for Celia. Being weak when she started the journey West, she never got strong or felt well until the following spring. Her baby was cross, making it more difficult for her.

Soon after they arrived in the Salt Lake Valley in August of 1852 they settled in Kaysville, Utah. They were the first in that locality to make cane molasses and to keep honey bees. They also raised the first fruit orchard. Celia was a most excellent helpmeet in all ways. They prospered and became quite well-to-do.

Celia was the mother of ten children. She raised eight of them to adulthood. Some of her children had poor health which kept her at home a great deal. This and her natural modesty and retiring disposition caused her to do less public work than many of the sisters of her times. She was, however, a faithful Relief Society worker throughout her life. She was a teacher in Relief Society for a great many years and seldom missed a meeting.

Her two great characteristics were honesty and charity. Though the public knew little of her, the poor and the sick and the sorrowful knew her well. Her life was filled with kindness and helpfulness to all the needy. Her honesty was of the Golden Rule kind. She never traded or sold anything that she did not give a little over measure. She did not want to take advantage of anyone. Among her family and friends she was dearly beloved. Many people said that Celia was the best woman they have ever known.

Celia passed away at her home in Kaysville on October 22, 1898. She and her husband are buried side-by-side in the Kaysville, Utah Cemetery.

ELIZABETH DEAN RAYMOND

No Photo Available

BIRTHDATE: 23 Apr 1811
Norwalk, Fairfield, Connecticut
DEATH: 2 Nov 1850
Council Bluffs, Iowa
PARENTS: Samuel Dean
Phebe Thurston
PIONEER: died at Winter Quarters
SPOUSE: Samuel J. Raymond
MARRIED: 1828
DEATH SP: 4 Dec 1876

CHILDREN:
George Alford, 14 Dec 1829 (died as an infant)
Julia Sophia, 9 Feb 1831
Benjamin Franklin, 26 Nov 1833
Harriet, 12 Aug 1836 (died as an infant)
Anna Leticia, 12 Aug 1849

Elizabeth and her husband, Samuel, were living in Hempstead, Long Island, New York in the 1840's when the Mormon missionaries came to their town. According to an account written by her daughter, Julia, Elizabeth had to be coaxed by her husband to attend the meeting and hear the strange new doctrine, but she believed it and was baptized before he was.

When a branch of the church was organized on Long Island, her husband became the branch president. Later he was called to go to Nauvoo to help build the temple.

Elizabeth and her teenage daughter, Julia, went to work at housework by the week to earn enough to gather with the Saints at Nauvoo. After they had earned what they could and sold most of their household goods, Elizabeth said a tender goodbye to her aged mother, and with her daughter Julia and son Benjamin, took the train to Brooklyn to Brother Orson Pratt's office. They then traveled by steamer, canal boat and wagon to Nauvoo.

The exodus to the West was beginning and the next few months of their lives were spent in camps and traveling in wagons from one place to the next. Often her husband was away, helping with the exodus or working to earn money for their journey. At times when they stopped to find work, Elizabeth and Julia would take turns working and staying in camp with Benjamin. Elizabeth could earn a dollar and a half a day; while Julia's wage was only fifty cents.

They made their way to Council Point and stayed with the saints at Winter Quarters, waiting for the chance to go West. Elizabeth was expecting a baby and was not well all winter. Julia took care of her and the new baby daughter when she arrived.

When the baby was about fifteen months old, Elizabeth passed away at the age of thirty-nine, in November, 1850. Julia writes, "That was the first real sorrow I have ever known."

Elizabeth Dean Raymond was a faithful Latter-day Saint who gave her life for her faith.

HANNAH CHAPMAN CHESTER GOODWORTH BABCOCK RAYMOND

BIRTHDATE: 2 Mar 1813
Ousefleet, Yorkshire, England
DEATH: 15 Feb 1898
Soda Springs, Bannock, Idaho
PARENTS: William Chapman
Merry Drury
PIONEER: 26 Sep 1856
E. Ellsworth Handcart Company
SPOUSE I: Thomas Chester
MARRIED: 28 Jan 1833
DEATH SP: 11 Sep 1844
Crowle, Lincolnshire, England

CHILDREN:
James, Nov 1834 (died)
Mary Ann, Oct 1835 (died)
Ann, 12 Feb 1836
Thomas, 2 Jan 1838
Frances, 26 Apr 1840
Emma, 5 Jun 1842 (died)
William, 3 May 1843

SPOUSE II: Joseph Goodworth
MARRIED: 29 Oct 1845
Hull, Yorkshire, England
DEATH SP: 11 May 1853
Crowl, Lincolnshire, England

CHILDREN:
Richard Brooks, 25 Mar 1846
Joseph, 16 Jan 1849
Frederick, 24 Jul 1850

SPOUSE III: Adolphus Babcock
MARRIED: 25 May 1858
Spanish Fork, Utah (divorced)
DEATH SP: 15 Mar 1872
Spanish Fork, Utah Co., Utah

CHILD:
Hannah Alice, 8 Apr 1858

SPOUSE IV: Charles Jeremiah Raymond
MARRIED: 7 Nov 1865
Salt Lake City, Salt Lake Co., Utah
DEATH SP: 2 Dec 1883
Soda Springs, Idaho
CHILDREN: None

Hannah grew up in a family of ten children. She was married to Thomas Chester at the age of nineteen. Seven children were born to them in nine years. Three of their children died in childhood. Sixteen months after the birth of their last child her husband, Thomas, died from an abscessed knee. At the age of thirty-one she was widowed with four children to raise.

About a year later she married Joseph Goodworth who was thirteen years younger that she was. To this union three sons were born. Then her second husband died of kidney disease.

In 1853, Hannah, at the age of forty now had been twice widowed and had seven living children to raise and support.

Hannah had accepted the Gospel of the Church of Jesus Christ of Latter-day Saints and decided to take advantage of the Perpetual Emigrating Fund and emigrate to America and to Utah.

As Hannah made plans for her departure she had three Chester children and three Goodworth children for whom she was responsible. All of these children were signed up with the P.E.F. but ship records show that Frances and William Chester did not accompany her to America. Story has it that the Grandfather Chester was bitterly opposed to her religion and to her emigrating. One account says that an elderly gentleman was seen walking away from the ship with the boy, William, by the hand. At any account the two children did not emigrate with her even though their names appeared on the ships passenger list. Hannah never saw Thomas or Frances again.

They sailed on the ship, "Enoch Train," arriving in Boston on April 30, 1856. During the voyage, diphtheria broke out. Hannah, a nurse, helped to care for the sick and bury the dead at sea. This was the first shipload of emigrants who would participate in crossing the Plains with handcarts to Utah.

From Boston they boarded a train for New York, then westward to Iowa. They arrived in Iowa City on May 12th, and spent almost four weeks preparing, enduring, and waiting for the trek across the Plains. Finally, the first handcart company left on June 9th, under their assigned leader, Edmund Ellsworth.

When the company arrived in Florence, Nebraska, they spent about two weeks regaining strength, repairing the carts, and readying themselves for the thousand mile journey that lay ahead. Hannah, her young sons; ages six, seven, and ten, and her daughter, Ann, walked almost the entire distance, approximately twelve hundred miles. Richard, the ten year old, pushed the handcart while his mother pulled. The company arrived in Salt Lake City September 26, 1856 and from there she moved south with the Saints.

Hannah's history for the next years is very sketchy. It appears that she had to farm the boys out as she could not afford to keep them. Her daughter, Ann, married Benjamin Ashby in 1857 and moved to Bountiful.

It is reported that she found work as a housekeeper with the Adolphus Babcock family. He, a widower, and his children lived in Spanish Fork, Utah. She gave birth to their only child, Hannah Alice Babcock, before their marriage. Shortly thereafter, the two separated.

In 1865, Hannah was sealed to Charles Jeremiah in Salt Lake City at the Endowment House. The Raymonds then made their home in Bear Lake Valley, Idaho. With them were her son, Frederick, Charles' son, Albert, and Hannah Alice (Babcock).

In a personal letter, Hannah is quoted as saying that for the first time in her life she had found happiness.

Hannah and her husband were among the first pioneers in Bear Lake County. Later, the family moved to Soda Springs, Idaho.

In the Summer of 1874, Hannah's son, William, and his family arrived from England and they made their home in Soda Springs near his mother. Her youngest daughter, Hannah Alice, had by this time married and she also made her home near her mother.

Hannah helped organize the first Relief Society in this area and served as one of the first counselors. The Relief Society was reorganized in 1879 and Hannah Raymond became the president. This organization remained intact for fifteen years at which time Hannah was released at the age of eighty-three.

She was also cited by Dr. Ellis Kackley as one of the ladies around the Soda Springs community who helped nurse his patients.

Her husband died in 1883. Hannah bore the additional burden of losing her eye sight, but she continued to live in her home doing her own work even though she eventually went blind.

In life she was kind yet earnest. A task was never beset by enough draw-backs to daunt her valliant spirit when she knew her cause was just. While she married many times she spent the most of her years alone to fulfill the many acts of kindness and deeds of daring that come with building homes on frontiers and facing deprivation and stress. With all, she was cheery and felt that "the Lord was good."

Hannah Raymond passed away on February 15, 1898, at age eighty-four, in Soda Springs and was buried in the Chester plot in the Cedar Cemetery.

HANNAH MORGAN EVANS RAYMOND

No Photo Available

BIRTHDATE: (chr.) 3 Jun 1785
Rumsey, Glamorganshire, Wales
DEATH: 1870
Kaysville, Davis Co., Utah
PARENTS: John Morgan
Mother's name unknown
PIONEER: 2 Oct 1855
E. Bunker Handcart Company
SPOUSE I: Edward Evans
MARRIED: 9 Dec 1804
Wales
DEATH SP: 3 Sep 1832
Lisvane, Wales

CHILDREN:
Mary, 1805 (died as a child)
Mary, 1809 (died as a child)
Mary, 1815
Thomas, 4 Sep 1818
John, 1823

SPOUSE II: Mr Raymond
MARRIED: a few years before her death
DEATH SP: Not given
CHILDREN: None

Hannah was born in Wales in 1785 to John Morgan, but her mother's name is unknown. She married Edward Evans in 1804 in Wales. She had two daughters whom they named Mary, but they died as children. Her third child was also named Mary, and then she had two sons.

Hannah's husband died in 1832 in Wales.

Hannah was more than seventy years of age when she crossed the Plains of America. She came with the Edward Bunker Handcart Company in the third company. She travelled with her son, Thomas, his wife Mary, and their five children. They arrived in the Salt Lake Valley on October 2, 1855.

She had walked the whole distance until they reached Echo Canyon. She then asked to ride because she was so tired. The captain of the group reminded her that he had thought she could not make it walking all the way. This angered her so that she strode off ahead of the company. Her family thought they would overtake her and help her, but they saw no more of her. When they entered theValley, she was there to greet them. Some men with a load of logs had come upon her and gave her a ride into Salt Lake City.

She comforted the family when one year old Joseph sickened and died on the Plains. She helped her daughter-in-law with the children, and when her son died a year after arriving in Utah, she helped his widow care for the family, the three older ones being children of a former wife. A new baby was born into this family a few months after their arrival in Utah.

Hannah had experienced much in her lifetime. She married a Mr. Raymond a few years before she died. No details are available about her at that time.

Hannah died sometime in 1870 around eighty-five years of age, a stalwart, woman, one of great stamina, compassion, and integrity. She was a brave woman who put her heart and soul into her religious beliefs and was a great example of courage and faith to those who have followed her.

ELIZABETH SIMMONS READ

No Photo Available

BIRTHDATE: 14 Jun 1825
London, England
DEATH: 11 May 1904
Ogden, Weber Co., Utah
PARENTS: Isaac Simmons
Elizabeth Hastings
PIONEER: Sep 1853
SPOUSE: William Smith Read
MARRIED: 20 Apr 1852
St. Louis, Missouri
DEATH SP: 1 Dec 1891
Ogden, Weber Co., Utah

CHILDREN:
Sarah Ann, 21 May 1853
William Smith Jr., 26 Jun 1855
Joseph Reform, 30 Aug 1857 (died as a child)
Josiah George, 2 Jan 1859
Tryphena Maria, 30 Mar 1861
Annie Rebecca, 10 Jun 1864
Oscar Isaac, 19 Feb 1867

Elizabeth was born in London, England in 1925. At the age of sixteen she became a member of the Congregational Church, giving up dancing, of which she was very fond. She remained a faithful member of this church for five years, but thought there must be more in religion than she knew. She heard of a meeting of the Mormons, and secretly attended. She was converted and baptized as a member of the Church of Jesus Christ of Latter-day Saints on a cold November day, when the ice had to be broken before she could enter the water.

Soon after joining the Church her mother died. She made arrangements to come to America with the John Hart family in 1853. She stayed in St. Louis for two years, and met and married William Smith Read in April, 1852, at the home of Brother Hart.

In 1853, they left St. Louis for the Salt Lake Valley. Thirteen days into the journey her first child, a little girl, was born. They settled in Ogden, Weber County, Utah, where they raised their family and endured all the hardships of the early settlers.

At one time, Elizabeth nearly lost her life being in a dugout after a long, heavy rain, and it caved in on her. She was dug out nearly lifeless. Through all these trials she remained cheerful and faithful to the end. Even though she had little schooling she continued to study all subjects, had a good memory, and was gifted in writing poetry.

Elizabeth passed away in Ogden, Weber, Utah in 1904 at the age of seventy-nine years.

MARIA LOUISA PICKETT TOLMAN READ

BIRTHDATE: 28 Nov 1856/57
St. Louis, Missouri
DEATH: 27 Mar 1930
Marion, Cassia Co., Idaho
PARENTS: George Pickett
Priscilla Clark
PIONEER: 1859 or 1860
SPOUSE: Cyrus Ammon Tolman
MARRIED: 12 Dec 1878
(later divorced)
DEATH SP: May 1911
Emmett, Idaho

CHILDREN:
Mannie Picket, 7 Jan 1876
Mary Elizabeth (Glenn), 7 Jan 1880
George Orion, 11 Jun 1882

SPOUSE II: George Franklin Read
MARRIED: 1 Jun 1891/1893
DEATH SP: 23 May 1950/1951

CHILDREN:
Robert Lock, 20 Aug 1895
Waldemar Pickett 19 Jul 1897
Ulea Jane, 26 Feb 1899

Maria Louisa was born in November, in 1856 in St. Louis, Missouri to George and Priscilla Clark Pickett. She arrived in the Salt Lake Valley in 1860. She grew up in Tooele, Tooele County, Utah.

Maria's father had died April 2, 1857 in St. Louis. Her mother then married her husband's brother-Maria's Uncle became her stepfather. Maria gave birth to Mannie Picket on January 4, 1876. The father is listed as William Gill Mills, but he and Maria were never married. Mannie was born in Granite, Salt Lake County, Utah.

Maria married Cyrus Ammon Tolman in 1878, and they lived in Tooele where she had one son and one daughter. She and Cyrus were later divorced.

In 1891, Maria married George Franklin Read. She had two sons and a daughter in this family. Maria's son, Mannie, was married in 1896, and had nine children in his family which gave Maria a large posterity; which was added to by her other children. They all honor her name.

Maria Louisa was baptized into the Church of Jesus Christ of Latter-day Saints on June 7, 1878, and was endowed on December 12, 1878.

Her husband, Cyrus, passed away in 1911 in Idaho. Maria Louisa passed away in March, 1930, in Marion, Idaho at the age of seventy-three years. She is buried in the cemetery in Cassia, Idaho. Her second husband, George Franklin Read lived until 1950 or 1951.

SARAH BRIMLEY READ

No
Photo
Available

BIRTHDATE: 30 May 1793
Kempston, Buckingston, England
DEATH: 18 Jun 1862
Slaterville, Weber Co., Utah
PARENTS: John Brimley
Mary Smith Brimley
PIONEER: 9 Nov 1856
James Willie Handcart Company
SPOUSE: William M. Read
MARRIED: 18 Dec 1814
North Crawley, England
DEATH SP: 1856
Near Laramie, Wyoming

CHILDREN:
William Smith, 1 Dec 1816
Amelia, 2 Oct 1818
Joel, 13 Jan 1820
James, 18 Jan 1822
Naomi, 1 Nov 1824
Josiah, 3 Oct 1825
Jesse, 6 Jan 1827
John Brimley, 27 Dec 1830
Tryphena, 25 Sep 1832
Ezra, 15 Dec 1836
Joseph Paul, 25 Jan 1839

Sarah was born in England. Little is known about her early life.

She married William M. Read of North Crawley, England on December 18, 1814. They became the parents of eleven children; three daughters and eight sons, all born in England. The family accepted the Gospel and were baptized into the Church of Jesus Christ of Latter-day Saints.

Sarah and William emigrated to America in 1851 soon after the death of their daughter, Tryphena. They traveled with their youngest daughter and her small son. They arrived in New Orleans and then sailed up the Mississippi to St. Louis, Missouri, arriving sometime in 1853. They remained in St. Louis to earn enough money to make the journey. Their three youngest sons, John Brimley, Ezra and Joseph Paul emigrated with them.

While in St. Louis, Ezra contracted cholera and became a victim. He was buried in an unmarked grave. Sarah and William were now in their sixties. They felt they must push on to the Salt Lake Valley. They joined the ill-fated James G. Willie Handcart Company of 1856.

William died somewhere along the route close to the present site of Laramie, Wyoming. Sarah and her children were among those rescued by help sent by President Brigham Young. They arrived in the Salt Lake Valley on November 9, 1856.

Her eldest son, William Smith Read, had settled in the Ogden area so Sarah and the children went to him. Sarah recovered from her ordeal and continued to keep house, administer to the sick and do whatever was needed for the next six years. She was adept at all the skills needed for her new life: sewing, quilting and cooking.

After walking the eight or nine miles to her son John Brimley Read's house in Slaterville and after partaking of a good meal, she curled up by the fireplace as she complained of a small pain and just wanted to rest awhile before retiring.

Sarah died quietly by the fireplace on June 18, 1862 at the age of sixty-nine years. She loved the Gospel dearly and possessed a great testimony. She had given her all to help settle Zion.

ANNA MAGDALENA WINTSCH REBER

BIRTHDATE: 28 Apr 1842
Kinderausen, Switzweland
DEATH: 18 Apr 1880
Santa Clara, Washington, Utah
PARENTS: Heinrich Wintsch
Elisabeth Mueller
PIONEER: Fall 1863
Wagon Train Company
SPOUSE: Samuel Reber
MARRIED: abt 1863
Payson, Utah Co., Utah
DEATH SP: 4 Mar 1910
Littlefield, Mojave Co., Arizona

CHILDREN:
Harmenia Ann, 13 Jul 1864
Henrietta, 28 Jan 1867
Matilda, 5 Mar 1869
Samuel, Jr., 4 Apr 1871
Joseph Hyrum, 12 Aug 1873
Otilla Lucy, 16 Jun 1876
Mary Elizabeth, 29 Jul 1879

Anna Magdalena Wintsch Reber was born April 28, 1842 in Kinderausen, Zurich, Switzweland. Anna was the only one of her family who embraced the Gospel.

She emigrated to Utah in 1863. She joined a wagon train in Florence, Nebraska. One of the leaders of the group was Samuel Reber. He had been called on a mission to go with ox-teams to the East and get emigrants. Anna and Samuel met on his third trip to Florence, Nebraska. Anna arrived in the Salt Lake Valley the Fall of 1863. Many of the emigrants from Switzerland were sent to the Santa Clara settlements in the Southern part of Utah near St. George, in Washington County, Utah.

Anna and Samuel decided to marry as they were on their journey to Santa Clara. The marriage was performed at Payson, Utah. On February 17, 1877, they were sealed as husband and wife in the St. George Temple. They became the parents of seven children; five daughters and two sons.

Anna met the hardships and challenges of pioneer life with faith and courage. She passed away soon after the birth of her last baby, a daughter Mary Elizabeth. She was thirty-eight years old. Her husband passed away in 1924 at Littlefield, Mojave County, Arizona.

ELIZABETH HANCOCK REDD

No
Photo
Available

BIRTHDATE: 1 Jan 1797
Stump Sound, North Carolina
DEATH: 28 Nov 1853
Spanish Fork, Utah Co., Utah
PARENTS: Zebedee Hancock
Abigail Taylor
PIONEER: Sep 1850
James Pace Co. Wagon Train
SPOUSE: John Hardison Redd
MARRIED: 27 Mar 1826
North Carolina
DEATH SP: 15 Jun 1858
Spanish Fork, Utah Co., Utah

CHILDREN:
Harriet, 1827
Edward Ward, 31 Jan 1828
Ann Moriah, 26 Jul 1830
Ann Elizabeth, 16 Dec 1831
Mary Catherine, 4 Jan 1834
Lemuel Hardison, 31 Jul 1836
John Holt, 13 Jun 1837
Benjamin Jones, 20 Jun 1842

Elizabeth was born in North Carolina. An ancestor, Will Hancock, was a member of the North Carolina Assembly. Elizabeth married John Hardison Redd on March 27, 1826. The ancestors of both John and Elizabeth were prominent among the original settlers along the Atlantic Coast in the South. They became the parents of eight children.

In the year 1838, John and Elizabeth and their children moved to Murfreesborough, Rutherford County, Tennessee. They purchased a plantation with slaves to operate it. The next four years were very successful ones in plantation production of tobacco.

In 1842, they were converted to the Church of Jesus Christ of Latter-day Saints. This new found faith helped them understand that all men are born free. They were baptized and did not hesitate to legally free each of their slaves. Four of their former slaves followed them West that they might continue in their household.

Elizabeth and John sold their plantation and moved to Nauvoo in 1844. They were there when the Prophet Joseph Smith was killed. They were there when Brigham Young was choosen to lead the Saints. Elizabeth and John received their Patriarchal Blessings from Hyrum Smith on April 3, 1844. They were driven out of Nauvoo with the other Saints.

They came West in the James Pace Company. They had no trouble with Indians but they did survive a buffalo stampede. Several of their number perished from Cholera and Whooping Cough. Both John and their fourteen year

old son, Lemuel, contracted Cholera but they were both fortunate enough to recover. They arrived in the Salt Lake Valley, September 20, 1850, settling in Spanish Fork about three miles above the present City and began building a home and a sawmill.

Elizabeth was a courageous pioneer mother. She had been reared with slaves to jump to her every whim. What a change it was when she took a life as a frontier woman; Indian troubles, the hard work of reclaiming the soil, the struggle to bring water to the land, quest for lumber to build the fort, caring for her children in often dangerous times. They spent their energies to eke out a living which took its toll on Elizabeth.

On May 5, 1851, their youngest daughter, Mary Catherine, became ill. She died before evening. Her death was a great heartache to her family. On November 25, 1853 their son, John Holt, died from injuries he received when he was thrown from a horse. Elizabeth was heartbroken. She couldn't eat. She went to bed and it is said she turned yellow.

Elizabeth passed away on November 28, 1953 and was buried in the Redd Graveyard (now Pioneer Graveyard) in Spanish Fork, Utah County, Utah.

LETTICE BROWN ECKERSALL CROSSLEY REDFORD

BIRTHDATE: 22 Feb 1814
Pilkington, Whitefield, England
DEATH: 1 Mar 1900
Mt. Sterling, Cache Co., Utah
PARENTS: Joseph Eckersall
Betty Brown
PIONEER: 20 Aug 1868
Chester Loveland Wagon Train
SPOUSE I: William Crossley
MARRIED: abt 1835
Pilkington, England
DEATH SP: 2 Jul 1837
England

CHILD:
Betty, 19 Nov 1836

SPOUSE II: Robert Patefield Redford
MARRIED: 12 Apr 1841
Manchester Cathedral, Lanc., England
DEATH SP: 1 Jul 1865
Wellsville, Cache Co., Utah

CHILDREN:
Joseph Smith, 21 Feb 1842
John, 16 Mar 1844
Ann, 27 May 1846
Abraham, 1 Sep 1849
Robert, 18 Aug 1852
Ephraim, 6 Jul 1855 (died in 1865)

Lettice Redford was born in Pilkington, Whitefield, Lancaster, England, the youngest of six children. Her mother died when Lettice was but six months old. After three years, her father remarried. As the children became old enough to work they did their share to keep the family together. Lettice and her sister, Alice, did the housework and cooked as well as work in the cotton factory.

Lettice grew into a beautiful young woman with expressive brown eyes and dark hair. She had a typical English personality, a romantic and loveable temperament and a talent for singing. She sang leading solo parts in the church choir.

Lettice married William Crossley about 1835. They became the parents of one child, a daughter Betty. Her husband died of consumption on July 2, 1837, leaving Lettice heartbroken. She and her eight month old daughter returned to live with her father and Lettice returned to her job at the cotton factory to help with expenses.

Lettice was returning home from work one evening when she was attracted to a crowd in the street and joined them. She listened intently to the missionaries and secretly attended their meetings. Her father was bitter toward the Mormons and their religion. She was baptized into the Church of Jesus Christ of Latter-day Saints on July 30, 1840. Her father turned her out of his house and forbid her to take her daughter with her. She found refuge with a good neighbor for some time. Lettice was the only member of her family to join the Mormon Church.

She met and married Robert Patefield Redford on April 12, 1841, in the Manchester Cathedral, England. Both were twenty-seven years old. They became parents of five sons and one daughter, all born in England. Her first daughter, Betty, died in 1850 at sixteen years of age. Her husband owned a green grocery business but when they became members of the Mormon Church they could not make a substantial living because of the persecution against the members of the Church.

Her husband decided he would go first to Utah and earn the money to send for his family. Lettice never saw her husband again. He died in Utah in 1865. Three of her children emigrated to America before she did and one of her sons sent money for Lettice and two sons to emigrate. They left Liverpool on June 30, 1868 on the steamer "Minnesota." Her youngest son had died at the age of ten in England. They joined the Chester Loveland Company and arrived in the Salt Lake Valley on August 20, 1868. Lettice had been ill for most of the journey.

She lived with her son John in Wellsville, Utah for a short time. She lived the remainder of her life with her son, Robert and his family in Mt. Sterling in south Wellsville. She passed away in her sleep a week following her eighty-sixth birthday. She was buried near her husband, Robert Redford.

PATIENCE VAY LAMBERT REDFORD

No Photo Available

BIRTHDATE: (chr.)28 Oct 1787
Crathorne Parish, England
DEATH: 18 Apr 1865
Wellsville, Cache Co., Utah
PARENTS: Joseph Vay
Mother's name not verified
PIONEER: 9 Sep 1850
Benjamin Hawkins Wagon Train
SPOUSE: Richard Lambert
MARRIED: 6 Oct 1811
Manchester, Lancashire, England
DEATH SP: 22 Dec 1833
Burnley, Lancashire, England

CHILDREN:
Elizabeth, 8 Sep 1813
Hannah, 25 Jun 1817
John, 31 Jan 1820
Richard, 17 Nov 1822
Joseph, 22 Apr 1826

SPOUSE II: Robert Patefield Redford
MARRIED: 29 Nov 1856
Salt Lake City, Salt Lake Co., Utah
DEATH SP: 23 Jul 1865
Wellsville, Cache Co., Utah
CHILDREN: None

Patience was born in England, she was christened in Crathorne Parish, Manchester, Lancashire, England. Little is known of her childhood.

Patience's natural ability toward nursing kept her busy, helped out her income and did much to mold her character. She married Richard Lambert when she was twenty-five years old. He was forty. They became the parents of five children; four sons and one daughter. Patience was kept busy caring for her children, nursing and caring for mothers at childbirth and helping care of their children until the new mother was able to resume her role.

In spite of all her tender, loving care her husband passed away on December 22, 1833 of dropsy, now known as Bright's disease. It was a sad Christmas. Her youngest child was just seven years old.

The Mormon missionaries came to the Lambert home in October, 1838. Patience learned that she and her husband and children could all be joined together in eternal life if they remained faithful and were worthy. In October, 1839, Patience and her children were baptized into the Church of Jesus Christ of Latter-day Saints.

They left England on the first ship chartered by the Church to transport converts to the United states on a ship named "Brittania."

During the six years of their stay in Nauvoo, Patience had her family with her and lived in happiness with work and faith. Her nursing ability was greatly needed among the Saints and helped in sustaining her family. When the mobs forced them out of their homes they crossed the Mississippi

River. They had to sleep on the cold, frozen ground. They moved to St. Joseph, Missouri and were again forced to leave their homes by mobs. They finally earned enough money to buy equipment and provisions for the westward trek across the Plains to the Salt Lake Valley. They traveled in covered wagons in the Benjamin Hawkins' Wagon Company. They walked all the way, arriving in the Salt Lake Valley on September 9, 1850.

In 1856, Patience married an English convert, Robert Patefield Redford. They traveled north to help settle Cache Valley, Utah. They stopped at Wellsville, Utah because they liked the location. They built a log cabin with a sod roof.

Patience was very kind to her neighbors and they helped her and taught her how to make quilts. She was a small woman who looked fragile but was nevertheless hale, hearty, active and helpful all her days.

This honorable pioneer passed away at seventy-nine years of age on Januray 29, 1865.

MARIAN BROWN LEBRUN REDINGTON

BIRTHDATE: 18 May 1834
Ribbsford, Worcester, England
DEATH: 11 Mar 1915
Oxford, Idaho
PARENTS: Francis Brown
Mary Ann Hayes
PIONEER: 29 Aug 1863
John R. Murdock Wagon Train
SPOUSE: John Redington
MARRIED: 1 Dec 1860
England
DEATH SP: 3 Apr 1910
Oxford, Idaho

CHILDREN:
Marian Elizabeth, 4 Sep 1861
Kate Emily, 29 Nov 1863
Annie Sarah, 21 Jul 1866
John Walter, 26 Feb 1868
George Robert, 11 Jun 1873
Alice Maud, 17 Apr 1875

Marian was born in 1834 in England. They crossed the ocean for America on the ship "John J. Boyd" with William Cluff as company leader. They crossed the Plains in the John Murdock Wagon Company and arrived in the Salt Lake Valley on August 29, 1863.

Marian had married John Redington in the parish church of Claimes, about three miles from the city of Worcester, England. They were also married according to the Church of Jesus Christ of Latter-day Saints on December 2, 1860. They had six children born to them; four daughters and two sons.

Marian led a long and useful life in service of the Church and its organizations. She always enjoyed reading, singing, and dancing.

This family must have moved to Idaho where both Marian and her husband John passed away. John Redington passed away on April 3, 1910 in Oxford, Idaho. Marian passed away five days later on March 11, 1915. She was nearly eighty-one years of age.

She was a great pioneer woman of courage who left her homeland of England for her religious beliefs. She lived her religion and was an example for others who have followed after her.

ELIZABETH ALBANIA GARRETT MIDGELY REECE

BIRTHDATE: 13 Dec 1847
Coventry, England
DEATH: 23 Jul 1934
Aberdeen, Idaho
PARENTS: William Garrett
Maria Maycock
PIONEER: 24 Sep 1862
Homer Duncan Co Wagon Train
SPOUSE I: Thomas Midgely
MARRIED: 1868
Salt Lake Endowment House
DEATH SP: 20 Dec 1907

CHILDREN: None

SPOUSE II: David Reece
MARRIED: 6 Jul 1880
DEATH SP: 20 Dec 1907

CHILDREN:
William Lewis, 20 May 1881
Virginia Maria, 27 Oct 1882
David, 21 Jan 1885

Elizabeth Albania was born in 1847 at Willenhall, near Coventry, Warwickshire, England. She emigrated to America with her parents when she was almost nineteen years of age. They traveled across the Plains of America with the Homer Duncan Wagon Company which arrived in the Salt Lake Valley on September 28, 1866. Their conversion to the Church encouraged their gathering.

Elizabeth married her first husband Thomas Midgely in 1868 in the Endowment House in Salt Lake City. They had no children. There is no record of his birth or his death.

She later married David Reece on July 6, 1880. She had three children from this marriage.

Elizabeth was a skilled dress maker and she made her living spinning and weaving cloth and making clothes. She was an accomplished singer and sang with many choruses and choirs. She was a faithful member of the Church of Jesus Christ of Latter-day Saints. She loved her religion and enjoyed participating with the members wherever she went.

She and her husband, David Reece were pioneers to the Aberdeen, Idaho community where they helped develop the area. Elizabeth had learned in her early life how to work hard and to accomplish much, a trait which helped her throughout her life. She was a great pioneer woman of faith and fortitude to be honored by those who follow her.

MARY CURTIS REED

BIRTHDATE: 15 May 1821
Conneaut, Erie Co., Pennsylvania
DEATH: 3 May 1888
Logan, Cache Co., Utah
PARENTS: Nahum Curtis
Millicent Waite
PIONEER: 8 Oct 1848
Wagon Train Company
SPOUSE: Calvin Reed
MARRIED: 11 Jul 1841
Nauvoo, Hancock Co., Illinois
DEATH SP: 25 Oct 1895
St. David, Cochise Co., Arizona

CHILDREN:
Olive Marian, 27 Jun 1842 (died as a child)
Nahum Calvin, 21 Jan 1844 (died as an infant)
Mary Mahala (Crockett), 16 Jun 1845
Heber Curtis, 7 Sep 1847
Hyrum Tillison, 17 May 1853 (died as a child)
Adelia Millicent (Hanchett), 7 Jul 1856
Clarinda Athelia, 9 Aug 1861 (died as a child)

Mary was born in Pennsylvania in 1821. Mary's education began in Michigan, and continued when they moved to Far West. She was taught by her school teacher sister, and learned to read and write. As a young girl, Mary was given the gift of tongues about twelve years of age. She had it on several occasions throughout her life.

At one meeting when she heard the Prophet Joseph Smith reiterate his thrilling testimony, and he said, "All who will with honest hearts receive the restored Gospel, shall receive the Holy Ghost with the signs that follow the believer, as in the days of Jesus and the Apostles; and now you may test me as a true or false prophet." Tears dropped down the cheeks of this timid little girl as she uttered forth by the power of the Holy Ghost choice words of unknown tongue, which thrilled her whole being, and fulfilled remarkably the words of Jesus Christ as uttered to his disciples, and thus fulfilled in our presence. She was eight years old the day when Joseph was baptized by Oliver Cowdery. Mary was baptized when she was about ten years old. She also remembered the Haun's Mill Massacre.

Mary Curtis and Calvin Reed were married on July 11, 1841 in Nauvoo, Illinois. They had seven children born to their family. Four of them died as children, Nahum died the day he was born.

Mary was a homemaker who did whatever she could to provide for her children. When the Mormon Battalion was organized, Calvin was to go with them, but because of illness, he was discharged. He and his family had a wagon and two yoke of oxen and had food for their journey West. They were careful so it would last. Once when they were to cross the river, Calvin forgot to unhatch the steer from the wagon. A board broke loose as they approached the river. One steer floundered with pain as someone had spit tobacco in its eye. When they threshed around, someone pulled the pin from the wagon tongue which released the steers. Mary was sitting on the seat of the wagon and the water rose up to her armpits. She raised her baby as high as she could to keep her dry. Why the wagon didn't go under was a miricle. Some thought that there might have been a sheet of ice beneath the water; all were saved and rescued. The oxen leaving the wagon lightened the load and all were saved and rescued by others. They arrived in the Salt Lake Valley on October 8, 1848.

They had been at Haun's Mill when the marauders came to the area. A neighbor had directed them down a road away from the Curtis family. In her journal, Mary wrote, " We did not die as they wished, but as a people, and as Saints of God, we grew in numbers."

Her husband married two other women. Sometimes they lived together and at other times each had her own home. They moved around the Utah areas.

In 1849, the Gold excitement was on. Miners came through and brought provisions they sold to the pioneers. They never suffered for bread, for they each had a small piece twice every day. They travelled to California for the gold, and reached San Bernardino on May 17, 1853. They moved back to Payson, and at one time her husband moved to Arizona for awhile.

Mary's health began to fail. She concluded her last days doing temple work. She did some in the St. George Temple, and some in the Logan Temple.

Mary Curtis Reed passed away on May 3, 1888 in Logan, Cache County, Utah. Her husband died over seven years later. His death was in Arizona.

Mary had endured many things in her lifetime. She was always grateful for the Gospel of Jesus Christ and she was an example of righteous living, a great example for her posterity who have followed her.

MATILDA EVE PETTIT REED

No
Photo
Available

BIRTHDATE: 4 Apr 1837
Hempsted, New York
DEATH: 20 Mar 1869
Utah
PARENTS: Ethan Pettit
Margaret Ellsworth
PIONEER: 1848
SPOUSE: Levi Ward Reed
MARRIED: 1852
Salt Lake City, Salt Lake, Utah
DEATH SP: 30 Nov 1893
North Point, Utah

CHILDREN:
Mathilda Eve (Baldwin), 29 Jul 1853
Mary Rosean (Rudy), 1 Aug 1854
Ira Allen, 1 Jan 1856
Rebecca Elizabeth, 14 Aug 1857 (died at age 12)
Caroline Augusta (Langford), Apr 1859
Levi Albert, 12 Nov 1860
Laura Margaret, (Evans) 4 May 1862
Tamson Leona, 30 Oct 1863 (died at age 8)
Harriet (Ericson), 17 Apr 1865
Clarissa (Larson), 16 Feb 1867
Rachel, Larson 30 Oct 1868

Matilda Eve was born in 1837 in New York state, the oldest of eight children. She and her family were pioneers of 1848, arriving when Matilda was eleven years old.

When Matilda was a child, she had a disease known as black canker, and she lost the sight in one eye. In spite of this handicap, she had the reputation of being an excellent cook and a good seamstress. She was a small woman with brown hair and grey eyes.

Matilda married Levi Ward Reed in 1852. When they were first married, Matilda and Levi lived in a house on Pugsley Street, where their first two children were born. Levi, having come from land along a river bank which seemed more desirable, chose to settle on the Jordan River banks. They secured land known as North Point, becoming one of the first to dwell on the west side of the river. Land there proved to be excellent for gardening purposes and they built up a home that was for many years a veritable beauty spot producing all manner of fruits and vegetables.

Matilda had eleven children. In 1869, she and her children contracted measles. On March 20th, of that year, Matilda passed away. Two of the children died of the same disease; her fourth child, Rebecca, died eight days after her mother when nearly twelve years of age, and Tamzon Leone, her eighth child, died March 29th, nine days later of the same disease. This left baby Rachel just four and a half months old, motherless.

This family had been very happy living by the Jordan River and enjoying the productive land there. They raised gardens, cattle and chickens. Matilda was almost thirty-two years of age, and already had had a full, hard life. She had

remained faithful and strong in her faith, and she surely endured with great fortitude the experiences which came into her life.

REBECCA BEARCE REED

No
Photo
Available

BIRTHDATE: 30 Sep 1785
New Milford, Connecticutt
DEATH: 10 Feb 1848
Pottawattamie Co., Iowa
PARENTS: Josiah Bearce
Freelove Canfield
PIONEER: 1848
Died on way to Utah
SPOUSE: John Reed
MARRIED:
Cheshire, New Hampshire
DEATH SP: Oct 1846
Long Point, Bonaparte, Iowa

CHILDREN:
Thomas Henry Green, 15 May 1808 (raised as their own son)
Lee, 27 Jan 1810
Caroline (Beckworth), 1 Nov 1812
Clarissa (Hancock), 18 Dec 1814
John H., 12 Dec 1815
William Willard, 11 Mar 1817
Suzanna, 12 Dec 1819 (died as a child)
Joel Goss, 22 Apr 1824
Lydia Rebecca (Steed), 15 May 1827
Laura Lucinda (Lyman), 22 May 1829
Levi Ward, 15 Nov 1831
Ira Beckwith, 25 Jun 1835

Rebecca was born in New Milford, Lichfield County, Connecticut on September 30, 1785. They lived in New Hampshire later after her marriage. She married John Reed about 1805.

Their first four children were all born dead and no names and dates were given. They raised Thomas Green as their own child. Their next four children were born in Acworth, New Hampshire. Lee lived to be about eighty-five years of age and died in Farmington, Utah. Caroline married and lived until 1872, the age of about sixty years. Clarisa married and traveled to Salt Lake City where she died at fifty-five years of age. William Willard lived to be seventy years old. Suzanne died about two years of age from scalding. Her birthdate is not known. The family must have traveled toward the West as their next child, John's birth is not known but he died in 1846 in Keokuk, Iowa. Joel, Lydia Laura, Levi and Ira were all born in Ohio, Ira was born in Kirtland, the others in Rome. Rebecca had given birth to 15 children.

The parents, Rebecca and John both died en route to Utah. John died first in October of 1846. He was buried on the Des Moines River. He was sixty-three years old. Rebecca died one year and four months later in February of 1848. She was buried at Mt. Pisgah, Iowa. They had started out in 1846. Their children, Levi, Ira, Clarissa, arrived in the Salt Lake Valley in November of 1848. Their other children in the family came to Utah at a later time.

Rebecca was a brave pioneer woman to have continued on her trek after the death of her husband. Her desire to join the Saints was a strong, and a driving force in her life. She also died having given her all, literally, for her religion, her family and her love for the Lord. She is remembered for her valiant spirit by those who have followed her.

CAROLINE REEDER

No
Photo
Available

BIRTHDATE: 24 Sep 1839
Linstead Parva, Suffolk, England
DEATH: 15 Oct 1856
near Three Crossings, Wyoming
PARENTS: David Reeder
Lydia Balls
PIONEER: 1856
James Willie Handcart Company
SPOUSE: Not married

CHILDREN: None

Caroline was born in England. Her mother died when Caroline was sixteen days old. Aunt Millie Page came and cared for baby Caroline and the family until she died. Grandmother Sarah Sones Balls helped with the family until Caroline's sister, Eliza, was old enough (eleven or twelve years old) to assume the task of housekeeper for the family and care of Caroline. Later, her sister Mary also assisted in taking care of the children and caring for the home. Mary was four years old when Caroline was born. Caroline was the sixth child in the family.

In 1851, when Caroline was twelve years old, the family joined the Church of Jesus Christ of Latter-day Saints. On May 1, 1856, Caroline left home with her father, her brother Robert and her sister Eliza and her three daughters to emigrate to Utah. They set sail on the ship "Thornton" with Captain Collins, leaving from Liverpool.

They arrived in New York, June 14, 1856, and went by rail to Iowa City, Iowa. They stayed three weeks making handcarts and tents. They were part of the James G. Willie Handcart Company.

Caroline, age seventeen, helped care for her sister's three daughters as they traveled, helping them to keep up with the carts. She helped push and pull the handcarts, also. When their rations grew short they reduced them from day to day by common consent. Nights were getting colder and some would sit down by the roadside and die. As many as thirteen people were buried in one grave.

Caroline, at the end of the day, gathered some sage brush to bring into camp. She sat down to rest, leaning on her bundle, exhausted. They found her chilled and dying.

They carried her into camp but she died without gaining consciousness. She was buried in an unmarked grave near Three Crossings, Sweetwater, Wyoming. She died the evening of October 15, 1856. Her death was a great loss to her family. They had to hurry on in threatening weather and colder nights on the Windriver Pass. Nearly 100 pioneers died during the journey to the Salt Lake Valley. The Company reached the Valley on November 9, 1856.

LYDIA WILKINSON REEDER

BIRTHDATE: 16 Aug 1841
Chediston, Suffolk, England
DEATH: 22 Jul 1884
Hyde Park, Cache Co., Utah
PARENTS: Nathaniel Wilkinson
Lydia Daines
PIONEER: 27 Aug 1860
D. Robinson Handcart Company
SPOUSE: Robert Reeder
MARRIED: 15 Apr 1861
Hyde Park, Cache Co., Utah
DEATH SP: 22 Dec 1917
Hyde Park, Cache Co., Utah

CHILDREN:
Robert William, 15 Jun 1864
George David, 9 Jun 1866
Martin Charles, 3 Jun 1871
Amanda Lydia (Richards), 3 May 1873
Rose Harriet (Jeffs), 24 Jun 1875

Lydia was born in England. She was the eighth and last child of Lydia and Nathaniel Wilkinson. Lydia's mother attended one of the first meetings held by the missionaries of the Church of Jesus Christ of Latter-day Saints in the Chediston, England area and embraced their message. She and her husband were baptized in 1851. Lydia was baptized on April 20, 1853.

In 1855, in company with other Saints, Lydia, her parents, two brothers and a sister began their journey to Zion. They arrived in New York on January 1, 1856. The family lived in New Jersey for the next three years then moved to Omaha, Nebraska. Here Lydia's father died. Lydia's brother, Robert, and her sister, Harriet, were now married.

When it was time to leave Omaha for the trek Westward, Lydia, her mother and a brother joined with the Seamons family with the Daniel Robinson Handcart Company. After enduring many hardships, Lydia with her mother and brother arrived in Utah on August 27, 1860. They moved to Hyde Park, Cache County, Utah. Her brother, Robert, provided them shelter until they could build for themselves a log home.

On April 15, 1861, Lydia married Robert Reeder in Hyde Park. He had lived in the same Parish in England where Lydia had lived and they may have been acquainted there. However, it was not until their friendship in Hyde

Park was made that they moved toward marriage. They were sealed in the Salt Lake City Endowment House on Novemebr 14, 1862.

Their home was in Hyde Park on the corner which at present is known as Lee Park. They became the parents of five children; three sons and two daughters. Not much is known about Lydia's early life and little about her life in Hyde Park.

She had the reputation of being very fastidious about her personal appearance and a very good homemaker. She built a good friendship with her husband's second wife, Ellen Flatt. She was also diligent in her attendance at church meetings and teaching her children the Gospel.

Lydia was a tall but frail person. After the birth of her fifth child, her health declined. On July 22, 1884, she passed away of dropsy in Hyde Park. She is buried in the Hyde Park Cemetery.

CHRISTINA AMELIA HESSELL CRISMON REES

BIRTHDATE: 27 Jun 1852
Kingsborg, Ostrgt, Sweden
DEATH: 16 Apr 1903
Spanish Fork, Utah Co., Utah
PARENTS: Peter Hessell
Margaret Swenson
PIONEER: before 1866
Handcart company
SPOUSE I: Charles Crismon
MARRIED: 12 Oct 1867
(later divorced)
DEATH SP: 23 Mar 1893
Lehi, Maricopa, Arizona

CHILD:
Annie Telula, 31 Jan 1871

SPOUSE II: Joseph Alexander Rees
MARRIED: 24 Jun 1872
Salt Lake City, Salt Lake Co., Utah
DEATH SP: 21 Mar 1922
Santaquin, Utah Co., Utah

CHILDREN:
Amelia Elizabyh (Bissell), 22 May 1873
David Alex, 5 Mar 1875 (died as an infant)
Alfred Cornelius, 9 Feb 1876
Augusta Margaret, 8 Mar 1878 (died as a child)
Sarah Sylvia (Harmon), 12 Sep 1880
Mary Ann (Reynolds), 25 Apr 1883
Elina Maud Layphon (Nelson), 8 Aug 1885
Esther Leona (Loewe), 17 Nov 1887
Bessie Ethel (Higgenbotham), 10 Dec 1889
Zella H. (Robbins), 16 Mar 1891
Octavia D. (Carson), 1 Jun 1894
Leah J., 7 Jan 1897 (died as an infant)

Christina Amelia was born in 1852 in Sweden. She had a brother, Frans, who died in infancy. Amelia came to

Utah before August, 1866 and was married to Charles Crismon on October 12, 1867 in the Endowment House. They later divorced. He died on March 23, 1893 at Lehi, Maricopa County, Arizona.

Christina Amelia married Joseph Alexander Rees on June 24, 1872 in the Endowment House. He passed away on March 21, 1922 in Santaquin, Utah. She had one daughter with Charles Crismon, and twelve children with Joseph Rees; ten girls and two boys.

Christina Amelia had arrived in Utah before 1866, when she and her mother, Anna Margareta Svensdotter Hessell came with one of the first handcart companies. They pulled the handcart and walked the entire way. Her father came later with an ox-train.

Joseph and Christina settled in Grantsville, Utah where their first four children were born. They moved to Spanish Fork, Utah by 1880, where their remaining children were born. Joseph Alexander Rees wrote the following about his dearly beloved wife, "During the whole of our married life she proved herself to be a true and noble wife, kind to my children, loyal to her friends and a dear devoted mother to her 13 children who loved her dearly." This is a great tribute to a great lady, one who is revered for her greatness by those who have followed her. She was indeed a great pioneer woman of faith and fortitude.

Christina Amelia Hessell Crismon Rees passed away on April 16, 1903 in Spanish Fork, Utah the area she had known for so many years. She was almost fifty-one years of age and had children who were still young to be cared for by her husband who lived nineteen years longer. He was buried in Santaquin, Utah after his death March 21, 1922.

EMILY VAUGHAN REES

BIRTHDATE: 15 Jul 1852
Cwmbach, South Wales
DEATH: 19 Jan 1919
Ogden, Weber Co., Utah
PARENTS: David Vaughan
Winefred Williams
PIONEER: 1863
Brother Bullock's Wagon Train
SPOUSE: Moroni Rees
MARRIED: 28 Jun 1869
Salt Lake Endowment House
DEATH SP: 2 Oct 1931
Ogden, Weber Co., Utah

CHILDREN:
Emily Maria (Thomas), 29 Apr 1871
Moroni Vaughan, 14 Jun 1873
David James, 29 Jan 1876
Mary Ellen (Thomas), 29 Dec 1877
Phillip Morgan, 16 May 1880
George Arthur, 25 Feb 1882
Gomer Vaughan, 8 Nov 1883
Gwennie (Miller), 17 Sep 1885
Thomas Richard, 1 Dec 1890

Emily was born in Cwbach, Glamorganshire, South Wales on February 25, 1852. She was the eighth and last child in the family. When she was eight years old, she was baptized.

Her father, brother and family came to America in a sailing vessel in 1860. Her father obtained work in about three months after arriving in America in the coal mines. After working about one week, her father met with an accident which later caused his death. He was very sickly and left to earn enough money to send for the rest of his family in 1861.

Emily, her mother and the rest of the family were six weeks on the ship. They stayed in New York about one month, then traveled to Minersville, Ohio, where the family members were all reunited. Two of Emily's sisters were able to come to Salt Lake with other families to help with their children. Her mother worked with the sick all the time to help make a living for the family.

After staying in the east for two years, Emily and the rest of the family arrived in Salt Lake in 1863 in Brother Bullock's Wagon Company. Emily, her sister and father walked all the way. They were instructed by the captain to not go far from the train for fear of Indian attacks. The wagons were all pulled by oxen. Emily's mother and one sister rode all the way as the sister was ill and needed her mother's care. This sister died three months after their arrival in Utah.

Emily was married to Moroni Rees June 28, 1869 in the Salt Lake Endowment House. They had nine children-six sons and three daughters. In November, after their marriage, Emily and Moroni moved to Malad, Idaho to try to make a living at freighting and farming. They endured many hardships trying to make a living on the dry farms. They later moved into a big stone house at Cherry Creek.

In 1904, Emily and Moroni retired from farming and moved with their two youngest children to Ogden, Utah. They made many trips to Malad to their children there. Emily always went to help her children when they had new babies. They also made trips to Provo to see their daughter, Mary Ellen.

A few days after one of these trips, Emily took very sick and she died suddenly on January 19, 1919. She is buried in the Ogden City Cemetery. She was about sixty-six years old. Her husband lived almost eleven years longer. What a wonderful example of uncomplaining faith this dear woman was. She is revered by her posterity.

EMMA DAVID REES

BIRTHDATE: 31 Jul 1840
Velinvole, Llanelly, Wales
DEATH: 10 Jan 1915
Spanish Fork, Utah Co., Utah
PARENTS: Morgan David
Elizabeth Bowen
PIONEER: 19 Sep 1852
Capt. William's Wagon Train
SPOUSE: Alfred Rees
MARRIED: 14 Aug 1859
Spanish Fork, Utah Co., Utah
DEATH SP: 11 Jul 1910
Spanish Fork, Utah Co., Utah

CHILDREN:
Alfred John, 12 May 1861
Ann (Burt), 6 Jul 1863
Elizabeth Emma (King), 6 Sep 1865
Margaret, 22 Feb 1868 (died as an infant)
Thomas David, 16 Jan 1870
Hannah (Phillips), 5 Oct 1872
Mary (Rickers Nave), 5 Mar 1875
Emma Jane (Harward), 10 Jul 1878
Leonora (Hansen), 26 May 1881
Vivian (Morgan), 15 Apr 1885 (twin)
Child, 15 Apr 1885 (twin - stillborn)

Emma was born in 1840 in Wales. Her parents joined the Church of Jesus Christ of Latter-day Saints in 1846. They started their sojourn to the United States on February 14, 1849 in the ship 'Troubador' to Liverpool. and then from Liverpool they sailed on the ship "Hartley," March 8, 1849, landing at New Orleans. Her mother, oldest sister and a child of this sister all died of cholera. The father and five daughters remained there in St. Louis until 1852 when they started their westward journey. They stayed in Council Bluffs for ten weeks and then continued on and arrived in the Salt Lake Valley on September 18, 1852. Emma was baptized in St. Louis in June of 1850. They crossed the Plains by ox-team and settled in Spanish Fork, Utah.

Emma married Alfred Rees, a member of the Third Handcart Company on August 14, 1859. They later were endowed in the Endowment House on October 20, 1865. They were married for fifty-one years and had ten children, nine reached maturity.

Emma's daughter, Ann, died in 1890, leaving three boys ranging in age from three to eight years of age. Emma took care of them until they reached maturity.

Few women would attempt the things Emma accomplished. She is among the most notable pioneer women of Utah. No night was too stormy for her to go to another in distress. She was an angel of mercy in sickness and death. She was serene in the most trying difficulties. She seemed to have magnetism in her hands.

Emma was a community-minded woman. She took care of the ill, went to their homes even where there were contagious diseases, where no one else would go. There were no undertakers in the community during early pioneer days and she was called upon to attend to that type of service. When a death occurred, she would make clothing, dress them and place them in the caskets. She was always careful to not bring any disease home to her own children. She bathed herself in a solution of carbolic acid water and changed her clothing in an old granary near their home. Emma also helped with many births. She also headed numerous committees and designed floats for parades. She was an ardent supporter of women's suffrage and helped organize the local unit in Spanish Fork and worked hard for the franchise of women in the state of Utah.

Emma David Rees passed away on January 10, 1915, loved and respected at the age of seventy-five.

MARGARET DAVIES REES

BIRTHDATE: 1 Nov 1818
Carmarthen, Wales
DEATH: 23 May 1898
Wales, Utah
PARENTS: Henry Davies
Sarah Davies
PIONEER: 2 Oct 1856
Edward Bunker Handcart Co.
SPOUSE: Thomas John Rees
MARRIED: 10 Sep 1836
Merthyr Tydfil, Wales
DEATH: 24 Mar 1882
Fairview, Utah

CHILDREN:
Henry Davis, 24 May 1837
Ann, 11 Jul 1839
Alfred, 11 Dec 1841
Sarah Jane, 9 May 1844
Helena, 5 Nov 1846
Nephi, 26 Jan 1849
Maria, 9 Mar 1851
Lenora, 2 Aug 1853
Daniel Ephraim, 11 Dec 1855
Thomas Davis, 26 Oct 1857
John Davis, 8 Sep 1861

Margaret was born in Wales in 1818. She was well educated as a school teacher and a seamstress. She married Thomas John Rees in 1836. Since her husband was Branch President, her home became an open house for missionaries and for meetings of the members.

The family left Liverpool, 19 Apr 1856, on the ship "Samuel Curling," arriving in Boston in May. They took cattle cars to Iowa City, Iowa. With her husband and eight children, she crossed the plains in the handcart. She traveled 1300 miles in three-and-a-half months, walking and pulling a handcart containing the bedding, clothing, cooking utensils and food for a family of ten. They left Iowa City 23 Jun and came into the Valley 2 Oct 1856.

In the fall of 1859 the family moved to Wales, Utah. Here Margaret's eleventh child was born and a permanent home established. Her husband's health was poor, so she made clothing for other families to help provide a living. She was the first Relief Society President in Wales, Utah. She raised ten children to adulthood.

MARGARET JOHN JENKINS REES

BIRTHDATE: 16 Dec 1837
Carveleth, Wales
DEATH: 3 Mar 1912
Wales, Sanpete, Utah
PARENTS: Henry Jenkins
Martha John Jenkins
PIONEER: 2 Oct 1856
Edward Bunker Handcart Co.
SPOUSE: Henry Davis Rees
MARRIED: 29 Mar 1859
Spanish Fork, Utah
DEATH: 16 Sep 1908
Wales, Sanpete, Utah

CHILDREN:
Martha Ann, 12 May 1860
Henry J., 21 Nov 1861
Thomas J., 7 Nov 1863
Margaret, 24 Sep 1865
Mary, 17 Dec 1867
Sarah, 18 Dec 1869
Helena, 14 Dec 1871
Alfred J., 21 Aug 1874
Katherine, 19 Sep 1876
Nephi John, 19 May 1878
Theodore J., 5 Feb 1881

Margaret was born in 1837 in Wales. She was baptized at thirteen years, in 1851. She attended a church singing school where she met her future husband.

The family left England, sailing on the ship "Samuel Curling." After arriving in Boston, they took cattle cars to Iowa City, and joined the handcart company. Food was in short supply, which caused the death of her father. She helped bury him and build a fire on top of the grave to keep the animals away. They arrived in the valley in 1856.

In 1859, she married Henry Davis Rees, at Spanish Fork, Utah. They moved to Wales, Utah and lived in a dugout the first winter. Margaret spun wool, wove cloth and knitted stockings. She prepared meals, sewed, washed, ironed, made cheese, butter and soap. She helped other women at childbirth, sewed for and prepared the bodies for burial.

Margaret and Henry saw that their children had schooling, including higher learning. She served as counselor in the Relief Society. She helped to raise four of her grandchildren who had been left motherless. Henry died in 1908 and Margaret died in 1912.

MARGARET JONES REESE

BIRTHDATE: 27 Sep 1809
Aberdare, Wales
DEATH: 9 Sep 1892
Bloomington, Bear Lake, Idaho
PARENTS: John Jones
Ann Davis
PIONEER: 2 Oct 1856
E. Bunker Handcart Company
SPOUSE: Thomas Reese
MARRIED: 31 Dec 1838
Aberdare, Wales
DEATH SP: 2 Feb 1847
Wales

CHILDREN:
George, 26 Jul 1840
Anne, 4 Jan 1842
Lotwick, 1 Mar 1845

Margaret was born and raised in Aberdare, Glamorganshire, Wales where her father worked as a collier.

She married Thomas Reese, who was also a collier. They became the parents to three children. In 1845, a missionary named Dan Jones visited their home and they became baptized as members of the Church of Jesus Christ of Latter-day Saints. The missionaries were frequent visitors at their home.

Two years later in 1847, Thomas was killed in a coal mine in Wales. Margaret was only thirty-seven when she was a left a widow with three children to raise. The family wanted to move to Zion, but were unable to do so until 1856.

On April 19, 1856, they sailed on the ship, "Samuel Curling." After landing in Boston, they rode in cattle cars on the train to Council Bluffs, Iowa. They were organized into the Third Handcart Company with Edward Bunker as their captain. They had very little food and clothing and suffered many hardships as they crossed the Plains. They arrived in the Salt Lake Valley on October 2, 1856.

They spent the winter in Salt Lake City. The next spring, they moved to Willard where they lived for seven years.

In 1864, her son, Lotwick was called by Brigham Young to go into Bear Lake County to help settle the territory. Margaret went with him. When they arrived, there were only three other wagons in the valley.

In helping to build this small settlement, they suffered many hardships and inconveniences, but with the help of everyone, the community grew. They cleared the sagebrush, planted crops, and raised what food they could. Margaret made everything they wore, including underwear, coats, and hats. She knit long stockings at night by the light of a kerosene lamp. She did all she could to make their home comfortable.

Margaret was very strong in her beliefs in the Church. She accepted callings and helped others who were in need whenever she could. After each of her children were grown and married, she lived with each family for a time. She passed away at the home of Lotwick in Bloomington at the age of eighty-three years.

MARTHA EYNON REESE

BIRTHDATE: 12 Nov 1834
Landshipping, Pembroke, Wales
DEATH: 22 May 1923
Logan, Cache Co., Utah
PARENTS: Richard Eynon
Sarah Morris
PIONEER: Fall 1855
Charles Helper Co. Wagon Train
SPOUSE: David Reese
MARRIED: Spring 1855
on board ship "Chimborazo"
DEATH SP: 13 Feb 1910
Logan, Cache Co., Utah

CHILDREN:
Valeria Shirley, 12 May 1856
Sarah Ann, 14 Apr 1858
David Henry, 25 Nov 1860
Martha Elizabeth, 26 Dec 1862
Omea Lewis, 8 Nov 1867
Homa, 25 Oct 1871
Eynon, 15 Mar 1876

Martha was born in South Wales. Her parents and Martha and some of her brothers and sisters joined the Church of Jesus Christ of Latter-day Saints in 1847.

After her father died, Martha and two of her sisters worked and helped with the financial expenses of their sad, widowed mother.

Martha had a desire to emigrate to Utah to be with the Saints. She was the first of her family to emigrate on April 10, 1855. She fell in love with a Welshman, David Reese, aboard the ship "Chimboraza." They were married by Elder John Stevenson. They were seven weeks crossing the Atlantic Ocean, landing at Castle Garden, New York in 1855. They joined the wagon train of Charles Helper and arrived in the Salt Lake Valley the Fall of 1855.

They spent the first winter in the Valley between Farmington and Salt Lake City. They moved to Willard, Utah and built their home. They were visited by Indians several times but had little trouble with them. Chief Washakie took dinner at their house one day. Martha could understand the language of the Indians. It was analogous to the Welsh language, her native tongue. She taught the Indians to make gloves, cook, sew clothes and wash clothing. One day a savage peeked through her window and raised his bow to shoot one of her babies. Martha grabbed an old rusty revolver and pointed it toward the savage and he fled, fearing for his life.

Shortly after settling in Logan, Martha gave her husband permission to marry a German widow. He built her a home on the farm where she raised her children. Martha had been a seamstress in Wales and was handy with a needle. She sewed beautiful clothing for herself and her family. They operated a livery stable with many fine buggies and plenty of horses to ride and drive. Martha and her husband built a skating rink and were able to make needed money.

The aim of Martha and David in coming to America was to build up the Church of Jesus Christ of Latter-day Saints. Their whole lives were spent in this direction.

Martha's husband passed away in 1910. During the years that she was a widow she sewed lovely beaded pouches for each child, grandchild and great-grandchild.

Martha passed away on May 22, 1923 in Logan, Utah. She was eighty-nine years old.

MARY MORGAN REESE REES

No
Photo
Available

BIRTHDATE: 5 Nov 1821/22)
Merthyre Tydil, Wales
DEATH: 29 Nov 1907
Brigham City, Box Elder, Utah
PARENTS: William Morgan
Elizabeth "Betsy" Davis
PIONEER: by 1853/1854
SPOUSE: John D. Reese/Rees
MARRIED: 4 Jul 1842
St. Mary's Church, Ireland
DEATH SP: 19 Mar 1880
Malad, Idaho

CHILDREN:
William, 7 Jan 1842
Mary Jane (Boothe), 21 May 1843
David Morgan, 27 Jul 1845
Joseph, 4 May 1847 (died as an infant)
Elizabeth, 8 May 1848 (died as an infant)
Hyrum, 30 Apr 1849 (died as an infant)
Meredith, 7 Jun 1851 (died as an infant)
Agnes Priscinda (Morgan), 25 Oct 1854
Martha Ann (Thomas), 31 Mar 1856
John Willard, 5 May 1859
Brigham Lorenzo, 5 Nov 1862 (died as an infant)
Edmond, 1 Jul 1864 (died as a child)
Rachel May (Thomas), 1 May 1866

Mary was born in 1821 or 1822 in Wales, she was the second of eleven children born in this family. All of them were born in Wales.

When they were grown, the children went to work to help support the family. Mary was employed as a maid in different homes of nobility. Once when Mary and another maid were left alone in a home, they heard footsteps following behind them but could see no one. They were frightened and sat huddled together until others returned home. Their employers made them promise not to tell anyone about this, even though others had heard noises at different times. Mary did not stay long there as she had no desire to work in a haunted house. She later went to Ireland with a family for whom she worked. While there a young man, John D. Rees, whom she had known and kept company with in Wales, came to Ireland to see her. They went for a walk in the afternoon, and he persuaded her to marry him. They went into a little church and asked the minister to marry them.

There were no witnesses for the marriage so they asked a stranger from the street to witness the ceremony. This was July 4, 1842. They decided to keep their marriage secret, so they could both work, and married women were not employed as maids. John returned to Wales. Her marriage was a secret no longer, as the gentleman who was their witness, told a pleasant dinner story of the marriage of their little maid. When called in to see the lady of the house later, Mary said it was true and that her husband had returned to Wales. Mary was liked very much, so the lady said she could stay as long as she cared to.

Mary and John got together, and they had a home and family. Missionaries of the Church of Jesus Christ of Latter-day Saints visited them, and Mary was very much impressed with their message, but John was not much interested. He was not, however, bitter, and Mary was free to go to the meetings and she was soon converted. John encourage her to study it carefully to be sure it was right. She gained a testimony of its truthfulness, and decided to be baptized without telling until later. The baptism was to be held in the evening, so Mary gathered some clothes together, tied them in a bundle, and laid them by the bushes by the gate the day before. When she was ready to leave, her husband asked where she was going and she answered "to a meeting," and he said,"I think I'll go with you this evening." She told him she would be happy to have him go with her, and she was determined to carry out her plan if possible. When she picked up her bundle she was compelled to tell him she was going to be baptized. He made no objection. He became more interested after she was baptized, and he was soon converted and baptized.

Desirous of emigrating to America, they saved and worked hard and sailed in 1850. Their money took them as far as Council Bluffs, where they lived for about three years while John worked as a blacksmith. Indians were sometimes a problem.

After living in Council Bluffs for three years, they had enough money to buy six oxen, a wagon, and enough food and clothing to continue their journey to the Salt Lake Valley.

They lived in Salt Lake City for a short period of time and were then called to help settle Brigham City. One of the first things they did there was to build a rock wall around an area for protection from Indians.

While they still lived in a wagon box, Mary gave birth to a baby girl. They were soon able to move into a warm home her husband built. The next year, food was scarce and they survived on sego and roots, and the babies could not eat that kind of food and were becoming weak. A good brother, had a fresh cow and although he had a family who needed the milk, he and his good wife supplied the babies of the settlement with milk which spared their lives.

One of Mary's hardest trials came when her husband asked to take another wife. He took several wives and Mary met that trial, trusting in the Lord for strength to carry on.

Her husband was called on a mission to Wales in April, 1866, leaving wives and families to carry on while he was away. When he returned, he brought an organ from New York, which was a happy surprise for the families. He was later called to go to Malad, Idaho as a councilor to the President of the Branch there. He took his fourth wife with him, but he didn't live very long. He contracted typhoid fever and passed away in 1880, at the age of sixty-five years.

After his death, and with her children all married, Mary lived alone in the same home that was built for her when they first settled in Brigham City. She was very interested in temple work, and she and her family did some temple work in the Logan Temple for all the dead whose names she could obtain.

Mary Morgan Reese/Rees was the mother of thirteen children, six of whom died in infancy or childhood, and of the seven remaining, three of them died leaving families, before Mary's death. She died in Brigham City, Utah on November 23, 1907 at the age of eighty-six.

Mary was a true, faithful pioneer woman who had experienced much leaving her homeland of Wales for the harsh land of the American West. She is honored by her posterity for her faith and fortitude, and her example of good, christian living.

SARAH GRIFFITHS REESE

BIRTHDATE: 15 Feb 1833
Amroth, South Wales
DEATH: 3 May 1918
Benson, Cache Co., Utah
PARENTS: William Griffiths
Mary Williams
PIONEER: 12 Sep 1861
John Murdock / Milo Andrus Co.
SPOUSE: Charles Reese
MARRIED: 6 Sep 1856
Amroth, South Wales
DEATH SP: 17 Sep 1904
Benson, Cache Co., Utah

CHILDREN:
William Griffiths, 15 Aug 1857
Charles Albert, 16 Nov 1859
Isaac Reese, 6 Oct 1861
Thomas Heber, 17 Sep 1862
Matthew Henry, 24 Nov 1864
John, 5 Jan 1867

Andrew James, 28 Nov 1868
George Willard, 7 Oct 1870
Richard Osmond, 12 Oct 1871
Herbert Manti, 12 Aug 1873
Alma Victor, 11 May 1875
Moses Martin, 9 May 1878

Sarah was born in Amroth, Wales at the Slade Grist Mill owned and operated by her father. She was the tenth of twelve children. When she was fourteen years old her father was accidently killed and her mother died two years later of grief.

When she was coming home from work one day, she heard two missionaries from the Church of Jesus Christ of Latter-day Saints preaching the Gospel. After hearing their message for the first time she said, "I have heard the truth." Though she had much opposition, never in her life did her testimony change. She was baptized on March 10, 1853.

Through Church and social functions she met Charles Reese. They courted and were married in 1856. Their great desire was to emigrate with the Saints.

In March, 1860, Sarah and her husband and two small sons left Liverpool, England on the ship "Underwriter. " They arrived in New York and proceeded onto Missouri where Charles worked in the coal mines to get the money to travel West. While in Missouri Sarah became very ill with cholera and Charles was told by the doctor that she may not live. Sarah said, "Get out my Patriarchal Blessing. It says there that I will go to Zion and there raise a large family. The Doctors don't know everything." Sarah and her husband became the parents of twelve sons; one died in infancy and four died in childhood.

In the Spring of 1861, they came West with the Andrus-Murdock Company. They arrived in the Salt Lake Valley on September 12, 1861. They continued on to Willard, Utah. They moved to Hyde Park, in Cache County the next Spring where they lived and prospered for several years.

They moved in 1870 to homestead land on the East Bank of the Bear River, later known as Benson. Here was an area to be developed from the start. Roads, canals, schools and churches needed to be built.

In all phases of civic and religious activity Sarah did her part. She was a Relief Society President for ten years. Under her leadership they helped the building fund by saving Sunday eggs which they sold for cash. They held bazaars, dances, sold refreshments, made clothing for workmen and made quilts. She also sewed burial clothes and clothing for needy families.

Seven of Sarah's sons lived to maturity. Her desire was to raise a strong family that would be contributors to this great land. She was a loving, caring mother. Among her numerous posterity are Educators, Doctors, Attorneys, Legislators, Farmers, Businessmen; all following her example in rearing responsible children. All honor her name. Sarah passed away in Benson, Utah on May 3, 1918.

MARY ANN STORER WALTON REEVES

BIRTHDATE: 15 Feb 1812
Birmingham, England
DEATH: 11 Aug 1888
Brigham City, Box Elder, Utah
PARENTS: William Storer
Elizabeth Floyd
PIONEER: 21 Aug 1852
Christopher Layton Wagon Train
SPOUSE I: Edward Walton
MARRIED: 12 Mar 1840
England
DEATH SP: 14 Oct 1848
England

CHILDREN:
Fredrick, 21 Apr 1841
Mary Ann Elizabeth (Cheney), 18 Nov 1843

SPOUSE II: William Reeves
MARRIED: 1851
DEATH SP: 10 Mar 1900 (or 20 Mar 1902)

CHILD:
William Moroni, 1852 (died as an infant)

Mary Ann was born in 1812 in England, the youngest of six children in her family. Her family belonged to the English Gentry Class, and Mary Ann grew up in a lovely old English estate with its wealth, culture and ease. Servants did the menial tasks. The daughters in the family were reared to be ladies, had a knowledge of books, did fine embroidery and loved music. Mary Ann chose the harp as her special study and became efficient on her beloved instrument.

In 1840, Mary Ann married Edward Walton, a young Englishman of her own class. Their new home was one of the well-ordered homes of the well-to-do English. They had two children born to them, a son and a daughter. On October 14, 1848, Edward Walton died, leaving Mary Ann the full responsibility of her home and her two young children.

A few years later, she met and in 1851, married William Reeves, a young man who was employed in Queen Victoria's Palace. He was a carpenter by trade, and he took care of the gardens where he shared information about the beautiful flowers there. His hobbies were music, pictures and flowers, and people thought being in the Queen's garden was how he developed his fine taste.

William Reeves was a member of the Church of Jesus Christ of Latter-day Saints, having been converted by missionaries from the Church of Jesus Christ of Latter-day Saints who had come to England. Through his ardent faith and his belief, Mary Ann too, became interested in his Church, and it was not long before she became a member.

William felt he could not ask her to share his earnest desire to go to America. Mary Ann saved him the need of courage to ask , and it was she who proposed that they leave their old life behind and cast their lot with the Saints who sought spiritual wealth which their new faith gave, rather than the comforts and luxuries of their well-established homes. Mary Ann's family bitterly resented her joining the 'despised' Mormon Church, and the disgrace it brought to their family. Mary Ann's mother died without knowing of her daughter's departure.

William and Mary Ann sailed for America on the "S. S. Ellen Maria," in February, 1852. After fifty-five days, they arrived at New Orleans. Accompanying them, of course, were Mary Ann's two children whom William loved and cared for as his very own, and their baby son, William. They traveled to Florence, Nebraska where they joined the Christopher Layton Wagon Company and set out for Zion.

Cholera broke out in the camp, and claimed their baby son. He was not yet one year old. He was buried along the trail in the Black Hills country. William also became ill with cholera and was given up to die. His grave was dug, but when the captain came along and asked who the grave was for, and was told for Brother Reeves, he said, "He can't die, I can't get along without him." He administered to William and gave him water, and the next day they continued on.

They were three months on the plains enduring many hardships, including storms, shortage of food, Indians, illness. At one time, Mary Ann was buried in a barrel of dirty clothes to protect her from the Indians. They arrived in the Salt Lake Valley on August 21, 1852, just over six months from the day they left England.

They lived in the vicinity of Salt Lake City for three years, suffering the hardships of those early days with poor houses, scarcity of food, with none of the comforts of life. Mary Ann learned to knit, spin flax and card wool to make their clothing.

They moved twelve miles north to the settlement of Centerville, where they made their home for the rest of Mary Ann's life. They soon gathered the necessities of life, and little by little, added some of the comforts and beauties they had known in their home in England for which they longed. Sometimes when Mary Ann became homesick for her friends and family in England, William sang to her "I'll Take You Home Again Kathleen" which comforted her.

They collected seed, plants and shrubs brought from England and other lands, and made the first real show flower garden in Centerville. Inside the home, Mary Ann kept many of her early home customs. She did not have the servants, but her kindly husband, remembering her old life, always prepared her breakfast for her.

The Sabbath Day was kept very strictly in their home. Food was prepared, shoes were polished, and clothing was laid out on Saturday.

When the railroad was built and came through, William and Fredrick made the building into a hall for theaters and dancing which furnished amusements for the Centerville young people and many who came from surrounding towns for the entertainment and fun. William took pride in having the best music he could get. He had a noted violinist come with his orchestra on many occasions.

In 1872, John and Sarah Coles came from England and settled in Centerville. Their eldest daughter, assisted William and Mary Ann. This daughter, Sarah, became William's second wife two years later, and she and William had six children born to them.

Throughout her life, Mary Ann remained a true and staunch member of the Church, she never regretted that sacrifice she had made when she left her family, home, and wealth behind her to face the new world to worship and to rear her children.

Mary Ann passed away on August 11, 1888, at the age of seventy-seven years and was buried in the Centerville Cemetery. William passed away on March 10, 1900 at Wellsville, Cache County, Utah and was buried in Brigham City.

These were great pioneers who left much for their new-found religions without regrets. They remained faithful, staunch and true to their beliefs. They are honored for their faithfulness and their example of giving up material things for religious, spiritual beliefs which were more important to them.

AGNES WESTERN REID

BIRTHDATE: 30 May 1841
Tiverton, Devonshire, England
DEATH: 2 Jan 1920
Oasis, Millard Co., Utah
PARENTS: Samuel R. Western
Ann Winsborough
PIONEER: 1866
Warren Snow Co. Wagon Train
SPOUSE: John Whirk Reid
MARRIED: 24 Apr 1865
Meadow, Millard Co., Utah
DEATH SP: 22 Jul 1910
Oasis, Millard Co., Utah

CHILDREN:
George, 11 Feb 1866
Ann Mariah, 27 Jan 1867
John William, 14 Jan 1869
Agnes Emma, 4 Jan 1871
Elizabeth Ann, 29 Dec 1873
Samuel Western, 6 May 1875 (twin)
Mary Jane, 6 May 1875 (twin)
Thomas George, 30 Apr 1877
Ada Adalade, 17 Jan 1879
Daniel Oscar, 1 Sep 1880

Agnes was born in England. When she was twelve years old she joined the Church of Jesus Christ of Latter-day Saints. She was the first of her father's family to emigrate to Utah.

She left Birmingham, England on her twenty-third birthday in 1864. She was fourteen weeks on the ocean, arriving at New Orleans, Louisiana. She then sailed up the Mississippi River and Missouri River to where the wagons were being prepared prior to the 1,300 mile journey to the Salt Lake Valley. She had to wait several weeks before beginning the long trek across the Plains. She joined the Warren S. Snow Wagon Company. She wore out all of her shoes walking all the way. She wrapped her feet in cloth, clothes or anything available as they traveled West. They did not reach the Valley until the middle of November, 1866. Help was sent out to meet them as they were snowed in along the trail.

Agnes had an Uncle John Western living in Meadow, Millard County, Utah but she had to stay in Salt Lake City until there was a group of people going that way.

John Whirk Reid was living in Beaver, Utah. He made several trips to Salt Lake City for freight for the local stores. Agnes' Uncle John, in Meadow, had feed and camping for travelers and while camping at Western's place John Reid met and won the hand of Agnes and got her Uncle's consent to their marriage. They were married on April 24, 1865 in Meadow. They were later sealed in the Salt Lake City Endowment House.

Agnes' mother had brought a platter with her when she came from England to Utah. She gave that platter to Agnes and it had been handed down for six generations. It is a prized possession of Betty Jeanne Mitchell Moran.

Agnes went through many trials and privations in the early days of the Mormon Church. She was a good singer and sang in the choirs wherever she lived. The Reids were very diligent in performing their duties in the Church. They were always anxious to bear their testimonies of the Gospel whenever the opportunity came to them. One of their sons, Thomas George, served a mission in England.

Agnes passed away on January 2, 1920 in Oasis, Millard County, Utah. Speakers at her funeral spoke in praise of the life she had lived and of her faithful labors in the Church. She died as she had lived in full faith of the Gospel and a glorious resurrection.

ANN HUDSON RICHARDSON VANCE REID

BIRTHDATE. 18 Mar 1837
Longwatton, England
DEATH: 28 Feb 1900
Salt Lake City, Salt Lake, Utah
PARENTS: Jonathan Hudson
Mary Barker
PIONEER: 16 Oct 1863
Rosel Hyde Handcart Company
SPOUSE: John Richardson
MARRIED: England
DEATH SP: 20 Oct 1863
Salt Lake City, Salt Lake, Utah

CHILD:
Hannah (Vance), 21 Jun 1855

SPOUSE II: William Perkins Vance
MARRIED: 10 Mar 1865
DEATH SP:
CHILDREN: None

SPOUSE III: John T. Reid
MARRIED:
DEATH SP:
CHILDREN: None

When a missionary from the Church of Jesus Christ of Latter-day Saints visited her home, Ann Hudson was greatly impressed with his message. She was baptized and longed to come to America with her daughter, Hannah. Her brother, Joseph Hudson, and uncle, John Richardson, also wanted to come to Zion. They left Liverpool on a ship called "Cynosure," a vessel which had been condemned. Elder George Q. Cannon blessed the ship, that it would make a safe voyage, which it did, and they arrived in New York on July 20, 1863.

Because the Civil War was being waged, they were put in not-too-clean cattle cars for the trip to Council Bluffs. They joined the Rosel Hyde Handcart Company and arrived in the Salt Lake Valley on October 16, 1863. John Richardson had been ill most of the way, and died just two days after arriving in Salt Lake.

Ann kept busy trying to find ways to support herself and her child. Two years later Brigham Young advised a young batchelor to marry Ann, to help raise her ten year old daughter. He was William P. Vance, a probate judge in Summit County. They were married on March 10, 1865. Later, because Ann was past child-bearing age, William was advised to marry her daughter, Hannah, and they were married on October 19, 1874. They had four children born to them, and later went to St. George to help colonize there.

Ann continued to live in Salt Lake City, and sell fruits and vegetables, eggs, and feathers for pillows. On June 30, 1898, she was sealed to John T. Reid.

One day she was going somewhere in her buggy when her horse became frightened and ran away with her. It ran near a tree and a limb knocked her off, killing her instantly. Thus ended the life of a beautiful, courageous lady, February 28, 1900.

ANN MACFARLANE REID

No
Photo
Available

BIRTHDATE: 7 Feb 1835
Sterling, Scotland
DEATH: 10 Apr 1867
Beaver City, Beaver Co., Utah
PARENTS: John MacFarlane
Annabellia Sinclare
PIONEER: prior to 1854
SPOUSE: Thomas Hand Reid
MARRIED: 9 Feb 1854
Salt Lake City, Salt Lake, Utah
DEATH SP: 7 May 1920
Hanna, Duchesne Co., Utah

CHILDREN:
Elizabeth ((Thayne), 28 Nov 1854
Thomas George, 29 Jan 1857
Annabel (Thayne), 12 Nov 1858
John MacFarlane, 12 Dec 1860
William, 18 Jun 1863
James, 28 Jul 1865

Ann was born in Sterling, Scotland. Ann was converted to the Church of Jesus Christ of Latter-day Saints in 1846. She had a desire to emigrate to the Salt Lake Valley to be with the members of the Church. The date she left Scotland is not known. Little information regarding Ann's youth, conversion and family is known.

Ann became the wife of Thomas Hand Reid on February 9, 1854. The marriage was performed by Patriarch John Smith in Salt Lake City, Utah. The exact date of Ann's arrival into the Salt Lake Valley is not known. However, records indicate that it was prior to 1854. Her husband was a convert of the Mormon Church in England. He had arrived in the Valley two years before Ann. They became the parents of six children; four sons and two daughters.

It is not recorded where they made their first home in Utah. Ann died in Beaver City, Utah on April 10, 1867 at the age of thirty-two years, just nine months after the death of her youngest child. Ann was buried beside her baby, James, in the Beaver City Cemetery. He had lived only nine days.

ELIZABETH JACKSON REID

BIRTHDATE: 17 Jan 1851
Manchester, Lancashire, England
DEATH: 19 Mar 1934
Orangeville, Emery Co., Utah
PARENTS: Thomas Jackson
Alice Crompton
PIONEER: 1 Sep 1856
Groesbeck Co. Wagon Train
SPOUSE: John Kirkwood Reid
MARRIED: 5 Jan 1868
Salt Lake City, Salt Lake, Utah
DEATH SP: 6 Apr 1926
Orangeville, Emery Co., Utah

CHILDREN:
Margaret, 21 Mar 1870
John Thomas, 6 Apr 1871
Alice, 14 Jul 1872
Elizabeth Cynthia, 9 Nov 1873
Edward Jackson, 23 Jun 1875
Minnie, 31 Dec 1876
Milly May, 7 May 1878
Eliza Jane, 6 Feb 1880
William Jackson, 14 Dec 1881
Robert Jackson, 5 Aug 1884
Lucy, 1 Apr 1886
Joseph Royal, 15 Jul 1888
Alexander Terrance, 29 Nov 1890
Clairmont Jackson, 4 May 1892
Rhea, 6 May 1894

Elizabeth was born in England. Her family had joined the Church of Jesus Christ of Latter-day Saints and desired to emigrate to America. Elizabeth was five years old when she traveled across the Atlantic Ocean with her mother and five other children. Their journey lasted six weeks, finally landing at Castle Garden, New York (now Ellis Island). Her father had emigrated earlier to prepare the way. The family traveled by ox-teams in the Grosbeck Company.

They settled in Salt Creek, now know as Nephi, Utah. After a short time, the family moved to Payson, Utah where Elizabeth was reared. Her mother was a midwife and nurse. Elizabeth took the responsibility of raising the family, cooking and sewing.

She married John Kirkwood Reid on January 5, 1868 in the Endowment House in Salt Lake City. Both were eighteen years old. She had met John when she was eleven years old. She knew then that one day they would marry. They became the parents of fifteen children.

In 1877, they were called to help settle the Castle Valley area in East Central Utah. It was the last settlement authorized by Brigham Young. John built a crude dugout for his family of seven children. When John returned to Manti to bring more supplies Elizabeth cared for the children. They had little food. Their wheat had coal oil spilled on it. Elizabeth cleaned it the best she could and ground it in a coffee mill and prepared it in the most palatable way she could for the children to eat. Also, in her husband's absence a cloudburst swept over the Valley. Water was pouring around and soon in the dugout. She tried to divert the water with a shovel. Fortunately, a stranger passing by heard their cries. He built a dike, diverting the flooding water and rescued the family.

When the first ward was organized Elizabeth served as the first Secretary in the Relief Society for six years. Then she served as the first counselor in the Stake Relief Society for many years. She traveled many miles visiting families.

Elizabeth was a petite woman, about five feet tall, never wieghing more than a hundred pounds. She was healthy, nonetheless. She was considered a natural home-maker. In spite of her large family her home was always clean and neat. The children were clean, well dressed in clothes she made herself. The children would gather the wool from sagebrush. Elizabeth would clean, card and spin it to make clothes for her growing children.

When the family outgrew the log cabin, a frame house was built. They opened the first store in Orangeville in 1879. Elizabeth spent the later part of her life working in her flower gardens, making quilts and needlework.

Elizabeth passed away in her sleep at the age of eighty-three in 1934.

ELIZABETH WHORK REID

No Photo Available

BIRTHDATE: 3 Mar 1791
Scotland
DEATH: 1876
Salt Lake City, Salt Lake, Utah
PARENTS: William Whork
Agnes McWilliam
PIONEER: abt 1852
SPOUSE: George Reid
MARRIED: 14 May 1817
DEATH SP: 3 Feb 1851
Scotland

CHILDREN:
Jane (White), 11 May 1819 (twin)
Agnes (Morgan), 11 May 1819 (twin)
William W. 22 May 1822
Peter Kelly, 4 Jun 1824
Thomas Hand, 7 Jul 1826
George, 14 Oct 1829
John W. 12 Jul 1831
Elizabeth (Miller), 1 Feb 1834(6)

Elizabeth was born in Scotland in 1791. She became the wife of George Reid, and the mother of eight children.

Elizabeth was baptized into the Church of Jesus Christ of Latter-day Saints by Thomas Hand Reid, her son, in the River Bladnuck, on December 31, 1851, and was confirmed by Elder Joseph Mascwell by the river side there, and then came to Salt Lake City. Elizabeth received her endowments and was sealed to her husband George in 1867.

Elizabeth lived a faithful life and passed away in 1876 and is buried in the Salt Lake City Cemetery.

JANE DYRE REID

No
Photo
Available

BIRTHDATE: 3 Apr 1806
Belfast, Antrium, Ireland
DEATH: 1 Oct 1858
Payson, Utah Co., Utah
PARENTS: Samuel Dyre
Ann McClure
PIONEER: 1852
Wagon Train Company
SPOUSE: William Reid
MARRIED: 1826
Ireland
DEATH SP: 24 Nov 1866
Payson, Utah

CHILDREN:
Samuel, 4 Jun 1828
Ellen, 4 Aug 1830
Rebecca (Tavsig), 3 May 1832
Robert, 8 Mar 1835
Thomas, 1837
Anna Jane (Judd), 4 Nov 1840
Edward, 1843
Fanny Mary (Sargent), 16 Jul 1847

Jane was born in Belfast, Ireland. Little is known of her childhood. She married William Reid in 1826. By 1840 they had moved to Liverpool, England. Sometime in 1849 the family was baptized into the Church of Jesus Christ of Latter-day Saints.

Jane and William became the parents of eight children; four boys and four girls. Their first two children probably died sometime before the family emigrated to America. They were six weeks on the ocean voyage and landed on May 4, 1849 on the bank of the Brandywine River. Their son, Edward, age about six years, died while they were at sea but they waited to bury him on the banks of the River.

The family stayed in Tennessee for about two years. They finally made the trip to Utah in 1852. They settled in Manti, Utah. The family now consisted of the parents, one boy, Robert, about seventeen years old and three girls: Rebecca, age twenty; Anna Jane, age twelve; and Fanny Mary "May" about five years old.

Nothing is recorded of Jane's life as a pioneer but she certainly must have worked hard and suffered the trials that the pioneers were subjected to.

In the 1860 Census, Jane's husband, William, was listed as a tanner. Jane seemed to be proficient in making medicines from roots and herbs and taught this art to her daughter, Fanny Mary. William Reid is reported to have been a farmer and stock raiser in addition to his tanning business.

Jane passed away at the age of sixty in Payson or Manti, Utah. It is not known if she died before or after her husband. He is listed as having died after 1861 in Payson, Utah.

MARY ADELAIDE COX REID

No
Photo
Available

BIRTHDATE: 28 Aug 1848
Silver Creek, Iowa
DEATH: 2 Jun 1908
Manti, Sanpete Co., Utah
PARENTS: Frederick W. Cox
Jemima Losee
PIONEER: 28 Sep 1852
SPOUSE: William Taylor Reid
MARRIED: 23 Nov 1869
Manti, Sanpete Co., Utah
DEATH SP: 28 Feb 1904
Manti, Sanpete Co., Utah

CHILDREN:
Clare William, 1 Dec 1872
Edgar Thomas, 13 Mar 1877
Mary Adelaide, 1 Jun 1879 (died as a child)
Alice (Bird), 13 Jul 1882

Mary Adelaide was born in 1848 in Silver Creek, Pottawattamie County, Iowa. She was one of six girls and two boys in her family. They lived in Pottawattamie County, Iowa. Her father had several wives in polygamous marriages. When the officials of the government opposed such marriages, her father was ordered to move two of his wives outside of the county and they would leave him alone.

This he did, so Mary's mother and her children lived in a small cabin which had at one time been a stable. Her father lived in town, and her mother with another family lived in the same cabin.

Mary's extended, large families left for Utah and arrived on September 28, 1852. About a week after their arrival, they continued on to Manti. Mary's parents and family members had been baptized into the Church of Jesus Christ of Latter-day Saints in 1840. They had lived a short time in Nauvoo, and her parents had received their endowments on January 27, 1846 in the Nauvoo Temple, and Mary had been born in the covenant.

Mary Adelaide married William Taylor Reid November 22, 1869 as his second wife. He was eighteen years older than Mary. He had emigrated from Ireland in 1862 and had come to Salt Lake City. Mary and William had four children, one of whom died as a young child. William had eight children by his first wife, Jane McEwan.

William was very active in the communities where they resided. He was county clerk for many years in Manti. In his church callings he served as Bishop and in other callings. In Manti, they had many friends and relatives from their earlier home areas.

Mary Adelaide was a kind, loving mother. She had experienced many pioneer trials in her lifetime. She was a faithful and stalwart pioneer who accepted whatever circumstances came along.

Mary passed away on June 2, 1908 just before her sixtieth birthday. She left a posterity of two sons, and one daughter who honor her pioneer faith and fortitude.

MARY B. RUSH RUSH REID

BIRTHDATE: 28 May 1806
Washington, Mason, Kentucky
DEATH: 26 Feb 1898
Snowville, Box Elder Co., Utah
PARENTS: Elijah Rush
Elizabeth Robertson
PIONEER: 1852
SPOUSE I: Mr. Rush
MARRIED: Unknown
DEATH SP: Unknown

CHILDREN:
Mary Ann, 1836
George Washington Alexander, 1838

SPOUSE II: Jesse Porter Reid
MARRIED: 23 Aug 1840
Nauvoo, Hancock Co., Utah
DEATH SP: 1891/1892
North Ogden, Weber Co., Utah

CHILDREN:
Elijah Clinton, 10 Oct 1844
Laura Emily (Johnston), 27 Sep 1850

Mary was born in 1806 in Kentucky. She was married to a Mr. Rush by whom she had two children Mary Ann and George Washington Alexander. Her husband then died.

In 1840, Mary met and later married Jesse Porter Reid in Nauvoo, Illinois. His first wife, Elizabeth, had died leaving him with two young children John and Mary Jane.

Jesse had been baptized into the Church of Jesus Christ of Latter-day Saints on August 8, 1833. He took his family to Missouri and then to Illinois to help build up Zion. He had been driven from his home in Missouri, and lost his land which he had legally bought and paid for. His wife had died in Illinois.

Following their marriage, after they added one more to their family, they began their westward trek. A second child was born to them in Iowa, Laura Emily. Mary had the six children to care for, and she did it well, and willingly. It was said of her "she was a good mother and showed no partiality among the four children. She and Jesse became the parents of two more children."

As they continued their trek, the Saints were not weakened by the persecutions and trials of the mobs, their poverty, disease, or inclement weather, but became stronger

and drawn together in their support of one another. They had learned that Zion was 'in the heart.' This family proved to be faithful, and did not turn back when the going became difficult. It is not known exactly when they arrived in Utah. Jesse's father was a pioneer of 1852, and Jesse's family may have accompanied them in the Warren Snow Wagon Company.

In Utah, Jesse Porter and Mary Rush Reid bought land and built a home on the beautiful sunny, foothill slopes of Mt. Ben Lomond in North Ogden, Utah. Tall timber grew in the area which became timber for most of the first pioneer homes in North Ogden. Their log home looked over the Ogden Valley from its elevated homestead.

Jesse was the first school master in North Ogden. He was an excellent teacher who was respected and loved by his students. He walked down the hill each morning and up the hill every night after school, in rain or sunshine, deep snow or below-freezing weather.

Mary's daughter, Laura Emily married, and died shortly after the birth of her third child. Her husband died three years later leaving the three orphaned children. Mary left North Ogden for the summer to care for these three in Stone, Idaho. Jesse visited Stone but missed his valley. Jesse continued to teach school in North Ogden, and Mary was like the mother hen caring for her flock of chickens. Mary decided to live in Snowville, Jesse stayed in Ogden.

Mary cared for the children well, her house was clean, and she was a good cook. It is said that Jesse married again in his old age, and this wife preceded him in death.

Jesse passed away alone in North Ogden in 1891 or 1892, at the age of eighty-one years.

Mary Rush Reid passed away in Snowville, Box Elder County, Utah in Mar of 1898. She was just two months short of being ninety-two years of age.

She was a true, brave pioneer woman of faith and fortitude, who never relinquished her responsibilities as a mother to many, and she provided a great example for those who have followed her. She is honored for her faith and fortitude and her long life of service to others.

SARAH SHIELDS REID

BIRTHDATE: 12 Jul 1828
DunDonald, Ireland
DEATH: 1 Aug 1889
Manti, Sanpete Co., Utah
PARENTS: Hugh Shields
Catherine Downey
PIONEER: 12 Sep 1861
John Murdock Co. Wagon Train
SPOUSE: Edward Reid
MARRIED: 23 Aug 1853
Belfast, Ireland
DEATH SP: 19 Nov 1920
Price, Carbon Co., Utah

CHILDREN:
Hugh Shields, 11 Jun 1854
John Shields, 15 Mar 1857
Edward Shields, 11 Jul 1859
Fanny Mary, 17 Sep 1862
Sarah, 2 Mar 1865
Ann Elizabeth, 26Apr 1868 (died at age 10)
Agnes Jane, 4 Jul 1871

Sarah was born in 1828 in Ireland. She was a beautiful girl living in Ireland when she met her husband Edward Reid. He had joined the Church of Jesus Christ of Latter-day Saints in 1847 and was a missionary in Ireland, England, Scotland and Wales for twelve years before the family moved to Utah in 1861. They had been married on August 23, 1853 in Belfast.

Sarah's family were members of the wealthier class and she was accustomed to an easy life, but she gave up her family and followed her husband in his travels and in his missionary work. He was a tailor by trade, and she was an expert needlewoman. Three sons were born to them during their missionary work in Great Britain.

They finally boarded the packet ship, "Monarch of the Sea," eventually arriving in the Salt Lake Valley in 1861. They lived in Payson and Salt Lake City where Edward did tailoring and farming. Four daughters were born to them in Payson. Two daughters Sarah age twelve, and Ann Elizabeth age ten died of diphtheria.

In about 1880, this family moved to Dover, near Payson, where Sarah's husband and sons tried to farm. The soil was poor, and the work was so hard that they decided to move to Manti by 1886.

Sarah had a great desire to do temple work in Manti, but she passed away there at the age of sixty-one before she could accomplish much. She passed away on August 1, 1889 in Manti, Sanpete County, Utah. Her family were great pioneers who helped settle Payson and Manti as they served the Lord throughout their lives beginning as missionaries in Great Britain from 1847 to 1861. They are honored for their faith and fortitude by their posterity.

JULIA ANN KILGORE YORK PERRISH REIDHEAD

BIRTHDATE: 23 Oct 1833
Reedsville, Oxford Co., Maine
DEATH: 29 Jun 1931
Phoenix, Maricopa Co., Arizona
PARENTS: Aaron Mareon York
& Hannah Carter York
PIONEER: 01 Oct 1850
Joseph A. Young Wagon Train
SPOUSE: George W. Perrish
MARRIED: 1850
DEATH SP:

CHILDREN:
Geneva, 4 Sep 1852 (died as an infant)
George Henry, 22 Jul 1854

SPOUSE II: John Reidhead
MARRIED: 24 Oct 1863
DEATH SP: 14 Aug 1916
Woodruff, Arizona

CHILDREN:
Lucretia Jane, 4 Aug 1864 (died 7 months)
Julia Ann, 15 Nov 1865
John, 11 Feb 1867
Alanson, 23 Jan 1871
Katie Louisa, 13 Jan 1872
Moris, 3 Mar 1874 (died at age 4)

Julia Ann was four years old when her parents joined the Church of Jesus Christ of Latter-day Saints in 1837. In 1839, they moved to Missouri with the Kirtland Camp. They lived a short time in Sugarbush, Missouri; in Lima, Illinois; and Nauvoo, Illinois.

Each time shortly after they were settled, they were driven from their homes by angry mobs. In Lima, all of their possessions had been destroyed when the mob burned their home down.

Julia was thirteen years old when her family moved to Mt. Pisgah, where they remained for four years. Julia's family crossed the Plains with the Joseph A. Young Wagon Company and arrived in the Salt Lake Valley on October 1, 1850.

When Julia Ann was seventeen, she married George Washington Perrish the year they arrived in the Valley.

Her first child was born in Salt Lake City and only lived a few days. Her second son was born in Provo and was ten months old when his father was called on a mission to Australia in 1855. He was disfellowshipped and never returned. Julia worked hard to support herself and her son for eight years.

She married John Reidhead who was a widower with three children of his own. They moved to Fountain Green and shortly after, a cancer broke out on her forehead which disfigured her face. Her husband entered into plural marriage in 1865.

They moved from Sanpete County back to Provo. They moved to Brigham City, Showlow, Taylor, and Woodruff; all in Arizona. In each of these places she served in the Relief Society Presidency. She also served as a Sunday School teacher for twenty-three years teaching all ages.

In 1883, Julia Ann, her husband, and two youngest children visited in St. George, Utah to work in the temple for three months. Her husband passed away in Woodruff, Arizona in 1916 and Julia Ann passed away at Phoenix, Arizona at the home of her daughter on June 29, 1931.

LYDIA RIPLEY BADGER REMINGTON

BIRTHDATE: 16 Mar 1831
Charleston, Orleans Co., Vermont
DEATH: 9 May 1888
Dry Fork, Uintah Co., Utah
PARENTS: John Badger
Lydia Chamberlain
PIONEER: 1850 Wagon Train
SPOUSE: Jerome N. Remington
MARRIED: 22 Jan 1848
DEATH SP: 10 Dec 1877
Paradise, Cache Co., Utah

CHILDREN:
Ernest Badger, 26 Oct 1848
Lydia Eugenia, 1 Jun 1851
Jerome Eugene, 5 Sep 1852
Harriet Amelia, 7 Feb 1854
Rodney Badger, 2 Jan 1856
Helen Maria, 13 Dec 1857
Joseph Fuller, 11 Oct 1859
Nancy Roxana, 8 Oct 1861
Marion Vilate, 8 Apr 1863
John Bradley, 25 Aug 1865
Phebe Violet, 2 Sep 1866
Laura Ellen, 4 Oct 1867

Lydia was born in Vermont in 1831. Her parents were baptized into the Church of Jesus Christ of Latter-day Saints the year after she was born so she grew up adhering to the rules of the religion.

Her family gathered with the Saints in Kirtland in 1836 or 1837 and Lydia attended school in the upper story of the Kirtland Temple but when the mob hostility increased, the Mormons fled into Far West.

Her family built a home in Nauvoo where she unknowingly watched history in the making. She saw the Prophet Joseph many times and heard him preach at Nauvoo in the Bowery, watched as the corner stone of the temple was laid, admired the Prophet at the head of the Nauvoo Legion and left Nauvoo in the early exodus of 1846.

As a child of seven or eight, she was baptized, comforted and protected by her parents as much as they were able before each of them passed away from illnesses exaggerated by exposure, her father, died that fall.

She lived with her uncle about seven miles from Winter Quarters, where she met and married Jerome the January before she was sixteen.

She traveled across the Plains to Salt Lake with her two year old baby to protect and entered the Salt Lake Valley the fall of 1850.

Lydia lived in Salt Lake in the 14th Ward for ten years and saw many of the wonders of the Church take place.

She saw the stream of men making the gold rush to California in 1849, the ground breaking and laying of the corner stone for the temple in 1853, she suffered through the devastating locust plague of 1855 and left her home with the thousands of other saints in June of 1858 fleeing from the approach of Johnston's Army.

They settled in Paradise, Cache County on a ten acre farm in 1860 and suffered many hardships. Indians forced them to move to another thirty acre farm four miles away called New Paradise. She was almost constantly pregnant and lost three consecutive infants soon after their birth. She lived in fear of Indians and in the most primitive frontier conditions and saw the death of her husband in 1877 moved to Uintah County with her family and contributed to the community there.

Lydia was a small boned, fleshy woman with no teeth, and couldn't adjust to the three sets of false teeth she tried to wear. She had thick hair she kept short. She had strength, honesty, leadership and adaptability. She was set apart as a midwife and helped many infants into this world. Her testimony was founded on personal acquaintances with the Prophet and increased steadily until her death in 1888 in Dry Fork, Utah.

ANE KIRSTINE PEDERSEN REYNOLDS

BIRTHDATE: 6 Mar 1842
Faurholt, Albaek, Denmark
DEATH: 16 Jan. 1913
Mt. Pleasant, Sanpete Co., Utah
PARENTS: Peder Laursen
Ane Thomasen
PIONEER: 22 Sep 1861
Samuel Wooley Wagon Train
SPOUSE: William F. Reynolds
MARRIED: 27 Oct 1861
Salt Lake City, Salt Lake, Utah
DEATH SP: 14 Apr 1904
Sanford, Conejoe Co., Colorado

CHILDREN:
Anna Elizabeth, 23 Aug 1862 (died at 2 days)
Laura Alice, 4 Aug 1863
Clara Cornelia (Kofford), 21 Mar 1865
Lilliam Elnora (Johnson), 13 Mar 1867
Asa Fletcher, 9 Nov 1869
Carlos Marion, 10 Jan 1872
William Irvine, 27 Jun 1875
Levi William, 17 Nov 1878
Annie Ervina, 25 Jan 1875/1877

Ane Kirstine was born in Faurholt, Albaek, Hjorring, Denmark, 1842, her mother was forty-four years old when she, her very much loved sixth daughter, was born and she was christened at home three days after her birth.

Missionaries of the Church of Jesus Christ of Latter-day Saints entered Denmark in 1850 to find many waiting for the truth and thousands were converted as soon as they heard the glad message. But there was persecution from those who believed the State Religion, (Lutheran) was the only one that should be permitted on Danish soil. Tormenting the hapless Mormons was a common thing and on March 28, 1855, thirteen year old Ane Kirstine and her mother, now fifty-seven, were baptized. Her father was never converted.

Because of their beliefs and the persecution, the Saints wanted to join the people of the Church in Zion. It took six years of preparation and then nineteen year old Ane Kirstine, gathering her courage, stepped aboard the "Monarch of the Sea," with nearly a thousand other converts, for the thirty-three day voyage to New York. She was on her way to Utah.

The converts entered the United States to find the Civil War in progress It became harder to migrate across the land to reach Florence, Nebraska, the gathering place, to begin the trek West and rail transportation many times was reduced to piling the converts in cattle cars for the long, long trip across country.

At the beginning of July, Ane Kirstine, along with 338 others, left Nebraska in the wagon train captained by Samuel A. Woolay for the nine weeks of weary, dirty, sun-burn and wind whipped trek to the Salt Lake Valley. They arrived on Sunday, September 22, 1861. Pleasant Grove was where Ane Kirstine was sent soon after arriving.

William Fletcher was a widower with six children, all needing a woman's care. Ellis age fourteen, William age twelve, George Washington age ten, Anna Eliza age eight, James C. age 5, and Sara Elizabeth just two years old, all took her into their hearts in a short time and it was not long before the children convinced each adult to marry the other. It did not take coaxing, because Ane loved them too.

In August, of the next year, Ane Kirstine had her own little daughter that tragically died two days later, the next August the family moved to Mt. Pleasant, in Sanpete County the area was in need of settlers. Hating to give up her home and the town she so loved, they did it anyway, it was a calling.

Soon after settling Laura Alice was born. A sickly baby, she hardly knew a well day and lived only one year. Ane and William went on to have seven more children, they lived a frontier life of danger, hard work, worship and contentment with the good of living.

William took three other wives as time went on. Anna Hawley, Neleene Thompson and Elizabeth Hawley. He preceded Anne Kirstine in death by ten years. She passed away two months before her seventy-first birthday.

ANNA HAWLEY REYNOLDS

No Photo Available

BIRTHDATE: 15 Jul 1829
Yarmouth, Ontario, Canada
DEATH: 28 Jan 1861
Pleasant Grove, Utah Co., Utah
PARENTS: William J. Hawley
Ellis Smith
PIONEER: 9 Oct. 1852
James C. Snow Co. Wagon Train
SPOUSE: William F. Reynolds
MARRIED: 22 Feb 1846
DEATH SP: 14 Apr 1904

CHILDREN:
Ellis, 20 Jan, 1849
William, 11 Aug 1849 (died at age 1)
George Washington, 11 Jul 1851
Ann Eliza, 18 Dec 1853
James Cyrus, 23 May 1856
Sarah Elizabeth, 3 Dec 1858

Anna was born in Yarmouth, Province of London, Ontario, Canada in 1829 to loving parents, the fourth of eight children. At Yarmouth, where Anna was born, her parents owned and ran an English-style inn with their own baker, barber, bootblack and bar a place much patronized by English and Canadian gentlemen as they traveled. There are indications of political problems, and government intervention, what ever the reason, the Hawleys and most of their friends moved across the border into the United States.

The Hawleys went first to Detroit, Michigan, then Royalton where a sister was born and died. They moved to Davies County, Iowa when Anna was about nine years old and she grew into a lovely young lady who caught Williams heart and at nineteen, William married the girl he adored and the young couple settled in the Drakesville Area where their first two children were born. The loss of her second baby was a devastating blow to the couple.

About this time the Mormon wagon trains began to pass by. Many of the neighbors refused the weary souls water to refresh themselves and their thirsty animals, but the Hawleys sympathized and made the travelers welcome. Their message of the Gospel was listened to and embraced which caused their neighbors to deride and reject the family. Their baptism by Ezra T. Benson was done in the dark of night to escape the mob retaliation.

Anna and Richard were in Pottawatamie, Iowa for the birth of their third child and when the persecutions worsened, all haste was used in procuring the needed supplies and equipment to cross the Plains, every one worked toward this end and by early June of 1852, five wagons containing the Hawleys, and the Reynolds were pulling out of Kanesville, Iowa in an ox train headed for Utah. Anna was twenty-three with one year old George Washington Reynolds in her arms and her two and a half year old daughter, Ellis, riding in the wagon.

William and Anna chose to settle in Battle Creek (Pleasant Grove) to be near the Hawleys on North Street, here she lived the rest of her life.

Two years passed, Anna who had not been physically strong to begin with became ill. Looking out the window at the snow upon the mountain, Anna cried out, "Oh, for a ball of that snow." William, trying to sooth his fevered wife walked for half a day to the snow line and back with snowballs wrapped in heavy sacks carried in a pail for his adored wife.

On January 27, Anna, drifted into a coma, remaining in this state for hours, suddenly she opened her eyes. "I am not going now" she announced in a clear voice, "I have so much to tell you, I have been to a heavenly sphere have seen such glorious things." But they hushed her to get her strength back, thinking she had more time. She passed away the next day without being able to tell of her vision.

CHRISTINA MCNEIL REYNOLDS

BIRTHDATE: 22 Sep 1832
Glasgow, Lanark, Scotland
DEATH: 1 Aug 1901
So. Cottonwood, Salt Lake, Utah
PARENTS: Daniel McNeil
Christina Taylor
PIONEER: 9 Nov 1856
James Willie Handcart Company
SPOUSE: Warren Ford Reynolds
MARRIED: 28 Jun 1857
DEATH SP: 10 Jul 1900
So. Cottonwood, Salt Lake, Utah

CHILDREN:
Christine Elizabeth, 11 Apr 1858
Asa Daniel, 14 Nov 1859
Margaret Ann, 1 May 1863
Charles Robert, 4 Jun 1865
William Warren, 28 Jan 1870
Sarah L., 29 Sep 1872
Gladys Caroline, 14 Sep 1874

Christina was born in Scotland in 1832. As a young girl of seventeen, independent of thought and positive in her actions, she was baptized by John Gray on October 2, 1849.

The Mormon faith was not kindly received in Scotland at the time and Christina was told to leave the house and never return. Keeping fast to her beliefs, she would have to prepare her own way to Utah, which took seven years.

The Perpetual Emigrating Fund helped many of the 764 Saints that boarded the "Thornton," on May 4, 1856, under the charge of James G. Willie, with the fire of Immigration blazing in their hearts. They were going to Zion. The orderly, crowded, event laden voyage ended nearly six weeks later in a New York harbor. Making their way by rail they began the historic trek in Iowa City, Iowa.

John Chislett was elected Sub Captain and the 500 Saints of the Willie Company were divided into groups of 100 with the third hundred, principally of Scottish decent.

Each 100 had five round tents that held twenty persons to a tent. There was one handcart to every five persons with each person limited to seventeen pounds of clothing, bedding and personal possessions. One Chicago wagon drawn by three yoke of Oxen went with each hundred, it hauled provisions and tents, the young men were distributed among different families to help them and some one appointed to come last to help those in need.

Several carts were drawn by young girls exclusively and two tents were occupied by those girls with no male companions.

The first leg, from Iowa City, Iowa, to Florence, Nebraska, 277 miles away and of three weeks duration, was made with light handcarts to prepare the travelers and help build their strength. They rested in Florence for repairs and reinforcements.

Starting at the late date of August 18, things went smoothly, except the carts began breaking down and using bootlace, tin kettles, and bacon grease for the axles was all they had to repair with. It was the beginning of their bad luck. A herd of buffalo stampeded toward them taking the cattle with them, never to be recovered. With so many oxen gone wagons were pulled by half a team. Food supplies ran out, clothing and bedding were inadequate for the early storms and soon death's stamp could be seen on exhausted, faces and it became unusual to leave a camp with out a burial.

They were rescued, history tells of the men who braved the horrible storms and with their own lives in peril, found the Willie Company and helped them into the Salt Lake Valley, to families who would nurse them back to health.

By summer of the next year, Christina, who survived the ordeal, had become acquainted with Warren Ford Reynolds and married him as his second wife, a marriage of forty-four years and seven children.

She and his first wife Edna, raised their children together, as they lived next to each other in harmony and love. Her joy was her children, her church and her home, each of which she gave her very best.

EDNA MARIA MERRELL REYNOLDS

BITHDATE: 25 Dec 1828
Cutter, Wayne Co., New York
DEATH: 28 Mar 1896
So. Cottonwood, Salt Lake, Utah
PARENTS: Hosea Merrell Mary
Ann Saxton Merrell
PIONEER: 20 Sep 1848
SPOUSE: Warren Ford Reynolds
MARRIED: 3 Jan 1846
DEATH SP: 10 Jul 1900
So. Cottonwood, Salt Lake, Utah

CHILDREN:
John William, 10 May 1850
Edward Decator, 22 Apr 1852
Edna Josephine, 19 Apr 1854
Mary Alice, 23 May 1856
Philinda Marie, 10 Sep 1858
Anna Eliza, 12 Jan 1862
Artamisea Ellen, 19 May 1864
Warren Hosea, 28 Jan 1866
Rosina Isabella, 27 Oct 1867
Rachel Amanda, 10 Jul 1871

Edna Maria was born in New York in 1828. Of French decent, Edna's forefathers had fled from France, cast their lot with the Puritans and settled in Salisbury, County of Wilshire, England. They came to America in the early 1600's and settled in New York state where Edna was born.

Hosea Merrell moved his family "out west" to Michigan and it was there that Edna met Warren Ford Reynolds. They were married when Edna was eighteen years old and shortly after decided to go to Nauvoo, Illinois. While there, they were baptized in the Mississippi River on April 15, 1846, by Elder Surryne.

Edna, with her husband and the Merrell family left Nauvoo by wagon, joining the 12,000 Saints who had crossed the river in an endless chain evacuating that city. Only those too ill or poor remained in Nauvoo.

With a company of Saints they arrived in the Salt Lake Valley on September 20, 1848. Edna and her husband settled in South Cottonwood and later built a home on Big Cottonwood Creek. Ten children were born to the couple.

The James G. Willie Handcart Company was rescued in 1856 and the poor freezing survivors were harbored with families until they were returned to health. Perhaps this is where Christina McNeil became acquainted with the Reynolds family. Edna made room for this second wife, June 28, 1857, they shared the same historical experiences because they lived side by side and raised their children together in love and harmony. Fleeing from their home at the threat of Johnston's Army, and returning to settle permanently in South Cottonwood.

She dug sego lilies to eat to survive, fought crickets and grasshopper plagues, and may have hid her husband from the law to escape the arrest of polygamy.

Edna, as described by her husband, was a wonderful woman. She raised her children to manhood and womanhood and made fine citizens of them. When she passed away at the age of sixty-seven it was said by one of the speakers at her funeral "Sister Reynolds had many friends and no enemies. She was a consistent Latter Day Saint, a true wife and noble mother ever ready to succor the needy, and cheer those who were gloomy or downcast." Warren Ford Reynolds was born in Avon, Livingston County, New York on June 7, 1823.

ELIZABETH MARIA STORR REYNOLDS

BIRTHDATE: 23 May 1855
Fredrickstad, Norway
DEATH: 23 Dec 1942
Vernal, Uintah Co., Utah
PARENTS: Nicoli Storr
Annie Boletta Borson
PIONEER: Sep 1869
Wagon Train Company
SPOUSE: William G. Reynolds
MARRIED: 6 Jan 1872
Heber City, Wasatch Co., Utah
DEATH SP: 29 Apr 1920
Vernal, Uintah Co., Utah

CHILDREN:
Roseltha Melissa, 23 Jan 1874
George Bardwell, 19 Dec 1875
Agnes Matilda, 29 May 1878
Alice Melvina, 19 Nov 1880
William Clark, 29 Jan 1883
Emma Jean, 5 Aug 1885
Della Mildred, 22 Apr 1888
Raymond, 1 Jul 1890
Essie Pearl, 14 Nov 1992
Inez Elizabeth, 9 Sep 1898

Elizabeth Maria was born May 23, 1855 in Fredrickstad, Norway. She never really knew her father. Her mother married and had four children, then later four more children by another husband.

Elizabeth joined the Church of Jesus Christ of Latter-day Saints when eight years old, but when her mother came to America she was left behind with her grandmother and two little sisters. They later came to America and joined with her mother in Omaha to come across the Plains. They traveled by wagon and ox team and had to walk most of the way. Their feet bled from the rocky terrain. They arrived in the Salt Lake Valley in September, 1869, and settled in Mill Creek, Utah.

At age seventeen, she married William George Reynolds, January 6, 1872. They made their home in Heber City at first, later moving to Vernal, Utah where they lived in a one-room cabin. It was the very cold winter of 1879/80 when the thermometer dropped to 40 below. Rations were short, and diphtheria took many lives. Elizabeth nursed the sick, but always bathed out in the cold and changed her clothing before rejoining her family.

Elizabeth had a wonderful sense of humor and could find things to laugh at even at the hardest trials. "Every cloud has a silver lining," she said. She did not have the opportunity to go to school as a young girl, and so she attended school with her three oldest children, while her two babies played on the lawn. Later in her life she raised a granddaughter when her daughter, Alice, passed away.

Elizabeth passed away in Vernal on December 23, 1942. Her husband preceded her in death on April 29, 1920, also in Vernal, Uintah County, Utah.

MELISSA BARDWELL REYNOLDS

BIRTHDATE: 5 Sep 1825
Nunda, Livingston, New York
DEATH: 10 Jul 1904
PARENTS: Joel Bardwell
Jane Bush
PIONEER: 1853
SPOUSE: William Pitt Reynolds
MARRIED: 6 Oct 1841
Erie, Pennsylvania
DEATH SP: 13 Nov 1900

CHILDREN:
Abigail Mary (Okes), 2 Sep 1842
Roseltha Melissa (Pearce), 13 Sep 1844
Emma Jane (Workman), 6 Dec 1847
William George, 18 Nov 1849
Welcome, 7 Jul 1851 (died as an infant)
Ammon Brown, 30 Aug 1853
Francis Joel, 6 Jul 1856 (died as an infant)
Wealthy Ann (Brown), 22 Nov 1858
Moses Adelbert, 15 Jun 1860 (died as an infant)
Isabell Rosina (Shirts), 8 May 1862
Belden Moroni, 8 May 1862
Clarissa Adelaide (Campbell), 7 Feb 1865
Elinor Evelina (Johnson), 4 Aug 1868
Susan Lueanna, 13 Mar 1870 (died as a child)

Melissa was just past seventeen, when she eloped with her twenty-five year old boyfriend, William Pitt Reynolds. They went from their little village of Nunda, to Erie, Pennsylvania a trip of about 100 miles. They rousted out a preacher who performed the ceremony for them on October 6, 1841.

Melissa's energetic manner was not quelled at all by the fact that she was bald from an illness she suffered in her childhood which caused her hair to fall out, and never grow back. She wore a small lace cap on her head.

When she was very young, Melissa's mother died, leaving her and her sister motherless. Her father soon

married Eunice Bolster who died in a short time, and he then married Susan Williams and she also died shortly. A fourth marriage was to Harriet who became the mother role very well, and the little ones loved her.

Melissa and William settled down in Nunda, and began their family. The Mormon missionaries came to their community, and this couple became interested in their message.

By 1848, Melissa and William moved to Michigan. They had joined the Church, and focused on moving to the West to help build up Zion in the Rocky Mountains. They remained in Michigan for five years preparing for the trek West. Melissa and her family started west in 1853. They traveled the 1,700 miles to reach Winter Quarters, and were so impressed with the captain of their company, that they named their son after him, Ammon Brown.

Beginning their journey, Melissa became ill and feared she would not be able to complete the journey. She insisted that their wagon carry enough lumber to build a casket for her burial on the plains. Her health actually improved on the journey and she lived nearly fifty years longer.

They arrived in the Salt Lake Valley in 1853, and William was called to run a saw mill in the Cottonwood Canyon where they remained for two years then moved to Provo. Around 1861, they moved to the Heber Valley, establishing the first gristmill there.

In 1880, they again became pioneers and moved into the Ashley Valley in the Uintah Basin. William was sixty-four and Melissa fifty-five years of age. They followed two of their sons and two of their daughters who had moved there. They constructed the first grist mill in the valley.

She wrote articles for the "Woman's Exponent," but signed only her initials on these, and did not reveal her writing activities even to her family. After about five years, one of her daughters learned by chance of her mother's authorship and was scolded for her curiosity.

William and Melissa Reynolds were sealed in the Endowment House in Salt Lake City in 1879. Later in their lives they were devoted temple workers, often traveling by team and wagon to do temple work in the Salt Lake, Manti, and Logan Temples.

Melissa passed away on July 10, 1904 at the age of seventy-eight years and was buried in the Maesar Cemetery. William had preceded her by four years when he passed away in 1900.

Their numerous posterity salute this courageous couple who made pioneering a continuing, lifelong pursuit, as they helped build the communities in four valleys in Utah.

PHOEBE JANE RAMSEY REYNOLDS

No
Photo
Available

BIRTHDATE: 10 Jan 1813
Cumberland, Tennessee
DEATH: sometime, 1852
PARENTS: William Ramsey
Sarah Ramsey
PIONEER: before 1850
SPOUSE: John Reynolds
MARRIED: 28 Jan 1828
DEATH SP: 7 Jul 1872
Beaver, Beaver Co., Utah

CHILDREN:
Martha Minerva (Norton), 3 Feb 1829
Sarah Ann, 6 Dec 1330
Josiah Anderson, 2 Oct 1831
Squire, 4 Nov 1833
Thursey Jane, 14 Feb 1836
Mary Elizabeth, 2 Oct 1838
Emma, 2 Feb 1841
William S., 15 Mar 1842
John Taylor, 3 Aug 1844
Enoch, 14 Feb 1847
Phoebe Jane, 22 Mar 1850

Phoebe Jane married John Reynolds when she was just fifteen years of age. They were married on January 28, 1828. They moved to Missouri where their first six children were born. They were in Marion, Cole Counties, and then in Independence, Missouri.

They had heard the Gospel of Jesus Christ of Latter-day Saints from some of the first missionaries of the Church. They were baptized in March, 1838 and joined with the Saints from then on. When the Saints were driven from their homes in Missouri by the terrible persecutions of the violent mobs who were trying to destroy the Church at that time, John and Phoebe and family were driven from their home and possessions and were forced to leave everything they owned and flee for their lives. About all they could take with them was their newly found faith, their trust in the Lord and in the Prophet Joseph Smith, their love for each other and for their Church.

After leaving Missouri, they came to Nauvoo, Illinois with the Prophet Joseph Smith and Brigham Young and others to help build up that beautiful city and temple. Phoebe and John were sealed to each other as man and wife for time and all eternity there by President Brigham Young on February 3, 1846. Two years prior to this time, the Prophet had been murdered by the mobs which had followed them and caused so much sorrow. Because of their grief, they moved to a small town near Nauvoo for a short time. She had another child while there making this her ninth child and she was just thirty-one years old. They returned to Nauvoo to help finish the temple. By July, 1846, the Battle of Nauvoo raged and the Saints were driven from that city and their temple fell into the hand of the mob in September of 1846.

Driven at the point of bayonettes by the mobs, the Reynolds family was again homeless, with many of their fellow Church members killed during these times. They, however escaped across the frozen Mississippi River in their covered wagon. They traveled to Kids Grove, Iowa, a distance from Council Bluffs. It was at the Winter Quarters of the Camp of Israel, in a covered wagon that Phoebe gave birth to her tenth child. They remained there until instructed to emigrate by President Young, in late 1848 or 1850. Her eleventh child was born in Utah in 1850.

In the Spring of 1852, Phoebe Jane's husband joined in the gold Rush to California. He left Phoebe Jane in Salt Lake with some of her family, a daughter married, one had married, had children and died in 1851, and her two sons were twenty and eighteen years old.

Some time during the year of 1852, Phoebe Jane passed away, leaving seven children still at home, the youngest just two years old. She was about thirty-nine years of age, had had eleven children, and had shared in the persecutions of the Church and the hardships of travel to Utah. She was truly a Utah pioneer.

The daughters of her family took care of the children until John returned from the gold fields one and a half years later. John had married again, having three polygamous wives. He passed away in 1872 in Beaver, Utah.

MARY ELIZABETH BROUGH REX

BIRTHDATE: 20 Nov 1858
London, Staffordshire, England
DEATH: 30 May 1939
Randolph, Rich Co., Utah
PARENTS: Samuel Brough
Elizabeth Bott
PIONEER: 15 Oct 1863
Samuel D. White Wagon Train
SPOUSE: William Rex
MARRIED: 6 Oct 1874
DEATH SP: 6 Apr 1927
Randolph, Rich Co., Utah

CHILDREN
William Thomas, 5 Jul 1875
Charles, 11 Jan 1877
Alfred George, 21 Jun 1878
Mary Elizabeth, 16 Jun 1880
Clive Celeste, 3 Nov 1881
Samuel, 6 Apr 1883
Arthur Henry, 11 Oct 1884
John Oseland, 15 Dec 1887
Percy Harold, 30 Sep 1889
Ada Estella, 13 Feb 1892
Myrtle, 13 Jul 1894
Alfreda, 6 Nov 1895
Hyrum Mack, 30 Nov 1901

Mary Elizabeth Brough was born in England in 1858 and at the age of four and a half years boarded the ship "Cynosure" with her parents bound for America. They left in a company of 750 Saints under the direction of David M. Stewart and after a voyage of forty-nine days in over crowded conditions, with shortages of every kind, they landed in New York Harbor on July 19, 1863.

The company traveled part way from New York to Florence Nebraska in cattle cars then had four weeks to rest and outfit themselves. They began their journey to the Salt Lake Valley under Captain Samuel D. White.

Mary, just one month away from five years old, had traveled for fifty days in open weather, walking many miles, some out of boredom, some so as to empty the wagons as they were hauled up grades by the laboring oxen and many as the wagons were let down steep grades, anchored by men holding ropes to keep the wagon from overtaking its own team. They arrived in the Valley on October 15, 1863. Snow had fallen.

For the next decade Mary grew up in Salt Lake City and just before her sixteenth birthday married William Rex in the Endowment House on October 6, 1874 and the couple settled in Randolph, Utah.

Mary Elizabeth dedicated the next twenty-seven years of her life to the thirteen children born to them, nine boys and four girls. Four children were left in her complete charge when her husband left to serve his mission.

She had the unsurmountable grief of the deaths of two children from measles. The little ones died so closely together that they were buried in the same grave.

She served her church well, working in the Young Women's organization and Relief Society. She loved to sing and sang in the ward choir for over fifty years.

Mary Elizabeth Rex was a provident home maker keeping both vegetable and flower gardens along with many berry bushes for bottled fruit and jams and she always made the traditional buns for Easter and brought some to each of her families for Good Friday.

Her testimony of the Gospel was fervent and enduring, her contribution to the many posterity who have followed in her footsteps.

ELIZA LEWIS BEECH RHEAD

BIRTHDATE: 4 Nov 1824
Longport Staffordshire, England
DEATH: 26 May 1895
Coalville, Summit Co., Utah
PARENTS: Thomas Lewis
Mary Ann Astbury
PIONEER: 20 Sep 1861
Ansel P. Harmon Wagon Train
SPOUSE: John Beech
MARRIED: 25 Dec 1842
Longport, England
DEATH SP: 5 Jul 1847
England

CHILDREN:
Mary Ann , 9 Jan 1844 (died as a child)
Thomas Lewis, 27 Aug 1846

SPOUSE II: Josiah Rhead
MARRIED: 9 Apr 1850
Longport, England
DEATH SP: 21 Nov 1887
Coalville, Summit Co., Utah

CHILDREN:
Edward Henry, 9 Jan 1851
Josiah Earl, 19 Apr 1853 (died as an infant)
Eliza Persis (Farnsworth), 9 May 1855
James Bourne, 17 Mar 1858
William George, 20 Jul 1860
Sarah Ann (Salmon), 22 Dec 1862
Elizabeth Jane, 12 Dec 1865 (died as a child)
Josiah Lewis, 8 May 1868

Eliza was born in 1824. She was the seventh child and third daughter born in the family. As a young girl, Eliza learned stay (corset) making, and worked some in the potteries, and she later established a stay-making business of her own.

Her great-grandfather Astbury, had introduced flint into the earth-ware paste, which discovery "had done more to improve, the quality and possibilities of English Earthenware than any other, and his productions are greatly valued today." One of the first two pieces he made using flint in the paste was brought to America in 1861 and is in the LDS Church Museum on Temple Square.

Eliza readily accepted the teaching of the Mormon Elders and was baptized as a member of the Church of Jesus Christ of Latter-day Saints on July 10, 1840 by Apostle George A, Smith, and was confirmed by Apostle Wilford Woodruff.

On December 25, 1842, Eliza married, John Beech, a potter by trade. They had a daughter and a son born to them. Her daughter, Mary Ann, died at four years of age. Her husband, John died five years after their marriage. Leaving Eliza with the two children to care for, she worked in the stay business for three years to support them.

On April 9, 1850, Eliza married Josiah Rhead, a moral, sober, industrious, and honest man who had also joined the Church in 1849. To this couple were born eight more children. Their four month old son died in 1853. This family remained in England for six years.

In 1856, plans were made to emigrate to America to the headquarters of the Church. They did not take Eliza's ten year old son, Thomas Beech, and left him with her sister. Five years after this family left England, Thomas with his Aunt, left England on April 25, 1861 for America. They arrived in Florence, Nebraska on June 2, 1861.

Eliza and Josiah and their two children Edward and Eliza, left England on the ship "Horizon," May 25, 1856. They arrived at Iowa City on July 8, 1856, joining the Edward Martin Handcart Company by July 26, 1856.

Josiah became ill, and he and his family were left to their fate by the roadside as the handcart company moved on. The Rhead family stayed in the area of Newton until the following spring, and then went to Fort Des Moines, Iowa in hopes of getting work at the pottery there.

Money was still scarce, yet the family was able to save some money from Josiah's work and Eliza took in washing and acted as a cook at the Des Moines House. They purchased a light spring wagon, a yoke of cows, and started for Florence, Nebraska, to join an emigrant train bound for Utah. Eliza and Josiah'a family arrived there about three weeks after her son Thomas Lewis had arrived. A great reunion was held when Eliza met her fifteen year-old son, a fine youth, and her beloved sister who had cared for him these five years.

On July 8, 1861, the family joined the Ansel P. Harmon Company to again travel West. By September 20, they reached Hoytsville, Summit County, Utah. Here they traded a yoke of cows for a ten acre farm on Chalk Creek. To another man, Josiah traded his best suit of clothes brought from England, for a one-room log cabin which he moved to the farm. They were soon located in their own home on their own farm.

Josiah Rhead related their journey across the Plains this way. "We were about ten weeks on our journey, we had a pleasant trip and plenty of provisions; we had a good time in general, free from sickness. We started to cross the Plains in one of the poorest outfits that ever crossed, and finally came in with one of the best."

The following was written on the cover of their light wagon:

"Don't scorn this wagon, if you please,

Although it's old, it giveth ease.

In crossing o're these Western Plains,

It saves us having many pains."

The wheels of the light wagon were later sold to Joel Lewis, who used them to make a push car which was used to haul coal out of the first coal mine in the territory of Utah.

In the Spring of 1862, the family moved to Salt Lake City for a time where Josiah and his son worked in the potteries. Her son, Thomas Lewis Beech, went to help raise cotton in Utah's Dixie, at a salary of 100 dollars a year. Two daughters were soon born to them, the second one Elizabeth Jane died as a child.

They later moved to the Coalville area where they eventually moved into a six-room brick home on a farm.

Eliza Lewis Beech Rhead, after much heart break, hard work, doing for others with love and compassion, raised a wonderful family. She never lost her testimony of the Church of Jesus Christ of Latter-day Saints. She was always active. She held many positions in the Church organizations, and at the time of her death she was the Stake President of the Young Ladies Mutual Improvement Association of the Summit Stake of Zion, a position she had held for eighteen years, while also being active in the Relief Society.

Eliza passed away, May 26, 1895, in Coalville at the age of seventy-one years. She had been a widow for eight years. What a great faithful, courageous woman she was. Her posterity look forward to the Eternities when they can meet her and express their love to her for her faithfulness and her courage in being a pioneer in their new Zion.

ALICE EVANS DAVIES ANTHONY RHEES

No Photo Available

BIRTHDATE: 1 Jan 1807
Merthyr Tydfil, Wales
DEATH: 11 Feb 1868
Ogden, Weber Co., Utah
PARENTS: Rees Evans
Mary Whilding
PIONEER: 10 Oct 1853
Joseph W. Young Wagon Train
SPOUSE I: David Davies
MARRIED: 10 Apr 1826
Merthyr Tydfil, Wales
DEATH SP: 19 Oct 1832

CHILDREN:
Margret, 15 Aug 1830
David, abt 1831 (died at age 12)

SPOUSE II: John Anthony
MARRIED: 23 Feb 1935
Merthyr Tydfil, Glamorganshire, Wales
DEATH SP: abt 1851
Llangonoyd, Glamorganshire, Wales

CHILDREN:
Mary Jane, 11 Dec 1836
John, abt 1838 (died at age 13)
Catherine, 17 Dec 1840 (died as an infant)
Jane, abt 1842
Ann, abt 1844
Anthony, 25 Sep 1845 (died at age 6)
Evan, 21 Jul 1848 (died at age 4)

SPOUSE III: David Edward Rhees
MARRIED: 13 Feb 1853
on board ship, "Jersey," Atlantic Ocean
DEATH SP: Utah

Alice was born and married in Merthyr Tydfil, Glamorganshire, Wales. She was nineteen years old when she married David Davies. They had two children before he died at the age of thirty-four.

Alice married John Anthony who was a widower with whom she had seven children. They were called to endure a lot of sadness with the death of so many of their children. Her son, David died in a mine accident at the age of twelve. Their son, John, was killed in a mine explosion at the age of thirteen. All of her children died young except her daughters, Margret and Mary Jane.

In 1845, their daughter, Mary Jane, became interested in the Church of Jesus Christ of Latter-day Saints and desired to join. Alice and John were much opposed and tried to hinder her from joining. A few years later, Alice became very ill. At Mary Jane's insistence, she finally consented to have the elders come to administer to her. She received immediate relief which resulted in her joining the Church in 1849. This brought about her separation from her husband, John.

After the death of her last son, Evan, Alice and Mary Jane decided to emigrate to Zion. They boarded the ship, "Jersey," at Liverpool, England. On the ship, both Mary Jane and Alice married while crossing the Atlantic Ocean. Alice married a man who was ten years younger than she. They landed in New Orleans on March 21, 1853.

They crossed the Plains with the Joseph W. Young Wagon Company and arrived in the Salt Lake Valley on October 10, 1853, settling in Ogden, Utah.

Alice suffered greatly with her daughter when Mary Jane lost four of her children in death in the fall of 1865 due to diphtheria.

ELIZA PARRATT RHEES

BIRTHDATE: 13 Jan 1848
Hoxton, Essex, London, England
DEATH: 6 Feb 1937
PARENTS: John Parratt
Jane Body
PIONEER: 15 Sep 1866
William Chipman Wagon Train
SPOUSE: Charles Horatio Rhees
MARRIED: 7 Dec 1866
Salt Lake City, Salt Lake, Utah
DEATH SP: 23 Dec 1911
Pleasant View, Weber Co., Utah

CHILDREN:
Reuben Thomas, 18 Nov 1867
Charles Herbert, 3 May 1869
Chancey Willard, 8 Dec 1870

William, 28 May 1872
Ellen, 14 Jun 1873
Son, 25 Apr 1874 (died as an infant)
Son, 10 Mar 1875 (died as an infant)
Daughter, 4 Jan 1876 (died asan infant)
Elizabeth, 10 Oct 1876 (stillborn)
Daughter, 20 Aug 1878 (died as an infant)
Miriam, 13 Jul 1885

Eliza was born in England. Her parents both died of cholera, leaving six children without home or parents. Eliza was the only one of her family who lived with her Uncle and Aunt John an Jaffe Latham. They were very kind to her. They had joined the Mormon Church.

They kept a key in their house for the Mormon missionaries, among whom was Charles H. Rhees. Eliza would bathe the feet of the Elders when they returned from tracting. She was also baptized into the Mormon Church. She loved to sing and had a beautiful voice. She was the Branch Choir Leader. At fifteen years of age Eliza found work at corset making.

Eliza emigrated to Utah with her seventy year old Aunt Jane Latham. The sailed on an old merchant ship the "Caroline." It was neither comfortable nor convenient. They took rail to the Missouri River the same day that they arrived in New York. They joined the William H. Chipman Wagon Company at Nebraska. Eliza walked most of the way, wearing out two pair of shoes.

They had overcome many troubles with the Indians, losing most of their herd of oxen, horses and cows, baggage being burned. But, Eliza wrote that she was thankful for Heavenly Father's protecting care over the thousand miles of rough roads. The Company arrived in the Salt Lake Valley on September 15, 1866.

Three days after their arrival, they were met by Charles H. Rhees who took them to Ogden, Utah where his first wife, Elizabeth, gave them every welcome. Eliza became the plural wife of Charles on December 7, 1866. She said that she and Elizabeth got along in peace and never made trouble with each other of any kind.

They moved to a one-room log home in Pleasant View. Later, they worked hard to build a three-room brick and rock house with floors in two rooms. She was the mother of eleven children. All of her children died in infancy except three sons. She wrote that at the birth of her third son pans were held above her bed to catch the rain water that came through the roof.

Eliza fought off grasshoppers from a ripe wheat field. They gave them trouble for seven years. She said that they were blessed because they paid their tithing. There was no doubt in her mind that Heavenly Father had sent seagulls to save their crops. After twenty-three years of married life the war waged against pologamy made Eliza move into her own home that her husband built for her.

Eliza had been trained to be self supportive and underwent the hardships of pioneer life uncomplainingly and cheerfully. She was a competent seamstress and spent most of her time making clothes. She served as a counselor in the Relief Society for sixteen years and as President of the Primary and YWMIA. She was a tireless and devoted worker among the sick. She always seemed to bring comfort and peace to others.

She wrote many poems and told stories of pioneer days in Utah. They continued to improve their farm, ending up with eighty acres of land on the bench now known as Pleasant View.

Eliza's husband passed away in 1911. Eliza passed away at the home of her son, Chancey and his wife on February 6, 1937.

ELIZABETH BUDD RHEES

BIRTHDATE: 17 Sep 1837
Carnock Wilts, England
DEATH: 25 Jan 1910
Ogden, Weber Co., Utah
PARENTS: William Budd
Mary Ann Watts
PIONEER: 23 Sep 1863
Daniel Carn Co. Wagon Train
SPOUSE: Charles Horatio Rhees
MARRIED: 21 May 1863
Liverpool, England
DEATH SP: 24 Dec 1914
Pleasant View, Weber Co., Utah

CHILDREN:
Elizabeth, 1 Sep 1864 (died as an infant)
Charles, 7 May 1866 (died as a child)
Ann, 8 May 1868 (died at birth)
Rufus, 17 Oct 1869
Lorenzo, 6 Mar 1872
Alice Eliza, 29 Mar 1874
Amy, 18 Feb 1876
Helen, 16 Mar 1879

Elizabeth was born in 1837 in England. She was converted to the Mormon religion by reading the "Voice of Warning." She was baptized in the presence of Elders from Zion including Charles H. Rhees who presided over the West Lavington District.

At the end of his first three year mission to England, Elizabeth and Charles were married in Liverpool, England by Elder George Q. Cannon with permission of Brigham Young on May 21, 1863. That same day they sailed for New York. He was thirty years of age and Elizabeth was not yet twenty-six. They arrived at New York about six weeks later and made their way to Winter Quarters, Nebraska, where they joined the Daniel Carn Wagon Company and went by ox-team to Ogden, Utah, arriving on September 3, 1863.

Being a city girl, Elizabeth was not prepared for the rigors of pioneer life. She, unwittingly, turned down a pair of heavy walking boots purchased by her husband, which he returned to the store. Everyone who could walk had to do so except the patrol men who rode horses. Elizabeth walked the entire distance. Her fine city footwear was soon in holes and tattered from trudging over rugged terrain of clay, rocks, sand, up hill and down, and wading through numerous creeks.

At one point in the trail, she managed to climb into the back of a covered wagon as the driver pulled into a deep and wild stream. Unluckily, a small piece of her apron peeked through the opening of the wagon cover. A patrol rider spied it, and forced Elizabeth to get down into the deep and wild stream. Frightened, she waded back stream and pulled herself upon the bank. She sought a better crossing, but found none. Later, when she was missed by those who had gone on, that same man rode back to find her. He carried her over the stream. She walked all the way to Ogden, and on September 23, 1863, she arrived at her pioneer one-room home, her feet shoeless and bleeding.

Elizabeth honored her religion all her life. She gave permission for her husband to take Eliza Parrott as second wife, because she had been acquainted with Eliza in England, and she welcomed her into the one-room cabin. Three months later, both wives were sealed to him in the Endowment House, with vows that there would never be any trouble between them, a vow that was never broken.

Elizabeth had become the mother of two children who were happy together. Lizzie often rocked Chattie in their rocking chair. At twenty months of age, Charlie took sick and died.

Lizzie was not well after his death. It became apparent that she was sinking away. Elizabeth cradling her in her arms, walked the floor when suddenly Lizzie brightened and turned her head and cried "Chattie Chattie." Her mother looked to see the chair slightly rocking but saw no one. Lizzie was gone-exactly one month to the day after little Charlie had died, leaving a precious testimony.

Early in 1868, they decided to move to Pleasant View where they purchased 200 acres. They first moved Elizabeth into a dugout in the hillside, and returned the next day with Eliza and her baby son. Elizabeth became ill and was confined to bed for a month and on May 8 1868, her third child, Ann, died at birth. Finally a lean-to home was built.

In 1882, Charles was called to a mission of three years. He left eight children ages fifteen and under, and two wives. They lived harmoniously together. Shortly after his return, he was called on a third mission to England.

The family prospered well and replaced some of their old furniture and made other improvements inside and out. With the laws against polygamy, the families were always on guard. These two wives lived together for twenty-three years. The family divided when C. H. Rhees had finished his third mission in 1889, and built a sixroom brick house. Eliza and her three sons moved into the new home. Elizabeth and her family remained in the old rock home.

Elizabeth had always encouraged the children to attain as much book learning as possible. When a daughter, Amy had finished her school in Ogden, she attended the academy at Logan, where she graduated with honors and became a school teacher.

Elizabeth Budd Rhees passed away on January 25, 1910 at eighty-two years of age, in Ogden, Utah. Her husband passed away five years later.

These families left a great posterity who honor them for their great examples of courage, faith and fortitude-faith in their leaders, and fortitude in doing what was asked of them in their Church and by their leaders.

MARY ANN JONES RHODES

BIRTHDATE: 30 Oct 1862
London, Middlesex, England
DEATH: 27 Dec 1958
Ogden, Weber Co., Utah
PARENTS: Richard Jones
Naomi Parsons
PIONEER: 4 Oct 1863
Thomas E. Ricks Wagon Train
SPOUSE: Joseph Rhodes
MARRIED: 22 Dec 1881
Salt Lake City, Salt Lake, Utah
DEATH SP: 20 Jan 1947
Ogden, Weber Co., Utah

CHILDREN:
Joseph William, 27 Oct 1882
Margaret Ann, 20 Sep 1885
Thomas David, 23 Apr 1887
Naomi Elizabeth, 18 Mar 1889
Sarah Myrtle, 10 Oct 1891
Sophie Lillias, 17 Nov 1893
Charles, 16 Nov 1895
Bessie, 8 Aug 1898
Inez Viola, 11 Apr 1901
Mary Ann, 19 Jul 1904
Boy, (stillborn)

Mary Ann Jones Rhodes was born in London, England. There were seven children in the family. Her parents had joined the Mormon Church ten years earlier, in 1852.

Her family set sail from England on June 4, 1863 on the ship "Amazon," arriving six weeks later in the New York Harbor. They journeyed by rail to St. Joseph, Missouri. They went by boat up the Missouri River to Florence, Nebraska where the Church teams were met. They purchased two teams of oxen and wagons and traveled with the Thomas E. Ricks Wagon Company. They arrived in the Salt Lake Valley on October 4, 1863, four months from the time they had left England and three weeks before Mary Ann's first birthday.

Brigham Young sent them north and they located in North Ogden, Weber County, Utah. Here Mary Ann spent her girlhood. She attended school in the first schoolhouse built in North Ogden.

Money was hard to obtain. Her Father sometimes made her shoes from heavy cloth and on stormy days would carry her to and from school on his back. When Mary Ann was thirteen years old her mother died at age forty-six. She had been an invalid for seven years. Mary Ann was very close to her mother. She had been by her bedside most of the illness and when she died it was very hard for her. Mary Ann lived with a brother and his family for awhile, and then another, until she was old enough to work and make her own living.

When she was sixteen years old, she went to Manti, Utah to work. She was present when the corner stone of the Manti Temple was laid. She returned to North Ogden to care for her father's six children when their mother died.

Mary Ann married Joseph Rhodes on December 22, 1881 in the Salt Lake City Endowment House. They became the parents of eleven children. They made their first home in North Ogden, then lived in other areas for periods of time; Warm Springs, Montana; Liberty, Utah; North Ogden, again; back to Montana then Liberty then Ogden, Utah. In Montana they lost their house to fire.

Mary Ann opened her home to the Missionaries when they lived in Montana. She washed and mended their clothes and always made them welcome. She organized a Sunday School and she taught the children and one of the Missionaries taught the adults.

Mary Ann was set-apart to help care for the sick, attend births and deaths. She served in church callings wherever the family lived. She served in a Relief Society Presidency, as a visiting teacher and as a Sunday School teacher. Her husband passed away in 1947, after sixty-six years together.

When she was eighty-eight years old she was chosen Queen of the Ogden Pioneer Days Centennial Celebration in 1950. She rode in the parade, dressed in a beautiful white dress, on a white float, looking as stately as any Queen.

Mary Ann enjoyed fairly good health until her death in 1958, at the age of ninety-six, in Ogden, Weber Co., Utah.

ANN OLIVER RICE

BIRTHDATE: 5 Aug 1852
Laudifglen, Morganshire, Wales
DEATH: 18 May 1932
Pleasant View, Weber Co., Utah
PARENTS: Francis Oliver
Elizabeth Bailey
PIONEER: 25 Sep 1866
John D. Holliday Wagon Train
SPOUSE: James Rice
MARRIED: 22 Mar 1870
Salt Lake Endowment House
DEATH SP: 4 Sep 1890
Pleasant View, Weber Co., Utah

CHILDREN:
Zenophen Zachariah, 1 Apr 1871
Francis Albert, 6 Nov 1872
Elizabeth Augusta, 21 Nov 1874
Marion Evelyn Almeda, 26 Jun 1876
Gertrude Oratia Beatrice, 1 Jul 1879
Thomas Henry, 17 Apr 1881
Joseph Lewis, 22 Apr 1884
Emily Ann Jane, 22 Jun 1886

Ann was born to parents who had already accepted the gospel of the Church of Jesus Christ of Latter-day Saints. After much difficulty and sacrificing, the family managed to migrate to America. They sailed on the ship, Columbia, and arrived in New York on January 1, 1857. They lived in Green County of New York for six years, then moved to Connecticut for three years, then to Massachusetts for a year. While in Massachusetts, Ann lost her eyesight from being hit by a rock in the back of her head at the age of fourteen.

On June 25, 1866, her family left Massachusetts to cross the Plains to the Salt Lake Valley. They traveled with Captain John Holliday's Wagon Company and arrived in the Valley on September 25, 1866. Both her sister and her mother died while crossing the Plains.

Ann worked for Mr. Hugh Finley, the match maker in Salt Lake City. She boxed the matches for him in exchange for a place to live and board. In 1869, she moved to North Ogden to live with her father and stepmother.

In 1870, she became the second wife of James Rice. James homesteaded some land on the Pole Patch and built a five-room house and barn out of logs. Ann and her children husked the corn they harvested and traded it to Boyle Furniture in Ogden. The husks were used for filling mattresses. Ann would knit stockings, mittens, and sweaters for the family. The first wife did all the sewing for the two families.

With her children holding on to her skirt, Ann walked the mile each Sunday from Pole Patch to Pleasant View Ward. She taught her children to read because she needed some one to read to her. She could give a whole evening of entertainment by singing old songs, reciting poems, and telling jokes.

After James and his first wife died, she was left alone and she did much of her work alone. When milking the cows, she would call out their names and the cows would come to her to be milked. In her seventy-seventh year, she knit a pair of slippers for each member of the Relief Society of the ward. She had knit over 400 large pairs of slippers and 300 small pair of slippers and pin cushions.

Ann lived with her daughter, Emily Beck, on the farm until she died at the age of seventy-nine years.

ELIZABETH ALMIRA BABBITT RICE

BIRTHDATE: 18 May 1830
Painesville, Lake Co., Ohio
DEATH: 27 Jun 1907
Parker, Fremont Co., Idaho
PARENTS: Lorin W. Babbitt
Almira Castle
PIONEER: Summer of 1849
SPOUSE: Leonard Gurley Rice
MARRIED: 18 Mar 1849
Kanesville, Iowa
(Winter Quarters)
DEATH SP: 1886

CHILDREN:
Leonard Babbitt, 1 Apr 1850
Lorin Henry, 6 May 1851 (died as a child)
Laurn Gurley, 11 Jun 1853
Son, 21 Jul 1854 (stillborn)
Lemuel Jerome, 30 Nov 1855
Anna Ida (Wilcox), Jul 1856
Lester Kelsey, 27 Feb 1857 (died as an infant)
Llewelyn Ira, 1 Aug 1858 (died as a child)
Elizabeth Caroline (Jenkins), 13 Dec 1859
John S. 24 Jan 1861 (died as a child)
Oscar South, 24 Apr 1863
Hyrum Smith, 25 Sep 1865

Elizabeth Almira was born in Ohio in 1830. Most of her life she was called "Libby." Her family were taught the Gospel and joined the Church of Jesus Christ of Latter-day Saints.

She lived in Nauvoo as a child where her formal schooling was listed as nineteen and one half days. She learned to read, write clearly and she loved reading the Bible and the Book of Mormon. She had a fond memory of living near the Joseph Smith family in Kirtland, and Nauvoo. She rememberd when the Prophet Joseph Smith hoisted her upon his strong shoulders and pranced off a few paces playing horse for her. Her family always had full faith in Joseph Smith as,a Prophet, and in the restoration of the Church of Jesus Christ of Latter-day Saints.

Her father was a carpenter on the Kirtland Temple and while there, he made a chest from scraps of lumber left over after the temple was finished. This was a cherished possession of Libby's.

Libby remembered the dark days in Nauvoo, when the Prophet and his brother were killed in Carthage Jail. Also, she testified seeing the mantle of Joseph Smith as it fell on Brigham Young at the great meeting held in Nauvoo.

Mob violence was familiar to her, as a mob came to their dwelling and ordered the family outside. Their father was away, her mother bedfast, so the frightened children ran outside lead by Libby. She grabbed a kettle and put it over her sister's head, her mother was pitched out into the yard where she lay in agony as she watched flames destroy their home and belongings. Her mother died, September 10, 1845, as a result of that violence.

Libby's father was guard and custodian of the Nauvoo Temple, and he was one of the last Saints to leave Nauvoo when they were forced out. He kept the temple key as a precious keepsake. (It is now in the Church treasures of the Nauvoo Temple.)

In the Fall of 1848, eighteen year old Elizabeth Almira Babbitt was in Kanesville, Iowa, awaiting emigration to Zion. She met again her childhood friend, Leonard Gurley Rice, a handsome nineteen year old young man who had recently returned from Utah to help escort a train of emigrants across the Plains. They fell in love and were married by Orson Hyde on Sunday evening on March 18, 1849.

They left on their honeymoon-their journey to the land of Zion. She walked hundreds of miles driving their two steers and two milk cows, milking them night and morning. Leonard was a scout and assigned as a cattle and horse herdsman. He took his turn at night on guard duty. They arrived in the Salt Lake Valley in the summer 1849. Libby brought her kitten, Kitty White, which proved to be valuable with the many, many mice.

Len and Libby settled in Farmington, Utah, into a one-room cabin with dirt floor and sod roof, a fireplace, and one paneless window. Split logs with ropes criss-crossed became the bed, also table, and stumps acted as chairs, and her treasured Kirtland chest held her few dishes.

Libby had eleven children, five died as children, and another son was killed in a snow slide at the age of twenty-five. Five sons and one daughter grew to maturity. She also raised an Indian girl the freighters discovered beside its slain mother after a battle between United States soldiers and Bannock Indians. This was Ann Ida who was sealed to Len and Libby. She took in another child in the year of her forty-eighth birthday, and at age sixty-two she cared for her son's five children after the death of their mother.

For their first twelve or more years in Utah, Len spent most of his time helping Saints reach the land of Zion. Self-sufficient aptly describes Libby. She milked cows, raised farm animals and chickens, had an orchard and a garden which produced food for their family and she shared with others. Most everything she had was a product of her own making, from clothing to straw mattresses to feather pillows, and comforters. She did beautiful hand sewing and never used a machine. She was very thrifty. Once a hen left the nest with one egg unhatched, and she put the egg inside her blouse or 'bask' to keep it warm until it hatched.

Elizabeth understood well the need for plural marriage and she lived in love and peace with her husband's two other wives and their large families. She accepted it when her husband was called on a two year mission to England when she was seven months pregnant and also had a family of six to care for. She also understood the importance and sacredness of temple work. She witnessed the dedication of the Nauvoo Temple with her parents in October, 1845. She was sealed to her husband in the Endowment House in Salt Lake City by Brigham Young on April 21, 1857. She kept the Word of Wisdom and taught it to her children. She paid a full tithing faithfully, and made the other offerings.

Libby spent the last years of her life among a few of her children in Parker, Idaho where she passed away June 27, 1907 at the age of seventy-seven years and was buried there. Her husband had preceded her in death by twenty-one years. He had been imprisoned because of polygamy and developed pneumonia in the cold damp cell and died a few weeks later. Their large posterity honor them for their faithful examples, and for their lives so representative of the Savior Jesus Christ.

ELIZABETH ANN MORRIS BUTLER RICE

BIRTHDATE: 13 Jun 1817
Port-Y-Ates, Carmarthen, Wales
DEATH: 30 Nov 1897
Escalante, Garfield Co., Utah
PARENTS: Richard Morris
Elizabeth Jones
PIONEER: 2 Oct. 1856
E. Bunker Handcart Company
SPOUSE I: Richard Butler
MARRIED: 20 Sep 1841
Myrther, Tydfil, Wales
DEATH SP: 26 Jul 1849
Wales

CHILDREN:
Elizabeth (Gates Campbell), 21 Jun 1842
John Thomas, 22 May 1844 (died at age 11)
Jane Thomas, 20 Feb 1846 (died at age 9)
William Richard, 16 May 1848

SPOUSE II: Ira Rice
MARRIED: 20 Nov 1856
DEATH SP: 14 Apr 1868
CHILDREN: None

Elizabeth Ann was the first of six children. When Ann's mother died, thirteen year old Ann effectively became mother to her brothers and sisters. Later her father married a widow with three children, but the new wife couldn't take the extra burden and persuaded him to desert his first family.

Ann and her next youngest sister, Margaret tried to provide for them all; house of children only, trying to find fuel, searching for food, in 18th Century Wales, Their plight was discovered and they were adopted and Ann found a good compassionate home.

At the age of twenty-four, she married Richard Butler, four years her junior, a coal miner at Merthyr Tydfil. Glamorganshire, Wales

Two or three years after their marriage, they were converted to the Church of Jesus Christ of Latter-day Saints by Elders John Corrill and Elias Higby and were well aquainted with Heber C. Kimball.

They began to save in preparation to join the Saints in Utah. Like many others, it took two years of saving plus selling much of what they owned to gather the necessary amount which was paid in advance to the Mormon Elder in charge of the journey.

Ann and Richards preparations were cruelly interrupted by the deaths of John and Jane one month of each other in June and July of 1855. They picked up the pieces of their lives and continued their quest. Then their goal was attained, their passage paid, and all their worldly good ready for their departure aboard the vessel "Sam Curling." Now Richard and the two babies became ill with cholera and all three died, one of the babies died two days before the ship was to sail.

With heart wrenching decision, the agreement was made, Ann would take the two surviving children and continue on, leaving their precious baby's burial in the care of her steadfast sister.

Even the voyage seemed cursed to Ann, during it a terrible storm lasting for days buffeted the ship, breaking at least one mast, apparently the ship was sinking, all were praying, the captain gave the two Priesthood leaders charge of the ship and they, Dan Jones and Thomas John Rees, through the power of the Priesthood, commanded the wind and waves to cease and the storm abated. The ship did complete its journey to Boston.

They left Iowa City on June 23, 1856 with the Edward Bunker Handcart Company. By July 30, they left Winter Quarters, soon Elizabeth became ill with cholera and was too sick to walk and Captain Bunker refused to let her ride in one of the supply wagons. Ann, Elizabeth and William Richard were left alone on the vast Plains to die alone. They knelt to pray, soon a wagon wheel or axle broke down on the wagon forcing the whole company to camp for the night. Ann and her children were able to catch up, the day and nights rest allowed her to doctor Elizabeth and by next morning they were able to continue the journey.

Ann continued living her life as an example of faith and fortitude, she was called to many infant settlements to help establish them. By now she had married Ira Rice. Their combined strength allowed them to surmont all the obstacles such pioneering placed upon them. She served her community as a Midwife, set apart by Heber C. Kimball and she was a choir member until her death. She helped hundreds of babies come into the world and was affectionately known as "Grandma Rice."

LUCY WITTER GEER RICE

BIRTHDATE: 23 Feb 1824
Perry, Ashtubula Co., Ohio
DEATH: 28 Mar 1899
Lewiston, Cache Co., Utah
PARENTS: Moses Geer
Sarah Thomas
PIONEER: 29 Sep 1847
Edward Hunter Co. Wagon Train
SPOUSE: William Kelsey Rice
MARRIED: 6 Oct 1844
Nauvoo, Hancock Co., Illinois
DEATH SP: 6 Jul 1913
Centerville, Davis Co., Utah

CHILDREN:
Ellen Marion, 13 Sep 1846
William Kelsey,, Jr., 22 Aug 1848
Lucy Augusta, 5 Mar 1850
Sarah Minerva, 13 Oct 1852
Ira Moses, 21 Jul 1854
Elizabeth Adalaide, 15 Mar 1856
Marietta, 14 Feb 1858
Kelsey Leonard, 28 Aug 1859
Juliette, 18 Mar 1861
Rosetta Ann, 12 Jun 1863
John Asaph, 19 Sep 1865
Lonna Adella, 23 Oct 1867

Lucy was eight years old when her father and older sister, Sarah, and she were baptized as members of the Church of Jesus Christ of Latter-day Saints. Lucy and her sister became expert seamstresses and helped the family financially with their sewing.

Lucy married William Kelsey Rice at the home of Joseph Smith in Nauvoo, Illinois. The newly weds were among the first to leave Nauvoo and cross the Mississippi River. Their first camp was called Sugar Creek where winds howled and snow flew. Sickness and death also camped there.

While her husband returned to Nauvoo for supplies, their first child was born in a wagon covered with boughs. Their next camp was Mount Pisgah. They arrived in the Salt Lake Valley on September 29, 1847 with the Edward Hunter Wagon Company and spent the winter in the Old Fort.

She brought a crayon box filled with potatoes the size of walnuts which were immediately planted after they arrived in the Valley. They were all saved and used as seed the following year.

In the Spring of 1849, they moved to Farmington, Utah. They had a two-room home in which she taught school. Lucy was a good seamstress. She made dresses, men's clothing, and even coats. She used the wool from her husband's sheep. She would clean the wool, card it, spin it into thread, and weave the threads into cloth. She raised flax which she cured, spun, and wove into cloth. She made soap from every scrap of meat rind or bone she could obtain. She and her family raised a good garden and willingly shared the vegetables with neighbors.

Besides raising her own twelve children, she raised two Indian children who were saved by her husband when he saw they were about to be killed by other revengeful Indians.

Lucy passed away in Lewiston, Utah at the age of seventy-five.

MARGARET BUCKWALTER WICKLE RICE

BIRTHDATE: 12 Nov 1828
Westinantmeal, Pennsylvania
DEATH: 10 Oct 1918
Bates, Teton Co., Idaho
PARENTS: John Buckwalter
Sarah Shuler
PIONEER: 1852 Handcart Com.
SPOUSE I: Lemuel L. Wickel
MARRIED: 1847
St. Louis, Missouri
DEATH SP: 4 Jun 1850
St. Loius, Missouri

CHILDREN:
Henry Lemon, 21 Aug 1848

SPOUSE II: Leonard Gurley Rice
MARRIED: 2 Jan 1853
Salt Lake City, Salt Lake Co., Utah
DEATH SP: 13 Sep 1886
Farmington, Davis Co., Utah

CHILDREN:
Rolley Leonard, 20 Oct 1853
William Lewis, 10 Dec 1855
Adelbert Leo, 4 Jul 1859
Edwin, 20 Dec 1861
Margret, 5 Nov 1865
Martha (Drake), 28 Jun 1868 (twin)
Mary (Beecher), 28 Jun 1868 (twin)

Margaret was born on November 12, 1828 in Westinantmeal, Chester County, Pennsylvania. When she was eleven years old she and her family joined the Church of Jesus Christ of Latter-day Saints. She knew and loved the Prophet Joseph Smith.

She suffered with the rest of the Saints when he was martyred. When she and her family were driven out of Nauvoo they had no money. A kind man gave them a ride on his steamboat to St. Louis, Missouri. Here she married Lemon Wickel. They had a son whom they named Henry. Her husband died of cholera.

After working for two years, she and her mother, brother and sisters had saved enough money to emigrate to Utah. They walked across the Plains. When Margaret and her family had lived in Nauvoo, Illinois, she had a special

friend by the name of Elizabeth Babbitt. How thrilled she was to meet her friend in Salt Lake City, after their arrival in the Valley in 1852. They had pulled and pushed a hand-cart across the Plains.

A short time later, Margaret became the second wife in plural marriage to Elizabeth's husband, Leonard Gurley Rice. In the coming years, she and Elizabeth were sister wives; they shared their husband, their children and their hopes and dreams.

Margaret was of noble character, deeply religious and always concerned for the needs of others. She was known by her friends and relatives as an extremely saintly woman. She loved to read Church books. Her cleanliness was a legend with those who knew her. She went to live with her sons.

They had moved to Cassia County, Idaho in 1882. Later she settled in the Teton Valley and lived with her daughter, Martha Rice Drake. She was sixty-one years old when she filed on a homestead next to her son-in-law, Asa Drake. To 'prove up' she needed to have a house, clear land, plant, and build fences. With the help of Asa, she did that. Her hands were never idle; gardens grew, wheat was ground and eggs, butter and cheese were always on hand.

Margaret died at the age of ninety in Bates, Teton, Idaho. She was buried at Victor, Idaho.

MARGARET MATHEWS RICE

No Photo Available

BIRTHDATE: 11 Jun 1849
Swansea Glanbar, South Wales
DEATH: 18 Feb 1926
PARENTS: Hopkin Mathews
Margaret Morris
PIONEER: 4 Oct 1856
E. Bunker Handcart Company
SPOUSE: Oscar North Rice
MARRIED: 15 Nov 1869
Logan, Cache Co., Utah
DEATH SP: 7 Sep 1880
Logan, Cache Co., Utah

CHILDREN:
Leonard Adelbert, 23 Aug 1874
Hopkin Ira, 26 May 1876
Margaret Elizabeth (Fuhriman), 3 Jul 1878
Ethel Irene (Dattage), 20 Apr 1881

Margaret was born in Swansea Glanbar Ganshire, South Wales, the third child in the family of Hopkin and Margaret Mathews. Her parents had joined the Mormon Church before Margaret was born, so she was born in the Church. She was not baptized until she was ten years old because they moved from place to place and her father was unable to perform the baptism due to ill health. She was one of three children born to her parents while her father and mother were on a seven year mission. She has vague recollections of being on the streets with her parents during their missionary labors.

Margaret was in her seventh year when her parents with their family of five children bade farewell to their native land to gather with the Saints in far-off Utah. The family took passage on the "Samuel Curling," a sailing vessel. After six weeks on the ocean they landed at Boston, Massachusetts on May 23, 1856. They boarded the train at Boston, traveling in sheep cars until they could change to more comfortable cars, finally arriving in Iowa City, Iowa. They camped here for three weeks while waiting for their handcart to be prepared.

They started on their journey, July 30, 1856, with the Edward Bunker Handcart Company. Margaret walked every day, often crying with hunger and weariness. Captain Bunker took her on his shoulder and carried her across the streams so she would be safe and dry. They made good time crossing the Plains. They arrived in the Salt Lake Valley about October 4th, having completed the entire journey from Wales to Salt Lake City in a little less than six months. They remained in Salt Lake one week, then they moved to Ogden where they made their home.

While living at Ogden, Utah, Margaret had the opportunity of attending school for a short time. She won her first book, a McGuffey reader, because she could spell Philadelphia, Delaware and Pennsylvania correctly.

In July, 1859, the family moved to Cache Valley. There were no boys in the family old enough to help support the family so Margaret and her sister, Mary, did farm work or anything that could be found to be done. She worked willingly and cheerfully. The year she was fourteen years old she and her sister did as much field work as two men.

She chose to become the plural wife of Oscar N. Rice on November 15, 1869. She was twenty years of age. They became the parents of four children, their first baby was a son who died after two months. She and her husband lived together happily for only a few years.

In September, 1880, her husband contracted pneumonia and passed away. He had been a devoted husband and a loving father. Margaret gave birth to her fourth and last child the following April.

Margaret was an active member of Relief Society almost from its organization. She had much sorrow and many trials to endure, especially since her widowhood, but she managed to keep her children together and see them grow to adulthood. She was excellent in caring for the sick.

Margaret became a confinement nurse and was very successful during her later years. She passed away on February 18, 1926, after being a widow for forty-six years.

SARAH ANN HARRINGTON RICE

No Photo Available

BIRTHDATE: 30 Jan 1800
Glocester, Rhode Island
DEATH: 1847
Polk, Iowa
PARENTS: Benjamin Harrington
Ruth Harrington
PIONEER: 1847 - 1850
died crossing the plains
SPOUSE: Ira Rice
MARRIED: 1825
Ontario, New York
DEATH SP: 14 Apr 1868
Washington, Washington, Utah

CHILDREN:
Harriet (Lamoreaux), abt 1826
Benjamin, abt 1827 (died at age 13)
Leonard Gurley, 3 Sep 1829
Henriette, 1831 (died as a child)
Sarah Ann, 1833 (died as a child)
Oscar North, 19 Oct 1835
Adeline Bowen, 24 Sep 1837
Adelbert, 1839
Caroline (McGuire), 1841
Deliah, 1842 (died as a child)
Hyrum Smith, 15 May 1844
Ephraim, 1846 (died as a young child - drowned)

Sarah was born in Rhode Island on January 30, 1800 to Benjamin Harrington. She married Ira Rice in 1825 in Ontario, New York. Sarah Ann had twelve children born to her. Five of her children died as infants or as young children. Her last child, Ephraim died by drowning at Des Moines Iowa when about five years of age.

Sarah Ann died in 1847 also in Polk, Iowa, leaving three young children and the others not too old for her husband to care for.

Sarah Ann had been the second wife of Ira, his first wife, Minerva Saxton, had had five children, and she had died about 1824 leaving the five children. Sarah Ann became the step mother of her five children in addition to the twelve she had herself.

After Sarah Ann's death, Ira married Elizabeth Ann Morris on November 20, 1856. Elizabeth Ann was a handcart pioneer who had two children and then had lost her husband. There were no children of this union.

Ira and his three wives were faithful members of the Church, following the Saints from Michigan to Nauvoo, Illinois and to Iowa, and finally to Utah. Sarah Ann and Ira had their endowments and sealing in the Nauvoo Temple on December 22, 1845.

Sarah was a true pioneer who gave up her life truly living the Gospel of Jesus Christ and was an example for those who have followed after her.

ELIZA ANN GRAVES RICH

BIRTHDATE: 3 Jun 1811
Waterford, Caledonia, Vermont
DEATH: 02 Jun 1879
Paris, Bear Lake Co., Idaho
PARENTS: Reuben Graves
Phoebe Palmer
PIONEER: 2 Oct 1847
Charles C. Rich Wagon Train
SPOUSE: Charles Coulson
Rich
MARRIED: 6 Jan 1845
Nauvoo, Hancock Co., Illinois
DEATH SP: 17 Nov 1883
Paris, Idaho

CHILDREN:
Mary Bratton, 11 Feb 1846
Eliza Ann, 14 Nov 1848
Fances Phoebe, 30 Jun 1850

Eliza Ann was born in Vermont, the oldest of three children. As a girl she was never strong and robust and could not do heavy work. Her aunt taught her the seamstress trade. This was before the sewing machine was invented and making men's suits was a hard job when it all had to be done by hand.

When Eliza was twenty years of age, she stood "five feet two inches tall and weighed ninety-eight pounds. She was a small but a very independent young lady, skilled in her trade and ready to face the world. She moved with her parents to Erie City, Pennsylvania where they made their home. She and her mother opened up a successful tailoring business.

They were at the height of their business career when they heard the Gospel and became members of the Church of Jesus Christ of Latter-day Saints. Their doors were always open to the Elders, and they did all in their power to help them in their labors. During this period she met her future husband, Charles C. Rich.

In 1841, Eliza with her mother and sister gathered with the Saints in Nauvoo, Illinois. She established a tailoring business and was known as the best seamstress in Nauvoo.

In January, 1845, Eliza became the second wife of Charles C. Rich in plural marriage. Before they were driven from Nauvoo by mobs, Eliza'a first child was born.

It was a cold, stormy day when they planned to leave Nauvoo. Her husband came into the room and looked at the frail little woman and tiny baby. He said, "Eliza, I can't take you. It would mean certain death to you and the baby. What shall we do?" Eliza answered, 'Bless me, Charles, and if you promise me I will be safe, I am not afraid." He did bless her that she and the baby would come to them and reach safety with the Saints. Eliza's mother stayed with her and the baby until they were strong enough to join her husband. It was a happy reunion.

In the Spring of 1847, they left Winter Quarters, Nebraska to journey across the Plains and find a home in the West.

The journey across the Plains, although full of trials and hardships, had many pleasant events to remember in after years. Eliza drove a wagon and ox-team across the Plains. Her mother rode in the wagon and cared for the baby. Eliza gave birth to two more girls, one died in infancy. They arrived in the Salt Lake Valley on Ocotber 2, 1847. They bought a ranch in Centerville, Utah.

Eliza was happy in that quiet and peaceful place. She worked hard spinning, weaving cloth, sewing and knitting, not only for her two girls but for other members of the Rich family. She was content to stay in Centerville while her husband answered a call to settle San Bernardino, California and while he completed a mission to Europe. He was an Apostle for the Church and had heavy assignments. When the call came for her husband to settle the Bear Lake Valley in 1864, Eliza helped him in that effort.

She was the first Relief Society in the Paris, Idaho First Ward. Her skilled fingers prepared the burial clothes for the members who died.

The hard winters were beginning to tell on Eliza; her health was beginning to fail. She was independent in spirit until the last. She passed away on June 2, 1879. She was buried in the Cemetery in Paris, Idaho, the only wife of Charles C. Rich to precede him in death.

ELIZABETH HOWARD STANDAGE THACKHAM RICH

No Photo Available

BIRTHDATE: 13 Sep 1792
Rachdale, England
DEATH: 1870
Richmond, Cache Co., Utah
PARENTS: James Howard
Elizabeth Dearden
PIONEER: 19-24 Sep 1847
Daniel Spencer Co. Wagon Train
SPOUSE I: William Standage
MARRIED: abt 1815
DEATH SP: 21 Mar 1850

CHILDREN:
William, 1818/19
Henry, 26 F6b 1818

SPOUSE II: William Thackham
MARRIED: 1820
DEATH SP: 1830 England

CHILDREN:
James, 1825
John, 13 Mar 1827
Anna Elizabeth, 1829 (died as a child)

SPOUSE III: Joseph Rich
MARRIED: 18 Jan 1853
Salt Lake City, Salt Lake Co., Utah
DEATH SP: 23 Jul 1866
Paris, Idaho
CHILDREN: None

Elizabeth was born in Rochdale, England in 1792. At about age twenty-two, she married William Standage. They made their home in England where they became the parents of two children.

Elizabeth left William and married William Thackham in 1820. They became the parents of three children. William Thackham passed away in about 1830.

Elizabeth and her family joined the Church of Jesus Christ of Latter-day Saints. They emigrated to America, joined the Saints in Nauvoo and then at Council Bluffs.

While she was there, her son, Henry Standage joined the Mormon Battalion and left his wife Sophronia Armenia Scott Reeves without house or tent, three dollars in money, very few possessions and one dow. Before he left, Henry asked Ira Eldridge to take his mother, Elizabeth, into the Eldridge home, to which Mr. Eldridge agreed.

Elizabeth came to Utah in the Daniel Spencer 1st 100, the Ira Eldridge 2nd 50, and the Isaac Haight first 10. They arrived in Utah the 19-24 of September of 1847.

When Henry returned to Utah from his Mormon Battalion service, he found his wife Sophronia, his mother Elizabeth and his brother, John Thackham, waiting for him. They had been among the first settlers of Salt Lake City.

In 1853, Elizabeth married Joseph Rich. They made their home in Richmond, Cache Valley, Utah. It was there in 1870, at the age of seventy-eight, that Elizabeth passed away.

Elizabeth had been a brave pioneer woman to have left England with her children, traveled across America with them to Council Bluffs, and traveled to Utah in her fifty-fifth year of age, celebrating that birthday just a few days before entering the Valley. She is honored by those who have followed after her for her great faith and fortitude.

ELIZABETH STOCK RICH

BIRTHDATE: 21 Sep 1848
Port Elizabeth, South Africa
DEATH: 18 Apr 1930
St. Charles, Bear Lake Co., Idaho
PARENTS: John Stock
Jane Adams
PIONEER: 5 Oct 1860
William Budge Co. Wagon Train
SPOUSE: Hyrum Smith Rich
MARRIED: 29 Jun 1867
Salt Lake City, Salt Lake, Utah
DEATH SP: 17 Aug 1924
St. Charles, Bear Lake Co., Idaho

CHILDREN:
Sarah Jane, 17 Nov 1868
Hyrum Smith, Jr., 26 Sep 1870
Edwin Coulsen, 20 Oct 1872
Orson Stock, 9 Oct 1874
Orissa Elizabeth, 13 Jun 1877
Aaron Adam, 25 Jun 1879
Luetta Ann, 19 Aug 1881
Ethel May, 4 Mar 1884
Verba Leola, 11 May 1886
Elmer John, 29 May 1888
Ray Charles, 13 May 1890
Elva Lauvon, 22 Apr 1893

Elizabeth Stock Rich was born at Port Elizabeth, South Africa. Her father and grandparents were emigrants from England to South Africa in 1820, where they pioneered in Cape Colony. Her father owned whaling vessels and they became very wealthy. Elizabeth had a monkey that she loved very much and would dress it up in her doll clothes.

After her parents heard the true Gospel they gave up all they had to emigrate to the Salt Lake Valley and start a new life with the Mormon Church. They traveled a distance of 16,000 miles. They sailed from Port Elizabeth to New York and came the rest of the way by team and wagons.

It took them seven months from Port Elizabeth to Utah. They traveled with the William Budge Wagon Company in 1860. On the Plains they encountered Indians on several occasions. They arrived in the Salt Lake Valley on October 5, 1860. The family went to Paris, Idaho in 1864 and lived in a two-room log cabin.

Elizabeth met Hyrum Smith Rich and became his bride on June 29, 1867 at Salt Lake City, Utah. They became the parents of twelve children. They also took care of Elizabeth's sister who was seven months old when her mother died.

Their first four children were born in Paris, Idaho. When their oldest child was six years old they moved to Fish Haven, Idaho where her husband became Bishop of the ward. Here they lived for four years. Next they purchased a farm in southern St. Charles on the shores of beautiful Bear Lake. They built a big home. Here their other eight children were born. Here they had the great sorrow of losing their son, Aaron.

Elizabeth spent a lot of time knitting stockings and mittens for her large family. She made dresses and front aprons for the girls. She liked to cook. They had lots of good times in the family and all got along very well. Elizabeth lived on their farm for many years. She did temple work in the Logan Temple in Utah. Elizabeth was a kind, patient and loving person.

Elizabeth's husband passed away on Aug 17, 1924 at St. Charles. Elizabeth passed away on April 18, 1930, also at St. Charles, at the age of eighty-two.

EMELINE GROVER RICH

BIRTHDATE: 30 Jul 1831
Freedom, Cattaraugus, New York
DEATH: 4 May 1917
Paris, Bear Lake Co., Idaho
PARENTS: Thomas Grover
Caroline Whiting
PIONEER: 2 Oct 1847
Charles C. Rich Wagon Train
SPOUSE: Charles Coulson Rich
MARRIED: 2 Feb 1846
Nauvoo, Hancock Co., Illinois
DEATH SP: 17 Nov 1883
Paris, Bear Lake Co., Idaho

CHILDREN:
Thomas Grover, 30 Dec 1849
Caroline Whiting, 22 Jan 1852
Nancy Emeline, 19 Feb 1854
Landon Jedediah, 11 Mar 1858
Samuel Joseph, 1 May,1860
Heber Charles Chase, 8 Aug 1863
Joel Hezekiah, 17 Oct 1865
George Quayle, 17 Mar 1869

Emaline was born in New York. Her mother died when Emeline was nine years old, leaving her father with six girls under the age of twelve.

Her parents had joined the Church of Jesus Christ of Latter-day Saints before Emeline was born. The family attended the dedication of the Kirtland Temple. They were persecuted and driven from their home in Missouri to find a new home in Nauvoo, Illinois.

Emeline, at the age of nine years, found employment in the homes of Nauvoo. At the age of fifteen she was working in the home of Charles Coulson Rich, an Apostle of the Mormon Church.

Before they were driven from Nauvoo by the angry mobs, Emeline became the fifth wife of Charles Rich. Less than two weeks after her marriage, Emeline joined the Rich families who were among the first groups of Saints to leave Nauvoo. They began their journey across the Plains to the Salt Lake Valley on June 14, 1847. She drove an ox-team from Winter Quarters to Utah. She walked all the way and missed but one day's driving. Her husband's love and kindness was her encouragement on the long journey. They entered the Salt Lake Valley on October 2, 1847. They lived first in tents and wagons.

When her husband was called to colonize the San Bernardino Valley in California, Emeline was one of three of his wives who accompanied him. All of them walked; Emeline carried her little baby. She had two more children in this Valley.

When their mission was over, they returned to Utah and Emeline and her three children moved into a log house on the "upper road" in Centerville, Utah. Here, in the next ten years, she gave birth to three more children. One was born the day her husband left for a mission to Europe. He had

left Emeline and her family in a very poor condition. She depended almost entirely for a living on her skill as a seamstress.

When her husband returned from his European Mission, Brigham Young called him and his families to settle the Bear Lake Valley in Idaho. Here, Emeline really felt "rooted" in a log cabin with three rooms, dirt floors, muslin at the windows, a fireplace and a roof of willows, straw and a thick covering of earth.

Emeline helped make the first American flag to float over Bear Lake for the 4th of July in 1864. Another great blessing came to her later in life. Brigham Young set her apart to administer to the sick and to act as a nurse and midwife. Her success in obstetrics was remarkable.

In 1880, her husband was stricken with a paralytic stroke. He experienced several more strokes and passed away in 1883. After his death Emeline Grover Rich received great joy and satisfaction in doing work for her departed family in the Logan Temple.

After a long, busy and useful life, she passed away as she had lived, honored, trusted and loved by all. Through all the vicissitudes and sorrows that she met throughout her life her faith in God and her devotion to her family, husband and friends never wavered. She kept the faith with herself and with God.

Emeline passed away on May 14, 1917 at the age of eighty-six at her home in Paris, having been ill only a few hours before her death.

HARRIET SARGENT RICH

BIRTHDATE: 23 Oct 1832
Fountain Co., Indiana
DEATH: 18 Jul 1915
Centerville, Davis Co., Utah
PARENTS: Abel M. Sargent
Sarah Edwards
PIONEER: 2 Oct 1847
Charles C. Rich Wagon Train
SPOUSE: Charles Coulson Rich
MARRIED: 28 Mar 1847
Winter Quarters, Nebraska
DEATH SP: 11 Nov 1883
Paris, Bear Lake Co., Idaho

CHILDREN:
Franklin David, 25 Apr 1849
Adelbert Coulson, 6 Dec 1851
Tunis Harriet, 28 Mar 1855
Abel George, 1 Feb 1857
Martha Caroline, 25 Feb 1859
Harley Thomas, 6 Nov 1863
Luna Rosetta, 13 Apr 1865
Morgan Jesse, 20 Jan 1868
Alvin Orlando, 2 Jan 1870
Drusilla Sarah, 14 Aug 1871

When Harriet was eighteen years old the family moved to Ohio where the Mormon Church was located. They followed the Church from one location to another; Missouri and Nauvoo, Illinois. Harriet remembers the murder of Joseph and Hyrum Smith as a sad and horrible incident in her life that she never forgot.

Before her family was driven out of Nauvoo, Harriet lived in the home of Charles C. Rich and his first wife, Sarah Pea Rich, to care for their children. She was not quite fifteen years old. The family moved to Mount Pisgah, Iowa and from there to Winter Quarters, Iowa. to prepare for the journey to the Salt Lake Valley.

Harriet married Charles Rich in Winter Quarters on March 28, 1847, and she became the sixth and last wife. As they made their way across the Plains, Harriet drove an ox-team. The company arrived in the Salt Lake Valley on October 2, 1847.

Harriet endured many hardships of pioneer life; helping to fight the crickets and helping to establish the settlement of the Valley.

She matured into a beautiful woman; she was talented and gifted with a beautiful singing voice. Her home rang with music of the guitar and the organ. All her children were gifted with musical talent.

Harriet was one of three of her husband's wives who accompanied him on his mission to settle the San Bernardino Valley, California. She loved the valley and the climate; they prospered and were happy.

Her husband was an Apostle of the Mormon Church and had many responsibilities. They returned to the Salt Lake Valley and settled in Centerville, Utah where they engaged in farming. Their daughter, Tunis, had died on the journey from San Bernardino. This was a great sadness to Harriet who had now lost two children.

Her husband was called to fulfill a mission in Europe, taking him away for two and one-half years. During this time, the wives and their children became very close and engaged in the task of helping each other and supporting their father and husband in his work for the Church.

After his return, in the Fall of 1863, they were called to settle the Bear Lake Valley. Her last four children were born there. The winters were long and hard. Harriet often said that this was the hardest mission of them all. She was very close with her children. She would make any sacrifice for their benefit. She resided there for the remainder of her life.

Harriet passed away while visiting at the home of her daughter, Drusilla, in Centerville, Utah on July 18, 1915. She was buried in the family plot in Paris, Bear Lake County, Idaho.

She was a beautiful lady in her old age as she was as a young girl; beautiful also in spirit. She was devoted to her children and to the memory of her great husband, who had passed away on November 11, 1883.

LYDIA POND RICH

BIRTHDATE: 9 Oct 1834
Whitetrow, Wiltshire, England
DEATH: 10 Dec 1911
Morgan, Morgan Co., Utah
PARENTS: Thomas Pond
Ann Garrett
PIONEER: 29 Sep 1853
Texas Independent Wagon Train
SPOUSE: John Henry Rich
MARRIED: 26 Dec 1852
DEATH SP: 1 Aug 1916
Richville, Morgan, Utah

CHILDREN:
Franklin John, 24 Aug 1853
James Thomas, 1 Jan 1855
William Henry, 4 Sep 1857
Lydia Melissa, 31 Oct 1859
Louisa Ann, 7 Jan 1862
Lucy Jane, 12 Nov 1864

Lydia's parents were strictly honest and taught their children the same. Her father died when Lydia was eight years old, leaving her mother with seven children. Lydia was the youngest. She, with her family, moved to Trowbridge, England, a manufacturing town of the finest woolen cloth. As a young girl, she worked in these mills.

It was here at the age of sixteen she heard the message of the restored gospel. She was baptized into the Church of Jesus Christ of Latter-day Saints. Soon after she joined the Church she became acquainted with John H. Rich and their courtship ripened into marriage. They were married on December 26, 1852.

Lydia and her husband were the only ones in their families who had joined the Church. They left their native land and turned their faces Zionward. They left from Liverpool, England on February 5, 1853 on the ship "Jersey." They landed in New Orleans, Louisiana, after being on the ocean six weeks and three days.

They then journeyed to Florence, Nebraska and started on their journey to the West about the middle of June. They traveled by wagon with the Texas Independent Company. When they reached the Black Hills she gave birth to a baby boy on August 24, 1853. They arrived in the Salt Lake Valley on September 29, 1853.

They experienced the hardships of getting settled in a new home, living the first winter with a family of Thomas Thurston in Centerville, Utah. Their room had a dirt floor and no windows. She tells it was here that she learned to make bread and butter. In the spring they moved into the settlement or fort. Her husband worked for their living and soon got them a home.

They moved a number of times, living in Centerville, Utah and then to the area where they would spend the rest of their lives, Weber Valley, which is now Morgan County, Utah.

Lydia, along with her husband, was prominent in the Church and the community. She was active in many positions in the Church. One of them was as the Stake Relief Society President when the Stake was organized in 1878. She also served as Ward Relief Society President, which she held until 1889, but continued on as Stake President for many years after that. Her words at the time of her calling were, "I shall never forget when my name was called for me to take this responsible position. I said to our dear sister Eliza R. Snow, I am not capable for that place." She said, "You will be and fill it with honor."

Near the end of her life she said that she had passed through many trials, but they had given her experiences that have been as gems by the wayside. Through all, her faith was increased. Her desire was to be faithful to the truth to the end of her life. She was so until the day she died at seventy-six years.

She left a posterity who have been stalwarts in the Church and filled many responsible positions. They honor her name and have brought honor to her name.

MARIA BENTLEY CHRISTIAN LINFORD RICH

No Photo Available

BIRTHDATE: 10 Apr 1813
Gravely, England
DEATH: 2 Oct 1885
North Ogden, Weber Co., Utah
PARENTS: William Christian
Mary Bentley
PIONEER: 9 Nov 1856
J. G. Willie Handcart Company
SPOUSE I: John Linford
MARRIED: 24 Jun 1833
Gravely, England
DEATH SP: 19 Oct 1856
Sweetwater River, Wyoming

CHILDREN:
Maria Mary, 1834 (died as an infant)
James Henry, 1836
George John, 1838
William, 1840 (died as an infant)
Joseph William, 1842
Amasa Christian, 1845

SPOUSE II: Joseph Rich
MARRIED: 26 Jul 1857
Salt Lake City, Salt Lake Co., Utah
DEATH SP: Not given
CHILDREN: None

Maria Rich was born in Gravely, Cambridgeshire, England, the seventh of thirteen children. She married John Linford on June 24, 1833 in England. They became the parents of six children all born in England, one daughter and five boys. Two of their babies died in infancy.

They heard of the Mormon Church through John Fielding who was a missionary in their town of Gravely. Maria and John were some of his first converts. They were baptized on December 9, 1842. They had embraced the Gospel wholeheartedly. Because of their baptism, they suffered severe persecution. John lost his business of making shoes and boots because family and friends turned against him. Maria stood by him without a murmur in his hour of trial.

They stayed in England until 1856 when they set sail on May 4, on the ship "Thornton." They made their way to Iowa City, Iowa and joined the James G. Willie Handcart Company. They numbered 500 pioneers leaving Iowa City on July 15, 1856 with 120 handcarts and 6 wagons.

On the journey West sixty-eight people died, Maria's husband John being one of them. He took cold on the camping grounds at Iowa City and gradually grew worse until he could not walk. Maria and her sons had to pull him in their handcart together with their bedding and cooking utensils. As they got into the Rocky Mountains the snow began to fall and the cold was intense. John, in his much weakened condition, could not stand it and he died on the banks of the Sweetwater River in Wyoming on October 19, 1856.

Maria said that her son George, a teenager, was at times the only able bodied man in their company. The snow was deep on the ground, the streams of water were very cold and the elderly women could hardly be persuaded to cross them. They said they would rather die. George would often carry them through the water on his back. They finally arrived in the Salt Lake Valley on November 9, 1856. Scouts had been sent by Brigham Young to rescue them.

The following year, July 26, 1857, Maria married Joseph Rich. He was the father of the Apostle Charles C. Rich. They were married by Brigham Young in his office.

In 1864, they moved to Bear Lake Valley in a company led by Apostle Rich who had been called to settle that area. They made their home in Paris, Idaho.

Maria served as the Relief Society President for a number of years. In 1884, Maria journeyed to North Ogden to visit two of her sons. While she was there, she was taken sick and passed away on October 2, 1885.

MARY ANN PHELPS RICH

BIRTHDATE: 6 Aug 1829
near Peoria, Tazewell, Illinois
DEATH: 17 Apr 1912
Paris, Bear Lake Co., Idaho
PARENTS: Morris Phelps
Laura Clark
PIONEER: 2 Oct 1847
Charles C. Rich Wagon Train
SPOUSE: Charles Coulson Rich
MARRIED: 6 Jan 1845
Nauvoo, Hancock Co., Illinois
DEATH SP: 17 Nov 1883
Paris, Bear Lake Co., Idaho

CHILDREN:
Laura Esphena, 25 Sep 1848 (died as an infant)
Mary Ann (Pomeroy), 15 May 1850
William Lyman, 9 Aug 1852
Morris Marion, 7 Aug 1854 (twin - died as a child)
Minerva Marian (Woolley), 7 Aug 1854 (twin)
Amasa Mason, 25 Oct 1856
Paulina Phelps, 21 Apr 1859 (died as a child)
Ezra Clark, 18 Aug 1864
Edward Israel, 9 Apr 1868
Jacob Phelps, 4 Dec 1877 (stillborn)

Mary Ann was born in 1829 in Illinois. Her family joined the newly-formed Church of Jesus Christ of Latter-day Saints in August, 1831, and moved to Jackson County, Missouri that winter.

They suffered the hardships and persecutions heaped upon the Saints from then on. They were driven from their home in the winter of 1833-1834 into Clay County, Missouri and from there to Caldwell County, and finally threatened with extermination and were expelled from the state. Mary was just four years old when her father was imprisoned and her mother, with her four little children had to drive her own team and wagon to escape to Illinois. The winter was bitterly cold, and they all suffered much. The family was later reunited and settled in Montrose, Iowa, across the Mississippi River from Nauvoo, Illinois. She had known Joseph Smith who had blessed her when a small child.

As a young girl, Mary became expert at spinning and weaving. Her mother died when Mary was just twelve years of age, in 1842. Mary lived and worked in the home of Charles C. and Sarah P. Rich doing weaving and helping care for their children while parents worked in the temple.

When Mary was just over fifteen years of age she married Charles Coulson Rich as his third wife with the consent and approval of his first wife.

When the Saints were forced to abandon Nauvoo, Mary never faltered nor complained about the hardships and suffering on the westward trek. She walked and drove their ox-team on the more than 1,000 mile trek. Charles was in charge of this company of 100 wagons. They arrived in the Salt Lake Valley on October 2, 1847.

Before leaving Nauvoo, they had received their endowments in the temple upon its completion, and while crossing the Plains, as Mary stated, "The spirit of the Lord was greatly manifested during that winter and we all enjoyed the privilege of having our endowments and sealings, and I received all these blessings in the Nauvoo Temple in common with my husband and family."

Three of Brigham Young's wives were in their company traveling to Utah. The co-captain of the group had died so the full responsibility of the group rested with Charles C. Rich. Also on the trip was another of his wives and she and Mary drove the wagon.

Their first winter in the Valley was difficult. Her husband had six wives and six children at that time. All worked together to survive. In February, 1849, Charles was ordained one of the Twelve Apostles, bringing new responsibilities for him.

In the Fall of that year, Mary and Charles and his two other wives were called to go to California by the southern route to find a place for Saints to settle as they came from the Islands of the sea. They lived there for six years and purchased some property that had some old houses on it; an area about twenty-five square miles. They returned to Utah in April, 1857, under much better conditions than when they left originally for San Bernardino, California.

Charles maintained a home in Salt Lake City for his first wife, but the others moved to Centerville, Utah. Mary's health had broken down some and she was better after her return to Utah to a climate somewhat cooler.

Her husband was called to preside over the European mission and left most of his families in Utah. By 1863, after his return from England, he was called to help settle the Bear Lake area. Thirty families were called to go to that area.

By 1864, they helped settle Paris, Fish Haven, St. Charles, Bloomington, Montpelier and Liberty. Mary's father had arrived and settled Montpelier with his family. Here, Charles built a little log room for each of his wives with some land. Mary's last children were born there.

In 1880, Charles C. Rich had a stroke and Mary went to Salt Lake to help care for him. It took much patience and care which they did with love and affection. She said of the experience where several wives helped, "I could never see the beauty of polygamy as I saw it then, for no one wife could have taken care of him as we did."

Mary was a true and faithful Latter-day Saint. Her family members were well educated, some of them becoming doctors. A son-in-law was also a medical doctor. Some attended the Univeriity of Utah in Salt Lake City, so she moved there to provide homes for them. Many sons fulfilled missions.

Mary passed away in Paris, Idaho on April 17, 1912 at the age of four months less than eighty-three years of age. She was truly a great pioneer woman who left a wonderful legacy to her numerous posterity who have followed her, many of whom have excelled in emulating her life.

NANCY O'NEAL RICH

No Photo Available

BIRTHDATE: 24 Apr 1782
Boone Co., Kentucky
DEATH: 5 Oct 1847
Salt Lake City, Salt Lake, Utah
PARENTS: Charles J. O'Neal
Janet/Jane Shaw
PIONEER: 2 Oct 1847
Joseph Rich Co. Wagon Train
SPOUSE: Joseph Rich
MARRIED: 23 Jun 1808
Kentucky
DEATH SP: 23 Jul 1866
Paris, Bear Lake Co., Idaho

CHILDREN:
Charles Coulson, 21 Aug 1809
Artimissa (Wixom), 22 Sep 1811
Jane Ann (Green), 5 Nov 1813
Minerva (Earl), 5 Jan 1816
Nancy (Porter), 3 Dec 1821

Nancy was born in 1782, in Boone County, Kentucky. In the late 1700's, her family started from Pennsylvania, to the settlement of Cincinnati, Ohio. They took their worldly possessions and supplies for a year with them.

The boats were built large and strong, to help protect the passengers from menacing Indians, and renegade whites as well. Nancy was the second daughter and fourth child in her family who had originally come from Ireland. Six more children were born later.

This family had sold their land, had loaded cattle, sheep, pigs, chickens and provisions. They also had brought tools, guns, ammunition, a spinning wheel, iron pots, pewter dishes, knives, clothes, and some treasured books, including a Bible. They had high hopes and courage as they faced the dangerous unknown. They moved across the Ohio River into Boone County, Kentucky, where their children were raised. Huge forests covered the land and wild animals roamed. The O'Neal children probably grew up with Indians as playmates. Early settlers worked together for the good of all. Friendship grew between the O'Neal family and the Thomas Rich family.

Joseph and Nancy were married on June 23, 1808. Joseph's brother married Margaret, and after her death, he married her sister, Jane.

Joseph and Nancy lived just a short distance east of their families where their first child, their only son, Charles Coulson Rich was born in 1809. They soon moved across the river to Indiana. Joseph built blockhouses for the settlers, he cleared land, built a cabin and planted crops. Nancy carried out the woman's traditional share of the household chores. They cleared land, quilted, husked corn, helped others with the work and socialized at the same time.

They participated in frontier social events, such as dancing, foot racing, and holiday celebrations. Indians ceased to be a menace, and more settlers came.

In 1815, Joseph Rich became the Constable of the township, which brought justice to horse thieves, hog thieves, keepers of billiard tables, and disorderly citizens, punished with whippings or with fines.

In Indiana, four daughters joined the family. The children's schooling was at home by their mother, Nancy. Some were sent away for further schooling. The girls were kept busy weaving, spinning, sewing clothes, making soap, candles, and tendering lard, boiling the family wash, and preparing meals from the abundant venison.

The family next moved to Illinois where Joseph bought 567 acres at $2.00 per acre. They farmed here. Charles, age twenty, taught school in the winter. They built a nice, comfortable home for their nearly-grown family, and enjoyed their home and their homemade furniture.

Joseph, Nancy, Charles, and Minerva were baptized on April 1, 1832, and confirmed at the water's edge. The Spirit of God seemed to rest upon them, and their minds and hearts were open. Greater light and knowledge came to them. The rest of their family were eventually baptized.

The Rich family moved to western Missouri, joined Zion's Camp, purchased land in Caldwell County and finally went to Far West, Missouri, where they built houses.

Many trials and persecutions came upon them. Mobs harrassed them, Joseph was imprisoned, and finally, after losing everything, they were forced to leave and they managed to reach Quincy, Illinois in 1839. Their daughters and their families were also in this area. Minerva, their daughter, had a daughter born, and then shortly after she died from complications of childbirth. Her husband raised their two older children, but he asked Nancy to raise the baby which she did.

The Rich family finally reached Mt. Pisgah, Iowa, by March, 1847. They had had their endowments in the Nauvoo Temple after their hard work completing the temple. They left Winter Quarters, June 14, 1847, with Charles in charge of their group.

During their travels West, Nancy became seriously ill from mountain fever or pneumonia, as the weather turned cold and stormy. Loving hands did all they could to help her. As they were finally entering the Salt Lake Valley Nancy asked to be raised up to see it, and she was pleased as she viewed their new home. This was her last pioneer stop in the long life on the frontier.

On October 2, 1847, they camped at the Pioneer Fort, now Pioneer Park. Hastily, they put up a tent, made a bed for Nancy, but she died Tuesday, October 5, 1847 late in the afternoon about 5:00 pm. She was the first white woman to die in the Valley and was buried next to Jedediah M. Grant's wife, Caroline, who had died on the trail and was brought to the Valley for burial.

Joseph Rich, Nancy's husband, was left to raise their seven year old granddaughter. He moved with his son to Bear Lake Country in 1865 where he died the next year in Paris, Idaho.

They were great pioneers who experienced all the trials and tribulations of pioneer life without wavering in their faith, or in helping, develop the West-true valiant pioneers who are honored by all who have followed.

SARAH DEARMON PEA RICH

BIRTHDATE: 23 Sep 1814
Glass Prairie, St. Clair, Illinois
DEATH: 12 Sep 1893
Salt Lake City, Salt Lake, Utah
PARENTS: John Pea
Elizabeth Knighton
PIONEER: 2 Oct 1847
Charles C. Rich Wagon Train
SPOUSE: Charles Coulton Rich
MARRIED: 11 Feb 1837
Far West, Caldwell Co., Missouri
DEATH SP: 17 Nov 1883
Paris, Bear Lake Co., Idaho

CHILDREN:
Sarah Jane, 4 Mar 1839
Joseph Coulson, 16 Jan 1841
Artemesia, 15 Jan 1843 (died at 9 months)
Charles Coulson Jr., 2 Sep 1844
John T., 15 Dec 1846
Elizabeth, 6 Oct 1849
David Patten, 8 Apr 1853
Benjamin E., 7 Nov 1855
Frederick Carmel, 19 Jul 1859

Sarah was taught to be thrifty in her youth. She would pick the flax and cotton from the field, prepare it, spin it, and weave it into cloth. For many years she was the weaver of the family. Her family were religious Methodist.

In 1835, two Elders came to their home and invited them to read the "Book of Momon." The family was converted and were baptized as members of the Church of Jesus Christ of Latter-day Saints.

They moved to Far West where Sarah met and married Charles Coulton Rich. Many times they had the privilege of hearing Joseph Smith speak.

They were very happy until persecution from mobs began. Charles took a prominent part in the Crooked River Battle and was forced to flee into the wilderness for his life. Sarah took seven families into her home at this time and all of them suffered the persecution as the mob was trying to obtain information of where to locate Charles.

With the help of her father, she moved to Quincy, Illinois and joined her husband. She gave birth to her first child a few days after her arrival. They also took Lewis Thompson, a boy nine years to raise. In November, 1839, they moved to Nauvoo as soon as Charles had built a home

for them. They enjoyed six years of building Zion before they were again driven from their home on February 12, 1846.

Sarah accepted the principle of polygamy, welcomed, and even helped to select the other wives. She and her husband had nine children of their own. They also took in two Judson orphans to raise.

Charles moved his families to Winter Quarters where they prepared to cross the Plains on June 14, 1847. Charles Rich was in charge of this company and they arrived in the Great Salt Lake Valley on October 2, 1847. They lived in the fort until their homes of logs from the canyons were built. Her husband was away on missions constantly, gone to California, England, etc. She had to move her family to Provo at the time of Johnston's Army to the Saints.

They were called to settle the Bear Lake area where she resided for three years and then returned to her home in Salt Lake City. She remained there forty years and owned one of the first fruit orchards in Utah Territory. Sarah was a teacher in the Relief Society from the time of its first organization until her death which occurred while visiting her son, Fred Rich, in Salt Lake City, Utah.

SARAH JANE PECK RICH

BIRTHDATE: 15 Sep 1825
Bainbridge, New York
DEATH: 29 Nov 1893
Paris, Bear Lake Co., Idaho
PARENTS: Benjamin Peck
Phoebe Crosby
PIONEER: 2 Oct 1847
Charles C. Rich Wagon Train
SPOUSE: Charles Coulson Rich
MARRIED: 9 Jan 1845
Nauvoo, Hancock Co., Illinois
DEATH SP: 17 Nov 1883
Paris, Bear Lake Co., Idaho

CHILDREN:
Hyrum Smith, 8 Oct 1846
Henrietta, 30 Jul 1849
Orson, 6 Oct 1851 (twin)
Orissa, 6 Oct 1851 (twin)
Samantha, 18 Oct 1853
Henry Benjamin, 15 Dec 1855
Lorenzo Ether, 22 Apr 1858
Phoebe J., 27 Apr 1860
Julia Ann, 7 Aug 1863
Wilford Woodruff, 10 Jan 1866
Walter Peck, 18 Jan 1869

Sarah's father was a river man who acted as a pilot going up and down the river. He died when she was four years old. Her mother supported their family as a tailoress. Her mother became a member of the Church of the Church of Jesus Christ of Latter-day Saints.

Her mother married Joseph Knight, Sr. and taught Sarah the principles of the Gospel. At the age of twenty-one, she became the fourth wife of Charles C. Rich.

A little more than a year later, she bid a last and sad farewell to her beloved Nauvoo. They arrived in Mount Pisgah three months after leaving Nauvoo. Sarah gave birth to her son, Hyrum, here.

On June 14, 1847, the Rich family started for Winter Quarters where they made preparations to cross the Plains. They traveled with seventeen persons and three teamsters in the Charles C. Rich Wagon Company and entered the Salt Lake Valley on October 2, 1847.

Her husband was a very busy man both in a civic and church capacity. Sarah and the other wives had to be largely responsible for their own lives as well as that of their children.

Charles purchased a farm in Centerville where Sarah was privileged to live. She raised a garden and fruit trees and sewed to support her family. She raised many chickens and ducks and sold the large eggs. Her husband, with three of his younger wives, had gone to San Bernardino to help settle the area.

In 1864, when their family was called by Brigham Young to settle the Bear Lake Valley, she had to leave her comfortable home situated in the heart of church activities near good schools and colleges in order to pioneer another valley. Each wife had their own home to protect them from the wet and cold.

Sarah was an excellent knitter and prepared the wool from the time it left the sheep's back until it became warm mittens, stockings, and sweaters for her family. She also made quilts and was a natural homemaker. Her home became a gathermg place for young people who were always welcome. She was the mother of eleven children. Only five sons lived to maturity.

Sarah Jane passed away in Paris, Idaho at the age of sixty-eight and is buried near her husband.

AGNES HILL RICHARDS

BIRTHDATE: 6 Jun 1808
Johnston, Renfrewshire, Scotland
DEATH: 30 Mar 1886
Mendon, Cache Co., Utah
PARENTS: Alexander Hill
Elizabeth Curry
PIONEER: 23 Sep 1851
John G. Smith Wagon Train
SPOUSE: John Kenny Richards
MARRIED: Spring 1831
DEATH SP: 15 Nov 1889

CHILDREN:
Elizabeth Hill, 13 Jan 1832 (died at age 3)
John, 1834 (stillborn)

Elizabeth Angelique, 22 Jul 1835
Mary, 14 May 1837
John Hill, 2 Jun 1839
Joseph Hill, 5 Dec 1841
Agnes, 2 Nov 1843
Rachel, 27 Jul 1846
Hyrum Thomas, 22 Mar 1849
Alexander Willard Hill, 10 Nov 1851
Daniel Brigham Hill, 14 Nov 1853

Agnes was born in Scotland and emigrated with her parents to Canada in 1819. In the beginning of the year 1831, she married John Kenny Richards of Quebec. She gave birth to her first child, Elizabeth, in 1832. Her little daughter died when a kettle of boiling maple syrup fell on her as she sat on the hearth stone. Not long after that, a disasterous fire occurred when the couple was absent from their home and all of its contents were lost.

In April of 1840, Agnes was baptized by Samuel Lake and became a member of the Church of Jesus Christ of Latter-day Saints. Around the beginning of September, 1842, she, her husband, and their four small children went to Nauvoo, Illinois. She was privileged to see and hear the Prophet Joseph Smith and Hyrum Smith preach on many occasions.

They experienced the joys of building Zion until they were chased from their home in Nauvoo on July 27, 1846, and under the sweltering noon day sun gave birth to a baby girl, Rachel. After rejoining with her husband, they made their long tedious journey through the unblazed woods, swamps, and over the prairie of Iowa until they arrived at Winter Quarters late in the fall of 1846.

On April 22, 1851, they resumed their journey westward with the John G. Smith Wagon Company. After enduring great trials and hardships, they arrived in the Salt Lake Valley on September 23, 1851.

They went to live in Mill Creek where her last two children were born. In 1859, they moved to Cache Valley in two covered wagons and arrived in Mendon, Utah on Christmas Day.

Agnes was an industrious, frugal, yet generous woman. Their clothing was made from wool sheared from the sheep by her husband and sons. She and her daughters washed, picked, carded, spun, and dyed the yarn for weaving into clothes. Many evenings were spent knitting stockings, sewing carpet rags, and patching quilts around the hearth stone by candle light.

Agnes passed away of pneumonia on March 30, 1886 and is buried in Mendon Cemetery.

AGNES MUIR FINDLAY RICHARDS

No
Photo
Available

BIRTHDATE: 26 Jan 1853
Crofthead Linlithgoushire,
Scotland
DEATH: 25 Nov 1919
Mendon, Cache Co., Utah
PARENTS: Walter Muir
Mary Bell Ross
PIONEER: 9 Oct 1866
Wagon Train Company
SPOUSE I: Williams Findlay
MARRIED: 14 Dec 1868
DEATH SP: 15 May 1869

CHILD:
Mary Elizabeth (Sorensen), 4 Oct 1869

SPOUSE II: Hyrum Thomas Hill Richards
MARRIED: 18 Apr 1876
Salt Lake Endowment House, Utah
DEATH SP: 18 Oct 1915
Mendon, Cache Co., Utah

CHILDREN:
Agnes (Hancock), 19 May 1877
Jane (Hughes), 25 Apr 1879
Rebecca, 13 jul 1881
Rachel Marilla (Buist Christensen), 12 Apr 1883
Emma Janette, 27 Dec 1884
Annie Laurie (Hughes), 13 Jan 1888
Bertha Viola, 26 Feb 1890
Hyrum John, 30 Jan 1892
Mahonri Moriancumor, 16 May 1896

Agnes' father was a Presbyterian Minister but in 1859, when Agnes was six years old,her family joined the Church of Jesus Christ of Latter-day Saints. Her father died in 1860 in Scotland.

On May 26, 1866, Agnes with her mother, brothers and two sisters, sailed from Liverpool on the sailing ship, "Arkright," bound for America. They arrived in New York City on July 6, 1866. By train they went to Montreal, Canada, and arrived at the banks of the Missouri River July 22, 1866. On July 25, 1866, their long journey West began. Progress was slow and arduous with travel by foot and by oxen and wagons. They arrived in Salt Lake City on October 9, 1866. After a short stay in Salt Lake City they moved to Mendon, Cache County, Utah. ,

On December 14, 1868, at the age of sixteen, Agnes married Williams Findlay. He died five months later on May 15, 1869. On October 4, 1869, her daughter, Mary Elizabeth, was born. In one year Agnes was a bride, widow and a mother.

After the death of her husband she taught school and even milked cows on the Hansen Ranch near Collinston, to help support her family.

On April 18, 1876, she married Hyrum Thomas Hill Richards in Salt Lake City. He was a mercantile and grain merchant.

Agnes enjoyed handwork of all kinds; knitting, crocheting and quilting. She was active in the Church. She served as a Relief Society teacher. She taught the Adults class in Sunday School and enjoyed singing in the choir.

Agnes passed away on November 25, 1919 in Mendon after a brief illness of pneumonia. She was buried in the Mendon Cemetery in Cache County, Utah.

ANN JONES VALLELEY CASH RICHARDS

BIRTHDATE: 27 Dec 1801
Wem, Shropshire, England
DEATH: 31 Jan 1877
Sugar House, Salt Lake Co., Utah
PARENTS: Joseph Jones
Mary Hayward
PIONEER:3/11 Sep 1855
J. Hindley or E. Stevenson Com.
SPOUSE I: John Valleley
MARRIED: abt 1819
DEATH SP: Not given

CHILDREN:
Margaret, abt 1820
John, abt 1822

SPOUSE II: James Cash
MARRIED: Unknown
DEATH SP: 1 Jun 1850
CHILDREN: None

SPOUSE III: Samuel Whitney Richards
MARRIED: sealed 19 Mar 1857
DEATH SP: 26 Nov 1909
CHILDREN: None

Ann was christened on December 27, 1801, and was born in Tilley, Shropshire, England. Ann married John Valleley about 1819 and had two children. At some point, Ann moved to Liverpool to work. She was supposedly a widow. It is not known what happened to her husband and children.

While in Liverpool, Ann met James Cash, who was a member of the Church of Jesus Christ of Latter-day Saints. James had a daughter, Mary Ellen, who had been born September 30, 1844 to him and his wife, Francis Brims. Francis had died November 24, 1846 leaving James to care for his two-year-old daughter. Apparently Ann married James Cash, but no record of marriage is found in civil or church records.

On June 1, 1850, James Cash died, according to the Liverpool Branch Church records. On June 31, 1850, Ann Cash, widow, was baptized in the Church of Jesus Christ of Latter-day Saints.

Journals of Samuel Whitney Richards and his brother, Franklin Dewey Richards show that Ann Cash was the housekeeper of the mission office in Liverpool. Their records show that Ann and her stepdaughter, Mary Ellen , sailed from Liverpool on the ship "Juventa," and finally arrived in the Salt Lake Valley on September 3, 1855. They were taken to the home of Samuel Whitney Richards. Samuel's Journals show that Mary Ellen's marriage, divorce, remarriage, birth of a child occurred. Ann Cash, known affectionately as "Auntie Cash" must have been in frail health. References showed she needed to be waited upon.

On March 19, 1857, Ann Jones Valleley Cash was sealed to Samuel Whitney Richards, who was twenty years her junior. She served as a grandmother figure in the homes of Samuel's wives. She is listed as being his sixth wife. At least once, Ann was called upon to prepare the body of an infant child of Samuel's for burial.

Ann passed away on January 31, 1877, at the Sugar House farm of Samuel, where she was living at the time. Her obituary praised her as "A Saint in love and faith of the Gospel of Jesus Christ." She was a pioneer woman of great faith and fortitude.

ELIZABETH JOHN RICHARDS

BIRTHDATE: 27 Nov 1837
Dowlais, South Wales
DEATH: 11 May 1912
Escalante, Garfield Co., Utah
PARENTS: John Harris
Jane Harris
PIONEER: 4 Oct 1864
William S. Warren Wagon Train
SPOUSE: Morgan Richards
MARRIED: 17 Feb 1857
Wales
DEATH SP: 25 Oct 1912
Escalante Garfield Co., Utah

CHILDREN:
William John, 22 Nov 1857 (died at age 5)
Alice Howell (Williams), 6 Apr 1860
John, 25 Aug 1862
William Morgan, 29 Jan 1865
Thomas, 15 May 1867
Franklin Dewey, 24 Feb 1870
Harriet Jane, 27 Apr 1873 (died as a child)
Edward, 16 Mar 1876
Elizabeth (Owens), 8 Dec 1878
Mary Ceclia (Mainelly), 16 Dec 1881

Elizabeth was born in South Wales in 1837. Elizabeth married Morgan Richards in Wales in 1857. They had ten children born into their family. Her husband was baptized into the Church of Jesus Christ of Latter-day Saints in July 18, 1843. Elizabeth was baptized on December 8, 1855. They were endowed in the Endowment House on January

11, 1868 in Salt Lake City. Her husband, Morgan, was also born in Wales.

Their first three children were born in Wales. Their oldest son, William John, died in England while they were waiting to board a ship for America. They left England on May 21, 1864 on the ship, "General McClellan," with 802 converts coming to America. During their voyage, the ship caught fire and hit an iceberg. They arrived in New York June 23, 1864.

As they had crossed the Plains, they left on July 22, 1864 in a company of sixty-five wagons and 329 people. Elizabeth traveled with her daughter Alice Howell, and her husband was with another wagon train helping with threshing machines. They arrived in the Salt Lake Valley on October 4, 1864.

They moved to the area of Farmington, Davis County, Utah, where their next two children were born. They moved to Panaca, Nevada, where Franklin Dewey was born. Their final area was in Panguitch, Garfield County, Utah, where the last four of their children were born. Escalante was their final home.

They had experienced many of the trials of pioneering, as they moved several places helping to colonize the territory. Elizabeth was truly a faithful, strong, pioneer woman who experienced much for her faith in Jesus Christ. She was an example for those who have followed after her.

Elizabeth passed away in Escalante, Garfield, Utah on May 11, 1912 at seventy-four years, five months, and fourteen days of age.

ELIZABETH MCCLENAHAM RICHARDS

BIRTHDATE: 12 Jun 1809
Pendleton, Kentucky
DEATH: 22 Nov 1893
Union, Salt Lake Co., Utah
PARENTS: Elizah McClenaham
Elizabeth Kemp
PIONEER: 12 Oct 1849
Silas Richards Co. Wagon Train
SPOUSE: Silas Richards
MARRIED: 5 Nov 1829
Sidney, Ohio
DEATH SP: 17 Mar 1884
Union, Salt Lake Co., Utah

CHILDREN:
Frances Maria (Brady), 20 Dec 1830 (twin)
Elizabeth Ann, 20 Dec 1830 (twin - died at age 16)
Sarah Jane (Morrell), 30 May 1833
Isabel, 20 Aug 1837 (died as an infant)
Martha (Cox), 20 May 1839
Lucy Ann (Brady), 23 Jun 1842

Elizabeth McClenaham was born in 1809 in Kentucky to Elijah and Elizabeth McClenahan. She married Silas Richards on November 5, 1829 in Sidney, Shelby County, Ohio.

Elizabeth and Silas were introduced to the Church of Jesus Christ of Latter-day Saints about ten years after they were married. They were baptized on April 25, 1840 They sold their property and moved from Ohio to Illinois to be nearer to the Saints. They assisted greatly, both financially and manually, to the building of the Nauvoo Temple. They received their endowments on February 7, 1846, and were sealed on February 7, 1852 in the Endowment House. Their endowments were in the Nauvoo Temple before they left that area.

They were well acquainted with Joseph Smith and Emma, and also Hyrum and his wife. Their deaths were difficult for Elizabeth and Silas to bear. They suffered with the other Saints the persecutions and were finally forced to move West. Their home and farm were valued at more than $3,000, and they were able to get only $800 for it. They took what livestock and property they could and moved to Council Bluffs.

They bought a house and farm, and were there for three years. One of their twins suffered from the hardships of the move and died shortly after they arrived. Elizabeth and Silas were devastated from this loss. Silas became Branch President, and Elizabeth was called on many times to feed and house church officials, sometimes having thirty or more people in her home to feed and prepare beds for. She was noted for looking after the physical necessities of life. An Apostle gave her a blessing and promised her she would never want for bread, nor would her posterity as long as they kept the commandments of God. This she did and taught her children to revere and respect God as well.

In 1849, they began their westward trek across the Plains. Silas was captain, so Elizabeth and her daughters had to drive their wagon and herd their cattle mostly alone. They arrived in late October in the Utah Valley and settled in Little Cottonwood Creek area. They pitched a tent in a blinding snow storm, found a place for their cattle.

Silas was the Bishop of Union and was the first school teacher. Elizabeth was again called upon to entertain and care for General Authorities often, but she loved it and enjoyed making them comfortable.

Elizabeth was the first Relief Society President in their ward, a position she held until her death. She spent much time assisting the sick and distressed, and preparing and laying out the dead. Elizabeth and her daughters worked hard harvesting vegetables and sugar cane. They sheared sheep, made wool, spun and dyed their yarn, wove cloth and made their own clothes by hand.

The Brady family were neighbors and good friends. In 1855, Silas took Keziah France as his second wife-she was fourteen years old, and Silas was her school teacher. Two of Silas and Elizabeth's daughters married Marion Brady, a brother of Keziah.

Elizabeth was a great lady and was loved and admired by all who knew her, especially by her daughters and their families. She passed away on November 22, 1893 in Union, a part of Salt Lake County, Utah. She was eighty-four years of age and had experienced much during her pioneering life from Kentucky to Utah.

ELIZABETH WHITTAKER CAIN RICHARDS

BIRTHDATE: 4 Aug 1828
Blakedown, Worcester, England
DEATH: 27 Mar 1880
Salt Lake City, Salt Lake, Utah
PARENTS: Thomas Whittaker
Sophia Turner
PIONEER. : 27 Sep 1847
Edward Hunter Co. Wagon Train
SPOUSE I: Joseph Cain
MARRIED: 1 Feb 1847
England
DEATH SP: 20 Apr 1857
Salt Lake City, Salt Lake, Utah

CHILDREN:
Elizabeth Turner, 14 Apr 1848
Joseph Moore,

SPOUSE II: Samuel Whitney Richards
MARRIED: 27 Jan 1859
Salt Lake City, Salt Lake, Utah
DEATH SP: 26 Nov 1909
CHILDREN: None

Elizabeth was born in 1828 in England. Her parents taught the children in her family to do what was right, from their early childhood. They were good, moral people, although not too involved in the Church of England.

Elizabeth's mother died suddenly, and her sister came home from Liverpool to care for the children. Sophia, the sister, had been taught the gospel of the Church of Jesus Christ of Latter-day Saints by John and she was anxious to teach the principles to her siblings, all of whom joined the Church and later emigrated to America. Two of her sisters, Sophia and Harriet, became wives of John Taylor.

Elizabeth met Joseph Cain while he was on a mission in England. They were married on February 1, 1847 , and they sailed to America immediately following. They arrived in the Salt Lake Valley on September 27, 1847, and settled near Samuel Whitney Richards. Joseph and Samuel became close friends and partners in many business ventures including cattle grazing, mills, and stores in Salt Lake.

Elizabeth was the mother of two children. She and Joseph also raised a foster daughter, Louie/Louise, who was the daughter of a friend, financially unable to care for her.

Elizabeth was involved in church activities. She worked diligently in the Relief Society, being a member of that organization when it was first organized in her ward. She was always known throughout her neighborhood as a charitable person, always extending. her hand to comfort and give assistance to others.

Elizabeth's husband, Joseph, passed away on April 20, 1857. Two years later she married his best friend and partner, Samuel Whitney Richards. Together she and Samuel continued the business partnership which Joseph had begun. Elizabeth was Samuel's sixth wife.

Elizabeth passed away on March 26, 1880, in Salt Lake City, Utah. She was married to Samuel for nearly twenty-one years before her death. She was fifty-one years old when she passed away.

Elizabeth was a courageous pioneer woman who experienced much for her faith in Jesus Christ.

HELENA LYDIA ROBINSON RICHARDS

BIRTHDATE: 27 Apr 1835
Douglas, Isle of Mann, England
DEATH: 18 Jul 1883
Cokeville, Lincoln, Wyoming
PARENTS: John Robinson
Elizabeth Maltby
PIONEER: 3 Sep 1855
John Hindley Co. Wagon Train
SPOUSE: Samuel W. Richards
MARRIED: 16 Feb 1856
Salt Lake City, Salt Lake, Utah
DEATH SP: 26 Nov 1909
Salt Lake City, Salt Lake, Utah

CHILDREN:
Martha Helena, 18 Feb 1857
Elizabeth Sophia, 4 Mar 1859
John Robinson, 4 Sep 1860
Jane Ida, 21 May 1862
Sylvia, 29 Feb 1864 (died as an infant)
Albert George, 11 May 1865
Maud, 10 Nov 1866
Franklin Richard, 11 Sep 1868
Minnie Bertha, 6 Mar 1871
Edwin Charles, 7 Jun 1873 (died as an infant)
Estella, 27 Jul 1874
Daughter, 1 Jun 1875 (died day of birth)

Helena Lydia was born in 1835 in England, on the Isle of Mann, England. Her parents were moderately wealthy, and she was brought up with an appreciation of the finer things of life. Her father was a carpenter and an Architect. This family was brought up with an Independent Faith.

In 1840, John Taylor came to the Isle of Mann to preach the Gospel of the Church of Jesus Christ of Latter-day Saints. Helena's mother received it with great joy and was baptized by Brother Taylor. Helena, and her half-sister, Jane, (who was eight years older than Helena) also joined the Church, but their father never joined.

On February 16, 1855, Helena and Jane left home to join the Saints. They traveled to Liverpool where they were detained for two weeks. They then sailed on the ship "Siddons," with about 500 Saints aboard. They were about eight weeks at sea, and landed at Philadelphia on April 22nd. John Taylor met them, and then sent them to St. Louis, then to the outfitting grounds where they joined the team of John Hindley and about sixty wagons. Captain Hindley became very ill, and Jane Robinson became his nurse.

Samuel and Helena were married on February 16, 1856 in the President's Office in Salt Lake City, Utah. Samuel was also married to a fourth wife, Jane Elizabeth Mayer, at the same time. Helena was the third wife. She lived with Samuel and his other wives for a time, and also with her friend, Elizabeth Cain, wife of Joseph Cain. At one time she lived in a little cabin on South Temple between first and third east.

When polygamists were being hunted by government agents, Samuel took Helena and her children to Spring Ranch, a dry farm near Cokeville, Wyoming. To be isolated on the ranch was very hard on Helena. She was an outgoing person, had sung on the stage of the Salt Lake Theater, and loved fine things.

Before moving to Wyoming, Helena taught lessons on her melodian to some of her husband's children in their Salt Lake Home. It appears that she was able to take her melodian with her as Samuel's journal often mentions that Helena was teaching music lessons at neighboring Smith's Fork.

Helena was never able to cope completely with plural marriage, and not having Samuel to herself. She made one trip back to the Isle of Mann to visit her parents. It is not known when she went, but she left her children in the care of her second wife, Mary Ann Parker. Helena was gone about six months on her journey.

Helena had twelve children, three of whom died as infants. She died while at the ranch in Wyoming. It was July 17, 1883. She had been faithful to her new-found Church and its leaders, had been a good mother to a large family, and had been charitable to those around her. She was a great pioneer woman who suffered much, went without much, and survived only to the age of forty-eight years. A great posterity honor her pioneering spirit and fortitude.

IDA LULU STENHOUSE RICHARDS

BIRTHDATE: 8 Mar 1857
New York City, New York
DEATH: Unknown
PARENTS: Thomas Stenhouse
Fanny Warn
PIONEER: 16 Sep 1859
Edward Hunter Co. Wagon Train
SPOUSE: Richard S. Richards
MARRIED: abt 1882 or 83
DEATH SP: Unknown

CHILDREN:
Laurence S., 1884
Vyvyan Warren, 30 Jul 1886
Evan Matthew, 31 Dec 1889
Muriel, abt 1892

Ida Lulu was born in 1857 in New York City, New York to Thomas Brown (Holmes) Stenhouse and Fanny Warn, when her father was presiding over the Eastern States Mission. She came to the Salt Lake Valley as a child of just over two years of age, with her parents and five siblings. During their years in Salt Lake City, her family entertained many visiting dignitaries.

Ida left Salt Lake City in 1875. Although a baptized member of the Church, in her late teen years, she began attending the St. Mark's Episcopal Church in Salt take City. Her records were transferred from St. Mark's to San Francisco in 1875.

Ida married Richard Sloane Richards in Salt Lake City or San Francisco. Her husband had been born in Warwickshire, Birmingham, England on November 9, 1846. It is thought her first son was born in San Francisco, California. The remainder of Ida's married life was spent in England where she and Sloane raised four children. Warren was born in Wales, attend Oxford University and was a Welsh schoolmaster. Evan was born in Brentford, Middlesex, England, and Muriel was born about 1892 also in Breatford Middlesex, England.

When Ida crossed the American Plains, they traveled with the Edward Hunter Wagon Company of 350 people and fifty-four wagons. They left Florence, Nebraska on June 26, 1859 and arrived in the Salt Lake Valley on September 16, 1859. Ida must have met him in San Francisco, or possibly in Salt Lake City.

Ida's death date is not known, but it is assumed she died in England.

JANE ELIZABETH MAYER RICHARDS

No
Photo
Available

BIRTHDATE: 5 May 1833
Cheltenham, England
DEATH: 15 May 1867
Salt Lake City, Salt Lake, Utah
PARENTS: John Mayer
Henrietta Cheek
PIONEER: 1854
SPOUSE: Samuel W. Richards
MARRIED: 16 Feb 1856
Salt Lake City, Salt Lake, Utah
DEATH SP: 26 Nov 1909
Salt Lake City, Salt Lake, Utah

CHILD:
Phineas Henry, 29 May 1857

Jane's family became converts to the Church of Jesus Christ of Latter-day Saints following the missionary labors of Samuel Whitney Richards. Jane sailed from England on Arpil 4, 1854 on the ship, "Germanicus." She probably crossed the Plains that year.

She became the fourth wife of Samuel Whitney Richards on February 16, 1856, at the same time he married his third wife. She gave birth to one son.

Jane Elizabeth returned to the eastern states to see her family and to show off her little boy. Jane convinced her husband to let her stay for a year and during this time her son died.

Eventually, Jane was able to return to Salt Lake City, Utah.

She is described as five feet two inches tall, with blue eyes, fair complexion, and light brown hair. Jane had a cheerful spirit, a noble heart, a truthful nature, and a deep trust in God.

She passed away at the age of thirty-six on May 15, 1867 in Salt Lake City, Utah.

JANE SNYDER RICHARDS

BIRTHDATE: 31 Jan 1823
Permelia, Jefferson, New York
DEATH: 17 Nov 1912
Ogden, Weber Co., Utah
PARENTS: Isaac Snyder
Lovisa Comstock
PIONEER: 19 Oct 1848
Willard Richards Wagon Train
SPOUSE: Franklin D. Richards
MARRIED: 18 Dec 1842
DEATH SP: 9 Dec 1899
Ogden, Weber Co., Utah

CHILDREN:
Wealthy Lovisa, 2 Nov 1843
Isaac Phineas, 23 Jul 1846

Franklin Snyder, 20 Jun 1849
Josephine, 25 May 1853
Lorenzo Maeser, 5 Jul 1857
Charles Comstock, 16 Sep 1859

John Willard, 15 Jul 1867
Albert Franklin, 21 Jun 1872
William Ernest, 30 Sep 1875
Leo Warren, 8 Feb 1878

Jane was baptized in January 1840 in Lake LaPorte, Illinois by her brother, Robert. She had been very ill. As soon as she came out of the waters of baptism, becoming a member of the Church of Jesus Christ of Latter-day Saints, she was healed.

After she married Franklin Dewey Richards in 1842, he was sent on several missions for the Church. They lived in Nauvoo until the Saints were forced to leave. She gave birth to her second child during this exodus.

After her husband returned from his mission in England, they left with the Willard Richards Wagon Company and crossed the Plains. Mary arrived in Salt Lake Valley on October 19, 1848.

They lived in Salt Lake City for several years until they were required to leave due to the arrival of the Johnston's Army. They went to Provo during this time.

Later, they moved to Ogden where her husband was asked to be the Probate Judge. Jane was set apart as the President of the Ogden Relief Society. In July 1877, she was set apart to preside over the Relief Societies of Weber Stake. She filled this position for thirty-one years.

Jane accompanied her husband on many trips. While in New York, she obtained much genealogical information of her immediate ancestry, which made it possible for her to do a considerable amount of temple work in their behalf.

She served as the Vice President of the Utah Board of Lady Managers of the Chicago World's Fair and spent several months there during the Fair.

She honored and dignified every position she held and faithfully performed many public duties.

KEZIAH FRANCES BRADY RICHARDS

BIRTHDATE: 14 Apr 1841
Nauvoo, Hancock Co., Illinois
DEATH: 7 Jun 1922
Union, Salt Lake Co., Utah
PARENTS: Lindsay A Brady
Elizabeth Ann Hendrickson
PIONEER: 17 Sep 1850
Warren Foote Co. Wagon Train
SPOUSE: Silas Richards
MARRIED: 6 Feb 1855
Salt Lake Endowment House
DEATH SP: 17 Mar 1884
Union, Salt Lake Co., Utah

CHILDREN:
Frances Ann, 30 Nov 1859
Cynthia Ellen, 13 Sep 1861
Silas Newton, 21 Oct 1863
Eliza Snow, 14 Mar 1865

Keziah was born to parents who had been converted to the Church of Jesus Christ of Latter-day Saints and had moved to Nauvoo, Illinois. They were acquainted with the Prophet, Joseph Smith and enjoyed living in Nauvoo.

When Keziah was nearly five years old, her famly was driven from Nauvoo. They settled in Winter Quarters for four years then started for the Rocky Mountains early in the summer of 1850. After many days of toil and sorrow, the Brady family arrived in the Salt Lake Valley on September 17, 1850 in the Warren Foote Wagon Company. Their family was sent to Union near Little Cottonwood Creek.

Keziah was baptized by Silas Richards in Salt Lake City on April 25, 1851 and was confirmed a member of the Church by her father.

Keziah became the second wife of Silas when she was fifteen years old and he was forty-eight. She continued attending school for four years before the birth of her first child. They became the parents of eight children.

Keziah made their own clothes from the wool taken from their own sheep. She also had a little buttery. The buttery had a small pebble ditch running through it where the cool water kept the milk and the butter cool all summer. She made their own soap for washing their clothes, and was always baking bread.

She took in three little orphaned sisters and raised them. Keziah was of a kind, sweet disposiotn.

She passed away at the age of eighty-one in Union, Salt Lake County, Utah.

LOUISA LULU GREENE RICHARDS

BIRTHDATE: 8 Apr 1849
Kanesville, Iowa
DEATH: 8 Sep 1944
Salt Lake City, Salt Lake, Utah
PARENTS: Evan M. Greene
Susan Kent
PIONEER: 1852 Wagon Train
SPOUSE: Levi Willard Richards
MARRIED: 16 Jun 1873
Salt Lake Endowment House
DEATH SP: 30 Mar 1914
Salt Lake City, Salt Lake, Utah

CHILDREN:
Mary Greene, 27 Jun 1874 (died at age 2)
Mabel Greene, 24 Jun 1877 (died at 3 weeks)
Levi Greene, 27 Jul 1875
Willard Greene, 17 Mar 1880
Evan Greene, 22 Feb 1884
Heber Greene, 22 Oct 1885
Sarah Greene, 25 Mar 1888

Louisa was born in Kanesville, Iowa, 1849. Her parents had joined the Church of Jesus Christ of Latter-day Saints in the 1830's and emigrated to Kirtland, Ohio.

After the expulsion from Nauvoo, Illinois in 1846, the family migrated to Winter Quarters and Kanesville. They journeyed to the Salt Lake Valley in 1852. Louisa was the eighth of thirteen children. She was between three and four years old when her family crossed the Plains.

Although Louisa was young, she remembered well the many of the dangers and hardships which which they met and endured on that long, tedious journey. She survived a run-away wagon, and being nearly drowned in the Missouri River.

The family settled first in Provo, Utah.

In 1859, they moved to Grantsville, Utah. In 1864, they moved to Smithfield in Cache Valley, Utah.

Her father taught his children to read and write. At the early age of fourteen she was composing dramatic dialogues and poems. She contibuted poems to the "Salt Lake Herald" and became noted for her literary abilities. She assumed the the editorship of the "Sunday Gazette" in the fall of 1869, in Smithfield, Utah.

Louisa felt impressed that the young girls in the Church should have their own magazine. President Brigham Young gladly appointed Louisa the mission and blessed her in it. The magazine was named "Woman's Exponent." Louisa also was President of the Retrenchment Association for young women in Smithfield, Utah.

During her five years as editor (1872-77), Louisa had married Levi Willard Richards in 1873. They became the parents of seven children; four sons and three daughters. Two daughters died in infancy and one in early childhood. Her four sons grew to manhood, distinguisting themselves in their professions.

Louisa often published under the nom de plume of "Lula." She came to be known as Lula Greene Richards. Louisa's niece, Persis Louisa Young, came to live with the family and help in the home. She was married to Levi Willard Richards as a polygamous wife in 1884.

Louisa continued to write as she reared her family. She published in the Exponent, Relief Society Magazine, Children's Friend, Era and the Young Woman's Journal. She conducted a department of the Juvenile Instructor under the heading "Our Little Folks." In 1904, she published a book of verse entitled "Branches That Run Over the Wall." She won the first, second and third prize in a poetry contest honoring the anniversary of the birth of the Prophet Joseph Smith.

While rearing her family and writing, Louisa also served as President of the Young Ladies Mutual Improvement Association for her ward in Salt Lake City; as an officer of the Relief Society of that ward; as a member of the General Board of the Primary Association; as a member of the General Board of the Deseret Sunday School Union.

She was an officiator in the Salt Lake Temple from the time of its dedication in 1893 until 1934.

After the death of her husband, Louisa lived with her neice and sister wife, Persis. Louisa's sweet disposition seemed to make it a pleasure for many of the church officials to visit her at her home in her later years.

Louisa passed away on September 8, 1944, after a full and active life. She was truly one of the great ladies of her period and contributed much to the testimonies of the women of the Church. Louisa is buried in the Salt Lake Cemetery beside her husband.

Typical of her life, her thoughts and her writing is the little verse with which Louisa ended a biographical sketch she had written of her mother:

> To humbly follow where the Savior trod,
>
> And keep the narrow way that leads to God;
>
> I need no better guide, I ask no other
>
> Than the dearest lessons taught by thee, My mother.

MARY ANN PARKER RICHARDS

BIRTHDATE: 4 Nov 1839
Chaigley, Lancaster, England
DEATH: 20 Dec 1914
Salt Lake City, Salt Lake, Utah
PARENTS: John Parker
Alice Woodace Whitaker
PIONEER: 28 Aug 1852
John Parker Indep. Wagon Train
SPOUSE: Samuel W. Richards
MARRIED: 14 Feb 1855
Salt Lake City, Salt Lake, Utah
DEATH SP: 26 Nov 1909
Salt Lake City, Salt Lake, Utah

CHILDREN:
Joseph William, 25 Jan 1856 (died at age 6)
Alice Parker, 29 Oct 1857
Wealthy Dewey, 10 Feb 1860
Maria Ann, 17 Aug 1862
Ellen May, 21 Sep 1864
Caroline Dewey, 22 Oct 1866
Whitney Samuel, 20 Feb 1869
Edith Vilate, 25 Feb 1872
Willard Parker, 27 Apr 1874
Florence Elizabeth, 20 Oct 1876 (died at age 2)

Mary Ann was nearly four when her mother died. On January 17, 1845, her father sailed from England to join the Mormon Saints in Nauvoo, taking his three little ones without any relative to assist him in their care. They came by way of New Orleans and landed at Nauvoo on April 2, 1845. They lived with her grandparents who were already living in Nauvoo. He married a widow with seven children. Shortly after their marriage, they were driven from Nauvoo. They went to St. Louis to earn enough money to buy provisions they needed to travel West and remained in St. Louis for six years.

In the Spring of 1852, her father sold his business and brought the first threshing machine into Utah. They arrived in Salt Lake Valley on August 28, 1852. They went into the business with their threshing machine. They built an adobe home in which they often had dancing parties.

Mary Ann married Samuel Whitney Richards as his second wife. She had ten children in all and cared for the three children of Samuel's first wife after she died. Her husband spent much time in the mission field. She was left to care for her family and oversee their affairs. She also became the peacemaker between Samuel's six wives and often cared for their children.

In the early seventies, she moved with her family to Dixie Country, where her parents were living and remained there for seven years. She returned with her husband to Salt Lake City where she made her home in Salt Lake City, Utah.

In 1895, she accompanied her husband to the Eastern States remaining with him while he presided over that mission for two years. She was a mother to the elders and made many friends.

Wherever she was, her home was always a gathering place for relatives, friends, converts, and emigrants. She liked to work in the temple whenever it was possible for her to do so. Her whole life was one of service until she passed away at the age of seventy-five.

MARY HASKINS PARKER RICHARDS

BIRTHDATE: 8 Sep 1823
Chaigeley, Lancashire, England
DEATH: 3 Jun 1860
Salt Lake City, Salt Lake, Utah
PARENTS: John Parker
Ellen Haskins
PIONEER: 1849 Wagon Train
SPOUSE: Samuel W. Richards
MARRIED: 29 Jan 1846
Nauvoo, Hancock Co., Illinois
DEATH SP: 26 Nov 1909
Salt Lake City, Salt Lake, Utah

CHILDREN:
Mary Amelia,
Samuel Parker,
Sylvester Alonzo,
Iantha Adelia,
Ianthus,
Male child,

Mary was born in England, 1823. Her parents were some of the first converts to the Church of Jesus Christ of Latter-day Saints in England. Early church meetings were held in the Parker home and they cared for Heber C. Kimball during a period of his illness.

Her parents wished to be united with other Saints so they emigrated to the United States and made their home in Nauvoo, Illinois. Three months later Mary and her brother decided to emigrate to Nauvoo, also. Mary was thirteen years old when she walked from her home to the seaport, boarded the ship and sailed for America on December 23, 1838. She had mixed feelings as she parted from other members of her family and her friends and finally gave vent to tears she endeavored to conceal.

In Nauvoo, Mary became a member of the newly organized Relief Society.

She married Samuel Whitney Richards on January 29, 1846 in the Nauvoo Temple; they both became ordinance workers. When the Saints were driven out of Nauvoo, Mary resided with her husband's parents at Winter Quarters, Iowa while her husband spent part of that time serving a mission in Great Britain for their beloved Church.

The main group of the Richards family left Winter Quarters in 1848 in the company headed by Samuel's Uncle, Willard Richards. By necessity to procure funds, Mary and Samuel remained behind for another year and worked a farm. Their first child, Mary Amelia, was three months old when they crossed the great Plains and joined the Saints in Salt Lake City in 1849.

Mary and Samuel's home was located close to her father-in-law Phinehas Richards. Four more children were born to their union.

Mary carried heavy responsibilities while her husband served so faithfully in his church and civic work. Mary was a loving mother whose greatest concern was the welfare of her lovely children.

She was a talented writer. Her poetry and journals depict pioneer life in the early period of the Church. The last few years of her life Mary was in poor health and passed away during childbirth on June 3, 1860.

She was thirty-five years old. She is buried in the Salt Lake City Cemetery.

MARY HOWELLS LLEWELLYN RICHARDS

BIRTHDATE: 4 May 1807
Merthyr, Tydvil, Wales
DEATH: 11 Feb 1880
Goshen, Utah Co., Utah
PARENTS: Hugh Howells
Elizabeth Howells
PIONEER: 2 Oct 1856
E. Bunker Handcart Company
SPOUSE: Edmund Llewehyn
MARRIED: 10 May 1834
Merthyr, Tydvil, Wales
DEATH SP: 23 Nov 1847

CHILDREN:
Edmund, 22 Jun 1835
John, 8 Mar 1838
Ann, 21 Apr 1839
Elizabeth, 21 Apr 1842 (died at age 1)
Elizabeth, 22 Oct 1846

SPOUSE II: Wlliam Richards
MARRIED: 27 Dec 1861 (for tirne only)
DEATH SP:
CHILDREN: None

Mary Howells was born in 1807, in Merthyr, Tyvil, Glamorganshire, Wales. She had one older sister, Ann who was born two years earlier. Mary's father was an iron, miner in Wales. Mary was working as a baker when she met and married Edmund Llewellyn who was a block layer. He died when their youngest child was thirteen months old.

Mary heard the missionaries and was baptized in 1846. Ten years later Mary and her four living children left their home in Wales and went to Liverpool, England to find passage to America. They left on the "Sam Curling" on April 19, 1856 with a total of 700 passengers known as "The Welsh Company." Her children at that time were Edmund age twenty-one, John age eighteen, Ann age seventeen and Elizabeth age ten. The two boys were baptized while emigrating to Utah. Their fare for passage was five pounds each. They were on the ship for five weeks and each person over eight years old was required to bring his own bed and bedding as well as cooking and eating utensils and a tin vessel that would hold three quarts of water. They also needed a box or a barrel to carry everything in. The rations they were given for each adult per week were: 3 1/2 pounds of bread, 1 1/2 pounds oatmeal, 1 pound of pork, 1 1/4 pounds of beef, 1 pound of flour, 1 1/2 pounds of rice, 1 1/2 pounds peas, 2 pounds of potatoes, 1 pound of sugar, 2 ounces of tea, 2 ounces of salt, 1/2 once of mustard, 1 1/4 ounce of pepper and 1 gallon of vinegar. They also reecived 3 quarts of water daily with some extra water provided for cooking.

The ship landed in Boston on the 23rd of May. They traveled from there on cattle trains 300 miles to Iowa City where they waited three weeks for their hand carts to be made. All were expected to help make provisions for the journey. When the carts were finished, they started their long journey pushing and pulling their handcarts to the land of Zion.

Mary and her children suffered many hardships along with the others in the handcart company which consisted of sixty-four hand carts. Many were sick and many died along the way but somehow Mary and her children were spared. They reached the Salt Lake Valley on October 2, 1856 and settled in Goshen, Utah County.

A memorial was written as a tribute to her and given at her funeral. Some excerpts follow: She was beloved and respected by all who knew her. We recognize her as a much respected fellow member, a woman of great integrity, one who was devoted by her faith and works to her religion and her God. The elders always found a welcome at her hospitable board and speak in high terms of her active willingness to aid the progress of this work. All who knew her will acknowledge her honesty of purpose as it was apparent to everyone. She was one who could not be turned aside from the gospel of Christ. Her conviction of truth was clear and her attachment to the revealed religion as taught by Joseph Smith in these latter days was sincere. She was truly a mother in Israel and a true follower of Christ. We resolve that while her death touches our hearts, it arouses our deeper desires to continue faithful and exemplify her precepts and example that our last days may be like hers. She was full of faith in the hereafter of a glorious resurrection.

MARY JULIA JOHNSON RICHARDS

BIRTHDATE: 24 Sep 1841
Illinois
DEATH: 20 Dec 1928
Provo, Utah Co., Utah
PARENTS: Joseph Ellis Johnson
Harriet Snider
PIONEER: 27 Sep 1861
Sixtus Johnson Co. Wagon Train
SPOUSE: Heber John Richards
MARRIED: 09 Apr 1862
Salt Lake City, Salt Lake, Utah
DEATH SP: 12 May 19__
Provo, Utah Co., Utah

CHILDREN:
Mary, 20 Jan 1863
Amelia, 24 Jan 1867
Harriet, 15 Feb 1870
Julia, 20 May 1872
Jennetta, 13 Jun 1875
Rhoda, 13 Jun 1878
Alice, 24 Oct 1880
Blanch, 9 Mar 1886

When Mary Julia was just a baby, her folks were forced to flee from their home with what they could pack into two bags. She grew up in the Council Bluff area where her family had many businesses including print shops, bakeries, drug stores, and nurseries. They were in the business of furnishing goods to the people who were on their way to California, Oregon, and Utah.

In 1861, they decided to cross the Plains with the Sixtus E. Johnson Wagon Company. Mary Julia was twenty years old when she arrived in the Salt Lake Valley. She had driven the commissary wagon across the Plains.

After her arrival, she fell in love with and married Heber John Richards. Mary and Heber John lived in the Seventeenth Ward for a year before her husband was sent on a mission to England. Upon his return, Brigham Young asked him to return to the East and study surgery. Again,

Mary Julia was left home alone. Eventually they became the parents of eight girls.

In 1890, the family spent a year and a half in Europe. After returning to Utah, the family moved to Provo.

Mary survived her husband and lived close to her daughters until her death at the age of eighty-seven.

MARY THOMPSON RICHARDS RICHARDS

BIRTHDATE: 21 Oct 1827
Hudgill,Cumberlahd, England
DEATH: 10 Sep 1905
Riverside, Box Elder Co., Utah
PARENTS: John Thompson
Phebe Robson
PIONEER: 19 Oct 1848
W. Richards & B. Young Com.
SPOUSE I: Willard Richards
MARRIED: 27 Jan 1846
Nauvoo, Hancock Co., Illinois
DEATH SP: 11 Mar 1854
Salt Lake City, Salt Lake, Utah

CHILDREN:
Phoebe Amelia, 7 Jun 1851
Jennetta, 22 Oct 1852

SPOUSE II: Franklin D. Richards
MARRIED: 6 Mar 1857
DEATH SP: 9 Dec 1899
Salt Lake City, Salt Lake Co., Utah

CHILDREN:
Myron John, 22 May 1858
Wealthy, 22 Mar 1861
Mary Alice "Mamie," 5 Jul 1863
Wilford Woodruff, 8 May 1866

Mary was born in England, eldest child and only daughter of her parents. Her father was a tailor by trade and Mary learned her seamstress skills from him. She made men's clothing and gloves and learned to reinforce men's trousers with leather in places where they received the most wear. These skills blessed her life and that of her children later in her life.

Mary was very sensitive to the thoughts and feelings of others. She loved her religion and tried to live up to its teachings, holding sacred her covenants. She and her parents and a brother were converted to the Church of Jesus Christ of Latter-day Saints about 1837. A few years later, they made preparations to emigrate to America under the Emigration Fund program. Their sailing across the Atlantic Ocean was a great hardship. By the time they reached Nauvoo, Illinois, they were exhausted and their vitality greatly depleted.

Mary married Dr. Willard Richards as a plural wife on January 27, 1846 at Nauvoo, Illinois. The same year the Saints were driven out of their beloved city of Nauvoo. Mary arrived in the Salt Lake Valley on October 19, 1848 with the Willard Richards and Brigham Young Wagon Company. Mary and Willard became the parents of two daughters. Her husband died at the early age of fifty years on March 11, 1854.

Brigham Young suggested that Willard's nephew, Franklin D. Richards, marry his Uncle's widow, Mary, for time only, so they could raise up children to Willard. Mary and Franklin D. became the parents of four children, two sons and two daughters.

Franklin D. moved four of his wives to Farmington, Utah. Each had a modest cottage and a small acreage of land large enough for a vegetable garden and an orchard, a place to keep a cow and perhaps a pig. These women had a hard time trying to make ends meet. They thanked God for what they had and did the best they could to live righteously and to bring their children up in such a way as to be a credit to the Church and the State. Mary's husband was an Apostle in the Church and was away much of the time attending to Church affairs.

Mary helped to bolster her finances by doing tailoring for the public. Her sewing had to be done by hand, but she was an expert at this. After the Logan Temple was finished, Mary had a great desire to do ordinance work there. She would stay for a week at a time where she did work for her dead. It was a great pleasure for her.

Her husband, Franklin D., passed away on December 9, 1899 in California. Mary became a worker in the Logan Temple for twenty years before her death. She was Matron for many years under Temple President Mariner W. Merrill.

Mary passed away on September 10, 1905 at the home of her son Myron at Riverside, Box Elder County, Utah. Her funeral and burial took place in Farmington, Utah. She was a much beloved woman. At her prior request, Apostle Melvin Ballard sang, "I Know That My Redeemer Lives." Mary's death left a great void in the family circle.

NANNY LONGSTROTH RICHARDS RICHARDS

BIRTHDATE: 15 Apr 1828
Arncliffe, Yorkshire, England
DEATH: 7 Jan 1911
Salt Lake City, Salt Lake, Utah
PARENTS: Stephen Longstroth
Ann Gill
PIONEER: Fall 1854
Willard Richards Wagon Train
SPOUSE I: Willard Richards
MARRIED: 25 Jan 1846
Nauvoo, Hancock Co., Illinois
DEATH SP: 11 Mar 1854
Salt Lake City, Salt Lake, Utah

CHILDREN:
Alice Ann, 24 Mar 1849

Mary Asenath, 18 Nov 1850
Stephen Longstroth, 29 Jul 1853

SPOUSE II: Franklin D. Richards
MARRIED: 6 Mar 1857
Salt Lake City, Utah
DEATH SP: 9 Dec 1899

CHILDREN:
Minerva Edmeresa, 11 May 1858
George F. Richards, 23 Feb 1861
William Fredrick Richards, 27 Apr 1866

Nanny Richards was born in England, 1828. Her parents were among the first in England to join the Church of Jesus Christ of Latter-day Saints. The whole family passed through much affliction and were persecuted because of their beliefs. Nanny was baptized in England in 1839.

The family became friends of Apostle Williard Richards who was in England on a Church mission. When he became ill they nursed him to better health in their home. Nanny was present at the Coronation of Queen Victoria, in England.

When Nanny was fourteen years old, her family emigrated to Zion. They left England on February 5, 1842 and arrived in New Orleans, Louisana. They journeyed up the Mississippi River, stopping at St. Louis, Missouri for a season while her father, who was a cabinet maker by trade, earned enough money to pay their way to Nauvoo, Illinois.

They lived in Nauvoo until they were driven from their homes by the mobs. Nanny was sealed to Willard Richards as a plural wife on January 25, 1846. They were married in the Nauvoo Temple on the same day as her older sister, Sarah, who was also one of Willard Richards' ten wives. Nanny was present at the meeting where the mantle of the Prophet Joseph fell upon Brigham Young's shoulders. It made such an impression on her that she never wavered in her faith and devotion to knowing God's will in all things.

She made her way to the Great Salt Lake Valley in 1848 with Willard Richards and Brigham Young Companies. Her first baby was born on March 24, 1849 in a wagon on South Temple Street, opposite the Temple Block, known as Richards Street. It was a terrible stormy night with deep snow drifts. Later, her husband built a long adobe house which faced south and placed his many families in this home. Here, Nancy gave birth to two more children.

Willard Richards passed away on March 11, 1854. Times were very hard for the family but they raised and sold much of the fruit from their trees which surrounded their home.

Nanny married Franklin D. Richards on March 6, 1857. They became the parents to three children. Nanny's sister, Sarah, died in 1858 at age thirty-two. Nanny carried a tremendous responsibility as she assumed the responsibility of her own children, three of her sister's children and two children from Willard's first wife, who had died in Nauvoo. She cared for three families; this was the greatest trial of her life.

Every day was wash day, with ten in the family the clothes were drying on lines everyday. Nanny made butter and crackers. They lived on sego lilies, greens, mushrooms and the fish the boys caught.

When Nanny was seventeen years old she was given a Patriarchal Blessing by Patriarch John Smith who told her that "prophets, seers and revelators should proceed forth from her." She was a faithful wife to two apostles, Willard and Franklin D. Richards. She was the mother of Apostle George F. Richards, and grandmother of two apostles, Stephen L. Richards and LeGrande Richards and great-grandmother to other apostles.

Nanny passed away on Janury 7, 1911 in Salt Lake City, Utah. She was one of the greatest pioneer women.

PERSIS GOODALL YOUNG RICHARDS

BIRTHDATE: 15 Mar 1806
Watertown, Jefferson, New York
DEATHl 16 Sep 1894
Salt Lake City, Salt Lake, Utah
PARENTS: Joel Goodall
Mary Swain
PIONEER: 13 Oct 1850
Edward Hunter Co. Wagon Train
SPOUSE I: Lorenzo Dow Young
MARRIED: 6 Jun 1826
Watertown, Jefferson, New York
DEATH SP: 21 Nov 1895
Salt Lake City, Salt Lake, Utah

CHILDREN:
William Goodall, 21 Feb 1827
Joseph Watson, 12 Jan 1829
Lucy Ann, 27 Nov 1832 (died at age 4)
Harriet Maria, 21 Jul 1834
John Royal, 30 Apr 1837
Franklin Wheeler, 14 Feb 1839
Lorenzo Zabriski, 2 Mar 1841
Lucius James, 12 Jul 1843 (twin - died at age 1)
Lucia Jane, 12 Jul 1843 (twin - died at age 1)
Brigham Willard, Sep 1844
Frances Elizabeth, 27 Jun 1845 (died as an infant)

SPOUSE II: Levi Richards
MARRIED: 27 Jan 1848
Nauvoo, Hancock Co., Illinois
DEATH SP: 18 Jun 1876
Salt Lake City, Salt Lake Co., Utah
CHILDREN: None

Persis was raised according to the standards of Quakers. She acquired a good education and was always anxious to learn. She married Lorenzo Dow Young when she was twenty years old.

They were converted to the Church of Jesus Christ of Latter-day Saints after the birth of their son. Upon conversion her parents disowned her. They were with the Saints through the good times and the bad times of Kirtland, Ohio, Missouri, and Illinois.

In the Spring of 1832, her husband was called on a mission to his native state of New York. Upon his return, he and his brother bought a family boat and with their families, they floated down the Ohio River to join the Saints in Missouri. They stopped along the way, due to Persis' illness and each time they waited for her to recover, they found people who were anxious to learn of the Gospel. They arrived in Kirtland in March of 1833.

Due to persecution of angry mobs, their family was compelled to move again and again. Lorenzo took a plural wife and traveled with her and some of his children in the first company to come across the Plains.

Persis always resented that she was left behind in Winter Quarters and never became a part of Lorenzo's family in Utah.

Persis attended Hebrew School under conditions of poverty and hardships with a family of little ones to care for, to attend classes, and prepare lessons. It was no small task. Her teacher told her she was the best student in the class because she was always prepared.

On January 27, 1848, Persis became the plural wife of Levi Richards. This plural relation proved to be an unusual blessing. There was a unity of no ordinary quality prevailing there.

RHODA RICHARDS

BIRTHDATE: 8 Aug 1784
Framingham, Massachusetts
DEATH: 17 Jan 1879
Salt Lake City, Salt Lake, Utah
PARENTS: Joseph Richards
Rboda Howe
PIONEER: 19 Oct 1848
Willard Richards Wagon Train

Rhoda was a bright, sensible, beautiful, young girl. Rhoda suffered a great deal with sickness during her young life. She spent much of her life mothering other people's children, particularly those of her kindred.

She had been engaged to a young man who died very soon before they were to have been married.

Rhoda's cousins Brigham and Joseph Young, came to the family home in Richmond, Massachusetts and earnestly preached the Gospel of the Church of Jesus Christ of Latter-day Saints to them. Four of the Richards family were baptized as members of the Church and then moved to Kirtland, then later to Nauvoo, Illinois.

The Richards family left Nauvoo with the other Saints in 1846 and lived at Winter Quarters until 1848. When her brother, Willard, returned from his first journey across the Plains, he took Rhoda back to Utah with him.

After their arrival in Salt Lake Valley, Levi Richards was called on a mission to Europe. His wife went with him. They left their son, Levi, Jr., in Rhoda's charge for five years. Rhoda also cared for the two children of her brother, Willard.

The first year after they arrived in the Salt Lake Valley, they lived in a wagon box. In later years they lived with her brothers and always helped with the utmost tenderness in rearing their children and with the many other tasks of the busy mothers.

She lived for some time in the Lion House at the time her cousin, Brigham Young, lived there. Later, she had a little home of her own built by her brother, Willard.

Rhoda lived to be ninety-four years old. She was ever cheerful, busy with her weaving, spinning, and knitting. She was ardent in her religious beliefs and welcome everywhere because of her winning sweetness.

SARAH GRIFFITH RICHARDS

BIRTHDATE: 26 Dec 1802
Monmouth, Monmouth, England
DEATH: 7 Jun 1892
Salt Lake City, Salt Lake, Utith
PARENTS: David Griffith, Jr.
Mary Steed
PIONEER: Fall 1853
SPOUSE: Levi Richards
MARRIED: 25 Dec 1843
Nauvoo, Hancock Co., Illinois
DEATH SP: 18 Jun 1876
Salt Lake City, Salt Lake, Utah

CHILD:
Levi Richards, 12 Jun 1843

Sarah was born in the old monastery where her mother's people had lived for many years. The Steeds were Catholic priests in a time when England had been Protestant. Catholics were very looked down upon and persecuted.

Her father was a shoemaker and had served in the British Army, but was not established well enough to make a good living. They were invited to live with Mary's parents in the monastery. Her father died when she was three years old, so they remained at the monastery until her grandfather made other arrangements with his brother, Thomas, to care for them and to help with their educational expenses.

After fifteen years of widowhood, her mother remarried to John Evans who was a baker and confectioner of Hereford. The family moved to London for two years. Sarah went into service with a family who took her to the Continent where she had the opportunity to study history, geography, needlework, penmanship, art, and music. The harp and guitar were her favorite instuments.

Five years later, at age twenty-four, she qualified to be a governess. She became the governess of Norman Hill for her Uncle Thomas and later a governess for the family of Mr. Greenall who lived in Liverpool.

At this time, her mother and stepfather were investigating the Church of Jesus Christ of Latter-day Saints. Sarah was also interested and became baptized.

She became aquainted with Levi Richards who was serving a mission and helping to arrange passage for saints to emigrate to Nauvoo, Illinois. Levi encouraged her to emigrate to America. When Levi returned to Nauvoo after his mission, an attachment grew between them and they were married by Brigham Young in Nauvoo on Christmas Day, 1843. They were blessed with one son, Levi Willard.

Sarah, her husband, and their frail son who was not yet a year old, were driven with the rest of the Saints from Naucoo in Febraury 1846. They made their way to Council Bluffs, Nebraska. They remained there for two years and as they were preparing to go West, Brigham Young called them to go to England on a mission as a couple. He told them that their son would not live if they took him with them and suggested they let him go west with the Richards family under the care of Levi's sister, Rhoda Richards.

They served on this mission for five years. In 1853, they returned to the United States on the ship "Cambria." They landed in East Boston on May 18, visited with relatives in Massachusetts, and then came to the Salt Lake Valley in the fall of 1853. Their son, Levi, hardly knew the parents he had not seen for five years. They settled in the area of Salt Lake City where Richard's Street now runs.

Levi passed away in 1876 at his home, and Sarah lived until June 7, 1892.

SUSAN SANFORD PEIRSON RICHARDS

BIRTHDATE: 13 Dec 1831
Richmond, Massachusetts
DEATH: 2 Mar 1878
PARENTS: William Peirson
Nancy Richards
PIONEER: 15 Jul 1852
Franklin Richads Wagon Train
SPOUSE: Franklin D. Richards
MARRIED: 26 Jun 1853
Salt Lake City, Salt Lake, Utah
DEATH SP: 9 Dec 1899

CHILDREN:
Nancy Eliza, 1 Dec 1857
Albert Damon, 30 Apr 1860
William Peirson, 18 May 1864

Susan born in Richmond, Massachusetts. She was the youngest of six children; two sisters and three brothers. Their home was humble with hard working parents and a large and good farm. Her mother was an apt housekeeper and taught Susan the value of work, thrift and courage. She learned to knit, sew, and do other good work. She helped her mother keep up their house and prudently cared for the produce on their farm. Her mother had cancer and Susan was a great help to her. They were very close.

Susan learned of the true Gospel of Jesus Christ from her mother's cousin, Brigham Young. She was baptized a member of the Church of Jesus Christ of Latter-day Saints on April 19, 1840. There was contention in their home as her father and brothers did not embrace the Gospel. Her father was one of the "selectmen" of Richmond, active in civic as well as other religious affiliations. Her two sisters left on February 1, 1841 to join the Saints. Susan stayed with her mother and helped with the physical work.

During her teen age years, she attended school, learning to read, write, spell and to do mathematics. She became a beautiful penman. Susan was only five feet tall, weighed 110 pounds, was of average build and had dark hair and blue eyes.

In the Spring of 1852, Susan and her mother left their home and started to Zion with her cousin Franklin D. Richards. He was returning from the Europe Mission of the Church. Her mother passed away and was buried near the Platte River in either Wyoming or Nebraska near the Liberty Pole. Her mother's death was a great sorrow to Susan. She continued on to Utah with the Franklin D. Richards Company. Her faith never faltered. She relied on her cousin for comfort, guidance and support. They arrived in the Salt Lake Valley on July 15, 1852.

Susan lived with her sister, Amelia. She presented her Uncle Willard Richards with a quart of apple seeds she and her mother had saved when drying apples at home in Richmond. From these seeds many apple trees grew in Utah.

Susan received her Temple Endowment on November 6, 1852. Her fondness for Franklin Richards increased, and she was married and sealed to him on June 26, 1853. He was in the mission field much of the time. Susan was a quiet person who did not make any fuss.

Even though her husband was not home much, his timely advice and counsel was heeded, and his family felt his spirit and love for them. Susan and Franklin became the parents of three children; two sons and one daughter.

Susan went to Hoytsville, Wanship Valley, to live with one of Franklin's other wives. The Indians caused problems so they gathered in groups for protection. This resulted in them moving to Wanship to be near neighbors.

Susan spent the remainder of her life in Wanship. Susan and her children benefited from her father's estate when he died.

Susan was a calm, quiet and courageous mother and wife. She was educated and taught her children. She did beautiful knitting and sewing. She made temple aprons to sell. She was president of the Relief Society in Wanship; also the Secretary. She taught her children well in the knowledge of the Gospel.

During her life she experienced many trials. At age forty-seven she contracted pneumonia and passed away on March 2, 1878 in Wanship, Summit County, Utah.

WEALTHY DEWEY RICHARDS

BIRTHDATE: 6 Sep 1786
Pittsfield, Massachusetts
DEATH: 18 Oct 1853
Salt Lake City, Salt Lake, Utah
PARENTS: Samuel Dewey, III
Milley McKee
PIONEER: 19 Oct 1848
Willard Richards Wagon Train
SPOUSE: Phineas Richards
MARRIED: 24 Feb 1818
Richmond, Massachusetts
DEATH SP: 25 Nov 1874
Salt Lake City, Salt Lake,Utah

CHILDREN:
Abraham, 9 Dec 1819 (died at birth)
Moses, 7 Sep 1819 (died at birth)
Betsey, 13 Jun 1820 (died at birth)
Franklin Dewey, 2 Apr 1821
George Spencer, 8 Jan 1823 (died at age 15)
Samuel Whitney, 9 Aug 1824
Maria Wealthy, 17 Jun 1827
Joseph William, 25 May 1829 (died at age 17)
Henry Phineas, 30 Nov 1831

Wealthy was born in Pittsfield, Berkshire County, Massachusetts, 1786. Wealthy's parents were descendents of prominent families in the settlements of Connecticut and other New England states. Her parents were devout members of the Congregational Church.

She had always lived in a home of refinement and had been well educated with a love of learning. She was quite intelligent and was called "a dictionary."

Wealthy became the wife of Phineas. She was skilled in sewing, cooking, and other arts of homemaking necessary to young women at that day. Their first three children died in infancy.

Her husband became a convert to the Church of Jesus Christ of Latter-day Saints by his cousin, Brigham Young. Her son, George Spencer, was killed at the Haun's Mill Massacre on Shoal Creek, Missouri.

Shortly afterward, her sons, Franklin and Samuel left home to serve as missionaries. After Phineas returned home from serving his third mission, Wealthy finally accepted the gospel and became a member.

Her family followed the church to Nauvoo, Illinois where they lived for two and one half years. They made a fine home and worked to complete the temple. Wealthy and her daughters braided straw and fashioned it into hats and bonnets. They were able to supplement the family income in this manner.

They were driven from Nauvoo and forced to live in a tent across the Mississippi River for a year of misery and hardship. Seeking a peaceful home, they began the trek to Salt Lake Valley in July, 1848, with the Willard Richards Wagon Company. Her son, Joseph joined the Mormon Battalion as a drummer, became ill, and died at Pueblo, Colorado.

Wealthy's health had weakened during her stay at Winter Quarters. She had been forced to spend the first year living in a tent in the bitter cold, with a poor diet. She also suffered emotionally at the loss of her two young sons for the gospel's sake.

When Phineas traveled to help colonize the Sanpete Valley in Utah County, she remained at home in Salt Lake City. Five years after arriving in the Salt Lake Valley, she passed away on October 18, 1853.

ANGELINE KING RICHARDSON

BIRTHDATE: 25 Nov 1813
Greenwich, Stueben, New York
DEATH: 10 Apr 1880
Ogden, Weber Co., Utah
PARENTS: Ebenezer N. King
Elizabeth "Betsy" Jacocks
PIONEER: 1850
Willie Brown Co. Wagon Train
SPOUSE: Ebenezer Richardson
MARRIED: 1833
DEATH SP: 27 Sep 1874

CHILDREN:
Mary Amanda, 24 Aug 1834
Albert Ebenezer, 2 May 1837
George Allen, 24 Dec 1839
Eliza, 17 Mar 1843
Josiah, 16 Apr 1844
Alma, 19 Jan 1845
Lois, 1846 (died as a child)
Jane, 1848 (died as an infant)
Emmaline Lafanny, 1 Sep 1850
Sylvester, 14 Feb 1852
Alonzo, abt 1854 (died as an infant)
John, abt 1856 (died as an infant)

Angeline was born in 1813 in New York. She and her family arrived in Salt Lake with the Willie Brown Company in about October, 1850. Angeline was baptized a member of the Church of Jesus Christ of Latter-day Saints in 1834, by the Prophet Joseph Smith. Her brother, Sam King, gave her a team and wagon to help her follow the Saints. She then began with her family, a long trip to Zion which ended sixteen years later with their Utah arrival. She did not see any of her parents or Family again.

A granddaughter said of her "I could write a book of the fine, kind, courageous life she lived. It would take a strong testimony of the Gospel to go through the trials she did. She had many trials to endure. It was she who lead the way for us, to happiness. She had strength and wisdom to work very hard, moving with the Saints, driven with a family of young children. Their problems were many and their faith in God helped them finish, leaving fine examples for us to follow."

Angeline was the first of four wives of Ebenezer Richardson. She gave birth to twelve children, four of whom died as children. She had six children with her when crossing the Plains. Two little daughters were laid to rest at Winter Quarters. Leaving two silent graves was a diffcult task. After arriving in the Salt Lake Valley, Angeline gave birth to four more children.

Her husband was called to serve as mission president in South Africa in 1857, leaving her with most of the responsibilities. She arose to the call to be head of the home during his absence and did a wonderful job.

Angeline loved her family and was a good manager. Her last thirteen years were spent living with her son, Josiah and daughter-in-law Sarah. Never a cross word was ever spoken between these two great ladies.

Both she and her husband never wavered from the truths they embraced when becoming baptized into the Church in 1834. They followed the prophet through all the trials in New York, Ohio, Missouri, and Illinois. And, of course, eventually they ended up in the Great Salt Lake Valley in Utah.

Her posterity owe much to this great elect lady who passed away on April 10, 1880 in Ogden, Weber County, Utah at the age of sixty-six years.

LAVINA STEWART RICHARDSON

No Photo Available

BIRTHDATE: 8 Jun 1824
Jackson Township, Ohio
DEATH: 1 Dec 1852
Payson, Utah Co., Utah
PARENTS: Philander B. Stewart
Sarah Scott
PIONEER: fall 1852
T. Tryon Prairie Schooner Comp.
SPOUSE: Shadrach Richardson
MARRIED: 1839
DEATH SP: 18 Jun 1892
Benjamin, Utah Co., Utah

CHILDREN:
Adelaine, abt 1842 (died as a child - after 1850)

Emerson, 9 Jun 1843 (died at age 7)
John, abt 1844 (died at age 4)
Olive, abt 1846 (died at age 1)
Shadrach Montgomery, 11 Mar 1848
Marcus, Dec 1849 (died at age 1)
William Wilshire, 2 Nov 1851
John, 1 Dec 1852 (stillborn)

Lavina was born in 1824 in Ohio, the twelfth child born into that family of eight daughters and four sons. Their first four children had died in their teens or early twenty's, before Lavina was born. Her faithful mother and her family had migrated west.

Lavina spent her youth in Ohio, where she married Shadrach Richardson in 1839, at fifteen years of age. They settled in Keg Creek, Iowa. She gave birth to seven children, five of whom died in infancy or early childhood. Just two of these children survived, and Shadrach was four years of age, and William just two years of age when their mother died in childbirth on December 1, 1852.

The Stewart and Richardson families had become acquainted as they migrated from Kentucky to Illinois to Iowa. A Stewart son had married a Richardson daughter and a Richardson son married Lavina Stewart, brothers and sisters from the same families.

Shadrach and Lavina started West after news of the California gold rush reached Iowa. Taking what belongings they could carry in a covered wagon, along with their two little boys, they traveled west with the Truman Tryon Company and arrived in Utah in the fall of 1852.

Weary and foot-sore, hoping to go to California to strike it rich, they arrived in Payson, Utah to visit their sister and brother there. The trials and hardships of the arduous journey proved too much for Lavina. She passed away on December 1, 1852, as did her seventh child who was born and died that same day. He had been named John.

Shadrach, alone, had the care of his two and four year old sons. The mercy and kindnesses of their dear relatives and the good people of Payson helped Shadrach survive. His desire to continue to California vanished, and he stayed in Utah with his family members Polly and Benjamin, who were wonderful helpers and support for him.

Lavina was baptized into the Church of Jesus Christ of Latter-day Saints in 1844. Shadrach joined the Church in 1855 and remained an active member the remainder of his life. Lavina had been a fine example of hard work, endurance, patience, industry and helpfulness; all qualities learned in the large family in which she was raised. She did not have the opportunity to rear her two sons, but her influence was felt in their lives. Their father remarried a widow in 1860 and she passed away in 1868 leaving him a widower once more with four additional children to care for.

Lavina's love of God and her great faith in Him was an outstanding influence in her family. She truly qualifies as "A Woman of Faith and Fortitude among Utah Pioneers."

MARY ANN DARROW RICHARDSON COX RICHARDSON

BIRTHDATE: 28 Feb 1818
Hebron, Washington, New York
DEATH: 13 Jan 1872
Springville, Utah Co., Utah
PARENTS: Stephen Darrow
Harriet Burbank
PIONEER: 3 Aug 1853
Wagon Train Company
SPOUSE I: Edmund Richardson
MARRIED: 2 Aug 1840
Salem, New York
DEATH SP: 27 Mar 1874
Juab Co., Utah

CHILDREN:
Emma Lynette, 31 Oct 1341
George Alvin, 4 Sep 1846

SPOUSE II: Frederick Walter Cox
MARRIED: 9 Jan 1858
Manti, Sanpete Co., Utah
DEATH SP: Not given

CHILDREN:
Charles Edmund, 13 Oct 1858
Sullivan Calvin, 26 Jan 1861

SPOUSE III: Edmund Richardson
MARRIED: Not given
DEATH SP: Not given
CHILDREN: None

Mary Ann was born in Hebron, Washington County, New York in 1818. During her teen years she worked in a cloth factory and learned the weaving trade which she later taught to others.

When twenty-two years old she married Edmund Richardson. After five years, they decided to join a group of Presbyterians who were going to Oregon. She wove a wagon cover for their wagon. They arrived in St. Joseph where they waited six weeks for other family members to join them. There were eleven wagons in their company. They walked much of the way and the trek took about three months.

As they traveled West, wagons broke down and oxen died. This made them feel they would not be able to reach Oregon. They felt the solution for them was to travel from Sublett's Cutoff, and go the 160 miles across the perilous desert facing Indians and the terrible Mormon dangers. Theirs was a three week trip to Salt Lake City.

They settled on the west bank of the Jordan River, they hoped far enough away from the city to be safe from the Mormons, yet near enough to afford protection from the Indians. They knew nothing of the Mormons except the vile things they had heard from Mormon haters.

Before their supper was ready, a barefoot boy forded the shallow river on a pony, dismounted at their camp, and graciously offered a pail of fresh milk. His mother had seen their campfire and thought fresh milk might be refreshing to the weary travelers.

The family obtained work in the mills near-by to sustain themselves. Through association with Mormon neighbors, accepting dinner with them, they quickly decided this was the truth and were baptized on October 3, 1853. They later received a call from Brigham Young to go to Manti to aid the struggling pioneers there.

Mary Ann's home was on the outskirts of town. One day an Indian, painted, came to her door insolently demanding food. She had just taken some biscuits from the oven and placed them on the hearth. She gave him some, but he demanded more. She refused, he went to snatch some more, but Mary Ann stopped him as he raised a long handled knife to strike her, she raised a fire shovel, and when he met her blazing eyes he left. A neighbor who had seen this, fainted, but Mary Ann went on about her work.

President Young visited their area and talked about having large families, saying that as many children as possible should be born to give more spirits their bodies. Without looking at her husband, Mary Ann knew that his head was bowed. He knew, by the pressure of her hand upon his, that she loved him despite their eight childless years following the births of their two children. They spoke to him about having their two children sealed to them, and he said their other children will be born under the covenant. Deep feelings surfaced in Edmund's thoughts. Earlier, he had followed the teachings of his earlier religion and had become a eunuch; more children was an impossibility.

President Young advised them to have a civil divorce and have Mary Ann married into polygamy so she could have more children who would become Edmund's because of their eternal sealing. What a difficult decision this was as these two deeply loved each other. Through prayer, and a revelation to them it was right, they did comply. From a list of five men, Mary Ann selected one, Fredrick Walter Cox. They proceded this way and she had two additional children born to her and Mr. Cox.

President Young recognized the good people these were and said to them "Brother and Sister Richardson, the teachings and work of the devil have taken away your posterity, but the teachings and authority of Christ can restore it, if you are willing to make a great sacrifice for it."

Because any children from this marriage were to be raised for Edmund Richardson, and also for protection for Brother Cox during the polygamist persecutions, Mary Ann retained her Richardson name and lived in the Richardson home. Edmund voluntarily moved out, went to work in the Tintic mines, and sent regular checks or alimony to support his family, and Mary Ann continued her weaving.

As Mary Ann watched Edmund drive away into the loneliness of the next few years, she whispered these words after him "Greater love hath no man than this: that he giveth his life for another."

She taught her children well. Her son, Charles Edmund, became a lawyer and later on he was a lawyer for the Saints in Mexico. Mary Ann's best teaching was her example. She always tried to build fine attitudes and good conduct in her children.

Near Mary Ann's end of her life, she fervently prayed that she might live until her children could take care of themselves. She often said she "expected another call soon." She was excited about doing temple work. Arrangements were made to go to the Endowment House to accomplish this request. She worried that Charles Edmund was too young to help her with this work. She asked if a boy of twelve years of age was too young to have his own endowments so he could help in the endowments. Daniel H. Wells then in charge, asked him many questions about his beliefs in the Gospel. Elder Wells gave his consent after hearing his faithful responses. This made it possible to do the temple work, which made Mary Ann extremely happy. She then remarked when the work was done, that she was not going to stay much longer, though she seemed to be in good health. Soon after this, she was stricken with pneumonia and passed away on january 13, 1872 in Springville, Utah about sixty-four years of age.

Mary Ann Richardson had been a faithful Latter-day Saint. She was one who had given up much when the spirit testified of the rightness of her extreme situation.

She was indeed a faithful pioneer woman who set an example in all she did.

MERAB STONE RICHARDSON

BIRTHDATE: 26 Sep 1845
New Haven, Connecticut
DEATH: 4 Feb 1913
Inkom, Bannock Co., Idaho
PARENTS: Amos Pease Stone
Amelia Bishop
PIONEER: 30 Sep 1850
Capt. Thomas Rich Wagon Train
SPOUSE: Thomas Richardson
MARRIED: 1864
Salt Lake Endowment House
DEATH SP: 17 Dec 1924
Pocatello, Idaho

CHILDREN:
Mary Amelia, 5 Oct 1865 (died as a child)
Thomas Ives, 30 Nov 1866
Amos, 13 Aug 1869 (died as a child)
James Albert, 15 Sep 1870 (died as a child)
John, 20 Feb 1873
George, 14 Oct 1875 (died as a child)
Merab Vilette (Morgan), 17 Oct 1876
Emily (Dille), 2 Apr 1879
Clara Minerva (Sorensen), 6 Aug 1881
Nathan, 9 Jun 1883 (died as a child)
Robert Howard, 17 Jun 1884
Anna, 14 May 1887 (died as a child)

Merab was born in 1845 in the state of Connecticut, the fourth child born into the family. Her mother died in December, 1845, leaving her father with the four young children. They had joined the Church of Jesus Christ of Latter-day Saints in December, 1844, in Connecticut.

They were making arrangements to leave for the West when her mother died. Amos married again in February, 1846, and left for the West in March leaving baby Merab with her Aunt Merab Bradley. Amos reached Council Bluff on June 15, where he bought several acres of land and built two cabin by 1847. In April, 1848, he left on a mission to the eastern states. When he returned in the fall, he brought his daughter, Merab with him.

This family left in June, 1850, for the 'Valley of the Mountains," with two wagons, three yoke of oxen and one yoke of cows. They arrived at the Platte River on June 4th, where their wagon company of fifty wagons was divided into three companies. Thomas Rich was the Captain of their group and they arrived in the Great Salt Lake Valley on September 30, 1850. Five days later they settled in Sessionville (later named Bountiful) ten miles north of Salt Lake. In 1857, they moved to Ogden where they made a permanent home.

Merab had the advantage of a liberal education because her father hired private teachers if a school wasn't available. She had an astute mind and a natural flair for nursing and in this she was very generous with her time and talents and her neighbors benefitted from her training and experience.

While she was living with the Davis Bartholomew family (her aunt and uncle), she met and married Thomas Richardson. He was twenty and she nineteen years of age. They were married in the Endowment House in 1864 and had a wedding reception in the ward meeting house.

Merab was a woman of great faith and fortitude. At one time her three month old baby daughter was pronounced dead from a severe attack of whooping cough. Merab picked up her child and ran to the field where her father-in-law was irrigating. He saw her coming, raised his right hand and began walking toward her praying as he went. When he reached her, the baby was breathing again. Returning to the house, the doctor said, "I told her the child was dead." Her father-in-law, Thomas Richardson replied, "This child will live to be a mother in Zion." She grew to womanhood, married and had seven children.

They lived in several towns in the northern part of Utah. While living in Corinne, an elderly Indian came to their home very ill with blood poisoning in one leg and burning up with fever. His leg was inflamed and enormously swollen. They prepared a cot for the Indian with clean covering, they gave him a bath, put on clean clothes, and cleansed the abcess with carbolic acid and sterile water. The Indian directed them to gather a lot of leaves from the squaw bush, and some berries and limbs and boil them. This was used as a poultice and the abcess finally cleared up after several days. Months later, the Indian returned with an old rag in which were some nuggets of gold which he gave to Merab in gratitude for her saving his life. She exchanged these for flour which lasted them for most of the year.

Merab's husband served a mission to the Indians on the Malad River in Idaho and Box Elder County of Utah in 1877-1879. He learned several Indian languages and became friends with them. The family moved to Blue Creek and kept a general merchandise store. Indians brought goods to them, which they sold to secure items to restock their store.

Thomas moved his family to Pocatello Junction in 1882 where he built a house on the land the railroad company had acquired from the Indians. With the help of a young Indian girl and a Chinese cook, Merab provided meals for some of the construction men.

Merab's daughter said of her, "I sincerely believe that, without a doubt, my mother was the most refined and gracious woman I ever knew. Her life was filled with kindness and deeds of charity. . . She was handicapped physically, having been dropped from a table when a small infant, and the vertebrae at the lower end of her spine was injured. Her neck, shoulders and back were very straight, but because of the injury, it was thought she would never be able to give birth to a living child. However, she had twelve children, six of whom grew to maturity."

Merab passed away on February 4, 1913 at Inkom, Bannock County, Idaho at the age of seventy-six years. She was a true pioneer who experienced much in her lifetime of the hardships of crossing the Plains, of meager rations, of hard work and endurance beyond expectations. She is honored by her posterity who have learned from her life, and joy in their relationship.

Her husband, Thomas passed away on December 22, 1924 also in Inkom, Idaho.

SARAH ANN KNIGHT RICHARDSON

BIRTHDATE: 15 Aug 1846
Pottawattamie Co., Iowa
DEATH: 16 Feb 1926
Plain City, Weber Co., Utah
PARENTS: John Knight
Millie Watson
PIONEER: 1852 Wagon Train
SPOUSE: Josiah Richardson
MARRIED: 22 Dec 1862
Plain City, Weber Co., Utah
DEATH SP: 13 Apr 1933
Plain City, Weber Co., Utah

CHILDREN:
Josiah Albert, 2 Sep 1863
Sarah Millie, 22 Mar 1865
George, 19 Nov 1867
Edgar William, Mar 1869
Louise Angeline, (chr.) 1 Apr 1870
John James, 3 Mar 1871 (died as a child)

Mary Bell, 22 Sep 1874 (died as a child)
Ada Emiline, 16 Aug 1876 (died as a child)
Ida Ellen, 16 Aug 1876 (died as a child)
Wallace Howard, 27 Nov 1878
Alberdine, 27 Mar 1880
Esther Ann, 22 Feb 1882
Ruth Catherine, 7 Oct 1883
Ebenezer, 8 Sep 1885
Lola Evelyn, 5 Oct 1887
Oscar G., 20 May 1890

Sarah Ann was born in 1846 in Pottawattamie County, Iowa. She came to Utah with her family by ox-team in 1852 when she was around six years of age. She attended school at Slaterville and spent her vacations spinning wool.

She married Josiah Richardson in Plain City, Utah on December 22, 1862, at the age of sixteen. They were later sealed in the Salt Lake Endowment House. She gave birth to sixteen children and then raised three of Josiah's second wife's children upon her death.

At age sixty, Sarah took a grandchild and raised her from the age of three weeks old until she married. Sarah was loyal to her husband, was faithful in her testimony, and gave great service to the Church.

Sarah was Relief Society President for twenty years at Malad, Ammon, Tilden, and Cove, Oregon. She always took her children to church, taught a class, raised them with, prayer in their home. She knew much sorrow in her lifetime, burying nine of the twenty children she raised before her death.

While serving as Relief Society President, she was called by the Church to take a nursing course. This she did in Idaho Falls. She served well in this capacity and was loved by all.

Her health broke, and the time came that she could no longer see, read or serve as she was used to doing. She asked for the Lord to take her home, and so this happened on February 16, 1926 when she was over seventy-nine years of age. She was buried in Plain City with six of her children by her side.

Sarah Ann was indeed, a faithful pioneer woman who contributed much to her family, her Church, and to the communities in which she resided. Her posterity honor her for the great example she was for all.

SARAH JANE HONE RICHARDSON

BIRTHDATE: 10 Aug 1861
Coventry, England
DEATH: 10 Apr 1928
Benjamin, Utah Co., Utah
PARENTS: David Hone
Sarah Adams
PIONEER: 23 Sep 1862
Omer Duncan Co. Wagon Train
SPOUSE: William Richardson
MARRIED: 16 Oct 1879
Springville, Utah Co., Utah
DEATH SP: 9 Jun 1929
Benjamin, Utah Co., Utah

CHILDREN:
William Wilshire, 26 Jul 1880
Sarah Elizabeth (Burgin), 21 Apr 1882
George Arthur , 29 May 1884 (died as a child)
Lavina (Hicks), 8 Oct 1885 (twin)
Rosina (Huber), 8 Oct 1885 (twin)
Ada (Wootton), 25 Feb 1888
Albert, 17 Oct 1890
Acel, 12 Jan 1893
Shadrach, 20 Mar 1895 (stillborn)
Milo, 6 Apr 1896
Marcellus, 3 Dec 1899 (stillborn)
Ezra David, 7 Dec 1902

Sarah Jane was born in Coventry, Warwickshire, England, in 1861. She was the first child born to them in England.

Sarah Jane was baptized into the Church of Jesus Christ of Latter-day Saints on August 30, 1884. Her parents had been baptized in 1857, and this family came to America aboard the boat "John J. Boyd," taking forty-four days for the journey.

From New York they crossed the Plains of America, and joined the Omer Duncan Wagon Company arriving in the Salt Lake Valley on September 23, 1862 when Sarah Jane was just one year of age. While crossing the Plains along the north side of the Platte River, an incident occurred which nearly destroyed part of the family. The mother, Sarah, was resting under the wagon to escape the intense noon day heat. The wagon train 'suddenly took fright.' Mr. Hone's quick action and foresight saved Sarah as he pulled her from beneath the wagon, badly lacerating his arm from his shoulder to his elbow. His wife and child were saved by his heroic action.

Upon their arrival in Utah, they moved south to Utah valley. They made their home first in Provo. They lived there during the Indian wars. Her father could not fight in the wars, but he helped those who did by caring for their families and farms at home, sacrificing everything they possessed for others. Sarah Jane grew up in these trying circumstances. There were five brothers born into this family in Utah. Sarah Jane spent her early life helping her mother with the chores of the home and farm.

Sarah Jane married William Wilshire Richardson on October 16, 1879 in Springville, Utah. Their marriage was later solemnized in the Logan Temple where they journeyed by ox-team in 1885 since she was baptized in 1884. This was a tiresome journey, but they wanted to show total commitment to the faith they had joined. Sarah Jane gave birth to twelve children. Two sons were stillborn, and one died at nearly five years of age.

Sarah Jane lived most of her life on the farm in Provo or Benjamin where all of her children were born. She died and is buried in Benjamin, Utah County, Utah.

Her husband died in 1929 in Benjamin, surviving his wife just over one year. They are buried in the Benjamin Cemetery.

Being the mother of nine living children took courage and fortitude. Three of their children went on missions for the Church; William Jr. went to the Central States, Sarah Elizabeth went to the Northwestern States, and Ezra went to the Australian Mission. So many posterity have been influenced by this stalwart pioneer woman.

VIOLET ELLEN KNIGHT RICHARDSON

BIRTHDATE: 9 Apr 1850
Council Bluffs, Iowa
DEATH: 15 Mar 1931
Ogden, Weber Co., Utah
PARENTS: John Knight, Jr.
Mary Millie Watson
PIONEER: 9 Oct 1852
Independent Co. Wagon Train
SPOUSE: William A.Richardson
MARRIED: Jan 1867
Salt Lake City, Salt Lake, Utah
DEATH SP: 26 May 1923
Ogden, Weber Co., Utah

CHILDREN:
William Alma, 14 May 1868
Millie May (Dudley), 7 Jul 1870
John, 4 May 1874
Josiah , abt 1875 (died as a child)
Charles, 26 Aug 1876
Ada Francis (Cowan), 8 Jun 1881
Walter, 29 Oct 1884
Eva Angelina (Fairweather), 14 Mar 1887
Wallace, 6 Sep 1889
Opal, 12 Apr 1893

Violet Ellen was born in Council Bluffs, Iowa, in 1850. When just two years old, she and her family crossed the Plains. Violet's father owned their own wagons and outfit. After resting a few days from the long and ardous journey to the Salt Lake Valley, the family moved north into Weber County and settled at Brigham's Fort, known today as Five Points. In 1853, they moved a few miles west to the new community of Slaterville, where they engaged in farming.

Violet, at the age of seventeen, fell in love and married a very handsome farmer by the name of William Alma Richardson. They, too, settled in Slaterville and followed the occupation of farming. Violet was a true and faithful wife and mother and shared loyally with her husband in all their trials and activities subsequent to the settling of the western country.

The year her tenth child was born, Violet also became a grandmother. Just before her fifth had been born, her little son Josiah, just two years old, was playing on a porch they were building and a board fell on him killing him instantly. She grieved greatly over the loss of her little boy for years.

Violet was interested in astronomy and loved to look into the sky and learn about the stars, their formation and what they meant, and the beautiful moonlit night was her greatest fascination.

She was an exceptionally good cook. Biscuits graced her table at least at one meal each day and sometimes more. Her black currant jam was an envy of the community. Fresh baked bread and jugs of milk were always the evening meal. She was very thrifty. Money seemed to mean nothing to her and she once made the remark that money could do as much harm as good. All she needed was the necessities of life-her luxuries were her family.

During World War I her son, Wallace, was assigned to go to France. When stationed in California, she went to see him off. In 1911, a granddaughter took her to visit another son in Portland. These were the only trips she ever took away from home.

Violet was ambitious and had wonderful health and always said she wanted to live to be eighty years old, and she passed away on March 15, 1931 just before her eighty-first birthday.

She was a faithful pioneer woman of great fortitude, an example to all.

MARY SUFLING RICHES

BIRTHDATE: 3 Nov 1813
East Ruston, Norfolk, England
DEATH: 12 Apr 1888
Salt Lake City, Salt Lake, Utah
PARENTS: Mathew Sufling
Martha Robison
PIONEER: 15 Sep 1861
Ira Eldredge Co. Wagon Train
SPOUSE: John Riches
MARRIED: 1839
DEATH SP: 3 Jul 1884
Salt Lake City, Salt Lake, Utah

CHILDREN:
Hannah, 21 Dec 1841
Isaac, 4 Sep 1844
John, 19 Oct 1849

Mary was a bible scholar. She read the book well, yet lacked the confidence to write. After she married John Riches, they moved to Brumstead Hall, a parish three miles from her birthplace.

They farmed here and came in contact with some missionaries from the Church of Jesus Christ of Latter-day Saints. They were converted and baptized members.

In 1861 they sold their belongings and sailed on the ship, "Manchester." They arrived in Castle Gardens and were transferred to the train cars on which they traveled until they reached St. Joseph. They joined the Ira Eldredge Company to make the journey across the Plains. They arrived in the Salt Lake Valley on September 15, 1861. Mary and her husband were employed by A. O. Smoot and moved to his dwelling on South Temple. They built their own log cabin and continued working for Smoot for four years.

In 1869, they moved to five acres of land on the State Road just below the present 17th South. By the end of the year, they were able to buy three five acre plots of ground. They worked very hard taming the land.

Mary's husband passed away in 1884 and the sons carried the burden of the farm labors. Mary was well known in the area as a good cook and was in demand at the farmers' houses at harvest time to cook for the men who worked on the farm. She was thrifty and provident.

Mary passed away on April 12, 1888 in Salt Lake City.

LOUISA SHILL RICHINS

BIRTHDATE: 22 Jun 1829
Syde, Gloucester, England
DEATH: 28 Apr 1993
Mesa, Maricopa, Arizona
PARENTS: Robert C. Shill
Prudence Golding
PIONEER: fall 1854
SPOUSE: Charles Wager Richins
MARRIED: 27 Jan 1851
DEATH SP: 27 Aug 1903
Colonia Diaz, Mexico

CHILDREN:
Hannah Louisa, 9 Sep 1852
Charles Robert, 25 Mar 1856
Wellington, 18 Jan 1858
Prudence Priscilla (Bond), 8 Jan 1860
Golden Freeman, 31 Mar 1861
Orson Oriel, 2 Apr 1862
Rebecca Louise (Blackburn), 26 Mar 1864
Infant, 18 Sep 1866 (stillborn)
Judith Shill, 11 Sep 1867
Marland Golding, 14 Mar 1871

Louisa was born in England, 1829. She was the youngest of twelve children. She was baptized on July 17, 1846, just after she turned seventeen years old.

She and her brother, Charles Goulding, converted Charles Wager Richins who became her husband on January 27, 1851, when she was twenty-one. They made their home in Gloucester, where their first child was born.

Charles emigrated in the Joseph W. Young Wagon Company, arriving in the Salt Lake Valley on October 10, 1852. One year later he sent for Louisa and their daughter. They sailed from Liverpool on April 8, 1854 on the steamship "Marshfield," landing at New Orleans, Louisiana on May 29, 1854, arriving in the Salt Lake Valley in the Fall of 1854.

Charles and Louisa lived in Salt Lake City for seven years. In 1860, they were called to settle Henefer, Summit County, Utah. Charles took a second wife Esther Stowe Ovard. They lived in the "Big House" together.

After the manifesto, Charles took his third wife to Mexico and Louisa returned to Arizona and bought five acres of land with the money Charles gave her. From time to time, she would visit him in Mexico.

Louisa was an herb doctor and a midwife. She attended many of the women, in the settlements at the birth of their children, receiving no pay, but serving only for the love of serving. Occasionally she was asked to help in the care of sick animals which she willingly did.

Louisa loved to write letters and became an ardent stamp collector by saving the postage stamps from all those she received. She was a quiet stately woman with small beautiful hands. She was small in stature and always dressed neatly. She commonly wore a blouse and shirt or a very plain dress, dark laced shoes and a sun bonnet.

Louisa passed away from a stroke on April 28, 1902 in Mesa, Arizona at the age of sixty-three. Charles outlived her ten years, passing away in Colonia Diaz, Chihuahua, Mexico.

MARY JANE JONES RICHINS

BIRTHDATE: 5 Jun 1858
Nettleton, England
DEATH: 24 Mar 1947
Grouse Creek, Box Elder, Utah
PARENTS: Robert Jones
Harriet Tipper
PIONEER: Sep 1866
William Chipman Wagon Train
SPOUSE: Albert Francis Richins
MARRIED: 16 Nov 1874
Salt Lake Endowment House
DEATH SP: 26 Apr 1932
Ogden, Weber Co., Utah

CHILDREN:
Albert Sidney, 8 Aug 1875
Eliza Harriet, 9 Oct 1876

George Robert, 26 Oct 1878
Louisa Emmaline, 24 Oct 1882
William Alma, 29 Jun 1885
Wilford Francis, 20 Nov 1887
Orson Chester, 10 Dec 1889
Joseph Ether, 29 Jan 1892
Newell Richins, 1 Jun 1894
Wellington Irvin, 29 Apr 1897
Orita Ellen, 12 Nov 1899
Nola Mary, 13 Sep 1903

Mary Jane's parents embraced the Gospel in England when the children were very young. Her mother died when she was five year old. In April of 1866, Robert and his three children left Nettleton, England and came to America on the ship, "John Bright."

After they landed in New York, they traveled by way of New Haven, Montreal, Detroit, Chicago, and then to St. Joseph, Missouri. They sailed the Missouri River to Wyoming. They camped there and Mary Jane was baptized in the Sweetwater River on July 7, 1866.

They joined the William Henry Chipman Wagon Company to reach the Salt Lake Valley. Her father had been very ill with Mountain Fever and lay in the wagon for several days while the children had to be responsible for their belongings.

Indians had killed many people in the wagon company that preceded them, took ninety-one head of cattle, shot them with arrows, and left them to die. It was a very gruesome sight and terrifying experience for the whole company. They were met in Echo, Utah by her father's relatives and taken to live with them for the first winter.

Mary Jane's father remarried and moved his family to Henefer, Utah, where she lived until she married Albert Francis Richins.

Five couples from Henefer decided to move to Grouse Creek to settle the area. They lived in a dugout until they could build their home of logs. They did quite well as the years went on.

Mary did hand sewing for some of the settlers and earned enough money to buy flour. She did washing for the sheep herders to earn money to buy the first wooden floor she had. They had to learn how to appease the Indians in the area. Mary would trade food she raised in the garden for pine nuts the Indians had gathered. She supplemented the family income by raising chickens and turkeys, and helping to run a store.

She helped support her husband on a two year mission when there were still nine children at home with the youngest child only two months old. She raised eleven of her children to maturity, then raised a granddaughter.

EMMA ORTON RICHMOND

No
Photo
Available

BIRTHDATE: 9 Dec 1842
DesMoines, Iowa
DEATH: 16 Sep 1902
PARENTS: William Reed Orton
Rebecca Huey
PIONEER: 1851
SPOUSE: Joseph B. Richmond
MARRIED: 3 May 1863
DEATH SP: 10 Jun 1916

CHILDREN:
Polly Ann, 6 Feb 1864
Almeda, 25 Jun 1865
Emma Jane, 31 Jan 1867
Sonoma, 25 Aug 1868
Joseph Thomas, 22 May 1870
William Reed, 30 Nov 1871
Everett Burrows, 25 Dec 1873
Maude, 16 Sep 1875
Harriet Rebecca, 29 Mar 1877
Jesse, 27 Feb 1879
Florence, 29 Jan 1881
Fred Garfield, 1 Nov 1883
Ray, 7 Dec 1884.

Emma's family experienced sore trials and hardships because they were "Mormons" but they stayed faithful and true. Her parents received their endowments on Jaunary 29, 1846 and were sealed for time and all eternity on January 30, 1846 in the Nauvoo Temple just before the Saints were driven out of their homes into Iowa.

The Ortons stayed in Iowa several years and crossed the Plains to Utah in 1851. Emma was eight years old. Her quiet, but energetic family spent a year in Salt Lake City and then moved to Provo.

Emma and her sister, Jane, married brothers and these two couples lived in Payson for a while, then Emma and Joseph moved to Provo. They had two farms, one on the bench and one in the river bottoms. They raised fruit, cattle, grain and hay. They lived in a log cabin and added rooms as they family increased in size.

Emma's life was spent as a homekeeper. Her house was always in order. She taught her thirteen children to work for there was plenty to do and very little money. Emma said very little, but what she said she meant. Emma corded and spun and made men's suits and all her children's clothing when they were young. Honesty was taught as one of the main principles of life.

The older children of the family cleared the sagebrush from the land to make it ready for the crops. She would prepare hot meals and walk two miles to the farm and there they would have their dinner together. Much fruit was dried such as apples and ground cherries. Emma sold some to make some extra money. She cured all of the meat the family used during the year. They saved money in many ways. For instance, on baking day the neighbors all used the same bacon rind to grease their pans. The oldest daughter had the job of going around to grease all the pans.

The last few years of her life Emma was not well and could do very little work. She died at the age of sixty years, leaving a vacant spot in the life of her companion, Joseph.

ELEANOR MARTIN RICKS

BIRTHDATE: 20 Dec 1807
Clark Co., Kentucky
DEATH: 26 Feb 1882
Logan, Cache Co., Utah
PARENTS: Christopher Martin
Anna Turner
PIONEER: 24 Sep 1848
Heber C. Kimball Wagon Train
SPOUSE: Joel Ricks
MARRIED: 17 May 1827
Trigg Co., Kentucky
DEATH SP: 15 Dec 1888
Logan, Cache Co., Utah

CHILDREN:
Thomas Edwin, 21 Jul 1828
Lewis, 20 Dec 1830
Sally Ann, 28 Dec 1832
Clarinda, 10 Jan 1835
Temperance R., 4 Jan 1837
William, 10 Jan 1839
Jonathan, 23 Jan 1841
Mary Elizabeth, 19 Jan 1843
Josiah, 27 May 1845
Joel Martin, 15 Oct 1850 (died as an infant)
Nathan, 17 Jan 1853

When Eleanor was twelve years old, her father moved to Trigg County. She married Joel Ricks on May 17, 1827. In 1829, they moved to Olive, Madison, Illinois where they received the gospel of the Church of Jesus Christ of Latter-day Saints and were baptized as members on June 6, 1841. Soon afterward, they moved to Nauvoo where they had a home behind the temple. They were endowed in the Nauvoo Temple.

They left all they had worked for in Nauvoo because of the persecution they were called upon to endure. The family crossed the Mississippi River on April 27, 1846 and crossed the territory of Iowa. At regular intervals, these companies tarried for a few days to plow and sow large tracts of land which would be harvested by those who followed.

They arrived near Council Bluffs where they made temporary residence on Silver Creek until the spring of 1848. At that time, they joined a great wagon company under the leadership of Heber C. Kimball. Her husband served as a captain of ten wagons as they crossed the Plains. They arrived in the Great Salt Lake Valley on September 24, 1848.

Their family located in Mill Creek Canyon, known as Mueller Park Canyon just east of Bountiful. Her husband helped Heber C. Kimball erect a saw mill.

In the Spring of 1849, they moved to Centerville. Nine children were born to Eleanor and Joel before crossing the Plains. Two more children were born to them in Centerville. Their family moved to Cache county in 1859 and built their home in Logan.

Whenever the church authorities visited Logan, they went to the Ricks' home. Eleanor kept an immaculate home and was an excellent cook. Eleanor's handiwork was admired by all. She knitted lace collars, curtains, and valances on her beds. She knitted bedspreads. She raised beautiful flowers. She knit socks to pay for her contribution to build the temple. She made a home of peace that brought much happiness to those who knew and loved her. Eleanor helped her husband in all of his activities. He was a patriarch in the church and it became her job to help write and record the blessings.

Eleanor passed away on February 25, 1882 and was buried in the Logan Cemetery.

ELIZABETH JANE SHUPE RICKS

No Photo Available

BIRTHDATE: 14 Aug 1841
Pleasant Valley, Wythe, Virginia
DEATH: 1 Jul 1889
Rexburg, Madison Co., Idaho
PARENTS: John Witstein Shupe
Martha Ann Thomas
PIONEER: 8 Aug 1853
Wagon Train Company
SPOUSE: Thomas Edwin Ricks
MARRIED: 27 Mar 1857
Salt Lake City, Salt Lake, Utah
DEATH SP: 28 Sep 1901
Rexburg, Fremont, Idaho

CHILDREN:
Willard, 24 Apr 1861
Martha Jane, 1 Jul 1863
Emma, Jul 1865
John, 10 May 1868
Lewis, 4 Feb 1871
Orson, 23 Apr 1873
Millie, 6 Feb 1875
May, 16 May 1877
Nathan, 21 Jul 1879
Eleanor, 3 Sep 1881

Elizabeth Jane was born in Virginia, the oldest of all her parents' children. The missionaries of the Church of Jesus Christ of Latter-day Saints found her family and taught them the true Gospel.

Her grandparents Shupe and her parents were baptized. In September, 1843, her parents and grandparents moved to Illinois to be near the Saints. Two years later they moved to Nauvoo, Illinois. Her grandfather and father worked as blacksmiths and wagon makers. Her father died at the early age of twenty-seven. Elizabeth Jane's mother later married Elijah Shaw April 5, 1850.

They came to Utah in 1853 when Elizabeth Jane was twelve years old. The company they traveled with is not known by the family. The first winter they lived in West Jordan and the following spring they moved to Centerville, Utah where they lived for five years. In 1859, they moved to North Odgen, Utah.

When Elizabeth Jane was fifteen years old, Thomas E. Ricks asked her step-father for her hand in marriage. Elizabeth accepted a bit reluctantly. She became one of his five plural wives on March 27, 1857. It appears that Thomas let his young wife grow up because she didn't have any children until she was almost twenty years old. She and Thomas became the parents of ten children; three died in childhood. Her second child, Martha Ann, developed an illness that crippled her for life. She never walked but did learn to feed herself. She lived sixty-six years and her mother took care of her until she died.

Her husband was a wealthy man. He was called by the Church to lead a colony and settle the upper Snake River Valley in 1882. He took Elizabeth Jane, his third wife, to Idaho to start the new settlement. Elizabeth Jane had one of the two houses in the settlement. She cooked for the men, sometimes as many as twenty besides her own family. She was very hospitable and never turned anyone from her door. Later, a bigger home was built that had a real shingle roof. The back part of the home was a post office and a store that the family took care of.

Elizabeth Jane was active in church and community service. She was a very talented woman and was certainly outstanding in every aspect.

The hardships of pioneer life took their toll on Elizabeth Jane. She passed away only six years after coming to Rexburg, Idaho on July 1, 1889. She had helped to build the town of Ricksburg and make the settlement a success. The name of this new town was to be Ricksburg, but the papers were changed and when papers came back from the State of Idaho the name had been changed to Rexburg. However, at a later date the College was named Ricks College.

Elizabeth Jane was very unassuming but would have been honored that the College was named for her husband and that she had a part in that.

ELLEN MARIA YALLOP RICKS

BIRTHDATE: 8 Apr 1848
Great Yarmouth, England
DEATH: 19 Jul 1924
Sugar City, Madison Co., Idaho
PARENTS: Ephriam Yallop
Mary Ann West
PIONEER: 4 Sep 1866
Thomas E. Ricks Wagon Train
SPOUSE: Thomas Edwin Ricks
MARRIED: 29 Nov 1866
Salt Lake City, Salt Lake, Utah
DEATH SP: 28 Sep 1901
Rexburg, Madison Co., Idaho

CHILDREN:
Ephraim, 16 Sep 1867
Alfred, 28 Nov 1869
Ernest, 23 Sep 1871
Ellen, 16 Dec 1873
Charlotte, 29 Dec 1875
Edith, 5 Mar 1878
Elizabeth Jane, 30 May 1881
Josiah, 23 Aug 1883
Zina, 27 Dec 1886

Ellen was born in England. She was the eighth and last child. When Ellen was a year old her mother died and several years later her father married a widow with two grown daughters, who were very unkind to the little motherless girl.

Ellen was the only one of her family to join the Church of Jesus Christ of Latter-day Saints. When the family was having general house cleaning she became acquainted with a cleaning lady who was a Mormon and here she learned about the true Gospel. Her stepmother felt it was a disgrace to live in the same house with a Mormon so her father said one or the other would have to move. Ellen Maria replied that she would be the one to go.

She left home that night and soon found employment in Hull, England. She worked for a year and made enough for her emigration fare to America. Just prior to leaving England, her stepmother's heart had softened and Ellen Maria was invited to return home and they assisted in fitting her out for her journey.

Ellen Maria was only nineteen years old when she left her English home in the company of four other girls all bound for Zion. The sailed on the ship "John Bright." She crossed the Plains by ox-team in the Captain Thomas E. Ricks Company.

Despite their hardships there was much time to laugh. She often took the dignified Captain Ricks' favorite riding horse and caused him to hasten after her in hot pursuit when she galloped over the Plains. Two months after she reached the Salt Lake Valley they were married in the Endowment House in Salt Lake City on November 29, 1866. They had arrived in the Salt Lake Valley on September 4, 1866. Ellen

Maria became his fifth wife in plural marriage. They became the parents of nine children; one died in childhood.

Ellen Maria had been given a good education and training in industry and careful management of the home. She taught these traits to her children. She was a wonderful homemaker and manager. She devoted much of her time in service to the Lord.

In 1884, she and her husband and children began pioneer life in the Snake River Valley in Idaho. Here she took her place with the other pioneer families sharing their joys and sorrows, work and pleasures.

In the year 1891, she was called to be President of the YLMIA of Bannock Stake, which comprised Bingham, Pocatello, Bannock, Fremont, Rigby, Yellowstone and the Teton Stakes. She spent many years presiding over this vast territory, traveling by wagon, buggy or horses. She labored year around for the benefit of the girls in this scattered land. Sometimes she was away from home two or three weeks at a time.

When her husband passed away, Ellen Maria moved to Sugar City, Idaho where her son, Alfred, was a bishop and she lived with him and his family.

For the rest of her life she did genealogy and temple work for over 1,000 of her people. She said this was the greatest joy that ever had come to her.

Ellen Maria passed away on July 19, 1924 in Sugar City, Idaho and was buried in the Sugar City Cemetery.

MARTHA BITTER RICKS

BIRTHDATE: 29 Aug 1860
New York City, New York
DEATH: 12 Jun 1946
Rexburg, Madison Co., Idaho
PARENTS: Traugott Bitter
Rosine Wilhelmina Aust
PIONEER: 23 Sep 1861
Joseph Young Co. Wagon Train
SPOUSE: Hyrum Ricks
MARRIED: 1 Apr 1880
Salt Lake City, Utah
DEATH SP: 13 Aug 1924
Rexburg, Madison Co., Idaho

CHILDREN:
Martha May, 30 Jan 1881
Hyrum, 30 Jul 1883
Daniel, 9 Mar 1886
Wilford Albert, 6 May 1888
Pearl, 30 Apr 1891
Ruby, 16 Sep 1893
Wilhelmina, 23 Apr 1896
Benjamin Marion, 7 Nov 1898
Leo Milton, 9 Sep 1900
Constance, 30 Aug 1902
Leland Nephi, 17 Dec 1905

Martha was born in New York City, New York. She was her parents' first child. When she was about nine months old her parents joined the Church of Jesus Christ of Latter-day Saints.

Their desire was to emigrate to Utah and live with the Saints. They joined the wagon-train of Captain Joseph Young and left Florence, Nebraska on July 8, 1861. They arrived in the Salt Lake Valley on September 23, 1861. Martha was almost a year old when she made the journey across the Plains with her family. They lived in Salt Lake City until the Fall of 1862 then moved to St. George, Utah. They lived there for one year then returned to Salt Lake City. In the Fall of 1864, they moved to Logan, Utah.

Martha became a member of the first YLMIA in 1875. She was soon called to be a teacher in that organization at the age of fifteen years. She was called to be a member of the Tabernacle Choir under the direction of Evan Stephans and later Alex Lewis.

At the age of nineteen she married Hyrum Ricks, a son of President Thomas E. Ricks and Tabitha Hendricks Ricks. They were married on April 1, 1880 in the Salt Lake City Endowment House. They became the parents of eleven children, all born in Logan, Utah.

In 1888, her husband was called on a mission to England. They had a little store and Martha decided to see if she could make a living in the grocery business while her husband served his mission. She called the Elders of the Church to administer to her children many times while her husband was away.

On July 2, 1894, Martha and Hyrum settled all of their business in Logan and moved to Rexburg, Idaho. They helped Hyrum's father, Thomas E. Ricks, build up the City of Rexburg. They became farmers.

Shortly after their arrival, Martha was chosen First Counselor in the YLMIA of the Second Ward. She also acted as the agent for the Young Woman's Journal. Martha held these positions for five years, then she was chosen to be the Ward Primary President. They started bazaars and made enough money to buy pictures for the chapel of the Ward. She served as President of the Primary until she was called to be on the Stake Primary Board. She was chosen Secretary of the Relief Society of the Third Ward in the year 1912. In 1913, she was chosen as a class leader in the YLMIA of the Third Ward. After three years she was called to be the President of the YLMIA.

She was released in September, 1918, when she went to Logan to help her sick parents. On her return from Logan she was asked to be Relief Society President. They held bazaars and parties so they had enough funds to help buy a new piano for the Ward and Chapel lights. She held this position for seven years while she was caring for an invalid sister and a sick husband.

When her husband passed away in 1924 she still had two children who were not married. Martha passed away on June 12, 1946 at the home of her daughter, Constance.

On June 15, 1946 she was buried by her husband in the Rexburg Cemetery.

RUTH CAROLINE DILLE RICKS

No Photo Available

BIRTHDATE: 11 Jan 1847
Huntingport, Iowa
DEATH: 17 Feb 1922
Logan, Cache Co., Utah
PARENTS: David Buele Dille
Harriet Lucretia Welch
PIONEER: Oct 1850
Captain Bennett Wagon Train
SPOUSE: Thomas Edwin Ricks
MARRIED: 6 Dec 1863
DEATH SP: 28 Sep 1901
Rexburg, Madison Co., Idaho

CHILDREN:
Harriet, 23 Jun 1867
Caroline, 16 Oct 1869
David, 28 Sep 1871
Rose Maude, 12 Jul 1874
Harvey Chapman, 22 Jun 1882

Ruth's mother died in Iowa as the family were starting across the Plains. Her father soon married, but it was not a happy marriage and the children suffered because of the relationship. She had one sister and four brothers. Her sister and two brothers died while crossing the Plains. One brother died near Ogden, Utah from eating poisoned turnips.

Ruth was three years old when she crossed the Plains journeying to the Salt Lake Valley. They arrived in the Salt Lake Valley by wagon with the Captain Bennett Company October, 1850. This was probably an Independent Wagon Company. Many independent companies came in 1850.

Ruth and her brother were very lonely in their young years as their father was very active in the Church of Jesus Christ of Latter-day Saints as well as filling a mission for the Church in Europe. They lived in Ogden, Utah to help build up that City.

On December 6, 1863, at the age of sixteen years, Ruth was married to Thomas E. Ricks. He and Ruth's father were good friends. Her father thought Thomas would be a good husband for his daughter since he was a man of much means and was kind and considerate to all.

Ruth was the fourth wife of Thomas Edwin Ricks in plural marriage. Thomas was thirty-five years old. They became the parents of five children; three girls and two boys; one child died in childhood. All of the children were born in Logan, Utah.

Ruth loved Logan and the Church work she was called to do. She found many friends and for the first time in her life she felt secure in her surroundings.

When her husband was called to settle the Upper Snake River Valley in Idaho, Ruth decided to stay in Logan. She continued in her many church activities and when her family were on their own she started working in the Logan Temple as an officiator where she worked for many years. She was one of Logan's earliest pioneer settlers, coming when she was a mere child. She was one of the most active workers in all projects and organizations for the church and the community.

Her husband passed away on September 28, 1901 in Rexburg, Idaho. Ruth passed away on February 17, 1922 in Logan and was buried on February 20, 1922 in the Logan Cemetery.

SARAH BERIAH FISKE ALLEN RICKS

BIRTHDATE: 1 Sep 1819
Potsdam, New York
DEATH: 12 Jun 1891
Logan, Cache Co., Utah
PARENTS: Varnum Fiske
Sarah Eames
PIONEER: 14 Sep 1852
Wagon Train Company
SPOUSE I: Ezra Hale Allen
MARRIED: 25 Dec 1837
DEATH SP: 27 Jun 1848

CHILDREN:
Cynthia Amorette, 19 Apr 1839
Jerusha Elvira, 23 Mar 184 1 (died at age 1)
Alexander Hamilton, Jul 1843 (died as an infant)
Alexander Alma, 28 Sep 1845

SPOUSE II: Joel Ricks
MARRIED: 26 Oct 1852
DEATH SP: 15 Dec 1888
Logan, Cache Co., Utah

CHILDREN:
Ezra Varnum, 13 Jul 1853
Sarah Beriah, 17 Jan 1855 (died at age 14)
Ellen Jane, 30 Mar 1856
Joel, 21 Jul 1858
Adelia, 24 Oct 1860 (died at age 3)
Esther Adeline, 28 Oct 1862

Sarah was a descendant of an early Massachusetts family. She obtained a basic education by attending public schools in Potsdam, New York.

In 1837, she married Ezra H. Allen and moved to his home in Madrid in 1841, they heard the missionaries from the Church of Jesus Christ of Latter-day Saints and her husband was baptized. They sold their land and prepared to go to Nauvoo in April of 1843. She was baptized a member in May, 1843. By this time, Sarah had given birth to four children and two of them had died.

In 1846, they were driven from Nauvoo and settled in Council Bluffs when her husband, Ezra, was called to serve in the Mormon Battalion. In 1849, while he was returning home from California, he was killed by Indians. His friends brought her a bag of gold dust he had worn around his neck. She had been teaching school in his absence and in 1852, she used this gold to purchase a covered wagon, oxen, and hired a teamster to bring her family to the Great Salt Lake Valley. They arrived on September 14, 1852.

Sarah became the second wife of Joel Ricks, a close friend of her husband's, on October 26, 1852. They lived in Centerville, Farmington, and then moved to Cache Valley. Six children were born to this union. She endured crickets, Johnston's Army, and hardships pioneer life brought. She washed, carded, and spun wool from her husband's sheep.

They moved into a new home in 1866. Then as she gathered the comforts of life, she had more time to work more for the church. In May, 1870, she was called as secretary of the Relief Society. In May of 1874, she was chosen as President. For the next ten years, she spent her time visiting the sick and caring for the needs of the sick and poor.

Sarah was a talented and poetic woman. Many of her poems and writings were published in local publications. She was instrumental in doing much family history. She did temple work and had a desire to see her family records completed.

TABITHA HENDRICKS RICKS

BIRTHDATE: 30 Sep 1830
Simpson Co., Kentucky
DEATH: 6 Mar 1924
Rexburg, Madison Co., Idaho
PARENTS: Samuel Hendricks
Rebecca Doris Hendricks
PIONEER: 24 Sep 1848
Heber C. Kimball Wagon Train
SPOUSE: Thomas Edwin Ricks
MARRIED: 18 Aug 1852
DEATH SP: 28 Sep 1901
Rexburg, Madison Co., Idaho

CHILDREN:
Sarah Catherine, 4 Jun 1853
Thomas Edwin, 3 Dec 1855
Joseph, 22 Jan 1857
Hyrum, 24 Jul 1858
Heber, 27 Apr 1860 (twin)
Brigham, 27 Apr. 1860 (twin)
Mary Elizabeth, 19 Aug 1861
William, 25 Scp 1863
Alice, 23 May 1865
James, 20 Dec 1867
Samuel, 20 Feb 1870
George, 2 Jan 1876

Tabitha was born in Kentucky in 1830, the eleventh child of a family of thirteen. When she was five her mother died as well as the baby and the broken hearted father soon moved his family of twelve children to Minden, Louisiana where Susannah spent her early childhood.

When she was thirteen, her sister's husband, Neriah Lewis, came to visit and persuaded her father to let her go to Illinois with him for better schooling. Tabitha's Aunt Drusilla Hendrick came for a visit and taught them about the Mormons.

Neriah moved his family to Nauvoo in July 1844, just two weeks after the Prophet Joseph was killed, during the worst time of Nauvoo's history and was run out of the state with the Saints. In 1848, Tabitha joined the Kimball Wagon Company, and out of necessity, drove a team of three oxen and a cow attached to the baggage wagon, from Winter Quarters to Salt Lake Valley. She was baptized six days into the journey.

Once in Utah, wanting more education, she milked cows for a man in Centerville to pay for schooling for three years.

Tabitha and Thomas Ricks were married in the fall just before she turned twenty-two, by Heber C. Kimball. They bought a farm in Centerville of twenty-five acres where they built a little adobe and log home.

Their first two children were born in Centerville, the next two in Farmington. Many days and nights were spent with her husband absent. Thomas, active in frontier settlement, was also a minute man for the communities protection and was gone a lot.

With their first four children they were called to help settle Logan where their last eight children were born. She was busy doing all the necessary work for making meals (from the growing to the plucking of feathers) and clothing (from the wool to the wearing) plus she raised silkworms and did her church work.

Her home, a block from the temple, was three stories high with two porches. Such a big house accommodated borders; Stake people who came to do temple work (once with out special invitation, seventeen bishops were present at the same time) and always welcomed the Church leaders. At one time or another she entertained each of the Apostles of the Church. Apostle Wilford Woodruff said, "There was no place that suited him so well as Grandma Ricks who was known for her delicious pies." (Thirty for one occasion.)

When Thomas was called to settle the Snake River Valley, Tabitha went to Rexburg to live permanently. Her life was one of unconditional love and service; a steadfast pioneer woman, and a worthy mate for her truly noble husband who passed away twenty years before her, and was buried by her side.

TAMAR LOADER RICKS

BIRTHDATE: 8 Sep 1833
Aston Rowant, England
DEATH: 1 Feb 1924
Sugar City, Madison Co., Idaho
PARENTS: James Loader
Amy Britnell
PIONEER: 30 Nov 1856
Martin Handcart Company
SPOUSE: Thomas Edwin Ricks
MARRIED: 27 Mar 1857
DEATH SP: 28 Sep 1901
Rexburg, Madison Co., Idaho

CHILDREN:
Amy Eliza, 11 Dec 1858
Sarah Eleanor, 6 Feb 1861
Joel, 12 Feb 1863 (died as an infant)
Ann Ricks, 17 Nov 1864 (died as a child)
Maria Loader, 23 Aug 1867
Clarinda, 15 Feb 1872 (died as a child)
Luamelia, 24 Nov 1874 (died at age 16)

Tamar was born in Aston Rowant, Oxfordshire, England in the cottage on the estate of Sir Henry Lambert, a wealthy land owner, where her father labored as head gardener. She was raised in a loving home, enjoyed a happy childhood and a Christian upbringing, the family being members of the Church of England.

When her father joined the Church of Jesus Christ of Latter-day Saints around 1850, Sir Lambert gave him one year to give up the peculiar faith then the family was ejected from the estate and his children from the school. Tamar had been working for some time in London an a clerk in a store.

Tamar's parents with six of their children, sailed for America in December of 1855, but she remained in Liverpool with her sister, Zilpah and husband John Jaques, who was helping to direct saints emigrating to America. They left six months later, May 25, 1856, on the ship "Horizon." With mixed emotion she sadly bid England good by and turned her attention to the joyful participation of the work of God. She was twenty-five years old.

They docked in Boston the last of June and proceeded to Iowa where she joined her parents, brothers and sisters and they were assigned to the Edward Martin Handcart Company, pushing a handcart to Utah. By the time they reached Florence, Nebraska, the exposure and physical exhaustion had made her so ill she was bent over and could not straighten up. She was given a blessing by Apostles' John Taylor and Franklin Richards, that she would walk before reaching the valley's of Utah. For part of the journey Tamar was pulled in a handcart. One month into the journey her father died at Ash Hollow.

Bitter, frequent storms, scarce provisions to the point of starvation and the always present exhaustion brought it's own peace to so many, death. Of those who survived, many lost extremities from freezing before they were met by the relief wagons at the Platte River. On November 30, they reached the Salt Lake Valley and the families who would nurture them until they were well.

One of the rescuing teamsters was twenty-eight year old Thomas Ricks. Tamar was offered a home with his family and five months later she became his second wife in polygamy.

Her first child was born in Farmington, where they lived for two years before moving to Cache Valley. The rest of her children were born there, one son and five daughters. Her son died an infant and two daughters died in childhood.

She lived in Logan twenty-five years, saw it grow and prosper then fifty-one year old Tamar left friends and family to help her husband with his calling to colonize in the upper Snake River Valley in 1884. The community was called Rexburg and once again she helped subdue the wilderness.

A dainty lady, with rose colored cheeks and twinkling blue eyes who loved to dress neatly, Tamar always made one feel welcome. She lived a widow's life for twenty-three years in her own home until at the age of eighty-three she was taken into her daughter's home where she passed away seven years later.

MARY CATHERINE PRISCOTT RIDD

BIRTHDATE: 6 Dec 1866
Devonport, Devonshire, England
DEATH: 8 Jul 1951
Salt Lake City, Salt Lake, Utah
PARENTS: James Priscott
Mary Gunn
PIONEER: 15 Sep 1858
John Gillespie Co. Wagon Train
SPOUSE: William James Ridd
MARRIED: 21 Mar 1888
DEATH SP: 11 Nov 1920
Salt Lake City, Salt Lake, Utah

CHILDREN:
John Williams, 9 Mar 1889
Clifford James, 7 Oct 1890
Ruth Leona, 27 May 1892
Earl Stanford, 14 May 1894
May Evalyn, 7 Aug 1895
William Prescott, 7 Sep 1897
Marie Christmas,
Grant Raymond, 11 Aug 1900
Lorna Doone, 20 Mar 1903
Girl living,

Mary Catherine was born in England in 1866 and as a nineteen month infant was carried aboard the packet ship "Constitution," by her parents, to leave Liverpool, England at one o'clock Wednesday, June 24, 1868.

Elder Harvy H. Cluff was in charge of the orderly group of 457 converts who boarded the ship for a crowded voyage to New York where a train brought the immigrants to Benton, Wyoming for the last leg of their month long journey.

When the trip by rail was accomplished, her parents were assigned to a wagon train. The John Gillespie Wagon Company of 500 pioneers began, on August 24, 1868, their three week trek to the Salt Lake Valley. The third to the last wagon train carrying converts to Zion.

Although the trek was short, the oxen still traveled three miles an hour. Walking was sometimes better than the rough, bumpy, rock jolting, road rutted, dusty ride. Streams must be crossed, mountains climbed and descended with double teams pulling or holding back loaded wagons to keep them from becoming runaway's. At these times every one piled out to walk to spare the burdened animals. Rain got down right miserable and wind blew dust into your eyes. They reached the city in mid September, Mary Catherine had been traveling for seventy-seven days.

She grew up to marry James Ridd in the Logan Temple, when she was twenty-one years old, The two lived in Salt Lake City where all of their ten children were born. Her address was 1470 South Main Street.

It was a hard time for the Mormons, the United States Government was pressing and attached much of the church property making the quality of life poor for the citizens of Utah. The manifesto against Polygamy was causing trouble for some of its leaders and they were put in prison.

Mary's first son was born the year the Trolley lines were put down Main Street, the second, Clifford, was born just as polygamy was being abandoned and the first free public school was begun. And Ruth Leona was surely carried to the temple grounds to see the forty year old effort of building the temple come to fruition as it was dedicated.

Mary and William James raised their children in Salt Lake City. She was about thirty-nine at the birth of her last child doing all the work required in providing for and raising ten children, and mourning the two who preceeded her in death. She was a responsible hard working member of her church possessing the spirit that enriched the Mormon effort in settling the West.

Mary was active in Relief Society in the 22nd Ward and the old Jefferson Ward and a member of the Finance Committee of the Jefferson Ward.

At the last, her son, Clifford, took her into his home where she passed away at the age of eighty-four. She was one of the last of the noble pioneers.

MARY ANN EAGLES RIDDLE

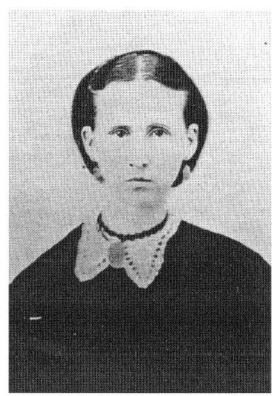

BIRTHDATE: 5 Nov 1845
Nauvoo, Hancock Co., Illinois
DEATH: 14 Apr 1899
Provo, Utah Co., Utah
PARENTS: Elias Eagles
Mary Ann Crook
PIONEER: 1850's
SPOUSE: Isaac Riddle
MARRIED: 29 Aug 1863
DEATH SP: 1 Sep 1906
Provo, Utah Co., Utah

CHILDREN:
Lydia Ann (Holdaway), 15 Sep 1866
Sophronia, 15 Feb 1869 (died at age 8)
Lillie Cornelia (Holdaway Baum), 19 Feb 1871
Wallace Monroe, 24 Dec 1872
Charles Edward, 23 Feb 1874
John Elias, 25 Feb 1876
Isaac Andrew, 10 Apr 1879 (died at age 7)

Mary Ann was born in Nauvoo in 1845, the Prophet Joseph had been killed the spring of the previous year and the exodus was hard upon them.

She was a toddler when the citizens were scourged from Nauvoo, and a child playing at camp time, gathering buffalo chips for fire, riding inside the wagon when it rained and walking with sore feet glad for the noon day rest and the early camp time, when she crossed the plains.

Her family made their way into the Salt Lake Valley and suffered the extreme hardships that every family endured and the business of survival thrust children into maturity at very early ages.

When Mary Ann was eighteen she married as a plural wife into the families of Isaac Riddle. She was his third wife. Each of their seven children were born in Beaver, Beaver County, Utah. Wallace Monroe was a Christmas Eve gift to the family.

Isaac's business ventures proved very successful, enabling his families many benefits. He owned several ranches and grist mills and his four families moved often. At one time he built a double house on the Riddle Ranch in Antimony. Mary Ann Eagles with her family lived in one side and Mary Roland with her family lived in the other, an arrangment they did not share for long because Isaac had other ranches and properties and his wives were capable managers who cooked for the ranch hands and made butter and cheese for sale.

Deepest grief came to the mother when her second child, little Sophronia died the spring she was eight years old, then nine years later, when her youngest son, Isaac's namesake, died on the ranch in Antimony the winter he was seven. The ranch was too isolated, too lonely, and Isaac moved his wife into Manti where he had business interests. The grieving parents needed the solace of the Lord and their broken hearts were healed by working in the temple, which they faithfully did for six years.

After about ten years in Manti, Isaac and Mary Ann moved to Provo (where Isaac could see to his investments in the Springville Roller mills). Mary Ann lived in one of the three homes built by Isaac on sixth north between second and third east, known as Riddle Row.

She had been suffering from a "stomach ailment" and became so ill two years after moving that Isaac wrote to his granddaughter Madora, the oldest daughter of Joselina, and she came to Provo to care for "Aunt Ann." Her condition worsened and she passed away on April 14, 1899 at age fifty-three. She is buried in the Provo City Cemetery.

MARY ANN LEVI RIDDLE

No
Photo
Available

BIRTHDATE: 30 Jun 1835
Canada
DEATH: 3 Mar 1872
Beaver, Beaver Co., Utah
PARENTS: Fredrick Levi
Julia Ann Karl
PIONEER 1852
SPOUSE: Isaac Riddle
MARRIED: 6 Mar 1853
DEATH SP: 1 Sep 1906

CHILDREN:
George Henry, 6 Mar 1854 (died as an infant)
Mary Ann, 7 Dec 1855
Isaac Jamison, 17 Dec 1857
Joselina, 11 Jul 1859
Madora, 9 Jun 1862
Laura, 28 Dec 1863

Mary Ann was born in Canada in 1835. When the Saints prepared to exodus into the Rocky Mountains, word was sent to the Canadian Mormons and those who would follow were advised that now was the time. Many packed immediately and in groups of wards or families, accepted the advice and joined the Church of Jesus Christ of Latter-day Saints in Iowa prepared for the trip West.

Twenty-one companies of Saints left Kanesville, Iowa within a two month period the summer of 1852, consisting of 3,782 people in a great migration to Utah and Mary Ann Levi, age seventeen was among them.

The spring after arriving, two months before her eighteenth birthday, she married Isaac Riddle in North Ogden. Their first baby, born on their first year anniversary, died shortly after birth and Mary Ann was so ill she was not expected to live. Isaac was called to Southern Utah for a mission among the Indians and only at Mary Ann's constant insistence and his strong faith, could he leave her.

It was not his last absence from home. Mary Ann's attitude that it was "his duty and they would trust in the Lord for help and guidance" gave Isaac the freedom of choice, to complete the missions he was asked to do. Mary Ann lived in Ogden with her family while he filled his missions.

When Isaac returned after two years, the couple sold their farm and moved to Santa Clara where they had a sawmill. In two years they again moved, to Pine Valley and lived in a dugout where their third child was born.

Joselina was the baby when they moved to Gunlock, Washington County in 1859, and settled into a permanent home, but the flood of 1862 took all they had except a few horses and a few head of cattle. Discouraged over this disaster, they moved to Pinto Creek, starting over again, but only for three years. They moved to Beaver County built a house and stayed for the next thirteen years.

Four months before Madora was born, Isaac took a plural wife, Mary Ann Eagles, and the families' lived in Beaver where each of her seven children were born.

Isaac and Mary Ann Levi were very strong in the Mormon faith and served diligently to further the work. They helped in building the temples in St. George and Manti, both physically and financially and both were recognized for their generosity in the building of the Salt Lake Temple.

She and her husband worked very hard and were successful in their missionary efforts, especially among the Indians. Their business ventures prospered, enabling Isaac to support his polygamous families and give his children an education.

At the very young age of thirty-six, Mary Ann passed away, her youngest child was eight and her oldest surviving child, sixteen. She was desirous for her children to have a good education and Isaac moved his families to Provo, to be nearer the university, the temple and his business interests.

MARY CAROLINE TURNBAUGH LANGFORD RIDDLE

BIRTHDATE: 25 Apr 1842
Pittsfield, Pike Co., Illinois
DEATH: 29 Aug. 1914
Provo, Utah Co., Utah
PARENTS: Isaac Turnbaugh
Parthena Davis
PIONEER: 13 Aug 1852
James Bay Co. Wagon Train
SPOUSE I: James H. Langford
MARRIED: 14 Sep 1856
(divorced 5 Feb 1880)
DEATH SP: 29 May 1908
Colonia Oaxaca, Sonora, Mexico

CHILDREN:
Mary Caroline (Kimball), 7 Apr 1858
Eliza Ann (Johnson Culverwell), 17 Aug 1859

James Harvey Jr., 27 May 1861
Thomas Fountain, 16 Jan 1863
William Bethurem, 21 Mar 1865
Isaac Fielding, 16 Dec 1868
Susan Parthena (Godbe), 25 Dec 1869
John Russell, 20 Sep 1870
Richard Henry, 17 Apr 1872
Sarah Eveline (or Sadie Adalaid), 11 Apr 1874
Jefferson Jones, 20 Nov 1875

SPOUSE II: Isaac Riddle
MARRIED: After 1880
DEATH SP: 1 Sep 1906
Provo, Utah Co., Utah
CHILDREN: None

Mary Caroline was born in Illinois in 1842. Her mother was Mormon and two years after her first husband died she married Isaac Turnbaugh. Isaac wanted to go to California and Mary's mother persuaded him to join a pioneer company to travel with so they were absorbed into the James W. Bay Company, the same company that Mary's future husband traveled with.

The Turnbaugh's never made it to California. They stopped in Centerville, Utah. Mary Caroline's father joined the Church and they stayed.

When Mary Caroline married James Harvey Langford, he was twenty-five and she was only fifteen. They settled in Willard, Box Elder County, where five of their eleven children were born.

In 1865, they moved to Panaca, Washington County, Utah (now Nevada) where the last six of her eleven children were born. Mary was thirty-three years old at the birth of her eleventh child.

Coming from a pioneering background, enabled Mary Caroline to cope with and manage the frontier ways necessary to survive and care for her many children. Her ability as a mother and homemaker is attested to by her children who all grew to adulthood.

She was a woman of ability and was chosen to learn midwifery. She delivered many of the babies in Panaca and many of her own grandchildren. Of all the babies she delivered safely, she was unable to save the life of her own daughter, Mary Caroline Kimball. Mary Caroline and Isaac were bringing their daughter to Panaca to attend her when she would deliver. The soon-to-be mother fell off the back of the wagon, went into labor and died during childbirth. The baby died soon after they returned to Panaca.

When she delivered her grandson, Ernest Langford, the son of James Harvey Jr., the marshals came to the house and tried to take her daughter-in-law, Rose Ellen, to testify in court against her polygamous husband. Mary Caroline grabbed a shotgun and dared them to arrest her and the marshals left!

Mary Caroline divorced James Harvey when her youngest child was not much over four years old. She married the second time in a polygamous marriage, to Isaac

Riddle, whom she also divorced some years later. During this marriage she did considerable temple work in the Manti Temple.

She was a slim woman most of her life. In her later years she lived in Provo where she passed away at the age of seventy-two, and was buried in the Manti Cemetery.

MARY MCDONALD RIDER

BIRTHDATE: 1 Aug 1845
Formal Lintrathen, Scotland
DEATH: 19 Feb 1931
Kanab, Kane Co., Utah
PARENTS: William McDonald
Christina Wallace
PIONEER: 25 Sep 1866
John D. Halliday Wagon Train
SPOUSE I: James Mayberry
MARRIED: Unmarried
DEATH SP: Drowned at sea

CHILD:
James McDonald, 17 Jul 1862

SPOUSE II: John Rider
MARRIED: 27 Jul 1867
DEATH SP: Not given

CHILDREN:
John McDonald, 23 Apr 1868
William McDonald, 14 Mar 1870
Francis James, 10 Feb 1872
Thomas , 28 Jan 1874
David Benjamin, 17 Aug 1875
Mary Jane (Townsend), 28 May 1877
Louisa Ellen , 15 Apr 1879
Rachel Ann (Wright), 15 Jul 1881
Oscar Leonard, 28 Jan 1883
Florence May (Ford), 10 Apr 1885
Wallace Henry, 11 May 1887 (twin)
Christine Eliza (andrus), 11 May 1887 (twin)
Rowland Wandle, 28 Sep 1890

Mary was born in Formal Lintrathen, Forforshire, Scotland in 1845, the daughter of a tenant farmer. When she was ten years old her mother joined the Church of Jesus Christ of Latter-day Saints against the wishes of her father. Soon after, Mary was baptized.

In her sixteenth year, Mary and James Mayberry of Scotland had a baby son, James. James Sr. drowned at sea.

In 1866, alone, Mary sailed on board the "American Congress" with 350 others bound for Zion. On board she met John Rider, another Mormon emigrant bound for Utah. Docking in New York the company proceeded half way, (to Wyoming, Nebraska) by rail to begin the trek of over 600 miles to Salt Lake City, mostly walking because the wagon was loaded with their possessions and provisions.

In a summer wedding of the next year, John and Mary were married. Three years later the couple were called to help establish Fort Kanab in southern Utah. The first effort to settle the region a few years earlier had been recalled. The Indians had become so hostile, so many cattle lost and some men killed that Kanab had been vacated in 1867 and the settlers called to safety.

This time the settlement held and Mary began raising her large family of thirteen children. She gathered hops and dried them, thus supplying yeast for the town of Kanab. She welcomed visitors into her home and shared her very best with those who came. The harvest from her garden and fruit trees was bottled, and served her family well, providing their food through the winters.

Her relatives watched her dance the Highland Fling and thrilled to listen to her stories of Scotland and the many conversions with her family of the Gospel. Mormonism was not easily accepted in the beginning and courage was needed to belong to and practice the faith.

The six week voyage was less than easy and sometimes the trip overland on the railroad was done in cattle cars.

Mary passed away in Kanab at the age of eighty-five and twelve of her fourteen children, those who survived her, attended her funeral.

ELIZABETH BLAKE RIDING

BIRTHDATE: 22 Jan 1849
Salisbury, Wiltshire, England
DEATH: 21 Apr 1908
St. George, Washington, Utah
PARENTS: Benjamin F. Blake
Harriet Hollis
PIONEER: Sep 1853 by wagon
The Ten Pound Wagon Train
SPOUSE: Henry Hale Riding
MARRIED: abt 1870
Salt Lake City, Salt Lake, Utah
DEATH SP: 21 Oct 1900
St. George, Washington, Utah

CHILDREN:
Henrietta, 23 May 1871
Elizabeth Jane, 30 Jul 1873
Mary Ann, 20 Sep 1875
Wiliiam Henry, 12 Sep 1877
Franklin Taylor, 19 Sep 1879
Seth Thomas, 15 Aug 1881
Alma Blake, 29 Jan 1884
Amos, 10 Oct 1885
Harriet, 23 Jul 1888

Elizabeth Riding was born in England. She was just four years old when her family emigrated to Salt Lake City to join the Saints. Her parents had joined the Church of Jesus Christ of Latter-day Saints in 1851 in England.

They set sail on the ship "Falcon," on March 28, 1953, arriving in New Orleans, Louisiana. It took them twelve days to travel up the Mississippi River to Keokuk, Iowa where they bought a wagon and outfit to cross the Plains to Utah. They arrived in the Salt Lake Valley, September of 1853.

Elizabeth was too young to understand such a hard journey. She loved Salt Lake City and her growing up years there in the Church.

She was twelve years old when her family was called on a mission to St. George, Utah. It was a long journey, taking several days by wagon and arriving there in December, 1861. They camped at the old adobe yard for several months until the town could be laid out and the lots drawn for. Her father's lot was at 1st East and first South.

He built his family a nice home and had three cabinet shops and the family prospered. It was a hard life compared to what they had known in England but the Church meant everything to them and nothing was too hard to endure for it. Her father was a master furniture builder, upholsterer and paper hanger. Her mother was a master seamstress who had made clothes for Queen Victoria in England.

Elizabeth fell in love with Henry Hale Riding who had also been born in England. She was twenty-one years old and he was twenty-five years old at the time of their marriage in the Endowment House in Salt Lake City about 1870. They became the parents of nine children; two died in childhood. Her husband married a second wife in plural marriage.

He passed away on October 21, 1900 in St. George, Washington County, Utah. He was fifty-five years old. Their children were grown by this time. Elizabeth got a thorn in her finger, got blood poisoning from it and passed away on April 21, 1908; eight years after her husband.

Elizabeth was a faithful pioneer, a loving wife and mother.

Edwin Taylor Hale, 17 Mar 1853
Thomas Edward, 22 Jun 1856
Ellen Lister Hale, 26 May 1861

Mary Ann was born in Burley, Lanchester, England. She married Christopher Lister Riding in 1840. They heard the gospel of the Church of Jesus Christ of Latter-day Saints and were baptized members early in their marriage. It took nearly seven years to save enough to move to America. By then they had three children and their first born had died.

In 1848, Mary and her husband, with their two children crossed the ocean and were able to travel as far as St. Louis, Missouri. Their lack of funds compelled them to remain there a few years to be able to purchase a wagon, yoke of oxen, two cows, and supplies to sustain their family while crossing the Plains. They arrived in the Salt Lake Valley in 1852.

Christopher and Mary purchased a lot at 175 South Main where the Walker Bank now stands. Mary built a two-room adobe home.

When Johnston's Army was approaching, their family moved to Provo. While there, her husband was called to settle in Dixie. On the way to Dixie, Mary and her children settled in Cedar City while Christopher went on to help settle Santa Clara. During the flood of 1862, he lost everything and moved to St. George where Mary joined him. At first, Mary's family of six children lived in a dugout with a thatched willow roof.

Mary's father, in England, tried for many years to get her to forsake the Church and return home. He left property to her that would have provided her with a life of ease. She chose, instead, to live in these primitive conditions where they fought snakes and scorpions.

Mary passed away in April of 1885 in St. George, Washington County, Utah.

MARY ANN HALE RIDING

No Photo Available

BIRTHDATE: 26 Jun 1816
Burley, Lanchester, England
DEATH: 1 Apr 1885
St. George, Washington, Utah
PARENTS: Henry Hale
Mary Ann Taylor
PIONEER: 1852
SPOUSE: Christopher L. Riding
MARRIED: 1840
Burley, Lanchester, England
DEATH SP: 30 Nov 1887
St. George, Washington, Utah

CHILDREN:
Lister Hale, 7 Sep 1841
Thirza Hale, 14 May 1843
Henry Hale, 7 Sep 1845
Alfred Hale, 11 Jul 1848
Mary Eleanor, 1850

ANN WEAVER RIGBY

No Photo Available

BIRTHDATE: 4 Jun 1816
Ulneswalton, England
DEATH: 18 Feb 1853
Salt Lake City, Salt Lake, Utah
PARENTS: James Weaver
Esther Sumner
PIONEER: 22 Sep 1848
SPOUSE: Barnett/Bernard Rigby
MARRIED: 25 Dec 1839
Leyland, Lancashire, England
DEATH SP: 9 Mar 1871
Salt Lake City, Sak Lake, Utah

CHILDREN:
George, 21 Sep 1839
Enoch, 20 Jan 1841
Susanna, 5 Nov 1843
James, 12 Nov 1845
Edward, 12 Nov 1845

Esther, 25 Oct 1848
Ann, 2 Dec 1850
Barnett, 9 Nov 1851

After Ann's birth, her family moved to Eccleston, an adjoining parish. On Christmas Day, 1839, Ann married Bernard Rigby.

Bernard and his father's family joined the Church of Jesus Christ of Latter-day Saints in 1840. As soon as they were financially able, Ann and her husband sailed on the ship, "Sheffield," and landed in New Orleans. They took a boat up the Mississippi River to Nauvoo. They built a home and began farming. Ann's first little boy died soon after their arrival in Nauvoo.

Ann was baptized and endowed on the same day in Nauvoo on Febraury 2, 1846. Three children were born to them while in Nauvoo, but the twins died when their family was being driven from their home in Nauvoo. They stayed in Council Bluffs until 1848 and were assisted by Brigham Young and other brothers at the Elkhorn River as they were crossing the Plains. They arrived in the Salt Lake Valley on September 22, 1848.

During their first winter in the Salt Lake Valley, they had to live in a leaking covered wagon where Ann gave birth to her daughter, Esther. They were a resourceful couple and soon had a nice adobe home in Farmers Ward. They made molasses out of sugar beets, carded and spun wool to make their clothes, and gleaned wheat from the fields to make their bread. Ann taught her children to work hard but to enjoy it. She taught her daughters to knit and sew.

Ann passed away at the age of thirty-seven. She was a devoted church member and held family evenings with her children where they were taught the Gospel and were encouraged to develop their musical talents.

BETSY ANN WADE RIDING RIGBY

CHILDREN:
Thomas, 1850
Seth Thomas, 4 Jun 1852
James Lister, 5 Apr 1860
Margaret Ann, 18 Dec 1862
William Edward, 17 Jan 1868

BIRTHDATE: 24 May 1827
Colne, Lancashire, England
DEATH: 10 Feb 1895
Salt Lake City, Salt Lake, Utah
PARENTS: Thomas Riding
Eleanor Lister
PIONEER: 1848
SPOUSE: Seth Rigby
MARRIED: 26 Jan 1852
Salt Lake Endowment House
DEATH SP: 6 Sep 1892
Salt Lake City, Salt Lake, Utah

Betsy Ann was the last child, born to her parents. She was christened on June 24, 1827 being given her maternal great-grandmothers name as her own middle name.

Betsy Ann anxiously accepted the gospel of the Church of Jesus Christ of Latter-day Saints at an early age in her native land of England. On May 18, 1845, being eighteen years old, she was baptized by her older brother, Christopher Lister Riding.

Wishing to be a part of the Saints gathering in America, she left behind her immediate family, and came across the ocean single and alone. Bearing few possessions, she did manage to bring with her some reminders of home, including a sampler stitched by her older sister who had passed away a few years earlier. As the Saints began to move westward, Betsy Ann continued with them, walking the entire way.

At a tender age and having endured all the trials of a pioneer on her own, she entered the Salt Lake Valley and was soon married to Seth Rigby who was one of the first pioneers to settle in Utah. At the time of her eternal sealing to her newlywed husband, she compassionately served as proxy for the sealing of Seth's first wife who was buried in Nauvoo along with two young children. She was a devoted wife and homemaker, helping with the farming and sharing the gospel with family and friends.

ELIZABETH ELLISON RIGBY

BIRTHDATE: 21 May 1804
Ince, Wigon Parish, Lancashire,
England
DEATH: 12 May 1886
Centerville, Davis Co., Utah
PARENTS: John Ellison
Margaret Ellison
PIONEER: 3 Sep 1860
James D. Ross Co. Wagon Train
SPOUSE: Aaron Rigby
MARRIED: 25 Jul 1824
DEATH SP: 14 Apr 1867
Centerville, Davis Co, Utah

CHILDREN:
Moses, (chr.) 13 Mar 1825 (died at 16 months)
Alice, (chr.) 30 Oct 1826
Margaret, (chr.) 1 Jun 1829
John, 16 Mar 1832
Samuel, (chr.) 2 Mar 1834
Elizabeth A., 29 Oct 1836
Ellen, 15 Aug 1839
Elizabeth B., 19 Aug 1843

Elizabeth was born in Ince, Wigon Parish, England, a thriving center of coal mines, cotton and linen mills. The girls worked in the mills, the boys in the mines, when they were old enough.

Elizabeth taught the children to make their own feather beds from the geese they raised. They were taught by missionaries from the Church of Jesus Christ of Latter-day Saints to read, their textbooks the Book of Mormon and the Journal of Discourses. Elizabeth gave assistance to the missionaries, taking them into her home, feeding and helping clothe them.

She paid her tithing, fast offerings, temple and emigration fund, and in 1855 her son John sailed to America to prepare the way for the family. Five years later when the emigration fund was paid, the family sailed March 28, 1860, on the picket ship "Underwriter" from Liverpool. Her daughter Alice and family followed in 1864, but her daughter, Lizzie, did not come.

The family left Florence, Nebraska, June 17, 1860, arriving in the Salt Lake Valley on September 3, 1860. Her son, John, met them and took them to their Centerville home, a two-room log cabin on forty acres.

Elizabeth adjusted to her new home and environment of farming. Sugar cane was the principal crop. Her courage was strong and her faith continued to grow.

Her husband, Aaron, passed away on April 11, 1867 and she followed him in death on May 12, 1886, both buried in Centerville, Davis County, Utah.

FANNY JORDAN RIGBY

BIRTHDATE: 8 Oct 1852
Gasport, Hampshire, England
DEATH: 10 Jul 1932
Fairview, Sanpete Co., Utah
PARENTS: James F. Jordan
Sarah Cannon
PIONEER: 1 Sep 1855
Secrist & Guyman Wagon Train
SPOUSE: James Rigby
MARRIED: 21 Mar 1870
Salt Lake City, Salt Lake, Utah
DEATH SP: 23 Sep 1929
Fairview, Sanpete Co., Utah

CHILDREN:
James Leonard, 12 Jan 1871
Fanny May, 16 May 1872
LeRoy, 20 Nov 1875
Charles Martin, 20 Jul 1877
Joseph Clark, 18 Nov 1880
Mary Edna, 20 Nov 1882
William Fredrick, 27 Mar 1885
Samuel Bills, 1 Feb 1888
Franklin Edgar, 26 Jan 1890
Lewis Lavern, 17 Apr 1892

Fanny was the daughter of the local Baptist Preacher. Their family became converted members of the Church of Jesus Christ of Latter-day Saints and decided to gather with the Saints in America. They sailed from Liverpool, England on the ship "Siddons," for America. They arrived on April 25, 1855 in Philadelphia, Pennsylvania. Their family crossed the Plains with the Jacob F. Secrist Wagon

Company. There was much sickness in this company which cost the life of their captain. Noah T. Guymon was appointed to serve as captain for the remainder of the journey. They arrived in the Salt Lake Valley on September 1, 1855.

The family lived in the tenth ward for nine years. Fanny's father was a cooper by trade. He often worked in the saw mill. Her family moved to Clover Creek where he engaged in the livestock business.

Fanny married James Rigby in the Endowment House in Salt Lake City. They became parents of ten children.

Thet moved their family to Saint John in Tooele County, Utah with the livestock business and then to Fairview in Sanpete County where he was in the sheep business. James and Fanny owned a ninety acre farm.

She kept a beautifid yard with beautiful flowers and a garden in which she raised vegetables and fruit. Fanny labored diligently as a Relief Society worker, but spent most of her time at home raising her children.

GRACE LIPTROT RIGBY

BIRTHDATE: 13 Jan 1841
Bedford, Leigh, Lancashire, England
DEATH: 30 Mar 1886
Hooper, Weber Co., Utah
PARENTS: William Liptrot
Elizabeth Hesketh
PIONEER: 4 Oct 1863
SPOUSE: John Rigby
MARRIED: 16 Sep 1860
Deane, Lancashire, England
DEATH SP: 29 Nov 1918
Hooper, Weber Co., Utah

CHILDREN:
John Thomas, 10 Oct 1865
William Henry, 29 Nov 1866 (died at age 13)
Joseph, Liptrot, 8 Jun 1869 (died at age 3)
Wilmur Liptrot, 3 Oct 1871
Hyrum Liptrot, 12 Oct 1874
Alma Liptrot, 29 Dec 1876
Elizabeth Liptrot, 1 Jul 1880

Grace was born to farming parents. She learned the alaphabet and numbers at her mother's knee while stitching a sampler. Her mother taught her to do beautiful embroidery work. Her mother died when Grace was sixteen years old. Grace was apprenticed as a seamstress in England. She was baptized a member of the Church of Jesus Christ of Latter-day Saints on June 17, 1852.

Grace married John Rigby, a coal miner, in September, 1860. After their marriage, John was baptized into the Church. Soon after that, they made plans to emigrate to America. They sailed on the ship "Cynosure," on May 30, 1863. They crossed the Plains and arrived in Salt Lake City on October 4, 1863.

They went to Ogden to settle. Grace raised peach and apple trees and currant bushes. She was very happy when she got her first sewing machine. It was run by a hand wheel instead of a treadle. She made all of the family's clothing. She frequently tailored men's suits for ZCMI. She also taught sewing to the Relief Society sisters and assisted neighbors with her expert ability.

From her home, she witnessed the railroad coming through Ogden in 1869. It sounded like old times in England. Their land was right on the edge of the railroad. They soon sold their property and moved to Hooper, where Grace and her sons helped John build a house.

Grace had a good singing voice. She used to tell Bible stories and sing songs to her children. She was bright and alert and had a sence of fun. Her health was very frail, but she did all that she could while on earth to further the work of the Gospel. She used every bit of energy she had to help others and care for her family.

Grace passed away at the age of forty-five, leaving her husband and five children. She was buried in the Hooper Cemetery.

LUCY ANN WRIGHT RIGBY

BIRTHDATE: 4 Feb 1844
Harborough, Magna, England
DEATH: 31 Aug 1929
Centerville, Davis Co,Utah
PARENTS: James Wright
Mary Ann Stean
PIONEER: 29 Sep 1866
Daniel Thompson Wagon Train
SPOUSE: John Rigby
MARRIED: 8 Nov 1867
Salt Lake Endowment House
DEATH SP: 18 Aug 1879
Centerville, Davis Co., Utah

CHILDREN:
Mary Ann, 18 Sep 1868
Elizabeth, 14 Oct 1879
Alice, 23 Dec 1872
Frank "L," 29 Mar 1875
William Lowe, 9 Apr 1877
Lucy Emma, 4 May 1879 (twin)
Esther Ellen, 4 May 1879 (twin)

Lucy Ann was born in a little village three miles north of Rugby it was Harborough, Magna, Warwickshire in England. Her mother was a milliner and dressmaker who sewed for Queen Victoria. Lucy often accompanied her father to work so her mother could concentrate on her sewing. When her parents were introduced to the gospel of the Church of Jesus Christ of Latter-day Saints, they were converted members of the Church. She was twelve years old at this time.

At fourteen, Lucy Ann began working outside of the home and became a professional cook. This helped her to save the money needed to emigrate to Utah at the age of twenty-two. She sailed on the ship, "Arkwright," to America. They docked in New York, then traveled, by train, boat, and foot to Wyoming, Nebraska. She crossed the Plains with the Daniel Thompson Wagon Company. She earned her way by cooking and washing for a family of ten whose mother was ill. They arrived in the Salt Lake Valley on September 19, 1866. In Salt Lake City, she went to work for Joseph W. Young, then later, for William Capener.

While working for the Capeners, she met John Rigby who was Mrs. Capener's brother. After they were married, they moved to Centerville. She worked side-by-side with her husband as they cleared away the brush, tilled the soil, tended the flocks, and operated their molasses mill.

Lucy Ann became a widow at the age of thirty-five with seven children to raise. Lucy supported her family by raising cows, chickens, and fruit. She often traded butter and eggs for groceries and clothes.

She served as a counselor in the first Primary in north Centerville. She was a teacher in Sunday School for many years. She was the first president of the Woman Suffrage Movement in Centerville. She loved to have groups in her home to have fun by singing, having corn husking bees, peach cutting bees, making molasses candy, and quilting parties.

Lucy Ann passed away at the age of eighty-five.

MARY CAROLINE CLARKE RIGBY

BIRTHDATE: 27 May 1863
Rhosllanerchrugog, North Wales
DEATH: 1 Nov 1958
Bancroft, Caribou Co., Utah
PARENTS: Amos Clarke
Ann Johnston
PIONEER: 5 Sep 1866
Samuel D. White Wagon Train
SPOUSE: George Clark Rigby
MARRIED: 1 Mar 1883
Salt Lake Endowment House
DEATH SP: 1 Apr 1921
Newton, Cache Co., Utah

CHILDREN:
Mary Ann, 18 Oct 1884
George Amos, 17 Aug 1886
Moses William, 11 Aug 1888
Miriam, 11 Aug 1888
Elmer Clarke, 13 Mar 1890
Ida Lavinia, 27 Jan 1892
Edna Orella, 7 Mar 1894
Harold Edward, 5 Aug 1896
Heber Golden, 14 Sep 1898
Liberty Lula, 4 Jul 1900
Sterling Clarke, 4 Jun 1903
Milton Thomas, 7 Jun 1905
Murland Frederick, 7 Jun 1905
Gwendolyn, 9 Oct 1908

Mary was born in Rhosllanerchrugog, Donbigshire, North Wales, 1863. She, with her parents and four brothers and sisters, left Liverpool, England in April 30, 1866 on the "John Bright" sailing vessel with 747 people and Collins M. Gillet as company leader.

After a hard, rough voyage of six weeks they landed in New York. Remained there a short time making the preparations needed to continue their journey. They made their way West and joined the Samuel D. White Wagon Company which left Wyoming, Nebraska on July 7, 1866 with 231 people and 46 wagons. After a long and tedious journey of eight weeks they arrived in the Salt Lake Valley.

Mary married George Clark Rigby on March 1, 1883, in the Endowment House. She became the mother of fourteen children, there being two sets of twins. Miriam died nine days after her birth.

Mary was a counselor in the first Primary of her ward, a counselor in the Relief Society, a visiting teacher, and sang in the ward choir. She traveled around the valley with her father to help teach the singing parts to the people as they prepared to sing in Logan at the Jubilee each year. She attended the dedication of the Logan Temple, May 17, 1884. For many years she did work in the temple.

Her husband was called to Great Britian on a mission in 1893, leaving her with the responsibility of their five young children, the oldest nearly nine. She never questioned the call. She and her husband saw that the children had a good education and did missionary work.

After her husband's early death in 1921, she continued to devote her life to her children, especially to the younger ones living at home. She was very interested in their advancement and lived in Logan and Salt Lake to further their education. The twins both received their doctors degrees, one in dentistry, one in medicine. The girls graduated from Utah State University and one son served a mission. Mary made many trips by airplane to enjoy the association of her family from California to Chicago, and from New York to New Orleans.

Mary was honored by the Daughters of the Utah Pioneers, as an original pioneer, at their yearly conventions, and on April 7, 1956, when she was ninety-two years old, she was asked to speak at the annual convention.

Mary passed away on November 1, 1958, mentally alert, at the age of ninety-five in Bancroft, Idaho at the home of a daughter. She was buried November 5, in Newton, Utah.

MARY CLARK RIGBY

BIRTHDATE: 8 Sep 1833
Rainbow, Cheshire, England
DEATH: 27 Jul 1871
Newton, Cache Co., Utah
PARENTS: William Clark
Elizabeth "Betty" Bradbury
PIONEER: 17 Oct 1853
John Brown Co. Wagon Train
SPOUSE: William F. Rigby
MARRIED: 9 Aug 1852
Hatfield, Herefordshire, England
DEATH SP: 13 Mar 1901
Logan Cache Co., Utah

CHILDREN:
John, 16 Nov 1854 (died at birth)
Mary Jane (Roskelley), 28 Jun 1857
William "Will" Frederick, 9 Oct 1859
George Clark, 23 Feb 1862
Margaret (Roskelley), 12 Feb 1864
Lavinia Clark (Card), 28 Feb 1866
Martin Clark, 23 May 1868
Sarah , 26 Jul 1871 (died as a young child - 28 Sep 1872)

Mary was born in England, 1833. Her mother died when she was only four years old, and her father died when she was seven. She went to live with her brother and worked in a silk factory. She was baptized in 1849, despite the opposition of her brothers, and was married to William F. Littlewood in 1852. (Littlewood was his mother's surname. William eventually adopted the surname Rigby, that of his natural father, later in life, at the suggestion of Brigham Young.) They continued to live with her brother while saving money to emigrate to Utah.

They Left England on the ship "Camillus," and arrived in New Orleans in 1853. They then crossed the Plains with the wagon company directed by Captain John Brown. The next year her first child, a boy, was born and died. Their next two children were born while they lived in Lehi.

In the Spring of 1860, they moved to Wellsville, a new settlement in Cache Valley. They were involved with the building of this settlement. Mary was adept at making soap and sold or traded her surplus to other settlers. She and her husband helped organize a dramatic company to entertain the new community. Mary was a good actress.

Mary's husband was called as the bishop of Clarkston, still further north in Cache Valley, and then of Newton, a few miles east-southeast of Clarkston. Four more children were born during this time. In addition, Mary and William answered the call to live the order of polygamy and several additional wives were added to the family.

Tragically, Mary passed away at age thirty-seven, after giving birth to her eighth child. She was the first person buried in the Newton Cemetery in 1871.

SARAH ANGELINE CLARKE RIGBY

BIRTHDATE: 17 Jun 1861
Rhosllanerchrugog, Wales
DEATH: 10 Apr 1919
Newton, Cache Co., Utah
PARENTS: Amos Clarke
Ann Johnstone
PIONEER: 11 Sep 1866
Samuel D. White Wagon Train
SPOUSE: William F. Rigby
MARRIED: 28 Apr 1881
Salt Lake City, Salt Lake, Utah
DEATH SP: 5 Feb 1907
Cache Junction, Cache Co., Utah

CHILDREN:
William Frederick, III, 28 Apr 1882 (died as child-17 Sep 1883)
Persis Sarah, 2 Dec 1883
Lettie Elizabeth (Jenkins), 18 Aug 1885
George Ora, 5 Aug 1887
Samuel Marriner, 13 Sep 1889
Edith Viola (Cooley), 13 Apr 1892
David Leroy, 1 Mar 1894
Rulon Robert, 29 Jan 1896
Oprah Vendeline (Fabricius), 14 Sep 1898
Martin Amos, 13 May 1901
Lula Anne (Larsen), 1 Mar 1903
Ray Clarke, 9 Jun 1906

Sarah was born in Rhosllanerchrugog, Denbighshire, Wales in 1861. Her parents were baptized as members of the Church of Jesus Christ of Latter-day Saints in 1855 and emigrated with five children on the ship "John Bright" in 1866. Sarah was only five when she crossed the Plains. Her family lived in Salt Lake City for three years.

They moved to Newton in 1869, where a balcksmith was needed for the new community. As a girl, she helped her father with farming chores, and did washing, ironing and sewing for other families to add to her family's income.

Sarah had a beautiful alto voice and sang with her sisters and father. She had the Welsh love of singing. She traveled with her father, teaching songs for the Sunday School Jubilee.

Sarah Angeline married William Frederick Rigby, Jr., also of Newton, in 1881. Her first son died at age eighteen months and a daughter was born while her husband was serving a mission in the Southern States.

Sarah served as the Young Women's Association President for several years early in her married life. She was the mother of twelve children.

Her husband passed away in 1907 after being hit by a train, leaving her a widow with eleven living children. Her youngest was seven months old. Her oldest son died the next year after being thrown beneath a wagon.

Sarah Angeline's health gradually failed and she suffered from cancer. Sarah passed away in 1919 at the age of fifty-eight.

SARAH HASLAM RIGBY

BIRTHDATE: 14 Jun 1835
Little Heaton, England
DEATH: 29 Sep 1916
Newton, Cache Co., Utah
PARENTS: John Haslam
Alice Hulme
PIONEER: 29 Aug 1863
John R. Murdock Wagon Train
SPOUSE: William Rigby
MARRIED: 3 Mar 1864
Salt Lake City, Utah
DEATH SP: Sep 1901
Wellsville, Cache Co., Utah

CHILDREN: None

Sarah was born in Little Heaton, Lanacashire, England, 1835. She was the eldest of three children. Her father died when the children were very young. Sarah's mother married Joseph Eckersley. They had six daughters and one son.

Being the eldest child of the family, Sarah went to work at an early age. She wove cloth and later learned the tailoring business. They were always very poor, but they were an industrious family and learned the meaning of work early in their lives. All the older members of Sarah's family were baptized into the Church of Jesus Christ of Latter-day Saints on May 24, 1847.

In 1854, Sarah's brother, William, emigrated to Zion. Through his efforts all the family was able to emigrate to be with the Saints. In 1861, Sarah's brother, Henry, emigrated. Then, in 1863 the family was finally able to sail for America on April 30, 1863.

They landed in New York City, then took crowded train cars for a two week miserable trip to Florence, Nebraska. They joined the John R. Murdock Wagon Company for the trek across the Plains. They walked most of the way. However, the younger children were able to ride in a wagon on top of a piano one teamster was taking to the Salt Lake Valley. They arrived in the Valley on August 29, 1863.

They camped in a tent on City Creek for a week until William arrived from Wellsville, Utah with a team and wagon. Henry met them in Wellsville. He was dressed so poorly that Sarah cried when she saw him and as soon as possible she made him some shirts out of some skirts she had brought with her. They stayed the first winter in the fort at Wellsville in a log cabin with dirt floors and a roof covered with willows. They had beds of straw. Her stepfather built a loom so that Sarah's mother could weave cloth in exchange for food. In the Spring, Sarah went to work at the home of William and Mary Rigby.

On March 3, 1864, Sarah married William Rigby in the Salt Lake City Endowment House in plural marriage. Elder Heber C. Kimball officiated.

After her marriage, Sarah lived in the same house with her husband's first wife, Mary, and their three children. Three years later she moved to Clarkston, Utah because her husband had been called to be the bishop there.

In 1872, she moved to Newton, Utah when her husband was called to be bishop there. Her husband built a rock house for his family in Newton. Just a few months after they had moved into the home, her husband's first wife, Mary, died giving birth to a daughter whom she named Sarah because of her love for her husband's second wife, Sarah.

Sarah was not able to have children of her own but she raised Mary's six children with a great deal of love. The children felt that Sarah was a true mother to each one of them. They loved and respected her as their mother. She always anticipated their needs and met them with understanding and caring. She never locked her door until all of her children were safe at home at night.

William was called on a mission to England in 1885. Sarah and the children took care of her husband's nursery business so all the families could have an income. When William returned from his mission he was arrested for polygamy and spent five months in the Utah Penitentiary. Sarah was substitute mother and father to all of William's families. They never had enough money or conveniences. Pioneer life was a hard one for Sarah and the children.

After her husband passed away 1901, Sarah became the head of the home. All the children paid her great love and respect and admiration and regularly visited her. She was never an invalid, but her health failed gradually for twenty years before she passed away at the age of eighty-one years; her life was filled with service to others. She was buried in the Newton Cemetery in Cache County, Utah.

SOPHIA ECKERSLEY RIGBY

BIRTHDATE: 8 Jun 1848
Lark Mill, Middleton, England
DEATH: 3 May 1928
Logan, Cache Co., Utah
PARENTS: Joseph Eckersley
Ann Hulme
PIONEER: 26 Aug 1863
John R. Murdock Wagon Train
SPOUSE: William F. Rigby
MARRIED:
DEATH SP: 13 Mar 1901

CHILDREN:
Joseph Eckersley, 27 Jul 1867
Henry Eckersley, 26 Aug 1869
Alice Eckersley, 24 Sep 1871
Martha Eckersley, 20 Sep 1873
Samuel Eckersley, 6 Feb 1876
Zina Eckersley, 21 Feb 1878
David Eckersley, 1 Mar 1880

James Eckersley, 25 Aug 1881
Elmer Eckersley, 15 Jul 1884
Willard Eckersley, 28 Oct 1885
Ella, 23 Apr 1888
Eva, 23 Apr 1888
Moroni, 27 Feb 1891
Leatha, 23 Oct 1892

Sophia was born in Lark Mill, Middleton Lancashire, England, 1848. At a young age, she worked in the silk mills winding bobbins. After her family joined the Church of Jesus Christ of Latter-day Saints and had sufficient money, they sailed to America on the ship "John J. Dye," in 1863. The family of Joseph Eckersley joined the John R. Murdock Wagon Company to cross the Plains. When they arrived, her step brother came with a big wagon and moved their family to Wellsville, Utah. Each member of the family had to work so they could support themselves.

William F. Rigby and his wife and family were living in Wellsville at this time. Sophia went to work for him in his home and on his farm picking potatoes and doing household work. Here she became well acquainted with him and became his fourth wife on June 25, 1865 at the age of seventeen. In 1871, William also married Sophia's younger sister, Mary Ann.

At the time Sophia was president of the Relief Society in Newton, William was forced to spend a great deal of his time on the underground as he was being chased by the United States Marshalls for polygamy. The women had to take care of themselves. They raised gardens and worked together to run the household and care for the ranch when William was not there.

Later, William moved Sophia to Rexburg, Idaho, then to Teton Valley, Wyoming. Life was harder as they were living on a homestead in a small cabin with many children and never enough room.

Sophia was Stake Relief Society President for nine years when the stake was organized. She was a beautiful singer and enjoyed her work in the choir and led the singing when there were public gatherings.

After William's death, she moved to Logan to work in the temple. Sophia passed away at the age of eighty.

SUSANNA HARTLEY RIGBY

No
Photo
Available

BIRTHDATE: 23 Dec 1791
Leyland, Lancashire, England
DEATH: 1 Feb 1859
Salt Lake City, Salt Lake, Utah
PARENTS: Barnett Hartley
Ann Ditchfield
PIONEER: 1848
Barnett Rigby
SPOUSE: Edward Rigby
MARRIED: 26 Feb 1811
Croston, Lanacashire, England
DEATH SP: 21 Oct 1846
Iowa

CHILDREN:
Sarah, 17 Feb 1811
James, 27 Jun 1813
Bernard, 10 Aug 1815
John, 4 Jan 1818
Seth, 23 Apr 1820
Robert, 24 May 1823
Edward, 17 Mar 1825
Peter, 11 Nov 1827
Oliver, 17 Apr 1830
Ann, 11 Sep 1832
Thomas, 1835
William, 8 Aug 1838

Susanna's family lived in the little village of Euxton where her father rented three cottages or dwelling houses. She married Edward Rigby on February 26, 1811 in the Leyland Parish Church. At that time, Edward was a weaver. She became the mother of twelve children.

Susanna and Edward were visited by missionaries from the Church of Jesus Christ of Latter-day Saints and were converted in 1838. She received a patriarchal blessing on September 24, 1840, by Peter Melling in Leyland.

Things were difficult financially for the Rigbys. When the call came to gather in Nauvoo, Susanna, Edward, and their family sailed across the ocean in 1841. On Susanna's birthday in 1845, they received their endowments in the Nauvoo Temple. She did temple work for her relatives.

They were driven from Nauvoo in 1846 by mobs of angry men. Two small children and her daughter, Sarah, died on the trek West. Sarah was run over by the wagon and oxen as she tried to climb into a wagon.

The Rigby family stayed in Council Bluffs for a time and her husband, Edward, died in Iowa at the age of fifty-seven.

The 1850 census shows Susanna and her son, William, living with the Seth and Barnett Rigby families. On January 24, 1852, Susanna was sealed to her husband in the Endowment House.

Susanna lived ten years after she came to the Valley, and passed away at the age of sixty seven on February 1, 1859.

ADELINE AMARILLA HAMBLIN LITTLEFIELD RIGGS

BIRTHDATE: 18 Sep 1823
Munson, Geagua Co., Ohio
DEATH: 20 Jul 1895
Kanab, Kane Co., Utah
PARENTS: Isaiah Hamblin
Daphne Haines / Haynes
PIONEER: 12 Sep 1850
Aaron Johnson Co. Wagon Train
SPOUSE I: Lyman O. Littlefield
MARRIED: 31 Jan 1846
DEATH SP: Not known

CHILD:
Charles Hamblin, 25 Apr 1847

SPOUSE II: John Ensign Riggs
MARRIED: 17 Dec 1851
Tooele, Tooele Co., Utah
DEATH SP: 22 Dec 1893
Kanab, Kane Co., Utah

CHILDREN:
Albert Ensign, 14 Nov 1852
Adeline Edwina, 2 Nov 1854
Herbert Edwin, 2 Nov 1854
Brigham Adelbert, 30 Apr 1857
Wallace Amasa, 19 Jan 1860
Mary Agnes, 29 Nov 1863

Adeline was into the Church of Jesus Christ of Latter-day Saints in 1844. She was married to Lyman Omer (Oman) Littlefield on January 31, 1846.

In 1850, Adeline and her son, joined seven other family members in Pottawattamie County, Iowa for the trip across the Plains. Mary traveled with the Aaron Johnson Wagon Company and arrived in the Salt Lake Valley on September 12, 1850.

They went immediately on to the Tooele Valley Settlement. Adeline taught school to help with the family's welfare.

She married John Ensign Riggs and they continued to live in Tooele until they were called by Brigham Young to help build in Santa Clara in southern Utah.

In 1871, they were called to settle Kanab, Kane County, Utah. Adeline was a nurse and midwife. She filled an admirable mission with limited herbs and medicines. She nursed men, women, and children in their very difficult frontier environment. She was a serious minded woman and loved peace and harmony in the home.

She was a regular partcipant in Relief Society and other LDS church functions. She loved to spend her precious "free" time reading.

DORTHE HANSEN NIELSEN RIGGS

BIRTHDATE: 6 Sep 1846
Klavsebolle, Denmark
DEATH: 16 Apr 1883
Millville, Cache Co., Utah
PARENTS: Hans I. Nielsen
Johanne C. Hansen Allerup
PIONEER: 1861
John Woolley Handcart Comp.
SPOUSE: John Riggs
MARRIED: 27 Dec 1864
Salt Lake City, Salt Lake, Utah
DEATH SP: 20 Feb 1809
Millville, Cache Co., Utah

CHILDREN:
John Levi, 25 Jun 1866
Joseph William, 13 Jun 1868
Dorthe Elizabeth, 24 Dec 1869
Uhanna Christine, 9 Feb 1872
Martha Amelia, 8 Aug 1874
James Standren, 3 Aug 1876
Walter, 6 May 1878
Theodore King, 5 Apr 1883

Dorthe was born on September 6, 1846 at Klavsebolle, Denmark, the daughter of Hans I. Nielsen and Johanne Christine Hansen Allerup. She came to the Salt Lake Valley with her parents in 1861 in the John Woolley Handcart Company.

Dorthe was married to John Riggs on December 27, 1864 in the Endowment House in Salt Lake City. She was a pioneer wife and mother who raised eight children, and owned and operated a farm in Cache Valley.

Dorthe was a beautiful loving woman, very good at keeping up her home and supplying the needs of her family.

Dorthe passed away in Millville, Cache County, Utah on April 16, 1883. Her husband John passed away on February 20, 1909, also at Millville, Cache County, Utah.

JANE KILTON BULLOCK RIGGS

BIRTHDATE: 4 Sep 1819
Grafton, New Hampshire
DEATH: 5 Sep 1910
Provo, Utah Co., Utah
PARENTS: Benjamin Bullock
Dorothy Kimball
PIONEER: Sep 1851
Capt. McPherson's Wagon Train
SPOUSE: John Riggs
MARRIED: 8 Oct 1843
Moira, Franklin Co., New York
DEATH SP: 26 Mar 1992
Provo, Utah Co., Utah

CHIDREN:
Martha Hart, (adopted)
Amos Gardner, (adpted)
Susan Jane, 12 Aug 1845 (died at age 12)

Mary Ruth, 16 May 1847 (died as an infant)
Dorothy "Dollie" Melissa, 21 Jan 1849
Julia Maria, 21 Nov 1851 (died at 18 months)
Martha Adeline, 31 May 1854
John Gideon Benjamin, 2 Nov 1856 (died at 7 months)
Mariette, 5 Mar 1859
Jane Kilton, 30 Oct 1861 (died at age 2)
Cyrus, (adopted)

Jane was born in Grafton, Grafton County, New Hampshire, 1819. When she was five years old, her parents moved to New York State, settling in Moira.

At the age of thirteen, she started teaching in her own town for seven years. She received eight dollars a month and boarded with trustees, staying a month in each home. She bought one hundred head of sheep with the money she earned from teaching. She went home at spring break and learned her mother had become a convert to the Church of Jesus Christ of Latter-day Saints. She was ashamed at first, then became converted herself by a missionary named John Riggs.

Jane and John Riggs were married on October 8, 1843. She sold wool from her own sheep to buy cloth to make a suit for her husband's wedding.

Jane and John Riggs moved to Nauvoo, Illinois, where they rented a small room while John worked on the temple, there. After the martyrdom in 1844, they moved to Green Plains which is south of Nauvoo. After their home was burnt to the ground before their eyes by a mob, they moved back to Nauvoo and lived with five other families. The following spring, they moved west to Council Bluffs. The family caught smallpox all at the same time, Their adopted son, Amos Gardner, died.

They remained in Council Bluffs for five years until they could gather the means with which to journey across the Plains. In 1847, John went back to Quincy, Illinois to complete his medical studies while Jane cared for the farm and the family. In 1851, they traveled in Captain McPherson's Wagon Train Company which arrived in the Salt Lake Valley in September of 1851.

They stayed in Salt Lake City for one week, went south to Provo, and made plans to go to California. She had a dream in which a messenger told her to stay where she was, that Provo is the right place.

They lived with about fifty other families inside the fort until they built a four-room adobe home. Jane joined the first Relief Society organized in Provo in 1857. Her husband's work as a doctor tied her to home so she could not take an active part in the Relief Society, but she always assissted in charitable ways and ministered temporal blessings to the needy.

Jane gave birth to eight children, three of whom grew to maturity. Her husband was a doctor in Provo for many years. She was greatly loved by all who knew her. She lived to be ninety-one years old.

SARAH KING HILLMAN COONS RIGGS

BIRTHDATE: 24 Aug 1789
Cambridge, Washington Co.,
New York
DEATH: 25 May 1870
Salem, Utah County, Utah
PIONEER: Oct 1852
Allen Weeks Wagon Company

ELIZABETH LOTT RILEY

BIRTHDATE: 15 Feb 1827
Bedford Co., Tennessee
DEATH: 14 Jul 1888
Clear Creek Cyn, Sevier, Utah
PARENTS: Stephen Lott
Mary Sasnett
PIONEER: 1851
SPOUSE: William W. Riley
MARRIED: Before 1850
Illinois
DEATH SP: 24 Jun 1899
Richfield, Sevier Co., Utah

CHILDREN:
Charity Emmeline, 18 Jan 1850
George Wallace, 20 Jun 1852
William Steven, 21 Dec 1853
John Henry, 14 Sep 1855
Elizabeth Moriah, 2 Sep 1857
Mary Jane, 29 Mar 1859
Joseph Davis, 12 Oct 1860
Hyrum Smith, 19 Oct 1862
Melissa Ellen, 28 Dec 1864
Brigham Young, 22 Oct 1866
Samuel Heber, 7 Nov 1869

Elizabeth was born in Tennessee, but had moved to Illinois with her family by the time she was five years old. When she was about twelve years old, her mother died. Her father made arrangements for his children to be raised in other homes. Elizabeth and her two sisters lived with their Aunt Charity Sasnett and her husband William Wommack Riley.

Elizabeth eventually married William as his second wife. Eleven children were born to Elizabeth and William.

Elizabeth worked hard to help sustain their large family. She and her children gleaned thirty bushels of wheat heads at one time. She also gathered and dried ground cherries which she sold at ten cents per pound. All of her family's clothing was produced by Elizabeth. She had a loom to weave the cloth which she later sewed into garments. She carded her own wool, spun it into yarn, and knit her family's stockings and mittens. Trousers for her sons were often made from seamless sacks with stripes going down each side. She gathered straw and braided it into hats. She made all her pillow and feather beds from the feathers of geese, swan, and wild ducks. Elizabeth's excellent homemaking skills and hard work provided most of life's necessities for her family.

HARRIET EMMETT RILEY

BIRTHDATE: 29 Jan 1824
Downham, , England
DEATH: 20 Jun 1903
Ogden, Weber Co., Utah
PARENTS: John Emmett
Sarah Boothman
PIONEER: 3 Sep 1852
Abraham O. Smoot Wagon Train
SPOUSE: James Riley
MARRIED: 1844
Lancaster, England
DEATH SP: 7 Jun 1905
Ogden, Weber Co., Utah

CHILDREN:
Sarah Ann, 22 Sep 1845
George Heber, 1 Oct 1848
John Willard, 29 Mar 1951
Mary Ann, 20 Dec 1853
Harriet Marinda, 6 Jul 1859
Olive Jane, 3 Feb 1862
Elizabeth Alice, 4 Feb 1964
Janies Evan, 20 Nov 1867

Harriet became converted and was baptized as a member of the Church of Jesus Christ of Latter-day Saints. She worked to send money to Reuben Hadlock for passage to the United States. When they went to Liverpool to board the ship, they found he had disappeared with the money for the entire group. She had to return home and start saving again.

She finally emigrated with the help of the Perpetual Emigration Fund.

When they reached Florence, Nebraska, her husband contracted cholera. She traded her treasured silk dress for a bottle of whiskey for his medicine and doctored him. He recovered.

Harriet helped push a handcart across the Plains in the Abraham O. Smoot Wagon Company. Sometimes she pushed it alone while her husband was hunting for stray cattle. They arrived in the Salt Lake Valley on September 3, 1852.

They moved to Ogden, Utah to settle. When Johnston's Army came into the Valley, her husband was at Echo Canyon prepared for battle if it became necessary. She prepared her home to be burned and took her children to Provo Valley. She was a woman og great diligence, determination, courage, and trust in the Lord.

SUSAN ANN STOKER RILEY

BIRTHDATE: 16 Nov 1844
Nauvoo, Hancock Co., Illinois
DEATH: 21 Mar 1920
Burlington, Big Horn, Wyoming
PARENTS: William Stoker
Almira Winegar
PIONEER: 20 Sep 1852
SPOUSE: Thomas Katen Riley
MARRIED: 6 Apr 1863
DEATH SP: Oct 1923

CHILDREN:
Mary Almira (Martell), 29 Dec 1864
William Alfred, 24 May 1867 (died as a child)
Thomas Katen, Jr., 25 Apr 1870
Rhoda Jane, 17 Jul 1872
Susan Ann, 10 Jul 1875
Sarah Alnora, 23 Jan 1878
Margaret Ellen, 1 Mar 1880
Christine Archibald, 26 Oct 1882
Effie Pearl, 28 Apr 1885
Michael Clarence, 9 Feb 1888

Susan Ann was born in Nauvoo, Illinois in November, 1844, the third child and first daughter. The Stokers, along with other Saints, were forced to leave their homes and flee to Iowa where they lived at Mt. Pisgah for some time.

Her family joined the Isaac Stewart Company in June, 1852 for their trek West. A baby sister had been born and died at Mt. Pisgah, and one brother was four and Emily Jane, her sister was just three weeks old. They arrived in the Salt Lake Valley on September 20, 1852. They visited relatives in Bountiful, and then moved to Spanish Fork (called Palmyra at that time). There they settled on twenty acres of land. In 1856, her father built a two-room adobe home with a mud roof for his family.

It was in Spanish Fork that Susan Ann met Thomas Katen Riley, a member of the Martin Handcart Company. They were married on April 6, 1863 when both were just nineteen years of age. They had ten children born to them, one died as a child.

In 1876, they were called to settle the Big Muddy. They sold their farm, bought two wagons and two teams of mules. Mary Almira, just twelve years old, drove one wagon with their supplies, and the rest of the family rode in the other one.

They returned for a time to Spanish Fork, then were called to go to southern Utah and Arizona where Thomas was in charge of the railroad, and Susan and the girls cooked

for the workers. Thomas took a second wife, and they had one little girl who died at age four.

Susan's oldest daughter was married in 1885, and after the wedding celebration, Thomas and Susan, along with their other children, left the next morning for Ashley, Uintah Basin, Utah. They lived there for about five years where they had a very nice home and a large, productive fruit orchard.

Thomas worked at many trades and enjoyed the challenges, and was happy to move on. On a beautiful spring morning in 1893, with tears dimming their eyes, the family once again left their home. With their children who were still at home, they moved to the Big Horn Territory, Wyoming. The journey took more than a month, and was very difficult. It was never ending prairie, badlands and hills. Several other families had joined them by the time they arrived. At first they lived in a tent for the summer.

Thomas built a cabin without floors, windows and a door made from a wooden frame with a deer hide stretched across it. In the spring, a city was laid out. Farms were homesteaded and a canal was built, a Sunday School was begun with Thomas Riley as Superintendent, and in 1894 a ward was organized. Susan was active in church and in community affairs.

It was in Burlington, Big Horn, Wyoming, that Thomas and Susan finally settled down and found contentment.

Susan passed away on March 21, 1920, and Thomas passed away on October 5, 1923, they both were in their seventies.

They were faithful and had much courage to go where they were asked to go and to make the most of every situation. They are honored for their great pioneering, spirit, and their faith in following their Church leaders.

ANN ANDERSON RINGROSE

No Photo Available

BIRTHDATE: abt 1795
Ireland
DEATH: 29 March 1878
Ogden, Weber Co., Utah
PARENTS: Alexander Anderson
Hannah McGovern
PIONEER: abt 1855
SPOUSE: William Ringrose
MARRIED: abt 1812
England
DEATH SP: 29 Aug 1850
Willenhall, England

CHILDREN:
Thomas, 1813
Richard, 22 Oct 1814
Samuel Henry, 4 Dec 1815
Mary Ann, 16 Aug 1818
William, 22 Jan 1821
Elizabeth, 3 Aug 1823
Ann, 11 Mar 1826

Rebecca, 22 Jun 1828
Thomas, 6 Jun 1831
Charlotte, 22 Jun 1835
Hannah, 14 Apr 1837

Nothing is known of Ann's childhood years. She was married about 1812 to William Ringrose. They were married about 1812 and had eleven children.

Ann's husband passed away on August 29, 1850 of a spinal injury. She was baptized a member of the Church of Jesus Christ of Latter-day Saints on June 26, 1853 and eventually five of her children joined the Church.

Ann left England for Utah in company with her son, Samuel Ringrose, and his family, and her daughter, Hannah. They sailed from Liverpool to New Orleans on the ship, "Clara Wheeler," arriving in,New Orleans in January, 1855. It is presumed that Ann came on to Utah that same year.

After Ann arrived in the Salt Lake Valley, she moved to Ogden. She received her endowments on June 6, 1863 in the Endowment House the same day her son, Richard, was endowed and sealed to his wife, Ann Maycock. She remained a faithful member of the Church for the remainder of her life.

Ann Anderson Ringrose was eighty-three when she passed away in Ogden, Weber County, Utah.

ANN MAYCOCK RINGROSE

No
Photo
Available

BIRTHDATE: 30 Jun 1810
Willenhall, England
DEATH: 5 Jan 1890
Harrisville, Weber Co., Utah
PARENTS: John Maycock
Elizabeth Smith
PIONEER: 24 Sep 1862
Homer Duncan Co. Wagon Train
SPOUSE: Richard Ringrose
MARRIED: 19 Jul 1835
Coventry, England
DEATH SP: 11 Jan 1880
Ogden, Weber Co., Utah

CHILDREN:
Elizabeth Ann, 13 Apr 1838
Samuel, 10 Oct 1840
Charles, 27 Jan 1843
Lucy, 22 Apr 1846
Sarah Ann, 3 Feb 1851
Mary Ann, 9 Jul 1852

Ann was the youngest of thirteen children born to her parents. On July 19, 1835, Ann married Richard Ringrose. They had six children.

Ann was converted and baptized into the Church of Jesus Christ of Latter-day Saints in the Coventry Branch on December 2, 1853. Her husband had been baptized a few weeks earlier. Ann, her husband, and their three daughters sailed on the ship, "William Tappscott," arriving in New

York on June 15, 1860. They were detained in quarantine until June 20, due to the outbreak of smallpox.

After a steamboat journey to Albany, these Saints traveled by train to St. Joseph, Missouri. Their family remained in the Midwest for two years before they traveled West with Captain Homer Duncan's Wagon Company. They arrived in the Salt Lake Valley on September 24, 1862.

Ann and Richard settled in Ogden, Utah, following their arrival into Utah. Ann and her husband were endowed and sealed in the Endowment House on June 6, 1863.

Following her husband's death, Ann lived the last decade of her life as a widow.

Ann passed away in Harrisville, Utah in her eightieth year. She was buried in Ogden beside her husband.

ANN BOYACK RIRIE

BIRTHDATE: 15 May 1830
Dundee, Forfarshire, Scotland
DEATH: 7 Sep 1914
Ogden, Weber Co., Utah
PARENTS: James Boyack
Elizabeth Mealmaker
PIONEER: 24 Oct 1855
Milo Andrus Co. Wagon Train
SPOUSE: James Ririe
MARRIED: 23 Nov 1855
Salt Lake Endowment House
DEATH SP: 17 Jun 1905
Ogden, Weber Co., Utah

CHILDREN:
Margaret Ann, 26 Feb 1857
James Boyack, 22 Oct 1858
David, 21 Nov 1860
William, 24 Nov 1862 (died as an infant)
Alexander, 24 Oct 1863
Elizabeth, 25 Oct 1865
George, 23 Jan 1868 (died as a child)
Isabelle, 25 Feb 1870 (twin)
Mary, 25 Feb 1870 (twin - died as an infant)
Joseph, 27 Feb 1872 (twin)
Hyrum, 27 Feb 1872 (twin)
Agnes, 27 Mar 1874

Ann was born in Willenhall, Warwickshire, England, 1830. The Boyack family lived on a small farm near Dundee and sold milk from their farm to many of the families who lived in the town. The children delivered the milk and also herded the sheep along the banks of the streams.

The family was converted and baptized into the Church of Jesus Christ of Latter-day Saints in 1842, when Ann was twelve years old. Ann worked in a delicatessen shop and became a very good cook.

They left Scotland in the Spring of 1855, when Ann was twenty-five years old. They spent three months on a small sailing vessel. After arriving in the United States, they crossed the Plains in the Milo Andrus Wagon Company, which arrived in the Salt Lake Valley on October 24, 1855.

The family settled in Spanish Fork and lived in very humble circumstances because two thirds of the grain in Utah was destroyed that summer and a large black bug was devouring the potatoes.

Ann married James Ririe on November 23, 1855 after a three week courtship. They began their married life in a house that James had built in Springville.

Life was very difficult at first, but improved after Johnston's Army settled in the area. James was able to sell some of his surplus potatoes and wheat at the army camp. He also sold watermelon pies which Ann baked.

They had sheep and after James sheared the sheep, Ann prepared the wool for spinning, weaving, and then made their clothing. They were parents to twelve children.

They decided to move to North Ogden, then later to west Ogden where they lived for many years. People were always welcome in their home. James' brother came, to live with them for ten years. Then James sent for his sister to come live with them, which she did for twenty-one years. In their later years, James and Ann moved to Ogden to live.

James passed away on June 17, 1905. Ann passed away nine years later.

ZILLAH JANE PLAYER RISER

BIRTHDATE: 13 Aug 1851
near Chimney Rock, Nebraska
DEATH: 15 Feb 1923
Salt Lake City,. Salt Lake, Utah
PARENTS: William J. Player
Nancy Hamer
PIONEER: Oct 1851
Alfred Cordon Co. Wagon Train
SPOUSE: George C. Riser, Jr.
MARRIED: 25 Dec 1871
Salt Lake City, Salt Lake, Utah
DEATH SP: 17 Jul 1942
Salt Lake City, Salt Lake, Utah

CHILDREN:
Nellie Christiana (Brough), 1 Feb 1873
George Christian, III, 16 Aug 1875
William Denton, 23 Jan 1878 (died as a child)
Orson Fritz, 12 Jun 1882
Irene Pearl (Richardson), 16 Feb 1885
Sidney Bismark, 12 Mar 1887
Wilford Lawrence, 28 Mar 1889
Lillian Leona (Dooly), 6 Sep 1892

Zillah Jane was born on August 13, 1851 on the Plains of Nebraska. Her parents were moving west from Ferryville, Iowa along the north side of the Platte River toward Utah. She was a third generation of the Player and Hamer pioneer families. She was named after her two grandmothers, Jane Thornley Hamer, and Zillah Sanders Brown Player.

Jane Hamer had arrived in Utah in 1851, with Zillah's family, and Zillah Player arrived in 1862 when Zillah Jane was about eleven years old. That was the first time she had met this Player grandmother.

Zillah Jane grew up in Great Salt Lake City where she attended school, and church with her Hamer and Haslem cousins, and the Kelser and Riser children.

On Christmas Day in 1871, at age twenty years, Zillah Jane Player married George C. Riser, Jr. They were married by the mayor of Great Salt Lake City, Daniel H. Wells. Zillah Jane and George built their home on the south side of Zillah Jane's parents' lot on 500 West.

George's father had married a second wife, and an uncle also had two wives. They lived next door to the young Riser family. Zillah Jane did not approve of polygamy and would not allow a polygamist into her home. Consequently, Zillah Jane was not popular with her husband's family.

Zillah Jane and George encouraged their children to not only be industrious, but to attend school also. Three of their sons graduated from the University of Utah. Two became prominent in the mining industry in Utah and the western states.

Zillah Jane was very interested in political activities. Whenever election time came around, Zillah Jane enthusiastically went all out and hung banners and bunting all over her home. She was involved with the Democratic party.

Zillah Jane Player Riser passed away at her daughter, Lillian Dooly's home on 2100 South in Salt Lake City on February 15, 1923. George had lived over two more decades, when he passed away in 1942, also in Salt Lake City.

These were two pioneers of faith and fortitude who helped in the development of Salt Lake City from this early period of time. They are honored by their posterity for their contributions and their examples.

MARTHA BRIGHT RITCHIE

BIRTHDATE: 11 Jun 1844
Nauvoo, Hancock Co., Illinois
DEATH: 15 Dec 1929
Marriott, Weber Co., Utah
PARENTS: John Bright
Sarah Webb
PIONEER: abt 1850
Wagon Train Company
SPOUSE: James Ritchie
MARRIED: Jul 1863
Salt Lake City, Salt Lake, Utah
DEATH SP: 27 Feb 1902

CHILDREN:
Annie, 1 May 1864
Susan, 11 Jan 1866
Alice, 16 Nov 1868
Thomas Henry, 29 Mar 1868
William 4 Apr 1871
Eliza Ellen, 27 Mar 1873
Emily, 20 Dec 1874
Rachel, 25 Jun 1876
Margaret, 4 Nov 1877
Charlotte, 29 Aug 1880
Brigham, 3 Sep 1882
Martha, 19 Dec 1884

Martha was born at Nauvoo, Illinois. She was just seven months old when her mother died, leaving three little girls. Their father was unable to care for them so they were put out among neighbors. At the time the Saints were driven from Nauvoo, their father took the children to Iowa. They remained there until Martha was six years old.

They journeyed across the Plains in an ox-cart. They suffered many hardships. Martha walked most of the way. They arrived in the Salt Lake Valley about 1850.

They lived in Salt Lake City a short time and then moved to Kaysville, Utah. They lived there a year then moved to Riverdale in Weber County. After a two year stay they moved to South Weber, Davis County.

While living in South Weber, Martha became the second wife of James Ritchie in plural marriage. Her sister was his first wife. Martha and James were married in the Endowment House in Salt Lake City on on July 18, 1863. They moved to Marriott, Weber County where Martha resided most of her life. She was the mother of twelve children; three boys and nine girls.

Martha and James homesteaded a farm at Salt Creek, now known as Warren. During this time she lived in a dugout with a horse blanket for a door.

Her first real home was a one-room log cabin with dirt floor and dirt roof which leaked when it rained. The story is told how the children had to borrow pans and pots from the neighbors because their mother was having a baby and it was raining so hard they were having a hard time keeping mother and baby dry.

Martha made candles and her own soap from waste fats. They slept on ticks filled with straw. They got their water from a well. They kept their butter and milk in the well in buckets to keep cool in the summer time. They used gourds to drink from. Many a time the children were put to bed so the clothes could be washed. Often they would go barefoot, especially during the summer. One pair of shoes had to last a child a year; worn to church and school only.

To get material for clothing, Martha would shear the sheep, wash the fleece, card and dye it. Then, she would spin the fleece into yarn for stockings and cloth. It was a joyous day when her husband would buy her a bolt of "store-bought" material.

Martha knitted hundreds of yards of lace; it was so beautiful it won prizes at the State Fair. Her hands were never idle. Christmas was a happy time for the children even though they didn't get very much. Molasses candy was a treat.

Martha served as a midwife. She did not have any special training, but she had a kind spirit and much first hand knowledge. She was very humble and had a lot of faith. She would pray for her sick children and call the Elders to administer to them. They had great faith in Heavenly Father. The children were happy growing up and they grew to be good people and lived righteous lives. They didn't have much but they learned to work and share and love each other.

Martha passed away on December 15, 1929 and was buried in Ogden, Weber County, Utah.

RUTH JAMES ROACH

BIRTHDATE: 12 Apr 1835
Llangeler, Carmarthen, Wales
DEATH: 21 Sep 1894
Spanish Fork, Utah Co., Utah
PARENTS: Evan James
Hannah Powell
PIONEER: 15 Dec 1856
John A. Hunt Co. Wagon Train
SPOUSE: William Roach
MARRIED: 23 Aug 1857
Spanish Fork, Utah Co., Utah
DEATH SP: 9 Jun 1893
Spanish Fork, Utah Co., Utah

CHILDREN:
William James, 13 Apr 1858
John Walter, 7 Feb 1860
Evan David, 15 Dec 1861
Elizabeth Ann, 18 Feb 1863
Walter Thomas, 11 May 1865
Ruth, 1 Dec 1867
Margaret Hannah, 10 Feb 1870
Sarah Jane, 19 May 1872
Thomas David, 13 Dec 1874
Joseph Hyrum, 5 Dec 1877

Ruth's mother died when Ruth was about three years old. Her father was a basket maker by trade and was not able to earn much money. When Ruth was old enough, she worked outside the home. She was working with the Morris Jenkins family when they heard the Gospel and wanted to go to Salt Lake Valley.

When Ruth was nineteen years old, she sailed on the ship, "Samuel Curling," with the Jenkins family. On May 24, 1856, they traveled on the railroad to Iowa City. She crossed the Plains in John A. Hunt's Wagon Company. They were experiencing terrible hardships at the time they passed the Edward Martin Handcart Company. The early snowstorm caused much suffering and misery. Their food was scarce. They were met by rescue parties and finally arrived in the Salt Lake Valley on December 15, 1856.

Their first home was a little dugout where their first child was born. They later built a small two-room adobe home in the Fourth Ward. They were the parents of ten children. Ruth was fully occupied taking care of these children. In 1882, the children all had typhoid fever, but all got well through the nursing care of their mother and with the help of the Lord.

Ruth passed away at the age of fifty nine in Spanish Fork, Utah County, Utah.

ALICE TATTERSALL ROBB

BIRTHDATE: 7 Mar 1853
Lancashire, England
DEATH: 11 Apr 1918
Paragonah, Iron Co., Utah
PARENTS: James Tattersall
Mary Alice Benson Tattersall
Riley Marsden
PIONEER: 1868
SPOUSE: Thomas Robb
MARRIED: 27 Feb 1871
Salt Lake Endowment House
DEATH SP: 22 Jun 1931
Paragonah, Iron Co., Utah

CHILDREN:
Mary Ellen, 14 Jul 1872
James, 24 Jul 1874
Thomas William, 2 May 1880
Margaret, 20 Apr 1883

Alice's father died when she was only three years old. Her mother married William Riley. As a girl, Alice worked in a cloth factory. While working there, she mashed two of her fingers so they never had normal nails.

Alice's grandparents and her mother were members of the Church of Jesus Christ of Latter-day Saints when Alice was born. When she was fifteen, she came to America and walked all the way across the Plains. Alice and her mother moved to Parowan in 1868. Alice's step father didn't come with them and her mother married William Marsden.

Alice lived with her Uncle Richard Benson. All her life she had a nice voice for singing. As a girl she sang in the choir in England and now she sang in the choir in Parowan.

Alice married Thomas Robb by taking a five week trip to the Endowment House in Salt Lake City, and back to Parowan. They moved to Paragonah and lived in a little log home.

Alice was the first president of the Young Ladies Mutual Improvement Association in Paragonah which was organized in 1869. She also served in the Relief Society as a counselor. She would spend as high as a week at a time with sick people, leaving her oldest daughter and husband

to care for the home and children. People were always welcome in her home.

Alice was a gentle, kind, and loving mother and grandmother. Alice died of a stroke at age sixty-five.

ANN TURNER ROBB

BIRTHDATE: 20 Jan 1827
Birse, Aberdeenshire, Scotland
DEATH: 6 Feb 1901
West Weber, Weber Co., Utah
PARENTS: John Turner
Isabella Smith
PIONEER: 2 Sep 1868
Daniel McArthur Wagon Train
SPOUSE: James Robb
MARRIED: 24 Jan 1847
Birse, Scotland
DEATH SP: 22 Jul 1875
West Weber, Weber Co., Utah

CHILDREN:
Jane "Jennie," 11 Jul 1847
Isabella (Duncan), 8 May 1849
Elizabeth (Purrington), 16 Nov 1854
Ann, 2 Mar 1856
James, 23 May 1861
John, 21 Jun 1863
Jessie, 21 Dec 1865
Margaret (McFarland), 6 Dec 1868
Alexander Charles, 20 Aug 1871

Ann was born in Scotland in 1827. She was the youngest child in the family of six. Ann married James Robb on January 24, 1847 in Birse, Aberdeenshire, Scotland. Ann and James had nine children.

This family left Benton, Wyoming on August 14, 1868 and were on the Plains on their trek West for twenty days.

In Utah, they began farming in the West Weber area. Seven years after their arrival in Utah, Ann's husband James, and their twelve year-old son, John, drowned. It was July 22, 1875.

Following these deaths, Ann was forced to find help to run the farm to support her family. Her youngest child was not yet four years of age. Ann did not remarry, but struggled to take care of the necessities of life for her family.

Ann passed away at the age of seventy-four years, having been a widow for twenty-six years. Both Ann and James are buried in West Weber, Utah where they had lived after coming to the West and settling there.

She was truly a fine example of pioneer women of faith and fortitude. She knew what had to be done to survive, and she did it with all her might, mind and strength. She is honored by her posterity for her courage, for her faith, and her determination to succeed.

AGNES NANCY (OR NANCY ANN) MCALLISTER ROBBINS

No
Photo
Available

BIRTHDATE: 1806
Newry, Armagh, Ireland
DEATH: 26 Apr 1856
Salt Lake City, Salt Lake Utah
PARENTS: James McAllister
Sarah Watson
PIONEER: Sep/Oct 1855
SPOUSE: Edward Robbins, Jr.
MARRIED: abt 1833
England
DEATH SP: 23 Jun 1851
St. Louis, Missouri

CHILDREN:
James, 21 Nov 1834
Joseph, 6 Jan 1837
Edward, abt 1839 (died as a child)
Mary, 27 Jul 1841
Sarah, abt 1843 (died as a child)
Jane, abt 1845 (died as a child)
Cyrus William, 5 Oct 1849

Agnes Nancy (or Nancy Ann) was born in Ireland in 1806. There is little information about her before her marriage.

She married Edward Robbins Jr. about 1833. He had been born in England—an English father and an Irish mother. Nancy had seven children, three of whom died in childhood.

Nancy and Edward joined the Church of Jesus Christ of Latter-day Saints and were baptized on November 29, 1847 in Westbromich. On September 5, 1849, Edward set sail from Liverpool, England with Nancy's blessings. He left her with the care of their three children, with another one expected in a month, and his eighty-seven year-old widowed mother. They longed to go to America, and decided that he should go to earn enough to bring the rest of the family later. Their humble home was filled with the spirit and no sacrifice seemed too great.

It was from St. Louis that Nancy received the Doctor's report telling of Edward's death from cholera on June 23, 1851. He passed away never having seen his last son.

She never gave up the dream that she and Edward shared. With long and hard work, and with much scrimping, she and her family started for Utah in 1855. Nancy's mother-in-law, Mary Richards Robbins, was then very old, but she was still anxious to go with the family. With courage, the ill-equipped family started out, the youngest child under six years and the oldest ninety-three.

The trip was difficult at best, but though her faith was strong and her spirit willing, her poor old body was worn out and Mary R. Robbins died and was buried along the trail at Ash Hollow, near Laramie, Wyoming. Nancy's dream of joining the main body of the Saints was realized as she arrived in the Salt Lake Valley in the fall of 1855.

Her hard life and sacrifice took their toll, and she didn't live long after arriving in the Valley. She passed away on April 28, 1856, just about six months after her arrival. She had survived long enough to realize the dream of she and her husband.

The letters written by him to her before she left England show much tenderness, faith, and desire to be together again. The following are some quotes from his letters which show his love, concern and above all his great faith. "If I did not know that it is the work of God I would soon be in Old England again, but knowing that we are to serve the Lord by sacrifice, I am determined to go ahead." . . . "My dear Nancy, I feel the want of you here more than ever I did before and I trust it will not be long before wee are again Eunighted never to part again. I would never wish any man to part with his family as it is a great sacrifice and if I had known as much before leaving England I fear I would not be strong enough to accomplish it. But what is done has been done for the gospel sake and I know if we keep faithful the Lord will work out our redemption and we will be spedily eunighted once more, I will come to a close by praying our father in heaven to Bless you and our dear children is my constant prayer. " (Written in his own words.) "I am now firmer in the faith than when I left you . . . . I send my love to you, kiss my Mary a hundred times for me and also Cyrus. May God bless him and you all and preserve you in my prayer."

ELLEN ARBON ROBBINS

BIRTHDATE: 20 Jul 1840
Gravely, England
DEATH: 24 Oct 1924
Snowville, Box Elder Co., Utah
PARENTS: James Arbon/Arborn
Susan Arbon
PIONEER: 1862
SPOUSE:: Joseph Robbins
MARRIED: 1 Mar 1863
Provo, Utah Co., Utah
DEATH SP: 21 Sep 1912
Snowville, Box Elder Co., Utah

CHILDREN:
Ellen Marie, 6 Dec 1863 (died as an infant)
Joseph Arbon, 23 May 1865
Edward James, 16 Feb 1867
Mary Jane, 1 Nov 1868
Arnold Henry, 18 Oct 1870
William Thomas, 23 Mar 1872
Cyrus McAllister, 21 Nov 1873
Agnes Eliza (Larkin), 17 May 1876
Alfred Newman, 21 Sep 1878
Myron Wilford, 17 May 1881
Susan-Arnetta (LaPray), 2 Apr 1883

Ellen was born in Gravely, Cambridgeshire, England on July 20, 1840. She spent a happy childhood with her parents and her family although it was associated with hard work. Opportunities for education were not accessible so Ellen grew up unlearned in the things of the world, but not in the things of God, as she was one of His chosen children.

Ellen was baptized along with her sisters on June 20, 1856 when sixteen years of age. She had learned the meaning of hard work as much of her time was spent in the fields helping her father. She went to work in London and Aunsbury, England where she learned the joys and sorrows of being an English house maid. The few pennies she made were choice because it was through her savings that she was able to come to Zion the land of promise. Just before she left, her brother was killed by a horse, and she gave her mother part of her savings for his funeral expenses.

In 1862, Ellen left her home and family and emigrated to America. After crossing the rolling sea, she met some friends and traveled across the Plains by ox-team. She settled in Provo where she met Joseph Robbins on the plains, he being a teamster.

Ellen and Joseph were married at Provo and later went to the Endowment House in Salt Lake City, She spent the first years of her married life in Provo. She buried two children there. They next moved to Willard with their third child, their small son Edward. In Willard, three more sons and a daughter came to their home. Happy days were spent in this pleasant little Utah town in spite of the many hardships they had.

They later moved to Snowville where three more children joined the family. Ellen became the mother of eleven children. This made for a lot of work maintaining the family. She also did a great deal of church work. She attended the laying of the corner stones of the Salt Lake Temple and the dedication of both the Salt Lake and the Logan Temples. She held many positions in the Relief Society for many years.

Ellen Robbins passed away on October 24, 1924 at Snowville. She had been a faithful, pioneer woman who had the fortitude to do what she needed to do in order to maintain her large family. She is honored by her posterity for the examples she had been for them in their own lives.

JANE ADELINE YOUNG ROBBINS

BIRTHDATE: 17 Dec 1834
Kirtland, Geauga Co., Ohio
DEATH: 9 Apr 1907
Salt Lake City, Salt Lake, Utah
PARENTS: Joseph Young
Jane Adeline Bicknell
PIONEER: 1 Oct 1850
Joseph Young Co. Wagon Train
SPOUSE: Charles B. Robbins
MARRIED: 22 Nov 1855
Salt Lake Endowment House
DEATH SP: 10 Nov 1905
Logan, Cache Co., Utah

CHILDREN:
Charlotte Adeline (Matthews), 22 Dec 1856
Henry, 18 Jan 1859
John Young, 16 Mar 1860
Alice Edna (Dumbeck), 25 Nov 1862
Joseph Burtis, 28 Jun 1867
Seymour Bicknell, 20 Dec 1869
LeGrand 24 Feb 1872
George Young, 2 Feb 1875

Jane Adeline was born in Kirtland, Ohio, on December 17, 1834. She was the oldest of eleven children born to the first of her father's five wives. Her father was the elder brother of President Brigham Young. As a child she was a member of the Nauvoo, Illinois Third Ward.

Jane was not quite four years old when she was with her family at the Haun's Mill massacre. She lived through the persecutions and extermination from Missouri and then from Nauvoo.

She was fifteen years old when her family crossed the Plains. They left Kanesville, June 15, 1850 in her father's wagon train company. They arrived in the Salt Lake Valley on October 1, 1850.

At the age of twenty-one, Jane married Charles Burtis Robbins. Her uncle, Brigham Young, performed the marriage in the Endowment House. They lived in Salt Lake City where their first four children were born. They then moved to Logan where five more children were born into their family. They were all raised in Logan, Utah.

Jane gave her permission for her husband Charles to take two additional wives. He married Martha Allen in 1865 and they had three children, and then Harriet Vilate Pitkin in 1878, and they had four children.

Jane Adeline Young Robbins passed away on April 9, 1907 in Salt Lake City at over seventy-two years of age. Charles had died about one and a half years before her death.

Jane had experienced much of hardships and persecutions as she had pioneered the West in Salt Lake City and in Logan Utah. She is to be honored by her posterity for her great faith and for her courageous fortitude in withstanding the adversities she encountered. She was a great pioneer woman of Utah.

JANE CARTER HARRIS ROBBINS

BIRTHDATE: 16 Feb 1840
Prince Rock, England
DEATH: 7 Aug 1933
Stone, Oneida Co., Idaho
PARENTS: Edwin Carter
Ann Stockdale
PIONEER: 4 Sep 1859
George Rowley Handcart Co.
SPOUSE I: William M. Harris
MARRIED: 4 Jul 1858
Williamsburg, New York
DEATH SP: 11 Apr 1870
Curlew Sinks, Box Elder, Utah

CHILDREN:
Charles Edwin, 21 Jul 1859
Mary Jane, 4 Nov 1861
Adaline, 4 Nov 1863 (died as an infant)
Sarah Ellen, 18 Dec 1864
William James, 8 Oct 1866
Lucy Ann, 19 Nov 1868

SPOUSE II William Robbins
MARRIED: 14 Jul 1872
Hansel Spring, Box Elder Co., Utah
DEATH SP: 29 May 1933
Salt Lake City, Salt Lake Co., Utah

CHILDREN:
Hilda, 16 Oct 1872
Rosella, 28 Jun 1873 (died as an infant)
Hubert Bross, 29 Jun 1874
Arthur William, 18 Sep 1876
Walter James, 10 Sep 1878
Avis, 6 Oct 1880 (twin - died as infant)
Rebecca, 6 Oct 1880 (twin - died as infant)
Pearl, 9 Oct 1883

When Jane was two years old, her father was killed in a stone quarry when a blast of dynamite was set off without warning. Her mother remarried four years later. Jane's stepfather had a severe stroke and was bedfast for several years.

During all these trials and hardships, the Carter family heard the gospel of the Church of Jesus Christ of Latter-day Saints and began making preparations to leave England.

On May 4, 1856, their family boarded the ship, "Thornton," and sailed for America. After they arrived in Castle Gardens, New York, they remained in New York for five years to earn enough money to buy provisions to cross the Plains. Here, Jane worked in a tailor shop.

Jane married William Morton Harris on July 4, 1858. They were counseled to go to Florence, Nebraska to prepare for their journey across the Plains. They made their handcart while waiting for orders to continue their trek. They joined George Rowley's Handcart Company. Jane gave birth to her first son at Chimney Rock, Nebraska and had to ride in the wagon called "The Great Western" for several days until she recovered. They arrived in the Salt Lake Valley on September 4, 1859.

They settled in Kaysville, Utah for a couple of years. They moved to Mill Creek where Jane's last four children were born. William wanted to raise his children on a farm, so in 1860, he and his brother-in-law homesteaded on farmland in Curlew Valley which is near Snowville, Utah.

On April 11, 1870, William died of complications of lead poisoning associated with his printing trade.

Two years after his death, Jane married William Moran Robbins. They lived on the farm in Curlew where they worked vigorously to provide for their thirteen children. Five children were from her first husband and eight children were from her second husband. They lived on the farm in Curlew Sinks for five years and later moved to a farm three miles from Snowville.

Jane served in the Relief Society and Primary for many years. Later she served as President of the Snowville Ward Primary. She was ninety-three years old when she passed away at the home of her son, Hulbert Robbins.

MARTHA ALLEN ROBBINS

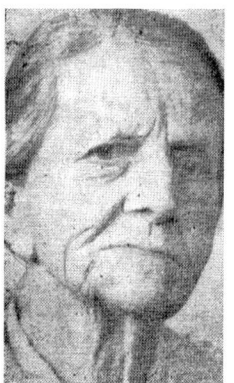

BIRTHDATE: 26 Sep 1841
Cold Ash, Berkshire, England
DEATH: 21 Sep 1939
Kaysville, Davis Co, Utah
PARENTS: John Allen
Hannah Willis
PIONEER: 26 Sep 1861
SPOUSE: Charles B. Robbins
MARRIED: 7 Jul 1865
Salt Lake City, Salt Lake, Utah
DEATH SP: 10 Nov 1905
Logan, Cache Co., Utah

CHILDREN:
Frank Allen, 27 Sep 1867
Florette, 12 Jul 1869
Martha, 27 Mar 1871

Martha was a brilliant student in England and earned tokens of commemoration from the Queen of England and the English schools she attended. She sailed on the packet ship, "Manchester," with her widowed mother, two brothers, and two sisters. They arrived in New York on May 16, 1861. They traveled from New York to Council Bluffs, Iowa where they joined a group of Saints to cross the Plains. They arrived in Salt Lake City on September 26, 1861.

Martha lived with the Bishop family in Tooele as their housekeeper. She also worked for Sarah Daft. Eventually, Martha went to Logan to help her married sister. This is where she met Charles Burtis Robbins.

After Martha and Charles were married in the Endowment House in Salt Lake City, Utah, they spent time at Promontory Point where Charles had a contract with the railroad.

After her husband passed away in 1905, Martha traveled back east to the World's Fair in St. Louis and several trips to Chicago. She also traveled to California several times. She loved nature, beautiful sunsets, and the grand mountains. She lived with her grand daughter for the last ten years of her life. She still took daily walks and helped with housework at the age of ninety.

Martha passed away at the age of ninety-five in Kaysville, Utah.

MARY ANN CAMPBELL RICHARDS ROBBINS

No
Photo
Available

BIRTHDATE: 1760 1762
Ballyton, Newtonards, Ireland
DEATH: 5 Oct 1855
Ash Hollow, Near Laramie, Wyoming
PARENTS: Michael Campbell
Nancy or Agnes Creighton
PIONEER: Oct 1855
Milo Andrus Co. Wagon Train
SPOUSE I: Mr. Richards
MARRIED: (later divorced)
DEATH SP. Unknown

CHILDREN: (birthdates unknown)
Nancy,
Ellen,

SPOUSE II: Edward Robbins
MARRIED: 1797 / 1798
DEATH SP: 1815
Belfast, Antrim, Ireland

CHILDREN:
Ann Marie (McWherter), 1798
Ellen Jane (Bailey Ramsden), Jun 1800
Catherine (Broomhead), 9 Jun 1802
Joseph, 1804
Edward Jr., 1806

Mary Ann Campbell was born in England in 1760, in Ballyton, Newtonards, Down, Ireland. She divorced her first husband on grounds of cruelty and cared for her two daughters alone.

In 1797, Mary Ann, now thirty-seven, married Edward Robbins,(his third marriage), and began another family. Edward, an enlisted man in the British Army, went with his regiment to Ireland during the Irish Rebellion. Mary Ann, with her two infant daughters, went with him. Her third daughter, Catherine, was born in Market Hill, Armagh. Their two sons were born in New Ray, of the same county. The family moved often. When Mary Ann's husband died in Boyne, he was buried in the Bell Wire Church Yard.

The fifty-five year old widow moved her family to West Bromwich, Staffordshire, where Ann Marie died, unmarried. Ellen Jane and Catherine married. Joseph, left home and was never heard from again. Edward Jr. married Nancy Agnes McAllister of Scotland, and took his mother into his home with his family.

This was the status of Mary Ann's decedents when the Gospel found them in 1839-1840. Cyrus H. Wheelock was one of the missionaries sent from Nauvoo, among his first converts was Catherine's husband, William Broomhead and his family. All of Mary Ann's children were attracted to the message and were baptized. At the age of ninety-two, Mary Ann was baptized on June 15, 1852 at the West Bromwich Bathe by John Taylor.

Edward, thinking to obtain employment in America, there by bringing his family over also, left England in 1849, but this was not to be. After writing encouraging letters of promise of comfort once they reached America, Edward was stricken with cholera and died on June 26, 1851. Four years later, and with help from relatives, they were able to arrange their passage to America.

In a company headed by Israel Barlow, Mary Ann with Edward's wife and children set sail on April 22, 1855 aboard the ship, "Samuel Curling," bound for Zion. To the delight of everyone, Mary Ann was on her feet dancing when music was played, and coins were tossed to her in compliment.

They docked in New York 27th of May. In Kansas, they met Mary Ann's oldest daughter's family who was prepared to continue the journey to Utah with them.

Because of her age and fortitude, for her journey Brigham Young provided a light conveyance with all the necessary supplies to insure her comfort and strict orders that her needs should be attended to in order for her to arrive in good health in spite of her advanced age.

All went well at first, but circumstances changed and about 200 miles from Salt Lake, she passed away in the back of a heavy wagon and was buried with little ceremony. Her absence was keenly felt by those awaiting her arrival when the company reached it's destination. But it was felt that her reward was sure in the Kingdom of God.

MARY CHILDE ROBBINS

BIRTHDATE: 15 Apr 1830
Much Wen Lock, England
DEATH: 28 Jul 1914
Gunnison, Sanpete Co., Utah
PARENTS: James Childe
Ann Childe
PIONEER: abt 1861
SPOUSE: James Robbins
MARRIED: 1 Mar 1859
Coventry, England
DEATH SP: 17 Jan 1886
Denver, Colorado

CHILDREN:
George John, 22 Dec 1859
Ellen Marie (Kearns), 22 Sep 1862
William, 2 Feb 1865
Melissa Emily (Peterson), 28 Jan 1867
John George, 8 Jun 1870
Emma Estella (Belitz), 22 Nov 1876

Mary was born in England in 1830. She married James Robbins on March 1, 1859 in Coventry, England at almost twenty-nine years of age. Before her marriage she was listed as being a servant according to the census records of England. James had been married before and had four children-Caroline age nine, James age eight, Sarah Charlotte age six, and Mary Ann age five.

James, his four children, Mary and her child all set sail for America on the ship "Wyoming" and arrived in Philadelphia on October 16, 1860. The wagon train with which they came west has not been identified. Mary was baptized on November 17, 1860. When they arrived in Utah they were sealed and received their endowments on December 20, 1862 in the Endowment House.

Mary and James' first home was in American Fork in a dug out. They must have lived there for a time, and later moved to Gunnison, Sanpete County in Utah.

Mary passed away in Gunnison, on July 28, 1914 at the age of eighty-four years. She had led an adventurous life by leaving England, crossing the Plains to a new, desert land. She was truly a pioneer woman of faith and fortitude to be honored by her posterity for her strength and courage, as well as her faith. She was buried on July 31, 1914 in the Mt. Olivet Cemetery in Salt Lake City, Utah.

Her husband had passed away many years before, leaving her a widow for twenty-eight years. He had died in Denver, Colorado, and was also buried in Salt Lake City.

HARRIET BEMIS ROBERDS

BIRTHDATE: 3 Apr 1838
Kirtland, Ohio
DEATH: 28 Apr 1918
San Bernardino, California
PARENTS: Alvin Bemis
Jerusha Gurnsey
PIONEER: Fall 1851
SPOUSE: Thomas R. Roberds
MARRIED: 23 Jan 1859
San Bernardino, California
DEATH SP: 5 May 1915
San Bernardino, California

CHILDREN:
William Harrison, 27 Mar 1860
Rosie, 10 Nov 1861
Dorthella Ann, 10 Jan 1863 (twin)
Nellie Dorthella, 10 Jan 1863 (twin)
Harriet Jerusha, 4 Apr 1864
John Thomas, 17 Dec 1865
Frances Georgina, 2 Apr 1867
Albert Franklin, 10 Dec 1868
Eli Thomas, 17 Apr 1871 (twin)
Geroge Richard, 17 Apr 1871 (twin)
Alvin Nephi, 14 Jul 1873
Walter Jasper, 18 Jan 1875
Berdie Maybelle, 5 Jun 1876

Harriet Bemis was born in Kirtland Ohio in 1838, the eighth born into a family of eleven children. Jerusha and her husband, Alvin Bemis, moved around New York as their circumstances demanded for the growth of their family's welfare. Their first seven children were born in New York then it seems they followed the Church of Jesus Christ of Latter-day Saints into Kirtland where Harriet was born in the spring of 1838.

The year of 1838, was the beginning of the end for the Saints in Kirtland, the Prophet left on January 12th, never to return and soon the inhabitants of that city would follow out of survival for themselves and their families.

Driven to Nauvoo for a scant eight years, then on to Winter Quarters and finally to the Rocky Mountains. Some must wait for the opportunity and finances before they could leave and two more children were born into the Bemis family as they waited in Kirtland but by 1844, they had moved to Lee County, Iowa where the last baby was born and died that year.

Harriet's father died in Lee County when she was ten years old, it would take three more years before her mother would find the wherewithal to grant her dead husband wish, to see the family safely into Zion.

In 1851, with the remaining ten children, she started westward from Council Bluffs. Arriving in Ogden the family stayed for three more years, until in 1854 when they joined other colonists for the journey to San Bernardino, California.

After their arrival in the Golden State, sixteen year old Harriet helped her mother and brothers as they settled on 240 acres of land near Lytle Creek Wash.

When Harriet was twenty-one years old, she fell in love with and married Richard Thomas Roberds, a young man exactly one year to the day older than she, they shared the same day of birth.

Thomas had traveled to Utah with his parents when he was eleven by way of Pueblo, Colorado and spent the winter there, then on to Hardscrabble, Utah for another year. They started for Salt Lake Valley in a party of twelve wagons driving two hundred head of loose stock and reached Salt Lake City in the Fall of 1848. They built log cabins and spent the winter among the Mormons. After a year of raising grain, Thomas' parents decided to go to California. En route the Roberds and others found a spring in the vicinity of Hangtown, (Diamond Spring) in northern California and mined for several years before they ventured on to San Bernardino where they settled and Thomas met and married Harriet Bemis.

Harriet had children who were raised in the "country that knew no winter," but the floods of 1862 wiped out her family's home on Lytle Creek. It was relocated on another section of the ranch only to be threatened by floods once again. Her mother and brothers solved the problem by building on higher ground.

Her older brother Samuel while on a logging trip in the mountains near San Bernardino, was killed by a she bear defending her cubs. Nephi, a younger brother was killed by Indians on a cattle round up in the Mojave desert in 1866, and her mother died when Harriet was thirty-six years old.

Harriet lived to be eighty years old. She had lived through the events of the pony express, the telegraph, the railroad and the motor car, so far away from the covered wagon that had bumped and rocked over the Plains and mountains and that had carried her into her future.

ANN SOPHIA ROLLINS BECKSTEAD ROBERTS

BIRTHDATE: 5 Mar 1831
Bangor, Penobscot, Maine
DEATH: 13 May 1885
Annabella, Sevier Co., Utah
PARENTS: Enoch P. Rollins
Sophia Wing Philbrook Lambert
PIONEER: 16 Oct 1852
Eli B. Kelsey Co. Wagon Train
SPOUSE I: Sidney M. Beckstead
MARRIED: 11 Jun 1850
Bellevue, Sarpy Co., Nebraska
DEATH SP: 7 Aug 1864
Nebraska

CHILDREN:
Mary Lucetta, 1847 (died as an infant)
Sarah Ann, 14 Mar 1851

Sabra Jane, 20 Oct 1853
Lillian Sophia, 7 Sep 1855
Mary Emily, 6 Dec 1857
Rosetta, 11 Aug 1859 (died at age three)
Loretta Delancy, 26 Sep 1861 (died at 16 months)
Cordelia, 28 Oct 1863 (died at 11 months)

SPOUSE II: Edward Killick Roberts
MARRIED: 19 Apr 1869
Salt Lake City, Salt Lake Co., Utah
DEATH SP: 3 Jun 1915
Annabella, Sevier Co., Utah

CHILDREN:
Melinda Elvina, 12 Feb 1870
Sidney Enoch, 5 Nov 1871

Ann's parents heard the gospel in the autumn of 1837. Most of the family was baptized as members of the Church of Jesus Christ of Latter-day Saints on February 8, 1841 in East Pelham, New York. Ann's father worked in various towns to make enough money to support his growing family.

In August of 1843, they left New York State and made their way to Akron, Ohio where they stayed to reimburse their funds. Ann passed through many of the hardships and persecutions of the early church members. When they were living on the banks of the Mississippi River, the mob ordered them to leave or be killed. Four families crossed the river to safety at Montrose, Iowa. The family endured much sickness and privation in the spring of 1848 as they started for Council Bluffs.

In 1849, Ann went to visit a sister in St. Louis. On her return to Nauvoo, she witnessed the burning of the temple. She returned to Council Bluffs on October 16, 1852,

Ann married Sidney Marcus Beckstead. They lived with his mother for two years and their first child was born there. They traveled across the Plains in the Eli B. Kelsey Wagon Company and arrived in the Great Salt Lake Valley on October 16, 1852.

Sidney and Ann settled in West Jordan where the ground proved unprofitable. They moved several times to find employment. They lived in East Weber, Mountain Green, West Jordan, and Riverdale. Two of their daughters died from Scarlet Fever and were buried in West Jordan.

At the time of Johnston's Army passing through the valley to Camp Floyd, they kept a Traveler's Rest on the State Road about a mile and a half from Draper. They lived for a short time in Spanish Fork, then built a home in Payson, then moved again to Santaquin.

In 1864, Sidney was called to go to the Missouri River to help some Saints cross the Plains. On the return trip he was accidently shot and was buried by the Platte River.

Ann taught school in order to make a living for her family. She taught at West Jordan one year and then returned to Payson and taught school there.

In Payson, she married a widower, Edward Killick Roberts. They had two children. She was a very patient, faithful wife. She had much courage and endurance having moved fourteen times in the twelve years before Sidney's death. She was active in the Primary, and Relief Society. She kept family records and was greatly interested in genealogy.

EMELINE MATHEWS ROBERTS

No Photo Available

BIRTHDATE: 7 Feb 1837
McComb, McDonough, Illinois
DEATH: 17 Apr 1867
Payson, Utah Co., Utah
PARENTS: Anson J. Mathews
Elizabeth Burgess
PIONEER: 1848
Independent Wagon Company
SPOUSE: Edward K. Roberts
MARRIED: 19 Apr 1850
Salt Lake Endowment House
DEATH SP: 3 Jun 1915
Annabella, Sevier Co., Utah

CHILDREN:
Eliza,Emeline, 2 Aug 1851
Susannah, 5 Jun 1853
Julia Sophia, 17 Oct 1854
William Edward, 19 Nov 1856 (died at age 1)
Elizabeth Elenor, 14 Aug 1858 (died at age 3)
Joseph Samuel, 31 Aug 1860 (died at age 6)
Mary Amanda, 8 Apr 1863
George Hannibal, 13 Feb 1865
John Henry, 17 Apr 1867 (died at 4 months)

Emeline was born in McComb, Illinois. She was the youngest child in a family of eight children. Four of her brothers and sisters died as children leaving Emeline with two older brothers and one older sister.

The family joined the Church of Jesus Christ of Latter-day Saints. Emeline moved with her parents to Nauvoo, Illinois. In 1848, Emeline and her parents traveled independently to Utah.

After Emeline's marriage in 1850 to Edward Killick Roberts, Emeline moved several times. Her first child was born in Mill Creek. The second child was born in Santaquin, the third and fourth children were born in Salt Lake City. Her fourth child, William, died shortly before he was one year old. Emeline's last five children were born in Payson.

She did not live to see her children inasmuch as she passed away while giving birth to her ninth child. Emeline was buried in Payson City Cemetery.

EMILY JAMES ROBERTS

BIRTHDATE: 18 Mar 1858
Scranton, Pennsylvania
DEATH: 20 Mar 1936
Paradise, Cache Co., Utah
PARENTS: William James
Sarah James
PIONEER: 7 Jun 1860
Daniel Robinson Handcart Com.
SPOUSE: John T. Roberts
MARRIED: 15 Nov 1875
DEATH SP: 28 May 1922

CHILDREN:
John James, 22 Jan 1877
Elizabeth (Hirst), 10 Feb 1879
Sarah Maria, 8 Jun 1881 (died as a child)
Rosabelle, 29 Aug 1883 (died as a child)
William James, 4 Nov 1887
Joseph James, 26 Nov 1889
Emily (Pearce), 22 Mar 1892

Emily was born in 1859 in Pennsylvania. They arrived in the Salt Lake Valley on June 7, 1860, a part of a handcart company led by Captain Daniel Robinson. They walked and pulled their handcarts, packed with luggage, 1,200 miles from Florence, Nebraska to the Salt Lake Valley.

Emily married John Thompson Roberts on November 15, 1875 when she was seventeen years of age. To them were born seven children; three sons, and four daughters.

Early in her life, Emily had become an expert at sewing and knitting. For many years she spun the yarn from the wool of sheep they raised, and then made cloth for dresses, shirts and even the pants her family wore. Emily also sewed for her neighbors and she made burial clothing. She knitted mittens, and socks which she sold to help care for her family needs. She was an excellent cook and could easily make a meal from the meager food available to the family. They moved to Hyrum, Utah.

Emily was always active in the Church of Jesus Christ of Latter-day Saints, and she served for many years as a Sunday School and Relief Society teacher. Her three sons were called to go on missions. To each one she said, "Go and we will find a way to care for you."

Her faith had no bounds and her courage never wavered. She was a faithful, true, pioneer woman who had much strength and fortitude to do her best. This trait she passed on to her posterity for which they are grateful.

EMMA DOROTHY BELL ROBERTS

BIRTHDATE: 18 Mar 1844
Nauvoo, Hancock Co., Illinois
DEATH: 9 Jan 1911
Vernal, Uintah Co., Utah
PARENTS: John Watson Bell
Ann Fish
PIONEER: Oct 1855
Gilbert & Garrish Freight Wagon
SPOUSE: Ephraim H. Roberts
MARRIAGE: 2 Nov 1861
Provo, Utah Co., Utah
DEATH SP: 14 Jul 1911
Naples, Uintah Co., Utah

CHILDREN:
Ephraim Bell, 31 Jan 1863
John Homer, 27 Aug 1865
Andrew Bethul, 4 Feb 1867
William Evermont, 21 Oct 1869
Myron Theodore, 31 Dec 1871
Marion Howard, 1 Jan 1872
George Henry, 30 Jul 1874
Ernest Alma, 10 Nov 1876
Alfred LeRoy, 9 Dec 1878
Frank Edward, 12 Apr 1881
Sylvia May, 12 Oct 1883
Don Watson, 25 May 1886

Emma Dorothy's parents joined the Church of Jesus Christ of Latter-day Saints in New Castle, England and emigrated to Nauvoo, Illinois in 1843. The family left Nauvoo with the Saints in 1846 and moved on to Council Bluffs, Iowa where they lived five years. Because of poor health, her father was advised to precede them in going to Utah.

A year later, in 1854, Emma's mother and her seven children joined a company of Saints in which to cross the Plains. Because her oxen had strayed, the company would not wait for them. After she located the oxen, she and her family followed the company. When they were being ferried across the Missouri River, one of her wagons, not properly blocked, rolled backward into the river. They lost most of their clothing and provisions. She started her wagons again toward Utah. The family traveled alone for two weeks until they overtook a government freight train and traveled with them until they reached Laramie, Wyoming. From there, they journeyed with the Gilbert and Garrish Freight Train into the Salt Lake Valley and arrived in October 1855.

The family received permission to glean the wheat fields and were able to gather eighteen bushels of wheat. Emma's father met them in Salt Lake and took his family to Provo where he was working as a tailor. Emma worked for different families.

She married Ephraim Horace Roberts who was a potter by trade. They had two children before they moved to Mona, Utah in 1866, where ten more children were born.

In 1893, they moved to Ashley, Utah where they rented a two-room log house. They made pottery in the north room and lived in the south room until they could build a larger log home with a separate potters shop. Emma had the responsibility to display and sell the pottery.

Emma Dorothy also worked in the Naples Ward Relief Society for many years. They discontinued their business because the men contracted poisoning of the lungs due to the lead used in making the pottery. They built a new house and converted their old home and shop into a dance hall.

HANNAH ROBERTS ROBERTS

BIRTHDATE: 27 Mar 1847
Eglwysbach, Wales
DEATH: 10 Apr 1878
Logan, Cache Co., Utah
PARENTS: Hugh Roberts
Mary Owens
PIONEER: 1864
Jeremy & Bywater Wagon Train
SPOUSE: Robert David Roberts
MARRIED: 6 Jun 1870
Salt Lake City, Salt Lake, Utah
DEATH SP: 10 Aug 1925
Logan, Cache Co., Utah

CHILDREN:
David Robert, 30 Mar 1871
Hugh, 22 May 1876

Hannah's family had joined the Church of Jesus Christ of Latter-day Saints while she was quite young. She was not allowed to attend school because she was a member of this new church.

When Hannah was seventeen years old, her family sailed the ocean and journeyed to their outfitting place in America.

The Civil War was still raging. They were threatened and mistreated by some of the soldiers. Hannah's mother had become very ill from drinking river water. Hannah rode in the wagon to cradle her mother's head in her lap as they traveled the rough bumpy trail. Their wagon broke down just west of Fort Bridger and their wagon train went on without them. After the repairs were made, they traveled on to Henefer where they were met by relatives. They remained in Henefer until her mother recuperated.

In November of 1864, they moved on to Salt Lake City. Jobs were scarce, so in July 1865, they moved to Smithfield in Cache County, Utah.

Hannah married David Roberts and they had two sons. Following Hugh's birth, she contracted a cold through some teeth that she had extracted. She never recovered from the effects. She weakened and grew slowly worse until she passed away at the age of thirty-one.

HARRIET ANN HEFFORD / EFFORD ROBERTS

BIRTHDATE: 16 May 1818
Apperly, England
DEATH: 16 Nov 1895
Kaysville, Davis Co., Utah
PARENTS: Thomas Efford
Mary Ann Ellis
PIONEER: 1850
Independent Wagon Company
SPOUSE: Levi Roberts
MARRIED: 18 Aug 1835
Deerhurst, England
DEATH SP: 22 Jan 1894
Kaysville, Davis Co., Utah

CHILDREN:
Henry B., 16 Jun 1836
Caroline B., 30 Oct 1838
Phoebe Ann, 22 Jan 1842
Marinda, 10 Apr 1845
Harriet Ann, 8 Sep 1848
Mary Jane, 13 Dec 1851
Matilda, 2 Jan 1854
Lucy Ann "Ellen," 1 Nov 1855

Harriet Ann was born and spent her early life in Apperly, Gloucestershire, England. She married Levi Roberts in Deerhurst, Gloucestershire, England, 1840. They were soon baptized as members of the Church of Jesus Christ of Latter-day Saints.

In 1841, they and their two children emigrated to America. They traveled on the ship, "North America," and landed in New Orleans. They traveled by boat up the Mississippi River to Nauvoo. While they lived in Nauvoo, two more children were born to them. Harriet Ann was a faithful wife and a loving mother. She encouraged her husband in performing his duties.

They were a part of the exodus leaving Nauvoo amidst so much persecution. After they reached Mt. Pisgah, Levi was called to serve in the Mormon Battalion. Even though she was very ill, she encouraged him to defend his country. After the war ended and her husband returned to Winter Quarters, they moved on to Council Bluffs, Iowa. They remained there until they had the necessary equipment to travel across the Plains. They traveled with Captain Pearson's Independent Wagon Company and arrived in the Salt Lake Valley in the Fall of 1850.

They settled in Kaysville where her husband built a four-room home of logs. In 1865, he built another home of logs which has since been moved to the Pioneers Trails Village by 'This is the Place Monument' in Salt Lake City.

Harriet had been patient and uncomplaining through the many years that she had been a hopeless invalid. She was known as a faithful, steadfast, and consistent woman. She passed away at the age of eighty-seven.

HARRIET MCEVERS ROBERTS

BIRTHDATE: 3 Sep 1808
Isle of Mott, Franklin, Vermont
DEATH: 27 Feb 1876
Provo, Utah Co., Utah
PARENTS: Charles McEvers
Tamma Knapp
PIONEER: Fall 1851
Wagon Train Company
SPOUSE: Horace Roberts
MARRIED: 5 Jun 1828
Morgan Co., Illinois
DEATH SP: 25 Dec 1868
Provo, Utah Co., Utah

CHILDREN:
Maria Louisa, 11 Nov 1829
Homer, 1 Jan 1831
Susan, 16 Feb 1834
Jane Cecilia, 4 Jun 1836
Ephraim Horace, 13 Jun 1838
Harriet Emily, 9 May 1841
Charles Daniel, 14 Oct 1843
Morris Geraldus, 26 May 1848
Laura Celestia, 8 Aug 1850

Harriet was born on the Isle of Mott in Vermont. She married Horace Roberts in Morris County, Illinois. They were the parents of five children by the time they joined the Church of Jesus Christ of Latter-day Saints in 1840. They were driven from their home and their property was taken from them.

In 1841, they went to live in Nauvoo. When they arrived, the prophet Joseph Smith advised them to build a pottery to make crockery for the Saints. As they made the crockery, they also helped to build the city and temple of Nauvoo. They were able to receive their endowments in the Nauvoo Temple.

After the martyrdom of the Prophet and his brother, they were again driven from their home. They went by team of oxen and wagon to Winter Quarters where they were sealed for eternity by Brigham Young in their home in February, 1848. Their four year old son was drowned in the Missouri River on April 26, 1848. They traveled with the Saints across the Plains and arrived into the Salt Lake Valley and settled in Provo, Utah County, in 1851.

The Prophet Brigham Young advised them to build another pottery. They were kept very busy with their business and raising their children.

Harriet passed away on February 27, 1876 in Provo, Utah County, Utah.

JANE ELIZA GRAVES ROBERTS

No Photo Available

BIRTHDATE: 21 Sep 1832
Yarmouth, Norfolk, England
DEATH: 1 May 1929
Provo, Utah Co., Utah
PARENTS: Daniel Graves
Elizabeth Sarah Baker
PIONEER: 1856 Wagon Train
SPOUSE: Horace Roberts
MARRIED: 11 Dec 1856
Salt Lake Endowment House
DEATH SP: 24 Dec 1868
Provo, Utah Co., Utah

CHILDREN:
Emaline Elizabeth (Cooper), 24 Oct 1857
Son, abt 1859

Jane Eliza was born in 1832 in England. She was the sixth of twelve children in the family and only two of them are known to have grown to maturity. Her mother died in 1838, and her father married Mary Newman in 1840. They were the parents of two children.

According to family history, Daniel Graves was a tutor for Queen Victoria's children. He had great interest in education and was well known for his penmanship. This interest in education prompted him to teach his two daughters to read and write. "Commoners" were not interested in taking an educated woman as a wife, and the titled gentry were not interested in marrying a commoner, educated or not.

Missionaries from the Church of Jesus Christ of Latter-day Saints approached the Graves family in England, and Daniel joined the new church and prepared to emigrate to the new world.

On 17 Apr 1855, Daniel and Mary, his second wife, boarded the "Chadarozo" at Liverpool, England bound for the United States of America with their five children and with Jane Eliza and her sister Elizabeth who were then twenty-three and twenty-seven years old.

Horace Roberts, who had come to Provo in 1851 to build a pottery, was listed as surety for Jane Eliza's passage in keeping with the Perpetual Emigration Fund to help bring new members to Zion.

Jane Eliza brought with her from England a set of Wedgewood China, Blue Willoware pattern. As they crossed the Plains in the wagon train, as it became necessary to lighten the load, she carried her china rather than leave it alongside the trail. This china was her dowry, all she had of her gentile past to offer a potential husband in this wild new country. Three dinner plates are all that remain of her set of Wedgewood.

Upon reaching Provo, Jane Eliza lived with Horace and Harriet Roberts at the family home. Her education became an asset for her rather than a hindrance, and she began teaching school.

On December 11, 1856, Jane Eliza became Horace Roberts' third polygamous wife. They had two children Emaline Elizabeth and possibly a son.

An 1880, census shows Jane Eliza living with the family of H. C. Southworth in Provo's third ward.

In 1901, the Utah County Infirmary opened and Jane Eliza was one of the first patients. After her treatment was completed, she became an aid. She lived and worked at the infirmary until her death on May 1, 1929. According to a yellowed newspaper clipping, she was the oldest woman in Utah when she died, as the paper listed her age as 117. If the birth date listed in her genealogy is correct, she was only ninety-seven years old. She is buried in the Provo City Cemetery.

During her lengthy pioneer life, she experienced much of the early history of Utah. She was truly a pioneer woman of faith and fortitude.

JANNET JONES ROBERTS

BIRTHDATE: 30 May 184
Dinas, Llantrisant, South Wales
DEATH: 25 Jul 1878
Bloomington, Bear Lake, Idaho
PARENTS: Llewellyn G. Jones
Mary Jannet John
PIONEER: prior to 1864
SPOUSE:: William Roberts
MARRIED: abt 1863
Farmington, Centerville, Utah
DEATH SP: 11 Aug 1881
Bloomington, Idaho

CHILDREN:
William Jones, 21 Feb 1864
Charles Llewellyn, 19 Sep 1865
Mary Elizabeth, 29 Jul 1867
David Ephraim, 3 Apr 1869
Griffith, 27 Jan 1871
Thomas John, 6 Jul 1873
Lydia (Loveland), 8 Jul 1875
Jenett, 21 Jul 1876
Child Roberts, 1878

Jannet (Jannett, Janett, Janet, Jennet) was born in 1841 in South Wales. Wales is a beautiful country, a land of high mountains and rushing streams. It has rich deposits of coal, and there is also farm land. Jannet's father could have gone into the coal mines to work to assist the family. Jannet was the first child born into her family. She was one of eight in the family. Her father and mother worked hard and the children also helped as they could.

In the Fall of 1840, Mormon missionaries went to Wales introducing the new religion of the Church of Jesus Christ of Latter-day Saints. Most of their children emigrated to America before the parents did. They established homes in the farming area of Bloomington, Idaho. The parents joined their family members in 1868.

In 1867, President Young asked for help from the Utah Saints to aid the thousands of converts who were coming to Utah. Aid was sent from Utah and Idaho.

It is not known exactly when Jannet came to Utah but she married William Roberts about 1863 in Centerville or Farmington in Utah. They moved to the Bloomington and Franklin, Idaho areas where their nine children were born. One of Janet's brothers, David, prepared a home for their parents as they emigrated in 1868 and they were happy to reunite with their family members.

William Roberts had emigrated from England. Together he and Jannet made a living through their hard work. Jannet helped as she could. She was a good mother to her children. She served others.

Jannet Jones Roberts passed away on July 25, 1878 in Bloomington at the age of thirty-seven years, possibly as she gave birth to her last child. Her husband died just over three years later, leaving their children ages from five through seventeen years of age.

Jannet Roberts was a brave young pioneer mother who had left England and Wales after joining the Mormon Church. She had indeed been a faithful pioneer woman of Utah, and of Idaho.

MARGARET CURTIS SHIPP ROBERTS

BIRTHDATE: 17 Dec 1849
St. Louis, Missouri
DEATH: 13 Mar 1926
Brooklyn, Kings, New York
PARENTS: Theodore Curtis
Margaret Morgan
PIONEER: Utah from California
SPOUSE I: Milford Bard Shipp
MARRIED: 1 Dec 1867
Salt Lake City, Salt Lake, Utah
DEATH SP: 14 Mar 1918
Salt Lake City, Salt Lake, Utah

CHILDREN:
Walter Curtis, 20 Feb 1869
Carl Lynn, 30 Apr 1872
Milfordetta, 17 Oct 1874
Louisa Caroline, 6 Aug 1876
Margaret Curtis, 14 Feb 1878
Morgan Farnsworth 4 Nov 1880
Gross Agnew, 23 Feb 1882
Wallace Bruce, 1883
Theodore Clair, 1885

SPOUSE II: Brigham Henry Roberts
MARRIED: Apr 1890
Salt Lake City, Salt Lake Co., Utah
DEATH SP: 27 Sep 1933
Salt Lake City, Salt Lake Co., Utah
CHILDREN: None

As an infant, Margaret traveled with her parents around Cape Horn to San Francisco. Then their company traveled overland to Salt Lake City. She attended Brigham Young's school with his children. Her mother died when she was seventeen.

Margaret married Milford Bard Shipp and encountered many challenges as his plural wife. In 1875, Brigham Young encouraged her to attend medical school in Philadelphia. She received her medical degree eight years later in March, 1883. Her children were left in the care of Ellis Reynolds Shipp who was also a plural wife of Milford Bard Shipp.

Margaret was talented as a physician and maintained a very successful practice in Salt Lake City. She trained many nurses over a period of thirty years. She also wrote articles for magazines and journals, and was asked to speak on many occasions.

A cancellation of her sealing to Milford Shipp was granted by Wilford Woodruff on June 15, 1888. She continued to support herself and her children through her medical practice. Of her nine children, only three lived to adulthood.

In 1890, Margaret married Brigham Henry Roberts in the Salt Lake Temple. She remained active in church and community affairs. In 1922, she joined her husband in the Eastern States Mission Headquarters while he served as Mission President.

Margaret passed away in Brooklyn at age seventy-six from pneumonia. She is one of the few women whose funeral was held in the Salt Lake Tabernacle.

Margaret was known as a woman of intelligence, kindness, personal magnetism, and unquestioning faith. She was a lover of art, poetry, music, and all that is elevating. She had been married to B. H. Roberts for more than thirty-six years when she passed away.

MARIA ANN DALLIMORE WORLTON ROBERTS

BIRTHDATE: 29 Jan 1847
Twerton, Bath, England
DEATH: 7 Nov 1930
Henefer, Summit Co., Utah
PARENTS: George Dallimore
Harriet Harris
PIONEER: 1863
Richard Ballantyne Wagon Train
SPOUSE I: James T. Worlton
MARRIED: 14 Nov 1863
Salt Lake City, Salt Lake, Utah
DEATH SP: 6 Feb 1885
Morgan, Morgan Co., Utah

CHILD:
William Albion, 24 Nov 1864

SPOUSE II: George Roberts
MARRIED: 11 Oct 1868
Salt Lake City, Salt Lake Co., Utah
DEATH SP: 4 Feb 1930
Henefer, Summit Co., Utah

CHILDREN:
Abigail, 27 Jun 1869
Harriet, 28 Jan 1872 (died as an infant)
George Jr., 23 Dec 1872
Robert William, 24 Apr 1875
Emma Jane, 30 Sep 1877
James Dallimore, 18 Nov 1879
Lulu Bell, 13 Mar 1882
Herbert Leason, 5 Aug 1885
Anna Almeda, 28 Aug 1887

Maria Ann was born in 1847 in Twerton, Bath, Somerset, England. She was baptized into the Church of Jesus Christ of Latter-day Saints on the same day as her brother and sister, July 29, 1856. She was nine years old at the time. Her parents had been baptized earlier.

Education was important to her family, and her father, a carpenter, saw to it that his children all attended school. Little is known about her life in England, but it is known that the spirit of gathering to "Zion" was strong among the Church members at that time, and Maria Ann, age sixteen, was the first of her family to venture to the promised land, with the aid of the Perpetual Emigration Fund.

The frail, tiny, fragile-looking young girl began her difficult journey to America, and it is assumed that she knew other church members from her home who emigrated at the same time. She left England on the ship "Amazon" on June 4, 1863 with 895 Saints on board. She crossed the Plains in 1863, and one history says she came with the Richard Ballantyne Wagon Company.

Almost immediately after her arrival in the Salt Lake Valley, Maria went to Lehi and she became the second wife of James Trimbrell Worlton who had children older than she was. He, was forty-two and she was sixteen.

They moved to Morgan, Utah. Elizabeth, the first wife had lost a two month old baby boy while crossing the Plains and she never quite got over the grief of his death, and was unable to have more children. She cared for Maria's little William as Maria was forced to work in the potato fields.

While helping lay railroad tracks through Morgan, George Roberts met the tiny young woman who was to become his wife. He felt protective towards her even though he had learned she was married with a child. He objected to her working so hard.

Maria divorced Mr. Worlton and later married George Roberts in 1868 at age twenty-one and George was nineteen. In order to marry, she had to give up her four year old son before she could obtain the divorce. Maria knew her son felt security in the only home he had known so she gave the child to the Worltons and never made contact with her son again.

George and Maria first settled in Henefer, where he farmed and developed the land and engaged in many other occupations. His major occupation was blacksmithing. Maria and George had nine children born to them; four sons and five daughters, one died shortly after birth. This kept Maria extremely busy.

Because George was successful in his many businesses, Maria's life was not as hard as other at that time. It is said that George took a cup of hot tea to Maria before she got up each morning, and he called her 'pullet' because she was so petite and moved with short quick steps.

George and Maria were active in the community but broke away from the Church that had brought them to Utah. Their children were not raised with religious training. They did not participate in any church.

George and Maria celebrated their Golden Wedding Anniversary on OCtober 11, 1819 with a party in their big house, their home for about twenty-five years. They then moved to a smaller home for their remaining years. They both passed away in Henefer, Summit County, Utah. George passed away in February and Maria in November of 1930.

Maria was a pioneer woman who experienced much in her lifetime coming to Utah from England at the age of sixteen years and living here until eighty-four years of age. She is honored for her courage, hard work, and sacrifice.

MARY ANN "POLLY" BULLOCK WILLIAMS HARTLEY ROBERTS

BIRTHDATE: 19 Sep 1829
Moira, Franklin Co., New York
DEATH: 18 Aug 1901
PARENTS: Benjamin Bullock III
Dorothy "Dolly" Kimball
PIONEER: 1854
Wagon Train Company
SPOUSE I: Judge Williams
MARRIED: Not given
DEATH SP: Not given

CHILDREN: None

SPOUSE II: Jesse Thompson Hartley
MARRIED: Not given
DEATH SP: Not given
CHILD:
Jesse, 27 Nov 1854 (died as an infant)

SPOUSE III: Benjamin Morgan Roberts
MARRIED: 23 Nov 1856
DEATH SP: 1891

CHILDREN:
Benjamin Morgan, Jr., 12 Aug 1857
Samuel Kimball, 19 Nov 1858

Isaac Bullock, 24 Feb 1860
Mary Jane (Farrer), 18 Oct 1862
Dorothy Melissa (Carter), 5 Mar 1863
John Riggs, 29 Oct 1865
Sarah Ann, 11 Jun 1866 (died as a child)
Sarah Ann, 10 Mar 1867
Martha Elizabeth (Nelson), 5 Feb 1868
Electa, 17 Apr 1870, (died as an infant)
Joseph Bullock, 25 Jun 1871

Martha Ann "Polly" Bullock was born in 1829 in the state of New York. She was the fourth child in the family. Her childhood was a happy one. She was taught how to work and to take responsibility in the home. She attended school, and received a good education as offered to the young people of that day.

At an early age, Mary Ann married Judge Williams in Moira, New York, but when the family left Nauvoo, because of religious differences, they parted company. The story is told that he gave her a little bag of gold as a parting gift and wished her well.

Mary Ann soon met a young darkeyed, dark haired man by the name of Jesse Thompson Hartley whom she married. Tragedy came to her family when her father passed away. Her father's death was a shock to Mary Ann who was in Kansas City with her husband.

They were making preparations to leave for the West when tragedy struck again when Jesse T. Hartley, her husband, was shot and killed. Mary was grief stricken. Her family was gone, her father dead and now her husband. She was expecting her first child. He was born shortly after her arrival in the Salt Lake Valley. He was named after his father. Nine months later, this little son died. Mary was indeed bereft. She found comfort with her sister, Jane, and her three brothers. Jane was located in Provo, and Mary Ann joined her there.

One of Mary Ann's brothers, Isaac, was called to preside over a mission for the Church at Fort Supply, Wyoming near Fort Bridger. He was to plant gardens, raise cattle, and build up the area to provide help for those coming from the East. It was also a mission to the Shoshone Indians as well.

On December 14, 1856, thirty-one year old Isaac married Electa Wood, later married a second wife, Ann, and took his two wives, and his widowed sister Mary Ann, on his mission to Fort Supply.

It was at Fort Supply that Benjamin Morgan Roberts was serving a mission among the Shoshone Indians. Benjamin met the wife of his choice in Mary Ann. It took persuasion on his part, and they were married on November 23, 1856; he was twenty-nine and she was twenty-seven years old. They began their life together in that area, and their first child was born in 1857, and it is said he was the first white child born in Wyoming.

When Johnston's Army came, they took possession of this place. These pioneers were called home. Later they were called on a mission to the Muddy. They were returning home to Provo when Indians stole their mules and left them stranded near Cedar City. They finally returned to Provo when Mary Ann was expecting her last child, and Benjamin was forty-four years of age.

Mary Ann lived with her youngest daughter following the death in 1891 of her husband. Mary Ann passed away at age seventy-two on August 18, 1901.

Mary Ann was truly a great pioneer woman who loved the Lord, and had faith to follow wherever she was called to go. She left a great posterity who honor her for this faith and for her great fortitude in overcoming the difficulties she encountered during her lifetime.

MARY KNOWLTON CORAY ROBERTS

BIRTHDATE: 22 Apr 1848
Atchon, Missouri
DEATH: 21 May 1923
Vernal, Uintah Co., Utah
PARENTS: Howard Coray
Martha Jane Knowlton
PIONEER: 1850
John Sharp Co. Wagon Train
SPOUSE: Orville Clark Roberts
MARRIED: 24 Jul 1868
Provo, Utah Co., Utah
DEATH SP: 12 Dec 1912

CHILDREN:
Orville Clark, 24 Oct 1869
Howard Daniel, 10 Jul 1871
Harriet Virginia, 7 Apr 1873
Mary Eliza, 13 Aug 1876
Martha Jane, 15 Jun 1878
Frank Homer, 10 Apr 1880
Daphne Helena, 3 Dec 1882
Don Carlos, 12 Jun 1885
Louis Demont, 17 Sep 1888

Mary was born in Missouri in 1848. Her story must begin with a little about her parents. Her father was a private secretary for the Prophet Joseph Smith, and her mother was a teacher. Her mother was asked to help the Prophet's mother write the life story of her son. Martha sat every day by the bed and wrote as Sister Smith told her the story. It became the book titled "The History of Joseph Smith by his Mother Lucy Mack Smith."

This family lived in Nauvoo, and when the troubles came there, they left, crossed the river with the Saints, stayed a while and planted crops along the way, and Martha also ran a ferry while her husband farmed, to they did not reach Salt Lake City, Utah until 1850. Their daughter, Mary, was born in 1848 near Winter Quarters. Many babies and old folks died during that winter.

Mary and her family reached the Salt Lake Valley. Her father then became a clerk for President Young. When

Johnston's Army came, the family moved south. Mary's family was raised in Provo, Utah, where her father and mother both taught school.

As a child, Mary was always quick to help others. She helped her family in the fields, but she was never as strong as most, and one day during the grasshopper famine, she fainted. Upon being questioned, her parents learned that she had been dividing her rations with her little sister. When she was a teenager, she and her sister sheared the wool from their pet sheep, colored and spun the wool into thread, and wove it into cloth for their Christmas dresses, which were all hand made.

At age seventeen, Mary began teaching school. She was a true friend to others and she was remembered for her kind, understanding smile.

Mary Coray married Orville Clark Roberts in Provo, Utah on July 24, 1868. Before this time, Clark had played an important part in the building up and the settling of Utah by crossing the Plains thirteen times assisting the Saints. He was an express rider for Col. Conover, and had carried messages for the government to the Indians. He had been shot twice, and had his horses shot from under him, but he was a strong, fearless young man. He became a friend to the Indians and learned their language.

Following their marriage, they went to live on a ranch near Mona in Juab County where they lived until 1880. They were called to help settle the southern part of the state. It was a hard journey to make with six small children, but they went, and Mary left a sick mother.

One year later Mary returned over that terrible trail to return to be with her mother until she passed away. Mary then returned to her family by riding the train from Ogden, through Denver, and on down to the end of the road, Durango, Colorado. Clark had built a two-room log house in Mancos, Colorado and was at the depot to greet Mary on her return home. Mary had great joy and relief at once more being with her dear husband.

They made their home in Mancos, where she gave birth to three more children. There was no help for women having children except the help neighbors could give, and the help of the Lord.

Clark built a new home for his family which was the first all lumber house in their area. They were happy with their new home. Clark began to lose his health. The exposures he had suffered in his early life showed its effect, and he became almost crippled with rheumatism. He felt a warmer climate would help him so he sold out and moved to New Mexico. He finally gave up his work. Mary took over the responsibility of supporting the family and did so until each became independent and began to care for her.

Clark passed away on December, 1912, and after his death, Mary lived with one or another of her children, wherever she thought she was needed.

Mary Coray Roberts passed away in 1923, after a long life of teaching in all the Church organizations and leaving lasting impressions for good on all who knew her. She was indeed, a truly great pioneer woman of faith and fortitude, qualities she passed on to her posterity who honor her name.

MARY OWENS ROBERTS

BIRTH DATE: 15 Oct 1806
Llanrwst, Denbighshire, Wales
DEATH: 9 Jan 1894
Liberty, Bear Lake Co., Idaho
PARENTS: Thomas Owens
Mary Hughes Morris
PIONEER: 16 July 1884
Capt. John Warren Wagon Train
SPOUSE: Hugh Roberts
MARRIED: 4 May 1830
Llanrwst, Denbighshire, Wales
DEATH SP: 13 Oct 1892
Liberty, Bear Lake Co., Idaho

CHILDREN:
Jane, 10 Oct 1830
Robert Owen, 20 Nov 1832
Elizabeth, 6 Mar 1835
Owen, 19 Mar 1837 (died at age 10)
Catherine, 12 Apr 1839
Margaret, 17 May 1841
Mary, 22 Nov 1843
Hannah, 27 Mar 1847
John, 16 Apr 1849
Thomas, 3 Apr 1851 (died at age 3)

Soon after Mary was born her parents separated. Her mother married her stepfather, Robert Griffith Humphreys, who helped raise her, along with her seven half-brothers and half-sisters. Her family not having very much money caused all the older children to go out to work at an early age. Mary became a servant girl. This enabled her to purchase many articles in the way of household needs.

When she met and married Hugh Roberts, she had saved up quite a lot of furniture including a large clock that stood on the floor. She was an excellent cook and home maker, which greatly aided her in the rearing of her family.

Mary Owens Roberts and her children, that were old enough, and living at the time; were all baptized on July 14, 1849 by Elder Able Evans. At this time in England all families belonging to the Church of Jesus Christ of Latter-day Saints were bitterly and severely persecuted. The Mormon children were excluded from the schools, and ostracized. Also many people withdrew their patronage from Hugh's shoe business, which made it difficult for the family to obtain a livelihood. But they never wavered in their faith.

On one occasion, Hugh and another elder was seized by a mob, dragged under a bridge, and there they were preparing to hang them with ropes. The women followed and raised such a strong remonstrance, (particularly his daughter, Catherine, who rushed up to him and clinging to him said to the mob, "You shall NOT hang my father.") The mob dispersed giving a warning and a threat that Elders preaching Mormonism in the neighborhood again would suffer death.

It was due to this persecution and the desire to go to Zion that Hugh, Mary, and most of their family left their native land and migrated to America on May 21, 1864 on board the "McClellan."

Mary, her husband, and family still did not find it easy in the free land of America. The Civil War was on and mobs here also were persecuting the Mormons. They had to travel up the Hudson River to Albany, New York and there go by train to Erie, Pennsylvania, where the train was put on a boat bound for Canada.

The Roberts family traveled on their journey westward, returning to the United States at Detroit, Michigan, then proceeded on to St. Joseph, Missouri, where they camped in a large warehouse. Here they took a boat again up the Missouri River. The river was shallow in places and the boat run into sand bars and got stuck in the mud and the passengers would have to get off and walk. Sometimes for considerable distances.

Finally they reached a place called Wyoming, which was located on the west bank of the Missouri River where they were put off to be outfitted to cross the great Plains to Zion. It was midnight and a terrible storm was raging, and they sought shelter under a large choke-cherry bush until morning. It was here that Mary Owens became thirsty during the night and drank some of the river water, and became very ill during the balance of the journey.

When morning came the family was provided with four yoke of oxen, with three families to each wagon, to go West in the John Warren Wagon Company.

After traveling about three days cholera broke out in the camp, but passed by the Roberts family. Also when about half-way over the Plains they came upon the camping place of some mule-team freighters and found all seven men were massacred by the Indians. Some soldiers were burying their bodies.

The family passed safely over the Platte River and stopped at Fort Laramie, Wyoming to get some medicine for Mary who was quite sick from drinking river water. Also to make some repairs on their wagon.

The family finally arrived in Salt Lake City, Utah on October 5, 1864. Here they were rewarded for all their hardships and trials. They raised their family, and worshiped their God in their own way and unafraid.

MARY PEAT ROBERTS

BIRTHDATE: 18 Nov 1829
Horsley, Derbyshire, England
DEATH: 21 Apr 1870
Salt Lake City, Salt Lake, Utah
PARENTS: Job Peat
Elizabeth Fletcher
PIONEER: 26 Aug 1866
Capt. Andrew Scott Wagon Train
SPOUSE: Samuel Roberts
MARRIED: 18 May 1852
Derby, England
DEATH SP: 18 May 1919
Afton, Wyoming

CHILDREN:
Thomas Haworth, 4 Dec 1852
Eliza, 8 Oct 1855
Katherine, 25 Mar 1857
Arthur, 13 Jun 1859
Walter, 6 Mar 1862
Mary, 2 Jan 1865 (died as a child)
Samuel, 2 Sep 1866
William Peat, 4 Jan 1869
Joseph Peat, 21 Apr 1870 (died as an infant)

Mary was born in 1829 in Horsely, Derbyshire, England as the third child in the family of eight children. She was a beautiful girl with brown, curly hair.

Mary married Samuel Roberts on May 18, 1852. They had nine children, six sons, and three daughters. After their marriage, they lived in Derby for three years and then decided to move to London where Samuel could make a more profitable living.

Samuel had learned his father's business as a photographer, book seller and news agent. In London he worked for a newspaper. They moved into a lodging house and kept boarders and roomers. Many of the Mormons in London, lived with them, called it home, and taught them the Gospel. They worked hard, and were happy enjoying the blessings of the gospel.

By 1865, they were seriously thinking of migrating to America. Word had been sent out by Brigham Young for the Saints of God to hasten to the valleys of the Rocky Mountains to help build up Zion.

On May 23, 1866, together with about 350 other Saints, Mary and Samuel and their family of six children sailed on the ship "American Congress" bound for America. After forty-two days on the ocean, they landed, in New York on July 4th. They took the trains from New York to Wyoming, Nebraska arriving there July 14th. The journey was hard on Mary, as she was almost eight months pregnant, and her baby, Mary, was just one and half years old.

They left Nebraska on August 8th, with Captain Andrew Scott's Wagon Company and began the next part of their long and difficult journey. Children old enough and able had to walk. Their eldest son, age fourteen, walked the entire trip. All had chores in camp like gathering fuel for fires, and carrying water. Mary, being heavy with child, rode part of the way as she took care of baby Mary. Samuel, their son, was born near Ft. Laramie on September 2, 1866 with only their faith, and the angels of the wagon train to help.

The weather was very cold as they reached the mountainous country, and their food supply had been rationed. At South Pass, the Saints encountered a, terrible snow storm and the Saints suffered because of insufficient clothing, no dry fuel, and short food supply. Regardless, they were anxious to reach Zion, and it was a happy day when they entered the Great Salt Lake Valley and could see houses, farms, and buildings in the city of Zion, a change from the endless desert and prairie.

Mary was weak because of these necessities being lacking, and the lack of care in childbirth. Mary, their baby daughter, was very ill. In the Valley, the family of Daniel H. Wells, the mayor of the city, took this family to their home for a period of time, and cared for them. Daniel had known them when he served his mission in England.

After a short time, the family moved into a small home on 2nd Avenue. They just settled in their home for about six weeks, when their little daughter, Mary died. This was another incident which tried their faith, Samuel found employment with the Deseret News, which provided food and clothing for his family. The sons earned what few pennies they could to help out by doing chores for neighbors. With great joy, Mary and Samuel were sealed in the Endowment House on November 30, 1867. On January 4, 1869, their eighth child was born.

The family prospered and were happy in their new homeland. Their ninth child was born, but with sadness, he and the beloved wife and mother, Mary Peat Roberts, passed away on April 21, 1870. Mary was forty years of age. She was truly a great pioneer woman of faith and fortitude who left a great legacy for her posterity.

PAMELIA EMMA BENSON ROBERTS

BIRTHDATE: 28 Feb 1842
Nauvoo, Hancock Co., Illinois
DEATH: 10 Feb 1892
Salt Lake City, Salt Lake, Utah
PARENTS: Ezra T. Benson
Pamelia Andrus
PIONEER: 22 Oct 1849
George A. Smith Wagon Train
SPOUSE: Bolivar Roberts
MARRIED: 23 Nov 1867
Salt Lake City, Salt Lake, Utah
DEATH SP: 11 Aug 1893
Salt Lake City, Salt Lake, Utah

CHILDREN:
Bolivar, 26 Feb 1865
Eliza Adula, 21 Dec 1866 (twin - died as an infant)
Daughter, 21 Dec 1866 (twin - died as an infant)
Don Carlos, 18 Feb 1868 (died as an infant)

Harry L., 1871
Don Carlos, 1876
Frank Taft, 4 Dec 1878

Pamelia Emma, daughter of Ezra T. Benson and Pamelia Andrus, was born on February 28, 1842 in Nauvoo, Hancock County, Illinois. On April 11, 1856, at the age of fourteen, Pamelia was taken with her brother, Charles Augustus Benson, for their endowments at the Endowment House. They had left Nauvoo, Illinois for Utah and traveled with the George A. Smith Wagon Company and arrived in Utah on October 22, 1849.

On November 23, 1867, Pamelia married Bolivar Roberts in Salt Lake City, Utah. She gave birth to seven children, three of whom died as infants the day they were born or the next day. She had one set of twin daughters both who died the day they were born. Their oldest son, lived until 1890 and was unmarried. Their son Harry died in San Francisco, California, in 1915, and is buried in the Salt Lake City Cemetery. The second Don Carlos was born in 1876, married Louise Hunt. She died in 1931, and he died in 1926 in Salt Lake City, Utah. Their last child was Frank Taft who was born in 1878. He married Catherine Chapman Culmer, He died in 1942 and is buried in Fresno, California.

Pamelia Roberts lived until February 10, 1892 when she passed away in Salt Lake City. She was eight days short of her fiftieth birthday. Her husband, Bolivar passed away one year and one half after she did. They were pioneers who came to Utah at an early age and remained here their lifetimes and helped develop the Utah territory.

SARAH ANN ROWELL ROBERTS

No
Photo
Available

BIRTHDATE: 23 May 1810
Monroe, Fairfield, Connecticut
DEATH: 10 Feb 1892
Kanosh, Millard Co., Utah
PARENTS: David Rowell
Sarah B1ackman
PIONEER: 1852
Capt. A. Bates & A. Cummings
SPOUSE: Sidney Roberts
MARRIED: 26 May 1830
Nauvoo Temple, Illinois
DEATH SP: 30 Apr 1874
Kanosh, Millard Co., Utah

CHILDREN:
Edna Mariah, 10 Jan 1831
George Henry, 3 Aug 1833
Lucinda Victoria, 7 Mar 1838
Susan Elizabeth, 3 Sep 1843 (died at age 5)
Joshua, 21 Nov 1845
Sarah Josephine, 1 Apr 1848
Sidney John Benedict, 14 Aug 1853

Sarah Ann's ancestors left England and emigrated to the Colonies as early as 1542, settling in the Connecticut and Massachusetts area.

Sarah married Sidney Roberts in May of 1830. Missionaries from the Church of Jesus Christ of Latter-day Saints began preaching the gospel in this area. Sidney and Sarah Ann accepted their message and were baptized. Due to the persecution of their neighbors and former friends, they decided to join the Saints in Nauvoo, Illinois.

They arrived in Illinois at the height of the mob persecution of the Saints there. Sidney's craftsmanship was in great demand because he had the skills of a blacksmith, carpenter, wagon maker and repairman. He was also clever at inventions.

Sarah and Sidney were among the first to be endowed and sealed in the Nauvoo Temple on January 23, 1846. They were also baptized for a number of their kindred dead. Sarah Ann took pride in her husband's work and would upholster or help him in any way she could. For five years they helped many emigrants with their wagons and machinery.

They came West in 1852 with the wagon train which was captained by Amos Bates and Alfred Cummings. Sidney acted as the company blacksmith. When they reached the Valley, they rented a house on the Salt Lake Short Line. Later, they bought a farm in Big Cottonwood Canyon.

Because of his skills, Sidney was sent to Mill Creek to help colonize there and to help build the great paper mill of the Church. Sarah supported her husband in the practice of polygamy when he married his second wife, Caroline.

Sarah gave generously of her services as a practical nurse and a midwife. Skillfully, she upholstered a wagon and a carriage which her husband made. She did temple work for the dead. She enjoyed weaving. Some time before 1870, they moved their family to Millard County and settled on Corn Creek, a little hamlet about seven miles from Kanosh. Later, they left Corn Creek and settled in Kanosh where they built a comfortable home and blacksmith shop.

Sarah was a widow for eighteen years and was eighty-two years old at the time of her death.

WILHELMINE FREDRIKKE KOFOED ROBBINS ROBERTS

BIRTHDATE: 22 Jul 1850
Arnager Parish, Denmark
DEATH: 28 Jun 1931
Burley, Idaho
PARENTS: Hans Ancher Kofoed
Cocilie Munch (Monk/Munk)
PIONEER: 4 Sep 1859
George Rowley Handcart Comp.
SPOUSE I: Wilson C. Robbins
MARRIED: 2 Mar 1866
Weston, Franklin Co., Idaho
DEATH SP: 8 Sep 1892
Weston, Franklin Co., Idaho

CHILDREN:
Lorenzo Wilson, 9 Jan 1867
Milton, 16 Sep 1868
Louisa Minnie (Fleming McClure), 22 Jul 1870
Willard Hans, 16 Dec 1872
Luvana Cecelia (Hooper), 28 Mar 1875

SPOUSE II: William More Roberts
MARRIED: 3 Oct 1885
Montpelier, Bear Lake Co., Idaho
DEATH SP: 29 Oct 1909

CHILDREN:
William Robert, 5 Oct 1887
Charles R., 15 Jul 1893

Wilhelmine "Minnie" Fredrikke Kofoed was born in Arnager Parish, Nylaraker, Bornholm, Denmark in 1850. Her parents were among the first on the Isle of Bornholm to join the Church of Jesus Christ of latter-day Saints and were promptly disinherited. Her parents, disposing of all their belongings, had enough money for the family of eight children and their blind grandmother, to book passage on the "Westmoreland" plus enough to purchase a good team and wagon to get them across the Plains of America.

They set to sea 6:00 a. m. the morning of April 25, 1857 for the thirty-six day voyage that ended dreadfully. The Captain charged much more for the passage than originally agreed upon and the fine team and wagon had to be sold with the money given to the Captain. They were put ashore with little money in a strange land and a language they did not understand.

Traveling by rail to Iowa City they joined others to travel to Florence, Nebraska where the Kofoed's stayed for two years working for money to complete their journey. Minnie attended school, and it was difficult for the seven year old to learn the language as she went at her studies. An older sister, Michelle, fell in love, married and stayed in Omaha. Their blind grandmother, Anne Madsen, became very ill and died.

The faith of the family was sorely tried, undernourished to the point of starvation, their body's reaction to the bread they were able to bake because of a kindness of Mr. Hire, made them ill and the family was down with chills and fever. Fearing the family had small pox, the towns people drove them to the outskirts of the settlement. Again, with the kindness of the owner, they were able to live in an old shack which provided meager shelter and little protection from the cold.

Minnie's father put his money with another man's and they bought a handcart. Her mother was to ride on the handcart with the other woman, but was never allowed to "because she couldn't speak the language" and the Kofoed's walked every step from Nebraska to Utah, most of the time barefoot because their wooden shoes had worn out. Minnie was nine years old.

They lived in Lehi for five years then settled in Weston, Idaho where a living was eked out among the sage brush, rocks and some times hostile Indians.

When she was sixteen, Wilhelmine married Wilson as his second wife, their baby Lorenzo was the first white child born in Weston. The marriage lasted fifteen years and she raised their five children in polygamy.

They separated in 1881 and Minnie went to work as cook for a railroad gang. When the gang moved to Montpelier, Idaho she went also and met and married William More Roberts.

Wilhelmine and William had two boys, the second died about four years of age. William was killed in a railroad accident after a few short years of marriage. In her later life, Minnie lived with her children, taking turns living with each child. She passed away at her son's home in Burley Idaho one month before her eighty-first birthday.

ELIZABETH EDWARD ROBERTSON

No
Photo
Available

BIRTHDATE: 25 Aug 1802
Kirkhillooks, Glenisla, Scotland
DEATH: 28 Nov 1850
Council Bluffs, Iowa
PARENTS: Thomas Edward
Agnast / Agnes Lindsay
PIONEER: Died en route
buried in Council Bluffs, Iowa
SPOUSE: John Robertson
MARRIED: 27 Jul 1823
Glenisla, Forfarshire, Scotland
DEATH SP: 17 Jul 1832
Scotland

CHILDREN:
William, 3 Jul 1824
Thomas, 5 Aug 1825
Peter, 1826
James, 22 Sep 1827
John, 23 Oct 1829
Alexander, 11 Apr 1831
Margaret, 9 Apr 1833
Charles Ogilvy, 25 Dec 1837

Elizabeth was the third child born, she was welcomed by a brother named William and a sister named Ann. A third daughter named Jean was born in January, 1804, eighteen months after Elizabeth was born. Elizabeth's mother died during the birth of baby Jean. Six years later, in 1810, Elizabeth's father passed away. Elizabeth was only eight years old. After the death of their father, the Edward children lived with their grandfather and grandmother Edward.

Elizabeth became the sweetheart of a tall thin man named John Robertson. She and John were married July 27, 1823, just a month before her twenty-first birthday. John was thirty years old. The couple farmed and ran an inn in a house named Faulds. They also took up the wool trade to supplement their income.

During the busy years of beginning and maintaining a family, all went well financially as long as the price of wool was good. When the price of wool dropped, the family's income was very sparce.

On July 17, 1832, John died, leaving Elizabeth to raise five sons and a baby which was to be born early in the spring. Elizabeth's and John's daughter, Margaret, was born April 9, 1832. This child, however, did not live to be a year old.

According to a history written by Jessie Robertson Wadley, the following incident was remembered of those perilous times: "Some kind neighbors helped with the wool and all creditors agreed to take proportionate parts of a sale that was forced by one creditor except the dissenting creditor himself. No one came to the sale except the dissenting creditor and the auctioneer, who advised Elizabeth to call in her neighbors. They came and bought household goods and gave them back to her. She continued to operate the inn which enabled her to send her sons to school and to pay off all of her debts except to the man who had forced the sale."

Elizabeth's two oldest sons found employment some distance from their home and became acquainted with Mormon missionaries while away at work. William and Thomas soon became converted to the Church of Jesus Christ of Latter Day Saints and were both baptized September 30, 1847. They asked the missionaries to teach the rest of the family the new gospel. The family was taught and baptized by Elders Hugh Findley and William Gibson. James, John, and Alexander were baptized January 25, 1848. Charles and Elizabeth were baptized in 1849. After joining the Church, the family decided to sell their home and furnishings and go to America to join with Saints in the west.

The journey began with a trip by train to Glasgow where they bought passage on a steamer to Liverpool. In Liverpool, they boarded the ship, "Argo," along with many other saints and left for America, January 10, 1850. The ship's quarters were extremely small and unsanitary. The voyage was scheduled to take four to five weeks, however, due to stormy weather, the journey lasted nearly nine weeks.

It was reported that the ship nearly wrecked near the coast of Cuba on one of the few calm nights of the voyage. A sudden flash of light in the sky came from out of nowhere, and illuminated the sea to reveal a huge rock just ahead of the ship. The captain, Charles Mills, was able to change course just in time to avoid striking the rock.

Elizabeth and her family landed in New Orleans where they boarded a river steamer called the 'Uncle Sam'. They traveled two weeks on the Mississippi River to St. Louis, and continued their trip on a steam boat named Robert Cambell up the Missouri River to Council Bluffs, Iowa.

Elizabeth and her sons settled in a place called Kanesville for a time, in the river bottoms, in order to find work and save money to finance the trip West. The family forever regretted their stay there because they all became ill with chills and fever and were sick for most of that year.

Elizabeth never recovered, she passed away on November 28, 1850, at the age of forty-eight, and was buried in an unmarked grave. Her sons made the journey across the Plains and remained true and faithful to the gospel and to the determination she exemplified throughout her life.

SARAH ANN CORDINGLY ROBERTSON

BIRTHDATE: 19 Dec 1834
Idle, Yorkshire, England
DEATH: 22 Mar 1913
Orderville, Kane Co., Utah
PARENTS: Thomas Cordingly
Mary Lee Cordingly
PIONEER: 5 Oct 1854
Wagon Train Company
SPOUSE: Thomas Robertson
MARRIED: 19 Dec 1854
DEATH SP: Summer of 1887
Spanish Fork, Utah Co., Utah

CHILDREN:
Levi Thomas, 28 Sep 1854 (died as a child)
Sarah Ann, 5 Oct 1856 (died as an infant)
Margaret Alice, 1858 (died as an infant)
Seth Cordingly, 18 Mar 1859
Edward Lee, 1861
Mary Elizabeth, 1864 (died as an infant)
Isaac, 17 May 1868
John Franklin, 18 Sep 1870
Lydia Matilda (Palmer), 12 Jan 1873
Helen Jane (Palmer), 16 Mar 1875
Charles Thomas, 23 Aug 1877
Emma (Heaton), 23 Jul 1880
Ronald Straum, 20 Nov 1884

Sarah Ann was born in Yorkshire, England in 1834. Her parents were baptized into the Church of Jesus Christ of Latter-day Saints in 1842. Her family had cared for Elder Lorenzo Barnes during his last illness. He was the first missionary in this dispensation to die in a foreign land.

Sarah came to America with her family when she was ten years old. After living in St. Louis for a few years, the Cordingly family started for Utah with the Hans Peter Olsen Wagon Company. They walked and came by ox-teams and arrived in the Salt Lake Valley on October 5, 1854.

Thomas Robertson, a young man who had worked in her father's foundry, accompanied them. Sarah Ann and Thomas were married on December 19, that same year in Salt Lake City. They made their first home in Palmyra, Utah.

Sarah Ann's husband, a blacksmith, helped protect the fort from Indians, but they were kind to the Indians and were liked by them. One Indian brought fresh-caught fish for breakfast many times. This family moved on to help settle the towns of Spanish Fork, Mona, and Kanab, Utah.

Sarah Ann gave birth to eight children, four of whom had died, when they were called to Orderville, not far from Kanab. It was almost impossible to get there. Sarah said, "I just felt like this was the last straw and I couldn't endure more." But their faith in the Gospel and their belief that they should never refuse to go where the Lord called them gave them strength to help establish a town where the United Order was successful.

Sarah Ann was head of the sewing department for the Order. After the Order broke up, her husband still ran his blacksmith shop and Sarah did her sewing for most everyone in town. She received mostly food and cloth for her pay.

In 1887, Thomas became very ill and was taken to Spanish Fork, then to Salt Lake City on the train. A week after he had died and was buried in Spanish Fork. Sarah Ann was left with eight children to support, including a two year old son.

Doing much sewing by candlelight, to support her family, she eventually lost her sight. Even after becoming blind, she pieced each of her children a star pattern quilt top. Her granddaughters threaded pin cushions full of needles and stacked quilt blocks in order, so she could continue making the quilt blocks by hand.

After being a widow for twenty-six years, Sarah Ann Cordingly Robertson passed away on March 22, 1913 in Orderville, Utah. Her body rests in a little cemetery alongside of other pioneers of southern Utah.

Sarah Ann was a faithful pioneer woman who endured much, who contributed much to others, and who left a great posterity who honor her name.

ANN FULLWELL ROBINS

No Photo Available

BIRTHDATE: 16 Jun 1782
Pensham, Worcestershire, England
DEATH: 27 Oct 1861
Kaysville, Davis Co., Utah
PARENTS: James Fullwell
Elizabeth Greaves
PIONEER: 1850 Wagon Train
SPOUSE: Richard Robins
MARRIED: 1 Dec 1808
England
DEATH SP: 21 January 1849
St. Louis, Missouri

CHILDREN:
Edmund, 24 Apr 1809
William, Died in Jun 1835
James, 18 Jan 1818
Ann, died in 1841
Thomas Fullwell, 13 Aug 1824

Ann was the first of seven children born to her parents. After she married Richard Robins they made their home in the Gloucestershire area. There they heard the gospel message preached to the members of the United Brethern by Elder Wilford Woodruff in 1840. Ann, Richard, their three sons, and their grandson, Edmund Jr. were baptized within a few weeks.

Ann and Richard had suffered the loss of two of their adult children, William and Ann. The gospel message was especially meaningful to them.

It was Ann's greatest desire to have her family leave England and join the Saints in Zion. The first one of the family to emigrate was James. He married Elizabeth Lambert in December 1840 and they sailed from Bristol in January, 1841. They lived in Nauvoo and were endowed in the Nauvoo Temple February 2, 1846. Her grandson, Edmund Jr., was also endowed in Nauvoo in 1846. After the exodus from Nauvoo, he traveled to St. Louis. He met Ann and Richard there when they arrived from England in 1848, with their son, Thomas, and his family. Richard had become ill on the journey and died in St. Louis on January 8, 1849. Ann continued her journey with her family.

They traveled to the Salt Lake Valley in 1850 with an independent wagon company. When they arrived in the Valley, Thomas went south to settle. Edmund Jr. and James stayed in Kaysville. Ann's desire to have all of her family come to Zion was slowly being realized.

It wasn't long before her eldest son, Edmund Sr., and his family arrived from England and settled in Kaysville. This completed the emigration of her family. Her joy was complete. She had the gospel, her children and grandchildren were all baptized; those who were old enough were endowed.

She spent her last years devoted to her family and her church. She carried out her church assignments with quiet devotion, always being helpful, never seeking praise.

Ann was seventy-nine when she died in the Fall of 1861. Hers is the first recorded burial in the Kaysville Cemetery in Davis County, Utah.

ANN (OR ANNA) JOHNSON ROBINS

BIRTHDATE: 27 Feb 1821
Leigh, Worcestershire, England
DEATH: 12 Jul 1873
Scipio, Millard Co., Utah
PARENTS: William Johnson
Elizabeth Ann Johnson
PIONEER: abt 1851
SPOUSE: Thomas F. Robins
MARRIED: 20 Aug 1844
Leigh, Worcestershire, England
DEATH SP: 6 Jun 1895
Scipio, Millard Co., Utah

CHILDREN:
Emily Ann, 20 Aug 1845
Mary Agnes Lenora, 12 Aug 1848
Emma Jane, 16 Dec 1851
Adeline Elizabeth, 4 Sep 1854
(Thomas) Leonard Acamus, 24 Jan 1856
William Alvin, May 1858
Willard Richard, 17 Oct 1859
Annette Harriet, 1862

Ann was born in 1821 in England. She was the third child born into the family. She was baptized a member of the Church of Jesus Christ of Latter-day Saints on January 31, 1841.

Ann married Thomas Fullwell Robins on August 20, 1844 in Leigh, Worcestershire, England. The family came to Utah in about 1851.

They first made their home in Battle Creek (now Pleasant Grove) until about 1856. The entire family bundled into a covered wagon, with all their belongings and moved to San Bernardino, California. They lived there one year and then returned to Holden, Millard County, Utah in 1857. They lived there until 1861 when they moved to Round Valley, (now Scipio, Millard County). They helped organize and settle this valley.

Eight children were born to this couple. Two were born while they lived in England, the third was born in Council Bluffs, Iowa, and the rest were born in Utah.

Ann was a loving wife, and a kind, devoted mother. Although she was a frail, sickly woman, one was always welcome at her hearth. No one was ever turned away hungry or cold. She was a quiet, well mannered lady with a heart of gold.

Together with her husband, they helped subdue the West, and made it the wonderful place they and many others called home.

Ann passed away on July 12, 1873, at the age of fifty-two years in Scipio, and was buried in the old Southeast Cemetery there. Her husband, Thomas, passed away on June 6, 1895, also in Scipio and his buried in the same cemetery.

These were true pioneer of the Utah territory. They are honored for their faith and fortitude for their untiring efforts.

ELIZABETH LAMBERT ROBINS

BIRTHDATE: 19 March 1819
Wellington Heath, Herefordshire, England
DEATH: 15 March 1886
Kaysville, Utah
PARENTS: William Lambert
Fanny Francis
PIONEER: 5 Oct 1850
Wagon Train
SPOUSE: James Robins
MARRIED: 1840
England
DEATH: 8 August 1907
Kaysville, Utah

CHILDREN:
Elizabeth Ann, 6 Dec 1847
James Edmund, 7 Nov 1850
Mary Jane, 7 Nov 1850
Isabel, 25 Sep 1853
Charles William, 3 Sep 1855
Thomas Hyrum, 17 Mar 1858

Elizabeth and James left Bristol, England, on the ship "Caroline" in February, 1841, with Thomas Clark as clerk of the company. They disembarked at Quebec and then proceeded by water and land. They arrived in Nauvoo May 1, 1841. They had both been baptized in England in 1840 before they were married. The exact dates of their baptisms were not recorded, only the year. In the Nauvoo Temple on February 2, 1846, they were endowed and then joined the mass exodus from Nauvoo. They were sealed on April 1, 1854, in the Endowment House in Salt Lake City.

Elizabeth gave birth to their first child, Elizabeth Ann, at Winter Quarters on December 6, 1847. In 1848 they moved to Council Bluffs and began their preparations for the trek across the plains. Elizabeth Ann was an active toddler and Elizabeth was expecting their second child when they started their journey in the early summer of 1850. A young boy, Joseph Halford, was orphaned at Council Bluffs, and Elizabeth took him in and raised him as one of her own.

They arrived in the Valley on October 5, 1850. Five weeks later, Elizabeth gave birth to twins, a boy and a girl. The next spring the family moved north to Kays Creek, later

known as Kaysville. They were one of the first families to settle in that area. Three more children were born there, a girl and two boys.

Elizabeth was talented in music and had a fine singing voice. She and James appeared on special programs and entertained at informal gatherings. She was fully active in her church duties.

Elizabeth was very happy when her sister, Hannah Green, and son, George, came from England in 1877. Elizabeth had seen none of her own family since leaving England in 1841. Hannah was a great help to the family when Elizabeth's health began to fail.

Elizabeth's son, Thomas, was on a mission in the Southern States when she died on March 16, 1886, at the age of sixty-seven. She had been ill for a long time before her death. She is buried in the Kaysville Cemetery.

MARIA ABELONE NIELSEN ROBINS

BIRTHDATE: 10 Jun 1857
Svenberg, Fuene, Denmark
DEATH: 5 Feb 1955
Scipio, Millard Co., Utah
PARENTS: Peter C. Nielsen
Mette Kristine Ditlevsen
PIONEER: 8 Oct 1866
Andrew H. Scott Wagon Train
SPOUSE: Thomas L. A. Robins
MARRIED: 28 Apr 1876
Scipio, Millard Co., Utah
DEATH SP: 23 Oct 1951
Scipio, Millard Co., Utah

CHILDREN:
Mattie Ann (Miner), 31 Jul 1876
Emma Jane (Herbert), 23 Nov 1878
Leonard Fullwell, 22 Jan 1883
Coniston Douglas, 16 Apr 1886
Willard Leroy, 21 Jan 1889
Clark "Tim," 8 Apr 1893
Gladys (Frampton Day), 3 Oct 1895
Alta (Stewart), 26 Dec 1899

Maria left her home in Denmark when she was eight years old and came with her father and mother, three sisters and two brothers across the ocean by ship and on to Deseret by covered wagon. She walked the entire distance across the Plains. Her youngest brother died soon after they were on their long journey across the Plains, and that was a source of much heartache.

After her marriage to Leonard Robins in 1876, they moved to some acreage which they secured under the Homestead Act, and there they built a log house and began their life together. Besides rearing her own eight children, Maria helped care for six of her grandchildren who also lived in her home until their adulthood.

She was a very intelligent person, and although she received only six weeks of schooling, she was an excellent reader and had an intuitive knowledge of mathematics, weights, and measures. This came in very handy when marketing farm animals and produce, and keeping mothers aware of the weight of their growing babies.

She had a perfect memory and was a source of information for anyone trying to find the exact date of a birth, marriage, death, or any important statistic. Her accuracy was proven time and time again.

She would wash the raw wool from the sheep, cord. and spin it into yarn. This yarn was used in many ways to provide the clothing for her family. She knit many things with speed and precision and also did some weaving of material. She was an excellent seamstress and one of her church callings was to make burial clothes for the dead. This also included, when appropriate, all of the priesthood robes. She was a visiting teacher as long as her health would permit.

Maria and her husband celebrated their seventy-fifth wedding anniversary with all eight of their children present.

ABIGAIL PARSONS ROBINSON

No
Photo
Available

BIRTHDATE: 13 Jul 1793
Cushing, Lincoln Co., Maine
DEATH: 1 Nov 1857
Burchcreek, Weber Co., Utah
PARENTS: William Parsons
Sarah Pearson
PIONEER: 04 Oct 1847
Parley P. Pratt Co. Wagon Train
SPOUSE: John Robinson, Sr.
MARRIED: 9 Jul 1814
Cushing, Lincoln Co., Maine
DEATH SP: 16 Feb 1887
Burchcreek, Weber Co., Utah

CHILDREN:
Mary Ann, 20 Oct 1814
William James, 30 Aug 1817
Niven, 4 Feb 1821
Benjamin, 24 Sep 1822
Cyrus, 12 Nov 1824 (lost at sea age 22)
Eveline Permelia, 19 Dec 1827
John Robinson, Jr., 9 Nov 1829
Sarah Abigail, 22 Sep 1833
Isaac Parsons, 17 Mar 1835
Lawrence, 18 Oct 1837

Two years after the outbreak of the War of 1812, Abigail married John Robinson, Sr. in Cushing, Maine. He was a wealthy sea captain who was owner of one ship and part owner in several other ships.

On one of his trips, he met a missionary from the Church of Jesus Christ of Latter-day Saints and was converted to the gospel. He and his family were baptized on July 4, 1844 in Warren, Maine. He sold his interest in his ships and land holdings and took a fortune with him as the family sailed to New Orleans and then sailed up the

Mississippi River to Nauvoo. They built a home and settled down to a business life.

The Saints were planning on their westward move, so John learned the skills of making wagon wheels. Many of the Saints had their wagons fitted with wheels, though they had no funds to pay.

Then the Robinson family left Nauvoo and joined the Saints at Winter Quarters. Here, they built and operated a general store, giving much assistance to the Saints who were making preparations for their journey. Abigail tells of how her husband gave much of their fortune to the needy Saints during their hardships at Winter Quarters.

On June 10th, they left Winter Quarters in the company called "The First Immigration" led by Parley P. Pratt. It was so large, they had to regroup into smaller groups after they had gone 150 miles. While coming down Emigration Canyon, their wagon broke down and they had to wait for repairs. So their arrival into the Salt Lake Valley was on October 4, 1847.

John and Abigail lived with their family in Salt Lake City for a short time. John was counselled by Church leaders to settle in the Jordan area. Her husband was the first bishop of the ward. In 1852, Abigail and her family supported him on a mission in Nova Scotia, the eastern most province of Canada. He was sixty years old at this time. While there, he visited his relatives in Maine and collected many names of his ancestors in order to have their temple work done. When he returned from his mission, she also supported him in his decision for plural marriage in 1853. They moved to south Ogden area near Burch Creek.

On November 1, 1857, when Abigail was sixty-four, she passed away of smallpox in their log cabin. She was wrapped in a blanket and buried at night without benefit of a casket.

AGNES MCGHIE ROBINSON

BIRTHDATE: 24 Jul 1843
Dairy, Ayr, Scotland
DEATH: 20 Jun 1919
Salt Lake City, Salt Lake, Utah
PARENTS: Wilham McGhie
Elizabeth Collins
PIONEER: 1 Oct 1854
Wagon Train Company
SPOUSE: Andrew Robinson
MARRIED: 8 May 1882
Mill Creek, Salt Lake Co., Utah
DEATH SP: 12 Dec 1892

CHILDREN: None known

Agnes was born in Scotland, 1843. She was the sixth of eight children in her family.

After being converted and baptized into the Church of Jesus Christ of Latter-day Saints on December 3, 1852, her family decided to emigrate to America. Agnes was ten years old when she boarded the ship, "Windemere" to cross the ocean.

After their arrival in New Orleans, they made their way to Kansas City and joined the Daniel Garn Wagon Company, leaving on July 2, 1854 and arriving in Utah on October 1, 1854. They settled in Mill Creek, Salt Lake County, Utah.

At the age of thirty-eight, Agnes married Andrew Robinson on May 8, 1882. Andrew was widower with seven children. Later, he also married Jane Burt.

Agnes was blind. She passed away on june 20, 1919 and is buried in the Salt Lake Cemetery.

ALICE COUPE ROBINSON

BIRTHDATE: 18 Dec 1818
Haslingden, Lancashire, England
DEATH: 30 May 1847
Pottawattamie Co., Iowa
PARENTS: James Coupe
Ann Holden
PIONEER: 1846
"Poor Company" Wagon Train
SPOUSE: John R. Robinson
MARRIED: 5 Mar 1842
on board a ship
DEATH SP: 9 Aug 1891
Paragonah, Iron Co., Utah

CHILDREN:
Sarah Ann (Holyoak), 22 Dec 1842
Richard Ammon, 18 May 1845

Alice left her homeland of England while a young woman. She crossed the Atlantic Ocean in a sailing vessel and was married on board the ship. They arrived in Nauvoo in 1842.

Alice shared her home with her father, James Coupe and her half-sister, Jane Coupe. She assisted in building up Nauvoo, and did ordinance work for her deceased family.

Alice went through the mobbings. She stayed in Nauvoo to help others get ready for the exodus until she was forced out of Nauvoo soon after the "Battle of Nauvoo," which took place on September 12, 1846.

Alice and her family camped with the "poor" company in the Mississippi River bottoms until relief wagons sent by the Camps of Israel returned to get them. She was present there and helped gather quail when that miracle occurred on October 9, 1846.

Alice tended her sick husband and assisted him, her two young children, and her young half-sister, Jane as they travelled by wagon to join the Mormon Pioneers in their trek across Iowa. She became ill and asked Jane to take care of her children.

Alice Coupe Robinson passed away somewhere in Pottawattamie County, Iowa on May 30, 1847. She was stalwart and faithful throughout her life, always sharing what little she had.

ELIZABETH WOOTTON ROBINSON

BIRTHDATE- 5 Nov 1835
Staffordshire, England
DEATH: 13 Nov 1899
Kanab, Kane Co., Utah
PARENTS: George Wootton
Ann Wootton
PIONEER: 1849
Ezra T. Benson Co. Wagon Train
SPOUSE: Richard S. Robinson
MARRIED: Fall 1853/1854
American Fork, Utah Co., Utah
DEATH SP: 8 May 1902
Sink Valley, Kane Co., Utah

CHILDREN:
Richard Joseph, 4 Sep 1854
Elizabeth Ann (Westewover), 1 Jun 1856
Edward "G," 3 Dec 1857
John Wootton, 13 Sep 1860
Emma Jane, 23 Feb 1861 (died as a child)
William Alfred, 6 Dec 1863
Armitta Kate (Brinkerhoff), 24 Oct 1865
George Heber, 15 Apr 1867
Oscar Attewell, 15 Feb 1869
Mary Ellen (Brown), 14 Oct 1871
Sarah Blanche (Hamblin) 2 Oct 1873
Martha Amy (Stewart Dalton), 26 Dec 1875
Ell, 26 Dec 1875

Elizabeth was born in 1835 in the Potteries area, Staffordshire, England. Not much is known about her childhood, but she and her mother came to America in 1842 on the ship, "Henry." They were six weeks on the ocean. Ann's brother and his family and the Robinson family were also on the same ship, and the two families became neighbors in Nauvoo.

They spent their first winter in St. Louis, and traveled to Nauvoo in the spring of 1843. In 1849, Elizabeth was with the Ezra T. Benson Wagon Company traveling to Utah. They settled in American Fork, Utah.

Elizabeth married Richard Smith Robinson, the eldest son of Edward Robinson and Mary Smith. (His mother died in Nauvoo, and Elizabeth's brother John had also died there. Edward had married John's widow Ann before coming across the Plains.)

Elizabeth and Richard went to the Indian mission at Harmony, Utah just out of Cedar City following their marriage. In 1855, they were in Santa Clara associating with Jacob Hamblin. In 1856, the went to Pinto, Wahington County, Utah as the only settlers there during the winter of 1856-1857. They lived in cellars covered with willows and clay for their homes, a branch of the Church was organized with Richard presiding, and they lived there for about twenty years.

Richard took two other wives in polygamy, Mary Ann Eccles in 1860 (she had ten children), and Mary Kate (she had one child who died), and Elizabeth had twelve children, three of whom died young. These other wives were frail, so much of the responsibility of caring for the children rested with Elizabeth. She never complained, but took care of the sick, and did all the sewing, making shirts for all the men and boys. Richard brought fabric each time he went to Salt Lake. Elizabeth sewed for herself and the other wives. She was a help-mate and comfort to her husband and family all the days of her life.

In 1876, they were called to settle Upper Kanab and run a dairy. They suffered the drudgery of ranch life. Night after night, the women were burning the candle sewing, patching, darning, and running the spinning wheel. Men milked 150 cows and made cheese. Every fall, Richard made a trip to Salt Lake City with the cheese and produce, and purchased dry goods, clothing, and Christmas toys. Each trip took a month to complete. A teacher was hired for the children a few months during the winters.

Elizabeth had worn herself out in caring for such a large family, but she never complained, so no one realized the seriousness of her illness at the age of sixty-two. She passed away in February of 1898.

A great posterity honor Elizabeth for her great faith and fortitude, and her charity in serving those around her. She was, indeed, a great pioneer woman of Utah.

ELSIE PERMELIA STODDARD ROBINSON

BIRTHDATE: 12 Dec 1845
Nauvoo, Hancock Co., Illinois
DEATH: 31 Mar 1907
Thatcher, Arizona
PARENTS: Amos Stoddard
Leah Fickes
PIONEER: 15 Oct 1850
Stoddard Indepen. Wagon Train
SPOUSE: Isaac Payson Robinson
MARRIED: 29 May 1863
Salt Lake City, Salt Lake, Utah
DEATH SP: 2 Apr 1917
Thatcher, Arizona

CHILDREN:
Isaac, 23 Apr 1864
Leah Lois (Brindenhall), 4 Jan 1866
Joseph Martin, 2 Jul 1867
Mary Annie (Brundage), 9 Dec 1868
Cyrus, 14 Sep 1870
Franklin, 7 Jun 1872
Emily (Taylor), 1 Jan 1874
Wilford 3 Sep 1875
Elsie Permelia (Kleinman), 5Jan 1878
Effie (Montierth), 13 Apr 1880
Orson Hyde, 14 Nov 1881
Zina (Dana), 12 Dec 1883
Jennie, 29 Aug 1886 (died as a child)

Elsie Permelia was born in Nauvoo, Illinois on December 12, 1845. When she was four years of age, her family emigrated to Utah with the Latter-day Saints.

She was too young to realize the trials and hardships that her parents and family went through while crossing the Plains; she could remember just a few incidents.

She was just one of four children in the family of three girls and one boy, who was crippled. As Elsie became old enough, she had to work hard to help get food enough to live on. Many time she went to the hills and dug sego lilies for her breakfast. Her parents drank tea which sold for $5.00 per pound, and she worked for a week to be able to purchase a pound of tea for them, or to work for one yard of calico. She worked for months to get one primer book for herself. She was permitted to go to school only six weeks of her life, but she taught herself to read.

Elsie, a charming young lady of nineteen years, fell in love with Isaac Payson Robinson. Their courtship lasted but a few days. They were married on May 29, 1863, and left the town of Burch Creek where she and her family had been living.

Isaac bought a small acreage in Strawberry Creek. Here he built a large one-room cabin of logs where eleven of their twelve children were born. Isaac raised sheep and cattle, and Elsie had chickens, and made butter which she marketed at Ogden where she sold forty pounds of butter weekly. That money, with her egg money, helped provide food and clothing for their large family.

After years of struggle, they began to feel prosperity when Isaac was called by President Brigham Young to help start a colony in Graham County, Arizona. Being an obedient servant, he sold and gave away what they had and in December, 1834, with two covered wagons and six horses began the trip to Arizona. They were four months on the road and it was bitter cold and there was much snow which fell. They lost horses, their children became ill, and they had little flour to make bread.

With all these problems, Elsie was not one to complain. Indians were at times on the rampage, a tent was their home, and food was scarce. Elsie, her husband, and all the children who were old enough, toiled and worked hard to make ends meet and to begin again. In 1886, another girl was born but she lived just two years.

Elsie had taught herself to read and really enjoyed the Book of Mormon and the Doctrine and Covenants. They made a two very large roomed home, cleared the land, planted a lot of trees, and soon they had shade and a nice place to live,

Elsie passed away on March 31, 1907 in Thatcher, Graham County, Arizona at the age of sixty-one years. Her husband, Isaac, passed away on April 2, 1917 also in Thatcher, Arizona.

A great posterity honor these faithful pioneers who helped settle Utah and Arizona.

EMMA SCHOFIELD ROBINSON

BIRTHDATE: 12 Oct 1853
Stayleybridge, Cheshire, England
DEATH: 27 Jan 1932
Paragonah, Iron Co., Utah
PARENTS: John Schofield
Isabelle Banks
PIONEER: Oct 1864
Joseph S. Rawlins Wagon Train
SPOUSE: John R. Robinson Jr.
MARRIED: 9 Oct 1873
Salt Lake Endowment House
DEATH SP: 9 Feb 1939 at
Paragonah, Iron Co., Utah

CHILDREN:
Emma Jane, 6 Jul 1874
Mary Isabelle, 10 Nov 1875
Margaret Alice, 29 Jun 1877
John Rowlandson, III, 13 Jun 1879
Hyrum Banks, 25 Feb 1882
Sarah Lucinda, 12 Aug 1884
Arnold Schofield, 8 Jul 1887
Lula Elizabeth, 3 Aug 1888
Ellis Raymond, 13 Oct 1891
Joseph Milton, 25 Jul 1894

Emma started to school in England when she was very young. She was excellent in spelling and composition and was up with her class in other studies. She learned how to knit, crochet, and sew as a young girl, which was a great help to her in rearing her family.

She left Salt Lake for Beaver with her family in 1865. She and another girl drove sheep most of the way. She attended school in Beaver. She worked in different homes to earn her board and keep. She cleaned, tended children, and cooked. This helped her to be an excellent housewife.

She later moved to Paragonah with her mother. This is where she met her husband and raised her family.

She made lace for trimming articles of clothing, knit stockings, and made beautiful quilts.

Emma was very active in the Church. She was a Relief Sociaty visiting teacher for many years. She was Relief Society President from 1897 to 1904. She was a Primary President and a teacher for several different classes. She helped care for the sick. She helped prepare the dead for burial by washing the body and sewing clothes.

She was a very good wife, mother, and grandmother. She was a good cook and helped her children and grandchildren to be the same.

JANE COUPE ROBINSON

BIRTHDATE: 27 Feb 1832
Haslingdon, Grange, England
DEATH: 12 Dec 1909
Paragonah, Iron Co., Utah
PARENTS: James Coupe
Alice Collinge
PIONEER: 1852
Capt. Isaac Bullock Wagon Train
SPOUSE: John R. Robinson
MARRIED: 24 Aug 1847
Pottawattamie Co., Iowa
DEATH SP: 9 Aug 1891,
Paragonah, Iron Co., Utah

CHILDREN:
James Coupe, 9 Oct 1849
William, 21 Mar 1852
John Rowlandson, Jr., 6 Apr 1855
Jane Elizabeth (Schofield), 24 Mar 1857
Alice, (Topham), 3 Apr 1859
Mary Lucinda (Topham), 8 May 1861
Thomas, 19 Sep 1863
Margaret, 21 Oct 1865
Joseph, 18 Feb 1868
Hyrum, 17 Mar 1870
Eliza May (Morris), 1 May 1872
Emma Josephine (Jones Smith), 4 Jan 1875
George Albert, 26 Oct 1876

According to family tradition, Jane promised her half-sister on her death bed to care for her children. A short time later, at the age of fifteen, she married her brother-in-law and raised those two children along with thirteen of her own. They were always made to feel that they were full brothers and sisters.

They arrived in Parowan, Iron County, Utah late in the year 1852, and after the first Indian troubles were over, they settled permanently in Paragonah, Utah.

Jane did a great deal of weaving. She also clerked in the family store which was located in the cellar of her home which sold groceries and other small necessary items. She did all of the sewing and knitting for her large family.

Jane and her husband took in members of a Cottam family traveling to St. George when other members of the community feared to do so becasue they had whooping cough. It is interesting to note that none of her five small children contracted the disease.

Jane was a courageous, trustworthy, God-fearing woman who spent years in the service of the Relief Society and in helping others less fortunate than herself.

Jane Coupe Robinson passed away at the age of seventy-seven, and is buried in the Parowan Cemetery beside her husband.

JEMIMA PARKES ROBINSON

BIRTHDATE: 23 Sep 1831
Derby, Derbyshire, England
DEATH: 4 Jan 1908
Payson, Utah Co., Utah
PARENTS: William Parkes
Mary Brentnall
PIONEER: 24 Oct 1854
Daniel Garn Co. Wagon Train
SPOUSE: Joseph Robinson
MARRIED: 26 Nov 1853
Derby, Derbyshire, England
DEATH SP: 26 Jun 1915
Canutillo, New Mexico

CHILDREN:
Elizabeth Annie, 1 Apr 1857
Jemima Mary, 1 May 1859 (died at age 18)
Joseph William, 24 Oct 1860 (died at age 12)
Samuel John, 10 Dec 1863
Jedde James, 27 Sep 1865
Josephine Parkes, 9 Aug 1868

Jemima began working in a silk spinning mill before her sixth birthday. She continued this work until she came to Utah with her husband in 1854.

Before working in the mill, she attended an infant's school for a short time where she learned her "letters." With this start, she became well educated through her own efforts. Her family heard the gospel, studied it, and eventually were baptized. Jemima was baptized on December 9, 1848 at the age of seventeen.

While performing church duties and attending meetings in her new church, she met Joseph Robinson. They were married November 26, 1853 in Derby, England. They sailed on the ship, "Windemere," where they endured sea sickness, a terrific storm on the ocean, and a fire aboard the boat. After their ten week voyage, they landed safely in America. They joined the Daniel Garn Wagon Company and her husband was asked to leave earlier to drive cattle.

Jemima was assigned to travel with a family having six children. Jemima arrived in the Salt lake Valley on October 24, 1854 and was happily reunited with her husband.

Their first child was born the following spring in Salt Lake City. Rumors of the invasion of Johnston's Army caused Brigham Young to order the evacuation of Salt Lake, so Jemima and her family moved to Payson. They lived in a large cellar basement along with some other families. Soon they were able to purchase a city lot and build a one-room log and dugout house with a dirt floor.

For a number of years, Joseph operated a cooperative water power sawmill eight miles up Payson canyon. This took him away from home a great deal of the time.

Although Jemima's health was often poor, she and the children assumed much of the responsibility and work at home. There were cows, calves, and chickens to be fed. Honey had to be extracted about once a week in season.

The garden and orchard had to be cultivated and irrigated. Butter, fruit, and vegetables took much time to produce and get to market. In 1880, Joseph was called on a mission to England. During his absence, she was able to support him on his mission and make improvements on the farm, repaint their home, all of the other many things that had to be done.

Joseph went to Old Mexico with a number of others. Jemima kept the home in Payson and kept things ready so when any of the family came back, they would have a home. She contracted pneumonia in December of 1907 and quietly passed away on January 4, 1908.

LAURINDA MARIA ATWOOD PINKHAM ROBINSON

BIRTHDATE: 3 May 1821
Mansfield, Tolland, Connecticut
DEATH: 1 Mar 1895
Farmington, Davis Co., Utah
PARENTS: Elisha Atwood
Anna Hartshorn
PIONEER: 09 Oct 1848
Amasa Lyman Co. Wagon Train
SPOUSE I: Sumnar Pinkham
MARRIED: Not given
DEATH SP: Not given

CHILDREN:
Delveret "Dee," 15/18 Jun 1844

SPOUSE II: Joseph Lee Robinson
MARRIED: 21 Mar 1847
Winter Quarters, Douglas, Nebraska
DEATH SP: 1 Jan 1893
Uintah, Weber Co., Utah

CHILDREN:
Jane Geneva, 14 Jul 1848
Nathan Benjamin, 5 Aug 1850
Josephine Elnora, 9 Nov 1852
Mary, 13 Nov 1854
Laurinda Eliza, 7 Sep 1 5
Jedediah Nephi, 1 Dec 1857
Annette Lowella, 25 May 1860 (twin)
Janette Orilla, 25 May 1860 (twin)

Laurinda's parents were converts to the Church of Jesus Christ Latter-day Saints. She was baptized a member while a young girl. She and her parents moved to Nauvoo where her father helped to build the Nauvoo Temple and where they suffered persecution because of their beliefs.

Laurinda was married to Sumnar Pinkham and had one child with him. He refused to go West when the Saints were driven from Nauvoo. Laurinda went with her parents to Winter Quarters. In 1847, she was married to Joseph Lee Robinson as his third wife in Winter Quarters. Their first child, Jane, was born while they were crossing the Plains.

They arrived in the Salt Lake Valley with the Amasa Lyman Wagon Company on October 9, 1848.

The next spring, they moved to Farmington where her husband was the first bishop. They had to move south due to the threat of invasion from Johnston's Army. Later they pioneered Mountain Green where they helped build a new meeting house, home, and schoolhouse, besides grubbing out a new farm.

Laurinda was left alone most of the time to take care of the children, farm, and stock because of the various duties of her husband. They raised cows, sheep, turkeys, ducks, and chickens. She made cheese and butter from the milk. She made clothing by processing the wool into thread which she wove into material, dyed it formed men's suits and women and children's clothing. She had a sweet singing voice.

After eight years, they moved back to Farmington where she worked many years as a teacher in the Relief Society. Brigham Young asked her to plant Mulberry Trees and raise silkworms. She did so and made the first silk dress in Utah. It was then sent to the World's Fair. She also spun the silk fringe used on the curtains for the St. George Temple.

Laurinda had nine children. One of her sons went on a mission and another son was killed by Indians. She had the power of healing and through the power of God could heal any of her children when they were ill.

LUCINDA VICTORIA ROBERTS ROBINSON

BIRTHDATE: 7 Mar 1838
Monroe, Fairfield, Connecticut
DEATH: 11 Jun 1917
Mountain Green, Morgan, Utah
PARENTS: Sidney Roberts
Sarah Ann Rowell
PIONEER: 1852
A. Bates & A. Cummings Comp.
SPOUSE: John Robinson Jr.
MARRIED: 24 Jan 1853
Big Cottonwood, Salt Lake, Utah
DEATH SP: 4 Oct 1891
Mountain Green, Morgan, Utah

CHILDREN:
John Heber, 4 May 1854
Sarah Cornelia, 15 Apr 1856
Henry Eugene, 7 Nov 1858
Lillis Sabina, 10 Mar 1861
Isaac Morgan, 7 May 1863
Joseph Franklin, 13 Dec 1865
George Hyrum, 28 Nov 1868
Margaret Valentine, 14 Feb 1871
Sidney Orson, 15 Jan 1874
Niven Lawrence, 23 Nov 1876
William Edward, 13 Aug 1879
Alonzo Rowell, 19 Mar 1883

Lucinda's parents gave her religious training and taught her to be a great homemaker. Her family was among the early converts of the Church of Jesus Christ of Latter-day Saints about the time Lucinda was born. They joined the movement to Nauvoo, Illinois at the height of the mob persecution.

She was a little girl at the time of the building of the temple. She can remember seeing Prophet Joseph Smith in military uniform. The family went north on the Mississippi River in a steam boat to Iowa City. They lived there for five years as her father helped many emigrants with their wagons and machinery.

In 1852, the family journeyed West with the Bates and Cummings as captains. When they arrived in Salt Lake Valley, they were sent to Mill Creek to help build the great paper mill of the Church there.

It was in Mill Creek that Lucinda met and married John Robinson, Jr. He had been helping her father build the mill near Big Cottonwood Canyon.

They first made their home in West Jordan. In 1854, Brigham Young sent them to colonize East Weber, known as Burchcreek. In 1859, after Johnston's Army was settled, John and Lucinda moved their family to Mountain Green where they cleared the land of brush and rocks, built roads, and worked hard to produce the food needed to support their family.

They learned they could make a good living by selling firewood and logs. Then the railroad needed ties to support the train tracks. They got to a point where they had enough produce to sell in Ogden. Lucinda was handy with the spinning wheel and made much of the material thread, yardage goods, stockings, rugs, and bedding of the home. She taught her daughters these skills as well.

Lucinda held positions in the Relief Society, Sunday School, and Primary organizations of the Church. She had a deep testimony of the truthfulness of the Gospel of Jesus Christ. She acted as a school trustee. She performed vicarious work for her ancestors in the Logan Temple. She had a keen memory of the scriptures. She was also an outstanding businesswoman in her community.

LUCY MARIA MILLER ROBINSON

BIRTHDATE: 10 Jan 1837
near Quincy, Illinois
DEATH: 20 Apr 1877
Farmington, Davis Co., Utah
PARENTS: Henry W. Miller
Elmira Pond
PIONEER: 1852
Wagon Train Company
SPOUSE: Oliver Lee Robinson
MARRIED: 26 Nov 1854
Farmington, Davis Co., Utah
DEATH SP: 19 Aug 1886
Farmington, Davis Co., Utah

CHILDREN:
Joseph Oliver, 13 Oct 1855 (died as an infant)
Lucy Maria, 22 Nov 1856
Loren Jay, 2 Feb 1859
Oliver LeGrande, 28 Oct 1860
Eugene Delacy, 11 Aug 1862
Alice Almira, 14 May 1864
James Henry, 8 Nov 1865
Sarah Jane, 25 Nov 1867
Annie Amelia, 8 Apr 1870
Helen Moselle, 23 Jul 1872 (died at 18 months)
Lillian Estelle, 16 Sep 1876

Lucy was two years old when her parents joined the Church of Jesus Christ of Latter-day Saints. As a young girl, she shared the hardships of the Saints. Her father was asked by Brigham Young to stay at Winter Quarters to raise wheat and take care of emigrants. He finally brought his family to Utah in the summer of 1852 being the captain of their own company. They settled in North Cottonwood (now Farmington), Utah.

When Lucy was seventeen years old, she married Oliver Lee Robinson. She shared her husband in polygamy with four other wives.

Lucy had the first treadle sewing machine in Farmington and sewed for the family, relatives, and friends. She paid for her machine by sewing tucks and hemming ruffles for the women of the community. She was a natural nurse. She had many talents. She was a good business manager and even took care of her husband's business affairs while he served a mission.

Before her husband returned from his mission to the Southern States, Lucy passed away at the age of thirty-nine. Her husband's third wife and Lucy's older daughters raised the children.

LYDIA FOSTER ROBINSON

BIRTHDATE. 9 Jan 1831
Nelson, New Hampshire
DEATH: 25 Sep 1872
Hooper, Weber Co., Utah
PARENTS: Stephen Foster
Sophia Briggs
PIONEER: 1852
SPOUSE:: Joseph Lee Robinson
MARRIED: 16 Feb 1853
Salt Lake City, Salt Lake, Utah
DEATH SP: I Jan 1893
Uintah, Weber Co., Utah

CHILDREN:
Amos Gilbert, 6 Jul 1854
Lydia Ann, 21 Feb 1856 (died at age 13)
George Alva, 3 Jan 1858
Emma Sophia (Clark), 16 Mar 1860
Stephen, 6 May 1862 (died at age 16)
William Foster, 9 Feb 1864

Lydia was born in 1831 in Nelson, Cheshire, New Hampshire. Her parents were of sturdy New England, Puritan stock. Their home was in the southwest corner of New Hampshire.

Her family was contacted by missionaries from the Church of Jesus Christ of Latter-day Saints, and they were baptized in the Gilsum Branch. Lydia was baptized in September, 1844. Her father was ordained to the Melchizedek Priesthood by Brigham Young and Orson Pratt.

Four months later on November 12, 1844, her father was accidently killed in an accident with his team and wagon. Her family moved to Kanesville, Iowa which was an emigration center for the Saints. From this point they were organized for the trek to Utah in 1852. It is not known with which group Lydia and her family traveled, but they arrived in Utah in 1852.

Before their first year in Salt Lake was up, Lydia married Joseph Lee Robinson on February 16, 1853 as his fourth wife. In his journal he wrote, "I received in Holy Wedlock Lydia Foster, an amiable young woman of 22 from the hands of the Prophet Brigham Young for which blessing I thank my God." Joseph had met Lydia on one of his several trips to Salt Lake from Parowan with George A. Smith. He recorded later of going to the house of the Lord and receiving their endowments. Lydia received her patriarchal blessing from Patriarch John Smith on November 9, 1853.

Lydia became acquainted with many of Joseph's first families as they lived in close proximity in Farmington. The three wives were very compatible and each had respect for the others. Their homes were short distances of each other and their families worked and visited as time permitted, especially when Joseph was on his Church assignments to and from Salt Lake and Parowan with George A. Smith.

When Lydia's first child was born, Joseph wrote in his journal, "My fourth wife, Lydia, bore me a son . . . Mother and child doing well, thank God." Lydia's first daughter was born in 1856, but she died at age thirteen. He wrote of her, "She was greatly beloved by her parents and friends. We mourn her loss. . . "After her next child, a son, was born Joseph wrote, "A fine child, my tenth son born to me, and my twentieth child." Lydia had a fourth child, a daughter, and a 5th and 6th sons, Stephen, the fifth, died as a child less than a year after birth.

In 1870, Joseph Lee moved Lydia from her Farmington home to a house built of logs and adobe in Hooper, Weber County, Utah. Her children attended school in an adobe school house there. Joseph married again, a widow with children and she lived not far from Lydia. Thus Lydia had another wife to become acquainted with and to share their routines and duties. Their acquaintance was not a long one. Lydia passed away in Hooper on September 25, 1872.

Joseph Lee's wives called Lydia "Gentle Lydia . . . always wanting to do her full share and more . . . so kind to everyone . . . so good and so wise." Joseph recorded her passing with some of these thoughts. "Lydia Foster departed this life, dropping off to sleep a few minutes before 1:00 o'clock. She closed her eyes, was quiet and breathed for a few minutes. . and left this troublesome world . . . Farewell dear."

Lydia's children lived with their father or other family members. They married and had large families who honor this brave pioneer woman for her faith and fortitude throughout life.

MARIA WOOD ROBINSON

No Photo Available

BIRTHDATE: 5 Jan 1806
Booneville, Oneida, New York
DEATH: 1 Dec 1872
Farmington, Davis Co., Utah
PARENTS: Zephaniah Wood
Ann Carpenter
PIONEER: Oct 1848
Lyman Co. Wagon Train
SPOUSE: Joseph Lee Robinson
MARRIED: 23 Jul 1832
Booneville, Oneida, New York
DEATH SP: 1 Jan 1893
Uintah, Weber Co., Utah

CHILDREN:
Oliver Lee, 8 Jul 1833
Ebenezer Jay, 19 Oct 1835
Anna Maria, 8 Jun 1838
Joseph, 31 Oct 1840 (died as a child)
Zephania, 21 Sep 1843 (died as a child)
Mary Elizabeth, 12 Jun 1845 (died as a child)
Joseph Elijah, 2 Feb 1849

Maria was born in 1806 in Booneville, New York. Maria was a woman of great faith. It became difficult for her to convert to the Church of Jesus Christ of Latter-day Saints because of her family's pressures. It was five years after her husband joined the Church before she was baptized. Following her conversion, she never wavered.

When polygamy was presented to her, it took prayer and searching her own soul. She did accept four other women as wives to her husband, and she gave love and support to all.

In writing about Maria Wood's life, an author "learned to love and respect this dear one, she was a lady born-she was fit to be a queen and in reality we believe she will be-just that." (from the publication "The Five Branches of Love" by Mary West Riggs). "She was a true helpmate to her husband, she was slow to accept all things even to religion-it came slow to her-but when it came she was truly and sincerely a Latter-day Saint . . . Because the Father knew, He gave to her a beautiful testimony which remained always with her. This came with the hardest trial of life to women-but to her she was allowed to see its beauty, its

truth. She it was, who helped timid Susan to know and to understand. Who kept prejudice from entering into her husband's heart. She loved the entire family she feared only inadequate finance which Joseph feared also."

Maria was the first wife, and Joseph Lee Robinson also married Susan McCord, Laurinda Atwood, Lydia Foster, and Mary Taylor.

Maria was truly a woman of great faith, and great fortitude who helped in the taming of the Utah territory. Her marriage to Joseph began a family of Robinsons that numbers many thousands at the present time.

Honor and deepest appreciation is expressed to her with gratitude for her willingness, her humility and her love for her life.

Maria Wood Robinson passed away on December 1, 1872 in Farmington, Davis County, Utah. Joseph's fourth wife had passed away in September, 1872 in Hooper, Utah. A great posterity honor these brave pioneers.

MARY POLLARD ROBINSON

BIRTHDATE: 6 Oct 1831
Eastwood, England
DEATH: 6 Sep 1902
Coalville, Summit Co., Utah
PARENTS: Robert Pollard
Mary Beniston
PIONEER: 19 Oct 1862
Horton D. Haight Wagon Train
SPOUSE: James Robinson
MARRIED: 28 Jul 1849
Eastwood, England
DEATH SP: 10 Mar 1898
Coalville, Summit Co., Utah

CHILDREN:
Brigham, 16 Jun 1850
Susannah (Birch), 15 Dec 1851
Elizabeth (Foulger), 29 Sep 1853
Sariah (Wilde), 15 Jan 1856
James, Jr. 8 Mar 1858
Francis John, 3 Jul 1859
William Springthorpe, 8 Aug 1862
William Samuel, 29 Nov 1863
Eli Oswald, 8 Apr 1866
Mary Hannah (Wilde Cox), 10 Mar 1868/1869
Robert Emanuel, 6 Apr 1870
Annie (Cox), 7 Apr 1872
Fredrick Solomon, 28 Feb 1875
Rose Emma (Robinson), 20 Aug 1879

Mary was born in Eastwood, Nottinghamshire, England. She came across the ocean on the ship "William Tappscott." Then traveled with the Horton D. Haight Wagon Company, and arrived in the Salt Lake Valley on May 14, 1862.

She was amoung the first residents of Coalville, Summit County, Utah. She was the other of fourteen children, and raised ten to maturity. She also raised a grandson, George Robinson, after the death of his mother. Her husband, James, lost his leg in a coal mining accident, consequently she took on the responsibility of running the farm with the help of her children.

Mary was a gifted seamstress and did beautiful handiwork. She was an excellent cook and homemaker.

Mary had an incredible courage, faith, love, and endurance, and rose above her overwhelming adversities.

MARY TAYLOR UPTON SIMMONS ROBINSON

BIRTHDATE: 6 Nov 1835
Coton-in-the-Elms, England
DEATHDATE: 20 Mar 1899
Ucon (Willow Creek) Idaho
PARENTS: Joseph Taylor
Harriet Sidwell
PIONEER: 30 Nov 1856
Edward Martin Handcart Comp.
SPOUSE I: William Upton
MARRIED: 12 Nov 1855
Derbyshire, England
DEATH SP: 11 Nov 1856
Martins Cove, Wyoming

CHILDREN: None

SPOUSE II: William Bert Simmons
MARRIED: 15 Mar 1857
Salt Lake City, Salt Lake Co., Utah
DEATH SP: 20 Aug 1866
Uintah, Weber Co., Utah

CHILDREN:
Joseph Taylor, 11 Feb 1858
George Albert, 10 Oct 1859
Alphonzo Bert, 3 Jul 1861
Eli Thomas, 10 Dec 1862
Mary Ann, 17 Feb 1865

SPOUSE III: Joseph Lee Robinson
MARRIED: 2 Feb 1867
Salt Lake Endowment House, Utah
DEATH SP: 1 Jan 1893
Uintah, Weber Co., Utah

CHILDREN:
Lee Sidwell, 16 Feb 1868
Samuel Taylor, 16 Oct 1869
Harriet Alice, 1 Oct 1871
Lucy, 4 Oct 1874

When Mary, her husband, and both of her parents arrived from England they traveled to Iowa City to join the Saints. Here they were assigned to the Edward Martin Handcart Company which left Iowa City, on August 25, 1856.

Winter came early presenting many trials and tribulations to the saints. Mary's father died on the Plains on October 8, 1856. The following month on November 11th, she lost both her mother and husband, at Martins Cove, Wyoming. By the dates recorded her husband died one day before their first wedding anniversary.

When the relief wagons arrived at the stranded handcart company, Mary's feet were black and her legs frozen. William Bert Simmons took her, unconscious, in his wagon to his home. There he and his wife, Amanda, nursed her back to health so skillfully that she lost not even a toe.

On March 15, 1857, about four months after arriving in the Valley she married William Simmons in President Brigham Young's office. She was blessed with five children.

When William became so very ill, Joseph Lee Robinson was called to administer to William. Joseph said that the Lord told him that should this man die he would have to take this young family and care for them. He didn't see how he could with all the other families he had. Mary lost her husband leaving her with children ages eight to eighteen months. Five months later she married Joseph Robinson and they have four children.

Troublesome times came to those who lived in polygamy. To relieve this situation and to get a better start in life for her children, Mary made the decision to go to the Snake River Valley.

Mary was lead soprano in the Ogden choir. She learned the trade of sewing and dressmaking as a young girl from an uncle who was a tailor. She served as counselor in the Relief Society Presidency in Willow Creek Ward in Idaho when it was organized in 1888. Served in various church positions.

Mary was a pioneer in the Snake River Valley country which was a desolate area at that time. She passed away at the age of sixty-four in Ucon (Willow Creek) Idaho.

ELIZABETH SQUIRES ROBISON

No Photo Available

BIRTHDATE: 24 Dec 1802
Nicholson, Pennsylvania
DEATH SP: Oct 1890
Hatton, Millard Co., Utah
PARENTS: Stephen Squires
Margaret McGee
PIONEER: 1849
SPOUSE: William H. Robison
MARRIED: 23 Jan 1823
DEATH SP: 27 Nov 1846
Winter Quarters, Nebraska

CHILDREN:
Margaret, 19 Aug 1824
William, Dec 1825
Twins, Feb 1827 (stillborn)

Jane, 17 Feb 1828
James Henry, 24 Aug 1830
Rosetta, 26 Apr 1833
Julia Ann, 14 May 1836
Clarinda, 26 Oct 1838
Charles William, 10 Dec 1841
Theodora, 21 Jul 1844
Sara Elizabeth, 15 May 1847

Elizabeth was born in 1802 in Nicholson, Wyoming, (Nicerson Township, Luzern) Pennsylvania. She was number ten of twelve children born in her family. Her parents had lived in New Jersey, Pennsylvania, and New York. (One record says she was born in New York.)

At age twenty, Elizabeth married William Henry Robison on January 23, 1823. They made their home in New York where seven children were born to them. They moved to Michigan where two more were born.

"The spirit of gathering" came to them after their conversion to the Church of Jesus Christ of Latter-day Saints. This resulted in the family moving to Nauvoo where child number ten was born. They suffered the expulsion and persecutions of the Saints there and were forced to move with the Saints to Winter Quarters, Iowa, where they built a house. William passed away while they were there on November 27, 1846.

Elizabeth and her family continued to travel to Utah and arrived in Salt Lake Valley in 1849, after the birth of her last child on May 15, 1847. Elizabeth had twelve children born to her.

Elizabeth's family lived for a time in Weber and then when her son was sent south to Millard County, Elizabeth and family settled, in Corn Creek, later called Hatton. They were joined in 1871 by Elizabeth's son, Charles and his family. The two brothers farmed and ran cattle together.

Elizabeth was a devoted mother and continued to do all she could for her family's welfare. She passed away at age eighty-seven in October, 1890, after being a widow for forty-three years.

Elizabeth is revered by her posterity for her great faith, and her fortitude in continuing on with her dreams and goals, and coming to help in the settling of the Utah Territory.

LILLIS ALVIRA (ANDRE) ROBISON

BIRTHDATE: 12 May 1832
Middleton, Pennsylvania
DEATH: 12 Dec 1921
Hinckley, Utah
PARENTS: Michael Andre
Alvira (Almira) Chapman
PIONEER: 16 Jul 1854
Independent Family Wagon Train
SPOUSE: Benjamin Hancock Robison
MARRIED: 12 May 1853
Crete, Illinois
DEATH SP: 24 Dec 1892
Millard Utah

CHILDREN:
Willis Eugene, 1 Mar 1854
Son, 1855
Benjamin Franklin, 7 Dec 1856
William Henry, 3 Jul 1858
Loretta Alvira, 29 May 1860
Edson Albert, 24 Jul 1863
Adelia Lillis, 10 Apr 1866
Martha Lorinda, 30 Jan 1368
Son, 17 Jun 1872

Lillis was born in Pennsylvania in 1832. Sometime during her youth her family moved to Crete, Illinois. It was here she met and married Benjamin Hancok Robison on her twenty-first birthday, 12 May 1853.

All the Robison families decided to go to the Salt Lake Valley They were detained until Lillis had her first son, Willis Eugene, 1 Mar 1854. Although Lillis didn't want to go, when she was well enough to travel, they started for the Salt Lake Valley, arriving 16 Jul 1854.

They settled in Chalk Creek for seven years. While living in the fort, Lillis gave birth to three more sons, one of whom died at birth. A littla girl, Loretta, was born about the time the family left the fort, but she only lived six months.

Benjamin married 18-year-old Susannah Turner. Lillis gave birth to three more children and Susannah eventually had nine.

When Benjamin and Susannah moved to Millard County, Lillis stayed in Fillmore, kept the farm and raised her family. One time when a traveler tried to steal one of her little pigs, she shot the pistol she had carried for years. He dropped the pig and ran for his life.

Benjamin died Christmas Eve 1892 at age fifty-one.

As Lillis grew older she lived for extended periods with her married children but chose to live out her days with her oldest son in Hinckley, Utah. Lillis died 12 Dec 1921 at age eighty-nine.

LUCRETIA HANCOCK ROBISON

BIRTHDATE: 24 Aug 1807
Shrewsbury, Rutland, Vermont
DEATH SP: 31 Aug 1899
Fillmore, Millard Co., Utah
PARENTS: Benjamin Hancock
Lucretia Proctor
PIONEER: 16 Jul 1854
Perrigrine Session Wagon Train
SPOUSE: Joseph Robison
MARRIED: 5 Feb 1829
Clay, Onondago, New York
DEATH SP: Jun 1869
Fillmore, Millard Co., Utah

CHILDREN:
Alfred, 30 Nov 1829
Benjamin, 9 Nov 1831
Joseph Vicory, 30 Dec 1832
Alvin Locke, 9 Mar 1834
Emily, 24 Jun 1835 (died at age 1)
William Henry, 3 Jul 1837
Mary, 13 Apr 1839 (died an infant)
Lucretia Proctor, 18 May 1841
Proctor Hancock, 5 Mar 1843
Almon, 15 May 1845 (died at age 14)
Albert, 8 Apr 1847
Adelia, 21 Dec 1848
Franklin Alonso, 21 Jul 1851

Lucretia's parents were typical New Englanders, making their own soap, candles, syrup, and sugar. They wove their cloth, sheared the wool and spun it into yard to knit stockings. As a child, she was required to spin seven knots. She was always industrious and was the happiest when she was busy. Her mother died when Lucretia was eighteen years old. She took care of the home and the five surviving siblings until her father remarried.

At age twenty-two, she married Joseph Robison. They became the parents to thirteen children. They lived with Joseph's father for a few years, then went to live with Lucretia's father for a couple of years.

In 1835, they purchased land in Shroeple, Oswego County, New York. They heard rumors of a young man named Joseph Smith starting a new religion. They eventually were baptized members of the Church of Jesus Christ of Latter-day Saints and began making preparations to join the members of the church in Nauvoo.

In 1844, they began their journey and had crossed the eastern boundary of Illinois when they were advised not to proceed any further because of the persecution of the Saints in the Nauvoo area. Joseph and Lucretia bought 160 acres of prairie land and an additional twenty acres of heavily wooded land in Crete, Missouri. They split rails, fenced their property, and built a home where they remained for ten years.

In 1854, they felt it was time to join with the Saints in the Rocky Mountains. Their independent company was well equipped for the long trip with seven reinforced wagons pulled by strong, well trained horses and oxen. They arrived in the Salt Lake Valley on July 16, 1854.

Joseph and Lucretia accepted the assignment to move to Fillmore to help build the settlement. They lived within the fort for seven years as protection from the Indians. It took them two years to build their rock home south of the fort. They farmed their ground and raised cattle. They planted an orchard. She planted a garden of vegetables and flowers.

Lucretia made friends with some of the Indians. When they asked for bread, she invited them in and taught them how to make their own bread. She sent for beads for the squaws to weave.

She was anxious to have her children receive a good education. She sent to Beaver for a teacher who held school in an upstairs room of their rock home. Other children from the community also came to the school.

After the death of her husband in 1868, she was a widow for thirty years. She welcomed death on August 31, 1899. She had given to church, her family, and the world everything she had to give.

LUCY ADELINE (ADALINE) HARDY ROBISON

BIRTHDATE: 3 Dec 1846
Nauvoo, Hancock, Illinois
DEATH: 14 Feb 1937
Fillmore, Millard, Utah
PARENTS: Joseph Hardy
Lucy Thorndyke Blanden Hardy
PIONEER: before 1865
SPOUSE: Charles William Robison
MARRIED: 3 Dec 1865
Hooper, Weber, Utah
DEATH: 25 Sep 1910
Hatton, Millard, Utah

CHILDREN:
Charles Franklin, 20 Mar 1868
Lois Rosetta, 23 Jul 1870
Pamela Ann, 24 Mar 1872
Joseph Henry, 17 Jun 1875
Bert Leonidus, 31 Jul 1878
Orson Alfonzo, 14 Aug 1881
William Adelbert, 26 Sep 1887

Lucy Adeline Hardy was born in Nauvoo, Illinois in 1846 to Joseph and Lucy Hardy. Her family traveled as pioneers to Utah and settled in Hooper. On 3 Dec 1865, at age twenty (on her birthday) she married Charles William Robison His mother and family had settled in Weber.

In 1866, Brigham Young called them to go to St. Charles, Idaho to help settle that area. Two children were born to them while in St. Anthony. In 1871, They went south to Corn Creek, now Hatton, in Millard County where his brother Henry and family had settled. They bought a farm and a house and he and his brother farmed and ran cattle together. Lucy had five more children while they lived there. Charles was an excellent farmer. They cured their own meat, smoked it and wrapped it in clean sacks and buried it in the wheat bin. They made molasses for all the people in Hatton, and they always kept a thirty gallon barrel in their cellar.

In the autumn of 1905, Charles had an accident and never walked again without crutches. He died 25 Sep. 1910 in Hatton. Lucy remained independent, and with the help of her youngest son, Adelbert, continued farming for a living. Lucy passed away at age eighty, in 1937, having been a widow for over twenty-six years. She was living in Fillmore at the time of her passing. She was a great pioneer woman of faith and fortitude and her posterity honor her for her diligence, faith, and hard work.

MARY ELIZABETH GROVER SIMMONS ROBISON

BIRTHDATE: 13 Apr 1833
Freedom, Cattaraugus, New York
DEATH: 28 Sep 1921
Upper Preston, Bingham, Idaho
PARENTS: Thomas Grover
Caroline Whiting
PIONEER: 2 Oct 1847
Charles C. Rich Wagon Train
SPOUSE I: William A. Simmons
MARRIED: 26 Apr 1850
Salt Lake City, Salt Lake, Utah
DEATH SP: 30 Sep 1857
Echo Canyon, Summit Co., Utah

CHILDREN:
George Alpheus, 25 Feb 1851 (died as an infant)
Mary Elizabeth, 2 Feb 1852
Amanda Almeda, 8 Sep 1853
Adeline Grover, 8 Feb 1855
William Carlos, 22 Dec 1856
Alice Simmons, 14 May 1858

SPOUSE II: David Robison
MARRIED: 26 Dec 1860
North Morgan, Morgan Co., Utah
DEATH SP: 11 Sep 1907
Lorenzo, Jefferson Co., Idaho

CHILDREN:
David G., 14 Oct 1861 (died at age 4)
Emma Jane G., 2 Mar 1863 (died at age 2)
Thomas Grover, 17 Dec 1865 (died as an infant)
Heber C., 20 Nov 1866
Emeline, 5 May 1868 (died as an infant)
Caroline, 27 May 1869
Charles, 16 Feb 1871 (died at age 7)
Eliza Ann, 2 Feb 1874
Joel Grover, 13 Nov 1875

Mary Elizabeth's parents joined the Church of Jesus Christ of Latter-day Saints in 1831. In 1836, the family moved to Kirtland, Ohio where her father worked on the temple.

Mary's mother died in 1840 and her seven daughters were taken into the homes of the Saints to be cared for. Mary Elizabeth was taken into the home of Prophet Joseph Smith until the prophet was martyred. She was then placed in the home of her Aunt Polly Duell.

On February 16, 1846, Mary Elizabeth left Nauvoo, Illinois on a flatboat which overturned in the Mississippi River. They moved first to Mt. Pisgah, then to Winter Quarters. In the Spring of 1847, they traveled with the Charles C. Rich Wagon Company to cross the Plains. Her older sister had married Charles C. Rich. They all arrived in the Salt Lake Valley in the Fall of 1847 and experienced the hardships of that first winter.

In the Spring of 1848, they moved to Centerville, Utah. The crickets ate most of their crops that year. Their next move in 1849 was to Farmington, Utah.

Mary married William Alpheus Simmons. They moved to Mormon Island in California for a while, then moved to San Bernardino to help settle the area. They returned to Utah in 1854 and lived in Bountiful, and back to Farmington, again. William was accidentally killed on September 30, 1857. They had six children born to their union.

Mary took in a boarder named David Robison. On December 26, 1860, they were married. They moved to North Morgan, Utah where nine children were born. Her first three children by David died within a few days of each other in the winter of 1865-1866.

Mary was called many times to take care of the sick and assisted as a midwife in many deliveries throughout her long life.

In August 1879, Mary, David, and David's plural wife, Johanna, and their children moved to settle Star Valley, Wyoming. In 1882, they moved to Gray's Lake, and finally in 1884, they moved to Lyman. Mary helped organize the first Relief Society and served as the first President.

Mary lived another fourteen years beyond her husband. She passed away at the age of eighty-eight on September 28, 1921.

MARY JANE WAITE ROBISON

BIRTHDATE: 12 Jan 1836
Cleveland, Ohio
DEATH: 18 Mar 1922
Pleasant Grove, Utah Co, Utah
PARENTS: John Waite
Jane Caldwell
PIONEER: 16 Oct 1852
Eli Kelsey Co. Wagon Train
SPOUSE: Lewis Robison
MARRIED: 5 Oct, 1855
DEATH SP: 1 Nov 1883
Pleasant Grove, Utah Co. Utah

CHILDREN:
Seth Milton, 11 May 1858
Minerva, 29 Jul 1860
Emma Lnora, 11 Oct 1862
Daniel Hanmer, 28 Apr 1865
Inez Melissa, 30 May 1868
Guy Kellogg, 3 Apr 1871

Mary Jane was born in Ohio in 1836, her mother joined the Church of Jesus Christ of Latter-day Saints, but no record exists to indicate that her father ever joined. Sixteen year old Mary Jane, with her mother and sister, Lucena, came to Utah by ox-team and wagon, with the Eli Kelsey Wagon Company arriving in the Salt Lake Valley in October of 1862.

In the fall of her nineteenth year, she became the second wife of Lewis Robison and for the first two years of her married life, lived at Fort Bridger where her first little boy was born. We can imagine the excitement that existed the time they were at Fort Bridger with almost every traveler passing through, the Indians and traders coming to the fort nearly every day and the United States Government constantly challenging them.

When Johnston's approaching army threatened, they packed all their belongings, burned the fort and retreated south.

After Guy was born, Lewis was called to operate a sawmill in American Fork Canyon and so thirty-six year old Mary Jane took her family and went with him. She cooked for thirty men who worked at the mill and on the railroad using the money she earned to help better her   family's lives, and by being frugal, they were able to get many things they could never before afford.

Her grandchildren could remember the buckskin gloves that she made. She purchased buckskin from the Indians from which she cut, sewed and beaded beautiful gloves, They sold for about nine dollars a pair, a very good price for the times.

Mary Jane loved her family, always wanting the best for them and the grandchildren loved to visit her and enjoy her cheerful, pleasant ways. The family lived in harmony, the wives agreeable to each other, They were all convinced

that if the Lord sanctioned polygamy, then He would help them make it work and it did.

Lewis died when Mary Jane was forty-seven years old. Her youngest child, twelve, would need her support and the oldest, Seth at age twenty-five would do his best for the family. Her years as a widow equaled those of her married life. She died at the age of eighty-six loved by all her family and friends.

NANCY ELLEN WAGAMAN ROBISON

BIRTHDATE: 1801
Quincy, Franklin, Pennsylvania
DEATH: 14 Nov 1883
Morgan,, Morgan Co., Utah
PARENTS: Andrew Wagaman
Catherine Rock
PIONEER: 27 Aug 1860
Daniel Robison 9th Handcart Co.
SPOUSE: Alexander Robison
MARRIED: 1828
DEATH SP: 23 Jan 1879
Quincy, Franklin, Pennsylvania

CHILDREN:
Nancy Ellen, 1823 (died as an infant)
Hannah Labelle, 15 Sep 1825
David, 2 Apr 1827
William, 18 Apr 1829
Daniel, 21 Mar 1831
Catherine, 18 Aug 1833
Eliza, 27 Oct 1835
Lenna, 10 Oct 1839
Franey Wagaman, 28 Jul. 1841
Ephraim, 28 Febe 1844
Mary Ann, 15 Oct 1845
Ephraim, 24 Feb. 1848

Nancy Ellen was born in Pennsylvania in 1801. She married Alexander in her home town of Quincy when she was twenty-seven and the couple were the parents of twelve children. Her first little girl died in the same year she was born and their tenth child died an infant also, ten grew to adulthood, married and had families of their own,

During the year 1854, when Nancy was fifty-three years old, they heard the testimony of elder Angus M. Cannon, a missionary from Utah and were converted to the Church of Jesus Christ of Latter-day Saints.

In May of 1860, Mary Ellen and Alexander left Pennsylvania with three sons, one daughter and their families, William age thirty-one, Daniel age twenty-nine, and Eliza age twenty-five, and David age thirty-three.

Leaving their cozy comfortable homes, their orchards and gardens, they traveled by rail and water the 2,000 miles to Florence, Nebraska and camped there for two weeks while arraignments were being made for a handcart company.

Daniel was appointed captain of the Ninth Handcart Company, the next to last handcart company to cross the Plains.

Ellen now fifty-nine and Alexander sixty were fortunate to meet Mr. Green, a merchant from Salt Lake City. He had several wagons loaded with goods and he invited Alexander and Ellen to drive a team of horses and four oxen with a load of merchandise and food to sell. They were in the Charles C. Rich Handcart Company, which followed the company. Upon arriving in the Salt Lake Valley after a successful journey, they were given room and board for the winter in exchange for caring for Mr. Green's buggy team.

In the Spring of 1861, their youngest son, Ephraim, took them to Farmington where they rented a one-room adobe house with a fireplace and one window. Food was scarce and many a meal consisted of the small potatoes given to them by compassionate neighbors. Lunch, when they went to the mountains for wood to chop, were those small potatoes boiled, with salt.

It took Alexander and Ephraim three years to scrape up enough money to buy a yoke of oxen and the front running gear of an old wagon. On this they built a small cart. They placed all their belongings on the cart and Nancy Ellen sat on the top of it all. Ephraim got on one side of the oxen and Alexander on the other. They walked over the mountain to Morgan in Morgan County, Utah, A distance of twenty miles, and spent their remaining years there.

Nancy passed away four years after her husband at the age of eighty-two. She had used her life in service of others, first her children, (she was either tending a new baby or expecting one for the first twenty years of her married life and was forty-seven at the birth of her last child), then in between family obligations, she gave her time to the Church filling many callings with honor and was a faithful tithing payer.

SELINA HAYWARD CHAFFEE ROBISON

BIRTHDATE: 26 Dec 1820
Susquehanna, Pennsylvanaia
DEATH: 17 Nov 1861
Fillmore, Millard Co., Utah
PARENTS: David Chaffee
Lucy Perrin
PIONEER: 1850 Wagon Train
Capt. Peter Robison
SPOUSE: Peter Robison
MARRIED: 6 Oct 1839
Gilvert Mills, New York
DEATH SP: 20 Oct 1902
Garrison, Millard Co., Utah

CHILDREN:
Maryette, 24 Aug 1841 d. 1847
David Peter, 17 Sep 1846 (died as an infant - 1847)
Cornelia Celina, 17 Sep 1848
Charles, 23 Aug 1850

Joseph Millard, 29 Mar 1852
Lucy Matilda, 2 Apr 1854
Sarah Johanna, 18 Jul 1856
James Henry, 27 May 1859
George Samuel, 18 Nov 1860

Selina (Celina) was born on December 26, 1820 in Susquehanna, Pennsylvania, the daughter of David Chaffee and Lucy Perrin. She had a good education and was able to teach school in Oswego County at the age of eighteen years,

She was married to Peter Robison on October 6, 1839 in Gilvert Mills, Oswego County, New York while she was still teaching. She became the mother of nine children, however the first two died as infants.

The family came across the Plains by wagon in 1850. Her husband was appointed wagonmaster of their company by President Brigham Young.

The family settled in Millard County in a town called Petersburg, or Hatton. This location was thought to be too harsh for fruit trees, and so was relocated a few miles to the east and named Kanosh.

Child-bearing was hard on Selina, and she passed away just one year after her last child was born, on November 17, 1861, in Fillmore, Utah. Her husband passed away on October 20, 1902 in Garrison, Millard County, Utah.

SUSANNAH TURNER ROBISON

BIRTHDATE: 3 Feb 1847
Milltown, Somerset, New Jersey
DEATH: 15 Apr, 1938
Salt Lake City, Salt Lake, Utah
PARENTS: David Turner
Rose Collier
PIONEER: 18 Sep 1861
John Murdock Co. Wagon Train
SPOUSE: Benjamin H. Robison
MARRIED: 26 Mar 1864
DEATH SP: 22 Dec 1882

CHILDREN:
Birdie Susannah, 7 Mar 1865
Mary Lucretia, 27 May 1866
Joseph Hancock, 5 Jan 1868
Almon David, 8 Dec 1869
Rose May, 21 Aug 1871
Benjamin Hancock, 14 Dec 1873
John Collier, 5 Dec 1875
Martha Alzina, 1 Apr 1879
George Albert, 9 Dec 1880
Edward Lorenzo, 26 Dec 1882

Susannah was born in New Jersey in 1847, the fourth child in a family of eleven. Her parents had come from Yorkshire, England dissatisfied with the direction of their religion, were seeking more and decided to come to America with their two children. Their third girl, Martha, was born in their new home, Milltown, New Jersey, where Susannah was also born.

"Schooling and luxuries were not to be had," Susannah writes "and from very early life I had responsibilities." She worked at the factory where her father was supervisor. At the age of seven she was put to work threading the shuttles and became so apt that she became "very popular," and worked there until she was fourteen.

When her father heard the message of the Church of Jesus Christ of Latter-day Saints of John Taylor and Wilford Woodruff, immediately he decided it was what he had come to America for. "It seemed we had entered into a new world" . . . "and to join the Saints in the land of Zion was our first and only object. The family was large but each of us, having the same thought in view, toiled and saved for the same purpose until it was accomplished."

Reaching Omaha, Nebraska before the Murdock Company was organized meant a three week wait of camping out under very poor circumstances, especially for their mother with a three week old baby. As they left to begin their journeys "little did we realize the joy or sadness that might come to us."

Her mother,, became ill with mountain fever, it was thought she would not survive, but she did. Susannah carried her baby brother many miles and said "foot sore" applied to them, "many times when we removed our shoes, the skin would come off with them." Through the long tedious journey their prayers were answered,. the family arrived intact.

The Robison's were sent to Fillmore and were befriended by Brother Chandler Holbrook who fed them their first meal eaten inside a house in over ninety days.

Thoroughly destitute, the family found employment, Susannah in the home of Daniel Thompson, where she stayed for a time and then at the home of Benjamin H. Robison. In 1863, Benjamin was called to Millard County to help the settlers and for the convenience of all, Brigham Young advised they marry which they did and "never regretted the act."

Returning to Fillmore five years later they settled permanently in their simple pioneer home. Ten children were born to them and "with all our duties they were a happy united family striving always to be worthy of the guiding influence and blessings of the Lord.

Susannah was thirty-five years old with nine children when on Christmas Eve 1882, her husband died. Two days later her tenth child was born. For fifty-six years she lived a widow's life caring for her ten children. Through it all she worked in the church and worked in the temple for the last twenty-three years of her life.

ELIZA JANE SKEEN ROBSON

No
Photo
Available

BIRTHDATE: 13 Jun 1849
Keg Creek, Pottawattamie, Iowa
DEATH: 14 Jan. 1888
Plain City, Weber Co., Utah
PARENTS: Joseph Skeen
Maria Amanda Dolby
PIONEER: 1851
SPOUSE: James P. Robson
MARRIED: 3 May 1865
DEATH SP: 27 Apr 1887
Plain City, Weber Co., Utah

CHILDREN:
James Lyman, 3 Nov 1866
Luella, 18 Jan 1869
Mary Maria, 8 Feb 1871 (died at age 8)
Rhonda Jane, 22 Nov 1873
Margaret Eliza, 14 Apr 1876
Joseph Lester, 16 Mar 1878 (died at age 1)
John Elmer, 6 Sep 1884
Charles Patterson, 31 Dec 1887 (died at 9 months)

Eliza Jane was born in Iowa in 1849, the sixth child in the Skenn family (named for two of her fathers sisters) and the only daughter of three girls to live to maturity. Her father had returned from service with the Mormon Battalion, rented a farm at Pottawattamie, and worked toward crossing the Plains.

When she was a two year old toddler the family made the last lap of the journey to the Salt Lake Valley and located at Lehi, Utah. Three years later her mother died and she early learned of sorrow and the dissolution of a motherless home.

Rhoda Sanford, a close neighbor, and sympathetic widow with five children soon won their affection, and three months after her mother's death their two families combined to give Eliza two big sisters and in time a baby brother. During March of 1859, Joseph Skeen moved his family north to Weber County and pioneered the waste land.

One month before her seventeenth birthday, Eliza married James Robson, a brother of her step-sister's husband and the two established a home a mile and a half north of the village. The busy farm life, care of the growing family activities of ward and church and association with family and friends filled their lives to overflowing. Grief followed the deaths of two of her children in the flue out break of 1879.

It was spring and James was busy preparing the soil for planting. This morning he brought his horse and plow to the rear of the house and began preparing the soil for spring planting. About noon Eliza Jane stepped to the door to call James in for dinner. She saw the harness had become loosened from the plow and he was stooping over to make the connection close in behind the old trusted work horse.

Suddenly the horse leaped forward and then with a vicious kick struck James to the ground, he died the next day.

Heartbroken Eliza Jane carried on during the summer keeping up her home and family and preparing for the new baby soon to come, but the shock and weary burdens she carried proved too heavy and she passed away soon after the birth of her son, Charles Patterson.

Eliza Jane passed away at the age of thirty-eight years, leaving her oldest son, James Lyman Robson just past twenty-one in charge of the farm and Luella age nineteen, in charge of the new baby who lived only nine and a half months.

Twenty-two years of companionship, love and devotion had cemented their lives so closely that they could not be long separated. Reunited, James and Eliza Jane sleep side by side in the cemetery at Plain City, Weber County, Utah.

LEANNAH ROBISON ROCK

BIRTHDATE: 10 Oct 1839
Tomstown, Pennsylvania
DEATH: 21 Oct 1909
Hibbard, Fremont Co., Idaho
PARENTS: Alexander Robison
Nancy Ellen Wagaman
PIONEER: Fall of 1860
Wagon Train Company
SPOUSE: Henry Rock
MARRIED: 17 Dec 1858
Tomstown, Pennsylvania
DEATH SP: 6 Mar 1908
Hibbard, Fremont Co., Utah

CHILDREN:
Elizabeth, 15 Jul 1859
Amanda, 2 Sep 1861
Henry, Jr., 9 Mar 1863
William, 24 Aug 1864
Jared, 24 Aug 1866
David, 5 Sep 1868
James Wellington, 19 Jan 1870
Nancy Ellen, 30 Nov 1871
Harry, 17 Jun 1875
Albert, 29 Jan 1879
Ernest, 29 Nov 1880

Leannah was born on October 10, 1839 in Tomstown, Franklin County, Pennsylvania. She was raised on a farm and was able to help grow and harvest food for their livelihood.

Leannah attended a one-room school when weather and farm work permitted her too. In 1855, her family first heard the missionaries from the Church of Jesus Christ of Latterday Saints. In 1856, they joined the Church and made plans to come to Zion.

She married Henry Rock on December 17, 1858 in Tomstown, Franklin County, Pennsylvania.

in 1860, Henry and Leannah and her parents and Henry's widowed mother joined an independent wagon company and crossed the plains, walking most of the way. Leannah's parents were called to settle Morgan County, where they operated a farm.

Henry and Leannah first lived in the Mill Creek area, where Henry's mother lived. They later moved to Davis County and finally to Morgan County, all in Utah. Leannah had ten more children, all of them born in Utah.

The family moved to Hibbard, Idaho, where Henry passed away on March 6, 1908. Leannah passed away on October 21, 1909, also at Hibbard, Franklin County, Idaho.

MARY ANN NEFF ROCKWELL

No
Photo
Available

BIRTHDATE: 5 Aug 1829
Strasburg, Pennsylvania
DEATH: 28 Sep 1866
Salt Lake City, Salt Lake, Utah
PARENTS: John Neff
Mary Barr
PIONEER: 2 Oct 1847
SPOUSE: Orrin Porter Rockwell
MARRIED: 1848
DEATH SP: 9 Jun 1878
Jedediah Grant Co. Wagon Train

CHILDREN:
Talitha, 1848
William, 1852
Mary Amanda, 11 Mar 1855
John Orrin, 23 Oct 1858
Letitia Barr, 4 Aug 1864
Joseph Neff, 24 Aug 1866

Mary Ann was born in Strasburg, Lancaster County, Pennsylvaniain 1829 and was thirteen when her parents heeded the message of the Mormon Elders and were baptized. After a visit in Nauvoo with the Prophet Joseph Smith, her well-to-do parents returned home to Pennsylvania and sold all of their wordly goods. They journeyed back to Nauvoo to join the Saints and arrived there just in time to begin the exodus West.

The Neff family settled in East Mill Creek where John Neff built a grist mill and established a comfortable home. Orrin Porter Rockwell and John Neff (several years his senior) became good friends and frequently invited Orrin and the Neffs to dine at the home of Mrs. Wooley, where John's pretty daughter, Mary Ann age twenty-two, caught Rockwell's eye. Though sixteen years older than she, he was healthy and rock hard from his outdoor life.

On May 3, 1854, Mary Ann and Orrin Porter Rockwell were sealed in the Salt Lake Endowment House. The ceremony was performed by Brigham Young.

Orrin established the "Hot Springs and Brewery Hotel" and stable near the 'Point of the Mountain and he and his family lived at their ranch in Lehi. Mary Ann made the home a cheery blend of warmth and comfort for their five children and Orrin.

Brigham Young enjoyed his hospitality as did the young stage drivers who became friends with the family. When one of the young drivers was killed brutally by the Indians, it so affected Mary Ann that she could no longer stay at the ranch, so her husband closed it up and moved his wife and family to Salt Lake City.

The family enjoyed their new home and neighborhood in Salt Lake. About one year later, on August 24, 1866, Mary Ann gave birth to their sixth child. There were complications. Her condition worsened and when her heart gave out, she passed away at the age of thirty-seven. The infant died two weeks later.

Her husband mourned her passing, for she was a gentle, calming influence in his sometimes turbulent life. A token of his esteem for his wife, a beautiful lemon-colored, elaborately embroidered fringed silk shawl from India, is now in the possession of the Daughters of the Utah Pioneers and can be viewed in the museum.

ANGELINE HODGEKINS HORNE ROCKWOOD

BIRTHDATE: 19 Feb 1820
Noblesborough, Lincoln, Maine
DEATH SP: Jul 1902
Centerville, Davis Co., Utah
PARENTS: Frank Hodgkins
Sarah Boyd
PIONEER: 12 Oct 1849
Silas Richards Co. Wagon Train
SPOUSE I: Moses Horne
MARRIED: 8 Nov 1835
Friendship, Lincoln Co. , Maine
DEATH SP: 1845
Nauvoo, Hancock Co., Illinois

CHILDREN:
Linda Ann, 6 Jul 1836
Sarah Elizabeth, 13 Jul 1839

SPOUSE II: Albert Perry Rockwood
MARRIED: 21 Jan 1846
Nauvoo, Hancock Co., Illinois
DEATH SP: 26 Nov 1879
Salt Lake City, Salt lake Co., Utah

CHILDREN:
Nancy Angeline, 24 Dec 1849
Moses Perry, 1 3 Nov 1853

Angeline was born in Maine in 1820. She married Moses Horne on November 18, 1835. They were the parents of two children. Angeline and Moses moved to Nauvoo. In 1845, Moses was killed in a stone quarry cutting stone for the Nauvoo Temple. His superviser

promised to take care of the family of anyone that was killed at the quarry.

True to his word Albert Perry Rockwood married Angeline Hopkins as her second husband and his third wife on August 21, 1846. By the next February, they were among the Saints that fled across the frozen Mississippi River for refuge.

Albert went with Brigham Young in the first group of pioneers leaving his wives and children in Winter Quarters. He returned the second time and took some of his family. Then again the third time for the last two wives and their children. Angeline was in this group. Leaving Winter Quarters in the Spring of 1849 in the Silas Richards Wagon Company, arriving in the Salt Lake Valley on October 12, 1849. Angeline had two more children, both born in Salt Lake City.

Angeline passed away in July, 1902 at Centerville, Davis County, Utah.

JULIANE SOPHIA OLSEN ROCKWOOD

BIRTHDATE: 3 Nov 1836
Uvelse Fredericksborg, Denmark
DEATH SP: 7 Feb 1914
Salt Lake City, Salt Lake, Utah
PARENTS: Ole Olsen
Mette Larsen
PIONEER: Oct 1862
John R. Murdock Wagon Train
SPOUSE: Albert P. Rockwood
MARRIED: 11 Apr 1863
Salt Lake City, Salt Lake, Utah
DEATH SP: 26 Nov 1879
Salt Lake City, Salt Lake, Utah

CHILDREN:
Nancy Matilda, 17 Jun 1864
Luther C., 30 Dec 1864
Timothy, 21 Feb 1866
Mary Emma, 4 May l868
Samuel, 22 May 1870
Ole Olsen, 28 Dec 1873
Frederick, 12 Aug 1874
Julius Apollos, 5 Mar 1878

Juliane was born in Denmark in 1836. She was the second of six children. Her father died on October 15, 1858, leaving her mother to raise the six children.

Juliane emigrated to America in the spring of 1862. She sailed on the ship "Humbolt" landing in New York Noon May 20, 1862. Then they went on to Florence, Nebraska. She joined the John R. Murdock Wagon Company arriving in the Salt Lake Valley in October, 1862.

After spending the night alone in the wagon because she didn't have anyone to greet her, she found work as a domestic maid at the home of Elder John VanCott for seven months. She then married Albert Perry Rockwood as his fourth wife on April 11, 1863. They were the parents of eight children but only two lived to adulthood.

At the time of their marriage, Albert was warden of the Utah Territorial Penitentiary on 14th East and 21st South in Salt Lake City. They lived in the wardens house outside the gates and she served as prison matron. Their first five sons were born here but four of the five died either at birth or within a few short months.

In 1871, the United States Marshall took over the penitentiary and Albert didn't think he should have the territorial prisoners so he moved them to 9th West and North Temple street. Juliane moved with him. Two more children were born here, one of whom died at birth.

During these times two of her sisters had emigrated to the Salt Lake Valley. Karen Marie had married and moved to Richmond, Utah and Maren Matilda was employed in the household of Brigham Young.

After the matter of the penitentiary had been resolved, Juliane moved to an adobe house on 6th East and 6th South a short time, then moved into the Rockwood town house at 1st South and 3rd East with Albert's first and fifth wives and their children.

In 1876, Albert was appointed Teritorrial Fish Commissioner and again Juliane and her two sons moved to the Rockwood farm on 11th East and 21st South where the fish hatcheries were. Here her last son Julius was born.

Albert Rockwood passed away on November 26, 1879 leaving Juliane with three small sons. Maren yet unmarried moved to the farm to help her. Maren attended to the inside chores, Juliane raised strawberries, raspberries, potatoes, and other garden products and sold them to provide a living.

Her son, Frederick, also died in 1886 leaving her two sons and her sister, Maren. In 1905, her sons built her an new home just south of the old one. Her sister Maren died on April 20, 1912. Juliane moved to a small apartment at the rear of Julius's home on Lincoln street.

She was a brave courageous woman. She served as counselor in Relief Society for several years and was visiting teacher. She would take her horse and wagon and cover a twenty-two square mile area. On her fiftieth birthday the ward gave her a chair in recognition of her faithfulness and compassionate service.

Juliane passed away on February 7, 1914 in Salt Lake City, Utah at the age of seventy-eight.

NANCY HAVEN ROCKWOOD

BIRTHDATE: 13 Jun 1805
Holliston, Massachusetts
DEATH: 23 Jan 1876
Salt Lake City, Salt Lake, Utah
SPOUSE: John Haven
Elizbeth Howe
PIONEER: 21 Sep 1848
Brigham Young Wagon Train
SPOUSE: Albert P. Rockwood
MARREID: 3 Apr 1827
Holliston, Massachustts
DEATH SP: 26 Nov 1879
Salt Lake City, Salt Lake, Utah

CHILDREN:
Elizabeth Perry, 28 Dec 1827
Ellen Ackland, 23 Mar 1829
Albert Haven, 29 Sep 1831
Miriam Mariah, 16 Feb 1834
Mary Ann, 16 Feb 1834
Albert Nelson, 19 Feb 1841

Nancy was born in Holliston, Middlesex County, Massachusetts in 1805. Nancy married Albert Perry Rockwood on April 3, 1827. They were the parents of six children, five born in Hollistor and one born in Nauvoo.

In May, 1838, the family left Holliston for Missouri. In September, 1838, they were in St. Louis, then on to Far West. On January 25, 1839 they were in Quincy, Illinois.

The time spent in Quincy was a difficult time for the little family because two of the three surviving children died leaving only Ellen.

In 1840, they moved to Commerce, Illinois. Albert opened a dry good store and Nancy made beautiful straw hats to sell. Another son, Albert Nelson, was born here. But the happiness didn't last long. On July 18, 1843 young Albert also died.

On September 13, 1845, their daughter, Ellen, married Brigham Young. By the next February, they were among the Saints who fled across the frozen Mississippi river for refuge. They went on to Winter Quarters in Iowa.

Albert Rockwood left with Brigham Young in the first group of pioneers, leaving Nancy and Ellen in Winter Quarters until June, 1848, when they left with Brigham Young's second group.

Nancy was courageous and industrious woman. She passed away on January 23, 1876 in Salt Lake City, Utah at the age of seventy-one.

JANE MORGAN RODEBACK

BIRTHDATE: 28 Mar 1811
Newlin, Chester, Pennsylvania
DEATH SP: 15 Sep 1890
Hoytsville, Summit Co., Utah
PARENT'S: Benjamin Morgan
Mary Fisher
PIONEER: 1852
Lt. Johnson's Indep Wagon Train
SPOUSE: Charles Rodeback
MARRIED: 18 Oct 1838
Newlin, Chester, Pennsylvania
DEATH SP: 1 Jun 1907
Hoytsville, Summit Co., Utah

CHILDREN:
Mary Ann, 30 Jun 1839
Lorenzo, 28 Dec 1840
Sarah Jane, 16 Aug 1842
Josephine Eleanor, 18 Aug 1845
Rebecca Hellen, 21 Jul 1847
Frances Isabelle, 11 Oct 1848
Charles LaVant, 29 Nov 1851
David Morgan, 22 Jul 1855

Jane was born in Newlin, Pennsylvania. She married Charles Rodeback and gave birth to her first two children in the same town in which she was born.

In May, 1841, they sold their farm and moved to Nauvoo, Illinois to be with the Saints and help in the construction of the temple. Her family was driven from their comfortable home in Nauvoo, away from the temple they worked so hard to build, away from the place where two of her children were buried. They moved first to Winter Quarters, then to Council Bluffs, and again to Kanesville, Iowa.

In 1851, Jane was left alone while her husband drove a team and wagon to Utah for David Wilkins. He took up two lots in Salt Lake City and returned to Kaneville for his family. In the Spring of 1852, they crossed the Plains and arrived in Salt Lake City.

After their arrival into the Valley, they continued to endure hardships. Sometimes, their food consisted of weeds and greens they could gather, roots, and sego lily bulbs. They endured the grasshopper plague and the "Move South" when Johnston led a United States army to the Salt Lake Valley.

After they returned to Salt Lake City, they were called to settle an area in Summit County which was later named Hoytsville. They built a home from the stone they found in the area, When they had trouble with the Indians, they had to move to the fort for protection.

In 1875, Charles was called to serve a mission and Jane was left to care for their home and property. Their son lived close by, so she was not completely alone.

Jane was a valiant Pioneer who faced many trials in her life, but gained strength from placing her faith in the gospel of Jesus Christ. She was devoted to her family, church, and community.

MARY ANN CLAYTON RODEBACK

BIRTHDATE: 30 Jan 1855
Sheffield, Yorkshire, England
DEATH: 13 Mar 1931
Lehi, Utah Co., Utah
PARENTS: Albert Clayton
Frances Higgenbotham
PIONEER: 1862 Wagon Train
SPOUSE: Charles L. Rodeback
MARRIED: 16 Oct 1872
DEATH SP: 12 May 1919
Provo, Utah Co., Utah

CHILDREN:
Charles Albert, 8 Aug 1873
Mary Frances, 12 Nov 1874
Elizabeth Jane, 9 Oct 1876
David, 26 Jan 1878
Clara Alice, 14 Apr 1881
Lenora Rodeback, 13 Aug 1883
James Henry, 16 Feb 1886
Edmund, 17 Mar 1888
John William, 13 Oct 1890
Beatrice, 21 Oct 1892
George Washington, 11 Dec 1894
Fern, 6 Dec 1896
Noah, 31 Mar 1900

Mary Ann's parents joined the Church of Jesus Christ of Latter-day Saints in England and emigrated to the United States with their children. As a child, she suffered in the cold of winter, the heat of summer, and lack of food at times. Her father, brother, and sister died before they were able to cross the Plains.

In 1862, her mother was able to bring her remaining two children across the Plains to the Salt Lake Valley. Her mother married Henry Olpin, a widower, and they lived in Salt Lake City for several years before they moved to Morgan.

They were endowed and sealed together on June 30, 1873 in the Edowment House in Salt Lake City. They built a log house in Hoytsville. Mary Ann was the mother of thirteen children who were all raised in this home. The family endured many hardships and trials that were a part of their lives in those trying times.

In later years, Mary Ann and her husband moved to Provo with their younger children. She was a good neighbor and helped others in times of sickness, sorrow, and death. She was devoted to her family, the church, and the community where she lived.

PHEBE BEAGLE RODEBACK

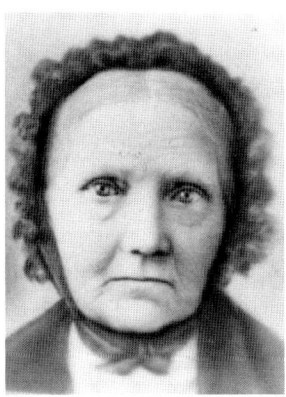

BIRTHDATE: 25 Jun 1811
Uchland, Chester, Pennsylvania
DEATH: 17 Sep 1898
Cedar Fort, Utah Co., Utah
PARENTS: Henry Beagle
Margaret Evans
PIONEER: Oct 1852
Warren Snow Co. Wagon Train
SPOUSE: James Rodeback
MARRIED: 24 May 1832
DEATH SP: 25 May 1875

CHILDREN:
Edward Hunter, 30 May 1833
Phoebe Ann, 2 Nov 1835
Margarett, Jun 1839
John, Jun 1841
Lorenzo Barnes, 11 Mar 1843
Rebecca H., 2 May 1846
Catherine Angeline, 14 Nov 1849
Sarah Jane, 20 Feb 1853
James, 20 Feb 1853

Her father, not knowing how to care for so young a child, bound her out to friends, an innkeeper and his wife of Philadelphia. At a young age she was taught to wait on customers. She was given a fine education and was brought up in the Quaker church.

At the age of eighteen, she was released from her bond and went to work in the home of Edward Hunter. Here, she met James Rodeback who was an apprentice wheelwright in Mr. Hunter's employ, and who later became her husband. As soon as James served his apprenticeship they were married, May 24, 1832.

When Phebe's father heard she was investigating the Church of Jesus Christ of Latter-day Saints, he offered to build them a new home and set them up in business if they would have nothing to do with "those Mormons," but if she went with them she would never see or hear from him again. She never did. Phebe and James were baptized on August 10, 1839 by Lorenzo Barnes.

They moved to Nauvoo on April 6, 1846; less than a month before their daughter, Rebecca, was born in a covered wagon just outside of Nauvoo.

They moved on to Council Bluffs, Iowa where they stayed a few years before joining the Warren Snow Wagon Company, which arrived in the Salt Lake Valley in October of 1852. From here the family moved to Pleasant Grove. for about three years and then to Cedar Fort.

Shortly after moving to Cedar Fort she began holding Sunday School classes in her home. She continued to hold them until a regular Sunday School was organized in 1863 with James as Superintendant and she as an assistant. She also served in the Relief Society Presidency.

Until a school was organized, Phebe called the children together and held school in her home.

Phebe passed away on September 17, 1898 at eighty-seven years of age.

ELIZABETH GEORGIANA QUILLEY READ RODWELL

BIRTHDATE: 22 Sep 1805
Basing Hampshire, England
DEATH: 5 Oct 1882
Nephi, Juab Co., Utah
PARENTS: William Quilley
Hannah Evemay
PIONEER: 30 Nov 1856
Edward Martin Handcart Comp.
SPOUSE: Samuel George Read
MARRIED: 1836
St. Dunstan's Church, England
DEATH SP: 8 Dec 1893
Salt Lake City, Salt Lake, Utah

CHILDREN:
Clara Elizabeth Quilley, 16 Jul 1839
Alicia Quilley, 20 Oct 1840
Samuel Milford, 13 Oct 1841
Thisbe Quilley, 26 Apr 1845
Walter Pyramus, 8 Aug 1848

SPOUSE II: John Rodwell
MARRIED: 10 Jan 1863
Salt Lake City, Salt Lake Co., Utah
DEATH SP: Not given
CHILDREN: None

Elizabeth was an intelligent, gracious, ambitious person. When she heard the true Gospel of the Church of Jesus Christ of Latter-day Saints, she and all except her youngest child were baptized as members of the Church.

They left England with a large group of emigrants on the ship, "Horizon." After they arrived in Boston, Massachusetts on June 20, 1856, they went by train to Iowa City. They had difficulty in obtaining handcarts and those handcarts they could buy were quickly made with green wood. As the wood dried, the cart fell apart. They were assigned to the Edward Martin Handcart Company.

Elizabeth tucked some medical supplies and herbs in the corner of her handcart. She also kept a few dry twigs and grass so she could readily start a fire. Her knowledge of the herbs and medicine kept her family quite well.

On August 8, 1856, their youngest son, Walter, wandered away from the company and became lost. Her husband stayed behind to find Walter. Elizabeth went on ahead pulling the handcart with her two daughters, Alicia age sixteen, and Thisbe age eleven, pushing from behind.

Their handcart company suffered terribly by being caught in early snow without ample food and clothing. Elizabeth was called upon to help relieve what suffering she could through her nursing skills and the few medical supplies she brought with her. In November, the Martin Handcart Company was rescued and carried into the Salt Lake Valley.

Elizabeth worked for Brigahm Young as a nurse and helper in his household. She also did nursing throughout the Valley. In 1858, Elizabeth and her daughter, Thisbe, went back across the Plains and found her husband was in love with a widow. Heartbroken, she agreed to give her husband a divorce and he was to try one more time to locate their son.

In the summer of 1861, after Walter had been found, Walter drove an oxen-team with his mother and sister, Thisbe, to Salt Lake City. This was Elizabeth's third crossing of the Plains.

Elizabeth married John Rodwell. When they moved to Nephi, Elizabeth delivered babies and nursed the sick for many years. She passed away in Nephi and was buried in the Salt Lake City Cemetery.

ELIZABETH HOLLIS ROE

No
Photo
Available

BIRTHDATE: 24 Dec 1812
Marshfield, England
DEATH: 24 Jul 1855
crossing the Plains
PARENTS: John Hollis
Mary Mason
PIONEER:
unknown Wagon Train,
SPOUSE: James Roe
MARRIED: 24 Mar 1840
Radford, England
DEATH SP: 16 Nov 1853
Radford, England

CHILDREN:
Emma (Taylor Watts), 5 Jun 1842
Mary (Halse), 19 Feb 1846
Isabella Jane (Boyd), 16 Aug 1847
Charles John, 6 Aug 1850

Elizabeth was born in Marshfield, Nottinghamshire, England in 1812. She married James Roe on march 24, 1840 in Radford, Nottinghamshire, England. They were the parents of four children. Her husband passed away on November 16, 1853.

Elizabeth and her children left Liverpool for the United States on the ship "Germanicus." Elizabeth had money to cover their expenses and enough lace to start a business on their arrival. She also hired a lady to help her. They landed in New Orleans on June 12, 1854. The next day they took a steam boat for St. Louis, Missouri.

Elizabeth passed away while crossing the Plains. The lady she hired returned to England. The children's money was stolen and so was the lace, they were pennieless. They

were separated and raised by different families after they arrived in the Salt Lake Valley.

ANN EVANS ROGERS

No
Photo
Available

BIRTHDATE: 3/4 Jul 1830
Merthyr Tydvil, South Wales
DEATH: 28 Feb 1892
Benson, Cache Co., Utah
PARENTS: William Evans
Mary Ann Pugh
PIONEER: 27 Aug 1859
James Brown Co. Wagon Train
SPOUSE: Thomas Rogers
MARRIED: 1850
near St. Louis, Missouri
DEATH SP: 5 Nov 1891
Benson, Cache Co., Utah

CHILDREN:
John, 19 Feb 1851
William, 18 Mar 1853
Thomas, 12 Mar 1855
Mary Jane, 28 Apr 1857
Elizabeth Ann, 28 Nov 1859
Henry Toles, 19 Jan 1862
Celestia Melissa, 5 Apr 1864
Martha Maritta, 20 Apr 1866
Marcus Evan, 20 Aug 1868
Charles George, 11 Sep 1872

Ann was born in Merthyr Tydvil, Monmouthshire, South Wales. She was baptized a member of the Church of Jesus Christ of latter-day Saints in 1844, the only one in her family to join. She sang in the choir in Wales under the direction of Elex Lewis.

She sailed from England on January 13, 1849, on the ship "Osprey," and arrived in New Orleans on April 1, 1849.

Ann met and married Thomas Rogers in 1850 in St. Louis, Missouri. They had ten children born to them, the first four while they lived in Missouri, the other six in Utah-one in Bountiful, four in Hyde Park, and the last one was born in Benson, Utah.

In the company of Captain James Brown, Ann and Thomas traveled to the West. They left Florence, Nebraska on June 13, 1859 with 253 Saints and 59 wagons. They arrived in the Salt Lake Valley on August 27, 1859. On November 28, of that year, Ann gave birth to her daughter, Elizabeth Ann.

They had stayed in St. Louis, for nine years before their trek to Utah. They moved to the northern part of the state where their remaining children were born.

Both Ann and her husband passed away in Benson, Cache County, Utah. Thomas passed away on November 5, 1891 and Ann passed away on February 28, 1892 within four months of each other.

They had been great pioneers in helping settle the northern part of Utah Territory. Their posterity honor them for their faithfulness and perseverance in helping in these pioneering endeavors.

AURELIA READ SPENCER ROGERS

BIRTHDATE: 4 Oct 1834
Deep River, Connecticut
DEATH: 19 Aug 1922
Farmington, Davis Co., Utah
PARENTS: Orson Spencer
Catherine Curtis
PIONEER: Oct 1848
Brigham Young Wagon Train
SPOUSE: Thomas E. Rogers
MARRIED: 27 Mar 1851
DEATH SP: 1896

CHILDREN:
Orson Thomas, 24 Jan 1852
Andrew Locy, 19 Dec 1854
Ellen Aurelia (Squires), 1 Jul 1857
Howard, 27 Jul 1859 (died as a child)
George, 29 Mar 1861
Clarence Albert, 8 Mar 1863 (died as a child)
Lucy Isabella (Avery), 4 Oct 1865
Catherine Mary, 9 Mar 1868 (died as an infant)
Joseph, 7 Apr 1869 (died as an infant)
William Ernest, 31 May 1871 (died as an infant)
Esther Leone (Stewart), 16 Sep 1872
Curtis Wilson, 23 Dec 1874

Aurelia was born in Connecticut, 1834. She was one of nine children in this family. Her father was a Baptist Minister in that town, and then in Massachusetts. In 1840, their Uncle Daniel Spencer introduced them to Mormonism. They and the Spencer families, joined the Church, disposed of their property, and started for Nauvoo in 1841. Times were different for them without a salary. They opened a store there.

Aurelia's mother died March 12, 1846, when they had moved to Iowa. Her father built a log house near Winter Quarters, and then he left on a mission to preside over the mission in England and to edit the "Millenial Star." The oldest sister, Ellen, and some friends named the Bullocks, were left to care for this family.

In the Spring of 1848, the Bullock family took these Spencer children with them to Salt Lake Valley. A young pioneer in this caravan named Thomas Rogers, cast glances at Aurelia as they journeyed. Orson Spencer married Martha Knight while in England. He later went on two more missions and married two other wives.

Aurelia Spencer and Thomas Rogers were married 27 Mar 1851. They settled in Farmington, Utah. Their first home was made of logs, had six windows, two rooms, a fireplace, and wood floors. They eventually had twelve children, five of whom died in infancy, the others lived to maturity.

In November, 1871, Aurelia was called to be the secretary of the Relief Society, a position she held until 1893.

In August, 1878, she presided over the Primary Association in Farmington. She had felt the boys of the community were too unruly and a little bit rowdy, and she felt the parents were too busy building homes, making a living, and developing farm lands to be concerned about their children and about going to church. Aurelia talked to the Bishop, prayed a lot about it, talked with Eliza R. Snow, the president of the Relief Society who talked with President John Taylor, and he approved the plan for a separate organization for the children. As a result, the first Primary Association of the Church was formed with its opening meeting held on August 25, 1878, in the Old Rock Church in Farmington, which still stands today and has the mural of that first primary in the Chapel. By 1880, Louie B. Felt became the first general president of all the Primary Associations of the Church. Aurelia had traveled throughout the Church in Utah and Idaho helping to organize these early primaries.

Aurelia also became a delegate to the Women's suffrage meetings in Georgia and Washington, D. C. in 1894 and 1895. In 1897, she was honored for her many contribution to the youth of the Church during the General Church Conference. She always bore a strong testimony of the Gospel, and held true to her teachings of the Divinity of the Savior.

A story is related of a fire that burned in Farmington in 1902 in a home where Aurelia sometimes stayed. Some of her clothes were in an upper room. She joined the water brigade passing buckets to help put out the fire. With a sick feeling, she remembered she had also left the Primary records on a table close to the window. She felt more of a loss at the thought of losing the records than anything else. This loss haunted her. She returned to the home to try to gather information to write the history of the Primary again. Thrilling news awaited her there. The Bishop of the ward had felt prompted to go through the window of the room. The smoke was so dense he nearly suffocated. As he reached near the window, he felt the cover of the table, drew it toward him and gathered up the corners and the books and boxes within it and passed them outside. The Primary records were saved by the providence of God.

Aurelia Rogers had the large family who have given her a great posterity. They honor her for her love, her caring and charity for others, and for her ability to lead others to be concerned and to do good. She is a great example for all.

Aurelia passed away on August 19, 1922 in her eighty-eighth year. Her husband had passed away in 1896, both had lived long, productive lives as pioneers of Utah. They both died in Farmington, Utah.

Upon her passing, the Deseret News said of her: "The sweetness and unselfishness of Mrs. Rogers' natural disposition, her abundant faith, hope and charity and unassumed humility, won for her the respect and love of young and old." She was a great lady, a great example of pioneer motherhood to be emulated by those who have followed her.

DIANNAH LOVINA DONAGHE ROGERS

BIRTHDATE: 4 Dec 1836
Warsaw, Benton, Missouri
DEATH: 4 Jun 1906
Provo, Utah Co., Utah
PARENTS: Hugh C. Donaghe
Eliza Linn Lindsey
PIONEER: 1861 Horseback
SPOUSE: Ruel Mills Rogers
MARRIED: 8 Dec 1853
Enterprise, McDonald, Missouri
DEATH SP: 6 Feb 1903

CHILDREN:
Susan Ann, 21 May 1855
Ronaldo Mace, 21 Feb 1857
Madona Frances, 15 Feb 1859
Ruel Mills, 5 Nov 1862
Althea Lovina, 3 Oct 1864
Roswell Medwin, 20 Mar 1867
Colenda Chrilla, 12 Apr 1869
Allie Zittella, 13 Sep 1871
Roxie Miriam, I Aug 1874
Nellie Evelyn, 22 Jun 1877

Diannah was born in Warsaw, Missouri to wealthy parents who were slave owners. She married Ruel Mills Rogers who was practicing physician.

When the Civil War broke out, they had no desire to take sides in the country's disputes. Quietly, they prepared provisions to slip away by covered wagon to join the Saints in Utah.

They had traveled many miles before they noticed they were being pursued by officers of the law. They welcomed them, fed them, visited with them, then let them drink the liquor they carried among their provisions. After the officers fell asleep, Diannah, Ruel, and their children left all of their provisions, took the officers' horses, and slipped away toward their destination. They encountered Indians who turned out to be friendly. They arrived in Utah in 1861 and located in Draper where Dr. Rogers practiced medicine.

Diannah was the mother of ten children. They lived in Moroni, on a farm on Provo Bench, and later on, in Pleasant Grove. Ruel had two other plural wives.

Diannah studied medicine and became licensed on March 4, 1893 to practise medicine in the field of midwifery. She was a great help her husband and the people of the community. She moved to Provo where she passed away on June 4, 1906 at the age of seventy years.

EDA HOLLISTER ROGERS

BIRTHDATE: 19 Aug 1801
Sharon, Litchfield, Connecticut
DEATH: 6 Mar 1877
Richmond, Cache Co., Utah
PARENTS: Samuel Hollister
Experience Smith
PIONEER: 1849
SPOUSE: Noah Rogers
MARRIED: 8 Oct 1819
DEATH SP: 31 May 1846
Mount Pisgah

CHILDREN:
Russell, 17 May 1820/21
Theodore, 3 Feb 1824
David, 24 May 1828
Chancey Foster, 23 Aug 1829
Henrietta, 30 May 1832
Elisha Henry, 17 May 1834
Clarissa Marina, 27 Mar 1836
Nephi Rogers, 10 May 1838

At the age of eighteen, Eda married Noah Rogers. Following their marriage, they moved to New York, where Noah studied to become a physician.

When Eda and Noah Rogers joined the Church of Jesus Christ of Latter-day Saints in February of 1837, Noah gave up his practice as a physician, so he could put all his time in promoting and teaching the gospel. Eda Rogers endured many hardships in helping promote the "work of the Lord" in the early days of the Church. Eda had to face many of the persecutions inflicted upon the Saints.

In April Conference, 1843 Noah Rogers was called on a mission to Vermont. Eda was to be left to support and raise the family at a time when persecutions were intense. Soon after this he was called with others to open up a mission in the Sandwich Islands (Hawaii). The separation was particularly difficult because communication was sparce and unreliable by mail. There would not be any consistent communication with Eda through the duration of his mission.

He returned to Nauvoo from his mission on December 29, 1845, finding Eda and his family, along with the body of the Saints, driven out of the city and living on the outskirts.

While on their journey Westward Eda's husband Noah took sick, was ill for ten days, then passed away.

When Eda Rogers left Nauvoo she had a butter churn which she cherished very much so she took it along with her and somewhere along the way, someone took it out of her wagon. This made her feel very badly as she was afraid she would never find it again. When she did find it someone had used it to put fish in, and although she washed and scrubbed, she couldn't get the fish smell out of it. She filled it with dirt and let it stand for awhile and "Mother Earth" cleaned the smell out so that she was able to use it again.

Their trials and tribulations were typical of Pioneer life filled with many hardships, heartache and discouragement. She arrived in the Salt Lake Valley in 1849.

After reaching the Valley, Eda worked six weeks for six yards of calico which she used to make her a dress. In those days calico cost sixty cents a yard and she valued her dress beyond expression.

She passed through the trying ordeals the Saints had to go through because of the voracious grasshoppers. Her family was forced to live on scanty rations. They had to live on Sego roots which they dug for a long time. They didn't taste bread for over six months. They had the money to buy flour but there was no flour to buy. Eda wintered her cow on bark her children whittled from willows they used for firewood. She also took the straw from her bed ticks to feed the cow so she would have milk for her family until spring.

ELIZA WATTON ROGERS

No Photo Available

BIRTHDATE: 1 Apr 1823
Birmingham, Warwick, England
DEATH: 1878
Farmington, Davis Co., Utah
PARENTS: James Watton
Selena Humphreys
PIONEER: 15 Sep 1852
John Tidwell Co. Wagon Train
SPOUSE: Telemachus Rogers
MARRIED: 5 Feb 1843
New Orleans, Orleans, Louisiana
DEATH SP: Not given
Farmington, Davis Co., Utah

CHILDREN:
Manassa, 13 Nov 1843
Eliza Jane, 27 Nov 1844
James Ephraim, 18 Jul 1848
Selena Mariah, 7 Oct 1854
Julia Etta, 24 Nov 1857
Telemachus, 27 Jan 1860

Eliza was born in Birmingham, Warwick, England. Her mother died and her father married Mary Ann Sherry Watton. They became converted to the Church of Jesus Christ of Latter-day Saints and were desirous to emigrate to the United States.

Eliza married Telemachus Rogers in New Orleans, Louisiana on February 5, 1843. Eliza, her husband, and two children together with her father and stepmother crossed the Plains in the John Tidwell Wagon Company. Her husband was one of the blacksmiths of the company and was much needed throughout the entire trek. Sometimes he had to

stay behind to repair a wagon for someone. He was also the best hunter and always returned with buffalo meat for the company to eat. They arrived in the Salt Lake Valley on September 15, 1852.

They settled in Farmington, Davis County, Utah, where Elizabeth mothered her six children. Her husband immediately put to work making plows and other farm implements which were in great demand by the settlers. They received many nice articles in trade for their services. They were able to build a lovely home with a lovely orchard and garden.

Eliza loved young people and they would often congregate at her home. She was an immaculate house-keeper.

Eliza and her husband did a great deal to help build the community of Farmington. Eliza still looked like a young girl when she died at the age of fifty-two of Pneumonia. She is buried in the Farmington City Cemetery.

EMMA HIGBEE ROGERS

BIRTHDATE: 2 Nov 1836
Caldwell Co., Missouri
DEATH: 23 Jul 1925
Mesa, Maricopa Co., Arizona
PARENTS: Isaac Higbee
Kesiah String
PIONEER: 23 Sep 1848
Heber C. Kimball Wagon Train
SPOUSE: Henry Clay Rogers
MARRIED: 19 Oct 1856
Provo, Utah Co., Utah
DEATH SP: 8 Mar 1902
Lehi, Maricopa Co., Arizona

CHILDREN:
Henry Collins, 16 Aug 1857
Charles Ross, 8 Sep 1859
Anna Keziah, 19 Mar 1862
Joseph Higbee, 20 Apr 1864
David John, 9 Oct 1866
George Samuel, 12 Feb 1868
Martha Amelia, 4 May 1871
Willis, 17 Aug 1873
Isaac Higbee, 27 Nov 1875
Emma Amanda, 6 Sep 1879
Hester Caroline, 30 Jan 1882

Emma was born on the banks of the Missouri Rivir. Her parents joined the Church of Jesus Christ of Latter-day Saints in Ohio and endured severe hardships. They made many moves because of the persecutions. Emma's mother died when she was five years old.

They crossed the Plains with the Heber C. Kimball Wagon Company and arrived in the Salt Lake Valley on September 23, 1848.

In 1849, the Isaac Higbee family was called by Brigham Young to help establish a new settlement on the

Provo River. In 1856, she married Henry Clay Rogers and they became the parents of eleven children.

In 1876, Brigham Young called this family to help settle Arizona. Emma experienced all the sorrows and pleasures in building new communities. She did her part in helping to establish peace with the Indians.

Emma was always cheerful, patient, kind, and always willing to shoulder any responsibility in order to accomplish the work of the Lord. She loved the Gospel and was a faithful member of the Church, working in the Relief Society and supporting her husband in all his church duties.

HANNAH JONES ROGERS

BIRTHDATE: 14 Jul 1831
Birchwood Cradley, England
DEATH: 27 Jan 1892
Deseret, Millard Co., Utah
PARENTS: James Jones
Mary Jones Jones
PIONEER: 19 Oct 1847
Willard Richards Wagon Train
SPOUSE: Theodore Rogers
MARRIED: 6 Mar 1852
Salt Lake Endowment House
DEATH SP: 21 May 1901
Salt Lake City, Sait Lake, Utah

CHILDREN:
Theodore William, 21 Feb 1853
John, 26 Aug 1854
Mary Amelia, 23 Aug 1856
Hannah Lucretia, 30 Oct 1858
Theodosia, 4 Feb 1861
Henry, 20 Jan 1863
Washington, 4 Jul 1865
James Noah, 28 Sep 1871

Hannah was born in England, the youngest child in a family of seven childen. Her father was a manufacturer of boots and shoes.

When Hannah and her family heard the teachings of the Church of Jesus Christ of Latter-day Saints they were converted and wanted to join with others in America, or Zion. They sacrificed their assets in England and set sail in January, 1844. Hannah was eleven. Two of the married brothers stayed in England.

The voyage was difficult. En-route she and the other children had measles. Then her mother became ill and died about a month into their voyage. Hannah was told by the captain of the ship that they would wrap the body in cloth and put weights on it so that it would go swiftly and deeply into the ocean where it would not be disturbed by sharks and other difficulties. Hannah felt the loss of her mother deeply.

After reaching port in New Orleans, the family took the 1,500 mile trip up the Mississippi River to the city of Nauvoo to join with the Church. There Hannah's two brothers, John and Herbert, got discouraged and left by boat down the Mississippi to go back to England; both became ill of typhoid fever and died. Her father, one brother Peter, Hannah and her sister Mary were all that were left of the family in the United States.

In spite of the turmoil that the martyrdom, June 27, 1844 brought to Nauvoo, these stalwarts stayed on. Their father James wrote: "If our family have suffered death in the bodies, the noble part is still existing, their spirits have returned to God."

While beginning the trek Westward on August 8, 1846, Hannah's father died and they buried him wrapped in the bark of a tree. His grave was shallow, beside the trail in the state of Iowa. At age fifteen, she was hardly consolable; she felt very much alone.

A very kind man, Willard Richards, finally persuaded her to continue West with him and his wife, Amelia. They reached the Salt Lake Valley in 1847. There Hannah lived with the Richards family. She gleaned wheat in the fields after the harvest. At one time she obtained ten bushels of grain which brought her $10.00. She was able to spend this "fortune" on clothing for herself, and learned to be very frugal. Before he died her father had given her a calf, and now she had two calves.

When Hannah was twenty-one, she met and married the capable young man, Theodore Rogers. They moved to Provo, where they acquired a farm on a site which later became the Union Pacific depot. Here her first son was born.

The family was called to go to St. George, but when they reached Fillmore they received instructions to remain there. Their first home was in the old Cedar Fort , then in a log house, and finally in a new brick house as they began to prosper through their industry.

Hannah learned all the skills of pioneer life. She baked bread for her family in a bake skillet over an open fire. She carded bats for quilts and did some spinning. She knitted stockings, mittens, and caps for her children. She pieced quilt covers from cast-off clothing, and used woolen bats for making bedding needed by the family. Her old spinning wheel and bake skillet are preserved among the relics in the old State House at Fillmore in the Daughters of the Utah Pioneers exibit.

A tragic event happened when Hannah's three-year-old daughter, Theodocia, died of burns suffered when her dress caught fire from the open fireplace.

Through all of the trying circumsatnces, Hannah Jones Rogers was a kind, patient, loving woman who bore her trials with little complaint. At times she spoke longingly of England; keeping in touch by writing letters to her loved ones there. Although her faith had been sorely tried many times, she remained true to the Church.

For this little, diligent, and frail woman, the strenuous pioneer life finally caused her health to fail. She suffered for nearly two years with dropsy and finally passed away at the age of sixty. Hannah had survived to be the last of her family who had left England to come to America those many years before.

JANET BROWN ROGERS

No Photo Available

BIRTHDATE: 17 Mar 1844
Hunterfield, Scotland
DEATH: 1 Oct 1923
Salt Lake City, Salt Lake, Utah
PARENTS: John Brown
Mary Young
PIONEER: 1864
SPOUSE: Alexander Rogers
MARRIED: 1864
(sealed in Endowment House
25 Aug 1866)
DEATH SP: Unknown

CHILDREN:
Alexander Jr., 16 Aug 1865
John Brown, 5 Aug 1867 (died)
James, 12 Sep 1869
Mary Ellen (Bell), 4 Nov 1872
William Wallace, 4 Oct 1875
Robert Bruce, 21 Apr 1880
Edgar Allen, 25 Jun 1883

Janet was born in Scotland in 1844. She came to Utah with her parents in 1864 when she was about twenty years of age. The details of the trip are unknown.

Shortly after their arrival in the Salt Lake Valley in 1864, Janet married Alexander Rogers. On August 25, 1866, they were sealed in the Endowment House by Heber C. Kimball. Janet had six sons, and one daughter. One son, John, preceded her in death.

Janet passed away on October 1, 1923 at seventy-nine years of age. She was buried in the Mt. Olivet Cemetery in Salt Lake City, Utah. She was survived by her daughter, five sons, and fifteen grandchildren as well as her husband.

Janet's health had been failing for more than a year and she was seriously ill for about three weeks before she died. Janet had lived in Salt Lake City for fifty-nine years. Her husband was a past grand master of the Odd Fellows of Utah and a charter member of the B. P. O. Elks lodge of Salt Lake.

Janet had experienced much of the development of Salt Lake City and the Territory of Utah, as a great pioneer.

JEMIMA BROWN ROGERS

BIRTHDATE: 13 Apr 1803
Erlestoke, Wiltshire, England
DEATH: 25 Jan 1891
North Ogden, Weber Co., Utah
PARENTS: Thomas Brown
Jane Baker
PIONEER: 9 Nov 1856
James Willey Handcart Company
SPOUSE I: not given
MARRIED: 8 Jun 1854
England
DEATH SP: Unknown

CHILD:
Thomas B., 27 Dec 1824

SPOUSE II: Francis Baker Rogers
MARRIED: England
DEATH SP: 8 Jun 1854
Bath, England

CHILD:
Elizabeth (Sharp), 13 Sep 1847

Jemima was born in England in 1803. She had two brothers, Joseph and Robert and two half-brothers, George and Edward. The family moved to Bath, Somersetshire, England. She received little education, and grew up under the stern necessity of work.

She participated in the local celebration of Queen Victoria's coronation in June, 1837.

Jemima was left a widow when her son, Thomas, was just a child. She later married Francis B. Rogers, but was left a widow the second time when her husband, Frank, died on June 8, 1854 in Bath, England.

Jemima saved all she could, and the help of her son, Thomas, who was already in Utah. She and her adopted daughter, Elizabeth, a girl about eight or nine years old, sailed from Englmd on the ship "Thorton" for the "promised land." There was twenty-three years difference between her two children, Thomas and Elizabeth.

Jemima and "Lizzie" joined the James G. Willey Handcart Company to cross the Plains. Their carts were made of green timber and it wasn't long before they dried out and commenced to fall apart necessitating repairs and caused further delays. Along with the cold, snow and not enough food or clothing, this made a very hard trip for fifty-three year old Jemima.

Jemima used all the exta clothing and covering she had to keep little Lizzie from freezing to death and by so doing she suffered such exposure herself that her scalp was so badly frozen that all her hair fell out. She wore various little black lace caps all of the rest of her life.

She raised her daughter, Lizzie, to be a very fine young lady, who married James Sharp, mayor of Salt Lake City.

Jemima lived with them in a mansion on Bingham Street until about 1885. At which time she moved to North Ogden and lived with her son, Thomas and his family, until she passed away on January 25, 1891 at the age of eighty-seven.

MARTHA COLLINS ROGERS

BIRTH DATE: 22 Aug 1793
Berkshire, Franklin Co., Vermont
DEATH: 18 June 1881
Provo, Utah Co., Utah
PARENTS: Names not given
PIONEER: 1852
SPOUSE: David White Rogers
MARRIED: 5 Dec 1811
Montreal, Lower Canada
(Sealed in the Nauvoo Temple
6 Feb 1846)
DEATH SP: 21 Sep 1881
Provo, Utah Co., Utah

CHILDREN:
Susanna Mehitable, 5 Jul 1813
Edward William, 5 Dec 1814
Charles Addison, 28 Jul 1816
Amelia Ann, 21 Apr 1818
Ross Ranson, 11 Feb 1821
Glezen Filmore, 2 Dec 1822
Hesther "Ester" Ann, 23 Mar 1825
Hannah Caroline, 26 Mar 1827
David Preson, Jul 1829
Sally Maria, 10 Jan 1832
Henry Clay, 10 Oct 1833

In the Fall of 1830, Martha and her family of six children were living in Dunkirk, New York, when she received a letter from her husband requesting that she and the children join him in New York City.

At this time Martha was almost destitute of means. However, she set about the task with that energy that always characterized all of her actions in overcoming obstacles that presented themselves when a lone woman starts on a journey of 600 miles with little or no means. They started in a wagon carrying their luggage and the livestock trudging along the road toward Buffalo. Her neighbors wept with sorrow to see her leave. Martha was greatly loved by all who knew her.

They also traveled by canal boat and a towboat. She had to request payment of the passage money when they arrived in New York. She stayed on board with the luggage, while two of her sons jumped off the boat and went in search of their father to pay for their passage.

Martha had a remarkable dream which was responsible for the deep interest she manifested in the new faith. She dreamed that she was in the middle of a heavy washing, when she heard a knock at the door and rather vexed, she opened the door and was accosted by two men who asked for her husband, declaring that they had a message of great importance to deliver. One was large and dark with a pleasant, intelligent countenance, while the other man was a small man, but very earnest. The dream, however had long since passed from her mind, when one morning while engaged in a heavy washing, she was bothered by a knocking at the door and rather disturbed, she went to answer the door when she recognized to her surprise, the two men of her dream. They asked for her husband and she informed them he was not at home and would not return until evening. They promised to return, saying they had a message of importance for him.

When they visited the Rogers family the next day, the dream of Martha was fulfilled, for she beheld the men of her dream and when they explained the gospel truths, the family was converted.

MARY ANN MEYER ROGERS

BIRTHDATE: 9 Apr 1833
Bucyrus, Crawford Co., Ohio
DEATH: 16 May 1923
St. George, Washington, Utah
PARENTS: George Meyer
Ann Yost
PIONEER: 23 Sep 1848
Heber C. Kimball Wagon Train
SPOUSE: David Rogers
MARRIED: 20 Feb 1853
Salt Lake City, Salt Lake, Utah
DEATH SP: 29 Dec 1904
St. George, Washington, Utah

CHILDREN:
Velleda Mary, 20 Nov 1855
Erazma Meyer, 28 Feb 1856
David Meyer, 23 Mar 1858
Julia Ann, 11 Oct 1860
Sarah Jane, 3 Aug 1863
Emma, 8 Jun 1866
Mary Elizabeth, 3 Aug 1869
Diantha, 24 Oct 1872
George Milton, 16 Feb 1877

Mary Ann was born in Bucyrus, Ohio. Her father moved to Indiana to farm. They came in contact with missionaries from the Church of Jesus Christ of Latter-day Saints and were baptized as members of the Church. They moved to Nauvoo for a short time and then moved on to Punca which is a little further west than Winter Quarters. At that time, Mary Ann worked for Lydia Knight.

They crossed the Plains in the Heber C. Kimball Wagon Company. After much tribulation, they arrived in the Salt Lake Valley on September 23, 1848. Their family went to Sessions Settlement where they made a house of sod for the first winter.

Mary Ann helped her father bring logs from the canyon to build their new home. Her family moved into the home, but Mary Ann continued working for Sister Pace and helped to milk cows and make cheese.

When Mary Ann married David Rogers, they lived in Mill Creek Canyon while running a saw mill for Peter White. In 1861, they were called to settle the Dixie area. They stopped on the banks of the Virgin River where they lived until they were flooded from the home.

They moved to St. George and built a home. Mary Ann taught school to her children and some of the neighbors' children. She was a wonderful cook and always had a start of yeast for everyone. She carded, spun, and wove her cloth, dried fruit for the winter, made molasses from sugar cane, and also raised a little tobacco. These items were taken up north and traded for things they needed.

David and Mary Ann raised a family of eight children. Mary Ann worked in all church organizations and for many years in the St. George Temple.

MARY JANE COLLINS ROGERS

BIRTHDATE: 21 Jun 1837
Missouri
DEATH: 6 Jun 1889
Ogden, Weber Co., Utah
PARENTS: John Collins
Polly Minerva Chapman
PIONEER: 1862
Independent Wagon Train Comp.
SPOUSE: Alma Denton Rogers
MARRIED: 1 5 Jun 1861
Fort Smith, Arkansas
DEATH SP: 5 Nov 1918
Lewiston, Cache Co., Utah

CHILDREN:
Sallie Columbia, 13 Jun 1862
Mary Minerva, 3 Dec 1863
Laura Etta, 28 Apr 1865
Alma Hernando, 10 Jun 1868
Susan Katherine Augustus, 3 Dec1869
Nancy Dillard, 25 Jul 1870
Adolphus Dion, 7 Dec 1873
Theron Actavious Lewelllyn, 14 Jun 1876
Adolphus Dio, 15 Apr 1878

Mary Jane was born in Missouri in 1837. When she was four years old her family moved to Arkansas. Mary and her brothers and sisters contracted Mountain Fever. The disease was fatal to her brother and left her blind.

Mary Jane and her mother supported a family of six children as dress makers.

Mary Jane married Alma Denton Rogers on June 15, 1861. They obtained a wagon and were camping in Pea Ridge, Arkansas during a Civil War battle in this place. It was here she gave birth to her first daughter, Sallie. It was here the family was taken prisoners but released when they found out she was blind.

The family came to the Salt Lake Valley in the Fall of 1862 in an independent wagon train. Mary Jane was the mother of nine children, two of whom died as babies.

Though blind Mary Jane did all her housework, cooking and making of the family clothes. She could recognize each of her children by their footsteps. Mary Jane made fancy dresses and quilts as well as doing knot work, making shawls and stockings. She made knitted lace and copied different patterns by feeling them. She could thread the finest needle with no difficulty.

In Coalville, Utah a squaw came to Mary Jane's house and ask her to thread a needle by making signs. After seeing the blind woman thread a needle she gave her daughter a string of beads.

Mary Jane learned brail , but not many books were available at that time. She played the church hymns on the accordion.

Mary Jane passed away on June 6, 1889 at the age of fifty-two in Ogden, Weber County, Utah.

REBECCA ADAMS ROGERS

BIRTHDATE: 29 Nov 1798
Birmingham, Warwick, England
DEATH: 3 Nov 1864
Salt Lake City, Salt lake, Utah
PARENTS: Stephan Adams
Elizabeth Reaves
PIONEER: 2 Nov 1864
Warren S. Snow Wagon Train
SPOUSE: William Rogers
MARRIED: 10 Aug 1823
Kings Norton, England
DEATH SP: 10 May 1834
Birmingham, Warwick, England

CHILDREN:
Mary Ann, 4 Apr 1824
William, 20 Mar 1826
Thomas, 30 Nov 1827
Susannah (Woolley), 11 Jun 1829
Mary Rebecca (Thorne), 7 May 1831
Ann (Meyhew Moore), 3 Aug 1832
Emma (Gillespie Shaw), 24 Sep 1834

Rebecca Adams was born on March 29, 1798 in Birmingham, Warwick, England. She was a pretty, rosy-cheeked girl of twenty years when she went to work in the home of the wealthy silversmith, Thomas Rogers.

As time passed the Rogers second son, William, fell in love with Rebecca, and they were married in 1822 against his parents wishes. After that, the parents never acknowledged their son or his children, even at his death.

Rebecca became the mother of seven children: Mary Ann, who died at age three; William; Thomas; Susannah; Ann; Mary Rebecca; and Emma. Emma was born just a few months after her father's death. William Rogers died suddenly of pneumonia on May 10, 1834.

Her son, Thomas, brought the Elders into her home, and they all joined the Church of Jesus Christ of Latter-day Saints except William, the eldest son. They desired to come to Zion, but could not all come at once. Thomas came first, in 1853; then Susannah came in 1960.

In 1863, Ann and Emma made the trip; finally Rebecca and her daughter, Mary, started in 1864. They sailed on the ship "Hudson" bound for New York, with John M. Kay in charge of the Saints. Her son William, stayed behind in England.

They were delayed for many weeks in Winter Quarters waiting for wagon trains to take them West. The trip was very hard on Rebecca because the season was so well advanced, and the snows of Wyoming delayed them further. Her hands and feet were frozen, though they came into the Valley on November 2, 1864.

Rebecca passed away, on November 3, 1864. It was a great disappointment to her children who were here, not to be able to see their mother, after waiting so long. Rebecca is buried in the Salt Lake City Cemetery.

RUTH PAGE ROGERS

BIRTHDATE: 1 May 1823
Downs Township, New Jersey
DEATH: 20 May 1907
PARENTS: Daniel Page
Mary Socwell
PIONEER: 4 Oct 1852
Springville Co. Wagon Train
SPOUSE: Samuel H. Rogers
MARRIED: 21 Feb 1853
Lehi, Utah Co., Utah
DEATH SP: 20 Sep 1891
Snowflake, Arizona

CHILDREN: None

Ruth was born in Downs Township, Cumberland County, New Jersey in poverty and hardship made even more miserable by accidents and illness that required her father to ask family and friends to care for and feed his children. Ruth went to live with her grandmother, Sarah Page, when she was three years old. When she was older, she went back home to help care for her mother and the younger children while her father was working in Pennsylvania.

They were so poor, they were constantly having difficulty in meeting their needs. Ruth worked outside the home and gave her money to her parents to help support the family.

In 1843, most of their family was baptized as members of the Church of Jesus Christ of Latter-day Saints. Almost seven years later, Ruth had purchased enough clothing to be

able to travel West. Her family didn't want her to travel alone, so they decided it was time to join the Saints in the west. They traveled to Council Bluffs and worked for two more years to save money for the journey across the Plains.

Ruth traveled with the Wallace Raymond family in the Springville Company which consisted of fifty wagons. Ruth agreed to do the washing and cooking for this family in exchange for her traveling expenses. They had trouble with Cholera Indians, thirst, and snow before they arrived in the Salt Lake Valley on October 4, 1852.

Ruth found work in Jordan and started to look for the missionary who had converted their family. He had married his brother's widow and later asked Ruth to marry him as his second wife.

In October of 1853, George Albert Smith called Samuel on a mission to settle in Iron County where they lived for seventeen years. In 1855, grasshoppers attacked their crops and Ruth did washing in exchange for wheat. Ruth's younger sister, Lorana, married Samuel Rogers and the two women made straw hats to sell to the men.

In March of 1876, Ruth and her husband joined the United Order. Her days were filled with tending her own garden, fowl, and pigs. She did sewing and knitting, and cared for the sick. She was a part of the women's work parties which fed the threshers and gathered honey.

Samuel was called to settle Snowflake, Arizona in 1879. She followed him in 1881. She served as a counselor in the Eastern Arizona Stake Primary Presidency.

Although Ruth had no children, she mothered many. She served as a visiting teacher most of her adult life and donated many items to the poor and spent many hours nursing the sick.

MARY HARRISON FERRON ROGERSON

BIRTHDATE: 24 Jan 1803
Betham or Ingleton, England
DEATH: 26 Aug 1888
Parowan, Iron Co., Utah
PARENTS: James Holt Ferron
Mary Harrison
PIONEER: 9 Nov 1856
Edward Martin Handcart Comp.
SPOUSE: William Rogerson
MARRIED: 23 Dec 1826
Preston, Lancs., England
DEATH SP: 17 May 1879
Chorley, Lancs., England

CHILDREN:
Jane (Ollerton), 5 Mar 1827
Margaret Bridget, 9 Jan 1829
James, 11 Aug 1830
Bridget (Butt), 19 Sep 1832
William Valentine, 14 Feb 1834
Mary Elizabeth Ann (Ollerton), 1835
Mary Ann, 19 Mar 1835
Sarah Marinda, 14 Jun 1838

Josiah, 27 Jan 1841
Sarah Ann (Lister), 13 Aug 1843
John Edward, 28 Feb 1847

Mary was born in England in 1803. She married William Rogerson on December 23, 1826. They lived in Preston and were the parents of eleven children.

After Mary joined the Church of Jesus Christ of Latter-day Saints she had a strong desire to go to Zion even though her husband wouldn't.

Mary and her six unmarried children left their homeland and sailed on the ship "Horizon" for Boston on May 25, 1856. Leaving her husband and oldest daughter, Jane, and her family in England. Jane and her family came in 1864 but Jane died on the Plains.

Mary and her family joined the Edward Martin Handcart Company. When they reached Iowa hill her crippled son, James, decided he couldn't make it and went back to his father in England.

Mary quilted a petticoat that she wore across the Plains, it was made out of two layers of material, quilted together, by Mary, with needles, thread, crochet hooks, breast pins, handkercheifs, scarfs, pieces of lace, and many other little things.

Mary went through the hard cold times with the rest of the handcart company. But was lucky enough that her family and her reached the Salt Lake Valley alive on November 9, 1856. They were greeted by an old friend from England and taken to his home for a nice warm dinner.

Mary and her two youngest children went to Kaysville to keep house for another friend. Then Mary and her two daughters went to Iron county in February. Her sons had been standing in the door of their home when a friend, Father Baer, said he had a message from their mother, then went to the corner of the house and got her. She later returned to Salt Lake to another friend.

Then, in September, Mary went back to the rest of her family in Parawan, Utah. Although she lived in Parowan the next thirty years not much is known of her life there.

Mary suffered a lot with arthritis in her later years. But helped raise her daughter, Sarah Ann's children after she passed away. She was a kind, patient woman.

The last few years of her life she spent most of her time in bed in severe pain. Mary passed away on August 26, 1888 in Parowan at the age of eighty-five.

ELIZABETH WILLIAMS HATHAWAY ROLFE

BIRTHDATE: 29 Aug 1801
Levonia, Oxford Co., Maine
DEATH: 7 Jul 1879
Lehi, Utah Co., Utah
PARENTS: Gilbert Hathaway
Lydia Tolman
PIONEER: 25 Sep 1847
Abraham O. Smoot Wagon Train
SPOUSE: Samuel Jones Rolfe
MARRIED: 4 Mar 1818
Maine
DEATH SP. Jul 1869
Lehi, Utah Co., Utah

CHILDREN:
Gilbert Hathaway, 25 Aug 1820
Benjamin William, 7 Oct 1822
Peter Tolman Rolfe, 7 Sep 1824
Ianthis Jerome, 8 Sep 1825
Weltha H., 27 Apr 1829
Lydia Mandana, 26 Dec 1831
Horace Cowin, 4 Jan 1834
Samuel Jones, Jr. 3 Jan 1836
William Jasper, 8 Dec 1838
Mary Ann Elizabeth, 6 Feb 1844
David Lorenzo, Apr 1846

Elizabeth was born in Levonia, Maine. She helped with the work and learned the habits of dependability and frugality.

At age seventeen, she married Samuel Jones Rolfe. They went to live in Concord, New Hampshire. They moved to Rumford, Maine where they lived about fourteen years before they moved to Kirtland, Ohio in 1835. The persecution was so bad, they moved to Clayton, Illinois. By the time they moved to Nauvoo, Illinois, they had ten children.

Her husband helped to build the Kirtland Temple and the Nauvoo Temple. Their last child was born in Winter Quarters.

They traveled in the Abraham Owen Smoot Wagon Company, arriving in the Salt lake Valley on September 25, 1847.

It was quite a responsibility to provide food, clothing, and bedding in a wagon box for themselves and their children. They made dugouts to shelter themselves for the first winter in the Salt Lake Valley.

Elizabeth's husband passed away in 1867, leaving her a widow for fourteen years. She had a sincere testimony of the gospel for which she had given a full measure of devotion.

AMANDA MELVINA FRANCE ROLLINS

BIRTHDATE: 30 Jun 1839
Burns, Alleghany Co., New York
DEATH: 25 Feb 1916
Centerville, Davis Co., Utah
PARENTS: Joseph David and
Elizabeth Cady Card France
PIONEER: 1849
Capt. Roswell Hyde
SPOUSE:: Steuben Rollins
MARRIED: 10 Feb 1855
Salt Lake City, Salt Lake, City
DEATH SP: 5 Mar 1909
Centerville, Davis Co., Utah

CHILDREN:
Steuben Oscar, 10 Dec 1855
Joseph Henry, 15 May 1857
Moroni, 14 Feb 1859 (died as an infant)
Franklin, 9 Apr 1860 (died as an infant)
William Dewilton, 6 Mar 1861
Thomas Alonzo, 11May 1863 (died as a child)
Charles Ora, 23 Aug 1865
Elizabeth Alice, 21 Nov 1867
George Wallace, 20 Sep 1869
Amanda Melvina, 126 Oct 1871
Rhoda Eleanor, 2 Jan 1874
Sarah Lavantia (Blanche), 3 Sep 1876

Amanda's mother died in her twenty-sixth year, when Amanda was three years old. She was in bed with her two children, Amanda and a son, Dewilton, and when they called their mother, they found her dead. She had had a heavy cold for six weeks and hadn't been able to recover from her baby's death just twenty-three days previous. It is believed she died of Tuberculosis.

Amanda's father left the two living children with friends until he married again about a year later. Her father had joined the Church of Jesus Christ of Latter-day Saints. The family again together, traveled by boat to Chicago, Illinois. Her father bought a wagon and yoke of oxen, and went to Garden Grove, Iowa. They found her stepmother's sister sick in bed with her two children. They stayed there-all winter, and then went to Winter Quarters. Her father helped the first groups across the Elkhorn river, and he stood guard.

Her father bought more animals, including cows which provided milk and butter for their journey. Amanda helped milk the cows, gather wood for fires. She also helped drive the oxen. At Ft. Laramie they were stopped by the Indians. Cholera was raging and the Indians blamed the pioneers for bringing the disease among them. Her diary states, "The suffering of the Indians and the sight of their dead will stay with me as long as I live. The Indians would come and stand off a way from the wagons and hold a bunch of bitter weeds in front of their face, and would not take anything from us to eat, although they were starving to death. The company donated flour and sugar, powder and lead to kill their meat and we started on again. The first merchants that ever came to Utah were in our company and they donated to the Indians freely, hats, shirts, and shoes." They arrived in the Salt Lake Valley in 1849; four years on the way.

Amanda was ten years old and was put to work in the fields doing a man's work. The family settled in Centerville, Davis County and her father eventually became a wealthy man. He took three more wives in polygamy, and had a total of thirty-two children.

Amanda married Steuben Rollins when she was fifteen. They were married on February 10, 1855. Twelve children were born of this union. Three baby boys died in infancy.

Amanda was a member of the Relief Society for many years. She was especially chosen to do washings and anointings and the laying out of the dead. She was usually the last to consider her own needs. She was happy to see her children take part with other children in Primary and Sunday School. She taught them correct principles throughout their lives. She welcomed visiting teachers to her home, and she helped neighbors in need.

Amanda and Steuben had a long life together having celebrated their golden wedding anniversary seven years before they were parted by death.

Steuben passed away on March 5, 1909, and Amanda passed away seven years later on February 25, 1916. Like her mother, Amanda was found dead in bed. She was buried in Centerville.

Amanda was a pioneer woman of great faith, and much fortitude, one who handled the trials and tribulations of pioneer life well. She is honored by her numerous posterity for the great example she set.

EVELINE WALKER ROLLINS

BIRTHDATE: 16 May 1823
Winchester, Randolph, Indiana
DEATH: 25 Sep 1912
Lyman, Uintah Co., Wyoming
PARENTS: Oliver Walker
Nancy Cressy Walker
PIONEER: 9 Oct 1848
Amasa Lyman Co. Wagon Train
SPOUSE: James Henry Rollins
MARRIED: 4 Sep 1838
Shoal Creek near Far West
DEATH SP: 10 Feb 1899
Lyman, Uintah Co., Wyoming

CHILDREN:
Horace Alganon, 30 Jun 1839
John Henry, 17 Feb 1841
Mary Amelia, 27 Dec 1843
Ephraim Edward, 7 Jul 1845
Nancy Evaline, 16 Feb 1849
Melissa Keziah, 13 Jul 1851
Charles Lyman, 10 Nov 1854
James Watson, 24 May 1856
Ida Minerva, 2 Oct 1862

Evaline was baptized a member of the Church of Jesus Christ of Latter-day Saints at the age of eight. While still a child, she was healed of cholera by her faith in God and a blessing given to her by Joseph Smith, Sr. She and her husband, James Henry Rollins, were married near Haun's Mill just a few weeks before the massacre. Her husband was jailed with fifty other church brethren. It took her quite some time to arrange bail for that many men. She visited him in the Richmond, Missouri jail.

After they were reunited, they moved to Nauvoo and lived until they were driven from their home again. They crossed the Plains to the Salt Lake Valley with the Amasa Lyman Wagon Company and arrived about October 9, 1848.

In 1851, the family was instructed by Brigham Young to join the Amasa Lyman and Charles C. Rich Company to settle in San Bernardino, California.

In 1858, they were called back to Utah and left most of their possessions. They settled in Minersville where they remained until 1898. They moved to Lyman, Wyoming to be near their children who were now raising families of their own.

HANNA HULME ROLLINS

BIRTHDATE: 24 Nov 1834
Duckinfield, England
DEATH: 30 Sep 1896
Minersville, Beaver Co., Utah
PARENTS: William Hulme
Mary Winterbottom
PIONEER: 1849 or 1850
Wagon Train Company
SPOUSE: James Henry Rollins
MARRIED: 3 Mar 1851
Salt Lake City, Salt Lake, Utah
DEATH SP: 7 Feb 1899
Lyman, Uinta Co., Wyoming

CHILDREN:
Alonzo Leonilas, 29 Apr 1852
Caroline Elizabeth (Banks), 11 Feb 1854
George Woodville, 19 Mar1 856
Francis Robert, 18 Nov 1858
LoisAdelade (Colton), 6 Jan 1861
Phobe Alice, 29 Jan 1863
Isaiah Earnest, 14 Jul 1865
Jane Losaine Roberts, 28 Sep 867
Edwin William, 6 Oct 1869
Edgar Willard, 6 Oct 1869
Julian Bosman, 4 Jun 1872
Levi Marion, 8 Nov 1874
Hannah Burdett (Hollingshead), 27 Nov 1875

Hannah was born in England in 1834. She traveled to America on the ship "Hartley," with her father and sister, Alice, arriving in New Orleans on April 28, 1849.

The exact date of her arrival in Salt Lake Valley is unknown. It is assumed she came by wagon sometime in 1849 or 1850. She married James Henry Rollins on March 3, 1851 in Salt Lake City, Utah. They were the parents of thirteen children.

In 1851, along with her husband and others, she accompanied Apostle Amasa Lyman and Charles C. Rich to settle the San Bernardino Valley in California. She was also a early settler in Parowan and Minersville, Utah.

Hannah was active in church and civic affairs. She served on the board of apprizers for the Minersville Relief Society, and was a stockholder in the Minersville Reservoir and Irrigation Company. She was musically inclined and made sure some of her children were schooled in singing and playing musical instruments.

Hannah passed away in Minersville, Utah on September 30, 1896 at the age of sixty-one.

SOPHIA WING PHILBROOK LAMBERT ROLLINS

No Photo Available

BIRTHDATE: 12 Dec 1805
Hampton, Maine
DEATH: 11 Mar 1872
Payson, Utah Co., Utah
PARENTS: John Philbrook
Nancy Philbrook Philbrook
PIONEER: 16 Oct 1852
Eli Kelsey Co. Wagon Train
SPOUSE I: Abial Lambert
MARRIED: 1823
DEATH SP: 1827

CHILDREN:
William Henry, 16 Jun 1824
Elizabeth, 5 Mar 1826
Marinda, 28 Nov 1827

SPOUSE II: Enoch Perham Rollins
MARRIED: 29 Apr 1829
DEATH SP: 9 Nov 1877

CHILDREN:
Mary Jane, 25 Dec 1829
Ann Sophia, 5 Mar 1831
Sabra Sherburn, 8 Nov 1833
Abby Amanda, 10 Jul 1835
John Park, 1 Sep 1836
Loretta Delenay, 10 Aug 1838
Martha Philbrook, 30 Apr 1840
Orson Hyde, 27 Feb 1842
Franklin Wheeler, 31 Mar 1844
Charles Drowne, 11 Mar 1846

Sophia was born in Hampton, Maine to parents who belonged to the Methodist Church. In 1823, she married Abial Lambert, who was a sea captain. On his last voyage at sea, he contracted yellow fever and died. She was left with three children to raise.

She married Enoch Perham Rollins in 1829 and they were the parents of ten children. They became members of the Church of Jesus Christ of Latter-day Saints.

In August of 1843, they left New York State and made their way to Akron, Ohio where they had to stay until they earned enough means to continue to Nauvoo. Sophia and Enoch were sealed in the Nauvoo Temple in June of 1846.

They were driven from their homes in Nauvoo and had to cross the Mississippi River in a row boat. When they landed at Montrose, Iowa, they made a shelter of quilts propped upon a pole. She suffered much sickness, privation, no shelter, and a lack of food.

In May of 1852, their family crossed the Plains and arrived in Salt Lake Valley on October 16, 1852.

Sophia made homes in many parts of Utah, from Cache Valley to Goshen. After Enoch took a second wife and because Sophia suffered from a lingering illness that prevented her from living alone, she lived with her children the rest of her life.

While she was visiting her grandchildren in Payson, she passed away and was buried in the Payson City Cemetery.

ELIZABETH GASKELL ROMNEY

BIRTHDATE: 8 Jan 1809
Dalton-in-Furness, England
DEATH: 11 Oct 1884
St. George, Washington, Utah
PARENTS: Joseph Gaskell
Elizabeth Slater
PIONEER: 13 Oct 1850
Edward Hunter Co. Wagon Train
SPOUSE: Miles Romney
MARRIED: 6 Nov 1830
Dalton-in-Furness, England
DEATH SP: 3 May 1877
St. George, Washington, Utah

CHILDREN:
George, 14 Aug 1831
Elizabeth, 22 Nov 1833
Sarah, 22 Feb 1836
Joseph Gaskell, 30 Apr 1838
Ellen, 12 May 1840
Miles Park, 18 Aug 1843
Hiram Thomas, 1845
Mary Ann, 20/27 May 1847
Jane Agnes, 3 Jan 1850

Elizabeth was born in Dalton-in-Furness, Lancashire, England. At age twenty-one, she married Miles Romney who was a carpenter in northwestern England.

In 1837, they heard the gospel of the Church of Jesus Christ of Latter-day Saints from Orson Hyde. In September of 1839, they were baptized as members of the Church. After their baptism, meetings were held every Sunday morning in their home.

The family sailed from England in the ship, "Sheffield," on February 7, 1841. After they arrived in New Orleans, they traveled by boat up the Mississippi River to Nauvoo, Illinois.

When the Saints were expelled from Nauvoo, their family could not afford to go across the Plains, so they moved to Burlington, Iowa for a short stay, then to St. Joseph, Missouri, and finally to St. Louis where they remained until the Spring of 1850.

At that time, they crossed the Plains with the Edward Hunter Wagon Company and arrived in Salt Lake Valley on October 13, 1850. Elizabeth cared for her nine children and supported her husband financially and spiritually while he served a mission to his native England in 1856 to 1858.

In October, 1860, Brigham Young called their family to help build the settlements in Southern Utah. They settled in Grafton until it was flooded away. Then they settled in St. George where they built a comfortable home and had a hotel and grocery store. She was the keeper of the household and of the children while her husband was attending to his church and community obligations.

Elizabeth raised a garden and dried or bottled her fruits and vegetables. She would spin thread from cotton or wool in order to make clothing for her family. Elizabeth was blessed with many gifts and talents. She was a great comfort to the Saints and was blessed with the gift of healing.

Elizabeth passed away at the age of seventy-five.

HANNAH HOOD HILL ROMNEY

BIRTHDATE: 9 Jul 1842
Tosoronto, Ontario, Canada
DEATH: 1 Jan 1929
Colonia Juarez, Mexico
PARENTS: Archibald N. Hill
Isabella Hood
PIONEER: 15 Sep 1849
Wagon Train Company
SPOUSE: Miles Park Romney
MARRIED: 10 May 1862
Salt Lake Endowment House
DEATH SP: 26 Feb 1904
Colonia, Mexico

CHILDREN:
Isabell, 3 Mar 1863
Elizabeth, 16 Dec 1866
Mary Ann "Minnie," 31 Jan 1868
Miles Archibald, 9 Nov 1869
Gaskell, 22 Sep 1871
Stillborn, 1873
George Samuel, 12 Nov 1874
Ernest Van, 11 Oct 1877
Maggie, 25 Apr 1880
Eugene, 16 Sep 1883
Leo, 11 Par 1887

It is of interest to relate that few women of the Church of Jesus Christ of Latter-day Saints can boast of such an extended journey, or series of journies, as can be recorded of Hannah.

She was born in Tosoronto Township, Simcoe, Ontario, Canada. The trip from Canada to Nauvoo was by team all the way and this was true of the journey from Nauvoo to the Great Basin.

Later in life, when Miles P. Romney family were called to help establish settlements in St. George and later in Apache County, Arizona, the distance was covered by team and wagon.

When the family, years later, migrated to Old Mexico to make their homes, Hannah and her children made the perilous journey in covered wagons the entire distance from St. Johns, Arizona to Colonia Juarez, Mexico. This fact alone marks Hannah as one of the most courageous women of her generation and testifies more eloquently than words of her unwavering faith in the Gospel.

—Thomas C. Romney, Ph.D

She attended the first Sunday School organized in Salt Lake City. Brother- Ballantyne was the superintendent and she was also in the first 24th of July parade held in Salt Lake City.

Her husband left for England one month after their marriage. She supported herself and their first little girl for the the next three and a half years.

Hannah was president of the Relief Society in St. George. She was a counselor to Minerva Snow in the Stake Relief Society in St. George. Hannah willingly entered into polygamy with four other wives. She traveled alone with her children in a wagon from St. Johns, Arizona to the colonies of Mexico through Indian territory. Then, in Mexico, she served as the Primary President, teaching the children to sing and pray. She taught the girls to sew and crochet and the boys to be responsible citizens.

Hannah grew a fine garden and for eight years ran a farm in Casa Grandes with her sons. They raised hundreds of bushels of wheat and corn. She had chickens and turkeys and sold butter, eggs and molasses.

Hannah states in her autobiography, "Most of the way across the Plains I traveled bare-footed and bare-headed." From childhood to the end of her life, she suffered every hardship known to pioneer women.

MARGARET ANN THOMAS ROMNEY

BIRTHDATE: 22 Jan 1845
London, Mddlsex, England
DEATH: April 25, 1915
Salt Lake City, Salt Lake, Utah
PARENTS: Joseph K. Thomas
Margaret Spotswood
PIONEER: 13 Sep 1861
Wagon Train Company
SPOUSE: George Romney
MARRIED: 29 Aug 1863
Salt Lake City, Salt Lake, Utah
DEATH SP: 1 Feb 1920
Salt Lake City, Salt Lake, Utah

CHILDREN:
George Romney, Jr., 7 July 1864
Joseph, 3 Dec 1865
Ambrose F., 18 Jul 1867
Clarence, 22 May 1869
Margaret Charlotte, 21 Jul 1871
Charles, 4 Jan 1873
Katherine, 18 Mar 1875
Walter, 2 Apr 1878
Raymond Thomas, 14 Jan 1881
Reuben, 1 Feb 1883
Ardelle, 22 Nov 1884

Margaret Ann's father died when she was a child in London. She came to America with her widowed mother and brother, Charles J. Thomas, in 1861.

She was an actress on the Salt Lake Theater stage. It was there that her husband-to-be saw her in a production and fell in love with her.

Margaret Ann and George Romney were married August 29, 1863. She was his third wife. She said she loved and admired George so much that she would rather have a third of him than all of another man. Her husband was a very fair, loving man, who treated all three families evenly.

Margaret Ann's child, Ardelle, remembered that every Eastertime "Papa" would go to the three homes and take each family of the thirty-five children separately out shopping to buy new dress shoes for the year. She would wait by the door, eagerly anticipating his arrival for her special time!

Margaret Ann was the last survivor of the dramatic company that played the opening night in the Salt Lake Theater. There were two plays presented at the theater on that memorable night, "Bride of the Market" and "State Secrets." Margaret Ann, before her marriage, appeared in the latter play and sang a song during her appearance. Her brother, Charles, a former Tabernacle organist, led the orchestra that evening. Her daughter, Katherine Romney Stewart, later became the first woman Tabernacle organist. Margaret Ann's talents were very versatile, as she also played many comedy roles from 1904 until her death in 1915.

LAURINE EMILIA HANSEN RONNOW

No
Photo
Available

BIRTHDATE: 15 Apr 1845
Bodstrup, Svendborg, Denmark
DEATH: 12 Aug 1897
Mt. Pleasant, Sanpete Co., Utah
PARENTS: Carl C. Hansen
Margarethe Kirstine Clausen
PIONEER: Late summer of 1862
Orson Hyde Co. Wagon Train
SPOUSE: Christian P. Ronnow
MARRIED: 13 Nov 1862
Ephraim, Sanpete Co., Utah
DEATH SP: 11 Apr 1911
Panaca, Lincoln Co., Nevada

CHILDREN:
Charles Christian, 29 Jul 1865
Joseph, 21 Jun 1869
Annie Kristine, 17 Mar 1872
Christian Peter, 9 Febl 875
Erastus Frederick, 25 Augl 877
Clara Emilia, 10 Jan 1880
Lilith Margaret, 4 Oct 1882
Daniel Jorgen, 4 Dec 1884
Christiana Josephine, 11 Mar 1889

Laurine was born in Denmark in 1845. Her father died when she was nine years old. She was the oldest of three children. Her mother married Christian P. Ronnow when Laurine was fifteen years old.

Laurine crossed the Atlantic Ocean on April 5, 1862, with her mother, stepfather, brother and little sister. She crossed the Plains with wagon and handcart in the Orson Hyde Wagon Company, arriving in the Salt Lake Valley late summer of 1862. They then went to Ephraim to live.

Her mother was in ill health and after having a baby boy in September, 1862, she died two months later. The deeath of her mother left Laurine in a strange land speaking another language. She married her step-father, Christian Peter Ronnow on November 13, 1862. She took care of her baby brother until he died in February, 1863. Laurine's first child Charles Christian was born July 29, 1865.

In 1866, they moved to Panaca, Navada. Their first home there was one-room built of rough rock with a dirt roof. A shed with a willow roof was used as a kitchen in the summer. Her second child, Joseph was born on June 21, 1869. Her husband engaged in farming and the mercantile business. Two years later they built a three-room adobe house with a front and back porch. As the family enlarged so did the house to eight rooms. Seven children were born here.

She always sang the children to sleep and told them stories about Denmark. They were interested in education and all their children had a college education.

Laurine passed away on August 12, 1897 in Mt. Pleasant, Utah after a lingering illness of spinal trouble. She was fifty-two years old. Her husband said "we lived a happy life. Laurine was a true, faithful, deserving, kind and unselfish wife and mother."

MARGARETHE KIRSTINE HANSEN RONNOW

No
Photo
Available

BIRTHDATE: 28 Dec 1819
Helletoft, Svendborg, Denmark
DEATH: 11 Nov 1862
Ephraim, Sanpete Co., Utah
PARENTS: Clause Christensen
Anne Kerstine Rosmusdatter
PIONEER: Late summer 1862
Orson Hyde Handcart Company
SPOUSE I: Carl C. Hansen
MARRIED: 14 Jun 1847
DEATH SP: 16 Apr 1854
Tranekjaer, Castle, Denmark

CHILDREN:
Laurine Emilia (Ronnow), 15 Apr 1845
Sophus Frederick Alavia, 16 Apr 1846
Sophus Fredrick, 26 Apr 1852

SPOUSE II: Christian Peter Ronnow
MARRIED: 03 Feb 1862
DEATH SP: 11 Apr 1911
Panaca, Lincoln Co., Nevada

CHILDREN:
Pertno Josephine Caroline, 24 Mar 1861
Child, 1862 (died)
Christian Peter, 24 Sep 1862

Margarethe was born in Denmark in 1891. She married Carl Christian Hansen in Jun 1847. They were the parents of three children. Carl died on April 16, 1854, leaving Margarethe the children to raise alone.

Margarethe married Christian Peter Ronnow on Febraury 3, 1862 and they were the parents of three more children.

On April 5, 1862 Christian, Margarethe Laurine, Sophus Fredrick and Pertno Josephine sailed to America. On May 21, 1862 their second child died on the Atlantic Ocean.

They landed in New York, then trekked across the plains with wagon and handcart. Owing to ill health, Margarethe rode part of the time. Arriving in Salt Lake in the late summer of 1862. The family located temperarily in Fort Ephraim, Sanpete County, Utah.

On September 24, 1862, Margarethe gave birth to a baby boy named Christian Peter. A few months later she passed away on November 11, 1862 at the age of forty-three.

Margarethe was a very kind, hard working mother and wife.

Her second husband married the daughter of her first marriage.

MARY ELIZABETH SMITH ROOKER

BIRTHDATE: 6 Oct 1851
Mt. Pisgah, Pottawattamie, Iowa
DEATH: 22 Oct 1891
Heber City, Wasatch Co., Utah
PARENTS: Thomas C. Smith
Sarah Frampton
PIONEER: 1852
Company unknown
SPOUSE: John Bunyon Rooker,
MARRIED: 7 Mar 1866
Heber, Wasatch Co., Utah
DEATH SP: 15 Sep 1908
Center Creek, Wasatch Co., Utah

CHILDREN:
Sarah Emily (Muir), 24 Dec 1868
Mary Catherine (Harris), 2 Oct 1871
John Samuel, 9 Jun 1875
James William, 20 Jun 1879
Amanda Lavern (Blake), 26 Jun 1884
Thomas C., 16 Mar 1888

Mary was born in Iowa in 1851 and was the oldest of twelve and the only child not born in Utah. She was described by others as an "angel," who worked hard all of her life to help support her family.

Her family has settled in Springville for about eight years and then were called to settle in Heber City. She took in washing and sewing.

In Heber City, Mary Elizabeth met and married John Bunyon Rooker in 1866. They made their home in Heber City and became the parents of six children.

Her family remembers her faith and integrity, and the lessons of honesty, thrift, and industry that she taught them. Mary passed away at the age of forty, her youngest child was under the age of three.

PERMELIA EMILY WOOLDRIDGE HUNDLEY ROOKER

BIRTHDATE: 7 Mar 1801
Elbert Co., Georgia
DEATH: 31 Aug 1881
Center Creek, Wasatch Co., Utah
PARENTS: Thomas Wooldridge
Cheriah / Keziah Davis
PIONEER: Fall of 1858
Wagon Train Company
SPOUSE: Jordan Y. Hundley
MARRIED: 27 Oct 1817
Madison Co., Alabama
DEATH SP: 15 Sep 1908
Center Creek, Wasatch Co., Utah

CHILDREN:
Felix Noel, 25 Aug 1818
Catherine Ann (Sprouse), 9 May 1820
Thomas Agustus, 4 Jan 1824

SPOUSE II: Samuel McRae Rooker
MARRIED: 27 Jul 1835
DEATH SP: 16 Nov 1894

CHILDREN:
James William, 14 Jun 1836
Lucynthia Rebecca (Cole), 27 Sep 1837
John Bunyon, 25 Apr 1839

Permelia Emily was born in Georgia, 1801. She was one of seven children. Her mother passed away when she was very young. Her father married Mrs. Martha Easter Aycock and they had one child, Augusta B. born 1813 in Georgia.

At age sixteen, she married Dr. Joron Yarbrough Hundley in Alabama. They became the parents of at least three. Permelia married a second time at age thirty-four to Samuel McRae Rooker. They made their home in Mississippi, where they had three children.

At age fifty-seven, she was a pioneer to Springville, Utah County. They arrived late in 1858 in a small group of six to eight families. She and Samuel were among the first settlers of Old Fort Heber in the summer of 1859. She was also a pioneer in Texas and again in what is now Denver, Colorado.

She traveled by wagon from Aurora, Colorado to Springville. Several daughters accompanied Permelia and Samuel to Utah and settled in Heber Valley.

Permelia passed away at the age of eighty, after a very active pioneer life and is buried in Center Creek, Wasatch County, Utah. Samuel outlived her by thirteen years, passing away on November 16, 1894 in Center Creek, Utah.

CHARLOTTE ELIZABETH MELLOR ROPER

BIRTHDATE: 16 Jan 1842
Leicester, England
DEATH: 26 Jun 1886
Huntington, Emery Co., Utah
PARENTS: James Mellor
Mary Ann Payne
PIONEER: 30 Nov 1856
E. Martin Handcart Company
SPOUSE: John Henry Roper
MARRIED: 4 Feb 1957
Provo, Utah Co., Utah
DEATH SP: 28 Nov 1928
Fayette, Sanpete Co., Utah

CHILDREN:
Henry Hutchinson, 31 Aug 1858
Susanna, 23 Jul 1859
William, 2 Feb 1861

Salena, 23 Nov 1862
Sarah Ann, 13 Mar 1865
Mary Ann, 23 Feb 1867
Clara Althera, 15 Oct 1869
Charlotte Elizabeth, 4 Mar 1872
Charles Henry, 10 Jan 1874
George Albert, 8 Feb 1876
Benjamin Franklin, 8 Sep 1878
James Leo, 29 Dec 1882
Oliver Marion, 13 May 1884

When Charlotte was very young, she worked in a factory making bonnets for infants. Her parents heard the gospel preached in their area and were baptized as members of the Church of Jesus Christ of Latter-day Saints within a week. They began preparing to come to Utah. Her father had quit his job after securing passage for his family on the ship "Horizon." There were several delays before the ship and people were ready to leave. Her mother had just given birth to Siamese twins and was still very weak.

They were faced with two choices, either they could remain in England another year with no work, or they could risk a late journey across the Plains. They chose the latter, Her mother was smuggled aboard ship the eve before the ship left port.

When the Saints reached Boston, Massachusetts, they boarded a train to Iowa City, Iowa. They reached Iowa on July 8th. There, they were fitted out with the necessary equipment for the trip to cross the Plains. Her father obtained two handcarts to help carry his weak wife and the twins besides their belongings. They were with the Edward Martin Handcart Company.

This handcart company suffered through blizzards and so many hardships that at least 150 Saints perished, Brigham Young sent a group of men out to meet the company and asked those at home to take the survivors into their homes to care for them physically and spiritually. They arrived in the Salt Lake Valley on November 30, 1856.

Charlotte's legs had been frozen beyond use. The Roper family took her into their home and nursed her back to better health. She suffered the rest of her life with her feet which had been so badly frozen. This was the beginning of the romance between Henry and Charlotte. They were married February 4, 1857.

They lived in Provo, Lehi, Gunnison, and Lawrence, Utah. She spun wool for clothes.

Charlotte was a devoted mother and a faithful Latter-day Saint until her death at age forty-four. She passed away on June 26, 1886 at Lawrence and was buried in Huntington, Emery County, Utah.

MARY ANN GRAYSON ROPER

BIRTHDATE: 26 Oct 1824
Sheffield, Yorkshire, England
DEATH: 7 Mar 1897
Oak City, Millard Co., Utah
PARENTS: John Grayson
Hannah Ellis
PIONEER: 1859
SPOUSE: Henry Roper
MARRIED: 24 Oct 1843
Sheffield, Yorkshire, England
DEATH SP: 10 Nov 1906
Oak City, Millard Co., Utah

CHILDREN:
Wilford, 7 Sep 1844
Harry, 19 Oct 1846
John, 24 Jan 1848
Fredrick, 9 Feb 1850
Lizzie, 1 Nov 1851
Alvin, 17 Feb 1852
Twins, 20 Feb 1853 (stillborn)
Frank, 9 Sep 1855
Laura, 5 May 1857
Willie, 21 Jul 1858
Kate Platte (Walker), 23 Sep 1859
Nellie Grayson (Lyman), 13 Apr 1862
Charlie, 1 Oct 1865
Abel Mosley, 22 Feb 1868

Mary Ann was born in England in 1829. She married Henry Roper on October 24, 1843. Six children were born to them in England; Wilford, Harry, John, Fredrick, Lizzie, and Alvin. Only Harry and Alvin lived to come to Zion with them.

They landed in New Orleans on June 4, 1854, then to St. Louis, Missouri and then on to Alton, Illinois. Three more children were born in Illinois; Frank, Laura, and Willie. They all died in infancy.

At Red Butte, on the Platte River, another daughter was born. They named her Kate Platte.

In 1859, they drove a load of stoves for a freighting company to get to the Salt Lake Valley. Here, in the Valley, another daughter, Nellie Grayson, was born.

They settled in Scipio, Utah then to the new settlement in Deseret on the Sevier river. Two more children were born in Deseret; Charlie and Abel Mosley.

In the Fall of 1868, they moved to Oak City (Oak Creek), Utah. Henry set up a blacksmith shop and Mary Ann spent a great deal of time among the sick as she was an experienced midwife. Mary Ann helped her husband with the first post office in Oak City, serving as post masters for twenty-nine years.

Mary Ann passed away on March 7, 1897 at the age of seventy-three in Oak City, Millard County, Utah.

MARY ANN NIELSEN LIND ROSE

BIRTHDATE: 8 Apr 1826
East Uttrup, Aalborg, Denmark
DEATH: 27 Sep 1899
North Ogden, Weber Co., Utah
PARENTS: Niels Nielsen
Karen Jensen
PIONEER: 25 Sep 1868
Wagon Train Company
SPOUSE I: Jens C. A. Lind
MARRIED: I Apr 1847
Aalborg, Jutland, Denmark
DEATH SP: 6 Apr 1878
Weston, Oneida Co., Idaho

CHILDREN:
Larsina Marie, 13 May 1849 (died as an infant)
Niles Peter, 26 Jun 1850 (died as an infant)
Maria Magdalena, 20 Oct 1851
Jensina Katrina, 14 Mar 1853
Jenny, 26 Mar 1855
Caroline Harriette, 31 Aug 1857
Jens Christian Anton, 9 Jul 1860 (died as a child)
George Christian, 9 Jul 1863
Lewis Peter, 17 Jun 1865
Niels Marinus, 8 Jul 1867 (died as a child)
Mariane Christina, 19 Feb 1870

SPOUSE II: Wesley Rose
MARRIED: I Jun 1898
DEATH SP: Not given
CHILDREN: None

Mary Ann was born on April 8, 1826 at East Uttrup, Aalborg, Denmark. She married Jens Christian Anton Lind on April 1, 1847.

In the early 1850's Elders Erastus Snow and George P. Dykes brought the gospel to the Lind family and they embraced it. As soon as they became members of the Church of Jesus Christ of Latter-day Saints they suffered many persecutions.

They were eager to come to Utah and had saved money to pay their way, but loaned it to assist in the emigration of some of the other Saints and the loan was never repaid. Years later some of their Scandinavian friends who lived in Ephraim, Utah raised enough money to pay for the transportation for the Lind family.

On June 13, 1868 they left Copenhagen on the steamship "Hansia," to sail to England. From Liverpool, they sailed on the "Emerald Isle" to America. During this most unpleasant journey many of the emigrants became sick from the measles and bad water. Among those who died was the little thirteen-month-old son of Mary.

The crossed the Plains in 1868 with an ox-team and wagon, arriving in the Salt Lake Valley on September 25, 1868. They lived for a time at Ephraim and Levan, Utah and then moved to Bridgeport, Idaho.

Mary Ann's husband passed away on April 6, 1878 in Weston, Idaho. On June 1, 1898, Mary Ann married Wesley Rose. Mary Ann passed away on September 27, 1899 in North Ogden, Weber County, Utah.

MARY ANN SHERRY THAXTON WATTON ROSE

BIRTHDATE: Jan 27 1809
Rutherford Co., North Carolina
DEATH: Feb 1886
Famiington, Davis Co., Utah
PARENTS: Richard Sherry
Martha McKinney
PIONEER: 15 Sep 1852
SPOUSE: Williamson Thaxton
Pendleton, South Carolina
MARRIED: 23 May 23 1829
Allen Co., Kentucky
DEATH SP: Not given
Quincy, Adams, Illinois

CHILDREN:
James William Thaxton, 22 Aug 1832
Richard Cantley Thaxton, 4 Jan 1837

SPOUSE II: James Watton
MARRIED: 16 Apr 1849
St. Louis, Missouri
DEATH SP: 6 Feb 1810
Farmington, Davis Co., Utah
CHILDREN: None

SPOUSE III: Abraham Rose
MARRIED: between 1880 and 1884
DEATH SP: 9 Sep 1884
Farmington, Davis Co., Utah
CHILDREN: None

Mary Ann was born on January 27, 1809 in Rutherford County, North Carolina. She married Williamson Thaxton in Allen County, Kentucky on May 23, 1829. Shortly after their marriage, they moved to Fulton County, Illinois.

While living in Fulton County, her husband enlisted, along with about two dozen others from the area, in "The Black Hawk War." Records indicate, however, that the family was probably living in Quincy, Illinois, when Mary Ann's son, James William, was born. A few years after Williamson's service in the Black Hawk War, they moved to northwest Missouri where their son, Richard Cantley, was born. There is no known record of her husband, Williamson Thaxton, after January 1837. One source states that Mary Ann lived for some time as a widow in or about St. Louis, Missouri.

Mary Ann and her two sons were baptized members of the Church of Jesus Christ of Latter-Day Saints in about 1849. Mary Ann married James Watton on April 16, 1849, in St. Louis, Missouri, and within a year after their marriage, they relocated to Pottawotamie County, Iowa, where they prepared and waited for their trek West to Utah.

On June 4, 1852, the first of the company's wagons began moving out on the Westward journey. At that time, Mary Ann was forty-three years old, her husband was fifty-one, and her son, Richard Cantley, was fourteen.

In late June they had a small misfortune, "a stampede in the first ten caused by Widow Weldens horses running away but no damage done except the breaking an ox yoke belonging to Father James Watton." They traversed hundreds of miles over "sandy roads, hills and mud holes" and steep sandy bluffs, across rivers, wet, swampy ground, and muddy creeks, through heavy wind and rain storms, at times in heat almost too much both for man and beast," Nine members died and many others became ill with the dreadful cholera. Food was scarce during the journey, but they were able to obtain food from buffalo hunts. On August 3, they reached Laramie, Wyoming, and finally on September 15, they reached the Salt Lake Valley.

Mary Ann and her family settled in Farmington, Utah, where she lived the remainder of her life. She was a dedicated Church member.

On June 30, 1868, the Farmington Ward Relief Society was organized. Mary Ann's name was listed as one of the sisters admitted into the society at that time. Her donation to the society that day was one spool cotton and three eggs which was valued at twenty-one cents.

Mary Ann passed away in February of 1886 at the age of seventy-seven and was buried in the Farmington Cemetery.

HELENA JONSSON ERICKSSON ROSBERG / ROSEBERRY

BIRTHDATE: 11 Oct 1822
Hyby, Malmohus, Sweden
DEATH: 18 Dec 1899
Pima, Graham Co., Arizona
PARENTS: Jons Peter Ericksson
Johanna/Hannah Jeppson Persson
PIONEER: 4 Sep 1859
George Rowley Handcart Comp.
SPOUSE: Carl Nilsson Rosberg
MARRIED: 7 Apr 1849
Malmo, Sweden
DEATH SP: 14 Nov 1868
Weber Co., Utah

CHILDREN:
Carolina Helena, 14 Aug 1850
Anna Gustafa, 29 Jan 1853
Anna Maria, 2 Sep 1855
Neils Joseph, 10 Sep 1858
Emma Caroline, 10 Sep 1858
Hannah Helena, 2 Oct 1861
Charles Louis, 2 Oct 1861
Ellen Augusta, 26 Dec 1864
Louisa Christina, 26 Dec 1864

Helena Charlotte, 26 Dec 1864
Elizabeth, 8 Mar 1867

As a child, Helena had several injuries and felt the Lord had preserved her life for a purpose. She was never afraid of hard work and helped build her first home.

She married Carl Roseberry when she was twenty. She became baptized a member of the Church of Jesus Christ of Latter-day Saints, without her husband's permission. He made her life so miserable, she left him and went to Denmark for a few years. She was going to sail to America and decided to write to her husband a letter telling him where he could find her if he still wanted her. He went after her, joined the Church, and the family returned to Sweden.

They sailed from England in April, 1859, on the ship, "William Tappscott." They walked across the Plains to Utah with the George Rowley Handcart Company.

Helena fell from the handcart and broke her hip. Each evening, she had to lie on the ground very still while holding a twin in each arm until they arrived in the Salt Lake Valley on September 4, 1859. If it had not been for the rescue party from the Valley which came to meet them, they would not have lived.

They were sent to help colonize Sanpete County where they endured poverty, hunger, and Indians. She gave birth to another set of twins and a set of triplets among a total of eleven children.

In 1867, after her youngest child was born, they moved to Santaquin. Her husband was killed while working on the railroad leaving her with seven small children to raise.

When her son, Joseph, was called by President Young to go to Arizona in 1878, she went with him. They helped colonize in Arizona and Mexico. She donated $5.00 toward the building of a temple in Arizona.

Helena passed away in Pima, Arizona at the age of seventy-seven. She withstood great trials and tribulations for the sake of her posterity.

ALICE NEIBAUR ROSENBAUM

BIRTHDATE: 22 May 1841
Nauvoo, Hancock Co., Illinois
DEATH: 21 Mar 1914
Brigham City, Box Elder, Utah
PARENTS: Alexander Neibaur
Ellen Brieshel
PIONEER: 20 Sep 1848
Wagon Train Company
SPOUSE: Morris D. Rosenbaum
MARRIED: 2 Apr 1858
Salt Lake City, Salt Lake, Utah
DEATH SP: 19 Aug 1885
Mink Creek, Franklin Co., Idaho

CHILDREN:
Sarah, 23 Sep 1859
David, 11 Mar 1860

Ellen, 17 Nov 1862
Fanny, 6 Nov 1864
Alice, 22 Jan 1866
Morris, 30 Jul 1867
Alexander, 13 Sep 1869
Aaron, 17 Oct 1873
Joseph, 21 Jan 1874
Margaret, 15 Aug 1877
Leah, 16 Nov 1879
Abigail, 30 Mar 1882
Bertha, 26 Dec 1883

Alice was born in Illinois in 1841. Her father was a Jew and had studied to become a rabbi. He had studied medicine and dentistry, then married a Christian woman, and became converted to the Church of Jesus Christ of Latter-day Saints. After their conversion in 1841, they emigrated to Nauvoo where Alice was born. Her father instructed Joseph Smith in Hebrew and German. They came to the Great Salt Lake Valley in September of 1848. Her father began his practice as a dentist and also engaged in the manufacture of sulphur matches.

At age sixteen, Alice married Morris David Rosenbaum who came to Salt Lake City in 1854 and later joined the Church. They made their home in Salt Lake City where they became the parents of two children. They were sealed by Brigham Young on July 2, 1858.

In 1861, they went to Brigham City and bought a place. They added eleven more children to their family. They were one of the Pioneer Merchants of Brigham City. Alice gave permission for Morris to marry a widow, Abigail Harriet Snow Caldwell, (daughter of Lorenzo Snow).

In 1880, Morris was sent to preside over the North German Mission. The families worked hard and took care of themselves for the years their father was gone.

Morris passed away in Mink Creek, Idaho when his daughter, Bertha, was nearly two years old. Alice raised her family alone, was a widow for twenty-nine years before her death at age seventy-two.

JOSEPHINE JULIANE KAY ROSENGREN / ROSENGREEN

BIRTHDATE: 22 Dec 1848
Steesbakken, Vang, Norway
DEATH: 29 Sep 1925
Idaho Falls, Bonneville, Idaho
PARENTS: Bernt Olaus Kay
Anne Hansdatter
PIONEER: 8 Oct 1866
Andrew H. Scott Wagon Train
SPOUSE: Niels Rosengren
MARRIED: 14 Feb 1868
Salt Lake City, Salt Lake, Utah
DEATH SP: 4 Apr 1930

CHILDREN:
John Hyrum, 7 Jul 1870
Anne Christine, 29 Octl 872
Ida M. Hall, (adopted daughter)

Josephine was born in Steesbakken, Vang, Hedmark, Norway in 1848. When she was seventeen years old, she was the first of her family to emigrate to Salt Lake Valley. She joined the Andrew H. Scott Wagon Company, arriving in October, 1866,

Two years later, February 14, 1868, she married Niels Rosengren in Salt Lake City, Utah. They were the parents of two children and adoped a little girl named Ida M. Hall.

Josephine was a quiet woman, she engaged in a lot of temple work. When she was sixty-three she joined the Daughters of the Utah Pioneers in November, 1921

Josephine passed away on September 29, 1925 in Idaho Falls, Idaho when she was seventy-seven years of age and was buried in Logan, Cache County, Utah.

REBECCA HENDRICKS WATSON ROSKELLEY

BIRTHDATE: 2 Nov 1835
near Franklin, Kentucky
DEATH: 11 May 1880
Smithfield, Cache Co., Utah
PARENTS: James Hendricks
Drusilla Dorris
PIONEER: 4 Oct 1847
Jedediah Grant's Wagon Train
SPOUSE I: Hiram Abiff Watson
MARRIED: 23 Jim 1852
Salt Lake Endowment House
DEATH SP: 20 Apr 1909
Minneapolis, Minnesota

CHILD:
Hiram Abiff Jr., 8 Apr 1853

SPOUSE II: Samuel Roskelley
MARRIED: 23 Jul 1858
Salt Lake City, Salt Lake Co., Utah
DEATH SP: 10 Feb 1914
Smithfield, Cache Co., Utah

CHILDREN:
Rebecca (Hillyard), 22 Apr 1859
Sharlotte, 7 Oct 1860
Zina (Hyde), 18 Mar 1862
Samuel, 11 Aug 1863
James, 10 Jan 1865
William Hendricks, 4 May 1866
Joseph, 5 Jun 1868

Rebecca was born in Kentucky in 1835. Soon after Rebecca was born, her family moved to Clay County, Missouri. They moved to Nauvoo, Illinois in 1840. Then moved with the Saints to Winter Quarters. They joined the

Jedediah M. Grant Company to cross the Plains, arriving in Salt Lake Valley on October 4, 1847. They lived at the Warm Springs bath house North of Salt Lake City.

When Rebecca was sixteen and a half, she married Hiram A. Watson who was on his way through to California. When Hiram went back east on a mission he decided after a year he wanted her to come back there to live. She wouldn't so they were divorced and Rebecca was left to raise her son, Hiram, alone.

Rebecca waited for Samuel Roskelley to return from his mission to England. One month after his return, they were married on July 23, 1858 in Salt Lake City, Utah. They moved to Provo for a while but soon returned to Salt Lake City. The following spring they moved to North Mill Creek and bought a shingle mill with Samuel's brother-in-law, Thomas VanNay.

In the Spring of 1860, Samuel and Rebecca moved to Cache Valley to farm. In 1863, they moved to Smithfield, where Samuel was bishop.

Rebecca with her big house was responsible for entertaining visiting dignitaries while they were in Smithfield.

Samuel was made Mayor of Smithfield in 1870, in addition to the many offices he held in various companies. Thus, most of the rearing of the children fell on Rebecca. It has been said that Rebecca was a good manager, and considered the waste of time a grave thing.

Rebecca was made a counselor in both the YWMIA and the Primary which were organized in 1875.

SARAH MAUD BURTON ROSKELLEY

BIRTHDATE: 4 Oct 1861
Plymouth, Devonshire, England
DEATH: 24 Sep 1932
Smithfield, Cache Co., Utah
PARENTS: William G. Burton
Hannah Tregale
PIONEER: Sep 1868
William G. Burton Wagon Train
SPOUSE: Samuel Roskelley
MARRIED: 21 Dec 1885
Logan Temple, Cache Co., Utah
DEATH SP: 14 Feb 1914
Smithfield, Cache Co., Utah

CHILDREN:
Maul Ellen, 24 Feb 1887
Marriner W., 11 Aug 1888
Clara, 7 Apr 1891
Lorenzo, 27 Dec 1893
Gilbert, 28 Dec 1897

Sarah Maude's parents were early converts to the Church of Jesus Christ of Latter-day Saints. Her father was Secretary in the Devonport Branch, then later became the Branch President.

A young lad of fourteen, Samuel Roskelley, had been forced from his home because he had joined the Church. He was taken into the Burton home to live and work. On July 22, 1867, their family emigrated to America from Plymouth on board the steamer, City of Washington.

After they arrived in New York, Maude's father was placed in charge of a small company of Saints traveling to Salt Lake City. They went by railroad to the end of the line at Benton. They left Benton by ox-team September 1, 1868. They were the last Saints to cross the Plains in wagons.

The family moved to Piedmont, Wyoming and later to Evanston, Wyoming where her father worked on the railroad. Her father was Branch President, her mother was Relief Society President, and Maude, at age sixteen was the secretary of the Relief Society.

When the family moved to Logan, Sarah Maude was set apart as the president of the Logan First Ward Primary. She also served as secretary of the Relief Society in Logan. During this time she helped her father in his bakery.

Samuel Roskelley emigrated to America and came to pay his respects to his old friends. He and Sarah Maude fell in love and married in the Logan Temple.

Despite the hardships of their lives, Maude continued with her church work and served from 1886 to 1896 in the Stake Primary Presidency. Then she became the Stake President of the Relief Society until 1900. When they moved to Smithfield, she was President of the Primary again for three years and then was a counselor in the Benson Stake Relief Society for fourteen years. She also served as secretary of the Genealogical Committee of the Smithfield Second Ward.

Sarah Maud passed away peacefully in Smithfield, Utah at the age of seventy-one years.

MARTHA ANN NELSON PARKER ROSS

BIRTHDATE: 17 Oct 1818
Fayette Co., Illinois
DEATH: Oct 1889
Washburn, Barry Co., Missouri
PARENTS: Dr. Ambrose Nelson
Joyce Faulconer
PIONEER: Fall of 1852
Independent Co. Wagon Train
SPOUSE I: Thomas Bryant Parker
MARRIED: 25 Oct 1835
DEATH SP: 27 Jul 1850

CHILDREN:
Robert Pollack, 1836
Thomas Bryant, 1838
Ambrose Nelson, 1839
Joseph Faulconer, 1841
Elizabeth Joyce, 1842
Alma Mormon, 1844

Exile Liberty, 1846
Margaret Parker, 1848

SPOUSE II: James Melvin Ross
MARRIED: 14 Mar 1856
DEATH SP: 19 Nov 1896

CHILD:
Orpha Elvira Ross, 14 Feb 1857

After Martha's father died her mother married again, twice. It was with her second step-father, Cyrus Remmick, they moved to Missouri.

When Martha was seventeen years old, she married Thomas Bryant Parker, a widower with three children. Martha and Tom had eight children. Their home in Palmyra was a spacious, two-story building of tavern, where they took in travelers.

They joined the Church of Jesus Christ of Latter-day Saints in 1844 and when they sold their place in Palmyra and moved to Kanesville, Martha was eight months pregnant, and Tom was in bed with bad health, besides being crippled in the hip, his lungs were affected from a sickness of a few years before.

On arriving in Kanesville, they again bought and ran a tavern and place for travelers. In 1850, just before Thomas passed away, he made Martha Ann promise that she would bring the family to "Zion."

In 1852, Martha sold the tavern and farm. They left with Captain Reese and her brother, Napolean B. Nelson, who were going to California. (Her brother thought that Martha would go with him, but she said no and that she would be going with the Saints). Martha, with her five children, two wagons and oxen, ten cows and one horse, came on with the others that she met along the way.

After arriving in the Salt Lake Valley, Martha Ann moved to Spring City to settle. She lived there about a year. While living here the Indians stole their oxen and cows. During the Indian war, she moved to Manti where she remained for two years before moving to Provo.

In 1856, Martha Ann married Melvin Ross and they had one daughter.

Martha Ann and her brother went back to Missouri to see her mother, while there her son, Joseph, came on a mission and promised to bring her home, but she passed away before he could. Martha Ann is buried in Washburn, Missouri.

MARY ANN JACKSON WOODRUFF ROSS

BIRTHDATE: 18 Feb 1818
Liverpool, Lancashire, England
DEATH: 25 Oct 1894
Salt Lake City, Salt Lake, Utah
PARENTS: William Jackson
Elizabeth Lloyd
PIONEER: 25 Sep 1847
Abraham O. Smoot Wagon Train
SPOUSE I: Wilford Woodruff
MARRIED: 15 Apr 1846
Nauvoo Temple, Illinois
DEATH SP: 2 Sep 1898
San Francisco, California

CHILD:
James Jackson, 25 May 1847

SPOUSE II: David James Ross
MARRIED: 13 Dec 1857
Salt Lake City, Salt Lake, Utah
DEATH SP: 29 Aug 1909
Freedom, Wyoming

CHILDREN:
William Jackson, 12 Oct 1858
John L., Dec 1859

Mary Ann's mother died when Mary was nineteen years old and her father died when she was twenty-two.

Mary Ann joined the Church of Jesus Christ of Latter-day Saints on July 1, 1841. She emigrated to the United States in February, 1846, and arrived in New Orleans on March 25, 1846.

Mary Ann became the second wife of Wilford Woodruff when she was sealed to him on April 15, 1846 in the Nauvoo Temple. On the 16th day of May, she was with the Saints who were driven from Nauvoo. They crossed the river and traveled West to join other saints already in the wilderness.

In the fall of 1846, after the battalion left, the company went to Winter Quarters. On the 13th of June, she began her trek across the Plains with her nineteen day old baby in the Abraham Owen Smoot Wagon Company. They arrived in the Salt Lake Valley on September 25, 1847.

Her husband, Wilford, had traveled with the very first company of Saints, had built a log cabin of two large rooms for Mary Ann, their son, James, and Aphek Woodruff, Wilford's father. Then he returned back east to get his first wife and family. On December 13, 1853, the sealing of Mary Ann Jackson and Wilford Woodruff was canceled.

Mary Ann was sealed to David James Ross on December 13, 1857, as his plural wife. Her husband had disobeyed President Brigham Young when he gave credit to men wishing to purchase weapons. When the men did not pay, Brigham Young became angry and David James Ross fled from Utah to avoid payment. Mary Ann never saw or heard from him again.

Even though Mary Ann's life was full of trials and hardships, she remained true and faithful to the Gospel. She is loved and revered by her posterity.

She passed away at the age of seventy-six on October 25, 1894, and was buried in the northwest corner of Wilford Woodruff's Cemetery lot.

RACHEL SMITH ROSS

BIRTHDATE: 22 Aug 1813
Smith Co., Tennessee
DEATH: 19 Dec 1900
Joseph, Sevier Co., Utah
PARENTS: James Agee
Margaret Love Smith
PIONEER: 6 Sept 1850
Aaron Johnson Co. Wagon Train
SPOUSE: Thomas Ross
MARRIED: 30 Sep 1835
DEATH SP: 4 Oct 1898

CHILDREN:
James Andrew, 1836
Margaret Ann, 3 Mar 1838
Leah Lucinda, 4 Feb 1842
Mary Elizabeth, 4 Mar 1845
Nancy Jane, 11 Dec 1848
Thomas William, 25 Jun 1851
Robert Francis, 18 Oct, 1853
John Franklin, 15 May 1856

Rachel was a petite little lady of French and English decent. She was very precise, a place for everything and everything in its place. She scoured her kitchen and pantry floors with fine white sand. She was loveable and kind, always knew her own mind, never complaining.

She did a great deal of fancy work, crocheting, knitting, pieceing quilts, making hats of wheat straw from the field, and making soap. She wove the material and made men's suits and women's clothes.

Rachel became a member of the Church of Jesus Christ of Latter-day Saints in 1842.

When she was eighty-seven years old her son used to saddle her horse "Old Bird" set her on it, then walk the horse to his house.

Rachel passed away at the age of eighty-seven years and three months in Joseph, Sevier County, Utah.

SARAH ELIZABETH SMITH ROSS

BIRTHDATE: 22 Apr 1837
Middlesex, England
DEATH: 4 Dec 1920
Salt Lake City, Salt Lake, Utah
PARENTS: George Smith
Sarah Harris
PIONEER: 3 Sep. 1860
James D Ross Co. Wagon Train
SPOUSE: James Darling Ross
MARRIED: 8 Sep 1857
London, Middlesex, England
DEATH SP: 1 Oct 1878
Salt Lake City, Salt Lake, Utah

CHILDREN:
Sarah Darling, 20 Jun 1858
William George, 28 Feb 1860
Annie Louise, 12 Jul 1861
Grace Rose, 18 Mar 1864
Charles J., 28 Feb 1867
George J., 5 Oct 1869

Sarah Elizabeth was the oldest of seven children.

Sarah was baptized into the Church of Jesus Christ of Latter-day Saints when she was fourteen in 1851.

After losing his wife and infant son, James Darling Ross found peace and comfort in the Smith home. Because of her kindness and gentleness a romance blossomed, and James and Sarah were married in September, 1857.

Among the Saints leaving England in 1860 were three generations in the same family; (1) George Smith and his wife Sarah Harris, (2) James Ross and his wife Sarah Elizabeth, (3) their children, Sarah Darling and William George.

They sailed on the ship "Underwriter," March 6, 1860, arriving in New York, May 1, 1860, and in Winter Quarters. The James D. Ross Wagon Company left Winter Quarters on June 17, 1860 with 249 souls, thirty-six wagons, fourteen oxen and fifty-four cows. They arrived in the Salt Lake Valley on September 3, 1860 and camped in the 8th Ward Square (site of City and County building). They bought their first ground where the Govenor's Mansion now stands, paying about a $100.00.

Sarah Elizabeth was often requested to sing at funerals and Relief Society gatherings. Having been raised in a life of comfort she brought a lot of beautiful clothes but because the other women had so little she seldom wore them. Later she began giving them away for special occasions and some later ended up in quilt pieces. Sarah became an excellent seamstress and made burial clothes. She also made a yeast called "Live Yeast" she would trade for flour. She would then sell the flour to the bakers, and in this way earn money.

Sarah's husband passed away when she was forty-one with five children to raise alone. She did a great deal of sewing at night by candlelight which weakened her eyes and in 1885 someone without sufficient medical knowledge put drops in her eyes that caused blindness. She was blind for thirty-five years. She complained little nor did she blame or become bitter at the situation.

Because of her beautiful character, Sarah lived a comparatively happy and useful life, developing understanding, love and patience that come with trust in God. She developed the ability to sew, knit and crochet, and some of her work was supior to that of those who could see. She could thread a needle as quick if not quicker than most anyone.

For many years she lived with her youngest son, George, on the corner of 2nd Avenue and H Street. This son was later killed in Salt Lake City's first automobile accident on September 20, 1908.

Sarah Elizabeth passed away on December 4, 1920 at the age of eighty-three. survived by three of her six children.

MARY LLEWELLYN BURCHELL ROSSITER

BIRTHDATE: (chr.) 1 Aug 1813
Dudley, Worcester, England
DEATH: 23 Jan 1899
Fairfield, Utah Co., Utah
PARENTS: Samuel Llewellyn
Mary Llewellyn / Lewellen
PIONEER: 1858
SPOUSE I: Joseph Burchell
MARRIED: 18 Jul 1839
Birmingham, Warwick, England
DEATH SP: 27 Jul 1847
Dudley, Worcester, England

CHILDREN:
Henry Thomas Burchell, 4 Jun 1840
Charles Burchell, 1 Apr 1842
Emma Burchell, 13 Feb 1844
Abraham George Burchell, 25 Aug 1846

SPOUSE II: Solomon Rossiter
MARRIED: Bloomsburg, Pennsylvania (later divorced)
DEATH SP: 4 Jan 1878
Salt Lake City, Salt Lake Co., Utah
CHILDREN: None

According to her baptismal certificate Mary was living at Dudley, Worcester, England. She grew up in Dudley and married Joseph Burchell, a miner.

After missionaries came to Dudley, Joseph and Mary were baptized as members of the Church of Jesus Christ of Latter-day Saints, but their plans to emigrate were interrupted when six month old Abraham died of a lung problem. Joseph told Mary they must go to America no matter what. Then five months later Joseph died in a mine accident. Mary was devastated but was determined to keep

her promise. In 1848, she was again ready when her oldest son, Henry, died of convulsions.

Mary left England in December, 1848, with her two remaining children, and upon their arrival into the United States they settled in Bloomsburg, Pennsylvania. Here she married Solomon Rossiter, but they were divorced on March 7, 1857.

She then took her children, Charles and Emma, to St. Louis, and eventually crossed the Plains in 1858. She supported the family by sewing and doing housekeeping.

When her son, Charles, found work in Fairfield, Utah, near Camp Floyd, Mary moved there. Fairfield was a thriving little town, and she made a good living as a seamstress.

Mary and her family left the LDS Church and joined the Reorganites who had a branch in Fairfield. Her daughter, Emma, married but her son, Charles, never married, and lived with his mother until her death on January 23, 1899. Charles died the following year and they are both buried in Fairfield, Utah.

AMELIA ANN LONGHURST HEWLETT ROUNDS

BIRTHDATE: 10 Oct 1846
Deptford, Kent, England
DEATH: 2 Oct 1923
Roberts, Jefferson Co., Idaho
PARENTS: William Longhurst
Ann Preston
PIONEER: 26 Oct 1864
William Hyde Co. Wagon Train
SPOUSE I: Thomas Hewlett
MARRIED: 22 Apr 1865
Salt Lake City, Utah (Annulled)
DEATH SP: 8 Sep 1888
Salt Lake City, Salt Lake, Utah

CHILDREN: None

SPOUSE: William Carmer Rounds
MARRIED: 17 Oct 1868
Salt Lake City, Utah
DEATH SP: 17 Jul 1894
Coalville, Summit, Utah

CHILDREN:
Ambrose Edmund, 3 Aug 1869
Matilda Ann, 10 Sep 1871
William Henry, 20 Oct 1873
Clara Amelia, 11 Dec 1876
George Clarence, 21 Dec 1879
Rosella (Grow), 21 Jan 1882

Amelia was born in England in 1846. She was the oldest of ten children. She was a cheerful fun-loving girl.

Amelia was eighteen years old when her family sailed from Liveropool in June, 1864, on the "S. S. Hudson," arriving in New York, then by train to St. Joseph, Missouri. They encountered much Civil War destruction en route. They took a river boat to Nebraska. Then joined the William Hyde Wagon Company for the Salt Lake Valley, arriving on October 26, 1864.

They spent a bitter winter in a dug out, where her younger brother was born in January. Amelia hired out to do house work.

In 1865, Amelia married Thomas Hewlett in polygamy a brief and sad marriage which was soon annulled. Later she met and married William Carmer Rounds, a widower with three children. They were married on October 17, 1868, and moved to Bountiful. They were the parents of six children, two of whom died young.

William operated a sawmill near Morgan and Amelia often accompanied him to near by settlements when he played the violin for dances and taught square dancing. Theirs was a mobile life moving from canyon to Morgan and Davis Counties for the winter to enable the children to attend school.

In 1877, William took another wife in polygamy and they also had six children.

Amelia was President of the Retrenchment Society while they lived in Salt Lake for two years. She also worked as a dress maker and milliner.

In 1894, her husband passed away of a heart attack leaving her with the two youngest children to support. Her father, four brothers, and two sons were living in Idaho so she joined them to make a new life for herself.

Amelia's sons built her a one-room house with a dirt roof. Soon she opened a little shop in her home selling candies and handmade hats. Her skills as a seamstress and milliner were outstanding and her products a work of art.

In 1917, she left her home and lived her remaining years with her daughter, Rosella. She could still step-dance and still entertain as she harmonized on old English folk songs and ballads. This perky and petite English lady passed away on October 2, 1923 at the age of seventy-seven.

BETSY QUIMBY ROUNDY

BIRTHDATE: 29 Jun 1795
Lunenburg, Essex Co., Vermont
DEATH: 28 Mar 1880
Salt Lake City, Salt Lake, Utah
PARENTS: Moses Quimby
Hannah Kennedy
PIONEER: 1847
Second Co. Wagon Train
SPOUSE: Shadrach Roundy
MARRIED: 22 Jun 1814
Rockingham, Vermont
DEATH SP: 4 Jul 1872
Salt Lake City, Salt Lake, Utah

CHILDREN:
Lauren Hotchkiss, 21 May 1815
Julia Rebecca, 5 Apr 1817
Lorenzo Wesley, 18 Jun 1819
Lauretta, Nov 1821
Samantha, 2 Jun 1824
Jared Curtis, 5 Jan 1827
Almeda Sophia, 7 Mar 1829
William Felshaw, Nov 1831 (died at age 8)
Nancy Jane, 20 May 1836
Malinda, 23 Jun 1838 (died at age 3)

Betsy was born to a family where religion was practised extensively. She was gentle, refined, intelligent, long suffering, patient, and faithful.

Betsy married Shadrach Roundy, June 22, 1814, and they moved to Onondaga, New York where most of their children were born. It was there they heard of the gospel as revealed to the Prophet Joseph Smith. Their whole family was converted and baptized as members of the Church of Jesus Christ of Latter-day Saints. They had a strong desire to move closer to the leaders of the church.

Shadrach went to Utah with the first company of Saints in 1847 and returned for his family to take them to Utah with the second company. Betsy continued moving with main body of Saints until they reached the Salt Lake Valley.

Her attitude was courageous. She endured hardships cheerfully and stood steadfast to her husband and the gospel. Betsy was endowed with all the motherly instincts and talents that were necessary for making a frontier home. In the first years in Utah, besides keeping her own home and children, she mothered Myron and William Roundy, who were motherless.

After she had raised ten children, she brought up three orphaned girls; two of whom were her grand-daughters and the other girl was named Lydia White.

Betsy and her husband were in the mercantile business in Nauvoo. When they were driven to the West, they with other LDS leaders organized in January 1845 a Mercantile and Mechanical Association for the purpose of protecting themselves against hostile gentile competition. This organization lasted for a year and served as a pattern for them to follow when they organized the Zion's Co-operative Mercantile Institution twenty years later in Salt Lake City.

Betsy assisted her husband as he served as bishop of the Sixteenth Ward. Betsy was left a good share of the time caring for the family alone since her husband crossed the Plains five times helping the pioneers to come across. Betsy's life was a busy and most useful one. It came to a close on March 28, 1880 in Salt Lake City, Utah.

ELIZABETH JEFFORD DRAKE BALLAM DAVIS ROUNDY

BIRTHDATE: 16 Mar 1830
Axminister, Devonshire, England
DEATH: 30 Jan 1916
Salt Lake City, Salt Lake, Utah
PARENTS: George M. Drake
Hannah Jefford
PIONEER: 1859
SPOUSE I: Henry R. Ballam
MARRIED: 13 Jul 1852
London, England
DEATH SP: 1858
London, England

CHILDREN:
Elizabeth, 21 Mar 1853
William Kimball, 27 Jun 1854
Cyrus, 27 Jun 1856 (twin)
Sarah, 27 Jun 1856 (twin)
Mary Dana, 2 Dec 1857

SPOUSE II: Daniel George Davis
MARRIED: 29 Apr 1860 (later divorced)
DEATH SP: 12 Sep 1916
Los Angelos, California

CHILD:
George Madison Drake, 3 Dec 1860

SPOUSE III: Jared Curtis Roundy
MARRIED: 17 Jan 1879
DEATH SP: 22 May 1895
St. David, Arizona
CHILDREN: None

Elizabeth attended school at Miss Lord's Seminary at Lyne in England. Her father taught her to read the bible and to believe in God. When she was eight years old, she refused to attend church because the minister did not preach what Christ taught in the Bible. Her father died when she was ten years old.

She left home in 1851 for London to continue her search for the true church. She attended a service of the Church of Jesus Christ of Latter-day Saints in Aldenham Branch and recognized the speaker and his message from a dream she had received three times previously. She joined the Church.

Needing money to pay for her emigration, she worked as a seamstress in an exclusive store which made clothing for Queen Victoria.

She married Richard Ballam in London on July 13, 1852. They had five children, but only two survived to adulthood. She traveled to America on the ship, "Tuscarora," and arrived in Philadelphia, Pennsylvania on July 3, 1857. Soon after her arrival, she learned of the death of her husband in England. She again engaged in dress-making to earn money to take herself and her two children to Utah where they arrived in 1859.

Soon after her arrival, she married Daniel George Davis. She returned with him to his home in Washington, D. C. While there, Elizabeth was appointed a clerkship in the United States Treasury at the recommendation of General F. B. Spinner. She served in this capacity until she resigned to fight against the passing of the Cragin Bill, an anti-Mormon legislative Bill.

When her husband returned from fighting in the Civil War, he had changed considerably. She divorced him and returned to Utah with her three children.

She was instrumental in drafting a petition for the release of Brigham Young when he had been imprisoned for contempt of court in 1871. In 1874, she traveled to obtain 26,000 signatures for a petition to Congress asking for women's rights as citizens, declaring their allegiance to the constitution and their belief in God, and their belief in his revelation of the divinity of polygamy and celestial marriage. As she was traveling, she met and married Jared Curtis Roundy as his plural wife.

Elizabeth was appointed by Brigham Young to serve as chairman of the committee for the preparation of the celebration of the centennial of the United States. Her church activity never ceased. She traveled with Eliza R. Snow all over Utah organizing Relief Societies. She served as secretary of the Relief Society in the Fifteenth Ward for many years. She served as a missionary by both talking and writing to many people about the gospel.

At the age of sixty two, she painted a picture of Joseph and Hyrum Smith which was hung in the Salt Lake Temple for many years. She was a faithful worker in the temple for many years before she passed away at the age of eighty-six.

LOVISE JENNE ROUNDY

BIRTHDATE: 15 Jun 1832
Upper Canada, near Kingston
DEATH: 1917
Logan, Cache Co., Utah
PARENTS: Benjamin P. Jenne
Sarah C. Snyder Jenne Richards
PIONEER: 19 Oct 1848
Willard Richards Wagon Train
SPOUSE: Jared Curtis Roundy
MARRIED: 26 Feb 1852
Salt Lake City, Salt Lake, Utah
DEATH SP: 22 May 1895
Maricopa Co., Arizona

CHILDREN:
Evalyn Aurelia (Peck), 23 Nov 1852
Jared Curtis, 13 May 1855
Sarah Louise (Phillips), 17 Jan 1858
Shadrack Jenne, 9 Feb 1860
George Snyder, 10 Oct 1862
Ida May (Snyder), 14 Oct 1864
Roseanna (Gibbons), 22 Dec 1867

Franklin Spencer, Oct 1870
Maud Syrene (Thompson), 7 Jul 1875

Lovise was born in Canada in 1832. Her younger years were spent in Nauvoo, Illinois. Lovise knew and loved Joseph and Hyrum Smith.

When Lovise was fourteen years old, in 1846, they crossed the Mississippi River, stopped in Sugar Creek for three months, and earned the means to go on.

While in Winter Quarters, Lovise had Canker, scurvy and blackleg, crippling her for many months. Her little brother died in Winter Quarters. Lovise left Winter Quarters on July 5, 1848, with her Aunt Jane and Uncle Franklin D. Richards. Her younger sister also came with them. Although they had trouble and grew weary from the work and travel, Lovise loved seeing the buffalo, deer, antelope and many other things that were a novelty to her. They arrived in the Salt Lake Valley on October 19, 1848.

They started their gardens early the next spring, covering everything as it came out of the ground even if they had to use their clothing. Because of this, they had a good early garden. They fixed meals for the emigrants on their way to the gold mines for fifty cents a meal.

One time when they didn't have enough flour, they shelled a bucket of peas and took them to the emigrant camp and traded it for a bucket and large scarf full of flour which lasted a long time.

Lovise's parents came to Utah in 1849, but her father left and went on to California, leaving her mother to raise the children. She married Franklin D. Richards who cared for them.

Lovise taught school in 1850 through 1851. She married Jared Curtis Roundy and they lived in Centerville, utah nearly five years then moved to Carson Valley.

Lovise's husband, Jared, married again to Elizabeth Snyder, but they only lived together a short time. Then he married an older lady but not much is said of this marriage. He then married Nellie (EllenDrake). She lived in the same house with Lovise and was very good to her.

They lived in Wanship until the sheriff from Logan came and arrested the two ladies for polygamy. Nellie went to jail. So as soon as possible, Nellie and Jared went to Arizona. This is where Jared passed away eleven years later.

Lovise was the Stake Primary President and the children helped cheer her up. She held this position for eighteen years. She also worked in the Relief Society.

When Lovise was eighty-three years old, she was making rugs, bedspreads, fancy handbags and many other things. She couldn't be idle.

Lovise passed away at the age of eighty-five in Logan, Cache County, Utah, at her daughter's place.

MERCY ANN DEUEL ROUNDY

BIRTHDATE: 30 Jul 1845
Montrose, Lee Co., Iowa
DEATH: 10 May 1889
Kanarra, Iron Co., Utah
PARENTS: William Henry Deuel
Eliza Avery Whiting
PIONEER: 2 Oct 1847
Charles C. Rich Handcart Comp.
SPOUSE: Myron S. Roundy
MARRIED: 3 Dec 1864
Salt Lake Endowment House
DEATH SP: 1 Feb 1902

CHILDREN:
Myron Shadrach, 25 Sep 1865
William Wesley, 23 Oct 1867
Louis Napoleon, 27 Sep 1869
Eliza Adaline, 16 Oct 1871
Susannah Minerva, 31 Dec 1873
Byron Alma, 5 Feb 1876
Mercy Linett, 12 Aug 1878
Mary Jane, 13 May 1881
Francis Priscilla, 30 May 1883

Mercy was an accomplished seamstress; taught dressmaking, tailoring, and knitting. She fashioned costumes for the home theatre groups in which she always took a leading part.

She and her husband were pioneers for the second time when they were called to help settle the Kanarra Valley in 1866. Having a beautiful voice she was a member of the ward choir at age eleven and was a member of the Tabernacle Choir when she lived in Salt Lake City, Utah.

She studied obstetrics under Dr, Jacobson from Denmark and served as a midwife. Held positions in the Relief Society.

PRISCILLA PARRISH ROUNDY

BIRTHDATE: 20 Mar 1833
Elizabethtown, Leeds, Canada
DEATH: 10 Aug 1914
Venice, Sevier Co., Utah
PARENTS: Samuel Parrish
Fanny Dack
PIONEER: 24 Sep 1847
Daniel Spencer Co. Wagon Train
SPOUSE: Lorenzo W. Roundy
MARRIED: 22 Apr 1857
DEATH SP: 24 May 1876

CHILDREN:
Fanny Jane,
Sarah,
Samuel H.,

Joel Jesse,
Annie Isadore,
David Alonzo,
Lydia Annis,
Heber Lorenzo,

At a young age, Priscilla migrated with her family from Canada to Illinois. Her father bought a Book of Mormon and soon the missionaries converted and baptized them as members of the Church of Jesus Christ of Latter-day Saints. After several moves, they settled in Nauvoo.

At age eleven, Priscilla heard the prophet preach his last sermon. She experienced much persecution until they moved from Nauvoo and traveled to Council Bluffs. Her family crossed the Plains in the Daniel Spencer Wagon Company. She drove the cows until her father's illness caused her to drive the wagon. They arrived on September 24, 1847. In the following year, she was one of the many pioneers who fought the crickets and witnessed the miracle of the seagulls.

On April 22, 1858, she became the third wife of Lorenzo Wesley Roundy. Later, they moved to Kannaraville to help settle the country.

Priscilla was widowed when her husband was drowned in the Colorado River. She was the mother of eight children. She spun her own yarn and made clothing, hats, and most of her children's shoes.

She was Primary President for seventeen years and Relief Society President for seventeen years. She gave compassionate service to those less fortunate than she. Never wagering in her faith, and perseverance to accept whatever was her lot. She did a lot of temple work for her family and others.

Priscilla passed away at the age of eighty-one at the home of her daughter in Venice, Utah.

SUSANNAH WALLACE ROUNDY

BIRTHDATE: 12 Dec 1820
Perth, Lanark, Ontario, Canada
DEATH: 4 Jul 1892
Escalante, Garfield, Utah
PARENTS: Francis Wallace
Sarah Alexander
PIONEER: Aug 1847
Second Co. Wagon Train
SPOUSE: Lorenzo W. Roundy
MARRIED: 16 May 1847
Along the trail to Utah
DEATH SP: 24 May 1876
Colorado River, Arizona

CHILDREN:
Wallace Wesley, 16 Mar 1848
Malinda Elizabeth, 15 Jul 1849
Napoleon Bonapart, 5 Feb 1851
Matilda Ann, 14 Oct 1852
Celestia Almeda, 30 Jul 1854
Mary Isabell, 3 Feb 1857
Betsy, 2 Mar 1859 (died at age 7 - 30 Jun 1866)
Lorenzo Wesley Jr. 20 May 1861

Susannah was the first born of ten children. Her father was born in Ulster, Ireland about 1784 and her mother was also born in Ulster, Ireland in 1798. They both died in San Antonio, Texas.

It is not told in Susannah's history when her parents came to Canada, or where they were married. Susannah learned to cook, sew and help with outside chores at a very young age.

The gospel message was brought to her family by President John Taylor when she was only fourteen years old. She received the Book of Mormon and had to steal away in the woods to read it. Her parents were very much opposed to the Gospel but she and her sister, Matilda who was twelve, were converted; baptized as members of the Church of Jesus Christ of Latter-day Saints. The two left their home together and journeyed to Nauvoo, Illinois to be with the Saints.

All they had to leave home with was a loaf of bread and a cake of cane sugar. From the age of fourteen to twenty-seven, Susannah made her own living. She was head cook in the Charter Oak Stove Factory for three years.

She knew the Prophet Joseph and Hyrum Smith well. She worked in the home of Hyrum when the Prophet Joseph Fielding Smith was born. Susannah went to the Nauvoo Temple on February 3, 1846 to receive her own endowment just before it closed.

In 1847, Susannah joined the Barnard family who was preparing to go west. They left Nauvoo early that year. They had to cross the Missoun River in the ice and snow mid-zero weather. They spent the next several months at Winter Quarters where more preparations were made for crossing the Plains. Susannah and her sister, Matilda, helped with the knitting and weaving.

Susannah met Lorenzo Wesley Roundy when he was lured as a teamster for the Barnard farruly. Lorenzo's wife and baby son had recently died leaving him with a two-year-old son. Susannah had prayed often that she could meet a man who shared her belief in the Gospel and Lorenzo seemed to be that man.

Later, in the Spring of 1847, after Brigham Young and the first company of 148 people left on their way, the Barnards and their helpers, Susannah, Matilda and Lorenzo, along with about 100 others, began the long trek across the Plains.

There were many trials and hardships as they traveled slowly on their long and tiring journey, with Susannah and Matilda walking all the way. Somewhere on their weary way, Matilda became suddenly ill and died and was buried by the side of the trail. Susannah felt very much alone now but soon became very close friends with Lorenzo and he proved to be a great strength to her.

Susannah and Lorenzo were married on May 16, 1847, just after they began their journey. Their company arrived in the Salt Lake Valley in August, 1847. Lorenzo's father, Shadrach, came out from the valley to meet them on the trail and brought them into the Valley.

Susannah proved to be a very courageous, faithful and strong woman having walked from upper Canada to Nauvoo and then from Nauvoo to the Salt Lake Valley.

They made their home in Salt Lake for about a year then moved to Centerville, Utah. They were close friends with Brigham Yotmg who called on Lorenzo to serve in various capacities of the Church.

At this time it was suggested that Lorenzo take a second wife. In 1857, Lorenzo married Priscilla Parrish. It was not easy for Susannah to share him with someone else but she finally gave her consent. Life in Utah did not prove to be without hardships and hard work for the family. They lived through Indian raids and wars, and fighting crickets and grasshoppers plagues and severe winers.

In the early 1860's, Brigham Young called Lorenzo, along with others, to go to southern Utah and settle the area. Lorenzo took his two wives and families and moved to Kanab. During the time they were there they suffered great losses and many hardships because of the savage Indians who were plundering, fighting and stealing.

They were then told to move to Kanarra in Iron County. Life was somewhat more calm. Lorenzo was ordained and set apart to be the first bishop of that area and held that position until his death. That gave Susannah added responsibilities taking care of guests, helping with tithing, a good deal of which was produce and the many other duties of a bishop's wife.

They eventually had a lovely home with beautiful furnishings. Susannah was a spotless housekeeper and was proud to have President Brigham Young as a guest on his way to and from his winter home in St. George. Often she was left alone as Lorenzo was called to investigate locations for new settlements. His last trip was to Arizona which required them to cross the Colorado River at Lee's Ferry in the early spring when the water was turbulent and treacherous. Their boat capsized but all were saved except Lorenzo.

The news was a dreadful shock to Susannah and difficult for her to accept. She sold her home and moved to Widtsoe, Utah to be near one of her sons. She later moved to Escalante where she passed away at the age of seventy-two and is buried there.

ELIZABETH FLAKE ROWAN (ROWAN)

BIRTHDATE: 1834
Anson, Richmond, No. Carolina
DEATH: Date unknown
San Bernardino, California
PARENTS:
PIONEER: Oct 1848
SPOUSE: Charles H. Rowan
MARRIED: 15 Jul 1867
San Bernardino, California
DEATH SP: Unknown

No
Photo
Available

CHILDREN:
Byron Thomas, 26 Feb 1869
Alice Ann, 28 Mar 1870
Son, unknown

Elizabeth "Liz" was born in North Carolina, 1834. She was raised on the plantation of William Love of North Carolina.

When Agnes Love married James Madison Flake, her father, gave Liz to her as her personal maid. Liz at the time was five years of age. When the Flakes joined the Church of Jesus Christ of Latter-day Saints and journeyed to Nauvoo, Illinois in 1844, Liz accompanied them.

During the winter of 1846-1847 the family lived in a dugout in Winter Quarters, waiting to start the long journey across the Plains. Liz and the three mall sons of Mrs. Flake walked and drove the cattle all the way to Utah. They reached the Salt Lake Valley in October, 1848.

After the death of James M. Flake in 1850, Apostle Lyman outfitted a company to go to southern California to make a settlement. Many of Agnes' friends from Mississippi going with Agnes, her two sons and the ever-faithful Liz, were very helpful during the long, hot journey across the desert. Agnes drove the mules and carriage and Liz drove two yoke of oxen. When they arrived at the San Bernardino Rancho, Liz helped the two boys make adobes for the first house built by Mormons in the San Bernardino Valley in 1851.

Agnes became very ill, and one night as she grew weaker she called Liz to awaken the children. While the mother gave them wise council on how to live good lives, Liz went to bring two neighbor men. When she returned Agnes was dead. Liz could not control her grief and she cried in anguish. The men couldn't quiet her, then finally one of the men said, "You should be glad your mistress is gone, now she can't whip you anymore," Liz jumped to her feet and took the man by the shoulders and pushed him out of the door, anger still flashing from her eyes. "You can't talk like that about my mistress when she isn't able to defend herself. She was the best woman that lived; she was not mean to me; she never hit me; I love her better than anyone in the world. You can't stay in this house."

Liz kept the house and took care of the children until the Fall of 1855, when she and the boys went to live with the Amasa Lyman family. When Agnes' son William was leaving to go back to Utah, Liz told him to marry and she would come and serve him and his family the rest of her life. William told her she was to have her freedom and that she sould marry and raise a family of her own. She still didn't want her freedom, but William left, placing her in the care of an older African American who had crossed the Plains with them.

Liz married a man by the name of Charles H. Rowan, a free man who crossed the Plains to Utah, then drove a team from Utah to San Bernardino. He owned and operated a barber shop in the Grand Southern Hotel for over forty years. After their marriage they purchased a lot in the business section of town upon which was located some of the leading stores and shops. They made their home on the second floor of the building.

Liz and her husband became the parents of three children, two sons and one daughter who was named Alice. Alice became a schoolteacher and taught the white children at Riverside for three years. It had been said that this was the first time in the United States where an African-American girl taught in a white school.

When William Flake, son of her beloved Agnes married , December 30, 1858, in Cedar City, Utah. Liz sent him a valuable set of silverware, many pieces of which are owned and treasured by William's descendants.

Liz and her husband passed away in San Bernardino, California.

JANE ANN MARTIN ROWAN

No
Photo
Available

BIRTHDATE: 31 Jan 1827
Eatington, England
DEATH: 8 Jan 1862
So. Cottonwood, Salt Lake, Utah
PARENTS: Barnabus Martin
Sarah Bailey
PIONEER: Oct 1855
Wagon Train Company
SPOUSE: Matthew Rowan
MARREID: 6 Jun 1853
Worchester, Worchester, England
DEATH SP: 8 Jan 1866
So. Cottonwood, Salt Lake, Utah

CHILDREN:
Ammon, 21 Apr 1854 (died at age 17 - 12 Oct 1871)
Emma (McGhie), 15 Mar 1856
Matthew Martin, 28 Aug 1859

Jane was born in Eatington, Warwickshire, England in 1827. In March of 1853, Jane Martin was residing at the Wells, near Malvern, Worcestershire, working for Mrs. Coltsworth. Jane was a member of the Church of Jesus Christ of Latter-day Saints; the Leamington Branch.

In May of 1853, Jane met Matthew while he was on a mission for the Church. They were married on June 6, 1853. They were first married by Reverend Palmer Parson of the Watermans Church of Worchester, England. Later after a good dinner, the couple was married by Orson Pratt in their room. Their first child, Ammon, was born on April 21, 1854. Matthew Rowan was released from the Presidency of the Sheffield Conference in 1854, and at that time he had permission to emigrate. They left for Zion the next spring.

Jane Ann, Matthew and little Ammon sailed for America from Liverpool on April 20, 1855 on the ship "Samuel Curling" arriving in New York, then on to St. Louis, they arrived in the Salt Lake Valley the latter part of October in 1855. They rented a log cabin in Salt Lake City and a while later they moved to a farm in South Cottonwood.

In 1862, a sudden illness overtook Jane Martin and she passed away within 24 hours at the age of thirty-four years and eleven months.

ELIZABETH ANGELIQUE RICHARDS ROWE

No
Photo
Available

BIRTHDATE: 22 Jul 1835
Toronto, Ontario, Canada
DEATH: 2 Jan. 1927
Blackfoot, Bingham Co., Idaho
PARENTS: John K. Richards
Agnes Hill
PIONEER: Oct 1851
Capt. Wadsworth
SPOUSE: Manning Rowe
MARRIED 27 Jul 1854
DEATH SP: 23 Feb 1904
Mendon, Cache Co., Utah

CHILDREN:
Mary Ellen, 28 May 1855
David Manning, 30 Apr 1858
William Albert, 8 Dec 1860 (died at age 4)
John Franklin, 11 Jun 1863 died at age 2)
Hannah Agnes, 4 Oct 1868
Elizabeth Rachel, Jan 1871
Margaret Ruth, 30 Jul 1875

Elizabeth Angelique was born in Canada in 1835. She was five years old when her parents joined the Church of Jesus Christ of Latter-day Saints and a year later, 1841, they started for Nauvoo, Illinois. At Detroit she saw for the first time, the railroad. Wooden rails were laid ready to be cobbered with iron.

Arriving in Nauvoo in the early spring, they built a home on Young Street and Elizabeth was baptized by the Prophet's brother, William Smith. The Mobocrats, fearing the growing influence and power of the fastest growing city in Illinois, began their harassment that escalated into persecution and murder. The little children were horribly affected by the whippings and floggings,

Elizabeth and her father, riding horses home from the fields, saw the mobs as they were taking the Prophet Joseph and his brother, Hyrum, to the Carthage Jail. The unruly mob of men so frightened her she could not return home alone so her father, wanting to go with the Prophet, had first to take his little girl home to safety before he could go to the Prophet in jail.

After being driven from Nauvoo and spending a year in Winter Quarters, the Richards crossed the Missouri River to Honey Creek, named for the abundance of honey found there, built a temporary home and Elizabeth went to school; the extent of her formal education with a little exception.

In the Spring of 1851, the Richards had gathered enough supplies to see them through the long journey and sixteen year old Elizabeth, traveling with her uncle William Swapp in the group of fifty led by Captain Wadsworth, left Honey Creek for Zion, her parents would follow a month later.

The river was so high some of the wagons lost both supplies and teams trying to cross and they had to travel 300 miles out of their way to find a crossing. While en route one of the drivers broke his leg and sixteen year old Elizabeth had to replace him. She managed the clumsy oxen over the rough plains and the company reached the Salt Lake Valley in October, 1851. The Richards made their home in Salt Lake City.

Three years after their arrival into the Valley, Elizabeth had met and was married to Manning Rowe. The couple moved to Santaquin and lived there for two years.

Manning was called to guard Echo Canyon Pass when the threat of Johnston's Army loomed. He left before the crops were in and Elizabeth, with a babe in arms, harvested the crops by her self, having help only in hauling them to the house.

The following spring they traded land that the Walker building stands on today and moved to Mendon, Cache Valley arriving on April 10, 1860, living in the wagon box until space could be cleared and a home built. Slowly they acquired a few sheep and chickens and settled down to farming, making the wearisome journey to Salt Lake to sell their produce.

Elizabeth was of a retiring nature, a good house wife and mother. Her greatest grief came when her two sons, William and John were scalded by boiling molasses and died with in three days of each other.

Elizabeth cared for her sick husband many years and lived a widow's life for twenty-three years.

HANNAH MANNING ROWE

No Photo Available

BIRTHDATE: 3 Jul 1787
New Jersey, New York
DEATH: 15 May 1852
Salt Lake City, Salt Lake, Utah
PARENTS: Enoch Manning
Margaret Thorn
PIONEER: 19 Oct 1848
Willard Richards Wagon Train
SPOUSE: David Rowe
MARRIED: abt 1820
DEATH SP: 20 May 1855
Salt Lake City, Salt Lake, Utah

CHILDREN:
Mary Ann, 1821 (died as an infant)
Margaret, 6 Dec 1823
William, 20 Feb 1826
Ruth, 27 Mar 1828
Manning, 17 Jul 1830

Hannah spent her early life in New Jersey. Her family was well-to-do, so Hannah had many advantages. Hannah fell in love with David Rowe, who was not in the socials circles of society. When they were married, she did not receive her father's blessing nor her inheritance.

David and Hannah moved to Indiana where they purchased land. She was the mother of five children. She sat knitting by firelight making sure the children understood what their school master was teaching. She and her family were staunch Baptists.

When her son, William, was eighteen years old, he brought two missionaries from the Church of Jesus Christ of Latter-day Saints to their home. Only William accepted the gospel and was baptized. He moved to Nauvoo, Illinois. It was his desire to convert his parents. He promised to care for his parents as long as they lived. They sold their home and arrangements were made to move to Zion with the Willard Richards Wagon Company.

They located in Salt Lake City and fared well with the motherly care of Hannah. Though Hannah brought Baptist literature with her across the Plains, it was not long before she and the rest of the family who were not members of the Church became candidates for baptism into the Church.

On May 15, 1852, Hannah passed away. She died happy in the fulfillment of her desire that the "family circle" should not be broken again. The gospel had made that very clear to her.

ANN TAYLOR ROWLEY

BIRTHDATE: 24 Apr 1846
Arnolld, Nottingham, England
DEATH: 14 Jan 1901
Huntington, Emery Co., Utah
PARENTS: George Taylor
Mary Franks Smith
PIONEER: 25 Sep 1863
Peter Nebeker Co.Wagon Train
SPOUSE: Samuel Rowley
MARRIED: 23 Apr 1865
Parowan, Iron Co., Utah
DEATH SP: 8 Jan 1928
Huntington, Emery Co, Utah

CHILDREN:
Mary Ann, 6 Mar 1866
Samuel James, 12 Jan 1868
Hannah Eliza, 20 Jan 1870
Sarah Jane, 15 Jul 1872
Alice Loura, 11 Oct 1874
George Walter, 25 Jan 1877
John Taylor, 1 Sep 1879

Ann was born in England in 1846. In 1861, they arrived in Nauvoo another year to get enough money to bring the rest of the family over. They were all reunited for Christmas of 1862.

The family all worked for another eight months to earn enough money for wagons and supplies. In the Fall, 1863, they left New York by rail to Fort Laramie, Wyoming. They then came on to Salt Lake in the Peter Nebeker Wagon Company arriving in October, 1863.

Ann's parents and four of her family went to Summit, Iron County, Utah. After eight months they moved to Parawan. Ann went to work at the Muliner farm making butter, cheese, and caring for the family. Because of her sweet disposition and friendly personality she was loved and respected by all.

Ann married Samuel Rowley on April 23, 1865 in Parowan, Iron County, Utah.

Ann didn't receive an education when she was younger so after she had five children she went to school in the afternoon to learn to read and write. About 1877, Ann's father came to live the rest of his years with them.

On October 23, 1879, Ann, Samuel and family including a six week old baby, headed for the Escalante desert. The trip took six months and was one to the coldest winters in that area.

After six months of road building and hardships and suffering they reached San Juan on the evening of April 6, 1880. This turned out to be the first trip through Hole in the Rock.

The Indians stole the best horses and Samuel had to pay twenty-five dollars to get them back. During the winter of 1882, two year old John died of the measles. In June, 1884, they started back to Huntington but the Colorado River was too high to cross. So they moved to Mancus, Colorado. When the water was low enough they returned to Huntington.

Samuel purchased a homestead on Rowley flats, they planted fruit and shade trees.

Their younger son, Richard Edwin, was born on August 22, 1889. He passed away when he was seven years old. Ann passed away four years later on January 14, 1901 at the age of fifty-five.

Ann taught her family the value of work,and love. They knew she was always available when they needed her. Ann was a devoted Relief Society worker.

EMMA JAMES JOHNSON ROWLEY

BIRTHDATE: 8 Jun 1840
Pinvin Worchester, England
DEATH: 27 Mar 1926
Nephi , Juab Co., Utah
PARENTS: William James
Jane Haynes
PIONEER: 9 Nov 1856
James Willie Handcart Company
SPOUSE: Lorenzo Johnson
MARRIED: 1 Mar 1857
St. George Temple, Utah
DEATH SP: Not given

CHILDREN:
Emma Ozella, 17 Oct 1858
James Parley, 2 Sep 1860
Orissa Jane, 13 Jul 1862
Martha Sylvania, 3 Aug 1864
Maryann Viola, 17 Aug 1866
Sarah Maria, 20 Aug 1868
George Aaron, 2 May 1871/1872

SPOUSE II: John Rowley
MARRIED: 21 Apr 1873
DEATH SP: 7 Oct 1893
Pacheco, Mexico

CHILDREN:
Fanny Rozella, 13 Jun 1874
Lilly Malinda, 14 Apr 1876

When Emma was sixteen years old she left England with her family to join the Saints in Zion. At Iowa they joined the James G. Willie Handcart Company and enjoyed the first 200 miles of the trip. Then trouble with Indians, early snows, cold , and the lack of food caused extreme hardships.

Having worn out her shoes and going barefoot, Emma was given some hide from a dead oxen to wrap around her feet. When that also wore out, she kept the worn out pieces and would toast them over the fire to eat.

She continued having hard times while she raised her nine children. She crocheted, knitted, and did all kinds of beautiful handwork. She was talented in making beautiful paper flowers, especially roses. She took pride in her appearance and how she dressed. She always wore a bit of white lace at the neck of her dress and made sure her hat was placed just right.

Her faith and testimony remained strong to her death. She was heard saying that she would rather die than give up her testimony of the truthfulness of the restored Gospel of Jesus Christ.

GEORGINA ANN MARIAH BARNETT ROYLANCE

BIRTHDATE: 6 Jun 1854
Steeple Ashton, England
DEATH: 14 Oct 1931
North Ogden, Weber Co., Utah
PARENTS: George Barnett
Mary Ann Mathew
PIONEER: 2 Nov 1864
Warren Snow Co. Wagon Train
SPOUSE: James Roylance
MARRIED: 9 Oct 1871
Salt Lake Endowment House
DEATH SP: 2 Feb 1930
North Ogden, Weber Co., Utah

CHILDREN:
Mary Ann (Blodgett), 3 Sep 1873
James H., 17 Jan 1875
George W., 14 Nov 1876
William, 20 Jan 1878
Alma, 14 Feb 1880
Maria May (Garner), 1 Apr 1882
John, 15 Mar 1884
Racheal (Brown), 5 May1886
Rosena Virtue, 5 Jul 1888
Heber Thomas, 10 Mar 1891
Sarah Serena (Harrop), 27 Apr 1893

Georgina was born in England in 1854. When she was ten years old she left England with her father, mother, two sisters, her brother, and grandmother. Her baby sister died while they were on the ocean.

They crossed the Plains with the Warren Snow wagon train. On October 14, 1864 at Blade Butte her mother died, after they burried her they put enough sage brush to burn for four days on her grave, then lit it as they left, to keep the Coyotes away.

Her grandmother died ten days later at the Big Muddy. They arrived in the Salt Lake Valley on November 2, 1864.

Her father bought a place in Pleasant View. They were among the first settlers of Weber County. She was the oldest girl and became the housekeeper. Although only ten years old, she did the sewing and cooked the meals over an open fire. She didn't like to make bread, so she would coax her father into doing it for her.

One day her father went to the canyon to get wood and didn't get back at dark. She heard a noise outside thinking it was her father she ran to the window and just as she put her face to the window a man put his to the window on the outside. She was terribly terrified, but soon found it was a neighbor who stayed with them until her father returned.

When she was seventeen years old she married James Roylance and went to his mother's house to live. Later they built a large brick house where they lived the rest of their lives. They were the parents of thirteen children.

After John was born Georgina was very ill. The malady settled in her legs and feet. In order to save her life her husband amputated her foot because the doctor would not do it because he said "she would die any way." She was ill for another year then she would put her knee in the rocking chair and go about her work. It was about fifteen years before she could get an artifical foot.

About seven years before his death her husband lost his eyesight, Georgina faithfuly took care of him, even though she was almost seventy.

Georgina passed away a year and nine months after her husband on October 14, 1931 at the age of seventy-seven.

ISABELLA ROBERTS NEWBY ROYLANCE

BIRTHDATE: 3 Jan, 1844
Thornley, Durham, England,
DEATH: 31 Dec 1896
Nortb Ogden, Weber Co., Utah
PARENTS: John Newby
Isabella Smurthwaite
PIONEER: 29 Sep 1866
Thompson Company
SPOUSE: Hyrum Roylance
MARRIED: 4 May 1867
DEATH SP: 8 Aug 1914 North
Ogden, Weber Co., Utah

CHILDREN:
John Newby, 9 Jan 1868
Hyrum, 15 Nov, 1869
Rebecca, 8 Apr 1871
Elizabeth Ann, 6 Apr 1873
William Thomas, 14 Sep 1875
George Newby, 28 Jul 1878
Mary Yarwood, 5 Aug 1880
Josephine, 29 Jan 1883 (twin)
Joseph, 29 Jan 1883 (twin)
Rachel, 26 Oct 1885

Isabella, often helped her father in his shop, he was a tailor by trade. Missionaries from the Church of Jesus Christ of Latter-day Saints came to their village and preached the gospel, Isabella was baptized in 1859. Her family were active in the Church, and often entertained the missionaries in their home. Isabella's mother died in 1863 and her father died in 1865, leaving a large family.

About a year after the father's death, the four Newby sisters, Margaret, Mary Ann, Isabella, and Elizabeth migrated to the United States.

While in St Louis the girls realized that the fine silks and satins they brought with them from England were inadequate for wearing as they crossed the Plains. These fine, expensive clothes were exchanged at a sacrifice for heavier more coarse clothing suitable for their journey and for wearing in Utah. The Newby sisters, along with some of the other children gathered wood, and buffalo chips and such for fires.

The sisters arrived in North Ogden, where they made their homes. Isabella met and married Hyrum Roylance eight months after arriving in the Salt lake Valley. Isabella and her husband homesteaded a thirteen acre farm west of the North Ogden Cemetery, They raised purebred Hamiltonians and Percheron horses, Durham cattle and twenty choice milk cows. These were hand milked. They had a fruit orchard and berries.

Isabella was a very thrifty helper, always doing things that brought in money. A milk house was built over a cool spring near the house. Here milk would be set in pans, the cream would be skimed off, churned, molded into pounds of butter, and sold or delivered to customers, Isabella supplied the Brown Hotel in Ogden and the Hot Springs Resort. She also raised flocks of all kind of fowl; chickens, turkeys, geese, ducks, guinea hens, which she also provided for her customers.

The family had a two-story, rock and brick barn, that became famous for its barn dances. The peacocks were a novelty that attracted many visitors and passersby, greeting them with a screeching cry, warning the family there was company coming. The environment of lovely fields, gardens, berries, young orchards, and clear spring water contributed to the health and well being of the children and conducive to forming characters of honor, honesty, industry and integrity.

Isabella became ill in December, 1895, of what was called inflammation of the bowels; now it would be called appendicitis. The doctor operated on her at home on the dining room table, and she passed away on December 31, 1895. Isabella and her husband shared their means with neighbors in need, often leaving a side of beef and never telling them where it came from.

Isabella and her husband also contributed to the Perpetual Emigration Fund, which brought other Saints to the Valley. Excerpt from a letter Isabella and her sister wrote to their family in England, North Ogden, Utah

Territory, U.S. America

March 29, 1869

Dear Uncle and Aunt:

Times are good and lively here now. Two railroads being built through the territory, money and work plentiful, and goods cheap. The railroad track has been laid to this valley, and we can see the iron horse puffing daily as it passes by.

Accept the kind love of your affectionate nieces,

Isabella Rylands and Mary Ann Chadwick

LUCY CLUCAS ROYLANCE

BIRTHDATE: 19 Oct 1845
Shelton, Staffordshire, England
DEATH: 30 May 1903
Springville, Utah Co., Utah
PARENTS: Henry Clucas
Elizabeth Martin
PIONEER: 1855
Milo Andrus Co. Wagon Train
SPOUSE: William Roylance
MARRIED: 27 Mar 1864
DEATH SP: 3 Apr 1903
Springville, Utah Co., Utah

CHILDREN:
William Martin, 31 Mar 1865
John Henry, 8 Nov 1867
Lucy Elizabeth, 24 Jan 1872
Heber, 23 Jul 1873
Archie Walton, 13 Oct 1875
Nephi, 25 Dec 1880
Thomas Spranger, 20 Nov 1881
Nellie Mae, 16 Sep 1883
Frank Emmett, 20 Oct 1885
Lillie, 12 Dec 1890

Lucy's parents joined the Church of Jesus Christ of Latter-day Saints in 1840, at the time John Taylor was a missionary in the British Mission. She and her family sailed from Liverpool, England on April 22, 1855 on the ship "Samuel Curling." They arrived in New York harbor Tuesday, May 22, 1855.

They continued their travels on May 24, going by steamboat to Philadelphia. They left Philadelphia by train Friday, May 25, 1855 about noon and arrived in Pittsburg Sunday morning May 27, 1855. They continued their journey to St. Louis, Missouri thence to Atchinson, Kansas.

Lucy, with her parents, her brother and sister crossed the Plains to Utah in the Milo Andrus Wagon Company. She walked nearly the entire distance. On arriving President Brigham Young asked where they wanted to locate. Bishop Aaron Johnson was there and asked that they go to Springville. Lucy, ten years old, was left in Salt Lake City to stay with the Heber C. Kimball family until the family could get situated in Springville. Later Lucy's father, Henry, walked all the way to Salt Lake City to get her and bring her to Springville.

Lucy was a nurse-maid at Bishop Johnson's home for a long time. She became a fine practical nurse and was a help to many people as she carried out this much needed service.

Lucy married William Roylance on March 27, 1864. They lived in Springville and worked hard. She gleaned wheat and would thresh it out by hand by various methods to make their bran wheat bread. She raised various kinds of fruits and berries and a fine truck gardens much of which was sold to help the family finances.

One time, when the Indians were hostile, she heard a noise at her back door. As she opened the door an Indian attacked her with a knife. Only a neighbors quick response to her screams saved her life. The neighbor was a Mr. Harmon.

Lucy crossed a fence, which separated their backyard from the old Springville Cemetery to prepare the family plot for Decoration Day. This caused a hernia to strangulate which led to her death the day before Decoration Day at age fifty-seven.

MARTHA JANET / JENNET SMITH ROYLANCE

BIRTHDATE: 12 Aug 1837
Liberty, McKean, Pennsylvania
DEATH: 9/10 Apr 1890
Springville, Utah Co., Utah
PARENTS: Aaron Smith
Permelia Sweet
PIONEER: 29 Aug 1859
James S. Brown Wagon Train
SPOUSE: William J. Roylance
MARRIED: 1 Oct 1860
DEATH SP: 29 Jun 1895
Salem, Idaho

CHILDREN:
Aaron Willance, 9 Aug 1861
William George, 17 May 1863
Alma Thomas, 1 Mar 1865
Mary Jennet, 28 February 1867
Heber C. 30 March 1869
Harvey, 16 November 1871

We are unsure of the spelling of her middle name, (her daughter Mary Jennet claims it spelled the same as her name).

Martha was a school teacher and a milliner. The family credit her for their phenomenal musical inclinations, love of education and of the finer things of life. The family was a musical one, Alma played the guitar, Aaron played the violin, and became a wonderful music instructor. Martha played the organ, while the family sang together. Martha Jennet sang in many public preformances.

Martha and Willam J. Roylance, were divorced on September 26, 1872. After the divorce Martha went back to teaching school and millinery work taking back her maiden name.

Martha received a letter from her father in 1882 urgently pleading that it was "her important duty to leave the Mormon Church and get her children from under its base influence, for it is based on the Book of Mormon and not on the Bible." (Her father Aaron Smith was a minister in both the Baptist and the Universalist denominations). Martha would not and could not deny the truthfulness of the gospel. She passed away alone in April of 1890 in Springville, Utah County, Utah.

MARY ANN OAKES ROYLANCE

BIRTHDATE: 22 Jun 1810
Congleton, Cheshire, England
DEATH: 3 Jan 1892
Springville, Utah Co., Utah
PARENTS: Randall Oakes
Mary Lucas / Clucas
PIONEER 17 Sep 1850
Warren Foote Co. Wagon Train
SPOUSE: John Roylance
MARRIED: 1830
Great Peover, Cheshire, England
DEATH SP: 23 Sep 1887
Springville, Utah Co., Utah

CHILDREN:
Henry, 21 May 1831
Ann, 8 Oct 1833
George, 8 Feb 1836
Thomas, 17 Jan 1838
William, 1 Apr 1840
Elizabeth, 26 Aug 1842
Alma, 29 May 1845
Mary Frances, 8 Aug 1849
Sarah Jane, 19 Feb 1851
Olive, 25 Nov 1854

When Mary Ann was a youth, she learned to make cheese and butter in Cheshire which area is famous for its dairy products.

She married John Roylance in 1830 and they had four children by the time they joined the Church of Jesus Christ of Latter-day Saints.

They sailed from Liverpool on the ship, "Sheffield," and arrived in New Orleans on March 31, 1841. They went to Nauvoo and then moved on to Iowa to farm. They moved with the Saints in 1846 to Winter Quarters.

Her husband was called to join the Mormon Battalion. She was left with sick children and no tent. Bishop Joseph Lee Robinson had a log cabin built for her family with donated tithing labor from other Saints.

Mary came to the Salt Lake Valley with the Warren Foote Wagon Company. They moved to Springville to settle. Their family consisted of ten children. She also raised a boy, Alfred Gales, from age thirteen when his mother died.

Her home was her castle and she was an immaculate housekeeper. She whitewashed her cellar every year to store cheeses, butter, and poultry. She sold the dairy products two or three times a year in Salt Lake City in exchange for commodities they couldn't buy in Springville. She loved flowers and her vegetable garden was a joy to her family as well as the less fortunate.

Mary Ann served as second counselor in the first Relief Society Presidency in Springville which was organized September 12, 1868. She was also a visiting teacher. She was a faithful reader of the scriptures and could converse well on all principles of the gospel.

MARY YARWOOD HILL ROYLANCE

BIRTHDATE: 25 Mar 1807
Lower Peover, Cheshire, England
DEATH: 30 Mar 1892
North Ogden, Weber Co., Utah
PARENTS: Samuel Yarwood
Esther Culcheth
PIONEER: 24 Sep 1853
Claudius Spencer Wagon Train
SPOUSE I: James Hill
MARRIED: 5 Apr 1836
Manchester, Lancashire, England
DEATH SP: 21 Feb 1841
Birkenhead, England

CHILD:
William John, 16 Jan 1838
John Kinder, born 1840 (died shortly after birth)

SPOUSE II: William J. Roylance
MARRIED: 1842 Montroset Iowa
DEATH SP: 29 Jun 1895 Salem, Idaho

CHILDREN:
Hyrum, 4 Jul 1844
Rachel, 16 May 1848
James, 30 Nov 1849

Mary joined the Church of Jesus Christ of Latter-day Saints in 1841, while living in England, and entertained the Elders among whom were Brigham Young and Heber C, Kimball.

Six weeks after the death of her husband James Hill, Mary and her brother, Samuel and his family joined a group of Saints and sailed from Liverpool, England. It took three weeks to cross the atlantic ocean. On May 16, 1841 they arrived in New Orleans.

She met William Roylance in the group of Saints crossing the ocean. Mary witnessed the persecutions of the prophet Joseph Smith and his brother Hyrum at the hands of the mobs.

Mary and her family stayed in Nauvoo until the last days of the Mormon presence there. She remembers the mobs appearing September 10, 1846, and along with others were driven from their home. They eventually settled in Burlington Iowa, across the Mississippi river, thirty miles north of Nauvoo.

In May of 1853, the family started West arriving in the Salt Lake Valley, the 24th of September. Shortly after their arrival, the family moved to North Ogden. Mary and her family lived in a wagon until they could build a one-room log house. Their food consisted of mostly corn meal.

They were in North Ogden during the hard winter of 1856, the year the grasshoppers destroyed the crops. Mary and her family dug for sego roots and went to the hills for food for their cattle. Everyone suffered from the lack of food and many of the cattle died. On July 24, 1857, word came that an army under the command of General Johnston was on its way to exterminate the Mormons, and so again Mary and her family moved; this time south to Springville, After the army left, they returned to their home in North Ogden.

The family purchased a cow some sheep and chickens. They raised grain, alfalfa, and a garden. Their stack of hay began to disappear at night, so Mary, with the help of her children, carried all the hay in the stack, in her apron and put it in a small cellar they owned. This took them all afternoon working fast and hard but they had enough hay to keep their cow through the winter, and enjoyed milk and butter.

Mary was awarded a decree of divorce on September 17, 1864 from William J. Roylance, who had taken a second wife, Martha Jennet Smith, in 1860. Mary had received a handsome bonnet at the Relief Society Jubilee, March 17, 1892, for being the oldest member of the Relief Society in North Ogden, she was eighty-five years old.

She passed away on March 30, 1892 of old age. Mary was a hard working industrious woman. She was tall with blonde hair and blue eyes; and enjoyed mingling with people,and having a good time. Mary had a better than average education and taught her children and some of the grandchildren to read and write.

The story is related that the night before she passed away, she raised up in her bed and stretched out her hands as if reaching for someone. She described a person in white standing at the foot of her bed. The description was that of her father, Samuel Yarwood, who had come for her. She passed away the next morning.

MARTHA TIMOTHY GARDNER RUDY

BIRTHDATE: 13 Aug 1862
Platte River, Nebraska
DEATH: 23 Dec 1948
Orem, Utah Co., Utah
PARENTS: John G. Timothy
Martha Davis
PIONEER: Oct 1862
Capt. Jones Co. Wagon Train
SPOUSE I: Charles A. Gardner
MARRIED: 5 Dec 1878
Salt Lake City, Salt Lake, Utah
DEATH SP: Feb 1890

CHILDREN:
John Alma, 21 Dec 1880
Martha LaPrele (Hoeft), 5 May 1882
Mary Alice (Bingham), 2 Nov 1883
Rhoda, 11 Aug 1885
Mabel (Prysbyla), 12 Sep 1886
Janette (Hess), 5 May 1888
Cora Belle, 30 Nov 1889

SPOUSE II: Josiah Philip Rudy
MARRIED: 26 May 1891
Vernal, Uintah Co., Utah
DEATH SP: 19 Feb 1955
Springville, Utah Co., Utah

CHILDREN:
Cornelia (Wells Yuditsky), 21 Apr 1892
Josiah Lloyd, 27 Apr 1894
Czar Felix, 10 Mar 1896
Gala (Caldwell), 21 Apr 1897
Philip Owen, 26 Mar 1899
Olive (Long), 14 Dec 1900
Thelma (Young), 21 Sep 1902 (twin)
Delma (Long), 21 Sep 1902 (twin)
LaRue (Wardle), 2 Apr 1904
Wanda, 17 Jul 1906

Martha was born in a covered wagon along the Platte River in 1862. She was the oldest in the family. This left her the responsibility of helping with the rest of the family, especially when her mother was bed ridden for several years.

Her family first lived in Lehi, then moved to Provo Valley in the vicinity of Heber City. The city had just been laid out so her father got two lots and built their first home. Sometime later this house was traded for a yoke of oxen. In April, 1867, they moved to Round Valley. Her father didn't believe girls needed an education so she didn't get any.

On December 5, 1878, when she was sixteen years old, Matha married Charles Alma Gardner. Brother John's wife was bedfast at this time so they lived with them to help her. They had a one-room house with two beds, four chairs and one table. In May they went to the saw mill in Provo to haul logs for the summer, in November, they returned to Round Valley. The next summer they did the same thing. They bought a sixty acre farm where they lived for the next four years.

In July, 1886, Martha's mother came to visit and persuaded them to move to Ashley Valley.

In February, 1890, Alma went to the mountains to work in the mine. He passed away of heart failure fifteen days later, leaving Martha with seven children to care for. In December, 1890, the school teacher came to live at their house, helping with board money.

On May 26, 1891, Martha married the school teacher, Josiah Philips Rudy. They were the parents of ten children.

Her daughter, Gala, died in 1932. leaving six children motherless. Martha was the mother of seventeen children, and spent her life raising them and working along side her husband.

ABIGAIL GRAY RUMEL

BIRTHDATE: 19 Nov 1826
Salem, Massachusetts
DEATH: 19 Nov 1904
Salt Lake City, Salt Lake, Utah
PARENTS: John Gray
Abigail Caldwell
PIONEER: 1849
Reddeck N. Allred Wagon Train
SPOUSE: John H. Rumel
MARRIED: 11 Jul 1847
St. Louis, Missouri
DEATH SP: 19 May 1894

CHILDREN:
Mary Abba (Holman), 2 Oct 1848
John Henry, 26 Feb 1851
Ellen Cecilia (Wardrop), 25 Mar 1854
William, 1 Apr 1857
Orson, 27 Jul 1859
Frank, 7 Nov 1861
Alice (Margetts), 10 Dec 1864
Annie (Finlay), 29 Jul 1867

Abigail was born in Massachusetts in 1826. When she was older she moved to Nauvoo, Illinois. When she was twenty-one, she married John H. Rumel in St. Louis, Missouri on July 11, 1847.

They moved to Winter Quarters with their daughter, Abba in the Spring of 1849, then on to the Salt Lake Valley the same year, arriving about the middle of October. 1849.

In 1879, Abigail started a millinery shop, which she ran as a successful business for fifteen years. She had learned the trade from her mother, who learned it from her mother in France. Although she never used banks, she was a prosperous woman and always paid her bills. Her long life of good deeds made her one of the most loved women of the state. She was always commanding the respect and confidence of all who did buisness with her.

Within three years time she lost her husband and two children, her daughter, Ellen, passed away on December 24, 1891, son, John Jr., on February 5, 1892 and her husband, John, on May 12, 1894.

Abigail passed away on November 19, 1904 in Salt Lake City at the age of seventy-eight.

HENRIETTA EATON BLYTH BUTLER POWELL RUSSELL

BIRTHDATE: 6 Jun 1831
Newton Par or Dalkeith, Scotland
DEATH: 12 Aug 1924
Fillmore, Millard Co., Utah
PARENTS: Charles Blythe
Isabella Brown
PIONEER: 1 Oct 1856
John Banks Handcart Company
SPOUSE I: John Low Butler
MARRIED: 5 Sep 1857
Salt Lake City, Salt Lake, Utah
DEATH SP: 10 Apr 1861
Spanish Fork, Utah Co., Utah

CHILDREN:
Isabella Elizabeth, 11 Jun 1858
John William, 11 Aug 1861

SPOUSE II: John Powell
MARRIED: 18 Jun 1864
Salt Lake City, Salt Lake Co., Utah
DEATH SP: 3 Jun 1902
Fillmore, Millard Co., Utah

CHILDREN:
Sarah, 13 Apr 1865
Annie, 8 Sep1866
Henrietta, 11 Aug 1868
Lilly, 30 Mar 1870
Alma, 13 Jan 1872
May, 7 Mayl 873
Ellen, 1 Apr 1875

SPOUSE III: Allen Russell
MARRIED: 24 Oct 1906
Manti, Sanpete Co., Utah
DEATH SP: 11 Jul 1919
Fillmore, Millard Co., Utah
CHILDREN: None

Henrietta was born in Scotland in 1831. She was the fourth of nine children. She saved her money for passage on the ship "Emarld Green," for America in 1855, arriving in St Louis, Misouri. Henrietta heard that the Banks Company was taking handcarts as well as wagons. She got her handcart to carry her personal belongings and joined them arriving in the Salt Lake Valley on October 1, 1856.

Henrietta was sent to live with Bishop E. Hunter, and did house work for her board and room and some spending money. Two years later she married Bishop John Low Butler of Spanish Fork as his eighth wife. They had two children Isabella and John, who was born three months after his father died.

Four years later, Henrietta married John Powell on June 18, 1864 becoming his second wife. They were the parents of seven children.

John tried his hand at farming but the crops failed. The dam at Deseret went out and washed away all the crops. John moved his family to Meadow. The next spring, Henrietta hired someone to move her to Fillmore where John was living with his first wife. She found work washing clothes.

Henrietta wove cloth, carded wool, and knitted socks for her children. She taught her family to read. She made a point of learning a few lines of poetry everyday to improve her mind.

In September, 1864, John and Henrietta moved to St. George to do ordinance work in the temple. John Powell passed away on June 3, 1902.

Henrietta married Allen Russell on October 24, 1906. They lived in Manti, spending ten years working in the Manti Temple. Allen Russell passed away on July 11, 1919, again, Henrietta found herself a widow.

She was an example of spiritual integrety. Her life's efforts were given to raising her family and helping the needy. Henrietta passed away on August 12, 1924 in Fillmore, Utah at age ninety-three.

LOUISA MARIA FOSTER RUSSELL

BIRTHDATE: 25 Sep 1840
Glisum, Chsr., New Hampshire
DEATH: 19 Jul 1917
Grafton, Washington Co., Utah
PARENTS: Stephen Foster
Sophia Briggs
PIONEER: abt 1852
SPOUSE: Alonzo H. Russell
MARRIED: 18 Apr 1856
Salt Lake City, Salt Lake, Utah
DEATH SP: 7 Aug 1910
Grafton, Washington Co., Utah

CHILDREN:
Elisha Foster, 9 Aug 1857
Maria Louisa, 25 Sep 1859
Franklin Stephen, 13 Jan 1863
Emily, 5 Sep 1865
Albert, 29 Sep 1867
Alfred, 24 Feb 1870
Lorenzo, 10/20 Oct 1873
Oscar, 4 Sep 1876
Alvaretta, 10 Jan 1880

Louisa joined the Church of Jesus Christ of Latter-day Saints and crossed the Plains experiencing the many hardships all of the pioneers endured. She arrived in the Salt Lake Valley about 1852.

Louisa entered into plural marriage in 1856 and was the fourth wife of her sister's husband, Alonzo Haventon/Haverton Russell. Her first two children were born in Salt Lake City. The other seven children were born in Southern Utah.

Louisa lived in a tent obtained from Johnston's Army until a home could be built. This was quite a struggle. The tent was used for meetings and entertainment as well as living quarters for the two families. Louisa was a faithful wife and made the best of the conditions.

Louisa was industrious and made nice cloth. She would cord the wool and make the clothing for the family. Fruit trees were planted and soon they were bearing. She dried many bushels of fruit. She was a good cook making pies, cakes, and bread. Her specialty was molasses cookies.

She had a special gift of removing warts, but no one ever found out her secret. Louisa was a good step dancer. She enjoyed hearing her six sons orchestra play and entertain people.

Very dear to all her family, Louisa Maria would never put herself forward in public, but will always be loved by her relatives.

SAMANTHA JANE BUCKLAND RUSSELL

BIRTHDATE: 12 Sep 1825
Royalton, Windsor Co., Vermont
DEATH: 30 Mar 1893
Kamas, Wasatch Co., Utah
PARENTS: Joseph M. Buckland
Hannah Daggett
PIONEER: abt 1854
Wagon Train Company
SPOUSE: Charles L. Russell
MARRIED: 26 Jan 1845
Royalton, Windsor Co., Vermont
DEATH SP: 16 Feb 1901
Woodland, Summit Co., Utah

CHILDREN:
Esther Amelia (Alexander), 15 Nov 1845
Emily Charity, 22 Sep 1847
Ellen Elizabeth (Gines), 19 Sep 1849
Joseph Smith, 20 Oct 1851
Nancy Laurice (Richardson), 29 Apr 1854
Charles Lyman Jr., 8 Apr 1857
Samantha Jane (Woodward), 6 May 1860
Alonzo Buckland, Mar 1860
Evaline Vilate, (Woodward), 6 Sep 1863
Ruth Clarissa, 16 Jan 1866
William Buckland, 3 Mar 1869

Samantha was born in Vermont in 1825. She was the second of six children. Samantha's mother left her father before she was seven. Samantha had a very poor childhood. At one time Samantha and her mother were sold to work for a year for seventy four dollars.

Samantha married Charles L. Russell on January 26, 1845. He was thirty and she was twenty years old. They lived in Royalton for many years, here their first four children were born and seven-year-old daughter, Emily, died in September, 1853.

Their fifth child, Nancy, was born on board the "Sam Cloom" on the Missouri River, April 29, 1854. They left for the Salt Lake Valley on June 2, 1854.

While living in Bountiful a son, Charles Lyman Jr., was born in April, 1858. They then moved to Lambs Canyon. An eighth child Alonzo was born at Mountian Dell in 1860.

In the Spring of 1861, they moved to Kamas, being among the first nine families there. Because of Indian trouble they moved into the fort at Sage Bottoms for protection, where Ruth was born in January, 1866. On March 3, 1869, William their last child was born in Kamas. This was their only son to survive.

In 1878, two of their children died, Alonzo died of diptheria in January and twelve year old Ruth.

As a mid-wife Samantha delivered many babies. She was dependable and kind, due to her medical studies she was able to help with other illness.

On December 18, 1892, she helped deliver her grandaughter, but it was Samantha's last confinement case, she became ill and died of a cerebral hemorrhage on March 1893 at the age of sixty-eight.

KITTIE BELL RYAN

No Photo Available

BIRTHDATE: 18 Sep 1861
Brooklyn, Kings, New York,
DEATH: Sep 1863
near Platte River, Wyoming.
PARENTS: William T. Ryan
Janet Cochrane
PIONEER: 3 Sep 1863
Independent Co. Wagon Train
SPOUSE: Not married

Kittie Bell was the second child of thirteen children born to William Thomas Ryan and Janet Cochrane.

Kittie Bell, almost three years, her mother twenty-nine, and three month old baby sister, Alice, left Florence, Nebraska with a company of Saints in July, 1863, by ox-team to travel to Utah. The company captain assigned a teamster to drive the ox-team for Janet Cochrane. Kittie Bell rode most of the way. Her baby sister, three month old Alice, was carried by the teamster.

After they had travled for about six weeks, Kittie Bell became ill probably because of lack of proper food for small children and passed away on September 3, 1863.

They had traveled some 615 miles and Kittie Bell was buried near the Platte River in Wyoming. Her mother dressed her and wrapped her in a blanket and men in the company dug the grave.

It was about 416 miles from the end of the trek to the Valley of the Great Salt Lake Valley in 1863. Three started out but only two arrived. Her father and step-brother arrived later with the freight they were bringing to the Saints in Utah.

History written in 1994 by Yvonne Jones Perry a grand daughter of Kittie's sister, Alice. The information taken from Alice Ryan Jones' history as she told it to Yvonne, bible pages of births and deaths of the Ryan family in possession of Yvonne, and Mormon Emigration 1840-1869 by William Clayton.

JANE (JENNIE) MITTON RYDALCH

BIRTHDATE: 23 Nov 1819
Lingill, Horton-in-Ribblesdale,
Yorkshire, England
DEATH: 2 Feb 1894
Grantsville, Tooele Co., Utah
PARENTS: William Mitton
Mary Calvert
PIONEER: 10 Oct 1853
Joseph W. Young Wagon Train
SPOUSE: William C. Rydalch
MARRIED: 7 Oct 1848
DEATH SP: 13 Apr 1901
Grantsville, Tooele Co., Utah

CHILDREN
Robert, 7 Mar 1842
William, 19 Sep 1845
William, 25 Feb 1849
John, 3 Mar 1851
Thomas, 19 Nov 1852
Chester, 7 Nov 1855
Jethro, 5 Dec 1857
Richard, 8 May 1860
Mary Alice, 26 Mar. 1863
Jane Elizabeth, 1 Apr 1865

Jane "Jennie" was born in Lingill, Horton-in-Ribblesdale, Yorkshire, England in 1819. She was a young lady of twenty-one when Mormonism was beginning to be heard among the British. Many pure of heart were prepared spiritually to receive the Gospel of Jesus Christ of Latter-day Saints and embraced whole heartedly the ideals. They suffered the unkindness of unbelieving fellow townsmen, the bad press of the opposing clergy and even to being rejected and disowned by their own families. Convinced, they strived to immigrate to America and join the body of the Church in Zion.

At twenty-nine and the mother of two young sons she married William Rydalch six weeks before her twenty-ninth birthday. The little family moved to Hollifield, where their son, William, was born.

Moving to Hawkswick, they began to prepare themselves to leave the land of their heritage and immigrate to Utah. Their departure from England was after the birth of their fifth son, Thomas.

At times the converts were accompanied the whole of the journey by one leader, Joseph W. Young organized and escorted 345 souls aboard the ship "Elvira Owen" on February 15, 1853 for a nearly six week voyage.

Because of crowded conditions, the poorest of nutrition and unhealthy water, each voyage was ripe for the sickness of it's passengers.

Below deck, the immigrant' s little world was dark and confined. It was a discordant symphony of children crying, the retching and vomiting of the sea sick, the muttering and growing of despairing companions and, above all, the waves crashing against the hull and over the deck.

They docked in New Orleans in the middle of April and proceeded to Keokuk, Iowa where, on July 11, Joseph W. Young continued his mission of guiding 321 pioneers over plains, valley, mountains and through rivers of water and buffalo to the Salt Lake Valley eighty-two days later. The Rydalch family was sent to Grantsville, Tooele County, Utah, where the last five of their ten children were born.

Jennie Rydalch was an excellent home maker and cook, a feat attested to by the many Church officials who stayed at their home when duties took them to that area.

Active in her church callings and faithful to the end, Jennie preceded her husband in death by seven years and passed away at the age of seventy-four in a land far from her birth.

ANN HERBERT RYNEARSON

BIRTHDATE: 3 May 1831
Hardfordshire, England
DEATH: 10 Jun 1920
Salt Lake Co., Utah
PARENTS: Joseph Herbert
Mariah Brooks
PIONEER: 9 Nov 1856
James Willie Handcart Company
SPOUSE: Andrew J. Rynearson
MARRIED: 15 Mar 1857
DEATH SP: 23 Nov 1905
Woodland, Summit Co., Utah

CHILDREN:
Charles Herbert, 22 Apr 1853
John, 4 Mar 1858
Ann Elizabeth, 29 Apr 1859
Olive Molisse, 23 Sep 1860
Andrew Melvin, 20 Jan 1862

Harriet, 2 Dec 1864
Susin, 20 Apr1866
Josephine, 19 Nov 1867
Hannah Maria, 27 Apr 1863
Mary Jane, 7 Dec 1870

Ann was born in England in 1831. She had three brothers and one sister. As a young girl, she worked in the hop gardens by day and sewed kid gloves at night to help support the family.

When Ann was twenty-six, she and her sixteen year old sister, Hannah, along with three year old Charles sailed from Liverpool on may 3, 1856 on the ship "Thorton," arriving in New York on June 14th.

From New York they traveled to Iowa then crossed the Plains with the James G. Willie Handcart Company.

Ann pulled a handcart with all her belongings. After the third day Hannah grew ill so she pulled her also. When they reached Fort Laramie they waited for wagons from Salt Lake. They left most of their belongings there with the promise they would get them next spring. But never did.

Ann worked for Mr. Rockwod for a year then married Andrew Jackson Rynearson on March 15, 1857. They were the parents of nine children. They lived in Sugar House, then later bought a farm in Willow Creek, where she made her home until she died.

Her husband moved to Woodland in 1879 and left Ann the property to help support her family. She helped support the family by making trimmings for dresses, collars for coats, and many things by sewing "down" from ducks and geese.

Years later her parents and two brothers came to Utah also, which made her very happy.

Ann passed away on April 16, 1897 at the age of sixty-six in Salt Lake County, Utah.

Masters Alexander, 22 Sep 1868
Burrilla, 1 Aug 1870
Clara, 20 Aug 1871

SPOUSE II: Andrew Jackson Rynearson
MARRIED: 28 Jan 1875
DEATH SP: 23 Nov 1805

CHILDREN:
Wilford, 6 Oct 1878
Sarah Bertha, 18 Sep 1880
Ester Viola, 30 Jan 1883
Ruth, 16 Feb 1885
George Ruben, 1 May 1888
Eva, 6 Apr 1892

Sarah was born in Illinois in 1845. She was three years old when she came West with her family in 1848. They later moved to St. George, Utah. Sarah started her schooling when she was seven years old and in her own hand describes her vocation as "Home Dubes."

A month before her sixteenth birthday, May 12, 1861, Sarah and Emanuel Masters Murphy were married in Brigham Young's office. They were the parents of six children; two of whom died as infants.

When Emanuel passed away in 1871, Sarah was only twenty-six years old.

On January 28, 1875, Sarah married Andrew Jackson Rynearson, as his second wife. They settled in Woodland. They were the parents of six children also.

Sarah was a Sunday School teacher, Primary counselor a counslor and president of Relief Society, in the Woodland Ward. She was about five feet tall and weighed about 120 pounds.

Sarah passed away on June 10, 1920 at the age of seventy-five in Woodland, Summit County, Utah.

SARAH ELIZABETH ALEXANDER MURPHY RYNEARSON

BIRTHDATE: 14 Jun 1845
Nauvoo, Hancock Co., Illinois
DEATH: 10 Jun 1920
Woodland, Summit Co., Utah
PARENTS: Randolf Alexander
Myra Nix
PIONEER: 1848 with family
SPOUSE I: Emanuel M. Murphy
MARRIED: 12 May 1861
Salt Lake City, Salt Lake, Utah
DEATH SP: 1871

CHILDREN:
Nancy Myrza, 17 May 1862
Randolph, 12 Nov 1864
Joseph, 25 Oct 1866